INTERNATIONAL HISTORICAL STATISTICS

EUROPE
1750–2000

FIFTH EDITION

INTERNATIONAL HISTORICAL STATISTICS

EUROPE
1750–2000

FIFTH EDITION

B.R. MITCHELL

palgrave
macmillan

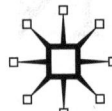 © Palgrave Macmillan, 2003

All rights reserved. No reproduction, copy or transmission of this
publication may be made without written permission.

No paragraph of this publication may be reproduced, copied or transmitted
save with written permission or in accordance with the provisions of the
Copyright, Designs and Patents Act 1988, or under the terms of any licence
permitting limited copying issued by the Copyright Licensing Agency,
90 Tottenham Court Road, London W1T 4LP.

Any person who does any unauthorised act in relation to this publication
may be liable to criminal prosecution and civil claims for damages.

The editor has asserted his right to be identified as the editor of this work
in accordance with the Copyright, Designs and Patents Act 1988.

First published 2003 by
PALGRAVE MACMILLAN
Houndmills, Basingstoke, Hampshire RG21 6XS and
175 Fifth Avenue, New York, N.Y. 10010
Companies and representatives throughout the world

PALGRAVE MACMILLAN is the global academic imprint of the Palgrave
Macmillan division of St. Martin's Press, LLC and of Palgrave Macmillan Ltd.
Macmillan® is a registered trademark in the United States, United Kingdom
and other countries. Palgrave is a registered trademark in the European
Union and other countries.

ISBN 0-333-99411-6   hardback
ISBN 0-333-99413-2   3-volume set

This book is printed on paper suitable for recycling and made from fully
managed and sustained forest sources.

A catalogue record for this book is available from the British Library.

Library of Congress Cataloging-in-Publication Data

Mitchell, B.R. (Brian R.)
   International historical statistics: Europe, 1750–2000 / B.R. Mitchell.–5th ed.
      p. cm
   Includes bibliographical references.
   ISBN 0-333-99411-6 (cloth)
      1. Europe—Statistics—History. I. Title.
HA1107 .M5 2003
314—dc21

                                                                    2002035257

   10   9   8   7   6   5   4   3   2   1
   12 11 10 09 08 07 06 05 04 03

Printed and bound in Great Britain by
Antony Rowe Ltd, Chippenham and Eastbourne

CONTENTS

Table number	Page number	
	vii	Introduction
	xv	Official Sources
	xix	Acknowledgements
	xxi	Weights and Measures: Conversion Ratios and Symbols
A	**1**	**POPULATION AND VITAL STATISTICS**
1	3	Population of Countries at Censuses (in thousands)
2	12	Population of Countries by Sex and Age Groups
3	48	Population of Major Districts (in thousands)
4	74	Population of Major Cities (in thousands)
5	78	Mid-year Population Estimates (in millions)
6	93	Vital Statistics: Rates per 1,000 Population
7	120	Deaths of Infants Under One Year Old (per 1,000 live births)
8	129	Emigration from Europe by Decades
9	130	Annual Migration Statistics (in thousands)
B	**143**	**LABOUR FORCE**
1	145	Economically Active Population by Major Industrial Groups (in thousands)
2	163	Unemployment
3	172	Industrial Disputes
4	186	Money Wages in Industry
5	194	Money Wages in Agriculture
C	**203**	**AGRICULTURE**
1	205	Area of Main Cereal, Potato and Sugar Beet Crops
2	261	Output of Main Cereal, Potato and Sugar Beet Crops
3	320	Area of Vineyards and Output of Wine
4	328	Area and Output of Mediterranean Crops
5	332	Numbers of Livestock
6	382	Output of Cows' Milk
7	388	Butter Output
8	392	Meat Output
9	398	Landings of Fish
10	402	External Trade in Corn
11	411	Exports of Agricultural, Fishing and Forestry Products
D	**419**	**INDUSTRY**
1	421	Indices of Industrial Production
2	428	Output of Coal (in millions of metric tons)
3	438	Output of Crude Petroleum
4	441	Output of Natural Gas
5	444	Output of Main Non-Ferrous Metal Ores
6	451	Output of Main Non-Metallic Minerals
7	453	Output of Iron Ore
8	457	Output of Pig Iron
9	467	Output of Crude Steel
10	474	Output of Aluminium
11	476	Imports and Exports of Coal by Main Surplus and Deficient Countries
12	487	Imports and Exports of Petroleum by Main Surplus and Deficient Countries
13	499	Imports and Exports of Iron Ore by Main Trading Countries

14	503	Raw Cotton Consumption Indicators
15	510	Cotton Spindles
16	513	Output of Cotton Yarn
17	517	Output of Cotton Tissues
18	521	Raw Wool Consumption Indicators
19	526	Output of Wool Yarn
20	530	Output of Wool Tissues
21	534	Output of Artificial and Synthetic Fibres
22	538	Linen Industry Indicators
23	541	Output of Sulphuric Acid
24	546	Timber Industry Indicators
25	550	Output of Motor Vehicles
26	554	Output of Beer
27	562	Output of Electric Energy
E	**569**	**EXTERNAL TRADE**
1	571	External Trade Aggregate Current Value
2	587	External Trade (by value) with Main Trading Partners
F	**671**	**TRANSPORT AND COMMUNICATIONS**
1	673	Length of Railway Line Open
2	684	Freight Traffic on Railways
3	697	Passenger Traffic on Railways
4	710	Merchant Ships Registered
5	731	Inland Navigation Traffic
6	735	Motor Vehicles in Use
7	745	Commercial Aviation
8	750	Postal and Telegraph Services
9	766	Telephone Services
10	776	Radio and Television Receiving Licences
G	**781**	**FINANCE**
1	783	Banknote Circulation
2	793	Deposits in Commercial Banks
3	800	Deposits in Savings Banks
4	811	Money Supply
5	816	Total Central Government Expenditure
6	825	Central Government Revenue and Main Tax Yields
H	**855**	**PRICES**
1	856	Wholesale Price Indices
2	863	Cost-of-Living/Consumer Prices Indices
I	**869**	**EDUCATION**
1	870	Children and Teachers in Schools
2	894	Number of Students in Universities
J	**903**	**NATIONAL ACCOUNTS**
1	905	National Accounts Totals
2	929	Proportions of National Product by Sector of Origin (%)
3	937	Balance of Payments

INTRODUCTION

Statistics are used nowadays not just as illustrations or to give a rough sense of proportions or magnitudes involved but as a major raw material of much economic history, especially of economic growth. Since the subject is by its very nature concerned with quantities, this is an inevitable and welcome development, though no sensible historian would ever claim that statistics can tell the whole story. Aggregative national statistics conceal local and regional detail which may be important in explaining the national picture, and no one doubts that an average may hide as much as it reveals.

In response to the demand for historical statistics, there has appeared since the late 1950s a number of collections for individual countries. The USA was the pioneer in this respect[1], followed by a majority of European countries. Not all are yet as complete as one would wish. Czechoslovakia (since World War II), Denmark, Italy, the Netherlands, Norway, Sweden, the USSR (since 1917), and Yugoslavia have all been covered more or less comprehensively by publications sponsored by their governments. The French have long designated occasional volumes of their *Annuaire Statistique* as Volumes Retrospectifs. In addition, the Bank of Finland has produced several *Studies on Finland's Economic Growth* which include many historical series, notably one by Riitta Hjerppe, which has been translated into English. Other countries have been covered unofficially—Austria-Hungary, Belgium, Germany, Spain and the United Kingdom.[2]

When the first edition of this book was conceived over thirty years ago, many of these publications had not appeared. The time then seemed ripe for gathering into one place the major statistical series for a number of different countries, especially in the light of burgeoning interest in comparative development. That interest has not abated and there still remains the need for a collection covering many countries. The objective of this volume is to fulfil this need—to provide economists and historians with a wide range of mainly economic statistical data without the difficulty of identifying sources and the considerable labour of extracting data from many different places, and of transforming variously defined annual figures into long comparable time-series.

There is a variety of statistical data going back into the Middle Ages for some countries but it is usually of a rather haphazard and incomplete nature—the output of precious metals, the trade of a particular port or in a particular commodity. In view of this and of the fact that modern economic growth is generally held to have begun with the British industrial revolution, which is dated at the earliest from the middle of the eighteenth century, it was decided to fix the starting date of this volume at 1750. This is not to imply that there are no useful statistics for earlier periods. It will be obvious even to the casual user of this work that there was no sudden beginning to the collection of large numbers of statistical series in the second half of the eighteenth century.

However, there is this to be said for 1750. With the single exception of price data for Spain and north-western Europe, few series of overall economic significance began before that date. The finishing date for most series in this edition is 1998, the latest date for which data were generally available at the time of compilation, although some series run to 2000. Even so, it must be realised that many of the statistics for the late 1990s are provisional and will be subject to revision in the future.

That there are pitfalls for the unwary user of statistics needs no saying and this is not the place to attempt to summarise those traps of which any introductory textbook will warn. However, there are certain problems of particular prominence in historical statistics to which attention may properly be drawn. The biggest single and most obvious problem is lack of availability of the data we should like to have, at any rate until the last four or five decades. There is a comparable though less apparent problem in the existence of data which *seem* to relate to the same things in different countries or at different times, but which do not in fact do so. Some sort of data are available in these cases but not the precise sort which we require. Basically, these are problems of definition. For example, in some times and places exports include bullion, in others they do not. Pig iron can include or exclude ferro-alloys; bank deposits may include those of other banks or they may not; corn output can be measured by volume or by weight; and so on. Often there is nothing one can do about this lack of uniformity except indicate its existence and warn against glib comparisons. One can find little comfort, however, in the fact that failure to observe such warning is one of the main reasons why statistics have sometimes been held to be worse than 'damned lies'! Kindred definitional difficulties are provided by the numerous changes in the boundaries of European countries during the 250 years covered here. These are plentifully referred to in the footnotes to the tables but to help the user a complete list of boundary changes for each country is given on pages ix–xiii.

Two problems are peculiar to historical statistics. The first is a mechanical one created by the variable and unknown efficiency of past collectors and compilers of statistics (including the present one), and their printers, and the impossibility of ever being able to check on these qualities. This is a situation with which one has to live, keeping a vigilant eye on one's credulity and endeavouring to estimate margins of error. Too often users of historical statistics–and we are nearly all guilty of this–take best-estimate figures for their calculations without working out the effects on their analysis of compounding margins of error.

The second peculiar problem concerns the purposes for which statistics were collected up to the end of the nineteenth century and indeed the purposes for which they are still compiled. William Robson has rightly said that 'the most important methodological development of the twentieth century' was 'the introduction of measurement in varying degrees in virtually every one of the social sciences'.[3] It was only with this development that there came much collection and publication of statistical material for its own sake. In some countries it began to happen a little before the end of the nineteenth century but it is generally true to say that most statistics prior to 1900 were by-products of taxation or military preparedness, although some of these, notably population censuses, had outgrown their origins some time before then. Many early series, therefore, have to be viewed with a measure of scepticism because there was clearly a premium on evading inclusion in the data. Registration of one's true age if one was a young man liable to military service, and the smuggling of dutiable imports, are only two of the most obvious examples. Understatement is not the only error to which early statistics were liable. Some counties found it convenient to inflate their population or wealth in order to impress potential enemies. There is no ready solution to all these difficulties. All one can do is to be careful and to keep a firm rein on credulity without resorting to stultifying total scepticism.

Anyone who looks carefully at the volumes of *British Historical Statistics* compiled by me and at the present work will be aware of a difference between them relating principally to the sources used. The British volumes provide more detail using more specialised sources. Working in Britain, these sources were readily available to me in a way in which similar sources for most other countries seldom have been. In the case of this book, therefore, the principal reliance has been on the official collections of statistics published by most governments well before the end of the nineteenth century, and on subsequent collections of historical statistics such as those referred to above. For the depth of coverage which could be included in the space available, this sort of source material is generally quite satisfactory.

However, two problems do arise from being thus confined. The first is the omission from statistical annuals of some statistics for some years—either through accidents of publication or because a series had ceased to be or had not yet become of clear general interest and significance. The second problem is the universal habit of government statistical services of changing the detail of coverage and of concepts from one yearbook to the next. Such changes often do occur in the collection of the statistics and there is nothing that can be done about it other than by indicating the break in continuity. Frequently, the changes relate only to presentation in the yearbook and access to more detailed sources can enable one to reconstruct the original format. With few exceptions, it has not been possible for me to do this in the tables that follow and as a result they undoubtedly contain more breaks in continuity than are strictly unavoidable. However, both this latter problem and the one caused by non-publication in statistical annuals have been mitigated to some extent by the co-operation which I have had from colleagues in various European universities and from officials of several national statistical offices and central banks. This assistance is acknowledged below and, where appropriate, in the notes to the tables. It must be stated that this is not to great extent a work of original research, in the sense that comparable time-series have been compiled where only the raw materials for such a compilation existed in the sources. It is, rather, almost entirely a collection of already published statistics, with many of their inconsistencies not eliminated.

These few general remarks are not intended as a critique of the usefulness of statistics in historical studies but as a warning against their careless and casual use in comparisons over time and between different countries. It has been rightly said that 'numbers are useful when they attain a level of subtlety and precision beyond that of words'[4]. Let the user of this volume be in no doubt of the need to seek for subtlety and of the difficulties in the way of precision.

Some of the problems peculiar to each topic are mentioned briefly in the introduction to each of the separate sections, but it must be pointed out that these are not intended to be comprehensive critiques of the statistics presented. To do this properly would require at least another volume. The intention here is only to draw the user's attention to the main types of difficulty in interpreting the statistics. The problems for each individual country are not generally dealt with unless they are outstandingly important. However, most of them are readily apparent from a careful use of the notes and footnotes to the tables.

Finally, there are the problems created by the division of previously sovereign political units - the U.S.S.R. and Yugoslavia. There is no completely satisfactory and consistent way of dealing with these. In many cases some of the statistical series shown are not available at present for long periods for the components into which these countries have been divided. This applies to the majority of economic statistics—to most of those pertaining to agriculture, industry and transport, and, almost by definition, overseas trade, prices, financial statistics and national accounts. In practice, only demographic data are available reasonably frequently for the period between 1945 (or, in some cases, 1919) and the date of division. These are shown here, where possible, for the separate components of Yugoslavia and the European parts of the Soviet Union; but in only a few cases are any other statistics included.

Boundary Changes

One of the main difficulties in using the historical statistics of Europe is caused by the numerous changes which have taken place in national boundaries. These are frequently referred to in the footnotes to the tables but to help the user a consolidated list of the changes follows here:

Albania	Part of the Turkish Empire until established as a separate state in 1913. It was occupied by Italy (and later by the Germans) from 1939 to 1944.
Armenia	i.e. eastern Armenia, which was part of the Russian Empire and later a Soviet Republic from 1828 to 1991.
Austria	Up to 1918 this name was given to the Cisleithanian part of the Habsburg monarchy, consisting of the provinces listed in table A3. The Italian provinces of the monarchy were sometimes included until their cession in 1859 (Lombardy) and 1866 (Venetia). In the period to 1815, and especially during the Napoleonic Wars, there were various changes in Austrian territory, which are not worth listing here, since the only statistics given for that period relate to central government finances. From 1815 to 1918 there were few changes, apart from the loss of Lombardy and Venetia. Krakow was incorporated in 1846, and Bosnia-Hercegovina was occupied in 1878 and formally annexed in 1908. Its statistics were not included with those of either Austria or Hungary, however.
	The Republic of Austria established in 1919 consisted of the old German-speaking provinces of Cisleithania, excluding parts of Carinthia, Styria, and Tirol. From 1922 it also included parts of what had previously been territories of the Hungarian Crown, combined into the new province of Burgenland. The republic was absorbed in Greater Germany from 1938 to 1945.
Azerbaijan	i.e. northern Azerbaijan, which was part of the Russian Empire and later a Soviet Republic from 1828 to 1991.
Belarus	Part of the Russian Empire and later a Soviet Republic (as Byelorussia) from the late 18th century to 1990. It was expanded after the Second World War by the inclusion of lands which were in Poland during the interwar period.
Belgium	Apart from the independent Principality of Liège, the territory later forming Belgium was ruled by the Austrians in the eighteenth century. In 1795 it was incorporated in revolutionary France, and in 1815 sovereignty was transferred to The Netherlands. Belgium's independence was established in 1830 by secession from The Netherlands, though in 1839 the Grand Duchy of Luxembourg was separated from the Belgian province of the same name and receded to The Netherlands and the province of Limburg was also divided. Since 1839 the Limburg was also divided. Since 1839 the only territorial change has been the acquisition of Eupen, Malmèdy, and surrounding districts from Germany in 1920. These were temporarily returned in 1940–1944.
Bosnia	Part of the Ottoman Empire until 1878, when it was occupied by Austria-Hungary, and *de jure* until 1908 when it was formally annexed. It became part of Yugoslavia in 1919 and so remained until its declaration of independence in 1991.
Bulgaria	Formerly part of the Turkish Empire, it was established as an independent country in 1878, covering approximately the northern two-thirds of the present territory. Much of the remainder became semi-independent, though under Turkish suzerainty, as Eastern Roumelia. This was united with Bulgaria in 1885. As a result of the two Balkan Wars in 1912–13, Southern Dobrudja was ceded to Romania, and a larger area in the south and west was acquired from Turkey, including part of eastern Thrace. This was enlarged in 1915, when Bulgaria entered the First World War on the side of the Central Powers, and a large part of Serbia was also seized. In 1916 Southern Dobrudja was also re-taken. In 1918 these wartime gains were all lost, together with the Aegean coastal strip won in 1913. Southern Dobrudja was permanently re-acquired in September 1940.

Czechoslovakia	Established in 1918/9 from the three Czech provinces of Cisleithania (Bohemia, Moravia, and Silesia) and the Slovak and Ruthene territories of the Hungarian Crown. These last (known as Sub-Carpathian Russia) were ceded to the U.S.S.R., along with a few Slovak villages, in 1945. A small area on the south bank of the Danube—the so-called Bratislava Bridgehead—was acquired from Hungary in 1947. From 1938 to 1945 Czechoslovakia was dismembered. The so-called Sudetenlands, along the frontier, were incorporated in Greater Germany; Teschen was seized by Poland; the remaining Czech lands were made a protectorate of Germany; and Slovakia was given nominal independence as a separate state.
Czechoslovakia/ Czech Republic	In 1992 Czechoslovakia was divided into two independent units, *viz* the Czech Republic and Slovakia.
Croatia	Part of the Habsburg Empire after its conquest from the Ottomans in the 18th century, it was attached to Hungary or Austria, though separately administered. From 1919 until its declaration of independence in 1990 it formed part of Yugoslavia.
Denmark	Denmark proper, and the Duchies of Schleswig, Holstein, and Lauenburg, were usually kept separate in the official statistics, though there are breaks in some series when the Duchies were ceded to Prussia in 1864. In 1920 the northern part of the old Duchy of Schleswig was returned to Denmark, and is known as South Jutland.
Estonia	Part of the Russian Empire from 1721 to 1917, and one of the Soviet Socialist Republics from 1940 to 1990. It was independent in the interwar period and has again been so since 1990.
Finland	Part of the Swedish Kingdom until 1809, though separately administered. It was then ceded to Russia, though as a Grand Duchy with an autonomous administration. This continued until 1917, the boundaries of the Grand Duchy being enlarged in 1809, 1811, and 1820 by the addition respectively of part of the Tornie River basin, of Viipuri province, and of Petsamo. Independence was declared in 1917 and established the following year. Petsamo, Viipuri, and certain other areas along the frontier were ceded to the U.S.S.R. in 1940, and though temporarily re-acquired in 1941–42, their cession was confirmed in 1945.
France	The boundaries of France were enlarged substantially during the Revolutionary and Napoleonic period, though most of the available statistics can be, and have been, given for the territory established in 1815. The main differences between this and the pre-Revolution territory were the inclusion of Gex and the exclusion of Philippeville and part of Wissembourg. In 1860 Savoy and Nice were acquired from Piedmont. From 1871 to 1918 Alsace (excluding the territory of Belfort) and Lorraine (excluding the areas organised as the department of Meurthe-et-Moselle) were ceded to Germany, and from 1940 to 1944 these districts were temporarily lost again. In 1947 Tende and Brigue were acquired from Italy.
Georgia	Absorbed in the Russian Empire between 1801 and 1864, it became one of the Soviet Republics after a short period of independence in 1918–21. It became independent again in 1990.
Germany	The German Empire was established in 1870, but many statistics for the area then covered have been synthesised for earlier years, though none prior to 1815. The boundaries then established for the state of Germany were only marginally changed to 1871, in which year most of Alsace and Lorraine were acquired. This was lost again in 1918, and various other territories were also ceded after the First World War. The mainly Polish provinces were taken from Germany in 1919; Danzig, Memel, northern Schleswig, and Eupen etc. were formally ceded in 1920, and eastern Upper Silesia was taken by Poland in 1922, following a plebiscite. In addition, Saarland was separately administered by France from 1920 to February 1935 (an arrangement which was followed again after the Second World War to the middle of 1959). During the period 1938–1941 various territories were incorporated in Greater Germany, but these were generally kept separate in the statistics. Four-power occupation was instituted following Germany's defeat in 1945, and during the next three or four years two *de facto* territories were established, which were formalised in 1949 as the Federal Republic of (West) Germany and the Democratic Republic of (East) Germany. East Berlin was included with the latter, and West Berlin, though not wholly incorporated in the former, is generally included in its statistics. Large parts of the pre-1939 eastern territories of Germany were ceded to Poland and the U.S.S.R. in 1945, but there have been only very minor boundary changes in the west and south. East Germany, the former D.D.R., was amalgamated into the Federal German Republic in 1990.

Greece	Formerly part of the Turkish Empire, Greece was established as an independent country in 1829, comprising the Morea, Euboea, the Cyclades Islands, and the mainland south of Arta and Thessaly. The Ionian Islands were ceded by Britain in 1864. In 1881 Thessaly and Arta were acquired from Turkey, though a small strip of the former was returned in 1897. In 1913 the present territories in Epiros, Macedonia, and western Thrace were acquired, along with Crete and most of the remaining Aegean islands except the Dodecanese. Eastern Thrace was added in 1919, though this was not confirmed until the treaty of Lausanne in 1923, when the loss (in 1921) of postwar acquisitions on the mainland of Asia Minor was also confirmed. The Dodecanese Islands were formally acquired from Italy in 1947.
Hungary	Up to 1918 this name could be given either to all the lands of the Hungarian Crown (i.e. Transleithania) or to the more restricted Ancient Kingdom. The former included Transylvania, the Banat and Backa, and the semi-autonomous Croatia-Slavonia, though from 1849 to 1868 the Banat and Backa (along with its associated military frontier regions) constituted the autonomous Voivodina, and Croatia-Slavonia was attached to Austria rather than Hungary. In 1868 the Voivodina was incorporated in Hungary, and Croatia-Slavonia returned to Hungarian domination, whilst in 1870 the latter's port of Fiume (Rijeka) was directly attached to Hungary. The remaining military frontier regions, which so long as they existed were always under Austria, were incorporated in Croatia-Slavonia in 1881.
	The territory of Hungary established in 1919 by the treaty of Trianon was greatly reduced compared with Transleithania, or even the Ancient Kingdom. The Slovak and Ruthene counties were lost to Czechoslovakia; Transylvania and several counties of Hungary proper, together with part of the Banat, were lost to Romania; the rest of the Banat, Backa, and parts of Hungary proper went to Yugoslavia. Finally, in 1922, the German-speaking western fringe was ceded to Austria. During 1939–1945 there were various enlargements of Hungarian territory, all of which were lost in 1945. In 1947 the Bratislava Bridgehead was ceded to Czechoslovakia.
Ireland	The twenty-six counties of southern Ireland became independent in 1921.
Italy	The Italian nation-state was established in 1860, though some statistics for the area covered by it have been synthesised for earlier years. Venetia was added to the original territory in 1866, and the Papal States in 1870. In 1919 South Tirol, the old Austrian Küstenland provinces, and the port of Zara (Zadar) in Dalmatia were acquired, and Fiume was added in 1922. In 1945 the last two, together with Istria and part of Venezia-Giulia were ceded to Yugoslavia. Trieste and its neighbourhood were disputed, and were in international occupation. This was ended in 1954, when the city and a strip of coast went to Italy, and the hinterland to Yugoslavia. In 1947 Tenda and Briga were ceded to France.
Latvia	Part of the Russian Empire from the 18th century to 1917, and one of the Soviet Republics from 1940 to 1990. It was independent in the interwar period and has been so again from 1990.
Lithuania	A much larger region than the present territory was incorporated in the Russian Empire by the 18th-century partitions of Poland. The present territory, independent from 1990, corresponds to that of the Soviet Republic of 1940–90. It includes Vilnius and its surroundings, which were part of Poland during the interwar period of independence.
Macedonia	Part of the Ottoman Empire until the Balkan War of 1912, it formed part of Serbia and then Yugoslavia subsequently, until its declaration of independence in 1991.
Moldova	The present territory, independent from 1990, corresponds to the Moldavian Soviet Socialist Republic constituted in 1940 from the largest part of Bessarabia and a strip of land on the east bank of the River Dniester. The latter, known as Transdniestria, has not yet been fully integrated.
Montenegro	Though formally under Turkey, it had much *de facto* independence even before 1878/80, when it was formally recognised. It was enlarged in 1878/80 and again in 1913.
Netherlands	Dutch independence was temporarily lost in the Napoleonic period, but re-established in 1814/5, when the old Austrian Netherlands and Liège were added to its territories. These revolted and became the independent kingdom of Belgium in 1830, though the Grand Duchy of Luxembourg and part of Limburg were formally re-acquired in 1839. The Grand Duchy was administered separately, and became independent in 1890 as a result of a difference in inheritance laws. Since 1839 the only boundary change has been the acquisition of the villages of Elten and Tuddern from Germany in 1949.
Norway	Part of the lands of the Danish Crown to 1814 and of the Swedish Crown from then to 1905, when it became independent. It was always administered as a separate unit.

Poland	There are no useful statistics for that part of the eighteenth century before Poland lost its independence in the partitions (the last one being 1795). It was re-established as an independent country in 1919, consisting of the former German territories of Posen, West Prussia, and part of Pomerania; the former Austrian territory of Galicia; and the former Polish provinces of Russia together with parts of Russia proper. To these were added eastern Upper Silesia in July 1922, and Teschen (taken from Czechoslovakia) in October 1938 (and returned in 1945). From October 1939 to March 1945 Poland was, in effect, dismembered, and when reconstituted its territory was shifted westwards by the cession to the U.S.S.R. of the eastern one-third of the pre-war lands, and the acquisition from Germany of most of East Prussia and of the territory east of the Oder and Neisse Rivers, including the port of Stettin (Szczecin). There was a minor exchange of territory with the U.S.S.R. in the Przemysl area in 1951.
Portugal	No territorial changes.
Romania	The separate principalities of Wallachia and Moldavia, under Turkish suzerainty, were united *de facto* in 1859. This was regularised in 1866, when Romania in practice acquired independence, though this was not formally recognised until 1878. At that date, Southern Bessarabia was ceded to Russia, and all except the southern part of Dobrudja was acquired from Turkey. In 1913 this southern part was acquired from Bulgaria. Romania entered the First World War in 1916, and in the treaty of Bucharest in 1918 lost Southern Dobrudja and many areas along the frontier with Hungary, but acquired Bessarabia from Russia. The losses were temporary, being reversed in 1919, and in 1920 Bukovina, part of the Banat, and Transylvania (including some counties of Hungary proper) were acquired in the break-up of the Habsburg Empire. In 1940 Southern Dobrudja was again ceded to Bulgaria (this time permanently), and Bessarabia and Northern Bukovina to the U.S.S.R. (also permanently, apart from the wartime seizure in 1941–43). Northern Transylvania was also lost to Hungary from 1940 to 1944.
Russia	Russian territorial acquisitions since 1750 have been very large, interrupted only in the period immediately following the 1917 Revolution. Russia received Polish territory in each of the three partitions (1772, 1793, and 1795), and acquired Turkish territory in the southern Ukraine, the Crimea, and the Kuban and Caucasia in 1774 and 1791. Georgia proper was acquired in 1801, Imeretia in 1810, Guria in 1829, Mingelia in 1857, Svanetia in 1858, and Abkhazia in 1864. Most of Azerbaijan was acquired in 1813. Yerevan and Nakhichevan were acquired in 1828, and the Kars region in 1878, which completed Russian territory in that area. Bessarabia was also acquired from Turkey, in 1812. The southern part was lost to Moldavia from 1856 to 1878, when it was re-acquired. The whole of it was lost to Romania from 1918 to 1940. In central Asia there were acquisitions pushing the frontier southwards and eastwards in 1864, 1865 (Tashkent), 1868 (Samarkand and Bukhara), 1871, 1873 (Khiva), 1876 (the Ferghana), 1881 (Askahabad), 1884 (Merw), and 1885. Finland, though always separately administered, was acquired in 1809. After the 1917 Revolution there were substantial territorial losses in Europe. Finland became independent, as did Estonia, Latvia, and Lithuania; Bessarabia was ceded to Romania, and the Polish provinces became part of independent Poland, taking with them parts of Russia proper. All these were re-acquired in 1939–40, except for central Poland and Finland (though Viipuri and Petsamo were recovered). These reacquisitions were confirmed in 1945, with minor adjustments on the Polish and Finnish frontiers. In addition northern Bukovina, taken in 1940 from Romania, was confirmed, and Sub-Carpathian Russia (Ruthenia) and the north-eastern part of East Prussia were added to the U.S.S.R. The U.S.S.R. was divided in 1990–91 into its component Republics. The area now known as Russia (strictly speaking the Russian Federation) corresponds to that of the former Russian Soviet Federated Socialist Republic. This includes much territory in Asia, but in most cases data for this cannot be shown separately.
Serbia	Established as an autonomous principality under Turkish suzerainty in 1817 and enlarged in 1833, Serbia became formally independent in 1878, when the Nis area was incorporated. In 1913 it was greatly enlarged by the addition of part of the Sanjak of Novi Pazar and much of Macedonia. In 1919 it formed the main nucleus of Yugoslavia.
Slovakia	See under Czechoslovakia for the period prior to its independence in 1992.
Slovenia	The greatest part of the country consists of what was the Austrian province of Carniola (or Krain) until 1918, together with parts of Styria and Istria. It was subsequently part of Yugoslavia until its declaration of independence in 1990.
Spain	No territorial changes.

Sweden	Apart from the acquisition of separately-administered Norway by the Swedish Crown from 1814 to 1905, and the loss of separately-administered Finland in 1809, there have been no territorial changes.
Switzerland	After various vicissitudes in the Napoleonic period (including incorporation in France), the federal system of the pre-Revolutionary cantons, as modified by the Act of Mediation of 1803, which ended the tributary status of certain areas, was restored. Moreover, the previously independent cantons of Geneva and Valais were added in 1815, and so was Neuchàtel, which had been (and anomalously continued to be until 1857) a fief of the Prussian Crown.
United Kingdom	Ireland was a separate kingdom until 1801, when it was incorporated. In 1921 the twenty-six counties of southern Ireland became independent. The term Great Britain as used in the tables refers to the United Kingdom excluding any Irish territory.
Ukraine	Part of the Russian Empire from the 18th century, it was one of the Soviet Republics from 1919 to 1990. Its western areas were included in Poland in the interwar period and partly in the Austrian province of Galicia before that.
Yugoslavia	Constituted in 1919 by adding to the previously independent Montenegro and Serbia, Croatia-Slavonia; part of the Banat, Backa, and parts of Hungary proper; and the former Austrian provinces of Carniola and Dalmatia (except Zara), together with parts of Carinthia and Styria. In 1945 Zara (Zadar), and other territories in the north-west were added, disputed parts near Trieste being finally acquired in 1954. Since 1990–91 the territory consists of Serbia (including Kosovo and Voivodina) and Montenegro.

Currency Changes

In addition to difficulties in comparing statistics over time which result from boundary changes, there are others caused by changes in currency units. It has not been possible to identify all of these prior to 1914, but the most important are listed below. Most of the others do not, in any case, matter so far as this volume is concerned, since in these cases statistics have been standardised in terms of later currency units.

Armenia	The dram replaced the rubel in November 1993 at the rate of 1 dram = 84 rubels.
Austria	1893; the florin (or gulden) was divided into two of a new currency unit, the krone. June 1925; a new unit, the schilling, was established, worth 10,000 kronen. 1947/8, a new schilling was issued, worth three old ones.[5]
Azerbaijan	The manat replaced the rubel in August 1992 at the rate of 1 manat = 10 rubels.
Belarus	The Belorussian rubel replaced the Soviet rubel at par in May 1992, and was itself replaced by a new rubel in August 1994 at the rate of 1 new rubel = 10 old.
Bosnia	The new Bosnian dinar replaced the Yugoslav dinar in October 1994 at the rate of 1 Bosnian dinar = 10, 000 old.
Bulgaria	March 1947, the value of the lev was doubled, the circulation being halved by decree. May 1952; a new lev was issued, worth 100 old leva.[5] January 1962; a new lev was issued, worth 10 old leva.
Croatia	The kuna replaced the dinar in May 1994 at the rate of 1 kuna = 1, 000 dinars.
Czechoslovakia	June 1953, a new korun was issued, worth 5 old koruna.[5]
Denmark	1873; the rigsdaler was divided into two of a new currency unit, the krone.
Estonia	The kroon replaced the rubel in June 1992 at the rate of 1 kroon = 10 rubels.
Finland	Swedish and Russian currency were both legal tender from 1809 to 1840, when the former was withdrawn. In 1864 Finnish marks were introduced alongside Russian currency, 4 marks equalling one rubel. January 1963; a new mark was issued, worth 100 old marks.
France	January 1960; a new franc was issued, worth 100 old francs.
Georgia	The lari replaced rubel coupons in September 1995 at the rate of 1 lari = 1 million coupon rubels.
Germany	November 1923; a new mark (the rentenmark) was issued, worth one million million old marks.[6]
West Germany	June 1948, a new unit, the Deutschmark, was established, worth 10 Reichsmarks.[1]

Greece   November 1944; a new drachma was issued, worth 50,000 million old drachmae. May 1954; a new drachma was issued, worth 1,000 old drachmae.

Hungary   1893, the florin (or gulden) was divided into two of a new currency unit, the krone. Dec. 1926; a new unit, the pengo, was established, worth 12,500 paper kronen. July 1946; a new unit, the forint, was established, worth 400,000 quadrillion pengos.

Latvia   The Latvian rubel was introduced at par with the Soviet rubel in May 1992, and was replaced in March-June 1993 by the lat at the rate of 1 lat = 200 rubels.

Lithuania   The talona replaced the Soviet rubel at par in May 1992, and was itself replaced by the lita in June 1993 at the rate of 1 lita = 100 talonai.

Macedonia   The denar replaced the Yugoslav dinar at par in May 1992. A new denar was introduced in May 1993 at the rate of 1 new denar = 100 old.

Moldova   The Moldovan rubel replaced the Soviet rubel at par in June 1992. It was itself replaced by the leuin November 1993 at the rate of 1 lei = 1, 000 rubels.

Poland   May 1924; a new unit, the zloty, was established, worth 1,800,000 marks. October 1950; a new zloty was issued, worth 100 old zlotys.[1] In January 1995 another new zloty was issued at the rate of 1 new = 10, 000 old.

Romania   1866; a new currency unit, the leu, was established, worth, one-quarter of a piastre. August 1947; a new leu was issued, worth 20,000 old lei.

Russia   1837; the silver rubel replaced the paper rubel as the basis of official statistics. It was worth approximately four times as much.

                  October 1922; a new currency unit, the chernovetz, was established, worth 10 old gold rubels, but paper rubels continued to circulate and depreciate. By March 1924, 1 chernovetz (later renamed rubel) equalled 50,000 million paper rubels.

Slovakia   The Slovak koruna replaced the Czechoslovak koruna at par in February 1993.

Slovenia   The tolar replaced the Yugoslav dinar at par in October 1991.

Ukraine   Still, in effect, using Soviet rubels, though a temporary coupon currency (the karbovanets) was issued at par in November 1992.

Yugoslavia   January 1966; a new dinar was issued, worth 100 old dinars.

                  January 1990; a further new dinar was issued, worth 10,000 of the previous dinars. It has been used in one or two tables because of retrospective revisions to the statistics.

                  In October 1993 another new dinar was issued at the rate of 1 new = 1 million old.

---

[1] U.S. Bureau of the Census, *Historical Statistics of the United States* (Washington, 1957). There have subsequently been three new editions.

[2] Riitta Hjerppe, *The Finnish Economy 1860–1985* (Helsinki, 1989); Alfred Hoffman & H. Matis, *Wirtschafts- und Sozialstatistik Oesterreichs-Ungarn* (Munich, 1978); P. Lebrun *et al*, *Histoire Quantitative de la Belgique au XIXe Siecle* (Brussells, various dates); Jurgen Kocka & Gerhard A. Ritter *et al*, *Sozialgeschichtliches Arbeitsbuch* (Munich, various dates); Albert Carrera *et al*, *Estadisticas Historic as de Espana* (Madrid, 1984); B.R. Mitchell., *British Historical Statistics* (Cambridge, 1988). Reference should be made to a major work on German historical statistics which is under way, viz. Wolfram Fischer, Franz Irsigler, Karl Heinrich Kaufhold & Hugo Ott, *Quellen und Forschungen zur Historishen Statistik von Deutschland*.

[3] W.A. Robson (ed.), *Man and the Social Sciences* (London, 1972)

[4] W. Paul Strassman, *Risk and Technological Innovation* (Ithaca, N.Y., 1959), p. 5.

[5] Privileged rates of exchange existed, usually for small sums, but the rate given here applied to most currency.

[6] This was a *de facto* change. It became *de jure* in October 1924 with the issue of the Reichsmark.

OFFICIAL SOURCES

The main sources used have been the official publications of the various European governments. In order to avoid excessive repetition of these in the notes to the tables, there follows a list of those used in more than one of the tables in this book:

Austria
Nachrichten über Industrie, Handel und Verkehr (1873–1908)
Österreichisches Statistisches Handbuch (1880–1917)
Republica of Austria (1945–1975)
Statistisches Handbuch für die Republik Österreich (1920–1937, 1950–)
Statistisches Handbüchlein für die Österreichische Monarchie (1861 and 1867)
Statistisches Jahrbuch der Österreichischen Monarchie (1861–1881)
Statistisches Jahrbuch für Österreich (1938)
Statistik des auswärtigen Handels (1891–1917)
Tafeln zur Statistik der Österreichischen Monarchie (1828–1859)
Übersichtstafeln zur Statistik der Österreichischen Monarchie für 1861 and 1862

Belgium
Annuaire Statistique de la Belgique (1870–)
Bulletin de la Commission Centrale de Statistique (1843–1928)
Documents Statistiques Recueillis et Publiés par le Ministre de l'Intérieur (1836–41; 1857–59)
Statistique Générale de la Belgique: Exposé de la Situation du Royaume (1841–50; 1851–60. 1861–75; 1876–1900)

Bulgaria
Annuaire Statistique du Royaume de Bulgarie (1910–1942)
Statistickeski Godishnik (1956–)

Czechoslovakia
Historická Statistická Rocenka c SSR (1985)
Manuel Statistique de la Republique Tchécoslovaque (1920–1932)
Statistical Digest of the Czechoslovak Republic (1948)
Statistical Handbook of the Czechoslovak Republic (London, 1942)
Statistická Príru ka Slovenska (1947–1948)
Statistická Rocenka (1934–1938, 1953–)
Statisticky Zpravodaj (1938–1947)
Zahrani ni Obchod c SR (1925–1939, 1947–)
Zahrani ni Obchod c ech, Moravya, Slezeka (1940–1945)
Zprávy Státního Úradu Statistického Republiky c eskoslovenské (1934–1947)

Denmark
Danmarks Historie, vol 9. (Copenhagen, 1985)
Meddelelser fra det Statistiske Bureau (1852–1861)
Sammendrag af Statistiske Oplysninger (1869–1893)
Statistisk Ärbog (1896–)
Statistisk Fjerde Raekke (1867–1959)
Statistisk Meddelelser (1862–1958)
Statistisk Ny Raekke (1845–1858)
Statistisk Tabelvaerk (1801–1849)
Statistisk Tredje Raekke (1860–1897)

Finland
Bidrag till Finlands Officiela Statistik (1886–1914)
Suomen Tilastollinen Vuosikinja (1883–)

France
Annuaire Statistique de la France (1878–)

Germany
Statistisches Jahrbuch für das Deutsches Reich (1880–1941)
Statistisches Jahrbuch der Deutschen Demokratischen Republik (1953–)
Statistisches Jahrbuch für die Bundesrepublik Deutschland (1952–)

Statistik des Deutsches Reich (1873–1939)
Statistik der Bundesrepublik Deutschland (1950–)
Die Wirtschaft des Auslands, 1900–1927

Greece   *Annuaire Economique de la Grèce* (1938)
              Annuaire Statistique de la Grèce/Statistical Yearbook of Greece (1930–1937, 1954–)

Hungary   *Magyar Statistikai Évkönyv* (1881–)

Iceland   *Tolfraedihandbok* (1930–)

Ireland   *Agricultural Statistics 1934–1956*
              Statistical Abstract of Ireland (1931–)

Italy   *Annali di Statistica* (1871–)
              Annuario Statistico Italiano (1878–)
              Cento Anno di Sviluppo Economico e Sociale dell' Italia
              Sommario di Statistiche Storiche Italiane, 1861–1955

Netherlands   *Bijdragen to de Statistiek van Nederland* (1894–)
              Jaarcijfers voor Nederland (1881–)
              Statistisch Jaarboekje (1851–1882)
              1899–1969: Zeventig Jaren Statistiek in Tijdreeksen

Norway   *Historisk Statistikk* 1968 and 1978
              Statistisk Ärbok (1879–)
              Statistisk Oversikter 1948

Poland   *Petit Annuaire Statistique de la Pologne* (1939)
              Rocznik Statystyczny (1920–1938, 1947–)

Portugal   *Anuario Estatistico* (1875–)

Romania   *Anuarul Statistic al României* (1904–1941, 1957–)
              Buletin Statistic General (1892–1939)
              Comertul Exterior al României (1871–)

Russia   *Annuaire de la Russie* (1904–1911)
              Celskoe Khozyistvo S.S.S.R. (1960)
              Narodnoe Khozyistvo S.S.S.R. (1932, 1956–)
              Promishlenost S.S.S.R.
              Statistika Rossieskoie Imperie (1887–1904)
              Statistieski Sbornik 1918–1966
              Strana Sovetov za 50 Let
              Vneshnaya Torgovilya S.S.S.R. 1918–1966

Spain   *Anuario de Estadistica Agraria* (1900–with gaps)
              Anuario Estadistico de España (1858–1867, 1915–1935, 1946–)
              Cuadro (later Estadistica) General del Comercio Exterior de España (1849–with gaps)
              Estadistica Minera (1861–with gaps)
              Memoria sobre el Movimento de la Poblacion de España (1858–1861, 1861–1870, 1900–1905)

Sweden   *Historisk Statistisk för Sverige* (3 parts in 4 volumes, 1955–1972)
              Statistisk Årsbok (1914–)
              Statistisk Tidskrift (1860–1913)

Switzerland   *Statistisches Jahrbuch der Schweiz* (1891–)

United Kingdom   *Annual Abstract of Statistics* (1946–)
Annual Statement of the Trade of the U.K (1854–1974)
Statistical Abstract for the Principal and Other Foreign Countries (1872–1912)[1]
Statistical Abstract of the United Kingdom (1854–1938)
Tables of Revenue, Population, Commerce, etc. (1833–1854)

Yugoslavia   *Annuaire Statistique du Royaume de Serbie* (1895–1908)
Matériaux pour la Statistique du Serbie (1888–1896)
Statisticki Godisnjak (1929–1940, 1954–)
Jugoslavija 1945–1964: Statisticki Pregled
Jugoslavija 1918–1988: Statisticki Godisnjak

---

[1]   Occasional collections of tables relating to foreign countries were published in Parliamentary Papers from 1844 to 1870, and have been used.

ACKNOWLEDGEMENTS

In compiling a volume of this kind I have inevitably contracted a large number of debts for the help which I have been given by a great variety of people. It is impossible to mention every single one of these here, and I hope that those who are not named below will accept this general expression of my gratitude.

My principal acknowledgement must be to my friend and former pupil, Hywel Jones, who collected much of the data for Russia in the original section and much also for other east European countries. In addition, for a time, he lived with the worksheets almost as intimately as I did myself and I sought his advice on numerous occasions.

Other former pupils who have helped me with the collection of data and to whom I am extremely grateful are Mrs Penelope Francks (*née* Gant), Willem Buiter, and Petr Kroslak, whilst I have received helpful advice in connection with this edition from Professor N. F. R. Crafts and Professor Vera Zamagni.

In the nature of our work we have been particularly demanding users of a number of libraries. The very willing response of their staff cannot go unacknowledged. Particular mention must be made of Mr Finkell and Mr Donald Ross of the Marshall Library, Cambridge, Mr Vickery, Mr Noblett and their staff in the Official Publications department of the Cambridge University Library, and Mr Spinney and his staff in the State Paper Room of the British Museum (including Mr Griscome and Mr Hopgood at the Woolwich Repository).

In the later stages of compilation I appealed to a number of individual scholars for help in filling gaps and to the government statistical services of almost every European country. For their assistance at this stage I would particularly like to thank Professor Lennart Jorberg of the University of Lund, Mrs Riitta Hjerppe of the University of Helsinki, Mr G. Radulescu, editor-in-chief of the *Enciclopedica Romana*, Dr Zofia Wysokinska of the University of Lodz and the directors and staff of the central government statistical services of Austria, Belgium Czechoslovakia, Finland, France, the German Federal Republic, Greece, Hungary, Ireland, Italy Luxembourg, the Netherlands, Norway, Poland, Portugal, and Sweden. Most of the data supplied by these services is acknowledged specifically in the tables, but some was transcribed from published source unavailable to me. In this connection I would like to make special mention of the help given by the central statistical services of Finland, the Netherlands, and Sweden. In addition some data, for which am very grateful, has been supplied by the Mission des Archives of the French Ministry of National Education, by the statistical service of the French Ministry of Industrial and Scientific Development, by the statistical information centre of the French Ministry of the Economy and of Finances, and by the director of the Groupement des Industries Sidérurgiques Luxembourgeoises.

I received financial assistance during the compilation the first edition of this volume which I am happy to acknowledge. The principal source has been the Social Science Research Council, which enabled me to employ Mr Jones and Mr Buiter, and which contributed to travelling expenses. In addition I have received help with travelling expenses from Trinity College, Cambridge. I am also grateful for the facilities which were made available to Mr Jones and myself by the Cambridge University Department of Applied Economics, and especially for the help of its librarian, Mrs Olga Peppercorn, Miss Marion Clark and the computing staff.

In addition to these personal acknowledgements, the author and publishers wish to thank the following, who have kindly given permission for the use of copyright material: Almqvist & Wiksell Forlag AB and Professor Jorberg for statistics from *Growth and Fluctuations of Swedish Industry 1869–1922*, and Professor Johansson for use of *The Gross Domestic Product of Sweden and its Composition 1861–1955*; Annales, Economics, Sociétes, Civilisations for use of an index from "The Industrial Production in France in the 19th Century" from *Annales E.S.C. No. 1/1970* by François Crouzet; Paul Bairoch and Université Libre de Bruxelles for statistics from *The Working Population and Its Structure* by P. Bairoch; Cambridge University Press for extracts from *National Income, Expenditure and Output of the United Kingdom 1855–1965* by C. H. Feinstein; Economic Commission for Europe for extract from *Growth and Stagnation in the European Economy* by Ingvar Svennilson; Harvard University Press for extracts from *Economic Elements in the Pax Britannica* by A. H. Imlah, *The Real National Income of Soviet Russia Since 1928* by A. Bergson; I.A.R.I.W. for extracts from *Review of Income & Wealth (1971)* by Frederic L. Pryor, by *Income and Wealth (Series V)* by Alexander Eckstein, *Income and Wealth (Series IX)* 1953 by I. Vinski; National Bureau of Economic Research for use of *The Growth of Industrial Production in the Soviet Union* by G. W. Nutter; Springer-Verlag New York Inc. for use of extracts from *Das Wachstum der Deutschen Wirtschaft seit der Mitte Das 19 Jahrhunderts* by W. G. Hoffman; W. Woodruff for extracts from *Impact of Western Man*.

The editor would also like to thank Andrew Whitelegg for his extensive research for the fourth edition, and to Nancy Webster for her painstaking work on this latest edition.

The publishers have made every effort to trace the copyright-holders but if they have inadvertently overlooked any they will be pleased to make the necessary arrangement at the first opportunity.

WEIGHTS AND MEASURES: CONVERSION RATIOS

The following is not a complete guide to all weights and measures used in Europe during the period covered by this volume. It is simply a list of those conversion ratios used in compiling the tables given here.

1 Imperial ton = 1.016047 metric tons
1 Zugthierlast (Switzerland) = 0.75 metric tons
1 Wiener centner = 0.056 metric tons
1 cantar = 0.056 metric tons
1 Zoll centner (Austria-Hungary) = 0.05 metric tons
1 pund (Denmark) or 1 pond (Netherlands) = 0.05 metric tons
1 Swedish centner (or 100 skalpund) = 0.0425 metric tons
1 skeppund (ores) = 0.253 metric tons
1 skeppund (pig iron) = 0.176 metric tons
1 skeppund (bar iron) = 0.1506 metric tons
1 pood = 0.016388 metric tons
1 tonde (coal) = 0.12 metric tons
1 tonde (butter) = 0.112 metric tons
1 ocque (or oke) = 0.001288 metric tons

1 dessiatine = 1.09 hectares
1 katastraljoch (Austria-Hungary) = 0.575464 hectares
1 tonde (land) = 0.551625 hectares
1 acre = 0.404686 hectares
1 stremma = 0.127 hectares

1 Danish mile = 7.532 kilometres
1 English mile = 1.609344 kilometres
1 verst = 1.067593 kilometres

1 last (Sweden and Netherlands) = 2 register tons
1 last (Finland) = 1.7985 register tons

1 eimer = 1, 767 hectolitres
1 bulk barrel (oil) = 1.636547 hectolitres
1 tunna = 1.45468 hectolitres
1 tonde (corn) = 1.391212 hectolitres
1 tonde (beer) = 1.3139 hectolitres
1 Lower Austrian metze = 0.618048 hectolitres
1 fanega = 0.546 hectolitres
1 Imperial bushel = 0.363677 hectolitres
1 chetvert = 0.2625 hectolitres
1 arroba (wine) = 0.1614 hectolitres
1 arroba (oil) = 0.1256 hectolitres
1 Imperial gallon = 0.0454596 hectolitres

SYMBOLS

··· = not available
- - = less than half the smallest digit used in the table
— = nil

A POPULATION AND VITAL STATISTICS

1.	Population of Countries at Censuses	page 3
2.	Population of Countries by Sex and Age Groups	page 12
3.	Population of Major Districts	page 48
4.	Population of Major Cities	page 74
5.	Mid-Year Population Estimates	page 78
6.	Vital Statistics Rates per 1,000 Population	page 93
7.	Deaths of Infants Under One Year Old Per 1,000 Live Births	page 120
8.	Emigration from Europe by Decades	page 129
9.	Annual Migration Statistics	page 130

The principal modern sources of population data are official censuses and registration records. In Europe, the earliest regular enumeration of national population dates from around the beginning of the period covered in this work. But outside Scandinavia (and some though by no means all the Italian states), systematic census-taking and civil registration of births, deaths, and marriages have been nineteenth- or even twentieth-century phenomena. Historical coverage of the different countries, therefore, varies widely in scope. There is also good reason to believe, unfortunately, that it varies in accuracy. The almost universal tendency of censuses is to under-enumerate, though published results may also have been deliberately inflated on occasion for political purposes. A proportion of vital events similarly escapes the registrar's net. But in most countries these tendencies have almost certainly declined over time, as officials have become more sophisticated, and as the population became more accustomed to procedures and less suspicious of their purpose. However, the increase in the number of town-dwellers living alone in recent decades, and, still more, the development of considerable immigration from poorer lands, may have reversed this process in some countries. Until the mid twentieth century[1] there was no means of knowing either the extent of understatement or its variation over time, so for the most part it is impossible to do more than guess at margins of error in the past. By and large, it seems safe to take all regular censuses after the first two or three in a series as accurate to within five per cent overall.[2] Isolated, sporadic censuses are probably rather less reliable in general.

Some kinds of information elicited in censuses are likely to be less accurate than others. Data about occupations present special difficulties, and these are considered in the next section. But the table in this section showing age-group data probably contains some of the largest margins of error of all. In addition to accidental errors, this information is peculiarly liable to deliberate falsification by respondents. When censuses were taken wholly or partly, or even only in popular belief, in connection with military service obligations, the male age-groups at risk might be seriously understated if the census officials were not particularly skilled. And at all times, vanity may have had some influence on the statistics. A further source of error, especially amongst illiterate people and in times of political disturbance, has been ignorance or incomplete knowledge. In many censuses, in the Balkan countries especially, right up to the interwar period, the number of people enumerated in single years of age was far higher for the ages 60, 70, 80, etc., or even for 65, 75, 85, than for 61, 72, 83, or other 'unrounded' ages. In the absence of birth certificates or other literary evidence, it seems that knowledge of one's exact age had often become only approximate by the later stages of life.

Boundary changes often affect the comparability of national and regional population data over time. But these are an obvious pitfall which few are likely to fall into unaware. A list of changes in national boundaries is given on pp. iii–iv, and changes in regional boundaries are indicated in footnotes. Less obvious, however, are the changes in the limits of the major cities whose populations are given in Table A4. As cities grow in population they generally grow in space, taking in areas which, while not usually uninhabited previously, were clearly not part of a city. This presents no conceptual problem, however, and the general rule adopted here has been to show the population statistics which apply to the city limits of the year to which they refer. However, a problem does arise when suburban areas which become functionally part of a central city remain administratively separate from it.

---

[1] The first occasion when this was possible was in 1950, when the US Bureau of the Census undertook a post-censal sample survey which indicated a net under-enumeration of about 1.4 per cent.

[2] Note, however, that in the case of Norway, the 1801 census is reckoned to be better than any other until 1865, though the other two early censuses (in 1769 and 1815) *were* the least good. [K. Ofstad, 'Population Statistics and Population Registration in Norway', *Population Studies* (1949).]

Wherever such separate areas are of significant size, this has been dealt with by including these areas with the centre as 'greater London', 'greater Paris', and so on.

In addition to periodic censuses, for the last century or more most countries have made annual estimates of their total populations, using primarily the registration statistics for births and deaths. Modern historical demographers have used the data furnished for earlier periods by the clerical records of baptisms and burials in some countries to construct acceptable estimates of population going back before the earliest census report. Much of this work applies, as yet, to areas smaller than the modern state and much is still ongoing. As a result, it is only the estimates for England which can be included here in Table A6, along with the later civil registration series. More national estimates will surely become available in time.

Demographers may find the vital statistics included here to be among the least sophisticated of such series that are available nowadays; but they have the merit, from the historical point of view, of being extant for much longer periods than the more refined measures. Even so, there is a serious question mark over their accuracy in many countries for some time after the their collection was begun. Drake reckons that there was between five and ten per cent under-registration in Norway in the eighteenth century, and that clerical errors may account for part of some of the very sharp fluctuations.[3] Presumably the same applies to Finland and Sweden, which exhibit similar characteristics and where a similar system of registration by the clergy of the state church was in operation. In England and Wales there were serious defects in the first two decades or so of civil registration[4], and O'Grada believes that in Ireland the records are incomplete for at least three or four decades after registration began.[5] On the whole, therefore, it would seem to be wise to assume at least some degree of unreliability in the early years of registration in every country. This applies to the USSR in the interwar period, quite possibly to Poland and Greece, and perhaps to other east European countries as well.

The vital statistics estimates derived for England from church records are, of course, even more speculative in principle, despite the rigorous attempts of the authors to test the robustness of the assumptions which they had to make. However, it seems possible to accept their claim that they are 'tolerably reliable', though if they are to be used for further calculation it is necessary to go back to the source to examine the details of their derivation.[6]

A variety of statistics on overseas migration is available for different countries, though much that is desirable is lacking altogether. Two tables on this subject have been included here. The first, A8, is essentially a work of synthesis, the result of extensive research into intractable material by Professor Woodruff. It is impossible to summarise this with sufficient brevity here; so that though the statistics are broadly accurate, anyone who intends to use them for further calculations should consult the source for details of definitions and methods of estimation. The other table, A9, presents some of the raw data on the subject, derived from national sources. A glance at the notes to the table should be enough to indicate how difficult it is to make comparisons between countries.

[3] M. Drake, 'The Growth of Population in Norway, 1735–1855', *Scandinavian Economic History Review* (1965).

[4] See D.V. Glass, 'A Note on Under-Registration in Britain in the Nineteenth Century', *Population Studies* (1951).

[5] Cormac O'Grada, 'The Population of Ireland 1700–1990: A Survey', *Annales de Demographie Historique* (1979).

[6] E.A. Wrigley & R.S. Schofield, *The Population History of England 1541–1871* (London, 1981), especially pp. 269–284. See also the discussion in B.R. Mitchell, *British Historical Statistics* (Cambridge, 1988), pp. 2–3.

A1 POPULATION OF COUNTRIES AT CENSUSES (in thousands)

Albania[66,67]

Date	Total	M	F
1930	1,003	...	...
1945	1,122	571	552
1950	1,219	626	593
1955	1,391	713	678
1960	1,626	835	791
1989	3,238	1,651	1,587

Austria: Cisleithania[1]

Date	Total	M	F
1818	13,381[2]	...	...
1821	13,964[2]	...	...
1824	14,519[2]	...	...
1827	15,131[2]	7,278[2]	7,854
1830	15,588[2]	7,502[2]	8,086
1834	15,714[2]	7,509[2]	8,205
1837	16,083[2]	7,710[2]	8,373
1840	16,575[2]	7,970[2]	8,606
1843	17,073[2]	8,219[2]	8,854
1846	17,613[2]	8,510[2]	9,104
1851	17,535[2]	8,399[2]	9,136
1857	18,225[2]	8,802[2]	9,422
1869	20,218[2]	9,814[2]	10,403
1880	22,144	10,820	11,325
1890	23,708	11,502	12,206
1900	25,922	12,624	13,298
1910	28,572	14,034	14,538

Austria: Bosnia & Hercegovina

Date	Total	M	F
1879	1,158	608	551
1885	1,360	729	631
1895	1,568	828	740
1910	1,898	995	903

Austria: Republic

Date	Total	M	F
1910	6,648	3,285	3,364
1923[3]	6,535	3,148	3,387
1934[4]	6,760	3,248	3,512
1951[4]	6,934	3,217	3,717
1961[4]	7,074	3,296	3,777
1971[4]	7,492	3,534	3,958
1981	7,555	3,572	3,983
1991	7,595	3,754	4,042
2000	8,110	3,974	4,136

Belgium

Date	Total	M	F
1816	4,166	...	...
1831	4,090[5]	...	...
1846	4,337	2,164	2,174
1856	4,530	2,272	2,258
1866	4,828	2,420	2,408
1880	5,520	2,758	2,762
1890	6,069	3,027	3,042
1900	6,694	3,325	3,369
1910	7,424	3,681	3,743
1920	7,406	3,644	3,761
	[6]	[6]	[6]
1930	8,092	4,007	4,085
1947	8,512	4,200	4,312
1961	9,190	4,497	4,693
1970	9,651	4,722	4,929
1981	9,849	4,810	5,038
1991	9,980	4,876	5,103
2001	10,273	5,034	5,239

Bulgaria

Date	Total	M	F
1881	2,008[7]	1,028[7]	980[7]
1888	3,154	1,605	1,549
1893	3,311	1,691	1,620
1900	3,744	1,910	1,835
1905	4,036	2,057	1,978
1910	4,338[8]	2,207[8]	2,131[8]
1920	4,847	2,421	2,426
1926	5,479	2,743	2,736
1934	6,078	3,054	3,024
1946	7,029	3,517	3,513
1956	7,614	3,799	3,814
1965	8,228	4,114	4,114
1975	8,728	4,358	4,370
1985	8,948	4,430	4,518
1992	8,487	4,171	4,317
2001[72]	8,124	3,981	4,143

Czechoslovakia

Date	Total	M	F
1910	13,599	6,613	6,983
1921	13,612	6,559	7,063
1930	14,730[9]	7,143[9]	7,586[9]
1946/7[10]	12,162	5,908	6,254
1950	12,338	5,997	6,342
1961	13,746	6,705	7,041
1970	14,345	6,989	7,356
1980	15,283	7,441	7,842
1991[68]	15,567	7,580	7,987
2001[73]	10,265	5,030	5,235
2001[74]	5,408	2,650	2,758

Denmark[11]

Date	Total	M	F
1769	798	398	400
1787	842	417	425
1801	929	460	469
1834	1,231	609	622
1840	1,289	636	653
1845	1,357	671	686
1850	1,415	696	719
1855	1,507	746	762
1860	1,608	797	811
1870	1,785	881	904
1880	1,969	967	1,002
1890	2,172	1,059	1,113
1901	2,450	1,193	1,256
1906	2,589	1,258	1,331
1911	2,757	1,338	1,419
1916	2,921	1,416	1,506
1921	3,104	1,511	1,593
	3,268[12]	1,592[12]	1,676[12]
1925	3,435	1,676	1,758
1930	3,551	1,736	1,814
1935	3,706	1,824	1,882
1940	3,844	1,900	1,944
1945	4,045	2,002	2,043
1950	4,281	2,123	2,158
1960	4,585	2,273	2,312
1970	4,938	2,451	2,486
1976	5,073	2,510	2,563
1991	5,124	2,528	2,596
2001	5,350	2,675	2,675

Estonia

Date	Total	M	F
1922	1,107	520	587
1934	1,126	529	597
1991	1,570	734	835
2000	1,369	643	726

See pp. 9–11 for footnotes

A1   Population of Countries at Censuses (in thousands)

Finland

Date	Total	M	F
1750	422	201	221
1760	491	236	255
1770	561	273	288
1775	610	298	312
1780	664	325	338
1785	679	333	346
1790	706	341	365
1795	771	375	396
1800	833	405	428
1805	896	435	460
	——[13]	——[13]	——[13]
1810	863[14]	414[14]	449[14]
1815	1,096	527	569
1820	1,178	567	610
1825	1,259[15]	607[15]	652[15]
1830	1,372	664	708
1835	1,394	675	719
1840	1,446	700	745
1845	1,548	751	796
1850	1,637	796	841
1855	1,689	819	870
1860	1,747	849	898
1865	1,843	899	944
1870	1,769	860	908
1875	1,913	935	978
1880	2,061	1,008	1,053
1890	2,380	1,172	1,209
1900	2,656	1,311	1,345
1910	2,943[16]	1,445[16]	1,499[16]
1920	3,148	1,533	1,617
1930	3,463	1,689	1,774
1940	3,696[17]	1,793[17]	1,903[17]
1950	4,030	1,926	2,104
1960	4,446	2,142	2,304
1970	4,598	2,220	2,378
1980	4,788	2,315	2,473
1985	4,911	2,378	2,533
1990[69]	4,998	2,426	2,572
2001[72]	5,187	2,542	2,645

France[18]

Date	Total	M	F
1801	27,349	13,312	14,037
1806	29,107[19]	14,313[19]	14,795[19]
1821	30,462	14,797	15,665
1831	32,569	15,950	16,619
1836	33,541	16,461	17,080
1841	34,230	16,898	17,319
1846	35,402	17,542	17,858
1851	35,783	17,795	17,988
1856	36,013[20]	17,857[20]	18,155[20]
1861	37,386	18,645	18,741
1866	38,067[21]	19,014[21]	19,053[21]
1872	36,103	17,983	18,120
1876	36,906	18,374	18,532
1881	37,406	18,657	18,749
1886	37,930	18,900	19,030
1891	38,133	18,932	19,201
1896	38,269	18,923	19,346
1901	38,451	18,917	19,534
1906	38,845	19,100	19,745
1911	39,192	19,254	19,938
	——[21]	——[21]	——[21]
1921	38,798	18,445	20,353
1926	40,228	19,310	20,919
1931	41,228	19,912	21,317
1936	41,183	19,797	21,386
1946	39,848	18,878	20,970
	——[22]	——[22]	——[22]
1954	42,781[23]	20,507[23]	22,274
1962	46,500	22,595	23,905
1968	49,655	24,197	25,458
1975	52,599	25,744	26,855
1982	54,273	26,493	27,780
1990	56,615	27,553	29,084
1999	58,620	28,724	29,896

Germany[24]

Date	Total	M	F
1816	22,377	...	...
1828	26,646	...	...
1834	28,237	...	...
1840	30,382	...	...
1852	33,413	...	...
1861	35,567	...	...
1864	37,804[24]	...	...
	39,392		
1871	41,059	20,157	20,907
1880	45,234	22,185	23,049
1890	49,428	24,231	25,198
1900	56,367	27,737	28,630
1910	64,926[25]	32,040[25]	32,886[25]
	58,451	28,824	29,627
1925[26]	63,181	30,583	32,598
1933[26]	66,030[27]	32,086[27]	33,944[27]
1939	69,460	33,912	35,405

East Germany (including East Berlin)

Date	Total	M	F
1939	16,745	8,191	8,555
1946	18,488	7,860	10,629
1950	18,388	8,161	10,277
1964	17,004	7,748	9,255
1971	17,068	7,865	9,203
1981	16,706	7,849	8,857

West Germany (including West Berlin)

Date	Total	M	F
1939	42,998	21,033	21,965
1946	46,560	20,804	25,756
1950[28]	50,787	23,711	27,076
1961	56,115	26,413	29,761
1970	60,651	28,867	31,784
1950	61,566	29,417	32,149

GERMANY

Date	Total	M	F
1990[69]	79,364	38,276	41,088
2001	82,195	40,276	41,919

See pp. 9–11 for footnotes

A1 Population of Countries at Censuses (in thousands)

Greece

Date	Total	M	F
1821	939	...	...
1828	753	...	...
1838	752	...	...
1843	915	...	...
1848	987	...	...
1853	1,036	...	...
1856	1,063	550	513
1861	1,097[29]	567[29]	529[29]
1870	1,458	754	704
1879	1,679	881	799
	——[30]	——[30]	——[30]
1889	2,187	1,134	1,054
1896	2,434[31]	1,267[31]	1,167[31]
1907	2,632[32]	1,325[32]	1,307[32]
1920	5,017	2,495	2,522
1928	6,205	3,076	3,128
1940	7,345[33]	3,658[33]	3,686[33]
1951	7,633	3,722	3,911
1961	8,389	4,091	4,297
1971	8,769	4,287	4,482
1981	9,740	4,780	4,960
1991	10,260	5,056	5,204
2001	10,575	5,182	5,393

Hungary: Transleithania[34]

Date	Total	M	F
1850	13,192[2]	6,520[2]	6,672
1857	14,349	7,379	6,970
1869	15,512	7,848	7,764
1880	15,739	7,800	7,939
1890	17,578	8,783	8,796
1900	19,255	9,582	9,672
1910	20,886	10,345	10,541

Hungary: Trianon Territory

Date	Total	M	F
1910	7,615	3,794	3,821
1920	7,990	3,876	4,114
1930	8,688	4,250	4,438
1941	9,317[35][36]	4,561[35][36]	4,756[35][36]
1949	9,205	4,423	4,781
1960	9,961	4,804	5,157
1970	10,322	5,004	5,318
1980	10,709	5,189	5,521
1990	10,450	5,023	5,427
2001	10,187	4,890	5,297

See pp. 9–11 for footnotes

Iceland

Date	Total	M	F
1769	46	21	25
1801	47	22	26
1840	57	27	30
1850	59	28	31
1860	67	32	35
1870	70	33	37
1880	72	34	38
1890	71	34	37
1901	78	38	41
1910	85	41	44
1920	95	46	49
1930	109	54	55
1940	121	60	61
1950	144	72	72
1960	177	90	88
1970	205	104	101
1980	229	116	114
1990[69]	255	128	127
2001[72]	284	142	142

Ireland[37]

Date	Total	M	F
1821	6,802[2]	3,342[2]	3,460
1831	7,767[2]	3,795[2]	3,973
1841	8,175[2]	4,020[2]	4,156
1851	6,552[2]	3,191[2]	3,362
1861	5,799	2,837	2,962
1871	5,412	2,640	2,773
1881	5,175	2,533	2,642
1891	4,705	2,319	2,386
1901	4,459	2,200	2,259
1911	4,390	2,192	2,198

Northern Ireland

Date	Total	M	F
1926	1,257	608	648
1937	1,280	623	657
1951	1,371	668	703
1961	1,425	694	731
1966	1,485	724	761
1971	1,536	755	781
1981	1,543	763	780
1991	1,573	766	807
2001	1,685	821	864

Republic of Ireland

Date	Total	M	F
1926	2,972	1,507	1,465
1936	2,963	1,520	1,448
1946	2,955	1,494	1,459
1951	2,961	1,507	1,454
1956	2,898	1,463	1,435
1961	2,818	1,417	1,402
1966	2,884	1,449	1,435
1971	2,978	1,496	1,482
1979	3,368	1,693	1,675
1981	3,443	1,729	1,714
1986	3,541	1,770	1,771
1991	3,524	1,759	1,765
1996	3,632	1,816	1,816

A1 Population of Countries at Censuses (in thousands)

Italy[38]

Date	Total	M	F
c 1770	14,689	…	…
c 1795	16,257	…	…
c 1800	17,237	…	…
c 1816	18,381	…	…
c 1825	19,727	…	…
1833	21,212	…	…
1838	21,975	…	…
1844	22,936	…	…
1848	23,617	…	…
1852	24,351	…	…
1858	24,857	…	…
1861	25,017[39]	…	…
1871	26,801	13,472	13,329
1881	28,460	14,265	14,194
1901	32,475	16,155	16,320
1911	34,671	17,022	17,650
1921	36,406[40]	17,940[40]	18,466[40]
	37,974	18,726	19,248
1931	41,177	20,134	21,043
1936	42,919[41]	21,068[41]	21,851[41]
1951	47,159[42]	22,961[42]	24,198[42]
	47,516	23,259	24,257
1961	50,624	24,784	25,840
1971	54,137	20,476	27,661
1981	56,557	27,506	29,051
1991	56,778	27,558	29,220
2001	57,691	28,269	29,422

Latvia

Date	Total	M	F
1925	1,845	860	985
1930	1,900	886	1,014
1935	1,950	912	1,038
1991	2,668	1,242	1,425
2000	2,372	1,091	1,281

Lithuania[43]

Date	Total	M	F
1923	2,029	968	1,061
1991[69]	3,736	1,769	1,967
2001	3,488	1,639	1,849

Luxembourg

Date	Total	M	F
1839	170	…	…
1843	180	…	…
1846	186	…	…
1849	190	…	…
1852	193	…	…
1855	189	…	…
		…	…
1864	203	…	…
1867	200	100	100
1871	198	98	99
1875	205	103	102
1880	210	105	104
1885	213	107	106
1890	211	105	106
1895	218	109	108
1900	236	122	114
1905	246	126	120
1910	260	134	126
1922	261	132	129
1930	300	154	146
1935	297	149	147
1947	291	145	146
1960	315	155	159
1966	335	165	170
1970	340	167	173
1981	365	178	187
1990	378	184	194
2001[72]	444	218	226

Netherlands

Date	Total	M	F
1816[44]	2,047	…	…
1829[45]	2,613	1,278	1,335
1839	2,861	1,401	1,460
1849	3,057	1,499	1,558
1859	3,309	1,629	1,680
1869	3,580	1,764	1,815
1879	4,013	1,983	2,030
1889	4,511	2,228	2,283
1899	5,104	2,521	2,584
1909	5,858	2,899	2,959
1920	6,865	3,410	3,455
1930	7,936	3,943	3,993
1940	8,923	4,454	4,469
1947	9,625	4,791	4,834
1960	11,556	5,754	5,802
1970[66]	13,119	6,550	6,570
1980[66]	14,091	6,994	7097
1991[66]	15,069	7,450	7,620
2001	16,032	8,016	8,016

Norway

Date	Total	M	F
1769	724	343	380
1801	883	423	461
1815	885	…	…
1825	1,051	511	540
1835	1,195	585	609
1845	1,328	652	676
1855	1,490	730	760
1865	1,702	836	866
1875	1,819	889	930
1890	2,001	966	1,035
1900	2,240	1,088	1,152
1910	2,392	1,156	1,236
1920	2,650	1,290	1,359
1930	2,814	1,372	1,442
1946	3,157	1,557	1,600
1950	3,278	1,625	1,653
1960	3,591	1,789	1,802
1970	3,874	1,926	1,948
1980	4,091	2,027	2,064
1990	4,247	2,100	2,148
2001	4,519	2,260	2,260

Poland[46]

Date	Total	M	F
1897/1900[47]	25,106	12,482	12,624
1921	27,177	13,133	14,044
1931	32,107[48]	15,619[48]	16,488[48]
1946	23,930	10,954	12,976
1950	25,008	11,928	13,080
1960	29,776	14,404	15,372
1970	32,642	15,854	16,789
1979	35,061	17,079	17,982
1984	37,026	18,026	19,000
1988	37,879	18,465	19,414
2001[72]	38,653	18,940	19,713

See pp. 9–11 for footnotes

A1   Population of Countries at Censuses (in thousands)

Portugal[49]

Date	Total	M	F
1768	2,410	...	...
1801	2,932	...	...
1821	3,026	...	...
1835	3,062	...	...
1838	3,224	...	...
1841	3,397[50]	...	...
	3,737		
1854	3,844	...	...
1858	3,923	...	...
1861	4,035[49]	...	...
1864	4,188	2,006	2,183
1878	4,551	2,176	2,375
1890	5,060	2,430	2,629
1900	5,423	2,592	2,832
1911	5,958	2,829	3,129
1920	6,087	2,910	3,177
1930	6,826	3,256	3,570
1940	7,722	3,712	4,010
1950	8,381	4,060	4,301
1960	8,889	4,254	4,635
1970	8,663	4,109	4,554
1981	9,883	4,738	5,095
1991	9,853	4,755	5,098
2001	10,231	4,911	5,320

Romania[51]

Date	Total	M	F
1899	5,957	3,027	2,930
1912	7,235[52]	3,656[52]	3,759[52]
1930	18,057[53]	8,887[53]	9,170[53]
1941	16,126	7,989	8,138
1948	15,873	7,672	8,201
1956	17,489	8,503	8,986
1966	19,103	9,351	9,752
1977	21,560	10,626	10,934
1992	22,786	11,207	11,578
2001[72]	22,397	10,975	11,422

Russia/U.S.S.R.[54,70]

Date	Total	M	F
1897[55]	126,367[56]	63,208[56]	63,159[56]
1926	147,028	71,053	75,985
1939	170,467[57]	81,665[57]	88,802[57]
1959	208,827	94,050	114,776
1970	241,720	111,399	130,321
1979	262,436	122,329	140,107
1989	286,731	135,300	151,400
1993[69]	148,146	69,528	78,618
2001[72]	144,837	68,073	76,764

Serbia[58]

Date	Total	M	F
1834	678	...	...
1840	830	...	...
1843	861	...	...
1846	915	...	...
1850	957	...	...
1854	999	...	...
1859	1,078	557	521
1863	1,109	572	537
1866	1,216	627	584
1874	1,354	696	658
1884	1,902[58][59]	973[58][59]	929[58][59]
1890	2,162	1,110	1,052
1895	2,312	1,187	1,126
1900	2,494	1,281	1,212
1905	2,689	1,382	1,306
1910	2,912	1,504	1,408

Spain[60]

Date	Total	M	F
1768/9	9,160	4,534	4,626
1787	10,268	5,109	5,159
1797	10,541	5,220	5,321
1857	15,455	7,664	7,791
1860	15,645	7,741	7,904
1877	16,622	8,126	8,496
1887	17,550	8,601	8,948
1897	18,109	8,779	9,329
1900	18,594	9,072	9,522
1910	19,927	9,674	10,253
1920	21,303	10,316	10,988
1930	23,564	11,498	12,066
1940	25,878	12,414	13,464
1950	27,977	13,470	14,507
1960	30,431	14,763	15,667
1970	33,824	16,505	17,319
1981	37,617	18,460	19,157
1991	38,872	19,036	19,836
2001	39,501	19,355	20,146

Sweden

Date	Total	M	F
1750	1,781	837	944
1760	1,924	912	1,012
1770	2,043	974	1,068
1775	2,021	967	1,054
1780	2,118	1,018	1,101
1785	2,150	1,037	1,113
1790	2,188	1,043	1,145
1795	2,281	1,093	1,188
1800	2,347	1,121	1,227
1805	2,427	1,167	1,261
1810	2,396	1,141	1,255
1815	2,465	1,177	1,288
1820	2,585	1,240	1,345
1825	2,771	1,333	1,438
1830	2,888	1,391	1,497
1835	3,025	1,462	1,564
1840	3,139	1,516	1,622
1845	3,317	1,604	1,713
1850	3,471	1,687	1,784
1855	3,641	1,765	1,876
1860	3,860	1,875	1,985
1870	4,169	2,017	2,152
1890	4,566	2,215	2,351
1890	4,785	2,317	2,468
1900	5,137	2,506	2,630
1910	5,522	2,699	2,824
1915	5,713	2,795	2,918
1920	5,905	2,898	3,006
1925	6,054	2,973	3,081
1930	6,142	3,021	3,121
1935	6,251	2,091	3,160
1940	6,372	3,160	3,211
1945	6,674	3,320	3,354
1950	7,041	3,505	3,535
1955	7,235	3,605	3,630
1960	7,495	3,739	3,757
1965	7,767	3,881	3,887
1970	8,077	4,034	4,043
1980	8,318	4,120	4,198
1985	8,360	4,128	4,232
1990	8,591	4,246	4,347
2001[72]	8,893	4,447	4,447

See pp. 9–11 for footnotes

A1 Population of Countries at Censuses (in thousands)

Switzerland

Date	Total	M	F
1837	2,190	1,085	1,105
1850	2,393	1,182	1,211
1860	2,507	1,235	1,272
1870	2,669	1,305	1,364
1880	2,846	1,395	1,451
1888	2,933[61]	1,426[61]	1,507[61]
	2,918	1,418	1,500
1900	2,315	1,627	1,688
1910	3,753	1,846	1,908
1920	3,880	1,871	2,009
1930	4,006	1,958	2,108
1940	4,266	2,060	2,205
1950	4,715	2,272	2,443
1960	5,429	2,663	2,766
1970	6,270	3,089	3,180
1980	6,366	3,115	3,251
1990[69]	6,712	3,278	3,434
2000	7,180	3,518	3,662

United Kingdom
Great Britain: England & Wales

Date	Total	M	F
1801	8,893	4,255	4,638
1811	10,164	4,874	5,291
1821	12,000	5,850	6,150
1831	13,897	6,771	7,126
1841	15,914	7,778	8,137
1851	17,928	8,781	9,146
1861	20,066	9,776	10,290
1871	22,712	11,059	11,653
1881	25,974	12,640	13,335
1891	29,003	14,060	14,942
1901	32,528	15,729	16,799
1911	36,070	17,446	18,625
1921	37,887	18,075	19,811
1931	39,952	19,133	20,819
1951	43,758	21,016	22,742
1961	46,105	22,304	23,801
1971	48,750	23,683	25,067
1981	49,155	23,873	25,281
1991	49,890	24,183	25,707
2001	52,042	25,327	26,715

Great Britain: Scotland

Date	Total	M	F
1755[63]	1,265	...	...
1801	1,608	739	869
1811	1,806	826	980
1821	2,092	983	1,109
1831	2,364	1,114	1,250
1841	2,620	1,242	1,378
1851	2,889	1,375	1,513
1861	3,062	1,450	1,612
1871	3,360	1,603	1,757
1881	3,736	1,799	1,936
1891	4,026	1,943	2,083
1901	4,472	2,174	2,298
1911	4,761	2,309	2,452
1921	4,882	2,348	2,535
1931	4,843	2,326	2,517
1951	5,096	2,434	2,662
1961	5,179	2,483	2,697
1971	5,229	2,515	2,714
1981	5,131	2,466	2,664
1991	4,998	2,392	2,607
2001	5,062	2,432	2,630

Yugoslavia

Date	Total	M	F
1921	11,985	5,880	6,105
1931	13,934[64]	6,892[64]	7,042[64]
1948	15,772	7,582	8,190
1953	16,937[65]	8,205[65]	8,732[65]
1961	18,549	9,043	9,506
1971	20,523	10,077	10,446
1981	22,425	11,084	11,341
1990[69,71]	23,818	11,780	12,037

Federal Republic of Yugoslavia

Date	Total	M	F
1991	10,496	5,248	5,248
2001[72]	10,645	5,323	5,323

See pp. 9–11 for footnotes

A1 Population of Countries at Censuses (in thousands)

NOTES

1. SOURCES: With the following exceptions all figures are taken from the official publications noted on p. xv:- Albania (1930), Estonia, Latvia, and Lithania—League of Nations, *Statistical Yearbook*; Finland (1775–1875) and Sweden (years ending in 5 to 1855)—J. Bertillon, *Statistique Internationale des Rencensements de la Population...* (Paris, 1899); Luxembourg (to 1852), Serbia (to 1859), and Switzerland (1837)—*Annuaire Internationale de Statistique* (The Hague, 1916); Scotland (1755)—J.G. Kyd, *Scottish Population Statistics* (Edinburgh, 1952).

2. A few of the figures given are official estimates rather than the results of complete censuses, but all were published as being comparable to the latter. The sole exception to this is Germany, for which estimates have been made for the period up to 1864 for the dates of the Prussian censuses. These are made on the basis of censuses in the various component states in years which were not always the same as that of the Prussian censuses, especially before 1834. This has been done because official published estimates include areas which were not incorporated in German states up to 1864.

3. No census was ever taken for Montenegro. Bertillon, *op cit.* above, and the *Annuaire Internationale de Statistique* (1916) give the following estimates of total population (in thousands):-

1857:120   1864:146   1897:228   1910:250.

The country was enlarged in 1878 by the acquisition of territory from Turkey.

4. Unless otherwise stated in footnotes, statistics are of population actually present.

FOOTNOTES

[1] The Italian provinces are not included.
[2] Civil population only.
[3] The census in Burgenland was on a different date from the other provinces.
[4] Resident population.
[5] In 1839 areas with a population of 326 thousand were ceded to the Netherlands.
[6] Between 1920 and 1930 three cantons were acquired from Germany.
[7] Between 1881 and 1888 Eastern Roumelia was added.
[8] Between 1910 and 1920 there were several boundary changes, involving the loss of Southern Dobrudja to Romania, and the gain of rather larger territories from Turkey.
[9] Between 1930 and 1946/7 Sub-Carpathian Russia (Ruthenia) and a few villages in Slovakia were ceded to the U.S.S.R.
[10] The censuses were on 4 October 1946 in Slovakia and 22 May 1947 in the Czech lands.
[11] The Duchies of Schleswig, Holstein, and Lauenburg are not included. Their total combined populations were as follows:-

1840: 849   1945: 889   1855: 969   1860: 1,004   1864: 1,010.

[12] From 1921 (2nd line) the part of Schleswig acquired from Germany in that year is included.
[13] In 1809 certain parishes in the Tornie River basin, with a population of 12 thousand, were added.
[14] In 1811 Viipuri province, with a population of 185 thousand, was added.
[15] The Greek Orthodox population was included for the first time in 1830, when it numbered 25 thousand.
[16] In 1820 Petsamo, with a population of 1.5 thousand, was added.
[17] Between 1940 and 1950 Viipuri and Petsamo were ceded to the U.S.S.R, but the population was moved to the remaining territory.
[18] Resident population. Estimates in the eighteenth century are as follows:-

1700: 19,669   1762: 21,769   1784: 24,800.

[19] In 1814/5 Philippeville and part of Wissembourg was excluded, and Gex was included. The total population in 1806 of the 1815 territory was 29,053 thousand.
[20] In 1860 Savoy and Nice were acquired from Italy. Their population in 1848 was 702 thousand.
[21] From 1871 to 1918 most of Alsace and Lorraine was incorporated in Germany and is not included here.
[22] In 1947 the villages of Tende and Brigue were acquired from Italy.
[23] Military personnel stationed overseas are subsequently included.
[24] The figures to 1864 (1st line) relate to the territories composing the German Empire in 1870, exclusive of areas ceded by Austria, Denmark, and France in 1860–1871. These latter are included from 1864 (2nd line).
[25] From 1910 (2nd line) the territories ceded after the First World War are excluded.
[26] The census in Saarland were in July 1937 and June 1935 respectively.
[27] It has been impossible to exclude a small part of Austria, incorporated in 1938, from the 1939 statistics, but all other territorial acquisitions in 1937–39 have been excluded.
[28] The census in Saarland was on a different date from the rest of Germany.
[29] In 1864 the Ionian Islands were acquired from Britain.
[30] In 1881 Thessaly and Arta were acquired from Turkey. Their population was 294 thousand.
[31] Between 1896 and 1907 a small strip of Thessaly was ceded to Turkey.
[32] Between 1907 and 1920 Epiros, Thrace, and part of Macedonia were acquired from Turkey.
[33] In 1949 the Dodecanese Islands were acquired from Italy. Their population in 1951 was 121 thousand.
[34] Including Croatia-Slavonia. Earlier figures are given by J. Kovacsis, "Situation Demographique de la Hongrie á la Fin du XVII Sicle, 1787–1815", *Annales de Démographie Historique* (1965) as follows (in thousands):-

1787: 7,117   1793: 7,141   1804: 7,961   1817: 8,314.

A1   Population of Countries at Censuses (in thousands)

Official estimates for 1843 and 1846 were 13,854 thousand and 14,542 thousand respectively. These appear to be too high. A. Fynes, *Statistik der Königreichs Ungarn* (Pesth, 1843) gives 12,880 for 1840.

[35] The population of Greater Hungary in 1941 was 13,644 thousand.

[36] In 1947 the Bratislava Bridgehead was ceded to Czechoslovakia.

[37] Earlier estimates are given by K.H. Connell, *The Population of Ireland 1750–1845* (Oxford, 1950) as follows (in thousands):-

1754: 3,191	1772: 3,584	1781: 4,048	1788: 4,389
1767: 3,480	1777: 3,740	1785: 4,019	1790: 4,591 1791: 4,753

[38] Statistics to 1861 are estimates made on the basis of censuses at different dates (but in the same year from 1833) in the various states which constituted the Kingdom of Italy in 1871.

[39] The census of 1861 gave the population in the area ruled by Italy at that time as follows (in thousands):-

Total   21,777;   Males   10,897;   Females   10,880

[40] From 1921 (2nd line) the territories acquired after the First World War are included.

[41] In 1945–7 territories in Istria and Piedmont were ceded to Yugoslavia and France.

[42] Subsequent statistics are of resident population.

[43] Excluding Memel.

[44] Excluding the Belgian provinces.

[45] Excluding the Belgian provinces, but including the part of Limburg ceded by Belgium in 1839.

[46] Earlier estimates for Russian Poland are given in J. Bertillon, *op.cit.* above, as follows (in thousands):-

	Total	Males	Females		Total	Males	Females
1815	2,600	...	...	1863	4,840	...	...
1823	3,702	...	...	1867	5,706	2,760	2,946
1835	4,060	...	...	1870	6,026	2,931	3,096
1854	4,852	...	...	1885	7,960	...	...
1858	4,764	2,298	2,466				

[47] Based on Austrian, German, and Russian data. The 1897 figures for Russian Poland are as follows (in thousands):-

Total   9,456;   Males   4,764;   Females   4,692.

[48] In 1945 Poland ceded large areas to the U.S.S.R. and acquired other large areas from Germany. In both cases much of the population was moved to the remaining territory of the ceding country.

[49] Statistics to 1861 are of resident population.

[50] To 1841 (1st line) the Azores and Maderia are not included.

[51] Earlier estimates, based on partial censuses, are available as follows (in thousands):-

	Total	Males	Females		Total	Males	Females
1844	3,578	...	...	1889	5,038	2,565	2,473
1859	3,865	...	...	1894	5,406	2,739	2,667

Part of Bessarabia was acquired from Russia in 1856, but returned in 1878, when Northern Dobrudja was acquired from Turkey.

[52] As a result of the Balkan Wars and the first World War, Romania acquired Southern Dobrudja, Bessarabia, Bukovina, Transylvania, part of the Banat, and parts of Hungary proper. The population of these areas in 1915 was estimated at 4,772 thousand.

[53] Between 1939 and 1941 there were several boundary changes. The statistics for 1941 given here relate to the territory established after the Second World War, the main changes from 1930 being the cession of Bessarabia and much of Bukovina to the U.S.S.R., and of Southern Dobrudja to Bulgaria.

[54] The statistics for 1897 are for the Russian Empire excluding Finland. Later statistics are for the U.S.S.R. Other official estimates are available as follows (in thousands):-

	Total	Males	Females	
1851	65,077	32,212	32,865	
1858	67,299	32,839	34,469	
1885	106,611	52,996	32,779	(164 thousand not distinguished by sex).

P.A. Khromov, *Economic Development of Russia in the 19th and 20th Centuries, 1800–1917* (Moscow, 1950) gives the following estimates at decennial intervals (in thousands):-

1800: 35,500	1830: 56,100	1860: 74,100	1890: 117,800
1810: 40,700	1840: 62,400	1870: 84,500	1900: 132,900
1820: 48,600	1850: 68,500	1880: 97,700	1910: 160,700.

[55] Statistics for the 50 Provinces of European Russia (i.e. excluding Finland, Poland, and the Caucasus) are as follows (in thousands):-

Total   94,215;   Males   46,448;   Females   47,767.

[56] The population of the areas of the former Empire excluded from the U.S.S.R. was 21,734 thousand in 1897 (excluding Finland).

A1 Population of Countries at Censuses (in thousands)

[57] The population of areas incorporated in the U.S.S.R. between 1939 and 1945 was approximately 22,200 thousand in 1939.
[58] Resident population to 1884.
[59] In 1878 Vranje, Nis, Pirot, and Toplica were acquired from Turkey. Their population was 303 thousand.
[60] Including the Canary Islands. A. Moreau de Jonnés, Statistique de l'Espagne (Paris, 1834) gives the following estimates (in thousands):-

1803: 10,351   1826: 13,953   1834: 14,660.

[61] From 1888 (2nd line) the statistics are of resident population.
[62] The Channel Islands and the Isle of Man are not included.
[63] Alexander Webster's census.
[64] Territories in Slovenia and Croatia, and the town of Zara (Zadar) were acquired from Italy in 1945.
[65] In 1954 the final boundary settlement with Italy added certain territories in the Trieste area.
[66] These are not census figures but estimates at 31 December.
[67] Estimated population in 1970: Males 1,097, Females 1,039, Total 2,136 thousand.
[68] Czech Republic 1993: Males 5017, Females 5313, Total 10,331; Slovakia 1991: Males 2574, Females 2700, Total 5274.
[69] Non-census Figures.
[70] Figures for ex-U.S.S.R. are as follows (except Latvia, Lithvania and Estonia):

		Total[69]	Male[69]	Female[69]
Armenia	1992	3,685	1,786	1,899
Azerbaijan	1989	7,021	3,423	3,597
Belarus	1992	10,265	4,819	5,446
Georgia	1989	5,401	2,562	2,839
Kazakhstan	1991	16,721	8,116	8,605
Kyrgistan	1992	4,452	2,183	2,268
Moldova	1992	4,351	2,076	2,275
Tajikistan	1989	5,092	2,530	2,562
Turkmenistan	1989	3,522	1,735	1,787
Uzbeckistan	1989	19,810	9,784	10,025
Ukraine	1992	51,802	24,004	27,797

[71] Figures for the former Yugoslavia are as follows:

		Total[69]	Male[69]	Female[69]
Bosnia-Hercegovena	1991	4,366	…	…
Croatia	1991	4,784	2,318	2,465
Macedonia	1992	4,351	2,076	2,274
Slovenia	1993	1,990	965	1,025
Yugoslavia	1991	10,394	…	…

[72] Estimates.
[73] Estimates for Czech Republic.
[74] Estimates for Slovak Republic.

A2 POPULATION OF COUNTRIES BY SEX AND AGE GROUPS (in thousands)

Key:- M = Males F = Females

ALBANIA

	1945		1950		1955		1960	
	M	F	M	F	M	F	M	F
0–4	88	75	91	84	115	107	148	138
5–9	84	71	81	72	88	81	...	...
10–14	69	58	76	66	80	70	...	...
15–19	47	50	64	54	76	65	...	71
20–24	30	40	56	48	63	54	...	65
25–29	35	36	41	41	55	48	...	54
30–34	30	33	38	36	40	40	...	48
35–39	34	34	35	33	37	36	...	40
40–44	26	27	30	31	34	33	...	35
45–49	28	27	24	23	29	30	...	32
50–54	...	...	23	24	22	22	...	29
55–59	...	...	15	18	20	23	...	22
60–64	...	...	16	19	14	18	...	...
65–69	...	...	13	15	14	16	...	...
70–74	99	101	9	11	10	13	...	...
75–79	...	...	6	7	7	9	...	...
80 & over	...	...	7	9	7	10	...	...
Unknown	...	...	1	1	3	4	...	2

A2 Population of Countries by Sex and Age Groups (in thousands)

AUSTRIA

1. Austrian provinces of the Hapsburg Empire[1]

	1869[2]		1880		1890		1900		1910	
	M	F	M	F	M	F	M	F	M	F
0–4	1,323	1,335	1,449	1,466	1,528	1,544	1,708	1,706	2,106	2,094
5–9	1,096	1,116	1,209	1,213	1,321	1,312	1,464	1,445	1,660	1,663
10–14	1,019	1,009	1,090	1,102	1,222	1,234	1,328	1,347	1,521	1,536
15–19	916	974	1,021	1,065	1,110	1,159	1,219	1,274	1,287	1,359
20–24	719	887	951	994	1,004	1,047	1,133	1,152	1,150	1,181
25–29	783	870	801	843	892	936	975	1,003	998	1,067
30–34	707	762	742	791	826	872	870	912	928	976
35–39	642	698	699	737	705	733	791	809	848	880
40–44	557	616	642	693	656	698	740	767	755	776
45–49	545	590	538	577	602	637	609	634	691	729
50–54	463	477	465	533	527	584	556	606	594	624
55–59	375	391	399	441	412	451	474	507	494	541
60–64	269	276	342	371	332	389	387	436	380	418
65–69	207	211	228	237	248	278	266	300	296	337
70–74	108	103	138	147	174	191	178	210	180	207
75–79	57	58	71	73	85	91	97	116	99	118
80 & over	28	29	36	40	45	51	61	75	47	62
Unknown	…	…	…	…	…	…	…	…	…	…

Republic of Austria

	1923[3]		1934		1951		1961		1971		1981		1991	
	M	F	M	F	M	F	M	F	M	F	M	F	M	F
0–4	281	275	237	231	271	259	298	285	304	289	221	210	232	219
5–9	226	225	273	266	261	252	249	239	329	314	244	235	236	225
10–14	315	312	299	292	276	267	263	251	300	286	307	293	232	219
15–19	318	316	196	196	224	216	263	254	260	252	334	324	262	246
20–24	302	311	293	296	244	243	265	252	268	260	305	302	333	312
25–29	249	289	294	300	224	294	207	202	246	241	259	259	351	338
30–34	222	263	288	298	159	213	229	232	254	249	268	261	313	309
35–39	216	251	237	278	203	260	211	282	205	202	245	241	261	262
40–44	207	233	203	247	242	295	147	200	225	230	254	248	263	260
45–49	195	215	196	238	254	287	194	254	204	277	201	200	240	243
50–54	169	180	184	214	227	267	224	281	142	198	214	224	246	249
55–59	145	156	168	197	177	233	226	267	175	239	186	265	184	195
60–64	117	131	136	156	149	201	186	241	189	258	123	185	187	214
65–69	86	100	104	122	124	168	132	199	169	233	138	212	152	242
70–74			72	88	92	128	96	153	117	188	127	212	93	163
75–79	101	129	30	52	56	80	63	104	66	129	88	162	82	158
80 & over			23	33	34	51	46	81	49	109	61	149	93	208
Unknown			5	7	2	2	…	…	…	…	…	…	…	…

see p. 45 for footnotes

A2   Population of Countries by Sex and Age Groups (in thousands)

BELGIUM

	1846 M	1846 F	1856 M	1856 F	1866 M	1866 F	1880 M	1880 F	1890 M	1890 F	1900 M	1900 F
0-4	254	251	245	244	291	289	344	339	353	351	394	389
5-9	240	234	224	221	254	251	309	305	330	327	347	345
10-14	217	207	222	216	223	221	279	274	316	313	325	323
15-19	197	193	217	210	214	210	256	252	301	296	324	321
20-24	198	196	201	192	204	203	232	231	279	264	305	301
25-29	165	162	179	173	190	186	196	194	231	230	276	275
30-34	151	150	170	166	169	166	175	176	205	207	242	240
35-39	144	141	151	147	158	149	175	173	175	175	211	211
40-44	134	127	138	136	147	142	159	159	156	158	186	189
45-49	128	123	126	124	127	124	138	137	154	156	166	173
50-54	91	100	116	111	116	116	127	126	136	139	135	142
55-59	65	83	101	99	100	101	112	114	113	116	128	136
60-64	61	72	68	75	88	87	90	94	97	102	106	114
65-69	49	56	46	59	71	72	69	75	78	86	80	88
70-74	34	38	33	41	38	45	50	56	53	60	57	65
75-79	21	24	21	25	20	28	31	34	31	37	35	42
80 & over	15	18	13	17	13	19	18	23	20	26	20	27
Unknown	...	...	...	...	...	...	...	...	...	...	...	...

	1910 M	1910 F	1920 M	1920 F	1930[4] M	1930[4] F	1947 M	1947 F	1961 M	1961 F	1970 M	1970 F	1981 M	1981 F
0-4	382	378	257	254	336	332	327	314	392	373	364	347	312	298
5-9	384	381	320	318	349	343	268	262	371	355	403	386	330	314
10-14	372	370	349	347	252	248	294	288	357	343	395	378	368	351
15-19	344	343	364	363	326	323	328	323	308	297	371	357	406	389
20-24	317	315	342	345	357	346	348	332	277	275	369	354	404	387
25-29	305	302	292	308	366	354	308	296	301	301	294	283	382	365
30-34	282	281	271	282	336	336	266	260	327	326	299	293	372	356
35-39	258	257	267	271	286	301	325	322	334	334	316	314	294	285
40-44	225	226	250	254	263	273	330	331	260	263	324	325	288	287
45-49	193	196	228	232	255	261	313	322	274	279	324	331	308	306
50-54	156	160	195	201	234	241	265	291	295	309	221	290	305	314
55-59	132	143	160	170	204	213	221	249	284	307	261	282	294	314
60-64	107	120	128	143	165	176	198	223	243	282	249	286	192	217
65-69	92	105	90	107	123	138	166	191	182	234	214	278	200	249
70-74	64	75	62	77	83	100	126	150	132	179	153	217	164	236
75-79	36	45	39	51	44	58	73	93	91	127	92	148	111	188
80 & over	23	32	22	32	27	41	44	58	70	108	74	133	85	183
Unknown	...	...	4	3	...	...	...	...	...	...	...	...	...	...

	1991 M	1991 F	1998 M	1998 F
0-4	306	291	309	295
5-9	307	292	313	298
10-14	311	297	307	293
15-19	337	323	315	303
20-24	375	360	337	328
25-29	411	395	377	364
30-34	399	386	413	399
35-39	372	359	400	389
40-44	358	345	371	361
45-49	275	271	357	348
50-54	278	283	273	272
55-59	284	298	266	276
60-64	266	294	263	285
65-69	236	285	238	280
70-74	128	176	198	262
75-79	118	194	102	158
80 & over	113	245	115	271
Unknown	...	...		

See p. 45 for footnotes

A2 Population of Countries by Sex and Age Groups (in thousands)

BULGARIA

	1881[5] M	F	1888 M	F	1892 M	F	1900 M	F	1905 M	F	1910 M	F	1920[16] M	F
0–4	147	141	274	263	246	239	276	270	295	290	314	307	253	243
5–9	184	172	217	209	259	251	247	245	269	264	294	288	315	303
10–14	109	104	178	164	198	186	238	229	239	232	267	255	330	312
15–19	64	87	130	135	146	142	208	202	209	207	211	212	271	268
20–24	68	66	83	94	109	111	137	132	182	176	182	185	213	221
25–29	83	90	89	99	100	105	121	123	134	133	177	173	165	178
30–34	65	61	81	96	85	97	109	110	114	114	128	122	138	163
35–39	80	69	108	101	104	94	108	94	118	101	119	106	151	160
40–44	54	37	95	86	85	83	82	85	85	86	94	92	108	117
45–49	48	39	91	67	85	68	82	71	81	75	85	78	95	96
50–54	24	20	61	56	68	63	66	73	65	77	66	79	87	92
55–59	30	32	48	39	54	42	68	53	84	62	80	64	83	91
60–64	19	16	45	43	53	48	64	58	67	63	68	64	67	70
65–69	22	20	29	25	30	24	38	28	45	33	46	37	51	45
70–74	10	8	28	29	28	27	31	29	34	31	37	33	41	41
75–79	11	11	15	13	13	11	12	10	15	13	17	13	21	18
80 & over	10	8	28	29	27	26	22	22	22	22	23	22	28	28
Unknown	...	...	3	2	2	2	...	...	...	...	...	...	1	1

	1926 M	F	1934 M	F	1946 M	F	1956 M	F	1965 M	F	1975 M	F	1985 M	F	1992 M	F
0–4	397	385	364	350	338	324	350	336	322	306	343	326	291	275	256	243
5–9	290	278	367	353	307	295	362	348	336	321	321	304	325	312	281	268
10–14	290	274	370	355	355	341	319	308	346	331	315	291	342	321	309	292
15–19	307	297	225	218	354	342	288	282	358	346	328	314	307	292	324	312
20–24	263	266	290	283	367	363	327	326	294	290	333	329	299	287	302	289
25–29	221	225	272	265	249	249	327	321	288	285	329	326	303	302	272	267
30–34	169	175	236	232	258	256	339	338	328	322	285	285	323	320	288	286
35–39	143	162	190	192	271	261	232	231	331	325	289	290	347	346	297	301
40–44	144	154	144	154	244	237	243	239	325	325	323	326	286	286	311	316
45–49	113	118	137	154	196	192	253	243	197	198	323	319	274	281	275	283
50–54	84	97	129	135	146	150	224	218	250	243	313	323	313	320	242	254
55–59	97	85	94	197	114	147	171	177	234	237	182	183	306	307	264	283
60–64	76	73	76	80	125	139	123	139	188	193	224	234	275	293	249	274
65–69	56	54	63	59	82	91	90	116	137	152	189	207	141	166	223	264
70–74	41	42	46	46	49	57	79	97	81	100	133	152	156	176	138	174
75–79	25	23	25	24	33	35	43	53	53	76	73	92	99	127	84	113
80 & over	28	28	27	27	30	33	32	40	47	63	54	74	65	95	80	121
Unknown	...	...	1	1	...	...	...	...	...	...	...	...	...	...	...	...

see p. 45 for footnotes

A2   Population of Countries by Sex and Age Groups (in thousands)

CZECHOSLOVAKIA

	1921 M	1921 F	1930 M	1930 F	1946/7[7] M	1946/7[7] F	1950 M	1950 F	1961 M	1961 F	1970 M	1970 F	1980 M	1980 F	1990[36] M	1990[36] F
0–4	526	511	713	697	582	562	640	616	587	560	548	522	689	658	544	520
5–9	698	693	769	753	471	458	522	506	665	636	566	539	665	636	585	559
10–14	784	777	476	465	446	436	429	420	661	635	584	556	545	521	692	662
15–19	733	746	684	684	512	504	471	464	538	523	659	630	561	535	652	624
20–24	645	681	737	731	525	544	489	499	442	432	639	616	578	552	542	519
25–29	494	568	669	683	410	422	507	533	448	445	508	502	644	624	554	530
30–34	422	494	574	624	393	413	289	301	481	491	417	418	620	606	577	556
35–39	394	453	454	525	505	519	485	502	501	527	433	439	493	494	632	619
40–44	367	414	391	460	466	484	480	494	309	327	459	479	402	411	594	591
45–49	348	384	360	416	414	446	439	460	427	450	474	512	413	430	467	482
50–54	315	345	327	378	316	373	352	401	457	482	278	303	425	463	368	396
55–59	261	286	297	336	249	303	261	319	394	432	393	434	418	483	367	413
60–64	220	258	241	277	209	261	213	271	305	374	382	438	224	275	347	426
65–69	158	189	179	211	165	207	168	218	204	285	289	369	296	378	304	419
70–74	103	132	127	160	120	155	122	161	136	203	189	287	273	341	141	212
75–79	55	71	70	93	73	94	77	102	86	134	99	177	135	234	149	254
80 & over	31	45	39	60	44	64	48	69	59	98	66	132	82	191	110	251
unknown	6	7	7	9	8	9	4	5	…	…	4	4	12	10	…	…

DENMARK[8]

	1801 M	1801 F	1834 M	1834 F	1840 M	1840 F	1850 M	1850 F	1860 M	1860 F
0–4	107	107	143	141	80	79	87	86	106	104
5–9					67	66	78	76	89	87
10–14	80	81	130	127	65	64	71	69	77	76
15–19					67	66	64	63	73	72
20–24	73	77	99	100	59	61	55	63	66	69
25–29					49	50	58	63	60	61
30–34	62	61	82	82	42	43	52	53	55	56
35–39					44	43	45	45	56	56
40–44	54	53	58	62	35	35	39	39	48	48
45–49					31	33	38	39	39	40
50–54	42	42	47	51	24	26	30	31	33	35
55–59					22	24	24	26	31	32
60–64	27	30	29	34	18	21	18	21	22	24
65–69					13	16	15	18	16	20
70–74	11	13	13	16	9	11	10	12	10	13
75–79					5	7	6	7	6	8
80 & over	2	4	3	5	3	5	4	5	4	6
unknown	…	…	…	…	…	…	…	…	…	…

See p. 45 for footnotes

A2 Population of Countries by Sex and Age Groups (in thousands)

DENMARK (Cont'd)

	1870 M	1870 F	1880 M	1880 F	1890 M	1890 F	1901 M	1901 F	1911 M	1911 F
0–4	112	110	128	125	140	138	154	152	168	165
5–9	97	94	108	106	127	124	136	134	153	150
10–14	92	91	100	98	115	112	128	126	145	143
15–19	83	82	89	88	98	97	119	118	127	127
20–24	70	74	81	87	80	90	100	106	108	119
25–29	65	68	71	76	71	81	85	92	99	110
30–34	58	62	61	66	70	78	75	83	92	100
35–39	56	57	57	61	64	68	67	74	80	86
40–44	51	52	52	55	54	59	66	73	70	77
45–49	50	51	48	49	52	54	57	62	61	69
50–54	42	43	43	45	46	49	50	55	59	66
55–59	33	34	41	43	39	42	43	48	50	55
60–64	25	29	33	36	34	37	37	41	41	47
65–69	21	24	23	27	30	34	29	34	33	38
70–74	13	16	15	19	20	24	21	24	24	29
75–79	8	10	10	13	11	14	14	18	15	19
80 & over	4	7	6	8	7	10	9	13	10	15
unknown	...	...	1	1	1	1	3	3	5	5

	1921[9] M	1921[9] F	1930 M	1930 F	1940 M	1940 F	1950 M	1950 F	1960 M	1960 F	1970 M	1970 F	1981 M	1981 F	1990 M	1990 F	1998 M	1998 F
0–4	173	169	157	154	162	157	214	204	202	193	200	190	157	150	149	142	177	167
5–9	169	167	169	165	150	146	201	193	189	180	200	191	186	179	137	131	169	160
10–14	170	168	166	162	155	151	160	155	190	181	188	179	197	187	162	155	146	139
15–19	156	156	164	164	167	164	148	144	211	201	191	181	205	195	188	180	149	143
20–24	137	148	156	162	160	161	148	148	194	187	215	203	190	182	203	193	179	174
25–29	119	130	140	150	161	162	157	160	153	150	190	180	191	182	206	195	195	188
30–34	109	119	129	141	157	160	155	157	139	140	153	148	208	199	190	181	219	208
35–39	102	110	115	124	142	147	156	158	141	144	140	140	197	188	188	181	197	189
40–44	93	99	104	113	129	137	152	155	151	156	142	143	153	149	207	200	189	183
45–49	80	84	96	103	112	119	136	142	148	151	151	155	136	137	185	179	187	183
50–54	68	75	87	92	99	106	121	130	147	151	142	146	134	138	143	143	206	201
55–59	57	64	72	76	88	94	103	111	137	145	141	147	137	145	125	129	153	153
60–64	52	60	59	65	76	80	87	95	115	128	126	138	126	137	118	128	123	129
65–69	40	47	45	52	58	62	72	79	93	109	100	118	112	130	111	130	103	115
70–74	29	35	36	42	40	46	55	59	69	84	74	95	90	116	89	113	89	110
75–79	19	22	22	26			34	38	46	57	49	66	58	88	67	99	68	98
80 & over	13	18	15	20			24	29	38	49	41	59	52	94	63	128	68	139
unknown	5	4	4	4	...	...	...	...	...	...	...	...	...	...	...	...	...	...

See p. 45 for footnotes

A2   Population of Countries by Sex and Age Groups (in thousands)

FINLAND

	1751 M	1751 F	1775 M	1775 F	1800 M	1800 F	1825 M	1825 F
0-9	57	59	82	83	110	110	159	161
10-19	42	43	64	63	78	81	113	116
20-29	35	38	49	52	68	72	107	113
30-39	22	23	37	39	55	60	85	90
40-49	18	21	30	33	42	46	65	73
50-59	15	18	18	20	27	31	44	52
60-69	9	13	11	13	16	19	24	32
70-79	5	7	5	7	7	8	8	12
80 & over	2	3	1	2	1	2	1	2
unknown	…	…	…	…	…	…	…	…

	1850 M	1850 F	1865 M	1865 F	1870 M	1870 F	1880 M	1880 F	1890 M	1890 F	1900 M	1900 F
0-4	114	114	133	131	112	111	146	143	163	161	178	174
5-9	90	91	99	98	98	98	120	120	139	138	150	148
10-14	77	79	92	92	90	89	92	92	126	124	144	142
15-19	71	73	85	86	85	87	96	96	115	113	133	130
20-24	72	74	79	82	78	81	87	87	88	88	120	118
25-29	68	69	68	70	73	76	82	83	90	91	108	107
30-34	60	62	60	64	62	65	72	75	79	80	82	82
35-39	50	52	59	63	53	57	67	71	75	76	83	84
40-44	40	43	54	58	52	56	56	59	65	69	72	74
45-49	40	44	46	50	45	49	46	50	60	64	67	70
50-54	36	40	37	40	37	42	44	49	48	53	57	62
55-59	29	33	27	32	27	32	37	43	38	44	50	56
60-64	19	24	25	30	19	23	27	34	33	40	37	43
65-69	14	19	18	23	15	19	18	23	25	31	27	33
70-74	9	13	11	15	9	13	9	13	15	20	19	25
75-79	4	7	4	7	4	7	5	8	7	10	11	15
80 & over	2	4	2	4	2	3	3	5	3	5	5	8
unknown	…	…	…	…	…	…	…	…	…	…	…	…

	1910 M	1910 F	1920 M	1920 F	1930 M	1930 F	1940 M	1940 F	1950 M	1950 F	1960 M	1960 F	1970 M	1970 F	1980 M	1980 F	1990 M	1990 F
0-4	202	197	177	171	171	165	172	166	257	246	208	199	173	166	163	156	1,721	1,830
5-9	176	172	181	175	183	177	161	156	193	184	224	215	194	187	154	147	1,956	1,863
10-14	161	158	165	159	188	183	173	168	167	162	251	241	203	195	176	169	1,925	1,821
15-19	143	140	179	172	167	164	176	171	158	154	189	183	216	205	194	186	2,132	2,037
20-24	137	135	179	175	144	148	153	154	165	162	159	153	228	217	195	186	2,131	2,070
25-29	125	123	155	155	127	130	158	162	148	161	148	141	169	162	207	196	2,147	2,130
30-34	112	111	134	139	122	124	158	162	124	144	155	153	146	142	229	215	2,102	2,112
35-39	100	99	117	122	112	114	134	141	135	152	140	146	139	136	170	162	2,112	2,116
40-44	76	76	112	117	99	102	113	125	137	152	117	139	146	148	144	142	2,196	2,145
45-49	75	77	101	105	88	91	94	106	115	131	126	147	130	149	134	134	1,508	1,465
50-54	63	67	87	93	64	68	82	96	94	114	125	146	106	132	137	144	1,434	1,432
55-59	56	61	72	81	61	68	69	84	74	93	100	122	109	138	116	143	1,460	1,533
60-64	44	52	50	58	48	56	56	72	59	82	75	103	101	133	88	124	1,373	1,537
65-69	35	43	42	53	38	47	42	58	43	66	53	78	72	105	82	124	1,203	1,484
70-74	22	29	28	39	25	33	25	37	29	49	36	60	46	79	64	109	665	888
75-79	12	17	18	26	15	21	16	26	17	31	20	39	25	48	36	73	625	1,009
80 & over	8	12	13	19	9	14	12	20	10	21	12	28	16	?	?	61	663	1,508
unknown	…	…	…	…	…	…	…	…	1	1	4	…	…	…	…	…	…	…

A2 Population of Countries by Sex and Age Groups (in thousands)

FRANCE

	1851 M	1851 F	1856 M	1856 F	1861[10] M	1861[10] F	1866 M	1866 F	1872[11] M	1872[11] F
0–4	1,684	1,640	1,749	1,700	1,830	1,790	1884	1,836	1,698	1,656
5–9	1,678	1,620	1,666	1,621	1,654	1,626	1,700	1,659	1,660	1,610
10–14	1,604	1,545	1,621	1,559	1,644	1,598	1,614	1,567	1,599	1,544
15–19	1,595	1,555	1,543	1,532	1,637	1,618	1,627	1,608	1,531	1,518
20–24	1,455	1,524	1,358	1,552	1,503	1,577	1,547	1,598	1,511	1,664
25–29	1,436	1,434	1,419	1,489	1,463	1,474	1,495	1,498	1,292	1,314
30–34	1,354	1,353	1,370	1,357	1,401	1,372	1,398	1,389	1,278	1,266
35–39	1,296	1,277	1,320	1,291	1,340	1,312	1,356	1,333	1,249	1,238
40–44	1,186	1,175	1,214	1,181	1,250	1,225	1,253	1,237	1,170	1,161
45–49	1,055	1,045	1,091	1,083	1,155	1,145	1,176	1,177	1,098	1,099
50–54	1,041	1,029	958	955	1,009	1,002	1,041	1,044	984	992
55–59	739	832	860	880	844	859	881	889	890	897
60–64	592	722	630	714	771	784	754	754	748	756
65–69	470	526	452	540	510	589	613	638	534	568
70–74	334	364	323	361	326	399	371	433	407	431
75–79	171	209	183	208	194	226	190	245	218	251
80 & over	104	139	100	132	114	144	115	150	113	155
unknown	...	...	...	...	...	...	...	...	...	...

	1876 M	1876 F	1881 M	1881 F	1886 M	1886 F	1891 M	1891 F	1896 M	1896 F
0–4	1,819	1,781	1,742	1,712	1,759	1,731	1,668	1,656	1,652	1,648
5–9	1,618	1,584	1,716	1,687	1,702	1,696	1,678	1,677	1,652	1,651
10–14	1,629	1,580	1,590	1,553	1,683	1,658	1,671	1,656	1,673	1,667
15–19	1,591	1,575	1,631	1,614	1,603	1,611	1,670	1,671	1,675	1,680
20–24	1,557	1,672	1,632	1,748	1,743	1,842	1,587	1,694	1,624	1,721
25–29	1,305	1,312	1,296	1,256	1,383	1,325	1,479	1,443	1,434	1,438
30–34	1,310	1,299	1,316	1,293	1,304	1,284	1,373	1,344	1,398	1,391
35–39	1,270	1,249	1,282	1,254	1,276	1,267	1,281	1,265	1,324	1,316
40–44	1,192	1,173	1,205	1,189	1,193	1,176	1,191	1,212	1,193	1,192
45–49	1,106	1,121	1,107	1,122	1,117	1,119	1,147	1,150	1,120	1,154
50–54	999	1,018	1,009	1,036	1,004	1,031	1,018	1,031	1,017	1,052
55–59	871	913	892	917	895	909	882	917	890	923
60–64	756	777	782	793	768	803	789	823	767	818
65–69	577	599	605	636	605	637	613	656	614	671
70–74	394	425	428	451	435	457	450	486	442	490
75–79	245	273	250	276	264	282	270	308	271	310
80 & over	144	182	174	211	168	201	165	212	175	225
unknown	...	...	...	...	...	...	...	...	...	...

A2 Population of Countries by Sex and Age Groups (in thousands)

FRANCE (*Cont'd*)

	1901[12]		1906		1911		1921[11]		1926	
	M	F	M	F	M	F	M	F	M	F
0–4	1,714	1,713	1,735	1,721	1,693	1,670	1,148	1,121	1,781	1,752
5–9	1,610	1,614	1,660	1,652	1,671	1,656	1,507	1,501	1,156	1,129
10–14	1,623	1,614	1,617	1,601	1,661	1,639	1,714	1,699	1,559	1,538
15–19	1,636	1,643	1,590	1,604	1,593	1,596	1,734	1,721	1,730	1,703
20–24	1,568	1,620	1,560	1,600	1,535	1,570	1,410	1,643	1,662	1,708
25–29	1,503	1,515	1,527	1,559	1,523	1,553	1,235	1,556	1,630	1,657
30–34	1,383	1,410	1,436	1,437	1,482	1,499	1,256	1,516	1,272	1,543
35–39	1,340	1,350	1,336	1,372	1,401	1,406	1,277	1,501	1,277	1,513
40–44	1,231	1,243	1,264	1,273	1,270	1,302	1,320	1,444	1,251	1,453
45–49	1,115	1,132	1,158	1,194	1,194	1,226	1,275	1,335	1,267	1,396
50–54	1,007	1,093	1,922	2,061	1,060	1,113	1,137	1,209	1,139	1,262
55–59	927	976			916	979	1,021	1,107	1,030	1,132
60–64	791	861	799	862	770	891	852	966	886	1,000
65–69	612	687	631	725	640	734	651	774	690	830
70–74	459	535	707	853	451	551	736	984	753	1,011
75–79	263	318			259	333				
80 & over	156	214	155	225	158	241	160	265	172	286
Unknown	...	...	...	...	...	...	...	...	...	...

	1931		1936		1946		1954		1962	
	M	F	M	F	M	F	M	F	M	F
0–4	1,756	1,715	1,604	1,584	1,397	1,351	2,028	1,953	2,061	1,985
5–9	1,790	1,746	1,697	1,678	1,384	1,364	1,832	1,765	2,047	1,974
10–14	1,185	1,147	1,768	1,735	1,560	1,536	1,358	1,315	2,125	2,046
15–19	1,560	1,518	1,147	1,123	1,631	1,615	1,471	1,443	1,603	1,541
20–24	1,721	1,667	1,485	1,474	1,634	1,643	1,621	1,561	1,417	1,338
25–29	1,798	1,699	1,674	1,643	1,046	1,070	1,629	1,573	1,601	1,514
30–34	1,624	1,648	1,715	1,659	1,384	1,419	1,537	1,526	1,674	1,616
35–39	1,259	1,534	1,556	1,606	1,558	1,569	991	998	1,641	1,629
40–44	1,227	1,460	1,182	1,467	1,566	1,565	1,497	1,504	1,243	1,250
45–49	1,184	1,404	1,143	1,398	1,363	1,481	1,499	1,520	1,220	1,262
50–54	1,175	1,324	1,089	1,326	1,009	1,350	1,421	1,469	1,418	1,482
55–59	1,078	1,187	1,058	1,240	940	1,250	1,348	1,348	1,351	1,453
60–64	895	1,031	933	1,080	845	1,153	835	1,199	1,130	1,332
65–69	722	872	727	892	739	997	721	1,068	754	1,154
70–74	506	659	530	699	552	772	549	860	571	940
75–79	291	414	311	453	317	497	389	618	389	704
80 & over	174	308	183	334	192	374	247	478	308	650
Unknown	...	...	...	...	...	...	...	...	...	...

See p. 45 for footnotes

A2 Population of Countries by Sex and Age Groups (in thousands)

FRANCE (Cont'd)

	1968 M	1968 F	1975 M	1975 F	1982 M	1982 F	1991 M	1991 F	1993 M	1993 F
0–4	1,772	1,699	1,753	1,672	1,607	1,523	1,970	1,830	1,913	1,826
5–9	2,136	2,055	2,138	2,047	1,951	1,870	1,955	1,863	1,945	1,859
10–14	2,104	2,025	2,197	2,103	2,204	2,079	1,925	1,821	2,006	1,912
15–19	2,147	2,070	2,162	2,080	2,231	2,131	2,132	2,036	2,013	1,926
20–24	1,935	1,851	2,128	2,084	2,125	2,107	2,131	2,070	2,194	2,145
25–29	1,481	1,382	2,264	2,126	2,105	2,090	2,148	2,130	2,171	2,161
30–34	1,594	1,514	1,595	1,466	2,222	2,152	2,102	2,112	2,154	2,167
35–39	1,708	1,646	1,554	1,468	1,857	1,766	2,112	2,116	2,125	2,143
40–44	1,671	1,656	1,658	1,613	1,473	1,413	2,197	2,145	2,191	2,165
45–49	1,530	1,561	1,663	1,649	1,554	1,523	1,508	1,465	1,791	1,753
50–54	953	1,006	1,567	1,636	1,589	1,622	1,434	1,432	1,384	1,377
55–59	1,354	1,469	972	1,040	1,475	1,581	1,460	1,533	1,414	1,482
60–64	1,249	1,423	1,148	1,318	1,175	1,334	1,373	1,537	1,393	1,553
65–69	1,062	1,308	1,093	1,349	807	1,003	1,704	1,484	1,206	1,472
70–74	686	1,090	882	1,214	901	1,245	665	888	891	1,192
75–79	428	819	556	937	655	1,049	625	1,009	512	809
80 & over	387	883	414	1,053	564	1,300	663	1,507	709	1,567
unknown	...	...	...	...	...	...	...	...		

GERMANY

	1871 M	1871 F	1880 M	1880 F	1890 M	1890 F	1900 M	1900 F
0–4	2,602	2,590	3,092	3,077	3,225	3,204	3,698	3,672
5–9	2,313	2,313	2,583	2,588	2,769	2,762	3,207	3,199
10–14	2,144	2,126	2,343	2,333	2,712	2,700	2,926	2,912
15–19	1,852	1,893	2,101	2,126	2,392	2,410	2,666	2,653
20–24	1,722	1,825	1,902	1,973	2,105	2,152	2,540	2,560
25–29	1,546	1,670	1,620	1,696	1,842	1,903	2,225	2,243
30–34	2,672	2,800	1,501	1,583	1,662	1,725	1,962	1,990
35–39			1,365	1,432	1,429	1,491	1,708	1,741
40–44	2,130	2,245	1,239	1,317	1,297	1,392	1,510	1,578
45–49			1,039	1,099	1,175	1,267	1,260	1,345
50–54	1,663	1,770	906	1,002	1,012	1,126	1,105	1,239
55–59			805	895	814	915	948	1,081
60–64	1,017	1,122	670	754	654	770	756	891
65–69			461	524	524	621	545	655
70–74	408	453	290	334	352	420	357	446
75–79			160	187	178	218	211	268
80 & over	66	83	79	97	90	119	114	154
Unknown	...	...	...	...	...	...	...	...

See p. 45 for footnotes

A2   Population of Countries by Sex and Age Groups (in thousands)

GERMANY (Cont'd)

	1910 M	1910 F	1925[13] M	1925[13] F	1933[13] M	1933[13] F	1939[14] M	1939[14] F
0–4	3,923	3,867	2,984	2,887	2,418	2,331	3,056	2,926
5–9	3,714	3,684	2,023	1,963	2,705	2,627	2,441	2,353
10–14	3,471	3,449	3,134	3,079	2,904	2,808	2,729	2,650
15–19	3,149	3,138	3,285	3,285	2,067	2,019	3,077	2,968
20–24	2,807	2,802	3,065	3,086	3,077	3,064	1,985	1,918
25–29	2,509	2,517	2,468	2,839	3,077	3,089	3,131	3,075
30–34	2,406	2,416	2,027	2,553	2,856	2,915	3,156	3,118
35–39	2,096	2,105	1,965	2,319	2,197	2,681	2,905	2,922
40–44	1,813	1,853	1,853	2,054	1,915	2,380	2,221	2,673
45–49	1,537	1,606	1,860	1,986	1,836	2,141	1,874	2,357
50–54	1,312	1,433	1,588	1,645	1,704	1,892	1,772	2,093
55–59	1,033	1,173	1,327	1,401	1,630	1,753	1,597	1,806
60–64	838	1,009	1,029	1,137	1,274	1,366	1,486	1,635
65–69	642	793	740	876	953	1,069	1,094	1,208
70–74	430	549	467	591	630	752	737	853
75–79	232	305	246	338	334	434	417	519
80 & over	130	187	135	200	186	278	230	329
Unknown	…	…	…	…	…	…	…	…

WEST GERMANY (including West Berlin)

	1946[15] M	1946[15] F	1950[13] M	1950[13] F	1961 M	1961 F	1970 M	1970 F	1980 M	1980 F
0–4			1,764	1,676	2,294	2,181	2,416	2,300	1,502	1,429
5–9	7,101	6,953	1,897	1,821	2,004	1,909	2,556	2,434	1,730	1,656
10–14			2,271	2,190	1,946	1,851	2,234	2,118	2,498	2,372
15–19			1,823	1,754	1,883	1,800	2,044	1,952	2,687	2,531
20–24	1,107	1,927	1,824	1,862	2,437	2,321	1,905	1,820	2,409	2,253
25–29	908	1,575	1,563	2,095	2,002	1,892	2,227	2,066	2,197	2,106
30–34	2,477	3,838	1,090	1,466	1,956	1,926	2,588	2,367	2,046	1,923
35–39			1,624	2,145	1,647	2,156	2,047	1,882	2,214	2,081
40–44	3,000	3,618	1,825	2,233	1,225	1,692	1,947	1,978	2,515	2,370
45–49			1,850	2,042	1,563	2,105	1,623	2,192	1,957	1,872
50–54	2,129	2,763	1,495	1,823	1,795	2,294	1,056	1,468	1,828	1,934
55–59			1,142	1,552	1,772	2,077	1,574	2,180	1,472	2,099
60–64	896	1,074	1,000	1,303	1,390	1,803	1,563	2,124	928	1,409
65–69			839	1,041	949	1,455	1,350	1,814	1,216	1,937
70–74	1,789	2,064	662	802	711	1,078	858	1,410	1,048	1,766
75–79			385	466	473	692	488	942	709	1,277
80 & over			209	286	350	512	391	738	463	1,135
Unknown	…	1	…	…	16	19	…	…	…	…

See p. 45 for footnotes

A2 Population of Countries by Sex and Age Groups (in thousands)

EAST GERMANY (including East Berlin)

	1946[16]		1950		1964		1971		1981	
	M	F	M	F	M	F	M	F	M	F
0–4	613	588	578	552	736	701	621	592	589	562
5–9	868	835	755	725	671	638	732	696	469	447
10–14	715	694	918	987	666	633	681	648	604	574
15–19	609	681	702	704	445	429	676	641	715	680
20–24	309	707	551	686	624	616	495	475	693	659
25–29	263	589	441	722	656	646	556	549	665	633
30–34	335	698	315	520	529	523	675	664	546	527
35–39	457	834	429	838	442	541	544	535	470	469
40–44	567	811	660	937	361	584	470	537	669	666
45–49	575	761	725	901	230	377	348	551	543	546
50–54	482	677	625	842	425	673	245	403	464	512
55–59	445	599	508	742	506	715	367	602	316	503
60–64	381	493	465	648	509	663	439	665	242	420
65–69	324	404	372	495	375	569	424	589	246	451
70–74	244	299	287	377	260	438	291	477	271	514
75–79	127	165	160	213	180	296	168	324	347	708
80 & over	65	100	77	121	133	216	133	254		
Unknown	…	…	…	…	…	…	…	…	…	…

BERLIN

	1946				1946	
	M	F		M	F
0–4	90	88	50–54	104	164
5–9	115	90	55–59	105	148
10–14	89	69	60–64	93	117
15–19	70	80	65–69	72	94
20–24	40	92	70–74	44	59
25–29	43	80	75–79	19	33
30–34	63	134	80 & over	7	18
35–39	96	168	Unknown	…	…
40–44	122	169			
45–49	119	170			

GERMANY

	1990	
	M	F
0–4	2,261	2,144
5–9	2,189	2,078
10–14	2,101	1,990
15–19	2,293	2,174
20–24	3,271	3,114
25–29	3,568	3,351
30–34	3,153	2,976
35–39	2,855	2,763
40–44	2,497	2,391
45–49	2,723	2,614
50–54	3,053	2,974
55–59	2,303	2,321
60–64	2,006	2,325
65–69	1,463	2,392
70–74	820	1,499
75–79	882	1,830
80 & over	836	2,150
Unknown	…	…

See p. 45 for footnotes

A2   Population of Countries by Sex and Age Groups (in thousands)

GREECE

	1861 M	1861 F	1870 M	1870 F	1879 M	1879 F	1889 M	1889 F
0–4			105	102	129	121	173	160
5–9			97	91	111	102	148	133
10–14	257	244	81	71	101	86	132	113
15–19			63	74	77	86	102	114
20–24	63	70	56	61	59	63	79	83
25–29	56	49	74	69	70	72	93	95
30–34	66	61	54	47	56	60	75	71
35–39			52	46	64	35	85	78
40–44	51	47	33	29	54	36	71	45
45–49			31	32	42	19	55	47
50–54	34	31	22	20	22	25	30	26
55–59			23	23	25	13	32	33
60–64	19	17	15	13	15	14	20	18
65–69			13	12	14	6	19	19
70–74	9	9	7	6	7	5	9	8
75–79			4	4	5	5	7	6
80 & over			3	3	3	3	4	4
unknown	...	...	...	...	...	...	...	...

	1907 M	1907 F	1920 M	1920 F	1928 M	1928 F	1940 M	1940 F
0–4	193	181	253	231	390	374	388	371
5–9	179	165	322	297	320	305	424	397
10–14	150	140	321	293	313	286	428	415
15–19	121	152	261	276	343	351	344	339
20–24	103	107	197	216	260	288	274	279
25–29	104	115	158	190	253	265	299	304
30–34	65	56	134	164	184	198	278	273
35–39	108	112	152	170	174	201	247	248
40–44	64	56	141	145	152	174	202	218
45–49	66	63	137	123	160	153	160	164
50–54	43	34	115	109	139	136	145	166
55–59	46	46	89	79	108	101	134	137
60–64	29	25	74	81	92	99	118	127
65–69	28	28	54	52	71	71	86	87
70–74	13	11	40	45	49	55	63	75
75–79	9	9	21	21	30	29	35	42
80 & over	5	6	22	26	26	33	47	44
unknown	...	...	...	...	...	...	...	...

A2 Population of Countries by Sex and Age Groups (in thousands)

GREECE (Cont'd)

	1950 M	1950 F	1961 M	1961 F	1971 M	1971 F	1981 M	1981 F	1991 M	1991 F	1998 M	1998 F
0–4	382	361	407	385	390	380	401	378	270	254	261	245
5–9	335	315	371	349	359	339	383	363	328	307	272	257
10–14	391	375	375	358	368	346	402	381	372	349	311	294
15–19	393	397	313	310	336	323	368	352	364	340	374	354
20–24	357	375	355	370	327	305	354	356	405	379	399	385
25–29	291	315	348	373	244	258	331	332	390	369	409	399
30–34	239	264	342	366	286	319	322	331	368	365	399	397
35–39	244	265	253	272	314	337	272	282	354	341	373	377
40–44	240	254	213	240	321	342	316	344	334	335	358	359
45–49	211	221	244	258	244	268	331	334	292	303	339	337
50–54	168	186	229	238	204	238	326	343	296	333	316	322
55–59	131	155	194	201	241	255	235	254	327	353	286	302
60–64	108	136	151	185	218	231	189	221	295	328	301	329
65–69	89	110	103	127	173	193	199	230	212	246	281	315
70–74	67	83	83	116	119	161	161	196	151	196	217	265
75–79	41	50	57	71	66	86	107	83	134	180	133	178
80 over	34	29	52	78	69	110	135	128	135	196	152	145
unknown	...	...	...	...	...	...	...	...	...	...		

HUNGARY

1. Ancient Kingdom of Hungary

	1869 M	1869 F	1880 M	1880 F	1890 M	1890 F	1900 M	1900 F	1910 M	1910 F
0–4	1,131	1,144	1,237	1,236	1,225	1,225	1,292	1,286	1,373	1,358
5–9	891	901	950	952	1,068	1,064	1,117	1,116	1,204	1,194
10–14	834	838	901	908	909	911	1,021	1,023	1,154	1,143
15–19	689	782	805	893	762	783	950	989	1,010	1,049
20–24	621	646	764	789	664	710	762	793	803	871
25–29	663	670	700	695	664	678	654	672	772	800
30–34	571	549	628	653	638	652	626	654	654	692
35–39	537	526	593	565	560	535	603	593	570	595
40–44	418	399	568	567	506	519	583	574	556	575
45–49	422	404	430	406	438	414	480	459	515	513
50–54	304	284	359	393	402	415	430	448	491	502
55–59	256	247	272	270	280	273	341	324	399	382
60–64	172	156	255	267	235	261	299	310	319	336
65–69	130	120	138	131	154	152	190	185	230	222
70–74	56	48	86	90	112	117	123	134	161	168
75–79	34	29	38	37	49	48	64	64	82	83
80 & over	17	15	25	27	29	33	43	49	49	59
Unknown	...	...	8	10	4	6	1	1	1	2

A2 Population of Countries by Sex and Age Groups (in thousands)

2. Hungary as established by the Treaty of Trianon

	1910 M	1910 F	1920 M	1920 F	1930 M	1930 F	1941 M	1941 F	1949 M	1949 F	1960 M	1960 F	1970 M	1970 F	1980 M	1980 F	1991 M	1991 F	1998 M	1998 F
0–4	488	483	336	327	444	438	396	386	408	392	424	406	363	341	440	419	314	300	275	259
5–9	425	421	433	433	454	444	399	390	383	372	467	448	334	316	394	373	322	308	315	301
10–14	415	412	458	456	311	303	428	422	371	364	400	387	423	401	360	339	404	386	316	346
15–19	372	381	419	426	413	421	448	442	389	387	378	375	470	448	332	314	426	404	448	427
20–24	307	321	350	405	416	423	283	298	383	400	330	349	396	383	418	399	361	345	368	352
25–29	297	299	285	341	373	377	387	395	366	407	355	368	372	369	462	445	309	300	322	314
30–34	255	257	250	298	339	364	408	404	228	259	367	386	326	346	389	380	353	350	315	316
35–39	224	224	243	276	267	311	363	360	357	393	358	396	349	363	363	365	432	433	406	414
40–44	207	207	217	240	235	275	325	347	324	351	212	239	358	379	315	340	377	383	369	391
45–49	184	180	194	200	225	253	251	293	308	326	338	377	346	386	332	354	324	341	307	338
50–54	173	175	182	185	196	217	214	256	246	296	309	340	202	229	331	364	283	323	264	317
55–59	148	145	156	153	167	176	197	229	188	233	276	305	309	356	308	362	267	318	219	293
60–64			134	140	146	153	160	186	167	213	217	265	264	311	170	209	256	320	204	288
65–69			101	103	113	116	124	139	131	164	148	201	213	262	237	307	221	307	160	259
70–74	296	311	61	68	80	87	92	102	90	113	110	154	145	204	171	241	127	195	107	199
75–79			33	35	46	51	54	61	53	65	70	99	78	127	104	164	102	176	42	88
80 & over			18	23	24	31	34	44	32	44	44	64	56	99	69	140	85	185	33	83
Unknown			2	2	1	1	1	1	...	...	...	...	...	...	...	...	...	...	...	...

IRELAND

1. The whole country

	1861 M	1861 F	1871 M	1871 F	1881 M	1881 F	1891 M	1891 F	1901 M	1901 F	1911 M	1911 F
0–4	352	342	331	322	292	284	239	232	225	218	221	215
5–9	310	302	320	312	315	307	258	250	228	223	222	216
10–14	306	291	322	307	315	301	280	270	234	225	217	210
15–19	329	344	259	273	274	285	276	274	235	238	215	208
20–24	298	317	214	244	232	246	224	221	217	227	191	185
25–34	367	391	343	390	296	338	286	312	321	336	312	324
35–44	277	319	260	284	263	296	227	261	234	249	273	264
45–54	262	286	225	252	214	229	218	241	195	219	198	196
55–64	205	224	205	220	172	192	163	171	169	182	138	145
65–74	87	97	112	113	106	108	93	99	96	95	144	170
75–79	35[17]	41[17]	39[17]	44[17]	47[17]	47[17]	44[17]	46[17]	38[17]	40[17]	53[17]	58[17]
80 & over	6[18]	8[18]	8[18]	9[18]	7[18]	8[18]	9[18]	10[18]	8[18]	8[18]	8[18]	8[18]
Unknown	3	1	2	2	2	1	1	1	...	...	...	...

See p. 45 for footnotes

A2 Population of Countries by Sex and Age Groups (in thousands)

2. Northern Ireland

	1926 M	1926 F	1937 M	1937 F	1951 M	1951 F	1961 M	1961 F	1966 M	1966 F	1971 M	1971 F	1981 M	1981 F	1991 M	1991 F
0–4	65	63	57	55	71	67	75	71	83	78	82	77	67	64	66	62
5–9	59	58	58	56	66	63	68	64	75	71	82	76	69	65	66	63
10–14	60	59	62	59	57	55	68	65	68	64	74	70	76	72	65	63
15–19	59	61	57	57	55	53	60	60	64	62	67	62	74	70	66	62
20–24	53	57	51	54	49	52	47	47	52	54	60	56	63	60	64	62
25–29	46	54	48	53	48	52	42	44	43	44	48	48	51	49	60	62
29–34	38	44	44	47	45	47	42	45	41	43	42	42	50	49	56	58
35–39	35	41	42	47	46	49	44	47	41	44	41	41	46	46	50	50
40–44	33	37	36	40	43	46	42	43	43	46	40	43	40	41	49	49
45–49	34	37	32	36	39	42	42	45	41	43	42	44	37	39	44	45
50–54	32	33	29	33	36	40	40	43	40	43	39	41	36	40	37	39
54–59	27	28	28	30	29	33	34	38	37	41	38	41	35	40	34	37
60–64	21	22	27	28	24	30	29	36	31	37	33	38	31	37	32	37
65–69	19	20	23	24	22	26	23	29	25	33	26	34	28	35	29	36
70–74	14	18	16	19	18	22	17	23	18	25	19	28	22	31	22	30
75–79	8	10	9	11	12	15	11	16	12	17	12	19	13	21	15	25
80 & over	6	8	6	8	8	11	10	15	10	16	10	17	10	22	12	29
Unknown	...	...	...	...	...	...	...	...	...	...	...	...	...	...	...	...

3. Southern Ireland (Irish Republic)

	1926 M	1926 F	1936 M	1936 F	1951 M	1951 F	1961 M	1961 F	1966 M	1966 F	1971 M	1971 F	1981 M	1981 F	1991 M	1991 F
0–4	146	142	136	132	160	153	153	147	161	155	162	154	181	172	140	131
5–9	149	140	136	133	144	138	147	141	152	147	162	155	179	170	166	156
10–14	151	145	144	139	133	128	148	141	146	140	152	146	175	166	179	173
15–19	146	140	138	130	126	115	120	114	133	126	137	131	167	160	176	170
20–24	125	116	135	120	105	97	80	78	95	91	110	105	140	136	142	131
25–29	107	109	113	104	100	99	72	73	75	74	88	85	124	122	115	113
30–34	93	91	94	89	96	95	75	78	74	73	77	75	118	114	120	122
35–39	87	88	97	96	102	99	82	85	77	78	75	74	99	95	118	115
40–44	86	83	84	79	94	86	85	86	81	82	76	76	85	81	117	112
45–49	87	82	81	76	82	79	89	86	84	83	80	81	78	74	94	92
50–54	86	77	79	74	83	80	82	75	84	81	80	79	75	74	84	80
55–59	67	59	75	68	65	64	69	68	76	71	78	76	73	76	69	68
60–64	54	52	68	62	61	61	65	67	62	62	68	66	68	71	66	70
56–69	52	50	60	53	54	53	51	52	55	59	54	57	64	70	57	68
70–74	38	45	41	45	49	51	44	49	42	48	45	54	48	55	50	62
75–79	21	25	25	28	32	33	30	34	29	34	28	34	29	39	36	49
80 & over	19	24	15	19	20	24	24	31	24	32	24	34	23	40	28	52
Unknown	...	...	...	...	...	...	...	...	...	...	...	...	...	...	...	...

A2 Population of Countries by Sex and Age Groups (in thousands)

ITALY

	1861 M	1861 F	1871[19] M	1871[19] F	1881 M	1881 F	1901 M	1901 F
0–4	1,495	1,465	1,571	1,526	1,751	1,688	2,147	2,061
5–9	1,189	1,157	1,483	1,434	1,530	1,479	1,812	1,750
10–14	1,084	1,056	1,369	1,320	1,383	1,327	1,714	1,674
15–19	959	1,079	1,176	1,241	1,301	1,334	1,495	1,526
20–24	915	934	1,169	1,176	1,213	1,233	1,305	1,335
25–29	912	945	1,027	1,046	1,050	1,078	1,071	1,134
30–34	720	705	957	967	1,015	1,042	995	1,054
35–39	850	842	835	829	886	891	952	983
40–44	571	541	848	845	893	902	894	926
45–49	602	611	700	683	692	689	810	827
50–54	438	403	700	682	723	738	760	797
55–59	434	444	449	430	539	532	664	674
60–64	270	247	487	485	542	548	560	587
65–69	220	225	288	268	301	284	414	422
70–74	118	107	225	217	248	244	297	302
75–79	80	79	102	91	117	103	172	168
80 & over	43	40	87	90	81	82	95	100
unknown	…	…	…	…	2	2	1	1

	1911 M	1911 F	1921[20] M	1921[20] F	1931 M	1931 F	1936 M	1936 F
0–4	2,197	2,116	1,813	1,736	2,328	2,246	2,218	2,140
5–9	1,911	1,840	2,062	1,989	2,278	2,205	2,210	2,148
10–14	1,862	1,808	2,131	2,058	1,619	1,567	2,233	2,180
15–19	1,560	1,673	1,879	1,862	2,032	2,014	1,562	1,529
20–24	1,393	1,521	1,627	1,703	1,910	1,914	1,979	1,955
25–29	1,131	1,309	1,307	1,500	1,565	1,650	1,833	1,841
30–34	1,023	1,146	1,206	1,374	1,350	1,520	1,536	1,584
35–39	931	1,018	1,093	1,214	1,139	1,370	1,323	1,470
40–44	884	947	1,023	1,079	1,071	1,273	1,113	1,322
45–49	846	881	947	966	992	1,131	1,031	1,217
50–54	805	838	841	860	904	980	948	1,079
55–59	690	703	775	781	809	856	842	915
60–64	624	652	687	713	694	743	730	783
65–69	477	479	518	527	597	635	588	641
70–74	334	347	385	401	430	468	463	504
75–79	184	185	220	220	256	282	282	321
80 & over	115	124	129	148	153	185	176	220
unknown	57	63	84	116	6	6	2	2

A2 Population of Countries by Sex and Age Groups (in thousands)

ITALY (*Cont'd*)

	1951[21] M	F	1961 M	F	1971 M	F	1981 M	F	1991 M	F
0–4	2,219	2,113	2,152	2,044	2,272	2,156	1,702	1,607	1,458	1,371
5–9	1,981	1,893	2,031	1,948	2,366	2,252	2,146	2,054	1,552	1,467
10–14	2,141	2,074	2,159	2,070	2,142	2,041	2,314	2,240	1,816	1,720
15–19	2,037	2,004	1,917	1,860	1,961	1,889	2,364	2,299	2,241	2,134
20–24	2,062	2,039	2,060	2,013	2,081	2,013	2,042	2,026	2,407	2,318
25–29	1,960	2,024	1,900	1,894	1,755	1,752	1,888	1,907	2,427	2,363
30–34	1,382	1,477	1,919	1,944	1,917	1,939	1,979	1,980	2,111	2,078
35–39	1,675	1,757	1,859	1,949	1,805	1,845	1,741	1,768	1,908	1,912
40–44	1,665	1,714	1,314	1,415	1,840	1,882	1,878	1,891	2,021	2,037
45–49	1,409	1,477	1,597	1,690	1,757	1,871	1,741	1,812	1,675	1,715
50–54	1,183	1,327	1,557	1,643	1,228	1,357	1,717	1,822	1,801	1,889
55–59	950	1,179	1,268	1,382	1,430	1,574	1,612	1,780	1,647	1,784
60–64	837	1,042	1,010	1,209	1,371	1,539	1,068	1,262	1,561	1,769
65–69	689	844	751	1,014	1,043	1,263	1,156	1,419	1,337	1,673
70–74	516	605	590	808	715	988	925	1,227	757	1,046
75–79	334	398	399	542	793	1,300	1,610		1,350	2,392
80 & over	220	290	301	424						
Unknown	...	...	...	...	...	...	...	...	...	...

NETHERLANDS

	1840 M	F	1849 M	F	1859 M	F	1869 M	F	1879 M	F	1889 M	F
0–4	190	188	173	171	202	199	234	232	276	273	299	294
5–9	158	154	175	171	181	177	197	193	225	225	256	255
10–19	293	290	308	305	320	315	335	331	390	387	456	455
20–29	229	241	262	271	274	283	276	288	300	306	347	359
30–39	184	193	201	210	230	237	238	247	249	257	270	277
40–49	145	157	157	167	176	183	201	205	214	219	225	230
50–54	135	155	117	132	127	138	145	155	169	177	182	191
55–59												
60–64			40	50	48	55	49	55	61	67	69	76
65–69			27	34	33	41	40	47	44	52	56	63
70–74	66	82	18	23	21	27	27	32	28	33	36	43
75–79			11	15	11	14	14	19	17	21	20	25
80 & over			7	10	6	9	8	11	10	13	12	16
Unknown	1	...	...	...	1	1	1	1	...	...	...	...

See p. 45 for footnotes

A2 Population of Countries by Sex and Age Groups (in thousands)

NETHERLANDS (*Cont'd*)

	1899 M	1899 F	1909 M	1909 F	1920 M	1920 F	1930 M	1930 F	1940 M	1940 F
0–4	334	328	373	365	396	381	427	409	434	415
5–9	290	287	338	331	377	367	427	412	419	399
10–14	271	267	311	306	363	354	384	372	418	402
15–19	244	243	279	277	341	334	374	370	422	408
20–24	220	227	246	251	298	301	351	359	376	366
25–29	186	197	217	226	263	271	320	331	362	363
30–34	167	175	201	211	233	242	283	295	340	351
35–39	150	154	175	184	213	220	252	263	311	323
40–44	127	129	156	163	196	204	224	232	274	285
45–49	119	121	138	142	171	178	203	209	242	253
50–54	99	104	114	118	146	153	184	190	212	219
55–59	94	99	103	107	127	133	155	161	186	192
60–64	79	86	80	87	97	102	126	132	160	167
65–69	58	65	70	76	77	84	100	106	124	131
70–74	41	48	50	57	54	60	66	71	87	94
75–79	26	32	28	35	35	40	41	46	54	60
80 & over	15	20	19	25	23	30	28	34	34	41
Unknown	...	...	...	...	...	...	...	...	...	...

	1947 M	1947 F	1960 M	1960 F	1970 M	1970 F	1980 M	1980 F	1991 M	1991 F	1998 M	1998 F
0–4	599	568	594	565	607	579	452	430	488	467	497	475
5–9	432	414	567	539	624	595	552	528	455	436	506	483
10–14	412	394	614	585	594	567	626	597	463	442	479	458
15–19	415	401	472	451	569	543	638	610	522	500	473	452
20–24	400	401	414	400	618	585	606	585	645	619	494	482
25–29	363	370	388	378	483	444	587	560	670	637	636	616
30–34	345	355	379	381	431	394	614	574	635	609	673	641
35–39	325	339	374	387	397	377	476	440	592	570	654	632
40–44	303	318	336	347	380	379	414	391	611	583	600	585
45–49	265	281	324	339	368	383	388	380	494	468	578	559
50–54	236	248	305	324	323	339	358	370	408	395	555	535
55–59	200	210	273	295	301	326	345	375	361	365	413	404
60–64	170	178	227	252	267	304	273	309	326	354	346	356
65–69	136	144	185	208	220	265	242	298	283	341	301	339
70–74	98	106	139	157	161	209	186	258	210	285	239	310
75–79	56	63	93	106	110	147	125	194	147	238	171	264
80 & over	36	43	73	88	97	182	13	199	135	307	147	388
Unknown	...	...	...	...	...	...	...	...	...	...		

A2 Population of Countries by Sex and Age Groups (in thousands)

NORWAY

	1801 M	1801 F	1855 M	1855 F	1865 M	1865 F	1875 M	1875 F	1890 M	1890 F	1900 M	1900 F
0–4	110	109	103	99	117	113	115	111	133	128	144	139
5–9			86	84	103	100	102	99	120	115	134	128
10–14	81	80	76	73	91	88	100	97	110	106	123	118
15–19			64	64	81	80	92	91	90	93	110	108
20–24	64	73	63	70	67	71	76	83	67	82	90	98
25–29			60	66	56	62	61	69	59	76	73	83
30–34	54	60	100	102	54	57	53	59	55	68	61	72
35–39					55	57	46	51	52	63	57	68
40–44	47	54	64	67	47	48	46	49	46	54	53	61
45–49					43	45	46	49	42	49	49	57
50–54	34	39	29	33	29	32	42	45	37	42	43	50
55–59			26	28	25	27	34	37	36	39	37	42
60–64	21	27	22	26	22	25	24	27	34	38	30	35
65–69			17	20	19	23	18	20	29	32	29	33
70–74	10	14	16	21	14	16	14	17	20	24	24	27
75–79					8	11	10	13	12	14	17	20
80 & over	3	4	5	7	5	8	8	11	8	12	12	16
Unknown	...	...	...	...	...	...	...	...	1	1	...	...

	1910 M	F	1920 M	F	1930 M	F	1946 M	F	1950 M	F	1960 M	F	1970 M	F	1980 M	F	1990 M	F	1998 M	F
0–4	144	138	150	144	121	116	151	144	164	155	158	150	169	160	133	126	141	134	147	155
5–9	143	138	143	138	142	137	111	107	137	130	155	147	161	152	157	151	132	125	149	157
10–14	137	132	140	135	145	140	103	99	109	105	163	154	157	150	171	162	137	131	131	138
15–19	120	118	135	133	137	133	116	113	104	100	135	129	155	148	162	154	163	156	130	136
20–24	90	100	118	123	122	124	134	130	117	112	107	103	162	152	158	151	174	165	142	146
25–29	73	87	100	105	110	118	137	136	133	129	101	98	134	126	156	148	165	156	168	173
30–34	70	81	82	90	104	110	128	127	132	131	114	110	105	102	163	153	163	155	168	176
35–39	62	70	70	80	91	96	120	121	126	124	130	127	99	97	135	127	157	149	157	164
40–44	54	63	67	75	76	84	109	114	116	118	129	129	111	108	105	102	163	153	155	160
45–49	51	61	58	65	64	74	101	107	105	111	122	121	126	124	97	96	123	118	147	155
50–54	48	56	50	58	62	69	88	93	96	103	111	114	123	126	107	106	97	97	147	153
55–59	43	50	46	55	52	59	70	78	81	87	98	106	113	117	117	120	93	95	106	106
60–64	36	41	40	48	43	51	57	67	64	73	86	96	98	108	109	119	96	102	85	90
65–69	29	35	34	41	36	45	48	56	50	60	68	77	81	96	94	107	100	115	82	92
70–74	21	26	25	31	29	36	38	45	41	49	49	59	62	80	72	92	78	100	77	95
75–79	17	20	17	21	20	26	23	31	27	34	32	42	42	56	47	71	57	83	64	92
80 & over	15	20	14	20	17	23	22	32	23	33	30	41	34	53	45	79	52	104	61	125
Unknown	...	...	...	...	1	1	2	2	...	...	...	...	...	...	...	...	...	...	...	...

A2   Population of Countries by Sex and Age Group (in thousands)

POLAND

	1921 M	1921 F	1931 M	1931 F	1950 M	1950 F	1960 M	1960 F	1970 M	1970 F	1978 M	1978 F	1991 M	1991 F	1997 M	1997 F
0–4	1,315	1,283	2,020	1,962	1,538	1,485	1,729	1,652	1,281	1,225	1,588	1,513	1,437	1,362	1,166	1,107
5–9	1,476	1,464	2,005	1,962	1,006	983	1,793	1,722	1,399	1,334	1,389	1,326	1,711	1,639	1,410	1,338
10–14	1,790	1,754	1,405	1,372	1,156	1,136	1,547	1,493	1,730	1,659	1,303	1,243	1,666	1,594	1,682	1,611
15–19	1,478	1,662	1,474	1,562	1,196	1,191	968	956	1,772	1,706	1,517	1,427	1,532	1,467	1,668	1,600
20–24	1,113	1,328	1,514	1,707	894	1,208	863	1,088	1,499	1,459	1,743	1,675	1,293	1,231	1,532	1,476
25–29	887	970	1,417	1,506	928	1,129	1,134	1,149	949	939	1,651	1,606	1,298	1,257	1,298	1,244
30–34	695	843	1,119	1,265	641	751	1,123	1,188	1,076	1,079	1,210	1,197	1,567	1,531	1,270	1,235
35–39	651	732	880	991	756	921	949	1,105	1,127	1,130	960	968	1,654	1,639	1,507	1,485
40–44	582	662	742	859	858	952	625	725	1,097	1,158	1,060	1,083	1,459	1,469	1,618	1,626
45–49	590	584	650	737	728	821	744	878	915	1,071	1,095	1,132	914	954	1,431	1,474
50–54	518	574	558	652	563	700	797	900	587	694	953	1,101	904	978	909	979
55–59	433	436	494	549	399	513	648	766	674	827	744	908	905	1,023	818	933
60–64			420	496	314	441	466	627	676	824	468	615	841	1,021	795	969
65–69	893	953	333	379	220	314	295	435	498	665	576	775	629	914	712	952
70–74			212	257	148	225	194	320	307	490	428	632	356	552	492	807
75–79			173	217	90	144	105	187	155	286	243	431	251	462	263	475
80 & over					62	118	69	144	102	232	144	336	240	550	229	537
Unknown	...	...	204[23]	15	28[24]	34[24]	35	36	10	10	9	9	...	...		

See p. 45 for footnotes

A2 Population of Countries by Sex and Age Groups (in thousands)

PORTUGAL

	1864		1875		1890		1900	
	M	F	M	F	M	F	M	F
0–4	246	237	321[29]	314[29]	298	291	324	313
5–9	219	210	239[28]	231[28]	283	272	310	300
10–14	259[27]	247[27]	220[28]	211[28]	271	254	295	285
15–19	161[28]	203[28]	189[28]	220[28]	225	237	251	265
20–24	156[28]	187[28]	170	195[28]	191	214	217	248
25–29	166[28]	194[28]	173[28]	206[28]	169	197	184	208
30–34	115[28]	129[28]	126[28]	145[28]	155	180	162	189
35–39	166[28]	182[28]	161[28]	183[28]	139	159	142	164
40–44	107[28]	113[28]	101[28]	114[28]	145	164	145	169
45–49	124[28]	139[28]	132[28]	153[28]	117	135	119	139
50–54	61[28]	71[28]	85[28]	98[28]	120	139	124	150
55–59	85[28]	106[28]	106[28]	122[28]	78	94	86	104
60–64	48[28]	55[28]	55[28]	59[28]	93	109	92	115
65–69	45[28]	55[28]	46[28]	58[28]	57	76	52	64
70–74	19[28]	22[28]	21[28]	26[28]	44	52	42	56
75–79	16[28]	20[28]	18[28]	23[28]	20	23	22	28
80 & over	9[28]	11[28]	10[28]	13[28]	16	22	19	27
unknown	3	3	3	3	9	10	6	6

	1911		1920		1930		1940	
	M	F	M	F	M	F	M	F
0–4	358	348	306	298	389	381	425	404
5–9	357	346	347	335	388	374	427	409
10–14	324	312	348	335	330	316	408	395
15–19	278	292	307	320	338	344	373	375
20–24	233	278	240	276	303	322	315	316
25–29	195	237	204	242	247	288	297	311
30–34	177	214	175	217	203	239	267	290
35–39	156	183	162	196	190	220	230	266
40–44	151	176	153	187	172	205	194	228
45–49	124	147	139	161	151	181	171	204
50–54	127	157	124	154	144	174	154	192
55–59	92	111	96	118	117	142	126	160
60–64	96	122	91	117	102	128	114	148
65–69	59	74	61	78	72	94	82	112
70–74	48	64	45	63	51	73	57	83
75–79	24	30	24	33	30	43	34	53
80 & over	21	32	20	32	22	39	26	50
unknown	7	7	13	15	6	7	11	13

A2 Population of Countries by Sex and Age Groups (in thousands)

PORTUGAL (*Cont'd*)

	1950 M	1950 F	1960 M	1960 F	1970 M	1970 F	1981 M	1981 F	1991 M	1991 F
0–4	454	435	424	403	402	387	405	387	296	279
5–9	406	392	400	385	432	417	440	423	345	323
10–14	406	394	393	385	411	402	435	419	386	370
15–19	404	407	341	354	355	375	434	425	421	406
20–24	380	382	316	343	298	330	386	383	413	400
25–29	335	347	304	326	241	277	337	343	408	405
30–34	263	278	288	302	250	284	308	321	362	365
35–39	273	294	268	287	263	292	269	296	317	328
40–44	248	277	225	243	261	290	273	301	290	309
45–49	211	249	229	250	243	270	278	309	251	283
50–54	176	215	210	241	209	235	268	302	251	284
55–59	146	186	173	211	206	234	249	283	247	288
60–64	126	169	136	177	184	226	199	233	228	275
65–69	95	135	105	144	140	186	182	226	198	249
70–74	99	100	79	116			139	193	143	193
75–79	41	66	50	81	192	314	82	135	108	165
80 & over	27	57	35	72			54	114	86	170
unknown	...	...	...	...	...	...	...	...	...	...

ROMANIA

	1899 M	1899 F	1912 M	1912 F	1930[30] M	1930[30] F	1930[31] M	1930[31] F	1956 M	1956 F	1966 M	1966 F	1977 M	1977 F	1993 M	1993 F
0–4	475	474	493	490	1,316	1,288	1,027	1,007	944	904	712	676	985	936	739	708
5–9	369	369	457	453	1,090	1,077	840	829	832	803	892	853	1,111	1,065	874	834
10–14	355	344	407	399	719	702	551	526	675	655	938	898	704	672	912	876
15–19	293	316	369	374	1,007	1,096	786	852	782	800	811	779	848	823	1,019	964
20–24	244	206	312	315	850	796	673	637	805	790	640	628	906	856	942	922
25–29	220	241	293	297	767	812	614	649	786	775	779	778	813	795	789	764
30–34	161	155	239	226	533	559	429	449	660	715	786	777	636	627	719	704
35–39	233	229	203	192	536	645	428	518	390	467	762	760	732	740	858	855
40–44	143	118	177	169	437	469	352	377	525	606	652	711	773	770	809	812
45–49	161	151	160	146	428	491	342	396	543	568	363	445	732	734	598	609
50–54	78	68	147	154	291	292	231	236	459	470	498	580	640	687	603	640
55–59	114	123	104	102	267	316	213	257	374	426	489	538	364	454	646	706
60–64	125	100	124	115	214	204	175	168	269	352	402	446	401	498	585	662
65–69	125	100	62	54	185	192	152	159	202	278	279	348	392	469	476	578
70–74	43	29	55	52	103	92	85	77	145	202	172	250	290	344	286	420
75–79			24	16	65	62	54	47	71	110	104	162	159	222	141	227
80 & over	11	7	29	23	34	35	29	29	40	66	64	112	89	155	177	289
Unknown	1	1	2	1	44	44	36	36	1	1	7	10	50	56	...	...

See p. 45 for notes

A2 Population of Countries by Sex and Age Groups (in thousands)

RUSSIA

	1897 M	1897 F	1926 M	1926 F	1939[33] M	1939[33] F	1959 M	1959 F	1970 M	1970 F	1987 (millions) M	1987 (millions) F	1993[37] M	1993[37] F
0–4	7,031	7,099	11,238	11,085	11,027	10,779	23,608	22,734	10,435	10,075	13.3	12.8	4.8	4.5
5–9	10,875	11,007	7,650	7,620	8,737	8,764			12,475	12,001	11.8	11.4	6.2	5.9
10–14			8,643	8,448	10,455	10,521	16,066	15,742	12,730	12,258	11.3	11.0	5.7	5.5
15–19	8,304	8,952	8,133	8,844	8,110	8,320			11,225	10,774	10.5	10.2	5.3	5.2
20–24			6,712	7,101	7,164	7,207	10,056	10,287	8,627	8,478	11.2	10.9	5.1	4.7
25–29	6,270	6,691	5,490	6,547	7,937	8,512	8,917	9,273	6,813	6,957	12.6	12.1	5.0	4.9
30–34			4,297	4,768	6,541	7,194	8,611	10,388	10,408	10,736	11.0	11.2	6.3	6.2
35–39	5,117	5,287	3,994	4,458	5,330	6,418	4,528	7,062	8,140	8,454	9.6	9.9	6.3	6.3
40–44			3,393	3,562	3,748	4,772	3,998	6,410	8,758	10,244	5.3	5.7	5.6	5.8
45–49	3,658	3,906	2,893	3,015	2,986	3,821	4,706	7,558	4,744	7,512	9.2	10.4	3.3	3.5
50–54			2,343	2,698	2,690	3,287	4,010	6,437	3,430	5,648	7.0	8.1	3.9	4.5
55–59	2,566	2,710	1,887	2,318	2,235	2,720	2,905	5,793	4,273	7,740	7.4	9.2	3.8	4.7
60–64			1,709	2,126	1,765	2,276	2,348	4,349			4.6	8.1	3.4	4.7
65–69	1,340	1,447	1,157	1,407	1,321	1,777	1,751	3,289	5,922	11,673	2.4	5.0	2.5	4.6
70–74			722	981	865	1,236					4.8	3.3	2.3	7.3
75–79	573	579	369	463	507	775	2,021	4,148	2,506	5,519				
80 & over			363	506	248	424	520	1,283	783	2,112				
Unknown	16	15	50	38	…	…	4	4	130	138	…			

SERBIA

	1890 M	1890 F		1890 M	1890 F
0–4	198	195	50–54	27	20
5–9	159	155	55–59	33	36
10–14	121	111	60–64	19	11
15–19	114	112	65–69	18	16
20–24	90	79	70–74	5	4
25–29	85	89	75–79	8	8
30–34	55	50	80 & over	7	6
35–39	75	73	Unknown	1	…
40–44	40	34			
45–49	55	53			

SPAIN

	1857 M	1857 F		1860 M	1860 F
0–1	222	213	0–1	209	200
1–7	1,284	1,258	1–5	927	896
8–15	1,286	1,237	6–10	844	823
16–20	666	740	11–15	795	765
21–25	607	660	16–20	683	786
26–30	728	751	21–25	620	663
31–40	1,156	1,136	26–30	672	720
41–50	761	784	31–40	1,185	1,174
51–60	544	577	41–50	832	841
61–70	308	318	51–60	545	583
71–80	92	97	61–70	328	331
81 & over	19	23	71–80	94	101
			81 & over	19	23

See p. 45 for footnotes

A2 Population of Countries by Sex and Age Groups (in thousands)

Spain (Cont'd)

	1877 M	1877 F	1887 M	1887 F	1900 M	1900 F	1910 M	1910 F
0–4	1,028	992	1,063	1,035	1,091	1,070	1,196	1,170
5–9	840	818	937	912	1,055	1,047	1,174	1,054
10–14	816	787	909	885	987	971	1,047	1,043
15–19	711	777	676	734	754	804	855	914
20–24	599	734	696	747	734	820	776	857
25–29	591	664	808[34]	883[34]	678	736	694	760
30–34	580	636	516	554	622	665	652	718
35–39	496	509	591	651	553	583	569	621
40–44	503	537	459	467	552	601	566	609
45–49	416	424	472	518	440	491	489	515
50–54	448	467	700	749	455	499	466	512
55–59	330	323			337	358	357	390
60–64	303	316	478	473	329	364	356	407
65–69	149	150			192	205	229	248
70–74	100	107	142	146	147	160	159	178
75–79	49	49			73	77	76	84
80 & over	34	45	22	30	69	66	55	77
Unknown	3	3	2	3	11	10	9	10

	1920 M	1920 F	1930 M	1930 F	1940 M	1940 F	1950 M	1950 F	1960 M	1960 F	1970 M	1970 F	1981 M	1981 F	1990 M	1990 F	1998 M	1998 F
0–4	1,130	1,120	1,324	1,283	1,137	1,111	1,318	1,255	1,514	1,456	1,658	1,560	1,572	1,485	1,085	1,012	988	924
5–9	1,175	1,153	1,313	1,272	1,390	1,370	1,251	1,184	1,377	1,323	1,652	1,591	1,712	1,585	1,285	1,197	1,014	956
10–14	1,157	1,148	1,153	1,308	1,376	1,365	1,180	1,147	1,369	1,309	1,543	1,474	1,702	1,606	1,593	1,504	1,131	1,075
15–19	1,003	1,081	1,080	1,108	1,248	1,297	2,649	2,710	2,389	2,312	1,363	1,337	1,662	1,609	1,688	1,596	1,425	1,358
20–24	859	955	1,053	1,097	1,015	1,167					1,279	1,262	1,481	1,457	1,684	1,610	1,670	1,605
25–29	750	833	933	988	952	1,107	2,066	2,255	2,365	2,450	1,117	1,119	1,285	1,263	1,621	1,580	1,669	1,611
30–34	704	771	803	851	929	994					1,022	1,049	1,232	1,223	1,432	1,422	1,613	1,579
35–39	594	646	686	745	826	908	1,737	1,951	1,920	2,076	1,200	1,208	1,123	1,127	1,256	1,248	1,495	1,486
40–44	617	679	656	697	734	808					1,150	1,180	1,015	1,037	1,208	1,216	1,325	1,330
45–49	506	550	558	602	628	702	1,443	1,618	1,599	1,803	1,054	1,083	1,161	1,192	1,072	1,085	1,206	1,219
50–54	490	532	530	583	572	622					805	907	1,104	1,158	988	1,034	1,135	1,169
55–59	396	421	424	479	466	530	992	1,187	1,235	1,463	752	880	969	1,047	1,088	1,163	950	1,003
60–64	475	430	385	443	423	513					683	811	731	883	977	1,088	961	1,068
65–69	237	270	281	321	309	392	828	1,194	1,027	1,478	571	712	635	818	806	957	937	1,090
70–74	173	207	192	234	208	269					380	1,534	521	704	549	763	755	961
75–79	86	100	102	132	124	167					413	689	585	997	404	633	510	751
80 & over	57	86	66	110	79	144									381	726	467	1,074
Unknown	34	34	25	23	...	...	7	7	16	48	...	...	1	1	...	...		

See p. 45 for footnotes

A2 Population of Countries by Sex and Age Groups (in thousands)

SWEDEN

	1751 M	1751 F	1760 M	1760 F	1770 M	1770 F	1780 M	1780 F	1790 M	1790 F	1800 M	1800 F
0–4	123	124	128	130	131	132	140	140	136	136	149	149
5–9	88	89	102	95	102	103	95	96	106	104	122	121
10–14	88	88	95	95	101	102	100	102	105	104	114	112
15–19	79	84	77	82	95	95	93	97	89	92	100	103
20–24	70	82	70	83	81	89	90	98	86	96	94	104
25–29	68	76	67	80	70	77	84	91	82	92	82	92
30–34	58	65	65	75	67	75	75	81	78	84	80	89
35–39	50	55	58	65	65	70	64	69	71	77	74	83
40–44	44	51	50	57	59	65	59	64	64	69	71	77
45–49	38	44	42	49	49	57	52	59	53	58	62	70
50–54	34	43	36	43	41	49	47	54	46	53	53	60
55–59	25	34	30	38	33	41	38	45	40	48	41	48
60–64	26	40	26	35	28	36	31	38	33	40	33	41
65–69	20	28	18	26	19	28	20	26	24	30	25	33
70–74	13	20	13	21	13	18	12	17	14	20	16	23
75–79	6	9	7	12	7	10	7	10	7	11	9	12
80 & over	6	9	5	9	6	9	4	7	4	7	4	7
Unknown	...	...	...	...	...	...	...	...	...	...	...	...

	1810 M	1810 F	1820 M	1820 F	1830 M	1830 F	1840 M	1840 F	1850 M	1850 F	1860 M	1860 F
0–4	141	141	168	167	193	192	194	193	219	216	259	255
5–9	120	120	129	130	168	168	173	171	184	184	205	203
10–14	119	118	116	116	144	144	163	164	168	168	177	186
15–19	111	114	115	117	129	131	165	166	169	170	177	177
20–24	93	106	110	115	107	111	133	137	154	158	154	159
25–29	86	97	104	110	106	110	115	119	148	153	150	156
30–34	82	91	88	97	102	106	97	102	123	128	138	146
35–39	69	77	78	87	93	100	94	100	104	110	138	145
40–44	66	76	72	82	76	87	87	95	86	93	111	119
45–49	61	70	58	67	65	77	77	88	80	89	90	101
50–54	54	63	54	64	58	70	61	74	72	83	69	80
55–59	47	55	46	58	44	55	49	62	60	73	62	74
60–64	35	44	38	48	37	49	42	56	45	60	52	64
65–69	24	30	28	38	28	39	26	36	30	43	40	53
70–74	15	21	17	24	19	27	18	27	20	31	23	34
75–79	9	12	8	12	10	16	10	16	10	16	12	19
80 & over	4	8	4	7	5	9	5	10	6	11	7	13
Unknown	...	...	...	...	...	...	...	...	...	...	...	...

A2 Population of Countries by Sex and Age Groups (in thousands)

SWEDEN (Cont'd)

	1870 M	1870 F	1880 M	1880 F	1890 M	1890 F	1900 M	1900 F	1910 M	1910 F
0–4	248	243	285	278	295	288	300	289	316	303
5–9	243	241	246	240	265	258	278	269	296	286
10–14	273	221	222	218	247	241	268	262	280	270
15–19	189	188	227	225	219	213	248	238	260	252
20–24	160	168	193	200	170	179	216	210	227	230
25–29	145	159	157	167	166	181	175	180	198	205
30–34	131	144	137	151	149	168	144	158	180	188
35–39	130	141	129	144	131	146	146	164	156	165
40–44	119	131	117	130	119	134	135	154	131	146
45–49	118	129	115	127	113	129	118	133	134	152
50–54	92	104	103	117	101	116	106	122	122	140
55–59	72	86	98	112	97	111	98	114	104	119
60–64	52	64	73	86	83	98	83	99	89	105
65–69	41	54	52	65	73	87	74	89	76	92
70–74	28	39	31	42	47	58	56	69	57	72
75–79	16	25	20	28	26	36	39	49	41	53
80 & over	8	15	11	20	15	24	22	32	31	44
Unknown	...	...	...	...	...	...	...	...	...	...

	1920 M	1920 F	1930 M	1930 F	1940 M	1940 F	1950 M	1950 F	1960 M	1960 F
0–4	288	276	231	223	227	218	312	297	260	245
5–9	292	281	267	257	209	200	302	288	274	259
10–14	302	289	278	268	227	220	230	222	313	298
15–19	283	274	284	274	264	255	211	205	303	291
20–24	257	252	280	275	273	264	230	229	236	230
25–29	223	230	250	256	276	269	269	264	220	216
30–34	200	213	228	236	275	270	274	268	236	234
35–39	180	191	204	217	248	251	275	269	269	265
40–44	166	176	187	202	223	230	272	268	271	265
45–49	144	154	169	180	197	208	242	247	269	265
50–54	120	134	154	163	177	190	213	222	261	261
55–59	119	137	130	140	155	166	183	197	226	235
60–64	103	122	104	118	134	145	156	173	191	206
65–69	82	100	95	113	105	116	129	143	152	173
70–74	62	76	74	90	74	87	100	112	116	138
75–79	42	55	47	59	54	67	64	72	78	94
80 & over	34	47	37	51	42	55	47	60	64	81
Unknown	...	...	...	...	...	...	...	...	...	...

A2 Population of Countries by Sex and Age Groups (in thousands)

SWEDEN (*Cont'd*)

	1970		1980		1990	
	M	**F**	**M**	**F**	**M**	**F**
0-4	297	281	235	224	290	275
5-9	293	279	284	271	250	237
10-14	273	258	296	281	253	241
15-19	282	270	296	282	288	275
20-24	339	323	283	271	308	293
25-29	326	301	296	283	317	299
30-34	252	237	338	322	296	281
35-39	226	219	322	301	299	287
40-44	238	235	245	235	333	322
45-49	266	264	218	216	314	299
50-54	260	259	226	230	236	231
55-59	253	256	246	254	205	210
60-64	234	245	234	246	204	220
65-69	187	211	211	234	209	235
70-74	140	169	175	211	178	216
75-79	91	122	116	162	134	185
80 & over	77	112	100	174	128	241
Unknown	...	...	...	...	...	...

A2 Population of Countries by Sex and Age Groups (in thousands)

SWITZERLAND

	1860 M	1860 F	1870 M	1870 F	1880 M	1880 F	1888 M	1888 F	1900 M	1900 F	1910 M	1910 F
0–4	137	138	148	148	167	167	162	161	189	189	203	201
5–9	115	116	141	141	150	149	155	155	169	168	197	197
10–14	117	117	128	129	137	138	153	154	157	157	188	187
15–19	121	122	110	112	134	135	135	136	159	156	180	177
20–24	111	117	102	114	114	122	117	127	148	153	155	161
25–29	97	103	103	112	98	101	108	117	137	136	153	151
30–34	94	99	95	103	95	99	91	98	118	120	145	145
35–39	84	88	87	91	94	98	85	91	107	111	129	128
40–44	73	77	82	87	86	91	81	88	93	98	109	113
45–49	67	69	73	77	75	79	79	86	76	81	97	103
50–54	60	64	61	66	68	74	68	76	69	78	80	89
55–59	53	55	54	57	58	64	57	64	65	73	62	71
60–64	41	43	45	48	44	50	49	56	52	62	52	63
65–69	27	28	35	37	34	37	38	43	39	46	43	53
70–74	20	21	22	22	23	25	22	25	27	32	29	36
75–79	10	10	10	10	13	14	12	14	15	18	16	20
80 & over	6	6	6	6	6	6	7	8	8	9	9	12
Unknown	2	2	8	7	…	…	…	…	…	…	…	…

	1920 M	1920 F	1930 M	1930 F	1941 M	1941 F	1950 M	1950 F	1960 M	1960 F	1970 M	1970 F	1980 M	1980 F	1990 M	1990 F	1998 M	1998 F
0–4	166	162	165	160	155	150	211	201	228	216	251	239	180	172	180	173	187	178
5–9	183	181	176	172	160	154	200	192	207	196	261	250	203	192	195	186	220	208
10–14	196	195	164	161	164	160	156	151	214	210	237	228	243	232	192	183	212	201
15–19	191	196	180	183	172	169	164	164	224	204	230	220	262	250	215	203	210	198
20–24	165	184	182	194	163	163	168	182	206	196	259	253	246	238	253	249	207	203
25–29	143	162	170	185	166	169	173	185	209	199	269	251	241	235	280	275	243	251
30–34	131	146	152	170	175	185	157	162	193	194	234	217	260	249	269	261	299	301
35–39	129	138	134	150	166	179	169	177	188	191	216	205	248	235	253	247	302	295
40–44	126	133	122	136	150	168	174	185	158	159	197	198	207	203	260	253	272	264
45–49	112	118	118	127	129	147	160	176	172	179	186	192	196	196	242	235	249	247
50–54	93	102	110	121	112	129	138	159	173	179	156	162	178	189	198	199	248	244
55–59	79	90	93	104	103	117	114	136	145	165	157	170	164	182	180	187	205	208
60–64	60	73	72	85	89	106	94	115	119	143	145	170	134	150	155	176	168	180
65–69	41	52	55	69	70	86	79	98	92	120	117	150	124	154	134	166	143	168
70–74	28	39	35	48	45	59	59	78	65	89	82	120	104	145	102	133	116	155
75–79	17	24	18	26	27	39	35	49	45	66	51	82	70	114	82	126	90	134
80 & over	10	15	11	18	15	24	21	35	33	54	39	72	55	116	85	180	97	201
Unknown	…	…	…	…	…	…	…	…	…	…	…	…	…	…	…	…		

A2 Population of Countries by Sex and Age Groups (in thousands)

UNITED KINGDOM

England and Wales

	1841[35]		1851		1861		1871		1881	
	M	F	M	F	M	F	M	F	M	F
0-4	1,048	1,058	1,177	1,171	1,355	1,346	1,536	1,535	1,758	1,763
5-9	953	952	1,050	1,042	1,173	1,172	1,351	1,356	1,569	1,579
10-14	880	852	964	949	1,060	1,045	1,221	1,204	1,402	1,398
15-19	782	805	873	884	958	975	1,085	1,096	1,268	1,279
20-24	723	827	796	871	860	969	952	1,053	1,112	1,216
25-29	611	672	699	771	734	835	843	937	981	1,067
30-34	565	602	618	658	662	725	746	814	840	905
35-39	435	450	533	556	590	634	641	700	745	797
40-44	436	452	474	494	551	583	590	640	673	726
45-49	314	325	394	406	453	478	507	546	548	604
50-54	307	327	346	363	392	414	456	489	486	536
55-59	190	202	255	271	299	315	346	372	382	425
60-64	209	231	227	254	266	291	295	328	341	387
65-69	121	139	152	176	176	201	205	236	232	271
70-74	104	120	115	135	128	153	150	174	158	192
75-79	56	64	65	81	72	89	82	100	90	113
80 & over	44	58	45	62	47	66	53	74	56	78
Unknown	...	...	...	...	...	...	...	...	...	...

	1891		1901		1911		1921		1931	
	M	F	M	F	M	F	M	F	M	F
0-4	1,775	1,778	1,855	1,861	1,936	1,918	1,682	1,640	1,510	1,480
5-9	1,693	1,702	1,739	1,748	1,847	1,850	1,767	1,752	1,678	1,645
10-14	1,611	1,613	1,671	1,671	1,748	1,752	1,837	1,823	1,620	1,587
15-19	1,465	1,486	1,608	1,639	1,655	1,682	1,728	1,775	1,710	1,725
20-24	1,247	1,399	1,473	1,648	1,503	1,673	1,448	1,703	1,699	1,795
25-29	1,111	1,239	1,328	1,496	1,456	1,623	1,340	1,620	1,629	1,728
30-34	978	1,050	1,158	1,274	1,376	1,501	1,281	1,520	1,433	1,622
35-39	866	916	1,035	1,111	1,261	1,352	1,273	1,472	1,283	1,520
40-44	746	802	898	953	1,075	1,158	1,223	1,378	1,229	1,434
45-49	642	695	760	813	926	1,000	1,162	1,244	1,187	1,367
50-54	550	611	636	693	768	834	971	1,043	1,116	1,265
55-59	413	471	498	555	608	670	782	849	987	1,081
60-64	357	416	410	480	477	543	601	681	778	879
65-69	260	312	282	347	366	441	449	537	578	693
70-74	185	233	196	251	237	317	281	376	377	494
75-79	102	132	113	151	128	183	159	234	204	296
80 & over	60	89	70	107	79	129	92	164	114	208
Unknown	...	...	...	...	...	...	...	...	...	...

A2 Population of Countries by Sex and Age Groups (in thousands)

UNITED KINGDOM
England and Wales (Cont'd)

	1951 M	1951 F	1961 M	1961 F	1971 M	1971 F	1981 M	1981 F	1991 M	1991 F
0-4	1,904	1,814	1,846	1,751	2,003	1,902	1,492	1,418	1,696	1,620
5-9	1,616	1,546	1,671	1,592	2,074	1,970	1,647	1,560	1,647	1,523
10-14	1,429	1,383	1,907	1,818	1,865	1,762	1,972	1,874	1,972	1,456
15-19	1,335	1,369	1,622	1,579	1,696	1,618	2,054	1,966	2,054	1,569
20-24	1,427	1,500	1,434	1,443	1,876	1,855	1,805	1,760	1,805	1,887
25-29	1,625	1,654	1,446	1,400	1,612	1,579	1,646	1,627	1,648	2,013
30-34	1,514	1,565	1,502	1,483	1,460	1,411	1,834	1,821	1,835	1,822
35-39	1,633	1,691	1,616	1,626	1,410	1,376	1,554	1,538	1,554	1,663
40-44	1,658	1,707	1,494	1,543	1,467	1,468	1,405	1,387	1,405	1,878
45-49	1,556	1,616	1,584	1,645	1,552	1,584	1,351	1,338	1,351	1,536
50-54	1,318	1,507	1,575	1,646	1,412	1,485	1,381	1,404	1,381	1,359
55-59	1,089	1,334	1,408	1,520	1,434	1,542	1,403	1,674	1,403	1,292
60-64	939	1,204	1,096	1,362	1,330	1,511	1,196	1,337	1,196	1,323
65-69	781	1,049	819	1,160	1,063	1,336	1,100	1,326	1,100	1,338
70-74	591	837	600	942	692	1,085	871	1,191	871	1,144
75-79	375	549	389	680	410	776	544	914	544	1,012
80 & over	226	418	295	612	327	805	368	960	367	1,313
Unknown	...	...	...	...	...	...	...	...	...	...

UNITED KINGDOM
Scotland

	1841[35] M	1841[35] F	1841 M	1841 F	1861 M	1861 F	1871 M	1871 F	1881 M	1881 F
0-4	174	169	189	183	212	205	231	225	258	252
5-9	159	155	172	168	184	179	205	200	228	222
10-14	151	146	163	155	165	158	190	182	206	199
15-19	128	142	146	154	150	157	167	168	190	189
20-24	113	141	129	152	127	153	138	154	167	177
25-29	93	113	104	126	101	132	116	139	137	152
30-34	86	102	89	105	91	111	100	120	112	125
35-39	65	77	76	89	79	96	85	105	98	114
40-44	67	79	71	83	74	89	80	96	91	106
45-49	46	53	57	66	62	73	67	80	74	89
50-54	45	56	54	65	56	68	61	74	67	81
55-59	29	34	37	44	43	51	48	58	51	62
60-64	34	43	33	45	41	53	43	55	46	60
65-69	17	22	22	29	24	33	29	38	31	42
70-74	16	21	18	24	18	26	23	32	23	33
75-79	9	11	10	14	11	15	12	17	13	19
80 & over	8	12	8	13	8	13	9	14	10	16
Unknown	3	2	...	...	3	...	...	...	...	...

See p. 45 for footnotes

A2 Population of Countries by Sex and Age Groups (in thousands)

UNITED KINGDOM
SCOTLAND (*Cont'd*)

	1891 M	1891 F	1901 M	1901 F	1911 M	1911 F	1921 M	1921 F	1931 M	1931 F
0–4	255	248	268	265	268	265	239	234	214	210
5–9	242	236	249	243	258	256	240	237	229	226
10–14	229	223	238	231	247	243	247	243	215	211
15–19	211	207	230	226	233	229	239	239	219	220
20–24	174	190	210	223	202	218	203	226	206	216
25–29	145	168	181	198	182	204	173	204	187	203
30–34	129	141	151	164	170	185	155	183	162	187
34–39	114	124	133	145	158	167	150	174	144	172
40–44	97	108	119	127	133	143	146	163	135	158
45–49	85	98	101	108	115	126	142	148	130	151
50–54	74	89	84	93	98	108	119	125	127	140
55–59	56	68	86	77	79	87	97	104	116	123
60–64	50	64	56	70	60	70	76	85	92	100
65–69	34	46	37	50	46	58	57	67	68	81
70–74	25	36	26	38	32	48	35	49	46	60
75–79	14	22	15	23	17	26	19	30	25	36
80 & over	10	17	10	18	10	19	12	23	13	25
Unknown	…	…	…	…	…	…	…	…	…	…

	1951 M	1951 F	1961 M	1961 F	1971 M	1971 F	1981 M	1981 F	1991 M	1991 F
0–4	241	230	240	229	228	216	158	150	162	155
5–9	203	195	215	206	240	228	176	168	162	155
10–14	196	191	230	219	227	216	218	207	160	152
15–19	173	189	187	187	199	193	228	219	169	163
20–24	172	192	159	174	197	194	200	195	184	190
25–29	187	194	161	166	158	158	172	170	190	202
30–34	166	179	163	170	148	152	180	178	183	192
35–39	178	191	171	177	147	153	150	151	167	171
40–44	180	190	153	167	151	157	141	147	177	179
45–49	169	181	164	179	157	166	139	146	147	150
50–54	141	167	164	178	140	156	140	150	136	144
55–59	116	145	147	165	143	163	138	151	130	141
60–64	98	127	113	146	134	159	114	137	124	141
65–69	83	109	83	121	107	141	106	135	111	135
70–74	66	86	60	94	68	111	83	120	80	113
75–79	42	56	40	65	39	76	51	92	58	97
80 & over	24	41	31	54	31	72	33	91	48	122
Unknown	1	1	…	…	…	…	…	…	…	…

See p. 45 for footnotes

A2 Population of Countries by Sex and Age Groups (in thousands)

YUGOSLAVIA

	1921 M	1921 F	1931 M	1931 F	1948 M	1948 F	1953 M	1953 F
0–4	612	585	1,000	971	840	808	1,046	1,002
5–9	705	671	898	858	858	828	769	738
10–14	768	727	563	535	915	883	818	787
15–19	624	628	643	642	866	857	891	866
20–24	495	546	701	670	668	782	873	850
25–29	363	413	588	587	478	585	664	771
30–34	337	430	485	516	360	426	483	583
35–39	327	381	360	399	543	594	341	412
40–44	300	354	326	399	499	501	521	566
45–49	245	257	300	339	425	468	481	497
50–54	245	263	260	311	297	357	402	439
55–59	204	199	210	225	244	326	280	349
60–64	195	202	193	215	210	274	211	285
65–69	122	112	150	151	164	222	178	243
70–74	92	94	108	116	103	131	123	169
75–79	48	44	56	56	64	85	70	98
80 & over	49	52	49	53	48	64	53	77
unknown	1	1	1	1	…	…	…	1

	1961 M	1961 F	1971 M	1971 F	1981 M	1981 F	1990[38] M	1990[38] F
0–4	990	947	918	877	958	905	887	830
5–9	1,023	978	938	893	945	893	936	878
10–14	936	897	959	914	918	869	958	905
15–19	694	684	1,013	971	945	900	935	885
20–24	797	784	900	854	952	908	922	877
25–29	825	823	649	642	973	921	944	905
30–34	767	792	762	761	867	828	943	905
35–39	563	682	803	799	635	629	958	916
40–44	343	414	738	767	746	746	792	771
45–49	423	492	540	663	769	775	642	734
50–54	483	515	323	399	694	739	708	735
55–59	409	442	383	465	494	632	694	744
60–64	311	373	414	467	281	369	566	674
65–69	184	246	315	369	303	398	379	547
70–74	136	202	206	276	281	359	175	264
75–79	86	125	94	145	276	418	183	289
80 & over	64	102	76	134			163	267
unknown	9	9	46	47	46	52	…	…

A2 Population of Countries by Sex and Age Groups (in thousands)

NOTES

1. SOURCES: With the following exceptions, all figures are taken from the official publications listed on p. xv. Czechoslovakia 1930 (ages over 60)—data supplied by the Federal Statistical Office of Czechoslovakia; Finland 1865 and Greece 1870, 1879, and 1889—J. Bertillon, *Statistique Internationale des Rencensements de la Population....* (Paris, 1899); Greece 1861—U.N., *The Aging of Populations and its Economic and Social Implications* (1956); Russia 1897—A.D. Webb, *New Dictionary of Statistics*, London, (1911); Russia 1926 and 1939—F. Lorimer, *The Population of the Soviet Union* (Geneva, 1946); Sweden 1751–1850—G. Sundbarg, *Statistisk Tidskrift*, 1908.
2. For fuller footnotes on territorial changes and on the nature of these statistics see table B.1.

FOOTNOTES

[1] Excluding Lombardy and Venetia.
[2] The statistics in 1869 relate to civil population only. The following classification of the civil population is available for 1857:-

	M	F		M	F
0–6	1,288	1,290	25–40	1,964	2,297
7–14	1,506	1,543	41–60	1,661	1,710
15–24	1,768	1,945	over 60	503	521

[3] 1st January in all provinces except Burgenland, for which the census was on 7th March.
[4] In 1930 and subsequently the eastern cantons ceded by Germany after the First World War are included.
[5] This does not include Eastern Roumelia. The figures given for the age group 5–9 are actually for 5–10, and older age groups are for 11–15, 16–20 etc. to 81 and over.
[6] The territory was enlarged between 1910 and 1920.
[7] Sub-Carpathian Russia (Ruthenia) and a few Slovak villages were ceded to Russia in 1945. The censuses were on 4th October 1946 in Slovakia and 22 May 1947 in the Czech lands.
[8] Denmark proper, excluding the Faroe Islands, Greenland, Iceland, and the Duchies of Schleswig, Holstein, and Lauenburg.
[9] Figures from 1921 onwards include the northern part of Schleswig, returned to Denmark by Germany after the First World War.
[10] Subsequently includes Savoy and Nice, acquired in 1860.
[11] Figures from 1872 to 1911 exclude most of Alsace and Lorraine, ceded to Germany in 1871 and reacquired in 1918.
[12] Subsequent figures are not census results but estimates at 1 January in each census year.
[13] Excluding Saarland.
[14] 1937 territory.
[15] Excluding West Berlin and Saarland.
[16] Excluding East Berlin.
[17] The figures are for the age-group 75–84.
[18] These figures are for the age-group 85 and over.
[19] Subsequent figures include Venetia.
[20] Subsequent figures include South Tirol and, up to 1936 (inclusive) Istria.
[21] Istria and certain other areas ceded to Yugoslavia and France after the Second World War are not subsequently included.
[22] The figures relate to the territory of the year in question. There were considerable boundary changes after the Second World War.
[23] Including 191 thousand soldiers in barracks.
[24] Excluding 394 thousand not tabulated by age or sex.
[25] Excluding civilian aliens, and including civilian nationals temporarily abroad. The classification in this year was based on year of birth rather than completed years of age.
[26] Including Madeira and the Azores.
[27] Age-group 10–15, comprising six years.
[28] These figures are for age-groups one year older than shown in the stub (i.e. 16–20 instead of 15–19, etc.)
[29] Age-group 1–5, comprising six years.
[30] The territory of Romania was much enlarged between 1912 and 1930.
[31] These figures are for the territory established after the Second World War.
[32] European Russia (excluding Finland and the Caucasus).
[33] These are estimates by F. Lorimer (see note 1 above).
[34] These figures are for the age group 25–30, comprising six years. Subsequent figures are for age-groups 31–35, 36–40 etc.
[35] These figures are only approximate.
[36] Figures for Czech Republic and Slovakia are as follows.

	Czech Republic (1993)		Slovakia (1991)	
	M	F	M	F
0–4	321	305	204	195
5–9	337	321	226	216
10–14	385	367	241	231
15–19	464	445	226	218
20–24	383	365	189	182
25–29	355	340	198	193
30–34	326	315	210	204

A2 Population of Countries by Sex and Age Groups (in thousands)

35–39	384	377	215	212
40–44	412	410	179	181
45–49	388	394	133	144
50–54	288	301	117	132
55–59	230	255	112	131
60–64	237	283	106	132
65–69	205	282	93	125
70–74	146	228	46	67
75–79	70	127	42	66
80 & over	82	195	34	69
Unknown	...	...	...	...

[37] Figures for former USSR as follows:

	Armenia (1992)		Azerbaijan (1989)		Belarus (1992)		Estonia (1993)		Georgia (1989)		Kazakhstan (1991)		Kyrgistan (1992)	
	M	F	M	F	M	F	M	F	M	F	M	F	M	F
0–4	194	183	444	417	381	360	51	48	238	227	954	918	318	307
5–9	199	190	390	369	427	411	58	56	224	216	890	869	289	284
10–14	176	168	348	332	388	376	55	54	220	212	814	800	240	236
15–19	156	151	365	328	367	361	54	52	218	201	745	712	218	218
20–24	144	139	330	357	337	343	57	52	203	210	680	616	194	180
25–29	147	160	336	371	377	378	51	50	226	241	726	725	177	181
30–34	165	181	272	289	442	439	56	56	201	215	723	724	174	176
35–39	129	147	189	200	390	395	55	57	174	188	591	606	134	138
40–44	95	107	112	120	342	357	51	55	124	136	461	483	100	104
45–49	53	62	123	133	210	224	40	45	139	157	259	282	48	48
50–54	81	93	170	186	283	328	43	50	164	182	446	498	81	88
55–59	76	87	137	148	262	327	40	50	141	163	257	298	67	76
60–64	74	85	97	120	256	347	36	50	130	167	268	370	62	78
65–69	48	62	39	68	164	308	26	46	57	103	128	253	36	59
70–74	16	29	24	52	78	171	14	32	39	84	67	153	16	34
75–79	12	24	23	47	51	136	9	22	33	68	55	148	11	27
80 & over	15	18	23	56	60	184	10	30	27	65	46	146	12	31
Unknown	...	...	...	...	...	...	...	...	...	...	...	...	...	...

	Latvia (1991)		Lithuania (1991)		Moldova (1992)		Tajikistan (1989)		Turkmenistan (1989)		Uzbekistan (1989)		Ukraine (1992)	
	M	F	M	F	M	F	M	F	M	F	M	F	M	F
0–4	102	98	149	142	199	191	457	444	283	276	1,630	1,585	1,779	1,694
5–9	100	97	146	141	219	212	353	344	233	228	1,319	1,292	1,971	1,903
10–14	89	86	135	131	192	188	297	290	205	202	1,138	1,117	1,838	1,778
15–19	92	87	137	132	179	178	263	262	188	178	1,003	1,001	1,887	1,831
20–24	96	89	143	134	147	141	227	236	161	165	911	921	1,719	1,681
25–29	101	98	156	149	146	157	219	222	157	164	890	894	1,790	1,801
30–34	102	103	151	152	180	192	162	163	124	128	696	697	1,995	2,041
35–39	90	94	124	127	166	176	118	120	90	94	503	510	1,833	1,922
40–44	82	88	110	118	151	163	71	68	52	53	286	286	1,697	1,823
45–49	74	83	103	115	77	90	80	71	54	54	318	308	1,099	1,249
50–54	84	98	101	120	105	126	82	83	56	58	323	328	1,818	2,149
55–59	68	86	92	117	93	114	68	74	46	51	266	296	1,262	1,518
60–64	62	90	80	114	84	110	56	64	37	47	216	268	1,349	1,836
65–69	37	79	54	96	58	94	27	42	17	31	97	172	882	1,691
70–74	22	45	29	55	38	62	17	29	11	22	60	124	431	982
75–79	19	47	24	53	22	40	14	23	9	18	58	107	338	924
80 & over	19	54	31	40	17	38	16	34	7	15	68	117	314	969
unknown	...	...	...	...	...	...	...	...	...	...	...	...	...	...

A2 Population of Countries by Sex and Age Groups (in thousands)

[38] Figures for former Yugoslavia as follows:

	Croatia (1991)		Maledonia (1992)		Slovenia (1993)		Yugoslavia (1991)
	M	F	M	F	M	F	
0–4	143	136	84	78	56	53	772
5–9	161	153	85	81	66	63	791
10–14	169	162	85	82	75	71	809
15–19	167	160	83	79	76	72	787
20–24	163	157	80	74	71	70	741
25–29	173	170	80	75	76	77	718
30–34	185	181	84	78	77	77	739
35–39	192	182	86	80	82	79	795
40–44	177	169	76	73	81	77	725
45–49	129	130	58	57	61	59	515
50–54	150	154	54	55	60	60	615
55–59	149	162	55	57	54	57	643
60–64	126	152	42	47	48	59	597
65–69	83	136	33	40	33	53	446
70–74	43	76	20	24	21	39	222
75–79	38	71	13	15	11	22	365
80 & over	34	74	11	14	15	35	
unknown	33	39	7	8	...	...	109

A3 POPULATION OF MAJOR DISTRICTS (in thousands)

AUSTRIA

(a) Habsburg Austria[3]

	1754	1780	1843	1846	1851	1857	1869	1880	1890	1900	1910
Lower Austria	930	1,570	1,453	1,531	1,538[1]	1,682[1]	1,991	2,331	2,662	3,100	3,532
Upper Austria	430		865	871	706[1]	707[1]	737	760	786	810	853
Salzburg	...	...			146[1]	147[1]	153	164	174	193	215
Styria	697	800	997	1,023	1,006	1,057	1,138	1,214	1,301	1,356	1,444
Tirol & Voralberg	385	680	848	866	858[1]	851[1]	886	913	929	982	1,092
Carinthia	272	288	777	796	319[1]	332[1]	338	349	361	367	396
Carniola	345	406			464[1]	452[1]	466	481	499	508	526
Küstenland	102	120	493	508	553[1]	521[1]	601	648	695	757	894
Dalmatia	...	...	406	418	394[1]	404[1]	457	476	527	594	646
Bohemia	1,972	2,868	4,319	4,410	4,386[1]	4,706[1]	5,141	5,561	5,843	6,319	6,770
Moravia	887	1,595	2,242	2,290	1,800[1]	1,867[1]	2,017	2,153	2,277	2,438	2,622
Silesia	155				439[1]	444[1]	513	565	606	680	757
Galicia	...	3,396	4,980	5,189	4,555[1]	4,597[1]	5,445	5,959	6,608	7,316	8,026
Bukowina	...				380[1]	457[1]	513	572	647	730	800

AUSTRIA

(b) Republic of Austria

	1910	1923	1934	1951	1961	1971	1981	1991
Lower Austria	1,425	1,427	1,447	1,400	1,374	1,421	1,428	1,511
Upper Austria	854	877	903	1,109	1,132	1,230	1,270	1,383
Salzburg	215	223	246	327	347	405	442	504
Styria	958	979	1,015	1,109	1,138	1,195	1,187	1,204
Tirol	305	314	349	427	446	544	587	654
Vorarlberg	145	140	155	194	226	277	305	342
Carinthia	371	371	405	475	495	527	536	560
Burgenland	292	286	299	275	271	272	270	273
Vienna	2,083	1,919	1,936	1,616	1,628	1,620	1,531	1,596

See pp. 72–3 for footnotes

A3 Population of Major Districts (in thousands)

BELGIUM

	1801	1806	1811	1816	1831	1846	1856	1866	1876	1880	1890	1900	1910	1920	1930	1947	1961	1970	1981	1990
Antwerp	246	285	282	295	350	406	434	466	538	577	700	819	969	1,017	1,173	1,281	1,444	1,538	1,576	1,605
Brabant	246	303	...	445	562	691	749	814	936	985	1,106	1,264	1,470	1,522	1,680	1,798	1,992	2,171	2,222	2,253
East Flanders	560	602	601	622	743	793	777	806	863	882	950	1,030	1,120	1,107	1,149	1,217	1,277	1,310	1,331	1,336
West Flanders	460	492	...	521	608	643	625	642	684	692	738	805	874	804	902	997	1,073	1,054	1,080	1,107
Hainaut	415	474	...	494	613	715	769	845	956	978	1,049	1,143	1,233	1,220	1,270	1,225	1,260	1,317	1,305	1,280
Liège	...	311	...	361	375	453	504	557	632	664	757	826	888	863	973[5]	964	1,011	1,003	1,004	1,001
Limbourg	...	...	...	330	319	186[3]	192	195	205	211	223	241	276	300	368	460	579	653	716	750
Luxembourg	...	...	...	320	306	186[4]	194	200	204	209	212	219	231	224	221	213	219	217	223	232
Namur	...	...	...	223	214	264	286	303	316	323	335	347	363	348	356	356	373	387	406	424

CZECHOSLOVAKIA

	1910	1921	1930	1946/7[7]	1950	1961	1970	1980
Bohemia, Moravia & Silesia	10,079	10,010	10,674	8,762	8,896	9,572	9,808	10,292
Slovakia	2,925	2,998	3,330	3,328[8]	3,442	4,174	4,537	4,991
Sub-Carpathian Russia (Ruthenia)	596	605	725					

See pp. 72–3 for footnotes

A3 Population of Major Districts (in thousands)

FRANCE

	1801	1831	1841	1851	1861	1872	1881	1891	1901	1911	1921	1931	1946	1954	1962	1968	1975	1982	1990
Ain	297	346[9]	356	373	370	363	363	357	350	342	316	323	307	312	328	339	376	419	471
Aisne	426	513	542	559	565	552	557	545	536	530	422	489	453	487	510	526	534	534	537
Allier	249	298	311	337	356	391	417	424	422	406	371	374	373	373	379	387	378	370	358
Alpes, Basses*	134	156	156	152	146	139	132	124	115	107	92	88	83	84	92	105	112	119	131
Alpes, Hautes	113	129	133	132	125	119	122	116	110	105	89	88	85	85	89	92	97	105	113
Alpes Maritimes					195	199	227	259	293	356	358	493	453	515	614	722	817	881	972
Ardèche	267	341	319	331	389	380	377	371	354	332	294	283	255	249	246	257	257	268	277
Ardennes	260[10]	291	319	331	329	320	334	325	316	319	278	294	245	280	297	309	309	302	296
Ariège	196	254	266	267	252	246	241	227	211	199	173	161	146	140	135	138	138	136	136
Aveyron	318[11]	359	375	394	396	402	415	400	382	369	333	324	308	293	287	282	278	279	270
Aube	231	246	258	265	263	256	255	256	246	241	228	243	235	241	252	270	285	289	289
Aude	225	270	284	290	284	286	328	317	314	301	287	297	269	268	268	278	272	281	299
Bouches-du-Rhône	285	359	375	429	507	555	589	631	734	806	842	1,012[12]	972	1,049	1,241	1,470	1,633	1,724	1,759
Calvados	452	495	496	491	481	454	440	429	410	396	385	401	400	443	477	520	561	590	618
Cantal	220	259	257	253	241	232	236	240	231	223	199	194	187	177	171	169	167	163	159
Charente	299	363	368	383	379	368	371	360	350	347	316	310	311	314	325	331	337	341	342
Charente-Maritime	399	445	460	470	481	466	466	456	452	451	418	415	416	448	471	484	498	513	527
Cher	218	256	274	306	323	335	351	359	346	338	305	294	286	284	291	305	316	320	322
Corrèze	244	295	306	321	310	303	317	328	318	310	274	264	255	243	239	238	240	241	238
Corsica[13]	164	198	221	236	253	259	273	289	296	291	282	297	268	247	276	274	290	240	250
Côte-d'Or	341	375	393	400	384	375	383	377	362	350	321	334	336	357	386	421	450	474	494
Côtes-du-Nord	504	599	608	633	629	622	628	619	609	606	558	540	527	503	498	506	526	539	538
Creuse	218	265	278	287	270	275	279	285	278	266	228	208	189	173	163	157	146	140	131
Dordogne	409	483	490	506	502	480	495	478	453	437	397	384	388	378	370	374	373	377	386
Doubs	216	266	286	297	296	291	311	303	299	300	285	306	298	327	383	426	471	477	485
Drôme	235	300	312	327	327	320	314	306	297	291	264	267	268	275	304	343	362	396	414
Eure	403	424	426	416	399	378	364	349	335	324	303	306	316	333	360	383	423	462	514
Eure-et-Loir	258	279	286	295	290	283	280	285	275	272	251	255	258	261	277	302	335	363	396
Finistère	439	524	576	618	627	643	682	727	773	810	763	744	725	728	739	769	804	828	839
Gard	300	357	376	408	422	420	416	419	421	413	396	407	381	397	433	479	495	530	585
Garonne, Haute	340[11]	428	468	482	484	479	478	472	448	432	425	442	512	526	592	691	777	825	926
Gers	258[11]	312	311	307	299	285	282	261	238	222	194	193	190	185	180	182	175	174	175
Gironde	503	554	568	614	667	705	749	794	821	829	819	853	858	897	936	1,009	1,061	1,128	1,214
Hérault	275	346	367	389	409	430	442	461	489	480	488	515	461	471	513	591	648	706	795

See pp. 72–3 for footnotes

A3 Population of Major Districts (in thousands)

France

	1801	1831	1841	1851	1861	1872	1881	1891	1901	1911	1921	1931	1946	1954	1962	1968	1975	1982	1990
Ille-et-Vilaine	489	547	549	575	585	590	615	627	614	608	559	563	578	587	610	653	702	750	799
Indre	206	245	253	272	270	278	288	293	289	288	260	248	252	247	249	247	249	243	238
Indre-et-Loire	269	297	306	316	324	317	329	337	336	341	328	335	350	365	393	438	479	506	529
Isère	436	550	589	603	578	576	580	572	569	556	526	584	574	626	726	768	860	937	1,016
Jura	288	313	317	313	298	288	285	273	261	253	229	229	216	220	224	233	239	243	249
Landes	224	282	288	302	301[14]	301	301	298	292	289	264	257	248	249	260	277	288	297	311
Loire	291	391	434	473	518	551	600	616	648	641	637	665	632	654	687	722	742	740	746
Loire Atlantique	369	470	487	536	580	602	626	645	665	670	650	652	665	734	794	861	934	995	1,052
Loire, Haute	230	292	298	305	306	309	316	317	314	304	269	252	228	216	210	208	205	206	207
Loir-et-Cher	210	236	249	262	269	269	276	280	276	271	252	242	242	240	248	268	284	296	306
Loiret	286	305	318	341	353	353	369	378	367	364	337	343	347	361	390	431	490	536	581
Lot	261[11]	285	288	296	296	281	280	254	227	206	177	167	155	148	149	151	151	155	156
Lot-et-Garonne	299[11]	347	347	341	332	319	312	295	279	268	240	248	265	266	272	291	293	299	306
Lozère	127	140	141	145	137	135	144	136	129	123	109	102	91	82	81	77	75	74	72
Maine-et-Loire	376	468	488	515	526	518	523	519	515	508	475	476	496	518	554	586	630	675	706
Manche	531	591	597	601	591	545	526	514	491	476	426	433	435	477	443	452	452	466	480
Marne	305	337	357	373	385	386	422	435	433	436	367	412	387	415	444	485	530	544	558
Marne, Haute	227	250	258	268	259	251	255	244	227	215	199	190	182	197	207	214	212	211	204
Mayenne	306	353	361	375	375	351	345	332	313	298	262	254	256	252	247	253	262	272	278
Meurthe[15]	338	416	445	450	429														
Meurthe et Moselle[15]						365	419	444	485	565	504	593	529	607	678	705	723	717	712
Meuse	270	315	326	329	306	385	290	292	283	278	207	216	189	207	218	210	204	200	196
Morbihan	401	434	448	478	487	490	522	544	563	578	546	538	507	521	527	540	564	591	620
Moselle[15]	348	417	440	460	446	(490)	(493)	(510)	(565)	(655)	589	693	622	769	923	971	1,006	1,007	1,011
Nièvre	233	282	305	327	333	340	348	344	324	299	270	255	249	240	243	248	245	240	233
Nord	765	990	1,085	1,158	1,303	1,448	1,603	1,736	1,867	1,962	1,788	2,029	1,917	2,099	2,274	2,418	2,511	2,521	2,532
Oise	351	398	399	404	401	397	405	402	408	411	388	407	397	435	482	541	606	662	726
Orne	396	442	442	440	423	398	376	354	327	307	275	274	273	275	278	289	294	295	293
Pas-de-Calais	506	655	685	693	724	761	819	874	955	1,068	990	1,205	1,169	1,277	1,348	1,396	1,403	1,412	1,433
Puy-de-Dôme	507	573	591	597	576	566	566	564	544	526	491	501	479	481	509	548	580	594	598
Pyrénées, Basses†	356	428	452	447	436[14]	427	434	425	426	433	403	423	416	420	469	509	535	556	578
Pyrénées Hautes	175	233	244	251	240	235	236	226	216	206	186	190	202	204	212	226	227	228	225
Pyrénées Orientales	111	157	174	182	182	192	209	210	212	213	218	239	229	230	252	282	300	335	364

See pp. 72–3 for footnotes

A3 Population of Major Districts (in thousands)

France

	1801	1831	1841	1851	1861	1872	1881	1891	1901	1911	1921	1931	1946	1954	1962	1968	1975	1982	1990
Rhin, Bas	450	540	560	587	578	(600)[16]	(612)[17]	(622)	(659)	(701)	652	688	673	708	764	827	882	916	953
Rhin, Haut		304	424	465	494	516	(459)[17]	(462)	(472)	(495)	(518)	469	517	472	510	544	585	635	671
Rhône	299	434	501	575	662	670	741	807	843	916[18]	957[18]	1,046[18]	919	967	1,110	1,326	1,430	1,445	1,508
Sâone, Haute		292	339	347	347	317	303	296	281	267	258	228	202	209	208	214	222	232	230
Sâone-et-Loire	453	524	552	575	582	598	626	620	620	604	555	539	507	511	530	550	570	572	559
Sarthe	388	457	471	473	466	447	439	430	423	419	389	385	412	420	441	462	490	505	514
Savoie					275	268	266	263	255	248	225	236	236	252	266	289	305	324	348
Savoie, Haute					267	273	274	268	264	255	236	253	271	294	333	379	448	495	568
Seine[50]	632	935	1,195	1,422	1,954	2,220	2,799	3,142	3,670	4,154	4,412	4,934	4,776	5,155	5,575	...	...	...	...
Seine-et-Marne	299	324	333	345	352	341	349	357	358	364	349	406	407	453	526	604	756	887	1,078
Seine-et-Oise[50]	422	448	471	484	513	580	578	629	707	818	922	1,366	1,415	1,709	2,302	...	...	...	...
Seine Maritime	610	694	737	762	790	790	814	840	854	877	881	905	846	942	1,025	1,114	1,173	1,193	1,223
Sèvres, Deux	242	295	310	324	329	331	350	354	342	338	310	308	313	313	317	326	336	343	345
Somme	459	544	560	571	573	557	551	546	538	520	453	467	441	464	482	511	538	545	547
Tarn	271	336	352	363	354	353	359	347	332	324	296	303	298	308	318	332	338	339	342
Tarn-et-Garonne	228[11]	242	239	238	233	222	217	207	196	183	160	164	168	172	175	184	183	190	200
Var	272	322	328	358	316[19]	294	289	288	326	331	323	377	371	413	485	556	626	708	815
Vaucluse	191	239	251	265	268	263	244	235	237	239	220	242	250	268	302	354	390	427	467
Vendée	243	330	356	384	396	401	422	442	441	439	397	390	394	396	403	421	451	483	509
Vienne	241	283	294	317	322	321	340	344	336	332	306	303	314	319	329	340	357	371	380
Vienne, Haute	245	285	293	319	320	322	349	373	382	385	350	336	336	324	329	342	352	356	353
Vosges	309	398	420	427	415	393[16]	407	410	421	434	384	378	342	373	380	388	398	396	386
Yonne	321	352	363	381	370	364	357	345	321	304	273	276	266	266	269	283	300	311	323
Territory of Belfort[17]						57	74	84	92	101	94	99	87	99	110	118	128	132	134
Ville de Paris															...	2,591	2,300	2,176	2,152
Yvelines															...	854	1,082	1,196	1,307
Essonne															...	673	923	998	1,084
Hauts-de-Seine															...	1,462	1,439	1,387	1,392
Seine-St.Denis															...	1,250	1,322	1,324	1,381
Val-de-Marne															...	1,121	1,216	1,194	1,215
Val-d'Oise															...	693	841	921	1,049

*Now named Alpes de Haut Provence.   †Now named Pyrénées Atlantique

See pp. 72–3 for footnotes

A3   Population of Major Districts (in thousands)

GERMANY

(a) Constituents of United Germany

	1816	1828	1834	1840	1852	1861	1864
Prussia	10,349	12,726	13,510	14,929	16,935	18,491	19,255
States later incorporated in Prussia[20]	2,154	2,617	2,793	2,960	3,104	3,193	3,257
Bavaria	3,655	4,088	4,247	4,371	4,559	4,690	4,807
Kingdom of Saxony	1,190	1,373	1,596	1,706	1,988	2,225	2,337
Württemburg	1,411	1,549	1,570	1,646	1,733	1,721	1,748
Baden	1,006	1,176	1,231	1,296	1,362	1,373	1,432
Hesse	607	718	761	812	854	857	853
Thuringian states[21]	709	802	855	896	960	1,004	1,035
Other states[22]	1,491	1,596	1,676	1,766	1,918	2,013	2,068

See pp. 72–3 for footnotes

A3 **Population of Major Districts** (in thousands)

(b) United Germany

	1864	1871[26]	1880	1890	1900	1910	1910[23]	1925	1933	1939[24]
Prussia[25]	23,582	24,689[26]	27,279	29,957	34,473	40,165	35,053	38,176	39,934	41,334
of which										
East Prussia	1,761	1,823	1,934	1,959	1,997	2,064	2,147	2,256	2,333	2,186
West Prussia	1,253	1,315	1,406	1,434	1,564	1,703	310	332	338	...
Posen	1,524	1,584	1,703	1,752	1,887	2,100				
Pomerania	1,438	1,432	1,540	1,521	1,635	1,717	1,719	1,879	1,921	2,394
Berlin	633	826	1,122	1,579	1,889	2,071	3,734	4,024	4,243	4,339
Brandenburg	1,984	2,037	2,267	2,542	3,109	4,093	2,429	2,592	2,726	3,008
Silesia	3,511	3,707	4,008	4,224	4,669	5,226	4,259	4,512	4,687	4,869
Saxony	2,045	2,103	2,312	2,580	2,833	3,089	3,105	3,293	3,401	3,618
Schleswig-Holstein	999	1,045	1,127	1,220	1,388	1,621	1,455	1,519	1,590	1,589
Hanover	1,926	1,961	2,120	2,278	2,591	2,942	2,985	3,223	3,368	3,458
Westphalia	1,667	1,775	2,043	2,429	3,188	4,125	4,089	4,784	5,040	5,209
Hesse-Nassau	1,388	1,400	1,554	1,664	1,898	2,221	2,287	2,475	2,585	2,675
Rhineland	3,372	3,579	4,074	4,710	5,760	7,121	6,463	7,214	7,632	7,906
Hohenzollern	65	66	68	66	67	71	71	72	73	74
Bavaria	4,775	4,863	5,285	5,595	6,176	6,887	6,882	7,380	7,682	8,223
Kingdom of Saxony	2,337	2,556	2,973	3,503	4,202	4,807	4,809	4,994	5,197	5,232
Württemberg	1,748	1,819	1,971	2,037	2,169	2,438	2,438	2,580	2,696	2,897
Baden	1,432	1,462	1,570	1,658	1,868	2,143	2,143	2,312	2,413	2,502
Hesse	817	853	936	993	1,120	1,282	1,282	1,347	1,429	1,469
Mecklenburg[26]	652	655	677	676	711	746	746	784	805	900
Oldenburg[27]	314	317	337	355	399	483	483	545	574	578
Brunswick	293	312	349	404	465	494	494	502	513	603
Bremen	104	122	157	180	225	300	300	339	372	450
Hamburg	279	339	454	623	768	1,015	1,015	1,153	1,218	1,712
Thuringian states[21]	1,035	1,067	1,170	1,272	1,420	1,586	1,509	1,607	1,660	1,744
Alsace-Lorraine	(1,584)	1,550	1,567	1,604	1,719	1,874				
Saarland[28]							652	770[29]	812[30]	842
Other states[31]	440	454	509	574	653	708	646	691	726	671

See pp. 72–3 for footnotes

A3 Population of Major Districts (in thousands)

(c) West Germany

	1939	1946	1950	1961	1970	1980
Schleswig-Holstein	1,589	2,573	2,595	2,317	2,494	2,605
Hamburg	1,712	1,403	1,606	1,832	1,794	1,650
Lower Saxony	4,540	6,228	6,797	6,641	7,082	7,246
Bremen	563	485	559	706	723	695
North Rhine-Westphalia	11,934	11,683	13,196	15,902	16,914	17,044
Hesse	3,479	3,974	4,324	4,814	5,382	5,589
Rhineland-Palatinate	2,960	2,741	3,005	3,417	3,645	3,639
Baden-Württemburg	5,476	5,817	6,430	7,759	8,895	9,233
Bavaria	7,084	8,791	9,185	9,515	10,479	10,899
Saarland	910	853	945	1,073	1,120	1,068
West Berlin	2,751	2,013	2,147	2,197	2,122	1,899

(d) East Germany

	1939	1946	1950	1964	1971	1981
Saxony-Anhalt	3,090	3,682	3,637	3,254	3,245	
Brandenburg	2,518	2,638	2,669	2,674	2,677	
Mecklenburg	1,572	2,313	2,253	2,062	2,096	
Saxony	5,668	5,792	5,945	5,486	5,292	
Thuringia	2,309	2,756	2,694	2,530	2,538	
East Berlin	1,588	1,175	1,189	1,071	1,086	1,158
Cottbus					862	885
Dresden					1,877	1,804
Erfurt					1,256	1,239
Frankfurt					681	707
Gera					739	742
Halle					1,925	1,829
Karl Marx18 Stadt					2,047	1,925
Leipzig					1,491	1,409
Magdeburg					1,320	1,267
Neubrandenburg					638	623
Potsdam					1,133	1,119
Rostock					859	890
Schwerin					598	590
Suhl					553	549

Germany

	1990
Baden Württemburg	9,726
Bayern	11,343
Berlin	3,420
Brandenburg	2,591
Bremen	679
Hamburg	1,640
Hessen	5,717
Mecklenburg	1,933
Lower Saxony	7,340
North Rhine-Westphalia	17,243
Rhineland-Palatinate	3,734
Saarland	1,070
Saxony	4,796
Saxony-Anhalt	2,890
Schleswig-Holstein	2,614
Thuringia	2,626

A3 Population of Major Districts (in thousands)

ITALY

(a) Constituents of United Italy

	circa 1770	circa 1800	circa 1816	circa 1825	1833	1838	1844/5	1848	1852	1857/8	1861
Mainland Sardinia[32]	2,481	2,661	3,243	3,494		3,449	3,992	3,773	...	3,800	3,812
Island of Sardinia						525		547	...	573	588
Lombardy	1,751	1,754	2,179	2,310	2,429	2,498	2,640	2,724	2,774	2,881	2,986
Veneto	1,698	1,845	1,953	1,941	1,963	2,094	2,236	...	2,315	2,294	2,339
Parma	400	415	427	433	466	474	494	495	503	502	504
Modena	300	388	373	404	438	485	507	576	598	610	602
Tuscany[33]	1,063	1,224	1,288	1,396	1,549	1,632	1,703	1,722	1,778	1,794	1,826
Papal States	1,609	2,310	2,355	2,435	2,732	...	2,930	3,019	...	3,125	3,180
Mainland Naples	4,094	4,985	4,914	5,600	5,933	6,149	6,383	6,610	6,830	6,963	6,787
Sicily	1,294	1,656	1,649	1,714	1,912	1,937	2,051	2,104	2,208	2,316	2,392

(b) United Italy

	1861	1871	1881	1901	1911	1921	1931	1936	1951	1961	1971	1981	1991
Piedmont	3,041[32]	2,900	3,070	3,317	3,424	3,384	3,498	3,506	3,612[35]	4,015[34]	4,544[34]	4,591[34]	4,418
Liguria	771	844	892	1,077	1,197	1,336	1,437	1,467	1,567	1,735	1,849	1,808	1,676
Lombardy	3,305	3,461	3,681	4,283	4,790	5,050	5,547	5,836	6,560	7,406	8,527	8,892	8,856
Venetia	(2,339)	2,643	2,814	3,134	3,527	4,200	4,123	4,288	3,918[35]	3,847	4,110	4,345	4,380
Emilia	2,047	2,114	2,183	2,445	2,681	3,033	3,218	3,339	3,544	3,667	3,841	3,958	3,909
Tuscany	2,006	2,152	2,209	2,549	2,695	2,766	2,892	2,974	3,293	3,286	3,471	3,581	3,530
Marches	883	915	939	1,061	1,093	1,148	1,218	1,278	1,364	1,347	1,359	1,412	1,429
Umbria	513	550	572	667	687	636	694	726	822	795	773	808	811
Latium	...	837	903	1,197	1,302	1,619	2,393	2,647	3,806	3,959	4,702	5,002	5,140
Abruzzi & Molise	1,213	1,283	1,317	1,442	1,431	1,433	1,499	1,601	1,685	1,564	1,483	1,546	1,580
Campania	3,110	2,755	2,897	3,160	3,312	3,547	3,487	3,699	4,795	4,761	5,055	5,463	5,630
Apulia	1,755	1,421	1,589	1,960	2,130	2,297	2,487	2,637	3,478	3,421	3,562	3,872	...
Basilicata	493	502	525	491	474	469	508	543	666	644	602	610	610
Calabria	1,140	1,206	1,258	1,370	1,402	1,512	1,669	1,772	2,167	2,045	1,963	2,061	2,070
Sicily	2,392	2,584	2,928	3,530	3,672	4,061	3,897	4,000	4,833	4,721	4,667	4,907	4,966
Sardinia	588	637	682	792	852	864	973	1,034	1,438	1,419	1,469	1,594	1,648
Trentino-Alto Adige							659	669	729	786	839	873	890
Friuli-Venezia Giulia						729	979	977	1,226[35]	1,166	1,210	1,234	1,197

See pp. 72–3 for footnotes

A3 Population of Major Districts (in thousands)

NETHERLANDS

	1830	1840	1849	1859	1869	1879	1889	1899	1909	1920	1930	1940	1950	1960	1970	1980	1990
Groningen	158	176	188	208	225	253	273	300	328	366	392	427	462	478	517	554	558
Friesland	205	228	247	274	292	330	336	340	360	383	400	428	468	480	522	584	610
Drenthe	64	72	83	95	106	119	131	149	173	210	222	250	285	314	367	418	455
Overyssel	179	198	216	235	254	274	295	333	383	439	521	585	682	783	921	1,018	1,050
Gelderland	310	346	371	404	433	467	512	567	640	730	829	938	1,101	1,288	1,506	1,694	1,864
Utrecht	132	145	149	160	174	192	221	251	289	342	407	490	584	687	801	895	1,063
North Holland	414	443	477	524	577	680	829	968	1,108	1,298	1,510	1,701	1,875	2,073	2,244	2,308	2,464
South Holland	480	526	563	619	688	804	950	1,144	1,391	1,679	1,958	2,174	2,425	2,726	2,969	3,084	3,325
Zeeland	137	151	160	166	178	189	199	216	233	245	248	254	272	284	306	348	366
North Brabant	349	378	396	408	429	466	510	554	623	734	898	1,052	1,267	1,513	1,788	2,051	2,276
Limburg	186	197	205	216	224	239	256	282	332	440	551	620	745	894	999	1,069	1,130
Hevoland	…	…	…	…	…	…	…	…	…	…	…	…	…	…	15	66	262

A3 Population of Major Districts (in thousands)

PORTUGAL

	1838	1858	1864	1878	1890	1900	1911	1920	1930	1940	1950	1960	1970	1981	1991
Viana de Castello				201	207	215	227	226	240	259	275	275	250	257	250
Braga	872	860	952	319	338	357	382	376	415	483	541	594	617	709	748
Porto				462	546	598	680	702	810	938	1,053	1,192	1,315	1,562	1,642
Vila Real	331	324	386	225	237	242	246	235	254	289	317	323	265	264	236
Braganca				169	180	185	192	170	185	213	227	230	177	184	158
Aveiro				257	287	303	336	344	382	430	477	522	546	623	654
Viseu				287	372	391	402	417	405	431	466	487	477	410	402
Coimbra	1,106	1,187	1,287	292	317	332	360	353	388	412	432	434	396	436	428
Guarda				228	250	261	272	256	268	294	304	276	212	206	188
Castelo Branco				174	205	217	242	239	266	300	320	311	252	234	215
Leiria				193	217	239	263	279	315	354	389	400	383	420	426
Santarem	791	755	836	221	255	283	323	332	379	422	453	462	435	454	445
Lisbon				498	611	710	853	934	907[36]	1,070	1,227	1,403	1,612	2,069	2,048
Portalegre				101	113	124	142	147	166	186	197	184	145	143	134
Evora	314	305	348	107	118	128	144	153	181	208	220	215	176	180	174
Beja				142	158	164	192	201	240	275	287	269	202	188	169
Algarve (Faro)	135	153	180	199	229	255	274	268	301	318	326	313	267	324	341
Azores	...	240	252	260	256	256	243	232	254	287	317	328	277	243	238
Madeira	...	99	112	131	134	151	170	179	212	250	267	268	253	253	253
Setubal[36]	...		...			...	...	...	234	269	324	376	464	658	713

See pp. 72–3 for footnotes

A3 Population of Major Districts (in thousands)

RUSSIA

(a) Fifty Provinces of European Russia

	1811	1838	1851	1863	1885	1897	1914
Archangel	210	230	234	284	316	347	484
Astrakhan	76	259	387	377	803	1,004	1,316
Bessarabia	300	790	874	1,026	1,527	1,935	2,657
Chernigov	1,260	1,300	1,375	1,487	2,076	2,298	3,132
Don Region	250	640	794	950	1,591	2,564	3,876
Ekaterinoslav	666	790	902	1,205	1,793	2,114	3,456
Estland	263	282	290	313	387	413	507
Grodno				894	1,321	1,603	2,048
Kovno				1,052	1,504	1,545	1,857
Mogilev	5,087	4,957	4,974	924	1,234	1,687	2,466
Minsk				1,001	1,647	2,148	3,036
Vilna				900	1,273	1,591	2,076
Vitebsk				777	1,235	1,489	1,953
Kaluga	987	915	941	965	1,174	1,133	1,477
Kazan	1,049	1,221	1,347	1,607	2,066	2,171	2,867
Kharkov	1,030	1,334	1,366	1,591	2,254	2,492	3,417
Kherson	370	766	889	1,330	2,027	2,734	3,745
Kiev	1,066	1,460	1,636	2,012	2,848	3,559	4,793
Kostromo	1,014	959	1,021	1,074	1,316	1,387	1,823
Kurland	510	503	539	574	668	674	798
Kursk	1,424	1,527	1,665	1,827	2,267	2,371	3,257
Livonia	715	740	822	925	1,208	1,299	1,744
Moscow	947	1,250	1,348	1,564	2,184	2,431	3,591
Nishegorod	1,043	1,071	1,127	1,285	1,469	1,585	2,067
Novgorod	766	825	891	1,006	1,194	1,367	1,672
Olonetz	245	239	263	297	333	364	466
Orel	1,228	1,366	1,407	1,534	1,964	2,034	2,782
Orenburg	788	1,771	1,713	1,843	3,118	3,797	5,270
Ufa							
Penza	869	988	1,056	1,179	1,471	1,471	1,912
Perm	1,113	1,489	1,742	2,139	2,650	2,994	4,008
Podolia	1,298	1,548	1,578	1,869	2,365	3,018	4,057
Poltava	1,625	1,622	1,689	1,911	2,653	2,778	3,792
Pskov	782	705	657	719	948	1,122	1,425

A3 Population of Major Districts (in thousands)

RUSSIA

(a) Fifty Provinces of European Russia

	1811	1838	1851	1863	1885	1897	1914
Ryazan	1,088	1,242	1,309	1,418	1,784	1,802	2,774
St. Petersburg	600	585	566	1,174	1,646	2,112	3,137
Samara	1,901	2,761	3,777	1,691	2,413	2,751	3,801
Saratov				1,687	2,222	2,406	3,269
Simbirsk				1,183	1,528	1,528	2,068
Smolensk	1,190	1,064	1,070	1,137	1,278	1,525	2,164
Tambov	1,267	1,592	1,667	1,975	2,608	2,684	3,530
Taurida	255	520	609	606	1,060	1,448	2,059
Tver	1,201	1,298	1,360	1,518	1,682	1,770	2,394
Tula	1,115	1,116	1,093	1,153	1,409	1,420	1,886
Vladimir	1,005	1,133	1,168	1,217	1,376	1,516	2,027
Volhynia	1,213	1,314	1,469	1,603	2,196	2,990	4,189
Vologda	703	748	864	975	1,199	1,342	1,752
Voronezh	1,180	1,507	1,630	1,938	2,569	2,531	3,631
Vyatka	1,120	1,512	1,819	2,221	2,859	3,031	3,927
Yaroslav	993	917	943	970	1,050	1,071	1,297
Other Districts							
Caucasus			2,709	4,158	7,285	9,289	12,717
Siberia			2,887	3,141	4,314	5,759	9,895
Steppe districts[38]	…	…	…	1,485	1,589	2,466	3,930
Central Asia	…	…	…	…	3,739	5,281	7,106

See pp. 72–3 for footnotes

A3 Population of Major Districts (in thousands)

(b) U.S.S.R.

	1926	1939	1959	1970	1979	1989
Armenia S.S.R.	881	1,282	1,763	2,492	3,031	3,288
Azerbaizhan S.S.R.	2,314	3,210	3,698	5,117	6,028	7,038
Belorussia S.S.R.	4,983	5,568	8,055[39]	9,002	9,500	10,200
Estonia S.S.R.			1,197	1,356	1,466	1,573
Georgia S.S.R.	2,677	3,542	4,044	4,686	5,015	5,443
Kazakh S.S.R.	6,074	6,146	9,295	13,009	14,684	16,536
Kirghiz S.S.R.	1,002	1,459	2,065	2,934	3,529	4,290
Latvia S.S.R.			2,093	2,364	2,521	2,680
Lithuania S.S.R.			2,711	3,128	3,398	3,690
Moldavia S.S.R.			2,884	3,569	3,947	4,338
R.S.F.S.R.	93,459	109,277	117,534[39]	130,079	137,551	147,400
Tadzhik S.S.R.	1,032	1,485	1,980	2,900	3,801	5,109
Turkmen S.S.R.	998	1,254	1,516	2,159	2,759	3,534
Ukraine S.S.R.	29,043	30,960	41,869[39]	47,127	49,755	51,707
Uzbek S.S.R.	4,565	6,282	8,106	11,799	15,391	19,905

See pp. 72–3 for footnotes

These are now Independent Countries. See table A1.

A3 Population of Major Districts (in thousands)

SPAIN

	1833[37]	1850[37]	1857	1860	1877	1887	1897	1900	1910	1920	1930	1940	1950	1960	1970	1981	1991
Almeria	235	292	316	315	349	339	345	359	380	358	342	360	357	361	378	405	455
Cadiz	325	358	383	391	429	430	434	439	446	513	508	600	700	819	878	1,002	1,078
Cordoba	315	349	352	359	385	421	444	456	499	565	669	761	782	798	731	717	754
Granada	371	427	442	441	479	485	478	492	523	574	644	738	783	769	742	762	790
Huelva	133	153	174	177	210	255	254	261	310	330	355	367	368	400	403	414	443
Jaen	267	307	346	362	423	438	464	474	527	592	674	753	766	736	668	627	637
Malaga	391	438	451	447	500	519	485	512	523	554	613	677	750	775	854	1,036	1,160
Sevilla	367	420	463	474	507	545	547	555	597	704	805	963	1,099	1,234	1,337	1,477	1,620
Andalusia	2,404	2,744	2,927	2,966	3,283	3,432	3,450	3,549	3,805	4,190	4,610	5,219	5,606	5,893	5,991	6,442	6,940
Huesca	215	247	258	263	252	255	239	245	248	251	243	232	236	234	222	220	207
Teruel	218	250	239	237	242	242	240	246	255	252	253	232	236	215	174	151	143
Zaragoza	301	350	384	393	401	415	413	422	449	495	536	595	622	657	757	842	837
Aragon	734	847	880	891	895	912	892	912	953	997	1,032	1,059	1,094	1,105	1,153	1,213	1,188
Asturias (Oviedo)	435	510	525	541	576	595	613	627	685	744	792	837	888	989	1,052	1,127	1,094
Alava	68	81	96	98	94	93	95	96	97	99	104	113	118	139	200	261	272
Guipuzcoa	109	142	156	163	167	182	192	196	227	259	302	332	374	478	626	693	676
Viscaya	111	150	161	169	190	236	290	311	350	410	485	511	569	754	1,041	1,181	1,155
Basque Provinces	288	373	413	429	451	510	577	604	674	767	892	956	1,061	1,371	1,867	2,135	2,104
Barcelona	442	534	714	726	837	903	1,035	1,055	1,141	1,349	1,801	1,932	2,232	2,878	3,915	4,619	4,654
Gerona	214	263	311	311	300	307	298	299	320	326	326	322	327	351	412	468	509
Lerida	151	197	307	315	285	285	275	275	285	315	314	297	324	334	347	355	353
Tarragona	233	290	321	322	330	349	334	338	338	355	351	339	357	363	433	516	542
Catalonia	1,040	1,284	1,652	1,674	1,752	1,844	1,942	1,966	2,084	2,345	2,791	2,891	3,240	3,926	5,107	5,958	6,059
Badajoz	306	336	405	404	433	482	491	520	593	645	702	743	816	834	702	635	650
Caceres	241	265	302	294	307	340	354	362	398	410	450	511	549	544	468	415	411
Extremadura	547	601	707	697	739	821	845	882	991	1,055	1,152	1,154	1,365	1,379	1,169	1,050	1,062
Corunna	436	511	552	557	596	614	631	654	677	709	768	883	956	992	1,031	1,083	1,096
Lugo	357	419	424	433	411	432	459	465	480	470	469	513	509	480	423	399	384
Orense	319	380	372	369	389	405	403	404	412	412	426	458	468	451	441	411	353
Pontevedra	360	420	483	446	452	443	448	457	495	533	568	642	672	680	781	860	897
Galicia	1,472	1,730	1,777	1,805	1,848	1,895	1,941	1,981	2,062	2,124	2,230	2,496	2,604	2,676	2,754	2,731	2,731

See pp. 72–3 for footnotes

A3 Population of Major Districts (in thousands)

Spain

	1833[37]	1850[37]	1857	1860	1877	1887	1897	1900	1910	1920	1930	1940	1950	1960	1970	1981	1991
Leon	267	289	349	340	350	381	384	386	395	412	442	493	546	585	563	518	526
Salamanca	210	240	264	262	286	314	317	321	334	322	339	390	412	406	380	368	358
Zamora	159	180	249	249	250	270	275	276	273	266	280	299	316	301	259	224	214
Leon	*636*	*709*	*861*	*851*	*885*	*965*	*977*	*982*	*1,003*	*1,000*	*1,061*	*1,182*	*1,273*	*1,291*	*1,201*	*1,110*	*1,098*
Albacete	191	196	201	206	219	229	233	238	265	292	333	374	397	371	341	334	342
Murcia	284	400	381	383	452	491	518	578	615	639	645	720	757	800	832	958	1,045
Murcia	*475*	*596*	*582*	*589*	*671*	*721*	*751*	*816*	*880*	*930*	*978*	*1,094*	*1,154*	*1,171*	*1,173*	*1,292*	*1,387*
Navarre	*230*	*280*	*297*	*300*	*304*	*304*	*303*	*308*	*312*	*330*	*346*	*370*	*383*	*402*	*467*	*507*	*519*
Cuidad Real	278	303	244	248	260	292	305	322	380	427	492	530	567	584	513	468	475
Cuenca	234	253	230	230	236	242	242	250	270	282	310	333	326	315	252	210	205
Guadalajara	159	200	199	205	201	202	199	189	209	201	204	206	203	184	150	143	146
Madrid	320	406	476	489	594	683	737	775	879	1,068	1,384	1,580	1,926	2,606	3,761	4,727	4,947
Toledo	282	330	329	334	335	360	370	377	413	443	489	480	527	522	478	472	489
New Castile	*1,273*	*1,492*	*1,478*	*1,505*	*1,627*	*1,778*	*1,853*	*1,923*	*2,151*	*2,421*	*2,879*	*3,129*	*3,560*	*4,211*	*5,154*	*6,021*	*6262*
Avila	138	133	164	169	180	193	198	200	209	209	221	235	251	238	212	179	174
Burgos	224	234	333	337	333	339	340	339	347	336	355	379	397	381	361	363	352
Logrono*	148	186	174	175	174	181	186	189	188	193	204	221	230	230	235	253	263
Palencia	148	180	186	186	181	189	193	192	196	192	208	217	233	232	202	187	185
Santander†	169	190	214	220	235	244	264	276	303	328	364	394	405	432	469	511	527
Segovia	135	155	147	146	150	154	156	159	168	167	174	189	201	196	162	149	147
Soria	116	140	148	150	154	152	148	150	156	152	156	160	161	147	117	99	94
Valladolid	185	210	244	247	247	267	276	279	284	281	302	333	348	363	413	490	494
Old Castile	*1,263*	*1,418*	*1,610*	*1,630*	*1,655*	*1,719*	*1,761*	*1,785*	*1,852*	*1,858*	*1,984*	*2,127*	*2,226*	*2,219*	*2,171*	*2,231*	*2,236*
Alicante	369	363	379	391	412	433	451	470	498	513	546	608	634	712	922	1,149	1,293
Castellon de la Plana	199	248	261	267	284	292	304	311	322	307	309	312	325	339	387	432	447
Valencia	389	500	607	618	679	734	776	807	884	926	1,042	1,257	1,348	1,430	1,770	2,066	2,118
Valencia	*957*	*1,111*	*1,240*	*1,275*	*1,374*	*1,459*	*1,532*	*1,588*	*1,704*	*1,745*	*1,897*	*2,177*	*2,307*	*2,481*	*3,078*	*3,647*	*3,857*
Balearic Islands	*229*	*253*	*263*	*270*	*289*	*313*	*302*	*312*	*326*	*339*	*366*	*407*	*422*	*443*	*533*	*685*	*709*
Las Palmas	...	...	...	...	...	...	...	157	193	206	251	321	375	454	549	756	767
Santa Cruz de Tenerife	...	...	...	...	...	...	...	202	251	251	304	360	418	491	576	688	725
Canary Islands	*200*	*258*	*234*	*237*	*281*	*292*	*335*	*359*	*444*	*458*	*555*	*680*	*793*	*944*	*1,125*	*1,445*	*1,493*

*Now named La Rioja. †Now named Cantabria See pp. 72–3 for footnotes

A3 Population of Major Districts (in thousands)

SWEDEN

District	1750	1760	1772	1795	1800	1810	1820	1830	1840	1850	1860	1870	1880	1890	1900	1910	1920	1930	1940	1950	1960	1970	1980	1990
Alveborg	126	120	127	148	153	152	170	198	219	246	269	279	289	276	280	288	300	313	329	359	375	403	425	441
Blekinge	35	40	54	60	62	69	79	86	96	108	118	126	137	143	146	149	147	145	145	146	144	154	154	150
Gävleborg	110[40]	120[40]	68	81	83	84	92	103	110	120	136	147	179	207	238	254	268	280	274	285	293	293	294	289
Göteborg & Bohus	80	81	88	111	117	117	135	154	165	188	214	232	262	298	337	381	425	457	486	557	625	715	711	740
Gotland	24	25	28	30	31	33	36	39	42	45	50	54	55	51	53	55	56	57	59	59	54	54	55	57
Halland	58	62	66	70	72	74	80	89	95	106	120	127	135	136	142	147	149	150	152	163	170	193	231	255
Jämtland	…[40]	…[40]	67[41]	79[41]	85[41]	36	37	42	46	52	61	70	84	100	111	118	134	135	139	144	140	125	135	136
Jönköping	104	113	116	113	114	116	122	137	150	163	171	180	196	194	203	214	228	232	242	271	285	307	303	308
Kalmar	89	105	116	130	130	138	150	166	185	202	221	233	245	233	228	228	231	231	228	237	236	241	242	241
Kopparberg	97	105	110	119	123	119	122	135	138	151	170	176	190	197	218	234	254	250	249	267	286	277	287	289
Kristianstad	91	94	100	113	117	121	135	150	166	190	210	222	231	222	219	228	241	246	248	259	256	264	280	289
Kronoberg	66	71	74	86	88	90	96	109	121	137	152	159	170	161	159	158	159	156	151	158	159	167	174	178
Malmöhus	106	108	116	137	142	154	177	200	222	253	284	316	349	369	409	457	487	511	530	582	626	719	743	779
Norrbotten	36[42]	41[42]	44[42]	68[42]	71[42]	32	37	44	49	59	69	76	91	105	135	161	183	200	216	241	262	255	267	264
Örebro	…[43]	…[43]	…[43]	95	95	95	100	116	125	138	152	168	182	183	195	207	219	219	226	247	262	277	274	272
Östergötland	128	133	141	155	158	163	173	188	207	222	233	254	267	267	279	294	306	307	317	348	358	382	393	403
Skaraborg	109	106	110	135	136	135	149	167	181	200	222	244	258	247	241	241	244	242	239	248	250	257	270	277
Södermanland	79	82	87	94	97	99	101	108	115	120	127	136	147	155	167	179	190	189	192	214	228	248	253	256
Stockholm City	54	69	72	75	76	65	76	81	84	93	112	136	169	246	301	342	419	502	591	744	809	747	647	679
Stockholm County	90	94	99	93	96	97	98	104	110	115	122	131	147	153	173	229	243	265	288	357	461	730	881	975
Uppsala	63	66	70	78	81	81	80	82	85	89	93	101	111	121	124	128	137	138	138	155	168	217	244	269
Värmland	172[43]	184[43]	194[43]	130	135	135	148	173	196	222	247	260	268	253	254	260	269	270	268	281	291	284	284	283
Västerbotten	…[42]	…[42]	…[42]	…[42]	…[42]	34	40	50	55	68	81	92	106	123	144	161	182	204	220	232	240	233	244	252
Västernorrland	…[40]	…[40]	…[41]	…[41]	…[41]	53	67	78	86	100	117	135	169	209	232	251	265	279	275	284	286	274	268	261
Västmanland	71	73	77	81	87	82	86	89	92	97	103	114	128	137	148	156	169	162	169	204	233	260	260	258

See pp. 72–3 for footnotes

A3 Population of Major Districts (in thousands)

SWITZERLAND

	1850	1870	1880	1888	1900	1910	1920	1930	1941	1950	1960	1970	1980	1990
Appenzell A.R.	44	49	52	54	55	58	55	49	45	48	49	49	48	52
Appenzell I.R.	11	12	13	13	13	15	15	14	13	13	13	13	13	14
Aargau	200	199	198	194	206	231	241	260	270	301	361	433	453	497
Basel Land	48	54	59	62	68	76	82	93	94	108	148	205	220	231
Basel City	30	47	64	74	112	136	141	155	170	196	226	235	204	192
Bern	458	502	530	537	589	646	674	689	729	802	890	983[51]	977[51]	949
Fribourg	100	110	115	119	128	140	143	143	152	159	159	180	185	208
Geneva	64	89	100	106	133	155	171	171	175	203	259	332	349	380
Glarus	30	35	34	34	32	33	34	36	35	38	40	38	37	38
Grisons	90	92	94	95	105	117	120	126	128	137	147	162	165	180
Lucerne	133	132	135	135	147	167	177	189	207	223	253	290	296	321
Neuchâtel	71	95	103	108	126	133	131	124	118	128	148	169	158	161
Nidwalden	11	12	12	13	13	14	14	15	17	19	17	26	29	33
Obwalden	14	14	15	15	15	17	18	19	20	22	23	25	26	29
St. Gallen	170	191	210	228	250	303	296	286	286	309	339	384	392	422
Schaffhausen	35	38	38	38	42	46	50	51	54	58	66	73	65	72
Schwyz	44	48	51	50	55	58	60	62	67	71	78	92	97	111
Solothurn	70	75	80	86	101	117	131	144	155	171	201	224	218	226
Ticino	118	122	130	127	139	156	152	159	162	175	196	245	266	290
Thurgau	89	93	99	105	113	135	136	136	138	150	166	183	184	205
Uri	15	16	24	17	20	22	24	23	27	29	32	34	34	34
Valais	82	97	100	102	114	128	128	136	148	159	178	207	219	255
Vaud	200	230	235	248	281	317	317	332	343	378	430	512	529	588
Zug	17	21	23	23	25	28	32	34	37	42	52	68	76	85
Zürich	251	284	316	337	431	504	539	618	675	777	952	1,108	1,123	1,157

A3 Population of Major Districts (in thousands)

UNITED KINGDOM

(a) England: Old Counties

	1801	1811	1821	1831	1841	1851	1861	1871	1881	1891[44]	1901	1911	1921	1931	1951	1961	1971
Bedfordshire	63	70	84	95	108	124	135	146	149	161	172	195	206	221	312	381	464
Berkshire	111	120	133	147	162	170	176	196	218	241	259	281	295	311	403	504	637
Buckinghamshire	108	118	135	147	156	164	168	176	176	187	197	219	236	271	386	488	588
Cambridgeshire	89	101	122	144	164	185	176	187	186	185	186	199	207	221	256	279[48]	303
Cheshire	192	227	270	334	396	456	505	561	644	755	842	962	1,020	1,088	1,259	1,369	1,546
Cornwall	192	221	261	301	342	356	369	362	331	323	322	328	321	318	345	342[48]	382
Cumberland	117	134	156	169	178	195	205	220	251	267	267	266	273	263	285	294	292
Derbyshire	162	186	214	237	272	296	339	379	462	511	596	679	709	750	826	878[48]	885
Devonshire	340	383	438	494	533	567	584	601	604	633	662	700	710	733	798	824	898
Dorsetshire	114	125	145	159	175	184	189	196	191	192	200	221	225	239	291	313	362
Durham	149	165	194	239	308	391	509	685	867	1,017	1,187	1,370	1,479	1,486	1,464	1,516	1,410
Essex[45]	200	218	249	272	295	310	319	337	338	377	405	488	554	643	847	1,104	1,358
Gloucestershire[49]	251	286	336	387	431	459	486	535	572	656	710	738	760	791	939	1,002	1,077
Hampshire[49]	219	246	283	314	355	405	482	544	593	694	801	953	1,008	1,103	1,293	1,433	1,675
Herefordshire	88	94	103	111	113	115	124	125	121	116	114	114	113	112	127	131	139
Hertfordshire[45]	97	110	128	140	155	165	171	188	194	214	242	290	311	373	562	788	925
Huntingdonshire	38	42	49	53	59	64	64	64	59	55	54	56	55	56	69	80[48]	203
Kent[45]	245	290	336	377	422	457	513	565	618	710	806	869	938	959	1,090	1,199	1,399
Lancashire	673	828	1,053	1,337	1,667	2,031	2,429	2,819	3,454	3,897	4,373	4,762	4,934	5,040	5,118	5,129	5,118
Leicestershire	130	150	174	197	216	230	237	269	321	376	438	477	494	542	631	683	772
Lincolnshire[45]	209	238	283	317	363	407	412	437	470	474	500	564	602	624	706	743[48]	809
London[45]	1,097	1,304	1,523	1,878	2,208	2,652	3,188	3,841	4,713	5,572	6,507	7,160	7,387	8,110	8,194	7,992	7,452
Monmouthshire	46	62	76	98	134	157	175	195	211	258	297	395	450	432	425	445	462
Norfolk	273	292	344	390	413	443	435	439	445	468	476	498	501	502	548	561	618
Northamptonshire	132	141	163	179	199	212	228	244	273	300	336	349	349	361	423	473[48]	469
Northumberland	168	183	213	237	266	304	343	387	434	506	603	697	746	757	798	821	796
Nottinghamshire	140	163	187	225	250	270	294	320	392	446	514	604	641	713	841	903	976
Oxfordshire	112	120	138	154	163	170	171	178	180	185	180	190	190	210	276	309	382
Rutland	16	16	18	19	21	23	22	22	21	21	20	20	18	17	21	24	27
Shropshire	170	185	198	214	226	229	241	248	248	237	240	246	243	244	290	297	337
Somerset	274	303	356	404	436	444	445	463	469	428	433	455	462	470	551	599	683
Staffordshire	243	295	346	409	509	609	747	858	981	1,053	1,184	1,286	1,356	1,434	1,621	1,734	1,858
Suffolk	214	234	272	296	315	337	337	349	357	362	373	394	400	401	443	472	546
Surrey[45]	85	96	109	120	136	142	165	208	247	271	325	393	423	507	747	906	1,003

See pp. 72–3 for footnotes

A3 Population of Major Districts (in thousands)

UNITED KINGDOM

(a) England: Old Counties

	1801	1811	1821	1831	1841	1851	1861	1871	1881	1891[44]	1901	1911	1921	1931	1951	1961	1971
Sussex	159	190	233	273	300	337	364	417	491	548	602	663	728	770	937	1,078	1,240
Warwickshire	207	229	274	337	402	475	562	634	737	921	1,087	1,250	1,393	1,533	1,862	2,025	2,082
Westmorland	41	46	51	55	56	58	61	65	64	66	64	64	66	65	67	67	73
Wiltshire	184	192	219	237	256	254	249	257	259	262	271	286	292	303	387	423	487
Worcestershire	146	169	194	223	248	277	307	339	380	337	360	380	398	420	523	570	693
Yorkshire																	
East Riding	111	133	154	168	194	219	238	265	309	342	385	433	461	483	511	527	543
North Riding	158	169	187	191	203	213	242	290	341	359	377	419	456	467	525	554	726
West Riding	591	684	833	1,013	1,195	1,366	1,553	1,882	2,237	2,521	2,843	3,131	3,270	3,446	3,586	3,645	3,785

A3 Population of Major Districts (in thousands)

(b) England: New Counties

	1961	1971	1981	1991		1961	1971	1981	1991
Avon	829	906	915	932	Leicestershire	706	800	845	867
Bedfordshire	383	464	507	524	Lincolnshire	469	503	551	584
Berkshire	517	631	681	734	Merseyside	1,718	1,657	1,512	1,404
Buckinghamshire	378	476	568	632	Norfolk	566	626	695	746
Cambridgeshire	437	506	579	645	Northamptonshire	398	469	528	579
Cheshire	730	867	930	956	Northumberland	274	280	299	305
Cleveland	526	568	568	550	North Yorkshire	575	627	667	702
Cornwall	343	382	432	468	Nottinghamshire	901	975	985	994
Cumbria	470	476	487	483	Oxfordshire	403	498	519	548
Derbyshire	847	887	910	928	Shropshire	298	337	376	406
Devon	797	823	898	1,009	Somerset	345	386	427	460
Dorset	500	554	595	645	South Yorkshire	1,303	1,323	1,304	1,263
Durham	605	607	607	593	Staffordshire	849	964	1,016	1,031
East Sussex	586	647	657	690	Suffolk	467	538	598	632
Essex	1,104	1,358	1,474	1,528	Surrey	906	1,002	1,004	1,018
Gloucestershire	426	467	502	528	Tyne & Wear	1,244	1,212	1,143	1,095
Greater London	7,992	7,452	7,678	...	Warwickshire	387	455	476	484
Greater Manchester	2,720	2,729	2,596	2,499	West Midlands	2,732	2,793	2,649	2,551
					West Sussex	492	594	662	702
Hampshire	1,151	1,373	1,466	1,541	West Yorkshire	2,005	2,067	2,037	2,014
Herefordshire & Worcestershire	492	560	632	677	Wiltshire	423	487	519	564
Hertfordshire	788	925	957	976					
Humberside	797	839	852	858					
Isle of Wight	96	110	119	124					
Kent	1,199	1,399	1,468	1,509					
Lancashire	1,261	1,345	1,377	1,384					

A3 Population of Major Districts (in thousands)

(c) Wales: Old Counties

	1801	1811	1821	1831	1841	1851	1861	1871	1881	1891[44]	1901	1911	1921	1931	1951	1961	1971
Anglesey	34	37	45	48	51	57	55	51	51	50	51	51	52	49	51	52	60
Brecknockshire	32	38	44	48	56	61	62	60	58	51	54	59	61	58	57	55	53
Caernarvonshire	42	50	58	67	81	88	96	106	119	116	123	123	128	121	124	122	123
Cardiganshire	43	50	58	65	69	71	72	73	70	63	61	60	61	55	53	54	55
Carmarthenshire	67	77	90	101	106	111	112	116	125	131	135	160	175	179	172	168	163
Denbighshire	60	64	76	83	88	93	101	105	112	121	134	147	158	158	171	174	185
Flintshire	39	46	54	60	67	68	70	76	81	77	81	93	107	113	145	150	176
Glamorganshire	71	85	102	127	171	232	318	398	511	688	861	1,122	1,254	1,229	1,203	1,230	1,257
Merionethshire	30	31	34	35	39	39	47	52	52	49	49	46	45	43	41	38	35
Montgomeryshire	48	52	60	67	70	67	67	68	66	58	55	53	51	48	46	44	43
Pembrokeshire	56	61	74	81	88	94	96	92	92	88	88	90	92	87	91	94	99
Radnorshire	19	20	23	25	25	25	25	25	24	22	23	23	24	21	20	18	18

(d) Wales: New Counties

	1961	1971	1981	1991		1961	1971	1981	1991
Clwyd	322	359	391	408	Mid Glamorgan	519	532	538	534
Dyfed	316	316	330	343	Powys	102	99	111	117
Gwent	424	441	440	442	South Glamorgan	380	390	384	393
Gwynedd	214	221	230	235	West Glamorgan	366	373	368	361

A3 Population of Major Districts (in thousands)

(e) Scotland[46] Old Counties

	1801	1811	1821	1831	1841	1851	1861	1871	1881	1891[44]	1901	1911	1921	1931	1951	1961	1971
Aberdeenshire	121	134	155	178	192	212	222	245	268	283	304	312	301	300	308	321[46]	320
Angusshire	39	107	113	140	170	191	204	238	266	278	284	281	271	270	275	278	280
Argyllshire	81	87	97	101	97	89	80	76	76	74	74	71	77	63	63	59	60
Ayrshire	84	104	127	145	164	190	199	201	218	226	254	268	299	285	321	343	361
Banffshire	37	38	44	48	50	54	59	62	63	61	60	61	57	55	50	46	44
Berwickshire	30	31	33	34	34	36	37	36	35	32	31	30	28	27	25	22	21
Buteshire	12	12	14	14	16	17	16	17	18	18	19	18	34[47]	19	19	15	13
Caithness-shire	23	23	29	35	36	39	41	40	39	37	34	32	28	26	23	27	28
Clackmannanshire	11	12	13	15	19	23	21	24	26	32	32	31	33	32	38	41	46
Dumfriesshire	55	63	71	74	73	78	76	75	76	74	73	73	75	75	86[46]	88	88
Dunbartonshire	21	24	27	33	44	45	52	59	75	98[46]	114	140	151[46]	148	164	185	238
East Lothianshire	30	31	35	36	36	36	38	38	39	37	39	43	47	47	52	53	56
Fifeshire	94	101	115	129	140	154	155	161	172	190[46]	219	268	293	276	307	321	327
Inverness-shire	73	78	90	95	98	97	89	88	90	90	90	87	82	82	85	83	90
Kincardineshire	26	27	29	31	33	35	34	35	34	36	41	41	42	41	47	26[46]	26
Kinross-shire	7	7	8	9	9	9	8	7	7	7	7	8	8	7	7	7	6
Kirkcudbrightshire	29	34	39	41	41	43	43	42	42	40	39	38	37	37	31[46]	29	28
Lanarkshire	148	191	244	317	427	530	632	765	904	1,136[46]	1,339	1,447	1,539[46]	1,586[46]	1,614	1,626	1,524
Midlothianshire	123	149	192	219	225	259	274	328	389	434	489	508	506	526	566	580	596
Morayshire	28	28	31	34	35	39	43	44	44	43	45	43	42	41	48	49	52
Nairnshire	8	8	9	9	9	10	10	10	10	9	9	9	9	8	9	8	11
Orkney	24	23	27	29	31	31	32	31	32	30	29	26	24	22	21	19	17
Peeblesshire	9	10	10	11	10	11	11	12	14	15	15	15	15	15	15	14	14
Perthshire	126	134	138	142	137	139	134	128	129	122[46]	123	124	126	121	128	127	127
Renfrewshire	79	93	112	133	155	161	178	217	263	225[46]	269	315	299[46]	289[46]	325	339	362
Ross & Cromarty	56	61	69	75	79	83	81	81	78	79	76	77	71	63	61	58	58
Roxburghshire	34	37	41	44	46	52	54	54	53[46]	53	49	47	45	46	46	43	42
Selkirkshire	5	6	7	7	8	10	10	14	26[46]	28	23	25	23	23	22	21	21
Shetland	22	23	26	29	31	31	32	32	30	29	28	28	26	21	19	18	17
Stirlingshire	51	58	65	73	82	86	92	98	112	119[46]	142	161	162	168	188	195	209
Sutherlandshire	23	24	24	26	25	26	25	24	23	22	21	20	18	16	14	14	13
West Lothianshire	18	19	22	23	27	30	39	41	44	53	66	80	84	81	89	93	108
Wigtownshire	23	27	33	36	39	43	42	39	39	36	33	32	31	29	32	29	27

See pp. 72–3 for footnotes

A3 Population of Major Districts (in thousands)

(f) Scotland: New Regions

	1961	1971	1981	1991		1961	1971	1981	1991
Borders	102	98	100	103	Highland	164	175	200	204
Central	245	263	273	267	Lothian	710	746	723	726
Dumfries & Galloway	146	143	145	148	Orkney	19	17	19	19
Fife	321	327	325	341	Shetland	18	17	27	22
Grampian	440	439	472	504	Strathclyde	2,854	2,576	2,405	2,248
					Tayside	398	398	392	384
					Western Isles	33	30	32	30

YUGOSLAVIA

	1948	1953	1961	1971	1981	1991[52]
Bosnia & Hercegovina	2,564	2,847	3,278	3,746	4,124	...
Croatia	3,780	3,936	4,160	4,426	4,601	
Macedonia	1,153	1,305	1,406	1,647	1,909	
Montenegro	377	420	472	530	584	615
Serbia	4,154	4,464	4,823	5,250	5,694	9,779
Kosovo	733	816	964	1,244	1,584	...
Voivodina	1,641	1,700	1,855	1,953	2,035	...
Slovenia	1,440	1,504	1,591	1,727	1,892	

A3   Population of Major Districts (in thousands)

NOTES

1. SOURCES:- As for table A.1, except that Austrian statistics for 1754 and 1780 are taken from P.G.M. Dickson, *Finance and Government under Maria Theresia, 1740-1780* (Oxford, 1987), and Russian statistics to 1914 are taken from A.F. Rashin, *Russian Population for 100 Years* (Moscow, 1956).
2. For fuller footnotes on territorial changes and on the nature of these statistics see table A.1.

FOOTNOTES

[1] Civil population only.
[2] The Italian provinces are included under Italy.
[3] Part of the province, with a population of 168 thousand, was ceded to the Netherlands in 1839.
[4] Part of the province (the Grand Duchy), with a population of 158 thousand, was ceded to the Netherlands in 1839.
[5] Eupen and Malmédy, with a population of 60 thousand in 1920, were acquired from Germany in 1921.
[6] Ceded to the U.S.S.R. in 1945.
[7] The census was in October 1946 in Slovakia and May 1947 in the Czech lands.
[8] Part of the district, with a population of 6 thousand in 1930, was ceded to the U.S.S.R. in 1945.
[9] The commune of Gex was acquired in 1815.
[10] Part of Rocroi canton was ceded to the United Netherlands in 1815.
[11] Tarn-et Garonne is estimated in 1801. It was formed out of Aveyron, Haute Garonne, Gers, and Lot-et-Garonne, and their populations are also consequently estimated in 1801.
[12] The population of Marseille (and hence of Bouches-du-Rhône) was overestimated by 191 thousand in 1931.
[13] The population of Corsica is overestimated, for a large number of people not normally resident were wrongly included. The overestimation was about 100 thousand in 1954 and 1962.
[14] A small part of Landes was transferred to Basses-Pyrénées in 1857.
[15] The parts of Meurthe and of Moselle annexed by Germany have constituted Moselle since 1872. The parts left to France have constituted Meurthe-et-Moselle.
[16] A small part of Vosges was transferred to Bas-Rhin in 1871.
[17] The Belfort Territory was part of Haut-Rhin until 1871.
[18] The population of Lyon (and hence of Rhône) was overestimated by 64 thousand in 1911, 102 thousand in 1921, and 120 thousand in 1931.
[19] Part of Var, with a population of 68 thousand, was transferred to Alpes-Maritimes in 1861.
[20] Hanover, Kurhessen, Nassau, Hesse-Homburg, and Frankfurt.
[21] Saxe-Weimar, Saxe-Meiningen, Saxe-Altenburg, Saxe-Coburg-Gotha, Schwarzburg-Rudolstadt, Schwarzburg-Sondershausen, Reuss (elder line), and Reuss (younger line).
[22] Mecklenburg-Schwerin, Mecklenburg-Strelitz, Oldenburg, Brunswick, Anhalt, Waldeck, Schaumburg-Lippe, Lippe, and the cities of Bremen, Hamburg, and Lübeck.
[23] Post-First World War boundaries
[24] The 1933 boundaries have been used so far as possible, but there are some unavoidable changes. The 1933 populations within the 1939 boundaries in these cases were as follows (in thousands):-

Prussia	39,692
Brandenburg	2,692
Pomerania	2,268
Silesia	4,710
Schleswig-Holstein	1.420
Hanover	3,237
Rhineland	7,960
Hamburg	1,676
Oldenburg	495
Other states	590.

[25] The principal change from part (a) of this table is the inclusion here of Schleswig-Holstein and Lauenburg, ceded by Denmark in 1864.
[26] i.e. both Mecklenburg-Schwerin and Mecklenburg-Strelitz.
[27] Including Birkenfeld and the Principality of Lübeck.
[28] Constituted out of part of Prussian Rhineland and part of Birkenfeld.
[29] The census was in July 1927.
[30] The census was in June 1935.
[31] Anhalt, Waldeck, Schaumburg-Lippe, Lippe, and (except in 1939) the city of Lübeck.
[32] Excluding Nice.
[33] Including Lucca.
[34] Including Valle d'Aosta province, which was formerly part of Piedmont, and had a population in 1951 of 94 thousand, in 1961 of 101 thousand, in 1971 of 109 thousand, in 1981 of 112 thousand, and in 1991 of 116 thousand.
[35] Territory from this province was ceded to France and to Yugoslavia after the Second World War.
[36] Setubal was part of Lisbon province prior to 1930.
[37] These are estimates on which too much reliance should not be placed.
[38] Urals, Turgai, Akmolinsk, and Semipalatinsk.
[39] Enlarged by territory incorporated in 1940–45.
[40] Västernorrland and Jamtland were included with Gävleborg in 1750 and 1760.
[41] Västernorrland was included with Jamtland in 1772, 1795, and 1800.

A3 Population of Major Districts (in thousands)

[42] Västerbotten was included with Norrbotten in these years.

[43] Örebro was included with Värmland in these years.

[44] The great majority of counties in England and Wales experienced some boundary change in 1891, on the establishment of Administrative Counties instead of the Ancient Counties. The most important of these, with the change effected (in thousands), were as follows:-

Cheshire	+25	Staffordshire	−30
Derbyshire	−17	Suffolk	−9
Gloucestershire	+56	Surrey	−20
Kent	+23	Sussex	−12
Lancashire	−30	Warwickshire	+116
Middlesex	−21	Worcestershire	−77
Norfolk	+13	Yorkshire: West Riding	14.
Somerset	−56		

[45] The population of the Country of London is for the Greater London Council area throughout. It has been deducted from the counties of which its was previously a part.

[46] All figures for Scotland relate to the counties as constituted at the time of the census concerned. The main transfers of population resulting from boundary changes were as follows (showing the population in thousands at the previous census of the area affected):-

1881	Roxburgh	−5;	Selkirky	+5		
1891	(these figures are at the 1891 census)				Dunbarton	+4;
	Fife	+3;	Lanark	+90;	Perth	−4;
	Renfrew	−66;	Stirling	−7;		
1921	Dunbarton	−4;	Lanark	+35;	Renfrew	−32
1931	Lanark	+15;	Renfrew	−15		
1951	Dumfries	+36;	Kirkcudbright	−6		
1961	Aberdeen	+20;	Kincardine	−20.		

[47] This figure was inflated because the 1921 census was taken during the holiday season.

[48] 1961 population for the 1971 area differed in these cases and was as follows:-

Cambridgeshire	277	Huntingdon & Peterborough	159	Worcestershire	623
Cornwall	343	Lincolnshire	744	Yorkshire: North Riding	665
Derbyshire	845	Northamptonshire	398	Yorkshire: West Riding	3,681
Devon	823	Shropshire	298		
Dorset	314	Staffordshire	1,689		
Durham	1,402	Warwickshire	2,017		

[49] Including the Isle of Wight.

[50] Between the 1962 and 1968 censuses the old departments of Seine and Seine-et-Oise were divided into the seven new departments listed at the end of the table.

[51] Including Jura Canton, which was formerly part of Bern and had a population of 67 thousand in 1970 and 65 thousand in 1980.

[52] Bosnia, Hercegovina, Croatia, Macedonia and Slovenia are separate countries. See Table A1. The figure for Serbia includes Kosovo and Voivodina, In which there was no independent census taken.

A4 POPULATION OF MAJOR CITIES (in thousands)

	circa 1750	1800/1	1850/1	1860/1	1870/1	1880/1	1890/1	1900/1	1910/1	1920/1	1930/1	1940/1[1]	1950/1	1960/1	1970/1	1980/1	1990/1	2000/1
Amsterdam	210	217	224	244	264	326	408	511	574	642	752	794	804	865	820	717	713	731
Antwerp[2]	46	62	88	117	127	169	224	273	302	334	576	595	584	643	671	790	668	447
Athens	10	12	31	41	45	63	108	111	167[07]	301	453[28]	481	565[3]	628[3]	867[3]	886[3]	772	...
Baku	...	...	...	14[63]	16	46[85]	87[88]	112	218	256	453[26]	809*	1,280	971*[59]	1,266*	1,046*	1,701[93]	1,787[99]
Barcelona	50	115	175	180	...	346	397	533	587	710	783	1,081	...	1,558	1,745	1,755	1,668	1,506[98]
Belfast	9	37[21]	103	122	174	208	273	349	387	...	415[26]	438[37]	444	416[4]	36	306	287	277
Belgrade	...	25	15	...	26[66]	30	54	69	91	112	267	...	368[48]	585	746	1,088	1,136	1,594[98]
Berlin	90	172	419	548	826	1,122	1,579	1,889	2,071	3,801[19]	4,243[33]	4,332	3,337[5]	3,261[5]	3,208[5]	3,057[5]	3,438	3,382
Birmingham	24	74	233	296	344	437	478	523	840	922	1,003	1,053	1,113	1,107	1,015	1,007[23]	994	977
Bologna	69	71[91]	73	75	116	104	...	152	173	211	246	270[36]	316	445	490	456	445	378
Bordeaux	67	91	131	163	194[72]	221	252	257	262	267	263	258[36]	258[54]	250[62]	267[68,6]	211[82]	210	219[99]
Bradford	...	13	104	106	147	194	266	280	288	291	299	288	292	296	294	457[23,6]	469	468
Bremen	28	40	53	67	83	112	126	163	247	258[19]	323[33]	342	445	565	582	556	552	542[99]
Bristol	45	64	137	154	183	207	289	339	357	377	404	419	443	436	427	391[23]	393	381
Brussels[7]	60	66[3]	251	281	314	421	500	599	720	685	840	913[38]	956	1,020	1,075	1,000	954	959
Bucharest	...	32	120	122	142	...	220	276[99]	341[12]	309[17]	631	648	886	1,226	1,475	1,929	1,934	2,054[99]
Budapest	...	54	178	187[57]	202	371	506	732	880	1,185	1,006	1,163	1,571*	1,805*	1,945*	2,059*	2,017	1,852[99]
Cologne	43	50	97	121	129	145	282	373	517	634[19]	757[33]	768	595	809	848	977	956	963[99]
Copenhagen	93	101	129	155	181	235	313	401	559	561	771*	890*	1,168*	1,262*	1,380*	1,382*	1,339	658
Donetsk (Stalino, Yuzovka)								32[97]	48	38	174[26]	462	...	699[59]	879	...	1,121	1,050[99]
Dniepropetrovsk (Ekaterinoslav)	...	9[11]	12	19	24	47[85]	47[88]	121	196	163	237[26]	501	...	660[59]	862	1,100	1,189	1,109[99]
Dortmund	...	4	11	23	44	67	90	142	214	295[19]	541[33]	537	507	648	640	609	600	590[99]
Dresden	52	60	97	128	177	221	277	396	548	529[19]	642[33]	625	494	492	502	517	488	478[99]
Dublin	90	165	272	250	246	250	245	373	305	399	419[26]	489[37]	522	537[8]	566	526	920	482[02]
Duisburg	3	4	9	13	31	41	59	93	229	244[19]	440[33]	431	411	504	455	559	537	521[99]
Düsseldorf	9	10	27	41	69	95	145	214	359	407[19]	499[33]	540	501	705	664	592	576	569[99]
Edinburgh	57	83	202	203	244	295	342	394	401	420	439	476	467	468	454	437[23]	438	449
Erevan	...	15	12	...	12	12	...	29[97]	33	...	65[26]	200	...	509[59]	767	1,055	1,200[93]	1250
Essen	...	4	9	21	52	57	79	119	295	439[19]	654[33]	660	605	730	698	650	626	601[99]
Florence	74	78	106	116	167	135	...	198	233	254	305	351	375	437	458	448	438	375
Frankfurt-on-Main	32	48	65	76	91	137	180	289	415	433[19]	556[33]	547	532	692	670	629	647	645[99]
Gdansk (Danzig)	46	53[16]	60	83	89	109	120	134	162	195	263[33]	266	170	286	364	457	465	459[99]
Geneva	22	22	31	41	44	49	52	59	58	56	124	124	145	176[9]	175[9]	176[9]	167	174[99]
Genoa	87	91[99]	120	129	130	180	...	235	272	316	608	635[36]	648	784	812	760	742	632
Glasgow	24	77	357	420	522	587	658	776	1,000	1,052	1,093	1,132	1,090	1,055	898	766[23]	687	578

See p. 77 for footnotes

A4 Population of Major Cities (in thousands)

	circa 1750	1800/1	1850/1	1860/1	1870/1	1880/1	1890/1	1900/1	1910/1	1920/1	1930/1	1940/1[1]	1950/1	1960/1	1970/1	1980/1	1990/1	2000/1
Gorky (Nizhne Novgorod)	9	14[11]	31	42[63]	41[67]	67[85]	73[88]	90[97]	109	106	222[26]	644	...	942[59]	1,170	1,367	1,441	1,350[99]
Gothenburg	8	13	26	37	56	76	105	131	168	202	243	281	354[10]	404[10]	451	431	399	467
The Hague	38	38	72	79	90	118	166	212	281	353	437	496	533[11]	605[11]	538[11]	457[11]	445	441
Hamburg	75	130	132	134	240	290	324	706	931	986[19]	1,129[33]	1,682	1,606	1,832	1,794	1,649	1,661	1,702[99]
Hanover	17	18	29	71	88	123	164	236	302	310[19]	444[33]	473	444	573	524	535	514	515[99]
Helsinki	..	9	21	19	26	43	62	91	147	189[19]	241	317	369[12]	453[12]	510[12]	483[12]	494	555
Kaliningrad (Königsberg)	60	61[16]	73	95	112	141	162	188	246	261[19]	316[33]	368	...	204[59]	297	366	410	427[99]
Kazan	20	54[11]	45	63[63]	79[67]	94	134	132[97]	188	148	179[26]	402	...	647[59]	869	1,011	1,104	1,102[99]
Kharkov	..	10[11]	25	52[63]	60[67]	101[79]	188[88]	175[97]	236	220	417[26]	833	...	934[59]	1,223	1,485	1,622	1,494[99]
Kiev	23	23[11]	50	68[63]	71[67]	166[85]	184	247[97]	505	366	514[26]	846	...	1,104[59]	1,632	2,248	2,643	2,663[99]
Krakow	20	24	50	42	50	66	75	91	150	184	221	255	347	479	583	718	751	741[99]
Kuibyshev (Samara)	..	4[11]	24	34[67]	34[67]	52	95[88]	92[97]	96	176	176[26]	390	...	806	1,045	1,238	1,239	1,160[99]
Leeds	16	53	172	207	259	309	368	429	453	408	483	497	505	511	496	705[23]	706	715
Leipzig	35	30	63	78	107	149	295	456	590	604[19]	713[33]	702	618	585	584	562	508	490[99]
Leningrad (Petrograd/ St. Petersburg)	150	336[11]	485	539[63]	667[69]	877	1,003[89]	1,267[97]	1,962	722	1,690[26]	3,191	...	3,321*[59]	3,950	4,676*	4,437	4,660[99]
Lisbon	148	180	240	224[64]	..	242[78]	301	356	435	486	594	702	790	817	760	807	678	565
Liverpool	22	80	376	444	493	553	630	704	753	805	856	822	789	747	610	510	474	493
Lodz	..	0.2	16	30	34	57	113	315[97]	408	452	605	665	593	708	762	836	847	811[99]
London[13]	675	1,117	2,685	3,227	3,890	4,770	5,638	6,586	7,256	7,488	8,216	8,700[38]	8,348	8,172	7,452	7,678	6,803	7172
Lvov (Lemberg)	25	39	68	70[57]	87	110	128	160	206	219	316	318	...	411[59]	553	688	807	786[99]
Lyon	114	110	177	319	323[72]	377	416	459	460	460	460	470[36]	471[14]	529[14]	528[14]	418[82,14]	415	453[99]
Madrid	109	160	281	271[57]	332	398	470[87]	540	600	751	834	1,089	1,618	2,260	3,146	3,188	2,991	2,882[98]
Manchester	18	90	303	339	351	462	505	645	714	736	766	728	703	661	544	449	433	393
Marseille	68	111	194	261	313[72]	360	404	491	551	586	610	620[36]	661[54]	778[54]	889[68]	879[82]	800	807[99]
Milan	124	135	242	242	262	322	..	493	579	836	992	1,116[36]	1,260	1,583	1,724	1,635	1,549	1302
Minsk	8	11[11]	24	30[63]	36[67]	58[85]	71[88]	91[97]	101	104	132[26]	239	...	509[59]	907	1,333	1,613	1,729[99]
Moscow	130	250	365	352[63]	612	748[82]	799[88]	989[97]	1,533	1,050	2,029[26]	4,137	...	5,046[59]	7,061*	8,203*	8,747	8,300[99]
Munich	32	40	110	148	169	230	349	500	596	631[19]	735[33]	828	832	1,085	1,294	1,299	1,237	1,194[99]
Nantes	57	72	96	104	114	124	123	133	171	184	187	195[36]	223[54]	246[62]	259[68]	247[82]	244	278[99]
Naples	305	427[96]	449	417	449	494	..	564	723	722*	839*	866*[36]	1,011*	1,183	1,233	1,211	1,208	1000
Nuremberg	30	30	54	63	83	100	143	261	333	353[191]	410[33]	431	362	455	474	484	495	486[99]
Odessa	2	6	90	119[63]	121[67]	194[77]	314	405[97]	506	428	421[26]	604	...	667[59]	892	1,072	1,096	1,002[99]
Oslo (Christiania)	7	10	28	40	67	119	151	228	243	258	253	275[38]	434[15]	476[15]	487	643[23]	745	773

A4 Population of Major Cities (in thousands)

	circa 1750	1800/1	1850/1	1860/1	1870/1	1880/1	1890/1	1900/1	1910/1	1920/1	1930/1	1940/1[1]	1950/1	1960/1	1970/1	1980/1	1990/1	2000/1
Palermo	118	139[15]	180	186	219	245	...	310	342	394	390	412[36]	491*	588	651	700	714	679
Paris	576	581	1,053	1,696	1,852[72]	2,269	2,448	2,714	2,888	2,907	2,891	2,830[36]	2,850[16]	2,790[16]	2,489[16]	2,189[82,16]	2,152	2,148[99]
Perm (Molotov)	6	3[11]	13	13	23[67]	32	39	45[97]	50	68	120[26]	255	...	629[59]	850	1,018	1,099	1,018[99]
Prague	59	75	118	143[57]	157	162	184	202	224[17]	677*	849*	928*[35]	922*[47]	1,005	1,080	1,193	1,212	1178
Riga	16	30	70	77[63]	102[67]	160	196[88]	256[97]	331	285[23]	378	393	...	580[59]	732	850	909	806[98]
Rome[18]	156	163[90]	175	184	244	300	...	463	542	692	1,008	1,156[36]	1,652	2,188	2,800	2,831	2,828	2656
Rostov-on-Don	...	4[11]	13	29[63]	39[67]	61[85]	67[88]	120[97]	121	233	308[26]	510	646[19]	600[59]	789	957	1,027	1,006[99]
Rotterdam	44	53	90	106	116	153	202	319	427	511	582	612	646[19]	729[19]	679[19]	579[19]	589	593
Rouen	67	85	104	104	104	106	102	116	125	124	123	123[36]	117[54,25]	123[62,25]	120[68,25]	105[82,25]	103	109[99]
Salonika	45	62	75	...	...	...	...	115	158	170	237	225	217[26]	251[26]	346[26]	406[26]	406	...
Saratov	8	27[11]	62	84[63]	93[67]	80	123	137[97]	206	189	220[26]	376	...	581[59]	757	873	899	879[99]
Seville	66	96	106	82[57]	...	129[77]	143[87]	148	155	206	218	239	375	442	548	654	653	702[98]
Sheffield	12	31	135	185	240	285	324	409	465	512	518	522	513	494	520	538[23]	520	513
Sofia	...	...	...	...	19	21	42	68	103	154	287[34]	401	435[46]	687*	877*	1,057*	1,220	1,192[96]
Stockholm	60	76	93	112	136	169	246	301	342	419	502	591	744[20]	807[20]	740[20]	647[20]	679	750
Strasbourg	40	49	76	82	86	105	124	151	179	167	181	193[36]	201[54,21]	229[62,21]	249[68,21]	252[82,21]	252	267[99]
Stuttgart	17	18	47[52]	56	92	117	140	177	286	309[19]	415[33]	460	498	638	633	582	584	581[99]
Szczecin (Stettin)	12	23	48[52]	64	76	92	116	211	232	233[19]	271[33]	269	159	269	337	388	413	417[99]
Toulouse	45	50	94	113	125[72]	140	150	150	150	175	195	213[36]	269[54]	324[62]	370[68]	354[82]	358	398[99]
Tiflis	...	30[25]	35[54]	61[63]	61[67]	90[85]	101[85]	161[97]	188	327	294[26]	519	695[59]	889	1,095	1,300[93]	1,310[27,99]	
Turin	57	78	135	178	208	254	...	336	427	502	597	629[36]	711	1,026	1,178	1,104	1,059	901
Ufa	...	9	13	17	20[67]	26[84]	30[88]	50[97]	103	93	99[26]	246	547[59]	771	1,009	1,097	1,096[96]	
Valencia	60	80	90	87[57]	...	138[77]	171[87]	214	233	244	275	451	509	505	654	752	719	739
Venice	149	134[02]	106	118[57]	129	129	...	152	161	192	260*	264*[36]	317*	347*	364*	333*	339	275
Vienna	175	247	444	476[57]	834	1,104	1,365	1,675	2,031	1,866[23]	1,874[34]	1,918	1,616	1,628	1,620	1,531	1,540	1,608
Volgograd (Stalingrad/ Tsaritsyn)	...	4[11]	...	7	12	31	38[88]	56[97]	78	90	15[26]	445	...	592[59]	818	948	1,006	996[99]
Warsaw	23	100	160	163[63]	252	339	454	638[97]	872	931	1,179	1,266	601	1,136	1,308	1,596	1,654	1,618[99]
Wroclaw (Breslau)	55	60	114	146	208	273	335	423	512	528[19]	625[33]	615	279	429	523	618	643	638[99]
Wuppertal	4	16	80[52]	106	146	189	242	299	339	314[19]	409[33]	398	363	421	419	394	384	371[99]
Zagreb (Agram)	...	13	14	17[57]	20	28	38	61	79	108	186	...	321[48]	438	574	650	704	1,047[99]
Zürich	11	12	17	20	57*	79*	94*	151	191*	207	250	336	390	440[22]	423[22]	370	342	337[99]

*= Suburbs included. Superior figure in italics show census dates where different. See p. 77 for footnotes

A4 Population of Major Cities (in millions)

NOTES

1. SOURCES:- The official publications noted on p. xv; early editions of the *Encyclopaedia Britannica* for some Russian cities in 1850, 1860, and 1870; and data supplied by various national statistical offices. Official estimates as well as census figures have been used. Where none is available for the 0/1 years, the nearest available date has been used and indicated.
2. The cities included in this table all had a population of 500,000 or more in 1960/1, or a population of 250,000 or more in 1900/1, with the exception of a few leading cities in countries which had few or none meeting these criteria.
3. The cities are in alphabetical order of their current name (or its English version where one exists). Older names by which they were known are given in brackets.
4. The statistics do not generally include the population of distinct suburbs, except where this seems most appropriate. Such cases are indicated in footnotes or by an asterisk. Normally the statistics apply to the boundaries of the day.

FOOTNOTES

* = suburbs included
[1] So many of the figures in this column are for 1939 that no special indication is given of this.
[2] Greater Antwerp throughout.
[3] The figures for Greater Athens in 1950/1, 1960/1, 1970/1, and 1980/1 were 1,379, 1,853, 2,540 and 3,027 respectively.
[4] Greater Belfast 529.
[5] East and West Berlin combined.
[6] The figures for Greater Bordeaux in 1954, 1962, 1968 and 1982 were 416, 462, 555 and 640 respectively.
[7] Greater Brussells throughout, except in 1800/1.
[8] Greater Dublin 593.
[9] The figures for Greater Geneva in 1960, 1970 and 1980 were 251, 321 and 335 respectively.
[10] The figures for Greater Gothenburg in 1950 and 1960 were 380 and 487 respectively.
[11] The figures for Greater Hague in 1950, 1960, 1970 and 1980 were 592, 737, 711 and 675 respectively.
[12] The figures for Greater Helsinki in 1950, 1960 and 1970 were 414, 566 and 803 respectively.
[13] Greater London throughout except for the 1750 figure.
[14] The figures for Greater Lyon in 1954, 1962, 1968 and 1982 were 650, 886, 1,075 and 1,221 respectively.
[15] The figures for Greater Oslo in 1950 and 1960 were 506 and 579 respectively.
[16] The figures for Greater Paris in 1954, 1962, 1968 and 1982 were 4,823, 7,369, 8,197 and 8,707 respectively.
[17] Greater Prague 586
[18] Greater Rome throughout.
[19] The figures for Greater Rotterdam in 1950, 1960, 1970 and 1980 were 716, 993, 1,066 and 1,018 respectively.
[20] The figures for Greater Stockholm in 1950, 1960, 1970 and 1980 were 928, 1,149, 1,345 and 1,386 respectively.
[21] The figures for Greater Strasbourg in 1954, 1962, 1968 and 1982 were 239, 302, 335 and 373 respectively.
[22] The figures for Greater Zürich in 1960, 1970 and 1980 were 630, 719 and 709 respectively.
[23] The following populations in 1970/1 correspond to the 1980/1 boundaries:- Belfast 417, Birmingham 1,098, Bradford 462, Bristol 438, Glasgow 982, Leeds 739, Oslo 645, Sheffield 573
[24] The figures for Greater Nantes in 1968 and 1982 were 394 and 465 respectively.
[25] The figures for Greater Rouen in 1954, 1962, 1968 and 1982 were 246, 325, 370 and 380 respectively.
[26] The figures for Greater Salonica in 1950/1, 1960/1, 1970/1 and 1980/1 were 297, 378, 557 and 706 respectively.
[27] 1999 Estimate.

A5   MID-YEAR POPULATION ESTIMATES (in millions)

	Finland	Norway	Sweden	U.K.:England[1]
1750	...	0.62	1.77	5.74
1751	0.43	0.63	1.79	5.77
1752	0.43	0.63	1.81	5.81
1753	0.44	0.64	1.83	5.86
1754	0.45	0.64	1.85	5.90
1755	0.45	0.65	1.87	5.94
1756	0.46	0.66	1.88	5.99
1757	0.47	0.66	1.89	6.02
1758	0.47	0.67	1.89	6.04
1759	0.48	0.68	1.90	6.06
1760	0.49	0.68	1.92	6.10
1761	0.50	0.69	1.93	6.15
1762	0.51	0.70	1.95	6.17
1763	0.51	0.70	1.95	6.16
1764	0.51	0.70	1.96	6.19
1765	0.52	0.71	1.97	6.25
1766	0.53	0.71	1.98	6.28
1767	0.53	0.71	2.00	6.29
1768	0.54	0.72	2.01	6.31
1769	0.55	0.73	2.03	6.36
1770	0.56	0.73	2.04	6.41
1771	0.56	0.74	2.05	6.45
1772	0.57	0.74	2.04	6.50
1773	0.58	0.73	2.00	6.55
1774	0.59	0.73	1.99	6.60
1775	0.60	0.73	2.01	6.67
1776	0.61	0.74	2.03	6.74
1777	0.62	0.75	2.05	6.81
1778	0.63	0.75	2.07	6.88
1779	0.64	0.76	2.08	6.95
1780	0.66	0.76	2.10	6.99
1781	0.66	0.77	2.13	7.04
1782	0.67	0.78	2.14	7.07
1783	0.67	0.78	2.14	7.13
1784	0.67	0.78	2.14	7.14
1785	0.68	0.78	2.15	7.22
1786	0.69	0.78	2.16	7.29
1787	0.70	0.79	2.17	7.37
1788	0.70	0.79	2.18	7.46
1789	0.71	0.80	2.19	7.54
1790	0.71	0.80	2.19	7.65
1791	0.71	0.81	2.19	7.74
1792	0.72	0.81	2.22	7.84
1793	0.73	0.82	2.24	7.94
1794	0.75	0.83	2.26	8.02
1795	0.76	0.84	2.28	8.10
1796	0.78	0.85	2.29	8.20
1797	0.79	0.86	2.31	8.29
1798	0.81	0.87	2.33	8.40
1799	0.82	0.88	2.35	8.50

A5 Mid-year Population Estimates (in thousands)

1800–1833

	Austria[2]	Denmark	Finland	France	Germany[4]	Ireland	Norway	Russia[18]	Sweden	U.K.: England & Wales	U.K.: Scotland
1800	...		0.83	...	...	...	...	35.5	2.35	8.61	...
1801	...		0.84	27.50	...	5.22	0.89	37.8	2.35	8.66₁	1.62
1802	...		0.86	27.88	...	5.29	0.88	38.1	2.36	9.13	1.64
1803	...		0.87	28.27	...	5.36	0.89	38.4	2.38	9.23	1.66
1804	...		0.88	28.98	...	5.43	0.89	38.7	2.40	9.37	1.68
1805	...		0.89	28.92	...	5.50	0.89	39.0	2.41	9.51	1.70
1806	...		0.90	29.17	...	5.57	0.90	39.3	2.43	9.66	1.72
1807	...		0.90	29.13	...	5.65	0.91	39.7	2.43	9.79	1.74
1808	...		0.89	29.15	...	5.72	0.91	40.0	2.43	9.92	1.76
1809	...		0.87	29.20	...	5.80	0.90	40.3	2.41	10.06	1.78
1810	...		0.86	29.28	...	5.88	0.90	40.7	2.40	10.19	1.80
1811	...		0.87	29.35	...	5.96	0.90	41.0	2.40	10.32	1.82
1812	...		1.06	29.37	...	6.04	0.90	41.4	2.41	10.48	1.85
1813	...		1.07	29.33	...	6.12	0.90	42.2	2.42	10.65	1.88
1814	...		1.08	29.34	...	6.20	0.90	43.4	2.43	10.82	1.90
1815	...	1.03	1.09	29.38	...	6.28	0.91	45.2	2.45	11.00	1.93
1816	...	1.04	1.11	29.48	...	6.36	0.92	45.9	2.48	11.20	1.96
1817	...	1.05	1.12	29.70	25.00	6.45	0.93	46.6	2.51	11.38	1.99
1818	29.81	1.07	1.14	29.88	25.37	6.54	0.95	47.2	2.53	11.55	2.01
1819	30.11	1.08	1.16	30.06	25.73	6.62	0.96	47.9	2.55	11.72	2.04
1820	30.50	1.10	1.17	30.25	26.10	6.71	0.97	48.6	2.57	11.90	2.07
1821	30.85	1.11	1.19	30.45	26.47	6.80	0.98	49.3	2.60	12.11	2.10
1822	31.22	1.12	1.20	30.70	26.85	6.89	1.00	50.1	2.63	12.32	2.13
1823	31.58	1.14	1.22	30.94	27.22	6.98	1.01	50.8	2.67	12.53	2.15
1824	31.97	1.15	1.24	31.19	27.57	7.08	1.03	51.5	2.70	12.72	2.18
1825	32.38	1.17	1.25	31.41	27.93	7.17	1.04	52.3	2.75	12.90	2.20
1826	32.83	1.18	1.27	31.60	28.26	7.27	1.06	53.0	2.79	13.07	2.23
1827	33.21	1.19	1.28	31.80	28.56	7.37	1.08	53.8	2.82	13.25	2.26
1828		1.20	1.30	32.00	28.86	7.46	1.09	54.6	2.84	13.44	2.29
1829		1.21	1.32	32.28	29.14	7.56	1.11	55.3	2.85	13.62	2.32
1830	34.08	1.21	1.35	32.37	29.39	7.66	1.12	56.1	2.88	13.80	2.34
1831	34.38	1.21	1.38	32.57	29.64	7.77	1.14	56.9	2.89	13.99	2.37
1832	...	1.21	1.38	32.73	29.91	7.81	1.15	57.7	2.91	14.16	2.40
1833	...	1.22	1.37	32.89	30.18	7.85	1.16	58.5	2.94	14.33	2.42

A5　Mid-year Population Estimates (in thousands)

1834–1854

	Austria[2]	Belgium[3]	Denmark	Finland	France	Germany[4]	Hungary[8]	Ireland	Netherlands	Norway	Russia[18]	Sweden	U.K.: England & Wales	U.K.: Scotland
1834	33.53	...	1.23	1.38	33.07	30.47	...	7.89	...	1.17	59.3	2.97	14.52	2.45
1835	...	4.19	1.24	1.39	33.26	30.80	...	7.94	...	1.19	60.2	3.00	14.72	2.47
1836	35.41₃	4.23	1.25	1.39	33.54	31.13	...	7.98	...	1.20	60.6	3.04	14.93	2.50
1837	16.15	4.26	1.26	1.39	33.69	31.45	...	8.02	...	1.21	61.0	3.07	15.10	2.52
1838	16.31	4.30₃	1.27	1.40	33.79	31.82	...	8.07	...	1.22	61.5	3.08	15.29	2.55
1839	16.49	...	1.28	1.42	33.94	32.22	...	8.11	2.64	1.23	61.9	3.10	15.51	2.57
1840	16.65	4.05	1.29	1.44	34.08	32.62	13.7[8]	8.16	2.88	1.24	62.4	3.12	15.73	2.60
1841	16.80	4.11	1.30	1.45	34.23	32.99	13.7[8]	8.20	2.91	1.25	62.9	3.16	15.93	2.62
1842	16.98	4.16	1.31	1.48	34.45	33.31	13.7[8]	8.22	2.94	1.27	63.5	3.19	16.13	2.65
1843	17.15	4.19	1.33	1.50	34.66	33.61	13.8[8]	8.24	2.97	1.29	64.0	3.22	16.33	2.68
1844	17.32	4.24	1.34	1.52	34.90	33.93	14.1[8]	8.28	3.00	1.30	64.6	3.26	16.53	2.71
1845	17.52	4.28	1.36	1.54	35.16	34.29	14.2[8]	8.29	3.04	1.32	65.2	3.30	16.7	2.74
1846	17.67	4.32	1.37	1.55	35.40	34.62	...	8.29	3.06	1.34	65.8	3.33	16.94	2.77
1847	17.63	4.34	1.38	1.57	35.47	34.79	...	8.02	3.05	1.35	66.5	3.35	17.15	2.80
1848	17.46	4.35	1.40	1.59	35.52	34.85	...	7.64	3.05	1.36	67.1	3.38	17.36	2.82
1849	17.41	4.37	1.41	1.61	35.55	35.01	...	7.26	3.06	1.38	67.8	3.42	17.56	2.85
1850	17.49	4.40	1.42	1.63	35.63	35.31	...	6.88	3.00	1.39	68.5	3.46	17.77	2.90
1851	17.63	4.45	1.44	1.65	35.80	35.63	...	6.51	3.05	1.41	69.0	3.50	17.98	2.92
1852	17.79	4.41	1.46	1.66	35.95	35.86	12.5	6.34	3.14	1.42	69.5	3.53	18.19	2.94
1853	17.92	4.53	1.47	1.67	36.07	35.99	12.7	6.20	3.15	1.42	70.1	3.55	10.40	2.96
1854	18.01	4.57	1.49	1.68	36.23	36.10	12.7	6.08	3.18	1.46	70.6	3.59	18.62	2.98

A5 Mid-year Population Estimates (in thousands)

1855–1899

	Austria[2]	Belgium	Bulgaria[10]	Denmark	Finland	France	Germany[4]	Greece	Hungary[8]	Ireland	Italy[9]	Netherlands
1855	17.94	4.60	...	1.51	1.69	36.08	36.14	...	12.7	6.01	...	3.21
1856	17.91	4.57	...	1.53	1.69	36.19	36.26	...	12.7	5.97	...	3.23
1857	18.10	4.55	...	1.55	1.69	36.30	36.53	...	12.8	5.92	...	3.27
1858	18.32	4.60	...	1.57	1.70	36.34	36.83	...	13.0	5.89	...	3.29
1859	18.53	4.65	...	1.59	1.72	36.50	37.19	...	13.1	5.86	...	3.31
1860	18.74	4.70	...	1.61	1.74	36.51_5	37.61	1.1	...	5.82	...	3.32
1861	18.92	4.76	...	1.63	1.76	37.39	38.00	1.1_{20}	...	5.79	...	3.35
1862	19.08	4.81	...	1.65	1.78	37.52	38.36	...	...	5.78	24.29	3.39
1863	19.27	4.86	...	1.67	1.79	37.71	38.76	...	...	5.72	24.47	3.43
1864	19.47	4.92	...	1.69	1.81	37.86	39.19	1.4	13.8	5.64	24.71	3.47
1865	19.65	4.96	...	1.71	1.83	38.02	39.55	1.4	13.9	5.59	24.97	3.51
1866	19.70	4.91	...	1.72	1.84	38.08	39.79	1.4	13.3	5.52	25.20	3.54
1867	19.74	4.86	...	1.74	1.83	38.23	40.03	1.4	13.3	5.49	25.34	3.57
1868	19.91	4.93	...	1.76	1.78	38.33_6	40.22	1.4	13.4	5.47	25.44	3.61
1869	20.11	4.99	...	1.78	1.73	36.82	40.49	1.4	13.5	5.45	25.59	3.61
1870	20.32	5.06	...	1.79	1.75	36.87	40.80	1.5	13.6	5.42	25.86	3.60
1871	20.51	5.10	...	1.81	1.79	36.19	41.00	1.5	13.8	5.40	25.95	3.63
1872	20.67	5.14	...	1.82	1.82	36.14	41.23	1.5	13.8	5.37	26.88	3.66
1873	20.74	5.21	...	1.84	1.85	36.34	41.56	1.5	13.4	5.33	27.05	3.69
1874	20.82	5.30	...	1.86	1.87	36.49	42.00	1.5	13.4	5.30	27.22	3.74
1875	21.01	5.37	...	1.87	1.90	36.66	42.52	1.6	13.4	5.28	27.38	3.79
1876	21.21	5.37	...	1.89	1.93	36.83	43.06	1.6	13.4	5.28	27.55	3.84
1877	21.40	5.37	...	1.92	1.96	37.00	43.61	1.6	13.6	5.29	27.71	3.89
1878	21.54	5.44	...	1.94	1.98	37.18	44.13	1.7	13.7	5.28	27.88	3.95
1879	21.71	5.51	...	1.96	2.11	37.32	44.64	1.7	13.7	5.27	28.04	4.01
1880	21.90	5.53	...	1.98	2.05	37.45	45.09	1.7	13.7	5.20	28.21	4.05
1881	22.05	5.55	2.88	1.99	2.07	37.59	45.43	1.7	13.88	5.15	28.38	4.09
1882	22.20	5.62	2.94	2.01	2.10	37.73	45.72	1.7	13.97	5.10	28.56	4.14
1883	22.36	5.69	3.00	2.03	2.13	37.86	46.02	1.7_{20}	14.09	5.02	28.77	4.20
1884	22.53	5.75	3.06	2.05	2.16	38.01	46.40	2.0	14.27	4.97	28.98	4.25
1885	22.70	5.82	3.12	2.08	2.19	38.11	46.71	2.0	14.44	4.94	29.19	4.31
1886	22.86	5.88	3.10	2.10	2.22	38.23	47.13	...	14.61	4.91	29.40	4.36
1887	23.05	5.94	3.14	2.12	2.26	38.20	47.63	...	14.76	4.86	29.61	4.42
1888	23.24	6.00	3.17	2.14	2.30	38.29	48.17	...	14.89	4.80	29.82	4.48
1889	23.44	6.06	3.20	2.16	2.33	38.37	48.72	2.2	15.06	4.76	30.04	4.53

A5 Mid-year Population Estimates (in thousands)

1890–1909

	Austria[2]	Belgium	Bulgaria[10]	Denmark	Finland	France	Germany[4]	Greece	Hungary[8]	Ireland	Italy[9]	Netherlands
1890	23.63	6.08	3.23	2.18	2.39	38.38	49.24	2.21	15.21	4.72	30.25	4.54
1891	23.81	6.10	3.26	2.19	2.41	38.35	49.76	…	15.32	4.68	30.46	4.59
1892	23.98	6.17	3.29	2.21	2.43	38.36	50.27	…	15.42	4.63	30.67	4.65
1893	24.15	6.22	3.34	2.23	2.45	38.38	50.76	…	15.54	4.61	30.88	4.70
1894	24.35	6.30	3.39	2.25	2.48	38.42	51.34	…	15.71	4.59	31.09	4.76
1895	24.54	6.38	3.44	2.28	2.51	38.40	52.00	…	15.88	4.56	31.30	4.83
1896	24.67	6.45	3.49	2.31	2.55	38.52	52.75	…	16.05	4.54	31.51	4.89
1897	25.03	6.54	3.55	2.34	2.59	38.60	53.57	…	16.23	4.53	31.72	4.97
1898	25.28	6.63	3.60	2.37	2.62	38.80	54.41	…	16.39	4.52	31.93	5.04
1899	25.53	6.71	3.66	2.40	2.66	38.90	55.25	…	16.56	4.50	32.14	5.11
1900	25.79	6.72	3.72	2.43	2.67	38.90	56.05	…	16.74	4.47	32.35	5.16
1901	26.05	6.75	3.77	2.46	2.69	38.98	56.87	…	16.92	4.45	32.53	5.22
1902	26.31	6.85	3.83	2.49	2.70	39.05	57.77	…	17.07	4.43	32.70	5.30
1903	26.55	6.94	3.89	2.52	2.73	39.12	58.63	…	17.21	4.42	32.83	5.39
1904	26.79	7.03	3.95	2.55	2.76	39.19	59.47	…	17.35	4.41	33.02	5.47
1905	27.00	7.12	4.00	2.57	2.79	39.22	60.31	…	17.47	4.40	33.19	5.55
1906	27.22	7.20	4.06	2.60	2.82	39.27	61.15	…	17.58	4.40	33.32	5.63
1907	27.48	7.28	4.12	2.63	2.86	39.27	62.01	…	17.72	4.39	33.51	5.71
1908	27.72	7.36	4.18	2.67	2.90	39.37	62.86	…	17.86	4.38	33.79	5.79
1909	27.96	7.42	4.24	2.70	2.93	39.43	63.72	…	18.02	4.39	34.12	5.84

A5 Mid-year Population Estimates (in thousands)

1855–1889

	Norway	Portugal	Romania	Russia[18]	Serbia	Spain	Sweden	Switzerland	U.K.: England & Wales	U.K.: Scotland
1855	1.48	...	...	71.1	...	...	3.62	...	18.83	2.98
1856	1.50	...	...	71.6	...	...	3.66	...	19.04	3.00
1857	1.52	...	...	72.1	...	...	3.68	...	19.26	3.01
1858	1.54	...	...	72.8	...	15.53	3.71	...	19.47	3.03
1859	1.57	...	...	73.9	...	15.58	3.76	...	19.69	3.04
1860	1.60	...	...	74.1	...	15.64	3.82	...	19.90	3.05
1861	1.61	...	3.94	73.6	...	15.70	3.89	...	20.12	3.07
1862	1.63	...	3.99	73.8	1.1	15.75	3.94	...	20.37	3.10
1863	1.65	...	4.03	74.3	1.1	15.81	3.99	...	20.63	3.13
1864	1.67	...	4.09	74.7	1.2	15.86	4.05	...	20.88	3.16
1865	1.69	...	4.11	75.1	1.2	15.92	4.09	...	21.14	3.18
1866	1.71	...	4.12	76.5	1.2	15.98	4.14	...	21.41	3.21
1867	1.72	...	4.13	79.9	1.2	16.03	4.18	...	21.67	3.24
1868	1.72	...	4.17	81.9	1.2	16.09	4.18	...	21.95	3.27
1869	1.73	...	4.22	83.4	1.3	16.14	4.18	...	22.22	3.31
1870	1.73	...	4.27	84.5	1.3	16.20	4.16	...	22.50	3.34
1871	1.74	...	4.31	85.4	1.3	15.92	4.19	2.68	22.79	3.37
1872	1.75	...	4.34	86.6	1.3	15.98	4.23	2.70	23.10	3.40
1873	1.77	...	4.35	87.9	1.3	16.03	4.27	2.71	23.41	3.44
1874	1.78	...	4.36	89.9	1.3	16.09	4.32	2.73	23.72	3.48
1875	1.80	...	4.38	90.2	1.4	16.14	4.36	2.75	24.04	3.51
1876	1.83	...	4.42	91.4	1.4	16.20	4.41	2.77	24.37	3.55
1877	1.85	...	4.46	92.2	1.4	16.59	4.46	2.79	24.70	3.59
1878	1.88	...	4.48	93.0	<u>1.4</u>	16.68	4.51	2.80	25.03	3.63
1879	1.90	...	4.51	95.3	1.7	16.77	4.54	2.82	25.37	3.67
1880	1.92	...	4.54	97.7	1.7	16.86	4.57	2.84	25.71	3.71
1881	1.92	...	4.58	100.0	1.8	16.95	4.57	2.85	26.05	3.74
1882	1.92	...	4.66	102.4	1.8	17.04	4.58	2.86	26.33	3.77
1883	1.92	...	4.73	104.7	1.9	17.14	4.59	2.87	26.63	3.80
1884	1.93	...	4.82	106.7	1.9	17.23	4.62	2.88	26.92	3.83
1885	1.94	...	4.91	108.8	2.0	17.32	4.66	2.90	27.22	3.86
1886	1.96	4.88	5.00	110.9	2.0	17.42	4.70	2.91	27.52	3.88
1887	1.97	4.92	5.08	113.1	2.0	17.51	4.72	2.92	27.83	3.91
1888	1.98	4.96	5.14	115.3	2.1	17.60	4.74	2.93	28.14	3.94
1889	1.98	5.00	5.22	116.6	2.1	17.68	4.76	2.94	28.45	3.97

A5 Mid-year Population Estimates (in thousands)

1890–1909

	Norway	Portugal	Romania	Russia[18]	Serbia	Spain	Sweden	Switzerland	U.K.: England & Wales	U.K.: Scotland
1890	2.00	5.05	5.29	117.8	2.2	17.76	4.77	2.95	28.76	4.00
1891	2.01	5.07	5.36	119.0	2.2	17.84	4.79	2.96	29.09	4.04
1892	2.03	5.11	5.41	120.2	2.2	17.92	4.80	3.00	29.42	4.08
1893	2.04	5.15	5.46	121.5	2.2	18.00	4.82	3.04	29.76	4.12
1894	2.06	5.18	5.52	122.7	2.3	18.08	4.85	3.08	30.10	4.17
1895	2.08	5.22	5.59	123.9	2.3	18.16	4.90	3.11	30.45	4.21
1896	2.11	5.26	5.67	125.1	2.4	18.24	4.94	3.15	30.80	4.25
1897	2.14	5.30	5.75	126.4	2.4	18.32	4.99	3.19	31.16	4.30
1898	2.17	5.33	5.83	128.4	2.4	18.40	5.04	3.23	31.52	4.34
1899	2.20	5.37	5.91	130.3	2.4	18.48	5.08	3.26	31.88	4.39
1900	2.23	5.42	6.00	132.9	2.5	18.53	5.12	3.30	32.25	4.44
1901	2.25	5.45	6.09	134.8	2.5	18.60	5.16	3.34	32.61	4.48
1902	2.27	5.50	6.16	136.6	2.6	18.72	5.19	3.38	32.95	4.51
1903	2.29	5.54	6.25	139.1	2.6	18.85	5.21	3.43	33.29	4.54
1904	2.30	5.60	6.34	141.6	2.7	18.99	5.24	3.47	33.64	4.56
1905	2.31	5.65	6.44	143.9	2.7	19.12	5.28	3.52	33.99	4.59
1906	2.32	5.69	6.53	146.4	2.7	19.25	5.32	3.56	34.34	4.62
1907	2.33	5.74	6.63	149.1	2.8	19.39	5.36	3.60	34.70	4.65
1908	2.35	5.79	6.73	152.5	2.8	19.52	5.40	3.65	35.06	4.68
1909	2.37	5.84	6.82	157.1	2.8	19.66	5.45	3.69	35.42	4.71

A5 Mid-year Population Estimates (in thousands)

1910–1939

	Albania	Austria[2]	Belgium[3]	Bulgaria[10]	Czecho-slovakia[12]	Denmark	Finland	France	Germany[4]	Greece	Hungary[8]	Ireland Republic	Ireland Northern
1910	...	28.20	7.44	4.31	...	2.74	2.96	39.54	64.57	...	18.18	4.38	
1911	...	28.42	7.46	4.37	...	2.77	3.00	39.62	65.36	...	18.33	4.38	
1912	...	28.63	7.52	4.43	...	2.80	3.02	39.67	66.15	...	18.49	4.37	
1913	...	28.85	7.60	4.50	...	2.83	3.05	39.77[5]	66.98	...	18.66	4.35	
1914	...	...	7.66	4.85	...	2.87	3.08	33.22	...	...	18.81	4.33	
1915	...	...	7.70	4.90	...	2.90	3.10	33.38	...	...	18.85	4.28	
1916	...	...	7.70	5.00	...	2.94	3.12	32.85	...	...	18.75	4.27	
1917	...	...	7.67	5.05	...	2.97	3.12	32.50	...	...	18.61[8] / 7.94	4.27	
1918	...	..[2]	7.60	5.10	...	3.01	3.12	32.83	...	...	7.89	4.28	
1919	...	6.42	7.57	5.15	13.53	3.04	3.13	31.97[6]	...	...	7.88	4.35	
1920	...	6.45	7.49	4.82	13.59	3.08[21]	3.17	39.00	...	...	7.95	4.36	
1921	...	6.50	7.44	4.90	13.66	3.28	3.21	39.24	...	...	8.03	4.35	
												Republic	Northern
1922	...	6.53	7.51	5.00	13.80	3.32	3.24	39.42	61.90	5.60	8.10	3.02	1.27
1923	...	6.54	7.57	5.10	13.93	3.36	3.27	39.88	62.31	6.00	8.17	3.01	1.26
1924	...	6.56	7.65[3]	5.21	14.07	3.39	3.30	40.31	62.70	6.00	8.23	3.00	1.26
1925	...	6.58	7.76	5.31	14.20	3.42	3.33	40.61	63.17	5.96	8.30	2.98	1.26
1926	...	6.60	7.84	5.42	14.31	3.45	3.36	40.87	63.63	6.04	8.38	2.97	1.25
1927	...	6.62	7.90	5.51	14.41	3.47	3.40	40.94	64.02	6.13	8.45	2.96	1.25
1928	...	6.64	7.97	5.59	14.50	3.50	3.42	41.05	64.39	6.21	8.52	2.94	1.25
1929	...	6.66	8.03	5.66	14.59	3.52	3.45	41.23	64.74	6.29	8.58	2.94	1.24
1930	...	6.68	8.08	5.73	14.68	3.54	3.48	41.61	65.08	6.37	8.65	2.93	1.24
1931	...	6.70	8.13	5.81	14.78	3.57	3.50	41.86	65.42	6.46	8.72	2.93	1.24
1932	1.00	6.72	8.19	5.88	14.89	3.60	3.53	41.86	65.72	6.54	8.78	2.95	1.25
1933	...	6.75	8.23	5.96	14.98	3.63	3.55	41.89	66.03	6.62	8.84	2.96	1.26
1934	...	6.76	8.26	6.04	15.06	3.67	3.58	41.95	66.41	6.73	8.91	2.97	1.26
1935	...	6.76	8.29	6.10	15.13	3.69	3.59	41.94	66.87	6.84	8.98	2.97	1.28
1936	...	6.76	8.32	6.15	15.19	3.72	3.63	41.91	67.35	6.94	9.04	2.97	1.28
1937	...	6.75	8.35	6.20	15.25[12] / 14.43	3.75	3.66	41.93	67.83	7.03	9.10	2.95	1.28
1938	1.05	6.75	8.37	6.25	14.60	3.78	3.69	41.96	... / 68.56	7.12	9.06	2.94	1.29
1939	1.06	6.65	8.39[3]	6.29	14.68	3.80	3.70	40.00	...	7.22	9.23	2.93	1.29

A5 Mid-year Population Estimates (in thousands)

1940–1964

	Albania	Austria[2]	Belgium[3]	Bulgaria[10]	Czecho-slovakia[12]	Denmark	Finland	France	Germany[4] East[13]	Germany[4] West[14]	Greece	Hungary[8]	Ireland Republic	Ireland Northern
1940	1.09	6.70	8.30	6.34[10]	14.71	3.83	3.70	39.00		...	7.32[15]	9.29	2.96	1.30
1941	1.09	6.74	8.28	6.71	14.67	3.86	3.71	37.80		...	7.4	9.34	2.99	1.31
1942	1.11	6.78	8.25	6.77	14.58	3.90	3.73	37.70		...	7.3	9.40	2.96	1.33
1943	...	6.81	8.24[3]	6.83	14.54	3.95	3.75	37.08		...	7.3	9.44	2.95	1.34
1944	...	6.83	8.29	6.88	14.59	4.00	3.78	36.50		...	7.3	9.50	2.94	1.36
1945	1.12	6.80	8.34	6.94	14.15	4.04	3.82	38.00	...	...	7.3	9.02	2.95	1.36
1946	1.13	7.00	8.37	7.00	12.92	4.10	3.90	40.32	18.06	46.19	7.4	9.04	2.96	1.35
1947	1.14	6.97	8.45	7.06	12.16	4.15	3.86	40.74	18.89	46.99	7.5	9.08	2.97	1.35
1948	1.16	6.95	8.56	7.13	12.34	4.19	3.91	41.21	19.07	48.25	7.8[15]	9.16	2.98	1.36
1949	1.18	6.94	8.61	7.19	12.34	4.23	3.96	41.60	18.89	49.20	7.48	9.25	2.98	1.37
1950	1.21	6.93	8.64	7.25	12.39	4.27	4.01	41.83	18.39	49.99	7.57	9.34	2.97	1.38
1951	1.24	6.93	8.68	7.26	12.53	4.30	4.05	42.16	18.35	50.53	7.65	9.42	2.96	1.37
1952	1.27	6.93	8.73	7.27	12.68	4.33	4.09	42.46	18.33	50.86	7.73	9.50	2.95	1.37
1953	1.30	6.93	8.78	7.35	12.82	4.37	4.14	42.75	18.18	51.35	7.82	9.59	2.95	1.38
1954	1.34	6.94	8.82	7.42	12.95	4.41	4.19	43.06	18.06	51.88	7.89	9.71	2.94	1.39
1955	1.38	6.95	8.87	7.50	13.09	4.44	4.23	43.43	17.94	52.38	7.97	9.82	2.92	1.39
1956	1.42	6.95	8.92	7.58	13.23	4.47	4.28	43.84	17.71	53.01	8.03	9.96	2.90	1.40
1957	1.46	6.97	8.99	7.65	13.36	4.49	4.32	44.31	17.52	53.66	8.10	9.84	2.88	1.40
1958	1.51	6.99	9.05	7.73	13.47	4.51	4.36	44.79	17.35	54.29	8.17	9.88	2.85	1.40
1959	1.56	7.01	9.10	7.80	13.56	4.55	4.39	45.24	17.30	54.88	8.26	9.94	2.85	1.41
1960	1.61	7.05	9.15	7.87	13.65	4.58	4.43	45.68	17.24	55.43	8.33	9.98	2.83	1.42
1961	1.66	7.09	9.18	7.94	13.78	4.61	4.47	46.16	17.12	56.17	8.40	10.03	2.82	1.43
1962	1.71	7.13	9.22	8.01	13.86	4.65	4.51	47.00	17.10	56.84	8.45	10.06	2.82	1.44
1963	1.76	7.18	9.29	8.08	13.95	4.68	4.54	47.82	17.15	57.39	8.48	10.09	2.84	1.45
1964	1.81	7.22	9.38	8.14	14.06	4.72	4.58	48.31	16.99	57.97	8.51	10.12	2.85	1.46

A5 Mid-year Population Estimates (in thousands)

1910–1944

	Italy[9]	Netherland	Norway	Poland[17]	Portugal	Romania[11]	Russia/USSR[18]	Spain	Sweden	Switzerland	U.K.: England & Wales	U.K.: Scotland	Yugoslavia[19]
1910	34.38	5.90	2.38	...	5.89	6.92	160.7	19.79	5.50	3.73	35.79	4.74	2.9
1911	34.68	5.98	2.40	...	5.96	7.03	163.9	19.93	5.54	3.78	36.14	4.75	2.9
1912	35.03	6.07	2.42	...	5.96	7.16	167.9	20.06	5.58	3.82	36.33	4.74	...
1913	35.42	6.16	2.45	...	5.97	7.29[11]	170.9	20.20	5.62	3.86	36.57	4.73	...
1914	35.86	6.28	2.47	...	5.98	7.56	175.1	20.33	5.66	3.90	36.97	4.75	...
1915	36.39	6.39	2.50	...	5.99	7.83	178.9	20.47	5.70	3.88	35.28	4.77	...
1916	36.71	6.52	2.52	...	6.00	...	181.5	20.61	5.74	3.88	34.64	4.79	...
1917	36.66	6.65	2.55	...	6.01	...	184.6[18]	20.74	5.78	3.89	34.20	4.81	...
1918	36.28	6.75	2.58	...	6.01	...	...	20.88	5.81	3.88	34.02	4.81	...[19]
1919	36.07	6.80	2.60	...	6.02	...	...	21.02	5.83	3.87	35.43	4.82	11.71
1920	36.37[9]	6.85	2.63	26.75	6.03	...	...	21.16	5.88	3.88	37.25	4.86	11.88
1921	...	6.92	2.67	27.15	6.08	15.58	...	21.30	5.93	3.88	37.93	4.88	12.06
1922	38.20	7.03	2.69	27.82	6.16	15.78	...	21.52	5.97	3.88	38.20	4.90	12.24
1923	38.50	7.15	2.71	28.16	6.24	15.99	...	21.74	6.00	3.88	38.45	4.89	12.42
1924	38.78	7.26	2.73	28.59	6.32	16.23	...	21.96	6.02	3.89	38.79	4.86	12.61
1925	39.11	7.36	2.75	29.27	6.40	16.49	...	22.19	6.04	3.91	38.93	4.87	12.80
1926	39.46	7.47	2.76	29.92	6.48	16.76	...	22.40	6.06	3.93	39.11	4.86	12.99
1927	39.81	7.58	2.77	30.29	6.55	17.02	...	22.63	6.08	3.96	39.29	4.85	13.18
1928	40.19	7.68	2.78	30.70	6.63	17.27	...	22.86	6.10	3.99	39.48	4.85	13.38
1929	40.55	7.78	2.79	31.08	6.71	17.54	...	23.10	6.11	4.02	39.60	4.83	13.58
1930	40.89	7.88	2.81	31.47	6.82	17.89	...	23.33	6.13	4.05	39.80	4.83	13.78
1931	41.25	8.00	2.82	31.93	6.88	18.04	...	23.57	6.15	4.08	39.99	4.84	13.98
1932	41.58	8.12	2.84	32.38	6.97	18.43	...	23.78	6.18	4.10	40.20	4.88	14.17
1933	41.93	8.24	2.86	32.81	7.06	18.65	...	24.12	6.20	4.12	40.35	4.91	14.37
1934	42.28	8.34	2.87	33.20	7.15	18.91	...	24.35	6.22	4.14	40.47	4.93	14.57
1935	42.63	8.43	2.89	33.60	7.24	19.09	...	24.57	6.24	4.15	40.64	4.95	14.77
1936	42.96	8.52	2.90	34.00	7.33	19.32	...	24.81	6.26	4.17	40.84	4.97	14.97
1937	43.27	8.60	2.92	34.36	7.41	19.53	...	25.05	6.28	4.18	41.03	4.98	15.17
1938	43.60	8.68	2.94	34.68[16]	7.50	19.75	...	25.28	6.30	4.19	41.21	4.99	15.38
1939	44.02	8.78	2.95	34.80[17]	7.60	19.93[11]	—[18]	25.52	6.32	4.21	41.46	5.01	15.60
1940	44.47	8.88	2.97	...	7.72	15.91[11]	191.7	25.76	6.36	4.23	41.86	5.06	...
1941	44.83	8.96	2.99	...	7.76	13.55	...	25.97	6.39	4.25	41.75	5.16	...
1942	45.10	9.04	3.01	...	7.83	13.61	...	26.19	6.43	4.29	41.90	5.17	...
1943	44.83	9.10	3.03	...	7.90	13.61	...	26.39	6.49	4.32	42.26	5.19	...
1944	44.94	9.17	3.06	...	7.98	13.70	...	26.60	6.56	4.36	42.45	5.21	...

A5 Mid-year Population Estimates (in thousands)

	Italy[9]	Netherland	Norway	Poland[17]	Portugal	Romania[11]	Russia/USSR[18]	Spain	Sweden	Switzerland	U.K.: England & Wales	U.K.: Scotland	Yugoslavia[19]
1945	45.09	9.26	3.09	...	8.05	13.68[11]	...	26.80	6.64	4.41	42.64	5.19	15.22
1946	45.38	9.40	3.13	23.77	8.12	15.79	...	27.02	6.72	4.47	42.70	5.17	15.44
1947	45.72	9.63	3.16	23.70	8.19	15.85	...	27.22	6.80	4.52	43.05	5.12	15.68
1948	46.05	9.80	3.20	23.98	8.26	15.89	...	27.44	6.88	4.58	43.50	5.15	15.90
1949	46.40	9.95	3.23	24.41	8.33	16.08	...	27.65	6.96	4.64	43.78	5.16	16.13
1950	46.77	10.11	3.26	24.82	8.40	16.31	181.0	27.87	7.01	4.69	44.02	5.17	16.35
1951	47.09	10.26	3.30	25.27	8.46	16.46	183.2	28.09	7.07	4.75	43.81	5.10	16.59
1952	47.34	10.38	3.33	25.75	8.50	16.63	186.4	28.53	7.12	4.81	43.95	5.10	16.80
1953	47.60	10.49	3.36	26.25	8.53	16.85	189.5	28.75	7.17	4.88	44.11	5.10	17.05
1954	47.90	10.61	3.39	26.76	8.57	17.04	192.7	28.98	7.21	4.93	44.27	5.10	17.28
1955	48.20	10.75	3.43	27.28	8.61	17.32	196.1	29.20	7.26	4.98	44.44	5.11	17.52
1956	48.47	10.89	3.46	27.81	8.65	17.58	199.6	29.43	7.32	5.04	44.67	5.12	17.68
1957	48.74	11.03	3.49	28.31	8.68	17.83	203.1	29.66	7.37	5.13	44.91	5.14	17.86
1958	49.04	11.19	3.52	28.77	8.72	18.06	206.8	29.89	7.41	5.20	45.11	5.16	18.02
1959	49.36	11.35	3.55	29.24	8.78	18.23	210.5	30.13	7.44	5.26	45.39	5.16	18.21
1960	50.20	11.49	3.58	29.56	8.94	18.40	214.2	30.45	7.48	5.36	45.77	5.18	18.40
1961	50.54	11.64	3.61	29.96	8.94	18.57	218.0	30.74	7.52	5.51	46.20	5.18	18.61
1962	50.88	11.81	3.64	30.32	9.02	18.68	221.5	31.07	7.56	5.67	46.66	5.20	18.82
1963	51.25	11.97	3.67	30.69	9.08	18.81	224.8	31.39	7.60	5.79	46.97	5.20	19.03
1964	51.67	12.13	3.69	31.16	9.12	18.93	227.8	31.72	7.66	5.89	47.32	5.21	19.22

1945–1964

A5 Mid-year Population Estimates (in thousands)

1965–1999

	Albania	Austria	Belgium	Bulgaria	Czecho-slovakia	Denmark	Finland	France	East Germany	West Germany	Greece	Hungary	Ireland Repub	Ireland Northern
1965	1.86	7.27	9.46	8.20	14.16	4.76	4.61	48.76	17.03	58.62	8.55	10.15	2.85	1.47
1966	1.91	7.32	9.53	8.26	14.24	4.80	4.64	49.16	17.07	59.15	8.61	10.18	2.88	1.48
1967	1.96	7.38	9.58	8.31	14.30	4.84	4.67	49.55	17.08	59.29	8.72	10.22	2.90	1.49
1968	2.02	7.41	9.62	8.37	14.36	4.87	4.63	49.91	17.08	59.50	8.74	10.26	2.91	1.50
1969	2.08	7.44	9.61	8.43	14.42	4.29	4.62	50.32	17.08	60.07	8.77	10.30	2.92	1.51
1970	2.14	7.47	9.64	8.49	14.33	4.93	4.61	50.77	17.06	60.65	8.79	10.34	2.94	1.53
1971	2.19	7.50	9.67	8.54	14.39	4.96	4.62	51.25	17.06	61.28	8.83	10.36	2.98	1.54
1972	…	7.54	9.71	8.58	14.46	4.99	4.64	51.70	17.04	61.67	8.89	10.39	3.02	1.54
1973	…	7.59	9.74	8.62	14.56	5.02	4.67	52.12	16.98	61.98	8.93	10.43	3.07	1.55
1974	…	7.60	9.77	8.68	14.69	5.04	4.69	52.46	16.92	62.05	8.96	10.47	3.12	1.55
1975	2.40	7.58	9.79	8.72	14.80	5.06	4.71	52.70	16.85	61.83	9.05	10.53	3.18	1.54
1976	2.45	7.57	9.81	8.76	14.92	5.07	4.73	52.91	16.79	61.51	9.17	10.59	3.23	1.54
1977	2.51	7.57	9.82	8.80	15.03	5.09	4.74	53.14	16.76	61.40	9.27	10.64	3.27	1.54
1978	2.56	7.56	9.83	8.81	15.14	5.10	4.75	53.38	16.76	61.31	9.36	10.67	3.31	1.55
1979	2.62	7.55	9.84	8.83	15.24	5.12	4.76	53.61	16.74	61.34	9.45	10.70	3.37	1.55
1980	2.67	7.55	9.85	8.86	15.31	5.12	4.78	53.88	16.74	61.56	9.64	10.71	3.40	1.56
1981	2.72	7.56	9.85	8.89	15.32	5.12	4.80	54.18	16.74	61.67	9.73	10.71	3.44	1.54
1982	2.78	7.57	9.86	8.92	15.37	5.12	4.83	54.48	16.70	61.64	9.79	10.70	3.48	1.54
1983	2.84	7.55	9.86	8.94	15.41	5.11	4.86	54.73	16.70	61.42	9.85	10.67	3.50	1.54
1984	2.90	7.55	9.85	8.96	15.46	5.11	4.88	54.95	16.67	61.18	9.90	10.64	3.53	1.55
1985	2.96	7.56	9.86	8.96	15.50	5.11	4.90	55.17	16.64	61.01	9.93	10.60	3.54	1.56
1986	3.02	7.56	9.86	8.96	15.53	5.12	4.92	55.39	16.62	61.05	9.97	10.56	3.54	1.57
1987	3.08	7.58	9.87	8.97	15.56	5.13	4.93	55.63	16.64	61.17	9.99	10.51	3.54	1.57
1988	3.14	7.60	9.90	8.99	15.58	5.13	4.95	56.12	16.67	61.42	10.01	10.46	3.54	1.58
1989	3.20	7.61	9.94	8.99	15.61	5.13	4.96	56.42		78.68 *(Germany)*	10.09	10.42	3.52	1.58
1990	3.26	7.71	9.97	8.99	15.64	5.14	4.99	56.73		79.37 *(Germany)*	10.16	10.38	3.50	1.59
1991	3.26	7.83	9.98	8.98	15.59	5.15	5.01	57.06		79.98 *(Germany)*	10.25	10.36	3.53	1.60
1992	3.36	7.88	10.06	8.54	10.32[22] *(Czech Republic[22])*	5.17	5.04	57.37		80.57	10.32	10.34	3.55	1.62
1993	3.39	7.99	10.08	8.47	10.33[22]	5.19	5.07	57.67		81.19	10.38	10.31	3.56	1.63
1994	3.54	8.03	10.06	8.44	10.33	5.20	5.08	57.90		81.42	10.42	10.26	3.58	1.65
1995	3.61	8.04	10.13	8.40	10.33	5.22	5.10	58.13		81.66	10.45	10.22	3.60	1.66
1996	3.65	8.05	10.13	8.36	10.31	5.26	5.12	58.37		81.89	10.47	10.19	3.62	1.69
1997	3.73	8.07	10.18	8.31	10.30	5.28	5.14	58.60		82.06	10.49	10.15	3.66	1.72
1998	3.79	8.07	10.21	8.25	10.29	5.30	5.15	58.85		82.02	10.51	10.11	3.70	1.73
1999	3.11	8.17	10.15	8.20	10.28	5.32	5.16	59.09		82.08	10.62	10.06	3.74	1.75

A5 Mid-year Population Estimates (in thousands)

1965–1999

	Italy	Netherlands	Norway	Poland	Portugal	Romania	Russia/USSR	Spain	Sweden	Switzerland	U.K.: England & Wales	U.K.: Scotland	Yugoslavia
1965	52.11	12.29	3.72	31.50	9.13	19.03	230.6	32.06	7.73	5.94	47.67	5.21	19.43
1966	52.52	12.46	3.75	31.70	9.11	19.14	233.1	32.39	7.81	6.00	47.97	5.20	19.64
1967	52.90	12.60	3.78	31.94	9.10	19.28	235.5	32.73	7.87	6.06	48.27	5.20	19.84
1968	53.24	12.73	3.82	32.30	9.11	19.72	238.3	33.08	7.92	6.13	48.51	5.21	20.03
1969	53.54	12.88	3.85	32.56	9.10	20.01	24.04	33.43	7.97	6.21	48.74	5.21	20.21
1970	53.82	13.04	3.88	32.53	9.04	20.25	242.8	33.78	8.04	6.27	48.89	5.22	20.37
1971	54.07	13.19	3.90	32.80	8.64	20.47	245.1	34.13	8.10	6.32	49.15	5.22	20.57
1972	54.38	13.33	3.93	33.07	8.63	20.66	247.5	34.49	8.12	6.38	49.33	5.21	20.77
1973	54.75	13.44	3.96	33.36	8.63	20.83	249.7	34.86	8.14	6.43	49.46	5.21	20.96
1974	55.11	13.54	3.99	33.69	8.75	21.03	252.1	35.22	8.16	6.44	49.47	5.22	21.16
1975	55.44	13.65	4.01	34.02	9.09	21.24	25.45	35.60	8.19	6.40	49.47	5.21	21.36
1976	55.72	13.77	4.03	34.36	9.35	21.45	256.8	35.97	8.22	6.35	49.46	5.20	21.57
1977	55.95	13.85	4.04	34.70	9.45	21.66	259.0	36.35	8.25	6.33	49.44	5.20	21.78
1978	56.15	13.94	4.06	35.01	9.56	21.85	261.3	36.77	8.28	6.33	49.44	5.18	21.97
1979	56.32	14.03	4.07	35.26	9.66	22.05	263.4	37.18	8.29	6.35	49.51	5.20	22.17
1980	56.43	14.14	4.09	35.58	9.77	22.20	265.5	37.54	8.31	6.32	49.60	5.19	22.30
1981	56.51	14.25	4.10	35.99	9.85	22.25	267.7	37.76	8.32	6.35	49.63	5.18	22.47
1982	56.64	14.31	4.11	36.23	9.93	22.48	270.0	37.98	8.32	6.39	49.60	5.17	22.64
1983	56.84	14.36	4.13	36.57	9.87	22.55	272.5	38.17	8.33	6.42	49.65	5.15	22.80
1984	57.00	14.42	4.14	36.91	9.89	22.62	275.1	38.34	8.34	6.44	49.76	5.15	22.97
1985	57.14	14.48	4.15	37.20	9.90	22.72	277.5	38.50	8.35	6.47	49.92	5.14	23.12
1986	57.25	14.56	4.17	37.46	9.91	22.82	280.2	38.67	8.37	6.50	50.07	5.12	23.27
1987	57.35	14.66	4.19	37.66	9.91	22.94	283.1	38.83	8.40	6.54	50.24	5.11	23.42
1988	57.44	14.76	4.20	37.86	9.90	23.05	283.7	39.00	8.44	6.59	50.39	5.09	23.56
1989	57.54	14.85	4.23	37.96	9.90	23.15	286.7	39.00	8.49	6.64	50.67	5.10	23.61
1990	57.66	14.95	4.24	38.12	9.89	23.20	288.6	39.02	8.56	6.71	50.87	5.10	23.64
1991	56.76	15.07	4.26	38.25	9.88	23.18	148.6[23]	39.02	8.62	6.80	51.10	5.11	10.41[24]
1992	56.86	15.18	4.29	38.36	9.86	22.78	148.7[23]	39.00	8.67	6.88	51.28	5.11	10.45[24]
1993	57.06	15.29	4.31	38.50	9.86	22.75	148.5[23]	39.08	8.72	6.94	51.44	5.12	10.49[24]
1994	57.20	15.38	4.32	38.54	9.90	22.73	148.0	39.14	8.78	6.99	51.39	5.14	10.51
1995	57.30	15.45	4.35	38.58	9.91	22.68	147.7	39.21	8.83	7.04	51.60	5.16	10.54
1996	57.38	15.53	4.38	38.61	9.92	22.60	147.7	39.27	8.84	7.07	51.80	5.17	10.57
1997	57.52	15.61	4.40	38.65	9.94	22.54	147.1	39.32	8.84	7.08	52.00	5.17	10.60
1998	57.36	15.70	4.43	38.66	9.95	22.50	146.5	39.37	8.85	7.11	52.23	5.18	10.61
1999	57.34	15.81	4.46	38.65	9.98	22.45	146.0	39.41	8.85	7.14	52.74	5.20	10.63

A5 Mid-year Population Estimates (in millions)

NOTES

1. SOURCES:- The main sources are the official publications listed on p. xv. In addition the following were used: Albania—League of Nations, *Statistical Yearbook* and United Nations, *Demographic Yearbook*; Russia to 1913—P.A. Khromov, *Economic Development of Russia in the 19th and 20th Centuries, 1800-1917* (Moscow, 1950); and U.K.: England to 1800 (1st line)—E.A. Wrigley & R.S. Schofield, *The Population History of England* (London, 1981).
2. The statistics relate, in principle, to the population actually present, though it is probable that in practice many figures, especially prior to 1890, were of normally resident population. Known exceptions are indicated in footnotes.

FOOTNOTES

[1] England only (excluding Monmouthshire) to 1801 (1st line).
[2] The Habsburg Empire to 1837 (1st line), Cisleithania from then to 1913, and the Republic (including Burgenalnd throughout) subsequently.
[3] *De jure* civil population. Parts of Limburg and Luxemburg ceded to the Netherlands are excluded from 1838, and the eastern communes ceded by Germany after the First World War are included from 1925 (except in 1940-43).
[4] Within the 1914 boundaries to 1913, and within the 1937 boundaries from 1922 to 1938.
[5] Subsequently including Savoy and Nice.
[6] Parts of Alsace-Lorraine ceded to Germany in 1871 and recovered after the First World War are excluded from 1869 to 1919. The figures for 1914-19 also exclude the invaded departments.
[7] Territory was acquired from Turkey in 1878, 1913, and after the First World War.
[8] Transleithania to 1917 (1st line), and the territory established by the Treaty of Trianon subsequently, as modified from 1947 by the cession of the Bratislava bridgehead to Czechoslovakia. The population of Croatia-Slavonia is not included here, except in 1841-45. It was as follows:-

1881	1.92	1888	2.14	1895	2.28	1902	2.42	1909	2.58
1882	1.94	1889	2.17	1896	2.30	1903	2.46	1910	2.61
1883	1.97	1890	2.19	1897	2.32	1904	2.49	1911	2.62
1884	2.00	1891	2.21	1898	2.34	1905	2.50	1912	2.65
1885	2.03	1892	2.22	1899	2.37	1906	2.52	1913	2.66
1886	2.06	1893	2.23	1900	2.40	1907	2.34	1914	2.68
1887	2.10	1894	2.25	1901	2.42	1908	2.58	1915	2.69

[9] Within the 1871 boundaries to 1920, the 1938 boundaries to 1943 (1st line), and the postwar boundaries subsequently.
[10] Within the 1939 boundaries to 1940. Including Southern Dobrudja subsequently.
[11] Within the original boundaries to 1915, except that Dobrudja is included in 1914 and 1915. Within the Treaty of Trianon boundaries from 1919 to 1939, and within the postwar boundaries subsequently, except that northern Transylvania is excluded in 1941-45.
[12] Within the 1937 boundaries to 1937 (1st line), and within the 1948 boundaries subsequently.
[13] Including East Berlin.
[14] Including West Berlin and Saarland.
[15] The figures for 1941-8 are based on provisional estimates. The Dodecanese Islands are included from 1949.
[16] At 1 January.
[17] Within the 1939 boundaries to 1939, and within the 1946 boundaries subsequently.
[18] The 50 provinces of European Russia to 1913, and the U.S.S.R. subsequently (including the territorial gains of 1940).
[19] Serbia to 1911, Yugoslavia as constituted in 1939 for 1919-39, and as constituted in 1953 subsequently.
[20] Including the Ionian Islands from 1864, and Thessaly and Arta from 1883.
[21] 1913 boundaries to 1920, including northern Slesvig subsequently.
[22] Czech Republic. Figures for Slovakia are: 1992, 5300; 1993. 5318.
[23] Russian Federation. Figures for ex. USSR are:

	Armenia	Azerbaijan	Belarus	Estonia	Georgia	Kazakhstan	Kyrgistan	Latvia	Lithuania	Moldova	Tajikistan	Turkmenistan	Ukraine	Uzbekistan
1991	3.61	7.20	10.27	1.57	5.43	16.81	4.45	2.66	3.74	4.36	5.46	3.75	52.00	20.90
1992	3.69	7.39	10.31	1.54	5.44	16.90	4.49	2.63	3.74	4.35	5.60	3.83	52.15	21.38
1993	3.73	7.39	10.36	1.52	5.45	16.96	4.53	2.59	3.73	4.36	5.74	3.92	52.18	21.86
1994	3.74	7.59	10.30	1.49	5.42	16.29	4.54	2.54	3.72	4.34	5.74	4.40	52.11	22.28
1995	3.76	7.68	10.28	1.48	5.41	16.06	4.59	2.51	3.71	4.34	5.83	4.50	51.72	22.69
1996	3.77	7.76	10.25	1.46	5.42	15.92	4.65	2.49	3.71	4.32	5.91	4.56	51.33	23.13
1997	3.78	7.83	10.22	1.45	5.12	15.75	4.72	2.46	3.70	3.65	5.92	4.23	50.99	23.56
1998	3.79	7.91	10.19	1.45	5.05	15.07	4.79	2.44	3.70	3.65	6.10	4.85	50.04	24.05
1999	3.79	7.98	10.15	1.41	5.39	14.94	4.86	2.43	3.69	4.38	6.23	4.38	50.10	23.95

A5 Mid-year Population Estimates (in millions)

[24] Yugoslavia (Montenego and Serbia) only. Figures for ex. Yugoslavia are:

	Bosnia-Hercegovina	Croatia	Macedonia	Slovenia
1991	4.16	4.78	2.04	2.00
1992	3.94	4.79	2.06	1.97
1993	3.70	4.78	2.12	1.99
1994	4.45	4.69	1.95	1.98
1995	4.18	4.66	1.96	1.98
1996	4.17	4.49	1.97	1.91
1997	4.20	4.57	1.99	1.98
1998	4.21	4.501	2.00	1.98
1999	3.84	4.554	2.01	1.98

A6 VITAL STATISTICS: RATES PER 1,000 POPULATION
B = Births   D = Deaths   M = Marriages

	Finland			Norway[1]			Sweden[1]		
	B	**D**	**M**	**B**	**D**	**M**	**B**	**D**	**M**
1749	…	…	…	33.0	27.9	…	33.8	28.1	17.1
1750	…	…	…	30.6	27.2	…	36.4	26.9	18.5
1751	44.3	24.6	21.8	35.0	27.0	…	38.7	26.2	18.5
1752	44.7	26.3	20.2	33.5	25.4	…	35.9	27.3	18.5
1753	44.1	26.1	19.0	34.8	23.4	…	36.1	24.0	17.4
1754	46.4	35.1	19.8	35.3	24.1	…	37.2	26.3	18.9
1755	46.9	30.7	18.8	33.5	25.1	…	37.5	27.4	18.3
1756	45.8	36.3	17.0	36.1	27.2	…	36.1	27.7	17.0
1757	43.3	36.2	16.0	34.5	22.1	…	32.6	29.9	15.9
1758	42.3	29.5	17.8	33.6	24.6	…	33.4	32.4	16.1
1759	44.5	28.1	19.6	32.3	19.5	…	33.6	26.3	19.5
1760	46.6	27.9	19.6	35.0	23.1	…	35.7	24.8	19.5
1761	45.8	28.3	16.8	35.9	24.4	…	34.8	25.8	18.9
1762	41.3	29.6	16.0	35.8	25.9	…	35.1	31.2	17.9
1763	43.0	41.0	16.0	34.5	38.8	…	35.0	32.9	17.3
1764	45.7	33.1	16.6	35.8	29.1	…	34.7	27.2	17.6
1765	42.9	29.7	16.2	34.5	30.2	…	33.4	27.7	16.3
1766	41.5	28.6	15.6	34.0	30.4	…	33.8	25.1	16.5
1767	40.7	29.1	15.6	35.1	25.1	…	35.4	25.6	16.5
1768	42.9	25.8	17.8	32.8	24.4	…	33.6	27.2	16.9
1769	42.4	28.3	16.8	33.7	23.7	…	33.1	27.2	16.3
1770	40.9	30.2	14.6	32.1	24.0	14.7	33.0	26.1	16.2
1771	38.0	26.1	15.2	31.6	23.2	13.5	32.2	27.8	15.5
1772	37.6	23.9	15.4	28.2	26.2	11.9	28.9	37.4	13.6
1773	37.9	21.5	17.0	25.0	48.1	12.0	25.5	52.5	15.5
1774	40.3	21.5	18.6	28.3	25.8	17.1	34.5	22.4	17.5
1775	40.4	25.6	17.2	33.8	23.6	18.6	35.6	24.8	18.9
1776	39.0	30.5	17.0	28.8	20.7	16.9	32.9	22.5	18.0
1777	40.1	32.0	17.6	31.3	21.0	16.8	33.0	24.9	18.1
1778	42.7	25.0	19.6	31.2	20.2	16.0	34.8	26.7	18.1
1779	43.2	21.9	18.2	31.5	27.4	18.2	36.7	28.5	17.3
1780	41.2	21.1	16.4	32.4	25.6	15.4	35.7	21.7	17.1
1781	37.7	26.5	15.2	31.4	20.9	16.1	33.5	25.6	15.7
1782	41.7	25.1	16.8	30.9	22.6	14.1	32.1	27.3	15.4
1783	40.0	31.2	16.2	27.6	24.8	16.2	30.3	28.1	16.0
1784	42.7	25.3	16.2	30.5	24.0	…	31.5	29.8	15.0
1785	39.8	30.3	15.6	28.9	33.3	…	31.4	28.3	15.6
1786	39.9	26.3	14.0	30.6	24.4	…	32.9	25.9	16.0
1787	40.4	23.7	15.4	29.2	22.8	…	31.5	24.0	15.9
1788	36.1	33.3	13.4	30.7	26.1	…	33.9	26.7	15.8
1789	34.2	37.7	15.2	30.6	30.6	…	32.0	33.1	15.9
1790	37.0	38.1	18.8	32.0	23.0	…	30.5	30.5	16.5
1791	36.0	40.9	23.4	32.7	23.0	…	32.6	25.5	21.7
1792	42.2	25.0	22.4	34.7	24.0	…	36.6	23.9	20.0
1793	43.8	25.6	19.4	34.1	22.1	…	34.4	24.3	17.8
1794	41.4	32.0	18.6	33.7	20.8	…	33.8	23.6	16.4
1795	42.1	23.6	15.8	32.3	22.6	15.5	32.0	27.9	15.2
1796	39.7	23.4	16.8	31.5	21.5	15.7	34.7	24.7	17.2
1797	41.2	20.2	16.4	32.7	22.4	16.2	34.8	23.8	16.9
1798	38.6	22.0	15.2	32.3	22.6	16.6	33.7	23.1	16.6
1799	38.7	27.6	15.4	32.5	20.9	15.7	32.0	25.2	14.7

See pp. 117–9 for footnotes

A6   Vital Statistics: Rates per 1,000 Population

1800–1849

	Austria[2]			Belgium			Denmark[4]			Finland		
	B	D	M	B	D	M	B	D	M	B	D	M
1800	...	...	...	...	...	...	29.9	28.5	18.8	37.6	25.5	16.4
1801	...	...	...	...	...	...	31.1	27.7	15.7	39.6	21.8	15.8
1802	...	...	...	...	...	...	32.2	23.2	18.4	39.2	22.3	14.6
1803	...	...	...	...	...	...	33.1	22.5	17.3	35.6	33.1	15.4
1804	...	...	...	...	...	...	32.2	23.7	17.6	39.1	25.0	15.8
1805	...	...	...	...	...	...	32.8	23.2	15.9	38.4	21.2	16.0
1806	...	...	...	...	...	...	30.2	22.3	14.8	35.7	21.9	15.2
1807	...	...	...	...	...	...	31.0	22.9	14.7	36.2	29.2	13.2
1808	...	...	...	...	...	...	30.6	25.2	14.5	30.4	60.5	10.0
1809	...	...	...	...	...	...	29.3	25.1	15.3	28.6	59.2	17.4
1810	...	...	...	...	...	...	30.3	22.7	17.6	40.5[5]	24.6[5]	23.6[5]
1811	...	...	...	...	...	...	30.5	24.4	17.5	36.4	30.8	18.2
1812	...	...	...	...	...	...	29.8	27.0	15.9	38.9	24.1	16.2
1813	...	...	...	...	...	...	29.1	22.8	16.1	35.6	27.3	15.0
1814	...	...	...	...	...	...	30.4	24.7	18.3	36.7	32.4	16.6
1815	...	...	...	...	...	...	34.1	21.6	20.4	37.5	26.0	17.4
1816	...	...	...	...	...	...	32.9	20.7	18.6	38.8	23.4	17.8
1817	...	...	...	...	...	...	32.8	19.0	15.4	39.0	24.0	17.2
1818	...	...	...	...	...	...	32.1	18.9	16.9	38.4	24.8	17.2
1819	...	...	...	...	...	...	32.5	19.5	16.7	36.1	27.2	15.2
1820	43.0	26.6	17.3	...	...	...	31.5	20.9	16.2	36.6	25.3	18.6
1821	41.4	25.7	15.8	...	...	...	32.1	24.0	16.1	41.4	22.9	19.0
1822	38.5	27.2	15.1	...	...	...	33.7	20.3	17.1	35.6	27.8	16.2
1823	39.6	28.8	14.5	...	...	...	32.6	17.7	15.7	40.3	24.2	17.8
1824	40.1	26.4	15.7	...	...	...	31.3	18.6	16.2	37.8	27.3	17.2
1825	40.3	26.9	15.6	...	...	...	31.3	19.2	16.7	38.5	26.1	16.4
1826	39.6	27.7	16.0	...	...	...	31.4	21.1	16.7	37.6	26.2	16.6
1827	38.6	28.9	17.2	...	...	...	29.2	20.0	15.4	36.7	21.5	18.2
1828	37.6	32.7	17.0	...	...	...	30.3	23.6	16.0	39.3	22.6	18.0
1829	36.1	31.4	17.4	...	...	...	29.6	28.8	16.6	38.7	26.3	16.6
1830	38.0	30.3	16.2	32.3	25.6	13.0	28.9	25.3	16.8	36.6	25.4	15.2
1831	35.6	42.2	14.5	33.0	24.0	15.1	29.7	30.1	16.0	35.2	28.5	17.2
1832	36.6	35.6	19.4	31.5	28.0	13.4	27.0	26.3	17.3	34.5	33.8	13.0
1833	40.4	31.8	17.3	33.2	26.8	12.9	32.2	23.3	17.2	30.2	46.4	13.6
1834	39.3	30.9	16.7	33.3	27.8	14.5	33.0	23.5	17.1	36.6	23.9	15.2
1835	38.5	30.2	16.2	34.0	24.0	16.1	31.7	22.9	16.2	34.3	24.7	14.0
1836	37.8	33.1	17.4	34.0	23.9	13.9	30.5	22.3	15.1	31.1	31.9	13.0
1837	39.7	33.2	17.5	33.4	27.6	15.1	30.0	21.7	15.2	31.6	28.4	14.6
1838	37.9	28.3	15.7	35.2[3]	25.5[3]	14.6[3]	29.8	20.0	13.1	31.8	22.5	14.2
1839	38.0	30.0	15.8	33.7	26.1	14.7	29.0	20.5	13.7	33.7	20.6	15.4
1840	38.6	30.4	15.9	34.2	25.0	15.1	30.4	21.0	14.6	34.7	22.1	15.6
1841	38.3	29.5	16.9	34.0	23.8	14.7	29.7	19.8	15.2	34.0	22.4	16.0
1842	41.2	30.8	16.3	32.6	24.9	14.0	30.1	20.2	15.4	37.2	21.9	16.6
1843	39.3	31.4	17.0	31.9	23.3	13.5	29.8	19.3	15.6	35.8	22.2	16.2
1844	39.7	28.9	16.4	31.8	22.5	13.9	30.3	19.3	16.3	35.0	21.8	16.2
1845	39.5	29.7	15.2	32.2	23.0	12.2	30.6	19.4	16.4	35.7	22.9	15.2
1846	37.0	28.9	16.0	27.8	25.1	11.9	30.1	21.5	16.1	33.2	25.1	14.8
1847	36.0	44.4	14.6	27.2	27.7	11.1	30.6	21.7	15.9	33.9	23.3	16.2
1848	32.7	41.3	17.8	27.7	24.0	13.3	30.6	21.1	15.0	36.5	23.8	18.6
1849	40.0	35.0	18.5	31.0	27.7	14.5	31.0	22.4	16.1	37.5	24.5	17.2

See pp. 117–9 for footnotes

A6 Vital Statistics: Rates per 1,000 Population

1800–1849

	France			Germany[6]			Netherlands[7]		
	B	D	M	B	D	M	B	D	M
1800	Years ending 22 September			...	...	...	...	...	...
1801	32.9	27.7	14.5	...	...	...	...	...	...
1802	33.0	27.7	14.6	...	...	...	...	...	...
1803	32.5	31.2	14.6	...	...	...	...	...	...
1804	31.3	31.0	14.3	...	...	...	...	...	...
1805	31.6	28.8	14.9	...	...	...	...	...	...
	Years ending 31 December								
1806	31.4	26.8	14.4	...	...	...	...	...	...
1807	31.8	27.6	14.6	...	...	...	...	...	...
1808	31.3	26.5	15.2	...	...	...	...	...	...
1809	32.0	25.0	18.4	...	...	...	...	...	...
1810	31.8	24.9	15.9	...	...	...	...	...	...
1811	31.6	26.1	13.1	...	...	...	...	...	...
1812	30.1	26.2	15.1	...	...	...	...	...	...
1813	30.5	26.4	26.4	...	...	...	...	...	...
1814	33.9	29.8	13.2	...	...	...	...	...	...
1815	32.5	26.0	16.7	...	...	...	...	...	...
1816	32.9	24.5	16.9	...	...	...	...	...	...
1817	31.8	25.3	13.9	39.5	26.7	19.5	...	...	...
1818	30.6	25.3	14.3	39.5	27.1	18.9	...	...	...
1819	32.9	26.1	14.3	41.5	27.9	18.5	...	...	...
1820	31.7	25.4	13.8	39.9	24.4	17.9	...	...	...
1821	31.7	24.3	14.6	40.8	22.9	17.0	...	...	...
1822	31.7	25.3	15.4	39.8	24.6	16.8	...	...	...
1823	31.2	24.0	16.9	38.8	24.5	15.9	...	...	...
1824	31.6	24.5	15.3	38.6	24.2	16.3	...	...	...
1825	31.0	25.9	15.5	39.1	24.5	16.9	...	...	...
1826	31.4	26.5	15.7	38.9	26.1	16.6	...	...	...
1827	30.8	24.9	16.1	36.1	26.4	15.8	...	...	...
1828	30.5	26.2	15.4	36.1	26.6	15.4	...	...	...
1829	30.0	25.0	15.6	35.3	27.8	15.5	...	...	...
1830	29.9	25.0	16.7	35.5	27.4	15.5	...	...	...
1831	30.3	24.6	15.1	35.0	30.4	14.4	...	...	...
1832	28.6	28.5	14.8	34.1	28.9	17.2	...	...	...
1833	29.5	24.7	16.0	36.7	28.5	17.4	...	...	...
1834	29.8	27.8	16.4	37.6	29.4	17.3	...	...	...
1835	29.9	24.5	16.6	36.4	26.2	16.5	...	...	...
1836	29.2	22.3	16.3	36.7	25.9	16.3	...	...	...
1837	28.0	25.3	15.8	36.3	29.1	16.4	...	...	...
1838	28.5	24.2	16.2	36.3	26.0	15.9	...	...	...
1839	28.2	22.7	15.8	36.4	27.2	16.1	...	...	...
1840	27.9	23.7	16.6	36.4	26.5	16.2	35.0	23.5	15.6
1841	28.5	23.2	16.5	36.4	26.2	16.4	35.5	23.3	15.0
1842	28.5	24.0	16.3	37.6	27.1	16.7	34.2	25.8	14.4
1843	28.2	23.1	16.5	36.0	26.9	16.4	33.8	23.1	14.2
1844	27.5	22.0	16.0	35.9	24.5	16.4	34.4	24.1	15.0
1845	27.9	21.1	16.1	37.3	25.3	16.3	34.2	23.2	15.0
1846	27.3	23.2	15.2	36.0	27.1	15.8	31.4	28.5	13.6
1847	25.4	23.9	14.1	33.3	28.3	14.4	28.6	31.1	12.6
1848	26.5	23.6	16.5	33.3	29.0	15.2	30.1	29.2	14.4
1849	27.7	27.4	15.7	38.1	27.1	16.4	34.2	31.2	16.4

See pp. 117–9 for footnotes

A6　Vital Statistics: Rates per 1,000 Population

1800–1849

	Norway			Sweden			United Kingdom: England and Wales		
	B	D	M	B	D	M	B	D	M
1800	...	...	...	28.7	31.4	14.9	...	...	...
1801	22.7	27.6	13.8	30.0	26.1	14.5	...	...	...
1802	27.6	24.9	15.3	31.7	23.7	15.7	...	...	...
1803	28.9	24.6	15.3	31.4	23.8	16.4	...	...	...
1804	27.7	23.2	15.9	31.9	24.9	16.1	...	...	...
1805	29.2	20.4	16.2	31.7	23.5	16.7	...	...	...
1806	29.6	20.7	16.2	30.8	27.5	16.1	...	...	...
1807	29.0	22.1	13.9	31.2	26.2	16.4	...	...	...
1808	26.9	26.4	11.6	30.4	34.9	16.2	...	...	...
1809	22.2	35.3	11.9	26.7	40.0	15.6	...	...	...
1810	26.3	26.8	15.8	33.0	31.6	21.5	...	...	...
1811	26.7	24.7	17.5	35.3	28.8	21.3	...	...	...
1812	29.1	21.3	17.4	33.6	30.3	18.3	...	...	...
1813	25.6	28.9	14.2	29.7	27.4	15.5	...	...	...
1814	24.2	22.2	12.9	31.2	25.1	15.0	...	...	...
1815	29.9	19.7	20.2	34.8	23.6	19.2	...	...	...
1816	35.1	19.3	20.5	35.3	22.7	18.6	...	...	...
1817	32.5	17.7	17.2	33.4	24.3	16.7	...	...	...
1818	30.8	19.1	16.3	33.8	24.4	16.9	...	...	...
1819	31.9	19.7	16.1	33.0	27.4	18.3	...	...	...
1820	33.3	18.9	18.0	33.0	24.5	16.9	...	...	...
1821	34.7	20.5	18.1	35.4	25.6	17.6	...	...	...
1822	32.9	19.5	17.9	35.9	22.6	18.6	...	...	...
1823	33.9	17.7	17.5	36.8	21.0	18.0	...	...	...
1824	32.5	18.5	16.3	34.6	20.8	17.7	...	...	...
1825	34.3	17.4	17.3	36.5	20.5	17.2	...	...	...
1826	34.8	18.5	16.5	34.8	22.6	16.2	...	...	...
1827	32.0	18.0	15.0	31.3	23.1	14.4	...	...	...
1828	31.8	19.4	15.3	33.6	26.7	15.8	...	...	...
1829	33.6	19.4	15.6	34.9	29.0	15.8	...	...	...
1830	32.3	19.7	15.4	32.9	24.1	15.5	...	...	...
1831	31.0	19.8	14.4	30.5	26.0	13.8	...	...	...
1832	29.9	18.5	13.6	30.9	23.4	14.4	...	...	...
1833	30.7	20.3	14.6	34.1	21.7	15.7	...	...	...
1834	31.7	22.4	15.1	33.7	25.7	16.0	...	...	...
1835	32.6	19.5	14.8	32.7	18.6	15.0	...	...	...
1836	29.4	19.2	14.0	31.8	20.0	14.3	...	...	...
1837	28.7	20.8	13.4	30.8	24.7	13.8	...	...	...
1838	27.7	19.9	12.4	29.4	24.1	12.2	30.3[8]	22.4[8]	15.4[8]
1839	26.7	21.6	12.9	29.5	23.6	13.5	31.8	21.8	15.9
1840	27.8	19.8	13.8	31.4	20.4	14.1	32.0	22.9	15.6
1841	29.8	17.3	15.3	30.3	19.4	14.3	32.2	21.6	15.4
1842	30.7	18.0	15.7	31.7	21.1	14.2	32.1	21.7	14.7
1843	30.2	17.9	15.8	30.8	21.5	14.4	32.3	21.2	15.2
1844	29.9	17.1	15.8	32.2	20.3	14.9	32.7	21.6	16.0
1845	31.2	16.9	16.0	31.5	18.8	14.6	32.5	20.9	17.2
1846	31.1	17.9	16.7	29.9	21.8	13.8	33.8	23.0	17.2
1847	30.8	20.3	14.6	29.6	23.7	13.6	31.5	24.7	15.9
1848	29.8	20.5	14.9	30.3	19.7	14.6	32.5	23.0	15.9
1849	32.0	18.3	15.4	32.8	19.8	15.7	32.9	25.1	16.2

See pp. 117–9 for footnotes

A6 Vital Statistics: Rates per 1,000 Population

1850–1899

	Austria			Belgium			Bulgaria			Denmark		
	B	D	M	B	D	M	B	D	M	B	D	M
1850	39.6	32.9	19.3	30.0	21.2	15.4	...	...	...	31.4	19.1	15.2
1851	39.2	29.8	17.5	30.3	21.4	15.0	...	...	...	30.1	18.4	19.7
1852	37.5	30.9	15.8	30.0	21.5	13.9	...	...	...	33.2	19.6	19.4
1853	37.2	31.9	15.4	28.3	22.2	13.5	...	...	...	31.6	25.0	18.3
1854	36.3	34.5	13.8	28.8	20.5	12.9	...	...	...	32.7	18.4	17.4
1855	32.2	43.9	12.8	27.7	24.7	13.0	...	...	...	31.9	20.0	17.0

Years ending 31 December

	Austria			Belgium			Bulgaria			Denmark		
1856	35.6	30.2	16.3	29.1	24.1	14.3	...	...	...	32.4	18.7	17.2
1857	39.4	28.2	16.7	31.6	22.8	16.5	...	...	...	32.9	21.8	17.8
1858	39.8	29.1	16.9	31.7	23.6	16.7	...	...	...	33.2	23.2	17.4
1859	40.7	29.2	14.1	32.4	24.2	16.0	...	...	...	33.6	20.3	16.7
1860	38.2	26.8	16.9	31.0	19.9	15.1	...	...	...	32.6	20.2	16.0
1861	37.4	29.8	16.0	31.1	22.5	14.3	...	...	...	31.6	18.4	14.9
1862	38.1	29.5	17.7	30.4	20.9	14.3	...	...	...	30.8	18.3	14.7
1863	40.6	29.9	16.9	32.2	22.3	14.8	...	...	...	30.9	18.1	15.0
1864	40.6	30.1	16.5	32.1	23.7	15.1	...	...	...	30.1	23.2	11.3
1865	38.0	30.5	15.6	31.6	24.7	15.2	...	...	...	31.1	23.0	17.8
1866	37.9	40.8	13.0	31.7	30.3	15.2	...	...	...	32.0	20.2	16.8
1867	36.8	29.4	19.4	32.6	21.9	15.8	...	...	...	30.3	19.8	15.3
1868	38.1	28.7	18.4	31.9	22.0	14.8	...	...	...	31.0	19.2	14.6
1869	39.6	29.0	20.8	32.0	22.1	15.0	...	...	...	29.3	19.0	14.7
1870	39.8	29.4	19.6	32.7	23.6	14.0	...	...	...	30.3	19.0	14.7
1871	38.7[9]	29.8[9]	18.8[9]	31.2	28.1	14.7	...	...	...	30.1	19.4	14.6
1872	38.9	32.6	18.6	32.7	23.5	15.7	...	...	...	30.3	18.4	15.0
1873	39.6	38.9	18.8	33.0	21.8	15.7	...	...	...	30.8	18.6	16.2
1874	39.6	31.7	18.0	33.1	20.9	15.4	...	...	...	30.9	20.0	16.4
1875	39.8	30.0	17.0	32.9	22.9	14.6	...	...	...	31.9	21.0	17.0
1876	40.0	29.8	16.6	32.7	21.6	14.1	...	...	...	32.6	19.7	17.1
1877	38.5	31.5	15.0	32.8	21.4	13.7	...	...	...	32.3	18.7	16.1
1878	38.4	31.6	15.2	31.9	21.7	13.5	...	...	...	31.6	18.4	14.8
1879	39.1	29.9	15.4	31.9	22.1	12.2	...	...	...	31.9	19.7	14.7
1880	37.5	29.7	15.2	31.0	22.3	14.1	...	...	...	31.7	20.4	15.2
1881	37.5	30.5	16.0	31.8	21.2	14.3	33.7	16.4	20.2	32.2	18.3	15.6
1882	39.0	30.8	16.4	31.6	20.5	14.0	36.7	19.1	19.4	32.3	19.2	15.4
1883	38.1	30.1	15.6	30.9	21.1	13.7	38.5	19.8	19.8	31.8	18.4	15.4
1884	38.6	29.3	15.8	30.9	21.2	13.6	38.5	17.2	17.6	33.3	18.3	15.6
1885	37.5	30.1	15.2	30.3	21.4	13.8	37.6	16.7	13.2	32.5	17.8	15.1
1886	37.9	29.4	15.6	29.9	21.3	13.5	32.6	19.2	18.4	32.4	18.1	14.2
1887	38.2	28.9	15.6	29.7	19.3	14.4	38.4[10]	18.2[10]	18.6[10]	31.7	18.2	14.0
1888	37.8	29.2	15.8	29.4	20.3	14.2	37.7	18.2	16.6	31.5	19.5	14.2
1889	37.8	27.3	15.0	29.4	19.8	14.5	36.7	18.5	16.0	31.2	18.5	14.2
1890	36.2	29.1	15.0	29.0	20.8	14.6	35.1	21.1	18.2	30.5	19.0	13.8
1891	38.2	28.0	15.4	30.0	21.2	15.0	39.1	26.7	18.2	31.0	20.0	13.6
1892	36.0	28.8	15.6	28.9	21.8	15.4	36.0	31.6	16.8	29.6	19.5	13.5
1893	37.9	27.1	15.8	29.5	20.3	15.2	35.0	27.6	13.2	30.8	19.0	14.0
1894	36.6	27.8	15.8	29.0	18.6	15.0	38.0	27.4	15.8	30.4	17.6	13.8
1895	37.9	27.5	16.0	28.5	19.5	15.5	40.7	26.5	18.4	30.3	16.9	14.1
1896	37.8	26.2	15.8	29.0	17.5	16.2	41.4	24.3	16.8	30.5	15.7	14.5
1897	37.2	25.5	16.0	29.0	17.2	16.5	42.5	25.6	16.6	29.8	16.6	14.9
1898	36.0	24.8	15.8	28.6	17.6	16.6	39.4	23.1	15.8	30.2	15.5	15.1
1899	36.8	25.2	16.4	28.8	18.8	16.5	40.7	24.8	17.6	29.7	17.3	15.0

see pp. 117–9 for footnotes

International Historical Statistics: Europe 1750–2000

A6 Vital Statistics: Rates per 1,000 Population

1850–1899

	Finland			France			Germany			Greece[13]		
	B	D	M	B	D	M	B	D	M	B	D	M
1850	35.7	26.3	16.2	26.8	21.4	16.7	37.2	25.6	17.0	...	...	...
1851	38.2	23.7	16.6	27.1	22.3	16.0	36.7	25.0	16.7	...	...	...
1852	35.0	30.0	14.4	26.8	22.6	15.7	35.5	28.4	15.3	...	...	...
1853	35.1	29.3	14.8	26.0	22.0	15.6	34.6	27.2	15.3	...	...	...
1854	37.5	25.9	15.6	25.5	27.4	15.0	34.0	27.0	14.1	...	...	...
1855	35.8	32.0	15.8	25.0	26.0	15.7	32.2	28.1	14.0	...	...	...
1856	36.3	34.0	15.8	26.3	23.1	15.7	33.5	25.2	15.0	...	...	...
1857	32.8	32.5	14.2	25.9	23.7	16.3	36.0	27.2	16.7	...	...	...
1858	36.5	29.7	15.4	26.7	24.1	16.9	36.5	26.8	17.0	...	...	...
1859	35.8	25.0	16.0	27.9	26.8	16.3	37.5	25.7	16.1	...	...	...
1860	36.4	24.8	17.8	26.2[11]	21.4[11]	15.8[11]	36.4	23.2	16.1	28.4	20.4	11.2
1861	37.8	23.8	17.2	26.9	23.2	16.3	35.7	25.6	15.5	29.5	20.9	11.0
1862	37.3	28.1	15.8	26.5	21.7	16.2	35.4	24.7	16.3	...	...	...
1863	36.2	29.6	14.8	26.9	22.5	16.0	37.5	25.7	17.0	...	...	...
1864	39.3	22.6	15.6	26.6	22.7	15.8	37.8	26.2	17.1	28.2	20.6	12.2
1865	34.2	24.9	14.0	26.5	24.7	15.7	37.6	27.6	17.9	29.4	21.4	13.2
1866	32.0	33.6	12.2	26.4	23.2	16.0	37.8	30.6	16.0	27.8	19.7	12.1
1867	32.3	38.1	12.8	26.2	22.7	15.7	36.8	26.1	18.2	30.1	20.0	12.0
1868	24.6	77.6	11.4	25.7	24.1	15.7	36.8	27.6	17.8	28.6	22.7	12.1
1869	33.7	25.2	19.8	26.0	23.6	16.5	37.8	26.9	19.0	28.8	22.6	13.1
1870	36.3	18.2	20.4	25.9[12]	28.4[12]	12.2[12]	38.5	27.4	15.4	28.1	21.9	12.3
1871	37.3	17.9	19.4	22.9	35.1	14.5	34.5	29.6	16.4	28.4	20.0	12.8
1872	36.4	19.7	17.4	26.7	22.0	19.5	39.4	29.0	20.6	28.6	20.6	11.8
1873	37.0	23.6	17.0	26.0	23.3	17.7	39.7	28.3	20.0	27.6	24.1	11.8
1874	37.9	24.1	18.0	26.2	21.4	16.6	40.1	26.7	19.1	29.2	19.3	12.4
1875	36.6	22.9	16.8	25.9	23.0	16.4	40.6	27.6	18.2	28.2	19.7	13.0
1876	36.7	21.9	16.4	26.2	22.6	15.8	40.9	26.4	17.0	29.6	19.4	13.2
1877	38.2	24.2	16.4	25.5	21.6	15.0	40.6	26.4	16.0	28.5	19.2	11.6
1878	35.4	24.1	15.4	25.2	22.5	15.0	38.9	26.2	15.4	27.2	18.5	11.4
1879	37.8	19.6	14.8	25.1	22.5	15.1	38.9	25.6	15.0	24.8	18.2	11.2
1880	36.5	23.9	15.4	24.6	22.9	14.9	37.6	26.0	15.0	24.4	17.9	11.0
1881	35.0	25.0	13.8	24.9	22.0	15.0	37.0	25.5	14.9	24.5[14]	18.9[14]	9.1[14]
1882	36.3	22.3	15.2	24.8	22.2	14.9	37.2	25.7	15.3	25.2	18.8	12.8
1883	35.9	20.8	15.6	24.8	22.2	15.0	36.6	25.9	15.3	25.0	20.1	13.2
1884	36.1	20.9	15.4	24.7	22.6	15.2	37.2	26.0	15.7	28.6	17.7	13.4
1885	34.2	22.0	14.6	24.3	22.0	14.9	37.0	25.7	15.8	28.5	19.9	13.0
1886	35.3	22.2	14.6	23.9	22.5	14.8	37.1	26.2	15.8	...	...	...
1887	36.2	19.0	15.2	23.5	22.0	14.5	36.9	24.2	15.6	...	...	...
1888	34.9	19.8	14.6	23.1	21.9	14.4	36.6	23.7	15.6	...	...	...
1889	33.4	19.6	13.8	23.0	20.7	14.2	36.4	23.7	16.0	34.1	24.5	12.4
1890	32.9	19.6	14.2	21.8	22.8	14.0	35.7	24.4	16.1	35.3	23.2	11.7
1891	34.3	21.2	13.8	22.6	22.9	14.9	37.0	23.4	16.1	...	...	...
1892	31.6	23.8	12.2	22.3	22.8	15.1	35.7	24.1	15.9	...	...	...
1893	30.1	21.0	11.6	22.8	22.5	14.9	36.8	24.4	15.8	...	...	...
1894	31.1	19.4	13.2	22.3	21.2	14.9	35.9	22.3	15.9	...	...	...
1895	32.9	17.9	14.8	21.7	22.2	14.7	36.1	22.1	15.9	...	...	...
1896	32.5	18.7	15.2	22.5	20.0	15.1	36.3	20.8	16.4	...	...	...
1897	32.3	17.7	15.6	22.2	19.4	15.1	36.0	21.3	16.7	...	...	...
1898	34.4	17.7	16.0	21.7	20.9	14.8	36.1	20.6	16.9	...	...	...
1899	33.7	20.2	14.8	21.8	21.0	15.2	35.8	21.5	17.1	...	...	...

See pp. 117–9 for footnotes

A6 Vital Statistics: Rates per 1,000 Population

1850–1899

| | Hungary[15] | | | Ireland | | | Norway | | |
	B	D	M	B	D	M	B	D	M
1850	...	...	...	...	...	...	31.0	17.2	15.3
1852	...	...	...	...	...	...	31.0	17.9	14.3
1853	...	...	...	...	...	...	32.0	18.3	15.6
1854	...	...	...	...	...	...	34.3	16.0	17.1
1855	...	...	...	...	...	...	33.4	17.2	16.2
1856	...	...	...	...	...	...	32.2	16.9	15.5
1857	...	...	...	...	...	...	33.0	17.1	15.1
1858	...	...	...	...	...	...	33.5	16.1	15.2
1859	...	...	...	...	...	...	34.8	17.0	15.4
1860	...	...	...	...	...	...	33.3	17.2	14.3
1861	39.7	32.2	18.8	...	...	...	30.7	19.5	13.6
1862	41.8	32.3	21.4	...	...	...	32.1	20.0	13.8
1863	44.3	33.9	19.9	...	...	...	32.7	18.9	14.3
1864	41.2	30.9	16.8	24.2	16.8	9.7	31.9	17.8	13.6
1865	41.8	30.3	19.0	25.9	16.9	11.0	31.9	16.6	13.7
1866	41.1	38.0	16.0	26.5	17.1	10.9	31.7	17.1	13.4
1867	38.0	32.8	20.4	26.3	17.6	10.8	30.1	18.5	12.9
1868	41.7	33.1	26.9	26.7	16.3	10.1	29.5	18.3	12.4
1869	41.9	31.3	21.7	26.7	16.9	10.0	28.9	17.2	12.3
1870	42.1	33.5	19.8	27.7	17.2	10.6	29.2	16.2	12.9
1871	42.8	40.1	20.4	28.1	16.8	10.7	29.3	16.9	13.3
1872	40.6	42.9	21.4	27.8	18.8	10.0	30.0	16.7	14.0
1873	42.4	62.9	22.4	27.1	18.9	9.6	29.9	17.0	14.5
1874	42.8	43.3	21.4	26.6	18.1	9.2	31.0	18.3	15.4
1875	45.4	37.7	22.2	26.1	19.0	9.1	31.5	18.8	15.7
1876	45.9	36.0	20.1	26.4	17.9	9.9	31.6	18.9	15.4
1877	43.3	36.9	18.5	26.2	18.2	9.3	31.7	16.9	15.1
1878	42.8	37.7	18.9	25.1	19.3	9.5	31.5	16.0	14.6
1879	45.7	36.3	20.8	25.2	20.1	8.7	32.1	15.1	13.5
1880	42.8	37.8	18.3	24.7	20.4	7.8	30.9	16.2	13.3
1881	43.2	35.1	20.0	24.5	17.9	8.5	30.0	17.0	12.8
1882	44.2	36.1	20.4	24.0	17.4	8.6	30.6	18.6	13.4
1883	45.0	32.2	20.8	23.5	19.4	8.5	31.0	17.0	13.2
1884	45.8	31.0	20.4	23.9	17.9	9.1	31.6	16.6	13.7
1885	44.9	32.3	19.8	23.5	18.7	8.6	31.5	16.5	13.4
1886	45.6	32.3	19.2	23.2	18.0	8.4	30.9	16.3	13.1
1887	44.3	34.5	18.0	23.1	18.4	8.6	31.4	16.2	12.7
1888	43.9	32.3	18.8	22.8	17.9	8.4	30.4	17.3	12.3
1889	43.8	29.9	16.4	22.7	17.4	9.0	29.6	17.8	12.5
1890	40.7[16]	32.5[16]	16.4[16]	22.3	18.2	8.9	30.4	18.0	12.9
1891	42.6	33.4	17.2	23.1	18.4	9.2	30.8	17.7	13.1
1892	40.6	34.7	18.4	22.5	19.4	9.3	29.6	17.9	12.6
1893	43.0	31.1	18.6	23.0	18.0	9.4	30.3	16.5	12.7
1894	41.6	30.4	18.4	22.9	18.2	9.4	29.6	16.9	12.6
1895	41.8[9]	29.7[9]	17.0[9]	23.3	18.5	10.1	30.4	15.6	12.8
1896	40.7	28.6	16.0	23.7	16.7	10.2	30.0	15.2	13.2
1897	40.5	28.1	16.2	23.5	18.5	10.1	30.0	15.4	13.3
1898	37.8	28.0	16.6	23.3	18.2	10.0	30.3	15.3	13.8
1899	39.2	27.3	18.0	23.1	17.7	9.9	29.9	16.8	14.1

See pp. 117–9 for footnotes

A6 Vital Statistics: Rates per 1,000 Population

1850–1899

	Portugal[18]			Romania[19]			Russia[21]		
	B	D	M	B	D	M	B	D	M
1850	...	...	...	...	...	...	...	...	...
1851	...	...	...	...	...	...	...	...	...
1852	...	...	...	...	...	...	...	...	...
1853	...	...	...	...	...	...	...	...	...
1854	...	...	...	...	...	...	...	...	...
1855	...	...	...	...	...	...	...	...	...
1856	...	...	...	...	...	...	...	...	...
1857	...	...	...	...	...	...	...	...	...
1858	...	...	...	...	...	...	...	...	...
1859	...	...	...	29.6	16.9	...	...	...	...
1860	...	...	...	31.6	20.3	...	...	...	...
1861	...	...	...	32.0	21.6	...	49.7	35.4	23.2
1862	...	...	...	32.0	21.8	...	51.1	34.0	21.8
1863	...	...	...	30.4	26.2	...	50.0	37.7	18.8
1864	...	...	...	36.0	26.0	...	52.9	38.7	...
1865	...	...	...	34.6	27.1	...	50.0	36.9	...
1866	...	...	...	31.3	38.0	11.6	...	...	...
1867	...	...	...	31.7	25.1	13.9	51.2	36.8	20.4
1868	...	...	...	33.4	25.1	14.6	48.8	39.7	19.2
1869	...	...	...	34.0	24.3	16.1	49.7	38.3	20.2
1870	...	...	...	34.4	26.1	14.4	49.2	35.0	20.8
1871	...	...	...	33.5	26.4	12.9	51.0	37.9	20.8
1872	...	...	...	32.0	30.5	16.5	50.0	41.2	20.8
1873	...	...	...	32.5	32.6	13.4	52.3	36.5	19.4
1874	...	...	...	34.3	34.9	14.2	51.4	35.2	19.6
1875	...	...	...	38.8	32.0	15.0	51.5	34.6	19.4
1876	...	...	...	37.0	28.3	14.2	50.6	34.9	16.8
1877	...	...	...	35.4	29.8	13.1	49.6	34.4	14.8
1878	...	...	...	31.5[20]	33.2[20]	15.9[20]	47.3	38.2	18.4
1879	...	...	...	37.1	29.2	20.5	50.2	34.8	20.4
1880	...	...	...	37.7	35.9	17.5	49.7	36.1	19.2
1881	...	...	...	41.5	26.7	18.2	49.1	34.1	19.6
1882	...	...	...	40.4	28.2	18.8	51.6	40.4	19.0
1883	...	...	...	42.8	26.0	19.8	50.6	37.5	19.2
1884	...	...	...	41.4	25.5	16.6	51.5	34.4	17.8
1885	...	...	...	43.1	25.0	16.0	50.0	35.8	17.2
1886	31.9	20.4	13.8	42.2	26.7	15.4	49.0	33.2	17.0
1887	33.7	22.1	14.0	41.0	30.5	15.2	49.5	33.8	18.0
1888	33.1	21.7	13.7	42.4	30.6	14.8	49.9	33.4	19.6
1889	33.7	22.5	14.0	40.6	27.2	15.6	51.6	35.5	17.6
1890	32.6	25.2	14.2	38.5	28.4	14.6	50.3	36.7	16.8
1891	32.0	22.8	13.7	42.3	30.1	16.6	50.6	35.8	17.2
1892	31.2	20.3	13.6	39.0	34.7	15.4	46.0	41.0	17.8
1893	31.9	21.4	13.2	40.5	30.8	14.8	48.8	34.4	17.8
1894	29.7	20.7	12.8	40.9	31.7	17.8	49.2	34.3	19.0
1895	30.0	20.8	12.7	42.3	27.6	14.8	50.1	35.5	18.6
1896	30.0	22.7	12.6	40.7	29.1	16.6	50.4	33.3	17.6
1897	30.4	21.9	13.7	42.9	29.6	14.4	50.0	31.7	18.2
1898	30.2	21.4	13.1	36.7	26.5	15.0	48.6	33.2	17.4
1899	29.9	20.2	13.6	42.0	27.5	16.8	49.3	31.2	18.6

See pp. 117–9 for footnotes

A6 Vital Statistics: Rates per 1,000 Population

1850-1899

	Serbia			Spain[23]			Sweden		
	B	D	M	B	D	M	B	D	M
1850	...	...	...	...	...	...	31.9	19.8	15.2
1851	...	...	...	...	...	...	31.7	20.7	14.7
1852	...	...	...	...	...	...	30.7	22.7	13.7
1853	...	...	...	...	...	...	31.4	23.7	14.4
1854	...	...	...	...	...	...	33.5	19.8	15.4
1855	...	...	...	...	...	...	31.8	21.5	15.0
1856	...	...	...	...	...	...	31.5	21.8	14.9
1857	...	...	...	...	...	...	32.4	27.6	15.5
1858	...	...	...	35.2	28.0	14.6	34.8	21.7	16.2
1859	...	...	...	38.4	28.8	14.6	35.0	20.1	16.6
1860	...	...	...	36.7	27.4	16.2	34.8	17.7	15.6
1861	...	...	...	39.0	26.6	16.6	32.6	18.5	14.5
1862	40.5	38.6	24.2	38.5	27.3	16.4	33.4	21.4	14.1
1863	43.0	35.1	30.2	37.8	29.2	15.8	33.6	19.3	14.5
1864	45.1	31.3	22.6	39.2	31.5	16.0	33.6	20.3	14.0
1865	46.7	25.5	24.2	38.6	33.8	16.2	32.8	19.4	14.1
1866	45.7	24.3	22.4	38.3	29.0	16.6	33.1	20.0	13.4
1867	44.8	25.7	20.9	38.5	30.4	14.8	30.8	19.6	12.2
1868	45.7	32.7	21.5	35.7	34.1	14.0	27.5	21.0	10.9
1869	45.2	29.7	23.8	37.0	34.1	17.0	28.3	22.3	11.3
1870	44.8	33.2	22.0	36.6	31.6	12.8	28.8	19.8	12.0
1871	43.2	32.4	20.6	...	...	...	30.4	17.2	13.0
1872	39.1	32.1	26.6	...	...	...	30.0	16.3	13.9
1873	42.4	32.6	22.0	...	...	...	30.8	17.2	14.6
1874	41.7	36.4	22.9	...	...	...	30.9	20.3	14.5
1875	45.8	31.3	21.9	...	...	...	31.2	20.3	14.1
1876	41.6	48.3	15.3	...	...	...	30.8	19.6	14.2
1877	33.3	33.6	25.3	...	...	...	31.1	18.7	13.7
1878	38.1[22]	33.4[22]	19.9[22]	36.1	30.5	14.2	29.8	18.1	12.9
1879	39.4	31.3	28.7	35.8	30.5	13.2	30.5	16.9	12.6
1880	40.7	31.5	23.5	35.5	30.1	12.4	29.4	18.1	12.6
1881	45.7	24.7	23.4	37.1	30.2	12.7	29.1	17.7	12.4
1882	44.4	23.1	24.2	36.2	31.4	12.1	29.4	17.4	12.7
1883	47.0	22.8	23.6	35.6	32.7	12.4	28.9	17.3	12.9
1884	47.6	25.0	21.4	36.7	30.6	13.2	30.0	17.5	13.1
1885	46.6	26.9	17.6	36.3	38.0	12.7	29.4	17.8	13.3
1886	42.0	29.6	23.6	36.7	29.2	12.7	29.8	16.6	12.8
1887	46.3	24.9	22.2	36.1	32.8	11.0	29.7	16.1	12.5
1888	45.7	24.4	21.8	36.4	30.1	11.2	28.8	16.0	11.8
1889	44.1	25.5	20.4	36.4	30.4	15.6	27.7	16.0	12.0
1890	40.3	25.3	19.9	34.4	32.1	15.8	28.0	17.1	12.0
1891	45.0	26.5	21.1	35.3	31.8	17.5	28.3	16.8	11.7
1892	42.4	33.5	19.0	35.8	30.6	16.9	27.0	17.9	11.4
1893	42.5	29.7	21.1	35.6	29.7	15.6	27.4	16.8	11.3
1894	42.5	28.1	21.9	34.8	30.3	15.6	27.1	16.4	11.5
1895	44.0	26.9	17.8	35.0	29.0	15.4	27.5	15.2	11.7
1896	41.2	27.0	17.7	35.9	29.6	14.5	27.2	15.6	11.9
1897	42.6	26.5	17.7	34.1	28.4	14.0	26.7	15.4	12.1
1898	35.1	22.9	18.3	33.3	28.2	13.6	27.1	15.1	12.3
1899	39.3	24.3	19.9	34.2	28.8	16.9	26.4	17.7	12.5

See pp. 117-9 for footnotes

A6 Vital Statistics: Rates per 1,000 Population

1850-1889

	Switzerland			United Kingdom: England and Wales			United Kingdom: Scotland		
	B	D	M	B	D	M	B	D	M
1850	...	...	...	33.4	20.8	17.2	...	...	...
1851	...	...	...	34.3	22.0	17.2	...	...	...
1852	...	...	...	34.3	22.4	17.4	...	...	...
1853	...	...	...	33.3	22.9	17.9	...	...	...
1854	...	...	...	34.1	23.5	17.2	...	...	...
1855	...	...	...	33.8	22.6	16.2	31.3[8]	20.8[8]	13.2[8]
1856	...	...	...	34.5	20.5	16.7	34.0	19.5	13.8
1857	...	...	...	34.4	21.8	16.5	34.3	20.6	14.2
1858	...	...	...	33.7	23.1	16.0	34.4	21.0	13.0
1859	...	...	...	35.0	22.4	17.0	35.0	20.3	13.9
1860	...	...	...	34.3	21.2	17.1	35.6	22.3	13.9
1861	...	...	...	34.6	21.6	16.3	34.9	20.3	13.6
1862	...	...	...	35.0	21.4	16.1	34.6	21.7	13.3
1863	...	...	...	35.3	23.0	16.8	35.0	22.9	14.3
1864	...	...	...	35.4	23.7	17.6	35.6	23.6	14.4
1865	...	...	...	35.4	23.2	17.5	35.5	22.3	14.8
1866	...	...	...	35.2	23.4	17.5	35.4	22.2	14.7
1867	...	...	...	35.4	21.7	16.5	35.1	21.3	13.9
1868	...	...	13.4	35.8	21.8	16.1	35.3	21.2	13.3
1869	...	...	14.4	34.8	22.3	15.9	34.3	23.0	13.4
1870	29.8	25.8	14.0	35.2	22.9	16.1	34.6	22.2	14.3
1871	29.0	27.6	14.6	35.0	22.6	16.7	34.5	22.2	14.3
1872	29.8	22.2	15.8	35.6	21.3	17.4	34.9	22.3	15.1
1873	29.7	22.7	15.4	35.4	21.0	17.6	34.8	22.4	15.5
1874	30.4	22.3	16.6	36.0	22.2	17.0	35.6	23.2	15.2
1875	31.8	24.0	18.0	35.4	22.7	16.7	35.2	23.3	14.8
1876	32.8	24.1	16.2	36.3	20.9	16.5	35.6	20.9	15.0
1877	32.0	23.5	15.8	36.0	20.3	15.7	35.3	20.6	14.4
1878	31.3	23.3	14.6	35.6	21.6	15.2	34.9	21.2	13.4
1879	30.5	22.6	13.8	34.7	20.7	14.4	34.3	20.0	12.8
1880	29.6	21.9	13.6	34.2	20.5	14.9	33.6	20.5	13.2
1881	29.8	22.4	13.6	33.9	18.9	15.1	33.7	19.3	13.9
1882	28.9	21.9	13.6	33.8	19.6	15.5	33.5	19.4	14.1
1883	28.5	20.4	13.8	33.5	19.6	15.5	32.8	20.2	14.1
1884	28.3	20.2	13.8	33.6	19.7	15.1	33.7	19.6	13.6
1885	27.7	21.3	13.8	32.9	19.2	14.5	32.7	19.3	13.1
1886	27.8	20.7	13.8	32.8	19.5	14.2	32.9	19.0	12.6
1887	27.9	20.2	14.2	31.9	19.1	14.4	31.8	19.0	12.7
1888	27.7	19.9	14.2	31.2	18.1	14.4	31.3	18.0	12.8
1889	27.7	20.3	14.0	31.1	18.2	15.0	30.9	18.4	13.3
1890	26.6	20.9	14.2	30.2	19.5	15.5	30.4	19.7	13.7
1891	28.2	20.6	14.4	31.4	20.2	15.6	31.2	20.7	13.9
1892	27.7	19.0	14.6	30.4	19.0	15.4	30.7	18.5	14.1
1893	27.9	20.1	14.4	30.7	19.2	14.7	30.8	19.3	13.2
1894	27.3	20.1	14.4	29.6	16.6	15.0	29.9	17.1	13.3
1895	27.3	19.2	14.6	30.3	18.7	15.0	30.0	19.4	13.5
1896	28.1	17.8	15.0	29.6	17.1	15.7	30.4	16.6	14.2
1897	28.3	17.7	15.6	29.6	17.4	16.0	30.0	18.4	14.4
1898	28.5	18.3	15.6	29.3	17.5	16.2	30.1	18.0	14.8
1899	29.0	17.7	15.6	29.1	18.2	16.5	29.8	18.1	15.0

See pp. 117-9 for footnotes

A6 Vital Statistics: Rates per 1,000 Population

1900–1949

	Albania			Austria[2]			Belgium			Bulgaria		
	B	D	M	B	D	M	B	D	M	B	D	M
1900	...	...	...	35.0	25.2	16.4	28.9	19.3	17.2	42.3	22.6	16.6
1901	...	...	...	36.6	24.0	16.3	29.4	17.2	17.4	37.7	23.3	17.6
1902	...	...	...	37.0	24.7	15.5	28.4	17.3	16.2	39.1	24.0	19.0
1903	...	...	...	35.2	23.8	15.6	27.5	17.0	15.7	41.3	22.9	19.0
1904	...	...	...	35.6	23.8	15.6	27.1	16.9	16.0	42.8	21.4	22.8
1905	...	...	...	33.8	25.1	15.6	26.2	17.5	15.8	43.5	21.7	21.5
1906	...	...	...	35.0	22.6	15.8	25.6	16.0	16.1	43.7	22.2	18.9
1907	...	...	...	34.0	22.7	15.1	25.2	15.4	16.0	43.3	22.2	19.7
1908	...	...	...	33.7	22.5	15.3	24.8	16.1	15.6	40.3	24.2	17.6
1909	...	...	...	33.4	22.9	15.1	23.5	15.4	15.3	40.4	26.5	18.2
1910	...	...	...	32.5	21.2	15.1	23.7	14.9	15.8	41.4	23.0	18.9
1911	...	...	...	31.3	21.9	15.2	22.8	16.0	15.9	39.9	21.4	18.7
1912	...	...	...	31.3	20.5	14.7	22.5	14.5	16.2	41.7	20.6	5.6
1913	...	...	...	29.7[2]	20.3[2]	13.5[2]	22.3	14.2	16.0	25.7	29.0	5.7
1914	...	...	...	...	...	...	20.4	14.2	10.7	45.1	20.7	12.6
1915	...	...	...	...	...	...	16.1	13.1	6.4	40.2	19.9	6.4
1916	...	...	...	...	...	...	12.9	13.1	7.9	21.3	20.8	2.2
1917	...	...	...	...	...	...	11.3	16.3	8.6	17.2	21.2	4.4
1918	...	...	...	14.1	26.4	13.1	11.3	20.8	11.5	21.2	32.0	9.6
1919	...	...	...	18.5	20.4	25.0	16.9	14.9	25.6	32.8	20.2	15.8
1920	...	...	...	22.7	19.0	26.6	22.2	13.9	28.8	39.9	21.4	14.1
1921	...	...	...	23.2	17.0	25.0	21.7	13.4	23.7	40.2	21.7	21.7
1922	...	...	...	23.1	17.4	22.8	20.4	13.9	22.0	40.5	23.6	21.2
1923	...	...	...	22.5	15.3	17.2	20.3	12.9	21.0	37.7	21.2	20.8
1924	...	...	...	21.7	15.0	16.2	19.8[24]	12.7[24]	20.8[24]	39.8	20.7	21.3
1925	...	...	...	20.6	14.4	15.4	19.6	12.8	19.1	36.9	19.2	19.8
1926	...	...	...	19.3	15.0	14.6	18.9	12.8	18.4	37.4	17.2	20.0
1927	...	...	...	17.9	15.0	14.6	18.2	13.0	18.1	33.2	20.3	18.6
1928	...	...	...	17.6	14.5	14.8	18.2	12.8	17.9	33.1	17.7	20.0
1929	...	...	...	16.8	14.6	15.4	18.1	14.4	17.8	30.6	18.1	19.7
1930	...	16.3	11.6	16.8	13.5	15.4	18.6	12.8	17.7	31.4	16.2	19.0
1931	...	...	...	15.9	14.0	14.8	18.1	12.7	16.2	29.5	16.9	19.2
1932	25.1	17.9	9.4	15.2	13.9	13.4	17.5	12.7	15.1	31.5	16.3	19.2
1933	...	...	...	14.3	13.2	13.0	16.3	12.7	15.8	29.2	15.6	18.8
1934	...	...	...	13.6	12.7	13.0	15.9	11.7	15.2	30.1	14.1	18.7
1935	...	...	...	13.1	13.7	13.6	15.2	12.3	15.2	26.4	14.6	15.8
1936	...	16.6	11.4	13.1	13.2	13.6	15.1	12.2	15.5	25.9	14.3	16.0
1937	...	19.5	11.2	12.8	13.3	13.8	15.0	12.5	15.2	24.3	13.6	16.6
1938	34.3	17.7	13.4	13.9	14.0	26.6	15.5	12.5	14.7	22.8	13.7	17.0
1939	27.9	15.0	10.0	20.7	15.3	35.2	15.0	13.2	13.1	21.4	13.4	18.2
1940	31.3	16.4	12.2	...	...	...	13.3[25]	15.1[25]	8.6[25]	22.2[26]	13.4[26]	18.0[26]
1941	28.0	16.6	12.6	...	...	...	11.9[25]	14.4[25]	12.8[25]	21.9	12.7	18.2
1942	...	14.2	14.0	...	...	...	12.8[25]	14.2[25]	15.0[25]	22.7	13.0	21.0
1943	...	...	...	...	...	...	14.6[25]	13.1[25]	12.6[25]	21.8	18.8	20.2
1944	...	...	...	...	...	...	15.0	15.1	10.9	22.0	18.4[27]	18.4
1945	...	...	...	...	...	...	15.3	14.5	19.9	24.1	16.2[27]	23.8
1946	...	...	...	15.9	13.4	18.0	17.5	13.2	21.7	25.6	12.2	22.0
1947	...	18.9	...	18.5	12.9	21.6	17.0	12.7	19.7	24.0	11.6	22.0
1948	...	16.1	...	17.7	12.1	20.6	17.2	12.0	18.5	24.6	11.4	22.2
1949	...	12.5	19.4	16.3	12.8	19.8	16.8	12.4	17.0	24.7	12.2	21.8

See pp. 117–9 for footnotes

A6   Vital Statistics: Rates per 1,000 Population

1900–1949

	Czechoslovakia			Denmark			Finland			France		
	B	D	M	B	D	M	B	D	M	B	D	M
1900	...	...	...	29.7	16.8	15.3	32.6	21.9	13.8	21.3	21.9	15.5
1901	...	...	...	29.7	15.7	14.2	33.2	21.1	13.8	22.0	20.1	15.6
1902	...	...	...	29.2	14.6	14.2	32.4	19.0	13.0	21.6	19.5	15.1
1903	...	...	...	28.7	14.6	14.2	31.5	18.5	13.0	21.1	19.3	15.1
1904	...	...	...	28.9	14.1	14.4	33.0	18.4	13.6	20.9	19.4	15.2
1905	...	...	...	28.4	15.0	14.4	31.8	19.1	13.4	20.6	19.6	15.4
1906	...	...	...	28.5	13.5	14.8	32.8	18.2	14.4	20.5	19.9	15.6
1907	...	...	...	28.2	14.1	15.2	32.8	18.8	14.4	19.7	20.2	16.0
1908	...	...	...	28.6	14.6	15.0	32.2	19.3	14.0	20.1	18.9	16.0
1909	...	...	...	28.2	13.3	14.8	32.8	17.4	13.4	19.5	19.1	15.6
1910	...	...	...	27.5	12.9	14.6	31.7	17.4	12.8	19.6	17.8	15.6
1911	...	...	...	26.7	13.4	14.4	30.8	17.4	12.6	18.7	19.6	15.6
1912	...	...	...	26.6	13.0	14.6	30.8	17.2	12.4	18.9	17.5	15.8
1913	...	...	...	25.6	12.5	14.4	28.8	17.1	12.6	18.8[12]	17.7[12]	15.0[12]
1914	...	...	...	25.6	12.5	13.8	28.7	16.6	12.0	18.1[30]	18.5[30]	9.8[30]
1915	...	...	...	24.2	12.8	13.0	27.0	16.9	11.6	11.8[30]	18.3[30]	4.2[30]
1916	...	...	...	24.4	13.4	14.4	25.7	17.6	12.4	9.5[30]	17.3[30]	6.2[30]
1917	...	...	...	23.7	13.2	14.0	25.9	18.8	12.8	10.4[30]	18.0[30]	9.1[30]
1918	...	...	...	24.1	13.0	15.2	25.4	30.4	9.6	12.1[30]	22.3[30]	10.4[30]
1919	22.4	18.3	27.4	22.6	13.0	16.4	20.5	20.2	12.0	13.0	19.0	28.6
1920	26.7	19.0	26.4	25.4	12.9	17.6	27.0	17.0	15.0	21.4	17.2	31.9
1921	29.2	17.7	24.2	24.0	11.0	16.2	25.9	14.9	15.0	20.7	17.7	23.2
1922	28.2	17.4	20.6	22.2	11.9	15.8	25.0	15.3	14.6	19.3	17.5	19.5
1923	27.3	15.0	18.8	22.3	11.3	16.0	25.3	14.7	14.6	19.1	16.7	17.8
1924	25.8	15.3	18.0	21.8	11.2	15.6	23.8	16.3	13.4	18.7	16.9	17.6
1925	25.1	15.2	18.4	21.0	10.8	15.0	23.7	14.4	13.4	19.0	17.4	17.4
1926	24.6	15.6	18.2	20.5	11.0	15.0	23.0	14.2	13.6	18.8	17.4	16.9
1927	23.3	16.0	18.0	19.6	11.6	15.0	22.5	15.4	14.4	18.2	16.5	16.4
1928	23.3	15.1	19.0	19.6	11.0	15.6	22.8	14.3	15.0	18.3	16.4	16.5
1929	22.4	15.5	19.0	18.6	11.2	15.8	22.2	15.9	14.6	17.7	17.9	16.2
1930	22.7	14.2	18.6	18.7	10.8	16.4	21.8	14.0	14.4	18.0	15.6	16.4
1931	21.5	14.4	17.6	18.0	11.4	16.2	20.7	14.1	13.8	17.5	16.2	15.6
1932	21.0	14.1	17.2	18.0	11.0	15.6	19.8	13.3	13.2	17.3	15.8	15.1
1933	19.2	13.7	16.6	17.3	10.6	17.6	18.4	13.6	13.8	16.2	15.8	15.1
1934	18.7	13.2	15.8	17.8	10.4	19.0	19.1	13.1	15.4	16.2	15.1	14.2
1935	17.9	13.5	15.2	17.7	11.1	18.6	19.6	12.7	16.0	15.3	15.7	13.6
1936	17.4	13.3	16.0	17.8	11.0	18.6	19.1	13.6	16.6	15.0	15.3	13.4
1937	17.2	13.3	16.6	18.0	10.8	18.2	19.9	12.8	18.0	14.7	15.0	13.1
1938	16.8[28]	12.8[28]	14.4[28]	18.1	10.3	17.8	21.0	12.8	18.4	14.6	15.4	13.1
1939	18.6	13.3	18.2	17.8	10.1	18.8	21.2	14.3	16.6	14.6	15.3[30]	12.3
1940	20.6	14.0	19.8	18.3	10.4	18.4	17.8	19.4	16.6	13.6[30]	18.0[30]	8.6[30]
1941	20.1	14.0	17.2	18.5	10.3	17.4	24.2	19.8	20.4	13.1[30]	17.0[30]	11.4[30]
1942	19.7	14.3	18.2	20.4	9.6	18.4	16.6	15.1	14.6	14.5[30]	16.6[30]	13.6[30]
1943	21.5	14.1	15.8	21.4	9.6	18.6	20.4	13.3	17.2	15.7[30]	16.0[30]	11.2[30]
1944	22.1[28]	15.0[28]	13.6[28]	22.7	10.2	18.6	21.3	18.9	16.8	16.1[30]	17.1[30]	10.5[30]
1945	19.5	17.8	15.0	23.5	10.5	18.0	25.5	13.1	23.6	16.2[30]	16.1[30]	19.8[30]
1946	22.7	14.1	20.2	23.4	10.2	19.6	27.9	11.8	26.2	20.9	13.5	25.7
1947	24.2[29]	12.1[29]	22.2[29]	22.1	9.7	19.2	28.0	11.9	22.6	21.3	13.1	21.0
1948	23.4	11.5	21.4	20.3	8.6	18.8	27.6	11.2	20.0	21.1	12.4	18.0
1949	22.4	11.9	21.2	18.9	8.9	17.8	26.1	11.2	17.6	20.9	13.7	16.4

See pp. 117–9 for footnotes

A6 Vital Statistics: Rates per 1,000 Population

	Germany			East Germany			Greece			Hungary		
	B	**D**	**M**	**B**	**D**	**M**	**B**	**D**	**M**	**B**	**D**	**M**
1900	35.6	22.1	17.0	...	...	...	...	...	...	39.4	27.0	17.8
1901	35.7	20.7	16.5	...	...	...	...	...	...	37.6	25.0	17.4
1902	35.1	19.4	15.8	...	...	...	...	...	...	38.6	26.9	17.2
1903	33.8	20.0	15.8	...	...	...	...	...	...	36.5	26.1	16.0
1904	34.1	19.6	16.1	...	...	...	...	...	...	37.0	24.8	18.0
1905	33.0	19.8	16.1	...	...	...	...	...	...	35.5	27.8	17.0
1906	33.1	18.2	16.3	...	...	...	...	...	...	36.1	24.9	17.6
1907	32.3	18.0	16.3	...	...	...	...	...	...	36.2	25.6	20.0
1908	32.1	18.1	15.9	...	...	...	...	...	...	36.7	25.0	18.6
1909	31.1	17.2	15.5	...	...	...	...	...	...	37.1	25.4	17.4
1910	29.8	16.2	15.4	...	...	...	...	...	...	35.4	23.4	17.4
1911	28.6	17.3	15.7	...	...	...	...	...	...	34.8	24.8	18.6
1912	28.3	15.6	15.8	...	...	...	...	...	...	36.0	23.0	17.4
1913	27.5	15.0	15.3	...	...	...	...	...	...	34.3	23.2	18.4
1914	26.8	19.0	13.6	...	...	...	...	...	...	34.5	23.4	14.4
1915	20.4	21.4[31]	8.2	...	...	...	...	...	...	23.7	25.3	13.0
1916	15.2[6]	19.2[31][6]	8.2[6]	...	...	...	...	...	...	16.8	20.9	6.8
1917	13.9	20.6[31]	9.4	...	...	...	...	...	...	16.0	20.7	8.2
1918	14.3[32]	24.8[31][32]	10.8[32]	...	...	...	...	...	...	15.3[15]	25.7[15]	13.8[15]
							...	...	...	16.3	26.4	15.2
1919	20.0	15.6	26.8	...	...	...	...	...	...	27.6	20.0	40.8
1920	25.9	15.1	29.0	...	...	...	...	...	...	31.4	21.4	26.2
1921	25.3[33]	13.9[33]	23.8[33]	...	...	...	21.2	13.6	11.2	31.8	21.2	23.2
1922	23.0	14.4	22.3	...	...	...	21.5	16.0	12.0	30.8	21.4	21.6
1923	21.2	13.9	18.9	...	...	...	19.0	17.0	14.8	29.2	19.5	19.2
1924	20.6	12.2	14.2	...	...	...	19.5	15.6	14.8	26.9	20.4	18.2
1925	20.8	11.9	15.5	...	...	...	26.3	14.9	16.2	28.3	17.1	17.8
1926	19.6	11.7	15.4	...	...	...	30.0	13.9	14.6	27.4	16.7	18.4
1927	18.4	12.0	17.0	...	...	...	28.8	16.3	14.4	25.8	17.8	18.2
1928	18.6	11.6	18.5	...	...	...	30.5	17.0	13.2	26.4	17.2	18.6
1929	18.0	12.6	18.4	...	...	...	28.9	18.4	14.2	25.1	17.8	18.2
1930	17.6	11.0	17.5	...	...	...	31.3	16.3	14.0	25.4	15.5	18.0
1931	16.0	11.2	16.0	...	...	...	30.8	17.7	14.0	23.7	16.6	17.6
1932	15.1	10.8	15.7	...	...	...	28.5	18.0	12.0	23.4	17.9	16.2
1933	14.7	11.2	19.3	...	...	...	28.6	16.8	14.0	21.9	14.7	16.6
1934	18.0	10.9	22.3	...	...	...	31.1	15.0	14.0	21.8	14.5	17.8
1935	18.9	11.8	19.5	...	...	...	28.2	14.8	13.4	21.1	15.3	17.0
1936	19.0	11.8	18.1	...	...	...	27.9	15.1	11.2	20.3	14.3	17.2
1937	18.8	11.7	18.3	...	...	...	26.2	15.0	13.0	20.0	14.2	17.8
1938	19.7	11.7	18.8	...	...	...	25.9	13.2	13.0	19.9	14.3	16.4
1939	20.4	12.3[31]	22.4	...	...	...	24.8	13.9	13.2	19.4	13.5[37]	17.4
1940	20.1	12.7[31]	17.6	...	...	...	24.5	12.8	9.0	20.0	14.3[37]	15.6
1941	18.1	12.1[31]	14.4	...	...	...	18.3[35]	17.1[35]	10.0[35]	19.0	13.2[37]	17.0
1942	14.9	12.0[31]	14.8	...	...	...	18.1[35]	26.0[35]	12.2[35]	19.9	14.6[37]	15.6
1943	16.0	12.1[31]	14.6	...	...	...	16.7[35]	15.3[35]	12.0[35]	18.4	13.5[37]	16.0[38]
1944	...	...	...	...	...	...	20.0[35]	15.2[35]	9.6[35]	...	...	...
1945	...	...	...	...	...	...	25.1[35]	11.7[35]	12.8[35]	18.7	23.4[37]	16.2
	West Germany[34]											
1946	16.1	13.0	17.6	10.4	22.9	13.8	28.2[35]	9.9[35]	14.0[35]	18.7	15.0	21.8
1947	16.4	12.1	20.2	13.1	19.0	17.4	27.4[35]	9.3[35]	13.2[35]	20.6[38]	12.9[38]	21.6
1948	16.5	10.5	21.4	12.8	15.2	19.2	27.0[35][36]	12.4[15][16]	11.2[35][36]	20.9	11.6	21.4
1949	16.8	10.4	20.4	14.5	13.4	20.2	18.6	7.9	11.2	20.6	11.4	23.4

See pp. 117–9 for footnotes

A6 Vital Statistics: Rates per 1,000 Population

1900–1949

	Ireland			Northern Ireland			Italy			Netherlands		
	B	D	M	B	D	M	B	D	M	B	D	M
1900	22.7	19.6	9.5	...	...	...	33.0	23.8	14.4	31.6	17.9	15.2
1901	22.7	17.8	10.1	...	...	...	32.5	22.0	14.4	32.2	17.2	15.4
1902	23.0	17.5	10.4	...	...	...	33.4	22.2	14.6	31.8	16.3	15.1
1903	23.1	17.5	10.4	...	...	...	31.7	22.4	14.4	31.6	15.6	14.7
1904	23.6	18.0	10.4	...	...	...	32.9	21.2	15.0	31.4	15.9	14.7
1905	23.4	17.1	10.5	...	...	...	32.7	22.0	15.4	30.8	15.3	14.6
1906	23.5	16.9	10.3	...	...	...	32.1	20.9	15.6	30.4	14.8	15.0
1907	23.2	17.6	10.3	...	...	...	31.7	20.9	15.6	30.0	14.6	15.2
1908	23.3	17.5	10.4	...	...	...	33.7	22.8	16.8	29.7	15.0	14.6
1909	23.4	17.1	10.3	...	...	...	32.8	21.7	15.6	29.2	13.7	14.2
1910	23.3	17.1	10.1	...	...	...	33.3	19.9	15.6	28.6	13.6	14.6
1911	23.2	16.5	10.7	...	...	...	31.5	21.4	15.0	27.8	14.5	14.4
1912	23.0	16.5	10.6	...	...	...	32.4	18.2	15.2	28.1	12.3	15.2
1913	22.8	17.1	10.2	...	...	...	31.7	18.7	15.0	28.2	12.3	15.8
1914	22.6	16.3	10.8	...	...	...	31.0	17.9	14.0	28.2	12.4	13.6
1915	22.0	17.6	11.1	...	...	...	30.5	22.3	10.2	26.2	12.5	13.4
1916	20.9	16.3	10.2	...	...	...	24.1	23.3	5.8	26.5	12.9	14.6
1917	19.7	16.6	9.6	...	...	...	19.5[39]	26.0[39]	5.4[39]	26.0[43]	13.1[43]	15.0
1918	19.8	17.9	10.3	...	...	...	18.2[39]	35.1[39]	6.0[39]	25.1	17.4	14.8
1919	20.0	17.6	12.2	...	...	...	21.5[40]	18.9[40]	18.6[40]	24.4	13.4	17.2
1920	22.8	14.8	12.0	...	...	...	32.2	19.0	28.2	28.6	12.3	19.2
	Southern Ireland											
1922	19.5	14.7	10.0	23.3	15.4	12.6	30.8	18.1	19.2	26.1	11.7	17.4
1923	20.5	14.0	10.4	23.9	14.7	12.5	30.0	17.0	17.4	26.2	10.2	16.0
1924	21.1	15.0	9.8	22.7	15.9	11.9	29.0	17.1	15.8	25.1	9.8	15.6
1925	20.8	14.6	9.2	22.0	15.7	12.2	28.4	17.1	15.2	24.2	9.8	14.8
1926	20.6	14.1	9.2	22.5	15.0	11.5	27.7	17.2	15.0	23.8	9.8	14.8
1927	20.3	14.8	9.0	21.3	14.6	11.5	27.5	16.1	15.2	23.1	10.2	15.0
1928	20.1	14.2	9.4	20.8	14.4	11.7	26.7	16.1	14.2	23.3	9.6	15.4
1929	19.8	14.6	9.2	20.4	15.9	12.0	25.6	16.5	14.2	22.8	10.7	15.
1930	19.9	14.3	9.4	20.8	13.8	12.2	26.7	14.1	14.8	23.1	9.1	16.0
1931	19.5	14.6	9.0	20.5	14.4	11.9	24.9	14.8	13.4	22.2	9.6	14.8
1932	19.1	14.6	8.8	19.9	14.1	11.1	23.8	14.7	12.8	22.0	9.0	13.8
1933	19.4	13.7	9.4	19.6	14.3	12.1	23.8	13.7	13.8	20.8	8.8	14.4
1934	19.5	13.2	9.6	20.1	13.9	13.0	23.5	13.3	14.8	20.6	8.4	14.6
1935	19.6	14.0	9.6	19.5	14.6	13.9	23.4	14.0	13.4	20.2	8.7	14.4
1936	19.6	14.4	10.0	20.3	14.4	14.3	22.4	13.8	14.8	20.2	8.7	15.0
1937	19.2	15.3	10.0	19.8	15.1	13.5	22.9	14.3	17.4	19.8	8.8	15.4
1938	19.4	13.6	10.2	20.0	13.7	13.4	23.8	14.1	15.0	20.5	8.5	15.4
1939	19.1	14.2	10.4	19.5	13.5	14.2	23.6	13.4	14.6	20.6	8.6	18.4
1940	19.1	14.2	10.2	19.5	14.6	15.1	23.5	13.6[41]	14.2	20.8	9.9	15.2
1941	19.0	14.6	10.0	20.5	15.2	18.3	20.9	13.9[41]	12.2	20.3	10.0	14.6
1942	22.3	14.1	11.8	22.3	13.3	17.6	20.5[42]	14.3[41][42]	12.8[42]	21.0[44]	9.5[44]	19.4
1943	21.9	14.8	11.8	23.5	13.4	15.1	19.9	15.2[41]	9.6	23.0	10.0[44]	14.4
1944	22.2	15.3	11.4	22.8	12.8	14.0	18.3	15.3[41]	9.6	24.0	11.8[44]	11.0
1945	22.7	14.5	11.8	21.3	12.3	15.4	18.3	13.6[41]	13.8	22.6	15.3[44]	15.6
1946	22.9	14.0	11.8	22.3	12.5	14.5	23.0	12.1	18.4	30.2	8.5	22.8
1947	23.2	14.8	11.0	23.2	12.6	14.1	22.3	11.5	19.4	27.8	8.1	20.4
1948	22.0	12.1	10.8	21.7	11.2	13.8	22.0	10.6	16.8	25.3	7.4	18.0
1949	21.5	12.7	10.8	21.2	11.5	13.4	20.4	10.5	15.6	23.7	8.1	16.6

See pp. 117–9 for footnotes

A6 Vital Statistics: Rates per 1,000 Population

1900–1949

	Norway			Poland[45]			Portugal[18]			Romania		
	B	D	M	B	D	M	B	D	M	B	D	M
1900	29.7	15.8	13.6	...	...	...	30.5	20.3	13.6	38.8	24.2	13.4
1901	29.9	15.0	13.1	...	...	...	31.3	20.9	13.9	39.3	26.2	14.2
1902	29.2	13.9	12.6	...	...	...	32.0	19.7	14.1	39.0	27.7	18.0
1903	28.6	14.8	11.9	...	...	...	33.0	20.1	13.9	40.1	24.8	17.4
1904	27.9	14.3	11.7	...	...	...	31.6	18.9	13.1	40.1	24.4	16.2
1905	27.1	14.8	11.5	...	...	...	31.8	20.0	13.3	38.3	24.7	15.8
1906	26.8	13.7	11.7	...	...	...	32.1	22.0	12.5	39.9	23.9	20.3
1907	26.3	14.3	12.0	...	...	...	30.7	19.7	12.3	41.1	26.3	21.0
1908	26.3	14.2	12.1	...	...	...	30.3	20.0	12.3	40.3	27.4	18.2
1909	26.8	13.6	11.9	...	...	...	29.9	19.2	12.3	41.1	27.4	18.4
1910	25.8	13.5	12.2	...	...	...	31.7	19.2	13.2	39.3	24.8	18.5
1911	25.7	13.2	12.4	...	...	...	38.6	22.0	13.8	42.3	25.3	21.0
1912	25.4	13.5	12.2	...	...	...	34.9	20.1	14.8	43.4	22.9	17.3
1913	25.1	13.3	12.5	...	...	...	32.5	20.6	11.7	42.1	26.1	18.3
1914	25.1	13.5	12.8	...	...	...	31.5	19.3	12.2	42.1	23.5	16.8
1915	23.6	13.4	12.8	...	...	...	32.6	20.5	12.0	40.5	24.5	14.3
1916	24.2	13.8	13.7	...	...	...	32.1	21.6	12.0	...	...	...
1917	25.1	13.6	14.2	...	...	...	31.4	22.3	11.1	...	...	...
1918	24.6	17.2	15.5	...	...	...	29.7	41.4	10.1	...[46]	...[46]	...[46]
1919	22.7	13.8	11.8	...	...	...	27.6	25.4	15.6	23.0	20.6	13.5
1920	26.1	12.8	14.0	...	...	...	33.6	23.7	17.6	33.7	25.9	25.8
1921	24.2	11.5	13.5	32.8	20.9	23.4	32.4	20.8	16.8	38.2	22.9	24.4
1922	23.3	12.1	12.8	35.3	19.9	22.9	33.1	20.4	16.3	37.2	22.8	20.6
1923	22.8	11.6	12.5	36.0	17.5	20.4	33.2	22.7	15.7	36.4	22.1	19.7
1924	21.3	11.3	12.2	35.0	18.2	18.8	32.8	20.0	14.6	36.7	22.5	18.2
1925	19.7	11.1	11.8	35.4	16.8	16.3	32.6	18.4	14.2	35.2	21.1	17.9
1926	19.6	10.8	11.5	33.1	17.8	17.2	33.5	19.8	14.8	34.8	21.4	18.3
1927	18.1	11.2	11.4	31.6	17.3	17.1	31.0	18.8	12.7	34.1	22.2	19.4
1928	17.9	10.9	12.0	32.0	16.4	19.2	31.9	18.7	13.7	34.7	19.6	17.7
1929	17.3	11.5	12.7	31.8	16.7	19.3	29.9	17.7	13.3	34.1	21.4	17.5
1930	17.0	10.6	12.9	32.3	15.6	19.1	29.7	17.1	14.0	35.0	19.4	18.6
1931	16.3	10.9	12.5	30.2	15.5	17.1	29.7	16.8	13.1	33.3	20.8	18.4
1932	16.0	10.6	12.4	28.9	15.0	16.7	29.9	17.1	13.0	35.9	21.7	19.0
1933	14.7	10.1	12.6	26.5	14.2	16.7	28.9	17.2	13.0	32.1	18.7	16.6
1934	14.6	9.9	13.4	26.6	14.4	16.7	28.4	16.6	13.3	32.4	20.7	18.4
1935	14.3	10.3	14.2	26.1	14.0	16.7	28.2	17.0	13.5	30.7	21.1	17.4
1936	14.6	10.4	15.4	26.2	14.2	16.7	28.1	16.3	12.7	31.5	19.8	18.4
1937	15.0	10.4	16.4	24.9	14.0	16.0	26.7	15.8	12.6	30.8	19.3	19.0
1938	15.4	10.0	16.6	24.3	13.7	16.1	26.6	15.4	13.0	29.6	19.2	17.6
1939	15.8	10.1	17.7	...	...	...	26.2	15.3	12.8	28.3[46]	18.6[46]	15.8[46]
1940	16.1	10.8	18.8	...	...	...	24.3	15.6	12.1	26.5[47]	19.1[47]	18.2[47]
1941	15.3	10.8	17.7	...	...	...	23.8	17.4	14.2	23.0[47]	19.3[47]	15.2[47]
1942	17.7	10.7	...	...	...	...	24.0	16.1	15.0	21.4[47]	19.5[47]	15.4[47]
1943	18.9	10.4	15.8	...	...	...	25.1	15.3	14.8	23.4[47]	18.1[47]	13.8[47]
1944	20.3	10.7	14.4	...	...	...	25.3	14.8	15.0	21.7[47]	19.6[47]	10.4[47]
1945	20.0	9.7	15.2	...	...	...	26.0	14.2	15.3	19.6[47]	20.0[47]	21.2[47]
1946	22.6	9.4	19.0	22.8	13.4	...	25.4	14.7	15.4	24.8	18.8	23.6
1947	21.4	9.5	18.9	26.2	11.3	...	24.5	13.3	16.5	23.4	22.0	19.6
1948	20.5	8.9	18.5	29.3	11.2	...	26.8	13.0	15.6	23.9	15.6	22.4
1949	19.5	9.0	17.0	29.4	11.6	22.4	25.5	14.1	15.7	27.6	13.7	23.2

See pp. 117–9 for footnotes

A6　Vital Statistics: Rates per 1,000 Population

	Russia[21]			Serbia			Spain			Sweden		
	B	D	M	B	D	M	B	D	M	B	D	M
1900	49.3	31.1	17.8	42.4	23.5	25.2	33.9	29.0	17.7	27.0	16.8	12.3
1901	47.9	32.1	17.2	38.0	21.0	16.6	35.0	27.8	16.9	27.0	16.1	12.1
1902	49.1	31.5	17.2	38.0	22.3	20.6	35.6	26.1	17.5	26.5	15.4	11.9
1903	48.1	30.0	17.8	40.9	23.5	19.0	36.4	25.0	16.4	25.7	15.1	11.6
1904	48.6	29.9	15.2	39.8	21.1	22.9	34.2	25.7	15.3	25.8	15.3	11.7
1905	45.0	31.7	15.2	37.3	24.8	19.8	35.1	25.7	14.3	25.7	15.6	11.7
1906	47.1	29.9	19.2	42.0	24.5	20.8	33.8	25.9	14.4	25.7	14.4	12.3
1907	47.5	28.4	18.0	40.0	22.4	21.2	33.3	24.4	14.1	25.5	14.6	12.4
1908	44.8	28.3	16.0	36.8	23.7	18.0	33.7	23.6	14.5	25.7	14.9	12.2
1909	44.7	29.5	16.0	38.7	29.3	18.8	33.1	23.7	13.2	25.6	13.7	11.9
1910	45.1	31.5	16.8	39.0	22.4	20.8	32.7	23.1	14.1	24.7	14.0	12.1
1911	45.0	27.4	16.0	36.3	21.8	20.6	31.5	23.4	14.3	24.0	13.8	11.8
1912	43.7	26.5	...	...	...	20.8	31.8	21.3	14.3	23.8	14.2	11.9
1913	43.1[21] 47.0	27.4[21] 30.2	...[21]	...	...	...	30.6	22.3	13.6	23.2	13.7	11.9
1914	...	...	...	...	...	...	29.9	22.2	13.2	22.9	13.8	11.6
1915	...	...	...	...	...	...	30.9	22.1	12.5	21.6	14.7	11.7
1916	...	...	...	...	...	...	29.1	21.4	13.3	21.2	13.6	12.2
1917	...	...	...	...	...	...	29.0	22.5	13.7	20.9	13.4	12.3
1918	...	...	...	...	...	...	29.3	33.3	13.5	20.3	18.0	13.3
1919	...	...	...	...	...	...	27.9	23.0	15.9	19.8	14.5	13.8
1920	30.9	...	...	...	...	...	29.5	23.4	16.6	23.6	13.3	14.6
1921	32.6	...	...	...	...	...	30.5	21.4	15.5	21.5	12.4	13.3
1922	33.4[21]	...	...	...	...	...	30.5	20.5	15.2	19.6	12.8	12.3
1923	38.8	...	...	...	...	...	30.5	20.7	14.5	18.9	11.4	12.6
1924	43.1	...	...	...	...	...	29.7	19.6	14.4	18.1	12.0	12.4
1925	44.7	...	...	...	...	...	29.1	19.2	14.3	17.6	11.7	12.4
1926	43.6	19.9	...	...	...	...	29.6	18.8	14.5	16.8	11.8	12.6
1927	43.2[21]	20.8[21]	...	...	...	...	28.1	18.6	14.1	16.1	12.7	12.8
1928	44.3	23.3	...	...	...	...	29.1	18.1	14.9	16.1	12.0	13.3
1929	...	...	...	...	...	...	28.3	17.6	14.6	15.2	12.2	13.7
1930	...	...	...	...	...	...	28.3	16.9	14.9	15.4	11.7	14.3
1931	...	...	...	...	...	...	27.6	17.4	14.9	14.8	12.5	13.9
1932	...	...	...	...	...	...	28.2	16.4	13.3	14.5	11.6	13.5
1933	...	...	...	...	...	...	27.7	16.4	12.3	13.7	11.2	14.0
1934	...	...	...	...	...	...	26.2	16.0	12.0	13.7	11.2	15.5
1935	30.1[21]	...	...	...	...	...	25.7	15.7	12.3	13.8	11.7	16.4
1936	33.6[21]	...	...	...	...	...	24.7	16.7	11.2	14.2	12.0	17.0
1937	38.7	18.9	...	...	...	...	22.6	18.9	11.4	14.4	12.0	17.7
1938	37.5	17.5	...	...	...	...	20.0	19.2	8.9	14.9	11.5	18.5
1939	36.5	17.3	...	...	...	...	16.5	18.4	11.3	15.4	11.5	19.4
1940	31.2	18.3	...	...	...	...	24.4	16.5	16.8	15.1	11.4	18.6
1941	...	...	...	...	...	...	19.6	18.6	14.6	15.6	11.3	18.2
1942	...	...	...	...	...	...	20.2	14.7	14.3	17.7	9.9	19.8
1943	...	...	...	...	...	...	22.9	13.2	13.2	19.3	10.2	19.4
1944	...	...	...	...	...	...	22.5	13.0	14.1	20.6	11.0	19.7
1945	...	...	...	...	...	...	23.1	12.2	14.4	20.4	10.8	19.4
1946	23.8	10.8	...	...	...	...	21.4	12.9	15.0	19.7	10.5	19.0
1947	...	...	...	...	...	...	21.4	12.0	16.5	18.9	10.8	17.5
1948	...	...	...	...	...	...	23.1	10.9	15.6	18.4	9.8	16.9
1949	...	...	...	...	...	...	21.5	11.4	14.2	17.4	10.0	15.9

See pp. 117–9 for footnotes

A6 Vital Statistics: Rates per 1,000 Population

1900–1949

	Switzerland			United Kingdom: England and Wales			United Kingdom: Scotland			Yugoslavia[48]		
	B	D	M	B	D	M	B	D	M	B	D	M
1900	28.6	19.3	15.4	28.7	18.2	16.0	29.6	18.5	14.6	...	...	...
1901	29.0	18.0	15.2	28.5	16.9	15.9	29.5	17.9	14.0	...	...	...
1902	28.5	17.0	14.8	28.5	16.3	15.9	29.3	17.3	14.2	...	...	...
1903	27.4	17.4	14.8	28.5	15.5	15.7	29.4	16.8	14.3	...	...	...
1904	27.3	17.5	14.6	28.0	16.3	15.3	29.1	17.1	14.1	...	...	...
1905	26.9	17.6	15.0	27.3	15.3	15.3	28.6	16.2	13.6	...	...	...
1906	26.9	16.6	15.4	27.2	15.5	15.7	28.6	16.4	14.3	...	...	...
1907	26.2	16.4	15.4	26.5	15.1	15.9	27.7	16.6	14.3	...	...	...
1908	26.4	15.8	15.2	26.7	14.8	15.1	28.1	16.6	13.5	...	...	...
1909	25.5	16.1	14.8	25.8	14.6	14.7	27.3	15.8	12.8	...	...	...
1910	25.0	15.1	14.6	25.1	13.5	15.0	26.2	15.3	13.0	...	...	...
1911	24.2	15.8	14.8	24.3	14.6	15.2	25.6	15.1	13.4	...	...	...
1912	24.2	14.2	14.6	23.9	13.3	15.6	25.9	15.3	13.7	...	...	...
1913	23.2	14.3	13.8	24.1	13.8	15.7	25.5	15.5	14.2	...	...	...
1914	22.4	13.8	11.4	23.8	14.0	15.9	26.1	15.5	14.8	...	...	...
1915	19.5	13.3	10.0	21.9	15.7[31]	19.4	23.9	17.1	15.2	...	...	...
1916	18.9	13.0	11.4	20.9	14.3[31]	14.9	22.8	14.7	13.1	...	...	...
1917	18.5	13.7	12.0	17.8	14.2[31]	13.8	20.1	14.4	12.6	...	...	...
1918	18.7	19.3	13.4	17.7	17.3[31]	15.3	20.2	16.3	14.3	...	...	...
1919	18.6	14.2	15.8	18.5	14.0[31]	19.7	21.7	15.6	18.3	...	...	...
1920	20.9	14.4	18.0	25.5	12.4	20.2	28.1	14.0	19.2	...	...	...
1921	20.8	12.8	16.8	22.4	12.1	16.9	25.2	13.6	16.1	36.7	20.9	26.0
1922	19.7	13.0	15.6	20.4	12.7	15.7	23.5	14.9	14.0	34.4	20.8	21.6
1923	19.4	11.8	15.2	19.7	11.6	15.2	22.9	12.9	14.4	34.8	20.3	20.8
1924	18.9	12.6	14.6	18.8	12.2	15.3	22.0	14.5	13.3	35.1	20.2	18.2
1925	18.5	12.2	14.4	18.3	12.1	15.2	21.4	13.5	13.3	34.2	18.7	19.2
1926	18.3	11.8	14.2	17.8	11.6	14.3	21.1	13.1	12.8	35.3	18.8	19.2
1927	17.5	12.4	14.4	16.6	12.3	15.7	19.9	13.6	13.4	34.3	21.0	18.8
1928	17.4	12.0	15.0	16.7	11.7	15.4	20.0	13.5	13.6	32.7	20.4	18.2
1929	17.1	12.5	15.6	16.3	13.4	15.8	19.2	14.7	13.6	33.3	21.1	18.8
1930	17.2	11.6	15.8	16.3	11.4	15.8	19.6	13.3	13.8	35.5	19.0	20.0
1931	16.7	12.1	15.8	15.8	12.3	15.6	19.0	13.3	13.5	33.6	19.8	18.0
1932	16.7	12.2	15.6	15.3	12.0	15.3	18.6	13.5	13.6	32.9	19.2	15.6
1933	16.4	11.4	15.6	14.4	12.3	15.8	17.6	13.2	13.9	31.5	17.0	15.4
1934	16.3	11.3	15.6	14.8	11.8	16.9	18.0	12.9	15.0	31.6	17.1	13.6
1935	16.0	12.1	14.6	14.7	11.7	17.2	17.8	13.2	15.3	29.9	16.9	15.0
1936	15.6	11.4	14.2	14.8	12.1	17.4	17.9	13.4	15.3	29.1	16.1	14.6
1937	14.9	11.3	14.6	14.9	12.4	17.5	17.6	13.9	15.4	28.0	16.0	15.6
1938	15.2	11.6	14.8	15.1	11.6	17.6	17.7	12.6	15.5	26.7	15.6	15.8
1939	15.2	11.8	15.0	14.8	12.1[31]	21.2	17.4	12.9	18.5	25.9	15.0	15.8
1940	15.2	12.0	15.4	14.1	14.4[31]	22.5	17.1	14.9	21.2	...	...	...
1941	16.9	11.1	17.0	13.9	13.5[31]	18.6	17.5	14.7	18.6	...	...	...
1942	18.4	10.9	17.2	15.6	12.3[31]	17.7	17.6	13.3	18.4	...	...	...
1943	19.2	11.0	16.6	16.2	13.0[31]	14.0	18.4	14.0	14.8	...	...	...
1944	19.6	12.0	16.0	17.7	12.7[31]	14.3	18.5	13.6	14.3	...	...	...
1945	20.1	11.6	16.2	15.9	12.6[31]	18.7	16.9	13.2	18.9	...	...	...
1946	20.0	11.3	17.4	19.2	12.0[31]	18.1	20.3	13.1	17.8	...[49]	...[49]	...[49]
1947	19.4	11.4	17.4	20.5	12.3	18.6	22.3	13.1	17.5	26.6	12.8	26.2
1948	19.2	10.8	17.2	17.8	11.0	18.2	19.7	12.0	17.2	28.1	13.5	25.6
1949	18.4	10.7	16.0	16.7	11.8	17.1	18.8	12.5	16.4	30.0	13.5	22.8

See pp. 117–9 for footnotes

A6   Vital Statistics: Rates per 1,000 Population

1950–1998

	Albania			Austria			Belgium			Bulgaria		
	B	D	M	B	D	M	B	D	M	B	D	M
1950	38.8	14.1	20.2	15.6	12.4	18.6	16.5	12.0	16.6	25.2	11.5	21.4
1951	38.5	15.2	20.2	14.8	12.7	18.2	16.4	12.4	16.2	21.1	10.7	17.6
1952	35.2	15.6	20.6	14.9	12.0	16.6	16.7	11.8	15.4	21.2	11.6	19.2
1953	40.9	13.7	19.4	14.8	12.0	15.6	16.7	12.1	15.4	20.9	9.3	18.6
1954	40.8	13.1	16.0	15.0	12.2	15.6	16.8	11.9	15.4	20.2	9.2	17.2
1955	44.5	15.1	16.4	15.6	12.2	16.4	16.7	12.2	15.5	20.1	9.1	17.0
1956	41.9	11.5	14.6	16.7	12.5	16.6	16.8	12.1	15.3	19.5	9.4	17.6
1957	39.1	11.8	16.2	17.0	12.8	16.2	17.0	11.9	15.1	18.4	8.6	17.4
1958	41.8	9.3	15.8	17.1	12.3	15.8	17.1	11.7	14.8	17.9	7.9	18.2
1959	41.9	9.8	14.8	17.7	12.5	15.8	17.4	11.4	14.3	17.6	9.5	17.2
1960	43.4	10.4	15.6	17.9	12.7	16.6	16.9	12.4	14.2	17.8	8.1	17.6
1961	41.2	9.3	22.6	18.6	12.1	17.0	17.2	11.6	13.6	17.4	7.9	16.8
1962	39.3	10.7	15.0	18.7	12.7	16.8	16.8	12.2	13.4	16.7	8.7	16.2
1963	39.1	10.0	15.0	18.8	12.8	16.2	17.1	12.5	13.4	16.4	8.2	16.4
1964	37.8	8.7	14.4	18.5	12.3	16.0	17.1	11.7	13.8	16.1	7.9	16.2
1965	35.2	9.0	15.0	17.9	13.0	15.6	16.4	12.1	14.0	15.3	8.2	16.0
1966	34.0	8.6	13.6	17.6	12.5	15.4	15.9	12.1	14.3	14.9	8.3	16.4
1967	35.3	8.4	17.2	17.4	13.0	15.4	14.7	12.0	14.2	15.0	9.0	17.4
1968	35.6	8.0	15.6	17.0	12.9	15.2	14.7	12.6	14.4	16.9	8.6	17.8
1969	35.3	7.5	14.8	16.3	13.3	15.8	14.6	12.5	15.0	17.0	9.5	17.4
1970	32.5	9.3	13.6	15.0	13.2	14.2	14.6	12.3	15.2	16.3	9.1	17.2
1971	33.3	8.1	14.0	14.5	13.0	12.9	14.4	12.3	15.2	15.9	9.7	16.3
1972	...	...	...	13.8	12.6	15.3	13.8	12.0	15.3	15.3	9.8	16.4
1973	...	...	...	12.9	12.2	13.1	13.3	12.1	15.2	16.2	9.5	17.2
1974	...	...	...	12.8	12.4	13.0	12.6	11.9	15.0	17.2	9.8	17.0
1975	...	...	...	12.4	12.7	12.3	12.2	12.2	14.6	16.6	10.3	17.2
1976	...	...	...	11.6	12.6	12.0	12.3	12.1	14.5	16.5	10.1	16.8
1977	...	...	...	11.3	12.2	12.0	12.4	11.4	14.1	16.1	10.7	17.0
1978	...	6.4	...	11.3	12.5	11.8	12.4	11.7	13.6	15.5	10.5	16.2
1979	27.5	6.7	...	11.4	12.2	12.0	12.6	11.4	13.3	15.3	10.7	15.8
1980	26.5	6.4	16.2	12.0	12.2	12.4	12.7	11.6	13.5	14.5	11.1	15.8
1981	26.5	6.6	...	12.4	12.3	12.6	12.7	11.5	13.2	14.0	10.7	15.0
1982	27.8	5.9	...	12.5	12.1	12.6	12.2	11.4	12.7	13.9	11.2	15.0
1983	26.0	6.1	...	11.9	12.3	14.8	11.9	11.7	12.1	13.8	11.4	15.0
1984	27.3	5.7	18.2	11.8	11.7	12.2	11.8	11.2	12.0	13.6	11.3	14.6
1985	26.2	5.8	17.0	11.6	11.9	11.8	11.6	11.4	11.9	13.3	12.0	14.8
1986	25.3	5.7	17.0	11.5	11.5	12.2	11.9	11.3	11.5	13.4	11.6	14.6
1987	25.9	5.6	17.8	11.4	11.2	20.2	11.9	10.7	11.5	13.0	12.0	14.4
1988	25.5	5.4	18.0	11.6	11.0	9.4	12.1	10.6	12.0	13.1	12.0	14.0
1989	24.6	5.7	17.2	11.7	10.9	11.2	12.2	10.8	13.0	12.5	11.9	14.0
1990	25.2	5.6	17.8	11.7	10.7	11.8	12.4	10.5	13.2	11.7	12.1	13.4
1991	23.8	5.5	15.2	12.1	10.7	11.2	12.6	10.5	12.2	10.7	12.3	10.8
1992	...	5.1	...	12.1	10.5	11.6	12.3	10.3	11.6	10.4	12.6	10.4
1993	...	...	...	11.9	10.3	11.2	12.0	10.6	10.8	10.0	12.9	10.0
1994	...	...	...	11.0	10.1	...	12.0	10.6	10.4	10.0	12.9	...
1995	20.0	5.0	...	11.0	10.1	...	11.4	10.5	10.7	8.6	12.7	...
1996	18.7	4.8	...	11.0	10.0	...	11.3	10.4	10.9	8.6	13.6	...
1997	16.5	4.9	6.8	10.4	9.8	...	11.3	10.2	10.6	7.7	14.0	...
1998	15.9	4.8	7.4	10.1	9.7	...	11.3	10.2	10.8	7.9	14.7	...

A6   Vital Statistics: Rates per 1,000 Population

1950–1998

	Czechoslovakia			Denmark			Finland			France		
	B	D	M	B	D	M	B	D	M	B	D	M
1950	23.3	11.5	21.6	18.7	9.2	18.2	24.5	10.2	17.0	20.5	12.7	15.8
1951	22.8	11.4	20.2	17.8	8.8	17.0	23.0	10.0	16.0	19.5	13.3	15.2
1952	22.2$_{50}$	10.6$_{50}$	17.6	17.8	9.0	16.4	23.1	9.5	15.8	19.3	12.3	14.8
1953	21.2	10.5	15.4	17.9	9.0	16.2	22.0	9.6	15.4	18.7	12.9	14.4
1954	20.6	10.4	15.8	17.3	9.1	15.8	21.5	9.1	15.6	18.7	12.0	14.6
1955	20.3	9.6	15.8	17.3	8.7	15.8	21.2	9.3	15.4	18.5	12.0	14.4
1956	19.8	9.6	17.6	17.2	8.9	15.4	20.8	9.0	15.4	18.4	12.4	13.5
1957	18.9	10.1	13.6	16.8	9.3	15.2	20.1	9.4	14.4	18.4	11.9	14.0
1958	17.4	9.3	14.8	16.5	9.2	15.0	18.6	8.9	14.4	18.1	11.1	13.9
1959	16.0	9.7	15.2	16.3	9.3	15.2	18.9	8.8	14.4	18.3	11.2	14.2
1960	15.9	9.2	15.6	16.6	9.5	15.6	18.5	9.0	14.8	17.9	11.3	14.0
1961	15.8	9.2	15.4	16.6	9.4	15.8	18.4	9.1	15.4	18.2	10.8	13.6
1962	15.7	10.0	15.6	16.7	9.7	16.2	18.1	9.6	15.2	17.7	11.4	13.5
1963	16.9	9.5	15.8	17.6	9.8	16.4	18.2	9.3	14.8	18.2	11.6	14.2
1964	17.2	9.6	15.8	17.7	9.9	16.8	17.7	9.4	15.2	18.2	10.7	14.4
1965	16.4	10.0	15.8	18.0	10.1	17.6	17.1	9.7	15.8	17.8	11.1	14.1
1966	15.6	10.0	16.2	18.4	10.3	17.2	17.0	9.5	16.8	17.6	10.7	13.8
1967	15.1	10.1	16.8	16.8	9.9	17.0	16.8	9.5	18.0	17.0	10.9	14.0
1968	14.9	10.7	17.2	15.3	9.7	16.2	15.9	9.7	17.4	16.7	11.0	14.2
1969	15.5	11.2	17.4	14.6	9.8	16.0	14.6	9.9	17.8	16.7	11.5	15.2
1970	15.9	11.6	17.6	14.4	9.8	14.8	14.0	9.6	17.8	16.7	10.6	15.6
1971	16.5	11.5	18.0	15.2	9.8	13.2	13.2	9.9	16.4	17.1	10.7	15.8
1972	17.4	11.1	18.6	15.1	10.1	12.4	12.7	9.5	15.4	16.9	10.6	16.2
1973	18.9	11.6	19.4	14.3	10.1	12.2	12.2	9.3	15.0	16.4	10.7	15.4
1974	19.9	11.7	19.2	14.1	10.2	13.2	13.3	9.5	14.8	15.3	10.5	15.0
1975	19.6	11.5	19.0	14.2	10.1	12.6	13.9	9.3	13.4	14.1	10.6	14.6
1976	19.3	11.4	18.6	12.9	10.6	12.2	14.1	9.5	13.6	13.6	10.5	14.2
1977	18.7	11.5	18.4	12.9	9.9	12.6	13.9	9.3	13.0	14.0	10.1	13.8
1978	18.4	11.6	17.8	12.2	10.4	11.2	13.5	9.2	12.6	13.8	10.3	13.4
1979	17.9	11.5	16.6	11.6	10.7	10.8	13.3	9.2	12.2	14.1	10.1	12.0
1980	16.3	12.2	15.4	11.2	10.9	10.4	13.2	9.3	12.2	14.9	10.2	12.4
1981	15.5	11.8	15.2	10.4	11.0	10.0	13.2	9.2	12.6	14.9	10.3	11.6
1982	15.2	11.8	15.2	10.3	10.8	9.6	13.7	9.0	12.6	14.6	10.0	11.4
1983	14.9	12.1	15.6	9.9	11.2	10.6	13.8	9.3	12.2	13.7	10.2	11.0
1984	14.7	11.9	15.6	10.1	11.2	11.2	13.3	9.2	11.6	13.8	9.9	10.2
1985	14.6	11.9	15.4	10.5	11.4	11.4	12.8	9.8	10.6	13.9	10.0	9.8
1986	14.2	12.0	15.4	10.8	11.3	12.0	12.3	9.6	10.4	14.1	10.0	9.6
1987	13.8	11.5	15.8	11.0	11.3	12.2	12.0	9.7	10.8	13.8	9.5	9.6
1988	13.8	11.4	15.2	11.5	11.5	12.6	12.8	9.9	10.6	13.8	9.4	9.8
1989	13.3	11.6	15.0	12.0	11.6	12.0	12.8	9.9	10.2	13.6	9.4	10.0
1990	13.4	11.7	16.8	12.3	11.9	12.2	13.1	10.0	9.8	13.4	9.3	10.2
1991	13.3	11.5	13.4	12.5	11.6	12.0	13.1	9.8	9.6	13.3	9.2	9.8
Czech Republic[54]												
1992	...	11.7	14.4	13.1	11.8	12.4	13.3	9.8	9.4	13.0	9.1	9.4
1993	...	11.5	12.8	13.0	12.1	12.2	12.8	10.1	9.2	12.3	9.2	...
1994	...	11.4	13.1	12.8	12.4	12.7	...	10.2	8.7	12.6	9.4	9.5
1995	9.3	11.4	14.6	13.3	12.1	12.4	12.3	9.6	9.0	12.5	9.1	9.7
1996	8.8	10.9	14.0	12.9	11.6	12.0	11.8	9.6	9.4	12.6	9.2	10.0
1997	8.8	10.9	13.7	12.8	11.3	12.5	11.5	9.6	9.2	12.4	9.0	9.9
1998	8.8	10.6	13.9	12.5	11.0	12.1	11.1	9.6	9.7	12.6	9.2	9.6

A6 Vital Statistics: Rates per 1,000 Population

	West Germany			East Germany			Greece			Hungary		
	B	D	M	B	D	M	B	D	M	B	D	M
1950	16.2	10.5	21.4	16.5	11.9	23.4	20.0	7.1	15.4	20.9	11.5	22.8
1951	15.7	10.8	20.6	16.9	11.4	21.2	20.3	7.5	16.6	20.2	11.7	19.8
1952	15.7	10.7	19.0	16.7	12.1	19.2	19.3	6.9	12.8	19.6	11.3	22.0
1953	15.5	11.3	18.0	16.4	11.7	17.4	18.4	7.3	15.6	21.6	11.7	19.0
1954	15.7	10.7	17.4	46.3	12.2	16.8	19.2	7.0	16.0	23.0	11.0	22.2
1955	15.7	11.1	17.6	16.3	11.9	17.4	19.4[51]	6.9[51]	16.6[51]	21.4	10.0	21.0
1956	16.1	11.3	18.0	15.9	12.0	17.2	19.7	7.4	13.8	19.5	10.5	19.4
1957	16.6	11.5	18.0	15.6	12.9	17.2	19.3	7.6	17.0	17.0	10.5	20.0
1958	16.7	11.0	18.2	15.6	12.7	17.8	19.0	7.1	16.9	16.0	9.9	18.6
1959	17.3	11.0	18.4	16.9	13.3	18.8	19.4	7.4	18.0	15.2	10.5	18.2
1960	17.4	11.6	18.8	17.0	13.6	19.4	18.9	7.3	14.0	14.7	10.2	17.8
1961	18.0	11.2	18.8	17.6	13.0	19.8	17.9	7.6	16.9	14.0	9.6	16.6
1962	17.9	11.3	18.6	17.4	13.7	19.4	18.0	7.9	16.7	12.9	10.8	16.2
1963	18.3	11.7	17.6	17.6	12.9	17.2	17.5	7.9	18.4	13.1	9.9	16.8
1964	18.2	11.0	17.4	17.2	13.3	16.0	18.0	8.2	17.9	13.1	10.0	17.4
1965	17.7	11.5	16.6	16.5	13.5	15.2	17.7	7.9	18.9	13.1	10.7	17.6
1966	17.6	11.5	16.2	15.7	13.2	14.2	17.9	7.9	16.6	13.6	10.0	18.4
1967	17.0	11.5	16.2	14.8	13.3	13.8	18.7	8.3	18.7	14.6	10.7	18.8
1968	16.1	12.2	14.8	14.3	14.2	14.0	18.3	8.4	15.0	15.0	11.2	18.6
1969	14.8	12.2	14.6	14.0	14.3	14.6	17.6	8.2	16.6	15.0	11.3	18.6
1970	13.4	12.1	14.6	13.9	14.1	15.4	16.5	8.4	15.4	14.7	11.6	18.8
1971	12.7	11.9	14.0	13.8	13.8	15.2	16.0	8.4	16.6	14.5	11.9	18.2
1972	11.3	11.8	13.4	11.8	13.8	15.6	15.9	8.6	13.6	14.7	11.4	18.8
1973	10.3	11.8	12.8	10.6	13.7	16.2	15.4	8.7	16.6	15.0	11.8	19.4
1974	10.1	11.7	12.2	10.6	13.5	16.2	16.1	8.5	15.2	17.8	12.0	19.0
1975	9.7	12.1	12.6	10.8	14.3	16.8	15.7	8.9	16.9	18.4	12.4	19.8
1976	9.8	11.9	11.8	11.6	13.9	17.2	16.0	8.9	14.0	17.5	12.5	19.0
1977	9.5	11.5	11.6	13.3	13.5	17.6	15.5	9.0	16.4	16.7	12.4	18.2
1978	9.4	11.8	10.8	13.9	13.1	16.8	15.7	8.7	15.5	15.8	13.1	17.4
1979	9.5	11.6	11.2	14.0	13.9	16.4	15.7	8.7	16.7	15.0	12.8	16.2
1980	10.1	11.6	11.8	14.6	14.2	16.0	15.4	9.1	12.9	13.9	13.6	15.0
1981	10.1	11.7	11.6	14.2	13.9	15.4	14.5	8.9	14.6	13.3	13.5	14.4
1982	10.1	11.6	11.8	14.4	13.7	15.0	14.0	8.8	13.8	12.5	13.5	14.2
1983	9.7	11.7	12.0	14.0	13.3	15.0	13.5	9.2	14.4	11.9	13.9	14.2
1984	9.5	11.3	11.8	13.7	13.3	16.0	12.7	8.9	11.1	11.8	13.8	14.0
1985	9.6	11.5	12.0	13.7	13.5	15.8	11.7	9.3	12.8	12.2	13.9	13.8
1986	10.3	11.5	12.2	13.4	13.4	16.6	11.3	9.2	11.7	12.1	13.8	13.6
1987	10.5	11.2	12.6	13.6	12.9	17.0	10.6	9.5	12.6	11.9	13.4	12.4
1988	11.0	11.2	13.0	12.9	12.8	16.4	10.7	9.3	10.4	11.9	13.2	12.4
1989	11.2	11.5	12.8	12.0	12.4	15.8	10.1	9.2	12.0	11.9	13.9	12.8
	Germany			**Incorporated into Germany**								
1990	11.4	11.5	13.0				10.2	9.3	11.8	12.1	14.1	12.8
1991	10.4	11.4	11.4				10.0	9.3	12.8	12.3	14.0	11.8
1992	10.0	11.0	11.2				10.1	9.5	9.8	11.8	14.4	11.0
1993	9.8	11.1	11.0				9.8	9.4	12.0	11.4	14.6	10.6
1994	9.7	11.3	11.1				9.6	9.5	11.7	11.3	14.1	9.8
1995	9.4	10.8	12.0				9.7	9.6	11.5	11.0	14.2	10.7
1996	9.7	10.8	11.8				9.6	9.6	11.9	10.3	14.0	11.4
1997	9.9	10.5	11.4				9.7	9.5	10.6	9.9	13.7	11.5
1998	9.7	10.4	11.7				9.6	9.8	12.0	9.6	13.9	11.9

A6 Vital Statistics: Rates per 1,000 Population

1950–1998

	Ireland			Northern Ireland			Italy			Netherlands		
	B	D	M	B	D	M	B	D	M	B	D	M
1950	21.4	12.7	10.8	21.0	11.6	13.3	19.6₄₂	9.8₄₂	15.4₄₂	22.7	7.5	16.4
1951	21.2	14.3	10.8	20.7	12.8	13.7	18.4	10.3	14.0	22.3	7.6	17.6
1952	21.9	11.9	10.8	20.9	10.8	13.5	17.8	10.0	14.2	22.3	7.4	16.8₅₂
1953	21.2	11.8	10.8	20.9	10.7	13.6	17.5	9.9	14.2	21.7	7.7	16.4
1954	21.3	12.1	10.8	20.8	10.9	13.2	18.0	9.1	14.8	21.5	7.5	16.6
1955	21.0	12.6	11.2	20.8	11.1	13.7	17.7	9.1	15.0	21.3	7.6	16.6
1956	21.0	11.7	11.6	21.1	10.6	13.4	17.7	10.1	14.8	21.3	7.8	17.0
1957	21.2	11.9	10.2	21.5	10.9	13.4	17.7	9.7	14.6	21.2	7.5	17.0
1958	20.9	12.0	10.6	21.6	10.8	13.2	17.6	9.3	15.2	21.2	7.6₅₃	16.4
1959	21.1	12.0	10.8	21.9	10.9	13.7	18.1	9.1	15.4	21.4	7.6	15.6
1960	21.5	11.5	11.0	22.5	10.8	13.9	18.1	9.6	15.4	20.8	7.7	15.6
1961	21.2	12.3	10.8	22.4	11.3	13.8	18.4	9.3	15.8	21.3	7.6	17.0
1962	21.8	12.0	11.0	22.7	10.6	13.8	18.4	10.0	16.0	20.9	8.0	15.8
1963	22.2	11.9	11.0	23.1	11.0	14.0	18.6	10.0	16.4	20.9	8.0	16.0
1964	22.4	11.4	11.2	23.6	10.5	14.6	19.5	9.4	16.0	20.7	7.7	17.0
1965	22.1	11.5	11.8	23.1	10.6	14.2	18.8	9.8	15.2	19.9	8.0	17.6
1966	21.6	12.2	11.6	22.5	11.1	14.5	18.4	9.3	14.4	19.2	8.1	18.0
1967	21.1	10.8	12.2	22.4	9.8	14.7	17.7	9.5	14.2	18.9	7.9	18.2
1968	20.9	11.4	13.0	22.1	10.6	15.0	17.3	9.9	14.0	18.6	8.2	18.4
1969	21.5	11.5	14.0	21.4	10.8	15.3	17.5	10.0	14.2	19.2	8.4	18.2
1970	21.9	11.4	14.1	21.0	10.8	16.2	16.8	9.6	14.6	18.3	8.4	19.0
1971	22.7	10.7	14.8	20.7	10.5	15.8	16.8	9.7	15.0	17.2	8.4	18.6
1972	22.7	11.4	14.8	19.4	11.0	15.4	16.3	9.6	15.4	16.1	8.5	17.6
1973	22.4	11.1	14.9	18.9	11.4	14.4	15.9	10.0	15.2	14.5	8.2	16.0
1974	22.1	11.2	14.6	17.6	11.2	13.9	15.7	9.6	14.6	13.7	8.1	16.2
1975	21.2	10.4	13.4	17.0	10.7	14.2	14.8	9.9	13.4	13.0	8.3	14.8
1976	21.0	10.6	12.8	17.1	11.1	12.8	13.9	9.8	12.6	12.9	8.3	14.0
1977	21.1	10.3	12.2	16.5	11.1	12.6	13.1	9.7	12.4	12.5	7.9	13.4
1978	21.2	10.2	12.8	17.1	10.5	13.4	12.6	9.5	11.8	12.6	8.2	12.8
1979	21.5	9.7	12.4	18.3	10.9	13.2	11.8	9.5	11.4	12.5	8.0	12.2
1980	21.9	9.7	12.8	18.5	10.9	12.8	11.3	9.8	11.4	12.8	8.1	12.8
1981	21.0	9.6	12.0	17.8	10.6	12.3	11.0	9.7	11.2	12.5	8.1	12.0
1982	20.3	9.3	11.6	17.6	10.4	12.6	10.9	9.4	11.0	12.0	8.2	11.6
1983	19.1	9.4	11.2	17.7	10.4	12.8	10.6	9.9	10.6	11.9	8.2	11.0
1984	18.2	9.1	10.4	17.9	10.1	13.1	10.3	9.4	10.4	12.1	8.3	11.0
1985	17.6	9.4	10.6	17.7	10.2	13.3	10.1	9.6	10.4	12.3	8.5	11.4
1986	17.4	9.5	10.4	18.0	10.3	13.1	9.7	9.5	10.4	12.7	8.6	11.4
1987	16.6	8.8	10.2	17.7	9.7	13.2	9.6	9.3	10.6	12.7	8.3	12.0
1988	15.3	8.9	10.2	17.5	10.0	12.6	9.9	9.3	11.0	12.6	8.4	12.0
1989	14.8	9.1	10.4	16.5	10.0	12.7	9.7	9.1	10.8	12.7	8.7	12.2
1990	15.1	9.0	10.4	16.7	9.7	12.1	9.8	9.4	10.8	13.2	8.6	12.8
1991	14.9	8.9	9.8	16.5	9.5	11.7	9.9	9.8	11.0	13.2	8.6	12.6
1992	14.5	8.7	9.0	15.9	9.3	11.5	9.9	9.5	10.6	13.0	8.6	12.4
1993	13.9	9.0	8.8	15.3	9.6	10.6	9.4	9.5	9.6	12.8	9.0	11.6
1994	14.1	9.5	8.4	15.1	9.4	10.7	9.5	9.6	9.7	12.9	9.0	11.7
1995	13.5	9.0	9.0	14.9	9.6	11.8	9.7	9.8	10.1	12.3	8.8	12.1
1996	13.9	8.8	10.1	15.2	9.8	11.6	9.8	9.4	10.2	12.2	8.9	12.6
1997	14.3	8.6	9.6	15.4	9.6	11.9	9.6	9.5	10.3	12.3	8.7	12.1
1998	14.5	8.5	9.9	15.2	9.8	11.6	9.7	9.4	10.6	12.7	8.8	12.3

A6 Vital Statistics: Rates per 1,000 Population

1950–1998

	Norway			Poland			Portugal			Romania		
	B	D	M	B	D	M	B	D	M	B	D	M
1950	19.1	9.1	16.7	30.7	11.6	21.6	24.3	12.2	15.5	26.2	12.4	23.4
1951	18.4	8.4	16.5	31.0	12.4	21.4	24.6	12.5	15.8	25.1	12.8	20.6
1952	18.8	8.5	16.5	30.2	11.1	20.8	24.9	11.8	15.8	24.8	11.7	20.4
1953	18.8	8.5	16.1	29.7	10.2	20.0	23.7	11.4	15.8	23.8	11.6	20.8
1954	18.5	8.6	15.9	29.1	10.3	19.6	23.1	11.1	16.2	24.8	11.5	24.2
1955	18.5	8.5	15.3	29.1	9.6	19.0	24.4	11.6	17.0	25.6	9.7	22.8
1956	18.5	8.7	14.5	28.1	9.0	18.8	23.4	12.4	15.2	24.2	9.9	23.4
1957	18.1	8.8	14.0	27.6	9.5	18.2	24.4	11.7	16.5	22.9	10.2	22.8
1958	17.9	9.0	13.6	26.3	8.4	18.4	24.4	10.5	16.8	21.6	8.7	23.4
1959	17.7	8.9	13.1	24.7	8.6	19.0	24.3	11.1	17.3	20.2	10.2	21.4
1960	17.3	9.1	13.2	22.6	7.6	16.4	24.2	10.8	15.7	19.1	8.7	21.4
1961	17.3	9.2	13.4	20.9	7.6	15.8	24.5	11.2	17.5	17.5	8.7	19.4
1962	17.1	9.4	13.2	19.8	7.9	15.0	24.5	10.8	15.7	16.2	9.2	19.8
1963	17.3	10.1	13.1	19.2	7.5	14.4	23.5	10.8	15.7	15.7	8.3	18.6
1964	17.8	9.5	13.5	18.1	7.6	14.8	23.8	10.6	16.0	15.2	8.1	18.0
1965	17.8	9.5	13.0	17.4	7.4	12.6	22.9	10.3	16.3	14.6	8.6	17.2
1966	17.9	9.6	14.8	16.7	7.3	14.2	22.2	10.8	16.5	14.3	8.2	17.8
1967	17.6	9.6	15.4	16.3	7.8	15.0	21.5	10.2	16.8	27.4	9.3	16.0
1968	17.6	9.9	15.4	16.2	7.6	16.0	20.6	10.0	16.1	26.7	9.6	15.0
1969	17.6	10.1	15.4	16.3	8.1	16.6	20.9	11.1	17.4	23.3	10.1	14.0
1970	16.6	10.0	15.2	16.6	8.1	17.?	20.0	10.3	18.0	21.1	9.5	14.4
1971	16.8	10.0	15.2	17.2	8.7	17.8	20.2	11.0	18.6	19.5	9.5	14.6
1972	16.3	10.0	14.6	17.4	8.0	18.6	19.5	10.1	17.2	18.8	9.2	15.2
1973	15.5	10.1	14.2	17.9	8.3	18.8	19.2	10.6	19.8	18.2	9.8	16.4
1974	15.0	9.9	13.8	18.4	8.2	19.0	18.9	10.7	18.0	20.3	9.1	16.6
1975	14.1	9.9	13.0	18.9	8.7	19.4	19.1	10.4	21.8	19.7	9.3	17.8
1976	13.3	10.0	12.6	19.5	8.8	19.0	19.3	10.6	21.0	19.5	9.6	18.2
1977	12.6	9.8	11.8	19.1	9.0	18.8	18.6	9.9	18.8	19.6	9.6	18.4
1978	12.7	10.0	11.6	19.0	9.3	18.7	17.1	9.8	16.6	19.1	9.7	18.4
1979	12.7	10.2	11.4	19.5	9.2	18.1	16.3	9.4	16.2	18.6	9.9	18.0
1980	12.5	10.1	10.8	19.5	9.9	17.2	15.8	9.6	14.6	18.0	10.4	16.4
1981	12.4	10.2	10.8	18.9	9.2	18.0	15.1	9.7	15.2	17.0	10.0	16.4
1982	12.5	10.1	10.6	19.4	9.2	17.4	15.2	9.3	14.8	15.3	10.0	15.6
1983	12.1	10.2	10.0	19.7	9.5	16.7	14.4	9.6	15.0	14.3	10.4	14.6
1984	12.1	10.3	10.0	18.9	9.9	15.5	14.2	9.6	13.8	15.5	10.3	14.6
1985	12.3	10.7	9.8	18.2	10.3	14.3	12.8	9.6	13.4	15.8	10.9	14.2
1986	12.6	10.5	9.8	17.0	10.1	13.8	12.4	9.4	13.6	16.5	10.6	...
1987	12.9	10.7	10.0	16.1	10.1	13.4	12.0	9.3	13.2	16.7	11.1	14.6
1988	13.7	10.8	10.4	15.5	9.8	13.0	11.9	9.6	14.4	16.5	11.0	15.0
1989	14.0	10.7	9.8	14.8	10.0	13.4	12.0	9.7	14.8	16.0	10.7	15.4
1990	14.4	10.8	10.4	14.3	10.2	13.4	11.8	10.4	14.6	13.6	10.6	16.6
1991	14.3	10.5	9.4	14.3	10.6	12.2	11.8	10.6	14.6	11.9	10.9	15.8
1992	14.0	10.4	9.0	13.4	10.2	11.4	11.7	10.3	14.2	11.4	11.6	15.4
1993	13.8	10.8	9.0	12.8	10.2	10.8	11.5	10.8	13.8	11.0	11.6	14.1
1994	13.7	10.6	9.1	12.6	10.1	10.7	11.0	10.3	14.1	12.1	11.7	13.8
1995	13.8	10.4	9.6	11.2	10.0	10.2	10.8	10.5	14.4	10.4	12.0	13.9
1996	13.9	10.0	9.7	11.1	10.0	10.4	11.1	10.8	13.9	10.2	12.7	14.6
1997	13.6	10.1	9.4	10.7	9.8	10.5	11.4	10.6	13.7	10.5	12.4	14.7
1998	13.2	10.0	9.5	10.2	9.7	10.2	11.4	10.7	14.1	10.5	12.0	15.1

A6 Vital Statistics: Rates per 1,000 Population

1950-1998

	Russia			Spain			Sweden		
	B	D	M	B	D	M	B	D	M
1950	26.7	9.7	...	20.1	10.8	15.0	16.5	10.0	15.5
1951	27.0	9.7	...	20.0	11.5	14.9	15.6	9.9	15.3
1952	26.5	9.4	...	20.7	9.6	15.5	15.5	9.6	15.0
1953	25.1	9.1	...	20.4	9.6	15.2	15.4	9.7	14.8
1954	26.6	8.9	...	19.8	9.0	15.9	14.6	9.6	14.7
1955	25.7	8.2	...	20.4	9.3	16.2	14.8	9.5	14.4
1956	25.7	7.6	...	20.5	9.7	17.5	14.8	9.6	14.1
1957	25.4	7.8	...	21.6	9.8	17.0	14.6	9.9	14.3
1958	25.3	7.2	...	21.7	8.6	16.9	14.2	9.6	13.7
1959	25.0	7.6	24.4	21.5	8.8	16.2	14.1	9.5	13.5
1960	24.9	7.1	...	21.6	8.7	15.6	13.7	10.0	13.4
1961	23.8	7.2	22.0	21.1	8.4	15.5	13.9	9.8	13.9
1962	22.4	7.5	20.0	21.1	8.8	15.3	14.2	10.2	14.3
1963	21.2	7.2	18.2	21.3	8.9	15.2	14.9	10.1	14.1
1964	19.6	6.9	17.0	21.8	8.5	14.7	16.0	10.0	15.3
1965	18.4	7.3	17.4	20.9	8.4	14.3	15.9	10.1	15.5
1966	18.2	7.3	17.8	20.5	8.4	14.2	15.8	10.1	15.7
1967	17.3	7.6	18.0	20.6	8.4	14.3	15.4	10.1	14.4
1968	17.2	7.7	17.8	20.0	8.4	14.1	14.3	10.4	13.3
1969	17.0	8.1	18.8	19.8	8.9	14.4	13.5	10.5	12.2
1970	17.4	8.2	19.6	19.5	8.3	14.7	13.7	9.9	10.8
1971	17.8	8.2	20.0	19.5	8.9	14.9	14.1	10.2	9.8
1972	17.8	8.5	18.8	19.4	8.1	15.3	13.8	10.3	9.8
1973	17.6	8.7	20.2	19.2	8.5	15.5	13.5	10.5	9.4
1974	18.0	8.7	20.8	19.5	8.4	15.3	13.5	10.6	11.0
1975	18.1	9.3	21.4	18.8	8.4	15.3	12.6	10.8	10.8
1976	18.4	9.4	20.2	18.8	8.3	14.5	12.0	11.0	10.9
1977	18.1	9.6	21.4	18.1	8.1	14.4	11.6	10.7	9.8
1978	18.2	9.7	21.4	17.3	8.1	14.0	11.3	10.8	9.1
1979	18.2	10.1	21.8	16.2	7.9	13.3	11.6	11.0	9.0
1980	18.3	10.3	20.5	15.2	7.8	11.8	11.7	11.0	9.0
1981	18.5	10.2	20.8	14.1	7.8	10.7	11.3	11.1	9.1
1982	18.9	10.1	20.5	13.6	7.8	10.2	11.1	10.9	8.9
1983	19.8	10.4	20.8	12.7	7.9	10.3	11.0	10.9	8.7
1984	19.6	10.8	19.2	12.3	7.8	10.3	11.3	10.9	8.8
1985	19.4	10.6	19.6	11.8	8.1	10.3	11.8	11.3	9.2
1986	20.0	9.8	19.6	11.2	7.9	10.5	12.2	11.1	9.3
1987	19.8	9.9	19.6	10.8	8.0	10.8	12.5	11.1	9.8
1988	18.8	10.1	18.8	10.7	8.2	11.0	13.3	11.5	10.4
1989	...	10.7	19.0	...	8.4	...	13.7	10.8	25.6
1990	13.4[55]	11.2[55]	18.8	10.3	8.6	11.2	14.5	11.1	9.4
1991	12.1[55]	11.4[55]	17.2	10.1	8.7	11.2	14.4	11.0	8.6
1992	10.7[55]	12.2[55]	14.2	10.2	...	11.2	14.2	10.9	8.6
1993	9.3[55]	14.3[55]	15.0	9.9	8.7	10.4	13.5	11.1	7.8
1994	9.1[55]	13.1[55]	14.9	9.7	8.6	10.3	12.6	11.0	8.1
1995	9.2[55]	14.9[55]	15.0	9.3	8.8	10.1	11.7	11.0	8.0
1996	8.8[55]	14.1[55]	14.7	9.2	8.9	10.6	10.8	10.6	7.9
1997	8.6[55]	13.7[55]	14.5	9.4	8.9	10.7	10.2	10.5	8.3
1998	8.8[55]	13.6[55]	14.1	9.3	8.9	10.8	10.0	10.5	8.5

A6 Vital Statistics: Rates per 1,000 Population

1950–1998

	Switzerland			United Kingdom England and Wales			United Kingdom: Scotland			Yugoslavia		
	B	D	M	B	D	M	B	D	M	B	D	M
1950	18.1	10.1	15.8	15.8	11.6	16.3	18.1	12.5	15.8	30.2	13.0	22.8
1951	17.2	10.5	15.8	15.5	12.5	16.5	17.8	12.9	16.2	27.0	14.1	20.6
1952	17.4	9.9	15.6	15.3	11.3	15.9	17.7	12.1	16.1	29.7	11.8	21.0
1953	17.0	10.2	15.4	15.5	11.4	15.6	17.8	11.5	16.0	28.4	12.4	19.6
1954	17.0	10.0	15.6	15.2	11.3	15.4	18.1	12.0	16.4	28.6	10.9	19.8
1955	17.1	10.1	16.0	15.0	11.7	16.1	18.1	12.1	16.9	26.9	11.4	18.6
1956	17.4	10.2	16.0	15.7	11.7	15.8	18.6	12.1	17.2	26.0	11.2	17.6
1957	17.7	10.0	16.2	16.1	11.5	15.4	19.1	11.9	16.7	23.9	10.7	17.4
1958	17.6	9.5	15.4	16.4	11.7	15.1	19.4	12.1	16.0	24.0	9.3	18.8
1959	17.7	9.5	15.2	16.5	11.6	15.0	19.2	12.2	15.7	23.4	9.9	18.0
1960	17.6	9.7	15.6	17.1	11.5	15.0	19.6	11.9	15.5	23.5	9.9	18.2
1961	18.3	9.5	15.6	17.6	11.9	15.0	19.5	12.3	15.7	22.7	9.0	18.2
1962	18.7	9.9	16.0	18.0	11.9	14.9	20.1	12.2	15.5	21.9	9.9	17.2
1963	19.3	10.1	15.4	18.2	12.2	14.9	19.7	12.6	15.2	21.4	8.9	16.6
1964	19.5	9.3	15.2	18.5	11.3	15.2	20.0	11.7	15.5	20.8	9.4	17.4
1965	19.1	9.5	15.4	18.1	11.6	15.6	19.3	12.1	15.5	21.0	8.8	18.0
1966	18.5	9.4	15.0	17.8	11.8	16.1	18.6	12.2	16.1	20.4	8.1	17.2
1967	17.9	9.2	15.2	17.3	11.4	16.0	18.5	11.4	16.2	19.6	8.8	17.0
1968	17.3	9.5	15.0	16.9	11.8	16.9	18.2	12.2	16.8	19.1	8.7	17.0
1969	16.7	9.5	15.2	16.4	12.0	16.3	17.3	12.3	16.6	18.9	9.3	17.2
1970	16.0	9.2	15.2	16.0	11.8	17.0	16.8	12.2	16.6	17.8	8.9	18.0
1971	15.5	9.3	14.4	15.9	11.5	16.5	16.6	11.8	16.3	18.3	8.7	17.8
1972	14.3	8.8	13.6	14.7	12.0	17.3	15.1	12.5	16.2	18.3	9.2	18.0
1973	13.6	8.9	12.6	13.7	11.9	16.2	14.3	12.4	16.1	18.1	8.6	17.6
1974	13.1	8.8	12.0	12.9	11.8	15.5	13.4	12.4	15.8	18.1	8.4	17.2
1975	12.2	8.7	11.0	12.2	11.7	15.4	13.1	12.1	15.1	18.2	8.7	16.8
1976	11.7	9.0	10.2	11.8	12.1	14.5	12.4	12.5	14.4	18.2	8.5	16.2
1977	11.5	8.8	10.4	11.5	11.6	14.4	11.9	11.9	14.4	17.7	8.4	16.4
1978	11.3	9.1	10.2	12.1	11.9	14.9	12.3	12.5	14.6	17.4	8.7	16.2
1979	11.3	9.0	10.8	12.9	12.0	14.9	13.1	12.6	14.7	17.1	8.6	16.0
1980	11.7	9.3	11.2	13.2	11.7	14.9	13.3	12.2	14.9	17.1	8.8	15.4
1981	11.6	9.3	11.2	12.8	11.6	14.2	13.3	12.3	14.1	16.4	9.0	15.4
1982	11.7	9.2	11.6	12.6	11.7	13.8	12.8	12.6	13.5	16.7	9.0	15.2
1983	11.5	9.3	11.8	12.7	11.7	13.9	12.6	12.3	13.6	16.4	9.6	15.0
1984	11.6	9.1	12.0	12.8	11.4	14.0	12.7	12.4	14.1	16.4	9.4	14.6
1985	11.5	9.2	12.0	13.1	11.8	13.9	13.0	12.5	14.2	15.9	9.2	14.2
1986	11.7	9.2	12.4	13.2	11.6	13.9	12.9	12.4	14.0	15.5	9.2	13.8
1987	11.7	9.1	13.2	13.6	11.3	14.0	13.0	12.1	14.0	15.3	9.2	14.0
1988	12.2	9.2	13.8	13.8	11.3	13.9	13.0	12.2	14.0	15.0	9.0	13.6
1989	12.2	9.2	13.6	13.6	11.4	13.7	12.5	12.1	13.9	14.2	9.3	13.4
1990	12.5	9.5	13.8	13.9	11.1	13.1	12.9	12.0	13.6	14.1	9.8	12.6
1991	12.7	9.2	14.0	13.7	11.1	12.0	13.1	12.0	13.2	...[56]	9.8[56]	11.8
1992	12.6	9.1	13.2	13.4	10.8	12.2	12.9	11.9	13.7	13.6[56]	10.0[56]	12.0
1993	12.1	9.0	12.4	12.1	11.2	11.6	12.4	12.5	13.0	13.4[56]	10.0[56]	11.6
1994	12.4	9.0	12.5	12.8	11.4	11.9	12.5	12.4	13.5	13.5	10.1	11.7
1995	11.7	9.0	12.7	12.5	10.9	12.4	12.1	12.6	13.7	13.1	10.2	11.6
1996	11.7	8.9	13.1	12.5	10.9	12.7	12.7	11.9	13.5	13.3	10.2	11.4
1997	11.2	8.5	12.8	12.3	10.7	12.1	13.1	11.8	13.4	13.0	10.6	11.3
1998	11.1	8.8	12.7	12.1	10.6	11.8	13.2	11.9	13.9	12.4	10.6	12.0

A6 Vital Statistics: Rates per 1,000 Population

NOTES

1. SOURCES:- The main sources are the official publications noted on p. xv and the United Nations, *Demographic Yearbook*, Albania to 1939—League of Nations, *Statistical Yearbook*; Russia to 1913—A.F. Rashin, *Naselenie Rossii za 100 let* (Moscow, 1956) the U.S.S.R. for the interwar period F. Lorimer, *The Population of the Soviet Union* (Geneva, 1946); and Serbia 1911–2-*Annuaire Internationale de Statistique* (The Hague, 1916).
2. In principle birth rates refer to live births and death rates do not include stillbirths.

FOOTNOTES

[1] Earlier, slightly less reliable data, are as follows:-

| | Norway | | Sweden | | | Norway | | Sweden | |
	Births	Deaths	Births	Deaths		Births	Deaths	Births	Deaths
1735	29.4	19.3	...	...	1742	26.3	69.3	31.5	39.0
1736	30.7	20.9	29.8	27.0	1743	28.5	29.2	30.1	43.7
1737	30.5	24.8	30.5	33.7	1744	30.1	22.1	35.1	25.3
1738	28.1	23.2	33.6	30.5	1745	32.8	18.8	36.9	23.3
1739	30.9	23.2	36.4	30.6	1746	28.2	21.2	34.8	26.4
1740	29.6	26.1	32.0	35.5	1747	33.0	23.9	34.6	27.5
1741	27.1	36.9	31.9	32.2	1748	32.9	33.1	33.5	26.0

[2] Cisleithania (excluding Lombardy and Venetia) to 1913. The present territory of the Republic subsequently.

[3] Parts of Limburg and Luxembourg were ceded to the Netherlands.

[4] Excluding the Duchies of Schleswig, Holstein, and Lauenburg.

[5] Of the territorial changes affecting Finland in 1809, 1811, and 1820 (referred to on p. viii) only the inclusion of Viipuri province in 1811 can have affected vital rates at all.

[6] Figures to 1916 apply to the German Empire as it was in 1913. This means that Alsace-Lorraine and Schleswig-Holstein are included throughout. Alsace-Lorraine is excluded from 1917. Other territorial changes are referred to in subsequent footnotes.

[7] The Grand Duchy of Luxembourg is excluded throughout.

[8] These figures are known to be underestimates. It is also known that registration was incomplete until the 1860's.

[9] Previously the figures apply to the civil population only.

[10] Figures from 1888 include Eastern Roumelia.

[11] Figures from 1861 include Savoy and Nice.

[12] Figures from 1871 to 1913 exclude the parts of Alsace and Lorraine ceded to Germany.

[13] The statistics for the period up to 1890 are known to be incomplete.

[14] Figures from 1882 include Thessaly and Arta.

[15] The Ancient Kingdom (excluding Croatia-Slavonia) up to 1918 (1st line). Subsequently the territory established by the treaty of Trianon and later adjusted. For statistics for Croatia-Slavonia see footnote 48.

[16] Figures from 1891 include Fiume.

[17] Venetia and the Papal States are included prior to their incorporation.

[18] Including the Azores and Maderia.

[19] The statistics for the period to 1878 are known to be incomplete.

[20] Figures from 1879 include northern Dobrudja but exclude southern Bessarabia.

[21] Figures to 1913 (1st line) apply to the 50 provinces of European Russia (excluding Finland, Poland and the Caucasus). The 2nd line for 1913 relates to the U.S.S.R. as constituted in 1924. The figures for 1920–22 relate to 20 European provinces, and those for 1923–27 to the European part of the U.S.S.R. Figures from 1928 apply to the U.S.S.R. as constituted at the time. The statistics for 1935–36 are estimates (see source).

[22] Figures from 1879 include Vranje, Nis, Pirot, and Toplica, acquired from Turkey.

[23] Including the Canary Islands.

[24] Figures from 1925 include Eupen, Malmédy, etc., acquired from Germany.

[25] 41 communes were excluded in these years. In addition, in 1940 the statistics for Tournai and Wavre are missing.

[26] Figures from 1941 include southern Dobrudja.

[27] Includes deaths in the armed forces stationed abroad.

[28] Figures from 1939 exclude Sub-Carpathian Russia (Ruthenia), and those from 1945 exclude 12 villages in Slovakia ceded to the U.S.S.R.

[29] Figures from 1948 include the Bratislava Bridgehead.

[30] Estimates were made for the departments affected by war. Military losses are excluded.

[31] Military losses are excluded.

[32] Figures from 1919 exclude territory ceded to Czechoslovakia, Denmark, and Poland (except in Silesia).

[33] Figures from 1922 exclude Eupen, Malmédy, etc., and part of Upper Silesia ceded to Poland.

[34] Rates for the same area in 1938 are as follows:- births: 19.5; deaths: 11.4; marriages 19.0.

[35] These statistics are less reliable than the remainder since 1920.

[36] Figures from 1949 include the Dodecanese Islands.

[37] Excludes deaths among the armed forces, but the rates were calculated on the basis of the population including the armed forces.

[38] Subsequently excludes the Bratislava Bridgehead, ceded to Czechoslovakia in 1947.

[39] Includes estimates for areas affected by the war.

[40] Figures from 1920 include territory acquired from Austria-Hungary.

[41] Deaths in the war zone and of military personnel abroad are not included.

A6   Vital Statistics: Rates per 1,000 Population

[42] Figures from 1943 are for the territory established after the Second World War, except that Trieste is not included until 1951.

[43] Up to 1917 children born alive but dying before registration were included in neither births nor deaths. Subsequently they were included in both.

[44] Deaths outside the country are normally included if registered within 1 year, but in these years deaths of deportees were excluded. Deaths among alien armed forces were also excluded.

[45] Boundaries of the day.

[46] From 1919 to 1939 the statistics apply to the territory established by the treaty of Trianon. In the following six years there were several boundary changes, but only two of them, made in 1940, were permanent, namely the cession of southern Dobrudja to Bulgaria, and of Bessarabia and northern Bukovina to the U.S.S.R. The figures for 1919 appear to be defective.

[47] Excluding northern Transylvania, temporarily ceded to Hungary, and Bessarabia and northern Bukovina (except when reconquered in 1943), ceded to the U.S.S.R. Statistics from 1946 are for present boundaries.

[48] Pre-First World War statistics for Croatia-Slavonia are as follows:-

	Births	Deaths	Marriages		Births	Deaths	Marriages
1881	42.9	31.1	21.6	1898	39.8	29.1	18.6
1882	43.4	31.2	22.4	1899	42.0	27.9	19.4
1883	45.3	33.3	22.8	1900	40.7	27.5	17.6
1884	46.0	32.7	23.0	1901	39.2	27.4	18.0
1885	46.1	30.1	22.4	1902	41.5	27.6	18.2
1886	47.4	28.5	20.2	1903	39.3	26.9	17.6
1887	45.5	30.1	18.0	1904	40.0	26.2	20.4
1888	44.8	30.8	18.6	1905	40.1	30.1	18.4
1889	46.0	30.5	16.8	1906	39.7	26.3	18.2
1890	39.6	33.0	17.2	1907	39.3	25.4	18.2
1891	43.0	32.9	17.6	1908	39.2	27.2	18.0
1892	41.2	39.5	19.2	1909	41.7	26.7	16.4
1893	42.6	33.7	19.8	1910	37.9	24.8	16.2
1894	43.0	32.6	20.2	1911	36.0	26.4	16.8
1895	43.8	30.9	17.0	1912	38.1	25.2	16.0
1896	41.6	32.5	18.0	1913	35.7	25.5	17.2
1897	41.8	32.6	17.4	1914	36.6	24.7	13.0

[49] Figures from 1947 include territory acquired from Italy.

[50] Figures from 1953 exclude unviable infants who die within 24 hours of birth.

[51] Statistics up to 1955 apply to the year of registration. Subsequently they apply to the year of birth, death, or marriage.

[52] The previous practice of including marriages abroad, if registered within 1 year, was subsequently discontinued.

[53] Up to 1958 deaths in refugee camps for Amboynese are excluded.

[54] Czech Republic. Figures for Slovakia are:

	B	D	M
1992	14.1	10.1	12.8
1993	13.7	9.9	11.6

[55] Russian Federation. Figures for ex-USSR are:

	Armenia			Azerbaijan			Belarus			Estonia			Georgia			Kazakhstan			Kyrgistan		
	B	D	M	B	D	M	B	D	M	B	D	M	B	D	M	B	D	M	B	D	M
1991	19.3	6.5	15.6	...	...	...	12.9	10.5	18.4	12.3	12.6	13.2	...	...	...	21.1	8.0	19.8	29.1	6.9	21.0
1992	19.1	7.0	12.4	...	...	...	12.4	10.3	15.4	11.7	13.0	11.4	...	...	...	20.0	8.1	17.4	28.6	7.2	18.2
1993	15.8	7.4	11.6	22.5	7.4	...	11.3	10.6	15.8	10.0	14.0	10.2	15.9	8.9	...	18.7	9.2	17.2	...	...	...

	Latvia			Lithuania		
	B	D	M	B	D	M
1991	13.0	13.1	16.8	15.0	11.0	19.4
1992	12.0	13.5	14.4	14.3	11.1	16.0
1993	10.3	15.2	11.2	12.5	12.4	12.8

	Moldova			Tajikistan			Turmenistan			Ukraine			Uzbekistan		
	B	D	M	B	D	M	B	D	M	B	D	M	B	D	M
1991	16.5	10.5	18.2	...	...	...	...	...	...	12.1	12.9	19.0	...	...	...
1992	16.0	10.2	18.0	...	...	...	...	...	...	11.4	13.4	...	33.3	6.5	22.0
1993	...	...	...	32.5	8.6	...	31.9	7.6	...	10.7	14.2	16.4	...	...	...

A6   Vital Statistics: Rates per 1,000 Population

[56]   Yugoslovia (Montenegro + Serbia). Ex-Yugoslovia are:

	Bosnia-Hercegovina			Croatia			Macedonia			Slovenia		
	B	D	M	B	D	M	B	D	M	B	D	M
1991	...	...	...	10.8	11.5	9.0	17.1	7.3	15.0	10.1	9.7	8.2
1992	...	...	...	9.8	10.8	9.2	16.2	7.8	15.0	10.2	9.7	9.2
1993	13.4	7.0	...	10.2	10.6	9.6	15.4	7.3	14.2	9.9	9.6	7.6

A7   DEATHS OF INFANTS UNDER ONE YEAR OLD PER 1,000 LIVE BIRTHS

1751-1799   1800-1849

Year	Sweden
1751	186
1752	222
1753	190
1754	206
1755	225
1756	220
1757	221
1758	209
1759	190
1760	179
1761	209
1762	239
1763	240
1764	207
1765	212
1766	209
1767	199
1768	220
1769	217
1770	209
1771	211
1772	239
1773	286
1774	167
1775	185
1776	174
1777	195
1778	211
1779	215
1780	164
1781	192
1782	188
1783	202
1784	195
1785	193
1786	202
1787	187
1788	207
1789	224
1790	209
1791	187
1792	193
1793	200
1794	181
1795	202
1796	193
1797	196
1798	184
1799	191

Year	Austria	Belgium	Denmark	France	Germany[3]	N'lands	Norway	Sweden	UK E & W
1800	...	...	...	...	...	...	...	240	...
1801	...	...	...	...	...	...	...	204	...
1802	...	...	...	...	...	...	...	182	...
1803	...	...	...	...	...	...	...	184	...
1804	...	...	...	...	...	...	...	185	...
1805	...	...	...	...	...	...	...	176	...
1806	190	...	...	...	...	...	...	230	...
1807	200	...	...	...	...	...	...	188	...
1808	194	...	...	...	...	...	...	220	...
1809	184	...	...	...	...	...	...	232	...
1810	186	...	...	...	...	...	...	193	...
1811	189	...	...	...	...	...	...	194	...
1812	182	...	...	...	...	...	...	204	...
1813	186	...	...	...	...	...	...	198	...
1814	201	...	...	...	...	...	...	195	...
1815	188	...	...	...	...	...	...	170	...
1816	178	...	...	...	...	...	...	184	...
1817	180	...	...	...	...	...	...	179	...
1818	181	...	...	...	...	...	...	169	...
1819	189	...	...	...	...	...	...	183	...
1820	184	...	...	...	...	...	...	163	...
1821	185	...	...	...	...	...	...	176	...
1822	198	...	...	...	...	...	...	162	...
1823	183	...	...	...	...	...	...	148	...
1824	192	...	...	...	...	...	...	156	...
1825	197	...	...	...	...	...	...	154	...
1826	195	...	...	...	...	...	...	172	...
1827	181	...	...	...	...	...	...	161	...
1828	188	...	...	...	...	...	...	170	...
1829	175	...	...	...	...	...	...	194	...
1830	237	...	...	182	...	...	...	181	...
1831	269	...	...	175	...	...	...	198	...
1832	243	...	...	182	...	...	...	166	...
1833	260	...	...	175	...	...	...	159	...
1834	271	192	...	209	...	...	...	174	...
1835	248	167	152	175	...	...	...	143	...
1836	236	173	162	168	292	...	134	153	...
1837	253	185	142	169	302	...	135	195	...
1838	240	190[2]	127	170	297	...	135	176	...
1839	255	185	147	160	285	...	158	164	151
1840	244	182	141	162	299	164	139	146	154
1841	251	152	142	158	300	171	115	159	145
1842	245	160	142	167	318	198	123	162	152
1843	259	149	129	157	287	169	118	159	150
1844	230	138	131	154	287	164	117	141	148
1845	247	145	139	144	289	168	118	149	142
1846	251	184	171	171	318	230	118	163	164
1847	...	156	153	159	286	208	120	173	164
1848	...	141	145	160	312	182	121	141	153
1849	243	147	145	173	285	169	99	142	160

See pp. 127-8 for footnotes

Abbreviations used where space demands:- Czech: Czechoslovakia; Den: Denmark; Ger: Germany; Gr: Greece; N'lands: Netherlands; Pol: Poland; Port: Portugal; Switz: Switzerland; UK: E & W: United Kingdom: England and Wales; UK: Scotland: United Kingdom: Scotland; Yug: Yugoslavia

A7 Deaths of Infants Under One Year Old per 1,000 Live Births

1850–1899

	Austria	Belgium	Bulgaria	Denmark	Finland	France	Germany	Hungary[10]	Ireland	Italy
1850	251	141	...	127	...	146	297[3]	...	...	...
1851	242	148	...	135	...	163	287	...	...	...
1852	242	147	...	137	...	162	298	229	...	...
1853	227	145	...	153	...	149	285	263	...	...
1854	273	149	...	121	...	179	291	264	...	...
1855	278[1]	161	...	126	...	175	285	268[11]	...	...
1856	241	148	...	122	...	170	253	245	...	...
1857	239	168	...	148	...	185	307	255	...	...
1858	250	164	...	142	...	177	289	246	...	...
1859	254	165	...	133	...	215	324	249	...	...
1860	237	139	...	136	...	150[5]	260	...	...	...
1861	264	164	...	126	...	190	...[8]	...	...	...
1862	250	150	...	131	...	163	...[8]	...	...	...
1863	259	157	...	125	...	180	298	...	...	232
1864	250	165	...	155	...	173	297	256	98	233
1865	270	189	...	145	...	191	332	224	98	229
1866	278	164	...	126	218	162	301	...	94	214
1867	253	128	...	134	223	171	312	...	97	223
1868	248	142	...	145	392	191	307	...	95	238
1869	242	130	...	125	141	177	293	...	93	215
1870	253	145	...	131	137	201[6]	298[3]	...	95	230
1871	255	173	...	129	141	228	330	...	91	227
1872	270	145	...	131	173	159	301	...	97	223
1873	290	142	...	126	184	178	307	...	96	214
1874	260	137	...	145	181	159	297[3]	...	94	224
1875	243	158	...	154	171	170	242[9]	...	95	215
1876	247	139	...	144	163	166	228	...	94	203
1877	258	131	...	130	161	157	225	...	92	208
1878	252	161	...	138	190	169	226	...	97	205
1879	240	159	...	131	138	158	218	...	101	207
1880	250	187	...	151	167	179	240	...	112	225
1881	250	155	...	121	186	166	224	...	91	192
1882	256	151	...	151	164	165	228	...	95	206
1883	253	154	...	138	149	165	232	...	98	198
1884	247	168	...	137	148	177	235	...	92	186
1885	255	150	...	128	162	161	226	...	95	194
1886	250	178	...	136	157	173	235	...	94	200
1887	244	137	...	131	132	160	217	...	95	193
1888	249	165	...	139	144	164	218	...	97	200
1889	236	160	...	141	142	155	226	...	94	184
1890	259	166	...	133	142	174	226	...	95	198
1891	243	162	...[4]	134	145	162	219	259	95	184
1892	259	169	144	140	169	181	230	275	105	186
1893	232	165	147	149	143	174	224	240	102	179
1894	251	152	142	134	140	157	219	247	102	186
1895	241	172	144	137	129	177	230	242	104	188
1896	230	142	134	126	143	149	208	226	95	177
1897	228	149	147	129	133	152	222	223	109	164
1898	224	160	143	123	128	168	210	226	110	171
1899	219	167	158	154	137	163	216	209	108	155

See pp. 127–8 for footnotes

A7 Deaths of Infants Under One Year Old per 1,000 Live Births

1850–1899

	Netherlands	Norway	Romania	Russia[12]	Serbia	Spain	Sweden	Switzerland	UK E & W	UK Scotland
1850	169	102	...	...	...	...	146	...	162	...
1851	179	108	...	...	...	...	152	...	153	...
1852	201	119	...	...	...	...	163	...	158	...
1853	187	103	...	...	...	...	161	...	159	...
1854	183	97	...	...	...	...	126	...	157	...
1855	199	103	...	...	...	...	145	...	153	125
1856	179	97	...	...	...	...	145	...	143	118
1857	212	100	...	...	...	...	165	...	156	118
1858	212	102	...	...	...	175	143	...	151	121
1859	227	104	...	...	...	191	143	...	153	108
1860	192	102	...	...	...	174	124	...	148	127
1861	196	113	...	...	...	168	137	...	153	111
1862	193	110	...	...	...	175	139	...	142	117
1863	184	106	...	...	...	190	133	...	149	120
1864	191	101	245	...	...	200	137	...	153	126
1865	220	103	219	...	...	201	135	...	160	125
1866	190	108	239	...	...	185	127	...	160	122
1867	197	122	194	243	...	188	140	...	153	119
1868	223	126	203	299	...	212	168	...	155	118
1869	192	111	193	275	...	196	146	...	156	129
1870	211	101	159	248	...	203	132	...	160	123
1871	227	99	144	274	...	...	114	222	158	130
1872	213	103	198	295	...	...	128	183	150	124
1873	206	106	191	262	...	...	129	200	149	125
1874	191	113	214	262	...	...	147	189	151	125
1875	220	115	203	266	...	...	149	197	158	132
1876	201	108	196	278	...	...	140	197	146	121
1877	188	107	190	260	...	...	126	191	136	115
1878	197	103	224	300	...	196	134	191	152	123
1879	182	92	185	252	...	191	111	181	135	108
1880	218	95	230	286	...	190	121	180	153	125
1881	182	97	177	252	...	189	113	187	130	113
1882	174	111	199	301	...	192	125	172	141	118
1883	187	97	175	284	...	204	116	164	137	119
1884	194	96	178	254	...	186	113	161	147	118
1885	169	93	170	270	...	192	114	173	138	121
1886	192	91	183	248	...	175	111	164	149	116
1887	163	88	193	256	...	199	103	162	145	122
1888	173	97	199	250	140	184	100	153	136	113
1889	176	110	191	275	155	...	107	159	144	121
1890	171	97	211	292	145	...	103	157	151	131
1891	169	97	209	272	167	...	108	163	149	128
1892	174	104	243	307	196	...	109	150	148	117
1893	164	89	217	252	175	...	101	152	159	136
1894	152	104	227	265	163	...	101	153	137	117
1895	167	96	201	279	158	...	95	159	161	133
1896	148	97	230	274	167	...	103	132	148	115
1897	148	96	215	260	167	...	99	141	156	138
1898	156	89	222	279	161	...	91	155	160	134
1899	149	107	198	240	152	...	112	136	163	131

See pp. 127–8 for footnotes

A7 Deaths of Infants Under One Year Old per 1,000 Live Births

1900–1949

	Austria	Belgium	Bulgaria	Czech	Den	Finland	France	Germany	East Germany	Gr	Hungary	Ireland	Nthrn Ireland
1900	231	172	132		128	153	160	229[19]		...	223	109	
1901	209	143	143		136	145	143	207		...	207	101	
1902	216	144	143		114	129	135	183		...	219	100	
1903	215	155	154		114	127	136	204		...	204	96	
1904	210	152	142		113	120	144	196		...	197	100	
1905	231	147	160		120	135	135	205		...	232	95	
1906	202	154	154		111	119	144	185		...	207	93	
1907	209	133	154		108	112	130	176		...	212	92	
1908	199	148	169		124	125	128	178		...	201	97	
1909	209	138	171		99	111	117	170		...	214	92	
1910	189	135	159		101	118	111	162		...	195	95	
1911	207	167	156		105	114	155	192		...	208	94	
1912	181	120	133		94	109	105	147		...	186	86	
1913	190[1]	130	...		92	113	112[6]	151		...	201	97	
1914	172	130[13]	...		99	104	111[17]	164		...	197	87	
1915	218	125	...		93	115	123[17]	148		...	264	92	
1916	192	116	...		101	110	117[17]	140[20]		...	219	83	
1917	186	140	...		99	118	129[17]	149		...	216	88	
1918	193	134[13]	146	...	76	116	146[17]	158[21]		...	217[10]	86	
1919	156	99	110	142	91	134	125[18]	145		...	164	88	
1920	...	110	146	178	91	96	123	131		...	196	83	
1921	...	122	183	173	77	95	121	134[22]		68	193	...	...
1922	156	114	155	166	82	99	90	130		82	198	69	77
1923	142	100	165	145	85	92	102	131		92	184	66	77
1924	128	95	150	148	84	107	90	108[23]		98	193	72	85
1925	119	100[14]	152	145	80	85	95	105		90	168	68	86
1926	123	104	127	154	84	86	102	102		75	167	74	85
1927	125	98	168	157	84	97	88	97		100	185	71	78
1928	120	94	149	146	81	84	97	89		94	177	68	78
1929	113	110	156	142	83	98	100	97		111	179	70	86
1930	104	100	138	137	82	75	84	85		99	153	68	68
1931	103	89	156	134	81	75	80	83		134	162	69	73
1932	106	94	150	137	72	71	82	79		123	184	72	83
1933	94	92	146	127	68	76	78	77		123	136	65	80
1934	92	82	131	128	64	73	74	66		112	148	63	70
1935	99	85	154	123	71	67	72	99		113	152	68	86
1936	93	86	144	124	67	66	72	66		114	139	74	77
1937	92	83	150	122	66	69	70	64		122	133	73	78
1938	80	81	144	121[15]	59	68	70	60		99	131	67	75
1939	73	82	139	98	58	70	68	72		118	121	66	71
1940	74	93[13]	136	99	50	88	91[17]	64		98	130	66	86
1941	70	92[13]	125	100	55	59	75[17]	...		...	116	74	77
1942	74	84[13]	131	111	47	67	77[17]	...		...	133	69	76
1943	79	75[13]	130	109	45	50	81[17]	...		...	116	83	78
1944	88	83	121	109[15]	48	69	82[17]	...		...	...	79	67
1945	162	100	145	137	48	63	114[17]	...[3]	...	...	169	71	68
1946	81	75	125	109	46	56	78	97	131	...	117	65	54
1947	78	69	130	89[16]	40	59	71	86	114	...	103[25]	68	53
1948	76	59	118	84	35	52	56	69	89	...[24]	94	50	46
1949	75	57	116	83	34	48	60	60	78	42	91	53	45

See pp. 127–8 for footnotes

A7   Deaths of Infants Under One Year Old per 1,000 Live Births

1900–1949

	Italy	N'lands	Norway	Pol[29]	Port[30]	Romania	Russia[12]	Serbia	Spain[32]	Sweden	Switz	UK E & W	UK Scotland	Yug [30] [33]
1900	174	155	91	...	...	197	252	150	204	99	150	154	128	...
1901	166	149	91	...	...	202	272	145	185	103	137	151	129	...
1902	172	130	74	...	...	212	258	151	180	86	132	133	113	...
1903	172	135	78	...	...	294	250	151	162	93	133	132	118	...
1904	161	137	75	...	...	...	232	135	173	84	140	145	123	...
1905	166	131	82	...	...	...	272	163	161	88	129	128	116	...
1906	161	127	69	...	...	...	248	143	174	81	127	132	115	...
1907	150	112	66	...	...	...	225	147	158	77	121	118	110	...
1908	150[27]	125	75	...	...	...	244	158	160	85	108	120	121	...
1909	157	99	70	...	...	...	248	181	154	72	115	109	108	...
1910	140	108	67	...	134	...	271	139	149	75	105	105	108	...
1911	157	137	65	...	...	...	237	...	162	72	123	130	112	...
1912	128	87	67	...	...	216	...	...	138	71	94	95	105	...
1913	138	91	64	...	160	233	...	...	155	70	96	108	110	...
1914	130	95	68	...	148	217	...	...	152	73	93	105	111	...
1915	148[26]	87	67	...	148	199	...		152	76	90	110	126	...
1916	166	85	64	...	154	...	...		147	70	78	91	97	...
1917	159	87	64	...	148	...	...		155	65	79	96	107	...
1918	196	103	63	...	209	...	...		183	65	88	97	100	...
1919	129[27]	93	62	...	182		...[31]		156	70	82	89	102	...
1920	127	83	58	...	164	221	...		114	63	84	80	92	...
1921	131	85	54	187	148	200	...		147	64	74	83	90	...
1922	128	77	55	167	144	207	...		142	63	70	77	101	...
1923	129	66	50	...	164	207	...		148	56	61	69	80	...
1924	126	61	50	...	144	201	...		140	60	62	75	98	...
1925	119	58	50	...	132	192	198		137	56	58	75	91	143
1926	127	61	48	...	144	194	172		128	56	57	70	83	143
1927	120	59	51	151	142	209	190		127	60	57	70	89	163
1928	120	52	49	145	...	184	155		126	59	54	65	86	150
1929	125	59	54	149	151	197	...		123	59	52	74	87	147
1930	106	51	46	143	144	176	...		117	55	51	60	83	153
1931	113	49	46	142	141	180	...		117	57	49	66	82	165
1932	110	46	47	144	147	185	...		112	51	51	64	86	167
1933	100	43	48	128	149	174	...		112	50	48	63	81	140
1934	99	43	39	141	144	182	...		113	47	46	59	78	150
1935	101	40	44	127	149	192	...		109	46	48	57	77	149
1936	100	39	42	141	140	175	...		109	43	47	59	82	137
1937	109	38	42	136	151	178	...		130	45	47	58	80	141
1938	106	37	37	140	137	183	...		120	43	43	53	70	140
1939	97	34	37	...	120	176[31]	...		135	40	43	51	69	132
1940	103	39	39	...	126	188	...		109	39	46	57	78	...
1941	115	44	43	...	151	166	...		143	37	41	60	83	...
1942	112[28]	40	36	...	131	178[31]	...		103	29	38	51	69	...
1943	115	40	35	...	133	184	...		99	29	40	49	65	...
1944	103	46	37	...	122	162	...		93	31	42	45	65	...
1945	103	80	36	...	115	188[31]	...		85	30	41	46	56	...
1946	87	39	35	...	119	164	...		87	27	39	43	54	...
1947	84	34	35	...	107	200	...		71	25	39	41	56	...
1948	72	29	30	111	100	143	...		64	23	36	34	45	...
1949	74	27	28	107	115	136	...		69	23	34	32	41	102

See pp. 127–8 for footnotes

A7   Deaths of Infants Under One Year Old per 1,000 Live Births

1950–1998

	Albania	Austria	Belgium	Bulgaria	Czech	Den	Finland	France	West Ger	East Ger	Gr	Hungary	Ireland	Nthrn Ireland
1950	...	66	53	95	78	31	44	52	55	72	35	86	46	41
1951	124	61	50	108	73	29	35	50	53	64	44	84	46	41
1952	100	52	45	98	56_{34}	29	32	45	48	59	48	70	41	39
1953	100	50	42	81	45	27	34	42	47	54	45	71	39	38
1954	98	48	41	86	38	27	31	41	44	50	50	61	38	33
1955	104	46	41	82	34	25	30	39	42	49	44_{35}	60	37	32
1956	82	43	39	72	31	25	26	36	39	47	39	59	36	29
1957	87	44	36	66	34	23	28	34	37	46	44	63	33	.29
1958	68	41	31	52	30	22	25	32	36	44	39	58	35	28
1959	77	40	30	56	26	22	24	30	34	41	41	52	32	28
1960	83	38	31	45	24	22	21	27	34	39	40	48	29	27
1961	80	33	28	38	23	22	21	26	32	34	40	44	31	27
1962	92	33	28	37	23	20	21	26	29	32	40	48	29	27
1963	91	31	27	36	22	19	18	26	27	31	39	43	27	27
1964	82	29	25	33	21	19	17	23	25	29	36	40	27	26
1965	87	28	24	31	26	19	18	22	24	25	34	39	25	25
1966	...	28	25	32	24	17	15	22	24	23	34	38	25	26
1967	...	26	23	33	23	16	15	21	23	21	34	37	24	23
1968	...	26	22	28	22	16	14	20	23	20	34	36	21	24
1969	...	25	21	31	23	15	14	20	23	20	32	36	21	24
1970	...	26	21	27	22	14	14	18	23	19	30	36	20	23
1971	...	26	20	25	22	14	14	17	23	18	27	35	18	23
1972	...	25	19	26	22	12	12	16	22	18	27	33	18	21
1973	...	24	18	26	21	12	11	15	23	16	24	34	18	21
1974	...	24	17	26	20	11	11	14	21	16	24	34	18	21
1975	...	21	16	23	21	10	10	14	20	16	24	33	18	20
1976	...	18	15	24	21	10	10	13	17	14	22	30	16	18
1977	...	17	14	24	20	9	9	11	16	13	20	26	16	17
1978	...	15	13	22	19	9	8	11	15	13	19	24	15	16
1979	...	15	12	20	18	9	8	10	14	13	19	24	13	15
1980	...	14	12	20	18	8	8	10	13	12	18	23	11	13
1981	...	13	11	19	17	8	7	9	12	12	16	21	11	13
1982	...	13	11	18	16	8	6	9	11	11	15	20	11	14
1983	...	12	11	17	16	8	6	8	10	11	15	19	10	12
1984	...	11	10	16	15	8	6	8	10	10	14	20	10	11
1985	...	11	9	15	14	8	6	8	9	10	14	20	9	10
1986	...	10	10	15	14	8	6	8	9	9	12	19	9	10
1987	...	10	10	15	13	8	6	8	8	9	13	17	7	9
1988	...	8	9	14	12	8	6	8	8	8	11	16	9	9
1989	...	8	9	14	11	8	6	8	8	8	...	16	8	8
									Germany					
1990	...	8	8	15	11	8	6	7	7		10	15	8	8
1991	...	8	8	17	12	8	...	7	7		9	16	8	8
					Czech Republic[37]									
1992	...	8	8	16	10	7	...	...	6		8	14	7	8
1993	...	7	8	16	9	6	5	...	6		9	17	6	9
1994	35	7	8	16	8	5	5	6	6		9	11	6	8
1995	30	5	6	15	8	5	4	5	5		8	11	6	7
1996	25	5	6	...	6	6	4	5	5		8	11	6	8
1997	22	5	6	18	6	5	4	5	5		8	10	6	9
1998	15	5	5	14	5	5	4	5	5		8	10	6	8

See pp. 127–8 for footnotes

A7   Deaths of Infants Under One Year Old per 1,000 Live Births

1950–1998

	Italy	N'lands	Norway	Poland	Port	Romania	Russia/ USSR	Spain	Sweden	Switz	UK E & W	UK Scotld	Yugo- slavia
1950	64[28]	25	28	108	94	117	81	64	21	31	30	39	119
1951	67	25	26	115	89	118	84	63	22	30	30	37	140
1952	63	23	24	95	94	105	75	55	20	29	28	35	105
1953	58	22[36]	22	88	96	96	68	53	19	30	27	31	116
1954	53	23	21	83	86	89	68	49	19	27	25	31	102
1955	51	22	21	81	90	78	60	51	17	26	25	30	113
1956	51	20	21	71	88	82	47	46	17	26	24	29	98
1957	50	18	21	77	88	81	45	47	18	23	23	29	102
1958	48	19	20	72	84	69	41	43	16	22	23	28	86
1959	45	18	19	72	89	76	41	42	17	22	22	28	92
1960	44	18	19	57	78	75	35	36	17	21	22	26	88
1961	41	17	18	54	89	69	32	37	16	21	21	26	82
1962	42	17	18	55	79	59	32	33	15	21	22	27	84
1963	40	16	17	49	73	55	31	32	15	20	21	26	78
1964	36	15	16	48	69	49	29	31	14	19	20	24	76
1965	36	14	17	42	65	44	27	30	13	18	19	23	72
1966	35	15	15	39	65	47	26	28	13	17	19	23	62
1967	33	13	15	38	59	47	26	32	13	17	18	21	61
1968	32	14	14	33	61	60	26	31	13	16	18	21	59
1969	30	13	14	34	55	55	26	29	12	15	18	21	57
1970	29	13	13	33	58	49	25	27	11	15	18	20	56
1971	28	12	13	30	50	42	23	24	11	14	18	20	50
1972	27	12	12	23	41	40	25	22	11	13	17	19	44
1973	26	12	12	28	45	38	26	20	10	13	17	19	44
1974	23	11	10	24	38	35	28	19	10	13	16	19	41
1975	21	11	11	25	39	35	25	19	9	11	16	17	40
1976	20	11	10	24	33	31	…	17	8	11	14	15	37
1977	18	10	9	25	30	31	…	16	8	10	14	16	36
1978	17	10	9	23	29	30	…	15	8	9	13	13	34
1979	16	9	9	21	26	32	…	14	7	8	13	13	33
1980	15	9	8	21	24	29	27	12	7	9	12	12	31
1981	14	8	8	21	22	29	…	12	7	8	11	11	31
1982	13	8	8	20	20	28	…	11	7	8	11	11	30
1983	12	8	8	19	19	24	26	10	7	8	10	10	31
1984	11	8	8	19	17	23	26	10	6	7	10	10	28
1985	10	8	8	18	18	26	26	9	7	7	9	9	28
1986	10	8	8	17	16	23	25	9	6	7	10	9	27
1987	10	8	8	17	14	22	25	9	6	7	9	9	25
1988	9	7	8	16	13	25	25	8	6	7	9	9	25
1989	9	7	8	16	12	27	27	…	6	7	8	9	24
1990	9	7	7	16	11	27	27	8	6	7	8	8	Yugo-
1991	8	7	6	15	11	23	18[38]	7	6	6	8	9	21[39]
1992	8	6	6	14	9	23	18[38]	7	5	6	8	9	16[39]
1993	7	6	5	13	9	23	20[38]	8	5	6	9	10	18[39]
1994	7	6	5	15	8	24	18	6	4	5	9	10	18
1995	6	6	4	14	8	21	18	6	4	5	8	10	17
1996	6	6	4	12	7	22	18	6	4	5	8	9	15
1997	6	5	4	10	6	22	17	5	4	5	7	9	14
1998	…	5	4	9	8	21	16	5	5	5	8	9	13

See pp. 127–8 for footnotes

A7 Deaths of Infants Under One Year Old per 1,000 Live Births

NOTE

SOURCES:- As for table A.6

FOOTNOTES

1 Cisleithania (excluding Lombardy and Venetia) to 1913, but excluding Dalmatia to 1855. From 1914 the statistics apply to the present Republic, except that Burgenland is not included until 1922. The figures to 1855 are for years ended 31 October.
2 Figures from 1839 exclude parts of Limburg and Luxembourg ceded to the Netherlands.
3 Bavaria only for 1836-50; Bavaria and the Kingdom of Saxony for 1851-70; Bavaria, Saxony, Baden, and Württenburg for 1871-74; Bavaria, Saxony, Baden, Württemberg, and Prussia for 1875-1900; German Empire and Republic for 1901-40; West Germany (including West Berlin and Saarland) since 1946. The Bavarian statistics up to 1869 were for years ended 30 September.
4 The sources contain statistics back to 1881, but they appear to be extremely defective before 1892.
5 Figures from 1861 include Savoy and Nice.
6 Figures from 1871 to 1913 exclude the parts of Alsace and Lorraine ceded to Germany.
7 The Bavarian figure for 1851 is 304.
8 Statistics for Saxony only are as follows:-

1860: 228;	1861: 294;	1862: 243:	1863: 230.

9 The figure without Prussia for 1875 is 308.
10 The Ancient Kingdom (excluding Croatia-Slavonia) to 1918, and subsequently the territory established by the treaty of Trianon. For statistics for Croatia-Slavonia see footnote 33.
11 Statistics to 1855 are for years ended 31 October.
12 Statistics to 1911 apply to the 50 provinces of European Russia (excluding Finland, Poland, and the Caucasus). Later statistics apply to the U.S.S.R.
13 Figures for some communes were missing.
14 Figures from 1925 include Eupen, Malmédy, etc.
15 Figures from 1939 exclude Sub-Carpathian Russia (Ruthenia), and from 1945 they exclude 12 villages in Slovakia which were ceded to the U.S.S.R.
16 Figures from 1948 include the Bratislava Bridgehead.
17 Estimates were made for departments affected by war.
18 Figures from 1920 are based on the numbers actually born alive, whereas previously they did not include those who died before registration. The figure for 1920 on the old basis is 118.
19 The figure for 1901 for the five states previously covered is 211.
20 The figures from 1917 exclude Alsace-Lorraine.
21 Figures from 1919 exclude territory ceded to Czechoslovakia, Denmark, and Poland (except in Silesia).
22 Figures from 1922 exclude part of Upper Silesia ceded to Poland.
23 Figures from 1925 exclude Eupen, Malmédy, etc.
24 Figures from 1949 include the Dodecanese Islands.
25 Figures from 1948 exclude the Bratislava Bridgehead.
26 Estimates were made for earthquake victims.
27 Figures from 1920 include territory acquired from Austria-Hungary.
28 Figures from 1943 are for the post-Second World War territory, except that Trieste is not included until 1951.
29 Boundaries of the day.
30 Including the Azores and Madeira.
31 Figures from 1919 to 1939 apply to the territory established by the treaty of Trianon. In 1940 this was reduced by the cession of Southern Dobrudja to Bulgaria (which proved permanent), of Bessarabia and northern Bukovina to the U.S.S.R. (which, apart from the reconquest in 1943, also proved permanent), and of northern Transylvania (which was recovered in 1945) to Hungary.
32 Including the Canary Islands.
33 Pre-First World War statistics for Croatia-Slavonia are as follows:-

1891	226	1897	213	1903	211	1909	195
1892	266	1898	201	1904	182	1910	191
1893	225	1899	187	1905	220	1911	201
1894	220	1900	198	1906	194	1912	184
1895	225	1901	195	1907	183	1913	203
1896	224	1902	200	1908	189	1914	181

34 From 1953 unviable infants who died within 24 hours of birth are excluded from both births and deaths.
35 Statistics to 1955 apply to the year of registration not year of death.
36 Up to 1953 infants of less than 28 weeks gestation born alive are excluded.
37 Czech Republic Figures for Slovakia: 1992 = 12.6, 1993 = 15.6

A7   Deaths of Infants Under One Year Old per 1,000 Live Births

[38]   Russian Federation Figures for ex-USSR:

	Armenia	Azer-baijan	Bel-arus	Est-onia	Geo-rgia	Lat-via	Lithu-ania	Kazakh-stan	Kyrgi-stan	Mold-ova	Tajiki-stan	Turkmeni-stan	Ukraine	Uzbeki-stan
1991	18.0	...	12.2	13.4	...	15.7	14.3	27.6	29.7	20.0	...	...	14.0	...
1992	18.9	...	12.4	15.8	...	17.6	16.5	26.3	31.6	18.6	...	...	14.1	37.6
1993	17.7	28.0	12.7	15.8	19.0	16.2	16.0	30.7	...	...	46.5	57.0	15.1	...
1994	15.1	26.2	13.3	14.5	16.7	15.7	14.2	27.4	29.6	22.9	42.4	...	14.7	28.4
1995	14.2	24.3	13.5	14.8	13.1	18.8	12.5	27.9	27.7	21.5	...	...	14.8	25.8
1996	15.5	20.8	12.6	10.4	17.4	15.9	10.1	25.9	26.6	20.5	...	...	14.5	24.7
1997	15.4	19.6	12.6	10.1	...	15.3	10.3	25.3	28.6	...	...	...	14.2	23.1
1998	14.7	16.6	11.2	8.9	12.4	15.0	9.3	21.8	26.0	17.9	...	33.2	12.9	...

[39]   Yugoslavia (Montenegro + Serbia). Figures for ex. Yugoslavia are:

	Croatia	Macedonia	Slovenia
1991	11.1	28.3	8.2
1992	11.6	30.6	8.9
1993	9.9	24.5	6.6
1994	10.2	22.5	6.5
1995	8.9	22.7	5.5
1996	8.0	16.4	...
1997	8.2	15.7	...
1998	8.2	...	...

A8 EMIGRATION FROM EUROPE BY DECADES (in thousands)

	1851 -60	1861 -70	1871 -80	1881 -90	1891 -1900	1901 -10	1911 -20	1921 -30	1931 -40	1941 -50	1951 -60
Austria–Hungary[1]	31	40	46	248	440	1,111	418	61	11[2]	...	53[3]
Belgium	1	2	2	21	16	30	21[4]	33	20[5]	29[6]	109
Denmark	...	8	39	82	51	73	52	64	100	38	68
Finland	...	...	...	26	59	159	67	73	3	7	32
France	27	36	66	119	51	53	32	4	5		155
Germany[7]	671	779	626	1,342	527	274	91	564	121[8]	618	872
Italy	5	27	168	992	1,580	3,615	2,194	1,370	235	467	858
Netherlands	16	20	17	52	24	28	22	32	4[8]	75[9]	341[10]
Norway	36	98	85	187	95	191	62	87	6	10[9]	25
Poland	...	...	...	...	...	...	...	634[11]	164[12]	...	...
Portugal	45	79	131	185	266	324	402	995	108	69[13]	346
Russia	...	...	58	288	481	911	420	...	...	...	...
Spain	3	7	13	572	791	1,091	1,306	560	132	166	543
Sweden	17	122	103	327	205	324	86	107	8	23	43
Switzerland	6	15	36	85	35	37	31	50	47	18[14]	23
United Kingdom and Ireland	1,313[15][16]	1,572[16]	1,849[16]	3,259	2,149	3,150	2,587	2,151	262	755[9]	1,454

NOTES

1. SOURCE:- W. Woodruff, *Impact of Western Man* (London, 1966)
2. Except as indicated in footnotes, this table refers to emigration outside Europe.

FOOTNOTES

[1] Republic of Austria from 1921 onwards.
[2] 1931–37.
[3] 1954–60.
[4] Excluding 1913–18.
[5] 1931–39.
[6] 1948–50.
[7] West Germany in 1941–50 and 1951–60.
[8] 1932–36.
[9] 1946–50.
[10] Excluding emigration to Dutch colonies.
[11] Incomplete figures.
[12] 1931–38.
[13] For the years 1941–49 emigration to European countries is included.
[14] For the years 1941–44 emigration to European countries is included.
[15] 1853–60.
[16] Excluding emigration direct from Irish ports.

A9 ANNUAL MIGRATION STATISTICS (in thousands)

key :E: Emigrants; I: Immigrants

	Austria		Belgium		Germany	Netherlands		Norway	Russia		UK	
	E	I	E	I	E	E	I	E	E	I	E	I
1815	...	...	...	...	...	...	...	...	...	...	2.1	...
1816	...	...	...	...	...	...	...	...	...	...	12.5	...
1817	...	...	...	...	...	...	...	...	...	...	20.6	...
1818	...	...	...	...	...	...	...	...	...	...	27.8	...
1819	1.3	4.9	...	...	...	...	...	...	...	...	34.8	...
1820	1.6	5.8	...	...	3.0	...	...	...	...	...	25.7	...
1821	2.7	6.0	...	...	2.8	...	...	...	...	...	18.3	...
1822	2.5	5.4	...	...	1.1	...	...	...	...	...	20.4	...
1823	2.3	3.0	...	...	1.3	...	...	...	...	...	16.6	...
1824	1.3	1.3	...	...	1.6	...	...	...	...	...	14.0	...
1825	0.9	0.8	...	...	3.2	...	...	0.1	...	...	14.9	...
1826	0.8	0.9	...	...	1.4	...	...	...	...	...	20.9	...
1827	0.8	1.0	...	...	1.2	...	...	...	...	...	28.0	...
1828	1.1	1.0	...	...	5.2	...	...	...	−0.5	0.4	26.1	...
1829	2.4	1.0	...	...	1.7	...	...	...	−1.6	1.3	31.2	...
1830	1.3[31] 2.0	0.8	...	...	5.5	...	...	...	−0.6	2.2	56.9	...
1831	1.7	0.5	...	...	7.2	...	...	...	−23.7	7.7	83.2	...
1832	1.4	1.1	...	...	11.2	...	...	...	−3.1	0.6	103.1	...
1833	1.5	1.4	...	...	7.7	...	...	...	−0.6	1.7	62.5	...
1834	1.8	0.7	...	...	19.5	...	...	...	0.1	0.9	76.2	...
1835	1.5	0.9	...	...	9.1	...	...	...	−2.4	2.3	44.5	...
1836	1.5	0.9	...	...	22.8	...	...	0.2	−1.2	1.9	75.4	...
1837	2.4	0.9	...	...	26.1	...	...	0.2	0.3	3.9	72.0	...
1838	1.8	0.9	...	...	12.9	...	...	0.1	−1.1	4.2	33.2	...
1839	1.5	1.0	...	...	23.1	...	...	0.4	−6.5	−0.1	62.2	...
1840	1.3	0.9	...	...	32.7	...	...	0.3	−3.4	0.5	90.7	...
1841	1.5	...	3.8	2.9	16.8	...	...	0.4	−2.5	2.0	118.6	...
1842	...	...	4.2	2.8	22.4	...	...	0.7	1.5	2.4	128.3	...
1843	1.5	1.1	3.9	4.1	15.8	0.1	...	1.6	−1.4	3.0	57.2	...
1844	...	...	4.2	2.7	22.8	0.2	...	1.2	−1.5	4.7	70.0	...
1845	...	...	6.5	3.0	37.8	0.7	...	1.1	−1.5	4.1	93.5	...
1846	1.5	1.1	...	...	63.4	1.8	...	1.3	0.4	6.9	129.9	...
1847	...	...	6.3	4.4	80.3	5.3	...	1.6	0.6	1.6	258.3	...
1848	...	...	5.0	5.4	62.6	2.2	...	1.4	−0.1	−0.8	248.1	...
1849	0.9	0.7	5.1	3.9	64.2	2.1	...	4.0	−13.1	−1.7	299.5	...

A9 Annual Migration Statistics (in thousands)

1850–1899

	Austria		Belgium		Bulgaria	Denmark		France		Germany
	E	I	E	I	E	E	I	E	I	E
1850	1.3	0.9	6.4	4.2	...	...	...	...	...	83.2
1851	4.7	1.0	6.1	4.1	...	...	...	...	...	78.8
1852	2.5	1.1	7.8	5.0	...	...	...	...	...	176.4
1853	9.5	3.3	9.5	4.9	...	...	...	...	...	150.6
1854	14.3[31] 7.1	1.9	8.0	5.0	...	...	...	...	...	239.2
1855	4.0	...	9.5	5.2	...	...	...	...	...	83.8
1856	2.8	...	13.3	5.6	...	...	...	...	...	80.9
1857	2.8	...	8.6	6.7	...	...	...	5.7	...	103.1
1858	2.1	...	8.1	7.8	...	...	...	3.7	...	56.8
1859	1.4	...	8.4	7.7	...	...	...	2.6	...	47.4
1860	2.0	...	9.3	8.3	...	...	...	3.5	...	57.9
1861	2.5	...	10.2	8.9	...	...	...	2.7	...	36.9
1862	1.6	...	9.5	9.2	...	...	...	2.3	...	31.3
1863	1.5	...	9.1	8.8	...	...	...	2.4	...	39.0
1864	2.3	...	10.7	9.2	...	...	...	3.1	...	60.7
1865	3.0	...	12.0	9.6	...	...	...	4.7	...	88.7
1866	3.8	...	14.3	10.6	...	...	...	5.6	...	120.4
1867	9.3	...	9.7	11.8	...	...	...	6.0	...	138.4
1868	4.1	...	9.9	11.2	...	...	...	6.4	...	58.9
1869	5.5	...	11.6	10.7	...	4.4	...	7.9	...	136.1
1870	5.9	...	7.3	16.6	...	3.5	...	4.6	...	122.2
1871	6.2[21] 9.2	...	13.2	16.7	...	3.9	...	5.9	...	76.2
1872	9.0	...	11.0	15.8	...	6.9	...	15.8	...	128.2
1873	10.3	...	8.0	15.8	...	7.2	...	8.4	...	110.4
1874	9.0[1]	...	8.2	16.8	...	3.3	...	7.2	...	47.7
1875	11.1	...	10.2	15.4	...	2.1	...	4.3	...	32.3
1876	10.8	...	13.1	14.4	...	1.6	...	2.2	...	29.6
1877	6.7	...	11.8	15.1	...	1.9	...	2.1	...	22.9
1878	5.1	...	11.6	14.3	...	3.0	...	2.3	...	25.6
1879	7.4	...	12.5	14.2	...	3.1	...	3.6	...	35.9
1880	21.0	...	15.1	16.5	...	5.7	...	4.6	...	117.1
1881	24.7	...	15.8	17.7	...	8.0	...	4.5	...	220.9
1882	18.1	...	16.3	18.1	...	11.6	...	4.9	...	203.6
1883	19.6	...	15.2	17.5	...	8.4	...	4.0	...	173.6
1884	21.0	...	14.0	16.6	...	6.3	...	6.1	...	149.1
1885	16.4[2]	...	13.2	18.3	...	4.3	...	6.1	...	110.1
1886	19.4[2]	...	17.0	19.8	...	6.3	...	7.3	...	83.2
1887	20.2[2]	...	17.5	19.3	...	8.8	...	11.2	...	104.8
1888	24.8[2][3]	...	23.0	21.2	...	8.7	...	23.3	...	104.0
1889	30.1[2]	...	23.2	22.2	...	9.0	...	31.4	...	96.1
1890	38.7[2]	...	21.7	21.5	...	10.3	...	20.6	...	97.1
1891	53.8[2]	...	19.0	20.7	...	10.4	...	6.2[31]	...	120.1
1892	50.3[2]	...	22.5	21.8	...	10.4	...	...	...	116.3
1893	48.8[2]	...	22.1	21.7	11.6	9.2	...	...	...	87.7
1894	18.8[2]	...	18.3	24.6	8.9	4.1	...	...	...	41.0
1895	46.0[2]	...	18.6	23.5	5.2	3.6	...	...	...	37.5
1896	51.5[2]	...	19.8	24.5	2.0	2.9	...	...	...	33.8
1897	25.1[2]	...	21.8	26.9	2.9	2.3	...	...	...	24.6
1898	32.3[2]	...	22.9	27.4	7.0	2.3	...	...	...	22.2
1899	55.9[2][4]	...	23.0	29.4	7.7	2.8	...	...	...	24.3

See pp. 141–2 for footnotes

A9   Annual Migration Statistics (in thousands)

1850–1899

	Hungary		Ireland		Italy		Netherlands		Norway	Poland	Portugal
	E	I	E	I	E	I	E	I	E	E	E
1850	...	...	...	...	...	...	0.8	...	3.7	...	...
1851	...	...	152.1[6]	...	...	...	1.2	...	2.6	...	...
1852	...	...	190.3	...	...	...	1.2	...	4.0	...	...
1853	...	...	173.1	...	...	...	1.6	...	6.1	...	...
1854	...	...	140.6	...	...	...	3.6	...	6.0	...	...
1855	...	...	90.9	...	...	...	2.1	...	1.6		
1856	...	...	90.8	...	...	...	1.9	...	3.2		
1857	...	...	95.1	...	...	...	1.7	...	6.4		
1858	...	...	64.3	...	...	...	1.2	...	2.5		1855–
1859	...	...	80.6	...	...	...	0.5	...	1.8		1865
1860	...	...	84.6	...	...	...	0.9	...	1.9		80.8
1861	...	...	64.3	...	...	...	0.8	...	8.9		
1862	...	...	70.1	...	...	...	0.8	...	5.3		
1863	...	...	117.2	...	...	...	1.1	...	1.1		
1864	...	...	114.2	...	...	...	0.7[31]	...	4.3		
1865	...	...	101.5	...	...	...	8.4	6.9	4.0		
1866	...	...	99.5	...	...	...	10.4	6.3	15.5[31]		6.0[7]
1867	...	...	80.6	...	...	...	11.0	6.8	12.8		7.2[7]
1868	...	...	61.0	...	...	...	9.8	7.4	13.2		6.7[7]
1869	...	...	66.6	...	134.9	...	14.8	7.5	18.1		8.4[7]
1870	...	...	74.9	...	107.2	...	8.5	7.8	14.8		10.4[7]
1871	0.3	...	71.2	...	122.5	...	11.7	7.0	11.4		12.7[7]
1872	0.6	...	78.1	...	146.3	86.5	12.7	8.1	13.3		17.3
1873	1.0	...	90.1	...	151.8	86.8	14.7	8.3	9.9		13.0
1874	0.9	...	73.2	...	108.2	79.0	9.8	8.4	4.4		14.8
1875	1.1	...	51.5	...	103.2	83.2	9.0	9.2	4.0		15.4
1876	0.6	...	37.6	...	108.8	73.6	8.6	9.9	4.4		11.0
1877	0.7	...	38.5	...	99.2	...	7.6	12.0	3.2[31]		11.1
1878	0.8	...	41.1	...	96.3	...	8.1	13.6	4.9		9.9
1879	1.8	...	47.1	...	119.8	...	10.4	14.0	7.6		13.2
1880	8.8	...	95.5	...	119.9	...	12.7	11.9	20.2		12.6
1881	11.3	...	78.4	...	135.8	...	18.8	13.9	26.0	...	14.6
1882	17.5	...	89.1	...	161.6	...	19.8	15.3	28.8	...	18.3
1883	14.8	...	108.7	...	169.1	...	16.8	14.4	22.2	...	19.3
1884	13.2	...	75.9	...	147.0	...	16.2	14.1	14.8	...	17.5
1885	12.3	...	62.0	...	157.2	...	15.0	13.7	14.0	...	15.0
1886	25.1	...	63.1	...	167.8	...	15.5	13.9	15.2	...	14.0
1887	18.3	...	82.9	...	215.7	...	17.5	13.5	20.7	...	16.9
1888	17.6[5]	...	78.7	...	290.7	...	19.0	13.4	21.5	...	24.0
1889	25.1	...	70.5	...	218.4	...	23.0	15.3	12.6	...	20.6
1890	31.5	...	61.3	...	217.2	...	19.0	13.1	11.0	19.3	29.4
1891	33.0	...	59.6	...	293.6	...	19.9	15.2	13.3	17.5	33.6
1892	35.1	...	50.9	...	223.7	...	21.4	15.9	17.0	13.1	21.1
1893	23.0	...	48.1	...	246.8	...	22.9	16.0	18.8	8.8	30.4
1894	8.0	...	35.9	...	225.3	...	21.1	15.7	5.6	5.6	26.9
1895	25.9	...	48.7	...	293.2	...	18.4	14.8	6.2	7.1	44.7
1896	24.6	...	39.0	...	307.5	...	23.2	16.6	6.7	6.2	28.0
1897	14.1	...	32.5	...	299.9	...	23.6	19.2	4.7	5.7	21.6
1898	22.8	...	32.2	...	283.7	...	25.4	19.3	4.9	7.8	23.5
1899	43.4	4.7	41.2	...	308.3	...	28.9	22.0	6.7	8.7	17.8

See pp. 141–2 for footnotes

A9 Annual Migration Statistics (in thousands)

	Russia		Serbia		Spain		Sweden		Switzerland		United Kingdom	
	E	I	E	I	E	I	E	I	E	I	E	I
1850	0.4	0.2	...	...	...	...	...	...	...	...	280.8	...
1851	1.7	2.1	...	...	...	...	1.1	...	...	...	336.0	...
1852	1.4	-3.8	...	...	...	...	3.3	...	...	...	368.8	...
1853	1.7	23.6	...	...	...	...	3.0	...	...	...	329.9	...
1854	-2.3	10.6	...	...	...	...	4.2	...	...	...	323.4	...
1855	3.0	-16.2	...	...	...	...	1.1	...	...	...	176.8	22.8
1856	-1.0	29.9	...	...	...	...	1.1	...	...	...	176.6	...
1857	-2.1	-5.2	...	...	...	...	1.8	...	...	...	212.9	...
1858	2.9	26.0	...	...	...	...	0.6	...	...	...	114.0	23.7
1859	37.9	31.3	...	...	...	...	0.3	...	...	...	120.4	19.9
1860	190.7	32.5	...	...	...	...	0.3	...	...	...	128.5	24.4
1861	20.7	46.8	...	...	...	...	2.3	...	...	...	91.8	32.0
1862	4.6	43.2	...	...	...	...	2.5	...	...	...	121.2	...
1863	1.5	38.9	...	...	...	...	3.1	...	...	...	223.8	17.6
1864	0.8	46.3	...	...	...	...	5.2	...	...	...	208.9	25.8
1865	3.4	72.6	...	...	...	...	6.7	...	...	...	209.8	33.5
1866	5.5	55.4	...	...	...	...	7.2	...	...	...	204.9	31.1
1867	4.5	58.7	...	...	...	...	9.3	...	...	...	196.0	36.6
1868	3.8	63.3	...	...	...	...	27.0	...	5.0	...	196.3	...
1869	-19.5	1.3	...	...	...	...	39.1	...	5.2	...	258.0	36.0
1870	20.7	34.9	...	...	...	...	20.0	...	3.5	...	256.9	41.5
1871	25.3	46.0	...	...	...	...	17.5	...	3.9	...	252.4	45.0
1872	10.3	66.9	...	...	...	...	15.9	...	4.9	...	295.2	41.7
1873	32.0	44.8	...	...	...	...	13.6	...	5.0	...	310.6	74.9
1874	33.5	72.8	...	...	...	...	7.8	...	2.7	...	241.0	118.1
1875	9.9	28.6	...	...	...	...	9.7	2.8	1.8	...	173.8	94.2
1876	1.3	35.3	...	...	...	...	9.4	3.2	1.7	...	109.5	71.4
1877	9.4	28.1	...	...	...	...	7.6	3.3	1.7	...	95.2	63.9
1878	0.2	76.9	...	...	...	...	9.0	2.8	2.6	...	112.9	54.9
1879	8.4	47.8	...	...	...	...	17.6	2.6	4.3	...	164.3	37.9
1880	-1.2	62.7	...	...	...	...	42.1	3.0	7.3	...	227.5	47.0
1881	24.8	46.9	...	...	...	...	46.0	3.0	10.9	...	243.0	52.7
1882	14.1	59.0	...	...	13.3	...	50.2	3.6	12.0	...	279.4	54.7
1883	23.6	47.7	...	...	3.9	...	31.6	4.2	13.5	...	320.1	73.8
1884	17.3	37.7	...	...	4.8	...	23.6	4.9	9.6	...	242.2	91.4
1885	9.7	51.0	...	...	0.6	...	23.5	5.5	7.6	...	207.6	85.5
1886	15.0	42.8	...	...	4.6	...	32.9	5.2	6.3	...	232.9	80.0
1887	18.9	11.3	...	...	14.2	...	50.8	4.6	7.6	...	281.5	85.5
1888	12.8	10.0	...	...	23.6	...	50.3	4.8	8.3	...	279.9	94.1
1889	36.5	7.5	4.9	22.9	72.4	...	33.4	5.5	8.4[31]	...	254.0	103.1
1890	40.9	4.7	2.9	15.4	11.1	...	34.2	6.0	7.7	...	218.1	109.5
1891	41.2	-6.7	4.5	7.3	5.2	...	42.8	6.1	7.5	...	218.5	103.0
1892	36.0	0.5	1.0	5.0	8.3	...	45.5	6.5	7.8	...	210.0	97.8
1893	48.5	2.0	2.2	0.5	19.8	...	40.9	7.4	6.2	...	208.8	102.1
1894	25.6	7.9	7.2	8.0	14.7	...	13.4	10.4	3.8	...	156.0	118.3
1895	27.6	17.1	3.2	4.7	64.5	...	19.0	8.5	4.3	...	185.2	109.4
1896	27.1	6.9	0.4	8.5	98.9	...	20.0	7.8	3.3	...	161.9	101.7
1897	24.3	18.1	1.7	13.8	-9.2	...	14.6	7.9	2.5	...	146.5	95.2
1898	31.6	27.3	8.0	18.2	-77.7	...	13.7	8.0	2.3	...	140.6	91.2
1899	40.7	14.9	7.6	15.7	-62.7	...	16.9	8.2	2.5	...	146.4	100.2

See pp. 141-2 for footnotes

A9   Annual Migration Statistics (in thousands)

	Austria E	Austria I	Belgium E	Belgium I	Bulgaria E	Czech E	Denmark E	Denmark I	Finland E	France E	France I
1900	62.6	...	25.1	29.3	7.8	...	3.6	...	10.4	...	...
1901	65.1	...	19.7	29.1	9.5	...	4.7	...	12.6	...	...
1902	93.7[8]	...	23.1	29.4	9.9	...	6.8	...	23.2	...	...
1903	102.3[9]	...	25.0	34.3	...	...	8.2	...	17.0	...	...
1904	79.0[10]	...	27.3	35.6	...	...	9.0	...	11.0	...	...
1905	123.7	...	28.0	36.9	...	...	8.1	...	17.4	...	...
1906	136.4	...	32.9	37.4	...	...	8.5	...	17.5	...	...
1907	177.4	...	32.4	38.9	...	...	7.9	...	16.3	...	...
1908	58.9	...	32.3	38.2	...	...	4.6	...	5.8	...	...
1909	129.8	...	35.2	39.7	...	...	6.8	...	19.1	...	...
1910	138.9	...	38.9	45.0	...	...	8.9	...	19.0	...	...
1911	91.9	...	33.0	41.1	...	...	8.3	...	9.4	...	...
1912	131.2	...	35.8	43.0	...	...	8.6	...	10.7	...	...
1913	194.5	...	41.3	45.5	...	...	8.8	...	20.1	...	...
1914	...	...	...	...	...	...	6.2	...	6.5	...	...
1915	...	...	...	...	...	...	3.3	...	4.0	...	...
1916	...	...	...	...	...	...	4.3	...	5.3	...	...
1917	...	...	...	...	...	...	1.6	...	2.8	...	...
1918	...	...	...	...	...	...	0.8	...	1.9	...	...
1919	...	...	57.8	50.0	...	...	3.3	...	1.1	...	...
1920	...	...	53.3	44.3	...	...	6.3	...	5.6	...	...
1921	5.2	...	27.4	24.4	...	...	5.3	...	3.6	...	...
1922	10.6	...	32.6	30.6	...	39.4	4.1	...	5.7	...	...
1923	15.5	...	31.1	34.7	...	32.3	7.6	...	13.8[31]	...	...
1924	2.7	...	31.9	51.3	...	54.4	6.3	...	5.4	...	...
1925	4.6	4.4	35.3	46.9	...	19.4	4.6	...	2.5	...	...
1926	3.9	3.9	36.2	44.5	...	26.1	5.8	...	6.0	...	...
1927	5.3	5.1	29.9	41.2	...	23.6	8.0[12]	...	6.1	...	...
1928	4.6	6.1	28.3	42.0	...	24.5	16.6	10.6	5.1	...	...
1929	4.9	7.4	29.2	55.6	...	30.7	14.6	11.6	6.4	...	...
1930	4.2	8.2	29.6	54.4	...	25.7	14.2	14.8	4.0	...	...
1931	2.6	6.3	19.3	32.0	10.7	9.6	9.6	16.3	0.7	...	...
1932	2.1	6.7	18.3	26.2	6.8	5.2	8.3	13.6	1.2	...	...
1933	1.4	4.8	16.2	19.3	5.7	4.7	7.5	12.1	0.7	...	...
1934	2.2	10.3	18.5	16.0	11.3	5.1	8.1	12.4	0.4	...	...
1935	...	6.3	16.2	16.4	28.7	5.7	8.9	11.7	0.6	...	...
1936	...	7.1	13.5	17.7	20.9	7.2	9.8	10.9	0.7	...	...
1937	...	6.9	14.2	22.2	20.4	14.8	9.5	10.0	1.5	...	...
1938	...	...	16.1	14.5	21.7	9.0	11.1	10.6	1.3	...	...
1939	...	...	18.0	11.8	29.1	...	11.3	13.9	1.0	...	...
1940	...	...	6.9	13.7	14.4	...	14.4	8.9	0.8	...	...
1941	...	...	3.2	13.8	18.5	...	6.2	7.7	0.7	...	...
1942	...	...	3.9	10.7	...	...	2.7	4.6	0.1	...	...
1943	...	...	3.6	5.2	...	...	3.2	3.7	—	...	...
1944	...	...	4.1	2.9	...	...	1.7	2.6	0.1	...	...
1945	...	...	19.4	12.6	...	...	5.1	6.8	—	...	...
1946	...	...	30.3	20.3	...	...	25.7	20.1	0.3	...	30.2
1947	0.4[11]	25.9[11]	47.5	19.5	...	...	28.6	21.7	0.3	...	73.2
1948	1.4	11.5	45.5	89.9	...	...	33.1	26.4	10.1	...	82.9
1949	0.7	5.0	44.0	31.8	...	...	25.9	24.5	7.7	...	85.4

See pp. 141–2 for footnotes

A9 Annual Migration Statistics (in thousands)

	Germany		Greece		Hungary		Ireland		Italy	
	E	I	E	I	E	I	E	I	E	I
1900	22.3	...	...	...	54.8	6.2	45.3	...	352.8	...
1901	22.1	...	...	...	71.5	8.5	39.6	...	533.2	...
1902	32.1	...	...	...	91.8	11.5	40.2	...	531.5	...
1903	36.3	...	...	...	119.9[17]	20.2	39.8	...	508.0	...
1904	28.0	...	...	...	97.3[18]	16.9	36.9	...	471.2	...
1905	28.1	...	...	...	170.4	17.6	30.7	...	726.3	...
1906	31.1	...	...	...	178.2	27.6	35.3	...	788.0	...
1907	31.7	...	...	...	209.2	51.2	39.1	...	704.7	...
1908	19.9	...	...	...	49.4[19]	53.8	23.3	...	486.7	...
1909	24.9	...	...	...	129.3	17.0	28.7	...	625.6	...
1910	25.5	...	...	...	119.9	24.7	32.5	...	651.5	...
1911	22.7	...	...	...	73.7	32.8	30.6	...	533.8	...
1912	18.5	...	...	...	120.5	23.6	29.3	...	711.4	...
1913	25.8	...	38.1	...	119.2	21.8	31.0	...	872.6	...
1914	11.8	...	...	...	...	...	20.3	...	479.2[31]	...
1915	0.5	...	...	...	...	...	10.7	...	146.0	...
1916	0.3	...	...	...	...	...	7.3	...	142.4	...
1917	...	...	...	...	...	...	2.1	...	46.5	...
1918	...	...	...	...	...	...	1.0	...	28.3	...
1919	3.1	...	...	12.0[15]	...	...	3.0	...	253.2	...
1920	8.5	48.6	12.2	7.7	...	...	15.5	...	614.6	...
1921	23.5	64.9	4.1	9.1	6.0[20]	...	13.6	...	201.3	124.0
1922	36.5	82.0	...	7.8	5.5	...	...	...	281.3	110.8
1923	115.4	48.2	15.3	9.5	5.1	...	...	...	390.0	119.7
1924	58.3	61.0	...	10.3	1.7	...	19.1	2.5	364.6	172.8
1925	59.5	78.0	3.6[16]	...	3.5	0.5	30.2	2.2	280.1	189.1
1926	62.7	76.4	6.7[16]	...	5.9	22.5	30.0	1.8	262.4	177.6
1927	59.3	88.8	9.3[16]	...	5.6	...	27.1	1.9	218.9[31]	140.4[31]
1928	56.0	103.3	...	...	5.5	...	24.7	2.2	150.0	98.9
1929	47.8	109.7	...	...	9.7	...	20.8	2.1	149.8	115.9
1930	36.5	129.2	...	...	6.2	...	16.0	2.6	280.1	129.0
1931	13.2	110.2	23.4	19.6	1.5	...	1.5	3.4	165.9	107.7
1932	10.3	106.6	26.6	19.0	0.8	2.2	0.8	4.1	83.3	73.2
1933	12.9	83.6	21.8	18.3	0.8	1.4	0.9	2.6	83.1	65.8
1934	14.2	89.0	26.0	22.2	0.9	1.7	1.0	1.7	68.5	49.8
1935	12.2	...	21.4	17.7	1.1	1.4	1.0	1.6	57.4	39.5
1936	15.2	...	17.2	14.5	1.1	1.0	1.3	1.5	41.7	32.8
1937	14.2	3.0	21.1	15.2	1.5	0.5	1.2	1.2	59.9	35.7
1938	22.7[13]	7.8	19.5	17.9	1.6	0.2	1.8	1.3	61.5	36.9
1939	25.5[13][14]	12.9[14]	15.6	27.7	2.1	0.2	1.1[21]	0.7[21]	29.5	87.3
1940	...	...	8.4	13.3	1.2	0.2	...	...	51.8	61.1
1941	...	...	...	...	0.4	0.1	...	...	8.8	46.1
1942	...	...	...	...	—	—	...	...	8.2[31]	20.5[31]
1943	...	...	...	...	...	...	...	...	...	...
1944	...	...	...	...	...	...	...	...	...	...
1945	...	...	...	...	...	...	...	...	...	...
1946	...	...	1.6	...	...	...	...	...	110.3	4.6
1947	...	...	4.9	...	2.1	0.9	...	...	254.1	65.5
1948	...	...	4.8	...	...	...	...	...	308.5	119.3
1949	...	...	4.3	...	...	...	...	...	254.5	118.6

See pp. 141–2 for footnotes

A9 Annual Migration Statistics (in thousands)

1900–1949

	Netherlands		Norway	Poland	Portugal	Romania		Russia		Serbia	
	E	I	E	E	E	E	I	E	I	E	I
1900	25.1	24.1	10.9	9.8	21.3	...	...	32.4	11.6	−1.6	6.9
1901	13.5	24.4	12.7	11.4	20.6	...	...	35.1	13.9	8.9	6.4
1902	14.8	24.5	20.3	9.1	24.2	...	...	30.8	10.7	9.3	17.2
1903	28.3	25.6	26.8	10.9[24]	21.6	...	...	62.0	9.9	7.3	10.9
1904	27.7	23.7	22.3	...	28.3	...	...	66.6	4.4	8.6	28.5
1905	27.5	25.2	21.1	...	33.6	...	...	92.9	2.3	10.5	13.5
1906	30.9	26.2	22.0	...	38.1	...	...	116.7	5.6	17.0	8.3
1907	38.4	27.3	22.1	35.6	41.9	...	...	89.9	13.2	14.2	15.6
1908	34.6	30.0	8.5	17.3	40.1	...	...	37.4	17.4	8.4	−5.1
1909	37.1	32.2	16.2	15.1	38.2	...	...	54.5	17.3		
1910	35.1	31.1	18.9	21.7	39.5	...	...	71.3	22.1		
1911	38.9	33.6	12.5	20.3	59.7	...	...	66.2	18.7		
1912	39.0	36.2	9.1	17.2	88.9	...	...	94.6	15.4		
1913	40.1	40.0	9.9	...	77.6	...	...	223.8	127.2		
1914	29.8	51.7	8.5	...	25.7	...	...	54.0	7.5	...	...
1915	17.1	32.5	4.6	...	19.3	...	...	−8.2	−6.1	...	...
1916	11.1	50.9	5.2	...	24.7	...	...	...	...	...	...
1917	8.8	50.5	2.5	...	15.7[31]	...	...	...	...	...	...
1918	20.6	22.7	1.2	...	11.9	...	...	...	...	...	...
1919	45.4	32.3	2.4	...	37.1	...	...	...	...	...	...
1920	63.1	41.6	5.6	...	64.8	...	...	...	...	...	...
1921	35.4	30.3	4.6	...	24.6	...	...	...	...	...	...
1922	34.4	43.0	6.5	46.8	39.8	...	...	...	...	...	...
1923	40.1	51.2	18.3	...	40.2	...	...	...	...	...	...
1924	50.2	41.3	8.5	26.1	29.7	...	...	...	...	...	...
1925	43.7	38.4	7.0	...	22.9	...	...	...	...	...	...
1926	41.9	48.2	9.3	49.9	47.1	21.7	1.3	...	...	...	...
1927	45.2	47.5	11.9	58.2	27.7	8.9	3.2	...	...	...	...
1928	48.4	48.6	8.8	64.6	34.3	12.0	4.2	...	...	...	...
1929	49.5	57.8	8.0	65.3	40.4	12.8	3.1	...	...	...	...
1930	56.7	66.7	3.7	76.0	23.2	10.9	3.6	...	...	...	...
1931	37.4	65.4	0.8	21.4	6.0	2.7	2.6	...	...	...	...
1932	38.6	55.9	0.4	35.5	5.9	1.4	2.0	...	...	...	...
1933	41.5	49.6	0.3	42.6	8.9	1.2	1.4	...	...	...	...
1934	44.5	43.7	0.5	53.8	7.5	1.4	1.0	...	...	...	...
1935	48.4	34.3	0.5	54.6	9.1	2.4	0.7	...	...	...	...
1936	48.3	32.5	0.5	102.5	12.5	1.6	0.4	...	...	...	...
1937	45.5	33.9	0.6	129.1	14.7	1.3	0.6	...	...	...	...
1938	48.2	33.1	0.8	...	13.6	1.7	0.4	...	...	...	...
1939	50.8	50.1	0.7	...	17.8	1.4	0.2	...	...	...	...
1940	26.4	19.5	0.3[23]	...	13.2	0.5	—	...	...	...	...
1941	17.3	10.7	...	...	6.3	0.5	—	...	...	...	...
1942	42.7[22]	8.3	...	...	2.2	...	...	...	...	...	...
1943	70.7[22]	8.8	...	...	0.9	...	...	...	...	...	...
1944	24.4[22]	5.3	...	...	2.4	...	...	...	...	...	...
1945	15.7[22]	29.1	...	...	5.9	...	...	...	...	...	...
1946	66.8	107.4	1.0	...	8.3	...	...	...	...	...	...
1947	65.9	54.4	1.5	...	12.8	...	...	...	...	...	...
1948	66.5	46.3	2.4	...	12.3	...	...	...	...	...	...
1949	58.2	36.3	2.7	...	17.3	...	...	...	...	...	...

See pp. 141–2 for footnotes

A9 Annual Migration Statistics (in thousands)

	Spain		Sweden		Switzerland		United Kingdom		Yugoslavia	
	E	I	E	I	E	I	E	I	E	I
1900	5.6	...	20.7	8.0	3.8	...	168.8	97.6	...	...
1901	3.8	...	24.6	7.6	3.9	...	171.7	99.7	...	...
1902	−6.6	...	37.1	6.8	4.7	...	205.7	104.1	...	...
1903	2.6	...	39.5	7.6	5.8	...	260.0	112.9	...	...
1904	30.1	...	22.4	9.3	4.8	...	271.4	144.6	...	...
1905	64.0	...	24.0	8.6	5.0	...	262.1	122.7	...	...
1906	52.9	...	24.7	9.6	5.3	...	325.1	130.5	...	...
1907	51.3	...	23.0	8.9	5.7	...	395.7	160.6	...	...
1908	71.4[31]	...	12.5	9.8	3.7	...	263.2	172.0	...	...
1909	111.1	...	22.0	8.1	4.9	...	288.8	149.1	...	...
1910	160.9	...	27.8	8.1	5.2	...	397.8	164.1	...	...
1911	139.7	...	20.0	7.8	5.5	...	454.5	192.7	...	...
1912	194.4	...	18.1	8.3	5.9	...	467.7	199.2	...	...
1913	151.0	...	20.3	8.4	6.2	...	469.6	227.6	...	...
1914	66.6	...	13.0	8.6	3.9	...	293.2	229.9	...	...
1915	50.4	...	7.5	6.4	2.0	...	104.9	129.7	...	...
1916	62.2	46.4	10.6	6.7	1.5	...	76.5	84.7	...	...
1917	43.1	37.7	6.4	5.8	0.7	...	20.6	21.0	...	...
1918	20.2	28.4	4.9	4.9	0.3	...	17.3	15.4	...	...
1919	69.5	47.2	7.3	7.8	3.1	...	180.2[31]	153.2[31]	...	...
1920	150.6	46.5	10.2	10.8	9.3	...	285.1	86.1	...	...
1921	62.5	76.4	9.0	8.6	7.1	...	199.5	71.4	13.0	...
1922	63.5	50.1	11.8	6.3	5.8	...	174.1[25]	68.0[25]	6.1	...
1923	93.2	32.1	29.2	5.8	8.0	...	167.6	58.9	11.5	...
1924	86.9	36.5	10.7	5.9	4.1	...	174.5	66.7	19.6[31]	4.8
1925	55.5	37.9	11.9	5.1	4.3	...	140.6	56.3	17.6	5.7
1926	45.1	39.9	13.0	5.4	4.9	7.1	166.6	51.1	18.2	5.6
1927	43.9	41.5	12.8	5.7	5.3	8.4	153.5	55.7	22.0	5.8
1928	48.6	38.6	13.5	5.6	4.8	9.7	136.8	59.1	21.8	5.8
1929	50.2	36.6	11.0	6.3	4.6	9.3	143.7	56.2	18.2	6.0
1930	41.6	41.6	5.7	7.5	3.6	10.4	92.2	66.2	13.6	7.6
1931	14.4	53.9	3.0	8.4	1.7	10.0	34.3	71.4	4.8	8.1
1932	10.2	47.5	2.1	9.0	1.3	9.3	27.0	75.6	2.5	6.0
1933	6.7	31.7	2.4	7.3	1.2	7.6	26.3	59.3	2.2	3.4
1934	15.7	20.0	2.4	5.7	1.2	2.3	29.2	49.8	2.9	2.3
1935	17.0	15.2	2.5	5.4	1.3	1.9	29.8	46.2	3.3	1.9
1936	...	...	2.4	4.7	2.0	1.9	29.8	47.2	3.9	1.9
1937	...	...	2.3	4.5	2.8	2.5	31.8	42.6	5.4	2.5
1938	...	...	2.1	5.8	2.0	2.0	34.1	40.6	5.7	2.1
1939	1.0	0.7	3.6	7.2	2.2	1.2	...	...	...	...
1940	2.9	2.1	3.1	6.8	1.1	0.9	...	...	...	...
1941	7.9	1.5	1.1	4.3	1.4	0.6	...	...	...	...
1942	3.4	0.8	0.9	3.1	0.3	0.6	...	...	...	...
1943	2.3	1.1	0.7	6.2	—	0.5	...	...	...	...
1944	2.0	1.7	0.5	13.3	—	0.1	...	...	...	...
1945	3.5	2.6	8.3	21.1	0.3	0.1	...	...	...	...
1946	7.5	5.1	6.9	31.4	1.8	2.4	166.6[26]	63.1[26]	...	...
1947	15.2	6.3	6.5	31.4	2.6	3.3	121.6	56.5	...	...
1948	20.9	6.1	9.8	32.9	3.6	4.2	157.3	61.4	...	...
1949	44.8	6.9	14.2	24.0	2.9	4.2	144.5	59.4	...	...

See pp. 141–2 for footnotes

A9 Annual Migration Statistics (in thousands)

1950–1969

	Austria E	Austria I	Belgium E	Belgium I	Denmark E	Denmark I	Finland E	France E	France I	West Germany E	West Germany I	Greece E	Italy E	Italy I	Netherlands E	Netherlands I	Norway E	Portugal E
1950	0.7	...	36.5	27.9	25.5	22.4	14.0	...	19.3	172.7	550.7	4.6	200.3	72.0	50.7	70.6	2.3	21.9
1951	3.6	...	43.0	60.0	29.0	20.3	19.6	...	26.3	248.6	386.2	14.2	293.1	91.9	58.8	37.6	2.9	33.7
1952	1.5	...	38.8	52.2	24.5	20.8	6.0	...	39.4	247.5	312.4	6.6	277.5	96.9	71.8	22.7	3.0	47.0
1953	1.8	0.7	38.1	40.1	18.4	19.3	5.1	...	20.2	151.4	500.3	8.8	224.7	103.0	57.5	37.6	2.5	39.7
1954	3.6	0.4	34.1	34.6	19.8	18.2	3.0	...[31]	16.4[31]	189.2	410.4	18.7	250.9	107.2	52.3	29.8	2.8	41.0
1955	5.1	1.0	32.8	51.1	26.8	18.7	1.8	173	225	190.9	510.7	29.8	320.1	141.9	43.1	39.0	2.6	29.8
1956	5.6	1.7	36.7	52.6	32.3	20.1	2.5	81.9	15.7	222.5	561.9	35.3	344.8	155.3	51.3	39.0	2.6[31]	27.0
1957	2.3	1.8	36.6	68.8	33.7	21.9	5.2	57.7	196	231.5	648.2	30.4	341.7	163.3	50.5	35.5	12.4	35.4
1958	1.5	0.8	40.3	47.1	25.2	23.2	5.6	59	143	210.7	539.6	24.5	255.5	139.0	44.7	54.4	11.3	34.0
1959	2.1	1.0	35.2	32.3	22.6	24.4	3.5	52	127	224.1	434.8	23.7	268.5	156.1	44.9	25.7	11.8	33.5
1960	2.1	1.0	32.2	42.2	23.6	26.6	1.8	58	138	259.9[27]	623.9[27]	47.8	383.9	192.2	48.9	33.1	18.7	32.3
1961	0.2	2.3	35.5	36.1	25.1	27.9	1.9	73	234	306.2	742.2	58.8	387.1	210.2	38.0	42.5	10.6	33.5
1962	0.5	2.7	33.1	52.7	24.2	27.9	3.6	155	340	355.4	607.4	48.1	365.60	229.1	37.2	51.1	12.5	33.5
1963	0.8	2.1	35.4	72.6	26.0	26.6	2.8	211	421	435.5	646.3	100.1	277.6	221.2	32.3	43.5	11.4	39.5
1964	1.1	2.5	38.2	92.3	25.8	27.1	3.6	226	471	486.1	763.7	105.6	258.5	190.2	38.9	55.5	14.3	55.6
1965	1.2	1.9	40.4	80.8	29.4	29.9	7.0	237	228	496.2	839.9	117.2	282.6	196.4	43.3	65.1	14.0	89.1
1966	1.2	2.6	40.8	71.1	28.1	29.8	9.9	220	256	614.1	745.7	86.7	296.5	206.5	46.5	69.3	13.4	120.2
1967	1.2	2.5	40.3	63.7	29.1	30.7	11.0	200	211	608.7	431.8	42.7	229.3	168.3	52.4	44.5	13.0	92.5
1968	1.4	2.7	44.3	57.1	30.1	26.7	12.2	198	231	407.9	686.1	50.9	215.7	150.0	47.7	53.7	13.6	80.5
1969	1.3	3.5	41.5	55.2	29.5	36.3	20.4	230	258	439.9	1,012.2	91.6	182.2	153.3	45.3[30] / 56.2	66.6[30] / 76.4	13.5	...

A9 Annual Migration statistics (in thousands)

1970–1993

	Austria E	Austria I	Belgium E	Belgium I	Denmark E	Denmark I	Finland E	France E	France I	West Germany E	West Germany I	Greece E	Italy E	Italy I	Netherlands E	Netherlands I	Norway E	Portugal E
1970	1.3	4.7	45.6	62.1	27.0	38.6	44.5	292	352	498.4	1,072.4	92.7	151.9	142.5	57.4	90.8	18.4	66.4
1971	1.5	4.9	37.3	62.7	31.6	35.0	18.5	372	409	557.0	987.7	61.7	167.7	128.6	62.0	95.1	12.7	50.4
1972	0.8	4.6	42.7	62.5	25.8	31.2	12.8	385	409	572.3	903.1	43.4	141.9	138.2	62.2	81.3	14.0	54.1
1973	0.6	4.2	40.4	64.3	29.7	41.9	10.3	435	476	583.9	967.9	27.5	123.8	125.2	63.6	84.7	13.9	79.5
1974	0.5	4.1	40.8	71.9	39.8	33.1	12.0	542	550	639.1	629.8	24.4	112.0	116.7	60.7	93.8	14.3	43.4
1975	0.2	4.1	40.2	69.9	40.7	31.9	12.2	596	592	655.3	456.1	20.3	92.7	122.8	55.2	127.3	14.8	24.8
1976	...	4.4	42.4	58.7	30.0	33.3	...	647	610	570.9	498.7	20.4	97.2	16.0	61.5	83.0	14.1	19.5
1977	...	5.0	41.8	55.3	26.9	327	...	774	776	507.2	539.9	16.5[32]	92.7	112.8	61.1	83.9	14.4	19.5
1978	...	5.9	42.8	52.6	26.7	32.1	...	820	821	460.5	575.9	...	85.6	89.9	61.1	89.2	14.9	22.1
1979	...	5.8	42.7	54.9	27.7	33.2	...	913	970	420.7	666.7	...	88.9	91.7	59.8	104.6	15.1	26.3
1980	...	...	41.3	54.7	30.9	33.5	10.0	1,099	1,185	441.1	752.1	...	84.9	90.5	59.5	112.5	14.7	25.2
1981	...	...	44.1	49.3	27.9	29.7	7.4	1,240	1,339	472.7	625.1	...	89.2	88.9	63.2	80.2	14.5	23.1
1982	...	...	43.9	44.7	28.2	28.3	6.8	1,312	1,317	496.1	420.8	...	71.5	98.3	67.5	70.7	14.7	17.1
1983	...	...	40.3	43.7	27.7	26.0	7.5	1,380	1,381	489.2	372.0	...	85.1	87.8	60.8	66.8	15.8	13.7
1984	...	...	39.0	47.0	29.0	25.1	...	1,573	1,564	606.5	452.7	...	48.9	77.0	58.9	66.9	15.9	14.0
1985	...	...	37.1	47.0	36.2	26.7	7.7	1,919	1,835	427.4	509.3	...	66.7	67.3	55.2	79.4	15.6	14.9
1986	...	...	37.4	49.0	38.9	27.9	8.3	1,308	1,263	409.8	596.7	...	57.9	56.0	54.7	87.4	16.7	13.7
1987	...	...	38.5	49.8	36.3	30.1	8.5	1,094	1,151	400.9	614.6	...	54.6	53.3	52.0	95.9	17.4	16.2
1988	...	...	34.9	48.5	35.1	34.5	8.3	1,069	1,272	421.9	903.9	...	...	...	55.8	91.2	19.8	18.3
1989	...	...	33.5	54.1	34.9	38.4	7.4	...	...	[33]999.9	[33]1185.5	...	51.1	39.1	59.7	98.9	27.3	...
										Germany								
1990	...	...	32.5	62.6	32.3	40.7	6.5	...	...	...	...	...	...	...	57.3	117.4	23.7	...
1991	...	...	33.7	67.5	32.6	43.6	5.9	...	...	985.9	1182.9	...	42.6	53.2	57.3	120.2	18.2	...
1992	...	...	33.7	66.8	31.9	43.4	6.0	...	...	1,163.5	1489.4	...	41.3	51.5	58.8	116.9	16.8	...
1993	...	...	34.2	63.7	32.3	43.4	...	...	...	942.5	1268.0	...	44.2	54.5	59.2	119.2	18.9	...

A9 Annual Migration statistics (in thousands)

	Spain		Sweden		Switzerland		United Kingdom	
	E	I	E	I	E	I	E	I
1950	59.1	9.6	12.9	27.9	2.7	4.5	130.3	66.0
1951	61.3	11.6	16.6	31.6	3.4	4.4	150.8	67.7
1952	63.0	19.5	15.0	26.3	3.6	4.3	165.9	68.7
1953	50.7	19.8	17.5	19.2	2.7	4.8	144.1	69.6
1954	59.3	18.6	13.8	20.8	2.3[31]	4.2[31]	135.7	82.6
					7.5	5.5		
1955	67.6	18.6	12.7	30.1	7.7	5.8	116.4	72.7
1956	57.0	17.4	14.7	28.0	8.2	5.8	129.8	64.1
1957	62.5	22.2	15.1	33.0	8.3	6.3	153.6	56.0
1958	54.5	29.5	14.2	22.1	7.9	6.7	105.1	61.0
1959	34.6	19.1	15.6	19.1	7.9	6.4	95.6	67.2
1960	33.2[29]	23.1	15.1	26.1	8.6	6.4	88.7	80.2
1961	34.3							
1961	36.5	24.2	15.0	29.6	8.6	7.3	91.0	83.7
1962	36.2	22.3	14.9	25.1	8.7	7.6	91.2	68.0
1963	25.9	22.3	15.3	27.0	8.9	7.7	107.2[31]	47.1[31]
1964	24.3	22.4	15.7	38.3	9.4	7.5	271.4	211.0
1965	21.4	21.2	16.0	49.6	10.2	7.7	284.3	206.3
1966	21.4	20.1	19.7	47.0	10.8	7.9	301.6	219.2
1967	19.3	18.6	20.0	30.0	10.9	8.5	309.0	225.0
1968	19.4	16.0	23.2	36.0	10.3	8.4	277.7	221.6
1969	20.0	13.7	20.4	64.5	11.2	8.5	292.7	205.6
1970	16.8	13.2	28.7	77.3	10.4	8.5	290.7	225.6
1971	14.4	11.6	39.6	42.6	10.0	8.8	240.0	199.7
1972	6.0	...	41.6	29.9	9.3	8.5	233.2	221.9
1973	5.1	...	40.3	29.4	10.0	8.0	245.8	195.7
1974	4.6	...	28.4	37.4	9.7	7.6	269.0	183.8
1975	3.9	...	27.2	44.1	9.8	6.8	238.3	197.2
1976	3.4	...	25.5	45.5	10.1	6.2	210.4	191.3
1977	3.2	...	21.1	44.0	10.2	6.7	208.7	162.6
1978	3.6	...	22.2	36.2	10.5	7.3	192.4	187.0
1979	4.2	25.7	23.5	37.0	10.9	7.8	188.6	194.8
1980	3.3	20.9	29.8	39.4	11.4[31]	8.1[31]	229.1	173.7
1981	5.8	9.4	29.4	32.3	97.7	121.4	233	153
1982	7.3	16.0	28.4	30.4	93.2	114.2	259	202
1983	...	17.5	25.3	27.5	91.3	96.5	185	202
1984	...	17.2	22.8	31.5	84.9	96.8	164	201
1985	...	20.1	22.0	33.1	85.1	98.9	174	232
1986	...	14.1	24.5	39.5	84.8	107.2	213	250
1987	...	16.9	20.7	42.7	86.3	112.7	210	212
1988	...	24.4	21.5	51.1	91.5	125.0	237	216
1989	...	33.9	21.5	65.9	96.6	130.2	205	250
1990	...	33.9	25.2	60.0	97.6	154.2	231	267
1991	...	24.3	24.7	49.7	103.3	164.7	239	267
1992	...	38.9	25.7	45.3	117.0	157.2	227	216
1993	...	33.0	29.9	61.8	105.0	144.5	215	212

See pp. 141–2 for footnotes

A9 Annual Migration Statistics (in thousands)

NOTES

1. SOURCES:- Four main sources have been used—I. Ferenczi *International Migration*, vol. 1 (New York, 1929); U.N., *Sex and Age of International Migrants: Statistics for 1918–1947* (1953); U.N., *Economic Characteristics of International Migrants: Statistics for Selected Countries, 1918–1954* (no date); and the annual U.N., *Demographic Yearbook*. In addition use was made of the official publications noted on pp. xv–xvii and statistics for Greece from 1946 to 1969 were supplied by the National Statistical Service of Greece.

2. The nature of the statistics varies greatly from country to country. Descriptions of the main characteristics (minor changes are indicated in footnotes) are as follows:-

Austria	1819–30—authorised migrants to and from Cisleithania and the Italian provinces; 1830–54—the same plus unauthorised migrants against whom proceedings were taken; 1854–71—authorised emigrants only (apparently) from Cisleithania; 1871–1913—intercontinental emigrants of Austrian citizenship via Hamburg and Bremen, and subsequently other ports (see footnotes); 1921 onwards—(a) intercontinental emigrants of Austrian citizenship embarking for non-European countries, Turkey, or Russia at Hamburg, Bremen, Cherbourg, le Havre, Antwerp, Amsterdam, and Genoa, and (b) aliens receiving immigrant work-permits, and their dependents. The movements of refugees are excluded.
Belgium	Departures and arrivals to and from foreign countries and Belgian colonies as recorded in local registers of resident population. These appear to have been incomplete before the late 1900's.
Bulgaria	Permanent emigrants who had been resident in the country.
Czechoslovakia	Citizens and resident aliens receiving emigrant passports.
Denmark	1869–1932—intercontinental emigration of citizens; 1933 onwards—migration to and from all overseas countries by citizens and resident aliens.
Finland	1900–1923—intercontinental emigration of all residents; 1924 onwards—emigration to all countries of all residents. (Incomplete figures are available in Ferenczi, *opp. 136-7.*, back to 1881.)
France	1857–91—steerage (or equivalent) passengers of French citizenship at le Havre, Bordeaux, Bayonne, and at various times other French ports; Immigration statistics from 1946 relate to permanent workers placed by the National Immigration Office, with migrants from Algeria added since 1955. Emigration statistics since 1955 relate solely to movements to Algeria.
Germany	1832–1939—intercontinental migration of citizens through German and the major foreign ports; 1946 onwards—all migrants to and from West Germany, including movements across the frontier with East Germany, and including short-term movements.
Greece	To 1940—all migrants of Greek citizenship or origin, except for the 1919–24 immigration figures, which are of aliens. 1946–53—all permanent transoceanic emigrants; 1954 onwards—all permanent emigrants.
Hungary	1871–1913—intercontinental emigrants of Hungarian citizenship via Bremen and Hamburg and, at various times, other ports (see footnotes).
Ireland	1851–1921—all natives who left Irish ports, including to Great Britain; 1924–33—citizens migrating other than to Europe and the Mediterranean area; 1934 onwards—the same plus British citizens. Statistics are not available after 1940, but see note 4 below.
Italy	1869–1913—intercontinental migration of citizens "in straitened circumstances"; 1914–17—intercontinental migration of manual workers, petty traders, and their families; 1928–42—intercontinental migration of all workers; 1943 onwards—all migration of citizens.
Netherlands	1843–65—intercontinental emigration of citizens via Dutch ports; 1865 onwards—departures and arrivals to and from overseas recorded in local registers of resident population. These were incomplete before 1920.
Norway	1821–1956—intercontinental emigration of citizens, though from 1866 to 1876 only emigrants to the U.S.A. are included; 1956 onwards—emigration to all countries of all residents.
Poland	1890–1913—permanent emigrants, other than to Russia, of all residents of Congress Poland; 1922–37—permanent emigration to all residents.
Portugal	1855–1917—intercontinental emigration of citizens; 1918 onwards—emigration to all countries of citizens.
Romania	All movements of citizens.
Russia	Emigration statistics relate to the outward balance of citizens crossing the frontiers, and immigration statistics to the inward balance of aliens. (Negative signs indicate net immigration of citizens and net emigration of aliens);
Serbia	As for Russia.
Spain	1851–1909—outward balance of passenger movements by sea; 1909 onwards—steerage (or equivalent) passengers, whether citizens or aliens, to destinations outside Europe.
Sweden	All residents moving to take up permanent residence.

A9   Annual Migration Statistics (in thousands)

Switzerland   1868–1954—emigration statistics relate to intercontinental movement of citizens and resident aliens; immigration statistics are of aliens only. (Statistics to 1889 are known to be incomplete.) 1954 onwards—emigrants and returned immigrants, of military age and Swiss citizenship only to 1980.

United   1815–76—intercontinental passengers to and from U.K. ports (including Irish ports);
Kingdom   1876–1919—intercontinental citizen passengers to and from U.K. ports;
             1920–63—intercontinental migration of U.K. and Commonwealth citizens for permanent residence;
             1964 onwards—all migration of U.K. and Commonwealth citizens, other than to and from Ireland.

Yugoslavia   Intercontinental migration of citizens, though emigration statistics since 1925 include a small number of resident aliens.

Break lines in the table which are not followed by a footnote number refer to the changes listed above.

3. A few series, deemed to be too short for inclusion in the table proper, are shown here (in thousands):-

Czechoslovakia—Immigrants (citizens and aliens)		Germany—Emigrants (citizens)			
1922	12.8	1844	24.0	1850	45.3
1923	7.2	1845	39.0	1851	56.5
1924	9.1	1846	56.5	1852	72.5
1925	7.7	1847	67.1	1853	55.7
1926	6.9	1848	44.4	1854	124.2
1927	7.2	1849	52.9		

4. Annual average net emigration from southern Ireland for intercensal periods is as follows (in thousands):-

1936–46	18.7
1946–51	24.4
1951–56	39.4
1956–61	42.4
1961–66	16.1
1966–71	10.8

FOOTNOTES

[1]   Bordeaux, le Havre, and Marseille were included from 1875.
[2]   A small proportion of Hungarians is included in these years.
[3]   Amsterdam, Antwerp, Genoa, Rotterdam, and the minor German ports were included from 1889, though the latter were dropped from 1899 without significantly affecting the series.
[4]   Bordeaux, le Havre, and Marseille were dropped from 1900.
[5]   Amsterdam, Antwerp, Genoa, and Rotterdam were included from 1889.
[6]   From 1 May.
[7]   Migrants from the Azores and Maderia are included.
[8]   Trieste was included from 1903.
[9]   Cherbourg and Fiume were included from 1904.
[10]   le Havre was included again from 1905.
[11]   From 1 March.
[12]   The occasion of this break is described in note 2. A comparable figure on the later basis for 1931 is 9.6 thousand;
[13]   Including Austria and Sudetenland.
[14]   To 31 August only.
[15]   From 1 April.
[16]   Intercontinental migrants only.
[17]   Fiume, Liverpool and Trieste were included from 1904.
[18]   le Havre was included from 1905.
[19]   Cherbourg was included from 1910.
[20]   From 1 October.
[21]   Excluding migrants through U.K. ports after June.
[22]   Including deportees.
[23]   To 30 April only.
[24]   Excluding emigrants from the towns, who numbered 2.1 thousand in 1902 and 13.0 thousand in 1904.
[25]   Migration via southern Irish ports was subsequently excluded.
[26]   These are known to be incomplete.
[27]   West Berlin is included from 1960.
[28]   Subsequent statistics are from the *Statistical Yearbook of the Netherlands* rather than the U.N. *Demographic Yearbook*
[29]   Previously excluding emigration by air.
[30]   This break occurs on a change of source from U.N. to national publications.
[31]   See note 2 above.
[32]   January to September only.
[33]   United Germany from this point onwards.

B LABOUR FORCE

1. Economically Active Population by Major Industrial Groups   page 145
2. Unemployment   page 163
3. Industrial Disputes   page 172
4. Money Wages in Industry   page 186
5. Money Wages in Agriculture   page 194

The statistics in this section cover a wide range of topics and come from a variety of sources. The occupation data for periods up to the 1960s were almost entirely derived by Professor Bairoch and his colleagues from national censuses of population. Therefore the problems of accuracy referred to in the last section also appear here. A more significant difficulty is the very considerable variations which have occurred in classifications, both between countries and over time. The distinction between an occupational and an industrial classification was seldom properly appreciated until well into the twentieth century. The treatment of retired persons was very variable, and so also was that of women working in agriculture or in other family-based economic units. When Jacques Bertillon came to put together his volume on nineteenth-century European population censuses for the International Institute of Statistics in 1899, he expressed the view that "the nomenclatures adopted by the different countries are so different that international comparisons would have been either very difficult or fallacious".[1] Professor Bairoch's group, having made every possible effort to achieve international and intertemporal comparability, in effect echo Bertillon, when they write that "because of the frequent changes in criteria and methods used in census taking ... it is practically impossible to come up with statistics that are perfectly comparable in time and space".[2] Rough comparisons of orders of magnitude are feasible, however, and the degree of precision has certainly improved over the last forty years, though differences between centrally-planned and market economies still need to be interpreted with great care.

Probably a still greater degree of heterogeneity is to be found in the unemployment statistics. Some come from trade union records (of both varying character and reliability and uncertain representativeness). Some derive from insurance scheme statistics (which can be almost as variable), and some from either total registration or sample surveys. In addition to variations in the definition of the unemployed, where percentages are shown they are also likely to be variations in the definition of the base, that is of the total workforce. It will be readily understood, therefore, that comparisons over time must be made with due regard to changes in the nature of the series, and that comparisons between countries must not be made without taking the differences in definitions into account. Availability of some indicator of the level of unemployment has varied from time to time, though there is rarely anything before the coming of modern, factory-based industry—certainly nothing that could be reproduced here. Generalised national insurance schemes became common only during the interwar period, but they have been subject to frequent changes which have broken the continuity of the figures.[3] Some of these changes have represented manipulations for political purposes, though perhaps the ultimate manipulation has been the virtual absence of any data for the centrally-planned economies of eastern Europe.

Data on industrial disputes are lacking for the centrally-planned economies, as they are likewise lacking for many periods and places with an authoritarian government. However, the statistics which do exist are reasonably homogeneous and reliable for each country individually, though comparisons between countries need to be made with care because of differences in reporting systems.

Wage data are notoriously intractable, and it is perhaps best to treat the indices shown here in Table B4 and B5 as little more than impressions of the general course of money wages. Apart from the well-known technical problems of index numbers dealt with in any textbook of statistics, there are problems in each country of availability and selection of data; of weighting different occupations and of the appropriateness (often taking the form of assessing obsolescence) of the chosen weights; of the differences between hourly, daily, or weekly wage rates and between weekly or longer-period earnings. Moreover, it must be stressed that these tables are concerned

---

[1] J. Bertillon, *Statistique internationale des rencensements de la population...*(Paris, 1899).

[2] P. Bairoch *et al*, *La population active et sa structure* (Brussels, 1968)

[3] For a discussion of the problems affecting the user of the British statistics, see W.R. Garside, *The Measurement of Unemployment* (Oxford, 1980).

with money wages, not real wages. To assess the latter, it is necessary to employ cost-of-living indices, such as are given in Table H.2 below, though these are not always available for all the periods for which there are wage data. In general, it must be emphasised that detailed comparisons between different countries require a degree of original research which it has not been possible to afford here. As yet there has been little scholarly effort devoted to this subject despite, or perhaps because of, its intermittent interest for journalists.[4]

---

[4]　A small beginning has been made in Peter Scholliers (ed.), *Real Wages in 19th and 20th Century Europe: Historical and Comparative Perspectives* (New York, etc., 1989), especially in the contribution by V. Zamagni.

B1 ECONOMICALLY ACTIVE POPULATION BY MAJOR INDUSTRIAL GROUPS (in thousands)[1]

AUSTRIA[4]   1857–2001

	Agriculture Forestry & Fishing	Extractive Industry	Manufacturing[2] Industry	Construction	Commerce Finance etc	Transport & Communications	Services[3]	Others Occupied
All								
1857	3,638[6]		1,225		111		698[9]	1,286[6]
1869	7,506	104[5]	1,859[5]	236	303	95	1,198[9]	215
Males								
1880	3,432[6]	108[5,7]	1,632[5,7]		241[8]	111	633[9]	454[6]
1890	4,165	130[5,7]	1,753[5,7]	273	289[8]	183	495[9]	
1900	4,083	184[5,7]	1,880[5,7]	357	333	246	582[9]	
1910	4,212	369[7]	2,361[7]		575[8]	375	654[9]	87
1920	638		778		269[8]		263[9]	21
1934	654	22			233[8]	134	205[9]	60
1939	655	26[5]	634[5]	251	131	172	283[9,8]	—
1951	513	48	632	256	157	159	233[9,8]	25
1961	362	47	652	314	181	173	261[8]	21
1971	228	25	681	246	277[8]	167	243	33
1981	152	22	745	266	359	180	300	—
1991	137	11	702	283	408	183	350	17
2001	116	9	598	329	579	199	383	16
Females								
1880	2,729[6]	10[5,7]	525[5,7]		79[8]	5	693[9]	428[6]
1890	4,305	14[5,7]	691[5,7]	20	89[8]	13	562[9]	
1900	4,123	10[5,7]	692[5,7]	16	126[8]	15	633[9]	
1910	4,294	53[7]	845[7]		349[8]	22	586[9]	169
1920	346		248		106[8]		89[9]	326
1934	350	1	244		148[8]	11	280[9]	35
1939	768	1[5]	260[5]	10	141	19	299[8,9]	—
1951	567	3	266	11	138	19	279[8,9]	14
1961	407	3	345[5]	19	189	25	354[8]	17
1971	199	2	327	15	328[8]	28	271	28
1981	138	4	335	27	460	38	376	—
1991	121	—	266	30	517	45	472	23
2001	104	1	207	33	714	63	581	19

B1   Economically Active Population by Major Industrial Groups (in thousands)[1]

BELGIUM   1846-2000

	Agriculture Forestry & Fishing	Extractive Industry	Manufacturing[2] Industry	Construction	Commerce Finance etc	Transport & Communications	Services[3]	Others Occupied
Males								
1846	681	44	329	41	45[10]	16[10]	117[10]	—
1856	712	63	400	62	53[10]	26[10]	132[10]	—
1866	705	93	466	68	67[10]	30[10]	145[10,11]	—
1880	674	104	513	84	149[10]	29[29]	206[10]	—
1890	640	130	604	93	217[10]	41[10]	268[10]	—
1900	616	166	738	131	264[10]	72[10]	271[10]	—
1910	585	192	807	185	182	184	256	—
1920	525	212	774	187	186	232	187	—
1930	505	201	987	238	277	242	304	—
1947	364	188	981	178	307	234	352	5
1961	213	109	961	246	306	220	446	5
1970[23]	133	49	902	283	450	211	439	47
1981	88		729	240	485	235	494	56
1990	74		604	221	510	213	619	30
2000	53	7	619	244	659	250	522	14
Females								
1846	342	4	310	...	23[10]	1[10]	57[10]	—
1856	354	10	317	...	32[10]	1[10]	115[10]	—
1866	372	15	275	1	37[10]	1[10]	151[10]	—
1880	387	10	259	1	88[10]	1[10]	176[10]	—
1890	268	9	256	1	96[10]	1[10]	207[10]	—
1900	249	7	321	1	122[10]	6[10]	225[10]	—
1910	217	8	383	2	111	7	342	—
1920	151	10	306	3	90	12	230	—
1930	141	6	346	3	166	12	310	—
1947	61	3	307	2	171	16	244	1
1961	41	1	285	4	212	19	345	1
1970	29	1	298	9	315	23	345	25
1981	26		206	11	122	35	525	36
1990	26		185	15	452	43	770	—
2000	19	1	188	18	558	68	849	24

BULGARIA   1910-2001

	Agriculture Forestry & Fishing	Extractive Industry	Manufacturing[2] Industry	Construction	Commerce Finance etc	Transport & Communications	Services[3]	Others Occupied
Males								
1910	929	2		158	67	28	84	15
1920	1,035	6		176	66	33	100	10
1934	1,348	8		220	75	47	149	58
1946	1,541	20		318	106	64	233	51
1956	1,317		482[12]	108	100	114	259[12]	24
1965	857		728	256	99	156	36	258
1975	499[55]	63	783[55,56]	288	135	231	367[56]	...
1985	393		950	328	126	235	420	...
1992	267	62	484	165	191	211	327	...
Females								
1910	892	—		20	1	...	28	...
1920	1,108	...		29	4	1	33	...
1934	1,397	—		46	6	1	54	29
1946	1,619	...		92	19	2	68	50
1956	1,346		176[12]	7	42	17	148[12]	9
1965	1,034		414	25	107	33	26	238
1975	551[55]	22	684[55,56]	62	252	68	443[56]	1
1985	379		828	79	296	80	473	...
1992	204	20	489	41	248	45	494	...
Total								
2001[57]	774	36	650	127	616	214	523	...

B1 Economically Active Population by Major Industrial Groups (in thousands)[1]

CZECHOSLOVAKIA   1921–2001

	Agriculture Forestry & Fishing	Extractive Industry	Manufacturing[2] Industry	Construction	Commerce Finance etc	Transport & Communications	Services[3]	Others Occupied
Males								
1921	1,666	150	1,598		255	223	350	55
1930[13]	1,447	129	1,428	362	362	266	421	65
1947	1,123	133	1,506		244	261	518	8
1961	716	1,440		459	180	288	407	—
1970	637	175	1,422	501	211	344	530	40
1980	602	1,761		603	267	331	585	38
1991	628	1,655		533	270	349	640	154
2001	158	55	875	388	539	252	419	3
Females								
1921	759	10	455		107	20	330	38
1930[13]	1,037	4	568	10	197	15	380	33
1947	1,084	10	536		133	25	259	13
1961	736	934		63	324	94	525	—
1970	506	29	1,129	97	478	148	714	12
1980	424	1,329		140	596	167	969	40
1991	365	1,233		121	636	182	1,140	133
2001	68	13	528	42	588	112	708	2

DENMARK   1850–2000

	Agriculture Forestry & Fishing	Extractive Industry	Manufacturing[2] Industry	Construction	Commerce Finance etc	Transport & Communications	Services[3]	Others Occupied
All								
1850[14]	654		291			57		98
Males								
1860[14]	366		177			38		48
1870[14]	411		192			58		54
1880[14]	478		231			75		67
1890[14]	463		268		82	35	71	90
1901	381	165		43	110		64	13
1911	403		231		91	48	55	18
1921	405		302		103	71	71	5
1930	438		365		137	84	68	11
1940	435	4	360	115	155	101	106	10
1950	397	4	402	128	176	117	130	15
1960	332	4	455	147	193	127	156	33
1970	189	3	435	198	249	124	216	51
1981	142	2	335	160	321	135	305	109
1991	121	3	386	177	351	140	341	19
2000	67	3	360	169	436	126	291	6
Females								
1860[14]	361		169			40		53
1870[14]	405		181			60		61
1880[14]	479		220			81		78
1890[14]	452		266		91	33	84	104
1901	150	67		...	21		117	8
1911	110		66		37	4	144	24
1921	69		66		44	9	204	11
1930	122		66		59	7	220	11
1940	127	...	123	1	86	14	330	4
1950	121	...	149	4	103	22	287	8
1960	35	...	155	4	120	24	306	3
1970	55	...	177	12	214	29	244	16
1981	52	...	148	19	278	40	562	97
1991	40	...	201	21	324	54	680	23
2000	23	...	165	15	341	50	663	7

B1   Economically Active Population by Major Industrial Groups (in thousands)[1]

FINLAND   **1754–2000**

	Agriculture Forestry & Fishing	Extractive Industry	Manufacturing[2] Industry	Construction	Commerce Finance etc	Transport & Communications	Services[3]	Others Occupied
All								
1754[15]	350		13		2	2	67	11
1769[15]	434		21		3	3	66	14
1805[15]	702		31		6	6	90	20
Males								
1880	260		39		6	17	37	...
1900	326	1	61	13	12	25	30	134
1910	568	...	103		15	26	19	92
1920	603	1	140		27	35	27	56
1930	634	1	158	28	38[8]	44	35	71
1940	629	3	224	39	48	60	55	93
1950	543	5	259	117	75	85	71	22
1960	466	6	292	166	106	102	89	5
1970	287	6	343	164	147	116	142	21
1980	168	9	361	143	169	132	177	28
1990	114	4	314	151	270	118	180	26
2000	93	3	348	136	327	128	221	5
Females								
1880	98		9		4	1	31	...
1900	103	...	20	...	5	1	34	68
1910	329	—	34		12	2	35	60
1920	429	—	51		23	5	47	55
1930	473	—	63	2	39[8]	7	65	55
1940	529	...	104	5	63	12	100	55
1950	369	1	162	6	85	22	156	7
1960	255	1	165	10	130	27	212	1
1970	142	1	200	12	252	35	242	8
1980	111	1	214	14	257	44	373	22
1990	83	...	165	18	339	47	451	26
2000	43	...	146	9	332	46	544	6

B1 Economically Active Population by Major Industrial Groups (in thousands)[1]

FRANCE 1856–1994

	Agriculture Forestry & Fishing	Extractive Industry	Manufacturing[2] Industry	Construction	Commerce Finance etc	Transport & Communications	Services[3]
Males							
1856	5,146	177[18]	2,002[18]	486	510	214	1,174[9]
1866[16]	5,299	145[18]	2,303[18]	561	525	276	1,372[9]
1866[17]	5,248	223[18]	2,019[18]	712	910	274	1,679[9]
1896[17]	5,741	224	2,903	543	783	552	1,811[9]
1901[17]	5,581	264	3,083	563	873	603	1,905[9]
1906[17]	5,525	279	3,169	539	972	631	1,913[9]
1911[17]	5,331	240	4,189		1,218	657	1,577[9]
1921	5,062	317	3,396	620	1,025	915	1,780[9]
1926	4,809	433	3,869	697	1,193	871	1,685[9]
1931	4,510	442	3,886	821	1,265	935	1,853[9]
1936	4,282	350	3,442	679	1,272	904	2,012[9]
1946	4,221	369	3,128	1,022	1,169	1,238	1,767[9]
1954	3,369	364	3,598	1,337	1,269	843	1,950[9]
1962	2,634	310	3,846	1,553	1,479	862	2,331
1968	2,120	234	4,058	1,990	1,890	970	1,816
1975	1,471	171	4,159	1,797	2,565	978	2,224
1982	1,163	123	3,801	1,648	2,734	1,005	2,525
1991	853	67	3,012	1,159	2,578	970	2,489
Females							
1856	2,159	17[18]	1,095[18]	16	228	10	889
1866[16]	2,237	14[18]	1,196[18]	18	260	14	923
1886[17]	2,598	30[18]	1,250[18]	61	504	21	1,179
1896[17]	2,760	6	1,716	2	510	161	1,219
1901[17]	2,664	6	1,926	2	791	213	1,427
1906[17]	3,330	6	2,059	1	642	241	1,422
1911[17]	3,241	6	2,496		835	60	1,082
1921	3,961	11	2,021	6	778	270	1,555
1926	3,391	16	2,000	6	780	160	1,487
1931	3,194	18	2,019	9	881	135	1,646
1936	2,922	8	1,695	8	859	132	1,698
1946	3,263	13	1,630	24	922	275	1,753
1954	1,826	9	1,642	53	875	177	1,954
1962	1,273	10	1,647	60	1,117	201	2,170
1968	1,013	7	1,696	102	1,477	252	2,377
1975	628	10	1,835	102	2,008	278	2,814
1982	598	11	1,633	126	2,339	325	3,441
1991	403	11	1,323	105	2,383	365	4,022
Total							
1994	1,048	66	4,330	1,443	6,056	1,397	7,734

B1   Economically Active Population by Major Industrial Groups (in thousands)[1]

GERMANY   1882–1939

	Agriculture Forestry & Fishing	Extractive Industry	Manufacturing[2] Industry	Construction	Commerce Finance etc	Transport & Communications	Services[3]	Others Occupied
Males								
1882	5,702	569	3,721	940	678	423	1,173	168
1895	5,540	789	4,565	1,340	930	598	1,596	150
1907	5,284	1,197	5,959	1,887	1,251	983	1,907	114
1925[19]	4,793	1,232	7,422	1,676	1,983	1,423	1,834	168
1933[19]	4,694	1,053	7,279	1,963	2,208	1,460	2,161	—
1939[20]	4,065	723	8,053	2,307	2,115	1,760	2,792	—
Females								
1882	2,535	22	995	6	176	14	443	67
1895	2,753	32	1,351	14	300	18	745	51
1907	4,599	48	1,875	19	549	43	1,069	42
1925	4,969	40	2,837	32	1,100	97	2,322	81
1933	4,685	30	2,688	40	1,409	92	2,570	—
1939	4,920	11	3,455	68	1,324	137	2,888	—

EAST GERMANY   1946–1971

	Agriculture Forestry & Fishing	Extractive Industry	Manufacturing[2] Industry	Construction	Commerce Finance etc	Transport & Communications	Services[3]	Others Occupied
Males								
1946	1,046	228	1,586	411	313	351	529	—
1950	962	370	1,782	432	333	356	526	7
1960[21]	772	2,061		453	321	356	486	—
1971[21]	529	153	1,829	525	293	357	728	—
Females								
1946	1,332	47	1,095	52	330	67	752	—
1950	1,097	54	920	43	384	78	566	13
1960[21]	630	1,311		40	606	178	834	—
1971[21]	431	46	1,356	89	638	198	1,044	—

West Germany   1946–1980

	Agriculture Forestry & Fishing	Extractive Industry	Manufacturing[2] Industry	Construction	Commerce Finance etc	Transport & Communications	Services[3]	Others Occupied
Males								
1946	2,735	614	4,087	1,125	898	1,035	1,629	—
1950	2,328	685	5,206	1,867	1,312	1,079	1,992	240
1961[22]	1,625	591	6,853	1,957	1,738	1,259	2,620	73
1970[22]	1,025	311	7,083	2,015	2,512	1,183	2,875	71
1980[22]	748	318	6,456	1,805	2,460	1,225	2,902	72
Females								
1946	2,852	43	1,467	50	617	124	1,878	—
1950	1,806	16	2,067	71	967	143	2,034	265
1961[22]	1,959	14	3,126	84	1,863	221	2,695	45
1970[22]	966	12	3,181	148	2,758	260	2,164	46
1980[22]	780	21	2,801	159	2,772	295	3,125	75

GERMANY   1992–2001

	Agriculture Forestry & Fishing	Extractive Industry	Manufacturing[2] Industry	Construction	Commerce Finance etc	Transport & Communications	Services[3]	Others Occupied
Males								
1992	525	158	6,186	1,614	3,388	1,265	4,708	—
2001	608	127	6,391	2,522	5,159	1,465	4,330	27
Females								
1992	390	16	2,538	220	3,880	437	5,345	—
2001	334	12	2,500	382	5,668	590	6,556	145

B1   Economically Active Population by Major Industrial Groups (in thousands)[1]

GREECE[23]   1920–2000

	Agriculture Forestry & Fishing	Extractive Industry	Manufacturing[2] Industry	Construction	Commerce Finance etc	Transport & Communications	Services[3]	Others Occupied
Males								
1920	817	8	235		147	77	117	122
1928	1,008	6	330		202	106	130	191
1951	1,152	13	340	74	199	135	273	144
1961	1,178	20	352	166	226	148	288	21
1971	834	20	426	255	342	199	228	26
1981	681	21	506	323	397	242	309	105
1990	495	21	514	255	524	229	380	18
2000	384	16	417	271	731	208	427	3
Females								
1920	109	1	59		4	1	47	123
1928	468	...	100		7	1	58	140
1951	215	1	121	1	21	3	115	32
1961	782	2	157	1	40	6	152	6
1971	478	2	153	2	99	13	121	39
1981	291	2	184	3	164	24	223	68
1990	398	2	232	4	336	29	341	32
2000	263	1	170	5	533	41	424	49

HUNGARY[24]   1857–2000

	Agriculture Forestry & Fishing	Extractive Industry	Manufacturing[2] Industry	Construction	Commerce Finance etc	Transport & Communications	Services[3]	Others Occupied
All								
1857	2,275		410			67	540	764[6]
1869	5,015	50	584	63	105	29	1,338	—
Males								
1880	3,547[6,25]	26[7]	714[7]		166		188[26]	443[6,26]
1890	3,954	44[7]	630[7]	93	145	76	321	185
1900	4,234	56[7]	758[7]	122	184	131	398	223
1910	4,332	72	1,204		246	193	386	196
1920	1,494	39	547		135	106	214	45
1930	1,560	35	714		170	104	188	64
1949	1,545	72	604	93	128	148	227	134
1960	1,171	145	803	273	156	245	237	137
1970	752	141	983	313	162	267	317	
1980	600	106	923	339	286	311	285	17
1990	574	840		265	179	290	445	—
2000	190	15	603	247	465	226	374	2
Females								
1880	973[6,25]	...[7]	715[7]		20		402	506[6]
1890	1,471	1[7]	95[7]	1	38	3	415	165
1900	1,821	1[7]	149[7]	3	42	6	429	133
1910	1,269	1	256		54	10	422	110
1920	632	1	132		49	12	198	49
1930	471	...	173		56	9	226	59
1949	651	3	189	3	66	17	137	138
1960	702	12	443	31	170	52	271	30
1970	471	22	750	57	258	78	419	
1980	340	20	752	74	409	102	501	5
1990	1,363	596		66	339	120	716	—
2000	61	4	408	21	497	86	648	2

B1   Economically Active Population by Major Industrial Groups (in thousands)[1]

IRELAND   **1841–1911**

	Agriculture Forestry & Fishing	Extractive Industry	Manufacturing[2] Industry	Construction	Commerce Finance etc	Transport & Communications	Services[3]	Others Occupied
Males								
1841	1,699	9[27]	303	72[27]	78		101	219[27]
1851	1,293	12[27]	257	58[27]	106		67	319[27]
1861	1,072	10[27]	231	66[27]	117		76	346[27]
1871	943	9[27]	194	58[27]	125		61	345[27]
1881	890	8[27]	164	56[27]	121		67	307[27]
1911	716	5	255		53	22	111	164
Females								
1841	145	…	686	…	33		281	…
1851	167	…	430	…	46		260	…
1861	101	…	335	…	46		334	…
1871	103	…	306	…	46		377	…
1881	96	…	215	…	39		412	…
1911	59	—	156		73	1	182	8

NORTHERN IRELAND   **1926–2001**

	Agriculture Forestry & Fishing	Extractive Industry	Manufacturing[2] Industry	Construction	Commerce Finance etc	Transport & Communications	Services[3]	Others Occupied
Males								
1926	133	3	107	22	51	21	50	4
1951	93	2	120	40	51	31	54	30
1961	68	1	112	41	54	28	70	
1971	48	1	113	54	55	31	110	
1981	27	11	77	37	65	19	79	7
1991	16	67		22	56	17	92	…
2001	18	…	76	60[58]	110	28	71	14
Females								
1926	16	—	95	…	19	1	50	1
1951	6	—	87	1	25	3	51	10
1961	3	…	73	1	32	3	60	
1971	2	…	49	…	67	2	80	
1981	1	1	38	2	48	4	103	4
1991	3	37		3	58	4	157	…
2001	3	…	26	4[58]	110	10	141	16

SOUTHERN IRELAND   **1926–2001**

	Agriculture Forestry & Fishing	Extractive Industry	Manufacturing[2] Industry	Construction	Commerce Finance etc	Transport & Communications	Services[3]	Others Occupied
Males								
1926	556	3	155		73	67	79	26
1936	542	3	100	62	68	67	98	47
1946	516	3	101	54	62	58	115	55
1951	436	10	140	95	103	54	98	10
1961	348	10	136	73	109	51	90	5
1971	259	11	171	98	139	54	92	7
1981	183	12	207	142	166	50	123	16
1991	142	6	158	77	166	52	135	134
2001	107	7	224	172	284	81	142	5
Females								
1926	122	—	33		35	2	143	8
1936	107	—	37	—	36	2	166	4
1946	81	—	35	—	37	1	172	8
1951	68	…	63	1	53	6	131	4
1961	42	…	62	1	55	7	118	1
1971	26	…	69	2	77	10	103	2
1981	13	…	72	3	108	14	135	6
1991	12	…	64	4	130	13	152	41
2001	13	1	94	8	287	30	259	11

B1 Economically Active Population by Major Industrial Groups (in thousands)[1]

ITALY · 1871–2001

	Agriculture Forestry & Fishing	Extractive Industry	Manufacturing[2] Industry	Construction	Commerce Finance etc	Transport & Communications	Services[3]	Others Occupied
Males								
1871	5,664	38	1,929		167	263	1,176	19
1881	5,498	59	1,446	836	247	310	904	876
1901	6,466	91	2,528		524	416	998	80
1911	6,112	110	2,877		723	530	844	78
1921	7,147	99	3,146		939	717	987	—
1931	6,545[28]		4,057[28]		1,039	767	951	
1936	6,412	126	2,707	974	1,156	667	865	190
1951	6,228		3,452	1,462	150	731	2,642	—
1961	4,150		6,333			4,135		—
1971	2,299		4,688	1,991	1,849	906	2,015	627
1981	1,430	739	3,572	1,769	2,817	1,093	2,165	610
1991	1,165	208	3,200	1,851	3,534	982	3,162	
2001	764	51	3,540	1,603	3,856	938	2,768	52
Females								
1871	3,036	…	1,358		33	8	567	4
1881	3,101	1	1,835	69	33	3	646	877
1901	3,200	1	1,370		113	8	592	67
1911	2,973	3	1,378		199	14	550	10
1921	3,117	1	1,245		231	22	632	—
1931	1,539[28]		1,252		280	27	805	
1936	2,431	2	1,342	5	449	35	955	29
1951	2,033		1,365	11	26	54	1,423	—
1961	1,507		1,553			1,841		
1971	943		1,635	35	961	86	1,423	348
1981	810	162	1,683	76	1,587	163	2,180	415
1991	658	19	1,531	106	2,128	167	2,880	—
2001	363	13	1,529	104	2,648	242	2,998	161

B1 Economically Active Population by Major Industrial Groups (in thousands)[1]

NETHERLANDS   1871–2001

	Agriculture Forestry & Fishing	Extractive Industry	Manufacturing[2] Industry	Construction	Commerce Finance etc	Transport & Communications	Services[3]	Others Occupied
Males								
1849	394	2	191	60	61	55	92	27
1859	389	2	214	67	67	68	107	27
1889	468	13	316	113	123	110	131	25
1899	512	14	389	130	179	103	129	34
1909	528	20	469	154	221	154	151	23
1920	551	42	610	184	272	208	192	29
1930	546	48	710	253	360	230	237	33
1947[11]	578	53	918	287	377	239	418	53
1960	406	60	1,121	374	448	269	469	94
1971	251	19	993	509	732	251	535	218
1981	233	7	903	447	745	279	874	45
1991	211	13	932	387	1,073	319	1,022	30
2001	158	8	887	468	1,564	358	927	96
Females								
1849	158	...	48	...	20	2	134	7
1859	79	—	44	...	18	1	161	5
1889	73	2	54	...	30	2	186	...
1899	80	2	72	...	40	3	234	...
1909	112	3	94	...	48	4	277	—
1920	90	3	128	1	76	10	321	1
1930	110	2	145	1	112	10	384	...
1947[11]	169	1	164	2	173	18	413	3
1960	41	1	208	5	222	22	428	2
1971	37	1	199	14	341	29	476	128
1981	43	1	179	26	469	42	782	21
1991	82	...	237	31	768	85	1,291	17
2001	73	1	263	40	1,232	129	1,573	94

NORWAY   1875–2000

	Agriculture Forestry & Fishing	Extractive Industry	Manufacturing[2] Industry	Construction	Commerce Finance etc	Transport & Communications	Services[3]	Others Occupied
Males								
1875	202[29]	4	92		25	42[29]	134[29]	24
1891	297		127			76[30]	25[30]	5
1900	288		177			94	28	13
1910	321	8	176		47	74	29	6
1920	336	15	233		66	84	34	4
1930	372	19	178	52	83	102	40	4
1946	367	9[31]	243[31]	121	84	117	81	11
1950	333	9	285	127	90	124	86	7
1960	261	9	302	131	113	147	116	5
1970	140	9	334	126	160	132	154	2
1980	114	10	325	146	221	132	240	9
1990	93	19	249	146	264	114	259	—
2000	64	28	230	135	365	117	264	2
Females								
1875	16[29]	—	33		4	...	224[29]	14
1891	87		50			15[30]	88[30]	4
1900	72		66			28	108	8
1910	53	...	61		37	4	125	4
1920	58	1	61		53	8	118	1
1930	41	1	59	...	62	6	146	...
1946	41	...[31]	78[31]	1	55	14	160	3
1950	27	...	83	2	60	16	139	1
1960	13	...	69	2	74	20	143	...
1970	30	...	73	3	131	25	141	1
1980	51	1	105	11	243	45	380	8
1990	36	5	88	14	284	50	480	—
2000	24	6	80	12	309	51	569	5

B1 Economically Active Population by Major Industrial Groups (in thousands)[1]

POLAND[36]   1897–2001

	Agriculture Forestry & Fishing	Extractive Industry	Manufacturing[2] Industry	Construction	Commerce Finance etc	Transport & Communications	Services[3]	Others Occupied
Males								
1897[32]	1,082	18	381	44	128	44	528[35]	15
1921[33]	5,148	85	941		375	227	589	161
1931	5,429	169	1,850		517	323	429	303
1950[34]	3,295	1,639[37]		448	365[37]	406[37]	665[37]	40
1960[34]	3,009	2,269[37]		711	341[37]	572[37]	852[37]	
1970	2,958	331	2,699	963	350[37]	851[37]	998[37]	
1978	2,759[55]	366	2,915[55]	1,229	384[37]	928[37]	1,225[37]	
1992	2,071	2,539		868	715	590	1,526	
2001	1,498	236	2,025	888	1,495	631	1,022	1
Females								
1897[32]	219	1	77	…	21	1	259[35]	14
1921[33]	5,122	8	232		144	17	365	—
1931	4,323	6	513		296	18	614	—
1950[34]	3,795	689[36]		71	279[35]	63[37]	599[37]	51
1960[34]	3,627	967[37]		80	459[37]	101[37]	918[37]	
1970	3,586	44	1,626	163	776[37]	217[37]	1,341[37]	
1978	2,660[55]	47	2,042[55]	253	990[37]	292[37]	1,871[37]	
1992	1,687	1,288		128	1,126	241	2,357	
2001	1,221	38	1,074	70	1,732	220	2,044	10

PORTUGAL   1890–2000

	Agriculture Forestry & Fishing	Extractive Industry	Manufacturing[2] Industry	Construction	Commerce Finance etc	Transport & Communications	Services[3]	Others Occupied
Males								
1890	1,076	4	297		72	50	81	—
1900	1,147	4	327		96	62	78	—
1911	1,127	9	393		125	73	122	—
1930	1,122	11	376		126	61	232	112
1940[38]	1,263	20	331	139	162	81	230	145
1950	1,348	24	455	165	206	106	242	6
1960	1,341	26	538	228	233	113	258	27
1970	824	12	492	253	298	130	396	71
1981	477	17	675	433	404	162	374	2
1990	425	33	663	372	536	172	486	1
2000	302	15	620	571	662	143	391	3
Females								
1890	487	…	298		31	2	6	—
1900	382	…	194		46	4	9	—
1911	335	…	155		30	3	173	—
1930	775	7	305		92	42	603	86
1940[38]	225	1	137	2	29	8	254	22
1950	242	2	175	1	34	8	273	2
1960	107	1	173	2	40	11	269	2
1970	179	…	261	3	103	18	233	32
1981	261	1	363	9	209	30	431	1
1990	420	3	497	12	400	40	617	1
2000	314	1	491	23	608	37	594	146

B1   Economically Active Population by Major Industrial Groups (in thousands)[1]

ROMANIA   1913–2001

	Agriculture Forestry & Fishing	Extractive Industry	Manufacturing[2] Industry	Construction	Commerce Finance etc	Transport & Communications	Services[3]	Others Occupied
Males								
1913	1,584	9	246		100	70	212	9
1930[39]	4,055	49	500	265	241	158	388	233
1956	3,380[40]		1,150[40]	242	227	259	426[40]	43
1966	2,531[55]		1,556[55]	493	240	375	477	4
1992	1,106	207	2,078	483	279	481	702	16
2001	2,284	131	1,217	378	570	397	742	…
Females								
1913	1,575	…	63		7	1	83	11
1930[39]	4,176	4	132	3	117	17	99	221
1956	3,898[40]		328[40]	23	122	38	284[40]	45
1966	3,390[55]		514[55]	44	184	62	491	3
1992	1,081	45	1,623	95	481	135	826	11
2001	2,243	19	1,007	52	713	122	823	…

RUSSIA/U.S.S.R.   1897–1999

	Agriculture Forestry & Fishing	Extractive Industry	Manufacturing[2] Industry	Construction	Commerce Finance etc	Transport & Communications	Services[3]	Others Occupied
Males								
1897[41]	15,077	155	2,920	671	1,051[36,45]	649	3,207[35]	227
1926[38]	36,170		3,487	356	900	1,195[44]	1,270[44]	610
1959	18,577[42]		22,866[43]		1,993[36,45]	—[43]	5,249[45]	133
1970	14,652		31,813[43]		2,086[36,45]	—[43]	8,945[45]	
1999	4,792	925	7,639	2,627	4,312	3,772	7,457	…
Females								
1897[41]	1,867	8	894	2	141[36,35]	21	1,777[35]	
1926[38]	35,565		1,171	8	257	98[44]	759[44]	866
1959	29,715[42]		14,400[43]		3,178[36,45]	—[43]	9,204[45]	58
1970	16,109		20,959[43]		5,798	—	15,612[45]	560
1999	2,353	285	5,453	818	6,328	1,715	11,932	…

B1 Economically Active Population by Major Industrial Groups (in thousands)[1]

SPAIN   1860–2001

	Agriculture Forestry & Fishing	Extractive Industry	Manufacturing[2] Industry	Construction	Commerce Finance etc	Transport & Communications	Services[3]	Others Occupied
Males								
1860	4,333	23	943		138	50	711	—
1877	4,112		755		144	208	511	—
1887[46]	4,033		921		167	115	345	—[46]
1900	4,324	76	775		226	133	437	190
1910	3,861		860		115	153	436	1,058
1920	4,217	130	1,284		349	219	489	283
1940	4,519	99	1,430	372	518	304	850	11
1950	4,853	171	1,543	570	594	402	799	152
1964	3,368	228	2,281	908	896	539	956	73
1970	2,646	124	2,405	1,196	1,347	605	1,126	126
1981	1,607	109	2,558	1,233	1,859	651	1,035	164
1991	1,105	76	2,285	1,467	2,145	678	1,541	133
2001	752	59	2,335	1,762	2,780	772	1,521	48
Females								
1860	—	—	224		—	—	110	—
1877	933		143		21	1	359	—
1887[46]	821		195		28	1	370	—[46]
1900	815	1	175		27	2	331	31
1910	359		174		20	2	352	107
1920	321	2	279		58	3	348	111
1940	262	1	309	2	71	6	466	—
1950	418	3	418	4	103	19	724	20
1964	809	1	797	9	451	30	695	21
1970	312	2	702	22	466	54	745	31
1981	247	7	660	27	695	71	1,013	59
1991	436	3	760	53	1,551	98	1,801	227
2001	267	5	769	88	2,377	193	1,844	373

B1   Economically Active Population by Major Industrial Groups (in thousands)[1]

SWEDEN   1860–2000

	Agriculture Forestry & Fishing	Extractive Industry	Manufacturing[2] Industry	Construction	Commerce Finance etc	Transport & Communications	Services[3]	Others Occupied
Males								
1860	510		164		15	21	79	—
1870	707		118			43	79	182[49]
1880	738		157			68	82	207[49]
1890	771		233				90	77
1900	772		362			125	81	113[49]
1910	758	13	467		82	106	114	47
1920	808	21	634		126	136	81	21
1930	799	37	704		170	169	98	18
1945	688	15	717	214	205	187[48]	182	34
1950	579	15[5]	802[5]	241	233	208	192	16
1960[47]	408	22	893	285	229	199	233	8
1970	221	18	777	319	341	199	325	6
1980	161	14	736	253	416	206	415	7
1990	111	10	684	287	536	216	466	5
2000	76	8	578	208	666	200	411	4
Females								
1860	154		10		6	—	78	—
1870	307		9			3		74
1880	332		17			5		90
1890	333		30			13		87
1900	336		51			23	103	106[49]
1910	258	—	85		38	6	176	49
1920	251	...	153		92	18	246	15
1930	242	...	186		149	22	295	2
1945	45	...	181	3	147	33[48]	329	8
1950	53	...[5]	205[5]	4	170	43	337	7
1960[47]	39	1	251	10	209	43	410	3
1970	56	1	245	13	318	48	523	2
1980	65	2	260	25	419	79	950	4
1990	38	2	268	26	497	103	1,222	1
2000	23	1	208	18	538	79	1,122	2

B1 Economically Active Population by Major Industrial Groups (in thousands)[1]

SWITZERLAND   1890–2000

	Agriculture Forestry & Fishing	Extractive Industry	Manufacturing[2] Industry	Construction	Commerce Finance etc	Transport & Communications	Services[3]	Others Occupied
Males								
1890	410		334		59	47	43	—
1900	405		435		69	52	47	—
1910	376	6	539		108	79	65	6
1920	386	6	557		118	83	77	3
1930	362[35]	7	638		123	78	124[35]	—
1941	385	7	520	136	128	70	146	30
1950	325	6	594	172	157	88	160	13
1960[38]	257	6	746	234	197	119	193	—
1970	178	6	826	272	350	139	199	4
1980	141	4	709	212	428	144	304	17
1990	139		654	316	594	165	370	—
2000	115		515	234	710	149	444	6
Females								
1890	148		217		36	2	22	—
1900	80		225		55	4	32	—
1910	101	...	270		86	6	138	3
1920	97	...	265		99	8	162	—
1930	51[35]	...	229		67	7	256[35]	—
1941	30	...	203	2	71	6	251	8
1950	30	...	228	4	96	10	267	6
1960[38]	23	...	275	5	149	16	286	—
1970	53	...	327	13	334	31	261	3
1980	50	...	262	10	394	39	341	11
1990	58		252	23	817	52	421	—
2000	66		178	33	585	75	766	4

B1　Economically Active Population by Major Industrial Groups (in thousands)[1]

U.K. (Great Britain)

	Agriculture Forestry & Fishing	Extractive Industry	Manufacturing[2] Industry	Construction	Commerce Finance etc	Transport & Communications	Services[3]	Others Occupied
Males								
1841[50]	1,458	218	1,816	376	94	196	459	474
1851	1,824	383	2,349	496	91	433	482	438
1861	1,818	457	2,609	593	130	579	564	511
1871	1,681	517	2,815	712	212	654	664	972
1881[51]	1,575	604	3,001	875	352	870	815	861
1891	1,475	751	3,460	899	449	1,104	860	1,009
1901	1,390	931	4,062	1,216	597	1,409	1,056	887
1911	1,489	1,202	4,688	1,140	739	1,571	1,361	741
1921	1,261	1,396	4,813	783	1,702	1,461	1,897	344
1931	1,181	1,272	4,958	1,108	2,314	1,563	2,267	137
1951	1,025	847	6,153	1,390	1,838	1,517	2,806	73
1961	777	728	6,308	1,597	2,066	1,486	3,136	135
1971	643	256	6,121	1,476	2,391	1,811	2,910	276
1981	425	334	4,631	1,478	2,496	1,465	2,857	98
1991	450	201	3,810	1,640	4,250	1,209	3,334	—
2001	305	104	3,596	1,858	5,132	1,512	2,952	104
Females								
1841[50]	81	7	639	1	1	4	1,041	41
1851	230	11	1,263	1	—	13	1,241	75
1861	164	6	1,456	1	2	11	1,537	80
1871	136	11	1,541	4	5	16	1,837	106
1881[51]	119	8	1,685	2	11	15	1,968	78
1891	81	7	1,948	3	26	20	2,317	89
1901	86	6	2,123	3	76	27	2,358	75
1911	117	8	2,430	5	157	38	2,560	98
1921	111	14	2,187	12	863	109	2,331	75
1931	76	9	2,355	14	1,021	110	2,644	44
1951	117	14	2,654	41	1,322	217	2,560	36
1961	97	21	2,666	69	1,773	230	2,861	64
1971	97	5	1,505	182	3,561	453	3,128	375
1981	90	20	1,867	127	2,441	329	4,270	77
1991	119	22	1,587	165	4,339	337	5,141	—
2001	86	11	1,226	200	4,748	495	5,785	114

YUGOSLAVIA

	Agriculture Forestry & Fishing	Extractive Industry	Manufacturing[2] Industry	Construction	Commerce Finance etc	Transport & Communications	Services[3]	Others Occupied
All								
1921	4,848		651[43]		133	—[43]	264	
Males								
1931	3,234		593		131	94	242	96
1948	3,322[52]		725		29[53]	112	547[53]	129
1953	3,079	106	649	224	161	151	375	16
1961	2,729	136	997	291	159	221	418	252
1971	2,270		1,093	364	287	283	507	23
1981	1,465		1,441	631	512	385	876	99
Females								
1931	1,865		124		39	8	64	38
1948	4,074[52]		183		8[53]	4	196[53]	180
1953	2,161	7	191	17	79	17	174	4
1961	2,019	8	374	26	106	28	310	60
1971	1,695		482	33	236	40	414	10
1981	1,218		768	58	520	60	109	36

B1 Economically Active Population by Major Industrial Groups (in thousands)[1]

NOTES

1. SOURCES:- The immediate source of all statistics (except the most recent) is P. Bairoch *et al, The Working Population and its Structure* (Institut de Sociologie, Universite Libre de Bruxelles, 1968). The original sources are described in detail there. The 1968/81 data come from I.L.O., *Yearbook of Labour Statistics*.
2. Professor Bairoch and his collaborators "tried to as great an extent as possible to unify the statistics in different countries during different periods", but were unable to achieve anything like perfect comparability. Comparisons between countries must be made with especially great caution owing to differences in classification, including differences in the definition of "economically active".
3. Where the original data were for an occupational rather than an industrial classification, this was usually transposed, with, of course, some degree of estimation involved. One exception is the statistics for Great Britain up to 1911, which are on an occupational basis.

FOOTNOTES

[1] Unless otherwise stated all statistics relate to the boundaries of the year in question.
[2] Unless otherwise stated, gas, water, electricity, and sanitary service workers are included under this heading.
[3] Except as otherwise indicated, armed forces are included under this heading.
[4] Cisleithania (excluding the Italian provinces) up to the First World War.
[5] Quarrying is included with "manufacturing industry".
[6] Many agricultural day-labourers were included in "others occupied".
[7] Metallurgy is included with "extractive industry".
[8] Includes catering services.
[9] Includes sanitary services.
[10] Some transport workers are included with both "Commerce, etc." and "Services".
[11] Military conscripts were assigned to their previous occupation in this year.
[12] Printing and publishing is included with "Services".
[13] 1945 territory.
[14] Statistics are of economically active heads of family and their dependants living in. Living out servants and their dependants and all servants of retired persons and rentiers were included in "Services".
[15] Statistics are of economically active heads of family and their dependants.
[16] Savoy and Nice are subsequently included.
[17] Excludes the parts of Alsace and Lorraine ceded to Germany.
[18] Gas, water, and electricity workers are included with "extractive industry".
[19] Excluding Saarland.
[20] 1937 territory.
[21] Including East Berlin.
[22] Including West Berlin.
[23] Conscripts in the armed forces are excluded.
[24] Transleithania up to the First World War.
[25] Excluding some family workers.
[26] Armed forces are included with "others occupied".
[27] These statistics cover workers of both sexes, but the number of females in extractive industry and in construction was negligible and was probably very small amongst "others occupied".
[28] Fishing is included with "manufacturing industry".
[29] Some agricultural workers were probably included with "services", as were some transport workers.
[30] Hotel workers were included with "commerce, etc.", and some transport workers were included with "services".
[31] Smelting is included with "extractive industry".
[32] Russian Poland only.
[33] Excluding Upper Silesia and part of Wilno.
[34] Excluding 394,000 persons in 1950 and 370,000 in 1960 who were not classified.
[35] Day labourers are included with "services".
[36] Catering is included with "commerce, etc.".
[37] Banks, urban transport, water, and sanitary services (and gas and electricity also in 1960) are included with "services".
[38] Excluding unemployed workers.
[39] Including rentiers and the retired.
[40] Forestry and fishing are included with "manufacturing industry", and gas, water, and sanitary services are included with "services".
[41] Excluding Poland.
[42] Including dependants.
[43] "Transport and Communications" are included with "Industry".
[44] "Communications" are included with "services".
[45] "Banking and finance" are included with "services".
[46] Excluding activities inadequately described.
[47] Excluding conscripts to the armed forces, persons unemployed for over four months, and persons seeking work for the first time.
[48] Excluding storage workers, who were distributed over various classes.
[49] Including railway workers, day labourers, servants living out, and probably in 1870 some inactive persons.
[50] Many who would later have been assigned to an occupation group were classed as unoccupied. The Islands in the British Seas are included in this year.

B1 Economically Active Population by Major Industrial Groups (in thousands)[1]

[51] Previously, retired persons who stated their former occupation were classified according to the latter.
[52] Includes all persons in agricultural households aged 14 and over who were capable of working.
[53] Clerical staff included with "services".
[54] In Russia in 1970 this includes persons employed in activities not adequately described.
[55] Fishing is included with "manufacturing industry".
[56] Workers in water supply are included in "services".
[57] Official estimates.
[58] Includes extractive industry.

B2 UNEMPLOYMENT (Numbers in thousands and Percentage of Appropriate Workforce)

1855–1886   1887–1929

Year	UK:GB %	Year	Austria No	Belgium No	Belgium %	Czech No	Denmark No	Denmark %	Finland No	France No	France %
1855	3.7	1887	...	...	...	...	...	...	...	...	...
1856	3.2	1888	...	...	...	...	...	...	...	...	...
1857	4.2	1889	...	...	...	...	...	...	...	...	...
1858	7.3										
1859	2.6	1890	...	...	...	...	...	...	...	...	...
		1891	...	...	...	...	...	...	...	...	...
1860	1.8	1892	...	...	...	...	...	...	...	...	...
1861	3.7	1893	...	...	...	...	...	...	...	...	...
1862	6.0	1894	...	...	...	...	...	...	...	...	...
1863	4.7										
1864	1.9	1895	...	...	...	...	...	...	...	...	7.0
		1896	...	...	...	...	...	...	...	...	6.7
1865	1.8	1897	...	...	...	...	...	...	...	...	6.9
1866	2.6	1898	...	...	...	...	...	...	...	...	7.3
1867	6.3	1899	...	...	...	...	...	...	...	...	6.6
1868	6.7										
1869	5.9	1900	...	...	...	...	...	...	...	...	6.8
		1901	...	...	...	...	...	...	...	...	7.8
1870	3.7	1902	...	...	...	...	...	...	...	...	9.9
1871	1.6	1903	...	...	...	...	9	...	...	...	9.4
1872	0.9	1904	...	...	...	...	10	...	...	...	10.2
1873	1.1										
1874	1.6	1905	...	...	...	...	11	...	...	...	9.0
		1906	...	...	...	...	5	...	...	...	7.6
1875	2.2	1907	...	...	...	...	6	...	...	...	7.0
1876	3.4	1908	...	...	...	...	10	...	...	...	8.6
1877	4.4	1909	...	...	...	...	12	...	...	...	7.3
1878	6.2										
1879	10.7	1910	...	...	...	...	11	10.7	...	...	5.8
		1911	...	3.0	...	...	10	9.5	...	...	5.7
1880	5.2	1912	...	3.0	...	...	8	7.6	...	...	5.4
1881	3.5	1913	...	4.0	...	...	8	7.5	...	...	4.7
1882	2.3	1914	...	...	...	...	13	9.9	...	...	...
1883	2.6										
1884	8.1	1915	...	...	...	...	10	8.1	...	...	...
		1916	...	...	...	...	7	5.1	...	...	...
1885	9.3	1917	...	...	...	...	15	9.7	...	...	...
1886	10.2	1918	...	...	...	...	38	18.1	...	...	...
		1919	147	...	...	...	32	10.9	...	...	...
		1920	58[2] / 19	...	...	...	17	6.1	...	13	...
		1921	12	35.0	11.5	72	57	19.7	...	28	...
		1922	49	12.9	4.2	127	50	19.3	...	13	...
		1923	110[1]	4.0	1.3	207	33	12.7	...	10	...
		1924	127	4.8	1.6	96	28	10.7	...	10	...
		1925	184	7.3	2.4	49	40	14.7	2.5	12	...
		1926	202	6.1	2.0	59	58	20.7	2.0	11	...
		1927	200	7.7	2.5	53	62	22.5	1.9	47	...
		1928	182	5.3	1.7	39	50	18.5	1.7	16	...
		1929	192	5.6	1.9	42	43	15.5	3.9	10	...

B2   **Unemployment** (Numbers in thousands and Percentage of Appropriate Workforce)

1887–1929

	Germany[8]		Hungary[9]	Ireland	Italy[10]	Netherland[11]	
	No	%	No	No	No	No	%
1887	...	0.2	...	...	...	...	...
1888	...	3.8	...	...	...	...	...
1889	...	0.2	...	...	...	...	...
1890	...	2.3	...	...	...	...	...
1891	...	3.9	...	...	...	...	...
1892	...	6.3	...	...	...	...	...
1893	...	2.8	...	...	...	...	...
1894	...	3.1	...	...	...	...	...
1895	...	2.8	...	...	...	...	...
1896	...	0.6	...	...	...	...	...
1897	...	1.2	...	...	...	...	...
1898	...	0.4	...	...	...	...	...
1899	...	1.2	...	...	...	...	...
1900	...	2.0	...	...	...	...	...
1901	...	6.7	...	...	...	...	...
1902	...	2.9	...	...	...	...	...
1903	...	2.7	...	...	...	...	...
1904	...	2.1	...	...	...	...	...
1905	...	1.6	...	...	...	...	...
1906	...	1.1	...	...	...	...	...
1907	...	1.6	...	...	...	...	...
1908	...	2.9	...	...	...	...	...
1909	...	2.8	...	...	...	...	...
1910	...	1.9	...	...	...	...	...
1911	...	1.9	...	...	...	...	2.5
1912	...	2.0	...	...	...	...	4.0
1913	...	2.9	...	...	...	...	5.0
1914	...	7.2	...	...	...	...	13.8
1915	...	3.3	...	...	...	16	12.0
1916	...	2.2	...	...	...	8	5.1
1917	...	1.0	...	...	...	14	6.5
1918	...	1.2	...	...	...	19	7.5
1919	...	3.7	...	...	...	27	7.7
1920	...	3.8[8]	...	...	...	29	5.8
1921	346	2.8	...	...	...	43	9.0
1922	215	1.5	...	...	...	45	11.0
1923	818	9.6	...	36	...	38	11.2
1924	927	13.5	...	36	...	28	8.8
1925	682	6.7	13	34	110	26	8.1
1926	2,025	18.0	13	25	114	25	7.3
1927	1,312	8.8	14	21	278	27	7.5
1928	1,391	8.4	15	22	324	22	5.6
1929	1,899	13.1[8]	15	21	301	28	5.9
		4.3					

B2 Unemployment (Numbers in thousands and Percentage of Appropriate Workforce)

1887–1929

	Norway[12]	Poland[13]		Romania[14]	Sweden[15]	Switz[16]	UK:GB[17]		Yugoslavia[14]
	%	No	%	No	%	%	No	%	No
1887	...	...	...	...	...	...	...	7.6	...
1888	...	...	...	...	...	...	...	4.9	...
1889	...	...	...	...	...	...	...	2.1	...
1890	...	...	...	...	...	...	...	2.1	...
1891	...	...	...	...	...	...	...	3.5	...
1892	...	...	...	...	...	...	...	6.3	...
1893	...	...	...	...	...	...	...	7.5	...
1894	...	...	...	...	...	...	...	6.9	...
1895	...	...	...	...	...	...	...	5.8	...
1896	...	...	...	...	...	...	...	3.3	...
1897	...	...	...	...	...	...	...	3.3	...
1898	...	...	...	...	...	...	...	2.8	...
1899	...	...	...	...	...	...	...	2.0	...
1900	...	...	...	...	...	...	...	2.5	...
1901	...	...	...	...	...	...	...	3.3	...
1902	...	...	...	...	...	...	...	4.0	...
1903	...	...	...	...	...	...	...	4.7	...
1904	3.9	...	...	...	...	...	...	6.0	...
1905	4.4	...	...	...	...	...	...	5.0	...
1906	3.2	...	...	...	...	...	...	3.6	...
1907	2.5	...	...	...	...	...	...	3.7	...
1908	3.7	...	...	...	...	...	...	7.8	...
1909	5.0	...	...	...	...	...	...	7.7	...
1910	2.9	...	...	...	...	...	...	4.7	...
1911	1.9	...	...	...	...	...	...	3.0	...
1912	1.3	...	...	...	...	...	...	3.2	...
1913	1.6	...	...	...	...	...	...	2.1	...
1914	2.4	...	...	...	...	...	...	3.3	...
1915	2.1	...	...	...	...	...	...	1.1	...
1916	0.8	...	...	...	...	...	...	0.4	...
1917	0.9	...	...	...	...	...	...	0.6	...
1918	1.4	...	...	...	...	...	...	0.8	...
1919	1.6	...	...	...	...	...	...	3.4	...
1920	2.3	...	...	...	...	...	...	2.0	...
1921	17.6	...	...	...	...	...	...	11.3	...
1922	17.1	...	...	...	...	...	...	9.8	...
1923	10.6	...	...	...	...	...	1,251	8.1	...
1924	8.5	...	...	...	...	...	1,113	7.2	...
1925	13.2	241	...	...	11.0	...	1,228	7.9	...
1926	24.3	217	...	...	12.2	3.4	1,385	8.8	...
1927	25.4	165	7.4	...	12.0	2.7	1,109	6.8	...
1928	19.1	126	5.0	10	10.6[15]	2.1	1,246	7.5	6
1929	15.4	129	4.9	7	11.2	1.8	1,240	7.3	8

B2 Unemployment (Numbers in thousands and Percentage of Appropriate Workforce)

	Austria[1]		Belgium[3]		Czech[4]	Denmark[5]		Finalnd[6]		France[7]
	No	%	No	%	No	No	%	No	%	No
1930	243	...	16.5	5.4	105	40	13.7	8.0	...	13
1931	300	...	41.1	14.5	291	53	17.9	11.5	...	64
1932	378	...	71.8	23.5	554	100	31.7	17.4	...	301
1933	406	...	62.4	20.4	738	97	28.8	17.1	...	305
1934	370	...	72.3	23.4	677	82	22.1	10.0	...	368
1935	349	...	65.5	22.9	686[4]	76	19.7	7.2	...	464
1936	350	...	49.2	16.8	623	79	19.3	4.8	...	470
1937	321	...	39.9	13.8	409	95	21.9	3.7	...	380
1938	245	...	53.7	18.4	...	98	21.3	3.6	...	402
1939	66	...	57.3[2]	19.3	...	89	18.4	3.3	...	418
1940	...	...	...	...	...	120	23.9	4.0	...	961
1941	...	...	...	...	...	130[18]	25.1[18]	3.4	...	395
						40	7.5			
1942	...	...	...	...	...	49	9.1	1.6	...	124
1943	...	...	...	...	...	34	6.3[19]	0.9	...	42
							10.7			
1944	...	...	...	...	...	25	8.3	2.0[6]	...	23
1945	...	...	117	...	...	47	13.4	5	...	68
1946	74[1]	...	48	...	...	28	8.9	1	...	57
1947	32	1.7	36	...	...	29[19]	8.9	...	...	46
						52				
1948	43	2.3	81	4.0	...	52	8.6	4	...	78
1949	91	4.6	174	8.6	...	59	9.6	26	...	131
1950	125	6.2	185	9.0	...	55	8.7	19	...	153
1951	116	5.7	159	7.6	...	63	9.7	6	...	120
1952	157	7.7	185	8.8	...	82	12.5	8	...	132
1953	184	9.0	192	9.2	...	61	9.2	29	...	180
1954	163	7.9	172	8.3	...	54	8.0	19	...	184
1955	118	5.4	118	5.8	...	66	9.7	9	...	160
1956	115[1]	5.1[1]	95	4.5	...	75	11.1	...	...	112
1957	108	4.7	81	3.9	...	71	10.2	...	...	81
1958	118	5.1	116	5.5	...	68	9.6	64	3.1	93
1959	107	4.6	132	6.3	...	44	6.1	46	2.2	141
1960	82	3.5	114	5.4	...	31	4.3	31	1.5	130
1961	64	2.7	89	4.2	...	29	3.9	27	1.2	111
1962	65	2.7	71	3.3	...	25	3.3	27	1.2	123
1963	71	2.9	59	2.7	...	33	4.3	32	1.5	140
1964	66	2.7	50	2.3	...	22	2.8	33	1.5	114
1965	66	2.7	55	2.4	...	18	2.3	31	1.4	142
1966	61	2.5	61	2.7	...	21	2.6	35	1.5	148
1967	65	2.7	85	3.7	...	25	3.2	63	2.9	196
1968	71	2.9	103	4.5	...	41	5.3	85	3.9	254
1969	68	2.8	85	3.7	...	31	3.9	61[6]	2.8[6]	223
1970	58	2.4	71	2.9	...	24	2.9	41	1.9	262
1971	52	2.1	71	2.9	...	30	3.7	49	2.3	338[7]
1972	49	1.9	87	3.4	...	30	3.6	55	2.5	383
1973	41	1.6	92[3]	3.6[3]	...	20[5]	2.4[5]	51	2.3	394
			111	2.9	...	22	0.9			
1974	41	1.5	121	3.1	...	52	2.1	39	1.7	498
1975	55	2.0	203	5.2	...	128	5.2	51	2.2	840

B2 Unemployment (Numbers in thousands and Percentage of Appropriate Workforce)

1930–1975

	Germany[8]		Greece[5]	Hungary[9]	Ireland[5]		Italy[10]		Netherland[11]		Norway[12]	
	No	%	No	No	No	%	No	%	No	%	No	%
1930	3,076	15.3	...	44	22	...	425	...	41[11] 74	7.8	...	16.6
1931	4,520	23.3	...	52	25[5]	...	734	...	138	14.8	...	22.3
1932	5,575	30.1	...	66	63	...	1,006[10]	...	271	25.3	...	30.8
1933	4,804	26.3	...	61	72	...	1,019	...	323	26.9	...	33.4
1934	2,718[8]	14.9[8]	...	52	104	...	964	...	333	28.0	...	30.7
1935	2,151	11.6	...	52	123	...	...	...	385	31.7	...	25.3
1936	1,593	8.3	...	52	100	...	...	...	414	32.7	...	18.8
1937	912	4.6	...	48	82	...	874	4.6	374	26.9	...	20.0
1938	429	2.1	...	47	87	...	810	4.3	354	25.0	...	22.0
1939	119	...	...	...	92	15.6	706[21]	3.8[21]	296	19.9[11]	...	18.3
1940	52	...	...	...	84	15.5	...	...	253		...	23.1
1941	...	...	...	...	75	14.6	...	...	175	...	...	11.4
1942	...	...	...	...	78	14.2	...	...	119	...	...	...
1943	...	...	...	...	67	12.5	...	...	...	...	...	...
1944	...	...	...	...	59	11.3	...	...	...	...	...	...
1945	...	...	...	...	59	10.6	...	...	137[23]	...	...	...
1946	...	...	...	...	60	10.6	1,324	...	89	...	...	3.6
	West Germany											
1947	...	...	...	...	56	9.3	1,620	8.3	47	...	...	3.1
1948	592[8]	4.2[8]	...	...	61	9.4	1,742[22]	8.9[22]	43	1.0	10	2.7
1949	1,230	8.3	...	...	61	9.0	1,673	8.6	63	1.5	8	2.2
1950	1,580	10.2	...	...	53	7.5	1,615	8.3	80	2.0	9	2.7
1951	1,432	9.0	...	...	50	7.3	1,721	8.8	93	2.3	11	3.6
1952	1,379	8.4	...	...	61[5]	9.1[5]	1,850	9.5	139	3.5	12	2.4
1953	1,259	7.5	...	...	71	9.6	1,947	10.0	107	2.7	14[12]	3.3
1954	1,221	7.0	...	...	62	8.1	1,959[10] 1,699	10.0[10] 8.8	76	1.9	13	2.2
1955	928	5.1	...	...	55	6.8	1,479	7.6	53	1.3	13	2.5
1956	761	4.0	38[20]	...	61	7.7	1,847	9.4	40	0.9	13	3.1
1957	662	3.4	87	...	70	9.2	1,643	8.2	52	1.2	15	3.2
1958	683[8] 769	3.5[8] 3.8	79	...	65	8.6	1,322	6.6	98	2.3	24	...
1959	540[8]	2.6[8]	89	...	62	8.0	1,117	5.6	77	1.8	23	...
1960	271	1.3	87	...	53	6.7	836	4.2	49	1.2	17	2.5
1961	181	0.7	76	...	47	5.7	710	3.5	35	0.9	13	2.0
1962	155	0.7	75	...	47	5.7	611	3.0	33	0.8	15	2.1
1963	186	0.8	70	...	50	6.1	504	2.5	34	0.9	18	2.5
1964	169	0.7	65	...	49	5.7	549	2.7	30	0.8	16	2.0
1965	147	0.6	64	...	49	5.6	714	3.6	35	0.9	13	1.8
1966	161	0.7	65	...	48	6.1	759	3.9	45	1.1	12	1.8
1967	459	2.1	83	...	55	6.7	679	3.5	90[11]	2.2[11]	11	1.2
1968	323	1.5	74	...	58	6.7	684	3.5	84	1.9	17	1.4
1969	17.9	0.9	66 52[5]	...	57	6.4	655 609[10]	3.4 3.2[10]	66	1.4	16	1.1
1970	14.9	0.7	49	...	65	7.2	1,111	5.4	56	1.1	12	0.8
1971	185	0.8	30	...	62	7.2	1,109	5.4	69	1.6	12	0.8
1972	246	1.1	24	...	72	8.1	1,297	6.4	115	2.8	15[12] 28	1.0[12] 1.7
1973	273	1.2	21	...	67	7.2	1,305	6.4	117	2.8	26	1.5
1974	582	2.6	27	...	71	7.9	1,113	5.4	143	3.5	25	1.5
1975	1,074	4.7	35	...	104	12.2	1,226	5.9	206	5.0	40	2.3

B2   Unemployment (Numbers in thousands and Percentage of Appropriate Workforce)

1930–1975

	Poland[13]		Port[23]	Rom[14]	Spain[14]		Sweden[15]	Switz[16]		UK:GB[17]		Yugoslavia[14]	
	No	%	No	No	No	%	%	No	%	No	%	No	%
1930	227	12.7	...	25	...	...	12.2	...	3.4	1,954	11.2	8	...
1931	300	14.0	...	36	...	...	17.2	...	5.9	2,647	15.1	10	...
1932	256	15.6	33	39	...	...	22.8	...	9.1	2,745	15.6	15	...
1933	250	16.7	25	29	352[21]	...	23.7	...	10.8	2,521	14.1	16	...
1934	342	16.3	35	17	407[21]	...	18.9	...	9.8	2,159	11.9	16	...
1935	382	11.9	42	14	697	...	16.1	...	11.8	2,036	11.0	18	...
1936	367	11.8	43[23]	14	...	...	13.6	81	13.2	1,755	9.4	19	...
1937	375	12.8	17	11	...	...	10.8	58	10.0	1,484	7.8	22	...
1938	348	8.8	17	7	...	...	10.9[15]	53	8.6	1,791	9.3	23	...
1939	...	...	18	9	...	...	9.2	37	6.5	1,514	5.8	24	...
1940	...	...	15	7	475	...	11.8	15	3.1	963	3.3	27	...
1941	...	...	14	6	450	...	11.3	9	2.0	350	1.2	...	...
1942	...	...	10	6	295	...	7.5	9	1.9	123	0.5	...	...
1943	...	...	5	6	225	...	5.7	6	1.4	82	0.4	...	...
1944	...	...	4	...	170	...	4.9	7	1.6	75	0.4	...	...
1945	...	...	3[23]	...	148	...	4.5	6	1.6	137	0.5	...	...
1946	79	...	2	...	178	...	3.2	4	1.0	374	1.9	...	...
1947	69	...	2	...	139	...	2.8	3	0.8	480	1.4	...	...
1948	79	...	2	...	117	...	2.8	3	0.6	310	1.3	...	...
1949	...	...	2	...	160	...	2.7	8	1.6	308	1.2[17] 1.6	...	...
1950	...	...	...	...	166	...	2.2	10	1.8	314	1.6	...	...
1951	...	...	...	...	144	...	1.8	4	0.8	253	1.3	...	...
1952	...	...	...	...	107	...	2.3	5	...	414	2.2	45	2.4
1953	...	...	...	...	107	...	2.8	5	...	342	1.8	82	4.0
1954	...	...	...	...	123	...	2.6	4	...	285	1.5	76	3.8
1955	31	...	...	...	112	...	2.5[15]	2.7	...	232	1.2	67	3.0
1956	...	...	...	...	106	...	1.7	3.0	...	257	1.3	99	4.3
1957	...	...	...	...	91	...	1.9	2.0	...	313	1.6	116	4.6
1958	...	...	...	...	81	...	2.5	3.4	...	457	2.2	132	4.9
1959	...	...	...	...	80	...	2.0	3.4	...	475	2.3	162	5.6
1960	37	...	...	...	114	...	1.4	1.2	...	360	1.7	159	5.1
1961	41	...	...	...	125	...	1.2	0.6	...	341	1.6	191	5.6
1962	46	...	...	...	98	...	1.3	0.6	...	463	2.1	237	6.7
1963	60	...	...	...	100	...	1.4	0.8	...	573	2.6	230	6.4
1964	65	...	...	...	130	...	1.1	0.3	...	381	1.7	213	5.6
1965	62	...	...	...	147	...	1.1	0.3	...	329	1.5	237	6.1
1966	58	...	...	...	123	...	1.4	0.3	...	360	1.5	258	6.7
1967	52	...	...	...	146	...	1.7[15]	0.3	...	560[13]	2.4[17]	269	7.0
1968	53	...	...	...	182	1.5	2.0	0.3	...	547	2.4	311	8.0
1969	71	...	...	...	159	1.3	1.7	0.1	...	539	2.3	331	8.2
1970	79	...	...	...	146	1.1	1.4	0.1	...	577	2.5	320	7.7
1971	82	...	...	...	190	1.5	2.0	0.1	...	752	3.4	291	6.7
1972	52	...	...	...	191	1.5	2.0	0.1	...	835	3.7	315	7.0
1973	28	...	...	...	150	1.1	1.9	0.1	...	588[17]	2.6[17]	382	8.1
1974	19	...	...	...	150	1.1	1.5	0.2	...	571	2.5	449	9.0
1975	15	...	...	...	257	1.9	1.4	10.2	0.8	902	3.9	540	10.2

B2 Unemployment (Numbers in thousands and Percentage of Appropriate Workforce)

1976–1999

Year	Austria[1] No	%	Belgium[3] No	%	Denmark[5] No	%	Finland[6] No	%	France[7] No	%	West Germany[8] / Germany[8] No	%	Greece[5] No	%	Ireland[5] No	%
1976	55	2.0	261	6.6	133	5.3	92	3.9	934[7] / 991	4.4	1,060	4.6	28	2.3	113	12.3
1977	51	1.8	301	7.4	164	6.5	140	5.9	1,122	4.9	1,030	4.5	28	2.1	111	11.8
1978	59	2.1	324	7.9	191	7.3	172	7.3	1,201	5.2	993	4.3	31	2.3	99	10.7
1979	57	2.0	341	8.2	162	6.1	143	6.0	1,361	5.9	876	3.8	32	2.2	89	...
1980	53	1.9	369	8.9	184	7.0	114[6]	4.7[6]	1,467	6.3	889	3.8	37	2.4	101	8.1
1981	69	2.4	454	10.9	243	9.2	121	4.9	1,750	7.4	1,272	5.5	43[5] / 149	2.7[5] / 4.0	128	10.1
1982	105	3.7	535	12.7	263	10.0	135	5.4	1,993	8.1	1,833	7.5	216	5.8	157	12.1
1983	127	4.5	589	14.0	283	10.5	138	5.5	1,974	8.3	2,258	9.1	302	7.9	193	14.7
1984	130	4.5	596	14.1	276	10.1	133	5.2	2,323	9.7	2,266	9.1	315	8.3	214	16.4
1985	139	4.8	558	13.3	252	9.2	129	5.0	2,442	10.2	2,304	9.3	304	7.8	231	17.7
1986	152	5.2	517	12.3	220	8.1	138	5.4	2,490	10.4	2,228	9.0	287	7.4	236	18.1
1987	164	5.6	501	11.9	222	8.0	130	5.1	2,532	10.6	2,229	8.9	286	7.4	247	18.8
1988	159	5.3	459	11.1	244	8.7	116	4.5	2,443	10.1	2,242	8.7	303	7.7	241	18.4
1989	149	5.0	419	10.1	265	9.4	89	3.5	2,323	9.4	2,147	8.0	296	7.5	231	17.9
1990	166	5.4	403	9.6	272	9.7	88	3.4	2,205	8.9	1,971	7.0	281	7.0	225	17.2
1991	185	5.8	429	10.2	296	10.6	193	7.6	2,349	9.4	2,601	8.3	301	7.7	254	19.0
1992	193	5.9	473	11.2	318	11.3	328	13.0	2,591	10.3	2,978	10.5	350	8.7	283	...
1993	222	6.8	550	13.0	349	12.4	444	17.7	2,911	11.6	3,418	12.0	398	9.7	294	...
1994	138	3.6	405	9.8	223	8.0	311	12.4	3,104	12.3	4,160	10.1	403	9.6	211	14.7
1995	144	3.7	390	9.3	195	7.0	293	11.6	2,931	11.6	4,035	8.8	424	10.0	177	12.2
1996	160	4.1	404	9.6	194	6.9	309	12.1	3,137	12.3	3,473	9.8	446	10.3	179	11.9
1997	165	4.2	375	8.9	174	6.1	315	12.3	3,192	12.4	3,890	9.7	440	10.3	159	11.9
1998	165	4.2	384	9.1	155	5.5	305	11.8	...	...	3,849	8.8	478	10.8	127	10.3
1999	146	3.8	375	8.6	...	...	306	11.9	...	...	3,503	8.8	...	...	97	5.7

Year	Italy[10] No	%	Netherlands[11] No	%	Norway[12] No	%	Poland[13] No	%	Spain[14] No	%	Sweden[15] No	%	Switzerland[16] No	%	UK: GB[17] No	%	Yugoslavia[14] No	%
1976	1,420	6.7	224	5.3	32	1.8	14		376	2.8	66	1.6	20.7	0.7	1,250	5.4	635	11.4
1977	1,538	7.2	218	5.1	27	1.5	12		540	4.1	75	1.8	12.0	0.4	1,345	5.7	700	11.9
1978	1,560	7.2	220	5.1	34	1.7	9		819	6.2	94	2.2	10.5	0.4	1,321[17]	5.6[17]	735	12.0
1979	1,686	7.7	225	5.1	38	2.0	6		1,037	7.9	88	2.1	10.3	0.4	1,025	3.9	762	11.9
1980	1,684	7.6	263	5.9	32	1.7	10		1,277	9.9	86	2.0	6.3	0.2	1,238	5.0	785	11.9
1981	1,895	8.4	401	9.1	40	2.0	26		1,566	12.1	108	2.5	6.0	0.2	2,040	8.0	809	11.9
1982	2,052	9.1	559	12.6	52	2.6	9		1,873	14.2	137	3.1	13.2	0.4	2,428	9.4	863	12.4
1983	2,264	9.9	702[11] / 801	15.5[11] / 17.1	69	3.4	5		2,199	16.5	151	3.5	26.3	0.9	2,673	10.4	910	12.8
1984	2,303	10.0	822	17.2	64	3.2	5		2,475	18.4	136	3.1	35.2[16]	1.1[16]	2,795	10.6	975	13.3
1985	2,382	10.3	761	15.9	53	2.6	4		2,642	19.5	125	2.8	30.3	1.0	2,184	10.8	1,040	13.8
1986	2,611	11.1	711	14.7	42	2.0	6		2,759	20.0	98[24]	2.2[24]	25.7	0.8	2,984	10.9	1,087	14.1
1987	2,832	11.9	686	14.0[25]	45	2.1	5		2,924	20.4	92	2.1	24.7	0.8	2,748	9.8	1,081	13.6
1988	2,885	12.0	433	6.5	69	3.1	...		2,858	19.3	78	1.8	22.3	0.7	2,223	7.8[25]	1,132	14.1
1989	2,865	12.0	390	5.8	106	4.9	...		2,550	17.2	67	1.5	17.5	0.6	1,799	6.3	1,201	14.9
1990	2,621	11.0	346	5.0	112	5.2	...		2,350	15.7	75	1.6	18.1	0.6	1,664	5.9	1,308	16.4[26]
1991	2,653	10.9	319	4.5	116	5.5	...		2,289	15.2	133	3.0	39.2	1.3	2,292	8.1	...	...
1992	2,799	11.5	336	5.3	126	5.9	...		2,260	14.9	233[25]	5.3[25]	92.3	2.5	2,779	9.9	...	...
1993	...	...	415	6.5	127	6.0	...		2,538	16.6	356	8.2	163.1[17]	4.5	2,919	10.4	...	...
1994	2,508	10.7	486	7.5	116	5.4	2,474		3,738	24.2	340	8.0	150.1	3.9	2,737	9.6	...	...
1995	2,639	11.3	464	7.0	107	4.9	2,277		3,583	22.9	333	7.7	129.0	3.3	2,460	8.6	...	...
1996	2,653	11.4	440	6.6	108	4.9	2,108		3,540	22.2	347	8.0	144.6	3.7	2,340	8.2	...	...
1997	2,688	11.5	375	5.5	93	4.1	1,923		3,356	20.8	342	8.0	162.1	4.1	2,037	7.1	...	...
1998	2,745	11.7	286	4.1	75	3.2	1,808		3,060	18.8	276	6.5	141.8	3.6	1,776	6.1	...	...
1999	2,669	11.4	222	3.2	75	3.2	...		...	...	...	...	...	...	...	...	...	...

B2 Unemployment (Numbers in thousands and Percentage of Appropriate Workforce)

NOTES

1. SOURCES:- I.L.O., *Yearbook of Labour Statistics*, and the official publications noted on p. xv., except that percentages to 1949 for UK: GB are from C.H. Feinstein, *National Income, Expenditure and Output of the United Kingdom, 1855-1965* (Cambridge, 1972) table 57.
2. The variety of different indicators of unemployment at different times and in different countries is clear from the footnotes. This should serve as a strong warning against incautious comparisons.

FOOTNOTES

[1] 1919-23—numbers given public relief; 1924-46—applicants for work at labour exchanges; 1947 onwards-registered unemployed. All figures are averages of monthly observations. There was a change in the scope of the data in 1957.

[2] The first figure is for January-April, before the Unemployment Assurance scheme came into force. The second figure is for May-December.

[3] 1911-39—average numbers of days' unemployment among insured workers, and percentages of possible days' work; 1945 onwards-average of monthly numbers of registered unemployed. There was a change in the scope of the data in 1973.

[4] Averages of monthly numbers of applicants for work at labour exchanges and private placement agencies, though excluding the latter from 1936.

[5] Averages of monthly numbers of insured workers unemployed. There was changes in the scope of the data in 1973 in the case of Denmark, 1970 and 1983 in the case of Greece, and 1932 and 1953 in the case of Ireland.

[6] 1925-44—applicants for work at labour exchanges; 1945 onwards—numbers seeking relief. There was a change in the scope of the data in 1981.

[7] Applicants for work to 1976 (1st line), though excluding certain people over 60 from 1972; official estimates of total unemployment from 1976 (2nd line).

[8] 1887-29—unemployed in trade unions; 1929 (2nd line) onwards—registered unemployed, being monthly averages except in 1948-59, when they were the numbers at 30 June or 30 September. Figures from 1949 onwards relate to the Federal Republic (excluding West Berlin and Saarland) to 1958 (2nd line). The latter was also excluded in 1921-34. The 1948 figure is for the British and American Occupation Zones. A series of "corrected" trade union percentage figures for 1903-49, by Galenson and Zellner, is given in Toni Pierenkemper, 'The Standard of Living and Employment in Germany, 1850-1980: An Overview', *Journal of European Economic History*, 16, 1 (1987) as follows:-

1903	4.7	1910	3.5	1923	10.2	1930	22.7	1937	6.9
1904	3.6	1911	3.1	1924	13.1	1931	34.3	1938	3.2
1905	3.0	1912	3.2	1925	6.8	1932	43.8	1939	0.9
1906	2.7	1913	4.2	1926	18.0	1933	36.2	1946	7.5
1907	2.9	1920	3.8	1927	8.8	1934	20.5	1947	5.0
1908	4.4	1921	2.8	1928	8.6	1935	16.2	1948	4.8
1909	4.3	1922	1.5	1929	13.3	1936	12.0	1949	8.3

[9] Averages of monthly numbers of applicants for work at labour exchanges, and, from 1930, private placement agencies.

[10] 1925-32—insured workers unemployed; 1933-54—numbers of registered unemployed; 1954 (2nd line) onwards—sample survey data. All figures are averages of monthly observations. There was a revision of the definition of unemployment from 1970 (2nd line).

[11] The numbers to 1983, and the percentages from 1948 to 1983 relate to registered unemployed, excluding married women who were not "breadwinners" prior to 1968. From 1983 (2nd line) they relate to persons seeking work for 20 hours or more per week. The figures are weekly averages to 1921 and monthly averages subsequently. The percentages to 1939 relate to the proportion of possible days' work lost owing to unemployment. They exclude persons on relief-work throughout. There was a change in the scope of the data in 1930.

[12] To 1972 the numbers are of registered unemployed and the percentages are of trade unionists unemployed. From 1972 (2nd line) data are from sample surveys. All figures are averages of monthly observations. There was a change in the scope of the data in 1954.

[13] Averages of monthly numbers of applicants for work.

[14] Averages of monthly numbers of registered unemployed.

[15] 1925-55—members of trade union benefit funds: 1956 onwards—sample survey data. There was a change in the scope of the data in 1929, 1939 and 1987. The figures are averages of monthly observations.

[16] The numbers relate to registered unemployed and the percentages to insured workers. The figures are averages of monthly observations. Those only partially unemployed are included from 1984.

[17] Numbers are averages of monthly figures of registered unemployed. It should be noted that there have been many changes in the scope of the data though revisions have preserved a measure of continuity except where indicated by a break line. The percentages to 1922 are based on trade union data. Subsequently they are National Insurance-based figures, using Feinstein's adjustments to 1949 (1st line).

[18] A different system was adopted on 1 June. The first figure is for January-May, the second for June-December.

[19] Temporarily unemployed workers are subsequently included.

[20] May-December only.

[21] December only.

[22] Excluding the third quarter.

[23] Registered unemployed, in December for 1937-45, otherwise average of all monthly figures.

[24] Prior to 1986: persons aged 16-74 years.

[25] Methodology revised: data not strictly comparable.

B2   Unemployment (Numbers in thousands and Percentage of Appropriate Workforce)

[26]   Figures for Croatia, Macedonia and Slovenia as follows

	Croatia		Macedonia		Slovenia	
	No	%	No	%	No	%
1991	254	8.0	165	...	75	8.2
1992	267	15.0	172	27.8	103	11.5
1993	...	...	175	29.3	129	14.4
1994	254	13.0	186	34.5	85	10.0
1995	...	...	216	36.7	70	9.0
1996	...	...	238	38.1	69	9.0
1997	...	...	253	40.2	69	9.0
1998	...	...	...	...	75	10.2

B3 INDUSTRIAL DISPUTES

	Austria[1]			Belgium			Czechoslavakia			Denmark		
	Number	Workers Involved (thou)	Days Lost (thou)	Number	Workers Involved (thou)	Days Lost (thou)	Number	Workers Involved (thou)	Days Lost (thou)	Number	Workers Involved (thou)	Days Lost (thou)
1888	...	...	...	...	...	...	...	...	...	...	...	...
1889	...	...	...	...	...	...	...	...	...	...	...	...
1890	...	...	...	...	...	...	...	...	...	...	...	...
1891	...	...	...	...	...	...	...	...	...	...	...	...
1892	...	...	...	...	...	...	...	...	...	...	...	...
1893	...	...	...	...	...	...	...	...	...	...	...	...
1894	159	44	...	...	...	...	...	...	...	...	...	...
1895	205	28	...	...	...	...	...	...	...	...	...	...
1896	294	36	...	139	23	...	...	...	...	...	...	...
1897	221	35	...	130	36	...	...	...	...	111	7	215
1898	255	40	...	91	13	...	...	...	...	147	7	123
1899	311	55	...	104	58	...	...	...	...	98	36	2,828
1900	303	105	...	146	32	...	...	...	...	82	8	218
1901	270	25	...	117	44	...	...	...	...	57	4	52
1902	264	37	...	73	10	...	...	...	...	68	2	133
1903	324	46	...	70	8	...	...	...	...	61	1	19
1904	414	64	...	81	12	...	...	...	...	86	3	69
1905	686	100	...	133	76	...	...	...	...	75	6	499
1906	1,083	154	...	207	25	...	...	...	...	90	4	68
1907	1,086	177	...	221	45	...	...	...	...	105	8	255
1908	721	79	...	101	14	...	...	...	...	122	8	85
1909	580	62	...	119	11	...	...	...	...	65	2	58
1910	657	55	...	108	26	...	...	...	...	71	2	61
1911	706	122	...	156	55	...	...	...	...	51	28	648
1912	761	121	...	202	61	...	...	...	...	60	4	50
1913	438	40	...	162	16	...	...	...	...	76	10	382
1914	260	33	...	...	...	...	...	...	...	44	3	56
1915	...	...	...	...	...	...	...	...	...	43	2	32
1916	...	...	...	...	...	...	...	...	...	66	13	241
1917	...	...	...	...	...	...	...	...	...	215	10	211
1918	...[1]	...[1]	...	...	...	...	...	...	...	253	9	182
1919	151	70	221	366	158	...	252	...	...	472	36	878
1920	329	199	927	506	289	...	614	...	...	243	22	690
1921	435	302	1,763	252	122	...	454	223	2,250	110	48	1,321
1922	381	307	1,635	169	85	...	290	331	3,975	31	49	2,272
1923	268	133	1,074	164	105	...	248	209	4,714	58	2	20
1924	401	286	2,295	186	83	...	334	98	1,362	71	10	175
1925	287	57	666	108	81	...	267	111	1,683	48	102	4,138
1926	186	25	233	137	70	...	163	49	735	32	1	23
1927	195	37	477	181	36	...	208	172	1,466	17	3	119
1928	242	44	563	191	72	...	280	102	1,728	11	0.5	11
1929	202	38	287	165	46	...	230	64	753	22	1	41

B3 Industrial Disputes

	Finland			France[19]			Germany[4][20]		
	Number	Workers Involved (thou)	Days Lost (thou)	Number	Workers Involved (thou)	Days Lost (thou)	Number	Workers Involved (thou)	Days Lost (thou)
1888	...	...	...	...	...	...	...	...	...
1889	...	...	...	...	...	...	...	...	...
1890	...	...	...	313	119	1,340	...	...	...
1891	...	...	...	267	109	1,717	...	...	...
1892	...	...	...	261	49	918	...	...	...
1893	...	...	...	634	170	3,175	...	...	...
1894	...	...	...	391	55	1,062	...	...	...
1895	...	...	...	405	46	617	...	...	...
1896	...	...	...	476	50	644	...	...	...
1897	...	...	...	356	69	781	...	...	...
1898	...	...	...	368	82	1,216	...	...	...
1899	...	...	...	739	177	3,551	1,311	265	3,381
1900	...	...	...	902	223	3,761	1,468	321	3,712
1901	...	...	...	523	111	1,862	1,091	149	2,427
1902	...	...	...	512	213	4,675	1,106	150	1,951
1903	...	...	...	567	123	2,442	1,444	251	4,158
1904	...	...	...	1,026	271	3,935	1,990	310	5,285
1905	...	...	...	830	178	2,747	2,657	966	18,984
1906	...	...	...	1,309	438	9,439	3,626	839	11,567
1907	176	...	596	1,275	198	3,562	2,512	575	9,017
1908	128	...	436	1,073	99	1,752	1,524	281	3,666
1909	51	...	252	1,025	167	3,560	1,652	291	4,152
1910	54	...	171	1,502	281	4,830	3,228	681	17,848
1911	51	...	291	1,471	231	4,096	2,798	896	11,466
1912	59	...	529	1,116	268	2,318	2,834	1,031	10,724
1913	70	...	74	1,073	220	2,224	2,464	655	11,761
1914	37	...	376	672	162	2,187	1,223	238	2,844
1915	...	...	...	98	9	55	141	48	46
1916	...	...	...	314	41	236	240	423	245
1917	483	...	1,495	696	294	1,482	562	1,468	1,862
1918	6	...	2	499	176	980	532	716	1,453
1919	39	...	160	2,026	1,151	15,478	3,719	2,761	33,083
1920	146	...	456	1,832	1,317	23,112	3,807	2,009	16,755
1921	76	...	120	475	402	7,027	4,455	2,036	25,874
1922	53	...	252	665	290	3,935	4,785	2,566	27,734
1923	50	...	262	1,068	331	4,172	2,046	1,917	12,344
1924	31	...	51	1,083	275	3,863	1,973	2,066	36,198
1925	38	3	113	931	249	2,046	1,708	1,115	2,936
1926	72	10	386	1,660	349	4,072	351	131	1,222
1927	79	13[3]	1,528	396	111	1,046	844	686	6,144
1928	71	21	502	816	204	6,377	739	986	20,339
1929	26	2	75	1,213	240	2,765	429	268	4,251

B3 Industrial Disputes

1888-1929

	Hungary			Ireland			Italy			Netherlands		
	Number	Workers Involved (thou)	Days Lost (thou)	Number	Workers Involved (thou)	Days Lost (thou)	Number	Workers Involved (thou)	Days Lost (thou)	Number	Workers Involved (thou)	Days Lost (thou)
1888	...	...	...	...	...	...	107	30	...	...	...	...
1889	...	...	...	...	...	...	133	25	...	...	...	...
1890	...	...	...	...	...	...	152	45	...	...	...	...
1891	...	...	...	...	...	...	164	44	...	...	...	...
1892	...	...	...	...	...	...	140	34	...	...	...	...
1893	...	...	...	...	...	...	154	25	...	...	...	...
1894	...	...	...	...	...	...	217	98	...	...	...	...
1895	...	...	...	...	...	...	243	104	...	...	...	...
1896	...	...	...	...	...	...	310	47	...	...	...	...
1897	...	...	...	...	...	...	379	46	...	...	...	...
1898	...	...	...	...	...	...	424	85	...	...	...	...
1899	...	...	...	...	...	...	1,701	430	...	...	...	...
1900	...	...	...	...	...	...	1,053	350	...	...	...	...
1901	...	...	...	...	...	...	617	136	...	122	...	...
1902	...	...	...	...	...	...	847	215	...	142	...	...
1903	...	...	...	...	...	...	715	155	...	163	...	...
1904	...	...	...	...	...	...	1,649	382	...	102	...	658
1905	...	...	...	...	...	...	2,268	581	...	132	...	123
1906	...	...	...	...	...	...	1,674	324	...	181	12	295
1907	...	...	...	...	...	...	1,071	189	...	154	12	458
1908	...	...	...	...	...	...	1,109	196	...	135	7	102
1909	...	...	...	...	...	...	1,255	386	...	189	8	297
1910	...	...	...	...	...	...	1,090	241	...	146	15	366
1911	...	...	...	...	...	...	907	465	...	217	21	442
1912	...	...	...	...	...	...	905	217	...	283	26	467
1913	...	...	...	...	...	...	599	174	...	427	55	912
1914	...	...	...	...	...	...	905	217	...	271	17	393
1915	...	...	...	...	...	...	608	180	...	269	17	118
1916	...	...	...	...	...	...	577	138	838	377	20	261
1917	...	...	...	...	...	...	470	175	849	344	32	545
1918	...	...	...	...	...	...	313	159	912	325	44	716
1919	...	...	...	...	...	...	1,871	1,555	22,325	649	62	1,057
1920	...	...	...	...	...	...	2,070	2,314	30,569	481	66	2,355
1921	...	...	...	...	...	...	1,134	724	8,180	299	48	1,282
1922	...	...	...	...	...	...	575	448	6,917	325	44	1,224
1923	...	...	...	131	21	1,209	201	66	296	289	56	1,216
1924	...	...	...	104	16	302	368	187	...	239	27	3,156
1925	...	...	...	86	7	294	618	308	...	262	34	781
1926	56	10	52	57	3	85	...	...	...	212₅	10₅	281₅
1927	84	25	295	53	2	64	169	19	...	230	14	202
1928	31	10	131	52	2	54	77	3	...	105	17	635
1929	63	15	149	53	5	101	83	3	...	226	21	890

B3 Industrial Disputes

	Norway			Poland			Romania			Spain[6]		
	Number	Workers Involved (thou)	Days Lost (thou)	Number	Workers Involved (thou)	Days Lost (thou)	Number	Workers Involved (thou)	Days Lost (thou)	Number	Workers Involved (thou)	Days Lost (thou)
1888	...	...	...	...	...	...	...	...	...	...	...	...
1889	...	...	...	...	...	...	...	...	...	...	...	...
1900	...	...	...	...	...	...	...	...	...	...	...	...
1901	...	...	...	...	...	...	...	...	...	...	...	...
1902	...	...	...	...	...	...	...	...	...	...	...	...
1903	...	...	...	...	...	...	...	...	...	...	...	...
1904	...	...	...	...	...	...	...	...	...	...	...	...
1905	...	...	...	...	...	...	...	...	...	...	...	...
1906	...	...	...	...	...	...	...	...	...	...	...	...
1907	...	...	...	...	...	...	...	...	...	...	...	...
1908	...	...	...	...	...	...	...	...	...	...	...	...
1909	...	...	...	...	...	...	...	...	...	...	...	...
1910	...	...	...	...	...	...	...	...	...	...	...	...
1911	...	...	...	...	...	...	...	...	...	...	...	...
1912	...	...	...	...	...	...	...	...	...	...	...	...
1913	...	...	...	...	...	...	...	...	...	...	...	...
1914	...	...	...	...	...	...	...	...	...	...	...	...
1905	...	...	...	...	...	...	...	...	...	153(130)	25	...
1906	...	...	...	...	...	...	...	...	...	145(122)	30	...
1907	...	...	...	...	...	...	...	...	...	152(118)	20	...
1908	...	...	...	...	...	...	...	...	...	182(127)	38	...
1909	...	...	...	...	...	...	...	...	...	147(78)	12	...
1910	...	...	...	...	...	...	...	...	...	246(151)	41	1,409
1911	...	...	...	...	...	...	...	...	...	311(118)	29	364
1912	...	...	...	...	...	...	...	...	...	279(171)	47	1,056
1913	...	...	...	...	...	...	...	...	...	284(201)	119	2,258
1914	...	...	...	...	...	...	...	...	...	212(140)	76	1,018
1915	...	...	...	...	...	...	...	...	...	169(91)	35	383
1916	...	...	...	...	...	...	...	...	...	237(178)	160	2,415
1917	...	...	...	...	...	...	...	...	...	306(176)	86	1,785
1918	...	...	...	...	...	...	...	...	...	463(256)	136	1,819
1919	...	...	...	...	...	...	...	...	...	895(403)	199	4,001
1920	...	...	...	...	...	...	...	...	...	1,060(424)	264	7,262
1921	...	...	...	...	...	...	...	...	...	373(233)	99	2,802
1922	26	2	91	...	...	...	...	...	...	488(429)	167	2,673
1923	57	25	796	...	...	...	...	...	...	458(411)	160	3,027
1924	61	63	5,152	929	582	7,137	88	12	212	165(155)	41	605
1925	84	14	667	538	150	1,322	73	20	210	181(164)	71	840
1926	113	51	2,205	590	146	1,423	88	20	326	96(93)	32	247
1927	96	22	1,374	635	237	2,483	51	7	58	107	95	1,312
1928	63	8	364	776	354	2,788	57	11	110	87	143	771
1929	73	5	197	510	222	1,072	127	31	412	96	67	314

B3 Industrial Disputes

	Sweden			Switzerland			United Kingdom			Yugoslavia		
	Number	Workers Involved (thou)	Days Lost (thou)	Number	Workers Involved (thou)	Days Lost (thou)	Number	Workers Involved (thou)	Days Lost (thou)	Number	Workers Involved (thou)	Days Lost (thou)
1888	...	...	...	...	...	...	517	119	...	...	...	...
1889	...	...	...	...	...	...	1,211	360	...	...	...	...
1890	...	...	...	...	...	...	1,040	393	...	...	...	...
1891	...	...	...	...	...	...	906	267	6,809	...	...	...
1892	...	...	...	...	...	...	700[8]	358[8]	17,382[8]	...	...	...
1893	...	...	...	...	...	...	615	634	30,468	...	...	...
1894	...	...	...	...	...	...	929	325	9,529	...	...	...
1895	...	...	...	...	...	...	745	263	5,725	...	...	...
1896	...	...	...	...	...	...	926	198	3,746	...	...	...
1897	...	...	...	...	...	...	864	230	10,346	...	...	...
1898	...	...	...	...	...	...	711	254	15,289	...	...	...
1899	...	...	...	...	...	...	719	180	2,516	...	...	...
1900	...	...	...	...	...	...	648	189	3,153	...	...	...
1901	...	...	...	...	...	...	642	180	4,142	...	...	...
1902	...	...	...	...	...	...	442	257	3,479	...	...	...
1903	142	25	642	...	...	...	387	117	2,339	...	...	...
1904	215	12	386	...	...	...	355	87	1,484	...	...	...
1905	189	33	2,390	...	...	...	358	94	2,470	...	...	...
1906	290	19	479	...	...	...	486	218	3,029	...	...	...
1907	312	24	514	...	...	...	601	147	2,162	...	...	...
1908	302	40	1,842	...	...	...	399	296	10,834	...	...	...
1909	138	302	11,800	...	...	...	436	301	2,774	...	...	...
1910	76	4	39	...	...	...	531	515	9,895	...	...	...
1911	98	21	570	85	...	...	903	962	10,320	...	...	...
1912	116	10	292	74	...	...	857	1,463	40,915	...	...	...
1913	119	10	303	64	...	...	1,497[9]	689[9]	11,631[9]	...	...	...
							1,459	664	9,804			
1914	115	14	620	31	...	...	972	447	9,878	...	...	...
1915	80	5	83	15	...	...	672	448	2,953	...	...	...
1916	227	21	475	38	...	...	532	276	2,446	...	...	...
1917	475	47	1,109	140	...	...	730	872	5,647	...	...	...
1918	708	61	1,436	268	...	...	1,165	1,116	5,875	...	...	...
1919	440	81	2,296	237	...	...	1,352	2,591	34,969	...	...	...
1920	486	139	8,943	184	...	...	1,607	1,932	26,568	...	...	...
1921	347	50	2,663	55	...	...	763	1,801	85,872	...	...	...
1922	392	76	2,675	104	...	...	576	552	19,850	...	...	...
1923	206	103	6,907	44	...	...	628	405	10,672	...	...	...
1924	261	24	1,205	70	...	...	710	613	8,424	60	5	76
1925	239	146	1,560	42	...	...	603	441	7,952	44	7	111
1926	206	53	1,711	35[7]	...	...	323	2,734	1,62,233	46	11	158
1927	189	10	400	26	2	34	308	108	1,174	78	8	239
1928	201	72	4,835	45	5	98	302	124	1,388	...	6	117
1929	180	13	667	39	5	100	431	533	8,287	14	2	13

B3 Industrial Disputes

	Austria			Belgium			Czechoslovakia			Denmark		
	Number	Workers Involved (thou)	Days Lost (thou)	Number	Workers Involved (thou)	Days Lost (thou)	Number	Workers Involved (thou)	Days Lost (thou)	Number	Workers Involved (thou)	Days Lost (thou)
1930	83	10	41	93	54	...	159	31	423	37	5	144
1931	56	12	100	73	20	...	254	50	499	16	4	246
1932	30	7	80	63	161	...	317	103	1,256	18	6	87
1933	23	6	65	86	35	...	209	37	289	26	0.5	18
1934	4	0.3	0.2	79	34	...	213	38	265	38	12	146
1935	2	0.1	0.2	150	99	...	219	40	490	14	0.8	14
1936	5	1.8	1.5	(111)[10]	(39)[10]	...	262	55	637	12	97	2,946
1937	5	1.5	0.4	209	82	...	430	121	1,119	22	1	21
1938	...	...	...	126	33	241	174	36	158	22	4	90
1939	...	...	...	68	43	...	...	...	...	19	0.5	16
1940	...	...	...	...	...	...	...	...	...	9	0.3	5
1941	...	...	...	...	...	...	...	...	...	2	0.1	3
1942	...	...	...	...	...	...	...	...	...	7	3	11
1943	...	...	...	...	...	...	...	...	...	17	6	24
1944	...	...	...	...	...	...	...	...	...	34	8	89
1945	...	...	...	160	140	563	...	...	...	35	9	66
1946	...	...	...	287	170	1,053	...	...	...	59	54	1,389
1947	...	...	...	473	301	2,212	...	...	...	29	8	467
1948	...	...	...	155	334	1,858	...	...	...	24	3	8
1949	...	...	...	99	48	830	...	...	...	17	3	10
1950	...	...	...	122[11]	148[11]	2,769	...	...	...	18	3	4
1951	...	32	84	163	121	593	...	...	...	12	2	4
1952	...	32	75	122	278	863	...	...	...	9	2	4
1953	...	13	38	115	117	412	...	...	...	8	0.4	2
1954	...	21	51	107	61	444	...	...	...	20	8	23
1955	...	26	58	143	119	1,002	...	...	...	13	6	10
1956	...	44	153	148	176	948	...	...	...	98	66	1,087
1957	...	20	46	115	339	3,789	...	...	...	14	3	7
1958	...	29	49	43	63	294	...	...	...	15	9	9
1959	...	47	51	57	123	983	...	...	...	23	6	18
1960	...	31	69	61[11]	19[11]	334	...	...	...	82	20	61
1961	...	39	114	38[11]	13[11]	92	...	...	...	34	153	2,308
1962	...	207	648	40	22	271	...	...	...	26	10	15
1963	...	17	34	48	18	247	...	...	...	19	7	24
1964	...	41	35	41	41	444	...	...	...	40	8	17
1965	...	146	151	63	19	70	...	...	...	37	14	242
1966	...	121	71	74	42	533	...	...	...	22	10	15
1967	...	7	16	58	38	182	...	...	...	22	10	10
1968	...	3	7	71	29	364	...	...	...	17	29	34
1969	...	17	19	88	25	162	...	...	...	48	36	56
1970	...	8	27	151	108	1,432	...	...	...	77	56	102
1971	...	2	4	184	87	1,240	...	...	...	31	6	21
1972	...	7	15	191	67	354	...	...	...	35	8	22
1973	...	78	160	172	62	872	...	...	...	205	337	3,901
1974	...	7	7	235	56	580	...	...	...	134	142	184
1975	...	4	6	243	86	608	...	...	...	147	59	100
1976	...	2	1	281	107	897	...	...	...	204	87	210
1977	...	...	...	220	66	664	...	...	...	228	36	230
1978	...	1	10	195	91	1,002	...	...	...	314	59	129
1979	8	1	1	215	56	615	...	...	...	218	157	173

B3   Industrial Disputes

	Austria			Belgium			Denmark		
	Number	Workers Involved (thou)	Days Lost (thou)	Number	Workers Involved (thou)	Days Lost (thou)	Number	Workers Involved (thou)	Days Lost (thou)
1980	9	24	17	132	27	217	225	62	187
1981	6	17	4	...	...	...	94	53	652
1982	2	...	...	...	...	...	180	53	93
1983	4	...	1	...	...	...	161	41	79
1984	2	...	1	...	...	...	157	51	132
1985	4	36	23	65	34	130	820	581	2,333
1986	11	3	3	...	...	...	215	57	93
1987	6	7	5	...	...	...	202	57	137
1988	—	—	—	64	23	194	157	30	96
1989	7	4	3	81	19	133	132	27	53
1990	9	5	9	33	10	103	232	33	98
1991	9	93	38	62	11	66	203	38	70
1992	3	18	23	35	26	120	151	33	63
1993	2	7	13	...	...	...	218	58	114
1994	—	—	—	30	5	71	240	36	75
1995	1	60	0.1	46	13	100	424	124	197
1996	—	—	—	60	20	146	930	65	76
1997	1	25	19	17	9	40	1,023	75	102
1998	—	—	—	484	19	87	1,258	502	3,173
1999	—	—	—	—	...	...	1,079	75	92

	Finland			France			Germany			Greece		
	Number	Workers Involved (thou)	Days Lost (thou)	Number	Workers Involved (thou)	Days Lost (thou)	Number	Workers Involved (thou)	Days Lost (thou)	Number	Workers Involved (thou)	Days Lost (thou)
1930	11	2	12	1,093	582	7,209	353	302	4,029	...	...	...
1931	1	0.1	...	286	48	950	463	297	1,890	...	...	...
1932	3	0.3	2	362	72	1,244	648	172	1,130	...	...	...
1933	4	1	10	343	87	1,199	(69)[12]	(13)[12]	(96)[12]	...	...	...
1934	46	6	90	385	101	2,393	...	...	...	...	...	...
1935	23	2	61	376	109	1,182	...	...	...	...	...	...
1936	29	3	35	16,907	2,423	...	...	...	...	...	...	...
1937	37	6	183	2,616	1,133	...	...	...	...	...	...	...
1938	31	4	111	1,220	324	...	...	...	...	...	...	...
1939	29	6	...	...	...	...	...	...	...	...	...	...
1940	4	0.5	...	...	...	...	...	...	...	...	...	...
1941	12	2	...	...	...	...	...	...	...	...	...	...
1942	...	...	...	...	...	...	...	...	...	...	...	...
1943	...	...	...	...	...	...	...	...	...	...	...	...
1944	...	...	...	...	...	...	...	...	...	...	...	...
							West Germany					
1945	102	36	358	...	...	...	...	...	...	...	...	...
1946	42	19	116	528	180	386	...	...	...	...	...	...
1947	228	113	480	2,285	2,998	22,673	...	...	...	...	...	...
1948	84	15	244	1,425	6,561	13,133	...	...	...	...	...	...
1949	48	54	1,195	1,426	4,330	7,129	892	58	271	...	...	...
1950	78	108	4,644	2,586	1,527	11,729	1,344[13]	79[13]	380[13]	206	129	434
1951	67	11	324	2,514	1,754	3,495	1,528	174	1,593	184	134	375
1952	43	9	54	1,749	1,155	1,733	2,529	84	443	114	52	110
1953	104	16	64	1,761	1,784	9,722	1,395	51	1,488	196	85	117
1954	36	19	116	1,479	1,319	1,440	538	116	1,587	172	49	39
1955	72	42	344	2,672	1,061	3,079	866	597	847	210	50	69
1956	43	451	6,971	2,440	982	1,423	268	52	1,580	...	...	...
1957	88	59	228	2,623	2,964	4,121	86	45	1,072	169	115	142
1958	50	14	45	954	1,112	1,138	1,484	202	782	113	92	109
1959	49	20	430	1,512	940	1,938	55[14]	22[14]	62[14]	100	42	59
1960	44	19	96	1,494	1,072	1,070	28	17	38	135	56	81
1961	51	45	41	1,963	2,552	2,601	119	20	61	115	53	188
1962	46	7	33	1,884	1,472	1,901	195	79	451	182	57	129
1963	66	105	1,380	2,382	2,646	5,991	187	316	1,846	227	101	331
1964	76	27	58	2,281	2,603	2,497	34	6	17	399	164	346

B3 Industrial Disputes

1965–1998

	Finland				France				Germany				Greece		
	Number	Workers Involved (thou)	Days Lost (thou)		Number	Workers Involved (thou)	Days Lost (thou)		Number	Workers Involved (thou)	Days Lost (thou)		Number	Workers Involved (thou)	Days Lost (thou)
1965	29	7	16		1,674	1,237	980		20	6	49		434	256	454
1966	150	66	123		1,711	3,341	2,523		205	196	27		609	349	712
1967	43	27	321		1,675	2,824	4,204		742	60	390		89	91	114
1968	68	27	282		...	...	...		36	25	25		...	...	...
1969	158	83	161		2,207	1,444	2,224		86	90	249		...	...	...
1970	240[18]	202[18]	233[18]		2,942	1,080	1,742		129	184	93		...	...	...
1971	838	403	2,711		4,318	3,234	4,388		624	536	4,484		...	...	...
1972	849	240	473		3,464	2,721	3,755		54	23	66		...	...	...
1973	1,009	678	2,497		3,731	2,246	3,915		732	185	563		...	...	...
1974	1,788	371	435		3,381	1,564	3,380		890	250	1,051		...	...	...
1975	1,530	215	284		3,888	1,827	3,869		201	36	69		14.2[21]	46[21]	21.8[21]
1976	3,282	513	1,225		4,348	2,023	5,011		1,481	169	534		947	301	788
1977	1,673	744	2,375		3,281	1,920	3,666			34	24		569	560	1,252
1978	1,237	165	32		3,195	705	2,200		1,239	487	4,281		616	471	987
1979	1,753	229	243		3,121	967	3,172		40	77	483		588	1,262	1,679
1980	2,238	413	1,606		2,118	501	1,523		132	45	128		726	1,408	2,907
1981	1,612	493	659		2,405	329	1,442		297	253	58		466	402	813
1982	1,240	167	208		3,113	398[25]	2,250		40	40	15		968	353	1,431
1983	1,940	422	720		2,837	38	1,321		114	94	41		675	224	555
1984	1,710	562	1,527		2,537	42	1,317		1,121	537	5,618		486	159	562
1985	848	171	174		1,901	23	727		53	78	34		453	786	1,094
1986	1,225	603	2,788		1,391	22	568		96	116	28		213	1,106	1,263
1987	802	99	131		1,391	19	511		119	155	33		381	1,271	1,733
1988	1,353	244	180		2,260	27	1,094		41	33	41		532	449	6,667
1989	606	157	204		1,743	20	800		306	44	100		312	796	9,338
1990	450	207	935		1,529	18	528		177	257	364		480	1,304	23,441
1991	270	128	458		1,318	19	497		367	208	154		161	476	5,839
1992	165	102	76		1,330	16	359		2,466	598	1,545		824	243	2,830
1993	125	23	17		1,351	20	511		413	29	84		596	183	1,602
1994	171	71	526		1,671	18	500		...	400	229		215	74	665
1995	112	127	869		2,066	43	784		...	183	247		110	52	449
1996	94	43	20		1,439	11	444		...	166	98		171	76	765
1997	91	28	103		1,607	121	392		...	13	52		125	45	391
1998	98	35	133		1,475	10	345		...	4	16		99	34	284

1930–1949

	Hungary				Ireland				Italy				Netherlands		
	Number	Workers Involved (thou)	Days Lost (thou)		Number	Workers Involved (thou)	Days Lost (thou)		Number	Workers Involved (thou)	Days Lost (thou)		Number	Workers Involved (thou)	Days Lost (thou)
1930	35	6	80		83	3	77		82	3	...		212	11	229
1931	38	11	190		60	5	310		67	4	...		215	28	766
1932	20	5	33		70	4	42		23	0.6	...		216	32	1,636
1933	31	10	125		88	9	200		34	0.8	...		184	15	483
1934	49	13	92		99	9	180		38	0.6	...		152	6	90
1935	50	17	111		99	10	288		43	0.6	...		152	13	244
1936	122	21	233		107	9	186		...	...	...		96	10[17] 9	77
1937	89	26	161		145	27	1,755		...	...	...		95	5	32
1938	64	9	105		137	14	209		...	...	...		141	8	125
1939	53	26	170		99	7	106		...	...	...		90	6	91
1940	35	33	370		89	8	152		...	...	...		23[15]	3[15]	43[15]
1941	3	0.8	1		71	5	77		...	...	...		...	...	...
1942	7	0.5	2		69	5	115		...	...	...		...	...	...
1943	8	0.5	1		81	6	62		...	...	...		...	...	...
1944	...	...	...		84	4	38		...	...	...		...	...	...
1945	9	6	7		87	9	244		...	...	...		118[16]	39[16]	161[16]
1946	17	26	57		105	11	150		...	...	...		270	75	682
1947	5	5	7		194	22	449		...	...	...		272	63	203
1948	...	...	...		147	17	258		...	...	...		183	19	131
1949	...	...	...		153	10	273		1,159	2,894	16,578		116	15	289

B3 Industrial Disputes

1950–1998

	Number	Ireland Workers Involved (thou)	Days Lost (thou)	Number	Italy Workers Involved (thou)	Days Lost (thou)	Number	Netherlands Workers Involved (thou)	Days Lost (thou)
1950	154	19	217	1,272	3,536	7,761	79	21	163
1951	138	25	545	1,190	2,145	4,515	85	15	67
1952	82	15	529	1,363	1,462	3,531	40	4	31
1953	75	7	82	1,415	4,678	5,828	58	11	30
1954	81	8	67	1,990	2,045	5,377	91	21	59
1955	96	12	236	1,981	1,383	5,622	63	24	133
1956	67	4	48	1,904	1,678	4,137	80	38	213
1957	45	4	92	1,731	1,227	4,619	37	2	7
1958	51	12	126	1,937	1,283	4,172	73	5	37
1959	58	9	124	1,925	1,900	9,190	48	8	14
1960	49	6	80	2,471	2,338	5,786	121	85	467
1961	96	27	377	3,502	2,698	9,891	43	10	25
1962	60	9	104	3,652	2,910	22,717	24	2	9
1963	70	16	234	4,145	3,694	11,395	104	30	38
1964	87	25	545	3,841	3,245	13,089	53	9	44
1965	89	40	556	3,191	2,310	6,993	60	23	55
1966	112	52	784	2,387	1,887	14,474	20	11	13
1967	79	21	183	2,658	2,243	8,568	8	2	6
1968	126	39	406	3,377	4,862	9,240	11	6	14
1969	134	62	936	3,788	7,507	37,825	28	12	22
1970	134	29	1,008	4,162	3,722	20,887	99	52	263
1971	133	44	274	5,598	3,891	14,799	15	36	97
1972	131	22	207	4,765	4,405	19,497	31	20	134
1973	182	32	207	3,769	6,133	23,419	7	58	584
1974	219	43	552	5,174	7,824	19,467	14	3	7
1975	151	29	296	3,601	14,110	27,189	5	0.3	0.5
1976	134	42	777	2,706	11,898	25,378	11	15	14
1977	175	34	442	3,308	13,803	16,566	44	44	247
1978	152	33	613	2,479	8,774	10,177	32	10	6
1979	140	50	1,465	2,000	16,237	27,530	57	37	309
1980	130	31	412	2,238	13,825	16,457	18	26	57
1981	117	32	434	2,204	8,227	10,527	11	9	24
1982	131	30	434	1,747	10,483	18,563[22]	12	70	215
1983	154	30	319	1,565	6,844	98,021	9	20	118
1984	192	31	386	1,816	7,357	60,923	16	16	29
1985	116	169	418	1,341	4,843	26,815	45	23	89
1986	102	50	309	1,469	3,607	39,506	35	17	39
1987	80	26	264	1,149	4,273	32,240	28	13	58
1988	65	10	143	1,769	2,712	23,206	38	5	9
1989	38	3	50	1,297	4,451	35,488	27	15	24
1990	49	49	10	1,094	1,634	41,448	29	25	207
1991	54	18	85	791	2,952	23,880	28	42	96
1992	38	13	191	903	3,178	22,216	23	52	85
1993	...	...	...	1,054	4,384	27,288	12	20	45
1994	28	5	25	861	2,614	33,374	17	21	47
1995	34	31	130	545	445	909	14	55	691
1996	32	13	114	904	1,689	1,930	12	8	7
1997	28	5	74	923	737	1,185	18	7	14
1998	34	8	37	1,103	435	580	22	30	33

B3 Industrial Disputes

	Norway			Poland			Romania				Spain[6]		
	Number	Workers Involved (thou)	Days Lost (thou)	Number	Workers Involved (thou)	Days Lost (thou)	Number	Workers Involved (thou)	Days Lost (thou)	Number		Workers Involved (thou)	Days Lost (thou)
1930	94	5	240	330	53	427	101	17	180	402(368)		287	3,745
1931	82	60	7,586	363	109	637	71	17	185	734(610)		288	3,843
1932	91	6	394	517	315	2,134	102	19	104	68(435)		444	3,590
1933	93	6	364	649	348	3,844	58	16	57	1,127(1,046)		937	14,441
1934	85	6	235	957	373	2,414	72	11	156[17]	594		742	11,103
1935	103	4	168	1,187	453	2,026	84	16	361				
1936	175	15	396	2,074	678	4,039	90	15	196	...		...	...
1937	195	29	1,014	2,107	567	3,323	70	7	73	...		...	...
1938	248	24	567	1,457	269	1,289	26	4	52	...		...	...
1939	81	16	860	...	...	...	...	...	...	...		...	...
1940	...	...	...	...	...	...						...	...
1941	...	...	...	...	...	...							
1942	...	...	...	...	...	...							
1943	...	...	...	...	...	...							
1944	...	...	...	...	...	...							
1945	16	4	65	...	...	...							
1946	39	5	79	...	...	...						...	...
1947	47	8	41	...	...	...							
1948	58	6	92	...	...	...				...		...	...
1949	47	9	105	...	...	...				...		...	...
1950	30	4	42	...	...	...	...	...	...			...	...
1951	28	4	36	...	...	...	...	...	...	...		...	...
1952	40	6	124	...	...	...	...	...	...	...		...	...
1953	55	5	41	...	...	...	...	...	...	...		...	...
1954	27	3	105	...	...	...	...	...	...	...		...	...
1955	22	10	108	...	...	...	...	...	...	...		...	...
1956	27	56	964	...	...	...	...	...	...	...		...	...
1957	18	3	27	...	...	...	...	...	...	...		...	...
1958	16	13	60	...	...	...	...	...	...	...		...	...
1959	18	2	48	...	...	...	...	...	...	...		...	...
1960	12	0.7	2	...	...	...	...	...	...	...		...	...
1961	19	23	423	...	...	...	...	...	...	...		...	...
1962	8	1	81	...	...	...	...	...	...				
1963	8	11	226	...	...	...	...	...	...	169		39	125
1964	3	0.2	1							209		119	141
1965	7	0.6	9	...	...	...	...	...	...	183		59	190
1966	7	1	5	...	...	...	...	...	...	132		37	185
1967	7	0.4	5	...	...	...	...	...	...	372		199	236
1968	6	0.5	14	...	...	...	...	...	...	309		131	241
1969	4	0.8	22	...	...	...	...	...	...	491		205	560
1970	15	3	47	...	...	...	...	...	...	1,547		440	1,092
1971	10	3	9	...	...	...	...	...	...	549		197	860
1972	9	1	12	...	...	...	...	...	...	710		236	587
1973	12	2	11	...	...	...	...	...	...	731		303	1,081
1974	13	22	318	...	...	...	...	...	...	2,009		557	1,749
1975	22	3	12	...	...	...	...	...	...	2,807		504	1,815
1976	35	22	138	...	...	...	...	...	...	3,662		2,556	12,593
1977	15	2	25	...	...	...	...	...	...	1,194		2,955	16,642
1978	14	4	63	...	...	...	...	...	...	1,128		3,864	11,551
1979	10	3	7	...	...	...	...	...	...	2,680		5,713	18,917

B3   Industrial Disputes

1980–1998

	Norway				**Spain[6]**		
	Number	Workers Involved (thou)	Days Lost (thou)		Number	Workers Involved (thou)	Days Lost (thou)
1980	35	19	104		2,103	2,287	6,178[23]
1981	17	4	28		1,993	2,006	5,146[23]
1982	12	25	281		1,810	1,059	2,788[23]
1983	9	1	6		1,451[23]	1,484[23]	4,417[23]
1984	21	31	104		1,498[23]	2,242[23]	6,358[23]
1985	11	7	66		1,092[23]	1,511[23]	3,224[23]
1986	16	166	1,031		914[24]	858[24]	2,279[24]
1987	10	2	13		1,497[24]	1,881[24]	5,025[24]
1988	15	8	83		1,193[24]	6,692[24]	11,641[24]
1989	14	11	17		1,094	1,396	3,739
1990	15	61	139		1,312	977	2,613
1991	4	...	2		1,645	1,984	4,537
1992	16	39	365		1,360	5,192	6,333
1993	12	7	34		1,209	1,077	2,141
1994	20	14	97		908	5,437	6,276
1995	11	10	51		883	573	1,457
1996	18	53	529		830	1,087	1,579
1997	6	1	7		744	650	1,837
1998	36	26	286		632	681	1,281

1930–1964

	Sweden			**Switzerland**			**United Kingdom**			**Yugoslavia**		
	Number	Workers Involved (thou)	Days Lost (thou)	Number	Workers Involved (thou)	Days Lost (thou)	Number	Workers Involved (thou)	Days Lost (thou)	Number	Workers Involved (thou)	Days Lost (thou)
1930	261	21	1,021	31	6	266	422	307	4,399		5	49
1931	193	41	2,627	25	5	74	420	490	6,983	5	1	14
1932	182	50	3,095	38	5	159	389	379	6,488	7	1	4
1933	140	32	3,434	35	3	69	357	136	1,072	8	3	14
1934	103	14	760	20	3	33	471	134	959	35	7	41
1935	98	17	788	17	0.9	15	553	271	1,955	141	26	221
1936	60	4	438	41	4	39	818	316	1,829	397	88	1,356
1937	67	31	861	37	6	115	1,129	597	3,413	238	53	911
1938	85	29	1,284	17	0.7	16	875	274	1,334	189	32	494
1939	45	2	159	7	0.2	4	940	337	1,356	...	...	...
1940	38	4	78	6	0.6	1	922	299	940	...	...	...
1941	34	2	94	15	0.7	14	1,251	360	1,079	...	...	...
1942	139	1	53	19	0.8	4	1,303	456	1,527	...	...	...
1943	167	7	94	19	1	12	1,785	557	1,810	...	...	...
1944	214	7	228	18	1	18	2,194	821	3,710	...	...	...
1945	163	133	11,321	35	4	37	2,293	531	2,835	...	...	...
1946	137	1	27	55	15	184	2,205	526	2,158	...	...	...
1947	81	57	125	29	7	102	1,721	620	2,433	...	...	...
1948	47	6	151	28	4	61	1,759	424	1,944	...	...	...
1949	31	1	21	12	0.9	41	1,426	433	1,807	...	...	...
1950	23	2	41	6	0.3	5	1,339	302	1,389	...	...	...
1951	28	15	531	8	1	8	1,719	379	1,694	...	...	...
1952	32	2	79	8	1	12	1,714	415	1,792	...	...	...
1953	20	26	582	6	2	61	1,746	1,370	2,184	...	...	...
1954	45	8	24	6	3	26	1,989	448	2,457	...	...	...
1955	18	4	159	4	0.4	1	2,419	659	3,781	...	...	...
1956	12	2	4	5	0.3	1	2,648	507	2,083	...	...	...
1957	20	2	53	2	0.1	1	2,859	1,356	8,412	...	...	...
1958	10	0.1	15	3	0.8	2	2,629	523	3,462	...	...	...
1959	17	1	24	4	0.1	2	2,093	645	5,270	...	...	...
1960	31	1	18	8	0.2	1	2,832	817	3,024	...	...	...
1961	12	0.1	2	...	...	...	2,686	771	3,046	...	...	...
1962	10	4	5	2	0.2	1	2,449	4,420	5,798	...	...	...
1963	24	3	25	4	1	71	2,068	591	1,755	...	...	...
1964	14	2	34	1	0.4	5	2,524	873	2,277	...	...	...

B3 Industrial Disputes

	Sweden			Switzerland			United Kingdom		
	Number	Workers Involved (thou)	Days Lost (thou)	Number	Workers Involved (thou)	Days Lost (thou)	Number	Workers Involved (thou)	Days Lost (thou)
1965	8	0.2	4	2	...	...	2,354	869	2,925
1966	26	29	352	2	...	...	1,937	531	2,398
1967	7	0.1	0.4	1	0.1	2	2,116	732	2,787
1968	7	0.4	1	1	0.1	2	2,378	2,256	4,690
1969	41	9	112	1	...	...	3,116	1,656	6,846
1970	134	27	156	3	0.3	3	3,906	1,793	10,980
1971	60	63	839	11	2	7	2,228	1,175	13,551
1972	44	7	11	5	0.5	2	2,497	1,726	23,909
1973	48	4	12	...	...	...	2,873	1,513	7,197
1974	85	17	58	3	0.3	3	2,922	1,622	14,750
1975	86	24	366	6	0.3	2	2,282	789	6,012
1976	73	9	25	19	2	20	2,016	670	3,284
1977	35	13	87	9	1	5	2,703	1,155	10,142
1978	99	8	37	10	1	5	2,471	1,003	9,405
1979	207	32	29	8	0.5	2	2,080	4,583	29,474
1980	212	747	4,478	5	4	6	1,330	842	11,964
1981	68	99	209	1	...	...	1,338	1,499	4,266
1982	46	5	2	1	0.1	0.6	1,572	2,103	5,312
1983	92	14	37	5	1	4	1,364	574	3,754
1984	206	24	31	2	0.1	0.7	1,221	1,464	27,135
1985	160	125	504	3	0.4	0.7	903	791	6,402
1986	75	69	696	1	...	0.1	1,074	720	1,920
1987	72	11	15	...	...	...	1,016	887	3,546
1988	144	95	797	4	0.1	0.9	781	790	3,702
1989	139	34	410	2	...	0.2	701	727	4,128
1990	126	73	770	2	0.5	4.0	630	298	1,903
1991	23	2	22	1	...	...	369	176	761
1992	20	18	28	3	0.2	0.7	253	148	528
1993	33	29	189	—	—	—	211	385	649
1994	13	21	52	8	6	14	205	107	278
1995	36	125	627	2	0.8	0.3	235	174	415
1996	9	9	61	3	5.0	7	244	364	1,303
1997	14	11	24	2	0.3	0.4	216	130	234
1998	13	0.5	1.6	7	16	24	166	927	282

B3 Industrial Disputes

NOTES

1. SOURCES:- I.L.O., *Yearbook of Labour Statistics* (since 1935), and the official publications noted on p. xv. Netherlands data of workers involved for 1906–9 and 1919–24 were supplied by the Dutch Central Office of Statistics, and Italian data for 1914–23 were supplied by the Italian Central Institute of Statistics.
2. Except as indicated in the footnotes, the number of workers involved and the days' work lost by them relate to all those clearly affected by a particular dispute, not just to those directly involved.
3. The reporting systems of countries differ considerably, and comparisons should not be made without taking these differences into account.

FOOTNOTES

[1] Cisleithania to 1914. In this period only workers directly involved are included.
[2] This column refers only to actual strikers.
[3] The figures are unknown for one dispute.
[4] The figures relate to West Germany after 1945.
[5] Previously disputes begun during the year; subsequently all disputes in being during the year.
[6] For the period to 1934 information about workers involved and days lost is not available for the total number of disputes recorded. The number of disputes to which the statistics in the second and third columns relate is shown in brackets in the first column.
[7] Previous statistics are taken from the records of the central employers' association or of the *union syndicale*, whichever shows the higher figure.
[8] Subsequently excludes strike involving less than ten workers or lasting less than one day, except when the number of days lost exceed one hundred.
[9] Southern Ireland is excluded from 1913.
[10] Excluding June & August, when the number of strikes was so great that records were never completely taken.
[11] Excluding general strikes and the political strike of 1950.
[12] First quarter only.
[13] Previously American and British Occupation Zones only.
[14] Subsequently includes West Berlin.
[15] January–May.
[16] May–December.
[17] Subsequently only workers directly involved are included.
[18] Previously excludes workers indirectly affected, though including days lost by these workers. Also previously excludes disputes lasting less than 4 hours, except when a loss of more than 100 days was involved.
[19] Earlier figures of estimated numbers of strikes (to 1864) and of actual numbers of strikes and strikers are given in Edward Shorter and Charles Tilly, *Strikes in France, 1830–1968* (Cambridge, 1974):

	Strikes		Strikes	Strikers (000)		Strikes	Strikers (000)
1830	40	1850	45	…	1870	116	88.2
1831	49	1851	55	…	1871	52	14.1
1832	51	1852	86	…	1872	151	21.1
1833	90	1853	109	…	1873	44	4.9
1834	55	1854	68		1874	58	7.8
1835	32	1855	168	…	1875	101	16.6
1836	55	1856	73	…	1876	102	21.2
1837	51	1857	55	…	1877	55	12.9
1838	44	1858	53	…	1878	73	38.5
1839	64	1859	58	…	1879	88	54.4
1840	130	1860	58	…	1880	190	110.4
1841	68	1861	63	…	1881	209	68.0
1842	62	1862	44	…	1882	271	65.5
1843	49	1863	29	…	1883	181	42.0
1844	53	1864	21	…	1884	112	33.9
1845	48	1865	58	27.6	1885	123	20.8
1846	53	1866	52	14.0	1886	195	35.3
1847	55	1867	76	32.1	1887	194	38.1
1848	94	1868	58	20.3	1888	188	51.5
1849	65	1869	72	40.6	1889	199	89.1

Shorter and Tilly's later statistics sometimes differ from those in the *Annuaire Statistique*, but not generally by significant amounts.

B3 Industrial Disputes

[20] Statistics of numbers of strikes for 1892–1913 are given in H. Kaelble and H. Volkmann, "Konjunktur und Streik während des Ubergangs zum Organisierten Kapitalismus in Deutschland", *Zeitschrift für Wirtschafts-und Sozialwissenschaften* (1972). These differ somewhat from those given in the table. They are as follows:-

1892	73	1900	852	1907	2,792
1893	116	1901	727	1908	2,052
1894	131	1902	861	1909	2,045
1895	204	1903	1,282	1910	3,194
1896	483	1904	1,625	1911	2,914
1897	578	1905	2,323	1912	2,825
1898	985	1906	3,480	1913	2,600
1899	976				

[21] September–December
[22] Hours of work lost subsequently.
[23] Excluding Catalonia
[24] Excluding the Basque Provinces.
[25] Subsequent statistics are based on monthly averages.

B4 MONEY WAGES IN INDUSTRY

Key to Part A:- a = daily wages in coal-mining to 1820 (1st line); average wages subsequently; b = gross weekly wages; c = unweighted average of weekly wages of compositors, builders and engineers and shift wages of coal hewers to 1880 (1st line), with Feinstein's index of average weekly wages in manufacturing subsequently; d = average wages in 5 industries; e = hourly wages of males; f = hourly wages of males in all activities to 1900, and daily wages subsequently

PART A: 1900 = 100   **1800–1887**

	France[1]	Germany[3]	U.K.:G.B.			Belgium	Denmark	France[1]	Germany[2]	Italy	Sweden	'UK:GB
	a	b	c			d	e	a	b	f	e	c
1800	34	26	...		1840	...	...	49	44	...	...	61
1801	35	26	...		1841	...	...	50	43	...	...	60
1802	35	26	66		1842	...	...	50	45	...	...	60
1803	36	27	...		1843	46	...	48	43	...	...	59
1804	37	27	...		1844	48	...	51	45	...	...	60
1805	39	30	...		1845	47	...	49	39	...	...	61
1806	39	30	...		1846	50	...	48	39	...	...	62
1807	40	28	...		1847	48	...	46	40	...	...	62
1808	41	28	...		1848	47	...	48	43	...	...	60
1809	42	28	...		1849	48	...	50	41	...	...	60
1810	43	28	...		1850	49	...	50	41	...	...	60
1811	43	29	...		1851	51	...	48	42	...	...	61
1812	43	29	...		1852	52	...	48	40	...	...	61
1813	43	31	...		1853	53	...	50	42	...	...	63
1814	43	31	68		1854	56	...	54	44	...	...	66
1815	42	33	...		1855	56	...	54	45	...	...	68
1816	42	35	...		1856	58	...	54	46	...	...	69
1817	42	33	...		1857	59	...	56	49	...	...	68
1818	42	32	...		1858	59	...	58	49	...	...	67
1819	42	33	58		1859	59	...	59	47	...	...	67
1820	41[4]	33	...		1860	60	...	60	48	...	...	69
1821	53	35	...		1861	61	...	62	50	...	41	70
1822	53	35	58		1862	62	...	64	50	...	45	70
1823	55	35	...		1863	65	...	64	50	...	45	70
1824	56	36	...		1864	67	...	64	51	...	42	71
1825	57 / 52	36	60		1865	70	...	64	51	...	45	73
1826	57	36	...		1866	72	...	66	54	...	44	77
1827	55	36	...		1867	72	...	68	54	...	45	75
1828	51	36	...		1868	72	...	69	56	...	49	74
1829	47	36	57		1869	74	...	71	58	...	52	74
1830	45	37	57		1870	75	47	72	60	...	49	75
1831	46	38	57		1871	75	47	71	63	65	51	78
1832	48	37	57		1872	83	50	75	77	69	57	83
1833	53	39	57		1873	91	58	76	88	69	61	88
1834	53	38	58		1874	89	63	76	85	73	66	88
1835	51	38	58		1875	88	66	77	83	73	67	86
1836	51	38	60		1876	85	66	78	76	77	64	86
1837	50	39	60		1877	79	63	79	71	81	67	86
1838	50	40	60		1878	81	61	81	72	81	63	83
1839	50	41	61		1879	79	61	82	69	81	59	81
					1880	82	63	88	70	85	63	80[5]
					1881	82	63	90	71	85	65	82
					1882	80	66	92	75	88	67	84
					1883	83	66	92	74	88	67	84
					1884	81	68	92	75	88	68	83
					1885	79	68	91	74	92	68	82
					1886	81	66	91	74	92	66	81
					1887	79	66	91	80	92	66	81

B4 Money wages in Industry

PART A: 1900 = 100   **1888–1914**

	Belgium d	Denmark e	France[1] a	Germany[2] b	Italy f	Sweden e	UK:GB c
1888	82	68	91	79	92	68	84
1889	82	68	92	80	96	72	85
1890	87	71	93	83	96	74	94
1891	86	74	93	83	96	75	95
1892	86	74	94	83	96	76	95
1893	84	76	95	86	96	78	94
1894	86	79	96	84	96	79	95
1895	85	79	96	85	96	80	95
1896	87	84	97	89	96	83	97
1897	88	87	98	94	100	87	98
1898	89	95	98	97	100	92	99
1899	93	97	100	101	100	96	101
1900	100	100	100	100	100[4]	100	100
1901	94	103	101	103	100	100	100
1902	96	103	100	103	103	102	100
1903	97	103	100	104	104	103	100
1904	97	105	101	106	104	107	100
1905	96	108	101	108	102	110	101
1906	99	111	105	114	106	116	103
1907	107	116	107	119	119	122	105
1908	103	121	108	121	119	125	103
1909	104	121	109	121	134	129	104
1910	108	124	110	125	131	135	105
1911	108	129	113	129	133	137	108
1912	114	134	116	135	137	142	110
1913	119	137[3]	117	138	143	144	113
1914	…	126	…	…	142	143	…

B4 Money wages in Industry

Key to Part B: a = average monthly earnings; b = daily wages of males in industry and transport; c = "general level" of wages in all activities; d = daily wages of insured males; e = hourly wages in manufacturing; f = hourly wages of males; g = unweighted mean of hourly wages in all sectors in Paris and in the provinces; h = gross weekly wages; i = monthly or weekly wages of adult males; k = hourly wages in engineering; l = average annual earnings in the Socialist sector of industry; m = daily earnings in industry, commerce and communications; n = average earnings of insured males involved in accidents; o = weekly average earnings of all wage-earners to 1920 (1st line) and basic weekly wages (average of June and December) subsequently

PART B: 1929 = 100[6]   1910-1938

	Austria	Belgium	Bulgaria	Czecho-slovakia[5]	Denmark	Finland	France	Germany	Hungary	Ireland
	a	b	c	d	e	f	g	h	e	k
								1914 = 100		
1910	...	...	...	...	...	...	...	...	...	...
1911	...	...	...	...	...	...	13	...	...	...
1912	...	...	...	...	...	...	...	...	...	...
1913	...	69	...	11	...	...	...	...	...	...
1914	...	...	...	...	37	7.7	...	100	...	...
1915	...	...	...	...	...	8.2	...	110	...	...
1916	...	...	...	...	...	10.9	17[7]	130	...	...
1917	...	...	...	...	50	15.7	...	160	...	...
1918	...	...	...	22	64	24.1	...	200	...	...
1919	...	...	...	39	112	35.5	...	340	...	...
1920	...	127	...	66	147	62	...	990[8]	...	...
1921	...	151	...	108	141	68	59	1,780[8]	...	...
1922	...	116	...	109	110	73	...	45,230[8]	...	...
1923	...	119	...	93	106	81	...	*[8]	...	...
								1929 = 100		
1924	...	106	...	91	112	84	65	54	...	...
1925	...	94	...	93	117	88	70	73	...	...
1926	...	91	...	94	105	93	84	76	...	...
1927	98	93	...	95	101	96	85	85	96	...
1928	96	97	93	98	100	100	88	97	98	...
1929	100	100	100	100[5]	100	100	100	100	100	...
										1931 = 100
1930	104	106	94	100	102	97	107	92	100	...
1931	102	99	91	98	102	85	107	81	96	100
1932	101	91	79	94	102	82	104	67	89	99
1933	97	88	84	89	102	93	103	68	84	99
1934	94	84	78	87	103	83	103	73	81	99
1935	...	81	78	85	104	84	100	75	77	99
1936	...	88	77	86	105	89	115	78	79	99
1937	...	97	85	...	105	97	146[7]	81	79	100
1938	...	103	90	...	111	103	167	85	84	106

* = 86.2 million million

B4   Money wages in Industry

PART B: 1929 = 100[6]   1910–1938

	Italy	Netherlands	Norway	Poland	Romania	Russia/ U.S.S.R.	Sweden	Switzerland	UK:GB	Yugo-slavia
	b	i	k	b	c	l	m	n	o	a
1910	...	...	31	...	...	...	...	...	...	...
1911	...	...	31	...	...	...	...	...	...	...
1912	...	...	33	...	...	...	...	...	...	...
1913	13	...	35	...	...	...	42	47	...	...
1914	19	...	37	...	3.6	...	43	...	55	...
1915	19	...	37	...	...	...	46	...	64	...
1916	22	...	38	...	...	...	51	...	73	...
1917	27	...	59	...	...	...	62	...	93	...
1918	33	...	86	...	...	...	90	78	116	...
1919	48	...	136	...	...	...	114	91	133[4]	...
1920	78	...	171[9]	...	...	...	130	103	152	...
1921	103	...	171	...	...	...	132	103	134	...
1922	99	...	130	...	...	...	96	97	104	...
1923	93	...	123	...	66	...	90	94	99	...
1924	93	...	131	...	76	...	91	97	102	...
1925	104	...	141	100	84	56[11]	93	97	103	3
1926	112	100	125	72	90	71[11]	94	98	103	...
1927	111	100	106	84	98	78[11]	94	98	101	...
1928	102	100	101	92	99	88	95	98	100	...
1929	100	100	100	100	100	100	100	100	100	...
										1930 = 100
1930	99	100	100	99	96	117	102	101	99	100
1931	92	100	97[9]	92	85	141	101	102	98	99
1932	87	93	98[9]	85	69	178	99	98	96	91
1933	84	93	98	77	63	196	96	96	95	86
1934	81	89	96	73	62	232	95	94	96	79
1935	78	25	95	71	61[10]	284	98	92	97	78
1936	78	85	95	70	100	...	99	90	99	80
1937	81	85	103	73	105	...	103	89	102	83
1938	85	89	113	77	107	433	109	93	105	85

B4   Money wages in Industry

Key to Parts C and D:- a = monthly earnings; b = daily wages of males in manufacturing; c = "general level" of wages to 1946, monthly earnings in the socialist sector subsequently; d = average daily wages in Slovakia to 1948 (1st line), monthly earnings in the entire socialist sector from then to 1953 and in the industrial part only subsequently; e = hourly wages in manufacturing; f = hourly wages of males; g = unweighted mean of hourly wages in all sectors in Paris and in the provinces to 1946 (1st line), with the average weighted in the source subsequently; h = monthly earnings in the socialist sector; i = gross weekly wages; k = hourly wages; l = monthly wages of males to 1943, and monthly earnings in the socialist sector of industry subsequently; m = daily wages in all activities; n = monthly or weekly wages of adult males; o = daily wages; p = hourly wages in industry, commerce and communications to 1950 (1st line). From then to 1971 (1st line) the figures relate to industry only, and subsequently is manufacturing only; q = average earnings of all wage-earners in June; r = basic weekly wages (average of June and December) to 1947 (1st line), and average weekly earnings of adult males in October subsequently.

PART C: 1955 = 100[6]   **1938–1970**

	Austria	Belgium	Bulgaria	Czecho-slovakia	Denmark	Finland	France	East Germany	Germany	Greece	Hungary
	a	b	c	d	e	f	g	h	i	k	l
	1938 = 100		1938 = 100	1938 = 100			1938 = 100		1938 = 100	1938 = 100	
1938	...	...	100	100	32	...	100	...	100	...	100
1939	...	...	104	96	33	4.6	102	...	102	...	111
1940	...	...	119	112	37	...	103	...	107	...	117
1941	...	...	132	147	39	...	118	...	114	...	140
1942	...	...	150	178	41	8.2	124	...	114	...	165
1943	...	...	167	210	44	9.5	133	...	...	...	236
1944	...	...	299	235	47	11	233	...	...	...	...
1945	...	...	499	265	50	...	380	...	...	...	...
							523		**West Germany**		
							1955 = 100		1955 = 100		
1946	...	...	570	416	55	26	22	...		...	...
								...		...	...
1947	175	71	...	504	58	36	30	...	...	...	...
			1955 = 100								
1948	278	78	...	70	67	52	46	...	49	...	52
1949	336	81	...	74	69	55	52	...	62	...	52
1950	378	83	...	81	73	66	57	...	69	...	60
1951	492	93	...	86	81	89	72	...	79	...	64
	553		...								
	1955 = 100		1955 = 100								
1952	89[12]	97	...	27	88	93	85	...	85	...	82
1953	88	95	89	89[4]	91	93	88	...	89	...	86
1954	93	97	95	94	96	96	93	...	93	...	96
1955	100	100	100	100	100	100	100	100	100	...	100
1956	105	106	101	104	108	111	109	103	107	...	107
1957	110	113	107	106	114	117	118	109	113	...	126
1958	117	115	110	108	119	123	132	117	118	...	127
1959	123	119	116	110	127	130	141	127	124	...	131
										1962 = 100	
1960	134	123	126	114	136	139	150	135	136	...	133
1961	146	127	131	117	152	149	161	141	150	96[13]	135
1962	155	135	134	117	168	157	176	143	165	100	137
1963	165	146	138	117	181	167	192	145	176	106	141
1964	180	161	141	121	197	188	206	149	190	117	145
1965	189	176	145	126	220	205	219	155	209	127	145
1966	212	191	151	129	247	221	232	158	221	143	152
1967	228	203	168	137	270	239	245	162	220	160	156
1968	242	215	179	148	302	266	272	169	235	171	159
1969	257	233	184	159	337	290	301	177	260	189	165
1970	281	260	194	164	374	321	331	185	300	200	175

B4 Money wages in Industry

	Ireland	Italy	Netherlands	Norway	Poland	Portugal	Russia/ U.S.S.R	Spain[15]	Sweden	Switz- erland	U.K.:G.B.	Yugo- slavia
	h	m	n	f	k	o	h	k	p	q	r	h
1938	47	1.1	38	33	...	...	...	...	...	...	39	...
1939	48	1.3	38	34	...	...	...	...	31	43	39	...
1940	48	1.5	41	36	...	...	46	...	33	45	45	...
1941	49	1.6	43	...	...	...	...	...	35	48	48	...
1942	49	1.8	43	...	...	...	...	...	39	55	52	...
1943	52	2.2	43	...	...	...	...	...	40	59	54	...
1944	54	3.7	43	40	...	...	...	...	41	63	57	...
1945	55	...	51	46	...	...	61	...	43	69	59	...
1946	57	19	63	53	...	...	66	...	46	76	64	...
1947	68	51	65	58	...	...	...	...	53	82	66₄ 59	...
1948	74	69	68	61	...	...	...	...	58	87	62	...
1949	81	73	70	64	...	...	...	...	59	88	64	...
1950	81	76	76	68	51	...	89	...	61₄ 59	88	68	...
1951	81	84	83	77	56	...	...	...	71	92	74	...
1952	91	88	84	86	62	...	...	...	84	95	80	...
1953	100	90	86	90	89	99	...	...	89	96	85	...
1954	100	94	95	95	95	98	...	...	92	97	92	...
1955	100	100₁₄	100	100	100	100	100	...	100	100	100	100
1956	108	105	105	108	111	103	103	...	109	105	107	109
1957	110	109	117	115	130	104	107	...	115	109	113	131
1958	112	115	122	120	138	109	109	...	122	113	115	137
1959	116	117	125	130	149	117	110	...	128	116	121	156
1960	124	121	135	136	153	124	112	...	136	123	130	187
1961	126	125	140	146	159	134	116	...	147	131	138	219
								1963 = 100				
1962	145	135	149	159	164	137	119	...	159	141	142	229
1963	147	150	159	168	172	143	122	100	170	152	150	280
1964	166	172	184	177	177	150	124	114	185	164	162	362
1965	169	186	202	193	183	170	128	133	204	176	176	501
1966	173	192	222	207	190	184	133	154	221	188	182	686
1967	189	200	237	222	199	198	140	177	239	199	192	755
1968	196	207	246	240	209	209	152	192	255	210	206	830
1969	220	220	270	263	215	...	160	213	277	222	223	959
1970	252	260	302	295	222	...	167	243	308	243	252	1,120

B4 Money wages in Industry

PART D: 1975 = 100   1970–1993

	Austria	Belgium	Bulgaria	Czecho-slovakia	Denmark	Finland	France	East Germany	West Germany	Greece	Hungary
	a	b	c	d	e	f	g	h	i	k	l
1970	53	47	84	84	47	44	51	85	68	46	75
1971	61	53	87	87	53	51	57	88	74	50	77
1972	68	60	89	91	59	58	63	91	80	54	81
1973	76	70	95	94	70	68	72	94	89	63	88
1974	88	85	97	97	84	82	85	97	96	80	94
1975	100	100	100	100	100	100	100	100	100	100	100
1976	109	111	101	103	111	117	116	105	108	129	106
1977	119	121	103	107	122	127	130	108	116	155	115
1978	126	128	107	111	133	138	146	112	122	192	125
1979	134	138	114	114	147	155	163	115	131	232	132
1980	144	151	127	116	161	170	189	117	138	295	139
1981	155	168	133	118	176	193	218	120	144	375	149
1982	165	178	137	121	194	214	248	122	149	500	158
1983	174	187	140	124	207	233	280	123	153	597	166
1984	183	195	144	127	216	255	297	126	158	755	188
1985	194	204	151	130	226	282	315	128	163	904	206
1986	203	205	160	132	235	300	328	133	168	1,019	219
1987	211	209	162	134	259	322	341	141	174	1,117	238
1988	219	215	175	137	275	340	350	145	181	1,323	338
1989	230	227	187	140	286	374	362		197	1,595	401
1990	247	237	223	145	298	407	397		207	1,904	502
1991	261	252	610	169	312	436	396	220		2,223	642
1992	276	263	1,493	208[17]	323	450	412	232		2,528	854
1993	290	274	2,316	260[17]	…	460	422	246		2,794	1,041

PART D: 1975 = 100   1970–1993

	Ireland	Italy	Netherlands	Norway	Poland	Portugal	Russia/U.S.S.R	Spain[15]	Sweden	Switz-erland	UK:GB	Yugo-slavia
	h	m	n	f	h	o	h	k	p	q	r	h
1970	49	44	55	53	63	…	82	38	66	59	48	38
1971	58	48	63	60	66	32	84	43	73	67	53	46
1972	63	52	70	65	70	37	87	50	91	75	61	54
1973	71	63	80	72	78	44	91	60	88	84	70	64
1974	85	79	90	86	89	70	96	75	98	94	82	82
1975	100	100	100	100	100	100	100	100	100	100	100	100
1976	115	122	108	117	110	125	105	130[15]	115	102	114	114
1977	134	146	119	129	119	146	107	148	124	106	123	135
1978	155	168	126	140	125	170	110	189	139	110	142	160
1979	183	198	131	143	136	202	112	231	151	114	165[16]	194
1980	211	243	138	157	156	248	115	272	167	120	187	240
1981	252	299	146	173	196	301	118	330	182	129	206	324
1982	288	350	157	191	295	359	121	381	192	138	225	412
1983	320	404	160	208	384	419	123	436	204	143	246	499
1984	355	449	162	226	454	500	127	491	227	147	266	763
1985	372	493	167	243	541	612	130	539	246	151	288	1,350
1986	409	515	170	268	654	730	134	592	263	159	307	2,767
1987	427	549	176	311	798	832	137	647	282	163	334	5,706
1988	445	582	179	328	1,487	927	146	699	304	169	360	15,382
1989	447	669	187	345	5,765	1,091	160	744	333	176	394	26,646
1990	482	727	194	349	27,065	1,404	…	861	367	186	427	…
1991	518	782	201	365	44,022	1,579	…	949	385	199	454	…
1992	542	807	204	397	72,799	…	…	1,031	413	208	469	…
1993	550	793	210	408		…	…	1,106	414	213	…	…

B4   Money wages in Industry

NOTES

1. SOURCES:- The main sources were I.L.O., *Year Book* (1931–34); I.L.O., *Yearbook of Labour Statistics* (since 1935); and the official publications noted on p. xv. In addition, the following were used:- France to 1820 (1st line)—F. Simiand, *Le salaire des ouvriers des mines de charbon en France* (Paris, 1907), and from 1820 (2nd line) to 1913—M. Lévy-Leboyer and François Bourguignon, *L'Économie française au XIX siécle* (Paris, 1985); Germany, 1871–1913—based on Ashok V. Desai, *Real Wages in Germany, 1871–1913* (Oxford, 1968) and J. Kuczynski, *Die Geschicte der Lage der Arbeiter unter dem Kapitalismus* (Berlin, 1961); Sweden to 1930—G. Bagge *et al, Wages in Sweden, 1860–1930* (London, 1933); U.K. to 1880 (1st line) and 1914–20 in part B—based on series in B.R. Mitchell, *British Historical Statiscs* (Cambridge, 1988) originally complied by A.L. Bowley, G.H. Wood, C.H. Feinstein, and B.R. Mitchell; U.K. 1880 (2nd line) to 1913—C.H. Feinstein, "New estimates of average earnings in the United Kingdom, 1880–1913", *Economic History Review* (2nd series, vol. XLIII, 4. 1990) and UK 1914–1919:—based on average annual earnings from C.H. Feinstein, *National Income, Expenditure and Output of the United Kingdom, 1855–1965* (Cambridge, 1972). The Polish figures for 1950–52 are based on data supplied by the Polish Central Statistical Office.
2. In principle, extractive and manufacturing industries and construction are covered in this table, except as otherwise indicated.
3. Only major changes in the scope of the data are indicated. Minor changes occur very frequently in most countries.
4. Allowance is made throughout this table for changes in the nominal value of currency units.

FOOTNOTES

[1]   Figures of hourly wages in Paris and in the provinces are available for a few years as follows (1901 = 100):-

	Paris		Paris	prov		Paris	prov		Paris	prov
1806	44	1853	...	51	1873	73	74	1900	99	...
1828	44	1856	63	...	1880	93	82	1906	108	108
1842	42	1857	...	57	1885	...	85	1911	111	112
1852	57	1862	70	...	1896	92	96			

[3]   Urban male workers only to 1913.
[4]   See key to series.
[5]   Bohemia only to 1929.
[6]   Unless otherwise indicated.
[7]   Paris data only in 1916 and provincial data only in 1937.
[8]   In December of each year.
[9]   Statistics to 1919 are for one month in late summer or autumn, whilst those for 1920, 1931, and 1932 are for one quarter only.
[10] There is no link between the earlier and the later indices. The value of the index for 1939 is 111.
[11] Statistics are for years ended 30 September.
[12] Second half-year only.
[13] November only.
[14] Minimum contract wages (including family allowances) subsequently
[15] Salaried workers are included to 1976.
[16] There was a change in classification in 1980.
[17] Czech Republic.

B5 MONEY WAGES IN AGRICULTURE

Key to series in part A: a = weekly wages of full-time labourers; b = annual earnings of labourers in real municipalities; c = daily wages (Markejång series); d = average yearly incomes of workers in agriculture, forestry and fishing.

PART A: 1770–1914: 1900 = 100

1770–1829

	UK England & Wales	Scotland
	a	a
1770–88	47	13[2]
1789	48	...
1790	49	23
1791	50	23
1792	52	23
1793	54	23
1794	56	24
1795	61	26
1796	67	27
1797	70	28
1798	72	28
1799	74	29
1800	76	30
1801	78	31
1802	79	31
1803	80	32
1804	86	36
1805	92	39
1806	96	42
1807	96	42
1808	96	42
1809	96	42
1810	96	42
1811	96	42
1812	96	42
1813	95	40
1814	94	39
1815	94	37
1816	93	37
1817	92	36
1818	90	35
1819	89	34
1820	87	34
1821	81	31
1822	71	28
1823	71	27
1824	66	27
1825	72	27
1826	72	28
1827	72	28
1828	72	28
1829	72	28

1830–1869

	Germany[1]	Norway	Sweden	UK England & Wales	UK Scotland
		b	c	a	a
1830	...	...	...	70	28
1831	...	...	...	72	28
1832	...	...	...	73	28
1833	...	...	...	74	28
1834	...	...	...	72	28
1835	...	...	...	70	30
1836	...	...	...	71	31
1837	...	...	...	72	34
1838	...	...	...	73	35
1839	...	...	...	75	38
1840	...	...	...	75	39
1841	...	...	...	75	42
1842	...	...	...	75	43
1843	...	...	...	75	45
1844	...	...	...	71	45
1845	...	...	...	65	44
1846	...	...	...	71	44
1847	...	...	...	71	44
1848	...	...	...	66	44
1849	...	...	...	66	44
1850	48	38	...	66[3] / 63	44
1851	49	...	...	62	44
1852	50	...	...	62	44
1853	51	...	...	67	50
1854	52	...	...	72	55
1855	53	50	...	74	58
1856	54	...	...	74	58
1857	55	...	...	74	55
1858	56	...	...	73	53
1859	57	...	...	72	53
1860	59	53	49	74	55
1861	59	...	51	75	55
1862	57	...	53	75	55
1863	60	...	52	74	55
1864	61	...	52	74	55
1865	62	60	52	76	55
1866	65	...	51	78	55
1867	64	...	48	80	55
1868	66	...	46	81	56
1869	66	...	46	79	60

B5   Money Wages in Agriculture

	Germany[1]	Norway a	Sweden b	U.K. England & Wales c	U.K. Scotland d
1870	68	57	48	80	62
1871	71	...	50	81	63
1872	79	...	59	86	68
1873	86	...	74	90	75
1874	88	...	77	94	80
1875	92	83	75	94	93
1876	93	...	76	95	98
1877	90	...	75	95	95
1878	84	...	63	95	90
1879	79	...	56	92	71
1880	79	71	60	92	70
1881	80	...	61	92	68
1882	80	...	67	92	74
1883	79	...	70	92	79
1884	79	...	70	92	78
1885	79	76	69	91	74
1886	79	...	65	90	71
1887	79	...	61	89	66
1888	80	...	62	89	66
1889	80	...	65	90	71
1890	82	78	69	91	75
1891	82	...	71	93	82
1892	83	...	74	93	86
1893	83	...	74	93	81
1894	86	...	74	92	85
1895	87	83	75	93	87
1896	88	...	76	93	87
1897	90	...	80	94	92
1898	94	...	87	95	90
1899	97	...	95	97	95
1900	100	100	100	100	100
1901	100	...	96	101	...
1902	102	...	95	101	...
1903	103	...	98	101	...
1904	105	...	99	101	...
1905	108	107	102	102	...
1906	111	...	108	...	...
1907	114	...	119	...	...
1908	116	...	123	...	...
1909	119	...	124	...	...
1910	121	134	126	103	...
1911	124	...	128	...	...
1912	128	...	131	...	...
1913	133	...	136	...	...
1914	...	173[4]	135	113	...

B5　Money Wages in Agriculture

Key to series in part B:- a = annual earnings of workers on whole-year engagements; b = average yearly incomes of workers in agriculture, forestry and fishing; c = weekly wages; d = annual wages of agriculture and forestry employees; e = daily wages; f = annual earnings of state employees in agriculture and forestry; g = day wages of casual workers in summer

PART B: 1914-1938: 1929 = 100　　　　　　　　　　　　　　　　　　　　　　　　　　　　**1914-1938**

	Czech[5]	Denmark a	Finland a	Germany[1] b	Hungary	Ireland c	Italy
1914	...	...	...	54[7]	...	...	...
1915	...	73	...	...	...	...	...
1916	...	...	...	...	...	...	...
1917	...	...	...	...	...	...	...
1918	...	103	...	...	...	...	...
1919	...	...	...	...	...	...	...
1920	...	...	...	...	...	...	...
1921	103	189	...	...	...	...	...
1922	...	...[6]	...	...	...	...	...
1923	...	131	...	...	...	...	...
1924	...	125	...	...	...	...	...
1925	92	143	...	74	...	105	...
1926	93	151	...	80	...	102	...
1927	97	127	93	85	...	102	109
1928	99	109[6] 106	98	92	105	99	101
1929	100	100	100	100	100	100	100
1930	100	104	100	105	91	98	93
1931	97	107	87	99	72	97	83
1932	96	100	69	82	63	94	75
1933	94	90	65	76	47	89	74
1934	...	90	72	78	44	84	71
1935	...	96	74	79	44	85	72
1936	...	107	80	81	48	87	73
1937	...	122	86	82	59	88	82
1938	...	135	110	84	...	109	86

B5 Money Wages in Agriculture

	Netherlands	Norway	Portugal	Romania	Russia	Sweden	U.K. England & Wales
		d	e	e	f	g	c
1914	...	...	...	...	...	64	53
1915	...	...	...	...	...	66	...
1916	...	74	...	...	...	80	...
1917	...	96	...	...	...	105	...
1918	...	131	...	...	...	151	96
1919	...	181	...	...	...	181	120
1920	...	226	...	...	...	198	136
1921	...	255	...	...	...	142	148
1922	...	211	...	...	...	106	107
1923	...	166	...	...	...	100	88
1924	...	153	...	...	...	101	88
1925	...	163	...	...	50	100	95
1926	100	151	...	...	63	100	99
1927	100	125	...	...	67	99	100
1928	100	109	...	...	78	99	100
1929	100	100	100	...	100	100	100
				1930 = 100			
1930	100	98	98	100	137	99	100
1931	95	92	89	75	200	98	100
1932	80	86	78	60	236	93	99
1933	75	81	80	59	271	93	97
1934	70	78	81	56	323	93	97
1935	70	78	81	57	395	95	99
				1955 = 100			
1936	70	81	82	62	...	16	101
1937	70	87	83	73	...	19	103
1938	70	102	83	...	...	21	108

B5 Money Wages in Agriculture

Key to series in Parts C and D: a = daily wages of permanent workers to 1954, monthly wages subsequently; b = daily wages to 1951 (1st line) and from 1955, monthly earnings in 1951 (2nd line) to 1954; c = monthly earnings on state farms; d = annual earnings of workers on whole-year engagements to daily wages subsequently; e = annual earnings to 1945, monthly earnings from 1946 to 1950, and hourly wages subsequently; f = monthly wages in April; g = weekly wages; h = weekly wages of males in November; i = not defined to 1942, and hourly wages including family allowances for 1949; k = weekly wages to 1954, hourly wages subsequently; l = monthly wages in summer in agriculture and forestry; m = daily wages; n = hourly wages; o = average minimum weekly wages for basic hours to 1947 (1st line) and average weekly earnings subsequently

PART C: 1938–1970: 1955 = 100   1938–1970

	Austria	Belgium	Bulgaria	Czech	Denmark	Finland	France	West Germany	Hungary	Ireland
	a	b	c	c	d	e	f	g	c	h
1938	...	...	...	...	18	2.9	...	...	...	32
1939	...	17	...	...	20	3.3	...	...	...	32
1940	...	...	...	...	21	3.4	...	...	...	35
1941	...	...	...	...	22	4.0	...	...	...	35
1942	...	...	...	...	25	5.1	...	...	...	39
1943	...	26	...	...	26	7.3	...	...	...	42
1944	...	31	...	...	34	9.7	...	...	...	47
1945	...	45	...	...	44	12$_9$	...	...	...	47
1946	...	60	...	...	54	28	...	...	...	53
1947	...	68	...	...	64	37	...	...	...	60
1948	...	71	...	...	63	50	...	...	...	66
1949	...	77	...	...	64	55	...	...	44	72
1950	64	80	...	...	66	81$_9$	...	65$_{10}$	45	72
1951	85	83$_9$ 86	...	...	71	86	63	81	57	80
1952	86	92	...	...	79	91	82	90	71	87
1953	86	95	82	...	87	91	88	92	79	95
1954	94$_9$	97$_9$	91	93	92	93	92	95	95	100
1955	100	100	100	100	100	100	100	100	100	100
1956	109	104	101	108	104	112	110	110	110	113
1957	116	106	110	112	103	118	123	119	125	113
1958	123	107	114	114	99	119	149	128	132	113
1959	124	109	118	120	102	124	168	136	137	120
1960	130	113	128	123	111	132	176	144	144	125
1961	148	118	128	126	125	136	183	160	147	128
1962	169	126	133	130	148	139	201	181	144	143
1963	180	136	137	130	171	160	223	198	151	143
1964	182	150	137	135	193	179	246	216	158	170
1965	221	166	146	142	218	204	263	239	158	188
1966	232	185	158	151	248	216	275	260	166	203
1967	257	194	171	160	274	234	299	266	173	211
1968	276	204	175	177	279	254	323	276	187	229
1969	295	216	177	192	287	268	369	296	201	270
1970	314	235	188	196	321	298	428	328	216	306

B5 Money Wages in Agriculture

	Italy	Netherlands	Norway	Poland	Portugal	Russia	Sweden[13]	U.K (GB)	Yugoslavia
	i	k	l	c	m	c	n	o	c
1938	1.1	23	...	...	38	...	21[11]	26	...
1939	1.2	25	15	...	37	...	21	26	...
1940	1.3	27	16	...	38	47	23	30	...
1941	1.5	30	18	...	41	...	26	36	...
1942	1.7	32	23	...	53	...	29	44	...
1943	...	33	28	...	62	...	33	45	...
1944	...	33	32	...	70	...	34	48	...
1945	...	43	36	...	75	46	38	51	...
1946	...	58	40	...	93	...	41	54	...
1947	...	60	50	...	107	...	46	61[9]	...
								62	...
1948	...	62	59	...	104	...	54	66	...
1949	77	67	66	...	101	...	56	69	...
1950	78	72	70	...	100	82	57[12]	71	...
								61	
1951	79	77	76	...	102	...	70	77	...
1952	83	80	84	...	103	...	88	82	...
1953	92	83	91	82	103	...	89	88	...
1954	97	93[9]	93	93	104	...	91	93	...
1955	100	100	100	100	100	100	100	100	1956=100
1956	105	105	106	110	125	...	106	107	100
1957	108	120	116	117	127	107	113	113	116
1958	113	133	121	131	133	114	120	120	131
1959	115	137	126	152	141	117[12]	125	123	147
1960	116	145	133	159	153	116	139	129	164
1961	121	148	142	166	159	124	154	135	195
1962	133	155	149	171	188	142	170	141	229[14]
1963	156	167	168	178	198	144	187	151	266
1964	178	192	179	185	224	151	201	157	338
1965	195	207	193	192	236	160	219	170	487
1966	206	226	218	204	252	172	241	179	716
1967	225	245	231	215	303	181	265[13]	187	835
1968	237	257	249	226	322	198	286	198	873
1969	262	280	264	234	356	200	310	215	1,004
1970	308	312	299	239	396	217	342	228	1,174

B5 Money Wages in Agriculture

PART D: 1970–93: 1975 = 100

1970–1993

	Austria	Belgium	Bulg-aria	Czecho-slovakia	Den-mark	Finland	France[17]	West Germany	Hungary	Ire-land	Italy	Neth-erlands	Norway	Poland	Port-ugal	Russia/USSR	Spain	Sweden	UK: GB	Yugo-slavia
	a	b	c	c	d	e	n	g	c	h	i	k	l	c	m	c	n	o	c	m
1970	56	47	76	81	35	35	[17]	61	83	43	34	46	54	58	42	80	...	58	42	35
1971	61	52	81	84	53	40	[17]	68	86	53	39	52	59	61	48	84	...	62	47	45
1972	67	58[15]	87	88	58[16]	49	[17]	73	89	58	46	64	64	68	54	88	...	69	53	53
1973	75	68	95	93	70	61	[17]	81	94	65	57	72	73	77	61	93	64	73	64	63
1974	88	83	95	97	83	77	73	93	101	81	75	86	87	88	80	98	85	82	80	84
1975	100	100	100	100	100	100	100	100	100	100	100	100	100	100	100	100	100	100	100	100
1976	110	113	104	103	111	119	117	110	107	118	125	111	119	129	114	106	123	115	113	116
1977	119	126	105	107	131	133	134	119	117	135	164	118	133	142	131	110	165	127	124	135
1978	127	134	113	110	141	146	...	125	126	157	194	127	143	151	154	113	204	135	141	156
1979	132	143	114	112	153	165	...	133	133	183	233	135	145	161	188	115	237	145	165	187
1980	138	153	117	116	167	182	...	143	142	219	286	142	170	182	224	118	274	161	195	232
1981	148	165	127	118	181	202[15]	...	149	152	...	349	148	186	251	303	121	317	174	217	328
1982	157	175	132	121	201	189	...	157	161	272	408	158	202	373	377	125	344	182	237	430
1983	165	208	128	125	220	203	...	163	167	...	481	161	215	429	441	133	386	195	261	507
1984	175	218	139	128	236	228	...	169	184	326	534	163	227	525	483	139	419	213	273	782
1985	187	225	136	131	240	247	...	174	198	...	598	168	247	618	...	144	456	226[18]	297	1,327
1986	197	230	146	133	244	270	...	178	212	370	628	173	266	734	...	151	489	276	313	2,670
1987	203	...	150	136	270	287	...	182	226[19]	...	663	175	290	858	...	156	536	302	329	5,463
1988	207	...	173	140	283	304	...	187	283	...	709	179	...	1,601	...	166	548	336	347	...
1989	219	...	198	144	296	339	...	197	328	...	766	184	...	6,298	...	184	609	361	366	...
								Germany												
1990	259	...	296	150	301	372	...	201	383	...	837	194	...	29,658	...	213	650	...	407	...
1991	238	...	690	166	...	412	...	210	452	...	853	202	...	50,954	...	360[20]	693	438	434	...
1992	240	...	1,050	...	...	421	...	222	545	...	941	214	...	76,901	...	3,202[20]	755	462	460	...
1993	214	...	1,696	...	...	413	...	228	679	...	903	217	...		...	...	795	455	480	...

B5   Money Wages in Agriculture

NOTES

1. SOURCES:- The main sources were the same as for table C. 4. In addition the following were used as a basis for the indices:—England & Wales to 1850 and Scotland to 1869—articles by A.L. Bowley and G.H. Wood in the *Journal of the Royal Statistical Society* (1898 and 1899); England & Wales from 1851 and Great Britain in Part III—Department of Employment and Productivity, *British Labour Statistics: Historical Abstract 1886-1968* (London, 1971); Scotland 1870-1900—R. Mollond & G. Evans, Scottish Farm Wages from 1870 to 1900, *Journal of the Royal Statistical Society* (1950); Germany to 1938—W.G. Hoffman, *Das Wachstum der Deutschen Wirtschaft seit der Mitte des 19 Jahrhunderts* (Berlin, etc., 1965); and Sweden to 1930—G. Bagge *et al*, Wages in Sweden, 1860-1930 (London, 1933). The Portuguese figure for 1946 is based on data supplied by the National Institute of Statistics.
2. Where wages are not specified as being hourly, daily, weekly, etc., there is no indication in the source as to which they were.
3. All statistics relate to adult males (normally "general hands") except where otherwise indicated.
4. Minor changes in the scope of the figures are not indicated.
5. Allowance is made throughout this table for changes in the nominal value of currency units. Average wages of Belgian male farm workers not provided with food were as follows at the general censuses of agriculture in the nineteenth century (in francs):- 1846 1.18; 1856 1.36; 1874 2.03; 1880 2.04; 1890 1.96; 1895 1.98. (These data were supplied by the Belgian National Institute of Statistics.) Lennart Jorberg, *A History of Prices in Sweden 1732-1914* (2 vols, Lund, 1972), gives the following quinquennial indices of the day wages of male agricultural workers in Sweden:-

1750/4 = 100		1860/4 = 100		1860/4 = 100	
1735/9	102	1805/9	29	1860/4	100
1740/4	92	1810/4	54	1865/9	92
1745/9	88	1815/9	62	1870/4	118
1750/4	100	1820/4	60	1875/9	134
1755/9	112	1825/9	62	1880/4	121
1760/4	163	1830/4	65	1885/9	121
1765/5	188	1835/9	65	1890/4	135
1770/4	172	1840/4	66	1895/9	154
1775/9	209	1845/9	66	1900/4	181
1780/4	218	1850/4	71	1905/9	213
1785/9	209	1855/9	97	1910/4	240
1790/4	227				
1795/9	309				

FOOTNOTES

[1] Statistics to 1938 relate to the average yearly incomes of workers in agriculture, forestry and fishing. The following indices of money wages in agriculture are given in J. Kuczynski, *Die Geschichte der Lage der Arbeiter under dem Kapitalismus* (Berlin, 1961):-

1900 = 100				1929 = 100			
1920-9	38	1870-9	80	1924	63	1929	100
1830-9	41	1880-9	88	1925	80	1930	99
1840-9	46	1890-9	97	1926	81	1931	98
1850-9	48	1900-9	106	1927	88	1932	87
1860-9	57	1910-4	121	1928	95		

[2] 1770.

[3] This break occurs on a change of source (see note 1 above).

[4] 1915.

[5] Moravia only.

[6] From 1923 to 1928 the figures relate only to workers aged 17-21 years.

[7] 1913

[8] These figures are for July 1918-May 1919, May 1919-April 1920, April-August 1920, and August 1920-August 1921.

[9] See key to series above.

[10] Monthly wages.

[11] Daily wages.

[12] Wider coverage of grades of worker subsequently.

[13] Males only from 1968, but the index has been scaled to be comparable in 1968.

[14] March and September only.

[15] The introduction of a new series, with no link to the old, means that direct comparability across this break is imperfect.

[16] Subsequently including the wages of female workers.

[17] The index from part C can be continued as follows (1955 = 100): 1971-442, 1972-464, 1973-544.

[18] Subsequently including holiday pay.

[19] Prior to 1988, net earnings after income tax deduction.

[20] Russian Federation.

C AGRICULTURE

1.	Area of Main Cereal, Potato, and Sugar Beet Crops	page 205
2.	Output of Main Cereal, Potato, and Sugar Beet Crops	page 261
3.	Area of Vineyards and Output of Wine	page 320
4.	Area and Output of Mediterranean Crops	page 328
5.	Numbers of Livestock	page 332
6.	Output of Cow's Milk	page 382
7.	Butter Output	page 388
8.	Meat Output	page 392
9.	Landings of Fish	page 398
10.	External Trade in Corn	page 402
11.	Exports of Selected Agricultural, Fishery, and Forestry Products	page 411

As with so many other official statistics, the first half of the nineteenth century saw the beginnings of those relating to agriculture in most of the countries of western Europe, and the second half saw their extension to eastern Europe. In some ways it is surprising that Britain, which during the Napoleonic Wars was the first country to face difficulties in feeding itself without substantial imports, was not the first to collect statistics of farm use. However, despite some attempts at that time,[1] it is clear that the necessary administrative machinery was lacking until around the middle of the nineteenth century when there was a good deal of opposition to the principle of government inquisition. This was not overcome where Great Britain was concerned—it had not applied to the gathering of statistics in Ireland—until the late 1860s or even, so far as output statistics were concerned, until the 1880s. Meanwhile, official agricultural statistics had begun in almost every other country in Europe, though not always on a regular annual basis.

There is no reason to believe that the official agricultural statistics are unreliable to any significant extent. Even in the USSR in the 1930s, when there was a deliberate attempt to hide some of the facts, this was not apparently achieved by outright falsification so much as by using the disguise of the so-called "biological" yield. In the early days of collection in any country, as with most statistical series, there were probably differences in interpretation amongst crop-reporters and officials, though these are most likely to arise over grass crops, which are not shown here. There is a fair amount of evidence that in countries like Britain crop estimates tend to understate year-to-year fluctuations by being somewhat too high in bad harvests and too low in good ones. In countries which are subject to more extreme climatic variations, such as Romania, it seems likely that an opposite tendency prevails; or, at any rate, that there is a tendency to exaggerate the impact of climatic disasters on total yields. However, neither of these sources of error appears to be of very great significance.[2]

Censuses of livestock population generally began at the same time as crop statistics, though regular annual estimates often came a little later. Only in the case of Portugal have they never been made. Statistics of the output of livestock products have generally been much later in appearance. The figures of numbers of livestock are a useful indicator of the size of this branch of agriculture, though only a rough one. Numbers at a particular date do not give a full picture of the output of meat, let alone of other animal products. Whether the date of the count is in summer or in winter will make some difference to overall numbers. In countries and at times when fodder crop production was insufficient to carry all the desired livestock through the winter this difference could be quite considerable. Then there is a point of more universal significance. The average age of flocks and herds has declined greatly since the nineteenth century, especially in western Europe. With this, the average annual output per animal has risen, especially in the case of meat. Some indication of this can be found in the tables of milk, butter, and meat output, though, as indicated, these do not go back in time nearly so far as one would like.

In addition to official agricultural statistics, this section also includes a table showing landings of fish in the major countries for which these are both significant and available, and two tables of the volume of external trade in some major products of the land. The first of these two, Table C 10, relates to cereals, and covers those countries where

---

[1] For a summary and assessment of these see W.E. Minchinton, 'Agricultural Returns and the Government during the Napoleonic Wars', *Agricultural History Review*, 1 (1953).

[2] For discussion of the British figures see B.R. Mitchell, *op.cit.*, p. 183.

either imports or exports have been of major significance for a substantial period of time. The second table is a miscellaneous collection of commodity exports, selected because of their importance to the countries concerned. Since all these commodities are relatively bulky in relation to their value, there does not seem to be any likelihood of illegal trade throwing any doubts on the accuracy of the statistics. It should be noted, however, that boundary changes sometimes affect comparability over time.

C1 AREA OF MAIN CEREAL, POTATO, AND SUGAR BEET CROPS (in thousands of hectares)

Key to abbreviations used where space demands:- Bwt = Buckwheat, MC = Mixed Corn, Ps = Potatoes, SB = Sugar Beet

ALBANIA 1929–1939

	Wheat	Rye	Barley	Oats	Maize
1929	30	2	5	11	61
1930	30	2	6	10	65
1931	29	2	5	10	62
1932	37	3	5	11	75
1933	43	3	6	11	77
1934	39	3	6	9	95
1935	39	2	4	9	85
1936	36	3	4	9	88
1937	40	4	6	12	92
1938	36	3	5	12	106
1939	48	4	6	15	104

AUSTRIA 1870–1907

	Wheat	Rye	Barley	Oats	Maize	Other Cereals	Potatoes	Sugar Beet
1870	997	2,085	1,119	1,748	313	...	850	122
1871	1,037	1,989	1,073	1,867	287	...	869	150
1872	945	1,942	1,090	1,917	295	...	887	168
1873	981	1,952	1,119	1,790	298	...	910	171
1874	979	1,958	1,107	1,810	313	...	933	163
1875	973	1,963	1,090	1,761	320	...	951	160
1876	1,037	1,965	1,115	1,787	319	...	976	168
1877	974	1,959	1,078	1,819	338	...	972	174
1878	998	1,947	1,058	1,790	335	...	973	185
1879	982	1,927	1,037	1,798	329	...	983	192
1880	994	1,850	1,079	1,796	343	...	995	209
1881	994	1,881	1,045	1,781	337	358	992	212
1882	1,017	1,924	1,019	1,759	352	327	985	222
1883	1,062	1,955	1,047	1,797	357	333	1,044	232
1884	1,107	1,986	1,075	1,834	362	339	1,084	242
1885	1,194	2,001	1,166	1,829	368	322	1,098	149
1886	1,174	2,018	1,118	1,868	363	300	1,090	180
1887	1,164	2,018	1,133	1,875	361	298	1,116	154
1888	1,186	2,022	1,131	1,874	363	297	1,107	194
1889	1,094	1,980	1,138	1,877	382	313	1,100	225
1890	1,147	2,007	1,116	1,874	372	291	1,079	245
1891	1,112	1,946	1,140	1,894	374	290	1,088	252
1892	1,125	1,975	1,112	1,873	367	284	1,099	256
1893	1,120	1,948	1,124	1,842	359	266	1,108	269
1894	1,098	1,955	1,136	1,879	326	269	1,098	286
1895	1,064	1,815	1,194	1,950	348	284	1,129	207
1896	1,059	1,841	1,178	1,917	346	371	1,152	247
1897	1,058	1,844	1,173	1,912	336	240	1,160	211
1898	1,056	1,831	1,168	1,901	341	241	1,182	210
1899	1,072	1,846	1,189	1,867	334	248	1,156	243
1900	1,065	1,706	1,234	1,899	333	150	1,168	240
1901	1,070	1,815	1,211	1,871	332	151	1,135	253
1902	1,058	1,836	1,216	1,832	329	154	1,138	196
1903	1,052	1,811	1,205	1,833	334	246	1,144	207
1904	1,115	1,931	1,184	1,822	338	250	1,277	218
1905	1,126	1,973	1,188	1,808	348	258	1,290	260
1906	1,161	2,023	1,177	1,834	343	262	1,314	239
1907	1,179	1,856	1,167	1,936	348	277	1,259	233

C1   Area of Main Cereal, Potato, and Sugar Beet Crops (in thousands of hectares)

AUSTRIA **1908–1959**

	Wheat	Rye	Barley	Oats	Maize	Other Cereals	Potatoes	Sugar Beet
1908	1,198	2,082	1,116	1,819	343	240	1,250	231
1909	1,191	2,078	1,131	1,851	336	249	1,233	212
1910	1,214	2,066	1,102	1,833	311	240	1,242	254
1911	1,215	2,027	1,097	1,878	303	226	1,258	249
1912	1,260	2,038	1,066	1,867	304	227	1,251	264
1913	1,213[2]	1,970	1,092	1,905[2]	286	217	1,276	255
1914	672	1,271[2]	700[2]	1,147	190[2]	124[2]	718[2]	243[2]
1915	745[2]	1,494[2]	757[2]	1,334[2]	201[2]	114[2]	901[2]	178[2]
1916	813[2]	1,568[2]	798[2]	1,469[2]	146[2]	127[2]	996[2]	195[2]
1917	...	...	...	...	...	...	...	...
1918	...[3]	...[3]	...[3]	...[3]	...[3]	...[3]	...[3]	...[3]
1919	150	290	94	245	42	23	97	5
1920	150	288	96	254	41	22	117	7
1921	153	307	108	269	45	26	133	8
1922	154[4]	307[4]	106[4]	266[4]	45[4]	28[4]	145[4]	9[4]
	186	338	127	285	60	31	163	11
1923	192	373	135	325	58	34	151	13
1924	195	376	138	309	60	34	167	10
1925	196	384	141	308	60	33	176	20
1926	202	394	147	315	62	34	178	20
1927	204	383	148	311	60	30	183	24
1928	208	379	156	301	58	28	189	30
1929	208	374	158	297	56	32	190	30
1930	205	375	174	312	58	35	189	35
1931	209	378	168	315	62	33	194	43
1932	216	387	171	307	67	37	202	43
1933	220	388	171	306	64	40	204	46
1934	232	382	167	303	65	39	202	50
1935	243	382	163	298	63	39	202	44
1936	253	373	163	289	64	41	210	38
1937	250	358	167	287	70	8	216	40
1938	250	366	168	287	73	8	215	47
1939	256	329	161	248	63	10	194	43
1940	213	276	182	247	65	15	190	41
1941	226	283	149	221	64	13	187	34
1942	208	247	152	216	65	17	175	32
1943	210	249	130	211	53	12	169	32
1944	208	239	128	204	48	13	174	30
1945	197	221	105	195	33	10	149	12
1946	200	229	115	199	52	20	156	16
1947	201	241	114	200	58	21	170	20
1948	203	239	108	200	57	21	175	22
1949	208	241	118	205	58	19	178	26
1950	218	249	134	208	59	17	184	29
1951	188	210	139	203	58	15	168	39
1952	203	213	139	200	60	14	170	40
1953	217	220	149	200	58	14	179	37
1954	238	218	150	191	58	15	177	43
1955	244	214	156	189	56	15	180	45
1956	251	214	168	187	51	15	181	43
1957	258	210	173	184	49	15	180	43
1958	263	206	173	178	49	16	178	51
1959	268	218	179	163	46	19	171	54

C1 Area of Main Cereal, Potato, and Sugar Beet Crops (in thousands of hectares)

AUSTRIA 1960–2000

	Wheat	Rye	Barley	Oats	Maize	Other Cereals	Potatoes	Sugar Beet
1960	277	171	209	161	58	20	180	45
1961	276	212	188	155	51	20	172	39
1962	270	209	193	151	54	21	169	48
1963	275	156	229	152	50	27	161	48
1964	283	166	227	143	50	27	158	53
1965	276	157	220	136	50	28	145	38
1966	314	144	230	126	55	32	137	47
1967	316	139	232	124	60	32	134	42
1968	306	142	238	119	74	32	130	44
1969	286	147	274	102	117	31	113	47
1970	275	136	290	102	124	34	110	44
1971	274	145	295	98	125	33	105	39
1972	274	144	296	96	132	32	101	48
1973	266	123	318	94	147	34	84	51
1974	269	123	319	92	149	34	82	54
1975	270	119	315	101	144	40	69	60
1976	289	120	325	95	160	38	73	56
1977	285	119	328	90	166	39	60	56
1978	286	109	355	89	178	37	57	44
1979	270	106	373	95	188	37	58	45
1980	269	109	374	92	193	...	53	51
1981	274	101	362	92	189	...	50	59
1982	289	100	340	91	198	...	46	58
1983	313	93	340	83	208	...	41	42
1984	315	94	329	78	207	...	41	51
1985	320	88	334	75	208	...	38	43
1986	324	83	333	73	217	...	35	28
1987	320	85	292	69	207	...	34	39
1988	292	88	292	69	201	...	33	38
1989	278	91	292	67	194	...	32	47
1990	265	87	288	66	189	...	35	50
1991	271	85	297	61	185	...	33	51
1992	246	69	275	55	173	...	33	54
1993	241	74	265	53	170	...	32	53
1994	241	77	253	49	179	...	30	52
1995	256	77	229	41	173	...	27	52
1996	248	51	260	42	201	...	26	53
1997	260	58	261	46	188	...	23	52
1998	264	59	266	41	171	...	23	50
1999	261	56	244	36	177	...	23	47
2000	294	52	224	33	188	...	24	43

C1   Area of Main Cereal, Potato, and Sugar Beet Crops (in thousands of hectares)

BELGIUM   **1846–1929**

	Wheat	Rye	Barley	Oats	Mixed Corn[1]	Buckwheat	Potatoes	Sugar Beet
1846	233	283	40	202	92	28	115	2
1856	367	292	45	219	100	25	150	8
1880	276	278	40	249	78	13	199	33
1895	180	283	40	249	52	5	185	54
1900	169	245	38	253	37	3	141	64
1901	166	251	38	249	37	3	144	62
1902	168	265	38	262	37	3	142	48
1903	144	254	32	286	33	3	146	54
1904	159	259	40	248	34	3	152	44
1905	163	267	38	237	33	2	146	64
1906	160	253	36	261	31	...	145	56
1907	159	260	37	248	30	...	143	53
1908	153	258	36	255	27	...	141	52
1909	158	258	35	250	26	...	140	58
1910	161	269	25	260	29	...	172	60
1911	161	262	34	259	28	...	157	59
1912	161	263	34	262	24	...	157	62
1913	159	259	34	272	26	...	160	52
1919	138	212	32	227	23	...	157	43
1920	124	217	36	237	23	...	148	53
1921	139	226	39	244	22	...	169	58
1922	122	215	33	290	15	...	180	60
1923	140	232	34	265	21	...	152	72
1924	138	227	32	265	21	...	159	81
1925	148	231	32	265	21	...	160	72
1926	143	226	35	270	21	...	161	64
1927	158	232	32	266	20	...	168	71
1928	172	232	31	270	20	...	166	64
1929	144[5]	229[5]	25	301[5]	19	...	171[5]	58[5]

BELGIUM   **1930–1949**

	Wheat	Rye	Barley	Oats	Mixed Corn	Potatoes	Sugar Beet
1930	166	232	34	273	19	163	57
1931	154	222	33	295	17	172	52
1932	156	227	36	288	17	176	53
1933	151	224	37	299	18	163	52
1934	150	214	38	294	18	160	55
1935	172	150	34	209	12	163	51
1936	172	156	30	216	12	160	48
1937	172	152	35	211	13	158	48
1938	174	154	31	213	12	147	49
1939	124	135	19	259	9	148	54
1940	146[6]	115[6]	23[6]	172[6]	10[6]	77[6]	...[6]
1941	178	126	30	167	10	105	48
1942	193	137	51	142	13	121	59
1943	203	158	77	125	14	116	54
1944	198[6]	141[6]	74[6]	128[6]	14[6]	103[6]	58[6]
1945	168	116	67	169	10	91	38
1946	138	105	62	190	10	79	44
1947	78	85	71	230	8	84	52
1948	143	86	77	189	6	88	45
1949	153	95	72	174	8	89	60

C1 Area of Main Cereal, Potato, and Sugar Beet Crops (in thousands of hectares)

BELGIUM   1950–2000

	Wheat	Rye	Barley	Oats	Mixed Corn	Potatoes	Sugar Beet
1950	174	89	84	178	7	98	63
1951	158	82	88	163	8	90	65
1952	166	82	90	165	7	87	64
1953	170	82	93	161	7	89	59
1954	184	82	76	152	8	93	57
1955	191	74	82	149	7	84	57
1956	188	68	91	158	4	86	62
1957	208	66	86	148	7	82	62
1958	219	69	95	142	8	81	66
1959	200	62	110	141	8	79	64
1960	203	63	105	141	7	79	63
1961	206	44	121	136	6	72	62
1962	209	39	128	125	4	68	57
1963	200	41	134	115	5	69	57
1964	216	42	128	105	4	61	64
1965	227	34	147	99	4	57	65
1966	212	30	160	91	4	59	67
1967	199	27	154	97	5	62	78
1968	203	27	154	87	5	55	90
1969	199	22	155	84	6	50	90
1970	181	20	169	72	6	46	89
1971	193	24	149	71	8	42	93
1972	204	21	149	67	8	37	101
1973	193	16	156	61	8	43	104
1974	190	13	149	60	8	40	105
1975	176	9	122	70	5	36	120
1976	195	15	139	48	8	38	96
1977	177	12	152	39	9	41	94
1978	178	15	153	32	9	35	110
1979	182	12	156	28	8	36	116
1980	179	10	153	28	8	38	117
1981	166	8	152	26	7	34	130
1982	170	7	131	34	6	37	124
1983	187	6	139	21	10	34	109
1984	177	7	136	19	9	36	117
1985	180	5	118	21	8	41	118
1986	181	4	128	14	8	40	113
1987	185	4	123	15	9	45	106
1988	186	3	120	16	8	41	109
1989	202	3	107	13	8	41	106
1990	205	3	92	8	8	48	108
1991	200	3	76	8	7	51	102
1992	201	2	73	8	7	58	101
1993	197	2	66	11	7	48	99
1994	212	3	72	13	7	52	95
1995	218	3	66	9	7	56	99
1996	214	2	63	10	6	61	98
1997	217	2	64	11	6	56	96
1998	222	3	67	9	6	59	94
1999	189	1	53	12	6	67	101
2000	221	2	59	9	6	67	91

C1   Area of Main Cereal, Potato, and Sugar Beet Crops (in thousands of hectares)

BULGARIA   **1898–1954**

	Wheat	Rye	Barley	Oats	Maize	Potatoes	Sugar Beet
1898	782	...	...	140	...	2	...
1899	826	148	214	137	447	2	1
1900	820	152	208	126	447	2	...
1901	815	...	...	...	...	...	...
1902	810	...	...	...	...	...	...
1903	807	169	229	162	488	2	
1904	915	175	233	185	486	2	...
1905	980	176	233	174	473	2	
1906	1,010	187	232	190	508	2	...
1907	977	182	232	190	498	2	...
1908	980	174	251	228	571	3	...
1909	1,040	202	241	197	607	3	2
1910	1,089	227	260	198	612	3	2
1911	1,118	221	251	181	632	3	3
1912	1,168	214	251	176	643	3	3
1913	999	194	211	153	579	3	5
1914	1,022	207	238	168	625	4	15
1915	973	219	249	163	657	5	8
1916	964	207	242	152	589	5	14
1917	1,004	184	244	141	565	7	15
1918	985	191	243	139	591	8	19
1919	832	184	196	115	585	6	9
1920	883	188	224	140	569	8	9
1921	904	189	212	134	575	8	12
1922	931	184	222	148	567	9	10
1923	932	172	220	150	552	10	12
1924	1,008	167	214	152	609	9	26
1925	1,030	184	222	144	640	10	...
1926	1,059	187	233	130	613	10	15
1927	1,082	188	227	132	681	12	21
1928	1,138	197	245	121	648	11	16
1929	1,077	217	219	157	800	11	19
1930	1,216	266	280	140	684	12	23
1931	1,236	243	245	119	680	13	12
1932	1,263	220	231	117	744	14	13
1933	1,253	209	244	132	727	14	12
1934	1,260	200	229	128	685	14	2
1935	1,104[7]	175[7]	203[7]	109[7]	718[7]	15[7]	7[7]
1936	1,196	198	217	121	669	16	5
1937	1,309	211	218	150	682	22	10
1938	1,395	188	225	144	700	20	12
1939	1,354	172	220	112	685	16	13
1940	1,319[8]	169[8]	189[8]	120[8]	674[8]	18[8]	17[8]
1941	1,362	182	231	174	806	25	20
1942	1,266	165	218	186	867	35	23
1943	1,348	169	212	167	789	39	29
1944	1,354	171	195	146	753	37	24
1945	1,283	151	169	145	728	30	31
1946	1,332	154	165	127	726	18	34
1947	1,260	162	191	156	760	14	18
1948	1,461	229	212	145	802	19	35
1949	...	...	...	...	...	...	31
1950	1,449	230	245	162	654	30	39
1951	...	...	...	...	...	...	32
1952	1,424	229	259	155	487	36	42
1953	...	...	...	...	...	...	...
1954	1,392	175	257	161	716	36	50

C1 Area of Main Cereal, Potato, and Sugar Beet Crops (in thousands of hectares)

BULGARIA

	Wheat	Rye	Barley	Oats	Maize	Potatoes	Sugar Beet
1955	1,368	167	289	159	742	31	48
1956	1,375	143	259	151	791	28	56
1957	1,439	133	253	162	759	31	63
1958	1,435$_9$ / 1,445	110	259	166	697	34	61
1959	1,402	91	267	181	736	37	65
1960	1,257	78	296	180	634	43	66
1961	1,317	71	305	160	635	41	67
1962	1,249	59	303	152	651	43	66
1963	1,188	57	343	133	660	43	68
1964	1,194	58	358	130	658	41	77
1965	1,145	46	372	119	555	37	66
1966	1,142	41	416	113	574	34	62
1967	1,064	31	387	120	567	33	61
1968	1,060	24	402	96	557	31	55
1969	1,039	24	412	76	578	29	59
1970	1,014	22	403	71	635	31	58
1971	1,013	19	434	75	655	29	45
1972	961	17	446	65	689	30	57
1973	934	15	458	46	623	27	61
1974	861	15	477	47	523	31	60
1975	819	17	575	50	652	30	78
1976	793	13	524	44	731	29	72
1977	774	13	529	57	702	34	72
1978	935	13	473	51	601	37	62
1979	958	16	468	53	666	39	62
1980	968	20	426	41	585	35	55
1981	1,032	27	382	46	563	36	56
1982	1,059	23	352	43	621	40	61
1983	1,128	25	323	34	596	41	33
1984	1,126	26	315	23	542	40	53
1985	1,067	32	260	29	435	40	50
1986	1,127	30	318	28	574	40	45
1987	1,085	29	295	28	497	37	41
1988	1,182	32	345	27	490	37	41
1989	1,138	25	360	38	563	40	40
1990	1,163	24	360	35	424	41	36
1991	1,200	25	383	36	560	43	38
1992	1,108	21	391	43	663	48	17
1993	1,268	19	328	30	560	45	12
1994	1,320	1,181	958	1,212	1,142	966	979
1995	15	14	15	18	18	20	20
1996	390	396	261	291	290	255	252
1997	53	36	35	41	45	33	42
1998	493	475	478	464	477	455	467
1999	47	56	40	44	51	52	53
2000	8	9	8	5	4	3	2

CZECHOSLOVAKIA

	Wheat	Rye	Barley	Oats	Maize	Potatoes	Sugar Beet
1920	637	906	695	802	152	607	210
1921	884	654	796	158	638	221	
1922	619	881	676	818	180	650	210
1923	610	860	687	842	181	637	232
1924	607	839	679	846	157	635	303
1925	618	847	694	838	157	640	307
1926	628	837	714	847	159	649	278
1927	642$_7$ / 751	821$_7$ / 996	712$_7$ / 708	855$_7$ / 840	159$_7$ / 140	651$_7$ / 717	294$_7$ / 288
1928	757	1,007	720	839	144	728	257
1929	819	1,089	744	870	135	761	246
1930	762	1,026	674	800	101	625	224
1931	797	983	717	797	94	679	186
1932	812	1,020	709	788	88	690	146
1933	885	1,023	661	773	87	700	145
1934	909	976	659	766	97	707	159
1935	929	990	644	748	96	706	157
1936	893	987	633	739	104	705	154

C1 Area of Main Cereal, Potato, and Sugar Beet Crops (in thousands of hectares)

CZECHOSLOVAKIA

1937–2000

	Wheat	Rye	Barley	Oats	Maize	Potatoes	Sugar Beet
1937	821	951	669	748	114	728	181
1938	897	1,016	659	763	180	763	136
1939	850	984	656	706	116	749	169
1940	746	708	754	799	121	728	200
1941	800	784	647	655	117	680	205
1942	871	861	659	636	120	707	190
1943	910	926	599	602	126	722	196
1944	912	915	549	572	118	727	203
1945	852	809	530	576	127	654	158
1946	900	786	546	600	121	640	175
1947	835	709	569	587[10]	128	600	183
1948	869	738	585	678	142	551	182
1949	797	710	572	630	129	569	194
1950	755	626	614	627	129	660	221
1951	740	552	634	569	139	666	244
1952	766	564	624	541	139	669	232
1953	748	534	649	547	149	636	232
1954	712	525	629	506	147	630	215
1955	720	513	642	526	160	621	216
1956	722	515	668	539	183	630	222
1957	742	519	670	536	169	629	227
1958	738	498	669	507	180	607	234
1959	720	476	672	507	187	585	242
1960	652	431	707	504	195	569	242
1961	643	463	696	494	201	515	252
1962	673	441	694	486	237	508	260
1963	720	426	692	453	213	503	259
1964	831	406	686	434	186	491	257
1965	826	411	667	422	161	444	230
1966	892	395	690	434	151	437	230
1967	929	321	712	481	150	408	206
1968	999	339	712	444	138	372	197
1969	1,054	275	780	432	127	325	183
1970	1,081	219	803	399	128	338	183
1971	1,103	234	851	359	142	332	189
1972	1,197	232	854	332	148	321	192
1973	1,235	225	873	280	169	305	199
1974	1,276	219	867	230	167	280	208
1975	1,183	191	980	222	158	251	219
1976	1,278	186	857	198	204	240	215
1977	1,287	212	856	174	203	237	216
1978	1,274	187	919	151	202	221	218
1979	1,111	166	1,042	149	206	216	218
1980	1,197	179	921	138	192	199	218
1981	1,090	171	996	160	178	200	219
1982	1,073	177	967	172	183	199	213
1983	1,192	203	822	154	204	193	211
1984	1,209	197	790	140	235	194	209
1985	1,221	182	799	126	224	188	208
1986	1,213	156	821	116	218	182	195
1987	1,217	142	840	109	220	180	191
1988	1,245	143	800	104	210	177	166
1989	1,239	175	751	103	190	170	183
1990	1,237	171	745	93	135	164	171
1991	1,204	128	792	89	166	168	168
1992	1,111	89	887	83	181	162	170
Czech Republic							
1993[51]	780	67	636	70	32	103	107
1994	811	79	640	76	27	77	91
1995	831	79	558	60	26	78	93
1996	798	64	600	66	33	86	104
1997	825	76	646	76	41	73	92
1998	912	72	578	58	33	73	81
1999	867	55	543	54	39	72	59
2000	970	43	495	50	47	69	61

C1 Area of Main Cereal, Potato, and Sugar Beet Crops (in thousands of hectares)

DENMARK   1861–1934

	Wheat	Rye	Barley	Oats	Mixed Corn	Potatoes	Sugar Beet
1861	62[11]	209[11]	303[11]	358[11]	34	31	...
1866	53	229	302	365	46	37	...
1871	57	248	304	371	55	43	...
1875	61	253	308	379	46	42	0.4
1876	62	254	308	381	49	42	0.3
1877	61	257	310	386	52	43	0.3
1878	60	259	312	390	55	43	0.5
1879	58	262	313	394	58	44	1.0
1880	57	265	315	398	62	44	1.3
1881	56	268	317	402	65	45	1.5
1882	55	270	314	405	69	46	2.5
1883	54	271	312	409	73	47	3.6
1884	53	273	309	412	77	48	6.4
1885	52	275	306	416	81	49	6.6
1886	51	277	303	419	85	50	7.7
1887	50	279	301	423	89	51	6.7
1888	49	281	298	426	93	52	6.9
1889	47	282	296	428	96	52	7.1
1890	45	283	293	429	100	52	7.3
1891	43	285	291	431	103	52	7.0
1892	41	286	289	433	103	52	6.8
1893	40	287	287	434	106	52	8.5
1894	38	288	284	436	110	52	12
1895	36	289	282	438	113	52	11
1896	34	291	280	439	120	52	13
1901	13	273	281	433	143	54	15
1907	41	276	234	403	170	54	16
1912	54	246	241	428	180	61	32
1915	67	211	260	414	180	67	32
1916	61	195	256	422	185	64	31
1917	53	177	240	397	195	58	31
1918	57	220	223	379	194	75	36
1919	52[12]	236[12]	237[12]	403[12]	202[12]	96[12]	42[12]
1920	73	227	253	441	201	92	39
1921	89	226	254	450	194	84	35
1922	96	221	270	453	188	83	24
1923	83	233	279	454	207	83	32
1924	60	188	302	462	232	72	39
1925	80	215	301	445	227	75	38
1926	102	208	312	424	237	77	30
1927	111	183	333	410	256	72	42
1928	102	146	355	404	297	63	46
1929	104[14]	152[14]	368[14]	392[14]	305[14]	64[14]	32[13] 30[14]
1930	101	149	376	388	304	68	33
1931	105	134	360	379	316	63	30
1932	99	120	345	398	318	70	38
1933	106	143	350	382	319	77	47
1934	114	153	340	382	338	77	48[15] 42

C1 Area of Main Cereal, Potato, and Sugar Beet Crops (in thousands of hectares)

DENMARK 1935-2000

	Wheat	Rye	Barley	Oats	Mixed Corn	Potatoes	Sugar Beet
1935	127	158	345	368	334	75	42
1936	120	132	369	378	325	76	38
1937	129	139	369	376	309	81	40
1938	132[14]	145[14]	397[14]	375[14]	302[14]	79[14]	38[14]
1939	134	137	421	376	304	70	40
1940	82	139	390	347	325	65	44
1941	84	195	383	348	326	74	48
1942	6	191	421	343	381	101	47
1943	49	224	398	336	334	105	46
1944	84	196	396	330	316	98	42
1945	87	161	408	336	304	107	39
1946	90	139	415	346	300	103	43
1947	24	105	466	343	321	106	44
1948	69	167	441	330	284	138	49
1949	83	195	455	308	285	106	63
1950	85	154	494	277	267	105	73
1951	81	119	519	274	262	105	71
1952	74	137	567	268	280	109	72
1953	71	131	622	244	284	107	61
1954	85	112	609	247	286	97	55
1955	67	77	611	266	306	94	40
1956	66	109	648	255	290	96	47
1957	64	116	691	236	288	88	54
1958	77	123	721	203	268	83	91
1959	88	121	752	204	264	87	55
1960	82	157	756	198	252	92	55
1961	105	183	799	195	254	72	39
1962	154	174	830	164	221	62	42
1963	135	116	938	186	195	64	69
1964	128	93	950	211	186	54	84
1965	126	88	1,041	203	138	41	60
1966	94	46	1,112	234	119	40	58
1967	90	37	1,170	243	97	37	53
1968	97	38	1,254	218	78	35	52
1969	98	38	1,305	205	58	34	52
1970	114	44	1,352	184	44	37	47
1971	121	42	1,370	186	39	32	49
1972	135	43	1,406	163	31	29	56
1973	123	42	1,445	129	23	32	63
1974	111	46	1,437	122	18	33	67
1975	102	49	1,443	111	15	31	86
1976	127	72	1,479	98	12	35	85
1977	116	89	1,528	78	11	38	85
1978	122	84	1,570	61	8	34	80
1979	114	70	1,622	39	5	32	78
1980	139	56	1,577	40	4	34	76
1981	148	50	1,541	42	4	36	78
1982	184	53	1,489	43	4	36	77
1983	242	77	1,347	29	3	30	72
1984	334	122	1,181	34	3	31	74
1985	339	126	1,094	42	...	30	73
1986	353	120	1,078	24	...	31	70
1987	398	136	943	20	...	30	67
1988	308	80	1,154	41	...	33	68
1989	446	101	997	27	...	34	67
1990	536	111	895	20	...	40	64
1991	519	80	839	21	...	43	65
1992	583	88	910	28	...	54	65
1993	621	79	721	26	...	46	66
1994	574	89	704	39	...	39	66
1995	610	96	715	31	...	42	68
1996	681	72	738	28	...	44	70
1997	689	84	720	26	...	39	69
1998	680	105	686	31	...	36	66
1999	638	51	728	26	...	38	63
2000	627	51	741	45	...	39	59

C1 Area of Main Cereal, Potato, and Sugar Beet Crops (in thousands of hectares)

FINLAND 1909-1962

	Wheat	Rye	Barley	Oats	Mixed Corn	Potatoes	Sugar Beet
1909	3.2	239	113	376	...	70	—
1910	3.2	240	110	399	6.7	73	—
1911	3.4	240	113	408	...	74	—
1912	3.4	239	113	414	...	74	—
1913	3.5	235	112	423	...	75	—
1914	4.0	235	110	431	...	77	—
1915	5.0	240	111	443	...	80	—
1916	6.6	236	113	446	...	81	—
1917	7.2	236	116	436	...	82	—
1918	7.5	238	115	438	...	81	—
1919	7.8	244	118	433	...	83	1
1920	8.7	233	116	395	8.5	71	1
1921	11	236	110	422	9.2	68	1
1922	15	237	112	427	11	67	1
1923	15	234	111	431	10	68	1
1924	15	238	110	425	10	67	1
1925	15	234	110	434	10	68	1
1926	16	229	110	441	10	69	2
1927	18	229	108	450	11	70	3
1928	19	222	110	461	12	70	3
1929	14	204	115	434	7.8	70	1
1930	14	208	115	439	10	71	1
1931	18	214	118	453	14	75	2
1932	24	218	125	455	14	77	2
1933	37	233	130	457	14	80	3
1934	51	246	132	475	15	83	3
1935	71	242	127	471	16	83	3
1936	84	233	130	450	16	87	3
1937	113	241	121	455	8.7	87	3
1938	131	236	121	463	9.6	85	5
1939	136	218	119	472	12	90	6
1940	141	186	114	427	9.8	81	3
1941	126	179	118	401	6.3	73	3
1942	127	159	108	377	4.8	67	2
1943	131	177	120	354	5.6	74	3
1944	127	162	136	314	6.1	69	4
1945	139	149	137	309	5.3	70	3
1946	158	147	140	321	5.5	77	4
1947	161	157	138	371	8.6	91	5
1948	166	144	132	404	15	104	6
1949	159	145	124	424	18	87	7
1950	189	133	115	437	15	96	10
1951	162	122	130	437	19	94	10
1952	137	119	146	473	19	97	11
1953	125	91	169	479	16	93	10
1954	150	93	165	487	17	88	15
1955	124	86	177	467	24	86	16
1956	133	89	193	464	28	93	15
1957	113	85	221	414	26	95	12
1958	127	76	223	442	25	86	13
1959	139	103	233	461	28	85	15
1960	181	111	213	490	24	86	15
1961	237	94	201	473	25	77	18
1962	286	82	205	456	31	74	20

C1   Area of Main Cereal, Potato, and Sugar Beet Crops (in thousands of hectares)

FINLAND   1963–2000

	Wheat	Rye	Barley	Oats	Mixed Corn	Potatoes	Sugar Beet
1963	239	76	262	444	35	77	16
1964	268	103	252	470	32	71	20
1965	267	111	252	472	29	73	20
1966	249	93	321	479	30	68	17
1967	252	96	346	455	31	65	18
1968	241	72	359	489	31	65	15
1969	204	70	373	483	28	58	13
1970	176	66	404	524	28	60	15
1971	173	59	408	540	26	50	17
1972	179	59	466	501	24	48	19
1973	188	52	458	528	22	46	22
1974	217	73	443	550	23	48	23
1975	219	38	464	572	20	49	24
1976	220	65	507	551	20	53	27
1977	131	47	583	465	24	46	31
1978	118	38	611	448	24	44	31
1979	99	37	633	451	15	43	33
1980	124	53	533	448	12	41	32
1981	112	45	502	444	13	39	32
1982	143	16	540	459	11	39	32
1983	160	47	550	449	13	45	33
1984	162	45	566	441	13	41	31
1985	157	31	646	411	9	39	31
1986	166	27	597	407	12	40	29
1987	147	38	660	404	11	43	30
1988	109	26	683	389	10	45	31
1989	151	69	517	446	11	45	31
1990	180	81	483	453	14	41	30
1991	118	10	541	343	12	36	32
1992	88	11	473	331	13	35	32
1993	99	23	459	331	13	36	33
1994	88	9	505	333	13	37	34
1995	101	21	516	329	13	36	35
1996	113	35	543	374	12	35	35
1997	125	23	589	369	12	33	35
1998	137	36	578	387	12	33	33
1999	118	12	581	404	14	32	35
2000	150	45	559	400	13	32	32

FRANCE   1815–1837

	Wheat	Rye	Barley	Oats	Maize	Buckwheat	Potatoes	Sugar Beet
1815	4,592	2,574	1,073	2,498	542	655	...	...
1816	4,472	2,541	1,100	2,469	560	658	...	...
1817	4,672	2,585	1,176	2,480	556	715	559	...
1818	4,623	2,575	1,147	2,461	576	668	568	...
1819	4,650	...	...	...	...	...	570	...
1820	4,684	2,697	1,356	2,556	582	645	574	...
1821	4,753	2,792	1,239	2,566	566	652	564	...
1822	4,798	2,789	1,223	2,589	562	645	568	...
1823	4,855	2,790	1,238	2,586	563	647	576	...
1824	4,884	2,751	1,235	2,573	569	648	620	...
1825	4,854	2,727	1,230	2,602	565	626	...	...
1826	4,895	2,722	1,223	2,647	578	633	...	...
1827	4,903	2,735	1,221	2,653	567	640	...	...
1828	4,948	2,739	1,221	2,680	572	659	...	...
1829	5,024	2,765	1,220	2,698	567	679	607	...
1830	5,012	2,696	1,295	2,761	581	659	610	...
1831	5,111	2,701	1,292	2,762	559	685	635	...
1832	5,160	2,669	1,285	2,756	599	681	668	...
1833	5,243	2,663	1,264	2,804	603	687	742	...
1834	5,303	2,599	1,284	2,724	596	691	790	...
1835	5,338	2,639	1,300	2,840	593[16]	701	804	...
1836	5,285	...	...	...	...	...	974	...
1837	5,408	...	...	...	...	...	789	...

C1 Area of Main Cereal, Potato, and Sugar Beet Crops (in thousands of hectares)

FRANCE

	Wheat	Rye	Barley	Oats	Maize	Buckwheat	Potatoes	Sugar Beet
1838	5,461	...	...	...	...	...	861	...
1839	5,384	...	...	...	...	...	878	...
1840	5,532	2,725	1,188	2,899	632	651	922	58
1841	5,563	...	...	...	...	...	970	...
1842	5,576	...	...	...	...	...	967	...
1843	5,664	...	...	...	...	...	1,016	...
1844	5,679	...	...	...	...	...	983	...
1845	5,743	...	...	...	...	...	1,014	...
1846	5,937	...	...	...	...	...	1,066	...
1847	5,979	...	...	...	...	...	991	...
1848	5,973	...	...	...	...	...	973	...
1849	5,966	...	...	...	...	...	932	...
1850	5,951	...	...	...	...	...	932	...
1851	5,999[17]	...	...	...	...	...	922	...
1852	6,985	2,451	1,041	3,263	602	709	829	111
1853	6,211	...	...	...	...	...	869	...
1854	6,408	...	...	...	...	...	894	...
1855	6,419	...	...	...	...	...	985	...
1856	6,468	...	...	...	...	...	897	...
1857	6,594	...	...	...	...	...	957	...
1858	6,640	...	...	...	...	...	983	...
1859	6,709	...	...	...	...	...	1,006	...
1860	6,711[18]	...[18]	...[18]	...[18]	...[18]	...[18]	1,010[18]	...[18]
1861	6,754	...	...	...	...	...	1,043	...
1862	7,473	1,928	1,087	3,324	586	669	1,234	136
1863	6,919	...	...	...	...	...	1,082	...
1864	6,880	...	...	...	...	...	1,099	...
1865	6,905	...	...	...	...	...	1,210	...
1866	6,916	...	...	...	...	...	1,110	...
1867	6,960	...	...	...	...	...	1,136	...
1868	7,063	...	...	...	...	...	1,129	...
1869	7,034	...	...	...	...	...	1,141	...
1870	6,924[19]	...[19]	...[19]	...[19]	...[19]	...[19]	...[19]	...[19]
1871	6,423	1,911	1,283	3,397	698	...	1,127	...
1872	6,938	1,888	1,068	3,145	698	...	1,151	...
1873	6,826	1,913	1,118	3,182	606	...	1,176	253
1874	6,874	1,844	1,083	3,246	650	...	1,169	...
1875	6,947	1,812	1,043	3,182	665	...	1,196	...
1876	6,859	1,820	1,038	3,257	661	...	1,251	...
1877	6,976	1,859	1,150	3,292	662	...	1,243	...
1878	6,843	1,810	1,003	3,313	615	...	1,264	...
1879	6,941	1,773	1,010	3,331	613	...	1,266	...
1880	6,880	1,839	1,036	3,472	624[16]	...	1,274	...
1881	6,950	1,777	1,024	3,479	608	...	1,343	220
1882	6,908	1,744	976	3,611	548	645	1,345	237
1883	6,804	1,720	1,066	3,729	630	630	1,389	226
1884	7,052	1,726	1,056	3,697	617	633	1,415	234
1885	6,957	1,673	966	3,689	561	628	1,437	104
1886	6,956	1,634	947	3,736	549	608	1,463	218
1887	6,967	1,624	934	3,720	558	623	1,488	194
1888	6,978	1,629	894	3,734	571	608	1,446	201
1889	7,039	1,599	873	3,759	558	591	1,455	226
1890	7,062	1,589	878	3,781	547	606	1,465	239
1891	5,754	1,499	1,223	4,243	558	624	1,493	260

C1 Area of Main Cereal, Potato, and Sugar Beet Crops (in thousands of hectares)

FRANCE   1892–1944

	Wheat	Rye	Barley	Oats	Maize	Buckwheat	Potatoes	Sugar Beet
1892	6,987	1,542	916	3,813	559	604	1,512	254
1893	7,073	1,530	875	3,842	567	584	1,529	259
1894	6,991	1,556	890	3,881	578	581	1,541	268
1895	7,002	1,534	891	3,969	585	577	1,542	237
1896	6,870	1,500	854	3,916	584	562	1,543	270
1897	6,584	1,452	858	3,991	585	552	1,548	270
1898	6,964	1,475	814	3,888	562	570	1,543	262
1899	6,940	1,489	806	3,939	561	586	1,565	279
1900	6,864	1,420	757	3,941	541	603	1,510	330
1901	6,794	1,412	744	3,886	547	601	1,546	339
1902	6,564	1,332	694	3,832	503	561	1,458	288
1903	6,479	1,297	697	3,844	502	553	1,436	283
1904	6,529	1,272	705	3,835	496	523	1,479	247
1905	6,510	1,269	707	3,812	502	523	1,487	317
1906	6,517	1,253	709	3,855	467	509	1,513	270
1907	6,577	1,240	713	3,871	500	503	1,522	276
1908	6,564	1,244	730	3,897	496	505	1,545	272
1909	6,596	1,227	734	3,927	495	500	1,547	286
1910	6,554	1,212	748	3,951	482	500	1,547	297
1911	6,433	1,174	772	3,991	425	461	1,559	297
1912	6,572	1,202	760	3,982	476	461	1,564	312
1913	6,542[20]	1,176[20]	760[20]	3,979[20]	458[20]	451[20]	1,548[20]	301[20]
1914	6,060	1,058	720	3,591	456	452	1,488	193
1915	5,489	935	637	3,263	378	433	1,345	104
1916	5,030	870	622	3,147	357	401	1,280	108
1917	4,191	742	687	2,958	343	378	1,370	100
1918	4,449[19,20]	706[19,20]	555[19,20]	2,720[19,20]	305[19,20]	311[20]	1,190[20]	85[20]
1919	4,708	813	608	2,953	301	329[19]	1,256[19]	96[19]
1920	5,094	869	664	3,350	336	352	1,441	122
1921	5,382	901	680	3,408	330	342	1,455	141
1922	5,290	888	693	3,436	320	356	1,464	153
1923	5,533	897	681	3,423	342	344	1,451	189
1924	5,512	889	714	3,495	342	363	1,463	229
1925	5,614	869	699	3,480	346	355	1,465	240
1926	5,249	793	691	3,512	337	349	1,461	254
1927	5,287	777	707	3,458	349	365	1,497	266
1928	5,243	769	711	3,503	344	342	1,473	282
1929	5,397	743	787	3,444	340	304	1,401	321
1930	5,374	747	745	3,424	337	321	1,429	324
1931	5,196	712	755	3,465	346	327	1,430	288
1932	5,434	701	720	3,387	340	329	1,413	309
1933	5,464	690	703	3,365	337	312	1,391	318
1934	5,404	685	732	3,322	340	308	1,410	337
1935	5,363	675	723	3,278	345	290	1,412	303
1936	5,206	661	743	3,291	342	286	1,422	311
1937	5,095	663	753	3,253	345	268	1,436	318
1938	5,050[21]	631[21]	759[21]	3,245[21]	340[21]	261[21]	1,425[21]	319[21]
1939	4,584	603	817	3,202	322	262	1,279	348
1940	4,252	515	695	2,681	278	221	1,061	242
1941	4,364	403	664	2,350	237	194	829	239
1942	4,280[21]	389[21]	638[21]	2,315[21]	232[21]	189[21]	777[21]	268[21]
1943	4,227	403	647	2,258	223	169	796	254
1944	4,163[21]	396[21]	622[21]	2,400[21]	217[21]	163[21]	797[21]	246[21]

C1 Area of Main Cereal, Potato, and Sugar Beet Crops (in thousands of hectares)

FRANCE

	Wheat	Rye	Barley	Oats	Maize	Buckwheat	Potatoes	Sugar Beet
1945	3,783	375	689	2,509	221	138	802	197
1946	4,131	442	731	2,509	244	114	852	250
1947	3,393	444	959	2,611	269	120	1,006	292
1948	4,231	565	820	2,439	294	124	1,047	309
1949	4,223	522	896	2,436	304	111	982	400
1950	4,319	504	962	2,353	325	99	988	395
1951	4,250	461	1,019	2,272	349	101	974	407
1952	4,297	431	1,075	2,275	349	93	938	424
1953	4,219	408	1,203	2,270	375	93	950	413
1954	4,491	405	1,231	2,154	411	84	955	380
1955	4,554	387	1,313	2,077	453	75	938	374
1956	2,745	371	2,283	2,277	653	74	962	376
1957	4,668	364	1,643	1,608	544	66	897	347
1958	4,615	347	1,782	1,487	590	60	884	365
1959	4,439	328	1,989	1,504	704	49	887	387
1960	4,358	299	2,089	1,427	824	46	880	428
1961	3,997	261	2,259	1,442	975	45	878	359
1962	4,571	243	2,177	1,356	866	41	852	352
1963	3,850	232	2,539	1,287	952	45	834	371
1964	4,388	220	2,360	1,094	893	35	680	425
1965	4,520	221	2,430	1,070	871	33	564	395
1966	3,992	198	2,642	1,094	964	28	526	295
1967	3,929	175	2,818	1,040	1,016	22	504	314
1968	4,090	163	2,781	949	1,024	18	459	404
1969	4,034	154	2,859	851	1,185	17	409	401
1970	3,746	135	2,953	799	1,486	16	401	403
1971	3,978	129	2,671	831	1,642	15	363	425
1972	3,958	128	2,674	762	1,877	13	301	448
1973	3,960	122	2,799	693	1,942	11	309	512
1974	4,140	114	2,714	670	1,907	11	305	534
1975	3,876	110	2,770	655	1,960	...	279	598
1976	4,274	117	2,780	652	1,394	...	273	613
1977	4,109	135	2,911	624	1,624	...	290	582
1978	4,167	138	2,813	611	1,802	...	269	556
1979	4,084	116	2,803	540	1,994	...	267	545
1980	4,590	129	2,647	532	1,754	...	224	549
1981	4,742	114	2,559	495	1,570	...	207	633
1982	4,843	111	2,388	518	1,611	...	207	562
1983	4,825	101	2,143	436	1,646	...	204	490
1984	5,106	100	2,108	440	1,742	...	205	525
1985	4,797	87	2,255	433	1,890	...	211	491
1986	4,859	81	2,088	312	1,889	...	201	449
1987	4,908	82	1,975	277	1,743	...	193	446
1988	4,824	79	1,916	273	1,970	...	183	432
1989	5,012	74	1,830	266	1,920	...	190	431
1990	5,143	67	1,549	222	1,549	...	190	475
1991	5,145	59	1,750	177	1,769	...	171	457
1992	5,080	55	1,800	168	1,869	...	184	461
1993	4,515	45	1,623	171	1,851	...	164	443
1994	4,574	44	1,405	166	1,663	8,900	165	437
1995	4,745	46	1,386	149	1,651	7,355	172	458
1996	5,040	49	1,535	140	1,734	7,585	175	460
1997	5,110	45	1,690	133	1,858	8,564	170	462
1998	5,234	46	1,631	202	1,799	10,085	164	456
1999	5,115	36	1,500	114	1,716	10,389	171	444
2000	5,250	32	1,535	103	1,765	15,057	169	410

C1   Area of Main Cereal, Potato, and Sugar Beet Crops (in thousands of hectares)

GERMANY[22]   1849–1924

	Wheat	Rye	Barley	Oats	Mixed corn & Buckwheat	Potatoes	Sugar Beet
1849	1,766	5,138	1,750	3,384	...	1,602	...
1855	1,844	5,408	1,737	3,575	...	1,848	...
1860	1,902	5,637	1,723	3,734	...	2,056	...
1870	1,964[22]	5,779[22]	1,636[22]	3,689[22]	...	2,396[22]	...
1871	2,170	5,833	1,683	3,777	...	2,517	...
1878	2,217	5,934	1,620	3,746	504	2,753	176
1879	2,306	5,929	1,625	3,746	506	2,758	174
1880	2,201	5,921	1,624	3,743	505	2,763	173
1881	2,195	5,913	1,633	3,745	525	2,768	233
1882	2,204	5,927	1,632	3,744	545	2,766	320
1883	2,294	5,812	1,751	3,763	566	2,906	337
1884	2,297	5,831	1,735	3,768	560	2,908	343
1885	2,294	5,842	1,742	3,767	555	2,921	349
1886	2,290	5,839	1,731	3,807	553	2,916	354
1887	2,291	5,842	1,731	3,810	547	2,918	360
1888	2,299	5,814	1,723	3,832	541	2,920	366
1889	2,322	5,802	1,685	3,887	531	2,918	372
1890	2,327	5,820	1,664	3,904	522	2,906	378
1891	2,213	5,480	1,807	4,155	514	2,923	383
1892	2,335	5,679	1,690	3,988	502	2,930	389
1893	2,391	6,012	1,594	3,907	491	3,037	395
1894	2,324	6,045	1,601	3,917	489	3,025	439
1895	2,270	5,894	1,663	4,029	494	3,050	407
1896	2,249	5,982	1,653	3,980	490	3,053	435
1897	2,247	5,967	1,644	3,999	486	3,068	443
1898	2,296	5,945	1,635	3,997	480	3,081	437
1899	2,340	5,871	1,641	4,000	473	3,131	461
1900	2,366	5,955	1,670	4,123	467	3,219	461
1901	1,896	5,812	1,859	4,411	463	3,319	468
1902	2,224	6,155	1,644	4,156	459	3,241	474
1903	2,107	6,013	1,700	4,290	455	3,238	481
1904	2,231	6,099	1,627	4,190	451	3,288	488
1905	2,260	6,146	1,633	4,182	447	3,317	494
1906	2,257	6,102	1,645	4,222	443	3,302	501
1907	2,053	6,043	1,702	4,377	438	3,297	508
1908	2,190	6,120	1,629	4,275	434	3,293	575
1909	2,130	6,131	1,646	4,310	430	3,324	621
1910	2,238	6,187	1,570	4,289	426	3,296	528
1911	2,256	6,136	1,585	4,328	422	3,321	535
1912	2,209	6,268	1,590	4,387	418	3,342	541
1913	2,246	6,414	1,654	4,438	414	3,412	548
1914	2,265	6,299	1,582	4,388	...	3,386	569
1915	2,262	6,411	1,620	4,615	...	3,572	400
1916	1,854	5,999	1,524	3,615	...	2,798	412
1917	1,679[22]	5,550[22]	1,461[22]	3,565[22]	...[22]	2,547[22]	402[22]
1918	1,589	5,747	1,365	3,266	490	2,728	402
1919	1,431	4,403	1,126	2,993	456	2,181	...
1920	1,540	4,325	1,198	3,244	388	2,450	...
1921	1,592	4,265	1,136	3,162	372	2,647	380
1922	1,501	4,142	1,152	3,202	366	2,721	409
1923	1,606	4,366	1,301	3,345	357	2,727	384
1924	1,588	4,259	1,446	3,525	373	2,760	394

C1   Area of Main Cereal, Potato, and Sugar Beet Crops (in thousands of hectares)

GERMANY   **1925-1944**

	Wheat	Rye	Barley	Oats	Mixed corn & Buckwheat	Potatoes	Sugar Beet
1925	1,677	4,708	1,435	3,452	343	2,809	403
1926	1,726	4,732	1,486	3,476	348	2,760	403
1927	1,859	4,721	1,488	3,486	405	2,814	434
1928	1,856	4,634	1,519	3,519	375	2,849	454
1929	1,722	4,727	1,552	3,490	383	2,867	455
1930	1,900	4,711	1,519	3,322	371	2,748	483
1931	2,281	4,366	1,619	3,183	374	2,744	381
1932	2,395	4,450	1,568	3,045	378	2,763	271
1933	2,431	4,524	1,585	2,882	383	2,744	304
1934	2,302[22]	4,491[22]	1,631[22]	2,785[22]	403[22]	2,733[22]	356[22]
1935	2,187	4,555	1,606	2,798	522	2,770	373
1936	2,153	4,514	1,635	2,778	518	2,798	389
1937	2,040	4,156	1,714	2,845	595	2,888	455
1938	2,094	4,263	1,673	2,697	591	2,893	502
1939	2,105	4,223	1,668	2,820	...	2,834	503
1940	1,897	4,975	1,686	2,843	...	2,813	537
1941	1,941	4,096	1,564	2,644	...	2,745	544
1942	1,715	3,381	1,501	2,809	...	2,777	547
1943	1,796	3,977	1,203	2,535	...	2,665	544
1944	1,781	3,851	1,179	2,438	...	2,764	543

C1 Area of Main Cereal, Potato, and Sugar Beet Crops (in thousands of hectares)

EAST GERMANY   **1946-1988**

	Wheat	Rye	Barley	Oats	Mixed corn & Buckwheat	Potatoes	Sugar Beet
1946	443	1,092	321	680	206	770	207
1947	335	1,180	298	655	230	732	213
1948	474	1,296	251	563	159	805	212
1949	469	1,304	253	530	139	813	217
1950	479	1,294	261	531	149	812	224
1951	464	1,277	264	553	155	831	224
1952	476	1,291	266	549	152	829	217
1953	420	1,223	317	585	154	833	213
1954	424	1,215	311	517	148	834	216
1955	400	1,074	337	536	132	843	215
1956	380	1,110	322	448	174	783	201
1957	420	1,098	321	455	208	810	219
1958	440	1,094	337	427	207	769	223
1959	435	1,031	354	410	210	771	234
1960	418	946	389	359	205	770	238
1961	377	825	432	351	247	682	218
1962	423	811	374	372	265	742	232
1963	426	820	424	315	252	747	232
1964	433	823	464	295	272	745	230
1965	491	822	497	260	234	725	221
1966	484	771	521	261	230	694	211
1967	533	746	553	270	212	686	209
1968	570	735	595	256	188	672	204
1969	560	690	642	272	182	604	192
1970	598	680	640	210	154	667	192
1971	633	668	656	230	132	658	211
1972	690	646	618	247	120	647	222
1973	696	646	692	228	102	650	229
1974	729	637	779	223	76	635	234
1975	689	593	929	243	59	574	266
1976	762	600	960	190	30	599	267
1977	732	619	997	153	19	587	269
1978	686	652	1,038	153	17	579	261
1979	712	678	945	136	18	549	254
1980	707	678	969	155	16	513	250
1981	675	656	964	172	17	505	261
1982	591	653	982	218	71	504	257
1983	754	713	889	163	18	483	238
1984	747	718	865	161	27	488	240
1985	744	690	882	178	25	475	233
1986	749	680	895	163	27	459	224
1987	748	655	891	149	17	448	219
1988	765	607	874	148	11	442	198
1989	777	624	895	143	...	431	217

Incorporated into West Germany

C1 Area of Main Cereal, Potato, and Sugar Beet Crops (in thousands of hectares)

WEST GERMANY 1949–2000

	Wheat	Rye	Barley	Oats	Maize	Mixed Corn & Buckwheat	Potatoes	Sugar Beet
1949	922	1,415	496	1,398	...		1,124	167
1950	1,013	1,363	613	1,158	...	249	1,141	193
1951	1,030	1,290	643	1,131	...	267	1,117	223
1952	1,193	1,356	707	1,112	...	285	1,147	222
1953	1,155	1,394	788	1,055	...	340	1,163	224
1954	1,107	1,530	733	943	...	450	1,190	254
1955	1,171	1,474	779	969	...	476	1,128	262
1956	1,153₂₃	1,483₂₃	851₂₃	951₂₃	...	495₂₃	1,135₂₃	269₂₃
1957	1,231	1,475	872	905	...	405	1,133	259
1958	1,315	1,503	881	837	...	412	1,074	284
1959	1,342	1,426	951	812	...	431	1,054	287
1960	1,396	1,318	980	748	...	454	1,042	294
1961	1,397	1,184	1,120	723	475	976	260	377
1962	1,319	1,092	1,138	805	13	531	963	290
1963	1,382	1,139	1,144	770	13	481	925	301
1964	1,447	1,146	1,153	766	18	467	851	327
1965	1,412	1,128	1,193	727	27	438	783	299
1966	1,389	1,021	1,288	777	31	433	732	294
1967	1,414	975	1,308	808	42	425	707	294
1968	1,464	962	1,330	821	58	450	659	290
1969	1,494	873	1,387	860	81	456	589	295
1970	1,493	865	1,475	825	99	426	597	303
1971	1,544	865	1,505	836	116	384	554	315
1972	1,626	843	1,549	808	118	359	503	331
1973	1,603	739	1,671	821	106	345	480	352
1974	1,631	708	1,665	851	108	335	467	369
1975	1,569	624	1,756	920	96	327	415	426
1976	1,632	663	1,735	856	102	287	415	440
1977	1,599	702	1,811	793	100	276	400	423
1978	1,619	651	1,951	749	116	246	355	402
1979	1,627	564	1,989	728	115	209	325	393
1980	1,668	547	2,002	691	119	187	306	395
1981	1,632	484	2,044	682	129	160	274	445
1982	1,578	407	2,021	723	160	175	265	418
1983	1,655	445	2,035	601	169	140	249	393
1984	1,634	439	2,060	555	182	125	244	405
1985	1,624	426	1,949	584	181	121	220	403
1986	1,648	414	1,947	506	187	110	210	390
1987	1,671	412	1,850	459	194	111	206	376
1988	1,743	378	1,836	474	199	103	199	379
1989	1,777	382	1,746	419	209	107	215	383
			Germany					
1990	2,438	1,057	2,584	479	228	149	606	615
1991	2,453	711	2,535	177	283	199	342	554
1992	2,598	615	2,408	168	296	229	361	554
1993	2,395	662	2,214	171	330	267	315	534
1994	2,446	723	2,070	392	346	283	323	503
1995	2,579	861	2,109	309	325	276	347	524
1996	2,594	809	2,208	302	372	289	336	516
1997	2,728	845	2,274	312	370	295	304	504
1998	2,802	926	2,181	264	341	270	297	503
1999	2,601	748	2,213	268	371	278	309	489
2000	2,971	843	2,072	237	361	288	304	452

C1   Area of Main Cereal, Potato, and Sugar Beet Crops (in thousands of hectares)

GREECE   1911–1969

	Wheat	Rye	Barley	Oats	Maize	Mixed Corn	Potatoes
1911	351	5.3	79	30	110	...	4.9
1912	...	...	...	...	...	...	...
1913	...[25]	...[25]	...[25]	...[25]	...[25]	...	...[25]
1914	440[25]	32[25]	135[25]	62[25]	196[25]	...	9.2[25]
1915	370	6.9	109	54	143	...	8.3
1916	362[25]	6.6[25]	120[25]	59[25]	155[25]	...	16[25]
1917	423	23	158	67	175	...	10
1918	442[25]	28[25]	167[25]	73[25]	170[25]	...	13[25]
1919	432	33	166	86	183	60	13
1920	436	30	156	65	189	56	10
1921	384[25]	31[25]	137[25]	66[25]	189[25]	52[25]	11[25]
1922	430	36	149	69	166	44	13
1923	430	23	147	76	154	45	12
1924	467	36	166	104	201	42	14
1925	465	43	177	101	201	41	12
1926	528	47	205	111	233	54	14
1927	499	47	188	103	197	48	11
1928	538	55	202	112	183	48	11
1929	501	52	145	102	203	34	7.6
1930	565	64	216	136	221	44	12
1931	605	69	223	139	250	53	14
1932	606	68	226	134	265	56	15
1933	693	74	224	138	261	55	18
1934	792	74	213	136	239	55	18
1935	846	73	206	139	223	52	19
1936	835	64	206	138	258	55	20
1937	857	68	212	145	279	58	25
1938	860	72	195	137	277	60	22
1939	926	54	180	137	258	60	22
1945	676	43	139	119	206	46	16
1946	751	58	170	122	264	55	26
1947	844	...	...	...	...	52	...
1948	843	57	205	141	246	56	29
1949	763	44	205	135	224	47	36
1950	867	55	206	147	248	42	34
1951	954	64	209	153	253	47	38
1952	965	66	215	153	255	44	39
1953	1,045	68	215	149	269	40	39
1954	1,045	62	211	138	253	36	40
1955	1,040	58	207	146	228	34	41
1956	1,062	53	206	147	228	32	40
1957	1,088	47	199	147	216	31	42
1958	1,111	43	195	143	204	28	39
1959	1,163	33	185	129	206	16	43
1960	1,142	29	181	128	210	18	38
1961	1,173	25	189	149	191	13	56
1962	1,193	22	185	144	166	12	57
1963	1,078	20	175	126	185	7	57
1964	1,263	18	167	119	150	7	58
1965	1,258	16	203	120	144	8	56
1966	1,132	14	284	118	139	6	55
1967	1,051	11	351	111	133	5	56
1968	1,098	8	332	92	147	4	54
1969	1,078	8	282	84	149	3	55

C1 Area of Main Cereal, Potato, and Sugar Beet Crops (in thousands of hectares)

GREECE   1970–2000

	Wheat	Rye	Barley	Oats	Maize	MC	Ps
1970	985	7	342	80	170	2	59
1971	979	7	381	81	166	2	51
1972	885	6	409	78	165	1	52
1973	845	5	413	72	160	1	56
1974	916	5	412	76	131	1	56
1975	926	5	395	70	128	1	57
1976	931	5	387	65	128	1	65
1977	939	4	361	57	123	1	70
1978	994	4	356	56	112	1	64
1979	990	4	384	54	123	1	63
1980	1,012	4	344	52	172	1	65
1981	1,065	4	304	52	176	1	62
1982	1,056	6	312	49	178	1	62
1983	984	7	329	43	192	1	64
1984	874	10	365	43	247	1	59
1985	875	12	312	43	238	1	56
1986	905	13	266	43	218	...	56
1987	886	18	241	44	262	...	55
1988	884	16	240	36	210	...	46
1989	888	17	245	36	245	...	55
1990	899	16	230	37	200	...	55
1991	1007	21	172	45	230	...	52
1992	948	18	171	43	211	...	51
1993	912	19	167	43	212	...	49
1994	902	19	163	44	212	...	49
1995	879	18	156	44	182	...	51
1996	865	18	154	43	213	...	50
1997	859	17	146	43	211	...	48
1998	855	16	139	44	214	...	48
1999	838	15	129	44	210	...	48
2000	860	15	122	46	215	...	47

HUNGARY[26]   1868–1897

	Wheat	Rye[27]	Barley	Oats	Maize	Potatoes	SB
1868	2,041	1,677	...	...	...	...	...
1869	2,158	1,609	788	890	1,404	334	15
1870	2,024	1,499	808	940	1,486	359	19
1871	1,884	1,510[27]	869	973	1,399	362	19
		1,535					
1872	2,020	1,500	882	1,032	1,478	362	19
1873	2,142	1,547	902	1,024	1,534	355	17
1874	2,246	1,455	947	1,048	1,603	360	21
1875	2,291	1,456	908	984	1,765	382	21
1876	2,603	1,641	1,078	1,240	2,038	501	26
1877	2,448	1,484	937	1,093	1,840	427	24
1878	2,503	1,559	1,006	1,155	1,894	466	25
1879	2,464	1,727	983	1,089	1,875	411	31
1880	2,411	1,301	978	1,018	1,866	361	37
1881	2,534	1,293	911	956	1,796	371	31
1882	2,494	1,293	999	993	1,894	386	33
1883	2,605	1,292	972	993	1,824	394	36
1884	2,751	1,304	995	995	1,856	412	39
1885	2,741	1,316	1,046	1,038	1,875	420	32
1886	2,664	1,302	1,044	1,053	1,914	426	38
1887	2,777	1,307	1,003	1,046	1,828	413	34
1888	2,770	1,282	981	1,045	1,865	439	41
1889	2,911	1,253	1,007	1,018	1,938	439	55
1890	2,979	1,239	1,008	993	1,932	433	66
1891	3,012	1,185	1,043	1,007	2,012	432	68
1892	3,064	1,248	1,043	1,004	2,089	458	73
1893	3,278	1,394	1,046	970	2,049	454	82
1894	3,204	1,244	1,056	986	2,022	460	91
1895	3,133	1,132	1,010	962	2,148	461	74
1896	3,126	1,135	1,010	938	2,082	444	75
1897	2,780	1,185	946	897	1,988	440	71

C1   Area of Main Cereal, Potato, and Sugar Beet Crops (in thousands of hectares)

HUNGARY[26]   1898-1949

	Wheat	Rye[27]	Barley	Oats	Maize	Potatoes	SB
1898	3,057	1,107	975	947	2,114	458	74
1899	3,158	1,143	1,116	964	2,129	456	73
1900	3,295	1,118	1,006	981	2,217	508	90
1901	3,317	1,136	1,013	982	2,199	506	91
1902	3,344	1,139	1,021	985	2,166	506	91
1903	3,445	1,130	1,039	1,023	2,268	537	95
1904	3,400	1,115	1,020	994	1,964	518	90
1905	3,417	1,131	1,033	1,017	2,123	537	94
1906	3,555	1,133	1,053	1,037	2,312	563	110
1907	3,266	1,065	1,103	1,074	2,441	570	110
1908	3,527	1,104	1,071	1,057	2,360	584	102
1909	3,252	1,062	1,157	1,091	2,453	602	112
1910	3,374	1,122	1,099	1,069	2,427	610	115
1911	3,381	1,089	1,107	1,074	2,465	621	139
1912	3,540	1,131	1,053	1,001	2,437	619	172
1913	3,211	1,055	1,193	1,209	2,663	644	182
1914	3,244	1,099	1,095	1,053	2,434	613	178
1915	3,351	1,063	1,145	1,080	2,513	637	107
1916	2,972	989	1,037	1,054	2,255	589	96
1917	3,067	1,003	966	999	2,197	599	110
1918	3,063[26]	974[26]	933[26]	960[26]	2,230[26]	482[26]	114[26]
1919	...	...	...	...	...	...	...
1920	1,077	597	512	325	816	254	31
1921	1,169	543	479	358	877	269	42
1922	1,426	673	463	328	989	257	42
1923	1,333	653	455	325	972	259	52
1924	1,416	663	408	287	995	248	68
1925	1,426	688	412	290	1,074	261	66
1926	1,500	700	425	275	1,065	251	63
1927	1,627	641	406	260	1,062	260	65
1928	1,677	651	413	264	1,062	265	67
1929	1,500	657	477	301	1,123	283	79
1930	1,695	652	458	246	1,054	272	74
1931	1,623	601	472	241	1,101	284	54
1932	1,535	629	469	234	1,176	299	42
1933	1,588	679	485	231	1,140	294	44
1934	1,537	642	478	224	1,124	290	45
1935	1,673	622	428	203	1,151	281	47
1936	1,630	650	470	214	1,137	297	49
1937	1,483	606	467	230	1,196	295	47
1938	1,619	632	454	224	1,174	291	44
1939	1,642	622	444	221	1,174	276	43
1940	1,407	541	410	245	1,146	279	56
1941	1,333	536	419	248	1,127	274	49
1942	1,416	537	415	233	1,085	265	47
1943	1,544	551	437	239	959	266	55
1944	1,539	541	448	240	1,049	266	60
1945	735	370	519	211	1,221	302	20
1946	1,091	454	464	202	1,159	256	54
1947	1,375	532	444	220	1,329	279	92
1948	1,366	614	434	215	1,325	274	112
1949	1,392	650	466	195	1,124	282	113

C1   Area of Main Cereal, Potato, and Sugar Beet Crops (in thousands of hectares)

HUNGARY[26]

1950–2000

	Wheat	Rye[27]	Barley	Oats	Maize	Potatoes	SB
1950	1,375	597	479	187	1,151	279	112
1951	1,394	575	447	151	1,153	203	118
1952	1,372	509	437	131	1,054	225	112
1953	1,320	436	407	124	1,161	199	125
1954	1,410	466	415	124	1,210	236	104
1955	1,358	447	404	121	1,291	230	112
1956	1,389	441	407	118	1,162	220	114
1957	1,247	421	482	172	1,346	241	83
1958	1,188	376	538	173	1,304	240	109
1959	1,116	353	541	170	1,358	230	122
1960	1,051	301	508	141	1,401	253	133
1961	1,014	268	522	110	1,340	240	130
1962	1,095	232	548	84	1,288	209	125
1963	1,005	209	486	90	1,289	232	118
1964	1,148	247	522	71	1,209	210	133
1965	1,125	246	501	57	1,218	207	121
1966	1,072	220	489	61	1,237	198	108
1967	1,160	204	447	55	1,237	169	104
1968	1,328	190	385	54	1,259	150	104
1969	1,324	183	381	48	1,255	140	97
1970	1,274	149	284	44	1,189	137	76
1971	1,273	127	298	45	1,321	129	73
1972	1,317	120	291	48	1,392	118	79
1973	1,294	107	287	37	1,461	106	92
1974	1,324	106	271	33	1,461	108	98
1975	1,251	104	257	45	1,413	100	127
1976	1,325	93	228	39	1,339	90	129
1977	1,311	91	224	32	1,281	99	122
1978	1,324	78	225	27	1,283	94	123
1979	1,135	69	262	44	1,352	76	112
1980	1,276	73	246	35	1,229	63	104
1981	1,151	74	286	55	1,163	61	122
1982	1,310	74	262	50	1,130	56	126
1983	1,355	72	277	48	1,102	50	109
1984	1,361	75	269	44	1,107	52	109
1985	1,358	85	279	44	1,053	50	107
1986	1,318	89	253	41	1,118	44	104
1987	1,301	94	205	40	1,144	43	117
1988	1,281	97	264	42	1,103	48	115
1989	1,242	97	283	45	1,105	72	120
1990	1,221	92	297	48	1,100	72	131
1991	1,158	94	357	51	1,154	78	158
1992	848	71	480	52	1,207	72	108
1993	986	72	436	56	1,270	91	100
1994	1,059	88	423	56	1,237	57	106
1995	1,108	77	393	53	1,033	57	125
1996	1,193	59	325	48	1,053	62	118
1997	1,248	67	370	52	1,059	64	98
1998	1,184	62	369	52	1,023	53	80
1999	734	40	334	71	1,115	56	66
2000	1,024	43	325	58	1,193	47	57

C1   Area of Main Cereal, Potato, and Sugar Beet Crops (in thousands of hectares)

CROATIA-SLAVONIA   1885–1916

	Wheat	Rye	Barley	Oats	Maize	Potatoes	Sugar Beet
1885	162	169	70	112	308	36	1
1886	162	175	69	111	313	43	1
1887	168	171	68	111	313	49	1
1888	175	168	67	107	320	53	1
1889	180	170	64	98	323	55	1
1890	188	169	67	97	330	55	1
1891	196	158	65	95	347	56	1
1892	206	157	68	95	351	58	1
1893	219	160	66	93	355	58	2
1894	227	156	69	93	365	59	1
1895	227	148	66	87	365	78	1
1896	237	149	69	92	366	59	1
1897	233	146	69	95	357	63	1
1898	245	147	71	100	391	85	1
1899	257	144	69	99	368	65	1
1900	269	137	74	100	371	67	1
1901	271	139	72	100	388	68	1
1902	278	128	70	99	379	72	1
1903	289	130	72	101	395	71	1
1904	295	128	70	100	395	72	1
1905	305	122	69	100	400	72	1
1906	298	114	67	102	407	73	2
1907	287	105	65	101	400	74	2
1908	307	97	65	100	406	73	2
1909	309	103	63	100	405	77	2
1910	320	105	64	97	403	78	3
1911	327	104	64	100	414	77	4
1912	335	97	63	96	423	79	4
1913	339	67	64	110	439	79	5
1914	342	90	62	103	428	84	8
1915	325	83	61	109	429	84	4
1916	306	68	59	112	419	82	3

IRELAND   1847–1882

	Wheat	Barley	Oats	Potatoes		Wheat	Barley	Oats	Potatoes
1847	301	135	891	115	1865	108	73	706	431
1848	…	…	…	…	1866	121	62	688	425
1849	278	142	834	291	1867	106	70	672	405
1850	245	130	867	354	1868	115	76	689	419
1851	204	136	886	352	1869	113	91	682	422
1852	143	117	924	355	1870	105	99	668	422
1853	132	122	873	364	1871	99	90	662	428
1854	166	102	828	401	1872	91	89	658	401
1855	180	96	858	397	1873	68	93	611	365
1856	214	76	824	447	1874	76	86	599	361
1857	227	88	802	464	1875	64	95	608	365
1858	221	79	802	469	1876	49	89	602	357
1859	188	74	802	486	1877	56	92	597	353
1860	189	74	796	474	1878	62	99	572	343
1861	162	82	809	459	1879	64	103	538	341
1862	144	79	800	412	1880	60	89	559	332
1863	105	71	791	414	1881	62	85	564	346
1864	112	71	735	421	1882	62	76	565	339

C1 Area of Main Cereal, Potato, and Sugar Beet Crops (in thousands of hectares)

IRELAND (Southern Ireland from 1922) 1883-2000

	Wheat	Barley	Oats	Potatoes	Sugar Beet		Wheat	Barley	Oats	Potatoes	Sugar Beet
1883	38	74	559	326	—	1940	123	53	276	149	25
1884	28	68	546	323	—	1941	187	66	316	173	32
						1942	233	75	355	172	22
1885	29	73	538	323	—	1943	206	85	379	165	34
1886	28	74	535	324	—	1944	260	68	382	167	33
1887	27	66	532	323	—						
1888	40	69	518	326	—	1945	268	69	338	157	34
1889	36	75	501	318	—	1946	260	58	336	158	32
						1947	235	59	334	155	25
1890	37	74	494	316	—	1948	210	49	356	156	27
1891	33	72	492	305	—	1949	147	64	278	142	24
1892	30	71	496	299	—						
1893	22	68	505	293	—	1950	148	50	248	136	24
1894	20	67	508	290	—	1951	114	68	251	130	24
						1952	103	91	247	125	22
1895	15	70	492	287	—	1953	143	76	231	125	26
1896	15	70	483	286	—	1954	197	66	216	118	30
1897	19	69	476	274	—						
1898	21	64	471	269	—	1955	145	86	221	116	22
1899	21	69	460	268	—	1956	138	96	212	115	24
						1957	164	124	187	108	29
1900	22	70	447	265	—	1958	170	125	185	106	34
1901	17	66	445	257	—	1959	114	135	187	105	28
1902	18	68	430	255	—						
1903	15	64	444	251	—	1960	148	133	172	95	28
1904	13	64	437	251	—	1961	140	146	149	86	32
						1962	127	164	140	85	32
1905	15	63	432	250	—	1963	94	133	134	83	36
1906	18	72	435	249	—	1964	87	143	117	74	32
1907	15	69	435	239	—						
1908	15	63	429	238	—	1965	74	188	115	70	27
1909	18	66	419	235	—	1966	53	187	98	68	22
						1967	77	183	96	65	26
1910	19	68	435	240	—	1968	90	184	88	59	26
1911	18	64	421	239	—	1969	83	198	77	55	25
1912	18	67	423	241	—						
1913	14	70	424	236	—	1970	95	214	68	57	26
1914	15	70	416	236	—	1971	90	235	60	52	30
						1972	68	252	52	44	34
1915	35	57	441	240	—	1973	58	243	50	48	30
1916	31	61	434	237	—	1974	55	246	44	40	26
1917	50	72	592	287	—						
1918	64	75	639	284	—	1975	45	245	49	41	33
1919	28	76	584	238	—	1976	50	259	40	47	34
						1977	48	289	35	53	35
1920	20	84	539	236	—	1978	49	307	31	41	36
1921	17₂₈	69₂₈	491₂₈	230₂₈	—	1979	49	324	28	41	35
1922	15	66	311	165	—						
1923	15	59	295	161	—	1980	53	366	25	40	33
1924	13	63	279	159	—	1981	49	357	23	36	35
						1982	57	332	23	37	35
1925	9	59	272	154	—	1983	59	313	23	34	36
1926	12	57	262	152	3.8	1984	77	304	25	36	35
1927	14	49	261	148	7.2						
1928	13	52	262	147	6.7	1985	78	298	23	33	34
1929	12	48	270	147	5.3	1986	76	283	21	30	37
						1987	57	276	20	30	37
1930	11	47	261	140	5.8	1988	60	266	20	28	33
1931	8.4	47	252	140	2.0	1989	62	263	19	26	32
1932	8.7	42	256	141	5.5						
1933	20	47	257	138	6.1	1990	74	236	23	26	33
1934	38	58	236	139	18	1991	86	193	21	21	33
						1992	91	184	20	22	31
1935	66	56	248	136	23	1993	77	177	20	22	32
1936	103	53	226	135	25	1994	74	170	21	21	35
1937	89	53	232	132	25						
1938	93	48	231	132	21	1995	71	179	20	22	35
1939	103	30	217	128	17	1996	86	181	21	24	32
						1997	94	190	21	18	32
						1998	84	191	19	19	33
						1999	68	192	20	18	34
						2000	84	181	18	14	32

C1   Area of Main Cereal, Potato, and Sugar Beet Crops (in thousands of hectares)

NORTHERN IRELAND   **1922–1993**

	Wheat	Barley	Oats	Potatoes		Wheat	Barley	Oats	Potatoes
1922	2.6	0.8	144	70	**1955**	0.5	2.0	102	47
1923	2.8	0.8	142	66	**1956**	1.1	2.5	104	51
1924	2.0	1.0	135	64	**1957**	1.6	5.2	96	42
					1958	1.6	6.5	88	40
1925	1.5	0.9	130	62	**1959**	1.0	11	81	39
1926	2.5	0.7	129	62					
1927	2.4	0.6	125	62	**1960**	1.4	24	82	35
1928	2.0	0.8	124	63	**1961**	2.0	45	74	31
1929	1.5	0.8	127	62	**1962**	1.7	52	66	31
					1963	1.0	60	59	33
1930	1.8	0.9	124	55	**1964**	1.3	67	51	29
1931	1.2	0.6	116	54					
1932	1.3	0.4	116	57	**1965**	1.5	74	39	25
1933	2.5	0.6	117	56	**1966**	1.2	70	33	23
1934	3.5	1.0	113	55	**1967**	1.0	62	33	23
					1968	0.8	56	30	20
1935	3.7	1.3	110	52	**1969**	1.1	55	23	17
1936	2.8	1.1	107	53					
1937	1.8	1.1	104	51	**1970**	1.2	50	18	19
1938	2.2	1.4	120	50	**1971**	1.0	57	15	17
1939	1.2	1.4	118	47	**1972**	0.9	51	12	15
					1973	0.6	48	10	14
1940	4.8	7.2	161	55	**1974**	0.6	49	9	12
1941	7.1	7.1	182	64					
1942	5.0	6.2	192	76	**1975**	0.6	50	9	11
1943	5.6	5.8	190	80	**1976**	0.6	50	7	14
1944	2.0	6.5	178	80	**1977**	0.4	52	6	19
					1978	0.6	56	5	14
1945	0.7	5.8	181	77	**1979**	0.5	52	4	14
1946	1.0	3.1	167	78					
1947	0.7	2.6	154	74	**1980**	0.4	52	4	15
1948	1.8	2.3	158	85	**1981**	0.4	51	3	13
1949	0.8	2.3	151	76	**1982**	1.0	47	3	14
					1983	1.5	45	3	13
1950	0.8	1.5	140	72	**1984**	3.1	45	3	14
1951	0.5	1.2	128	58					
1952	0.8	2.2	122	55	**1985**	5.0	46	3	13
1953	0.9	2.5	117	56	**1986**	3.8	47	2	12
1954	0.8	2.1	108	53	**1987**	5.0	44	3	12
					1988	4.9	42	3	12
					1989	4.9	40	3	10
					1990	5.8	37	3	11
					1991	5.9	38	3	11
					1992	7.4	37	2	11
					1993	6.7	39	2	9

C1 Area of Main Cereal, Potato, and Sugar Beet Crops (in thousands of hectares)

ITALY[29]

1872–1942

	Wheat	Rye	Barley	Oats	Maize	Rice	Potatoes	Sugar Beet
1872	4,737		478	380	1,717	232	70	...
1881	4,434	161	338	437	1,893	202	151	...
1890	4,407	141	332	453	1,912	193	174	...
1891	4,502	142	308	448	1,906	195	181	...
1892	4,530	144	313	450	1,903	198	194	...
1893	4,556	145	323	458	1,920	162	198	...
1894	4,574	142	303	466	1,901	165	200	...
1895	4,593	137	297	474	1,957	163	209	...
1896	4,581				1,956			...
1901	4,760	...	...	...	1,755	...	...	...
1902	4,750	...	...	...	1,700	...	...	...
1903	5,154	...	...	...	1,688	...	...	...
1904	5,397	...	...	...	1,941	...	...	...
1905	5,315	...	...	...	1960	...	...	...
1906	5,137	...	...	...	1,896	...	...	...
1907	5,230	...	...	...	1,814	...	...	...
1908	5,108	...	...	...	1,801	...	...	...
1909	4,709	122	250	503	1,636	144	283	45
1910	4,759	122	248	503	1,621	144	284	50
1911	4,752	122	248	514	1,616	145	288	53
1912	4,755	123	244	508	1,594	146	288	54
1913	4,744	124	251	506	1,574	146	292	62
1914	4,769	123	247	491	1,576	146	294	41
1915	5,060	119	246	489	1,573	144	293	50
1916	4,726	116	241	446	1,586	143	295	50
1917	4,272	113	190	448	1,559	138	296	47
1918	4,366[20]	109[20]	193[20]	491[20]	1,440[20]	138[20]	299[20]	43[20]
1919	4,287	111	194	457	1,501	132	309	52
1920	4,569	114	200	469	1,501	112	301	46
1921	4,767[29]	116[29]	219[29]	485[29]	1,504[29]	116[29]	309[29]	64[29]
1922	4,650	129	233	491	1,561	119	349	82
1923	4,676	127	230	495	1,533	123	348	90
1924	4,566	125	232	478	1,540	138	348	124
1925	4,724	126	233	486	1,554	144	346	57
1926	4,915	121	237	498	1,525	148	352	80
1927	4,976	124	236	487	1,520	142	354	88
1928	4,963	126	227	521	1,502	135	354	115
1929	4,773	124	234	523	1,505	137	351	116
1930	4,823	122	236	511	1,516	146	351	116
1931	4,809	123	218	464	1,396	145	349	112
1932	4,931	117	210	446	1,448	135	412	114
1933	5,094	114	207	448	1,431	134	399	82
1934	4,967	112	199	424	1,491	134	400	89
1935	5,005	110	199	428	1,445	138	406	92
1936	5,137	106	195	435	1,489	145	426	120
1937	5,173	105	195	435	1,471	145	422	134
1938	5,031	104	199	442	1,507	148	425	138
1939	5,225	105	201	420	1,459	157	427	147
1940	5,076	105	203	442	1,509	163	429	173
1941	4,970	107	207	445	1,451	167	450	151
1942	5,169	105	254	444	1,428	162	463	148
1943	5,342[29]	102[29]	276[29]	461[29]	1,390[29]	152[29]	474[29]	151[29]
1944	4,763	94	241	425	1,265	127	397	113

C1   Area of Main Cereal, Potato, and Sugar Beet Crops (in thousands of hectares)

ITALY   1943–2000

	Wheat	Rye	Barley	Oats	Maize	Rice	Potatoes	Sugar Beet
1945	4,481	94	239	434	1,307	97	392	29
1946	4,622	99	238	443	1,259	118	398	101
1947	4,499	98	242	480	1,228	132	419	110
1948	4,665[29]	99[29]	251[29]	476[29]	1,244[29]	143[29]	406[29]	113[29]
1949	4,729	99	250	469	1,239	129	390	131
1950	4,719	98	251	473	1,241	143	383	174
1951	4,728	96	251	462	1,267	156	386	198
1952	4,682	94	253	465	1,273	174	393	222
1953	4,770	93	250	457	1,272	176	393	210
1954	4,770	86	248	452	1,274	179	397	224
1955	4,852	80	244	434	1,237	169	391	258
1956	4,883	74	237	423	1,257	138	387	225
1957	4,911	71	229	420	1,251	126	386	210
1958	4,839	68	224	414	1,217	134	384	247
1959	4,665	68	221	412	1,193	136	386	287
1960	4,556	63	216	409	1,190	129	379	245
1961	4,345	60	220	428	1,197	123	379	227
1962	4,556	56	210	411	1,120	118	377	226
1963	4,394	53	204	400	1,121	115	386	230
1964	4,408	51	197	384	1,072	120	356	231
1965	4,288	48	186	367	1,028	126	348	282
1966	4,274	46	179	359	988	132	347	298
1967	4,012	46	181	358	1,017	144	339	345
1968	4,275	42	175	323	967	156	319	306
1969	4,218	38	175	312	999	169	306	291
1970	4,138	35	179	303	1,026	173	286	281
1971	3,910	29	185	277	934	175	237	254
1972	3,804	18	186	250	891	183	194	250
1973	3,590	18	203	238	890	190	182	235
1974	3,712	17	224	236	890	188	181	196
1975	3,545	17	249	239	897	174	179	271
1976	3,544	16	274	236	989	182	174	305
1977	2,796	15	290	225	983	186	185	254
1978	3,472	15	294	228	928	191	172	265
1979	3,452	15	308	222	937	183	169	285
1980	3,408	15	329	226	942	176	161	292
1981	3,259	14	336	222	988	169	153	330
1982	3,327	13	352	218	1,005	177	148	273
1983	3,333	11	385	207	982	182	139	225
1984	3,274	9	434	190	961	180	139	225
1985	3,034	9	468	182	923	186	138	232
1986	3,136	8	465	184	848	192	134	312
1987	3,087	8	445	177	768	190	131	302
1988	2,895	8	450	171	843	198	126	275
1989	2,944	8	471	169	804	206	125	302
1990	2,773	8	467	158	768	213	125	281
1991	2,683	8	472	146	859	205	111	277
1992	2,517	8	450	146	854	216	111	294
1993	2,299	8	436	138	934	229	95	262
1994	2,371	7	392	144	910	236	86	282
1995	2,482	7	374	135	942	239	89	284
1996	2,408	8	359	142	1,022	245	91	258
1997	2,366	8	357	151	1,039	233	91	295
1998	2,328	7	363	152	969	223	90	277
1999	2,387	4	354	142	1,028	221	86	284
2000	2,330	3	345	141	1,064	220	82	249

C1 Area of Main Cereal, Potato, and Sugar Beet Crops (in thousands of hectares)

NETHERLANDS

	Wheat	Rye	Barley	Oats	Buckwheat	Potatoes	Sugar Beet
1852	80	182	41	82	63	90	...
1853	71	182	43	86	64	87	...
1854	79	184	42	82	63	90	...
1855	73	183	44	91	64	96	...
1856	81	192	43	89	64	99	...
1857	83	190	43	81	65	100	...
1858	82	193	47	84	62	104	...
1859	85	196	43	84	67	101	...
1860	83	194	44	89	64	105	...
1861	83	189	41	97	68	107	...
1862	84	193	41	92	65	107	...
1863	88	195	42	93	64	110	...
1864	79	193	42	107	66	108	...
1865	82	193	41	97	67	106	...
1866	84	203	42	95	68	109	...
1867	79	200	47	105	68	111	...
1868	86	203	43	103	68	117	...
1869	90	206	47	105	68	119	...
1870	84	203	47	105	68	123	9
1871	57	164	58	140	74	127	11
1872	86	200	45	100	67	126	13
1873	87	197	55	104	66	134	15
1874	91	200	44	103	66	131	11
1875	95	202	49	112	66	132	15
1876	86	199	47	116	67	132	13
1877	90	200	46	118	65	137	14
1878	94	204	46	111	63	139	15
1879	93	201	48	114	55	142	16
1880	93	197	47	118	59	141	18
1881	89	196	47	119	56	141	16
1882	83	202	46	116	55	141	18
1883	87	199	49	119	54	142	20
1884	89	202	47	113	53	145	21
1885	85	204	50	115	52	142	16
1886	81	204	45	122	51	143	18
1887	85	204	45	115	48	147	19
1888	85	202	45	114	47	149	22
1889	85	203	44	115	46	148	24
1890	85	204	42	115	45	145	28
1891	59	184	45	153	44	150	23
1892	74	201	44	126	39	152	25
1893	71	202	42	126	38	152	28
1894	65	208	38	133	37	150	33
1895	62	210	39	131	36	151	35
1896	62	215	39	128	32	150	46
1897	62	213	36	134	31	151	39
1898	73	215	35	127	30	150	43
1899	72	214	36	128	29	156	46
1900	64	214	38	131	28	156	46
1901	55	216	36	135	27	156	49
1902	62	218	36	137	26	158	33
1903	56	218	32	144	24	151	40
1904	54	216	31	145	22	159	34

C1 Area of Main Cereal, Potato, and Sugar Beet Crops (in thousands of hectares)

NETHERLANDS   **1905–1956**

	Wheat	Rye	Barley	Oats	Buckwheat	Potatoes	Sugar Beet
1905	61	219	33	132	21	161	47
1906	57	218	29	139	19	161	42
1907	55	220	31	139	18	158	44
1908	57	222	30	140	17	159	48
1909	52	224	28	142	16	161	55
1910	55	222	28	141	14	162	56
1911	58	225	28	138	13	166	56
1912	58	228	27	138	12	172	65
1913	57	228	27	141	10	170	60
1914	60	228	27	141	10	171	63
1915	66	221	26	145	8	177	57
1916	55	200	24	139	7	...[30]	65
1917	49	189	21	155	8	...[30]	46
1918	61	119	24	159	8	...[30]	38
1919	68	201	23	158	8	...[30]	53
1920	62	199	23	160	7	...[30]	67
1921	73	202	25	155	5	179	74
1922	61	202	25	159	4	193	56
1923	62	210	24	154	3	161	67
1924	48	198	25	152	3	168	74
1925	53	201	30	148	2	170	66
1926	53	197	27	154	2	170	62
1927	62	197	27	149	1.2	173	70
1928	60	196	28	152	0.9	179	65
1929	45	197	31	160	0.7	182	55
1930	58	192	31	150	0.5	161	58
1931	78	180	29	149	0.5	164	37
1932	120	166	20	142	0.4	176	40
1933	137	165	18	136	0.5	153	47
1934	148	187	32	131	0.4	143	42
1935	154	210	41	128	0.3	139	41
1936	152	238	43	129	0.3	112	44
1937	119	231	49	153	0.2	123	43
1938	126	243	43	150	...	130	44
1939	124	225	41	163	...	134	46
1940	134	228	43	139	...	137	50
1941	137	241	47	109	...	169	45
1942	144	281	51	104	...	222	41
1943	149	317	46	114	...	226	44
1944	147	299	33	123	...	207	40
1945	119	216	48	148	...	181	18
1946	122	225	62	177	...	203	45
1947	86	181	68	163	...	216	51
1948	99	184	53	142	...	236	47
1949	104[31]	190[31]	49[31]	135[31]	...	197[31]	68[31]
	98	182	47	130		...	...
1950	91	175	69	141	...	175	67
1951	75	161	65	154	...	165	66
1952	82	184	69	153	...	170	63
1953	65	172	103	157	...	158	68
1954	110	167	63	143	...	170	79
1955	89	154	70	171	...	153	67
1956	86	171	74	154	...	146	69

C1 Area of Main Cereal, Potato, and Sugar Beet Crops (in thousands of hectares)

NETHERLANDS 1957–2000

	Wheat	Rye	Barley	Oats	Potatoes	Sugar Beet
1957	99	157	72	159	145	65
1958	111	145	82	137	140	81
1959	120	144	72	126	145	93
1960	128	153	69	115	148	93
1961	123	120	103	123	133	85
1962	133	107	100	119	130	77
1963	127	106	101	113	124	70
1964	151	106	87	103	124	79
1965	158	98	99	101	125	92
1966	148	74	120	99	131	92
1967	154	73	107	88	138	100
1968	153	75	107	76	147	104
1969	155	62	99	83	145	103
1970	142	57	105	55	158	104
1971	142	60	98	45	154	102
1972	156	54	83	33	149	113
1973	138	31	90	30	157	117
1974	130	22	73	33	158	109
1975	107	18	83	34	151	137
1976	131	21	62	25	161	139
1977	126	21	66	21	170	130
1978	121	17	71	25	162	131
1979	141	12	63	21	166	124
1980	142	10	53	18	173	121
1981	132	7	53	21	165	130
1982	131	6	44	24	166	134
1983	148	7	37	14	163	117
1984	145	6	34	12	160	129
1985	128	5	39	11	169	131
1986	117	4	42	6	167	138
1987	111	6	51	9	168	128
1988	114	7	63	13	161	123
1989	138	7	50	8	165	124
1990	139	9	39	3	175	125
1991	123	7	42	3	179	123
1992	127	6	34	4	186	121
1993	118	8	40	5	166	117
1994	122	6	44	6	171	115
1995	135	8	36	3	179	116
1996	142	7	36	2	185	117
1997	137	5	42	2	180	114
1998	139	6	40	2	127	113
1999	103	3	58	3	180	120
2000	137	6	47	2	180	111

C1 Area of Main Cereal, Potato, and Sugar Beet Crops (in thousands of hectares)

NORWAY[32]   1865–1964

	Wheat	Rye	Barley	Oats	Mixed Corn	Potatoes
1865	5.0	12	51	93	20	32
1875	4.6	15	57	93	21	36
1890	4.3	14	52	97	14	39
1900	5.0	13	40	97	7.6	37
1907	5.0	15	36	106	6.2	41
1910	5.0	15	36	107	6.1	42
1917	8.6	11	47	103	8.4	46
1918	17	15	63	138	12	53
1920	9.8	12	52	119	8.7	50
1923	10	11	50	103	8.1	46
1924	8.6	10	55	93	7.9	47
1925	8.9	9.0	56	97	7.6	47
1926	8.9	9.5	58	98	7.3	48
1927	9.9	9.3	61	97	6.8	50
1928	12	7.4	60	100	6.8	51
1929	12	7.4	54	97	5.5	46
1930	12	7.7	54	97	5.5	47
1931	12	6.2	56	96	5.5	47
1932	11	6.6	55	95	5.6	50
1933	11	6.3	57	98	5.8	49
1934	19	5.9	60	92	5.0	49
1935	24	6.2	62	87	4.5	50
1936	30	5.9	60	85	4.4	52
1937	32	5.9	60	85	4.5	52
1938	35	5.4	60	85	4.5	54
1939	41	3.2	47	87	4.9	51
1940	41	3.1	48	89	4.9	57
1941	46	3.7	56	93	7.4	63
1942	49	4.3	53	91	7.8	79
1943	48	3.9	51	92	6.8	81
1944	47	3.7	47	89	6.7	73
1945	48	2.7	42	86	5.4	65
1946	38	2.5	41	84	4.7	62
1947	29	1.3	39	76	3.8	57
1948	33	1.3	37	74	4	65
1949	31	1.0	40	76	4	58
1950	32	1.2	42	78	4	59
1951	24	0.6	55	77	4	59
1952	21	0.5	64	80	3	58
1953	17	0.6	81	72	3	56
1954	20	0.7	93	71	2	55
1955	18	0.6	101	68	3	56
1956	21	0.9	109	66	2	58
1957	14	0.6	135	61	2	55
1958	8.0	0.5	145	57	2	53
1959	9.3	1.1	141	65	2	55
1960	9.2	1.4	145	65	2	57
1961	9.7	0.9	154	62	2	53
1962	9.7	1.8	164	53	1	50
1963	7.0	1.1	179	44	1	52
1964	7.2	0.7	182	52	1	49

C1 Area of Main Cereal, Potato, and Sugar Beet Crops (in thousands of hectares)

NORWAY[32]   **1965-2000**

	Wheat	Rye	Barley	Oats	Mixed Corn	Potatoes
1965	4.3	0.6	189	46	1	48
1966	2	...	188	41	1	45
1967	3	1	179	45	1	40
1968	5	1	176	50	1	38
1969	4	1	185	54	1	35
1970	4	2	184	68	1	34
1971	3	1	179	84	1	31
1972	4	1	181	86	1	29
1973	5	2	172	101	1	29
1974	14	3	170	103	1	30
1975	16	1	180	103	...	25
1976	20	2	173	102	...	26
1977	21	2	179	99	...	26
1978	21	2	185	97	...	23
1979	17	1	196	95	...	20
1980	16	1	186	112	...	20
1981	13	1	174	118	...	20
1982	17	1	169	133	...	21
1983	23	1	181	119	...	21
1984	34	...	171	124	...	19
1985	39	...	171	129	...	19
1986	40	...	174	127	...	17
1987	58	...	163	123	...	18
1988	44	...	173	127	...	19
1989	38	...	175	132	...	19
1990	47	...	174	126	...	19
1991	53	...	181	133	...	18
1992	55	...	176	127	...	19
1993	70	...	173	106	...	18
1994	68	3	169	106	...	19
1995	66	4	175	93	...	18
1996	59	4	175	97	...	18
1997	59	4	175	95	...	18
1998	69	4	167	93	...	18
1999	52	2	183	91	...	15
2000	68	2	162	96	...	15

POLAND   **1919-1944**

	Wheat	Rye	Barley	Oats	Potatoes	Sugar Beet
1919	430	2,648	532	988	1,152	66
1920	725	2,928	787	1,667	1,644	71
1921	847	3,588	992	1,924	1,941	80
1922	1,042	4,543	1,143	2,379	2,189	109
1923	1,017	4,645	1,199	2,515	2,279	136
1924	1,073	4,417	1,218	2,585	2,331	163
1925	1,094	4,904	1,224	2,577	2,359	172
1926	1,314	5,687	1,113	1,972	2,394	185
1927	1,360	5,764	1,118	1,981	2,440	202
1928	1,290	5,341	1,156	2,038	2,505	234
1929	1,427	5,798	1,259	2,192	2,636	239
1930	1,645	5,895	1,234	2,187	2,672	185
1931	1,819	5,772	1,272	2,172	2,718	149
1932	1,726	5,646	1,207	2,220	2,715	116
1933	1,694	5,775	1,166	2,204	2,740	99
1934	1,746	5,639	1,177	2,190	2,762	112
1935	1,754	5,784	1,219	2,234	2,832	119
1936	1,742	5,831	1,187	2,255	2,893	121
1937	1,693	5,721	1,232	2,294	2,980	147
1938	1,754	5,895	1,178	2,277	3,030	150
1939	1,763[33]	5,967[33]	1,184[33]	2,320[33]	3,060[33]	164[33]
1940	1,195	4,852	931	1,770	2,781	293
1941	1,193	4,875	959	1,752	2,957	309
1942	1,088	4,345	1,071	1,838	2,651	338
1943	1,055	4,666	944	1,852	2,631	343
1944	1,050	4,418	917	1,798	2,672	329

C1   Area of Main Cereal, Potato, and Sugar Beet Crops (in thousands of hectares)

POLAND   1945–2000

	Wheat	Rye	Barley	Oats	Potatoes	Sugar Beet
1945	614	3,564	708	1,294	1,840	201
1946	700	3,083	748	1,100	1,665	170
1947	1,112	4,632	930	1,562	2,303	210
1948	1,384	5,088	863	1,756	2,478	224
1949	1,445	5,166	841	1,775	2,538	261
1950	1,480	5,080	835	1,698	2,616	287
1951	1,524	5,027	814	1,630	2,606	319
1952	1,488	4,954	827	1,691	2,619	349
1953	1,498	4,755	877	1,710	2,563	362
1954	1,559	4,799	839	1,634	2,648	381
1955	1,431	4,952	822	1,641	2,702	392
1956	1,464	4,964	777	1,595	2,714	364
1957	1,441	5,066	777	1,738	2,763	339
1958	1,474	5,213	742	1,709	2,758	358
1959	1,435	5,202	644	1,686	2,788	376
1960	1,361	5,122	717	1,641	2,876	401
1961	1,401	4,880	680	1,602	2,819	420
1962	1,393	4,700	663	1,584	2,910	430
1963	1,542	4,383	749	1,682	2,840	372
1964	1,640	4,417	745	1,574	2,845	444
1965	1,660	4,494	700	1,349	2,803	476
1966	1,679	4,331	683	1,398	2,732	435
1967	1,758	4,299	653	1,428	2,763	434
1968	1,886	4,300	634	1,395	2,747	414
1969	1,965	4,174	759	1,367	2,718	410
1970	1,985	3,413	924	1,531	2,732	409
1971	2,061	3,711	899	1,330	2,669	421
1972	2,048	3,543	1,017	1,359	2,656	438
1973	1,962	3,416	1,083	1,271	2,678	445
1974	2,002	3,137	1,230	1,182	2,684	440
1975	1,842	2,792	1,335	1,291	2,581	496
1976	1,832	2,934	1,210	1,115	2,466	555
1977	1,834	3,116	1,235	1,097	2,437	532
1978	1,852	3,030	1,203	1,030	2,360	523
1979	1,549	2,868	1,470	1,094	2,441	455
1980	1,609	3,039	1,322	997	2,344	460
1981	1,418	3,002	1,294	1,156	2,258	470
1982	1,456	3,273	1,237	1,086	2,178	493
1983	1,537	3,448	1,099	1,042	2,220	486
1984	1,706	3,545	1,055	934	2,147	473
1985	1,885	3,083	1,242	995	2,095	436
1986	2,025	2,760	1,335	924	2,009	423
1987	2,132	2,647	1,286	856	1,934	422
1988	2,179	2,325	1,250	850	1,866	412
1989	2,195	2,275	1,175	803	1,858	423
1990	2,281	2,314	1,174	747	1,835	440
1991	2,437	2,289	1,237	686	1,733	361
1992	2,405	2,034	1,198	667	1,757	376
1993	2,477	2,213	1,168	642	1,761	399
1994	2,407	2,436	1,032	618	1,697	400
1995	2,407	2,451	1,048	595	1,522	384
1996	2,480	2,415	1,129	625	1,342	453
1997	2,555	2,298	1,242	626	1,306	419
1998	2,631	2,291	1,138	561	1,295	400
1999	2,583	2,242	1,107	572	1,268	372
2000	2,635	2,130	1,096	566	1,251	333

C1 Area of Main Cereal, Potato, and Sugar Beet Crops (in thousands of hectares)

PORTUGAL[34]   1911–1964

	Wheat	Rye	Barley	Oats	Maize	Rice	Potatoes
1911	490	132	...	...	...	...	...
1912	...	107	...	...	...	...	...
1913	...	91	...	...	...	...	...
1914	376	...	...	...	238	...	11
1915	377	...	...	...	243	7.0	11
1916	376	...	...	...	234	7.3	...
1917	277	...	84	231	...	7.2	...
1918	410	298	78	225	271	15	29
1919	446	314	74	232	287	18	25
1920	444	215	60	183	297	7.3	26
1921	513	232	58	163	289	5.5	18
1922	468	239	76	253	341	5.8	21
1923	427	222	69	213	304	5.0	21
1924	420	270	78	225	266	9.8	28
1925	426	255	77	205	308	9.8	36
1926	430	239	75	202	315	11	36
1927	431	171	73	186	334	13	18
1928	446	163	72	195	351	13	19
1929	435	159	70	175	366	14	19
1930	453	165	69	174	364	14	27
1931	514	173	69	171	380	15	29
1932	591	148	78	186	376	11	31
1933	576	166	85	167	437	15	34
1934	544	141	50	163	430	24	33
1935	557	134	65	209	433	24	32
1936	468	157	78	266	428	18	32
1937	493	140	73	261	368	21	30
1938	459	134	75	250	393	19	31
1939	505	126	64	243	395	20	30
1940	502	116	61	208	394	22	30
1941	555	133	64	170	360	25	32
1942	578	152	81	214	377	26	46
1943	546	169	108	275	467	26	63
1944	605	225	114	252	498	25	61
1945	618	253	123	270	441	22	63
1946	654	287	128	292	502	26	64
1947	680	285	131	295	504	26	96
1948	698	280	130	312	523	28	87
1949	688	270	140	316	483	28	83
1950	680	265	146	292	494	27	88
1951	673	268	153	290	457	31	93
1952	708	267	157	293	488	34	90
1953	756	266	158	298	475	33	89
1954	779	255	157	293	469	36	89
1955	806	254	151	301	470	38	89
1956	786	254	154	302	487	39	89
1957	814	255	155	309	483	37	90
1958	812	253	152	303	479	35	85
1959	847	272	137	304	481	36	89
1960	738	269	120	302	468	37	92
1961	658	299	127	268	495	38	108
1962	728	309	134	288	503	37	102
1963	740	319	126	296	488	37	107
1964	685	312	110	242	496	38	109

C1 Area of Main Cereal, Potato, and Sugar Beet Crops (in thousands of hectares)

PORTUGAL[34]   **1965–2000**

	Wheat	Rye	Barley	Oats	Maize	Rice	Potatoes
1965	628	316	126	271	484	35	101
1966	523	282	111	218	473	35	101
1967	586	239	107	226	436	32	117
1968	614	239	135	224	438	33	105
1969	568	236	119	218	427	38	107
1970	602	233	105	193	418	42	112
1971	509	225	92	168	393	42	109
1972	480	226	89	168	390	43	112
1973	442	207	81	157	372	39	109
1974	462	210	94	171	360	33	112
1975	462	211	101	207	372	30	107
1976	532	219	143	215	349	22	116
1977	259	190	67	145	361	34	125
1978	355	213	86	177	367	33	119
1979	281	209	72	159	376	35	108
1980	351	206	79	175	377	35	114
1981	340	142	74	160	348	25	108
1982	353	138	77	170	278	34	114
1983	331	133	83	191	276	26	121
1984	293	130	84	194	251	30	123
1985	285	123	86	190	246	30	126
1986	292	115	87	194	252	32	119
1987	324	128	84	197	262	32	141
1988	296	121	74	167	255	33	117
1989	330	127	82	184	257	33	120
1990	178	102	53	106	261	33	122
1991	310	87	66	97	215	33	109
1992	280	75	67	75	181	21	110
1993	250	70	66	75	170	15	90
1994	235	66	58	75	177	24	90
1995	296	62	51	73	177	22	94
1996	237	61	46	71	185	28	88
1997	277	59	33	76	186	29	82
1998	149	51	26	48	193	27	86
1999	220	49	25	83	164	25	87
2000	234	45	22	85	154	24	78

ROMANIA   **1865–1903**

	Wheat	Rye	Barley	Oats	Maize		Wheat	Rye	Barley	Oats	Maize
1865	420	44	226	61	892	1890	1,510	167	518	179	1,743
1866	...	...	...	...	...	1891	1,543	122	526	185	1,693
1867	874	122	283	66	1,053	1892	1,496	133	560	226	1,822
1868	894	119	251	59	1,075	1893	1,304	143	594	252	1,839
1869	897	125	259	61	1,099	1894	1,393	160	559	263	1,768
1870	865	128	233	59	1,088	1895	1,438	218	553	271	1,846
1871	855	122	262	72	1,113	1896	1,505	243	608	282	1,939
1872	731	120	298	92	1,083	1897	1,595	226	677	288	1,855
1873	992	104	354	99	1,278	1898	1,454	193	655	306	2,120
1874	1,170	108	458	112	1,366	1899	1,662	189	639	310	2,017
1875	1,345	132	462	118	1,425	1900	1,590	164	438	255	2,035
1876	1,065	148	513	110	1,385	1901	1,637	211	504	265	2,128
						1902	1,486	173	508	321	2,182
1886	1,175	231	555	227	1,714	1903	1,606	158	531	427	2,072
1887	1,130	237	609	236	1,846						
1888	1,256	301	507	214	1,734						
1889	1,340	172	512	196	1,795						

C1 Area of Main Cereal, Potato, and Sugar Beet Crops (in thousands of hectares)

ROMANIA   1904–1956

	Wheat	Rye	Barley	Oats	Maize	Potatoes	Sugar Beet
1904	1,720	134	533	428	2,090	12	8.9
1905	1,958	161	529	373	1,976	11	12
1906	2,023	184	559	382	2,082	11	9.7
1907	1,714	147	510	352	1,929	9.8	6.6
1908	1,802	147	620	490	2,020	3.9	9.0
1909	1,689	137	549	485	2,123	8.7	11
1910	1,948	174	549	447	1,986	10	13
1911	1,931	132	507	401	2,035	12	14
1912	2,069	107	500	382	2,079	12	14
1913	1,623[35]	91[35]	563[35]	522[35]	2,147[35]	10[35]	13[35]
1914	2,112	84	568	428	2,066	11	15
1915	1,904	76	555	431	2,107	11	14
1916	1,960	81	588	432	2,046	14	12
1917	...[35]	...[35]	...[35]	...[35]	...[35]	...[35]	...[35]
1918	2,300	253	858	439	2,318	31	7.3
1919	1,728[35]	303[35]	786[35]	385[35]	2,732[35]	58[35]	3.4[35]
1920	2,023	316	1,400	966	3,295	97	5.6
1921	2,488	327	1,569	1,239	3,444	165	23
1922	2,650	267	1,727	1,334	3,404	143	22
1923	2,690	270	1,878	1,345	3,404	174	37
1924	3,172	271	1,851	1,237	3,621	189	54
1925	3,301	270	1,704	1,185	3,931	186	64
1926	3,327	296	1,552	1,078	4,059	179	82
1927	3,101	281	1,764	1,084	4,219	198	85
1928	3,206	296	1,749	1,116	4,455	206	57
1929	2,737	313	2,054	1,213	4,795	208	49
1930	3,056	392	1,975	1,087	4,427	190	46
1931	3,466	407	1,919	871	4,755	192	20
1932	2,870	348	1,787	792	4,776	191	18
1933	3,116	388	1,815	830	4,827	198	43
1934	3,079	369	1,753	827	5,005	204	37
1935	3,438	389	1,651	797	5,169	207	37
1936	3,432	421	1,611	804	5,260	216	29
1937	3,552	438	1,513	785	5,159	216	30
1938	3,818	482	1,278	651	4,997	193	48
1939	4,079[36]	488[36]	1,096[36]	589[36]	4,932[36]	207[36]	53[36]
1940	2,078	92	588	433	3,567	110	37
1941	2,283	88	522	438	3,251	112	55
1942	1,485	58	588	502	3,099	154	37
1943	2,148	84	587	527	3,012	172	60
1944	2,819[36]	174[36]	610[36]	640[36]	3,225[36]	221[36]	53[36]
1945	1,890[36]	107[36]	596[36]	627[36]	2,659[36]	191[36]	37[36]
1946	2,739	140	618	638	3,357	206	...
1947	1,660[37]	87[37]	410[37]	510[37]	4,308[37]	230[37]	56[37]
1948	2,545	113	479	566	3,673	172	67
1949	...	...	...	...	...	180[37]	64[37]
1950	2,785	204	534	520	2,853	229	72
1951	2,807	212	510	467	2,871	243	90
1952	2,776	207	502	473	2,960	243	100
1953	2,758	216	518	484	2,887	243	112
1954	2,457	195	438	435	3,302	250	107
1955	2,948	202	390	385	3,265	258	145
1956	2,894	172	300	340	3,571	256	139

C1   Area of Main Cereal, Potato, and Sugar Beet Crops (in thousands of hectares)

ROMANIA   **1957–2000**

	Wheat	Rye	Barley	Oats	Maize	Potatoes	Sugar Beet
1957	2,968	155	303	352	3,722	265	131
1958	2,973	140	292	311	3,645	271	141
1959	2,988	119	280	300	3,555	276	201
1960	2,837	98	266	270	3,572	292	200
1961	2,969	90	284	244	3,428	293	172
1962	3,043	77	251	174	3,107	299	155
1963	2,874	80	224	130	3,379	319	179
1964	2,959	91	196	89	3,319	306	190
1965	2,983	102	233	116	3,306	298	190
1966	3,035	91	246	138	3,288	306	194
1967	2,913	62	257	127	3,221	315	176
1968	2,817	44	292	132	3,344	316	185
1969	2,759	42	307	131	3,293	305	188
1970	2,321	45	288	131	3,084	286	170
1971	2,501	48	330	128	3,131	290	178
1972	2,523	42	327	121	3,197	296	197
1973	2,359	34	315	105	2,957	284	235
1974	2,396	33	403	85	2,963	295	219
1975	2,351	35	442	70	3,305	289	247
1976	2,389	40	410	45	3,378	301	235
1977	2,269	40	595	54	3,318	306	255
1978	2,284	40	722	48	3,179	305	249
1979	2,105	39	773	60	3,311	294	259
1980	2,244	35	809	51	3,288	286	238
1981	2,111	30	917	62	3,327	299	282
1982	2,155	36	943	88	3,055	271	269
1983	2,227	35	741	70	2,935	318	256
1984	2,360	30	672	67	3,091	312	280
1985	2,366	30	680	72	3,090	321	276
1986	2,545	35	575	80	2,976	348	270
1987	2,400	40	560	70	2,894	343	266
1988	2,500	37	660	75	3,200	330	280
1989	2,319	40	768	106	2,738	325	291
1990	2,230	40	749	144	2,470	335	300
1991	2,154	63	1018	210	2,575	235	202
1992	1,461	15	628	304	3,336	219	180
1993	2,282	26	637	365	3,066	249	97
1994	2,412	29	785	334	2,983	249	130
1995	2,481	21	582	239	3,109	244	133
1996	1,782	16	515	234	3,277	257	136
1997	2,409	16	627	219	3,038	255	129
1998	2,019	13	517	228	3,129	261	118
1999	1,676	11	416	248	3,013	274	65
2000	1,940	14	412	232	706	283	45

C1   Area of Main Cereal, Potato, and Sugar Beet Crops

RUSSIA/U.S.S.R. (in million hectares)[38]   **1872–1940**

	Wheat	Rye	Barley	Oats	Maize	Potatoes	Sugar Beet
1872	11.6	26.9	6.3	13.3	...	1.2	...
1881	11.7	26.1	5.0	14.1	...	1.5	...
1892	13.2	27.4	6.3	13.8	0.9	2.2	0.29
1893	13.2	25.3	6.4	13.4	0.9	2.3	0.33
1894	13.3[38]	25.6[38]	6.4[38]	13.3[38]	0.8[38]	2.3[38]	...[38]
	13.8	27.3	6.8	14.3	0.8	3.0	0.34
1895	13.4	27.1	6.8	14.8	0.8	3.1	0.35
1896	14.6	27.9	7.2	15.4	0.9	3.2	0.35
1897	14.9	27.3	7.4	15.7	0.9	3.3	0.40
1898	15.1	27.2	7.5	15.5	1.0	3.4	0.44
1899	15.9	27.6	7.5	15.6	1.0	3.5	0.48
1900	16.7	28.6	7.6	16.2	1.1	3.6	0.53
1901	17.5	28.7	7.8	16.5	1.1	3.8	0.54
1902	17.8	28.7	7.8	16.2	1.2	3.8	0.58
1903	18.2	29.0	8.3	16.4	1.1	3.9	0.54
1904	19.0	28.6	8.6	16.4	1.2	4.0	0.48
1905	20.0	28.2	8.7	16.7	1.2	3.8	0.54
1906	20.4	29.1	8.5	16.6	1.0	3.9	0.58
1907	19.0	28.7	8.8	16.5	1.2	4.0	0.62
1908	19.4	27.6	9.4	16.4	1.2	4.1	0.56
1909	19.7[38]	27.9[38]	9.3[38]	16.4[38]	1.2[38]	4.2[38]	...[38]
	29.0	29.4	11.7	19.0	2.1	4.4	0.56
1910	31.4	29.0	12.3	19.5	2.1	4.5	0.67
1911	32.4	29.9	12.5	19.6	2.0	4.6	0.79
1912	31.6	30.0	12.5	19.0	2.1	4.7	0.76
1913	33.5[38]	30.7[38]	13.6[38]	19.7[38]	2.1[38]	4.9[38]	0.72[38]
	31.6	25.8	10.8	16.9	1.3	3.1	0.65
1919	...	...	...	...	...	...	0.29
1920	19.2	19.1	6.7	11.3	1.2	2.5	0.16
1921	15.5	19.4	6.4	9.8	1.3	1.4	0.12
1922	10.5	21.5	3.8	7.3	2.2	2.5	0.18
1923	13.2	25.3	6.3	11.7	1.7	3.8	0.26
1924	21.3	27.8	7.3	12.8	2.4	4.7	0.38
1925	24.2	28.4	6.4	12.7	3.4	5.0	0.53
1926	28.7	29.2	7.4	15.2	3.0	5.2	0.54
1927	30.7	28.2	7.1	17.4	2.9	5.5	0.66
1928	27.7	24.6	6.9	17.2	4.4	5.7	0.77
1929	29.7	24.9	8.1	18.9	3.5	5.7	0.77
1930	33.8	28.9	7.4	17.9	3.7	5.7	1.04
1931	36.9	27.6	6.9	17.5	4.0	6.2	1.39
1932	34.5	26.2	6.8	15.4	3.7	6.1	1.54
1933	32.2	25.4	7.3	16.7	4.0	5.6	1.21
1934	35.2	24.0	8.5	18.0	3.7	6.1	1.18
1935	37.1	23.5	9.1	18.3	3.2	7.4	1.23
1936	39.0	21.9	9.2	18.1	3.1	7.6	1.26
1937	41.4	23.1	9.2	17.6	2.8	6.9	1.19
1938	41.5	21.6	9.2	17.9	2.1	7.4	1.18
1939	40.9[38]	17.8[38]	9.3[38]	18.4[38]	2.5[38]	...[38]	1.19[38]
1940	40.3	23.3	10.5	20.2	3.7	7.7	1.23

C1 Area of Main Cereal, Potato, and Sugar Beet Crops

RUSSIA/U.S.S.R. (in million hectares)   **1945-2000**

	Wheat	Rye	Barley	Oats	Maize	Potatoes	Sugar Beet
1945	24.9	20.5	9.6	14.4	4.2	8.3	0.83
1950	23.7	23.7	8.2	16.2	4.8	8.6	1.31
1953	48.3	20.3	9.2	15.3	3.5	8.3	1.57
1954	49.3	20.5	10.3	15.9	4.3	8.7	1.60
1955	60.5	19.1	9.3	14.8	6.2	9.1	1.76
1956	62.0	18.5	11.9	15.1	9.3	9.2	2.01
1957	69.1	18.1	9.2	14.0	5.8	9.8	2.11
1958	66.6	18.0	8.6	14.8	4.4	9.5	2.50
1959	63.0	17.1	8.3	14.3	3.5	9.5	2.75
1960	60.4	16.2	11.0	12.8	5.1	9.1	3.04
1961	63.0	16.8	11.7	11.5	7.2	8.9	3.12
1962	67.4	16.9	14.3	6.9	7.0	8.7	3.17
1963	64.6	15.0	18.4	5.7	7.0	8.5	3.75
1964	67.9	16.8	20.3	5.7	5.1	8.5	4.11
1965	70.2	16.0	18.3	6.6	3.2	8.6	3.88
1966	70.0	13.6	19.4	7.2	3.2	8.4	3.80
1967	67.0	12.4	19.1	8.7	3.5	8.3	3.80
1968	67.2	12.3	19.4	9.0	3.4	8.3	3.56
1969	66.4	9.2	22.5	9.3	4.2	8.1	3.38
1970	65.2	10.0	21.3	9.3	3.4	8.1	3.37
1971	64.0	9.5	21.6	9.6	3.3	7.9	3.32
1972	58.5	8.2	27.3	11.4	4.0	8.0	3.49
1973	63.2	7.0	29.4	11.9	4.0	8.0	3.55
1974	59.7	9.8	31.1	11.6	4.0	8.0	3.61
1975	62.0	8.0	32.5	12.1	2.7	7.9	3.67
1976	59.5	9.0	34.3	11.3	3.3	7.1	3.75
1977	62.1	6.7	34.5	13.0	3.4	7.1	3.76
1978	62.9	7.7	32.7	12.1	2.5	7.0	3.76
1979	57.7	6.5	37.0	12.2	2.7	7.0	3.73
1980	61.5	8.6	31.6	11.8	3.0	6.9	3.71
1981	59.2	7.6	31.8	12.5	3.5	6.9	3.63
1982	57.3	9.8	29.7	11.5	4.2	6.9	3.53
1983	50.8	10.3	31.7	12.4	3.9	6.9	3.49
1984	51.1	9.4	30.4	12.8	3.9	6.8	3.47
1985	50.3	9.4	29.0	12.6	4.5	6.4	3.41
1986	48.7	8.7	30.0	13.2	4.2	6.4	3.40
1987	46.7	9.7	30.6	11.8	4.6	6.2	3.40
1988	48.1	10.1	29.7	11.0	4.4	6.1	3.37
1989	47.7	10.7	27.6	10.7	4.1	6.0	3.35
1990	48.2	10.4	26.1	10.7	4.4	5.8	3.27
1991	45.9	8.5	28.7	10.7	3.9	6.0	3.16
1992[52]	24.6	7.5	14.5	8.5	0.8	3.4	1.44
1993	22.1	5.9	15.4	8.4	0.8	3.3	1.30
1994	22.1	3.9	16.4	8.3	0.5	3.3	1.1
1995	21.6	3.2	14.7	7.9	0.6	3.3	1.1
1996	22.5	4.1	11.8	6.6	0.6	3.4	1.1
1997	24.0	3.9	11.8	5.8	0.8	3.3	0.7
1998	19.9	3.2	7.1	4.0	0.5	3.2	0.7
1999	19.7	3.2	7.4	3.9	0.5	3.2	0.8
2000	19.7	3.4	6.9	4.0	0.7	3.2	0.7

C1 Area of Main Cereal, Potato, and Sugar Beet Crops (in thousands of hectares)
ESTONIA

1914–1940/1992–2000

	Wheat	Rye	Barley	Oats	Potatoes
1918		previously included in Russia			
1919	13	132	106	...	56
1920	15	152	120	...	
1921	13	155	114	146	66
1922	21	159	134	161	76
1923	23	164	126	153	72
1924	18	159	124	166	67
1925	21	155	115	150	69
1926	24	136	121	146	69
1927	27	148	119	146	71
1928	28	144	106	130	65
1929	33	133	114	150	62
1930	37	148	112	149	68
1931	40	144	113	148	68
1932	52	147	108	144	67
1933	63	151	104	139	68
1934	65	147	104	138	72
1935	63	145	105	139	74
1936	66	137	101	138	74
1937	68	149	89	145	76
1938	70	148	88	149	78
1939	75	151	84	144	89
1940–1991		included in Russia			
1992	47	62	288	46	45
1993	33	46	250	40	47
1994	34	22	219	36	40
1995	39	32	186	38	37
1996	46	31	148	49	36
1997	51	34	166	54	35
1998	67	39	167	60	33
1999	66	24	154	61	31
2000	69	29	165	53	31

LATVIA

1918–1940/1992–2000

	Wheat	Rye	Barley	Oats	Potatoes	Sugar Beet
1918			previously included in Russia			
1919	...	...	...	...	...	...
1920	16	197	124	216	49	...
1921	19	227	146	252	59	...
1922	28	236	157	273	69	...
1923	43	267	178	309	79	...
1924	43	266	179	334	75	...
1925	48	267	177	330	79	...
1926	49	251	190	321	82	...
1927	59	256	185	305	86	...
1928	66	258	146	239	78	...
1929	59	238	183	303	80	...
1930	72	267	177	320	94	...
1931	87	231	183	322	100	4
1932	103	240	185	325	102	9
1933	125	258	184	307	104	13
1934	142	268	180	300	108	14
1935	140	271	193	333	124	14
1936	129	258	189	339	120	12
1937	137	288	181	335	127	14
1938	141	287	178	348	138	14
1939	153	298	180	378	145	13
1940–1991			included in Russia			
1992	123	131	347	69	97	25
1993	153	188	270	49	98	12
1994	95	63	267	54	80	12
1995	110	40	203	46	75	10
1996	149	56	178	54	79	10
1997	152	63	195	59	70	11
1998	151	58	173	60	59	16
1999	146	47	147	47	50	15
2000	158	55	135	46	51	13

C1 Area of Main Cereal, Potato, and Sugar Beet Crops (in thousands of hectares)

LITHUANIA 1920–1940/1992–2000

	Wheat	Rye	Barley	Oats	Potatoes	Sugar Beet
1920			previously included in Russia			
1921	73	505	168	310	132	...
1922	79[39]	554[39]	169[39]	311[39]	132[39]	...
1923	82	583	175	331	143	...
1924	85	538	196	325	176	...
1925	112	542	205	345	163	...
1926	122	449	215	382	147	...
1927	120	502	197	310	139	...
1928	159	470	169	288	122	...
1929	198	451	214	350	132	...
1930	213	506	182	368	153	1
1931	194	509	197	368	169	3
1932	206	483	201	373	173	5
1933	202	490	207	343	179	4
1934	208	496	204	329	183	4
1935	217	513	206	340	176	7
1936	199	493	214	357	182	8
1937	211	509	214	349	184	8
1938	203	528	217	355	186	8
1939	202	497	209	348	177	9
1940–1991			included in Russia			
1992	284	164	612	62	114	33
1993	384	230	541	30	115	33
1994	270	204	620	55	117	27
1995	261	135	545	47	125	24
1996	348	152	474	52	125	31
1997	376	158	503	56	121	35
1998	360	174	463	50	136	30
1999	334	135	421	51	121	31
2000	370	133	353	44	109	28

C1   Area of Main Cereal, Potato, and Sugar Beet Crops (in thousands of hectares)

SPAIN[40]   1890–1945

	Wheat	Rye	Barley	Oats	Maize	Rice	Potatoes	Sugar Beet
1890	...	...	...	...	...	...	...	...
1891	2,654	633	979	227	320	...	...	...
1892	3,368	667	1,058	281	209	...	...	...
1893	3,219	751	1,072	275	291	...	...	...
1894	3,340	578	1,083	277	348	...	...	...
1895	3,179	667	1,033	240	327	...	...	...
1896	3,187	715	983	258	388	...	...	...
1897	3,858	778	1,258	242	440	...	...	...
1898	3,862	714	1,514	377	409	...	...	...
1899	3,663	748	1,402	377	470	...	...	...
1900	3,869	731	1,389	379	476	...	...	...
1901	3,712	797	1,336	382	468	...	...	...
1902	3,693	784	1,457	450	462	...	243	21
1903	3,635	781	1,433	452	373	...	...	...
1904	3,652	765	1,382	447	434	...	...	...
1905	3,593	750	1,350	453	465	...	...	...
1906	3,763	887	1,465	482	446	...	...	...
1907	3,698	902	1,441	480	449	...	241	...
1908	3,757	909	1,403	490	459	...	254	...
1909	3,783	833	1,408	497	465	37	...	24
1910	3,809	821	1,349	508	454	38	323	28
1911	3,928	804	1,444	513	463	38	...	33
1912	3,895	787	1,335	517	465	38	256	43
1913	3,903	776	1,566	547	447	39	...	59
1914	3,918	763	1,378	528	460	39	279	35
1915	4,062	737	1,532	568	466	40	297	40
1916	4,374	747	1,573	566	467	41	301	54
1917	4,185	730	1,621	566	476	43	339	59
1918	4,139	736	1,704	610	473	45	295	66
1919	4,200	732	1,722	646	477	45	326	54
1920	4,150	728	1,748	643	473	48	340	71
1921	4,203	723	1,754	638	477	46	319	54
1922	4,172	711	1,652	613	469	46	328	50
1923	4,245	729	1,837	645	472	46	306	62
1924	4,200	737	1,758	662	470	47	315	179
1925	4,339	747	1,786	728	474	49	...	114
1926	4,361	755	1,810	754	407	50	300	72
1927	4,381	736	1,802	773	462	49	309	62
1928	4,278	621	1,801	792	388	49	336	59
1929	4,299	615	1,817	744	407	48	369	61
1930	4,506	628	1,838	785	447	49	370	80
1931	4,551	613	1,879	804	426	46	415	112
1932	4,552	614	1,957	779	446	50	418	85
1933	4,520	591	1,875	766	432	47	425	83
1934	4,608	577	1,923	782	434	46	413	92
1935	4,554	572	1,841	748	440	47	419	71
1939	3,496	527	1,368	576	446	43	412	36
1940	3,535	551	1,562	646	452	54	430	64
1941	3,762	602	1,652	712	380	47	449	67
1942	3,776	609	1,669	774	354	47	466[41]	48
1943	3,736	630	1,698	792	326	48	400[41]	60
1944	3,710	630	1,669	728	316	49	370	62
1945	3,766	599	1,594	703	308	48	370	58

C1 Area of Main Cereal, Potato, and Sugar Beet Crops (in thousands of hectares)

SPAIN[40]

1946–2000

	Wheat	Rye	Barley	Oats	Maize	Rice	Potatoes	Sugar Beet
1946	3,950	598	1,569	674	325	50	362	71
1947	4,017	607	1,544	640	326	51	359	65
1948	4,041	618	1,504	629	332	52	358	93
1949	4,086	613	1,554	626	332	54	359	93
1950	4,080	617	1,546	624	330	58	363	87
1951	4,214	635	1,567	642	333	63	377	110
1952	4,262	626	1,615	591	345	65	335	179
1953	4,256	598	1,604	602	370	68	342	118
1954	4,260	613	1,604	608	369	71	355	91
1955	4,288	604	1,539	612	357	67	354	98
1956	4,305	607	1,575	617	369	66	364	112
1957	4,378	570	1,533	586	376	67	372	102
1958	4,365	554	1,513	579	389	65	373	133
1959	4,368	540	1,452	572	405	67	400	144
1960	4,234	509	1,428	556	428	66	395	145
1961	3,880	485	1,450	583	447	62	416	158
1962	4,252	486	1,449	549	430	63	409	166
1963	4,239	438	1,447	527	487	63	411	116
1964	4,137[42]	406[42]	1,381[42]	509[42]	514[42]	64[42]	365[42]	144[42]
1965	4,254	393	1,374	502	478	59	368	146
1966	4,185	384	1,338	469	482	59	375	157
1967	4,257	398	1,499	486	478	60	376	171
1968	3,958	366	1,923	508	523	60	382	174
1969	3,770	331	2,110	493	494	65	377	182
1970	3,754	313	2,220	467	530	64	398	217
1971	3,655	294	2,371	463	543	61	394	199
1972	3,587	278	2,519	467	534	59	401	207
1973	3,151	268	2,773	472	523	61	409	190
1974	3,163	249	3,027	475	501	61	407	142
1975	2,661	228	3,262	457	485	62	385	200
1976	2,772	234	3,240	455	432	64	391	293
1977	2,715	236	3,348	406	442	68	403	253
1978	2,752	228	3,519	442	443	68	371	235
1979	2,551	220	3,477	436	467	69	355	166
1980	2,698	217	3,575	458	454	68	335	183
1981	2,635	220	3,508	464	428	69	343	218
1982	2,662	212	3,615	442	418	68	338	259
1983	2,603	217	3,735	454	354	41	340	249
1984	2,306	231	4,023	479	440	73	348	220
1985	2,043	211	4,245	459	526	74	331	180
1986	2,114	221	4,340	393	524	78	297	196
1987	2,221	222	4,401	353	542	76	298	179
1988	2,339	221	4,257	345	556	80	282	157
1989	2,317	223	4,312	359	528	59	278	191
1990	2,006	207	4,359	349	477	89	270	170
1991	2,223	187	4,413	325	485	94	266	165
1992	2,243	180	4,112	314	393	86	257	163
1993	2,030	173	3,485	328	774	50	212	181
1994	1,969	154	3,800	348	342	67	201	183
1995	2,126	165	3,570	367	358	55	206	172
1996	2,012	167	4,390	391	440	105	182	157
1997	2,079	143	4,860	400	486	114	150	158
1998	1,913	124	4,100	413	459	113	136	149
1999	2,422	122	3,970	410	398	112	136	135
2000	2,370	111	4,249	427	425	115	123	131

C1 Area of Main Cereal, Potato, and Sugar Beet Crops (in thousands of hectares)

SWEDEN 1865–1921

	Wheat	Rye	Barley	Oats	Mixed Corn	Potatoes	Sugar Beet[43]
1865	48	363	214	428	71	128	7
1866	48	345	229	485	80	133	10
1867	48	338	228	504	77	130	8
1868	46	344	226	512	78	134	9
1869	48	352	226	509	76	137	9
1870	51	356	229	523	75	142	11
1871	57	356	229	528	76	143	12
1872	60	357	231	543	78	144	12
1873	63	355	231	557	77	148	11
1874	66	353	236	561	80	150	11
1875	67	353	239	582	79	151	12
1876	66	358	233	592	80	151	11
1877	68	359	232	610	82	154	11
1878	67	361	228	619	80	153	11
1879	68	371	232	630	83	154	12
1880	71	378	233	659	83	154	12
1881	70	380	235	666	84	155	12
1882	70	385	237	676	85	155	13
1883	71	384	233	683	85	155	13
1884	72	385	227	699	91	157	15
1885	73	375	220	734	98	153	17
1886	73	376	220	751	100	161	19
1887	73	377	224	775	101	156	20
1888	74	380	222	787	101	154	21
1889	76	382	220	797	103	155	23
1890	71	391	221	801	105	156	25
1891	71	396	221	806	108	156	27
1892	71	400	223	814	112	159	28
1893	71	403	219	818	116	158	32[43]
1894	71	402	219	818	117	158	22
1895	71	404	220	827	120	159	19
1896	71	407	218	819	122	158	28
1897	72	410	219	823	123	158	23
1898	74	411	221	823	125	158	23
1899	76	410	221	820	126	158	26
1900	78	411	217	825	130	155	29
1901	79	410	218	826	133	155	28
1902	82	412	215	824	135	155	24
1903	81	410	214	824	136	155	27
1904	81	411	213	828	139	154	24
1905	83	410	208	822	141	154	27
1906	85	411	204	813	149	152	31
1907	88	407	197	811	152	151	31
1908	91	404	195	809	155	153	32
1909	96	403	185	797	158	152	33
1910	97	402	182	792	162	152	35
1911	101	400	181[44]	790[44]	163[44]	153	29
1912	...	...	...	...	...	...	...
1913	117	371	182	789	172	152	29
1914	117	392	170	780	177	152	32
1915	127	388	170	795	186	152	32
1916	128	369	167	777	197	148	37
1917	133	331	176	782	251	158	31
1918	153	384	185	733	265	164	30
1919	141	372	168	712	262	163	36
1920	145	370	161	709	263	147	44
1921	145	370	160	709	262	147	49

C1   Area of Main Cereal, Potato, and Sugar Beet Crops (in thousands of hectares)

SWEDEN   **1922–1974**

	Wheat	Rye	Barley	Oats	Mixed Corn	Potatoes	Sugar Beet[43]
1922	144	353	173	728	270	162	17
1923	146	352	155	719	261	159	43
1924	131	264	173	773	280	158	41
1925	147	352	167	730	265	159	40
1926	155	339	179	739	271	160	5
1927	227	276	124	697	228	140	40
1928	227	276	114	693	226	140	43
1929	232	256	125	708	232	141	28
1930	262	241	132	660	268	136	37
1931	276	207	126	643	269	132	35
1932	278	212	110	673	234	138	40
1933	303	226	105	651	236	132	51
1934	290	236	100	660	239	132	51
1935	273	228	105	671	251	129	51
1936	281	215	104	671	258	133	51
1937	299	197	95	657	252	131	55
1938	308	189	101	661	253	133	51
1939	337	175	104	660	252	132	51
1940	309	171	107	635	284	135	54
1941	286	207	99	629	291	137	54
1942	279	249	112	597	278	142	53
1943	268	220	113	575	277	147	50
1944	274	201	96	551	277	138	55
1945	291	168	93	543	277	145	55
1946	303	157	90	531	277	143	55
1947	293	115	100	529	288	142	48
1948	316	160	88	489	281	148	47
1949	307	135	86	502	309	135	49
1950	339	127	94	502	318	130	54
1951	324	97	113	496	319	121	54
1952	328	123	152	496	321	127	54
1953	387	132	189	487	302	127	51
1954	432	149	166	474	299	120	60
1955	353	94	213	509	301	122	53
1956	397	123	240	535	291	122	50
1957	333	115	263	515	272	119	54
1958	282	92	293	532	255	114	51
1959	315[45]	97[45]	317[45]	536[45]	247[45]	119[45]	51[45]
	313	96	315	526	243	108	
1960	337	103	321	548	227	114	50
1961	273	74	356	558	221	99	49
1962	314	75	369	514	199	92	46
1963	244	40	482	517	191	94	41
1964	270	43	470	510	177	81	44
1965	288	63	498	478	156	73	43
1966	196	40	608	493	125	66	40
1967	256	62	571	488	103	67	39
1968	250	70	600	519	95	69	42
1969	267	73	639	513	84	65	40
1970	265	80	610	509	76	54	40
1971	246	83	604	526	69	50	40
1972	270	108	624	539	71	47	42
1973	292	96	642	509	77	46	42
1974	340	10	638	468	77	48	47

C1 Area of Main Cereal, Potato, and Sugar Beet Crops (in thousands of hectares)

SWEDEN 1975–2000

	Wheat	Rye	Barley	Oats	Mixed Corn	Potatoes	Sugar
1975	303	98	649	497	71	43	52
1976	397	124	595	483	68	45	53
1977	376	112	641	491	63	47	54
1978	297	83	722	486	62	44	53
1979	251	60	754	489	59	41	52
1980	297	69	694	484	60	40	52
1981	231	52	729	508	64	40	52
1982	293	57	677	509	66	40	54
1983	347	65	660	432	66	40	53
1984	326	65	687	458	69	39	53
1985	287	48	711	475	56	38	52
1986	321	40	681	487	50	37	52
1987	336	42	581	425	46	38	51
1988	259	35	567	447	38	39	51
1989	223	68	476	411	36	39	50
1990	335	71	461	358	37	39	50
1991	253	42	468	346	40	35	39
1992	264	33	432	342	47	38	48
1993	246	45	389	303	60	40	51
1994	252	39	449	341	54	33	53
1995	261	40	453	273	51	35	58
1996	335	34	469	284	43	37	59
1997	344	29	483	315	50	36	60
1998	398	35	445	311	62	34	60
1999	275	25	482	306	64	32	60
2000	401	35	409	291	58	33	55

SWITZERLAND 1908–1942

	Wheat[1]	Rye	Barley	Oats	Potatoes	Sugar Beet
1908	43	23	...	...	...	...
1909	42	24	5	33	...	...
1910	42	25	5	33	...	...
1911	42	24	5	33	47	0.5
1912	42[10] 66	25	5.0	33	47	—
1913	66	24	5.2	33	47	0.8
1914	64	25	6.0	34	47	0.8
1915	70	27	6.5	37	49	0.8
1916	83	18	6.8	26	55	0.5
1917	57	29	7.7	29	57	0.4
1918	87	29	9.0	35	60	0.4
1919	76	22	7.5	23	55	0.3
1920	68	20	7.2	23	50	0.7
1921	67	23	6.6	21	46	1.2
1922	61	22	6.5	21	45	1.2
1923	62	22	6.4	21	45	1.2
1924	62	22	6.3	20	45	1.3
1925	62	22	6.2	20	48	1.4
1926	65	20	6.5	20	48	1.5
1927	65	20	7	20	48	1.7
1928	65	20	7	20	48	1.6
1929	65	19	7.3	20	45	1.1
1930	67	20	7.2	20	49	1.2
1931	67	19	7.1	18	46	1.3
1932	68	19	7.0	17	47	1.4
1933	74	17	3.6	10	45	1.5
1934	79	16	4.2	10	46	1.5
1935	85	16	4.2	10	46	1.5
1936	88	16	4.3	11	47	1.7
1937	85	15	4.4	11	47	2.4
1938	86	15	5.0	11	47	2.9
1939	94	15	7.9	13	47	3.2
1940	88	10	11	21	50	3.1
1941	100	14	18	32	60	3.4
1942	108	14	22	34	71	3.9

C1 Area of Main Cereal, Potato, and Sugar Beet Crops (in thousands of hectares)

SWITZERLAND   1943-2000

	Wheat[1]	Rye	Barley	Oats	Potatoes	Sugar Beet
1943	119	16	26	38	83	4.8
1944	117	14	29	41	85	5.7
1945	112	13	32	44	84	5.6
1946	110	15	30	40	79	5.6
1947	105	13	27	35	67	5.5
1948	98	12	25	33	62	5.4
1949	95	12	24	31	53	5.5
1950	98	16	19	22	56	6.1
1951	98	16	20	24	55	5.9
1952	101	15	24	25	57	5.9
1953	95	15	25	26	57	5.8
1954	104	12	21	22	54	5.8
1955	109	11	22	21	51	5.5
1956	89	13	31	25	56	5.9
1957	105	11	25	19	52	5.9
1958	106	12	24	16	50	5.9
1959	112	13	25	16	50	5.3
1960	110	14	26	14	50	5.2
1961	116	11	29	15	48	5.1
1962	109	16	35	14	47	4.9
1963	108	16	32	12	45	6.9
1964	106	18	30	11	43	7.6
1965	107	15	31	10	37	8.4
1966	108	13	32	10	39	8
1967	100	15	31	9	38	9
1968	108	15	30	8	37	9
1969	107	11	37	10	33	9
1970	104	13	41	8	30	9
1971	97	13	39	10	28	9
1972	97	13	42	9	27	10
1973	91	11	44	10	25	10
1974	88	10	46	11	24	11
1975	90	6	45	13	25	11
1976	91	9	42	13	25	11
1977	89	9	44	11	24	12
1978	89	9	46	11	24	13
1979	86	9	48	10	24	14
1980	90	8	46	11	25	13
1981	87	7	50	12	25	14
1982	88	5	48	14	24	15
1983	91	4	51	11	24	15
1984	95	5	52	10	23	15
1985	97	4	51	10	20	14
1986	96	4	55	7	20	14
1987	95	4	51	8	20	15
1988	93	4	54	9	19	15
1989	99	4	55	11	20	14
1990	103	4	61	11	20	14
1991	98	5	59	11	19	14
1992	97	5	60	10	19	14
1993	97	7	62	11	19	14
1994	103	6	64	10	17	14
1995	102	7	61	8	17	14
1996	101	7	57	8	17	17
1997	98	4	60	8	15	19
1998	97	3	62	7	14	17
1999	94	3	65	6	14	17
2000	96	4	65	5	14	18

C1 Area of Main Cereal, Potato, and Sugar Beet Crops (in thousands of hectares)

UK: GREAT BRITAIN   1867–1919

	Wheat	Barley	Oats	Other Corn[46]	Potatoes
1867	1,363	914	1,113	367	199
1868	1,478	870	1,116	353	219
1869	1,492	911	1,126	419	237
1870	1,417	960	1,118	369	238
1871	1,446	966	1,099	405	254
1872	1,456	937	1,095	386	228
1873	1,412	945	1,083	387	208
1874	1,469	926	1,051	371	210
1875	1,352	1,016	1,078	378	212
1876	1,212	1,025	1,132	351	204
1877	1,282	979	1,115	352	207
1878	1,302	1,000	1,092	316	206
1879	1,170	1,079	1,075	312	219
1880	1,177	998	1,132	284	223
1881	1,136	988	1,174	283	234
1882	1,216	913	1,147	300	219
1883	1,057	928	1,204	299	220
1884	1,083	878	1,180	293	229
1885	1,003	913	1,190	290	222
1886	925	907	1,247	263	224
1887	938	844	1,250	265	227
1888	1,038	844	1,166	265	239
1889	991	859	1,169	249	234
1890	966	854	1,175	256	214
1891	934	855	1,173	245	216
1892	898	824	1,213	224	212
1893	768	840	1,284	223	214
1894	780	848	1,316	234	204
1895	573	877	1,334	211	219
1896	686	852	1,253	212	228
1897	764	824	1,229	201	204
1898	851	771	1,181	193	212
1899	810	802	1,198	188	222
1900	747	805	1,225	192	227
1901	688	798	1,212	188	234
1902	698	773	1,237	199	232
1903	640	752	1,271	195	228
1904	556	745	1,316	196	231
1905	727	694	1,235	199	246
1906	711	709	1,231	206	229
1907	658	693	1,264	217	222
1908	658	675	1,258	207	227
1909	738	673	1,207	224	233
1910	732	700	1,223	197	219
1911	771	647	1,219	213	231
1912	779	667	1,223	222[47]	248
1913	711	711	1,179	282	239
1914	756	688	1,153	214	248
1915	909	559	1,243	184	246
1916	799	608	1,244	168	226
1917	801	655[48]	1,335[48]	166[48]	265
1918	1,067	669	1,628	268	325
1919	931	681	1,487	288	255

C1 Area of Main Cereal, Potato, and Sugar Beet Crops (in thousands of hectares)

UK: GREAT BRITAIN

	Wheat	Barley	Oats	Other Corn[46]	Potatoes	Sugar Beet
1920	781	745	1,337	276	286	…
1921	826	650	1,279	249	288	…
1922	822	616	1,276	275	291	1.2
1923	728	601	1,192	234	244	3.2
1924	645	593	1,211	250	239	3.2
1925	626	595	1,131	205	257	6.9
1926	666	514	1,135	205	259	9.3
1927	689	472	1,072	192	267	23
1928	588	524	1,069	179	256	52
1929	559	494	1,110	191	269	94
1930	567	456	1,068	200	222	72
1931	505	452	1,006	184	233	95
1932	542	416	991	172	264	104
1933	704	328	951	171	272	148
1934	752	387	898	168	254	163
1935	758	351	909	166	240	152
1936	728	361	910	165	239	144
1937	741	366	826	134	239	127
1938	778	398	849	156	247	136
1939	713	409	864	154	238	140
1940	727	535	1,215	210	281	133
1941	909	590	1,417	401	391	142
1942	1,013	612	1,480	426	452	172
1943	1,397	717	1,300	443	483	169
1944	1,301	792	1,301	440	493	174
1945	919	891	1,337	405	488	169
1946	834	892	1,276	400	498	176
1947	875	831	1,185	369	465	160
1948	921	845	1,192	432	541	167
1949	794	831	1,165	470	454	170
1950	1,002	718	1,117	531[46]	427	174
				365		
1951	862	771	1,028	358	367	172
1952	821	921	1,044	359	346	165
1953	896	898	1,033	351	342	168
1954	994	833	939	259	330	177
1955	788	927	943	194	306	172
1956	927	938	934	178	322	172
1957	853	1,056	853	145	287	174
1958	892	1,108	809	121	292	178
1959	780	1,227	742	99	291	176
1960	849	1,341	717	88	300	177
1961	737	1,504	627	66	254	173
1962	911	1,561	549	57	267	172
1963	779	1,847	465	48	278	171
1964	892	1,970	405	40	286	179
1965	1,024	2,109	371	36	275	184
1966	905	2,411	334	32	248	180
1967	932	2,377	377	38	264	185
1968	977	2,345	352	47	259	188
1969	832	2,358	359	62	231	185
1970	1,009	2,193	358	77[46]	251	188
				78		
1971	1,096	2,232	347	61	239	191

C1   Area of Main Cereal, Potato, and Sugar Beet Crops (in thousands of hectares)

UK GREAT BRITAIN

1972–2000

	Wheat	Barley	Oats	Maize	Other Corn[46]	Potatoes	Sugar Beet
1972	1,126	2,237	303	...	68	222	190
1973	1,145	2,227	265	...	64	209	194
1974	1,232	2,165	244	...	61	203	195
1975	1,033	2,295	224	...	66[46]	193	195
1976	1,231	2,132	228	29	34	208	206
1977	1,077	2,352	189	35	33	214	203
1978	1,258	2,296	175	26	24	201	210
1979	1,372	2,295	132	25	21	190	214
1980	1,440	2,278	144	22	18	190	213
1981	1,491	2,276	140	18	16	179	210
1982	1,662	2,175	126	16	15	178	204
1983	1,694	2,098	105	15	14	182	199
1984	1,936	1,933	103	16	13	184	198
1985	1,897	1,919	131	20	14	178	191
1986	1,994	1,869	95	23	13	166	205
1987	1,989	1,785	96	23	12	165	203
1988	1,881	1,835	118	24	12	168	201
1989	2,083	1,652	119	25	12	176	...
1990	2,013	1,515	107	34	12	162	...
1991	1,981	1,393	103	44	13	177	...
1992	1,759	1,297	100	51	12	180	...
1993	1,759	1,164	92	73	9	171	...
1994	1,811	1,106	109	...	...	164	195
1995	1,859	1,192	112	...	...	171	196
1996	1,976	1,267	96	...	...	177	199
1997	2,036	1,359	100	...	...	166	196
1998	2,045	1,255	98	...	...	164	189
1999	1,847	1,179	92	...	...	178	183
2000	2,086	1,128	109	...	...	166	173

SERBIA

1893–1910

	Wheat	Rye	Barley	Oats	Maize	Potatoes
1893	317	60	92	106	532	8
1894	...	...	...	...	...	...
1895	...	...	...	...	...	...
1896	...	...	...	...	...	...
1897	280	37	75	100	448	6
1898	282	45	96	95	500	...
1899	404	59	114	101	546	...
1900	295	36	75	85	463	8
1901	305	38	79	91	506	8
1902	326	40	88	100	525	10
1903	348	43	95	108	534	10
1904	366	45	99	105	541	11
1905	372	48	108	104	553	11
1906	373	49	109	106	548	12
1907	368	44	101	96	550	11
1908	379	48	104	101	566	11
1909	378	50	114	108	584	11
1910	386	51	108	108	583	11

YUGOSLAVIA

1920–1929

	Wheat	Rye	Barley	Oats	Maize	Potatoes	Sugar Beet
1920	1,441	198	375	416	1,815	204	16
1921	1,497	187	368	406	1,880	209	17
1922	1,486	197	375	391	1,911	215	19
1923	1,555	187	361	375	1,802	213	27
1924	1,717	195	364	353	1,965	218	48
1925	1,743	198	358	343	2,072	231	33
1926	1,691	202	351	352	1,995	222	35
1927	1,830	209	391	379	2,066	226	41
1928	1,895	201	382	370	2,031	222	55
1929	2,110	238	427	386	2,318	233	59

C1   Area of Main Cereal, Potato, and Sugar Beet Crops (in thousands of hectares)

YUGOSLAVIA

1930–2000

	Wheat	Rye	Barley	Oats	Maize	Potatoes	Sugar Beet
1930	2,123	247	444	408	2,398	242	52
1931	2,141	244	431	379	2,388	236	44
1932	1,951	243	407	328	2,521	237	43
1933	2,079	256	429	376	2,538	249	30
1934	2,024	248	422	371	2,656	259	26
1935	2,150	252	422	372	2,472	257	29
1936	2,211	254	425	360	2,705	262	30
1937	2,130	254	417	346	2,691	258	21
1938	2,130	254	415	362	2,753	266	29
1939	2,203	254	416	357	2,681	263	46
1940	2,097	258	405	352	[2,827][49]	273	42
1948	1,887[50]	249[50]	319[50]	348[50]	2,370[50]	197[50]	79[50]
1949	1,791	258	313	358	2,240	234	90
1950	1,787	256	325	389	2,210	241	98
1951	1,766	287	331	339	2,360	226	100
1952	1,838	295	317	334	2,290	240	76
1953	1,889	298	360	339	2,410	245	84
1954	1,854	276	331	341	2,460	256	79
1955	1,907	278	338	321	2,470	261	70
1956	1,624	252	353	373	2,570	268	70
1957	1,974	256	408	402	2,590	285	83
1958	1,994	248	390	347	2,390	277	71
1959	2,134	236	378	338	2,580	290	82
1960	2,064	213	363	334	2,570	288	79
1961	1,964	180	371	355	2,513	292	83
1962	2,134	177	351	310	2,464	301	78
1963	2,144	157	350	315	2,411	321	98
1964	2,103	157	369	306	2,431	320	89
1965	1,683	146	405	321	2,553	320	82
1966	1,833	141	394	320	2,502	333	106
1967	1,883	138	343	301	2,512	330	102
1968	2,012	132	312	285	2,462	332	79
1969	2,021	124	300	272	2,399	330	95
1970	1,833	112	280	283	2,352	346	85
1971	1,930	110	280	265	2,425	326	85
1972	1,925	104	290	256	2,383	315	79
1973	1,657	96	328	251	2,377	317	86
1974	1,842	91	330	249	2,256	321	104
1975	1,615	84	360	270	2,363	314	107
1976	1,723	76	293	232	2,374	308	107
1977	1,604	69	306	231	2,321	315	122
1978	1,712	63	273	210	2,130	298	126
1979	1,524	59	292	209	2,251	296	140
1980	1,516	55	324	194	2,202	287	128
1981	1,386	54	310	194	2,297	291	147
1982	1,558	53	284	176	2,246	282	139
1983	1,609	51	280	168	2,264	274	141
1984	1,458	47	271	153	2,331	274	145
1985	1,438	45	264	151	2,400	274	150
1986	1,346	42	267	152	2,369	283	138
1987	1,455	41	263	140	2,218	271	164
1988	1,507	40	222	135	2,280	274	130
1989	1,479	37	242	144	2,279	294	142
1990	1,485	37	240	140	2,300	290	142
1991	1,547	35	245	130	2,166	285	143
1992[53]	677	10	115	77	1,515	110	91
1993	890	9	120	70	1,513	100	53
1994	908	9	…	74	1,388	113	71
1995	863	10	…	74	1,372	115	62
1996	583	10	…	86	1,439	117	70
1997	802	8	…	73	1,366	115	56
1998	796	9	…	71	1,351	116	54
1999	619	6	…	67	1,267	106	69
2000	652	6	…	63	1,207	104	45

C1   Area of Main Cereal, Potato, and Sugar Beet Crops (in thousands of hectares)

NOTES

1.   SOURCES:- The official publications noted on p. xv; International Institute of Agriculture, *Yearbook of Agricultural Statistics*; and F.A.O., *Yearbook of Food and Agricultural Statistics*. Belgian data for 1919–21 and for 1940 were taken from a pamphlet, *Statistiques Agricoles 1900–1961*, kindly sent to me by the Belgian National Institute of Statistics. Netherlands data for oats in 1852 and 1865 and for potatoes in 1852 were supplied by the Dutch Central Office of Statistics. Polish data for 1951 and 1952 were supplied by the Polish Central Statistical Office.

2.   Most statistics are of areas sown, or, to be more precise, of areas under crops on a particular date during the summer. Some series may be of areas harvested, and where this is known it is indicated in footnotes.

FOOTNOTES

[1]   Including spelt.

[2]   Excluding part of Küstenland and Galicia, and of Bukovina in 1914 and 1916.

[3]   Subsequent figures are for the Republic. Statistics for 1917 and 1918 are available for the provinces later forming the Republic, but including those parts of Carinthia, Styria and Lower Austria which were incorporated in Yugoslavia and Czechoslovakia. They are as follows (in thousands) with the 1913 figures for comparison:-

	Wheat	Rye	Barley	Oats	Maize	Other Cereals	Potatoes	Sugar Beet
1913	197	407	132	347	49	40	161	18
1917	166	332	109	283	49	35	133	9
1918	162	313	103	264	46	33	166	9

[4]   Subsequent figures include Burgenland, which was previously part of Hungary.

[5]   A different series was given in post-Second World War publications, as follows:-

	Wheat	Rye	Barley	Oats	Potatoes	Sugar Beet
1929	153	186	25	231	153	53

[6]   Figures for 1941–44 exclude the Eupen and Malmédy areas, and are reckoned to be underestimates owing to concealment by farmers.

[7]   There was a change in the basic of reckoning.

[8]   Subsequent statistics include southern Dobrudja, acquired from Romania in 1940.

[9]   Subsequently including spelt.

[10]   Subsequently including mixed corn.

[11]   The areas in 1837 can be estimated as follows, assuming the same ratios of seed used to areas as in 1861:-

Wheat	Rye	Barley	Oats	Buckwheat
24	206	233	215	25

[12]   Subsequent figures include South Jutland, acquired from Germany.

[13]   Prior to this a certain amount of fodder beet is included.

[14]   Statistics for 1930–38 are for rural communes only. Statistics which include the towns are available for 1933, as follows:-

Wheat	Rye	Barley	Oats	Mixed Corn	Potatoes
107	145	355	388	324	78

[15]   Subsequent statistics are of beets sown for sugar production only.

[16]   Prior to 1836, and from 1871 to 1880, millet is included.

[17]   Subsequent returns were made by cantonal commissions instead of mayors.

[18]   Subsequently includes Savoy and Nice.

[19]   From 1871 to 1918 the parts of Alsace and Lorraine ceded to Germany are excluded. Areas in these parts in 1919 were as follows:-

Wheat	Rye	Barley	Oats	Maize
104	41	47	98	3

[20]   Excluding the invaded departments from 1914–1918 (Italy in 1918 only).

[21]   From 1939 to 1944 parts of Alsace and Lorraine annexed by Germany are excluded, and in 1943 and 1944 Corsica is excluded.

[22]   From 1871 to 1917 Alsace-Lorraine is included. From 1918 to 1944 statistics relate to the boundaries of the day, except that Austria and the Sudetenland are never included. Saarland is included from 1935.

[23]   West Berlin and Saarland are not included until 1957, in which year the areas in these parts were as follows:-

Wheat	Rye	Barley	Oats	Mixed Corn	Potatoes
11	10	4	12	4	13

[24]   Statistics are available for 1860 for the boundaries of the day, as follows:-

Wheat	Rye	Barley	Oats	Maize	Mixed Corn
120	3	46	5	70	46

C1 Area of Main Cereal, Potato, and Sugar Beet Crops (in thousands of hectares)

25 The following boundary changes affected the area covered between 1911 and 1921:- 1911-4 parts of Thessaly, Epiros, Macedonia, and Thrace and some islands were acquired; 1914-5 Macedonia was temporarily lost; 1916-7 western Macedonia was recovered; 1918-9 present mainland frontiers were achieved, but Thrace was not included in the statistics; 1921-2 Thrace included.

26 Figures to 1918 apply to Transleithania (excluding Croatia-Slavonia). Subsequently they are for the territory established by the treaty of Trianon.

27 Including mixed corn, but excluding summer rye to 1871 (1st line).

28 Subsequently the 26 counties of what became the Republic of Ireland.

29 Figures to 1921 apply to the boundaries of 1871; for 1922-43 they apply to the 1924 boundaries; and from 1944 they apply to the boundaries of 1954, except that Trieste is not included until 1949.

30 The area of potatoes for human consumption is available for these and neighbouring years as follows:-

| 1915 | 144 | 1917 | 174 | 1919 | 180 | 1921 | 153 |
| 1916 | 172 | 1918 | 178 | 1920 | 173 | | |

31 Previously the statistics are of cadastral area, and subsequently of nett area.

32 Statistics for 1835 are available as follows:-

Wheat	Rye	Barley	Oats	Mixed Corn	Potatoes
0.7	6.1	33	70	16	15

33 Figures from 1940 are for postwar boundaries. Those for the war years are only rough estimates.

34 Excluding the Acores and Madeira.

35 The following boundary changes affected the area covered between 1913 and 1921:- 1914 Dobrudja acquired; 1918 Bessarabia acquired; 1920 Bukovina, Transylvania, part of the Banat, and parts of Hungary proper acquired.

36 Southern Dobrudja was ceded to Bulgaria in 1940. Bessarabia and northern Bukovina were ceded to the U.S.S.R. in 1940, but were temporarily reconquered in 1943 and are apparently included in the statistics for 1944. Northern Transylvania was ceded to Hungary in 1940 and was reacquired by 1946.

37 These statistics are described by the F.A.O. as "doubtful".

38 Figures to 1894 (1st line) apply to the 50 provinces of European Russia (excluding Finland, Poland, and the Caucasus). From 1894 (2nd line) to 1909 (1st line) Poland is also included, though the sugar beet statistics relate to the whole Russian Empire. From 1909 (2nd line) to 1913 (1st line) the figures apply to the whole Empire. From 1913 (2nd line) to 1939 they apply to the U.S.S.R. as constituted in 1924, except that for 1920-23 they exclude central Asia, Transcaucasia, and the Far East. From 1940 the figures apply to the present territory of the U.S.S.R.

39 Previously excluding Memel.

40 Figures are available for 1855 as follows:-

Wheat	Rye	Barley	Potatoes
2,959	1,199	1,288	204

41 Including potatoes in market gardens.

42 The basis changed from area sown to area harvested.

43 Figures to 1893 include fodder beet.

44 Small areas previously classified under this heading were subsequently put into a "pasture" category.

45 Subsequently excluding farms of less than 2 hectares.

46 Rye, mixed corn, beans, and peas to 1950 (1st line). Subsequently only rye and mixed corn for threshing, with maize from 1970 to 1975.

47 The Scottish component of field beans for fodder was no longer included.

48 Some fields previously classified as oats or barley are subsequently assigned to the Mixed Corn category.

49 Area sown rather than area harvested.

50 Territory was acquired from Italy after the Second World War.

51 Czech Republic. Figures for Slovakia are: Wheat, 397; Rye, 23; Barley, 247; Oats, 14; Maize, 146; Potatoes, 47; Sugar Beet, 33.

52 Russian Federation: Figures for ex-U.S.S.R. (excluding Estonia, Latvia + Lithuania) are as follows:

		Wheat	Rye	Barley	Oats	Maize	Potatoes	Sugar Beet
Armenia	1992	76	1	92	2	1	13	—
	1993	115	—	82	2	1	14	—
	1994	86	80	70	0.8	2	31	—
	1995	60	50	70	0.8	2	33	—
	1996	85	13	77	2	2	33	—
	1997	108	200	74	2	2	33	—
	1998	118	100	61	0.9	2	33	—
	1999	112	135	51	0.9	3	32	—
	2000	107	105	47	0.4	3	33	—
Azerbaijan	1992	435	1	175	2	12	29	—
	1993	499	1	189	3	10	30	—
	1994	453	1	160	2	10	18	—
	1995	396	2	165	3	11	16	—
	1996	461	3	150	2	8	21	—
	1997	538	2	100	0.5	8	27	—
	1998	506	0.7	59	—	10	33	—
	1999	423	0.1	56	0.3	28	38	—
	2000	495	—	108	0.5	32	52	—

C1 Area of Main Cereal, Potato, and Sugar Beet Crops (in thousands of hectares)

		Wheat	Rye	Barley	Oats	Maize	Potatoes	Sugar Beet
Belarus	1992	118	1.0	1.1	333	1	779	51
	1993	132	1.0	1.1	309	5	749	55
	1994	101	...	1.3	368	2	697	58
	1995	177	...	1.0	337	1	725	55
	1996	273	...	0.9	335	2	719	45
	1997	296	...	0.8	325	3	700	47
	1998	369	...	0.8	293	2	695	52
	1999	411	...	0.8	293	4	668	55
	2000	450	...	0.8	300	5	661	50
Georgia	1992	113	1	48	10	95	22	1
	1993	85	—	37	10	112	21	1
	1994	69	0.2	28	8	138	24	1
	1995	63	0.8	32	9	142	23	0.9
	1996	80	0.3	32	6	149	27	—
	1997	174	0.4	42	7	203	27	—
	1998	133	0.2	26	5	204	33	—
	1999	111	0.1	28	5	223	34	1
	2000	105	0.1	31	7	220	34	2
Kazakhstan	1992	13,800	629	5,650	456	126	247	85
	1993	12,700	528	7,000	549	117	244	45
	1994	12,086	297	5,650	613	104	...	55
	1995	11,291	148	3,934	407	70	...	45
	1996	11,223	81	3,281	421	73	...	50
	1997	10,661	66	2,777	337	61	...	...
	1998	9,127	42	1,763	174	62	...	...
	1999	8,736	19	1,700	139	66	...	...
	2000	10,050	30	1,625	189	75	...	...
Kyrgistan	1992	249	1	263	4	55	27	6
	1993	228	1	245	3	46	27	12
	1994	333	4.6	207	4	37	34	10
	1995	364	6.3	151	3	35	44	14
	1996	452	3.0	99	2	46	49	14
	1997	537	3.0	81	1	37	56	11
	1998	489	—	75	1	46	59	21
	1999	457	—	91	2	58	64	26
	2000	444	—	70	1	59	69	24
Moldova	1992	282	1	123	3	260	55	83
	1993	346	1	139	4	343	63	83
	1994	300	2	147	5	283	63	83
	1995	394	3	135	6	329	59	90
	1996	381	5	109	4	358	68	84
	1997	410	4	129	6	458	70	76
	1998	357	2	107	5	398	62	71
	1999	342	3	108	4	403	66	61
	2000	320	3	102	4	420	70	63
Tajikistan	1992	184	2	55	3	11	13	—
	1993	200	2	38	4	11	12	—
	1994	172	1	40	4	10	12	—
	1995	190	1	36	4	10	14	—
	1996	277	1	30	2	24	10	—
	1997	356	1	25	1	9	16	—
	1998	339	—	28	1	11	17	—
	1999	326	—	27	0.8	10	23	—
	2000	301	—	30	0.5	11	23	—
Turkmenistan	1992	192	2	61	—	39	3	—
	1993	256	—	84	—	47	3	—
	1994	262	—	86	...	44	3	—
	1995	437	—	47	...	35	4	—
	1996	584	—	25	...	20	4	—
	1997	496	—	94	...	18	4	—
	1998	500	—	60	...	15	6	—
	1999	600	—	50	...	10	5	—
	2000	700	—	45	...	10	6	—

C1   Area of Main Cereal, Potato, and Sugar Beet Crops (in thousands of hectares)

		Wheat	Rye	Barley	Oats	Maize	Potatoes	Sugar Beet
Ukraine	1992	6,300	499	3,400	492	1,100	1,700	1,400
	1993	5,700	499	5,700	510	1,300	1,500	1,500
	1994	4,507	476	5,092	604	652	1,527	1,467
	1995	5,479	604	4,413	560	1,161	1,531	1,449
	1996	5,892	627	3,425	482	671	1,549	1,260
	1997	6,508	696	3,704	554	1,637	1,577	1,005
	1998	5,641	702	3,562	550	908	1,513	893
	1999	5,932	624	3,475	529	689	1,551	900
	2000	5,162	637	3,689	481	1,279	1,630	746
Uzbekistan	1992	627	5	280	—	99	43	1
	1993	623	5	275	—	107	44	—
	1994	959	7	349	—	81	53	2
	1995	1,164	6	267	—	53	46	1
	1996	1,329	5	185	—	40	44	1
	1997	1,468	2	194	—	49	58	9
	1998	1,412	1	144	—	38	55	13
	1999	1,420	3	100	—	57	49	19
	2000	1,333	3	89	—	51	51	15

[53] Yugoslavia only. Ex-Yugoslavia figures as follows:

		Wheat	Rye	Barley	Oats	Maize	Potatoes	Sugar Beet
Bosnia-Hercegovina	1992	130	5	28	29	215	53	2
	1993	120	4	21	28	208	50	1
	1994	90	3	17	10	115	36	1
	1995	70	3	16	5	93	53	1
	1996	55	2	18	16	147	41	—
	1997	95	3	22	26	207	38	—
	1998	106	4	24	28	219	49	—
	1999	95	4	23	29	214	49	—
	2000	104	5	23	26	208	44	—
Croatia	1992	169	2	33	18	370	61	18
	1993	212	2	37	17	373	65	15
	1994	198	3	36	18	371	66	16
	1995	227	2	33	16	354	66	19
	1996	201	2	31	16	361	66	21
	1997	208	2	34	18	371	63	23
	1998	242	2	43	22	378	64	29
	1999	169	2	45	24	384	63	28
	2000	236	3	46	20	389	65	21
Macedonia	1992	112	11	55	4	44	13	2
	1993	117	11	56	3	45	13	2
	1994	122	10	60	4	43	14	2
	1995	130	9	55	3	42	14	1
	1996	117	7	49	3	42	14	2
	1997	115	7	51	3	40	14	2
	1998	114	7	54	3	32	14	2
	1999	115	7	51	3	46	13	2
	2000	122	5	50	2	37	13	2
Slovenia	1992	43	3	8	2	62	30	3
	1993	43	3	8	2	62	29	3
	1994	42	2	13	3	52	10	5
	1995	37	2	13	2	47	10	6
	1996	35	2	13	2	47	9	6
	1997	33	1	10	2	47	9	6
	1998	35	1	11	2	45	9	8
	1999	32	0.9	11	2	44	10	11
	2000	38	0.6	12	2	49	10	8

C2 OUTPUT OF MAIN CEREAL, POTATO, AND SUGAR BEET CROPS (in thousands of hectolitres or metric tons)

ALBANIA (thousands of metric tons)   1929–2000

	Wheat[1]	Rye	Barley	Oats	Maize
1929	31	3	5	12	63
1930	29	2	5	11	46
1931	32	2	5	9	70
1932	42	3	7	14	108
1933	65	5	9	12	109
1934	44	4	7	9	148
1935	42	3	4	9	115
1936	30	3	4	8	125
1937	45	4	6	11	137
1938	38	3	4	11	143
1939	50	3	5	13	123
1940	30	…	…	…	…
1941	37	…	…	…	…
1944	45	…	…	…	…
1945	41	…	…	…	…
1952	86	8	9	13	97
1953	127	14	16	26	159
1954	116	11	14	22	121
1955	123	15	14	22	177
1956	99	13	11	20	178
1957	125	15	10	17	223
1958	101	9	7	13	167
1959	105	9	9	15	209
1960	64	6	7	11	129
1961	98	7	9	12	164
1962	146	7	7	16	131
1963	62	5	8	11	198
1964	124	6	8	15	188
1965	115	7	7	14	175
1966	154	7	10	16	230
1967	176	7	11	18	263
1968	184	7	6	9	274
1969	210	7	7	11	265
1970	230	…	…	…	…
1971	138	…	…	…	…
1972	…	…	…	…	…
1973	166	…	…	…	…
1979	491	…	…	…	367
1980	496	…	…	…	277
1981	489	…	…	…	311
1982	524	…	…	…	342
1983	583	…	…	…	366
1988	633	…	…	…	233
1989	611	…	…	…	302
1990	615	…	…	…	302
1991	297	…	…	…	350
1992	234	…	…	…	278
1993	430	…	…	…	292
1994	420	4	9	20	196
1995	405	4	7	13	216
1996	271	3	3	13	214
1997	388	3	4	12	195
1998	395	3	3	15	189
1999	272	3	3	13	206
2000	330	4	4	14	215

C2 Output of Main Cereal, Potato, and Sugar Beet Crops (in thousands of hectolitres or metric tons)

AUSTRIA (Cisleithania)   **1842–1905**

	Wheat	Rye[2]	Barley	Oats	Maize	Other Corn	Potatoes	Sugar Beet
			thousands of hectolitres				thousands of metric tons	
1842	9,399	23,521	15,996	28,850	2,156	3,200	41,992	...
1843	9,439	23,523	16,205	28,852	2,211	3,173	40,616	...
1844	9,420	23,493	16,166	28,846	2,111	3,079	41,486	...
1845	9,634	23,534	16,173	30,171	2,677	3,571	40,687	...
1846	9,644	23,367	15,852	29,573	2,475	3,451	31,867	...
1847	9,662	23,373	15,773	29,593	2,572	3,509	32,700	...
1851	9,630	23,519	15,501	29,433	3,110	4,047	40,765	
1854	9,620	24,905	13,107	28,935	3,266	4,392	46,516	...
1857	12,587	29,527	16,745	31,148	4,616	4,942	44,245	...
1859	11,598	29,762	16,030	32,002	4,526	5,132	43,840	...
1868	11,819	24,166	16,189	29,987	3,996	5,112	64,405	...
1869	11,377	23,754	14,550	28,086	4,608	3,709	64,843	1,758
1870	12,835	27,401	16,226	28,530	4,250	3,637	83,008	2,215
1871	12,819	26,351	16,431	32,449	3,903	3,295	63,900	2,136
1872	11,285[1]	23,491	17,367	34,935	9,249	3,760	75,227	2,907
1873	10,053[1]	27,976	15,899	26,831	5,367	2,574	69,845	2,403
1874	14,804[1]	28,434	17,460	28,073	5,793	4,373	94,079	2,009[4]
1875	10,885	23,275	13,175	25,564	6,073	3,407	93,460	2,537
1876	12,720	21,240	18,134	33,082	5,918	4,134	91,283	2,678
1877	14,050	28,171	13,817	30,311	5,141	3,389	94,520	3,287
1878	15,927	29,995	17,086	34,570	6,793	4,581	91,856	3,734
1879	12,147	22,360	13,273	30,401	5,455	3,960	57,397	3,402
1880	14,302	22,753	17,809	32,680	6,021	3,110	85,770	4,092
1881	14,507	28,260	16,485	33,609	4,549	2,985	99,555	4,099
1882	15,698	29,062	17,231	32,272	5,514	2,284	85,883	4,618
1883	13,347	24,028	16,354	33,673	7,115	3,882	102,018	4,197
1884	15,441	27,090	18,230	38,009	5,992	3,539	99,292	4,766
1885	17,016	27,984	18,345	33,390	7,008	3,881	129,737	2,537
1886	15,734	27,043	18,768	39,730	6,766	3,280	117,590	3,298
1887	18,450	32,168	20,568	37,034	5,622	2,973	119,085	2,456
							thousands of metric tons	
1888	18,271	28,827	20,210	37,081	5,845	3,543	8,119	4,009
1889	13,525	25,042	16,137	28,524	5,806	2,863	9,033	5,025
1890	15,528	28,538	19,188	36,731	6,774	3,112	8,234	5,523
1891	14,474	24,676	19,478	38,569	6,756	3,005	6,309	5,385
1892	17,681	29,617	21,804	39,683	6,783	2,946	9,532	5,516
1893	15,386	27,854	18,502	31,503	5,468	2,607	8,343	4,923
1894	16,982	30,009	21,321	38,659	4,861	2,919	9,607	6,726
1895	14,720	23,539	20,824	40,013	6,597	3,435	9,845	4,230
			thousands of metric tons					
1896	1,136	1,877	1,227	1,599	448	3,341	8,818	5,935
1897	939	1,604	1,109	1,475	379	3,136	8,001	4,921
1898	1,276	2,026	1,382	1,869	417	4,406	11,614	4,719
1899	1,366	2,168	1,594	2,021	366	3,378	10,790	6,528
1900	1,114	1,394	1,339	1,714	392	3,526	11,702	5,228
1901	1,198	1,920	1,461	1,716	445	3,293	11,896	6,546
1902	1,351	2,096	1,607	1,821	342	2,695	11,654	4,686
1903	1,257	2,062	1,608	1,863	408	2,868	9,719	5,324
1904	1,462	2,330	1,455	1,591	318	2,930	10,840	4,072
1905	1,484	2,495	1,534	1,798	439	3,554	15,835	7,184

C2 Output of Main Cereal, Potato, and Sugar Beet Crops (in thousands of hectolitres or metric tons)

AUSTRIA (Cisleithania)

	Wheat	Rye[2]	Barley	Oats	Maize	Other Corn	Potatoes	Sugar Beet
				thousands of metric tons				
1906	1,585	2,523	1,655	2,243	462	3,386	13,997	6,372
1907	1,425	2,199	1,710	2,476	422	3,914	14,663	6,394
						thousand tons		
1908	1,691	2,880	1,513	2,091	385	213	12,951	5,814
1909	1,591	2,909	1,728	2,496	407	260	13,053	5,522
1910	1,567	2,771	1,472	2,063	439	242	13,366	7,062
1911	1,603	2,649	1,620	2,270	304	187	11,605	4,250
1912	1,895	2,981	1,707	2,430	389	185	12,542	7,924
1913	1,623	2,709	1,750	2,677	338	171	11,552	6,962
1914	1,035[6]	1,894[6]	1,273[6]	1,918[6]	274[6]	111[6]	7,758[6]	6,775[6]
1915	882[6]	1,545[6]	759[6]	1,072[6]	287[6]	68[6]	8,672[6]	4,619[6]
1916	757[6]	1,278[6]	850[6]	1,388[6]	145[6]	95[6]	6,234[6]	4,494[6]

AUSTRIA (Republic) (thousands of metric tons)

	Wheat[1]	Rye	Barley	Oats	Maize	Other Cereals	Potatoes	Sugar Beet
1917	163	278	72	158	71	23	895	90
1918	140	270	92	188	58	23	585	170
1919	139	230	83	197	54	14	545	75
1920	148	255	96	232	54	12	669	129
1921	178	335	119	276	64	19	833	94
1922	173[7]	320[7]	103[7]	249[7]	68[7]	17[7]	1,287[7]	126[7]
	202	345	122	266	88	21	1,398	173
1923	242	403	171	375	88	29	1,426	242
1924	231	411	157	332	94	29	1,647	433
1925	290	550	201	388	117	29	2,068	493
1926	257	475	198	435	97	26	1,298	481
1927	325	511	238	439	126	29	2,666	723
1928	352	506	282	462	108	33	2,488	725
1929	315	510	269	451	117	40	2,803	691
1930	327	524	267	401	121	43	2,653	973
1931	300	481	217	332	127	35	2,716	978
1932	322	615	274	390	132	35	2,666	1,020
1933	398	687	333	503	137	46	2,355	1,067
1934	362	575	295	467	155	45	2,749	1,409
1935	422	620	270	391	128	36	2,392	1,500
1936	382	473	278	427	171	43	2,369	912
1937	400	477	288	475	206	13	3,612	1,008
1938	441	591	306	435	200	14	3,257	1,133
1939	447	499	287	360	118	16	2,765	1,235
1940	285	313	280	344	135	19	2,605	875
1941	342	388	234	286	125	18	2,602	832
1942	276	270	222	271	116	21	2,252	744
1943	343	356	215	302	98	18	1,773	666
1944	294	279	181	250	84	15	1,751	576
1945	227	230	120	205	43	...	1,420	128
1946	228	244	112	188	85	20	1,533	225
1947	206	260	110	193	89	21	1,842	245
1948	261	289	125	225	100	23	2,069	360
1949	350	365	199	286	119	30	2,008	480
1950	384	388	230	223	120	25	2,548	821
1951	342	334	246	299	138	25	2,159	1,062

C2 Output of Main Cereal, Potato, and Sugar Beet Crops (in thousands of hectolitres or metric tons)

AUSTRIA (Republic) (thousands of metric tons)   **1952-2000**

	Wheat[1]	Rye	Barley	Oats	Maize	Other Cereals	Potatoes	Sugar Beet
1952	401	340	251	341	122	22	2,567	853
1953	499	421	320	360	151	27	3,293	1,058
1954	452	370	312	334	149	23	2,792	1,345
1955	549	416	346	364	152	28	3,005	1,439
1956	570	434	385	374	144	30	3,229	1,228
1957	574	400	392	340	149	29	4,034	1,655
1958	549	397	335	333	155	30	3,542	2,005
1959	589	417	405	312	146	38	2,946	1,951
1960	702	353	589	343	213	45	3,809	1,906
1961	712	472	512	335	198	45	3,395	1,250
1962	706	467	557	332	193	51	3,214	1,546
1963	690	322	617	342	194	64	3,499	2,090
1964	751	388	605	327	212	67	3,438	2,203
1965	661	315	523	274	187	60	2,539	1,462
1966	897	363	706	325	275	83	3,007	2,308
1967	1,045	377	772	336	316	88	3,049	2,006
1968	1,045	413	770	324	399	96	3,473	1,936
1969	950	440	934	288	698	95	2,941	2,005
1970	810	363	913	272	612	101	2,704	1,947
1971	974	448	1,016	284	721	102	2,717	1,590
1972	863	402	977	255	726	95	2,341	2,148
1973	939	400	1,087	284	966	112	2,117	2,220
1974	1,102	415	1,238	290	557	113	1,996	2,386
1975	945	347	1,006	306	981	122	1,579	3,134
1976	1,234	410	1,287	283	936	...	1,746	2,583
1977	1,072	351	1,212	279	1,159	...	1,352	2,721
1978	1,195	410	1,424	304	1,166	...	1,401	1,885
1979	850	278	1,129	273	1,347	...	1,494	2,145
1980	1,201	383	1,514	316	1,293	...	1,264	2,587
1981	1,025	320	1,220	304	1,374	...	1,310	3,007
1982	1,236	348	1,437	325	1,551	...	1,121	3,510
1983	1,417	348	1,449	292	1,454	...	1,012	2,020
1984	1,501	381	1,517	292	1,542	...	1,138	2,564
1985	1,563	339	1,521	284	1,727	...	1,042	2,407
1986	1,415	284	1,292	270	1,740	...	982	1,571
1987	1,451	309	1,177	246	1,685	...	879	2,128
1988	1,560	356	1,366	273	1,700	...	1,001	1,934
1989	1,363	381	1,422	249	1,491	...	845	2,641
1990	1,370	375	1,437	262	1,400	...	850	2,760
1991	1,375	350	1,427	226	1,571	...	790	2,522
1992	1,325	278	1,342	185	1,118	...	738	2,605
1993	1,018	292	1,100	191	1,359	...	715	3,000
1994	1,255	319	1,184	172	1,421	...	594	2,561
1995	1,304	314	1,065	162	1,473	...	724	2,885
1996	1,240	156	1,083	153	1,736	...	769	3,131
1997	1,352	207	1,258	197	1,842	...	677	3,012
1998	1,342	236	1,211	164	1,646	...	647	3,314
1999	1,416	218	1,152	152	1,699	...	712	3,217
2000	1,313	183	855	118	1,816	...	695	2,559

C2 Output of Main Cereal, Potato, and Sugar Beet Crops (in thousands of hectolitres or metric tons)

BELGIUM   **1846–1946**

	Wheat	Rye	Barley	Oats	Mixed Corn[1]	Potatoes	Sugar Beet
			thousands of hectolitres				thousands of metric tons
1846	3,584	2,055	1,143	4,770	3,317	15,292	78
1856	3,756	6,066	1,561	7,411	2,719	26,687	304
av. of			thousands of metric tons				
1871–80	432	417	78	389	114	2,487	1,123
1895	348	506	87	437	49[8]	2,681	1,715
1900	375	504	104	569	67	2,393	2,180
1901	385	538	106	589	69	2,751	1,168
1902	395	568	108	662	71	2,264	1,364
1903	336	553	85	702	62	2,356	1,458
1904	376	559	109	544	64	2,494	1,163
1905	338	542	98	490	57	1,556	2,101
1906	353	523	95	657	61	2,413	1,749
1907	431	597	112	667	67	2,400	1,454
1908	365	564	96	625	52	2,255	1,560
1909	397	588	100	628	53	2,459	1,590
1910	381	583	92	631	55	2,912	1,812
1911	429	619	97	628	57	2,747	1,507
1912	418	541	93	509	53	3,306	1,730
1913	402	571	92	696	55	3,201	1,392
1919	288	368	75	397	44	2,829	1,095
1920	280	462	94	492	46	2,257	1,438
1921	395	540	111	511	57	1,947	1,463
1922	289	467	75	519	22	3,931	1,699
1923	364	528	91	683	45	2,822	2,037
1924	354	525	81	642	41	2,866	2,489
1925	394	551	91	617	48	3,101	2,168
1926	348	511	92	736	43	3,001	1,683
1927	443	555	91	669	42	3,309	1,983
1928	490	588	95	704	46	3,634	1,828
1929	360	563	62	747	32	3,908	1,570
1930	360	473	83	555	31	2,962	1,865
1931	376	520	88	702	31	3,577	1,466
1932	419	601	102	760	36	4,439	1,736
1933	410	567	100	831	37	3,689	1,516
1934	439	565	105	807	39	3,262	1,690
1935	438	382	84	553	24	3,006	1,535
1936	440	357	79	553	24	3,225	1,491
1937	423	345	86	520	27	3,091	1,376
1938	548	385	89	621	27	3,258	1,202
1939	349	349	51	724	20	3,323	1,669
1940	...[9]	...[9]	...[9]	...[9]	...[9]	...[9]	...[9]
1941	374	290	75	331	16	2,152	1,295
1942	402	316	125	281	20	2,175	1,587
1943	534	332	181	315	25	2,270	1,769
1944	505[9]	314[9]	166[9]	305[9]	25[9]	2,121[9]	1,696[9]
1945	310	151	113	367	15	1,222	878
1946	366	222	147	496	18	1,477	1,099

C2 Output of Main Cereal, Potato, and Sugar Beet Crops (in thousands of hectolitres or metric tons)

BELGIUM (thousands of metric tons)   1947–2000

	Wheat	Rye	Barley	Oats	Mixed Corn[1]	Potatoes	Sugar Beet
1947	122	162	188	509	11	1,600	1,106
1948	344	184	172	385	10	2,133	1,598
1949	596	258	237	587	19	2,047	2,348
1950	547	240	261	506	15	2,318	2,675
1951	514	204	269	473	19	2,016	1,858
1952	565	221	273	463	17	2,124	2,194
1953	560	213	294	462	16	1,919	2,389
1954	575	245	247	452	17	2,634	2,132
1955	714	220	281	481	18	2,184	2,246
1956	597	196	288	484	10	2,034	2,204
1957	751	190	296	454	17	2,044	2,486
1958	779	200	318	443	20	1,914	2,832
1959	789	176	398	423	22	1,357	1,474
1960	773	183	382	450	19	1,894	3,063
1961	722	114	409	444	18	1,789	2,703
1962	735	117	499	427	12	1,872	2,019
1963	759	119	482	395	15	1,530	2,135
1964	900	133	516	373	13	1,755	3,114
1965	854	98	520	305	12	1,419	2,537
1966	650	76	486	293	12	1,475	2,586
1967	828	90	623	361	17	1,944	3,615
1968	839	87	574	315	18	1,566	4,108
1969	754	70	555	281	21	1,253	4,217
1970	708	61	526	194	21	1,373	3,868
1971	878	82	588	278	32	1,373	4,873
1972	916	72	637	244	29	1,106	4,319
1973	976	59	716	246	30	1,201	5,136
1974	1,004	46	699	222	31	1,460	4,465
1975	677	29	426	228	18	1,049	4,913
1976	891	47	610	129	24	714	4,600
1977	742	61	676	115	29	1,370	4,343
1978	956	57	765	136	36	1,262	5,224
1979	953	41	767	119	32	1,199	5,869
1980	853	38	807	109	26	1,181	5,315
1981	875	32	752	109	27	1,195	6,936
1982	1,010	30	791	133	28	1,310	7,430
1983	1,003	26	670	80	40	978	5,120
1984	1,248	32	873	92	45	1,332	5,763
1985	1,150	22	685	94	38	1,482	5,952
1986	1,257	19	793	39	38	1,401	5,886
1987	1,046	17	678	60	36	1,620	5,425
1988	1,252	14	738	55	37	1,614	6,109
1989	1,402	13	647	44	42	1,443	6,061
1990	1,266	13	532	34	36	1,665	6,418
1991	1,361	11	490	36	37	1,823	5,676
1992	1,329	9	450	36	36	2,428	5,957
1993	1,428	10	391	54	35	2,175	6,264
1994	1,554	13	406	64	39	2,303	5,702
1995	1,531	11	420	49	43	2,367	6,051
1996	1,908	11	455	49	41	2,806	6,125
1997	1,717	10	441	56	36	2,899	6,545
1998	1,832	7	375	32	37	2,456	5,366
1999	1,529	4	388	49	38	3,007	7,112
2000	1,634	8	387	47	39	3,033	5,311

C2 Output of Main Cereal, Potato, and Sugar Beet Crops (in thousands of hectolitres or metric tons)

BULGARIA (thousands of metric tons)   1899–1939

	Wheat	Rye	Barley	Oats	Maize	Potatoes	Sugar Beet
1899	589	118	145	84	520	21	10
1900	706	171	237	92	495	…	10
1903	968	197	278	165	580	9	4
1904	1,150	197	281	162	324	7	23
1905	951	181	249	136	461	8	22
1906	1,064	191	261	172	706	10	44
1907	641	99	147	108	358	8	25
1908	993	142	246	163	526	9	23
1909	873	175	203	136	520	9	21
1910	1,150	230	307	156	720	12	32
1911	1,314	228	270	151	777	14	65
1912	1,218	214	271	126	723	14	61
1913	1,184	205	250	126	736	14	80
1914	632	160	202	113	799	16	190
1915	967	187	267	126	746	19	76
1916	806	152	228	98	490	18	115
1917	791	137	219	87	443	18	97
1918	631	110	148	52	215	15	58
1919	817	156	102	84	647	22	176
1920	810	159	206	102	530	26	82
1921	1,148	155	185	97	416	28	118
1922	886	162	224	112	416	29	150
1923	986	174	241	133	682	33	153
1924	672	109	154	93	629	34	404
1925	1,126	182	263	112	656	37	5
1926	995	181	241	98	694	48	225
1927	1,146	177	280	94	532	38	295
1928	1,338	205	340	89	515	21	176
1929	903	186	204	137	940	44	262
1930	1,560	321	433	111	775	63	402
1931	1,737	271	345	103	889	71	201
1932	1,310	229	296	101	887	72	187
1933	1,509	246	352	130	951	81	296
1934	1,078	164	187	75	790	84	19
1935	1,304[10]	197[10]	282[10]	93[10]	1,009[10]	121[10]	154[10]
1936	1,643	208	322	136	872	109	80
1937	1,767	238	330	147	859	146	209
1938	2,149	188	355	89	532	64	129
1939	1,857	195	362	114	950	127	229

C2 Output of Main Cereal, Potato, and Sugar Beet Crops (in thousands of hectolitres or metric tons)

CZECHOSLOVAKIA (thousands of metric tons)   **1920–1969**

	Wheat	Rye	Barley	Oats	Maize	Potatoes	Sugar Beet
1920	717	837	811	866	245	5,003	4,781
1921	1,053	1,365	1,034	1,075	240	4,329	4,072
1922	915	1,298	1,009	1,039	251	9,069	5,240
1923	986	1,355	1,197	1,331	270	6,224	6,024
1924	877	1,136	971	1,204	260	6,514	8,374
1925	1,070	1,476	1,246	1,304	306	7,499	9,075
1926	927	1,166	1,143	1,380	266	5,047	6,599
1927	1,099[10]	1,252[10]	1,285[10]	1,458[10]	260	9,109[10]	8,124[10]
	1,285	1,523	1,277	1,428		10,074	7,959
1928	1,402	1,779	1,402	1,423	223	8,593	6,226
1929	1,440	1,834	1,395	1,494	231	10,696	6,209
1930	1,335	1,759	1,215	1,279	181	8,642	6,420
1931	1,092	1,368	1,071	1,220	164	9,408	5,238
1932	1,429	2,138	1,499	1,621	212	8,898	3,960
1933	1,937	2,048	1,346	1,546	112	7,894	2,913
1934	1,329	1,501	1,031	1,148	180	9,137	4,240
1935	1,640	1,603	1,058	1,001	150	7,400	3,651
1936	1,457	1,399	1,015	1,189	238	10,243	4,758
1937	1,374	1,471	1,114	1,359	280	11,913	5,986
1938	1,764	1,867	1,326	1,363	279	7,358	3,877
1939	1,572	1,729	1,193	1,265	264	9,971	5,067
1940	1,111	867	1,240	1,277	202	8,236	4,937
1941	1,160	981	910	844	193	8,931	4,775
1942	1,451	1,231	1,143	986	218	7,754	4,237
1943	1,561	1,536	1,021	965	207	5,440	3,981
1944	1,210[13]	1,214[13]	884[13]	744[13]	132[13]	6,815[13]	4,525[13]
1945	1,122	980	665	691	186	6,769	3,241
1946	1,320	1,136	766	825	203	9,159	4,341
1947	853	938	670	714[14]	132	4,678	2,407
1948	1,429	1,143	898	994	297	6,067	4,295
1949	1,556	1,316	1,023	1,062	240	5,772	4,283
1950	1,430	1,147	1,030	895	218	8,156	6,296
1951	1,476	1,015	1,143	929	302	7,356	5,203
1952	1,573	930	1,137	927	212	7,924	4,760
1953	1,566	954	1,247	869	430	9,702	5,588
1954	1,107	803	1,115	866	382	8,314	5,603
1955	1,473	968	1,291	974	391	7,905	6,152
1956	1,541	1,050	1,408	1,034	399	9,635	4,585
1957	1,525	948	1,362	899	445	8,756	6,775
1958	1,346	937	1,199	871	479	6,589	6,946
1959	1,649	967	1,467	929	503	6,334	4,946
1960	1,503	895	1,745	1,020	572	5,093	8,368
1961	1,666	994	1,581	959	461	5,331	6,894
1962	1,644	916	1,752	905	471	5,002	5,811
1963	1,766	880	1,620	797	578	6,506	8,018
1964	1,829	870	1,429	669	465	7,656	7,474
1965	1,992	822	1,399	630	393	3,678	5,662
1966	2,247	790	1,608	746	476	5,846	7,762
1967	2,516	689	1,936	968	421	6,037	7,663
1968	3,153	769	2,113	869	453	6,526	8,098
1969	3,257	687	2,499	969	495	5,180	5,809

C2 Output of Main Cereal, Potato, and Sugar Beet Crops (in thousands of hectolitres or metric tons)

CZECHOSLOVAKIA (thousands of metric tons)

1970–2000

	Wheat	Rye	Barley	Oats	Maize	Potatoes	Sugar Beet
1970	3,174	454	2,280	776	513	4,793	6,644
1971	3,878	619	2,851	902	524	4,621	5,832
1972	4,017	634	2,651	726	642	5,058	6,884
1973	4,646	690	2,962	740	619	5,087	6,163
1974	5,059	671	3,375	687	574	4,522	8,219
1975	4,202	530	3,114	591	843	3,565	7,734
1976	4,807	561	2,901	379	514	4,214	5,248
1977	5,214	641	3,207	454	792	3,760	8,232
1978	5,601	630	3,642	454	619	3,995	7,285
1979	3,736	486	3,604	401	949	3,725	7,645
1980	5,386	570	3,575	421	745	2,695	7,255
1981	4,325	544	3,392	431	706	3,743	6,989
1982	4,606	583	3,654	488	941	3,608	8,210
1983	5,820	751	3,276	473	722	3,177	6,041
1984	6,170	710	3,677	479	940	3,978	7,513
1985	6,023	620	3,538	473	1,114	3,450	7,746
1986	5,305	547	3,530	419	992	3,512	7,134
1987	6,154	496	3,551	406	1,160	3,072	6,697
1988	6,541	534	3,411	366	996	3,659	5,481
1989	6,356	708	3,550	330	1,000	3,167	6,390
1990	6,707	736	4,071	421	468	2,534	5,609
1991	6,205	484	3,793	346	862	2,718	5,515
1992	5,110	319	3,551	249	780	2,627	5,413
Czech Republic							
1993[45]	3,304	256	2,419	263	157	2,396	4,310
1994	3,713	276	2,419	208	91	1,231	3,240
1995	3,822	262	2,140	187	113	1,330	3,712
1996	3,727	204	2,262	214	169	1,800	4,316
1997	3,640	259	2,485	246	285	1,402	3,722
1998	3,845	261	2,093	179	201	1,520	3,479
1999	4,028	202	2,137	179	260	1,407	2,691
2000	4,084	150	1,629	136	304	1,476	2,809

DENMARK

1875–1904

	Wheat	Rye	Barley	Oats	Mixed Corn	Potatoes	Sugar Beet
	thousands of hectolitres						*thousand tons*
1875	1,759	5,956	8,154	10,798	1,194	4,183	...
1876	1,426	5,049	6,589	8,884	1,190	3,792	...
1877	1,706	5,614	6,968	9,121	1,336	3,030	...
1878	1,824	6,144	8,449	11,747	1,721	3,938	...
1879	1,649	5,237	7,229	10,540	1,626	2,266	...
1880	1,797	6,591	8,857	12,131	1,953	4,798	...
1881	977	6,110	7,688	10,797	1,762	4,403	...
1882	1,575	5,940	8,324	12,257	2,202	2,948	...
1883	1,588	6,230	7,353	10,760	2,004	5,653	...
1884	1,655	5,869	7,304	10,917	2,164	4,853	...
1885	1,806	6,307	7,359	11,996	2,431	5,378	...
1886	1,664	5,834	8,179	12,465	2,604	5,782	...
1887	1,886	6,079	7,712	11,233	2,763	6,039	...
1888	1,158	5,764	7,802	12,501	2,802	4,712	...
1889	1,478	6,390	6,563	9,885	2,554	4,393	...
1890	1,330	5,993	8,265	13,148	3,139	4,390	...
1891	1,470	6,888	7,980	12,134	3,167	5,076	...
1892	1,502	7,181	8,713	14,359	3,659	6,642	...
1893	1,359	6,922	6,095	9,813	2,593	7,588	...
1894	1,150	5,864	7,495	13,506	3,570	5,818	328
1895	1,222	6,483	7,680	14,179	3,816	7,281	349
1896	1,300	7,076	7,488	13,575	3,785	7,647	379
1897	1,224	6,384	6,756	12,411	3,577	7,108	387
1898	1,054	5,685	7,706	14,615	4,037	5,839	277
1899	1,288	6,469	7,645	13,065	3,826	6,643	332
1900	1,270	7,032	8,045	14,212	4,060	8,222	382
1901	1,332	5,851	7,852	13,183	4,619	7,753	449
1902	1,595	6,618	8,206	14,385	4,723	9,574	292
1903	1,572	6,803	8,225	14,510	4,783	8,900	401
1904	1,509	5,802	7,569	13,097	5,043	8,562	357

C2 Output of Main Cereal, Potato, and Sugar Beet Crops (in thousands of hectolitres or metric tons)

DENMARK   1905–1954

	Wheat	Rye	Barley	Oats	Mixed Corn	Potatoes	Sugar Beet
	thousands of hectolitres						thousand tons
1905	1,433	6,783	6,905	11,193	4,851	10,387	512
1906	1,466	6,635	7,039	13,646	5,490	10,120	475
1907	1,530	5,601	7,617	14,986	6,159	8,607	406
1908	1,522	6,756	7,106	14,250	5,967	10,484	434
1909	1,349	6,668	7,611	14,861	6,184	8,573	450
						thousand tons	
1910	1,925	6,352	7,832	14,816	6,252	832	742
	thousands of metric tons						
1911	155	449	514	764	351	823	734
1912	137	418	561	795	369	827	1,052
1913	182	432	596	829	384	1,070	930
1914	158	283	495	685	322	946	967
1915	217	338	618	760	360	1,073	825
1916	165	274	533	750	347	674	736
1917	117	225	389	547	275	888	883
1918	172	323	467	603	325	1,105	944
1919	161	379	534	691	379	1,445	1,017
1920	189[15]	318[15]	513[15]	684[15]	348[15]	1,194[15]	847[15]
	201	337	538	737	366	1,233	868
1921	303	310	600	757	367	1,366	869
1922	252	363	663	848	379	1,340	572
1923	241	385	707	916	443	1,238	765
1924	160	265	745	917	479	742	953
1925	265	349	796	956	508	1,311	1,209
1926	239	317	728	876	488	812	984
1927	256	263	786	883	556	565	1,095
1928	332	246	1,100	1,059	763	1,173	1,282
1929	320[16]	265[16]	1,112[16]	1,035[16]	772[16]	1,072[16]	907[16]
1930	278	255	1,051	998	750	984	1,069
1931	274	214	957	936	740	877	783
1932	299	222	1,009	1,055	794	1,304	1,033
1933	314	251	959	997	796	1,327	1,726
1934	350	274	956	987	809	1,373	1,047
1935	399	284	1,107	1,042	852	1,218	1,886
1936	307	199	898	836	636	1,289	1,817
1937	368	251	1,099	1,025	754	1,324	1,505
1938	461[16]	284[16]	1,359[16]	1,144[16]	795[16]	1,433[16]	1,363[16]
1939	383	262	1,103	1,024	781	1,349	1,572
1940	189	272	1,159	906	712	1,352	1,570
1941	193	306	914	721	573	1,316	1,765
1942	16	412	1,386	1,011	953	1,667	1,592
1943	179	507	1,288	1,036	861	1,942	1,460
1944	276	412	1,250	979	771	1,409	1,271
1945	280	311	1,259	995	737	1,609	1,290
1946	298	287	1,387	1,085	777	1,810	1,533
1947	55	179	1,329	872	702	1,826	1,455
1948	253	400	1,458	937	759	1,500	1,711
1949	300	469	1,571	982	764	1,794	2,130
1950	297	331	1,615	834	682	1,850	2,624
1951	273	270	1,767	847	687	1,950	2,455
1952	301	358	2,130	960	822	2,320	2,045
1953	283	331	2,180	823	813	1,885	2,487
1954	292	276	2,045	800	798	1,938	1,694

C2 Output of Main Cereal, Potato, and Sugar Beet Crops (in thousands of hectolitres or metric tons)

DENMARK (thousands of metric tons)   1955–2000

	Wheat	Rye	Barley	Oats	Mixed Corn	Potatoes	Sugar Beet
1955	254	191	2,200	863	836	1,442	2,022
1956	266	290	2,402	852	853	2,140	2,312
1957	273	313	2,560	786	829	1,781	3,064
1958	274	306	2,485	648	752	1,558	3,240
1959	364	289	2,338	568	602	1,731	1,593
1960	320	454	2,801	681	727	1,963	2,230
1961	434	514	2,808	684	759	1,490	1,397
1962	644	513	3,299	609	719	1,162	1,440
1963	495	319	3,399	671	619	1,334	2,598
1964	541	292	3,900	821	659	1,213	3,154
1965	564	265	4,125	780	479	937	1,883
1966	400	136	4,159	864	401	972	2,159
1967	421	118	4,382	904	328	857	2,139
1968	464	131	5,047	863	280	866	2,148
1969	428	126	5,255	765	200	663	2,008
1970	512	134	4,813	631	142	1,033	1,892
1971	585	150	5,458	701	132	750	1,999
1972	592	155	5,572	637	111	709	2,166
1973	542	140	5,432	444	75	748	2,521
1974	592	168	5,967	472	62	898	2,691
1975	519	163	5,156	367	46	666	3,140
1976	593	213	4,801	263	33	576	3,019
1977	606	324	6,142	270	48	954	3,543
1978	642	315	6,301	206	28	932	3,056
1979	590	257	6,662	163	19	844	3,092
1980	652	199	6,044	159	16	842	3,010
1981	835	208	6,044	176	14	1,053	3,225
1982	1,207	235	6,357	178	16	1,229	3,624
1983	1,548	315	4,423	85	9	853	2,616
1984	2,446	608	6,072		158	1,121	3,614
1985	1,996	560	5,251		168	1,073	3,516
1986	2,177	546	5,134		111	1,129	3,195
1987	2,284	513	4,292		95	957	2,632
1988	2,080	366	5,419		202	1,246	3,379
1989	3,224	487	4,959		115	1,242	3,302
1990	4,101	565	5,030		109	1,614	3,300
1991	3,670	395	5,041		116	1,462	3,231
1992	3,583	308	2,974		79	1,775	2,974
1993	4,350	339	3,407		120	1,500	3,622
1994	3,725	423	3,446		190	1,359	3,138
1995	4,481	495	3,899		158	1,441	3,130
1996	4,758	343	3,953		158	1,617	3,064
1997	4,965	453	3,887		150	1,545	3,367
1998	4,928	538	3,565		161	1,456	3,486
1999	4,471	248	3,675		129	1,502	3,545
2000	4,693	262	3,979		233	1,645	3,345

FINLAND (thousands of hectolitres)   1878–1891

	Wheat	Rye	Barley	Oats	Mixed Corn	Potatoes
1878	36	3,103	1,639	2,683	84	3,307
1879	34	3,741	1,901	2,999	91	3,619
1880	39	4,036	1,781	2,984	78	3,152
1881	32	2,511	1,884	2,948	94	4,686
1882	42	3,897	2,071	3,289	110	4,615
1883	43	4,320	2,073	3,619	128	4,902
1884	43	3,898	1,890	3,610	123	4,126
1885	42	3,855	1,861	3,699	129	4,975
1886	47	4,502	2,157	4,345	149	6,974
1887	55	4,589	2,158	5,015	168	6,712
1888	52	4,391	1,963	4,659	141	6,111
1889	53	4,527	2,177	4,784	162	7,115
1890	51	4,518	2,312	5,518	182	6,068
1891	44	4,377	1,788	4,282	119	5,850

C2   Output of Main Cereal, Potato, and Sugar Beet Crops (in thousands of hectolitres or metric tons)

FINLAND (thousands of hectolitres)   **1892–1944**

	Wheat	Rye	Barley	Oats	Mixed Corn	Potatoes
1892	40	3,243	1,470	4,583	111	3,801
1893	45	3,828	1,781	4,858	125	4,181
1894	52	4,301	2,030	4,918	151	6,066
1895	52	4,667	2,154	6,624	158	6,357
1896	43	4,817	2,097	6,174	167	6,508
1897	56	4,679	2,114	6,335	171	6,614
1898	56	4,578	2,018	6,713	177	5,968
1899	51	3,603	1,330	5,280	117	4,524
1900	56	4,044	1,634	6,239	148	5,415
1901	49	4,459	1,717	6,037	143	5,753
1902	28	3,115	1,279	5,353	108	5,391
1903	46	3,735	1,844	6,007	152	6,770
1904	47	3,652	1,732	5,989	122	5,450
1905	46	4,071	1,874	6,364	156	7,296
1906	53	4,203	1,895	6,911	151	7,200
1907	49	3,888	1,808	7,274	147	6,613
1908	39	3,945	1,800	6,456	189	5,707
1909	47	4,259	1,722	6,963	189	6,775
1910	44	3,632	1,736	7,106	200	6,127
1911	50	3,317	1,739	6,683	216	6,497
1912	42	3,657	1,795	7,416	261	6,630
1913	58	3,618	1,725	7,760	268	6,467
1914	69	3,979	1,521	6,897	211	6,603
1915	92	3,972	1,769	8,424	204	7,235
1916	87	3,488	1,721	7,776	161	6,930
1917	80	3,141	1,587	6,625	130	6,737

thousands of metric tons

	Wheat	Rye	Barley	Oats	Mixed Corn	Potatoes
1918	6	213	97	325	6	455
1919	7	220	99	357	6	492
1920	9	250	116	396	9	558
1921	16	297	133	506	12	623
1922	19	268	141	540	16	525
1923	19	239	85	582	10	462
1924	22	286	130	492	13	634
1925	25	348	141	587	14	723
1926	25	303	156	593	14	851
1927	29	328	143	633	16	758
1928	27	279	126	570	15	689
1929	21	265	141	514	11	721
1930	24	336	165	627	17	928
1931	31	315	166	670	22	978
1932	40	329	179	670	23	983
1933	67	373	179	636	22	1,282
1934	89	395	209	776	28	1,139
1935	115	350	116	609	24	1,269
1936	143	308	185	693	25	1,433
1937	209	431	176	728	15	1,388
1938	256	369	207	826	18	1,198
1939	231[17]	306[17]	189[17]	768[17]	19[17]	1,234[17]
1940	179	210	139	505	13	1,234
1941	147	220	118	454	7	745
1942	172	204	139	545	6	972
1943	177	208	161	475	7	1,081
1944	160	167	149	345	6	639

C2   Output of Main Cereal, Potato, and Sugar Beet Crops (in thousands of hectolitres or metric tons)

FINLAND (thousands of hectolitres)   **1945-2000**

	Wheat	Rye	Barley	Oats	Mixed Corn	Potatoes
1945	265	156	151	331	6	780
1946	178	144	151	334	6	891
1947	196	186	160	433	10	1,114
1948	265	199	214	640	24	1,950
1949	323	219	181	723	28	1,157
1950	296	215	176	702	26	1,273
1951	212	190	211	716	34	1,327
1952	227	183	224	809	33	1,504
1953	218	130	314	904	32	1,379
1954	235	132	262	774	27	1,090
1955	190	119	262	644	31	1,067
1956	199	124	286	659	35	1,693
1957	177	115	348	698	43	1,255
1958	215	111	406	799	44	1,381
1959	243	162	332	696	32	1,079
1960	368	186	440	1,109	52	1,717
1961	461	127	365	941	46	1,057
1962	422	101	270	616	36	950
1963	397	124	492	820	67	1,221
1964	463	163	370	742	41	850
1965	501	190	502	1,020	59	1,257
1966	368	119	597	881	52	1,066
1967	507	163	681	940	60	881
1968	516	134	718	1,064	51	908
1969	481	126	840	1,139	60	780
1970	409	131	933	1,330	65	1,136
1971	443	132	1,054	1,424	60	803
1972	463	119	1,140	1,245	56	716
1973	462	124	992	1,169	48	669
1974	593	134	963	1,113	49	525
1975	622	81	1,242	1,450	47	680
1976	654	178	1,553	1,573	56	948
1977	295	80	1,447	1,022	55	737
1978	241	74	1,565	1,082	55	746
1979	208	77	1,650	1,283	40	674
1980	357	124	1,534	1,258	34	736
1981	235	64	1,080	1,008	28	478
1982	435	35	1,599	1,320	29	601
1983	550	116	1,764	1,407	40	804
1984	478	92	1,715	1,321	40	745
1985	472	72	1,845	1,218	26	708
1986	529	71	1,714	1,174	32	773
1987	281	74	1,089	723	15	490
1988	285	49	1,612	857	23	854
1989	507	196	1,630	1,444	32	981
1990	627	224	1,770	1,662	44	881
1991	431	28	1,779	1,155	37	672
1992	212	27	1,331	998	35	673
1993	359	63	1,679	1,202	38	777
1994	337	22	1,858	1,149	39	726
1995	380	58	1,764	1,097	42	798
1996	459	87	1,860	1,261	36	766
1997	464	47	2,004	1,243	38	754
1998	397	49	1,316	975	36	590
1999	254	24	1,568	990	41	791
2000	538	108	1,985	1,413	44	785

C2   Output of Main Cereal, Potato, and Sugar Beet Crops (in thousands of hectolitres or metric tons)

FRANCE (thousands of metric tons)   1815–1867

	Wheat	Rye[18]	Barley[18]	Oats[18]	Maize[18] [19]	Buckwheat[18]	Potatoes[18]	Sugar Beet
1815	2,960	1,400	830	1,710	410	340	1,630	...
1816	3,250	1,490	890	1,810	290	230	1,960	...
1817	3,600	1,590	1,070	1,920	410	410	3,610	...
1818	3,950	1,750	840	1,400	430	210	2,220	...
1819	4,490	2,190	1,070	1,850	640	...	2,900	...
1820	3,330	1,800	1,240	1,960	410	500	3,090	...
1821	4,370	2,150	1,140	2,040	350	510	3,260	...
1822	3,810	1,920	900	1,660	420	540	3,140	...
1823	4,400	2,120	1,130	2,040	450	420	3,400	...
1824	4,630	2,120	1,090	2,120	410	470	3,540	...
1825	4,580	1,890	920	1,580	460	390	...	...
1826	4,470	2,110	980	1,780	500	480	...	...
1827	4,260	1,960	1,000	1,990	350	450	...	...
1828	4,410	2,120	1,030	1,960	440	630	...	...
1829	4,820	2,320	1,000	1,960	460	510	4,130	...
1830	3,960	1,910	1,280	2,460	510	480	4,170	...
1831	4,230	1,960	1,160	2,500	520	660	5,210	...
1832	6,010	2,700	1,190	2,190	280	390	3,800	...
1833	4,960	2,430	1,020	2,010	510	380	5,660	...
1834	4,650	2,090	1,120	2,130	590	660	5,780	...
1835	5,380	2,340	1,160	2,320	490[19]	330	5,470	...
1836	4,770	...	...	...	...	...	6,160	...
1837	5,090	...	...	...	...	...	5,770	...
1838	5,080	...	...	...	...	...	6,980	...
1839	4,870	...	...	...	...	...	6,460	...
1840	6,070	1,970	1,080	2,290	540	520	6,920	1,570
1841	5,360	...	...	...	...	...	8,930	...
1842	5,350	...	...	...	...	...	7,090	...
1843	5,520	...	...	...	...	...	7,870	...
1844	6,180	...	...	...	...	...	8,950	...
1845	5,400	...	...	...	...	...	5,920	...
1846	4,550	...	...	...	...	...	5,970	...
1847	7,320	...	...	...	...	...	7,600	...
1848	6,600	...	...	...	...	...	6,640	...
1849	6,810	...	...	...	...	...	6,750	...
1850	6,600	...	...	...	...	...	5,620	...
1851	6,450[20]	...	...	...	...	...	5,300	...
1852	7,140	1,790	1,110	2,940	590	650	4,170	3,220
1853	4,780	...	...	...	...	...	4,680	...
1854	7,290	...	...	...	...	...	5,250	...
1855	5,470	...	...	...	...	...	7,210	...
1856	6,400	...	...	...	...	...	6,130	...
1857	8,280	...	...	...	...	...	7,700	...
1858	8,250	...	...	...	...	...	8,310	...
1859	6,570	...	...	...	...	...	7,000	...
1860	7,620	...	...	...	...	...	6,690	...
1861	5,640	...	...	...	...	...	7,050	...
1862	8,240	1,770	1,330	610	670	10,270	4,430	...
1863	8,760	...	...	...	...	...	8,910	...
1864	8,340	...	...	...	...	...	8,440	...
1865	7,170	...	...	...	...	...	9,190	...
1866	6,380	...	...	...	...	...	7,360	...
1867	6,220	...	...	...	...	...	8,040	...

C2 Output of Main Cereal, Potato, and Sugar Beet Crops (in thousands of hectolitres or metric tons)

FRANCE (thousands of metric tons) 1868–1919

	Wheat	Rye[18]	Barley[18]	Oats[18]	Maize[18,19]	Buckwheat[18]	Potatoes[18]	Sugar Beet
1868	8,760	...	...	...	...	...	10,820	...
1869	8,100	...	...	...	...	...	9,430	...
1870	7,420[21]	...[21]	...[21]	...[21]	...[19,21]	...[21]	...[21]	...[21]
1871	5,200	1,940	1,650	4,040	580	620[21]	8,470	...
1872	9,060	2,110	1,290	3,570	830	...	8,380	...
1873	6,140	1,470	1,190	3,190	620	...	9,150	7,740
1874	9,980	2,010	1,280	3,360	790	...	11,240	...
1875	7,550	1,960	1,170	3,240	760	590	9,440	...
1876	7,160	1,920	1,130	2,870	510	...	8,650	...
1877	7,510	1,870	1,130	3,080	780	...	9,060	...
1878	7,150	1,780	1,030	3,660	770	...	8,410	...
1879	5,990	1,360	1,020	3,520	540	...	7,740	...
1880	7,550	1,870	1,220	3,990	710[19]	670	10,470	...
1881	7,570	2,370	1,120	3,620	610	...	10,130	7,570
1882	9,870	2,110	1,250	4,080	740	700	8,550	8,310
1883	7,930	1,770	1,290	4,400	690	700	10,340	8,340
1884	8,820	1,880	1,230	4,130	710	700	10,680	7,080
1885	8,520	1,740	1,110	4,060	640	550	11,250	5,480
1886	8,240	1,620	1,140	4,220	640	650	11,290	6,890
1887	8,710	1,690	1,090	3,760	750	530	11,710	5,120
1888	7,500	1,580	1,000	3,920	710	620	10,350	5,460
1889	8,320	1,660	990	3,990	660	580	10,700	7,140
1890	8,970	1,730	1,080	4,420	590	600	11,040	6,480
1891	5,880	1,540	1,620	4,970	670	640	11,170	6,530
1892	8,460	1,700	1,040	3,890	680	610	13,540	6,220
1893	7,560	1,630	770	2,860	670	550	11,840	6,050
1894	9,370	1,900	1,080	4,270	700	600	12,820	7,640
1895	9,240	1,820	1,080	4,400	670	620	12,920	6,380
1896	9,260	1,770	1,030	4,300	770	530	12,950	8,480
1897	6,590	1,210	900	3,680	770	580	11,320	7,760
1898	9,930	1,700	1,050	4,670	600	470	11,830	6,590
1899	9,950	1,710	1,020	4,470	650	500	12,350	7,230
1900	8,860	1,510	910	4,140	570	510	12,250	8,590
1901	8,460	1,480	870	3,700	680	560	12,020	9,020
1902	8,920	1,160	940	4,640	630	570	11,190	7,440
1903	9,880	1,480	980	5,000	650	630	11,610	7,900
1904	8,150	1,340	850	4,220	500	400	12,280	5,800
1905	9,110	1,490	910	4,440	610	520	14,260	9,550
1906	8,950	1,300	820	4,280	370	280	10,130	7,190
1907	10,380	1,430	970	5,120	610	470	13,940	7,180
1908	8,620	1,310	920	4,750	660	510	17,010	7,790
1909	9,780	1,410	1,040	5,560	660	530	16,680	8,220
1910	6,880	1,110	970	4,820	590	590	8,520	7,740
1911	8,770	1,190	1,090	5,070	430	210	12,770	5,760
1912	9,100	1,240	1,100	5,150	600	500	15,020	9,540
1913	8,690[22]	1,270[22]	1,040[22]	5,180[22]	540[22]	560[22]	13,590[22]	7,990[22]
1914	7,690	1,110	980	4,620	570	530	11,990	6,060
1915	6,060	840	690	3,460	430	460	9,400	1,740
1916	5,580	850	830	4,020	420	270	8,780	2,780
1917	3,660	630	810	3,110	380	380	10,410	2,710
1918	6,140	730	600	2,560	250	220	6,520	1,480
1919	4,970[21,22]	730[21,22]	500[21,22]	2,490[21,22]	250[21,22]	270[21,22]	7,730[21,22]	1,720[21,22]
	5,120	780	570	2,620	260	...	...	...

C2 Output of Main Cereal, Potato, and Sugar Beet Crops (in thousands of hectolitres or metric tons)

FRANCE (thousands of metric tons)   1920-1972

	Wheat	Rye[18]	Barley[18]	Oats[18]	Maize[18 19]	Buckwheat[18]	Potatoes[18]	Sugar Beet
1920	6,450	880	840	4,230	390	360	11,640	2,930
1921	8,800	1,130	830	3,550	260	250	8,310	2,440
1922	6,620	980	890	4,180	320	390	12,650	3,960
1923	7,500	930	980	4,890	320	320	9,920	4,460
1924	7,650	1,020	1,050	4,430	460	420	15,350	6,460
1925	8,990	1,110	1,030	4,760	510	410	15,200	5,980
1926	6,310	760	1,000	5,290	320	370	11,130	5,450
1927	7,520	860	1,100	4,980	530	420	17,530	6,760
1928	7,660	870	1,100	4,940	310	310	11,260	6,560
1929	9,180	930	1,300	5,420	470	340	16,170	7,880
1930	6,210	720	920	4,150	570	360	13,920	10,820
1931	7,190	750	1,040	4,590	630	370	16,300	7,230
1932	9,080	860	1,090	4,820	410	370	16,480	8,850
1933	9,860	900	1,150	5,670	430	300	14,820	8,710
1934	9,210	840	1,030	4,380	510	330	16,650	10,310
1935	7,760	750	1,030	4,460	570	280	14,320	8,280
1936	6,930	710	1,000	4,210	530	340	15,250	8,680
1937	7,020	740	1,020	4,350	510	230	15,880	8,670
1938	9,800[23]	810[23]	1,290[23]	5,460[23]	580[23]	240[23]	17,310[23]	7,980[23]
1939	7,300	750	1,360	5,270	610	290	14,410	11,570
1940	5,060	540	920	3,230	410	220	10,290	5,000
1941	5,580	360	780	2,700	300	180	6,940	5,600
1942	5,480[23]	340[23]	760[23]	3,000[23]	200[23]	85[23]	6,930[23]	7,210[23]
1943	6,380	340	710	2,810	190	95	6,530	6,120
1944	6,360[23]	330[23]	630[23]	2,580[23]	250[23]	84[23]	7,560[23]	5,070[23]
1945	4,210	270	660	2,600	160	85	6,060	4,470
1946	6,760	460	1,060	3,770	210	70	9,880	6,630
1947	3,270	380	1,120	2,810	200	63	10,960	5,890
1948	7,630	640	1,270	3,380	460	86	15,680	9,430
1949	8,080	650	1,430	3,220	190	66	9,650	9,610
1950	7,700	610	1,570	3,310	400	73	12,940	13,580
1951	7,120	490	1,660	3,690	690	88	12,070	11,830
1952	8,420	480	1,730	3,350	480	93	11,070	9,500
1953	8,980	470	2,240	3,660	800	95	13,640	12,540
1954	10,570	510	2,520	3,570	960	75	15,860	11,660
1955	10,360	440	2,670	3,640	1,090	54	13,750	10,980
1956	5,680	470	6,410	4,600	1,740	71	16,850	10,880
1957	11,080	480	3,630	2,580	1,390	64	13,900	11,250
1958	9,600	440	3,890	2,640	1,670	61	12,750	12,890
1959	11,540	470	4,930	2,810	1,820	51	12,210	7,760
1960	11,010	420	5,720	2,740	2,810	45	14,890	19,020
1961	9,570	350	5,410	2,590	2,470	56	14,190	13,240
1962	14,050	360	6,000	2,630	1,860	45	13,260	11,560
1963	10,250	360	7,380	2,880	3,870	46	15,820	13,950
1964	13,840	390	6,790	2,310	2,110	34	11,420	16,240
1965	14,760	387	7,378	2,509	3,420	34	11,068	16,961
1966	11,297	357	7,421	2,578	4,331	30	10,439	12,889
1967	14,288	344	9,874	2,821	4,139	27	10,231	12,769
1968	14,985	327	9,139	2,528	5,379	22	9,836	17,557
1969	14,459	309	9,452	2,309	5,723	22	8,860	17,900
1970	12,922	287	8,126	2,100	7,581	19	8,694	17,522
1971	15,482	294	8,910	2,540	8,954	19	8,829	19,951
1972	18,046	328	10,466	2,478	8,252	18	7,245	19,276

C2 Output of Main Cereal, Potato, and Sugar Beet Crops (in thousands of hectolitres or metric tons)

FRANCE (thousands of metric tons)

	Wheat	Rye[18]	Barley[18]	Oats[18]	Maize[18][19]	Buckwheat[18]	Potatoes[18]	Sugar Beet
1973	17,850	327	10,948	2,208	10,692	14	7,209	22,688
1974	19,141	311	10,037	2,081	8,692	15	7,356	21,556
1975	15,013	292	9,344	1,948	8,194	13	6,495	23,656
1976	16,126	310	8,530	1,431	5,617	...	4,193	22,869
1977	17,450	389	10,262	1,901	8,505	...	7,668	27,133
1978	20,968	435	11,321	1,865	9,525	...	7,326	24,488
1979	19,544	355	11,196	1,845	10,406	...	7,008	26,060
1980	23,781	408	11,692	1,924	9,323	...	6,609	28,442
1981	23,772	330	10,102	1,756	9,146	...	6,347	36,429
1982	25,358	326	10,036	1,802	10,446	...	6,642	32,331
1983	24,795	293	8,773	1,419	10,515	...	5,317	26,320
1984	33,026	347	11,512	1,875	10,434	...	6,126	28,752
1985	2,883	297	11,442	1,770	12,448	...	6,913	29,989
1986	26,472	234	10,105	1,067	11,675	...	6,267	25,873
1987	27,221	298	10,400	1,098	12,470	...	6,696	26,284
1988	29,677	276	10,086	1,074	14,200	...	6,344	28,606
1989	31,817	262	9,810	1,025	12,926	...	5,750	27,694
1990	33,363	248	10,067	875	8,996	...	6,000	29,925
1991	34,345	218	10,643	734	12,873	...	5,487	29,520
1992	32,507	208	10,476	694	14,886	...	6,676	31,675
1993	29,324	189	8,995	714	14,966	...	5,801	31,748
1994	30,500	174	7,649	685	12,958	26	5,463	29,036
1995	30,880	191	7,683	601	12,740	17	5,839	30,571
1996	35,949	221	9,519	622	14,530	15	6,249	31,211
1997	33,847	197	10,124	568	16,832	19	6,690	34,372
1998	39,809	216	10,591	888	15,206	26	6,053	31,156
1999	37,050	165	9,378	514	15,357	25	6,645	32,919
2000	37,355	146	9,717	459	16,073	37	6,652	31,131

GERMANY[24] (thousands of metric tons)

	Wheat	Rye	Barley	Oats	Mixed Corn & Buckwheat	Potatoes	Sugar Beet
1846	1,416	2,927	1,533	2,383	...	7,055	233
1857	1,944	6,325	1,945	2,948	...	9,166	316
1858	1,855	5,439	2,150	3,528	...	12,363	464
1949	1,902	5,647	2,065	3,391	...	11,390	556
1850	1,846	4,499	1,872	3,098	596	10,942	627
1851	1,747	4,318	1,912	3,382	593	7,123	853
1852	2,164	4,972	1,741	2,826	572	11,644	1,064
1853	1,836	4,733	1,866	3,372	573	9,060	1,010
1854	2,264	5,567	2,097	3,888	640	9,107	936
1855	1,524	3,894	2,067	3,804	516	10,146	984
1856	2,224	5,949	2,174	4,072	631	13,941	1,121
1857	2,456	6,059	1,585	2,408	528	16,501	1,467
1858	1,822	5,022	1,407	2,470	434	15,973	1,612
1859	2,109	4,694	1,514	3,336	483	14,667	1,861
1860	2,491	6,561	2,261	4,623	640	11,925	1,632
1861	2,326	5,374	2,118	4,118	558	14,212	1,574
1862	2,296	5,705	2,260	4,526	580	17,629	1,610
1863	2,504	6,542	2,052	3,858	569	20,717	1,895
1864	2,497	6,496	2,279	4,474	590	17,974	2,011
1865	2,186	5,645	2,089	4,002	513	21,592	2,205
1866	2,223	5,264	1,989	3,952	494	16,046	2,411
1867	1,981	5,076	1,956	3,946	460	17,664	2,439
1868	2,852	7,499	2,213	3,857	565	22,116	2,300
1869	2,652	6,307	2,201	4,110	530	20,077	2,300
1870	2,409[24]	6,247[24]	2,101[24]	3,973[24]	487[24]	20,366[24]	2,300[24]
1871	2,544	5,821	2,254	4,427	481	14,850	2,300
1872	2,750	6,251	2,264	4,554	497	25,510	2,251
1873	2,720	5,639	2,138	4,326	460	20,163	3,182
1874	4,267	7,051	2,217	4,302	495	26,452	3,529
1875	2,724	6,409	1,979	3,832	432	22,816	2,757
1876	2,562	5,774	1,992	4,202	413	23,914	4,161

C2 Output of Main Cereal, Potato, and Sugar Beet Crops (in thousands of hectolitres or metric tons)

GERMANY[24] (thousands of metric tons)   1877–1919

	Wheat	Rye	Barley	Oats	Mixed Corn & Buckwheat	Potatoes	Sugar Beet
1877	2,982	7,374	2,002	4,196	446	20,952	3,550
1878	3,503	8,190	2,770	6,101	552	27,613	4,488
1879	3,161	6,581	2,454	5,169	470	22,092	4,064
1880	3,236	5,862	2,550	5,128	466	22,795	4,738
1881	2,879	6,445	2,466	4,531	466	29,839	6,272
1882	3,441	7,112	2,676	5,429	552	21,132	8,769
1883	3,196	6,568	2,539	4,516	505	29,147	8,897
1884	3,377	6,414	2,672	5,124	525	28,091	10,399
1885	3,513	6,894	2,700	5,264	541	32,774	9,300
1886	3,550	7,182	2,752	5,901	568	29,433	8,370
1887	3,746	7,536	2,614	5,220	550	29,559	8,100
1888	3,270	6,512	2,688	5,595	523	25,608	7,891
1889	3,041	6,324	2,308	5,092	550	31,135	9,200
1890	3,743	6,926	2,712	5,934	536	27,316	10,623
1891	3,095	5,644	2,801	6,357	486	21,718	9,488
1892	3,987	8,064	2,873	5,743	550	32,728	9,790
1893	3,933	8,942	2,360	4,180	471	40,724	9,794
1894	3,876	8,343	2,849	6,580	548	33,609	12,537
1895	3,643	7,725	2,794	6,244	529	37,786	11,196
1896	3,845	8,534	2,727	5,969	502	32,329	12,616
1897	3,726	8,171	2,564	5,719	515	33,776	12,637
1898	4,122	9,032	2,829	6,754	533	36,721	11,569
1899	4,323	8,676	2,984	6,883	568	38,486	13,254
1900	4,307	8,551	3,002	7,092	546	40,585	16,013
1901	2,931	8,163	3,321	7,050	509	48,687	16,030
1902	4,383	9,494	3,100	7,467	574	43,462	12,940
1903	4,003	9,904	3,324	7,873	587	42,902	15,200
1904	4,259	10,061	2,948	6,936	555	36,287	12,340
1905	4,187	9,607	2,922	6,547	527	48,323	17,370
1906	4,399	9,626	3,111	8,431	571	42,937	16,480
1907	3,937	9,758	3,498	9,149	587	45,538	15,900
1908	4,212	10,737	3,060	7,695	560	46,393	14,630
1909	4,254	11,348	3,496	9,126	606	46,706	15,510
1910	4,249	10,511	2,903	7,900	545	43,468	18,150
1911	4,469	10,866	3,160	7,704	557	34,374	10,080
1912	4,768	11,548	3,482	8,520	594	50,209	17,330
1913	5,094	12,222	3,673	9,714	621	54,121	18,540
1914	4,343	10,427	3,138	9,038	...	45,570	16,919
1915	4,235	9,152	2,484	5,986	...	53,973	10,963
1916	3,288	8,937	2,797	7,025	...	25,074	10,145
1917	2,484[24]	7,003[24]	1,865[24]	3,716[24]	...[24]	34,882[24]	9,967[24]
1918	2,528[24]	6,676[24]	1,850[24]	4,381[24]	...[24]	24,744[24]	9,884[24]
1919	2,315	6,100	1,670	4,494	...	21,479	5,819

C2 Output of Main Cereal, Potato, and Sugar Beet Crops (in thousands of hectolitres or metric tons)

GERMANY[24] (thousands of metric tons)   1920–1944

	Wheat	Rye	Barley	Oats	Maize	Mixed Corn & Buckwheat	Potatoes	Sugar Beet
1920	2,434	4,972	1,800	4,870	…	…	28,249	7,964
1921	3,140[24]	6,798[24]	1,939[24]	5,004[24]	…	…[24]	26,149[24]	7,980[24]
1922	2,071	5,234	1,607	4,015	…	…	40,661	10,792
1923	3,057	6,682	2,361	6,107	…	…	32,580	8,696
1924	3,053	6,876	2,808	6,785	…	558	43,682	10,267
1925	3,878	9,272	2,989	6,423	…	595	47,976	10,326
1926	3,135	7,367	2,832	7,274	…	530	34,536	10,495
1927	3,931	7,859	3,149	7,299	…	650	43,183	10,854
1928	4,424	9,374	3,682	7,696	…	711	45,396	11,011
1929	3,850	8,971	3,499	7,946	…	743	43,660	11,091
1930	4,320	8,447	3,146	5,990	…	622	50,783	14,919
1931	4,804	7,348	3,320	6,478	…	660	46,815	11,039
1932	5,674	9,200	3,537	6,766	…	748	39,632	7,876
1933	6,342	9,600	3,815	6,911	…	788	46,031	8,579
1934	5,144[24]	8,369[24]	3,524[24]	5,300[24]	…	744[24]	48,371[24]	10,394[24]
1935	5,269	8,226	3,727	5,925	…	1,040	45,118	10,568
1936	4,975	8,125	3,739	6,180	…	1,033	50,956	12,096
1937	5,034	7,609	4,002	6,511	121	1,265	60,841	15,701
1938	6,250	9,467	4,673	7,003	179	1,409[25]	55,983	15,545
1939	4,956	8,404	3,726	6,143	106	1,291	51,867	16,770
1940	4,123	6,537	3,118	5,990	65	1,360	54,794	16,503
1941	4,285	7,320	3,135	5,045	48	1,395	45,238	16,086
1942	3,573	5,654	3,195	6,069	45	2,116	52,993	16,403
1943	4,341	7,745	2,632	5,389	42	1,397	39,127	14,607
1944	3,808	7,508	2,291	4,444	39	1,242	41,240	13,671

EAST GERMANY (thousands of metric tons)   1946–1969

	Wheat[1]	Rye	Barley	Oats	Mixed Corn	Potatoes	Sugar Beet
1946	776	1,403	504	1,111	242	10,404	4,065
1947	504	1,523	446	963	281	8,063	3,122
1948	999	1,950	428	809	204	12,419	4,584
1949	1,065	2,356	517	1,016	226	9,940	3,867
1950	1,214	2,418	587	1,127	282	14,706	5,754
1951	1,494	2,992	746	1,556	387	14,872	6,047
1952	1,442	2,864	685	1,430	369	13,935	6,336
1953	1,152	2,292	806	1,446	352	13,273	6,062
1954	1,081	2,394	749	1,128	305	15,520	6,952
1955	1,211	2,337	924	1,362	326	11,194	5,712
1956	1,086	2,299	834	1,112	411	13,565	4,324
1957	1,259	2,231	897	999	441	14,529	6,465
1958	1,363	2,368	931	1,143	500	11,498	6,976
1959	1,371	2,133	1,039	966	435	12,436	4,659
1960	1,456	2,126	1,269	1,007	516	14,821	6,837
1961	1,038	1,504	947	856	495	8,430	4,657
1962	1,315	1,726	1,164	1,054	675	13,284	4,970
1963	1,280	1,675	1,197	807	574	12,886	6,176
1964	1,348	1,890	1,496	774	675	12,872	6,003
1965	1,802	1,810	1,651	758	610	12,857	5,804
1966	1,521	1,642	1,525	703	525	12,823	6,611
1967	2,012	1,986	1,927	845	583	14,065	6,948
1968	2,377	1,936	2,121	864	530	12,639	6,998
1969	1,987	1,544	2,067	841	480	8,832	4,856

C2 Output of Main Cereal, Potato, and Sugar Beet Crops (in thousands of hectolitres or metric tons)

EAST GERMANY (thousands of metric tons)   **1970–1993**

	Wheat[1]	Rye	Barley	Oats	Mixed Corn	Potatoes	Sugar Beet
1970	2,132	1,483	1,926	558	343	13,054	6,135
1971	2,490	1,754	2,286	807	395	9,412	5,128
1972	2,744	1,904	2,592	890	379	12,140	7,223
1973	2,861	1,699	2,848	806	276	11,401	6,682
1974	3,154	1,949	3,422	922	254	13,404	6,959
1975	2,736	1,563	3,681	780	148	7,673	6,414
1976	2,715	1,455	3,456	506	58	6,816	5,106
1977	2,914	1,644	3,681	411	43	10,313	8,578
1978	3,147	1,895	4,135	595	47	10,777	7,569
1979	3,116	1,830	3,323	532	51	12,243	6,695
1980	3,098	1,917	3,979	582	46	9,214	7,034
1981	2,942	1,797	3,476	598	47	10,378	8,043
1982	2,739	2,119	4,055	848	259	8,883	7,193
1983	3,550	2,092	3,882	498	44	7,063	5,711
1984	3,903	2,510	4,138	700	98	11,908	7,820
1985	3,936	2,505	4,366	746	86	12,350	7,397
1986	4,195	2,406	4,293	666	101	9,997	7,747
1987	4,040	2,283	4,198	637	60	12,228	7,683
1988	3,699	1,785	3,798	507	30	11,546	4,625
1989	3,477	2,103	4,683	476	…	9,167	6,220

Included in
West
Germany

WEST GERMANY (thousands of metric tons)   **1949–1976**

	Wheat[1]	Rye	Barley	Oats	Maize	Mixed Corn & Buckwheat	Potatoes	Sugar Beet
1949	2,471	3,310	1,213	2,600	21	607	20,875	4,735
1950	2,614	3,021	1,472	2,545	17	537	27,959	6,975
1951	2,949	3,034	1,688	2,835	21	648	24,103	7,291
1952	3,291	3,119	1,757	2,616	16	686	23,854	6,845
1953	3,179	3,280	2,072	2,554	20	847	24,535	8,422
1954	2,892	4,098	1,920	2,473	20	1,187	26,769	9,013
1955	3,379	3,495	2,079	2,477	20	1,031	22,874	8,936
1956	3,487	3,735	2,310	2,451	20[26]	1,130	26,756	8,346
1957	3,843[26]	3,816[26]	2,504[26]	2,228[26]	16	1,534[26]	26,289[26]	9,690[26]
	3,870	3,838	2,513	2,250		1,537	26,488	9,692
1958	3,721[27]	3,748[27]	2,423[27]	2,172[27]	13	1,089[27]	22,850[27]	11,237[27]
	3,751						22,864	
1959	4,522	3,887	2,843	2,039	13	1,105	22,720	8,169
1960	4,965	3,798	3,221	2,179	20	1,349	24,559	12,325
1961	4,038	2,515	2,722	1,913	23	1,203	21,516	9,253
1962	4,592	2,966	3,744	2,333	43	1,554	25,104	9,525
1963	4,856	3,239	3,562	2,321	48	1,409	25,812	12,493
1964	5,203	3,609	3,915	2,308	63	1,453	20,624	12,863
1965	4,348	2,825	3,364	2,052	96	1,201	18,095	10,939
1966	4,533	2,696	3,869	2,340	127	1,259	18,839	12,468
1967	5,819	3,162	4,734	2,718	196	1,396	21,294	13,697
1968	6,198	3,189	4,974	2,893	287	1,527	19,196	13,633
1969	6,000	2,889	5,130	2,976	400	1,535	15,985	12,941
1970	5,662	2,665	4,754	2,484	507	1,226	16,250	13,329
1971	7,142	3,032	5,774	3,037	594	1,367	15,176	14,410
1972	6,608	2,917	5,997	2,888	564	1,270	15,038	14,656
1973	7,134	2,576	6,622	3,045	573	1,226	13,677	15,858
1974	7,761	2,560	7,048	3,482	521	1,282	14,549	16,499
1975	7,014	2,125	6,970	3,445	531	1,170	10,853	18,203
1976	6,702	2,100	6,487	2,497	480	868	9,808	18,930

C2 Output of Main Cereal, Potato, and Sugar Beet Crops (in thousands of hectolitres or metric tons)

WEST GERMANY (thousands of metric tons)   1977–2000

	Wheat[1]	Rye	Barley	Oats	Maize	Mixed Corn & Buckwheat	Potatoes	Sugar Beet
1977	7,235	2,540	7,582	2,714	579	960	11,368	20,649
1978	8,118	2,457	8,608	3,202	617	938	10,510	18,777
1979	8,061	2,114	8,184	2,994	741	777	10,205	18,337
1980	8,156	2,098	8,826	2,658	672	677	7,932	19,122
1981	8,313	1,729	8,687	2,678	832	587	8,422	24,383
1982	8,632	1,639	9,460	3,113	1,054	727	7,821	22,732
1983	8,998	1,599	8,944	2,068	934	469	6,299	16,295
1984	10,223	1,931	10,284	2,507	1,026	518	8,050	20,060
1985	9,866	1,821	9,690	2,807	1,204	527	7,905	20,813
1986	10,406	1,768	9,377	2,276	1,302	460	7,390	20,260
1987	9,932	1,599	8,571	2,008	1,217	344	6,836	19,049
1988	11,922	1,579	9,587	2,038	1,535	449	7,434	18,590
1989	11,032	1,797	9,716	1,534	1,574	460	7,948	20,767
Germany								
1990	15,787	4,001	14,073	2,115	1,545	695	16,616	29,878
1991	16,612	3,323	10,843	1,155	1,937	1,034	10,584	25,926
1992	15,542	2,422	10,476	998	2,139	1,144	10,897	27,150
1993	15,520	2,936	8,995	1,202	2,730	1,405	12,074	28,160
1994	16,539	3,451	10,903	1,663	2,446	1,365	10,635	24,211
1995	17,763	4,521	11,891	1,420	2,395	1,342	10,888	26,048
1996	18,922	4,214	12,074	1,605	2,913	1,269	13,558	26,064
1997	19,827	4,580	13,399	1,599	3,188	1,102	12,067	25,769
1998	20,187	4,775	12,512	1,279	2,781	1,270	11,711	26,787
1999	19,615	4,329	13,301	1,339	3,257	1,343	12,031	27,578
2000	21,634	4,208	12,201	1,087	3,324	1,407	13,694	27,870

GREECE (thousands of metric tons)[28]   1911–1952

	Wheat	Rye	Barley	Oats	Maize	Mixed Corn	Potatoes
1911	344	6	80	32	151	...	28
1912	...[28]	...[28]	...[28]	...[28]	...[28]	...	...[28]
1913	...	...	...	...	...	...	...
1914	357[28]	3[28]	103[28]	54[28]	239[28]	...	44[28]
1915	246	4	87	45	147	...	46
1916	220[28]	4[28]	86[28]	40[28]	120[28]	...	41[28]
1917	313	18	126	52	155	...	47
1918	374[28]	26[28]	158[28]	66[28]	164[28]	...	47[28]
1919	267	29	118	56	192	34	40
1920	305	26	135	61	204	40	50
1921	281[28]	27[28]	129[28]	54[28]	192[28]	38[28]	42[28]
1922	246	28	129	68	143	27	46
1923	239	16	117	58	162	32	51
1924	210	23	94	45	156	17	48
1925	305	40	151	79	173	24	41
1926	338	41	166	72	207	28	50
1927	353	38	158	68	130	27	33
1928	356	44	158	76	129	23	33
1929	311	34	104	61	178	18	35
1930	264	47	171	86	173	20	54
1931	306	46	156	77	159	29	63
1932	465	53	193	99	214	35	85
1933	773	71	230	134	273	47	113
1934	699	63	196	99	210	32	108
1935	740	55	194	100	192	30	104
1936	532	42	154	94	287	39	129
1937	818	65	219	134	323	44	193
1938	980	58	221	135	217	50	158
1939	923	48	185	127	256	45	187
1945	375	24	81	46	141	18	128
1946	729	57	163	89	190	34	230
1947	578	40	130	78	276	30	301
1948	770	43	215	108	229	40	320
1949	839	41	196	113	222	37	394
1950	850	48	200	120	195	32	347
1951	930	46	230	140	250	42	412
1952	1,050	56	213	116	230	34	453

C2 Output of Main Cereal, Potato, and Sugar Beet Crops (in thousands of hectolitres or metric tons)

GREECE (thousands of metric tons)[28]   **1953–2000**

	Wheat	Rye	Barley	Oats	Maize	Mixed Corn	Potatoes
1953	1,400	67	258	167	309	35	445
1954	1,219	51	253	150	254	32	442
1955	1,337	54	224	157	285	31	422
1956	1,245	47	229	148	238	29	456
1957	1,720	45	241	191	257	32	507
1958	1,786	41	266	175	225	23	469
1959	1,767	27	217	139	290	14	490
1960	1,666	28	240	149	288	15	423
1961	1,528	22	221	144	228	8	400
1962	1,722	20	232	152	215	8	403
1963	1,417	18	207	127	253	7	466
1964	2,088	18	242	139	249	6	544
1965	2,072	16	338	150	249	6	517
1966	2,020	15	563	167	275	5	531
1967	1,936	13	774	153	313	5	599
1968	1,568	8	471	98	344	3	603
1969	1,723	9	447	102	413	3	576
1970	1,931	9	737	107	511	2	756
1971	1,946	9	781	115	571	2	668
1972	1,768	8	874	113	584	1	689
1973	1,682	6	850	108	605	1	765
1974	2,152	7	969	120	458	1	778
1975	2,120	7	916	114	488	1	878
1976	2,376	9	944	104	505	1	1,018
1977	1,767	6	662	77	496	1	1,015
1978	2,704	6	891	94	523	1	908
1979	2,407	6	861	76	711	1	968
1980	2,970	7	911	83	1,279	…	1,084
1981	2,932	8	742	82	1,507	…	1,056
1982	3,039	11	823	82	1,550	…	1,021
1983	2,059	13	624	62	1,758	…	1,135
1984	2,316	18	854	66	2,162	…	1,051
1985	1,806	23	583	64	1,908	…	1,023
1986	2,389	29	838	80	1,994	…	971
1987	2,213	32	573	70	2,156	…	980
1988	2,183	44	605	68	2,251	…	960
1989	2,030	38	660	64	1,740	…	1,107
1990	1,580	30	400	47	1,700	…	1,100
1991	3,227	50	465	80	2,306	…	1,088
1992	2,344	42	436	73	2,048	…	1,020
1993	2,143	42	415	75	2,099	…	1,006
1994	2,470	39	416	82	2,071	…	968
1995	2,315	39	412	84	1,839	…	1,051
1996	1,882	35	356	80	2,110	…	980
1997	1,991	36	348	88	2,025	…	883
1998	1,880	41	326	83	1,816	…	876
1999	2,064	36	320	86	1,950	…	867
2000	2,183	32	303	87	2,037	…	883

HUNGARY[29]   **1851–1874**

	Wheat	Rye[30]	Barley	Oats	Maize	Potatoes	Sugar Beet
			thousands of hectolitres				thou.tons
1851	20,134	19,520	18,653	29,103	21,287	16,980	…
1854	21,358	24,072	15,645	31,370	34,057	22,264	…
1857	29,287	27,540	19,216	36,083	39,142	17,772	…
1859	27,922[29]	28,927[29]	19,300[29]	35,842[29]	38,338[29]	17,694[29]	…
1869	17,725	17,223	8,457	10,998	17,683	14,714	94
1870	22,260	17,728	11,132	12,777	21,821	12,159	138
1871	15,819	15,852[30]	12,256	14,110	12,323	11,327	117
		16,061					
1872	15,564	13,121	10,738	15,265	17,893	12,560	127
1873	14,076	7,977	9,900	12,426	12,240	8,418	82
1874	21,614	14,906	12,449	14,030	7,602	15,514	154

C2 Output of Main Cereal, Potato, and Sugar Beet Crops (in thousands of hectolitres or metric tons)

HUNGARY[29]

1875–1927

	Wheat	Rye	Barley	Oats	Maize	Potatoes	Sugar Beet
1875	17,243	12,809	7,609	7,829	28,138	14,447	124
1876	18,218	10,486	11,117	13,854	22,968	17,418	150
1877	25,316	15,345	12,043	14,038	20,425	15,681	155
1878	38,277	21,388	16,709	21,203	36,249	32,422	278
1879	18,434	10,480	9,200	10,480	23,243	15,851	261
1880	27,954	14,465	17,943	21,729	34,806	31,024	339
1881	31,327	16,759	14,065	16,847	28,866	30,395	597
1882	46,431	21,478	20,286	23,787	37,891	42,713	674
1883	31,909	16,677	13,849	18,029	30,740	43,285	738
1884	37,783	18,106	16,498	20,118	31,836	39,978	676
1885	40,108	17,642	19,141	19,187	38,447	38,607	595
1886	36,245	15,530	13,344	19,379	29,768	32,839	626
1887	51,421	21,263	19,636	21,672	25,979	32,602	500
1888	47,880	17,626	15,899	19,917	33,613	37,549	806
1889	32,959	14,981	12,164	15,379	36,083	40,101	1,109
1890	<u>52,165</u>	<u>20,235</u>	<u>18,647</u>	<u>18,777</u>	<u>31,685</u>	<u>29,755</u>	985
			thousands of metric tons				
1891	3,777	1,096	1,212	986	3,792	2,079	1,312
1892	3,865	1,332	1,161	979	3,026	2,774	1,337
1893	4,371	1,607	1,410	1,055	3,483	3,269	1,543
1894	3,962	1,558	1,311	1,088	1,780	2,838	1,461
1895	4,444	1,251	1,187	1,051	3,709	3,239	1,255
1896	4,127	1,334	1,328	1,084	3,334	3,609	1,512
1897	2,206	926	915	799	2,639	3,041	1,424
1898	3,490	1,180	1,248	1,142	3,236	3,729	1,495
1899	3,845	1,304	1,341	1,179	2,946	3,605	1,618
1900	3,843	1,113	1,173	1,025	3,243	4,497	1,979
1901	3,373	1,127	1,090	988	3,236	4,314	1,918
1902	4,651	1,361	1,358	1,202	2,656	3,852	1,951
1903	4,408	1,291	1,406	1,268	3,448	4,501	2,096
1904	3,731	1,198	1,087	911	1,509	3,005	1,591
1905	4,287	1,374	1,360	1,132	2,389	4,578	1,923
1906	5,373	1,415	1,519	1,273	4,138	4,874	2,649
1907	3,280	1,069	1,373	1,154	3,953	4,849	2,361
1908	4,142	1,219	1,226	1,018	3,712	3,796	2,067
1909	3,085	1,196	1,565	1,339	4,111	4,995	2,593
1910	4,619	1,329	1,168	1,026	4,769	4,816	2,873
1911	4,760	1,279	1,602	1,301	3,491	4,438	2,940
1912	4,717	1,375	1,527	1,114	4,488	5,384	4,796
1913	4,119	1,327	1,738	1,449	4,625	4,875	4,776
1914	2,864	1,077	1,421	1,256	4,377	5,315	4,014
1915	4,048	1,161	1,270	1,174	4,068	5,784	2,532
1916	3,055	950	1,130	1,228	2,370	4,361	2,007
1917	3,354	1,014	804	775	2,632	2,991	1,590
1918	<u>2,588</u>[29]	<u>824</u>[29]	<u>879</u>[29]	<u>667</u>[29]	<u>2,397</u>[29]	<u>3,122</u>[29]	<u>2,154</u>[29]
1920	1,032	514	472	324	1,274	2,072	640
1921	1,435	588	466	319	805	1,249	543
1922	1,489	639	483	327	1,238	1,320	711
1923	1,843	794	594	399	1,251	1,334	864
1924	1,403	561	320	228	1,883	1,535	1,274
1925	1,951	826	554	371	2,235	2,310	1,527
1926	2,039	798	555	360	1,944	1,875	1,445
1927	2,094	568	516	327	1,736	2,005	1,455

C2 Output of Main Cereal, Potato, and Sugar Beet Crops (in thousands of hectolitres or metric tons)

HUNGARY   **1928–1980**

	Wheat	Rye	Barley	Oats	Maize	Potatoes	Sugar Beet
1928	2,700	828	668	400	1,260	1,471	1,438
1929	2,041	798	683	411	1,794	2,168	1,607
1930	2,295	722	601	261	1,407	1,841	1,461
1931	1,975	550	476	194	1,518	1,447	966
1932	1,754	770	719	316	2,432	1,557	849
1933	2,622	956	841	358	1,809	1,856	944
1934	1,764	619	544	259	2,098	2,119	922
1935	2,292	728	556	246	1,418	1,393	769
1936	2,389	714	658	262	2,593	2,451	1,124
1937	1,964	618	557	270	2,759	2,559	1,013
1938	2,688	805	724	310	2,662	2,141	969
1939	2,689	762	652	321	2,185	2,026	918
1940	1,819	597	551	319	2,379	2,372	1,168
1941	1,886	560	603	339	1,806	2,192	906
1942	1,703	513	511	279	1,444	1,804	738
1943	2,279	669	705	352	1,246	1,821	726
1944	2,319	646	679	318	2,297	2,636	...
1945	658	304	442	171	1,871	1,691	178
1946	1,127	424	441	198	1,364	1,143	516
1947	1,152	430	399	167	1,781	1,061	1,159
1948	1,583	786	692	334	2,862	2,117	1,771
1949	1,830	750	690	240	...	1,920	1,240
1950	2,040	790	640	220	...	...	1,240
1951	2,350	790	723	188	2,833	2,050	2,000
1952	1,699	542	567	134	1,172	1,170	1,375
1953	2,182	562	757	164	2,602	1,900	2,850
1954	1,660	480	587	150	2,550	1,991	1,920
1955	2,131	544	794	176	2,912	2,467	2,241
1956	1,845	494	645	176	2,034	2,055	1,948
1957	1,959	487	962	263	3,233	2,707	1,878
1958	1,487	371	735	192	2,833	2,600	2,070
1959	1,909	443	1,093	256	3,558	2,366	2,679
1960	1,768	364	986	219	3,534	3,001	3,370
1961	1,936	310	984	152	2,727	1,830	2,356
1962	1,973	245	1,150	132	3,269	2,149	2,653
1963	1,593	228	875	123	3,582	2,298	3,434
1964	2,143	275	822	60	3,552	1,949	3,554
1965	2,443	288	1,012	63	3,564	1,485	3,452
1966	2,327	242	916	72	3,907	2,433	3,570
1967	3,004	225	934	86	3,522	1,507	3,356
1968	3,352	238	904	68	3,764	1,335	3,471
1969	3,579	235	908	80	4,754	1,590	3,303
1970	2,723	158	553	57	4,072	1,813	2,175
1971	3,922	182	785	91	4,732	1,797	2,023
1972	4,095	173	807	64	5,554	1,349	2,909
1973	4,502	178	874	72	5,963	1,355	2,754
1974	4,971	177	899	75	6,247	1,720	3,708
1975	4,007	147	701	92	7,172	1,630	4,089
1976	5,148	157	749	92	5,141	1,396	3,943
1977	5,319	144	708	69	6,007	1,650	3,890
1978	5,677	138	763	82	6,655	1,883	4,192
1979	3,709	93	710	93	7,396	1,512	3,927
1980	6,077	141	929	113	6,673	1,392	3,941

C2 Output of Main Cereal, Potato, and Sugar Beet Crops (in thousands of hectolitres or metric tons)

HUNGARY 1981–2000

	Wheat	Rye	Barley	Oats	Maize	Potatoes	Sugar Beet
1981	4,614	116	903	169	6,998	1,608	4,719
1982	5,762	117	871	123	7,959	1,459	5,371
1983	5,985	138	1,013	124	6,426	1,234	3,783
1984	7,392	193	1,220	156	6,686	1,551	4,360
1985	6,578	166	1,046	133	6,818	1,378	4,073
1986	5,793	172	857	126	7,261	1,264	3,760
1987	5,748	186	794	99	7,234	1,077	4,258
1988	7,026	255	1,183	138	6,256	1,407	4,511
1989	6,840	267	1,340	149	4,560	1,332	5,301
1990	6,159	266	1,359	158	4,500	1,200	5,674
1991	6,008	223	1,555	135	7,745	1,088	5,867
1992	3,453	136	1,723	147	4,405	1,020	2,928
1993	3,050	120	1,150	100	4,500	1,006	2,300
1994	4,874	193	1,558	131	4,761	946	3,370
1995	4,614	171	1,408	139	4,679	1,099	4,199
1996	3,912	98	921	112	5,989	1,308	4,677
1997	5,259	153	1,330	138	6,828	1,139	3,691
1998	4,898	129	1,305	132	6,143	1,148	3,361
1999	2,638	80	1,042	180	7,149	1,199	2,934
2000	3,692	86	900	97	4,984	864	1,980

CROATIA-SLAVONIA 1885–1916

	Wheat	Rye	Barley	Oats	Maize	Potatoes	Sugar Beet
	thousands of hectolitres						thou.tons
1885	1,884	2,055	920	1,712	3,945	140	4
1886	1,885	2,091	884	1,713	4,594	196	4
1887	1,892	1,957	790	1,500	3,751	244	4
1888	2,099	1,920	769	1,320	4,563	269	7
1889	1,723	1,686	644	859	4,355	300	8
1890	2,370	2,031	857	1,258	4,493	232	8
1891	2,325	1,537	738	1,306	5,466	224	8
1892	2,492	1,684	788	1,228	5,461	232	8
	thousands of metric tons						
1893	223	129	53	56	403	301	13
1894	240	141	62	78	320	279	7
1895	234	110	51	65	476	333	8
1896	261	144	65	78	465	263	5
1897	167	95	45	64	371	250	6
1898	310	155	77	102	529	352	6
1899	245	122	60	92	373	260	5
1900	300	113	63	81	475	365	7
1901	291	128	66	84	520	537	16
1902	327	134	71	91	388	355	13
1903	399	151	84	106	604	526	17
1904	268	94	50	71	289	253	9
1905	356	115	62	88	467	343	8
1906	282	94	60	80	520	350	20
1907	277	80	45	61	456	697	24
1908	360	111	56	62	515	575	24
1909	317	93	51	81	553	458	32
1910	311	80	46	58	654	775	49
1911	413	100	57	81	610	609	47
1912	308	69	43	51	611	590	44
1913	435	95	68	95	736	575	89
1914	341	77	51	84	657	537	165
1915	242	53	37	78	393	378	57
1916	223	35	35	91	312	272	46

incorporated in Yugoslavia

C2 Output of Main Cereal, Potato, and Sugar Beet Crops (in thousands of hectolitres or metric tons)

IRELAND (thousands of metric tons)   1847–1922

	Wheat	Barley	Oats	Potatoes		Wheat	Barley	Oats	Potatoes
1847	624	297	1,639	2,081	1885	56	147	921	3,227
1848	…	…	…	…	1886	51	141	934	2,711
1849	462	298	1,399	4,079	1887	52	105	770	3,626
					1888	69	138	896	2,563
1850	331	287	1,471	4,009	1889	73	165	896	2,894
1851	319	297	1,532	4,512					
1852	246	267	1,666	4,324	1890	72	156	904	1,839
1853	242	281	1,521	5,834	1891	71	168	957	3,086
1854	310	236	1,606	5,143	1892	60	146	918	2,626
					1893	45	141	985	3,113
1855	324	210	1,460	6,335	1894	42	143	980	1,903
1856	348	144	1,314	4,479					
1857	355	160	1,265	3,566	1895	30	145	926	3,528
1858	373	151	1,274	4,971	1896	33	160	864	2,744
1859	313	130	1,162	4,399	1897	37	132	826	1,522
					1898	51	151	949	2,989
1860	271	140	1,258	2,785	1899	47	155	909	2,804
1861	182	128	1,144	1,888					
1862	146	123	1,036	2,183	1900	46	141	890	1,872
1863	179	141	1,270	3,501	1901	40	148	903	3,426
1864	187	142	1,111	4,382	1902	44	180	952	2,770
					1903	32	132	854	2,401
1865	176	136	1,087	3,928	1904	28	119	873	2,684
1866	172	122	1,034	3,118					
1867	155	138	1,056	3,197	1905	39	156	882	3,478
1868	202	164	1,083	4,127	1906	42	157	911	2,704
1869	170	177	990	3,426	1907	36	152	872	2,282
					1908	38	155	927	3,251
1870	161	191	1,073	4,286	1909	48	182	986	3,254
1871	150	172	1,052	2,839					
1872	130	160	945	1,835	1910	47	149	955	2,917
1873	100	187	981	2,726	1911	45	155	859	3,754
1874	147	208	1,016	3,609	1912	43	158	971	2,588
					1913	35	174	960	3,799
1875	118	216	1,165	3,569	1914	39	176	919	3,501
1876	103	198	1,088	4,222					
1877	97	179	907	1,785	1915	88	128	996	3,770
1878	117	199	968	2,568	1916	77	142	905	2,472
1879	91	166	789	1,132	1917	124	171	1,374	4,220
					1918	154	182	1,472	3,925
1880	113	175	994	3,034	1919	67	177	1,242	2,791
1881	117	169	1,001	3,489					
1882	105	140	929	2,026	1920	39	162	906	2,018
1883	66	144	958	3,507	1921	42	126	766	2,597
1884	50	136	920	3,089	1922	42	152	828	3,486

IRELAND (thousands of metric tons)   1923–1934

	Wheat	Barley	Oats	Potatoes	Sugar Beet
1923	32	117	474	1,500	…
1924	28	125	490	1,516	…
1925	20	134	595	2,172	…
1926	31	146	649	1,963	87
1927	39	137	678	2,482	136
1928	32	134	648	2,282	143
1929	32	130	700	3,055	144
1930	30	120	642	2,375	161
1931	21	107	529	1,963	35
1932	23	108	637	3,063	152
1933	54	122	634	2,537	205
1934	104	148	570	2,586	492

C2 Output of Main Cereal, Potato, and Sugar Beet Crops (in thousands of hectolitres or metric tons)

IRELAND (thousands of metric tons)   1935–2000

	Wheat	Barley	Oats	Potatoes	Sugar Beet
1935	182	159	626	2,618	572
1936	213	124	525	2,460	600
1937	190	120	582	2,749	564
1938	201	112	568	2,500	401
1939	282	80	548	3,046	396
1940	318	141	736	3,168	648
1941	442	145	695	3,749	686
1942	520	175	780	3,170	367
1943	442	191	809	3,148	710
1944	555	154	792	3,055	602
1945	582	152	737	3,032	714
1946	470	123	700	3,279	502
1947	318	90	663	2,642	458
1948	416	102	805	3,328	603
1949	367	162	568	2,735	639
Republic of Ireland					
1950	333	121	537	2,920	538
1951	252	178	586	2,810	568
1952	266	253	587	2,719	555
1953	417	229	576	2,761	822
1954	497	179	482	2,284	681
1955	406	250	576	2,148	598
1956	433	319	544	2,649	636
1957	522	390	438	2,377	808
1958	351	336	456	1,880	797
1959	369	460	482	2,634	942
1960	469	442	426	1,829	950
1961	470	515	381	2,145	891
1962	439	603	396	2,117	930
1963	301	589	368	1,969	952
1964	272	652	313	1,526	893
1965	233	616	324	1,648	758
1966	185	638	283	1,679	704
1967	298	677	293	1,748	956
1968	408	531	286	1,625	1,092
1969	359	578	251	1,453	916
1970	381	782	207	1,468	982
1971	380	991	207	1,428	1,218
1972	270	981	179	1,070	1,113
1973	229	905	162	1,332	1,321
1974	245	1,038	157	1,112	926
1975	195	1,019	165	1,018	1,429
1976	200	922	130	1,180	1,468
1977	250	1,445	135	1,515	1,376
1978	247	1,320	124	1,070	1,456
1979	245	1,439	105	1,141	1,322
1980	272	1,701	91	880	1,156
1981	286	1,670	90	684	1,319
1982	400	1,676	100	869	1,659
1983	387	1,503	101	661	1,630
1984	602	1,770	141	870	1,694
1985	495	1,494	106	686	1,309
1986	424	1,428	102	619	1,274
1987	402	1,599	106	697	1,623
1988	475	1,606	113	694	1,334
1989	477	1,474	99	668	1,451
1990	603	1,337	136	687	1,550
1991	673	1,148	143	571	1,409
1992	713	1,167	136	642	1,397
1993	520	952	134	650	1,380
1994	572	910	128	642	1,390
1995	583	1,084	129	618	1,547
1996	771	1,225	146	733	1,476
1997	725	1,087	132	472	1,648
1998	673	1,073	119	482	1,640
1999	597	1,278	136	559	1,712
2000	706	1,129	128	395	1,380

C2 Output of Main Cereal, Potato, and Sugar Beet Crops (in thousands of hectolitres or metric tons)

NORTHERN IRELAND (thousands of metric tons)   1923–1993

	Wheat	Barley	Oats	Potatoes		Wheat	Barley	Oats	Potatoes
1923	6.3	1.8	280	931	1955	1.3	5.9	228	769
1924	4.3	2.0	272	842	1956	3.3	7.5	253	888
					1957	4.5	15	207	670
1925	3.5	2.3	278	1,187	1958	4.4	18	185	583
1926	6.2	1.6	297	1,086	1959	2.9	34	190	734
1927	5.8	1.5	280	1,074					
1928	5.0	2.0	281	1,173	1960	4.4	74	191	714
1929	3.9	1.8	291	1,142	1961	5.6	96	143	633
					1962	5.9	178	165	651
1930	4.7	2.1	281	870	1963	3.4	171	137	657
1931	2.8	1.3	230	709	1964	4.4	210	121	550
1932	3.4	1.1	294	1,144					
1933	6.2	1.5	267	964	1965	5.8	236	91	511
1934	9.9	2.5	278	938	1966	4.3	197	73	476
					1967	4.3	202	79	527
1935	9.9	3.3	264	901	1968	3.6	199	75	469
1936	7.4	2.8	263	798	1969	4.2	183	58	395
1937	4.5	2.6	247	882					
1938	5.8	3.4	295	722	1970	5	160	43	406
1939	3.0	3.1	274	878	1971	4	198	40	375
					1972	4	175	29	304
1940	13	15	384	1,047	1973	3	177	26	311
1941	18	17	439	1,241	1974	3	197	24	297
1942	12	14	435	1,251					
1943	12	13	400	1,306	1975	3	187	23	243
1944	4.5	15	385	1,087	1976	2	172	17	331
					1977	2	217	18	466
1945	1.5	13	389	1,106	1978	3	220	14	351
1946	2.2	7.5	382	1,577	1979	2	175	11	348
1947	1.4	4.6	269	1,040					
1948	4.8	6.6	398	1,693	1980	2	196	11	396
1949	2.1	6.5	360	1,453	1981	2	174	10	321
					1982	6	203	10	362
1950	2.0	4.1	313	1,365	1983	8	199	10	332[10]
1951	1.4	3.4	300	1,216	1984	22	222	10	413
1952	2.2	6.6	294	1,090					
1953	2.5	7.2	277	1,143	1985	11	162	6	296
1954	2.1	6.0	243	927	1986	21	192	7	325
					1987	31	206	11	340
					1988	32	192	11	339
					1989	32	168	12	339
					1990	40	166	12	339
					1991	41	170	14	317
					1992	53	168	10	322
					1993	37	138	9	257

ITALY (thousands of metric tons)[31]   1861–1874

	Wheat	Rye	Barley	Oats	Maize	Rice	Potatoes
1861	3,290	168	182	231	1,440	280	864
1862	3,300	196	203	239	1,268	167	912
1863	3,485	161	238	255	1,620	279	960
1864	3,380	148	218	275	1,590	288	1,027
1865	3,725	179	190	289	1,830	307	1,088
1866	3,943	148	228	285	2,010	329	1,040
1867	3,877	144	257	333	1,920	543	946
1868	4,307	158	287	313	2,400	525	1,056
1869	3,997	149	224	333	2,100	434	1,200
1870	4,039	162	197	337	1,860	550	1,248
1871	4,010	152	248	340	2,304	529	1,106
1872	3,861	137	356	324	2,496	474	1,151
1873	4,023	179	302	369	2,010	419	1,195
1874	3,917	102	278	365	2,523	433	1,051

C2 Output of Main Cereal, Potato, and Sugar Beet Crop (in thousands of hectolitres or metric tons)

ITALY (thousands of metric tons)[31]   1875–1927

	Wheat	Rye	Barley	Oats	Maize	Rice	Potatoes	Sugar Beet
1875	3,933	130	310	374	2,682	483	1,056	…
1876	3,806	139	317	372	2,971	507	1,109	…
1877	3,836	145	305	366	2,802	408	1,162	1.0
1878	3,675	133	297	395	2,392	673	1,186	1.6
1879	4,040	117	225	290	2,239	491	1,286	0.3
1880	4,702	176	327	347	2,093	498	1,151	1.0
1881	2,856	113	210	244	1,439	421	1,009	0.6
1882	4,261	144	268	296	1,886	396	1,110	1.8
1883	3,420	130	240	275	1,915	402	1,240	3.2
1884	3,390	121	226	285	2,421	399	1,279	6.2
1885	3,217	112	213	298	2,136	392	1,273	1.1
1886	3,293	116	219	280	2,200	433	1,198	1.5
1887	3,470	118	194	316	2,120	398	1,180	1.6
1888	3,026	100	173	268	1,844	255	1,069	3.9
1889	2,995	104	195	306	2,082	417	966	5.5
1890	3,613	112	255	335	1,902	315	1,202	6.7
1891	3,889	116	226	351	1,839	347	1,208	13
1892	3,180	108	185	304	1,830	363	970	8.9
1893	3,717	114	184	322	2,100	246	1,373	9.6
1894	3,442	109	194	300	1,512	287	1,073	17
1895	3,237	102	173	338	1,788	300	1,235	22
1896	3,992	125	234	326	2,028	207	1,278	19
1897	2,389	75	170	291	1,672	370	1,429	32
1898	3,775	119	156	317	2,021	371	1,504	49
1899	3,791	121	176	371	2,246	417	1,744	191
1900	3,903	127	204	333	2,359	595	1,521	476
1901	4,808	155	223	505	2,694	558	1,675	589
1902	3,991	132	230	343	1,941	532	1,786	756
1903	5,383	171	171	500	2,387	606	2,056	1,037
1904	4,896	146	165	490	2,428	606	2,138	622
1905	4,682	141	213	575	2,609	539	2,341	745
1906	5,149	162	189	528	2,494	580	2,531	844
1907	5,178	158	223	588	2,374	656	2,497	1,023
1908	4,448	140	234	563	2,573	590	2,689	1,627
1909	5,043	188	238	561	2,666	533	2,841	1,257
1910	4,064	156	212	370	2,729	491	2,545	1,619
1911	5,097	151	243	530	2,513	537	2,796	1,556
1912	4,390	151	187	366	2,647	493	2,534	1,729
1913	5,690	160	241	562	2,908	609	2,958	2,819
1914	4,493	150	154	294	2,816	611	2,749	1,352
1915	4,518	125	246	407	3,269	629	2,554	1,494
1916	4,676	150	225	337	2,188	583	2,442	1,347
1917	3,709	127	165	438	2,221	590	2,165	905
1918	4,856	149	216	587	2,055	587	2,331	1,146
1919	4,497	131	186	449	2,303	546	2,294	1,846
1920	3,744	130	131	313	2,396	506	2,351	1,300
1921	5,108[31]	161[31]	231[31]	489[31]	2,477[31]	528[31]	2,626[31]	2,097[31]
1922	4,255	137	171	388	2,012	521	2,128	2,507
1923	5,918	160	218	507	2,336	584	2,616	2,859
1924	4,479	151	180	424	2,767	663	2,852	4,433
1925	6,340	165	267	604	2,880	706	3,143	1,409
1926	5,808	160	229	517	3,092	762	3,366	2,517
1927	5,154	147	196	391	2,288	780	2,833	2,190

C2   Output of Main Cereal, Potato, and Sugar Beet Crops (in thousands of hectolitres or metric tons)

ITALY (thousands of metric tons)[31]   **1928–1979**

	Wheat	Rye	Barley	Oats	Maize	Rice	Potatoes	Sugar Beet
1928	6,017	161	229	616	1,702	708	2,170	2,965
1929	6,668	175	255	597	2,523	727	2,820	3,362
1930	5,433	155	238	467	2,979	694	2,631	3,433
1931	6,376	165	236	512	1,942	700	2,532	2,560
1932	7,286	160	243	552	3,011	687	3,492	2,435
1933	7,923	171	224	538	2,587	715	2,785	2,153
1934	6,238	142	201	469	3,198	688	3,024	2,719
1935	7,632	158	203	508	2,495	735	2,283	2,436
1936	6,112	132	193	478	3,051	734	2,638	2,613
1937	8,064	145	233	620	3,396	791	3,214	3,524
1938	8,184	138	248	629	2,940	817	2,942	3,281
1939	7,971	151	236	548	2,582	762	2,780	3,671
1940	7,104	152	219	571	3,428	929	3,299	5,246
1941	7,070	147	236	587	2,612	864	3,094	4,171
1942	6,575	140	234	487	2,455	793	2,997	3,689
1943	6,510[31]	126[31]	228[31]	441[31]	1,682[31]	643[31]	2,279[31]	3,199[31]
1944	6,451	114	221	435	2,183	416	2,303	3,124
1945	4,177	78	129	252	1,438	356	1,467	401
1946	6,126	106	231	461	1,909	489	2,343	2,317
1947	4,702	97	179	447	1,920	636	2,824	2,230
1948	6,166[31]	112[31]	230[31]	486[31]	2,250[31]	619[31]	3,025[31]	3,409[31]
1949	7,073	125	227	415	2,212	610	2,629	3,619
1950	7,774	131	295	558	1,924	706	2,432	4,468
1951	6,962	122	270	510	2,748	750	2,858	5,961
1952	7,876	127	267	508	2,396	930	2,717	5,897
1953	9,056	130	313	602	3,213	934	3,132	6,231
1954	7,283	115	278	546	2,963	869	3,202	6,592
1955	9,504	123	292	523	3,204	880	3,382	9,208
1956	8,681	107	275	506	3,411	648	3,418	7,055
1957	8,478	92	296	582	3,496	637	3,157	6,176
1958	9,815	105	296	568	3,670	737	3,668	7,681
1959	8,471	105	279	541	3,879	755	3,979	11,459
1960	6,794	93	232	431	3,813	622	3,818	7,818
1961	8,301	96	279	585	3,936	700	3,932	7,071
1962	9,497	93	285	597	3,263	663	3,561	7,148
1963	8,127	77	280	548	3,692	564	4,384	7,882
1964	8,586	86	252	466	3,957	624	3,823	7,966
1965	9,776	83	285	527	3,317	509	3,550	9,079
1966	9,400	83	253	477	3,510	621	3,860	11,259
1967	9,596	82	295	556	3,860	745	4,010	13,507
1968	9,590	75	258	390	3,991	639	3,960	11,457
1969	9,585	71	292	491	4,519	862	3,970	10,571
1970	9,689	69	315	486	4,754	817	3,668	9,518
1971	9,994	55	373	488	4,528	892	3,259	8,776
1972	9,421	38	390	440	4,789	755	2,949	11,177
1973	8,920	38	458	419	5,089	1,045	2,947	9,388
1974	9,695	37	559	462	5,043	997	2,903	7,711
1975	9,610	37	640	506	5,326	1,010	2,943	12,536
1976	9,516	35	755	439	5,320	917	2,974	15,452
1977	6,347	32	676	354	6,455	693	3,145	11,539
1978	9,333	36	827	468	6,221	971	2,843	11,521
1979	9,130	37	823	438	6,261	1,127	3,012	13,465

C2 Output of Main Cereal, Potato, and Sugar Beet Crops (in thousands of hectolitres or metric tons)

ITALY (thousands of metric tons)[31]   1980–2000

	Wheat	Rye	Barley	Oats	Maize	Rice	Potatoes	Sugar Beet
1980	9,295	36	957	456	6,443	985	2,976	13,675
1981	8,959	31	992	424	7,264	901	2,933	17,832
1982	9,124	32	1,096	363	6,884	1,017	2,620	11,621
1983	8,833	27	1,200	317	6,752	1,031	2,574	10,084
1984	10,227	25	1,640	440	6,857	1,018	2,503	11,598
1985	8,563	23	1,643	370	6,411	1,130	2,496	9,708
1986	9,260	22	1,566	406	6,461	1,141	2,602	15,136
1987	9,520	20	1,729	367	5,808	1,064	2,511	15,465
1988	8,134	18	1,583	388	6,365	1,112	2,376	13,540
1989	7,413	21	1,644	296	6,360	1,246	2,458	16,891
1990	8,109	21	1,703	307	5,864	1,282	2,479	13,800
1991	9,416	19	1,793	359	6,238	1,236	2,219	11,975
1992	8,938	23	1,741	333	7,413	1,314	2,509	14,762
1993	8,404	21	1,512	359	7,738	1,318	2,013	11,867
1994	8,251	20	1,467	355	7,483	1,361	2,021	12,629
1995	7,947	20	1,421	301	8,454	1,321	2,081	13,188
1996	7,987	20	1,350	350	9,548	1,424	2,055	12,114
1997	6,758	19	1,180	311	10,005	1,442	2,020	13,803
1998	8,338	20	1,379	378	9,031	1,394	2,194	13,382
1999	7,743	12	1,313	331	10,017	1,427	2,072	14,505
2000	7,464	9	1,262	318	10,138	1,186	2,053	11,530

NETHERLANDS   1842–1874

	Wheat	Rye	Barley	Oats	Buckwheat	Potatoes	Sugar Beet
			thousand hectolitres				thousand tons
1842	1,051	2,642	1,101	2,296	804	...	...
1843	1,455	3,365	1,169	2,612	941	...	...
1844	1,309	3,040	1,252	2,389	991	...	...
1845	1,168	2,927	1,284	2,735	990	...	...
1846	1,200	1,597	1,209	2,057	1,260	5,818	...
1847	1,747	3,776	1,545	2,796	981	9,836	...
1848	1,749	3,410	1,452	2,634	1,446	8,217	...
1849	1,539	3,687	1,373	2,858	1,016	11,492	...
1850	1,531	3,368	1,280	2,504	976	9,651	...
1851	1,583	3,085	1,217	2,285	1,314	10,230	...
1852	1,517	2,887	1,254	2,696	1,036	8,527	...
1853	855	2,577	1,261	2,851	1,394	7,571	...
1854	1,618	3,629	1,530	3,032	1,363	10,629	...
1855	1,190	3,064	1,428	3,356	1,293	9,912	...
1856	1,851	3,899	1,641	3,309	1,154	13,498	...
1857	1,891	3,956	1,431	2,402	870	12,979	...
1858	1,654	3,803	1,737	2,530	1,101	16,979	...
1859	1,610	2,732	1,195	2,496	1,253	11,557	...
1860	1,774	3,758	1,485	3,261	1,232	12,472	...
1861	1,572	3,332	1,823	3,526	1,472	6,737	...
1862	1,646	3,056	1,317	3,971	1,297	16,592	...
1863	1,978	3,766	1,497	3,494	935	17,690	...
1864	1,745	4,088	1,776	4,570	1,104	16,870	...
1865	1,702	3,629	1,514	3,720	1,368	16,857	...
1866	1,561	3,699	1,331	3,382	1,242	13,119	...
1867	1,329	2,309	1,533	4,020	1,482	15,165	...
1868	2,000	3,892	1,645	3,651	611	15,846	...
1869	2,073	3,823	1,750	3,704	953	16,122	...
1870	2,056	3,892	1,849	4,093	967	16,446	277
1871	1,190	2,453	2,037	5,697	1,366	13,291	331
1872	1,951	3,968	1,689	3,824	1,019	18,730	394
1873	1,834	2,860	1,655	3,917	951	17,900	331
1874	2,390	3,755	1,660	4,093	1,007	20,337	333

C2 Output of Main Cereal, Potato, and Sugar Beet Crops (in thousands of hectolitres or metric tons)

NETHERLANDS   1875–1929

	Wheat	Rye	Barley	Oats	Buckwheat	Potatoes	Sugar Beet
	thousand hectolitres						thousand tons
1875	2,250	3,567	1,938	4,599	1,235	19,811	499
1876	1,920	3,420	1,705	4,511	856	19,027	306
1877	1,753	3,612	1,413	4,136	1,244	17,079	298
1878	1,992	3,507	1,435	4,048	1,170	15,656	401
1879	1,770	3,368	1,449	4,232	867	10,332	314
1880	2,080	3,301	1,751	4,767	881	13,923	449
1881	1,658	2,970	1,541	4,189	780	22,817	382
1882	1,917	3,949	1,645	4,634	893	16,448	419
1883	1,984	3,825	1,800	4,030	911	24,871	579
1884	2,077	3,736	1,722	3,975	992	26,294	595
1885	2,232	4,079	1,929	4,595	464	23,931	402
1886	1,846	3,776	1,660	5,161	744	22,524	392
1887	2,428	4,855	1,846	4,273	427	27,052	443
1888	1,848	3,477	1,501	4,418	812	16,444	348
1889	2,281	3,990	1,708	4,714	840	23,073	773
1890	1,912	3,916	1,464	4,666	577	18,941	732
1891	1,235	2,918	1,575	6,531	558	16,001	421
1892	1,896	4,382	1,757	5,288	489	33,166	750
1893	1,752	4,363	1,681	4,345	547	31,585	758
1894	1,468	4,331	1,275	5,322	549	20,858	738
1895	1,509	4,510	1,512	5,471	623	26,306	1,029
1896	1,778	4,782	1,608	5,406	421	29,251	1,742
1897	1,512	4,204	1,317	5,682	557	27,461	1,152
1898	1,905	4,815	1,347	5,856	482	27,538	1,258
1899	1,796	4,570	1,399	5,660	431	33,723	1,603
1900	1,646	4,808	1,615	6,095	425	28,338	1,509
1901	1,491	4,997	1,366	6,514	342	33,446	1,828
1902	1,799	4,923	1,639	6,780	494	33,392	914
1903	1,500	4,924	1,347	7,087	476	25,864	960
1904	1,559	4,763	1,271	6,552	296	33,274	1,018
1905	1,709	4,843	1,414	5,654	411	30,673	1,599
1906	1,742	4,912	1,148	6,629	356	33,655	1,363
1907	1,876	5,104	1,442	7,377	325	33,267	1,306
1908	1,804	5,591	1,393	6,936	322	34,075	1,563
1909	1,465	6,221	1,174	6,823	289	34,279	1,497
1910	1,565	5,412	1,093	6,357	293	31,144	1,627
1911	1,942	5,677	1,204	6,246	133	36,462	2,005
1912	1,975	5,671	1,186	5,750	175	42,949	2,176
1913	1,820	5,954	1,104	6,663	169	38,503	1,665
1914	2,037	4,749	1,064	6,825	151	42,562	1,994
1915	2,498	5,679	1,191	7,292	100	44,663	1,714
1916	1,687	4,104	838	6,317	101	37,051	1,717
1917	1,392	4,673	761	6,293	97	43,690	1,458
1918	1,914	4,589	922	6,561	72	45,913	1,245
1919	2,064	5,185	831	6,520	86	44,896	1,494
1920	2,112	5,214	937	7,204	98	42,821	1,906
1921	3,017	6,339	1,163	7,048	46	37,829	2,708
1922	2,171	6,040	1,108	6,279	66	57,204	1,818
1923	2,189	5,135	1,040	6,569	43	37,650	1,720
1924	1,658	5,567	1,229	6,589	34	41,332	2,426
1925	1,997	5,866	1,230	6,410	26	46,977	2,224
1926	1,965	4,881	1,232	7,109	21	44,211	2,111
1927	2,205	4,826	1,159	6,672	15	37,441	1,826
1928	2,627	6,201	1,557	7,826	12	57,649	2,289
1929	1,958	6,547	1,715	8,134	9	60,961	2,060

C2 Output of Main Cereal, Potato, and Sugar Beet Crops (in thousands of hectolitres or metric tons)

NETHERLANDS 1930–1984

	Wheat	Rye	Barley	Oats	Buckwheat	Potatoes	Sugar Beet
			thousand hectolitres				thousand tons
1930	2,169	5,328	1,389	6,454	6	45,206	2,138
1931	2,417	5,068	1,131	6,243	6	42,095	1,029
1932	4,597	4,960	864	6,028	6	52,955	1,656
1933	5,488	5,582	803	6,312	7	44,894	1,948
1934	6,461	7,079	1,570	6,249	7	43,575	1,786
1935	5,964	6,595	1,814	6,115	4	39,547	1,526
1936	5,577	6,819	1,927	6,890	5	36,839	1,638
1937	4,556	6,869	2,128	7,730	4	39,229	1,582
1938	434	551	140	447	...	2,843	1,520
1939	417	603	146	449	...	3,050	1,716
1940	394	444	144	387	...	2,821	1,894
1941	381	448	141	224	...	3,451	1,653
1942	281	581	140	223	...	4,550	1,322
1943	341	608	113	253	...	4,200	1,574
1944	...	...	...	...	...	...	...
1945	218	206	93	252	...	2,591	449
1946	359	456	176	425	...	4,245	1,705
1947	194	318	135	433	...	4,611	1,577
1948	306	382	155	356	...	5,870	1,893
1949	425	517	184	521	...	4,605	2,943
1950	295	421	232	382	...	4,048	2,913
1951	269	459	197	492	...	3,793	2,444
1952	326	498	238	483	...	4,356	2,782
1953	250	433	279	485	...	3,685	2,977
1954	397	515	208	467	...	3,999	3,061
1955	350	465	264	582	...	3,907	2,984
1956	309	492	273	483	...	3,206	2,525
1957	393	458	292	505	...	3,741	2,689
1958	402	427	315	446	...	3,606	2,878
1959	494	386	268	319	...	3,141$_{40}$	3,098
					...	3,315	
1960	590	460	291	387	...	4,173	4,676
1961	482	301	385	431	...	3,720	3,854
1962	603	339	431	465	...	3,952	2,934
1963	530	313	387	424	...	3,854	2,691
1964	712	356	376	420	...	4,111	3,876
1965	691	250	373	363	...	3,230	3,573
1966	597	190	416	357	...	4,123	3,645
1967	739	239	447	365	...	4,840	5,074
1968	679	239	389	318	...	5,045	5,128
1969	677	207	389	322	...	4,704	5,002
1970	640	168	329	199	...	5,604	4,711
1971	706	209	373	206	...	5,749	5,024
1972	673	151	340	140	...	5,581	4,957
1973	725	105	383	134	...	5,771	5,592
1974	746	78	315	163	...	6,095	4,911
1975	528	63	336	158	...	5,003	5,927
1976	710	65	263	103	...	4,783	6,828
1977	661	74	287	94	...	5,752	6,329
1978	792	68	355	140	...	5,842	6,324
1979	836	49	288	109	...	6,277	5,491
1980	882	39	258	94	...	6,267	5,931
1981	882	29	249	115	...	6,445	7,061
1982	967	26	247	136	...	6,219	7,946
1983	1,043	26	177	61	...	5,412	5,446
1984	1,131	25	192	58	...	6,673	6,955

C2 Output of Main Cereal, Potato, and Sugar Beet Crops (in thousands of hectolitres or metric tons)

NETHERLANDS 1985–2000

	Wheat	Rye	Barley	Oats	Potatoes	Sugar Beet
1985	851	19	197	58	7,150	6,335
1986	940	19	262	40	6,857	7,707
1987	769	25	262	47	7,478	6,920
1988	827	28	302	60	6,742	6,737
1989	1,047	33	251	32	6,856	7,679
1990	1,076	36	219	16	7,036	8,623
1991	944	34	238	18	6,949	7,189
1992	1,017	34	204	19	7,595	8,251
1993	1,008	39	253	27	7,699	7,479
1994	981	27	228	28	7,088	6,149
1995	1,167	43	203	16	7,340	6,449
1996	1,269	38	235	11	8,081	6,416
1997	986	28	270	10	7,973	6,606
1998	1,072	30	215	11	5,249	5,505
1999	851	14	365	14	8,221	7,317
2000	1,183	29	288	13	8,127	6,727

NORWAY (thousands of metric tons) 1835–1932

	Wheat	Rye	Barley	Oats	Mixed Corn	Potatoes
1835	1.1	7.6	44	86	24	261
1845	1.5	10	62	112	33	394
1855	5.7	18	83	142	40	483
1865	7.6	17	81	133	34	529
1875	7.5	25	104	155	39	587
1889	7	24	97	166	27	591
1900	9	23	68	159	14	554
1901	8	23	59	137	11	592
1902	7	21	44	110	8	464
1903	8	23	66	152	12	609
1904	6	20	49	116	9	461
1905	8	28	68	171	12	709
1906	8	28	67	170	12	604
1907	7	25	52	125	8	483
1908	9	22	73	199	13	689
1909	9	26	63	156	10	565
1910	8	23	70	186	13	570
1911	9	23	67	156	10	606
1912	11	25	79	201	14	809
1913	12	22	85	192	15	750
1914	11	22	69	133	10	753
1915	12	17	77	173	13	549
1916	13	15	96	217	17	788
1917	14	15	94	194	16	846
1918	30	27	128	274	24	780
1919	23	23	110	233	20	991
1920	16	21	102	214	17	805
1921	16	22	79	179	14	701
1922	17	22	97	199	16	897
1923	16	20	74	133	11	721
1924	13	17	101	154	14	627
1925	13	16	113	175	16	939
1926	16	16	112	194	15	895
1927	17	15	102	184	12	605
1928	22	12	112	184	13	951
1929	20	14	99	176	11	900
1930	20	14	107	198	12	766
1931	16	10	92	138	8	774
1932	20	13	118	194	12	1,035

C2 Output of Main Cereal, Potato, and Sugar Beet Crops (in thousands of hectolitres or metric tons)

NORWAY (thousands of metric tons)   1933–1983

	Wheat	Rye	Barley	Oats	Mixed Corn	Potatoes
1933	21	11	100	180	11	977
1934	33	10	116	176	9	800
1935	51	12	123	182	10	916
1936	57	11	115	171	9	946
1937	68	11	129	188	10	861
1938	72	11	124	197	11	938
1939	78	6	103	201	12	807
1940	69	6	93	159	10	1,308
1941	76	7	106	164	15	1,068
1942	83	8	95	156	15	1,182
1943	79	7	92	171	14	1,378
1944	78	6	77	155	12	938
1945	86	4	81	165	11	1,112
1946	80	5	94	186	12	1,204
1947	46	2	81	132	7	919
1948	76	3	89	177	10	1,454
1949	67	2	86	163	10	1,099
1950	66	2	99	180	10	1,116
1951	40	1	123	170	9	1,015
1952	40	1	148	161	8	1,187
1953	39	1	206	179	7	1,249
1954	41	2	224	161	6	1,130
1955	32	1	209	114	5	981
1956	56	3	297	182	6	1,392
1957	30	1	315	136	4	1,010
1958	17	1	340	127	4	1,202
1959	20	2	304	118	4	1,071
1960	23	4	400	173	6	1,247
1961	27	3	428	174	5	1,222
1962	20	4	343	107	2	919
1963	18	3	463	113	3	1,218
1964	20	2	480	126	2	804
1965	12	2	485	113	2	1,134
1966	4	1	405	91	2	1,090
1967	11	2	485	123	2	807
1968	16	4	621	176	3	912
1969	11	4	486	140	1	763
1970	12	5	580	228	1	857
1971	10	5	569	279	2	708
1972	12	5	522	271	1	634
1973	20	7	535	349	2	672
1974	62	11	649	404	2	847
1975	52	4	445	259	1	435
1976	65	7	486	287	...	484
1977	78	8	630	360	...	605
1978	80	8	668	367	...	576
1979	67	4	649	361	...	473
1980	65	5	657	428	...	571
1981	58	3	607	463	...	529
1982	76	2	623	495	...	526
1983	97	3	569	401	...	470

C2 Output of Main Cereal, Potato, and Sugar Beet Crops (in thousands of hectolitres or metric tons)

NORWAY (thousands of metric tons) 1984–2000

	Wheat	Rye	Barley	Oats	Mixed Corn	Potatoes
1984	170	2	658	581	...	489
1985	170	3	601	494	...	440
1986	159	3	545	401	...	398
1987	249	4	566	466	...	370
1988	149	2	542	374	...	484
1989	140	3	614	423	...	455
1990	207	4	590	404	...	440
1991	246	5	663	568	...	415
1992	193	4	488	325	...	511
1993	379	12	640	371	...	455
1994	280	15	588	387	...	471
1995	312	14	547	353	...	400
1996	266	12	682	385	...	419
1997	256	10	663	359	...	470
1998	365	16	650	381	...	453
1999	230	6	624	355	...	380
2000	333	10	596	410	...	344

POLAND (thousands of metric tons) 1919–1963

	Wheat	Rye	Barley	Oats	Potatoes	Sugar Beet
1919	429	2,618	606	1,107	10,514	1,241
1920	619	1,871	840	1,873	18,096	1,385
1921	1,018	4,256	1,224	2,181	16,800	1,129
1922	1,153	5,014	1,297	2,506	33,219	2,671
1923	1,354	5,962	1,656	3,522	26,494	2,575
1924	884	3,655	1,208	2,412	26,870	3,211
1925	1,738	6,741	1,301	2,093	24,729	3,687
1926	1,429	5,182	1,214	1,941	21,380	3,725
1927	1,627	5,887	1,276	2,139	26,771	3,620
1928	1,612	6,110	1,527	2,498	27,661	4,921
1929	1,793	7,010	1,660	2,953	31,750	4,970
1930	2,240	6,958	1,464	2,348	30,902	4,717
1931	2,265	5,703	1,476	2,310	30,988	2,761
1932	1,346	6,111	1,401	2,391	29,975	2,379
1933	2,174	7,073	1,436	2,683	28,330	1,852
1934	2,080	6,464	1,453	2,551	33,470	2,567
1935	2,011	6,617	1,468	2,598	32,502	2,501
1936	2,133	6,364	1,401	2,640	34,281	2,555
1937	1,926	5,638	1,363	2,343	40,221	3,246
1938	2,172	7,253	1,371	2,657	34,558	3,162
1939	2,270[32]	7,630[32]	1,480[32]	2,880[32]	...[32]	...[32]
1940	1,778	5,984	1,437	2,586	45,207	7,670
1941	1,790	6,300	1,404	2,413	38,952	7,890
1942	1,332	5,272	1,665	2,758	38,328	8,000
1943	1,559	6,676	1,453	2,767	28,663	7,140
1944	1,349[32]	6,005[32]	1,256[32]	2,404[32]	34,230[32]	6,660[32]
1945	751	3,766	967	1,556	21,870	3,460
1946	619	2,763	674	1,017	18,710	2,983
1947	985	4,306	1,035	1,763	30,821	3,493
1948	1,620	6,304	1,010	2,402	26,756	4,228
1949	1,781	6,759	1,028	2,333	30,901	4,789
1950	1,888	6,488	1,081	2,127	36,130	6,377
1951	1,363	6,148	1,009	1,981	26,696	5,363
1952	2,013	6,173	1,176	2,348	27,725	6,158
1953	1,870	4,853	1,134	2,169	31,800	6,881
1954	2,002	5,844	1,085	2,073	35,662	6,950
1955	2,134	7,003	1,239	2,287	27,021	7,286
1956	2,121	6,558	1,131	2,259	38,052	6,428
1957	2,319	7,437	1,227	2,541	35,104	7,621
1958	2,321	7,329	1,210	2,670	34,800	8,427
1959	2,484	8,113	1,043	2,483	35,698	5,975
1960	2,303	7,878	1,310	2,774	37,855	10,262
1961	2,792	8,356	1,339	2,940	45,203	11,555
1962	2,700	6,685	1,315	2,740	37,817	10,075
1963	3,067	7,124	1,479	2,830	44,868	10,661

C2 Output of Main Cereal, Potato, and Sugar Beet Crops (in thousands of hectolitres or metric tons)

POLAND (thousands of metric tons)   1964–2000

	Wheat	Rye	Barley	Oats	Potatoes	Sugar Beet
1964	3,042	6,964	1,261	2,218	47,860	12,574
1965	3,422	8,202	1,468	2,541	43,263	12,314
1966	3,603	7,661	1,409	2,625	46,144	13,620
1967	3,934	7,645	1,412	2,818	48,620	15,521
1968	4,670	8,438	1,494	2,891	50,817	14,800
1969	4,710	8,167	1,948	3,063	44,935	11,321
1970	4,608	5,433	2,149	3,209	50,301	12,742
1971	5,456	7,827	2,451	3,195	39,801	12,557
1972	5,147	8,149	2,750	3,212	48,735	14,341
1973	5,807	8,268	3,159	3,220	51,928	13,664
1974	6,408	7,882	3,909	3,244	48,519	12,971
1975	5,207	6,270	3,638	2,920	46,429	15,707
1976	5,745	6,922	3,617	2,695	49,951	15,107
1977	5,308	6,249	3,396	2,552	41,148	15,640
1978	6,029	7,434	3,635	2,491	46,648	15,707
1979	4,187	5,201	3,731	2,186	49,572	14,154
1980	4,175	6,566	3,420	2,245	26,391	10,139
1981	4,203	6,731	3,540	2,730	42,562	15,867
1982	4,476	7,792	3,647	2,608	31,951	15,085
1983	5,165	8,781	3,262	2,377	34,473	16,364
1984	6,010	9,546	3,555	2,604	37,437	16,048
1985	6,461	7,600	4,086	2,682	36,546	14,664
1986	7,502	7,074	4,412	2,486	39,037	14,217
1987	7,942	6,816	4,335	2,428	36,252	13,989
1988	7,582	5,501	3,804	2,222	34,707	14,069
1989	8,462	6,216	3,909	2,186	34,390	14,374
1990	9,026	6,044	4,217	2,119	36,313	16,700
1991	9,270	5,899	4,257	1,873	29,078	11,412
1992	7,368	3,981	2,819	1,229	23,388	11,052
1993	8,243	4,992	3,255	1,493	26,271	15,621
1994	7,658	5,300	2,686	1,243	23,058	11,676
1995	8,668	6,288	3,279	1,495	24,891	13,309
1996	8,576	5,652	3,437	1,581	27,217	17,846
1997	8,193	5,299	3,866	1,630	20,776	15,886
1998	9,537	5,664	3,612	1,460	25,949	15,171
1999	9,051	5,181	3,401	1,446	19,927	12,564
2000	8,503	4,003	2,783	1,070	24,232	13,134

PORTUGAL (thousands of metric tons)[33]   1911–1936

	Wheat	Rye	Barley	Oats	Maize	Rice	Potatoes
1911	322	…	…	…	…	…	…
1914	191	…	…	…	…	…	…
1915	183	…	…	…	278	17	…
1916	206	81	28	57	263	21	171
1917	202	90	32	66	252	17	165
1918	261	123	32	66	237	23	152
1919	223	98	31	67	248	21	154
1920	282	131	39	89	298	24	169
1921	256	116	35	82	289	11	175
1922	272	138	40	84	296	20	180
1923	359	133	53	118	260	16	180
1924	288	133	45	91	296	18	193
1925	340	129	48	91	364	17	340
1926	233	92	32	69	312	18	259
1927	312	119	43	80	384	22	311
1928	205	101	31	73	363	20	262
1929	294	119	43	81	379	22	345
1930	368	125	52	113	425	25	565
1931	368	129	44	92	446	26	605
1932	151	120	46	92	367	26	672
1933	324	92	31	53	364	47	620
1934	672	125	44	112	304	55	556
1935	601	119	49	97	269	58	513
1936	235	90	35	84	284	64	517

C2 Output of Main Cereal, Potato, and Sugar Beet Crops (in thousands of hectolitres or metric tons)

PORTUGAL (thousands of metric tons)[33]   **1937–2000**

	Wheat	Rye	Barley	Oats	Maize	Rice	Potatoes
1937	399	96	39	98	320	85	596
1938	430	99	40	92	296	68	596
1939	516	99	39	91	365	72	606
1940	268	75	26	26	397	83	617
1941	449	91	49	82	418	89	625
1942	524	124	66	132	391	79	835
1943	295	99	48	70	481	74	891
1944	368	130	68	77	558	64	896
1945	315	122	48	78	363	45	743
1946	508	147	104	210	554	63	940
1947	348	151	73	112	474	86	1,024
1948	356	124	83	92	511	92	1,018
1949	405	149	94	104	342	78	790
1950	575	170	129	141	688	121	1,128
1951	580	194	137	148	615	141	1,390
1952	579	175	102	134	650	141	1,078
1953	690	183	105	131	499	140	1,120
1954	781	195	104	125	587	154	1,073
1955	508	155	72	82	583	183	1,104
1956	558	171	78	97	641	160	1,102
1957	797	203	101	128	427	162	1,196
1958	809	209	102	143	425	149	1,087
1959	623	175	66	89	487	163	866
1960	492	138	50	61	466	151	1,041
1961	430	119	52	65	632	177	1,056
1962	645	171	72	104	591	173	894
1963	592	216	61	98	523	166	1,145
1964	472	167	46	68	597	181	1,143
1965	612	209	72	99	459	137	888
1966	312	145	49	63	565	154	923
1967	637	175	73	111	577	146	1,296
1968	747	199	94	129	548	149	1,083
1969	454	167	54	79	553	176	1,126
1970	548	157	54	72	581	195	1,220
1971	794	168	85	125	526	162	1,124
1972	604	164	62	85	519	164	1,139
1973	517	134	57	79	509	168	1,086
1974	534	143	75	99	486	130	1,115
1975	601	145	86	121	451	133	1,013
1976	686	165	117	127	378	97	918
1977	224	103	39	60	442	95	1,201
1978	250	123	44	64	449	135	1,128
1979	248	113	41	69	461	145	1,021
1980	430	138	54	96	489	155	1,118
1981	315	126	41	72	377	112	829
1982	425	119	51	86	421	143	983
1983	327	92	54	99	424	109	905
1984	466	103	91	152	481	134	1,038
1985	397	97	65	119	531	147	1,136
1986	463	93	90	153	611	149	1,062
1987	534	108	80	79	655	144	1,178
1988	397	77	51	155	667	151	856
1989	615	106	84	81	666	147	1,063
1990	768	77	62	127	643	153	999
1991	618	80	124	79	656	170	1,370
1992	301	70	54	45	628	110	1,593
1993	367	59	70	61	586	85	1,352
1994	463	64	96	79	726	132	1,327
1995	360	36	53	58	766	125	1,436
1996	406	54	70	60	854	172	1,326
1997	330	41	29	44	913	164	1,049
1998	151	32	26	29	1,204	161	1,225
1999	373	56	29	100	935	152	1,367
2000	353	47	33	112	891	143	1,250

C2 Output of Main Cereal, Potato, and Sugar Beet Crops (in thousands of hectolitres or metric tons)

ROMANIA

1867–1927

	Wheat	Rye	Barley	Oats	Maize	Potatoes	Sugar Beet
	thousand hectolitres					thousand tons	
1867	10,230	1,039	2,947	740	12,845	...	...
1868	11,359	1,502	3,559	831	16,013	...	...
1869	8,343	1,326	2,796	823	15,709	...	...
1870	9,864	1,345	2,840	740	14,472	...	...
1871	9,404	1,270	3,306	1,021	15,130	...	...
1872	6,355	864	3,514	1,127	12,458	...	...
1873	10,219	736	4,919	1,586	11,626	...	...
1874	11,929	1,131	7,001	1,715	11,475	...	...
1875	11,836	925	3,375	1,005	22,510	...	...
1876	7,558	1,182	6,364	1,413	22,988	...	...
1886	12,221	2,264	5,105	3,585	25,533	...	...
1887	16,720	2,683	6,576	4,335	17,164	...	...
1888	20,352	5,145	8,104	3,786	22,189	...	...
1889	17,687	2,027	5,575	2,310	24,413	...	...
1890	18,267	1,671	5,699	2,678	21,440	...	...
1891	17,122	1,365	7,836	2,718	21,166	...	...
1892	22,591	1,637	7,227	3,905	32,433	...	...
1893	21,382	2,717	12,591	5,441	25,568	...	...
1894	15,323	2,032	5,985	3,520	10,605	...	...
1895	24,162	3,264	7,902	3,652	25,100	...	...
1896	25,139	4,308	11,182	5,469	23,078	...	...
1897	12,920	2,393	7,449	3,457	28,201	...	...
1898	20,644	2,684	10,478	6,118	35,833	...	...
1899	9,138	700	1,597	2,202	9,682	...	...
1900	19,875	2,119	5,122	3,064	29,920	...	...
1901	25,530	3,383	8,563	5,833	41,284	...	...
1902	26,905	2,454	8,683	10,241	24,219	...	...
1903	26,012	2,513	10,459	11,077	28,387	...	...
1904	18,937	776	4,076	4,443	6,901	93	145
1905	36,413	2,588	9,297	6,686	20,888	102	217
1906	40,127	3,136	11,819	9,220	46,004	126	192
1907	14,884	900	7,070	6,287	20,290	105	109
1908	19,316	930	4,536	6,065	27,801	117	167
	thousands of metric tons						
1909	1,602	79	449	405	1,903	104	208
1910	3,016	201	644	446	2,813	132	308
1911	2,603	157	569	402	3,004	154	263
1912	2,433	92	456	304	2,810	131	292
1913	2,291[34]	95[34]	602[34]	551[34]	3,111[34]	98[34]	282[34]
1914	1,260	50	537	367	2,783	102	225
1915	2,444	74	632	434	2,345	126	185
1916	2,137	...	654	420	...	...	...
1917	...[34]	...[34]	...[34]	...[34]	...[34]	...[34]	...[34]
1918	584	43	109	85	80	72	49
1919	1,797[34]	255[34]	689[34]	331[34]	3,591[34]	284[34,35]	34[34]
1920	1,669	240	1,472	992	4,624	609	89
1921	2,138	231	1,985	963	2,810	1,388	352
1922	2,504	234	2,042	1,336	3,044	1,116	331
1923	2,779	244	1,325	910	3,846	1,953	643
1924	1,917	151	670	610	3,949	1,669	873
1925	2,851	203	1,019	740	4,159	1,698	988
1926	3,018	286	1,685	1,159	5,840	1,941	1,285
1927	2,633	237	1,262	868	3,533	2,149	1,255

C2 Output of Main Cereal, Potato, and Sugar Beet Crops (in thousands of hectolitres or metric tons)

ROMANIA

	Wheat	Rye	Barley	Oats	Maize	Rice	Potatoes	Sugar Beet
1928	3,145	292	1,511	980	2,756	...	2,052	1,055
1929	2,715	337	2,740	1,359	6,386	...	2,484	893
1930	3,559	465	2,371	1,157	4,520	...	1,958	849
1931	3,682	355	1,414	670	6,063	...	2,008	310
1932	1,512	267	1,467	643	5,993	...	1,725	303
1933	3,241	446	1,884	806	4,554	...	1,502	678
1934	2,084	211	871	563	4,846	...	2,072	648
1935	2,625	323	924	594	5,379	...	2,022	627
1936	3,503	453	1,612	847	5,612	...	2,113	427
1937	3,760	451	917	513	4,752	...	2,107	498
1938	4,821	517	832	463	5,117	...	1,804	731
1939	4,453[36]	432[36]	816[36]	487[36]	6,051[36]	...	1,988[36]	855[36]
1940	1,376	53	496	371	3,743	...	744	518
1941	1,986	55	391	333	3,347	...	854	567
1942	855	25	332	337	2,182	...	1,199	335
1943	2,319	68	587	500	2,884	...	1,629	739
1944	3,289[36]	166[36]	451[36]	476[36]	4,128[36]	...	1,905[36]	714[36]
1945	1,066[36]	44[36]	267[36]	258[36]	1,099[36]	...	893[36]	201[36]
1946	1,609	62	233	282	1,007	...	675	342
1947	1,279[37]	66[37]	360[37]	...	5,279[37]	...	1,630[37]	600[37]
1948	2,397	85	280	375	2,260	...	717	597
1949	...	...	...	...	...	...	1,090[37]	...
1950	2,219	182	325	283	2,101	36	1,601	633
1951	3,521	229	526	389	3,100	45	2,141	1,430
1952	2,975	211	518	429	2,520	49	2,257	890
1953	3,964	262	612	494	3,225	55	2,355	1,300
1954	2,140	170	386	357	4,953	50	2,397	1,408
1955	3,006	214	445	374	5,877	35	2,608	2,000
1956	2,436	136	291	305	3,932	37	2,675	1,519
1957	3,701	152	417	392	6,338	36	3,058	2,043
1958	2,914	124	305	250	3,657	37	2,777	1,732
1959	4,001	128	449	315	5,680	55	2,897	3,446
1960	3,450	103	405	284	5,531	49	3,009	3,399
1961	3,990	104	468	275	5,740	31	2,875	2,911
1962	4,054	75	419	16?	4,932	20	2,597	2,180
1963	3,799	78	351	123	6,023	51	2,692	2,298
1964	3,824	92	348	79	6,692	54	2,640	3,668
1965	5,937	125	485	124	5,877	46	2,195	3,275
1966	5,065	100	483	170	8,022	56	3,352	4,368
1967	5,820	71	531	163	6,858	69	3,096	3,830
1968	4,848	48	590	114	7,105	60	3,707	3,936
1969	4,349	47	544	137	7,676	68	2,165	3,783
1970	3,356	43	513	117	6,536	65	2,064	3,175
1971	5,595	65	789	161	7,850	67	3,783	4,321
1972	6,041	58	839	111	9,817	45	3,672	5,581
1973	5,488	43	730	102	7,397	50	2,644	4,380
1974	5,007	42	916	91	7,440	53	4,119	4,947
1975	4,860	52	952	57	9,241	56	2,716	4,905
1976	6,724	49	1,231	55	11,583	97	4,788	6,911
1977	6,463	50	1,859	61	10,114	47	4,207	6,246
1978	6,243	57	2,307	57	10,208	58	4,465	5,845
1979	4,676	40	2,043	60	12,425	60	4,562	6,109
1980	6,427	40	2,466	47	11,153	39	4,135	5,562

C2 Output of Main Cereal, Potato, and Sugar Beet Crops (in thousands of hectolitres or metric tons)

ROMANIA 1981–2000

	Wheat	Rye	Barley	Oats	Maize	Rice	Potatoes	Sugar Beet
1981	5,310	35	2,571	65	11,892	49	4,447	5,441
1982	6,460	45	3,052	91	12,620	46	5,006	6,647
1983	5,205	45	2,193	80	11,982	84	6,209	4,819
1984	7,580	47	2,448	94	13,274	110	6,391	7,019
1985	5,666	45	1,850	102	11,903	138	6,631	6,446
1986	7,320	66	2,497	156	7,527	153	5,187	5,397
1987	9,672	55	3,231	100	7,182	115	4,141	5,217
1988	8,572	60	3,202	60	6,762	131	3,621	4,868
1989	7,880	55	3,436	168	6,810	70	4,420	6,771
1990	7,320	59	2,680	234	10,497	66	3,186	3,277
1991	3,473	80	2,951	258	6,828	31	1,873	4,703
1992	3,206	70	1,678	508	7,987	39	2,012	2,897
1993	5,314	59	1,553	554	9,343	36	3,709	1,776
1994	6,135	51	2,134	497	9,343	15	2,947	3,273
1995	7,667	43	1,816	404	9,923	24	3,020	2,655
1996	3,144	20	1,108	291	9,607	23	3,591	2,848
1997	7,156	29	1,889	325	12,687	11	3,206	2,726
1998	5,182	26	1,238	362	8,623	5	3,319	2,361
1999	4,658	21	1,018	390	10,935	4	3,957	1,415
2000	4,434	22	867	244	4,898	4	3,470	…

RUSSIA/U.S.S.R[38] 1870–1908

	Wheat	Rye	Barley	Oats	Maize	Potatoes	Sugar Beet
			(in millions of hectolitres)			(million tons)	
1870	99	278	58	265	…	146	…
1871	…	…	…	…	…	…	1.4
1872	57	199	43	198	…	135	2.0
1873	…	…	…	…	…	…	2.1
1874	…	…	…	…	…	…	1.7
1875	53	197	32	134	23	124	2.2
1876	…	…	…	…	…	…	3.2
1877	…	…	…	…	…	…	2.4
1878	…	…	…	…	…	…	2.6
1879	60	202	44	179	26	122	2.7
1880	…	…	…	…	…	…	…
1881	…	…	…	…	…	…	3.5
1882	…	…	…	…	…	…	3.8
1883	97	236	57	246	34	112	3.6
1884	118	303	59	221	7	130	4.0
1885	78	309	44	171	8	107	5.5
1886	71	291	59	251	9	123	4.7
1887	123	328	74	273	6	139	4.3
1888	130	311	70	240	9	129	4.6
1889	79	243	51	216	50	134	4.4
1890	94	197	72	238	107	146	4.9
1891	74	220	62	159	130	127	4.3
1892	106	258	74	192	97	203	3.7
1893	164	321	129	286	170	253	5.6
1894	161[38]	380[38]	105[38]	286[38]	84[38]	236[38]	5.4
	169	403	112	306	84	314	
			(in million metric tons)				
1895	8.4	19.6	4.9	10.4	0.6	21.1	5.5[44]
1896	8.7	19.3	4.9	10.4	0.4	23.2	5.7
1897	7.0	15.8	4.5	8.5	1.2	21.9	6.0
1898	9.7	17.9	6.0	8.9	1.0	23.2	6.0
1899	9.1	22.1	4.3	13.0	0.6	23.8	7.3
1900	9.2	22.7	4.5	11.5	0.6	25.3	6.4
1901	9.1	18.5	4.6	8.4	1.5	23.2	8.2
1902	13.1	22.4	6.4	12.6	1.0	27.5	8.6
1903	12.9	22.1	6.7	10.3	1.0	23.6	7.7
1904	11.3	24.6	6.7	15.2	0.5	24.0	6.4
1905	12.8	17.7	6.4	12.0	0.6	27.6	7.7
1906	9.9	15.9	5.8	8.8	1.5	25.1	10.1
1907	9.7	19.4	6.6	11.6	1.1	27.7	8.6
1908	11.0	19.0	7.0	11.7	1.3	28.4	8.2

C2 Output of Main Cereal, Potato, and Sugar Beet Crops

RUSSIA/U.S.S.R.[38]   1909–1965

	Wheat	Rye	Barley	Oats	Maize	Potatoes	Sugar Beet
				(millions of metric tons)			
1909	16.5[38]	22.0[38]	8.9[38]	15.0[38]	0.7[38]	31.5[38]	6.9
	23.0	22.9	10.9	16.9	1.4	32.8	
1910	22.8	22.2	10.6	15.5	2.6	36.6	13.2
1911	15.3	19.5	9.5	12.7	2.4	32.0	13.6
1912	21.8	26.7	10.8	15.8	2.4	38.0	10.7
1913	28.0[38]	25.7[38]	13.1[38]	18.2[38]	2.1[38]	35.9[38]	12.4[38]
1914	…	…	…	…	…	…	…
1920	8.7	9.4	4.7	7.0	1.1	20.9	0.7
1921	5.6[38]	10.2[38]	2.7[38]	5.2[38]	1.2[38]	20.6[38]	0.4[38]
1922	10.6	18.2	4.3	7.8	3.0	22.2	1.5
1923	12.3	19.8	5.7	8.4	3.2	34.7	2.6
1924	13.1	18.8	4.4	8.9	2.3	36.2	3.4
1925	20.8	22.8	6.0	11.5	4.5	38.6	9.1
1926	24.4	23.7	5.5	14.8	3.5	43.0	6.4
1927	21.6	24.2	4.5	13.1	3.1	41.2	10.4
1928	22.0	19.3	5.7	16.5	3.3	46.4	10.1
1929	18.9	20.4	7.2	15.7	3.0	45.6	6.3
1930	26.9	23.6	6.8	16.6	2.7	49.4	14.0
1931	20.5	22.0	5.2	11.0	4.8	44.8	12.0
1932	20.3	22.0	5.0	11.2	3.4	43.1	6.6
1933	27.7	24.2	7.9	15.4	4.8	49.3	9.0
1934	30.4	20.1	6.8	18.9	3.8	51.0	11.4
1935	30.8	21.4	8.2	18.3	2.8	69.7	16.2
1936	30.7	18.0	9.3	13.4	4.1	51.5	16.8
1937	46.9	29.4	10.6	21.9	3.9	65.6	21.9
1938	40.8	20.9	8.2	17.0	2.7	42.0	16.7
1939	…[38]	…[38]	…[38]	…[38]	…[38]	…[38]	21.0[38]
1940	31.8	21.1	12.0	16.8	5.2	76.1	18.0
1941	…	…	…	…	…	26.6	2.0
1942	…	…	…	…	…	23.5	2.2
1943	…	…	…	…	…	35.9	1.3
1944	…	…	…	…	…	54.6	4.1
1945	13.4	…	…	…	…	58.3	5.5
1946	…	…	…	…	…	55.6	4.3
1947	…	…	…	…	…	74.5	14.0
1948	…	…	…	…	…	95.0	12.9
1949	…	…	…	…	…	89.6	15.7
1950	31.1	18.0	6.4	13.0	6.6	88.6	20.8
1951	…	…	…	…	…	58.8	23.6
1952	43.9	…	…	…	…	69.2	22.2
1953	41.3	14.5	7.9	10.1	3.7	72.6	23.2
1954	42.4	15.6	7.8	10.8	3.7	75.0	19.8
1955	47.3	16.5	10.4	11.8	11.6	71.8	31.0
1956	67.4	14.1	12.9	13.2	9.9	96.0	32.5
1957	58.1	14.5	8.5	12.7	4.6	87.8	39.7
1958	76.6	15.8	13.0	13.4	10.2	86.5	54.4
1959	69.1	16.9	10.2	13.5	5.7	86.6	43.9
1960	64.3	16.4	16.0	12.0	9.8	84.4	57.7
1961	66.5	16.7	13.3	8.9	17.1	84.3	50.9
1962	70.8	17.0	19.5	5.7	15.5	69.7	47.4
1963	49.7	11.9	19.8	4.0	11.1	71.8	44.1
1964	74.4	13.6	28.6	5.5	13.8	93.6	81.2
1965	59.7	16.2	20.3	6.2	8.0	88.7	72.3

C2 Output of Main Cereal, Potato, and Sugar Beet Crops

RUSSIA/U.S.S.R.[38]   1966–2000

	Wheat	Rye	Barley	Oats	Maize	Potatoes	Sugar Beet
1966	100.5	13.1	27.9	9.2	8.4	87.9	74.0
1967	77.4	13.0	24.7	11.6	9.2	95.5	87.1
1968	93.4	14.1	28.9	11.6	8.8	102.2	94.3
1969	79.9	10.9	32.7	13.1	12.0	91.8	71.2
1970	99.7	13.0	38.2	14.2	9.4	96.8	78.9
1971	98.8	12.8	34.6	14.7	8.6	92.7	72.2
1972	86.0	9.6	36.8	14.1	9.8	78.3	76.4
1973	109.8	10.8	55.0	17.5	13.2	108.2	87.0
1974	83.9	15.2	54.2	15.3	12.1	81.0	77.9
1975	66.2	9.1	35.8	12.5	7.3	88.7	66.3
1976	96.9	14.0	69.5	18.1	10.1	85.1	99.9
1977	92.2	8.5	52.7	18.4	11.0	83.7	93.1
1978	120.9	13.6	62.1	18.5	9.0	86.1	93.5
1979	90.3	8.1	48.0	15.2	8.4	91.0	76.2
1980	98.2	10.2	43.5	15.5	9.5	67.0	81.0
1981	81.1	9.6	36.1	12.4	9.4	72.1	60.8
1982	84.3	14.8	43.0	16.8	14.7	78.2	71.4
1983	77.5	17.3	50.0	18.8	13.3	82.9	81.8
1984	68.6	14.0	41.8	19.2	13.6	85.5	85.4
1985	78.1	15.7	46.5	20.5	14.4	73.0	82.4
1986	92.3	15.3	53.9	21.9	12.5	87.2	79.3
1987	83.3	18.1	58.4	18.5	14.8	75.9	90.7
1988	84.4	18.5	44.5	15.3	16.0	62.7	87.9
1989	92.3	20.0	48.5	16.8	15.3	72.2	97.4
1990	109.6	24.3	56.6	18.8	9.9	63.7	81.2
1991	80.0	13.0	42.0	14.0	8.5	64.5	79.0
1992	46.2	13.8	27.0	11.2	2.1	38.2	25.5
1993	42.4	9.1	26.6	11.5	2.4	38.0	25.5
1994	32.1	5.9	27.0	10.7	0.8	33.8	13.9
1995	30.1	4.0	15.7	8.5	1.7	39.9	19.0
1996	34.9	5.9	15.9	8.3	1.0	38.6	16.1
1997	44.2	7.4	20.7	9.3	2.6	37.0	13.8
1998	27.0	3.2	9.7	4.6	0.8	31.4	10.7
1999	30.9	4.7	10.6	4.3	1.0	31.3	15.2
2000	34.4	5.4	14.1	6.0	1.5	34.0	14.0

ESTONIA (thousands of metric tons)   1919–2000

	Wheat	Rye	Barley	Oats	Potatoes
1919	12	125	98	...	519
1920	17	164	130	...	687
1921	14	185	125	162	782
1922	21	147	145	146	718
1923	20	166	89	115	682
1924	15	139	121	141	675
1925	22	183	115	127	650
1926	24	114	132	133	926
1927	29	171	94	98	742
1928	28	141	92	99	501
1929	34	146	124	149	753
1930	45	226	128	158	863
1931	47	148	129	164	855
1932	57	181	100	130	783
1933	67	222	81	116	949
1934	85	230	115	160	892
1935	62	173	92	134	893
1936	66	154	87	114	1,031
1937	76	212	81	139	986
1938	86	188	97	177	998
1939	85	228	90	149	874
1940–1991	76	191	83	148	1,047
			included in Russia		
1992	90	150	302	48	648
1993	100	114	399	51	652
1994	57	41	339	57	563
1995	77	58	279	80	537
1996	101	62	317	115	500
1997	111	72	312	115	437
1998	118	55	273	99	317
1999	88	39	186	71	404
2000	147	61	348	117	472

C2   Output of Main Cereal, Potato, and Sugar Beet Crops (in thousands of hectolitres or metric tons)

LATVIA (thousands of metric tons)   1919–2000

	Wheat	Rye	Barley	Oats	Potatoes	Sugar Beet
1919	...	...	...	...	...	...
1920	11	119	67	113	375	...
1921	21	249	141	245	674	...
1922	26	174	147	264	675	...
1923	45	274	131	230	578	...
1924	43	199	162	271	676	...
1925	59	315	178	304	751	...
1926	51	155	189	276	1,014	...
1927	72	259	130	177	717	...
1928	68	215	71	146	314	...
1929	64	241	208	340	1,080	...
1930	111	365	187	342	1,104	
1931	92	143	192	343	1,167	61
1932	144	300	193	323	1,205	184
1933	183	355	195	331	1,403	186
1934	219	412	218	389	1,446	339
1935	178	364	205	386	1,461	294
1936	144	286	165	284	1,612	244
1937	172	422	218	405	1,782	280
1938	192	379	221	447	1,751	231
1939	212	448	222	485	1,640	218
1940–1991	...	...	...	...	...	...
			included in Russia			
1992	324	295	426	60	1,167	...
1993	305	341	446	74	1,272	...
1994	199	113	481	88	1,045	228
1995	244	71	284	73	864	263
1996	358	113	372	101	1,081	258
1997	395	134	359	117	946	388
1998	385	105	322	104	694	597
1999	352	88	233	66	796	451
2000	427	111	261	80	747	408

LITHUANIA (thousands of metric tons)   1919–2000

	Wheat	Rye	Barley	Oats	Potatoes	Sugar Beet
1919	...	...	...	...	...	...
1920	...	...	...	...	...	...
1921	77	535	145	264	1,386	...
1922	89[39]	616[39]	234[39]	420[39]	1,848[39]	...
1923	81	607	173	331	1,630	...
1924	90	465	203	270	1,658	...
1925	144	663	245	285	1,581	...
1926	114	351	249	320	1,665	...
1927	144	538	188	243	1,264	...
1928	172	475	150	267	960	...
1929	254	560	268	439	1,853	...
1930	246	668	202	417	1,760	11
1931	227	412	241	410	1,996	45
1932	257	572	239	356	1,919	120
1933	223	552	232	331	1,824	52
1934	285	669	254	380	2,493	95
1935	275	641	252	400	1,774	136
1936	219	542	233	332	2,118	170
1937	221	607	274	388	2,510	186
1938	251	624	274	420	2,118	144
1939	257	659	257	409	2,354	170
1940–1991	...	...	...	...	...	...
			included in Russia			
1992	834	342	955	51	1,079	...
1993	919	437	842	36	1,200	...
1994	549	313	1,091	69	1,096	462
1995	637	239	892	67	1,593	692
1996	936	287	1,176	102	2,044	796
1997	1,127	348	1,194	112	1,830	1,002
1998	1,031	349	1,104	97	1,849	949
1999	871	261	741	67	1,708	871
2000	427	311	859	83	1,792	870

C2 Output of Main Cereal, Potato, and Sugar Beet Crops (in thousands of hectolitres or metric tons)

SPAIN[41] (thousands of metric tons)   1890–1944

	Wheat	Rye	Barley	Oats	Maize	Rice	Potatoes	Sugar Beet
1890	2,075	463	807	...	402	...	...	170
1891	1,962	430	778	133	501	...	...	210
1892	2,134	425	932	162	462	...	...	145
1893	2,414	534	1,004	172	531	...	...	170
1894	2,984	476	1,224	210	638	...	...	135
1895	2,202	440	907	150	559	...	...	85
1896	1,976	402	688	133	526	...	...	200
1897	2,549	474	995	182	530	...	...	410
1898	3,405	531	1,585	243	447	...	...	480
1899	2,659	541	1,175	219	652	...	...	491
1900	2,744	553	1,235	238	672	...	...	710
1901	3,726	721	1,738	331	654	174	...	553
1902	3,634	665	1,770	339	642	168	2,299	671
1903	3,510	572	1,401	333	447	189	...	843
1904	2,596	439	1,172	268	540	179	...	639
1905	2,518	673	1,000	323	810	217	3,091	678
1906	3,828	785	1,965	408	475	193	...	703
1907	2,731	687	1,167	247	645	216	...	978
1908	3,265	671	1,515	408	511	204	...	882
1909	3,922	886	1,716	498	671	207	...	667
1910	3,741	701	1,661	421	695	211	3,617	483
1911	4,041	734	1,890	492	730	216	...	812
1912	2,988	479	1,306	334	637	244	2,534	1,004
1913	3,059	709	1,493	368	639	223	...	1,341
1914	3,159	608	1,574	453	770	248	2,086	738
1915	3,923	728	1,839	528	643	235	2,750	836
1916	4,147	731	1,891	469	728	242	2,966	1,005
1917	3,883	615	1,697	480	746	236	3,088	1,217
1918	3,693	773	1,970	442	613	208	2,601	1,124
1919	3,518	592	1,782	478	649	303	2,749	705
1920	3,772	707	1,970	548	703	289	2,935	1,627
1921	3,950	714	1,945	517	632	262	2,782	1,816
1922	3,415	667	1,688	453	682	274	2,867	1,399
1923	4,276	713	2,436	587	608	243	2,599	1,220
1924	3,314	668	1,822	438	655	296	2,430	1,660
1925	4,425	760	2,154	631	717	306	...	1,460
1926	3,990	597	2,096	547	437	320	3,165	1,822
1927	3,912	674	2,008	569	663	310	3,610	1,520
1928	3,338	417	1,780	517	535	290	3,807	1,437
1929	4,198	583	2,119	665	630	304	4,623	1,599
1930	3,993	547	2,263	726	733	313	4,203	2,322
1931	3,659	536	1,975	605	670	266	4,677	2,856
1932	5,013	658	2,886	831	693	218	5,026	2,035
1933	3,762	526	2,177	592	660	295	4,782	1,982
1934	5,085	548	2,819	752	788	294	4,418	2,301
1935	4,300	489	2,113	571	736	293	4,337	1,577
1939	2,870	410	1,418	479	843	178	3,494	721
1940	2,161	351	1,396	474	742	269	3,413	1,350
1941	3,078	410	1,698	589	703	208	3,588	1,359
1942	3,662	518	2,381	789	524	207	3,681	931
1943	3,127	460	2,064	659	378	208	2,646	1,129
1944	3,769	515	2,150	598	538	239	3,302	1,183

C2   Output of Main Cereal, Potato, and Sugar Beet Crops (in thousands of hectolitres or metric tons)

SPAIN[41] (thousands of metric tons)   **1945-2000**

	Wheat	Rye	Barley	Oats	Maize	Rice	Potatoes	Sugar Beet
1945	2,263	277	1,031	297	472	206	2,664	958
1946	4,131	534	2,636	749	531	206	2,558	1,526
1947	3,180	431	1,725	469	490	237	2,835	1,213
1948	3,275	443	2,066	533	479	235	2,702	1,986
1949	3,035	489	1,635	448	331	263	2,814	1,512
1950	3,374	467	1,491	507	536	252	2,870	1,385
1951	4,266	514	2,151	552	607	285	4,550	2,436
1952	4,098	495	2,200	554	647	324	3,797	4,136
1953	3,026	406	1,476	435	707	393	3,717	2,379
1954	4,773	526	2,205	526	751	401	3,939	1,854
1955	3,991	493	1,718	506	616	389	4,081	2,267
1956	4,196	511	1,551	452	714	384	4,307	2,743
1957	4,900	496	1,881	535	771	388	3,954	2,285
1958	4,540	515	1,778	519	916	375	4,292	3,207
1959	4,635	533	2,092	524	959	386	4,588	3,919
1960	3,520	385	1,562	431	1,012	361	4,620	3,572
1961	3,431	351	1,744	495	1,067	394	4,918	4,423
1962	4,812	453	2,162	513	920	392	4,153	3,584
1963	4,860	424	2,071	466	1,171	399	5,075	2,750
1964	3,977	346	1,927	390	1,203	398	4,254	3,331
1965	4,715	349	1,892	370	1,142	350	4,079	3,678
1966	4,876	353	2,006	442	1,154	375	4,423	4,042
1967	5,650	336	2,576	492	1,195	366	4,490	4,282
1968	5,312	355	3,441	539	1,473	362	4,570	4,620
1969	4,624	320	3,969	547	1,507	417	4,789	4,980
1970	4,126	259	3,103	393	1,848	382	5,301	5,446
1971	5,449	272	4,784	582	2,056	361	4,865	6,412
1972	4,562	263	4,358	440	1,923	347	5,275	5,212
1973	3,966	252	4,402	425	2,038	387	5,579	5,501
1974	4,535	254	5,404	559	1,993	367	5,693	3,984
1975	4,303	241	6,728	609	1,794	379	5,338	6,337
1976	4,436	214	5,473	528	1,545	406	5,659	10,167
1977	4,064	228	6,766	418	1,892	379	5,881	8,307
1978	4,806	251	8,068	553	1,969	401	5,364	8,291
1979	4,082	221	6,252	456	2,212	427	5,637	5,124
1980	6,039	284	8,705	680	2,314	433	5,737	6,908
1981	3,408	212	4,758	445	2,157	444	5,470	7,941
1982	4,410	169	5,270	443	2,330	402	5,222	9,085
1983	4,268	253	6,662	464	1,803	224	5,163	9,619
1984	6,052	315	10,789	788	2,529	440	5,981	8,095
1985	5,329	273	10,698	680	3,414	462	5,927	6,619
1986	4,392	220	7,431	433	3,424	496	5,124	7,746
1987	5,791	319	9,836	502	3,557	483	5,552	7,937
1988	6,514	357	12,070	537	3,577	507	4,530	8,926
1989	5,468	332	9,394	507	3,328	342	5,366	7,333
1990	4,760	274	9,415	524	3,051	569	5,399	7,233
1991	5,468	237	9,262	404	3,233	582	5,182	6,679
1992	4,357	222	6,105	313	2,758	564	5,181	7,234
1993	5,002	304	9,520	405	1,699	316	3,977	8,650
1994	4,302	207	7,416	414	2,344	408	3,860	8,360
1995	3,138	168	5,047	231	2,590	330	3,914	7,438
1996	6,041	296	10,697	664	3,751	734	3,856	8,236
1997	4,676	212	8,550	521	4,452	776	3,254	8,530
1998	5,436	207	10,895	726	4,349	796	3,129	8,866
1999	5,084	220	7,434	531	3,769	845	3,367	8,162
2000	7,333	210	11,283	952	3,898	798	3,138	8,254

C2 Output of Main Cereal, Potato, and Sugar Beet Crops (in thousands of hectolitres or metric tons)

SWEDEN (thousands of metric tons)   1802-1858

	Wheat	Rye	Barley	Oats	Mixed Corn	Potatoes
1802	14	140	165	105	50	44
1803	15	167	171	85	49	41
1804	12	155	169	101	53	53
1805	14	158	157	100	51	56
1806	10	135	174	100	50	54
1807	14	160	167	93	47	51
1808	13	157	149	76	42	61
1809	15	206	183	105	58	78
1810	15	193	177	113	62	90
1811	13	156	168	100	51	84
1812	14	179	148	82	39	66
1813	16	181	178	83	49	102
1814	16	176	191	104	57	99
1815	17	172	201	106	59	122
1816	16	186	168	89	46	120
1817	16	159	185	107	55	144
1818	13	153	147	90	47	123
1819	18	196	160	93	45	142
1820	20	213	209	119	64	216
Av 1818-22	25	246	217	133	76	296
1824	31	286	234	139	82	404
1830	33	307	241	152	83	469
1835	36	319	230	156	86	517
1840	36	308	244	167	90	596
1845	44	353	273	199	120	676
1850	48	366	282	209	111	624
1854	52	405	295	273	105	690
1858	74	515	328	445	125	1,009

SWEDEN (thousands of metric tons)   1860-1878

	Wheat	Rye	Barley	Oats	Mixed Corn	Potatoes	Sugar Beet
1860	69	436	286	536	95	...	...
1861	58	332	287	493	95	...	...
1862	61	439	307	639	115	...	...
1863	70	441	280	489	88	...	...
1864	71	498	298	592	100	...	...
1865	59	420	265	495	86	...	...
1866	68	429	250	596	108	953	16
1867	41	297	201	564	94	656	13
1868	69	403	236	399	72	1,021	12
1869	81	515	330	708	125	859	14
1870	89	551	365	760	107	1,511	22
1871	86	483	377	853	130	1,019	23
1872	75	431	344	631	125	1,257	24
1873	98	516	311	797	108	927	31
1874	102	495	315	488	83	1,289	18
1875	95	518	375	816	119	1,301	17
1876	90	502	308	685	103	1,271	12
1877	74	395	258	740	99	1,000	8
1878	100	519	378	907	125	1,232	7

C2   Output of Main Cereal, Potato, and Sugar Beet Crops (in thousands of hectolitres or metric tons)

SWEDEN (thousands of metric tons)   **1879–1931**

	Wheat	Rye	Barley	Oats	Mixed Corn	Potatoes	Sugar Beet
1879	85	491	352	896	116	866	11
1880	105	568	382	917	128	1,501	19
1881	59	405	309	835	107	1,321	16
1882	103	522	403	1,035	137	903	19
1883	85	477	340	889	122	1,226	38
1884	110	566	372	985	143	1,178	47
1885	113	564	274	872	136	1,208	43
1886	110	529	346	960	153	1,257	54
1887	123	581	346	1,014	152	1,517	87
1888	102	509	303	1,036	142	1,003	93
1889	104	549	311	772	124	1,689	167
1890	108	562	356	1,205	184	813	224
1891	122	581	306	964	165	1,180	261
1892	124	614	338	1,221	194	1,340	314
1893	107	636	294	970	154	1,465	411
1894	118	471	323	1,178	190	1,070	564
1895	103	506	326	1,196	186	1,343	565
1896	130	631	321	942	173	1,486	770
1897	129	609	318	972	186	1,292	730
1898	129	541	335	1,217	205	893	514
1899	129	557	264	900	176	787	569
1900	150	669	333	1,193	227	1,587	819
1901	122	565	295	941	176	1,062	838
1902	127	579	280	957	190	1,349	608
1903	151	619	324	1,075	213	1,526	661
1904	143	538	317	866	207	1,204	570
1905	150	650	308	1,055	223	1,763	810
1906	182	686	341	1,192	275	1,605	986
1907	168	534	294	1,136	271	1,258	827
1908	191	665	356	1,273	301	1,792	938
1909	202	651	305	1,182	297	1,471	962
1910	209	622	330	1,290	308	1,604	1,068
1911	220	617	325	1,098	306	1,262	966
1912	212	586	308	1,274	320	1,530	846
1913	259	585	369	1,401	364	1,969	858
1914	242	680	265	806	217	1,704	967
1915	263	601	300	1,253	353	1,953	839
1916	246	642	298	1,239	369	1,497	937
1917	188	354	248	891	312	2,021	834
1918	242	490	252	814	375	1,833	812
1919	254	574	277	1,076	468	2,001	939
1920	281	570	243	1,015	451	1,628	1,039
1921	336	674	261	1,090	498	1,757	1,485
1922	259	562	294	1,120	499	1,929	456
1923	299	594	249	1,052	492	1,631	1,042
1924	185	276	288	1,033	493	1,418	914
1925	364	676	314	1,176	536	2,106	1,364
1926	331	587	326	1,271	531	1,953	142
1927	417	385	201	1,057	403	975	993
1928	499	431	209	1,168	467	1,708	1,096
1929	517	411	248	1,249	511	1,885	767
1930	567	436	240	1,121	529	1,759	1,215
1931	464	283	223	988	500	1,482	876

C2 Output of Main Cereal, Potato, and Sugar Beet Crops (in thousands of hectolitres or metric tons)

SWEDEN (thousands of metric tons)   **1932–1980**

	Wheat	Rye	Barley	Oats	Mixed Corn	Potatoes	Sugar Beet
1932	655	433	223	1,251	518	2,123	1,554
1933	717	462	199	1,099	475	2,031	1,839
1934	757	517	215	1,229	541	1,979	1,862
1935	643	430	222	1,239	564	1,757	1,866
1936	589	351	200	1,203	526	1,806	1,800
1937	689	374	189	1,241	539	1,838	2,077
1938	804	374	240	1,375	628	1,858	1,834
1939	861	354	232	1,271	591	1,809	1,900
1940	421	266	189	937	478	2,294	1,859
1941	331	279	158	776	421	2,071	1,844
1942	472	448	220	926	528	1,840	1,734
1943	524	405	233	850	495	2,171	1,868
1944	543	357	175	730	470	1,435	1,803
1945	588	276	169	755	463	1,659	1,814
1946	680	289	183	783	515	1,941	1,776
1947	399	142	176	678	432	1,758	1,493
1948	702	322	193	793	572	2,277	1,808
1949	698	277	178	840	648	1,720	1,770
1950	739	243	210	807	654	1,734	1,978
1951	471	169	248	794	665	1,630	1,732
1952	773	277	328	784	677	1,711	1,597
1953	987	297	469	945	716	1,727	1,997
1954	1,021	301	361	863	657	1,429	1,848
1955	717	170	407	597	528	1,285	1,663
1956	951	267	613	1,133	698	2,012	1,786
1957	711	230	557	847	548	1,498	2,103
1958	598	170	659	894	520	1,393	1,764
1959	836	211	664	787	486	1,411	1,733
1960	824	230	847	1,176	563	1,753	2,414
1961	839	164	945	1,394	545	1,526	2,264
1962	906	164	926	1,184	448	1,516	1,441
1963	696	75	1,155	1,156	428	1,908	1,574
1964	1,065	119	1,375	1,448	456	1,477	1,731
1965	1,038	169	1,437	1,340	410	1,542	1,340
1966	576	82	1,408	1,154	266	1,355	1,434
1967	1,130	195	1,564	1,396	259	1,399	1,798
1968	1,074	209	1,776	1,584	262	1,486	1,982
1969	917	182	1,575	1,129	177	931	1,470
1970	945	221	1,870	1,656	206	1,490	1,561
1971	977	296	1,993	1,834	198	1,242	1,706
1972	1,130	357	1,850	1,601	139	1,137	1,783
1973	1,312	316	1,736	1,188	160	947	1,781
1974	1,793	429	2,356	1,656	244	1,257	2,140
1975	1,455	322	1,903	1,321	165	837	1,992
1976	1,765	427	1,826	1,251	165	1,058	2,077
1977	1,522	338	1,966	1,416	153	1,279	2,199
1978	1,290	298	2,434	1,550	170	1,339	2,247
1979	1,003	196	2,346	1,524	148	1,284	2,206
1980	1,193	223	2,172	1,567	157	1,084	2,257

C2   Output of Main Cereal, Potato, and Sugar Beet Crops (in thousands of hectolitres or metric tons)

SWEDEN (thousands of metric tons)   **1981–2000**

	Wheat	Rye	Barley	Oats	Potatoes	Sugar Beet
1981	1,066	179	2,452	1,816	1,206	2,484
1982	1,490		2,378	1,663	1,036	2,336
1983	1,721	235	2,026	1,268	939	1,922
1984	1,776	246	2,733	1,904	1,307	2,508
1985	1,338	157	2,309	1,668	1,266[10]	2,156
1986	1,731	154	2,327	1,486	1,208	2,187
1987	1,558	137	1,907	1,440	958	1,697
1988	1,296	128	1,879	1,330	1,283	2,439
1989	1,751	319	1,870	1,455	1,179	2,654
1990	2,173	340	2,052	1,614	1,233	2,550
1991	1,481	165	1,935	1,426	1,029	1,628
1992	1,406	136	1,261	807	1,253	2,135
1993	1,764	233	1,749	1,348	1,150	2,300
1994	1,345	173	1,661	991	1,063	2,350
1995	1,556	206	1,793	947	1,074	2,479
1996	2,030	166	2,113	1,200	1,201	2,430
1997	2,056	139	2,086	1,274	1,214	2,430
1998	2,249	161	1,687	1,136	1,199	2,571
1999	1,659	117	1,853	1,055	991	2,753
2000	2,399	187	1,634	1,151	980	2,602

SWITZERLAND (thousands of metric tons)   **1909–1949**

	Wheat	Rye	Barley	Oats	Potatoes	Sugar Beet
1909	97	51	10	80	…	25
1910	75	41	9	63	650	15
1911	96	46	10	70	650	23
1912	87	43	9	58	660	—
1913	97	45	10	75	725	32
1914	89	44	12	75	520	32
1915	108	52	14	81	835	23
1916	111	33	13	60	500	20
1917	122	37	15	61	1,050	12
1918	142[12]	47	15	75	935	13
1919	139	40	14	40	760	8
1920	135	41	14	45	769	28
1921	138	46	12	44	691	42
1922	97	43	11	36	676	34
1923	142	48	12	44	686	32
1924	123	36	11	39	540	45
1925	139	48	12	39	740	43
1926	142	41	12	45	611	49
1927	143	40	12	42	695	50
1928	150	44	12	43	673	52
1929	144	40	14	41	778	37
1930	123	37	11	36	590	40
1931	138	36	12	34	750	38
1932	136	38	13	35	655	50
1933	176	36	7	21	746	61
1934	184	34	8	20	802	64
1935	204	27	8	21	656	59
1936	255	32	7	20	568	63
1937	202	34	8	24	846	86
1938	230	36	11	25	766	92
1939	200	30	13	26	620	108
1940	189	23	23	52	882	129
1941	244	31	40	81	1,084	121
1942	252	30	49	78	1,381	151
1943	293	36	58	94	1,707	154
1944	296	33	63	95	1,719	188
1945	258	28	76	110	1,613	213
1946	237	29	64	89	1,080	171
1947	218	25	55	74	1,230	161
1948	225	27	54	65	1,141	185
1949	290	30	65	88	764	204

C2 Output of Main Cereal, Potato, and Sugar Beet Crops (in thousands of hectolitres or metric tons)

SWITZERLAND (thousands of metric tons)   1950–2000

	Wheat	Rye	Barley	Oats	Potatoes	Sugar Beet
1950	253	38	44	52	1,132	235
1951	261	37	51	63	968	209
1952	279	39	61	70	1,192	203
1953	245	37	63	78	986	213
1954	346	45	62	67	1,312	219
1955	338	29	63	59	934	210
1956	217	36	94	69	1,288	224
1957	304	30	70	56	1,264	245
1958	337	39	71	47	1,311	282
1959	349	40	76	48	1,302	261
1960	378	47	76	44	1,291	230
1961	316	34	92	47	1,239	224
1962	318	65	125	49	1,127	168
1963	299	50	95	35	1,246	297
1964	388	63	105	38	1,206	362
1965	352	51	95	30	906	298
1966	348	46	107	33	1,049	366
1967	426	63	117	32	1,125	423
1968	416	58	112	30	1,098	453
1969	379	43	132	37	979	392
1970	346	49	142	29	977	379
1971	410	52	168	41	1,093	472
1972	410	50	156	37	824	396
1973	345	45	173	39	910	540
1974	411	40	210	55	929	518
1975	356	24	172	55	908	479
1976	401	42	183	49	769	587
1977	324	37	172	41	713	545
1978	409	44	215	55	893	633
1979	424	41	222	47	871	780
1980	394	35	212	53	853	674
1981	409	30	226	58	1,048	901
1982	424	23	236	60	960	834
1983	446	19	241	52	711	830
1984	597	29	312	53	923	859
1985	550	20	269	52	817	789
1986	492	19	230	30	743	761
1987	462	18	241	38	658	824
1988	559	19	299	48	748	923
1989	649	21	359	60	770	888
1990	572	19	347	55	760	965
1991	602	25	356	56	711	896
1992	546	28	359	52	741	907
1993	580	34	392	58	908	976
1994	584	31	394	52	634	841
1995	631	42	303	44	631	824
1996	679	45	333	46	812	1,143
1997	597	25	314	47	687	1,180
1998	616	23	336	41	560	1,125
1999	506	19	258	29	484	1,186
2000	586	23	283	27	600	1,408

C2   Output of Main Cereal, Potato, and Sugar Beet Crops (in thousands of hectolitres or metric tons)

UK: GREAT BRITAIN   **1884–1935**

	Wheat	Barley	Oats	Potatoes	Sugar Beet
		thousands of hectolitres			
1884	29,169	26,877	39,780	3,803	—
1885	28,214	28,819	39,405	3,250	—
1886	22,352	26,215	42,399	3,219	—
1887	27,027	23,746	39,012	3,622	—
1888	26,160	24,903	39,034	3,108	—
1889	26,619	24,519	41,251	3,646	—
1890	26,674	26,885	43,704	2,857	—
1891	26,228	26,229	40,868	3,102	—
1892	21,295	25,631	42,289	3,098	—
1893	17,908	21,649	41,050	3,532	—
1894	21,517	26,289	49,259	2,834	—
1895	13,519	24,964	44,418	3,651	—
1896	20,747	25,736	41,460	3,619	—
1897	19,979	24,296	42,489	2,650	—
1898	26,556	24,746	43,244	3,336	—
1899	23,829	24,624	41,726	3,126	—
1900	19,142	22,660	41,763	2,779	—
1901	19,076	22,221	40,039	3,730	—
1902	20,610	24,180	47,412	3,245	—
1903	17,325	21,627	45,339	2,961	—
1904	13,411	20,797	46,330	3,646	—
1905	21,419	21,131	42,341	3,823	—
		thousands of metric tons			
1906	1,686	1,495	2,283	3,484	—
1907	1,542	1,458	2,432	3,025	—
1908	1,472	1,328	2,224	3,981	—
1909	1,700	1,466	2,201	3,733	—
1910	1,526	1,360	2,200	3,533	—
1911	1,804	1,279	2,106	3,886	—
1912	1,520	1,214	1,893	3,231	—
1913	1,566	1,437	2,018	3,927	—
1914	1,733	1,389	2,066	4,096	—
1915	1,992	1,002	2,203	3,891	—
1916	1,584	1,128	2,134	3,085	—
1917	1,660	1,208	2,317	4,522	—
1918	2,467	1,320	3,013	5,446	—
1919	1,878	1,221	2,381	3,622	—
1920	1,539	1,413	2,251	4,458	—
1921	2,060	1,190	2,176	4,062	66
1922	1,770	1,114	1,963	5,286	56
1923	1,611	1,117	2,057	3,636	106
1924	1,435	1,161	2,235	3,598	183
1925	1,437	1,172	2,129	4,277	438
1926	1,382	1,041	2,276	3,721	1,135
1927	1,512	971	1,996	3,916	1,527
1928	1,349	1,140	2,181	4,618	1,392
1929	1,350	1,117	2,314	4,819	2,036
1930	1,145	845	2,020	3,661	3,109
1931	1,026	861	1,891	3,205	1,694
1932	1,184	846	2,029	4,521	2,268
1933	1,693	699	1,951	4,628	3,351
1934	1,879	830	1,789	4,536	4,161
1935	1,771	744	1,848	3,825	3,459

C2 Output of Main Cereal, Potato, and Sugar Beet Crops (in thousands of hectolitres or metric tons)

UK: GREAT BRITAIN   **1936–2000**

	Wheat	Barley	Oats	Potatoes	Sugar Beet
1936	1,497	741	1,750	3,865	3,503
1937	1,529	666	1,630	4,113	2,624
1938	1,990	915	1,729	4,475	2,226
1939	1,668	903	1,761	4,424	3,586
1940	1,654	1,106	2,554	5,461	3,227
1941	2,032	1,145	2,860	6,892	3,278
1942	2,597	1,455	3,175	8,293	3,986
1943	3,490	1,658	2,713	8,674	3,820
1944	3,184	1,765	2,615	8,155	3,319
1945	2,209	2,130	2,908	8,842	3,948
1946	1,997	1,987	2,568	8,752	4,595
1947	1,693	1,640	2,280	6,850	3,007
1948	2,394	2,053	2,612	10,295	4,388
1949	2,237	2,157	2,683	7,727	4,026
1950	2,646	1,734	2,422	8,295	5,302
1951	2,352	1,967	2,358	7,201	4,607
1952	2,342	2,365	2,523	6,884	4,304
1953	2,705	2,554	2,590	7,249	5,360
1954	1,810	2,274	2,236	6,516	4,594
1955	2,640	2,977	2,525	5,610	4,629
1956	2,888	2,838	2,273	6,766	5,252
1957	2,722	2,989	1,972	5,111	4,612
1958	2,750	3,203	1,987	5,062	5,834
1959	2,827	4,046	2,032	6,293	5,598
1960	3,036	4,235	1,900	6,559	7,331
1961	2,609	4,957	1,708	5,728	6,031
1962	3,968	5,688	1,610	6,108	5,398
1963	3,043	6,533	1,324	6,024	5,338
1964	3,789	7,311	1,225	6,514	6,318
1965	4,165	7,956	1,142	7,067	6,813
1966	3,470	8,527	1,048	6,104	6,599
1967	3,898	9,012	1,307	6,673	6,884
1968	3,466	8,071	1,149	6,403	7,118
1969	3,360	8,481	1,250	5,820	6,034
1970	4,231	7,369	1,175	7,076	6,412
1971	4,811	8,360	1,321	7,021	7,869
1972	4,775	9,070	1,219	6,222	6,216
1973	5,000	8,830	1,054	6,497	7,427
1974	6,127	8,936	931	6,494	4,587
1975	4,486	8,324	771	4,308	4,864
1976	4,737	7,476	747	4,458	6,325
1977	5,272	10,314	772	6,155	6,382
1978	6,610	9,628	692	6,980	7,081
1979	7,166	9,448	530	6,137	7,659
1980	8,454	10,127	590	6,708	7,380
1981	8,705	10,052	609	5,892	7,395
1982	10,311	10,753	564	6,514	10,007
1983	10,794	9,781	456	5,553[10]	7,494
1984	14,947	10,850	407	6,985	9,017
1985	12,035	9,579	607	6,597	7,717
1986	13,891	9,821	495	6,121	8,118
1987	11,908	9,019	441	6,420	7,991
1988	11,690	8,513	522	6,560	8,152
1989	14,030	8,070	525	6,262	8,115
1990	13,900	7,900	535	6,504	8,000
1991	14,363	7,627	523	6,267	7,673
1992	14,095	7,365	505	7,802	9,300
1993	12,753	6,013	477	7,069	8,988
1994	13,314	5,950	595	6,531	8,016
1995	14,310	6,833	617	6,407	8,431
1996	16,102	7,784	589	7,225	10,420
1997	15,020	7,830	577	7,125	11,084
1998	15,470	6,630	585	6,422	10,002
1999	14,870	6,580	540	7,131	10,584
2000	16,700	6,490	640	6,652	9,079

C2 Output of Main Cereal, Potato, and Sugar Beet Crops (in thousands of hectolitres or metric tons)

YUGOSLAVIA (Serbia to 1912) (thousands of metric tons)   1890–1956

	Wheat	Rye	Barley	Oats	Maize	Potatoes	Sugar Beet
1890	190	...	...	...	...	...	...
1891	220	...	...	...	...	...	...
1892	300	...	...	...	...	...	...
1893	238	33	55	47	460	22	...
1894	240	...	...	...	...	...	...
1895	240	...	...	...	...	...	...
1896	220	...	...	...	...	...	...
1897	365	48	92	142	865	43	...
1898	264	40	87	93	717	...	...
1899	319	42	85	72	659	...	...
1900	221	17	49	39	469	29	...
1901	220	20	50	50	480	30	...
1902	310	30	80	60	470	40	...
1903	300	30	70	60	490	40	...
1904	320	30	70	50	240	20	...
1905	310	30	80	50	540	30	...
1906	360	40	110	70	710	50	...
1907	230	20	70	40	450	20	...
1908	310	20	70	40	530	20	...
1909	439	45	138	85	873	38	75
1910	348	35	88	63	739	44	63
1911	417	43	100	73	674	59	92
1912	...	...	...	...	...	...	150
1920	1,171	155	287	323	2,569	1,118	205
1921	1,410	148	291	274	1,874	713	189
1922	1,210	115	241	265	2,281	864	313
1923	1,662	150	306	312	2,154	1,182	373
1924	1,572	141	293	302	3,795	1,039	1,063
1925	2,140	200	395	345	3,791	1,236	511
1926	1,944	189	376	358	3,410	954	592
1927	1,540	150	315	292	2,109	1,021	599
1928	2,811	191	394	366	1,819	863	929
1929	2,585	210	412	351	4,148	1,632	1,098
1930	2,186	199	404	285	3,465	1,471	745
1931	2,689	193	392	265	3,203	1,111	707
1932	1,455	212	392	269	4,793	1,391	733
1933	2,629	245	463	371	3,578	1,468	510
1934	1,860	195	410	333	5,154	1,844	480
1935	1,989	196	376	278	3,028	1,351	484
1936	2,924	203	423	333	5,181	1,628	618
1937	2,347	209	383	295	5,336	1,620	404
1938	3,030	227	421	327	4,756	1,711	557
1939	2,876	244	424	348	4,046	1,384	922
1940	1,887[42]	211[42]	371[42]	288[42]	4,380[42]	1,910[42]	783[42]
1948	2,532	251	353	345	4,075	1,480	1,498
1949	2,523	269	381	384	3,709	2,100	1,095
1950	1,833	219	266	195	2,093	1,048	851
1951	2,283	277	359	293	4,040	1,654	1,937
1952	1,683	225	258	216	1,470	1,149	512
1953	2,514	309	458	352	3,840	2,096	1,514
1954	1,384	191	253	233	3,000	1,876	1,219
1955	2,436	263	390	278	3,900	2,270	1,380
1956	1,603	205	344	324	3,370	2,190	1,130

C2 Output of Main Cereal, Potato, and Sugar Beet Crops (in thousands of hectolitres or metric tons)

YUGOSLAVIA (Serbia to 1912) (thousands of metric tons)

1957-2000

	Wheat	Rye	Barley	Oats	Maize	Potatoes	Sugar Beet
1957	3,103	280	604	484	5,660	3,310	2,030
1958	2,453	241	470	259	3,950	2,620	1,480
1959	4,134	265	575	404	6,670	2,760	2,420
1960	3,574	233	529	373	6,160	3,270	2,290
1961	3,174	191	571	432	4,550	2,690	1,730
1962	3,514	169	475	305	5,270	2,630	1,870
1963	4,143	156	524	345	5,380	3,030	2,670
1964	3,703	175	534	293	6,960	2,820	2,830
1965	3,462	156	682	338	5,920	2,380	2,620
1966	4,603	176	713	386	7,980	3,230	4,030
1967	4,823	171	606	363	7,200	2,800	3,680
1968	4,363	138	450	295	6,810	2,890	2,910
1969	4,882	135	459	308	7,821	3,440	3,636
1970	3,792	127	402	309	6,933	2,964	2,948
1971	5,605	134	464	312	7,443	2,952	2,961
1972	4,844	120	487	260	7,930	2,406	3,294
1973	4,750	118	676	298	8,253	2,974	3,338
1974	6,282	120	794	353	8,031	3,127	4,300
1975	4,404	98	703	368	9,389	2,394	4,213
1976	5,979	105	653	320	9,106	2,828	4,711
1977	5,595	87	650	309	9,870	3,034	5,287
1978	5,355	81	560	284	7,585	2,501	5,157
1979	4,512	81	631	283	10,084	2,724	5,924
1980	5,091	79	826	294	9,317	2,440	5,213
1981	4,270	75	720	311	9,807	2,774	6,224
1982	5,218	84	669	269	11,126	2,636	5,671
1983	5,525	83	661	248	10,719	2,580	5,666
1984	5,595	81	748	256	11,293	2,457	6,792
1985	4,859	77	704	252	9,896	2,413	6,268
1986	4,776	74	703	260	12,526	2,651	5,599
1987	5,272	69	504	232	8,863	2,210	6,238
1988	6,300	76	616	253	7,710	1,849	4,508
1989	5,599	75	702	279	9,415	2,359	6,797
1990	6,359	72	650	260	6,270	2,200	5,920
1991	6,500	71	726	796	11,557	2,465	6,366
1992[47]	2,137	16	754	250	4,311	711	2,730
1993[47]	3,027	16	250	130	4,237	592	1,304
1994	3,249	15	290	126	4,724	844	2,238
1995	2,949	17	307	138	5,828	986	1,694
1996	1,507	13	270	131	5,367	904	2,418
1997	2,920	15	342	134	6,939	1,066	2,043
1998	2,967	17	369	135	5,174	991	1,980
1999	2,035	10	300	122	6,140	865	2,428
2000	2,056	8	252	96	2,968	690	1,070

C2   Output of Main Cereal, Potato, and Sugar Beet Crops (in thousands of hectolitres or metric tons)

NOTES

1. SOURCES:- The main sources were as for table C1. Portugese data for 1915 and 1916 were supplied by the Portugese National Institute of Statistics.

2. Unless conversion was done in the source, statistics which were collected in units of volume have been left in volume measure here. The appropriate ratios for converting measures of volume into measures of weight vary slightly each year, and from country to country. The following table gives a guide to the ratios which may be used to calculate approximate weights, showing the weight in kilograms of 1 hectolitre of various crops:-

	Current British Convention	French 19th Century	Italian 19th Century	Danish 1911	Hungarian 1897	Portugese 1916–18
wheat	78.6	...	75	77.3	74.9	77.7
rye	67.3	71	65	73.7	69.3	74.2
barley	69.8	64	65	67.6	62.7	58.0
oats	52.4	47	41	50.3	43.2	46.0
maize	74.8	70	72	...	73.4	75.6
mixed corn	...	...	...	55.7	67.2	...
buckwheat	62.3	65	...	61.1	...	...
rice	...	...	51	...	...	...
potatoes	66.1	76	...	71.9	70.7	...

3. P.A. Khromov, *Economic Development of Russia in the 19th and 20th Centuries, 1800–1917* (Moscow, 1950) gives the following statistics of the total grain harvest in the 50 provinces of European Russia (excluding Finland, Poland, and the Caucasus) in million chetverts:-

1800–13 average	155	1865	182	1874	271
1834–40 average	179	1866	220	1875	208
1841–48 average	210	1870	282	1876	237
1857–61 average	220	1871	219	1877	267
1861	216	1872	242	1878	276
1864	199	1873	241		

FOOTNOTES

[1] Including spelt.
[2] Including spelt, except in 1872–74.
[3] Including spelt to 1916.
[4] Including spelt from 1917.
[5] Excluding Galicia, which had an output of 86 thousand tons in 1873.
[6] Galicia is excluded in 1914 and 1915, and about three-quarters of it in 1916. Küstenland is excluded in 1915 and 1916, and part of it in 1914. Bukovina is excluded in 1914 and 1916. The output of these districts in 1913 was as follows:-

	Wheat	Rye	Barley	Oats	Maize	Other Corn	Potatoes	Sugar Beet
Galicia	503	592	326	689	30	53	333	11
Küstenland	20	3	4	4	53	2	12	—
Bukovina	20	27	72	79	45	1	45	7

[7] Burgenland is not included until 1922 (2nd line). Figures for 1913 on the same basis as for 1917 and for 1923 are as follows:-

	Wheat	Rye	Barley	Oats	Maize	Other Corn	Potatoes	Sugar Beet
1917 basis	290	604	179	466	78	42	1,508	404
1923 basis	351	634	221	488	103	42	1,605	605

In all statistics for the Republic spelt is included in wheat instead of rye.

[8] Spelt only.
[9] Figures for 1941–44 exclude Eupen and Malmédy. They are known to be underestimates owing to concealment by farmers.
[10] The method of collection was changed.
[11] Subsequent figures include southern Dobrudja.
[12] Subsequently including spelt.
[13] Subsequently excludes Sub-Carpathian Russia (Ruthenia) and 12 villages in Slovakia ceded to the U.S.S.R.
[14] Subsequently includes mixtures of oats and barley.
[15] Subsequently includes South Jutland, acquired from Germany.
[16] Statistics for 1930–38 are for rural communes only. Figures including the towns are available for 1933, as follows:-

Wheat	Rye	Barley	Oats	Mixed Corn	Potatoes	Sugar Beet
319	255	974	1,013	808	1,349	1,781

[17] Subsequently excludes territory ceded to the U.S.S.R.

C2 Output of Main Cereal, Potato, and Sugar Beet Crops (in thousands of hectolitres or metric tons)

[18] Up to 1880 (1833 for potatoes and 1885 for buckwheat) the unit of collection was the hectolitre. Conversion was made to a measure of weight by the French authorities, using the fixed ratios given above.

[19] Millet is included with maize up to 1835 and from 1871 to 1880.

[20] Up to 1851 returns were made by mayors, who appear to have under-estimated in comparison with later returns made by cantonal commissioners.

[21] From 1871 to 1919 the parts of Alsace and Lorraine ceded to Germany are excluded.

[22] From 1914 to 1919 the invaded departments are excluded.

[23] From 1939 to 1944 parts of Alsace-Lorraine annexed by Germany are excluded, and in 1943 and 1944 Corsica is excluded.

[24] Statistics to 1870 apply to the territory later constituting the German Empire, exclusive of Alsace-Lorraine, which is included for 1871–1917. From 1919 to 1944 the statistics apply to the boundaries of the day, but always excluding Austria, the Sudetenland, and territories in Poland, Lithuania and France annexed in 1939–41. The main changes in this period were cessions to Czechoslovakia, Denmark, and Poland in 1919 and to Poland in 1922, and the return of Saarland in 1935.

[25] Subsequently mixed corn only.

[26] Subsequently includes Saarland.

[27] Subsequently includes West Berlin, which had a negligible effect on the statistics.

[28] The following are the changes in the area to which the statistics apply:- In 1913 new territories in the north and in the islands were acquired from Turkey. Macedonia was lost in 1915, and the western part of it recovered in 1917. In 1919 the postwar frontiers were achieved, but Thrace is not included in the statistics until 1922.

[29] Figures to 1859 apply to the whole Kingdom (including Croatia and the military frontier). Later statistics, to 1918, apply to Transleithania (excluding Croatia-Slavonia). From 1920 they apply to the territory established by the treaty of Trianon.

[30] Figures to 1871 (1st line) exclude summer rye.

[31] Up to 1921 the statistics apply to the 1871 boundaries. For 1922–43 they apply to the 1924 boundaries, and from 1944 they apply to post-Second World War territory, except that Trieste is not included until 1949.

[32] Statistics for 1940–44 relate to the pre-war boundaries, except for small areas incorporated in Germany. From 1945 they apply to the present territory.

[33] Mainland only. Earlier statistics for 1882–4, are as follows: (in thousand hectolitres):-

	Wheat	Rye	Barley	Oats	Maize
1882	2,054	1,718	773	294	4,255
1883	1,963	1,701	749	398	4,644
1884	1,960	1,694	666	359	4,481

[34] The following are the changes in the area to which the statistics apply:- 1914 Dobrudja acquired; 1918 Bessarabia acquired; 1920 Bukovina, Transylvania, part of the Banat, and parts of Hungary proper acquired.

[35] Exclusive of the output of intercropping, which normally constituted 10–20 per cent of the total.

[36] The following are the changes in the area to which the statistics apply:- Southern Dobrudja was ceded to Bulgaria in 1940. Bessarabia and northern Bukovina were ceded to the U.S.S.R. in 1940, but were temporarily reconquered in 1943 and are apparently included in the 1944 statistics. Northern Translyvania was ceded to Hungary in 1940 but reacquired by 1946.

[37] These statistics are described by the F.A.O. as 'doubtful'.

[38] The figures to 1894 (1st line) apply to the 50 provinces of European Russia (excluding Finland, Poland, and the Caucasus). From 1894 (2nd line) to 1909 (1st line) Poland is also included, except for sugar beet (see below). From 1909 (2nd line) to 1913 the statistics apply to the whole Russian Empire except Finland. For 1920–39 they apply to the U.S.S.R. as constituted in 1924, except that the figures for 1920 and 1921 (which, unlike the others, are not later revisions) exclude Turkestan, Transcaucasia, and the Far East. From 1940 the figures apply to the present territory of the U.S.S.R. The sugar beet statistics apply throughout to either the whole Empire except Finland or to the current territory of the U.S.S.R.

[39] Previously excluding Memel.

[40] Subsequently includes early potatoes.

[41] Output in 1855 in thousands of hectolitres was as follows:- wheat 66,148; rye 8,993; barley 27,794.

[42] Subsequently including territory ceded by Italy.

[43] The following figures are available for earlier years:-

1882	3	1884	20	1886	32	1888	37
1883	7	1885	26	1887	34	1889	49

[44] Previous statistics are of the quantities used in factories in the season beginning in the year indicated. The break is negligible.

[45] Czech Republic. Figures for Slovakia as follows: Wheat, 43; Rye, 67; Barley, 780; Oats, 22; Maize, 684; Potatoes 530; Sugar Beet 1,470.

[46] Russian Federation Ex. U.S.S.R. (except Estonia, Latvia & Lithuania) as follows:

		Wheat	Rye	Barley	Oats	Maize	Potatoes	Sugar Beet
Armenia	1992	192	1	141	2	4	322	—
	1993	165	1	130	2	5	350	—
	1994	152	0.1	69	0.6	5	417	—
	1995	153	0.1	89	0.8	4	428	—
	1996	201	- -	105	2	4	423	—
	1997	179	0.3	59	1	10	360	—
	1998	239	0.2	71	1	6	440	—
	1999	214	0.1	65	1	11	414	—
	2000	178	0.1	33	0.2	6	290	—

C2 Output of Main Cereal, Potato, and Sugar Beet Crops (in thousands of hectolitres or metric tons)

Russian Federation Ex. U.S.S.R. (except Estonia, Latvia & Lithuania) as follows:

		Wheat	Rye	Barley	Oats	Maize	Potatoes	Sugar Beet
Azerbaijan	1992	859	600	371	3	21	100	—
	1993	780	700	300	3	20	200	—
	1994	739	3	262	4	14	150	18
	1995	596	1	263	4	12	156	28
	1996	759	3	224	2	14	215	46
	1997	935	1	152	0.5	19	223	34
	1998	820	0.4	79	- -	29	313	41
	1999	866	0.2	106	0.5	100	394	42
	2000	1,150	- -	226	0.6	104	469	47
Belarus	1992	330	3,100	2,900	723	25	8,900	1,100
	1993	400	2,800	3,300	800	25	11,600	1,600
	1994	230	1,864	3,013	760	1	8,241	1,078
	1995	438	2,143	1,965	638	3	9,504	1,172
	1996	600	1,794	2,194	707	5	10,881	1,011
	1997	744	1,788	2,359	822	6	6,942	1,262
	1998	787	1,384	1,623	501	6	7,574	1,428
	1999	711	929	1,181	369	10	7,491	1,187
	2000	949	1,239	1,574	491	13	8,718	1,474
Georgia	1992	1	2	60	6	210	200	15.0
	1993	1	2	35	7	225	190	12.1
	1994	89	0.1	32	6	343	297	8
	1995	77	0.1	34	5	387	353	13
	1996	107	0.3	28	3	491	286	0.3
	1997	292	0.3	45	8	546	353	- -
	1998	145	0.1	20	3	420	350	- -
	1999	226	0.3	51	3	490	443	23
	2000	89	0.3	30	2	226	302	23
Kazakhstan	1992	18,200	533	8,500	727	368	2,600	11
	1993	12,500	400	6,800	600	300	2,300	900
	1994	9,052	264	5,497	882	234	2,040	433
	1995	6,490	84	2,208	250	136	1,721	371
	1996	7,678	29	2,696	359	122	1,656	341
	1997	8,955	51	2,583	286	111	1,472	128
	1998	4,746	14	1,093	73	167	1,263	225
	1999	11,242	17	2,265	194	198	1,695	294
	2000	9,074	48	1,664	182	249	1,693	273
Kyrgistan	1992	634	1	582	12	281	362	130
	1993	800	1	550	8	238	300	200
	1994	608	5	310	7	129	311	114
	1995	701	9	173	3	149	432	107
	1996	1,040	4	166	3	182	562	190
	1997	1,274	4	152	3	171	678	205
	1998	1,204	- -	162	3	228	773	429
	1999	1,109	- -	180	5	308	957	536
	2000	1,039	- -	150	3	338	1,046	450
Moldova	1992	926	18	405	7	634	311	1,900
	1993	1.4	20	481	11	1.4	300	1,900
	1994	658	2	325	7	629	475	1,527
	1995	1,278	5	338	9	979	400	2,084
	1996	784	8	141	4	1,037	383	1,917
	1997	1,345	8	288	9	1,831	440	1,880
	1998	913	4	215	9	1,239	372	1,452
	1999	800	4	183	5	1,140	329	1,009
	2000	770	3	152	3	1,091	342	1,800
Tajikistan	1992	3.0	2	42	3	32	167	—
	1993	3.6	—	40	3	30	100	—
	1994	182	1	25	2	18	134	
	1995	174	1	22	2	19	112	
	1996	400	0.7	17	0.4	90	108	
	1997	452	0.6	23	0.3	30	128	
	1998	388	0.4	26	0.4	36	175	
	1999	368	0.4	23	0.4	36	238	
	2000	283	0.2	21	0.2	25	303	

C2 Output of Main Cereal, Potato, and Sugar Beet Crops (in thousands of hectolitres or metric tons)

Russian Federation Ex. U.S.S.R. (except Estonia, Latvia & Lithuania) as follows:

		Wheat	Rye	Barley	Oats	Maize	Potatoes	Sugar Beet
Turkmenistan	1992	368	230	124	—	147	9	—
	1993	500	235	150	—	180	16	—
	1994	675	...	203	—	150	30	—
	1995	695	...	207	—	121	21	—
	1996	453	...	36	—	15	21	—
	1997	707	...	20	—	5	17	—
	1998	1,245	...	12	—	8	27	—
	1999	1,506	...	20	—	8	28	—
	2000	1,150	...	22	—	9	29	—
Ukraine	1992	19,500	1,200	1.0	1,200	2,900	20,200	28,800
	1993	22,000	1,200	1.4	1,500	3,800	21,000	33,700
	1994	13,857	941	...	1,385	1,539	16,102	28,138
	1995	16,273	1,207	...	1,116	3,392	14,729	29,650
	1996	13,547	1,092	...	731	1,837	18,410	23,009
	1997	18,404	1,348	...	1,062	5,340	16,701	17,663
	1998	14,937	1,140	...	777	2,301	15,405	15,523
	1999	13,585	919	...	760	1,737	12,723	14,064
	2000	10,160	968	...	880	3,848	19,838	13,199
Uzbekistan	1992	964	8	361	1	367	365	22
	1993	950	10	300	—	341	425	—
	1994	1,362	11	342	0.7	276	567	23
	1995	2,347	12	336	0.9	186	440	14
	1996	2,742	8	207	0.4	137	514	2
	1997	3,073	5	144	- -	139	692	86
	1998	3,556	2	83	- -	124	691	120
	1999	3,602	5	85	- -	168	656	...
	2000	3,522	5	80	- -	131	730	...

[47] Yugoslavia Ex–Yugoslavia figures as follows:

		Wheat	Rye	Barley	Oats	Maize	Potatoes	Sugar Beet
Bosnia Hercegovina	1992	400	10	72	40	839	296	96
	1993	300	9	60	36	850	230	55
	1994	313	8	44	22	460	255	40
	1995	239	7	42	11	372	377	42
	1996	166	5	47	36	588	347	0.6
	1997	287	7	58	59	830	338	- -
	1998	341	9	63	66	847	413	- -
	1999	258	9	56	62	984	438	- -
	2000	339	12	53	57	475	283	...
Croatia	1992	658	6	107	45	1,538	480	525
	1993	887	6	126	41	1,672	507	537
	1994	750	7	109	42	1,687	563	592
	1995	877	5	103	38	1,735	692	691
	1996	741	6	88	40	1,886	666	906
	1997	834	5	108	47	2,183	620	931
	1998	1,020	6	143	56	1,983	665	1,233
	1999	558	6	125	57	2,135	729	1,114
	2000	1,032	7	151	47	1,526	554	482
Macedonia	1992	300	1	127	5	130	138	61
	1993	240	3	112	5	110	90	43
	1994	336	15	149	5	133	134	54
	1995	381	15	152	4	166	156	55
	1996	269	11	97	3	142	157	79
	1997	294	11	120	3	157	158	72
	1998	337	14	142	4	141	180	58
	1999	377	11	126	4	200	165	67
	2000	299	7	110	3	127	164	56
Slovenia	1992	178	7	27	6	207	368	97
	1993	166	7	25	6	200	340	55
	1994	182	6	44	6	328	128	222
	1995	156	6	44	4	240	191	265
	1996	137	6	41	5	296	181	308
	1997	139	4	39	5	355	188	289
	1998	169	4	43	5	333	196	380
	1999	117	3	33	6	308	194	467
	2000	163	2	38	5	285	191	349

C3   AREA OF VINEYARDS AND OUTPUT OF WINE (in thousands of hectares and hectrolitres)

1840-1889

	Austria[1]		France[2]		Germany		Hungary[9]	
	V	W	V	W	V	W[5]	V	W
1840	...	...	2,145	27,700	...	...	...	...
1841	...	...	...	...	...	...	...	...
1842	...	3,523	...	...	...	...	...	15,848
1843	...	3,599	...	...	...	...	...	...
1844	...	3,454	...	...	...	...	...	...
1845	...	3,859	2,169	30,100	...	...	...	...
1846	...	3,793	...	...	...	2,880	...	...
1847	...	3,880	...	54,300	...	2,940	...	...
1848	...	...	...	51,600	...	2,980	...	...
1849	...	...	2,193	35,600	...	2,180	...	...
1850	...	...	2,182	45,300	...	1,690	...	...
1851	...	3,990	2,180	39,400	...	1,070	...	15,869
1852	...	...	2,190	38,000	...	1,650	...	...
1853	...	...	2,168	22,700	...	1,630	382	...
1854	...	4,754	2,173	10,800	...	420	...	10,363
1855	...	...	2,175	15,200	...	1,050	...	...
1856	...	...	2,170	21,300	...	1,020	...	...
1857	...	6,418	2,180	35,400	...	1,960	...	10,193
1858	...	...	2,184	53,900	...	3,590	...	...
1859	...	5,959	2,173	29,900	...	3,190	...	9,329
1860	...	...	2,205[3]	39,600[3]	...	1,720	...	...
1861	...	...	2,220	29,700	...	1,090	...	4,016
1862	...	...	2,321	48,600	...	2,530	...	4,885
1863	...	...	2,274	51,400	...	2,480	...	3,979
1864	...	...	2,256	50,700	...	1,100	...	3,116
1865	...	...	2,293	68,900	...	1,650	...	3,533
1866	...	...	2,287	63,800	...	3,000	...	2,799
1867	...	...	2,315	39,100	...	2,960	...	4,677
1868	...	4,845	2,332	52,100	...	4,440	...	4,995
1869	205	3,730	2,350[4]	70,000[4]	...	2,090	...	4,407
1870	205	2,721	2,238	54,500	...	2,310[6]	...	4,087
1871	206	3,212	2,369	56,900	...	2,170	425	4,622
1872	209	2,221	2,373	50,200	...	1,540	425[9]	2,864[9]
1873	204	1,859	2,381	35,700	...	1,720	358	3,675
1874	207	3,158	2,447	63,100	...	3,500	358	1,998
1875	205	6,426	2,421	83,800	...	4,500	359	6,260
1876	207	2,389	2,370	41,800	...	3,230	360	1,858
1877	202	3,202	2,346	56,400	...	2,460	360	3,905
1878	207	6,731	2,296	48,700	119	3,060	362	8,100
1879	207	2,929	2,241	25,800	119	990	362	6,314
1880	207	1,731	2,209	29,700	116	520	362	2,427
1881	207	3,036	2,069	34,100	119	2,670	361	4,231
1882	207	3,367	2,197	33,500	119	1,600	367	4,113
1883	207	3,474	2,096	36,000	120	2,810	364	4,336
1884	207	3,286	2,041	34,800	120	2,970	368	4,411
1885	229	4,001	1,991	28,500	120	3,730	368	6,025
1886	233	3,722	1,959	25,100	120	1,500	364	4,370
1887	233	4,702	1,944	24,300	120	2,390	353	5,512
1888	233	4,155	1,843	30,100	121	2,860	343	4,344
1889	235	4,106	1,818	23,200	121	2,020	334	4,997

C3 Area of Vineyards and Output of Wine (in thousands of hectares and hectrolitres)

1840–1889

	Croatia-Slavonia		Italy[10]		Portugal[11]	Romania		Spain
	V	W	V	W	W	V	W	W
1840	...	...	...	...	...	...	...	...
1841	...	...	...	...	...	...	...	...
1842	...	...	...	...	...	...	...	...
1843	...	...	...	...	...	...	...	...
1844	...	...	...	...	...	...	...	...
1845	...	...	...	...	...	...	...	...
1846	...	...	...	...	...	...	...	...
1847	...	...	...	...	...	...	...	...
1848	...	...	...	...	...	...	...	...
1849	...	...	...	...	...	...	...	...
1850	...	...	...	...	...	...	...	...
1851	...	...	...	...	...	...	...	...
1852	...	...	...	...	...	...	...	...
1853	...	...	...	...	...	...	...	...
1854	...	...	...	...	...	...	...	...
1855	...	...	...	...	...	...	...	...
1856	...	...	...	...	...	...	...	...
1857	...	...	...	...	...	...	...	...
1858	...	...	...	...	...	...	...	...
1859	...	...	...	...	...	...	...	...
1860	...	...	...	...	...	80	1,300	...
1861	...	...	...	19,200	...	...	...	...
1862	...	...	...	23,460	...	...	1,149	...
1863	...	...	...	19,800	...	...	961	...
1864	...	...	...	21,486	...	...	535	...
1865	...	average 783	...	22,696	...	95	558	...
1866	...	...	...	23,906	...	...	1,821	...
1867	...	...	...	25,116	...	...	979	...
1868	...	...	...	26,326	...	...	1,242	...
1869	...	...	...	27,536	...	...	1,102	...
1870	...	...	...	25,800	...	102	678	...
1871	...	...	...	28,500	...	102	1,684	...
1872	65	...	...	26,400	...	102	1,037	...
1873	...	...	...	28,900	...	...	...	...
1874	...	...	...	28,095	...	...	...	...
1875	...	...	...	28,260	...	110	...	...
1876	...	...	...	22,500	...	...	...	...
1877	...	...	...	25,440	...	...	...	...
1878	...	...	...	26,520	...	...	...	...
1879	...	...	...	26,081	...	...	...	...
1880	...	...	average 3,167	28,643	...	...	...	...
1881	...	...		25,832	2,244	...	...	...
1882	...	...	...	33,500	2,812	...	...	...
1883	...	...	...	35,934	2,527	...	...	...
1884	...	...	...	28,728	3,257	...	...	...
1885	68	1,197	...	31,918	...	...	...	20,500
1886	68	1,593	...	38,227	...	163	2,600	23,618
1887	68	1,274	...	34,532	...	...	...	23,013
1888	68	1,089	...	32,846	...	...	...	27,861
1889	67	618	...	21,757	...	146	3,076	29,876

C3   Area of Vineyards and Output of Wine (in thousands of hectares and hectrolitres)

1890–1944

	Austria[1]		Bulgaria		Czechoslovakia		France		Germany		Greece[7]		Hungary[9]	
	V	W	V	W	V	W	V	W	V	W[5]	V[8]	W[5]	V	W
1890	235	3,623	...	...	...	...	1,817	27,400	120	2,980	...	...	311	3,790
1891	245	2,998	...	...	...	...	1,764	30,200	119	750	...	...	254	1,367
1892	245	3,460	...	...	...	...	1,793	28,900	118	1,670	...	...	249	885
1893	251	4,535	...	...	...	...	1,821	50,700	116	3,820	...	...	226	1,044
1894	252	3,775	...	...	...	...	1,707	39,400	117	2,820	...	...	220	1,541
1895	253	3,583	...	...	...	...	1,661	26,900	116	2,010	...	1,600	203	2,143
1896	253	3,485	...	...	...	...	1,641	44,000	116	5,050	...	2,150	207	1,606
1897	253	2,775	...	...	...	...	1,624	31,900	117	2,780	...	1,200	205	1,256
1898	254	4,224	...	...	...	...	1,648	31,700	117	1,410	...	1,651	208	1,265
1899	255	3,368	111	...	...	...	1,632	46,800	117	2,000	...	1,254	214	1,918
1900	254	5,213	...	1,929	...	...	1,609	68,500	119	2,000	...	770	222	1,824
1901	254	4,796	...	...	...	...	1,618	60,100	120	2,000	...	1,100	227	2,901
1902	250	4,857	...	...	...	...	1,588	42,300	120	2,480	...	2,000	234	2,913
1903	250	3,766	81	1,078	...	...	1,588	35,200	120	3,790	...	1,300	239	2,705
1904	250	4,484	91	1,619	...	...	1,725	68,900	120	4,240	...	1,800	248	3,856
1905	249	5,337	91	1,462	...	...	1,744	57,900	120	3,860	...	1,100	258	3,519
1906	249	4,298	92	779	...	...	1,748	52,200	120	1,640	...	...	270	3,431
1907	238	4,250	89	867	...	...	1,649[14]	66,100[14]	119	2,490	...	...	276	3,408
1908	226	8,142	86	1,643	...	...	1,666	60,800	117	3,140	...	...	290	7,235
1909	230	6,253	85	1,319	...	...	1,637	54,600	115	2,020	...	...	298	3,649
1910	223	2,547	79	771	...	...	1,630	28,700	113	850	...	...	305	2,825
1911	222	3,837	68	551	...	...	1,606	45,000	110	2,923	97	3,231	312	4,616
1912	224	3,970	62	715	...	...	1,563	59,500	109	2,019	...	...	319	2,993
1913	219	4,353	54	609	...	...	1,550[15]	44,300[15]	106	1,005	...[17]	...[17]	324	3,316
1914	214[12]	3,615[12]	57	348	...	...	1,534	60,000	102	921	136[17]	3,845[17]	315	2,257
1915	198[12]	3,199[12]	52	476	...	...	1,533	20,400	97	2,699	108	3,392	315	3,039
1916	180[12]	1,697[12]	49	601	...	...	1,518	36,100	92	1,076	195[17]	2,747[17]	307	2,213
1917	39	1,046	49	660	...	...	1,516	38,300	94	1,956	172	3,027	305	5,609
1918	38	1,050[1]	47	678	...	...	1,512[15]	45,200[15]	92[6]	2,729	164[17]	3,174[17]	303[9]	5,701[9]
1919	38	288	43	781	...	...	1,505[4]	54,500[4]	69	1,741	178	2,667	...	...
1920	37[1]	295	44	426	19	333	1,518	59,300	73	2,440	140	1,749	190	2,450
1921	26	397	45	609	17	454	1,517	48,000	74	1,755	146[17]	1,873[17]	210	3,478
1922	25[1] / 30	827[1] / 938	48	669	17	595	1,527	76,800	74	3,406	122	1,794	216	4,614
1923	32	822	56	769	17	330	1,537	60,000	75	791	127	1,778	221	4,640
1924	32	305	63	959	16	262	1,550	70,900	74	1,804	124	2,301	222	1,363
1925	32	860	68	1,153	17	313	1,542	65,100	73	1,591	112	2,363	221	3,441
1926	34	462	73	1,526	17	140	1,525	42,600	73	989	114	2,692	221	1,293
1927	32	226	77	1,528	17	106	1,506	51,200	73	1,428	103	2,270	222	1,826
1928	38	775	79	1,713	17	323	1,516	60,300	73	2,053	122	3,075	222	3,083
1929	31	573	86	1,634	17	224	1,511	65,000	72	2,019	130[18] / 110	2,546	216	2,490
1930	35	1,202	88	1,556	18	474	1,527	45,600	71	2,814	123	2,209	213	4,022
1931	33	1,385	91	1,348	19	456	1,550	59,300	71	2,840	128	1,945	214	3,900
1932	30	1,078	93	1,415	19	434	1,541	49,600	72	1,722	142	3,950	212	3,557
1933	31	930	88	1,253	20	338	1,534	51,800	72	1,799	143	3,910	210	3,083
1934	32	909	93	1,511	21	329	1,555	78,100	73	4,525	145	3,700	211	2,542
1935	34	1,379	89	2,023	24	601	1,549	76,100	72	4,174	153	5,100	214	2,858
1936	38	984	88	825	25	525	1,511	43,700	72	3,315	152	1,940	214	4,539
1937	38	853	89	1,446	26[13]	432[13]	1,518	54,300	74	2,522	156	3,400	216	4,473
1938	40	1,045	89	2,346	...	...	1,513[16]	60,300[16]	73	2,445	157	4,680	218	3,309
1939	41	...	...	2,200	...	246	1,494	69,000	72	2,992	133	4,495	220	4,176
1940	39	270	135	777	16	181	1,470	49,400	67	1,086	...	...	223	863
1941	40	727	144	1,333	15	190	1,453	47,600	...	...	...	...	225	1,576
1942	40	512	146	2,042	16	225	1,434[16]	35,000[16]	...	...	...	...	229	4,205
1943	40	894	147	2,146	16	219	1,422	41,000	...	...	...	...	235	3,923
1944	40	625	151	2,241	16	189	1,403[16]	44,300[16]	...	...	...	...	...	...

C3 Area of Vineyards and Output of Wine (in thousands of hectares and hectrolitres)

1890–1944

	Hungary[1] Croatia-Slavonia		Italy[10]		Portugal[11]		Romania		Spain		Switzerland		Serbia/ Yugoslavia	
	V	W	V	W	V	W	V	W	V	W	V	W	V	W
1890	54	333	3,430	29,457	...	...	146	3,081	...	24,351	...	...	...	...
1891	61	251	3,444	37,177	...	...	160	3,557	...	24,271	...	...	...	...
1892	57	187	3,466	34,346	186	3,606	139	3,122	...	29,941	...	...	...	...
1893	53	189	3,435	32,679	...	...	146	1,300	...	21,616	...	...	61	421
1894	46	245	3,451	26,385	...	...	...	...	...	21,790	...	...	...	...
1895	43	292	3,462	24,901	...	6,500	145	3,373	...	21,383	28	888	...	...
1896	41	140	3,446	29,544	...	3,280	144	4,628	...	16,156	...	1,270	...	...
1897	42	196	...	29,427	...	4,000	154	3,200	...	15,351	...	1,015	68	941
1898	40	186	...	34,389	...	5,000	139	3,900	1,454	20,004	31	855	...	...
1899	40	351	...	34,093	...	3,200	148	2,061	1,419	21,148	30	868	68	285
1900	38	334	...	36,648	...	5,500	146	3,498	1,407	22,559	30	2,103	...	100
1901	37	542	3,990	46,513	...	6,000	133	891	1,401	22,399	32	1,200	...	100
1902	38	676	4,000	43,628	...	4,800	143	1,043	1,384	12,184	31	1,191	37	200
1903	39	572	4,010	36,953	...	3,000	133	1,861	1,441	14,850	29	989	35	200
1904	41	873	3,991	43,036	...	6,200	104	836	1,411	21,856	19	1,267	34	400
1905	43	741	4,046	30,836	...	4,100	90	1,760	1,461	17,704	28	840	32	400
1906	44	623	3,779	31,357	...	...	87	1,761	1,399	13,575	28	1,300	35	600
1907	40	805	3,768	56,749	...	...	83	968	1,367	18,384	27	682	35	500
1908	40	1,676	3,759	54,481	...	6,900	79	2,284	1,310	18,557	26	925	40	900
1909	42	1,199	4,455	65,035	...	...	74	1,270	1,298	14,716	16	409	32	394
1910	45	247	4,455	32,642	...	...	74	1,713	1,293	11,283	24	244	34	154
1911	46	872	4,453	47,527	...	4,075[19]	71	993	1,290	14,747	24	749	...	...
1912	46	554	4,431	49,164	...	...	70	1,590	1,260	16,466	23	659	...	...
1913	48	1,096	4,429	58,210	...	...	73[20]	1,519[20]	1,250	17,105	22	181	...	...
1914	48	971	4,413	47,965	...	...	71	661	1,241	16,168	21	368	...	...
1915	48	437	4,412	21,233	...	4,837	69	1,997	1,247	10,112	21	666	...	...
1916	31	521	4,336	43,412	...	4,583	75	...	1,284	23,396	20	331	...	...
1917	...	833	4,317	54,279	...	4,406	...[20]	...[20]	1,294	23,763	18	608	...	...
1918	...	...	4,136	40,657	...	4,270	83	1,724	1,317	22,568	19	705	...	...
1919	incorporated in Yugoslavia		4,264	38,999	...	5,133	86[20]	2,209[20]	1,320	20,525	19	590	...	...
1920			4,236	47,123	...	3,384	102	2,371	1,332	26,771	18	606	173	3,460
1921			4,218[10]	35,551[8]	...	4,607	...	...	1,331	19,204	18	479	172	3,150
1922			4,274	38,247	...	5,794	...	...	1,341	25,672	15	1,019	168	4,615
1923			4,273	57,993	...	6,131	204	5,435	1,342	22,078	14	748	167	4,414
1924			4,277	48,089	...	5,246	210	6,114	1,341	21,745	14	306	165	2,918
1925			4,264	48,876	...	5,672	235	7,585	1,353	26,698	14	357	178	4,097
1926			4,283	40,940	...	3,666	220	5,065	1,382	15,754	14	454	175	2,912
1927			4,279	39,151	...	9,267	240	7,101	1,398	28,325	14	309	178	2,855
1928			4,399	52,460	...	4,525	240	7,127	1,417	22,085	14	609	176	4,318
1929			4,294	46,910	351	6,600	240	5,046	1,389	24,998	13	746	181	2,910
1930			4,240	40,761	...	5,785	240	8,385	1,440	18,228	12	572	184	4,016
1931			3,947	40,025	...	7,380	240	8,748	1,427	19,074	11	525	199	4,494
1932			3,944	49,103	...	6,150	273	7,815	1,433	21,188	11	388	192	4,387
1933			3,945	35,035	...	9,200	273	7,514	1,417	19,764	11	240	195	2,853
1934			3,962	32,146	...	10,805	273	8,704	1,451	21,719	11	847	199	3,867
1935			3,958	47,616	...	5,924	273	10,458	1,465	17,037	11	1,100	207	5,418
1936			3,918	34,110	...	3,709	273	6,707	...	...	12	488	214	3,865
1937			3,907	36,582	...	8,049	365	10,663	...	...	11	469	215	2,903
1938			3,910	41,780	...	10,955	365	9,924	...	...	12	345	219	4,672
1939			3,936	42,550	...	7,720	...[21]	11,542[21]	1,358	20,151	12	733	223	4,738
1940			3,934	30,494	...	5,187	229	2,120	1,456	14,168	11	462	...	...
1941			3,947	36,671	...	7,374	...	7,491	1,395	16,944	11	826	...	...
1942			3,927	37,987	...	8,335	...	3,188	1,367	20,350	11	750	...	...
1943			3,932[10]	37,830[10]	...	14,007	...	6,750	1,370	21,945	11	747	...	...
1944			3,889	33,270	...	14,507	...	5,548	1,371	21,180	11	1,051	...	...

C3   Area of Vineyards and Output of Wine (in thousands of hectares and hectrolitres)

1945–2000

	Austria[1]		Bulgaria		Czechoslovakia		France		West Germany		Greece		Hungary[9]	
	V	W	V	W	V	W	V	W	V	W[5]	V[8]	W[5]	V	W
1945	36	881	155	2,361	16	236	1,434	28,600	…	…	129	2,400	239	3,335
1946	36	1,266	156	1,550	17	587	1,436	36,200	…	…	129	3,090	238	3,657
1947	35	1,053	…	4,300	19	419	1,440	44,200	…	…	…	3,770	237	2,364
1948	35	1,016	…	1,500	20	337	1,433	47,400	51	2,185	…	3,850	238	2,679
1949	35	971	…	426	19	290	1,437	42,900	51	1,363	…	4,140	…	3,173
1950	35	1,291	…	1,818	18	264	1,453	65,100	49	3,244	…	3,940	230	3,600
1951	36	1,104	…	2,270	19	267	1,450	52,900	53	3,114	…	3,500	228	3,226
1952	36	746	…	…	19	272	1,455	53,900	53	2,715	…	3,404	225	2,637
1953	37	826	146	…	18	266	1,455	59,100	55	2,457	…	3,860	216	1,786
1954	37	1,639	146	…	18	302	1,445	60,900	59	3,100	…	4,228	216	1,859
1955	37	1,164	146	…	19	328	1,435	61,100	60	2,408	…	3,575	201	3,368
1956	37	351	146	…	23	[304][22]	1,386	51,700	59	930	…	3,982	196	2,330
1957	37	1,415	158	…	32	370	1,335	33,300	59	2,264	…	4,016	196	3,260
1958	37	1,897	165	…	22	489	1,315	47,700	61	4,800	…	3,211	199	5,294
1959	35	728	174	…	24	257	1,323	60,300	64	4,303	…	3,274	201	3,257
1960	35	897	180	2,890	24	294	1,318	63,100	66	7,433	…	2,820	204	2,956
1961	36	1,328	182	2,800	24	325	1,285	48,600	67	5,094	142	3,350	204	3,508
1962	36	1,007	185	4,480	24	226	1,287	75,000	68	3,928	138	3,740	219	3,131
1963	40	1,827	189	4,620	25	346	1,271	57,500	69	6,034	134	2,567	229	4,243
1964	40	2,840	190	3,620	26	524	1,270	62,400	69	7,185	130	3,593	243	5,545
1965	45	1,387	192	4,740	27	281	1,263	68,417	69	5,035	129	4,057	247	2,425
1966	45	1,454	194	4,270	28	345	1,250	62,253	69	4,809	127	3,843	245	3,367
1967	46	2,594	200	3,511	29	746	1,240	62,026	69	6,069	125	3,948	240	4,789
1968	46	2,477	203	4,970	29	825	1,228	66,460	70	6,048	122	4,120	236	4,843
1969	46	2,265	201[18] 170	4,913	31	987	1,208	51,290	71	5,947	125	5,160	234	5,614
1970	47	3,096	169	4,086	32	991	1,200	75,402	74	9,889	…	4,532	230	4,379
1971	48	1,813	169	4,087	34	1,025	1,173	62,245	76	6,027	…	4,560	222	4,289
1972	48	2,596	166	3,787	36	1,090	1,174	59,469	78	7,456	…	4,820	218	5,034
1973	48	2,404	162	5,204	37	1,115	1,181	83,472	81	10,697	110	4,610	213	6,231
1974	50	1,665	164	4,442	38	1,151	1,179	76,431	83	6,805	98	4,570	210	4,258
1975	50	2,704	165	3,???	40	1,238	1,186	66,974	85	9,241	105	4,090	206	4,951
1976	50	2,901	162	5,372	41	1,325	1,189	74,145	86	8,659	105	4,070	200	4,511
1977	50	2,594	159	3,708	43	1,386	1,168	53,020	88	10,389	112	4,000	192	5,622
1978	56	3,366	157	4,524	43	1,417	1,141	58,905	89	7,297	103	4,360	186	4,752
1979	56	2,773	181	4,681	45	1,317	1,131	84,377	88	8,181	103	4,122	174	5,132
1980	60	3,086	175	4,092	45	1,421	1,081	86,762	89	4,635	101	4,499	168	5,694
1981	60	2,085	169	4,864	46	1,423	1,052	72,891	89	7,159	97	4,798	161[24] 136	3,891
1982	59	4,906	167	5,740	47	1,303	1,040	101,416	89	15,403	95	4,600	130	6,768
1983	59	3,698	148	4,549	47	1,378	1,022	88,470	90	13,041	94	5,014	128	6,261
1984	58	2,519	146	5,155	48	1,563	1,005	81,696	92	7,993	92	5,338	127	5,073
1985	58	1,126	144	3,859	48	1,763	995	87,686	93	5,402	91	4,416	125	2,890
1986	58	2,230	138	3,898	48	1,403	978	92,815	93	10,062	…	5,069	115	4,420
1987	58	2,184	137	3,909	48	1,403	967	89,848	93	8,942	…	4,470	113	3,260
1988	58	3,502	138	3,400	47	1,420	958	72,488	95	9,315	…	4,730	109	4,710
1989	58	2,580	139	2,570	35	1,390	948	69,340	94	14,490	…	5,030	110	3,710
									Germany					
1990	58	3,140	140	2,900	35	1,420	980	65,550	94	9,700	…	4,270	111	5,470
1991	54	3,090	138	2,550	35	1,550	902	65,040	99[27]	11,190	…	4,660	110	4,610
1992	54	2,590	137	2,010	34	1,340	904	…	100[27]	13,400	…	4,390	112	3,880
1993	54	2,700	120	1,800	10[26]	35[26]	901	…	102[27]	13,400	…	…	107	3,640
					in thousands of tonnes									
1994	54	265	113	130	11	50	899	5,485	104	1,041	128	305	101	369
1995	54	194	108	140	11	46	895	5,558	104	1,375	129	305	90	350
1996	49	211	111	238	11	49	887	5,965	102	864	124	411	100	419
1997	49	211	111	238	11	49	900	5,611	102	853	124	437	100	419
1998	48	270	112	196	11	56	873	5,427	102	1,083	124	454	99	434
1999	48	280	114	139	11	56	873	6,294	101	1,229	124	433	99	334
2000	48	280	110	139	11	56	874	5,880	101	1,125	124	430	85	300

C3 Area of Vineyards and Output of Wine (in thousands of hectares and hectolitres)

	Italy[10]		Portugal[11]		Romania		Russia/ U.S.S.R.[23]	Spain		Switzerland		Yugoslavia	
	V	W	V	W	V	W	W million hl.	V	W	V	W	V	W
1945	3,873	29,298	...	10,167	215[21]	6,357[21]	...	1,373	13,852	11	613	...	...
1946	3,873	33,750	...	6,689	...	5,450	...	1,378	17,345	11	731	...	...
1947	3,848	36,446	...	10,111	220	3,640	...	1,394	20,955	11	881	...	...
1948	3,842[10]	40,393[10]	...	8,176	212	3,410	...	1,420	14,184	11	791	223	4,100
1949	3,853	41,037	...	7,927	202	4,090	...	1,431	14,324	11	551	232	4,040
1950	3,924	41,049	...	8,725	223	4,250	...	1,444	14,469	11	721	234	3,350
1951	3,931	49,761	...	9,490	223	4,550	...	1,481	16,074	11	1,041	250	6,058
1952	3,900	44,854	...	5,802	227	4,090	3.2	1,497	17,889	11	678	256	3,151
1953	3,886	52,542	...	11,736	222	4,100	4.1	1,510	23,465	12	682	261	3,825
1954	3,884	50,474	296	12,185	218	4,100	4.6	1,481	17,498	13	698	274	2,851
1955	3,849	58,441	291	11,336	213	5,764	4.7	1,497	16,847	13	801	280	5,300
1956	3,841	62,981	287	10,965	222	2,622	5.1	1,524	21,144	13	445	273	3,220
1957	3,791	42,509	289	9,576	230	...	5.5	1,541	17,365	13	413	271	4,210
1958	3,800	67,994	318	8,585	240	...	6.2	1,567	19,834	12	654	275	5,780
1959	3,769	66,374	321	8,924	257	...	6.7	1,583	17,278	12	1,061	277	4,600
1960	3,722	55,318	323	11,458	271	5,600	7.8	1,606	21,257	12	1,104	273	3,350
1961	3,675	52,760	325	7,420	278	4,800	8.5	1,617	20,482	12	862	272	4,260
1962	3,623	69,569	330	15,268	263	6,700	10.1	1,627	24,508	12	837	270	5,150
1963	3,524	53,640	339	12,979	247	6,100	11.9	1,524	25,836	12	942	266	5,900
1964	3,437	66,945	342	13,595	256	5,800	12.7	1,534	34,860	12	975	263	5,850
1965	3,353	68,206	345	14,749	242	5,211	13.4	1,544	26,452	12	966	262	5,150
1966	3,270	64,796	346	8,928	253	5,566	15.9	1,548	30,749	12	832	259	5,690
1967	3,199	74,725	348	9,941[11]	264	5,240	18.0	1,584	23,310	12	961	257	5,230
1968	3,093	65,323	348	11,879	278	6,792	19.1	1,588	23,133	12	1,034	256	6,080
1969	2,772	71,658	348	8,270	288	6,848	24.0	1,592	24,619	12	796	255	7,060
1970	1,917	68,874	350	11,497	293	4,323	26.8	1,578	25,274	12	1,267	253	5,478
1971	1,918	64,271	...	9,000	299	6,350	28.0	1,476	24,325	12	882	252	5,546
1972	1,931	59,190	...	8,345	300	6,235	17.8	1,541	26,560	12	1,004	250	6,263
1973	1,919	76,716	...	11,177	300	9,223	28.0	1,574	39,999	13	1,299	249	7,701
1974	1,912	76,870	...	13,994	298	6,284	26.8	1,567	36,190	13	755	247	5,811
1975	1,908	69,830	...	8,979	296	7,270	29.7	1,611	32,465	13	830	247	5,419
1976	1,889	65,850	...	9,486	298	9,668	31.5	1,622	24,327	14	1,194	246	6,379
1977	1,843	64,142	...	6,908	291	9,108	30.7	1,637	21,820	14	1,300	246	6,297
1978	1,911	72,440	...	6,594	290	7,633	24.7	1,640	29,481	13	778	247	5,880
1979	1,781	84,384	...	14,415	256	8,863	29.4	1,632	48,205	14	1,108	246	6,743
1980	1,756	86,227	...	10,290	259	7,599	32.2	1,657	42,402	14	842	247	8,173
1981	1,715	70,296	...	9,095	257	9,957	34.4	1,657	33,667	14	255	240	6,887
1982	1,667[25] 1,283	72,487	...	10,207	260	13,069	34.9	1,657	37,433	14	1,840	246	8,576
1983	1,138	83,078	...	8,430[11] 8,330	256	9,487	35.1	1,645	30,913	14	1,612	242	7,877
1984	1,129	70,779	...	8,463	253	10,038	34.1	1,587	33,957	14	1,179	238	6,290
1985	1,102	62,195	...	9,634	249	5,349	26.5	1,552	32,382	14	1,250	232	4,614
1986	1,093	76,798	...	7,689	261	11,846	14.1	1,531	35,082	14	1,345	229	7,556
1987	1,082	75,822	...	10,740	265	8,055	14.7	1,481	39,976	14	1,100	229	6,417
1988	1,074	61,010	...	3,600	268	6,420	17.8	1,440	22,129	14	1,110	227	5,973
1989	1,065	60,330	...	7,440	212	3,580	19.3	1,473	31,290	15	1,700	227	4,860
1990	1,051	53,400	...	10,430	225	4,360	15.7	1,500	40,960	15	1,200	230	4,700
1991	993	59,790	...	9,830	225	5,010	18.0	1,379	31,340	15	1,250	203	6,100
1992	975	68,690	...	7,550	235	4,710	0.7[28]	1,480	35,730	15	1,240	65[29]	1,700[29]
1993	974	54,000	...	9,000	245	8,000	0.7	1,450	27,090	15	1,220	65[29]	1,550[29]
					in thousands of tonnes								
1994	926	5,928	360	662	225	537	296	1,150	1,871	15	119	88	306
1995	910	5,641	360	721	226	550	350	1,250	1,834	15	119	80	180
1996	896	5,877	251	953	252	580	280	1,300	2,987	15	120	82	349
1997	894	5,085	251	880	255	580	280	1,300	3,443	15	120	82	349
1998	874	5,714	257	358	251	500	218	1,118	3,022	15	117	71	258
1999	877	5,807	258	760	251	650	290	1,163	3,330	15	131	60	137
2000	876	5,781	257	603	241	580	290	1,200	3,413	15	128	60	197

C3 Area of Vineyards and Output of Wine (in thousands of hectares and hectolitres)

NOTE

SOURCES: The main sources are as for table C1, with additional material for Hungary and Romania from *Magyarorszag Szoloszeti Statistikaya 1860–1873*. The Czechoslovak output in 1952 was furnished by the Federal Statistical Office of Czechoslovakia.

FOOTNOTES

[1] Cisleithania (excluding Lombardy and Venetia) to 1916. Subsequent figures apply to the Republic, though Burgenland is not included until 1922 (2nd line), and for 1917–20 (area) and 1917–18 (output) the whole of Carinthia and Styria is included (i.e. including parts later incorporated in Yugoslavia). Figures for 1913 comparable with those for 1922 (2nd line) and after are 48 thousand hectares and 677 thousand hectolitres.

[2] Various estimates were made for earlier periods. The following appear in official publications:- Area 1829 2,003; 1835 2,119; Output 1788 25.0; 1808 28.0; 1827 36.8; 1829 31.0; 1830 15.3; 1835 26.5. J.C. Toutain, *Le produit de l'agriculture francaise de 1700 a 1958*, (Cahiers de l'I.S.E.A., 1961) makes the following estimates of annual average output (in million hectolitres):- 1701–10 65.4; 1751–60 21.3 to 47.4; 1771–80 26.3: 1781–90 15.8 to 33.5; 1803–12 35.4.

[3] Subsequently includes Savoy and Nice.

[4] From 1870 to 1919 the parts of Alsace and Lorraine ceded to Germany are excluded.

[5] Wine must.

[6] Figures for 1871–1918 include Alsace-Lorraine. The area and output in 1913 without Alsace-Lorraine are 79 thousand hectares and 825 thousand hectolitres.

[7] In 1860 there were 65 thousand hectares of vineyards and an output of 213 thousand hectolitres.

[8] These figures are of vineyards for wine.

[9] Figures to 1872 apply to the whole Kingdom. From 1873 to 1918 they exclude Croatia-Slavonia. And from 1920 they apply to the territory established by the treaty of Trianon.

[10] Up to 1921 the statistics apply to the 1871 boundaries. For 1922–43 they apply to the 1924 boundaries. Since 1943 they apply to the 1954 boundaries, except that Trieste is not included until 1949.

[11] Excluding Azores and Madeira to 1967, and excluding Azores from 1983 (2nd line).

[12] Part of Küstenland is excluded.

[13] Subsequently excluding Sub-Carpathian Russia (Ruthenia), which was ceded to the U.S.S.R. in 1945. Its area in 1937 was 4.6 thousand hectares and its output 140 thousand hectolitres.

[14] Figures to 1907 do not include Corsica.

[15] Figures for 1914–18 exclude the invaded departments.

[16] From 1939 to 1944 parts of Alsace-Lorraine annexed by Germany are excluded, and in 1943–44 Corsica is excluded.

[17] The following are the changes in the area to which the statistics apply:- In 1913 new territories in the north and in the islands were acquired from Turkey. In 1915 Macedonia was lost, and the western part of it was regained in 1917. In 1919 the post-war boundaries were achieved, but Thrace is not included in the statistics until 1922.

[18] Subsequently only vineyards in production.

[19] Excluding Santarem and Villa Real provinces.

[20] Southern Dobrudja was acquired in 1914, Bessarabia in 1918, and Bukovina, Transylvania, part of the Banat and part of Hungary proper in 1920.

[21] The wine-producing area was affected by the cession of northern Transylvania to Hungary in 1940. It was regained in 1946.

[22] Excluding production on state farms.

[23] The figure for 1940 was 2 million hectolitres.

[24] Subsequently only the area cultivated.

[25] Subsequently excluding secondary cultivation.

[26] Czech Republic. Slovakia = 24 (Area) 900 (Output).

[27] Germany.

[28] Russian Federation. Ex U.S.S.R. as follows

Armenia	1992	
	1993	
Azerbaijan	1992	
	1993	
Belarus	1992	
	1993	
Georgia	1992	0.1
	1993	0.1
Kazakhstan	1992	
	1993	
Kyrgistan	1992	
	1993	
Moldova	1992	0.1
	1993	0.1
Tajikistan	1992	
	1993	

C3   Area of Vineyards and Output of Wine (in thousands of hectares and hectolitres)

Turkmenistan	1992	
	1993	
Ukraine	1992	0.2
	1993	0.2
Uzbekistan	1992	
	1993	

[29] Yugoslavia. Figures for ex Yugoslavia as follows

	Bosnia-Hercegovina		Croatia		Macedonia		Slovenia	
	V	W	V	W	V	W	V	W
1992	5	170	56	2,060	32	1,360	20	550
1993	4	—	57	2,080	25	1,000	21	950
1994	4	4	53	255	30	88	21	83
1995	4	3	52	70	35	90	21	50
1996	3	5	58	196	27	101	20	93
1997	3	5	53	226	27	101	20	93
1998	4	7	55	228	29	123	17	85
1999	4	6	55	209	29	122	15	69
2000	4	5	55	209	29	122	15	69

C4   AREA AND OUTPUT OF MEDITERRANEAN CROPS (in thousands of hectares and thousands of metric tons)

Key:- A = Area; CF = Citrus Fruits; O = Output; OFF = Other Fresh Fruits

1861–1904

	Bulgaria Tobacco		Italy[1] Olives	CF	OFF	Tobacco	Romania Tobacco		Spain Olives	
	A	O	O	O	O	O	A	O	A	O[9]
1861	...	...	1,055	237	436	...	...	...	...	...
1862	...	...	1,908	240	473	...	...	...	...	...
1863	...	...	1,294	261	336	...	...	...	...	...
1864	...	...	2,055	276	297	...	...	...	...	...
1865	...	...	2,281	248	332	...	...	...	...	...
1866	...	...	1,974	314	481	...	...	...	...	...
1867	...	...	1,421	298	565	...	...	...	...	...
1868	...	...	1,810	270	556	3.5	...	...	...	...
1869	...	...	2,325	286	661	3.9	...	...	...	...
1870	...	...	2,179	279	632	3.7	...	...	...	...
1871	...	...	2,778	342	588	3.8	...	...	...	...
1872	...	...	2,069	350	677	4.4	...	...	...	...
1873	...	...	2,851	330	718	4.9	...	...	...	...
1874	...	...	2,269	325	652	4.9	...	...	...	...
1875	...	...	2,632	372	576	4.4	...	...	...	...
1876	...	...	2,351	407	588	5.7	...	...	...	...
1877	...	...	2,128	390	627	4.5	...	...	...	...
1878	...	...	2,022	431	576	5.1	...	...	...	...
1879	...	...	2,671	420	622	4.9	...	...	...	...
1880	...	...	2,384	402	725	5.5	...	...	...	...
1881	...	...	958	490	686	5.7	...	...	...	...
1882	...	...	1,575	483	606	5.1	...	...	...	...
1883	...	...	1,146	565	561	5.4	...	...	...	...
1884	...	...	1,635	560	591	6.0	...	...	...	...
1885	...	...	1,679	471	595	6.1	...	...	...	...
1886	...	...	2,283	511	579	5.3	...	...	...	...
1887	...	...	1,421	542	624	4.1	...	...	...	...
1888	...	...	2,185	570	710	2.2	...	...	...	...
1889	...	...	1,126	470	877	1.8	...	...	...	...
1890	...	...	2,266	620	965	2.3	4.7	2.6	...	136
1891	...	...	2,023	495	995	3.1	4.4	3.1	1,123	181
1902	...	...	1,263	491	820	4.5	6.1	5.1	1,123	364
1893	...	...	2,190	520	702	6.1	5.8	3.4	1,123	162
1894	...	...	1,600	556	711	5.9	5.6	2.3	1,123	169
1895	...	...	2,176	522	732	6.8	...	...	1,123	296
1896	...	...	1,468	543	799	5.9	5.7	4.1	1,123	45
1897	...	...	1,396	461	707	6.3	4.5	3.8	1,135	282
1898	...	...	1,918	529	761	5.7	2.3	2.6	1,135	176
1899	5	4	736	635	791	5.8	2.2	1.2	1,199	156
1900	...	4	1,220	668	899	6.2	4.6	4.1	1,253	143
1901	...	...	2,144	708	894	5.8	4.1	3.0	1,267	294
1902	...	...	1,240	775	847	5.0	4.1	2.8	1,272	226
1903	...	9	2,185	831	694	5.6	5.8	4.6	1,333	198
1904	...	5	1,133	662	892	6.2	6.3	1.8	1,327	161

C4 Area and Output of Mediterranean Crops (in thousands of hectares and thousands of metric tons)

| | Bulgaria | | Greece | | | | | Italy[1] | | | | |
| | Tobacco | | Cotton | | Tobacco | | Dried Grapes | Olives | | CF | OFF | Tobacco |
	A	O	A	O	A	O	O	A	O	O	O	O
1905	...	4	...	...	...	...	...	...	2,287	789	872	7.1
1906	...	6	...	...	...	...	...	...	746	740	1,228	7.0
1907	6	4	...	...	...	...	...	...	1,940	768	1,040	7.3
1908	5	3	...	...	...	...	...	...	424	902	1,125	6.8
1909	5	4	...	...	...	...	...	2,345	1,715	1,065	728	8.3
1910	8	6	...	...	...	...	...	2,331	723	966	1,070	9.1
1911	12	11	9.0	2.7	15	13	146	2,345	1,258	999	1,024	9.5
1912	9	6	...3	...3	...3	...3	...3	2,313	499	847	1,039	9.3
1913	6	5	...	...	...	...	...	2,291	905	1,113	1,179	8.1
1914	20	15	12₃	3.3₃	36₃	25₃	181₃	2,298	928	1,018	1,156	8.7
1915	22	16	6.8	1.9	18	13	161	2,308	788	964	1,497	9.0
1916	15	12	6.9₃	1.4₃	29₃	16₃	146₃	2,310	1,074	1,087	1,109	7.2
1917	25	15	4.9	1.3	40	28	142	2,301	1,100	803	1,583	4.9
1918	41	26	7.8₃	1.7₃	47₃	30₃	124₃	2,295	1,503	878	952	7.0
1919	32	22	10	2.2	37	30	133	2,293	596	842	1,366	7.8
1920	39	29	7.0	1.3	39	32	137	2,292	1,061	799	1,393	9.8
1921	23	16	5.2₃	1.2₃	29₃	23₃	130₃	2,290₁	1,183₁	780₁	1,070₁	14.9₁
1922	34	26	7.5	1.8	32	26	202	2,310	2,007	858	1,172	19.0
1923	53	40	12	2.4	62	58	151	2,310	1,412	783	1,177	23.1
1924	49	49	16	3.1	82	50	185	2,284	1,658	832	1,387	27.9
1925	51	40	15	3.2	80	61	178	2,295	1,063	843	1,192	36.4
1926	32	27	15	3.9	81	61	174	2,294	1,351	1,041	1,413	39.3
1927	24	22	15	2.7	92	63	170	2,280	1,147	839	1,332	32.8
1928	22	16	15	3.3	93	59	171	2,329	1,718	840	1,380	37.2
1929	38	33	20	3.3	101	69	139	2,258	1,824	957	1,359	34.0
1930	32	27	20	3.5	97	66	171	2,265	770	1,016	1,134	42.2
1931	35	32	18	3.0	84	43	101	2,091	1,378	839	1,320	49.0
1932	20	17	20	4.8	63	29	189	2,091	1,255	1,300	1,543	40.8
1933	27	25	29	6.9	78	55	167	2,078	957	859	1,403	39.0
1934	22	21	37	7.8	73	42	207	2,077	1,249	834	1,289	39.6
1935	35	28	45	11	80	46	213	2,074	1,331	725	1,255	38.6
1936	43	42	62	13	111	81	177	2,171	966	732	1,083	42.2
1937	39	35	72	16	95	69	189	2,173	1,701	691	1,248	42.9
1938	31	26	68	14	84	48	188	2,176	1,042	836	1,076	42.1
1939	43	41	65	14	97	48	175	2,183	2,027	693	1,303	43.2
1940	53₂	44₂	...	...	...	...	...	2,187	1,024	744	1,313	51.3
1941	52	39	...	...	...	...	...	2,187	1,269	785	1,271	53.5
1942	48	42	...	...	...	...	...	2,188	1,128	705	1,199	48.6
1943	54	38	...	...	...	...	...	2,208₁	914₁	684₁	1,334₁	33.5₁
1944	44	32	...	...	...	...	...	2,195	985	521	1,325	23.5
1945	46	23	28	6.9	46	23	60	2,195	663	554	1,237	17.1
1946	73	40	52	10	64	34	76	2,107	854	638	1,267	44.5
1947	62	48	42	12	80	45	112	2,263	1,592	735	1,692	76.4
1948	...	...	46	12	72	37	100	2,277₁	679₁	775₁	1,499₁	74.4₁
1949	...	...	57	48	75	46	126	2,286	1,150	670	2,027	71.8
1950	...	...	77	79	103	58	117	2,294	1,012	998	1,869	78.7
1951	...	...	87	89	96	63	107	2,316	2,148	905	2,136	79.5
1952	...	...	82	77	76	42	114	2,214	1,099	958	2,376	73.0
1953	...	...	89	95	88	63	123	2,196	2,011	1,023	2,380	68.3
1954	96	55	109	128	106	67	113	2,215	1,730	1,005	2,220	66.1

C4 Area and Output of Mediterranean Crops (in thousands of hectares and thousands of metric tons)

1955–1959

	Bulgaria		Greece					Italy[1]				
	Tobacco		Cotton		Tobacco		Dried Grapes	Olives		CF	OFF	Tobacco
	A	O	A	O	A	O	O	A	O	O	O	O
1955	90	55	166	189	129	97	107	2,256	1,153	1,059	2,710	72.3
1956	89	72	160	154	118	82	132	2,240	981	1,053	2,777	71.2
1957	94	57	156	191	122	109	144	2,233	2,010	1,117	2,431	77.1
1958	108	83	162	187	112	84	125	2,247	1,462	1,273	3,285	79.8
1959	119	99	131	170	102	80	137	2,298	1,654	1,230	3,869	90.3

1905–1944

	Portugal	Romania				Spain									
	Olive Oil	Tobacco		Olives		Citrus Fruits		Sugar Cane		Cotton		Tobacco	
	O	A	O	A	O	A	O	A	O	A	O	A	O
1905	...	7.7	3.9	1,315	149	...	...	...	...	...	...	...	...
1906	...	6.2	4.5	1,346	134	...	...	...	...	...	...	...	...
1907	...	8.8	7.1	1,353	306	...	...	...	...	...	...	...	...
1908	...	9.3	7.3	1,388	152	...	...	...	...	...	...	...	...
1909	...	8.3	5.5	1,395	240	...	...	...	...	...	...	...	...
1910		9.5	7.0	1,416	108[9] / 625	48[10]	...	...	189	...	...	...	...
1911	23	10	9.3	1,444	2,220	...	...	...	234	...	...	...	...
1912	...	9.3	6.0	1,448	355	...	...	4.0	152	...	...	...	...
1913	...	11[4]	9.5[4]	1,453	1,487	...	...	4.0	139	...	...	...	...
1914	...	11	7.7	1,465	1,181	51	...	...	72	...	...	...	...
1915	26	13	8.4	1,482	1,773	...	...	1.9	64	...	...	...	...
1916	26	10	...	1,487	1,147	...	...	1.6	44	...	...	...	...
1917	38	...[4]	...[4]	1,504	2,208	...	...	1.7	64	...	...	...	...
1918	27	13	6.1	1,559	1,394	...	...	1.9	86	...	...	...	...
1919	28	15[4]	12[4]	1,572	1,813	...	...	1.9	65	...	...	...	...
1920	18	24	17	1,571	1,662	...	...	1.9	73	...	...	...	...
1921	23	17	10	1,614	1,523	...	...	2.3	129	...	...	0.1	0.2
1922	29	21	13	1,613	1,540	...	...	2.6	120	0.5	...	0.2	0.4
1923	44	18	9.7	1,624	1,613	...	...	2.3	93	0.4	...	...	...
1924	40	31	22	1,655	1,745	...	...	3.1	108	1.5	0.9	...	...
1925	38	37	16	1,679	1,868	56	...	...	120	2.2	1.1	...	...
1926	16	30	18	1,694	1,291	57	1,219	...	...	4.6	2.2	...	...
1927	89	31	20	1,713	3,517	63	1,091	...	...	4.6	1.6	...	1.4
1928	26	28	15	1,787	971	63	1,190	2.4	141	7.8	2.1	2.1	2.9
1929	76	31	26	1,818	3,341	69	1,490	2.7	167	7.8	2.1	2.7	4.7
1930	18	34	24	1,882	619	75	1,255	3.8	232	18	4.8	4.8	7.9
1931	64	16	11	1,911	1,806	75	1,257	3.8	259	5.8	2.4	3.6	5.9
1932	39	10	7.1	1,878	1,836	78	1,230	3.4	202	8.2	3.1	4.1	7.5
1933	74	10	6.3	1,901	1,647	80	1,027	3.2	209	7.8	2.7	4.3	7.5
1934	22	10	5.9	1,905	1,579	78	1,024	3.1	194	10	5.6	4.1	7.4
1935	52	18	13	1,921	2,251	80	961	3.1	197	25	7.9	4.1	7.1
1936	27	18	15	...	...	...	...	...	...	...	...	...	...
1937	97	14	10	...	...	...	...	...	...	...	...	...	...
1938	33	17	12	...	...	...	...	...	...	...	...	...	...
1939	76	22[5]	14[5]	1,918	1,150	81	757	2.8	188	16	4.3	3.8	5.3
1940	34	13	10	1,936	1,445	82	801	2.6	181	19	4.7	5.0	7.2
1941	90	14	11	1,974	1,946	82	903	2.5	144	22	9.1	5.4	10
1942	38	18	11	1,971	1,301	86	829	2.1	97	33	13	6.5	8.3
1943	86	...	...	1,971	2,057	85	917	2.3	113	49	14	8.5	11
1944	36	22	15	1,967	1,322	85	1,109	2.6	137	60	17	9.0	13

C4 Area and Output of Mediterranean Crops (in thousands of hectares and thousands of metric tons)

1945–1959

	Portugal	Romania		Spain									
	Olive Oil	Tobacco		Olives		Citrus Fruits		Sugar Cane		Cotton		Tobacco	
	O	A	O	A	O	A	O	A	O	A	O	A	O
1945	40	21[5]	11[5]	1,976	973	84	960	3.0	126	36	5.6	8.7	9.8
1946	44	25	7.9	1,989	2,000	81	634	3.2	144	58	20	10	15
1947	92	24	...	1,993	2,556	81	800	3.3	166	28	9.5	7.4	13
1948	28	27	14	2,001	733	81	877	3.5	210	53	20	9.9	16
1949	97	...	...	2,008	1,924	82	756	3.9	271	37	9.6	9.9	15
1950	39	29	14	2,023	902	84	967	4.2	302	34	13	10	15
1951	104	34	25	2,049	2,951	89	1,097	4.2	283	44	25	15	20
1952	51	33	15	2,062	1,499	92	1,435	4.8	353	67	52	19	30
1953	120	36	24	2,077	1,790	93	1,080	5.2	422	88	60	21	32
1954	48	32	19	2,084	1,456	96	1,363	5.1	369	108	67	22	34
1955	67	35	26	2,130	1,350	97	1,178	5.0	388	164	110	20	33
1956	92	35	26	2,113	1,858	96	506	5.1	406	200	148	18	27
1957	99	40	36	2,122	1,614	102	1,313	5.1	364	160	106	17	25
1958	61	47	31	2,123	1,644	102	1,346	5.0	323	169	121	16	23
1959	90	36	26	2,145	2,228	109	1,662	5.1	324	225	191	16	23

1960–1999

	Bulgaria		Greece					Italy				
	Tobacco		Cotton		Tobacco		Dried Grapes	Olives		Citrus Fruits	OFF	Tobacco
	A	O	A	O	A	O	O	A	O	O	O	O
1960	87	62	165	184	94	64	120	2,311	2,106	1,238	3,906	79.5
1961	96	56	217	288	104	74	166	2,317	2,251	1,477	4,764	25.0
1962	120	107	278	270	122	89	201	2,321	1,741	1,238	4,766	46.3
1963	124	105	233	305	147	129	143	2,290	2,861	1,618	5,275	65.2
1964	131	150	141	225	143	134	163	2,294	1,878	1,804	5,511	78.9
1965	121	123	136	228	132	126	177	2,291	2,232	1,777	5,138	73.5
1966	117	132	133	260	126	104	183	2,287	1,808	2,029	6,002	73.1
1967	103	118	136	285	128	114	149	2,283	2,712	2,161	5,049	86.9
1968	114	115	141	228	112	89	195	2,257	1,933	2,510	5,285	74.1
1969	117	95	158	338	107	80	186	2,230	2,413	2,529	5,145	79.4
1970	118	108	143	328	98	95	169	2,253	2,124	2,400	5,776	78.4
1971	115	120	139	360	91	88	161	2,222	2,385	2,585	5,319	79.3
1972	122	158	174	395	84	86	137	2,199	1,870	2,546	5,285[7] / 5,271	84.3
1973	119	138	155	361	84	91	146	2,182	2,836	2,758	5,311	93.8
1974	123	140	154	370	84	83	179	2,180	2,323	2,934	5,154	92.7
1975	127	157	138	366	98	119	157	2,172	3,371	2,812	5,273	113
1976	121	162	150	329	114	142	138	2,165	1,851	3,072	5,875	109
1977	122	115	183	382	106	120	144	2,161	3,598	2,812	4,931	110
1978	115	136	160	408	102	129	138	2,156	2,308	2,787	4,983	110
1979	115	156	135	325	96	128	125	2,147	2,490	2,932	5,228	137
1980	108	120	142	357	89	118	138	2,139	3,700	2,847	5,458	126
1981	106	130	132	385	89	131	156	2,130	3,140	3,047	5,500	131
1982	103	145	139	308	93	138	153	2,121[8] / 1,047	2,208	2,568	145	
1983	108	109	174	394	91	116	176	1,254	4,553	3,805	5,864	156
1984	104	135	207	429	92	145	178	1,254	1,973	2,948	5,818	161
1985	102	120	236	498	97	150	179	1,207	3,581	3,558	5,231	166
1986	103	121	230	606	97	161	160	1,177	2,003	3,908	5,377	150
1987	90	133	202	535	95	155	121	1,175	3,582	2,395	5,617	162
1988	87	116	256	720	88	135	137	1,166	2,347	3,297	5,919	184
1989	73	81	278	782	81	126	150	1,153	3,194	3,361	5,549	197
1990	53	71	282	700	76	132	130	1,149	1,032	2,956	5,989	205
1991	53	72	240	720	82	162	90	1,134	4,117	3,170	5,296	193
1992	51	66	305	782	91	187	97	1,140	2,468	3,630	6,813	151
1993	39	59	341	700	81	168	91	1,133	3,065	3,326	5,918	149
1994	26	33	290	620	76	142	86	1,118	2,640	2,833	...	120
1995	14	19	330	714	65	149	94	1,107	3,289	2,608	...	124
1996	28	40	321	720	64	134	84	1,104	2,147	2,868	...	131
1997	42	61	317	707	66	137	78	1,124	3,591	2,918	...	131
1998	34	39	306	695	67	137	60	1,115	2,549	2,185	...	133
1999	26	34	329	734	65	140	81	1,128	3,765	2,902	...	126

C4   Area and Output of Mediterranean Crops (in thousands of hectares and thousands of metric tons)

1960–1999

	Portugal	Romania		Spain									
	Olive Oil	Tobacco		Olives		Citrus Fruits		Sugar Cane		Cotton		Tobacco	
	O	A	O	A	O	A	O	A	O	A	O	A	O
1960	85	22	16	2,148	2,367	115	1,617	5.1	320	250	217	18	30
1961	113	28	18	2,153	1,863	124	1,959	5.4	336	319	318	21	37
1962	52	38	26	2,167	1,641	132[6]	1,407	5.3	363	346	335	19	32
						114							
1963	99	41	40	2,194	3,124	124	2,082	5.0	354	263	285	18	27
1964	41	40	42	2,211	579	108	1,087	5.1	357	197	225	20	28
1965	72	38	35	2,220	1,664	114	1,999	5.1	458	198	249	21	34[6]
1966	38	38	40	2,154	2,108	122	2,284	5.3	430	234	267	13	21
1967	81	39	35	2,257	1,378	127	2,120	5.5	412	144	198	18	31
1968	53	36	33	2,224	2,282	129	1,874	5.5	407	136	229	14	26
1969	72	36	24	2,227	1,746	141	2,571	5	420	150	180	14	20
1970	67	34	23	2,196	2,107	154	2,069	6	421	91	160	15	26
1971	42	33	30	2,095	1,749	170	2,323	5	423	78	124	16	27
1972	54	39	38	2,137	2,323	173	3,034	5	369	122	177	18	27
1973	42	52	38	2,122	2,257	197	2,946	5	332	92	139	16	26
1974	48	53	39	2,085	1,648	201	2,737	4	321	101	161	14	23
1975	58	57	40	2,102	2,358	223	2,921	4	273	62	159	15	26
1976	43	53	64	2,097	2,139	216	2,704	4	280	56	125	16	29
1977	36	51	47	2,084	1,934	183	2,841	4	305	78	138	15	32
1978	47	50	41	2,069	2,781	186	2,810	4	287	43	97	16	30
1979	67	44	39	2,065	2,300	187	2,941	5	317	47	127	18	35
1980	44	44	37	2,057	2,255	193	2,952	4	350	58	189	20	37
1981	29	39	28	2,045	1,521	197	2,634	4	237	72	205	20	43
1982	95	35	33	2,046	3,338	198	3,012	4	274	49	159	22	42
1983	13	35	25	2,050	1,328	198	3,860	4	239	40	121	22	43
1984	56	35	37	2,039	3,525	207	2,510	4	241	60	165	22	43
1985	36	35	27	2,051	1,989	218	3,501	3	263	64	204	25	42
1986	54	34	35	2,063	2,557	211	3,852	3	224	79	253	22	38
1987	42	35	27	2,057	3,879	232	4,485	3	194	79	251	20	32
1988	17	34	32	2,035	2,224	237	4,239	2	192	137	372	29	34
1989	39	34	31	2,053	2,946	243	4,754	2	164	68	190	27	37
1990	44	34	32	2,121	3,043	240	4,794	2	170	82	234	23	34
1991	65	10	14	2,127	3,946	241	4,546	2	170	79	260	24	49
1992	26	7	8	2,141	2,371	246	5,190	2	167	75	210	24	45
1993	25	9	11	...	3,104	...	...	2	151	32	88	23	42
1994	36	10	13	2,094	2,800	250	5,076	2	139	...	60	18	44
1995	49	10	13	2,119	1,694	247	4,768	1	101	...	50	17	43
1996	46	9	12	2,126	4,517	250	4,212	1	51	...	136	18	44
1997	42	13	18	2,208	5,880	284	5,789	1	75	...	175	17	46
1998	38	13	18	2,194	4,279	284	5,126	1	111	...	153	15	44
1999	52	11	15	2,200	3,395	283	5,824	1	80	...	185	13	45

C4 Area and Output of Mediterranean Crops (in thousands of hectares and thousands of metric tons)

NOTE

SOURCES:- As in Table C1

FOOTNOTES

[1] Up to 1921 the statistics apply to the boundaries of 1871. For 1922—43 they apply to the 1924 boundaries; and from 1944 onwards to the 1954 boundaries, except that Trieste is not included until 1949.

[2] Subsequently includes southern Dobrudja.

[3] The following are the changes in the area to which the statistics apply:- In 1913 new territories in the north and in the islands were acquired from Turkey. In 1915 Macedonia was lost, but the western part of it was regained in 1917. In 1919 the post war boundaries were achieved, but Thrace is not included in the statistics until 1922.

[4] Southern Dobrudja was acquired in 1914, Bessarabia in 1918, and Bukovina, Transylvania, part of Banat, and parts of Hungary proper in 1920.

[5] Southern Dobrudja was ceded to Bulgaria in 1940. Bessarabia and northern Bukovina were ceded to the U.S.S.R. in 1940, and though temporarily reconquered in 1943, this does not appear to have affected these series. Northern Transylvania was ceded to Hungary in 1940, but was regained by 1946.

[6] There was a change in the basis of calculation.

[7] Subsequently excluding pomegranates and quinces.

[8] Subsequently excluding secondary cultivation.

[9] Olive oil output to 1910 (1st line).

[10] Oranges only. The area of oranges in 1902 was 42 thousand hectares.

C5 NUMBERS OF LIVESTOCK (in thousands)

Key to series:- H = horses; C = cattle; P = pigs; S = sheep; G = goats; Po = poultry; A&M = asses and mules; R = reindeer

AUSTRIA: Cisleithania   1842–1910

	H	C	P	S	G	Po
1842	1,116	4,984	...	6,745	...	...
1843	1,143	5,048	...	6,503	...	...
1844	1,144	5,044	...	6,540	...	...
1845	1,145	5,049	...	6,532	...	...
1846	1,152	5,203	...	6,541	...	...
1847	1,155	5,223	...	6,474	...	...
1807	1,123	5,126	2,156	5,640	1,065	...
1857	1,295	8,013	3,410	5,285	1,028	...
1869	1,390	7,425	2,551	5,026	979	...
1880	1,463	8,584	2,722	3,841	1,007	...
1890	1,548	8,644	3,550	3,187	1,036	...
1900	1,716	9,511	4,683	2,621	1,020	26,672
1910	1,803	9,160	6,632	2,428	1,257	35,981

AUSTRIA: Republic   1918–1964

	H	C	P	S	G	Po
1918	...	[1,842][1]	[1,270][1]	...	...	...
1919	[243][1]	[1,719][1]	[1,107][1]	...	...	...
1920	[236][2]	[2,190][2]	[1,247][2]	[450][2]	[320][2]	...
1923	[265][2]	[2,038][2]	[1,380][2]	[591][2]	[374][2]	[5,418][2]
1934	261	2,349	2,823	263	326	9,072
1938	247	2,579	2,868	315	349	9,304
1939	231	2,620	2,830	317	323	8,815
1940	226	2,582	2,190	342	305	7,622
1941	226	2,494	2,043	354	292	6,939
1942	221	2,505	1,772	402	300	5,972
1943	224	2,530	1,872	444	308	6,169
1944	240	2,536	1,697	460	281	5,648
1945	264	2,187	1,030	391	247	4,161
1946	274	2,206	1,490	399	272	4,326
1947	283	2,158	1,724	474	310	4,664
1948	284	2,109	1,618	454	316	4,140
1949	282	2,203	1,927	375	317	5,134
1950	283	2,281	2,523	362	323	6,972
1951	276	2,284	2,448	332	310	7,216
1952	267	2,347	2,701	319	311	8,002
1953	259	2,300	2,643	297	298	8,577
1954	245	2,304	2,803	278	280	9,193
1955	236	2,346	2,933	255	256	9,318
1956	222	2,325	2,727	227	227	9,401[3]
1957	200	2,297	2,917	207	209	9,767
1958	180	2,279	2,838	194	187	9,843
1959	163	2,308	2,845	185	175	10,155
1960	150	2,387	2,990	175	162	10,131
1961	135	2,457	2,995	169	149	10,278
1962	121	2,437	2,849	153	132	10,328
1963	109	2,311	2,925	145	120	10,609
1964	97	2,350	3,132	147	111	10,880

C5   Numbers of Livestock (in thousands)

AUSTRIA: Republic   1965–1999

	H	C	P	S	G	Po
1965	85	2,441	2,639	142	98	10,574
1966	75	2,497	2,786	138	94	11,021
1967	66	2,480	2,932	130	88	11,092
1968	59	2,433	3,094	126	77	11,510
1969	53	2,418	3,196	121	69	11,740
1970	47	2,468	3,445	113	62	12,335
1971	43	2,499	3,091	112	56	12,396
1972	40	2,514	3,256	119	51	12,600
1973	39	2,624	3,290	136	48	12,181
1974	40	2,581	3,517	154	46	12,410
1975	41	2,500	3,683	169	43	13,090
1976	41	2,502	3,878	174	40	13,495
1977	43	2,547	3,694	181	37	14,174
1978	45	2,594	4,007	192	36	15,074
1979	43	2,548	4,004	195	35	14,633
1980	40	2,577	3,706	191	32	14,307
1981	41	2,530	4,009	194	32	15,798
1982	41	2,546	3,981	199	32	15,525
1983	42	2,633	3,881	216	32	15,369
1984	41	2,669	4,027	220	30	15,103
1985	45	2,651	3,926	245	33	14,616
1986	44	2,637	3,801	256	31	14,369
1987	45	2,590	3,947	261	33	14,659
1988	44	2,541	3,874	256	32	13,742
1989	44	2,562	3,773	289	36	14,135
1990	48	2,584	3,688	309	37	13,139
1991	49	2,534	3,629	323	40	13,479
1992	57	2,532	3,720	312	39	12,872
1993	61	2,401	3,800	324	40	13,589
1994	65	2,334	3,820	334	47	13,589
1995	67	2,329	3,729	342	50	13,266
1996	72	2,326	3,706	365	54	13,157
1997	73	2,272	3,664	381	54	12,215
1998	74	2,198	3,680	384	58	13,950
1999	75	2,172	3,810	360	54	13,540

C5   Numbers of Livestock (in thousands)

BELGIUM   1816–1999

	H^4	C	P	S		H^4	C	P	S
1816	254	981	...	970	1941	230	1,759	444	186
1817	241	913	...	727	1942	230	1,407	526	216
1818	240	895	...	677	1943	223	1,392	485	213
1819	242	890	...	672	1944	238[7]	1,440[7]	635[7]	199[7]
1820	241	894	...	680	1945	257	1,539	735	177
1821	246	894	...	710	1946	262	1,652	776	144
1822	246	889	...	735	1947	251	1,588	648	107
1823	243	887	...	772	1948	240	1,688	912	113
1824	255	897	...	805	1949	234	1,902	1,361	121
1825	254	893	...	774	1950	227	2,020	1,234	116
1826	256	887	...	...	1951	234	2,127	1,427	124
1827	256	875	...	...	1952	227	2,151	1,382	114
1828	258	878	...	...	1953	203	2,168	1,161	44
1829	262[5]	899[5]	...	...[5]	1954	191	2,207	1,240	38
1840	247	913	421	733	1955	182	2,197	1,347	36
1845	295	1,204	496	663	1956	172	2,368	1,225	42
1856	277	1,258	458	583	1957	165	2,422	1,267	44
					1958	156[8]	2,495[8]	1,480[8]	47[8]
1866	283	1,242	632	586	1959	157	2,538	1,559	69
1880	272	1,383	646	365					
1895	272	1,421	1,163	236	1960	147	2,531	1,579	59
					1961	139	2,639	1,882	64
1900	242	1,657	1,006	...	1962	132	2,687	1,859	60
1901	245	1,646	1,015	...	1963	120	2,480	1,563	58
1902	247	1,647	1,137	...	1964	109	2,524	1,745	64
1903	249	1,720	1,183	...					
1904	246	1,782	1,155	...	1965	98	2,619	1,885	67
					1966	87	2,597	2,117	68
1905	245	1,788	1,047	...	1967	79[4]	2,611	2,392	65
1906	245	1,780	1,148	...	1968	81	2,674	2,504	84
1907	250	1,818	1,279	...	1969	76	2,713	3,094	85
1908	253	1,861	1,162	...					
1909	255	1,857	1,117	...	1970	67	2,715	3,835	66
					1971	60	2,643	3,925	66
1910	317	1,880	1,494	185	1972	58	2,750	4,298	69
1911	262	1,812	1,229	...	1973	55	2,896	4,720	74
1912	263	1,831	1,349	...	1974	53	2,889	4,666	81
1913	267	1,849	1,412	...					
					1975	52	2,805	4,679	83
1919	162	1,286	770	...	1976	49	2,823	4,813	82
1920	205	1,487	977	...	1977	44	2,823	4,935	84
1921	222	1,515	976	...	1978	40	2,870	4,992	91
1922	230	1,517	1,139	...	1979	37	2,894	4,987	84
1923	243	1,603	1,176	...					
1924	252	1,628	1,139	...	1980	33	2,896	5,011	86
					1981	31	2,859	5,076	79
1925	250	1,655	1,152	...	1982	30	2,896	5,113	83
1926	250	1,712	1,144	...	1983	29	2,965	5,188	97
1927	256	1,739	1,124	...	1984	28	2,989	5,269	1,09
1928	253	1,751	1,139	...					
1929	249	1,738	1,237	187	1985	26	2,943	5,412	124
					1986	24	2,967	5,763	128
1930	246	1,759	1,250	...	1987	23	2,950	5,881	133
1931	242	1,768	1,235	...	1988	22	2,967	6,233	129
1932	238	1,784	1,245	...					
1933	233	1,813	1,353	...	1989	21	3,127	6,350	188
1934	232	1,840	1,258	...	1990	21	3,249	6,700	192
					1991	21	3,264	6,550	175
1935	231	1,837	1,284	...	1992	22	3,222	6,823	181
1936	263	1,783	1,054	...	1993	23	3,252	7,089	179
1937	264	1,710	872	...	1994	30	3,289	6,948	167
1938	265	1,690	960	...					
1939	246	1,600	856	...	1995	39	3,369	7,053	161
					1996	45	3,363	7,225	161
1940	[286][6][7]	1,828[7]	633[7]	153[7]	1997	66	3,280	7,194	162
					1998	67	3,184	7,436	155
					1999	67	3,395	7,632	158

C5 Numbers of Livestock (in thousands)

BULGARIA

	H	C	P	S	Po
1890	344	1,426	462	6,868	...
1901	495	1,596	368	7,015	...
1905	538	1,696	465	8,131	...
1910	478[9]	1,606[9]	527[9]	8,669[9]	8,689[9]
1920	398	1,877	1,090	8,923	7,294
1926	482	1,817	1,002	8,740	10,118
1934	532	1,498	902	8,840	12,774
1939	507	1,449	752	9,413	...
1940	509[9]	1,511[9]	860[9]	9,182[9]	...[9]
1941	591	1,639	1,095	10,128	...
1942	594	1,755	1,061	8,847	7,661
1943	522	1,492	498	7,471	7,039
1944	478	1,390	675	6,390	6,649
1945	476	1,391	836	7,178	6,399
1946	499	1,631	719	8,916	11,412
1947	549	1,711	1,028	8,837	11,613
1948	...	...	825	8,266	11,380
1949	...	...	...	8,853	...
1950	...	...	...	7,820	...
1951	...	...	...	7,569	...
1952	473	1,625	1,058	7,569	11,592
1953	471	1,638	1,337	7,759	12,610
1954	467	1,591	1,436	7,867	12,851
1955	468	1,607	1,316	7,802	13,611
1956	472	1,602	1,413	7,829	13,817
1957	460	1,529	1,468	7,596	14,117
1958	431	1,442	1,993	7,742	14,302
1959	382	1,356	2,052	8,619	15,236
1960	334	1,284	2,266	8,769	21,666
1961	312	1,452	2,553	9,333	23,366
1962	301	1,582	2,331	10,161	22,800
1963	277	1,582	2,066	10,107	20,969
1964	256	1,494	2,097	10,308	21,922
1965	249	1,474	2,607	10,440	21,883
1966	240	1,450	2,408	10,312	20,845
1967	229	1,385	2,276	9,998	23,637
1968	224	1,363	2,314	9,905	27,726
1969	199	1,297	2,140	9,652	24,874
1970	182	1,255	1,966	9,223	29,590
1971	169	1,279	2,369	9,678	33,706
1972	159	1,379	2,806	10,127	34,102
1973	148	1,441	2,598	9,921	34,788
1974	142	1,454	2,431	9,765	36,939
1975	137	1,554	3,422	9,791	35,089
1976	133	1,656	3,889	10,014	38,061
1977	128	1,722	3,456	9,723	39,504
1978	126	1,736	3,399	10,144	41,080
1979	124	1,763	3,772	10,105	40,295
1980	120	1,787	3,830	10,536	41,003
1981	120	1,796	3,808	10,433	41,636
1982	119	1,807	3,844	10,726	40,563

C5 Numbers of Livestock (in thousands)

BULGARIA 1983–1999

	H	C	P	S	Po
1983	119	1,783	3,810	10,761	42,853
1984	119	1,778	3,769	10,978	43,078
1985	118	1,751	3,734	10,501	42,277
1986	120	1,706	3,912	9,724	39,227
1987	121	1,678	4,050	9,563	39,735
1988	123	1,649	4,034	8,886	41,424
1989	122	1,613	4,119	8,609	41,804
1990	119	1,575	4,352	8,130	36,338
1991	115	1,457	4,187	7,938	27,800
1992	114	1,310	3,141	6,703	21,707
1993	114	974	2,680	4,814	19,872
1994	113	750	2,071	3,763	17,111
1995	133	638	1,986	3,398	17,822
1996	151	632	2,140	3,383	17,349
1997	170	582	1,500	3,020	16,227
1998	126	612	1,480	2,847	14,766
1999	133	671	1,721	2,774	15,686

CZECHOSLOVAKIA 1920–1970

	H	C	P	S	G	Po
1920	591	4,377	2,053	986		
1925	740	4,691	2,539	861	1,245	17,886
1930	...	4,458	2,776	608	1,081	36,617
1931	...	4,451	2,576	531	...	...
1932	708	4,341	2,621	465	...	...
1933	701	4,405	3,430	476	877	...
1934	701	4,305	3,032	510	930	...
1935	695	4,283	2,745	547	957	39,232
1936	704	4,596	3,242	592	1,000	40,414
1937	...	4,938	3,900	644	1,072	43,493
1938	...	...	3,827	...	1,008	41,989
1939	641	4,728	3,123	519	1,052	37,577
1940	630	4,729	3,319	495	1,114	31,379
1941	631	4,609	2,766	466	1,127	26,664
1942	638	4,425	3,071	519	1,320	25,891
1943	602	4,383	2,933	490	1,408	26,275
1944	608[10]	4,358[10]	3,256[10]	519[10]	1,459[10]	23,610[10]
1945	649	4,143	2,362	510	1,509	...
1946	653	3,975	2,944	491	1,310	12,281
1947	630	3,275	2,566	386	1,115	13,478
1948	628	3,663	3,242	459	922	16,393
1949	629	4,213	4,218	531	982	17,794
1950	605	4,303	3,802	596	...	18,206
1951	572	4,376	4,234	800	...	18,690
1952	559	4,445	4,918	982	...	20,787
1953	544	4,082	4,174	1,017	...	21,094
1954	543	4,041	4,771	1,017	...	22,540
1955	543	4,107	5,285	1,000	899	23,367
1956	542	4,134	5,369	956	846	23,876
1957	517	4,091	5,435	889	790	24,250
1958	456	4,183	5,283	817	739	25,364
1959	389	4,303	5,687	727	696	27,569
1960	330	4,387	5,962	646	662	28,157
1961	292	4,518	5,895	603	616	28,805
1962	254	4,507	5,897	524	597	28,032
1963	227	4,480	5,845	527	588	30,093
1964	204	4,436	6,139	568	582	28,840
1965	188	4,389	5,544	614	559	27,752
1966	177	4,462	5,305	670	521	29,466
1967	166	4,437	5,601	770	477	31,208
1968	156	4,249	5,136	906	417	32,544
1969	144	4,223	5,037	977	364	34,871
1970	131	4,288	5,530	981	318	39,187

C5 Numbers of Livestock (in thousands)

CZECHOSLOVAKIA   1971–1999

	H	C	P	S	G	Po
1971	118	4,349	5,935	932	285	38,238
1972	100	4,466	6,093	889	241	39,170
1973	84	4,556	6,266	842	212	41,232
1974	71	4,566	6,719	811	174	39,476
1975	62	4,555	6,683	805	140	40,130
1976	57	4,654	6,820	797	121	44,142
1977	53	4,758	7,510	841	98	44,774
1978	49	4,887	7,601	865	83	46,957
1979	47	4,915	7,588	875	72	48,351
1980	45	5,002	7,894	910	63	47,283
1981	44	5,103	7,302	959	57	47,388
1982	44	5,131	7,126	990	52	49,212
1983	45	5,190	7,070	1,041	52	50,977
1984	46	5,150	6,743	1,068	55	48,519
1985	46	5,065	6,651	1,087	54	47,278
1986	46	5,073	6,833	1,104	52	48,726
1987	45	5,044	7,235	1,075	52	47,984
1988	44	5,075	7,384	1,047	50	48,849
1989	42	5,129	7,498	1,051	50	49,000
1990	42	4,923	7,090	1,030	52	49,000
1991	39	4,347	7,139	886	53	49,000
1992	34	2,512[78]	4,599[78]	254[78]	45[78]	24,830[78]

Czech Republic

	H	C	P	S	G	Po
1993[78]	19	2,113[78]	4,071[78]	186[78]	45[78]	24,970[78]
1994	18	2,161	4,070	196	45	24
1995	19	2,030	3,867	165	45	26
1996	19	1,989	4,016	134	42	27
1997	19	1,866	4,080	121	38	26
1998	20	1,701	4,013	93	35	28
1999	23	1,657	4,000	86	34	12

DENMARK   1861–1930

	H	C	P	S	Po
1861	325	1,121	304	1,749	…
1866	353	1,194	382	1,875	…
1871	317	1,239	442	1,842	…
1876	352	1,348	504	1,719	…
1881	348	1,470	527	1,549	…
1888	376	1,460	771	1,225	4,592
1893	411	1,696	829	1,247	5,856
1898	449	1,745	1,168	1,074	8,767
1903	487	1,840	1,457	877	11,555
1909	535	2,254	1,468	727	11,816
1914	567	2,463	2,497	515	15,140
1915	526	2,416	1,919	533	…
1916	515[11]	2,290[11]	1,983[11]	254[11]	…
1917	572	2,458	1,651	480	12,288
1918	545	2,124	621	470	9,884
1919	558	2,188	716	509	12,134
1920	563[12]	2,286[12]	1,008[12]	504[12]	13,997[12]
	602	2,504	1,116	540	14,395
1921	598	2,591	1,430	522	17,803
1922	576	2,525	1,899	442	19,184
1923	562	2,523	2,855	374	20,029
1924	548	2,667	2,868	303	20,284
1925	536	2,758	2,517	261	20,093
1926	548	2,838	3,122	233	18,524
1927	525	2,913	3,731	…	…
1928	519	3,016	3,363	…	…
1929	521[13]	3,031[13]	3,616[13]	193[13]	22,075[13]
1930	495	3,057	4,872	…	…

C5 Numbers of Livestock (in thousands)

DENMARK

	H	C	P	S	Po
1931	499	3,208	5,453	...	...
1932	496	3,237	4,886	...	...
1933	501	3,134	4,407	...	...
1934	506	3,062	3,061	...	...
1935	521	3,072	3,036	...	28,568
1936	536	3,108	3,497	...	...
1937	552	3,084	3,066	187	26,498
1938	565[13]	3,186[13]	2,842[13]	...[13]	27,863[13]
1939	594	3,326	3,183	147	33,296[14]
1940	575	3,279	3,269	...	24,568
1941	612	3,065	1,815	...	13,181
1942	613	2,919	1,211	186	10,507
1943	625	3,028	2,083	186	15,340
1944	639	3,188	2,084	203	16,836
1945	644	3,237	1,646	213	16,372
1946	653	3,167	1,768	170	17,890
1947	601	3,014	1,830	91	18,886
1948	574	2,826	1,448	77	22,806[14]
1949	532	2,949	2,684	65	25,868
1950	502	3,053	3,235	59	24,548
1951	465	3,110	3,189	56	22,250
1952	422	3,051	3,588	48	23,429
1953	399	3,068	4,310	39	24,571
1954	358	3,151	4,852	37	25,013
1955	309	3,180	4,598	33	22,959
1956	282	3,168	4,630	34	24,704
1957	254	3,214	5,409	34	23,060
1958	237	3,273	5,347	36	26,272
1959	212	3,379	6,074	42	26,506
1960	171	3,397	6,147	44	24,485
1961	125	3,593	7,095	47	30,575
1962	100	3,504	7,181	52	29,047
1963	81	3,343	7,334	61	25,281
1964	64	3,277	8,011	71	24,982
1965	53	3,345	8,591	93	20,264
1966	46	3,374	8,120	112	20,527
1967	42	3,282	8,486	122	18,595
1968	40	3,141	7,963	110	18,448
1969	42	3,000	8,022	90	18,421
1970	45	2,842	8,361	70	17,847
1971	47	2,723	8,626	57	16,220
1972	48	2,779	8,929	52	18,419
1973	50	2,957	8,423	55	16,124
1974	55	3,100	7,763	59	15,417
1975	58	3,060	7,682	61	15,262
1976	60	3,095	7,701	59	14,773
1977	61	3,099	7,925	56	14,943
1978	59	3,081	8,751	56	14,764
1979	56	3,035	9,342	54	15,016
1980	50	2,961	9,957	56	14,243
1981	44	2,914	9,799	55	15,331
1982	44[15]	2,873[15]	9,319[15]	58[15]	15,185[15]
	35	2,862	9,288	49	15,075

C5 Numbers of Livestock (in thousands)

DENMARK 1983–1999

	H	C	P	S	Po
1983	33	2,852	9,253	52	14,766
1984	33	2,750	8,717	55	14,415
1985	32	2,618	9,089	70	14,067
1986	30	2,495	9,321	89	14,008
1987	33	2,351	9,266	101	14,709
1988	34	2,323	9,217	124	14,768
1989	35	2,232	9,120	86	16,266
1990	35	2,241	9,280	100	15,498
1991	34	2,180	9,489	122	15,086
1992	29	2,115	10,345	102	18,259
1993	19	2,082	10,870	93	18,916
1994	18	2,105	10,923	145	19
1995	18	2,091	11,084	145	19
1996	20	2,093	10,842	170	19
1997	39	2,004	11,383	142	18
1998	38	1,977	12,095	156	18
1999	40	1,887	11,626	142	20

FINLAND 1881–1920

	H	C	P	S	Po[18]	R
1881	269	1,029	149	886	...	...
1882	273	1,070	151	921	...	...
1883	278	1,112	160	949	...	...
1884	282	1,140	165	961	...	...
1885	282	1,163	166	978	...	...
1886	286	1,222	178	1,020	...	...
1887	290	1,250	185	1,043	...	...
1888	285	1,254	178	1,021	...	...
1889	290	1,268	186	1,032	...	...
1890	293	1,305	194	1,054	...	...
1891	293	1,291	189	1,026	...	...
1892	290	1,287	176	996	310	106
1893	291	1,306	169	1,007	...	...
1894	297	1,364	178	1,028	...	...
1895	301	1,409	197	1,067	...	...
1896	303	1,456	215	1,092	...	...
1897	306	1,475	222	1,101	...	...
1898	307	1,485	224	1,080	...	...
1899	308	1,457	214	1,031	...	...
1900	311	1,428	211	985	...	...
1901	313	1,409	205	971	...	...
1902	316	1,406	210	942	...	...
1903	317	1,417	214	919	...	...
1904	315	1,451	216	936	...	...
1905	323	1,481	220	938	...	...
1906	326	1,475	219	912	...	...
1907	328[16]	1,491[17]	221	904	...	...
1908	281	1,149	...	...	...	...
1909	284	1,153	...	...	...	...
1910	301	1,199	422	1,330	...	...
1911	298	1,188	...	...	...	...
1912	298	1,189	...	...	...	...
1913	297	1,178	...	...	...	...
1914	294	1,167	...	...	...	...
1915	288	1,150	...	...	...	...
1916	276	1,111	...	...	...	...
1917	271	1,106	...	...	...	...
1918	262	1,076	...	815	...	...
1919	273	1,101	...	...	...	...
1920	313[16]	1,194[17]	374	1,704	879	53
	385	1,824				

C5 Numbers of Livestock (in thousands)

FINLAND 1921–1973

	H	C	P	S	Po[18]	R
1921	393	1,792	375	1,572	...	...
1922	398	1,844	378	1,571	1,113	63
1923	400	1,865	382	1,550	1,151	61
1924	403	1,864	376	1,485	1,204	61
1925	402	1,871	378	1,451	1,239	62
1926	400	1,860	391	1,414	1,258	67
1927	396	1,872	418	1,368	1,298	66
1928	394	1,917	435	1,319	1,363	59
1929	358	1,744	380	967	1,688	55
1930	357	1,810	395	1,024	1,907	64
1931	362	1,822	346	920	2,227	79
1932	360	1,806	414	965	2,741	84
1933	357	1,745	435	973	3,009	92
1934	358	1,767	496	982	2,975	96
1935	361	1,822	510	1,024	2,844	103
1936	369	1,879	459	1,025	2,879	100
1937	380	1,925	504	1,072	2,801	100
1938	390	1,954	531	1,073	2,766	107
1939	386[19]	1,938[19]	519[19]	1,000[19]	2,765[19]	93[19]
1940	348	1,470	311	729	1,865	77
1941	359	1,588	259	717	1,964	192
1942	358	1,551	213	677	1,403	172
1943	363	1,720	263	789	1,078	148
1944	358[20]	1,859[20]	364[20]	965[20]	1,082[20]	118[20]
1945	385	1,693	229	1,015	993	68
1946	381	1,674	254	1,099	1,172	84
1947	385	1,566	335	982	1,446	96
1948	382	1,451	304	999	1,918	107
1949	402[21]	1,538[21]	409[21]	1,067[21]	2,668[21]	138[21]
1950	409	1,782	446	1,220	3,524[22]	87
1951	382	1,814	442	1,096	3,871	124
1952	369	1,851	414	1,126	3,851	125
1953	339	1,809	434	998	3,667	152
1954	326	1,885	546	908	4,003	141
1955	313	1,902	523	749	4,059[18][22] / 5,858	174
1956	297	1,839	494	566	5,887	152
1957	275	1,838	589	457	6,241	162
1958	261	1,935	597	407	6,476	170
1959	254	1,949	524	381	5,478	171
1960	251	1,921	483	341	5,743	181
1961	235	2,057	534	307	6,460	202
1962	228	2,152	626	279	6,509	188
1963	220	2,195	577	238	6,842	176
1964	207	2,146	600	222	6,581	197
1965	184	2,028	595	199	6,878	193
1966	165	2,049	651	175	6,960	168
1967	141	2,036	771	173	7,284	177
1968	126[23]	2,071[23]	720[23]	155[23]	6,940[23]	185[23]
1969	101	1,981	797	159	7,248	137
1970	90	1,873	1,047	187	8,264	150
1971	73	1,865	1,183	175	8,293	174
1972	60	1,835	1,093	155	9,400	185
1973	48	1,884	1,190	145	9,600	195

C5 Numbers of Livestock (in thousands)

FINLAND   1974–1999

	H	C	P	S	Po[18]	R
1974	48	1,905	1,098	146	9,064	140
1975	44	1,843	1,078	124	8,638	156
1976	40	1,815	1,097	111	9,073	172
1977	38	1,762	1,191	105	8,689	193
1978	34	1,779	1,291	106	8,332	201
1979	32	1,736	1,332	113	8,477	206
1980	34	1,738	1,451	106	8,476	210
1981	33	1,766	1,506	103	6,907	204
1982	34	1,719	1,505	104	6,913	208
1983	35	1,681	1,466	104	7,609	180
1984	36	1,657	1,382	110	7,958	202
1985	37	1,608	1,295	112	7,469	209
1986	39	1,567	1,323	116	7,037	227
1987	40	1,498	1,342	126	6,791	230
1988	38	1,443	1,305	119	6,678	236
1989	40	1,379	1,327	108	6,338	256
1990	44	1,363	1,348	103	6,746	239
1991	45	1,315	1,290	107	5,441	260
1992	49	1,263	1,352	108	5,566	232
1993	49	1,232	1,309	120	5,547	215
1994	49	1,230	1,300	79	5,554	205
1995	50	1,185	1,295	80	5,561	226
1996	52	1,179	1,395	115	5,543	237
1997	55	1,150	1,467	150	5,230	230
1998	56	1,101	1,401	128	5,507	242
1999	56	1,086	1,351	106	5,998	239

FRANCE   1840–1910

	H	C	P	S	G
1840	2,818	11,762	4,911	32,151	964
1852	2,866[24]	11,911[24]	5,246[24]	33,282[24]	1,338[24]
1862	2,914[25]	11,813[25]	6,038[25]	29,530[25]	1,726[25]
1882	2,838	12,997	7,147	23,809	1,851
1883	2,852	11,794	5,847	21,640	1,462
1884	2,886	12,018	5,881	22,328	1,553
1885	2,911	13,105	5,881	22,617	1,483
1886	2,938	13,275	5,775	22,688	1,426
1887	2,909	13,395	5,979	22,880	1,545
1888	2,892	13,379	5,847	22,631	1,546
1889	2,881	13,518	6,038	21,997	1,505
1890	2,862	13,562	6,017	21,658	1,505
1891	2,883	13,662	6,096	21,792	1,480
1892	2,795	13,719	7,421	21,116	1,485
1893	2,768	12,154	5,861	20,276	1,466
1894	2,807	12,879	6,038	20,722	1,485
1895	2,812	13,234	6,306	21,164	1,510
1896	2,850	13,334	6,402	21,191	1,499
1897	2,899	13,487	6,263	21,445	1,496
1898	2,894	13,418	6,231	21,278	1,502
1899	2,917	13,551	6,305	21,358	1,504
1900	2,903	14,521	6,740	20,180	1,558
1901	2,926	14,674	6,758	19,670	1,529
1902	3,028	14,929	7,209	18,477	1,532
1903	3,082	14,105	7,561	17,954	1,563
1904	3,139	14,137	7,522	17,801	1,462
1905	3,169	14,316	7,559	17,783	1,477
1906	3,165	13,968	7,049	17,461	1,457
1907	3,095	13,940	6,995	17,460	1,421
1908	3,216	14,240	7,202	17,456	1,425
1909	3,236	14,298	7,306	17,358	1,418
1910	3,198	14,532	6,900	17,111	1,418

C5 Numbers of Livestock (in thousands)

FRANCE 1911–1963

	H	C	P	S	G
1911	3,236	14,436	6,720	16,425	1,424
1912	3,222	14,706	6,904	16,468	1,409
1913	3,222[26]	14,788[26]	7,036[26]	16,131[26]	1,435[26]
1914	2,205	12,668	5,926	14,038	1,308
1915	2,209	12,520	4,910	12,262	1,231
1916	2,246	12,342	4,362	10,845	1,177
1917	2,303	12,242	4,165	9,881	1,161
1918	2,233[25][26]	12,251[25][26]	4,377[25][26]	9,061[25][26]	1,197[25][26]
1919	2,413	12,374	4,081	8,991	1,175
1920	2,635	13,217	4,942	9,406	1,341
1921	2,706	13,344	5,166	9,600	1,361
1922	2,778	13,576	5,196	9,782	1,368
1923	2,848	13,749	5,406	9,925	1,353
1924	2,859	14,025	5,802	10,172	1,377
1925	2,880	14,373	5,793	10,537	1,378
1926	2,894	14,482	5,777	10,775	1,388
1927	2,927	14,941	6,019	10,693	1,405
1928	2,936	15,005	6,017	10,445	1,372
1929	2,986	15,631	6,102	10,452	1,885
1930	2,924	15,467	6,329	10,152	1,675
1931	2,919	15,434	6,398	9,845	1,488
1932	2,901	15,643	6,488	9,762	1,463
1933	2,878	15,830	6,769	9,730	1,448
1934	2,838	15,705	7,044	9,571	1,405
1935	2,810	15,670	7,043	9,558	1,316
1936	2,774	15,762	7,089	9,808	1,359
1937	2,742	15,804	7,117	9,994	1,447
1938	2,692[27]	15,622[27]	7,127[27]	9,872[27]	1,416[27]
1939	2,123	14,189	6,380	8,948	1,277
1940	2,115	14,381	4,978	8,182	1,246
1941	2,193	15,515	4,750	7,771	1,065
1942	2,190[27]	15,806[27]	4,405[27]	7,092[27]	1,084[27]
1943	2,120	14,516	3,656	6,615	931
1944	2,046[27]	13,480[27]	3,667[27]	6,224[27]	851[27]
1945	2,257	14,273	4,386	6,632	1,021
1946	2,354	15,100	5,334	7,259	1,146
1947	2,407	15,126	5,678	7,406	1,145
1948	2,418	15,434	6,424	7,510	1,236
1949	2,414[28]	15,432[28]	6,760[28]	7,480[28]	1,282[28]
1950	2,397	15,801	6,824	7,511	1,297
1951	2,380	16,235	7,222	7,585	1,294
1952	2,333	16,281	7,179	7,675	1,289
1953	2,287	16,911	7,287	7,839	1,278
1954	2,215	17,322	7,570	8,013	1,251
1955	2,161	17,572	7,729	8,216	1,280
1956	2,064	17,693	7,759	8,403	1,270
1957	1,982	17,924	8,131	8,573	1,240
1958	1,903	18,466	8,469	8,749	1,199
1959	1,825	18,735	8,357	8,942	1,164
1960	1,729	19,501	8,603	9,063	1,172
1961	1,617	20,583	9,217	8,924	1,176
1962	1,526	20,265	9,080	8,945	1,124
1963	1,357	20,041	8,967	8,626	1,069

C5 Numbers of Livestock (in thousands)

FRANCE

	H	C	P	S	G
1964	1,228	20,244	9,043	8,821	1,041
1965	1,114	20,640	9,239	9,056	1,014
1966	1,044	21,184	9,840	9,186	1,017
1967	874	21,679	10,693	9,510	924
1968	750[29]	21,566[29]	9,602[29]	9,794[29]	919[29]
1969	697	21,719	10,463	10,037	925
1970	626	21,723	11,483	10,239	924
1971	524	21,764	11,386	10,115	909
1972	447	22,509	11,387	10,442	899
1973	425	23,701	11,560	10,375	923
1974	413	24,119	12,031	10,568	959
1975	398	24,078	11,451	10,803	991
1976	398	23,840	11,509	11,046	1,021
1977	380	23,762	11,548	11,415	1,048
1978	374	23,906	11,340	11,642	1,080
1979	364	23,919	11,446	11,911	1,125
1980	307	23,548	11,563	12,969	1,226
1981	303	23,597	11,717	13,094	1,222
1982	299	23,828	11,724	13,118	1,208
1983	298	23,890	11,814	12,915	1,164
1984	294	23,475	11,744	12,618	1,106
1985	291	23,288	11,811	12,432	1,086
1986	287	22,893	12,419	12,044	1,090
1987	284	22,189	12,643	12,000	1,091
1988	287	21,780	12,480	12,000	1,103
1989	292	21,419	12,366	11,943	1,215
1990	292	21,446	12,239	11,970	1,240
1991	322	20,970	12,068	11,490	1,236
1992	340	20,328	12,564	12,068	1,121
1993	345	20,112	13,383	12,564	1,071
1994	332	20,099	14	11,505	1,055
1995	338	20,524	15	10,320	1,069
1996	338	20,661	15	10,556	1,188
1997	340	20,664	15	10,463	1,202
1998	347	20,023	15	10,316	1,200
1999	348	20,265	15	10,240	1,199

GERMANY

	H	C	P	S	G	Po
1816	...	9,317	3,243	...	...	...
1819	...	9,914	3,322	...	...	...
1822	...	9,877	3,593	...	...	...
1825	...	10,371	4,105	...	...	...
1828	...	10,424	3,832	...	...	...
1831	...	10,844	4,037	...	...	...
1834	...	11,661	4,514	...	...	...
1837	...	12,098	4,502	...	...	...
1840	...	12,755	5,245	...	...	...
1843	...	12,605	4,919	...	...	...
1846	...	13,155	5,116	...	...	...
1849	...	13,102	5,735	...	...	...
1852	...	13,107	4,751	...	...	...
1855	...	13,265	4,786	...	...	...
1858	...	13,160	5,884	...	...	...
1861	...	13,417	5,995	...	...	...
1864	...	14,011	7,279	...	...	...
1867	...	13,536[31]	8,349[31]	...	...	...

C5 Numbers of Livestock (in thousands)

	H	C	P	S	G	Po
1872	...	14,307	8,549	...	...	...
1873	3,352	15,777	7,124	24,999	2,320	...
1882	...	14,141	11,047	...	...	...
1883	3,523	15,787	9,206	19,190	2,641	...
1892	3,836	17,556[30]	12,174	13,590	3,092	...
1900	4,195	18,940[30]	16,807	9,693	3,267	64,102
1904	4,267	19,332[30]	18,921	7,907	3,330	...
1907	...	...	...	...	...	76,625
1912	...	...	...	...	...	82,164
1913	4,558	20,994	25,659	5,521	3,548	...
1914	3,435	21,829	25,341	5,471	3,538	...
1915	3,342	20,317	17,287	5,073	3,438	...
1916	3,304	20,874	17,002	4,979	3,940	65,178
1917	3,324[31][32]	20,095[31][32]	11,052[31][32]	4,954[31][32]	4,315[31][32]	58,995[31][32]
	3,257	19,650	10,778	4,918	4,210	57,347
1918	3,425	17,650	10,271	5,347	4,321	51,305
1919	3,465	16,318	11,518	5,341	4,140	...
1920	3,588	16,807	14,179	6,150	4,459	60,955
1921	3,683[32]	16,851[32]	15,879[32]	5,890[32]	4,331[32]	68,015[32]
	3,666	16,791	15,818	5,891	4,296	67,160
1922	3,650	16,316	14,678	5,566	4,140	65,200
1923	...	16,653	17,226	6,094	4,658	...
1924	3,855	17,326	16,895	5,735	4,360	71,706
1925	3,917	17,202	16,200	4,753	3,796	71,504
1926	3,873	17,221	19,423	4,080	3,484	75,705
1927	3,810	18,011	22,899	3,819	3,225	79,418
1928	3,718	18,414	20,106	3,635	2,890	84,509
1929	3,617	18,033	19,944	3,480	2,625	92,154
1930	3,522	18,470	23,442	3,504	2,581	98,232
1931	3,451	19,124	23,080	3,499	2,516	92,449
1932	3,395	19,139	22,859	3,405	2,503	93,538
1933	3,397	19,739	23,891	3,387	2,588	96,901
1934	3,360[33]	19,198[33]	23,170[33]	3,483[33]	2,494[33]	94,416[33]
	3,370	19,266	23,298	3,487	2,556	94,972
1935	3,390	18,938	22,827	3,928	2,501	94,145
1936	3,410	20,088	25,892	4,341	2,634	97,036
1937	3,434	20,504	23,847	4,692	2,630	93,261
1938	3,443	19,911	23,481	4,809	2,509	97,130
1939	3,023	19,948	25,240	4,852	2,306	97,117
1940	3,128	19,663	21,578	4,862	2,174	96,631
1941	3,093	19,432	18,303	4,984	2,030	82,117
1942	3,096	19,102	15,025	5,196	2,213	74,248
1943	3,142	19,598	16,549	5,671	2,330	77,171
1944	3,232	20,286	15,336	6,802	...	...

C5 Numbers of Livestock (in thousands)

EAST GERMANY 1946–1989

	H	C	P	S	G	Po
1946	646	2,767	1,969	748	899	...
1947	649	2,782	2,074	686	1,072	...
1948	665	2,879	2,616	723	1,398	...
1949	695	3,317	4,322	900	...	...
1950	723	3,615	5,705	1,085	1,628	22,726
1951	745	3,808	7,088	1,240	1,578	26,584
1952	749	3,936	9,100	1,428	1,327	27,230
1953	727	3,796	8,208	1,550	1,136	25,834
1954	695	3,793	8,367	1,712	961	26,782
1955	669	3,760	9,029	1,807	860	27,300
1956	641	3,719	8,326	1,893	764	28,732
1957	624	3,744	8,255	2,019	694	31,391
1958	607	4,145	7,504	2,111	625	33,138
1959	560	4,465	8,283	2,115	547	38,604
1960	447	4,675	8,316	2,015	439[34]	36,910[34]
1961	403	4,548	8,864	1,930	446[35]	35,879[34]
1962	369	4,508	8,045	1,792	388[34]	35,626[34]
1963	341	4,614	9,289	1,899	397	39,581
1964	306	4,682	8,759	1,972	353	38,210
1965	272	4,762	8,878	1,963	302	37,988
1966	250	4,918	9,312	1,928	278	37,070
1967	219	5,019	9,254	1,818	236	37,976
1968	188	5,109	9,523	1,794	204	38,802
1969	148	5,171	9,237	1,696	158	42,565
1970	127	5,190	9,648	1,598	135	43,034
1971	106	5,293	9,995	1,607	113	43,343
1972	94	5,379	10,361	1,657	96	43,658
1973	82	5,482	10,849	1,742	78	45,667
1974	76	5,585	11,519	1,847	65	47,530
1975	70	5,532	11,501	1,883	53	47,122
1976	68	5,471	11,291	1,870	42	48,444
1977	66	5,549	11,757	1,927	34	48,258
1978	66	5,572	11,734	1,965	29	50,240
1979	66	5,596	12,132	1,979	25	51,444
1980	70	5,772	1,287	2,038	23	51,611
1981	76	5,749	12,869	2,169	23	54,392
1982	81	5,690	12,107	2,198	22	51,356
1983	88	5,768	13,057	2,359	24	53,018
1984	101	5,848	13,191	2,527	22	51,317
1985	105	5,826	12,945	2,587	22	50,680
1986	105	5,804	12,840	2,647	21	50,216
1987	104	5,720	12,503	2,656	19	50,719
1988	102	5,710	12,464	2,634	19	49,430
1989	107	5,724	12,013	2,603	19	...

included in West Germany

C5   Numbers of Livestock (in thousands)

WEST GERMANY   **1948–1999**

	H	C	P	S	G	Po
1946	…	…	…	…	…	…
1947	…	…	…	…	…	…
1948	1,617	10,569	6,755	2,491	1,428	28,221
1949	1,629	10,883	9,698	2,020	1,445	44,218
1950	1,570	11,149	11,890	1,643	1,347	51,801
1951	1,455	11,375	13,603	1,666	1,302	54,271
1952	1,360	11,641	12,979	1,544	1,153	54,768
1953	1,271	11,641	12,435	1,352	1,024	59,097
1954	1,172	11,521	14,525	1,226	891	58,856
1955	1,099	11,553	14,593	1,188	766	56,040
1956	1,025	11,815	14,408	1,146	660	57,680
1957	967[33]	11,948[33]	15,418[33]	1,127[33]	567[33]	60,161[33]
	974	12,009	15,495	1,135	587	60,962
1958	912	12,127	14,734	1,113	498	62,327
1959	814	12,480	14,876	1,084	414	64,083
1960	710	12,867	15,776	1,035	352	63,983
1961	634[36]	13,277[36]	17,207[36]	1,010[36]	292[36]	69,267[36]
	636	13,281	17,218	1,011	292	69,447
1962	560	13,355	16,869	981	236	69,253
1963	493	13,014	16,643	899	189	76,014
1964	417	13,053	18,146	841	150	80,616
1965	360	13,680	17,723	797	122	85,246
1966	312	13,973	17,682	812	105	91,998
1967	283	13,981	19,033	810	89	91,388
1968	264	14,061	18,732	830	75	91,866
1969	254	14,286	19,323	841	60	98,955
1970	253	14,026	20,969	843	50	101,545
1971	265	13,638	19,985	850	43	102,181
1972	283	13,892	20,028	908	40	102,174
1973	320	14,364	20,452	1,016	38	99,143
1974	325	14,430	20,234	1,040	…	91,538
1975	341	14,493	19,805	1,094	…	90,826
1976	355	14,496	20,589	1,091	…	90,462
1977	377	14,763	21,386	1,135	36	92,563
1978	378	15,007	22,641	1,136	…	90,371
1979	380	15,050	22,374	1,146	…	87,862
1980	382	15,070	22,553	1,179	…	87,139
1981	364	14,992	22,310	1,108	…	80,509
1982	369	15,098	22,478	1,172	…	83,033
1983	354	15,552	…	1,218	…	78,304
1984	370	15,688	23,617	1,300	…	82,295
1985	…	15,627	24,282	1,296	…	74,996
1986	368	15,305	24,503	1,383	…	76,269
1987	…	14,887	23,670	1,414	…	…
1988	375	14,659	22,589	1,464	…	76,884
1989	375	14,563	22,165	1,533	…	72,035
			Germany			
1990	484	20,287	31,819	3,239	…	106,053
1991	491	20,970	26,063	2,488	…	106,055
1992	492	20,328	26,075	2,369	…	95,632
1993	496	20,112	26,044	2,360	…	101,139
1994	599	18,671	26,075	2,368	92	101,139
1995	652	15,962	24,698	2,340	95	101,139
1996	652	15,889	23,737	2,394	100	104,000
1997	670	15,760	24,283	2,324	105	102,731
1998	600	15,227	24,795	2,302	115	105,000
1999	524	14,942	26,293	2,280	125	107,700

C5 Numbers of Livestock (in thousands)

GREECE[37]   1860-1966

	H	A&M	C	P	S	G	Po
1860	83[37]	99[37]	259[37]	134[37]	2,540[37]	2,408[37]	...
1899	159	230	417	80	4,568	3,339	...
1911	149[37]	212[37]	298[37]	227[37]	3,545[37]	2,638[37]	2,819[37]
1914	64[37]	207[37]	331[37]	138[37]	2,614[37]	1,650[37]	1,585[37]
1916	212[37]	423[37]	435[37]	302[37]	4,790[37]	3,482[37]	4,663[37]
1917	218	395	571	351	5,548	3,575	3,794
1918	186[37]	355[37]	649[37]	365[37]	5,468[37]	3,473[37]	4,453[37]
1919	...	...	...	...	...	...	...
1920	201	364	659	416	5,811	3,418	5,073
1921	177[37]	371[37]	675[37]	404[37]	5,789[37]	3,717[37]	5,410[37]
1922	211	377	754	407	5,961	4,212	5,777
1923	194	355	671	334	5,643	3,674	5,956
1924	259	422	844	390	6,623	4,169	6,072
1925	270	437	854	452	6,636	4,103	7,860
1926	281	457	925	510	6,951	4,669	7,313
1927	277	464	909	453	6,442	4,579	7,738
1928	290	493	910	419	6,920	4,919	8,693
1929	323	528	831	276	5,806	4,179	...
1930	317	497	837	335	6,799	4,637	8,635
1931	325	512	868	423	7,072	4,626	9,037
1932	324	524	875	472	6,927	4,678	10,063
1933	341	544	914	507	7,427	4,952	11,502
1934	347	551	950	584	7,910	5,207	11,251
1935	361	556	957	624	8,185	5,286	11,246
1936	359	589	986	607	8,440	5,514	12,067
1937	372	597	998	465	8,451	5,288	12,330
1938	363	588	967	430	8,139	4,356	11,945
1939	...	...	1,103	358	7,795	3,499	11,945
1940-3	...	...	...	...	...	...	...
1944	194[37]	381[37]	505[37]	280[37]	5,300[37]	2,700[37]	8,200[37]
1945	200	411	533	330	5,600	2,900	7,816
1946	220	455	561	400	6,000	3,130	8,377
1947	241	504	693	480	7,116	3,535	8,324
1948	237	520	709	509	6,767	3,527	8,516
1949	246	562	751	537	6,785	3,629	8,748
1950	279	621	815	582	6,905	3,710	9,050
1951	292	651	846	636	7,326	3,958	10,010
1952	305	668	873	587	7,784	4,139	10,506
1953	315	692	904	603	8,254	4,510	11,278
1954	317	704	917	603	8,738	4,643	12,056
1955	326	716	957	621	8,970	4,795	12,748
1956	332	726	981	641	9,275	4,894	13,595
1957	333	731	1,005	640	9,195	4,939	14,122
1958	331	734	1,028	631	9,255	5,010	14,656
1959	328	731	1,046	638	9,374	5,066	13,873
1960	327	729	1,074	628	9,353	5,064	14,337
1961	337	715	1,069	547	8,962	4,603	15,030
1962	329	695	1,060	513	8,899	4,389	17,161
1963	318	687	1,034	483	8,513	4,153	17,851
1964	306	675	1,017	486	8,097	3,990	18,535
1965	294	654	1,046	558	7,819	3,895	22,424
1966	279	635	1,082	553	7,829	3,945	25,707

C5   Numbers of Livestock (in thousands)

GREECE[37]

	H	A&M	C	P	S	G	Po
1967	265	609	1,094	492	7,874	4,042	25,626
1968	267	587	1,038	392	7,724	4,005	25,916
1969	255	599	997	383	7,680	4,054	26,133
1970	232	537	952	446	7,535	4,130	24,558
1971	216	515	986	504	7,686	4,185	29,005
1972	194	487	1,055	590	7,906	4,261	31,050
1973	180	467	1,232	826	8,367	4,472	29,959
1974	166	442	1,240	761	8,274	4,476	30,417
1975	158	431	1,184	709	8,361	4,608	29,218
1976	149	416	1,115	819	8,300	4,566	30,348
1977	138	397	1,036	866	8,075	4,508	28,529
1978	125	377	975	892	8,029	4,512	29,979
1979	116	356	932	948	8,043	4,532	29,747
1980	105	341	881	993	8,048	4,755	29,881
1981	95	325	830	1,017	8,144	4,526	29,846
1982	86	308	792	1,059	8,227	4,637	30,553
1983	80	293	755	1,065	8,252	4,744	29,388
1984	74	276	725	1,061	8,258	4,816	29,424
1985	67	261	722	1,009	8,342	4,935	28,324
1986	62	247	761	1,130	8,617	5,218	27,584
1987	65	258	741	1,139	8,613	5,282	26,892
1988	60	255	731	1,226	8,670	5,339	27,295
1989	60	251	687	1,160	8,723	5,970	27,578
1990	60	248	634	1,143	8,660	5,904	26,767
1991	50	187	616	1,125	9,759	5,918	...
1992	45	170	629	1,040	9,694	5,832	...
1993	45	160	608	1,143	9,659	5,449	...
1994	38	140	579	1,013	8,706	5,378	27,844
1995	36	127	578	1,009	8,802	5,379	27,979
1996	35	115	581	994	8,869	5,525	27,683
1997	33	112	580	987	8,896	5,570	27,800
1998	32	100	580	998	8,884	5,600	28,266
1999	31	106	583	933	8,930	5,520	28,453

HUNGARY[38]

	H	C	P	S	Po
1842[39]	1,554	5,607	4,958	[20,017]	...
1857	1,964	4,291	4,088	11,087	...
1884	1,749	4,879	4,804	10,595	...
1895	1,997	5,830	6,447	7,527	...
1911	2,001	6,184	6,416	7,698	...
1924	850	1,896	2,458	1,814	...
1925	876	1,920	2,633	1,891	...
1926	865	1,847	2,520	1,804	...
1927	903	1,805	2,387	1,611	...
1928	918	1,812	2,662	1,566	...
1929	892	1,819	2,582	1,573	...
1930	860	1,785	2,362	1,464	
1931	865	1,814	2,715	1,440	
1932	846	1,819	2,361	1,210	
1933	820	1,697	1,899	1,056	
1934	803	1,678	2,502	1,087	
1935	807	1,756	3,176	1,228	
1936	794	1,742	2,554	1,350	
1937	798	1,756	2,624	1,484	
1938	814	1,882	3,110	1,629	17,617
1939	...	...	...	...	...
1940	865	2,068	4,390	1,510	...
1941	844	2,049	3,949	1,254	...
1942	900	2,365	4,670	1,709	...
1943	...	...	...	...	...

C5 Numbers of Livestock (in thousands)

HUNGARY[38]

	H	C	P	S	Po
1944	...	...	...	...	...
1945	329	1,070[40]	1,114	328	...
1946	399	1,100[40]	1,327	370	...
1947	490	1,479[40]	1,894	508	...
1948	651	1,993[40]	2,771	579	...
1949	600	1,942	3,316	910	...
1950	712	2,222	5,542	1,049	18,181
1951	697	2,009	4,298	1,143	18,830
1952	698	2,091	4,740	1,481	18,190
1953	681	2,236	4,977	1,637	16,616
1954	683	2,075	4,454	1,869	23,040
1955	711	2,128	5,818	1,857	23,536
1956	729	2,170	6,056	1,930	23,880
1957	720	1,973	4,996	1,873	24,878
1958	724	1,937	5,338	2,050	26,114
1959	717	2,004	6,225	2,155	26,698
1960	628	1,971	5,356	2,381	26,844
1961	463	1,957	5,921	2,643	27,349
1962	374	1,987	6,409	2,850	27,345
1963	339	1,906	5,428	3,043	28,283
1964	323	1,883	6,358	3,305	21,266
1965	321	1,964	6,963	3,400	29,209
1966	295	1,973	5,799	3,270	31,325
1967	287	2,014	6,005	3,274	30,738
1968	274	2,096	6,609	3,311	27,351
1969	249	2,006	5,970	3,277	34,253
1970	231	1,933	5,970	3,024	35,097
1971	219	1,882	7,594	2,054	35,400
1972	204	1,893	6,858	1,936	30,678
1973	189	1,930	8,011	1,813	32,744
1974	163[41]	2,017[41]	8,293[41]	2,021[41]	33,154[41]
1975	156	1,904	6,953	2,039[41]	38,667
1976	147	1,887	7,854	2,350	43,449
1977	144	1,949	7,850	2,619	43,260
1978	134	1,966	8,011	2,863	43,294
1979	126	1,925	8,355	2,927	41,240
1980	120	1,918	8,330	3,090	42,764
1981	112	1,945	8,296	3,140	42,787
1982	112	1,922	9,035	3,180	45,397
1983	111	1,907	9,844	2,977	41,267
1984	102	1,901	9,237	2,832	40,962
1985	98	1,766	8,280	2,465	38,376
1986	95	1,725	8,687	2,337	37,176
1987	88	1,664	8,216	2,336	36,222
1988	76	1,690	8,327	2,216	35,607
1989	75	1,598	7,660	2,069	34,190
1990	77	1,571	8,000	1,865	31,121
1991	76	1,420	5,993	1,808	28,912
1992	75	1,159	5,364	1,752	30,535
1993	75	1,002	5,002	1,280	26,542
1994	71	999	5,002	1,252	30,813
1995	78	910	4,356	947	33,906
1996	71	928	5,032	977	31,458
1997	79	909	5,289	872	27,692
1998	72	871	4,931	858	30,983
1999	70	873	5,479	909	30,557

C5   Numbers of Livestock (in thousands)

IRELAND   1841–1898

	H	C	P	S	Po
1841	...	1,863	1,413	2,106	8,459
1847	558	2,591	622	2,186	5,691
1848	...	...	...	...	...
1849	526	2,771	795	1,777	6,328
1850	527	2,918	928	1,876	6,945
1851	522	2,967	1,085	2,122	7,471
1852	525	3,095	1,073	2,614	8,176
1853	540	3,383	1,145	3,143	8,661
1854	546	3,498	1,343	3,722	8,630
1855	556	3,564	1,178	3,602	8,367
1856	573	3,588	919	3,694	8,908
1857	600	3,621	1,255	3,452	9,491
1858	611	3,667	1,410	3,495	9,563
1859	629	3,816	1,266	3,593	10,252
1860	620	3,606	1,271	3,542	10,061
1861	614	3,472	1,102	3,556	10,371
1862	603	3,255	1,154	3,456	9,917
1863	580	3,144	1,067	3,308	9,649
1864	562	3,262	1,058	3,367	10,424
1865	548	3,498	1,306	3,694	10,682
1866	536	3,746	1,497	4,274	10,890
1867	524	3,708	1,235	4,836	10,335
1868	525	3,647	870	4,901	10,603
1869	528	3,734	1,082	4,651	10,802
1870	533	3,800	1,461	4,337	11,159
1871	538	3,976	1,621	4,233	11,717
1872	541	4,059	1,389	4,263	11,738
1873	532	4,147	1,044	4,485	11,863
1874	527	4,125	1,099	4,442	12,068
1875	526	4,115	1,252	4,254	12,139
1876	535	4,117	1,425	4,009	13,619
1877	553	3,998	1,469	3,988	13,566
1878	562	3,985	1,269	4,095	13,711
1879	572	4,068	1,072	4,018	13,783
1880	557	3,922	850	3,562	13,430
1881	548	3,957	1,096	3,256	13,972
1882	539	3,987	1,430	3,072	13,999
1883	534	4,097	1,348	3,219	13,382
1884	535	4,113	1,307	3,245	12,747
1885	547	4,229	1,269	3,478	13,851
1886	549	4,184	1,263	3,366	13,910
1887	557	4,157	1,408	3,378	14,461
1888	565	4,099	1,398	3,627	14,486
1889	574	4,094	1,381	3,789	14,857
1890	585	4,240	1,570	4,323	15,408
1891	593	4,449	1,368	4,723	15,276
1892	606	4,531	1,113	4,828	15,336
1893	614	4,464	1,152	4,421	16,097
1894	623	4,392	1,389	4,105	16,181
1895	630	4,358	1,338	3,913	16,370
1896	629	4,408	1,405	4,081	17,538
1897	610	4,465	1,327	4,158	17,777
1898	591	4,487	1,254	4,288	17,687

C5 Numbers of Livestock (in thousands)

IRELAND 1899–1921

	H	C	P	S	Po
1899	580	4,507	1,363	4,365	18,234
1900	567	4,609	1,269	4,387	18,547
1901	565	4,673	1,219	4,379	18,811
1902	580	4,782	1,328	4,216	18,504
1903	596	4,664	1,384	3,945	18,154
1904	605	4,677	1,315	3,828	18,257
1905	609	4,645	1,164	3,749	18,549
1906	604	4,639	1,244	3,715	18,977[42]
1907	596	4,676	1,317	3,817	24,327
1908	605	4,792	1,218	4,126	24,031
1909	599	4,700	1,149	4,133	24,105
1910	613	4,689	1,200	3,980	24,339
1911	616	4,712	1,415	3,907	25,448
1912	618	4,848	1,324	3,829	25,526
1913	614	4,933	1,060	3,621	25,701
1914	619	5,052	1,306	3,601	26,919
1915	561	4,844	1,205	3,600	26,089
1916	599	4,970	1,290	3,764	26,473
1917	598	4,909	947	3,744	22,245
1918	619	4,863	974	3,627	24,424
1919	625	5,029	978	3,513	...
1920	624	5,023	982	3,586	...
1921	...	5,197	977	3,708	...

SOUTHERN IRELAND 1922–1947

	H	C	P	S	Po
1922	487	4,375	938	2,794	17,246
1923	487	4,278	1,286	2,666	17,278
1924	473	4,268	987	2,726	16,982
1925	460	3,991	732	2,813	17,279
1926	434	3,947	884	3,003	21,367
1927	424	4,047	1,178	3,120	21,584
1928	429	4,125	1,183	3,263	21,714
1929	433	4,137	945	3,375	22,089
1930	448	4,038	1,052	3,515	22,900
1931	450	4,029	1,227	3,575	22,782
1932	446	4,025	1,108	3,461	22,536
1933	441	4,137	931	3,405	22,505
1934	429	4,086	968	2,931	19,984
1935	420	4,019	1,088	3,042	19,485
1936	424	4,014	1,017	3,062	20,312
1937	429	3,955	934	3,000	19,491
1938	442	4,056	959	3,197	19,630
1939	445	4,057	931	3,048	19,551
1940	459	4,023	1,049	3,071	19,975
1941	459	4,150	764	2,909	17,393
1942	452	4,084	519	2,693	17,365
1943	454	4,136	434	2,560	17,097
1944	459	4,246	381	2,663	18,330
1945	465	4,211	426	2,581	18,314
1946	452	4,146	479	2,423	18,276
1947	438	3,950	457	2,094	17,304

C5 Numbers of Livestock (in thousands)

SOUTHERN IRELAND 1948–1999

	H	C	P	S	Po
1948	421	3,921	457	2,058	20,790
1949	402	4,127	675	2,192	22,077
1950	391	4,322	645	2,385	21,132
1951	367	4,376	558	2,616	18,838
1952	342	4,309	719	2,857	19,379
1953	329	4,397	882	2,930	19,114
1954	313	4,504	958	3,113	16,062
1955	296	4,483	799	3,269	16,076
1956	276	4,537	747	3,439	16,362
1957	258	4,417	900	3,720	14,502
1958	244	4,466	948	4,174	14,078
1959	234	4,684	852	4,412	13,904
1960	224	4,741	951	4,314	13,047
1961	207	4,713	1,056	4,528	12,843
1962	196	4,741	1,111	4,671	11,870
1963	190	4,860	1,102	4,691	11,888
1964	180	4,962	1,108	4,950	11,627
1965	172	5,359	1,266	5,014	11,405
1966	158	5,590	1,014	4,664	10,793
1967	143	5,586	985	4,239	10,593
1968	134	5,572	1,063	4,077	10,492
1969	125	5,688	1,116	4,006	10,335
1970	124	5,956	1,192	4,082	11,231
1971	117	6,134	1,323	4,189	11,777
1972	112	6,438	1,199	4,260	11,734
1973	103	6,970	1,108	4,261	11,339
1974	98	7,215	923	4,060	10,707
1975	89	7,168	796	3,683	9,536
1976	83	6,954	925	3,475	9,532
1977	80	7,124	939	3,534	9,336
1978	76	7,125	1,056	3,385	9,557
1979	...	7,178	1,154	3,376	9,358
1980	68	6,909	1,030	3,292	9,903
1981	65	6,760	1,021	3,332	9,168
1982	61	6,760	1,057	3,431	9,461
1983	60	6,859	1,081	3,583	9,171
1984	58	6,872	1,035	4,074	8,822
1985	58	6,907	1,004	4,487	8,914
1986	56	6,718	1,003	5,012	8,795
1987	54	6,647	999	5,595	8,781
1988	53	6,604	979	6,656	8,941
1989	53	...	961	4,991	8,496
1990	53	...	99	5,782	8,933
1991	53	...	1,069	6,001	9,920
1992	53	...	1,346	5,988	10,062
1993	53	...	1,423	6,125	10,266
1994	48	6,308	1,487	5,991	10,966
1995	40	6,410	1,498	5,775	11,906
1996	45	6,532	1,542	5,583	11,221
1997	52	6,757	1,665	5,391	11,233
1998	50	6,992	1,717	5,634	10,991
1999	76	7,093	1,800	5,624	11,636

C5   Numbers of Livestock (in thousands)

NORTHERN IRELAND   **1922–1974**

	H	C	P	S	Po
1922	...	800	118	425	...
1923	122	748	196	464	6,682
1924	117	736	140	509	6,814
1925	112	667	112	484	6,733
1926	109	666	158	529	7,916
1927	107	697	236	600	7,898
1928	105	738	229	624	7,979
1929	104	700	192	655	8,309
1930	104	673	216	704	8,808
1931	103	681	236	794	8,691
1932	104	715	220	792	9,371
1933	102	734	271	750	10,150
1934	101	769	380	761	10,292
1935	100	799	458	818	10,085
1936	99	770	522	835	10,570
1937	98	730	570	829	10,182
1938	99	732	561	893	10,193
1939	97	753	627	895	10,220
1940	97	732	475	854	9,122
1941	97	787	351	812	12,933
1942	95	827	271	742	14,601
1943	90	832	257	683	15,430
1944	88	886	237	672	16,646
1945	85	919	249	654	17,471
1946	77	913	312	640	19,841
1947	75	934	334	527	21,029
1948	68	966	335	575	24,234
1949	61	980	458	645	24,242
1950	55	990	523	717	20,724
1951	45	961	585	672	17,838
1952	40	941	676	795	16,456
1953	37₄₃	936	759	895	14,608
	33				
1954	30	942	820	930	11,386
1955	28	904	686	870	11,272
1956	24	918	653	873	11,536
1957	21	972	742	929	11,737
1958	19	980	700	980	12,250
1959	16	964	848	1,011	11,886
1960	13	998	985	1,099	10,393
1961	11	1,075	1,033	1,183	10,214
1962	...	1,109	1,182	1,209	9,595
1963	...	1,110	1,190	1,140	9,283
1964	...	1,112	1,152	1,094	10,557
1965	...	1,116	1,248	1,074	10,394
1966	...	1,189	1,057	1,054	10,864
1967	...	1,235	975	1,012	11,944
1968	...	1,207	1,012	962	12,059
1969	...	1,243	1,033	935	12,942
1970	...	1,320	1,069	966	13,966
1971	...	1,384	1,157	975	14,664
1972	...	1,444	1,047	1,004	14,870
1973	...	1,536	1,015	964	12,693
1974	...	1,620	839	937	11,818

C5 Numbers of Livestock (in thousands)

NORTHERN IRELAND

	H	C	P	S	Po
1975	...	1,626	645	934	12,056
1976	...	1,548	698	926	12,109
1977	...	1,565	625	957	11,070
1978	...	1,548	683	974	11,936
1979	...	1,541	722	1,000	11,884
1980	...	1,507	691	1,061	11,389
1981	...	1,436	627	1,139	11,486
1982	...	1,429	640	1,234	10,979
1983	...	1,472	651	1,324	10,513
1984	...	1,507	615	1,450	10,775
1985	...	1,514	617	1,590	10,061
1986	...	1,471	617	1,701	9,924
1987	...	1,429	607	1,858	10,380
1988	...	1,439	619	2,073	10,331
1989	...	1,485	590	2,341	9,545
1990	...	1,546	591	2,534	10,136
1991	...	1,552	589	2,592	11,013
1992	...	1,576	588	2,657	11,950
1993	...	1,578	594	2,611	12,991

ITALY[44]

	H	A & M	C[40]	P	S	G
1861	432	839	3,230	2,092	8,038	2,151
1862	399	757	3,086	1,840	7,456	1,992
1863	374	693	2,975	1,626	6,979	1,862
1864	358	643	2,900	1,452	6,609	1,758
1865	350	620	2,858	1,317	6,347	1,680
1866	350	611	2,852	1,220	6,194	1,627
1867	417	642	3,270	1,534	6,443	1,649
1868	437	669	3,343	1,511	6,508	1,649
1869	466	716	3,454	1,539	6,685	1,676
1870	505	782	3,606	1,618	6,975	1,730
1871	552	839	3,784	1,707	7,521	1,793
1872	579	884	3,932	1,777	7,596	1,839
1873	601	917	4,047	1,833	8,013	1,877
1874	615	940	4,132	1,874	8,173	1,906
1875	624	952	4,187	1,899	8,277	1,925
1876	626	953	4,209	1,910	8,323	1,936
1877	622	943	4,202	1,905	8,313	1,938
1878	622	940	4,162	1,886	8,245	1,931
1879	626	942	4,298	1,924	8,319	1,951
1880	633	952	4,505	1,983	8,436	1,979
1881	645	968	4,783	2,064	8,596	2,016
1882	660	1,014	4,930	2,094	8,611	2,027
1883	684	1,038	5,047	2,109	8,576	2,029
1884	702	1,055	5,133	2,109	8,488	2,023
1885	714	1,064	5,189	2,094	8,352	2,007
1886	721	1,064	5,215	2,065	8,163	1,983
1887	720	1,059	5,213	2,021	7,923	1,951
1888	714	1,045	5,175	1,962	7,633	1,909
1889	702	1,024	5,110	1,888	7,292	1,859
1890	684	995	5,014	1,800	6,900	1,800
1891	686	1,009	4,981	1,755	6,681	1,780
1892	688	1,023	4,965	1,725	6,524	1,775
1893	692	1,033	4,964	1,710	6,428	1,785
1894	696	1,043	4,979	1,709	6,393	1,811
1895	701	1,051	5,011	1,722	6,420	1,851

C5 Numbers of Livestock (in thousands)

ITALY[44] 1896–1949

	H	A & M	C[40]	P	S	G
1896	708	1,056	5,060	1,750	6,504	1,907
1897	715	1,060	5,124	1,793	6,655	1,978
1898	723	1,063	5,204	1,850	6,865	2,064
1899	732	1,063	5,302	1,922	7,137	2,165
1900	742	1,062	5,415	2,008	7,478	2,282
1901	753	1,075	5,544	2,109	7,863	2,413
1902	764	1,086	5,690	2,224	8,317	2,560
1903	777	1,093	5,819	2,320	8,777	2,672
1904	790	1,098	5,931	2,396	9,243	2,750
1905	805	1,099	6,028	2,453	9,714	2,793
1906	843	1,150	6,108	2,491	10,191	2,802
1907	877	1,196	6,171	2,509	10,674	2,776
1908	907	1,235	6,218	2,508	11,163	2,715
1909	933	1,269	6,284	2,519	11,552	2,658
1910	954	1,297	6,337	2,541	11,841	2,686
1911	972	1,319	6,408	2,576	12,031	2,718
1912	986	1,335	6,487	2,622	12,120	2,781
1913	995	1,345	6,574	2,680	12,110	2,875
1914	1,000	1,350	6,668	2,750	12,000	3,000
1915	903	1,288	6,482	2,585	11,998	3,029
1916	837	1,252	6,338	2,461	11,956	3,052
1917	804	1,240	6,238	2,379	11,875	3,070
1918	803	1,253	6,180	2,337	11,752	3,083
1919	833	1,292	6,165	2,338	11,744	3,080
1920	896	1,356	6,193	2,379	11,744	3,080
1921	990[44]	1,446[44]	6,264[44]	2,461[44]	11,754[44]	3,083[44]
1922	992	1,452	6,624	2,585	11,945	3,093
1923	1,000	1,460	7,000	2,750	12,100	3,100
1924	1,012	1,471	7,226	3,081	12,220	3,103
1925	1,029	1,484	7,346	3,229	12,303	3,103
1926	1,050	1,500	7,400	3,493	12,350	3,100
1927	1,042	1,487	7,297	3,574	12,109	2,641
1928	1,021	1,462	7,214	3,572	11,465	2,286
1929	988	1,423	7,149	3,487	10,851	2,037
1930	942	1,371	7,104	3,318	10,268	1,893
1931	919	1,342	7,080	3,287	9,716	1,854
1932	896	1,316	7,075	3,261	9,291	1,824
1933	874	1,291	7,090	3,239	8,933	1,804
1934	854	1,268	7,123	3,223	8,822	1,792
1935	834	1,247	7,176	3,212	8,778	1,789
1936	816	1,227	7,248	3,206	8,863	1,795
1937	796	1,224	7,300	2,814	9,095	1,804
1938	791	1,228	7,680	2,940	9,467	1,828
1939	781	1,221	7,892	3,303	9,875	1,867
1940	762	1,109	8,242	3,474	9,852	1,818
1941	743	998	8,501	3,645	9,829	1,770
1942	769	995	8,385	3,725	9,422	1,727
1943	710[44]	919[44]	7,326[44]	3,391[44]	8,194[44]	1,571[44]
1944	651	845	6,248	3,067	6,966	1,415
1945	628	806	5,885	3,044	6,845	1,411
1946	641	803	6,229	3,316	7,532	1,559
1947	691	840	7,277	3,894	8,727	1,859
1948	792[44]	1,123[44]	7,848[44]	3,949[44]	10,130[44]	2,360[44]
1949	799	1,157	8,180	4,404	10,366	2,594

C5 Numbers of Livestock (in thousands)

ITALY[44]   **1950-1999**

	H	A & M	C[40]	P	S	G
1950	798	1,169	8,350	4,055	10,295	2,491
1951	769	1,166	8,395	3,512	10,142	2,255
1952	734	1,158	8,708	4,215	10,002	2,113
1953	706	1,136	9,008	4,368	9,892	1,981
1954	669	1,126	8,831	3,745	9,452	1,798
1955	617	1,035	8,686	3,760	9,042	1,731
1956	573	965	8,440	3,863	8,568	1,679
1957	496	931	8,476	3,921	8,543	1,590
1958	474	919	8,649	3,900	8,626	1,549
1959	446	892	9,062	3,845	8,393	1,471
1960	430	860	9,399	4,148	8,343	1,440
1961	408	833	9,827	4,335	8,231	1,381
1962	390	780	9,520	4,478	8,065	1,309
1963	367	736	9,152	4,684	7,857	1,278
1964	348	701	8,608	5,029	7,762	1,236
1965	341	688	9,183	5,409	7,866	1,228
1966	331	627	9,386	5,176	8,000	1,139
1967	321	600	9,503	5,292	8,212	1,140
1968	319	548	9,539	6,186	8,285	1,124
1969	310	510	10,024	7,298	8,206	1,045
1970	296	481	9,563	9,224	8,138	1,031
1971	271	438	8,721	8,980	7,948	1,019
1972	254	400	8,611	8,196	7,846	976
1973	249	343	8,738	8,201	7,809	948
1974	250	311	8,408	8,814	7,995	958
1975	253	287	8,153	8,888	8,152	940
1976	264	277	8,446	9,097	845	948
1977	264	259	8,737	9,420	8,694	960
1978	267	243	8,487	8,921	8,973	980
1979	273	227	8,639	8,807	9,110	978
1980	272	210	8,719	8,928	9,277	1,009
1981	272	208	8,734	9,015	9,592	1,029
1982	256	166	8,797	9,132	9,257	1,059
1983	253	160	9,019	9,252	10,745	1,174
1984	246	155	9,113	9,041	11,098	1,149
1985	248	150	9,106	9,169	11,293	1,189
1986	253	142	8,908	9,278	11,451	1,201
1987	249	136	8,819	9,383	11,456	1,206
1988	256	128	8,794	9,360	11,623	1,214
1989	269	119	8,737	9,254	11,569	1,246
1990	288	84	8,746	9,520	11,575	1,229
1991	316	60	8,004	8,549	10,435	1,314
1992	330	50	7,783	8,307	10,403	1,321
1993	338	50	7,683	8,200	10,370	1,346
1994	323	40	7,459	8,348	10,461	1,378
1995	324	40	7,164	8,023	10,682	1,448
1996	315	37	7,265	8,061	10,668	1,373
1997	305	34	7,163	8,171	10,943	1,419
1998	290	29	7,166	8,281	10,894	1,347
1999	288	29	7,129	8,323	10,898	1,331

C5 Numbers of Livestock (in thousands)

NETHERLANDS 1816–1884

	H	C[45]	P	S		H	C[45]	P	S
1816	189	975	...	677	**1864**	255	1,335	295	930
1820	209	1,027	...	692	**1865**	254	1,314	296	967
1825	200	944	...	638	**1866**	254	1,272	322	1,076
					1867	255	1,361	303	1,027
1830	193	967	...	638	**1868**	253	1,368	290	950
					1869	254	1,402	300	927
1840	217	1,066	...	781					
1844	220	1,057	...	613	**1870**	252	1,411	329	900
					1871	252	1,376	319	868
1851	270	1,249	237	803	**1872**	248	1,377	320	855
1852	239	1,251	239	836	**1873**	253	1,432	360	902
1853	234	1,237	234	832	**1874**	259	1,469	352	936
1854	240	1,145	240	858					
					1875	260	1,457	339	941
1855	235	1,255	236	821	**1876**	266	1,439	352	891
1856	235	1,260	239	782	**1877**	270	1,413	360	885
1857	237	1,279	261	779	**1878**	275	1,471	360	909
1858	236	1,213	251	768	**1879**	279	1,462	337	898
1859	239	1,227	261	802					
					1880	278	1,470	335	848
1860	243	1,288	271	866	**1881**	271	1,434	376	792
1861	247	1,335	281	870	**1882**	270	1,428	404	745
1862	250	1,374	279	882	**1883**	269	1,437	421	704
1863	254	1,381	299	894	**1884**	269	1,474	427	753

NETHERLANDS 1885–1931

	H	C[45]	P	S	Hens
1885	270	1,510	442	774	...
1886	273	1,531	458	803	...
1887	274	1,526	490	804	...
1888	274	1,494	485	778	...
1889	276	1,490	494	772	...
1890	273	1,533	579	819	...
1891	272	1,532	547	811	...
1892	271	1,529	544	752	...
1893	265	1,485	571	688	...
1894	264	1,509	640	665	...
1895	266	1,543	662	679	...
1896	269	1,583	656	706	...
1897	274	1,621	654	729	...
1898	280	1,641	714	737	...
1899	285	1,647	738	755	...
1900	295	1,656	747	771	4,343
1901	302	1,649	764	752	4,561
1902	304	1,647	823	709	4,673
1903	296	1,667	883	654	4,935
1904	295[46]	1,690[46]	862[46]	607[46]	...[46]
1910	327	2,027	1,260	889	9,778[47]
1918	378	2,049	600	642	...
1919	362	1,969	450	437	...
1921	364	2,063	1,519	668	9,661
1930	299	2,366	2,018	485	24,637
1931	...	...	...	...	25,915

C5 Numbers of Livestock (in thousands)

NETHERLANDS

	H	C[45]	P	S	Hens
1932	...	...	2,736	...	26,671
1933	...	2,877	2,113	...	...
1934	269	2,830	2,082	642	34,540
1935	288	2,639	1,524	680	28,482
1936	295	2,570	1,679	655	27,788
1937	300	2,627	1,406	608	27,704
1938	312	2,763	1,538	654	29,646
1939	322	2,817	1,553	690	32,805
1940	326	2,690	1,288	574	34,908
1941	319	2,659	948	508	7,740
1942	337	2,441	491	574	3,683
1943	309	2,058	545	451	3,868
1944	...	2,190	...	...	...
1945	302	2,277	769	489	...
1946	305	2,410	1,040	558	10,915
1947	316	2,367	857	460	13,959
1948	303	2,313	871	425	17,405
1949	279	2,543	1,301	465	20,288
1950	256	2,726	1,864	390	23,465
1951	254	2,867	1,939	360	25,361
1952	245	2,862	1,847	383	23,830
1953	249	2,934	1,968	424	27,558
1954	242	3,026	1,975	407	31,951
1955	222	2,995	2,378	381	30,673
1956	210	2,962	2,332	433	35,557
1957	201	3,105	2,529	496	35,154
1958	195	3,204	2,472	543	37,797
1959	196	3,396	2,590	522	43,199
1960	187	3,507	2,955	456	42,410
1961	171	3,623	2,860	438	49,917
1962	162	3,817	2,800	482	45,890
1963	149	3,695	2,923	468	44,597
1964	137	3,567	3,268	443	45,551
1965	123	3,751	3,752	484	42,279
1966	105	3,968	3,918	558	45,285
1967	89	4,030	4,295	529	44,511
1968	...	4,116	4,683	552	45,400
1969	...	4,277	4,755	554	49,091
1970		4,366[48]	5,650[48]	610[48]	56,209[48]
		4,314	5,533	575	55,375
1971	...	4,201	6,158	572	60,125
1972	...	4,306	6,233	592	58,430
1973	...	4,675	6,425	657	60,328
1974	...	4,979	6,719	749	62,388
1975	...	4,956	7,279	760	68,053[49]
					59,482
1976	...	4,964	7,507	780	59,795
1977	...	4,877	8,288	800	59,898
1978	...	4,990	9,172	841	60,116
1979	...	5,149	9,722	895	63,195
1980	...	5,226	10,137	858	65,219
1981	...	5,191	10,315	815	67,936
1982	...	5,241	10,254	776	69,231
1983	...	5,411	10,656	772	63,840

C5 Numbers of Livestock (in thousands)

NETHERLANDS

	H	C[45]	P	S	Hens
1984	...	5,516	11,146	765	65,538
1985	...	5,248	12,383	814	71,491
1986	...	5,123	13,481	868	73,325
1987	...	4,895	14,349	985	77,243
1988	...	4,710	13,934	1,169	74,385
1989	...	4,606	13,820	1,405	71,437
1990	...	4,731	13,634	1,702	74,371
1991	...	4,876	13,788	1,800	75,193
1992	...	4,794	13,727	1,954	79,675
1993	...	4,629	13,709	2,000	77,961
1994	97	4,716	14,565	1,766	76,421
1995	100	4,654	14,397	1,674	78,548
1996	107	4,557	13,958	1,627	79,113
1997	112	4,411	14,253	1,465	79,940
1998	114	4,283	13,446	1,394	78,276
1999	116	4,206	13,567	1,401	76,791

NORWAY

	H	C	P	S	Po
1836	113	644	80	1,029	...
1846	132	843	89	1,447	...
1855	154	950	113	1,596	...
1865	149	953	96	1,705	...
1875	152	1,017	101	1,686	...
1890	151	1,007	121	1,418	...
1900	173[50]	950[50]	165[50]	999[50]	1,659[50]
1907	164	1,088	307	1,390	1,411
1917	202	1,150	238	1,295	1,884
1918	211	1,046	207	1,400	1,676
1923	193	1,131	237	1,525	2,638
1924	186	1,114	249	1,507	3,018
1925	184	1,151	253	1,529	3,173
1926	183	1,200	303	1,595	3,053
1927	183	1,210	300	1,608	2,994
1928	182	1,221	283	1,654	3,092
1929	177	1,224	289	1,533	2,929
1930	177	1,251	339	1,588	3,098
1931	177	1,310	317	1,692	3,324
1932	179	1,342	304	1,736	3,503
1933	180	1,340	420	1,764	3,544
1934	181	1,295	550	1,698	3,513
1935	183	1,328	410	1,737	3,437
1936	186	1,348	410	1,749	3,472
1937	190	1,343	445	1,739	3,481
1938	193	1,399	429	1,778	3,526
1939	204	1,455	362	1,744	3,438[51]
1940	206	1,400	400	1,700	3,000
1941	207	1,280	270	1,660	2,340
1942	208	1,250	220	1,695	1,500
1943	218	1,220	145	1,715	1,200
1944	227	1,255	220	1,795	1,200
1945	231	1,220	195	1,760	1,200
1946	238	1,267	257	1,707	1,433
1947	225	1,225	259	1,698	2,047
1948	206	1,175	248	1,630	2,726
1949	198	1,224	419	1,736	3,711
1950	191	1,237	422	1,812	3,912
1951	184	1,231	386	1,929	3,321
1952	175	1,152	418	1,987	3,197
1953	168	1,150	379	1,985	3,385
1954	159	1,181	406	1,952	3,563

C5 Numbers of Livestock (in thousands)

NORWAY   1955–1999

	H	C	P	S	Po
1955	150	1,171	464	1,922	3,482
1956	142	1,112	507	1,826	3,954
1957	133	1,103	459	1,821	3,838
1958	126[52]	1,116[52]	423[52]	1,810[52]	3,477[52]
1959	117	1,105	475	1,806	3,039
1960	109	1,129	492	1,842	3,108
1961	102	1,180	534	1,855	2,924
1962	94	1,159	550	1,864	2,717
1963	86	1,122	515	1,881	2,595
1964	77	1,102	536	1,941	2,502[51]
1965	67	1,059	568	1,989	3,278
1966	61	1,041	568	2,096	3,774
1967	53	996	590	2,067	3,876
1968	47	1,008	610	1,946	3,716
1969	42	973	658	1,874	3,872
1970	35	943	642	1,753	3,746
1971	31	932	682	1,681	3,804
1972	27	940	737	1,635	3,838
1973	25	966	766	1,648	3,997
1974	24	955	747	1,632	4,121
1975	22	915	669	1,639	3,822
1976	22	921	698	1,667	3,798
1977	21	945	658	1,874	3,836
1978	20	953	705	1,845	3,758
1979	18	971	687	1,919	4,156
1980	18	976	666	1,979	3,469
1981	16	1,017	776	2,155	3,462
1982	15	1,009	775	2,227	3,683
1983	16	975	795	2,272	3,682
1984	16	976	719	2,351	4,413
1985	16	971	697	2,415	4,106
1986	16	967	738	2,339	4,083
1987	17	946	779	2,254	4,030
1988	17	932	746	2,207	3,977
1989	17	949	697	2,183	3,656
1990	19	953	708	2,211	3,763
1991	21	984	721	2,363	3,671
1992	21	1,008	766	2,316	3,689
1993	21	1,003	745	2,316	3,729
1994	22	980	748	2,462	3,695
1995	22	998	768	2,524	3,656
1996	23	1,006	768	2,558	3,461
1997	24	1,018	692	2,448	3,240
1998	26	1,036	689	2,399	3,206
1999	26	1,046	439	2,294	3,181

POLAND   1921–1938

	H	C	P	S	Po
1921	3,289	8,063	5,287	2,193	...
1924	...	...	...	...	35,000
1927	4,069	8,601	6,329	1,918	...
1928	...	...	...	...	...
1929	4,047	9,057	4,829	2,524	...
1930	4,103	9,400	6,047	2,492	50,000
1931	4,124	9,786	7,321	2,599	...
1932	3,940	9,461	5,844	2,488	...
1933	3,773	8,985	5,753	2,557	...
1934	3,764	9,258	7,091	2,554	...
1935	3,760	9,759	6,723	2,802	...
1936	3,825	10,200	7,060	3,024	...
1937	3,889	10,572	7,696	3,188	...
1938	3,916[53]	10,554[53]	7,525[53]	3,411[53]	50,420[53]

C5 Numbers of Livestock (in thousands)

POLAND

	H	C	P	S	Po
1945	1,395[54]	3,323[54]	1,697[54]	707[54]	...
1946	1,730	3,911	2,674	727	19,365
1947	2,016	4,746	4,700	983	26,598
1948	2,297	5,748	5,100	1,410	46,061
1949	2,652	7,072	6,120	1,945	49,406
1950	2,800	7,200	9,350	2,199	46,240
1951	2,870	7,200	8,450	2,574	...
1952	2,745	7,255	8,648	2,895	...
1953	2,722	7,385	9,730	3,330	...
1954	2,650	7,687	9,788	4,170	...
1955	2,560	7,912	10,888	4,243	53,700
1956	2,547	8,353	11,561	4,223	...
1957	2,623	8,265	12,325	4,040	...
1958	2,733	8,210	11,959	3,882	...
1959	2,839	8,353	11,209	3,778	...
1960	2,805	8,695	12,615	3,662	71,858
1961	2,730	9,168	13,434	3,494	77,825
1962	2,657	9,590	13,617	3,251	75,770
1963	2,620	9,841	11,653	3,056	79,270
1964	2,593	9,940	12,918	3,022	81,434
1965	2,554	9,947	13,779	3,061	80,288
1966	2,590	10,391	14,251	3,164	81,026
1967	2,643	10,768	14,233	3,321	80,117
1968	2,673	10,940	13,911	3,328	84,269
1969	2,633	11,049	14,357	3,229	85,498
1970	2,585	10,844	13,446	3,199	87,561
1971	2,501	11,076	15,243	8,180	88,854
1972	2,422	11,453	17,347	3,110	92,875
1973	2,373	12,192	19,782	3,050	94,227
1974	2,312	13,023	21,496	3,023	96,583
1975	2,237	13,254	21,311	3,175	99,795
1976	2,151	12,879	18,847	3,430	79,193
1977	2,062	13,019	20,051	3,934	83,708
1978	1,891	13,115	21,717	4,248	83,696
1979	1,856	13,036	21,224	4,221	84,901
1980	1,780	12,649	21,326	4,207	81,165
1981	1,726	11,797	18,480	3,886	71,281
1982	1,734	11,912	19,471	3,899	67,244
1983	1,600	11,269	15,587	4,104	62,439
1984	1,537	11,197	16,657	4,534	69,271
1985	1,404	11,055	17,614	4,837	72,347
1986	1,272	10,919	18,949	4,991	59,234
1987	1,141	10,523	18,546	4,739	63,101
1988	1,051	10,322	19,605	4,377	66,188
1989	973	10,733	18,835	4,409	66,000
1990	941	10,049	19,464	4,158	70,000
1991	939	8,844	21,868	3,234	60,000
1992	900	8,221	22,086	1,870	58,000
1993	841	7,643	18,860	1,268	54,000
1994	622	7,696	19,467	869	44,292
1995	636	7,306	20,418	713	46,395
1996	569	7,136	17,964	552	43,977
1997	558	7,307	18,135	491	53,285
1998	561	7,029	19,168	453	51,120
1999	551	6,455	18,537	392	50,017

C5   Numbers of Livestock (in thousands)

PORTUGAL[55]   **1925–1999**

	H	A&M	C	P	S	G
1925	80	325	768	1,117	3,684	1,557
1934	86	388	778	1,139	3,224	1,257
1940	81	361	832	...	3,890	1,196
1955	68	359	895	1,419	3,593	707
1972	30	264	1,072	1,977	2,420	741
1979	24	178	1,173	2,450	2,081	733
1990	26	250	1,343	2,531	5,567	857
1991	24	241	1,323	2,526	5,672	878
1992	23	215	1,329	2,591	5,729	869
1993	24	198	1,324	2,603	5,798	851
1994	25	205	1,311	2,666	5,991	836
1995	23	190	1,285	2,430	5,900	819
1996	25	177	1,267	2,375	5,800	799
1997	22	162	1,299	2,394	6,300	781
1998	24	143	1,284	2,385	5,800	785
1999	19	143	1,266	2,350	5,850	750

ROMANIA   **1800–1950**

	H	C	P	S	Po
1860	461	2,608	1,057	4,410	...
1875	391	1,833	804	4,191	...
1884	533	2,376	886	4,655	...
1888	564	2,406	797	4,973	...
1890	595	2,520	926	5,002	...
1895	671	2,138	1,079	6,848	...
1900	864	2,589[56]	1,709	5,655	...
1911	825[57]	2,667[57]	1,022[57]	5,270[57]	...
1916	1,219[58]	2,873[58]	1,382[58]	7,811[58]	...
1919	1,380	4,634	2,290	7,791	...
1920	1,485	4,730	2,514	8,690	...
1921	1,687	5,521	3,132	11,194	...
1922	1,802	5,746	3,147	12,321	...
1923	1,828	5,549	2,925	12,481	...
1924	1,845	5,399	3,133	13,612	...
1925	1,815	5,049	3,088	12,950	...
1926	1,877	4,798	3,168	13,582	...
1927	1,942	4,553	3,076	12,941	...
1928	1,945	4,436	2,832	12,801	...
1929	1,959	4,334	2,413	12,406	...
1930	1,809	3,834	2,323	11,921	...
1931	1,988	4,080	3,222	12,356	...
1932	2,034	4,189	2,964	12,294	...
1933	...	...	...	...	...
1934	...	...	...	...	...
1935	2,167	4,327	2,970	11,838	...
1936	2,025	4,171	3,030	11,809	39,709
1937	2,065	4,184	3,170	12,372	38,282
1938	2,158	4,161	3,165	12,768	34,666
1939	2,043[58]	4,254[58]	2,926[58]	12,851[58]	35,406[58]
1940	1,095	2,643	1,770	8,288	22,036
1941	1,103	2,765	1,655	8,003	23,055
1942	1,113[58]	[3,087][40][58]	2,001[58]	8,093[58]	22,151[58]
1943	978	[3,315][40]	1,906	7,478	20,383
1944	...	...	...	...	...
1945	748[58]	2,484[58]	1,020[58]	5,628[58]	11,872[58]
1946	768	3,048	1,406	7,088	...
1947	...	...	...	...	...
1948	932	4,183	1,591	10,634	15,263
1949	917	4,164	1,967	10,303	14,014
1950	971	4,309	2,211	9,834	17,507

C5 Numbers of Livestock (in thousands)

ROMANIA   1951–1999

	H	C	P	S	Po
1951	1,073	4,778	2,587	11,599	27,207
1952	1,073	4,674	3,654	10,914	27,223
1953	...	...	...	...	...
1954	1,067	4,477	4,088	10,145	27,500
1955	1,120	4,630	4,370	10,882	29,500
1956	1,150	4,800	4,950	11,120	33,000
1957	1,200	4,600	3,900	10,500	35,000
1958	1,309	4,470	3,249	10,374	35,000
1959	1,223	4,394	4,008	10,662	35,000
1960	1,110	4,450	4,300	11,200	37,000
1961	1,000	4,530	4,300	11,500	38,000
1962	1,013	4,707	4,665	12,285	44,692
1963	780	4,566	4,518	12,168	34,150
1964	709	4,637	4,658	12,400	38,358
1965	689	4,756	6,034	12,734	39,910
1966	689	4,935	5,365	13,125	40,085
1967	705	5,198	5,400	14,109	43,966
1968	715	5,332	5,752	14,380	47,148
1969	703	5,136	5,853	14,298	47,618
1970	668	5,216	6,359	13,818	54,333
1971	654	5,528	7,742	14,071	61,262
1972	631	5,767	8,785	14,455	64,496
1973	610	5,897	8,987	14,302	66,511
1974	557	5,983	8,566	13,929	67,672
1975	562	6,126	8,813	13,865	78,626
1976	576	6,357	10,193	14,331	91,503
1977	550	6,306	9,744	14,463	89,019
1978	570	6,511	10,337	15,612	99,725
1979	566	6,513	10,899	15,820	95,417
1980	555	6,485	11,542	15,865	97,800
1981	598	6,303	12,464	17,288	109,244
1982	...	6,246	12,644	16,921	111,047
1983	...	6,752	14,347	18,451	119,237
1984	...	7,039	14,777	18,637	123,962
1985	672	7,077	14,319	18,609	124,770
1986	686	6,692	13,651	17,342	120,149
1987	693	6,703	14,095	17,219	125,322
1988	693	6,559	14,328	16,839	127,304
1989	702	6,416	14,351	16,210	127,564
1990	663	6,291	11,671	15,435	113,968
1991	670	5,381	12,003	14,062	121,379
1992	749	4,355	10,954	13,879	106,032
1993	721	3,683	9,852	12,079	87,725
1994	751	3,957	9,262	11,499	76,532
1995	784	3,481	7,758	10,897	70,157
1996	806	3,496	7,959	10,381	80,524
1997	816	3,435	8,235	9,663	78,478
1998	822	3,235	7,097	8,938	66,620
1999	839	3,143	7,194	8,409	64,480

C5   Numbers of Livestock (in thousands)

RUSSIA/U.S.S.R.[59] (in millions)   1866–1999

	H	C	P	S		H	C	P	S
1866	15.5	21.0	9.4	44.2	1940	17.7	47.8	22.5	66.6
					1941	21.1	54.8	27.6	80.0[60]
1870	15.6	21.4	9.1	45.3	1942	10.0	31.6	8.3	70.5
					1943	8.2	28.3	6.1	61.4
1877	17.6	27.3	10.8	51.8	1944	7.8	33.8	5.5	63.2
1882	20.0	23.8	9.2	47.5					
1883	17.9	23.6	9.4	46.7	1945	9.9	44.1	8.8	70.5[60]
					1946	10.7	47.6	10.6	58.5
1888	19.7	24.6	9.2	44.5	1947	10.9	47.0	8.7	57.7
1889	...	...	...	...	1948	11.0	50.1	9.7	63.3
					1949	11.8	54.8	15.2	70.4
1890	19.8	25.5	9.6	46.1					
1891	17.3	25.3	9.6	39.8	1950	12.7	58.1	22.2	77.6
1892	16.6	24.0	8.8	40.0	1951	13.8	57.1	24.4	82.6
1893	...	...	...	...	1952	14.7	58.8	27.1	90.5
1894	16.7	24.1	8.8	37.3	1953	15.3	56.6	28.5	94.3
					1954	15.3	55.8	33.3	99.8
1895	17.0	24.5	9.2	38.2					
1896	18.8	29.5	13.3	46.4	1955	14.2	56.7	30.9	99.0
1897	18.8	30.7	12.9	45.8	1956	13.0	58.8	34.0	103.3
1898	19.1	30.2	12.0	46.3	1957	12.4	61.4	40.8	108.2
1899	19.6	30.9	11.6	45.5	1958	11.9	66.8	44.3	120.2
					1959	11.5	70.8	48.7	129.9
1900	19.7	31.7	11.8	47.6					
1901	20.2	31.9	12.1	38.8	1960	11.0	74.2	53.4	136.1
1902	20.5	32.2	11.6	47.8	1961	9.9	75.8	58.7	133.0
1903	20.3	31.8	11.4	46.9	1962	9.4	82.1	66.7	137.5
1904	20.7	31.9	12.0	46.5	1963	9.1	87.0	70.0	139.7
					1964	8.5	85.4	40.9	133.9
1905	20.8	31.2	11.5	45.4					
1906	20.5	30.5	11.9	42.2	1965	7.9	87.2	52.8	125.2
1907	20.5	29.7	11.6	40.7	1966	8.0	93.4	59.6	129.8
1908	20.6	29.7	11.4	39.9	1967	8.0	97.1	58.0	135.5
1909	21.3	30.5	11.3	39.9	1968	8.0	97.2	50.9	138.4
					1969	7.5	95.7	49.0	140.6
1910	21.9	31.3	12.0	40.7					
1911	21.8	31.0	12.7	40.2	1970	7.4	95.2	56.1	130.7
1912	22.1	31.0	12.6	39.6	1971	7.4	99.2	67.5	138.0
1913	22.8	32.0	13.5	41.4	1972	7.1	102.4	71.4	139.9
1914	21.3[59]	30.4[59]	13.0[59]	38.9[59]	1973	6.8	104.0	66.6	139.1
					1974	6.7	106.3	70.0	142.6
1915	...	...	...	...					
1916	34.2	51.7	17.3	82.5	1975	6.4	109.1	72.3	145.3
1917	34.5	51.6	18.6	91.7	1976	6.4	111.0	57.9	141.4
1918	33.9	50.8	19.3	80.2	1977	6.0	110.3	63.1	139.8
1919	32.3	48.6	18.4	78.7	1978	5.8	112.7	70.5	141.0
					1979	5.7	114.1	73.5	142.6
1920	30.3	45.9	16.3	77.3					
1921	28.7	43.7	15.4	75.7	1980	5.6	115.1	73.9	143.6
1922	25.7	40.9	13.1	68.2	1981	5.6	115.1	73.4	141.6
1923	23.3	41.8	10.4	62.9	1982	5.6	115.9	73.3	142.4
1924	24.0	47.3	14.6	69.1	1983	5.6	117.2	76.7	142.2
					1984	5.7	119.6	78.7	145.3
1925	25.2	51.2	18.4	78.6					
1926	26.9	54.0	18.1	85.8	1985	5.8	121.0	77.9	142.9
1927	29.1	56.5	18.7	90.3	1986	5.8	120.9	77.8	140.8
1928	32.1	60.1	22.0	97.3	1987	5.9	122.1	79.5	142.2
1929	32.6	58.2	19.4	97.4	1988	5.9	120.6	77.4	140.8
					1989	5.9	119.6	78.1	140.7
1930	31.0	50.6	14.2	85.5					
1931	27.0	42.5	11.7	62.5	1990	5.9	118.4	78.9	138.4
1932	21.7	38.3	10.9	43.8	1991	5.9	115.6	75.4	132.9
1933	17.3	33.5	9.9	34.0	1992[79]	2.6	52.2	35.4	52.2
1934	15.4	33.5	11.5	32.9	1993[79]	2.5	54.6	31.5	41.2
					1994	2.5	48.9	28.5	40.6
1935	14.9	38.9	17.1	36.4					
1936	15.5	46.0	25.9	43.8	1995	2.4	43.2	24.8	31.8
1937	15.9	47.5	20.0	46.6	1996	2.3	39.7	22.6	25.3
1938	16.2	50.9	25.7	57.3	1997	2.2	35.1	19.1	20.3
1939	17.2[59]	53.5[59]	25.2[59]	69.9[59]	1998	2.0	31.5	17.3	16.4
					1999	1.8	28.4	17.2	13.4

C5 Numbers of Livestock (in thousands)

ESTONIA

	H	C	P	S	Po
1919	165	407	150	420	...
1920	165[61]	443[61]	261[61]	530[61]	...
1921	...	...	...	...	...
1922	199	527	272	745	...
1923	210	513	338	666	...
1924	208	502	288	609	...
1925	224	555	339	720	676
1926	226	599	333	666	748
1927	230	634	354	667	779
1928	228	651	327	659	810
1929	205	604	279	476	946
1930	204	627	290	467	979
1931	207	669	323	479	1,034
1932	208	692	303	514	1,104
1933	210	682	277	541	1,115
1934	212	676	282	552	1,093
1935	218	725	289	593	1,109
1936	216	731	245	584	1,147
1937	209	639	379	651	1,465
1938	219	661	385	650	1,477
1939	219	706	442	696	1,614
1992	8	708	799	143	6,000[81]
1993	7	615	772	144	3,000[81]
1994	5	463	684	83	3,186
1995	5	420	543	62	3,082
1996	5	370	448	50	2,875
1997	4	343	298	39	2,325
1998	4	326	306	36	2,602
1999	4	307	326	28	2,636

LATVIA

	H	C	P	S	Po[62]
1919	...	...	...	...	...
1920	261	768	481	978	...
1921	283	800	482	1,132	...
1922	303	811	402	1,162	...
1923	341	911	487	1,488	...
1924	340	905	458	1,235	...
1925	352	916	487	1,182	...
1926	365	955	521	1,152	...
1927	369	967	535	1,128	...
1928	365	961	535	1,090	...
1929	356	978	382	906	1,854
1930	359	1,026	523	873	2,378
1931	366	1,117	712	923	2,708
1932	366	1,153	582	984	2,922
1933	370	1,156	586	1,114	2,995
1934	375	1,158	686	1,209	3,038
1935	384	1,275	803	1,347	3,634
1936	389	1,261	674	1,352	3,757
1937	392	1,210	739	1,334	3,668
1938	400	1,224	814	1,361	3,957
1939	415	1,272	892	1,470	4,322
1992	28	1,383	1,246	184	9,000[81]
1993	28	1,144	867	165	4,000[81]
1994	26	678	704	114	4,127
1995	27	551	501	86	3,700
1996	27	538	553	72	4,198
1997	26	509	460	41	3,791
1998	23	477	430	29	3,551
1999	19	434	421	26	3,209

C5   Numbers of Livestock (in thousands)

LITHUANIA   1921-1999

	H	C	P	S[63]	Po
1921	409	849	1,343	1,073	...
1922	455	1,021	1,514	1,228	...
1923	505	1,285	1,697	1,413	...
1924	482	1,252	1,564	1,399	...
1925	497	1,339	1,488	1,455	...
1926	535	1,397	1,441	1,573	...
1927	617	1,128	1,010	1,410	...
1928	611	1,199	1,060	1,468	2,214
1929	588	1,160	944	1,125[63]	2,010
1930	562	1,034	1,207	604	2,262
1931	592	1,121	1,338	606	2,805
1932	589	1,154	1,234	625	3,083
1933	580[64]	1,156[64]	1,236[64]	630[64]	2,950
1934	545	1,152	1,232	1,258	2,200
1935	545	1,132	1,223	1,220	2,087
1936	547	1,149	1,210	1,275	2,177
1937	549	1,163	1,184	1,289	2,230
1938	550	1,164	1,187	1,241	2,240
1939	521	1,104	1,117	1,224	1,997
1940	557	1,189	1,161	1,263	2,237
1992	78	2,197	2,180	58	16,000[81]
1993	78	1,701	1,360	52	8,000[81]
1994	81	1,384	1,196	45	8,200
1995	78	1,152	1,260	40	8,300
1996	78	1,065	1,270	32	8,000
1997	81	1,054	1,128	28	7,300
1998	78	1,016	1,200	24	7,423
1999	74	922	1,159	15	6,749

SERBIA   1890-1910

	H	C	P	S	G
1890	163	819	909	2,964	510
1896	170	915	904	3,094	...
1901	185	957	960	3,062	432
1906	174	963	908	3,160	510
1910	153	957	866	3,819	63

SPAIN[65]   1859-1918

	H	A&M	C	P	S	G	Hens
1859	382	1,415	1,869	1,608	18,687	3,145	
1865	673	...	2,905	4,265	22,055	4,430	
1888	310	995	1,460	1,162	13,773	2,650	
1891	...	...	2,218	1,928	13,359	2,534	
1905	498	1,431	2,075	1,744	13,026	2,386	
1906	441	1,546	2,497	2,080	13,846	2,440	
1907	457	1,584	2,212	2,031	13,728	2,808	
1908	446	1,622	2,452	2,120	16,119	3,355	
1909	495	1,699	2,317	2,296	15,471	3,285	
1910	520	1,754	2,369	2,424	15,117	3,216	
1911	546	1,741	2,541	2,472	15,726	...	
1912	526	1,758	2,562	2,571	15,830	...	
1913	542	1,797	2,879	2,710	16,441	...	
1914	525	1,825	2,743	2,810	16,128	...	
1915	512	1,777	2,926	2,883	15,995	...	
1916	489	1,752	3,071	2,814	16,012	...	...
1917	558	1,967	3,233	3,929	17,227	...	...
1918	577	1,966	3,174	4,107	17,735	...	...

C5 Numbers of Livestock (in thousands)

	H	A&M	C	P	S	G	Hens
1919	594	2,083	3,397	4,229	19,337	3,971	...
1920	...[65]	...[65]	...[65]	...[65]	...[65]	...[65]	
1921	722	2,433	3,718	5,152	20,522	4,298	25,103
1922	...	...	...	...	...	...	...
1923	626	2,132	3,435	4,728	18,550	3,804	...
1924	634	2,147	3,436	4,160	18,460	3,804	...
1925	698	2,363	3,794	5,267	20,067	4,749	26,777
1929	598	2,160	3,660	4,773	19,370	4,525	...
1930	...	...	...	...	...	...	...
1931	563	2,179	3,654	5,102	20,047	4,008	...
1932	803	2,623	4,163	5,018	16,571	4,624	...
1933	568	2,190	3,569	5,412	19,093	4,575	...
1935	808	2,655	4,215	5,134	17,526	4,692	29,799
1939	555	1,922	3,739	6,942	21,779	6,692	29,591
1940	592	1,990	3,899	5,613	24,237	6,249	26,721
1942	602[66]	1,914[66]	4,152[66]	4,974[66]	23,489[66]	6,109[66]	25,499
1948	607	1,826	3,300	2,668	15,921	4,272	18,716
1950	642	1,821	3,112	2,688	16,344	4,135	23,819
1955	598[66]	1,754[66]	2,742[66]	2,793[66]	15,933[66]	3,097[66]	23,370
1960	506	1,844	3,640	6,032	22,622	3,300	32,388
1961	...	...	...	...	...	...	...
1962	440	1,897	3,683	6,118	20,099	2,599	40,032
1963	397	1,770	3,671	6,055	19,868	2,336	40,973
1964	345	1,382	3,723	5,011	17,617	2,284	35,211
1965	321	1,221	3,712	4,931	17,073	2,196	38,486
1966	304	1,118	3,721	5,770	16,761	2,279	42,736
1967	313	1,190	3,914	6,824	16,648	2,449	44,991
1968	308	1,102	4,021	6,673	16,726	2,504	47,911
1969	304	1,027	4,215	7,488	17,024	2,529	48,892
1970	282	901	4,282	7,621	17,005	2,551	...
1971	266	841	4,169	7,423	16,668	2,448	...
1972	261	736	4,235	8,048	15,950	2,368	...
1973	266	687	4,495	9,112	16,238	2,403	...
1974	256	630	4,438	8,671	15,599	2,230	43,099
1975	251	580	4,335	8,662	15,195	2,293	...
1976	262	534	4,384	9,248	14,776	2,178	...
1977	255	507	4,538	9,804	14,536	2,206	...
1978	257	485	4,601	10,496	14,522	2,283	...
1979	242	407	4,469	10,531	13,800	2,091	
1980	242	387	4,495	11,263	14,180	1,977	
1981	246	363	4,450	10,850	14,678	2,170	
1982	250	337	4,874	12,023	16,456	2,522	
1983	253	329	4,964	12,364	16,755	2,595	
1984	254	305	4,942	11,962	17,053	2,573	
1985	252	288	4,930	11,960	16,954	2,635	
1986	248	257	5,086	13,387	17,641	2,828	
1987	241	269	5,095	17,303	20,310	2,888	
1988	250	241	5,052	16,941	22,544	2,900	
1989	241	241	5,188	16,002	22,739	4,574	
1990	241	241	5,331	16,100	24,037	3,663	
1991	241	273	5,126	18,260	24,625	2,972	
1992	263	263	4,976	18,234	24,615	2,837	
1993	263	263	5,018	18,188	23,872	2,947	
1994	248	263	5,018	18,234	23,872	2,901	
1995	248	263	5,248	19,288	23,058	3,157	
1996	248	263	5,512	18,731	21,323	2,605	
1997	246	263	5,925	18,517	23,982	2,935	
1998	246	263	5,884	19,397	24,857	3,007	
1999	246	263	5,951	21,668	24,190	2,779	

C5   Numbers of Livestock (in thousands)

SWEDEN[67]   **1815–1919**

	H	C	P	S		H	C	P	S
1815	406	1,545	...	1,294	**1884**	476	2,327	477	1,410
1820	417	1,601	...	1,347	**1885**	480	2,366	516	1,442
1823–27	381	1,621	514	1,440	**1886**	485	2,381	548	1,444
					1887	481	2,331	571	1,378
1828–32	385	1,658	525	1,413	**1888**	482	2,349	610	1,350
1833–37	384	1,674	514	1,466	**1889**	480	2,331	621	1,338
1838–42	391[68]	1,700[68]	514[68]	1,453[68]	**1890**	487	2,399	645	1,351
1843–47	383	1,788	555	1,531	**1891**	489	2,420	655	1,345
					1892	494	2,483	682	1,352
1848–50	382	1,807	555	1,547	**1893**	495	2,474	717	1,324
1851–55	399[68]	1,919[68]	564[68]	1,592[68]	**1894**	501	2,516	769	1,319
1856–60	401	1,917	458	1,644[69]	**1895**	506	2,540	787	1,313
1861	435	1,987	379	1,741[69]	**1896**	512	2,555	789	1,299
1862	438	2,000	379	1,737[69]	**1897**	517	2,548	803	1,297
1863	439	2,010	378	1,764[69]	**1898**	523	2,582	816	1,291
1864	442[68]	2,035[68]	384[68]	1,775[69][68]	**1899**	525	2,583	811	1,284
1865	428	1,924	380	1,590	**1900**	533	2,583	806	1,261
1866	437	1,983	387	1,645	**1901**	539	2,594	809	1,232
1867	434	1,977	362	1,622	**1902**	542	2,577	808	1,196
1868	401	1,742	300	1,409	**1903**	546	2,586	816	1,167
1869	421[68]	1,874[68]	339[68]	1,539[68]	**1904**	547	2,546	797	1,106
1870	428	1,966	354	1,595	**1905**	555	2,550	830	1,074
1871	438	2,026	383	1,636	**1906**	564	2,600	872	1,051
1872	446	2,103	401	1,660	**1907**	566	2,629	879	1,022
1873	456	2,181	422	1,695	**1908**	575	2,685	895	1,010
1874	447	2,094	399	1,565	**1909**	581	2,730	922	1,022
1875	459	2,186	415	1,609	**1910**	587	2,748	957	1,004
1876	461	2,189	432	1,589	**1911**	588	2,690	951	946
1877	459	2,163	426	1,534	**1912**	...[70]	...[70]	...[70]	...[70]
1878	465	2,211	431	1,536	**1913**	...	...	...	...
1879	466	2,237	416	1,503	**1914**	660	3,069	1,023	1,205
1880	465	2,228	419	1,457	**1915**	672	2,884	891	1,146
1881	459	2,192	419	1,377	**1916**	701	2,913	1,065	1,198
1882	470	2,257	431	1,388	**1917**	715	3,020	1,030	1,344
1883	473	2,287	455	1,412	**1918**	715	2,584	634	1,409
					1919	716	2,551	717	1,564

SWEDEN   **1927–1939**

	H	C	P	S	Po
1927	620	2,899	1,387	708	9,504
1928	...	...	...	...	...
1929	...	...	...	...	...
1930	653	3,060	1,522	652	
1931	656	3,109	1,614	635	...
1932	612	2,920	1,495	468	11,304
1933	611	2,890	1,563	443	...
1934	609	2,890	1,456	449	...
1935	611	2,919	1,293	444	...
1936	616	2,950	1,322	429	...
1937	633	2,986	1,425	353	...
1938	617	3,036	1,371	406	...
1939	616	2,976	1,316	373	11,192

C5 Numbers of Livestock (in thousands)

SWEDEN 1940-1999

	H	C	P	S	Po
1940	617	2,889	1,315	329	11,208
1941	612	2,757	1,001	403	10,697
1942	591	2,546	845	435	6,993
1943	594	2,790	989	520	8,049
1944	604	2,859	1,054	558	9,093
1945	599	2,843	1,079	516	9,696
1946	593	2,869	1,165	482	11,000
1947	551	2,797	1,189	421	12,395
1948	487	2,625	1,195	349	14,023
1949	465	2,584	1,238[71]	311	12,448
1950	440	2,648	1,263	279	12,241
1951	412	2,610	1,324	228	12,329
1952	383	2,509	1,374	223	11,722
1953	359	2,531	1,422	209	11,591
1954	335	2,560	1,614	202	11,819
1955	312	2,575	1,568	177	11,697
1956	276	2,397	1,555	154	11,302
1957	255	2,426	1,855	143	11,274
1958	244	2,543	2,031	139	11,307
1959	229[72]	2,580[72]	2,202[71 72]	146[72]	12,553
	211	2,471	2,161	129	
1960	192	2,392	1,830	140	11,925
1961	178	2,465	1,963	155	11,701
1962	163	2,551	1,998	165	10,061
1963	149	2,422	1,791	184	9,907
1964	133	2,311	1,865	218	9,997[73]
					9,615
1965	109	2,250	1,884	220	8,778
1966	93	2,211	1,898	238	8,048
1967	78	2,083	2,016	267	8,106
1968	69	2,062	2,086	327	9,898
1969	67	2,043	2,065	342	8,452
1970	61	1,926	2,074	335	7,836
1971	55	1,833	2,281	330	8,356
1972	53	1,829	2,428	332	8,277
1973	52	1,890	2,374	347	7,823
1974	50	1,910	2,375	372	8,004
1975	49	1,879	2,446	368	7,714
1976	48	1,863	2,468	389	7,554
1977	...	1,878	2,556	390	7,066
1978	...	1,892	2,605	387	7,480
1979	...	1,911	2,604	383	8,400
1980	...	1,935	2,618	392	8,642
1981	...	1,939	2,617	403	8,281
1982	...	1,938	2,601	430	8,392
1983	...	1,902	2,584	437	7,291
1984	...	1,878	2,593	437	6,730
1985	...	1,837	2,589	426	11,069
1986	...	1,716	2,439	407	11,422
1987	...	1,656	2,234	397	10,820
1988	...	1,662	2,274	395	10,998
1989	...	1,688	2,264	401	11,159
1990	...	1,718	2,264	406	11,311
1991	...	1,773	2,201	419	11,759
1992	...	1,831	2,279	448	12,008
1993	...	1,830	2,390	471	11,466
1994	86	1,827	2,328	484	8,093
1995	83	1,777	2,313	462	7,912
1996	85	1,790	2,349	469	7,897
1997	87	1,781	2,351	442	7,606
1998	87	1,739	2,286	421	7,516
1999	87	1,713	2,115	437	7,860

C5 Numbers of Livestock (in thousands)

	H	C	P	S	G	Po
1866	100	993	304	447	375	...
1876	101	1,036	335	368	396	...
1886	89	1,213	395	342	416	...
1896	109	1,307	567	272	416	...
1901	125	1,340	555	219	355	...
1906	135	1,498	549	210	362	...
1911	144	1,443	570	161	341	...
1916	137	1,616	545	173	359	...
1918	129	1,531	366	230	356	2,386
1919	124	1,433	465	265	350	...
1920	130	1,382	546	241	334	...
1921	134	1,425	640	245	330	3,247
1926	140	1,587	637	170	289	4,116
1929	140	1,609	924	184	236	...
1931	140	1,609	926	185	238	4,864
1932	...	...	...	...	...	...
1933	...	1,684	897	...	...	...
1934	...	1,660	1,003	...	...	...
1935	...	1,590	1,088	...	...	...
1936	140	1,569	878	176	220	5,544
1937	...	1,638	936	...	...	...
1938	...	1,701	923	...	...	...
1939	...	1,711	880	...	...	...
1940	...	1,695	959	...	...	4,641
1941	144	1,584	764	198	215	3,752
1942	144	1,493	670	196	207	3,042
1943	146	1,517	629	204	218	3,725
1944	147	1,497	600	209	218	3,775
1945	149	1,461	698	193	205	4,492
1946	152	1,472	655	196	208	5,051
1947	147	1,451	710	182	189	5,025
1948	142	1,424	767	183	187	5,800
1949	138	1,478	887	183	185	6,100
1950	134	1,530	908	170	180	6,300
1951	131	1,607	892	192	148	6,240
1952	131	1,682	1,007	190	145	6,260
1953	128	1,635	1,017	185	142	6,280
1954	126	1,593	950	195	145	6,260
1955	120	1,583	1,038	195	120	6,240
1956	117	1,646	1,162	201	113	6,420
1957	113	1,643	1,160	201	112	6,405
1958	108	1,664	1,190	202	110	6,420
1959	103	1,687	1,226	200	113	6,420
1960	100	1,746	1,351	210	...	5,980
1961	95	1,761	1,335	227	89	5,965
1962	90	1,782	1,235	227	89	5,880
1963	82	1,716	1,314	230	85	5,750
1964	76	1,698	1,426	240	82	5,800
1965	73	1,773	1,672	249	78	6,331
1966	67	1,796	1,514	266	75	6,586
1967	62	1,835	1,620	236	73	6,657

C5 Numbers of Livestock (in thousands)

SWITZERLAND 1868–1999

	H	C	P	S	G	Po
1968	59	1,855	1,849	280	72	6,211
1969	56	1,869	1,799	290	71	6,345
1970	53	1,907	1,753	291	...	6,361
1971	50	1,823	1,836	292	...	5,963
1972	47	1,841	1,879	301	...	6,021
1973	47	1,911	2,136	336	69	6,698
1974	48	1,973	2,065	359	...	6,536
1975	47	1,965	1,964	366	...	6,121
1976	47	2,005	2,005	377	...	6,138
1977	46	2,005	2,065	368	...	6,053
1978	46	2,024	2,115	383	80	6,688
1979	45	2,038	2,062	361	...	6,337
1980	45	2,031	2,205	353	...	6,146
1981	45	1,954	2,071	335	...	5,956
1982	45	1,944	2,093	333	...	...
1983	46	1,933	2,191	355	79	6,082
1984	48	1,943	2,004	361	...	...
1985	46	1,926	1,988	357	...	...
1986	48	1,902	1,973	365	...	...
1987	48	1,858	1,917	355	...	...
1988	49	1,837	1,941	367	72	...
1989	48	1,850	1,869	371	69	6,856
1990	49	1,848	1,787	395	68	6,529
1991	52	1,829	1,723	409	65	...
1992	54	1,783	1,706	415	58	...
1993	55	1,745	1,692	424	57	6,227
1994	51	1,755	1,660	439	57	6,445
1995	46	1,756	1,611	437	52	6,064
1996	43	1,772	1,580	442	53	6,251
1997	46	1,673	1,395	420	58	6,352
1998	46	1,641	1,487	422	60	6,566
1999	46	1,608	1,452	423	62	6,731

C5 Numbers of Livestock (in thousands)

UNITED KINGDOM: Great Britain

	H	C	P	S		H	C	P	S
1867	…	4,993	2,967	28,919	1920	1,580	6,713	2,122	19,744
1868	…	5,424	2,309	30,711	1921	1,601	6,660	2,651	20,490
1869	…	5,313	1,930	29,538	1922	1,552	6,869	2,450	20,122
					1923	1,485	7,017	2,798	20,621
1870	1,267	5,403	2,171	28,398	1924	1,426	7,059	3,427	21,729
1871	1,254	5,338	2,500	27,120					
1872	1,258	5,625	2,772	27,922	1925	1,350	7,368	2,799	23,094
1873	1,276	5,965	2,500	29,428	1926	1,307	7,451	2,345	24,062
1874	1,312	6,125	2,423	30,314	1927	1,249	7,486	2,888	24,608
					1928	1,204	7,240	3,167	23,968
1875	1,340	6,013	2,230	29,167	1929	1,160	7,191	2,509	23,661
1876	1,375	5,844	2,294	28,183					
1877	1,389	5,698	2,499	28,161	1930	1,118	7,086	2,454	23,965
1878	1,413	5,738	2,483	28,406	1931	1,091	7,274	2,945	25,580
1879	1,433	5,856	2,092	28,157	1932	1,067	7,591	3,350	26,412
					1933	1,052	7,914	3,236	25,901
1880	1,421	5,912	2,001	26,619	1934	1,034	7,973	3,526	24,183
1881	1,425	5,912	2,048	24,581					
1882	1,414	5,807	2,510	24,320	1935	1,021	7,860	4,074	24,243
1883	1,411	5,963	2,618	25,068	1936	1,013	7,853	4,040	24,205
1884	1,414	6,269	2,584	26,068	1937	1,005	7,909	3,883	24,712
					1938	1,002	8,030	3,822	25,882
1885	1,409	6,598	2,403	26,535	1939	987	8,119	3,767	25,993
1886	1,425	6,647	2,221	25,521					
1887	1,428	6,441	2,299	25,959	1940	959	8,361	3,631	25,465
1888	1,420	6,129	2,404	25,257	1941	962	8,153	2,207	21,445
1889	1,421	6,140	2,511	26,632	1942	917	8,248	1,872	20,764
					1943	871	8,428	1,571	19,700
1890	1,433	6,509	2,774	27,272	1944	829	8,616	1,631	19,435
1891	1,488	6,853	2,889	28,733					
1892	1,518	6,945	2,138	28,735	1945	796	8,697	1,903	19,496
1893	1,525	6,701	2,114	27,280	1946	756	8,716	1,644	19,718
1894	1,529	6,347	2,390	25,862	1947	703	8,633	1,294	16,186
					1948	635	8,840	1,816	17,589
1895	1,545	6,354	2,884	25,792	1949	557	9,263	2,364	18,847
1896	1,553	6,494	2,879	26,705					
1897	1,526	6,500	2,342	26,340	1950	494	9,630	2,463	19,714
1898	1,517	6,622	2,452	26,743	1951	432	9,512	3,306	19,311
1899	1,517	6,796	2,624	27,239	1952	374	9,303	4,287	20,860
					1953	333	9,508	4,406	21,560
1900	1,500	6,805	2,382	26,592	1954	300	9,777	5,431	21,943
1901	1,511	6,764	2,180	26,377					
1902	1,505	6,556	2,300	25,766	1955	274	9,764	5,157	22,078
1903	1,537	6,705	2,687	25,640	1956	233	9,989	4,821	22,721
1904	1,560	6,858	2,862	25,207	1957	208	9,909	5,232	23,868
					1958	189	9,976	5,695	25,125
1905	1,572	6,987	2,425	25,257	1959	…	10,328	5,135	26,601
1906	1,569	7,011	2,323	25,420					
1907	1,556	6,912	2,637	26,115	1960	157	10,772	4,739	26,772
1908	1,546	6,905	2,823	27,120	1961	…	10,861	5,009	27,784
1909	1,553	7,021	2,381	27,618	1962	…	10,749	5,540	28,289
					1963	…	10,605	5,670	28,204
1910	1,545	7,037	2,350	27,103	1964	…	10,515	6,227	28,563
1911	1,481	7,114	2,822	26,495					
1912	1,441[74]	7,026	2,656	25,058	1965	…	10,826	6,731	28,837
	1,611				1966	…	11,017	6,282	28,903
					1967	…	11,106	6,131	27,874
1913	1,607	6,964	2,234	23,931	1968	…	10,944	6,375	27,042
1914	1,609	7,093	2,634	24,286	1969	…	11,131	6,750[76]	25,669
1915	1,487	7,288	2,579	24,598	1970	…	11,261	7,020	25,114
1916	1,567	7,442	2,314	25,007	1971	…	11,420	7,567	25,006
1917	1,583	7,437	2,051	24,043	1972	…	12,040	7,572	25,873
1918	1,586	7,410	1,825	23,353	1973	…	12,910	7,965	26,979
1919	1,600	7,424	1,936	21,534					

C5 Numbers of Livestock (in thousands)

UNITED KINGDOM: Great Britain

	H	C	P	S	Po[75]		H	C	P	S	Po[75]
1974	...	13,583	7,705	27,562	127,854	**1985**	...	11,397	7,248	34,037	118,906[77]
											111,229
1975	...	13,091	6,886	27,336	124,515	**1986**	...	11,063	7,320	35,315	112,750
1976	...	12,522	7,249	27,339	130,113	**1987**	...	10,728	7,335	36,843	120,234
1977	...	12,434	7,132	27,239	123,860	**1988**	...	10,433	7,361	38,869	122,546
1978	...	12,122	7,045	28,798	126,037	**1989**	...	10,354	7,510	38,281	120,366
1979	...	12,048	7,142	28,946	124,460						
						1990	...	10,424	7,450	39,310	124,636
1980	...	11,918	7,123	30,385	123,716	**1991**	...	10,220	7,597	39,405	127,241
1981	...	11,702	7,201	30,958	120,800	**1992**	...	10,163	7,609	39,953	124,013
1982	...	11,815	7,383	31,833	124,384	**1993**	...	10,084	7,754	39,727	130,175
1983	...	11,818	7,523	32,746	117,105	**1994**	174	11,834	7,892	43,295	130,027
1984	...	11,707	7,074	33,352	116,681						
						1995	175	11,733	7,627	42,771	130,939
						1996	176	11,913	7,590	41,530	140,000
						1997	177	11,633	8,072	42,823	145,000
						1998	178	11,519	8,146	44,471	137,800
						1999	180	11,423	7,284	44,656	153,590

YUGOSLAVIA

	H	C	P	S	G	Po
1921	1,062	4,951	3,350	7,002	1,553	...
1922	1,044	4,058	2,887	8,462	1,801	...
1923	1,063	3,870	2,497	7,639	1,730	...
1924	1,054	3,784	2,518	7,619	1,718	...
1925	1,106	3,768	2,802	7,907	1,811	13,679
1926	1,117	3,706	2,806	7,933	1,721	13,697
1927	1,120	3,729	2,770	7,736	1,739	13,839
1928	1,109	3,654	2,663	7,722	1,750	13,810
1929	1,140	3,728	2,675	7,736	1,804	15,143
1930	1,161	3,812	2,924	7,953	1,731	16,272
1931	1,169	3,872	3,133	8,426	1,928	16,425
1932	1,157	3,812	2,863	8,510	1,872	16,820
1933	1,187	3,876	2,656	8,600	1,871	17,014
1934	1,206	3,990	2,792	8,868	1,881	17,858
1935	1,201	3,982	2,932	9,211	1,896	17,761
1936	1,216	4,074	3,126	9,568	1,906	18,356
1937	1,249	4,169	3,180	9,909	1,901	19,114
1938	1,264	4,267	3,451	10,137	1,890	19,419
1939	1,273	4,225	3,504	10,154	1,866	19,226

C5   **Numbers of Livestock** (in thousands)

YUGOSLAVIA   **1947-1999**

	H	C	P	S	Po
1947	879	3,928	3,485	9,192	...
1948	973	4,246	3,439	9,970	...
1949	1,050	5,278	4,135	11,654	19,354
1950	1,097	5,248	4,295	10,046	20,207
1951	1,095	4,740	3,917	10,276	17,174
1952	1,103	4,834	3,999	10,522	20,440
1953	1,126	5,007	4,527	11,404	19,665
1954	1,193	5,097	4,310	12,112	25,450
1955	1,242	5,290	4,780	11,979	24,873
1956	1,296	5,206	4,655	11,360	25,938
1957	1,307	4,947	3,705	10,622	25,992
1958	1,296	4,860	4,226	10,626	28,508
1959	1,274	5,038	5,657	11,249	27,721
1960	1,272	5,297	6,210	11,449	30,343
1961	1,200	5,702	5,818	10,823	28,878
1962	1,226	5,884	5,161	11,143	28,304
1963	1,175	5,355	5,013	10,056	29,939
1964	1,140	5,094	6,100	9,707	32,473
1965	1,109	5,219	6,985	9,433	31,429
1966	1,131	5,584	5,118	9,868	31,685
1967	1,134	5,710	5,525	10,329	35,153
1968	1,126	5,693	5,865	10,346	35,974
1969	1,109	5,261	5,093	9,730	37,142
1970	1,076	5,029	5,544	8,974	40,854
1971	1,048	5,138	6,562	8,703	44,954
1972	1,015	5,148	6,216	8,326	44,584
1973	964	5,366	6,342	7,774	49,206
1974	945	5,681	7,401	7,852	54,685
1975	922	5,872	7,683	8,175	54,991
1976	864	5,755	6,536	7,831	54,764
1977	812	5,641	7,326	7,484	59,031
1978	759	5,542	8,452	7,514	60,398
1979	701	5,491	7,747	7,339	61,513
1980	617	5,436	7,502	7,354	63,055
1981	573	5,474	7,867	7,384	65,690
1982	515	5,464	8,431	7,398	67,408
1983	505	5,351	8,370	7,452	69,680
1984	463	5,341	9,337	7,458	74,008
1985	438	5,199	8,673	7,678	70,453
1986	409	5,034	7,821	7,693	78,281
1987	384	5,030	8,459	7,819	79,696
1988	362	4,881	8,323	7,829	78,598
1989	340	4,759	7,396	7,564	74,872
1990	314	4,705	7,231	7,596	73,524
1991	630	4,527	7,338	7,431	30,212[80]
1992[80]	89[80]	1,975[80]	3,844[80]	2,715[80]	26,038[80]
1993[80]	82[80]	1,991[80]	4,092[80]	2,752[80]	23,293[80]
1994	82	1,809	3,693	2,635	20,311
1995	96	1,950	4,192	2,671	23,491
1996	93	1,926	4,446	2,656	24,287
1997	90	1,899	4,216	2,566	23,542
1998	86	1,894	4,150	2,402	26,188
1999	76	1,831	4,372	2,195	26,492

C5 Numbers of Livestock (in thousands)

NOTES

1. SOURCES:- The main sources were as for table D1. Bulgarian statistics for sheep in 1946–51 were supplied by Professor Michael Kaser's group at St. Anthony's College, Oxford and are derived from B. Simov *et al*, *Virzstanoviavane; irazvitie na promishlenostta v N R B, 1944–1948* (Sofia, 1968). Dutch statistics for horses in 1865–69 and for cattle in 1965 and 1868–69 were supplied by the Netherlands Central Office of Statistics. Romanian statistics for 1949, 1950, 1954, and 1957 were supplied by Mr. G. Radulescu, Editor-in-Chief of the *Enciclopedica Romana*.

2. With some exceptions, indicated in footnotes, statistics were taken in either summer or winter, as follows:- SUMMER: Denmark, Finland, France, Great Britain, Hungary (to 1911), Ireland, Italy, Netherlands, (from 1910), Norway (from 1900), Poland, the Baltic States, Spain (from 1939) and Sweden. WINTER: Austria, Belgium, Bulgaria, Czechoslovakia, Germany, Greece, Hungary (from 1945), Netherlands (to 1904), Norway (to 1890), Romania, Russia, Spain (to 1935), Switzerland, and Yugoslavia.

FOOTNOTES

[1] The whole of Carinthia, Lower Austria, Styria, and Tirol is included in these figures, but Burgenland is not.

[2] Excluding Burgenland, which had the following livestock in 1923 (in thousands):-

Horses	Cattle	Pigs	Sheep	Goats	Poultry
18	125	93	6	8	491

[3] Subsequently excluding turkeys and guinea fowl.

[4] Horses used in agriculture to 1967, except in 1940 (see footnote 6).

[5] Figures to 1829 exclude the whole of Limburg and Luxembourg.

[6] This figure is of all horses. The comparable figure for 1941 is 269.

[7] Figures for 1941–44 exclude Eupen and Malmédy, and are underestimates because of concealment by farmers.

[8] Previous statistics relate to holdings of one hectare or more, whilst there is no limit for later figures. However, some smallholdings are undoubtedly omitted.

[9] Between 1910 and 1920 southern Dobrudja was ceded to Romania and rather larger areas were acquired from Turkey. From 1941 southern Dobrudja is again included.

[10] Subsequently excludes Sub-Carpathian Russia (Ruthenia) and 12 villages in Slovakia, ceded to the U.S.S.R. in 1945.

[11] These statistics are for February instead of in the summer.

[12] Subsequently includes South Jutland.

[13] For 1930–38 the statistics relate to rural communes only. Figures including the towns are available for 1933 as follows:- (in thousands)

Horses	Cattle	Pigs	Sheep	Fowls
520	3,185	4,477	179	26,625

[14] For 1940–48 the statistics for fowls relate to rural communes only. In 1949 the number of fowls in the towns was 706 thousand.

[15] Subsequently excluding holdings of less than 5 hectares.

[16] From 1908 to 1920 (1st line) the statistics relate only to horses over three years old. This figure is not given for 1907, but the number of 'horses' (as opposed to 'colts') was 286 thousand.

[17] From 1908 to 1920 (1st line) the statistics relate only to cattle over two years old. This figure is not given for 1907, but the number of 'bulls' and 'cows' (as opposed to 'young cattle') was 1,185 thousand.

[18] Over six months old only, except from 1955 (2nd line).

[19] Subsequent statistics apparently relate to a different time of year from the earlier ones.

[20] Subsequent statistics compare to ones taken on 1 September in 1932 and 1938, which differ from the continuous series given here, and are as follows (in thousands):-

	Horses	Cattle	Pigs	Sheep
1932	348	1,713	361	879
1938	381	1,849	487	1,022

[21] Figures for 1945–49 were taken at 1 March. Figures from 1950 have been taken at 15 June.

[22] Revised figures for 1950 and 1955 are given in the 1967 *Statistical Yearbook of Finland*, but not for the intervening years. The revised figures are 3,381 in 1950 and 3,945 in 1955.

[23] Previously on holdings above quarter of a hectare, and subsequently on those over 1 hectare.

[24] Subsequently includes Savoy and Nice.

[25] Figures for 1870–1918 exclude the parts of Alsace and Lorraine ceded to Germany.

[26] Figures for 1914–18 exclude the invaded departments.

[27] Parts of Alsace-Lorraine annexed by Germany are excluded from 1939 to 1945, and Corsica is excluded in 1943–44.

[28] Subsequently includes Tende and Brigue.

[29] Subsequent statistics were collected in December rather than summer or autumn.

[30] W.G. Hoffman, *Das Wachstum der Deutschen Wirtschaft seit der Mitte des 19 Jahrhunderts* (Berlin, etc., 1965) gives different figures for cattle as follows (in thousands):-

1892	15,690;	1900	16,906;	1904	16,917

[31] Figures for 1872 to 1917 (1st line) include Alsace-Lorraine.

C5   Numbers of Livestock (in thousands)

[32] Figures for 1917 (2nd line) to 1921 (1st line) apparently relate to the 1921 boundaries (i.e. including Eastern Upper Silesia, but excluding other territory ceded after the First World War). Statistics for 1913 for the comparable area to 1921 (2nd line) are as follows (in thousands):-

	Horses	Cattle	Pigs	Sheep	Goats	Poultry
	3,806	18,474	22,533	4,988	3,164	71,907 (in 1912).

[33] Subsequently including Saarland.
[34] Excluding the Kleintierhaltung in Berlin.
[35] This is a mid-year rather than an end-year figure.
[36] Subsequently including West Berlin.
[37] Statistics apply to the territory of the day (see p. xi). However, Macedonia is excluded in 1916 and eastern Macedonia in 1917 and 1918, and Thrace is not included until 1922.
[38] Transleithania (excluding Croatia-Slavonia) to 1911. Later statistics are for the territory established by the treaty of Trianon. The following figures are available for Croatia-Slavonia (in thousands):-

	Horses	Cattle	Pigs	Sheep	Goats
1857	130	357	417	195	29
1895	311	909	883	596	22
1911	350	1,135	1,164	850	96

[39] These are estimates, of which that for sheep is believed to be excessive.
[40] Including buffaloes.
[41] December instead of March.
[42] Subsequently the coverage of young poultry was much improved.
[43] Subsequently horses used for agriculture purposes only.
[44] Statistics up to 1921 apply to the 1871 boundaries. For 1922–43 they apply to the 1924 boundaries, and from 1944 they apply to the 1954 boundaries, except that Trieste is not included until 1949.
[45] The following earlier figures of cattle are available (in thousands):-

1804	903;	1807	978

[46] Subsequent statistics were taken in late spring or summer, whereas earlier ones were at 31 December.
[47] *Jaarcijfers* for 1921 gives a figure of 6,710, whilst the one given here appears in later issues. It is likely, however, that the difference does not spring from a revision but from greater coverage of the later series.
[48] Subsequently excluding holdings of less than 10 Standard Farm Units.
[49] Subsequently layers and broilers only.
[50] Subsequent statistics were taken in autumn or summer, and, until 1959, were for rural communes only, whereas earlier ones were at 31 December and included the towns.
[51] Figures for 1940–64 are of hens only, and from 1965 they are of hens and cocks only.
[52] Subsequent statistics include urban municipalities.
[53] Subsequent figures are for the post war territory.
[54] Unofficial estimates of doubtful validity.
[55] Mainland only.
[56] Including buffaloes.
[57] Dobrudja was acquired in 1913.
[58] Figures for 1919 to 1939 apply to the interwar territory. Southern Dobrudja was ceded to Bulgaria in 1940. Bessarabia and northern Bukovina were ceded to the U.S.S.R. in 1940, though temporarily reconquered in 1943. Northern Transylvania was ceded to Hungary from 1940 to 1945.
[59] Figures to 1914 are for the 50 provinces of European Russia (excluding Finland, Poland, and the Caucasus). From 1916 to 1939 they are for the U.S.S.R. boundaries of 1924, and subsequently for the boundaries of the day.
[60] Figures for 1942–45 include goats.
[61] Excluding the district of Petseri to 1920.
[62] Fowls over six months only.
[63] Figures to 1929 include goats.
[64] Subsequent figures were taken in June (as were those of fowls throughout), whereas earlier ones were taken in December.
[65] Statistics prior to 1921 are originally from a variety of sources and are clearly not always comparable with each other. Earlier statistics given in J.V. Vives, *An Economic History of Spain* (Princeton, 1969) are as follows (in thousands):-

	Horses	Asses & Mules	Cattle	Pigs	Sheep	Goats
1797	23	...	1,650	1,200	11,700	2,500
1803	140	450	2,680	2,100	12,000	...

[66] Excluding suckling animals in 1948–1955.

C5   Numbers of Livestock (in thousands)

67   The following earlier statistics are available (in thousands):-

	Horses	Cattle	Sheep
1805	397	1,468	1,214
1810	405	1,516	1,243

68   Excluding the town of Stockholm in 1843 to 1855 and in 1865–1869.
69   Including goats, which numbered 173 thousands in 1851–5 and 133 thousand in 1865.
70   Subsequent statistics were taken in summer or early autumn, whereas earlier ones are for the years' end.
71   Subsequent statistics to 1959 were collected in April rather than June.
72   Subsequent statistics relate only to farms of two hectares and over.
73   Subsequent only fowls and chickens.
74   Earlier statistics are of horses used in agriculture, later ones of all horses on agricultural holdings.
75   The Scottish component excludes geese, and also, in 1968 and 1969, ducks.
76   Changes in the basis of collection affected comparability, but only to a significant extent for pigs and poultry.
77   Subsequently excluding turkeys.
78   Czech Republic. Figures for Slovakia are

	H	C	P	S	G	Po
1992		1,182	2,269	561	11	15,000 (FAO estimates)
1993	13	916	2,179	397	12	12,000 (FAO estimates)
1994	11	993	2,179	411	10	12,200
1995	10	916	2,037	397	11	14,200
1996	10	929	2,076	428	9	13,400
1997	10	892	1,985	418	21	14,100
1998	10	803	1,809	417	15	14,222
1999	10	704	1,592	326	17	13,117

79   Russian Federation. Figures for ex-U.S.S.R. are:

		Horses	Cattle	Pigs	Sheep
Armenia	1992	...	499	84	854
	1993	...	499	81	724
	1994	11	502	82	720
	1995	12	504	82	620
	1996	12	508	80	590
	1997	13	510	54	566
	1998	13	466	57	532
	1999	12	469	86	508
Azerbaijan	1992	35	1,716	140	5,088
	1993	33	1,791	123	4,701
	1994	35	1,621	48	4,357
	1995	38	1,633	33	4,376
	1996	43	1,682	30	4,434
	1997	49	1,780	23	4,648
	1998	53	1,844	21	5,103
	1999	56	1,913	26	5,735
Belarus	1992	212	6,577	4,703	373
	1993	215	6,221	4,308	336
	1994	215	5,851	4,181	271
	1995	220	5,403	4,005	230
	1996	229	5,054	3,895	204
	1997	232	4,855	3,715	155
	1998	233	4,801	3,686	127
	1999	229	4,685	3,698	106
Georgia	1992	20	1,216	782	1,400
	1993	20	1,130	688	1,350
	1994	20	929	365	920
	1995	21	944	367	754
	1996	24	974	353	674
	1997	26	1,008	333	600
	1998	28	1,027	330	525
	1999	30	1,050	365	521

C5   Numbers of Livestock (in thousands)

Russian Federation. Figures for ex-U.S.S.R. are:

		Horses	Cattle	Pigs	Sheep
Kazakhstan	1992	1,510	9,084	2,794	33,908
	1993	1,500	9,576	2,591	33,732
	1994	1,777	9,347	2,445	33,312
	1995	1,636	8,073	1,983	24,273
	1996	1,557	6,860	1,623	18,786
	1997	1,310	5,425	1,036	13,000
	1998	1,083	4,307	879	9,693
	1999	986	3,957	891	8,691
Kyrgistan	1992	315	1,095	299	9,200
	1993	310	1,122	247	8,490
	1994	322	1,062	169	7,103
	1995	299	920	118	4,924
	1996	308	869	114	4,075
	1997	314	848	88	3,545
	1998	320	885	93	3,220
	1999	325	910	105	3,308
Moldova	1992	48	1,000	1,753	1,239
	1993	51	971	1,487	1,294
	1994	55	916	1,165	1,366
	1995	59	832	1,061	1,411
	1996	61	726	1,041	1,320
	1997	63	646	950	1,264
	1998	66	551	798	1,029
	1999	68	452	806	1,008
Tajikistan	1992	48	1,222	56	2,172
	1993	53	1,244	46	2,081
	1994	50	1,250	46	2,078
	1995	48	1,199	32	1,958
	1996	47	1,147	6	1,805
	1997	45	1,082	2	1,663
	1998	45	1,050	1	1,620
	1999	46	1,037	1	1,600
Turkmenistan	1992	20	777	237	5,380
	1993	22	1,004	212	6,000
	1994	20	1,104	159	6,000
	1995	18	1,181	128	6,100
	1996	17	1,199	82	6,150
	1997	17	959	65	5,400
	1998	16	950	55	5,500
	1999	16	880	48	5,650
Ukraine	1992	717	23,728	17,839	7,259
	1993	707	22,457	16,175	6,597
	1994	716	21,607	15,298	6,118
	1995	737	19,624	13,946	4,793
	1996	756	17,557	13,144	3,209
	1997	753	15,313	11,236	2,193
	1998	737	12,759	9,479	1,539
	1999	721	11,721	10,083	1,198
Uzbekistan	1992	113	5,113	654	8,275
	1993	123	5,275	529	8,407
	1994	120	5,431	391	9,360
	1995	145	5,484	350	9,053
	1996	146	5,204	208	8,352
	1997	146	5,100	100	7,340
	1998	150	5,200	70	7,706
	1999	155	5,225	80	7,840

C5 Numbers of Livestock (in thousands)

[80] Yugoslavia. Figures for ex-Yugoslavia are:

		H	C	P	S	Po (FAO)
Bosnia-Hercegovina	1992	70	500	590	854	8,000
	1993	56	425	550	718	8,000
	1994	17	570	300	600	6,000
	1995	18	519	290	520	5,000
	1996	17	390	180	473	4,000
	1997	19	412	162	378	3,000
	1998	19	426	372	581	3,574
	1999	20	442	350	632	3,507
Croatia	1992	27	590	1,183	539	13,000
	1993	22	590	1,262	524	12,000
	1994	22	519	1,347	444	9,523
	1995	21	493	1,175	453	10,724
	1996	21	462	1,196	426	9,818
	1997	19	451	1,175	452	9,884
	1998	16	443	1,166	427	9,039
	1999	13	438	1,361	488	9,951
Macedonia	1992	65	285	173	2,531	4,000
	1993	62	280	182	2,420	4,000
	1994	62	280	185	2,459	4,685
	1995	62	281	172	2,466	4,880
	1996	66	283	175	2,319	3,361
	1997	66	295	192	1,814	4,033
	1998	60	298	184	1,805	3,500
	1999	60	290	196	1,550	3,339
Slovenia	1992	11	484	529	28	11,000
	1993	8	504	602	21	11,000
	1994	9	478	592	29	8,000
	1995	8	477	571	39	5,000
	1996	8	496	592	43	4,150
	1997	8	486	552	53	4,773
	1998	10	446	578	72	6,208
	1999	12	453	592	72	7,150

(Poultry = FAO estimates).

[81] FAO Estimate.

C6 OUTPUT OF COWS' MILK (in thousands of tons)

Netherlands

1903	2,439	**1908**	2,619	**1912**	2,877	**1916**	3,217
1904	2,314	**1909**	2,530	**1913**	2,943	**1917**	2,650
1905	2,423	**1910**	2,706	**1914**	3,026	**1918**	1,944
1906	2,536	**1911**	2,680	**1915**	3,125	**1919**	2,162
1907	2,576						

	Austria*	Belgium	Bulgaria[2]	Czech*	Denmark[4]	Finland	France*	Germany*[7]	East Germany*	Hungary*[8]	Ireland[9]
1920	...	...	...	...	2,703	...	...	...	...	...	...
1921	...	...	...	...	3,333	...	...	...	...	...	...
1922	...	...	...	...	3,519	...	...	...	...	...	...
1923	...	...	...	...	3,833	...	12,067	...	...	...	...
1924	...	...	...	...	4,238	...	...	...	...	...	...
1925	...	...	...	...	4,348	13,098	...	...	...	...	...
1926	...	...	...	...	4,529	...	12,571	...	...	...	2,357
1927	...	...	...	...	4,678	...	...	...	...	...	...
1928	...	...	...	...	4,777	...	...	21,315	...	...	...
1929	...	2,914	...	...	5,075	2,133	14,282	22,826	...	...	2,376
1930	2,492	2,958	...	...	5,272	...	...	21,508	...	...	...
1931	...	2,975	...	...	5,565	...	...	23,610	...	...	...
1932	...	3,110	...	...	5,485	...	...	24,226	...	...	...
1933	...	3,150	...	...	5,390	...	...	24,720	...	...	...
1934	2,622	3,131	...	...	5,320	2,387	...	24,450	...	...	2,320
1935	...	3,104	...	...	5,120	2,435	14,692	24,200[7]	...	345	2,357
1936	...	3,174	...	4,633	5,275	2,475	...	25,400	...	411	2,311
1937	2,369	2,928	...	4,616	5,300	2,663	14,828	25,445	...	460	2,292
1938	...	3,090	...	...	5,400	2,682	13,751	25,120	...	455[8] 1,572	2,268
1939	1,983	2,834	541	3,877	5,300	2,307	14,192	25,360	...	...	2,348
1940	1,925	...	533	3,194	4,622	2,028[5]	10,645[6]	24,440	...	...	2,184
1941	1,945	2,128	413	2,846	3,621	1,761	9,767[6]	...	...	...	2,264
1942	1,947	2,089	144	2,403	3,338	1,460	8,489[6]	22,531	...	...	2,212
1943	2,020	2,152	184	1,984	3,813	1,502	8,106[6]	22,810	...	...	2,240
1944	1,888	2,100	154	1,897[3]	4,010	1,633	7,412[6]	...	...	...	2,217[9]
1945	1,375	1,121	113[2]	2,049	4,271	1,611	7,892[6]		...	...	2,264
1946	1,387	2,194[1] 2,323	...	2,649	4,595	1,500	10,600	**West Germany**	...	...	2,170
1947	1,250	2,525	...	2,417	4,106	1,700	10,300	...	...	...	2,020
1948	1,553	2,729	...	2,258	4,058	1,930	11,100	8,555	2,025	866	2,104
1949	1,748	3,216	...	2,618	4,883	2,175	13,700	11,316	2,560	...	2,306
1950	2,085	3,392	...	3,272	5,403	2,450	15,500	13,861	3,580	1,446	2,409
1951	2,296	3,453	...	3,555	5,233	2,652	16,500	15,171	3,805	1,452	2,278
1952	2,311	3,524	271	3,587	4,998	2,862	15,500	15,812	4,392	1,424	2,245
1953	2,424	3,711	267	3,244	5,378	2,946	17,500	16,741	4,239	1,364	2,381
1954	2,539	3,836	300	3,264	5,394	2,914	18,600	17,054	4,702	1,455	2,451
1955	2,533	3,893	381	3,521	5,124	2,865	18,035	16,907	5,077	1,526	2,437
1956	2,613	3,859	456	3,711	5,068	3,085	19,600	17,007	4,986	1,576	2,550
1957	2,732	3,916	524	3,742	5,344	3,153	20,660	17,263[7] 17,378	5,286	1,779	2,695
1958	2,752	3,931	593	3,764	5,147	3,155	21,115	17,977	5,656	1,949	2,629
1959	2,777	3,940	673	3,771	5,426	3,322	20,300	18,497	5,826	1,990	2,493
1960	2,842	4,113	745	3,830	5,399	3,486	22,972	19,250	5,730	1,955	2,671
1961	2,901	4,123	813	3,945	5,524	3,624	23,816	19,872[7] 19,996	5,612	1,897	2,784
1962	3,005	4,166	772	3,664	5,355	3,644	24,332	20,307	5,216	1,805	2,877
1963	3,049	4,031	797	3,535	5,086	3,758	25,363	20,714	5,569	1,803	2,892
1964	3,128	3,873	926	3,763	5,233	3,825	25,260	20,841	5,751	1,854	3,009

C6 Output of Cows' Milk (in thousands of tons)

	Austria*	Belgium	Bulgaria	Czech*	Denmark	Finland	France*	West Germany*	East Germany*	Greece	Hungary*	Ireland
1965	3,209	3,958	1,000	3,924	5,367	3,769	26,780	21,183	6,371		1,761	3,142
1966	3,216	3,952	1,098	4,169	5,306	3,693	28,016	21,322	6,728		1,549	3,232
1967	3,360	4,080	1,211	4,335	5,193	3,559	29,355	21,717	6,904	521	1,975	3,461
1968	3,351	4,129	1,199	4,554	5,122	3,596	30,444	22,121	7,227	510	1,933	3,671
1969	3,341	4,132	1,206	4,751	4,872	3,599	30,031[20]	22,216	7,232	528	1,888	3,684[10]
												3,050
1970	3,328	3,962	1,252	4,794	4,630	3,310	27,276	21,856	7,091	553	1,863	2,983
1971	3,281	3,819	1,291	4,924	4,556	3,293	27,639	21,165	7,150	557	1,808	3,060
1972	3,286	3,879	1,308	5,123	4,636	3,286	28,846	21,490	7,515	555	1,810	
1973	3,138	3,850	1,344	5,430	4,729	3,107	29,291	21,265	7,738	646	1,957	3,371
1974	3,149	3,959	1,411	5,503	4,818	3,056	29,470	21,508	8,076	660	2,020	3,239
1975	3,182	3,869	1,435	5,463	4,918	3,164	29,686	21,604	8,095	710	1,979	3,485
1976	3,240	3,843	1,456	5,400	5,045	3,278	29,536	22,165	8,092	716	2,085	3,747
1977	3,320	3,872	1,549	5,530	5,139	3,231	30,215	22,523	7,939	678	2,142	4,032
1978	3,368	4,022	1,619	5,641	5,324	3,225	30,850	23,296	8,226	661	2,336	4,556
1979	3,384	4,034	1,802	5,664	5,225	3,242	31,776	23,907	8,198	674	2,457	4,644
1980	3,518	4,033	1,829	5,909	5,117	3,275	32,250	24,779	8,321	666	2,548	4,567
1981	3,625	4,060	1,899	5,918	5,037	3,190	32,417	24,858	8,202	657	2,681	4,542
1982	3,689	4,083	2,001	5,931	5,217	3,170	33,059	24,565	7,678	613	2,741	4,952
1983	3,737	4,170	2,092	6,496	5,427	3,236	33,630	25,465	8,203	610	2,809	5,333
1984	3,769	4,119	2,162	6,763	5,234	3,124	33,984	26,151	8,729	575	2,800	5,564
1985	3,797	4,097	2,118	6,883	5,099	3,174	33,436	25,674	9,044	570	2,713	5,655
1986	3,776	4,217	2,172	7,015	5,111	3,071	34,110	26,350	9,358	643	2,763	5,452
1987	3,818	4,056	2,181	6,921	4,860	2,938	33,312	24,436	9,235	628	2,817	5,362
1988	3,763	3,900	2,168	6,963	4,739	2,753	26,606	23,974	9,204	630	2,873	5,330
1989	3,778	3,917	2,135	7,101	4,747	2,753	25,984	24,243	9,504	680	2,862	5,382
1990	3,791	3,810	2,112	6,931	4,730	2,730	26,561	23,725	9,100	670	2,897	5,605
1991	3,848	3,808	1,760	5,826	4,640	2,566	25,759	29,063		695	2,490	5,345
1992	3,907	3,775	1,589	5,785	4,605	2,475	25,324	28,191		660	2,301	5,389
1993	3,997	3,762	1,350	3,454[21]	4,660	2,462	24,935	28,200		695	2,070	5,314
1994	3,279	3,605	1,198	3,134	4,442	2,512	25,322	27,866		720	1,936	5,337
1995	3,148	3,644	1,165	3,125	4,676	2,468	25,438	28,607		738	1,979	5,347
1996	3,034	3,681	1,163	3,134	4,695	2,431	25,109	28,779		740	1,975	5,297
1997	3,090	3,477	1,197	2,787	4,632	2,462	24,917	28,702		737	1,989	5,256
1998	3,256	3,682	1,327	2,716	4,668	2,447	24,834	28,378		769	2,107	5,091
1999	3,349	3,649	1,388	2,818	4,665	2,477	24,892	28,334		777	2,106	5,121

C6   Output of Cows' Milk (in thousands of tons)

1920–1944

	Netherlands	Norway[1]	Poland[12]	Russia (million tons)	Spain	Sweden[15]	Switz[16]	U.K.*[17]
1920	2,513	...	...	...	...	...	...	...
1921	2,981	...	...	19.2[13]	...	...	...	...
1922	3,080	...	...	...	...	...	...	...
1923	3,401	...	...	...	...	...	2,452	...
1924	3,627	...	...	26.2	...	...	2,542	...
1925	3,726	...	...	...	...	...	2,574	...
1926	3,982	...	...	...	...	...	2,752	...
1927	4,167	...	...	...	...	...	2,709	...
1928	4,263	...	...	31.0	...	...	2,830	...
1929	4,351	...	...	29.8	...	1,990	2,688	...
1930	4,418	1,223	...	27.0	1,374	2,162	2,615	...
1931	4,544	...	...	23.4	...	2,165	2,625	...
1932	4,607	1,258	...	20.6	...	2,157	2,709	5,864
1933	4,732	...	9,265	19.2	1,499	2,196	2,784	5,958
1934	4,778	1,312	...	20.8	...	2,372	2,808	5,958
1935	4,996	1,302	...	21.4	...	2,455	2,732	5,958
1936	5,165	1,352	...	23.5	...	2,653	2,673	6,174
1937	5,340	1,364	...	26.1	...	2,778	2,706	6,165
1938	5,325	1,373	10,310	29.0	...	2,962	2,792	6,099[17]
1939	5,512	1,413	...	27.2	...	3,156	2,693	8,483
1940	5,194	1,522	...	26.6[14]	...	3,102	2,618	7,752
				33.6				
1941	4,089	...	...	...	1,424	2,722	2,471	7,396
1942	3,117	...	...	...	...	2,516	2,261	7,522
1943	2,715	...	...	...	1,977	2,829	2,219	7,855
1944	2,583	...	...	...	...	3,106	2,115	8,019

C6 Output of Cows' Milk (in thousands of tons)

1945–1999

	Italy*	Netherlands	Norway	Poland[12]	Romania*	Russia (million tons)	Spain	Sweden	Switzerland[16]	U.K.*	Yugoslavia*
1945	...	2,546	1,078	...[12]	...	26.4	...	3,375[15] 4,284	2,120	8,241	...
1946	4,547	3,911	1,259	2,793	...	27.7	...	4,625	2,160	8,549	...
1947	3,704	3,918	1,319	3,399	...	30.2	...	4,489	2,060	8,348	...
1948	4,202[18]	4,687	1,393	...	...	33.4	...	4,402	2,285	9,174	...
1949	4,917	5,464	1,525	...	...	34.9	...	4,647	2,441	9,754	...
1950	5,277	5,771	1,610	...	...	35.3	...	4,852	2,573[16] 2,521	10,479	1,440
1951	5,469	5,679	1,632	...	...	36.2	1,789	4,705	2,636	10,039	...
1952	5,450	5,601	1,558	9,091	1,573	35.7	1,967	4,438	2,648	10,156	1,283
1953	5,691	5,830	1,574	9,293	1,508	36.5	2,077	4,420	2,693	10,764	1,502
1954	6,122	5,863	1,540	9,613	1,698	38.2	2,068	4,275	2,791	10,974	1,548
1955	6,644	5,725	1,548	9,903	1,830	43.0	1,930	4,062	2,787	10,436	1,701
1956	6,459	5,822	1,541	10,278	1,714	49.1	2,076	3,935	2,814	11,616	1,857
1957	6,784	5,876	1,566	11,043	1,798	54.7	2,151	4,034	2,870	11,972	2,159
1958	6,913	6,134	1,514	11,859	2,007	58.7	2,045	3,980	2,890	11,429	2,192
1959	7,283	6,299	1,537	12,302	2,794	61.7	1,950	3,860	2,967	11,092	2,300
1960	7,356	6,721	1,614	12,488	2,951	61.7	2,075	3,926	3,084	12,080	2,283
1961	7,559	6,952	1,603	12,759	3,083	62.6	2,221	3,977	3,066	12,642	2,249
1962	7,501	7,283	1,641	12,861	2,887	63.9	2,237	3,927	3,113	12,923	2,220
1963	6,721	7,020	1,656	12,641	2,734	61.2	2,364	3,782	3,092	12,600	2,170
1964	7,063	6,971	1,642	12,592	2,742	63.3	2,380	3,640	3,014	13,399	2,238
1965	7,757	7,151	1,643	13,331	2,972	72.6	2,418	3,655	3,095	12,862	2,303
1966	8,369	7,242	1,680	14,221	3,437	76.0	2,726	3,538	3,131	12,661	2,513
1967	8,280	7,520	1,709	14,480	3,835	79.9	3,014	3,318	3,252	13,059	2,607
1968	8,352	7,791	1,769	14,642	3,565	82.3	3,373	3,301	3,300	13,509	2,633
1969	8,148	7,915	1,731	14,758	3,511	81.5	3,180	3,180	3,193	13,750[10] 12,747	2,626
1970	8,225	8,238	1,704	14,948	3,549	83.0	3,664[19] 4,456	2,932	3,183	12,971	2,567
1971	8,428	8,392	1,744	15,147	3,593	83.2	4,395	2,879	3,140	13,305	2,581
1972	8,987	8,951	1,807	15,765	3,887	83.2	4,652	2,997	3,214	14,171	2,814
1973	8,939	9,354	1,803	16,243	3,390	88.3	4,940	3,033	3,274	14,402	3,105
1974	8,805	9,915	1,800	16,667	3,387	91.8	5,084	3,112	3,339	13,993	3,487
1975	8,676	10,221	1,820	16,375	3,458	90.8	5,139	3,168	3,375	13,934	3,654
1976	8,856	10,490	1,874	16,519	3,826	89.7	5,374	3,247	3,452	14,419	3,846
1977	9,110	10,612	1,868	16,935	4,212	94.9	5,520	3,249	3,489	15,200	4,072
1978	9,360	11,367	1,902	17,105	4,369	94.7	5,732	3,298	3,518	15,913	4,132
1979	9,727	11,562	1,934	16,942	4,365	93.2	5,842	3,394	3,647	15,918	4,285
1980	9,904	11,785	1,943	16,480	4,148	90.9	6,053	3,465	3,655	15,974	4,342
1981	9,814	12,148	1,963	15,326	3,601	88.9	6,063	3,496	3,682	15,862	4,484
1982	9,979	12,750	2,019	15,278	3,365	91.0	6,131	3,654	3,663	16,759	4,602
1983	10,128	13,240	1,996	16,081	3,853	96.5	6,259	3,714	3,733	17,261	4,610
1984	10,176	12,782	1,993	16,730	4,060	97.9	6,438	3,774	3,856	16,227	4,580
1985	10,237	12,559	1,948	16,433	4,191	98.6	6,442	3,675	3,845	16,057	4,684
1986	10,155	12,665	1,955	15,778	4,073	102.2	6,157	3,515	3,863	16,234	4,525
1987	10,192	11,698	1,987	15,532	4,075	103.8	5,947	3,461	3,761	15,358	4,598
1988	10,093	11,425	1,972	15,420	4,270[8]	106.8	5,812	3,446	3,768	14,981	4,700
1989	9,905	11,354	1,961	16,404	3,223	108.1	5,801	3,356	3,892	14,903	4,609
1990	10,676	11,180	1,959	16,170	3,305	108.7	6,100	3,523	3,772	15,284	4,369
1991	10,534	11,050	1,908	14,442	3,511	100.0	5,699	3,200	3,917	14,763	4,254
1992	10,364	10,909	1,898	13,153	3,359	47.2[22]	5,730	3,168	3,873	14,701	1,763[23]
1993	10,103	11,010	1,893	12,680	3,559	46.4[22]	5,800	3,349	3,927	14,780	1,889[23]
1994	10,673	10,873	1,933	12,222	4,295	41.9[22]	6,030	3,421	3,887	14,991	1,897
1995	11,259	11,294	1,908	11,642	4,645	39.1[22]	6,203	3,304	3,913	14,844	1,947
1996	11,575	11,013	1,902	11,696	4,686	35.5[22]	6,133	3,258	3,862	14,808	2,000
1997	11,752	10,922	1,884	12,123	4,638	33.8[22]	5,837	3,276	3,867	14,841	2,082
1998	11,833	10,995	1,804	12,596	4,441	32.9[22]	6,104	3,277	3,894	14,632	2,131
1999	11,736	11,174	1,790	12,284	5,076	31.9[22]	6,300	3,299	3,852	15,014	1,825

C6 Output of Cows' Milk (in thousands of tons)

NOTES

1. SOURCES:- Statistics for Denmark prior to 1929 are based on estimates in E. Jensen, *Danish Agriculture* (Copenhagen, 1937). All other statistics are taken from the official publications noted on p. xv or from the International Institute of Agriculture and the F.A.O. *Statistical Yearbooks.*
2. The basis on which the statistics are collected varies from country to country and over time, so that comparisons must be made with caution. In principle, the statistics include milk fed to young animals, except for countries marked with an asterisk or as indicated in footnotes.
3. Where necessary, conversions from liquid measure have been made on the assumption that the specific gravity of milk is 1.031.
4. A rather different series of milk production (i.e. milk sold off farms) is given for Finland back to 1860 in Pentti Viita, *Maataloustuotanto Suomessa 1860–1960* (Helsinki, 1965) as follows:-

1860	447	1875	656	1890	963	1905	1,384	1920	1,496
1861	445	1876	679	1891	917	1906	1,418	1921	1,585
1862	408	1877	680	1892	948	1907	1,542	1922	1,682
1863	427	1878	721	1893	986	1908	1,530	1923	1,680
1864	447	1879	735	1894	1,123	1909	1,529	1924	1,761
1865	456	1880	701	1895	1,292	1910	1,541	1925	1,900
1866	489	1881	638	1896	1,312	1911	1,519	1926	1,969
1867	447	1882	709	1897	1,389	1912	1,644	1927	2,071
1868	447	1883	725	1898	1,403	1913	1,676	1928	2,061
1869	484	1884	746	1899	1,290	1914	1,612	1929	2,098
1870	520	1885	776	1900	1,326	1915	1,524	1930	2,204
1871	539	1886	828	1901	1,260	1916	1,606	1931	2,256
1872	553	1887	837	1902	1,204	1917	1,461	1932	2,239
1873	565	1888	854	1903	1,302	1918	1,195	1933	2,271
1874	610	1889	892	1904	1,345	1919	1,275	1934	2,340

FOOTNOTES

[1] Including Luxembourg from 1946 (2nd line).
[2] Figures for 1939–45 are for deliveries to dairies only.
[3] Subsequently excludes Sub-Carpathian Russia (Ruthenia) and 12 villages in Slovakia ceded to the U.S.S.R. in 1945.
[4] Including South Jutland from 1920. The following earlier estimates are given in E. Jensen, *op. cit.* in note 1 (converted to thousands of tons):-

1861	758	1888	1,765	1903	2,723
1871	1,090	1893	2,022	1909	3,525
1881	1,438	1898	2,241	1914	3,602

[5] Subsequently excluding milk produced in the towns.
[6] Excluding parts of Alsace-Lorraine annexed by Germany, and, in 1943-44, Corsica.
[7] Saarland is excluded to 1935 and from 1948 to 1957 (1st line). West Berlin is included from 1961 (2nd line).
[8] Figures to 1938 (1st line) are probably are only of deliveries to dairies.
[9] Statistics to 1944 are for years ended 31 May following that indicated.
[10] Subsequently excluding milk fed to livestock.
[11] Figures to 1940 are for years ended 30 June.
[12] There was a substantial change of territory in 1945.
[13] The figure is for the 1924 boundaries of the U.S.S.R. Earlier figures on the same basis are:- 1913–24.1; 1917–24.2.
[14] Statistics from 1940 (2nd line) are for the territory established after the Second World War.
[15] Statistics to 1945 (1st line) are of deliveries to dairies only.
[16] Including goats' milk to 1950 (1st line).
[17] Great Britain only to 1938, and excluding milk fed to livestock.
[18] Subsequently including Trieste.
[19] Milk fed to livestock is not included previously.
[20] This break results from a revision in methods of assessment.
[21] Czech Republic. Slovakia = 1,277
[22] Russian Federation. Ex-U.S.S.R. figures are

Armenia	1992	376	Azerbaijan	1992	800x
	1993	200		1993	700
	1994	406		1994	784
	1995	418		1995	827
	1996	421		1996	843
	1997	425		1997	882
	1998	445		1998	947
	1999	452		1999	993

C6 Output of Cows' Milk (in thousands of tons)

Belarus	1992	3,287	Lithuania	1992	2,245
	1993	3,270		1993	2,500
	1994	4,691		1994	2,559
	1995	5,510		1995	2,670
	1996	5,070		1996	2,441
	1997	4,908		1997	2,400
	1998	5,132		1998	2,378
	1999	5,232		1999	2,411
Estonia	1992	919	Moldova	1992	1,128
	1993	808		1993	967
	1994	817		1994	899
	1995	864		1995	826
	1996	913		1996	733
	1997	945		1997	646
	1998	968		1998	589
	1999	909		1999	569
Georgia	1992	500	Tajikistan	1992	475
	1993	426		1993	500
	1994	429		1994	446
	1995	475		1995	370
	1996	521		1996	170
	1997	600		1997	220
	1998	608		1998	240
	1999	647		1999	280
Kazakhstan	1992	5,210	Tukmenistan	1992	400
	1993	5,490		1993	181
	1994	5,252		1994	715
	1995	4,576		1995	727
	1996	3,584		1996	755
	1997	3,295		1997	755
	1998	3,364		1998	765
	1999	3,535		1999	875
Kyrgistan	1992	900	Ukraine	1992	18,995
	1993	800		1993	18,199
	1994	872		1994	17,935
	1995	864		1995	17,060
	1996	885		1996	15,592
	1997	893		1997	13,540
	1998	959		1998	13,532
	1999	1,041		1999	13,140
Latvia	1992	1,479	Uzbekistan	1992	3,679
	1993	1,219		1993	2,800
	1994	1,314		1994	3,620
	1995	1,399		1995	3,550
	1996	1,462		1996	3,309
	1997	1,286		1997	3,370
	1998	1,215		1998	3,459
	1999	1,200		1999	3,500

[23] Yugoslavia: Ex-Yugoslavia figures are

	Bosnia-Hercegovina	Croatia	Macedonia	Slovenia
1992	705	709	117	380
1993	560	602	118	480
1994	400	600	119	577
1995	316	593	133	608
1996	385	621	138	593
1997	427	622	137	599
1998	516	635	179	634
1999	569	631	180	649

C7   BUTTER OUTPUT (in thousands of metric tons)

1900–1934

	Austria	Belgium	Denmark[2]	Finland	France	Germany	Ireland	Italy	Netherlands	Norway	Russia/USSR	Sweden	Switzerland	U.K.[10]
1900			72											
1901			79											
1902			81											
1903			92						60					
1904			95						54					
1905			95						57					
1906			96						60					
1907			106						61					
1908			112						62					
1909			113						59					
1910			112						65					
1911		55	113						62					
1912		55	109						67					
1913			112						69					
1914			117						70					
1915			111						73					
1916			105						74					
1917			91						63					
1918			58						46				13	
1919			62₃						51				12	
1920		46	85						57					
1921		49	105						60					
1922		49	120						65					
1923		51	132						69					
1924		52	140						73					
1925		60	141						75				13	
1926		61	152						83				14	
1927		62	162						85				13	
1928		63	166	21			33	42	85	3		41	15	
1929		60	179	24	220	310	36	42	87	4		48	16	
1930		62	190	27		345	35	42	87	4		55	17	49₁₀ / 7
1931		61	195	28	219	380	31	43	85	6		54	14	
1932		65	188	26	213	420	31	43	85	8		51	23	
1933		70	185	24	218	448	34	44	85	9		55	24	
1934	22	67	183	24	236	451₅	39	45	88	9		62	28	12

C7 Butter Output (in thousands of metric tons)

1935–1959

	Austria	Belgium	Denmark[2]	Finland	France	Germany	Ireland	Italy	Netherlands	Norway	Russia/USSR	Sweden	Switzerland	U.K.[10]
1935	23	62	173	24	243	452	42	50	96	9	⋮	63	27	21
1936	23	65	180	28	⋮	496	43	45	100	11	⋮	67	25	27
1937	23	63	183	30	208	517	39	55	101	12	⋮	73	24	19
1938	⋮	64	189	33	⋮	508	39	58	101	15	⋮	80	29	21
1939	31	61[1]	183	34	196[4]	548	36	60	109	18	⋮	84	27	22
1940	42	⋮	163	24	170[4]	627	33	61	106	13	⋮	81	23	16
1941	45	24	124	20	154[4]	⋮	34	54	100	8	⋮	78	22	8
1942	44	28	109	14	145[4]	⋮	31	49	71	11	⋮	72	18	10
1943	43	33	125	16	149[4]	⋮	30	38[8]	55	9	⋮	79	19	9
1944	41	21	129	17	123[4]	⋮	29	35	49	7	⋮	87	19	10

Germany — East[6] / West[5,7]

	Austria	Belgium	Denmark[2]	Finland	France	Germany (E / W)	Ireland	Italy	Netherlands	Norway	Russia/USSR	Sweden	Switzerland	U.K.[10]
1945	20	19	132	25	125	⋮ / ⋮	31	37	39	4	⋮	94	18	8
1946	25	22	141	31	152	54 / 226	28	38	53	6[9] / 15	⋮	100[9] / 106	20	11[10] / 20
1947	21	25	125	32	143	⋮ / 174	26	45	53	17	⋮	101	16	15
1948	22	⋮	120	40	180	45 / 174	29	47	71	17	⋮	95	14	17
1949	25	26[1] / 66	156	48	193	⋮ / 237[7] / 242	35	53	84	19	⋮	101	15	19
1950	25	72	179	53	225	71 / 259	37	58	94	19	⋮	111	19	25
1951	25	72	168	56	250	85 / 276	33	60	84	17	⋮	108	25	14
1952	29	74	154	62	235	97 / 271	33	60	74	16	382	95	22	16
1953	30	83	173	65	276	96 / 288	36	61	83	18	389[9] / 501	99	24	25
1954	32	91	181	65	305	109 / 303	40	62	82	14		94	29	28
1955	30	91	164	59	300	144 / 290	38	65	74	16	575	86	26	25
1956	33	89	165	74	325	141 / 301	44	63	77	18	675	83	27	34
1957	40	89	175	78	345	152 / 311	50	63	77	21	754	88	29	44
1958	40	90	159	80	340	158 / 359[5] / 362	48	62	92	18	779	87	31	36
1959	38	87	168	86	335	161 / 376	39	66	81	17	845	79	33	20

C7 Butter Output (in thousands of metric tons)

1955–1998

	Austria	Belgium	Denmark[2]	Finland	France	East Germany	West Germany	Ireland	Italy	Netherlands	Norway	Russia/ USSR	Sweden	Switz	U.K.
1960	39	89	167	93	385	175	406	46	67	100	20	848	84	35	45
1961	38	88	171	96	405	178	432	49	71	97	19	894	84	32	56
1962	39	97	167	96	405	160	449	50	70	102	20	940	92	35	65
1963	40	90	149	102	432	168	465	50	52	94	21	884	85	35	48
1964	42	85	156	105	427	173	472	56	56	88	20	952	80	30	28
1965	45	89	166	101	475	197	484	65	64	102	20	1,184	80	33	41
1966	45	85	160	101	492	206	489	67	70	99	24	1,157	75	34	34
1967	47	88	154	96	538	209	502	73	68	97	23	1,177	65	41	41
1968	46	98	160	102	575	220	524	78	68	118	26	1,165	66	38	54
1969	45	98	144	101	513	215	510	78	67	112	23	1,065	63	32	58
1970	42	92	131	87	481	216	494	73	67	121	19	1,067	50	29	65
1971	39	85	124	84	474	225	462	75	71	125	20	1,122	46	29	67
1972	43	92	136	83	539	249	489	78	79	163	22	1,176	56	31	96
1973	42	88	146	80	550	250	510	84	79	169	23	1,350	56	31	97
1974	42	92	137	78	543	266	508	73	71	172	21	1,360	58	34	54
1975	41	93	139	74	559	273	518	84	62	204	20	1,320	56	35	48
1976	41	90	139	82	531	278	542	98	67	202	23	1,356	61	35	90
1977	43	84	131	73	537	273	533	102	72	179	24	1,500	62	34	135
1978	39	98	140	73	538	281	563	119	77	211	20	1,472	63	33	164
1979	37	97	131	74	575	275	567	122	79	203	20	1,420	65	37	161
1980	40	88	113	74	598	280	576	111	76	181	22	1,388	66	35	170
1981	41	92	109	72	580	273	542	112	72	183	23	1,318	64	35	172
1982	41	93	121	70	619	266	551	133	76	216	25	1,403	69	33	216
1983	45	105	131	84	622	291	622	158	78	271	27	1,563	73	35	241
1984	43	102	104	80	632	309	567	165	81	241	25	1,588	78	38	206
1985	41	97	110	72	606	316	505	160	80	230	23	1,605	75	38	202
1986	42	100	112	72	640	321	566	153	80	265	23	1,700	68	37	222
1987	38	86	96	68	571	310	464	134	84	199	24	1,755	66	34	176
1988	35	72	94	61	516	306	392	125	83	170	22	1,805	62	36	140
1989	40	83	92	62	539	313	398	139	81	180	23	1,808	67	39	130
1990	41	88	94	62	550	286	391	151	79	175	20	1,802	74	38	138
1991	42	77	70	59	486	556		146	103	163	21	1,570[11]	60	40	112
1992	43	72	62	57	451	477		134	101	149	19	7,460[12]	59	39	98
1993	43	70	59	55	443	486		140	98	148	18	7,000[12]	69	39	109
1994	43	73	59	53	444	461		127	93	129	16	488	56	41	155
1995	41	91	54	53	453	486		142	94	132	16	421	57	42	127
1996	42	97	57	54	473	480		142	81	128	14	323	57	40	120
1997	42	107	50	50	466	442		139	93	135	18	277	59	40	139
1998	42	112	49	50	463	426		141	91	140	27	265	53	41	137

C7 Butter Output (in thousand of metric tons)

NOTE

SOURCE:- International Institute of Agriculture and F.A.O. *Statistical Yearbooks*, and the official publications noted on p. xv.

FOOTNOTES

[1] Figures for 1940 to 1949 (1st line) are of butter made in factories only.
[2] Earlier estimates are given in E. Jensen, *Danish Agriculture* (Copenhagen, 1937), and in E. Lindhard, *'Danmarks Landbrug, 1875–1925'*; *Lantbruck i Norden, 1875–1925* (Gothenburg, 1926), as follows (converted, where necessary, into thousands of tons):-

| 1861 | 24 | 1876 | 42 | 1888 | 65 | 1898 | 84 |
| 1871 | 36 | 1881 | 49 | 1893 | 75 | | |

[3] Subsequently including southern Jutland.
[4] Excluding the parts of Alsace-Lorraine annexed by Germany and, in 1943–44, Corsica.
[5] Saarland is excluded to 1934 and from 1946 to 1958 (1st line).
[6] Butter made in factories only.
[7] Figures from 1946 to 1949 (1st line) are for butter made in factories only.
[8] Subsequent figures are for the 1954 boundaries.
[9] Earlier figures are of butter made in factories only.
[10] Figures for 1930 (2nd line) to 1946 (1st line) are of butter made in factories only.
[11] Russian Federation: Figures for ex-U.S.S.R. as follows

	Armenia	Azerbaijan	Belarus	Georgia	Kazakhstan	Kyrgistan	Moldova	Tajikistan
1992	150F	2,500F	130,000F	700F	70,000F	9,000F	16,700	4,000F
1993	150F	2,400F	125,000F	700F	65,000F	8,000F	9,300	4,000F
1994	200	1,400	73,600	- -	46,500	3,900	8,300	1,500
1995	100	1,500	65,000	- -	30,400	2,000	5,600	700
1996	100	300	60,900	- -	15,300	1,100	3,900	200
1997	100	500	71,700	- -	7,200	1,500	2,600	200
1998	100	400	74,200	- -	4,700	1,500	2,600	100

	Turkmenistan	Ukraine	Uzbekistan	Estonia	Latvia	Lithuania
1992	4,000	302,888	17,312	26,849	31,757	49,200
1993	4,000	311,793	12,000F	23,114	33,000	53,000
1994	3,200	253,700	14,400	18,900	9,700	31,200
1995	1,900	221,900	10,500	15,600	6,400	32,300
1996	1,000	163,100	4,400	20,700	7,500	34,800
1997	900	116,500	4,000	17,500	7,800	34,700
1998	700	112,700	3,500	17,500	9,200	35,700

[12] Russian Federation: FAO estimate.

C8 MEAT OUTPUT (in thousands of metric tons)

1929–1959

	Austria	Belgium	Bulgaria	Czechoslovakia	Denmark[4]	Finland	France[6]	Germany[10]	East[11]	West[10]	Greece	Hungary	Ireland[14]	Italy
1929	...	257	...	474	...	87	1,310	3,151			...	...	...	800
1930	...	266	...	473	...	89	1,258	3,132			...	...	...	666
1931	...	277	...	483	...	95	1,229	3,232			...	...	...	703
1932	...	285	...	462	...	96	1,276	3,109			...	...	...	658
1933	...	307	46	435	...	97	1,342	3,151			...	...	...	679
1934	...	308	46	493	457	99	1,395[7] / 1,610	3,515[10]			...	...	...	634
1935	...	312	45	407	424	101	1,688	3,429			...	...	158	...
1936	...	302	47	380	397	99	1,702	3,375			...	...	163	...
1937	...	316	44	...	429	102	1,648	3,586			...	...	156	...
1938	...	303	44	...	393	109	1,651[8]	3,677			49	...	148	...
1939	...	296	43	426	407	126	1,516	...			...	...	154	...
1940	...	243	43	341	379	114	984	...			...	...	166	...
1941	...	135	49	310	278[5]	79	779	...			...	...	193	...
1942	...	147	42	285	271	64	734[8]	...			...	...	179	...
1943	...	101	23	289	282	77	609	...			...	...	145	...
1944	...	90	20	257	...	105	611[8]	...			...	...	143[14]	...
1945	...	90	31	240	332	90	822	...			50	...	143	320
1946	...	129	16	282	388	103	1,293		...	...	54	...	146[15] / 162	463
1947	...	152	25[2]	420	416	108	1,380		...	829	...	...	152	382
1948	...	187	...	259	298	109	1,500		...	833	...	...	135	478
1949	137	280	...	289	391[5] / 370	112	1,805		349	1,097	64	...	140	511
1950	196	315	...	...	437	103	1,901		625	1,490	62	...	146	511
1951	233	316	...	...	493	116	1,835		845	1,697	64	...	153	491
1952	260	344	...	...	481	112	1,985		1,019	1,818	79	109	177	570
1953	280[1]	356	...	...	574	114	2,190		1,177	1,938	85	118	190	609
1954	331	372	...	312	625	129	2,370		1,125	2,916	94	118	215	620
1955	343	381	...	353	633	133	2,455		1,202	2,179	107	128[3]	183	646
1956	354	385	...	392	611	130	2,500		1,199	2,213	116	161	170	703
1957	357	379	209	413	669	136	2,515		1,271	2,352	120	166	202	700
1958	375	400	256	415[3] / 709	666	133	2,470 / 2,509		1,280	2,461[10]	126	179	218	778
1959	376	413	231	716	713	131	2,673		1,266	2,519	134	376	224	853

C8 Meat Output (in thousands of metric tons)

1960–1974

	Austria	Belgium	Bulgaria	Czech	Denmark	Finland	France[6]	Germany[10] West[10]	Germany[11] East[11]	Greece	Hungary	Ireland[14]	Italy
1960	391	427	210	733	753	129	2,780	2,600[12] / 2,947	1,363	139	354	247	898
1961	410	418	243	761	756	131	2,928	3,077[10]	1,407	140	393	289	1,010
1962	434	450	262	775	811	150	3,093	3,292	1,225	152	410	285	1,056
1963	466	458	242	775	826	157	2,994[9] / 2,692	3,329	1,346	160	399	293	979
1964	436	420	263	831	845	167	2,605	3,391	1,494	169	391	280	979
1965	439	451	296	913	899	166	2,809	3,415	1,578	188	417	297	970
1966	435	490	311	881	928	159	2,862	3,443	1,660	206	406	310	1,049
1967	450	538	327	925	956	182	3,017	3,525	1,731	206	407	377	1,109[20] / 1,395
1968	403	576	352	978	925	175	3,056	3,786	1,798	208	469	360	1,560
1969	410	599	326	925	881	201	2,869	3,819	1,825	221	439	386	1,610
1970	414	695	301	955	911	213	2,971	3,969	1,800	233	438	400	1,725
1971	437	729	324	1,005	960	242	3,152	4,150	1,867	246	501	437	1,782
1972	435	753	364	1,066	937	239	3,060	3,952	2,001	265	538	410	1,746
1973	437	798	361	1,083	960	223	3,048	3,915	2,094	287	530[13] / 834	393	1,799
1974	475	884	352	1,141	983	245	3,416	4,202	2,245	336	940	514	1,859

C8   Meat Output (in thousand of metric tons)

1929–1974

	Neth'l	Norway[17]	Poland	Portugal[18]	Rom	Russia/ U.S.S.R[23] (million tons)	Spain	Sweden	Switz	U.K.[27]	Yugo-slavia[29]
1929	411	85	582	44	209	5.8	189	139	155	1,221	...
1930	412	...	586	44	187	4.3	184	159	151	1,154	...
1931	503	93	702	...	193	3.9	171	174	151	1,157	...
1932	512	...	690	51	169	2.8	161	174	159	1,217	...
1933	447	94	649	...	196	2.3	150	171	171	1,274	...
1934	437	102	647	53	228	2.0	147	185	173	1,316	...
1935	408	97	683	51	230	2.3	152	177	173	1,383	...
1936	413	98	738	58	229	3.7	...	189	158	1,402	...
1937	369	100	800	52	220	3.0	...	212	154	1,360[27]	...
1938	365	101	...	56[18]	237	4.5	...	219	163	...	...
1939	419	63	...	68	234[21]	5.1	...	234	198	...	440
1940	347	64[17]	...	67	172	3.9[24] / 4.7	74	251	200	...	...
1941	240	...	...	60	81	...	65	214	170	...	...
1942	188	...	...	43	99[21]	...	55	113[26] / 149	136	...	...
1943	...	...	...	49	119	...	85	188	132	...	...
1944	...	...	...	63	...[21]	...	...	...	126	...	...
1945	...	...	...	61	34[19]	2.6	...	...	118	934	...
1946	174	73	...	49	...	3.1	62	246	119	901	...
1947	194	82	...	51	...	2.5	54	262	141	762	283
1948	158[15]	68	...	73	...	3.1	82	242	137	787	312
1949	219	90	...	81	...	3.8	110[25]	277	165	952	347
1950	331	102	...	75	...	4.9	432	291	179	1,133	366
1951	381	99	...	72	...	4.7	436	312	176	1,157	329
1952	370	103	...	78[19] / 91	...	5.2	416	308	188	1,293	329
1953	397	100	...	93	...	5.8	398	305	198	1,348	398
1954	422	106	1,093	102	...	6.3	421	313	197	1,653	431
1955	467	122	1,213	99	...	6.3	413	334	198	1,559	454
1956	470	116	1,364	96[16] / 141	...	6.6	424	308	210	1,637	469
1957	496	117	1,496	142	...	7.4	449	326	220	1,680	493
1958	489	112	1,607	136	...	7.7	451	353	217	1,718	498
1959	501	116	1,479	148	...	8.7	483	364	221	1,673	575
1960	583[16] / 680	120	1,503	156	...	8.7	540	337	236	1,713	635
1961	640	127	1,623	162	...	8.7	532	338	246	1,867	644
1962	697	133	1,653	162	...	9.5	522	374	254	1,945	509
1963	752	121	1,571	150	260	10.2	587	375	255	1,981	657
1964	696	121	1,565	147	277	8.3	670	364	260	1,961	679
1965	786	130	1,733	162	302	10.0	577	368	276	1,993	776
1966	793	131	1,785	173	322	10.7	699	395	284	2,011	709
1967	864	130	1,817	160	395[22] / 679	11.5	766	397	289	1,983	780
1968	944	132	1,826	184	742	11.6	793	397	320	1,988	858
1969	935	141	1,882	217	717	11.8	822	401	328	1,976	806
1970	1,065	138	1,825	210	735	12.3	940	398	337	2,100	847
1971	1,155	140	1,841	200	753	13.3	935	401	350	2,149	922
1972	1,099	147	2,064	206	873	13.6	901	404	355	2,122	875
1973	1,130	152	2,270	221	994	13.5	1,104	394	370	2,073	857
1974	1,293	162	2,535	230	1,069	14.6	1,281	425	387	2,310	1,012

C8 Meat Output (in thousands of metric tons)

1975–1998

Year	Austria	Belgium	Bulgaria	Czechoslovakia	Denmark	Finland	France	East Germany	West Germany	Greece	Hungary	Ireland	Italy	Netherlands	Norway	Poland	Portugal	Romania	Russia/USSR	Spain	Sweden	Switzerland	UK	Yugoslavia
1975	482	848	428	1,096	970	241	3,416	2,412	4,168	346	996	565	1,799	1,302	161	2,478	256	1,055	15.0	1,204	431	380	2,290	1,052
1976	492	837	493	1,071	959	251	3,517	2,382	4,294	356	908	489	1,883	1,345	151	2,337	236	1,104	13.6	1,213	447	399	2,160	1,052
1977	492	842	453	1,121	988	247	3,373	2,318	4,283	362	1,002	552	2,021	1,369	164	2,271	250	1,215	14.7	1,309	457	415	2,130	1,160
1978	504	879	455	1,175	1,050	261	3,438	2,375	4,546	369	998	567	2,051	1,440	165	2,505	278	1,223	15.5	1,336	459	411	2,133	1,256
1979	535	919	487	1,184	1,153	271	3,713	2,386	4,710	353	1,029	579	2,207	1,528	170	2,549	273	1,346	15.4	1,465	470	428	2,222	1,251
1980	623	952	493	1,210	1,218	283	3,753[28]	2,478	4,801	381	1,065	642	2,300	1,564	172	2,397	295	1,343	15.1	1,534	480	452	2,305	1,226
1981	642	974	520	1,234	1,232	303	3,910	2,604	4,738	370	1,055	506	2,285	1,648	181	1,861	322	1,361	15.2	1,579	484	434	2,225	1,253
1982	656	941	530	1,124	1,223	302	3,796	2,416	4,650	366	1,098	539	2,283	1,644	186	2,120	327	1,205	15.4	1,676	491	454	2,184	1,274
1983	656	979	493	1,190	1,290	305	3,827	2,444	4,746	359	1,184	554	2,382	1,709	180	2,023	308	1,279	16.4	1,671	484	446	2,346	1,280
1984	681	1,036	533	1,231	1,282	296	4,020	2,583	4,880	364	1,263	588	2,470	1,830	179	1,975	305	1,367	17.1	1,708	484	445	2,387	1,401
1985	687	1,034	542	1,247	1,320	300	3,797	2,713	4,838	366	1,165	632	2,462	1,885	183	2,192	295	1,340	18.0	1,682	494	458	2,419	1,324
1986	681	1,053	589	1,256	1,389	299	3,657	2,776	5,048	339	1,118	692	2,420	1,929	186	2,461	305	1,350	18.9	1,733	462	458	2,329	1,317
1987	678	1,094	573	1,281	1,385	300	3,768	2,802	5,064	334	1,171	673	2,476	2,061	196	2,494	317	1,347	19.7	2,146	428	444	2,421	1,399
1988	686	1,111	679	1,330	1,385	282	3,834	2,800	4,969	327	1,137	644	2,501	2,346	196	2,543	317	1,381	20.0	2,383	431	446	2,288	1,388
1989	634	1,130	629	1,397	1,319	291	3,693	1,953	4,757	363	1,355	639	2,597	2,249	185	4,298	359	1,396	19.8	...	452	456	2,215	1,216
1990	627	1,042	610	1,364	1,359	307	3,789	...	5,171	360	1,308	734	2,660	2,349	191	4,493	398	1,555	18.6	4,827	446	444	2,277	1,540
1991	612	1,308	559	1,227	1,431	301	3,921	6,114		360	1,286	825	2,677	2,335	190	4,533	433	1,713	..[31]	4,887	411	449	2,352	1,515
1992	615	1,327	561	1,198	1,542	296	4,185	5,532		360	1,133	862	2,698	2,363	200	4,313	427	1,430	8.6[31]	4,920	411	439	2,260	547[32]
1993	605	1,380	468	829[30]	1,667	278	4,073	5,009		369	995	850	2,601	2,509	221	3,940	440	1,453	7.7	...	436	426	2,161	507[32]
1994	757	1,380	343	643	1,712	280	3,890	5,064		353	682	753	2,619	2,294	206	2,111	438	1,114	5.7	2,849	454	394	2,387	794
1995	723	1,405	366	674	1,677	265	3,975	5,052		343	650	779	2,603	2,218	208	2,354	435	950	4.8	2,925	456	404	2,409	899
1996	767	1,436	388	667	1,673	270	4,072	5,160		344	781	836	2,670	2,223	217	2,483	450	880	4.6	3,118	460	385	2,094	986
1997	754	1,377	342	621	1,697	281	4,088	5,054		339	715	865	2,633	1,958	221	2,323	461	916	4.1	3,238	482	373	2,135	883
1998	776	1,373	342	615	1,795	282	4,040	5,254		342	717	902	2,598	2,244	221	2,245	467	859	3.8	3,326	483	380	2,209	933

C8 Meat Output (in thousand of metric tons)

NOTES

1. SOURCES:- International Institute of Agriculture and F.A.O. *Statistical Yearbooks*, and the official publications noted on p. xv. Finnish statistics to 1954 are from Pentii Viita, *Maataloustuotanto Suomessa 1860–1960* (Helsinki, 1965).
2. W.G. Hoffman, *Das Wachstum der Deutschen Wirtschaft seit der Mitte des 19 Jahrhunderts* (Berlin, etc., 1965) gives the following estimates for Germany for the period 1816–1938, relating to the territory of Imperial Germany in 1914 for the period 1816–1913 (except that Alsace-Lorraine is only included from 1871), and to the boundaries of the day for 1924–39 (in thousands of metric tons):-

1816	338	1845	761	1862	1,019	1879	1,515	1896	2,482	1913	3,183
1819	368	1846	779	1863	1,093	1880	1,515	1897	2,523	1924	2,602
1822	390	1847	704	1864	1,239	1881	1,507	1898	2,611	1925	2,699
1825	453	1848	730	1865	1,195	1882	1,581	1899	2,764	1926	2,786
1928	458	1849	766	1866	1,189	1883	1,641	1900	2,803	1927	3,106
1831	485	1850	838	1867	1,113	1884	1,745	1901	2,712	1928	3,406
1834	545	1851	803	1868	1,153	1885	1,774	1902	2,575	1919	3,331
1835	611	1852	740	1869	1,198	1886	1,822	1903	2,704	1930	3,335
1836	641	1853	756	1870	1,172	1887	1,889	1904	2,901	1931	3,513
1837	624	1854	752	1871	1,245	1888	2,014	1905	2,878	1932	3,369
1838	637	1855	715	1872	1,242	1889	1,934	1906	2,847	1933	3,391
1839	659	1856	808	1873	1,317	1890	1,915	1907	2,835	1934	3,758
1840	664	1857	889	1874	1,440	1891	1,899	1908	3,177	1935	3,616
1841	696	1858	974	1875	1,443	1892	1,930	1909	3,199	1936	3,495
1842	785	1859	957	1876	1,453	1893	2,044	1910	3,200	1937	3,732
1843	641	1860	1,012	1877	1,389	1894	2,051	1911	3,357	1938	3,776
1844	687	1861	991	1878	1,480	1895	2,216	1912	3,274		

3. Earlier Figures are available for Finland, as follows:

1860	41	1875	42	1890	59	1905	75	1920	87	
1861	42	1876	45	1891	58	1906	73	1921	92	
1862	40	1877	40	1892	55	1907	76	1922	93	
1863	37	1878	41	1893	51	1908	77	1923	95	
1864	39	1879	48	1894	55	1909	74	1924	93	
1865	39	1880	49	1895	60	1910	80	1925	91	
1866	42	1881	37	1896	66	1911	83	1926	90	
1867	40	1882	38	1897	70	1912	85	1927	93	
1868	31	1883	43	1898	74	1913	85	1928	94	
1869	31	1884	43	1899	72	1914	86			
1870	36	1885	43	1900	71	1915	85			
1871	43	1886	49	1901	68	1916	78			
1872	36	1887	54	1902	68	1917	80			
1873	36	1888	52	1903	67	1918	73			
1874	36	1889	50	1904	70	1919	75			

4. In general, meat from animals other than cattle, pigs, and sheep is not included, though national practice has varied. Where a change is known to have occurred it is indicated in the footnotes.

FOOTNOTES

[1] Figures from 1954 are ones which were revised later. From the size of the break here it appears that there were substantial revisions. The unrevised figure for 1954 is 285.
[2] Previous figures are of slaughterings in towns only.
[3] Previous figures are of commercial production only.
[4] Earlier estimates are given in E. Lindhard, *'Danmarks Landbrug, 1875–1925', Landbrukt i Norden, 1975–1925* (Gothenburg, 1926), as follows (in thousands of tons):-

1871	116	1888	146	1903	242	1918	175
1876	124	1893	164	1909	261	1923	357
1881	129	1898	194	1914	359	1924	365

[5] Figures for 1942 to 1949 (1st line) include allowance for the weight of animals exported alive.
[6] Excluding horsemeat.
[7] Earlier figures are of meat on which slaughter tax was paid.
[8] Figures for 1939–44 exclude the parts of Alsace-Lorraine annexed by Germany, and those for 1943–44 exclude Corsica.
[9] Earlier figures include lard.
[10] Up to 1934 and from 1947 to 1957 (1st line) Saarland is excluded. West Berlin is also excluded from 1947 to 1961. In 1962 production there was 26 thousand tons.
[11] Statistics are of the live weight of meat animals slaughtered.
[12] There was a change in the assessment of pork weights.

C8 Meat Output (in thousand of metric tons)

[13] There was a great increase in the recorded production of pig meat.
[14] Figures to 1944 are for years ended 31 May.
[15] Subsequent statistics do not include meat from imported animals.
[16] Subsequently including lard.
[17] Figures to 1940 are for years ended 30 June.
[18] Mainland only up to 1938.
[19] Earlier statistics are of slaughterings in public slaughterhouses.
[20] Subsequent statistics include estimates of unregistered slaughterings.
[21] Southern Dobrudja was ceded to Bulgaria in 1940. Bessarabia and northern Bukovina were ceded to the U.S.S.R. in 1940, but were reconquered temporarily in 1943, and may be included in the 1943 and 1944 figures. Northern Transylvania was ceded to Hungary in 1940 but regained by 1946.
[22] Later revisions were not carried further back than 1967.
[23] Earlier statistics are available as follows (in millions of tons):-

1913 (1924 boundaries)	4.1
1917	4.3
1921	3.3
1924	3.4
1928	4.9

[24] Figures from 1940 (2nd line) are for the territory established after the Second World War.
[25] Earlier figures are for commercial production in 50 provincial capitals only.
[26] Earlier figures relate only to inspected slaughterhouses.
[27] Figures to 1937 are for Great Britain only.
[28] There was a change in the method of assessment.
[29] Including goat meat.
[30] Czechoslovakia Republic. Slovakia = 399
[31] Russian Federation. Ex-U.S.S.R. as follows.

	Armenia	Azerbaijan	Belarus	Georgia	Kazakhstan	Kyrgistan	Moldva	Tajikistan
1992	67	118	950	111	1,266	216	234	69
1993	43	124	869	104	1,309	199	180	68
1994	43	68	641	94	1,052	177	...	58
1995	41	66	582	114	867	167	...	53
1996	45	71	554	124	740	169	...	45
1997	40	76	563	111	623	164	...	30
1998	38	79	568	116	554	167	...	32

	Turkmenistan	Ukraine	Uzbekistan	Estonia	Latvia	Lithvania
1992	96	3,399	468	108	245	377
1993	58	2,815	408	84	168	404
1994	100	2,387	483	63	124	199
1995	104	2,035	491	62	112	182
1996	97	1,855	447	54	67	175
1997	98	1,664	474	49	63	177
1998	87	1,575	497	51	62	151

[32] Yugoslavia. Ex-Yugoslavia as follows.

	Bosnia-Hercegovina	Croatia	Macedonia	Slovenia
1992	119	188	37	138
1993	103	207	45	135
1994	52	90	40	123
1995	34	78	36	123
1996	37	74	26	117
1997	20	72	26	113
1998	16	63	23	98

C9 LANDINGS OF FISH (in thousands of metric tons)

	Denmark	France	Germany	Iceland	Italy[8]	Netherlands	Norway[3]	Sweden	United Kingdom
1860	...	...	...	...	38	...	...	...	...
1861	...	...	...	...	40	...	...	...	...
1862	...	...	...	...	42	...	...	...	...
1863	...	...	...	...	42	...	...	...	...
1864	...	...	...	...	44	...	...	...	...
1865	...	...	...	...	43	...	...	...	...
1866	...	...	...	...	47	...	21	...	...
1867	...	...	...	...	47	...	22	...	...
1868	...	...	...	...	47	...	20	...	...
1869	...	...	...	...	47	...	19	...	...
1870	...	...	...	...	47	8	25	...	...
1871	...	...	...	...	47	10	25	...	...
1872	...	...	...	...	50	8	23	...	...
1873	...	...	...	...	47	12	25	...	...
1874	...	61	...	...	47	11	23	...	...
1875	...	57	...	...	47	10	24	...	...
1876	...	67	...	...	47	11	22	...	...
1877	...	67	...	...	51	14	29	...	...
1878	...	...	...	...	55	11	21	...	...
1879	...	71	...	...	55	17	21	...	...
1880	...	76	29	...	60	22	23	...	...
1881	...	...	29	...	62	20	20	...	...
1882	...	61	29	...	62	24	20	...	...
1883	...	78	30	...	61	24	24	...	...
1884	...	92	30	...	65	34	24	...	...
1885	...	93	31	...	72	29	19	...	...
1886	...	93	31	...	74	38	22	...	...
1887	...	...	32	...	73	37[2]	15	...	...
						48			
1888	...	88	32	...	78	41	22	...	592
1889	...	100	34	...	84	54	23	...	653
1890	...	93	34	...	85	56	22	...	649
1891	...	...	32	...	89	43	26	...	611
1892	...	...	40	...	91	71	25	...	636
1893	...	...	41	...	91	67	24	...	689
1894	...	97[1]	48	...	95	65	23	...	714
		118							
1895	...	128	62	...	88	58	22	...	715
1896	...	181	71	...	92	64	22	...	747
1897	...	158	59	...	98	41	25	...	706
1898	...	162	88	...	94	63	21	...	805
1899	...	133	67	...	80	34	24	...	760
1900	...	148	97	...	82	53	29	...	745
1901	...	156	122	...	77	70	28	...	805
1902	...	132	120	...	72	93	29	...	913
1903	...	128	144	...	83	107	29	...	943
1904	...	139	149	...	80	100	27	...	1,030
1905	...	137	140	46	82	76	31	...	1,024
1906	...	148	155	49	87	93	33	...	1,044
1907	...	137	179	55	90	107	39	...	1,205
1908	...	165	181	59	103	86	35[3]	...	1,152
							421		
1909	...	151	185	56	124	101	522	...	1,136

C9 Landings of Fish (in thousands of metric tons)

1910–1914

	Denmark	France	Germany	Iceland	Italy[8]	Netherlands	Norway[3]	Sweden	United Kingdom
1910	44	170	194	61	118	98	529	...	1,162
1911	53	129	190	66	109	86	581	...	1,198
1912	58	111	204	87	104	66	655	...	1,200
1913	61	127	217	93	100	99	597	...	1,224
1914	52	82	...	93	90	65	618	107	896

1915–1946

	Den-mark	Faroes	France[8]	Germany	Iceland	Italy	Neth'l	Norway	Poland	Port-ugal	Russia/USSR	Spain	Sweden	U.K.
1915	67	...	65	...	109	71	82	575	...	...	...	...	31	440
1916	93	...	65	...	128	64	95	515	...	...	...	...	45	418
1917	63	...	65	...	104	55	...	541	...	...	...	...	48	396
1918	65	...	67	...	98	66	13	611	...	...	...	...	84	445
1919	89	...	115	...	128	88	111	657	...	...	...	...	...	868
1920	64	...	126	...	137	102	86[2]	484	...	...	...	...	97	1,096
1921	62	...	111[4] / 230	...	140	112[8]	84	438	...	...	...	...	68	856
1922	51	...	223	...	183	120	75	563	...	...	...	...	69	923[10]
1923	68	17	241	...	184	114	85	571	...	...	...	...	88	862
1924	69	16	251	274	254	109	108	617	...	...	...	...	75	1,054
1925	79	17	253	261	269	107	86	622	...	...	...	...	72	983
1926	76	20	267	294	201	113	102[2] / 201	799	...	...	...	268	77	971
1927	84	21	270	298	323	118	213	792	...	165	...	231	80	1,021
1928	95	24	257	324	342	124	246	894	...	200	...	254	88	1,061
1929	89	27	286	337	348	129	231	976	...	150	954	182	82	1,111
1930	93	32	291	368	417	135	243	994	...	185	...	286	87	1,152
1931	88	31	307	388[6] / 347	363	140	259	740	6	202	...	309	88	1,041
1932	90	29	309	339	345	144	210	910	9	175	...	320	87	1,025
1933	85	27	317	387	398	146	195	1,055	14	155[9]	...	322	102	985
1934	89	23	333	401	371	148	219	683	15	217	...	388	101	981
1935	87	21	294	478	310	167	197	924	17	223	...	...	107	1,044
1936	87	19	319	599	301	170	233	1,031	23	203	...	...	112	1,095
1937	88	28	358	672	368	173	263	904	14	190	1,583	...	121	1,142
1938	87	29	444[5]	718	352	175	236	1,065	13	241	1,523	299	144	1,097[11] / 816
1939	101	...	187	542	307	177	171	1,043	...	201	...	370	133	607
1940	119	...	136	...	410	160	...	1,081	...	195	...	440	90	200
1941	156	...	147	...	309	127	96	811	...	192	...	435	113	144
1942	163	...	117	...	412	100	78	755	...	201	...	453	125	178
1943	192	...	93	...	463	85[8]	71	643	...	254	...	445	144	178
1944	173	...	81[5]	...	546	79	...	648	...	251	...	482	129	192

				East	West									
1945	...	...	214[6]	...	...	366	100	...[6]	756[12]	3	244[6]	...	553	153[6]	324[11] / 522
1946	197	...	245	...	265	413	115[6] / 160	190	945	23	306	...	594	184	944

C9 Landings of Fish (in thousands of metric tons)

1947–1998

	Den-mark	Faroes	France[8]	Germany East	Germany West	Iceland	Italy	Neth'l	Norway	Poland	Port-ugal	Russia/ USSR	Spain	Sweden	U.K.
1947	206	97	317	...	302	506	160	295	1,196	40	282	...	581	179	1,037[11] / 1,172
1948	226	92	438	...	409	516	157	294	1,504	47	292	1,485	547	194	1,206
1949	258	100	435	...	501	437	179[8]	264	1,297	49	281	1,827	598	182	1,159
1950	251	98	432	...	553	386	186	258	1,468	66	307	1,627	604	187	989
1951	293	93	464	...	679	440	185	294	1,839	88	307	1,977	619	183	1,086
1952	324	87	468	...	663	437	212	314	1,815	92	363	1,888	617	204	1,105
1953	343	89	497	62	764	458	208	343	1,557	107	425	1,983	643	200	1,122
1954	359	89	479	63	704	480	218	339	2,068	118	439	2,258	666	201	1,070
1955	425	106	497	69	815	518	218	320	1,813	127	425	2,495	770	220	1,100
1956	463	116	516	75	801	548	220	298	2,201	139	472	2,616	762	197	1,050
1957	533	106	492	97	792	517	212[6] / 248	301	1,746	139	470	2,531	777	222	1,015
1958	598	107	501	93	743	605	246	314	1,442	145	456	2,621	845	238	999
1959	674	87	556	106	768	655	254	320	1,575	162	428	2,756	859	268	989
1960	581	109	571	114	674	610	250	315	1,543	184	475	3,051	970	254	924
1961	638	120	568[7] / 751	130	619	716	282	346	1,523	186	500	3,250	988	267	893
1962	785	144	744	150	633	833	257	322	1,332	180	526	3,616	1,108	293	944
1963	848	137	742	189	647	785	290	361	1,388	227	540	3,977	1,332	341	961
1964	871	139	780	225	624[6]	973	325	388	1,623	264	604	4,476	1,213	387	974
1965	841	145	768	231	633	1,199	354	377	2,312	298	554	5,100	1,355	380	1,047
1966	851	165	805	223	657	1,240	369	353	2,872	335	506	5,349	1,380	330	1,068
1967	1,070	173	820	288	662	898	373	315	3,266	339	540	5,777	1,460	351	1,026
1968	1,467	166	803	302	683	601	364	323	2,856	407	506	6,082	1,533	328	1,040
1969	1,275	176	701	316	652	690	371	323	2,491	408	457	6,498	1,522	278	1,083
1970	1,226	208	764	322	613	734	387	301	2,980	469	464	7,244	1,539	295	1,099
1971	1,401	207	758	338	508	685	405	321	3,075	518	463	7,337	1,505	238	1,107
1972	1,443	208	774	336	419	727	425	348	3,124	544	445	7,752	1,529	227	1,076
1973	1,465	247	797	365	478	902	401	344	2,910	580	478	8,614	1,569	227	1,130
1974	1,835	247	790	363	526	945	426	326	2,578	679	430	9,255	1,498	214	1,079
1975	1,767	286	784	376	442	995	406	351	2,484	801	375	9,970	1,512	215	970
1976	1,912	342	778	279	454	986	420	285	3,365	750	346	10,132	1,469	213	1,027
1977	1,806	310	743	212	432	1,374	372	313	3,407	655	307	9,351	1,389	190	997
1978	1,740	318	768	198	412	1,567	399	324	2,593	571	253	9,000	1,373	193	1,031
1979	1,721	267	745	222	357	1,645	426[13] / 479	324	2,658	601	243	9,050	1,255	206	906
1980	2,011	275	788	235	307	1,515	506	340	2,409	640	270	9,516	1,315	241	847
1981	1,852	242	775	245	331	1,442	514	434	2,552	630	260	9,566	1,357	265	883
1982	1,927	249	752	236	313	789	546	505	2,501	608	255	9,991	1,474	264	912
1983	1,863	330	782	237	306	839	551	506	2,836	735	248	9,817	1,413	269	852
1984	1,848	347	770	226	327	1,535	578	432	2,466	719	285	10,593	1,441	282	848
1985	1,765	374	832	201	225	1,680	589	504	2,119	683	299	10,523	1,483	240	901
1986	1,849	353	874	212	202	1,659	568	455	1,914	645	402	11,260	1,489	215	858
1987	1,706	391	849	196	202	1,633	560	456	1,949	671	395	11,160	1,526	215	952
1988	1,972	360	888	179	209	1,759	576	398	1,840	655	347	11,332	1,593	251	946
1989	1,929	309	850			1,502	551	453	1,908	565	332	11,310	1,560	258	824
1990	1,518	289	863	391		1,508	525	460	1,745	473	322	10,389	1,400	260	771
1991	1,793	247	816	303		1,050	552	444	2,168	457	326	7,047[14]	1,320	245	820
1992	1,995	271	817	307		1,577	557	439	2,547	506	300	5,611[14]	1,330	315	827
1993	1,534	262	831	316		1,718	552	487	2,561	423	274	4,461[14]	1,290	348	898
1994	1,916	253	904	273		1,560	599	529	2,585	460	270	3,780	1,262	394	964
1995	2,044	297	892	298		1,616	627	522	2,802	451	265	4,374	1,365	412	1,003
1996	1,723	324	846	312		2,064	575	511	2,960	369	266	4,730	1,358	379	975
1997	1,866	345	855	319		2,210	553	550	3,223	391	229	4,715	1,382	364	1,016
1998	1,599	397	810	334		1,686	562	657	3,259	277	232	4,518	1,420	416	1,057

C9 **Landings of Fish** (in thousands of metric tons)

NOTES

1. SOURCES:- France to 1920, Iceland, Italy, Norway, and the U.K. from the official publications noted on p. xv. Germany from W.G. Hoffman, *Das Wachstum der Deutschen Wirtschaft seit der Mitte des 19 Jahrhunderts* (Berlin, 1965); Netherlands to 1920 from data supplied by the Netherlands Central Office of Statistics; all others from League of Nations and United Nations *Statistical Yearbooks* and F.A.O., *Yearbook of Fisheries Statistics*.
2. The definitions of fish landings vary from country to country, but except as indicated in footnotes they are consistent for each country. For France prior to 1961, the Netherlands since 1946, and the U.K. throughout, fish landed at foreign ports are not included; and for the Netherlands since 1946 fish landed at Dutch ports by foreign ships are included. Otherwise the statistics relate to fish caught by the ships of the country concerned.

FOOTNOTES

[1] Figures to 1894 (1st line) are of cod, herring and mackerel only.
[2] Statistics to 1887 (1st line) are of pickled herring only. From 1887 (2nd line) to 1920 they are of all salted herring. Subsequently all kinds of fish are included, but from 1921 to 1926 (1st line) they exclude coastal fisheries.
[3] Statistics to 1908 (1st line) are of the value of the catch in million kroner.
[4] Figures from 1894 (2nd line) to 1921 (1st line) are of cod, herring, mackerel, tunny, and sardines only.
[5] Figures for 1939–1964 exclude some molluscs.
[6] There is a change in the method of estimation.
[7] Subsequently includes that part of the catch which was landed abroad.
[8] Figures to 1921 apply to the 1871 boundaries. For 1922–43 they apply to the 1924 boundaries, and from 1944 to the boundaries of 1954, except that Trieste is not included until 1950.
[9] Previous statistics exclude that part of the catch which was recorded in numbers not in weight.
[10] Subsequent statistics do not include southern Ireland. Statistics for Great Britain alone in 1922 and 1923 were respectively 902 and 860 thousand tons.
[11] Statistics for 1938 (2nd line) to 1945 (1st line) are for England and Wales only, and from 1945 (2nd line) to 1947 (1st line) they are for Great Britain.
[12] Subsequent statistics are converted to round fresh weight.
[13] The reason for this break is unknown.
[14] Russian Federation. Figures for ex-U.S.S.R. as follows.

	Azerbaijan	Belarus	Estonia	Georgia	Kazakhstan	Latvia	Lithuania	Turkmenistan	Ukraine	Uzbekistan
1992	39	15	132	40	80	157	192	40	525	28
1993	36	14	146	37	75	142	119	37	371	23
1994	19	8	124	8	48	139	151	17	311	17
1995	11	6	132	4	50	150	149	11	414	14
1996	7	7	109	3	46	143	130	9	450	7
1997	6	5	124	3	34	106	198	9	403	11
1998	5	5	119	3	24	103	223	8	491	10

C10   EXTERNAL TRADE IN CORN (in thousands of metric tons or hectolitres)

Key:- (a) = thousand hectolitres; (b) = thousand metric tons; I = Imports; E = Exports

1750–1799

	Great Britain[1] I (a)	Great Britain[1] E (a)	Sweden[17] I (a)[31]
1750	...	2,764	3,439
1751	...	1,929	2,030
1752	...	1,251	2,680
1753	...	876	4,369
1754	...	1,039	4,691
1755	...	689	7,091
1756	...	300	6,024
1757	413	35	3,843
1758	58	26	3,109
1759	...	663	2,004
1760	...	1,146	1,411
1761	...	1,286	1,638
1762	...	858	5,267
1763	...	1,251	5,988
1764	...	1,155	9,816
1765	305	486	8,102
1766	32	480	5,875
1767	1,449	15	6,141
1768	1,015	20	8,097
1769	12	150	6,603
1770	—	218	5,036
1771	9	29	3,815
1772	73	20	7,891
1773	166	23	5,734
1774	841	47	2,200
1775	1,632	265	1,060
1776	61	614	4,058
1777	678	256	5,339
1778	308	410	5,094
1779	15	646	5,717
1780	12	652	4,537
1781	465	300	9,274
1782	236	422	10,813
1783	1,699	151	15,052
1784	631	259	15,839
1785	323	387	11,745
1786	148	596	11,361
1787	172	352	8,135
1788	433	241	7,328
1789	329	407	9,350
1790	649	90	6,622
1791	1,364	207	4,429
1792	64	873	3,074
1793	1,425	224	3,306
1794	954	451	3,219
1795	913	55	728
1796	2,557	73	2,448
1797	1,344	160	5,394
1798	1,155	175	10,091
1799	1,347	113	7,176

1800–1849

	Austria-Hungary[2] I (b)	Austria-Hungary[2] E (b)	Denmark[3] I (a)	Denmark[3] E (a)	France[4] I (a)	France[4] E (a)
1800	...	...	...	...	...	...
1801	...	...	...	...	...	...
1802	...	...	...	...	...	...
1803	...	...	...	...	...	...
1804	...	...	...	...	...	...
1805	...	...	...	...	...	...
1806	...	...	...	...	...	...
1807	...	...	...	...	...	...
1808	...	...	...	...	...	...
1809	...	...	...	...	...	...
1810	...	...	...	...	...	...
1811	...	...	...	...	...	...
1812	...	...	...	...	...	...
1813	...	...	...	...	...	...
1814	...	...	...	...	...	...
1815	...	...	...	...	...	...
1816	...	...	...	...	...	...
1817	...	...	...	...	...	...
1818	...	...	...	...	...	...
1819	...	...	...	...	1,305	186
1820	...	...	...	1,745	662	173
1821	...	...	...	2,514	609	63
1822	...	...	...	2,041	1	72
1823	...	...	...	2,010	1	90
1824	...	...	...	2,814	1	218
1825	...	...	...	2,925	951	799
1826	...	...	...	2,560	90	541
1827	...	...	...	2,428	5	20
1828	...	...	...	3,268	88	16
1829	...	...	...	2,308	130	17
1830	...	...	...	2,089	154	10
1831	...	...	...	1,877	85	20
1832	...	...	...	2,291	335	17
1833	...	...	...	3,021	1	18
1834	...	...	...	3,511	...	20
1835	...	...	...	2,560	...	21
1836	...	...	...	1,966	17	23
1837	...	...	...	2,239	21	25
1838	...	...	...	2,416₃ / 1,168	8	49
1839	...	...	...	1,769	88	59
1840	...	...	...	2,131	168	15
1841	...	...	...	1,784	12	64
1842	37	78	...	1,333	42	64
1843	74	67	138	1,798	152	22
1844	67	126	57	2,559	186	28
1845	65	73	62	2,674	56	33
1846	66	57	51	2,975	369	18
1847	98	84	366	2,758	757	15
1848	71	8	17	3,801	94	144
1849	...	...	40	4,430	...	222

C10 External Trade in Corn (in thousands of metric tons or hectolitres)

1800–1849

	Norway[5]	Russia[6]	Sweden[17]		U.K.: Great Britain	
	I	E	I	E	I	E
	(b)	(a)	(a)[31]	(a)[31]	(a)	(a)
1800	...	...	1,824	...	3,680	64
1801	...	...	8,692	...	4,145	81
1802	...	...	4,452	...	1,885	433
1803	...	...	3,696	...	1,088	224
1804	...	...	4,979	...	1,341	183
1805	...	...	1,140	...	2,679	227
1806	...	...	3,439	...	902	87
1807	...	...	1,798	...	1,178	73
1808	...	...	779	...	247	285
1809	...	...	4,409	...	1,327	90
1810	...	...	3,701	...	4,559	221
1811	...	...	4,600	...	977	285
1812	...	...	6,245	...	847	134
1813	...	...	13,061	...	1,626	...
1814	...	...	6,931[17]	...	2,481	323
1815	...	...	2,853	63	1,117	663
1816	...	...	3,004	12	966	355
1817	...	...	2,467	1	3,171	925
1818	...	...	7,423	14	4,928	172
1819	...	...	5,853	55	1,821	131
1820	...	...	423	378	2,897	276
1821	...	...	60	425	2,057	582
1822	...	...	372	62	1,487	465
1823	...	...	29	11	1,233	425
1824	...	...	49	218	1,286	180
1825	...	...	39	115	2,292	113
1826	...	...	2,305	44	2,609	58
1827	...	...	5,120	137	2,071	166
1828	53	...	11	1,338	4,102	221
1829	49[5]	...	13	675	6,371	218
1830	...	...	432	344	6,417	108
1831	...	...	1,533	664	8,343	192
1832	...	...	1,077	125	3,648	844
1833	...	...	51	2,013	3,392	279
1834	...	...	23	1,985	2,853	463
1835	72	...	739	1,390	2,185	390
1836	87	...	60	633	2,505	748
1837	108	...	1,182	372	3,226	896
1838	89	...	8,504	1	5,594	463
1839	110	...	1,911	496	9,050	125
1840	83	...	133	830	7,351[7] / 635	253
1841	78	...	757	1,680	596	...
1842	81	468	1,506	1,854	661	...
1843	76	586	463	983	251	...
1844	100	761	379	1,709	477	...
1845	59	699	744	4,468	354	...
1846	68	1,115	1,359	2,675	647	...
1847	83	2,755	153	2,665	1,749	...
1848	109	1,037	70	4,038	1,238	...
1849	117	925	317	6,081	1,758	...

C10 External Trade in Corn (in thousands of metric tons or hectolitres)

1850–1899

	Austria-Hungary[2]		Denmark[3]		France[4]		Germany[11]
	I	E	I	E	I	E	I
	(b)	(b)	(a)	(a)	(b)	(b)	(b)
1850	...	...	83	4,083	...	326	...
1851	156	56	152	3,288	8	364	...
1852	235	39	95	3,531	20	177	...
1853	275[8]	24[8]	180	3,437	359	78	...
1854	332	58	194	3,570	418	19	...
1855	225	122	124	4,575	276	14	...
1856	138	233	198	3,104	658	13	...
1857	125	169	208	3,364	291	30	...
1858	133[2]	117[2]	129	3,302	137	484	...
1859	123	108	115	4,003	105	613	...
1860	102[2]	352[2]	267	3,217	55	362	692
1861	111	435	482	3,662	1,027	92	547
1862	120	418	442	3,123	472	42	671
1863	116	212	411[3]	4,511[3]	185	62	360
1864	176	216	121	3,242	61	154	384[11]
1865	92[2]	487[2]	193	4,980	26	358	516[12]
1866	104	429	279	4,018	63	515	536
1867	105	1,029	333	3,813	694	43	1,357
1868	121	1,385	565	2,695	831	51	1,284
1869	110	819	393	3,359	139	66	876
1870	155	427	366	4,766	424[10]	31[10]	1,037[11]
1871	190	632	308	4,104	1,044	12	1,077[12]
1872	462	281	289	4,623	421	312	1,170
1873	619	340	675	3,241	519	223	1,639
1874	743	446	956	2,640	821	171	2,010
1875	202	592	882	2,732	354	492	1,891
1876	289	651	1,156	2,637	534	253	2,571
1877	529	947	2,473	1,512	349	388	3,155
1878	488	897	1,960	2,752	1,398	62	2,844
1879	521	961	1,643[7]	3,626[7]	2,234	33	3,217
			234	289			
1880	786	730	159	307	2,040	31	1,642
1881	652	687	143	192	1,319	33	1,878
1882	663	1,117	138	175	1,341	22	2,090
1883	528	755	213	155	1,073	28	2,175
1884	555	589	217	114	1,127	19	2,715
1885	651	695	197	150	688	20	2,195
1886	250	643	167	160	746	14	1,443
1887	216	780	235	129	924	8	2,025
1888	94	1,015	285	114	1,175	15	1,713
1889	97	794	281	88	1,185	17	2,801
1890	183	774	289	84	1,101	13	3,037
1891	109	764	255	90	2,066	10	3,002
1892	102	770	264	121	1,945	19	3,233
1893	203	852	317	95	1,026	30	2,783
1894	522	635	487	94	1,279	38	3,890
1895	395	485	470	45	500	21	3,795
1896	279	663	452[9]	66[9]	190	27	5,028
			447	52			
1897	678	576	619	50	549	28	4,914
1898	1,246	512	633	58	2,009	60	5,581
1899	296	665	650	61	159	31	4,922

C10 External Trade in Corn (in thousands of metric tons or hectolitres)

	Italy[13]	Norway[5]	Romania[15]	Russia[6]	Spain[16]	Sweden[17]		U.K.
	I	I	E	E	I	I	E	I
	(b)	(b)	(b)	(b)	(b)	(a)[31]	(a)	(b)
1850	...	113	...	992	...	2,074	5,041	1,450
1851	...	105	...	1,153	...	5,721	3,278	1,551
1852	...	101	...	1,824	...	4,903	2,169	1,246
1853	...	95	...	2,556	...	2,384	3,790	1,712
1854	...	73	...	637	...	754	6,932	1,291
1855	...	88	...	145	...	702[17]	10,705	1,060
1856	...	102	...	1,713	55	4,877	6,710	1,577
1857	...	133	...	1,770	226	4,863	10,242	1,555
1858	...	100	...	2,142	152	1,169	15,787	1,876
1859	...	114	...	2,367	9	748	17,197	1,715
1860	...	127	...	2,343	...	1,216	16,499	2,401
1861	214	154	...	2,342[6]	...	6,959[7]	19,363[7]	2,709
				2,437		63[17]	94[17]	
						78	135	
1862	323	122	...	2,716	...	54	106	3,240
1863	450	150	...	1,744	...	54[17]	150	2,590
1864	764	162	...	...	...	72[17]	149	2,030
1865	443	135	...	2,535	...	28	196	2,215
1866	379[13]	136	...	3,097	...	46	167	2,782
1867	282	110	...	3,807	27	122	217	2,961
1868	224	154	...	3,090	457	148	129	3,033
1869	233	160	...	2,592	138	130	174	3,624
1870	270[14][13]	172	...	5,212	63	62	323	3,338
1871	290[14]	129	...	5,825	65	32	326	3,845
1872	330	152	...	4,065	29	72	262	4,737
1873	269	156	...	5,147	...	94	253	4,259
1874	364	183	...	6,697	16	199	254	4,163
1875	311	188	...	5,703	22	133	242	4,867
1876	329	193	...	6,402	40	129	316	5,355
1877	210[13]	241	...	7,590	9	276	229	5,620
1878	346	210	...	10,621	60	226	307	6,021
1879	488	190	...	10,022	121	177	366	6,135
1880	230	191	...	5,897	30	149	322	5,996
1881	147	211	...	6,020	20	211	226	5,627
1882	165	190	...	8,639	276	223	292	5,673
1883	232	200	1,310	8,869	238	293	304	6,476
1884	355	197	1,034	9,223[7]	99	281	202	4,977
1885	724	229	1,375	5,301	112	328	251	6,170
1886	936	202	1,308[15]	4,258	150	244	285	5,367
1887	1,016	198	1,573	6,028	314	273	268	5,876
1888	670	256	1,673	8,394	243	223	191	6,234
1889	873	251	1,990	7,173	145	227	119	6,510
1890	645	220	1,937	6,425	160	211	72	6,773
1891	464	251	1,754	5,975	155	190	183	6,462
1892	697	206	1,709	2,945	139	238	112	6,616
1893	861	249	2,507	6,103	419	259	217	6,867
1894	487	268	1,805	9,694	425	371	139	7,707
1895	658	272	1,744	8,671	203	251	75	7,866
1896	737[13]	298	2,299	7,553	187	237	62	8,223
1897	456	296	1,692	7,227	142	193	21	7,702
1898	915	316	2,180	6,922	59	244	40	8,252
1899	516	338	874	4,907	373	342	39	8,240

C10 External Trade in Corn (in thousands of metric tons or hectolitres)

1900–1944

	Austria-Hungary		Denmark[3]		France[4]		Germany[11]
	I	E	I	E	I	E	I
	(b)	(b)	(b)	(b)	(b)	(b)	(b)
1900	298	529	593	60	159	40	4,815
1901	379	533	548	53	194	27	5,503
1902	313	660	622	44	288	24	5,468
1903	388	770	558	51	505	18	5,753
1904	751	449	697	51	236	25	5,064
1905	758	616	631	57	201	44	6,375
1906	266	569	809	47	320	46	6,541[11]
1907	138	513	681	53	382	39	6,753
1908	131	417	567	61	85	52	5,393
1909	956	351	653	38	149	81	6,513
1910	438	390	635	75	653	37	6,765
1911	593	111	674	86	2,170	25	8,110
1912	844	212	759	93	727	40	7,390
1913	898	457	863	89	1,570	31	7,561
1914	882	154	578	91	1,790	92	…
1915	…	…	936	…	2,105	157	…
1916	…	…	590	…	2,921	48	…
1917	…	…	298	…	2,406	37	…
1918	…	…	3	17	2,014[10]	25[10]	…
1919	…	…	252	12	2,382	35	…[11][20]
	Austria						
	I(b)						
1920	321		269	22	2,415	33	1,482
1921	592		543	55	1,120	46	4,921
1922	408		644	49	679	83	3,264[21]
1923	468		948	26	1,429	85	…
1924	603		1,042[9]	72[9]	1,496	114	…
			1,063	72			
1925	646		941	61	1,223	15	3,962
1926	677		748	104	485	64	5,158
1927	658		1,288	65	2,178	11	7,791
1928	600		1,173	77	1,461	6	6,183
1929	636		815	79	1,431	6	4,832
1930	764		1,414	46	1,070	914	3,450
1931	922		1,897	46	2,388	626	2,585
1932	851		1,616	23	1,753	186	3,002
1933	910		1,207	33	488	194	1,517
1934	913		852	100	537	466	1,687
1935	721		824	76	545	916	1,000[20]
1936	679		852[9]	81[9]	438	400	353
			843	81			
1937	856[2]		985[3]	178[3]	326	87	387
			996	178			
1938	692		667	121	413[10]	135[10]	391
1939	…		343	94	526	801	…
1940	…		260	3	662	305	…
1941	…		5	29	427	19	…
1942	…		49	17	211	462	…
1943	…		—	56	…	301	…
1944	…		—	11	150[10]	329[10]	…

C10 External Trade in Corn (in thousands of metric tons or hectolitres)

1945–1949

	Austria	Denmark[3]		France[4]		West Germany[20,22]
	I	I	E	I	E	
	(b)	(b)	(b)	(b)	(b)	
1945	...	—	38	664	66	...
1946	...	42	87	2,000	43	...
1947	...	106	120	558	122	...
1948	354	287	221	1,180	83	...
1949	770	450[18]	175[18]	645[18]	268[4]	...
			195	1,780	388	...

1950–2000

	Austria[2]	Denmark[3]		France[4]		W. Germany[29]	E. Germany[23]
	I	I	E	I	E	I	I
	(b)	(b)	(b)	(b)	(b)	(b)	(b)
1950	634	412	151	1,265	1,042	3,162	251
1951	940	296	105	1,294	849	4,713	364
1952	929	249	326	1,517	390	4,737	334
1953	652	157[19]	353[19]	1,161	496	3,377	349
1954	564	1,042	177	850	1,667	5,566	328
1955	892	859	253	747	2,913	4,292	555
1956	658	952	341	2,500	1,754	6,413	606
1957	640	561	205	1,087	3,097	5,641	1,078
1958	658	920	469	988	1,868	4,895	1,292
1959	858	1,463	246	1,097	1,364	5,454[20]	1,335
1960	888	1,292	163	744	2,700	5,155	1,520
1961	523	826	185	872	4,193	5,474	1,250
1962	709	1,211	250	1,253	3,199	7,706	1,238
1963	590	647	334	1,319	5,240	4,906	1,023
1964	729	1,013	215	1,351	7,006	5,702	1,303
1965	955	950	498	1,600	7,144	6,453	1,225
1966	875	920	373	1,518	7,472	6,729	1,350
1967	524	834	265	1,353	7,148	6,790	1,184
1968	435	646	219	1,169	10,376	6,267	1,075
1969	277	346[18]	469[18]	1,266	12,374	6,295	1,311
		242	405				
1970	227	395	351	1,122	10,364	7,890	2,084
				1,043	10,284		
1971	367	746	228	805	11,532	8,186	1,867
1972	211	491	339	709	14,454	8,597	2,040
1973	281	427	352	905	16,294	8,385	1,594
1974	179	462	668	654	17,530	7,164	1,219
1975	168	262	1,013	1,295	13,229	6,606	1,130
1976	190	598	592	1,513	14,020	8,423	1,691
1977	174	614	703	1,843	11,012	6,751	1,100
1978	98	384	1,363	2,270	14,762	6,471	687
1979	96	367	1,020	1,565	16,987	5,255	811
1980	160	355	1,139	1,570	19,637	5,034	476
1981	128	509	542	1,746	22,125	4,995	794
1982	127	377	725	2,482	19,379	4,977	731
1983	97	510	873	1,889	23,078	4,209	1,543
1984	109	364	1,492	1,747	25,168	4,444	1,657
1985	151	494	1,549	1,216	28,717	6,482	1,219
1986	135	349	1,905	1,058	25,439	5,170	227
1987	151	357	1,749	1,130	27,241	4,462	546
1988	179	211	2,200	951	28,195	4,181	650
1989	132	171	2,108	917	29,168	4,524	295
1990	152	140	3,250	922	30,898	3,987	150
1991	164	207	2,708	1,206	29,456	3,545	
1992	177	534	2,539	968	32,655	3,313	
1993	275	644	2,046	1,231	34,332	3,579	
1994	233	480	1,580	1,229	26,848	3,321	
1995	265	468	2,400	1,072	28,447	3,382	
1996	349	442	2,026	1,253	27,254	3,588	
1997	327	440	2,026	1,412	28,204	2,742	
1998	428	555	1,930	1,445	28,764	2,673	
1999	416	762	2,006	1,329	34,859	3,068	
2000	...	...	...	...	...	...	

C10 External Trade in Corn (in thousands of metric tons or hectolitres)

1900–1949

	Hungary[24] E (b)	Italy[13] I (b)	Norway[5] I (b)	Romania[15] E (b)	Russia[6] E (b)	Spain[16] I (b)	Sweden[17] I (b)	U.K.[1] I (b)
1900	...	732	318	1,376	5,947	223	374	8,128
1901	...	1,046	313	2,172[15] 2,300	6,702	144	246	8,404
1902	...	1,178	360	2,612	8,526	70	431	8,462
1903	...	1,173	455	2,408	9,532	91	435	9,200
1904	...	806	391	1,520	9,435	223	472	9,244
1905	...	1,172	383	2,385	7,056	885	381	9,055
1906	...	1,374[13]	379	3,156	8,506	526	345	8,986
1907	...	933	356	3,108	6,646	117	272[17]	9,178
1908	...	790	356	1,698	5,605	79	352	7,995
1909	...	1,332	348	2,135	11,226	96	378	8,972
1910	...	1,442	377	2,137	12,639	161	401	9,044
1911	...	1,391	387	3,859[15]	10,488	134	344	9,118
1912	...	1,790	304	2,787[15]	7,524	42[16] 218	490[17] 507	9,748
1913	...	1,811	326	2,745	9,084	782	350	9,939
1914	...	1,016	323	2,034	5,335	636	350	8,797
1915	...	2,252	309	677	300	579	585	8,392
1916	...	1,831	344	[1,791][25]	[343][26]	423	369	8,258
1917	...	1,916	270	...	...[6]	108	150	7,021
1918	...	1,542	161	...	2	197	116	4,493
1919	1	2,105[13]	330	1	—	554	233	5,673
1920	3	2,118	349	939	4	688	270	7,719
1921	444	2,800	310	1,453	3	915[16]	363	7,184
1922	181	2,681	386	1,165	1[27]	608	228	7,907
1923	363	2,789	409	1,708	728[27]	318	581	8,273[1]
1924	910	2,131	461	1,259	2,576[27]	301	597	9,503
1925	763	2,242	395	789	569[27]	545	455	7,548
1926	1,014	2,146	421	1,631	2,016[27]	385	460	7,481
1927	725	2,308	454	2,825	2,099[27]	309	576	8,875
1928	693	2,745	382	965	289[27]	654	694	7,977
1929	1,071	1,765[13]	365	1,595	178	634	565	8,412
1930	840	1,935	463	3,085	4,764	135	488	8,320
1931	576	1,485	540	3,182	5,056	175	660	10,001
1932	316	1,056	451	2,456	1,727	580	530	8,892
1933	968	466	493	1,741	1,684	106	426	9,413
1934	646	469	444	865	769	62	225	9,280
1935	415	550	458	1,091	1,517	53	120	9,212
1936	694	535	408	1,951	321	...	154	9,882
1937	736	1,658	492	2,118	1,277	...	295	9,546
1938	656	291	457	1,259	2,054	...	258	9,178
1939	1,179	648	551	1,896[15]	277[6]	[385][28]	98	8,519
1940	487	691	162	1,080	1,155	712	186	8,506
1941	290	86	178	135	...	707	11	6,228
1942	243	83	134	34	...	407	119	3,676
1943	287	...	336	42	...	458	32	3,375
1944	161	...	77	92	...	388	23	2,988
1945	...[24]	...[13]	408	...	...	438[16]	66	4,337
1946	...	1,206	356	...	1,700	346	136	3,766
1947	23	1,062	280	...	800	307	167	4,968
1948	...	1,891	512	...	3,200	388	250	6,742
1949	317	1,667	450	...	2,400	296	195	6,108

C10 External Trade in Corn (in thousands of metric tons or hectolitres)

	Hungary[24] E (b)	Italy[13] I (b)	Norway[5] I (b)	Romania[15] E (b)	Russia[6] E (b)	Spain[16] I (b)	Sweden[17] I (b)	U.K.[1] I (b)
1950	324	1,051	565	...	2,900	301	246	5,178
1951	383	1,557	478	...	4,100	283	448	6,498
1952	249	1,272	443	...	4,500	116	529	6,647
1953	260	1,133	548	...	3,100	584	121	7,055
1954	318	259	421	...	3,900	815	106	5,812
1955	419	761	526	...	3,700	96	409	7,080
1956	258	645	523	...	3,215	150	327	7,267
1957	24	534	377	...	7,413	278	205	7,328
1958	112	191	425	476	5,100	136	421	8,445
1959	109	59	451	223	7,009	278	616	8,453
1960	95	583	460	731	6,818	218	421	8,046
1961	167	2,434	481	1,208	7,481	1,576	303	8,219
1962	78	449	503	1,068	7,814	1,347[16] 1,357	389[17] 369	9,040
1963	79	301	503	1,409	6,260	1,541	396	7,873
1964	90	540	538	1,234	3,513	2,059	308	7,672
1965	200	926	537	882	4,330	2,359	184	7,969
1966	56	1,168	580	1,303	3,557	3,449	227	7,515
1967	204	847	582	2,339	4,248	3,308	153	7,788
1968	148	1,356	545	1,562	5,406	2,492	146	7,957
1969	488	1,427	519[30] 547	1,377	7,205[30] 8,049	2,436	95	8,567
1970	700[24] 859	1,164	834	373	6,918	2,214	113	9,252
1971	159	1,607	649	704	9,573	3,171	73	8,669
1972	549	1,284	783	902[15] 905	5,091	2,596	75	8,102
1973	550	2,030	879	1,128	5,812	2,978	148	7,467
1974	1,862	2,544	766	713	8,475	4,705	300	6,947
1975	1,310	1,612	634	1,164	4,414	4,772	110	7,189
1976	1,714	2,451	828	1,633	2,384	4,060	84	8,264
1977	1,027	2,987	713	2,052	4,676	5,034	76	8,409
1978	871	3,570	664	1,853	2,455	5,237	79	6,795
1979	644	2,934	694	646	3,903	5,134	93	6,109
1980	931[24]	3,134	836	1,576	2,287	6,136	126	5,305
1981	1,445	3,016	748	1,600	2,628	6,027	214	4,145
1982	1,608	3,416	780	1,202	2,224	7,615	111	3,717
1983	1,405	2,801	483	533	2,266	6,512	120	3,218
1984	1,491	4,019	396	344	2,195	4,063	117	2,731
1985	2,265	4,536	291	845	1,851	4,166	110	3,271
1986	2,174	5,259	562	373	1,599	3,246	138	3,476
1987	1,502	4,617	556	527	1,827	1,943	263	3,473
1988	2,076	4,904	566	362	1,657	3,416	188	3,318
1989	1,856	5,632	545	276	1,669	2,224	118	3,671
1990	1,348	4,666	378	...	1,539	3,020	112	4,116
1991	1,700	6,510	196	...	589	4,016	115	4,310
1992	4,248	6,313	336	...	3[32]	3,783	151	4,696
1993	343	5,023	302	...	1,627[32]	4,955	207	5,706
1994	1,086	6,014	668	8	1,627	5,047	211	3,321
1995	4,109	6,875	445	851	2,338	7,730	108	2,866
1996	642	8,335	634	1,746	695	5,961	150	2,571
1997	2,582	8,260	406	798	802	6,390	115	3,200
1998	4,451	8,315	442	891	2,111	6,709	212	3,230
1999	2,676	8,082	535	1,025	987	6,885	234	3,151
2000	...	...	...	...	...	...	...	...

C10   External Trade in Corn (in thousands of metric tons or hectolitres)

NOTES

1.   SOURCES:- Apart from France 1819–26, which comes from M. Block, *Statistique de la France* (Paris, 1860), all figures are taken from the official publications noted on p. xv with gaps filled from League of Nations and United Nations, *International Trade Statistics*, International Institute of Agriculture, *Yearbook of Agricultural Statistics*, and F.A.O., *Trade Yearbook*.
2.   Except as indicated in footnotes, the statistics are of 'special' trade—i.e. exports of domestic produce or imports for consumption.

FOOTNOTES

[1]   Figures to 1840 (1st line) are for Great Britain, and include trade with Ireland. Subsequently they are for the U.K., southern Ireland being treated as external from April 1923. Statistics to 1840 (1st line) are of wheat and flour only. Subsequently they are of barley, maize, oats, and wheat.
[2]   All statistics relate to the boundaries of the day, except that Dalmatia was not included until 1861. All cereals are covered, together with cereal preparations from 1938.
[3]   Figures to 1838 (1st line) include the Duchies of Schleswig, Holstein, and Lauenburg as part of Denmark. From 1838 (2nd line) to 1863 they are not included, but trade *with* them is ignored. Statistics for 1864–73 are for years ended 31 March following that indicated. Up to 1863 flour, meal, the minor grains, and peas are included. Subsequently (except as indicated in footnote 18) the statistics are of barley, maize, oats, rye, and wheat, and, from 1936 (2nd line), rice.
[4]   Figures to 1949 (1st line) are of wheat and flour only. Subsequentlly they cover all cereals and to 1970 (1st line), cereal preparations.
[5]   All grains except rice. Data is lacking for Finmark and Nordland provinces in 1829.
[6]   Figures to 1861 (1st line) are of barley, oats, rye, and wheat only. There were substantial territorial losses between 1917 and 1921 and gains between 1940 and 1945.
[7]   Subsequently in thousands of metric tons.
[8]   Earlier statistics are for years ended 31 October. The 1853 figures cover 14 months.
[9]   Up to 1896 (1st line) and from 1924 (2nd line) to 1936 (1st line) the statistics are of 'general' rather than 'special' trade.
[10]   Alsace-Lorraine is excluded to 1871–1918 and for 1939–44.
[11]   Figures to 1 March 1906 apply to the Zollgebiet. Subsequently they are for the Empire or Republic. Schleswig-Holstein is included from 1865 and Alsace-Lorraine from 1871 to 1918. Statistics cover all grain except buckwheat and rice.
[12]   From 1 July 1865 to December 1871 maize is not included.
[13]   Wheat only. Transit trade is included in 1877 and probably earlier, but not subsequently. There were changes in the composition of 'special' trade in 1897, 1907, and 1930. The main territorial changes were the inclusion of Venetia in 1867, the Papal States in 1871, and the acquisitions from Austria-Hungary in 1920, and the loss of territory to Yugoslavia in 1945.
[14]   Including oats and maslin.
[15]   Barley, maize, rye, and wheat to 1901 (1st line), with oats from 1901 (2nd line) and all other cereals from 1972 (2nd line). Malt is also included from 1887 to 1911. There were substantial territorial gains in 1913 and 1920, and losses in 1940.
[16]   Wheat only to 1912 (1st line). Barley, maize, oats, rye and wheat from 1912 (2nd line) to 1921. Barley, maize, and wheat from 1922 to 1945, with maslin also from 1946 to 1962 (1st line). Subsequently all cereals and preparations.
[17]   Including Finland to 1814. Data for imports relate to barley, oats, rye, and wheat to 1861 (2nd line), with wheat flour and rye flour included from 1861 (3rd line). Malt is included from 1856 to 1863, but imports had been negligible for many years previously. Maize is included from 1908 although barley is excluded for 1908 to 1912 (1st line). From 1912 (2nd line) to 1962 (1st line) statistics are of all imports of grains and flour, and subsequently they are of all cereals. Exports are of oats only to 1861 (2nd line) and of barley, oats, rye, and wheat subsequently.
[18]   From 1949 (2nd line) to 1969 (1st line) flour, meal etc. is included. There is no break in the import series in 1949.
[19]   Subsequently does not include trade with the Faroe Islands and Greenland.
[20]   Saarland is treated as external from 1920 to 18 February 1935 and from 1946 to 4 July 1959.
[21]   From July 1922 eastern Upper Silesia was transferred to Poland.
[22]   Excluding West Berlin.
[23]   Wheat only.
[24]   Barley, maize, oats, rye, wheat, and flour to 1945. Subsequently to 1970 (1st line) maize, wheat, and flour; all grains and flour from then to 1980, and all grains thereafter.
[25]   January–September only.
[26]   Exports across the European frontier only.
[27]   Figures for 1922–28 are for economic years ending in the year indicated. Exports for October–December 1928 were 1 thousand tons.
[28]   April–December only.
[29]   All cereals and flour.
[30]   Subsequently all cereals and cereal preparations.
[31]   The original data to 1861 (1st line) were given in barrels, and have been converted on the basis of 1.649 hectolitres to the barrel.
[32]   Russian Federation.

	Kazakhstan	Ukraine
1992	1,000	5,206
1993	600	5,027
1994	3,173	2,076
1995	4,073	2,263
1996	3,190	3,345
1997	3,889	1,684
1998	3,186	4,074
1999	4,145	6,143
2000	...	5,027

C11 EXPORTS OF AGRICULTURAL, FISHING AND FORESTRY PRODUCTS (in units indicated)

Key:- (a) = thousand metric tons; (b) = thousand score; (c) = thousand hectolitres; (d) = million cubic metres; (e) = millions; (f) = thousands

1830–1879

	Denmark			Finland		France	Greece		Italy	
	Butter (a)	Eggs (b)	Meat (a)	Wood (f)	Wood Pulp (a)	Wine (c)	Currants (a)	Tobacco (a)	Citrus Fruits (a)	Wine (c)
1830	1.9	...	...	...	...	875	...	...	...	...
1831	1.6	...	0.2	...	...	806	...	...	...	...
1832	1.4	...	0.1	...	...	1,303	...	...	...	...
1833	1.4	...	0.2	...	...	1,338	...	...	...	...
1834	1.5	...	0.2	...	...	1,393	...	...	...	...
1835	1.7	...	0.3	...	...	1,301	...	...	...	...
1836	2.2	...	0.4	...	...	1,305	...	...	...	...
1837	2.0	...	0.4	...	...	1,114	...	...	...	...
1838	2.1	...	0.4₁ 1.3	...	...	1,453	...	...	...	...
1839	1.9	...	2.2	...	...	1,194	...	...	...	...
1840	2.0	...	2.0	...	...	1,334	...	...	...	...
1841	2.0	...	1.9	...	...	1,478	...	...	...	...
1842	1.5	...	1.3	...	...	1,368	...	...	...	...
1843	1.2	...	1.1	...	...	1,430	...	...	...	...
1844	1.3	...	0.6	...	...	1,403	...	...	...	...
1845	1.2	...	1.0	...	...	1,491	...	...	...	...
1846	1.3	...	0.9	...	...	1,360	...	...	...	...
1847	1.5	...	0.9	...	...	1,488	...	...	...	...
1848	1.2	...	1.0	...	...	1,548	...	...	...	...
1849	1.5	...	1.0	...	...	1,872	...	...	...	...
1850	2.1	...	1.7	...	...	1,911	...	...	...	...
1851	1.4	...	1.4	...	...	2,269	...	...	...	...
1852	2.4	...	1.3	...	...	2,439	...	...	...	...
1853	1.1	...	1.2	...	...	1,976	...	...	...	...
1854	1.7	...	1.4	...	...	1,330	...	...	...	...
1855	1.4	...	1.4	...	...	1,215	...	...	...	...
1856	1.5	...	1.3	...	...	1,275	...	...	...	...
1857	1.2	...	1.6	...	...	1,124	...	...	...	...
1858	1.0	...	1.0	...	...	1,620	31	1.1	...	...
1859	0.9	...	1.6	...	...	2,519	28	0.6	...	...
1860	1.7	...	2.2	310	...	2,021	40	1.0	...	...
1861	2.4	8	1.7	339	...	1,858	36	1.1	5	255
1862	2.9	10	1.7	303	...	1,894	40	0.4	46	217
1863	4.4	15	2.1	452	...	2,084	38	0.4	69	468
1864	4.0	26	3.1	406	...	2,336	36	1.3	66	236
1865	4.9	35	7.6	617	...	2,868	52	1.3	70	275
1866	5.0	70	5.4	515	...	3,274	60	0.6	91₃	359₃
1867	4.5	31	5.1	474	...	2,591	65	0.9	67	299
1868	4.0	27	5.4	597	...	2,806	60	0.7	72	241
1869	6.3	32	5.5	617	...	3,063	56	1.1	88	287
1870	7.6	56	9.4	522	...	2,866₈	47	0.4	77₃	240₃
1871	7.2	340	7.5	555	...	3,319	75	0.8	88	243
1872	10.6	690	5.6	783	...	3,430	62	1.6	88	609
1873	11.6	1,427	7.2	894	1	3,981	77	1.1	84	309
1874	14.8	1,184	7.9	1,127	3	3,232	79	1.4	72	272
1875	13.5	1,595	6.4	1,001	2	3,730	81	1.4	96	363
1876	16.0	1,398	5.8	1,553	3	3,331	...	...	93	507
1877	13.2	944	6.1	1,605	2	3,102	...	...	101	363
1878	11.4	1,201	5.9	1,043	3	2,795	...	...	98	537
1879	11.7	1,310	5.7	995	3	3,047	...	...	100	1,077

C11 Exports of Agricultural, Fishing and Forestry Products (in units indicated)

1880–1929

	Denmark			Finland			France	Greece		Ireland	Italy	
	Butter	Eggs	Meat	Wood[2]	Wood pulp	News-print	Wine	Currants	Tobacco	Meat	Citrus Fruits	Wine
	(a)	(b)	(a)	(f)	(a)	(a)	(c)	(a)	(a)	(a)	(a)	(c)
1880	12.5	1,992	7.2	1,570	3	…	2,488	…	…	…	93	2,206
1881	12.3	1,860	6.6	1,221	1	…	2,572	…[10]	…[10]	…	129	1,760
1882	14.3	2,390	7.5	1,461	2	…	2,618	…	…	…	120	1,332
1883	17.2	2,814	12.2	1,380	3	…	2,541	…	…	…	159	2,629
1884	16.6	3,643	16.8	1,444	6	…	2,472	…	…	…	173	2,381
1885	17.8	3,624	13.2	1,490	6	…	2,603	…	…	…	152	1,481
1886	20.2	4,652	15.2	1,207	7	…	2,709	…	…	…	125	2,354
1887	24.1	5,547	21.2	1,088	9	…	2,402	…	…	…	230	3,603
1888	30.2	5,039	36.0	1,238	8	…	2,118	…	…	…	165	1,829
1889	34.4	5,839	35.8	1,371	11	…	2,167	…	…	…	194	1,439
1890	44.6	6,686	30.9	1,263	14	…	2,162	…	…	…	191	936
1891	45.7	7,170	37.4	1,595	13	…	2,049	…	…	…	135	1,179
1892	45.3	7,939	43.6	1,486	13	…	1,845	116	2.6	…	171	2,449
1893	49.0	7,027	52.0	1,824	20	…	1,569	147	2.7	…	198	2,363
1894	59.0	7,950	53.4	2,262	21	…	1,721	161	2.4	…	215	1,943
1895	59.0	7,906	68.3	2,288	19	…	1,697	155	1.9	…	221	1,711
1896	60.6[6]	9,826[6]	82.0[6]	2,648	19	…	1,784	165	2.9	…	237	1,656
	50.8	9,624	78.0									
1897	53.0	12,228	69.4	2,958	17	…	1,775	111	2.3	…	224	2,396
1898	60.7	13,202	77.7	3,005	20	…	1,636	124	2.0	…	197	2,503
1899	61.2	15,058	84.7	3,164	18	…	1,717	126	2.9	…	239	2,430
1900	61.3	16,612	84.7	3,382	24	…	1,905	74	3.8	…	201	1,827
1901	66.8	19,014	79.0	3,374	26	…	2,022	109	4.3	…	244	1,335
1902	69.8	21,530	95.3	3,452	26	17	2,052	120	4.6	…	320	1,389
1903	80.1	23,244	101	4,467	37	18	1,726	119	5.7	…	310	2,163
1904	81.5	21,406	121	4,924	59	24	1,643	112	7.0	…	347	1,211
1905	79.9	20,733	110	4,550	61	25	2,606	112	5.9	…	310	987
1906	79.4	19,765	107	4,505	56	28	2,110	125	8.1	…	347	814
1907	85.7	20,106	122	4,330	61	33	2,788	123	6.8	…	382	1,041
1908	88.9	21,254	141	4,733	64	33	2,273	101	4.9	…	368	1,364
1909	89.2	19,207	129	4,718	71	36	2,280	105	6.0	…	369	1,588
1910	88.5	20,363	131	4,788	87	46	2,318	112	5.8	…	381	2,033
1911	89.6	21,513	146	5,109	114	54	1,569	125	8.5	…	389	1,179
1912	85.2	19,226	173	5,317	138	57	2,060	…[11]	…	…	368	1,177
1913	91.0	22,734	163	6,687	127	70	1,659[9]	96[12]	10[12]	…	437	1,787
1914	95.3	22,863	188	3,533	97	72	1,155	…	…	…	442	2,045
1915	101.6	24,097	182	592	100	72	1,003	…	…	…	335	961
1916	95.8	24,058	135	714[2]	101[7]	78	689	…	…	…	316	623
				192	94							
1917	61.5	22,190	114	125	54	68	460	…	…	…	206	1,230
1918	14.7	16,388	20	268	80	16	434[8,9]	…	…	…	136[3]	2,780[3]
1919	36.6	16,935	13	3,108	130	31	1,180	…	…	…	210	725
1920	74.8	27,310	68	4,049	170	90	2,136	104	27	…	236	874
1921	92.1	32,407	103	3,234	173	94	1,801	102	26	…	271	913
1922	95.5	36,756	146	4,921	235	130	1,034	87	37	…	225	891
1923	112	39,962	210	5,468	261	127	1,503	120	21	…	224	830
1924	123	41,624	216	5,969	377	135	2,251	109	42	…	301	2,559
1925	123	40,334	231	5,979	367	149	1,556	95	42	32	384	1,455
1926	133	41,610	221	5,950	406	144	1,834	95	55	33	372	1,051
1927	143	42,243	275	7,495	466	155	1,279	96	53	41	405	1,036
1928	148	39,450	292	6,611	611	172	1,375	95	49	54	304	922
1929	159	39,285	271	6,565	645	174	1,382	84	50	44	323	974

C11 Exports of Agricultural, Fishing and Forestry Products (in units indicated)

	Denmark			Finland			France	Greece		Ireland	Italy	
	Butter	Eggs	Meat	Wood[2]	Wood pulp	News-print	Wine	Currants	Tobacco	Meat	Citrus Fruits	Wine
	(a)	(b)	(a)	(f)	(a)	(a)	(c)	(a)	(a)	(a)	(a)	(c)
1930	169	43,112	350	5,299	633	188	1,088	86	49	35	405	1,032
1931	172	48,716	442	4,470	786	191	820	80	43	37	385	1,672
1932	158	55,236	434	4,363	937	201	703	88	35	25	308	803
1933	151	53,517	335	5,397	1,006	226	725	87	35	26	417	999
1934	150	56,279	261	6,162	1,051	260	725	98	37	28	343	993
1935	138	58,613	225	5,950	1,214	280	721	101	50	35.5	313	944
1936	146	70,088	200	6,405	1,359	342	825	101	40	34.6	269	1,438
1937	153	80,645	227	6,289	2,470	382	862	113	42	30.7	371	1,872
1938	158	77,916	214	5,069	1,246	358	1,032	104	49	31.7	356	1,441
1939	150	85,675	230	3,886	1,298	422	916	...	...	29.1	414	1,477
1940	108	67,172	174	1,328	266	61	482	...	...	38.6	353	1,697
1941	53	27,427	89	1,235	517	51	1,646	...	...	50.2	383	1,837
1942	36	5,371	38	1,348	281	58	1,589	...	...	25.2	240	1,300
1943	50	1,861	69	1,633	273	103	1,942	...	...	11.9	...	...
1944	53	2,500	121	579	186	44	937	...	...	12.2	...	...
1945	61	7,857	75	691	164	56	766	...	...	19.0	...[3]	...[3]
1946	78	9,811	96	2,387	450	208	728	...	...	15.1	85	323
1947	87	14,497[13]	90	3,386	633	246	582	...	...	7.1	201	489
		(a)										
1948	106	40.8	70	3,340	800	289	620	64	18	6.0	281	633
1949	138	80.5	154	3,830	921	348	744	85	28	12.1	357	684
1950	156	95.5	249	3,827	1,056	379	984	88	25	38.0	369	1,072
1951	140	85.4	299	4,840	1,191	382	1,892	65	32	49.4	344	980
1952	117	89.6	292	4,158	865	392	2,275	86	41	78.4	350	1,223
1953	137	97.2	370	3,560	991	402	2,786	106	49	86.9	330	1,207
1954	141	105.5	408	4,145	1,149	392	3,034	119	52	107.9	389	1,180
1955	129	107.7	428	4,788	1,312	470	3,024	104	55	63.9	354	1,185
1956	121	100.0	378	4,223	1,317	537	3,227	96	49	53.4	423	1,884
1957	118	103.0	451	4,449	1,336	551	2,282	121	69	70.4	451	1,912
1958	115	107.1	454	4,259	1,344	585	1,305	100	62	84.8	386	1,850
1959	118	107.7	484[21]	4,950	1,459	576	2,084	99	55	82.1	459	1,453
1960	118	84.7	526	5,635	1,594	691	3,282	106	61	104	403	2,156
1961	120	67.3	538	5,415	1,601	846	4,113	99	66	134	464	2,112
1962	115	50.7	594	4,541	1,709	870	3,528	124	47	130	443	2,313
1963	102	39.2	636	4,306[2]	1,927	882	4,358	137	62	135	415	2,471
1964	104	30.2	638	4,680	2,125	989	3,688	115	70	124	515	2,319
1965	116	23.4	688	4,124	1,999	1,101	3,493	125	73	136	562	2,636
1966	112	23.8	688	3,790	2,218	1,193	3,880	124	73	146	483	2,569
1967	104	22.8	712[21]	3,481	2,124	1,151	3,462	108	88	215	498	2,592
1968	107	21.0	711	3,962	2,224	1,161	3,620	110	70	194	534	2,851
1969	100	25.0	666	4,478	2,217	1,156	3,954	138	71	207	610	2,324
1970	87	20.3	679	4,702	2,057	1,187	4,132	125	63	217	508	4,831
1971	77	13.9	732	4,758	1,507	1,168	4,963	125	59	241	495	8,468
1972	87	11.3	803	4,910	1,611	1,310	5,869	142	74	226	455	13,348
1973	100	12.4	709	5,256	1,664	1,321	7,275	92	46	217	239	9,538
1974	101	10.1	697	4,323	1,338	1,137	6,596	106	67	275	371	9,579
1975	98	11.1	709	2,857	948	776	6,352	113	51	330[22] / 311	412	12,942
1976	92	6.3	652	3,850	1,101	866	7,153	132	56	227	487	13,006
1977	90	3.1	717	4,355	1,181	840	8,318	111	53	313	489	10,912
1978	88	2.9	757	5,470	1,531	1,113	7,667	125	70	317	326	12,513
1979	83	4.1	841	6,638	1,865	1,394	8,634	110	55	311	336	18,657

C11   Exports of Agricultural, Fishing and Forestry Products (in units indicated)

1980–2000

	Denmark			Finland			France	Greece		Ireland	Italy	
	Butter	Eggs	Meat	Wood	Wood pulp	News-print	Wine	Currants	Tobacco	Meat	Citrus Fruits	Wine
	(a)	(b)	(a)	(f)	(a)	(a)	(c)			(a)	(a)	(c)
1980	72	2.0	850	6,939	1,939	1,432	9,240	100	70	408	330	15,065
1981	71	2.3	914	5,411	1,685	1,542	9,205	90	58	273	250	19,289
1982	75	5.6	919	4,600	1,458	1,339	9,435	103	65	268	255	19,443
1983	81	3.7	944	4,932	1,572	1,467	10,880	112	78	302	269	13,720
1984	66	2.8	946	4,821	1,561	1,676	11,401	167	88	281	245	15,751
1985	59	1.2	972	4,898	1,534	1,643	11,892	141	87	334	374	16,847
1986	66	2.1	985	4,555	1,469	1,470	13,082	131	89	417	345	10,513
1987	70	1.0	971	4,894	1,599	1,437	13,576	112	110	419	226	10,897
1988	60	0.9	993	5,052	1,680	1,203	13,238	67	84	370	184	11,153
1989	55	4.4	1,024	4,537	1,653	1,079	13,209	102	106	440	228	12,569
1990	50	7.5	1,034	4,156	1,461	1,203	12,494	99	123	410	226	15,779
1991	49	6.0	1,052	4,276	1,348	1,159	12,334	57	121	440	223	13,179
1992	48	5.5	1,234	4,268	1,334	999	11,604	73	119	530	173	12,461
1993	48	3.0	1,284	6,188	1,456	1,252	10,695	71	119	528	220	13,963
1994	49	3.4	1,416	5,701	1,493	1,252	11,618	...	113	758	...	...
1995	48	8.0	1,264	5,924	1,302	1,099	11,391	...	141	775	...	...
1996	54	9.6	1,282	5,370	1,542	1,051	...	...	152	670	...	...
1997	44	9.9	1,434	4,981	1,751	1,211	...	...	116	647	...	...
1998	43	9.7	1,463	4,732	1,635	1,199	...	...	114	700	...	...
1999	40	8.3	1,479	4,452	1,882	1,223	...	...	120	828	...	...
2000	40	13.4	1,473	4,301	1,681	1,144	...	...	118	765	...	...

1830–1864

	Norway				Portugal		Russia	Spain		Sweden		
	Fish	Timber	Paper	Wood pulp	Cork	Wine	Sugar	Oranges	Wine	Timber	Paper	Wood pulp
	(a)	(d)	(a)	(a)				(e)	(c)	(d)	(a)	(a)
1830	56	...	...	...	...	...	...	...	...	...	...	...
1831	67	...	...	...	...	...	...	...	...	...	...	...
1832	79	...	...	...	...	...	...	...	...	...	...	...
1833	91	...	...	...	...	...	...	...	...	...	...	...
1834	80	...	...	...	...	...	...	...	...	...	...	...
1835	72	...	...	...	...	...	...	...	...	...	...	...
1836	68	1.2	...	...	...	...	...	...	...	...	...	...
1837	95	1.1	...	...	...	...	...	...	...	...	...	...
1838	61	1.2	...	...	...	...	...	...	...	...	...	...
1839	68	1.4	...	...	...	...	...	...	...	...	...	...
1840	93	1.3	...	...	...	...	...	...	...	...	...	...
1841	78	1.3	...	...	...	...	...	...	...	...	...	...
1842	83	1.3	...	...	...	...	...	...	...	...	...	...
1843	63	1.3	...	...	...	...	...	...	...	...	...	...
1844	102	1.3	...	...	...	...	...	...	...	...	...	...
1845	85	1.4	...	...	...	...	...	...	...	...	...	...
1846	104	1.4	...	...	...	...	...	...	...	...	...	...
1847	89	1.1	...	...	...	...	...	...	...	...	...	...
1848	78	0.9	...	...	...	...	...	...	...	...	...	...
1849	106	1.0	...	...	...	...	...	...	...	...	...	...
1850	84	1.1	...	...	...	...	...	55	590	...	...	...
1851	107	1.3	...	...	...	...	...	70	654	...	...	...
1852	88	1.3	...	...	...	...	...	45	708	...	...	...
1853	89	1.5	...	...	...	...	...	51	877	...	...	...
1854	77	1.5	...	...	...	...	...	62	1,075	...	...	...
1855	87	1.5	...	...	...	...	...	84	1,062	...	...	...
1856	93	1.5	...	...	...	...	...	217	1,050	...	...	...
1857	89	1.5	...	...	...	...	...	106	1,572	...	...	...
1858	84	1.5	...	...	...	...	...	122	888	...	...	...
1859	103	1.6	...	...	...	...	...	150	1,013	...	...	...
1860	113	1.6	...	...	...	...	...	209	1,317	...	0.2	...
1861	93	1.7	...	...	...	...	...	117	1,151	1.2	0.1	...
1862	126	1.8	...	...	...	...	...	243	1,159	1.3	0.6	...
1863	125	1.9	...	...	...	...	...	157	1,137	1.4	0.1	...
1864	119	2.0	...	...	...	...	...	101	1,288	1.6	0.2	...

C11 Exports of Agricultural, Fishing and Forestry Products (in units indicated)

1865–1912

	Norway				Portugal			Russia	Spain		Sweden		
	Fish	Timber	Paper	Wood pulp[18]	Cork	Pres Sardines	Wine	Sugar	Oranges	Wine	Timber	Paper	Wood pulp
	(a)	(d)	(a)	(a)	(a)	(a)	(c)	(a)	(a)	(c)	(d)	(a)	(a)
1865	130	2.2	...	...	...		...	...	134	1,040	2.0	0.4	...
1866	123	2.1	...	...	...		...	...	190	1,062	1.9	0.5	...
1867	125	2.0	...	...	...		...	...	298	1,254	2.1	1.1	...
1868	128	2.1	...	...	...		...	...	189	1,750	2.5	1.4	...
1869	168	2.1	...	...	...		...	...	272	1,733	2.4	1.5	...
1870	146	2.1	...	1	...		...	...	229	1,421	2.6	1.8	...
1871	114	2.3	...	2	...		...	...	445	1,584	2.7	1.9	...
1872	183	2.2	...	3	...		...	...	582	1,868	3.1	1.9	5.8
1873	134	2.3	...	4	17		402	...	507	2,548	3.1[14] 3.4	2.5	6.7
1874	152	2.0	...	6	19		531	...	590	1,980	3.1	3.0	5.6
1875	158	1.6	...	9	12		583	...	440	1,968	2.9	3.4	5.2
1876	154	2.0	...	12	16		528	8	627	1,746	3.4	4.7	5.9
1877	146	1.7	1	15	14		571	64	677	2,169	3.6	4.0	6.1
1878	133	1.6	1	19	11		425	5	638	2,793	3.0	5.3	5.2
1879	140	1.5	2	21	11		419	3	683	3,699	3.3	7.0	9.8
1880	132	1.9	3	26	17	...	593	...	789	6,079	3.7	7.1	9.5
1881	172	1.8	2	43	19	...	701	1	600	6,872	3.8	5.4	9.0
1882	130	1.9	3	67	23	...	778	2	939[13] 117	7,514	4.3	6.0	9.2
1883	109	2.0	3	81	20	...	870	...	99	7,524	4.5	6.5	10
1884	128	2.0	4	88	22	...	820	2	105	6,400	4.1	6.7	11
1885	130	1.8	4	103	21	2.6	1,501	48	71	7,078	4.3	7.8	16
1886	156	1.7	4	110	22	5.6	1,963	62	82	7,266	4.1	8.6	26
1887	179	1.8	4	139	23	7.4	1,467	75	86	8,234	4.3	9.8	29
1888	166	1.9	5	171	21	6.8	1,731	91	94	8,979	5.0	11.3	39
1889	178	2.0	5	185	24	4.7	1,475	81	98	8,589	5.1[15] 5.2	11.3	52
1890	168	1.9	7	202	23	6.9	914	53	101	9,418	5.2	16	64
1891	141	1.9	10	228	22	9.4	826	124	65	11,307	5.5	19	86
1892	188	1.9	15	212	23	9.8	1,002	48	89	6,736	5.2	21	74
1893	210	1.7	19	231	23	7.9	770	37	91	5,165	5.3	19	82
1894	162	1.7	22	250	23	5.8	611	86	160	4,126	5.5	24	85
1895	167	1.7	28	260	27	8.7	682	93	235	5,348	5.5	25	122
1896	148	1.8	35	298	28	9.4	761	222	215	6,665	5.1	28	150
1897	205	2.1	39	313	32	10.0	782	133	277	5,343	6.4	29	151
1898	195	2.0	41	325	29	11.5	863	119	238	6,409	6.5	31	153
1899	160	2.0	44	365	25	8.3	830	127	311	4,842	6.6	39	186
1900	159	2.0	47	392	27	9.6	829	205	260	3,869	6.7	50	205
1901	162	1.8	48	390	29	10	791	128	285	2,339	6.0	58	209
1902	181	2.0	49	454	28	13	839	130	369	1,968	6.4	80	251
1903	169	2.1	53	453	31	15	780	240	396	2,431	6.6	93	316
1904	152	1.8	60	453	35	14	729	180	409	2,285	6.1	103	342
1905	152	1.8	69	453	27	16	900	100	314	3,072	6.0	122	336
1906	172	2.0	92	515	38	19	908	97	393	2,463	6.3	138	361
1907	197	1.9	94	568	41	17	910	179	469	2,385	5.9	146	456
1908	200	1.5	108	605	35	17	842	298	466	2,568	5.2	143	490
1909	263	1.3	124	612	36	18	863	204	468	2,346	4.7	137	491
1910	279	1.3	139	649	43	19	1,156	148	497	2,518	5.5	166	652
1911	272	1.2	126	637	43	23	1,165	452	442	2,987	5.5	176	736
1912	261	1.1	151	707	46	25	1,146	375	563	3,203[5]	5.8	204	812

C11 Exports of Agricultural, Fishing and Forestry Products (in units indicated)

1913–1962

	Norway				Portugal			Russia	Spain		Sweden		
	Fish	Timber	Paper	Wood pulp[18]	Cork	Pres Sardines	Wine	Sugar	Oranges	Wine	Timber	Paper	Wood pulp
	(a)	(d)	(a)	(a)	(a)	(a)	(c)	(a)	(a)	(c)	(d)	(a)	(a)
1913	296	1.0	181	721	89	25	1,090	...	569	3,126	6.3	216	847
1914	257	0.9	182	746	...	...	...	...	478	2,422	5.1	190	800
1915	339	1.4	207	740	...	...	...	...	456	1,637	5.3	228	872
1916	309	1.4	100	701	...	...	...	...	383	4,433	6.2	265	870
1917	302	1.0	80	420	...	...	2,070	...	246	6,285	3.5	183	620
1918	228	0.7	112	525	...	...	1,505	...	173	2,620	3.7	155	624
1919	257	0.9	107	529	...	...	1,478	...	349	6,142	5.0	170	808
1920	375	0.9	184	607	...	...	1,029	...	258	4,930	5.4	299	881
1921	267	0.5	82	372	...	...	709	...	434	3,116	3.0	191	482
1922	281	1.0	216	612	123	38	2,536	...	401	2,960	5.9	295	1,047
1923	315	0.9	211	705	109	53	1,538	...	461	3,050	5.8	331	896
1924	283	0.8	196	672	110	44	1,360	15	671	3,470	5.3	378	1,221
1925	266	0.9	284	638	122	34	1,042	28	715	2,900	5.4	404	1,188
1926	284	0.8	257	726	137	32	947	25	717	2,990	4.9	420	1,303
1927	292	0.7	300	729	123	33	864	110	620	5,030	5.7	425	1,455
1928	282	0.8	309	792	123	35	1,499	136	859	5,952	5.9	411	1,327
1929	335	0.8	314	879	140	34	945	127	793	3,786	6.6	489	1,789
1930	329	0.6	294	850	100	35	818	102	1,085	3,489	5.4	444	1,641
1931	234	0.4[16]	172	648	93	45	756	320	855	3,349	3.9	485	1,567
1932	251	347	277	871	90	44	755	76	882	1,975	4.0	473	1,292
1933	260	271	257	836	123	29	767	38	978	2,503	4.7	516	1,916
1934	194	258	258	950	124	34	743	49	885	1,550	4.7	556	1,999
1935	219	257	286	753	136	40	854	76	700	1,313	3.6	609	2,103
1936	240	268	290	878	153	43	879	163	...	...	4.2	607	2,280
1937	254	290	322	958	...	...	799	134	...	...	4.5	664	2,552
1938	227	235	240	768	114	30	838	114	...	...	3.6	474	1,981
1939	259	289	307	780	...	41	992	25	[111][20]	[263][20]	3.9	601	2,331
1940	224	161	121	421	...	36	701	34	325	419	2.3	...	1,044
1941	201	230	76	391	...	50	601	...	313	198	2.4	190	756
1942	183	64	29	198	...	33	791	...	231	271	1.8	237	659
1943	164	27	40	167	67	38	625	...	203	555	1.0	194	439
1944	179	55	20	67	53	34	484	...	249	699	0.8	207	297
1945	89	21	59	59	65	27	564	...	263	384	2.8	245	1,569
1946	259	123	245	249	82	36	1,303	28	139	358	3.2	521	1,804
1947	301	169	260	344	159	27	825	18	174	361	2.2	627	1,797
1948	350	151	279	505	139	31	999	15	274	831	2.8	682	1,680
1949	333	217	278	655	124	17	1,170	63	426	1,370	3.8	711	1,893
1950	221	213	299	776	177	17	1,009	97	421	768	4.0	865	2,091
1951	282	230	302	825	196	22	1,212	124	727	744	4.5	926	2,010
1952	287	237	244	779[18]	124	30	1,136	138	777	704	4.1	668	1,630
1953	237	304	213	593	126	32	1,067	195	1,004	1,030	4.9	841	2,166
1954	299	209	230	654	123	42	1,295	208	809	1,545	4.7	985	2,229
1955	329	216	216	669	132	53	1,626	210	1,000	1,190	5.3	1,086	2,302
1956	342	252	242	681	114	47	1,856	174	379	1,413	4.9	1,221	2,547
1957	323	317	255	674	102	40	1,808	191	459	1,481	5.5	1,301	2,470
1958	288	278	244	653	117	49	2,286	200	732	3,272	4.3	1,329	2,358
1959	310	206	294	683[18]	127	60	1,582	197	784	1,349	4.9	1,471	2,679
1960	271	208	300	814	138	54	1,605	243	941	1,200	4.8	1,700	2,932
1961	192	185	328	765	129	61	1,632	414	906	1,531	4.5	1,804	2,729
1962	216	152	302	772	131	59	1,502	792	1,121	1,769	4.6	1,881	2,839

C11 Exports of Agricultural, Fishing and Forestry Products (in units indicated)

1963–2000

	Norway				Portugal			Russia/ U.S.S.R	Spain		Sweden		
	Fish	Timber	Paper	Wood pulp[18]	Cork	Pres sardines	Wine	Sugar	Oranges	Wine	Timber	Paper	Wood pulp
	(a)	(d)[16]	(a)	(a)	(a)	(a)	(c)	(a)	(a)	(c)	(d)	(a)	(a)
1963	211	171[17] 319	354	791	143	53	1,748	802	670	1,825	4.9	2,086	3,209
1964	195	379	389	878	144	55	2,270	348	1,337	2,013	5.6	2,327	3,476
1965	218	335	402	869	139	61	2,455	604	1,155	2,185	5.3	2,293	3,333
1966	229	251	415	851	116	55[19] 73	2,768	993	1,278	2,426	5.0	2,398	3,614
1967	217	252	479	825	99	68	2,520	1,032	1,188	2,659	5.5	2,430	3,519
1968	227	194	595	921	92	62	2,418	1,300	1,021	2,384	6.4	2,784	3,588
1969	297	401	1,040	952	103	48	2,418	1,081	1,029	2,581	6.8	3,133	3,669
1970	338	258	1,072	993	99	45	2,051	1,079	1,441	3,333	6.9	3,328	3,742
1971	296	266	1,025	777	97	40	2,019	1,002	1,195	3,647	7.5	3,315	3,308
1972	317	286	1,034	827	108	42	1,965	50	1,400	3,865	8.4	3,600	3,685
1973	303	635	1,080	996	97	45	2,096	43	1,646	4,078	9.4	4,107	4,735
1974	262	595	1,118	977	86	30	1,870	95	1,540	4,631	7.4	4,301	4,613
1975	278	390 232	833	621	67	30	2,073	53	1,510	5,175	5.3	3,118	3,329
1976	298	441	933	678	67	36	1,880	73	1,526	6,078	6.6	3,681	2,569
1977	295	236	869	595	65	38	1,684	81	1,465	5,537	6.1	4,017	3,201
1978	297	298	949	643	54	43	1,377	162	1,459	3,710	6.8	4,614	3,845
1979	329	465	1,074	611	60	41	1,403	226	1,552	6,400	6.9	5,035	3,499
1980	291	428[23] 333	1,104	562	65	43	1,612	152	1,336	5,781	5.9	4,801	3,030
1981	342	191	1,078	603	54	35	1,366	169	1,354	6,138	5.6	4,895	2,876
1982	358	301	1,042	530	44	39	1,353	247	1,400	4,926	7.5	4,646	2,464
1983	408	361	1,122	572	46	42	1,422	152	1,239	6,033	8.5	4,939	3,068
1984	426	364	1,290	614	44	41	1,481	189	2,026	6,641	8.0	5,316	3,246
1985	416	252	1,356	653	37	39	1,417	164	1,335	6,810	7.9	5,455	3,008
1986	489	236	1,298	619	37	35	1,501	301	2,354	5,529	7.7	5,790	2,933
1987	546	223	1,345	654	35	29	1,573	159	1,948	4,784	7.5	6,251	3,030
1988	579	327	1,347	644	35	29	1,580	213	1,885	4,645	6.6	6,382	3,183
1989	650	686	1,465	636	32	35	1,577	171	1,848	5,206	6.8	6,435	2,913
1990	716	632	1,476	589	30	34	1,574	133	1,986	4,627	6.4	6,613	2,768
1991	843	643	1,464	570	26	34	1,677	50	1,962	6,753	6.8	6,431	2,777
1992	877	809	1,388	546	26	28	2,549	61[24]	2,221	7,385	8.1	6,646	2,817
1993	1,051	870	1,597	512	11	27	2,135	...[24]	2,557	9,993	9.9	7,026	2,865
1994	...	...	998	585	...	...	2,379	137	1,359	9,611	9.8	5,763	2,837
1995	...	...	1,181	600	...	...	1,862	147	1,361	9,418	9.6	5,545	2,560
1996	...	...	1,071	543	...	...	1,974	245	1,280	9,578	9.4	5,527	2,678
1997	...	...	1,102	532	...	...	2,481	47	1,247	8,365	9.0	6,101	2,871
1998	...	...	1,106	552	...	...	2,673	48	1,260	7,459	8.7	6,244	2,878
1999	...	...	1,159	562	...	...	2,301	147	1,223	9,632	9.5	6,771	2,969
2000	...	...	1,285	551	...	...	2,067	169	1,416	8,737	9.8	7,102	3,072

C11 Exports of Agricultural, Fishing and Forestry Products (in units indicated)

NOTES

1. SOURCES:- The main sources were the official publications noted on p. xv with gaps filled from the League of Nations and United Nations, *International Trade Statistics*, and the F.A.O., *Trade Yearbook*. Finnish statistics of wood and pulp to 1916 (1st line) are taken from Erkki Pihkala, *Finland's Foreign Trade 1860–1917* (Bank of Finland, Helsinki, 1969).
2. Except as indicated in footnotes, the statistics are of 'special' trade, i.e. exports of domestic produce.
3. Swedish data for timber are available for 1738–1860 in *Historisk Statistik för Sverige*, vol. 3, but in a variety of units of measurement.

FOOTNOTES

[1] Figures to 1838 (1st line) include the Duchies of Schleswig, Holstein, and Lauenburg as part of Denmark. From 1838 (2nd line) to 1863 they are not included, but trade *with* them is ignored.
[2] Figures to 1916 (1st line) are of pitprops, square timber, sawn logs, and sawn timber. From 1916 (2nd line) to 1963 (1st line) they are of pitprops, square timber, deals, boards, etc., but not plywood or veneers. From 1963 (2nd line) they are of all sawn or planed wood.
[3] Venetia was included from 1867, the Papal States from 1871, and the territories acquired from Austria from 1919. Statistics from 1946 relate to the 1954 boundaries.
[5] From 1865 (2nd line) to 1912, full-bodied wines other than 'sherry and similar types' are excluded.
[6] Figures to 1896 (1st line) are of 'general' trade.
[7] This break is occasioned by a change of source (see note 1).
[8] The parts of Alsace and Lorraine ceded to Germany are excluded from 1871 to 1918.
[9] Figures for 1914–18 exclude the occupied departments.
[10] Arta and part of Thessaly were acquired in 1881.
[11] Subsequent statistics cover all dried grapes.
[12] Previous statistics are for Old Greece, subsequent ones for the enlarged country, though the boundaries were not fully stabilised until 1923.
[13] Subsequent statistics are in thousands of metric tons.
[14] Previously only covers beams, deals, planks, and rafters, but subsequently includes masts, spars, and pitprops.
[15] Subsequently including staves.
[16] Subsequent statistics are in thousands of cubic metres.
[17] Subsequently includes floated timber.
[18] Statistics to 1959 (1st line) are of mechanical and sulphite wood pulp only, mechanical pulp being reckoned at wet weight up to 1952 and subsequently at dry weight. From 1959 (2nd line) the figures are of all pulp and waste paper.
[19] Subsequently covers all prepared and preserved fish.
[20] April–December only.
[21] From 1960 to 1968 excluding dried meat from animals other than pigs. This amounted to 6 thousand tons in 1960, and 5 thousand tons in 1968.
[22] Subsequently only fresh, chilled and frozen meat
[23] Subsequently sawn conifers only.
[24] Russian Federation, Ukraine = 1992, 180; 1993, 180.

D INDUSTRY

1.	Indices of Industrial Production	page 421
2.	Output of Coal	page 428
3.	Output of Crude Petroleum	page 438
4.	Output of Natural Gas	page 441
5.	Output of Main Non-ferrous Metal Ores	page 444
6.	Output of Main Non-metallic Minerals	page 451
7.	Output of Iron Ore	page 453
8.	Output of Pig Iron	page 457
9.	Output of Crude Steel	page 467
10.	Output of Aluminium	page 474
11.	Imports and Exports of Coal by Main Surplus and Deficient Countries	page 476
12.	Imports and Exports of Petroleum by Main Surplus and Deficient Countries	page 487
13.	Imports and Exports of Iron Ore by Main Trading Countries	page 499
14.	Raw Cotton Consumption Indicators	page 503
15.	Cotton Spindles	page 510
16.	Output of Cotton Yarn	page 513
17.	Output of Cotton Tissues	page 517
18.	Raw Wool Consumption Indicators	page 521
19.	Output of Wool Yarn	page 526
20.	Output of Wool Tissue	page 530
21.	Output of Artificial and Synthetic Fibres	page 534
22.	Linen Industry Indicators	page 538
23.	Output of Sulphuric Acid	page 541
24.	Timber Industry Indicators	page 546
25.	Output of Motor Vehicles	page 550
26.	Output of Beer	page 554
27.	Output of Electric Energy	page 562

Apart from Table D1, which gives synthetic indices of overall industrial production, and Table D15, showing the number of cotton spindles, all the tables in this section relate to the physical input or output and the volume of external trade of major commodities which possess an adequate degree of homogeneity to allow aggregation and meaningful comparisons between countries. Inevitably, these are mostly basic commodities: raw materials or manufactures at an intermediate stage, rather than finished goods; yarn and cloth rather than clothing; metals rather than machinery (of which the only example included here is motor vehicles). The picture that this selection of statistics is likely to give of industrial development is necessarily biassed and partial. Until recent decades there is little that could be added to them in the way of continuous statistical series for the output of finished products, though perhaps a little more could be done for external trade.

Probably enough has been written about the problems of constructing indices of industrial production for most users to be aware of the pitfalls. Even given all the desired basic information, an index which reflects accurately the composition of industrial output in any year will not, in a changing world, have precisely the right weighting of activities for another year. Where the components of an index are expressed in terms of values rather than volume, changes in relative prices will be an added source of possible misrepresentation. Changing the weights and linking indices is one solution to this problem, and often the best one; but it takes away exact precision of comparability. Such precision, however, can easily become unreal and meaningless where new commodities and activities are added to, and sometimes displace, old ones. Moreover, when much of the available statistical data consist of raw materials used there is always a problem in capturing numerically that part of the growth of industrial production which takes the form of increasing output per unit of input. Changes in quality are also difficult, if not impossible, to capture. All worthwhile indices of industrial production, then, are compromises between relevance and exact comparability over time. The skill of the constructor is in picking the base-years and linking points which produce least distortion, and appear to represent best the reality of industrial activity and change. Judgement on these matters inevitably contains subjective elements, and it is safe to say that there is no objectively perfect index. That said, how useful are the good indices in encapsulating change! Even so, one must never lose sight of the fact that percentage rates of change are not themselves of much significance if one is unaware of the absolute size of the base from which they are derived.

The bulk of the tables in this section are reasonably straightforward. Most of the commodities covered are fairly homogeneous, though hardly one is perfectly so. The main sources of such variations which are not obvious are referred to in the notes following each table and in the footnotes. A great many other commodities could have been included for the period since the late 1940s, using either national or United Nations sources but very few of these could have been carried back to earlier years. Since the United Nations publications are fairly widely available there seemed to be no great advantage in including them.

D1 INDICES OF INDUSTRIAL PRODUCTION

Key:- (a) 1913 = 100; (b) 1937 = 100; (c) 1950 = 100; (d) Soviet official index 1937 = 100; (e) Moorsteen — Powell index 1937 = 100; (f) 1929 = 100

1801–1849

	France (a)	United Kingdom (a)		France (a)	Spain (a)	United Kingdom (a)
			1825	19.7	...	13
1801	...	6.6	1826	20.8	...	13
1802	...	6.9	1827	21.3	...	13
1803	...	7.1	1828	20.9	...	14
1804	...	7.3	1829	21.1	...	14
1805	...	7.4	1830	21.0	...	15
1806	...	7.6	1831	20.4	8.4	15
1807	...	7.8	1832	21.5	...	16
1808	...	7.9	1833	22.9	...	16
1809	...	8.1	1834	23.1	...	17
1810	...	8.2	1835	23.0	10.3	17
1811	...	8.4	1836	23.2	...	18
1812	...	8.5	1837	22.8	...	19
1813	...	8.6	1838	24.2	...	19
1814	...	8.8	1839	22.9	...	20
1815	19.2	9.0	1840	24.3	...	20
1816	19.5	9.2	1841	25.6	...	21
1817	19.9	9.5	1842	26.7	11.9	22
1818	21.3	9.8	1843	28.3	12.8	22
1819	19.5	10	1844	28.4	15.3	23
1820	20.7	10	1845	29.7	16.5	24
1821	21.9	11	1846	30.6	16.8	24
1822	21.4	11	1847	29.7	15.5	25
1823	20.2	12	1848	26.7	16.6	26
1824	21.8	12	1849	32.2	19.0	27

D1   Indices of Industrial Production

	Austria (a)	France (a)	Germany (a)	Italy (a)	Russia (a)	Spain (a)	Sweden[2] (a)	U.K. (a)
1850	...	33.5	9.5	...	...	20.7	...	28
1851	...	31.1	9.8	...	...	23.1	...	29
1852	...	34.8	10.0	...	...	23.7	...	30
1853	...	36.5	9.9	...	...	23.6	...	31
1854	...	34.2	9.7	...	...	23.3	...	32
1855	...	37.3	10	...	...	24.8	...	33[3]
								26.3
1856	...	38.1	11	...	...	26.9	...	28.1
1857	...	35.3	12	...	...	27.8	...	29.1
1858	...	38.2	12	...	...	28.6	...	28.5
1859	...	36.6	12	...	...	29.7	...	30.0
1860	...	39.1	13	...	8.8	31.2	...	31.7
1861	...	38.7	13	32	8.5	32.4	15	31.7
1862	...	37.0	13	32	6.8	31.0	16	32.4
1863	...	37.8	15	32	7.3	32.0	17	32.5
1864	...	41.2	15	32	7.6	32.1	17	35.0
1865	...	39.9	16	33	7.5	33.2	19	37.3
1866	...	40.4	17	35	9.8	32.6	18	38.7
1867	...	40.2	17	37	10.0	35.0	18	36.4
1868	...	43.8	18	37	9.7	31.6	20	36.4
1869	...	44.4	19	40	11	32.8	24	35.8
1870	...	40.0	19[1]	40	11	35.0	25	40.2
1871	...	41.3	21	39	12	38.8	19	43.5
1872	...	45.8	24	40	12	41.5	20	44.8
1873	...	43.8	26	44	12	46.8	20	45.3
1874	...	46.5	27	46	13	44.0	23	46.4
1875	...	47.1	27	46	14	45.9	24	46.7
1876	...	47.7	28	46	14	47.2	25	47.5
1877	...	46.5	27	46	14	49.7	25	47.4
1878	...	47.4	28	44	18	48.6	24	47.3
1879	...	46.0	27	44	18	47.6	25	45.6
1880	28.6	49.4	26	42	18	49.1	25	50.3
1881	31.8	54.1	27	47	22	53.8	29	53.5
1882	33.1	55.3	27	47	21	55.2	30	55.7
1883	37.0	54.5	29	47	23	59.3	29	56.5
1884	38.3	52.5	30	49	22	59.0	32	54.4
1885	36.4	52.0	31	51	24	60.1	34	52.1
1886	39.0	52.9	31	49	25	55.5	32	51.0
1887	40.3	53.7	33	53	28	53.8	34	55.1
1888	39.6	55.6	35	51	26	56.3	36	58.3
1889	42.9	58.4	39	51	29	60.4	37	62.4
1890	46.8	57.3	40	51	32	62.5	40	63.3
1891	50.0	60.3	41	47	34	62.5	43	64.1
1892	50.6	63.6	42	47	35	65.8	45	61.0
1893	51.9	61.5	43	47	40	71.8	48	60.0
1894	55.8	62.7	45	51	40	69.1	52	63.5
1895	57.8	59.5	49	53	44	68.8	51	66.5
1896	58.4	64.4	50	51	46	70.6	57	71.4
1897	59.1	66.7	53	53	49	66.8	58	73.4
1898	63.6	68.6	56	53	54	73.9	62	77.0
1899	64.3	71.3	58	56	60	78.5	66	80.1

D1 Indices of Industrial Production

	Austria (a)	Belgium (b)	Bulgaria (b)	Czech (b)	Denmark (b)	Finland (b)	France (a)	Germany (a)	Greece (b)	Hungary (b)	Ireland (b)
1900	64.9	...	...	...	...	14	67.9	61	...	...	...
1901	68.2	52	...	...	...	14	67.7	59	...	...	...
1902	68.2	60	...	...	...	13	66.3	60	...	...	...
1903	68.8	62	...	...	...	15	70.8	65	...	...	...
1904	69.4	63	...	...	...	15	66.9	68	...	...	...
1905	73.3	64	...	...	...	16	74.6	70	...	...	...
1906	76.6	67	...	...	...	18	76.1	73	...	...	...
1907	87.7	69	...	...	...	19	79.3	79	...	...	...
1908	85.7	66	...	...	...	19	77.8	78	...	...	...
1909	83.8	72	...	...	...	19	83.1	81	...	...	...
1910	84.4	75	...	...	...	21	81.1	86	...	...	...
1911	89.0	79	...	...	...	24	88.8	91	...	...	...
1912	97.4	84	...	...	...	26	102.3	97	...	...	...
1913	100	83	...	...	...	29	100	100[10] / 84	...	...	...
1914	...	...	...	...	...	23	...	69	...	...	...
1915	...	...	...	...	...	28	...	56	...	...	...
1916	...	...	...	...	...	30	...	54	...	...	...
1917	...	...	...	...	...	22	...	52	...	...	...
1918	...	...	...	...	...	13	(b)	48	...	...	...
1919	...	...	...	...	...	20	56[7]	32	...	...	...
1920	...	61	...	...	...	26	61	46	...	...	...
1921	...	54	...	62	...	26	54	56	...	...	...
1922	(b)	67	...	57	...	32	77	60	...	...	...
1923	62	79	...	60	...	37	87	39	...	...	...
1924	64	87	...	79	...	39	108	59	...	...	...
1925	74	82	...	82	...	42	107	69	57	...	...
1926	74	96	...	80	...	46	125	67	55	...	63
1927	84	106	...	92	63	51	109	84	61	74	...
1928	92	115	...	99	68	57	126[8] / 111	85	65	75	...
1929	94	115	...	104	74	61	123	85	66	77	69
1930	80	97	...	93	79	56	123	74	68	73	...
1931	66	88	...	84	74	51	105	60	71	67	70
1932	58	73	...	66	67	53	91	50	67	63	...
1933	59	76	...	63	77	58	99	56	73	68	...
1934	66	76	...	69	87	70	92	71	83	76	...
1935	75	83	...	73	92	77	88	82	93	82	...
1936	81	90	103[5]	83	96	86	95	91	92	91	98
1937	100	100	100	100	100	100	100	100	100	100	100
1938	101[4]	81	108	...	100	106	92	107	109	98	103[12]
1939	...	86	115	...	107	101	...	113	116	...	...
1940	...	...	128	...	87	31	...	109	...	...	...
1941	...	...	136	...	83	83	...	112	...	...	...
1942	...	...	131	...	87	36	56[9]	113	...	...	...
1943	...	...	114[6]	...	89	100	49[9]	127	...	...	75
1944	...	...	...	...	88	93	35[9]	125	...	...	78
1945	...	...	...	...	75	98	45[9]	...	37[11]	...	89
								East — West			
1946	...	73	...	...	102	112	76	38 — ...	62	...	106
1947	...	91	...	...	117	124	89	49 — ...	78	...	117
1948	92	100	230	108	128	140	103	64 — 63	85	...	133
1949	123	100	307	123	137	147	112	79 — 90	101	125	152

D1 Indices of Industrial Production

	Italy	Netherlands	Norway	Poland	Romania	Russia/USSR		Spain	Sweden	U.K.[15]	Yugo-slavia
	(a)	(b)	(b)	(b)	(b)	(b)		(a)	(a)	(a)	(b)
1900	61	…	…	…	…	63		80.7	68	80.1	…
1901	61	…	…	…	…	65		81.2	70	80.3	…
1902	67	…	…	…	…	69		85.6	73	81.7	…
1903	67	…	…	…	…	67		84.8	77	80.0	…
1904	70	…	…	…	…	69		80.9	80	81.0	…
1905	74	…	…	…	…	61		81.5	81	85.7	…
1906	79	…	…	…	…	69		87.0	89	89.3	…
1907	90	…	…	…	…	73		92.1	92	91.0	…
1908	93	…	…	…	…	74		95.3	90	83.7	…
1909	95	…	39	…	…	77		90.0	83	84.3	…
1910	95	…	45	…	…	86		93.0	97	85.5	…
1911	95	…	46	…	…	91		95.1	99	91.5	…
1912	102	…	55	…	…	95		104	103	93.9	…
1913	100	…	59	…	…	100		100	100	100	…
	(b)				…	(d)	(e)	(f)	(b)		
	57					17	…	63.2	46		
1914	54	…	60	…	…	…	…	63.0	44	93.7	…
										(b)	
										57.4	
1915	71	…	65	…	…	…	…	65.8	48	58.6[16]	…
1916	71	…	67	…	…	…	…	68.9	50	55.4	…
1917	63	…	56	…	…	12	…	67.6	42	51.7	
1918	61	…	51	…	…	…	…	68.8	35	50.0	
1919	59	…	53	…	…	…	…	63.8	39	55.1	
1920	59	…	60	…	…	…	…	66.8	44	61.2[15]	…
										60.0	
1921	54	…	43	…	…	5	…	67.5	34	48.9	
1922	61	…	53	…	…	…	…	68.7	40	56.5	…
1923	66	…	59	…	…	…	…	77.1	44	59.9	
1924	73	…	63	…	…	8	…	81.0	50	66.5	…
1925	83	73	69	67	49	12	…	84.3	51	69.1	…
1926	83	75	61	66	57	17	…	89.0	56	65.3	…
1927	80	83	63	81	64	19	…	91.6	58	75.3	…
1928	88	95	69	92	71	22	37	100.3	63	73.3	…
1929	90	97	77	92	76	27	43	100	66	76.9	…
1930	85	99	78	81	74	33	53	105.3	68	73.6	…
1931	77	93	60	71	78	40	57	94.5	64	68.9	…
1932	77	82	72	58	67	45	58	93.6	59	68.6	…
1933	82	88	72	63	78	48	61	92.6	60	73.1	…
1934	80	90	75	71	94	57	70	94.7	73	80.4	…
1935	86	88	83	77	93	70	83	97.9	81	86.6	…
1936	86	89	91	85	99	90	99	…	89	94.4	…
1937	100	100	100	100	100	100	100	…	100	100	100
1938	100	101	100	109	100	112	104	…	101	97.3	108
1939	109	110	107	…	…	130	111	…	110	…	115
1940	110	104[13]	92	…	…	131	116	83.9	100	…	…
1941	103	89[13]	90	…	…	…	…	78.5	98	…	…
1942	89	70[13]	82	…	…	…	…	83.7	103	…	…
1943	69	64[13]	78	…	…	…	…	86.6	108	…	…
1944	42	43[13]	64	…	…	136	…	91.4	115	…	…
1945	29	31[13]	57	…	…	120	77	86.9	113	…	…
1946	71	77	97	…	…	100	81	96.7	137	99.7	90
1947	91	98	115	…	…	122	93	95.1	140	105.0	138
1948	99	116	128	150	84	151	114	99.6	150	114.0	171
1949	109	129	137	177	…	185	137	97.7	155	120.7	192

D1 Indices of Industrial Production

	Austria	Belgium	Bulgaria	Czech	Denmark	Finland	France	East Germany	West Germany	Greece	Hungary	Ireland
1949	37	60	15	27	51	41	43	23	28	30	23	55
1950	43	61	18	31	56	44	45	29	35[17]	38	30	63
1951	49	69	22	35	58	51	51	36	41	44	38	64
1952	50	66	26	41	55	48	51	41	45	43	46	64
1953	51	64	29	45	58	52	52	46	48	49	52	68
1954	58	70	32	47	63	59	57	51	54	60	54	72
1955	67	75	34	52	64	65	64	55	63	63	54	74
1956	71	80	40	57	65	67	69	59	68	64	49	71
1957	75	80	46	63	69	69	75	63	71	69	56	68
1958	77	76	53	70	71	67	77	70	73	76	63	70
1959	81	77	64	78	80	72	78	79	79	77	70	76
1960	90	83	73	87	86	82	85	85	88	84	78	81
1961	94	88	81	95	90	91	90	90	93	89	87	88
1962	96	93	91	101	98	96	95	96	97	91	94	94
1963	100	100	100	100	100	100	100	100	100	100	100	100
1964	108	107	111	104	113	107	107	107	110	111	107	108
1965	113	109	127	112	120	115	109	113	116	121	111	113
1966	118	111	142	121	122	121	116	121	117	140	118	118
1967	119	113	161	129	126	125	119	129	114	146	125	127
1968	128	119	177	135	130	132	123	137	125	159	138	141
1969	142	131	194	141	147	151	136	146	141	178	139	152
1970	154	135	213	154	152	169	145	155	150	196	152	159
1971	163	139	233	165	155	171	155	164	153	218	162	165
1972	176	148	254	176	167	193	163	174	159	249	171	173
1973	184	156	277	188	175	207	175	186	170	287	183	172
1974	194	162	299	189	167	215	179	199	167	283	198	197
1975	182	146	330	213	153	206	167	211	158	295	207	189
1976	193	159	350	225	164	208	181	223	171	326	216	206
1977	201	159	374	238	166	210	183	234	172	333	231	223
1978	206	162	399	249	169	221	187	245	177	358	242	241
1979	221	170	421	259	175	243	195	256	185	380	249	256
1980	227	168	439	268	175	262	197	268	184	382	244	252
1981	225	164	462	274	175	270	193	281	179	385	251	259
1982	224	164	454	276	180	271	193	290	173	388	257	258
1983	226	167	505	285	186	280	193	302	174	387	260	277
1984	237	171	526	296	203	293	147	314	179	396	267	312
1985	248	174	542	307	212	304	199	328	185	409	269	323
1986	251	176	564	316	221	307	199	340	189	408	274	334
1987	253	180	587	323	214	320	203	351	190	403	285	366
1988	264	189	627	330	217	333	211	362	197	424	285	406
1989	280	198	610	335	228	348	221	...	215	432	271	444
1990	300	205	509	322	229	346	225		226	420	249	464
1991	304	200	395	241	233	314	225		232	416	200	479
1992	302	200	334	212	238	320	225		228	413	181	524
1993	295	190	325	...	231	335	219		212	401	185	554
						1990 = 100						
1994	93.6	94.7	...	69.8	111	108	99.1		93.9	95.6	84.0	133.4
1995	112.3	100.6	100.0	75.9	116	115	101.5		95.9	97.9	87.9	160.8
1996	113.4	101.4	105.1	77.4	118	119	102.4		96.5	99.1	90.9	173.0
1997	120.6	106.0	94.6	80.8	124	130	106.2		99.8	100.8	100.9	198.6
1998	130.5	109.6	82.6	83.3	127	140	111.7		104.1	106.7	113.4	228.9
1999	138.5	110.8	...	80.9	129	148	114.0		105.7	110.0	125.2	252.7

D1   Indices of Industrial Production

1949-1999
1963 = 100

	Italy	Neth-erlands	Norway	Poland	Portugal	Rom-ania	Russia/U.S.S.R (a)	Russia/U.S.S.R (b)	Spain	Sweden	Switz-erland	U.K.[15]	Yugo-slavia
1949	29	42	51	18	...	...	21	137	32	55	...	66	34
1950	33	47	56	23	...	16	26	156	37	57	...	70[19]	35
1951	37	49	60	29	...	...	30	176	42	60	...	72	34
1952	39	49	60	34	...	...	33	189	48	58	...	71	33
1953	42	54	63	40	47	33	37	205	50	59	...	75	37
1954	46	59	67	44	...	...	42	228	52	61	...	79	42
1955	51	64	70	49	56	40	47	254	54	65	...	83	47
1956	54	68	74	54	61	45	52	279	59	67	...	83	52
1957	58	71	76	59	64	48	57	302	64	70	...	85	57
1958	60	71	76	65	69	53	63	345	66	71	71	84	63
1959	67	79	80	71	73	58	70	358	67	75	77	88	70
1960	77	87	87	79	80	68	77	379	72	83	84	95	77
1961	84	90	91	88	88	78	84	407	81	89	91	96	84
1962	92	95	95	95	92	89	93	...	91	94[18]	95	97	93
1963	100	100	100	100	100	100	100	...	100	100	100	100	100
1964	101	110	109	109	112	114	107	...	112	110	105	108	116
1965	109	116	115	119	119	129	117	...	126	118	108	112	125
1966	121	123	121	128	127	143	127	...	142	122	112	113	131
1967	131	129	126	138	134	163	139	...	151	125	116	114	130
1968	140	143	132	149	147	182	151	...	163	131	121	120	138
1969	145	156	139	163	158	200	162	...	188	140	131	123	153
1970	155	170	145	175	170	227	175	...	207	149	143	124	167
1971	154	180	150	189	177	255	189	...	215	151	146	125	185
1972	161	188	159	211	198	284	202	...	250	155	149	127	198
1973	177	200	168	233	227	325	216	...	289	164	157	138	210
1974	185	205	173	261	238	373	233	...	316	173	159	136	233
1975	168	195	185	286	218	418	250	...	295	167	139	129	246
1976	189	206	185	310	234	465	262	...	301	167	140	133	254
1977	191	208	183	329	267	522	278	...	317	156	148	140	278
1978	195	179	179	341	279	570	290	...	324	155	148	143	302
1979	208	182	185	348	302	615	301	...	327	164	151	149	326
1980	219	182	181	345	322	656	311	...	331	164	159	139	340
1981	216	178	179	300	327	674	321	...	328	160	158	135	354
1982	209	171	179	296	340	681	330	...	324	158	152	137	354
1983	202	176	178	315	342	713	346	...	333	166	151	143	359
1984	209	186	189	333	338	760	358	...	336	178	155	143	379
1985	212	193	192	346	345	797	371	...	342	182	164	151	389
1986	219	193	196	362	366	858	389	...	353	182	170	154	405
1987	228	195	199	374	380	897	402	...	369	191	172	159	405
1988	241	195	198	393	401	930	417	...	380	193	183	165	407
1989	250	207	217	380	464	702	423	...	397	197	189	171	407
1990	250	213	219	279	518	544	420	...	397	198	194	171	138
1991	247	218	225	242	518	426	_385_	...	394	189	196	164	333
1992	245	218	239	248	509	407		...	384	185	194	164	...
1993	241	217	248	262	493	420		...	364	192	194	167	...

——————— 1990 = 100 ———————

	Italy	Neth-erlands	Norway	Poland	Portugal	Rom-ania	Russia/U.S.S.R	Spain	Sweden	Switz-erland	U.K.[15]	Yugo-slavia
1994	101.5	105.3	120.1	112.9	94.9	59.9	51.3	98.3	101.9	101.0	104.5	40.5
1995	107.0	108.5	127.2	123.8	99.4	65.5	49.4	102.9	112.1	103.1	106.3	42.4
1996	106.0	111.1	134.1	135.5	100.8	69.2	47.4	102.2	114.7	103.0	107.4	45.5
1997	109.6	111.3	138.7	150.7	103.3	64.6	48.1	109.2	122.8	107.8	108.5	49.6
1998	111.6	114.0	137.8	157.7	107.4	53.6	45.5	115.1	127.9	111.8	109.4	51.3
1999	111.7	116.5	137.5	165.3	110.8	48.9	...	118.1	129.1	115.5	109.9	38.9

D1   Indices of Industrial Production

NOTES

1. SOURCES:- Austria 1880–1913 Richard Rudolph, 'The Role of Financial Institutions in the Industrialization of the Czech Crownlands, 1880–1914', unpublished doctoral dissertation, Department of History, University of Wisconsin (1968), p. 23. Belgium to 1937—The I.R.E.S. index, quoted in C. Carbonnelle, 'Recherches sur l'évolution de la production en Belgique de 1990 à 1957', *Cahiers Economiques de Bruxelles* (1959). Finland to 1949—Reino Hjerppe *et al*, *Suomess Teollisuus ja Teollinen Käsityö 1900–1965* (Helsinki, 1976) France to 1913—F. Crouzet, 'Un indice de la production industrielle francaise au XIXe siecle', *Annales (Economies, Societes, Civilisations)* (1970). Germany to 1913—W.G. Hoffman, *Das Wachstum der Deutschen Wirtschaft seit der Mitte des 19 Jahrhunderts* (Berlin, etc., 1965). Germany 1913 to 1944—D. Petzina *et al*, *Sozialgeschichtlich Arbeitsbuch, III* (Munich, 1978). Italy to 1947—*Annali di Statistica*, serie VIII vol. 9. Russia to 1913—R.W. Goldsmith, 'The Economic Growth of Tsarist Russia, 1860–1913', *Economic Development and Cultural Change* (1961). Russia 1928–61 (second column)—R. Moorsteen & R.P. Powell, *The Soviet Capital Stock, 1928–1962* (Homewood, III,. 1966). (This is a combined index of the separate indices published on pp. 622–4 of civilian industries, munitions industries, and construction, using their weights in 1937.) Spain to 1949—Albert Carreras, "La Produccion Industrial Española 1842–1981...," *Revista de Historia Economica* (1984). U.K. to 1855—W.G. Hoffman, *British Industry, 1700–1950* (Oxford, 1955). U.K. 1855–1949—C.H. Feinstein, *National Income, Expenditure and Output of the United Kingdom, 1855–1965* (Cambridge, 1972). All other statistics are from the official publications noted on p. xv, or from the League of Nations and United Nations, *Statistical Yearbooks*.
2. Another index of industrial production in France, covering periods of years since the late 18th century, is given by T. Markovitch, *L'industrie francaise de 1789 a 1964—conclusions generales* (Cahiers de l'I.S.E.A., 1966), as follows (1938 = 100):-

1781–90	6.3	1865–74	28.8	1925–34	93.9
1803–12	7.1	1875–84	33.9	1935–38	97.5
1815–24	9.4	1885–94	39.4	1946–49	116.4
1825–34	12.4	1895–1904	47.8	1950–54	141.8
1835–44	16.5	1905–13	57.8	1955–59	187.7
1845–54	19.5	1920–24	67.9	1960–64	246.4

In a revised edition (1987) he also gives an annual index from 1815.

3. The bases of many official indices have been changed quite frequently in the last 20 or 30 years. Where this has happened, the old and the new indices have been crudely spliced together.

FOOTNOTES

[1] From 1871 to 1917 including Alsace—Lorraine.
[2] The index to 1913 is of the value of the output of manufactures and handicrafts at constant prices.
[3] This break is occasioned by the change of source (see note 1).
[4] First 9 months only.
[5] July–December only.
[6] January–July only.
[7] On the 1913 = 100 basis the 1919 figures is 57.
[8] A much more complete index begins in 1928.
[9] Excluding Alsace-Lorraine.
[10] Subsequently 1937 = 100.
[11] May–December only.
[12] A series published in the first U.N. *Statistical Yearbook*, but not given in the retrospective tables published in the Irish *Statistical Abstract*, gave the following figures for 1938–43:-

1938	98	1940	101	1942	77
1939	103	1941	94	1943	78

[13] These are described as 'rough estimates'.
[14]
[15] The statistics from 1920 (2nd line) relate to Great Britain and Northern Ireland.
[16] On the 1913 = 100 basis the figure for 1915 is 95.5.
[17] On the all-Germany 1937 = 100 basis the 1950 figure for West Germany alone is 64.
[18] Previously does not include electricity and gas.
[19] The official index has been spliced onto Feinstein's.

D2 OUTPUT OF COAL (in millions of metric tons)
HC = Hard Coal   BC = Brown Coal

1815–1859

	Austria[1]		Belgium	France[3]	Germany		Hungary[4]		Spain		UK[5]
	HC	BC			HC	BC	HC	BC	HC	BC	
1815	...		...	0.9	...	...		...	...	...	22.3
1816	...		...	...	...	...		...	...	...	...
1817	...		...	...	1.3	...		...	...	...	...
1818	...		...	...	1.3	...		...	...	...	...
1819	0.1		...	...	1.2	...		...	...	...	...
1820	0.1		...	1.1	1.3	...		...	...	...	...
1821	0.1		...	...	1.4	...		...	...	...	...
1822	0.1		...	...	1.5	...		...	...	...	...
1823	0.1		...	...	1.5	...		...	...	...	...
1824	0.2		...	...	1.6	...		...	...	...	...
1825	0.2		...	1.5	1.6	...		...	...	...	...
1826	0.2		...	...	1.6	...		...	...	...	...
1827	0.2		...	1.7	1.7	...		...	...	...	...
1828	0.2		...	1.8	1.7	...		...	...	...	...
1829	0.2		...	1.7	1.7	...		...	...	...	...
1830	0.2		...	1.9	1.8	...		...	...	...	30.5
1831	0.2		2.3	1.8	1.7	...		...	...	...	31.5
1832	0.2		2.3	2.0	1.9	...		...	...	...	32.1
1833	0.2		2.5	2.1	2.1	...		...	...	...	32.9
1834	0.2		2.4	2.5	2.1	...		...	...	...	33.8
1835	0.3		2.6	2.5	2.1	...		...	...	...	35.2
1836	0.3		3.1	2.8	2.3	...		...	...	...	36.4
1837	0.3		3.2	3.0	2.7	0.5		...	...	...	37.8
1838	0.3		3.3	3.1	2.9	0.6		...	...	...	39.3
1839	0.4		3.5	3.0	3.0	0.7		...	0.02	...	40.8
1840	0.5		3.9	3.0	3.2	0.7		...	0.02	...	42.6
1841	0.5		4.0	3.4	3.4	0.6		...	...	...	43.8
1842	0.6[1] 0.5		4.1	3.6	3.8	1.0		...	0.04	...	44.2
1843	0.5		4.0	3.7	3.6	0.9		...	...	...	46.0
1844	0.6		4.4	3.8	3.8	1.0		...	0.03	...	47.6
1845	0.7		4.9	4.2	4.4	1.2		...	0.04	...	51.1
1846	0.8		5.0	4.5	4.6	1.3		...	...	...	53.1
1847	0.8		5.7	5.2	4.8	1.5		...	0.04	...	54.0
1848	0.9		4.9	4.0	4.4	1.7		...	0.05	...	56.6
1849	0.9		5.3	4.0	4.6	1.8		...	...	...	59.3
1850	0.9		5.8	4.4	5.3	1.5		...	0.06	...	62.5
1851	0.7	0.4	6.2	4.5	5.9	1.9	0.1	0.1	...	...	65.2
1852	0.7	0.5	6.8	4.9	6.6	2.2	0.1	0	...	...	68.3
1853	0.8	0.6	7.2	5.9	7.3	2.6	0.1	0.1	...	...	71.2
1854	0.9	0.7	7.9	6.8	8.6	2.7	0.1	0.1	0.09	0.02	75.1
1855	1.0	0.8	8.4	7.5	10.2	2.9	0.1	0.1	0.09	...	76.4
1856	1.1	1.0	8.2	7.9	11.0	3.3	0.1	0.1	0.09	...	79.0
1857	1.3	1.0	8.4	7.9	11.5	3.8	0.1	0.2	...	...	81.9
1858	...[2]	...[2]	8.9	7.4	12.5[28]	3.6[28]	...[2]	...[2]	0.11	...	80.3
1859	1.6	1.1	9.2	7.5	10.6[28]	3.5[28]	0.2	0.2	...	...	82.8

D2 Output of Coal (in millions of metric tons)

1860–1909

	Austria[1]		Belgium	Bulgaria	France[6]	Germany[7]		Hungary[4]		Italy[8]	
	HC	BC		BC		HC	BC	HC	BC	HC	BC
1860	1.7	1.5	9.6	...	8.3	13.6	4.8	0.2	0.2	...	
1861	2.0	1.6	10.1	...	9.4	14.1	4.6	0.3	0.2	...	
1862	2.3	1.7	9.9	...	10.3	15.6	5.1	0.3	0.3	...	
1863	2.2	1.8	10.3	...	10.7	16.9	5.5	0.3	0.3	...	
1864	<u>2.2</u>	<u>1.9</u>	11.2	...	11.2	19.4	6.2	<u>0.3</u>[6]	<u>0.2</u>[6]	...	
1865	2.5	2.0	11.8	...	11.6	21.8	6.8	0.4	0.3	...	
1866	2.3	1.9	12.8	...	12.3	21.4	6.5	0.5	0.3	...	
1867	2.9	2.4	12.8	...	12.7	23.8	7.0	0.4	0.5	...	
1868	3.3	2.8	12.3	...	13.3	25.7	7.2	0.5	0.4	0.1	
1869	3.5	3.1	12.9	...	13.5	26.8	7.6	0.5	0.6	0.1	
1870	3.8	3.5	13.7	...	<u>13.3</u>[6]	26.4	7.6	0.5	0.6	0.1	
1871	4.4	4.2	13.8	...	13.3	<u>29.4</u>[7]	<u>8.5</u>[7]	0.6	0.9	0.1	
1872	4.1	4.8	15.7	...	15.8	33.3	9.0	0.6	0.9	0.1	
1873	4.5	5.8	15.8	...	17.5	36.4	9.8	0.7	0.9	0.1	
1874	4.5	6.4	14.7	...	16.9	35.9	10.7	0.6	0.8	0.1	
1875	4.6	6.9	15.0	...	17.0	37.4	10.4	0.6	0.8	0.1	
1876	4.9	6.9	14.3	...	17.1	38.5	11.1	0.7	0.9	0.1	
1877	4.9	7.1	13.9	...	16.8	37.5	10.7	0.7	0.9	0.1	
1878	5.1	7.2	14.9	...	17.0	39.6	10.9	0.7	0.9	0.1	
1879	5.4	7.9	15.4	...	17.1	42.0	11.4	0.7	0.9	0.1	
1880	5.9	8.4	16.9	...	19.4	47.0	12.1	0.8	1.0	0.1	
1881	6.3	9.0	16.9	...	19.8	48.7	12.9	0.8	1.1	0.1	
1882	6.6	9.0	17.6	...	20.6	52.1	13.3	0.8	1.3	0.2	
1883	7.2	9.9	18.2	...	21.3	55.9	14.5	0.9	1.5	0.2	
1884	7.2	10.0	18.1	...	20.0	57.2	14.9	0.9	1.6	0.2	
1885	7.4	10.5	17.4	...	19.5	58.3	15.4	1.0	1.6	0.2	
1886	7.4	10.9	17.3	...	19.9	58.1	15.6	0.9	1.6	0.2	
1887	7.8	11.6	18.4	...	21.3	60.3	15.9	0.8	1.7	0.3	
1888	8.3	12.9	19.2	...	22.6	65.4	16.6	0.9	1.9	0.4	
1889	8.6	13.8	19.9	...	24.3	67.3	17.6	0.9	2.0	0.4	
1890	8.9	15.3	20.4	...	26.1	70.2	19.0	1.0	2.3	0.4	
1891	9.2	16.2	19.7	...	26.0	73.7	20.5	1.0	2.4	0.3	
1892	9.2	16.2	19.6	...	26.2	71.4	21.2	1.1	2.6	0.3	
1893	9.7	16.8	19.4	...	25.7	73.9	21.6	1.0	2.9	0.3	
1894	9.6	17.3	20.5	0.1	27.4	76.7	22.1	1.0	3.2	0.3	
1895	9.7	18.4	20.5	0.1	28.0	79.2	24.8	1.1	3.5	0.3	
1896	9.9	18.9	21.3	0.1	29.2	85.7	26.8	1.1	3.8	0.3	
1897	10.5	20.5	21.5	0.1	30.8	91.1	29.4	1.1	3.9	0.3	
1898	10.9	21.1	22.1	0.1	32.4	96.3	31.6	1.2	4.5	0.3	
1899	11.5	21.8	22.1	0.1	32.9	102	34.2	1.2	4.3	0.4	
1900	11.0	21.5	23.5	0.1	33.4	109	40.5	1.4	5.1	0.5	
1901	11.7	22.5	22.2	0.1	32.3	109	44.5	1.4	5.2	0.4	
1902	11.0	22.1	22.9	0.1	30.0	107	43.1	1.2	5.1	...	0.4
1903	11.5	22.2	23.8	0.1	34.9	117	45.8	1.2	5.3	...	0.3
1904	11.9	22.0	24.2	0.1	34.2	121	48.6	1.2	5.5	...	0.3
1905	12.6	22.7	23.3	0.2	35.9	121	52.5	1.1	6.1	...	0.4
1906	13.5	24.2	25.1	0.1	34.2	137	56.4	1.2	6.4	...	0.5
1907	13.8	26.3	25.3	0.2	36.8	143	62.5	1.3	6.5	...	0.4
1908	13.9	26.7	23.1	0.2	37.4	148	66.6	1.2	7.2	...	0.5
1909	13.7	26.0	25.1	0.2	37.8	149	68.7	1.4	7.7	...	0.6

D2 Output of Coal (in millions of metric tons)

	Netherlands[9]	Romania	Russia	Serbia HC	Serbia BC	Spain HC	Spain BC	Sweden[10]	U.K.
1860	...	...	0.3	...	...	0.3	...	...	87.9
1861	...	...	0.4	...	...	0.3	...	...	89.2
1862	...	...	0.3	...	...	0.4	...	...	91.1
1863	...	...	0.4	...	...	0.4	...	...	95.7
1864	...	...	0.4	...	...	0.4	...	...	99.1
1865	...	...	0.4	...	...	0.5	...	...	102
1866	...	...	0.4	...	...	0.4	...	...	105
1867	...	...	0.4	...	...	0.5	...	...	106
1868	...	...	0.4	...	...	0.5	...	...	108
1869	...	...	0.6	...	...	0.5	...	...	111
1870	...	...	0.7	...	...	0.6	...	...	115
1871	...	...	0.8	...	...	0.6	...	...	121
1872	...	...	1.1	...	...	0.7	...	...	125
1873	...	...	1.2	...	...	0.7	...	...	130
1874	...	...	1.3	...	...	0.7	...	0.1	129
1875	...	...	1.7	...	...	0.7	...	0.1	135
1876	...	...	1.8	...	...	0.7	...	0.1	136
1877	...	...	1.8	...	...	0.7	...	0.1[10]	136
1878	...	...	2.5	...	...	0.7	...	0.1	135
1879	...	...	2.9	...	...	0.7	...	0.1	136
1880	...	...	3.3	...	...	0.8	...	0.1	149
1881	...	...	3.5	...	...	1.2	...	0.1	157
1882	...	...	3.8	...	...	1.2	...	0.1	159
1883	...	...	4.0	...	...	1.0	...	0.2	166
1884	...	...	3.9	...	...	1.0	...	0.2	163
1885	...	...	4.3	...	...	0.9	...	0.2	162
1886	...[9] 0.1	...	4.6	...	...	1.0	...	0.2	160
1887	0.1	...	4.5	...	...	1.0	...	0.2	165
1888	0.1	...	5.2	...	...	1.0	...	0.2	173
1889	0.1	...	6.2	...	...	1.1	...	0.2	180
1890	0.1	...	6.0	...	...	1.2	...	0.2	185
1891	0.1	...	6.2	...	...	1.3	...	0.2	188
1892	0.1	...	6.9	...	...	1.4	...	0.2	185
1893	0.1	...	7.6	0.1	...	1.5	...	0.2	167
1894	0.1	...	8.8	...	0.1	1.7	...	0.2	191
1895	0.1	...	9.1	...	0.1	1.7	...	0.2	193
1896	0.1	...	9.4	...	0.1	1.9	0.1	0.2	198
1897	0.1	...	11.2	...	...	2.0	0.1	0.2	205
1898	0.1	0.1	12.3	...	0.1	2.4	0.1	0.2	205
1899	0.2	0.1	14.0	...	0.1	2.6	0.1	0.2	224
1900	0.3	0.1	16.2	0.1	0.1	2.6	0.1	0.3	229
1901	0.3	0.1	16.5	...	0.1	2.7	0.1	0.3	223
1902	0.4	0.1	16.5	...	0.1	2.7	0.1	0.3	231
1903	0.5	0.1	17.9	...	0.1	2.7	0.1	0.3	234
1904	0.4	0.1	19.6	...	0.1	3.0	0.1	0.3	236
1905	0.5	0.1	18.7	...	0.1	3.2	0.2	0.3	240
1906	0.5	0.1	21.7	0.1	0.2	3.2	0.2	0.3	255
1907	0.7	0.1	26.0	0.1	0.2	3.7	0.2	0.3	272
1908	0.9	0.1	25.9	0.1	0.2	3.9	0.2	0.3	266
1909	1.1	0.2	26.8	0.1	0.2	3.9	0.3	0.2	268

D2 Output of Coal (in millions of metric tons)

1910–1964

	Austria[1] HC	Austria[1] BC	Belgium	Bulgaria HC	Bulgaria BC	Czechoslovakia HC	Czechoslovakia BC	Denmark	France[6]	Germany[7] HC	Germany[7] BC
1910	13.8	25.1	25.5	...	0.2	...	...	...	38.4	153	69.5
1911	14.4	25.3	24.6	...	0.2	...	...	...	39.2	161	73.8
1912	15.8	26.3	24.5	...	0.2	...	...	...	41.1	175	80.9
1913	16.5	27.4	24.4[11] / 22.8	...	0.4	[14.1][12]	[23.1][12]	...	40.8	190	87.2
1914	15.5	23.6	16.7	...	0.4	[13.5][12]	[20.0][12]	...	27.5	161	83.7
1915	16.3	22.1	14.2	...	0.5	[14.3][12]	[18.4][12]	...	19.5	147	87.9
1916	...	...	16.9	...	0.6	15.5	19.4	...	21.3	159	94.2
1917	...	...	14.9	...	0.8	14.5	18.3	...	28.9	168	95.5
1918	...[1]	...[1]	13.9	...	0.7	12.0	16.3	...	26.3[6]	158[7]	101[7]
1919	...	...	18.5	...	0.6	10.3	17.3	...	22.4	117[15]	93.6
1920	0.1	2.7	22.1	...	0.7	11.4	20.0	...	25.3	108	112
1921	0.1	2.5	21.8	...	0.9	12.0	21.3	...	29.0	114	123
1922	0.2	3.1	21.2	...	1.0	10.5	19.2	...	31.9	119[16]	137[16]
1923	0.2	2.7	22.9	0.1	1.0	12.3	16.3	...	38.6	62.2	118
1924	0.2	2.8	23.4	0.1	1.2	15.2	20.5	...	45.0	119	124
1925	0.1	3.0	23.1	0.1	1.2	12.6	18.6	...	48.1	133	140
1926	0.2	3.0	25.2	0.1	1.1	14.2	18.5	...	52.5	145	140
1927	0.2	3.1	27.6	0.1	1.2	14.0	19.6	...	52.9	154	151
1928	0.2	3.3	27.6	0.1	1.4	14.6	20.4	...	52.4	151	166
1929	0.2	3.5	26.9	0.1	1.6	16.5	22.5	...	55.0	163	174
1930	0.2	3.1	27.4	0.1	1.5	14.5	19.2	...	55.1	143	146
1931	0.2	3.0	27.0	0.1	1.4	13.2	17.9	...	51.0	119	133
1932	0.2	3.1	21.4	0.1	1.7	11.0	15.8	...	47.3	105	123
1933	0.2	3.1	25.3	0.1	1.5	10.6	15.0	...	48.0	110	127
1934	0.3	2.9	26.4	0.1	1.6	10.8[13]	15.1[13]	...	48.7	125[15]	137
1935	0.3	3.0	26.5	0.1	1.6	10.9	15.1	...	47.1	143	147
1936	0.2	2.9	27.9	0.1	1.6	12.2	15.9	...	46.2	158	161
1937	0.2	3.2	29.9	0.1	1.7	16.8[14]	17.9[14]	...	45.4	185[14]	185[14]
1938	0.2	3.3	29.6	0.1	1.9	15.8	16.0	...	47.6[6]	186	195
1939	0.2	3.5	29.8	0.2	2.0	18.8	19.4	...	50.2	188	212
1940	0.2	3.7	25.5	0.2	2.6	21.0	22.3	0.2	41.0	184	225
1941	0.2	3.5	26.7	0.2	2.8	21.1	22.4	1.0	43.9	187	236
1942	0.2	3.5	25.1	0.2	3.4	22.8	24.1	1.8	43.8	188	246
1943	0.2	3.7	23.7	0.2	3.8	24.6	27.6	2.6	42.4	190	253
1944	0.2	3.7	13.5	0.1	2.9	23.2	26.8	2.2	26.6[6]	166	229

	Austria[1] HC	Austria[1] BC	Belgium	Bulgaria HC	Bulgaria BC	Czechoslovakia HC	Czechoslovakia BC	Denmark	France[6]	East Germany HC	East Germany BC	West Germany[15] HC	West Germany[15] BC
1945	0.1	2.1	15.8	0.1	3.4	11.7[14]	15.4[14]	2.3	35.0	...		35.5	24.3
1946	0.1	2.4	22.9	0.1	3.4	14.2	19.5	2.3	49.3	2.5	108	53.9	51.6
1947	0.2	2.8	24.4		4.2	16.2	22.4	2.8	47.3	2.7	102	71.1	58.7
1948	0.2	3.3	26.7	0.1	4.1	16.7	23.6	2.4	45.1	2.8	110	87.0	64.9
1949	0.2	3.8	27.9	0.2	5.1	17.0	26.5	1.6	53.0	3.0	124	103	73.8
1950	0.2	4.3	27.3	0.2	5.8	17.4	27.5	0.8	52.5	2.8	137	111	77.4
1951	0.2	5.0	29.7	0.2	6.2	17.3	30.2	1.6	55.0	3.2	151	119	84.9
1952	0.2	5.2	30.4	0.2	7.2	19.1	33.3	1.6	57.4	2.8	158	123	85.2
1953	0.2	5.6	30.1	0.3	8.1	18.9	34.3	0.8	54.5	2.6	173	124	86.2
1954	0.2	6.3	29.2	0.3	8.6	19.9	37.9	0.7	56.3	2.6	182	128	89.5
1955	0.2	6.6	29.9	0.3	9.1	20.6	40.8	0.8	57.4	2.7	201	131	92.2
1956	0.2	6.7	29.5	0.4	9.8	21.8	46.3	1.4	57.4	2.7	206	134	97.0
1957	0.2	6.9	29.0	0.4	10.7	22.5	51.0	2.6	59.1	2.8	213	133	98.7
1958	0.1	6.5	27.1	0.4	11.6	23.9	56.8	2.4	60.0	2.9	215	133[15]	95.5
1959	0.1	6.2	22.8	0.5	13.9	25.1	53.7	2.7	59.8	2.8	215	142	95.4
1960	0.1	6.0	22.5	0.6	15.4	26.2	58.4	2.7	58.2	2.7	225	142	98.0
1961	0.1	5.7	21.5	0.6	17.0	26.2	65.3	2.5	55.3	2.7	237	143	99.0
1962	0.1	5.7	21.2	0.6	19.1	27.1	69.5	2.6	55.2	2.6	247	141	103
1963	0.1	6.1	21.4	0.7	20.3	28.2	73.3	2.5	50.2	2.5	254	142	108
1964	0.1	5.8	21.3	0.6	23.8	28.2	75.6	2.2	55.3	2.3	257	142	113

D2 Output of Coal (in millions of metric tons)

1910–1964

	Greece[17]	Hungary[4] HC	BC	Italy[8] HC	BC	Netherlands HC	BC	Norway[13]	Poland[19] HC	BC	Portugal HC	BC
1910	...	1.3	7.7	...	0.6	1.3	—	...	...	...	...	—
1911	—	1.3	8.2	...	0.6	1.5	—	...	...	...	...	—
1912	—	1.3	8.3	...	0.7	1.7	—	...	...	...	...	—
1913	...	1.3	9.0	...	0.7	1.9[10]	—	...	...	...	...	—
1914	...	1.1	8.1	...	0.8	2.0	—	...	...	...	...	...
1915	...	...	...	...	0.9	2.3	—	...	...	...	0.1	...
1916	0.1	1.2	7.9	...	1.3	2.7	—	...	...	...	0.1	...
1917	0.2	1.2$_4$	7.6$_4$	...	1.7	3.1	...	...	...	...	0.2	...
1918	0.2	...	...	...$_8$	2.1$_8$	3.5	1.5	0.1	...	...	0.2	...
1919	0.2	...	...		1.1	3.5	1.9	0.1	...	...	0.1	...
1920	0.2	0.8	4.8	0.1	1.6	4.1	1.4	0.1	31.7	0.2	0.1	...
1921	0.2	0.7	5.5	0.1	1.0	4.2	0.1	0.1	29.9	0.3	0.1	...
1922	0.1	0.9	6.2	0.2	0.8	4.9	...	0.2	34.6[19]	0.2	0.1	...
1923	0.1	0.8	6.9	0.2	1.0	5.6	0.1	0.2	36.1	0.2	0.1	...
1924	0.1	0.7	6.3	0.1	0.9	6.2	0.2	0.3	32.3	0.1	0.1	...
1925	0.1	0.8	5.5	0.2	1.0	7.1	0.2	0.3[18]	29.1	0.1	0.1	...
1926	0.2	0.8	5.8	0.2	1.2	8.8	0.2	0.3	35.7	0.1	0.2	...
1927	0.1	0.8	6.2	0.2	0.9	9.5	0.2	0.3	38.1	0.1	0.2	...
1928	0.1	0.8	6.5	0.1	0.7	10.9	0.2	0.3	40.6	0.1	0.2	...
1929	0.2	0.8	7.0	0.2	0.8	11.6	0.2	0.3	46.2	0.1	0.2	...
1930	0.1	0.8	6.2	0.2	0.6	12.2	0.1	0.2	37.5	0.1	0.2	...
1931	0.1	0.8	6.1	0.2	0.4	12.9	0.1	0.2	38.3	...	0.2	...
1932	0.1	0.9	5.9	0.3	0.4	12.8	0.1	0.3	28.8	...	0.2	...
1933	0.1	0.8	5.9	0.3	0.4	12.6	0.1	0.3	27.4	...	0.2	...
1934	0.1	0.8	6.2	0.4	0.4	12.3	0.1	0.3	29.2	...	0.2	...
1935	0.1	0.8	6.7	0.4	0.5	11.9	0.1	0.3	28.5	...	0.2	...
1936	0.1	0.8	7.1	0.8	0.8	12.8	0.1	0.3	29.7	...	0.2	...
1937	0.1	0.9	8.1	1.0	1.1	14.3	0.1	0.3	36.2	...	0.3	...
1938	0.1	1.0	8.3	1.0	1.3	13.5	0.2	0.3	38.1	...	0.3	...
1939	0.1	1.1	9.4	1.1	2.0	12.9	0.2	0.3	[23.2][20]	...	0.3	...
1940	0.2	1.2	10.2	1.0	3.4	12.1	0.2	0.3	[47][21]	...	0.4	0.1
1941	0.2	1.3	11.0	1.2	3.2	13.4	0.2	0.1	[58][21]	...	0.4	0.1
1942	0.4	1.2	11.2	1.4	3.5	12.3	0.3	...	[65][21]	...	0.5	0.1
1943	0.4	1.4	10.8	1.0	2.3	12.5	0.4	...	[70][21]	...	0.4	0.1
1944	0.2	1.3	8.4	0.2	0.9	8.3	0.2	...	[54][21 19]	...[19]	0.4	0.1
1945	0.1	0.7	3.6	0.1$_8$	1.5$_8$	5.1	0.1	...	[20.2][22]	...	0.4	0.2
1946	0.1	0.7	5.6	0.1	2.7	8.3	0.5	0.1	47.3	1.5	0.4	0.1
1947	0.1	1.1	7.7	0.2	3.1	10.1	0.5	0.3	59.1	4.8	0.4	0.1
1948	0.1	1.2	9.4	0.1	1.8	11.0	0.3	0.4	70.3	5.0	0.4	0.1
1949	0.2	1.4	10.5	0.1	1.9	11.7	0.2	0.5	74.1	4.6	0.4	0.1
1950	0.2	1.4	11.9	0.1	1.7	12.2	0.2	0.4	78.0	4.8	0.4	0.1
1951	0.2	1.6	13.7	0.1	2.0	12.4	0.2	0.5	82.0	4.9	0.4	0.1
1952	0.3	1.7	16.8	0.1	1.9	12.5	0.2	0.5	84.4	5.1	0.4	0.1
1953	0.4	2.0	19.0	0.1	1.8	12.3	0.3	0.4	88.7	5.6	0.5	0.1
1954	0.7	2.4	19.1	0.1	1.7	12.1	0.2	0.3	91.6	5.9	0.4	0.1
1955	0.8	2.7	19.6	...	1.5	11.9	0.3	0.3	94.5	6.0	0.4	0.1
1956	0.8	2.4	18.2	0.1	1.5	11.8	0.3	0.4	95.1	6.2	0.4	0.1
1957	1.0	2.3	18.9	0.1	1.4	11.4	0.3	0.4	94.1	6.0	0.5	0.2
1958	1.2	2.6	21.6	...	1.5	11.9	0.3	0.3	95.0	7.5	0.6	0.2
1959	1.5	2.7	22.6	...	1.9	12.0	0.2	0.3	99.1	9.3	0.5	0.2
1960	2.5	2.8	23.7	...	1.5	12.5	...	0.4	104	9.3	0.4	0.2
1961	2.5	3.1	25.1	...	2.2	12.6	...	0.4	107	10.3	0.5	0.2
1962	2.6	3.3	25.3	...	2.5	11.6	...	0.5	110	11.1	0.4	0.2
1963	3.6	3.7	26.8	...	1.9	11.5	...	0.4	113	15.3	0.4	0.1
1964	3.9	4.1	27.4	...	1.7	11.5	...	0.4	117	20.3	0.4	0.1

D2 Output of Coal (in millions of metric tons)

	Romania[23]		Russia/U.S.S.R.[25]		Spain		Sweden	UK	Serbia/Yugoslavia[27]	
	HC	BC	HC	BC					HC	BC
1910	...	0.1	25.4		3.8	0.2	0.3	269	...	0.2
1911	...	0.2	28.4		3.7	0.3	0.3	276	...	0.3
1912	...	0.2	31.1		3.9	0.3	0.4	265	0.3	
1913	...	0.2	36.0[25]		4.0	0.3	0.4	292	...	
			28.0	1.1						
1914	...	0.2	30.8	1.1	4.1	0.3	0.4	270		...
1915	—	0.3	30.0	1.4	4.4	0.3	0.4	257		...
1916	—	0.3	32.5	2.0	5.1	0.5	0.4	260		...
1917	...	...	29.0	2.3	5.4	0.6	0.4	252		...
1918	...[23]	...[23]	11.5	1.5	6.5	0.7	0.4	231		...
1919	0.2	1.4	7.7	1.7	5.7	0.5	0.4	233		...
1920	0.2	1.4	6.7	2.0	5.4	0.6	0.4	233	0.1	2.8
1921	0.2	1.6	7.5	2.0	5.0	0.4	0.4	166[26]	0.1	3.0
1922	0.3	1.9	9.3	2.0	4.4	0.3	0.4	254	0.1	3.6
1923	0.3	2.2	10.5	2.2	6.0	0.4	0.4	280	0.1	4.0
1924	0.3	2.5	14.6	1.7	6.1	0.4	0.4	271	0.1	4.0
1925	0.3	2.6	14.9	1.6	6.1	0.4	0.3	247	0.2	4.0
1926	0.3	2.7	23.4	2.4	6.5	0.4	0.4	128	0.2	4.0
1927	0.4	2.8	29.5	2.8	6.6	0.4	0.4	255	0.3	4.5
1928	0.4	2.6	32.5	3.1	6.4	0.4	0.4	241	0.4	4.7
1929	0.4	2.7	36.6	3.5	7.1	0.4	0.4	262	0.4	5.2
1930	0.3	2.1	43.3	4.5	7.1	0.4	0.4	248	0.4	4.9
1931	0.3	1.6	50.7	6.0	7.1	0.3	0.3	223	0.4	4.4
1932	0.2	1.5	57.5	6.9	6.9	0.3	0.3	212	0.4	4.1
1933	0.2	1.3	67.5	8.9	6.0	0.3	0.3	210	0.4	3.8
1934	0.2	1.6	82.8	11.4	5.9	0.3	0.4	224	0.4	3.9
1935	0.3	1.7	95.3	14.3	6.9	0.3	0.4	226	0.4	4.0
1936	0.3	1.7	109	17.6	3.3	0.2	0.5	232	0.4	4.0
1937	0.3	1.9	110	18.1	2.1	0.2	0.5	244	0.4	4.6
1938	0.3	2.5	115	18.5	5.6	0.2	0.4	231	0.4	5.3
1939	0.3	2.2	125	21.3	6.6	0.2	0.4	235	0.4	5.6
1940	0.3	2.4	140	25.9	8.9	0.6	0.5	228	0.4	6.9
1941	0.3	2.2	...	...	8.8	0.8	0.6	210	...	...
1942	0.3	2.4	...	...	9.3	1.1	0.6	208	...	...
1943	0.3	2.6	...	...	9.7	1.2	0.6	202	...	...
1944	0.2	2.1	...	...	10.4	1.2	0.6	196	...[27]	...[27]
1945	0.2	1.8	99.4	49.9	10.6	1.3	0.6	186	0.2	3.4
1946	0.2	1.8	114	49.8	10.7	1.3	0.5	193	0.8	6.0
1947	0.2	2.1	132	51.0	10.5	1.3	0.4	200	1.1	8.2
1948	0.2[24]	2.7[24]	150	58.2	10.4	1.4	0.4	211	1.0	9.7
	2.0	0.9								
1949	...	...	169	66.4	10.6	1.3	0.3	219	1.3	10.8
1950	2.8	1.2	185	75.9	11.0	1.3	0.3	220	1.2	11.7
1951	3.2	1.4	202	79.5	11.3	1.5	0.3	226	1.0	11.0
1952	3.4	1.8	215	85.9	12.1	1.6	0.3	228	1.0	11.1
1953	3.3	2.2	224	96.1	12.2	1.8	0.3	227	0.9	10.3
1954	3.2	2.4	244	103	12.4	1.8	0.3	227	1.0	12.7
1955	3.4	2.8	277	113	12.4	1.8	0.3	225	1.1	14.1
1956	3.5	3.0	304	125	12.9	1.9	0.3	226	1.2	15.9
1957	3.6	3.4	329	135	13.9	2.5	0.3	227	1.2	16.8
1958	3.9	3.5	353	140	14.4	2.7	0.3	219	1.2	17.8
1959	4.1	3.8	365	138	13.5	2.1	0.3	209	1.3	19.8
1960	3.4	3.4	375	135	13.8	1.8	0.3	197	1.3	21.4
1961	3.8	3.5	377	129	13.8	2.1	0.2	194	1.3	22.8
1962	4.1	4.0	386	131	12.7	2.5	0.1	201	1.2	23.5
1963	4.4	4.3	395	137	12.9	2.6	0.1	199	1.3	26.1
1964	4.5	4.9	409	14.5	12.2	2.6	0.1	198	1.3	28.2

D2 Output of Coal (in millions of metric tons)

1965-1998

	Romania		Russia/USSR		Spain		UK	Yugoslavia	
	HC	BC	HC	BC	HC	BC	HC	HC	BC
1965	4.7	5.6	428	150	12.9	2.8	192	1.2	28.8
1966	4.8	6.6	439	146	12.9	2.7	179	1.1	28.2
1967	5.1	7.9	451	144	12.4	2.7	178	0.9	25.6
1968	5.5	9.3	456	138	12.3	2.8	170	0.8	25.9
1969	5.9	11.1	467	140	11.6	2.7	156	0.7	25.8
1970	6.4	14.1	476	148	10.8	2.8	147	0.6	27.8
1971	6.8	13.8	488	153	10.7	3.1	149	0.7	30.2
1972	6.6	16.5	499	156	11.1	3.1	122	0.6	30.3
1973	7.2	17.7	511	157	10.0	3.0	132	0.6	31.9
1974	7.1	19.9	524	161	10.5	2.9	110	0.6	33.0
1975	7.3	19.8	538	164	10.8	3.4	129	0.6	34.9
1976	7.1	18.7	548	164	10.5	4.2	124	0.6	36.3
1977	7.1	19.6	555	167	11.9	5.8	122	0.5	36.8
1978	7.4	21.8	557	166	11.5	8.3	122	0.5	39.2
1979	8.1	24.7	554	165	11.9	10.7	121	0.4	42.5
1980	8.1	27.1	553	163	13.1	15.5	130	0.4	46.6
1981	8.3	28.6	544	160	14.7	20.9	127	0.4	51.5
1982	7.2	30.7	555	163	15.7	23.9	125	0.4	54.3
1983	7.8	36.7	558	158	15.4	24.5	119	0.4	59.0
1984	8.0	36.0	556	156	15.6	24.3	51.2	0.4	64.7
1985	8.7	37.9	569	157	16.1	23.8	94.0	0.4	68.1
1986	8.5	38.0	588	163	15.9	22.4	108	0.4	68.4
1987	8.8	38.5	595	165	14.1	20.5	104	0.4	70.8
1988	8.9	42.6	599	172	14.3	17.6	102	0.4	70.5
1989	8.3	53.0	477	163	14.5	21.9	98	0.3	74.3
1990	4.4	33.7	474	156	14.7	21.1	94	0.3	75.6
1991	3.8	28.6	414	152	13.9	19.6	95	0.3	58.3
1992	4.1	33.7	193[31]	127[31]	14.7	18.7	84	...[32]	40.0[32]
1993	1.1	38.5	190[31]	113[31]	14.0	17.4	68	...[32]	37.4[32]
1994	1.4	39.1	177	95	14.0	15.5	49	.08	38.2
1995	1.1	39.9	177	86	13.5	14.8	53	.07	39.9
1996	1.3	40.5	167	90	13.6	13.6	50	.08	38.3
1997	1.7	32.0	159	85	13.7	12.6	48	.09	40.5
1998	1.6	34.2	157	79	13.9	12.4	49	.10	42.1

	Austria[1]		Belgium	Bulgaria		Czechoslovakia		Denmark	France	East Germany	
	HC	BC	BC	HC	BC	HC	BC	HC	HC	HC	BC
1965	0.1	5.4	19.8	0.6	24.5	27.6	73.2	2.1	54.0	2.2	251
1966	...	5.3	17.5	0.5	24.7	26.7	74.1	2.0	52.9	2.0	249
1967	...	4.6	16.4	0.5	26.7	25.9	71.4	1.3	50.6	1.8	242
1968	—	4.2	14.8	0.4	28.3	25.9	74.9	0.8	45.1	1.6	247
1969	—	3.8	13.2	0.4	28.6	27.1	79.3	0.4	43.5	1.3	255
1970	—	3.7	11.4	0.4	28.9	28.1	81.8	0.1	40.1	1.0	261
1971	—	3.8	11.0	0.4	26.6	28.7	84.8	—	35.8	0.9	263
1972	—	3.8	10.5	0.4	26.9	27.8	85.6	—	32.7	0.8	248
1973	—	3.6	8.8	0.4	26.5	27.7	81.8	—	28.4	0.8	246
1974	—	3.6	8.1	0.3	24.0	27.9	82.8	—	25.7	0.6	243
1975	—	3.4	7.5	0.3	27.5	28.0	87.1	—	25.6	0.5	247
1976	—	3.2	7.2	0.3	25.2	27.7	90.3	—	25.1	0.5	247
1977	—	3.1	7.1	0.3	24.9	27.4	94.0	—	24.4	0.3	254
1978	—	3.1	6.6	0.3	25.5	27.8	95.7	—	22.4	0.1	253
1979	—	2.7	6.1	0.3	28.0	28.0	96.9	—	21.1	—	256
1980	—	2.9	6.3	0.3	29.9	27.7	95.7	—	20.7	—	258
1981	—	3.1	6.1	0.2	29.0	27.0	96.4	—	21.5	—	267
1982	—	3.3	6.5	0.2	32.0	27.1	98.9	—	20.0	—	276
1983	—	3.0	6.1	0.2	32.1	26.4	102	—	19.6	—	278
1984	—	2.9	6.3	0.2	32.1	25.9	105	—	19.0	—	296

(continued overleaf)

D2 Output of Coal (in millions of metric tons) (contd.)

	Austria[1]		Belgium	Bulgaria		Czechoslovakia		Denmark	France	East Germany	
	HC	BC	BC	HC	BC	HC	BC	HC	HC	HC	BC
1985	—	3.1	6.2	0.2	30.7	25.7	102	—	17.0	—	312
1986	—	3.0	5.6	0.2	35.0	25.2	103	—	16.5	—	311
1987	—	2.8	4.4	0.2	36.6	25.7	102	—	16.3	—	309
1988	—	2.1	2.5	0.2	33.9	25.5	99.9	—	12.9	—	310
1989	—	2.1	1.9	0.2	34.1	25.1	92.3	—	12.3	—	301
1990	—	2.5	1.0	0.1	31.5	22.6	83.7	—	10.5	—	280
1991	—	2.1	0.6	0.1	28.3	19.5	80.8	—	10.1	Included in Germany	
						Czech Republic[29]					
1992	—	1.8	0.2	0.3	30.1	18.9[29]	68.1	—	9.5		
1993	—	1.7	—	0.3	28.8	18.4[29]	66.9	—	8.6	—	
	BC										
1994	1.4		0.7	0.1	28.6	17.4	66.0	—	8.1		
1995	1.3		0.6	0.2	30.6	17.1	57.9	—	8.5		
1996	1.1		0.5	0.1	28.1	16.5	59.6	—	7.7		
1997	1.1		0.4	0.1	26.9	16.0	57.4	—	6.3		
1998	1.2		0.5	0.1	27.3	17.2	56.1	—	6.0		

	West Germany		Greece	Hungary[4]		Italy	Nether- lands	Norway	Poland		Portugal	
	HC	BC	BC	HC	BC	BC	HC		HC	BC	HC	BC
1965	135	104	5.1	4.4	27.1	1.4	11.4	0.4	119	22.6	0.4	0.1
1966	126	99.2	5.0	4.4	26.0	1.6	10.1	0.4	122	24.5	0.4	0.1
1967	112	97.7	5.3	4.1	23.0	2.9	8.1	0.4	124	23.9	0.4	...
1968	112	102	5.8	4.2	22.0	2.1	6.7	0.3	129	26.9	0.4	...
1969	112	108	6.7	4.1	22.4	2.2	5.6	0.4	135	30.9	0.4	...
1970	111	108	7.7	4.2	23.7	2.7	4.3	0.5	140	32.8	0.3	—
1971	111	105	10.9	3.9	23.5	2.6	3.6	0.4	145	34.5	0.3	—
1972	102	110	11.3	3.7	22.2	1.5	2.8	0.5	151	38.2	0.3	—
1973	97.3	119	13.1	3.4	23.4	2.2	1.7	0.4	157	39.2	0.2	—
1974	94.9	126	14.3	3.2	22.6	2.0	0.8	0.4	162	39.8	0.2	—
1975	92.4	123	17.9	3.0	21.9	2.0	—	0.5	172	39.9	0.2	—
1976	89.3	135	22.6	2.9	22.3	2.0	—	0.5	179	39.3	0.2	—
1977	84.8	123	23.6	2.9	22.5	1.8	—	0.4	186	40.8	0.2	—
1978	83.9	124	21.7	3.0	22.7	1.9	—	0.3	193	41.0	0.2	—
1979	86.3	131	23.6	3.0	22.7	2.1	—	0.3	201	38.1	0.2	—
1980	87.1	130	23.2	3.1	22.6	1.9	—	0.3	193	36.9	0.2	—
1981	88.5	131	27.3	3.1	22.9	2.0	—	0.4	163	35.5	0.2	—
1982	89.0	127	27.4	3.0	23.0	1.9	—	0.4	189	37.6	0.2	—
1983	82.2	124	30.6	2.8	22.4	1.7	—	0.5	191	42.5	0.2	—
1984	79.4	127	32.5	2.6	22.5	1.8	—	0.5	192	50.4	0.2	—
1985	82.4	121	35.9	2.6	21.4	1.9	—	0.5	192	57.7	0.2	—
1986	80.8	114	38.1	2.3	20.8	1.0	—	0.4	192	67.3	0.2	—
1987	82.4	109	44.6	2.4	20.5	1.0	—	0.4	193	73.2	0.3	—
1988	79.3	109	48.3	2.3	18.6	1.0	—	0.3	193	73.5	0.2	—
1989	77.4	110	51.9	2.1	17.9	1.0	—	0.4	178	71.8	0.3	—
	Germany											
1990	76.4	108	51.9	1.7	15.8	1.0	—	0.3	148	67.6	0.3	—
1991	72.7[30]	280[30]	52.7	1.7	15.3	0.9	—	0.3	140	69.4	0.3	—
1992	72.1	242	55.1	1.3	14.5	0.7	—	0.4	132	66.9	0.2	—
1993	64.2	222	54.8	0.9	13.7	1.0	—	0.3	130	68.1	0.2	—
1994	57.6	241	56.7	—	14.1	0.3	—	0.3	133	66.7	0.1	—
1995	58.8	193	57.6	—	14.6	0.4	—	0.3	136	63.5	—	—
1996	53.1	187	59.8	—	15.1	0.3	—	0.2	137	63.8	—	—
1997	51.2	177	58.9	—	15.6	0.1	—	0.4	137	63.1	—	—
1998	50.6	185	57.4	—	16.4	0.2	—	0.5	139	64.2	—	—

D2   Output of Coal (in millions of metric tons)

NOTES

1. SOURCES:- Belgium 1831–1913—A. Wibail, 'L'évolution économique de l'industrie charbonnière Belge depuis 1831', *Bulletin de l'Institute des Sciences Economiques* vol. IV no. 1 (1934). Germany 1817–1849—based on the indices in W.G. Hoffman, *Das Wachstum der Deutschen Wirtschaft seit der Mitte des 19 Jahrhunderts* (Berlin, etc., 1965). Germany 1850–1914—based on Wolfgang Fischer, *Statistik der Bergbauproduktion Deutschlands, 1850–1924* (St. Katherinene, 1989). Russia to 1921 (except 1913) (2nd line)—W. Nutter, *The Growth of Industrial Production in the Soviet Union* (Princeton, 1962). U.K. 1815 based on estimate in M.W. Flinn, *The History of the British Coal Industry* vol. 2. (Oxford, 1984); U.K. 1830–72—estimates in Roy Church, *ibid*, vol. 3 (Oxford, 1986); U.K. 1873–1937—based on B.R. Mitchell, *British Historical Statistics* (Cambridge, 1988); U.K. 1938 onwards—based on Ministry of Fuel and Power (later Ministry of Power) *Statistical Digest* and its successors, and its *Supplement* for 1945. All other figures are taken from the official publications noted on p. xv with a few gaps filled from the U.N. *Statistical Yearbook*.
2. Lignite is counted as brown coal, except as indicated in footnote. Where there is no other indication, output was of hard coal entirely.
3. The calorific power of different types of coal varies quite substantially, even within the two broad categories of hard and brown coal. The relation between these two is conventionally taken to be that brown coal has 60 per cent of the heating value of hard coal in Czechoslovakia, France, and Hungary, but only 50 per cent in other countries.

FOOTNOTES

[1] Figures to 1842 (1st line) include Hungary and the Italian provinces. From 1842 (2nd line) to 1918 they apply to the Kingdom of Austria, and subsequently to the Republic. The outputs of the Austrian provinces in Italy prior to 1866 were as follows (all brown coal, in thousands of tons):-

1842	7	1848	19	1854	26	1860	7
1843	10	1849	16	1855	21	1861	7
1844	9	1850	—	1856	19	1862	16
1845	12	1851	11	1857	19	1863	7
1846	17	1852	20	1858	—	1864	11
1847	19	1853	55	1859	7	1865	7

Lombardy was lost after 1859, and the statistics for the rest of the period are for Venetia alone. Data to 1864 are for years ended 31 October.

[2] Total output of hard and brown coal for the whole Austro-Hungarian Empire was 2,911 thousand tons.

[3] Hard coal and lignite. Earlier figures are given in M. Block, *Statistique de la France* (Paris, 1860) as follows (in thousands of tons):-

1787	215;	1802	844;	1811	774.

[4] Hungarian output is included with Austrian prior to 1842. From 1842 to 1917 the statistics apply to the whole Kingdom of Hungary, and subsequently to the Republic.

[5] M.W. Flinn, *op. cit.* in note 1 above, gives the following earlier estimates (converted to thousand metric tons):-

1700—3,033	1750—5,314;	1775—8,992;	1800—15,286

[6] From 1871 to 1918 and from 1939 to 1944 parts of Alsace and Lorraine ceded to Germany are excluded.

[7] From 1871 to 1918 parts of Alsace-Lorraine are included.

[8] Statistics to 1918 apply to the boundaries of 1871. From 1919 to 1945 they apply to the boundaries of 1924, and subsequently to the boundaries of 1954.

[9] Figures to 1886 (1st line) relate to state-owned mines only, and from 1886 (2nd line) to 1913 (1st line) they relate to Limburg province only.

[10] Data to 1877 are for years ended 31 October.

[11] This break is probably occasioned by a change from unscreened to screened production figures, and by the exclusion in later years of colliery consumption.

[12] This production is also included in the statistics for Austria.

[13] One mine was transferred from the brown to the hard coal category.

[14] For 1938–45 Sudetenland is excluded from Czechoslovakia and included in Germany.

[15] From 1920 to 1934 and from 1945 to 1958 Saarland is excluded. Statistics for that district are as follows (in thousands of tons):-

1920	9,410	1928	13,107	1945	3,463	1952	16,236
1921	9,575	1929	13,579	1946	7,898	1953	16,418
1922	11,240	1930	13,236	1947	10,541	1954	16,818
1923	9,192	1931	11,367	1948	12,567	1955	17,329
1924	14,032	1932	10,438	1949	14,262	1956	17,090
1925	12,990	1933	10,561	1950	15,091	1957	16,455
1926	13,681	1934	11,318	1951	16,279	1958	16,423

[16] From July 1922 eastern Upper Silesia is excluded.

[17] The output is entirely of lignite.

[18] The entire output comes from Spitzbergen. Up to 1925 the statistics cover only coal shipped from the island.

[19] Statistics relate to the boundaries of the day, except that eastern Upper Silesia is included in 1920-22 and except as indicated in footnote 21.

[20] First half-year only.

D2 Output of Coal (in millions of metric tons)

[21] These are rough estimates, and include most of the Ostrava–Karvina coalfield, which was part of Czechoslovakia prior to 1940 and after 1944.

[22] April–December

[23] Coal mines in Transylvania were acquired in 1919.

[24] This break is apparently caused by the transfer of the Jin Valley coalfields from the brown to the hard coal category.

[25] Figures from 1913 (2nd line) to 1940 apply to the 1923 boundaries of the U.S.S.R. Subsequent boundary changes do not signify.

[26] Subsequently excluding the very small production of southern Ireland.

[27] Data to 1912 are for Serbia. There were coal mines in the territory acquired from Italy in 1945, and the 1939 output of the postwar territory was 1,410 thousand tons.

[28] Excluding Hesse, Hanover and, in 1859, Saxony.

[29] Czech Republic Slovakia:- BC–1992 3,352, 1993 3547.

[30] Germany (United).

[31] Russian Federation. Ex-USSR as follows

	Kazakhstan HC	Kazakhstan BC	Kyrgistan HC	Kyrgistan BC	Uzbekistan HC	Uzbekistan BC	Estonia HC	Estonia BC	Ukraine HC	Ukraine BC
1992	126	4.1	1.0	1.1	0.2	4.5	—	18.8	128	5.8
1993	112	4.7	0.7	0.9	0.1	3.7	—	14.9	112	4.1
1994	100	4.8	0.7	0.5	0.2	3.6	—	14.5	91.3	3.1
1995	80	3.7	0.5	0.3	- -	2.9	—	13.3	81.5	2.3
1996	73	3.6	0.3	0.2	- -	2.7	—	14.7	74.1	1.6
1997	70	2.4	0.5	0.2	- -	2.8	—	14.4	75.5	1.4
1998	69	2.7	0.6	0.1	- -	2.9	—	14.6	77.6	1.5

[32] Yugoslavia. Ex-Yugoslavia as follows

	Bosnia-Hercegovina BC	Croatia HC	Macedonia BC	Slovenia BC
1992	15.0	0.1	7.0	5.6
1993	…	0.1	7.3	5.1
1994	14.0	0.1	6.9	4.9
1995	16.4	0.1	7.2	4.8
1996	16.4	0.1	7.1	4.8
1997	16.4	- -	6.7	4.9
1998	15.7	- -	6.8	5.0

D3 OUTPUT OF CRUDE PETROLEUM (in millions of metric tons)

	Austria[1]	Germany[2]	Hungary[3]	Netherlands	Poland[6]	Romania	Russia/USSR[8]
1895	0.2	...	...	—	...	0.1	6.9
1896	0.3	...	...	—	...	0.1	7.1
1897	0.3	...	...	—	...	0.1	7.6
1898	0.3	...	...	—	...	0.2	8.6
1899	0.3	...	...	—	...	0.2	9.3
1900	0.3	...	...	—	...	0.2	10.7
1901	0.4	...	...	—	...	0.3	12.0
1902	0.5	...	...	—	...	0.3	11.6
1903	0.7	0.1	...	—	...	0.4	11.1
1904	0.8	0.1	...	—	...	0.5	11.7
1905	0.8	0.1	...	—	...	0.7	8.3
1906	0.7	0.1	...	—	...	1.0	8.9
1907	1.1	0.1	...	—	...	1.1	9.8
1908	1.7	0.1	...	—	...	1.1	10.4
1909	2.1	0.1	...	—	...	1.4	11.2
1910	1.8	0.1	...	—	...	1.3	11.3
1911	1.5	0.1	...	—	...	1.6	10.5
1912	1.1	0.1	...	—	...	1.9	10.4
1913	1.1	0.1	...	—	...	1.8	10.3[8]
							9.2
1914	[0.7][1]	0.1	...	—	...	1.8	9.2
1915	[0.6][1]	0.1	...	—	...	1.6	9.4
1916	...	0.1	...	—	...	1.2	10.0
1917	...[1]	0.1[2]	...[3]	—	...	0.7	8.8
1918	...	...	...	—	...	1.0	4.1
1919	...	...	...	—	...	0.9	4.4
1920	...	...	...	—	0.8	1.1	3.9
1921	...	...	...	—	0.7	1.2	3.8
1922	...	...	...	—	0.7	1.4	4.7
1923	...	0.1	...	—	0.7	1.5	5.3
1924	...	0.1	...	—	0.8	1.9	6.1
1925	...	0.1	...	—	0.8	2.3	7.1
1926	...	0.1	...	—	0.8	3.2	8.3
1927	...	0.1	...	—	0.7	3.7	10.3
1928	...	0.1	...	—	0.7	4.3	11.6
1929		0.1	...	—	0.7	4.8	13.7
1930	...	0.2	...	—	0.7	5.8	18.5
1931	...	0.2	...	—	0.6	6.8	22.4
1932	...	0.2	...	—	0.6	7.3	21.4
1933	...	0.2	...	—	0.6	7.4	21.5
1934	...	0.3	...	—	0.5	8.5	24.2
1935	...	0.4	...	—	0.5	8.4	25.2
1936	...	0.4	...	—	0.5	8.7	27.4
1937	...	0.5	...	—	0.5	7.2	28.5
1938	0.1	0.6	...	—	0.5	6.6	30.2
1939	0.1	0.7	0.1	—	0.3[5]	6.2	30.3
1940	0.4	1.1	0.3	—	...	5.8	31.1[8]
1941	0.7	0.9	0.4	—	...	5.5	...
1942	0.9	0.7	0.7	—	...	5.7	...
1943	1.1	0.7	0.8	—	...	5.3	...
1944	1.2	0.1	[0.8][4]	—	...[6]	3.5	...

D3 Output of Crude Petroleum (in millions of metric tons)

1945–1949

	Austria[1]	West Germany[2]	Hungary[3]	Netherlands	Poland[6]	Romania	Russia/USSR[8]
1945	0.4	0.5	0.7	...	[0.1][7]	4.6	19.4
1946	0.8	0.6	0.7	0.1	0.1	4.2	21.7
1947	0.9	0.6	0.6	0.2	0.1	3.8	26.0
1948	1.0	0.6	0.5	0.5	0.1	4.1	29.2
1949	1.1	0.8	0.5	0.6	0.2	4.7	33.4

1950–1998

	Austria[1]	France	West Germany	Hungary	Italy	Netherlands	Norway	Poland	Romania	Russia/U.S.S.R	U.K.	Yugo-slavia
1950	1.7	0.1	1.1	0.5	...	0.7	—	0.2	5.0	37.9	...	0.1
1951	2.3	0.3	1.4	0.5	...	0.7	—	0.2	6.2	42.3	...	0.1
1952	2.8	0.3	1.8	0.6	0.1	0.7	—	0.2	8.0	47.3	0.1	0.2
1953	3.2	0.4	2.2	0.8	0.1	0.8	—	0.2	9.1	52.8	0.1	0.2
1954	3.4	0.5	2.7	1.2	0.1	0.9	—	0.2	9.7	59.3	0.1	0.2
1955	3.7	0.9	3.1	1.6	0.2	1.0	—	0.2	10.6	70.8	0.1	0.3
1956	3.4	1.3	3.5	1.2	0.6	1.1	—	0.2	10.9	83.8	0.1	0.3
1957	3.2	1.4	4.0	0.7	1.3	1.5	—	0.2	11.2	98.3	0.1	0.4
1958	2.8	1.4	4.4	0.8	1.5	1.6	—	0.2	11.3	113	0.1	0.5
1959	2.5	1.6	5.1	1.0	1.7	1.8	—	0.2	11.4	130	0.1	0.6
1960	2.4	2.0	5.5	1.2	2.0	1.9	—	0.2	11.5	148	0.1	0.9
1961	2.4	2.2	6.2	1.5	2.0	2.0	—	0.2	11.6	166	0.1	1.3
1962	2.4	2.4	6.8	1.6	1.8	2.2	—	0.2	11.9	186	0.1	1.5
1963	2.6	2.5	7.4	1.8	1.8	2.2	—	0.2	12.2	206	0.1	1.6
1964	2.7	2.8	7.7	1.8	2.7	2.3	—	0.3	12.4	224	0.1	1.8
1965	2.9	3.0	7.9	1.8	2.2	2.4	—	0.3	12.6	243	0.1	2.1
1966	2.8	2.9	7.9	1.7	1.8	2.4	—	0.4	12.8	265	0.1	2.2
1967	2.7	2.8	7.9	1.7	1.6	2.3	—	0.4	13.2	288	0.1	2.4
1968	2.7	2.7	8.0	1.8	1.5	2.1	—	0.5	13.3	309	0.1	2.5
1969	2.8	2.5	7.9	1.8	1.5	2.0	—	0.4	13.2	328	0.1	2.7
1970	2.8	2.3	7.5	1.9	1.4	1.9	—	0.4	13.4	353	0.1	2.9
1971	2.5	1.9	7.4	2.0	1.3	1.7	0.3	0.4	13.8	377	0.1	3.0
1972	2.5	1.5	7.1	2.0	1.2	1.6	1.6	0.3	14.1	400	0.1	3.2
1973	2.6	1.3	6.6	2.0	1.0	1.5	1.6	0.4	14.3	429	0.1	3.3
1974	2.2	1.1	6.2	2.0	1.0	1.5	1.7	0.6	14.5	459	0.1	3.5
1975	2.0	1.0	5.7	2.0	1.0	1.4	9.2	0.5	14.6	491	1.2	3.7
1976	1.9	1.1	5.5	2.1	1.1	1.4	13.8	0.4	14.7	520	11.4	3.9
1977	1.8	1.0	5.4	2.2	1.1	1.4	13.6	0.4	14.6	546	37.4	4.0
1978	1.8	1.1	5.1	2.2	1.5	1.4	17.0	0.3	13.7	572	52.9	4.1
1979	1.7	1.2	4.8	2.0	1.7	1.3	18.8	0.3	12.3	588	76.6	4.1
1980	1.5	1.2	4.6	2.0	1.8	1.3	24.5	0.3	11.5	603	78.9	4.2
1981	1.3	1.7	4.5	2.0	1.5	1.3	23.4	0.3	11.6	609	87.9	4.4
1982	1.3	1.6	4.3	2.0	1.7	1.6	24.5	0.2	11.7	613	100	4.3
1983	1.3	1.7	4.1	2.0	2.2	2.6	30.5	0.2	11.6	616	111	4.1
1984	1.2	2.1	4.1	2.0	2.2	3.1	34.7	0.2	11.5	613	121	4.0
1985	1.1	2.6	4.1	2.0	2.3	3.7	38.3	0.2	10.7	583	122	4.1
1986	1.1	2.9	4.0	2.0	2.5	4.6	42.5	0.2	10.1	599	121	4.1
1987	1.1	3.2	3.8	1.9	3.9	4.3	49.5	0.1	9.5	607	118	3.9
1988	1.2	3.4	5.6	1.9	4.8	3.9	56.6	0.2	9.4	606	109	3.7
1989	1.2	3.2	5.4	2.0	4.7	3.4	72.6	0.2	9.2	589	87	3.8
			Germany									
1990	1.2	3.0	3.6	2.0	4.7	3.5	79.6	0.2	8.0	553	88	3.6
1991	1.3	3.0	3.7[9]	1.8	4.3	3.3	91.4	0.2	6.8	...	87	...
1992	1.2	2.9	3.3[9]	1.8	4.5	2.8	104.4	0.2	6.6	399[10]	89	1.2[11]
1993	1.2	2.8	3.1[9]	1.6	4.6	2.7	111.8	0.2	6.7	353[10]	94	1.1[11]
1994	1.1	2.7	2.9	1.5	4.8	3.4	125	0.2	6.7	316	119	1.0
1995	1.0	2.5	2.9	1.6	5.2	2.7	134	0.2	6.7	305	121	1.1
1996	0.9	2.1	2.8	1.4	5.4	2.2	153	0.3	6.6	299	122	1.0
1997	0.9	1.7	2.8	1.3	5.9	2.0	152	0.3	6.5	304	119	0.9
1998	1.0	1.5	2.6	1.2	6.1	1.8	156	0.2	6.4	308	116	0.7

D3 Output of Crude Petroleum (in millions of metric tons)

NOTES

1. SOURCES:- The official publications noted on p. xv with a few gaps filled from U.N. *Statistical Yearbooks*. Czechoslovak figures for 1947, 1949, and 1950 were supplied by the Federal Statistical Office of Czechoslovakia.
2. Output from oil shale is not included in this table.
3. Earlier statistics are available for some countries, and were given in previous editions of this work, but, except for Russia from 1875, the amounts were negligible. The Russian figures are as follows (in million tons):
4. Bulgaria (since 1955), Czechoslovakia (from its foundation), France (from 1919 to 1949), Italy (from unification to 1949), U.K. (from 1939 to 1949), and Yugoslavia (from 1935 to 1949) produced trivial amounts not shown here. These were given in previous editions of this work.

FOOTNOTES

[1] Cisleithania to 1917, except in 1914 and 1915 when the statistics are for Galicia only. Later statistics are for the Republic.
[2] Includes Alsace-Lorraineto 1917.
[3] Transleithania (including Croatia-Slavonia) to 1917, and subsequently the territory established by the treaty of Trianon.
[4] First 9 months only.
[5] First half-year only.
[6] The territory in Galicia ceded to the U.S.S.R. in 1945 contained the main Polish oilfields.
[7] April–December only.
[8] Figures to 1913 (1st line) apply to the Russian Empire. From 1913 (2nd line) to 1940 they apply to the 1923 territory of the U.S.S.R., and subsequently to the post-Second World War Boundaries.
[9] Germany (United).
[10] Russian Federation. Ex-USSR as follows

	Armenia	Azerbaijan	Belarus	Georgia	Kazakhstan	Kyrgistan	Moldova	Tajikistan	Turkmenistan	Ukraine	Uzbekistan
1994	—	9.3	2.0	—	18.5	0.08	—	0.03	3.3	4.2	5.5
1995	—	8.9	1.9	—	17.9	0.08	—	0.02	3.5	4.0	5.1
1996	—	8.8	1.8	—	21.0	0.1	—	0.02	4.0	4.0	4.9
1997	—	8.8	1.8	—	23.4	0.08	—	0.02	4.4	4.1	5.1
1998	—	8.7	1.6	—	25.6	0.09	—	...	4.9	4.2	4.8

[11] Yugoslavia. Ex-Yugoslavia as follows.

Croatia	
1992	2.0
1993	1.9
1994	1.5
1995	1.5
1996	1.4
1997	1.4
1998	1.2

D4 OUTPUT OF NATURAL GAS (in millions of cubic metres)

1913–1959

	Austria	Czech	France	Germany		Hungary	Italy	Neth'l	Poland	Romania	Russia/ U.S.S.R	U.K.	Yugo- slavia
1913	...	...	...	...		—	6	—	...	104	29	—	...
1914	...	...	...	...		—	6	—	...	115	...	—	...
1915	...	...	...	...		—	6	—	...	106	...	—	...
1916	...	...	...	...		—	6	—	...	93	...	—	...
1917	...	...	...	...		—	7	—	...	...	...	—	...
1918	...	...	...	...		—	7	—	...	...	...	—	...
1919	...	...	...	...		—	9	—	...	144	...	—	...
1920	...	...	...	...		—	8	—	405	171	...	—	...
1921	...	...	...	...		—	8	—	400	181	...	—	...
1922	...	...	...	...		—	7	—	403	250	22	—	...
1923	...	...	...	...		—	7	—	390	287	25	—	...
1924	...	...	...	...		—	7	—	438	362	28	—	...
1925	...	...	...	...		—	7	—	535	370	140	—	...
1926	...	...	...	...		—	6	—	481	377	228	—	...
1927	...	...	...	...		—	6	—	454	439	271	—	...
1928	...	- -	- -	...		—	6	—	460	613	304	—	...
1929	...	2	- -	...		—	7	—	467	807	331	—	2
1930	—	3	- -	...		...	—	9	—	487	1,206	520	—
1931	—	1	- -	...		...	—	12	—	474	1,383	847	—
1932	- -	1	- -	...		...	2	13	—	437	1,456	1,049	—
1933	- -	1	- -	...		...	2	14	—	462	1,500	1,066	—
1934	15	1	- -	...		12	2	15	—	469	1,814	1,533	—
1935	- -	1	- -	...		14	3	12	—	485	1,914	1,791	—
1936	- -	1	- -	...		22	3	13	—	483	2,130	2,053	—
1937	- -	2	- -	...		21	4	15	—	531	2,007	2,179	—
1938	1	2	- -	...		18	8	17	—	584	1,860	2,200	—
1939	...	1	- -	...		30	13	20	—	332[4]	1,702	2,200	—
1940	...	2	- -	...		...	32	28	—	...	1,661	3,219[7]	—
1941	...	2	- -	...		...	38	42	—	...	1,575	...	—
1942	...	1	3	...		...	47	55	—	...	1,791[6]	...	—
											1,333		
1943	...	1	46	...		...	70	55	—	...	1,412	...	—
1944	149	1	66	...		...	78	49	—	...	930	...	—
				Germany East	Germany West								
1945	...	2	85	...	71	77	42	—	102[5]	1,304	3,278	—	3
1946	...	3	110	...	109	91	64	—	149	1,332	3,750	—	9
1947	...	...	147	...	78	101[3]	94	1	148	1,176	4,590	—	12
1948	241	5	174	...	67	320	117	6	157	2,346	5,070	—	8
1949	...	12	228	...	54	370	249	7	136	...	5,240	—	8
1950	470	37	246	...	68	379	510	8	182	3,350	5,761	—	15
1951	483	74	282[1]	...	84[2]	405[57]	966	9	277	4,044	6,252	—	13
1952	448	155	258	...	57	500	1,433	16	313	4,952	6,384	—	14
1953	555	168	233	...	58	549	2,280	25	319	5,595	6,869	—	24
1954	625	172	251	...	87	558	2,967	100	358	5,826	7,512	—	28
1955	748	173	256	...	240	545	3,627	145	393	6,169	8,981	—	34
1956	745	274	306	...	367	452	4,466	169	436	6,756	12,067	—	38
1957	759	772	439	...	357	411	4,987	166	419	7,460	18,583		421
1958	820	1,246	682	24	344	379	5,175	208	384	8,506	28,085	1	46
1959	1,128	1,482	1,645	23	388	334	6,118	226	418	9,305	35,391	1	50

D4 Output of Natural Gas (in millions of cubic metres)

1960–1993

	Austria	Czech	France	East Germany	West Germany	Hungary	Italy	Neth'l	Norway	Poland	Romania	Russia/ U.S.S.R.	U.K.	Yugo-slavia
1960	1,469	1,428	2,846	26	448	342	6,447	330	—	541	10,143	45,303	1	53
1961	1,556	1,390	4,010	38	481	324	6,862	449	—	723	10,914	58,981	3	69
1962	1,635	1	4,740	53	616[2] / 807	340	7,150	499	—	791	12,907	73,525	4	95
1963	1,699	1,080	4,861	101	1,171	611	7,267	569	—	945	14,262	89,832	6	191
1964	1,764	970	5,090	108	1,808	784	7,684	835	—	1,180	15,483	108,566	6	274
1965	1,724	902	5,048	133	2,639	1,108	7,800	1,743	—	1,312	17,281	127,666	13	330
1966	1,874	987	5,161	116	3,390	1,552	8,767	3,311	—	1,290	18,616	142,962	3	402
1967	1,797	897	5,563	107	4,338	2,045	9,300	6,991	—	1,463	20,502	157,445	472	462
1968	1,630	959	5,682	143	6,487	2,687	10,408	14,056	—	2,402	21,737	169,101	2,019	584
1969	1,483	976	6,506	343	8,912	3,235	11,960	21,848	—	3,672	22,740	181,121	5,060	730
1970	1,897	929	5,880	1,232	12,645	3,469	13,171	31,617	—	4,975	23,629	197,945	11,110	977
1971	1,891	977	7,149	2,853	15,365	3,705	13,348	43,742	—	5,164	25,251	212,398	18,462	1,151
1972	1,963	907	7,517	5,055	17,690	4,110	14,062	58,385	—	5,601	26,212	221,386	26,565	1,242
1973	2,270	804	7,546	7,012	19,378	4,821	15,242	70,815	—	5,811	27,753	236,326	28,903	1,329
1974	2,207	736	7,628[8]	7,732	20,195	5,101	15,228	83,725	—	5,528	28,643	260,553	34,825	1,447
1975	2,359	694	79,716	7,270	18,280	5,182	14,579	90,853	—	5,963	31,826	289,268	36,257	1,554
1976	2,144	746	76,817	8,622	18,747	6,082	15,643	97,302	—	6,699	34,716	320,953	38,419	1,730
1977	2,393	774	83,011	8,504	19,217	6,611	13,717	96,899	3,139	7,296	36,765	346,003	40,307	1,897
1978	2,414	918	85,319	9,012	20,579	7,346	13,702	88,730	14,891	7,991	37,015	372,194	38,501	1,935
1979	2,312	612	84,080	9,013	20,652	6,521	13,466	93,636	21,581	7,335	35,369	406,597	39,232	1,857
1980	1,903	415	81,734	8,087	8,938	6,142	12,531	91,153	25,973	6,329	36,521	435	37,294	1,820
1981	1,437	453	76,909	9,000	19,161	6,011	13,961	84,617	26,162	6,172	38,440	465	37,410	1,651
1982	1,324	457	71,388	6,464	16,823	6,641	14,519	72,035	25,534	5,555	38,866	501	37,841	1,703
1983	1,213	406[9] / 587	72,152	7,661	17,726	6,510	12,991	76,536	25,831	5,491	38,569	536	38,700	2,090
1984	1,272	712	68,541	8,042	16,213	6,911	13,902	77,251	27,375	6,087	38,293	587	38,529	1,998
1985	1,164	685	58,632	7,676	14,720	7,456	14,158	80,721	26,699	6,390	38,192	643	42,971	2,400
1986	1,112	706	45,711	7,315	14,109	7,022	15,893	74,037	28,102	5,824	37,891	686	45,304	2,447
1987	1,167	766	42,388	7,025	16,099	7,126	16,218	74,247	29,868	5,781	38,920	727	47,641	2,887
1988	1,265	900	…	6,396	15,009	6,272	16,511	65,610	29,855	5,713	36,515	770	45,755	3,015
1989	1,486	903	…	—	…	6,175	…	71,715	30,745	5,377	32,723	796	…	…
1990	…	699	…	16,016 *(Germany)*		5,040	17,296	72,238	27,642	3,866	28,334	815	49,549	…
1991	1,329	576	…	… *(Germany)*		5,057	…	81,666	27,425	…	24,451	…	…	…
1992	1,440	368	…	17,761 *(Germany)*		5,325	…	82,020	29,419	4,015	21,790	…	55,944	846[10]
1993	1,488	…	…	17,675 *(Germany)*		…	19,473	83,652	28,867	4,634	…	…	65,336	824[10]

Russia/U.S.S.R. figures from 1980 onward are in thousand millions.

D4 Output of Natural Gas (in millions of cubic metres)

NOTES

1. SOURCES:- The official publications noted on p. xv and the League of Nations and United Nations *Statistical Yearbooks*, and U.N., *World Energy Supplies*.
2. Except as incidated in footnotes, the statistics in this table relate to natural gas from gasfields only, and exclude methane from coalfields.
3. Trivial amounts were produced in Italy prior to 1913 and in Bulgaria since 1965. These were given in previous editions of this work. The following earlier figures are available for Romania (in million cubic metres) :-

1910 33;   1911 70;   1912 82.

FOOTNOTES

[1] This break is unexplained, but may be due to the earlier inclusion of methane from coal mines.
[2] From 151 (1st line) to 1962 (2nd line) natural gas from oil wells is excluded.
[3] Previously excludes repressured gas.
[4] First half-year only.
[5] April–December only.
[6] This break is unexplained, but may be due to the subsequent exclusion of gas from oil wells.
[7] Figures to 1940 apply to the 1923 boundaries of the U.S.S.R., and later figures to the post-Second World War boundaries.
[8] Subsequent statistics are in million kilowatt hours. The conversion ratio appears to be about 10.8 kWh per cubic metre.
[9] This break occurs as a change from national to U.N. sources
[10] Yugoslavia only.

D5   OUTPUT OF MAIN NON-FERROUS METAL ORES (in thousands of metric tons)

1750–1804

Year	Copper[1] U.K.	Tin[3] Germany	Year	Copper[1] U.K.	Tin[3] Germany	Year	Copper[1] U.K.	Tin[3] Germany
1750	9.6	2.9	1770	31.3	3.0	1788	...	3.4
1751	11.2	2.3	1771	28.3[2]	2.9	1789	...	3.5
1752	12.3	2.6		3.4		1790	...	3.2
1753	13.2	2.6	1772	3.5	3.2	1791	...	3.5
1754	14.2	2.8	1773	3.4	2.9	1792	...	3.9
			1774	3.7	2.5	1793	...	3.3
1755	14.4	2.8				1794	...	3.4
1756	16.3	2.8	1775	3.7	2.7			
1757	17.3	2.8	1776	3.6	2.7	1795	...	3.5
1758	15.2	2.8	1777	3.5	2.8	1796	5.1	3.1
1759	17.0	2.7	1778	3.5	2.8	1797	5.3	3.3
			1778	3.1	2.6	1798	5.7	2.9
1760	16.1	2.8	1779	3.8	2.7	1799	5.0	2.9
1761	17.3	2.4						
1762	16.4	2.6	1780	2.9	3.0	1800	5.3	2.6
1763	18.2	2.8	1781	3.6	2.7	1801	5.4	2.4
1764	21.8	2.7	1782	3.5	2.6	1802	5.3	2.7
			1783	4.4	2.6	1803	5.7	3.0
1765	17.1	2.8	1784	4.5	2.7	1804	5.5	3.0
1766	21.6	3.1						
1767	18.8	2.9	1785	4.5	2.9			
1768	24.1	2.7	1786	4.9	3.5			
1769	27.1	2.9	1787	...	3.3			

1805–1836

Year	Copper Germany	Copper U.K.	Lead Spain	Lead U.K.	Tin U.K.	Zinc Germany
1805		6.3	...	...	2.8	...
1806		7.0	...	...	2.9	...
1807		6.8	...	...	2.5	...
1808		6.9	...	...	2.4	...
1809		6.9	...	...	2.5	...
1810		5.8	...	...	2.0	...
1811		6.2	...	...	2.4	...
1812		6.8	...	...	2.4	...
1813		7.0	...	...	2.4	...
1814		6.5	...	...	2.7	...
1815		6.6	...	...	3.0	...
1816		6.8	...	...	3.4	...
1817		6.6	...	...	4.2	...
1818		6.9	...	...	4.1	...
1819		6.9	...	...	3.4	...
1820	...	7.6	...	...	3.0	...
1821	...	8.6	...	...	3.4	...
1822	...	9.2	...	...	3.3	...
1823	...	8.0	...	...	4.3	...
1824	...	7.9	...	...	5.1	...
1825	...	8.3	...	...	4.4	...
1826	...	9.1	...	...	4.7	...
1827	...	10.5	...	...	5.6	...
1828	...	10.1	...	...	5.0	...
1829	...	9.9	...	...	4.5	...
1830	...	11.1	...	...	4.5	...
1831	...	12.4	...	...	4.4	...
1832	...	12.3	...	...	4.4	...
1833	...	11.4	...	...	4.1	...
1834	...	11.4	...	...	4.0	...
1835	...	12.5	...	...	4.3	...
1836	...	11.8	...	...	4.1	...

D5 Output of Main Non-ferrous Metal ores (in thousands of metric tons)

	Copper		Lead		Tin	Zinc
	Germany	U.K.	Spain	U.K.	U.K.	Germany
1837	32	11.0	...	...	4.9	51
1838	33	11.7	...	...	...	56
1839	36	12.7	...	...	...	52
1840	30	11.2	...	...	...	53
1841	32	10.2	...	...	...	66
1842	36	10.1	...	...	...	82
1843	37	11.1	...	...	...	96
1844	37	11.4	...	...	...	110
1845	35	13.1	...	53.5	...	127
1846	40	12.1	...	51.0	...	139
1847	43	12.2	...	56.6	...[5]	131
1848	41	13.1	...	55.8	10.3	127
1849	40	12.3	...	59.6	10.9	131
1850	45	12.0	47.6	65.5	10.5	151
1851	56	12.4	...	66.1	9.6	154
1852	70	11.9	...	66.0	9.8	185
1853	71	12.0	...	62.0	9.0_5	165
					5.9	
1854	70	12.2_2	...	65.0	6.0	182
1855	72	21.6	42.1	66.5	6.1	219
1856	80	24.6	...	74.3	6.3	231
1857	74	17.7	...	68.5	6.7	223
1858	74	14.7	...	69.4	7.0	250
1859	80	16.1	...	64.2	7.2	284

	Bauxite	Copper			Lead			Tin	Zinc	
	France	Germany	Spain	U.K.	Germany	Spain[4]	U.K.	U.K.	Germany	Italy
1860	...	93	2.7	16.3	...	64.5	64.3	6.8	310	...
1861	...	106	1.7	15.5	...	62.4	66.6	7.6	334	0.2
1862	...	124	2.9	15.0	...	62.8	70.1	8.6	334	0.2
1863	...	142	3.3	14.4	...	72.3	69.3	10.2	292	0.3
1864	...	157	2.9	13.5	...	65.4	68.2	10.3	313	0.2
1865	...	153	3.6	12.1	...	62.0	68.3	10.2	335	0.7
1866	...	164	3.5	11.4	...	67.9	68.5	10.2	353	1.5
1867	...	179	...	10.4	96	...	69.5	8.8	369	6.4
1868	...	202	...	10.8	95	...	72.1	9.4	370	51.0
1869	...	217	...	8.4	101	...	74.5	9.9	405	80.5
1870	...	207	...	7.3	106	85.8	74.6	10.4	367	92.8
1871	...	217	...	6.4	97	...	70.2	11.1	335	56.4
1872	...	282	...	5.8	94	...	61.4	9.7	420	80.9
1873	...	292	...	5.3	101	...	55.1	10.1	445	79.0
1874	...	263	...	5.0	104	...	59.7	10.1	451	64.7
1875	...	279	...	4.7	114	119.6	58.3	9.8	468	62.0
1876	...	305	...	4.8	121	...	59.6	8.6	534	66.0
1877	...	344	...	4.6	147	...	62.4	9.7	577	88.8
1878	...	374	...	4.1	153	...	58.9	10.3	597	62.7
1879	...	399	...	3.6	149	...	52.4	9.7	590	73.4
1880	...	481	...	3.8	160	79.8	57.8	9.1	633	85.3
1881	...	524	...	4.0	165	...	49.4	8.8	660	72.2
1882	...	567	...	3.6	178	88.3	51.1	9.3	695	91.4
1883	...	613	...	2.6	170	99.3	44.1	9.5	678	100.6
1884	...	593	...	3.5	163	83.3	40.7	9.7	632	105.0

D5 Output of Main Non-ferrous Metal ores (in thousands of metric tons)

1885–1914

	Bauxite	Copper			Lead			Tin	Zinc	
	France	Germany	Spain	U.K.	Germany	Spain[4]	U.K.	U.K.	Germany	Italy
1885	...	621	...	2.8[6]	158	89.0	38.3	9.5	681	107.9
1886	...	496	...	...	159	106.0	40.1	9.5	705	107.5
1887	...	508	...	...	158	119.0	38.5	9.4	901	93.1
1888	...	531	...	...	162	129.0	38.2	9.4	668	87.3
1889	...	573	...	...	170	136.9	36.2	9.1	709	97.1
1890	...	596	...	...	168	140.3	34.1	9.8	759	110.9
1891	...	588	...	...	159	145.7	37.7	9.5	794	120.7
1892	...	568	...	...	163	152.3	30.0	9.4	800	129.7
1893	...	585	...	...	168	157.1	30.2	9.0	788	132.8
1894	...	588	...	...	163	152.6	30.2	8.5	729	132.8
1895	...	633	...	...	162	160.8	29.5	6.8	706	121.2
1896	...	717	6	...	158	167.0	31.3	4.9	730	118.2
1897	...	701	7	...	150	166.4	27.0	4.5	664	122.2
1898	...	703	6	...	149	167.4	25.8	4.7	642	132.1
1899	...	734	4	...	144	162.6	24.0	4.1	665	150.6
1900	...	748	5	...	148	172.5	24.8	4.3	639	139.7
1901	77	777	7.9	...	153	169.2	20.3	4.6	648	135.8
1902	97	762	7.3	...	168	177.6	18.0	4.5	703	132.0
1903	134	773	7.7	...	166	175.0	20.3	4.4	683	157.5
1904	76	798	8.1	...	164	185.8	20.1	4.2	716	148.4
1905	103	794	8.2	...	153	185.6	20.9	4.5	731	147.8
1906	118	769	9.1	...	141	185.4	22.7	4.6	705	155.8
1907	158	771	9.9	...	147	186.5	24.9	4.5	698	160.5
1908	171	727	14.6	...	157	188.1	21.3	5.1	706	152.3
1909	130	799	17.5	...	160	180.0	22.9	5.3	724	129.9
1910	196	926	17.4	...	149	190.5	21.8	4.9	718	146.3
1911	255	869	18.3	...	140	189.9	18.3	5.0	700	139.7
1912	259	969	22.5	...	143	232.6	19.5	5.3	770	149.8
1913	309	942	24.0	...	145	193.9	18.4	5.4	773	158.3
1914	...	884	13.3	...	129	143.6	19.7	5.1	637	145.9

1915–1932

	Bauxite			Copper		
	France	Hungary	Yugoslavia	Germany	Spain[4]	Yugoslavia
1915	...	...	...	1,023	22.3	...
1916	...	...	...	1,282	20.8	...
1917	...	...	...	1,140	25.6	...
1918	...	...	...	1,009	21.7	...
1919	159	...	...	630	23.4	...
1920	267	...	...	575	11.3	54
1921	95	...	10	623[4]	22.0	76[3]
				15.5		4.0
1922	236	...	31	17.5	10.0	5.2
1923	394	...	33	18.2	13.2	6.8
1924	389	...	19	22.7	16.6	8.1
1925	502	...	79	23.8	21.3	7.3
1926	511	4	132	27.7	23.9	9.7
1927	653	340	100	27.3	28.7	13
1928	636	396	49	26.2	28.7	15
1929	678	389	103	29.0	28.5	21
1930	609	32	95	27.0	23.0	24
1931	404	90	65	29.8	23.0	24
1932	401	112	67	30.7	15.6	30

D5 Output of Main Non-ferrous Metal ores (in thousands of metric tons)

1933-1969

	Bauxite			Copper		
	France	Hungary	Yugoslavia	Germany	Spain[4]	Yugoslavia
1933	491	72	81	31.5	17.3	40
1934	529	185	85	28.0	13.8	44
1935	513	211	216	30.2	11.8	39
1936	650	329	292	29.1	22.7	39
1937	691	533	354	29.9	17.1	39
1938	684	540	406	30.0[7]	23.2	42
1939	709	496	319	23.9	10.4	42
1940	489	558	283	24.8	7.2	...
1941	587	781	...	23.6	8.2	...
1942	640	889	...	24.0	14.4	
1943	916	998	...	24.4	17.9	...
1944	666	...	...	25.0[7]	18.3	...
				East Germany[8]		
1945	258	44	...	...	14.7	...
1946	449	101	71	3.0	19.0	22
1947	680	340	88	4.0	17.0	37
1948	804	446	144	5.9	19.3	37
1949	785	861	347	7.6	20.4	34
1950	808	578	206	8.3	19.5	40
1951	1,146	753	498	8.5	20.8	32
1952	1,119	1,207	613	11.0	24.9	33
1953	1,156	1,394	478	15.8	22.7	28
1954	1,287	1,260	687	20.7	24.2	27
1955	1,494	1,241	791	19	27.3	25
1956	1,462	892	881	18	31.9	25
1957	1,690	907	888	21	33.6	30
1958	1,830	1,049	733	23	47.7	30
1959	1,757	938	816	24	58.4	32
					54.9[4]	
1960	2,067	1,190	1,025	24	8.2	35
1961	2,225	1,366	1,232	25	9.6	30
1962	2,194	1,468	1,332	26	7.9	46
1963	2,029	1,363	1,285	24	6.8	49
1964	2,433	1,477	1,293	23	9.9	52
1965	2,662	1,477	1,574	22	9.8	56
1966	2,811	1,429	1,887	19	8.8	63
1967	2,813	1,650	2,131	19	8.6	66
1968	2,713	1,959	2,072	19	8.4	70
1969	2,773	1,934	2,128	15	10	82

D5   Output of Main Non-ferrous Metal ores (in thousands of metric tons)

1915–1964

	Lead			Tin	Zinc			
	Germany	Spain[4]	U.K.	U.K.	Germany	Italy	Poland	Yugoslavia
1915	121	171.5	15.7	5.0	585	80.6	...	...
1916	137	174.4	12.8	4.8	630	94.0	...	...
1917	125	172.9	11.5	4.0	630	79.5	...	...
1918	125	169.7	11.1	4.0	535	67.1	...	...
1919	85	101.5	10.5	3.3	342	65.6	...	...
1920	97	121.4	11.2	3.1	353	96.0	43	...
1921	84_9	135.9	5.3	0.7	355_9	63.5_2	70	...
						27.6		
1922	63_2		8.5	0.4	98_2	40.2	94	...
					40.1			
1923	23.0	127.5	9.7	1.0	31.7	52.9	104	
1924	36.5	141.8	11.1	2.0	58.4	58.9	101	
1925	42.8	153.6	12.0	2.4	69.3	69.6	124	
1926	53.9	149.5	14.7	2.4	104.4	74.7	129	
1927	57.6	144.0	15.7	2.6	141.6	85.4	108	
1928	57.6	131.0	14.3	2.8	144.4	84.8	100	4.8
1929	60.5	142.8	18.0	3.3	142.5	87.0	105	4.7
1930	68.7	123.3	19.6	2.5	138.7	79.6	100	7.5
1931	54.3	109.6	22.8	0.6	105.2	47.1	60	15.5
1932	51.0	105.4	31.8	1.4	75.3	32.2	27	23.1
1933	53.7	88.4	38.3	1.6	104.4	29.1	42	28.5
1934	58.9	72.2	51.9	2.0	131.7	46.1	55	31.2
1935	60.0	71.4	39.8	2.1	140.9	62.2	53	31.0
1936	64.0	41.1	29.5	2.1	156.5	68.2	55	30.5
1937	75.0	32.0	25.5	2.0	165.6	73.7	72	47.7
1938	89.3_7	31.8	28.8_10	2.0	196.4_7	107.7	70	44.5
			30.2					
1939	96.0	26.0	16.8	1.7	190.2	106.0	...	33.1
1940	95.6	46.0	13.8	1.6	261.8	81.6	...	31.8
1941	101.5	46.9	8.1	1.5	287.0	70.7	...	...
1942	102.4	37.9	5.5	1.4	277.7	75.9	...	...
1943	107.4_7	33.6	4.2	1.4	297.5_7	67.9	...	...
1944	...	30.4	4.0	1.3	...	21.2	...	...
	West Germany				**West Germany**			
1945	...	27.1	2.9	1.2	...	10.3	...	7.7
1946	...	29.6	2.6	0.8	...	25.4	46	22.4
1947	...	32.1	2.9	0.9	...	57.8	57	35.0
1948	25.6	22.1	2.3	0.9	53.6	73.5	71	36.7
1949	40.9	27.4	2.2	0.9	57.8	74.3	108	43.9
1950	44.8	34.9	3.1	0.9	70.2	87.0	114	48.4
1951	50.4	41.2	4.2	0.9	75.3	102	118	44.1
1952	51.6	41.8	6.0	0.9	80.7	112	125	47.8
1953	63.0	48.8	8.4	1.1	116.1	106	138	60.0
1954	67.7	56.1	9.3	1.0	121	118	142	57.2
1955	68.1	61.2	8.3	1.1	120	120	156	55.7
1956	66.3	58.8	8.0	1.1	122	123	153	57.5
1957	72.0	61.2	8.7	1.0	126	130	159	58.1
1958	61.9	69.8	4.6	1.1	117	137	163	60.0
1959	53.0	68.6	2.4[6]	1.3	106	132	168	60.7
1960	50.0	71.6	...	1.2	114	131	176	56.4
1961	49.7	77.7	...	1.2	122	136	182	59.9
1962	49.8	72.2	...	1.2	113	131	181	61.1
1963	52.8	67.3	...	1.2	108	105	181	88.3
1964	48.9	58.0	...	1.2	111	116	187	91.8

D5 Output of Main Non-ferrous Metal ores (in thousands of metric tons)

1965–1969

	Lead			Tin	Zinc			
	Germany	Spain[4]	U.K.	U.K.	Germany	Italy	Poland	Yugoslavia
1965	48.5	53.8	…	1.3	109	114	190	91.8
1966	55.4	65.9	…	1.3	107	118	193	85.2
1967	59.4	52.6	…	1.5	114	125	196	90.0
1968	52.5	64.1	…	1.8	117	142	203	95.5
1969	39.3	78.4	…	1.6	116	132	208	96.7
		71.7						

1970–1998

	Bauxite			Copper			Lead		Tin	Zinc			
	France	Hungary	Yugo-slavia	East Germany	Spain	Yugo-slavia	West Germany	Spain	U.K.	West Germany	Italy	Poland	Yugo-slavia
1970	2,992	2,022	2,098	18	10	89	40	73	1.7	127	109	242	101
1971	3,117	2,090	1,959	15	34	93	41	70	1.8	132	98	194	99
1972	3,281	2,358	2,197	20	33	130	38	69	3.3	121	102	200	97
1973	3,299	2,600	2,167	18	33	138	34	64	3.6	123	78	203	97
1974	2,938	2,751	2,370	16	39	150	30	64	3.2	116	78	203	95
1975	2,563	2,890	2,306	16	31	138	32	58	3.3	116	76	210	103
1976	2,330	2,918	2,033	17	36	136	32	66	3.3	115	81	215	107
1977	2,059	2,949	2,044	15	36	144	31	65	3.8	116	70	221	112
1978	1,978	2,899	2,566	14	37	151	22	71	2.8	89	62	231	104
1979	1,969	2,976	3,012	12	36	138	25	72	2.4	117	54	237	102
1980	1,921	2,950	3,138	12	42	131	23	87	3.0	121	40	217	95
1981	1,824	2,914	3,249	13	51	133	22	84	3.9	111	43	201	89
1982	1,610	2,627	3,668	12	48	127	23	73	4.2	106	39	184	84
1983	1,595	2,917	3,500	12	55	124	23	82	4.1	113	43	189	87
1984	1,527	2,994	3,347	12	63	128	21	97	5.0	113	42	191	86
1985	1,452	2,815	3,250	12	57	135	20	87	5.2	118	45	191	89
1986	1,379	3,022	3,459	13	51	140	17	82	4.3	104	26	184	95
1987	1,388	3,101	3,394	13	16	139	19	82	3.6	99	33	186	87
1988	978	2,906	3,034	10	14	131	18	75	3.4	76	38	183	91
1989	550	2,644	3,252	9	29	104	9	63	3.8	64	42	170	89
				Germany			Germany						
1990	490	2,559	2,953	3	14	139	9	59	3.4	58	43	155	84
1991	9	2,013	…	…	9	137	…	44	2.3	…	43	145	…
1992	—	1,721	792[11]	…	9	…[11]	…	30	2.0	…	36	152	6[11]
1993	—	1,561	…	…	4	…	3	25	1.7	92	33	151	…
1994	128	1,360	…	…	5	84.8	…	24	1.6	…	21	151	7
1995	131	1,015	…	…	22	87.6	…	31	1.9	…	23	155	12
1996	165	1,056	323	…	36	82.5	…	24	1.9	…	10	159	18
1997	164	743	470	…	39	87.4	…	23	2.1	…	8	158	19
1998	80	909	226	…	37	84.6	…	19	0.3	…	3	158	20

D5 Output of Main Non-ferrous Metal ores (in thousands of metric tons)

NOTES

1. SOURCES:- Germany 1837–59—based on indices in W.G. Hoffman, *Das Wachstum der Deutschen Wirtschaft seit der Mitte des 19 Jahrhunderts* (Berlin, etc., 1965). Great Britain 1750–1938—B.R. Mitchell. *British Historical Statistics* (Cambridge, 1988), where the original sources are given. All other statistics are taken from the official publications noted p. xv or from the League of Nations and United Nations *Statistical Yearbooks*.
2. So far as possible, the statistics in this table are of metal content. Deviations from this are indicated in the footnotes.

FOOTNOTES

[1] Prior to 1854 the statistics relate only to copper sold publicly in Cornwall and Devon.
[2] Statistics up to this point are of crude ore.
[3] This series is available almost continuously back to the mid-16th century, and then at wider intervals to 1199.
[4] Statistics to 1960 (1st line) are said to be refined metal production from native ores, whilst latter figures are of the Cv content of ores. It is probably that smeltes production of imported ores was also included in the earlier series.
[5] The figures for 1848 to 1853 (1st line) are of crude ore.
[6] The quantities are insignificant after this date.
[7] Figures for 1939–44 include Austria and annexed territories in the East (which include the Polish lead and zinc mines.)
[8] Output in West Germany is small.
[9] Subsequently excluding eastern Upper Silesia, ceded to Poland in mid-1922.
[10] Subsequently including metal from lead concentrates.
[11] Yugoslavia. Ex-Yugoslavia as follows.

	Bauxite		Copper	Zinc
	Croatia	Macedonia	Macedonia	Slovenia
1992	122	—	41	9
1993	7	—	39	7
1994	3	—	39	2
1995	1	—	41	0
1996	1	—	47	0
1997	—	—	47	0
1998	—	—	39	0

D6 OUTPUT OF MAIN NON-METALLIC MINERALS (in thousands of metric tons)

1861–1909

	Germany Potassium Salts	Italy Sulphur
1861	2	166
1862	20	165
1863	59	183
1864	117	181
1865	93	172
1866	145	198
1867	153	199
1868	181	201
1869	232	201
1870	292[1]	204
1871	375	200
1872	490	239
1873	451	274
1874	430	251
1875	529	207
1876	581	276
1877	812	260
1878	770	305
1879	662	376
1880	666	360
1881	906	373
1882	1,201	446
1883	1,189	447
1884	969	411
1885	921	426
1886	945	374
1887	1,080	342
1888	1,235	377
1889	1,186	371
1890	1,275	369
1891	1,371	396
1892	1,351	419
1893	526	418
1894	1,644	406
1895	1,522	371
1896	1,781	426
1897	1,946	497
1898	2,209	502
1899	2,493	564
1900	3,051	554
1901	3,535	563
1902	3,285	539
1903	3,631	554
1904	4,085	528
1905	5,044	569
1906	5,542	500
1907	5,749	427
1908	6,099	445
1909	7,042	435

1910–1959

	France Potash	Germany Potassium Salts	East Germany Potash	Italy Sulphur
1910	...	8,312	...	430
1911	...	9,607	...	414
1912	...	11,161	...	389
1913	...	11,957	...	386
1914	...	8,230	...	378
1915	...	6,980	...	358
1916	...	8,730	...	269
1917	...	8,953	...	212
1918	...	9,283[1]	...	234
1919	...	7,888	...	226
1920	...	11,390	...	264
1921	145	9,196	...	274
1922	212	13,079	...	167
1923	262	11,351	...	256
1924	272	8,105	...	295
1925	312	12,085	...	264
1926	367	9,415	...	271
1927	371	11,080	...	306
1928	407	12,499	...	296
1929	492	13,328	...	324
1930	506	11,967	...	351
1931	368	8,051	...	353
1932	326	6,416	...	350
1933	332	7,363	...	377
1934	356	9,617	...	343
1935	347	11,673	...	312
1936	369	11,765	...	328
1937	490	14,460	...	344
1938	581	16,442	...	380
1939	614	15,900	...	356
1940	230	16,200	...	331
1941	673	17,230	...	299
1942	619	16,810	...	227
1943	664	16,970	...	138
1944	467	16,100	...	78
		West Germany		
1945	145	...	...	75
1946	574	...	...	144
1947	633	...	...	158
1948	684	5,270	...	175
1949	799	7,291	...	201
1950	902	8,927	1,336	213
1951	872	10,847	1,409	216
1952	928	12,585	1,346	231
1953	904	12,587	1,378	218
1954	1,081	15,576	1,463	197
1955	1,189	16,107	1,552	185
1956	1,327	15,544	1,556	171
1957	1,402	16,200	1,604	179
1958	1,479	16,664	1,650	157
1959	1,462	17,422	1,644	121

D6   Output of Main Non-metallic Minerals (in thousands of metric tons)

1960-1969   1915-1969

	France Potash	West Germany Potassium Salts	East Germany Potash	Italy Sulphur
1960	1,535	18,642	1,666	81
1961	1,712	19,509	1,675	70
1962	1,722	18,413	1,752	54
1963	1,722	18,537	1,845	43
1964	1,807	20,588	1,857	29
1965	1,808	22,209	1,926	36
1966	1,736	21,483	2,006	14
1967	1,780	19,850	2,206	10
1968	1,683	20,187	2,293	7
1969	1,770	20,310	2,346	1

1989-1998

	France Potash	Germany Potash	Italy Sulphur
1989	1,291	2,880	315
1990	1,404	2,100	297
1991	1,224	3,902	280
1992	1,236	3,461	280
1993	960	2,711	300
1994	936	2,793	300
1995	799	3,278	...
1996	751	3,332	...
1997	725	3,423	...
1998	730	3,200	...

NOTES

1.   SOURCES:- The official publications noted on p. xv. The German figures for 1914-16 and 1939-44 were calculated by means of the index in W.G. Hoffman, *Das Wachstum der Deutschen Wirtschaft seit der Mitte des 19 Jahrhunderts* (Berlin, etc. 1965).
2.   Statistics of potash derived from potassium salts mined in Germany are available in the source for part of the period covered here. The weight of potash averages a little over 12 per cent of the weight of the salts.

FOOTNOTE

[1]   Figures for 1870-1918 include Alsace.

D7 OUTPUT OF IRON ORE (in thousands of metric tons)

	Austria[1]	France	Germany	Italy[2]	Lux	Norway	Spain	Sweden	U.K.
1822	...	...	175	...	...	...	...	...	...
1823	...	...	163	...	...	...	...	...	...
1824	...	...	149	...	...	...	...	...	...
1825	...	...	192	...	...	...	...	...	...
1826	...	...	229	...	...	...	...	...	...
1827	...	...	220	...	...	...	...	...	...
1828	...	...	235	...	...	...	...	...	...
1829	...	...	206	...	...	...	...	...	...
1830	...	...	235	...	...	...	...	...	...
1831	...	...	263	...	...	...	...	...	...
1832	...	...	266	...	...	...	...	...	...
1833	...	...	260	...	...	...	...	...	...
1834	...	...	263	...	...	...	...	...	...
1835	...	830	280	...	...	...	...	...	...
1836	...	897	286	...	...	...	...	236	...
1837	...	973	343	...	...	...	...	256	...
1838	...	1,013	372	...	...	...	...	248	...
1839	...	1,032	401	...	...	...	...	258	...
1840	...	995	429	...	...	...	...	261	...
1841	...	1,044	486	...	...	...	...	265	...
1842	...	2,566	486	...	...	...	...	285	...
1843	...	2,418	401	...	...	...	...	256	...
1844	...	2,382	372	...	...	...	...	247	...
1845	...	2,460	429	...	...	...	...	234	...
1846	...	...	601	...	...	...	...	264	...
1847	...	3,464	629	...	...	...	...	288	...
1848	...	...	687	...	...	...	...	289	...
1849	...	1,766	658	...	...	...	...	294	...
1850	...	1,821	830	...	...	...	...	281	...
1851	502	1,774	715	...	...	...	...	322	...
1852	525	2,081	801	...	...	...	...	324	...
1853	547	3,319	887	...	...	...	...	317	...
1854	581	3,847	1,230	...	...	...	...	317	...
1855	599	3,876	1,345	...	...	...	...	359	9,707
1856	663	4,608	1,716	...	...	...	...	376	10,651
1857	695	4,495	1,945	...	...	...	...	364	9,777
1858	...	3,933	1,602	...	...	...	...	368	8,170
1859	...	...	1,087	...	...	...	...	361	8,006
1860	...	3,033	1,259	...	...	...	173	395	8,153
1861	...	3,198	1,545	83	...	24	130	429	7,332
1862	...	3,366	1,831	105	...	24	213	430	7,683
1863	...	3,278	2,003	137	...	19	223	448	8,752
1864	...	3,137	2,117	134	...	44	253	464	10,227
1865	...	3,011	2,546	142	...	50	192	497	10,069
1866	...	3,162	2,489	154	...	25	180	483	9,820
1867	696	2,772	2,603	141	...	19	254	485	10,182
1868	681	2,684	2,918	117	722	20	385	535	10,332
1869	688	3,131	3,147	112	924	17	311	596	11,694
1870	835	2,614[3]	2,918[4]	89	912	21	436	616	14,602
1871	864	1,852	3,376	86	990	7	586	663	16,902
1872	928	2,782	4,720	163	1174	33	722	732	16,089
1873	1,040	3,051	4,835	259	1,332	29	812	832	15,833
1874	906	2,517	3,690	280	1,443	30	423	926	15,083

D7   Output of Iron Ore (in thousands of metric tons)

1875–1879

	Austria[1]	France	Germany	Italy[2]	Lux	Norway	Spain	Sweden	U.K.
1875	705	2,506	3,690	228	1,091	29	520	822	16,075
1876	555	2,393	3,519[5]	232	1,197	21	885	797	16,998
1877	539	2,426	3,717	230	1,263	17	1,578	739	16,965
1878	666	2,470	4,051	190	1,411	12	1,706	677	15,978
1879	628	2,271	4,245	187	1,614	8	1,754	645	14,611

1880–1922

	Austria[1]	France	Germany	Italy[2]	Lux	Norway	Poland	Rom-ania	Russia[6]/ USSR	Spain	Sweden	U.K.	Yugo-slavia
1880	697	2,874	5,065	289	2,173	7	...	...	...	3,565	775	18,315	...
1881	619	3,032	5,439	421	2,162	6	...	...	...	3,503	826	17,726	...
1882	903	3,467	5,787	242	2,477	2	...	...	...	4,726	893	18,321	...
1883	882	3,298	6,181	204	2,576	2	...	...	...	4,526	885	17,662	...
1884	974	2,977	6,554	225	2,451	...	...	...	...	3,907	910	16,397	...
1885	931	2,318	6,509	201	2,648	...	...	...	...	3,933	873	15,665	...
1886	796	2,286	6,051	209	2,434	...	...	...	...	4,167	872	14,336	...
1887	847	2,579	6,701	231	2,650	2	...	...	...	5,556	903	13,308	...
1888	1,009	2,842	7,402	177	3,262	1	...	...	...	4,618	960	14,825	...
1889	1,115	3,070	7,832	173	3,171	1	...	...	...	4,854	986	14,779	...
1890	1,362	3,472	8,047	221	3,359	1	...	...	1,736	6,055	941	14,002	...
1891	1,231	3,579	7,555	216	3,102	1	...	...	1,940	5,123	987	12,983	...
1892	993	3,707	8,169	214	3,370	1	...	...	1,986	5,134	1,294	11,495	...
1893	1,109	3,517	8,106	191	3,352	1	...	...	2,041	5,450	1,484	11,383	...
1894	1,215	3,772	8,434	188	3,958	...	...	...	2,411	5,352	1,927	12,565	...
1895	1,385	3,680	8,437	183	3,913	1	...	...	2,851	5,514	1,904	12,817	...
1896	1,449	4,062	9,404	204	4,759	2	...	...	3,130	6,763	2,039	13,921	...
1897	1,614	4,582	10,117	201	5,349	4	...	...	4,024	7,420	2,087	14,009	...
1898	1,734	4,731	10,552	190	5,349	4	...	...	4,444	7,197	2,303	14,404	...
1899	1,725	4,986	11,975	237	6,014	5	...	...	5,790	9,398	2,435	14,693	...
1900	1,894	5,448	12,793	247	6,171	18	...	...	6,001	8,676	2,610	14,253	...
1901	1,963	4,791	12,115	232	4,455	42	...	...	4,652	7,907	2,795	12,472	...
1902	1,744	5,004	12,834	241	5,130	54	...	...	3,925	7,905	2,897	13,641	...
1903	1,716	6,220	15,221	375	6,010	53	...	...	4,219	8,304	3,678	13,936	...
1904	1,719	7,023	15,699	409	6,348	45	...	...	5,193	7,985	4,085	13,995	...
1905	1,914	7,395	16,848	367	6,596	63	...	...	4,976	9,077	4,366	14,825	...
1906	2,254	8,481	19,505	384	7,229	109	...	...	5,345	9,449	4,503	15,749	...
1907	2,540	10,008	20,204	518	7,493	141	...	...	5,452	9,896	4,480	15,984	...
1908	2,632	10,057	18,426	539	5,799	120	...	...	5,578	9,272	4,713	15,272	...
1909	2,490	11,890	19,712	505	5,794	40	...	...	5,171	8,786	3,886	15,042	...
1910	2,628	14,606	22,446	551	6,263	102	...	...	5,742	8,667	5,549	15,470	...
1911	2,766	16,639	23,820	374	6,060	221	...	...	6,995	8,774	6,151	15,768	...
1912	2,927	19,160	27,200	582	6,511	408	...	...	6,935	9,139	6,699	14,011	...
1913	3,039	21,918	28,608	603	7,333	545	...	...	9,537[6] 9,214	9,862	7,476	16,254	...
1914	2,281	11,252	20,505	706	4,900	652	...	...	7,660	6,820	6,589	15,107	...
1915	2,547	620	17,710	680	6,140	715	...	...	5,940	5,618	6,883	14,463	...
1916	...	1,681	21,334	942	6,958	418	...	...	7,250	5,857	6,987	13,712	...
1917	...	2,035	22,465	994	4,502	303	...	...	5,330	5,551	6,217	15,084	...
1918	...[1]	1,672[3]	18,392[4]	694[2]	3,131	96	...	...	590	4,693	6,624	14,847	...
1919	...	9,413	6,154	613	3,112	91	113	90	4,640	4,981	12,451	...	...
1920	...	13,922	6,362	390	3,704	79	184	80	170	4,768	4,519	12,911	10
1921	711	14,201	5,907	279	3,032	57	306	91	140	2,602	6,464	3,534	16
1922	1,112	21,106	5,928	311	4,489	259	410	95	190	2,772	6,201	6,978	37

D7 Output of Iron Ore (in thousands of metric tons)

	Austria[1]	France	Germany	Italy[2]	Lux	Norway	Poland	Rom-ania	Russia[6]/USSR	Spain	Sweden	U.K.	Yugo-slavia
1923	1,211	23,349	5,118	341	4,080	386	455	99	410	3,456	5,588	11,050	245
1924	714	29,044	4,457	219	5,334	522	288	103	940	4,613	6,500	11,228	347
1925	1,030	35,598	5,923	496	6,678	425	210	107	2,220	4,443	8,169	10,306	139
1926	1,094	39,318	4,793	505	7,756	213	317	103	3,430	3,182	8,466	4,160	369
1927	1,599	45,482	6,626	503	7,266	479	546	97	4,810	4,960	9,661	11,387	336
1928	1,928	49,191	6,475	625	7,027	531	736	84	6,133	5,771	4,669	11,443	440
1929	1,891	50,728	6,374	715	7,571	746	659	90	7,997	6,547	11,468	13,427	428
1930	1,181	48,571	5,741	718	6,649	772	477	93	10,663	5,517	11,236	11,813	431
1931	512	38,559	2,621	561	4,765	575	285	62	10,591	3,190	7,071	7,748	133
1932	307	27,599	1,340	412	3,313	374	77	8	12,086	1,760	3,299	7,446	27
1933	267	30,245	2,592	508	3,362	474	164	14	14,455	1,815	2,699	7,582	53
1934	467	32,015	4,343	485	3,828	567	247	84	21,509	2,094	5,253	10,757	180

	Austria[1]	France	Germany	Italy[2]	Lux	Norway	Poland	Rom-ania	Russia[6]/USSR	Spain	Sweden	U.K.	Yugo-slavia
1935	0.8	32.0	5.3	0.6	4.1	0.8	0.3	0.1	26.8	4.0	7.9	11.1	0.2
1936	1.0	33.3	6.7	0.8	4.9	0.8	0.5	0.1	27.8	2.3	11.2	12.9	0.5
1937	1.9	37.8	8.5	1.0	7.8	1.0	0.8	0.1	27.8	1.3	15.0	14.4	0.6
1938	2.7	33.1	11.1[7]	1.0	5.1	1.4	0.9	0.1	26.6	2.5	13.9	12.0	0.6
1939	3.0	33.0[3]	13.2	0.9	5.9	1.3	...	0.1	26.9	3.6	13.8	14.7	0.7
1940	3.2	12.7	17.2	1.2	4.9	0.6	0.8	0.1	29.9	2.6	11.3	18.0	...
1941	2.9	10.6	15.6	1.3	6.9	0.6	0.9	0.2	...	2.3	10.5	19.3	...
1942	3.0	12.8	13.3	1.1	5.1	0.3	0.8	0.2	...	2.2	9.7	20.2	...
1943	3.2	16.9	12.6	0.8	5.3	0.2	0.7	0.3	...	2.1	10.8	18.8	...
1944	3.0	9.4[3]	10.3[7]	0.4	2.9	0.3	0.7	0.2	...	2.2	7.3	15.7	...
			West Germany										
1945	0.3	7.7	...	0.1[2]	1.4	0.1	...	0.1	15.9	1.9	3.9	14.4	...
1946	0.5	16.2	3.9	0.1	2.2	0.1	0.4	0.1	19.3	2.4	6.9	12.4	0.4
1947	0.9	18.7	4.4	0.2	2.0	0.1	0.5	0.1	23.3	2.4	8.9	11.3	0.7
1948	1.2	23.1	7.3	0.5	3.4	0.2	0.7	0.2	28.0	2.5	13.3	13.3	0.9
1949	1.5	31.4	9.1	0.6	4.1	0.3	0.7	0.3	32.6	2.8	13.7	13.6	0.8
1950	1.9	30.0	10.9	0.5	3.8	0.3	0.8	0.4	39.7	3.0	13.6	13.2	0.7
1951	2.4	35.2	12.9	0.6	5.6	0.3	0.9	0.5	44.9	3.3	15.4	15.0	0.6
1952	2.7	40.8	15.4	0.8	7.2	0.8	1.0	0.6	52.6	3.8	16.9	16.5	0.7
1953	2.8	42.4	14.6	1.0	7.2	1.2	1.3	0.7	59.6	4.0	17.0	16.1	0.8
1954	2.7	43.8	13.0	1.1	5.9	1.1	1.6	0.6	64.3	3.8	15.3	15.8	1.1
1955	2.8	50.3	15.7	1.4	7.2	1.3	1.9	0.6	71.9	4.8	17.4	16.4	1.4
1956	3.3	52.7	16.9	1.7	7.6	1.5	2.0	0.7	78.1	5.8	18.9	16.5	1.7
1957	3.5	57.8	18.3	1.6	7.8	1.5	2.0	0.6	84.3	5.2	19.9	17.2	1.9
1958	3.4	59.5	18.0	1.3	6.6	1.6	2.2	0.7	88.6	5.0	18.3	14.8	2.0
1959	3.4	60.9	18.1	1.2	6.5	1.5	2.0	1.1	94.0	4.6	18.4	15.1	2.1
1960	3.5	67.0	18.9	1.3	7.0	1.7	2.2	1.5	106	5.6	21.7	17.4	2.2
1961	3.7	66.6	18.9	1.2	7.5	1.7	2.4	1.7	118	6.1	23.6	16.8	2.2
1962	3.8	66.3	16.6	1.2	6.5	1.9	2.4	1.7	128	5.8	22.5	15.5	2.2
1963	3.7	57.9	12.9	1.0	7.0	2.0	2.6	2.3	138	5.1	23.6	15.2	2.3
1964	3.6	60.9	11.6	0.9	6.7	2.1	2.7	1.9	146	5.1	26.6	16.6	2.3
1965	3.5	59.5	10.8	0.8	6.3	2.5	2.9	2.5	153	5.8	29.4	15.7	2.5
1966	3.5	55.1	9.5	0.8	6.5	2.5	3.1	2.7	160	5.1	28.0	13.9	2.5
1967	3.5	49.2	8.6	0.7	6.3	3.4	3.1	2.8	168	5.1	28.3	12.9	2.6
1968	3.5	55.2	7.7	0.7	6.4	3.7	3.0	2.7	177	6.2	32.4	13.9	2.7
1969	4.0	55.4	7.5	0.8	6.3	3.9	2.8	3.0	186	6.2	33.2	12.3	2.7

D7 Output of Iron Ore (in thousands of metric tons)

1970–1998

	Austria[1]	France	West Germany	Italy[2]	Lux	Norway	Poland	Rom-ania	Russia[6]/ USSR	Spain	Sweden	U.K.	Yugo-slavia
1970	4.0	56.8	6.8	0.8	5.7	4.0	2.6	3.2	195	7.0	31.5	12.0	3.7
1971	4.2	55.9	6.4	0.7	4.5	4.1	2.1	3.5	203	7.3	34.4	10.2	3.7
1972	4.1	54.2	6.1	0.6	4.1	3.9	1.7	3.4	208	6.5	34.0	9.0	4.0
1973	4.2	54.2	6.4	0.5	3.8	4.0	1.4	3.2	216	6.9	34.7	7.1	4.7
1974	4.2	54.3	5.7	0.6	2.7	3.9	1.3	3.3	224	7.8	36.2	3.6	5.0
1975	3.8	49.6	4.3	0.6	2.3	4.1	1.2	3.1	235	8.6	30.9	4.5	5.2
1976	3.8	45.2	3.0	0.5	2.1	4.0	0.7	2.8	241	7.6	29.9	4.6	4.3
1977	3.4	36.6	3.5	0.5	1.5	3.6	0.7	2.5	242	7.9	24.8	3.7	4.5
1978	2.8	33.5	1.6	0.4	0.8	3.8	0.5	2.5	246	8.2	21.1	4.2	4.6
1979	3.2	31.6	1.7	0.2	0.6	4.1	0.2	2.4	242	8.5	26.2	4.3	4.6
1980	3.2	29.0	1.9	0.2	0.6	3.9	0.1	2.3	245	8.9	26.9	0.9	4.5
1981	3.0	21.6	1.6	0.1	0.4	4.1	0.1	2.3	242	8.4	23.1	0.7	4.8
1982	3.3	19.4	1.3	0.2	…	3.5	…	2.1	244	7.6	14.7	0.5	5.1
1983	3.5	16.0	1.0	0.1	…	3.5	…	2.0	245	7.4	13.8	0.4	5.0
1984	3.6	14.8	1.0	0.3	…	3.8	…	1.9	247	8.0	17.8	0.4	5.3
1985	3.7	14.5	1.0	…	…	3.5	…	2.3	248	6.5	20.5	0.3	5.5
1986	3.0	12.4	0.7	…	…	3.6	…	2.4	250	6.1	20.5	0.3	6.6
1987	2.3	11.2	0.2	…	…	3.1	…	2.3	251	4.5	19.7	0.3	6.0
1988	2.3	10.0	0.1	…	…	2.6	…	2.3	250	4.3	20.4	0.2	5.5
1989	2.4	9.4	0.1	…	…	2.3	…	2.4	241	4.6	21.7	—	5.1
1990	2.3	8.7	—	…	…	2.2	…	2.0	236	3.0	19.9	—	4.1
1991	2.1	7.5	0.1	…	…	2.4	…	1.5	199	3.9	19.3	—	2.6[8]
1992	1.6	5.7	…	…	…	2.3	…	1.3	…	…	…	—	3.7
1993	1.4	3.5	…	…	…	2.4	…	0.9	…	…	…	—	2.4
1994	0.5	1.7	…	…	…	1.7	—	0.2	141	0.9	12.7	—	…
1995	0.7	1.4	…	…	…	1.5	—	0.2	44	1.0	13.7	—	…
1996	0.5	1.4	…	…	…	1.1	…	0.1	41	0.5	13.6	—	…
1997	0.5	0.1	…	…	…	0.3	…	0.1	41	- -	13.9	—	…
1998	0.4	—	…	…	…	0.4	…	0.1	42	- -	13.3	—	…

NOTES

1. SOURCES:- Germany 1817–76—based on the index in W.G. Hoffman, *Das Wachstum der Deutschen Wirtschaft seit der Mitte des 19 Jahrhunderts* (Berlin, etc., 1965). Luxembourg 1868–75—data supplied by the Service Central de la Statistique et des Etudes Economiques. Russia 1913 (2nd line) to 1927—G.W. Nutter, *Growth of Industrial Production in the Soviet Union* (Princeton, 1962). U.K. 1855–1938—based on B.R. Mitchell and Phyllis Deane, *Abstract of British Historical Statistics* (Cambridge, reprinted edition, 1971), where the original sources are given and discussed (see pp. 128–9). All other statistics are taken from the official publications noted on p. xv with a few gaps filled from the British Iron & Steel Federation *Statistical Year Books*.
2. These statistics relate to the weight of crude ores, not to their metal content. Figures of the latter for recent years are available in the U.N. *Statistical Yearbooks*.

FOOTNOTES

[1] Cisleithania (excluding the Italian provinces) to 1918, and the Republic subsequently.
[2] Statistics to 1918 apply to the 1871 boundaries. For 1919–45 they apply to the 1924 boundaries, and from 1946 to the boundaries of 1954.
[3] From 1871 to 1918 and from 1940 to 1944 the parts of Alsace and Lorraine ceded to Germany are excluded.
[4] For 1871–1918 includes Alsace-Lorraine.
[5] The figures to 1876 are based on an index (see note 1), and the last digit cannot be regarded as accurate.
[6] Figures to 1913 (1st line) apply to the Russian Empire. From 1913 (2nd line) to 1940 they apply to the 1923 boundaries of the U.S.S.R., and subsequently to the post-Second World War territory.
[7] For 1939–44 includes Polish Upper Silesia.
[8] Yugoslavia.

D8 OUTPUT OF PIG IRON (in thousands of metric tons)

	1780–1804						1805–1829				
	Austria[1]	France	Germany	Russia[2]	U.K.[3]		Austria[1]	France	Germany	Russia[2]	U.K.[3]
1780	...	...	...	110	...	1805	...	...	...	149	250
1781	...	...	...	106	...	1806	...	...	...	146	270
1782	...	...	...	109	...	1807	...	...	...	144	290
1783	...	...	...	112	...	1808	...	...	...	145	300
1784	...	...	...	109	...	1809	...	...	...	146	350
1785	...	...	...	116	...	1810	...	...	...	144	400
1786	...	...	...	122	...	1811	...	...	...	145	360
1787	...	...	...	124	...	1812	...	...	...	134	360
1788	...	...	...	125	...	1813	...	...	...	130	370
1789	...	...	...	123	...	1814	...	...	...	123	400
1790	...	...	...	128	90	1815	...	...	...	...	340
1791	...	...	...	137	100	1816	...	...	...	...	270
1792	...	...	...	121	100	1817	...	...	...	132	260
1793	...	...	...	134	110	1818	...	...	...	127	280
1794	...	...	...	130	110	1819	...	113	...	132	280
1795	...	...	...	135	120	1820	...	...	...	135	320
1796	...	...	...	123	120	1821	...	...	...	159	390
1797	...	...	...	130	140	1822	...	...	...	153	360
1798	...	...	...	138	160	1823	...	...	85	149	450
1799	...	...	...	154	170	1824	...	198	85	140	550
1800	...	...	...	160	180	1825	...	199	95	158	580
1801	...	...	...	167	200	1826	...	206	100	157	520
1802	...	...	...	160	220	1827	...	216	105	184	690
1803	...	...	...	153	230	1828	73	221	105	178	700
1804	...	...	...	160	240	1829	...	217	120	188	690

D8 Output of Pig Iron (in thousands of metric tons)

	1830–1857					1858–1884			
	Austria[1]	Belgium	Finland	France		Austria[1]	Belgium	Finland	France
1830	...	...	...	266	1858	...[4]	324	13	872
1831	...	90	...	225	1859	221	319	12	864
1832	...	93	...	225					
1833	...	95	...	236	1860	225	320	15	898
1834	...	100	...	269	1861	230	312	9	967
					1862	250	357	12	1,091
1835	...	115	...	295	1863	237	392	13	1,157
1836	...	135	...	308	1864	202[5]	450	13	1,213
1837	...	150	...	332					
1838	...	132	...	348	1865	191	471	14	1,204
1839	...	100	...	350	1866	178	482	18	1,260
					1867	215	423	14	1,229
1840	...	95	...	348	1868	263	436	17	1,235
1841	113	90	...	377	1869	278	534	19	1,381
1842	114	96	...	399					
1843	115	98	...	423	1870	279	565	20	1,178[7]
1844	130	107	...	427	1871	292	609	21	860
					1872	313	656	19	1,218
1845	134	135	...	439	1873	371	607	24	1,382
1846	151	189	...	522	1874	332	533	25	1,416
1847	156	248	7	592					
1848	146	162	5	472	1875	303	542	21	1,448
1849	141	149	6	414	1876	273	491	26	1,435
					1877	259	471	22	1,507
1850	155	145	5	406	1878	293	465	14	1,521
1851	159	168	6	446	1879	286	453	18	1,400
1852	172	179	7	523					
1853	182	230	10	661	1880	320	608	22	1,725
1854	197	285	8	771	1881	380	625	22	1,886
					1882	435	727	22	2,039
1855	213	294	11	849	1883	522	783	18	2,069
1856	228	322	9	923	1884	540	751	23	1,872
1857	244	302	12	992					

D8 Output of Pig Iron (in thousands of metric tons)

	German[6]	Hungary[9]	Italy[10]	Luxembourg	Norway[12]	Russia[2]	Spain[14]	Sweden[14]	U.K.[3]
1830	110	...	...	...	...	187	...	...	680
1831	120	...	...	...	...	194	...	...	600
1832	130	...	...	...	...	174	...	...	630
1833	135	...	...	...	...	159	...	...	730
1834	140	...	...	...	...	167	...	...	790
1835	155	...	...	...	...	175	...	...	930
1836	160	...	...	...	...	181	...	107	970
1837	175	...	...	...	...	191	...	109	1,030
1838	170	...	...	...	...	181	...	110	1,120
1839	185	...	...	...	...	182	...	116	1,250
1840	190	...	...	...	...	189	...	125	1,400
1841	185	24	...	...	...	179	...	121	1,330
1842	180	28	...	12	...	188	...	122	1,080
1843	185	28	...	...	...	190	...	133	1,220
1844	180	28	...	...	...	185	...	117	1,560
1845	190	32	...	13	...	187	...	98	2,200
1846	230	30	...	14	...	215	...	127	2,210
1847	230	40	...	24	...	195	...	138	2,000
1848	210	...	...	18	...	198	...	143	2,090
1849	190	...	...	19	...	190	...	119	2,170
1850	210	...	...	13	...	228	...	142	2,250
1851	230	38	...	11	...	207	...	145	2,500
1852	270	37	...	...	...	215	...	150	2,700
1853	310	59	...	14	...	238	...	146	2,900[3]
1854	390	58	...	...	...	231	...	146	3,119
1855	420	63	...	...	...	251	...	188	3,270
1856	500	72	...	15	...	259	15	159	3,644
1857	540	87	...	17	...	213	...	151	3,718
1858	500	...[4]	...	...	...	277	...	177	3,511
1859	460[8]	97	...	...	...	271	...	183	3,773
1860	529	88	...	...	...	298[2]	21	185	3,888
						336			
1861	592	85	27	7	...	320	35	170	3,772
1862	696	98	29	...	...	251	48	200	4,006
1863	813	108	24	17	...	279	45	187	4,582
1864	905	117[5]	21	...	...	300	51	241	4,845
1865	988[6]	101	17	27	...	300	50	227	4,882
1866	977	97	20	46[11]	6	305	39	230	4,597
				70					
1867	1,034	95	22	80	7	289	42	254	4,837
1868	1,184	132	20	80	5	325	43	263	5,050
1869	1,313	127	18	100	4	330	34	292	5,533
1870	1,261[7]	124	20	130	4	359	54	300	6,059
1871	1,424	133	17	140	3	359	54	299	6,733
1872	1,828	147	24	160	2	400	56	339	6,850
1873	1,991	163	29	250	1	380	43	346	6,671
1874	1,666	162	29	240	1	379	38	328	6,087
1875	1,759	160	28	270	2	428	37	351	6,467
1876	1,615	127	19	231	1	443	44	352	6,661
1877	1,718	129	16	215	1[12]	400	47	345	6,715
1878	1,899	141	19	248	1	418	67	341	6,483
1879	1,965	118	12	261	1	433	69	343	6,091

D8   Output of Pig Iron (in thousands of metric tons)

	Germany[6]	Hungary[9]	Italy[10]	Luxembourg	Norway[12]	Russia[2]	Spain[14]	Sweden[14]	U.K.[3]
1880	2,468	144	17	261	1	449	86	406	7,873
1881	2,620	164	28	294	1	471	114	430	8,275
1882	3,004	176	25	377	1	479	120	399	8,725
1883	3,135	176	24	335	1	482	140	423	8,666
1884	3,235	195	18	366	1	510	124	431	7,937

	Austria	Belgium	Czech	Finland	France	Germany	Hungary[9]	Italy[10]
1885	499	713	...	24	1,631	3,268	216	16
1886	485	702	...	17	1,517	3,128	235	12
1887	512	756	...	20	1,568	3,532	193	12
1888	586	827	...	20	1,683	3,813	204	12
1889	617	832	...	15	1,734	3,963	239	13
1890	666	788	...	24	1,962	4,100	299	14
1891	617	684	...	23	1,897	4,096	305	12
1892	631	753	...	24	2,057	4,351	310	13
1893	663	745	...	21	2,003	4,428	319	8
1894	742	819	...	21	2,070	4,700	330	10
1895	779	829	...	23	2,004	4,770	349	9
1896	817	959	...	26	2,340	5,564	401	7
1897	888	1,035	...	33	2,484	6,009	420	8
1898	958	980	...	27	2,525	6,367	469	12
1899	996	1,025	...	27	2,578	7,160	471	19
1900	1,000	1,019	...	31	2,714	7,550	456	24
1901	1,030	764	...	31	2,389	6,964	451	16
1902	992	1,069	...	30	2,405	7,450	435	31
1903	971	1,216	...	23	2,841	8,800	416	75
1904	988	1,283	...	16	2,974	8,860	388	89
1905	1,120	1,311	...	22	3,077	9,507	421	143
1906	1,222	1,363	...	16	3,314	10,833	420	135
1907	1,384	1,378	...	15	3,590	11,390	440	112
1908	1,467	1,270	...	12	3,401	10,505	523	113
1909	1,465	1,616	...	9	3,574	11,092	530	208
1910	1,505	1,852	...	8	4,038	13,111	502	353
1911	1,596	2,046	...	9	4,470	13,845	518	303
1912	1,760	2,301	...	10	4,939	15,600	553	380
1913	1,758	2,485	[1,228][13]	9	5,207	16,761	623	427
1914	1,353	1,454	[928][13]	10	2,736	12,481	494	385
1915	1,429	68	[953][13]	8	584	10,190	388	378
1916	1,477	128	[1,218][13]	9	1,311	11,327	453	467
1917	1,933	8	[1,061][13]	9	1,408	11,601	447	471
1918	...[1]	...	781	6	1,293	10,680[7]	...[9]	314[10]
1919	60	251	663	7	1,333[7] 2,412	6,284	...	240
1920	100	1,116	737	10	3,434	7,044[16]	...	88
1921	226	876	577	10	3,417	7,845	71	61
1922	321	1,613	335	12	5,229	9,396[17]	98	158
1923	342	2,148	817	9	5,432	4,936	124	236
1924	267	2,844	983	11	7,693	7,812	116	304
1925	380	2,543	1,166	11	8,494	10,177	93	482
1926	332	3,368	1,088	9	9,432	9,644	189	513
1927	433	3,709	1,260	10	9,273	13,103	300	489

D8 Output of Pig Iron (in thousands of metric tons)

1928-1939

	Austria	Belgium	Czech	Finland	France	Germany	Hungary[9]	Italy[10]
1928	458	3,857	1,569	9	9,981	11,804	285	507
1929	459	4,041	1,645	7	10,300	13,240	368	671
1930	297	3,365	1,437	3	10,035	9,695	257	537
1931	145	3,198	1,165	5	8,199	6,063	160	510
1932	95	2,749	450	7	5,537	3,932	66	461
1933	88	2,710	499	5	6,234	5,247	93	518
1934	133	2,953	600	2	6,151	8,717[1]	140	529
1935	193	3,030	811	6	5,789	12,846	186	633
1936	248	3,161	1,140	4	6,230	15,302	306	762
1937	388	3,843	1,627[15]	16	7,855	15,960	358	801
1938	551	2,426	1,675	28	6,012	18,045	335	864
1939	...	3,059	...	29	7,376	17,478	409	1,005

1885-1919

	Lux	Netherlands	Norway	Poland	Romania	Russia[2]	Spain[14]	Sweden[14]	U.K.	Yugo-slavia
1885	420	...	—	...	...	528	159	465	7,534	...
1886	301	...	—	...	...	531	148	442	7,122	...
1887	492	...	1	...	...	613	134	457	7,681	...
1888	524	...	1	...	...	667	186	457	8,127	...
1889	562	...	- -	...	...	741	179	441	8,457	...
1890	560	...	1	...	...	928	192	456	8,031	...
1891	545	...	- -	...	...	1,005	197	490	7,525	...
1892	587	...	1	...	...	1,073	193	486	6,817	...
1893	558	...	- -	...	...	1,150	232	453	7,089	...
1894	680	...	- -	...	...	1,333	243	463	7,546	...
1895	695	...	- -	...	...	1,455	236	463	7,827	...
1896	899	...	- -	...	...	1,624	261	494	8,799	...
1897	870	...	- -	...	...	1,883	317	538	8,937	...
1898	955	...	- -	...	...	2,244	262	532	8,748	...
1899	983	...	- -	...	...	2,713	296	498	9,572	...
1900	971	...	- -	...	...	2,937	310	526	9,104	...
1901	916	...	- -	...	...	2,870	331	528	8,056	...
1902	1,080	...	1	...	...	2,601	326	538	8,818	...
1903	1,218	...	1	...	...	2,491	380	507	9,078	...
1904	1,198	...	- -	...	...	2,975	358	529	8,834	...
1905	1,368	...	- -	...	...	2,736	390	539	9,762	...
1906	1,460	...	...	...	...	2,722	321	604	10,347	...
1907	1,485	...	—	...	...	2,822	355	616	10,276	...
1908	1,300	...	—	...	...	2,827	404	568	9,202	...
1909	1,553	...	—	...	...	2,900	429	445	9,685	...
1910	1,683	...	—	...	...	3,047	373	604	10,173	...
1911	1,729	...	- -	...	...	3,598	409	634	9,679	...
1912	2,252	...	- -	...	...	4,203	403	699	8,891	...
1913	2,548	...	- -	...	...	4,641[2] 4,216	425	730[14] 742	10,425	...
1914	1,827	...	7	...	...	4,137	431	652	9,067	...
1915	1,591	...	9	...	...	3,764	440	777	8,864	...
1916	1,951	...	6	...	...	3,804	498	758	9,062	...
1917	1,529	...	6	...	...	2,964	358	857	9,488	...
1918	1,267	...	9	...	...	597	387	779	9,253	...
1919	617	...	2	407	12	117	294	509	7,536	...

D8 Output of Pig Iron (in thousands of metric tons)

	Lux	Netherlands	Norway	Poland	Romania	Russia[2]	Spain[14]	Sweden[14]	U.K.	Yugo-slavia
1920	693	...	3	412	19	116	251	484	8,164	6
1921	970	...	2	444	33	117	347	320	2,658	12
1922	1,679	...	2	480[17]	31	180	210	274	4,981	16
1923	1,407	...	4[12] 26	520	39	314	400	301	7,560	24
1924	2,157	69	64	336	46	670	497	533	7,424	15
1925	2,363	118	87	315	64	1,309	528	459	6,362	3
1926	2,559	143	97	327	63	2,203	487	495	2,497	19
1927	2,732	204	123	618	63	2,961	590	455	7,410	23
1928	2,770	258	141	684	70	3,282	557	438	6,716	29
1929	2,906	254	154	706	72	4,021	749	524	7,711	31
1930	2,473	273	145	478	69	4,964	616	496	6,291	35
1931	2,053	257	119	347	26	4,871	473	418	3,834	38
1932	1,960	236	103	199	9	6,161	296	282	3,631	10
1933	1,888	253	112	306	2	7,110	330	346	4,202	31
1934	1,955	258	127	382	62	10,430	363	558	6,065	33
1935	1,872	254	130	396	82	12,490	341	613	6,527	21
1936	1,987	274	168	586	97	14,400	226	632	7,845	44
1937	2,513	312	181	720	127	14,487	132	693	8,629	50
1938	1,551	267	174	880	133	14,650	436	714	6,869	116
1939	1,838	284	191	[652][19][21]	119	14,520	473	691	8,108	113

D8 Output of Pig Iron (in thousands of metric tons)

	Austria[1]	Belgium	Bulgaria	Czech	Denmark	Finland	France	Germany	E. Germany	Hungary[9]	Italy
1940	679	1,790	—	1,582	...	25	3,683	13,955	...	427	1,062
1941	646	1,422	—	1,528	...	22	3,351	15,441	...	448	1,038
1942	784	1,269	—	1,576	...	28	3,838	15,332	...	418	887
1943	961	1,631	—	1,679	...	42	4,921	15,972	...	417	648
1944	928	719	—	1,565[15]	...	99	2,893	13,369	...	296	233[10]
								W. Germany			
1945	102	735	—	576	12	35	1,177	...	...	44	65
1946	58	2,161	—	961	18	77	3,444	2,083	124	160	177
1947	279	2,817	—	1,423	23	66	4,886	2,265	132	301	318
1948	613	3,929	1	1,645	31	90	6,559	4,663	274	384	449
1949	838	3,749	3	1,885	39	99	8,345	7,140	313	420	393
1950	883	3,695	3	1,951	51	64	7,761	9,473	337	465	504
1951	1,049	4,868	5	2,057	33	101	8,750	10,697	342	534	953
1952	1,173	4,790	9	2,306	36	108	9,769	12,877	660	631	1,102
1953	1,321	4,232	6	2,781	36	79	8,666	11,654	1,078	734	1,222
1954	1,354	4,625	7	2,790	40	74	8,841	12,512	1,318	857	1,256
1955	1,506	5,385	8	2,982	55	114	10,960	16,482	1,517	883	1,625
1956	1,737	5,770	10	3,282	56	103	11,480	17,577	1,574	768	1,873
1957	1,960	5,581	54	3,563	59	128	11,916	18,358	1,663	837	2,072
1958	1,818	5,519	91	3,774	44	101	11,967	16,659[16]	1,775	1,100	2,060
1959	1,837	5,967	177	4,244	59	108	12,472	21,602	1,898	1,121	2,098
1960	2,232	6,553	192	4,696	73	137	14,145	25,739	1,995	1,259	2,683
1961	2,262	6,454	206	4,971	66	152	14,566	25,431	2,031	1,320	3,056
1962	2,118	6,740	223	5,177	69	331	13,959	24,251	2,075	1,397	3,556
1963	2,106	6,899	265	5,254	69	332	14,306	22,909	2,150	1,399	3,741
1964	2,204	8,044	457	5,716	73	597	15,863	27,182	2,260	1,499	3,498
1965	2,200	8,367	695	5,868	75	940	15,770	26,990	2,338	1,584	5,488
1966	2,195	8,230	930	6,269	76	936	15,590	25,413	2,448	1,640	6,289
1967	2,140	8,902	1,028	6,822	76	1,025	15,710	27,366	2,525	1,669	7,294
1968	2,474	10,371	1,111	6,918	76	811	16,455	30,305	2,333	1,659	7,826
1969	2,816	11,211	1,134	7,009	77	1,231	18,215	33,764	2,098	1,760	7,781
1970	2,964	10,845	1,252	7,548	68	1,164	19,228	33,627	1,994	1,835	8,332
1971	2,849	10,403	1,378	7,961	68	1,029	18,354	29,990	2,027	1,984	8,536
1972	2,846	11,777	1,562	8,360	41	1,183	19,016	32,002	2,151	2,070	9,415
1973	3,006	12,655	1,610	8,534	...	1,412	20,304	36,828	2,202	2,110	10,032
1974	3,443	13,020	1,528	8,905	...	1,381	22,519	40,221	2,280	2,298	11,686
1975	3,056	9,081	1,560	9,281	...	1,368	17,921	30,074	2,456	2,229	11,350
1976	3,318	9,877	1,612	9,475	...	1,319	19,024	31,849	2,528	2,233	11,631
1977	2,965	8,910	1,664	9,715	...	1,764	18,257	28,959	2,626	2,300	11,410
1978	3,077	10,128	1,539	9,944	...	1,903	18,497	30,148	2,548	2,343	11,341
1979	3,702	10,776	1,501	9,529	...	2,087	19,415	35,167	2,386	2,381	11,327
1980	3,485	9,845	1,583	9,819	...	2,072	19,159	33,873	2,458	2,227	12,150
1981	3,477	9,791	1,571	9,903	...	2,017	17,274	31,876	2,441	2,207	12,260
1982	3,115	7,831	1,617	9,525	...	1,998	15,047	27,621	2,149	2,194	11,537
1983	3,320	8,033	1,674	9,466	...	1,956	13,770	26,598	2,207	2,059	10,313
1984	3,745	8,968	1,621	9,561	...	2,093	15,039	30,666	2,357	2,109	11,631
1985	3,704	8,719	1,754	9,562	...	2,023	15,405	31,919	2,578	2,109	12,062
1986	3,349	8,048	1,651	9,573	...	2,016	13,982	29,443	2,738	2,069	11,961
1987	3,451	8,242	1,437	9,788	...	2,218	13,449	28,918	2,754	2,124	11,335
1988	3,665	9,147	1,484	9,706	...	2,173	14,786	33,016	2,786	2,103	11,349
1989	3,823	8,863	1,141	9,911	...	2,284	15,072	33,048	2,736	1,984	12,012
1990	3,452	9,416	943	8,640	...	2,283	14,412	30,324		1,682	12,024
1991	3,439	9,353	837	8,253	...	2,332	14,148	30,024		1,311	10,992
1992	3,067	8,524	998	4,889[22]	...	2,452	13,056	27,577		1,176	10,608
1993	3,000	8,179	...	4,511[22]	...	2,595	12,660	26,323		1,407	11,196
1994	3,320	8,976	1,470	5,274	...	2,597	13,008	29,632		1,595	11,161
1995	3,878	9,204	1,607	5,263	...	2,242	13,758	29,599		1,515	11,677
1996	3,416	8,604	1,504	4,898	...	2,457	12,987	27,340		1,496	10,321
1997	3,966	8,064	1,643	5,276	...	2,784	14,399	30,462		1,140	11,477
1998	4,021	8,616	1,500	4,980	...	2,916	13,896	29,705		1,259	10,791

D8   Output of Pig Iron (in thousands of metric tons)

	Lux'bg	Neth'l	Norway	Poland	Romania	Russia[2]	Spain[14]	Sweden	Switzerland	U.K.	Yugo-slavia
1940	1,059	169	147	915[20]	122	14,902	579	787	5	8,337	122
1941	1,343	176	123	1,081	118	...	536	749	10	7,512	...
1942	1,692	152	111	1,128	162	...	535	770	12	7,850	...
1943	2,268	94	145	1,169	226	...	584	828	15	7,302	...
1944	1,348	99	124	1,095[21]	141	...	551	887	29	6,845	...
1945	317	25	51	219	54	8,803	479	785	3	7,221	12
1946	1,365	187	135[18]	726	66	9,862	491	719	12	7,886	8
1947	1,818	288	146	867	...	11,223	503	725	12	7,910	171
1948	2,624	442	202	1,134	186	13,742	522	803	36	9,425	183
1949	2,372	434	234	1,391	...	16,389	615	860	32	9,651	202
1950	2,499	454	226	1,533	320	19,175	664	837	34	9,788	226
1951	3,157	524	245	1,616	336	21,909	650	905	40	9,824	262
1952	3,076	539	273	1,836	381	25,071	763	1,103	40	10,900	288
1953	2,722	593	278	2,359	448	27,415	800	1,057	41	11,354	281
1954	2,800	610	246	2,663	429	29,972	877	1,001	35	12,074	368
1955	3,085	670	355	3,112	570	33,310	964	1,247	54	12,670	531
1956	3,316	662	452	3,506	583	35,754	913	1,412	41	13,381	647
1957	3,368	701	565	3,682	686	37,040	962	1,543	45	14,512	735
1958	3,285	917	523	3,864	737	39,600	1,302	1,414	34	13,183	779
1959	3,444	1,139	623	4,374	846	42,972	1,675	1,501	40	12,784	900
1960	3,786	1,346	720	4,563	1,014	46,757	1,886	1,627	50	16,016	1,016
1961	3,834	1,456	757	4,770	1,099	50,893	2,077	1,895	50	14,984	1,042
1962	3,597	1,571	724	5,311	1,511	55,265	2,101	1,957	50	13,912	1,103
1963	3,587	1,708	749	5,395	1,706	58,691	1,911	2,017	42	14,826	1,060
1964	4,191	1,947	894	5,643	1,924	62,377	1,903	2,354	30	17,551	1,076
1965	4,145	2,364	1,090	5,760	2,019	66,184	2,338	2,451	25	17,740	1,177
1966	3,963	2,209	1,139	5,855	2,198	70,264	2,107	2,397	25	15,962	1,217
1967	3,963	2,588	1,232	6,581	2,456	74,812	2,687	2,567	24	15,396	1,256
1968	4,308	2,821	1,431	6,676	2,992	78,788	2,783	2,702	22	16,695	1,286
1969	4,872	3,460	1,491	6,856	3,477	81,634	3,300	2,768	25	16,653	1,288
1970	4,814	3,594	1,251	7,111	4,210	85,933	4,165	2,842	28	17,672	1,377
1971	4,588	3,759	1,313	7,331	4,381	89,256	4,825	2,815	32	15,416	1,630
1972	4,671	4,289	1,372	7,579	4,890	92,327	5,928	2,587	28	15,316	1,949
1973	5,091	4,707	1,506	7,896	5,713	95,933	6,271	2,782	26	16,938	2,109
1974	5,469	4,804	1,583	7,952	6,081	99,868	6,904	3,181	35	13,903	2,316
						million tons					
1975	3,889	3,970	1,565	7,926	6,602	103	6,842	3,508	35	12,131	2,196
1976	3,756	4,265	1,584	8,078	7,415	105	6,626	3,196	23	13,435	2,118
1977	3,568	3,922	1,242	9,827	7,784	107	6,621	2,500	27	12,232	2,127
1978	3,721	4,613	1,310	11,409	8,155	111	6,243	2,557	35	11,434	2,301
1979	3,801	4,814	1,652	11,296	8,879	109	6,454	3,116	30	12,898	2,610
1980	3,568	4,328	1,428	11,682	9,013	107	6,364	2,596	33	6,316	2,668
1981	2,889	4,600	1,720	9,140	8,857	108	6,259	1,972	33	9,554	3,081
1982	2,587	3,617	1,370	8,357	8,637	107	5,997	1,928	10	8,389	2,924
1983	2,316	3,747	1,620	9,457	8,191	110	5,426	2,167	10	9,560	3,096
1984	2,768	4,926	1,549	9,799	9,558	111	5,319	2,391	54	9,562	3,159
1985	2,754	4,819	1,518	9,613	9,212	110	5,457	2,603	66[26]	10,458	3,419
1986	2,650	4,628	1,315	10,381	9,329	114	4,862	2,592	147	9,785	3,363
1987	2,305	4,575	1,130	10,310	8,673	114	4,804	2,480	140	12,110	3,158
1988	2,519	4,994	1,207[23]	10,264	8,203	115	4,691	2,494[25]	134	13,163	3,276
1989	2,684	5,163	240	9,492	9,052	114	5,464	2,648	141	11,832	2,899
1990	2,645	4,960	54	8,640	6,355	110	5,733	2,696	129	12,492	2,460
						thousand tons					
1991	2,463	4,697	61	6,516	4,525	46,638[24]	5,600	2,851	105	12,060	526[27]
1992	2,255	4,849	70	6,480	2,925	44,021[24]	5,076	2,883	102	11,520	512[27]
1993	2,412	5,405	73	6,336	3,189	39,339[24]	5,000	2,850	82	11,616	62[27]
1994	1,927	5,443	70	6,866	3,496	36,480	5,447	3,036	88	11,943	17
1995	1,028	5,530	70	7,373	4,203	39,676	5,106	3,020	97	12,236	109
1996	829	5,544	71	6,540	4,025	37,079	4,127	3,130	100	12,830	565
1997	438	5,805	70	7,295	4,557	37,277	3,927	3,072	100	13,056	907
1998	—	5,562	70	6,129	4,541	34,582	4,236	3,156	100	12,746	792

D8 Output of Pig Iron (in thousands of metric tons)

NOTES

1. SOURCES:- Germany to 1859—based on the index in W.G. Hoffman, *Das Wachstum der Deutschen Wirtschaft seit der Mitte des 19 Jahrhunderts* (Berlin, etc. 1965). German wartime statistics, and those for most East European countries, and all statistics for Luxembourg from 1866 onwards are taken from the British Iron and Steel Federation (later British Steel Corporation), *Statistics of the Iron and Steel Industries* (later *Statistical Year Book*). Earlier statistics for Luxembourg were supplied by the Groupement des Industries Sidérurgiques Luxembourgeoises. Finnish statistics to 1899 were supplied by the Central Statistical Office of Finland, those for 1846–70 being taken from Eevert Laine, *Suomen Vuoritiomi, 1809–1884*. Russian statistics to 1860 (1st line) are from S.G. Strumilin, *Istoriia Chernoi Metallurgii v S.S.S.R.* I (Moscow, 1954), and those from 1860 (2nd line) to 1913 (1st line) are from P.A. Khromov, *Economic Development of Russia in the 19th and 20th Centuries, 1800–1917* (Moscow, 1950). U.K. to 1853—based on Philip Riden, "The Output of the British Iron Industry before 1870," *Economic History Review* 2nd series xxx, 3 (1977). All other statistics are taken from the official publications noted on p. xv.
2. Output of ferro-alloys is normally included in these statistics.
3. T.J. Markovitch, *L'industrie francaise de 1789 á 1964* (Cahiers de l'I.S.E.A., 1966) gives the following averages of French output (in thousands of metric tons):-

    1781–90 141;   1803–12 200;   1815–24 150

    S.G. Strumilin, *op. cit.* gives the following statistics for years before his continuous series begins (in thousands of metric tons):-

    1720 10;   1730 16;   1740 25;   1750 33;   1760 60;   1770 84

    Philip Riden, *loc. cit.* above, gives the following estimates for periods before his continuous series begins (in thousands of Imperial tons):-

av.	1720–4	27	1735–9	27	1750–4	28	1765–9	40	1780–4	62
	1725–9	29	1740–4	26	1755–9	31	1770–4	40	1785–9	80
	1730–4	28	1745–9	27	1760–4	34	1775–9	48		

FOOTNOTES

[1] Figures to 1918 are for Cisleithania (excluding Lombardy and Venetia), and later figures are for the Republic. Decennial averages for 1819–48 for the whole Austro-Hungarian Empire are available as follows (in thousands of tons):-

    1819–28 73;   1829–38 103;   1839–48 164

Statistics for Lombardy and Venetia are available as follows (in thousands of tons):-

1841	6.4	1845	6.3	1849	8.1	1853	9.4
1842	6.3	1846	10.2	1850	...	1854	8.6
1843	6.4	1847	7.5	1851	14.3	1855	8.5
1844	5.4	1848	7.4	1852	10.9	1856	10.4
						1857	9.9

[2] Figures to 1860 (1st line) apply to the 50 provinces of European Russia (excluding Finland, Poland, and the Caucasus). From 1860 (2nd line) to (1st line) they are for the whole Russian Empire. From 1913 (2nd line) to 1940 they are for the 1923 boundaries of the U.S.S.R., and later figures are for the post-Second World War boundaries.
[3] The statistics to 1853 are estimates in thousand Imperial tons.
[4] Output for the whole Austro-Hungarian Empire was 373 thousand tons.
[5] Statistics to 1864 are for years ended 31 October. Output for the whole Austro-Hungarian Empire in November and December 1864 was 56 thousand tons.
[6] Including Luxembourg to 1865.
[7] From 1871 to 1919 (1st line) the parts of Alsace and Lorraine ceded in 1871 are excluded From France, and (except in 1919) are included in Germany. The output of this district can be derived from German sources (in thousands of tons):-

1881	305	1890	640	1900	1,524	1910	2,723
1882	359	1891	635	1901	1,447	1911	2,908
1883	371	1892	734	1902	1,630	1912	3,149
1884	410	1893	726	1903	1,974	1913	3,864
1885	432	1894	804	1904	2,070		
1886	429	1895	829	1905	2,169		
1887	516	1896	920	1906	2,423		
1888	543	1897	928	1907	2,512		
1889	563	1898	994	1908	2,182		
		1899	1,290	1909	2,315		

[8] Previous figures are based on an index (see note 1) and are rounded to the nearest 5 to 1844 and the nearest 10 from 1845–59.
[9] Figures to 1918 are for Transleithania (including Croatia-Slavonia), and later figures are for the territory established by the treaty of Trianon. Ferro-alloys are not included until 1950.
[10] Figures to 1918 are for the boundaries of 1871. For 1919–45 they apply to the 1924 boundaries, and from 1946 to the 1954 boundaries. Ferro-alloys are not included.
[11] Previous statistics apparently relate to wrought and cast iron. Earlier figures are available as follows (in thousand tons):-

    1806 24;   1811 14

D8 Output of Pig Iron (in thousands of metric tons)

[12] Including castings to 1877, but excluding ferro-alloys to 1923 (1st line).
[13] This is also included in Austrian output.
[14] Excluding ferro-alloys (to 1913 (1st line) in the case of Sweden).
[15] Teschen is excluded from 1938 to 1944
[16] From 1921 to 1924 and 1946 to 1958 Saarland is excluded. The output of this district was as follows (in thousand tons):-

1921	896	1930	1,912	1946	247	1953	2,382
1922	1,157	1931	1,515	1947	653	1954	2,497
1923	929	1932	1,349	1948	1,134	1955	2,879
1924	1,345	1933	1,592	1949	1,582	1956	3,031
1925	1,450	1934	1,827	1950	1,684	1957	3,166
1926	1,625			1951	2370	1958	3,103
1927	1,771			1952	2,550		
1928	1,936						
1929	2,105						

[17] Eastern Upper Silesia was transferred from Germany to Poland from July 1922.
[18] Subsequently excluding production for use in the producers's own works, and also excluding ferro-silicon converted to 45%Si.
[19] First half-year only.
[20] Excluding central Poland.
[21] From 1940 to 1944 Teschen (previously and subsequently part of Czechoslovakia) is included. Figures from 1945 are for the postwar boundaries, which include what was formerly German Silesia.
[22] Czech Republic. Slovakia: 3205 (1993).
[23] Change in source.
[24] Russian Federation. Ex-USSR are as follows.

Ukraine	1991	34,638
	1992	33,565
	1993	25,970
	1994	20,837
	1995	18,314
	1996	18,110
	1997	21,060
	1998	21,239

[25] Including Foundry Pig Iron.
[26] Includes Pig Iron for Steel making.
[27] Yugoslavia. Ex-Yugoslavia as follows.

Croatia	1992	40
	1993	40
	1994	40
	1995	20
	1996	—
	1997	—
	1998	—
Macedonia	1992	13
	1993	20
	1994	20
	1995	20
	1996	20
	1997	20
	1998	20

D9 OUTPUT OF CRUDE STEEL (in thousands of metric tons)

1860–1909

	Austria[1]	Belgium	France	Germany	Italy	Luxembourg	Russia[3]	Spain	Sweden	U.K.
1860	...	...	...	...	...	...	1.6	21	...	...
1861	...	...	...	...	...	...	1.9	33	...	...
1862	...	...	...	...	...	...	2.0	41	...	...
1863	...	...	...	...	...	...	2.0	53	...	...
1864	...	...	...	...	...	...	3.5	45	...	...
1865	...	...	...	...	...	...	4	43	...	...
1866	...	...	...	...	...	...	4	33	...	...
1867	...	...	...	...	...	...	6	40	...	...
1868	...	...	...	...	...	...	10	37	...	...
1869	...	...	...	...	...	...	8	36	...	...
1870	22	...	84	126	...	...	9	36	12	...
1871	36	...	80	143	...	...	7	43	9	334
1872	55	...	130	189	...	...	9	42	16	417
1873	77	...	156	248	...	...	9	32	16	582
1874	97	...	217	325	...	...	9	23	21	640
1875	89	54	239	318	...	...	13	25	19	719
1876	90	80	231	340	...	...	18	34	21	841
1877	97	100	250	391	...	...	44	44	17	901
1878	85	120	282	463	...	...	64	45	19	998
1879	86[2]	110	339[2]	510	...	...	210	44	20[2]	1,025
1880	124	132	389	690	3	...	307	49	37	1,316
1881	134	142	422	900	4	...	293	54	49	1,807
1882	155	183	458	1,070	3	...	248	66	58	2,143
1883	165	179	522	1,060	3	...	222	59	65	2,040
1884	320	186	503	1,140	5	...	207	53	67	1,802
1885	289	155	554	1,203	3	...	193	53	77	1,917
1886	268	155	428	1,315	24	21	242	78	78	2,300
1887	310	216	493	1,681	73	57	226	97	111	3,093
1888	402	232	592	1,793	118	70	222	87	114	3,357
1889	433	254	626	1,999	158	97	259	111	136	3,628
1890	516	221	683	2,135	108	97	378	137	168	3,636
1891	495	222	744	2,452	76	111	434	135	172	3,208
1892	516	260	825	2,653	57	103	515	129	160	2,967
1893	578	273	790	3,034	71	129	631	139	167	2,997
1894	671	406	818	3,617	55	131	703	147	168	3,161
1895	753	408	876	3,891	50	135	879	105	197	3,312
1896	898	599	1,181	4,697	66	137	1,022	122	257	4,198
1897	949	617	1,325	4,887	64	144	1,225	147	274	4,558
1898	1,084	654	1,434	5,279	87	170	1,619	116	264	4,639
1899	1,146	731	1,499	5,872	109	166	1,897	153	272	4,933
1900	1,170	655	1,565	6,461	116	185	2,216	199	300	4,980
1901	1,099	516	1,425	6,137	129	257	2,228	168	269	4,983
1902	1,167	769	1,568	7,466	135	315	2,184	166	286	4,988
1903	1,162	969	1,840	8,430	187	372	2,434	193	318	5,115
1904	1,257	1,091	2,096	8,564	201	366	2,766	201	333	5,108
1905	1,459	1,227	2,255	9,669	270	398	2,266	247	368	5,905
1906	1,608	1,395	2,451	10,700	391	435	2,496	280	398	6,566
1907	1,731	1,467	2,767	11,619	430	444	2,671	325	420	6,628
1908	2,018	1,198	2,723	10,726	537	461	2,698	297	438	5,381
1909	1,963	1,580	3,039	11,515	662	535	2,940	254	313	5,976

D9 Output of Crude Steel (in thousands of metric tons)

	Austria[1]	Belgium	France	Germany	Italy	Luxembourg	Russia[3]	Spain	Sweden	U.K.
1910	2,174	1,892	3,413	13,100	732	598	3,314	261	472	6,476
1911	2,348	2,028	3,837	14,303	736	716	3,949	286	471	6,566
1912	2,708	2,442	4,429	16,355	918	947	4,503	297	515	6,905
1913	2,611	2,403[4]	4,687	17,609	934	1,326[12]	4,918[3]	242	591	7,787
		2,467								
1914	...	1,396	2,802	13,810	911	1,136	4,466	356	507	7,971

	Austria[1]	Belgium	Bulgaria	Czech	Denmark	Finland	France	Germany		Ireland	Hungary	Italy
1915	...	99	...	...	...	...	1,111	12,278		...	...	1,009
1916	...	99	...	...	...	...	1,784	14,871		...	...	1,269
1917	...	10	...	...	...	...	1,991	15,501		...	...	1,332
1918	...[1]	11	...	...	...	...	1,800	14,092		...	...	933[11]
1919	...	334	...	786	...	...	1,293[7]	8,710[7]		...	...	732
							2,156	7,847				
1920	...	1,253	...	973	...	6	2,706	9,278[8]		...	62	774
1921	297	789	...	918	...	15	3,099	9,997[9]		...	166	700
1922	481	1,565	...	721	...	24	4,538	11,714		...	257	983
1923	500	2,297	...	1,180	...	25	5,222	6,305		...	283	1,142
1924	370	2,875	...	1,350	...	29	6,670	9,835		...	239	1,359
1925	464	2,549	...	1,475	...	29	7,464	12,195		...	231	1,786
1926	474	3,339	...	1,345	...	28	8,617	12,342		...	325	1,780
1927	551	3,680	...	1,689	...	12	8,349	16,311		...	472	1,596
1928	636	3,905	...	1,973	...	30	9,479	14,517		...	486	1,960
1929	632	4,110	...	2,193	...	26	9,716	16,245		...	514	2,122
1930	468	3,354	...	1,817	...	28	9,444	12,536		...	369	1,743
1931	323	3,105	...	1,514	...	18	7,816	8,291		...	316	1,409
1932	205	2,790	...	672	...	35	5,638	5,771		...	180	1,396
1933	226	2,731	...	734	...	36	6,577	7,617		...	228	1,771
1934	309	2,944	...	940	...	38	6,155	11,923[8]		...	315	1,850
1935	364	3,023	...	1,178	...	45	6,255	16,447		...	446	2,209
1936	418	3,168	...	1,538	20	42	6,686	19,208		...	553	2,025
1937	650	3,863	...	2,301[6]	20	48	7,893	19,849		...	665	2,087
1938	673	2,279	...	1,800	26	76	6,137	22,656[10]		...	647	2,323
1939	780	3,104	...	2,421	...	77	7,950	23,733[10]		...	733	2,283
1940	766	1,894	...	2,265	...	77	4,413	21,540		...	750	2,258
1941	804	1,624	...	2,316	...	62	4,310	20,836		...	782	2,063
1942	897	1,380	...	2,332	...	84	4,488	20,480		...	784	1,934
1943	1,054	1,670	...	2,514	...	97	5,127	20,758		...	776	1,727
1944	1,013	634	...	2,543[6]	...	93	3,092	18,318[10]		...	694	1,026
								West[8]	East			
1945	172	749	...	993	46	86	1,661	...	...	...	129	395[11]
1946	187	2,297	...	1,677	52	89	4,408	2,555	153	...	343	1,153
1947	357	2,882	...	2,286	58	77	5,733	3,060	...	...	597	1,691
1948	648	3,920	5	2,621	72	103	7,236	5,561	398	...	770	2,125
1949	835	3,849	5	2,806	76	111	9,152	9,156	643	...	860	2,055
1950	947	3,777	5	3,122	123	102	8,652	12,121	999[19]	...	1,048	2,362
									1,257			
1951	1,028	5,054	7	3,455	161	127	9,835	13,506	1,748	14	1,290	3,063
1952	1,058	5,067	6	3,754	176	147	10,867	15,806	2,249	15	1,459	3,535
1953	1,283	4,497	18	4,366	180	147	9,997	15,420	2,573	16	1,543	3,500
1954	1,653	4,973	62	4,270	199	175	10,627	17,434	2,701	15	1,491	4,207

D9 Output of Crude Steel (in thousands of metric tons)

1955–1969

	Austria[1]	Belgium	Bulgaria	Czech	Denmark	Finland	France	Germany		Ireland	Hungary	Italy
								West[8]	East			
1955	1,823	5,852	74	4,474	237	177	12,592	21,336	2,816	18	1,629	5,395
1956	2,078	6,312	130	4,882	240	194	13,398	23,189	3,046	19	1,415	5,908
1957	2,509	6,233	159	5,166	262	204	14,096	24,507	3,277	22	1,375	6,787
1958	2,393	5,980	211	5,509	255	186	14,616	22,785[8]	3,430	25	1,627	6,271
1959	2,512	6,410	230	6,136	292	232	15,219	29,435	3,615	23	1,759	6,762
1960	3,163	7,141	253	6,768	317	254	17,281	34,100	3,750	30	1,887	8,229
1961	3,101	6,960	340	7,043	323	277	17,570	33,458	3,867	28	2,053	9,124
1962	2,970	7,297	423	7,639	367	304	17,240	32,563	4,048	19	2,333	9,490
1963	2,947	7,279	461	7,600	359	326	17,556	31,597	4,051	20	2,374	10,157
1964	3,194	8,796	475	8,377	396	371	19,780	37,339	4,264	53	2,365	9,793
1965	3,221	9,229	588	8,599	412	359	19,604	36,821	4,313	53	2,520	12,660
1966	3,193	8,917	699	9,124	405	347	19,585	35,316	4,485	56	2,649	13,639
1967	3,023	9,716	1,239	10,002	401	411	19,655	36,744	4,592	65	2,739	15,890
1968	3,467	11,573	1,461	10,555	457	729	20,410	41,159	4,695	68	2,902	16,963
1969	3,926	12,837	1,515	10,802	482	967	22,511	45,316	4,824	81	3,033	16,428

1915–1946

	Lux'bg	Netherlands	Norway	Poland	Portugal	Romania	Russia[3]/ USSR	Spain	Sweden	Switz	U.K.	Yugo-slavia
1915	980	—	…	…	—	…	4,120	387	600	—	8,687	
1916	1,312	—	…	…	—	…	4,276	323	614	—	9,136	…
1917	1,087	—	…	…	—	…	3,080	470	581	—	9,873	…
1918	888	—	…	…	—	…	402	303	545	—	9,692	…
1919	369	—	…	…	—	…	199	241	491	—	8,021	…
1920	585	—	…	981[13]	—	40	194	…	437	—	9,212	23
1921	754	—	…	841[13]	—	45	220	306[18]	212	—	3,762	27
							360					
1922	1,394	—	…	1,004[13]	—	68	318	231	311	—	5,975	44
1923	1,201	—	7	1,135	—	82	615	463	271	—	8,618	51
1924	1,887	—	7	681	—	87	993	540	501	—	8,333	41
1925	2,086	—	8	782	—	101	1,868	626	475	—	7,504	53
1926	2,244	—	9	788	—	112	2,911	608	495	—	3,654	64
1927	2,471	—	11	1,244	—	130	3,592	671	499	—	9,243	73
1928	2,567	—	17	1,438	—	153	4,251	777	576	—	8,657	84
1929	2,702	—	25	1,377	—	161	4,854	1,007	694	—	9,791	98
1930	2,270	—	22	1,237	—	157	5,761	929	611	—	7,444	86
1931	2,035	—	11	1,037	—	113	5,620	648	539	—	5,286	92
1932	1,956	—	26	564	—	103	5,927	534	528	—	5,345	71
1933	1,845	—	31	883	—	145	6,889	508	630	—	7,138	90
1934	1,932	10	32	856	—	175	9,693	647	862	—	8,992	90
1935	1,837	20	52	949	—	213	12,588	595	896	—	10,017	100
1936	1,981	20	59	1,149	—	220	16,400	373	977	—	11,974	125
1937	2,510	39	70	1,468	—	239	17,730	167	1,105	—	13,192	169
1938	1,437	57	68	1,441	—	276	18,057	574	972	5	10,565	227
1939	1,762	110	68	504[14][15]	—	268	17,564	584	1,151	—	13,433	235
1940	1,042	153	69	1,168[16]	—	261	18,317[3]	804	1,145	40	13,183	258
1941	1,249	187	59	2,005	1	…	…	689	1,156	74	12,510	…
1942	1,569	157	63	2,091	1	…	…	644	1,228	82	13,150	…
1943	2,159	157	65	2,440	1	351	…	676	1,214	92	13,240	…
1944	1,269	…	50	1,950[15]	1	…	…	657	1,197	113	12,337	…
1945	259	…	37	488[17]	1	118	12,252	576	1,203	107	12,014	67
1946	1,295	137	58	1,219	1	157	13,346	641	1,203	34	12,899	202

D9 Output of Crude Steel (in thousands of metric tons)

1947–1969

	Lux'bg	Netherlands	Norway	Poland	Portugal	Romania	Russia[3]/ USSR	Spain	Sweden	Switz	U.K.	Yugo-slavia
1947	1,714	196	66	1,579	2	183	14,534	608	1,191	102	12,929	311
1948	2,453	334	74	1,955	2	353	18,639	624	1,257	120	15,116	368
1949	2,279	428	77	2,304	2	459	23,291	720	1,370	124	15,803	401
1950	2,451	490	81	2,515	2	555	27,329	815	1,437	130	16,554	428
1951	3,077	554	88	2,787	2	644	31,350	818	1,504	144	15,890	434
1952	3,002	685	98	3,179	3	698	34,492	904	1,666	156	16,681	442
1953	2,659	862	111	3,604	3	717	38,128	897	1,759	157	17,891	515
1954	2,828	929	121	3,949	2	628	41,434	1,100	1,840	150	18,817	616
1955	3,225	981	171	4,426	3	766	45,272	1,213	2,127	166	20,108	805
1956	3,456	1,051	290	5,014	4	779	48,698	1,243	2,399	171	20,990	887
1957	3,493	1,185	350	5,304	4	864	51,176	1,346	2,483	234	22,047	1,049
1958	3,379	1,438	371	5,663	4	934	54,920	1,560	2,407	244	19,880	1,119
1959	3,663	1,670	426	6,160	4	1,420	59,971	1,823	2,821	251	20,510	1,299
1960	4,084	1,942	490	6,681	5	1,806	65,294	1,919	3,189	275	24,695	1,442
1961	4,113	1,971	499	7,234	6	2,126	70,756	2,340	3,530	297	22,441	1,532
1962	4,010	2,087	488	7,684	5	2,451	78,307	2,311	3,573	318	20,820	1,596
1963	4,032	2,342	542	8,004	222	2,704	80,231	2,492	3,837	322	22,880	1,588
1964	4,559	2,646	614	8,573	250	3,039	85,038	3,150	4,447	345	26,643	1,677
1965	4,585	3,138	676	9,088	273	3,426	91,021	3,516	4,689	347	27,421	1,769
1966	4,390	3,256	730	9,850	271	3,670	96,907	3,847	4,757	428	27,686	1,867
1967	4,481	3,402	795	10,454	316	4,088	102,224	4,521	4,760	445	24,257	1,832
1968	4,834	3,707	812	11,007	313	4,751	106,537	4,971	5,069	453	26,255	1,997
1969	5,521	4,721	849	11,291	399	5,541	110,330	5,981	5,377	500	26,822	2,220

D9 Output of Crude Steel (in thousands of metric tons)

	Austria	Belgium	Bulgaria	Czech	Denmark	Finland	France	West Germany	East Germany	Hungary	Ireland	Italy
1970	4,079	12,609	1,800	11,480	473	1,167	23,773	45,040	5,053	3,108	80	17,277
1971	3,960	12,444	1,947	12,064	471	1,025	22,859	40,314	5,350	3,111	80	17,452
1972	4,070	14,532	2,121	12,727	498	1,456	24,054	43,706	5,670	3,274	77	19,815
1973	4,238	15,523	2,246	13,158	449	1,615	25,264	49,521	5,892	3,327	116	20,995
1974	4,699	16,224	2,188	13,640	535	1,656	27,023	53,232	6,165	3,467	110	23,803
1975	4,068	11,584	2,265	14,323	559	1,618	21,530	40,414	6,472	3,673	81	21,836
1976	4,477	12,145	2,460	14,693	723	1,644	23,221	42,415	6,740	3,652	58	23,446
1977	4,093	11,256	2,589	15,064	686	2,196	22,094	38,985	6,850	3,723	47	23,334
1978	4,335	12,624	2,470	15,294	864	2,333	22,841	41,253	6,976	3,877	69	24,283
1979	4,917	13,464	2,482	14,817	805	2,463	23,360	46,040	7,023	3,908	72	24,300
1980	4,624	12,344	2,565	15,225	734	2,509	23,176	43,838	7,308	3,764	2	26,501
1981	4,656	12,299	2,484	15,270	613	2,427	21,258	41,610	7,467	3,643	32	24,778
1982	4,258	10,182	2,584	14,992	560	2,414	18,402	35,880	7,168	3,702	61	24,009
1983	4,411	10,266	2,831	15,024	492	2,416	17,582	35,729	7,219	3,616	141	21,810
1984	4,870	11,414	2,878	14,831	548	2,632	19,000	39,787	7,573	3,750	166	24,110
1985	4,660	10,781	2,944	15,036	528	2,518	19,008	40,497	7,853	3,646	203	23,898
1986	4,292	9,803	2,965	15,112	632	2,586	17,865	37,134	7,967	3,713	208	22,882
1987	4,301	9,844	3,045	15,416	606	2,669	17,693	36,248	8,243	3,621	220	22,859
1988	4,560	11,240	2,875	15,380	649	2,796	19,122	41,023	8,131	3,583	200	23,760
1989	5,004	10,956	2,899	15,468	624	2,899	16,800	41,076	7,824	3,220	324	25,176
1990	4,548	11,424	2,188	14,880	610	2,840	19,020	38,436		2,730	325	25,452
1991	4,404	11,340	1,615	12,072	633	2,873	18,432	38,784		1,900	293	25,032
1992	3,936	10,332	1,551	7,349[20]	591	3,062	18,024	38,876		1,541	257	24,744
1993	4,152	10,176	1,941	6,732[20]	603	3,239	17,112	37,620		1,752	326	25,848
1994	4,398	11,331	2,491	7,075	720	3,420	18,242	40,963		1,932	288	26,212
1995	4,991	11,606	2,724	7,003	660	3,176	18,101	42,051		1,860	312	27,907
1996	5,390	10,817	2,457	6,519	732	3,301	17,633	39,792		1,878	336	24,391
1997	6,359	10,739	2,628	6,593	792	3,734	19,767	10,591		1,690	336	25,870
1998	6,525	11,425	2,237	6,061	792	3,929	20,126	10,218		1,940	355	25,782

	Lux'bg	Neth'l	Norway	Poland	Portugal	Romania	Russia[3] USSR	Spain	Sweden	Switz	U.K.	Yugo-slavia
1970	5,462	5,042	869	11,795	385	6,517	116	7,394	5,494	524	28,291	2,228
1971	5,241	5,083	885	12,738	409	6,803	121	7,794	5,263	532	24,153	2,453
1972	5,457	5,585	918	13,476	431	7,401	126	9,564	5,248	543	25,293	2,588
1973	5,294	5,625	950	14,057	497	8,161	131	10,809	5,651	584	26,594	2,676
1974	6,448	5,840	956	14,565	357	8,840	136	11,646	5,972	593	22,323	2,836
1975	4,625	4,822	907	15,004	384	9,549	141	11,115	5,613	420	20,098	2,916
1976	4,566	5,190	909	15,639	389	10,733	145	11,085	5,168	545	22,274	2,757
1977	4,329	4,927	711	17,841	341	11,457	147	11,270	3,953	656	20,411	2,377
1978	4,791	5,591	812	19,257	366	11,779	151	11,469	4,314	651	20,311	3,454
1979	4,954	5,805	911	19,218	411[19] 649	12,909	149	12,254	4,643	886	21,464	3,537
1980	4,624	5,271	866	19,485	663	13,176	148	12,553	4,231	929	11,277	3,634
1981	3,790	5,472	847	15,719	555	13,005	148	13,020	3,795	934	15,573	3,977
1982	3,510	4,354	768	14,795	602	13,055	147	13,449	3,946	835	13,704	3,840
1983	3,294	4,484	895	16,236	674	12,593	153	13,262	4,204	835	14,986	4,134
1984	3,987	5,739	920	16,533	690	14,437	154	13,379	4,674	978	15,121	4,244
1985	3,945	5,517	930	16,126	665	13,795	155	14,679	4,851	987	15,722	4,338
1986	3,705	5,283	836	17,144	717	14,276	161	11,905	4,719	1,075	14,725	4,565
1987	3,302	5,082	837	17,145	750	13,885	162	11,691	4,683	866	17,414	4,476
1988	3,661	5,518	869	16,873	832	14,314	163	11,886	4,779	988	18,950	4,584
1989	3,720	5,676	670	15,096	761	14,411	160	12,397	4,488	1,064	18,744	4,500
1990	3,480	5,408	368	13,644	717	9,761	154	12,658	4,452	1,105	16,464	3,576
1991	3,384	5,168	431	10,440	547	7,130	73[21]	12,700	4,236	955	16,632	…[22]
1992	3,072	5,437	440	9,864	749	5,376	62[21]	12,161	4,416	1,050	16,008	87[22]
1993	3,288	6,000	501	9,936	775	5,446	54[21]	12,858	4,596	1,260	16,464	…[22]
1994	3,073	6,172	456	11,112	744	5,943	48,812	13,440	4,956	1,100	17,286	…
1995	2,613	6,409	503	11,892	828	6,697	51,590	13,932	4,920	850	17,604	…
1996	2,501	6,326	511	10,668	871	6,216	49,253	12,166	4,908	750	17,992	…
1997	2,580	6,641	564	11,592	905	6,790	48,502	13,677	5,148	1,000	18,510	…
1998	2,477	6,377	639	9,916	854	6,405	43,673	14,819	5,172	1,000	11,681	…

D9 Output of Crude Steel (in thousands of metric tons)

NOTES

1. SOURCES:- The same as for table D7, except that Austria-Hungary 1880–1913 and Spain 1884–1904 are taken from I. Svennilson, *Growth and Stagnation in the European Economy* (Geneva, 1954), and Russia to 1950 is taken from G.W. Nutter, *Growth of Industrial Production in the Soviet Union* (Princeton, 1962).
2. Except as indicated in footnote 2, and except for Russia to 1913 (1st line), which includes wrought iron, the statistics in this table relate to the types of steel produced by the Bessemer, Siemens-Martin, and later-invented processes. The following statistics of the output of crucible steel and wrought iron for France for the period 1824–69 (in thousands of tons) were supplied by the Ministry of Industrial and Scientific Development:-

1824	142	1836	210	1848	283	1859	543
1825	144	1837	225	1849	252	1860	562
1826	151	1838	226	1850	257	1861	669
1827	149	1839	233	1851	268	1862	781
1828	151	1840	240	1852	320	1863	807
1829	154	1841	271	1853	474	1864	834
1830	148	1842	292	1854	535	1865	811
1831	146	1843	318	1855	579	1866	868
1832	148	1844	326	1856	588	1867	835
1833	158	1845	355	1857	586	1868	894
1834	183	1846	373	1858	553	1869	1,014
1835	210	1847	390				

The following averages of the output of steel and steel manufactures for Sweden for the period 1833–65 (in thousands of tons) were supplied by the Swedish Central Office of Statistics:-

1833	8	1846–50	11	1856–60	20
1836–40	9	1851–55	18	1861–65	28
1841–45	11				

FOOTNOTES

[1] Figures to 1918 are for the whole Austro-Hungarian Empire, Hungary's proportion growing from about 20 per cent in 1880 to about 30 per cent in 1913. After 1918 the figures are for the Republic.

[2] Previous figures are of Bessemer steel only.

[3] Figures to 1913 (1st line) are for the whole Russian Empire except Finland. From 1913 (2nd line) to 1940 they apply to the 1923 territory of the U.S.S.R. Later figures are for the post-Second World War territory.

[4] This break occurs on a change of source (see note 1 to table E8).

[5] This is also included in the Austro-Hungarian output.

[6] From 1938 to 1944 Teschen is excluded.

[7] Up to 1918 the parts of Alsace-Lorraine ceded to Germany in 1871 are included in Germany rather than in France. Subsequently they are included in France.

[8] From 1921 to 1934 and from 1946 to 1958 Saarland is excluded. Its output during these periods was as follows (in thousands of tons):-

1921	987	1928	2,073	1946	291	1953	2,684
1922	1,313	1929	2,209	1947	708	1954	2,805
1923	1,064	1930	1,935	1948	1,228	1955	3,165
1924	1,485	1931	1,538	1949	1,757	1956	3,374
1925	1,582	1932	1,463	1950	1,898	1957	3,439
1926	1,737	1933	1,676	1951	2,603	1958	3,460
1927	1,895	1934	1,950	1952	2,823		

[9] In July 1922 eastern Upper Silesia was transferred from Germany to Poland.

[10] For 1939–44 includes Sudetenland, and for 1940–44 parts of Poland also.

[11] Figures to 1918 apply to the boundaries of 1971. For 1919–45 they apply to the boundaries of 1924, and from 1946 to the boundaries of 1954.

[12] Previous figures do not include castings.

[13] It is not clear whether or not the output of eastern Upper Silesia prior to July 1922 is included here.

[14] First half-year only.

[15] For 1940–44 includes Teschen, which was previously and subsequently part of Czechoslovakia. From 1945 the figures apply to the postwar territory.

[16] Excluding central Poland.

[17] February–December only.

[18] Previously rolled iron and steel.

[19] Previously steel ingots only.

[20] Czech Republic. Slovakia: 4,498 (1992); 3,922 (1993).

D9 Output of Crude Steel (in thousands of metric tons)

[21] Russian Federation. Ex. USSR as follows.

Kazakhstan	1991	6
	1992	6
	1993	4
	1994	3
	1995	3
	1996	3
	1997	4
	1998	4
Ukraine	1991	45
	1992	42
	1993	33
	1994	25
	1995	23
	1996	23
	1997	26
	1998	25

[22] Yugoslavia. Ex. Yugoslavia as follows.

Croatia	1991	214
	1992	102
	1993	74
	1994	63
	1995	45
	1996	46
	1997	70
	1998	6
Macedonia	1991	209
	1992	162
	1993	133
	1994	67
	1995	31
	1996	21
	1997	27
	1998	45
Slovenia	1991	275
	1992	392
	1993	349
	1994	424
	1995	408
	1996	94
	1997	99
	1998	98

D10 OUTPUT OF ALUMINIUM (in thousands of metric tons)

1890–1917   **1918–1944**

	France	Germany	Italy	Norway	U.K.		France	Germany	Italy	Norway	U.K.
1890	...[2]	...	...	...	...	1918	12	...	1.7	...	...
1891	...	...	...	...	...	1919	10	...	1.7	...	...
1892	0.1	...	...	...	...						
1893	0.1	...	...	...	...	1920	12	19	1.2	...	8.1
1894	0.3	...	...	...	...	1921	8	19	0.7	...	5.1
						1922	7	16	0.8	...	7.1
1895	0.4	...	...	...	...	1923	14	16	1.5	13	9.1
1896	0.4	...	...	...	...	1924	16	19	2.1	20	8.1
1897	0.5	...	...	...	...						
1898	0.6	...	...	...	...	1925	18	26	1.9	21	9.7
1899	0.8	...	...	...	...	1926	24	31	1.9	24	3.1
						1927	25	28	2.5	21	9.7
1900	1.0	...	...	...	...	1928	26	32	3.5	25	9.7
1901	1.2	...	...	...	...	1929	29	33	7.4	29	8.1
1902	1.4	...	...	...	...						
1903	1.6	...	...	...	...	1930	25	31	8.0	27	13
1904	1.6	...	...	...	...	1931	18	27	11	21	14
						1932	14	19	13	18	10
1905	1.9	...	...	...	...	1933	14	19	12	15	11
1906	3.4	...	...	...	...	1934	15	37	13	15	13
1907	4.7	...	0.3	...	...						
1908	4.7	...	0.6	...	...	1935	22	71	14	15	15
1909	6.1	...	0.8	...	...	1936	30	98	16	15	16
						1937	35	128[3]	23	23	19
1910	6.4	...	0.8	...	...	1938	42	166	26	29	23
1911	7.4	...	0.8	...	...	1939	53	199	34	31	25
1912	10	...	0.8	...	...						
1913	13	0.8	0.9	...	7.6	1940	60	211	39	28	19
1914	10	...	0.9	...	...	1941	64	234	48	18	23
						1942	45	264	44	20	48
1915	6	...	0.9	...	...	1943	46	250	46	24	57
1916	10	...	1.1	...	...	1944	26	244[3]	17	20	36
1917	11	...	1.7	...	...						

1945–1964

	France	West Germany	Italy	Norway	Poland	U.K.
1945	37	...	43[4]	5	...	32
1946	48	...	11	17	...	32
1947	53	...	25	22	...	29
1948	64	...	33	31	...	30
1949	54	29	26	36	...	30
1950	61	28	37	47	...	30
1951	90	74	49	52	...	28
1952	106	100	52	53	...	28
1953	113	107	55	56	...	31
1954	120	129	58	64	...	32
1955	129	137	62	75	20	25
1956	150	147	63	99	...	28
1957	160	154	77	104	...	30
1958	169	137	74	126	...	27
1959	173	151	75	148	...	25
1960	238	169	84	168	26	29
1961	279	173	83	175	48	33
1962	294	178	81	209	48	35
1963	298	209	91	219	47	31
1964	316	220	116	268	48	32

D10 Output of Aluminium[1] (in thousands of metric tons)

	France	West Germany	Italy	Norway	Poland	U.K.
1965	341	238	124	276	47	36
1966	364	244	129	330	55	37
1967	361	253	128	361	92	39
1968	366	257	142	468	93	38
1969	372	263	145	502	97	34
1970	381	309	146	522	99	40
1971	384	427	136	530	119	100
1972	394	448	149	557	102	171
1973	359	533	184	620	102	252
1974	393	689	212	648	102	293
1975	383	678	190	595	103	308
1976	385	697	206	618	103	334
1977	400	742	260	623	104	350
1978	391	740	271	639	100	346
1979	395	742	269	664	97	359
1980	432	731	271	653	95	374
1981	436	729	274	634	66	339
1982	390	724	233	637	43	241
1983	361	743	196	713	44	252
1984	342	777	230	781	46	288
1985	368	745	224	740	47	275
1986	386	765	243	758	47	276
1987	382	738	233	852	47	294
1988	328	744	226	838	48	300
1989	329	742	220	867	48	297
1990	325	720	232	...	46	290
1991	255	690[5]	218	...	46	294
1992	414	603[5]	161	...	44	244
1993	425	552[5]	156	...	47	240
1994	709	559	551	906	50	319
1995	618	430	590	919	56	456
1996	617	358	561	923	52	468
1997	641	349	631	977	54	497
1998	669	375	690	1,058	54	492

NOTES

1. SOURCES:- The official publications noted on p.xv supplemented (for Germany) by the League of Nations *Statistical Yearbooks*.
2. Secondary production has, in recent years, been much more important than primary production in the United Kingdom. Figures of this for 1942–80 can be found in B.R. Mitchell *British Historical Statistics* (Cambridge, 1988).

FOOTNOTES

[1] Primary production, excluding metal derived from scrap.
[2] Output began in 1862, but did not exceed 15 tons per year until 1890.
[3] Figures for 1938–44 include Austria and the annexed territories in the East.
[4] Subsequent figures are for the boundaries of 1954.
[5] Germany

D11 IMPORTS AND EXPORTS OF COAL BY MAIN SURPLUS AND DEFICIENT COUNTRIES (in thousands of metric tons)

Key:- I = Import; E = Exports; NI = Net Imports

1827–1869

	Austria[1]		Belgium		Denmark[10]	Finland	France	
	I	E[2]	I[4]	E[4]	I[5]	I	I[5]	E[5]
1827	...	...	...	...	...	...	542	5
1828	...	...	...	...	...	...	584	5
1829	...	...	...	...	...	...	554	6
1830	...	...	...	...	...	...	637	6
1831	...	...	3	470	...	...	548	7
1832	...	...	12	319	...	...	576	22
1833	...	...	12	576	...	...	702	23
1834	...	...	24	648	...	...	747	23
1835	...	...	16	696	...	...	803	21
1836	...	...	22	774	...	...	999	26
1837	...	...	28	789	...	...	1,144	34
1838	...	...	35	776	...	...	1,227	35
1839	...	...	28	746	...	...	1,219	33
1840	...	...	30	779	...	...	1,291	37
1841	...	...	28	1,015	...	...	1,619	49
1842	29	21	35	1,015	...	...	1,669	58
1843	24	36	31	1,086	51	...	1,663	62
1844	28	39	11	1,243	60	...	1,756	52
1845	33	44	9	1,543	79	...	2,207	66
1846	36	7	11	1,356	85	...	2,194	54
1847	40	53	10	1,827	65	...	2,549	53
1848	36	40	10	1,461	118	...	2,144	49
1849	...	...	11	1,665	102	...	2,394	38
1850	...	...	9	1,987	128	...	2,833	42
1851	85	59	10	2,057	118	...	2,927	35
1852	121	58	8	2,104	126	...	3,096	41
1853	179[3]	72[3]	13	2,332	136	...	3,530	46
1854	64	109	53	2,626	173	...	4,130	100
1855	63	129	69	2,974	171	...	4,952	112
1856	90	138	89	2,866	245	...	5,070	100
1857	156	117	146	2,887	250	...	5,368	120
1858	208	189	108	3,091	185	...	5,672	131
1859	222[1]	198[7]	110	3,145	236	...	5,759	178
1860	234[1]	279[1]	97	3,450	205	14	6,160	200
1861	268	294	93	3,379	295	27	6,290	283
1862	317	370	79	3,289	256	27	6,218	260
1863	343	323	73	3,328	285	29	6,120	315
1864	344	397	67	3,783	244	18	6,633	343
1865	367[1]	386[1]	75	4,071	383	23	7,213	343
1866	287	481	184	4,520	353	26	8,230	406
1867	394	731	444	4,081	345	23	7,983	356
1868	587	809	253	4,295	409	33	7,975	394
1869	687	821	223	4,269	356	26	8,304	381

D11   Imports and Exports of Coal by Main Surplus and Deficient Countries (in thousands of metric tons)

	Greece I	Italy I[5]	Neth'l NI[5]	Norway I[5]	Russia I[7]	Spain I	Sweden I[4]	Switz I[4]	U.K. E
1816	...	...	...	...	...	...	...	...	242
1817	...	...	...	...	...	...	...	...	257
1818	...	...	...	...	...	...	...	...	276
1819	...	...	...	...	...	...	...	...	242
1820	...	...	...	...	...	...	...	...	255
1821	...	...	...	...	...	...	...	...	267
1822	...	...	...	...	...	...	...	...	292
1823	...	...	...	...	...	...	...	...	258
1824	...	...	...	...	...	...	...	...	287
1825	...	...	...	...	...	...	...	...	318
1826	...	...	...	...	...	...	...	...	354
1827	...	...	...	...	...	...	...	...	375
1828	...	...	...	...	...	...	...	...	364
1829	...	...	...	4	...	...	...	...	377
1830	...	...	...	3	...	1	...	...	512
1831	...	...	...	2	...	1	...	...	519
1832	...	...	...	...	...	1	...	...	597[8]
1833	...	...	...	...	...	2	...	...	639
1834	...	...	...	...	...	2	...	...	620
1835	...	...	...	6	...	2	...	...	741
1836	...	...	...	7	...	8	...	...	926
1837	...	...	...	9	...	14	...	...	1,124
1838	...	...	...	19	...	9	...	...	1,324
1839	...	...	...	15	...	18	...	...	1,455
1840	...	...	...	17	...	14	15	...	1,618
1841	...	...	...	22	...	38	15	...	1,861
1842	...	...	...	27	...	54	30	...	2,007
1843	...	...	...	24	...	65	22	...	1,849
1844	...	...	...	25	...	76	22	...	1,725
1845	...	...	...	37	...	103	33	...	2,482
1846	...	...	1,082	37	...	106	31	...	2,428
1847	...	...	1,458	39	...	98	30	...	2,028
1848	...	...	1,375	50	...	111	52	...	2,742
1849	...	...	1,256	40	...	123	58	...	2,775
1850	...	...	1,182	52	...	186	76	...	3,264
1851	...	...	1,175	56	...	192	82	...	3,352
1852	...	...	1,419	56	...	202	81	...	3,535
1853	...	...	1,571	62	...	246	86	...	3,818
1854	...	...	2,241	89	...	207	105	...	4,186
1855	...	...	1,752	97	...	208	119	...	4,839
1856	...	...	1,780	114	...	285	180	...	5,728
1857	...	...	1,589	115	...	321	231	...	6,587
1858	...	...	1,398	101	...	337	193	55	6,393
1859	...	...	1,328	123	...	433	260	78	6,893
1860	...	...	1,808	126	...	453	259	114	7,163
1861	...	240	1,660	162	...	472	336	160	7,682
1862	...	446	2,138[6]	140	...	515	343	177	8,140
1863	...	390	1,536	137	...	566	343	177	8,133
1864	...	555	1,273	180	...	543	363	216	8,674
1865	...	456	1,443	178	...	473	375	263	9,003
1866	...	524	1,579	195	650	522	385	260	9,800
1867	64	516	1,510	233	803	507	355	254	10,214
1868	32	580	1,580	237	577	522	416	290	10,666
1869	73	650	1,630	207	803	510	363	280	10,397

D11   Imports and Exports of Coal by Main Surplus and Deficient Countries (in thousands of metric tons)

1870–1919

	Austria		Belgium		Bulgaria	Denmark[10]	Finland	France	
	I	E	I[4]	E[4]	I[4]	I[5]	I	I[5]	E[5]
1870	927	925	229	3,753	...	431	33	6,045[11]	395[11]
1871	1,364	1,047	204	4,186	...	448	41	5,950	329
1872	1,588	1,167	219	5,357	...	429	33	7,709	577
1873	1,785	1,681	696	4,960	...	433	31	8,029	695
1874	1,627	2,161	464	4,501	...	468	45	7,433	747
1875	1,628	2,703	725	4,710	...	550	30	8,282	672
1876	1,576	2,750	833	4,399	...	581	33	8,221	727
1877	1,499	2,755	678	4,091	...	574	40	7,882	614
1878	1,665	2,921	721	4,466	...	545	46	8,201	594
1879	[2,272][4]	[3,278][4]	740	4,832	...	616	27	8,880	539
1880	2,204	3,700	934	5,375	...	702	34	9,941	603
1881	2,148	3,643	1,040	5,392	...	743	33	10,222	601
1882	2,146	3,469	1,059	5,387	...	797	41	10,868	457
1883	2,368	4,047	1,302	5,438	...	916	38	11,707	510
1884	2,478	4,103	1,257	5,473	...	912	49	11,678	500
1885	2,508	4,102	1,260	5,187	...	955	76	10,917	506
1886	2,664[9]	4,489[9]	1,025	5,181	...	915	43	10,381	610
	2,723	4,540							
1887	2,885	4,783	1,036	5,518	...	939	42	10,565	595
1888	3,271	6,162	1,063	5,528	...	1,056	37	10,551	629
1889	3,423	6,542	1,025	5,817	...	1,128	51	9,981	943
1890	3,628	7,505	1,787	5,914	...	1,081	69	11,603	941
1891	3,937	7,687	1,766	6,043	...	1,163	71	11,690	906
1892	3,625	7,490	1,684	5,882	...	1,157	61	11,557	896
1893	4,171	7,520	1,583	6,281	...	1,130	60	11,401	898
1894	4,502	7,643	1,707	5,992	...	1,282	71	11,644	801
1895	5,052	7,903	1,896	5,992	...	1,328	74	11,510	963
1896	5,664	8,338	1,955	5,973	...	1,744[10]	95	11,594	904
						1,626			
1897	5,674	8,956	2,288	5,973	...	1,743	176	11,975	1,021
1898	6,022	9,371	2,386	6,124	...	1,810	164	11,917	1,101
1899	5,881	9,795	3,152	6,104	...	1,979	255	13,370	1,026
1900	6,931	8,942	3,601	6,939	17	1,940	204	16,177	927
1901	6,461	9,129	3,102	6,363	27	2,020	134	15,441	719
1902	6,342	8,815	3,497	6,574	20	2,074	125	15,132	843
1903	6,457	9,063	3,908	6,388	28	2,159	167	14,802	959
1904	6,768	8,758	4,085	6,485	36	2,329	171	14,562	1,207
1905	7,008	9,227	4,659	6,161	42	2,265	189	14,007	1,858
1906	8,009	9,596	5,858	6,288	44	2,466	203	18,742	1,448
1907	10,394	10,049	5,801	6,020	77	2,198	302	19,431	1,224
1908	17,920	11,120	5,876	6,161	134	2,727	496	19,166	1,162
1909	10,877	9,546	6,338	6,651	112	3,017	447	20,023	1,256
1910	18,593	10,952	7,211	6,551	114	2,771	362	19,892	1,370
1911	11,611	7,974	8,402	6,826	184	2,951	456	21,445	1,432
1912	12,099	8,447	9,524	6,697	158	3,499	519	20,704	1,952
1913	14,656	8,125	10,451	6,738	108	3,590	586	25,323	1,500
1914	10,762	6,263	...	...	219	3,618	229	18,057	737
1915	...	...	...	...	...	3,890	7	19,735	114
1916	...	...	...	...	6	3,705	30	20,422	117
1917	...	...	...	...	23	2,125	16	17,453	126
1918	...	...	...	...	180	2,228	27	16,835[11]	1,851[11]
1919	...	...	...	...	1	2,323	43	22,100	523

D11 Imports and Exports of Coal by Main Surplus and Deficient Countries (in thousands of metric tons)

1870–1919

	Germany		Greece	Italy	Netherlands	Norway
	I[4]	E[4]	I	I[5]	NI[5]	I[5]
1870	...	...	76	942	1,810	235
1871	...	...	112	791	1,820	227
1872	2,268	3,820	66	1,037	1,950	243
1873	1,456	4,022	73	960	1,860	242
1874	1,809	4,197	56	1,031	1,710	301
1875	1,876	4,523	60	1,060	1,960	380
1876	2,105	5,287	...	1,454	2,260	334
1877	2,026	5,009	...	1,330	2,300	450
1878	1,931	5,825	...	1,325	2,440	404
1879	1,894	6,012	...	1,524	2,630	423
1880	2,059[14]	7,236	...	1,738	2,910	462
	5,140					
1881	5,017	7,458	...	2,073	2,921	477
1882	5,112	7,632	...	2,180	2,950	524
1883	5,500	8,705	...	2,351	3,269	564
1884	5,763	8,817	...	2,605	3,262	575
1885	6,024	8,956	...	2,957	3,416	661
1886	6,645	8,655	...	2,927	3,448	644
1887	7,099	8,781	...	3,583	3,496	623
1888	8,464	9,460	...	3,873	3,898	718
1889	10,207	8,847	...	3,999	3,784	820
1890	10,671	9,145	...	4,355	3,647	767
1891	11,839	9,536	...	3,917	4,256	891
1892	11,138	8,971	139	3,878	4,029	903
1893	11,370	9,677	120	3,724	4,069	900
1894	11,674	9,739	122	4,696	4,107	1,061
1895	12,298	10,361	117	4,305	4,081	1,121
1896	13,115	11,599	141	4,081	4,395	1,136
1897	14,183	12,390	133	4,260	4,604	1,230
1898	14,270	13,989	170	4,432	4,530	1,233
1899	14,837	13,943	89	4,860	4,605	1,478
1900	15,344	15,276	155	4,947	5,001	1,520
1901	14,406	15,266	155	4,839	4,873	1,413
1902	14,308	16,101	124	5,406	4,771	1,547
1903	14,729	17,390	149	5,547	5,054	1,529
1904	14,968	17,997	131	5,905	5,417	1,508
1905	17,345	18,157	102	6,474	5,541	1,513
1906	...[12]	19,551[12]	95	7,673	6,011	1,544
1907	22,685	20,061	159	8,300	6,049	1,749
1908	20,244	21,191	273	8,452	5,996	2,073
1909	20,365	23,351	210	9,304	6,158	2,096
1910	18,594	24,257	270	9,339	6,331	2,159
1911	17,983	27,406	341	9,596	6,613	2,187
1912	17,646	31,145	...	10,057	7,433	2,474
1913	17,527	34,598	504[15]	10,834	8,264	2,483
1914	...	...	...	9,759	7,334	2,764
1915	...	...	...	8,369	6,712	3,095
1916	...	...	...	8,065	5,610	2,833
1917	...	...	...	5,038	...	1,226
1918	...[13]	...[13]	...	5,841	1,326	1,574
1919	...	...	...	6,227	3,506	1,791

D11 Imports and Exports of Coal by Main Surplus and Deficient Countries (in thousands of metric tons)

1870–1919

	Portugal I[5]	Romania I	Russia/U.S.S.R[7] I	Russia/U.S.S.R[7] E	Spain I	Sweden[4] I	Switz I	UK E
1870	...	...	845	...	624	465	321	11,341
1871	...	...	1,238	...	599	495	393	12,404
1872	182	...	1,062	...	641	601	459	12,916
1873	260	...	833	...	624	599	436	12,272
1874	186	...	1,037	...	588	643	440	13,596
1875	426	...	1,041	...	702	788	465	14,203
1876	418	...	1,498	...	770	832	542	15,942
1877	239	...	1,481	...	836	870	514	15,120
1878	228	...	1,821	...	829	723	487	15,240
1879	253	...	1,486	...	841	723	521	15,993
1880	317	...	1,922	...	938	959	603	18,178
1881	322	...	1,791	...	1,023	908	559	19,061
1882	381	62	1,730	...	1,157	1,033	619	20,246
1883	405	131	2,267	...	1,297	1,049	690	22,019
1884	428	144	1,913[7] / 1,992	...	1,357	1,157	702	22,713
1885	394	139[9]	1,823	...	1,339	1,253	740	23,074
1886	433	155	1,867	...	1,421	1,224	749	22,462
1887	446	170	1,575	...	1,408	1,244	813	23,632
1888	482	203	1,742	...	1,502	1,414	827	26,043
1889	559	195	2,081	...	1,615	1,643	914	27,946
1890	600	241	1,748	...	1,718	1,657	994[14] / 1,116	29,199
1891	622	335	1,748	...	1,863	1,757	1,276	29,970
1892	604	301	1,669	...	1,870	1,746	1,252	29,514
1893	529	341	2,006	...	1,747	1,747	1,024	28,153
1894	632	312	2,265	...	1,841	1,984	1,290	32,266
1895	599	313	2,246	...	1,725	1,968	1,385	32,224
1896	615	327	2,351	...	1,883	2,050	1,514	33,477
1897	652	367	2,529	...	1,853	2,300	1,598	35,921
1898	745	414	2,995	...	1,441	2,458	1,714	35,621
1899	764	319	4,481	...	1,783	3,135	1,851	41,841
1900	883	158	4,500	...	1,992	3,130	2,057	44,796
1901	861	221	3,671	...	2,163	2,870	1,871	42,549
1902	950	180	3,378	...	2,309	2,984	1,888	43,852
1903	918	177	3,500	...	2,266	3,288	2,052	45,671
1904	939	168	3,890	...	2,307	3,481	2,160	46,998
1905	914	170	4,145	...	2,352	3,411	2,267	48,239
1906	1,060	184	4,394	...	2,427	3,856	2,511	56,492
1907	1,158	346	4,093	...	2,136	4,402	2,924	64,622
1908	1,156	281	4,416	...	2,219	4,693	2,921	63,551
1909	1,173	228	4,363	...	2,353	4,341	2,947	64,089
1910	1,191	240	4,709	...	2,315	4,453	2,838	63,081
1911	1,148	253	5,303	...	2,372	4,288	3,145	65,636
1912	1,337	...	6,088[7] / 5,305	...	2,678[9]	4,774	3,197	65,478
1913	1,392	419	7,748	...	3,098	5,375	3,387	74,578
1914	1,211	...	4,552	...	2,876	5,077	3,111	59,987
1915	1,071	...	658	...	1,905	5,056	3,312	44,234
1916	950	...	948	...	2,151	5,333	3,152	38,967
1917	402	...	753	...	1,167	2,024	2,270	35,558
1918	215	...	17	...	528	2,486	2,142	32,263
1919	647	...	...	...	901	2,210	1,736	35,816

D11   Imports and Exports of Coal by Main Surplus and Deficient Countries (in thousands of metric tons)

	Austria[1]	Belgium		Bulgaria	Czechoslovakia		Denmark[10]	Finland	France	
	I	I[4]	E[4]	I	I[4]	E[4]	I[5]	I	I[5]	E[5]
1920	3,995[14]	2,184	2,056	1	1,299	4,289	2,711	90	32,516	35
1921	5,749	6,160	7,666	4	1,097	6,258	2,561	87	25,336	2,171
1922	5,085	5,623	4,585	8	626	4,990	3,638	243	32,211	2,655
1923	5,023	9,089	3,634	14	919	4,606	3,967	525	33,451	2,929
1924	5,765	10,041	3,377	23	1,068	5,129	4,651[10] 4,651	619	34,785	2,775
1925	5,272	11,498	3,997	18	1,775	4,660	4,041	612	30,460	2,801
1926	5,125	10,633	5,328	12	1,737	6,298	3,945	567	29,109	3,006
1927	5,601	12,569	4,481	7	2,015	5,722	5,023	1,034	30,422	2,675
1928	5,712	12,098	5,868	7	2,827	5,593	4,588	1,076	29,985	3,202
1929	6,658	15,295	5,271	9	2,861	5,961	5,552	1,170	36,575	4,080
1930	4,823	13,809	5,467	9	2,247	4,756	5,059	917	36,420	2,911
1931	4,625	12,279	7,270	4	2,239	4,146	5,303	1,068	32,714	2,831
1932	3,508	9,190	5,039	4	1,959	3,301	4,983	1,060	25,464	2,086
1933	3,118	7,463	4,975	4	1,399	3,353	4,937	1,137	25,619	1,921
1934	3,083	7,290	5,177	3	1,479	3,703	5,180	1,298	24,535	1,885
1935	3,028	6,490	5,647	4	1,506	3,416	5,437	1,222	22,002	1,528
1936	2,925	6,916	6,511	3	1,370	3,513	5,838[10] 5,800	1,724	22,907	1,333
1937	3,393	9,939	5,636	3	1,443	5,130	6,016	2,232	30,890	1,034
1938	...	6,899	6,576	4	1,921	...	5,396	1,778	22,724	1,215
1939	...	...	...	3	...	...	6,015	1,421	18,078	1,185
1940	...	...	...	1	...	...	4,117	690	8,020	304
1941	...	...	...	4	...	...	3,700	1,064	2,120	700
1942	...	...	...	...	...	...	2,995	901	3,137	702
1943	...	...	...	...	...	...	3,535	1,308	4,758	19
1944	...	...	...	...	...	...	3,737	905	3,682	56
1945	...	...	...	...	...	...	1,499	111	5,326	53
1946	2,367	...	...	...	...	...	3,836	938	10,973	409
1947	3,831	7,557	2,082	...	1,049	1,604	4,296	1,499	17,195	460
1948	5,872	5,873	1,551	...	2,221	2,936	3,582	2,415	21,020	415
1949	6,212	3,687	1,796	...[26]	3,335	3,583	4,919	1,200	22,575	1,160
1950	5,678	3,594	3,154	36	3,966	3,461	6,676	1,929	14,861	2,401
1951	6,039	5,844	2,527	36	4,313	2,387	6,114	2,384	20,098	2,093
1952	5,057	5,465	3,578	41	4,063	2,706	6,250	2,601	20,110	1,718
1953	4,550	5,702	5,031	43	4,785	2,588	6,302	2,026	16,231	2,564
1954	5,960	7,410	6,577	45	4,406	2,530	6,788	2,319	17,044	3,072
1955	5,300	7,843	8,339	49	4,060	2,924	7,673	2,642	18,179	6,440
1956	5,646	9,185	6,008	40	3,451	3,085	5,805	2,708	24,382	2,551
1957	6,049	9,863	5,384	142	2,292	3,475	4,609	3,085	26,671	2,421
1958	6,166	9,726	3,860	174	2,576	3,817	4,439	2,484	21,306	2,074
1959	4,627	9,154	3,049	289	2,355	4,115	4,139	2,862	17,588[5] 16,314	1,735[5] 1,691
1960	5,295	8,645	3,166	320	2,402	4,955	5,478	3,166	15,979	1,613
1961	4,815	8,809	3,560	812	3,355	5,301	5,159	3,047	16,778	1,505
1962	5,125	9,359	3,477	1,219	4,023	5,501	5,508	2,985	16,508	1,557
1963	5,778	12,015	3,144	1,568	4,346	5,883	5,594	2,543	22,813	1,176
1964	5,465	11,837	2,980	2,293	5,044	5,886	5,119	3,307	19,713	1,103
1965	5,292	11,550	2,490	2,820	4,538	5,398	4,486	3,349	17,150	1,092
1966	4,962	10,425	1,741	3,183	4,030	5,617	4,657	2,772	15,896	989
1967	4,735	10,110	2,033	3,524	4,162	5,632	4,341	2,792	15,449	925
1968	4,885	11,714	1,595	3,594	4,623	5,860	4,709	2,754	15,763	1,088
1969	4,752	12,403	1,425	4,288	4,624	6,488	4,251	3,224	16,376	2,047
1970	5,515	13,359	1,191	5,308	4,569	6,720	3,812	4,064	17,600	2,095
1971	4,325	10,274	1,124	6,230	5,447	6,895	2,451	3,645	16,830	1,511
1972	4,700	10,795	1,180	6,113	5,535	6,982	2,357	3,385	15,171	1,608
1973	4,804	12,104	1,102	6,122	5,299	7,318	3,196	3,804	16,467	1,958
1974	5,113	14,837	1,019	6,301	5,168	7,627	3,831	4,916	21,325	1,775

D11 Imports and Exports of Coal by Main Surplus and Deficient Countries (in thousands of metric tons)

	Germany		E.Germany	Greece	Hungary		Italy	S.Ireland	Neth'l	Norway
	I	E[4]	I[5]	I	I[5]	E[5]	I[5]	I	NI	I[5]
1920	2,704[13]	7,305[13]	...	212	...	...	5,620	...	3,125	1,827
1921	3,580[13]	...[13]	...	244	603	191	7,471	...	3,977	1,066
1922	14,614[13]	5,062[13]	...	227	788	309	8,834	...	4,822	2,070
1923	26,808[17]	1,209[17]	...	321	838	267	9,134	...	3,916	2,165
1924	15,280[17]	2,795[17]	...	461	1,133	271	11,170	2,521	4,482	2,444
1925	9,903	13,646	...	630	1,189	512	10,513	2,275	4,187	2,375
1926	4,882	38,035	...	551	1,219	677	12,258	1,784	2,592	1,970
1927	7,894	26,878	...	714	1,513	309	14,059	2,537	3,191	2,678
1928	10,176	23,895	...	695	1,661	288	12,698	2,444	2,269	2,607
1929	10,691	26,769	...	785	1,860	409	14,603	2,501	2,834	2,976
1930	9,150	24,383	...	827	1,237	385	12,937	2,540	1,892[21]	2,737
									3,710	
1931	7,568	23,123	...	778	869	381	11,094	2,452	2,623	2,424
1932	5,662	18,312	...	734	384	346	8,778	2,341	1,655	2,538
1933	5,738	18,444	...	596	330	232	9,562	2,302	684	2,635
1934	6,639[13]	21,937[13]	...	757	419	179	12,737	2,375	1,006	2,669
1935	5,930	26,774	...	744	367	214	14,590	2,281	473	2,810
1936	6,104	29,493	...	869	465	207	9,264	2,514	414	3,040
1937	6,651	39,659	...	895	580	253	12,927	2,604	89	3,462
1938	6,412	30,769	...	897	524	287	12,140	2,524	373	2,929
1939	...	...	...	...	...	...	11,276	2,922	1,936	3,561
1940	...	...	...	...	...	...	12,530	2,802	...	1,853
1941	...	...	...	...	...	...	11,582	1,512	...	1,361
1942	...	...	...	...	...	...	10,793	1,065	...	1,427
1943	...	...	...	...	...	...	...	1,032	...	1,709
1944	...	...	...	...	...	...	...	746	...	1,420
	West Germany[18]									
1945	...	...	...	...	...	...	...	935	...	1,124
1946	...	5,145	...	...	...	...	5,713	1,297	2,740	1,826
1947	...	5,974	...	...	...	...	9,154	1,533	3,285	2,380
1948	1,957	9,453	...	247	...	...	8,610	1,724	2,788	2,015
1949	3,099[18]	13,189[18]	...	290	940	120	8,952	1,658	3,340	1,745
1950	5,089	15,740	9,038	284	944[20]	47	8,597	1,994	3,891	1,832
					899					
1951	10,148	13,665	8,726	382	944	126	11,036	2,203	4,540	1,790
1952	12,407	12,700	9,865	292	1,427	211	9,484	1,843	4,538	1,174
1953	10,103	14,168	12,351	283	1,673	428	9,320	1,773	4,288	1,166
1954	9,121	17,003	13,503	255	2,017	698	9,195	1,831	5,297	1,018
1955	16,931	13,186	13,086	323	1,996	527	10,403	1,947	5,761	1,285
1956	19,757	12,844	12,437	236	1,895	217	10,820	1,518	−685	1,469
1957	22,567	13,573	12,592	282	3,525	31	11,760	1,275	6,375	1,133
1958	17,210[13]	12,614	15,098	250	2,276	94	9,323	1,401	4,519	966
1959	9,576	16,565[13]	16,535	192	2,245	58	8,288	1,616	3,043	861
1960	8,072	19,515	16,086	235	2,402	63	10,417	1,687	3,057	1,040
1961	8,281	19,002	16,731	236	2,614	137	10,344	1,810	2,678	990
1962	9,029	19,857	17,574	213	2,623	143	11,152	1,506	4,670	927
1963	9,986	18,551	17,866	287	3,703	278	11,780	1,474	5,642	1,051
1964	8,659	15,804	19,169	302	4,366	189	10,935	1,323	4,795	1,044
1965	8,451	14,919	17,887	430	3,687	184	11,295	1,307	2,422	1,045
1966	8,156	17,248	17,477	398	2,434	196	12,550	1,353	2,654	1,114
1967	7,998	18,773	14,885[19]	238	2,793	218	11,134	1,278	2,834	1,055
			11,153							
1968	7,079	21,466	9,127	286	2,664	241	11,132	1,245	3,766	1,234
1969	7,959	18,693	9,527	370	2,751	335	11,937	1,167	3,695	1,283
1970	10,241	16,874	11,315	448	3,245	93	12,224	1,230	2,836	1,309
1971	8,574	15,011	11,018	398	3,219	105	11,856	1,052	1,937	1,088
1972	8,233	13,888	10,678	531	2,888	135	11,044	910	1,400	944
1973	8,360	14,673	11,540	696	2,667	141	11,011	861	2,185	997
1974	7,200	18,363	10,242	887	2,632	110	12,550	901	3,435[28]	1,260

D11 Imports and Exports of Coal by Main Surplus and Deficient Countries (in thousands of metric tons)

1920–1974

	Poland		Portugal	Romania	Russia/U.S.S.R.[7]		Spain	Sweden[4]	Switz	UK[29]	Yugo-slavia
	I[5]	E[5]	I[4]	I	I	E	I	I	I	E	I[4]
1920	2,691	147	600	...	37	—	369	3,172	2,647	25,332	...
1921	3,525[22]	335[22]	643	...	251	—	1,080	1,693	1,634	25,057	...
1922	2,477	5,439	934	40	605[24]	—	1,644	3,156	2,220	65,228	316
1923	267	12,913	794	195	496[24]	—	1,196	3,879	2,783	80,734	308
1924	389	11,416	939	228	319[24]	—	1,430	4,715	2,602	62,640	334
1925	243	8,158	988	273	48[24]	—	1,667	4,240	2,739	51,632	546
1926	122	14,437	879	201	306[24]	—	1,013	3,967	2,707	20,927	441
1927	237	11,226	1,076	187	472[24]	—	2,005	5,837	3,045	51,970	449
1928	248	13,035	1,146	159	...	—	1,888	5,175	3,029	50,854	531
1929	315	14,071	1,139	238	66	1,400	2,084	6,259	3,462	61,234	664
1930	164	12,697	1,236	168	64	1,900	1,681	5,970	3,148	55,755	585
1931	142	14,073	1,100	116	107	1,700	1,200	5,974	3,290	43,436	450
1932	147	10,425	916	105	53	1,800	918	5,826	3,280	39,523	354
1933	174	9,274	1,099	68	15	1,800	798	6,054	3,165	39,695	292
1934	150	10,251	1,110	79	26	2,200	1,125	6,747	3,118	40,296	343
1935	173	9,214	1,161	59	36	2,200	1,155	7,000	3,088	39,335	430
1936	169	8,720	1,080	62	...	1,800	...	7,694	3,178	35,073	305
1937	95	11,372	1,318	77	...	1,300	...	8,938	3,486	40,985	413
1938	180	11,947	960	90	...	400	...	7,713	3,337	36,431	...
1939	...	...	1,177	...	- -	200	...	8,682	3,967	37,509	...
1940	...	...	763	...	3,414	...	125	5,721	2,677	19,961	...
1941	...	...	686	...	...	...	141	4,803	2,216	5,166	...
1942	...	...	491	...	...	...	182	3,890	1,909	3,631	...
1943	...	...	515	...	...	...	174	4,803	1,945	3,683	...
1944	...[23]	...[23]	574	...	...	...	90	3,562	1,369	2,648	...
1945	...	...	471	...	...	...	55	362	239	3,378	...
1946	...	...	536	...	7,900	500	75	3,455	1,536	4,526	...
1947	...	[19,338][16]	927	...	8,300	1,000	17	5,064	2,522	1,074	...
1948	102	32,222	767	...	7,800	800	507	7,017	2,638	10,674	...
1949	—	28,131	871	...[26]	9,400	1,200	998	5,949	2,021	14,139	...
1950	—	32,089	693	90	8,800	1,000	726	7,145	2,675	13,768	...
1951	—	31,197	642	135	8,000	100	538	8,442	3,378	7,932	...
1952	—	30,116	464	248	8,700	200	993	8,011	2,805	11,940	...
1953	—	30,134	580	337	8,900	2,300	1,168	5,841	2,345	14,196	689
1954	—	30,505	469	504	9,800	2,800	975	5,190	2,796	13,936	835
1955	—	30,444	512	665	8,700	2,900	647	5,869	2,790	12,429	1,121
1956	15	25,964	480	702	6,400	4,100	336	5,519	3,323	8,679	1,466
1957	551	19,398	558	765	3,400	7,000	628	5,187	3,484	7,140	1,749
1958	1,128	23,465	400	705	3,800	8,100	1,108	3,387	2,481	4,291	1,147
1959	2,209	23,843	332	822	4,400	9,200	844	3,299	2,393	3,535	1,535
1960	1,185	25,038	392	1,006	4,800	10,500	346	3,767	2,710	5,226	1,688
1961	1,502	25,064	566	873	4,700	12,900	503	3,462	2,375	5,687	1,672
1962	1,552	25,111	548	1,397	4,900	15,900	1,851	3,454	2,442	4,787	1,616
1963	1,742	24,979	668	1,524	5,100	16,800	1,918	3,405	2,964	8,002	1,691
1964	1,831	26,898	652	1,569	5,100	19,200	1,951	3,645	2,090	5,964	2,219
1965	1,846	28,567	645	1,543	6,800	18,800	1,722	3,110	1,770	3,856	2,298
1966	1,621	29,825	760	1,715	7,300	18,600	1,452	3,154	1,397	3,752	2,008
1967	1,436	30,090	689	1,773	7,800	19,200	1,554	2,697	1,052	2,625	1,581
1968	1,392	32,414	623	2,119	6,900	21,137	2,279	2,807	986	3,558	1,868
1969	1,389	30,755	687	2,518	7,200	23,239	2,378	2,672	873	4,486	1,952
1970	1,405[25] 1,096	35,072	739	2,841	7,100	24,300	3,651	2,868	827	3,363	2,022
1971	1,264	36,260	470	2,871	8,400	24,800	3,040	2,642	568	2,695	2,259
1972	1,157	39,062	545	2,936	9,700	24,400	3,306	2,193	391	1,749	2,191
1973	1,165	43,605	470	3,908	10,000	24,400	3,506	2,522	371	2,693	2,468
1974	1,203	48,284	322	4,028	9,700	26,000	3,737	3,100	536	1,865	2,658

D11   Imports and Exports of Coal by Main Surplus and Deficient Countries (in thousands of metric tons)

1975–1997

	Austria	Belgium		Bulgaria	Czechoslovakia		Denmark	Finland	France	
	I	I	E	I	I	E	I	I	I	E
1975	4,284	10,159[27]	923[27]	6,593[27]	5,188	7,648	4,279	4,734	20,413	1,291
		6,629	398	6,272						
1976	4,372	7,274	351	6,185	5,209	7,482	4,363	3,703	21,765	1,636
1977	3,885	6,475	324	6,257	5,619	6,975	5,707	5,181	23,785	1,428
1978	3,790	7,007	225	6,201	5,591	7,251	6,261[25]	5,719	25,589	1,331
							6,134			
1979	4,550	9,622	319	6,360	5,492	6,905	7,575	6,034	29,960	2,143
1980	4,518	10,139	441	6,732	5,058	7,349	9,953	5,899	32,740	1,309
1981	4,659	10,057	700	7,051	4,423	6,395	10,908	6,763	30,161	1,699
1982	4,863	10,484	694	7,227	4,980	6,904	9,685	5,824	24,801	1,602
1983	4,729	7,510	620	7,087	5,028	6,854	8,559	5,519	20,254	1,494
1984	5,573	9,318	1,025	7,200	4,565	6,628	9,830	4,807	23,825	1,833
1985	5,759	9,320	871	8,054	4,686	6,665	12,788	6,327	21,278	1,698
1986	5,396	8,521	1,045	7,294	4,896	6,355	12,212	6,563	18,553	1,240
1987	5,558	9,133	942	7,268	4,235	5,589	12,104	6,131	14,780	1,328
1988	5,219	11,065	856	6,451	4,781	5,813	10,359	5,554	13,829	2,164
1989	4,982	12,658	802	6,240	4,503	2,215	10,740	5,565	15,943	1,200
1990	4,843	14,161	668	5,790	4,635	1,489	9,944	6,101	19,389	968
1991	5,120	14,421	960	4,507	5,819	2,373	12,809	5,173	21,808	1,251
1992	4,859	14,014	669	3,674	2,559[30]	5,426[30]	11,942	4,263	21,903	900
1993	4,111	11,894	645	4,235	1,939[30]	5,301[30]	10,467	5,933	14,231	1,109
					Czech Republic					
1994	2,997	12,392	...	...	1,730	6,450	...	8,087	...	...
1995	2,976	12,036	...	...	2,661	6,976	...	5,887	...	...
1996	3,660	11,371	...	...	3,174	6,731	...	6,250	...	...
1997	...	11,863	...	...	2,263	6,634	...	7,471	...	...

	West Germany		E. Germany	Greece	Hungary		Italy	S. Ireland	Netherlands	Norway
	I	E	I	I	I	E	I	I	I	I
1975	7,894	15,195	9,411	763	2,808	103	12,580	697	4,879	1,111
1976	7,536	13,480	9,023	606	2,657	60	11,954	639	5,532	1,112
1977	7,968	15,019	9,123	457	3,154	66	12,287	878	6,577	910
1978	8,039	19,548	8,532	402[25]	2,640	41	11,836	849[25]	6,020[25]	930
				378				839	5,330	
1979	9,379	16,334	11,618	458	3,066	21	13,989	1,245	6,694	1,316
1980	11,266	13,539	9,964	484	3,115	...	16,675	1,205	7,658	1,283
1981	13,049	12,458	7,799	172	3,054	...	18,665	1,289	8,451	1,200
1982	13,316	10,919	6,761	391	3,206	...	18,003	1,239	9,314	1,280
1983	11,775	11,631	6,018	536	2,943	...	15,926	1,427	8,165	1,085
1984	11,462	11,975	5,447	1,119	2,556	...	20,365	1,395	10,540	1,406
1985	12,333	9,714	6,828	2,093	3,704	...	21,160	1,913	12,148	1,636
1986	12,492	8,100	8,846	1,786	3,636	...	20,570	2,625	12,904	1,393
1987	10,357	6,841	9,005	1,841	2,654	...	20,339	2,943	13,484	1,266
1988	9,077	5,806	7,688	1,534	2,845	...	19,225	3,460	14,176	1,339
1989	6,501	6,022	4,570	1,193	2,475	...	21,098	3,338	13,137	1,304
	Germany									
1990	5,909	...	Included	1,380	1,978	...	20,015	3,136	16,232	1,247
1991	9,542	...	in	1,407	2,012	...	20,427	3,125	15,058	1,086
1992	15,441	2,934	West	2,132	1,284	...	18,010	3,046	15,295	1,087
1993	13,090	1,609	Germany	1,337	1,251	...	14,600	2,907	15,328	1,179
1994	...	...		...	1,935	...	15,308	4,733	16,792	...
1995	...	...		...	1,761	...	18,267	2,538	17,438	...
1996	...	...		...	1,893	...	16,332	2,487	17,528	...
1997	...	...		...	1,742	...	15,250	3,053	18,997	...

D11 Imports and Exports of Coal by Main Surplus and Deficient Countries (in thousands of metric tons)

1975–1997

	Poland		Portugal	Romania	Russia/U.S.S.R.		Spain	Sweden[4]	Switzerland	U.K.[29]	Yugo-slavia[4]
	I	E	I	I	I	E	I	I	I	E	I
1975	1,096	45,058	410	4,594	9,818	26,143	4,391	2,834	321	2,182	2,809
1976	1,080	45,138	457	4,933	9,376	26,813	...	3,118	306	1,436	2,926
1977	1,044	45,422	497	5,032	9,121	28,193	4,151	2,152	316	1,941	3,016
1978	945	45,517	543	6,285	9,880	...	3,640[25] 3,392	1,965	317	2,266	3,327
1979	945	46,486	468	6,171	9,512	...	4,208	2,752	524	2,339	3,620
1980	1,012	34,387	432	6,516	6,700	25,300	5,697	2,649	773	4,042	3,634
1981	1,072	16,674	419 352	6,390	3,834	...	7,068	2,312	1,033	9,513	4,025
1982	972	30,182	365	5,672	8,869	...	7,214	3,157	595	7,389	3,692
1983	1,021	36,778	428	6,832	11,564	...	5,940	3,341	458	6,344	4,190
1984	1,031	44,712	493	6,451	12,834	...	7,031	4,253	660	2,440	3,806
1985	1,060	37,794	1,552	6,554	10,373	28,300	8,465	5,281	585	2,558	4,485
1986	1,150	35,860	1,782	6,556	11,693	33,536	8,764	4,873	706	2,748	4,260
1987	1,092	33,235	2,542	6,296	9,583	35,454	8,856	4,248	606	2,342	4,190
1988	1,085	35,021	2,990	5,765	11,875	39,385	8,766	4,226	493	1,737	3,945
1989	926	28,943	3,554	5,782	9,957	42,551	10,569	4,199	372	2,039	3,469
1990	560	28,065	4,669	4,981	8,681	35,438	10,455	3,889	509	2,307	3,259
1991	54	19,534	4,254	2,966	193	25,961	12,988	3,498	395	1,824	2,200
1992	126	19,602	4,482	5,786	39,723[31]	34,078[31]	14,279	3,373	177	973	70[32]
1993	129	22,968	4,766	2,666	28,300[31]	27,400[31]	12,776	3,494	148	1,095	60[32]
1994	...	...	4,417	3,746	...	...	12,454	3,012	...	...	...
1995	...	...	5,349	4,727	...	...	11,482	3,448	...	...	...
1996	...	...	4,776	4,719	...	...	13,761	3,140	...	...	...
1997	...	...	5,160	5,242	...	...	12,370	3,231	...	...	...

NOTES

1. SOURCES:- Belgium to 1912—A. Wibail, L'evolution economique de l'industrie charbonniere Belge depuis 1831 '*Bulletin de l'Institute des Sciences Economiques* VI 1 (1934). Bulgaria and Romania from 1950, U.N., *World Energy Supplies*. Czechoslovakia 1949–52—supplied by the Federal Statistical Office of Czechoslovakia. Finland 1943 and 1945—supplied by the Central Statistical Office of Finland. U.K. to 1938—based on B.R. Mitchell, *British Historical Statistics* (Cambridge, 1988), where the original sources are given. All other statistics are taken from the official publications noted on p. xv, with gaps filled from the League of Nations, *International Trade Statistics* and the United Nations, *Yearbook of International Trade Statistics*.
2. Exports from England & Wales for 1697–1791 and from Great Britain for 1792–1808 can be found in E.B. Schumpeter, *English Overseas Trade Statistics, 1697–1808* (Oxford, 1960), and, in uniform Imperial measure, in B.R. Mitchell, *op. cit*. They include shipments to Ireland, however.
3. Where no indication is given in the footnotes, statistics in this table are of hard coal only.

FOOTNOTES

[1] Figures to 1914 apply to the Austro-Hungarian customs area. This included Lombardy to 1859, and Venetia to 1865. It did not include Dalmatia until 1861. Figures from 1920 are for the Republic of Austria.

[2] Lignite is included, but not coke.

[3] These figures are for the 14 months from 1 November 1852, previous statistics being for years ended 31 October.

[4] Coke is included.

[5] Coke and lignite are included (converted to coal equivalent in the case of France prior to 1959).

[6] Re-exports are not deducted prior to 1863, but they were extremely small.

[7] Figures to 1884 (1st line) relate to European Russia (except Finland) and include coke, lignite and peat. From 1884 (2nd line) to 1912 (1st line) they are for the Empire (except Finland), still including coke, lignite and peat. From 1912 (2nd line) to 1918 they are for the Empire, but are of coal only. From 1920 the figures are for the U.S.S.R.

[8] Coke is not subsequently included.

[9] Coke is subsequently included.

[10] Figures from 1896 (2nd line) to 1924 (1st line) and from 1936 (2nd line) onwards are net of re-exports.

[11] Figures for 1871–1918 treat Alsace-Lorraine as foreign.

[12] Prior to March 1906 the statistics exclude trade via the free ports.

[13] Significant changes in the area covered by the statistics were as follows:- Alsace-Lorraine was lost in 1918; West Prussia, Posen, and the Saarland were lost in 1921, and eastern Upper Silesia in July 1922. Saarland was recovered in February 1935, excluded again in 1945, and reincorporated in West Germany on 5 July 1959.

[14] Lignite is subsequently included.

[15] There were major territorial acquisitions between 1913 and 1920.

[16] Excluding lignite.

[17] These are incomplete figures owing to the French occupation of the Ruhr.

D11   Imports and Exports of Coal by Main Surplus and Deficient Countries (in thousands of metric tons)

[18] Figures for 1946-49 exclude the French Occupied Zone.
[19] Lignite is subsequently excluded.
[20] Subsequently only coke-oven coke is included.
[21] Bunker coal is not subsequently included with exports.
[22] Eastern Upper Silesia was acquired in July 1922.
[23] There were major territorial changes, including the acquisition of the whole of Silesia.
[24] These figures are for the economic years, ended 30 September.
[25] Subsequently excluding briquettes.
[26] Subsequent statistics are expressed in coal equivalent.
[27] Subsequently hard coal only.
[28] Net imports in 1975 were 3,881 thousand tons.
[29] Imports, insignificant before 1971, were subsequently as follows (in thousands of metric tons):-

1971	4,164	1975	5,083	1979	4,375	1983	4,360	1986	10,554
1972	4,996	1976	2,837	1980	7,334	1984	8,894	1987	9,781
1973	1,668	1977	2,439	1981	4,290	1985	12,732	1988	11,993
1974	3,541	1978	2,352	1982	4,063				

[30] Czech Republic Slovakia = 5,500 (1992) (IMPORT)
5,193 (1993) (IMPORT)
[31] Russian Federation Ex-USSR as follows

		I	E
Armenia	1992	141	
	1993	8	
Azerbaijan	1992	27	
	1993	13	
Belarus	1992	1,616	
	1993	1,644	
Estonia	1992	258	
	1993	52	
Georgia	1992	236	
	1993	156	
Kazakhstan	1992	4,260	42,459
	1993	2,473	33,821
Kyrgistan	1992	1,354	1,024
	1993	946	531
Latvia	1992	813	
	1993	552	
Lithuania	1992	919	
	1993	304	
Moldova	1992	2,489	194
	1993	1,938	
Tajikistan	1992	122	186
	1993	56	80
Turkmenistan	1992	269	
	1993	135	
Ukraine	1992	11,465	5,088
	1993	8,930	4,126
Uzbekistan	1992	1,674	
	1993	590	

[32] Yugoslovia. Ex-Yugoslovia as follows

		I	E
Croatia	1992	759	
	1993	633	
Macedonia	1992		
	1993		
Slovenia	1992	14	
	1993	20	

D12 IMPORTS AND EXPORTS OF PETROLEUM BY MAIN SURPLUS AND DEFICIENT COUNTRIES
(in thousands of metric tons)

1856–1904

	Austria[1]		Bulgaria	Denmark	Finland	Germany	Italy	Netherlands
	I	E	I	I	I	I	I	I
1856	...	...	...	...	...	...	...	...
1857	...	...	...	...	...	...	...	...
1858	...	...	...	...	...	...	...	...
1859	...	...	...	...	...	...	...	...
1860	...	...	...	...	...	...	...	...
1861	...	...	...	...	...	...	...	...
1862	...	...	...	...	...	...	...	...
1863	...	...	...	0.5	...	...	...	3.9
1864	3.4	0.3	...	1.7	...	...	1.2	8.2
1865	3.3[1]	0.7[1]	...	2.2	...	12	8.4	5.6
1866	4.8	0.5	...	2.2	0.1	33	12	9.7
1867	6.4	0.5	...	3.8	0.1	61	19	12
1868	12	0.6	...	4.8	0.3	72	35	16
1869	20	0.7	...	5.0	0.4	91	30	15
1870	32	0.9	...	5.3	0.9	96	39	18
1871	41	1.2	...	5.4	1.0	125	43	20
1872	47	0.9	...	5.9	0.8	121	42	21
1873	65	0.8	...	7.5	2	172	35	28
1874	69	0.8	...	10	2	155	44	29
1975	81	0.4	...	8	1	201	45	34
1876	109	0.4	...	10	2	212	44	34
1877	104	0.4	...	14	3	250	50	41
1878	105	0.3	...	9	2	251	47	42
1879	93	0.3	...	19	2	252	59	44
1880	115	1.0	...	8	3	213	58	49
1881	148	0.7	...	18	4	291	60	54
1882	125	2.2	...	16	4	343	61	60
1883	110	2.1	...	17	5	370	64	68
1884	135	5.1	...	21	4	463	74	75
1885	141	3.1	...	19	6	482	93	77
1886	129	2.6	...	25	5	438	72	85
1887	113	1.6	8	21	6	509	76	90
1888	120	2.0	6	25	7	564	70	90
1889	140	3.4	9	29	9	626	71	99
1890	129	4.2	13	29	9	647	71	104
1891	140	2.6	12	39	10	676	86	114
1892	150	2.4	11	38[2] / 33	10	743	84	123
1893	164	4.4	14	45	12	765	91	129
1894	143	6.0	17	37	10	785	90	141
1895	137	14	11	45	13	811	83	150
1896	87	43	12	47[3] / 35	15	854	96	152
1897	92	37	16	37	16	895	91	160
1898	81	29	14	40	17	906	89	169
1899	98	32	12	44	20	911	85	162
1900	44	51	16	42	19	938	86	169
1901	41	37	15	45	21	927	69	180
1902	41	55	12	46	22	939	69	190
1903	39	89	15	49	23	980	68	193
1904	43	136	21	53	24	980	69	181

D12   Imports and Exports of Petroleum by Main Surplus and Deficient Countries (in thousands of metric tons)

1905–1909

	Austria[1]		Bulgaria	Denmark	Finland	Germany	Italy	Netherlands
	I	E	I	I	I	I	I	I
1905	44	209	14	53	28	959[12]	67	189
1906	35	245	20	52	25	971	65	200
1907	37	227	14	58	28	1,021	78	199
1908	21	378	18	61	30	1,052	91	197
1909	23	505	21	74	32	983	101	197

1856–1899

	Norway	Portugal	Romania	Russia	Spain	Sweden	Switz	U.K.[5]
	I	I	E	E	I[4]	I	I	I
1856	—	...	...	...	...	—	...	0.3
1857	—	...	...	...	...	—	...	2.9
1858	—	...	...	...	...	—	...	3.3
1859	—	...	...	...	...	—	...	0.6
1860	—	...	...	...	...	—	...	- -
1861	—	...	...	...	...	—	...	1.3
1862	- -	...	...	...	...	—	...	20
1863	0.1	...	...	...	...	—	...	29
1864	0.2	...	...	...	...	0.7	...	17
1865	0.3	...	...	...	...	0.9	...	12
1866	0.6	...	...	...	...	1.6	...	25
1867	0.8	...	...	...	...	1.6	...	18
1868	1.1	...	...	...	...	3.4	...	17
1869	1.5	...	...	...	1	3.3	...	21
1870	2.3	...	...	...	2	5.0	15	27
1871	3.5	...	...	...	1	5.4	22	35
1872	3.1	...	...	...	2	6.6	19	25
1873	5.2	...	...	...	1	8.4	27	65
1874	5.5	...	...	...	2	9.0	...	84
1875	5.2	...	...	...	4	9.1	15	76
1876	5.9	...	...	...	1	10	18	98
1877	8.9	...	...	...	4	11	18	132
1878	5.5	...	...	...	2	11	21	118
1879	6.6	...	...	...	11	14	21	169
1880	7.4	...	...	...	25	12	23	152
1881	9.3	...	...	...	47	17	26	231
1882	7.7	7.9	...	...	35	18	28	233
1883	9.0	5.4	18	59	41	19	27	275
1884	11	9.6	22	113	44	24	33	207
1885	10	9.1	21	177	57	25	27	289
1886	11	9.4	15	246	45	28	32	278
1887	10	9.4	16	311	43	28	33	302
1888	13	10	18	573	59	26	36	369
1889	15	11	19	734	33	45	39	402
1890	14	12	12	788	51	38	41	411
1891	16	12	18	889	55	42	44	510
1892	23	14	20	939	45	42	48	509
1893	24	14	17	987	55	49	52	606
1894	29	15	17	880	44	47	53	637
1895	28	14	16	1,059	44	59	56	692
1896	36	13	17	1,058	40	52	63	742
1897	40	14	21	1,046	35	66	66	725
1898	37	14	27	1,115	33	64	66	857
1899	42	15	48	1,392	24	74	69	938

D12 Imports and Exports of Petroleum by Main Surplus and Deficient Countries (in thousands of metric tons)

1900–1909

	Norway I	Portugal I	Romania E	Russia E	Spain I[4]	Sweden I	Switz I	U.K.[5] I
1900	40	14	49	1,442	43	80	71	996
1901	47	20	58	1,558	36	78	72	991
1902	45	18	76	1,534	35	84	74	1,113
1903	59	21	126	1,783	32	96	74	1,117
1904	51	18	164	1,837	29	97	75	1,180
1905	44	19	220	945	29	105	73	1,172
1906	42	19	333	661	49	107	76	1,169
1907	44	21	428	733	25	112	79	1,188
1908	65	21	463	797	29	144	83	1,342
1909	63	22	424	796	38	141	81	1,399

1910–1944

	Austria[1] I	Austria[1] E	Belgium I	Belgium E[7]	Bulgaria I	Czech I	Denmark I	Finland I	France[11] COI	France[11] ROI	France[11] E	Germany COI	Germany ROI	Germany E
1910	36	451	...	...	22	....	89	33	...	...	...	1,014	...	...
1911	39	400	...	...	20[8]	....	98	34	...	...	...	987	...	...
1912	39	610	...	...	18	...	110	35	...	...	...	1,118	...	...
1913	51	494	389	...	26	...	125	36	...	...	...	1,034	...	...
1914	41	309	...	...	25	...	124	26	...	...	...	...	...	...
1915	...	145	...	...	13	...	120	29	...	...	...	...	...	...
1916	...	344	...	...	7	...	129	32	...	...	...	...	...	...
1917	...	...	...	...	2	...	64	25	...	...	...	...	...	...
1918	...[1]	...[1]	...	...	6	...	18	...	...	...	...	...	...	...
1919	...	...	...	...	20	...	132	41	...	...	...	...	...	...
1920	80	...	...	...	6	...	169	12	...	...	...	...	...	...
1921	96	...	...[6]	...	22	52	145	17	...	...	...	...	...	...
1922	104	...	208	...	31	65	218	21	...	...	...	...	...	...
1923	104	...	308	...	39	120	260	27	...	...	...	...	492	...
1924	160	...	358	...	36	146	319[3 9] / 301	33	...	...	...	...	772	...
1925	142	...	381	...	44	133	312	29	...	...	...	...	1,167	...
1926	169	...	378	...	48	144	374	30	...	...	...	...	1,388	...
1927	183	...	366	...	51	173	387	35	106	2,233	117	...	1,684	144
1928	238	...	632	...	60	196	419	44	188	2,867	141	...	2,001	142
1929	260	...	706	...	77	194	438	36	198	3,069	113	...	2,531	199
1930	314	...	733	...	79	356[8] / 404	527	38	460	3,397	107	...	3,271	298
1931	312	...	759	...	75	411	555	32	450	3,724	80		2,935	355
1932	257	...	821	...	64	399	575	44	985	3,523	144		2,453	288
1933	327	...	832	...	66	362	565	36	2,799	3,018	280		2,647	286
1934	259	...	1,038	...	66	370	604	43	3,977	1,801	554		3,094	216
1935	284	...	879	...	76	400	573	46	5,316	1,074	586		3,863	...
1936	294	...	1,190	...	75	423	656[3] / 644	68	6,018	1,485	556		4,246	...
1937	269	14	1,186	...	89	485	686	209	6,140	1,623	663		4,335	...
1938	...	...	1,124	404	88	...	833	234	6,968	1,325	664		4,986	...
1939	...	...	...	...	100	...	852	260	6,149	1,177	496		...	...
1940	...	...	...	...	102	...	154	100	3,655	656	338		...	...
1941	...	...	...	...	73	...	60	83	18	284	82		...	...
1942	...	...	...	...	...	...	69	96	...	227	8		...	...
1943	...	...	...	...	...	...	51	97	...	166	1		...	...
1944	...	...	...	...	...	...	47	50	...	125	...		...	...

D12   Imports and Exports of Petroleum by Main Surplus and Deficient Countries (in thousands of metric tons)

1945–1964

	Austria[1]		Belgium		Bulgaria	Czech	Den-mark	Finland	France[11]			West Germany			East Germany
	I	E	I	E[7]	I	I	I	I	COI	ROI	E	COI	ROI	E	I
1945	...	...	...	...	...	...	150	25	299	1,789	32	...	...	...	1
1946	...	...	...	...	1,842	...	623	149	2,686	2,694	384	...	...	...	...
1947	14	...	2,094	776	1,430	318	1,123	318[10] / 357	5,029	2,102	753	...	...	...	...
1948	54	14	2,224	741	...	395	1,148	514	7,729	1,202	1,063	2,523	...	...	...
1949	93	38	2,048	488	...	574	1,212[9] / 1,325	408	11,812	665	2,332	1,087	...	...	...
1950	86	48	2,448	466	...	393	1,860	542	14,135	412	3,448	1,950	...	...	406
1951	82	23	3,706	764	...	563	1,989	609	18,073	633	5,123	3,206	509	...	433
1952	55	34	4,543	1,966	...	652	2,007	719	21,222	728	7,201	3,574	683	540	451
1953	45	79	4,978	2,005	...	605	2,161	801	22,000	482	7,235	4,560	963	1,008	723
1954	109	96	5,809	1,664	343	935	2,596	943	23,640	751	6,498	5,985	1,369	1,585	1,016
1955	381	163	7,101	1,863	331	1,060	3,249	1,118[16] / 682	24,832	952	6,111	7,111	2,847	2,130	1,105
1956	318	399	8,320	2,350	378	1,176	3,701	944	25,013	1,285	5,668	7,999	5,108	2,680	1,156
1957	425	307	8,617	2,170	479	1,609	3,868	1,480	24,062	2,744	4,546	8,158	5,709	2,053	1,424
1958	792	220	9,540	2,697	518	1,645	4,380	1,803	28,318	1,749	6,666	10,889	6,478	2,498	1,479
1959	945	182	9,576	3,289	698	2,076	4,537	1,861	29,171	2,125	6,512	16,895	5,531	2,856	2,025
1960	1,210	151	10,078	3,389	915	4,969[15]	5,154	2,624	31,023	2,687	7,074	23,056	6,725	3,531	2,579[17] / 2,677
1961	1,703	94	11,147	3,202	1,182	2,785	5,889[9] / 5,816	2,923	35,018	2,462	8,178	29,293	6,959	5,561	3,183
1962	2,272	210	12,779	3,523	1,661	...	7,336	3,465	37,161	3,070	7,526	33,202	12,634	5,268	3,484
1963	2,750	225	16,387	5,136	2,152	4,217	8,078	3,554	43,257	4,047	6,956	40,078	14,425	6,628	4,171
1964	3,000	211	18,073	5,116	3,154	...	9,858	5,390[16]	49,192	4,415	7,822	51,276	14,388	7,795	5,380

1910–1932

	Greece	Hungary		Italy		Netherlands		Norway	Poland		Portugal
	I	I	E	I	E	I	E	I	I	E	I
1910	...	...	...	99	...	198	...	65	...	...	22
1911	...	...	...	143	...	201	...	72	...	...	22
1912	...	...	...	141	...	204	...	82	...	...	22
1913	...	...	...	150	...	214	...	80	...	...	32
1914	...	...	...	161	...	360	...	91	...	...	28
1915	...	...	...	169	...	175	...	63	...	...	27
1916	...	...	...	216	...	152	...	108	...	...	29
1917	...	...	...	232	...	104	...	59	...	...	29
1918	...	...	...	287	...	5	...	44	...	...	11
1919	...	5	...	241	...	418	...	120	...	...	31
1920	...	17	...	247	...	481	...	85	1	93	30
1921	...	43	...	204	...	422	...	88	1	231	20
1922	...	60	...	291	...	501	...	150	...	292	39
1923	...	83	...	349	...	621	...	152	15	317	60
1924	...	93	...	376	...	686	...	185	3	355	64
1925	74	77	...	428	...	674	...	185	5	273	62
1926	88	133	...	466	...	777	...	181	2	381	74
1927	111	166	...	537	...	935	...	202	3	196	87
1928	127	192	...	607	...	915	...	222	4	187	113
1929	148	208	...	699	...	897	...	270	7	185	111
1930	161	249	...	739	...	1,010	...	270	8	122	126
1931	165	165	...	702	...	1,119	...	303	5	148	126
1932	182	147	...	674	...	954	...	373	- -	161	125

D12 Imports and Exports of Petroleum by Main Surplus and Deficient Countries (in thousands of metric tons)

1933–1964

	Greece	Hungary		Italy		Netherlands		Norway	Poland		Portugal
	I	I	E	I	E	I	E	I	I	E	I
1933	183	175	...	642	...	1,015	...	433	3	155	141
1934	209	234	...	725		953	...	484	...	148	163
1935	244	174	...	842	...	1,094	27	460	...	118	197
1936	281	258	...	692	...	1,240	50	470	...	110	175
1937	324	280	...	1,376	...	1,505	69	542	...	77	192
1938	81	209	...	1,682	...	1,724	70	581	7	...	193
1939	...	...	...	2,031	...	...	...	679	...	...	209
1940	...	...	...	1,262	...	...	...	242	...	...	219
1941	...	...	...	348	...	...	...	186	...	...	181
1942	...	...	...	527	...	...	...	163	...	...	43
1943	...	...	...	...	...	...	...	156	...	...	87
1944	...	...	...	...	...	...	...	161	...[13]	...[13]	110
1945	...	...	...	...	...	...	...	172	...	...	186
1946	...	...	...	357	...	...	...	577	190	...	359
1947	...	...	...	1,787	...	2,315	113	949	238	...	566
1948	159	...	...	2,420	...	2,664	215	1,299	384	...	587
1949	197	11	29	3,188	...	3,641	11289	1,306	337	...	527
1950	1,074	32	8	5,289	...	6,220	3,340[20]	1,390	473	1	565
1951	1,152	218	28	7,461	1,376	7,309	3,976	1,775	755	7	742
1952	1,236	293	52	9,978	2,890	7,962	4,698	1,985	844	24	961
1953	1,236	403	61	12,922	5,145	8,615	5,178	2,158	950	50	977
1954	1,390	359	43[18] 63	15,939	6,578	11,527	7,440	2,248	1,186	59	1,297
1955	1,493	312	154	17,590	5,874	13,770	8,721	2,819	1,431	125[21] 155	1,462
1956	1,520	461	89	18,915	5,773	15,622	9,495	3,003	1,489	137	1,503
1957	1,606	1,221[19] 1,249	176	19,981	5,742	15,988	9,839	2,944	1,786	69	1,644
1958	1,817	1,211	273	22,826	6,687	18,508	11,514	3,019	1,874	142[21]	1,705
1959	2,046	1,324	357	25,560	8,304	17,874	10,172	3,183	2,204	178	1,829
1960	2,379	1,557	487	30,628	9,222	21,744	12,786	3,633	2,504	196	1,941
1961	2,484	1,643	486	35,788	10,438	24,600	13,272	4,423	3,034	274	1,992
1962	2,989	1,790	577	43,345	11,635	25,283	13,848	5,138	3,703	555[21] 573	2,067
1963	3,395	2,234	475	49,890	12,809	26,063	12,354	5,559	4,250	589	2,245
1964	3,317	2,579	553	57,513	14,926	30,077	13,296	5,982	4,637	586	2,483

1910–1919

	Romania	Russia/U.S.S.R.			Spain		Sweden	Switz	United Kingdom			Yugo-slavia
	E	I	COE	ROE	I	E[7]	I	I	COI	ROI	E	I
1910	582	...		859	31	...	140	85	1,350	...		...
1911	674	...		855	33	...	165	87	1,428	...		...
1912	851	...		839	32	...	152	91	1,618	...		...
1913	1,056	...		947	39[4] 88	...	180	87	1,907	...		...
1914	640	...		528	76	...	144	56	2,526			
1915	...	...		78	92	...	149	45	2,299	...		...
1916	...	...		41	91	...	163	39	1,764	...		...
1917	...	...		34	72	...	51	28	3,230	...		...
1918	...	...		2	56	...	40	20	5,174	...		...
1919	...	...		...	109	...	163	...	2,788	...		...

D12   Imports and Exports of Petroleum by Main Surplus and Deficient Countries (in thousands of metric tons)

1920-1964

	Romania	Russia/U.S.S.R.			Spain		Sweden	Switz	United Kingdom			Yugoslavia
	E	I	COE	ROE	I	E[7]	I	I	COI	ROI	E	I
1920	246	- -		- -	161	...	190	68	17	3,436	257	...
1921	362	...		7	139	...	145	43	413	4,111	109	...
1922	433	...	52[14]		136	...	178	85	883	3,820	351	74
1923	413	...	84[14]		154	...	218	92	1,360	3,798	484	72
1924	436	...	712[14]		217	...	255	107	1,888	4,224	634	74
1925	785	5	1,373[14]		238	...	302	88	2,313	3,967	872	100
1926	1,494	...	1,474[14]		263	...	330	90	2,185	5,185	609	112
1927	1,913	...	2,086[14]		345	...	358	169	2,702	5,250	631	133
1928	2,344	...	2,783[14]		411	...	441	201	2,024	6,038	633	143
1929	2,817	...	3,859		461	...	479	240	1,980	6,341	805	154
1930	3,784	2	295	4,418	610	...	577	265	1,874	7,202	668	206
1931	4,572	...	382	4,842	725	...	639	308	1,400	6,894	520	107
1932	4,975	...	629	5,489	727	...	714	367	1,498	6,941	521	152
1933	5,594	1	536	4,394	652	...	773	381	1,596	7,563	521	137
1934	6,222	...	459	3,856	924	...	814	418	1,935	8,407	637	128
1935	6,221	...	207	3,162	878	...	931	418	1,985	8,502	736	119
1936	6,228	...	218	2,448	...	...	1,008	400	2,080	8,864	680	158
1937	5,168	...	68	1,861	...	...	1,185	393	2,143	9,279	772	143
1938	4,126	142	188	1,200	...	...	1,335	414	2,308	9,541	601	...
1939	...	76	26	500	...	...	1,488	428	2,201	8,873	541	...
1940	...	69	...	874	...	...	541	284	1,589	10,161	221	...
1941	...	...	...	...	...	...	131	111	992	12,275	54	...
1942	...	...	...	...	...	...	108	87	600	9,942	67	...
1943	...	...	...	...	...	...	147	72	535	14,684	38	...
1944	...	...	...	...	...	...	137	58	695	19,891	80	...
1945	...	...	...	...	608	39	196	30	964	15,056	171	...
1946	...	500	...	500	528	5	1,836	394	2,214	12,428	410	...
1947	...	1,000	...	800	1,727	...	3,098	726	2,514	10,762	654	...
1948	...	800	...	700	1,840	...	3,334	883	4,715	13,408	347	...
1949	...[27]	1,700	100	800	2,214	...	3,048	875	6,145	11,637	508	...
1950	2,850	1,825	300	726	3,550	20	3,767	1,057	9,394[23]	10,055[23]	1,212	460
1951	3,450	2,096	900	1,421	3,683	23	4,892	1,119	16,970	9,943	3,467	421
1952	4,650	2,954	1,300	1,687	4,278	32	5,083	1,238	23,195	6,057	5,528	332
1953	5,400	3,636	1,500	2,642	4,745	142	5,538	1,322	26,163	6,113	7,510	533
1954	5,500	3,176	2,100	4,186	4,981	96	6,476	1,617	28,526	6,718	7,955	543
1955	5,840	3,587	2,916	4,894	5,447	110	8,084	1,892	28,301	8,652	6,375	518
1956	5,580	3,569	3,897	5,968	6,368	101	9,771	2,508	29,067	9,571	7,838	603
1957	5,250	2,673	5,923	7,505	8,938	281	9,400	2,548	28,416	11,003	6,388	667
1958	4,956	2,745	9,083	8,679	9,420	635	10,597	2,953	34,289	11,191	8,525	654
1959	5,642	3,000	12,485	12,462	9,048	539	10,862	3,063[22]	39,868	12,957	8,353	711
1960	5,717	2,870	17,825	14,902	8,795	776	13,210	3,940	45,331	14,023	9,215	595
1961	5,766	2,367	23,388	17,220	9,867	691	13,340	4,317	49,744	11,996	7,825	433
1962	5,589	2,095	26,279	18,574	11,837	877	14,606	5,018	53,189	15,946	9,893	1,021
1963	5,465	2,011	30,243	20,676	12,537	908	16,129	6,787	54,732	18,511	9,880	935
1964	5,787	1,820	36,691	19,500	15,148	1,143	17,975	7,047	60,349	18,914	9,232	1,053

D12 Imports and Exports of Petroleum by Main Surplus and Deficient Countries (in thousands of metric tons)

1965–1997

	Austria		Belgium		Bulgaria	Czech	Denmark	Finland	France		
	I	E	I	E[7]	I	I	I	I	COI	ROI	E
1965	2.8	0.2	20.0	5.4	3.6	6.1	10.7	5.5	58.6	3.7	10.0
1966	3.7	0.1	21.9	5.6	4.1	6.5	12.4	7.1	62.8	4.9	13.0
1967	3.7	0.1	23.3	5.5	4.8	7.4	13.0	8.2	72.3	4.8	12.6
1968	5.0	0.1	29.6	7.9	5.8	7.8	14.5	9.1	77.2	5.2	11.5
1969	5.4	0.2	34.3	11.6	7.4	9.4	17.8	10.2	86.3	5.3	11.8
1970	6.8	0.1	36.5	10.2	8.3[25] 8.2	9.8	20.7	12.9	100	6.4	10.7
1971	7.9	0.2	38.7	9.6	9.7	11.5	20.5	12.1	105	8.1	11.8
1972	8.6	0.2	51.5	13.4	10.3	12.6	21.6	13.1	121	8.9	12.4
1973	9.8	0.2	44.4	14.8	11.2	14.2	21.2	13.9	137	7.3	13.4
1974	8.9	0.1	39.4	11.4	12.1	14.7	20.0	13.9	130	6.9	11.2
1975	8.5	0.2	35.4	13.6	12.3	15.8	18.7	11.0	107	7.9	11.4
1976	10.0	0.2	38.4	13.6	12.7	17.1	18.5	14.2	123	9.1	12.5
1977	9.5	0.2	41.8	16.8	12.6	18.3	18.9	14.8	118	8.3	14.8
1978	10.5	0.2	40.2	14.1	14.5	18.6	18.4[26] 18.2	13.5[26] 13.4	116	9.6	14.4 7.3
1979	11.2	0.1	42.4	14.2	14.9	18.8	17.6	15.8	126	12.1	17.6
1980	11.3[26] 11.0	0.1	41.5[26] 41.2	17.1[26] 16.7	...	19.3	14.2	15.8	110	18.4	16.2
1981	9.6	0.1	37.8	15.9	...	18.3	11.5	13.4	90.3	18.6	16.1
1982	8.4	0.1	36.6	15.0	...	17.3	11.3	12.3	76.5	22.5	12.2
1983	7.9	0.1	31.0	15.5	...	17.1	10.8	13.2	68.8	22.6	11.2
1984	8.5	0.3	35.3	15.5	...	17.2	10.6	12.2	72.0	19.8	13.4
1985	8.8	0.8	31.1	12.4	...	16.9	10.7	12.9	68.5	22.3	15.0
1986	9.2	0.5	39.0	16.5	...	16.9	10.1	13.6	66.0	27.0	15.4
1987	9.3	0.4	38.6	16.6	...	17.0	9.5	14.6	62.1	31.2	13.5
1988	9.2	0.4	39.4	18.2	...	16.4	9.4	12.1	66.0	28.4	11.6
1989	9.5	0.4	40.5	20.4	...	16.6	8.7	11.5	65.7	24.9	9.8
1990	10.0	0.4	41.3	20.1	...	13.4	10.0	11.1	69.6	24.5	11.9
1991	10.3	0.4	45.0	22.3	...	11.2	11.1	11.7	72.9	26.0	11.8
1992	10.4	0.5	46.1	21.9	...	6.6[29]	16.1	11.3	71.0	24.5	11.9
						Czech Republic					
1993	10.4	0.7	45.2	23.9	...	6.1[29]	16.7	10.9	74.7	22.0	14.0
1994	...	...	...	22.5	...	6.4	...	9.8	75.4	25.1	13.1
1995	...	...	...	20.8	...	7.0	...	8.4	75.7	21.9	11.4
1996	...	...	...	23.9	...	7.6	...	9.5	83.1	22.0	14.0
1997	...	...	...	22.7	...	7.0	...	9.9	86.9	19.5	...

D12 Imports and Exports of Petroleum by Main Surplus and Deficient Countries (in thousands of metric tons)

	East Germany	West Germany			Greece	Hungary		Italy		Netherlands	
	I	COI	ROI	E	I	I	E[7]	I	E	I	E[7]
1965	6.5	59.1	15.7	7.1	4.8	2.6	0.5	70.0	21.2	33.2	14.5
1966	7.3	67.7	17.5	7.7	4.7	3.4	0.6	79.6	26.4	36.9	16.5
1967	7.8	72.0	19.1	8.2	5.3	3.5	0.9	90.6	26.1	40.2	18.2
1968	9.3	85.7	20.5	9.9	5.1	3.8	1.0	91.5	27.5	42.6	19.4
1969	10.3[15] 9.3	89.6	25.1	9.7	6.2	4.4	1.0	105	30.8	54.3	27.6
1970	10.3	98.8	30.4	10.7	6.6	5.3	0.8	116	32.3	75.2	38.8
1971	10.9	100	33.5	10.7	7.4	5.6	0.3	120	32.4	80.0	41.0
1972	14.9	103	36.2	10.6	9.5	6.7	0.6	125	33.2	98.6	50.7
1973	16.0	110	40.3	11.5	15.9	7.5	0.5	131	33.5	110	53.3
1974	16.4	103	35.5	11.3	15.6	7.8	0.3	124	27.4	69.2	44.3
1975	17.0	88.4	36.3	8.2	13.8	9.2	0.4	106	18.4	64.4	42.9
1976	18.0	97.7	40.2	8.4	15.9	9.6	0.4	111	18.8	63.8	46.5
1977	19.0	96.3	38.8	8.5	14.7	10.0	0.5	110	21.5	76.2	45.4
1978	19.9	94.4	46.5	8.5[27] 7.3	16.1	11.9	0.3	119[26] 118	26.7[26] 26.5	70.6[26] 69.8	41.4[26] 40.8
1979	20.7	107	36.5	7.4	21.2	11.6	0.4	120	24.3	76.6	43.1
1980	21.9	96.9	32.4	8.1	23.3	10.2	0.6	108	14.9	66.8	38.9
1981	22.7	79.2	30.2	7.8	21.8	9.3	0.7	103	15.2	56.0	34.8
1982	21.7	72.5	32.2[25] 31.2	8.3[25] 6.1	18.7	10.3	...	98.0	17.4	56.3	37.0
1983	22.6	65.2	36.0	5.7	16.0	10.4	...	97.3	14.1	59.3	40.7
1984	23.2	66.9	36.1	5.1	15.0	10.4	...	89.8	12.3	58.1	40.5
1985	22.8	64.2	40.0	4.5	14.7	9.1	...	93.7	14.4	58.2	41.5
1986	22.2	66.6	46.4	3.3	19.7	9.3	...	99.2	18.2	59.8	44.9
1987	20.9	63.8	44.7	3.2	18.5	10.0	...	100	15.9	62.0	44.1
1988	20.5	72.0	38.9	4.8	18.7	8.6	...	94.1	15.5	76.7	43.1
1989	21.1	66.2	36.1	5.6	19.4	7.8	...	100	12.7	78.8	45.3
1990	21.0	71.9	36.3	7.4	20.3	7.8	...	105	17.3	77.4	43.7
		Germany									
1991	Included in	88.7	40.3	6.8	19.2	5.9	...	103	19.3	76.0	43.4
1992	West Germany	99.0	37.7	11.2	21.0	6.6	...	110	19.7	77.6	41.5
1993		99.6	37.8	12.6	19.7	7.6	...	97.9	21.2	77.6	43.1
1994		107	37.1	15.7	13.4	5.8	...	75.6	19.4	56.6	49.2
1995		100	37.0	...	11.4	5.9	...	73.0	17.1	59.8	49.7
1996		104	39.2	14.0	17.8	5.5	...	74.5	15.9	61.5	49.4
1997		101	40.3	12.7	10.8	5.4	...	78.0	19.1	61.2	49.7

D12   Imports and Exports of Petroleum by Main Surplus and Deficient Countries (in thousands of metric tons)

	Norway		Poland		Portugal	Romania		Russia/U.S.S.R.		
	I	E	I	E	I	COI	ROE	I	COE	ROE
1965	5.8	1.2	5.5	1.0	2.6	...	5.4	1.7	43.4	20.6
1966	6.7	1.1	5.7	0.5	2.4	...	5.4	1.5	50.3	22.9
1967	6.9	1.2	6.5	0.7	2.7	...	5.1	1.2	54.1	24.5
1968	7.9	1.6	8.1	1.5	2.9	0.8	5.1	1.0	59.2	26.5
1969	8.8	1.7	8.9	1.7	3.4	1.4	4.6	2.4	63.9	26.4
1970	10.8	2.1	9.4	1.3	4.3	2.3	4.9	4.4	66.8	25.6
1971	9.7	2.0	10.3	1.1	4.8	2.9	4.8	6.0	74.8	26.2
1972	10.7	4.0	12.0	1.7	4.9	2.9	4.6	8.6	76.2	26.7
1973	11.6	3.6	14.2	1.3	5.0	4.1	4.5	4.0	85.3	28.3
1974	10.6	4.0	13.6	1.2	6.6	4.5	1.0	5.2	80.6	30.8
1975	8.8	10.3	16.4	1.6	5.7	5.1	5.7	7.3	93.1	32.0
1976	11.0	16.2	18.3	2.7	6.4	8.5	7.5	7.1	111	32.6
1977	11.8	15.9	19.7	2.2	6.4	8.8	6.3	7.2	120	34.6
1978	10.7	18.7[15] 18.7	20.0	1.9	7.0	12.9	7.1	7.1	114	44.2
1979	10.8	18.7	20.5	1.5	8.2	14.3	7.0	7.2	122	42.8
1980	10.0	23.2	20.8	1.6	8.6	16.0	8.3	7.6	122	44.3
1981	7.2	20.5	17.4	0.8	8.0[26] 8.0	12.9	7.7	7.7	121	46.0
1982	6.8	20.7	16.4	0.6	9.3	10.9	6.1	10.6	128	50.4
1983	5.0	25.6	17.5	1.4	9.0	12.4	8.7	14.4	128	53.5
1984	5.2[28] 5.1	30.1	16.9	0.4	9.8	13.5	10.0	15.2	126	57.5
1985	4.4	32.6	17.2	0.5	8.5	14.6	9.2	14.4	117	49.7
1986	5.6	35.4	17.8	0.4	10.3	15.0	9.0	16.6	129	56.8
1987	5.6	41.7	17.5	0.5	9.6	16.0	8.8	16.2	137	59.2
1988	1.2	48.1	18.2	0.8	9.6	16.5	8.9	19.8	144	61.0
1989	0.9	63.6	17.5	0.7	9.7	21.8	13.3	13.3	127	55.1
1990	1.4	66.6	15.8	1.1	10.6	16.0	8.6	8.2	109	49.1
1991	1.5	80.8	13.9	1.3	9.6	8.4	2.5	—	56	37.8
1992	1.0	91.4	23.7	0.9	11.2	6.6	2.2	10.7[30]	142[30]	43.6[30]
1993	1.3	98.6	25.9	1.1	10.9	7.6	2.6	10.3[30]	127[30]	43.6[30]
1994	0.9	111	13.7	0.9	13.4	8.1	4.0	...	...	...
1995	1.4	122	12.7	0.8	13.2	8.7	3.8	...	...	...
1996	1.3	137	13.0	...	11.1	7.1	2.9	8.9	116	56.6
1997	1.5	138	13.4	...	12.7	6.2	2.7	7.9	117	60.6

D12 Imports and Exports of Petroleum by Main Surplus and Deficient Countries (in thousands of metric tons)

	Spain		Sweden	Switz	United Kingdom				Yugo-slavia
	I	E[7]	I	I	COI	ROI	COE	ROE	I
1965	16.2	1.3	19.1	8.2	66.7	20.5	...	10.8	1.3
1966	19.2	1.2	22.5	8.9	71.3	22.2	0.1	12.0	2.4
1967	24.7	2.3	22.6	9.4	74.4	24.5	0.8	11.6	3.2
1968	31.5	5.4	26.2	10.8	82.6	22.5	0.4	14.2	3.6
1969	30.8	4.8	29.2	11.6	94.4	20.7	0.6	14.2	3.9
1970	31.8	4.6	32.7	12.9	102	20.9	1.4	17.1	5.4
1971	36.2	3.9	31.1	13.4	109	20.0	1.8	16.6	5.8
1972	39.7	4.6	29.6	13.4	107	20.3	3.3	16.1	5.2
1973	42.6	4.1	29.7	14.6	115	20.6	2.9	17.0	9.4
1974	45.4	2.2	28.9	13.4	113	15.9	1.0	15.2	8.6
1975	43.1	1.8	30.6	12.2	88.5	14.7	1.1	14.0	8.2
1976	50.0	2.2	30.6	12.9	88.6[23]	14.4[23]	3.4[23]	16.5[23]	9.0
					87.0	16.1	3.3	16.6	
1977	49.1	2.2	31.4	13.0	68.6	16.3	15.3	15.2	10.8
1978	48.9	1.6	28.5	13.4	65.5	14.7	23.1	14.3	11.8
1979	51.5	1.3	32.3	12.9	57.9	16.0	38.8	14.4	13.1
1980	50.6	0.8	30.4	12.7	44.8	14.1	38.5	16.1	11.0
1981	49.3	1.4	25.2	11.3	33.0	14.4	52.5	14.2	10.4
1982	47.4	4.1	24.3	10.6	28.3	17.2	60.3	14.5	9.9
1983	49.7	8.2	25.7	12.1	22.8	17.4	68.3	15.9	10.5
1984	49.6	8.8	21.1	11.8	25.0	28.5	75.9	16.4	11.0
1985	46.6	8.0	22.6	12.0	26.9	25.0	79.6	18.9	10.2
1986	49.3	12.0	22.4	13.3	32.6	22.9	81.8	20.2	11.5
1987	49.4	9.1	22.5	11.7	33.1	20.5	80.6	18.5	12.0
1988	52.1	9.9	22.7	12.0	32.8	21.2	70.0	18.6	13.3
1989	49.4	9.2	22.2	11.7	38.3	18.6	49.1	15.8	11.7
1990	50.6	9.7	23.2	12.6	41.6	20.5	54.0	16.7	12.0
1991	50.9	11.3	22.8	13.1	45.3	20.4	52.4	18.9	10.2
1992	54.0	9.5	23.6	13.0	46.4	19.3	54.4	19.7	2.0[31]
1993	51.4	9.4	23.4	12.0	50.5	17.5	60.2	22.9	0.5[31]
1994	50.6	11.5	17.9	...	39.8	17.4	77.6	...	...
1995	53.5	10.0	16.4	...	40.3	14.5	79.0	...	...
1996	50.0	...	19.8	...	40.9	14.4	76.4	...	...
1997	53.3	12.0	22.7	...	41.4	14.5	69.8	...	...

D12 Imports and Exports of Petroleum by Main Surplus and Deficient Countries (in thousands of metric tons)

NOTES

1. SOURCES:- Finland to 1917—Erkki Pihkala, *Finland's Foreign Trade 1960-1917* (Bank of Finland, Helsinki, 1969). Finland 1943 and 1945—supplied by the Central Statistical Office of Finland. Netherlands imports 1914-21—supplied by the Netherlands Central Office of Statistics. Poland imports 1928-48 and exports 1950-58—supplied by the Polish Central Statistical Office. U.K. to 1980—based on B.R. Mitchell, *British Historical Statistics* (Cambridge, 1988), and the original sources given there. All other statistics are taken from the official publications noted on p. xv, with gaps filled from the League of Nations, *International Trade Statistics* and the United Nations, *Yearbook of International Trade Statistics*.
2. Except as indicated in headings or footnotes, crude oil and refined products are aggregated.

FOOTNOTES

[1] Figures to 1916 are for the Austro-Hungarian customs area, which excluded Venetia from 1866. Later figures are for the Republic of Austria.
[2] Figures to 1892 (1st line) include other oils than petroleum.
[3] From 1896 (2nd line) onwards, except for 1924-36, the statistics are of net imports.
[4] Figures 1913 (1st line) are of crude oil only.
[5] Converted, where necessary, from the original fluid measure on the basis of 1 metric tons = 256 gallons.
[6] Subsequently including Luxembourg.
[7] Refined products only.
[8] Previously refined products only.
[9] From 1924 (2nd line), except for 1949-61, lubricating oils are excluded.
[10] A broader classification is used subsequently.
[11] Prior to 1927 statistics are available only in value terms in official sources. T.J. Markovitch, *L'industrie francaise de 1789 à 1964* (Cahiers de l'I.S.E.A., 1966) gives the following annual averages of net imports of crude oil (in thousands of tons):-

1855-64	15	1885-94	192	1920-24	352
1865-74	22	1895-1904	230	1925-34	1,560
1875-84	67	1905-13	117		

[12] Prior to 1909 excludes trade of the Free Ports.
[13] The Galician oilfields were in the part of Poland ceded to the U.S.S.R. in 1945.
[14] These figures are for economic years, ended 30 September, Exports in October-December 1928 were 796 thousand tons.
[15] Subsequently crude oil only.
[16] From 1955 (2nd line) to 1964 (1st line) motor spirit and kerosene are excluded.
[17] Figures to 1960 (1st line) do not include heating oil.
[18] Figures to 1954 (1st line) are of gas oil only.
[19] Figures from 1949 to 1957 (1st line) for imports and 1970 (1st line) for exports do not include kerosene.
[20] Figures to 1950 do not include lubricating oil.
[21] Figures to 1955 (1st line) and from 1959 to 1962 (1st line) are of fuel oil and motor fuel only.
[22] A new classification brought more items under the heading "petroleum products" from 1960.
[23] Refinery feedstocks were transferred from the "refined" to the "crude" category from 1950 and back again in 1976.
[24] Subsequently including crude oil.
[25] Subsequently excluding lubricating oils, etc.
[26] Subsequently excluding residuals.
[27] Subsequently refined products only.
[28] Subsequently excluding some refined products.
[29] Czech Republic. Slovakia = 4.2 (1992) (IMPORTS)
    4.2 (1993) (IMPORTS)
[30] Russian Federation Ex-USSR as follows

		I	COE	ROE				I
Armenia	1992				Lithuania	1992		4.1
	1993	0.2				1993		5.2
Azerbaijan	1992	1.3	1.1					
	1993	1.2						
Belarus	1992	19.75	1.1	2.7				
	1993	12.37	0.3	—				
Georgia	1992	0.7						
	1993	0.2						
Kazakhstan	1992	11.5	13.6					
	1993	8.4	11.7					
Kyrgistan	1992							
	1993							

D12   Imports and Exports of Petroleum by Main Surplus and Deficient Countries (in thousands of metric tons)

		I	COE	ROE
Moldova	1992			
	1993			
Tajikistan	1992	0.2		
	1993	—		
Turkmenistan	1992	1.1		
	1993	0.3		
Ukraine	1992	36.3		3.5
	1993	19.7		
Uzbekistan	1992	4.2		
	1993	4.1		

[31] Yugoslavia. Ex-Yugoslavia as follows

		I
Croatia	1992	2.7
	1993	3.7
Macedonia	1992	1.0
	1993	1.1
Slovenia	1992	0.7
	1993	0.5

D13 IMPORTS AND EXPORTS OF IRON ORE BY MAIN TRADING COUNTRIES (in thousands of metric tons)

Key:- E = Exports; I = Imports

1847-1899

	Belgium[1]	France		Germany	Norway	Spain	Sweden	United Kingdom
	I	I	E	I	E	E	E	I
1847	...	14	—	...	...	...	...	...
1848	...	11	—	...	...	...	...	...
1849	...	30	—	...	...	...	...	...
1850	...	34	—	...	...	3	...	...
1851	...	18	—	...	...	10	...	...
1852	...	21	—	...	...	8	...	...
1853	...	27	—	...	...	4	...	...
1854	...	47	—	...	...	9	...	...
1855	...	55	—	...	...	12	...	11
1856	...	102	1	...	...	16	...	—
1857	−61	165	15	...	...	18	...	17
1858	−69	154	31	...	...	19	...	29
1859	−97	164	31	...	...	21	1.9	29
1860	−120	268	70	1	...	32	2.3	23
1861	−93	309	64	−4	0.3	40	5.7	23
1862	−66	375	65	−67	1.2	56	6.1	37
1863	−16	436	67	−143	0.4	72	5.6	63
1864	38	458	92	−155	2.5	62	7.7	75
1865	74	477	153	−160	2.2	57	17	78
1866	150	450	137	−78	5.7	53	14	58
1867	171	492	150	−50	6.0	81	10	88
1868	260	554	195	132	10	116	12	116
1869	387	592	239	−189	16	55	10	133
1870	389	489[2]	145[2]	216[2]	17	253	13	211
1871	432	378	136	247	3	391	12	329
1872	612	670	337	124	15	747	19	815
1873	524	722	354	356	19	800	24	984
1874	630	807	215	−68	29	700	25	766
1875	663	833	180	−386	22	336	27	466
1876	505	844	106	−473	14	682	15	683
1877	567	979	81	−476	6.0	1,258	13	1,159
1878	593	933	80	−821	1.2	1,346	14	1,192
1879	424	943	67	−744	0.5	1,062	13	1,102
1880	611	1,177	123	−656	0.1	2,822	30	2,675
1881	802	1,308	106	−817	0.2	3,122	24	2,490
1882	863	1,432	129	−836	0.4	4,025	20	3,338
1883	1,245	1,501	105	−1,087	5.7	4,226	32	3,242
1884	1,297	1,413	120	−918	0.7	3,968	40	2,775
1885	1,237	1,420	90	−859	1.4	3,797	26	2,868
1886	1,262	1,159	104	−1,019	0.2	4,188	19	2,924
1887	1,452	1,155	281	−709	2.5	5,216	42	3,826
1888	1,693	1,312	296	−1,049	0.4	4,464	117	3,619
1889	1,650	1,447	266	−945	1.1	5,052	119	4,096
1890	1,473	1,612	288	−685	0.4	5,709	188	4,544
1891	1,342	1,438	299	−576	0.8	4,344	174	3,232
1892	1,454	1,684	305	−620	0.1	4,800	320	3,842
1893	1,514	1,631	302	−780	0.5	4,785	484	4,131
1894	1,684	1,638	248	−466	1.6	4,976	831	4,485
1895	1,532	1,651	237	−463	1.5	5,175	800	4,521
1896	1,680	1,862	239	−55	2.1	6,273	1,151	5,525
1897	2,134	2,138	300	−44	4.2	6,885	1,401	6,065
1898	1,869	2,032	236	583	4.6	6,558	1,440	5,556
1899	2,303	1,951	292	1,045	13	8,613	1,628	7,168

D13 Imports and Exports of Iron Ore by Main Trading Countries (in thousands of metric tons)

1900–1944

	Belgium[1] I	Czech I	France I	France E	Germany I	Norway E	Poland I	Spain E	Sweden E	UK I
1900	2,108	...	2,119	372	860	27	...	7,823	1,620	6,399
1901	1,441	...	1,663	259	1,980	39	...	6,894	1,761	5,638
1902	2,182	...	1,563	423	1,089	49	...	7,560	1,729	6,543
1903	2,654	...	1,833	714	1,881	42	...	7,692	2,827	6,415
1904	2,918	...	1,739	1,219	2,620	45	...	7,292	3,066	6,199
1905	2,940	...	2,152	1,356	2,386	61	...	8,590	3,317	7,463
1906	3,113	...	2,016	1,759	3,778[3]	81	...	9,282	3,661	7,949
1907	3,096	...	2,000	2,148	4,572	133	...	8,636	3,522	7,765
1908	2,896	...	1,455	2,384	4,665	110	...	7,253	3,654	6,155
1909	3,912	...	1,204	3,908	5,512	39	...	8,180	3,196	6,431
1910	4,588	...	1,319	4,895	6,864	89	...	8,284	4,414	7,134
1911	5,155	...	1,352	6,177	8,239	181	...	7,345	5,087	6,449
1912	5,527	...	1,455	8,324	9,810	441	...	8,469	5,521	6,708
1913	6,360[1] 7,085	...	1,412	10,068	11,406[1] 14,019	569	...	8,907	6,440	7,561
1914	...	...	702	4,829	...	468	...	6,095	4,787	5,797
1915	...	...	271	95	...	426	...	4,509	5,992	6,296
1916	...	...	628	75	...	405	...	5,046	5,537	7,045
1917	...	...	508	127	...	198	...	5,138	5,818	6,289
1918	...	...	119[2]	68[2]	...[2]	97	...	4,345	4,464	6,688
1919	...	...	304	1,697	...	33	...	3,703	2,417	5,284
1920	2,450	656	485[6]	4,910[6]	5,915[6]	226	...	4,631	3,729	6,605
1921	1,680[4]	561	460	5,301	6,521	180	...	1,825	4,337	1,918
1922	3,594	318	380	9,468	11,014[7]	285	240	2,752	5,322	3,529
1923	6,523	1,065	534	9,854	2,377[8]	359	668	3,371	4,958	5,954
1924	9,034	1,003	725	12,287	3,076[8]	525	259	3,827	5,948	6,022
1925	9,050	1,084	1,242	9,227	11,540	425	294	3,618	8,800	4,452
1926	10,847	1,034	1,368	11,234	9,553	128	273	1,857	7,656	2,122
1927	12,678	1,067	1,047	14,665	17,409	380	710	4,758	10,716	5,247
1928	13,727	1,669	998	17,055	13,794	546	504	5,421	5,093	4,511
1929	14,057	2,079	1,141	16,389	16,953	735	...	5,595	10,899	5,780
1930	12,915	1,862	1,012	15,080	13,890	632	...	3,724	9,387	4,204
1931	10,675	1,604	782	12,407	7,071	348	...	1,873	4,496	2,153
1932	9,482	379	335	10,061	3,452	343	112	1,310	2,219	1,824
1933	9,836	389	561	10,986	4,572	481	...	1,411	3,151	2,751
1934	10,261	520	941	12,641	8,265	683	137	1,778	6,870	4,429
1935	10,583	791	443[6]	16,632[6]	14,061[6]	786	270	1,893	7,719	4,620
1936	10,718	822	392	18,252	18,469	995	381	1,744	11,198	6,057
1937	12,407	1,945	921	19,321	20,621	1,026	625	848	13,565	7,152
1938	9,394	1,360[5]	437	15,515	21,927	1,497	665	1,145	12,685	5,247
1939	10,113	1,205	...	...	...	1,182	...	1,261	13,650	5,393
1940	3,209	900	...	...	...	239	...	800	10,137	4,635
1941	1,470	1,278	...	...	...	505	...	559	9,539	2,332
1942	1,127	1,085	...	...	...	568	...	672	8,625	1,953
1943	4,631	1,279	...	...	...	342	...	591	10,257	1,924
1944	736	563	...	...	...	243	...[10]	528	4,598	2,207

D13 Imports and Exports of Iron Ore by Main Trading Countries (in thousands of metric tons)

1945–1997

	Belgium	Czech	France		West Germany	East Germany	Norway	Poland	Spain		Sweden	UK
	I	I	I	E	I	I	E	I		E	E	I
1945	1,845	55[5]	…	…	…	…	4	…		261	1,229	4,136
1946	5,984	…	102	5,582	…	…	5	…		789	5,316	6,707
1947	6,784	…	199	6,636	51	…	51	1,200		730	8,504	6,955
1948	9,511	1,824	261[6]	6,312[6]	2,429	…	183	1,616		817	11,518	8,876
1949	9,404	1,963	469	7,587	4,518[9]	…	204	1,617		990	12,783	8,832
1950	8,620	2,195	195	8,009	4,870	5	283	1,918		936[11] / 1,550	12,943	8,527
1951	11,808	2,560	353	10,599	7,371	145	269	2,170		2,254	15,246	8,887
1952	11,058	2,986	436	10,013	9,642	398	679	2,625		2,434	15,878	9,847
1953	11,862	3,038	989	10,391	10,048	622	1,010	3,097		2,097	14,686	11,157
1954	12,819	3,700	312	11,484	8,754	812	993	4,105		1,628	14,221	11,797
1955	15,054	3,926	553	14,144	14,325	1,237	1,306	4,407		2,838	15,813	13,065
1956	15,749	3,903	645	14,398	17,825	695	1,338	4,776		4,352	17,474	14,550
1957	16,078	4,923	982	14,651	19,122	815	1,324	5,914		4,616	17,661	16,167
									I[12]	E		
1958	16,872	5,164	1,004	15,568	16,962	910	1,224	5,750	498	2,223	14,935	13,106
1959	18,305	6,385	957[6]	20,379[6]	20,036[6]	1,019	1,017	6,213	278	1,084	15,617	13,564
1960	20,752	7,211	1,520	27,155	33,654	1,190	1,310	7,320	33	3,151	19,888	18,257
1961	20,652	7,970	1,713	25,855	32,673	1,096	1,209	7,670	214	1,067	20,434	15,206
1962	21,204	8,319	1,915	25,683	29,140	1,260	1,348	8,104	234	1,188	19,599	13,104
1963	19,765	9,333	3,505	21,204	27,081	1,334	1,287	8,806	93	1,294	20,486	14,164
1964	23,012	9,309	3,642	22,091	35,097	1,405	1,629	9,087	94	1,650	24,689	18,290
1965	23,899	9,553	3,985	20,747	35,567	1,452	1,444	9,274	362	1,234	24,885	18,594
1966	21,552	9,336	4,304	18,195	31,519	1,456	1,505	9,429	575	571	22,545	16,199
1967	22,006	10,366	4,889	17,537	32,180	1,550	2,506	10,056	598	814	23,396	16,333
1968	26,490	11,147	5,051	18,271	40,024	1,424	2,880	11,106	594	1,169	29,037	17,872
1969	27,517	10,716	6,973	18,515	43,813	1,320	2,872	11,575	971	1,676	31,986	18,462
1970	29,169	12,724	9,694	18,643	48,128	1,490	3,117	11,843	2,431	2,037	27,972[13]	20,174
1971	28,152	12,592	9,438	18,304	40,684	1,561	2,902	12,430	3,428	2,345	26,549	17,456
1972	28,078	13,152	11,648	19,072	40,845	1,601	3,083	12,548	4,147	1,896	28,069	17,361
1973	32,417	13,211	11,644	19,454	50,489	1,775	3,163	13,668	5,116	1,661	33,293	22,868
1974	33,430	13,985	15,953	19,833	57,770	1,802	2,809	15,609	5,280	2,962	33,503	19,952
1975	25,520	14,802	13,276	15,991	44,828	2,118	3,267	15,423	6,206	1,960	23,511	15,782
1976	26,979	15,400	14,139	15,758	47,157	2,053	2,867	15,829	6,149	2,187	22,415	18,578
1977	21,522	15,970	15,499	11,842	40,049	2,267	2,739	16,943	4,899	1,466	19,230	15,542
1978	24,243	15,600	14,697	11,225	42,514	2,046	3,122	17,198	4,628	2,025	22,614	15,453
1979	26,144	12,459	17,433	10,172	52,160	2,033	3,436	18,872	5,195	1,995	26,546	17,842
1980	22,156	12,819	18,717	8,646	50,174	2,088	2,778	20,150	4,757	2,088	21,248	8,530
1981	21,135	12,166	16,574	6,378	44,612	2,335	3,667	15,870	4,698	1,147	18,014	14,848
1982	18,613	11,640	14,995	5,836	39,171	1,932	2,334	13,493	4,620	1,869	12,654	10,783
1983	17,519	11,683	12,636	5,031	35,801	1,842	3,088	13,787	4,202	1,580	14,194	13,395
1984	19,628	11,108	16,088	4,752	42,924	1,971	3,220	17,110	4,224	1,973	17,615	14,434
1985	18,986	11,268	16,294	4,628	45,320	2,681	2,685	16,973	5,023	2,128	18,303	15,655
1986	17,978	11,264	16,190	4,168	42,045	2,598	2,565	16,644	4,406	1,790	17,220	14,807
1987	18,113	10,366	15,055	3,739	39,910	2,525	2,559	17,116	5,952	2,015	16,763	18,196
1988	20,252	10,058	18,727	3,725	45,169	2,375	1,794	16,644	5,670	…	17,722	17,934
1989	19,487	9,765	19,906	3,024	47,283	…	2,019	13,441			17,484	15,421
1990	20,348	10,123	18,285	3,280	43,890	Included in West Germany	2,149	12,066			16,398	12,539
1991	19,489	12,028	17,189	3,153	43,440		2,157	…			15,251	15,580
								Millions				
1992	18,004	…	16,406	2,875	41,474		2,410	8.0			…	15,852
1993	15,776	…	…	…	35,505		2,659				…	14,562
1994	17,011	7,368	…	…	42,773		…	8.8			15,393	14,157
1995	15,331	9,146	…	…	43,316		…	8.4			16,918	15,679
1996	12,996	8,079	…	…	39,376		…	10.8			15,173	…
1997	11,161	7,383	…	…	41,782		…	9.8			15,794	…

D13 Imports and Exports of Iron Ore by Main Trading Countries (in thousands of metric tons)

NOTES

1. SOURCES:- Belgium to 1913—A. Wibail, "L'évolution é conomique de la sidérurgie Belge de 1830á 1913", *Bulletin de l'Institut des Sciences Economiques* V, 1 (1933). France 1866–1922—supplied by the Direction Nationale des Statistiques de Commerce Extérieur. Poland 1828–34 and 1950–53—supplied by the Polish Central Statistical Office. Sweden 1867–1883—L. Jörberg, *Growth and Fluctuations of Swedish Industry, 1869–1912* (Lund) (1961). All other statistics are taken from the official and other publications noted on pp. xv–xvii with gaps filled from League of Nations, *International Trade Statistics*, United Nations, *Yearbook of International Trade*, and the British Iron & Steel Federation, *Statistical Year Book*.
2. The statistics are of crude weight, not iron content.

FOOTNOTES

[1] Figures to 1913 (1st line) are of net imports.
[2] From 1871 to 1918 Alsace-Lorraine was part of Germany rather than France.
[3] Up to March 1906 the free ports were not included with Germany.
[4] Including Luxembourg from 1 May 1922.
[5] From 16 March 1939 to 30 April 1939 Sudetenland is excluded, and the Czech lands and Slovakia were treated as independent of each other. The figures given here are aggregates of the separate statistics of each.
[6] From 1921 to February 1935 and from April 1948 to July 1959, Saarland was included with France rather than Germany.
[7] Eastern Upper Silesia was transferred from Germany to Poland in July 1922.
[8] These figures are incomplete owing to the French occupation of the Ruhr.
[9] Figures for 1947–49 are of the American and British Occupation Zones only.
[10] Poland acquired the whole of Silesia in 1945.
[11] Figures to 1950 do not include exports of iron concentrates.
[12] Prior to this date imports were negligible.
[13] Excluding a negligible amount of pyrites.

D14 RAW COTTON CONSUMPTION INDICATORS (in thousands of metric tons)

1750–1804

Year	Sweden[1]	U.K.
1750	--	1.0
1751	--	1.3
1752	--	1.5
1753	--	1.9
1754	0.1	1.4
1755	--	1.7
1756	--	1.2
1757	--	0.8
1758	--	0.9
1759	--	1.0
1760	--	0.8
1761	--	1.2
1762	--	1.3
1763	--	1.1
1764	--	1.7
1765	--	1.7
1766	--	3.1
1767	--	1.6
1768	--	1.8
1769	--	1.8
1770	--	1.5
1771	--	1.1
1772	--	2.2
1773	--	1.1
1774	--	2.4
1775	--	2.8
1776	0.1	2.7
1777	0.1	2.9
1778	--	2.7
1779	0.1	2.5
1780	0.1	3.0
1781	--	2.3
1782	0.1	5.2
1783	0.1	4.3
1784	0.1	5.1
1785	0.1	8.2
1786	0.1	8.7
1787	0.1	10.1
1788	0.1	8.9
1789	0.1	15
1790	0.1	14
1791	0.1	13
1792	0.1	15
1793	0.1	8
1794	0.1	10
1795	0.1	11
1796	0.2	14
1797	0.1	10
1798	--	14
1799	--	19
1800	0.1	24
1801	0.1	24
1802	0.1	25
1803	0.2	24
1804	0.2	28

1805–1859

Year	Austria[4]	Belgium[1]	Finland[1]	France[3,5]	Germany[3]	Neth'l[3]	Russia[6]	Spain	Sweden[1]	U.K.[2]
1805	...	...	...	...	...	...	...	...	0.1	27
1806	...	...	...	...	...	...	...	...	0.1	26
1807	...	...	...	...	...	...	...	...	0.1	33
1808	...	...	...	...	...	...	...	...	...	19
1809	...	...	...	...	...	...	...	...	0.8	40
1810	...	...	...	...	...	...	...	...	1.8	56[2]
1811	...	...	...	...	...	...	...	...	0.4	40
1812	...	...	...	...	...	...	1.4	...	0.1	33
1813	...	...	--	...	...	...	0.7	...	0.1	35
1814	...	...	--	...	...	...	0.5	...	...	33
1815	...	...	--	...	...	...	0.8	...	0.1	37
1816	...	1.3	--	...	...	...	0.6	...	...	40
1817	...	0.8	--	...	...	...	0.8	...	0.1	49
1818	...	1.8	0.1	...	...	...	1.1	...	0.1	50
1819	...	2.2	0.1	...	...	...	1.6	...	0.2	49
1820	...	1.1	--	...	...	...	0.6	...	0.2	54
1821	...	2.0	--	...	...	...	1.0	...	0.2	59
1822	...	2.2	--	...	...	...	1.6	...	0.1	66
1823	...	2.1	--	...	...	...	1.3	...	0.2	70
1824	...	1.2	--	...	...	...	0.9	...	0.1	75
1825	...	2.4	--	...	...	...	1.0	...	0.1	76
1826	...	3.2	0.1	...	...	...	1.7	...	0.2	68
1827	...	3.1	--	...	...	...	1.1	...	0.2	89
1828	4.7	2.3	--	...	...	...	1.5	...	0.2	99
1829	5.9	4.8	--	...	...	...	2.2	...	0.2	99
1830	6.4	3.0	--	...	...	...	1.9	...	0.2	112
1831	5.6	1.0	--	28	...	...	1.7	...	0.3	119
1832	8.7	2.5	0.1	34	2.4	...	2.1	...	0.4	126
1833	8.1	3.1	--	36	1.8	...	2.3	...	0.3	130
1834	8.2	2.2	--	37	7.5	...	2.5	3.4	0.3	137
1835	8.7	4.8	--	39	4.5	...	3.6	2.9	0.4	144
1836	12	6.7	--	44	7.6	...	4.2	3.6	0.5	157
1837	13	7.0	0.1	44	10.2	...	4.3	4.3	0.4	166
1838	13	6.9	0.1	51	9.0	...	5.4	5.2	0.6	189
1839	12	4.1	--	40	6.8	...	5.8	3.8	0.6	173
1840	12	9.1	0.1	53	12.8	...	6.5	8.4	0.8	208
1841	14	7.6	...	56	11.1	...	5.1	8.4	0.8	199
1842	18	6.1	...	57	12.1	...	8.4	4.9	1.2	197
1843	21	7.5	...	60	15.3	...	7.7	2.6	1.1	235
1844	19	7.2	...	59	13.3	...	9.6	7.0	1.4	247
1845	24	8.7	0.3	60	17.0	...	12	17	1.4	275
1846	25	6.2	0.3	64	16.0	-1.7	12	...	1.4	279
1847	24	7.6	0.3	45	13.8	1.6	14	...	2.1	200
1848	16	8.2	0.4	45	15.4	2.8	20	...	3.4	262
1849	25	13	0.4	64	19.8	0.4	26	12	2.8	286
1850	29	10	0.3	59	17.1	-0.2	20	16	2.0	267
1851	24	10	...	58		1.2	23	15	3.4	299
1852	35	12	...	72		2.0	30	16	3.7	336
1853	32	11	0.7	75	average	5.0	32	16	4.5	345
1854	32	11	0.5	72	26	0.8	27	17	6.7	352
1855	34	11	0.6	76		-1.0	25	17	6.7	381
1856	39	13	--	84		-1.3	36	28	7.6	404
1857	36	11	0.9	73	average	3.1	40	17	5.5	375
1858	40	12	0.1	80	40	-3.9	44	21	4.5	411
1859	37[4]	13	0.4	82	48	9.7	48	24	6.9	443

D14   Raw Cotton Consumption Indicators (in thousands of metric tons)

1860–1914

	Austria[4]	Belgium[1]	Finland[1]	France[3]	Germany[3]	Italy[1]	Neth'l[3]	Portugal[1]	Russia[6]	Spain	Sweden[1]	Switz[1]	UK[2]
1860	45[4]	15	1.4[7] 1.8	115	67	...	3.6	...	47	24	8.2	33	492
1861	44	15	1.6	110	74	12.4	−2.3	...	43	27	7.7	29	457
1862	19	5	0.3	28	38	3.8	−1.4	...	14	13	1.3	19	205
1863	16	7	0.5	45	40	4.1	6.6	...	18	17	0.7	20	230
1864	18	7	0.5	56	37	3.2	1.4	...	27	14	1.7	23	251
1865	22[4]	12	0.8	61	46	2.8	−1.8	...	26	15	3.2	24	328
1866	25	15	0.9	99	57	6.0	4.5	...	48	19	4.7	34	400
1867	37	16	1.3	74	67	9.9	4.4	...	54	21	5.7	34	439
1868	40	16	1.2	99	73	11	4.5	...	42	22	4.9	41	450
1869	42	16	1.8	94	64	12	3.0	...	53	20	5.6	42	426
1870	45	16	1.4[8]	59[5]	81[5]	15	5.0	...	46	27	6.4	38	489
1871	58	26	1.6[8]	99	112	27	13	...	68	35	10	54	547
1872	48	24	1.8[8]	80	111	20	18	2.0	59	28	5.7	42	536
1873	43	18	1.7[8]	55	118	24	5.2	2.0	58	27	8.2	38	565
1874	48	20	2.2	94	127	31	5.8	1.6	76	38	10	41	579
1875	52	18	2.3	101	114	19	5.5	2.1	85	34	6.0	22	557
1876	56	19	1.9	103	135	20	10	2.0	77	39	10	24	581
1877	57	20	2.0	85	117	24	5.2	2.7	73	34	8.8	19	558
1878	57	22	2.3	80	111	27	12	2.4	118	36	7.0	16	541
1879	66	22	2.3	90	123	37	9	2.8	106	37	6.8	23	522
1880	64	23	3.0	89	137	47	14	3.4	94	45	9.2	22	617
1881	72	30	2.8	109	139	49	10	3.3	149	45	10	25	649
1882	67	25	3.1	111	138	63	9	3.3	127	46	10	23	661
1883	95	24	3.0	116	169	67	18	4.0	147	54	13	29	692
1884	85	25	3.3	97	160	66	13	3.7	121	53	10	27	672
1885	72	17	2.6	108	156	79	17	4.2	124	49	11	23	589
1886	83	21	3.3	111	161	68	9	5.1	137	46	11	20	658
1887	95	23	3.2	121	198	76	12	5.0	184	46	11	27	680
1888	83	21	2.8	95	179	75	9	5.5	137	42	12	22	692
1889	87	14	4.2	124	225	90	8	6.0	171	64	12	29	709
1890	105	32	4.4	125	227	102	12	8.2	136	50	13	27	755
1891	106	34	4.1	154	237	93	14	7.2	152	61	15	25	756
1892	108	21	4.7	179	219	98	12	7.4	164	61	13	24	702
1893	110	35	2.9	138	227	99	11	11	187	59	11	22	650
1894	119	35	5.6	160	254	120	11	11	190	68	18	25	727
1895	122	22	4.4	141	267	108	12	13	201	71	14	26	755
1896	117	29	5.2	134	242	113	16	10	224	59	14	24	743
1897	123	38	6.7	189	273	120	14	13	225	76	18	24	740
1898	143	43	5.8	176	322	133	20	15	233	65	19	26	799
1899	132	35	6.2	175	295	131	19	16	264	86	16	24	799
1900	127	35	6.4	159	279	123	18	16	262	66	17	24	788[10]
1901	138	33	5.6	185	327	135	20	13	264	78	17	25	712
1902	147	45	5.9	187	336	147	22	15	286	85	18	25	741
1903	152	54	5.3	219	370	154	19	14	295	80	18	26	733
1904	156	40	5.9	176	382	155	21	15	299	71	17	27	674
1905	164	48	6.3	202	394	165	24	16	273	76	19	26	822
1906	168	54	7.8	205	385	183	22	13	296	87	21	26	841
1907	206	62	8.1	229	454	218	29	17	319	92	21	28	900
1908	181	49	7.7	232	429	207	29	16	347	95	21	26	870
1909	193	67	7.7	260	448	191	22	15	349	71	17	27	827
1910	173	63	6.8	158	383	175	20	16	362	73	21	24	740
1911	201	126	8.0	252	437	190	29	18	351	90	20	27	858
1912	224	141	8.7	276	507	214	35	18	421	93	22	30	972
1913	210	140	8.8	271	478	202	36	18	424[6] 223	88	22	31	988
1914	172	...	6.9	160	...	191	29	15	...	84	23	24	942

D14 Raw Cotton Consumption Indicators (in thousands of metric tons)

	Austria[4]	Belgium[1]	Bulgaria[1]	Czech[3]	Finland[1]	France[3]	Germany[3]	E. Germany	Greece[1]	Hungary[1]	Italy[1]
1915	123	...	- -	...	8.9	219	...	...	...	...	291
1916	...	...	- -	...	12.4	226	...	...	...	...	254
1917	...	...	- -	...	4.0	254	...	...	...	...	179
1918	...[4]	...	0.2	...	0.6	136[5]	...[5]	...	...	...	130
1919	...	51	- -	...	6.4	201	...	...	...	...	179
1920	10	101	0.2	62	6.5	202	139	...	...	0.2	179
1921	23	61	- -	89	7.2	189	...	...	...	0.9	158
1922	24	65	- -	71	7.5	240	218	...	...	2.2	178
1923	22	76	0.2	75	7.3	235	215	...	...	3.1	185
1924	24	72	0.2	104	5.9	281	316	...	...	3.0	201
1925	34	95	0.4	137	8.1	317	413	...	...	5.2	237
1926	26	92	0.8	101	8.8	344	327	...	...	5.5	239
1927	34	115	1.4	148	9.6	327	508	...	...	7.6	209
1928	31	111	1.7	125	9.0	315	388	...	...	9.1	233
1929	26	111	1.9	123	7.7	358	393	...	...	13	245
1930	22	100	2.7	113	7.1	361	346	...	...	15	205
1931	22	101	3.1	93	7.2	222	303	...	...	16	171
1932	20	80	3.8	81	7.6	244	358	...	...	18	190
1933	25	101	4.8	71	9.2	349	419	...	...	23	220
1934	28	100	7.2	79	14	223	349	...	...	26	187
1935	33	121	6.3	78	13	222	356	...	...	24	149
1936	38	128	8.3	95	13	329	318	...	...	29	101
1937	39	136	10.4	111	15	298	350	...	...	27	166
1938	...	124	12.0	71[9]	14	288	353	...	...	27	159
1939	...	64	9.5	44	12	239	...	...	...	26	111
1940	...	45	5.3	10	10	282	...	...	...	16	108
1941	...	1	1.7	10	4	...	...	...	...	7.2	4
1942	...	1	- -	2	- -	...	...	...	...	0.3	1
1943	...	...	0.9	0.5	- -	...	...	...	...	3.9	...
1944	...	...	0.5	-[9]	- -	...	...	...	...	0.8	...
1945	...	52	2.3	4	6	218	...	...	5	0.2	...
1946	—	67	13	20	9	188	...	...	13	12	187
1947	11[4]	98	...[1]	60[3]	11	221	...	...	3[1]	26[1]	206
							W. Germany[3]				
1948	14	71[1] / 88	...	54	10[1] / 12	190[3] / 242	94	...	19	26	205[1] / 180
1949	17	80	...	60	8	231	127	...	18	30	207
1950	20	87	...	60	11	252	189	...	21	30	203
1951	21	103	22	65	12	272	235	43	25	30	214
1952	21	88	26	69	13	266	209	54	24	33	193
1953	17	80	29	59	13	249	233	65	23	50	187
1954	20	93	33	65	14	290	265	75	26	51	190
1955	23	92	33	72	13	275	271	87	25	51	174
1956	23	90	34	76	14	264	286	87	23	43	166
1957	23	98	35	80	16	298	310	89	26	34	192
1958	26	81	36	89	14	305	311	92	28	44	187
1959	25	82	41	92	15	254	294	98	28	43	189
1960	26	90	48	98	18	298	319	100	26	51	222
1961	28	93	47	102	17	303	325	102	30	55	226
1962	28	86	50	106	16	285	303	104	31	59	227
1963	25	86	52	105	16	278	283	100	34	62	231
1964	25	87	54	103	16	283	285	93	35	65	227
1965	26	79	56	104	17	258	286	93	38	73	191
1966	25	75	61	108	15	267	282	92	44	76	218
1967	23	66	65	111	17	268	255	91	46	78	241
1968	21	65	72	111	16	243	258	89	44	74	223
1969	23	66	74	108	16	244	255	89	46	69	221

D14   Raw Cotton Consumption Indicators (in thousands of metric tons)

	Neth'l[3]	Poland[1]	Portugal[1]	Romania[1]	Russia/USSR[6]	Spain	Sweden[1]	Switz[1]	UK[2]	Yugo[1]
1915	40	...	18	0.1	...	143	121	38	876[11]	...
1916	38	...	16	...	...	102	28	27	894	...
1917	10	...	14	—	...	97	7	22	816	...
1918	- -	...	15	—	...	60	7	8	680	...
1919	32	...	7	0.2	...	74	17	27	692	...
1920	29	23	12		...	80	23	23	783	14
1921	31	37	14	0.5	...	82	13	26	484	38
1922	31	65	14	1.4	...	83	18	23	639	42
1923	32	58	16	1.8	...	83	19	28	618	45
1924	25	43	13	1.9	...	79	21	31	621	50
1925	42	55	14	1.5	...	86	20	34	730	57
1926	45	66	16	1.1	...	82	23	30	684	69
1927	53	79	17	2.7	...	96	24	36	706	69
1928	49	76	17	...	208	74	25	32	689	70
1929	53	66	16	3.3	238	76	22	32	679	76
1930	52	61	18	3.3	257	99	23	31	577	88
1931	52	55	15	3.0	338	95	24	26	447	81
1932	35	51	21	3.7	395	106	25	29	570	86
1933	39	61	22	5.0	379	98	23	34	534	105
1934	42	68	22	5.7	420	102	32	32	600	146
1935	40	66	23	6.0	437	99	28	29	572	149
1936	50	71	21	9.4	596	...	32	30	631	168
1937	63	72	30	17	717	...	34	38	649[12]	207
1938	53	...	28	20	893	...	36	31	503	216
1939	61	...	19	13	...	...	47	42	597	181
1940	...	...	24	13	849[6]	74	20	22	630	...
1941	...	...	23	7.9	...	52	16	12	438	...
1942	...	...	23	0.4	...	66	32	1.7	426	...
1943	...	...	18	1.4	...	88	18	0.1	401	...
1944	...	...	33	1.0	...	84	35	0.2	365	...
1945	...	...	24	...	312	116	12	19	325	...
1946	53	...	39	...	...	70	19	38	369	...
1947	54	69	26	...	...	57	17	32	370	...
1948	45[3]	—[1]	33[1]	—[1]	...	75	26[1]	26[1]	443	30
	48	73	33	18			25	31		
1949	53	78	33	13	821	91	25	29	443	34
1950	61	87	36	17	953	59	28	30	461	35
1951	65	90	35	22	1,265	53	29	34	464	30
1952	58	90	39	24	1,360[6]	68	27	36	311	26
					911					
1953	64	91	38	50	965	75	26	32	377	26
1954	70	92	42	51	1,019	69	29	36	404	27
1955	72	94	46	54	1,106	76	30	38	354	34
1956	73	95	44	49	1,084	86	29	36	330	38
1957	74	92	43	46	1,171	100	30	40	344	42
1958	72	101	45	50	1,236	103	30	42	292	42
1959	71	108	46	51	1,301	103	28	34	289	43
1960	77	116	55	52	1,344	121	28	39	278	48
1961	82	125	66	56	1,344	126	28	42	250	52
1962	77	128	66	65	1,355	139	27	42	221	54
1963	78	125	69	67	1,366	119	23	41	226	72
1964	76	132	74	69	1,431	114	21	41	237	72
1965	77	145	80	71	1,496	114	21	43	230	81
1966	71	150	83	73	1,550	126	20	40	212	89
1967	67	150	78	74	1,626	126	17	40	181	90
1968	62	143	80	76	1,691	98	17	40	180	90
1969	62	141	85	80	1,713	119	15	41	177	91

D14 Raw Cotton Consumption Indicators (in thousands of metric tons)

	Austria[4]	Belgium[1]	Bulgaria[1]	Czech[3]	Finland[1]	France[3]	W. Germany[3]	E. Germany	Greece[1]	Hungary[1]	Italy[1]
1970	23	70	75	105	13	248	254	93	49	72	221
1971	23	66	70	108	14	237	234	92	53	76	201
1972	23	62	75	108	14	235	240	91	61	72	200
1973	22	57	72	112	13	231	233	97	77	74	187
1974	22	58	73	113	13	233	238	83	82	75	195
1975	19	46	69	114	12	202	209	81	90	79	180
1976	21	44	67	108	13	203	222	83	114	77	195
1977	24	39	68	108	13	208	209	83	125	79	200
1978	21	31	68	117	12	184	176	83	131	70	182
1979	22	35	65	117	12	179	169	87	143	68	212
1980	24	41	60	119	13	184	172	89	153	69	228
1981	22	34	60	105	10	162	171	98	142	77	202
1982	22	32	63	111	10	165	190	102	144	66	224
1983	21	38	65	123	10	165	207	102	151	60	229
1984	20	39	63	123	10	160	214	99	156	63	253
1985	20	41	58	121	7	155	216	96	163	63	260
1986	19	46	55	130	6	156	224	97	172	62	288
1987	22	51	54	133	6	154	235	101	173	61	321
1988	24	48	54	127	6	145	220	104	169	61	314
1989	23	43	65	123	4	141	202	89	165	65	310
1990	24	46	65	123	4	124	206	72	170	58	315
1991	25	40	39	97	2	113	223		180	41	333
1992	32	39	26	63	2	100	178		180	30	320

	Neth'l[3]	Poland[1]	Portugal[1]	Romania[1]	Russia/ USSR[6]	Spain	Sweden[1]	Switz[1]	UK[2]	Yugo[1]
1970	59	145	90	80	1,756	113	14	42	172	92
1971	55	150	93	87	1,821	111	12	43	161	90
1972	52	152	104	93	1,843	119	9	43	138	90
1973	47	150	109	100	1,843	124	9	41	141	92
1974	46	152	120	103	1,865	119	9	41	121	94
1975	37	147	106	98	1,886	115	8	38	111	98
1976	32	152	104	102	1,879	119	6	40	107	103
1977	34	152	108	102	1,879	125	6	47	106	108
1978	27	152	102	102	1,923	115	6	44	90	112
1979	22	158	110	104	1,919	117	6	45	97	111
1980	22	170	128	106	1,925	102	6	50	87	108
1981	16	134	130	125	1,746	91	4	50	46	106
1982	17	132	135	123	1,678	87	7	47	45	103
1983	14	134	142	98	1,693	100	7	54	50	112
1984	10	135	147	90	1,813	105	6	59	46	124
1985	11	140	159	102	1,951	110	6	59	46	128
1986	11	151	167	106	2,028	133	6	65	48	120
1987	11	158	178	98	1,996	151	5	63	49	115
1988	9	160	187	89	1,985	153	5	76	45	116
1989	7	166	191	81	2,003	135	5	64	41	912
1990	8	137	190	81	1,995	154	5	61	33	98
1991	5	88	154	78	1,275[1]	145	5	62	23	77
1992	4	72	150	65	1,239[1]	144	5	61	14	70

D14 Raw Cotton Consumption Indicators (in thousands of metric tons)

NOTES

1. SOURCES:- Statistics prior to 1948 are taken from the official publications noted on p. xv with occasional gaps filled from League of Nations sources, with the following exceptions:- Belgium to 1830—R. Demoulin, *Guillaume Ier et la transformation économique des Provinces Belges* (Liège, 1938). Finland to 1860 (1st line)—Per Schybergson, *Hantverk och fabriker. Finlands konsumtionsvaruindustrii 1815–1870* (transcribed by the Central Statistical Office of Finland). Finland 1860 (2nd line) to 1917—Erkki Pihkala, *Finland's Foreign Trade 1860–1917* (Bank of Finland, Helsinki, 1969). Germany to 1850, K.F.W. Dieterici, *Statistische Uebersicht der Wichtigsten Gegenstände...*, (Berlin, 1838–52). Russia to 1913 (1st line)—P.A. Khromov, *Economic Development of Russia in the 19th and 20th Centuries, 1800–1917* (Moscow, 1950). Russia 1913 (2nd line) to 1953 (1st line)—G.W. Nutter, *The Growth of Industrial Production in the Soviet Union* (Princeton, 1962). U.K. to 1936—based on B.R. Mitchell, *British Historical Statistics* (Cambridge, 1988), where the original sources are given. Statistics from 1948 (except Russia to 1953) are taken from the United Nations, *Statistical Yearbooks*, the original source being the International Cotton Federation. These latter are for years ended 31 July.
2. Where statistics of cotton consumption are available they have been preferred. Otherwise statistics of imports minus re-exports are given, or, failing that, "special" trade imports—i.e. imports *intended* for home consumption. In the last resort statistics of total imports have been given.
3. Estimates of consumption in thousands of bales are available back to 1907 in publications of the International Federation of Master Cottonspinners, though with a gap for the wars and immediate postwar periods. They were given in measure of weight for the year ended 31 July 1939 in the U.N. *Statistical Yearbook* as follows (in thousands of tons):-

Austria	39	Germany	234	Romania	20
Belgium	70	Greece	18	Spain	30
Bulgaria	16	Hungary	28	Sweden	30
Czechoslovakia	43	Italy	144	Switzerland	31
Finland	13	Netherlands	56	United Kingdom	583
France	281	Poland	76	Yugoslavia	20
		Portugal	22		

FOOTNOTES

[1] Figures to 1947 or 1948 (1st line) are of "special" imports, and subsequently of estimated consumption for years ended 31 July.
[2] Estimated consumption. From 1948 they are for years ended 31 July.
[3] Figures to 1947 or 1948 (1st line) are of net imports, and subsequently of estimated consumption for years ended 31 July.
[4] Figures to 1915 are for the whole Austro-Hungarian customs area. Lombardy was excluded from 1860 and Venetia from 1866, and Dalmatia was not included until 1861. Figures from 1920 are for the Republic of Austria. Austria-Hungarian statistics are of net imports. Republic statistics are of "special" imports to 1947 and subsequently of estimated consumption for years ended 31 July.
[5] T.J. Markovitch, *L'industrie francaise de 1789 à 1964* (Cahiers de L'I.S.E. A, 1966) gives the following figures for averages of years (in thousands of tons):- 1781–90—4.0; 1815–24—19.0; 1825–34—34. For 1871–1918 Alsace-Lorraine is included with Germany rather than France.
[6] Figures to 1859 are of total imports of raw cotton. From 1860 to 1913 (1st line) they are said to be raw cotton consumption, though to begin with they are the same as imports. From 1913 (2nd line) to 1953 (1st line) the figures are of ginned cotton consumption, and subsequently they are of raw cotton consumption for years ended 31 July. The figures to 1913 (1st line) apply to the Russian Empire (excluding Finland). From 1913 (2nd line) to 1940 they are for the 1923 boundaries of the U.S.S.R., and subsequently for the postwar territory.
[7] This break occurs on a change of source (see note 1).
[8] These figures exclude imports by rail.
[9] From March 1939 to 1944 the Sudetenland is excluded.
[10] Figures for 1900–14 are for years ended 31 August.
[11] Subsequent figures are for years ended 31 July.
[12] Subsequent figures are for 52 week periods as close to the calendar year as possible.
[13] Russian Federation. Ex'-USSR as follows

Armenia	1992	6
	1993	5
Azerbaijan	1992	30
	1993	30
Belarus	1992	33
	1993	32
Estonia	1992	44
	1993	30
Georgia	1992	19
	1993	15
Kazakhstan	1992	39
	1993	39
Kyrgistan	1992	26
	1993	26

D14 Raw Cotton Consumption Indicators (in thousands of metric tons)

Lativa	1992	13
	1993	12
Lithuania	1992	22
	1993	20
Moldova	1992	36
	1993	32
Tajikistan	1992	32
	1993	32
Turkmenistan	1992	7
	1993	15
Ukraine	1992	208
	1993	171
Uzbekistan	1992	205
	1993	207

D15 COTTON SPINDLES (in thousands)

1834-1970

	Austria[1]	Belgium	Czechoslovakia	France	Germany	East Germany[2]	Italy
1834	800	200	...	2,500	626[8]	...	...
1852	1,400	400	...	4,500	900	...	...
1861	1,800	612	...	5,500	2,235	...	...
1867	1,500	625	...	6,800[7]	2,000[7]	...	450
1877	1,558	800	...	5,000	4,700	...	880
1882/3	1,950	840	...	4,800	4,800	...	1,150
1886/7	2,070	...	...	...	5,060	...	...
1891/2	2,400	930	...	5,040	6,071	...	1,686
1904	3,450	880[6]	...	6,150	8,434	...	2,435
1908	4,000	1,200	...	6,700	9,900	...	4,200
1913	4,909[1]	1,492	...	7,400[7]	11,186[7]	...	4,600
1920[3]	1,140	1,572	3,584	9,400	9,400	...	4,515
1921	...	1,548	3,082	9,600	9,400	...	4,506
1922	...	1,630	3,549	9,600	9,500	...	4,580
1923	1,023	1,683	3,508	9,600	9,605	...	4,570
1924	1,051	1,741	3,460	9,359	9,464	...	4,570
1925	1,038	1,788	3,471	9,428	9,500	...	4,771
1926	1,032	1,854	3,568	9,511	10,480	...	4,833
1927	1,025	1,936	3,629	9,567	10,800	...	5,086
1928	1,014	2,070	3,663	9,770	11,153	...	5,189
1929	955	2,156	3,673	9,880	11,250	...	5,210
1930	817	2,172	3,636	10,250	11,070	...	5,342
1931	768	2,164	3,638	10,350	10,591	...	5,397
1932	767	2,156	3,622	10,144	10,233	...	5,384
1933	758	2,087	3,627	10,144	9,850	...	5,338
1934	774	2,106	3,627	10,170	10,109	...	5,493
1935[4]	765	2,091	3,625	10,157	...	...	5,477
1936	776	2,008	3,611	10,016	...	...	...
1937	777	1,995	3,548	9,932	10,247	...	...
1938	742	1,993	3,357	9,783	10,323	...	5,395
1939	742	1,984	3,330	9,794	12,225[9]	...	5,324
					West Germany		
1950	546	1,802	2,331	8,148	5,785	750	5,566
1951	561	1,844	2,340	8,110	6,168	850	5,661
1952	571	1,857	2,380	8,110	6,244	890	5,736
1953	577	1,833	2,380	7,964	6,279	890	5,781
1954	607	1,835	2,420	7,698	6,100	980	5,750
1955[3]	608	1,752	2,450	7,618	6,005	1,000	5,698
1956	596	1,661	2,480	5,547	5,954	1,000	5,726
1957	607	1,601	1,893	6,257	5,855	1,100	5,574
1958[5]	579	1,581	1,900	6,280	6,120	1,150	5,212
1959	579	1,521	1,950	6,071	5,948	1,150	4,854
1960	576	1,493	1,950	5,802	5,909	1,150	4,611
1961	565	1,470	2,055	5,467	5,817	1,150	4,522
1962	563	1,463	2,089	5,418	5,605	1,357	4,453
1963	559	1,446	2,066	4,645	5,403	1,518	4,449
1964	557	1,387	2,042	4,563	5,214	1,586	4,466
1965	503	1,337	2,102	4,299	5,091	1,586	4,424
1966	480	1,215	2,151	4,189	4,926	1,586	4,287
1967	453	1,121	2,124	4,105	4,672	1,586	4,324
1968	435	1,080	2,133	3,788	4,529	1,625	4,325
1969	416	1,068	2,124	3,621	4,349	1,625	4,125
1970	415	985	2,095	3,588	4,262	1,675	4,121

D15 Cotton Spindles (in thousands)

1834–1970

	Netherlands	Poland[2]	Portugal	Russia[2]	Spain	Switzerland	UK
1834	....	....		700[12]		580	10,000
1852	....	....		....		900	20,977[17]
1861	40	....		1,000[13]		1,350	30,387
1867	....	....		2,500[14]		1,000	34,215
1877	....	....		....		1,854[16]	44,207[18]
1882/3	250		110	4,400	1,865	1,900	....
1886/7	....		....			....	44,348[19]
1891/2	260	....	160[11]	6,000	2,050	1,722	44,509[20]
1904	....		230	7,146[21]	2,600	1,600	47,857[21][22]
1908	386	...	378	7,900	1,850	1,500	52,818
1913	479	...	480	9,212[15]	2,000	1,398	55,653
1920[3]	598	1,400	482	7,200	1,800	1,536	58,692
1921	630	1,161	400	....	1,806	1,531	56,141
1922	720	1,200	487		1,806	1,519	56,605
1923	669	1,200	487	7,246	1,813	1,513	56,583
1924	686	1,101	503		1,813	1,515	56,750
1925	817	1,172	503	....	1,813	1,517	57,116
1926	921	1,375	503	....	1,817	1,529	57,286
1927	1,002	1,372	503	6,945	1,873	1,518	57,325
1928	1,111	1,544	503	7,311	1,897	1,525	57,136
1929	1,160	1,557	503	7,465	1,875	1,504	55,917
1930	1,167	1,554	503	7,624	1,875	1,446	55,207
1931	1,215	1,555	503	....	2,070	1,381	54,246
1932	1,213	1,706	453	....	2,070	1,346	51,891
1933	1,224	1,818	446	9,200	2,070	1,303	49,001
1934	1,236	1,696	452	9,800	2,070	1,295	45,893
1935[4]	1,219	1,684	452	9,800	2,070	1,287	43,756
1936	1,218	1,683	464	9,800	2,070	1,236	42,307
1937	1,221	1,704	471	9,900	2,070	1,272	39,938
1938	1,206	1,715	469	10,050	2,070	1,248	37,340
1939	1,241	1,764[10]	444	10,350	2,000	1,249	36,322
1950	1,170	1,067	536	9,483	2,210	1,156	29,580
1951	1,170	1,085	782	9,750	2,210	1,162	28,968
1952	1,170	1,185	949	9,900	2,206	1,165	27,933
1953	1,234	1,220	875	9,900	2,226	1,158	27,232
1954	1,232	1,260	886	10,150	2,240	1,158	26,454
1955[3]	1,099	1,275	896	10,150	2,335	1,189	25,183
1956	1,077	1,310	962	10,100	2,364	1,188	23,972
1957	1,059	1,340	998	10,147	2,364	1,199	22,487
1958[5]	1,041	1,925	1,055	10,712	2,608	1,192	19,889
1959	1,032	1,954	1,088	10,800	2,700	1,177	14,104
1960	1,020	2,001	1,101	10,800	2,589	1,169	9,710
1961	1,013	2,019	1,125	11,500	2,711	1,168	9,465
1962	985	1,955	1,138	12,202	2,648	1,126	8,053
1963	987	1,973	1,155	12,300	2,580	1,120	6,475
1964	960	1,965	1,112	12,000	2,612	1,132	6,077
1965	907	1,967	1,198	12,707	2,580	1,114	5,345
1966	821	2,076	1,212	13,427	2,420	1,040	5,092
1967	656	2,086	1,249	14,173	2,176	1,027	3,790
1968	637	2,042	1,323	14,507	2,117	978	3,822
1969	552	2,083	1,335	14,604	2,101	965	3,635
1970	563	2,108	1,357	14,694	2,210	941	3,486

D15 Cotton Spindles (in thousands)

NOTES

1. SOURCES:- 1834-67, all countries except Russia in 1840 and 1857, the U.K. in 1850, 1861 and 1867, and Italy in 1867—D.S. Landes in the *Cambridge Economic History of Europe*, vol. VI, part 1. Russia in 1840—M.G. Mulhall, *Dictionary of Statistics* (4th edition, London, 1899). Russia in 1857, Switzerland in 1876, and all statistics for 1904—S.J. Chapman, *The Cotton Industry and Trade* (London, 1905). Italy in 1867—*L'Industria Tessile Cotoniera in Italia dai suoi Inizia ad Oggi* (Rome, 1952). 1877, all countries except Switzerland and the U.K.—*Annali di Statistica*, serie II, vol. 13. 1882/3, all countries except the U.K.—T. Ellison, *The Cotton Trade of Britain* (London, 1886). 1891-2, all countries except the U.K.—F. Merttens in *Transactions of the Manchester Statistical Society* (April 1894). 1904—all countries except the U.K.—J.A. Todd, *The Cotton World* (London, 1927) U.K. in 1850-1903—*Reports of H.M. Inspectors of Factories*, published in the Sessional Papers of Parliament. 1908-1970—publications of the International Federation of Cotton and Allied Textile Industries (under various names).

2. In principle, the statistics in this table relate to spinning spindles, except as indicated in footnotes. Rayon spinning spindles are included.

FOOTNOTES

[1] The figures to 1913 apply to the whole Austro-Hungarian Empire.
[2] Statistics from 1950 are estimated. (From 1920 in the case of Russia).
[3] From 1920 to 1934 and 1955 to 1957 the count was made on 31 July.
[4] From 1935 to 1954 the count was made on 31 January.
[5] From 1958 the count was made on 31 December.
[6] In 1898.
[7] From 1871 to 1918 Alsace-Lorraine is included in Germany rather than France.
[8] In 1836.
[9] This figure probably applies to Greater Germany (i.e. including Austria and Sudetenland).
[10] There were substantial territorial changes in 1945.
[11] In 1894.
[12] *Circa* 1840.
[13] In 1857.
[14] In 1870.
[15] Figures to 1913 are for the whole Russian Empire, including Finland.
[16] In 1876.
[17] In 1850.
[18] In 1878. According to Ellison (*op. cit.* in sources) this figure may have related to machines in use only.
[19] In 1885. According to Ellison (*op, cit.* in sources) this figure may have related to machines in use only.
[20] In 1890.
[21] In 1903.
[22] Figures to 1903 include doubling spindles, which numbered 3,952 thousand in 1903.

D16 OUTPUT OF COTTON YARN (in thousands of metric tons)

	Austria	Belgium	Bulgaria	Czechoslovakia	France	Germany[3]	East Germany[6]	Greece	Hungary[6]	Italy
1920	...	...	...	...	...	...	...	...	...	148
1921	...	...	...	...	...	...	...	...	...	133
1922	...	...	...	...	...	...	...	...	...	156
1923	18.1	...	...	...	...	...	...	6.2	...	164
1924	16.6	...	...	...	...	...	...	6.0	...	173
1925	26.6	...	...	...	...	316	...	...	...	199
1926	23.0	...	...	...	...	267	...	7.7	...	199
1927	29.0	...	...	...	...	366	...	...	...	179
1928	27.2	74.3	...	...	...	355	...	7.9	...	196
1929	23.7	68.8	1.3	...	280	...	...	8.2	...	220
1930	19.9	61.3	2.2	...	238	...	...	9.6	...	184
1931	17.7	51.7	2.7	...	193	...	...	10.1	...	153
1932	18.0	44.6	3.1	...	180	...	...	10.1	...	169
1933	18.4	46.4	4.5	...	235	350	...	12.5	...	191
1934	22.9	43.4	6.5	83.9	...	...[4]	...	14.2	...	173
1935	26.9	61.3	6.2	...	...	359	...	13.5	...	171
1936	31.4	66.3	8.8	41.2[1]	...	369	...	15.2	...	140
1937	32.5	72.5	10.1	88.7	...	369	...	15.8	...	187
1938	31.0	75.1	...	...	250	411	...	15.8	21.0	178
1939	...	...	11.5	...	...	...	...	17.1	...	192
1940	...	...	...	...	...	...	...	...	...	178
1941	...	...	...	...	60[2]	...	...	...	...	115
1942	...	...	...	...	36	...	...	...	...	76
1943	...	...	...	...	28	...	...	...	...	49
1944	...	...	...	...	14	...	...	0.9	...	17
						West Germany				
1945	...	...	...	...	63[2]	...	...	8.2	...	[10][8]
1946	4.6	62.8	...	37.0	172	44	...	14.1	8.9	135
1947	8.7	74.5	...	54.7	204	79	...	15.4	18.8	180
1948	12.4	85.9	15.9	68.1	224	119	...	15.4	23.9	189
1949	18.1	89.7	16.5	75.8	228	228	...	18.0	28.6	209
1950	19.4	106.3	16.4	77.4	251	282	24.0	19.8	32.8	216
1951	21.8	117.7	19.8	75.2	271	324	39.4	21.7	37.9	231
1952	17.4	91.2	25.0	68.1	256	292	51.1	20.3	43.9	203
1953	18.9	99.8	26.4	63.3	270	343	58.9	21.6	42.7	193
1954	21.2	112.5	27.7	67.4	295	369	61.8	23.9	44.9	203
1955	23.5	107.6	30.2	76.2	265	373	63.1	23.5	47.2	175
1956	23.9	108.6	31.3	81.7	281	396	62.2	23.7	37.7	190
1957	25.8	111.4	33.2	87.5	313	418	60.6	27.0	45.1	212
1958	26.5	86.3	36.3	94.5	308	393	64.2	23.4	46.4	199
1959	25.2	97.5	46.8	98.2	282	398[4]	66.9	22.4	48.0[7]	214
									38.5	
1960	26.6	103.2	49.0	102.2	315	421	72.6	23.9	47.0	239
1961	28.4	103.4	49.9	106.4	315	403	79.6	26.5	51.1	239
1962	27.0	94.9	52.7	109.9	296	383	82.9	29.3	53.0	249
1963	25.4	93.9	55.7	106.9	298	373	78.6	30.5	57.2	251
1964	25.7	94.4	57.7	105.5	300	381	81.0	31.4	59.5	240
1965	24.4	85.2	60.6	108.1	267	382[5]	79.0	34.9	63.9	201
						295				
1966	22.9	79.9	63.7	112.2	289	281	77.6	36.8	63.6	251
1967	20.1	70.7	67.3	112.3	268	251	77.0	38.5	64.8	247
1968	19.5	72.5	69.8	112.0	257	255	73.3	36.2	62.8	233
1969	20.6	75.3	71.1	110.6	267	252	69.4	39.8	57.6	254
1970	20.8	74.8	73.7	113.9	270	239	68.5	41.9	56.7	247
1971	21.4	69.7	75.3	118.6	266	221	66.9	46.4	55.5	225
1972	21.3	66.8	78.8	121.5	275	222	61.8	51.9	55.8	238
1973	20.6	65.4	80.2	123.6	280	215	59.1	65.3	57.5	237
1974	20.4	64.7	79.7	126.0	279	214	57.9	69.5	57.9	236

D16 Output of Cotton Yarn (in thousands of metric tons)

	Netherlands	Poland[12]	Portugal	Romania	Russia/ U.S.S.R.[16]	Spain	Sweden[12]	Switzerland	U.K.[12]	Yugo-slavia
1920	...	...	...	...	15	32.1	...	...	...	...
1921	...	...	...	...	22	27.3	...	...	...	...
1922	...	...	...	...	72	35.4	...	...	...	...
1923	...	...	...	...	87	26.6	...	...	...	...
1924	...	...	...	...	116	33.4	...	...	...	...
1925	...	...	...	...	197	33.4	...	...	...	...
1926	39.4	...	...	...	252	29.5	...	...	...	...
1927	44.2	...	...	...	284	34.5	...	...	...	...
1928	48.3	60	...	...	324	30.3	22.1	...	...	...
1929	50.0	51	...	...	354	30.8	20.7	...	...	...
1930	49.2	47[7] 60	...	...	287	33.0	21.4	...	...	...
1931	43.5	55	...	...	314	32.2	19.0	...	...	...
1932	32.7	54	...	...	355	32.5	23.7	...	...	...
1933	37.9	62	...	...	367	30.5[11]	23.7	...	...	...
1934	38.7	70	...	...	388	...	27.7	...	...	...
1935	39.9	72	...	...	384	...	26.6	...	557	...
1936	45.3	78	...	...	480	...	29.0	...	594	...
1937	55.5	78	...	...	533	...	28.7	...	616	...
1938	51.7	64	20.8	16.5	529	...	27.5	...	476	...
1939	57.8	...	21.6	...	562	...	28.5	...	495	18.9
1940	47.1	...	22.6	...	650	49	28.2	...	540	...
1941	21.5	...	25.3	...	...	42	22.6	...	409	...
1942	15.1	...	21.0	...	...	57	20.7	...	363	...
1943	13.5	...	17.3	...	...	73	19.3	...	355	...
1944	...	...[9]	19.4	...	...	65	20.1	...	334	...
1945	...	[14][10]	24.8	...	303	75	24.2	...	301	2.4
1946	34.4	47	28.9	...	...	85	24.5	...	336	23.7
1947	46.9	59	29.0	...	...	60	22.7	24.3	336	28.7
1948	54.9	82	31.9	21.4	568	65	24.3	26.5	413	27.8
1949	62.1	91	30.7	...	...	60	26.3	25.4	417	29.2
1950	67.6	92	35.6	29.2	663	58	28.1	28.7	433	29.9
1951	69.7	95	31.7	34.2	...	52	28.3	31.2	439	26.9
1952	62.8	95	35.8	38.5	...	64	25.7	29.4	314	25.9
1953	74.0	104	34.9[13] 36.3	41.9	899	68	26.2	28.3	376	27.7
1954	78.3	109	42.7	42.7	971	64	27.9	32.5	399	34.1
1955	79.6	115	44.6	45.6	1,038	65	26.9	32.9	356	38.2
1956	80.8	116	42.9	43.0	977	70	27.2	32.6	337	38.9
1957	82.9	123	44.6	44.5	1,016	75	28.1	37.3	347	42.6
1958	79.0	135	47.1	47.1	1,063	96	26.7[7]	35.1	304	45.2
1959	81.6	146	46.5	48.2	1,124	90	25.3	31.1	292	47.0
1960	87.3	153	56.5	51.6	1,169	95[7] 116	25.4	36.2	285	50.6
1961	87.2	165	62.3	59.6	1,165	132	25.2	38.8	266	55.3
1962	84.3	163	63.7	69.7	1,192	134	23.4	37.5	237	68.6
1963	84.5	160	70.0	70.5	1,220	128	20.8	37.1	238	74.9
1964	88.4	179	74.1	74.0	1,274	127	19.6	38.5	247	82.0
1965	81.7	187	79.7	78.3	1,292	121	18.7	39.2	237	86.0
1966	79.9	193	80.6	80.4	1,323	132	17.2	36.4	225	92.5
1967	68.8	194	79.6	84.3	1,373	129	15.4	36.2	190	93.1
1968	70.5	194	84.4	93.0	1,421	111	14.1	37.2	190	94.7
1969	69.0[7] 54	198	88.0	102.0	1,438	144	13.2	39.4	191	96.0

D16 Output of Cotton Yarn (in thousands of metric tons)

	Austria	Belgium	Bulgaria	Czech	France	West Germany	East Germany[6]	Greece	Hungary[6]	Italy
1975	16.4	44.3	78.9	129	232	192	59.1[12] 123[15]	79.4	61.2	200
1976	20.7	53.5	78.8	123	253	208	138	110	58.5	234
1977	20.1	40.7	86.2	125	238	178	135	101	60.1	212
1978	17.7	40.7	84.4	129	228[14] 172	163	136	116	62.8	226
1979	18.6	47.7	85.5	134	171	161	135	128	60.6	242
1980	18.4	47.4	87.4	135	171	170	136	135	59.9	231
1981	17.4	40.6	87.3	137	149	146	135	128	58.2	216
1982	15.8	45.9	85.8	139	149	168	135	128	55.7	225
1983	16.9	45.7	85.2	140	149[14] 199	181	135	137	56.5	217
1984	17.2	46.7	83.5	140	201	194	138	134	56.7	230
1985	15.3	47.8	82.7	142	195	203	138	132	57.9	221
1986	15.3	50.7	85.1	143	193	205	141	130	59.2	230
1987	18.4	56.8	88.1	145	196	226	146	143	62.8	261
1988	16.7	45.3	86.0	147	201	197	152	143	62.0	259
1989	15.7	46.1	82.5	147	182	193	152	128	59	267
1990	16.7	50.7	72.2	146	170	190		134	55	271
						Germany				
1991	18.1	47.8	31.0	99	154	185		128	30	261
1992	19.2	46.0	25.5	71	150	169		112	24	245
1993	23.2	47.2	24.2	61	154	154		...	22	244
1994	22.2	48.1	23.7	60	179	123		120	16	220
1995	22.0	48.6	27.6	64	162	90		121	14	218
1996	21.6	47.9	26.0	58	154	91		124	...	222
1997	21.4	46.5	28.2	62	160	98		222	17	225
1998	22.0	44.9	26.9	65	168	88		...	14	...

	Netherlands	Poland[12]	Portugal	Romania	Russia/ U.S.S.R.[16]	Spain	Sweden[12]	Switzerland	U.K.[12]	Yugo-slavia
1970	52	208	91.5	109.0	1,435	143	11.5	40.7[7]	184	102
1971	47	214	82.6	121.3	1,495	139	9.5	39.5	162	100
1972	44	212	92.3	129.6	1,505	142	8.3	39.9	154	101
1973	40	215	147	144	1,535	138	8.2	39.2	153	103
1974	39	214	106	157	1,557	139	7.4	39.9	140	108
1975	29	212	91	145	1,573	71[7]	6.3	33.0	125	107
1976	35	218	89	165	1,583	70	6.9	43.6	133	117
1977	30	219	97	171	1,597	69	5.6	44.7	125	121
1978	22	224	93	175	1,627	94	5.3	41.9	118	118
1979	19	214	109	175	1,623	101	5.1	46.1	118	120
1980	16	217	119	183	1,636	110	4.9	48.8	90	117
1981	12	195	117	189	1,645	102	4.5	47.8	67	118
1982	13	173	126	187	1,634	108	4.8	50.3	67	121
1983	9.1	177	136	171	1,658	106	5.2	52.9	67	121
1984	7.5	179	140	169	1,688	94	5.7	56.5	64	129
1985	9.1	184	139	170	1,742	99	5.4	57.5	65	133
1986	8.4	195	147	181	1,747	105	4.8	61.9	64	137
1987	8.9	198	151	172	1,725	108	4.9	61.3	67	140
1988	7.3	206	152	16.5	1,764	103	4.3	57.1	60	136
1989	4.8	196	157	156	1,760	104	4.1	45.8	44	125
1990	3.5	127	149	130	1,705	103	4.4	50.1	30	...[19]
1991	2.5	73	138	92	1,118[18]	97	4.6	45.1	20	...[19]
1992	2.5	84	94	65	709[18]	96	3.9	41.0	...	18[19]
1993	...	94	...	63	513[18]	...	...	39.6	...	...
1994	...	68	122	62	265	129	3.4	38.3	...	...
1995	...	65	119	61	199	146	3.0	31.1	...	...
1996	...	63	121	62	147	...	3.2	33.5	...	...
1997	...	71	123	43	175	...	2.2	...	...	...
1998	...	61	123	36	149	...	1.6	...	...	...

D16 Output of Cotton Yarn (in thousands of metric tons)

NOTES

1. SOURCES:- The official publications noted on p. xv with gaps filled from League of Nations and United Nations, *Statistical Yearbooks*, and Russian statistics to 1945 and in 1950 taken from G.W. Nutter, *The Growth of Industrial Production in the Soviet Union* (Princeton, 1962).
2. Except as indicated in footnotes, tyre cord yarns are excluded, and yarn made from waste and from mixed fibres of more than 50 per cent cotton are included.

FOOTNOTES

[1] Subsequently including tyre cord yarn.
[2] Alsace-Lorraine is excluded from 1941 to June 1945.
[3] The following statistics are available for Germany before 1914 (in thousands of tons): 1907 359; 1908 355; 1909 369.
[4] Prior to 1935 and from 1946 to 1959 Saarland is excluded.
[5] Previously mixed yarns of less than 50 per cent cotton are included.
[6] Excluding yarn made from waste.
[7] The cause of this break is not given.
[8] May–December.
[9] There were substantial territorial changes in 1945.
[10] April–December.
[11] Figures to 1934 are for Catalonia only.
[12] Including tyre cord yarn (from 1975 (2nd line) in the case of East Germany).
[13] Subsequently including yarns of mixed fibres including tyre cord yarns of these materials.
[14] Pure cotton yarn only from 1978 (2nd line) to 1983 (1st line).
[15] Subsequently including thread.
[16] Earlier figures are available for Russia as follows:-

　　　　　　　　　1913 271　　　1917 211　　　1918 118　　　1919 19.

[17] Czech Republic. Slovakia = 1992 17　　1993 2.
[18] Ex.-U.S.S.R. as follows:

	Armenia	Azerbaijan	Belarus	Estonia	Georgia	Kazakh-stan	Kyrgi-stan	Latvia	Moldova	Tajiki-stan	Turkmeni-stan	Ukraine	Uzbeki-stan
1992	...	22	45	22	—	39	25	6	26	19	5	124	109
1993	...	22	35	13	—	35	14	5	—	18	5	59	110
1994	0.4	20	13	14	0.8	20	9	2	0.2	13	5	30	108
1995	0.2	19	10	16	0.6	4	3	3	0.1	13	11	18	103
1996	0.3	13	11	20	0.4	3	4	4	0.1	20	21	9	105
1997	—	8	10	23	0.2	2	3	4	0.1	9	23	6	114
1998	0.1	3	19	24	0.1	2	2	5	0.1	14	29	11	...

[19] Yugoslavia. Ex Yugoslavia as follows.

	Croatia	Macedonia	Slovenia
1991	14	9	11
1992	11	9	10
1993	...	7.4	10
1994	6.9	6.3	10.5
1995	6.7	3.9	9.8
1996	4.2	4.4	8.8
1997	5.4	2.9	...
1998	5.1	3.4	...

D17 OUTPUT OF COTTON TISSUES (in units shown)

1921-1967

			Thousands of metric tons							
	Austria	Belgium	France	Germany	Greece	Italy	Netherlands	Portugal	Spain	Sweden
1921	...	...	...	...	...	94	...	...	...	...
1922	...	...	...	...	...	101	...	...	...	...
1923	...	...	...	...	...	105	...	...	...	...
1924	...	...	...	...	...	122	...	...	...	...
1925	...	...	...	...	...	134	...	...	...	...
1926	...	...	...	...	...	130	...	...	...	...
1927	...	...	...	...	...	116	...	...	...	...
1928	...	63.1	177	288	...	126	...	...	...	14.9
1929	...	61.4	181	...	...	135	...	...	...	14.9
1930	...	49.0	177	...	20	110	...	...	...	15.7
1931	...	45.0	148	...	22	95	...	...	...	14.1
1932	...	38.7	145	...	22	95	...	...	...	18.1
1933	...	38.6	167	284	24	110	...	...	...	15.7
1934	86.9	34.0	138	...	27	103	...	...	...	18.1
1935	93.0	51.0	138	...	27	104	...	...	...	18.6
1936	99.8[1]	51.9	158	271[3]	27	84	...	...	...	20.0
	12.0			204						
1937	13.0	53.2	151	...	29	90	...	...	...	20.1
1938	12.0	49.5	149	222	28	94	57.0	16.8	...	19.9
1939	...	...	...	...	40	85	...	...	...	20.2
1940	...	...	...	...	...	75	...	17.5	42.7	20.7
1941	...	...	...	...	...	27	...	19.1	36.0	14.4[8]
1942	...	...	...	...	...	10	...	17.9	49.0	15.4
1943	...	...	...	...	...	9	...	14.4	63.4	13.9
1944	...	...	...	...	...	1	...	15.5	55.8	13.8
				West Germany						
1945	...		31	...	19	[7][4]	...	19.8	64.5	17.5
1946		54.7	101	28	30	82	30.9	23.3	73.8	18.5
1947	5.6	68.7	134	51	45	100	44.5	23.0	51.6	18.3
1948	8.4	62.7	150	76	55	113	45.5	25.7	56.4	20.3
1949	12.1	59.5	155	145	61	110	53.0	24.6	51.5	22.0
1950	13.4	73.5	195	189	92	118[5]	58.9	28.8	50.0	23.5
						157				
1951	14.4	79.1	206	217	98	168	60.1	27.3	45.2	23.7[7]
									23.4	
1952	12.0	61.9	192	209	87	146	55.0	30.1	55.3	21.9
1953	12.8	66.6	202	238	96	147	59.9	30.3	52.0	21.9
1954	13.8	77.1	218	252	110	158	63.5	34.5	46.1	22.8
1955	15.1	74.1	193	259	99	137	62.9	35.1	45.9	23.0
1956	15.5	79.6	197	277	105	144	64.8	34.5	47.9[7]	23.0
									69.6	
1957	16.8	84.6	226	287	119	160	66.0	34.5	67.7	24.2
1958	17.6	67.2	234	274	124[1]	157	60.6	35.5	71.7	23.5[7]
					14					
1959	16.7	74.7	225	275	13	166	63.3	36.5	69.6	22.6
1960	18.4	84.4	240	289	15	183	71.3	40.4	79.1[7]	22.6
									92.6	
1961	19.7	81.6	236	280[3]	17	182	70.3	42.2	102.1	22.8
				238						
1962	18.8	79.4	233	223	18	194	65.7[6]	42.2	108.3	22.0
							62.9			
1963	18.7	82.3	233	208	19	202	63.1	46.1	104.0	19.8
1964	18.9	85.8	231[2]	206	19	184	64.5	49.4	109.5	20.6
			242							
1965	19.1	75.4	210	206	24	146	58.5	52.2	109.3	19.0
1966	20.4	74.0	224	199	22	178	55.2	51.3	119.5	16.8
1967	18.6	68.4	210	178	22	179	52.6	52.5	122.9	15.4

D17 Output of Cotton Tissues (in units shown)

1913-1967

	millions of linear metres					millions of square metres			
	Bulgaria	Czech	Poland	Russia	UK	E. Germany	Hungary	Romania	Yugo
1913	...	...	...	2,582	...	...	...	...	...
1917	...	...	...	1,205	...	...	...	...	...
1918	...	...	...	932	...	...	...	...	...
1919	...	...	...	153	...	...	...	...	...
1920	...	...	...	120	...	...	...	...	...
1921	...	...	...	151	...	...	...	...	...
1922	...	...	...	347	...	...	...	...	...
1923	...	...	...	642	...	...	...	...	...
1924	...	...	...	923	...	...	...	...	...
1925	...	...	...	1,678	...	...	...	...	...
1926	...	...	...	2,273	...	...	...	...	...
1927	...	...	...	2,480	...	...	...	...	...
1928	...	...	42.6	2,678	...	...	...	...	...
1929	...	...	36.3	2,996	...	...	...	...	...
1930	... / 40.1	...	32.6[7]	2,351	...	...	...	...	...
1931	...	...	35.1	2,242	...	...	...	...	...
1932	...	...	30.4	2,694	...	...	...	...	...
1933	...	...	36.1	2,732	...	...	...	...	...
1934	...	43.6[9]	41.0	2,733	...	...	...	...	...
1935	...	...	45.1	2,640	2,805	...	...	...	...
1936	...	...	49.7	3,270	...	...	...	...	...
1937	...	...	51.5	3,448	3,328	...	...	...	...
1938	...	...	...	3,460	...	...	...	104	...
1939	34	...	...	3,763	...	...	...	...	111
1940	...	...	...	3,954	...	...	...	...	...
1941	...	...	...	...	1,966	...	...	...	...
1942	...	...	...	...	1,620	...	...	...	...
1943	...	...	...	...	1,640	...	...	...	...
1944	...	...	...[10]	...	1,507	...	...	...	...
1945	...	...	[11][11]	1,616	1,407	...	...	...	...
1946	...	...	207	1,901	1,487	...	...	...	89
1947	...	...	258	2,541	1,484	...	...	...	148
1948	58	264	349	3,150	1,768	...	147	91	161
1949	...	318	406	3,601	1,833	...	166	...	153
1950	83	347	436	3,899	1,941	74	177	140	146
1951	94	363	468	4,768	2,014	122	204	173	123
1952	106	359	468	5,044	1,546	153	212	200	112
1953	114	328	494	5,285	1,704	169	207	197	132
1954	119	329	521	5,589	1,823	198	224	210	166
1955	132	342	561	5,904	1,629	201	234	243	174
1956	142	351	556	5,456	1,474	211	181	192	183
1957	153	370	570	5,587	1,493	205	208	188	207
1958	170	404	599	5,788	1,307	217	218	207	219
1959	209	424	637	6,149	1,223	241	226[7] / 213	218	229
1960	218	446	667	6,387	1,183	254	225	248	257
1961	227	467	710	6,425[12] / 4,875	1,129	264	247	282	269
1962	243	478	693	4,914	957	289	265	299	312
1963	251	467	696	5,071	927	267	275	301	348
1964	269	463	761	5,366	946	250	293	302	378
1965	291	478	811	5,494	928	244	305	319	394
1966	299	494	844	5,703	837	244	317	339	416
1967	307	492	823	5,916	681	247	313	357	378

D17 Output of Cotton Tissues (in units shown)

	Austria	Belgium	France	West Germany	Greece	Italy	Netherlands	Portugal	Spain	Sweden
				thousands of metric tons						
1968	18.3	68.7	199	186	23	174	48.5	57.3	104.9	14.2
1969	19.0	70.8	206	190	23	177	47.6	56.2	119.5	13.1
1970	17.9	70.3	197	182	19	175	44.6	44.9	120.7	11.0
1971	17.9	71.7	197	179	21	163	38.2	50.5	119.4	10.0
1972	18.8	73.8	205	189	24	162	37.1	50.5	123.3	9.1
1973	16.6	72.5	208	188	25	171	36.9	54.0	129.9	9.3
1974	15.6	67.7	205	182	28	182	38.2	59.1	132.5	8.8
1975	13.7	55	175	166	30	160	32.3	50	131	7.3
1976	17.4	63	190	199	30	181	38.7	52	132	7.8
1977	16.0	49	182	170	29	171	34.7	53	132	7.0
1978	14.8	46	175	160	28	175	28.5	54	132	6.2
1979	15.9	52	176	160	29	198	25.9	58	105	6.2
1980	16.3	51	171	163	39	204	22.9	61	106	6.5
1981	15.4	47	156	146	39	216	17.5	64	101	7
1982	13.8	53	160[13] 224	159	38	212	15.3	64	79	7
1983	16.1	51	214	169	42	206	11.0	69	88	7
1984	16.8	51	212	177	34	231	12.0	73	80	8
1985	16.4	53	194	189	40	226	11.3	74	82	8
1986	15.6	55	189	185	48	227	10.9	75	81	8
1987	17.1	54	189	193	53	224	9.7	78	89	7
1988	16.8	49	179	182	53	216	8.3	78	92	2
				Germany						
1989	16.8	56	140	176	55	225	10.3	78	98	2
1990	18.0	58	138	170	…	225	10.5	76	97	—
1991	19.2	56	126	178	…	212	10.2	71	98	—
1992	19.2	52	123	148	…	188	8.8	49	95	—
1993	15.6	52	116	136	…	180	…	…	…	—
				millions of square metres						
1994	83	…	691	635	94	1,521	…	421	622	…
1995	89	…	723	444	72	1,585	…	418	689	…
1996	14	…	684	466	85	…	…	401	695	…
1997	15	…	695	489	91	…	…	410	670	…
1998	16	…	712	506	82	…	…	445	663	…

	Bulgaria	Czechoslovakia	Poland	U.K.	East Germany	Hungary	Romania	Russia/USSR	Yugo
		millions of linear metres				**millions of square metres**			
1968	319	480	834	6,116	668	250	290	377	401
1969	335	469	845	6,208	662	237	270	410	415
1970	319	501	881	6,152	628	248	258	437	390
1971	324	524	904	6,397	559	244	267	482	391
1972	323	537	901	6,421	513	242	275	531	374
1973	333	553	868	6,578	453	243	308	571	361
1974	347	550	884	6,624	410	248	318	612	365
1975	372	555	928	405	246	317	591	6,634	376
1976	359	531	948	374	274	319	677	6,779	385
1977	371	533	951	368	272	332	703	6,811	384
1978	353	544	935	380	270	328	717	6,967	410
1979	349	557	905	365	262	306	707	6,977	418
1980	346	560	903	314	277	295	748	7,068	386
1981	354	574	805	278	286	287	732	7,171	377
1982	366	583	692	261	288	282	738	7,145	372
1983	367	585	744	255	298	280	709	7,286	379
1984	368	598	812	265	294	278	697	7,523	318
1985	351	606	831	274	298	287	700	7,677	344
1986	349	607	821	275	308	292	731	7,777	358
1987	353	600	749	245	287	292	710	7,945	366
1988	361	591	783	219	304	294	689	8,106	351
1989	357	592	760	113	304	247	709	8,906	339
1990	291	580	428	166	213	206	536	8,647	…
1991	126	408	286	155		133	437	5,649[15]	46[16]
1992	90	362	239	…	**Germany**	86	289	3,799[15]	38[16]
		Czech Republic[14]							
1993	72	282	229	…		78	271	2,822[15]	26[16]
1994	83	340	321	…	635	76	294	1,631	24[16]
1995	86	358	263	…	444	66	275	1,401	19[16]
1996	93	330	295	…	466	…	212	1,120	22[16]
1997	85	346	303	…	489	79	173	1,374	19[16]
1998	98	337	275	…	506	44	170	1,241	23[16]

D17   Output of Cotton Tissues (in units shown)

NOTES

1. SOURCES:- The official publications noted on p. xv with gaps filled from League of Nations and United Nations, *Statistical Yearbooks* and O.E.C.D., *Statistical Bulletins*, and Russian statistics to 1934 taken from G.W. Nutter, *The Growth of Industrial Production in the Soviet Union* (Princeton, 1962).
2. Except as indicated in footnotes, fabrics of mixed fibres with cotton predominating are included in this table.

FOOTNOTES

[1]   Previous figures are in million square metres.
[2]   Subsequent figures include cloth of mixed fibres, which has previously been excluded.
[3]   Figures for 1928, 1933, and 1936 (1st line) are of total output in cotton factories. Figures from 1936 (2nd line) to 1961 (1st line) are of cotton yarn input to weaving mills. From 1961 (2nd line) the figures are of output of cloth containing 50 per cent or more of cotton.
[4]   May–December.
[5]   Figures to 1950 (1st line) do not include cloth of mixed fibres.
[6]   Figures to 1962 (1st line) are of cotton and mixed yarn input to weaving mills.
[7]   The reason for this break is not given.
[8]   Previous statistics are known to be not quite complete.
[9]   This figure is in thousands of metric tons.
[10]   Previous statistics are in thousands of metric tons. There were substantial territorial changes in 1945.
[11]   April–December.
[12]   Subsequent statistics are in million square metres.
[13]   Subsequently sales from factories.
[14]   Czech Republic

Slovakia	1993	101
	1994	76
	1995	90
	1996	57

[15]   Russian Federation. Ex-USSR as follows.

	Armenia	Azerbaijan	Belarus	Estonia	Geo-gia	Kazakh-stan	Kyrgi-stan	Latvia	Lithuania	Moldova	Tajiki-stan	Turkmeni-stan	Ukraine	Uzbeki-stan
1992	5	114	119	111	…	135	119	45	106	150	58	29	509	474
1993	2	115	92	55	…	136	65	22	89	1	57	29	262	482
1994	—	78	25	74	2	85	49	—	42	1	34	20	145	433
1995	—	58	34	90	1	21	21	2	35	2	28	17	87	456
1996	1	24	45	120	1	21	25	6	35	—	17	18	54	445
1997	—	17	48	130	—	14	20	9	62	—	8	14	28	425
1998	—	7	72	127	—	10	13	12	64	—	13	15	57	…

[16]   Yugoslavia.

D18 RAW WOOL CONSUMPTION INDICATORS (in thousands of metric tons)

1816–1869

	Austria-Hungary[1] NI	Belgium I	France[2] C	Germany O	Italy O	I	United Kingdom O[3]	NI[4]
1816	...	...	...	11.1	...	...		3.4
1817	...	...	...	...	...	...		6.4
1818	...	...	...	...	...	...		11.2
1819	...	...	...	12.6	...	...		7.3
1820	...	...	...	...	...	...		4.4
1821	...	...	...	...	...	...		7.4
1822	...	...	...	14.3	...	...		8.6
1823	...	...	...	...	...	...		8.7
1824	...	...	...	...	...	...		10.1
1825	...	...	...	17.0	...	...		19.5
1826	...	...	...	...	...	...		6.8
1827	...	...	...	...	...	...		12.8
1828	...	...	...	18.1	...	...		13.2
1829	...	...	...	...	...	...		9.0
1830	...	...	...	...	...	...		13.0
1831	...	...	...	17.8	...	...		12.3
1832	...	...	...	...	...	...		10.6
1833	...	...	...	...	...	...		14.8
1834	...	...	...	19.5	...	...		19.7
1835	...	...	...	...	...	...		15.2
1836	...	...	...	...	...	...		27.1
1837	...	...	...	23.5	...	...		19.5
1838	...	...	...	...	...	...		20.3
1839	...	...	...	...	...	...		23.6
1840	...	2.9	...	25.9	...	...		19.8
1841	...	3.9	...	...	...	...		20.5
1842	−3.3	4.1	...	...	...	...		15.3
1843	−3.1	3.8	...	26.5	...	...		17.2
1844	−4.5	3.9	...	...	...	...		24.9
1845	−4.1	4.7	...	...	...	...		29.5
1846	−1.8	3.4	...	27.9	...	...		25.6
1847	−2.8	4.1	...	...	...	...		23.7
1848	−1.7	3.3	...	...	...	...		27.4
1849	...	4.6	...	27.7	...	...		24.1
1850	0.2	4.2	...	...	...	...		21.7
1851	1.3	5.2	...	...	...	...		27.7
1852	11	5.7	...	28.9	...	...		31.1
1853	−4.3[2]	5.6	...	...	...	...		45.8
1854	6.7	5.9	...	...	...	...		31.2
1855	0.9	8.3	...	27.0	...	...		24.3
1856	−2.5	10.3	...	...	...	...		34.1
1857	2.5	11.2	...	...	...	...		35.5
1858	−1.3	10.2	...	28.1	...	...		39.2
1859	−4.6	13.2	...	...	...	...		43.2
1860	−1.3	14.0	...	...	...	...		48.2
1861	0.2	16.4	...	32.5	8.0	8.2		35.0
1862	−3.2	18.6	99	...	7.7	3.7		51.5
1863	−7.1	14.4	...	...	7.0	3.5		47.8
1864	−5.8	20.9	...	36.6	6.6	4.9		65.0
1865	−7.2	28.0	...	...	6.4	4.9	68	54.7
1866	−5.7	29.9	...	...	6.2	4.6	66	74.0
1867	2.7	35.1	...	36.2	6.4	6.7	74	83.5
1868	−0.1	47.4	...	...	6.5	4.6	78	62.6
1869	0.9	47.0	...	...	6.7	6.7	75	58.7

D18   Raw Wool Consumption Indicators (in thousands of metric tons)

1870–1924

	Austria-Hungary[1]	Belgium	France[2]	Germany		Italy		United Kingdom	
	NI	I	C	O	NI	O	I	O	NI
1870	1.1	41.7	···[6]	···[6]	...	7.0	4.7	72	73.3
1871	4.7	52.5	...	...	...	7.5	4.4	69	79.9
1872	6.6	53.4	...	34.2	...	7.8	6.0	71	73.2
1873	−4.5	53.4	...	...	...	8.0	5.2	75	85.3
1874	3.4	51.1	...	...	...	8.2	6.3	76	86.2
1875	1.8	45.8	163	...	...	8.4	6.8	74	82.8
1876	3.9	51.9	...	...	...	8.7	8.4	71	94.3
1877	7.1	49.0	...	...	...	9.1	8.2	69	96.6
1878	10.8	46.5	...	...	...	9.5	6.5	69	87.8
1879	11.7	43.3	...	...	...	9.6	8.5	69	71.7
1880	7.3	49.3	173	...	53.4	9.7	7.3	68	94.8
1881	12.1	45.5	...	...	65.3	9.9	9.5	63	77.3
1882	15.4	57.0	168	30.1	75.1	9.9	7.5	59	95.6
1883	13.6	48.4	...	...	78.2	10.7	9.5	58	90.4
1884	15.8	36.4	...	...	93.8	10.6	10.1	60	105
1885	13.8	43.8	200	...	88.7	10.4	11.1	62	97
1886	9.5	39.2	227	...	95.7	10.2	12.1	62	119
1887	19.6	44.4	211	...	100.9	10.1	11.1	61	109
1888	15.2	38.1	205	...	118.7	9.9	9.4	61	126
1889	15.4	44.2	218	...	129.0	9.8	9.8	60	143
1890	16.1	35.0	210	...	119.6	9.7	8.2	63	124
1891	19.7	42.2	227	...	136.6	9.6	9.0	67	145
1892	21.8	32.8	230	23.8	151.4	10.0	9.8	69	134
1893	20.1	44.9	237	...	139.7	9.7	8.9	69	143
1894	23.7	37.8	241	...	150.3	9.6	9.4	64	157
1895	23.7	48.5	230	...	172.0	9.8	12.4	61	158
1896	23.5	49.3	266	...	161.1	10.1	10.8	62	166
1897	22.9	41.8	243	...	152.8	10.3	10.9	63	149
1898	24.1	46.3	262	...	167.8	10.6	10.2	63	183
1899	22.9	62.4	265	...	168.6	10.7	13.4	64	160
1900	21.7	42.0	203	18.3	130.2	10.8	12.7	64	203
1901	26.7	53.4	262	...	140.7	11.0	14.5	63	171
1902	31.0	55.2	241	...	150.4	11.2	16.9	62	145
1903	27.8	53.9	243	...	155.0	11.4	15.4	60	129
1904	30.4	52.8	214	15.8	158.6	12.0	15.6	60	125
1905	26.8	63.9	221	15.9	154.3	12.6	14.9	59	139
1906	29.6	61.2	244	15.9	162.0	13.2	16.3	59	158
1907	33.1	67.2	244	16.2	171.7	13.9	18.5	59	190
1908	35.7	59.5	231	15.7	166.6	14.5	21.2	61	163
1909	40.3	59.6	276	15.3	178.7	15.0	22.0	64	161
1910	40.5	161.3	273	14.8	181.5	15.4	23.3	65	196
1911	42.2	154.2	271	14.2	183.4	15.6	23.2	62	211
1912	42.0	156.8	255	13.6	200.7	15.8	27.2	...	193
1913	33.5	149.5 50	266	13.3	182.2	15.7	28.6	...	214
1914	36.4	...	210	...	...	15.6	20.8	...	174
1915	...	...	88	...	...	15.6	60.8	...	354
1916	...	...	93	...	...	15.5	61.4	...	257
1917	...	...	78	...	...	15.5	41.1	...	268
1918	...	...	60[6]	...	...	15.9	42.8		180
1919	...	...	174	···[6]	...	16.4	33.6		390
1920	...	...	168	...	...	16.4	33.1		288
1921	...	...	155	...	···[7]	16.5	23.2	av	178
1922	...	33	305	...	191	16.7	45.7	48	273
1923	...	51	260	...	133	16.9	42.3		124
1924	...	49	225	14.3	147	17.0	42.1	48	160

D18 Raw Wool Consumption Indicators (in thousands of metric tons)

1925–1974

	Belgium	France	Germany		Italy		United Kingdom	
	I	C	O	NI	O	I	O	NI
1925	43	246	11.9	134	17.2	41.7	50	153
1926	52	286	10.2	147	17.3	53.2	52	191
1927	62	303	9.6	208	17.0	47.8	54	190
1928	57	269	9.1	171	16.1	59.7	52	180
1929	68	199	8.7	169	15.2	64.7	51	182
1930	65	306	8.1	156	14.4	60.3	50	210
1931	47	250	8.1	141	13.6	53.9	51	250
1932	39	254	8.1	144	13.0	77.3	54	254
1933	36	301	8.0	158	12.6	91.8	54	243
1934	30	193	8.1	143	12.4	71.8	52	217
1935	55	221	9.1	124	12.3	57.5	49	239
1936	63	197	10.1	103	11.5	21.0	49	269
1937	64	194	11.1	103	11.8	45.1	49	235
1938	65	232	12.1	139[7]	12.3	37.7	50	265
1939	...	207	12.1	...	12.8	32.1	51[8]	305
							31	
1940	...	118	...	...	13.0	22.6	41	784
1941	...	...	...	...	12.8	2.9	36	141
1942	...	...	...	...	12.2	0.9	33	185
1943	...	...	...	...	10.2	...	28	121
1944	...	...	...	...	9.1	...	27	230

West Germany

	c[8]		c[8,9]		c[8]			
1945	...	56	...	...	8.7	...	26	188
1946	...	280	...	...	9.6	...	28	158
1947	38	215	...	14	11.2	59	23	202[12]
								186
1948	30	190	...	21[9]	13.6	62	23	219
1949	32	179	5.1	41	16.0	54	25	223
1950	37	190[8]	4.1	58	16.0	57	26	235
		115						
1951	28	90	4.2	53	15.5	44	25	180
1952	26	97	3.9	60	15.1	57	28	172
1953	32	114	3.4	70	15.0	60	29	221
1954	29	116	3.1	69	14.2	54	32	209
1955	29	111	3.0	76	13.8	51	30	216
1956	35	126	2.9	80	12.2	58	31	216
1957	37	141	2.9	82	12.2	73	34	218
1958	33	113	2.9	63	12.5	68	35	202
1959	36	121	2.9[10]	68	12.7	75	38	231
			4					
1960	40	129	4	69	12.7	90	35	218
1961	38	127	4	68	12.7	85	39	214
1962	46	123	4	67	12.3	93	39	203
1963	44	125	4	70	12.3	89	37	208
1964	43	111	4	65	12.0	84	38	190
1965	44	107	3	66	12.0	86	38	183
1966	43	119	3	68	12.3	110	39	176
1967	36	98	3	56	12.2	99	39	163
1968	40	109	3	67	11.9	96	36	178
1969	42	121	3	75	12.0	107	31	175
1970	40	125	3	68	11.7	93	31	153
1971	30	136	3	74	11.3	88	31	141
1972	31	138[11]	2	77	11.0	97[11]	31	152
		146				103		
1973	23	117	2	54	11.1	92	32	137
1974	20	105	2	39	11.4	86	33	113

D18   Raw Wool Consumption Indicators (in thousands of metric tons)

1975–1993

	Belgium I[13]	France C	West Germany C	Italy O	C	O	U.K. C
1975	24	107	54	11.6	89	33	111
1976	32	125	67	11.9	119	32	120
1977	31	117	57	12.1	113	30	113
1978	31[13]	105[13]	59[13]	12.4	113[13]	32	109[13]
	32	59	78		111		99
1979	33	59	71	12.6	134	32	98
1980	34	59	72	12.8	138	34	85
1981	30	53	66	13.1	133	33	81
1982	35	46	57	12.7	116	33	81
1983	41	44	59	12.7	111	33	82
1984	40	45	63	12.8	127	37	84
1985	38	43	62	12.9	130	40	85
1986	37	38	61	13.5	125	40	89
1987	33	36	63	13.3	140	42	96
1988	34	33	58	13.6	140	44	104
1989	39	28	60	13.8	134	47	97
1990	36	22	52	14.0	138	48	94
1991	…	…	…	14.5	…	47	88
1992	…	…	…	13.7	…	47	92
1993	…	…	…	13.0	…	44	90

D18 Raw Wool Consumption Indicators (in thousands of metric tons)

NOTES

1. SOURCES:- Germany, output to 1959—W.G. Hoffman, *Das Wachstum der Deutschen Wirtschaft seit der Mitte des 19 Jahrhunderts* (Berlin, etc., 1965). U.K., output to 1927 and net imports to 1938—B.R. Mitchell, *British Historical Statistics* (Cambridge, 1988), where the original sources are given. All other statistics are taken from the official publications noted on p. xv with gaps filled from League of Nations, *International Trade Statistics* and *Statistical Yearbooks* and United Nations, *Statistical Yearbooks*.
2. Except as indicated in footnotes, the output figures relate to the weight unwashed, and the trade figures to all kinds of unmanufactured wool and animal hair. Belgian import statistics include wool tops.

FOOTNOTES

[1] The following rough estimates of output are derived from official sources plus *The Textile Mercury Wool Year Book* (1908–14) (in thousand tons):- 1835–44–31; 1845–54–27; 1855–64–29; 1865–74–35; 1875–84–22; 1885–94–20; 1895–1904–19; 1905–13–19

[2] T.J. Markovitch, *L'industrie francaise de 1789 á 1964* (Cahiers de l'I.S.E.A. 1966) gives the following estimates of output and of net imports (in thousand tons):-

	O	NI		O	NI		O	NI		O	NI
1781–90	30.0	6.0	1825–34	58.1	8.4	1855–64	60.0	50.4	1885–94	52.3	177.2
1801–14	48.0	6.0	1835–44	64.3	17.4	1865–74	47.3	99.5	1895–1904	40.1	03.0
1815–24	58.1	5.8	1845–54	66.6	24.0	1875–84	45.7	138.2	1905–13	34.0	21.3

[3] Estimates of average annual output are given in B. R. Mitchell, *op.cit* above, for the following periods (converted to thousands of metric tons):-

1775	36	1820–4	50	1835–9	54	1850–4	61
1776–99	41	1825–9	52	1840–4	57	1855–9	64
1800–19	45	1830–4	54	1845–9	59	1860–4	66

[4] Earlier figures of imports to England and Wales (to 1791) or Great Britain, including those from Ireland, are as follows:-

1772	0.7	1781	1.1	1790	1.5	1799	2.3	1808	1.1
1773	0.7	1782	0.5	1791	1.3	1800	3.8	1809	3.1
1774	1.0	1783	1.2	1792	2.0	1801	3.4	1810	5.0
1775	0.7	1784	0.7	1793	0.9	1802	3.5	1811	2.2
1776	0.9	1785	1.4	1794	2.0	1803	2.7	1812	3.2
1777	1.3	1786	0.7	1795	2.2	1804	3.7	1813	...
1778	0.2	1787	1.9	1796	1.6	1805	3.9	1814	7.1
1779	0.3	1788	1.9	1797	2.1	1806	3.3	1815	6.8
1780	0.8	1789	1.2	1798	1.1	1807	5.3	1816	3.7

[5] Subsequent figures are of net imports.
[6] From 1871 to 1918 Alsace-Lorraine is included in Germany rather than France.
[7] Figures for 1922–1938 are of gross imports, but exports were very small.
[8] Subsequent statistics are of virgin clean wool only.
[9] Figures for 1947–48 are for the British and American Occupation Zones only.
[10] The reason for this break is not given.
[11] Subsequently including consumption outside the wool industry.
[12] Subsequent statistics are of the consumption of virgin clean wool.
[13] Subsequently all data have been recalculated to show consumption at the spinning stage rather than at the carding stage. The Belgian series is changed from imports to consumption.

D19   OUTPUT OF WOOL YARN (in thousands of metric tons)

1925–1974

	Austria	Belgium	Bulgaria	Czechoslovakia	France	Germany	East Germany	Greece	Hungary
1925	...	...	...	...	...	123	...	...	...
1926	...	...	...	...	...	...	...	...	...
1927	...	...	...	...	...	...	...	...	...
1928	...	...	...	...	...	136	...	...	...
1929	...	...	0.4	...	...	...	...	...	...
1930	...	...	0.9	...	...	...	...	0.5	...
1931	...	...	0.6	...	...	...	...	0.4	...
1932	...	...	0.6	...	...	...	...	0.5	...
1933	...	...	0.5	...	...	136	...	0.6	...
1934	...	...	0.4	35.0	...	...	...	0.7	...
1935	...	...	0.3	...	...	133	...	0.7	...
1936	...	...	0.5	15.9	...	138	...	1.1	...
1937	13.5	...	0.6	27.2	...	155	...	0.9	...
1938	10.8	25.8	...	...	118	177	...	0.8	11.6
1939	...	...	0.8	...	...	...	...	1.8	...
1940	...	...	...	...	...	...	...	0.9	...
1941	...	...	...	...	...	...	...	0.9	...
1942	...	...	...	...	[43][1]	...	...	...	...
1943	...	...	...	...	[33][1]	...	...	...	...
1944	...	...	...	...	20	...	...	...	...

West Germany

	Austria	Belgium	Bulgaria	Czechoslovakia	France	Germany	West Germany	Greece	Hungary
1945	...	...	...	...	39	...	...	...	...
1946	...	30.9	...	...	92	20	...	2.0	1.8
1947	3.8	42.3	...	29.5	116	28	...	2.0	6.0
1948	6.8	34.1	5.2	32.0	132	38	...	2.7	7.9
1949	9.3	35.6	6.2	35.4	123	65	...	3.4	8.3
1950	11.0	40.2	7.0	34.4	127	92	9.8	6.2	12.1
1951	11.5	34.1	6.7	32.3	120	95	14.2	5.1	13.7
1952	9.3	29.8	7.7	35.2	110	90	14.1	4.5	11.7
1953	10.5	37.6	8.3	31.8	120	106	20.1	5.0	8.7
1954	10.9	38.8	8.7	29.2	128	105	27.1	4.1	11.4
1955	11.8	41.6	9.4	32.2	129	115	19.5	3.8	13.4
1956	12.4	45.3	11.1	31.8	142	118	21.5	4.1	9.8
1957	12.2	47.1	11.0	33.0	154	124	20.9₅ / 69.0	4.7	12.1
1958	10.4	38.1	11.7	37.2	134	106	73.0	4.8	13.1
1959	11.5	46.5	15.6	38.5	136	113	79.7	7.3	13.0
1960	12.5	50.8	16.4	39.3	143	118	80.1	10.0	14.9
1961	13.4	54.1	15.5	41.1	147	114	78.0	9.4	15.7
1962	13.6	58.6	16.3	42.0	146	114	79.1	9.4	16.5
1963	13.8	64.4	17.4	40.9	158	115	76.0	11.0	16.7
1964	13.2	62.3	17.3	40.1	147	117	73.3	11.7	16.9
1965	12.9	64.6	17.4	41.7	130	120₂ / 91	71.7	8.2	16.7
1966	13.7	69.7	18.4	42.9	146	91	70.9	9.5	17.6
1967	12.5	61.0	19.6	42.9	127	70	71.0	8.9	18.0
1968	12.8	72.6	20.6	42.5	130	79	66.9	7.5	16.4
1969	13.5	81.3	23.1	43.2	145	87	67.3	8.3	14.7
1970	12.3	81.2	24.3	45.5	143	79	68.2	11.1	14.2
1971	12.3	90.3	25.4	47.3	152	85	64.4	10.7	14.7
1972	12.4	89.1	27.1	48.1	155	87	62.4	12.4	13.5
1973	12.0	84.0	29.0	49.3	152	65	62.8	10.7	13.2
1974	10.3	78.7	30.5	50.3	143	55	58.7	10.9	11.8

D19 Output of Wool Yarn (in thousands of metric tons)

	Italy	Netherlands	Poland	Romania	Russia[4]/U.S.S.R	Spain	Sweden	U.K.	Yugoslavia
1925	...	...	...	...	29	...	...	...	...
1926	...	...	...	...	36	...	...	...	...
1927	...	...	...	...	44	...	...	...	...
1928	...	...	31.8	...	50	...	10.5	...	...
1929	...	...	29.8	...	57	...	10.3	...	...
1930	...	...	23.2	...	71	...	10.2	...	...
1931	...	8.5	25.3	...	73	...	8.7	...	...
1932	...	8.4	21.3	...	71	...	9.6	230	...
1933	...	9.1	23.6	...	68	...	10.8	228	...
1934	...	8.4	26.4	...	61	...	12.6	239	...
1935	...	7.0	30.1	...	66	...	12.3	...	...
1936	...	8.5	33.0	...	73	...	13.3	...	...
1937	...	9.4	34.2	...	77	...	14.0	249	...
1938	71	9.7	...	7.0	80	...	10.5	212	...
1939	...	14.0	...	...	90	...	11.7	...	6.2
1940	...	15.0	...	...	83	14.7	15.1	...	...
1941	...	13.3	...	...	...	14.9	11.9[6]	...	...
1942	...	9.6	...	...	...	15.1	12.6	...	...
1943	...	7.4	...	...	...	15.2	12.6	...	...
1944	...	...	...	...	...	15.0	13.5	...	...
1945	...	...	[7.6][3]	...	40	13.5	15.6	...	...
1946	60	15.0	22.2	...	50	17.5	16.8	...	8.9
1947	83	19.0	23.8	...	64	16.8	16.8	184	10.8
1948	83	21.9	33.2	8.2	82	13.6	18.7	228	13.0
1949	93	23.5	38.6	...	96	8.8	18.8	240	13.3
1950	108	23.7	41.9	12.8	102	10.0[5] / 11.3	18.3	252	13.9
1951	103	18.7	45.8	15.6	115	8.3	16.1	227	13.4
1952	106	19.7	44.4	15.6	125	10.7	13.4	206	10.3
1953	115	21.8	50.2	17.0	137	13.8	15.8	243	7.7
1954	124	23.1	50.1	16.9	159	11.6	14.9	244	8.7
1955	129	23.9	52.0	17.7	168	12.5	14.1	244	10.7
1956	130	24.9	53.0	17.3	180	13.8	14.1	241	12.2
1957	146[2] / 112	24.1	54.7	17.4	188	13.7	15.1	244	14.8
1958	107	21.8	56.5	17.5	201	14.1	13.7	224	16.7
1959	134	24.9	58.6	17.2	213	12.2	12.9	247	17.3
1960	161	24.5	58.5	19.4	221	13.0[5] / 19.3	13.2	249	20.6
1961	156	24.7	60.3	21.9	232	24.6	12.6	239	19.8
1962	168	24.6	62.4	20.5	241	25.7	12.5	236	19.3
1963	172	25.9	59.7	22.5	243	27.5	12.2	251	26.4
1964	165	25.0	63.9	24.1	236	29.0	12.2	254	26.7
1965	159	23.2	65.5	24.8	236	31.0	10.7	249	31.8
1966	192	24.0	69.2	26.3	258	31.7	9.7	243	35.2
1967	178	20.9	75.1	28.3	282	32.3	9.4	228	32.1
1968	173	20.7[7] / 15	77.7	30.4	302	32.9	8.2	246	29.6
1969	173	17	81.6	32.3	322	36.9	7.2	243	33.9
1970	167	16	84.4	35.7	350	36.5	5.1	227	37.9
1971	166	14	87.7	38.4	371	37.4	4.4	224	39.4
1972	180	15	87.4	41.5	377	37.0	4.0	232	42.4
1973	200	14	88.8	46.0	393	37.3	3.0	235	41.9
1974	203	12	92.3	49.2	408	34.0	2.6	210	40.4

D19 Output of Wool Yarn (in thousands of metric tons)

1975–1998

	Austria	Belgium	Bulgaria	Czechoslovakia	France	W. Germany	E. Germany	Greece	Hungary
1975	8.8	71.2	31.5	52.6	134	51	62.4	15.4	10.1
1976	9.1	81.1	34.0	52.7	145	60	83.6	16.5	9.8
1977	9.3	76.9	34.9	54.0	155	54	79.1	15.5	10.6
1978	8.7	74.0	43.0	53.6	136	53	77.4	20.0	11.0
1979	8.2	76.3	35.6	55.1	138	56	76.2	19.2	11.5
1980	9.9	80.8	35.9	55.6	134	60	76.5	17.3	12.3
1981	9.7	78.6	36.9	57.3	133	52	74.8	16.3	12.9
1982	8.8	73.7	37.9	58.0	122	47	75.8	15.0	11.5
1983	8.6	86.7	37.8	58.4	116	46	76.4	14.5	10.8
1984	9.2	92.4	36.5	57.5	114	49	75.5	13.3	10.9
1985	9.8	90.6	35.1	55.1	112	56	75.0	12.5	10.5
1986	9.6	86.2	35.2	55.7	98	55	76.0	15.1	10.5
1987	8.0	84.9	41.0	55.4	88	53	76.9	12.5	10.0
1988	8.1	90.2	38.2	55.6	76	49	79.1	9.0	8.8
1989	9.6	97.4	35.7	55.3	22	46	79.9	9.3	6.0
1990	8.8	88.2	29.8	52.3	60	40	...	11.0	4.0
1991	8.7	87.8	18.4	33.1	58		43	9.7	3.3
1992	8.3	80.6	15.8	21.9[8]	20		43	9.6	1.5
1993	...	70.5	15.2	17.5[8]	47		35		1.3
1994	8.5	71.4	14.1	17.9	32		34	4.8	1.1
1995	8.8	69.3	14.0	16.8	28		31	6.4	1.3
1996	9.0	67.1	12.9	17.2	15.8		26	13.9	1.5
1997	8.7	69.5	11.6	15.9	...		26	12.8	...
1998	...	72.8	7.3	13.3	...		23	12.6	...

1975–1998

	Italy	Netherlands	Poland	Romania	Russia/U.S.S.R	Spain	Sweden	U.K.	Yugoslavia
1975	214	9	103	50.8	417	28.5[5] 16.2	2.4	188	41.8
1976	286	11	106	55.8	429	16.2	2.4	189	44.2
1977	284	10	107	60.8	437	20.0	2.0	187	46.1
1978	289	9	107	67.6	447	31.8	1.9	183	44.5
1979	325	9	107	70.9	450	29.0	1.9	174	43.4
1980	320	8	107	73.7	456	31.8	1.8	141	53.7
1981	310	7	88	75.0	453	31.8	1.6	131	56.2
1982	285	7	75	77.6	449	28.3	1.7	115	53.0
1983	291	6	81	78.8	447	33.3	1.6	121	51.1
1984	318	6	83	73.4	433	31.3	1.5	127	52.2
1985	326	5	84	72.0	421	27.1	1.2	134	50.6
1986	294	5	83	77.0	421	27.1	0.6	148	51.9
1987	284	4	80	75.9	428	23.5	0.4	156	53.5
1988	291	4	84	76.2	439	26.3	0.3	152	50.0
1989	302	3	77	66.5	443	28.2	0.3	64	48.3
1990	285	3	55	58.9	427	23.1	0.2	50	...
1991	307	2	37	49.1	207[9]	24.8	...	42	...
1992	324	2	34	40.2	153[9]	25.4	...	...	62[10]
1993	319	...	36	43.6	117[9]	...	...	...	...
1994	496	...	37	35.6	112	21.6	...	...	...
1995	477	...	34	31.7	107	19.0	...	...	...
1996	448	...	36	31.7	29	17.5	...	...	...
1997	469	...	33	27.8	28	19.4	...	...	...
1998	419	...	27	20.2	24	20.3	...	...	...

D19 Output of Wool Yarn (in thousands of metric tons)

NOTES

1. SOURCES:- The official publications noted on p. xv with gaps filled from League of Nations and United Nations, *Statistical Yearbooks*, and the Russian statistics to 1936 taken from G.W. Nutter, *The Growth of Industrial Production in the Soviet Union* (Princeton, 1962).
2. In principle, the output of mixed yarn with more than 50 per cent wool content is included in this table.

FOOTNOTES

[1] Excluding Alsace-Lorraine.
[2] Certain mixed yarns are not subsequently included.
[3] April–December.
[4] G.W. Nutter, *op. cit.* in note 1, gives the following figures for earlier years, the first figure for 1913 applying to the Russian Empire and the second to the U.S.S.R. territory of 1923:-

1893	18	1908	70	1913	$\frac{110}{47}$
1895	29	1910	74	1918	25
1900	55	1911	75	1919	10
1905	65	1912	82		

[5] The reason for this break is not given. The figure for 1950 comparable to the later series for East Germany is 51.8
[6] Previous statistics do not include yarn spun on commission.
[7] Subsequently only yarns for industrial use.
[8] Czech Republic

Slovakia	1992	35.8	1993	29.6	1994	3.7	1995	3.3	1996	2.6

[9] Russian Federation. Ex-USSR as follows:

	Armenia	Azerbaijan	Belarus	Estonia	Kyrgi-stan	Latvia	Moldova	Tajiki-stan	Turkmeni-stan	Ukraine	Uzbeki-stan
1991	2.1	6.4	35	3.1	12.7	10.1	5.9	4.6	3.0	41.2	4.3
1992	1.3	4.1	30	1.6	10.3	6.2	3.2	4.3	2.0	35.8	4.8
1993	0.9	2.8	28	0.2	8.3	4.0	2.9	4.0	3.0	29.6	5.3
1994	0.2	1.0	22	0.2	4.7	5.3	2.8	1.5	2.0	15.8	4.9
1995	0.2	1.4	12	0.1	3.0	2.0	1.7	0.6	4.0	8.8	3.3
1996	0.2	0.1	13	0.2	2.3	3.6	1.5	0.3	5.1	4.5	2.7
1997	0.1	0.1	16	0.3	2.1	3.1	1.2	0.8	4.8	4.5	2.3
1998	0.1	0.2	16	0.4	1.3	3.2	1.2	1.1	3.0	3.2	...

[10] Ex-Yugoslavia countries as follows:

	Croatia	Macedonia	Slovenia
1991	3.6	8.1	4.5
1992	3.7	7.0	5.1
1993	3.8	5.4	5.0
1994	3.6	4.9	4.9
1995	3.2	3.9	2.9
1996	2.5	4.0	0.9
1997	1.9	4.4	...
1998	1.5	3.8	1.1

D20 OUTPUT OF WOOL TISSUES (in units stated)

	Austria	Belgium	France	Germany	Italy	Netherlands	Portugal	Sweden
				Thousands of metric tons				
1928	...	...	...	...	...	...	...	8.0
1929	...	...	...	...	...	...	...	8.1
1930	...	...	...	...	...	...	...	8.4
1931	...	...	...	...	...	...	...	7.2
1932	...	...	...	...	...	...	...	8.0
1933	...	...	...	...	...	...	...	8.3
1934	...	...	...	...	...	...	...	10.4
1935	...	...	...	...	...	...	...	10.2
1936	...	...	...	60.0	...	...	...	11.5
1937	10.8	...	...	...	...	...	...	11.6
1938	6.0	12.8	71.8	64.8	45.3	17.4	...	9.5
1939	...	...	...	...	...	...	...	10.7
1940	...	...	...	...	...	...	7.0	12.9
1941	...	...	...	...	...	...	8.0	10.4
1942	...	...	...	...	...	...	7.5	9.2
1943	...	...	...	...	...	...	5.0	9.5
1944	...	...	...	...	...	...	6.2	9.9
				West Germany				
1945	...	...	...	...	...	...	7.0	11.1
1946	...	19.5	46.5	13.2	39.9	17.0	7.2	12.3
1947	2.7	22.5	64.8	18.7	45.0	21.6	8.6	12.9
1948	4.3	19.4	77.0	25.6	49.4	25.8	9.7	14.2
1949	6.3	21.4	76.1	43.4	47.2	25.8	8.3_2	15.1
							2.5	
1950	7.2	26.4	75.0	60.2	59.1	24.2	3.2	14.2
1951	7.8	25.0	72.2	65.1	51.5	20.2	4.1	13.8
1952	6.1	20.2	67.0	58.4	64.8	21.4	3.6	11.3
1953	5.2	24.2	62.6	68.1	64.4	23.2	4.2	13.3
1954	5.5	25.1	66.0	65.9	79.9	25.0	4.2	11.8
1955	5.9	28.5	63.5	71.7	77.7	26.7	4.1	11.0
1956	5.7	30.8	67.6	72.0	82.6	27.3	4.1	11.6
1957	5.2	30.0	76.6	74.8	85.8	26.3	4.3	11.2
1958	4.6	24.7	73.1	63.9	76.4	25.2	4.2	10.1
1959	4.6	29.2	67.7	67.1_1	84.5	28.8_1	4.5	10.6_3
				162		71		6.6
1960	4.9	29.3	67.8	171	82.4	68	5.0	6.5
1961	5.1	33.4	69.2	169	78.6	70	4.9	6.0
1962	5.8	35.2	69.8	169	80.1	68	5.0	5.8
1963	6.2	36.3	77.2	151	77.4	71	5.5	5.3
1964	5.8	38.9	75.6	148	70.8	72	5.8	4.8
1965	5.7	38.3	60.1	157	52.5	67	6.0	4.6
1966	6.6	40.8	67.0	152	99.2	69_3	5.9	3.8
						35		
1967	6.1	36.1	63.5	122	92.3	28	6.1	4.0
1968	6.8	35.0	54.4	142	98.2	30	6.8	3.9
1969	6.9	37.6	69.9	142	98.7	30	7.3	3.6
1970	6.0	39.2	63.6	126	99.6	27	8.3	2.7
1971	5.9	41.7	68.0	131	97.0	29	8.8	1.6
1972	6.6	43.9	71.3	141	107.5_8	26	9.2	1.6
					146			
1973	6.8	37.3	71.6	124	164	24	10.7	1.0
1974	6.4	30.5	67.5	99	157	21	10.3	0.7

D20 Output of Wool Tissues (in units stated)

	millions of linear metres					millions of square metres			
	Bulgaria	Czech	Poland	Russia[7]	E. Germany	Hungary	Romania	U.K.	Yugoslavia
1927	...	...	...	103	...	...	...	...	...
1928	...	...	15.8	117	...	...	...	...	...
1929	...	...	11.7	129	...	...	...	...	...
1930	...	...	8.6[5] 14.4	115	...	...	...	...	...
1931	...	...	13.2	108	...	...	...	...	...
1932	...	...	10.3	89	...	...	...	...	...
1933	...	...	11.7	86	...	...	...	...	...
1934	...	12.1	14.5	78	...	...	...	...	...
1935	...	...	17.7	84	...	...	...	268	...
1936	...	7.8	21.6	102	...	...	...	...	...
1937	...	17.2	20.9	108	...	...	...	290	...
1938	...	...	...	113	...	20	12.3	...	...
1939	5.3	...	...	122	...	...	...	...	12.4
1940	...	...	...	120		...	...	...	...
1941	...	...	...	...		...	...	...	...
1942	...	...	...	...		...	...	...	...
1943	...	...	...	...		...	...	216	...
1944	...	...	...	...		...	...	178	...
1945	...	...	[5.1][6]4	54	...	...	...	177	...
1946	...	...	23	71	...	...	...	204	16
1947	...	19.6[4]	33	95	...	...	...	212	22
1948	5.4	40	42	124	...	20	11.8	244[2] 347	29
1949	...	48	50	149	...	23	...	367	26
1950	8.9	48	56	155	...	27	23	376	24
1951	8.2	47	61	176	...	31	28	350	23
1952	9.2	48	63	190	...	23	27	316	20
1953	10.4	40	71	209	...	16	29	344	17
1954	10.0	35	71	243	43	21	30	346	20
1955	11	39	76	252	32	26	31	343	26
1956	13	37	76	268	27	20	31	332	28
1957	13	38	76	284	29	24	29	330	34
1958	14	43	78	303	34	25	28	292	33
1959	19	46	80	326	43	24	28	305	38
1960	19	46	79	369	48	27	32	307	46
1961	17	48	78	382	49	29	37	295	43
1962	18	48	83	396	48	30	34	274	42
1963	19	46	84	403[1] 636	39	29	38	272	48
1964	19	43	90	618	39	30	41	272	53
1965	20	44	91	607	39	29	41	270	55
1966	22	45	91	669	40	31	44	253	58
1967	22	46	90	723	39	32	50	246	52
1968	23	45	94	774	36	36	52	246	50
1969	26	46	99	814	36	24	55	239	49
1970	27	49	99	849	37	27	63	215	57
1971	28	53	99	888	37	26	70	186	59
1972	29	57	100	890	37	24	74	184	59
1973	30	56	107	919	37	23	83	192	60
1974	33	63	117	940	37	25	94	175	66

D20 Output of Wool Tissues (in units stated)

	Austria	Belgium	France	Italy	Portugal	Sweden
			thousands of metric tons			
1975	5.7	30.1	63.2	158	8.1	0.5
1976	5.4	34.0	61.8	186	8.1	0.4
1977	5.3	27.4	61.1	185	7.4	0.4
1978	4.8	27.6	59.5	186	8.2	0.4
1979	4.6	30.7	62.1	211	10.4	0.4
1980	5.7	35.7	59.8	170	10.2	0.5
1981	5.2	35.6	54.4	170	9.5	0.5
1982	5.1	33.4	49.7	154	8.8	0.6
1983	4.5	35.9	47.8	161	9.5	0.6
1984	4.4	38.1	47.2	171	9.8	0.6
1985	4.4	35.7	49.7	177	11.9	0.5
1986	4.3	35.7	48.4	160	13.1	0.4
1987	3.7	33.9	42.9	155	12.6	0.4
1988	3.2	35.8	43.5	163	10.3	0.3
1989	3.0	36.5	40.5	163	11.3	0.3
1990	3.0	34.2	33.1	149	12.0	0.2
1991	2.0	31.4	32.6	153	10.2	—
1992	2.0	31.9	30.3	158	5.2	—
1993	1.0	28.3	24.0	152		
			million square metres			
1994	3	20	37	443	9	…
1995	2	19	34	433	8	…
1996	3	16	36	431	6	…
1997	3	18	39	427	6	…
1998	4	21	35	426	8	…

	Bulgaria	Czecho-slovakia	Poland	East Germany	West Germany	Hungary	Nether-lands	Romania	Russia/ U.S.S.R	U.K.	Yugo-slavia
	millions of linear metres					**millions of square metres**					
1975	38	68	124	37	99	22	23	96	956	151	66
1976	36	61	125	39	104	22	21	105	986	143	67
1977	36	61	124	39	96	24	17	119	989	150	79
1978	35	58	124	38	97	25	14	123	993	144	73
1979	37	58	123	38	97	24	12	125	979	138	71
1980	39	58	121	39	109	27	12	128	971	118	92
1981	40	60	106	39	96	29	8.6	128	973	97	96
1982	42	61	92	40	82	26	4.9	142	951	100	94
1983	49	62	99	39	79	23	4.4[9] 2.7	144	911	94	96
1984	42	62	103	41	87	24	3.1	123	872	91	99
1985	42	60	105	41	104	23	4.4	131	841	91	101
1986	47	59	103	42	102	22	4.7	140	842	93	110
1987	44	58	100	44	99	18	3.8	139	854	90	105
1988	34	59	101	47	104	17	4.2	133	876	89	104
1989	34	59	97	…	109	21	4.5	141	890	25	100
1990	31	59	65	…	108	11	4.4	107	865	20	…
1991	17	44	44	121		7	4.2	100	492[11]	39	27[12]
1992	15	34	33	119		4	4.4	69	351[11]	37	24[12]
		Czech Republic									
1993	16	30[10]	32	…		3	…	68	269[11]	33	16[12]
1994	21	34	51	95		1	3.8	65	114	38	13[12]
				million square metres							
1995	20	32	50	87		1	2.9	68	107	39	11[12]
1996	18	30	50	87		1	2.5	50	67	42	11[12]
1997	17	28	49	87		—	2.0	34	63	37	10[12]
1998	19	29	45	79		—	2.0	22	52	35	9[12]

D20 Output of Wool Tissues (in units stated)

NOTES

1. SOURCES:- The official publications noted on p. xv with gaps filled from League of Nations and United Nations, *Statistical Yearbooks*, and the Russian statistics to 1934 taken from G.W. Nutter, *The Growth of Industrial Production in the Soviet Union* (Princeton, 1962). The Czech figures for 1949 and 1950 were supplied by the Federal Statistical Office of Czechoslovakia.
2. Except as indicated in footnote 5, statistics in this table include cloths of mixed yarns in which wool predominates.

FOOTNOTES

[1] Subsequent statistics are in million square metres.
[2] Previous statistics are in million linear metres.
[3] The reason for this break is not given.
[4] Previous statistics are in thousands of metric tons.
[5] Previous statistics are of pure wool cloth only.
[6] April–December.
[7] G.W. Nutter, *op. cit.* in note 1, gives an estimate for 1913 for the 1923 territory of the U.S.S.R. of 105 million metres.
[8] Subsequently including woollen blankets.
[9] Subsequently pure wool cloth only.
[10] Czech Republic.
[11] Ex-U.S.S.R. countries as follows: (million square metres)

	Armenia	Azerbaijan	Belarus	Kazakhstan	Kyrgistan	Moldova	Turkmenistan	Ukraine	Uzbekistan
1992	2.9	7.3	39.4	22.9	10.9	0.2	3.0	76.5	0.9
1993	0.8	5.8	40.0	20.1	9.4	0.1	3.0	59.7	1.2
1994	2.0	2.0	20.0	10.0	4.0	...	3.0	26.4	1.0
1995	1.0	1.0	8.0	3.0	2.0	...	3.0	19.2	1.0
1996	—	—	8.0	2.0	3.0	...	3.0	12.5	1.0
1997	—	—	9.0	2.0	3.0	...	3.0	14.0	—
1998	—	—	10.0	1.0	2.0	...	3.0	8.9	—

[12] Ex-Yugoslavia countries as follows: (million square metres)

	Croatia	Macedonia	Slovenia
1991	5	10	15
1992	6	9	15
1993	7	7	13
1994	7	5	10
1995	7	6	7
1996	5	4	3
1997	3	4	...
1998	2	4	...

D21 OUTPUT OF ARTIFICIAL AND SYNTHETIC FIBRES (in thousands of metric tons)

1910-1969

	Austria	Belgium	Czech	Finland	France	Germany	E. Germany	Italy	Netherlands
1910	...	...	...	...	1.2	...		...	...
1911	...	...	...	...	...	...		...	...
1912	...	...	...	...	...	...		...	...
1913	0.7	1.4	...	...	2.9	2.1		0.2	...
1919	...	...	...	...	...	...		0.3	...
1920	...	...	...	...	1.5	...		0.7	...
1921	...	...	...	...	...	...		1.5	...
1922	0.7	3.0	0.3	...	2.9	5.0		2.6	1.1
1923	1.1	3.5	0.9	...	4.0	6.5		4.8	1.8
1924	1.0	4.0	0.6	...	6.0	10.5		10.5	2.0
1925	1.5	5.0	1.0	...	6.5	11.8		13.9	2.7
1926	1.3	6.0	0.9	...	7.9	11.2		16.7	4.5
1927	1.7	7.5	1.5	...	9.5	18.7		24.4	5.8
1928	1.5	6.6	1.7	...	13.6	22.2		25.0	6.8
1929	1.4	6.1	2.0	...	19.0	28.1		32.3	8.0
1930	0.8	5.8	2.3	...	23.2	29.3		30.1	8.0
1931	...	4.4	2.8	...	20.7	30.6		34.3	8.5
1932	0.4	4.3	2.6	...	24.0	28.2		32.5	9.0
1933	0.4	5.1	2.7	...	26.9	32.8		38.3	8.7
1934	0.9	5.9	3.6	...	27.9	46.2		48.7	9.9
1935	0.9	6.3	2.8	—	30.2	62.0		69.6	9.6
1936	0.9	6.6	3.4	—	30.0	88.3		89.0	10.0
1937	1.0	7.8	4.3	—	35.1	157		119	10.9
1938	1.1	5.8	2.7	- -	32.9	219		119	9.3
1939	5.9	6.8	2.7	0.8	32.5[2]	273		140	...
1940	20.8	6.2	5.4	0.2	26.6	308		163	...
1941	32.7	9.4	6.2	- -	49.3	373		181	...
1942	32.7	8.6	7.4	0.9	54.1	401		144	...
1943	31.8	12.3	13.1	2.5	55.1	401		102	12.0
1944	21.1	6.1	15.0	5.2	26.5	300		30.6	9.4
					West Germany[3]				
1945	1.5	5.0	3.6	3.6	22.4[2]	21.8	...	3.3	...
1946	2.3	20.3	12.5	5.4	46.4	28.7	...	42.9	9.5
1947	4.2	20.9	18.9	5.9	56.6	103	...	74.0	20.5
1948	10.8	21.6	22.4	6.3	74.4	103	44.2	65.8	25.8
1949	17.6	19.0	25.9	6.2	73.3	129	...	86.6	29.8
1950	32.8	23.1	26.2	7.8	84.1	163	87.4	104	33.3
1951	43.7	30.2	27.9	8.7	106.8	185	97.5	133	36.7
1952	32.7	19.4	32.8	9.3	77.7	144	106	79	32.8
1953	30.9	28.4	36.6	11.3	97.8	175[3]	114	110	38.1
1954	39.0	32.2	37.5	16.1	112	196	120	133	42.8
1955	41.9	33.1	49.1	17.0	121	229	123	140	46.3
1956	44.7	34.4	49.2	17.1	121	243	126	162	45.5
1957	50.3	36.7	47.7	19.9	140	258	138	162	47.8
1958	50.9	28.8	54.8	15.2	149	228	143	156	48.8
1959	55.8	30.9	58.0	14.1	142	262	147	181	52.6
1960	58.1	34.0	61.9	16.4	164	282	145	195	58.4
1961	51.4	37.0	68.0	18.5	175	296	151	216	60.4
1962	55.7	40.3	73.1	18.3	191	337	156	253	64.8
1963	60.5	42.1	75.5	22.1	223	373	157	278	75.5
1964	64.7	45.6	80.8	25.4	241	422	159	314	89.2
1965	67.9	49.3[1]	80.3	29.4	217	456	161	297	102.5
1966	66.3	55.7	85.3	33.4	235	493	173	324	110.4
1967	66.8	57.2	91.4	30.6	219	496	184	335	97.2
1968	76.4	57.9	91.9	35.4	249	622	189	387	113
1969	81.5	57.7	94.3	35.0	288	715	194	442	128

D21 Output of Artificial and Synthetic Fibres (in thousands of metric tons)

	Norway	Poland	Romania	Russia	Spain	Sweden	Switz	U.K.	Yugoslavia
1913	—	...	—	...	—	—	0.1	5.2	...
1922	—	0.2	—	...	—	—	0.9	5.9	...
1923	—	0.4	—	...	—	—	1.7	6.9	...
1924	—	0.5	—	...	—	0.1	1.5	10.0	...
1925	—	0.6	—	...	—	0.1	2.4	12.2	...
1926	—	0.9	—	...	—	0.1	3.3	10.4	...
1927	—	1.6	—	...	—	0.1	4.1	15.8	...
1928	—	2.4	—	0.2	0.5	0.2	4.5	20.6	...
1929	—	2.6	—	...	0.9	0.2	4.6	21.4	...
1930	—	2.7	—	...	1.2	0.2	4.6	21.2	...
1931	—	3.6	—	...	1.4	0.3	4.6	23.8	...
1932	—	3.5	—	2.8	1.8	0.3	4.0	31.5	...
1933	—	3.8	—	...	2.5	0.3	4.2	36.6	...
1934	—	4.7	—	...	2.6	0.5	4.6	40.5	...
1935	—	5.7	—	...	3.2	0.7	3.7	53.9	...
1936	—	5.9	0.3	8.0	1.8	1.0	5.0	63.1	...
1937	0.1	7.5	0.6	8.6	1.4	2.1	5.5	67.3	...
1938	0.1	10.2₄	0.8	0.9	0.9	2.5	5.5	61.1	...
1939	0.2	8.1	1.2	11.5	1.5	2.9	5.5	77.0	...
1940	0.3	11.8	0.9	11.1	3.1	3.6	5.5	76.7	...
1941	0.3	14.5	1.0	...	4.1	5.0	8.4	61.9	...
1942	0.5	17.2	1.2	...	5.5	8.4	15.6	54.9	...
1943	0.5	20.0	2.0	...	6.6	12.7	17.7	56.4	...
1944	0.5	16.8	1.1	...	8.3	16.5	18.2	60.1	...
1945	0.3	...	1.4	1.1	7.4	13.6	16.4	62.8	...
1946	2.4	8.7	1.3	3.2	14.8	14.9	16.7	80.9	...
1947	3.3	11.9	1.4	6.7	16.4	11.2	17.0	91.8	...
1948	7.1	18.0	1.3	11.1	16.4	12.1	17.5	106	...
1949	11.8	22.3	1.4	17.0	18.6	12.8	16.8	131	...
1950	13.5	24.9	1.4	24.2	24.5	14.1	17.3	168	...
1951	14.3	27.4	1.9	34.1₅	23.6	17.4	18.8	174	...
1952	11.6	32.0	2.5	49.4	31.9	11.9	19.1	128	...
1953	14.4	41.3	2.2	62.3	32.3	14.0	22.6	190	...
1954	16.5	48.2	2.5	78.9	39.5	17.5	22.7	203	...
1955	15.7	54.0	2.6	110	46.9	18.5	24.7	214	...
1956	14.4	59.0	2.6	129	50.1	22.7	25.6	219	...
1957	16.1	62.9	2.7	149	51.5	26.1	25.5	225	—
1958	13.4	65.9	3.0	166	51.5	26.4	23.4	224	10.1
1959	14.5	68.6	3.4	180	49.4	28.6	26.0	234	19.7
1960	14.3	77.6	4.1	211	59.7	28.5	29.0	269	21.1
1961	12.9	82.5	4.6	251	52.9	30.8	29.9	259	19.8
1962	17.3	84.6	4.9	277	63.6	31.8	33.4	284	21.0
1963	20.3	87.3	5.7	309	72.2	31.9	38.3	326	21.1
1964	23.8	94.3	6.3	361	80.5	36.6	41.3	374	22.0
1965	26.0	102	20.9	408	71.8	38.4	47.5	391	22.2
1966	24.3	108	34.3	458	75.0	35.7	46.0	400₆	28.6
1967	26.2	115	47.3	511	70.4	38.1	51.8	434	29.3
1968	29.4	122	53.6	554	88.2	36.6	58.0	539	36.5
1969	30.6	129	56.5	584	113	35.4	58.9	554	38.5

D21 Output of Artificial and Synthetic Fibres (in thousands of metric tons)

	Austria	Belgium	Czech.	Finland	France	W Germany	E. Germany	Italy	Netherlands[9]
1970	86.5	57.4	100	39.6	256	723	209	425	126
1971	102	56.9	109	38.8	345	785	210	488	142
1972	107	54.5	117	39.8	369	801	229	498	149
1973	116	54.5	125	38.5	400	980	255	547	...
1974	122	49.5	131	38.7	364	940	266	492	...
1975	101	23.1	140	35.6	288	767	280	413	...
1976	131	49.2	147	36.3	337	915	291[10] 357	536	...
1977	129	45.2	153	45.3	326	847	460	496	...
1978	138	58.2	163	48.8	323	881	459	506	...
1979	140	64.3[8]	152	54.7	312	924	452	520	...
1980	141	126	165	55.7	262	879	442	502	...
1981	142	120	169	50.6	259	913	461	576	...
1982	131	100	180	57.3	247	844	463	552	...
1983	139	89	186	61.3	240	908	461	569	...
1984	142	86	189	69.9	239	934	471	639	...
1985	142	100	197	66.2	221	963	470	690	...
1986	139	107	193	59.1	201	951	447	699	...
1987	136	142	197	60.4	198	983	451	704	...
1988	136	111	204	68.6	196	997	...	710	...
1989	140	132	201	45.1	245	105	...	694	...
1990	146	119	201	35.7	267	116	...	729	...
1991	111	125	155	29.9	276		117	705	...
1992	122	113	47	34.5	352		106	728	...
1993	74	61	39	41.4	289		79	674	...

	Norway	Poland	Romania	Russia	Spain	Sweden	Switz.	U.K.	Yugoslavia
1970	28.0	136	76.6	623	118	36.1	60.4	599	40.8
1971	28.2	149	95.3	676	137	37.7	70.1	613	54.7
1972	28.9	160	99.6	746	176	38.5	79.8	647	77.0
1973	29.4	176	116	830	200	38.1	80.8	731	84.1
1974	28.9	186	143	887	197	37.1	75.6	628	88.2
1975	18.4	213	148	955	172	20.6	69.2	562	82.4
1976	26.1	229	179	1,020	205	31.6	81.1	618	85.6
1977	24.7	237	183	1,088	218	33.5	82.4	552	96.6
1978	28.4	240	192	1,131	250	37.0	87.3	607	101
1979	29.3	231	205	1,101	271	37.0	92.4	596	137
1980	28.3	244	200	1,176	259	35.0	86.2	450	140
1981	28.2	182	220	1,213	292	33.8	85.0	395	139
1982	20.0	179	211	1,255	281	38.0	80.4	334	151
1983	—	201	218	1,353	270	40.1	86	389	147
1984	—	210	234	1,401	279	40.1	98	383	197
1985	—	210	258	1,394	315	33.4	100	330	195
1986	—	204	303	1,480	298	24.8	93	288	198
1987	—	210	289	1,517	290	24.5	88	277	198
1988	—	214	297	1,554	299	17.5	96	280	198
1989	—	221	276	1,595	296	15.8	99	273	196
1990	—	135	209	...	303	12.6	82	273	183
1991	—	105	142	309	283	8.5	...	267	...
1992	—	104	113	245	286	8.2	...	262	...
1993	—	108	101	170	256	...	...	241	...

D21 Output of Artificial and Synthetic Fibres (in thousands of metric tons)

NOTE

SOURCES:- The official publications noted on p. xv with gaps filled from the League of Nations and United Nations, *Statistical Yearbooks*, and from O.E.C.D., *Statistical Bulletins*.

FOOTNOTES

1 Subsequently including tow for cigarette filters.
2 From 1940 to 1945 Alsace-Lorraine is excluded.
3 Figures for 1946–53 are of production for sale only.
4 Subsequent figures apply to the boundaries established in 1945.
5 Previously excluding synthetic fibres, which amounted to 2.3 thousand tons in 1953.
6 Previously the statistics of continuous filament were of deliveries rather than output. The effect of the change is to raise the series by about 1 per cent.
7 Subsequently exluding acetate fibres.
8 Benelux subsequently.
9 See under Belgium for figures from 1980.
10 This break is not explained in the source but is occasioned by an increase in the non-cellulosic continuous fibres component.

D22 LINEN INDUSTRY INDICATORS (in thousands of metric tons)

1760–1889

Year	UK Flax & Hemp Input	Year	UK Flax & Hemp Input	Year	Austria/Hungary Flax & Hemp 1	Belgium Flax & Hemp 1	Germany Linen Yarn Output	UK Flax & Hemp Input
1760	26	1800	78	1840	...	...	...	133[3] 131
1761	36	1801	85	1841	...	...	...	136
1762	83	1802	74	1842	164	...	...	121
1763	39	1803	89	1843	154	...	...	148
1764	41	1804	94	1844	158	...	...	166
1765	40	1805	85	1845	160	...	...	157
1766	37	1806	89	1846	149	...	...	139
1767	37	1807	92	1847	154	...	...	129
1768	41	1808	70	1848	...	...	...	157
1769	43	1809	96	1849	...	...	...	188
1770	47	1810	99	1850	...	...	50	189
1771	58[1]	1811	74	1851	158	...	53	163[4] 157
1772	43	1812	93	1852	...	...	51	155
1773	43	1813	...	1853	...	...	50	170
1774	47	1814	86	1854	138	...	51	128
1775	43	1815	100	1855	...	...	51	130
1776	45	1816	79	1856	...	12	51	154
1777	47	1817	93	1857	154	...	49	164
1778	48	1818	103	1858	...[2]	...	51	132
1779	54	1819	83	1859	145	...	50	138
1780	47	1820	82	1860	...	...	50	143
1781	48	1821	80	1861	...	...	50	144
1782	59	1822	101	1862	...	...	55	165
1783	42	1823	107	1863	143	...	48	148
1784	52	1824	99	1864	...	...	46	168
1785	48	1825	104	1865	...	...	47	171
1786	49	1826	85	1866	152[2]	39	47	147
1787	55	1827	102	1867	169	...	47	144
1788	66	1828	98	1868	156	...	52	170
1789	62	1829	94	1869	158	...	49	151
1790	56	1830	103	1870	148	...	55[5]	200
1791	56[1]	1831	102	1871	143	...	47	213
1792	73	1832	110	1872	...	...	45	175
1793	70	1833	116	1873	137	...	54	200
1794	72	1834	104	1874	133	...	54	205
1795	72	1835	101	1875	110	...	50	173
1796	76	1836	144	1876	139	...	44	149
1797	66	1837	122	1877	131	...	47	188
1798	76	1838	158	1878	150[4]	...	50	159
1799	85	1839	147	1879	137	...	49	159
				1880	148	61	44	172
				1881	141	60	41	173
				1882	13	54	46	178
				1883	140	35	48	155
				1884	145	32	47	151
				1885	135	23	43	160
				1886	133	20	38	132
				1887	153	38	41	149
				1888	126	54	41	175
				1889	131	52	44	174

D22 Linen Industry Indicators (in thousands of metric tons)

Year	Austria/Hungary Flax & Hemp 1	Belgium Flax & Hemp 1	France Yarn Output	Germany Linen Yarn Output	U.K Flax & Hemp 1	Year	Belgium Flax & Hemp 1	France Yarn Output	Germany Linen Yarn Output	U.K Flax & Hemp 1
1890	142	55	...	46	171	1940	...	...	...	181
1891	140	61	...	43	149	1941	...	18.9[11]	...	128
1892	151	63	...	26	145	1942	...	17.4[11]	...	117
1893	150	52	...	42	145	1943	...	14.1[11]	...	110
1894	138	64	...	42	161	1944	...	8.4[11]	...	140
									West Germany[7]	
1895	153	74	...	44	203	1945	...	7.7[11]	...	111
1896	150	62	...	41	156	1946	...	17.0	...	97
1897	140	55	...	37	161	1947	91	18.2	...	118
1898	151	59	...	39	167	1948	82	20.7	...	127
1899	148	73	...	40	148	1949	104	19.5	5	92
1900	151	...	...	33	141	1950	122	24.0	5	127
1901	154	...	...	31	145	1951	135	29.7	7	139
1902	155	...	...	36	139	1952	156[6]	31.0	7	118
1903	183	...	...	42	163	1953	138	28.5	8	125
1904	150	...	...	32	161	1954	159	31.0	9	126
1905	188	...	...	42	168	1955	189	28.3	10	142
1906	209	...	...	31	155	1956	196	29.3	9	129
1907	176	...	...	32	186	1957	196	31.0	10	140
1908	161	...	...	30	172	1958	123	30.3	9	118
1909	158	...	...	30	164	1959	120	26.6	9[7]	130
1910	161	...	...	29	167	1960	134	30.5	9	133
1911	138	155	...	30	170	1961	184	30.7	9	113
1912	158	176	...	34	202	1962	180	28.8	9	126
1913	146	140	...	31	196	1963	205	26.0	8	126
1914	112	...	...	...	170	1964	257	24.9[12]	7	124
								12.9		
1915	...	...	...	...	179	1965	247	20.8	8	110
1916	...	...	...	...	189	1966	191	22.5	6	98
1917	...	...	...	...	164	1967	152	17.5	6	88
1918	...	...	...	...	139	1968	141	15.9	6	85
1919	...	62	...	...[5]	86	1969	107	15.5	5	84
1920	...	125	...	19	135	1970	55	16.7	5	85[10]
										39
1921	...	62	...	21	54	1971	59	16.2	5	27
1922	...	63	...	23	85	1972	81	14.2	4	33
1923	...	91	...	20	99[8]	1973	94	14.0	4	30
1924	...	119	...	20	124	1974	76[9]	14.3	4	23[9]
1925	...	136	41.6	18	105	1975	62	11.4	3	13
1926	...	163	47.8	11	112	1976	54	11.3	4	16
1927	...	164	47.2	19	129	1977	51	9.8	3	10
1928	...	212	45.4	13	107	1978	84	9.2	2	12
1929	...	177	39.0	7	121	1979	84	11.1	2	12
1930	...	137	40.4	7	107	1980	72	9.8	...	9
1931	...	96	37.4	6	107	1981	61	9.8	...	7
1932	...	97	32.7	8	94	1982	49	9.2	...	8
1933	...	66	35.0	11	94	1983	55	8.5	...	9
1934	...	68	29.7	20	125	1984	66	8.9	...	10
1935	...	146	26.8	19	120	1985	71	7.7	...	12
1936	...	154	27.2	17	137	1986	84	5.9	...	8
1937	...	166[6]	28.6	20	138	1987	71	6.7	...	12
1938	...	205	29.3	23	123	1988	74	7.1	...	12
1939	...	...	...	...	149	1989	79	6.5	...	8
									Germany	
						1990	68	5.3	...	11
						1991	68	5.3	...	9
						1992	52	5.1	...	8
						1993	52	6.8	...	13

D22   Linen Industry Indicators (in thousands of metric tons)

NOTES

1. SOURCES:- Germany to 1938—based on the 1907 census output (given in *Statistisches Jahrbuch, 1913*) and the index in W.G. Hoffman, *Das Wachstum der Deutschen Wirtschaft seit der Mitte des 19 Jahrhunderts* (Berlin, etc., 1965), pp. 368–70. U.K. hemp component—E.B. Schumpeter, *English Overseas Trade, 1697–1808* (Oxford, 1960), the *Return relating to Flax and Hemp* (P.P. 1854 LXV and similar previous returns), and the *Annual Statement of Trade*. U.K. flax component to 1935—based on the 1913 net imports and domestic output (from *Annual Statement of Trade and Agricultural Statistics* respectively) and the index in the endpapers of W.G. Hoffman, *British Industry, 1700–1950* (Oxford, 1955). All other statistics are from the official publications noted on p. xv.

2. Except as indicated in footnotes, input of raw material in any year is taken to be domestic output plus imports minus exports and re-exports. No allowance can be made for stock changes or for wastage.

3. T.J. Markovitch, *L'Industrie française de 1789 à 1964* (Cahiers de l'I.S.E.A., 1966) gives annual average figures of French flax and hemp consumption for the following periods (in thousand tons):-

1781–90	77.5	1825–34	96.5	1855–64	109.7	1885–94	61.3
1803–12	73.0	1835–44	104.4	1865–74	103.2	1895–1904	39.5
1815–24	80.0	1845–54	97.8	1875–84	91.4	1905–13	32.7

FOOTNOTES

[1] Figures to 1771 apply to England & Wales only. From 1772 to 1791 they are for Great Britain only.

[2] Lombardy was excluded from 1859 and Venetia from 1866.

[3] Figures to 1840 (1st line) have not had the small re-exports of hemp deducted.

[4] Previous statistics include jute.

[5] From 1871 to 1918 Alsace-Lorraine is included in Germany rather than France. German statistics for 1920–38 apply to the 1924 territory.

[6] Only from 1938 to 1952 are the small re-exports of hemp deducted.

[7] Saarland is excluded from 1949 to 1959.

[8] Southern Ireland is excluded from 1 April 1923.

[9] Later figures exclude hemp, of which 4 thousand tons were imported by Belgium and 6 thousand tons by the U.K. in 1974.

[10] Subsequently the hemp component comprises true hemp only, not sisal etc.

[11] Linen only.

[12] Tow appears to have been excluded subsequently. Comparable figures back to 1952 are as follows:-

1952	18.6	1956	17.8	1960	16.2
1953	16.1	1957	18.1	1961	14.8
1954	18.1	1958	16.6	1962	13.1
1955	15.5	1959	13.7	1963	13.0

D23 OUTPUT OF SULPHURIC ACID (in thousands of metric tons)

1860-1919

	Austria[1]	Belgium	France	Germany	Italy[3]	Neth'l	Russia[4]	Spain[15]	Sweden	Switz	U.K.[5]
1860	...	...	...	...	...	...	5	...	...	...	...
1865	...	...	...	...	...	...	7	...	...	380	
1866	...	...	...	...	...	...	...	...	...	...	...
1867	...	...	125	75	...	...	...	...	...	...	
1868	...	...	...	...	...	...	...	...	...	...	
1869	...	...	...	...	...	...	...	...	...	...	
1870	...	...	...	...	...	...	8	...	...	...	590
1871	...	...	...	43	...	...	...	...	...	...	
1872	...	...	...	47	...	...	...	...	...	...	
1873	...	...	...	45	...	...	...	...	...	...	
1874	...	...	...	55	...	...	...	...	...	...	
1875	...	...	...	86	...	...	16	...	...	...	730
1876	...	...	...	85	...	...	...	...	...	...	...
1877	...	...	...	86	...	...	...	...	...	...	
1878	23	30	200	92	...	...	...	...	...	...	
1879	...	...	...	112	...	...	...	...	...	...	
1880	...	...	...	130	...	...	23	...	...	...	900
1881	...	...	...	214	...	...	...	...	...	...	
1882	...	...	...	237	...	...	...	...	...	...	
1883	...	...	...	245	...	...	...	...	...	...	
1884	...	...	...	285	...	...	...	...	...	...	
1885	...	...	...	283	...	...	37	...	...	...	890
1886	...	...	...	292	...	...	...	...	...	...	
1887	...	...	...	316	...	...	...	...	10	...	
1888	...	...	...	330	...	...	44	...	16	...	
1889	...	...	...	389	...	...	...	...	13	...	
1890	49	...	...	420	...	...	40	...	17	...	870
1891	...	...	...	423	...	...	...	...	18	...	
1892	...	...	...	446	...	...	37	...	28	...	
1893	...	...	...	477	59	...	44	...	27	...	
1894	...	...	...	511	72	...	...	...	31	...	
1895	...	...	...	504	96	...	52	...	35	...	770
1896	...	...	...	553	111	...	...	...	40	...	
1897	...	...	...	584	129	...	60	...	37	...	
1898	...	...	...	636	139	...	...	...	39	...	
1899	...	...	...	689	165	...	...	...	36	...	
1900	100	165	625	703	230	...	106	...	35	...	1,010
1901	...	...	...	708	235	...	...	...	41	...	...
1902	...	...	...	798	252	...	...	1	42	...	
1903	...	...	...	836	263	...	...	1	59	...	
1904	...	...	...	998	278	...	...	1	48	...	
1905	...	...	...	1,059	302	...	178	2	53	...	
1906	113	...	...	1,129	365	...	...	5	95	...	
1907	...	...	...	1,159	425	...	...	8	117	...	
1908	...	...	...	1,151	524	...	...	9	64	...	
1909	...	...	...	1,223	590	...	...	7	46	...	
1910	...	...	...	1,381	645	...	250	10	73	...	
1911	...	...	...	1,500	596	...	275	12	79	...	
1912	...	...	...	1,650	635	...	284	26	79	...	
1913	350	420	900	1,727	645	320	292[4] 121	21[15]	84	30	1,082
1914	...	...	...	1,506	630	...	...	26	84	...	...
1915	...	...	...	1,138	626	...	...	39	76	...	
1916	...	...	...	...	...	...	...	110	76	...	
1917	...	...	...	1,104	...	...	...	131	55	...	
1918	...	...	...	1,009[2] 848	624[3]	...	...	61	45	...	
1919	...	...	...	442	365	...	17	57	65	...	...

D23   Output of Sulphuric Acid (in thousands of metric tons)

1920–1974

	Austria	Belgium	Bulgaria	Czech	Denmark	Finland	France	Germany	E. Germany	Greece	Hungary	Ireland[12]
1920	...	...	...	...	...	...	...	792[8] 367	...	...	...	...
1921	...	...	...	...	...	...	...	954[9] 862	...	...	...	...
1922	...	...	...	...	...	1.2	...	1,040	...	...	...	...
1923	...	...	...	...	...	7.8	...		...	...	...	...
1924	...	...	...	...	...	10	...	744	...	...	...	...
1925	44	462	...	114	...	11	1,500	961	...	...	50	...
1926	...	...	...	...	...	11	...	1,239	...	...	...	...
1927	...	...	...	...	3	11	...	1,448	...	...	...	42
1928	...	...	...	...	3	21	...	1,555	...	...	...	48
1929	...	496	...	221	3	19	1,032	1,704	...	...	...	58
1930	...	585	...	...	3	15	...	1,475	...	25	...	57
1931	...	396	...	...	3	12	...	1,105	...	16	...	45
1932	...	344	...	...	3	15	...	939	...	14	...	40
1933	...	...	...	...	3	18	...	1,213	...	15	...	37
1934	...	625	...	...	4	20	...	1,307[8]	...	29	...	40
1935	...	...	...	...	4	22	...	1,574	...	46	...	44
1936	...	...	...	...	5	24	...	1,765	...	49	...	52
1937	28	...	...	165	5	25	...	2,050	...	43	...	54
1938	32	749	...	...	7	29	1,272	2,272	...	52	40	55
1939	35	...	...	...	6	27	...	2,716	...	58	...	...
1940	22	...	...	...	5	25	...[6]	2,140	...	...	...	...
1941	24	...	...	...	3	14	458	2,362	...	...	...	...
1942	24	...	...	...	4	18	365	2,514	...	...	...	...
1943	43	...	...	...	4	26	342	2,543	...	...	...	...
1944	54	...	...	...	6	26	153	2,199	...	...	...	...
								West Germany[10]				
1945	6	122	...	...	5	30	277[6]	...	...	14	...	...
1946	4	545	...	123	4	54	840	342	108	35	...	50
1947	6	729	...	192	5	61	1,069	517	...	41	20	55
1948	6	829	...	215	5	66	1,275	761[10]	190	39	33	53
1949	8	780	...	219	7	89	1,151	1,139	...	50	59	53
1950	9	880	...	252	11	94	1,215	1,466	300	41	62	62
1951	10	934	8	258	9	117	1,450	1,703	354	71	71	70
1952	16	846	12	278	8	120	1,191	1,740	370	60	94	58
1953	28	767	14	311	9	135	1,180	1,897	446	59	120	51
1954	35	966	15	341	10	133	1,378	2,092	531	96	111	66
1955	69	1,143	19	383	10	133	1,473	2,279	592	119	124	66
1956	74	1,116	29	422	10	153	1,535	2,530	611	88	101	65
1957	80	1,073	40	445	10	163	1,600	2,723	640	106	115	60
1958	117	1,133	64	463	9	148	1,786[7] 1,824	2,917	650	90	130	54
1959	121	1,249	91	513	13	168	1,890	2,938[11]	689	141	148	73
1960	140	1,423	123	553	18	187	2,046	3,170	730	135	164	95
1961	150	1,322	192	599	12	229	2,205	3,103	819	131	189	129
1962	160	1,233	247	643	12	238	2,271	3,101	861	125	212	...
1963	200	1,249	269	725	13	333	2,394	3,316	919	120	267	...
1964	217	1,348	291	893	17	356	2,702	3,602	937	138	322	...
1965	193	1,488	318	933	24	383	2,916	3,751	985	236	378	...
1966	229	1,362	353	982	16	480	3,073	3,834	973	379	393	...
1967	241	1,484	360	1,012	14	549	3,227	3,778	988	504	424	...
1968	269	1,746	472	977	16	597	3,349	4,210	1,078	551	446	...
1969	277	1,837	498	1,034	22	678	3,527	4,481	1,104	665	454	...
1970	289	1,794	502	1,110	22	843	3,682	4,435	1,099	623	457	...
1971	286	1,932	514	1,174	17	783	3,923	4,388	1,076	728	468	...
1972	300	2,460	514	1,176	16	1,004	4,114	4,735	1,045	813	566	...
1973	303	2,595	561	1,209	15	937	4,383	5,069	1,058	912	648	...
1974	...	2,590	761	1,211	16	1,229	4,689	5,130	1,005	886	657	...

D23 Output of Sulphuric Acid (in thousands of metric tons)

	Italy	Neth'l	Norway	Poland	Portugal	Romania	Russia[4]	Spain[15]	Sweden	Switz	U.K.	Yugoslavia
1920	352	...	...	...	...	...	...	98	91	...	...	...
1921	420	...	...	...	...	...	11	163	63	...	...	...
1922	485	...	...	...	...	...	...[14]	138	61	...	...	...
1923	767	...	...	...	...	...	45	173	79	...	...	...
1924	632	...	...	...	...	...	89	179	88	...	...	...
1925	800	350	...	...	...	...	100	202[15]	114	30	848	...
1926	823	...	...	...	...	...	145	219	111	...	...	...
1927	820	...	...	185	...	25	176	178	108	...	861	...
1928	704	...	...	222	...	25	211[14]	179	121	...	900	...
1929	835	375	...	233	...	27	265	110	129	...	930	...
1930	831	320	...	165	...	48	396	151	140	...	813	...
1931	633	380	...	120	...	40	464	128	130	...	682	...
1932	562	430	...	99	...	...	552	114	121	...	763	...
1933	678	460	...	121	...	38	627	127	127	...	772	...
1934	774	380	...	139	...	39	782	162	127	...	864	...
1935	804	280	...	112	...	39	994	261	152	...	912	...
1936	957	360	...	135	...	39	1,197	81	147	...	1,012	...
1937	1,026	430	...	181	...	39	1,369	...	163	...	1,068	...
1938	1,076	474	40	189	78	44	1,544	87	167	120	960	...
1939	1,284	460	...	...	82	45	1,625	118	171	...	1,086	25
1940	1,255	195	...	...	80	...	1,587[4]	168	158	...	1,215	11
1941	1,136	57	...	...	73	...	...	158	148	...	1,219	...
1942	766	72	...	...	84	...	...	[128][16]	144	...	1,305	...
1943	547	92	...	...	58	...	...	[74][16]	185	...	1,271	...
1944	175	...	...	...	107	...	...	125[15] / 276	221	...	1,289	...
1945	122	...	...	[36][13]	113	...	781	369	229	...	1,236	5
1946	525	276	30	124	113	...	725	288	262	120	1,349	26
1947	845	312	35	155	116	...	996	367	242	120	1,354	32
1948	975	376	40	222	136	28	1,479	353	281	140	1,577	44
1949	1,160	396	57	276	141	...	1,845	403	305	150	1,687	45
1950	1,276	438	69	...	148	52	2,125	456	333	119	1,832	40
1951	1,460	542	68	277	194	60	2,372	565	342	147	1,632	39
1952	1,505	559	67	348	186	60	2,662	640	327	120	1,530	36
1953	1,601	584	67	370	204	68	2,919	650	342	84	1,905	40
1954	1,824	687	79	419	209	74	3,292	721	395	120	2,075	59
1955	1,943	690	78	450	228	92	3,798	799	397	180	2,131	72
1956	2,046	720	83	481	202	95	4,323	859	399	128	2,287	107
1957	2,064	715	77	499	239	122	4,569	980	422	125	2,373	124
1958	2,031	761	71	573	266	144	4,803	1,072	387	121	2,277	125
1959	2,145	812	88	610	311	199	5,081	1,141	404	129	2,467	128
1960	2,299	860	87	685	320	226	5,398	1,132	410	160	2,745	130
1961	2,446	827	90	794	341	248	5,718	1,236	421	163	2,705	234
1962	2,551	818	90	852	352	326	6,132	1,499	448	122	2,775	286
1963	2,711	854	104	888	417	343	6,885	1,462	475	148	2,927	391
1964	2,890	976	110	1,001	408	417	7,647	1,528	524	159	3,185	472
1965	2,979	1,090	124	1,062	413	541	8,518	1,616	579	194	3,358	435
1966	3,369	1,058	139	1,139	412	619	9,367	1,781	603	169	3,168	542
1967	3,524	1,170	214	1,213	403	679	9,734	1,796	604	164	3,234	552
1968	3,489	1,376	262	1,314	430	773	10,159	2,067	632	149	3,335	549
1969	3,465	1,511	310	1,516	430	838	10,665	2,152	703	164	3,287	649
1970	3,327	1,562	312	1,901	463	994	12,059	2,021	709	168	3,352	696
1971	3,097	1,496	314	2,252	398	1,047	12,775	2,454	769	165	3,459	752
1972	3,033	1,537	355	2,568	379	1,162	13,685	2,325	945	165	3,449	791
1973	3,036	1,546	382	2,914	326	1,311	14,855	2,595	938	...	3,886	882
1974	3,219	1,674	381	3,333	420	1,358	16,663	2,919	940	...	3,855	863

D23 Output of Sulphuric Acid (in thousands of metric tons)

	Belgium	Bulgaria	Czechoslovakia	Denmark	Finland	France	West Germany	East Germany	Greece	Hungary
1975	1,844	854	1,245	21	1,034	3,758	4,157	1,002	920	630
1976	1,891	857	1,240	17	1,016	3,959	4,668	957	920	616
1977	2,011	860	1,276	16	982	4,501	4,678	927	1,111	633
1978	2,112	974	1,195	57	849	4,584	4,671	971	1,181	644
1979	2,299	998	1,253	68	1,048	4,957	5,067	952	1,151	588
1980	2,151	852	1,285	36	1,039	4,952	4,777	958	1,088	590
1981	1,974	920	1,315	20	1,058	4,412	4,832	948	980	573
1982	1,718	916	1,252	21	1,032	4,166	4,411	920	1,000	571
1983	1,898	861	1,244	20	1,145	4,325	4,340	926	1,016	606
1984	2,247	908	1,246	27	1,165	4,531	4,309	885	1,155	549
1985	2,107	810	1,298	36	1,207	4,322	4,199	883	1,086	520
1986	1,957	807	1,292	23	1,100	3,956	4,105	883	952	540
1987	2,069	689	1,264	33	870	3,960	4,070	867	912	573
1988	2,136	840	1,249	91	1,179	4,081	4,053	799	987	512
1989	1,956	846	1,142	122	1,129	4,187	4,028	835	1,023	502
1990	1,906	522	1,089	90	1,010	3,771	3,221	431	950	263
1991	1,936	356	682	37	1,015	3,627	3,064		841	141
1992	1,906	404	522[17]	38	1,087	2,871	...		617	99
1993	1,593	409	383[17]	...	1,179	2,357	...		...	77
							Germany			
1994	...	428	337	5	1,084	2,227	2,781		623	80
1995	...	454	340	25	1,159	2,382	1,387		753	114
1996	...	525	345	19	1,288	2,263	1,225		1,544	94
1997	...	556	333	...	2,182	2,243	1,370		1,655	89
1998	...	499	327	...	2,496	2,231	1,601		1,672	62

	Italy	Netherlands	Norway	Poland	Portugal	Romania	Russia/ USSR	Spain	Sweden	Switz- erland	U.K.	Yugo- slavia
1975	3,006	1,292	328	3,413	399	1,448	18,645	3,624	793	...	3,166	871
1976	2,896	1,402	405	3,179	309	1,555	20,015	2,958	767	...	3,271	842
1977	2,946	1,572	384	3,268	476	1,523	21,104	3,284	816	122	3,405	874
1978	2,945	1,680	381	3,172	380	1,655	22,411	2,965	807	115	3,453	902
1979	2,955	1,744	386	2,983	633	1,750	22,364	2,950	764	...	3,498	975
1980	2,827	1,726	354	3,019	636	1,756	23,033	3,052	660	...	3,381	1,186
1981	2,544	1,726	407	2,776	546	1,814	24,095	2,875	838	...	2,889	1,248
1982	2,221	1,609	412	2,676	472	...	23,801	2,940	786	...	2,587	1,183
1983	2,540	1,451	440	2,786	431	1,941	24,714	2,995	890	...	2,629	1,300
1984	2,636	1,609	460	2,769	553	1,915	25,338	3,683	927	...	2,654	1,471
1985	2,724	1,508	448	2,863	497	1,835	26,037	3,391	958	...	2,525	1,489
1986	2,605	1,209	484	2,965	448	1,971	27,847	3,577	1,014	...	2,330	1,595
1987	2,724	956	516	3,149	331	1,693	28,531	3,318	992	...	2,180	1,592
1988	2,499	1,144	796	3,154	293	1,825	29,372	3,440	962	...	2,257	1,713
1989	2,212	...	...	3,115	289	1,687	28,726	3,325	902	...	1,977	1,617
1990	2,038	...	...	1,721	260	1,111	27,267	2,848	855	...	...	...
1991	1,853	...	...	1,088	51	745	11,597[18]	1,628	928	...	...	...[19]
1992	1,733	...	615	1,244	...	572	9,704[18]	1,724	...	...	...	302[19]
1993	1,430	...	...	1,145	...	527	8,243[18]	...	...	...	...	...
1994	1,975	...	...	1,452	12	491	6,334	1,375	487	...	1,266	24[19]
1995	2,161	500	...	1,861	13	477	6,946	2,847	507	...	1,293	87[19]
1996	2,214	418	...	1,761	10	422	5,764	2,265	572	...	643	231[19]
1997	2,214	356	...	1,741	11	329	6,247	2,817	566	...	613	177[19]
1998	2,097	429	...	1,707	15	229	5,840	3,134	548	...	716	211[19]

D23 Output of Sulphuric Acid (in thousands of metric tons)

NOTES

1. SOURCES:- Austria 1878–1906 and U.K. 1865–1900—L.F. Haber, *The Chemical Industry during the Nineteenth Century* (Oxford, 1952), quoting, for Austria, J. Glaser, *Die Chemische Industrie österreichs und ihre Entwicklung.* Czechoslovakia. 1925–51—supplied by the Federal Statistical Office of Czechoslovakia. Germany 1867, France 1867–1925, Belgium 1867–1925, Netherlands 1913–25—T.J. Kreps, *The Economics of the Sulphuric Acid Industry* (Stanford, 1938), where the original sources are cited. Austria, Hungary, and Switzerland in 1925—League of Nations, *The Chemical Industry* (Geneva, 1927). Russia to 1950—G.W. Nutter, *The Growth of Industrial Production in the Soviet Union* (Princeton, 1952). Sweden to 1907—supplied by the Swedish Central Office of Statistics. All other statistics are taken from the official publications noted on p. xv, with gaps filled from League of Nations and United Nations, *Statistical Yearbooks.*
2. So far as possible, except as indicated in footnote 3, output is given in terms of 100% H_2SO_4.
3. With the exceptions of Germany, Italy, and Spain, all statistics prior to 1914 are estimates.

FOOTNOTES

[1]   Figures to 1913 apply to the whole Austro-Hungarian Empire.
[2]   Subsequently excluding Alsace-Lorraine and Posen.
[3]   Figures to 1918 are of acid of unknown grade, but clearly not 100% H_2SO_4. If the figure for 1918 were on the same basis as 1919 it would be 390 thousand tons when converted to the 100% H_2SO_4 basis.
[4]   Figures to 1913 (1st line) apply to the whole Russian Empire. From 1913 (2nd line) to 1940 they apply to the 1923 territory of the U.S.S.R., and subsequently to the territory established after the Second World War.
[5]   It is not clear whether the estimates to 1900 are in thousands of Imperial or metric tons, but in view of their tentative nature it is not of much concern. Considerably lower estimates are given in T.J. Kreps, 1900, (*op cit.* in note 1) for 1867 and 1878, *viz.* 155 and 600 thousand tons respectively.
[6]   From 1941 to 1945 Alsace-Lorraine is excluded.
[7]   Subsequent figures include residual acid.
[8]   From 1920 (2nd line) Saarland, Danzig, and Mernel are excluded. Saarland is reincluded from 1 March 1935.
[9]   From 1921 (2nd line) eastern Upper Silesia is excluded.
[10] Figures to 1946–48 are for the American and British Occupation Zones only.
[11] From 1945 to 1959 Saarland is excluded.
[12] Years ended 30 June.
[13] May–December. There were substantial boundary changes in 1945.
[14] Figures for 1923 to 1928 are for years ended 30 September.
[15] Figures to 1944 (1st line) are of production for sale. Estimates of total production in 1913/4 and in 1924/5 by T.J. Kreps, *op. cit.* in note 1, are 60 and 320 thousand tons respectively.
[16] Excluding Valencia and Alicante provinces.
[17] Czech Republic.
[18] Russian Federation. Ex-U.S.S.R. as follows:

	Azerbaijan	Belarus	Kazakhstan	Ukraine	Uzbekistan
1991	552	998	2,815	4,186	2,393
1992	269	616	2,349	3,000	1,476
1993	141	399	1,568	1,843	1,361
1994	56	291	681	1,646	805
1995	24	437	695	1,593	1,016
1996	31	549	653	1,577	984
1997	53	698	635	1,438	870
1998	24	640	605	1,354	...

[19] Yugoslavia. **Ex**-Yugoslavia as follows:

	Croatia	Macedonia	Slovenia
1991	187	102	86
1992	278	95	121
1993	178	86	125
1994	206	72	123
1995	233	82	116
1996	223	99	103
1997	202	105	109
1998	164	101	128

D24 TIMBER INDUSTRY INDICATORS (in units shown)

Key:- a = thousand metric tons, b = million cubic metrs, c = thousand cubic metres, d = thousand standards

	1848–1879						**1880–1909**			
	Finland	**Germany**	**Sweden**				**Finland**	**Germany**	**Sweden**	
	Wood Pulp[1]	Working Wood output	Timber Cut	Wood Pulp			Wood Pulp[1]	Working Wood output	Timber Cut	Wood Pulp
	(a)	(b)	(c)	(a)			(a)	(b)	(c)	(a)
1848	...	5.5	...	—						
1849	...	4.9	...	—						
1850	...	5.7	...	—		1880	...	10.8	1,125	17
1851	...	5.6	...	—		1881	...	11.6	884	23
1852	...	6.1	...	...		1882	...	12.3	945	21
1853	...	5.8	...	...		1883	...	13.7	952	19
1854	...	6.0	...	...		1884	- -	14.5	845	27
1855	...	6.1	...	—		1885	- -	14.5	1,063	28
1856	...	7.3	...	—		1886	- -	14.2	871	36
1857	...	7.6	...	—		1887	1	15.4	907	47
1858	...	7.6	...			1888	1	15.5	1,112	52
1859	...	6.7	...	...		1889	4	16.2	1,248	79
1860	...	7.0	...	—		1890	5	17.3	988	95
1861	...	7.9	...	—		1891	5	17.8	1,108	117
1862	...	8.7	...	—		1892	6	19.9	1,214	117
1863	...	9.2	...	—		1893	8	16.2	1,094	140
1864	...	8.8	...	...		1894	9	20.8	1,308	181
1865	...	8.6	...	—		1895	9	17.6	1,322	215
1866	...	8.1	...	—		1896	9	20.1	1,709	277
1867	...	7.8	...	—		1897	10	19.7	1,900	313
1868	...	9.0	...	—		1898	13	19.3	2,139	335
1869	...	11.7	...	3		1899	13	20.0	2,130	341
1870	...	10.8[2]	498	3		1900	14	19.8	2,258	318
1871	...	10.7	577	4		1901	19	19.7	1,766	334
1872	...	12.0	553	5		1902	18	20.9	1,877	395
1873	...	12.5	635	8		1903	25	24.0	2,056	437
1874	...	12.6	508	7		1904	23	23.7	1,860	459
1875	...	11.5	401	8		1905	30	22.7	2,100	525
1876	...	13.0	621	10		1906	57	23.2	2,148	560
1877	...	10.2	592	12		1907	64[1] 181	23.5	2,337	577
1878	...	10.5	499	7		1908	146	24.1	2,224	750
1879	...	10.4	359	11		1909	184	26.1	2,572	680

D24 Timber Industry Indicators (in units shown)

	Finland		Germany		Norway			Russia/U.S.S.R	Sweden	
	Rough Sawn Timber (d)	Wood Pulp (a)	Working Wood (b)	Wood Pulp (a)	Sawn & Planed (b)	Wood Pulp (a)	Timber Floated (b)	Sawn Wood (b)	Timber Cut (c)	Wood Pulp (a)
1910	...	231	31.3	...	...	...	...	...	3,194	941
1911	758	240	28.2	...	...	...	...	...	3,214	967
1912	...	273	28.7	...	...	...	...	...	3,331	1,135
1913	...	299	...	620	...	681	...	14	3,813	1,186
1914	628	282	...	...	...	...	...	...	3,914	1,135
1915	417	307	...	...	...	...	...	...	4,823	1,216
1916	320	342	...	...	...	...	...	...	4,937	1,324
1917	219	246	...	...	...	...	...	...	4,361	1,024
1918	131	157	...$_2$	...	...	...	...	...	4,802	920
1919	261	228	...	...	...	...	...	...	4,160	949
1920	464	324	...	400	...	654	...	...	3,418	1,299
1921	609	352	...	390	...	371	6,057	...	1,927	777
1922	726	458	...	430	...	612	1,507	...	3,967	1,303
1923	963	542	...	1,134	...	697	2,780	...	3,921	1,372
1924	952	566	22.2	1,307	...	659	4,841	...	3,869	1,696
1925	997	624	25.7	1,650	...	812	4,683	...	4,664	1,733
1926	1,153	675	23.6	1,698	...	755	4,048	...	4,542	1,927
1927	1,282	777	24.9	1,891	1,258	819	4,257	13	4,384	2,103
1928	1,229	896	25.8	1,986	1,502	882	4,202	14	4,876	1,900
1929	1,059	973	24.3	2,056	1,484	958	5,262	17	5,180	2,540
1930	819	1,076	23.7	2,088	1,374	931	5,321	22	5,360	2,447
1931	691	1,084	19.5	1,805	1,110	551	2,736	24	5,099	2,198
1932	706	1,263	15.9	1,709	1,023	900	2,016	24	4,973	1,996
1933	897	1,379	23.1	1,769	946	855	3,332	27	5,778	2,563
1934	1,137	1,568	27.7	2,011	1,133	983	4,145	31	5,378	2,870
1935	960	1,728	27.7	2,153	1,177	861	4,022	34	4,995	2,978
1936	1,016	1,976	34.4	2,367	1,284	993	3,372	40	5,190	3,180
1937	1,151	2,191	39.3	2,564	1,384	1,096	4,184	34	5,084$_6$	3,524
									(b)	
									44.0	
1938	848$_3$	2,110$_3$	47.2	2,553	1,396	900	5,630	...	39.8	3,061
1939	662	1,612	...	...	1,525	965	2,281	34	39.1	3,137
1940	309	657	...	...	1,765	581	3,357	35	42.1	1,967
1941	359	678	...	...	1,806	597	2,999	...	44.9	1,302
1942	369	662	...	...	1,490	494	2,572	...	44.2	1,751
1943	450	830	...	...	1,089	432	2,376	...	51.3	1,278
1944	368	664	...	...	905	320	2,451	...	38.8	1,298
			West Germany							
1945	490	781	...	...	759	254	1,732	15	48.9	1,999
1946	565	1,195	...	239	1,247	510	2,658	16	44.4	2,736
1947	687	1,458	...	344	1,491	631	3,467	19	45.8	2,825
1948	764	1,621	29.1	529	1,600	816	3,768	30	36.7	3,003
1949	804	1,572	26.5	774	1,945	893	4,713	...	40.8	2,881
1950	892	1,912	21.7	918	1,938	1,015	3,663	50	34.0	3,160
1951	1,040	2,190	22.3	997	1,767	1,086	3,740	56	38.7	3,369
1952	746	1,879	21.8	901	2,115	1,009	4,874	61	41.7	3,029
1953	842	1,928	18.9	1,034	2,179	1,078	4,260	66	34.7	3,210
1954	977	2,420	18.6	1,192	2,213	1,035	3,985	69	41.5	3,641
1955	1,017	2,750	23.4	1,274	2,251	1,259	3,746	76	41.6	3,883
1956	772	2,841	19.3	1,337	2,372	1,247	3,922	77	41.9	4,105
1957	835	3,065	20.5	1,376	2,348	1,313	4,253	82	41.7	4,251
1958	987	3,063	20.7	1,340	2,265	1,282	3,865	94	40.9	4,083
1959	1,034	3,181	21.8	1,385	2,034	1,381	3,348	104	36.3	4,389
1960	1,341	3,699	20.4	1,451	2,237	1,533	3,434	106	43.1	4,949
1961	1,295	4,297	21.9	1,440	2,039	1,525	3,134	104	44.3	5,178

D24   Timber Industry Indicators (in units shown)

1962–2000

	Finland		Germany		Norway			Russia/U.S.S.R		Sweden	
	Rough Sawn Timber (d)	Wood Pulp (a)	Working Wood (b)	Wood Pulp (a)	Sawn & Planed (b)	Wood Pulp (a)	Timber Floated (b)	Sawn Wood (b)	Wood Pulp (a)	Timber Cut (b)	Wood Pulp (a)
1962	1,137	4,419	23.0	1,403	1,926	1,500	2,808	105	...	46.3	5,190
1963	1,195[4]	4,825·	18.5	1,435	1,970	1,594	2,462	106	...	43.3	5,676
	5,582								...		
1964	5,779	5,330	21.0	1,390	2,499	1,798	2,481	111	...	49.7	6,366
1965	5,708[5]	5,575	21.7	1,390	2,598	1,826	2,238	111	...	49.7	6,678
1966	4,944	5,498	23.6	1,410	2,403[8]	1,794	1,648	107	4,568	48.9	6,543
					1,649						
1967	5,130	5,508	23.6	1,444	1,816	1,798	1,490	109	4,973	54.2	6,792
1968	4,993	5,704	20.9	1,559	1,747	2,000	1,326	110	5,321	48.0	7,081
1969	5,689	6,062	23.8	1,672	1,910	2,088	1,042	112	5,563	51.8	7,627
1970	6,224	6,222	25.4[7]	1,732	1,969	2,182	1,005	116	6,550	58.8	8,142
			28.2								
1971	7,515	5,991	28.3	1,677	1,969	1,977	1,036	119	6,896	63.5	7,734
1972	7,475	6,284	23.8	1,707	2,017	2,061	888	119	7,413	56.4	8,314
1973	8,140	6,678	30.7	1,760	2,312	2,063	769	117	7,730	58.5	9,462
1974	7,504	6,603	32.0	1,849	2,288	2,371	809	115	8,295	60.5	9,745
1975	4,931	5,188	26.1	1,531	2,084	1,657	972	116	8,585	56.2	8,414
1976	5,757	5,395	28.6	1,845	2,020	1,771	909	113	8,984	53.2	8,378
1977	7,000	5,256	29.4	1,862	2,021	1,509	730	109	9,228	45.3	7,656
1978	7,608	6,088	28.1	1,842	2,093	1,433	524	106	9,391	45.0	8,557
1979	9,650	7,050	27.3	1,946	2,357	1,528	587	100	8,732	45.9	9,083
1980	10,230	7,246	30.3	1,996	2,463	1,494	502	98	8,824	46.7	8,699
1981	8,260	7,344	29.4	2,021	2,462	1,608	546	98	9,067	48.3	8,530
1982	7,300	6,714	29.0	2,005	2,262	1,523	551	97	9,222	49.4	7,706
1983	7,995	7,163	26.1	2,081	2,312	1,641	389	97	9,803	52.2	8,668
1984	8,232	8,031	29.1	2,222	2,364	1,864	...	97	10,100	51.7	9,293
1985	7,300	7,977	31.2	2,203	2,230	1,978	...	98	10,374	50.7	9,123
1986	7,110	7,929	29.2	2,219	2,258	1,954	...	101	...	51.9	9,395
1987	7,530	8,462	28.7	2,260	2,360	1,949	...	102	...	52.5	9,988
1988	7,790	9,001	29.5	2,358	2,358	1,974	...	103	...	53.4	10,074
1989	7,763	8,998	31.8	2,418	2,492	1,938	...	105	...	53.8	10,093
1990	7,503	8,773	68.4	2,339	2,413	1,925	...	105	...	52.9	9,203
1991	5,983	8,466	31.6[9]	2,436	2,263	1,864	...	79[10]	...	51.4	9,063
1992	6,983	8,627	27.7	2,275	2,362	1,769	...	65[10]	...	53.5	8,908
1993	7,679	9,314	28.3	2,032	2,362	1,943	...	40[10]	...	51.2	9,293
1994	10,220	10,054	...	...	2,415	2,287	...	31	3,917	...	10,487
1995	9,860	10,180	...	...	2,210	2,557	...	27	5,073	...	10,506
1996	9,710	9,785	...	...	2,420	2,342	...	22	3,817	...	10,166
1997	11,360	11,181	...	...	2,520	2,434	...	21	3,750	...	10,816
1998	12,240	11,976	...	...	2,525	2,493	...	20	3,991	...	10,549
1999	12,708	12,208	...	...	2,336	2,426	...	19	5,109	...	10,693
2000	13,320	12,539	...	...	2,463	2,520	...	20	5,944	...	11,545

D24 Timber Industry Indicators (in units shown)

NOTE

SOURCES:- Finland to 1923—supplied by the Central Statistical Office of Finland, Germany to 1938—W.G. Hofman, *Das Wachstum der Deutschen Wirtschaft seit der Mitte des 19 Jahrhunderts* (Berlin, etc., 1965). Russia to 1956—G.W. Nutter, *The Growth of Industrial Production in the Soviet Union* (Princeton, 1962). Sweden to 1899—supplied by the Swedish Central Office of Statistics. All other statistics are taken from the official publications noted on p. xv, with gaps filled from the League of Nations and United Nations, *Statistical Yearbooks*.

FOOTNOTES

[1] Figures of mechanical pulp are not included until 1907 (2nd line). The only earlier figure available for this type is for 1904, when output was 67 thousand tons.
[2] From 1871 to 1918 Alsace-Lorraine was included.
[3] Subsequently excluding Viipuri and Petsamo, ceded to the U.S.S.R. in 1940.
[4] Subsequently in million cubic metres.
[5] The method of collecting the statistics was changed.
[6] Figures to 1937 (1st line) are for state forests only. From 1937 (2nd line) they include private forests, exclude bark which was previously included, and are in million cubic metres.
[7] Subsequently including wood for fuel.
[8] Subsequently sawn wood only.
[9] Germany.
[10] Russian Federation.

D25 OUTPUT OF MOTOR VEHICLES (in thousands)

1920–1969

	Czechoslovakia		France[1]		Germany		East Germany		Italy		Netherlands	
	CV	PC	CV	PC	CV	PC	CV	PC	CV	PC	CV	PC
1920	...	...	40		...	...	...	...	...	...	...	...
1921	...	...	14	41	...	...	...	...	...	...	...	...
1922	...	...	26	49	...	...	...	...	...	...	...	...
1923	...	...	38	72	...	...	...	...	...	...	...	...
1924	...	5		48		97	...	...	...	...	...	...
1925	5		56	121	10	39	...	...	3.6	46	...	...
1926	7		33	159	5	32	...	...	3.3	61	...	...
1927	2	8	46	145	12	85	...	...	3.6	51	...	...
1928	3	10	36	187	21[3]	102[3]	...	...	3.7	54	...	...
					30	108						
1929	3	12	42	212	32	96	...	...	3.2	52	...	...
1930	4	13	38	194	19	77	...	...	4.5	42	...	...
1931	4	12	34	167	15	63	...	...	2.6	26	...	...
1932	3	10	28	136	8	43	...	...	3.1	27	...	...
1933	1	8	30	159	13	92	...	...	3.5	38	...	...
1934	1	8	24	157	27	147	...	...	4.4	41	...	...
1935	1	7	22	143	42	205	...	...	9.5	41	...	...
1936	1	10	24	180	57	244	...	...	17	36	...	...
1937	2	13	25	177	62	269	...	...	16	61	...	...
1938	2	11	45[1]	182[1]	63	275	...	...	12	59	...	...
1939	...	...	...	...	...	...	...	...	13	56	...	...
1940	...	...	...[2]	...[2]	...	...	...	...	26	22	...	...
1941	...	...	44	11	...	...	...	...	28	11	...	...
1942	...	...	36	3	...	...	...	...	21	9	...	...
1943	...	...	19	—	...	...	...	...	17	4	...	...
1944	...	...	10[2]	—[2]	...	...	...	...	12	2	...	...

West Germany[4]

	CV	PC	CV	PC	CV	PC	CV	PC	CV	PC	CV	PC
1945	...	...	33	2	...	...	...	...	8	2	...	...
1946	3.0	3.8	65	30	13	10	...	...	18	11	...	...
1947	8.4	9.4	70	66	13	10	...	...	17	25	...	...
1948	7.2	18.0	98	100	27[4]	30[4]	0.4	2.6	15	44	...	...
1949	5.8	20.8	98	188	55	104	1.2	3.5	21	65	...	...
1950	6.0	24.5	100	257	82	219	6.2	7.2	29	100	...	...
1951	11.5	17.1	133	314	93	277	11	11	30	118	...	...
1952	10.1	6.3	130	370	106	318	12	12	25	114	...	...
1953	11.4	7.3	130	368	96	388	18	14	32	143	1.3	...
1954	12.9	5.4	163	437	113	561	20	20	36	181	1.5	...
1955	10.5	12.5	172	553	140	762	22[5]	22[5]	39	231	1.9	...
1956	11.0	25.1	179	649	159	911	24	28	36	280	2.5	...
1957	10.3	34.6	204	724	166	1,040	20	36	34	318	1.8	...
1958	11.5	43.4	204	924	181	1,307	16	38	34	369	1.6	—
1959	11.5	50.6	198	1,085	208	1,503	16	53	30	471	3.0	3.9
1960	13.3	56.2	234	1,136	230	1,817	13	64	49	596	4.1	15
1961	16.4	58.8	217	1,028	235	1,904	12	70	66	694	5.1	13
1962	17.2	64.3	230	1,307	234	2,109	8	72	69	878	5.0	24
1963	15.4	56.5	255	1,482	240	2,414	10	84	75	1,105	5.4	17
1964	13.9	42.1	264	1,351	247	2,650	12	93	62	1,029	6.5	30
1965	16.5	77.7	242	1,374	230	2,733	15	103	72	1,104	6.1	30
1966	18.0	92.7	263	1,761	205	2,830	21	107	84	1,282	7.2	33
1967	19.9	111.7	258	1,752	172	2,296	23	112	104	1,439	7.1	49
1968	22.6	125.5	243	1,833	229	2,862	25	115	119	1,545	9.0	58
1969	23.6	132.4	291	2,168	274	3,437	27	121	119	1,477	11.1	61

D25 Output of Motor Vehicles (in thousands)

	Poland		Romania		Russia/U.S.S.R.		Spain		Sweden		United Kingdom		Yugoslavia	
	CV	PC	CV	PC	CV	PC	CV	PC	CV	PC	CV	PC	CV	PC
1920	—	—	...	...	...	...	—	—		—	...	...	...	...
1921	—	—	...	...	...	...	—	—		—	...	...	...	...
1922	—	—	...	...	...	...	—	—		—	...	...	...	...
1923	—	—	...	...	...	...	—	—		—	24	71	...	...
1924	—	—	...	...	...	...	—	—		—	30	117	...	...
1925	—	—	...	...	—	...	—	—		0.3	35	132	...	...
1926	—	—	...	...	—	...	—	—		0.3	44	154	...	...
1927	—	—	...	...	—	...	—	—		0.8	47	165	...	...
1928	—	—	...	...	1	0.1	—	—		1.2	47	165	...	...
1929	—	—	...	...	2	0.2	—	—	1.3	0.5	57	182	...	...
1930	—	—	...	...	4	0.2	—	—		2.3	67	170	...	...
1931	—	—	...	...	4	—	—	—		2.3	67	159	...	...
1932	—	—	...	...	24	—	—	—		2.9	61	171	...	...
1933	—	—	...	...	39	10	—	—		2.7	66	221	...	...
1934	—	—	...	...	55	17	—	—		3.2	86	257	...	...
1935	—	—	...	...	78	19	—	—		3.4	92	338	...	...
1936	—	—	...	...	132	4	—	—	3.0	1.5	114	354	...	...
1937	—	—	...	...	182	18	—	—	4.8	1.8	114	390	...	...
1938	—	—	...	...	184	27	—	—	4.8	2.2	104	341	...	...
1939	—	—	...	...	182	20	—	—		7.6	97[1]	305[1]	...	...
1940	—	—	...	...	140	6	—	—	...	1.8	132	1.9	...	...
1941	—	—	...	...	...	...	—	—	...	0.1	140	5.1	...	...
1942	—	—	...	...	...	...	—	...	...	0.1	155	5.5	...	...
1943	—	—	...	...	...	...	—	—	...	0.2	148	1.6	...	...
1944	—	—	...	...	...	...	—	—	...	0.3	131	2.1	...	...
1945	—	—	...	...	70	5	—	—	...	0.5	123	17	...	...
1946	—	—	...	...	96	6	—	—	6.0	2.0	146	219	...	...
1947	—	—	...	...	123	10	—	—	8.0	4.0	155	287	...	...
1948	—	—	...	...	177	20	—	—	7.8	4.2	173	335	...	...
1949	0.2	—	...	...	277	46	0.2	—	5.7	5.3	216	412	...	...
1950	0.8	—	...	...	294	65	0.2	—	7.8	8.9	261	523	...	...
1951	2.6	0.1	...	...	235	54	0.4	—	9.9	13	258	476	...	...
1952	6.9	1.6	...	...	248	60	0.3	—	11	11	242	448	...	...
1953	11	1.6	...	...	300	77	0.4	0.5	11	19	240	595	...	...
1954	13	1.7	...	...	354	95	0.4	6.1	16	28	269	769	...	...
1955	13	4.0	...	...	400	108	1.7	14	18	33	340	898	...	...
1956	13	5.8	...	...	441	98	4.7	18	19	38	297	708	...	...
1957	15	8.0	...	...	467	114	7.1[6]	23	19	52	288	861	...	...
1958	14	12	...	...	490	122	16	33	22	69	313	1,052	...	...
1959	18	14	...	...	480	125	18	39	17	96	371	1,190	...	...
1960	24	13	...	...	501	139	17	42	20	109	458	1,353	...	...
1961	25	14	...	...	533	149	30	56	22	108	460	1,004	...	...
1962	29	16	...	...	561	166	41	71	22	126	425	1,249	...	...
1963	34	18	10	18	590	173	53	83	21	147	404	1,608	14	3
1964	35	20	12	26	604	185	61	124	23	162	465	1,868	16	3
1965	34	26	13	33	613	201	74	160	25	182	455	1,722	17	4
1966	38	28	12	32	655	230	89	255	25	174	439	1,604	19	5
1967	40	27	12	36	697	251	86	279	20	194	385	1,552	23	6
1968	45	39	13	44	750	280	76	317	21	222	409	1,816	28	8
1969	52	48	14	51	785	294	74	380	28	245	466	1,717	33	19

D25 Output of Motor Vehicles (in thousands)

1970–1998

	Czechoslovakia		France[1]		W. Germany		E. Germany		Italy		Netherlands	
	CV	PC	CV	PC	CV	PC	CV	PC	CV	PC	CV	PC
1970	24.5	143	292	2,458	296	3,529	27	127	135	1,720	11.7	67
1971	25.1	149	316	2,694	265	3,692	28	134	116	1,701	13.0	78
1972	25.6	154	335	2,993	276	3,513	30	140	107	1,732	12.3	87
1973	27.5	164	394	3,202	277	3,643	33	147	135	1,825	12.8	95
1974	30.1	169	418	3,045	228	2,840	37	155	142	1,631	12.4	69
1975	33.4	175	346	2,951	247	2,905	38	159	110	1,349	10.6	60
1976	36.7	179	455	3,388	291	3,548	38	164	119	1,471	11.5	59
1977	38.6	159	450	3,559	276	3,796	40	167	143	1,490	14.2	45
1978	40.1	175	455	3,620	267	3,901	40	171	148	1,509	11.7	62
1979	43.2	182	462	3,730	282	3,943	40	171	151	1,481	15.9	89
1980	45.7	184	505	3,488	317	3,530	40	177	165	1,445	16.5	81
1981	45.9	181	474	2,953	274	3,590	42	180	183	1,254	12.0	78
1982	47.3	174	467	3,086	266	3,771	41	183	156	1,296	13.2	91
1983	43.2	178	462	3,228	269	3,875	41	188	180	1,395	11.6	106
1984	46.9	180	424	2,909	237	3,783	45	202	160	1,439	13.4	109
1985	48.0	184	459	2,817	262	4,165	47	210	185	1,384	14.0	108
1986	50.2	185	507	3,011	267	4,269	47	218	179	1,653	15.2	119
1987	51.2	172	516	3,283	244	4,348	44	217	200	1,712	17.5	125
1988	50.5	164	550	3,456	258	4,312	42	218	231	1,883	19.3	120
1989	49.7	189	594	3,415	274	4,536	41	217	254	1,971	19.3	133
1990	52.4	191	554	3,293	315	4,634	33	145	248	1,873	13.8[10]	122

					Germany							
					CV	PC						
1991	30.0	177	477	3,190	356	4,647			247	1,632	13.0[10]	84
1992	15.2[9]	...[9]	506	3,526	326	4895			210	1,475	12.5[10]	95

Czech Republic[9]

1993	10.0[9]	...[9]	383	2,837	240	3875			161	1,116	16.8	80
1994	11.0	...	356	2,965	230	3,961			...	1,340	...	92
1995	11.9	...	321	2,744	224	4,222			...	1,422	...	98
1996	12.3	...	387	2,871	219	...			...	1,244	...	103
1997	14.5	...	426	2,962	216	4,713			...	1,563	...	97
1998	14.8	...	438	3,005	230	4,875			...	1,379	...	109

	Poland		Romania		Russia/U.S.S.R.		Spain		Sweden		United Kingdom[1]		Yugoslavia	
	CV	PC	CV	PC	CV	PC	CV	PC	CV	PC	CV	PC	CV	PC
1970	53	65	37	24	815	344	77	455	32	272	458	1,641	17	63
1971	60	86	37	30	862[7]	529	68	460	31	292	459	1,742	17	60
1972	67	91	39	38	651	730	84	612	34	321	408	1,921	18	71
1973	77	115	39	60	687	917	104	719	38	345	417	1,747	17	99
1974	80	133	36	68	729	1,119	115	721	43	331	403	1,534	15	115
1975	85	164	39	68	765	1,201	101	711	52	336	381	1,268	19	132
1976	79	216	38	71	788	1,239	94	770	52	341	372	1,333	22	139
1977	76	279	39	77	810	1,280	121	1,010	51	264	398	1,316	21	179
1978	75	326	38	81	842	1,312	135	1,006	46	290	384	1,223	20	194
1979	71	350	37	74	861	1,314	134	990	57	314	408	1,070	24	206
1980	67	351	35[8] 32	88	874	1,327	131	1,048	60	268	389	924	23	186
1981	54	240	19	92	877	1,324	115	877	52	306	230	955	20	180
1982	48	228	33	104	866	1,307	119	944	47	323	269	888	20	158
1983	52	269	18	90	860	1,315	119	1,110	46	374	233	1,045	21	168
1984	55	278	18	125	850	1,327	121	1,137	59	378	225	909	19	187
1985	57	283	20	134	926	1,332	153	1,220	60	402	256	1,048	20	177
1986	55	290	14	124	942	1,326	173	1,290	66	415	229	1,019	19	198
1987	56	293	13	129	958	1,332	248	1,444	70	416	247	1,143	18	218
1988	57	293	17	141	974	1,262	313	1,498	79	259	317	1,227	18	226
1989	53	285	14	144	900	1,217	344	1,651	84	240	326	1,308	14	227
1990	43	266	8	100	...	1,259	302	1,696	77	216	274	1,302	10	289
1991	22	167	8	84	378[11]	1,030[11]	244	1,787	77	178	222	1,340	...[12]	...[12]
1992	19	219	4	74	410[11]	963[11]	256	1,817	...	205	240	1,291	4[12]	22[12]
1993	20	334	4	93	390[11]	956[11]	...	...	...	...	...	...	...[12]	...[12]
1994	23	338	...	56	...	798	...	2,146	...	193	...	1,654	...	8
1995	21	366	...	70	...	835	...	2,254	...	198	...	1,735	...	8
1996	19	441	...	97	...	868	...	2,334	...	203	...	1,707	...	9
1997	16	520	...	109	...	986	...	2,278	...	219	...	1,818	...	10
1998	15	592	...	104	...	840	...	2,469	...	214	...	1,709	...	12

D25 Output of Motor Vehicles (in thousands)

NOTES

1. SOURCES:- The official publications noted on p. xv with gaps, filled from the League of Nations and United Nations, *Statistical Yearbooks* and O.E.C.D. *Statistical Bulletins*. Russian statistics to 1947 are taken from G.W. Nutter, *The Growth of Industrial Production in the Soviet Union* (Princeton, 1962) and Swedish statistics for 1925–28, 1930–36, and 1939 are based on data supplied by the Swedish Central Office of Statistics.
2. Except as indicated in footnotes, the statistics relate to the production of complete vehicles, other than motor cycles. They do not include the assembly of imported parts.
3. Available pre-1920 statistics are as follows (in thousands) France: all vehicles: 1905–14; 1910–38; 1913–45

		1907	1908	1909	1910	1911	1912
Germany:	CV	0.4	0.4	0.6	0.8	1.4	1.8
	PC	3.9	4.6	7.3	9.4	11.7	16.1

FOOTNOTES

[1] Figures to 1938 or 1939 are for years ended 30 September.
[2] Figures for 1941–44 exclude Alsace-Lorraine.
[3] Chassis production for export is not included until 1929 (2nd line).
[4] Figures to 1946–48 are for the American and British Occupation Zones only.
[5] Subsequently excluding military vehicles.
[6] Previously excluding three-wheeled vehicles.
[7] Subsequently excluding wheeled tractors.
[8] Subsequently excluding buses.
[9] Czech Republic:

Slovakia	1993	5(PC)
	1994	8
	1995	22
	1996	32
	1997	42
	1998	125

[10] Tractors not included.
[11] Russian Federation.

		CV	PC
Ukraine	1991	37	156
	1992	42	135
	1993	29	140
	1994	33	94
	1995	28	59
	1996	26	7
	1997	23	2
	1998	25	26

[12] Yugoslavia.

		CV	PC
Slovenia	1991	2	79
	1992	—	84
	1993	...	74
	1994	...	88
	1995	...	89
	1996	...	92
	1997	...	95
	1998	...	98

D26   OUTPUT OF BEER (in thousands of hectolitres)

1750–1804   **1805–1859**

	U.K.[1]			Austria[2]	Belgium	France	Germany	U.K.[1]
1750	948	1805	...	...	...	...	1,230
1751	955	1806	...	...	...	...	1,238
1752	939	1807	...	...	...	...	1,254
1753	1,098	1808	...	...	...	...	1,249
1754	927	1809	...	...	...	...	1,233
1755	918	1810	...	...	...	...	1,267
1756	942	1811	...	...	...	...	1,293
1757	889	1812	...	...	...	...	1,276
1758	915	1813	...	...	...	...	1,171
1759	940	1814	...	...	...	...	1,210
1760	1,003	1815	...	...	...	...	1,313
1761	988	1816	...	...	...	...	1,284
1762	945	1817	...	...	...	...	1,147
1763	918	1818	...	...	...	...	1,162
1764	920	1819	...	...	...	10,200	1,215
1765	890	1820	...	...	...	11,100	1,156
1766	897	1821	...	...	...	11,300	1,202
1767	879	1822	...	...	...	11,500	1,236
1768	896	1823	...	...	...	11,300	1,300
1769	897	1824	...	...	...	11,900	1,298
1770	898	1825	...	...	...	12,300	1,369[1]
1771	900	1826	...	...	...	12,400	1,476
1772	898	1827	...	...	...	12,000	1,423
1773	904	1828	...	...	...	11,700	1,358
1774	864	1829	...	...	...	11,100	1,394
1775	897	1830	...	...	...	11,100	1,264
1776	922	1831	...	4,687	...	12,800	...
1777	938	1832	...	4,755	...	11,400	...
1778	956	1833	...	5,114	...	12,000	...
1779	981	1834	...	5,570	...	12,200	...
1780	1,021	1835	...	5,575	3,381	12,700	...
1781	1,009	1836	...	5,632	...	12,800	...
1782	1,053	1837	...	5,639	...	13,200	...
1783	931	1838	...	5,772	...	12,900	...
1784	1,000	1839	...	5,577	...	12,900	...
1785	985	1840	...	5,309	4,241	13,100	...
1786	963	1841	4,424	5,161	...	13,800	...
1787	1,023[1]						
	1,064	1842	4,662	5,221	...	15,000	...
1788	1,051	1843	4,450	4,843	...	13,600	...
1789	1,059	1844	4,714	5,731	...	13,100	...
1790	1,089	1845	5,016	5,537	4,700	14,400	...
1791	1,144	1846	...	5,338	...	13,600	...
1792	1,221	1847	3,816	4,550	...	11,600	...
1793	1,244	1848	4,228	5,230	...	13,000	...
1794	1,207	1849	...	5,277	...	14,000	...
1795	1,211	1850	...	5,544	4,048	14,600	...
1796	1,302	1851	5,771	5,669	4,449	14,500	...
1797	1,369	1852	...	5,586	4,523	13,400	...
1798	1,372	1853	...	5,382	5,048	13,800	...
1799	1,378	1854	4,790	5,089	4,959	12,500	...
1800	1,169	1855	4,885	5,130	5,871	12,700	...
1801	1,107	1856	5,835	5,603	6,649	13,300	...
1802	1,151	1857	6,733	6,235	7,088	15,400	...
1803	1,244	1858	6,950	6,996	6,807	16,500	...
1804	1,206	1859	7,133[2]	7,167	6,697	17,400	...

D26 Output of Beer (in thousands of hectolitres)

	Austria[2]	Belgium	Bulgaria	Denmark[3]	France	Germany	Hungary[7]	Italy[8]
1860	6,507	6,555	...	...	6,573	17,000	626	...
1861	5,806	6,503	...	...	6,798	17,200	490	...
1862	7,037	6,424	...	...	6,963	18,800	572	...
1863	7,831	6,911	...	...	7,051	20,700	489	...
1864	7,374	7,217	...	...	7,212	21,800	464	...
1865	7,295	7,562	...	...	7,686	23,700	597	...
1866	7,144	7,289	...	...	8,078	23,600	552	...
1867	6,855	6,951	...	...	7,007	22,700	439	...
1868	7,291	7,393	...	...	7,327	21,900	539	...
1869	7,915	7,267	...	...	7,528	23,900	589	...
1870	9,304	7,794	...	...	6,499[4]	23,700[4]	689	...
1871	10,028	7,721	...	...	6,400	26,500	799	...
1872	11,445	8,789	...	...	7,146	31,800[5] / 32,945	759	...
1873	12,685	9,189	...	...	7,414	36,989	765	
1874	11,744	9,360	...	...	7,345	38,194	580	...
1875	11,536	9,674	...	...	7,356	38,936	597	...
1876	11,671	9,688	...	...	7,604	38,857	506	...
1877	11,101	9,268	...	...	7,743	38,269	438	...
1878	10,815	9,171	...	...	7,565	37,425	508	...
1879	10,707	8,683	...	...	7,375	37,184	474	112
1880	10,530	9,239	...	...	8,227	38,497[6] / 38,572	427	116
1881	11,530	9,317	...	...	8,625	39,109	456	127
1882	11,655	9,094	...	...	8,306	39,324	487	131
1883	11,877	9,312	...	...	8,619	40,873	547	122
1884	12,392	9,703	...	...	8,493	42,374	645	144
1885	12,486	9,367	...	...	8,010	41,857	669	168
1886	11,961	9,461	...	...	7,979	45,068	630	145
1887	12,718	10,160	...	...	8,234	47,100	631	175
1888	12,621	10,160	...	...	7,952	47,696	522	138
1889	12,938	10,631	...	...	8,383	54,420	503	158
1890	13,570	10,771	...	...	8,491	52,830	547	156
1891	14,038	10,770	...	730	8,306	53,205	645	132
1892	15,151	10,927	...	737	8,937	54,780	1,239	99
1893	16,248	11,383	...	743	8,938	55,623	1,322	94
1894	16,514	11,551	...	790	8,443	55,369	1,587	95
1895	17,275	12,230	35	825	8,867	60,695	1,416	115
1896	18,621	12,778	38	909	8,991	61,621	1,676	107
1897	19,060	13,186	32	956	9,233	66,378	1,597	109
1898	19,207	13,707	52	982	9,558	67,968	1,604	133
1899	19,574	14,280	59	1,042	10,396	69,500	1,566	145
1900	20,023	14,617	41	1,018	10,712	70,857	1,448	163
1901	20,104	14,660	45	1,072	10,423	71,157	1,415	162
1902	19,628	14,431	52	950	10,410	67,699	1,238	176
1903	19,227	14,804	61	949	10,944	68,976	1,317	217
1904	19,820	15,317	69	983	11,392	70,241	1,516	220
1905	19,099	15,750	90	907[3]	10,705	72,755[19] / 68,591	1,501	305
1906	20,420	16,399	122	2,588	11,594	69,031	1,688	360
1907	20,915	16,283	156	2,549	11,349	69,535	1,882	447
1908	21,885	15,932	145	2,646	11,749	66,961	2,157	548
1909	19,735	15,354	140	2,441	11,352	63,754	1,908	567
1910	20,849	16,019	160	2,579	12,239	64,465	2,185	598
1911	22,149	17,032	...	2,663	14,350	70,353	2,706	721
1912	22,709	16,899	213	2,449	12,656	67,872	2,951	673
1913	21,082	16,727	166	2,466	12,844[14]	69,200	2,988	652
1914	20,076	...	242	2,527	9,056	59,373	3,074	526

D26 Output of Beer (in thousands of hectolitres)

	Norway[9]	Romania[10]	Russia[11]	Serbia	Sweden	Switzerland	U.K.
1870	208	...	...	...	...	...	...
1871	232	...	...	...	...	...	...
1872	247	...	...	...	...	...	...
1873	315	...	...	...	...	...	...
1874	358	...	...	...	...	...	...
1875	431	...	...	...	...	...	...
1876	414	...	...	...	...	...	...
1877	423	...	...	...	...	...	...
1878	426	...	...	...	...	...	...
1879	366	...	...	...	...	...	...
1880	363	...	...	...	...	...	...
1881	355	24	...	...	...	...	44,955
1882	356	20	...	...	...	...	45,057
1883	381	20	...	...	...	...	44,784
1884	369	24	...	...	...	...	46,036
1885	374	18	...	...	950	895	45,176
1886	300	18	...	...	1,040	1,004	45,239
1887	302	24	...	...	1,070	1,115	46,216
1888	350	28	...	42	1,285	1,102	46,507
1889	347	23	...	39	1,340	1,158	49,755
1890	427	26	...	46	1,305	1,295	52,100
1891	492	30	...	43	1,475	1,383	52,757
1892	467	...	...	50	1,480	1,460	52,470
1893	480	32	...	55	1,525	1,522	52,520
1894	475	36	...	66	1,608	1,512	52,743
1895	420	42	...	61	1,744	1,702	53,574
1896	414	42	5,364	55	2,102	1,880	56,284
1897	457	53	5,657	55	2,253	2,003	57,791
1898	555	63	5,374	68	2,531	2,118	59,218
1899	606	91	5,913	70	2,958	2,143	61,214
1900	589	81	5,872	71	2,894	2,166	60,010[19]
1901	559	53	5,744	63	3,125	1,963	59,144
1902	529	48	5,706	71	2,941	1,999	58,674
1903	437	60	6,682	76	3,062	2,079	58,160
1904	417	78	6,674	76	3,176	2,115	56,971
1905	428	86	7,291	68	3,208	2,265	55,403
1906	426	112	8,796	82	3,293	2,393	56,506
1907	419	135	9,300	90	3,152	2,436	56,360
1908	418	178	8,760	108	3,120	2,441	54,885
1909	450	186	9,253	112	2,734	2,346	53,843
1910	462	186	10,198	...	2,583	2,507	54,777
1911	502	176	10,990	...	2,776	3,003	57,113
1912	529	265	10,666	...	2,658	2,997	56,682
1913	514	324[26]	11,612[11]	...	2,745	2,969	58,836
1914	550	299	8,064	...	2,827	2,811	56,870

D26 Output of Beer (in thousands of hectolitres)

	Austria[2]	Belgium	Bulgaria	Czech	Denmark	Finland	France	Germany		Greece	Hungary	Ireland
1915	16,040	8,139	216	...	2,425	...	5,824	45,862		...	3,054	...
1916	11,910	7,086	161	...	2,581	...	7,705	36,835		...	2,972	...
1917	...[2]	5,391	73	...	2,306	...	7,115	23,837[4]		...	977	...
1918	1,179	4,930	12	...	1,669	...	6,375[14]	24,825[20]		...	1,262[7]	...
1919	...	9,488	20	4,420	2,374	...	10,785	29,458[21]		...	...	...
1920	3,049	10,408	139	5,889	2,662	...	11,548	23,438		...	491	...
1921	3,040	12,536	219	6,554	2,471	...	12,254[4]	33,993[22]		119	443	...
1922	3,371	15,643	204	6,123	2,133	...	16,802	...		85	768	...
1923	3,000	14,491	222	7,273	2,294	...	20,235	...		62	354	...
1924	4,590	14,919	217	8,581	2,264	...	20,396	38,149		128	421	...
1925	5,054	14,650	125	9,215	2,415	...	19,688	47,560		160	612	3,998
1926	5,330	13,960	91	9,713	2,258	...	19,121	48,342		97	455	3,741
1927	5,210	13,257	77	9,998	2,132	...	19,237	51,619		95	690	3,519
1928	5,256	14,928	72	11,062	2,014	...	16,312	54,995		80	671	3,370
1929	5,275	15,377	84	11,611	2,119	...	21,145	58,078		98	601	3,524
1930	5,385	16,662	51	11,417	2,291	...	20,761	48,560		87	446	3,710
1931	4,385	18,377	47	10,377	2,212	...	21,000[15]	37,137		76	310	3,357
1932	3,058	15,558	91	9,556	2,005	105	16,250[15]	33,570		63	184	2,861
1933	2,522	14,667	60	7,952	2,024	141	19,195[15]	34,144[21] 34,891		58	165	3,013
1934	2,419	14,717	46	7,996	2,161	191	29,211	36,858		73	167	3,034
1935	2,287	14,109	32	7,744	2,209	233	24,709	39,762		85	185	3,193
1936	2,304	14,384	39	7,562	2,332	297	23,133	39,897		93	220	3,089
1937	2,136	14,228	69	8,316[12]	2,353	368	24,250	43,602		95	241	2,895
1938	...	13,835	96	6,283	2,267	405	23,080[16]	48,108[23]		97	288	2,365
1939	...	12,912	129	6,634	2,356	373	18,231	51,268[23]		93	...	2,346
1940	...	10,232	...	5,989	1,865	473	18,148[16]	48,723[23]		83	...	2,240
1941	...	5,791	...	6,248	2,083	423	14,902	47,024		19	...	2,574
1942	...	5,097	...	6,273	1,957	411	13,137	42,512		...	...	2,110
1943	...	4,860	...	5,748	2,217	534	14,168[17]	43,363		...	...	2,066
1944	...	4,817	...	5,585[12]	2,492	582	13,044[16][18]	...		...	...	2,319

								West	**East**			
1945	...	7,870	...	7,421[13]	2,831	591	9,256	...		45	343	2,705
1946	2,004	10,802	...	7,426	2,764	593	10,491	...[24]		86	166	2,746
1947	1,374	12,595	...	8,846	3,159	605	12,866	11,989		89	371	2,430
1948	1,745	11,340	298	8,160	3,236	669	8,325	10,685		107	494	2,708
1949	2,232	10,494	...	9,695	3,433	705	8,717	13,424		137	472	2,944
1950	2,877	10,140	381	10,779	3,540	776	7,851	17,057	3,800	203	777	3,035
1951	3,051	9,929	322	11,144	3,370	878	7,617	22,533	5,739	242[19] 183	981	3,071
1952	3,821	10,171	388	11,438	3,125	881	8,388	25,849	6,992	226	1,250	3,089
1953	4,211	10,210	422	10,982	3,287	896	8,396	28,768[19] 25,869	8,391	204	1,686	3,036
1954	4,087	9,667	549	10,204	3,257	889	8,834[18]	27,247	10,617	233	1,989	3,130
1955	4,305	9,998	584	10,486	3,388	932	12,575	30,912	11,772	286	2,354	3,208
1956	4,612	9,769	584	11,099	3,374	902	13,064	33,917	11,073	301	2,408	3,385
1957	4,942	10,185	599	12,472	3,525	908	15,153	38,886	12,954	333	2,735	3,192
1958	5,120	10,148	750	12,577	3,528	860	17,573	40,941	12,885	357	3,065	3,253
1959	4,885	10,600	873	13,604	3,938	894	18,734	44,300[24]	13,658	376	3,318	3,252
1960	5,269	10,110	1,075	14,093	4,023	917	17,261	47,324	13,424	435	3,555	3,391
1961	5,703	10,514	1,220	14,911	4,236	966	18,154	51,492	13,682	444	3,781	3,622
1962	5,885	10,309	1,322	15,705	4,273	935	18,205	55,215	13,078	411	3,826	3,461
1963	6,397	10,734	1,460	16,581	4,439	986	17,850	59,156	13,180	361	4,080	3,396
1964	6,671	11,330	1,376	17,827	4,765	996	20,252	66,521	13,772	401	4,228	3,463
1965	6,896	11,092	1,717	18,801	4,567	1,180	19,795	67,439	13,633	530	4,440	3,466
1966	7,286	11,278	1,935	19,375	5,561	1,178	20,220	70,206	14,004	723	4,635	3,478
1967	7,623	11,723	2,169	19,393	6,007	1,395	20,647	71,342	14,582	772	4,801	3,468
1968	7,305	11,894	2,402	20,066	6,019	1,581	19,962	73,231	15,014	783	4,814	3,774
1969	7,365	12,478	2,726	20,817	6,523	2,381	20,781	78,795	15,982	735	4,896	3,727

D26 Output of Beer (in thousands of hectolitres)

	Italy[8]	Neth'l	Norway[9]	Poland	Portugal	Romania[10]	Russia/ U.S.S.R.[11]	Spain	Sweden[8]	Switz.	U.K.	Yugoslavia
1915	600	...	511	...	...	325	...	...	2,619	2,130	48,564	...
1916	620	...	615	...	...	329	...	...	2,631	1,703	44,959	...
1917	411	...	564	...	...	...	...	279	2,372	1,241	27,088	...
1918	505[8]	...	412	...	...	...[26]	...	266	1,499	842	21,294	...
1919	949	...	583	...	...	41	...	297	1,542	922	36,108	...
1920	1,157	...	894	...	...	169	...	303	2,040	1,068	44,846	...
1921	1,369	...	869	1,659	...	314	...	349	2,072	1,362	40,403	550
1922	1,188	...	847	1,840	...	792	...	349	1,824	1,355	34,808	620
1923	1,465	...	809	...	...	[786][10]	...	419	1,960	1,451	32,666[27]	...
1924	1,281	...	712	1,641	...	737	2,276	438	2,070	1,581	33,928	...
1925	1,218	1,944	746	1,651	...	642	2,513	442	1,417	1,835	34,144	...
1926	1,296	2,033	667	1,690	...	872	4,084	616	1,455	2,044	32,949	...
1927	983	2,058	558	2,097	...	929	4,141	601	1,502	2,058	32,569	...
1928	1,127	...	502	2,511	...	985	3,907	603	1,470	2,338	41,019	1,301
1929	902	2,319	502	2,786	...	771	3,400	744	1,503	2,541	40,749	1,189
1930	672	2,280	506	2,516	...	595	3,700	794	1,642	2,610	39,765	1,582
1931	433	2,103	415	1,928	...	419	3,920	359	1,614	2,621	35,415	1,204
1932	422	1,807	420	1,400	...	358[10]	4,210	719	1,563	2,526	30,147[28]	824
1933	372	1,609	391	1,058	...	342	4,315	745	1,265	2,419	31,761	558
1934	289	1,512	397	1,172	...	510	4,568	763	1,205	2,471	33,996	485
1935	497	1,373	406	1,065	...	514	5,186	793	1,302	2,321	35,685	451
1936	577	1,262	443	1,179	...	506	7,436	...	1,349	2,047	36,659	483
1937	613	1,298	481	1,407	64	596	8,960	...	1,481	2,136	39,127	700
1938	709	1,382	480	1,502	65	605	10,310	...	1,588	2,135	40,153	886[29]
1939	830	1,508	504	...	69	637[26]	10,740[11]	770	1,752	2,185	41,785	427
1940	815	1,764	607	...	82	770	12,130	611	1,563	2,461	41,731	...
1941	633	2,247	477	...	115	1,274	...	82	1,294	2,010	47,626	...
1942	299	2,076	65	...	126	1,062	...	583	1,350	1,401	47,740	...
1943	...	2,286	—	...	132	1,003[26]	...	616	1,285	1,018	49,026	...
1944	347	1,848	2	...	142	...	...[11]	645	1,285	868	51,507	...
1945	696[8]	1,157	25	...	158	...	4,050	669	1,376	1,059	53,463	...
1946	898	1,873	446	...	150	...	5,690	465	1,478	1,183	50,046	54
1947	919	1,852	518	1,529	170	...	6,840	861	1,660	1,693	48,774	682
1948	892	1,514	471	1,615	183	418	7,075	503	1,670	1,732	46,126	1,187
1949	1,200	1,336	550	2,532	163	...	9,835	460	1,721	1,895	43,002	1,411
1950	1,383	1,413	598	3,458	129	871	13,080	604	1,756	1,993	41,182	1,144
1951	1,299	1,603	664	3,790	126	954	15,170	744	1,753	2,110	41,056	1,188
1952	1,581	1,611	687	4,231	135	1,184	16,080	1,157	1,785	2,361	40,914	922
1953	1,495	1,832	651	4,978	150	1,245	18,330	1,299	1,969	2,362	40,888	568
1954	1,690	1,978	655	5,246	150	1,362	18,890	1,375	2,041	2,340	39,058	801
1955	1,566	2,321	750	5,170	205	1,308	18,470	1,683	2,238	2,572	39,850	804
1956	1,833[8]	2,485	764	5,195	204	1,312	18,070	1,827	2,121	2,686	39,801	770
1957	1,697	2,733	759	5,692	218	1,557	19,650	2,371	2,089	2,966	40,505	1,043
1958	1,959	2,941	782	6,106	297	1,512	19,910	2,897	2,777	3,156	39,376	1,230
1959	2,071	3,398	817	6,590	328	1,480	23,190	3,295	2,752	3,293	41,634	1,262
1960	2,489	3,552	843	6,732	379	1,633	24,979	3,433	2,795	3,127	43,369	1,630
1961	3,055	3,802	904	7,055	415	1,927	26,667	4,100	2,798	3,748	45,333	1,860
1962	3,779	3,965	874	6,563	322	2,128	28,184	4,667	2,724	4,004	45,660	1,788
1963	3,689	4,408	977	7,254	373	2,256	28,088	5,688	2,959	4,136	46,276	2,241
1964	4,268	4,965	981	7,580	501	2,384	28,296	6,906	2,987	4,580	48,472	2,669
1965	4,547	5,402	1,071	7,735	502	2,665	31,690	7,497	3,039	4,396	48,447	2,995
1966	5,179	5,695	1,137	8,297	660	3,028	34,371	8,352	3,141	4,586	49,470	4,051
1967	5,553	6,571	1,226	8,956	749	3,311	36,126	9,418	3,279	4,685	50,210	4,367
1968	5,384	6,849	1,338	9,453	857	3,511	38,300	10,260	3,755	4,510	51,433	4,752
1969	5,748	7,841	1,442	9,992	1,000	3,707	39,706	10,755	4,251	4,657	53,861	5,344

D26 Output of Beer (in thousands of hectolitres)

1970-1998

	Austria	Belgium	Bulgaria	Czecho-slovakia	Denmark	Finland	France	West Germany	East Germany	Greece	Hungary	Ireland
1970	7,391	13,015	3,047	21,178	7,122	2,424	20,871	81,609	16,642	777	5,006	3,885
1971	7,697	12,876	3,234	22,274	7,815	2,383	20,955	84,474	18,057	807	5,027	4,155
1972	8,038	13,495	3,390	22,498	8,445	2,500	20,395	85,881	18,445	1,010	4,963	4,200
1973	8,208	14,691	3,760	22,270	9,023	2,597	22,664	87,450	19,412	1,170	5,860	4,402
1974	7,765	14,604	4,242	22,138	8,408	2,489	22,098	87,688	19,308	1,470	6,456	4,492
1975	7,557	13,797	4,516	22,628	8,881	2,494	22,660	88,426	20,380	1,380	6,619	5,000
1976	7,783	14,544	4,695	22,629	8,328	2,455	24,585	91,391	21,202	1,380	6,765	4,300
1977	7,778	13,819	4,927	22,442	8,450	2,732	23,540	90,017	21,705	1,800	6,998	4,400
1978	7,720	13,395	5,165	22,058	8,056	2,526	22,781	87,919	22,297	1,990	7,233	...
1979	7,771	13,681	5,303	23,601	8,307	2,698	22,793	87,851	23,061	2,460	7,412	...
1980	7,698	14,291	5,254	23,393	9,168	2,822	21,289	89,569	23,633	2,560	7,841	...
1981	8,181	13,811	5,128	23,934	9,747	2,840	21,852	90,857	24,091	3,100	7,987	...
1982	8,313	14,629	5,477	24,912	10,122	2,804	22,409	91,183	25,404	2,930	7,882	...
1983	8,403	14,224	5,505	24,957	11,038	2,905	22,086	91,626	25,313	2,850	7,830	4,223
1984	8,440	14,311	5,764	23,768	8,671	2,956	20,280	87,725	24,500	2,970	7,962	4,214
1985	8,836	13,931	5,838	22,354	8,286	3,170	19,300	88,375	24,288	3,262	8,740	4,352
1986	9,017	13,715	6,023	22,789	9,064	3,285	19,000	89,129	24,316	3,103	8,963	4,479
1987	8,638	13,988	6,212	22,228	8,754	3,427	18,000	87,804	24,128	3,461	9,045	4,360
1988	8,938	13,792	6,332	22,670	9,160	3,789	17,800	88,166	24,521	4,524	9,420	4,624
1989	9,174	13,164	6,720	23,333	9,217	3,947	...		24,843	3,869	9,722	5,094
1990	9,799	14,141	6,507	21,966	9,362	4,151	19,109		15,885	3,961	9,918	5,236
1991	9,971	13,799	4,880	20,579	...	4,418	18,654	112,071		3,772	9,570	...
				Czech Republic[30]								
1992	10,176	14,259	4,695	18,982	9,775	4,685	18,512	114,089		4,025	9,162	...
1993	11,465	...	4,247	17,366	9,435	4,579	18,291	111,075		...	7,877	...
1994	10,070	15,055	4,792	17,876	9,410	4,524	17,688	113,428		4,376	8,082	...
1995	9,474	15,110	4,331	17,687	9,903	4,702	18,311	111,875		4,024	7,697	8,132
1996	9,445	14,408	4,402	18,057	9,591	4,980	17,140	108,938		3,766	7,270	10,765
1997	9,303	14,758	3,031	18,558	9,181	4,840	...	108,729		3,950	6,973	12,095
1998	8,837	14,763	3,796	18,289	8,044	4,341	...	106,993		...	7,163	12,580

	Italy	Nether-lands	Norway[9]	Poland	Portugal	Romania	Russia/ U.S.S.R.	Spain	Sweden	Swit-zerland	U.K.	Yugo-slavia
1970	5,938	8,772	1,517	10,372	1,345	4,375	41,857	12,307	4,374	4,733	55,165	6,665
1971	6,285	9,492	1,656	11,211	1,365	4,951	44,131	12,184	4,469	4,821	56,850	8,327
1972	6,524	9,875	1,687	11,809	1,504	5,051	45,861	12,332	4,406	4,494	57,737	9,345
1973	8,598	11,066	1,821	12,788	2,529	5,621	50,809	14,755	4,507	4,710	60,582	9,704
1974	8,064	11,642	1,869	12,442	2,975	6,480	54,003	15,483	4,386	4,631	63,057	9,429
1975	6,493	12,430	1,875	12,901	3,194	7,449	57,050	16,626	4,562	4,342	64,565	8,454
1976	7,377	13,862	1,875	12,318	2,812	7,625	59,152	17,127	4,793	4,239	65,635	8,685
1977	7,402	13,993	1,867	12,069	2,795	7,918	61,861	17,273	4,703	4,033	65,239	9,588
1978	7,939	14,650	1,926	11,378	3,610	8,980	64,138	21,930	4,153	3,998	66,418	10,005
1979	9,115	15,387	1,923	11,293	3,786	9,842	63,315	20,785	4,104	4,022	67,419	11,254
1980	8,718	15,683	1,974	11,155	3,780	9,897	61,330	20,609	3,867	4,082	64,830	11,712
1981	9,016	16,639	2,131	10,514	4,035	9,730	62,976	19,296	3,684	4,201	61,721	12,163
1982	10,543	16,180	2,013	10,617	3,608	9,911	64,673	19,122	3,694	4,205	59,786	13,469
1983	10,320	17,330	1,911	10,306	4,265	9,928	66,081	20,823	3,705	4,171	60,324	12,398
1984	9,201	17,050	1,944	9,867	3,682	9,845	65,385	21,464	3,616	4,078	60,105	10,925
1985	10,381	17,530	1,991	11,078	3,795	9,847	65,721	22,475	3,784	4,076	59,655	10,656
1986	11,372	17,990	2,134	11,300	4,128	10,603	48,907	23,510	3,979	4,087	59,439	11,643
1987	11,503	17,550	2,198	11,900	4,977	10,364	50,711	24,788	4,106	4,045	59,895	12,054
1988	11,589	17,437	2,238	12,500	5,619	10,655	55,811	26,141	4,391	4,049	60,156	11,970
1989	10,615	18,908	2,229	12,082	6,874	11,513	60,182	27,546	4,722	4,121	54,950	11,286
1990	11,248	20,055	2,281	11,294	6,919	10,527	62,507	27,940	4,711	4,143	70,800	...
1991	11,049	19,863	...	13,633	6,309	9,803	...	26,482	4,663	4,137	...	5,622
1992	10,489	20,419	2,273	14,139	6,860	10,014	...	24,279	4,969	4,020	...	4,714
1993	9,873	20,709	...	12,585	...	9,929	...	...	5,087	3,804	...	3,018
1994	10,258	21,200	...	14,099	6,902	9,047	21,800	25,587	5,379	3,828	66,161	5,043
1995	10,616	22,380	2,255	15,205	7,220	8,768	21,400	25,396	5,471	3,672	59,337	5,611
1996	9,559	22,670	...	16,667	6,958	8,118	20,800	24,520	5,318	...	61,262	5,987
1997	10,379	23,780	2,396	19,281	6,766	7,651	26,100	24,786	5,078	...	64,736	6,106
1998	11,073	23,040	1,833	21,017	7,072	9,989	33,500	22,428	4,765	...	60,806	6,630

D26 Output of Beer (in thousands of hectolitres)

NOTES

1. SOURCES:- Belgium 1868 and 1869—supplied by the Belgian National Institute of Statistics. France to 1834—T.J. Markovtich, *L'industrie francaise de 1789 à 1964* (Cahiers de l'I.S.E.A., 1966). Germany to 1872 (1st line)—W.G. Hoffman, *Das Wachstum der Deutschen Wirtschaft seit der Mitte des 19 Jahrhunderts* (Berlin, etc., 1965), using the index of beer output. Greece to 1928—estimated from data supplied by the National Statistical Service of Greece. Russia to 1955—G.W. Nutter, *The Growth of Industrial Production in the Soviet Union* (Princeton, 1962). All other statistics are taken from the official publications noted on p. xv with gaps filled from the League of Nations and United Nations, *Statistical Yearbooks*.
2. Except as indicated in footnotes, all types of beer have been aggregated in this table, though for the U.K. from 1881 to 1932 the statistics are expressed in the source in terms of standard barrels of 36 gallons at a gravity of 1,055 degrees.
3. Home-brewed beer is not covered in this table.

FOOTNOTES

[1] Figures to 1787 (1st line) apply to England & Wales, and from 1787 (2nd line) to 1830 to Great Britain. They are for years ended 24 June in 1750–52; years ended 5 July from 1753 to 1825; and years ended 5 January from 1826 to 1830.

[2] Figures to 1859 apply to the whole Austro-Hungarian Empire. From 1860 to 1917 they apply to Cisleithania, and subsequently to the Republic. Up to 1937 they are for years ended 31 August.

[3] Figures to 1905 are for taxed beer only. Figures for tax-free beer are for years ended 31 May, and are as follows (in thousands of hectolitres):-

1892	1,200	1896	1,333	1900	1,516	1903	1,495
1893	1,236	1897	1,389	1901	1,490	1904	1,556
1894	1,267	1898	1,400	1902	1,534	1905	1,591
1895	1,282	1899	1,503				

[4] From 1871 to 1917 Alsace-Lorraine is included in Germany rather than France, though not included in the French statistics until 1922.

[5] This break occurs on a change of source (see note 1).

[6] Small areas outside the main tax districts are included for the first from 1880 (2nd line).

[7] Figures to 1918 apply to Transleithania, and subsequently to the territory established by the treaty of Trianon. Up to 1938 they are for years ended 31 August.

[8] Figures to 1918 apply to the boundaries of 1871. For 1919–45 they apply to the boundaries of 1924, and subsequently to the boundaries of 1954. Up to 1956 they are for years beginning 1 July.

[9] Strong beer only.

[10] From 1881 to 1922 and from 1934 to 1943 the figures are for years ended 31 March following that indicated. The figure for 1923 is for 9 months beginning 1 April, and that for 1932 is for 15 months ended 31 March 1933.

[11] Figures to 1913 (1st line) apply to the Russian Empire. From 1913 (2nd line) to 1939 they apply to the territory of the U.S.S.R. in 1923. In 1940 they include territories incorporated in 1939–40, and from 1945 they apply to the present territory.

[12] Figures to 1938–44 are for the Czech lands only.

[13] Year beginning 1 July.

[14] Figures to 1914–18 exclude the invaded departments.

[15] The figures to 1931 and 1932 are for years ended 31 March following that indicated, and the figure to 1933 is for 9 months beginning 1 April.

[16] Figures for 1939–44 exclude Haut Rhin, together with for 1941–44 the rest of Alsace-Lorraine.

[17] Excluding Corsica.

[18] Figures for 1945–54 are known to be incomplete.

[19] The method of measurement was changed.

[20] Subsequently excluding Eupen, Malmedy, etc., Posen, West Prussia, and Danzig.

[21] Subsequently excluding Memel, northern Schleswig, and (until 1933) Saarland.

[22] Subsequently excluding eastern Upper Silesia.

[23] From 1939 to 1944 includes Memel, and from June 1940 to 1944 Eupen, Malmedy, etc.

[24] From 1947 to 1959 Saarland is excluded.

[25] Years ended 30 September.

[26] Southern Dobrudja is included from 1914 to 1939; Bessarabia and Bukovina from 1920 to 1939; and Transylvania and the Banat from 1920, except for certain parts of northern Transylvania in 1940–43.

[27] Southern Ireland is excluded from 1 April 1923.

[28] See note 2.

[29] Figures to 1938 are of consumption rather than production.

[30] Czech Republic, Slovakia = 1992 3686; 1993 3967.

[31] Russian Federation. Ex-USSR as follows

	Armenia	Azerbaijan
1991	419	5,159
1992	149	1,855
1993	70	1,478
1994	70	1,114
1995	53	1,022
1996	29	1,013
1997	50	1,016
1998	132	1,011

D26 Output of Beer (in thousands of hectolitres)

	Belarus	Estonia	Georgia	Kazakhstan	Kyrgistan	Latvia	Lithuania	Moldova	Tajikistan	Turkmenistan	Ukraine	Uzbekistan
1991	3,389	68	...	3,133	445	1,295	1,412	660	364	5	13,093	1,759
1992	2,736	143	...	2,301	310	859	1,426	410	135	4	10,997	1,434
1993	2,146	242	...	16,568	191	546	1,164	297	82	3	9,086	1,363
1994	1,889	477	63	...	121	638	1,353	...	67	218	9,087	1,291
1995	1,518	492	65	...	121	653	1,093	...	47	113	7,102	724
1996	2,013	459	48	...	141	645	1,139	...	6	17	6,025	677
1997	2,413	543	79	...	141	715	1,413	...	6	44	6,125	619
1998	2,604	744	74	...	130	721	1,559	...	9	29	6,842	...

[32] Ex-Yugoslavia countries as follows: (thousands of hectolitres)

	Croatia	Macedonia	Slovenia
1991	2,248	928	2,203
1992	2,720	861	1,783
1993	2,481	952	1,978
1994	3,122	984	2,075
1995	3,166	993	2,087
1996	3,292	...	2,223
1997	3,607	...	2,138
1998	3,759	...	2,000

D27 OUTPUT OF ELECTRIC ENERGY (in giga Watt hours)

1900–1944

	Austria[1]	Belgium	Bulgaria[2]	Czech[1]	Denmark	Finland[1,3]	France	Germany[1]	Greece[1]	Hungary[1,7]	Ireland[1,8]
1900	...	...	...	...	...	...	...	1.00	...	...	...
1901	...	...	...	...	...	...	0.34	1.30	...	...	...
1902	...	...	...	...	...	...	0.37	1.40	...	...	...
1903	...	...	...	...	...	...	0.43	1.60	...	...	...
1904	...	...	...	...	...	...	0.48	2.20	...	...	...
1905	...	...	...	...	...	...	0.53	2.60	...	...	...
1906	...	...	...	...	...	...	0.60	2.70	...	...	...
1907	...	...	...	...	...	...	0.67	3.20	...	...	...
1908	...	...	...	...	...	...	0.75	3.90	...	...	...
1909	...	...	...	...	...	...	0.85	4.80	...	...	...
1910	...	...	...	...	...	...	1.02	5.40	...	...	...
1911	...	...	...	...	...	...	1.23	6.00	...	...	...
1912	...	...	...	...	...	...	1.48	7.40	...	...	...
1913	...	...	...	0.96	...	...	1.80	8.00	...	...	...
1914	...	...	...	...	...	...	2.15	8.80	...	...	...
1915	...	...	...	...	...	...	1.90	9.80	...	...	...
1916	...	...	...	...	...	...	2.18	11.00	...	...	...
1917	...	...	...	...	...	...	2.40	12.00	...	...	...
1918	...	...	...	...	...	...	2.70[4]	13.00[4,6]	...	...	...
1919	...	...	...	1.16	...	...	2.90	13.50	...	...	...
1920	1.77	1.20	...	1.37	0.25		3.50[5] 5.80	15.00	0.08	...	...
1921	1.78	1.30	...	1.40	0.26		6.50	17.00	0.09	...	...
1922	1.84	1.41	...	1.36	0.27		7.30	17.00	0.10	...	...
1923	1.91	1.59	...	1.48	0.31	0.33	8.17	15.40	0.11	0.34	...
1924	2.02	1.83	0.02	1.76	0.34	0.53	9.95	17.30	0.12	0.36	...
1925	2.14	2.19	0.03	1.96	0.38	0.54	11.14	20.33	0.13	0.44	...
1926	2.19	2.70	0.04	2.10	0.42	0.61	12.44	21.22	0.14	0.52	...
1927	2.31	3.13	0.05	2.38	0.46	0.69	12.58	25.14	0.16	0.60	...
1928	2.40	3.60	0.07	2.75	0.50	0.76	14.25	27.87	0.18	0.65	...
1929	2.55	4.14	0.09	2.50	0.56	1.00[3]	15.60	30.66	0.17	0.70	0.06
1930	2.50	4.29	0.10	...	0.58	1.21	16.85	29.10	0.22	0.72	0.12
1931	2.40	4.11	0.11	...	0.66	1.26	15.67	25.79	0.26	0.71	0.15
1932	2.30	3.75	0.12	...	0.66	1.48	14.95	23.46	0.28	0.69	0.17
1933	2.39	3.79	0.13	2.24	0.75	1.69	16.40	25.66	0.29	0.73	0.19
1934	2.46	3.91	0.14	2.43	0.83	1.85	16.74	30.66	0.31	0.81	0.21
1935	2.60	4.33	0.14	2.59	0.87	2.10	17.47	35.70[6] 36.71	0.37	0.90	0.24
1936	2.68	4.80	0.17	2.97	0.98	2.32	18.47	42.49	0.40	0.98	0.28
1937	2.89	5.39	0.20	3.55[17] 4.12[18]	1.10	2.79	20.08	48.97	0.44	1.06	0.31
1938	2.99	5.13	0.23	[2.16]	1.14	3.11	20.80	55.33	0.47	1.11	0.38
1939	3.42	5.43[16]	0.27	[2.47]	1.07	3.11	22.10[4]	61.38	0.50[20] 0.31	1.23	0.41
1940	3.81	4.19	0.30	[2.65]	0.87	1.71	20.68	62.96	0.29	...	0.44
1941	4.20	4.82	0.30	...	1.00	1.78	20.28	70.00	0.22	...	0.45
1942	4.68	4.99	0.32	...	1.09	1.93	20.03	71.50	0.18	...	0.41
1943	5.10	5.06	0.34	...	1.13	3.14	21.07[6]	73.94	0.16	1.81	0.44
1944	5.81	3.71	0.31	...[18]	1.05	2.73	16.03[4]	...	0.15	...	0.40

D27 Output of Electric Energy (in giga Watt hours)

	Italy[1,9]	Neth'l[1]	Norway[10]	Poland[1,11]	Port-ugal[1,24]	Romania[1]	Russia[12]/U.S.S.R.	Spain[1]	Sweden[1,13]	Switz[1,14]	U.K.[15]	Yugo-slavia
1895	0.03	...	...	...	...	...	...	...	...	...	...	...
1896	0.05	...	...	...	...	...	...	...	...	...	0.1	...
1897	0.05	...	...	...	...	...	...	...	...	...	0.1	...
1898	0.08	...	...	...	...	...	...	...	...	...	0.1	...
1899	0.10	...	...	...	...	...	...	...	...	...	0.2	...
1900	0.14	...	...	...	...	...	...	...	...	...	0.2	
1901	0.16	...	...	...	...	...	...	0.19	0.1	...	0.4	
1902	0.22	...	...	...	...	...	...	0.20	0.1	...	0.5	
1903	0.30	...	...	...	...	...	...	0.21	0.1	...	0.6	
1904	0.40	...	...	...	...	...	...	0.22	0.2	...	0.8	
1905	0.45	...	...	...	...	...	...	0.23	0.2	...	1.0	
1906	0.55	...	...	...	...	...	...	0.24	0.2	...	1.2	
1907	0.70	...	...	...	...	...	...	0.25	0.3	...	1.43[15]	
1908	0.95	...	...	...	...	...	...	0.29	0.4	...	1.6	...
1909	1.15	...	...	...	...	...	...	0.33	0.6	...	1.7	
1910	1.30	...	...	...	...	...	...	0.36	0.8	...	1.9	
1911	1.50	...	...	...	...	...	...	0.42	0.8	...	2.1	
1912	1.80	...	...	...	...	...	...	0.46	1.2	...	2.4	
1913	2.00	...	...	...	...	...	2.04[12] 1.95	0.50	1.45[13]	...	2.5	
1914	2.20	...	...	...	...	...	...	0.53	...	...	3.0	...
1915	2.58	...	...	...	...	...	...	0.57	...	...	3.5	...
1916	2.93	...	...	...	...	...	2.58	0.71	...	...	4.1	
1917	3.43	...	...	...	...	...	...	0.85	...	...	4.7	
1918	4.00[9]	...	...	...	...	...	...	0.82	...	...	4.9	
1919	4.30	0.61	...	...	...	...	...	0.67	2.43	...	4.9	
1920	4.00	0.71	5.30	...	0.10	...	0.50	0.96	2.61	2.80	5.4[15] 8.54	...
1921	4.69	0.77	5.60	...	0.11	...	0.52	0.87	2.22	2.65	8.41	...
1922	4.54	0.91	6.00	...	0.12	...	0.78	1.04	2.68	3.00	9.27	
1923	4.73	1.05	6.20	1.52	0.13	0.15	1.15	1.19	2.99	3.30	10.27	
1924	5.61	1.19	6.60	1.51	0.14	0.16	1.56	1.35	3.52	3.70	11.26	...
1925	6.45	1.33	7.00	1.67	0.15	0.24	2.93	1.54	3.67	3.99	12.11	...
1926	7.26	1.49	7.30	1.96	0.17	0.39	3.51	1.62	4.01	4.40	12.74	...
1927	8.39	1.72	7.70	2.32	0.19	0.42	4.21	1.77	4.39	4.73	14.50	
1928	8.74	1.96	8.10	2.62	0.22	0.54	5.01	2.41	4.41	5.04	15.63	...
1929	9.63	2.26	7.80	3.05	0.24	0.57	6.22	2.43	4.97	5.28	16.98	0.75
1930	10.67	2.47	7.63	2.91	0.26	0.55	8.37	2.61	5.12	5.17	17.69	...
1931	10.47	2.58	7.40	2.60	0.27	0.52	10.69	2.68	5.09	5.05	18.22	0.78
1932	10.59	2.59	7.20	2.26	0.29	0.54	13.54	2.80	4.90	4.79	19.46	0.78
1933	11.65	2.66	7.25	2.40	0.30	0.59	16.36	2.90	5.34	4.93	21.20	...
1934	12.60	2.80	7.14	2.62	0.33	0.75	21.01	3.03	6.03	5.35	23.42	0.72
1935	13.80	2.84	7.84	2.82	0.36	0.87	26.23	3.27	6.90	5.69	25.93	0.63
1936	13.65	3.12	7.99	3.08	0.37	0.96	32.84	2.80	7.43	6.05	28.87	0.80
1937	15.43	3.49	8.33[10] 9.19	3.63	0.42	1.08	36.17	2.47	7.98	6.84	31.93	0.91
1938	15.54	3.69	9.78	3.98	0.43	1.15	39.37	2.75	8.16	7.04	33.77	1.09
1939	18.42	4.06	10.47	[2.06][21]	0.45	1.21[22]	43.20	3.11	9.05	7.13	35.81[23] 26.28	1.10
1940	19.43	3.78	9.22	...	0.46	1.13	48.31[12]	3.62	8.62	8.05	28.35	...
1941	20.76	3.65	9.42	...	0.48	1.17	...	3.89	9.12	8.29	31.75	...
1942	20.23	3.61	...	...	0.47	1.27[22]	...	4.44	9.80	7.97	34.88	...
1943	18.25	3.57	...	...	0.48	...	...	4.78	11.04	8.68	36.12	...
1944	13.54[9]	2.97	...	...	0.51	...	...	4.72	12.43	8.52	37.41	...

D27 Output of Electric Energy (in giga Watt hours)

1945-1997

	Austria[1]	Belgium	Bulgaria[2]	Czecho-slovakia[1]	Denmark	Finland[1]	France	West Germany[1]	East Germany[1]	Greece[1]	Hungary[1,7]	Ire-land[1,8]
1945	3.18	3.53[16]	0.40	4.46	0.98	2.96	18.37	...	...	0.21	0.69	0.48
1946	4.34	6.11	0.44	5.62	1.38	2.94	22.83	22.00	11.54	0.29[20] 0.31	1.16[7]	0.57
1947	3.90	7.05	0.48	6.66	1.68	2.87	25.81	27.75	...	0.41	...	0.62
1948	5.33	7.69	0.55	7.52	1.84	2.96	28.85	34.08	14.60	0.51	2.23	0.71
1949	5.51	7.95	0.70	8.28	1.98	3.57	29.93	40.65	...	0.61	2.36	0.78
1950	6.35	8.27	0.82[2]	9.28	2.22	4.18	33.03	46.10	19.47	0.70	3.00	0.97
1951	7.38	9.25	1.02	10.30	2.55	4.61	38.15	53.73	21.46	0.85	3.51	1.03
1952	8.03	9.26	1.35	11.63	2.69	4.77	40.57	58.67	23.18	0.97	4.20	1.16
1953	8.76	9.59	1.56	12.36	2.77	5.40	41.46	62.88	24.25	1.03	4.62	1.29
1954	9.85	10.34	1.73	13.61	3.28	5.71	45.57	70.46	26.04	1.17	4.82	1.46
1955	10.75	10.95	2.07	15.01	3.88	6.84	49.63	78.87	28.70	1.35	5.43	1.57
1956	11.72	11.85	2.39	16.59	4.02	6.66	53.83	87.82	31.18	1.55	5.20	1.64
1957	12.46	12.61	2.66	17.72	3.70	7.74	57.43	94.65	32.74	1.69	5.45	1.77
1958	13.56	12.52	3.02	19.62	3.87	7.97	61.60	98.24	34.87	1.86	6.48	1.89
1959	14.79	13.18	3.87	21.88	4.37	7.92	64.51	106.20	37.25	2.04	7.09	2.09
1960	15.97	14.12	4.66	24.45	5.18	8.63	72.12	116.42[19] 118.99	40.31	2.28	7.62	2.26
1961	16.63	14.97	5.41	26.96	4.97	10.44	76.49	127.29	42.52	2.52	8.38	2.45
1962	17.81	16.41	6.04	28.73	5.78	11.59	83.09	138.36	45.06	2.81	9.12	2.71
1963	18.44	17.76	7.18	29.86	6.99	11.58	88.25	150.39	47.45	3.22	9.67	2.89
1964	20.36	19.43	8.70	31.98	7.32	12.46	93.78	164.84	51.03	3.86	10.58	3.23
1965	22.24	20.37	10.24	34.19	7.38	13.61	101.44	172.34	53.61	4.40	11.18	3.54
1966	23.82	21.52	11.76	36.47	9.31	15.51	106.11	177.88	56.87	5.76	11.86	3.84
1967	24.44	22.60	13.63	38.62	9.48	16.40	111.64	184.68	59.69	6.67	12.49	4.24
1968	25.71	25.06	15.45	41.63	12.10	17.36	117.92	203.28	63.23	7.43	13.16	4.74
1969	26.35	27.63	17.23	43.13	16.57	19.28	131.52	226.05	65.46	8.43	14.07	5.24
1970	30.04	28.96	19.51	46.16	18.86	21.19	140.71	242.61	67.65	9.82	14.54	5.91
1971	28.75	31.60	21.02	47.24	17.54	20.84	149.00	259.63	69.42	11.56	14.99	6.29
1972	29.39	35.66	22.27	51.40	19.37	22.30	163.65	274.77	72.83	13.12	16.32	6.75
1973	31.32	39.12	21.95	53.47	18.00	24.94	174.48	299.00	76.91	14.82	17.64	7.29
1974	33.88	40.76	22.81	56.03	17.65	26.52	180.40	311.71	80.29	15.02	18.98	7.62
1975	35.20	39.02	25.24	59.28	18.69	25.13	178.51	301.80	84.57	16.15	20.47	7.85
1976	35.33	45.00	27.75	62.75	19.22	27.88	194.87	333.65	89.15	17.86	22.05	8.65
1977	37.68	44.77	29.71	66.50	20.73	31.56	202.56	335.32	92.00	19.00	23.40	9.28
1978	38.07	48.36	31.38	69.10	19.16	33.87	217.29	353.36	95.96	21.05	25.55	10.16
1979	40.64	49.65	32.37	68.09	20.47	37.34	231.06	372.18	96.84	22.10	24.51	10.77
1980	41.97	51.02	34.83	72.73	25.16	38.71	246.67	368.77	98.81	22.65	23.87	10.57
1981	42.89	48.18	36.97	73.50	18.13	39.07	264.54	368.81	100.72	23.43	24.22	11.01
1982	42.89	47.94	40.46	74.75	22.07	39.35	266.46	366.88	102.91	23.27	24.77	10.79
1983	42.62	49.91	42.64	76.28	22.16	40.35	283.37	373.81	104.93	22.26	25.79	11.13
1984	42.38	51.85	44.67	78.39	22.58	43.31	309.81	394.88	110.09	24.82	26.30	11.52
1985	44.53	54.18	41.63	80.63	29.00	47.32	328.57	408.70	113.83	27.74	26.80	11.99
1986	44.65	55.50	41.82	84.77	30.60	48.91	346.30	408.27	115.29	28.24	28.06	[9.04][8]
1987	50.52	60.00	43.47	85.82	29.27	50.91	360.74	418.26	114.18	30.09	29.75	13.05
1988	49.02	61.91	45.04	87.37	27.96	53.07	373.31	431.16	118.33	33.17	29.22	13.23
1989	50.17	63.90	44.33	87.53	22.36	53.38	387.10	440.89	118.98	34.46	29.59	13.85
1990	50.41	67.16	42.14	86.63	25.76	53.68	398.60	449.49	117.29	35.00	28.41	14.51
1991	51.47	68.13	38.92	83.27	36.33	56.95	433.30	\{ ... \}		35.81	29.98	15.15
				Czech Republic[26]								
1992	51.18	68.34	35.61	59.29	30.85	56.63	441.40	...		37.41	31.61	16.01
1993	52.67	67.11	38.10	58.88	33.73	58.83	454.10	...		38.40	32.78	16.41
1994	53.30	72.28	38.13	58.70	24.74	41.45	65.64	476.20	526.9	44.95	33.51	17.11
1995	56.58	74.46	41.79	60.84	26.31	38.20	63.89	493.78	534.9	46.12	34.01	17.88
1996	54.83	76.45	42.72	64.26	25.28	54.98	75.86	51.30	545.3	51.92	35.09	19.18
1997	56.85	78.94	42.80	64.59	24.82	48.38	69.17	51.54	546.4	48.81	35.39	20.68

D27 Output of Electric Energy (in giga Watt hours)

1945–1997

	Italy[1,9]	Neth'l[1]	Norway[1]	Poland[1,11]	Port-ugal[1,24]	Romania[1]	Russia[12]/ U.S.S.R.	Spain[1]	Sweden[1]	Swit-[1,14] zerland	U.K.[1]	Yugo-slavia[1]
1945	12.65	1.83	...	...[11]	0.55	...	43.26	4.17	13.54	9.60	36.40	0.83
1946	17.48	3.70	11.31	5.71	0.64	...	48.57	5.41	14.20	10.07	40.34[23] 49.50	1.14
1947	20.57	4.64	11.99	6.61	0.72	...	56.49	5.97	13.46	9.77	50.80	1.45
1948	22.69	5.58	12.07	7.51	0.81	1.50	66.34	6.11	14.08	10.43	54.80	2.06
1949	20.78	6.34	15.00	8.15	0.87	1.86	78.26	5.63	16.04	9.76	57.40	2.19
1950	24.68	7.42	16.92	9.42	0.94	2.11	91.23	6.92	18.18	10.48	63.30	2.41
1951	29.22	7.91	17.65	10.51	1.04	2.47	104.02	8.30	19.35	12.25	69.37	2.55
1952	30.84	8.60	18.48	11.98	1.34	2.89	119.12	9.42	20.55	12.89	71.48	2.70
1953	32.62	9.60	18.80	13.68	1.38	3.44	134.33	10.05	22.44	13.47	75.10	2.98
1954	35.57	10.59	21.27	15.47	1.66	3.70	150.70	10.48	23.96	13.18	81.88	3.44
1955	38.12	11.19	22.60	17.75	1.89	4.34	170.23	11.92	24.72	15.45	89.10[25]	4.34
1956	40.59	12.45	23.11	19.50	2.18	4.93	191.65	13.67	26.63	14.90	95.77	5.05
1957	42.73	13.37	25.72	21.16	2.17	5.44	209.69	14.52	28.97	15.89	99.97	6.25
1958	45.49	13.85	27.34	23.96	2.67	6.18	235.35	16.35	30.35	16.89	107.34	7.36
1959	49.35	14.97	28.51	26.38	2.99	6.82	265.11	17.35	32.23	18.18	114.80[25]	8.11
1960	56.24	16.52	31.12	29.31	3.26	7.65	292.27	18.61	34.72	19.07	129.07	8.93
1961	60.56	17.62	33.59	32.25	3.61	8.66	327.61	20.88	38.32	22.30	137.51	9.92
1962	64.86	19.26	37.74	35.38	3.83	10.09	369.28	22.91	40.62	21.34	150.80	11.28
1963	71.34	20.98	39.46	36.96	4.30	11.68	412.42	25.90	40.66	22.01	162.62	13.54
1964	76.74	22.98	43.94	40.61	4.76	13.85	458.90	29.53	45.40	22.86	170.95	14.19
1965	82.97	25.01	48.95	43.80	4.63	17.22	506.67	31.72	49.11	24.46	182.77	15.52
1966	89.99	27.87	48.35	47.39	5.59	20.81	544.57	37.70	50.66	27.96	188.21	17.17
1967	96.83	30.06	52.87	51.26	5.93	24.77	587.70	40.64	53.84	30.55	194.01	18.70
1968	104.01	33.62	59.70	55.52	6.22	27.83	638.66	45.85	56.25	30.55	206.92	20.64
1969	110.45	37.14	57.02	60.05	6.84[24]	31.51	689.05	52.12	58.08	29.67	220.91	23.37
1970	117.42	40.86	57.61	64.53	7.49	35.09	740.93	56.49	60.64	33.17	230.14	26.02
1971	124.80	44.90	63.56	69.89	7.93	39.45	800.36	62.52	66.55	32.78	237.11	29.51
1972	135.26	49.55	67.61	76.47	8.90	43.44	857.43	68.90	71.68	31.30	243.90	33.23
1973	145.52	52.63	73.05	84.30	9.82	46.78	914.61	76.27	78.08	37.16	261.76	35.06
1974	148.91	55.35	76.70	91.60	10.75	49.06	975.75	80.86	75.13	37.41	253.25	39.46
1975	147.33	54.26	77.49	97.17	10.70	53.72	1,038.6	82.00	80.57	42.99	252.28	40.04
1976	163.55	58.14	82.13	104.10	9.78	58.27	1,111.4	89.25	86.42	36.24	255.98	43.57
1977	166.54	58.28	72.43	109.36	13.78	59.86	1,150.1	92.69	90.02	45.90	262.01	48.58
1978	175.04	61.60	81.00	115.56	14.60	64.26	1,201.9	98.33	92.90	42.35	267.38	51.25
1979	181.26	64.46	89.12	117.47	16.71	64.93	1,238.2	104.70	95.20	45.55	278.74	54.97
1980	185.74	64.81	84.10	121.87	15.26	67.49	1,293.9	109.20	96.69	46.63	264.86	59.43
1981	181.66	64.05	93.40	115.00	13.90	70.14	1,326.0	110.02	103.30	50.12	258.74	60.36
1982	184.44	60.31	93.16	117.58	15.27	68.92	1,367.0	113.57	100.05	50.75	253.81	62.32
1983	182.88	59.65	106.37	125.82	18.16	70.26	1,419.1	114.67	109.39	50.47	257.02	67.56
1984	182.67	62.80	106.67	134.79	20.02	71.67	1,493.0	118.11	123.84	47.71	261.53	73.01
1985	185.74	62.95	103.29	137.71	19.01	71.82	1,544.1	125.60	137.14	53.46	274.43	74.80
1986	192.33	67.16	97.28	140.29	20.22	75.48	1,598.9	129.15	138.65	54.42	278.50	77.92
1987	201.37	68.42	104.28	145.83	20.10	74.08	1,664.92	133.39	146.57	56.60	279.70	80.79
1988	203.56	69.60	110.06	144.37	22.41	75.28	1,705.00	123.57	146.53	57.52	265.71	83.65
1989	210.75	73.05	119.20	145.47	25.55	75.85	1,722.00	146.59	143.91	51.66	291.75	86.31
1990	216.89	71.87	121.85	136.34	28.53	64.31	1,726.00	151.75	146.54	52.38	297.47	85.91
1991	222.04	74.25	111.01	134.71	29.87	56.91	...	155.70	147.38	54.13	300.59	78.88
1992	226.24	77.20	117.51	132.75	30.09	54.19	1,008.45	158.50	146.44	55.91	298.47	36.49[28]
1993	222.79	76.99	120.10	133.87	31.20	55.48	956.59	156.53	144.31	58.13	301.79	34.16[28]
1994	231.87	79.67	113.39	135.34	31.37	55.13	875.91	161.51	143.04	66.50	324.50	34.52[28]
1995	242.73	80.83	123.13	138.99	33.26	59.26	860.02	167.1	147.03	63.08	335.63	37.17[28]
1996	244.07	85.09	104.75	143.16	34.52	61.35	847.2	174.5	139.38	57.06	347.05	38.09[28]
1997	250.77	86.64	111.55	142.76	34.18	57.14	834.10	190.2	149.86	62.80	344.95	40.31[28]

D27 Output of Electric Energy (in giga Watt hours)

NOTES

1. SOURCES:- Germany 1900–24 is based on the index in W.G. Hoffman, *Das Wachstum der Deutschen Wirtschaft seit der Mitte des 19 Jahrhunderts* (Berlin, etc., 1965). Sweden 1900–12 is based on capacity figures in L. Jorberg, *Growth and Fluctuations of Swedish Industry, 1869–1912* (Lund, 1961). U.K. to 1920 (1st line) is based on the 1907 Census of Production and statistics drawn from Garcke's *Manual of Electricity Undertakings* (London, 1896–1921). All other statistics are taken from the official publications noted on p xv with gaps filled from the League of Nations and United Nations, *Statistical Yearbooks*, and O.E.C.D., *Statistical Bulletins*.
2. Except as indicated in footnotes, the statistics are of net output (i.e. exclusive of electricity consumed in the power stations).
3. The negligible production figures for Italy prior to 1895 are given in the first two editions of this work, and the Industrial Commodity Statistical Yearbook.

FOOTNOTES

[1] Statistics are of gross output (to 1969 2nd line in the case of Finland).
[2] Figures to 1950 are of public supply only.
[3] Figures to 1929 (1st line) are of public supply only.
[4] Alsace-Lorraine is included in Germany up to 1918, and in France from 1919 onwards, except in 1940–44.
[5] Previous figures are rough estimates based on major companies only.
[6] From 1919 to 1935 (1st line) Saarland is excluded.
[7] Figures to 1946 are of public supply only.
[8] Figures are of public supply only, and are for years ended 31 March following that indicated to 1985. The 1986 figure is for April–December.
[9] Figures to 1918 apply to the 1871 boundaries. For 1919–45 they apply to the 1924 boundaries, and from 1946 to the 1954 boundaries. They are for years ended 30 June.
[10] Figures to 1937 (1st line) are of consumption rather than production. Subsequently they are of gross output.
[11] There were major territorial changes in 1945. Statistics up to then exclude production at plant with less than 100 kWh capacity. Subsequently they exclude production at plant with less than 1,000 kWh capacity.
[12] Figures for 1913 (1st line) are for the Russian Empire. From 1913 (2nd line) to 1940 they are for the U.S.S.R. territory of 1923, and subsequently for the present territory.
[13] Figures to 1912 are rough estimates based on capacity installed.
[14] Years ended 30 September.
[15] Figures to 1920 (1st line) are rough estimates of sales, except for the Census of Production figure for 1907. Subsequently they are of gross output.
[16] For 1940–45 output for own industrial use is measured gross instead of net, making the statistics about 3 per cent higher.
[17] Previously excluding output from small power stations.
[18] The figures for 1938–40 exclude the Sudetenland. A series for 1937–45 for Slovakia is given in *Statisticka Prirueka Slovanska* (1947) as follows:-

1937	0.43	1940	0.51	1943	0.71
1938	0.41	1941	0.59	1944	0.64
1939	0.48	1942	0.64	1945	0.33

[19] West Berlin is included from 1960 (2nd line).
[20] Figures from 1939 (2nd line) to 1946 (1st line) are of public supply only.
[21] First half-year only.
[22] Southern Dobrudja, Bessarabia, and northern Bukovina are excluded from 1940, and northern Transylvania is excluded for 1940–42.
[23] Figures from 1939 (2nd line) to 1946 (1st line) are of the output of authorised undertakings and of railways in Great Britain only.
[24] Excluding the Azores and Madeira to 1969.
[25] This break results from a revision in the production statistics of industrial producers. The reduction in 1960 amounted to 0.28. A revised figure was also published for 1955, viz. 88.43.
[26] Czech Republic.
[27] Russian Federation. Ex-USSR as follows

	Armenia	Azer-baijan	Belarus	Estonia	Georgia	Kazakh-stan	Kyrgi-stan	Latvia	Lithuania	Moldova	Tajiki-stan	Turkmeni-stan	Ukraine	Uzbeki-stan
1992	9.0	19.76	37.60	11.83	11.47	82.70	11.89	3.83	18.70	11.25	16.82	13.18	252.52	50.91
1993	6.3	19.05	33.37	9.12	9.7	77.44	11.09	3.92	14.12	10.37	17.74	12.64	229.91	49.15
1994	5.6	17.58	31.39	9.15	6.8	66.39	12.93	4.44	10.02	8.22	16.98	10.49	202.92	47.80
1995	5.5	17.05	24.92	8.69	6.9	66.66	12.35	3.97	13.89	6.06	14.76	9.80	194.31	47.45
1996	6.2	17.08	23.72	9.10	7.2	58.65	13.76	3.12	16.79	6.12	13.91	10.10	181.98	45.42
1997	6.0	16.97	26.05	9.22	7.1	52.00	12.60	4.50	15.63	5.28	14.00	9.40	178.00	46.00

D27 Output of Electric Energy (in giga Watt hours)

[28] Yugoslavia. (Ex-Yugoslavia as follows)

	Bosnia-Herzegovina	Croatia	Macedonia	Slovenia
1992	11.68	8.89	6.1	12.09
1993	11.00	9.36	6.0	11.69
1994	1.92	8.28	5.5	12.63
1995	2.20	8.86	6.1	12.65
1996	4.08	10.55	6.5	12.77
1997	4.98	9.69	6.7	13.16

E EXTERNAL TRADE

1. External Trade Aggregate Current Values   page 571
2. External Trade with Main Trading Partners   page 587

Because it has long been an important source of revenue to governments, external trade provides more statistical material at an earlier date for most countries than does any other economic activity. Indeed some statistics go back to mediaeval times. These are all partial, however, for it was not until some of the rising nation-states of the seventeenth century began to see external trade as an instrument of policy that the statistics covered more than the goods on which duties could be conveniently levied. In any case, in all countries the customs duties were practically always 'farmed' until the late eighteenth century, though the central government took over in England as early as 1696.

Unfortunately for modern users of the trade statistics, it was the standard practice until some time in the nineteenth century to record the aggregate values of trade in terms of officially fixed values for each commodity (or, at any rate, for most commodities). Since these were not always kept up to date, the aggregates tended to become increasingly misleading as a representation of the actual values of imports and exports at any time.[1] For this reason, the statistics are only shown here from the time when declared or computed actual values were used, or from which consistent and reliable estimates of these values have been made.

Most continental European countries have recorded their external trade in two forms: 'general' trade and 'special' trade. The former includes all commodities entering or leaving the country; the latter relates only to commodities intended for internal use or to commodities which have been in some sense 'produced' within the country. It is the latter, the 'special' trade, which has been shown in this section whenever possible. It must be noted, however, that the exact definition of 'special' trade has not been rigidly fixed, though the scope for major variations is obviously lacking. Moreover, statements of origin or of intention to sell can be both honestly and dishonestly mistaken. These sources of unreliability or lack of true comparability in the figures are not likely to be of very great significance. Perhaps more important, at any rate in the early part of the nineteenth century, is the inherent defect in trade statistics which results from smuggling. Probably this has never been entirely absent wherever there have been sizeable tariffs on articles which are valuable in relation to their bulk. For the eighteenth and early nineteenth centuries, when tariff levels were generally quite high and preventive staff were not usually either well-paid or efficient, the tales of extensive smuggling seem to be well justified.[2] The approach to free trade in the middle two decades of the nineteenth century must have rendered much of this activity redundant. By the time tariffs were once again raised, policing was much more effective than it had been earlier, though certainly never completely proof against smuggling of small valuable items such as watches. For practical purposes, then, it seems possible to take the statistics in this section as reasonably, though not perfectly, accurate from the middle of the nineteenth century onwards.

It is clear that one major influence on the course of these statistics has been the changes which have taken place in price levels, above all since 1914. It has not been found practicable to include a list showing variations in the exchange rates of European countries for the whole period, though these obviously have a bearing on any comparative analysis of external trade. An idea of the changing price levels in each country for at least the crucial period since 1914 can be got from section H below, coupled with the alterations in the internal value of the currency unit listed on p. xii above.

Table E2, showing the trade of each country with others which have at various times been its chief trading partners, presents its own peculiar problems. The main difficulty is that the records of no two countries tell precisely the same story about their trade with each other. The chief reason for this is confusion between countries of shipment, of consignment, and of origin. Different systems have been used at various times in most countries but even when allowance can be made for this, it is clear that the system supposedly in use has not always been followed with precise accuracy in every case.

---

[1]   This problem in relation to the English statistics is admirably set out in G.N. Clark, *Guide to English Commercial Statistics, 1696–1782* (London, 1938). Belgium, France, the Netherlands, and the Scandinavian countries operated similar systems up to some point in the middle of the nineteenth century.

[2]   Discussion of the problem of smuggling so far as Britain is concerned can be found in G.D. Ramsay, *English Overseas Trade during the Centuries of Emergence* (London, 1957), pp. 166–206, and in W.A. Cole, 'Trends in Eighteenth Century Smuggling', *Economic History Review*, second series X, 3 (1958) and in a later comment by Hoh-Cheung and Lorna H. Mui in ibid., XXVIII, 1 (1975).

It would be extremely useful to have statistics showing a breakdown of the trade between various countries by major commodity groups. Unfortunately, changes in definition occur in the published statistics of every country with great frequency, and to produce reasonably consistent and comparable figures for even one country is a considerable enterprise.[3] Reluctantly, therefore, such commodity statistics have been omitted. They are available for recent periods in the publications on trade of the United Nations and of the OECD, and on an individual country basis in the volumes of historical statistics noted on p. viii and in works such as those of Walther Hoffman and his associates.[4] Data on the volume of external trade in a few commodities can be found in sections C and D above.

---

[3] As I discovered when compiling tables for the Overseas Trade chapter of the *Abstract of British Historical Statistics* (Cambridge, 1962).
[4] W.G. Hoffman *et al*, *Das Wachstum der Deutschen Wirtschaft seit der Mitte des 19 Jahrhunderts* (Berlin, etc., 1965), pp. 149–165.

E1 EXTERNAL TRADE AGGREGATE CURRENT VALUE (in millions)

1796–1844

Year	Austria/Hungary[1] (kronen)		Denmark (Kronen)		Finland (marks)		France[3] (francs)		Russia (paper rubels)		Spain[6] (pesetas)		Sweden (kroner)		United Kingdom (pounds)		
	I	E	I	E	I	E	I	E	I	E	I	E	I	E	I	DE	R
1796	...	...	...	...	...	...	...	...	...	...	...	...	...	...	40	30	9
1797	...	...	...	...	...	...	...	...	...	...	...	...	...	...	34	28	9
1798	...	...	...	...	...	...	...	...	...	...	...	...	...	...	50	32	11
1799	...	...	...	...	...	...	253	300	...	...	...	...	...	...	51	37	9
1800	...	...	...	...	...	...	323	272	...	...	...	...	...	...	62	38	15
1801	...	...	...	...	...	...	415	305	...	...	...	...	...	...	69	41	13
1802	...	...	...	...	...	...	465	325	46	63	...	...	...	...	55	46	13
1803	...	...	...	...	...	...	430	347	45	67	...	...	...	...	54	37	9
1804	...	...	...	...	...	...	441	380	43	59	...	...	...	...	57	38	11
1805	...	...	...	...	...	...	492	375	46	72	...	...	...	...	61	38	10
1806	...	...	...	...	...	...	477	456	43	63	...	...	...	...	53	41	9
1807	...	...	...	...	...	...	393	376	33	54	...	...	...	...	54	37	8
1808	...	...	...	...	...	...	320	331	...	...	...	...	...	...	52	37	7
1809	...	...	...	...	...	...	288	332	...	...	...	...	...	...	74	47	14
1810	...	...	...	...	...	...	339	366	...	...	...	...	...	...	89	48	13
1811	...	...	...	...	...	...	299	328	...	...	...	...	...	...	51	33	7
1812	...	...	...	...	2	5	308	419	76	139	...	...	...	...	56	42	9
1813	...	...	...	...	6	6	251	354	122	132	...	...	...	...	...	...	...
1814	...	...	...	...	6	7	239	346	113	194	...	...	...	...	81	46	25
1815	...	...	...	...	5	7	199	422									
1816	...	...	...	...	6	9	243	548	114	219	...	...	...	...	71	52	17
1817	...	...	...	...	7	10	332	464	129	200	...	...	...	...	50	42	13
1818	...	...	...	3	7	10	336	502	167	295	...	...	...	...	61	42	10
1819	...	...	...	3	6	9	295	460	181	256	...	...	...	...	81	47	12
1820	...	...	...	7	4	7	335	543	177	215	...	...	...	...	56	35	10
1821	...	...	...	8	4	6	394	405	245	223	...	...	...	...	54	36	10
1822	...	...	...	7	5	6	426	385	208	200	104	108	...	...	46	37	10
1823	...	...	...	7	5	7	362	391	157	188	110	109	...	...	45	37	8
1824	...	...	...	8	5	8	455	441	160	198	113	88	...	...	52	35	7
1825	...	...	...	10	6	9	534[3]	667[3]	179	205	168	89	...	...	51	38	8
			...				401	544	191	245	142	138	...	...	74	39	8
1826	...	...	...	9	7	9	436	461	194	190	137	85	...	...	50	32	7
1827	...	...	...	17	5	11	414	507	208	238	137	104	...	...	59	37	7
1828	...	...	...	13	6	9	454	511	201	206	125	106	...	...	57	37	7
1829	...	...	...	14	7	9	483	504	216	227	130	113	...	...	54	36	7
1830	...	...	...	17	8	9	489	453	198	272	116	97	...	...	56	38	6
1831	137	160	...	19	6	8	374	456	177	244	113	122	...	...	62	37	7
1832	159	179	...	17	9	9	505	507	196	261	93	89	21	22	53	37	7
1833	163	182	...	16	9	10	491	560	193	249	126	135	21	25	59	40	7
1834	162	172	...	19	10	10	504	511	218	229	106	118	22	24	65	42	8
1835	184	177	...	19	12	11	520	577	223	227	142	115	23	28	68	47	9
1836	199	193	...	20	13	11	565	629	237	282	168	144	26	28	84	53	9
1837	195	180	...	24	13	12	569	514	252	264	129	129	25	26	70	42	9
1838	207	211	...	25	11	15	657	659	248	313	141	115	29	33	80	50	9
1839	207	212	...	29	11	12	651	677	249	341	148	151	29	32	91	53	10
									million new paper rubels[5]								
1840	222	217	...	30	13	13	747	695	78.1	85.4	143	140	27	31	91	51	10
1841	213	224	37	28	17	14	805	761	80.8	89.3	138	124	31	34	84	52	10
1842	223	217	36	27	15	14	847	644	84.6	85.0	148	135	29	27	76	47	8
1843	235	219	35	29	16	15	846	687	75.0	82.2	134	125	26	25	71	52	8
1844	242	230	45	45	16	16	867	790	78.5	93/4	157	151	26	32	79	59	8

E1   External Trade Aggregate Current Value (in millions)

	Austria/Hungary[1] (kronen)		Belgium[2] (francs)		Bulgaria (leva)		Denmark (kroner)		Finland (marks)	
	I	E	I	E	I	E	I	E	I	E
1845	244	226	...	...	...	...	55	44	18	15
1846	266	214	217	149	...	...	61	52	20	14
1847	269	236	241	171	...	...	71	58	19	15
1848	176	97	182	151	...	...	55	43	20	13
1849	185	125	207	179	...	...	63	42	22	15
1850	334	220	237	264	...	...	67	48	23	16
1851	316	273	218	200	...	...	67	47	31	19
1852	419	292	267	230	...	...	57	50	20	20
1853	[415][8]	[457][8]	298	294	...	...	66	61	24	20
1854	438	458	343	389	...	...	78	77	18	9
1855	497	488	385	344	...	...	95	87	25	13
1856	602	528	435	370	...	...	99	82	38	21
1857	586	485	435	414	...	...	99	66	44	23
1858	617	551	440	381	...	...	61	51	31	22
1859	538	585	451	413	...	...	75	62	31	25
1860	458[1]	614[1]	517	470	...	...	79	59	38	27
1861	472	615	556	453	...	...	84	62	49	33
1862	430	666	587	502	...	...	81	61	63	34
1863	525	606	610	534	...	...	82[10]	58[10]	61	39
1864	545	703	684	596	...	...	70	50	51	38
1865	558	730	756	602	...	...	116	92	65	41
1866	490	761	747	643	...	...	120	94	51	38
1867	589	815	775	597	...	...	135	91	58	43
1868	775	858	864	657	...	...	129	89	62	48
1869	841	876	904	692	...	...	126	87	70	50
1870	872	791	921	690	...	...	126	113	68	50
1871	1,082	935	1,277	889	...	...	143	113	76	61
1872	1,228	776	1,278	1,051	...	...	163	136	93	68
1873	1,166	847	1,423	1,159	...	...	200	140	107	89
1874	1,255	1,006	1,293	1,115	...	...	209[10]	156[10]	137	94
									197	174
1875	1,099	1,102	1,307	1,102	...	...	210	152	146	86
1876	1,069	1,190	1,449	1,064	...	...	208	160	128	100
1877	1,111	1,333	1,426	1,082	...	...	205	144	138	106
1878	1,104	1,309	1,473	1,112	...	...	175	137	118	89
1879	1,113	1,368	1,526	1,190	32	20	182	141	105	95
1880	1,227	1,352	1,681	1,217	48	33	208	177	127	124
1881	1,284	1,463	1,630	1,303	58	32	224	162	142	108
1882	1,308	1,563	1,608	1,326	42	34	226	161	153[11]	120[1]
1883	1,250	1,500	1,552	1,343	49	46	255	167	147	118
1884	1,225	1,383	1,426	1,338	51	35	246	150	137	112
1885	1,116	1,344	1,347	1,200	44	45	223	133	108	89
1886	1,078	1,397	1,335	1,182	64	50	188	139	97	77
1887	1,137	1,346	1,432	1,241	65	46	221	154	105	76
1888	1,066	1,458	1,534	1,244	66	64	245	157	111	90
1889	1,178	1,532	1,556	1,459	73	81	268	173	132	102
1890	1,221	1,543	1,672	1,437	85	71	268	195	140	92
1891	1,227	1,573	1,800	1,519	81	71	294	209	146	103
1892	1,245	1,445	1,537	1,369	77	75	280	208	145	93
1893	1,341	1,611	1,575	1,356	91	91	284	198	126	113
1894	1,400	1,591	1,575	1,304	99	73	307	222	138	135
1895	1,445	1,484	1,680	1,385	69	78	312	217	150	142
1896	1,412	1,548	1,777	1,468	77	109	319	219	172	158
1897	1,511	1,532	1,873	1,626	84	60	326	243	202	167
1898	1,640	1,615	2,045	1,787	73	67	367	239	237	178
1899	1,609	1,862	2,260	1,949	60	53	400	270	251	183

E1 External Trade Aggregate Current Value (in millions)

	France (francs)		Germany[13] (marks)		Greece[4] (drachmas)		Italy[15] (litre)		Netherlands (gulden)	
	I	E	I	E	I	E	I	E	I	E
1845	856	848	...	...	...	...	...	...	...	...
1846	920	852	...	...	...	...	...	...	162	118
1847	956	720	...	...	...	...	...	...	169	126
1848	474	690	...	...	...	...	...	...	181	124
1849	724	936	...	...	21	13	...	...	180	127
1850	791	1,068		...	...	...	...	...	188	137
1851	765	1,158	...	...	23	12	...	...	200	144
1852	989	1,257	...	...	22	9	...	...	205	157
1853	1,196	1,542	...	...	18	8	...	...	204	154
1854	1,292	1,414	...	...	19	6	...	...	244	193
1855	1,594	1,558	...	...	24	10	...	...	249	217
1856	1,990	1,893	...	...	27	23	...	...	294	225
1857	1,873	1,866	...	...	33	22	...	...	300	231
1858	1,563	1,887	...	...	36	22	...	...	313	231
1859	1,641	2,266	...	...	41	22	...	...	288	242
1860	1,897	2,277	...	...	48	24	...	...	316	251
1861	2,442	1,926	...	...	43	25	821	478	335	273
1862	2,199	2,243	...	...	39	25	830	576	329	253
1863	2,426	2,643	...	...	50[4]	20[4]	902	633	351	287
1864	2,523	2,924	...	...	49	22	984	573	381	344
1865	2,642	3,088	...	...	67	37	965	558	403	344
1866	2,794	3,181	...	...	69	37	869	613	425	338
1867	3,027	2,826	...	...	67	43	884	732	439	340
1868	3,304	2,790	...	...	66	36	895	786	469	368
1869	3,153	3,075	...	...	75	42	935	791	461	391
1870	2,867[12]	2,802[12]	...	...	76	34	895	755	507	399
1871	3,567	2,873	...	...	87	56	961	1,075	586	460
1872	3,570	3,762	...	...	88	50	1,183	1,162	617	514
1873	3,555	3,787	...	...	82	57	1,261	1,131	682	508
1874	3,508	3,701	...	...	88	58	1,296	978	718	538
1875	3,537	3,873	...	...	102	67	1,207	1,022	713	533
1876	3,989	3,576	...	...	87	53	1,307	1,208	750	541
1877	3,680	3,436	...	...	96	52	1,142[15]	934[15]	809	563
1878	4,176	3,180	...	...	91	57	1,062	1,021	847	582
1879	4,595	3,231	...	...	102	56	1,252	1,072	840	630
1880	5,033	3,468	2,814	2,923	98[4]	60[4]	1,187	1,104	840	630
1881	4,863	3,561	2,962	3,030	116	70	1,240	1,165	920	690
1882	4,822	3,574	3,099	3,224	143	76	1,227	1,152	992	752
1883	4,804	3,452	3,221	3,259	121	83	1,288	1,188	1,073	684
1884	4,343	3,232	3,236	3,190	116	74	1,319	1,071	1,129	841
1885	4,088	3,088	2,923	2,854	114	76	1,460	951	1,092	891
1886	4,208	3,249	2,874	2,976	117	79	1,458	1,028	1,103	950
1887	4,026	3,246	3,109	3,136	132	103	1,605	1,002	1,137	992
1888	4,107	3,247	3,253	3,207	109	96	1,175	892	1,272	1,115
1889	4,317	3,704	4,015	3,167	133	108	1,391	951	1,245	1,094
1890	4,437	3,753	4,162	3,335	121	96	1,319	896	1,300	1,088
1891	4,768	3,570	4,151	3,176	140	107	1,127	877	1,356	1,141
1892	4,188	3,461	4,010	2,954	119	82	1,173	958	1,282	1,134
1893	3,854	3,236	3,962	3,092	91	88[14]	1,191	964	1,409	1,117
1894	3,850	3,078	3,942	2,961	110	74	1,095	1,027	1,461	1,115
1895	3,720	3,374	4,119	3,318	108	73	1,187	1,038	1,444	1,178
1896	3,799	3,401	4,307	3,525	116	72	1,180[15]	1,052[15]	1,635	1,338
1897	3,956	3,598	4,681	3,635	116	82	1,192	1,092	1,706	1,479
1898	4,472	3,511	5,076	3,757	138[14]	88	1,413	1,204	1,796	1,516
1899	4,518	4,153	5,463	4,217	131	94	1,507	1,431	1,917	1,583

E1 External Trade Aggregate Current Value (in millions)

1845–1899

	Norway (kroner)		Portugal[18] (milreis or escudos)		Romania[20] (piastres)		Russia (rubels)		Spain[6] (pesetas)	
	I	E	I	E	I	E	I	E	I	E
1845	...	...	...	...	...	...	83.2	92.2	152	152
1846	...	...	...	...	...	...	87.0	102	172	169
1847	...	...	...	...	...	...	89.2	148	165	195
1848	...	...	...	...	...	...	90.8	88.0	170	129
1849	...	...	...	...	...	...	96.2	95.9	153	137
1850	...	...	...	...	...	...	93.9	98.1	174	164
1851	43	43	...	...	...	...	104	97.4	169	145
1852	43	42	...	...	...	...	101	115	185	136
1853	49	46	...	...	...	...	102	148	192	188
1854	55	42	...	...	...	...	70.4	65.3	215	131
1855	61	45	...	...	...	...	72.7	39.5	257	323
1856	67	48	...	...	...	...	123	160	332	323
1857	63	46	...	...	...	...	152	170	376	336
1858	45	42	...	...	...	...	149	151	380	204
1859	56	48	...	...	...	...	159	166	317	247
1860	63	53	...	...	...	...	159	181	375	272
1861	79	49	27	14	...	...	167	177	454	305
1862	75	55	...	...	...	274	153	180	464	246
1863	80	61	...	...	175	308	155	155	565	295
1864	77	50	...	...	143	366	175	187	568	321
1865	90[17]	54[17]	25	20	...	...	164	209	472	261
1866	105	69	27	19	108	94	205	223	426	296
1867	97	70	26	17	132	124	265	245	359	381
1868	105	69	25	18	150	189	261	227	448	390
1869	93	78	23	18	133	169	342	264	385	434
					(lei)					
1870	103	81	25	20	72	158	336	360	394	337
1871	102	81	27	21	90	173	369	369	456	439
1872	137	105	29	23	85	159	435	327	602	496
1873	167	121	34	24	92	136	443	364	414	585
1874	186	121	28	23	123	135	471	432	528	508
1875	177	103	36	24	101	145	531	382	478	538
1876	167	118	35	23	166	235	478	401	529	452
1877	190	109	32	25	336	141	321	528	496	569
1878	140	92	32	20	307	217	596	618	482	536
1879	132	89	34	21	254	239	588	628	522	544
1880	151	109	35	25	255	219	623	499	624	737
1881	165	121	36	21	275	207	518	506	574	759
1882	160	123	37[19]	25[19]	269	245	567	618	707	768
1883	161	116	31	23	360	221	562	640	838	838
1884	159	112	33	22	295	184	537	590	701	721
1885	146	102	33	23	269	248	435	538	695	766
1886	135	103	37	26	296	255	427	484	726	623
1887	134	107	37	21	315	266	400	617	690	760
1888	158	122	38	23	310	256	386	784	676	817
1889	192	133	42	23	368	274	432	751	828	851
1890	209	131	44	22	363	276	407	692	845	876
1891	223	130	40	21	437	275	372	707	742	962
1892	200	126	31	25	381	285	400	476	644	998
1893	205	136	38	23	430	371	400	599	615	906
1894	206	132	36	24	422	294	554	669	754	904
1895	223	137	40	27	305	265	526	689	707	915
1896	240	148	40	26	338	324	586	689	807	1,244
1897	264	168	40	27	356	224	560	730	902	1,349
1898	280	159	49	31	390	283	618	733	826	1,314
1899	310	159	51	29	333	149	661	627	1,025	1,088

E1 External Trade Aggregate Current Value (in millions)

	Sweden (kronor)		Switzerland (francs)		United Kingdom (pounds)			Serbia (dinars)	
	I	E	I	E	I	DE	R	I	E
1845	26	37	...	...	88	60	9	...	...
1846	28	37	...	...	87	58	9	...	...
1847	31	46	...	...	112	59	12	...	...
1848	35	32	...	...	88	53	8	...	...
1849	38	36	...	...	101	64	12	...	...
1850	36	36	...	...	103	71	12	...	...
1851	42	40	...	...	110	74	13	...	...
1852	44	41	...	...	110	78	13	...	...
1853	52	52	...	...	149[7]	99	17[7]	...	...
1854	79	79	...	...	152	97	19	...	...
1855	85	96	...	...	144	96	21	...	...
1856	106	92	...	...	173	116	23	...	...
1857	85	78	...	...	188	122	24	...	...
1858	57	59	...	...	165	117	23	...	...
1859	74	79	...	...	179	130	25	...	...
1860	79	86	...	...	211	136	29	...	...
1861	107	80	...	...	217	125	35	...	...
1862	97	87	...	...	225	124	42	...	...
1863	96	92	...	...	249	147	50	...	...
1864	95	94	...	...	275	160	52	...	...
1865	105	108	...	...	271	166	53	...	...
1866	112	106			295	189	50		
1867	133	127	...	...	275	181	45	26	25
1868	134	118	...	...	295	180	48	30	38
1869	132	123	...	...	295	190	47	27	34
1870	140	152	...	...	303	200	44	28	31
1871	163	159	...	...	331	223	61	28	28
1872	207	200	...	...	355	256	58	29	33
1873	261	219	...	...	371	255	56	27	32
1874	297	225	...	...	370	240	58	32	35
1875	261	204	...	...	374	223	58	31	35
1876	283	223	...	...	375	201	56	...	...
1877	300	215	...	...	394	199	53	...	...
1878	232	184	...	...	369	193	53	...	...
1879	213	185	...	...	363	192	57	42	39
1880	271	236	...	...	411	223	63	46	35
1881	282	222	...	...	397	234	63	43	40
1882	293	254	...	...	413	241	65	48	40
1883	328	256	...	...	427	240	66	50	40
1884	320	239	...	...	390	233	63	51	40
1885	337	246	756	666	371	213	58	40	38
1886	296	228	799	667	350	213	56	52	41
1887	291	247	837	671	362	222	59	36	36
1888	323	282	827	673	388	235	64	35	39
1889	372	302	907	695	428	249	67	35	39
1890	376	304	954	703	421	264	65	38	46
1891	368	323	932	672	435	247	62	43	52
1892	359	328	869	658	424	227	64	37	46
1893	332	328	828	646	405	218	59	41	49
1894	345	298	826	621	408	216	58	35	46
1895	343	311	916	663	417	226	60	28	43
1896	357	340	994	688	442	240	56	33	53
1897	399	358[22]	1,027	693	451	234	60	45	56
1898	446	345	1,065	724	471	233	61	41	57
1899	503	358	1,160	796	485	255[24]	65	46	66
						264			

E1 External Trade Aggregate Current Value (in millions)

	Albania (gold francs)		Austria/Hungary (kronen)		Belgium[2] (francs)		Bulgaria[9] (leva)		Czechoslovakia (koruna)	
	I	E	I	E	I	E	I	E	I	E
1900	...	...	1,696	1,942	2,216	1,923	46	54	...	...
1901	...	...	1,653	1,885	2,221	1,828	70	83	...	...
1902	...	...	1,720	1,914	2,381	1,926	71	104	...	...
1903	...	...	1,877	2,130	2,656	2,110	82	108	...	...
1904	...	...	2,048	2,089	2,782	2,183	130	158	...	...
1905	...	...	2,146	2,244	3,068	2,334	122	148	...	...
1906	...	...	2,341	2,380	3,454	2,794	108	115	...	...
1907	...	...	2,502	2,457	3,774	2,334	125	126	...	...
1908	...	...	2,398	2,255	3,327	2,848	130	112	...	...
1909	...	...	2,746	2,319	3,704	2,810	160	111	...	...
1910	...	...	2,853	2,419	4,265	3,407	177	129	...	...
1911	...	...	3,192	2,404	4,509	3,580	199	185	...	...
1912	...	...	3,557	2,734	4,958	3,952	213	156	...	...
1913	...	...	3,407	2,770	5,050	3,716	189	93	...	...
1914	...	...	2,902	2,095	...	...	...	...	...	...
1915	...	...	3,800	1,335	...	...	...	...	...	...
1916	...	...	6,009	1,540	...	...	...	...	...	...
1917	...	...	...	...	...	...	...	...	...	...
1918	...	...	...	...	...	...	...	...	...	...
1919	...	...	...	...	5,246	2,300	964	552	...	...
			Austria (schilling)							
1920	18	2	2,450	1,342	12,942	8,862	2,255	2,056	23,912	28,515
1921	18	2	2,446	1,302	10,198	7,273	2,976	2,801	23,685	29,458
1922	12	3	2,529	1,589	9,229[2]	6,234[2]	4,066	5,926	13,498	19,633
1923	23	8	2,765	1,616	13,205	9,725	5,154	4,343	10,821	13,903
1924	20	12	3,448	1,970	17,712	13,865	5,678	5,876	15,855	17,035
1925	22	17	2,833	1,923	17,881	14,807	7,284	6,242	17,618	18,821
1926	25	12	2,766	1,703	23,063	19,999	6,247	5,618	15,277	17,857
1927	25	11	3,082	2,036	29,139	26,697	6,129	6,627	17,962	20,135
1928	32	15	3,230	2,200	32,060	30,954	7,041	6,231	19,208	21,224
1929	39	15	3,263	2,189	35,624	31,880	8,325	6,397	19,988	20,499
1930	33	12	2,699	1,851	31,094	26,159	4,587[9] / 4,588	6,191[9] / 6,191	15,715	17,474
1931	30	8	2,161	1,291	23,971	23,179	4,659	5,934	11,801	13,149
1932	23	5	1,384	764	16,343	15,123	3,383	3,383	8,158	7,392
1933	16	6	1,148	775	15,243	14,288	2,846	2,846	6,125	5,923
1934	12	4	1,153	857	14,022	13,795	2,247	2,535	6,392	7,288
1935	14	6	1,206	895	17,446	16,126	3,009	3,253	6,743	7,947
1936	17	7	1,249	952	21,707	19,745	3,151	3,910	7,915	8,036
1937	19	10	1,454	1,217	27,892	25,516	4,662	5,020	10,982	11,983
1938	23	10	...	...	23,069	21,671	4,930	5,578	[6,889][25]	[8,511][25]
	(leks)									
1938	1,004	339								
1939	...	...	...	...	19,811	21,934	5,197	6,065	25	25
1940	...	...	...	...	8,292[2]	10,808[2]	7,028	7,019	25	25
1941	...	...	...	...	7,283	5,308	10,239	9,234	25	25
1942	...	...	...	...	6,357	4,598	12,929	13,437	25	25
1943	...	...	...	...	6,209	8,421	15,131	16,271	25	25
1944	...	...	...	...	3,588	5,289	6,478	11,357	25	25
1945	81	22	...	...	13,763[2]	3,986[2]	5,820	12,397	[777][25]	[500][25]
1946	102	95	...	...	57,184	29,836	17,514	14,942	10,308	14,283
1947	1,513	237	1,191	842	85,559	61,655	21,416	24,533	28,920[26]	28,550
									(new koruna)	
1948	909	417	3,900	1,984	87,518	74,121	37,741	36,351	4,906	5,422
1949	645	291	6,366	3,229	81,858	80,092	...	...	5,170	5,805

E1 External Trade Aggregate Current Value (in millions)

	Denmark (kroner)		Finland (marks)		France (francs)		Germany[13] (marks)	
	I	E	I	E	I	E	I	E
1900	416	282	270	195	4,698	4,109	5,769	4,611
1901	397	291	215	184	4,369	4,013	5,421	4,431
1902	434	318	233	199	4,394	4,252	5,631	4,678
1903	444	352	268	212	4,802	4,252	6,003	5,015
1904	466	359	267	215	4,502	4,451	6,354	5,223
1905	483	391	268	247	4,779	4,867	7,129	5,732
1906	559	394	314	280	5,627	5,265	8,021[29]	6,359[29]
1907	601	417	379	265	6,223	5,596	8,745	6,847
1908	551	440	364	243	5,640	5,051	7,663	6,399
1909	567	444	367	255	6,246	5,718	8,519	6,597
1910	577	485	384	288	7,174	6,234	8,927	7,475
1911	623	537	445	318	8,066	6,077	9,683	8,106
1912	739	597	470	338	8,231	6,713	10,674	8,967
1913	777	637	495	402	8,421	6,880	10,751	10,097
1914	718	780	380	282	6,402	4,869	...	...
1915	1,029	979	578	256	11,036	3,937	...	...
1916	1,250	1,177	963	498	20,640	6,214	...	...
1917	1,024	970	1,232	440	27,554	6,013	...	...
1918	910	710	505	227	22,306[12]	4,723[12]	...[12]	...[12]
1919	2,394	740	2,510	880	35,799	11,880	...[30][31]	...[30][31]
1920	2,943	1,591	3,627	2,926	49,905	26,894	3,929	3,709
1921	1,549	1,410	3,586	3,389	22,754	19,772	5,732	[2,976][32]
1922	1,456	1,176	3,970	4,468	24,275[11]	21,379[11]	6,301	6,188
1923	1,907	1,539	4,600	4,393	32,859	30,867	4,808[31]	5,338[31]
							6,150	6,102[33]
1924	2,218	1,976	4,716	4,971	40,163	42,369	9,132	6,674
1925	1,937	1,789	5,520	5,574	44,095	45,755	12,429	9,284
1926	1,528	1,406	5,668	5,637	59,598	59,678	9,984	10,415
1927	1,578	1,447	6,386	6,324	53,050	54,925	14,114	10,801
1928	1,647	1,541	8,013	6,245	53,436	51,375	13,931	12,055
1929	1,715	1,616	7,001	6,430	58,221[28]	50,139[28]	13,359	13,486
1930	1,656	1,524	5,226	5,404	52,511	42,835	10,349	12,036
1931	1,410	1,260	3,457	4,457	42,206	30,436	6,713	9,592
1932	1,104	1,086	3,502	4,631	29,808	19,705	4,653	5,741
1933	1,225	1,164	3,926	5,298	28,431	18,474	4,199	4,872
1934	1,307	1,176	4,775	6,226	23,097	17,850	4,448[30]	4,178[30]
1935	1,287	1,213	5,332	6,240	20,974	15,496	4,156	4,270
1936	1,442	1,327	6,211	7,223	25,414	15,492	4,228	4,778
1937	1,649[27]	1,541[27]	9,162	9,380	42,391	23,939	5,495	5,919
	1,674	1,569						
1938	1,625	1,535	8,488	8,398	46,065	30,590	5,449	5,264
1939	1,740	1,578	7,568	7,710	43,785	31,590	5,207	5,653
1940	1,377	1,517	9,164	2,875	45,770	17,511	5,012	4,868
1941	1,311	1,278	10,200	4,321	24,936	15,777	6,925	6,840
1942	1,210	1,053	11,731	5,991	25,952	29,664	8,691	7,560
1943	1,225	1,338	12,874	8,713	13,960	35,407	8,258	8,588
1944	1,167	1,361	8,910	6,332	9,769	25,557	...	...

	Denmark (kroner)		Finland (marks)		France (francs)		West Germany (marks)		East Germany (valuta marks)	
	I	E	I	E	I	E	E	I	E	I
1945	696	904	6,793	5,228	57,027	11,399	...	...	...	...

million new marks

1946	2,848	1,618	243	231	264,737	101,388	...	...	...	...
1947	3,090	2,313	470	432	397,135	223,321	...	...	...	...
1948	3,424	2,731	664	553	672,673	434,047	3,164	1,817	...	...
1949	4,211	3,560	663	644	926,326	783,906	7,330	3,806	1,315	1,387

E1 External Trade Aggregate Current Value (in millions)

	Greece[4] (drachmae)		Hungary (pengos)		Ireland (pounds)		Italy[15] (litre)		Netherlands (gulden)	
	I	E	I	E	I	E	I	E	I	E
1900	131	103	...	...	...	...	1,700	1,338	1,968	1,695
1901	141	94	...	...	...	...	1,718	1,374	2,047	1,734
1902	137	80	...	...	...	...	1,723	1,464	2,172	1,828
1903	137	86	...	...	...	...	1,813	1,483	2,278	1,951
1904	137	91	...	...	...	...	1,878	1,564	2,420	1,986
1905	142	84	...	...	...	...	2,016	1,694	2,584	1,994
1906	145	124	...	...	...	...	2,514[15]	1,894[15]	2,524	2,084
1907	149	118	...	...	...	...	2,881	1,938	2,692	2,212
1908	155	111	...	...	...	...	2,913	1,718	2,824	2,181
1909	138	102	...	...	...	...	3,112	1,855	3,137	2,455
1910	161[19]	145[19]	...	...	...	...	3,246	2,065	3,265	2,632
1911	174	141	...	...	...	...	3,389	2,190	3,333	2,732
1912	158	146	...	...	...	...	3,702	2,383	3,613	3,113
1913	178[4]	119[4]	...	...	...	...	3,646	2,497	3,918	3,083
1914	319	179	...	...	...	...	2,923	2,195	2,889	2,505
1915	289	218	...	...	...	...	4,704	2,512	2,111	1,749
1916	399	155	...	...	...	...	8,390	3,053	1,883	1,347
1917	223	113	...	...	...	...	13,990	3,276	970	821
1918	734[4]	297[4]	...	...	...	...	16,039	3,305	618	386
1919	1,522	764	...	...	...	...	16,623	6,004	2,835	1,426
1920	2,177	682	484	191	...	...	26,822	11,628	3,345	1,722
1921	1,764	944	604	295	...	...	16,914	8,043	2,267	1,385
1922	3,170[4]	2,489[4]	626	383	...	...	15,741	9,160	2,032	1,230
1923	6,076	2,544	491	392	...	...	17,157	10,950	2,017	1,312
1924	8,039	3,266	815	667	69	51	19,373	14,270	2,366	1,689
1925	10,177	4,574	865	848	63	44	26,200	18,170	2,455	1,809
1926	9,967	5,440	941	877	61	42	25,879	18,544	2,443	1,749
1927	12,600	6,040	1,182	808	61	44	20,375	15,519	2,550	1,900
1928	12,417	6,331	1,211	826	60	46	21,920	14,444	2,688	1,990
1929	13,276	6,960	1,064	1,039	61	47	21,303[15]	14,767[15]	2,766	2,005
1930	10,524	5,799	823	912	57	45	17,347	12,119	2,427	1,728
1931	8,763	4,165	539	570	50	36	11,643	10,210	1,896	1,315
1932	7,870	4,576	329	335	43	26	8,268	6,812	1,306	850
1933	8,426	5,155	313	391	36	19	7,432	5,991	1,254	754
1934	8,831	5,474	345	404	39	18	7,675	5,224	1,079	736
1935	10,766	7,095	402	452	37	20	7,790	5,238	978	711
1936	11,847	7,384	437	504	40	23	6,039	5,542	1,071	796
1937	15,548	9,546	484	588	44	23	13,943	10,444	1,605	1,204
1938	14,759	10,149	417	522	41	24	11,273	10,497	1,460	1,079
1939	12,281	9,200	493	604	43	27	10,309	10,823	1,560	1,006
1940	12,243	9,079	603	516	47	33	13,220	11,519	1,023	649
1941	4,384	3,899	740	799	30	32	11,467	14,514	744	635
1942	12,589	5,405	946	1,152	35	33	14,038	16,047	482	617
1943	28,182	10,202	1,148	1,300	26	28	...	...	420	641
1944	...	11,328	809	950	29	30	...	...	...	...
1945	2,830	1,225	...[34]	...[34]	41	36	...	...	...	...
	(tho m drachmae)		**(forints)**							
1946	515	202	371	420	72	39	...	...	2,205	816
							(tho m lire)			
1947	930	387	1,459	1,045	131	40	937	341	4,279	1,893
1948	1,822[4]	470[4]	1,975	1,933	137	49	844	576	4,965	2,719
1949	2,048	575	3,382	3,293	130	61	883	641	5,332	3,851

E1 External Trade Aggregate Current Value (in millions)

	Norway (kroner)		Poland[35] (zlotys)		Portugal (escudos)		Romania (lei)		Russia/U.S.S.R. (rubels)	
	I	E	I	E	I	E	I	E	I	E
1900	311	173	...	...	60	31	217	280	626	716
1901	287	165	...	...	58	28	292	354	593	762
1902	290	181	...	...	56	28	283	375	599	860
1903	293	193	...	...	59	31	270	356	682	1,001
1904	292	193	...	...	62	31	311	262	651	1,006
1905	312	218	...	...	61	29	338	457	635	1,077
1906	344[17]	246[17]	...	...	60	31	422	491	801	1,095
1907	362	229	...	...	61	30	431	554	847	1,053
1908	355	219	...	...	67	28	414	379	913	998
1909	366	243	...	...	65	31	368	465	906	1,428
1910	402	283	...	...	70	36	410	617	1,084	1,449
1911	469	298	...	...	68	34	570	692	1,162	1,591
1912	526	336	...	...	75	34	638	642	1,172	1,519
1913	552	393	...	...	89	35	590	671	1,374	1,520
1914	567	410	...	...	69	27	504	452	...	...
1915	868	677	...	...	76	34	333	570	1,131	397
1916	1,354	988	...	...	129	56	...	...	2,675	579
1917	1,661	791	...	...	137	55	...	...	...	...
									(new rubels)	
1918	1,253	755	...	...	178	83	...	...	82.5	6.4
1919	2,584	782	...	...	229	107	3,762	104	2.5	0.1
1920	3,033	1,247	...	...	691	222	6,980	3,448	22.5	1.1
1921	1,464	638	...	...	933	225	12,145	8,263	165	15.8
1922	1,314	787	845	655	1,252	444	12,325	14,039	[213][39]	[49.8][39]
1923	1,343	831	1,117	1,196	2,299	684	19,514	24,575	117[39]	105[39]
1924	1,537	1,066	1,479	1,266	2,958	949	26,265	28,361	183[39]	293[39]
1925	1,379	1,048	1,666	1,397	2,484	861	30,098	29,025	567[39]	453[39]
1926	1,093	812	1,549[19]	2,253[19]	2,342	736	37,128	38,224	593[39]	552[39]
			1,547	2,253						
1927	977	685	2,892	2,515	2,662	723	33,840	38,111	560[39]	633[39]
1928	1,023	683	3,362	2,506	2,679	1,029	[31,641][38]	[27,030][38]	741[39]	621[39]
1929	1,073	752	3,111	2,813	2,529	1,073	29,626	28,960	691	724
1930	1,065	684	2,246	2,433	2,408	945	22,951	28,517	830	813
1931	861	467	1,468	1,879	1,675	812	15,426	22,189	867	636
1932	690	569	862	1,084	1,722	792	11,451	16,710	552	451
1933	665	558	827	960	1,918	802	11,739	14,166	273	389
1934	737	578	799	975	1,973	909	13,209	13,656	182	328
1935	825	605	861	925	2,296	924	10,848	16,756	189	288
1936	927	685	1,003	1,026	1,997	1,030	12,638	21,703	242	243
1937	1,293	823	1,254	1,196	2,362	1,203	20,163	31,359	229	295
1938	1,193[17]	787[17]	1,300	1,185	2,304	1,142	18,694	21,525	245	230
1939	1,366	808	[766][36]	[781][36]	2,078	1,338	...	...	168	104
1940	948	612	...	...	2,449	1,619	...	...	246	240
1941	1,125	575	...	...	2,469	2,973	30,576	41,286	278	179
1942	944	492	...	...	2,500	3,941	44,907	52,816	182	66
1943	1,008	539	...	...	3,342	4,035	89,988	71,132	173	67
1944	722	517	...	...	3,939	3,166	...	...	199	115
1945	1,206	326	...[37]	...[37]	4,083	3,237	...	...	260	302
1946	2,197	1,202	583	506	6,896	4,586	334,253	102,569	692	588
1947	3,820	1,820	1,281	985	9,494	4,310	...	...	670	694
1948	3,721	2,061	2,066	2,125	10,362	4,295	...	...	1,102	1,177
1949	4,221	2,137	2,530	2,475	9,047	4,094	...	...	1,340	1,303

E1   External Trade Aggregate Current Value (in millions)

	Spain[6] (pesetas)		Sweden (kronor)		Switzerland[23] (francs)		United Kingdom (pounds)			Serbia/Yugoslavia (dinars)	
	I	E	I	E	I	E	I	DE	R	I	E
1900	1,089	1,222	526	391	1,111	836	523	291	63	54	66
1901	1,144	1,159	460	353[22]	1,050	837	522	280	68	44	66
1902	1,085	1,138	502	392	1,129	874	528	283	66	45	72
1903	1,176	1,192	530	441	1,196	889	543	291	70	58	60
1904	1,179	1,253	572	415	1,240	891	551	301	70	61	62
1905	1,206	1,279	574	450	1,380	969	565	330	78	56	72
1906	1,037	1,334	638	504	1,469	1,071	608	376	85	44	72
1907	1,047	1,344	674	525	1,687	1,153	646	426	92	71	81
1908	1,015	1,166	598	482	1,487	1,038	593	377	80	76	78
1909	960	1,138	614	473	1,602	1,098	625	378	91	74	93
1910	1,092	1,255	669	493	1,745	1,196	678	430	104	85	98
1911	1,219	1,396	690	664	1,802	1,257	680	454	103	115	117
1912	1,349	1,509	783	760	1,979	1,358	745	487	112	106	84
1913	1,581[6]	1,552[6]	847	817	1,920	1,376	769	525	110	…	78
1914	1,093	881	727	772	1,478	1,187	697	431	95	…	…
1915	1,190	1,509	1,143	1,316	1,680	1,670	852	385	99	…	…
1916	1,422	1,515	1,139	1,556	2,379	2,448	949	506	98	…	…
1917	1,616	2,522	759	1,350	2,405	2,323	1,064	527	70	…	…
1918	1,777	2,299	1,233	1,350	2,401	1,963	1,316	501	31	…	…
1919	2,378	2,929	2,534	1,576	3,533	3,298	1,626	799	165	…	…
											687
1920	5,475	1,710	3,314	2,278	4,243	3,277	1,933	1,334	223	3,466	1,321
1921	2,663	1,999	1,259	1,097	2,296	2,140	1,086	703	107	4,122	2,461
1922	2,863	1,562	1,114	1,154	1,914	1,762	1,003[40]	720[40]	104[40]	6,422	3,691
1923	3,469	1,817	1,295	1,142	2,243	1,760	1,096	767	119	8,310	8,049
1924	3,540	2,169	1,424	1,261	2,504	2,070	1,277	801	140	8,222	9,539
1925	3,364	2,297	1,446	1,360	2,633	2,039	1,321	773	154	8,753	8,905
1926	2,679	2,249	1,490	1,420	2,415	1,836	1,241	653	125	7,632	7,818
1927	2,696	2,148	1,584	1,617	2,564[23]	2,023[23]	1,218	709	123	7,286	6,400
1928	3,028	2,518	1,708	1,575	2,719	2,133	1,196	724	120	7,835	6,445
1929	3,895	2,506	1,783	1,812	2,731	2,098	1,221	729	110	7,595	7,922
1930	3,895	3,250	1,662	1,550	2,564[23]	1,762[23]	1,044	571	87	6,960	6,780
1931	2,977	2,525	1,428	1,122	2,251	1,349	861	391	64	4,800	4,801
1932	2,985	1,757	1,155	947	1,763[23]	801[23]	702	365	51	2,860	3,056
1933	2,241	1,488	1,096	1,079	1,594	853	675	368	49	2,883	3,378
1934	2,690	1,517	1,305	1,302	1,435	844	731	396	51	3,573	3,878
1935	3,018	1,381	1,476	1,297	1,283	822[23]	756	426	55	3,700	4,030
1936	…	…	1,633	1,514	1,266	882	848	441	61	4,077	4,376
1937	…	…	2,123	2,000	1,807	1,286	1,028	521	75	5,234	6,272
1938	…	…	2,082	1,843	1,607	1,317	920	471	62	4,975	5,047
1939	…	…	2,499	1,889	1,889	1,298	886	440	46	4,757	5,521
	1,475[6]	1,983[6]									
1940	2,069	1,315	2,004	1,328	1,854	1,316	1,152	441	26	…	…
1941	1,966	1,863	1,674	1,345	2,024	1,463	1,145	365	13	…	…
1942	2,161	2,249	1,780	1,319	2,049	1,572	1,206	391	11	…	…
1943	3,250	3,142	1,814	1,172	1,727[23]	1,629	1,885	337	13	…	…
1944	2,956	3,422	1,677	853	1,186	1,132	2,360	327	18	…	…
1945	3,085	3,150	1,084	1,758	1,225	1,474	1,517	436	51	…	…
										(new dinars)	
1946	2,302	2,909	3,386	2,547	3,423	2,676	1,301[11]	915[11]	50	509	676
1947	4,341	3,353	5,220	3,240	4,820	3,268	1,798	1,142	60	2,076	2,046
1948	5,127	3,959	4,945	3,979	4,999	3,435	2,075	1,578	65	3,831	3,712
1949	4,969	4,163	4,333	4,250	3,791	3,457	2,278	1,787	59	3,685	2,484

E1 External Trade Aggregate Current Value (in thousand millions)

1950-1999

	Albania (leks)		Austria (schillings)		Belgium (francs)		Bulgaria (new leva)		Czechoslovakia (koruna)		Denmark (kroner)	
	I	E	I	E	I	E	I	E	I	E	I	E
1950	1.1	0.3	9.2	6.5	98	83	...	...	4.6	5.6	5.9	4.6
1951	2.0	0.5	14.0	9.6	128	133	...	...	6.5	6.1	7.0	5.8
1952	1.6	0.7	14.0	10.8	123	123	0.18	0.20	6.3	6.3	6.6	5.9
1953	2.0	0.5	13.3	13.2	122	113	0.23	0.24	6.3	7.2	6.9	6.2
1954	1.3	0.5	17.0	15.9	128	116	0.23[26]	0.27	6.7	7.2	8.1	6.6
1955	2.1	0.6	23.1	18.2	143	139	0.29	0.28	7.6	8.5	8.1	7.3
1956	1.9	0.9	25.3	22.1	164	159	0.29	0.35	8.5	10.0	9.1	7.7
1957	2.7	1.5	29.3	25.4	172	160	0.39	0.43	10.0	9.8	9.4	8.1
1958	3.9	1.5	27.9	23.9	157	153	0.43	0.44	9.8	10.9	9.3[27]	8.7[27]
											9.4	9.0
1959	4.3	1.7	29.8	25.2	173	165	0.68	0.55	11.5	12.4	11.1	9.7
1960	4.1	2.4	36.8	29.1	198	190	0.74	0.67	13.1	13.9	12.5	10.3
1961	3.6	2.4	38.6	31.3	211	196	0.78	0.77	14.6	14.7	12.9	10.6
1962	3.2	2.0	40.3	32.9	228	217	0.92	0.90	14.9	15.8	14.7	11.5
1963	3.5	2.4	43.6	34.5	256	242	1.1	0.98	15.6	17.7	14.7	13.2
1964	4.9	3.0	48.4	37.6	297	280	1.2	1.1	17.5	18.5	18.1	14.7
1965	...	...	54.6	41.6	325	320	1.4	1.4	19.2	19.4	19.5	16.0
1966	...	...	60.5	43.8	359	342	1.7	1.5	19.7	19.8	20.7	16.9
1967	...	...	60.0	47.0	364	354	1.8	1.7	19.3	20.6	21.9	17.7
1968	...	...	64.9	51.7	420	409	2.1	1.9	22.2	21.6	24.3	19.8
1969	...	...	73.5	62.7	501	504	2.0	2.1	23.7	23.9	28.6	22.7
1970	...	...	92.3	74.3	570	580	2.1	2.3	26.6	27.3	33.1	25.2
1971	...	...	104	79.0	629	620	2.5	2.6	28.9	30.1	34.2	27.3
1972	...	...	121	89.7	682	711	2.8	2.8	30.9	32.6	35.5	31.4
1973	...	...	138	102	856	870	3.2	3.2	35.8	35.3	47.0	37.5
1974	...	...	168	133	1,161	1,100	4.2	3.7	44.0	41.2	60.5	46.9
1975	...	...	163	131	1,131	1,057	5.2	4.5	50.7	46.7	59.7	50.0
1976	...	...	206	152	1,369	1,266	5.4	5.2	56.0	52.1	75.0	55.0
1977	...	...	235	162	1,448	1,345	6.1	6.0	63.2	58.2	79.6	60.4
1978	...	...	232	176	1,526	1,410	6.8	6.6	68.1	63.6	81.4	65.3
1979	...	...	270	206	1,784	1,661	7.4	7.7	75.8	70.2	98.3	78.2
1980	...	...	316	226	2,101	1,890	8.3	8.9	81.5	80.2	111	97.0
1981	...	...	335	252	2,310	2,062	10.0	9.9	86.3	87.7	126	116
1982	...	...	333	267	2,653	2,393	11.0	10.9	94.2	95.3	141	130
1983	...	...	348	277	2,821	2,651	12.0	11.8	103	104	149	147
1984	...	...	392	315	3,196	2,992	12.8	13.0	114	115	172	165
1985	...	...	431	354	3,318	3,168	14.1	13.7	120	120	192	180
1986	...	...	408	342	3,065	3,070	14.4	13.3	200	198	185	172
1987	...	...	412	342	3,110	3,100	14.1	13.8	204	202	174	175
1988	...	...	451	383	3,394	3,382	13.9	14.4	209	214	174	182
1989	...	...	515	429	3,884	3,943	12.5	13.5	215	217	195	186
1990	...	...	556	466	4,016	3,944	10.2	10.5	238	215	196	205
1991	...	...	592	479	4,116	4,024	45.1	57.4	294	321	207	216
1992	...	...	594	488	4,023	3,970	104.4	86.2	354	329	212	230
1993	...	...	566	468	3,875	4,129	119.2	99.0	366[47]	385[47]	191	247

Million US$ Dollars

Czech Republic

1994	603	139	55,340	45,031	130,081	143,674	4,144	3,947	17,500	16,234	34,882	41,422
1995	713	202	29,646	25,515	159,713	175,881	5,662	5,359	25,306	21,686	45,090	49,763
1996	841	207	67,324	57,824	163,680	175,455	6,850	6,602	29,002	20,160	44,435	50,101
1997	649	139	64,785	58,598	157,280	171,903	5,315	5,323	27,188	22,751	44,044	47,720
1998	828	205	68,187	62,746	162,208	177,662	4,974	4,296	28,813	26,417	45,427	47,481
1999	1,140	264	68,757	63,408	160,770	176,140	5,430	3,937	28,667	26,834	44,157	48,457

E1 External Trade Aggregate Current Value (in thousand millions)

	Finland (marks)		France (francs)		East Germany (valuta marks)		West Germany (marks)		Greece (drachmae)		Hungary (forints)	
	I	E	I	E	I	E	I	E	I	E	I	E
1950	0.89	0.81	1,073	1,078	2.0	1.7	11.4	8.4	2,141	452	3.7	3.9
1951	1.6	1.9	1,615	1,484	2.6	3.0	14.7	14.6	5,975	1,524	4.6	4.6
1952	1.8	1.6	1,592	1,416	3.2	3.1	16.2	16.9	5,193	1,798	5.4	5.1
1953	1.2	1.3	1,458	1,406	4.1	4.1	16.0	18.5	7,156	3,397	5.7	5.8
									(new drachmae)			
1954	1.5	1.6	1,522	1,510	4.6	5.4	19.3	22.0	9.9	4.6	6.2	6.1
1955	1.8	1.8	1,674	1,736	5.0	5.4	24.5	25.7	11.5	5.5	6.5	7.1
1956	2.0	1.8	$1,976_{28}$ $1,978$	$1,623_{28}$ $1,623$	5.9	5.6	28.0	30.9	13.9	5.7	5.6	5.7
1957	2.3	2.1	2,267	1,889	6.9_{34}	7.7_{34}	31.7	36.0	15.7	6.6	8.0	5.7
1958	2.3	2.5	2,357	2,153	7.2	8.0	31.1	37.0	16.9	7.0	7.4	8.0
			(new francs)									
1959	2.7_{34}	2.7_{34}	25.1	27.7	8.5	9.0	35.8_{30}	41.2_{30}	17.0	6.1	9.3	9.0
1960	3.4	3.2	31.0	33.9	9.2	9.3	42.7	47.9	21.1	6.1	11.5	10.3
1961	3.7	3.4	33.0	35.7	9.5	9.6	44.4	51.0	21.4	6.7	12.0	12.1
1962	3.9	3.5	37.1	36.4	10.1	10.0	49.5	53.0	21.0	7.5	13.5	13.0
1963	3.9	3.7	43.1	39.9	9.8	11.4	52.3	58.3	24.1	8.7	15.3	14.2
1964	4.8	4.1	49.7	44.4	11.1	12.3	58.8	64.9	26.6	9.3	17.5	15.9
1965	5.3	4.6	51.0	49.6	11.8	12.9	70.4	71.7	34.0	9.8	17.8	17.7
1966	5.5	4.8	58.6	53.8	13.5	13.5	72.7	80.6	36.7	12.2	18.4	18.7
1967	5.8	5.2	61.1	56.2	13.8	14.5	70.2	87.0	35.6	14.9	20.8	20.0
1968	6.7	6.9	68.8	62.6	14.2	15.9	81.2	99.6	41.8	14.0	21.2	21.0
1969	8.5	8.3	89.1_{11}	77.0_{11}	17.3	17.4	98.0	114	47.8	16.6	22.6	24.5
1970	11.1	9.7	106	99.6	20.4	19.2	110	125	58.7	19.3	29.4	27.2
1971	11.7	9.9	118	114	20.8	21.3	120	136	62.9	19.9	35.1	29.4
1972	13.1	12.1	136	131	22.9	23.9	129	149	70.4	26.1	34.1	35.6
1973	16.6	14.6	166	160	27.3	26.2	145	178	103	42.8	37.3	42.0
1974	25.7	20.7	255	220	33.9	30.4	180	231	132	60.9	51.0	46.9
1975	28.0	20.2	231	223	39.3	35.1	184	222	172	74.4	61.5	52.2
1976	28.6	24.5	308	266	45.9	39.5	222	257	223	93.8	230	205
1977	30.7	30.9	346	312	49.9	41.8	235	274	252	101	267	239
1978	32.2	35.2	368	345	50.7	46.2	244	285	288	124	301	241
1979	44.2	43.4	457	415	56.4	52.4	292	314	357	144	309	282
1980	58.2	52.8	571	470	63.0	57.1	341	350	453	221	300	281
1981	61.3	60.3	654	549	67.0	65.9	369	397	494	238	314	299
1982	64.8	63.0	758	606	69.9	75.2	376	428	666	286	325	324
1983	71.5	69.7	800	695	76.2	84.2	390	432	848	393	365	374
1984	74.5	80.9	904	813	83.5	90.4	434	488	1,084	543	391	414
1985	81.5	84.0	963	871	86.7	93.5	464	537	1,413	629	410	425
1986	77.6	82.6	888	864	90.5	91.5	414	526	1,582	790	425	406
1987	82.2	87.6	945	890	86.6	89.9	410	527	1,759	881	444	433
1988	92.1	90.9	1,054	998	87.2	90.2	440	568	1,757	776	461	492
1989	105.5	99.8	1,217	1,103	...	...	547	682	2,629	1,231	524	571
1990	103.0	101.3	1,267	1,142	Included in		573	681	3,138	1,281	545	604
1991	87.7	92.8	1,297	1,200	West Germany		644	666	3,922	1,585	856	764
1992	94.9	107.5	1,264	1,227			637	671	4,442	1,808	878	844
1993	103.4	134.1	1,135	1,167			549	604	5,052	1,934	1,158	795
					Million US$ Dollars							
1994	23,214	29,658	230,639	236,072			384,746	429,075	21,489	9,392	14,383	10,689
1995	28,114	39,573	276,981	287,334			444,554	508,398	25,509	10,970	15,046	12,435
1996	29,265	38,435	235,122	241,072			458,810	524,228	27,398	9,480	15,856	12,647
1997	29,786	39,318	271,945	290,285			445,682	512,503	27,718	8,656	20,652	18,613
1998	32,301	42,963	290,273	306,096			471,447	543,431	...	...	25,596	22,955
1999	30,727	40,666	289,925	300,161			472,171	541,090	...	...	27,920	24,947

E1 External Trade Aggregate Current Value (in thousand millions)

1950–1999

	Ireland (million pounds/punts)		Italy (lira)		Netherlands (gulden)		Norway (kroner)		Poland (zlotys)		Portugal (escudos)		Romania (new lei)	
	I	E[10]	I	E	I	E	I	E	I	E	I	E	I	E
1950	159	72	926	753	7.8	5.4	4.8[42]	2.8[42]	2.7	2.5	7.9	5.3	1.5	1.3
1951	205	82	1,355	1,030	9.7	7.4	6.3	4.4	3.7	3.0	9.5	7.6	...	...
1952	172	102	1,460	867	8.5	8.0	6.2[43]	4.0[43]	3.5	3.1	10.0	6.8	...	...
1953	182	114	1,513	942	9.0	8.2	6.5	3.6	3.1	3.3	9.5	6.3	...	...
1954	120	115	1,524	1,024	10.9	9.2	7.3	4.2	3.6	3.5	10.1	7.3	...	...
1955	204[41] 208	110	1,695	1,160	12.2	10.2	7.8	4.5	3.7	3.7	11.5	8.2	2.8	2.5
1956	183	108	1,984	1,341	14.2	10.9	8.7	5.5[44]	4.1	3.9	12.7	8.6	...	...
1957	184	131	2,296	1,595	15.6	11.8	9.1	5.9	5.0	3.9	14.4	8.3	...	...
1958	199	131	2,010	1,611	13.8	12.2	9.4[17]	5.3[17]	4.9	4.2	13.8	8.3	2.9	2.8
1959	213	131	2,105	1,821	15.0	13.7	9.4	5.8	5.7	4.6	13.7	8.4	3.0	3.1
1960	226	153	2,953	2,280	17.2	15.3	10.4	6.3	6.0	5.3	15.7	9.4	3.9	4.3
1961	261	181	3,265	2,614	18.7	15.7	11.5	6.7	6.7	6.0	18.9	9.4	4.9	4.8
1962	274	174	3,797	2,918	19.4	16.6	11.9	6.9	7.5	6.6	16.8	10.6	5.6	4.9
1963	308	197	4,745	3,159	21.6	18.0	13.0	7.7[45]	7.9	7.1	18.9	12.0	6.1	5.5
1964	349	222	4,533	3,724	25.5	21.0	14.2	9.2	8.3	8.4	22.4	14.8	7.0	6.0
1965	372	221	4,611	4,500	27.0	23.1	15.8	10.3	9.4	8.9	26.6	16.6	6.5	6.6
1966	373	244	5,368	5,024	29.0	24.4	17.2	11.2	10.0	9.1	29.4	17.8	7.3	7.1
1967	392	285	6,142	5,441	30.2	26.4	19.6	12.4	10.6	10.1	30.5	20.2	9.3	8.4
1968	497	333	6,429	6,366	33.6	30.2	19.3	13.8	11.4	11.4	33.9	21.9	9.7	8.8
1969	590	372	7,792	7,330	39.8	36.1	21.0	15.7	12.8	12.6	37.3	24.5	10.4	9.8
			(million million lira)											
1970	655	433	9.4	8.3	48.6	42.6	26.4	17.5	14.4	14.2	45.5	27.3	11.8	11.1
1971	755	539	9.9	9.4	52.3	49.8	28.7	18.0	16.2	15.5	524	30.2	12.6	12.6
1972	838	647	11.3	10.8	55.4	53.9	28.8	21.6	19.6	18.1	60.7	35.3	14.5	14.4
1973	1,138	869	16.3	19.7	66.6	66.9	36.0	27.1	26.1	21.4	74.8	45.4	17.4	18.6
1974	1,627	1,122	26.7	19.8	87.8	88.0	46.6	34.7	34.8	27.6	11.8	58.0	25.6	24.2
1975	1,704	1,447	25.2	22.9	88.0	88.7	50.5	37.9	41.7	34.2	97.7	49.3	26.5	26.5
1976	2,338	1,859	36.7	31.2	104	106	60.5	43.3	46.1	36.6	131	55.1	30.3	30.5
1977	3,091	2,518	42.4	40.0	112	107	68.6	47.3	48.6	40.7	191	77.7	34.9	34.9
1978	3,713	2,963	47.9	47.5	114	108	60.2	57.1	50.9	44.7	230	106	40.6	36.8
1979	4,828	3,478	64.6	59.9	135	128	69.3	68.5	54.3	50.2	332	176	48.8	43.5
1980	5,421	4,082	85.6	66.7	152	147	83.6	91.7	58.3	51.9	473	232	59.0	51.0
1981	6,578	4,778	104	86.0	164	171	89.7	104	51.2	44.3	609	257	55.7	56.4
1982	6,816	5,691	116	99.2	167[11]	177[11]	99.7	113	869	951	754	332	44.0	53.3
1983	7,367	6,944	122	111	174	184	98.4	131	970	1,060	899	509	130	173
1984	8,912	8,897	148	129	199	211	113	154	1,210	1,336	1,161	761	161	228
1985	9,428	9,743	173	150	216	226	133	171	1,595	1,691	1,327	972	148	192
1986	8,621	9,374	149	145	185	197	150	134	1,964	2,116	1,442	1,082	136	164
1987	9,155	10,723	162	150	184	188	152	145	2,876	3,236	1,965	1,311	133	168
1988	10,213	12,301	180	168	196	204	151	146	5,272	6,012	2,581	1,582	122	182
1989	12,284	14,597	210	193	221	229	163	187	14,864	19,476	3,024	2,016	135	168
1990	12,469	14,337	218	204	229	239	170	212	90,513	136,055	3,603	2,336	210	135
1991	12,851	15,019	226	210	237	249	165	220	164,259	157,716	3,808	2,354	406	320
1992	13,195	16,629	232	219	236	246	161	218	219,950	179,687	4,093	2,465	1,891	1,376
1993	14,748	19,642	231	264	226	244	170	226	340,183	257,568	3,889	2,469	4,471	3,658
						Million US$ Dollars								
1994	25,910	34,155	169,179	191,431	141,317	155,554	27,303	34,685	21,383	17,042	27,304	18,006	7,109	6,151
1995	33,068	44,638	206,025	233,980	176,873	196,276	32,973	41,995	29,050	22,895	33,314	23,211	10,278	7,910
1996	35,900	48,670	206,969	250,355	180,642	197,420	35,616	48,958	37,137	24,440	35,178	24,606	11,435	8,085
1997	39,233	53,449	210,283	240,424	178,132	194,909	35,713	48,547	42,308	25,751	35,063	23,972	11,280	8,431
1998	44,620	64,572	218,255	242,147	187,733	201,363	36,196	39,649	46,494	27,191	38,534	24,813	11,821	8,300
1999	46,535	70,544	216,626	230,199	187,529	200,290	34,047	44,892	45,903	27,397	38,461	23,864	10,392	8,505

E1   External Trade Aggregate Current Value (in thousand millions)

1950–1999

	Russia/U.S.S.R (rubels)		Spain[6] (pesetas)		Sweden (kronor)		Switzerland (francs)		United Kingdom (pounds)			Yugoslavia (new dinars)	
	I	E	I	E	I	E	I	E	I	DE	RE	I	E
1950	1.3	1.6	4.3	4.3	6.1	5.7	4.5	3.9	2.6[11]	2.2[11]	0.08	2.9	1.9
1951	1.8	2.1	4.2	5.1	9.2	9.2	5.9	4.7	3.9	2.6	0.13	4.8	2.2
1952	2.3	2.5	5.7	4.5	8.9	8.1	5.2	4.7	3.5	2.6	0.14	4.7	3.1
1953	2.5	2.7	6.5	5.2	8.2[46]	7.7	5.1	5.2	3.3	2.6	0.10	4.9	2.3
1954	2.9	2.9	6.7	5.1	9.2	8.2	5.6	5.3	3.4	2.6	0.10	4.2	3.0
1955	2.8	3.1	6.8	4.9	10.3	8.9	6.4	5.6	3.9	2.9	0.12	5.5	3.2
1956	3.3	3.3	8.4	4.8	11.4	10.1	7.6	6.2	3.9	3.1	0.14	5.9	4.0
1957	3.5	3.9	9.4	5.2	12.6	11.1	8.4	6.7	4.0	3.3	0.13	8.3	4.9
1958	3.9	3.9	9.6	5.3	12.2	10.8	7.3	6.6	3.7	3.2	0.14	8.6	5.5
1959	4.6	4.9	47.7	29.9	12.5	11.4	8.3	7.2	4.0	3.3	0.13	8.6	6.0
1960	5.1	5.0	43.3	43.5	15.0	13.3	9.6	8.1	4.5	3.6	0.14	10.3	7.1
1961	5.2	5.4	65.5	42.6	15.2	14.2	11.6	8.8	4.4	3.7	0.16	11.4	7.1
1962	5.8	6.3	94.2	44.2	16.2	15.1	13.0	9.5	4.5	3.8	0.16	11.1	8.6
1963	6.4	6.5	117	44.1	17.6	16.6	14.0	10.4	4.8	4.1	0.15	13.2	9.9
1964	7.0	6.9	135	57.3	19.9	19.0	15.5	11.4	5.5	4.3	0.15	16.5	11.2
1965	7.3	7.4	180	58.0	22.6	20.5	15.9	12.9	5.8	4.3	0.17	16.1	13.6
1966	7.1	8.0	214	75.2	23.7	22.1	17.0	14.2	6.0	5.3		19.6	15.8
1967	7.9	8.7	211	84.7	24.3	23.4	17.8	15.2	6.4	5.2		21.3	15.6
1968	8.5	9.6	245	111	26.5	25.6	19.4	17.3	7.9	6.4		22.5	15.8
1969	9.3	10.5	294	133	30.5	29.4	22.7	20.0	8.3	7.3		26.7	18.4
1970	10.6	11.5	330	167	36.3	35.1	27.9	22.1	9.0	8.1		35.9	21.0
1971	11.2	12.4	346	206	36.2	38.2	29.6	23.6	9.8	9.2		48.8	27.2
1972	13.3	12.7	438	245	38.6	41.7	32.3	26.1	11.1	9.8		55.0	38.0
1973	15.5	15.8	562	303	46.3	53.2	36.6	29.9	15.9	12.5		76.7	48.5
1974	18.8	20.7	884	408	72.8	70.5	42.9	35.4	23.2	16.6		128	64.7
1975	26.7	24.0	932	441	74.0	72.0	34.3	33.4	24.0	19.6		131	69.2
1976	28.7	28.0	1,169	583	84.0	90.2	36.9	37.0	31.1	25.3		125	82.9
1977	30.1	33.3	1,350	775	90.2	85.7	43.0	42.2	36.2	32.0		164	89.4
1978	34.6	35.7	1,431	1,001	92.7	98.2	42.3	41.8	39.5	35.4		182	103
1979	37.9	42.4	1,704	1,221	123	118	48.7	44.0	46.9	40.6		266	129
1980	44.5	49.6	2,451	1,493	142	131	60.9	49.6	49.8	47.4		411	245
1981	52.6	57.1	2,976	1,890	146	145	60.1	52.8	51.2	51.0		430	298
1982	56.4	63.2	3,475	2,234	174	168	58.1	52.7	57.0	55.6		557	428
1983	59.6	67.9	4,177	2,847	200	211	61.1	53.7	66.1	60.7		771	629
1984	65.4	74.4	4,629	3,778	219	243	69.0	60.7	79.0	70.5		1,497	1,280
1985	69.4	72.7	5,073	4,104	245	260	74.7	66.6	85.0	78.4		2,259	1,976
1986	62.6	68.3	4,891	3,802	233	265	73.5	67.0	86.2	73.0		3,108	2,724
1987	60.7	68.1	6,030	4,196	257	281	75.2	67.5	94.0	79.8		5,633	5,152
1988	65.0	67.1	7,040	4,686	280	305	82.4	74.1	107	81.7		17,371	16,590
												Million Dinars	
1989	72.1	68.7	8,396	5,135	317	333	95.2	84.3	122	93.7		46,293	41,403
1990	70.7	60.7	8,915	5,643	324	340	96.6	88.3	126	103.7		186,683	144,437
												Million New Dinars	
1991	76.0	80.8	9,672	6,226	301	333	95.0	87.9	119	104.9		9,136	7,780[49]
1992			10,205	6,606	291	326	86.7	86.1	126	108.5		6,119	4,014[49]
	Dollars												
1993	26.8[48]	44.3[48]	10,402	7,982	332	388	83.8	86.6	137	120.9		...	...
					Million US$ Dollars								
1994	50,518	67,542	92,189	72,929	51,732	61,352	64,085	66,238	226,172	204,009		...	...
1995	60,945	81,096	113,317	91,043	64,751	79,816	77,006	78,061	265,321	242,036		...	...
1996	62,278	88,599	121,794	102,002	72,898	84,904	74,471	76,205	287,537	262,004		4,102	1,842
1997	73,660	88,288	122,721	104,368	65,710	82,956	71,075	72,506	306,591	281,082		4,799	2,368
1998	60,476	74,888	133,153	109,231	68,256	84,739	73,885	75,439	314,033	271,849		4,622	2,604
1999	40,429	74,663	144,438	109,966	68,431	84,771	75,440	76,124	317,958	268,254		...	...

E1 External Trade Aggregate Current Value

NOTES

1. SOURCES:- Finland to 1859—Kauko E. Joustela, *Suomen Venäjänkauppa autonomisen ajan alkupuollskolla vv. 1809-65* Helsinki, 1963). Finland 1860-1917 Erkki Pihkala, *Finland's Foreign Trade, 1860-1917* (Bank of Finland, Helsinki, 1969). Germany to 1939—W.G. Hoffman, *Das Wachstum der Deutschen Wirtschaft seit der Mitte des 19 Jahrhunderts* (Berlin, etc.), 1965). Germany 1940-49—supplied by the Federal German Statistical Office. Russia to 1913—P.A. Khromov, *Economic Development of Russia in the 19th and 20th Centuries, 1800-1917* (Moscow, 1950). Sweden 1832-42—supplied by the Swedish Central Office of Statistics. U.K. imports and re-exports to 1953—estimates in A.H. Imlah, *Economic Elements in the Pax Britannica* (Cambridge, Mass., 1958). All other statistics are taken from the official publications noted on p. xv with gaps filled from the League of Nations, *International Trade Statistics* and the United Nations, *Yearbook of International Trade.*
2. Except as indicated in footnotes, statistics are of merchandise trade only, and are of 'special' rather than 'general' trade—i.e. imports for domestic consumption, and exports of domestic origin plus re-exports of commodities originally entered for domestic consumption.
3. Imports are normally valued c.i.f., and exports f.o.b.

FOOTNOTES

[1] The Austro-Hungarian customs area did not include Dalmatia until 1861, and it excluded Bosnia-Herzegovina throughout. Otherwise it conformed to the boundaries of the day of the Hapsburg Empire. Statistics from 1920 apply to the Republic of Austria.

[2] From May 1922 to 31 August 1940, and since 1 May 1945, the statistics apply to the Belgium-Luxembourg customs area. Gold movements are included.

[3] E. Levasseur, *Histoire du Commerce de la France* (Paris, 1912) quotes the following statistics from Arnould, *De la balance du commerce* for period averages during the *ancien régime* (in million livres):-

	I	E		I	E		I	E
1716-20	92.3	122.5	1740-48	182.6	238.5	1765-76	333.3	391.6
1721-32	115.8	148.4	1749-55	275.5	341.2	1777-83	345.7	337.8
1733-35	123.3	154.2	1756-63	174.6	148.9	1784-88	567.7	493.9
1736-39	167.6							

Statistics to 1825 (1st line) are of 'general' trade.

[4] The following are the main boundary changes affecting the trading area of Greece:- 1864 Ionian Islands acquired; 1881 Arta and much of Thessaly acquired; 1914 Crete, Epiros, and part of Macedonia acquired; 1919 Thrace acquired, but the eastern part was returned to Turkey in 1923; 1949 Dodecanese Islands acquired.

[5] The revaluation of the paper rouble in terms of silver was approximately four times.

[6] These are partly estimated series, consistent except for the inclusion of gold from 1814 and the treatment of Ceuta, Mehilla and the Canary Islands as part of Spain from 1940 (2nd line).

[7] The values of imports are re-exports to 1853 are estimates (see note 1). All imports are included, whether for home consumption or for re-export.

[8] These figures are for the 14 months beginning 1 November 1852. Previous statistics are for years ended 31 October.

[9] Statistics are of 'general' trade, though re-exports are in fact negligible. Gold movements are included up to 1930 (1st line).

[10] Figures for 1864 to 1874 are for years beginning 1 April.

[11] There is a slight break owing to changes in the method of valuation.

[12] From 1871 to 1918 Alsace Lorraine was included in Germany rather than France.

[13] Statistics are available back to 1871, but not on a consistent basis, and incomplete statistics go back to 1834 for the Zollverein.

[14] Previous statistics are based on officially determined, but variable values.

[15] Transit trade is included in 1877 and probably earlier. It is excluded subsequently, but there were alterations in definition affecting the composition of 'special' trade in 1897, 1907, and 1930.

[16] Including very small amounts of re-exports.

[17] Figures to 1938 and from 1959 are of 'general' trade. For the period to 1865 they are calculated on the basis of fixed estimated prices. Up to 1906 in-transit trade for Sweden is included in both imports and exports.

[18] Including Maderia and the Azores.

[19] Previous statistics include gold movements.

[20] Figures to 1910 and from 1950 are of 'general' trade, but in 1910 they did not differ from those of 'special' trade.

[21] Figures for 1849-53 exclude trade in tobacco.

[22] Statistics of exports to Norway are incomplete for the period 1898-1901.

[23] After 1930 re-exports (though not direct transit trade) are included in both imports and exports. All gold movements are included to 1927. From 1928 gold for banking purposes is excluded, and from 1936 (exports) and 1944 (imports) all gold is excluded. From 1933 to 1939 the repair and finishing trades are included.

[24] The value of new ships sold abroad is subsequently included.

[25] The 1938 figures are for January-September and the 1945 figures for May-December. For the intervening period the following statistics are available for the separate parts of the country (in million koruna):-

Czechoslovakia (less Sudetenland)	Imports	Exports	Protectorate (continued)	Imports	Exports
Oct-Dec 1938	1,501	1,723	1944	1,829	4,701
Jan-15 March 1939	2,194	2,292	Jan-Apri 1945	213	432

E1   External Trade Aggregate Current Value

Bohemia, Moravia, Silesia Protectorate			Slovakia		
16 Mar–Dec 1939	4,103	4,312	16 Mar–Dec 1939	1,555	2,200
1940	4,764	4,215	1940	2,873	3,175
1941	3,654	4,248	1941	3,486	3,191
1942	2,695	4,085	1942	4,751	4,704
1943	2,583	5,149	1943	5,183	5,832

26   Imports as well as exports are subsequently valued f.o.b.
27   Strictly speaking the statistics to 1937 (1st line) are not of 'special' trade, but of 'general' imports less re-exports (at import value) and 'general' exports less re-exports (at export value). Statistics from 1958 (2nd line) are of 'general' trade.
28   There were slight changes in the basis of collection.
29   Prior to 1 March 1906 the free ports of Hamburg, Cuxhaven, Bremerhaven, and Geestemunde were not included in the German customs area.
30   From 1920 to March 1935 and from 1945 to July 1959 Saarland is not included in Germany (or West Germany).
31   Figures for 1920 to 1923 (1st line) are in 1913 values instead of current values.
32   May–December only.
33   Reparations in kind are not previously included. In 1924 they amounted to 122 thousand gold marks.
34   The figures are subsequently of 'general' trade.
35   Figures to 1939 include the Free City of Danzig.
36   January to July only.
37   Statistics are subsequently of 'general' trade, both imports and exports being valued f.o.b. at official exchange rates.
38   Including bullion.
39   The figure for 1922 is for 9 months to 30 September, and the statistics for 1923–28 are for years ended 30 September. In the last quarter of 1928 (not shown here) imports were 159 and exports 170 million roubles.
40   Trade with southern Ireland is treated as external from 1 April 1923.
41   Revised estimates for the parcel post were not carried back beyond 1955.
42   Spitzbergen is subsequently treated as an integral part of Norway.
43   Partly worked gold, and coins of gold and silver, are subsequently no longer included.
44   Subsequently including whale-oil etc. delivered direct from fishing grounds.
45   Subsequently includes floated timber.
46   Subsequently includes unmanufactured gold and silver, and coins.
47   Czech Republic. Slovakia = 195 (I); 168 (E).
48   Russian Federation
49   Yugoslavia

E2 EXTERNAL TRADE (by value) WITH MAIN TRADING PARTNERS

AUSTRIA-HUNGARY (in million kronen)

1891–1916

	Germany		British East Indies		Italy		Russia[1]		U.K.		U.S.A.	
	I	E	I	E	I	E	I	E	I	E	I	E
1891	448	855	96	9	68	94	56	36	129	107	47	21
1892	462	804	93	10	84	107	48	33	123	92	50	28
1893	493	856	104	15	102	115	62	47	134	135	58	24
1894	516	835	88	14	100	105	86	58	149	142	63	26
1895	518	767	80	13	95	125	94	54	151	127	75	34
1896	515	804	85	14	94	120	88	55	147	148	85	35
1897	541	798	83	24	110	119	112	52	138	141	112	34
1898	565	841	84	33	118	116	136	64	139	149	134	29
1899	599	983	87	36	119	143	87	81	148	165	125	32
1900	635	1,016	84	46	114	147	89	72	149	201	153	38
1901	635	978	95	60	104	136	86	73	137	187	129	33
1902	652	988	89	46	110	148	96	75	143	173	136	40
1903	697	1,091	112	34	122	153	114	80	155	227	163	46
1904	767	1,037	130	62	105	157	120	72	155	182	182	41
1905	804	1,114	125	69	107	161	138	65	157	200	204	53
1906	906	1,133	164	73	116	178	151	69	189	231	215	59
1907	979	1,177	185	51	123	193	138	78	239	222	239	67
1908	995	1,047	136	56	118	228	127	72	216	231	222	58
1909	1,068	1,045	174	58	123	233	181	77	219	241	231	84
1910	1,154	1,062	214	69	131	228	167	91	229	224	237	81
1911	1,263	1,038	220	52	142	222	209	96	229	216	290	58
1912	1,406	1,213	199	63	162	239	229	91	245	257	349	64
1913	1,367	1,211	233	95	169	216	202[1]	103[1]	217	270	323	70
1914	1,190	1,009	196	47	182	190	135	70	148	132	224	63
1915	1,648	975	24	—	204	35	26	25	6	—	221	17
1916	2,384	1,153	4	—	5	—	134	77	2	—	19	4

E2   External Trade (by value) with Main Trading Partners

AUSTRIA (in million schillings)   1922–1959

Year	Czechoslovakia I	E	Germany I	E	Hungary I	E	Italy I	E	Poland I	E	Switzerland I	E	U.K. I	E	U.S.A. I	E	Yugoslavia I	E
1922	596	163	575	248	282	206	131	168	118	147	130	75	59	56	207	22	104	199
1923	633	168	508	228	301	134	193	167	171	129	159	119	66	73	176	29	142	213
1924	780	217	537	279	402	174	250	205	259	194	197	131	108	85	192	41	151	205
1925	566	215	479	316	318	162	122	208	249	164	127	93	105	72	222	42	134	176
1926	554	208	483	222	361	172	144	180	252	73	130	108	103	69	151	61	166	153
1927	565	240	543	412	298	203	140	192	270	106	157	114	135	76	192	64	176	157
1928	593	279	667	440	279	191	114	196	301	123	167	138	146	81	217	76	131	165
1929	591	303	704	374	328	168	119	207	291	107	149	124	120	99	198	75	132	169
1930	480	228	581	333	285	122	107	176	217	84	116	110	93	102	144	49	149	150
1931	367	156	495	224	198	93	94	109	178	57	94	95	76	93	96	25	96	100
1932	213	83	290	139	136	72	68	76	106	33	49	61	37	29	56	15	108	58
1933	158	63	236	130	135	81	51	87	77	52	44	64	37	35	62	19	104	57
1934	160	67	209	145	129	98	50	91	73	35	45	64	51	47	62	13	98	53
1935	156	66	204	145	115	96	57	127	77	38	40	51	54	39	71	17	82	54
1936	144	71	216	157	118	95	59	129	74	49	39	47	55	53	78	23	77	49
1937	160	88	238	184	132	112	80	173	67	53	48	70	67	65	87	31	115	67
1947	156	78	210	37	34	36	89	138	63	23	160	212	109	45	40	44	26	18
1948	270	149	228	115	117	73	288	369	120	29	220	264	143	148	173	102	223	97
1949	391	233	764[2]	250[2]	202	140	574	766	242	122	214	187	287	137	1,843	96	179	217
1950	399	398	1,528	996	199	237	722	1,214	425	199	380	341	713	244	2,138	363	214	262
1951	464	509	2,351	1,369	282	151	742	1,348	528	421	604	586	1,642	845	3,116	577	341	288
1952	434	417	3,009	2,171	242	214	878	1,528	541	385	521	554	1,341	754	2,553	551	619	556
1953	287[3]	227[3]	3,737[3]	2,609[3]	173[3]	166[3]	970[3]	2,158[3]	557[3]	403[3]	581[3]	593[3]	1,376[3]	1,181[3]	1,652[3]	820[3]	348[3]	564[3]
	247	227	3,762	2,510	125	167	967	2,306	527	407	564	549	766	908	1,655	765	248	544
1954	224	195	6,106	3,728	363	305	1,436	2,829	533	465	766	694	817	616	1,488	734	439	634
1955	395	279	8,173	4,557	502	392	1,837	3,059	634	464	1,001	837	1,035	665	2,431	898	386	558
1956	459	494	8,602	5,159	496	507	2,057	3,685	668	712	1,252	1,222	1,068	792	3,262	1,154	391	597
1957	490	587	11,094	6,119	391	614	2,321	4,467	857	832	1,443	1,374	1,218	630	3,659	984	489	677
1958	472	486	10,915	6,052	529	510	2,104	4,062	772	815	1,204	994	1,213	578	2,818	1,177	458	681
1959	546	472	11,979	6,671	619	677	2,339	4,140	730	521	1,305	1,142	1,375	647	2,032	1,484	535	708

E2 External Trade (by value) with Main Trading Partners

AUSTRIA (in million schillings to 1974, thousand million schillings subsequently)

1960–1997

	Czechoslovakia		Germany		Hungary		Italy		Poland		Switzerland		U.K.		U.S.A.		Yugoslavia	
	I	E	I	E	I	E	I	E	I	E	I	E	I	E	I	E	I	E
1960	598	764	14,706	7,810	693	695	2,963	4,847	813	526	1,594	757	1,819	820	2,703	1,284	719	1,011
1961	608	835	16,553	8,585	546	678	3,060	4,764	721	691	1,808	825	1,942	958	2,287	1,200	621	902
1962	651	798	17,071	9,177	784	734	3,302	5,036	848	759	2,003	2,369	2,039	934	2,249	1,273	654	874
1963	732	706	18,006	9,093	848	991	3,377	5,750	1,052	526	2,238	2,337	2,342	1,347	2,064	1,311	778	882
1964	770	751	20,215	10,481	703	1,125	3,606	4,624	1,037	612	2,632	2,963	2,581	1,716	2,497	1,493	690	990
1965	988	967	22,815	11,899	814	1,102	4,512	4,481	1,180	829	3,018	3,109	2,987	1,616	2,400	1,739	725	1,013
1966	913	1,146	25,670	11,707	983	1,012	4,575	4,712	1,106	931	3,623	3,556	3,470	1,846	2,624	2,005	1,168	998
1967	972	1,072	25,014	10,444	884	1,252	4,717	5,580	958	1,042	4,387	4,067	3,614	2,613	2,096	2,010	1,200	1,501
1968	1,207	1,207	26,879	12,094	1,052	1,351	4,657	5,332	1,061	1,015	4,856	4,746	3,995	3,280	2,171	2,393	1,174	1,948
1969	1,596	1,566	30,352	15,197	1,254	1,598	4,829	6,345	1,198	1,097	5,598	5,956	4,859	3,566	2,193	2,855	1,176	2,323
1970	1,753	1,606	38,053	17,357	1,549	2,089	6,032	7,189	1,506	1,161	6,820	7,698	6,252	4,552	3,155	3,043	1,296	3,444
1971	2,123	1,733	42,844	18,111	1,548	2,222	6,973	7,329	1,361	1,249	7,740	8,820	6,914	5,661	3,869	3,185	1,186	3,332
1972	2,000	1,648	50,480	20,120	1,975	2,162	8,700	8,625	1,586	1,825	8,743	10,362	7,310	6,993	3,902	4,040	1,224	2,870
1973	2,214	1,984	57,460	22,186	2,551	2,581	10,137	10,731	1,710	2,492	10,255	11,162	7,127	7,744	4,225	4,243	1,432	3,956
1974	3,092	2,872	67,455	26,227	3,256	5,072	11,893	12,760	2,388	4,345	11,549	13,341	7,151	8,528	4,835	4,646	1,712	6,819
thousand million schillings																		
1975	3.3	3.3	65.3	28.6	2.4	4.7	13.2	10.4	2.6	5.8	11.0	10.3	6.5	7.3	4.8	3.2	1.4	6.0
1976	3.1	3.2	84.6	35.6	3.1	4.5	17.0	13.9	2.7	6.7	13.0	11.0	7.5	7.4	6.2	4.0	1.7	5.5
1977	3.3	3.5	99.2	43.0	3.3	5.0	20.5	14.6	2.4	5.9	14.0	11.5	8.1	7.5	7.0	5.0	1.8	6.0
1978	3.5	3.2	100	51.3	2.6	5.4	20.6	15.5	2.2	5.4	14.2	13.7	7.2	8.7	7.0	5.3	1.6	6.1
1979	4.3	2.9	114	62.5	3.2	4.7	25.1	20.2	2.7	5.8	14.5	15.2	7.9	9.2	8.5	5.2	2.2	8.2
1980	5.8	3.1	129	69.8	4.4	4.9	28.7	24.8	3.1	6.1	15.8	17.0	8.7	8.3	10.7	4.9	2.6	7.4
1981	6.3	3.3	130	73.3	5.0	6.7	27.9	25.3	2.6	3.5	16.0	18.6	7.8	10.5	13.7	6.5	2.5	7.6
1982	7.3	4.2	135	78.3	4.8	6.4	28.7	24.2	3.2	2.3	15.9	18.7	7.3	11.5	12.5	7.8	2.9	7.8
1983	7.4	3.6	145	85.3	5.9	6.1	31.0	24.6	3.6	3.1	16.5	18.9	7.5	11.3	11.7	8.2	3.5	7.2
1984	7.8	3.5	157	93.1	8.1	7.0	33.8	29.5	5.0	3.4	17.4	21.7	8.4	13.8	13.7	12.9	4.4	7.7
1985	8.3	3.9	176	107	8.5	9.2	35.5	31.8	4.8	4.3	19.4	23.9	9.8	16.3	16.0	16.5	4.7	8.2
1986	6.5	4.0	179	112	6.6	7.8	36.5	31.8	4.3	3.4	19.8	26.8	9.4	15.3	13.1	13.8	4.0	7.7
1987	5.9	3.9	182	119	6.2	6.6	38.7	35.5	4.0	3.0	19.4	25.4	9.9	15.6	14.2	12.2	3.9	6.8
1988	6.0	4.7	201	134	6.4	6.8	40.3	39.9	4.2	3.7	19.9	27.6	11.2	18.1	15.3	13.5	4.7	7.8
1989	6.7	5.0	225	148	7.8	8.7	46.2	45.3	4.4	5.2	21.3	31.1	12.9	19.3	18.6	14.9	6.0	9.2
1990	6.4	8.6	243	171	8.7	10.5	50.3	45.8	5.0	4.4	23.7	32.4	14.3	18.1	20.2	14.9	6.4	12.4
1991	7.4	9.2	253	187	11.5	14.5	52.3	44.9	5.7	7.5	24.7	30.6	16.0	17.3	23.4	13.5	5.8	9.6
1992	11.1	13.8	255	194	11.9	15.6	51.2	42.9	5.0	7.1	23.8	28.9	16.1	17.4	23.4	12.8	5.1[84]	9.3[84]
1993	9.1[83]	11.3[83]	234	182	10.8	16.5	50.9	36.9	4.7	6.4	23.1	28.8	15.4	15.3	24.8	15.4	—	—
Million US$ Dollars																		
1994	992.6[83]	1,181.1[83]	22,133.2	17,177.4	1,128.1	1,763.7	4,881.8	3,657.9	454.1	529.6	2,253.4	2,869.0	1,602.5	1,427.1	2,418.6	1,568.6	—	—
1995	1,240.5[83]	1,535.4[83]	28,631.2	21,523.4	1,234.8	2,057.8	5,788.4	4,939.7	617.3	744.7	2,569.8	3,289.5	1,955.6	1,797.5	2,792.5	1,598.8	—	—
1996	1,355.9[83]	1,676.9[83]	28,844.5	21,636.4	1,807.9	2,299.1	5,923.9	4,819.2	534.6	855.6	2,442.2	3,144.9	2,027.5	2,045.1	3,000.1	1,840.9	—	—
1997																		

E2 External Trade (by value) with Main Trading Partners

BELGIUM (in million francs)

1844–1879

	Argentina I	Argentina E	France I	France E	Germany I	Germany E	India I	India E	Netherlands I	Netherlands E	Russia I	Russia E	U.K. I	U.K. E	U.S.A. I	U.S.A. E
1844	...	...	...	...	...	...	...	...	...	...	...	...	...	...	...	...
1845	2	—	43	82	27	33	...	...	37	33	23	1	42	16	20	3
1846	1	—	47	69	32	29	...	...	34	22	22	1	27	13	13	3
1847	2	—	45	72	31	36	...	...	41	28	32	1	37	13	17	6
1848	2	—	38	49	21	27	...	...	38	27	15	1	27	29	12	5
1849	3	—	43	56	23	31	...	...	36	29	13	1	39	34	20	7
1850	4	—	51	67	25	40	...	...	39	31	13	2	37	37	17	10
1851	3	1	55	66	25	37	...	...	40	31	12	2	41	32	12	10
1852	6	1	55	80	28	44	...	...	45	36	22	3	49	36	20	9
1853	6	1	62	99	37	45	...	...	51	42	28	4	47	60	21	15
1854	8	2	57	119	48	46	...	...	68	52	18	1	47	119	27	18
1855	12	2	60	132	66	36	...	...	75	49	2	—	67	78	23	11
1856	22	3	73	146	61	47	...	...	78	57	19	2	77	59	28	15
1857	37	2	76	158	46	69	...	...	82	58	27	5	73	67	31	15
1858	23	1	106	139	38	62	...	...	84	59	30	6	86	59	19	13
1859	34	2	110	150	41	60	...	...	93	59	26	8	78	77	22	11
1860	41	4	110	162	59	74	...	...	102	62	28	6	83	95	24	10
1861	42	3	97	174	72	69	...	...	114	60	33	7	91	76	27	5
1862	45	2	139	178	76	75	...	...	109	63	31	7	85	103	23	12
1863	28	3	150	187	73	76	...	...	112	74	22	11	109	103	26	6
1864	36	3	179	217	81	84	...	...	129	82	24	4	119	115	29	9
1865	83	4	203	239	72	83	...	...	113	70	40	14	146	134	19	7
1866	72	4	197	265	89	81	...	...	88	80	30	8	141	130	38	10
1867	56	2	196	236	102	91	...	...	97	68	48	15	131	122	37	9
1868	71	3	201	273	112	108	...	...	122	75	47	13	142	120	36	7
1869	67	3	233	258	116	121	...	...	134	81	46	22	145	129	39	11
1870	50	3	233	231	122	139	...	...	141	82	43	22	159	147	42	11
1871	63	5	247	297	230	209	...	...	171	103	64	12	233	193	87	9
1872	77	8	316	321	169	240	...	...	165	121	63	12	230	238	81	14
1873	71	7	336	380	172	266	...	...	179	132	73	13	263	242	136	16
1874	50	5	326	343	167	243	...	...	171	157	92	15	204	222	123	19
1875	48	4	356	344	172	244	...	...	170	150	81	18	249	209	71	17
1876	58	4	353	314	196	244	...	...	185	165	115	19	249	192	111	11
1877	64	8	354	296	215	223	...	...	197	166	82	25	213	228	122	11
1878	54	7	323	329	237	220	...	...	187	146	130	23	194	250	176	9
1879	40	7	309	372	220	248	...	...	202	156	145	17	200	230	230	20
1880	39	5	335	399	245	234	18	—	237	151	127	13	255	247	271	36
1881	33	11	336	415	229	251	50	—	245	160	118	11	240	254	223	43

E2 **External Trade (by value) with Main Trading Partners**

BELGIUM (in million francs)

1882–1924

	Argentina		France		Germany		India		Netherlands		Russia		U.K.		U.S.A.	
	I	E	I	E	I	E	I	E	I	E	I	E	I	E	I	E
1882	46	12	318	441	243	227	72	2	238	163	139	10	198	262	185	45
1883	48	10	307	415	233	229	81	3	210	177	134	8	198	274	160	43
1884	62	17	277	412	185	236	65	3	188	176	124	8	185	252	161	40
1885	55	11	259	322	176	215	69	3	197	186	93	6	164	238	120	33
1886	60	15	251	330	152	196	69	4	200	175	74	9	172	236	160	41
1887	69	18	283	335	157	210	47	4	199	168	96	6	188	240	165	49
1888	55	22	289	343	179	212	56	5	216	172	150	6	183	256	120	52
1889	57	42	323	353	174	258	64	9	205	217	113	11	198	300	118	43
1890	75	17	316	359	182	265	77	10	206	208	114	10	213	268	157	51
1891	87	12	327	379	180	313	122	9	197	229	116	8	199	266	200	55
1892	68	14	300	311	168	313	61	13	179	190	74	6	183	235	207	53
1893	83	15	278	310	180	301	71	15	201	177	98	17	198	242	135	50
1894	90	14	282	285	185	294	76	16	174	155	105	22	178	235	126	42
1895	93	14	300	284	199	311	53	20	175	165	117	22	193	267	133	47
1896	85	19	311	288	215	327	55	21	177	171	110	31	206	291	174	49
1897	68	17	297	298	234	363	47	17	155	184	139	41	276	302	232	60
1898	100	21	311	332	245	451	92	18	165	203	126	41	284	242	303	52
1899	148	20	390	346	285	486	85	15	169	215	132	44	312	235	280	65
1900	119	21	375	426	324	427	40	18	196	218	126	31	301	359	267	79
1901	100	21	351	351	300	415	71	25	199	201	106	29	227	342	336	78
1902	104	14	386	357	331	429	85	22	208	218	148	33	241	359	276	89
1903	185	22	412	393	340	459	117	29	229	233	219	38	248	365	266	93
1904	199	42	466	347	351	505	142	26	241	269	212	27	255	392	222	86
1905	240	48	518	372	410	570	104	35	245	261	238	33	284	366	242	92
1906	238	66	605	548	465	642	104	28	260	273	234	36	352	410	299	108
1907	243	72	652	530	460	701	175	29	299	304	211	38	395	411	318	80
1908	311	60	517	465	450	680	96	29	290	282	203	38	353	364	341	73
1909	320	90	563	499	495	730	168	35	283	311	326	41	362	409	277	107
1910	278	129	747	669	576	881	188	32	293	328	364	67	419	458	231	117
1911	272	84	739	695	602	959	268	35	298	352	318	67	436	498	341	114
1912	306	93	908	752	703	1,007			357	368	272	83	506	595	414	145
1913	317	91	1,000	762	762	940	241	48	357	321	267	88	519	545	420	106
1914	...	...														
1919	211	10	938	590	100	667	108	7,383	448	28	7	1,416	241	1,416	241	1,087
1920	833	142	2,318	2,527	952	1,282	621	113	778	1,037	19	3	2,185	1,454	2,280	316
1921	714[4]	108[4]	1,785[4]	1,639[4]	1,409[4]	1,097[4]	359[4]	102[4]	952[4]	954[4]	28[4]	6[4]	1,198[4]	1,343[4]	1,615[4]	222[4]
1922	[467][5]	[138][5]	[1,347][5]	[1,114][5]	[870][5]	[609][5]	[122][5]	[104][5]	[703][5]	[456][5]	[6][5]	[1][5]	[931][5]	[769][5]	[747][5]	[147][5]
1923	956	362	2,866	2,019	916	458	388	231	1,381	1,206	38	2	2,212	1,902	1,479	874
1924	1,469	434	3,791	2,196	1,614	1,576	636	359	1,815	1,704	120	4	2,400	2,916	1,985	1,087

E2 External Trade (by value) with Main Trading Partners

BELGIUM[4] (in million francs)   1925–1959

	Argentina		France		Germany		India		Netherlands		Russia/U.S.S.R		U.K.		U.S.A.	
	I	E	I	E	I	E	I	E	I	E	I	E	I	E	I	E
1925	1,420	438	3,727	2,189	1,640	1,829	686	307	1,890	1,589	148	82	2,232	2,902	2,174	1,208
1926	1,681	516	4,912	2,834	2,504	2,487	761	463	2,385	2,274	238	8	2,668	3,839	2,625	2,277
1927	2,348	772	5,925	3,071	3,610	4,521	664	694	3,104	2,893	218	8	3,384	4,877	3,200	2,421
1928	2,230	1,109	6,666	3,967	3,994	4,246	821	793	3,707	4,120	205	51	3,613	5,246	3,098	2,422
1929	2,347	941	6,939	4,016	4,908	3,812	882	797	4,134	4,043	210	103	3,980	5,806	3,407	2,155
1930	1,551	712	5,516	4,121	5,181	2,987	797	575	4,047	3,348	605	77	2,838	4,998	3,106	1,289
1931	1,268	407	4,172	4,070	4,047	2,390	428	467	3,514	2,969	470	56	1,955	4,917	2,099	1,149
1932	1,034	306	2,658	2,930	2,748	1,553	296	441	2,327	1,946	366	33	1,413	2,367	1,411	715
1933	910	331	2,581	2,934	2,473	1,448	368	289	1,742	1,767	462	52	1,372	1,792	1,201	720
1934	949	453	2,339	2,410	2,004	1,628	347	280	1,437	1,549	384	117	1,098	2,002	1,004	594
1935	1,259	591	2,725	2,960	2,133	1,583	439	360	1,636	1,845	562	189	1,393	2,400	1,296	991
1936	1,189	597	2,898	3,520	2,476	2,064	637	391	1,936	2,360	632	298	1,959	2,888	1,475	1,572
1937	1,766	388	3,443	4,401	3,175	2,779	412	428	2,275	2,818	748	449	2,307	3,455	2,368	1,909
1938	951	687	3,310	3,324	2,599	2,648	642[6] 597	364[6] 357	2,075	2,610	783	444	1,833	2,973	2,489	1,443
1939	1,222	775	3,073	2,862	2,378	1,999	408	334	1,868	3,444	253	148	1,610	3,027	1,928	1,983
1940	535[4]	247[4]	1,285[4]	2,089[4]	1,322[4]	1,181[4]	157[4]	166[4]	1,009[4]	2,071[4]	—[4]	…[4]	695[4]	1,116[4]	834[4]	705[4]
1941	—	—	1,266	1,201	3,979	2,369	—	—	883	1,331	…	…	7	7	39	—
1942	—	—	1,913	1,052	2,988	2,894	1	—	716	835	…	…	1	1	7	—
1943	—	—	2,092	1,085	2,798	6,453	—	—	600	670	…	…	—	—	3	—
1944	—	—	1,116	445	1,630	4,266	—	—	409	355	—	—	6	—	4	—
1945	528[4]	9[4]	2,061[4]	1,360[4]	519[4]	1[4]	173[4]	—[4]	460[4]	847[4]	12[4]	—[4]	3,314[4]	67[4]	2,526[4]	748[4]
1946	2,149	1,044	7,718	4,454	1,483	173	588	100	2,970	4,495	52	9	9,669	1,934	11,618	3,230
1947	2,865	1,855	9,698	7,638	2,282[2]	945[2]	1,501[76]	697[76]	5,022	7,867	377	82	7,932	6,055	22,662	2,711
1948	3,666	3,878	7,665	6,971	4,881	3,268	1,043	1,022	7,189	11,444	2,199	886	8,478	6,665	15,647	4,452
1949	2,197	2,145	8,248	5,983	5,281	8,381	780	1,171	7,587	11,727	248	1,313	7,218	7,494	14,781	4,188
1950	1,468	501	11,042	7,626	7,892	5,631	917	696	9,779	18,561	552	1,027	9,426	6,426	15,253	6,992
1951	1,375	1,843	13,104	12,141	11,186	8,042	1,400	869	13,916	23,789	854	669	10,627	13,319	20,558	10,501
1952	1,050	1,208	12,451	9,096	13,289	11,719	966	945	16,216	18,745	579	742	10,050	13,588	18,070	9,213
1953	2,421	248	13,405	9,062	14,868	10,513	779	1,021	16,620	20,121	836	827	10,955	8,785	12,438	11,544
1954	2,921	1,008	15,259	11,109	17,358	11,116	594	1,228	17,068	24,174	1,398	1,216	10,680	7,252	13,129	9,275
1955	1,220	1,163	17,693	13,897	19,703	16,335	1,237	1,146	18,811	28,766	1,471	846	12,059	8,928	15,673	12,183
1956	1,685	769	19,482	16,904	24,340	16,059	786	2,449	21,363	34,659	1,792	1,586	13,227	10,090	20,429	15,090
1957	2,047	2,778	20,428	17,564	26,730	16,286	689	1,969	24,302	36,215	1,746	1,410	14,079	8,884	21,247	13,113
1958	2,232	3,144	18,137	16,141	26,840	17,606	595	1,870	24,581	31,515	1,262	883	11,572	8,690	15,497	14,076
1959	2,368	2,121	21,552	14,719	28,226	22,103	534	778	27,171	35,008	1,637	375	14,342	9,743	16,252	21,786

E2 External Trade (by value) with Main Trading Partners

1960–1997

BELGIUM[4] (in thousand million Francs)

	Argentina		France		Germany		India		Netherlands		Russia/U.S.S.R		U.K.		U.S.A.	
	I	E	I	E	I	E	I	E	I	E	I	E	I	E	I	E
1960	2.3	1.4	26.9	19.6	33.7	29.8	0.7	1.2	29.4	40.1	1.4	1.0	14.6	10.5	19.6	17.9
1961	2.4	1.4	31.1	22.1	37.6	30.2	0.8	0.9	32.3	45.9	1.8	1.4	15.9	10.3	18.7	18.1
1962	3.5	0.9	33.2	26.8	42.6	38.2	0.8	0.8	33.7	49.3	2.3	1.3	18.4	10.8	22.6	20.7
1963	3.3	0.4	38.5	35.2	49.2	44.8	0.8	1.1	37.7	54.6	2.6	0.7	21.1	13.9	23.6	20.6
1964	3.1	0.5	43.8	42.3	58.7	57.9	0.9	1.1	44.0	64.1	2.5	0.7	22.7	13.8	26.2	22.5
1965	3.1	0.7	49.8	46.4	69.1	69.7	1.3	1.6	48.3	70.4	2.3	1.1	24.4	15.3	27.5	26.6
1966	3.9	0.4	55.8	55.2	77.6	72.0	1.3	1.9	52.5	76.0	3.0	1.3	26.6	16.1	28.5	29.6
1967	4.2	0.4	55.8	63.2	78.1	69.8	1.5	2.0	54.2	75.8	3.0	2.0	25.1	16.7	29.6	29.4
1968	3.7	0.6	63.6	75.8	86.6	85.5	2.0	1.8	60.8	85.9	3.3	2.4	30.1	17.8	34.5	38.5
1969	4.0	0.9	79.4	106	116	115	2.1	2.0	71.2	97.4	2.9	2.6	34.8	20.2	38.3	34.3
1970	4.7	1.0	97.6	115	133	140	1.6	2.1	83.3	113	3.9	2.7	33.2	21.41	50.2	35.1
1971	4.2	1.1	111	123	158	157	1.7	1.7	103	123	5.0	3.2	38.9	22.41	40.2	41.3
1972	3.7	1.4	133	144	166	180	1.8	2.4	109	132	4.6	4.1	43.6	31.5	38.4	43.4
1973	4.4	1.2	161	181	212	206	1.9	2.3	138	155	6.9	8.2	55.9	40.3	48.4	48.8
1974	4.6	2.3	200	220	257	236	2.3	3.7	192	189	10.5	14.3	66.8	59.3	75.5	61.6
1975	3.3	3.0	197	202	248	235	2.0	5.7	192	181	11.0	12.8	70.2	68.4	71.7	43.1
1976	5.0	1.0	223	266	306	294	3.8	5.8	241	215	11.6	11.7	92.1	76.3	83.7	45.0
1977	5.0	1.4	230	257	322	302	7.5	9.4	245	226	14.5	9.8	113	92.0	87.2	56.6
1978	5.4	1.9	250	268	351	322	9.7	14.3	250	232	14.8	11.0	128	102	88.1	58.2
1979	5.1	3.4	279	318	394	373	7.1	11.7	297	268	17.4	13.8	141	135	119	61.9
1980	4.6	3.7	303	367	413	402	6.6	10.7	345	287	32.5	18.1	169	160	161	63.3
1981	4.7	2.9	316	396	435	414	7.8	20.0	394	303	36.3	21.9	171	178	166	87.2
1982	6.6	2.5	367	464	543	489	9.7	27.0	472	340	67.9	24.5	186	231	187	105
1983	10.7	2.8	396	483	582	560	13.3	29.4	512	378	71.4	34.0	244	261	181	136
1984	16.0	2.2	467	552	637	590	10.9	38.0	601	417	108	31.6	280	296	188	181
1985	11.9	2.0	499	601	696	589	11.6	41.8	615	451	74.0	37.3	296	310	188	201
1986	10.5	2.6	486	615	709	606	11.8	36.2	548	461	46.8	22.2	256	267	155	163
1987	7.3	2.6	488	634	756	615	12.5	38.5	533	466	48.0	18.4	244	261	148	161
1988	9.6	2.3	522	676	829	657	19.4	50.8	602	498	45.9	19.2	259	316	150	168
1989	11.7	1.8	578	807	912	744	27.9	64.0	685	540	46.5	21.2	306	370	183	190
1990	9.8	1.4	635	798	711	599	23.7	49.0	704	537	47.1	15.0	331	342	179	170
1991	8.7	2.5	649	767	968	955	22.7	47.1	709	551	43.5	17.2	344	311	198	151
1992	6.8	3.2	663	764	962	907	20.3	45.3	705	544	15.4[85]	7.1[85]	310	311	177	153
1993	7.6	4.5	606	790	808	871	27.2	63.5	608	543	39.2[85]	20.2[85]	351	351	206	197
									Million US$ Dollars							
1994	...	...	20,178.0	26,068.3	25,331.7	28,773.4	940.6	1,863.0	22,146.9	18,069.5	1,431.3	752.9	11,806.4	11,605.1	6,639.7	6,887.6
1995	...	...	23,486.8	29,299.9	32,001.8	34,715.8	1,117.1	2,580.6	27,160.4	21,499.4	1,346.6	1,041.8	13,540.8	13,179.8	8,576.9	6,248.8
1996	...	...	23,825.7	28,964.0	31,281.3	33,014.7	1,202.8	2,461.7	29,210.5	21,841.8	1,263.3	1,272.0	14,347.5	14,873.8	9,564.0	6,964.4
1997	...	...	21,375.8	26,825.0	28,270.7	30,808.3	1,181.9	2,826.7	27,097.4	20,079.4	1,397.2	1,537.6	13,836.6	16,393.8	11,483.0	8,075.2

E2 External Trade (by value) with Main Trading Partners

BULGARIA (in million leva)[7]

1885–1913

	Austria-Hungary		France		Germany		Italy		Russia		Turkey		U.K.	
	I	E	I	E	I	E	I	E	I	E	I	E	I	E
1885	11	1	2	5	2	1	1	2	3	–	5	9	11	12
1886	17	2	4	10	2	–	1	1	4	–	11	29	18	5
1887	15	4	4	6	3	–	1	1	3	–	10	25	22	6
1888	18	3	4	14	4	–	1	1	3	–	10	28	20	10
1889	22	4	3	18	4	1	1	2	5	–	10	31	21	13
1890	33	6	3	19	4	1	1	2	5	–	10	22	20	15
1891	34	3	4	24	5	–	1	1	5	–	10	17	16	17
1892	28	3	3	20	8	13	2	3	3	–	10	22	18	7
1893	33	2	4	14	12	16	2	2	3	–	10	25	20	17
1894	35	3	4	9	12	12	3	1	5	–	13	27	20	12
1895	22	3	3	13	9	13	2	1	3	–	9	23	15	14
1896	22	3	3	14	9	20	3	2	4	–	10	22	18	33
1897	22	4	4	9	11	8	3	1	4	–	9	11	23	17
1898	20	10	4	7	9	7	3	2	3	–	7	17	17	10
1899	18	4	3	5	9	4	3	1	2	–	6	21	12	10
1900	13	6	3	5	6	6	3	1	4	–	5	18	8	6
1901	17	7	4	5	10	9	4	3	4	–	10	24	14	16
1902	18	8	4	8	9	11	5	3	3	–	11	15	15	24
1903	23	10	3	8	11	9	6	3	4	–	12	23	15	20
1904	38	14	11	8	20	12	8	5	6	–	17	26	19	25
1905	33	19	7	9	21	12	7	4	3	–	17	21	20	13
1906	28	8	5	9	16	15	6	4	5	–	18	22	20	15
1907	35	8	7	7	20	17	6	3	5	–	18	27	21	21
1908	36	6	7	6	21	12	5	4	6	–	19	33	23	10
1909	39	12	11	5	29	14	5	3	6	–	21	37	27	8
1910	48	8	15	9	34	14	7	2	7	–	21	44	23	15
1911	48	11	25	11	40	23	9	4	7	–	16	29	30	24
1912	51	16	15	8	44	25	13	9	10	–	14	17	32	16
1913	55	14	13	5	37	17	7	4	32	1	6	4	17	8

E2 External Trade (by value) with Main Trading Partners

BULGARIA (in million leva)[7]

1919–1954

	Austria		Czechoslovakia		France		East Germany		West Germany		Germany		Italy		Russia/U.S.S.R.		Turkey		U.K.	
	I	E	I	E	I	E	I	E	I	E	I	E	I	E	I	E	I	E	I	E
1919	—	18	39	81	6	21	...	...	...	...	...	...	346	68	...	...	147	64	105	21
1920	66	149	73	203	198	100	...	...	...	...	...	...	625	284	24	1	408	79	311	53
1921	263	107	148	155	301	135	...	...	...	...	...	...	611	303	3	59	116	528	449	16
1922	340	216	155	105	279	309	...	...	...	...	870	713	497	522	14	122	299	1,034	604	30
1923	423	512	165	158	495	514	...	...	...	...	1,014	286	846	521	20	4	199	532	812	28
1924	590	531	316	385	419	632	...	...	...	...	1,126	867	789	502	19	1	176	225	724	26
1925	702	461	570	350	493	311	...	...	...	...	1,430	1,131	1,020	771	32	2	199	224	959	28
1926	541	429	748	407	481	321	...	...	...	...	1,369	1,095	865	679	27	—	131	112	709	42
1927	502	1,058	600	313	447	383	...	...	...	...	1,290	1,529	894	486	20	—	151	173	736	66
1928	567	915	757	183	540	349	...	...	...	...	1,494	1,739	1,070	686	18	1	159	296	732	121
1929	635	803	748	304	680	329	...	...	...	...	1,850	1,912	888	670	27	1	189	161	739	100
1930	311[7]	478[7]	430[7]	396[7]	425[7]	321[7]	...	...	...	...	1,065[7]	1,621[7]	623[7]	514[7]	22[7]	—[7]	94[7]	80[7]	376[7]	128[7]
1931	335	993	431	274	328	234	...	...	...	...	1,084	1,748	638	542	3	—	90	80	617	59
1932	208	507	292	104	227	90	...	...	...	...	900	880	344	424	12	1	75	48	358	86
1933	137	277	106	99	96	93	...	...	...	...	841	1,025	281	258	11	1	27	18	152	50
1934	107	135	85	91	86	53	...	...	...	...	902	1,083	176	233	10	—	30	36	143	53
1935	193	149	294	224	43	60	...	...	...	...	1,608	1,562	94	285	7	1	19	16	141	142
1936	181	116	244	128	39	80	...	...	...	...	1,940	1,860	19	142	4	—	25	25	146	454
1937	166	202	244	279	164	81	...	...	...	...	2,699[8]	2,163[8]	246	211	1	—	25	32	232	695
1938	...	...	292	255	182	83	...	...	...	...	2,563	3,284	370	422	2	—	44	32	348	267
1939	...	...	227	217	62	53	...	...	...	...	3,403	4,110	357	368	5	—	42	39	...	...
1944	...	...	225	134	24	76	...	...	...	...	4,676	9,965	26	1	1	112	181	74	...	...
1945	...	...	3	8	2	3	...	...	...	...	269	60	1	—	4,632	11,626	315	282	...	...
1946	...	...	[789][7]	[1,223][7]	[17][7]	[476][7]	...	...	...	...	[61][7]	[21][7]	[29][7]	[76][7]	[9,850][7]	[8,064][7]	[341][7]	[278][7]	...	...
1947	...	...	...	...	...	...	...	...	...	...			...	...	...	...	...	...	...	...
1948	20	62	106	88	13	17	16	41	...	—			23	17	...	...	...	...	...	...
1949	...	...	...	...	...	...	...	...	...	...			...	...	510	437	6	6	15	6
1950	...	...	...	...	...	...	...	...	...	...			...	...	...	...	...	...	...	...
1951	50	48	136	145	5	1	77	75	8	12			4	5	...	...	...	...	...	...
1952	...	...	...	...	...	...	...	...	...	...			...	...	...	...	...	...	...	...
1953	...	...	...	...	...	...	...	...	...	...			...	...	614	665	4	9	21	22
1954	28	68	183	144	6	7	169	201	38	39			6	14	613	734	9	11	39	35

E2 External Trade (by value) with Main Trading Partners

BULGARIA (in million leva)[7]   1955–1997

Values 1955–1993 in **million new leva**; values 1994–1997 in **Million US$ Dollars**.

Year	Austria I	Austria E	Czechoslovakia I	Czechoslovakia E	France I	France E	East Germany I	East Germany E	West Germany I	West Germany E	Italy I	Italy E	Russia/U.S.S.R. I	Russia/U.S.S.R. E	Turkey I	Turkey E	U.K. I	U.K. E
1955	38	35	283	173	9	11	157	221	42	37	7	6	807	812	8	9	32	13
1956	46	37	246	219	29	25	226	269	54	53	13	11	706	1,001	8	8	50	21
1957	43	46	220	319	36	30	219	174	98	65	32	42	1,190	1,366	7	12	35	13
1958	31	31	246	277	37	33	267	202	104	84	30	36	1,314	1,364	8	9	21	22
1959	73	44	360	288	62	28	348	319	322	102	113	64	1,949	1,765	7	5	69	27
1960	11	13	72	64	9	6	82	66	44	22	8	11	389	360	2	3	13	8
1961	21	10	65	71	12	6	99	89	25	25	12	9	416	394	1	2	9	7
1962	26	10	71	75	13	15	79	94	26	34	17	22	518	454	1	3	14	10
1963	31	10	95	82	18	11	114	95	39	41	21	23	586	522	3	4	20	11
1964	25	20	74	86	30	11	105	96	60	37	29	37	656	610	3	4	17	15
1965	36	15	90	107	30	8	99	127	80	48	38	46	689	718	5	4	22	21
1966	37	27	91	74	56	16	122	126	154	48	48	68	827	776	5	7	37	25
1967	46	25	115	94	41	25	148	138	79	65	74	65	916	904	4	6	23	26
1968	38	25	97	104	57	21	176	142	84	63	67	51	1,107	1,046	6	6	24	31
1969	36	24	93	119	29	25	179	174	53	63	65	57	1,139	1,146	6	5	23	34
1970	42	19	113	102	52	44	184	203	57	60	67	67	1,118	1,261	6	5	52	29
1971	46	26	151	118	59	27	213	219	69	59	71	71	1,297	1,399	6	7	38	44
1972	34	26	175	135	29	28	271	219	91	73	71	81	1,448	1,597	8	4	41	29
1973	49	26	183	132	35	38	278	267	138	88	71	95	1,646	1,750	10	9	48	29
1974	83	33	170	150	71	41	380	294	291	92	100	77	1,831	1,872	16	18	70	35
1975	93	28	165	206	125	49	347	317	410	76	135	62	2,653	2,481	13	39	74	25
1976	81	45	234	257	106	64	372	393	312	106	88	57	2,958	2,818	11	64	64	29
1977	75	40	254	267	110	65	443	471	281	94	94	62	3,461	3,250	23	54	60	28
1978	82	39	268	276	82	76	465	457	308	109	91	68	4,047	3,584	13	36	43	24
1979	114	52	296	265	110	75	487	445	314	134	102	110	4,336	4,020	4	111	83	38
1980	137	82	310	274	147	96	548	487	397	227	119	127	4,743	4,445	12	94	99	127
1981	153	55	418	355	151	127	552	579	487	226	143	135	5,451	4,768	18	107	170	130
1982	173	47	425	413	117	165	634	582	490	197	151	146	6,134	5,616	25	93	128	104
1983	197	39	492	471	96	142	681	646	464	197	107	99	6,951	6,618	26	126	106	108
1984	182	54	506	526	140	107	713	677	472	226	125	67	7,580	7,230	35	218	107	202
1985	206	50	583	626	177	61	712	701	547	199	163	68	7,898	7,776	11	152	179	238
1986	212	29	653	610	123	71	746	742	699	145	160	110	8,098	8,154			175	74
1987	218	31	697	673	99	59	804	757	695	160	165	82	8,056	8,437			162	76
1988	219	36	752	666	95	48	818	750	686	142	156	103	7,454	9,006			135	97
1989	193	48	630	594	131	70		752	633	184	185	89	6,767	8,917			147	117
1990	165	45	479	467	75	55		305	386	142	197	82	5,827	6,763			171	59
1991	2,115	563	535	492	959	827	*Included in West Germany*		3,146	2,728	1,883	1,549	19,508	28,552			1,631	1,113
1992	3,185	1,136	1,687	690[86]	2,462	2,361			12,529	6,993	5,082	5,293	23,961[87]	16,430[87]			2,599	2,854
1993	3,478	1,165	1,743	588[86]	3,211	7,629			15,205	6,776	6,036	6,114	39,487[87]	15,098[87]			7,755	3,187
1994	121.4	50.0	55.5[86]	15.7[86]	114.7	97.3			537.3	320.1	222.7	272.7	1,100.7	479.4	78.3	180.9	135.1	97.0
1995	156.9	45.8	75.5[86]	18.5[86]	157.3	152.9			697.0	457.8	326.6	436.5	1,583.9	536.1	99.8	385.1	147.4	167.2
1996	123.2	50.3	65.9[86]	23.3[86]	162.7	127.0			575.1	442.0	318.6	493.1	1,694.2	480.0	96.0	384.3	105.1	140.9
1997	118.0	54.0	63.0[86]	18.6[86]	156.5	133.6			563.2	468.1	347.2	575.1	1,374.8	391.8	101.6	442.3	126.9	130.6

E2 External Trade (by value) with Main Trading Partners

CZECHOSLOVAKIA (in million koruna)   1920–1959

Year	Austria I	Austria E	Germany I	Germany E	East Germany I	East Germany E	West Germany I	West Germany E	Hungary I	Hungary E	Poland I	Poland E	Romania I	Romania E	Russia/U.S.S.R. I	Russia/U.S.S.R. E	U.K. I	U.K. E	U.S.A. I	U.S.A. E
1920	3,042	9,678	5,604	3,331					656	2,512	399	1,425	308	732	138	126	1,009	813	4,111	544
1921	1,983	7,835	5,862	3,061					926	3,066	384	1,424	482	1,175	72	133	1,342	2,104	4,547	771
1922	986	3,969	3,700	4,118					684	1,589	324	605	430	523	21	93	652	1,347	2,286	932
1923	667	2,639	4,488	3,205					353	714	376	358	186	405	6[9]	9[9]	337	1,219	714	557
1924	1,244	3,524	6,435	4,131					880	1,135	723	558	467	796	80	73	448	1,586	889	719
1925	1,296	3,252	7,140	5,347					1,121	1,178	1,238	659	369	850	33	404	654	1,535	1,174	756
1926	1,131	2,904	5,635	4,780					1,028	1,228	1,097	364	481	835	80	156	605	1,540	765	845
1927	1,280	3,069	6,539	5,721					963	1,622	1,023	662	663	908	154	190	800	1,520	1,232	1,012
1928	1,442	3,124	7,410	5,670					849	1,468	1,264	851	537	871	191	279	830	1,478	1,148	1,170
1929	1,565	3,074	7,675	4,691					967	1,306	1,299	888	473	700	257	259	817	1,423	1,089	1,472
1930	1,211	2,439	6,011	3,572					930	1,004	880	639	562	596	302	328	579	1,378	786	977
1931	851	1,796	4,791	2,493					134	289	619	379	566	341	278	489	434	1,356	484	805
1932	450	1,039	2,869	1,454					121	201	375	189	335	302	164[9]	121[9]	339	406	926	507
1933	299	721	1,774	1,170					167	190	191	167	177	221	113	77	280	360	464	428
1934	325	769	1,707	1,618					128	154	235	145	186	271	96	32	331	466	355	494
1935	310	754	1,536	1,224					133	139	252	264	260	383	73	104	367	547	400	615
1936	355	716	1,834	1,230					144	157	221	169	362	380	91	181	475	723	483	729
1937	457	877	1,904	1,801					161	227	279	315	532	654	125	94	695	1,039	961	1,112
1946	407	627	107	998					589	382	28	141	192	189	1,352	1,713	916	420	853	1,083
1947	507	1,023	276	526					569	801	690	479	246	391	1,946	1,395	3,376	1,840	2,955	1,250
1948	898	1,539	858	1,264					1,037	1,111	2,024	2,643	1,471	1,190	5,888	6,006	3,816	1,358	1,820	1,168
1949	177	281			151	146	105	200	203	236	385	518	271	273	1,272	1,358	420	129	..	..
1950	208	185			215	297	112	180	245	240	417	631	153	273	1,384	1,425	302	284	..	..
1951	232	199			392	256	131	90	348	355	644	617	233	266	1,815	1,833	242	295	..	..
1952	180	168			353	371	67	126	447	548	595	702	270	294	2,298	2,092	220	204	..	..
1953	113	103			438	441	61	106	529	507	722	733	259	794	2,476	2,313	167	208	—	14
1954	97	93			542	584	121	127	558	484	581	607	271	305	2,522	2,510	159	192	3	20
1955	120	135			705	574	119	124	555	461	548	740	300	270	2,631	2,900	202	163	4	25
1956	155	144			851	1,010	280	364	467	424	554	714	205	252	2,808	3,085	193	178	5	39
1957	180	148			1,039	952	431	395	528	547	432	563	192	267	3,856	2,866	261	248	10	44
1958	150	140			1,167	1,134	445	386	651	557	515	683	161	272	3,253	3,579	233	211	7	54
1959	160	163			1,260	1,282	417	439	626	620	590	827	306	436	4,305	4,229	353	256	13	72

E2 External Trade (by value) with Main Trading Partners

CZECHOSLOVAKIA (in million koruna)

	Austria I	Austria E	East Germany I	East Germany E	West Germany I	West Germany E	Hungary I	Hungary E	Poland I	Poland E	Romania I	Romania E	Russia/U.S.S.R. I	Russia/U.S.S.R. E	U.K. I	U.K. E	U.S.A. I	U.S.A. E
1960	271	195	1,427	1,408	428	489	676	804	796	924	463	458	4,539	4,742	390	274	40	89
1961	264	215	1,656	1,583	450	512	978	750	1,016	1,181	389	554	4,723	5,136	442	311	61	68
1962	254	201	1,644	1,655	440	483	1,004	900	1,044	1,447	433	634	5,626	5,964	438	292	51	71
1963	253	210	1,675	1,599	333	545	944	1,099	1,052	1,408	381	725	6,067	6,886	601	362	76	98
1964	255	244	1,829	1,915	506	594	1,057	1,138	1,392	1,388	537	669	6,572	6,924	663	419	98	99
1965	349	306	2,073	1,995	633	664	1,234	952	1,502	1,791	679	496	6,874	7,364	528	434	139	147
1966	446	282	2,291	2,141	584	678	1,237	952	1,294	1,703	664	500	6,585	6,627	691	485	307	203
1967	381	333	2,305	2,294	595	739	1,086	1,097	1,434	1,691	623	644	6,950	7,035	520	480	133	195
1968	505	384	2,877	2,362	729	861	1,305	1,205	1,785	1,668	787	718	7,460	7,257	575	507	118	163
1969	635	518	2,988	2,590	1,060	1,309	1,375	997	1,873	1,787	1,001	769	7,957	8,096	564	557	133	129
1970	735	544	3,208	3,285	1,513	1,501	1,313	1,438	1,942	2,196	976	1,122	8,703	8,795	669	575	196	169
1971	761	698	3,578	3,319	1,781	1,662	1,428	1,789	1,925	2,507	890	1,076	9,780	9,529	769	621	209	157
1972	738	720	3,891	3,552	1,721	1,689	1,759	1,732	2,358	3,019	1,017	1,169	10,266	11,061	694	659	417	174
1973	969	776	4,550	3,948	2,101	2,086	2,171	1,898	2,911	3,608	1,291	1,165	10,737	11,188	810	813	788	220
1974	1,479	1,142	5,269	4,470	3,030	2,488	2,621	2,272	3,557	3,742	1,413	1,247	11,997	12,258	1,336	1,247	796	320
1975	1,618	1,110	6,188	5,720	3,271	2,579	2,662	2,738	4,847	4,127	1,424	1,516	16,276	15,387	1,133	971	756	180
1976	1,756	1,230	6,568	6,550	3,198	2,748	3,336	3,356	5,032	4,902	1,650	1,759	18,230	17,696	1,143	788	1,472	218
1977	2,537	1,410	7,039	7,084	3,713	3,052	3,700	3,328	5,380	5,345	2,251	2,071	21,402	19,995	1,301	951	858	220
1978	2,606	1,422	8,109	7,544	4,088	3,409	3,821	3,833	5,720	5,713	2,482	2,310	23,844	22,018	1,564	922	737	308
1979	2,159	1,861	8,411	7,207	4,787	4,037	4,336	3,974	6,220	5,654	2,490	2,528	26,886	25,001	1,658	1,181	1,690	286
1980	2,424	2,628	8,522	7,476	4,408	5,189	4,608	4,310	6,190	6,026	2,335	2,427	29,384	28,516	2,349	1,357	1,657	395
1981	2,544	2,586	8,533	8,418	4,334	5,144	4,760	4,415	5,575	5,843	2,108	2,214	34,463	33,005	1,670	1,304	955	379
1982	3,063	2,863	8,948	8,635	4,408	4,841	5,133	5,089	5,933	5,949	2,477	2,434	40,917	38,745	1,535	1,005	895	330
1983	2,940	2,817	10,635	9,315	4,659	4,928	5,146	5,523	6,411	7,327	2,383	1,881	47,574	43,421	1,321	1,139	593	351
1984	2,251	2,911	11,783	10,107	4,731	5,365	6,387	5,688	8,193	8,134	2,320	1,981	53,230	49,606	1,376	1,256	305	488
1985	2,680	3,107	11,469	10,992	5,091	5,401	6,952	5,666	9,609	9,169	2,525	2,456	55,345	52,305	1,472	1,237	285	505
1986	3,458	2,857	12,030	10,873	6,149	5,655	6,844	6,247	10,954	10,632	2,572	2,630	56,794	52,948	1,484	1,269	300	448
1987	3,803	2,824	12,922	11,642	7,013	5,668	6,579	7,020	12,532	12,006	2,572	2,630	55,521	54,553	1,430	1,484	192	460
1988	4,112	3,295	13,649	11,705	7,252	6,138	7,166	7,240	13,747	13,739	2,995	2,631	52,023	57,177	1,686	1,634	305	485
1989	11,830	9,938	16,746	14,257	20,213	18,685	10,294	8,641	18,485	18,438	3,561	3,938	63,729	66,439	4,731	4,396	813	1,413
1990	23,124	12,717	19,499	9,172	32,132	28,372	8,147	8,841	20,370	13,394	1,732	2,518	51,410	54,159	6,862	5,521	1,368	1,639
[88] 1991 Czech Republic	23,124	18,631	Included in West Germany		59,630	80,659	5,676	13,989	14,458	23,326	982	3,210	93,489	62,428	6,182	6,143	5,427	3,195
[88] 1992	26,594	17,910			78,424	81,456	…	…	…	11,906	…	…	15,393[89]	10,468[89]	…	…	14,828	…
[88] 1993	29,181	22,874			95,193	98,358	…	…	…	10,217	…	…	35,908[89]	16,406[89]	…	…	11,242	…

Million US$ Dollars

	Austria I	Austria E	West Germany I	West Germany E	Hungary I	Hungary E	Poland I	Poland E	Romania I	Romania E	Russia/U.S.S.R. I	Russia/U.S.S.R. E	U.K. I	U.K. E	U.S.A. I	U.S.A. E
1994	1,207.1	1,013.1	3,795.5	4,153.1	170.9	363.3	426.2	548.6	46.4	…	1,256.5	548.2	452.3	392.6	506.8	302.6
1995	1,747.5	1,426.4	8,015.7	8,144.9	218.5	378.3	683.1	966.9	57.1	…	1,879.2	632.8	953.4	687.9	853.2	415.5
1996	1,594.0	1,411.2	8,262.1	7,892.0	275.6	390.7	806.5	1,205.4	72.6	…	2,059.9	692.8	1,043.0	551.8	940.0	463.2
1997	1,646.9	1,461.4	8,672.0	8,131.6	355.0	427.1	870.9	1,305.1	91.7	…	1,843.3	771.4	1,054.9	688.8	1,030.4	583.3

E2 External Trade (by value) with Main Trading Partners

DENMARK (in million kroner)

1874–1911

	France		Germany		Norway		Sweden		U.K.		U.S.A.	
	I	E	I	E	I	E	I	E	I	E	I	E
1874	4	—	83	59	10	15	26	24	58	71	4	—
1875	5	—	84	50	8	18	26	22	64	73	2	—
1876	4	—	88	53	6	16	27	26	59	76	4	—
1877	3	1	85	53	5	12	24	26	54	64	8	—
1878	3	2	76	48	5	11	20	21	41	63	8	—
1879	3	2	73	54	5	9	19	20	47	64	11	1
1880	4	1	80	67	6	16	28	27	53	76	18	1
1881	5	1	91	62	6	18	25	28	59	64	19	2
1882	4	1	97	60	7	12	32	27	59	73	12	4
1883	5	2	102	59	7	11	42	30	65	82	17	4
1884	5	1	99	58	8	10	39	27	63	68	15	4
1885	6	2	94	52	6	9	36	23	54	63	16	2
1886	4	2	76	50	6	8	30	23	49	72	13	2
1887	5	2	91	60	5	7	36	22	57	77	15	3
1888	5	1	100	36	6	7	38	18	62	111	10	2
1889	8	2	100	41	7	7	41	20	73	126	14	2
1890	7	2	100	59	6	7	43	22	68	129	21	2
1891	9	2	111	68	6	9	47	23	69	132	19	2
1892	10	1	104	67	5	9	49	26	68	136	29	1
1893	5	1	110	47	4	7	44	24	69	144	20	1
1894	6	2	119	66	5	8	50	23	69	153	14	1
1895	7	1	122	66	6	7	47	22	71	155	10	2
1896	8	2	126	58	6	9	51	22	78	170	17	2
1897	11	2	129	66	7	10	52	27	79	171	48	2
1898	9	1	134	56	8	10	53	33	97	200	64	2
1899	11	1	144	67	7	11	52	35	101	216	78	7
1900	15	2	154	68	8	12	53	38	108	233	78	7
1901	13	1	147	68	9	13	47	40	88	249	87	9
1902	14	3	166	79	8	13	56	40	88	269	71	16
1903	16	4	190	90	10	14	56	37	95	294	80	17
1904	16	1	214	105	9	13	54	40	90	283	74	16
1905	14	2	207	128	10	15	59	42	100	280	100	21
1906	18	2	234	124	12	14	63	48	111	291	129	26
1907	17	1	258	129	14	19	67	53	135	312	124	27
1908	16	1	238	122	11	22	58	46	109	337	113	25
1909	16	1	256	133	11	19	58	40	114	330	86	31
1910	16	3	242	125	7	11	56	23	117	341	52	9
1911	17	3	266	160	8	16	67	31	115	353	63	8

E2 External Trade (by value) with Main Trading Partners

DENMARK (in million kroner)

1912–1949

	France I	France E	Germany I	Germany E	Norway I	Norway E	Sweden I	Sweden E	U.K. I	U.K. E	U.S.A. I	U.S.A. E
1912	19	3	314	182	9	19	69	33	136	373	69	9
1913	21	3	328	179	9	19	71	34	135	410	87	9
1914	18	6	265	301	17	23	83	38	145	432	84	12
1915	13	6	200	487	28	32	93	68	253	385	314	12
1916	20	2	265	691	40	56	117	63	337	351	311	9
1917	14	2	244	490	31	79	135	113	286	265	214	4
1918	4	2	316	308	47	128	235	187	196	52	38	2
1919	53	8	335	265	48	137	195	231	814	164	599	29
1920	65	22	532	326	73	184	190	358	888	672	754	91
1921	43	30	462	211	41	82	98	139	305	826	343	43
1922	46	38	477	89	33	86	105	94	341	763	224	15
1923	61	17	651	105	40	76	115	131	407	1,063	254	29
1924	81	14	649	364	41	64	129	169	446	1,187	294	29
1925	72	13	583	402	43	76	114	148	307	1,088	337	10
1926	67	10	504	291	30	65	98	112	186	859	263	12
1927	59	9	509	321	22	50	106	108	217	877	251	9
1928	64	12	567	342	28	68	109	108	240	919	227	10
1929	69	12	591	340	38	67	125	109	263	967	239	19
1930	69	16	591	262	41	77	123	102	251	951	194	10
1931	53	21	491	179	22	68	91	85	219[10]	815[10]	154	6
1932	29	15	296	150	24	33	63	66	255	729	88	5
1933	36	14	287	158	29	31	89	58	356	781	76	8
1934	41	15	288	189	28	42	103	76	407	740	82	11
1935	36	12	292	206	33	55	90	82	479	732	70	9
1936	16	20	376	280	43	53	101	84	542	744	79	12
1937	20[11]	10[11]	407[11]	298[11]	38[11]	79[11]	103[11]	102[11]	642[11]	825[11]	93[11]	29[11]
	18	10	404	297	38	71	102	82	638	824	87	29
1938	20	22	399[12]	304[12]	41	41	107	74	562	861	128	17
1939	28	16	470	369	40	56	127	77	573	827	128	21
1940	5	2	770	1,089	48	45	67	56	150	190	93	2
1941	–	–	1,021[12]	977[12]	58	99	99	66	1	1	1	–
1942	1	1	848	693	59	77	136	75	–	–	–	–
1943	1	1	869	990	68	79	97	73	–	–	–	10
1944	2	–	908[12]	1,090[12]	57	68	38	62	–	–	–	–
1945	4	29	159	183	91	115	153	72	107	310	23	34
1946	76	62	118	73	143	102	201	173	1,289	514	256	51
1947	101	60	108	37	158	125	213	209	671	627	605	99
1948	109	116	119	39	149	176	226	205	889	831	494	147
1949	202	170	105	232	157	188	289	188	1,339	1,564	672	112

E2 External Trade (by value) with Main Trading Partners

DENMARK (in million kroner) 1950–1997

Year	France I	France E	Germany I	Germany E	Norway I	Norway E	Sweden I	Sweden E	U.K. I	U.K. E	U.S.A. I	U.S.A. E
1950	503	136	571	787	206	163	471	273	1,869	1,931	544	119
1951	402	296	895	729	262	249	594	307	1,818	2,224	745	164
1952	322	178	1,032	732	248	244	592	301	1,830	2,262	552	279
1953	302	184	1,268	708	249	211	646	323	1,994	2,492	309	409
1954	365	124	1,562	841	279	253	744	429	2,157	2,400	396	490
1955	441	157	1,517	1,220	268	304	722	517	2,077	2,413	635	531
1956	339	245	1,754	1,398	321	310	809	524	2,206	2,340	904	562
1957	396	195	1,801	1,553	335	300	840	706	2,286	2,229	924	662
1958	317[13]	255[13]	1,845[13]	1,725[13]	328[13]	416[13]	935[13]	640[13]	2,111[13]	2,228[13]	842[13]	790[13]
1959	408	229	2,350	1,924	370	440	1,073	700	2,359	2,519	1,042	969
1960	549	167	2,728	2,061	406	461	1,183	914	1,820	2,701	1,220	695
1961	588	297	2,877	2,142	518	525	1,395	970	1,834	2,573	1,037	789
1962	589	239	3,145	2,193	612	588	1,722	1,106	2,045	2,787	1,219	860
1963	558	402	3,082	2,217	526	532	1,755	1,377	2,134	3,007	1,296	830
1964	743	490	3,713	2,353	597	801	2,310	1,703	2,482	3,380	1,566	884
1965	724	437	4,125	2,700	738	906	2,570	1,971	2,583	3,502	1,657	1,064
1966	746	502	4,203	2,395	801	1,046	2,808	2,103	2,842	3,812	1,628	1,312
1967	858	483	4,196	2,077	977	1,269	3,160	2,395	3,034	3,998	1,881	1,219
1968	1,030	528	4,562	2,396	1,024	1,425	3,627	2,959	3,294	4,080	2,054	1,577
1969	1,207	612	5,440	2,831	1,183	1,532	4,438	3,561	3,917	4,362	2,195	1,853
1970	1,415	594	6,128	3,125	1,281	1,735	5,188	4,096	4,513	4,605	2,426	1,948
1971	1,365	639	5,895	3,105	1,258	1,852	5,272	4,009	4,312	4,841	2,672	1,987
1972	1,376	728	5,697	3,178	1,419	1,844	4,851	4,054	3,739	5,055	2,156	2,118
1973	1,872	1,277	9,525	6,200	2,182	2,520	7,443	5,293	5,222	7,214	3,163	2,712
1974	2,140	1,509	10,500	7,548	2,519	2,746	7,815	7,126	5,264	7,548	3,437	2,559
1975	2,247	1,581	11,775	6,648	2,892	3,489	8,489	10,624	6,117	9,414	3,615	2,579
1976	2,849	2,300	15,635	7,900	3,513	3,702	10,623	8,685	7,665	9,418	3,853	3,144
1977	3,352	2,613	15,628	9,162	3,758	4,468	10,434	8,643	8,721	8,468	4,554	3,432
1978	3,523	2,991	16,810	11,070	3,384	4,032	10,519	8,300	9,237	11,571	4,236	3,647
1979	4,588	3,785	19,135	13,510	4,019	4,660	12,319	10,394	11,500	11,524	5,055	3,697
1980	4,739	4,920	20,127	18,055	4,502	5,985	13,969	11,927	13,263	13,694	6,988	4,262
1981	5,039	5,473	23,053	19,017	5,360	7,083	14,957	13,084	14,832	15,454	10,545	6,047
1982	5,741	7,017	28,694	22,381	5,207	8,295	16,376	13,910	15,210	18,046	9,381	7,490
1983	6,700	8,079	29,701	25,354	6,136	9,380	19,634	15,411	15,829	19,786	8,020	10,694
1984	7,656	7,317	35,002	26,644	7,067	10,516	23,945	18,874	15,459	21,228	8,930	15,915
1985	8,527	7,925	40,384	28,871	7,747	12,071	24,991	21,692	18,010	21,908	11,339	18,149
1986	9,322	8,914	43,625	28,925	6,747	13,075	22,784	19,481	14,026	20,096	9,700	14,558
1987	9,273	9,714	41,006	29,719	7,377	12,972	21,267	20,115	13,273	20,195	9,306	12,385
1988	8,642	10,426	39,907	31,934	7,798	12,413	21,378	20,958	12,320	21,746	10,472	10,671
1989	9,720	12,387	43,390	35,946	8,577	11,699	23,605	25,061	13,365	24,912	13,468	11,482
1990	10,420	12,952	43,738	42,375	9,205	12,267	22,593	27,591	14,886	23,126	12,152	10,482
1991	12,975	13,421	45,518	51,428	11,674	12,704	22,400	26,300	16,641	23,590	13,045	10,576
1992	11,404	13,712	46,997	56,765	10,964	13,767	22,009	25,239	16,693	24,171	11,506	10,155
1993	10,602	13,952	44,857	58,262	9,889	16,156	20,820	23,392	15,345	23,044	9,189	12,301
							Million US$ Dollars					
1994	1,811.5	1,955.4	7,249.5	8,302.8	1,709.9	2,483.3	3,891.7	3,918.2	2,191.4	3,036.8	1,715.8	1,953.4
1995	2,220.7	2,360.7	9,186.0	10,219.4	2,120.7	2,771.4	5,024.7	4,404.2	2,810.6	3,537.1	1,942.6	1,727.6
1996	2,240.5	2,174.3	8,697.6	9,699.3	2,205.3	2,994.6	4,969.5	4,734.1	2,897.5	4,006.9	2,033.5	1,759.9
1997	2,451.9	2,293.4	9,466.1	9,673.7	2,291.5	2,926.3	5,597.3	5,355.3	3,308.0	4,404.2	2,216.2	1,961.8

E2 External Trade (by value) with Main Trading Partners

FINLAND (in million marks)

1827–1864

	Germany		Russia[14]		Sweden		U.K.		U.S.A.	
	I	E	I	E	I	E	I	E	I	E
1827	…	…	2	2	…	…	…	…	…	…
1828	…	…	2	2	…	…	…	…	…	…
1829	…	…	3	2	…	…	…	…	…	…
1830	…	…	4	2	…	…	…	…	…	…
1831	…	…	3	2	…	…	…	…	…	…
1832	…	…	5	3	…	…	…	…	…	…
1833	…	…	3	3	…	…	…	…	…	…
1834	…	…	4	3	…	…	…	…	…	…
1835	…	…	5	3	…	…	…	…	…	…
1836	…	…	6	3	…	…	…	…	…	…
1837	…	…	9	3	…	…	…	…	…	…
1838	…	…	6	3	…	…	…	…	…	…
1839	…	…	5	3	…	…	…	…	…	…
1840	…	…	7	5	2	2	…	…	…	…
1841	…	…	8	5	2	2	…	…	…	…
1842	…	…	6	5	3	2	…	…	…	…
1843	…	…	8	5	2	2	…	…	…	…
1844	…	…	9	5	2	…	…	…	…	…
1845	…	…	9	7	2	1	…	…	…	…
1846	…	…	9	6	2	1	…	…	…	…
1847	…	…	8	6	2	1	…	…	…	…
1848	…	…	8	6	2	1	…	…	…	…
1849	…	…	9	6	2	1	…	…	…	…
1850	…	…	10	7	2	1	…	…	…	…
1851	…	…	11	9	1	2	…	…	…	…
1852	…	…	11	9	2	2	…	…	…	…
1853	…	…	12	10	2	1	…	…	…	…
1854	…	…	12	6	4	3	…	…	…	…
1855	15	…	17	7	6	6	3	5	…	…
1856	15	2	18	7	8	4	4	5	1	…
1857	14	2	24	8	5	3	4	5	3	…
1858	12	2	14	9	3	2	5	4	2	…
1859	10	2	14	11	3	3			5	…
1860	11	2	15	12	4	3	5	6	6	…
1861	14	2	22	13	4	5	5	7	9	…
1862	16	3	33	14	5	4	4	7	8	…
1863	16	2	33	18	5	3	6	9	6	…
1864	14	3	27	18	4	3	4	9	7	…

E2 External Trade (by value) with Main Trading Partners

FINLAND (in million marks)

1865–1899

	Germany		Russia		Sweden		U.K.		U.S.A.[15]	
	I	E	I	E	I	E	I	E	I	E
1865	18	3	34	17	5	3	4	11	8	—
1866	10	3	28	12	5	2	4	9	7	—
1867	12	2	36	26	4	3	4	8	5	—
1868	11	3	36	26	5	4	5	9	5	—
1869	15	5	31	26	6	4	13	9	6	—
1870	16	4	22	21	8	5	9	10	5	—
1871	18	5	20	16	7	5	9	10	7	—
1872	22	6	23	16	9	5	15	14	7	—
1873	24	6	34	26	10	8	20	20	9	—
1874	37	6	63	37	13	8	21	24	8	—
1875	39	6	68	41	13	6	21	18	11	—
1876	34	9	65	36	10	9	16	24	2	—
1877	35	7	77	35	9	9	16	21	1	—
1878	28	5	67	41	8	6	13	27	2	—
1879	25	6	57	50	6	5	12	14	3	—
1880	35	7	58	51	10	10	15	18	4	—
1881	41	5	68	50	11	8	17	32	4	—
1882	43	8	72	55	14	8	16	23	2	—
1883	40	7	67	48	13	10	17	24	3	—
1884	34	7	68	44	11	11	21	25	—	—
1885	30	4	50	40	9	8	13	18	2	—
1886	24	5	47	34	8	7	12	14	1	—
1887	28	6	46	31	8	31	15	13	—	—
1888	35	8	50	32	8	9	14	18	1	—
1889	38	8	54	37	9	9	19	23	4	—
1890	45	6	47	36	12	7	23	18	2	—
1891	47	7	53	36	10	6	22	19	5[15]	—
1892	42	8	61	33	9	5	17	21	1	—
1893	36	8	50	40	7	5	14	25	1	—
1894	49	9	48	44	9	5	17	33	1	—
1895	53	10	51	49	9	6	19	36	—	—
1896	59	11	55	48	10	5	24	47	—	—
1897	66	13	73	48	12	6	29	51	—	—
1898	75	15	82	51	15	8	38	54	1	—
1899	81	17	86	55	14	7	41	54	—	—

E2 External Trade (by value) with Main Trading Partners

FINLAND (in million marks)

1900–1934

	Germany		Russia/USSR		Sweden		U.K.		U.S.A.	
	I	E	I	E	I	E	I	E	I	E
1900	90	17	101	57	13	7	34	58	1	—
1901	67	16	87	55	11	6	26	52	—	—
1902	85	19	94	59	11	6	22	61	—	—
1903	98	20	103	53	11	8	27	64	2	—
1904	95	20	105	58	12	7	27	64	—	—
1905	101	27	95	68	13	8	29	75	—	—
1906	124	29	96	33	16	9	36	86	—	—
1907	153	31	111	73	19	10	46	84	—	—
1908	146	26	99	68	20	9	47	82	—	—
1909	145	32	117	72	18	10	41	78	—	—
1910	160	35	110	80	19	12	46	86	—	—
1911	173	47	138	89	21	14	62	88	—	—
1912	187	49	132	99	25	15	68	88	—	—
1913	203	52	140	113	28	17	61	109	—	—
1914	118	21	145	126	40	24	34	68	—	—
1915	7	—	385	204	164	62	5	...	—	—
1916	—	—	607	480	324	30	1	...	—	—
1917	—	—	626	428	580	16	1	1	—	—
1918	101	98	48	18	140	27	30	15	6	21
1919	157	82	6	1	321	71	676	377	639	21
1920	611	139	1	8	385	239	1,003	1,252	795	193
1921	1,206	372	1	56	267	406	709	1,142	614	275
1922	1,316	388	19	139	248	292	867	1,653	609	291
1923	1,564	271	216	85	264	253	848	1,816	584	343
1924	1,411	454	221	221	294	248	884	2,001	629	301
1925	1,760	747	74	430	358	237	937	2,062	812	296
1926	1,975	715	108	220	418	219	727	2,162	801	365
1927	2,075	999	209	319	523	194	924	2,539	981	341
1928	2,962	988	126	269	657	138	990	2,208	1,179	409
1929	2,683	925	119	211	540	126	912	2,441	873	453
1930	1,937	674	132	243	390	142	715	2,103	638	412
1931	1,210	375	96	99	287	132	435	1,991	372	413
1932	1,003	386	178	70	345	120	641	2,166	269	444
1933	1,081	521	184	100	387	116	808₁₆	2,429₁₆	289	462
1934	988	631	274	101	501	161	1,090	2,913	412	429

E2 External Trade (by value) with Main Trading Partners

FINLAND (in million marks)

1935–1964

	Germany		Russia/USSR		Sweden		U.K.		U.S.A.	
	I	E	I	E	I	E	I	E	I	E
1935	1,088	595	161	67	599	306	1,291	2,905	405	561
1936	1,201	719	125	37	785	392	1,502	3,462	518	667
1937	1,804	1,228	133	58	1,127	463	2,062	4,189	775	740
1938	1,723	1,244	106	44	1,111	405	1,862	3,701	774	773
1939	1,663	1,276	64	27	1,203	484	1,449	2,793	763	984
1940	1,888	1,554	194	9	2,232	274	623	85	1,251	150
1941	5,601	2,343	131	56	1,857	377	34	—	615	42
1942	8,654	3,982	2	—	969	262	1	—	22	—
1943	9,851	5,978	--	—	688	210	--	—	2	—
1944	6,464	4,273	--	—	712	442	--	—	2	--
	million new marks		million new marks		million new marks		million new marks		million new marks	
1945	106	—	1,293	1,546	3,501	832	727	1,839	3	99
1946	—	—	52	46	24	22	52	62	47	16
1947	5	1	53	56	23	26	82	136	111	52
1948	5[2]	5[2]	83	83	32	31	168	160	80	54
1949	6	20	75	100	44	27	147	178	51	50
1950	39	45	71	62	59	34	207	190	53	76
1951	147	133	119	155	87	58	327	575	97	128
1952	226	145	220	275	106	63	347	373	140	86
1953	93	92	261	335	53	41	192	290	61	95
1954	102	116	271	337	69	43	286	352	70	90
1955	159	165	260	317	87	34	359	435	93	104
1956	240	154	283	342	110	38	416	382	132	119
1957	259	188	403	424	134	66	402	460	128	107
1958	386	269	419	428	193	89	401	548	125	115
1959	481[13]	292[13]	475[13]	448[13]	243[13]	86[13]	420[13]	623[13]	136[13]	154[13]
1960	660	366	500	450	354	153	539	776	195	158
1961	784	437	503	409	422	192	563	748	208	148
1962	795	422	538	628	474	203	596	716	201	189
1963	695	442	653	590	458	209	592	791	189	191
1964	831	477	846	498	612	266	711	951	233	238

E2 External Trade (by value) with Main Trading Partners

FINLAND (in million marks)

1965–1997

Year	West Germany / Germany I	West Germany / Germany E	Russia/U.S.S.R. I	Russia/U.S.S.R. E	Sweden I	Sweden E	U.K. I	U.K. E	U.S.A. I	U.S.A. E
1965	996	512	755	725	737	343	808	944	265	273
1966	942	535	856	682	781	423	887	989	252	308
1967	939	450	931	896	892	508	880	1,091	227	303
1968	1,034	722	1,135	1,062	1,066	751	1,023	1,421	233	401
1969	1,410	836	1,097	1,173	1,434	1,157	1,391	1,537	347	498
1970	1,881	1,029	1,377	1,151	1,924	1,543	1,735	1,715	483	453
1971	1,974	1,029	1,624	1,050	2,130	1,611	1,808	1,906	505	470
1972	2,360	1,247	1,520	1,492	2,489	2,142	1,817	2,218	577	578
1973	3,075	1,511	2,002	1,705	3,270	2,223	1,875	2,880	788	652
1974	3,946	1,779	4,640	2,835	4,719	3,394	2,263	3,971	1,901	766
1975	4,414	1,740	4,737	4,069	5,105	3,687	2,497	2,967	2,114	642
1976	4,571[80]	2,408[80]	5,132[80]	4,903[80]	5,201[80]	4,350[80]	2,277[80]	3,493[80]	2,154[80]	659[80]
1977	4,208	3,119	6,050	6,016	4,099	4,862	2,665	3,663	1,435	1,370
1978	4,356	3,547	6,066	6,276	4,656	5,143	2,961	4,432	1,624	1,387
1979	5,706[80]	4,779[80]	8,632[80]	5,987[80]	6,113[80]	6,975[80]	3,819[80]	5,678[80]	2,219[80]	1,850[80]
1980	7,332	5,606	12,233	9,302	7,023	8,718	5,004	5,941	3,373	1,667
1981	7,442	5,510	14,378	14,924	6,920	8,059	4,934	6,424	4,578	2,230
1982	8,586	5,700	15,910	16,805	7,870	7,547	4,642	6,827	3,947	2,008
1983	9,464	6,669	18,389	18,244	7,996	8,635	4,766	7,200	4,043	2,860
1984	10,386	7,758	17,274	15,397	9,194	9,961	5,788	9,738	3,734	6,615
1985	12,180	7,779	17,153	18,099	9,621	11,085	5,848	9,076	4,401	5,308
1986	13,159	8,016	11,933	16,774	10,558	12,228	5,056	8,667	3,722	4,480
1987	15,130	9,581	12,462	13,523	11,205	13,090	6,192	9,990	4,539	4,523
1988	14,866	9,842	10,592	13,563	11,765	12,835	5,942	11,863	5,616	5,245
Germany										
1989	15,483	10,027	11,116	13,958	12,215	13,135	6,370	11,955	5,821	5,355
1990	17,508	12,568	10,202	12,884	13,407	14,456	7,823	10,724	6,974	5,898
1991	14,834	14,331	7,455[90]	4,521[90]	10,806	12,884	6,739	9,613	6,002	5,648
1992	16,085	16,804	6,700[90]	3,020[90]	11,133	13,769	8,215	11,518	5,792	6,365
1993	16,924	17,633	7,836[90]	6,059[90]	10,545	14,861	9,113	14,033	7,503	10,504
Million US$ Dollars										
1994	3,425.4	3,883.2	1,968.3	1,530.7	2,435.3	3,177.5	1,924.6	2,996.9	1,780.5	2,101.2
1995	4,584.7	5,306.8	2,121.4	1,917.4	3,415.2	4,036.4	2,420.7	4,110.3	2,127.8	2,658.2
1996	4,634.3	4,796.0	2,137.2	2,439.7	3,680.8	4,264.1	2,728.8	4,052.6	2,257.7	3,189.8
1997	4,497.7	4,416.5	2,264.3	2,951.3	3,746.3	3,963.4	2,420.8	4,019.8	2,266.2	2,822.0

E2 External Trade (by value) with Main Trading Partners

FRANCE (in million francs)

1842–1876

	Algeria		Belgium		Germany		Italy		Spain		U.K.		U.S.A.	
	I	E	I	E	I	E	I	E	I	E	I	E	I	E
1842	3	45	99	52	90	76	127	101	39	72	154	159	176	82
1843	2	41	91	44	56	67	115	64	26	62	86	87	144	66
1844	2	63	104	46	58	75	117	68	32	74	90	99	134	102
1845	3	89	117	58	54	81	103	74	32	68	85	110	141	96
1846	4	94	102	49	56	81	149	80	36	74	79	113	141	100
1847	3	83	111	59	62	76	119	80	36	71	72	127	128	132
1848	2	73	64	66	24	49	65	68	21	64	29	190	101	117
1849	14	79	91	84	34	57	103	85	27	69	59	200	147	147
1850	5	76	104	101	38	62	101	94	35	71	69	226	123	178
1851	16	94	101	124	38	64	106	103	31	61	66	278	122	134
1852	18	103	124	122	48	56	133	107	32	65	86	250	168	163
1853	25	118	140	123	66	57	148	101	44	69	92	317	158	217
1854	33	118	133	124	61	56	135	86	51	67	133	280	193	182
1855	37[17]	156[17]	146[17]	131[17]	84[17]	69[17]	147[17]	99[17]	66[17]	93[17]	244[17]	251[17]	205[17]	204[17]
1856	53	104	197	151	118	77	155	105	97	81	285	317	176	247
1857	39	108	204	182	121	108	218	146	107	96	337	372	223	324
1858	31	89	176	168	144	142	166	136	106	102	322	387	189	258
1859	29	97	149	166	105	147	168	155	49	112	262	426	178	210
1860	58	153	177	167	134	182	173	184	69	105	308	599	240	250
1861	61	131	224	157	194	184	180	189	73	129	438	456	363	82
1862	41	125	259	206	141	231	194	183	55	137	526	620	96	100
1863	52	127	268	211	156	235	207	247	55	170	592	800	81	94
1864	76	129	285	229	176	248	231	285	57	169	567	891	69	75
1865	71	136	304	258	186	256	242	284	54	157	600	991	49	108
1866	67	130	305	262	221	225	237	238	63	124	637	1,141	192	173
1867	68	115	381	255	286	259	321	187	90	103	578	907	141	156
1868	72	144	354	272	303	253	329	178	88	109	580	879	150	126
1869	64	130	316	295	256	305	321	230	104	97	551	910	175	193
1870	47	110	272	311	103	104	235	201	74	91	525	851	218	307
1871	80	132	476	410	161	199	442	153	107	102	839	819	190	313
1872	138	141	440	479	358	410	375	229	124	113	666	936	205	333
1873	149	140	475	470	311	463	346	230	141	110	597	925	200	291
1874	113	136	409	524	316	414	289	204	130	139	596	992	242	296
1875	109	146	439	527	349	427	323	219	94	141	627	1,074	190	264
1876	123	149	404	446	389	431	415	216	96	155	652	1,038	265	230

E2 External Trade (by value) with Main Trading Partners

FRANCE (in million francs)   1877–1914

	Algeria		Belgium		Germany		Italy		Spain		U.K.		U.S.A.	
	I	E	I	E	I	E	I	E	I	E	I	E	I	E
1877	122	138	409	446	373	395	342	186	109	133	576	1,063	258	217
1878	120	129	411	410	419	344	349	170	149	138	582	919	488	207
1879	122	139	415	429	413	344	358	180	183	150	601	834	716	276
1880	127	162	457	465	438	363	398	181	343	159	665	914	731	332
1881	92	161	472	453	455	383	434	210	371	168	703	901	506	319
1882	96	165	508	457	477	339	361	200	367	158	724	966	390	365
1883	96	155	492	471	462	326	427	177	372	171	697	907	353	350
1884	102	147	463	457	417	328	369	172	298	153	617	844	280	275
1885	124	168	405	437	374	300	263	177	361	162	537	832	272	254
1886	125	189	419	448	335	298	309	193	398	173	526	858	293	282
1887	134	153	414	481	322	316	308	192	357	149	476	820	325	271
1888	158	174	419	473	333	308	181	119	378	172	529	864	248	256
1889	201	179	475	571	338	342	134	144	355	195	538	996	307	274
1890	208	195	501	538	351	342	122	150	353	153	627	1,026	317	329
1891	187	207	487	500	366	364	124	126	412	81	589	1,013	486	248
1892	195	190	387	502	337	355	132	133	278	35	530	1,027	534	240
1893	142	185	395	505	323	336	151	128	208	14	493	965	317	205
1894	208	199	372	478	310	325	122	98	176	109	481	916	327	186
1895	246	203	288	497	310	334	115	134	213	109	496	1,002	283	289
1896	197	218	282	501	308	340	127	115	288	100	511	1,033	314	225
1897	238	216	288	513	309	380	132	151	247	99	486	1,136	438	242
1898	224	226	315	549	334	394	138	143	326	82	506	1,024	623	210
1899	271	260	332	606	360	457	159	192	239	148	591	1,242	427	255
1900	166	259	422	598	427	465	149	156	220	135	675	1,230	510	255
1901	198	259	358	562	402	444	140	155	157	121	602	1,201	457	253
1902	254	269	330	634	418	487	154	175	148	125	567	1,283	425	248
1903	263	287	325	631	444	513	152	172	167	122	556	1,195	540	255
1904	234	315	306	678	429	555	151	190	164	111	524	1,217	483	251
1905	216	327	313	764	477	629	154	213	180	111	593	1,260	512	295
1906	244	355	377	804	583	640	182	247	171	131	751	1,299	588	402
1907	291	393	427	861	638	650	194	264	169	126	884	1,373	671	396
1908	273	399	410	749	608	617	165	242	149	128	794	1,183	657	315
1909	272	397	439	903	661	726	165	293	180	124	888	1,266	728	474
1910	447	439	470	1,004	861	804	189	344	195	141	931	1,279	614	456
1911	426	490	543	1,024	980	795	190	278	231	136	994	1,220	827	380
1912	427	569	541	1,144	999	822	209	302	230	140	1,049	1,365	890	431
1913	331	553	556	1,108	1,069	867	241	306	282	151	1,116	1,457	895	423
1914	313	445	318	602	614	511	174	215	193	112	857	1,165	795	377

E2 External Trade (by value) with Main Trading Partners

FRANCE (in million francs-new francs from 1960)

1915–1949

Year	Algeria I	Algeria E	Belgium I	Belgium E	Germany I	Germany E	Italy I	Italy E	Spain I	Spain E	U.K. I	U.K. E	U.S.A. I	U.S.A. E
1915	547	368	23	36	8	—	433	388	581	140	3,038	1,101	3,028	446
1916	539	520	7	57	6	—	717	782	884	190	5,969	1,123	6,163	622
1917	683	524	5	69	6	—	815	971	1,348	207	6,808	1,018	9,771	682
1918	624	604	5	36	5	—	818	780	578	183	6,396	1,083	7,140	420
1919	1,224	959	1,111	1,534	755	1,560	1,017	678	1,464	388	8,803	2,117	9,218	893
1920	1,054	2,290	3,325	4,479	2,668	1,502	1,283	1,249	1,052	970	10,318	4,238	10,866	2,256
1921	1,112	1,415	1,732	3,250	2,615	1,877	616	686	490	563	2,943	3,192	3,539	2,193
1922	984	1,716	1,796[18] / 1,880	4,015[18] / 4,194	1,446	1,970	774	797	366	518	3,273	3,979	3,845	2,007
1923	1,284	2,128	2,533	5,721	1,174	1,080	1,140	1,173	651	899	5,040[19]	6,363[19]	4,851	2,473
1924	1,653	2,613	2,734	7,222	2,051	3,959	1,481	1,481	900	1,168	4,773	7,899	5,586	3,151
1925	1,727	2,981	3,349	7,742	2,346	3,833	1,727	2,225	877	1,456	5,688	9,266	6,377	3,094
1926	2,702	3,369	4,876	9,525	4,925	4,384	2,231	2,623	1,073	1,765	6,142	10,594	7,820	3,673
1927	2,601	3,426	3,980	8,263	4,170	6,630	1,550	2,064	1,444	1,622	6,330	9,000	6,807	3,152
1928	2,832	3,965	4,040	7,955	5,004	5,623	1,525	2,129	1,619	1,694	5,309	7,935	6,177	3,033
1929	2,990	4,501	3,920	7,224	6,613	4,743	1,516	2,209	1,442	1,588	5,859	7,625	7,160	3,335
1930	3,300	4,564	4,199	5,442	7,937	4,155	1,527	1,681	1,508	1,129	5,298	6,894	6,148	2,435
1931	3,428	3,976	3,633	3,582	6,142	2,749	1,437	992	1,405	685	3,851	5,088	3,800	1,543
1932	3,291	3,271	2,447	2,240	3,613	1,699	630	595	717	387	2,464	1,983	2,900	957
1933	3,865[3]	3,310[3]	1,965[3]	2,140[3]	3,037[3]	1,714[3]	621[3]	496[3]	686[3]	377[3]	2,178[3]	1,695[3]	2,857[3]	868[3]
1934	2,813	3,083	1,469	1,978	2,226	1,989	484	552	498	396	1,649	1,565	2,190	836
1935	2,330	2,578	1,406	1,816	1,738	1,051	405	596	339	300	1,583	1,639	1,788	718
1936	2,843	2,693	1,643	1,857	1,774	667	215	138	473	288	1,803	1,958	2,526	880
1937	3,807	3,290	3,060	3,146	3,492	1,565	571	632	315	425	3,389	2,753	4,033	1,535
1938	4,864	3,780	3,160	4,181	3,153	1,851	578	485	192	389	3,239	3,559	5,277	1,683
1939	4,760	3,702	3,046	3,921	2,089	1,036	500	317	79	138	2,978	4,153	5,841	2,268
1940	4,879	2,817	2,666	1,820	99	652	821	258	429	230	3,679	2,137	8,485	1,209
1941	6,612	3,046	1,699	2,038	3,915	6,247	503	500	262	224	146	113	505	125
1942	5,707	3,354	1,471	3,188	7,519	17,795	422	299	542	205	13	137	142	3
1943	36	—	1,717	3,651	8,380	29,189	143	45	235	199	33	151	65	—
1944	39	16	811	1,938	4,807	22,418	25	—	224	90	30	75	1,407	—
1945	1,933	2,682	1,583	2,809	1,665	114	103	—	247	171	5,064	323	27,175	593
1946	24,627	13,358	10,267	20,263	12,785	2,342	2,349	653	218	60	15,095	5,339	83,860	6,399
1947	36,897[20]	31,645[20]	19,238[20]	26,286[20]	15,160[20]	5,850[20]	2,736[20]	2,165[20]	20[20]	3[20]	12,466[20]	15,452[20]	120,082[20]	5,979[20]
					West Germany									
1948	80,496	67,308	25,248	31,261	35,964	23,376	11,379	4,606	4,209	863	18,834	31,828	118,679	15,813
1949	80,822	107,770	32,212	45,129	68,444	39,292	17,091	15,833	12,672	7,009	32,819	70,109	162,657	15,739

E2 External Trade (by value) with Main Trading Partners

FRANCE (in thousand million francs — new francs from 1960)

1950–1997

	Algeria I	Algeria E	Belgium I	Belgium E	West Germany I	West Germany E	Italy I	Italy E	Spain I	Spain E	U.K. I	U.K. E	U.S.A. I	U.S.A. E
1950	92	122	49	69	70	84	37	28	9.8	11	40	99	132	44
1951	98	164	77	86	102	70	48	35	13	14	57	134	182	88
1952	114	179	62	80	115	79	34	38	18	19	60	85	160	55
1953	108	159	60	85	110	99	23	45	17	24	67	76	135	64
1954	116	173	71	100	120	123	25	58	17	20	70	84	133	54
1955	133	208	92	119	154	177	37	67	16	31	76	125	160	73
1956	133	216	107	125	199	166	50	65	12	25	108	97	239	78
1957	161	299	118	141	250	202	56	75	16	26	97	103	301	90
1958	190	412	126	136	274	225	55	73	29	35	84	103	237	126
1959	168[20]	471[20]	133[20]	187[20]	365[20]	363[20]	88[20]	132[20]	18[20]	30[20]	98[20]	105[20]	212[20]	229[20]
1960	2.5	5.4	1.8	2.5	4.9	4.7	1.2	2.0	0.3	0.4	1.1	1.7	3.7	2.0
1961	2.9	4.4	2.0	3.0	5.6	5.4	1.5	2.4	0.4	0.6	1.5	1.8	3.6	2.1
1962	3.2	2.8	2.5	3.1	6.5	6.3	2.0	2.7	0.5	0.8	1.9	1.7	3.8	2.1
1963	2.8	2.7	3.3	3.6	7.8	6.6	2.6	3.7	1.1	1.1	2.6	2.0	4.4	2.1
1964	3.0	2.4	3.9	4.3	9.1	7.7	3.1	3.4	1.4	1.4	2.7	2.3	5.6	2.3
1965	2.8	2.5	4.2	4.8	9.4	9.6	3.6	3.6	0.7	1.7	2.6	2.3	5.4	2.9
1966	2.7	2.2	5.1	5.5	11.3	10.4	4.7	4.4	0.8	1.9	2.9	2.5	5.9	3.3
1967	2.6	2.0	5.7	5.6	12.3	9.7	5.3	5.2	0.8	1.9	2.9	2.9	6.0	3.3
1968	2.8	2.3	7.2	6.4	14.7	11.6	6.6	5.8	0.9	1.7	3.0	3.0	6.5	3.8
1969	3.1	2.4	10.2	8.4	20.0	15.9	9.0	8.1	1.2	2.2	4.0	3.2	7.6	4.2
1970	3.5	3.1	11.9	10.9	23.4	20.5	9.8	11.1	1.5	2.5	4.8	3.8	10.5	5.3
1971	1.3	2.8	12.9	12.7	26.4	24.3	11.7	12.4	2.0	2.8	5.3	5.2	10.0	6.1
1972	1.7	2.4	15.4	15.0	30.2	27.8	13.8	15.1	2.7	3.3	6.6	7.0	11.0	7.0
1973	2.1	3.3	19.3	18.4	37.7	30.9	15.0	18.8	3.6	4.6	7.7	10.1	13.8	7.5
1974	4.8	6.2	25.7	24.9	48.9	37.9	19.0	25.6	5.1	6.5	11.3	14.4	19.7	10.8
1975	3.2	8.1	22.0	22.8	43.6	37.0	20.3	21.6	5.3	5.9	11.0	14.6	17.5	8.8
1976	3.3	7.0	29.5	27.1	59.2	46.0	27.5	29.1	7.5	6.9	15.1	16.1	22.6	12.1
1977	3.9	8.8	31.1	31.1	64.1	53.3	33.2	32.7	9.7	8.1	18.1	20.2	24.1	16.1
1978	3.2	6.9	34.1	35.6	70.0	59.8	37.4	37.6	11.2	8.3	20.3	25.0	26.9	19.2
1979	4.9	8.2	41.1	40.9	82.8	71.7	46.1	47.6	13.4	11.2	25.6	32.0	34.4	20.4
1980	7.4	11.1	47.5	43.9	92.2	75.4	53.4	58.6	16.5	13.1	30.8	32.7	45.3	20.8
1981	13.0	12.8	48.8	45.5	105	81.4	58.6	62.4	17.9	15.9	35.9	39.1	52.3	30.3
1982	25.8	14.0	58.5	52.3	128	89.6	72.8	68.4	23.1	18.8	46.0	43.9	59.7	34.3
1983	23.4	18.6	64.2	59.3	135	108	79.4	74.1	27.0	22.1	56.8	52.7	61.8	43.8
1984	24.8	23.6	74.3	69.8	147	119	89.2	88.6	30.7	26.2	72.8	64.4	69.9	65.9
1985	20.8	21.8	82.3	73.9	159	131	96.8	95.3	36.5	29.3	79.0	71.6	73.2	75.3
1986	11.5	15.9	83.9	74.9	172	133	103	97.0	36.9	33.8	57.7	72.6	67.0	61.1
1987	8.5	11.8	88.7	79.9	187	143	111	104	41.2	45.5	67.2	75.5	67.6	62.5
1988	8.3	9.4	96.3	86.7	208	158	123	118	44.4	51.8	76.9	94.3	81.5	70.7
1989	9.4	12.8	111.8	97.7	235.2	176.5	140.3	133.4	54.2	63.0	86.8	94.3	93.7	72.4
1990	10.5	14.7	111.7	107.2	238.7	196.8	146.5	129.9	59.6	72.5	91.8	103.2	103.2	69.5
1991	12.0	12.3	109.5	108.7	235.4	223.4	142.2	132.3	66.5	81.8	100.9	107.8	124.5	76.5
1992	9.9	11.8	108.9	112.9	236.1	215.7	134.5	134.1	68.2	87.9	97.4	113.3	129.4	80.0
1993	7.8	11.9	102.1	101.6	202.1	204.0	140.1	110.3	62.5	77.0	92.2	111.1	99.6	83.5

million US $ dollars

	Algeria I	Algeria E	Belgium I	Belgium E	West Germany I	West Germany E	Italy I	Italy E	Spain I	Spain E	U.K. I	U.K. E	U.S.A. I	U.S.A. E
1994	1,496.6	2,414.0	20,791.1	20,431.0	40,657.4	39,975.0	22,999.7	21,926.8	13,929.2	16,691.7	18,219.3	23,112.4	19,476.2	16,423.0
1995	1,509.2	2,855.6	24,506.2	24,258.1	50,549.4	50,152.2	27,283.6	27,405.3	17,811.9	20,880.1	21,897.7	26,292.9	21,320.2	16,763.6
1996	1,720.5	2,460.5	23,345.4	24,147.4	48,265.9	49,120.4	28,125.1	26,420.9	19,176.8	22,712.2	23,128.9	26,853.1	22,420.9	17,311.9
1997	2,168.7	2,290.5	21,414.3	22,759.6	44,115.2	44,979.0	26,070.5	26,309.8	17,727.1	22,763.1	22,229.3	28,640.8	23,358.3	18,446.3

E2 External Trade (by value) with Main Trading Partners

GERMANY (in million marks)

1880–1913

Year	Austria-Hungary		Belgium		France[23]		Italy		Netherlands		Russia[24]		Sweden[21]		U.K.		U.S.A.[25]	
	I	E	I	E	I	E	I	E	I	E	I	E	I	E	I	E	I	E
1880	402	291	195	164	246	285	63	52	190	227	336	213	23	61	351	438	...	...
1881	433	316	215	169	253	319	57	71	247	240	333	183	26	59	365	449	...	...
1882	503	326	238	171	245	342	53	74	271	259	391	193	28	63	397	513	115	192
1883	476	336	273	174	248	313	62	84	239	256	410	184	28	72	480	552	136	144
1884	426	325	293	163	244	283	83	87	236	230	414	169	31[21] / 18	73[21] / 59	507	514	125	176
1885	384	284	280	147	218	248	76	85	213	225	345	151	21	59	452	453	122	155
1886	404	286	277	155	222	249	90	84	212	230	264	148	20	52	453	443	106	212
1887	422	296	278	161	213	219	91	99	231	234	362	132	27	50	461	491	143	231
1888	446[22]	299[22]	271[22]	172[22]	214[22]	219[22]	111[22]	81[22]	247[22]	271[22]	456[22]	200[22]	35[22]	54[22]	496[22]	480[22]	153[22]	236[22]
1889	530	319	336	137	271	209	149	102	284	249	552	197	50	71	665	647	317	395
1890	583	332	314	151	258	231	140	93	307	258	542	206	46	91	601	690	397	417
1891	570	331	249	153	251	237	133	87	270	268	581	263	52	73	565	679	403	358
1892	564	321	207	141	255	201	134	90	209	234	383	240	55	67	548	629	535	347
1893	572	339	188	148	239	201	149	84	212	240	353	185	61	71	565	670	427	354
1894	572	353	170	150	211	188	125	81	188	243	544	195	63	73	512	632	450	270
1895	513	374	177	159	223	202	138	82	161	245	569	221	63	76	536	676	483	368
1896	547	400	173	168	230	201	132	89	159	262	635	364	74	78	551	713	528	383
1897	583	406	182	189	246[23] / 243	210[23] / 210	146	88	181	263	708[24] / 700	372[24] / 346	87	92	568	699	652	397
1898	627	426	197	187	261	205	161	92	181	278	727	410	103	105	566	741	876	333
1899	716	450	243	207	298	216	193	112	197	321	702	397	104	135	673	801	894	377
1900	704	486	215	253	303	277	181	123	209	364	717	325	104	137	719	862	1,004	440
1901	684	464	183	236	272	249	178	123	192	372	716	318	84	110	553	907	986	385
1902	696	480	194	261	304	253	189	125	195	392	760	344	80	118	557	958	893	449
1903	724	500	206	268	330	272	196	131	187	417	826	379	90	131	594	982	935[25] / 943	469[25] / 495
1904	703	555	231	277	365	274	187	141	212	410	819	315	99	147	615	985	943	495
1905	752	580	273	312	402	293	211	164	246	433	1,091	368	119	156	718	1,042	992	542
1906	811[22]	649[22]	291[22]	356[22]	434[22]	383[22]	231[22]	241[22]	242[22]	443[22]	1,070[22]	406[22]	150[22]	177[22]	825[22]	1,067[22]	1,237[22,25]	637[22,25]
1907	813	717	297	343	454	449	285	303	228	452	1,108	438	172	187	977	1,060	1,320	653
1908	752	737	262	323	420	438	236	311	231	454	946	450	145	174	697	997	1,283	508
1909	755	767	290	349	485	455	288	289	253	454	1,364	445	142	156	723	1,015	1,263	606
1910	759	822	326	391	509	543	275	324	259	499	1,387	547	164	191	767	1,102	1,188	633
1911	739	918	340	413	524	599	285	348	298	532	1,634	625	183	192	809	1,140	1,343	640
1912	830	1,035	387	493	552	689	305	401	345	609	1,528	680	214	197	843	1,161	1,586	698
1913	827	1,105	345	551	584	790	318	394	333	694	1,425	880	224	230	876	1,438	1,711	713

E2 External Trade (by value) with Main Trading Partners

GERMANY (in million marks)

1923–1943

	Austria		Belgium		France		Italy		Netherlands		Russia/U.S.S.R.		Sweden		U.K.		U.S.A.	
	I	E	I	E	I	E	I	E	I	E	I	E	I	E	I	E	I	E
1923	131[26]	305[26]	85[26]	112[26]	186[26]	67[26]	150[26]	245[26]	201[26]	685[26]	92[26]	73[26]	95[26]	271[26]	1,015[26]	557[26]	1,172[26]	475[26]
1924	134	313	204	106	694	114	372	240	426	648	126	89	121	286	827[27]	612[27]	1,709	491
1925	176	320	415	344	558	489	496	425	743	996	205	250	269	342	944	937	2,196	604
1926	116	311	343	418	378	670	388	486	543	1,127	323	266	234	401	576	1,163	1,603	744
1927	211	366	548	441	806	562	528	462	698	1,119	433	330	370	409	963	1,178	2,073	776
1928	232	425	474	489	741	693	467	547	710	1,175	379	403	253	431	894	1,180	2,026	796
1929	202	441	447	609	642	935	443	602	701	1,355	426	354	350	476	865	1,306	1,790	991
1930	181	360	325	601	519	1,149	365	484	561	1,206	436	431	304	494	639	1,219	1,307	685
1931	114	275	222	464	342	834	268	341	384	955	304	763	158	424	453	1,134	791	488
1932	65	160	146	302	190	483	181	223	273	633	271	626	95	228	259	446	592	281
1933	58	121	139	278	184	395	166	227	232	613	194	282	103	191	238	406	483	246
1934	66	107	161	236	177	282	185	246	264	482	210	63	134	198	206	383	373	158
1935	71	108	126	202	154	253	188	278	196	404	215	39	153	207	256	375	241	170
1936	77	109	139	212	99	255	209[28]	241[28]	169	396	93	126	192	230	264	406	232	172
1937	93	123	198[29]	288[29]	156[29]	313[29]	221[29]	311[29]	216[29]	468[29]	65[29]	117[29]	232[29]	277[29]	309[29]	432[29]	282[29]	209[29]
1938	...	...	154	190	159	229	284	349	208	460	53	34	267	275	309	374	455	157
1939	...	...	129	161	78	129	287[28]	362[28]	177	504	30[30]	31[30]	262	377	181	228	198	125
											129	134						
1940	...	...	243	131	...	315	508	724	406	440	396	217	346	403	—	—	16	11
1941	...	...	562	385	752	546	938	1,192	640	695	325	272	477	455	—	—	8	3
1942	...	...	705	293	1,404	560	1,022	1,305	857	534	—	—	410	423	—	—	—	—
1943	...	...	681	308	1,416	—	781	950	824	427	—	—	386	477	—	—	—	—

E2 External Trade (by value) with Main Trading Partners

EAST GERMANY (in million valuta marks)[32]

1950–1988

	Bulgaria		Czechoslovakia		West Germany[33]		Hungary		Poland		Russia/U.S.S.R.	
	I	E	I	E	I	E	I	E	I	E	I	E
1950	...	...	...	...	255	333	...	...	...	...	...	...
1951	...	...	...	...	183	148	...	...	...	...	...	...
1952	...	...	...	...	193	139	...	...	...	...	...	...
1953	76	84	245	238	263	293	144	179	470	456	1,926	1,821
1954	104	100	323	307	436	440	202	197	470	562	1,918	2,465
1955	130	89	297	394	551	573	261	194	482	520	1,773	2,166
1956	144	136	443	461	614	647	165	200	440	584	2,340	3,391
1957	112	125	499	590	772	860	198	266	432	635	3,092	3,401
1958	128	155	610	662	799	888	305	275	356	641	2,941	3,553
1959	191	213	666	733	960	965	347	368	440	784	3,883	3,955
1960	230	290	785	807	898	1,014	393	396	457	773	4,024	3,884
1961	277	352	916	962	857	922	436	418	430	875	4,497	3,830
1962	320	268	944	912	823	885	414	473	455	979	5,234	4,590
1963	305	411	907	964	829	1,021	400	512	456	1,050	4,926	5,361
1964	338	366	1,049	1,056	1,078	1,113	472	522	608	988	5,087	5,811
1965	394	409	1,103	1,226	1,107	1,235	521	532	589	1,132	5,061	5,505
1966	455	442	1,234	1,301	1,469	1,288	637	592	649	1,175	5,815	5,361
1967	480	525	1,336	1,328	1,288	1,249	644	771	692	1,195	5,954	5,913
1968	514	637	1,381	1,689	1,228	1,410	720	813	942	1,224	6,269	6,583
1969	617	641	1,545	1,741	1,954	1,535	889	779	1,103	1,324	7,326	6,962
1970	714	665	1,920	1,850	2,162	1,888	931	1,124	1,230	1,673	8,170	7,315
1971	761	749	1,987	1,973	2,153	2,142	1,066	1,286	1,275	1,920	7,954	8,139
1972	768	912	2,122	2,240	2,624	2,204	1,274	1,219	1,543	2,282	8,009	9,615
1973	959	1,034	2,360	2,637	2,436	2,499	1,618	1,155	2,236	2,576	8,638	9,889
1974	992	1,189	2,517	3,035	2,987	3,010	1,685	1,703	2,408	2,640	10,147	9,956
1975–86											...	
1987	2,554	2,623	6,394	6,842	26,805	28,371	4,386	4,762	4,597	5,401	41,541	36,886
1988	2,721	3,072	6,853	7,987	25,701	28,969	4,749	5,629	6,124	6,228	34,470	33,486

E2   External Trade (by value) with Main Trading Partners

WEST GERMANY (in million marks to 1969, thousand million marks subsequently)

1948–1969

	Austria		Belgium		France		Italy		Netherlands		Russia/USSR		Sweden		U.K.		U.S.A.	
	I	E	I	E	I	E	I	E	I	E	I	E	I	E	I	E	I	E
1948	32	121	80	263	11	223	68	69	122	224	4	—	94	75	129	256	1,574	102
1949	44	229	418	403	91	514	318	217	402	368	3	—	295	241	182	380	2,588	160
1950	178	312	405	677	690	612	507	486	1,246	1,164	1	—	637	531	489	361	1,735	430
1951	237	500	610	987	621	973	549	674	1,022	1,456	2	—	803	974	498	878	2,722	989
1952	369	627	943	1,196	606	1,077	643	632	1,170	1,345	17	1	927	1,239	525	955	2,505	1,044
1953	407	668	850	1,308	780	1,084	744	1,240	1,251	1,657	66	7	811	1,173	645	788	1,655	1,243
1954	565	1,034	867	1,580	965	1,194	843	1,341	1,526	2,059	93	53	904	1,476	847	858	2,228	1,227
1955	697	1,359	1,385	1,733	1,445	1,458	1,044	1,434	1,770	2,422	151	112	1,103	1,779	866	1,026	3,202	1,611
1956	781	1,417	1,343	2,106	1,345	1,947	1,223	1,656	2,002	2,876	224	289	1,276	1,956	1,147	1,257	3,970	2,074
1957	902	1,761	1,316	2,145	1,547	2,253	1,553	2,000	2,258	3,246	409	250	1,486	2,169	1,135	1,407	5,629	2,494
1958	916	1,847	1,409	2,453	1,595	2,164	1,698	1,853	2,500	2,995	386	303	1,411	2,266	1,361	1,460	4,193	2,642
1959	998[31]	1,960[31]	1,776[31]	2,489[31]	2,761[31]	2,970[31]	2,182[31]	2,202[31]	3,124[31]	3,465[31]	443[31]	383[31]	1,533[31]	2,285[31]	1,630[31]	1,661[31]	4,576[31]	3,776[31]
1960	1,152	2,444	2,441	2,890	3,998	4,202	2,631	2,847	3,638	4,210	673	778	1,804	2,593	1,956	2,147	5,974	3,723
1961	1,247	2,686	2,355	3,262	4,618	4,777	3,043	3,385	3,762	4,755	796	823	1,930	2,614	1,965	2,122	6,097	3,454
1962	1,376	2,757	2,765	3,583	5,270	5,440	3,735	4,106	4,196	4,883	861	826	2,000	2,670	2,351	1,954	7,033	3,858
1963	1,369	2,938	3,359	4,142	5,495	6,432	3,700	5,462	4,789	5,718	835	614	2,014	2,981	2,472	2,212	7,942	4,195
1964	1,524	3,295	4,305	4,879	6,270	7,424	4,468	4,593	5,350	6,736	937	774	2,304	3,259	2,782	2,717	8,066	4,785
1965	1,712	3,798	5,416	5,558	7,843	7,792	6,562	4,499	6,826	7,371	1,101	586	2,742	3,573	3,141	2,804	9,196	5,741
1966	1,695	4,219	5,607	6,421	8,617	9,216	6,680	5,657	6,870	7,988	1,153	541	2,389	3,574	3,155	3,129	9,177	7,178
1967	1,477	4,097	5,436	6,439	8,488	10,050	6,436	6,890	7,275	8,628	1,100	792	2,167	3,534	2,932	3,472	8,556	7,859
1968	1,766	4,420	6,799	7,444	9,778	12,242	8,066	7,568	8,810	10,114	1,175	1,094	2,489	3,850	3,407	4,028	8,850	10,835
1969	2,190	4,857	8,987	9,277	12,697	15,118	9,491	9,260	11,256	11,522	1,306	1,582	2,897	4,369	3,913	4,591	10,253	10,633

E2 External Trade (by value) with Main Trading Partners

WEST GERMANY (in million marks to 1969, thousand million marks subsequently)

1970–1997

thousand million marks

	Austria		Belgium		France		Italy		Netherlands		Russia/USSR		Sweden		U.K.		U.S.A.	
	I	E	I	E	I	E	I	E	I	E	I	E	I	E	I	E	I	E
1970	2.3	5.7	10.4	10.3	13.9	15.5	10.8	11.2	13.3	13.3	1.3	1.5	3.1	4.7	4.3	4.5	12.1	11.4
1971	2.5	6.4	11.6	11.6	15.9	17.0	12.7	11.5	15.8	14.5	1.3	1.6	3.1	4.6	4.4	5.4	12.4	13.1
1972	2.7	7.5	13.0	12.3	18.2	19.4	13.9	12.6	17.6	15.2	1.4	2.3	3.2	5.0	4.6	7.0	10.8	13.8
1973	3.0	8.4	14.2	14.7	19.0	23.1	14.0	15.0	20.7	18.3	2.0	3.1	3.6	5.9	5.2	8.4	12.2	15.1
1974	3.5	10.2	15.9	17.6	20.9	27.3	15.0	18.7	25.2	23.5	3.3	4.8	4.3	7.9	6.3	11.0	14.0	17.3
1975	3.8	9.8	15.7	18.9	22.1	26.0	17.2	16.2	25.7	22.2	3.2	4.8	5.5	8.1	6.9	10.1	14.2	13.1
1976	5.1	12.5	19.1	20.3	25.8	33.7	18.9	19.0	30.6	24.8	4.4	6.8	7.0	9.0	8.5	12.2	17.5	14.4
1977	6.1	14.5	19.6	21.5	27.3	33.6	20.7	18.7	30.8	27.5	4.6	6.5	7.9	8.8	10.4	14.6	17.0	18.2
1978	7.1	14.6	20.5	23.7	28.3	34.9	23.2	19.4	30.7	28.4	5.4	6.3	9.5	7.7	12.1	16.9	17.4	20.2
1979	8.4	16.5	23.4	26.8	33.2	40.0	25.8	24.5	35.8	31.3	7.4	6.6	6.2	9.1	17.2	21.0	20.3	20.8
1980	9.8	19.3	24.5	27.5	36.6	46.6	27.1	29.9	39.1	33.3	7.5	7.9	7.2	10.1	22.9	22.9	25.7	21.5
1981	10.3	20.0	24.7	28.9	40.1	51.9	27.6	31.3	44.3	33.9	9.2	7.6	7.7	10.4	27.5	26.2	28.4	26.0
1982	11.1	20.6	25.5	31.1	42.9	60.1	28.7	32.4	45.9	36.1	11.4	9.4	7.5	11.3	27.0	31.3	28.2	28.1
1983	12.6	22.1	28.1	31.8	44.6	55.6	31.6	32.1	48.1	37.9	11.8	11.2	8.4	11.3	27.1	35.4	27.7	32.8
1984	13.7	24.3	28.8	34.0	45.8	61.3	34.2	37.7	53.0	42.1	14.4	10.8	9.9	13.0	33.3	40.6	31.1	46.8
1985	15.3	27.4	29.1	37.0	49.3	64.0	37.2	41.8	58.3	46.3	13.6	10.5	10.9	14.7	37.2	46.0	22.3	55.5
1986	16.4	28.1	29.2	37.2	47.1	62.3	38.1	42.9	47.8	45.5	9.3	9.4	10.0	14.7	29.8	44.6	26.9	55.2
1987	17.3	28.4	29.1	38.8	47.5	63.6	39.2	46.1	44.9	46.1	7.3	7.8	10.0	15.8	29.4	46.6	25.6	49.9
1988	20.2	32.4	31.2	42.0	53.1	71.3	40.2	51.7	45.4	49.2	6.9	9.4	10.7	16.7	30.4	52.9	29.1	45.7
1989	22.6	35.8	35.4	46.4	61.8	85.2	45.8	60.1	52.7	55.0	8.5	11.5	13.1	18.8	35.2	60.1	38.5	46.8
GERMANY																		
1990	24.7	37.2	40.1	48.1	65.8	84.6	52.2	60.3	56.6	54.9	9.1	10.4	13.4	17.1	37.4	55.3	37.2	47.0
1991	26.9	39.6	45.9	48.7	78.9	87.5	59.7	61.3	62.7	56.0	14.2[91]	17.7[91]	14.5	15.0	42.7	50.7	42.2	41.7
1992	28.0	39.9	44.8	49.6	76.4	87.0	58.5	62.4	61.2	55.7	12.9[91]	13.9[91]	14.1	14.6	43.6	51.9	42.4	42.7
1993	26.4	37.3	34.0	42.7	65.4	77.3	48.2	47.5	50.0	48.3	13.0[91]	15.9[91]	12.5	12.7	35.4	50.3	40.3	46.7
									Million US$ Dollars									
1994	18,194.1	24,570.7	23,532.8	28,927.1	42,243.2	51,329.4	32,085.8	32,416.1	31,929.2	32,618.0	8,164.3	6,643.5	9,500.2	8,690.9	23,918.7	34,258.2	27,591.7	33,512.3
1995	18,195.1	29,110.6	30,734.7	34,324.3	51,076.7	61,364.3	39,734.8	39,747.8	40,669.2	39,894.3	9,499.9	7,197.1	12,841.5	9,745.1	30,453.0	43,299.1	31,616.5	38,170.3
1996	18,104.2	30,231.2	29,169.4	33,100.9	48,969.6	58,431.3	38,777.8	39,421.2	40,578.1	40,059.4	10,245.9	7,601.7	12,656.0	9,696.5	31,531.0	42,298.4	32,876.3	39,921.4
1997	16,007.1	26,514.7	26,867.3	29,792.5	45,785.3	54,520.4	34,031.9	37,746.6	37,041.3	35,807.5	9,896.0	9,488.1	11,911.5	8,267.2	30,370.8	43,302.9	33,807.3	44,232.7

E2 External Trade (by value) with Main Trading Partners

GREECE (in million drachmae)   1851–1889

	Austria-Hungary		France		Germany		Italy		Russia		Turkey		U.K.		U.S.A.	
	I	E	I	E	I	E	I	E	I	E	I	E	I	E	I	E
1851	4	3	2	…	…	…	…	…	1	…	8	1	6	7	…	…
1852	3	2	2	2	…	…	…	…	1	1	10	1	4	3	…	…
1853	3	[2][34]	2	[1][34]	…	…	…	…	…	[1][34]	6	[1][34]	5	[2][34]	…	…
1854	…	…	2	…	…	…	…	…	1	…	8	1	6	7	…	…
1857	9	5	5	2	…	…	…	…	1	1	8	3	9	11	1	…
1858	8	4	7	3	…	…	…	…	1	1	8	4	10	11	1	…
1859	8	3	7	3	…	…	…	…	2	—	11	4	10	11	1	1
1860	8	4	8	2	…	…	…	…	4	1	10	4	14	13	1	1
1861	8	3	9	2	…	…	…	…	4	—	9	4	12	14	1	1
1862	7	3	10	1	…	…	…	…	2	—	9	6	11	13	…	…
1863	8	3	11	1	…	…	…	…	4	1	12	4	15	12	…	…
1864	9	3	10	1	…	…	…	…	2	1	11	5	16	12	…	…
1865	10	7	11	3	…	…	…	…	6	2	15	7	24	20	1	1
1868	…	…	16	7	…	…	12	7	…	…	13	8	29	26	…	…
1871	…	…	13	6	…	…	8	2	16	5	17	7	34	45	…	…
1872	…	…	…	…	…	…	…	…	…	…	…	…	…	…	…	…
1873	…	…	…	…	…	…	…	…	…	…	…	…	…	…	…	…
1874	16	8	18	3	…	…	7	2	14	2	21	8	39	46	…	…
1883	34	9	18	24	…	1	6	3	17	2	18	6	37	36	…	…
1887	17	7	10	22	3	4	6	2	34	1	17	4	31	42	…	4
1888	16	8	11	18	4	3	4	1	25	1	13	4	29	41	2	5
1889	19	9	12	33	5	3	5	3	26	2	25	10	10	33	3	3

E2 External Trade (by value) with Main Trading Partners

GREECE (in million drachmae)   1890–1913

	Austria-Hungary		France		Germany		Italy		Russia		Turkey		U.K.		U.S.A.	
	I	E	I	E	I	E	I	E	I	E	I	E	I	E	I	E
1890	17	9	10	21	6	2	5	2	21	1	19	10	33	33	2	6
1891	19	7	13	6	7	3	4	2	27	3	21	8	40	50	3	4
1892	16	6	11	15	9	3	4	3	15	2	22	5	34	33	2	5
1893	13	7	7	14	8	5	2	2	17	2	15	3	25	36	2	6
1894	14	8	8	10	9	2	3	5	29	5	9	8	30	22	3	2
1895	14	6	7	8	8	5	2	7	28	5	10	7	31	17	4	2
1896	12	7	9	7	10	3	3	4	24	8	14	8	29	18	5	3
1897	12	8	12	8	8	5	3	5	29	2	9	5	29	27	4	4
1898	17	8	12	10	11	5	5	4	33	2	16	7	42	28	5	4
1899	15	8	10	11	10	5	6	4	33	1	16	7	26	27	4	6
1900	15	8	13	7	12	10	6	4	32	1	11	4	27	39	4	8
1901	17	9	14	9	12	7	6	4	31	1	12	5	31	29	3	6
1902	21	9	11	8	11	6	6	5	31	2	12	6	29	20	3	4
1903	19	10	12	12	11	6	6	4	31	–	14	5	29	22	2	5
1904	20	11	10	9	13	7	7	4	27	3	16	7	30	21	2	4
1905	19	8	10	7	14	8	6	4	28	1	16	5	28	24	3	6
1906	17	11	10	8	15	11	7	5	27	5	14	7	28	38	4	9
1907	19	11	11	8	14	11	6	8	25	2	13	6	31	33	7	11
1908	18	13	11	11	15	10	6	9	22	2	14	6	36	27	7	6
1909	17	10	10	8	12	10	6	6	27	1	12	6	31	25	5	9
1910	20	12	10	15	14	15	7	14	36	4	11	5	35	33	4	11
1911	24	14	10	14	13	16	7	4	34	3	9	5	41	34	4	13
1912	28	17	9	20	14	15	7	12	24	2	9	6	38	28	4	13
1913	29	13	11	14	13	12	6	4	35	3	4	1	43	28	3	9

E2 External Trade (by value) with Main Trading Partners

GREECE (in million drachmae to 1938, thousand million drachmae 1947–53)

1919–1953

	France		Germany		Italy		Russia		Turkey		U.K.		U.S.A.	
	I	E	I	E	I	E	I	E	I	E	I	E	I	E
1919	135	41	—	6	165	43	3	16	61	87	411	193	350	81
1920	222	36	26	53	215	56	14	–	60	54	532	136	456	99
1921	135	30	88	140	156	53	4	–	35	50	294	201	393	175
1922	201	125	184	524	276	205	1	–	90	55	445	422	677	660
1923	429	123	275	474	448	319	94	–	199	30	863	703	1,221	243
1924	663	156	468	860	883	490	82	1	209	28	1,273	480	1,111	594
1925	860	286	826	840	1,001	879	234	7	245	56	1,534	621	1,826	1,078
1926	840	339	756	1,189	739	1,079	255	4	253	34	1,168	635	1,621	1,284
1927	979	359	936	1,286	833	1,276	339	7	268	33	1,709	627	2,007	1,312
1928	867	314	1,071	1,627	646	1,039	340	2	259	19	1,795	828	1,957	1,256
1929	903	426	1,250	1,613	753	1,272	281	5	339	14	1,688	816	2,088	1,118
1930	780	403	1,099	1,392	659	838	356	20	392	11	1,365	748	1,651	875
1931	573	259	1,072	588	537	696	583	27	481	13	1,153	629	842	724
1932	395	236	758	690	450	786	794	19	265	9	1,076	1,113	1,089	485
1933	364	433	864	918	478	721	649	30	274	23	1,210	973	492	642
1934	588	147	1,291	1,231	430	534	438	69	253	51	1,470	952	552	805
1935	184	192	1,997	2,109	394	423	487	71	218	61	1,658	897	667	1,202
1936	224	250	2,674	2,681	59	132	552	66	177	40	1,889	899	846	1,057
1937	266	241	4,134	2,960	437	601	244	69	202	56	1,668	922	652	1,580
1938	229	296	4,256	3,904	501	525	365	32	273	66	1,926	843	1,070	1,731

in thousand million drachmae

	France		Germany		Italy		Russia		Turkey		U.K.		U.S.A.	
	I	E	I	E	I	E	I	E	I	E	I	E	I	E
1947	[2.2][35]	[1.9][35]	[2.3][35]	—	[7.8][35]	[10.0][35]			[11.4][35]	[0.3][35]	[14.9][35]	[20.0][35]	[41.5][35]	[14.1][35]
1948	29	26	85	14	83	67	...	...	56	10	137	121	859	66
1949	95	62	79	60	84	42	...	...	97	4	186	120	847	109
1950	75	24	171	90	132	22	...	...	54	6	265	68	695	75
1951	311	170	561	305	547	138	...	...	122	13	576	221	1,767	209
			West Germany											
1952	409	157	630	539	614	113	—	–	73	45	515	290	1,136	228
1953	496	199	958	868	1,195	310	5	43	210	78	771	396	1,146	406

E2 External Trade (by value) with Main Trading Partners

GREECE (in million new drachmae to 1979, thousands million subsequently) 1954–1997

	France I	France E	W.Germany / Germany I	E	Italy I	E	Russia/U.S.S.R I	E	Turkey I	E	U.K. I	E	U.S.A. I	E
1954	652	333	1,602	1,113	1,538	585	44	110	65	37	1,098	578	1,376	454
1955	711	484	1,927	1,371	1,313	803	58	66	69	38	1,271	541	2,098	708
1956	724	761	2,220	1,133	1,260	632	145	205	105	24	2,010	538	2,344	677
1957	937	444	2,957	1,702	1,549	543	318	271	70	19	1,743	589	2,571	906
1958	920	893	3,442	1,422	1,497	418	428	503	39	12	1,677	531	2,324	947
1959	633	448	3,273	1,254	1,193	452	537	353	82	13	2,022	571	1,757	790
1960	959	290	3,351	1,129	1,215	377	850	565	53	11	2,150	577	2,845	818
1961	1,316	339	3,859	1,262	1,387	227	597	563	41	27	2,273	522	2,431	971
1962	1,668	397	3,986	1,366	1,610	637	610	577	103	49	2,512	725	2,017	576
1963	1,499	316	4,404	1,681	1,800	447	852	672	102	43	2,517	680	2,538	1,646
1964	1,869	496	5,260	1,977	2,154	549	822	725	95	14	2,842	679	3,029	1,346
1965	2,885	515	5,866	2,238	3,094	501	1,096	807	233	6	3,106	760	3,381	936
1966	2,581	723	6,335	2,415	3,680	603	1,142	849	182	5	3,601	707	3,935	1,279
1967	2,836	1,367	6,732	2,343	3,683	1,477	1,125	915	122	5	3,266	743	3,003	1,953
1968	3,161	460	7,708	2,750	4,307	1,872	814	743	100	13	4,047	583	3,203	1,428
1969	3,265	1,118	9,216	3,296	4,299	1,610	910	901	271	36	4,267	765	4,557	1,623
1970	4,274	1,086	10,901	3,887	4,916	1,933	1,087	1,035	181	19	5,064	1,147	3,479	1,448
1971	4,640	1,864	12,264	4,008	5,781	1,710	937	611	167	21	4,617	851	4,172	1,783
1972	5,751	2,175	14,688	5,639	7,703	2,635	1,271	1,072	360	145	4,912	862	4,367	2,550
1973	7,771	2,837	20,061	9,245	9,379	4,064	1,320	1,310	666	496	5,794	2,998	8,619	2,757
1974	9,354	3,633	21,418	12,861	11,282	5,201	1,798	2,421	746	421	6,248	3,501	12,102	3,687
1975	10,323	5,396	27,265	15,881	14,171	6,130	3,328	2,824	23	98	8,290	3,626	12,689	3,767
1976	12,338	6,292	32,184	20,026	18,347	8,619	6,411	3,062	54	240	9,925	3,883	15,085	5,361
1977	15,285	7,007	38,110	21,631	22,668	7,128	4,235	3,792	67	475	13,913	5,074	12,881	4,705
1978	17,824	8,276	43,933	25,747	28,402	13,443	9,678	3,493	234	292	13,904	5,379	14,886	5,421
1979	22,747	8,801	53,605	28,402	33,540	14,101	7,610	2,037	739	1,170	20,493	7,456	17,464	8,026

in thousand million drachmae — (from 1980 the W.Germany column is labelled **Germany**)

	France I	France E	Germany I	E	Italy I	E	Russia/U.S.S.R I	E	Turkey I	E	U.K. I	E	U.S.A. I	E
1980	28.0	16.3	63.1	39.6	37.1	21.5	6.4	3.9	0.5	0.9	20.7	9.1	20.8	12.5
1981	32.2	16.0	96.8	43.3	47.8	16.9	18.3	4.1	1.2	0.7	24.3	11.9	25.3	20.7
1982	47.1	19.9	114	54.3	61.5	25.1	14.8	9.4	1.2	0.6	24.3	13.7	28.2	25.4
1983	57.7	29.2	146	78.8	75.4	53.0	21.7	12.6	2.5	1.3	34.9	19.0	31.0	24.6
1984	74.6	46.8	180	107	104	73.3	57.3	13.7	3.3	6.4	42.8	34.1	31.8	45.1
1985	90.9	50.2	240	126	132	71.2	73.5	19.5	3.5	7.6	53.4	43.6	44.4	51.3
1986	128	74.9	336	187	183	107	39.8	10.9	4.0	6.3	65.7	53.8	47.9	56.1
1987	138	75.9	390	214	216	142	44.0	10.3	5.9	13.9	85.8	72.5	48.5	59.9
1988	141	66.9	355	195	255	110	37.5	12.8	7.3	8.2	86.9	59.8	67.5	48.7
1989	181	108.0	522	256	391	249	39.9	22.7	19.7	13.9	152.7	90.6	89.4	69.9
1990	254	121.9	646	277	483	211	56.9	20.1	22.9	18.2	165.1	92.7	115.5	71.3
1991	305	118.8	760	377	557	263	72.6	16.0	30.6	19.2	209.9	107.8	168.3	90.2
1992	354	136.0	914	445	641	346	85.0[92]	23.8[92]	27.5	25.4	247.1	132.2	161.9	72.9
1993	399	119.6	854	459	707	255	126.0[92]	52.7[92]	31.8	34.0	307.1	110.3	188.1	86.5

Million US$ Dollars

	France I	France E	Germany I	E	Italy I	E	Russia/U.S.S.R I	E	Turkey I	E	U.K. I	E	U.S.A. I	E
1994	1,731.9	501.7	3,522.0	1,983.1	3,576.0	1,299.1	548.4	243.3	170.8	138.2	1,335.8	550.7	688.0	455.4
1995	2,106.3	597.4	4,289.7	2,421.8	4,849.0	1,544.0	703.0	269.8	209.7	221.0	1,683.3	667.5	840.4	343.7
1996	2,280.4	598.5	4,147.0	2,207.2	4,973.3	1,597.8	694.2	360.5	231.3	354.0	1,912.6	706.4	940.8	454.8
1997	2,260.5	447.1	3,522.0	1,650.8	4,166.4	1,333.2	613.8	411.8	291.0	431.8	1,598.1	666.7	960.7	487.2

E2 External Trade (by value) with Main Trading Partners

HUNGARY (in million pengos to 1938, million forints 1949-1959)

1920-1959

	Austria		Czechoslovakia		Germany / East Germany		West Germany		Poland		Romania		Russia/USSR	
	I	E	I	E	I	E	I	E	I	E	I	E	I	E
1920	244	115	91	26	41	21			...	...	4	3	...	...
1921	227	157	176	47	78	27			...	...	21	14	...	...
1922	180	145	149	57	104	35			28	10	45	44	...	...
1923	126	171	118	45	70	24			31	7	50	34	...	...
1924	188[36]	242[36]	204[36]	160[36]	102[36]	53[36]			45[36]	17[36]	64[36]	35[36]	...	...
1925	193	283	209	198	132	89			42	38	69	34	...	...
1926	186	325	212	171	157	114			49	14	76	35	...	...
1927	207	281	286	157	216	107			54	28	85	37	...	...
1928	196	282	272	145	237	98			49	27	96	45	...	...
1929	140	316	229	170	213	121			51	17	96	47	...	...
1930	95	256	173	153	175	94			30	12	73	29	...	...
1931	67	170	49	24	131	73			25	7	65	20	...	...
1932	51	101	34	23	74	51			7	3	41	11	...	...
1933	62	106	32	29	62	44			4	4	24	13	...	...
1934	81	99	24	20	63	90			4	3	30	20	...	...
1935	76	86	19	21	91	108			4	4	54	24	...	...
1936	72	87	22	20	113	115			5	4	59	24	...	...
1937	87	99	30	21	125	141			5	5	48	25	...	...
1938	47	95	27	22	124	143			6	5	40	21	—	—
1949	229	230	348	333	26	61	189	239	179	135	138	184	725	820
1950	210	198	382	407	96	284	367	287	365	316	261	298	908	1,115
1951	128	197	606	614	263	157	201	218	425	376	206	171	1,180	1,516
1952	212	192	857	677	464	353	194	200	395	420	262	220	1,387	1,741
1953	188	152	819	822	476	422	186	187	332	378	240	301	1,664	2,198
1954	302[37]	242	788[37]	885	616[37]	574	322[37]	238	298[37]	341	194[37]	178	1,719[37]	2,018
1955	326	313	662	928	602	762	462	353	336	375	220	228	1,178	1,795
1956	257	242	648	734	533	452	313	410	291	266	152	142	1,271	1,418
1957	291	195	925	890	825	582	344	351	415	257	200	142	2,779	1,244
1958	236	277	897	1,085	838	885	416	401	376	394	161	177	2,281	1,864
1959	351	320	1,035	1,023	1,063	1,050	455	570	469	458	267	213	3,002	2,449

E2 External Trade (by value) with Main Trading Partners

HUNGARY (in million forints to 1979, thousands million forints subsequently)

1960–1997

	Austria		Czechoslovakia		East Germany		West Germany		Poland		Romania		Russsia/U.S.S.R.	
	I	E	I	E	I	E	I	E	I	E	I	E	I	E
1960	405	377	1,313	1,103	1,185	1,182	648	525	582	535	487	304	3,556	3,011
1961	371	304	1,214	1,617	1,231	1,295	642	614	681	700	286	335	4,183	3,896
1962	433	407	1,480	1,608	1,375	1,231	582	626	786	831	459	428	4,892	4,600
1963	571	403	1,761	1,557	1,560	1,255	744	676	937	921	421	399	5,076	5,023
1964	587	401	1,815	1,750	1,564	1,431	943	796	1,118	991	487	494	5,839	5,755
1965	607	463	1,579	2,105	1,540	1,586	909	934	1,037	1,233	456	337	6,496	6,168
1966	565	572	1,562	2,012	1,780	1,849	1,080	1,001	1,076	1,234	387	353	6,073	6,184
1967	754[78]	556[78]	1,786[78]	1,798[78]	2,278[78]	1,924[78]	1,218[78]	868[78]	1,309[78]	1,193[78]	463[78]	436[78]	6,949[78]	7,201[78]
1968	643	477	1,882	2,083	2,304	2,016	900	905	1,321	1,133	477	429	7,593	7,910
1969	734	642	1,684	2,343	2,234	2,636	971	1,191	1,390	1,379	571	533	8,400	8,462
1970	956	759	2,333	2,381	3,074	2,644	1,549	1,630	1,701	1,623	814	632	9,767	9,272
1971	1,126	749	2,945	2,328	3,813	2,842	1,797	1,613	1,797	2,209	956	793	11,984	10,249
1972	1,045	935	2,909	2,955	3,600	3,481	2,568	1,955	1,789	2,525	807	821	11,821	12,839
1973	1,321	1,303	3,058	3,714	3,232	3,220	4,707	2,608	1,823	2,587	1,135	1,272	12,710	14,034
1974	2,526	1,638	3,819	4,300	4,845	4,767	4,873	2,819	2,354	2,730	1,233	1,866	14,522	14,989
1975	2,302	1,224	4,616	4,377	6,367	5,650	4,411	2,771	3,029	2,728	2,164	1,459	21,549	20,273
1976	11,029	7,473	14,669	15,331	20,209	18,624	22,112	16,607	10,121	9,007	5,388	5,571	63,174	61,906
1977	12,559	8,646	14,728	17,295	21,926	22,079	29,069	21,122	11,792	11,605	7,000	7,148	73,614	72,612
1978	15,350	7,937	17,483	16,126	23,433	20,456	37,614	20,831	12,635	11,630	7,030	6,636	84,784	74,349
1979	16,132	9,638	16,349	19,812	22,908	22,878	37,521	26,850	12,321	12,953	7,912	7,904	90,652	79,205

thousand million Forints

	Austria		Czechoslovakia		East Germany		West Germany		Poland		Romania		Russsia/U.S.S.R.	
	I	E	I	E	I	E	I	E	I	E	I	E	I	E
1980	16.2	12.2	15.4	17.1	20.8	19.1	35.1	27.5	11.0	12.0	6.4	6.8	83.0	82.3
1981	18.3	13.0	15.4	18.0	21.1	20.7	37.3	26.0	10.6	10.1	6.3	6.1	90.0	100
1982	16.2	12.3	17.1	18.1	22.3	19.9	36.3	23.6	12.7	12.2	6.4	5.1	96.1	109
1983	16.9	16.4	18.7	18.1	24.4	22.0	37.3	27.9	15.9	14.8	6.7	4.8	104	118
1984	19.7	21.4	19.6	21.5	24.9	24.5	41.8	31.0	17.3	16.6	6.9	6.0	114	125
1985	25.6	22.9	20.1	24.1	26.3	25.8	46.5	38.8	19.0	16.3	7.1	7.3	122	143
1986	27.1	22.4	22.7	24.7	29.3	26.8	54.4	35.6	20.7	17.7	8.3	8.4	135	142
1987	29.4	24.8	25.0	22.6	29.5	25.1	64.5	44.5	18.4	15.4	8.5	7.6	132	147
1988	34.1	28.8	24.0	27.2	30.3	26.6	65.5	55.2	19.2	16.8	8.4	8.6	118	139
1989	45.0	37.1	27.0	29.0	32.5	30.8	83.9	68.0	17.2	18.1	8.5	8.3	115	144
1990	54.2	45.3	25.4	25.0	32.3	18.8	94.8	101.9	13.1	10.0	4.9	10.7	104	122
1991	114.2	82.9	35.5	16.5	Included in		183.1	205.3	16.2	15.7	5.3	9.9	131	102
1992	126.3	90.1	37.7	22.9	West Germany		206.9	233.9	14.2	11.3	5.6	14.9	148[93]	111[93]
			Czech Republic											
1993	184.3	122.7	36.6[94]	20.8[94]	355.6	143.6	359.1	318.5	20.4	23.4	12.5	20.9	184[95]	85[95]

Million US$ Dollars

	Austria		Czech Republic		East Germany		West Germany		Poland		Romania		Russsia/U.S.S.R.	
	I	E	I	E	I	E	I	E	I	E	I	E	I	E
1994	1,748.3	1,163.9	347.4	197.7	369.7	213.2	3,402.9	3,017.5	193.3	222.0	119.0	197.2	1,745.8	807.0
1995	1,663.7	1,303.3	364.0	207.4	382.2	251.0	3,628.2	3,686.8	248.5	337.1	130.2	357.5	1,839.8	822.8
1996	1,535.6	1,394.7	487.4	289.7	399.6	241.7	3,819.8	3,814.8	298.4	387.8	146.5	277.6	2,020.5	776.6
1997	2,213.9	2,138.2	481.9	302.9			5,694.9	7,033.2	355.3	500.4	149.7	304.8	1,833.5	947.4

E2 External Trade (by value) with Main Trading Partners
IRELAND (in million pounds)

1924–1997

1924–1959 (Germany column shown as *West Germany* from 1948; I = imports, E = exports)

Year	Germany I	Germany E	Britain I	Britain E	N. Ireland I	N. Ireland E	U.S.A. I	U.S.A. E
1924	0.7	0.1	48	43	7.9	7.5	3.7	0.2
1925	0.9	0.1	44	37	6.8	6.5	3.2	0.3
1926	2.3	0.2	40	35	6.5	5.7	5.0	0.3
1927	1.5	0.4	41	38	6.4	5.1	4.7	0.5
1928	1.8	0.3	40	39	6.2	5.3	3.8	0.3
1929	1.6	0.7	42	39	6.1	5.2	4.8	1.0
1930	1.3	0.7	40	36	5.8	4.8	3.9	1.2
1931	1.2	0.1	36	31	5.0	3.9	2.0	0.4
1932	1.3	0.1	29	22	3.8	3.0	1.3	0.1
1933	1.8	0.2	23	16	2.1	2.2	1.1	0.2
1934	2.3	0.2	24	14	2.0	2.3	1.9	0.1
1935	1.3	0.5	25	16	1.8	2.0	1.4	0.2
1936	1.3[3]	0.6	27[3]	19	1.6[3]	2.3	1.9[3]	0.3
1937	1.4	0.8	21	20	0.6	2.2	2.9	0.2
1938	1.4	0.9	21	20	0.6	2.5	4.7	0.1
1939	1.5	…	20	23	0.8	2.7	3.6	0.3
1940	…	…	23	28	0.6	3.4	4.1	0.5
1941	…	—	24	28	0.6	3.4	2.3	0.7
1942	…	—	21	27	1.0	5.1	3.0	0.3
1943	…	—	19	23	0.5	4.9	3.6	0.3
1944	…	—	13	24	0.8	5.7	3.0	0.3
1945	…	—	13	28	0.9	6.9	4.0	0.4
1946	…	—	19	29	1.6	7.2	8.5	0.6
1947	…	—	36	27	2.2	7.5	29	0.3
West Germany								
1948	…	0.1	52	35	2.2	7.6	11	0.4
1949	0.5	0.4	71	46	2.3	8.4	19	0.5
1950	1.9	1.5	72	54	2.4	8.5	21	1.3
1951	4.6	1.2	82	58	2.7	11	25	3.2
1952	5.4	0.9	93	73	2.6	14	18	3.2
1953	5.3	0.9	85	86	2.4	17	16	2.4
1954	7.3	1.8	90	86	2.7	17	12	2.2
1955	9.6	1.5	97	81	3.0	15	18	3.0
1956	8.0	2.3	105	68	3.4	15	14	3.2
1957	7.0	3.3	101	79	8.6	22	11	4.0
1958	8.0	2.8	96	80	8.4	21	14	7.5
1959	10	3.5	104	77	8.9	19	14	9.9

[3] Break in series.

1960–1997 (I = imports, E = exports)

Year	Germany I	Germany E	Great Britain I	Great Britain E	N. Ireland I	N. Ireland E	U.S.A. I	U.S.A. E
1960	12	3.7	105	92	7.4	20	19	11
1961	14	5.6	119	111	14	23	20	13
1962	19	5.3	125	105	11	23	21	14
1963	20	5.8	142	111	14	30	18	14
1964	24	9.0	162	129	16	29	27	10
1965	24	12.0	174	127	15	27	30	9
1966	22	9.5	179	141	14	28	35	17
1967	25	6.9	179	170	18	35	32	26
1968	36	8.1	237	195	21	43	38	49
1969	43	10.8	289	201	25	50	55	57
1970	46	13	322	235	30	57	49	60
1971	55	14	348	289	26	66	65	60
1972	64	30	397	327	31	67	63	61
1973	93	54	534	393	43	82	78	86
1974	126	66	706	530	52	104	105	109
1975	120	115	768	628	64	154	122	91
1976	161	161	1,067	743	84	162	200	139
1977	202	216	1,363	993	126	190	275	157
1978	266	248	1,674	1,151	162	248	312	183
1979	361	305	2,202	1,359	212	266	411	167
1980	374	399	2,531	1,463	223	300	474	216
1981	496	454	2,935	1,589	334	332	768	304
1982	524	532	2,965	1,790	308	418	878	406
1983	587	687	3,026	2,064	313	498	1,083	565
1984	678	903	3,483	2,476	339	588	1,466	866
1985	729	985	3,706	2,606	321	605	1,602	954
1986	772	1,022	3,248	2,604	340	598	1,365	816
1987	765	1,203	3,439	3,044	377	619	1,555	834
1988	881	1,369	3,910	3,592	392	757	1,623	950
1989	1,075	1,610	5,028	4,896	489	776	1,973	1,153

Million US$ Dollars

Year	Germany I	Germany E	Great Britain I	Great Britain E	N. Ireland I	N. Ireland E	U.S.A. I	U.S.A. E
1990	1,041	1,679	5,266	4,834	500	816	1,815	1,175
1991	1,058	1,906	5,320	4,799	496	789	1,921	1,309
1992	1,104	2,122	5,602	5,232	468	825	1,869	1,368
1993	1,072	2,605	5,361	5,589	419	706	2,530	1,790
1994	1,816.6	4,837.0	9,347.8	9,615.4	…	…	4,709.9	2,858.2
1995	2,256.2	6,328.6	11,498.3	11,140.1	…	…	5,717.2	3,641.8
1996	2,452.2	5,844.8	12,430.2	11,428.3	…	…	5,537.3	4,302.7
1997	2,328.2	6,688.0	13,216.4	12,946.7	…	…	5,870.7	6,052.5

E2 External Trade (by value) with Main Trading Partners

ITALY (in million lire)

1861-1894

Year	Austria-Hungary		France		Germany		Switzerland		U.K.		U.S.A.[42]	
	I	E	I	E	I	E	I	E	I	E	I	E
1861	158	66	219	184	8	1	84	146	191	26	31	3
1862	139	56	233	188	4	5	81	136	192	95	16	17
1863	147	70	267	235	5	4	74	115	203	88	6	10
1864	152	78	294	204	4	2	72	91	179	93	9	16
1865	121	78	346	187	6	5	64	76	184	86	8	3
1866	94[38]	60[38]	315	215	5	6	59	97	190	93	18	25
1867	146	125	258	280	6	4	62	105	179	73	33	21
1868	169	140	230	290	8	5	61	121	205	85	41	31
1869	155	106	261	266	10	3	49	122	232	117	38	30
1870	147	133	224[39]	203[39]	13	5	49	135	240[40]	116[40]	39	35
1871	172	197	201	393	13	8	52	157	283	143	51	32
1872	215	220	326	442	15	8	49	176	294	135	45	29
1873	225	222	363	446	24	14	41	160	302	111	50	29
1874	250	208	391	366	28	19	41	108	281	132	48	28
1875	233	191	367	382	37	24	31	109	298	140	43	29
1876	264	187	412	542	40	21	33	150	309	134	49	21
1877	234[41]	154[41]	322[39,41]	401[39,41]	25[41]	17	26[41]	80[41]	296[40,41]	126[40,41]	40[41]	27[41]
1878	196	173	268	464	39	21	32	98	237	97	54	36
1879	194	207	295	438	46	24	29	107	256	95	72[42]	61[42]
1880	181	166	300	476	88	78	34	102	259	84	76	55
1881	218	151	329	524	66	68	36	135	307	83	63	57
1882	189	147	310	458	85	73	44	130	290	92	69	61
1883	200	135	300	500	109	86	52	123	298	92	58	59
1884	200	108	282	415	110	109	66	118	300	89	60	55
1885	222	93	288	367	119	104	71	109	314	71	72	46
1886	223	93	311	446	129	108	81	88	275	71	55	52
1887	249	92	326	405	166	115	65	88	306	79	64	66
1888	137	84	156	170	145	80	58	214	264	115	77	61
1889	159	90	167	165	156	91	62	230	314	113	75	76
1890	144	84	163	161	141	119	55	169	320	111	82	77
1891	122	93	144	150	134	131	48	150	262	115	74	74
1892	122	106	169	147	144	145	49	173	245	113	79	100
1893	120	120	159	148	147	146	51	188	252	104	96	82
1894	115	126	131	144	140	143	43	206	249	122	107	91

E2 External Trade (by value) with Main Trading Partners

1895–1929

ITALY (in million lire)

	Austria-Hungary		France		Germany		Switzerland		U.K.		U.S.A.[42]	
	I	E	I	E	I	E	I	E	I	E	I	E
1895	133	114	162	136	144	170	46	187	235	115	124[42]	102[42]
1896	132[41]	121[41]	134[41]	153[41]	145[41]	160[41]	45[41]	170[41]	230[41]	110[41]	122[41]	86[41]
1897	134	137	161	116	150	179	42	185	223	114	125	93
1898	130	144	116	146	157	192	40	185	254	117	166	107
1899	161	159	152	202	194	236	49	247	300	148	168	118
1900	191	144	167	169	203	221	57	207	359	154	226	121
1901	178	131	179	175	206	235	57	205	279	151	234	140
1902	176	127	184	168	222	246	57	260	287	143	211	177
1903	176	154	193	171	236	226	59	274	282	132	212	166
1904	187	137	188	171	252	206	49	258	319	134	239	191
1905	195	144	205	182	287	222	50	320	348	130	238	226
1906	226[41]	140[41]	228[41]	213[41]	394[41]	252[41]	65[41]	366[41]	450[41]	132[41]	311[41]	240[41]
1907	249	158	256	198	527	301	73	349	523	156	393	236
1908	301	145	276	204	521	245	80	297	501	132	405	204
1909	309	156	329	199	504	307	80	217	491	168	390	272
1910	290	165	334	218	525	293	84	216	476	210	363	264
1911	289	185	327	206	550	301	78	204	510	223	415	247
1912	294	219	390	223	626	328	85	219	577	264	515	262
1913	265	221	283	231	613	343	87	249	592	261	523	268
1914	234	197	206	174	503	319	77	232	505	306	443	262
1915	46	119	240	438	230	204	118	314	849	391	1,749	283
1916	1	—	595	738	12	—	209	632	1,977	447	3,415	315
1917	- -	—	993	912	18	—	249	605	2,165	483	6,192	244
1918	2	—	1,234	1,207	16	—	191	410	2,666	727	6,641	169

	Austria		France		Germany		Switzerland		U.K.		U.S.A.	
	I	E	I	E	I	E	I	E	I	E	I	E
1919	106	275	760	1,403	88	85	370	786	2,444	773	7,350	630
1920	654	621	1,904	1,696	1,097	574	575	1,505	4,609	1,379	8,689	939
1921	445	510	1,070	967	1,293	814	287	831	1,680	795	5,711	1,084
1922	327	222	1,151	1,365	1,246	972	331	1,208	2,022	1,117	4,398	1,018
1923	326	335	1,324	1,581	1,308	697	372	1,201	2,204	1,211	4,608	1,523
1924	467	686	1,474	1,823	1,524	1,565	408	1,612	2,169	1,493	4,648	1,239
1925	673	666	2,358	2,024	2,253	2,025	521	1,635	2,728	1,852	6,196	1,896
1926	634	562	2,136	2,111	2,956	2,215	592	1,509	1,881	1,755	5,608	1,934
1927	507	485	1,799	1,284	2,108	2,233	539	1,255	1,826	1,528	3,958	1,641
1928	464	434	2,060	1,362	2,303	1,856	546	988	1,794	1,404	4,012	1,521
1929	483[41]	427[41]	2,044[41]	1,304[41]	2,737[41]	1,777[41]	549[41]	1,051[41]	2,040[41]	1,461[41]	3,561[41]	1,718[41]

E2 External Trade (by value) with Main Trading Partners

ITALY (in million lire)

1930–1964

	Austria		France		Germany		Switzerland		U.K.		U.S.A.	
	I	E	I	E	I	E	I	E	I	E	I	E
1930	412	378	1,504	1,234	2,258	1,555	548	929	1,677	1,190	2,538	1,327
1931	291	315	825	1,119	1,588	1,091	401	771	1,099	1,201	1,327	1,046
1932	186	190	482	517	1,151	778	310	578	743	736	1,108	688
1933	175	131	413	459	1,143	729	721	483	727	689	1,115	529
1934	190	122	437	352	1,248	834	293	438	707	529	957	388
1935	272	134	471	305	1,427	851	246	338	568	431	879	423
1936	370	193	128	190	1,617	1,086	233	345	52	156	895	550
1937	632	289	491	442	2,589[43]	1,503[43]	412	508	561	641	1,539	784
1938	…	…	254	328	3,016	2,202	376	495	728	587	1,338	782
1939	…	…	154	243	3,030	1,899	336	530	568	518	979	773
1940	…	…	125	290	5,139	3,558	470	718	419	276	1,219	393
1941	…	…	207	219	6,890	7,106	534	1,087	3	—	91	5
1942	…	…	119	181	8,374[43]	7,639[43]	519	627	2	—	18	—
					135,485	86,685						
1948	13,050	10,283	7,893	23,058	17,590	16,577	25,764	44,232	27,812	45,490	317,701	51,337
1949	20,016	18,492	21,470	36,188	39,726	54,284	26,732	35,598	34,593	67,018	311,041	26,392
1950	25,481	19,977	41,764	65,313	75,887	73,799	33,465	47,813	51,129	85,755	217,884	47,699
1951	32,164	21,049	58,511	92,656	99,906	80,246	42,022	57,731	50,075	138,551	284,477	70,535
1952	42,159	24,019	58,942	56,734	136,730[2]	87,977[2]	55,134	56,106	83,384	71,153	307,529	87,185
1953	55,142	25,703	75,909	49,121	179,619	103,865	63,447	64,047	116,934	67,751	202,821	90,080
1954	64,457	35,628	97,534	60,449	203,679	115,159	58,260	73,988	102,633	80,967	186,510	80,221
1955	70,283	42,858	108,367	67,539	214,733	145,664	57,344	84,415	90,545	84,065	253,094	99,585
1956	82,854	48,319	100,203	95,912	247,558	179,983	63,556	100,217	107,163	86,621	325,368	125,897
1957	98,902	53,102	121,425	101,087	281,161	224,706	66,329	121,932	121,845	99,224	427,060	161,904
1958	93,262	45,761	94,690	84,558	243,321	226,850	64,163	122,302	109,213	109,213	357,981	177,463
1959	91,949	51,084	162,082	112,089	292,911	295,072	70,966	13,549	116,655	135,741	234,053	215,978
1960	112,133	69,614	248,679	172,116	418,835	375,761	86,259	152,614	151,865	156,312	418,360	239,662
1961	110,996	72,943	299,505	199,671	509,370	465,487	93,423	179,196	179,730	175,730	539,691	238,786
1962	116,145	78,159	334,283	269,066	642,051	562,036	104,327	206,695	239,922	174,779	553,281	275,592
1963	131,866	82,114	460,587	328,058	813,232	564,231	121,170	212,673	290,911	169,112	651,598	298,180
1964	105,814	87,776	446,498	406,490	738,468	707,188	114,999	227,452	248,097	207,833	615,781	316,927

E2 External Trade (by value) with Main Trading Partners

ITALY (in thousand million lire)   1965–1997

	Austria		France		West Germany		Switzerland		U.K.		U.S.A.	
	I	E	I	E	I	E	I	E	I	E	I	E
1965	101	104	452	464	681	953	107	244	214	211	621	387
1966	107	110	542	583	858	1,007	125	252	251	239	657	465
1967	127	116	655	676	1,060	960	142	259	271	263	665	540
1968	122	109	728	801	1,148	1,189	156	286	273	281	748	681
1969	145	117	968	1,061	1,462	1,440	185	328	313	264	886	795
1970	167	143	1,235	1,065	1,861	1,780	209	390	353	313	967	846
1971	176	173	1,399	1,267	1,998	2,129	212	441	362	362	892	918
1972	205	273	1,772	1,536	2,286	2,486	243	488	395	463	931	1,062
1973	333	290	2,442	1,880	3,302	2,821	371	607	560	648	1,352	1,111
1974	451	399	3,509	2,498	4,734	3,662	549	825	809	1,025	2,037	1,504
1975	393	483	3,355	3,025	4,316	4,293	583	862	840	1,047	2,194	1,490
1976	645	736	4,975	4,684	6,231	5,884	890	1,160	1,283	1,495	2,893	2,010
1977	807	1,015	5,895	5,715	7,140	7,413	1,153	1,602	1,582	2,106	2,950	2,666
1978	900	1,126	6,970	6,774	8,313	9,037	1,441	1,954	1,912	2,876	3,239	3,385
1979	1,262	1,507	9,032	8,873	11,107	11,336	1,773	2,562	2,613	3,916	4,381	3,877
1980	1,615	1,788	11,858	10,094	14,180	12,211	2,175	2,952	3,784	4,064	5,921	3,555
1981	1,878	1,914	12,938	11,686	16,191	13,351	3,301	3,455	4,012	4,999	7,032	5,841
1982	1,954	2,141	14,531	15,104	18,656	15,489	3,984	3,961	4,601	6,221	7,863	6,989
1983	2,150	2,602	15,380	16,252	19,387	18,331	4,735	4,574	4,749	7,019	7,266	8,523
1984	2,698	2,912	18,436	18,078	23,666	20,782	6,100	5,246	6,384	8,716	9,111	14,045
1985	3,084	3,294	21,546	21,003	28,742	24,172	6,667	6,070	8,540	10,424	10,294	18,357
1986	3,188	3,447	21,705	22,704	30,468	26,355	6,485	6,608	7,606	10,298	8,474	15,604
1987	3,731	3,794	23,592	24,571	34,076	27,959	7,718	7,082	8,514	11,193	8,619	14,456
1988	4,320	4,129	26,734	27,677	39,217	30,211	8,063	7,868	9,168	13,417	10,054	14,834
1989	4,846	4,637	30,842	31,413	44,496	32,718	9,089	8,617	10,173	15,204	11,444	16,615
1990	4,968	4,962	30,979	33,320	46,189	38,686	9,926	9,206	11,372	14,404	11,099	15,516
					Germany							
1991	4,938	5,280	31,981	31,851	47,223	44,019	10,003	8,810	12,835	13,968	12,617	14,441
1992	5,069	5,422	33,550	32,060	50,047	44,662	10,444	8,717	13,284	14,391	12,141	15,281
1993	6,609	5,140	34,822	31,639	51,630	44,967	10,417	11,925	16,957	13,535	12,348	20,489
					Million US$ Dollars							
1994	3,761.8	4,670.3	2,278.1	24,851.6	32,310.9	36,119.2	8,254.9	7,169.3	10,265.8	12,337.4	7,803.3	…
1995	4,751.3	5,487.4	28,317.3	30,018.9	38,962.2	43,248.4	9,100.2	8,771.2	12,390.7	14,292.8	9,890.9	…
1996	4,803.3	5,965.3	28,245.2	32,042.4	38,555.7	44,089.2	8,853.4	9,269.3	13,761.9	16,325.5	10,170.7	…
1997	4,778.1	5,403.3	27,478.6	29,010.6	37,441.3	38,960.2	8,120.1	8,215.0	13,948.0	16,938.0	10,376.3	…

E2 External Trade (by value) with Main Trading Partners

NETHERLANDS (in million florins)

1846–1879

	Belgium		Dutch East Indies		Germany[44]		Russia		U.K.		U.S.A.	
	I	E	I	E	I	E	I	E	I	E	I	E
1846	10	15	48	11	21	29	8	6	35	25	6	2
1847	14	20	48	9	20	31	16	10	32	26	5	4
1848	13	16	51	9	19	33	9	4	47	34	5	4
1849	15	18	55	8	23	30	12	3	35	35	7	3
1850	23	21	50	10	27	27	10	3	37	39	4	5
1851	31	22	52	12	23	33	9	3	40	38	4	5
1852	23	21	63	16	24	37	12	3	40	41	6	4
1853	21	20	53	19	28	32	17	2	45	47	5	4
1854	36	26	61	25	37	48	12	–	53	54	6	3
1855	22	40	63	18	44	56	–	–	51	56	6	4
1856	28	29	74	22	50	63	15	5	56	59	8	5
1857	42	29	67	37	51	29	18	5	57	60	7	4
1858	51	30	69	23	52[44]	69[44]	14	4	60	54	8	7
1859	42	34	70	25	50	67	13	5	56	61	9	5
1860	39	33	73	32	56	70	19	5	67	64	11	5
1861	30	40	76	39	62	80	19	5	79	61	12	3
1862	35	34	76	28	68	80	18	3	68	62	6	3
1863	41	44	66	23	74	95	9	8	91	72	6	3
1864	40	54	78	53	83	98	13	4	94	91	5	2
1865	48	55	73	27	97	121	11	4	118	98	3	4
1866	46	40	79	41	99	121	14	8	125	89	4	3
1867	44	38	79	44	90	122	23	4	130	84	6	3
1868	56	53	83	31	99	136	15	4	147	94	7	5
1869	55	62	76	28	109	136	15	4	131	108	8	4
1870	56	67	81	32	103	144	23	4	174	106	10	3
1871	79	65	80	31	104	183	33	5	195	112	26	4
1872	97	74	67	35	113	201	23	6	220	109	22	5
1873	91	76	82	45	131	230	27	3	247	115	30	4
1874	87	77	77	36	137	222	39	8	228	117	30	5
1875	105	80	77	41	155	227	37	21	242	125	21	4
1876	102	86	73	42	154	221	43	15	225	124	30	5
1877	107	90	74	48	186	217	57	8	206	132	39	4
1878	117	90	69	53	193	232	63	10	217	131	52	3
1879	112	94	56	42	208[44]	259[44]	83	8	219	129	54	9
					221	270						

E2 External Trade (by value) with Main Trading Partners

NETHERLANDS (in million florins)   1880–1914

	Belgium		Dutch East Indies		Germany		Russia		U.K.		U.S.A.	
	I	E	I	E	I	E	I	E	I	E	I	E
1880	104	101	56	47	246	266	46	9	212	147	81	16
1881	111	109	53	42	289	304	47	7	244	160	61	16
1882	124	113	53	40	312	349	77	9	276	156	43	38
1883	141	115	81	36	322	333	90	5	258	132	61	19
1884	146	130	76	43	302	407	94	4	317	187	66	22
1885	162	128	97	45	297	401	77	5	269	229	56	26
1886	158	138	90	45	314	414	75	5	262	255	67	46
1887	161	131	114	41	302	420	95	3	246	293	79	49
1888	157	146	118	47	318	530	126	5	341	298	62	38
1889	177	140	143	69	269	511	113	5	297	285	76	22
1890	195	148	160	53	271	517	121	6	284	271	98	24
1891	186	150	225	64	271	552	119	4	270	296	93	21
1892	184	160	177	63	271	504	39	3	267	326	149	23
1893	176	168	193	57	279	551	89	6	264	256	155	22
1894	161	155	225	54	285	557	175	5	246	260	132	22
1895	166	154	202	52	293	596	198	5	238	268	111	38
1896	174	164	239	53	302	700	223	6	256	290	167	47
1897	186	166	218	60	304	790	249	7	270	322	234	45
1898	209	161	261	64	342	814	164	8	269	338	279	44
1899	206	159	289	68	335	834	205	8	277	349	297	61
1900	208	176	273	64	386	911	145	11	288	383	284	65
1901	226	175	324	62	466	901	160	8	248	426	303	79
1902	233	193	349	61	565	895	210	10	237	457	234	107
1903	228	213	337	62	603	972	230	8	257	461	232	106
1904	259	221	376	68	555	1,039	333	11	253	433	232	97
1905	254	227	400	71	638	1,066	319	12	264	410	241	81
1906	264	260	337	68	614	1,058	216	10	309	466	315	86
1907	286	285	437	82	599	1,159	209	12	325	446	294	86
1908	471	281	405	89	692	1,081	280	13	296	490	322	81
1909	290	289	425	88	743	1,279	558	14	293	500	291	100
1910	301	330	494	114	820	1,319	433	16	325	545	295	85
1911	324	319	456	126	902	1,357	367	18	339	555	331	105
1912	344	371	496	154	1,046	1,555	292	25	354	605	362	136
1913	352	340	529	163	1,133	1,478	366	31	341	684	443	131
1914	246	219	395	143	877	1,125	188	22	327	602	301	164

E2 External Trade (by value) with Main Trading Partners

NETHERLANDS (in million florins)

1915–1949

	Belgium		Dutch East Indies/Indonesia		Germany		Russia/USSR		U.K.		U.S.A.	
	I	E	I	E	I	E	I	E	I	E	I	E
1915	63	114	379	132	608	714	--	1	396	476	331	117
1916	59	53	388	111	566	520	2	1	358	396	273	102
1917	22	63	..	..	246	317	..	..	192	306	199	37
1918	13	20	5	11	321	154	..	..	52	74	24	14
1919	225	177	329	163	433	578	21	29	588	208	549	57
1920	321	181	240	264	903	421	5	2	555	328	526	77
1921	229	172	129	206	649	254	3	5	318	357	392	47
1922	191	176	103	132	609	168	6	5	327	307	271	62
1923	220	142	114	111	501	187	22	3	310	368	256	69
1924	255	153	135	107	577	495	46	10	306	414	271	58
1925	276	166	137	137	594	470	35	17	394	468	276	71
1926	273	146	145	128	668	381	39	3	232	483	258	80
1927	270	158	117	130	654	466	31	4	252	460	268	65
1928	302	174	141	182	730	468	23	4	259	437	266	69
1929	286	207	147	187	842	451	38	3	263	406	272	71
1930	259	195	97	144	768	360	59	4	230	380	211	49
1931	198	174	72	89	620	252	72	89	160	317	148	34
1932	135	118	60	47	400	179	36	5	118	160	86	29
1933	131	106	51	31	396	161	35	5	113	128	78	32
1934	114	86	58	31	312	180	27	8	102	137	69	28
1935	112	80	57	32	249	131	23	11	96	148	65	42
1936	129	101	79	44	247	119	22	17	114	170	73	58
1937	192	142	126	94	338	179	40	22	146	253	137	74
1938	171	114	102	100	311	157	32	23	127	238	154	46
1939	231	98	91	101	369	139	22	22	127	230	147	46
1940	152	63	54	42	324	311	4	11	56	78	135	12
1941	89	63	6	--	518	502	--	1	--	--	2	--
1942	52	44	--	--	327	485	--	--	--	--	--	--
1943	41	44	--	--	285	536	3	1	--	--	--	--
					West Germany							
1946	302	170	20	26	56	52	1	--	372	89	536	59
1947	522	296	197	133	97	58	..	..	422	243	1,198	61
1948	732	424	334	200	267	160	9	11	492	393	862	85
1949	762	511	406	392	361	411	59	19	621	627	879	130

E2 External Trade (by value) with Main Trading Partners

1950–1997

NETHERLANDS (in million florins)

	Belgium I	Belgium E	Indonesia I	Indonesia E	West Germany I	West Germany E	Russia/U.S.S.R. I	Russia/U.S.S.R. E	U.K. I	U.K. E	U.S.A. I	U.S.A. E
1950	1,437	727	510	300	961	1,109	9	2	820	790	899	271
1951	1,774	1,095	755	402	1,205	1,029	53	6	845	1,178	1,071	449
1952	1,451	1,251	543	440	1,184	1,118	97	19	782	1,002	1,085	536
1953	1,556	1,266	494	291	1,441	1,150	119	86	897	879	900	694
1954	1,841	1,293	528	233	1,832	1,459	88	125	936	1,060	1,284	627
1955	2,205	1,411	369	258	2,155	1,755	115	59	1,039	1,263	1,652	602
1956	2,680	1,543	440	315	2,547	1,979	160	30	1,158	1,273	1,976	679
1957	2,816	1,826	454	274	2,902	2,191	150	73	1,255	1,280	2,049	604
1958	2,459	1,830	308	111	2,691	2,337	156	41	1,017	1,455	1,554	688
1959	2,747	2,009	272	98	3,098	2,964	240	46	1,132	1,470	1,651	787
1960	3,155	2,184	236	100	3,712	3,452	169	45	1,183	1,676	2,279	754
1961	3,549	2,373	149	48	4,313	3,630	144	72	1,335	1,564	2,073	702
1962	3,804	2,444	73	37	4,469	4,025	132	116	1,405	1,755	2,199	724
1963	4,163	2,694	55	33	5,247	4,649	171	86	1,577	1,727	2,348	736
1964	4,911	3,207	344	43	6,200	5,661	129	54	1,830	1,923	2,813	812
1965	5,299	3,438	118	400	6,392	6,428	192	106	1,758	2,011	2,768	882
1966	5,509	3,690	120	353	7,211	6,576	175	91	1,771	2,009	3,295	1,112
1967	5,568	3,886	166	355	7,670	6,885	187	241	1,674	2,330	3,208	1,241
1968	6,047	4,320	136	216	8,876	8,393	196	169	1,844	2,579	3,671	1,579
1969	7,046	5,031	164	189	10,626	10,718	247	202	2,319	2,754	3,862	1,631
1970	8,187	5,942	171	178	13,164	13,873	210	165	2,815	2,981	4,737	1,832
1971	7,334	6,960	183	174	14,386	16,438	228	163	2,967	3,553	5,126	1,960
1972	8,584	8,130	190	168	15,021	18,273	256	205	2,874	3,962	4,519	2,019
1973	9,763	9,694	262	221	18,542	21,812	357	218	3,439	5,278	5,937	2,373
1974	11,665	12,362	317	225	23,232	26,515	632	455	4,790	8,018	7,944	3,509
1975	11,510	12,280	314	409	22,354	26,941	768	523	5,097	8,121	8,771	2,440
1976	13,165	15,656	364	566	25,178	32,763	1,021	462	6,472	8,805	9,585	3,011
1977	13,363	15,719	510	624	27,423	33,089	1,060	500	7,504	8,007	9,546	3,675
1978	14,392	16,088	404	476	29,042	33,344	1,154	454	7,660	8,099	9,845	3,582
1979	16,522	19,765	528	409	32,681	38,929	1,695	610	10,535	10,744	11,350	3,587
1980	17,737	22,080	544	929	33,944	44,004	2,535	1,012	12,466	11,576	13,434	3,686
1981	18,628	24,487	583	678	35,203	50,273	4,410	1,535	14,004	14,112	15,567	5,495
1982	18,518	25,061	415	602	36,949	52,146	6,839	1,128	15,732	16,358	15,320	5,739
1983	19,023	25,671	676	770	38,766	56,095	7,492	1,524	15,353	16,438	15,505	7,894
1984	22,360	29,392	782	876	43,708	62,516	7,003	971	17,299	19,888	17,718	10,574
1985	26,641	31,902	792	534	48,326	67,684	7,658	1,128	21,542	21,409	17,834	11,842
1986	26,286	28,058	631	664	48,888	55,687	2,548	818	15,213	20,094	14,569	9,334
1987	26,734	27,191	632	512	49,012	51,405	2,765	832	14,188	19,340	13,307	8,133
1988	28,806	29,953	814	827	51,650	53,403	2,235	943	15,107	21,939	15,004	8,746
1989	31,625	33,553	934	403	56,903	59,176	2,798	1,429	17,439	25,412	18,714	10,433
1990	31,959	35,097	946	858	58,807	66,140	2,789	1,047	18,761	24,336	18,046	9,562
1991	33,341	35,574	1,026	711	60,227	73,316	2,023[96]	1,241[96]	20,385	23,211	18,350	9,569
1992	33,511	35,658	1,260	729	60,509	73,197	...	...	20,521	23,260	19,179	9,716
1993	33,581	35,123	1,531	1,067	59,586	70,809	...	...	20,420	22,615	18,322	9,982
						Million US$ Dollars						
1994	14,690.3	18,050.7	1,009.7	369.7	28,787.7	38,267.0	940.1	1,243.0	11,379.5	12,533.9	10,268.0	5,360.5
1995	17,247.0	21,162.6	1,084.4	733.5	34,168.2	46,123.3	1,296.7	1,576.7	14,614.3	15,183.0	13,292.0	5,680.5
1996	16,563.6	21,240.8	1,181.9	398.2	32,896.0	45,896.3	1,573.8	1,589.3	14,365.0	14,846.8	13,497.4	5,469.9
1997	15,285.0	20,995.5	1,038.4	528.4	29,075.8	46,095.0	1,824.1	1,921.0	16,240.4	17,810.6	16,121.4	7,109.3

E2 External Trade (by value) with Main Trading Partners

NORWAY (in million kroner)

1866–1899

	Denmark		France		Germany		Netherlands		Sweden		Great Britain/U.K.[46]		U.S.A.	
	I	E	I	E	I	E	I	E	I	E	I	E	I	E
1866	14	3.9	5.8	9.3	31	10	3.0	6.5	5.8	5.5	28	19	0.4	0.4
1867	17	3.7	3.2	8.7	30	10	2.6	5.7	4.9	6.4	24	21	0.1	0.1
1868	19	3.8	3.8	8.2	33	12	2.6	6.2	6.1	4.6	24	21	0.1	–
1869	18	4.6	3.9	9.5	29	13	2.8	7.0	5.3	5.9	21	22	–	–
1870	18	4.5	2.8	7.8	27	12	3.1	6.4	8.5	7.9	26	24	0.1	0.1
1871	15	5.0	2.6	6.6	25	13	3.4	6.2	9.7	7.9	28	25	0.1	–
1872	22	6.2	6.0	10.5	31	18	4.4	7.4	11	11	41	30	0.1	–
1873	19	6.0	10.1	12.4	42	20	5.8	8.7	12	12	53	40	0.4	0.1
1874	20	7.8	8.9	10.7	49	19	6.8	7.3	13	15	55	38	2.0	–
1875	21	5.9	8.7	7.7	47	18	5.9	6.2	13	13	52	29	2.4	0.1
1876	19	5.9	10.6	10.5	45	19	6.9	6.7	14	15	45	36	2.1	–
1877	18	5.0	9.4	9.3	54	18	7.9	6.5	14	12	50	34	3.9	–
1878	15	4.3	4.7	6.6	42	16	6.3	4.7	12	9	36	28	3.8	0.1
1879	14	5.0	3.9	6.2	35	17	5.3	5.6	12	9	37	25	2.3	0.3
1880	18	5.9	6.2	8.5	39	14	5.9	6.0	13	14	42	39	1.9	0.2
1881	20	6.6	9.7	8.3	45	16	6.6	7.3	15	14	42	41	2.9	0.1
1882	15	7.1	5.4	10.2	50	16	5.6	6.6	19	15	43	38	2.6	0.2
1883	13	5.6	5.9	8.8	47	17	5.3	5.4	19	14	42	40	6.2	0.3
1884	13	6.1	5.5	9.5	46	15	5.4	5.4	17	13	42	37	6.4	0.3
1885	11	4.9	4.6	7.8	42	12	4.8	5.4	16	13	37	34	7.4	0.4
1886	10	4.4	3.6	7.5	38	13	4.7	5.3	17	14	34	34	6.0	1.5
1887	9	4.7	3.4	7.6	35	14	5.0	5.1	17	14	35	35	7.2	1.1
1888	9	6.0	3.2	8.9	43	16	5.8	5.7	19	17	44	40	6.3	1.4
1889	9	4.8	4.7	8.0	48	17	7.5	6.4	22	21	60	44	7.9	1.9
1890	9	5.3	5.8	7.1	55	18	8.1	6.2	23	20	66	42	9.2	2.1
1891	12	5.1	5.7	9.9	56	16	8.2	6.0	25	19	63	43	14.7	1.7
1892	11	4.4	7.4	7.2	55	16	9.0	5.9	27	20	53	44	9.5	1.8
1893	10	4.5	3.7	8.1	56	16	8.9	6.2	28	21	56	48	10.4	2.0
1894	9	4.4	3.6	7.9	56	15	8.1	6.5	29	21	58	45	8.9	1.1
1895	9	4.8	4.4	6.1	59	17	8.5	6.7	34	23	64	48	7.8	0.7
1896	11	4.8	5.2	7.0	64	18	9.9	7.6	38	23	63	56	11	0.8
1897	13	7.2	4.1	7.4	71	22	9.6	8.9	42	26	68	65	12	0.9
1898	14	6.9	5.1	6.9	82	23	12.0	9.3	24	15	81	66	14	1.3
1899	17	6.5	4.2	6.9	88	22	14.0	9.3	26	16	89	66	19	0.9

E2 External Trade (by value) with Main Trading Partners

NORWAY (in million kroner)

1900-1934

	Canada[45]		Denmark		France		Germany		Netherlands		Sweden		Great Britain/U.K.[46]		U.S.A.	
	I	E	I	E	I	E	I	E	I	E	I	E	I	E	I	E
1900	...	...	17	7.3	5.2	8.2	85	23	15	11	27	15	93	74	17	2.0
1901	...	...	19	6.8	4.4	8.3	77	20	13	10	24	15	79	70	18	1.5
1902	...	...	18	7.6	5.3	9.3	79	25	15	11	24	16	77	75	12	2.2
1903	...	...	17	8.6	5.6	7.1	79	25	13	16	31	16	68	79	12	2.4
1904	...	...	17	8.2	4.3	7.3	83	27	14	18	34	14	75	77	9	3.6
1905	...	...	21	9.7	4.5	9.9	87	31	14	20	38	15	78	82	8	4.6
1906	...	...	20	11.3[47]	6.0	10.0[47]	88	36[47]	15	24[47]	41[47]	16[47]	96[46,47]	95[46,47]	14	5.4[47]
1907	...	...	25	12.1	6.6	8.9	101	35	18	14	23	15	105	88	15	7.1
1908	...	...	27[48]	9.4[48]	7.3[48]	10[48]	112[48]	33[48]	17[48]	14[48]	20[48]	12[48]	94[48]	85[48]	18[48]	5.9[48]
1909	0.5	0.4	20	6.0	9.5	12	117	35	13	8	21	17	89	78	28	18.0
1910	0.5	0.8	20	6.9	11	11	133	43	14	11	25	22	103	84	29	24
1911	0.5	0.8	22	7.6	12	11	148	51	17	12	31	20	127	82	31	26
1912	0.6	1.2	27	8.4	15	13	168	55	20	18	35	21	148	88	34	29
1913	0.8	1.2	28	9.2	12	14	176	67	21	18	46	26	146	98	39	30
1914	1.1	1.0	29	18	11	10	151	76	22	16	47	35	159	105	73	45
1915	0.3	0.7	33	30	14	28	155	193	37	18	75	67	254	187	184	33
1916	- -	0.8	69	41	23	79	176	292	47	14	132	68	374	274	338	32
1917	3.2	0.5	104	20	31	82	156	150	45	10	162	56	431	302	551	22
1918	- -	- -	129	42	14	113	138	85	22	26	221	97	363	311	200	7
1919	24	1.5	140	46	54	44	156	205	52	14	190	71	781	221	753	34
1920	56	1.7	192	76	79	86	323	137	84	29	189	80	995	389	691	98
1921	35	2.3	96	37	30	32	271	84	62	11	126	50	377	174	277	80
1922	4	2.4	104	36	29	55	283	76	59	14	128	52	294	229	243	90
1923	21	3.9	90	41	32	53	308	78	66	14	91	52	294	251	224	112
1924	31	5.3	76	47	34	67	312	104	81	23	99	65	366	289	211	132
1925	41	3.3	84	46	36	72	280	107	75	28	93	62	311	302	195	111
1926	24	4.0	82	30	43	49	223	81	54	16	83	52	212	229	156	95
1927	27	4.3	53	22	31	23	197	86	53	16	79	39	199	198	134	73
1928	31	4.4	73	27	26	29	217	93	61	16	87	37	197	178	121	65
1929	19	4.2	65	32	21	38	261	98	49	19	97	42	222	200	112	74
1930	14	2.8	74	37	23	38	229	82	44	26	89	44	247	171	103	55
1931	11	2.0	70	19	24	27	198	54	35	18	89	30	174[46]	129[46]	66	33
1932	10	1.8	34	25	24	35	147	69	29	20	58	32	149	144	58	51
1933	16	2.2	32	24	21	32	139	70	29	25	56	38	152	114	46	60
1934	19	2.6	42	23	22	27	141	79	25	19	80	44	169	140	64	55

E2 External Trade (by value) with Main Trading Partners

NORWAY (in million kroner) — 1935–1954

Year	Canada[45] I[48]	Canada[45] E[48]	Denmark I[48]	Denmark E[48]	France I[48]	France E[48]	Germany I[48]	Germany E[48]	Netherlands I[48]	Netherlands E[48]	Sweden I[48]	Sweden E[48]	Great Britain/U.K.[46] I[48]	Great Britain/U.K.[46] E[48]	U.S.A. I[48]	U.S.A. E[48]
1935	33	2.9	43	25	29	28	140	79	20	14	82	50	147	146	67	65
1936	37	2.7	37	30	30	42	163	90	24	17	105	55	165	162	78	80
1937	39	2.6	59	29	43	44	219[43] / 225	107[43] / 113	33	28	138	66	236	207	110	80
1938	46[49]	2.5[49]	42[49]	34[49]	36[49]	52[49]	220[49]	122[49]	39[49]	21[49]	137[49]	69[49]	193[49]	194[49]	119[49]	61[49]
1939	57	2.3	50	34	44	36	259	118	35	27	140	86	230	195	147	84
1940	21	0.5	35	36	14	15	340	283	13	10	95	79	98	79	108	15
1941	– –	–	76	45	4	6	757	340	10	22	73	55	: :	–	4	–
1942	– –	–	62	48	18	8	623	357	9	7	60	47	: :	–	1	–
1943	– –	–	83	62	6	6	683	388	5	3	67	48	: :	–	1	–
1944	– –	–	59	50	5	5	458	418	2	1	48	30	: :	–	: –	–
1945	60	0.3	149	83	– –	18	69[43]	116[43]	2	4	362	50	223	10	143	8
1946	133	6.1	107	130	65	86	123	64	49	52	225	143	425	125	477	63
1947	102	23.5	183	141	152	115	70	49	117	93	322	194	737	264	950	89
1948	127	6.0	185	122	169	136	101	113	125	112	492	180	682	325	497	158
1949	118	6.5	182	150	217	130	163[2] / 133	155[2] / 137	154	83	593	194	900	388	553	149
1950	88	8.6	185	198	314	129	199	315	219	126	701	217	1,073	505	589	273
1951	228	21	229	236	286	229	423	341	273	189	756	371	1,442	876	785	316
1952	275	25	248	225	228	172	698	354	260	127	863	388	1,246	813	698	312
1953	279	17	207	231	223	136	1,047	332	296	122	855	341	1,365	708	554	414
1954	283	13	248	270	235	171	1,109	426	429	154	1,144	397	1,471	797	611	359

E2 External Trade (by value) with Main Trading Partners

NORWAY (in million kroner)

	Canada		Denmark		France		West Germany		Netherlands		Sweden		U.K.		U.S.A.	
	I	E	I	E	I	E	I	E	I	E	I	E	I	E	I	E
1955	314	16	292	238	272	187	1,086	506	416	158	1,260	409	1,579	980	667	416
1956	407	25	293	289	323	257	1,525	653	404	189	1,214	546	1,639	1,055	825	466
1957	412	20	288	328	338	261	1,556	780	526	242	1,474	589	1,588	1,171	803	398
1958	423[49]	22[49]	414[50] / 416[49]	323[50] / 330[49]	308[49]	212[49]	1,892[49]	746[49]	645[49]	196[49]	1,494[49]	520[49]	1,447[49]	1,028[49]	639[49]	476[49]
1959	451	29	421	379	297	181	1,903	852	653	188	1,525	554	1,262	1,182	661	597
1960	510	26	429	400	337	162	2,030	864	595	238	1,663	763	1,570	1,422	873 / 875[51]	428 / 428[51]
1961	533	32	528	525	352	215	2,275	898	603	223	1,884	811	1,811	1,375	798	549
1962	492	42	547	606	447	248	2,108	1,050	574	206	2,041	924	1,781	1,183	850	738
1963	487	41	778	540	474	270	2,207	1,168	662	244	2,492	1,048	2,083	1,361	893	751
1964	510	49	793	629	481	371	2,234	1,353	715	310	2,704	1,309	1,876	1,849	1,058	853
1965	588	68	862	741	689	321	2,497	1,416	715	353	3,349	1,620	1,903	1,834	1,104	914
1966	671	88	997	791	532	335	2,757	1,497	758	314	3,227	1,709	2,350	2,111	1,283	990
1967	590	82	1,228	978	589	340	2,676	1,545	763	346	3,816	1,944	2,782	2,398	1,257	1,004
1968	821	91	1,314	977	651	342	2,673	1,816	616	391	3,711	2,098	2,390	2,666	1,473	1,140
1969	801	88	1,374	1,146	793	505	3,136	2,288	755	483	3,986	2,456	2,809	2,713	1,644	1,081
1970	1,251	89	1,646	1,262	777	634	3,796	3,148	864	573	5,317	2,840	3,257	3,145	1,922	1,007
1971	1,315	134	1,846	1,329	807	809	4,067	2,792	850	532	5,502	3,063	3,459	3,364	1,721	1,268
1972	1,019	209	1,979	1,561	1,057	695	3,955	2,708	1,255	684	5,394	3,405	3,359	4,089	1,713	1,560
1973	1,084	360	2,305	2,054	1,794	872	5,034	2,994	1,916	916	6,248	4,080	3,722	4,886	2,216	1,444
1974	1,316	276	2,631	2,822	1,445	1,164	6,696	3,636	1,955	1,301	8,780	6,083	4,678	5,768	3,787	1,847
1975	976	304	2,934	2,745	1,898	1,371	7,920	3,727	2,280	1,266	9,725	6,011	4,898	9,184	3,609	2,191
1976	1,106	530	3,341	3,057	2,219	1,098	9,381	4,122	3,319	1,564	11,111	6,137	5,926	12,891	3,956	2,031
1977	1,007	310	3,930	2,905	3,320	1,454	10,193	4,463	2,234	1,787	12,374	5,842	8,385	13,977	4,189	1,922
1978	801	238	4,001	3,060	1,953	1,665	8,549	7,538	2,319	1,638	11,014	5,722	7,185	19,982	4,064	2,856
1979	1,410	402	4,277	3,671	2,582	1,630	9,645	9,737	2,432	1,992	12,286	7,712	9,571	24,969	4,993	2,756
1980	2,011	374	5,158	3,816	3,027	2,097	11,598	15,480	2,827	3,362	13,999	8,506	12,266	37,897	6,791	2,729
1981	1,747	390	5,452	4,156	3,135	2,221	13,179	18,698	2,871	3,833	14,738	9,378	12,195	41,659	8,272	3,872
1982	1,354	457	6,174	4,270	3,365	2,501	15,495	22,915	3,412	6,587	17,054	10,435	11,822	41,291	9,148	3,173
1983	1,706	1,568	6,375	4,791	3,544	3,447	14,506	24,310	3,532	9,102	18,485	13,192	10,264	46,092	8,995	5,742
1984	2,414	863	7,215	5,498	5,175	4,987	16,368	26,824	3,898	9,878	19,414	15,023	11,610	55,994	10,135	7,858
1985	2,512	625	8,962	6,165	5,536	8,952	21,297	26,549	4,686	10,360	23,669	15,017	13,223	61,040	9,554	8,723
1986	2,001	706	10,704	5,970	6,109	4,639	25,419	25,313	5,726	8,119	26,950	13,377	13,195	36,784	10,288	7,304
1987	1,877	1,166	11,734	7,394	5,618	7,338	23,556	21,448	5,843	10,342	28,758	16,111	13,618	38,638	9,813	8,244
1988	2,547	2,114	11,430	7,777	5,025	10,531	20,518	18,105	5,913	9,884	26,540	17,250	11,722	38,131	10,005	8,879
1989	3,514	4,129	10,858	8,754	5,335	16,591	20,560	20,970	5,442	12,418	24,805	23,153	12,124	50,098	12,121	12,364
							Germany									
1990	3,704	5,203	11,226	10,247	6,327	16,315	23,571	23,447	6,702	16,538	26,493	24,572	15,110	55,396	14,952	13,374
1991	3,625	5,858	12,093	12,405	6,312	16,528	23,368	24,368	8,673	17,450	25,480	22,784	14,380	58,325	12,857	10,275
1992	2,911	5,681	12,137	11,880	6,538	16,800	23,361	28,721	6,384	15,592	24,988	20,461	15,028	52,870	13,818	11,067
1993	3,454	5,236	12,704	9,944	7,311	17,902	23,167	29,472	7,003	19,221	24,195	19,731	15,645	55,707	13,792	13,481
								Million US$ Dollars								
1994	534.0	1,152.9	2,015.6	1,639.4	1,105.7	2,827.0	3,802.9	4,322.3	1,158.4	3,302.8	4,094.4	3,260.3	2,830.6	7,231.6	2,009.8	2,345.1
1995	703.3	1,576.6	2,473.2	2,099.0	1,446.1	3,246.6	4,558.0	4,981.1	1,457.8	3,977.4	5,048.3	4,119.1	3,203.7	8,362.0	2,189.4	2,569.1
1996	741.3	1,980.5	2,654.6	2,237.2	1,444.1	4,320.6	4,592.0	5,456.8	1,528.4	5,436.3	5,855.3	4,540.6	3,191.3	9,713.4	2,220.8	3,626.8
1997	620.4	2,307.2	2,518.1	2,449.6	1,459.0	4,119.7	4,842.9	5,283.7	1,549.0	5,539.7	5,606.8	4,268.7	3,369.7	9,357.8	2,383.9	3,004.8

E2 External Trade (by value) with Main Trading Partners

POLAND (in million zloty)[52]

1922–1959

	Czechoslovakia		Germany		East Germany		West Germany		Russia/U.S.S.R.		U.K.		U.S.A.	
	I	E	I	E	I	E	I	E	I	E	I	E	I	E
1922	55	31	312	324					3	21	59	27	132	6
1923	54	58	487	605					5	23	91	70	171	7
1924	85	100	510	547					5	11	110	133	184	7
1925	91	157	511	559					9	39	133	115	230	10
1926	78[53]	196[53]	367[53]	573[53]					13[53]	42[53]	161[53]	386[53]	270[53]	15[53]
1927	167	253	737	805					100	45	271	306	373	19
1928	213	296	903	859					39	39	314	227	467	19
1929	228	296	850	877					40	81	265	288	384	31
1930	170	216	606	627					46	129	178	294	271	22
1931	100	144	359	315					36	125	104[10]	318[10]	155	13
1932	46	90	173	176					19	29	75	178	104	10
1933	36	48	146	168					18	60	83	185	110	16
1934	33	50	109	162					18	26	86	192	121	23
1935	35	53	124	140					15	11	117	181	123	43
1936	36	49	143	145					16	9	142	222	119	67
1937	44	52	182[8]	173[8]					15	4	149	219	149	101
1938	41	43	299	286					10	1	148	216	158	63
1946	..[54]	..[54]	..[54]	..[54]					..[54]	..[54]	..[54]	..[54]	..[54]	..[54]
1947	25	59	34	42					318	282	109	54	204	6
1948	212	173	124	164					472	443	166	174	119	3
1949	278	213			189	259	45	75	474	481	338	251	58	17
1950	352	233			308	352	66	55	770	616	255	213	20	45
1951	338	350			542	353	77	59	965	722	414	271	6	33
1952	371	334			478	410	66	51	1,100	989	252	173	—	45
1953	329	381			512	445	60	64	1,054	1,098	232	242	2	53
1954	320	309			546	450	74	60	1,347	1,316	270	215	6	73
1955	319	301			487	500	92	113	1,254	1,122	279	312	10	92
1956	412	305			541	430	226	212	1,377	1,081	260	317	10	95
1957	309	244			660	501	221	200	1,688	1,034	358	255	223	107
1958	378	290			622	426	269	284	1,336	1,061	332	275	407	107
1959	452	323			749	548	267	312	1,809	1,252	346	347	284	122

E2   External Trade (by value) with Main Trading Partners

POLAND (in million zloty to 1981 (1st line) and thousand million exchange zloty subsequently)

1960–1997

Million zloty (1960–1981, 1st line)

Year	Czechoslovakia I	Czechoslovakia E	East Germany I	East Germany E	West Germany I	West Germany E	Russia/U.S.S.R. I	Russia/U.S.S.R. E	U.K. I	U.K. E	U.S.A I	U.S.A E
1960	509	452	746	499	268	274	1,861	1,561	355	396	337	126
1961	651	587	811	439	251	310	1,959	1,940	407	416	484	142
1962	795	583	940	470	237	301	2,311	2,275	473	416	314	169
1963	772	579	1,014	482	219	321	2,589	2,470	418	451	347	165
1964	773	783	943	658	271	337	2,570	2,887	329	514	453	221
1965	976	834	1,085	613	326	404	2,914	3,126	386	510	121	275
1966	933	713	1,121	642	239	440	3,167	2,965	640	580	178	317
1967	941	811	1,168	703	375	425	3,684	3,607	712	591	204	348
1968	914	982	1,185	917	472	471	4,043	4,168	700	588	193	340
1969	979	1,082	1,280	1,111	505	510	4,801	4,486	736	554	196	368
1970	1,242	1,059	1,599	1,314	573	723	5,445	5,003	764	609	233	371
1971	1,429	1,094	1,832	1,239	790	800	5,701	5,549	780	611	324	425
1972	1,696	1,338	2,211	1,530	1,570	977	5,856	6,683	910	685	404	471
1973	1,985	1,676	2,412	2,187	3,069	1,431	6,363	6,914	1,247	855	1,045	632
1974	2,067	2,056	2,558	2,080	4,155	1,743	7,817	7,875	1,675	1,234	1,573	861
1975	2,249	2,742	3,131	3,151	3,360[81] / 3,399	1,778[81] / 1,894	10,557	10,766	2,227	968	1,959	778
1976	2,712	2,862	3,516	3,635	4,036	2,451	11,744	11,080	2,266	1,057	2,765	937
1977	2,969	3,087	3,688	3,794	3,565	2,754	14,107	12,900	2,741	1,143	1,812	1,214
1978	3,169	3,302	4,030	3,684	3,508	3,262	15,227	15,139	2,921	1,416	2,238	1,464
1979	3,166	3,619	4,177	3,640	3,571	3,790	16,984	17,745	2,347	1,610	2,342	1,307
1980	3,346	3,571	3,849	3,572	3,957	4,465	19,323	16,181	2,031	1,678	2,351	1,298
1981	3,190	3,150	3,700	3,196	2,948	3,686	21,664	14,449	1,224	1,331	2,460	1,107

thousand million exchange zloty

Year	Czechoslovakia I	Czechoslovakia E	East Germany I	East Germany E	West Germany I	West Germany E	Russia/U.S.S.R. I	Russia/U.S.S.R. E	U.K. I	U.K. E	U.S.A I	U.S.A E
1981	49	48	57	49	70	88	332	221	32	32	59	26
1982	51	51	59	45	61	81	329	287	27	34	11	19
1983	62	55	67	51	66	92	357	331	35	52	13	18
1984	74	75	77	62	90	120	440	395	44	55	20	29
1985	96	104	97	85	145	146	549	480	57	72	20	35
1986	124	132	115	103	195	198	638	585	63	74	13	45
1987	177	195	157	137	335	350	790	802	105	142	38	90
1988	336	359	265	264	687	747	1,228	1,475	222	302	103	156
1989	846	1,075	...	...	2,337	2,757	2,688	4,048	664	1,263	201	540
1990	276	5,282	...	...	15,586	32,503	15,369	19,767	4,382	9,227	1,259	3,527
1991	5,487	7,284			43,596	46,427	23,193	17,312	6,531	11,210	3,717	3,923
1992	6,941	6,854			52,582	5,649	18,702[98]	9,925[98]	14,732	7,704	7,473	4,149
1993	6,329[97]	6,217[97]			9,529	9,351	23,098[98]	11,922[98]	19,662	11,086	17,413	7,539

Million US$ Dollars

Year	Czechoslovakia I	Czechoslovakia E	East Germany I	East Germany E	West Germany I	West Germany E	Russia/U.S.S.R. I	Russia/U.S.S.R. E	U.K. I	U.K. E	U.S.A I	U.S.A E
1994	350.3	342.5	161.5	166.7	5,289.4	5,117.3	1,271.2	644.5	1,085.0	609.4	1,000.3	407.4
1995	474.5	429.4	185.3	169.2	5,843.9	6,114.6	1,440.0	902.9	1,102.9	769.7	754.2	582.9
1996	891.7	698.2	380.8	279.4	7,736.6	8,777.5	1,959.8	1,274.2	1,502.7	916.9	1,140.4	622.7
1997	1,150.5	847.2	432.5	280.0	9,166.3	8,417.3	2,525.8	1,653.8	2,186.9	960.8	1,645.9	563.7

E2 External Trade (by value) with Main Trading Partners

PORTUGAL (in million escudos)

1861–1894

	France		Germany		Portugese Colonies		Spain		U.K.		U.S.A.	
	I	E	I	E	I	E	I	E	I	E	I	E
1861	3.0	0.4	0.3	0.2	0.8	0.6	2.4	1.3	14	8	0.8	0.1
1862–68	...	...	...	...	...	...	...	...	...	...	...	...
1869	3.1	1.0	0.3	0.2	0.6	0.6	1.9	1.4	10	10	1.1	0.2
1870	2.4	0.8	0.4	0.2	1.0	0.8	1.8	1.8	13	12	1.7	0.2
1871	2.2	0.9	0.3	0.4	0.5	0.7	2.0	1.6	16	12	1.5	0.4
1872	3.8	0.4	0.5	0.7	0.8	0.6	2.8	1.8	15	13	1.2	0.2
1873	4.1	1.0	1.0	0.5	0.8	0.5	2.5	1.8	19	14	0.9	0.2
1874	4.4	1.0	0.6	0.9	0.8	0.9	1.3	1.4	13	12	1.3	0.3
1875	5.9	1.3	0.8	0.8	0.8	1.1	2.3	1.3	18	14	2.3	0.4
1876	5.5	2.2	0.6	0.9	0.8	1.0	2.1	1.3	18	12	2.1	0.4
1877	5.2	2.1	1.1	0.9	0.8	0.8	2.1	1.6	14	12	2.1	0.8
1878	4.7	1.0	1.2	0.6	0.4	0.7	2.5	1.2	15	11	2.3	0.3
1879	4.3	1.2	1.6	0.8	0.7	0.7	2.5	1.1	13	11	6.0	0.3
1880	4.1	1.5	1.9	1.1	0.7	0.8	2.1	1.8	15	11	5.3	0.6
1881	4.4	2.6	2.5	0.7	0.7	0.6	2.2	1.6	15	9	5.5	0.6
1882	4.1	2.8	2.7	0.9	0.7	0.6	2.0	1.5	15	12	5.7	0.7
1883	...	...	...	...	...	...	...	...	...	...	...	...
1884	...	...	...	...	...	...	...	...	...	...	...	...
1885	4.5	6.5	3.7	1.1	0.7	0.6	1.6	1.2	12	6.0	4.6	0.6
1886	5.1	9.5	4.7	1.3	0.8	0.6	2.6	1.2	12	6.7	5.0	0.6
1887	5.0	4.8	4.5	1.6	0.7	0.6	2.3	1.2	12	6.8	5.3	0.6
1888	5.0	5.2	4.7	1.9	0.8	0.9	2.6	0.9	12	7.8	4.9	0.6
1889	6.0	3.8	5.4	2.0	0.8	1.0	3.2	1.1	14	8.5	3.7	0.5
1890	6.9	1.5	6.3	2.1	0.8	1.1	2.9	0.9	13	8.0	5.1	0.7
1891	5.3	1.3	5.2	2.3	0.9	1.3	2.5	0.9	12	7.5	5.3	0.8
1892	3.4	1.0	2.8	2.2	0.9	1.6	1.7	1.4	10	8.7	6.0	0.9
1893	3.8	0.9	4.4	2.0	1.0	2.1	2.9	1.4	11	6.6	7.3	0.8
1894	3.8	0.8	4.3	2.1	1.0	2.2	3.0	2.5	10	6.7	5.8	0.5

E2 External Trade (by value) with Main Trading Partners

PORTUGAL (in million escudos)

1895–1929

	France		Germany		Portugese Colonies		Spain		U.K.		U.S.A.	
	I	E	I	E	I	E	I	E	I	E	I	E
1895	4.0	0.7	5.2	2.1	1.1	2.6	3.8	3.2	11	7.2	6.8	0.5
1896	3.9	0.6	5.6	2.0	1.1	2.9	3.8	3.2	12	7.2	4.4	0.5
1897	3.5	0.9	5.3	2.2	1.0	3.5	4.2	3.9	12	7.4	4.6	0.6
1898	4.7	1.0	6.6	2.2	1.2	5.0	4.5	4.1	16	8.8	7.0	0.5
1899	4.4	0.7	7.3	2.1	1.2	5.5	3.6	3.4	17	7.8	8.1	0.5
1900	5.0	1.0	8.6	2.2	1.5	5.5	4.6	4.7	19	7.9	9.0	0.6
1901	5.7	0.8	9.0	2.1	1.4	3.8	5.3	4.4	18	8.3	7.6	0.6
1902	5.7	0.8	9.2	2.1	1.6	3.4	6.0	4.6	17	8.3	4.0	0.7
1903	5.6	0.9	9.9	2.0	1.7	4.9	5.4	5.4	17	8.0	6.2	0.7
1904	6.0	0.8	10.5	2.4	1.8	5.3	5.6	6.0	18	7.0	4.4	0.6
1905	6.1	0.7	9.6	2.3	1.9	4.9	5.2	4.1	17	7.3	3.5	0.5
1906	6.4	1.0	10.0	2.5	1.6	4.5	4.3	5.0	17	7.9	4.7	0.4
1907	6.7	0.7	11.0	2.5	2.0	4.5	4.1	4.9	19	7.4	6.1	0.6
1908	6.2	0.7	10.0	2.3	2.1	4.1	4.8	5.4	18	7.0	7.2	0.6
1909	5.8	0.8	10.0	2.3	2.1	5.2	4.6	5.5	17	7.3	6.9	0.9
1910	6.2[56]	0.9[56]	11.0[56]	3.3[56]	2.6[56]	6.3[56]	4.7[56]	5.1[56]	20[56]	8.0[56]	7.4[56]	1.1[56]
1911	5.2	1.4	12.0	3.3	2.6	4.7	5.1	5.8	19	6.9	5.8	0.8
1912	6.9	1.7	12.0	3.0	1.9	4.9	4.5	5.2	21	7.3	7.8	1.0
1913	7.6	1.3	16.0	3.4	2.9	5.0	3.8	5.5	23	7.6	9.9	1.2
1914	5.5	1.1	10.0	1.5	3.1	5.2	2.1	2.2	21	8.2	9.0	1.4
1915	4.7	3.0	0.6	0.1	4.0	7.5	3.9	2.5	30	9.4	15	1.5
1916	6.4	13	0.1	...	6.7	10	8.6	3.4	58	13	27	2.8
1917	9.3[56]	17[56]	0.8[56]	—[56]	28[56]	13[56]	15[56]	10[56]	58[56]	12[56]	42[56]	7.7[56]
1918	8.7[56]	22[56]	0.8[56]	...[56]	22[56]	16[56]	29[56]	13[56]	65[56]	30[56]	63[56]	3.7[56]
1919	11	21	0.3	0.1	20	10	20	3.0	98	28	46	4.9
1920	53	28	26	2.8	24	32	35	10.6	26	51	118	16
1921	78	21	61	10	42	31	53	9.5	292	49	164	17
1922	101	107	127	18	52	74	46	15	437	85	116	24
1923	185	130	248	27	111	100	69	23	768	152	257	45
1924	109	73	466	84	197	130	105	25	979	255	303	42
1925	231	89	340	64	172	102	82	33	720	252	227	39
1926	269	64	395	53	160	83	114	29	574	218	318	46
1927	283	51	364	71	181	87	163	27	689	210	326	28
1928	250	163	349	117	205	112	72	32	822	220	298	59
1929	237	119	382	118	199	136	71	46	679	251	340	77

E2 External Trade (by value) with Main Trading Partners

PORTUGAL (in million escudos)

1930–1959

	France		Germany		Portugese Colonies		Spain		U.K.		U.S.A.	
	I	E	I	E	I	E	I	E	I	E	I	E
1930	206	130	354	90	192	103	114	30	516	203	324	53
1931	125	150	265	82	178	81	54	22	396	189	167	37
1932	114	125	237	76	178	110	57	42	401	165	191	51
1933	98	78	250	76	200	121	71	41	542	180	181	56
1934	95	89	269	107	216	104	71	44	451	216	193	49
1935	122	92	287	126	189	114	92	42	592	215	260	54
1936	101	115	281	124	201	106	68	27	418	273	229	74
1937	110	123	354	131	262	154	25	57	427	258	248	94
1938	141	94	387	149	233	140	12	55	393	236	266	61
1939	140	66	276	121	253	173	6	26	395	359	219	121
1940	100	120	39	29	476[56]	293[56]	16	93	422	471	586	235
1941	47	36	200	565	655[56]	400[56]	66	49	375	526	629	547
1942	35	37	313	960	1,016[56]	566[56]	99	76	309	1,147	388	226
1943	36	51	481	855	1,109[56]	562[56]	132	99	516	1,229	464	388
1944	18	11	314	361	1,257[56]	742[56]	178	111	433	788	476	714
1945	36	211	14	1	1,527[56]	759[56]	159	55	445	573	778	551
1946	203	163	34	3	2,068[56]	1,036[56]	182	83	943	659	1,714	685
1947	391	103	51	13	740	1,103	141	76	1,122	635	2,993	495
1948	350	156	37	65	869	1,143	82	63	2,313	756	2,351	437
1949	589	236	74	125	1,059	1,050	79	43	2,206	759	1,615	418
1950	397	256	298	195	1,286	1,332	68	88	1,353	925	1,235	690
1951	509	317	516	352	1,104	1,711	160	106	1,459	1,483	1,434	1,016
1952	472	287	724	426	1,528	1,728	79	51	1,592	831	1,367	990
1953	510	216	1,037	450	1,392	1,659	67	33	1,452	787	935	1,036
1954	694	282	1,378	504	1,716	1,788	52	134	1,507	1,092	838	753
1955	877	436	1,665	637	1,569	1,927	63	47	1,615	1,262	1,102	839
1956	957	548	2,039[2]	615[2]	1,515	2,109	96	144	1,729	1,238	1,313	786
1957	1,190	425	2,408	566	1,687	2,156	99	94	1,909	1,163	1,561	703
1958	1,062	548	2,431	641	2,031	2,262	58	60	1,780	940	970	687
1959	1,029	356	2,416	700	1,931	2,397	143	80	1,753	949	830	816

E2 External Trade (by value) with Main Trading Partners

PORTUGAL (in million escudos to 1974, thousand million escudos subsequently)

1960–1997

	France		West Germany		Portugese Colonies[82]		Spain		U.K.		U.S.A.	
	I	E	I	E	I	E	I	E	I	E	I	E
1960	1,307	319	2,677	857	2,239	2,384	138	95	1,868	1,284	1,152	1,049
1961	1,462	401	2,982	810	2,354	2,153	228	120	2,907	1,263	1,431	1,111
1962	1,584	507	2,684	855	2,110	2,364	197	275	2,500	1,277	1,499	1,392
1963	1,511	607	2,867	904	2,680	2,829	255	266	2,588	1,627	1,671	1,411
1964	1,579	740	3,400	1,125	3,297	3,673	453	456	3,007	2,340	2,364	1,559
1965	1,998	764	4,322	1,339	3,616	4,111	721	453	3,448	2,922	2,151	1,755
1966	2,208	905	4,486	1,134	3,901	4,179	740	426	4,024	3,327	2,347	2,032
1967	2,092	937	4,591	1,074	4,290	4,781	1,361	360	4,164	4,330	2,094	2,027
1968	2,348	1,007	5,290	1,258	5,265	5,416	1,407	343	4,410	4,611	2,469	2,309
1969	2,675	1,278	5,861	1,570	5,496	6,027	1,597	423	5,168	5,158	1,814	2,314
1970	3,176	1,245	7,050	1,728	6,717	6,688	1,983	442	6,369	5,570	3,251	2,374
1971	3,469	1,357	8,204	1,889	6,944	6,490	2,501	515	7,150	6,751	3,614	2,928
1972	3,848	1,825	8,983	2,550	7,045	5,165	3,021	732	7,884	8,048	5,391	3,785
1973	5,192	2,344	10,794	3,417	7,539	6,740	4,061	1,011	8,516	10,792	6,117	4,430
1974	9,160	3,449	15,863	4,647	12,415	6,372	5,365	1,200	10,930	13,234	11,088	5,761
					thousand million escudos							
1975	7.5	3.3	11.0	5.0	5.1	4.1	4.1	1.3	8.7	10.5	12.3	3.6
1976	10.9	4.6	15.2	5.9	3.3	2.7	6.1	1.2	12.2	10.2	12.9	3.7
1977	15.4	6.2	23.7	9.2	2.5	5.1	9.2	1.6	19.8	14.2	19.4	5.2
1978	20.7	9.6	31.9	14.0	1.8	6.0	12.5	2.3	23.2	19.4	27.2	7.5
1979	28.4	17.1	41.8	21.6	3.7	9.1	19.3	5.1	30.7	31.4	39.0	10.8
1980	34.5	24.5	55.8	31.4	3.1[82] / 2.2	14.0[82] / 13.8	26.1	8.3	41.6	34.3	52.3	13.2
1981	47.4	32.3	66.9	32.0	2.5	19.4	40.1	7.3	49.2	37.1	72.9	13.4
1982	65.5	44.1	89.3	42.9	3.4	16.5	45.4	11.7	58.6	49.1	81.5	20.4
1983	74.1	68.8	103	67.8	4.1	22.7	46.0	20.3	68.7	75.3	127	30.9
1984	91.7	94.6	118	104	8.4	33.8	82.8	33.5	77.8	117	156	67.2
1985	107	124	152	133	15.8	37.9	98.0	40.2	100	141	129	89.6
1986	145	164	205	159	12.1	23.3	157	71.7	108	154	101	83.3
1987	221	207	294	201	7.9	27.1	231	118	158	184	94.8	84.3
1988	294	177	372	232	6.1	42.9	336	177	211	228	110	93.7
1989	350	251	435	316	8.1	56.3	434	251	225	250	133	120
1990	412	362	570	389	12.5	64.1	514	310	273	283	141	113
1991	455	338	570	450	14.6	79.1	603	351	285	254	130	90
1992	526	352	615	473	15.6	110.6	678	367	292	275	123	86
1993	...	...										
			Germany			*Million US$ Dollars*						
1994	3,468.3	2,645.9	3,761.0	3,400.9	...	...	5,384.7	2,639.7	1,775.1	2,085.6	978.8	929.2
1995	3,964.8	3,294.6	4,952.1	5,033.2	...	...	7,118.3	3,559.8	2,216.2	2,596.8	1,099.6	1,056.1
1996	3,782.2	3,376.6	5,285.4	4,413.6	...	...	7,666.3	3,425.9	2,295.1	2,567.7	1,082.1	1,087.0
1997	3,550.3	3,199.0	4,952.0	4,546.5	...	...	7,568.3	3,207.6	2,317.5	2,755.1	1,080.0	1,099.8

E2 External Trade (by value) with Main Trading Partners

ROMANIA (in million lei)[57]

1871–1904

	Austria–Hungary		France		Germany		Russia		U.K.	
	I	E	I	E	I	E	I	E	I	E
1871	30	27	9	21	7	1	1	7	25	20
1872	..	..	..	..	..	..	..	..	..	..
1873	34	34	15	19	10	8	4	5	19	17
1874	48	56	16	10	6	-	3	2	33	13
1875	40	39	16	24	5	-	2	2	25	19
1876	79	74	28	32	15	1	5	4	27	41
1877	180	90	39	6	40	-	27	5	37	12
1878	168	67	16	19	20	1	28	5	53	40
1879	125	69	16	18	19	2	11	6	51	38
1880	126	83	18	28	24	1	6	4	57	56
1881	135	72	23	19	32	2	6	5	51	82
1882	135	75	23	27	30	6	9	8	45	98
1883	154[57]	72[57]	37[57]	19[57]	44[57]	5[57]	9[57]	8[57]	79[57]	89[57]
1884	130	70	24	17	43	-	10	9	58	62
1885	121	84	14	12	42	3	9	13	52	85
1886	94	35	15	29	73	3	10	13	71	117
1887	54	21	25	20	90	9	9	8	87	154
1888	51	14	28	19	83	7	7	5	85	144
1889	49	17	33	13	108	16	10	5	102	141
1890	53	9	40	17	109	13	9	5	98	161
1891	71	23	42	10	140	31	14	3	115	144
1892	89	32	31	11	114	33	8	3	84	121
1893	110	37	35	8	118	131	11	4	94	80
1894	115	43	34	10	117	58	9	7	84	79
1895	86	42	26	6	81	26	10	9	59	75
1896	93	33	26	9	96	17	8	6	73	112
1897	97	55	24	5	99	7	8	4	79	55
1898	109	86	26	7	111	13	8	5	76	38
1899	96	38	22	6	91	10	7	6	60	11
1900	69	44	16	8	56	19	6	5	31	17
1901	71	49	19[57]	10	84	40	6	6	56	24
1902	70	44	17	11	80	20	6	6	55	41
1903	74	49	16	10	78	15	9	6	43	31
1904	93	53	18[57]	9	92	20	8	6	45	26

E2 External Trade (by value) with Main Trading Partners

ROMANIA (in million lei)[57]

1905–1938

	Austria–Hungary		Czechoslovakia		France		Germany		Russia/U.S.S.R.		U.K.	
	I	E	I	E	I	E	I	E	I	E	I	E
1905	96	41	...	...	17	19	92	35	9	4	51	32
1906	119	32	...	...	19	28	142	24	10	3	63	53
1907	105	33	...	...	20	32	148	56	9	6	70	86
1908	95	26	...	...	23	28	141	25	13	8	67	40
1909	86	115	...	...	24	28	125	27	11	4	58	35
1910	98	37	...	...	26	47	138	24	12	6	57	34
1911	137	63	...	...	35	49	184	33	14	7	86	56
1912	139	95	...	...	39	50	240	43	17	6	88	43
1913	138	96	...	...	34	64	238	52	13	4	56	45
1914	133	135	...	...	28	27	183	47	11	3	56	36
1915	93	339	...	...	17	—	89	176	29	2	21	—
(Austria)												
1919	168	6	35	22	438	11	4	—	—	—	529	
1920	770	254	250	142	971	138	134	41	—	—	1,394	224
1921	2,050	392	1,065	407	1,653	929	1,087	353	1	—	1,681	994
1922	1,968	995	1,156	1,124	728	1,355	2,422	822	—	245	1,096	332
1923	3,057	2,569	1,619	1,082	1,292	2,613	4,429	1,788	2	2	1,801	1,174
1924	4,421	3,913	3,028	2,630	2,123	1,778	5,051	1,615	5	—	2,583	1,645
1925	4,948	4,347	4,273	2,742	2,333	1,665	4,996	2,462	...	—	3,152	2,369
1926												
1927	4,500	5,025	4,716	2,031	2,618	1,364	7,645	7,096	33	—	2,841	2,232
1928												
1929	3,715	2,733	4,020	1,789	1,641	1,296	7,135	8,005	43	1	2,160	1,867
1930	2,679	2,589	1,370	1,985	1,707	1,959	5,777	5,364	42	—	1,874	3,230
1931	1,395	2,368	1,923	1,557	1,244	2,411	4,589	2,543	40	—	1,305	2,246
1932	583	1,063	1,458	1,161	1,681	2,170	2,832	2,054	—	—	1,285	2,324
1933	1,078	933	1,155	679	1,238	1,753	2,181	1,503	—	—	1,744	2,182
1934	1,303	1,243	1,312	741	1,463	1,322	2,048	2,264	—	—	2,147	1,368
1935	1,175	2,108	1,408	990	783	689	2,580	2,802	—	—	1,064	1,615
1936	1,695	1,874	1,449	1,528	747	1,760	4,566	3,855	6	—	929	3,132
1937	1,722	2,138	3,267	2,590	1,243	1,813	5,853	6,054	38	52	1,907	2,783
1938	...	...	2,465	2,059	1,444	1,006	6,908[8]	5,707[8]	22	20	1,529	2,386

E2 External Trade (by value) with Main Trading Partners

ROMANIA (in million valuta lei to 1980, thousand million current lei subsequently)

1958–1997

	Austria		Czechoslovakia		France		East Germany		West Germany		Russia/U.S.S.R.		U.K.	
	I	E	I	E	I	E	I	E	I	E	I	E	I	E
1958	34	36	234	136	94	92	217	181	134	158	1,523	1,412	45	39
1959	31	40	295	210	61	84	269	213	113	144	1,408	1,500	65	52
1960	59	94	383	376	149	117	311	323	277	263	1,596	1,689	107	90
1961	88	101	458	341	152	131	352	318	380	300	1,793	2,107	308	138
1962	109	89	532	350	124	168	334	280	480	310	2,223	2,060	264	131
1963	107	134	609	330	143	193	386	251	458	323	2,396	2,477	300	145
1964	153	145	579	451	272	158	411	426	527	322	2,958	2,531	250	190
1965	143	146	418	572	295	131	375	430	663	379	2,365	2,631	263	183
1966	183	128	418	554	341	308	506	400	889	445	2,379	2,459	274	270
1967	321	141	541	522	481	327	555	419	1,537	579	2,562	2,597	307	385
1968	279	176	603	677	484	298	545	463	1,031	634	2,789	2,734	603	337
1969	297	183	652	845	564	321	507	728	1,027	724	…	2,730	611	294
1970	357	329	951	791	674	364	691	635	959	1,004	3,005	3,173	593	307
1971	365	298	896	735	807	503	920	781	887	1,253	2,908	2,399	690	305
1972	373	284	964	825	784	529	1,044	1,364	956	1,369	3,203	3,869	789	367
1973	452	450	987	1,091	839	611	1,125	1,322	2,096	1,722	3,449	4,120	635	480
1974	645	732	1,047	1,184	839	804	1,340	1,510	3,921	2,350	3,757	4,085	1,442	1,204
1975	895	598	1,285	1,162	941	748	1,569	1,340	2,847	2,192	4,579	5,279	879	624
1976	940	686	1,316	1,369	1,266	891	2,174	2,079	2,020	2,624	5,305	5,559	823	745
1977	984	638	1,730	1,884	1,188	867	2,535	2,570	2,653	2,545	6,655	6,687	985	660
1978	1,160	690	1,966	2,062	1,479	942	2,825	2,732	3,300	2,932	6,521	6,469	948	891
1979	…	…	…	…	…	…	…	…	…	…	…	…	…	…
1980	1,197	731	1,929	1,843	1,473	1,550	2,634	2,971	3,782	4,343	9,222	9,969	1,112	764
1981	2.9	3.4	4.3	3.8	7.1	6.2	6.9	7.0	9.4	12.1	30.0	30.3	3.9	3.5
1982	2.0	2.6	4.5	4.6	2.1	4.7	7.6	6.9	6.1	12.1	23.0	25.8	3.3	2.9
1983	1.4	3.2	4.1	4.9	1.8	5.5	8.1	7.7	4.6	10.8	29.0	30.1	2.1	4.7
1984	1.6	4.0	4.2	4.9	2.7	6.4	8.8	9.3	6.5	16.1	31.9	35.3	3.4	5.1
1985	1.2	3.3	4.9	5.0	2.0	5.0	8.6	8.2	5.0	14.4	33.3	41.1	2.7	5.2
1986	1.1	3.0	5.0	5.2	1.7	5.2	8.5	9.1	4.4	10.4	45.4	38.3	2.2	4.5
1987	1.1	3.2	5.0	4.9	1.1	3.7	8.4	8.2	3.3	10.6	40.1	36.8	1.1	4.6
1988	0.8	3.2	5.1	5.9	1.1	5.0	9.3	8.2	2.7	9.6	38.6	39.6	0.9	4.3
1989	0.9	2.7	6.2	5.2	0.8	4.0	9.9	9.0	2.9	10.9	42.5	38.0	1.1	4.1
1990	3.5	1.6	6.6	4.3	4.0	4.6	Included in West Germany		24.0	14.9	49.5	34.1	3.9	2.9
1991	16.6	9.5	5.1	3.2	15.2	13.7			45.1	38.1	74.3	73.2	13.7	11.3
1992	186	105	79	27	475	171			826	479	798[100]	415[100]	188	158
1993	191	105	36[99]	[99]	507	219			1,031	700	764[100]	220[100]	171	185
1994	192.2	96.4	50.0	…	359.1	315.8			1,258.6	985.9	980.9	207.3	220.8	200.2
1995	308.8	154.8	61.7	…	532.0	456.5			1,766.2	1,434.2	1,228.7	157.9	299.7	235.9
1996	339.9	169.2	82.1	…	555.5	459.8			1,949.4	1,486.0	1,432.1	164.3	324.2	247.3
1997	304.0	177.6	104.6	…	648.5	465.3			1,850.7	1,419.0	1,356.2	249.8	387.8	299.3

Unit notes: values for 1981–1991 are in thousand million lei; Czechoslovakia data from 1993 are for the Czech Republic[99]; France and later columns 1992–1993 are in Million Dollars; 1994–1997 are in Million US$ Dollars.

E2 External Trade (by value) with Main Trading Partners

RUSSIA (in millions rubels)[58]

1832–1875

	Austria–Hungary		China		France		Germany		Romania		U.K.	
	I	E	I	E	I	E	I	E	I	E	I	E
1832	12	14	...	...	13	11	36	25	...	...	60	96
1833	11	15	8	7	13	11	30	20	...	...	58	111
1834	11	11	7	7	13	11	44	18	...	...	64	106
1835	12	11	7	7	14	8	36	17	...	...	71	90
1836	11	15	5	9	16	11	35	22	...	...	79	130
1837	12	12	8	4	18	10	42	22	...	...	81	114
1838	12	14	8	8	19	10	39	18	...	...	79	85
1839	12	14	9	9	22	13	43	25	...	...	73	80
1840	11[58]	13[58]	9[58]	9[58]	31[58]	16[58]	46[58]	21[58]	...	...	76[58]	134[58]
1847	3	5	...	...	9	21	14	14	...	...	22	47
1848	3	3	...	...	8	3	14	5	...	...	26	40
1849	3	5	...	...	9	5	14	6	...	...	27	41
1850	3	5	...	...	8	4	13	7	...	...	25	42
1851	7	5	...	...	8	3	20	10	...	...	27	39
1852	6	6	...	...	9	7	19	12	...	...	25	43
1853	6	8	4	4	8	15	22	16	...	...	28	66
1854	5	8	7	6	4	3	24	20	...	...	9	12
1855	7	6	7	7	1	--	43	18			1	--
1856	9	7	6	6	6	17	41	23			22	64
1857	7	7	8	6	9	14	38	22			39	72
1858	8	6	7	6	11	16	33	18			41	66
1859	7	7	8	6	10	13	36	21	2	1	45	76
1860	8	6	7	6	11	12	37	25	2	3	44	85
1861	8	6	8	5	12	20	38	25	2	3	48	76
1862	7	6	9	5	11	11	42	31	1	2	36	82
1863	5	5	7	3	9	11	39	27	1	2	43	67
1864	8	6	6	4	10	15	42	28	1	2	53	87
1865	6	7	5	5	10	16	58	32	2	3	49	98
1866	8	6	5	5	10	17	78	35	1	3	59	102
1867	13	7	6	4	15	18	105	42	1	2	75	108
1868	11	9	...	...	13	21	120	46	1	3	79	106
1869	11	10	6	3	21	22	137	56	3	7	98	123
1870	10	14	8	4	19	34	136	76	3	3	107	170
1871	17	14	7	3	12	34	163	75	3	2	97	172
1872	24	20	...	...	19	22	171	77	4	3	120	143
1873	20	25	12	4	25	27	167	110	4	1	129	129
1874	21	33	11	3	20	33	181	136	2	2	128	136
1875	26	17	11	3	33	38	221	110	2	2	134	131

E2 External Trade (by value) with Main Trading Partners

RUSSIA (in million rubels)[58]

1876–1913

	Austria–Hungary		China		France		Germany		Romania		U.K.	
	I	E	I	E	I	E	I	E	I	E	I	E
1876	23	27	...	...	18	30	198	120	3	2	104	132
1877	20	50	...	...	10	24	148	197	1	3	93	148
1878	27	40	...	...	20	83	263	175	1	5	162	191
1879	20	33	...	...	20	83	267	187	2	9	146	184
1880	23	33	...	...	21	53	274	138	2	10	150	148
1881	23	28	...	...	20	53	220	149	1	8	108	156
1882	30	33	...	...	20	51	214	178	2	7	125	210
1883	26	25	...	...	23	39	169	189	2	5	134	210
1884	21	31	...	...	19	39	176	183	2	8	123	152
1885	22	27	...	...	14	34	144	142	3	4	95	154
1886	17	24	...	...	12	25	135	119	2	3	108	140
1887	12	24	...	...	13	36	113	152	2	4	92	182
1888	15	23	3	...	13	53	122	182	1	5	6	279
1889	18	28	1	...	18	35	124	190	1	7	96	258
1890[58]	17	27	14	...	16	42	114	176	1	7	87	192
1890	18	30	29	3	17	49	115	178	2	7	93	204
1891	16	34	29	5	17	49	103	193	2	9	83	180
1892	15	24	28	5	18	35	102	138	1	5	101	119
1893	23	35	33	4	29	72	101	133	1	6	118	155
1894	27	40	39	4	28	56	143	148	2	8	133	175
1895	24	35	42	5	23	50	176	179	2	10	120	175
1896	23	30	41	6	23	58	190	184	2	8	111	161
1897	19	39	39	6	25	64	180	175	1	11	104	151
1898	24	42	40	6	27	69	202	179	2	13	115	140
1899	31	27	44	8	28	60	231	164	2	7	130	129
1900	27	26	46	7	31	57	217	188	2	5	127	146
1901	25	30	47	10	28	61	211	179	2	10	103	157
1902	24	36	52	9	27	55	208	203	2	16	99	189
1903	27	37	56	22	28	76	242	233	2	16	114	218
1904	21	41	52	23	27	62	228	235	2	10	103	230
1905	20	46	61	32	26	64	240	255	1	10	97	249
1906	21	45	97	58	29	77	298	285	1	18	106	225
1907	24	43	90	26	29	73	337	291	2	14	115	229
1908	27	49	93	23	36	65	348	279	3	13	120	221
1909	27	61	75	22	50	89	363	387	2	16	128	289
1910	35	50	79	20	61	94	450	391	2	15	154	315
1911	34	68	82	26	57	91	488	491	3	30	155	337
1912	33	73	76	31	56	98	532	454	2	20	142	328
1913	28	51	59	23	45	79	512	356	1	17	136	210

E2. External Trade (by value) with Main Trading Partners

RUSSIA/USSR (in million rubels).[58]

1918–1954

	China		Czechoslovakia		France		Germany		Hungary		Poland		Romania		U.K.	
	I	E	I	E	I	E	I	E	I	E	I	E	I	E	I	E
1918	5	–	–	–	2	–	–	1	–	–	–	–	–	–	9	2
1919	–	–	–	–	–	–	–	–	–	–	–	–	–	–	–	–
1920	–	–	–	–	–	–	5	–	–	–	–	–	–	–	5	–
1921	[–][59]	[–][59]	[1][59]	[–][59]	[1][59]	[–][59]	[66][59]	[7][59]	[–][59]	[–][59]	[6][59]	[1][59]	[3][59]	[–][59]	[42][59]	[14][59]
1922	–	–	–	–	6	–	43	34	–	–	7	3	–	–	29	23
1923	–	–	–	–	–	1	48	52	–	–	2	2	–	–	38	66
1924	9	4	2	–	2	12	36	52	–	–	2	2	–	2	38	66
1925	13	7	17	–	7	17	81	69	–	–	8	3	–	–	87	152
1926	24	14	15	–	15	31	138	88	–	–	8	3	–	1	102	173
1927	24	15	9	2	17	42	127	138	1	–	10	15	–	1	79	173
1928	36[59]	19[59]	14[59]	3[59]	28[59]	32[59]	195[59]	152[59]	1[59]	–[59]	6[59]	12[59]	–[59]	1[59]	37[59]	122[59]
1929	27	18	14	7	25	33	153	169	1	–	15	10	–	–	43	159
1930	19	22	21	3	23	35	197	161	–	–	30	11	–	1	63	220
1931	13	20	28	4	12	22	322	101	1	–	24	6	–	1	58	209
1932	14	19	8	1	3	23	257	79	–	–	4	4	–	1	72	109
1933	17	14	4	1	4	18	116	67	–	–	10	4	–	–	24	68
1934	7	5	2	1	9	17	23	77	–	–	4	3	–	–	25	54
1935	6	5	5	1	14	14	17	52	1	1	2	3	–	–	18	68
1936	7	7	8	2	8	18	55	21	–	–	2	3	–	–	17	65
1937	7	6	2	3	5	15	34	18	–	–	1	2	–	–	11	95
1938	14	7	3	2	6	9	11	15	–	–	–	1	–	–	30	64
1939	18	6	3	1	3	5	10	11	–	–	–	1	–	–	19	23
1940	17	9	4	1	–	–	71	125	–	1	–	–	–	1	2	–
							East Germany	West Germany								
1946	56	11	29	26	1	34	45	–	10	9	98	96	20	27	8	28
1947	72	69	35	40	–	10	20	–	16	15	123	94	25	34	32	39
1948	81	112	122	128	–	7	56	–	26	31	156	120	82	43	24	123
1949	129	180	185	185	2	3	132	1	60	75	168	123	90	100	33	61
1950	170	349	181	198	4	3	144	–	75	114	189	217	125	103	36	92
1951	298	431	228	261	7	8	295	–	103	110	238	280	125	129	70	142
1952	372	499	269	327	10	8	329	2	127	135	316	326	176	203	112	117
1953	427	628	281	314	19	16	435	2	155	142	331	296	207	199	48	81
1954	521	683	286	316	32	41	556	10	150	138	304	372	175	191	47	100

E2 External Trade (by value) with Main Trading Partners

RUSSIA/U.S.S.R. (in million rubels)[58]

1955–1995

	China		Czechoslovakia		France		East Germany		West Germany		Hungary		Poland		Romania		U.K.	
	I	E	I	E	I	E	I	E	I	E	I	E	I	E	I	E	I	E
1955	579	674	348	320	33	54	456	431	21	26	132	104	258	389	189	241	64	152
1956	688	660	357	336	46	63	564	514	61	38	109	114	255	322	212	191	67	133
1957	664	490	347	496	43	60	688	776	56	65	96	225	230	388	171	226	101	159
1958	793	571	461	402	73	78	734	720	65	59	146	181	239	339	210	226	66	131
1959	990	859	524	543	90	79	801	927	108	80	186	234	285	438	225	209	82	149
1960	763	735	587	568	117	66	836	947	179	107	223	280	348	442	252	235	97	173
1961	496	331	628	587	108	72	788	1,088	161	107	294	323	429	478	307	263	115	204
1962	465	210	742	694	139	77	966	1,235	184	121	350	370	508	535	314	337	106	192
1963	372	169	856	764	64	93	1,173	1,183	134	118	381	399	553	596	369	359	117	194
1964	283	122	872	811	62	95	1,195	1,247	178	112	433	443	646	594	379	444	93	215
1965	203	173	932	833	103	100	1,156	1,227	120	129	464	491	703	654	397	363	137	262
1966	129	158	828	805	144	117	1,114	1,266	125	167	461	454	660	723	365	348	152	297
1967	51	45	884	871	170	130	1,271	1,275	147	173	537	527	812	821	382	355	178	273
1968	33	53	891	934	265	124	1,445	1,356	205	189	602	608	928	945	411	375	246	330
1969	26	25	1,003	999	126	127	1,466	1,565	298	199	647	630	1,012	1,079	405	429	216	384
1970	20	22	1,111	1,083	287	126	1,557	1,738	321	223	722	758	1,135	1,215	474	445	223	418
1971	63	65	1,109	1,122	260	179	1,591	1,581	401	242	718	811	1,131	1,190	469	393	184	373
1972	98	89	1,220	1,110	312	172	1,823	1,479	508	236	877	800	1,330	1,157	518	416	166	328
1973	104	103	1,445	1,392	455	280	2,167	1,908	785	495	1,118	1,003	1,598	1,485	628	534	179	556
1974	101	103	1,447	1,441	518	379	2,050	2,064	1,326	840	1,094	1,082	1,664	1,753	584	552	190	658
1975	113	97	1,977	2,110	837	518	2,763	3,114	2,036	968	1,689	1,732	2,515	2,557	861	734	385	618
1976	135	180	2,224	2,321	923	774	2,779	3,219	1,981	1,168	1,721	1,772	2,485	2,751	830	770	407	825
1977	130	118	2,437	2,901	904	820	3,066	3,661	1,745	1,223	1,960	2,067	2,872	3,196	1,022	1,004	375	958
1978	175	164	3,059	3,002	974	839	3,711	3,982	1,969	1,498	2,430	2,396	3,600	3,450	979	971	669	857
1979	157	175	3,183	3,363	1,198	1,426	3,917	4,217	2,284	2,218	2,414	2,741	3,718	3,838	1,068	1,078	811	1,093
1980	147	170	3,536	3,648	1,510	2,242	4,327	4,873	2,989	3,096	2,757	2,982	3,596	4,406	1,510	1,350	953	859
1981	94	83	4,097	4,392	1,662	2,530	5,145	5,538	2,698	3,643	3,294	3,314	3,215	4,942	1,670	1,783	857	647
1982	103	120	4,726	5,059	1,266	2,296	5,769	6,444	2,909	4,074	3,742	3,716	4,092	4,824	1,681	1,427	751	815
1983	233	256	5,421	5,871	1,728	2,422	6,596	6,798	3,360	4,066	4,007	4,058	4,787	5,274	1,665	1,640	632	1,185
1984	561	468	6,017	6,591	1,777	2,447	7,367	7,481	3,376	4,536	4,434	4,321	5,297	6,069	1,755	1,807	819	1,393
1985	933	877	7,441	7,673	1,811	2,449	8,532	8,617	3,664	4,787	5,479	5,135	6,241	7,339	2,572	2,195	784	1,371
1986	912	909	6,559	6,935	1,130	1,538	7,131	7,870	2,869	2,874	4,875	4,670	6,130	6,802	2,416	2,818	515	1,272
1987	720	696	6,626	6,513	1,045	1,459	6,804	7,338	2,567	2,395	4,873	4,421	6,071	6,032	2,251	2,440	1,109	1,524
1988	813	942	6,856	6,422	1,194	1,451	6,910	7,714	3,596	2,286	4,825	4,270	6,723	6,031	2,470	2,535	777	1,986
1989	1,084	1,329	6,610	6,255	1,218	1,349	Included in West Germany		11,355	9,310	4,813	4,187	7,410	5,771	2,489	2,681	1,009	958
1990	3,278	2,391	10,031	8,803	3,155	4,647			22,579	12,114	7,126	6,927	12,764	7,908	1,784	4,731	2,718	5,294
1991	3,048	2,883	4,198	5,082	2,481	3,865			13,923	10,637	2,312	3,032	3,473	4,037	1,571	1,718	1,201	4,091
			Czech Republic						Million US$ Dollars									
1992	952.0	2,888.9	429.9	1,278.9	1,009.5	1,330.2			5,675.2	6,375.5	761.2	1,407.8	945.8	1,414.2	⋯	474.7	895.8	4,258.7
1993	865.4	3,431.8	438.2	1,904.9	1,083.9	1,543.2			6,483.1	6,049.1	842.1	1,804.4	1,321.4	2,002.9	736.2	894.2	1,099.6	3,187.1
1994	1,003.9	4,750.4	534.7	1,939.1	1,277.6	1,602.5			5,213.5	7,080.3	657.9	1,978.1	928.4	2,477.9	⋯	⋯	1,146.3	3,543.9
1995	1,261.4	3,981.4	585.8	1,822.2	1,594.7	1,626.1			6,643.3	6,531.1	920.6	1,853.7	1,354.4	2,514.6	739.6	⋯	1,505.4	3,054.6

E2 External Trade (by value) with Main Trading Partners

SERBIA (in million dinars)

1884–1912

	Austria–Hungary		Germany		Italy		Russia		U.K.	
	I	E	I	E	I	E	I	E	I	E
1884	32	34	7.6	0.1	1.3	—	0.4	—	4.1	—
1885	30	32	2.3	0.1	1.3	0.1	0.9	—	3.4	0.2
1886	37	36	2.0	0.1	0.7	0.1	0.7	—	4.1	0.1
1887	27	32	1.3	0.5	0.5	0.1	0.8	—	3.2	—
1888	24	33	1.5	1.1	0.5	—	1.1	—	3.5	0.1
1889	23	34	2.1	0.8	0.5	—	1.1	—	3.7	0.2
1890	23	39	2.9	0.8	0.4	—	1.1	—	4.9	0.2
1891	26	46	4.3	0.9	1.0	—	0.8	—	5.2	—
1892	22	41	3.8	1.2	0.7	—	0.7	—	3.8	—
1893	24	43	4.1	1.7	1.5	0.1	0.7	—	4.5	—
1894	21	41	2.8	2.0	0.6	—	0.7	—	3.6	—
1895	17	39	1.9	1.6	0.4	—	1.3	—	2.4	—
1896	19	47	3.6	2.5	0.5	—	0.4	—	4.1	—
1897	26	49	4.8	3.7	0.5	—	0.5	—	6.5	—
1898	23	51	4.3	2.2	0.7	—	0.3	—	3.8	—
1899	27	55	4.8	5.9	0.9	—	0.7	—	5.7	—
1900	26	57	15	3.9	0.8	—	0.2	0.1	3.8	0.6
1901	23	56	6.8	4.1	0.9	0.1	0.7	0.9	3.9	0.6
1902	25	58	6.8	5.5	1.0	0.3	0.7	0.1	4.8	1.1
1903	35	51	7.1	3.1	1.2	0.1	0.7	—	4.9	0.3
1904	37	55	8.1	2.6	1.0	—	1.1	—	5.0	—
1905	33	65	6.3	2.1	0.8	0.1	0.8	—	5.3	—
1906	22	30	10	19	0.9	0.6	1.2	0.2	4.6	0.1
1907	26	13	20	33	2.3	4.9	0.4	3.1	10.2	2.3
1908	32	22	21	14	2.3	3.5	1.0	—	8.8	0.5
1909	18	29	29	16	2.3	3.0	1.9	—	7.6	0.1
1910	16	18	35	22	3.6	1.1	1.8	—	11.4	1.7
1911	47	48	31	29	4.9	4.4	3.4	0.1	9.5	0.1
1912	48	36	31	18	3.4	3.8	1.3	0.1	8.5	— —

E2   External Trade (by value) with Main Trading Partners

SPAIN[60] (in million pesetas)

1849–1884

	Argentina		Cuba		France		Germany		U.K.		U.S.A.	
	I	E	I	E	I	E	I	E	I	E	I	E
1849	5.2	2.2	26	23	32	24	1.7	1.9	25	40	15	7
1850	2.4	1.9	22	25	53	33	2.6	0.6	29	35	21	6
1851	2.4	1.6	25	28	48	31	2.6	1.0	37	32	20	7
1852	3.1	2.3	35	32	48	36	1.8	1.0	37	40	22	7
1853	1.4[61]	3.3	26[61]	37	53[61]	48	1.9[61]	2.6	38[61]	64	22[61]	15
1854	2.6	8.2	36	39	43	60	1.1	5.3	40	76	28	14
1855	3.4	5.6	45	47	86	84	--	2.3	37	105	30	10
1856	2.5	7.1	40	47	121	68	1.5	4.2	48	70	41	15
1857	2.6	6.9	37	57	135	86	2.7	7.4	81	63	39	17
1858	3.3	6.6	42	57	117	68	3.7	3.1	84	49	37	13
1859	1.7	8.3	39	59	89	57	1.6	3.3	73	64	39	16
1860	2.3	8.2	41	56	95	62	0.7	2.3	93	80	52	19
1861	3.8	9.0	46	59	180	81	0.5	3.2	141	94	36	6
1862	11.2	11	53	58	156	63	0.4	3.3	105	77	12	10
1863	3.7	10	59	62	190	64	1.5	11.1	108	95	15	9
1864	3.0	13	55	63	185	101	1.3	6.5	133	103	15	7
1865	3.4	11	54	56	141	89	0.6	6.4	107	94	15	8
1866	3.1	8	45	58	110	93	0.2	3.2	72	95	14	10
1867	2.9	10	40	52	175	83	0.1	7.1	86	85	21	9
1868	2.2	11	43	54	212	70	0.1	2.4	116	88	24	11
1869	..	..	..	..	..	..	..	..	..	..	..	..
1870	..	..	..	..	..	..	..	..	..	..	..	..
1871	3.2	12	40	70	129	78	2.4	6.7	206	177	66	23
1872	8.5	18	37	67	117	89	1.2	7.9	148	218	55	28
1873	12.7	15	40	68	99	123	4.5	10.6	216	230	48	22
1874	8.2	16	51	61	144	104	5.9	8.7	180	165	70	20
1875	10.5	21	28	86	150	74	3.5	5.7	195	156	61	16
1876	8.2	10	38	70	164	91	7.3	7.9	144	179	60	12
1877	3.6	14	27	82	142	91	14	6.1	168	210	61	16
1878	3.5	13	23	63	173	120	13	6.7	141	175	65	15
1879	4.7	16	33	68	170	162	28	5.8	142	174	97	14
1880	4.9	15	29	70	270	232	43	7.2	135	211	95	22
1881	6.3	17	23	63	207	255	51	8.7	135	200	83	21
1882	6.6	16	23	68	221	310	83	7.1	171	235	92	28
1883	7.7	17	27	59	235	303	87	10.1	187	204	101	22
1884	8.4	19	20	53	192	255	89	7.6	164	168	90	18

E2 External Trade (by value) with Main Trading Partners

SPAIN (in million pesetas)[60]

1885–1919

	Argentina		Cuba		France		Germany		U.K.		U.S.A.	
	I	E	I	E	I	E	I	E	I	E	I	E
1885	10.3	18	40	65	199	316	95	12	119	162	91	15
1886	9.3	19	39	69	245	339	103	12	113	156	95	19
1887	6.0[60]	19[60]	37[60]	61[60]	235[60]	309[60]	83[60]	10[60]	114[60]	185[60]	100[60]	22[60]
1888	8.0	17	36	65	212	352	58	12	122	179	76	14
1889	8.6	23	35	83	264	386	54	15	161	207	102	15
1890	11	15	45	86	292	426	44	11	195	218	79	25
1891	11	8	37	115	327	457	43	10	238	176	87	15
1892	14	10	50	145	231	259	23	11	194	174	91	16
1893	13	10	30	128	204	206	20	14	155	179	87	16
1894	18	8	22	117	206	175	22	9	153	177	93	13
1895	14	10	30	136	235	238	34	6	155	198	85	13
1896	9[3]	10[3]	56[3]	256[3]	218[3]	282[3]	44[3]	9[3]	155[3]	226[3]	73[3]	11[3]
1897	14	11	27	253	147	254	53	21	155	264	99	12
1898	6	13	19	67	118	322	44	18	142	252	94	10
1899	25	13	21	74	158	250	65	26	241	281	120	13
1900	31	13	5	57	147	217	78	32	249	277	106	17
1901	25	13	3	58	145	179	80	35	199	274	120	19
1902	21	11	6	52	153	175	89	46	188	310	116	18
1903	22	17	7	66	161	220	95	41	185	316	118	26
1904	28	24	5	81	143	213	94	45	173	310	102	28
1905	44	30	5	73	160	208	85	37	168	318	119	35
1906	36	44	4	61	168	177	93	47	175	292	141	35
1907	24	40	4	63	158	198	99	60	181	296	136	39
1908	26	50	5	50	203	212	106	54	197	270	139	41
1909	35	52	4	54	198	239	115	48	206	267	122	62
1910	41	64	4	56	198	260	116	56	204	263	110	66
1911	27	69	2	55	164	281	129	61	168	237	130	58
1912	40	71	3	64	183	258	138	74	201	236	155	67
1913	111	70	2	65	204	328	185	74	245	232	167	72
1914	38	41	6	52	134	251	108	42	219	233	147	64
1915	86	68	10	58	94	531	21	--	363	264	298	63
1916	60	85	19	71	110	567	3	--	326	285	454	96
1917	48	95	16	63	145	588	1	--	100	202	777	106
1918	85	113	12	43	88	343	--	--	67	168	142	50
1919	122	67	14	44	111	492	4	5	183	206	392	98

E2 External Trade (by value) with Main Trading Partners

SPAIN (in million pesetas)[60]

1920–1959

Year	Argentina I	Argentina E	Cuba I	Cuba E	France I	France E	Germany I	Germany E	U.K. I	U.K. E	U.S.A. I	U.S.A. E
1920	134	97	17	81	219	280	86	16	214	219	331	78
1921	212	127	32	57	362	361	276	43	368	401	767	135
1922	123	99	89	56	198	211	279	45	448	326	481	156
1923	...	...	...	...	...	...	...	...	...	...	...	...
1924	119	100	10	105	349	346	233	99	441	424	514	175
1925	173	94	9	83	281	256	180	104	289	360	432	164
1926	137	80	10	73	344	266	181	86	216	360	401	212
1927	107	85	11	70	382	413	230	173	294	374	513	212
1928	166	121	29	64	419	522	286	158	311	375	513	211
1929	152	128	14	78	351	457	288	157	356	399	436	258
1930	53	175	20	65	270	470	284	181	301	387	412	227
1931	35	56	12	20	107	194	147	87	132	212	201	74
1932	59	39	9	15	74	133	100	66	99	192	161	52
1933	20	27	9	12	64	132	96	60	84	157	137	54
1934	18	22	9	14	66	96	99	68	86	142	147	52
1935	22	32	8	15	51	69	123	75	95	128	147	56
1940	88	6	23	6	20	31	24	14	19	90	87	47
1941	106	5	4	4	14	16	51	162	21	40	39	42
1942	58	10	2	2	14	35	117	137	30	72	16	24
1943	75	23	1	3	15	9	171	227	31	122	93	77
1944	85	37	3	5	13	17	81	153	24	239	112	135
1945	89	34	22	11	12	12	17	2	36	257	158	178
1946	92	21	28	17	5	4	2	1	78	119	162	160
1947	259	46	29	22	1	– –	2	4	77	130	107	76
1948	352	29	32	25	130	57	– –	8	130	165	96	105
1949	188	37	15	19	89	125	12	29	117	184	126	65
1950	32[60]	37[60]	10[60]	23[60]	94[60]	79[60]	49[60]	27[60]	85[60]	176[60]	158[60]	189[60]
1951	32	12	19	37	125	121	59	84	112	304	209	203
1952	21	5	22	29	162	147	160	127	177	247	292	49
1953	28	1	22	29	188	116	214	192	190	231	221	158
1954	12	5	26	28	164	96	212	157	195	237	346	149
1955	3	3	39	34	205	110	192	198	192	223	351	143
1956	6	7	36	31	156	89	246	159	215	205	615	181
1957	6	9	44	36	140	100	219	201	229	246	688	134
1958	20	9	57	37	181	149	231	151	207	235	577	144
1959	19	8	23	24	135	80	255	196	167	241	573	180

E2 External Trade (by value) with Main Trading Partners

SPAIN (in million pesetas to 1969, thousand million pesetas subsequently)

1960–1996

thousand million pesetas

Year	Argentina I	Argentina E	Cuba I	Cuba E	France I	France E	W. Germany I	W. Germany E	U.K. I	U.K. E	U.S.A. I	U.S.A. E
1960	272	314	620	592	3,376	3,445	4,455	6,540	3,639	7,535	8,426	4,337
1961	387	499	554	264	5,730	3,385	7,276[2]	6,465[2]	4,917	7,218	16,493	4,225
1961							7,115	6,283				
1962	1,575	397	511	82	8,945	4,052	12,402	6,570	8,954	7,059	18,641	4,721
1963	3,323	511	1,302	549	12,715	4,322	15,713	5,386	11,615	7,070	19,178	4,744
1964	1,404	1,045	3,934	1,881	16,627	6,817	18,804	7,794	13,177	8,217	21,172	5,785
1965	3,488	863	1,868	2,293	19,596	6,429	25,374	7,928	16,588	7,795	31,602	6,932
1966	6,818	1,836	2,289	4,713	23,818	8,323	31,626	8,504	20,102	8,140	36,537	8,818
1967	7,709	2,069	2,317	1,692	24,197	8,504	29,361	8,728	18,238	8,567	35,562	12,362
1968	6,046	1,491	2,837	1,298	24,014	9,740	32,061	11,495	19,698	11,336	41,313	19,529
1969	7,452	3,073	2,969	2,751	30,067	12,836	39,634	14,291	22,481	11,962	50,965	19,957
1970	7.5	3.4	2.5	2.6	33.2	17.3	41.9	19.7	23.5	14.7	62.8	23.6
1971	10.4	3.1	1.9	2.0	34.2	22.3	42.2	25.1	27.3	17.4	54.0	31.5
1972	5.4	2.6	1.2	1.2	42.3	28.9	53.8	28.7	33.9	20.6	69.4	40.0
1973	8.8	3.3	3.2	2.3	57.1	38.7	76.6	35.6	35.7	24.3	90.5	41.9
1974	14.5	3.7	9.9	3.6	75.5	51.5	99.7	45.1	45.3	37.4	137	47.9
1975	10.8	3.0	18.0	10.2	77.7	60.3	95.5	47.2	49.8	33.6	148	46.3
1976	11.8	2.0	6.1	13.9	91.3	84.6	123	63.8	58.5	42.3	166	59.5
1977	24.3	9.8	11.9	11.6	113	124	136	82.0	71.3	49.0	163	76.2
1978	33.0	12.7	8.1	7.7	130	166	142	107	77.0	64.6	190	92.7
1979	37.3	27.5	6.9	13.4	165	197	163	126	96.1	78.8	212	85.1
1980	17.5	26.8	6.5	13.5	202	247	201	153	115	105	319	79.4
1981	22.2	29.3	6.0	16.0	239	271	242	163	133	131	413	127
1982	27.2	19.0	12.1	11.6	278	368	329	182	171	127	482	142
1983	36.2	18.8	134	12.9	344	44.5	366	260	257	151	496	207
1984	47.9	16.9	14.1	28.8	398	556	458	351	281	336	519	356
1985	47.6	17.3	210	49.1	471	637	538	392	330	348	556	408
1986	29.9	23.0	12.7	40.9	586	687	749	446	382	336	488	349
1987	24.1	9.0	12.8	23.6	773	785	974	500	425	398	501	342
1988	31.2	16.4	9.5	24.3	942	864	1,130	561	498	455	627	367
1989	41.2	12.3	10.8	25.3	1,157	1,001	1,139	616	549	517	762	385
1990	48.9	17.2	8.1	30.1	1,309	1,162	1,463	758	602	510	748	330
1991	64.1	26.0	9.5	29.4	1,464	1,243	1,559	992	728	474	770	297
1992	77.3	46.3	8.6	20.7	1,631	1,347	1,676	1,043	745	503	750	317
1993	46.3	78.7	8.3	24.1	1,700	1,466	1,515	1,133	753	638	739	373

(W. Germany figures become **Germany** from 1991 onwards)

Million US$ Dollars

Year	Argentina I	Argentina E	Cuba I	Cuba E	France I	France E	Germany I	Germany E	U.K. I	U.K. E	U.S.A. I	U.S.A. E
1994	688.7	904.0	...	289.5	16,148.2	14,746.5	13,511.5	10,397.4	7,259.7	6,016.5	5,818.6	3,606.6
1995	816.1	956.8	...	395.9	19,523.9	18,401.5	17,286.5	13,809.8	8,812.3	7,160.9	6,750.2	3,799.7
1996	865.9	1,314.4	...	464.0	21,959.9	20,602.5	18,228.5	14,920.1	10,195.4	8,425.9	7,526.6	4,239.5

E2 External Trade (by value) with Main Trading Partners

SWEDEN (in million kronor)   1830–1864

	Denmark[66,67]		France		Germany		Netherlands		Norway		U.K.		U.S.A.	
	I	E	I	E	I	E	I	E	I	E	I	E	I	E
1830	2.2	2.6	0.4	3.0	4.5	2.1	0.3	0.8	2.8	0.9	2.6	5.9	1.2	3.7
1831	...	...	...	...	...	...	...	...	...	...	...	...	...	...
1832	1.8	2.8	0.6	2.1	4.4	2.8	0.3	0.6	2.4	0.8	2.2	4.4	1.6	4.5
1833	2.2	3.1	0.6	2.2	4.3	3.1	0.4	1.1	2.6	1.1	2.1	6.1	1.7	5.0
1834	2.2	2.6	0.4	3.0	4.6	2.9	0.3	0.8	2.8	0.9	2.6	5.9	1.2	3.7
1835	2.3	2.8	0.6	2.5	5.1	2.6	0.4	1.0	2.4	1.1	2.9	7.0	1.6	6.0
1836	1.6	2.8	0.5	1.8	7.6	3.0	0.4	0.9	2.7	1.0	2.5	6.9	2.1	7.3
1837	2.5	2.8	0.5	3.0	5.8	4.1	0.4	1.1	3.5	1.5	2.4	6.4	1.6	3.1
1838	3.0	3.3	0.5	3.1	8.0	7.2	0.4	1.4	2.9	1.0	2.3	6.9	1.9	5.2
1839	2.0	3.3	0.5	2.4	8.2	3.8	0.5	1.1	2.6	1.5	3.1	6.9	1.9	6.8
1840	2.0	4.1	0.4	2.1	7.4	5.0	0.3	0.7	4.2	1.4	2.8	7.3	1.7	3.9
1841	2.5	3.5	0.5	2.2	7.9	6.1	0.8	1.5	4.0	1.5	4.0	7.4	1.7	4.3
1842	2.5	3.7	0.6	2.5	8.4	10.5	0.6	0.7	3.6	1.2	4.9	6.4	2.0	2.4
1843	1.9	3.6	0.8	2.9	5.6	7.7	0.5	0.7	2.6	1.2	4.1	5.6	1.2	1.5
1844	1.7	3.6	0.6	2.8	7.9	5.3	0.5	0.8	3.9	2.1	4.5	8.5	0.9	2.7
1845	2.0	4.2	0.6	3.9	12.3	4.8	0.5	0.7	3.2	2.0	3.6	13	1.3	2.5
1846	2.5	4.9	0.7	5.3	8.1	5.6	0.5	0.6	3.9	1.6	4.2	11	1.3	1.5
1847	2.5	7.8	0.6	4.2	18.1	7.3	0.6	0.7	4.4	2.2	5.3	15	1.7	3.3
1848	2.4	4.2	0.6	1.5	7.9	11.2	0.7	0.6	4.4	2.6	5.0	10	2.9	3.8
1849	2.4	4.4	0.9	2.6	7.9	7.4	1.1	1.0	4.7	2.2	5.7	12	4.0	2.7
1850	2.6	5.5	0.7	3.1	8.2	5.3	0.8	0.7	3.5	1.2	5.0	12	2.5	3.8
1851	3.6	5.7	0.5	3.1	10	6.0	0.8	0.6	4.6	0.9	6.3	16	3.6	2.9
1852	3.3	6.0	0.8	4.3	10	7.0	0.6	0.5	4.1	0.8	6.8	15	3.0	2.0
1853	4.8	10.7	1.1	6.0	27	11	0.9	1.7	6.4	1.4	13	35	5.5	2.6
1854	3.9	10.7	1.1	4.6	34	12	0.9	2.1	6.0	3.4	14	35	4.9	3.3
1855	4.7	11.5	1.2	5.4	31	14	1.9	8.6	8.4	6.3	18	40	2.9	2.9
1856	6.7	9.1	1.4	6.3	30	23	2.7	2.9	8.7	4.0	19	33	6.9	3.5
1857	4.8	8.2	1.4	8.4	24	20	1.5	1.1	8.9	2.7	15	25	6.4	3.0
1858	4.4	5.4	1.1	5.6	20	8	1.2	1.9	5.2	2.3	11	24	2.9	2.0
1859	4.7	6.8	2.4	7.7	23	13	1.6	2.0	5.4	3.6	16	32	5.5	2.9
1860	5.9	7.1	1.8	7.7	27	8	3.3	2.8	5.6	4.5	17	42	6.5	2.7
1861	7.2	6.6	1.5	10.4	30	7	4.7	2.0	5.6	3.1	23	36	6.4	0.8
1862	8.2	7.7	1.8	9.8	39	8	3.5	2.0	5.8	2.3	20	40	0.2	1.1
1863	10.4	7.7	2.6	9.4	35	8	2.4	4.1	4.6	2.2	22	46	0.1	1.2
1864	8.4	6.6	2.3	9.4	28	7	4.4	2.8	5.7	2.2	24	49	0.9	2.5

E2 External Trade (by value) with Main Trading Partners

SWEDEN (in million kronor)

1865–1899

	Denmark[66,67]		France		Germany		Netherlands		Norway		U.K.		U.S.A.	
	I	E	I	E	I	E	I	E	I	E	I	E	I	E
1865	10	7.7	3.7	11	33	8	4.6	4.4	5.9	3.6	31	53	0.7	1.1
1866	10	7.7	3.2	13	32	9	4.2	4.0	6.6	4.2	36	54	0.7	2.8
1867	26	11	4.2	18	31	12	4.4	4.4	7.4	3.6	29	63	1.0	3.9
1868	...	...	...	...	...	...	...	...	...	...	...	...	...	...
1869	...	...	...	...	...	...	...	...	...	...	...	...	...	...
1870	31	9	4.1	17	33	9	10.2	4.4	10	7.0	32	84	1.1	4.9
1871	25	15	4.1	14	43	11	8.9	6.7	9	7.2	52	79	6.0	6.7
1872	31	19	5.9	18	55	15	6.8	6.1	12	6.5	77	105	2.9	8.6
1873	37	22	9.4	19	62	18	9.9	5.3	13	7.4	95	121	8.0	7.0
1874	54	32	10.7	20	63	14	11.3	5.2	15	7.5	91	127	8.3	2.1
1875	49	25	10.1	25	55	13	9.2	4.9	15	7.1	92	109	2.5	1.1
1876	51	24	11.6	25	58	16	10.9	11.7	17	7.0	98	120	5.8	0.8
1877	49	22	9.3	25	67	14	12.1	10.6	15	6.7	87	117	6.9	0.7
1878	42	21	8.0	26	57	12	10.7	5.1	12	7.1	63	93	7.6	0.5
1879	48	21	5.5	28	52	13	9.2	5.7	11	6.4	59	92	6.2	1.1
1880	56	24	6.5	29	62	17	8.4	6.1	17	8.0	78	124	11.8	2.9
1881	52	22	7.8	28	77	21	7.7	10.4	17	8.2	74	107	9.8	0.4
1882	52	25	7.6	33	84	18	9.1	7.7	19	10.6	78	127	6.2	1.6
1883	57	32	7.6	31	91	19	9.3	9.9	21	9.2	86	129	9.5	0.3
1884	53	33	8.5	29	89	18	6.6	8.9	22	11	89	112	5.4	1.7
1885	50	31	8.2	24	101	19	6.7	9.0	24	10	85	122	8.6	0.8
1886	42	26	6.8	21	92	21	6.1	9.3	23	11	77	111	8.7	2.6
1887	47	32	6.2	27	89	24	5.5	8.5	23	12	74	110	6.6	2.8
1888	42	35	6.7	30	94	27	6.9	14	28	14	94	130	4.2	1.1
1889	45	34	7.6	24	116	36	9.0	13	34	16	111	142	5.9	1.4
1890	44	33	7.9	24	118	37	9.6	16	33	18	109	137	8.2	0.9
1891	45	37	9.1	34	120	38	8.5	13	34	17	99	146	13	0.7
1892	44	40	9.6	19	116	48	9.2	17	35	18	95	150	13	2.4
1893	40	37[63]	6.2	29[63]	113	44[63]	7.0	17[63]	31	16[63]	86	151[63]	11	0.7[63]
1894	40	38	8.5	32	120	39	3.7	18	27	15	98	124	12	--
1895	38	41	7.9	25	116	43	8.3	18	29	18	98	131	11	0.1
1896	46	42	7.2	29	118	44	8.8	20	29	20	99	144	9	0.7
1897	49	43	7.6	31	135	46	8.5	24	33	21[64]	121	150	7	0.2
1898	59	43	8.0	28	158	50	10	25	21	6	139	149	10	0.1
1899	61	43	9.0	29	184	55	10	26	20	6	155	157	10	—

E2 External Trade (by value) with Main Trading Partners

SWEDEN (in million kronor)

1900–1934

	Denmark[66,67]		France		Germany		Netherlands		Norway		U.K.		U.S.A.	
	I	E	I	E	I	E	I	E	I	E	I	E	I	E
1900	63	48	9.7	30	188	65	11	30	22	7	177	169	9	—
1901	65	47	8.9	26	169	60	12	23	23	Z64	132	150	11	..
1902	63	55	9.3	28	197	63	13	24	24	24	130	150	10	..
1903	64	61	9.5	31	206	71	16	24	25	32	139	162	13	..
1904	73	58	10.3	30	222	72	18	24	23	35	149	149	9	..
1905	40	50	16	30	220	85	14	23	23	31	140	159	41	10
1906	42	55	20	37	231	97	15	26	25	35	159	171	60	12
1907	46	58	23	40	238	109	17	17	23	25	177	182	61	14
1908	43	46	19	37	210	103	15	15	21	25	152	169	60	10
1909	40	45	23	36	213	97	16	14	21	24	157	156	48	16
1910	45	55	28	42	230	124	18	16	21	29	164	191	53	23
1911	46	66	31	49	240	134	19	24	20	38	161	196	55	24
1912	50	67	33	53	274	171	20	19	24	43	189	223	60	32
1913	54	71	35	66	290	179	21	19	26	54	207	238	77	34
1914	52	73	29	33	239	175	19	19	29	49	184	258	78	41
1915	70	80	24	31	251	486	27	43	51	76	214	330	322	34
1916	80	94	24	97	420	438	22	61	61	115	164	320	214	75
1917	113	113	16	64	288	352	23	80	52	163	65	216	96	50
1918	203	182	13	86	448	293	42	113	98	211	149	253	83	19
1919	249	160	63	126	269	131	60	61	77	200	669	512	646	62
1920	313	137	96	187	500	185	78	95	90	183	915	825	779	129
1921	120	88	45	52	325	119	45	42	43	107	218	327	243	97
1922	90	84	32	105	314	103	39	55	37	80	268	285	167	133
1923	108	81	38	89	342	90	52	35	36	73	284	359	214	128
1924	124	83	45	93	353	133	57	48	40	55	308	363	227	153
1925	124	84	49	84	378	206	59	56	49	65	291	367	219	143
1926	122	91	55	90	460	189	59	41	47	64	221	386	199	173
1927	133	100	54	67	485	271	58	59	42	78	264	448	201	175
1928	119	103	59	90	531	198	69	70	45	86	275	393	252	166
1929	130	118	52	102	548	275	74	70	50	96	309	450	261	198
1930	114	112	56	93	533	225	66	57	52	95	263	395	229	161
1931	91	83	49	69	472	114	61	39	40	72	201	300	178	133
1932	76	62	30	56	339	90	47	32	38	61	194	242	125	100
1933	66	74	30	68	320	115	48	42	37	55	197	285	113	131
1934	80	88	39	68	350	186	63	46	44	84	255	328	154	128

E2 External Trade (by value) with Main Trading Partners

SWEDEN (in million kronor)

1935–1964

Year	Denmark[66,67] I	Denmark[66,67] E	France I	France E	Germany I	Germany E	Netherlands I	Netherlands E	Norway I	Norway E	U.K. I	U.K. E	U.S.A. I	U.S.A. E
1935	101	78	49	56	358	187	73	40	50	67	285	322	189	156
1936	105	84	50	72	399	241	84	44	53	103	314	374	223	188
1937	127	87	65	92	485[65]	315[65]	106	61	64	140	403	479	318	221
1938	125	91	62	61	499	335	115	69	65	123	380	451	339	166
1939	121	103	77	62	651	371	134	94	88	139	452	439	420	179
1940	72	50	25	18	794	494	50	45	77	112	170	120	310	55
1941	55	79	9	14	911	579	30	47	43	84	24	21	139	14
1942	53	110	7	9	842	550	25	27	36	69	13	28	91	25
1943	61	77	9	11	932	552	21	18	42	59	15	2	60	1
1944	72	39	6	3	819[65]	349[65]	17	12	21	28	16	6	51	2
1945	79	143	8	67	90	—	19	69	51	331	75	282	201	239
1946	141	175	117	161	7	—	98	175	125	185	487	426	919	190
1947	175[3,66] / 155	155[3,66] / 135	200[3] / 189	184[3]	110[3]	21[3]	184[3]	198[3]	166[3]	245[3]	701[3] / 444	527[3] / 491	1,814[3] / 1,640	365[3] / 349
1948	154	159	257	203	151	151	173	194	158	365	860	671	692	292
1949	156	208	238	191	314	338	213	226	169	417	743	726	416	247
1950	214	336	389	250	697	733	274	345	181	513	1,215	812	524	356
1951	233	414	467	522	1,314	989	432	501	301	542	1,491	1,752	863	475
1952	226	443	323	480	1,662[2] / 1,587	1,036[2] / 962	472	411	350	632	1,282	1,353	858	463
1953	256 / 327[67]	437 / 540[67]	384	361	1,492	881	507	454	292	620	1,337	1,451	657	513
1954	325	538	453	390	1,867	1,008	640	485	331	805	1,464	1,524	724	381
1955	375	518	501	465	2,260	1,183	731	548	330	867	1,413	1,749	1,009	440
1956	389	558	433	635	2,515	1,377	797	625	425	824	1,583	1,789	1,171	512
1957	520	587	387	572	2,769	1,569	849	671	463	1,090	1,741	1,980	1,608	529
1958	491	640	450	478	2,856	1,536	928	527	412	1,137	1,718	1,757	1,296	629
1959	492	738	493	435	2,850	1,725	964	558	434	1,141	1,717	1,713	1,317	910
1960	648	872	589	515	3,210	2,017	1,166	680	571	1,212	1,950	2,122	1,889	848
1961	696	1,071	570	610	3,359	2,234	1,110	789	620	1,385	2,141	2,118	1,718	704
1962	769	1,198	666	670	3,555	2,310	1,248	825	698	1,457	2,320	1,997	1,640	847
1963	986	1,273	681	781	3,771	2,341	1,280	839	792	1,861	2,623	2,238	1,765	920
1964	1,241	1,650	810	956	4,288	2,727	1,145	977	959	2,026	3,007	2,647	2,002	1,034

E2 External Trade (by value) with Main Trading Partners
SWEDEN (in million kronor) 1965–1997

	Denmark		France		West Germany / Germany		Netherlands		Norway		U.K.		U.S.A.	
	I	E	I	E	I	E	I	E	I	E	I	E	I	E
1965	1,417	1,851	940	1,001	4,880	2,967	1,221	1,065	1,227	2,409	3,326	2,722	2,150	1,241
1966	1,488	1,981	1,024	1,202	4,774	2,839	1,282	1,091	1,303	2,329	3,646	2,803	2,215	1,522
1967	1,694	2,211	1,180	1,092	4,693	2,577	1,181	1,010	1,450	2,799	3,569	3,123	2,258	1,720
1968	1,908	2,420	1,193	1,189	4,959	2,960	1,215	1,176	1,542	2,661	3,595	3,784	2,457	1,984
1969	2,339	2,939	1,310	1,534	5,809	3,447	1,315	1,315	1,793	2,911	4,218	3,839	2,615	1,856
1970	2,808	3,442	1,502	1,766	6,856	4,142	1,626	1,581	2,108	3,808	5,000	4,403	3,155	2,096
1971	2,888	3,794	1,407	1,941	6,847	4,302	1,468	1,680	2,249	3,924	5,097	5,170	2,884	2,494
1972	3,114	3,844	1,763	2,078	7,268	4,476	1,586	1,643	2,493	3,978	5,018	6,136	2,763	2,937
1973	3,538	5,250	1,892	2,712	9,153	5,392	2,281	2,131	3,182	5,021	5,727	7,860	3,055	3,217
1974	5,098	5,953	2,786	3,697	13,157	6,939	3,413	3,104	4,784	7,354	7,777	9,330	4,590	3,744
1975	5,285	6,213	3,129	3,443	14,348	7,196	3,479	2,909	4,960	8,032	8,183	7,857	4,887	3,760
1976	5,861	7,827	3,341	4,394	15,676	7,918	3,715	3,367	5,107	9,014	8,760	9,034	5,597	3,682
1977	6,121	8,058	3,500	4,319	16,882	8,657	4,067	3,727	5,194	10,908	9,651	9,353	6,435	4,603
1978	6,537	8,935	3,997	4,831	17,112	10,776	3,695	4,637	5,047	10,081	10,326	10,637	6,777	6,201
1979	8,098	10,663	5,254	6,332	21,248	13,330	5,559	5,609	6,656	11,218	14,903	13,629	9,005	7,022
1980	8,650	11,061	6,140	7,652	23,779	16,103	5,253	6,262	7,375	12,828	16,730	13,035	16,730	13,035
1981	8,992	11,244	5,626	7,726	23,684	16,371	5,548	6,524	8,973	13,898	17,481	14,460	11,814	8,884
1982	10,020	13,002	6,996	9,530	30,076	17,605	7,848	8,365	12,470	17,763	21,325	16,867	14,678	11,957
1983	12,318	17,743	9,261	10,502	34,317	23,915	8,314	10,052	14,961	21,286	27,749	22,863	16,704	18,554
1984	14,317	20,125	9,363	12,177	38,418	28,136	9,392	10,847	16,805	22,370	29,868	24,859	17,767	27,582
1985	16,572	21,489	11,353	12,553	43,861	29,901	9,532	11,460	15,968	27,255	33,161	25,767	20,506	30,228
1986	15,896	21,148	12,125	13,584	47,731	30,659	9,888	12,276	13,110	29,661	24,199	27,665	18,235	29,865
1987	17,360	20,893	13,259	15,061	56,261	33,351	10,588	13,801	15,176	30,270	23,545	28,674	17,793	30,067
1988	18,610	21,064	14,033	16,088	59,439	36,986	11,359	14,612	16,949	28,512	24,045	34,230	20,968	30,064
1989	21,773	22,095	16,816	17,724	63,896	42,310	13,236	16,633	22,159	27,308	25,608	37,277	25,894	30,935
1990	24,720	23,102	16,134	18,296	62,944	47,282	13,272	18,108	25,519	28,335	26,114	34,353	28,042	29,184
					Germany									
1991	23,455	23,489	14,608	18,399	56,538	50,474	13,042	18,136	23,013	28,084	25,041	31,002	25,620	26,731
1992	22,673	23,318	14,946	18,864	54,084	48,749	12,461	18,242	19,915	27,485	25,010	31,513	25,439	26,889
1993	24,432	25,769	17,947	20,875	59,888	55,783	15,543	19,716	21,533	31,632	31,618	39,814	30,372	32,612
							Million US$ Dollars							
1994	3,413.1	4,016.6	2,883.7	2,918.6	9,433.9	7,648.1	2,089.6	3,037.9	3,124.3	4,672.3	4,954.9	5,744.9	4,413.4	4,625.6
1995	4,597.4	5,077.2	3,414.8	4,118.6	12,725.5	10,249.5	4,671.3	4,365.8	4,620.6	6,102.6	6,087.4	7,559.1	3,520.3	6,302.5
1996	5,030.8	5,329.4	3,765.5	3,959.4	12,566.3	9,910.1	5,015.7	4,696.3	5,210.0	7,147.1	6,833.0	8,085.1	3,871.2	7,012.1
1997	4,720.9	5,063.8	3,735.3	3,801.4	12,078.4	9,161.5	5,003.2	4,605.4	5,034.6	6,894.4	6,378.7	7,576.1	3,906.5	6,870.0

E2   External Trade (by value) with Main Trading Partners

SWITZERLAND (in million francs)   1885–1919

	Austria-Hungary		France		Germany		Italy		U.K.		U.S.A.	
	I	E	I	E	I	E	I	E	I	E	I	E
1885	66	38	179	140	249	158	112	60	52	99	18	78
1886	92	36	188	139	261	160	119	58	46	104	21	87
1887	88	38	212	131	264	165	117	65	46	103	29	81
1888	96	33	203	142	254	165	116	51	44	105	22	87
1889	107	39	262	142	270	185	141	54	51	106	25	76
1890	102	39	226	124	295	182	129	50	52	107	29	83
1891	87	36	214	125	293	164	136	47	46	113	31	72
1892	68	37	179	103	227	162	140	46	42	117	41	76
1893	76	40	112	74	238	168	147	43	44	118	38	80
1894	80	39	110	73	243	157	144	38	43	118	35	72
1895	68	39	139	75	274	164	158	39	47	131	39	91
1896	71	40	178	81	305	172	137	39	52	147	39	71
1897	67	41	192	84	306	176	150	39	54	146	52	71
1898	66	42	204	83	315	194	156	39	51	148	73	74
1899	77	46	214	96	345	199	191	42	56	166	62	92
1900	69	46	207	110	350	202	162	44	62	176	57	96
1901	64	45	206	109	317	192	158	46	47	189	61	88
1902	71	47	217	112	324	203	178	51	54	186	62	109
1903	78	48	222	114	356	202	181	52	57	178	57	117
1904	82	52	239	108	377	211	169	54	58	172	54	106
1905	92	54	274	120	441	232	177	57	67	175	57	125
1906	92	64	281	109	480	277	201	70	84	176	59	136
1907	103	66	298	121	551	282	230	83	118	189	70	160
1908	99	65	284	117	513	240	172	92	87	179	61	112
1909	102	70	306	121	534	254	185	83	91	182	64	146
1910	111	80	347	130	566	270	203	86	113	200	69	144
1911	114	85	340	133	581	275	181	85	100	213	75	142
1912	122	89	376	138	647	307	193	91	117	230	84	136
1913	109	78	348	141	631	306	207	89	113	236	118	136
1914	103	67	221	115	481	275	194	83	76	234	108	122
1915	66	157	189	221	418	457	259	90	112	355	324	107
1916	45	195	236	401	472	709	390	150	160	424	565	133
1917	44	93	305	462	483	699	369	136	269	362	459	120
1918	61	101	280	466	620	445	222	97	248	269	354	99
1919	69	242	407	502	483	698	273	209	363	347	788	183

E2 External Trade (by value) with Main Trading Partners

SWITZERLAND (in million francs)

1920–1954

	Austria		France		Germany		Italy		U.K.		U.S.A.	
	I	E	I	E	I	E	I	E	I	E	I	E
1920	72	106	603	522	809	253	325	166	466	646	865	283
1921	32	88	321	239	440	195	200	74	156	349	385	586
1922	25	48	303	240	366	193	225	93	174	348	190	215
1923	31	65	395	214	417	124	232	101	182	363	178	210
1924	34	90	454	206	486	328	288	94	188	397	207	206
1925	41	70	499	173	471	368	266	104	281	422	227	192
1926	40	66	496	154	465	267	252	113	150	300	188	201
1927	46[53]	81[53]	475[53]	135[53]	542[53]	398[53]	226[53]	115[53]	192[53]	311[53]	220[53]	210[53]
1928	57	71	491	157	624	386	200	141	203	308	244	195
1929	55	68	490	182	698	349	203	158	169	290	239	208
1930	51[68]	55[68]	447[68]	183[68]	709[68]	278[68]	185[68]	120[68]	139[68]	265[68]	205[68]	144[68]
1931	43	45	362	156	660	198	180	94	99[10]	237[10]	164	92
									96	236		
1932	28	24	272	123	500	111	143	82	79	86	115	55
1933	36	23	244	142	461	139	134	80	91	88	90	58
1934	36	24	230	122	389	183	116	76	91	84	76	48
1935	29	22[53]	207	121[53]	338	170[53]	91	73[53]	76	78[53]	70	48[53]
1936	27	25	187	115	314	171	83	62	77	98	72	70
1937	44	38	245	140	403	200	117	102	113	144	126	112
1938	33	31	229	121	373	206	117	91	95	148	125	91
1939	...	...	275	140	440	192	135	81	109	165	133	130
1940	...	...	139	112	411	285	165	142	88	95	199	140
1941	...	...	76	93	656	577	245	186	14	23	151	108
1942	...	...	77	67	660	656	154	159	20	22	235	102
1943	...	...	78[53]	52	532[53]	598	131[53]	94	4[53]	36	56[53]	153
1944	...	...	52	24	433	293	29	5	1	34	21	141
1945	2	1	130	165	54	11	47	11	22	32	137	385
1946	42	20	355	282	45	8	228	156	197	58	548	453
1947	89	39	459	298	133	16	321	210	323	117	1,032	395
1948	106	73	391	329	323	69	299	227	356	140	954	456
1949	57	65	353	240	332	313	251	260	276	158	766	430
1950	63	82	511	858	497	362	324	520	370	137	626	515
1951	102	125	620	392	914	422	398	348	399	229	943	597
1952	97	107	512	330	959	496	379	442	336	233	837	703
1953	94	118	515	367	1,040	609	462	504	341	246	619	852
1954	108	135	643	389	1,253[2]	680[2]	546	466	317	267	710	641
					1,216	641						

E2 External Trade (by value) with Main Trading Partners

SWITZERLAND (in million francs)

	Austria I	Austria E	France I	France E	West Germany I	West Germany E	Italy I	Italy E	U.K. I	U.K. E	U.S.A. I	U.S.A. E
1955	128	169	770	385	1,507	755	613	463	336[19] / 333	303 / 298	828	650
1956	177	184	844	542	1,853	864	726	503	411	329	1,001	762
1957	208	210	886	578	2,193	961	936	541	450	366	1,197	765
1958	153	202	757	494	1,954	1,080	870	520	413	372	837	658
1959	176	220	932	501	2,808	1,242	951	593	617	414	875	815
1960	209	1,212	544	2,841	1,493	1,013	671	573	472	1,096	807	817
1961	287	306	1,489	664	3,664	1,578	1,212	746	681	510	1,199	911
1962	365	344	1,740	778	4,087	1,668	1,355	870	811	560	1,270	961
1963	359	369	2,006	915	4,419	1,722	1,454	1,052	927	645	1,206	1,039
1964	440	448	2,310	998	4,703	1,864	1,523	1,007	1,113	781	1,353	
1965	471	535	2,312	1,052	4,795	2,203	1,628	1,202	1,158	901	1,351	1,242
1966	545	643	2,394	1,223	4,997	2,142	1,684	1,180	1,287	918	1,534	1,528
1967	625	777	2,454	1,383	5,102	2,024	1,752	1,303	1,374	1,131	1,488	1,555
1968	732	843	2,521	1,496	5,737	2,463	1,937	1,513	1,422	1,291	1,737	1,780
1969	957	1,005	2,753	1,718	6,643	3,035	2,201	1,753	1,833	1,383	1,922	1,884
1970	1,251	1,152	3,362	1,807	8,349	3,289	2,623	2,074	2,167	1,585	2,372	1,963
1971	1,434	1,345	3,729	2,073	8,801	3,586	2,929	2,085	2,340	1,719	2,121	1,998
1972	1,671	1,543	4,381	2,330	9,681	3,922	3,129	2,174	2,364	2,036	2,234	2,263
1973	1,812	1,800	5,117	2,647	11,063	4,201	3,417	2,495	2,240	2,276	2,333	2,445
1974	2,109	2,326	5,886	3,109	12,479	4,843	3,930	2,823	2,502	2,539	2,806	2,501
1975	1,489	1,852	4,754	2,965	9,553	4,944	3,386	2,307	2,105	2,051	2,587	2,135
1976	1,511	1,973	4,891	3,366	10,470	5,761	3,564	2,758	2,483	2,182	2,520	2,521
1977	1,629	2,245	5,264	3,687	12,144	6,969	4,201	3,400	3,148	2,400	2,888	2,768
1978	1,649	1,939	5,286	3,612	12,233	7,537	4,148	2,634	3,378	2,869	3,171	2,974
1979	1,830	2,011	6,273	3,845	13,946	8,643	5,055	3,127	3,755	3,091	3,049	2,993
1980	2,184	2,271	7,462	4,548	16,766	9,750	5,845	3,899	5,073	3,134	4,105	3,552
1981	2,263	2,263	7,428	4,751	16,908	9,687	5,845	4,070	3,458	3,429	4,475	4,129
1982	2,154	2,142	6,657	4,729	17,262	9,572	5,733	3,973	3,181	3,268	4,153	4,095
1983	2,167	2,211	7,131	4,461	17,413	10,698	6,141	3,804	3,303	3,481	4,993	4,594
1984	2,431	2,359	7,565	5,023	20,128	11,853	6,808	4,461	4,975	4,835	4,563	5,943
1985	2,666	2,583	8,344	5,552	22,913	13,103	7,243	4,956	5,425	5,299	4,391	6,871
1986	2,897	2,605	8,424	6,065	24,267	14,146	7,487	5,161	5,375	5,182	3,970	6,343
1987	2,903	2,558	8,109	6,166	25,806	14,368	7,742	5,568	4,578	5,038	3,994	5,917
1988	3,182	2,693	8,746	6,936	28,056	15,481	8,356	6,160	4,691	5,820	4,561	6,294
1989	3,664	2,976	10,332	8,258	31,902	17,134	9,665	7,159	5,316	6,908	6,080	7,439
1990	3,807	3,265	10,708	8,748	32,529	19,307	10,159	7,850	5,083	6,573	5,921	6,977
1991	3,648	3,323	10,347	8,465	31,134	20,908	9,491	7,635	5,260	5,811	6,971	7,153
1992	3,608	3,365	9,987	8,726	30,880	21,593	9,248	8,058	5,336	6,063	5,866	7,866
1993	3,653	3,551	9,814	8,504	29,248	21,401	9,814	7,255	3,217	6,409	5,581	8,212
Million US$ Dollars												
1994	2,786.9	2,484.4	7,466.5	6,192.7	22,273.6	16,157.7	6,706.0	5,127.2	4,501.3	4,566.9	4,498.0	6,265.3
1995	3,388.9	2,908.9	9,129.8	7,776.2	27,023.3	19,437.6	8,121.1	6,192.6	4,447.6	4,972.1	5,130.4	7,073.6
1996	3,145.7	2,481.6	9,155.8	7,577.6	24,886.7	18,314.6	8,507.8	6,075.3	5,090.6	5,090.7	5,686.9	7,593.2
1997	2,862.8	2,333.3	8,336.8	6,915.1	22,948.7	17,031.7	7,455.3	5,684.6	4,921.1	4,415.2	6,345.6	7,993.4

E2 External Trade (by value) with Main Trading Partners

UNITED KINGDOM (in million pounds)

1827–1864

Year	Argentina I	Argentina E	Australia I	Australia E	Canada I	Canada E	France I	France E	Germany I	Germany E	India[70] I	India[70] E	Netherlands I	Netherlands E	New Zealand I	New Zealand E	Russia I	Russia E	U.S.A. I	U.S.A. E[69]
1827	...	...	...	0.3	...	1.4	...	0.4	...	4.8	...	3.7	...	...	...	...	...	1.4	...	7.0
1828	...	...	...	0.4	...	1.7	...	0.5	...	4.6	...	...	...	...	...	...	...	1.3	...	5.8
1829	...	...	...	0.3	...	1.6	...	0.5	...	4.7	...	...	...	...	...	...	...	1.4	...	4.8
1830	...	...	...	0.3	...	1.9	...	0.5	...	4.6	...	...	...	...	...	...	...	1.5	...	6.1
1831	...	...	...	0.4	...	2.1	...	0.6	...	3.8	...	...	...	...	...	...	...	1.2	...	9.1
1832	...	...	...	0.5	...	2.1	...	0.7	...	5.3	...	...	...	...	...	...	...	1.6	...	5.5
1833	...	...	...	0.6	...	2.1	...	0.8	...	4.5	...	2.6	...	2.2	...	...	...	1.5	...	7.6
1834	...	...	...	0.7	...	1.7	...	1.1	...	4.7	...	3.2	...	2.5	...	...	...	1.4	...	6.8
1835	...	...	...	0.7	...	2.2	...	1.5	...	4.8	...	4.3	...	2.6	...	...	...	1.8	...	10.6
1836	...	...	...	0.8	...	2.7	...	1.6	...	4.6	...	3.6	...	2.5	...	...	...	1.7	...	12.4
1837	...	...	...	0.9	...	2.1	...	1.6	...	5.0	...	3.6	...	3.0	...	...	...	2.0	...	4.7
1838	...	...	...	1.3	...	1.9	...	2.3	...	5.1	...	3.9	...	3.5	...	...	...	1.7	...	7.6
1839	...	...	...	1.7	...	3.0	...	2.3	...	5.4	...	4.7[70]	...	3.6	...	...	...	1.8	...	8.8
1840	...	...	...	2.1	...	2.8	...	2.4	...	5.6	...	5.2	...	3.4	...	...	...	1.6	...	5.3
1841	...	...	...	1.3	...	2.9	...	2.9	...	6.0	...	4.8	...	3.6	...	...	...	1.6	...	7.1
1842	...	...	...	1.0	...	2.3	...	3.2	...	6.6	...	4.4	...	3.6	...	...	...	1.9	...	3.5
1843	...	...	...	1.3	...	1.8	...	2.5	...	6.7	...	5.7	...	3.6	...	...	...	1.9	...	5.0
1844	...	...	...	0.8	...	3.0	...	2.7	...	6.7	...	6.9	...	3.1	...	...	...	2.1	...	7.9
1845	...	...	...	1.2	...	3.6	...	2.8	...	7.1	...	5.9	...	3.4	...	...	...	2.2	...	7.1
1846	...	...	...	1.5[71]	...	3.3	...	2.7	...	7.2	...	5.8	...	3.6	...	—	...	1.7	...	6.8
1847	...	0.2	...	1.6	...	3.2	...	2.6	...	6.8	...	4.8	...	3.0	...	0.1	...	1.8	...	11.0
1848	...	0.4	...	1.4	...	2.0	...	1.0	...	5.3	...	4.6	...	2.8	...	0.1	...	1.9	...	9.6
1849	...	1.4	...	2.0	...	2.3	...	2.0	...	6.1	...	6.2	...	3.5	...	0.1	...	1.6	...	12
1850	...	0.8	...	2.5	...	3.2	...	2.4	...	7.5	...	7.2	...	3.5	...	0.1	...	1.5	...	15
1851	...	0.5	...	2.6	...	3.8	...	2.0	...	7.7	...	7.0	...	3.5	...	0.2	...	1.3	...	14
1852	...	0.8	...	4.1	...	3.1	...	2.7	...	7.9	...	6.5	...	4.1	...	0.1	...	1.1	...	17
1853	...	0.6	...	14.3	...	4.9	...	2.6	...	8.2	...	7.3	...	4.5	...	0.2	...	1.2	...	24
1854	1.3	1.3	4.3	11.6	7.1	6.0	10	3.2	16	8.5	11	9.1	6.7	4.6	...	0.3	4.3	0.1	30	21
1855	1.1	0.7	4.5	6.0	4.7	2.9	9	6.0	16	9.9	13	9.9	6.5	4.6	...	0.2	0.5	—	26	17
1856	1.0	1.0	5.6	9.6	6.9	4.1	10	6.4	11	12	17	11	7.4	5.7	0.1	0.3	12	1.6	36	22
1857	1.6	1.3	5.8	11	6.4	4.3	12	6.2	14	13	19	12	7.2	6.4	0.2	0.4	13	3.1	34	19
1858	1.2	1.0	5.0	10	4.7	3.2	13	4.9	9	13	15	17	6.3	5.5	0.3	0.5	12	3.1	34	15
1859	1.6	1.0	5.5	11	5.5	3.6	17	4.8	11	12	15	20	6.7	5.4	0.3	0.6	14	4.0	34	23
1860	1.1	1.8	6.0	9	6.8	3.7	18	5.3	15	14	15	17	8.3	6.1	0.4	0.6	16	3.3	45	22
1861	1.5	1.4	6.4	10	8.7	3.7	18	8.9	14	13	22	16	7.7	6.4	0.5	0.9	13	3.0	49	9
1862	1.1	0.9	6.5	11	8.5	4.0	22	9.2	15	13	34	15	7.9	6.0	0.6	1.2	15	2.1	28	14
1863	1.2	1.3	6.4	11	8.2	4.8	24	8.7	14	14	48	20	8.7	6.3	0.7	2.0	12	2.7	20	15
1864	1.2	1.8	8.9	10	6.9	5.6	26	8.2	15	16	52	20	12.0	6.9	1.1	1.9	15	2.8	18	17

(Australia E, 1846: an alternative figure of 1.4 is also given.)

E2 External Trade (by value) with Main Trading Partners

UNITED KINGDOM (in million pounds)   1865–1899

	Argentina		Australia		Canada		France		Germany		India		Netherlands		New Zealand		Russia		U.S.A.	
	I	E	I	E	I	E	I	E	I	E	I	E	I	E	I	E	I	E	I	E
1865	1.0	2.0	9.0	12	6.4	4.7	32	9.1	17	18	37	18	12	8.1	1.3	1.6	17	2.9	22	21
1866	1.1	2.8	9.9	12	6.9	6.8	37	12	19	16	37	20	12	9.0	1.6	2.2	20	3.2	47	29
1867	0.9	2.8	11	8	6.8	5.9	34	12	19	21	26	22	11	9.4	1.7	1.5	22	3.9	41	22
1868	1.5	1.9	11	10	6.8	4.8	34	11	18	23	30	21	11	10.4	1.5	1.7	20	4.3	43	21
1869	1.3	2.3	11	12	7.7	5.2	34	11	18	23	33	18	13	10.8	1.6	1.9	17	6.5	43	25
1870	1.5	2.3	12	8	8.5	6.8	38	12	15	20	25	19	14	11.2	2.1	1.5	21	7.0	50	28
1871	2.0	2.5	12	9	9.3	8.3	30	18	19	27	31	18	14	14.1	2.5	1.4	24	6.6	61	34
1872	1.9	3.9	13	12	9.1	10.2	42	17	19	32	34	19	13	16.2	2.7	2.3	24	6.6	55	41
1873	2.6	3.7	14	14	11	8.6	43	17	20	27	30	21	13	16.7	3.2	3.4	21	9.0	72	34
1874	1.3	3.1	15	15	12	9.3	47	16	20	25	31	24	15	14.4	3.5	4.4	21	8.8	74	28
1875	1.4	2.4	17	16	10	9.0	47	15	22	23	30	24	15	13.1	3.5	3.9	21	8.1	70	22
1876	1.7	1.5	19	15	11	7.4	45	16	21	20	30	22	17	11.8	3.5	3.2	18	6.2	76	17
1877	1.7	2.1	18	16	12	7.6	46	14	26	20	31	25	20	9.6	3.7	3.3	22	4.2	78	16
1878	1.1	2.3	17	15	10	6.4	41	15	24	20	28	23	22	9.3	4.0	4.3	18	6.6	89	15
1879	0.8	2.1	17	13	10	5.4	39	15	22	19	25	21	22	9.4	4.5	3.6	16	7.6	92	20
1880	0.9	2.5	20	14	13	7.7	42	16	24	17	30	31	26	9.2	5.2	2.9	16	8.0	107	31
1881	0.6	3.3	22	18	11	8.4	40	17	24	17	33	29	23	8.9	5.1	3.7	14	6.2	103	30
1882	1.2	4.2	20	20	10	9.7	39	17	26	19	40	29	25	9.4	4.7	4.3	21	5.8	88	31
1883	0.9	4.9	20	20	12	9.2	39	18	28	19	39	32	25	9.5	5.8	3.9	21	5.0	89	27
1884	1.2	5.8	22	20	11	8.7	37	17	24	19	34	31	26	10.2	6.0	3.7	16	5.0	86	24
1885	1.9	4.7	18	21	10	7.2	36	15	23	16	32	29	25	8.9	5.1	3.9	18	4.2	87	22
1886	1.6	5.2	16	19	10	7.9	37	14	21	16	32	31	25	8.2	4.7	3.3	14	4.4	82	27
1887	2.2	6.2	18	17	11	8.1	37	14	25	16	31	31	25	8.2	5.7	3.1	16	4.2	83	30
1888	2.7	7.7	20	23	9	7.6	39	15	27	16	31	33	26	8.5	5.9	3.0	26	4.8	80	29
1889	2.0	10.7	20	20	12	8.1	46	15	27	19	36	31	27	9.7	6.8	3.2	27	5.3	96	30
1890	4.1	8.4	21	20	12	7.2	45	17	26	19	33	34	26	10.1	8.3	3.3	24	5.8	97	32
1891	3.5	4.2	23	22	13	7.2	45	16	27	19	32	31	27	9.5	8.2	3.4	24	5.4	104	28
1892	4.5	5.7	23	16	15	7.4	44	15	26	18	31	28	29	8.8	7.8	3.5	15	5.4	108	27
1893	4.8	5.5	22	12	13	7.2	44	13	26	18	26	29	29	9.2	8.1	3.3	19	6.4	92	24
1894	6.2	4.5	24	13	13	6.3	44	14	27	18	28	29	28	8.8	8.3	3.0	24	6.9	90	19
1895	9.1	5.4	25	14	13	5.8	48	14	27	21	26	25	28	7.4	8.4	3.1	25	7.0	87	28
1896	9.0	6.6	21	18	16	5.5	50	14	28	22	25	30	29	8.3	8.1	4.0	23	7.2	106	20
1897	5.8	4.8	21	17	20	6.2	53	14	26	22	25	27	29	8.9	8.6	4.0	22	7.5	113	21
1898	7.8	5.6	20	17	21	7.3	51	14	29	23	28	30	29	8.6	9.0	4.0	20	9.2	126	15
1899	11	6.2	24	18	21	8.1	53	15	30	26	28	31	31	9.4	9.7	4.5	19	11.7	120	18

E2 External Trade (by value) with Main Trading Partners

UNITED KINGDOM (in million pounds)

1900-1934

Year	Argentina I	Argentina E	Australia I	Australia E	Canada I	Canada E	France I	France E	Germany I	Germany E	India I	India E	Netherlands I	Netherlands E	New Zealand I	New Zealand E	Russia/U.S.S.R. I	Russia/U.S.S.R. E	U.S.A. I	U.S.A. E
1900	13	7.1	24	22	22	8.1	54	20	31	28	27	30	31	10.9	12	5.5	22	11.0	139	20
1901	12	6.8	24	21	20	11	51	17	32	24	27	35	33	9.1	11	5.6	22	8.7	141	18
1902	14	5.9	20	20	24	12	51	16	34	23	29	33	35	8.4	11	5.7	26	8.6	127	24
1903	19	8.0	17	16	27	11	49	16	35	24	32	35	35	8.7	14	6.4	31	9.1	122	23
1904	23	11	24	17	23	11	51	15	34	25	37	41	35	8.2	13	6.3	31	8.2	119	20
1905	25[72]	13[72]	27[72]	17[72]	26[72]	12[72]	53[72]	16[72]	36[72]	30[72]	36[72]	43[72]	36[72]	10[72]	13[72]	6.4[72]	33[72]	8.2[72]	116[72]	24[72]
1905	25	13	27	17	26	12	47	16	54	30	36	43	15	10	13	6.4	35	8.2	115	24
1906	24	19	29	20	29	14	47	20	56	34	38	45	16	12	16	7.4	32	8.9	131	28
1907	27	18	34	24	26	18	16	23	57	41	44	52	16	14	18	8.7	33	11	134	31
1908	36	16	29	23	25	13	42	22	55	33	30	49	17	12	15	8.8	30	13	124	21
1909	33	19	33	24	26	16	44	21	58	32	35	44	17	12	18	7.4	38	11	118	30
1910	29	19	39	28	26	21	44	23	62	37	43	46	19	13	21	8.7	44	12	118	31
1911	27	19	39	31	25	20	42	24	65	39	45	52	19	13	18	9.8	43	14	123	28
1912	41	21	36	35	28	24	46	26	70	40	52	58	21	14	20	10.4	41	14	135	30
1913	43	23	38	35	32	25	46	29	80	41	48	70	24	15	20	10.8	40	18	142	29
1914	37	15	37	34	32	18	38	26	47	23	43	63	24	13	23	9.4	28	14	139	34
1915	64	12	45	29	42	14	31	70	– –	...	62	46	23	18	30	9.4	21	13	238	26
1916	52	14	36	36	61	19	27	93	– –	– –	72	53	22	24	32	12.1	18	25	292	33
1917	48	13	64	22	85	17	23	112	– –	– –	67	60	20	21	29	7.0	18	49	376	33
1918	63	18	45	26	125	15	35	131	– –	– –	89	49	8	15	25	7.7	7	0.3	515	23
1919	82	21	111	26	118	17	49	147	1	15	108	71	22	34	53	9.6	16	13	542	34
1920	128	43	112	63	97	44	76	136	30	22	96	181	39	48	48	27	34	12	563	77
1921	68	28	68	46	64	20	53	44	21	18	44	109	39	27	49	15	3	2.2	275	44
1922	57[73]	23	65[73]	60	57[73]	26[73]	49[73]	49	27[73]	32[73]	48[73]	92	34[73]	35	49[73]	16	8	3.6	222[73]	56[73]
1923	65[73]	28[73]	49[73]	58[73]	56[73]	28[73]	59[73]	49[73]	35[73]	43[73]	67[73]	86[73]	37[73]	30[73]	43[73]	21[73]	9[73]	2.5[73]	211[73]	60[73]
1924	79	27	59	61	68	30	67	42	37	43	79	91	43	25	47	20	20	3.9	241	54
1925	69	29	73	60	73	29	65	31	48	44	80	86	46	25	51	23	25	6.2	245	52
1926	68	23	61	61	66	27	59	20	73	26	58	82	50	18	47	21	24	5.9	229	49
1927	77	27	53	61	57	30	63	24	60	42	66	85	45	21	47	20	21	4.5	200	45
1928	77	31	54	56	59	36	61	25	64	41	65	84	43	22	47	19	22	2.7	188	47
1929	82	29	56	54	48	36	57	32	69	37	63	78	42	22	48	21	27	3.7	196	46
1930	57	25	46	32	40	30	49	30	66	27	51	53	40	19	45	18	34	6.8	154	29
1931	53	15	46	15	35	21	41	23	64	18	37	32	35	14	38	11	32	7.3	104	18
1932	51	11	46	20	45	17	19	18	31	15	32	34	22	12	37	10	20	9.2	84	15
1933	42	13	49	21	48	18	19	18	30	15	37	33	19	12	37	10	18	3.3	76	10
1934	47	15	50	26	53	21	19	17	31	14	42	37	21	12	40	11	17	3.6	82	18

E2 External Trade (by value) with Main Trading Partners

UNITED KINGDOM (in million pounds)

1935–1964

	Argentina		Australia		Canada		France		Germany		India		Netherlands		New Zealand		Russia/U.S.S.R.		U.S.A.	
	I	E	I	E	I	E	I	E	I	E	I	E	I	E	I	E	I	E	I	E
1935	44	15	54	29	58	22	22	17	32	20	41	38	23	12	3.5	88	23	3.5	93	28
1936	45	15	61	32	77	24	26	18	35	21	52	34	25	12	44	17	19	3.1	114	31
1937	60	20	72	38	92	29	26	21	39	23	65	39	32	15	50	20	29	3.1	118	21
1938	39	19	72	38	81	24	24	15	32	22	56[74] / 50	36[74] / 34	29	13	47	19	20[75] / 29	6.5[75] / 11		
1939	47	20	62	32	82	23	27	14	19	12	49	30	30	14	42	16	17	8	118	28
1940	61	18	97	46	153	33	15	16			73	33	12	6	56	17	2	1	276	33
1941	52	16	46	38	194	39	–	–			57	32	–	–	56	15	1	23	409	32
1942	49	13	40	64	178	33	–	–			60	22	–	–	60	25	3	67	536	26
1943	58	10	33	44	285	32	–	–			60	18	–	–	50	19	2	54	1,104	20
1944	81	4	54	51	390	27	–	7			70	24	–	–	57	17	2	50	1,391	19
1945	48	6	53	50	323	28	2	27	2	3	68	33	1	6	63	15	4	28	610	19
1946	67	21	67	55	201	34	14	34	6	18	69	80	12	31	74	28	5	10	230	36
1947	131	35	97	72	239	45	31	24	19	21	95	92	26	31	90	43	8	12	297	48
1948	122	53	169	145	223	73	46	34	30	25	108[76] / 96	114[76] / 96	44	45	109	53	27	5	183	66
1949	77	51	213	189	225	80	75	33	38	27	99	117	65	53	117	65	16	9	222	57
1950	96	39	220	256	180	126	110	44	42	44	98	97	86	72	134	87	34	12	211	113
1951	86	28	254	324	261	137	135	55	78[2] / 75	50[2] / 50	153	115	128	74	165	111	60	4	380	137
1952	53	21	227	221	320	130	87	62	90	51	115	113	102	71	166	115	58	4	315	146
1953	99	15	294	213	306	157	82	66	70	59	113	115	89	94	170	100	40	3	253	159
1954	81	23	236	278	273	132	97	64	78	71	148	115	110	100	176	126	42	10	282	150
1955	87	24	264	284	344	141	137	72	91	77	159	130	133	106	180	139	63	23	420	183
1956	92	17	236	240	348	178	112	89	110	92	141	168	137	119	197	127	55	26	408	243
1957	108	33	248	236	320	195	110	88	125	105	158	176	132	118	183	140	71	37	483	244
1958	104	33	199	235	309	188	101	72	136	123	139	161	159	98	161	128	60	24	352	273
1959	106	40	223	223	312	208	104	77	144	142	143	171	160	113	183	98	63	27	371	361
1960	98	42	197	260	375	215	132	88	182	163	149	151	180	116	183	121	75	37	566	326
1961	75	51	174	201	349	222	143	112	194	171	145	152	173	138	160	124	85	43	484	280
1962	93	47	185	228	349	188	131	138	194	199	136	117	197	151	169	107	84	42	476	327
1963	89	25	206	236	369	173	154	181	208	213	141	137	209	168	173	115	91	55	498	340
1964	78	28	250	256	452	187	184	185	266	219	141	127	235	192	208	117	90	38	639	356

E2 External Trade (by value) with Main Trading Partners

UNITED KINGDOM (in million pounds)   1965–1997

	Argentina		Australia		Canada		France		Germany		India		Netherlands		New Zealand		Russia/U.S.S.R.		U.S.A.	
	I	E	I	E	I	E	I	E	I	E	I	E	I	E	I	E	I	E	I	E
1965	71	27	219	281	458	201	191	177	265	255	128	114	271	193	208	125	119	47	672	498
1966	71	23	208	255	425	215	212	197	302	253	119	95	291	196	187	126	125	50	723	625
1967	72	25	174	254	456	213	255	204	339	247	126	82	329	194	186	99	123	63	812	615
1968	52	34	211	317	513	259	312	235	436	323	135	72	393	242	197	103	158	103	1,064	879
1969	79	47[79] / 47	236	315[79] / 323	507	299[79] / 311	325	290[79] / 313	467	362[79] / 419	107	61[79] / 67	408	278[79] / 298	216	120[79] / 122	196	96[79] / 96	1,133	866[79] / 912
1970	66	44	260	346	682	288	368	339	549	505	105	73	459	377	203	129	211	102	1,174	945
1971	57	57	278	365	642	350	445	394	648	537	111	140	508	409	228	146	200	89	1,113	1,083
1972	77	51	284	319	607	380	604	512	841	591	112	141	614	451	252	147	117	90	1,188	1,209
1973	106	43	343	406	741	414	979	679	1,352	792	148	133	912	604	276	167	164	97	1,641	1,516
1974	93	50	313	607	940	495	1,346	917	1,909	1,033	203	129	1,640	989	243	259	225	110	2,270	1,785
1975	53	68	290	639	864	544	1,624	1,166	2,008	1,310	235	166	1,873	1,121	322	257	236	211	2,362	1,810
1976	92	64	413	701	1,169	630	2,093	1,749	2,773	1,856	356	208	2,432	1,511	331	256	460	241	3,092	2,454
1977	121	130	387	763	1,217	702	2,672	2,165	3,591	2,514	384	278	2,495	2,153	384	290	545	347	3,728	3,065
1978	153	115	370	854	1,134	737	3,198	2,496	4,498	3,086	322	348	2,518	2,251	434	268	489	423	4,149	3,485
1979	144	128	490	841	1,272	767	4,016	3,027	5,778	4,218	365	456	3,443	3,061	416	312	492	416	4,884	4,003
1980	116	173	499	816	1,412	752	3,849	3,595	5,067	5,654	318	529	3,398	3,839	409	251	422	449	6,019	4,554
1981	137	161	395	864	1,509	845	3,979	3,626	5,941	5,516	294	639	3,895	4,019	427	235	427	408	6,048	6,258
1982	58	37	493	1,041	1,436	852	4,267	4,492	7,406	5,412	379	805	4,512	4,643	539	322	645	356	6,624	7,475
1983	- -	4	564	941	1,523	974	5,042	5,651	9,666	6,069	367	805	5,104	5,441	486	286	730	445	7,497	8,486
1984	-	5	640	1,189	1,618	1,184	5,886	6,996	11,088	7,484	571	781	6,115	6,127	483	368	855	735	8,368	10,159
1985	2	4	741	1,373	1,653	1,694	6,636	7,771	12,655	8,966	434	895	6,553	7,345	533	397	727	536	9,925	11,519
1986	29	10	643	1,228	1,470	1,698	7,387	6,210	14,138	8,549	441	941	6,623	5,442	456	343	702	542	8,471	10,370
1987	65	10	673	1,224	1,569	1,938	8,382	7,781	15,783	9,404	537	1,090	7,148	5,856	487	378	875	492	9,135	11,013
1988	66	13	742	1,377	2,042	2,038	9,399	8,410	17,675	9,526	566	1,113	8,282	5,679	443	300	725	512	10,768	10,715
1989	98	14	866	1,712	2,285	2,168	10,885	9,636	20,257	11,367	702	1,383	9,661	6,738	437	400	833	681	13,521	12,185
1990	144	36	1,036	1,646	2,258	1,902	11,844	10,933	20,151	13,272	800	1,264	10,559	7,548	485	440	918	606	14,357	12,999
1991	135	70	867	1,356	1,919	1,701	11,114	11,856	17,871	14,713	777	1,017	10,115	8,278	391	260	901	355	13,705	11,347
1992	125	119	1,014	1,377	1,898	1,584	12,299	11,576	19,153	15,337	864	946	9,969	8,573	429	263	⋯	⋯	13,715	12,231
1993	141	179	997	1,600	1,854	1,842	13,124	11,690	19,454	15,472	1,090	1,150	8,778	7,804	496	332	822[101]	551[101]	16,329	15,350
										Million US$ Dollars										
1994	⋯	⋯	1,629.7	2,935.9	2,882.9	2,939.0	22,612.1	20,139.7	32,773.4	25,810.7	1,975.6	2,011.3	14,981.4	14,296.9	826.8	⋯	1,233.5	1,085.1	27,290.2	26,486.3
1995	⋯	⋯	1,753.1	3,348.1	3,756.9	2,859.0	25,038.9	23,390.2	40,247.3	31,141.1	2,266.3	2,655.8	17,628.9	18,867.5	910.2	⋯	1,524.9	1,373.7	32,129.4	29,071.8
1996	⋯	⋯	2,023.3	3,852.0	3,878.0	3,084.8	26,533.2	25,904.4	40,827.6	31,573.9	2,515.0	2,666.2	18,744.7	20,308.6	986.6	⋯	1,990.2	1,576.7	36,088.8	31,472.7
1997	⋯	⋯	2,246.4	4,021.4	4,183.8	3,531.6	28,331.0	26,285.8	41,151.0	32,585.7	2,657.7	2,580.6	19,932.4	22,000.2	946.4	⋯	2,419.2	2,019.0	41,156.5	35,007.6

E2 External Trade (by value) with Main Trading Partners

YUGOSLAVIA (in million dinars)

1920–1954

	Austria		Czechoslovakia		Germany		East Germany		West Germany		Italy		Russia		U.K.		U.S.A.	
	I	E	I	E	I	E	I	E	I	E	I	E	I	E	I	E	I	E
1920	714	563	322	68	50	99					1,271	358	2	...	244	3	82	5
1921	1,161	882	843	101	174	397					864	633	—	—	246	18	99	5
1922	1,861	848	1,278	299	462	311					1,005	1,126	1	—	459	70	225	17
1923	2,238	2,328	1,538	629	724	339					1,488	2,424	2	—	823	172	306	29
1924	1,626	2,333	1,650	944	682	389					1,688	2,757	8	1	874	132	321	51
1925	1,604	1,652	1,559	834	866	637					1,644	2,249	9	—	713	86	342	77
1926	1,533	1,610	1,427	939	918	724					1,054	1,960	9	6	439	68	309	50
1927	1,424	1,449	1,399	727	899	679					940	1,590	2	11	511	84	255	48
1928	1,355	1,154	1,402	580	1,067	779					939	1,680	3	4	447	102	385	60
1929	1,324	1,238	1,329	426	1,188	675					823	1,971	10	5	426	107	360	126
1930	1,171	1,199	1,225	556	1,221	791					783	1,919	8	—	412	104	285	58
1931	730	727	872	744	925	543					494	1,199	2	—	316	96	200	49
1932	384	676	447	403	506	345					362	705	2	5	213	65	127	29
1933	463	732	349	366	379	471					459	726	4	—	280	90	148	64
1934	442	634	418	437	497	598					555	798	6	2	331	181	230	157
1935	441	577	517	540	598	752					371	672	13	—	373	212	229	225
1936	420	640	626	540	1,088	1,039					102	137	5	—	347	432	260	214
1937	538	848	580	493	1,695	1,361					430	587	6	—	409	465	312	291
1938	342	306	530	398	1,618	1,814					445	324	3	—	431	485	299	256
1939	450	520	314	801	1,818	1,242					557	584	3	3	242	367	248	281
1946	607	438	1,827	4,324			302	17	—	—	784	920	2,418	7,022	43	168	222	152
1947	1,556	2,498	8,964	9,560			2,099	1,383	—	—	3,988	7,152	11,274	8,514	2,767	1,325	2,020	1,045
1948	4,420	5,595	16,103	13,962			3,938	1,576	—	—	9,229	7,879	10,223	13,640	4,361	6,177	3,217	2,363
1949	7,635	6,741	5,647	2,616			1,179	204	6,548	3,372	9,472	6,207	1,167	2,789	9,326	13,340	9,263	5,049
1950	5,242	4,788	—	—			—	—	11,909	5,960	6,148	5,097	—	—	5,026	8,779	14,591	6,443
1951	4,549	4,959	—	—			—	—	13,434	9,222	9,784	5,951	—	—	9,187	10,155	43,968	8,080
1952	7,696	7,819	—	—			—	—	22,678	17,493	9,407	10,778	—	—	7,624	10,437	21,609	10,843
1953	6,273	3,594	332	866			4,089	...	20,701	9,366	8,470	8,756	318	439	7,382	6,550	40,754	7,801
1954	6,562	5,941					67	275	17,172	14,204	7,107	10,516			7,129	6,814	28,446	6,869

E2 External Trade (by value) with Main Trading Partners

YUGOSLAVIA (in million dinars to 1979, thousand million dinars subsequently)   1955–1997

Year	Austria I	Austria E	Czechoslovakia I	Czechoslovakia E	East Germany I	East Germany E	West Germany I	West Germany E	Italy I	Italy E	Russia I	Russia E	U.K. I	U.K. E	U.S.A. I	U.S.A. E
1955	5,849	4,525	2,197	2,177	662	622	16,611	10,193	12,892	11,547	4,333	5,385	6,432	6,069	43,250	8,311
1956	5,804	5,179	3,616	2,455	950	1,308	14,216	14,746	12,309	13,712	21,139	12,669	9,787	5,867	38,767	8,223
1957	7,517	5,748	5,685	2,584	2,278	3,122	22,640	15,755	20,279	16,091	20,709	14,675	12,560	7,162	52,121	10,022
1958	7,608	5,661	8,213	5,853	7,881	7,907	24,065	12,529	19,189	16,173	17,345	10,922	10,839	10,366	40,198	9,889
1959	7,898	6,289	6,946	4,918	8,661	8,000	28,932	13,437	…	17,316	17,288	14,154	10,637	10,216	42,004	9,344
1960	11,237	8,990	7,874	7,724	11,207	13,915	36,973	15,230	28,545	22,431	17,081	15,803	13,624	12,988	26,549	11,589
1961	9,730	7,680	5,943	5,067	11,286	9,052	42,824	17,366	39,815	21,103	9,601	15,269	13,893	14,347	54,357	10,961
1962	9,619	8,060	7,728	6,404	10,906	10,601	29,933	21,360	31,378	28,902	17,742	12,988	14,573	14,768	54,862	15,669
1963	9,517	8,502	12,916	6,958	14,775	11,363	29,400	24,444	33,887	47,499	21,860	25,612	15,182	13,039	55,833	13,893
1964	10,435[77]	9,222[77]	24,662[77]	13,453[77]	21,805[77]	18,952[77]	34,002[77]	24,124[77]	52,341[77]	39,581[77]	30,034[77]	34,840[77]	20,609[77]	16,576[77]	51,908[77]	15,397[77]
1965	430	355	882	887	789	951	1,463	1,195	1,719	1,803	1,349	2,345	780	453	2,376	776
1966	471	559	1,165	845	1,099	905	1,934	1,423	2,106	2,163	1,822	2,422	1,098	549	2,498	936
1967	881	723	1,420	752	1,033	946	4,299	1,443	3,421	3,002	2,458	3,289	1,367	688	1,860	1,189
1968	1,420	757	1,752	932	1,164	940	5,450	2,061	4,567	3,858	3,200	3,528	1,481	1,032	1,535	1,518
1969	1,733	790	2,038	1,068	1,320	748	6,605	2,752	5,434	…	2,859	3,509	2,030	1,444	1,572	1,586
1970	2,580	860	2,576	1,516	1,262	868	9,642	3,358	6,426	4,328	3,285	4,106	3,036	1,644	2,723	1,521
1971	2,594	792	2,603	1,963	1,559	1,168	10,480	3,576	6,737	3,843	4,782	4,558	3,342	1,923	3,343	1,854
1972	2,443	1,008	2,556	2,179	1,704	1,383	10,271	4,485	6,800	5,237	4,811	5,600	2,788	1,818	3,374	2,555
1973	3,572	1,332	3,182	2,152	2,445	1,391	14,558	5,448	9,022	7,926	6,915	6,946	2,801	1,419	3,174	3,953
1974	6,087	1,624	5,035	3,486	2,932	2,303	23,126	6,181	15,141	7,288	12,781	11,422	3,882	1,172	6,022	5,367
1975	5,384	1,273	5,409	4,154	3,798	3,217	24,436	5,369	14,772	6,321	13,712	17,211	4,036	1,070	7,096	4,493
1976	4,219	1,711	5,558	3,923	3,716	3,281	20,956	7,242	12,927	10,132	17,034	19,411	5,142	1,005	6,256	6,001
1977	4,603	1,615	6,064	3,524	5,287	3,704	26,715	6,637	17,500	11,288	22,117	19,353	5,998	1,147	9,273	5,046
1978	6,192	1,926	6,755	4,489	4,752	4,425	32,869	8,621	15,086	9,691	25,085	25,440	6,181	973	11,221	6,771
1979	10,198	3,214	9,199	6,266	6,363	4,981	54,863	14,040	21,768	13,606	34,065	26,618	7,582	1,794	20,129	7,086
thousand million dinars																
1980	14.7	5.5	14.7	12.0	9.5	9.0	68.3	21.2	30.5	22.7	73.7	68.0	10.8	2.5	27.7	10.7
1981	15.1	6.3	17.9	14.9	12.6	10.2	66.7	23.7	35.2	27.6	81.0	99.5	12.4	2.8	26.1	10.6
1982	21.4	8.3	24.5	26.2	17.2	14.8	77.7	30.1	42.8	32.7	11.4	14.3	19.1	3.9	35.4	13.0
1983	27.2	13.6	43.3	41.0	26.6	24.1	10.3	51.2	62.1	51.1	156	171	15.7	9.8	49.1	21.9
1984	51.7	36.5	81.9	68.8	47.4	50.2	197	111	120	117	245	349	28.1	20.4	77.4	53.9
1985	71.8	48.4	107	92.5	69.7	56.5	295	162	191	181	367	631	43.2	33.3	144	85.9
1986	105	59.5	153	113	101	87.5	454	235	256	240	496	826	67.1	50.1	178	150
1987	228	170	260	199	166	166	938	559	544	638	984	1,125	128	109	330	336
1988	824	591	626	638	447	455	3,036	1,198	1,852	2,592	2,417	3,088	385	432	924	973
Million Dinars																
1989	1,994	1,284	1,533	1,307	1,307	942	7,815	4,748	4,896	6,257	6,734	8,983	816	1,139	2,223	1,931
1990	10,784	5,887	5,096	4,557	2,524	2,116	33,761	22,767	24,107	25,101	24,214	26,016	4,254	3,391	8,522	7,155
1991[102]	351	222	247	101			1,868	1,838	972	1,092	1,173[103]	1,373[103]	286	181	380	341
1992[102]	260	109	194	39			921	654	588	480	919[103]	848[103]	171	79	227	159
Million US$ Dollars																
1993[102]	…	…					…	…	…	…	…	…	…	…	…	…
1994[102]	…	…					…	…	…	…	…	…	…	…	…	…
1995[102]	164.5	68.9					578.8	417.0	370.3	302.0	580.8	538.2	106.5	49.7	145.5	100.2
1996[102]	123.5	26.7					523.8	146.4	434.6	180.6	224.6	156.4	98.0	27.5	119.4	33.1
1997[102]	156.2	37.7					644.5	218.0	482.1	272.4	453.6	176.5	92.0	71.8	133.6	15.6

(From 1990 the West Germany columns are headed **Germany**.)

E2 External Trade (by value) with Main Trading Partners

NOTES

1. SOURCES:- Finland to 1882 (plus trade with Sweden to 1885 and with the U.S.A. to 1891); the French statistics for 1842 (together with statistics of trade with Algeria in 1868 and 1871); the German statistics for 1940–49; the Polish statistics for 1951–54; and the Swedish statistics for 1832–41 were supplied by their respective central statistical offices, or the Direction Nationale des Statistiques de Commerce Exterieur in the case of France. Data for Bulgaria in 1939–46 were kindly supplied by Prof. Kaser's group, and are derived from P. Shapkerev, *Spisanie na Bulgarskoto ikonomichksko Dryzhestvo* 9–19 (1946). All other statistics are taken from the official publications noted on page xv with gaps filled from the League of Nations, *International Trade Statistics*, and the United Nations, *Yearbook of International Trade*.
2. In this table no attention is drawn to the changes of boundary in the trading partners of each country shown. (see page ix).
3. Except as indicated in footnotes, statistics are of merchandise trade only, and are of 'special' rather than 'general' trade—i.e. imports for home consumption, and exports of home origin plus re-exports of commodities originally entered for home consumption.
4. Except as indicated in footnotes, statistics are of countries of first or last consignment.

FOOTNOTES

1. Including Finland to 1913.
2. Subsequently West Germany only.
3. Subsequent statistics are of countries of origin or consumption.
4. From 1 May 1922 to 31 August 1940 and since 1 May 1945 the statistics are for the Belgium—Luxembourg customs area. Gold movements are included.
5. May–December only.
6. Subsequently excludes Burma.
7. Gold movements are included to 1930. The statistics for 1946 are for the first 9 months only and are in the pre-war currency, a new lev being introduced in 1947.
8. Including Austria from 1938 to 1946.
9. For 1924–32 the statistics relate to European Russia only.
10. Eire is included with the U.K. to 1931.
11. Strictly speaking, the statistics up to 1937 (1st line) are not of 'special' trade, but of 'general' imports less re-exports (at import value), and 'general' exports less re-exports (at export value).
12. Including Austria from July 1938 to May 1945, and the Protectorate of Bohemia, Moravia, and Silesia in 1942–44.
13. Subsequently 'general' trade, and countries of origin or consumption.
14. Statistics of Finnish trade with Russia are available back to 1812 as follows (in million marks):-

	Imports	Exports		Imports	Exports		Imports	Exports
1812	0.4	0.4	1817	2.9	0.7	1822	2.2	1.4
1813	2.8	0.4	1818	3.1	0.9	1823	1.7	1.5
1814	2.4	0.4	1819	3.6	0.9	1824	2.3	1.9
1815	1.4	0.4	1820	1.5	1.1	1825	3.3	1.9
1816	2.1	0.5	1821	1.4	1.3	1826	3.2	2.0

15. Figures to 1891 relate to the American continent, not the U.S.A.
16. Eire is included with the U.K. to 1933.
17. Figures to 1855 (1st line) are in officially fixed values.
18. Subsequently Belgium—Luxembourg.
19. Previously including Cyprus, Gibraltar, and Malta.
20. From 1948 to July 1959 Saarland is included as part of France.
21. Including Norway to 1884 (1st line).
22. The Hanse towns were treated as foreign to 1888, and the free port areas to March 1906. From this last date statistics relate to countries of origin or consumption (and consignment only if this is unknown).
23. Including Algeria and Tunisia to 1897 (1st line).
24. Including Finland to 1897 (1st line).
25. Porto Rico is included from 1904, and the Panama Canal Zone from 1906, to 1913.
26. Figures for 1923 are in post-inflation values.
27. Eire is included with the U.K. to 1924.
28. Ethiopia and Libya are included in 1937–39.
29. Austria was part of Germany in 1938–43.
30. Subsequently including the Baltic States.
31. Saarland was incorporated in West Germany from 6 July 1959. Whilst it had been part of the French customs area from 1948, trade between West Germany and Saarland is not here included with trade with France.
32. Trade was expressed in rubels to 1959, but the statistics have been converted on the basis of 1 rubel = 1.0502 valuta marks to 1957 and 4.6671 valuta marks for 1958–9.
33. Including West Berlin.
34. Excluding the value of currants.
35. The figures for 1947 are in thousands of U.S. dollars.
36. The original statistics were given in gold crowns up to 1924, were converted into paper crowns by the Hungarian statistical office retrospectively, and are here converted further into pengos.
37. Imports are valued f.o.b. from 1955.
38. Venetia is included as part of Italy from 1867.
39. Algeria is included with France for 1871–77.
40. Gibraltar and Malta are included with the U.K. to 1877, and British Asian possessions are included for 1871–77.
41. Transit trade is included in 1877 and probably earlier. It is excluded subsequently, but there are alterations in definition affecting the composition of 'special' trade in 1897, 1907, and 1930.

E2 External Trade (by value) with Main Trading Partners

[42] Canada is included with the U.S.A. for 1880-96.

[43] Austria is included with Germany for 1938-45.

[44] Statistics relate to trade with the Zollverein to 1858, but with Prussia only from 1859 to 1879 (1st line)

[45] Including Newfoundland throughout.

[46] U.K. up to 1906 and from 1932 onwards; Great Britain for 1907-31.

[47] Direct in-transit trade for Sweden is included in both imports and exports to 1906, and exports of transit goods from Sweden are included in other countries.

[48] For 1909-34 countries of purchase or sale.

[49] Statistics are of 'general' trade to 1938 and from 1959 onwards.

[50] Subsequently including the Faroë Islands and Greenland.

[51] Subsequently including Hawaii.

[52] Countries of origin or consumption.

[53] Gold movements are included up to 1927. In the case of Switzerland, gold other than for banking purposes continued to be included until 1935 (for exports) and 1943 (for imports).

[54] Subsequently 'general' trade, with both imports and exports valued f.o.b.

[55] Exclusive of the value of coal sent under special agreement.

[56] Figures to 1910 are by countries of origin and first destination (and consignment only if these are unknown). For 1911-37 they are by countries of purchase or sale. From 1938 they are by countries or origin or consumption, though there is apparently no break between 1937 and 1938. The Azores and Madeira are included as part of Portugal. The statistics for 1917 and 1918, supplied by the National Institute of Statistics, include re-exports, as do those for the colonies for 1940-46.

[57] Gold movements are included to 1883.

[58] Figures to 1890 (1st line) are for trade over the European frontier only. Statistics to 1840 are in paper rubels, and from 1847 to 1913 in silver or gold rubels. All figures for the Soviet period are in millions of new (1961) rubels.

[59] The figures for 1922 are for the 9 months to 30 September. Figures for 1923-28 are for years ended 30 September. Statistics for the last quarter of 1928 have been omitted.

[60] Including Ceuta and Melilla and the Canary Islands from 1951. Prior to 1888 transit trade cannot be excluded. Gold movements are included.

[61] Figures to 1853 exclude tobacco.

[62] Values to 1959 are in gold pesetas, which in terms of the official exchange rate of that year were equal to about 20 paper pesetas.

[63] A revaluation of exports in 1894 revealed overestimation previously.

[64] Exports to Norway are incomplete for 1898-1901.

[65] Austria is included with Germany for 1938-44.

[66] Iceland is included with Denmark to 1947 (1st line).

[67] The Faroe Islands are included with Denmark to 1954 (1st line).

[68] Re-exports (though not direct transit trade) are subsequently included in both imports and exports.

[69] Statistics of exports to the U.S.A. are available back to 1805 as follows (in million pounds):-

1805	11.0	1811	1.8	1817	6.9	1822	6.9
1806	12.4	1812	...	1818	9.5	1823	5.5
1807	11.8	1813	...	1819	4.9	1824	6.1
1808	5.2	1814	—	1820	3.9	1825	7.0
1809	7.3	1815	13.3	1821	6.2	1826	4.7
1810	10.9	1816	9.6				

[70] Ceylon is included with India to 1839.

[71] Previously all British possessions in the Pacific.

[72] Previously countries of purchase or sale.

[73] Southern Ireland is treated as foreign from 1 April 1923.

[74] Burma is included with India to 1938 (1st line).

[75] The Baltic states are included with Russia from 1938 (2nd line)

[76] Subsequently excluding Pakistan.

[77] Subsequent figures are in million new dinars, and there was also a change in the system of valuation.

[78] Subsequently countries of origin or destination instead of by the domicile of the contractor.

[79] Subsequently including re-exports.

[80] Statistics are of country of sale or purchase to 1976, country of origin or final destination in 1977-79, and country of consignment subsequently.

[81] Subsequently including West Berlin

[82] Former colonies in Africa only from 1980 (2nd line).

[83] Czech Republic. Slovakia = 3.1(I); 4.1 (E).

Slovakia (Million US$ Dollars)		
	Imports	Exports
1994	362.8	395.3
1995	521.0	552.7
1996	617.0	731.0

[84] Yugoslavia only.

	1992		1993	
	I	E	I	E
Slovenia	3.0	5.6	3.4	4.1
Croatia		2.0		2.8
Macedonia		.3		.5

E2   External Trade (by value) with Main Trading Partners

[85]   Russian Federation.
[86]   Czech Republic. Slovakia = 119 (I);   97 (E).

	Slovakia (Million US$ Dollars)				
	Import	Export		Import	Export
1994	9.9	...	1996	19.1	...
1995	18.9	...	1997	20.9	...

[87]   Russian Federation. Ex-U.S.S.R.

	1992		1993			1992		1993	
	I	E	I	E		I	E	I	E
Armenia	3	2	7	33	Latvia	25	30	120	61
Belarus	340	436	477	568	Lithuania	47	38	208	156
Georgia	9	13	76	289	Moldova	304	207	444	324
Estonia	9	15	45	40	Ukraine	5,120	3,358	6,974	3,887

[88]   Czech Republic.

	Austria		Hungary		Slovakia (Million US$ Dollars) Poland		Russia		U.K.	
	I	E	I	E	I	E	I	E	I	E
1994	381.5	351.4	110.8	365.7	157.5	189.3	1,194.7	277.6	105.7	85.6
1995	447.7	425.9	193.2	390.9	243.3	378.0	1,456.0	330.8	148.2	112.4
1996	509.4	533.9	217.0	403.3	269.5	426.9	1,933.1	307.8	203.2	135.3
1997	498.6	629.0	225.5	412.2	286.0	484.0	1,596.7	328.4	256.1	144.6

[89]   Russian Federation.
[90]   Russia. Estonia = 1993 761 (I);   1,883 (E).
[91]   Russian Federation.
[92]   Former U.S.S.R.
[93]   Former U.S.S.R.
[94]   Czech Republic. Slovakia = 37.5 (I),   15.2 (E)

	Slovakia (Million US$ Dollars)				
	Import	Export		Import	Export
1994	355.6	143.6	1996	382.2	251.0
1995	369.7	213.2	1997	399.6	241.7

[95]   Russia. Ukraine = 32.1 (I);   24.2 (E).
[96]   Former U.S.S.R.
[97]   Czech Republic : Slovakia = 2, 946 (I);   2955 (E)

	Slovakia (Million US$ Dollars)				
	Import	Export		Import	Export
1994	161.5	166.7	1996	380.8	279.4
1995	185.3	169.2	1997	432.5	280.0

[98]   Russian Federation : Ukraine = 1992   2,252 (I);   2,554 (E)   1993   3,615 (I);   3,381 (E).
[99]   Czech Republic. Slovakia = 23 (I);   6 (E).

	Slovakia (Million US$ Dollars)				
	Import	Export		Import	Export
1994	31.8	...	1996	59.1	...
1995	48.6	...	1997	72.2	...

[100]   Russian Federation.

	1992		1993			1992		1993	
	I	E	I	E		I	E	I	E
Belarus	4	2	10	2	Georgia	1	1	—	2
Latvia	1	1	1	1	Kazakhstan	4	5	7	11
Lithuania	1	—	4	1	Tajiristan	—	1	—	2
Moldova	121	72	87	94	Turkmenistan	3	3	7	7
Ukraine	148	104	133	105	Uzbekistan	2	7	2	6
Azerbaijan	—	—	6	1					

[101]   Russian Federation.
[102]   Yugoslavia.
[103]   Ex-U.S.S.R.

F TRANSPORT AND COMMUNICATIONS

1.	Length of Railway Line Open	page 673
2.	Freight Traffic on Railways	page 684
3.	Passenger Traffic on Railways	page 697
4.	Merchant Ships Registered	page 710
5.	Inland Navigation Traffic	page 731
6.	Motor Vehicles in Use	page 735
7.	Commercial Aviation	page 745
8.	Post and Telegraph Services	page 750
9.	Telephone Services	page 766
10.	Radio and Television Licences	page 776

Government has generally been involved more intimately in the provision of means of transport and communication than in agriculture or industry, at any rate until quite recently; and if not in its provision, then at least in its regulation. As a consequence, there is usually more statistical material available from the past than on most other subjects except external trade. Shipping was a matter of close concern to all major maritime powers. The railways were of obvious military as well as economic importance and were under government surveillance if not control from the beginning, even in Britain—something made easier by their need for government help in securing rights of way. Civil aviation was similarly controlled for a variety of reasons. Postal services were long recognised as a government function, though nowhere organised on modern lines until Hill's example of the penny post in the United Kingdom in 1840. Telegraphs fell naturally into the same niche, where they were not simply an adjunct of the railways. Telephones generally followed, except in some of the smaller countries, where they were pioneered by foreign (mostly American) private enterprise. In Europe, unlike North America, the potential social influence of radio led to its direct control by governments, to a consequent desire to find finance from users of radio services, and hence to the almost universal use, up to the 1960s at least and usually later, of licensing systems which produced a useful statistical by-product. The principal absentees from this list of government influence are inland navigation and road transport, which remain, in market economies at any rate, the fields about which least data are available.

Table F1, showing the length of railway line open to the public in each country, is fairly straightforward and has the merit of being an almost complete record from the beginning of railway operation. Up to about 1870, there is a great diversity of figures given for many countries in the various secondary sources which provided continent-wide comparisons. Part of this was due to boundary changes and part to misinformation about opening dates of some stretches of line. Where the source of the discrepancies could not be identified, the national statistical offices of the countries concerned have generally been most helpful in supplying definitive statistics. The other two tables on railways do not generally give figures from the very beginning of operation but some sort of national statistics were compiled from an early date in most countries. Initially, these tended to be simple totals of freight and passengers carried, often involving much double-counting where journeys took place over more than one system. Indeed, at this stage governments seem to have been more interested in financial than in traffic statistics, even where they were not running the railways. These statistics have not been included here, for they are often in a very confused state and require careful interpretation. The aggregate traffic statistics available are shown in Tables F2 and F3, and by the later part of the nineteenth century these increasingly came to include the more sophisticated figures of unit-distance carried.

The principal problems in using the shipping statistics in Table F4 arise from changes in the size of ships covered by different countries' registers, and from changes in the method of measuring capacity. In most countries there has been a lower limit of size below which vessels have not been included in the register; but this has changed from time to time, and it has differed between countries. So far as aggregate capacity is concerned, especially of mechanically-propelled vessels, this limit and the changes in it has made little impact. The numbers, especially of sailing ships, have sometimes fluctuated violently with changes in the limit. These are usually easily apparent and it is hoped that all are indicated in footnotes.

Changes in methods of measuring capacity are a more difficult problem. The two basic methods—gross and net, representing the inclusion and exclusion of space which cannot be used for paying traffic—are readily distinguished, especially in the case of mechanically-propelled vessels. In this table, the net measure has been preferred wherever such a series is available. However, these have become increasingly scarce since World War II. A less easily identifiable change took place in the British measurement system (generally used internationally) in the middle of the nineteenth century. The original system, established in 1773 though not statutorily enforced in Britain until 1786, was based on length and breadth only. In 1836, a new Act changed the system to cubic capacity but was optional to begin with. Old ships did not have to be remeasured and new ones did not have to use the new system until a further legal change in 1855. It is not clear in the British statistics how much change there was during the period 1836–55. G.S. Graham writes that "... although lengths were somewhat increased after 1836, the same general type of ship continued to be built until the new measurement law came into force in 1855".[1] The implication is that most of the change of system was concentrated in 1855 and if this was so one can only conclude that it had remarkably little effect on the tonnage recorded. This is surprising in view of the fact that the old system encouraged the building of ships of great depth, which would tend to result in an understatement of their carrying capacity.

Whatever the effect on the British statistics, it is usually completely unclear whether the statistics of other countries before 1855 were expressed in terms of the old or the new system of measurement. Probably, since most series were published retrospectively, it is best to assume that it was on the new.

Table F5 presents a selection of statistics on the volume of inland waterway traffic for those countries for which the data are both available and significantly large. Traffic across international borders on the main rivers of Europe is mostly concerned. Canal systems have usually been too fragmented in ownership for consistent and reliable data to have been available.

The statistics of motor vehicles in use, shown in Table F6, are reasonably uniform in definition so far as their main constituents are concerned. There are many minor variations at different times, mostly involving government-owned vehicles or special vehicles such as fire engines and ambulances. The data are, unfortunately, rather patchy for eastern Europe since World War II. However, the official statistics of these countries contain quite extensive information about both goods and passenger traffic flows on the state-owned road transport networks. None of this material has been included here because it is not generally available for the market economies.

Apart from some early statistics on civil air traffic from national sources, the main reliance in Table F7 has been on the publications of the International Civil Aviation Organization, which makes for a large measure of consistency. It should be noted that these data apply to airlines based in each of the countries concerned, not to the actual traffic at the countries' airports.

Postal statistics, and even those of telegrams, which one might expect to be reasonably uniform and homogeneous, exhibit very considerable divergencies between countries and over time. Mail is generally broken down into various categories—letters, postcards, newspapers, samples, packets, official communications—further divided into registered and unregistered, and sometimes into express and ordinary mail. Whether or not some of these categories are excluded from the officially published statistics (and especially from the summary statistics which have often been the only ones available) has varied much from country to country and from time to time. Another source of variation has been the treatment of international mail and telegrams, especially the transit between countries. It is hoped that all these sources of differences have been noted. Even where they are known they are a serious adverse influence on direct comparability.

Statistics of telephone calls, which in this edition have been shown separately in Table F10, are now supplemented by data on the number of telephones in use. These latter data have not always been produced in an entirely consistent fashion, but it is hoped that all changes have been noted. The measurement of calls, especially international, has been subject to some of the same variations as the mail. Problems have also arisen where calls over different distances have been measured in different units, and these have tended to get worse as telephone systems have become increasingly automated. It is hoped that as consistent series as possible have been included and that breaks in continuity have all been signalled. However, nothing can be done about the absence of statistics which has followed privatisation of the system in one or two cases.

F1 LENGTH OF RAILWAY LINE OPEN (in kilometres)

	Austria-Hungary	Belgium	Bulgaria	Denmark	Finland[2]	France	Germany	Greece	Ireland	Italy
1825	—	—	—	—	—	—	—	—	—	—
1826	—	—	—	—	—	—	—	—	—	—
1827	—	—	—	—	—	—	—	—	—	—
1828	—	—	—	—	—	17	—	—	—	—
1829	—	—	—	—	—	17	—	—	—	—
1830	—	—	—	—	—	31	—	—	—	—
1831	—	—	—	—	—	31	—	—	...	—
1832	—	—	—	—	—	52	—	—	...	—
1833	—	—	—	—	—	73	—	—	...	—
1834	—	—	—	—	—	141	—	—	...	—
1835	—	20	—	·	—	141	6	—	...	—
1836	—	44	—	—	—	141	6	—	...	—
1837	14	142	—	—	—	159	21	—	...	—
1838	32	258	—	—	—	159	140	—	...	—
1839	144	312	—	—	—	224	240	—	...	8
1840	144	334	—	—	—	410	469	—	21	20
1841	351	379	—	—	—	548	683	—	...	20
1842	378	439	—	—	—	645	931	—	...	49
1843	378	558	—	—	—	743	1,311	—	...	82
1844	473	577	—	—	—	822	1,752	—	...	133
1845	728	577	—	—	—	875	2,143	—	...	152
1846	900	594	—	—	—	1,049	3,281	—	...	259
1847	1,048	691	—	32	—	1,511	4,306	—	...	286
1848	1,071	780	—	32	—	2,004	4,989	—	585	379
1849	1,250	796	—	32	—	2,467	5,443	—	795	564
1850	1,357	854	—	32	—	2,915	5,856	—	865	620
1851	1,392	870	—	32	—	3,248	6,143	—	1,005	702
1852	1,392	901	—	32	—	3,654	6,605	—	1,140	705
1853	1,392	948	—	32	—	3,954	7,147	—	1,343	808
1854	1,433	1,072	—	32	—	4,315	7,571	—	1,444	1,081
1855	1,588	1,333	—	32	—	5,037	7,826	—	1,589	1,207
1856	1,790	1,417[1] / 1,442	—	86	—	5,852	8,617	—	1,702	1,360
1857	1,982	1,511	—	111	—	6,868	8,991	—	1,725	1,580
1858	2,401	1,692	—	111	—	8,094	9,650	—	1,913	1,777
1859	2,641	1,714	—	111	—	8,840[3]	10,593	—	2,037	2,236[3]
1860	2,927	1,729	—	111	—	9,167	11,089	—	2,195	2,404
1861	3,181	1,824	—	111	107	9,626	11,497	—	2,291	2,773
1862	3,351	1,906	—	168	107	10,522	12,048	—	2,573	3,109
1863	3,516	2,012	—	228	110	11,533	12,651	—	2,803	3,725
1864	3,554	2,094	—	307	110	12,362	13,114	—	2,889	4,162
1865	3,698	2,285	...	419	111	13,227	13,900	—	2,960	4,591
1866	3,965	2,511	...	478	111	13,915	14,787	...	3,074	5,258
1867	4,145	2,598	...	478	111	15,000	15,679	...	3,105	5,559
1868	4,533	2,730	...	592	111	15,835	16,316	...	...	5,933
1869	5,273	2,816	...	680	170	16,465[4]	17,215	9	...	6,124
1870	6,112	2,897	224	770	483	15,544	18,876[4]	12	...	6,429
1871	7,350	3,119	224	882	489	15,632	21,471	12	3,201	6,710
1872	8,508	3,224	224	905	489	17,438	22,426	12	3,367	7,044
1873	9,344	3,333	224	905	492	18,139	23,890	12	3,383	7,223
1874	9,668	3,432	224	1,121	492	18,744	25,487	12	3,425	7,707
1875	10,331	3,499	244	1,252	638	19,357	27,970	12	3,459	8,018
1876	10,775	3,589	224	1,367	852	20,034	29,305	12	3,473	8,422
1877	11,250	3,644	244	1,445	852	20,534	30,718	12	3,547	8,664
1878	11,297	3,741	224	1,445	852	21,435	31,471	12	3,638	8,755
1879	11,374	4,012	224	1,561	852	22,249	33,250	12	3,679	8,898

F1   Length of Railway Line Open (in kilometres)

1825–1879

	Netherlands	Norway	Portugal[61]	Romania	Russia[7]	Spain	Sweden	Switzerland	U.K.:GB
1825	—	—	—	—	—	—	—	—	43
1826	—	—	—	—	—	—	—	—	61
1827	—	—	—	—	—	—	—	—	66
1828	—	—	—	—	—	—	—	—	72
1829	—	—	—	—	—	—	—	—	82
1830	—	—	—	—	—	—	—	—	157[8]
1831	—	—	—	—	—	—	—	—	225
1832	—	—	—	—	—	—	—	—	267
1833	—	—	—	—	—	—	—	—	335
1834	—	—	—	—	—	—	—	—	480
1835	—	—	—	—	—	—	—	—	544
1836	—	—	—	—	—	—	—	—	649
1837	—	—	—	—	—	—	—	—	870
1838	—	—	—	—	27	—	—	—	1,196
1839	17	—	—	—	…	—	—	—	1,562[8]
1840	17	—	—	—	…	—	—	—	2,390[8]
1841	17	—	—	—	…	—	—	—	2,858
1842	17	—	—	—	…	—	—	—	3,122
1843	98	—	—	—	…	—	—	—	3,291
1844	109	—	—	—	…	—	—	—	3,600
1845	153	—	—	—	144	—	—	—	3,931[9]
1846	153	—	—	—	278	—	—	—	4,889[9]
1847	176	—	—	—	368	—	—	25	6,352[8]
1848	176	—	—	—	382	28	—	25	8,022
1849	176	—	—	—	…	28	—	25	8,918
1850	176	—	—	—	501	28	—	25	9,797
1851	176	—	—	—	1,004	76	—	25	10,090
1852	176	—	—	—	…	102	—	25	10,673
1853	204	—	—	—	1,049	191	—	25	10,958
1854	204	68	36	—	…	298	—	39	11,525
1855	311	68	36	—	…	440	—	210	11,744
1856	335	68	36	—	…	491	66	346	12,318
1857	335	68	36	—	1,170	640	209	519	12,919
1858	335	68	36	—	…	822	326	704	13,452
1859	335	68	36	—	1,336	1,120	447	937	14,069
1860	335	68	67	—	1,626	1,885	527	1,053	14,603
1861	…	68	67	—	2,238	2,358	571	…	15,210
1862	…	185	204	—	3,516	2,735	908	1,156	16,027
1863	…	185	455	—	3,521	3,574	1,014	…	17,038
1864	645	234	694	—	3,616	4,055	1,143	…	17,704
1865	776	270	694	…	3,842	4,832	1,305	1,322	18,439
1866	…	313	694	…	4,573	5,164	1,567	1,322	19,234
1867	…	313	694	…	5,038	5,231	1,687	1,322	19,837
1868	…	359	694	…	6,786	5,406	1,687	1,354	…
1869	…	359	694	…	8,166	5,426	1,727	…	…
1870	1,419	359	714	248	10,731	5,454	1,727	1,421	…
1871	1,488	414	774	316	13,641	5,472	1,817	1,439	21,558
1872	1,499	493	782	…	14,360	5,503	1,935	1,470	22,097
1873	1,551	493	795	…	16,206	5,636	2,321	1,470	22,513
1874	1,620	493	…	648	18,220	5,830	3,361	1,617	23,062
1875	1,620	549	954	921	19,029	6,094	3,679	1,962	23,365
1876	1,629	580	977	921	19,623	6,318	4,298	2,275	23,695
1877	1,694	811	…	921	21,092	6,512	4,837	2,451	23,951
1878	1,781	887[5]	1,078	921	22,371	6,702	5,193	2,557	24,273
1879	1,849	1,023	…	921	22,680	7,110	5,677	2,571	24,815

F1 Length of Railway Line Open (in kilometres)

	Austria-Hungary	Belgium	Bulgaria	Czech[10]	Denmark	Finland[2]	France
1880	11,429	4,112	224	...	1,584	852	23,089
1881	11,707	4,182	224	...	1,621	852	24,249
1882	11,937	4,294	224	...	1,762	852	25,576
1883	12,240	4,319	224	...	1,810	1,158	26,692
1884	13,153	4,366	224	...	1,936	1,158	28,722
1885	13,329	4,410	224[4]	...	1,936	1,178	29,839
1886	13,633	4,420	...	...	1,959	1,520	30,696
1887	14,164	4,446	...	...	1,865	1,553	31,446
1888	14,810	4,447	693	...	1,965	1,559	32,128
1889	15,111	4,470	693	...	1,965	1,842	32,914
1890	15,273	4,526	803	...	2,005	1,895	33,280
1891	15,583	4,517	803	...	2,033	1,897	33,878
1892	15,670	4,525	803	...	2,085	1,974	34,881
1893	15,927	4,527	838	...	2,122	2,098	35,350
1894	16,299	4,541	838	...	2,185	2,242	35,971
1895	16,420	4,572	861	...	2,231	2,391	36,240
1896	16,727	4,589	861	...	2,236	2,391	36,472
1897	17,315	4,590	985	...	2,465	2,473	36,934
1898	18,124	4,534	994	...	2,526	2,516	37,255
1899	18,780	4,562	1,436	...	2,754	2,649	37,494
1900	19,229	4,562	1,566	...	2,914	2,650	38,109
1901	19,531	4,543	1,566	...	2,986	2,653	38,274
1902	19,939	4,552	1,566	...	3,024	2,746	38,547
1903	20,369	4,557	1,567	...	3,078	2,962	39,105
1904	20,621	4,539	1,567	...	3,207	3,046	39,363
1905	21,002	4,550	1,567	...	3,207	3,046	39,607
1906	21,594	4,574	1,567	...	3,353	3,053	39,775
1907	21,701	4,604	1,591	...	3,365	3,056	39,963
1908	21,921	4,663	1,591	...	3,404	3,140	40,186
1909	22,377	4,668	1,694	...	3,403	3,252	40,285
1910	22,642	4,679	1,897	...	3,445	3,356	40,484
1911	22,749	4,679	1,934	...	3,691	3,421	40,635
1912	22,879	4,677	2,109	...	3,707	3,421	40,838
1913	22,981	4,676	2,109	...	3,868	3,560	40,770
1914	...	...	2,124	...	3,951	3,683	37,400
1915	...	...	2,124	...	3,977	3,685	36,400
1916	...	...	2,148	...	4,113	3,793	36,600
1917	**Austria**	...	2,148[4]	...	4,257	3,828	36,700
1918	...	...	2,203	13,077	4,251	3,906	36,400[4]
1919	6,263	4,727	2,203	13,065[10]	4,263[11]	3,984	37,700
1920	6,639	4,938	2,205	13,430	4,328	3,988	38,200
1921	6,639	4,964	2,205	13,448	4,976	3,990	41,800
1922	6,640	4,984	2,256	13,468	4,974	4,091	41,900
1923	6,625	5,018	2,256	13,465	4,969	4,240	42,000
1924	6,625	5,035	2,296	13,456	4,968	4,295	42,000
1925	6,638	5,085	2,296	13,491	5,067	4,524	42,100
1926	6,644	5,101	2,308	13,497	5,073	4,664	42,100
1927	6,677	5,100	2,309	13,533	5,126	4,827	42,200
1928	6,688	5,096	2,380	13,567	5,201	4,936	42,200
1929	6,687	5,099	2,417	13,608	5,243	5,040	42,300

F1   Length of Railway Line Open (in kilometres)

	Germany	Greece	Hungary	Ireland[13]	Italy	Netherlands
1880	33,838	12	...	3,816	9,290	1,841
1881	34,381	12	...	3,931	9,506	1,961
1882	35,081	12		3,969	9,753	2,007
1883	35,993	22		4,029	10,149	2,119
1884	36,780	70		4,066	10,591	2,247
1885	37,571	222		4,146	11,003	2,392
1886	38,525	474		4,238	11,823	2,453
1887	39,785	540		4,306	12,277	2,547
1888	40,827	602		4,401	13,037	2,598
1889	41,793	640		4,494	13,537	2,600
1890	42,869	697		4,496	13,629	2,610
1891	43,424	715		4,610	13,964	2,623
1892	44,177	906		4,662	14,487	2,623
1893	44,340	916		4,816	15,004	2,661
1894	45,462	916		4,902	15,492	2,661
1895	46,500	916		5,109	15,970	2,661
1896	47,433	949		5,117	16,053	2,742
1897	48,449	970		5,101	16,243	2,742
1898	49,830	1,003		5,114	16,352	2,777
1899	50,702	1,018		5,114	16,407	2,770
1900	51,678	1,033		5,125	16,429	2,771
1901	52,933	1,033		5,166	16,451	2,819
1902	53,843	1,117		5,175	16,723	2,851
1903	54,775	1,132		5,266	16,825	2,911
1904	55,817	1,335		5,307	16,912	2,924
1905	56,739	1,351		5,333	17,078	3,031
1906	57,584	1,372		5,415	17,380	3,046
1907	58,291	1,372		5,414	17,583	3,046
1908	59,241	1,427		5,415	17,723	3,070
1909	60,389	1,548		5,460	17,913	3,070
1910	61,209	1,573		5,476	18,090	3,190
1911	61,978	1,573		5,478	18,394	3,190
1912	62,734	1,584		5,480	18,632	3,256
1913	63,378[12]	1,584		5,491	18,873	3,305
	61,159					
1914	61,749	...[4]		...	19,125	3,339
1915	62,091	2,303		...	19,652	3,400
1916	62,347	2,328		...	20,046	3,400
1917	62,443[12]	2,346		...	20,198	3,400
	64,635					
1918	...[4]	2,373		...	20,262	3,403
1919	57,935[4]	2,383		5,531	20,304	3,451[14]
1920	57,545[4]	2,396	...	5,542	20,385	3,606
1921	57,652[4]	2,463	8,141	5,542	20,556	3,653
1922	57,245	2,463	8,566	5,542	20,760	3,663
1923	57,327	2,463	8,504	5,542	20,911	3,663
1924	57,546	2,463	8,508	5,525	21,010	3,623
1925	57,716	2,681	8,498	5,535	21,106	3,623
1926	57,864	2,681	8,522	5,535	21,349	3,627
1927	57,980	2,681	8,506	5,535	21,473	3,675
1928	58,223	2,679	8,617	5,517	21,598	3,676
1929	58,183	2,679	8,671	5,517	21,855	3,677

F1 Length of Railway Line Open (in kilometres)

	Norway	Poland[17]	Portugal[6]	Romania	Russia/U.S.S.R[7]	Serbia	Spain	Sweden	Switzerland	U.K.:G.B.
1880	1,057	...	1,144	921	22,865	—	7,491	5,876	2,571	25,060
1881	1,115	...	1,222	951	23,091	—	7,756	6,170	2,618	25,336
1882	1,327	...	1,482	1,089	23,429	—	7,853	6,305	2,829	25,751
1883	1,452	...	1,485	1,200	24,145	—	8,323	6,400	2,883	26,052
1884	1,562	...	1,524	1,271	25,007	253	8,702	6,600	2,890	26,309
1885	1,562	...	1,528	1,359	26,024	253	9,007	6,890	2,890	26,720
1886	1,562	...	1,529	1,402	27,345	398	9,334	7,277	2,927	26,891
1887	1,562	...	1,745	1,896	28,240	540	9,603	7,388	2,961	27,220
1888	1,562	...	1,871	2,135	29,428	540	9,643	7,527	3,010	27,501
1889	1,522	...	...	2,409	29,933	540	9,848	7,888	3,142	27,619
1890	1,562	...	1,932	2,424	30,596	540	10,163	8,018	3,243	27,827
1891	1,562	...	1,991	2,429	30,723	540	10,613	8,279	3,323	27,902
1892	1,562	...	2,104	2,470	31,202	540	10,972	8,461	3,412	28,067
1893	1,562	...	2,134	2,496	32,870	540	11,572	8,782	3,487	28,429
1894	1,611	...	2,151	2,513	35,206	540	11,926	9,234	3,544	28,765
1895	1,726	...	2,152	2,534	37,058	540	12,612	9,756	3,596	28,986
1896	1,752	...	2,156	2,818	39,546	562	12,945	9,896	3,655	29,144
1897	1,952	...	2,159	2,880	41,585	562	12,959	10,226	3,724	29,411
1898	1,952	...	2,159	2,916	44,622	562	13,049	10,360	3,798	29,762
1899	1,981	...	2,159	3,081[15]	49,870	571	13,135	10,708	3,859	29,828
1900	1,981	...	2,168	3,100	53,234	571	13,205	11,303	3,867[1] / 3,544	30,079
1901	2,057	...	2,171	3,149	56,452	593	13,416	11,574	3,688	30,385
1902	2,105	...	2,183	3,177	57,599	593	13,552	11,951	3,767	30,495
1903	2,303	...	2,201	3,179	58,362	675	13,694	12,362	3,925	30,860
1904	2,383	...	2,280	3,178	59,616	707	13,840	12,543	4,031	31,139
1905	2,490	...	2,294	3,179	61,085	707	14,037	12,647	4,086	31,456
1906	2,548	...	2,328	3,181	63,623	707	14,419	13,088	4,121	31,722
1907	2,561	...	2,374	3,186	65,500	695	14,465	13,248	4,224	31,796
1908	2,582	...	2,360	3,187	65,919	692	14,566	13,364	4,311	31,951
1909	2,847	...	2,439	3,186	66,345	695	14,595	13,604	4,385	32,026
1910	2,976	...	2,448	3,437	66,581	892	14,694	13,829	4,463	32,184
1911	3,085	...	2,868	3,479	68,027	949	14,925	13,942	4,534	32,223
1912	3,085	...	2,868	3,532	68,954	976[4]	15,126	14,171	4,640	32,266
1913	3,085	...	2,958	3,549	70,156[16][7] / 58,500	1,598	15,351	14,377	4,832	32,623
1914	3,165	...	2,976[6] / 3,115	3,588	62,300	...	15,533	14,360	4,876	...
1915	3,174	...	3,149	3,702	65,100	...	15,671	14,561	4,941	...
1916	3,177	...	3,161	3,169	69,300	...	15,879	14,648	5,037	...
1917	3,180	...	3,185	1,330	70,300	...	15,931	14,760	5,066	...
1918	3,236	...	3,207	3,123	71,300	...	15,964	14,852	5,079	...
1919	3,250	...	3,231	4,968	71,400	...	16,078	14,855	5,078	32,703
						Yugoslavia				
1920	3,286	13,763[17]	3,268	4,968[4]	71,600[7]	9,321	16,089	14,869	5,078	32,707
1921	3,286	15,356[4]	3,269	10,585	71,800[7]	9,340	16,214	14,893	5,080	32,691
1922	3,445	18,323	3,269	10,578[15]	71,900	9,340	16,330	15,109	5,083	32,717
1923	3,456	19,307	3,224	10,925	72,300	9,364	16,398	15,211	5,098	32,743
1924	3,456	19,318	3,224	10,925	74,500	9,547	16,514	15,424	5,101	32,767
1925	3,589	19,281	3,225	11,001	74,500	9,758	16,540	15,695	5,102	32,849
1926	3,603	19,260	3,225	11,109	75,700	9,803	16,652	15,793	5,135	32,857
1927	3,627	19,377	3,385	11,086	76,900	9,840	16,912	15,985	5,137	32,839
1928	3,835	19,495	3,386	11,060	76,900[7]	10,014	16,980	16,415	5,136	32,846
1929	3,835	19,533	3,407	11,130	76,900	9,996	17,232	16,436	5,136	32,641

F1 Length of Railway Line Open (in kilometres)

	Austria	Belgium	Bulgaria	Czechoslovakia	Denmark	Finland[2]	France
1930	6,710	5,125	2,441	13,610	5,294	5,128	42,400
1931	6,729	5,097	2,992	13,624	5,289	5,136	42,500
1932	6,717	5,134	3,030	13,621	5,291	5,224	42,500
1933	6,716	5,154	3,079	13,624	5,123	5,318	42,600
1934	6,701	5,145	3,143	13,612	5,176	5,455	42,600
1935	6,700	5,145	3,220	13,595	5,177	5,501	42,600
1936	6,702	5,138	3,236	13,595	5,152	5,510	42,600
1937	...	5,134	3,245	13,548	5,061	5,651	42,600
1938	...	5,128	3,352	...	5,000	5,740	42,600
1939	...	5,140	...	...	4,915	5,864	42,500
1940	...	5,038	...	...	4,915	4,596	40,600
1941	...	4,960	...	...	4,858	5,222	39,500
1942	...	4,890	...	...	4,861	5,670	39,800
1943	...	4,888	...	...	4,861	5,686	39,400
1944	...	5,102	...	...	4,861	4,220	39,400
1945	...	5,096	...	...[4]	4,861	4,513	40,500
1946	6,062	5,086	3,732	13,095	4,878	4,607	40,600
1947	...	5,049	...	13,095	4,878	4,713	41,100
1948	6,742	5,041	...	13,095	4,879	4,711	41,300
1949	...	5,050	...	13,124	4,822	4,641	41,300
1950	6,734	5,046	3,967	13,124	4,815	4,726	41,300
1951	6,738	5,046	...	13,132	4,770	4,815	41,200
1952	6,738	5,056	...	13,167	4,772	4,843	41,200
1953	6,703	5,041	...	13,162	4,740	4,880	41,200
1954	6,697	5,034	...	13,141	4,690	4,845	41,000
1955	6,698	4,935	4,091	13,168	4,575	4,918	39,800
1956	6,685	4,910	...	13,168	4,556	5,031	39,800
1957	6,612	4,854	4,108	13,168	4,441	5,100	39,600
1958	6,610	4,829	...	13,124	4,364	5,107	39,500
1959	6,600	4,715	4,146	13,139	4,343	5,284	39,400
1960	6,596	4,632	4,136	13,139	4,301	5,323	39,000
1961	6,586	4,620	4,163	13,139	4,220	5,327	38,700
1962	6,570	4,566	4,125	13,147	4,215	5,357	38,600
1963	6,566	4,544	...	13,165	4,020	5,363	38,500
1964	6,583	4,485	4,160	13,197	3,975	5,398	38,200
1965	6,580	4,485	4,094	13,301	3,901	5,470	37,890
1966	6,569	4,441	4,094	13,330	3,901	5,555	37,810
1967	6,542	4,364	4,158	13,332	3,438	5,619	37,460
1968	6,534	4,336	4,158	13,317	3,475	5,725	37,404
1969	6,510	4,282	4,196	13,315	3,198	5,724	36,742
1970	6,506	4,263	4,196	13,308	2,890	5,841	36,532
1971	6,495	4,165	4,231	13,296	2,890	5,910	35,624
1972	6,478	4,144	4,243	13,299	2,522	5,924	35,180
1973	6,477	4,081	4,245	13,293	2,493	5,936	34,812
1974	6,475	4,048	4,282	13,241	2,493	5,948	34,834
1975	6,468	4,004	4,290	13,215	2,493	5,957	34,787
1976	6,469	3,998	4,307	13,186	2,487	6,036	34,717
1977	6,468	3,998	4,295	13,190	...	6,089	34,597
1978	6,461	4,003	4,269	13,166	2,487[11]	6,079	34,522
					2,933		
1979	6,458	4,046	4,269	13,142	2,944	6,100	34,444

F1 Length of Railway Line Open (in kilometres)

	Germany	Greece	Hungary	Ireland[13]	Italy	Netherlands
1930	58,176	2,678	8,676	5,507	22,119	3,677
1931	58,178	2,677	8,676	5,512	22,571	3,639
1932	58,208	2,687	8,675	5,510	22,808	3,639
1933	58,185	2,687	8,662	5,485	22,892	3,621
1934	58,232[4]	2,687	8,659	5,467	23,158	3,576
	58,378[22]					
1935	58,841[22]	2,692	8,655	5,327	23,046	3,484
1936	58,967	...	8,657	5,296	22,890	3,387
1937	59,126	...	8,671	5,255	22,931	3,342
1938	59,882[19]	2,976	8,671	5,234	22,955	3,315
1939	61,940[19]	...	...	5,234	22,955	3,314
1940	...	...	...	5,205	22,992	3,314
1941	...	...	...	5,164	23,062	3,351
1942	...	...	...	5,164	23,227	3,170
1943	...	...	...	5,166	...	3,159
1944	...	...	5,094	...[4]	...	
1945	...	...	...	5,074	18,655	2,824
	East	**West**				
1946	...	...	...	5,074	20,637	3,079
1947	...	...	...	5,008	20,983	3,251
1948	...	...	...	5,008	21,399	3,347
1949	...	36,930	2,531	...	5,008	21,639	3,208
1950	12,895	36,924	2,553	8,756	4,965[13]	21,550	3,204
1951	...	36,863	2,554	8,812	4,862	21,711	3,210
1952	...	36,853	2,546	8,875	4,797	21,743	3,210
1953	...	36,853[20]	2,522	8,852	4,661	21,822	3,186
1954	15,500	37,136[21]	2,585	8,874₁	4,654	21,852	3,186
				10,164			
1955	16,134	37,009	2,605	10,298	4,519	21,923	3,178
1956	16,094	36,514	2,664	10,285	4,458	21,723	3,220
1957	16,121	36,060[22]	2,628	10,280	4,337	21,584	3,223
		36,602					
1958	16,093	36,518	2,628	10,297	4,136	21,516	3,227
1959	16,150	36,291	2,545	10,276	3,457	21,310	3,229
1960	16,174	36,019	2,583	10,307	3,289	21,277	3,253
1961	16,160	35,921	2,583	10,290	3,141	21,143	3,250
1962	16,159	35,638	2,583	10,336	2,831	20,972	3,251
1963	16,114	35,492	2,576	10,218	2,824	21,014	3,245
1964	16,108	35,374	2,576	10,274	2,824	20,885	3,238
1965	15,930	35,229	2,583	10,069	2,668	20,812	3,238
1966	15,730	34,476	2,573	10,075	2,474	20,381	3,232
1967	15,513	34,314	2,573	9,941	2,474	20,566	3,227
1968	15,237	34,037	2,571	9,692	2,472	20,358	3,148
1969	14,909	33,724	2,571	9,579	2,472	20,301	3,148
1970	14,658	33,010	2,571	9,514	2,517	20,212	3,148
1971	14,525	32,744	2,542	9,394	2,515	20,239	3,148
1972	14,384	32,604	2,543	9,289	2,515	20,198	2,834
1973	14,317	32,303	2,543	9,193	2,515[13]	20,174	2,832
1974	14,252	31,987	2,543	8,989	2,515	20,176	2,832
1975	14,298	31,892	2,476	8,740	2,334	20,176	2,790
1976	14,307		2,479	8,669	2,337	20,088	2,790
1977	14,215	31,578	2,479	8,523	2,337	20,122	2,788
1978	14,199	31,532	2,479	8,412	2,338	19,803	2,788
1979	14,164	31,540	2,479	8,327	2,321	19,719	2,788

F1   Length of Railway Line Open (in kilometres)

	Norway[5]	Poland[17]	Portugal	Romania	Russia/ U.S.S.R.[7] thousands	Spain	Sweden	Switzer-land	U.K.: G.B.	Yugo-slavia
1930	3,835	19,600	3,407	11,133	77.9	17,278	16,523	5,142	32,632	10,041
1931	3,835	19,891	3,420	11,120	81.0	17,286	16,474	5,136	32,638	10,252
1932	3,873	20,016	3,465	11,213	81.8	17,297	16,454	5,135	32,604	10,218
1933	3,873	20,142	3,468	11,206	82.6	17,446	16,543	5,136	32,580	10,208
1934	3,873	20,063	3,468	11,213	83.5	17,443	16,561	5,137	32,553	10,225
1935	3,964	20,085	3,475	11,194	84.4	17,437	16,596	5,132[25]	32,450	10,244
1936	3,998	20,181	3,491	11,216	85.1	...	16,532	5,163	32,400	10,293
1937	3,998	20,245	3,522	11,259	84.9	...	16,707	5,249	32,334	10,335
1938	3,988	20,438	3,581	11,310[4] 9,990	85.0[7]	...	16,710	5,240	32,216	10,419
1939	3,968	...	3,582	...	86.4	...	16,599	5,228	32,176	10,521
1940	3,968	...	3,586	...	106.1	17,446	16,610	5,221	32,094	...
1941	4,155	...	3,586	...	...	17,547	16,581	5,223	32,050	...
1942	4,155	...	3,586	...	62.9	17,756	16,583	5,216	32,031	...
1943	4,175	...	3,586	...	81.7	17,927	16,567	5,213	32,028	...
1944	4,276	...[4]	3,586	...	110.7	17,928	16,569	5,218	32,012	...[4]
1945	4,276	[17,938][23]	3,584	...	112.9	17,930	16,552	5,217	31,984	...
1946	4,376	23,218	3,584	10,020	114.1	17,930	16,552	5,222	31,981	9,900
1947	4,376	24,049	3,584 3,561[24]	...	115.5	17,932	16,552	4,219	31,968[26]	10,614
1948	4,471	24,259	3,561	10,677	115.8	17,928	16,528	5,181	31,540	11,331
1949	4,471	26,076	3,590	...	116.0	17,969	16,533	5,171	31,500	11,448
1950	4,469	26,312	3,590	10,853	116.9	18,071	16,516	5,152	31,336	11,541
1951	4,469	26,386	3,596	...	117.8	18,078	16,476	5,152	31,152	11,581
1952	4,470	26,606	3,597	...	118.6	18,187	16,459	5,125	31,022	11,548
1953	4,470	26,762	3,597	...	119.3	18,040	16,456	5,124	30,935	11,619
1954	4,454	26,999	3,597	...	120.3	18,096	16,396	5,119	30,821	11,622
1955	4,454	26,985	3,597	10,967	120.7	18,040	16,357	5,106	30,676	11,652
1956	4,485	27,003	3,597	...	120.7	17,895	16,177	5,106	30,618	11,735
1957	4,504	26,974	3,597	10,976	121.2	18,006	16,093	5,106	30,521	11,760
1958	4,474	27,040	3,597	10,989	122.8	18,091	16,019	5,114	30,333[27]	11,787
1959	4,493	27,017	3,597	10,998	124.4	18,139	15,790	5,117	29,747	11,882
1960	4,493[5]	26,904	3,597	10,981	125.8	18,033	15,399	5,117	29,562	11,867
1961	4,467	26,827	3,597	10,986	126.6	...	14,794	5,118	28,812[27]	11,867
1962	4,408	26,928	3,597	11,005	127.7	...	14,254	5,112	28,133	11,792
1963	4,408	26,920	3,597	10,998	128.6	...	14,063	5,112	27,330	11,857
1964	4,360	26,898	3,597	10,985	129.3	17,779	13,721	5,098	25,735	11,847
1965	4,348	26,862	3,597	10,979	131.4	17,561	13,433	5,074	24,011	11,839
1966	4,349	26,739	3,618	11,007	132.5	17,350	13,067	5,071	22,082	11,580
1967	4,294	26,638	3,617	11,023	133.3	17,362	12,907	5,059	21,198	11,351
1968	4,294	26,628	3,617	11,016	133.6	17,434	12,807	5,051	20,031	10,688
1969	4,294	26,574	3,592	11,006	134.6	16,841	12,543	5,018	19,170	10,456
1970	4,292	26,678	3,563	11,012	135.2	16,507	12,203	5,010	18,969	10,289
1971	4,292	26,717	3,563	11,012	135.4	16,350	12,171	5,010	18,738	10,332
1972	4,256	26,737	3,563	11,023	136.3	16,375	12,104	5,007	18,417	10,417
1973	4,257	26,587	3,563	11,019	136.8	15,976	12,104	4,992	18,227	10,398
1974	4,257	26,709	3,563	11,086	137.5	15,825	12,102	4,990	18,168	10,319
1975	4,257	26,702	3,563	11,039	138.3	15,839	12,065	4,994	18,118	10,068
1976	4,241	26,734	3,591		138.5	15,832	12,061	4,994	18,007	9,967
1977	4,241	26,832	3,592		139.8	15,758	12,077	4,995	17,973	9,967
1978	4,241	26,835	2,588	11,119	140.4	15,758	12,074	4,991	17,901	9,762
1979	4,239	27,271	3,588		141.1	15,742	12,006	4,991	17,735	9,381

F1 Length of Railway Line Open (in kilometres)

1980–2000

	Austria	Belgium	Bulgaria	Czechoslovakia	Denmark	Finland[2]	France
1980	6,459	3,978	4,267	13,131	2,944	6,098	34,362
1981	6,419	3,971	4,267	13,130	2,944	6,091	34,596
1982	6,416	3,930	4,273	13,142	2,944	6,092	34,599
1983	6,401	3,920	4,278	13,141	2,954	6,092	34,710
1984	6,359	3,842	4,279	13,114	2,965	6,000	34,688
1985	6,371	3,741	4,297	13,130	2,965	5,900	34,676
1986	6,385	3,667	4,294	13,116	2,965	5,899	34,639
1987	6,330	3,568	4,300	13,102	2,969	5,884	34,647
1988	6,338	3,554	4,300	13,103	2,837	5,884	34,563
1989	6,662	3,554	4,299	13,109	2,838	5,863	34,322
1990	6,658	3,513	4,299	13,111	2,838	5,846	34,322
1991	6,657	3,479	4,299	13,115	2,838	5,853	34,322
1992	6,657	3,432	4,294	9,439[29]	2,838	5,853	32,727
1993	6,651	3,410	4,291	9,451[29]	2,881	5,853	32,557
1994	5,749	3,568	4,300	…	2,770	5,924	34,322
1995	5,749	3,568	…	…	2,770	5,924	34,322
1996	5,624	3,410	4,294	…	2,838	5,864	34,074
1997	5,624	3,396	4,292	9,441	2,848	5,895	34,123
1998	5,636	3,368	4,292	9,440	3,358	5,859	32,027
1999	5,849	3,380	4,292	9,440	3,323	5,859	32,027
2000	6,123	3,437	4,294	9,435	2,859	5,865	31,939

	East Germany	Germany	West Germany	Greece	Hungary	Ireland	Italy	Netherlands
1980	14,248		31,497	2,479	8,142 / 8,033	2,321	19,814	2,760
1981	14,233		31,357	2,479	8,024	2,321	19,833	2,760
1982	14,231		31,236	2,479	8,025	2,319	19,780	2,760
1983	14,226		30,995	2,479	8,027	2,276	19,793	2,777
1984	14,226		30,720	2,479	8,030	2,276	19,750	2,777
1985	14,054		30,578	2,479	8,024	2,276	19,726	2,796
1986	14,005		30,418	2,479	8,026	2,276	19,563	2,789
1987	14,008		30,335	2,479	8,030	2,276	19,538	2,809
1988	14,024		30,129	2,479	8,025	2,276	19,566	2,828
1989		44,330		2,479	8,038	1,944	19,562	2,828
1990		44,118		2,484	8,038	1,944	19,588	2,780
1991		44,332		2,484	8,072	1,944	19,582	2,780
1992		44,467		2,484	7,996	2,812	19,465	2,753
1993		44,252		2,497	7,752	2,812	…	2,757
1994		45,468		2,479	7,765	1,947	20,011	2,828
1995		45,468		2,479	7,765	1,947	20,011	2,828
1996		45,457		2,503	7,785	1,947	19,503	2,757
1997		43,966		2,474	7,619	1,947	18,961	2,791
1998		43,966		2,474	7,606	1,947	19,437	2,739
1999		46,300		2,548	7,606	1,947	19,272	2,813
2000		40,826		2,548	7,606	1,947	19,394	2,739

F1 Length of Railway Line Open (in kilometres)

	Norway	Poland	Portugal	Romania	Russia/ U.S.S.R.[7] thousands	Spain	Sweden	Swit	U.K.: G.B.	Yugoslavia
1980	4,242	27,185	3,588	11,110	141.8	15,743[28] 13,542	12,006	5,000	17,645	9,465
1981	4,242	27,172	3,611	11,093	142.8	13,543	11,952	4,995	17,431	9,393
1982	4,242	27,158	3,617	11,125	143.3	13,572	12,362	4,997	17,229	9,389
1983	4,242	27,139	3,614	11,106	143.6	13,573	12,323	5,002	16,964	9,409
1984	4,242	27,070	3,614	11,169	144.1	...	12,063	5,010	16,879	9,279
1985	4,219	27,095	3,607	11,192	144.9	13,466	11,745	5,017	16,752	9,283
1986	4,219	26,848	3,607	11,221	145.6	12,721	11,745	5,016	16,670	9,246
1987	4,217	26,637	3,607	11,275	146.1	12,686	11,673	5,020	16,633	9,270
1988	4,175	26,545	3,608	11,298	146.7	12,550	11,555	5,020	16,599	9,349
1989	4,044	26,644	3,126[30]	11,343	146.7	12,710	11,501	5,020	16,587	9,567
1990	4,044	26,228	3,126	11,348	147.4	12,560	11,211	5,030	16,584	...
1991	4,027	25,848	3,117	11,365	147.5[31]	13,060	11,045	5,029	16,558	3,947[33]
1992	4,023	25,254	3,054	11,430	...	13,060	10,983	5,029	16,528	3,960[33]
1993	4,023	24,926	3,325	11,380	87.6[32]	13,060	10,884	5,029	16,536	3,960[33]
1994	4,223	26,250	3,625	11,275	158	15,430	12,000	4,418	16,914	...
1995	4,223	...	3,625	11,275	158	15,430	12,084	4,418	16,914	...
1996	4,026	25,528	3,068	11,365	154	14,400	12,000	5,763	16,888	...
1997	4,027	24,313	3,068	11,365	154	14,343	12,624	5,719	17,561	...
1998	4,023	24,313	3,072	11,365	154	15,172	11,837	5,249	16,878	...
1999	4,012	24,313	3,072	11,376	150	15,079	13,415	4,479	16,878	...
2000	4,012	23,420	2,850	11,385	150	13,950	12,821	4,492	16,878	...

NOTES

1. SOURCES:- In addition to the official publications noted on p. xv the following have been used:- Belgium to 1856 (1st line) and Spain to 1871—G. Stürmer, *Geschichte der Eisenbahnen* (Bromberg, 1872); Belgium 1856 (2nd line) to 1867—A. Scheler, *Annuarie Statistique et Historique Belge*; Finland to 1913—Matti Tapani Peltonen, *Liikewne Sciomessa 1860-1913* (Helsinki, 1983) Great Britain to 1938 and Ireland to 1913—B.R. Mitchell *British Historical Statistics* (Cambridge, 1988) where the original sources are given; Hungary to 1889—*Statistisches Nachrichten über die Eisenbahnender Österreichisch—Ungarischen Monarchie* (1890-1). Russia to 1913—P.A. Khromov, *Economic Development of Russia in the 19th and 20th Centuries, 1800-1917* (Moscow, 1950). The following data were supplied by their respective national statistical offices:- France to 1841; Greece 1950; Germany 1870-1914; Norway to 1914; Spain 1901 (2nd line) to 1914; and Sweden to 1914.
2. Except where otherwise indicated, the statistics are normally for the geographical length of line open at the end of each year. Narrow gauge lines are, in general, included, but not rack and similar mountain railways.
3. Statistics up to 1914 are, so far as possible, and except as indicated in footnotes, for 1913 boundaries.

FOOTNOTES

[1] These breaks occur on a change of source.
[2] Subsequently (throughout for Finland) statistics are of average length in use during the year.
[3] 104 km. of Savoy railways were transferred from Italy to France.
[4] These breaks occur as a result of territorial changes: See Introduction.
[5] At 30 June in 1878-1960.
[6] The statistics to 1914 (1st line) are of the average length of line (excluding local line) open during the year. Subsequent figures are of all lines open at year-end.
[7] Statistics to 1913 (1st line) are for the Russian Empire (exclusive of Finland). From 1913 (2nd line) to 1939 they are for the 1923 territory of the U.S.S.R., and from 1946 onwards for its postwar territory. Figures for 1921-28 are at 30 September.
[8] For 1831-39 and 1841-47 Ireland is included.
[9] At 30 June.
[10] Excluding the Kosice-Bohumin line in 1918 and 1919.
[11] The 1919 figure is of average length in use during the year. Subsequent statistics to 1976 relate to 31 March. From 1978 (2nd line) certain tramways open to goods traffic are included.
[12] Excluding narrow gauge lines from 1913 (2nd line) to 1917 (1st line).
[13] Including lines in both Northern Ireland and the Republic of Ireland. From 1950 to 1973 the Republic component is at 31 March in the year following that indicated.
[14] The reason for this break is not given in the source.
[15] At 31 March in the year following that indicated in 1900-22.
[16] By 1913 an additional 1,590 km. had been built, the exact date of construction of which was (and is) unknown.
[17] Including Danzig from 1921 to 1938.
[18] Subsequently excluding London Passenger Transport Board lines.

19   So far as possible these figures relate to the 1937 territory.
20   Hamburg Dock Railway (456 km.) is included from 1954.
21   The Salzgitter line (29 km.) is included from 1955.
22   Saarland, with 146 km., was reincorporated in 1935. In 1957 it was again included in West Germany having then 542 km.
23   Excluding narrow gauge lines (2,052 km, in 1946)
24   Subsequently lines exploited rather than lines in existence.
25   A new method of measurement was used subsequently.
26   Subsequently state railways only.
27   135 km was transferred to docks authorities in 1959 and 16 km was transferred back in 1962. The 16 km has here been included in the 1960 figure.
28   Excluding narrow gauge lines from 1980 (2nd line).
29   Czech Republic.Slovakia 3660.
30   Rectified figure.
31   Former USSR.
32   Russia. Ex-USSR as follows

	Armenia	Azer-baijan	Bel-arus	Est-onia	Geor-gia	Kazakh-stan	Kyrgi-stan	Lat-via	Lithu-ania	Mold-ova	Tajiki-stan	Turkmeni-stan	Ukraine	Uzbeki-stan
1990	...	...	...	...	...	...	...	...	...	...	480	...	...	...
1992	830	...	...	...	...	13,841	...	...	...	1,328	...	...	...	...
1993	...	2,125	5,488	...	1,583	...	370	2,413	...	...	...	2,187	23,631	3,380
1994	840	...	...	1,024	...	...	...	...	...	...	...	...	...	...
1995	...	...	...	...	...	...	...	2,400	2,000	...	...	...	23,350	...
1996	...	2,090	5,570	...	1,570	14,460	...	2,400	2,010	1,150	...	2,120	23,350	3,460
1997	825	2,125	5,488	1,018	1,583	13,841	370	2,412	2,002	1,328	480	2,187	23,350	3,380
1998	825	2,125	5,488	1,018	1,583	13,841	370	2,412	2,002	1,328	480	2,187	23,350	3,380
1999	825	2,125	5,563	1,018	1,583	14,400	370	2,412	2,002	1,328	480	2,187	23,350	3,380
2000	825	2,125	5,563	1,018	1,583	14,400	370	2,412	2,002	1,328	480	2,187	23,350	3,380

33   Yugoslavia. Ex-Yugoslavia

	Bosnia-Herc	Croatia	Macedonia	Slovenia
1991	1,021	...	...	1,195
1992	...	2,664	275	1,201
1993	...	2,699	922	...
1994	...	2,592	...	...
1995	...	...	...	...
1996	1,021	2,699	...	...
1997	1,021	1,907	699	1,201
1998	1,021	1,907	922	1,201
1999	1,021	2,296	922	1,201
2000	1,021	2,296	699	1,201

F2 FREIGHT TRAFFIC ON RAILWAYS (in stated units)

Key:- a = million metric tons; b = million ton-kilometres; c = thousand million ton-kilometres

1850–1894

	Austria[1]		Belgium[3]		Bulgaria	Denmark		Finland[3]		France	
	a	b	a	b	a	a	b	a	b	a	b
1850	1.4	...	1.3	...	...	...	...	...	...	4.3	...
1851	1.8	...	1.3	72	...	...	...	...	...	4.6[5]	462[5]
1852	2.3	...	1.5	72	...	...	...	...	...	5.4	...
1853	2.6	...	1.8	85	...	...	...	...	...	7.2	813
1854	3.3	...	2.3	104	...	...	...	...	...	8.9	1,143
1855	3.4	...	2.7	111	...	...	...	...	...	10.7	1,517
1856	4.0	...	2.6	115	...	...	...	...	...	12.9	1,868
1857	4.1	...	2.9	102	...	...	...	...	...	15.0	2,142
1858	5.2	...	3.3	148	...	...	...	...	...	17.7	2,391
1859	5.6	...	3.4	153	...	...	...	...	...	20.0[6]	2,729[6]
1860	7.2	...	3.8	160	...	...	...	...	...	23.1	3,120
1861	8.8	...	...	...	...	...	—	...	...	27.9[5]	3,809[5]
1862	8.8	...	...	...	...	...	...	—	0.8	27.3	3,884
1863	8.5	...	...	...	...	...	...	—	3.3	28.9	4,074
1864	9.6	...	5.3	...	...	...	...	—	2.0	31.1	4,626
1865	10.5	...	5.9	...	...	...	...	—	2.6	34.0	5,172
1866	10.9	...	6.5	...	...	...	...	—	2.9	37.4	5,826
1867	13.3[1]	...	6.5	...	...	0.2	...	—	2.9	38.6	5,845
	12.6										
1868	15.8	...	6.6	...	...	0.2	...	0.1	3.0	42.4	6,310
1869	17.2	...	7.1	...	...	0.3	...	0.1	3.8	44.0	6,271
1870	21.0	...	7.6	...	...	0.3	...	0.1	7.9	37.1[7]	5,057[7]
1871	[25.6][2]	...	11.0	...	...	0.4	...	0.2	18	37.8[5]	5,509[5]
1872	29.4	...	13.1	...	...	0.5	...	0.2	24	53.4	7,725
1873	36.9	...	13.8[3]	...	...	0.5	...	0.2	27	57.5	8,251
			28.8								
1874	36.0	...	24.7	...	...	0.6	...	0.3	32	56.7	7,926
1875	38.0	3,912	26.6	...	...	0.7	...	0.4	39	58.9	8,136
1876	40.6	4,088	26.3	...	...	0.9	...	0.4	46	61.8	8,326
1877	43.8	4,668	26.6	...	...	0.9	...	0.5	52	61.6	8,185
1878	44.8	4,590	27.7	...	...	0.8	...	0.4	45	63.1	8,400
1879	45.1	4,551	29.6	...	...	0.8[4]	...	0.4	41	69.0	8,999
1880	47.9	4,767	32.8	...	...	1.0	...	0.5	49	80.8	10,350
1881	51.9	5,015	34.1	...	...	1.1	...	0.5	52	84.6[5]	10,750
1882	56.0	5,661	36.1	...	...	1.2	...	0.6	69	88.7	10,840
1883	62.4	5,942	36.6	...	...	1.2	...	0.5	60	89.1	11,070
1884	61.2	5,810	35.2	...	...	1.4	...	0.6	61	80.4	10,480
1885	61.6	6,071	33.6	...	...	1.4	...	0.7	72	75.2	9,791
1886	62.6	6,128	34.8	...	...	1.4	...	0.6	69	73.4	9,314
1887	65.7	6,539	37.1	...	...	15	...	0.6	73	77.3	9,917
1888	73.5	7,282	40.4	...	...	1.5	...	0.7	90	82.4	10,410
1889	79.1	7,618	42.6	...	...	1.7	...	0.9	98	87.0	11,050
1890	84.4	8,214	43.0	...	...	1.8	...	1.0	104	92.5	11,760
1891	84.6	8,002	42.3	...	...	1.8	...	1.0	120	96.5[5]	12,290[5]
1892	85.3	7,710	41.2	...	...	2.0	...	1.0	127	95.7	12,120
1893	90.9	8,350	43.9	...	...	2.2	128	1.1	147	97.0	12,270
1894	92.9	8,398	45.5	...	0.4	2.3	139	1.1	151	99.1	12,480

F2 Freight Traffic on Railways (in stated units)

	Germany		Greece	Hungary[8]		Ireland	Italy[10]		Netherlands		Norway	
	a	b	a	a	b	a	a	b	a	b	a	b
1850	...	303	...	...	...	...	...	...	...	...	...	...
1851	...	394	...	...	...	...	...	...	...	...	...	...
1852	...	527	...	...	...	...	...	...	...	...	...	...
1853	...	621	...	...	...	...	...	...	...	...	...	...
1854	...	898	...	...	...	...	...	...	...	...	...	...
1855	...	1,095	...	...	...	...	...	...	...	...	0.1	...
1856	...	1,242	...	...	...	1.0	...	...	...	...	0.1	4
1857	...	1,531	...	...	...	1.1	...	...	...	...	0.1	5
1858	...	1,505	...	...	...	1.2	...	...	...	...	0.1	5
1859	...	1,475	...	...	...	1.4	...	...	...	...	0.2	5
1860	...	1,675	...	...	...	1.5	...	...	...	...	0.1	5
1861	...	1,998	...	...	...	1.7	...	...	...	...	0.2	6
1862	...	2,431	...	...	...	1.7	...	...	...	...	0.2	7
1863	...	2,777	...	...	...	1.8	...	...	...	...	...	...
1864	...	3,220	...	...	...	1.9	...	...	...	...	...	...
1865	...	3,672	...	...	...	2.0	...	...	...	...	...	...
1866	...	3,777	...	...	...	2.3	...	...	...	...	...	...
1867	...	4,527	...	...	...	2.6	...	...	...	...	0.3	16
1868	...	5,184	...	1.4	...	...[9]	...	...	...	...	0.3	18
1869	...	5,520	...	1.6	...	...	...	...	...	...	0.4	21
1870	...	5,876[7]	...	2.0	...	...	4.8	...	...	...	0.3	20
1871	...	6,400	...	3.0	...	3.0	5.2	...	...	...	0.3	19
1872	...	8,200	...	3.5	...	3.1	6.4	...	...	...	0.4	24
1873	...	9,900	...	4.1	...	3.2	7.4	...	...	...	0.5	30
1874	...	10,100	...	3.7	...	3.2	7.1	...	...	...	0.6	31
1875	...	10,400	...	4.1	...	3.4	7.2	...	...	...	0.6	33
1876	...	10,800	...	4.4	...	3.6	7.2	...	...	...	0.7	42
1877	...	11,000	...	5.4	...	3.7	7.5	...	...	...	0.7	44
1878	...	11,100	...	5.6	...	3.6	7.5	...	2.7	...	[0.3][11]	[19][16]
1879	...	11,900	...	6.7	...	3.7	8.4	...	2.8	...	0.5	33
1880	...	13,500	...	6.5	...	3.7	9.3[10]	...	4.0	...	0.6	38
1881	...	14,300	...	7.7	...	3.6	10.3	...	4.4	408	0.6	43
1882	...	15,600	...	8.7	...	3.9	11.0	...	5.0	472	0.8	57
1883	...	16,400	...	9.4	...	4.1	12.5	...	5.2	578	0.9	64
1884	...	16,800	...	10.6	...	3.9	13.4	...	5.2	523	0.9	68
1885	...	16,600	...	10.9	...	3.8	14.0	1,695	5.2	523	0.9	68
1886	...	17,200	...	12.1	...	3.7	14.7	1,779	5.1	541	1.0	68
1887	...	18,700	...	12.9	...	3.8	15.8	1,976	5.8	587	1.0	67
1888	200	20,400	...	13.6[8] 22.6	2,795	3.8	16.5	1,852	6.4	648	1.0	70
1889	214	22,100	0.1	24.0	2,716	4.2	17.2	1,972	6.9	658	1.2	84
1890	218	22,500	...	25.8	3,136	4.4	17.5	2,038	...	...	1.3	89
1891	231	23,400	...	27.8	3,429	4.5	17.2	1,994	6.6	735	1.3	89
1892	233	23,500	0.2	29.7	3,669	4.4	17.0	1,976	6.6	766	1.3	88
1893	...	24,700	0.2	35.0	4,212	4.3	16.9	1,946	7.5	842	1.4	94
1894	...	25,000	...	40.8	4,535	4.7	17.5	1,983	7.1	791	1.4	93

F2 Freight Traffic on Railways (in stated units)

1850–1894

	Portugal	Romania	Russia[12]	Serbia	Spain		Sweden	Switzerland	U.K: G.B.
	a	a	a	a	a	b	a	a	a
1850	...	...	...	...	...	...	...	...	...
1851	...	...	...	...	...	...	...	...	...
1852	...	...	...	...	...	...	...	...	...
1853	...	...	...	...	...	...	...	...	...
1854	...	...	...	...	...	...	...	...	...
1855	...	...	...	...	...	...	...	...	...
1856	...	...	...	...	...	...	...	...	64.8
1857	...	...	...	...	...	...	...	...	71.3
1858	...	...	...	...	...	...	...	...	73.1
1859	...	...	...	...	...	...	...	...	78.6
1860	...	...	...	...	...	...	...	...	89.8
1861	...	...	...	...	...	...	...	...	94.0
1862	...	...	...	...	...	...	...	...	93.4
1863	...	...	...	...	...	...	...	...	100
1864	...	...	...	...	...	...	...	...	110
1865	...	...	...	...	...	...	0.3	...	114
1866	...	...	...	...	...	...	0.3	...	124
1867	...	...	5.2	...	...	...	0.5	...	135[9]
1868	...	...	7.2	...	2.6	437	0.8	...	...
1869	...	...	...	...	2.7	454	1.6	...	...
1870	...	...	...	...	3.2	483	2.1	...	...
1871	...	...	...	...	3.5	542	2.1	...	169
1872	...	...	14.1	...	4.0	636	2.5	...	179
1873	...	...	18.7	...	3.9	625	3.0	...	191
1874	...	...	22.2	...	2.7	491	3.5	...	188
1875	...	...	25.5	...	3.2	618	5.1	...	199
1876	...	...	26.7	...	4.5	702	4.7	...	206
1877	...	0.8	...	...	5.7	855	4.7	...	212
1878	...	0.9	...	...	5.3	840	5.0	...	206
1879	...	0.8	...	...	5.0	832	4.5	...	212
1880	0.7	0.8	...	...	6.8	1,044	5.9	5.8	235
1881	0.7	1.0	...	...	6.4	1,000	6.7	5.7	245
1882	0.9	1.1	45.1	...	6.9	1,060	7.3	6.4	256
1883	...	1.3	49.9	...	8.9	1,381	7.6	7.1	267
1884	0.9	1.2	42.4	...	8.1	1,336	7.5	7.3	260
1885	1.0	1.5	42.9	...	7.9	1,304	7.6	7.5	258
1886	1.0	1.6	42.4	...	8.5	1,220	7.4	7.6	255
1887	1.1	2.1	50.1	...	8.9	1,173	7.6	8.3	269
1888	1.3	2.3	65.2	...	8.7	1,208	8.5	8.9	282
1889	1.6	2.6	75.1	...	8.8	1,251	9.9	9.4	298
1890	2.3	3.1	68.5	0.3	10.3	1,347	10.6	9.4	304
1891	2.0	3.4	70.6	0.3	9.7	1,288	11.2	9.7	311
1892	1.6	3.3	73.5	0.3	...	1,242	11.3	9.5	310
1893	1.5	4.2	79.4	0.4	...	1,327	12.0	10.3	293
1894	1.6	3.7	88.9	0.3	...	1,321	13.1	10.6	325

F2 Freight Traffic on Railways (in stated units)

	Austria[1]		Belgium		Bulgaria		Czech		Denmark		Finland[3]		France	
	a	b	a	b	a	b	a	b	a	b	a	b	a	b
1895	93.9	8,516	46.7	...	0.4	...	...	...	2.4	154	1.2	159	101	12.9
1896	100	9,017	49.6	...	0.7	...	...	...	2.7	173	1.4	180	104	13.2
1897	104	9,557	51.8	...	0.7	...	...	...	3.0	191	1.7	213	108	13
1898	111	10,451	47.4	...	0.8	55	...	...	3.6	220	1.9	240	114	14
1899	115	10,678	52.2	...	0.7	47	...	...	3.8	236	2.2	287	120[5]	13.7[5]
1900	119	11,128	55.1	...	0.7	50	...	...	4.2	267	2.5	343	83.4	16.0
1901	121	11,158	54.2	...	1.0	68	...	...	4.3	268	2.3	304	80.4	15.8
1902	120	11,104	56.9	...	0.9	74	...	...	4.5	273	2.3	317	81.0	15.7
1903	122	11,448	59.3	...	0.9	89	...	...	5.1	321	2.8	373	85.3	16.1
1904	125	11,694	60.5	...	1.3	129	...	...	5.3	333	2.9	376	85.5	16.2
1905	134	12,314	64.4	...	1.3	121	...	...	5.7	361	2.8	351	91.0	17.4
1906	145	13,347	70.2	...	1.2	123	...	...	6.2	383	3.1	376	95.1	18.2
1907	152	14,710	71.4	...	1.3	149	...	...	6.5	398	3.5	425	102	19.3
1908	155	14,982	67.9	...	1.3	140	...	...	6.9	421	3.6	435	103	20.0
1909	152	15,217	71.0	...	1.6	188	...	...	6.9	416[16] 462	3.7	443	107	20.8
1910	138	15,152	76.2	...	1.7	196	...	...	6.9	465	3.9	462	113	21.5
1911	146	16,365	80.8	...	2.3	270	...	...	7.3	492	4.5	558	121	22.7
1912	160	17,287	87.2	...	2.0	215	...	...	7.8	533	4.6	596	131	24.2
1913	...	...	88.4	5,729	1.9[13]	176[13]	...	...	8.8	578	5.0	649	136	25.2
1914	...	...	...	...	2.5	...	...	...	9.3	601	4.4	685	88.2	17.8
1915	...	...	...	...	2.0	...	...	...	10.0	705	5.2	1,279	71.5	16.5
1916	...	...	...	...	2.8	...	...	...	11.6	932	6.2	1,483	79.7	18.9
1917	...	...	...	...	3.5	...	...	...	11.5	902	4.9	1,216	83.7	20.2
1918	...[1]	...[1]	...	...	2.9[14]	...	...	...	10.4	748	1.9	298	64.7	20.1
1919	...	...	...	...	1.8	...[14]	[59.2][15]	[4,720][15]	11.5[16]	760[16]	4.1	616	77.0	20.7
1920	...	...	70.4	...	2.4	478	78.8	6,240	12.4	885	5.4	932	103[7]	25.9[7]
1921	...	...	66.9	...	2.9	535	81.4	6,636	11.9	849	5.2	835	137	26.0[7]
1922	27.4	...	78.3	5,044	3.3	601	74.7	7,072	9.8	649	6.9	1,135	157	28.6
1923	...	...	88.0	5,888	3.5	635	77.0	7,735	10.3	650	8.3	1,351	174	33.3
1924	22.7	...	97.9	7,011	4.1	706	90.0	9,808	10.7	681	8.2	1,337	199	37.2
1925	25.3	3,751	96.8	7,037	3.6	672	89.5	9,874	11.5	715	8.9	1,442	195	37.1
1926	...	3,940	109	8,272	3.8	660	88.9	10,249	10.1	647	10.1	1,630	208	40.4
1927	27.8	4,257	104	7,810	4.0	702	95.1	11,191	9.4	633	11.1	1,768	194	36.6
1928	29.1	4,240	110	7,808	4.4	741	104	11,980	9.7	647	11.5	1,837	208	39.2
1929	30.7	4,444	119	8,386	4.8	880	109	12,381	9.6	667	10.7	1,804	223	41.8
1930	27.2	3,813	105	7,133	4.6	853	94.3	10,476	10.2	723	9.6	1,592	224	40.9
1931	23.6	3,154	94.0	6,027	4.5	852	81.5	9,228	9.5	696	8.5	1,444	193	37.1
1932	19.2	2,584	76.2	4,534	4.3	813	62.6	7,218	8.5	647	8.8	1,481	161	31.9
1933	18.5	2,556	74.9	4,440	4.2[14]	809[14]	55.7	6,501	6.7	540	10.5	1,674	153	31.0
1934	22.0	2,743	75.5	4,483	[3.1]	[591]	60.8	7,141	7.3	579	12.6	1,966	148	29.7

F2 Freight Traffic on Railways (in stated units)

	Germany		Greece		Hungary[8]		Ireland	Italy		Netherlands		Norway		Poland	
	a	c	a	b[40]	a	b	a	a	b	a	b	a	b	a	b[26]
1895	260	26.6	0.3	...	31.9	4,395	4.8	18.6	2,028	7.8	873	1.4	96	...	...
1896	284	28.1	...	...	35.0	4,638	4.8	19.3	2,151	8.0	926	1.6	110	...	...
1897	301	30.3	...	...	35.7	4,772	5.1	20.4	2,296	8.6	976	1.8	125	...	...
1898	321	32.7	0.3	...	38.6	4,942	5.2	21.7	2,438	8.3	1,044	2.1	141	...	...
1899	341	35.1	0.3	...	39.9	5,020	5.3	23.9[23]	2,624[23]	9.3	1,090	2.2	149	...	...
1900	360	37.0	0.3	...	42.6	315	5.2	18.0	2,126	9.6	1,051	1.6	111	...	...
1901	353	35.4	0.4	...	43.0	5,381	5.2	19.5	2,234	10.3	1,163	2.3	154	...	...
1902	366	36.8	0.4	30	44.7	5,414	5.4	22.0	2,440	10.8	1,216	2.2	146	...	...
1903	392	39.6	0.5	...	46.4	5,582	5.7	23.7[23]	2,573[23]	10.8	1,219	2.5	158	...	...
1904	408	41.2	0.6	...	52.7	5,669	5.8	...[24]	...[24]	11.4	1,294	3.6	205	...	...
1905	444	44.6	0.5	...	51.9	6,041	5.8	25.7	4,893	11.6	1,281	3.7	209	...	...
1906	479	48.3	0.5	36	55.8	6,426	5.9	29.8	5,219	12.5	1,337	4.3	235	...	...
1907	515	51.3	0.6	...	61.5	6,935	6.2	32.6	5,621	12.5	1,320	4.4	240	...	...
1908	497	49.9	0.6	40	61.9	7,068	6.1	34.1	5,755	12.7	1,346	4.5	257	...	...
1909	526	52.8	0.6	...	66.9	7,557	6.3	35.6	6,065	13.1	1,354	6.1	339	...	...
1910	575	56.4	0.6	45	68.8	8,095	6.6	37.6	6,185	13.7	1,422	4.9	294	...	...
1911	617	62.6	0.7	49	78.8	8,999	6.7	39.1	6,486	15.4	1,851	5.8	336	...	...
1912	668	66.2	0.7	45	83.6	9,666	6.8	40.9	6,819	17.0	1,736	6.5	363	...	...
1913	677	67.7	0.7	50	87.2	9,914	6.8[9]	41.4	7,070	17.5	1,802	7.2	401	...	...
1914	529	...	0.8	56	...[8]	...[8]	5.7	37.7	7,144	15.1	1,622	7.7	419	...	...
1915	368	...	0.7	58	67.9	...	...	38.3	8,874	13.5	1,693	6.8	434	...	...
1916	416	...	0.8	65	78.2	11,778	...	40.5	11,083	14.0	1,712	6.4	502	...	...
1917	...[7]	...[7]	0.6	54	74.8	10,054	...	38.7	10,627	12.1	...	6.8	533	...	...
1918	387	...	0.8	51	74.5	9,911	...	39.0	10,266	12.0	...	5.9	486	...	...
1919	287[17]	...[17]	0.8	56	...[8]	...[8]	...	39.7	9,795	12.7	...	6.1	450	12.0	...
1920	337	...	0.7[21]	57[21]	...	...	...	38.8	8,620	16.7	...	6.1	498	17.0	...
1921	354	...	1.1	...	19.6	1,594	...	41.7	8,598	15.8	...	7.0	483	30.9	...
1922	470[18]	68.7[18]	1.0	...	26.1	2,288	...	48.4	9,877	14.7	...	7.9	493	43.9	10,041
1923	[289][19]	[42.7][19]	1.2	77	34.1	2,906	...[22]	54.1	10,463	14.6	...	9.1	550	76.0	10,521
1924	[343][19]	[47.9][19]	1.6	115	37.7	3,155	...	63.2	11,911	16.2	...	7.6	512	60.0[25] 63.0	10,984
1925	442	60.2	1.8	153	35.4	3,029	...	65.3	12,532	16.6	...	10.3	634	63.0	12,634
1926	472	65.4	1.8	157	33.5	2,909	3.1	65.0	12,386	20.0	...	9.9	611	69.0	16,227[26] 15,020
1927	529	73.3	1.7	150	39.1	3,399	3.6	61.9	10,995	20.4	...	9.8	610	79.0	17,560
1928	522[20] 525	73.9	1.7	150	40.6	3,420	3.6	64.5	11,666	22.0	...	8.5	590	86.0	20,161
1929	531	77.1	2.0	182	40.7	3,445	3.6	65.3	12,246	24.3	...	9.9	468	91.0	21,242
1930	438	61.6	2.5	211	38.8	3,345	3.4	55.4	10,991	22.7	...	11.6	717	74.0	18,296
1931	357	51.7	2.4	198	32.9	2,868	3.3	46.5	9,584	22.0	...	8.3	550	67.0	18,291
1932	308	44.8	2.1	180	23.9	2,487	2.9	40.7	8,612	18.3	...	6.0	455	51.0	13,539
1933	338	48.2	1.9	166	17.1	2,082	2.6	40.5	7,976	18.1	...	5.7	467	51.0	14,182
1934	403[17]	57.6[17]	2.1	188	19.6	2,449	3.1	43.0	7,883	17.4	...	5.8	465	57.0	16,234

F2 Freight Traffic on Railways (in stated units)

1895–1934

	Portugal	Romania[29]		Russia/U.S.S.R.[12]		Spain		Sweden		Switzerland		U.K.:G.B.		Serbia	
	a	a	b[28]	a	c	a	b	a	b	a	b	a	c	a	b
1895	1.7	3.5	...	91.6	...	...	1,469	14.8	...	11.1	...	335	...	0.3	...
1896	1.9	4.2	...	101	...	...	1,532	16.7	...	12.2	...	357	...	0.4	...
1897	2.0	3.9	...	118	27.6	11.6	1,711	18.5	...	13.0	...	375	...	0.4	...
1898	2.0	4.8	...	120[12] / 123	30.0[12] / 30.9	11.9	1,885	19.2	1,261	13.6	...	379	...	0.4	...
,1899	2.4	3.6	...	...	33.3	14.9	2,078	19.6	1,333	14.3	...	415	...	0.5	...
1900	2.7	4.0	...	154	38.9	16.4	2,182	21.6	1,450	14.5	...	427	...	0.5	...
1901	2.8	4.6[29]	...	155	39.2	16.0	2,124	21.5	1,460	13.8	...	417	...	0.5	...
1902	3.4	4.7	...	161	40.3	17.4	2,133	22.3	1,474	12.4	...	439	...	0.5	...
1903	3.8[27] / 3.6	5.0	...	179	44.8	16.6	2,586	25.7	1,847	12.2	...	445	...	0.6	...
,1904	3.6	4.2	...	181	47.7	16.7	2,446	27.6	1,989	12.8	...	451	...	0.6	...
1905	3.8	5.7	...	169	45.4	17.9	2,357	29.1	2,063	13.9	...	463	...	0.7	...
1906	4.0	6.1	...	191	49.3	19.1	2,400	32.0	2,237	15.5	1,077	491	...	0.8	...
1907	4.2	6.8	...	204	54.2	19.5	2,537	33.7	2,365	17.3	1,211	518	...	...	...
1908	4.3	6.4	...	209	53.5	19.6	2,526	33.1	2,343	16.8	1,151	494	...	...	...
1909	4.5	6.9	...	225	58.1	19.7	2,520	31.1	2,167	16.1	1,180	502	...	...	...
1910	4.8	8.2	...	235	65.8	20.9	2,669	37.0	2,663	17.3	1,249	516	...	...	...
1911	...	9.4	...	...	...	21.5	2,798	38.1[27] / 35.0	2,797[27] / 2,628	18.2	1,366	525	...	...	...
1912	...	8.8	...	...	...	23.2	3,106	38.5	2,913	19.6	1,437	522	...	...	...
1913	...	9.0	1,443	...[12] / 132	76.8[12] / 65.7	24.6	3,175	41.0	3,184	19.3	1,458	571[9] / 370	...	...	...
1914	5.6	8.1[30] / 9.9	...	123	62.9	29.0	2,954	39.5	3,132	17.1	1,391	...	...	...	...
1915	5.9	9.3	...	126	75.6	30.7	3,301	47.5	4,422	19.3	1,551	...	...	...	...
1916	6.6	4.3	...	147	91.2	35.1	3,808	53.4	5,538	21.4	1,661	...	...	...	...
1917	6.0	2.4	...	115	63.0	35.5	3,781	48.7	4,584	20.3	1,360	...	...	...	...
1918	5.5	1.7	...	37	14.1	35.2	3,852	44.1	3,992	19.3	1,173	...	...	...	...
1919	4.6	3.5	...	31	17.5	35.1	3,736	38.1	3,123	19.3	1,388	310	...	...	...
														Yugoslavia[32]	
1920	5.0	5.3[29]	...[29]	40	14.4	33.1	3,775	39.1	3,287	22.2	1,401	323	31.4	...	...
1921	5.7	...	...	37	15.7	32.8	3,781	27.1	2,371	16.9	1,081	272	21.7	...	...
1922	6.4	...	...	[40][31]	[16.1][31]	39.9	3,826	29.7	2,730	17.9	1,219	306	27.5	15.5	1,551
1923	5.9	16.5	2,560	58	23.5	35.8	4,105	32.7	2,877	19.6	1,274	349	31.0	18.1	2,019
1924	6.1	17.3	3,457	68	33.7	43.3	4,424	36.4	3,192	22.3	1,930	340	31.2	21.1	2,268
1925	5.6	20.1	3,151	84	47.4	41.5	4,483	38.1	3,446	22.4	1,904	321	30.0	21.4	2,435
1926	5.8	22.5	3,551	117	68.9	41.9	4,682	37.7	3,575	22.8	1,812	219	23.0	21.3	2,921
1927	5.6	23.7	3,713	136[31]	81.7[31]	45.7	4,845	41.7	3,932	24.3	2,005	327[9]	30.9[9] / 23.1	21.9[32]	3,194[32] / 3,252
1928	6.7	21.9	3,339	156	93.4	49.4	5,226	34.6	3,133	25.5	2,223	311	29.0	23.7	3,933
1929	7.0	23.0	3,541	188	113	49.9	5,700	46.1	4,585	26.5	2,358	335	30.8	24.7	4,298
1930	7.8	23.2	3,552	239	134	48.1	5,450	42.0	4,256	25.5	2,209	309	29.1	21.7	3,849
1931	6.3	21.0	3,450	258	152	...	5,115	30.8	3,465	24.9	2,043	273	26.7	19.3	3,411
1932	7.0	20.9	3,523	268	169	...	5,142	24.4	2,497	21.7	1,673	254	24.4	15.9	3,020
1933	7.2	20.8	3,798	268	170	...	4,803	25.0	2,517	21.4	1,678	255	24.6	15.6	3,048
1934	7.8	23.6	4,208	317	206	...	4,636	31.4	3,344	21.6	1,801	274	26.5	16.5	3,222

F2   Freight Traffic on Railways (in stated units)

	Austria[1]		Belgium		Bulgaria		Czechoslovakia		Denmark[16]		Finland[3]	
	a	b	a	b	a	b	a	b	a	b	a	b
1935	23.0	2,844	76.9	4,757	4.4	835	65.3	7,886	7.1	596	13.7	2,020
1936	22.3	2,877	85.1	5,331	4.6	875	63.5	8,563	7.0	603	15.2	2,239
1937	...	4,151	96.4	6,230	5.2	984	72.5	10,871	7.3	647	17.6	2,639
1938	...	...	82.5	5,144	5.7	1,078	...	9,308	7.2	651	15.3	2,305
1939	...	...	84.7	5,556	6.0	1,191	...	...	7.1	673	13.9	2,197
1940	...	...	40.2	3,332	7.0	1,489	...	...	8.2	853	10.4	2,173
1941	...	...	45.8	3,632	...	...	...	...	...	...	11.8	...
1942	...	...	40.5	3,168	...	...	...	...	...	...	13.3	...
1943	...	...	39.7	3,060	...	...	...	...	...	...	14.6	...
1944	...	...	15.6	1,096	...	...	...	...	20.2	1,969	11.6	...
1945	...	...	26.2	2,049	...	...	...	...	18.2	1,671	13.2	2,492
1946	...	...	52.0	4,695	...	...	57.4	9,268	15.1	1,363	16.2	3,221
1947	...	12,619	61.1	5,868	...	1,262	64.4	11,405	13.0	1,294	17.3	3,499
1948	27.4	17,341	64.0	6,153	9.8	1,717	74.4	14,279	12.1	1,383	17.1	3,495
1949	34.5	18,822	60.2	5,666	...	...	82.1	16,416	10.8	1,320	15.4	3,041
1950	35.9	18,820	60.8	5,462	14.0	2,580	96.0	18,634	9.3	1,228	16.8	3,465
1951	39.1	19,238	72.2	6,628	...	2,939	108	21,475	9.6	1,310	20.6	4,445
1952	37.4	19,261	66.6	6,067	17.9	3,140	119	24,404	10.2	1,446	18.0	3,960
1953	36.4	18,969	62.5	5,721	...	3,682	123	26,328	8.5	1,283	16.3	3,692
1954	41.3	20,843	61.9	5,635	...	3,840	128	28,457	8.0	1,249	18.9	4,118
1955	44.5	23,286	69.6	6,618	23.7	4,118	140	31,702	7.9	1,294	20.1	4,500
1956	45.7	24,103	70.6	6,922	25.5	4,484	149	34,279	7.8	1,298	18.8	4,437
1957	46.9	24,818	66.8	6,586	27.6	4,928	160	39,541	8.4	1,350	18.6	4,349
1958	42.0	23,972	57.8	5,830	...	5,243	174	42,674	8.2	1,325	16.9	4,076
1959	41.4	24,345	58.5	6,062	35.1	6,289	181	44,101	8.7	1,420	17.7	4,211
1960	45.4	26,685	60.8	6,303	38.4	6,981	194	47,407	8.4	1,417	19.8	4,873
1961	43.5	26,931	61.4	6,455	40.5	7,447	206	50,674	8.4	1,436	19.7	4,727
1962	43.9	27,908	62.3	6,467	40.4	7,876	207	52,224	8.4	1,494	19.3	4,917
1963	45.9	28,875	65.3	6,825	43.5	8,573	202	51,662	8.8	1,610	18.9	4,936
1964	45.3	29,081	66.6	6,925	51.5	9,969	214	55,391	8.7	1,498	20.0	4,871
1965	44.9	29,215	63.9	6,758	56.0	10,784	219	56,904	9.0	1,532	21.6	5,192
1966	44.7	29,836	59.3	6,234	60.7	11,449	224	57,652	8.3	1,488	21.9	5,619
1967	42.8	29,806	59.4	6,082	63.1	11,719	226	55,781	8.1	1,480	22.6	5,603
1968	43.3	29,431	63.3	6,675	62.8	12,198	227	56,710	7.8	1,453	22.3	5,633
1969	45.9	30,906	69.2	7,416	62.7	12,618	226	56,760	7.7	1,490	23.4	6,032
1970	50.0	32,971	71.2	7,816	68.1	13,858	237	60,995	8.5	1,729	24.8	6,279
1971	48.9	33,603	66.4	7,328	70.2	14,918	250	63,464	8.9	1,875	23.5	5,764
1972	49.5	34,165	69.3	7,490	72.9	15,825	260	65,512	8.7	1,907	25.2	6,514
1973	51.5	34,963	75.5	8,183	75.7	16,640	261	64,943	9.0	2,034	27.5	7,018
1974	54.1	36,579	82.1	9,146	78.0	17,309	266	67,951	9.6	2,227	28.3	7,493
1975	46.4	33,580	59.2	6,757	78.8	17,285	271	69,271	8.8	1,997	23.4	6,443
1976	46.9	36,002	60.0	6,648	76.6	17,055	276	70,748	7.9[16]	1,905[16]	24.2	6,552
1977	46.5	34,826	58.4	6,485	75.2	17,080	274	71,550	...[33]	...[33]	22.8	6,403
1978	44.9	34,384	63.2	7,119	75.0	17,148	278	72,359	...[33]	...[33]	23.3	6,332
1979	50.5	37,351	73.9	8,535	77.7	17,653	283	73,041	7.8	1,800	27.5	7,373
1980	51.6	38,966	71.1	7,999	77.8	17,681	286	72,640	7.5	1,720	30.5	8,341
1981	50.3	38,482	69.6	7,528	81.5	18,052	286	72,258	7.0	1,566	30.6	8,396
1982	50.0	38,639	62.4	6,788	83.9	18,276	289	71,585	7.0	1,657	29.3[34]	8,004[34]
											28.7	8,000
1983	50.3	38,372	63.3	6,570	82.6	18,060	292	73,069	7.2	1,633	29.3	8,091
1984	55.8	40,846	70.8	7,905	83.4	18,134	299	74,015	7.4	1,670	29.8	7,981
1985	58.2	41,841	72.4	8,254	82.9	18,172	293	73,598	7.9	1,768	30.8	8,067
1986	55.1	41,131	63.1	7,423	85.0	18,327	297	75,152	8.0	1,800	27.8	6,952
1987	54.7	40,703	64.0	7,266	82.5	17,842	291	73,525	7.6	1,644	30.1	7,403
1988	55.4	41,859	65.8	7,694	79.3	17,585	295	75,294	7.8	1,671	33.0	7,816
1989	58.6	44,048	65.9	8,049	77.3	17,034	284	71,985	8.0	1,723	33.7	7,958
1990	62.6	46,842	67.1	8,354	63.2	14,132	130	64,326	8.4	1,787	34.6	8,357
1991	64.7	50,061	64.5	8,153	35.2	8,685	...	49,933	8.5	1,858	31.1	7,634
1992	62.5	50,769	62.3	8,074	32.2	7,758	170[53]	31,116[53]	8.7	1,870	32.6	7,848
							Czech Republic[53]					
1993	60.3	49,295	57.7	7,568	31.4	7,702	120[53]	25,579[53]	8.8	1,751	37.9	9,259
1994	61.5	50,126	59.2	8,081	33.5	7,774	...	24,393	9.1	2,008	39.0	9,949
1995	62.7	51,079	58.4	7,287	35.1	8,595	...	25,395	8.9	1,985	38.0	9,293
1996	60.9	50,347	58.2	7,244	33.9	7,549	...	24,174	8.8	1,757	37.1	8,806
1997	61.5	50,678	59.7	7,465	33.4	7,444	...	22,173	9.0	1,983	39.2	9,856
1998	62.7	49,834	60.5	7,600	31.6	6,152	...	19,529	9.2	2,058	39.4	9,885

F2 Freight Traffic on Railways (in stated units)

1935–1998

	France		Germany		West Germany		Greece		Hungary		Ireland	
	a	c	a	c	a	c	a	b[40]	a	b	a	b
1935	139	27.1	448	64.1	...	...	2.1	203	19.4	2,390	3.3	
1936	148	29.5	497	71.4	...	...	2.4	244	21.4	2,635	3.2	
1937	157[35]	31.8[35]	547	80.6	...	...	...	265	24.1	3,015	3.2	
1938	133	26.5	574	89.0	...	...	2.6	324	25.2	3,056	2.9	
1939	141	29.3	...	...	...	...	...	353	...	...	3.3	
1940	102	24.0	...	...	...	...	...	397	...	...	3.4	
1941	112	28.4	...	...	...	...	...	...	...	...	3.9	
1942	103	27.4	...	...	...	...	...	...	...	...	3.9	
1943	95.0	24.1	...	...	...	...	...	...	...	...	4.3	
1944	42.2	9.6	...	...	...	...	...	...	...	...	4.5	
1945	69.3	17.8	...	...	...	...	...	...	...	...	4.4	
			East Germany									
1946	126	32.4	...	...	...	24.9	...	...	...	...	4.0	
1947	141	37.1	...	...	184	32.7	...	114	16.9	2,556	3.9	
1948	158	41.3	...	...	236[36]	41.9[36]	1.1	108	24.0	3,276	3.0	
1949	161	41.1	111	12.4	288	43.6	1.4	146	33.4	4,549	3.6	404
1950	152	38.9	129	15.1	291	43.1	1.9	195	41.8	5,424	3.6	414
1951	177	45.4	153	17.3	324	49.9	2.4	264	48.6	6,276	3.5[41]	409[41]
1952	174	44.0	158	19.1	331	49.9	2.5	317[40]	60.6	7,447	3.1	356
1953	163	40.3	182	22.1	313[38]	45.9[37] 46.6	2.3	335	69.6	8,179	3.4	382
1954	169	41.6	191	23.2	325[39]	47.6[39]	2.6	351	66.2	8,174	3.2	370
1955	192	46.9	208	25.2	367	52.9	2.5	303	70.8	8,807	3.2	383
1956	205	50.3	210	27.3	388[36] 414	56.4[36] 57.6	2.1	342	64.0	8,170	2.8	325
1957	217	53.7	220	28.6	423	57.8	2.4	373	73.7	9,496	2.6[22]	309[22]
1958	212	52.9	227	30.1	386	51.6	2.2	363	79.5	10,242	2.3	306
1959	213	53.4	229	31.6	396	53.6	2.1	361	87.4	11,703	2.4	317
1960	227	56.9	238	32.9	429	57.1	2.2	362	97.1	13,346	2.5	338
1961	230	58.8	249	34.7	424	58.2	2.5	410	99.7	13,865	2.4	332
1962	231	61.2	260	37.4	419	60.0	2.7	417	102	14,560	2.5	337
1963	240	63.0	261	37.6	431	64.5	2.8	445	106	15,371	2.5	340
1964	248	65.3	267	39.1	442	63.6	3.2	546	115	17,037	2.4	335
1965	239	64.6	260	38.9	422	61.0	3.3	570	115	17,297	2.4	377
1966	233	64.1	263	39.7	374	59.3	3.3	552	119	17,904	2.7	412
1967	229	62.9	253	38.5	319	57.4	3.4	563	118	18,512	2.9	480
1968	229	63.0	253	38.5	346	61.1	2.5	548	115	18,340	3.3	527
1969	243	67.2	252	39.4	380	69.4	2.5	587	113	18,420	3.2	505
1970	250	70.4	263	41.5	392	73.6	3.0	688	118	19,821	3.4	546
1971	240	67.0	263	44.0	362	67.2	3.4	748	120	20,322	3.7	578
1972	246	68.6	274	44.7	366	66.7	3.1	756	119	20,061	3.7	564
1973	258	73.9	281	46.8	386	69.3	3.3	798	123	21,318	3.7	568
1974	265	77.1	286	49.2	404	71.3	4.0	902	130	23,123	[2.2]⁴	[452]⁴¹
1975	219	64.0	289	49.7	329	57.3	4.0	931	132	23,541	3.4	561
1976	215	65.5	296	51.8	343	61.4	3.5	844	132	23,156	3.5	585
1977	203	63.3	299	52.2	324	57.9	3.5	855	135	24,181	3.6	587
1978	203	64.3	300	53.0	337	59.5	3.6	854	135	24,500	3.8	620
1979	213	67.6	302	54.4	371	68.1	4.1	841	134	24,661	3.8	619
1980	209	66.4	312	56.4	364	60.8	3.6	814	130	24,399	3.6	624
1981	187	61.4	315	55.8	346	63.5	3.0	693	131	24,342	3.6	678
1982	174	58.4	323	54.0	318	58.8	2.6	586	127	23,273	3.6	654
1983	166	56.6	326	54.9	310	57.3	3.5	670	124	23,079	3.3	582
1984	168	57.5	337	56.7	330	61.5	4.0	770	122	22,848	3.4	601
1985	162	55.8	348	58.7	335	65.5	4.2	733	118	22,309	3.4	601
1986	146	51.7	346	58.9	317	62.1	4.2	689	119	22,600	3.1	574
1987	142	51.3	345	58.8	307	60.2	3.8	591	115	21,732	3.0	563
1988	145	52.3	349	60.4	310	61.2	4.0	596	112	21,058	3.0	545
1989	147	53.3	339	59.0	315	63.3	4.0	658	105	19,819	3.1	556
1990	142	51.5	230	40.1	310	62.9	3.7	647	88	16,781	3.3	582
1991	140	51.5	**Included in West Germany**		419	82.2	3.5	605	67	11,937	3.3	600
1992	137	50.4			380	72.8	3.4	563	53	10,015	3.3	633
1993	118	45.9			329	66.6	3.4	523	44	7,708	3.1	575
1994	128	49.7			374	71.8	...	...	44	7,707	2.9	569
1995	124	49.1			375	70.9	...	...	47	8,422	3.0	602
1996	136	50.5			360	69.7	...	...	45	7,634	2.9	570
1997	141	54.8			381	73.7	...	...	49	8,149	2.7	522
1998	142	55.0			384	74.0	...	...	50	8,150	2.5	469

F2   Freight Traffic on Railways (in stated units)

	Italy[43] a	Italy[43] b	Netherlands a	Netherlands b	Norway a	Norway b	Poland a	Poland c	Portugal a	Portugal b	Romania[29] a	Romania[29] b[28]
1935	47.3	10,090	14.1		8.4	598	58.0	15.7	4.1[46]	...	24.6	4,370
1936	51.7	10,441	13.9	...	9.5	643	61.0	16.4	4.3[46]	588[46]	25.7	4,633
1937	57.6	11,524	16.1	2,256	11.9	771	76.0	19.9	4.2[46]	586[46]	26.8	4,934
								22.1[25]				
1938	54.4	11,554	14.6	2,040	13.3	825	78.0	22.4	6.2	523	27.6	4,950
1939	64.9	15,032	15.7	2,196	11.3	736	...	...	6.9	591	27.8[29]	4,888[29]
1940	70.2	19,981	19.0	2,664	7.8	616	...	...	7.5[27]	611	...	4,597
									4.3			
1941	72.7	24,080	19.3	2,700	5.1	651	...	...	4.5	657	...	5,516
1942	71.3	27,625	17.8	2,484	5.3	672	...	...	5.0	710	...	5,214
1943	35.1	...	17.0	2,376	6.6	739	...	...	5.1	711	...	4,942
1944	15.0[42]	...	10.6	1,488	6.3	715	...	...	5.3	729	...	3,679[29]
1945	28.4	8,903	5.3	2,040	4.3	592	...	...	5.2	688	...	...
1946	37.0	10,117	13.5	1,914	7.0[44]	842[44]	73.1	19.5	5.7	784	18.6	3,857[28]
												4,794
1947	42.2[24]	9,851[24]	16.1	2,267	10.0	1,062	93.7	21.3	4.6	733	...	...
	48.9	10,939										
1948	49.4	11,154	18.5	2,541	12.3	1,227	121	28.3	4.1	644	24.1	5,655
1949	50.6	10,478	19.9	2,787	13.6	1,386	140	32.7	3.6	569	...	...
1950	50.5	10,419	21.2	3,016	14.6[45]	1,379[45]	160	35.1	3.3	521	35.1	7,598
1951	58.0	11,733	22.6	3,256	14.9	1,409	176	38.5	3.5	585	38.1	8,743
1952	57.9	12,406	22.1	3,067	16.1	1,541	187	40.3	3.8	678	45.2	10,791
1953	58.1	12,618	23.7	3,252	15.2	1,377	211	44.6	3.5	642	53.1	12,554
1954	59.0	12,981	25.1	3,373	15.0	1,368	222	48.2	3.7	685	50.4	12,619
1955	64.6	14,685	25.6	3,440	15.7	1,448	236	52.0	3.9	723	59.0	14,675
1956	66.4	14,202	26.5	3,562	16.6	1,498	239	52.1	4.0	761	62.0	15,955
1957	65.9	14,395	25.2	3,398	16.4	1,532	249	55.3	4.0	773	65.3	17,044
1958	57.7	13,154	23.6	3,124	16.8	1,445	250	57.2	3.8	738	66.6	17,018
1959	61.4	14,422	24.6	3,210	15.7	1,421	265	61.7	3.8	751	69.0	17,475
1960	68.7	15,860	26.4	3,409	18.2[11]	1,579[11]	287	66.5	3.7	762	77.5	19,821
					19.3	1,638						
1961	67.2	15,518	26.4	3,391	19.6	1,725	298	69.7	3.7	736	85.3	22,207
1962	66.8	16,684	27.8	3,702	20.0	1,766	306	72.7	3.7	730	92.0	24,419
1963	69.0	17,076	31.0	4,093	20.3	1,817	313	74.4	3.8	766	99.6	26,755
1964	62.4	14,728	30.3	3,885	23.0	1,972	332	79.1	3.8	763	110	29,386
1965	61.7	15,289	27.4	3,522	25.3	2,136	341	81.0	3.7	755	114	30,981
1966	60.8	16,022	25.2	3,272	24.5	2,208	354	85.0	3.3	677	127	34,541
1967	58.5	17,096	25.5	3,235	27.0	2,409	366	88.5	3.4	727	137	37,297
1968	58.1	17,280	25.8	3,274	31.2	2,597	378	92.6	3.6	771	148	40,705
1969	57.6	17,282	26.3	3,433	30.2	2,717	374	95.0	3.5	737	155	44,031
1970	60.9	18,129	26.7	3,532	30.1	2,845	382	99.3	4.0	777	171	48,045
1971	56.7	17,284	23.3	3,233	28.8	2,610	398	104	3.8	813	185	50,840
1972	56.3	17,187	21.8	3,071	29.6	2,659	416	110	4.1	797	194	53,280
1973	57.2	17,637	23.6	3,463	31.9	2,846	431	116	4.3	819	206	57,103
1974	55.9	18,217	22.6	3,370	32.1	2,952	453	125	4.2	867	218	61,618
1975	45.7	14,885	17.7	2,721	25.8	2,626	464	129	3.3	754	228	64,803
1976	50.6[43]	16,376[43]	17.7	2,696	29.2	2,771	465	131	3.4	855	238	67,556
1977	52.3	17,577	17.7	2,805	23.9	2,631	481	135	3.7	885	248	70,035
1978	55.6	16,639	18.2	2,882	27.1	2,713	489	138	3.9	933	260	73,738
1979	58.8	17,742	21.8	3,376	33.5	3,085	480	135	3.4	872	273	76,031
1980	56.3	18,384	21.4	3,396	31.1	3,081	482	135	3.7	1,001	275	75,535
1981	51.0	17,115	20.4	3,320	26.3	2,886	402	110	3.7	1,003	274	75,251
1982	49.3	16,904	18.2	2,915	20.4	2,545	402	113	3.9	1,060	271	71,110
1983	49.0	16,746	17.4	2,782	19.4	2,459	415	118	4.5	1,044	280	72,316
1984	54.1	17,870	19.2	3,119	22.5	2,667	426	124	5.5	1,239	289	75,159
1985	52.6	17,968	20.4	3,269	25.9	2,932	419	121	5.3	1,196	283	74,215
1986	51.3	17,410	19.1	3,107	25.7	3,015	431	122	5.3	1,328	307	79,092
1987	54.3	18,427	18.6	2,995	23.6	2,822	429	121	5.7	1,485	304	78,070
1988	58.0	19,567	19.6	3,200	22.7	2,617	428	122	6.0	1,597	315	80,607
1989	61.8	20,587	19.4	3,108	21.5	2,780	388	111	6.9	1,718	306	81,131
1990	65.2	21,217	18.4	3,070	21.8	2,354	261	85	6.7	1,588	219	57,253
1991	66.9	21,680	17.8	3,038	18.6	2,674	228	65	7.7	1,783	146	37,853
1992	68.8	21,830	17.1	2,764	20.2	2,294	202	73	7.4	1,767	111	28,170
1993	65.6	20,226	16.7	2,681	20.0	2,872	139	78	6.8	...	99	25,170
1994	68.8	22,564	17.9	2,830	19.9	2,678	121	65	8.7	1,826	97	24,704
1995	70.5	24,050	18.5	3,097	20.0	2,715	123	69	9.3	2,342	109	27,179
1996	69.4	23,314	19.2	3,123	19.9	2,641	123	68	9.0	2,178	108	26,877
1997	...	...	22.4	3,406	19.7	2,401	124	69	10.3	2,632	98	24,789
1998	...	...	23.7	3,778	19.4	2,144	123	62	9.9	2,340	90	19,708

F2 Freight Traffic on Railways (in stated units)

	Russia/U.S.S.R.[12]		Spain		Sweden		Switzerland		U.K. GB[51]		Yugoslavia	
	a	c	a	b	a	b	a	b	a	c	a	b
1935	389	258	29.7	4,683	35	3,885	20.8	1,830	275	26.8	17.5	3,305
1936	483	323	…	…	39	4,543	19.1	1,543	285	28.5	17.9	3,334
1937	517	355	…	…	46	5,607	23.5	2,164	302	30.1	20.5	3,987
1938	516	371	…	…	41	5,206	20.7	1,710	269	26.6	22.1	4,315
1939	554[12]	392[12]	…	…	46	6,054	24.8	2,137	293	…	21.1	4,784
1940	593	415	…	…	45	7,210	28.4	3,180	299	…	…	…
1941	549	402	…	…	46	7,969	33.3	3,879	291	…	…	…
1942	290	228	26.5	4,271	48	8,477	32.8	3,668	300	39.0	…	…
1943	313	256	23.4	5,228	51	8,818	30.2	2,972	306	39.8	…	…
1944	371	297	20.0	5,594	48	8,121	26.3	1,433	297	40.0	…	…
1945	395	314	24.0	4,676	44	6,996	20.1	1,406	271	36.0	…	…
1946	453	335	24.7	4,881	47	8,087	24.8	1,846	267	33.7	19.5	…
1947	491	351	26.2	5,177	44	8,128	26.5	1,995	261[51]	33.0[51]	26.9	…
1948	620	446	22.7	6,396	46	8,459	25.0	2,080	277	35.4	36.2	7,434
1949	735	524	23.2	6,412	43	8,107	21.7	1,858	285	36.0	48.4	9,642
1950	834	602	23.5	7,305	44	8,640	24.0	2,229	286	36.2	46.1	9,944
1951	909	677	24.0	7,889	48	10,027	28.5	2,680	289	37.4	41.9	8,704
1952	997	741	26.5	8,536	46	9,633	26.3	2,476	289	36.6	37.9	8,383
1953	1,067	798	27.2	8,632	43	9,017	26.0	2,647	294	37.2	39.3	8,817
1954	1,131	857	29.0		43	9,235	28.1	2,868	288	36.1	43.7	9,571
1955	1,267	971	27.7	8,199	47	10,320	31.2	3,275	279	34.9	50.2	11,577
1956	1,371	1,079	29.1	8,589	49	10,969	35.6	3,537	281	35.1	52.1	11,869
1957	1,488	1,213	31.8	9,225	48	10,396	34.5	3,725	279	34.1	56.6	12,984
1958	1,617	1,302	32.4	9,292	43	9,475	31.9	3,500	247	30.1	57.2	13,031
1959	1,764	1,430	29.0	8,378	44	9,685	34.2	3,798	238	29.0	60.7	13,974
			27.1	7,128								
1960	1,885	1,504	43.2[47]	7,966[47]	50	10,928	39.0	4,346	252	30.5	65.2	15,191
1961	1,988	1,567	44.8	8,107	50	11,100	41.1	4,651	242	28.8	64.2	14,941
1962	2,077	1,646	43.7	8,454	49	11,064	43.4	4,907	232	26.3	63.6	15,033
1963	2,158	1,749	42.0	8,702	52	12,015	46.4	5,238	239	25.2	71.8	17,345
1964	2,289	1,854	43.1	9,157	59	12,919	49.1	5,271	243	26.2	76.5	18,258
1965	2,415	1,950	43.9	9,209	61	13,883	50.5	5,585	232	25.2	74.8	18,036
1966	2,482	2,016	41.8	8,901	59	14,062	50.7	5,784	217	24.2	71.6	17,518
1967	2,605	2,161	43.0	9,637	59	13,538	51.7	5,974	204	22.3	68.7	16,390
1968	2,706	2,275	43.4	9,255	65	14,798	52.7	6,113	211	24.0	68.4	16,372
1969	2,759	2,367	43.5	9,692	68	16,021	56.2	6,557	210	25.3	70.2	17,691
1970	2,896	2,495	43.1	10,339	66	17,311	60.2	7,035	209	26.8	75.4	19,253
1971	3,049	2,637	43.3	10,112	60	15,658	59.9	7,072	198	24.3	75.6	19,653
1972	3,172	2,761	46.5	10,753	62	16,214	61.3	7,178	178	23.4	72.3	19,179
1973	3,346	2,958	49.4	12,002	68	18,260	63.0	7,610	199	25.5	74.5	20,447
1974	3,497	3,098	51.2[48]	12,009[48]	73	19,598	61.2	7,451	178	24.2	81.5	23,081
1975	3,621	3,237	46.8		58	16,057	46.9	5,518	177	23.5	77.7	21,638
1976	3,655	3,295	46.8	11,159	59	16,238	50.0	6,044	178	23.1	73.7	21,017
1977	3,723	3,331	48.0	11,826	51	14,782	52.2	6,324	172	22.8	77.4	22,225
1978	3,776	3,429	45.0	11,078	50	14,764	51.4	6,553	172	20.0	80.8	23,378
1979	3,688	3,349	[43.0][49]	[10,015][49]	63	17,347	56.9	7,352	171	19.9	87.8	25,925
1980	3,728	3,440	46.6	11,100	57	16,648	59.7	7,799	155	17.6	84.9	25,018
1981	3,762	3,503	45.3	11,022	49	15,410	58.2	7,519	155	17.5	86.0	25,720
1982	3,725	3,464	42.9	10,928	44	14,331	54.3	6,873	143	15.9	85.7	26,166
1983	3,851	3,600	42.4	11,019	45	15,445	53.7	6,759	146	17.1	89.6	27,860
1984	3,909	3,639	42.1	12,077	50	17,776	50.5	7,276	79	12.7	91.7	28,731
							57.7					
1985	3,951	3,718	[41.2][50]	[12,077][50]	56	18,420	45.2[52]	7,436	123	15.4	90.7	28,719
1986	4,076	3,834	43.9	11,766	56	18,553	46.3	7,336	140	16.5	89.8	27,573
1987	4,067	3,825	40.2	11,942	54	18,406	45.7	7,192	142	17.3	84.2	26,070
1988	4,116	3,925	39.7	12,145	56	18,687	50.3	7,970	150	18.0	83.6	25,413
1989	4,017	3,852	40.7	12,048	56	19,156	53.1	8,661	143	16.4	71.0	25,800
1990	1,990	…	37.3	11,613	56	19,599	54.3	8,905	138	16.0	62.0	24,444
1991	3,435	…	32.7	10,755	54	18,815	53.1	8,769	136	15.3	…	5,760[56]
1992	…	…	28.7	9,513	53	18,609	49.8	8,316	122	15.5	…	4,409[56]
1993	1,346[55]	…	24.9	8,000	52	17,337	46.4	7,919	103	13.7	…	1,699[56]
1994	…	…	27.1	8,966	57	19,062	51.4	8,586	100	12.9	…	1,387
1995	…	…	29.2	10,419	59	19,390	52.0	8,626	101	13.1	…	1,460
1996	…	…	30.0	10,449	56	18,835	51.0	7,907	129	15.1	…	2,062
1997	…	…	31.5	11,488	57	19,114	…	…	139	16.9	…	2,432
1998	…	…	32.9	11,739	56	19,019	…	…	142	17.3	…	2,743

F2   Freight Traffic on Railways (in stated units)

NOTES

1. SOURCES:- Germany ton/kms to 1870—W. Fischer *et al, Sozialgeschichtliches Arbeitsbuch* I (Munich, 1982), 1871–1938—W.G. Hoffman, *Das Wachstum derDeutschen Wirtschaft seit der Mitte des 19 Jahrhunderts* (Berlin, etc., 1965); Great Britain and Ireland to 1980—based on B.R. Mitchell, *British Historical Statistics* (Cambridge, 1988), where the original sources are given; Greece 000 tons in 1938 and 1948-55—supplied by the National Statistical Service of Greece; Poland 1921 and 1922—supplied by the Polish Central Statistical Office; Russia 1941 and 1942—E.W. Williams, *Freight Transportation in the Soviet Union* (Princeton, 1962). All other statistics are taken from the official and other publications noted on p. xv.
2. It is not always clear whether traffic for the servicing of the railway is included or not, though there appears to be an indication whenever a change in this respect occurs.
3. The following earlier statistics are available (in thousands of tons):-

	Austria-Hungary	Belgium		Austria-Hungary	Belgium	France
1834	26	—	1841	181	166	1,060
1835	48	—	1842	230	194	1,480
1836	67	—	1843	301	333	1,530
1837	64	—	1844	332	560	1,940
1838	70	4	1845	383	691	2,310
1839	82	50	1846	592	778	2,520
1840	118	102	1847	931	1,005	3,600
			1848	867	939	2,920
			1849	1062	1,035	3,420

and in million ton/kms:-

	France	Germany		France	Germany
1840	38	3	1845	100	51
1841	...	8	1846	119	82
1842	...	14	1847	...	160
1843	...	26	1848	...	168
1844	81	33	1849	...	234

See also footnote 5 below.

FOOTNOTES

[1] Including Hungary to 1867 (1st line) and mixed lines subsequently until 1912. The Italian provinces are excluded throughout. From 1922 the statistics are for the Republic and relate to state operated lines only.
[2] Excluding the Kaschau-Oderberger line, which carried 274 thousand tons in 1870.
[3] State operated lines only (to 1873 (1st line) in the case of Belgium).
[4] Previously excluding small amounts of traffic in Holland-Falster.
[5] Revised figures are given here for 1900. In the source they are also given at decennial intervals for the period 1841-91 as follows:-

	thousand tons	million tons/kms		thousand tons	million tons/kms
1841	1,010	37	1871	27,800	5,530
1851	4,340	488	1881	56,200	10,600
1861	23,500	3,790	1891	63,100	11,800

[6] Savoy and Nice included subsequently.
[7] Alsace-Lorraine is excluded from France for 1870-1921 and included in Germany for 1871-1917.
[8] Transleithania to 1918. The figures to 1888 (1st line) are for purely Hungarian lines only. Subsequently they include traffic on mixed Austro-Hungarian lines, which is also included in the Austrian statistics (see footnote 1). Statistics for 1915-1918 are for years ended 30 June.
[9] New bases of collection were adopted in 1869, 1913, and 1928. In addition, Manchester Ship Canal rail traffic is excluded from 1913 (2nd line).
[10] Figures to 1880 (1st line) relate to goods trains only. Subsequently express traffic is included.
[11] First half-year only. Subsequent figures to 1960 (1st line) are for years ended 30 June.
[12] Figures to 1898 (1st line) apply to European Russia (exclusive of Finland). From 1898 (2nd line) to 1913 (1st line) they apply to the whole Empire, except Finland. From 1913 (2nd line) to 1939 they apply to the territory of the U.S.S.R. in 1923, and subsequently to the present territory.
[13] The territorial changes of the Balkan Wars were effective from 1914.
[14] For 1919-33 figures are for years ended 31 March following that indicated. The 1934 figures are for 9 months.
[15] Excluding the Kosice-Bohumin line.
[16] State-operated lines only to 1909 (1st line). From 1920 to 1976 the statistics are for years ended 31 March.
[17] Memel, Danzig, Posen, West Prussia, parts of Pomerania and Schleswig, Eupen, Malmedy, etc. and Saarland are excluded from 1920, though Saarland is reincorporated from 1935.
[18] Eastern Upper Silesia is excluded from July 1922.
[19] Excluding the occupied Rhineland.
[20] Previously excluding some private narrow gauge lines.

F2 Freight Traffic on Railways (in stated units)

21 The territorial gains in the north are included from 1921.
22 Subsequent statistics relate to railway systems based in southern Ireland, though their traffic in Northern Ireland is included. From 1958 the latter ceased when the state took over the southern part of the Great Northern Railway.
23 Figures for 1899–1903 are of freight charged at full car load rate only.
24 Statistics for 1905–1947 (1st line) are for years beginning 1 July and are for state-operated lines only. Figures are available for privately-operated lines as follows (calendar years throughout):-

		thousand tons	million ton/ kms		thousand tons	million ton/ kms		thousand tons	million ton/ kms
	1906	3,683	104	1930	9,137	109	1938	8,760	256
	1907	3,898	101	1931	7,161	154	1939	9,830	284
	1908	4,543	116	1932	6,493	141	1940	12,150	...
	1909	5,073	127	1933	5,967	131	1941	14,160	...
	1910	5,698	142	1934	5,770	143			
	1927	9,250	...	1935	5,950	143	1944	7,410	...
	1928	9,945	217	1936	7,530	185	1945	4,700	...
	1929	10,418	227	1937	9,350	271	1946	7,120	...

Figures for the state lines for the calendar year 1947 were as follows:- 41,202 thousand tons and 10,746 million ton/kilometres.

25 Tonnage figures to 1924 (1st line) and ton/kilometrage figures to 1937 (1st line) relate to standard gauge lines only.
26 Traffic for the servicing of the railways is included to 1926 (1st line).
27 The reason for this break is not given in the source.
28 State-operated lines only. All remaining private lines were nationalised in 1946.
29 For 1901–20 the figures are for years ended 31 March following that indicated. The newly-acquired territories are included after 1920. Bessarabia, northern Bukovina, and southern Dobrudja are excluded from 1940, and northern Transylvania is excluded for 1940–44.
30 Subsequently including traffic for the servicing of the railways, which had previously been excluded.
31 The figure for 1922 is for 9 months to 30 September, and the figures for 1923–27 are for years ended 30 September.
32 Figures to 1927 (1st line) are for state-operated lines plus the Southern Railway only.
33 The following statistics are available for 1977–8:- State lines for year ended 31 March 1977 7.5 m.tons; 1,875 m.tkm. State lines for year ended 31 March 1978 7.0 m. tons; 1,765 m.tkm. State lines for April–December 1978 5.0 m.tons; 1,278 m.tkm. Private lines for calendar year 1977 0.7 m.tons; 16 m.tkm. Private lines for calendar year 1978 0.7 m.tons; 16 m.tkm.
34 State-operated lines only from 1982 (2nd line).
35 State-operated lines only from 1938.
36 Saarland is excluded from 1949 to 1956 (1st line).
37 From 1946 to 1953 (1st line) the ton/km, statistics are for state-operated lines only.
38 Subsequently including the Hamburg Dock line.
39 Subsequently including the Salzgitter line.
40 Traffic for the servicing of the railways is included to 1952 (1st line).
41 Subsequent statistics to 1973 for the state lines are for years ended 31 March following that indicated. From 1958 this covered all lines in southern Ireland. The 1974 figures are for the period April–December, and those for 1975 are for the calendar year.
42 Excluding Allied military traffic.
43 State railways only from 1977.
44 From 1946/7 goods carried jointly by state and private lines are counted twice.
45 Including freight carried free of charge from 1951.
46 These figures are for the main six companies only.
47 Including narrow gauge lines subsequently.
48 A new method of reckoning was adopted in 1974.
49 Excluding the Basque Provinces and Catalonia.
50 Excluding private lines.
51 State railways only from 1948.
52 State railways only from 1985 (2nd line).
53 Czech Republic. Slovakia = 1993, 64(a); 14,304(b).

	Slovakia (million ton-kilometres)
1993	14,304
1994	12,236
1995	13,674
1996	12,017
1997	12,373
1998	11,754

54 Ex-Soviet Union
55 Russia. Ex-USSR figures as follows:

	million ton-kilometres											
	Armenia	Azerbaijan	Belarus	Estonia	Georgia	Kazakhstan	Kyrgistan	Lithuania	Moldova	Tajikistan	Ukraine	Uzbekistan
1994	378	3,312	27,963	3,612	955	146,778	629	7,996	3,533	2,169	200,422	19
1995	403	2,384	25,510	3,846	1,246	124,502	403	7,220	3,134	2,115	195,762	17
1996	351	2,778	26,018	4,198	1,141	112,688	481	8,103	2,897	1,719	160,384	20
1997	381	3,515	30,636	5,141	2,006	106,425	472	8,622	2,937	1,384	160,433	17
1998	420	4,702	30,370	6,079	2,574	99,371	466	8,265	2,575	1,458	158,693	16

F2 Freight Traffic on Railways (in stated units)

[56] Yugoslavia Ex-Yugoslavia as follows: (millions)

	Bosnia-Herz	Croatia	Macedonia	Slovenia
1991	1,946 (TKM)	. . .	. . .	. . .
1992	. . .	4.5 (Tons)	3.9 (Tons)	13.0 (Tons)
1993	. . .	11.6 (Tons)	3.4 (Tons)	12.6 (Tons)
		million ton-kilometres		
1994	. . .	1,563	151	2,448
1995	. . .	1,974	169	3,076
1996	. . .	1,717	271	2,550
1997	. . .	1,876	279	2,852
1998	. . .	2,001	408	2,859

F3 PASSENGER TRAFFIC ON RAILWAYS (in millions)

KEY:- P = passengers; PK = passenger kilometres

	Austria[1]		Belgium[2]	Denmark	Finland[3]		France		Germany	Hungary[7]	Ireland	Italy
	P	PK	P	P	P	PK	P	PK	PK	P	P	P
1834	0.002	...	...	...	—	—	...	...	...	...	...	...
1835	0.047	...	0.421	...	—	—	...	...	...	...	...	...
1836	0.079	...	0.871	...	—	—	...	...	...	...	...	...
1837	0.082	...	1.4	...	—	—	...	...	...	...	...	...
1838	0.272	...	2.2	...	—	—	...	...	...	...	...	...
1839	0.378	...	2.0	...	—	—	...	...	...	...	...	...
1840	0.353	...	2.2	...	—	—	...	...	62	...	...	...
1841	2.2	...	2.6	...	—	—	6.4[5]	112	97	...	...	...
1842	1.9	...	2.7	...	—	—	6.2	...	145	...	...	...
1843	2.7	...	3.1	...	—	—	7.4	...	185	...	2.1	...
1844	2.7	...	3.4	...	—	—	8.1	283	256	...	2.6	...
1845	2.6	...	3.5	...	—	—	8.9	247	308	...	3.4	...
1846	3.4	...	3.7	...	—	—	10.4	328	428	...	3.6	...
1847	4.9	...	3.7	...	—	—	12.8	...	547	...	3.8	...
1848	4.1	...	3.6	...	—	—	11.9	...	615	...	3.8[8]	...
1849	4.7	...	3.9	...	—	—	14.8	...	664	...	6.1	...
1850	6.5	...	4.2	...	—	—	18.7	...	783	...	5.5	...
1851	8.0	...	4.4	...	—	—	19.9[5]	797	865	...	5.6	...
1852	8.2	...	4.5	...	—	—	22.6	...	914	...	6.2	...
1853	8.3	...	4.7	...	—	—	24.7	1,155	935	...	7.1	...
1854	9.1	...	4.9	...	—	—	28.1	1,375	1,041	...	6.9	...
1855	9.5	...	5.3	...	—	—	32.9	1,822	1,090	...	7.2	...
1856	9.9	...	6.0	...	—	—	36.4	1,845	1,263	...	7.9	...
1857	10.5	...	6.5	...	—	—	41.6	1,994	1,457	...	8.4	...
1858	11.2	...	6.6	...	—	—	45.4	2,107	1,491	...	8.4	...
1859	15.7	...	7.1	...	—	—	52.4[4]	2,707[4]	1,637	...	9.4	...
1860	12.2	...	7.4	...	—	—	56.5	2,521	1,733	...	10.0	...
1861	12.2	...	...	...	—	—	61.9[5]	2,689	1,901	...	10.7	...
1862	12.9	...	...	...	- -	2.1	65.1	2,853	2,064	...	10.4	...
1863	13.2	...	...	...	0.1	3.5	70.2	3,006	2,360	...	11.5	...
1864	12.7	...	9.4	...	0.1	4.6	73.4	3,164	2,571	...	11.9	...
1865	12.8	...	10.7	...	0.1	4.3	81.5	3,328	2,676	...	13.2	...
1866	15.7	...	11.6	...	0.1	3.6	87.3	3,407	3,132	...	13.1	...
1867	12.1[1] 11.6	...	12.6	1.9	0.1	3.3	101.6	4,301	2,978	...	14.0	14.9
1868	13.8	...	12.8	2.1	0.1	3.3	102.9	3,899	3,236	0.7	...[9]	17.5
1869	16.8	...	13.6	2.6	0.1	3.6	111.2[6]	4,108[6]	3,534	1.2	13.3	...
1870	19.4	...	14.1[2]	2.9	0.4	1.8	102.6	4,272	4,447[6]	2.1	14.3	22.2
1871	[23.7][1]	...	18.3	3.1	0.6	32	95.7[5]	4,589	5,000	3.7	15.5	22.4
1872	31.7	...	23.2	3.5	0.8	42	111.5	4,278	5,000	5.4	16.3	25.5
1873	37.7	...	26.4[2] 40.2	3.9	0.9	44	116.5	4,347	5,700	5.9	16.3	26.3
1874	35.8	...	42.2	4.5	1.1	48	121.1	4,446	5,800	6.0	16.5	27.3
1875	35.8	...	48.4	5.0	1.2	59	131.3	4,786	6,000	5.5	16.9	28.0
1876	35.4	1,608	51.4	6.0	1.5	66	137.0	4,962	6,100	5.3	17.4	28.1
1877	32.8	1,522	52.0	6.2	1.4	67	138.8	4,870	6,100	5.0	17.3	28.1
1878	33.2	1,659	53.6	6.0	1.6	69	152.8	5,779	6,200	5.5	17.9	29.0
1879	33.7	1,614	53.9	5.8	1.8	68	150.5	5,254	6,100	5.8	16.4	30.4
1880	34.7	1,668	56.3	5.9	1.8	66	165.1	5,863	6,500	5.8	17.3	32.5
1881	36.8	1,628	57.2	6.2	1.7	64	179.7[5]	6,323[5]	6,800	6.2	17.6	34.0
1882	41.6	1,886	61.5	6.8	1.8	68	194.9	6,761	7,100	6.4	18.7	34.4
1883	47.4	2,660	63.7	7.6	1.8	68	207.2	7,040	7,400	7.1	19.3	36.8
1884	52.2	2,170	64.5	8.0	1.8	71	211.9	6,883	7,700	8.3	19.6	36.4

F3   Passenger Traffic on Railways (in millions)

| | Netherlands | | Norway | | Portugal | Romania | Russia[11] | Spain | Sweden | Switz | U.K.:G.B. |
	P	PK	P	PK	P	P	P	P	P	P	P
1838	...	...	...	...	...	...	...	...	...	...	5.4
1839	...	...	...	...	...	...	...	...	...	...	...
1840	...	...	...	...	...	...	...	...	...	...	...
1841	...	...	...	...	...	...	...	...	...	...	...
1842	...	...	...	...	...	...	...	...	...	...	...[8]
1843	...	...	...	...	...	...	...	...	...	...	21.7
1844	...	...	...	...	...	...	...	...	...	...	25.2
1845	...	...	...	...	...	...	...	...	...	...	30.4
1846	...	...	...	...	...	...	...	...	...	...	40.2
1847	...	...	...	...	...	...	...	...	...	...	47.9
1848	...	...	...	...	...	...	...	...	...	...	54.4[8]
1849	...	...	...	...	...	...	...	...	...	...	57.8
1850	...	...	...	...	...	...	...	...	...	...	67.4
1851	...	...	...	...	...	...	...	...	...	...	79.7
1852	...	...	...	...	...	...	...	...	...	...	82.8
1853	...	...	...	...	...	...	...	...	...	...	95.2
1854	...	...	...	...	...	...	...	...	...	...	104.3
1855	...	...	0.128	...	...	...	...	...	...	...	111.4
1856	...	...	0.161	5	...	...	...	...	...	...	121.4
1857	...	...	0.174	6	...	...	...	...	...	...	130.6
1858	...	...	0.168	5	...	...	...	...	...	...	130.7
1859	...	...	0.170	6	...	...	...	...	...	...	140.3
1860	...	...	0.152	5	...	...	...	...	...	...	153.5
1861	...	...	0.142	5	...	...	...	...	...	...	163.0
1862	...	...	0.160	6	...	...	...	8.2	0.8	...	170.0
1863	...	...	...	...	...	...	...	10.5	1.0	...	192.2
1864	...	...	...	...	...	...	...	11.4	1.0	...	217.4
1865	...	...	0.300	...	...	...	...	11.4	1.1	...	238.7
1866	...	...	...	...	...	...	...	11.0	1.3	...	261.2
1867	...	...	0.386	13	...	...	9	...	1.5	...	273.7
1868	...	...	0.388	14	...	...	10	...	...	...	...[9]
1869	...	...	0.613	19	...	...	...	...	2.4	...	298.6
1870	...	...	0.551	17	...	...	...	...	2.5	...	322.2
1871	...	...	0.584	19	...	...	21	11.5	2.6	...	359.7
1872	...	...	0.771	23	...	...	24	11.9	3.1	...	406.5
1873	...	...	1.5	46	...	...	27	10.8	4.0	...	439.0
1874	...	...	1.7	46	...	...	...	10.6	5.3	...	461.3
1875	...	...	1.5	43	...	...	28	12.2	6.5	...	490.1
1876	...	...	1.5	41	...	...	29	14.0	6.8	...	517.1
1877	...	...	1.4	41	...	1.3	...	13.2	7.3	...	532.3
1878	13.1	417	[0.608][10]	[19][10]	...	1.2	...	13.3	7.2	...	547.1
1879	13.4	421	1.4	44	...	0.7	...	14.2	6.2	...	546.3
1880	14.5	454	1.6	51	2.1	0.8	...	14.8	7.0	21.5	596.6
1881	15.2	469	1.8	56	2.2	1.0	...	...	7.1	21.7	608.4
1882	15.8	487	2.3	72	2.3	1.2	37	...	7.8	22.5	636.1
1883	16.0	542	2.7	84	2.5	1.4	38	...	8.6	23.9	664.4
1884	16.8	554	3.2	93	2.6	1.4	37	18.5	9.0	23.3	675.4

F3 Passenger Traffic on Railways (in millions)

	Austria[1]		Belgium		Bulgaria		Czechoslovakia		Denmark		Finland[3]	
	P	PK	P	PK	P	PK	P	PK	P	PK	P	PK
1885	55.6	2,246	65.5	...	...	...	...	...	8.3	...	1.8	76
1886	56.8	2,217	65.9	...	...	...	...	...	8.0	...	1.9	81
1887	57.3	2,255	68.8	...	...	...	...	...	9.2	...	2.1	93
1888	59.9	2,345	73.4	...	...	...	...	...	9.2	...	2.1	102
1889	64.0	2,437	76.3	...	...	...	...	...	9.5	...	2.2	104
1890	74.9	2,789	82.4	...	...	...	...	...	9.7	...	2.5	126
1891	85.0	3,078	86.5	...	...	...	...	...	10.3	...	2.6	137
1892	92.1	3,228	88.2	...	...	...	...	...	10.5	...	2.5	128
1893	97.3	3,513	92.1	...	...	...	...	...	12.1	303	2.6	132
1894	102.9	3,670	96.9	...	0.3	25	...	...	13.0	330	2.5	136
1895	106.4	3,847	99.6	...	0.4	27	...	...	13.4	336	3.0	149
1896	105.2	3,933	106.8	...	0.4	29	...	...	14.7	367	3.6	179
1897	109.5	4,034	114.4	...	0.5	36	...	...	15.2	387	4.3	222
1898	126.1	4,440	115.4	...	0.6	41	...	...	17.1	456	5.6	283
1899	142.3	4,894	129.0	...	0.6	45	...	...	19.5	522	6.2[16] / 6.4	319
1900	158.1	5,194	139.1	...	0.7	64	...	...	20.8	546	7.1	337
1901	169.6	5,323	139.8	...	0.7	55	...	...	22.6	590	7.5	338
1902	173.6	5,518	142.5	...	0.9	69	...	...	24.4	613	7.6	342
1903	176.5	5,339	148.9	...	1.0	76	...	...	24.1	607	8.7	382
1904	182.5	5,603	152.9	...	1.2	91	...	...	24.5	625	9.2	390
1905	189.9	5,864	163.4	...	1.4	100	...	...	24.2	631	10.1	426
1906	207.1	6,353	169.8	...	1.6	126	...	...	25.2	665	11.8	523
1907	223.7	6,789	181.2	...	1.8	132	...	...	27.2	705	12.4	518
1908	228.3	7,058	176.8	...	2.2	149	...	...	27.9	723	12.8	495
1909	242.0	7,446	178.4	...	2.8	197	...	...	28.6	747[15] / 869	13.4	528
1910	254.6	7,522	193.1	4,306	3.1	210	...	...	29.4	917	14.3	555
1911	276.6	7,955	198.9	...	3.5	234	...	...	30.2	923	15.0	593
1912	290.9	8,321	211.0	...	3.3	230	...	...	31.7	958	16.2	622
1913	...	...	224.3	6,242	1.9[12]	136[12]	...	...	32.5	950	18.1	704
1914	...	...	...	...	4.2	303	...	...	33.9	969	19.3	735
1915	...	...	...	...	3.5	285	...	...	34.3	959	17.6	773
1916	...	...	...	...	1.5	140	...	...	38.0	1,049	23.3	1,074
1917	...	...	...	...	1.6	126	...	...	42.2	1,191	29.0	1,194
1918	...[1]	...[1]	...	...	2.7	231	...	...	38.1	1,151	12.4	585
1919	...	...	112.7	...	5.4[13]	443[13]	[215.2][14]	[6,429][14]	42.3	1,231	13.0	679
1920	...	...	223.3	5,205	6.9	469	280.2	8,687	45.6	1,365	17.2	775
1921	78.7	2,628	240.2	...	8.2	529	294.1	10,467	45.0	1,389	18.0	683
1922	97.9	3,495	248.9	6,157	9.1	568	294.2	8,271	42.0	1,258	21.2	911
1923	84.6	3,055	262.5	6,609	8.3	509	291.3	8,171	42.2	1,290	25.0	1,024
1924	108.7	3,643	251.1	6,194	9.0	571	320.9	8,953	43.1	1,293	28.4	1,062
1925	117.7	3,990	245.0	6,049	8.4	539	325.0	9,305	45.0	1,364	21.6	908
1926	110.5	3,719	244.5	6,259	8.5	578	325.0	9,264	45.5	1,384	22.0	940
1927	108.1	3,612	237.8	5,781	8.1	536	314.9	8,483	42.8	1,298	22.3	983
1928	110.8	3,821	255.2	6,270	9.0	610	338.1	9,070	40.8	1,238	23.5	1,084
1929	104.9	3,666	264.8	6,365	9.4	647	343.6	9,178	42.1	1,263	23.2	1,094
1930	101.0	3,454	262.3	6,964	8.2	550	334.5	8,821	43.7	1,318	21.5	1,045
1931	89.1	3,137	242.0	5,810	7.7	532	293.8	7,829	44.4	1,366	19.6	907
1932	70.5	2,527	208.8	5,157	8.0	566	265.8	7,092	42.7	1,351	18.7	830
1933	60.0	2,284	202.9	5,058	7.2	510	240.5	6,492	39.0	1,223	17.5	817
1934	57.0	2,131	193.8	4,873	[5.4][13]	[395][13]	244.4	6,755	41.3	1,364	18.7[17]	890[17]

F3 Passenger Traffic on Railways (in millions)

| | France | | Germany | | Greece | | Hungary[7] | | Ireland |
	P	PK	P	PK	P	PK	P	PK	P
1885	214.5	7,025	...	7,900	...	...	9.1	...	19.1
1886	216.6	7,137	...	8,400	...	...	8.6	...	18.7
1887	217.8	7,212	...	8,700	...	...	8.1	...	19.5
1888	224.8	7,345	340	8,300	...	...	8.8[7]	742	19.9
							14.1		
1889	244.2	8,628	377	10,200	3.4	...	19.0	940	21.0
1890	241.1	7,943	426	11,300	...	...	29.2	1,237	21.4
1891	255.7[5]	8,286[5]	464	11,800	...	...	35.9	1,504	22.2
1892	288.1	9,243	488	11,900	5.0	...	41.1	1,672	22.6
1893	317.8	10,010	...	12,700	4.5	...	45.6	1,869	23.7
1894	336.5	10,330	...	12,900	...	...	49.6	2,027	24.5
1895	348.9	10,660	592	14,000	4.7	...	53.2	2,091	26.2
1896	363.0	11,150	646	15,200	...	...	57.5	2,207	26.6
1897	374.8	11,440	692	16,300	...	...	57.0	2,126	25.9
1898	385.9	11,820	756	17,700	5.7	...	60.3	2,248	26.6
1899	401.8[5]	12,340[5]	805	18,800	6.2	...	61.6	2,292	27.4
1900	430	14,000	856	20,200	6.2	...	64.4	2,320	27.7
1901	406	12,900	876	20,700	6.3	...	67.0	2,433	26.9
1902	410	13,100	891	21,200	6.8	129	68.6	2,431	28.2
1903	413	13,200	958	22,600	7.0	...	72.4	2,540	28.6
1904	420	13,600	1,030	24,000	7.3	...	78.5	2,738	29.0
1905	429	14,100	1,116	25,800	7.8	...	86.5	2,950	29.0
1906	445	14,700	1,209	27,900	8.2	156	96.1	3,356	29.2
1907	459	15,200	1,295	29,800	8.5	...	107.2	3,667	29.7
1908	464	15,900	1,362	31,300	8.3	157	111.7	3,756	29.0
1909	476	16,200	1,470	33,800	8.7	...	124.2	4,032	29.6
1910	492	16,800	1,541	35,700	9.0	181	140.0	4,404	30.7
1911	494	17,500	1,643	38,200	9.1	182	153.8	4,772	30.8
1912	509	18,100	1,744	40,200	10.4	233	164.1	5,055	29.2[9]
1913	529	19,300	1,798	41,400	12.6	297	166.1	5,022	31.3
1914	355	13,700	...	...	12.3	254	...[7]	...[7]	...
1915	209	8,800	...	...	13.4	279	160	...	...
1916	325	10,000	...	...	17.1	431	204.3	10,746	...
1917	352	10,100	...	...	14.1	334	237.3	10,671	...
1918	377	11,900	...[6]	...[6]	14.7	402	263.0	12,031	...
1919	463	20,200	...	...	15.0	450	...	...	...
1920	500[6]	22,100[6]	...[18]	...[18]	15.8[22]	447[22]	...[7]	...[7]	...
1921	661	25,700	...	...	17.9	...	111.8	2,534	...
1922	720	27,300	2,979[19]	75,600[19]	21.9	...	103.8	2,916	...[23]
1923	767	29,300	[2,382][20]	...	22.4	...	113.8	3,469	...
1924	772	28,400	[1,963][20]	44,600	26.7	...	111.1	3,423	...
1925	802	29,800	2,168	50,100	28.5	751	92.8	2,837	...
1926	777	28,300	1,877	44,000	27.0	720	104.9	2,838	23.3
1927	724	26,000	1,970	46,600	26.1	666	111.3	2,945	22.2
1928	745	27,000	2,071[21]	48,800	26.3	656	121.0	3,165	21.4
			2,088						
1929	765	28,200	2,057	48,100	28.1	679	125.4	3,171	22.5
1930	790	29,200	1,900	44,300	28.1	661	120.6	3,110	20.9
1931	773	29,000	1,636	37,700	26.8	608	110.8	2,744	20.1
1932	705	25,600	1,352	31,500	24.5	548	91.8	2,272	19.3
1933	661	24,600	1,284	30,700	24.3	531	55.4	1,783	17.7
1934	621	23,400	1,408[18]	35,500[18]	25.2	544	59.1	1,879	19.6

F3 Passenger Traffic on Railways (in millions)

	Italy		Netherlands		Norway		Poland		Portugal	Romania[22]	
	P	PK	P	PK	P	PK	P	PK	P	P	PK
1885	40.8	...	16.6	543	3.1	89	...	...	2.6	1.4	...
1886	42.7	...	16.8	547	3.1	92	...	...	2.9	1.6	...
1887	45.5	...	17.7	567	3.2	93	...	...	3.7	2.0	...
1888	49.3	...	18.5	581	3.2	92	...	...	4.4	2.1	...
1889	51.0	...	19.5	633	3.6	99	...	...	5.0	2.4	...
1890	50.9	...	...	...	4.0	107	...	...	6.0	2.9	...
1891	49.4	2,191	22.2	640	4.3	117	...	...	5.7	4.3	...
1892	50.1	2,175	22.5	648	4.7	126	...	...	5.9	5.4	...
1893	50.3	2,184	23.5	694	4.7_{25}	126_{25}	...	...	6.2	5.8	...
					5.7	134					
1894	51.7	2,275	24.4	709	6.0	138	...	...	6.7	6.0	
1895	52.6	2,302	25.3	738	6.3	146	...	...	7.2	5.9	...
1896	53.0	2,332	24.8	716	6.8	160	...	...	8.3	6.5	...
1897	54.0	2,407	25.0	724	7.4	172	...	...	9.6	5.7	...
1898	55.5	2,526	26.0	763	8.4	199	...	...	11.4	5.8	...
1899	57.9	2,571	27.9	815	9.4	220	...	...	11.4	7.1	...
1900	59.7	2,801	30.8	843	7.0	171	...	...	11.9	5.5	...
1901	61.1	2,775	32.7	962	9.9	234	...	...	12.6	5.3_{29}	...
1902	64.5	2,913	34.1	987	10.1	243	...	...	12.8	5.7	...
1903	67.7	3,041	35.9	1,043	9.9	235	...	...	13.5_{27}	5.6	...
									12.5		
1904	$..._{24}$	$..._{24}$	38.2	1,104	9.9	241	...	...	13.1	5.6	...
1905	85.1	4,178	38.8	1,170	9.8	235	...	...	13.4	6.6	...
1906	82.4	4,269	40.7	1,233	10.1	248	...	...	13.5	7.6	...
1907	88.8	4,365	41.0	1,248	10.4	257	...	...	13.2	8.2	...
1908	91.0	4,524	42.0	1,240	10.7	269	...	...	14.6	8.3	...
1909	92.5	4,532	43.2	1,271	15.4	386	...	...	15.2	9.2	...
1910	95.5	4,448	46.2	1,368	13.1	335	...	...	14.9	10.2	...
1911	99.2	4,500	44.9	1,176	14.3	371	...	...	...	11.4	...
1912	102.9	4,858	49.3	1,299	16.0	405	...	...	...	12.2	...
1913	106.0	5,000	54.1	1,433	17.8	462	...	...	...	11.1	...
1914	98.7	4,595	48.6	1,275	18.6	482	...	...	18.9	11.6	871
1915	93.2	5,028	60.0	1,458	18.7	508	...	...	20.0	...	...
1916	90.6	5,239	76.4	1,776	21.4	573	...	...	21.6	...	...
1917	82.1	5,201	64.4	...	25.8	678	...	...	17.9	...	...
1918	92.4	5,838	60.6	...	26.6	701	...	...	16.8	4.9	...
1919	118.3	6,407	60.2	...	30.2	773	61	...	19.1	14.2	...
1920	112.8	6,430	54.8	...	32.2	824	67	...	22.9	13.6_{29}	$..._{29}$
1921	111.3	6,640	55.4	...	28.4	741	130	...	23.6	...	...
1922	112.1	6,540	51.7	...	27.3	688	148	9,362	24.6	...	...
1923	115.1	7,028	49.4	...	27.9	695	169	9,552	24.9	17.2	3,331
1924	120.0	8,200	47.9	...	26.7	669	177_{26}	6,897	23.2	56.4	3,804
							178				
1925	129.0	8,000	47.2	...	23.7	623	164	6,366	24.9	50.7	3,412
1926	127.0	8,428	48.1	...	22.8	586	148	5,965	...	46.0	3,455
1927	123.3	8,144	52.3	...	20.1	530	161	6,307	30.0	40.4	3,150
1928	139.5	8,137	57.6	...	19.2	524	176	7,077	33.1	40.7	3,170
1929	143.7	8,071	58.8	...	18.1	502	167	7,073	33.3	38.8	3,047
1930	125.8	7,370	59.0	...	17.9	520	154	6,717	32.9	35.1	2,917
1931	108.0	6,528	56.2	...	17.6	532	136	5,474	30.2	31.6	2,630
1932	105.2	6,293	49.6	...	18.3	517	115_{27}	4,695	28.4	26.0	2,204
1933	106.6	6,991	50.1	...	18.7	529	139	4,754	28.3	27.1	2,297
1934	112.6	7,698	48.1	...	17.8	517	147	5,275	30.2	30.5	2,526

F3 Passenger Traffic on Railways (in millions)

	Russia/U.S.S.R.[11]		Serbia		Spain		Sweden		Switzerland		U.K.: G.B.
	P	PK	P	PK	P	PK	P[33]	PK	P	PK	P
		Thousand millions									
1885	37	...	...	...	17.7	...	9.7	...	24.0	...	678.1
1886	37	...	...	...	20.2	...	9.6	...	24.6	...	706.9
1887	37	...	...	...	20.1	...	10.1	...	25.6	...	714.2
1888	43	...	...	...	23.1	...	10.1	...	26.9	...	722.6
1889	43	...	...	...	24.7	...	11.1	...	29.2	...	754.2
1890	44	...	0.3	27	25.8	...	12.7	...	32.1	...	796.3
1891	48	...	0.4	33	27.9	...	13.6	...	34.6	...	823.3
1892	49	...	0.5	40	24.8	...	14.0	...	37.0	...	841.8
1893	52	...	0.5	40	33.7	...	14.8	...	39.7	...	849.5
1894	56	...	0.8	54	34.0	...	16.8	...	42.4	...	886.9
1895	61	...	0.7	43	34.3	...	18.3	...	45.0	...	903.5
1896	68	...	0.6	44	34.1	...	20.4	...	48.7	...	953.8
1897	75	9.2	0.6	39	25.7	...	22.7	...	52.5	...	1,004.5
1898	84[11] 85	10.0[11] 10.7	0.6	45	27.0	...	25.5	675	56.5	...	1,036.3
1899	94	11.3	0.7	51	29.0	...	28.7	761	60.1	...	1,079.3
1900	104	13.0	0.8	56	32.0	...	30.8	823	62.2	...	1,114.6
1901	113	13.3	0.7	50	33.4	...	33.3	875	60.1	...	1,145.5
1902	115	13.4	0.8	54	37.4	...	33.2	885	60.6	...	1,160.0
1903	123	14.6	0.8	55	39.6	...	36.3	968	68.2	...	1,166.6
1904	128	18.7	0.9	65	42.7	...	39.4	1,043	74.7	...	1,169.8
1905	122	19.5	1.0	75	42.6	...	41.7	1,097	81.6	...	1,170.0
1906	136	20.6	1.0	78	45.1	...	46.5	1,264	90.0	1,849	1,211.1
1907	149	18.9	...	...	47.3[32] 46.0	...	52.0	1,415	96.7	1,955	1,229.8
1908	162	20.4	...	...	47.2	...	54.2	1,441	101.5	2,027	1,249.1
1909	175	21.4	...	...	46.0	...	53.8	1,463	104.1	2,081	1,235.5
1910	195	23.2	...	...	48.9	...	58.3	1,573	109.1	2,307	1,276.0
1911	212	...	...	...	50.3	...	60.3	1,637	116.2	2,431	1,295.5
1912	245[11]	...[11]	...	...	54.0	...	63	1,728	122.4	2,518	1,265.2
1913	185	25.2	...	...	57.5	2,139	67	1,848	127.7	2,685	1,423.5[9] 1,199.3
1914	235	...	...	...	57.9	2,159	69	2,010	114.2	2,385	...
1915	264	...	...	...	62.6	2,136	70	2,145	107.1	1,980	...
1916	348	...	...	...	67.6	2,340	76[33]	2,403	121.7	2,222	...
1917	354	...	...	...	71.0	2,419	77	2,404	119.2	2,080	...
1918	386	...	...	...	75.5	2,567	79	2,243	103.3	1,936	...
1919	202	...	...	...	83.6	2,936	86	2,451	113.9	2,124	1,522.6
			Yugoslavia[31]								
1920	143	...	...	...	97.8	3,242	84	2,408	128.5	2,405	1,579.0
1921	84	11.3	...	...	105.0	3,428	75	2,161	120.0	2,223	1,229.4
1922	[77][30]	[9.9][30]	36.5	1,534	107.9	3,559	66	1,999	119.3	2,215	1,194.7
1923	122	13.9	38.0	1,628	115.0	3,629	64	2,045	127.5	2,351	1,235.6
1924	154	15.4	40.0	1,580	118.4	2,645	66	2,009	140.0	2,640	1,236.2
1925	212	19.0	40.0	1,629	117.9	3,680	66	2,038	146.4	2,819	1,232.6
1926	263	23.4	42.0	1,973	117.9	3,625	66	2,094	146.8	2,805	1,069.0
1927	254[30]	22.1[30]	46.2[31] 47.6	2,110[31] 2,137	114.6	3,491	66	2,166	157.8	3,017	1,174.7 1,195.9[34]
1928	291	24.5	50.4	2,274	113.4	3,515	67	2,221	166.5	3,225	847.1
1929	365	32.0	49.6	2,210	114.6	3,809	69	2,294	175.2	3,434	869.9
1930	558	51.8	47.6	2,297	117.1	3,844	70	2,435	176.5	3,528	844.3
1931	724	61.8	43.2	2,154	...	3,530	68	2,323	171.7	3,416	795.2
1932	967	83.7	36.4	1,800	...	3,540	65	2,261	161.0	3,219	777.3
1933	927	75.2	32.9	1,703	...	3,553	65	2,268	158.9	3,311	798.9
1934	945	71.4	31.6	1,647	...	3,443	69	2,479	157.5	3,286	829.7

F3 Passenger Traffic on Railways (in millions)

	Austria		Belgium		Bulgaria		Czechoslovakia		Denmark		Finland[3]	
	P	PK	P	PK	P	PK	P	PK	P	PK	P	PK
1935	55.8	2,185	198.7	5,648	7.2	518	236.5	6,429	49.2	1,454	10.6	954
1936	52.4	2,160	207.1	5,635	8.7	579	240.9	6,776	55.0	1,613	21.4	1,012
1937	...	2,407	221.9	6,148	10.2	685	268.7	9,239	61.2	1,654	23.3	1,149
1938	...	...	213.4	5,965	11.1	739	...	8,647	61.7	1,651	24.2	1,234
1939	...	...	191.9	5,394	12.2	784	...	...	62.2	1,729	24.7	1,372
1940	...	...	89.3	2,803	16.0	1,022	...	...	64.2	1,876	...	...
1941	...	...	139.8	4,137	16.5	1,322	...	...	...	...	...	...
1942	...	...	193.2	5,721	...	...	...	...	...	...	...	...
1943	...	...	206.4	6,055	...	...	...	...	...	...	...	...
1944	...	...	132.8	3,097	...	...	...	...	99.0	3,316	...	...
1945	...	...	219.2	4,977	...	...	...	...	113.7	3,483	63.2	3,239
1946	...	...	237.6	6,776	...	...	309.9	13,190	101.0	2,957	61.7	3,021
1947	...	3,545	240.4	7,210	...	2,628	350.6	14,654	120.1	3,420	61.7	2,908
1948	123.9	4,211	233.6	7,088	50.0	2,560	415.3	14,977	116.3	3,486	49.9	2,256
1949	111.9	4,111	223.6	7,116	...	...	429.4	15,264	112.7	3,476	44.8	2,091
1950	115.2	4,288	219.1	7,047	48.9	2,292	441.5	15,615	111.0	3,392	46.3	2,189
1951	123.9	4,671	226.7	7,253	...	2,278	480.9	17,253	112.5	3,301	45.6	2,310
1952	130.3	4,661	231.8	7,546	51.8	2,489	496.5	17,649	112.7	3,175	39.6	2,073
1953	135.7	5,032	228.7	7,528	...	2,405	488.8	17,852	118.9	3,339	37.1	2,060
1954	135.0	5,174	229.4	7,562	...	2,535	508.6	17,906	122.9	3,313	38.4	2,140
1955	147.5	5,569	235.4	7,846	58.7	2,784	524.0	18,791	123.5	3,319	39.5	2,261
1956	148.8	5,748	247.3	8,333	61.0	2,807	530.0	18,628	119.6	3,259	35.8	2,250
1957	150.0	5,902	253.3	8,555	60.8	2,707	541.3	19,048	120.2	3,204	34.0	2,249
1958	158.0	6,187	263.5	9,057	...	3,088	536.7	18,682	122.2	3,267	30.9	2,118
1959	159.3	6,309[35] / 6,534	255.0	8,519	71.5	3,243	557.6	18,574	125.1	3,308	34.0	2,273
1960	163.7	6,840	261.4	8,578	79.0	3,617	580.6	19,335	124.9	3,303	36.6	2,343
1961	166.0	6,765	265.1	8,693	81.8	3,839	587.5	19,978	123.0	3,363	39.2	2,603
1962	178.3	6,776	272.8	8,958	81.1	3,912	577.3	19,769	123.0	3,410	37.3	2,357
1963	180.9	6,862	276.3	9,009	82.5	4,021	564.2	19,037	120.7	3,374	30.9	1,953
1964	178.7	6,817	275.3	9,041	85.7	4,341	562.1	19,232	122.4	3,443	31.7	2,038
1965	176.3	6,667	273.5	8,975	90.0	4,655	569.1	19,748	125.2	3,473	31.2	2,050
1966	172.7	6,548	269.9	8,708	96.7	5,119	568.7	19,382	125.0	3,514	31.5	2,131
1967	164.8	5,934	265.0	8,534	100	5,429	578.1	19,750	123.8	3,505	29.8	2,153
1968	163.7	5,815	254.8[9]	8,177	101	5,707	549.1	18,965	122.7	3,348	27.6	2,201
1969	170.3	6,394	247.8	8,238	105	6,061	517.7	18,569	120.0	3,309	25.6	2,154
1970	170.2	6,478	246.8	8,260	106	6,223	486.1	16,884	119.8	3,477	23.4	2,156
1971	177.6	6,698	245.5	8,425	100	6,223	480.6	16,966	121.4	3,461	24.9	2,349
1972	191.8	6,768	240.3	8,168	101	6,700	443.9	15,798	121.0	3,723	27.0	2,594
1973	188.0	6,725	236.6	8,093	103	7,071	444.2	15,670	118.4[37]	3,572[37]	29.6	2,773
1974	188.6	6,790	237.3	8,279	105	7,453	418.8	15,066	115.1	3,414	32.8	3,047
1975	184.3	6,689	232.1	8,258	104	7,569	410.0	15,433	112.5	3,440	35.5	3,135
1976	183.3	6,712	227.2	8,191	102	7,499	384.6	14,531	106.4	3,415	37.0	2,985
1977	186.3	6,973	200.4[36]	7,667[36]	99	7,343	377.3	15,709	...[38]	...[38]	36.8	2,977
1978	184.0	7,308	170.8	7,136	99	6,710	361.1	15,909	...[38]	...[38]	37.3	2,983
1979	183.6	7,435	163.0	6,955	100	6,847	347.8	15,384	151.7	3,069	37.6	3,020
1980	184.3	7,586	163.7	6,963	100	7,055	352.1	15,402	141.8	3,992	39.3	3,216
1981	184.0	7,246	166.8	7,078	98	6,962	316.4	13,645	147.3	4,413	41.0	3,274
1982	184.7	7,217	162.6	6,879	97	7,092	330.9	15,085	146.7	4,734	41.4	3,326
1983	182.9	7,023	155.5	6,631	98	7,255	322.1	14,600	144.3	4,593	41.5	3,339
1984	174.4	7,004	149.9	6,444	102	7,538	324.3	14,615	145.2	4,618	41.0	3,276
1985	172.5	7,205	150.3	6,572	105	7,785	320.6	14,942	156.7	4,909	40.4	3,224
1986	173.2	7,332	139.1	6,069	109	8,004	329.6[55] / 422.3	15,310[55] / 19,935	156.2	4,876	34.8 / —[57]	2,676
1987	173.6	7,363	142.2	6,270	110	8,075	415.8	20,029	156.7	4,860	45.8	3,106
1988	175.4	7,783	143.1	6,348	108	8,143	415.4	19,408	154.1	4,733	46.2	3,147
1989	178.7	8,445	142.0	6,400	99	7,601	411.0	19,699	151.5	4,733	45.5	3,208
1990	185.7	8,575	142.4	6,539	102	7,793	...	19,335	156.8	4,851	46.0	3,331
1991	193.0	9,208	145.5	6,771	73	4,866	405.8	19,263	155.9	4,777	45.8	3,230
1992	195.2	9,561	145.0	6,798	76	5,393	395.9[56]	11,753[56]	160.0	4,648	45.1	3,057
							Czech Republic[56]					
1993	207.5	9,342	145.3	6,694	76	5,877	242.2[56]	8,548[56]	152.0	4,700	44.4	3,007
1994	211.7	9,384	145.0	6,638	75	5,059	238.6	8,481	155.6	4,847	44.5	3,037
1995	268.5	9,755	148.1	6,757	72	4,693	229.1	8,023	153.1	4,783	45.9	3,184
1996	273.7	9,824	148.6	6,788	76	5,065	233.6	8,111	152.8	4,718	47.0	3,254
1997	269.8	8,477	151.7	6,984	77	5,886	219.8	7,710	158.7	4,999	47.3	3,376
1998	268.3	8,313	152.5	7,097	73	4,740	216.7	7,001	162.6	5,369	48.0	3,377

F3   Passenger Traffic on Railways (in millions)

	France		Germany		E Germany		Greece		Hungary		Ireland[23]	
	P	PK	P	PK	P	PK	P	PK	P	PK	P	PK
1935	582	22,600	1,542	40,300			26.5	612	61.3	1,911	22.6	...
1936	577	23,300	1,667	44,300			28.8	714	66.1	2,045	20.5	...
1937	614[39]	27,000[39]	1,874	51,100			...[43]	775	72.1	2,221	20.0	...
1938	540	22,100	2,049	57,100			10.2	811	78.0	2,376	19.3	...
1939	481	20,500	...	...			...	842	...	...	19.8	...
1940	347	17,100	...	...			...	750	...	...	19.9	...
1941	454	17,100	...	...			...	...[43]	...	...	25.2	...
1942	579	23,200	...	...			...	...	...	...	23.6	...
1943	686	28,200	...	...			...	...	...	...	26.2	...
1944	433	15,000	...	...			...	...	...	...	26.4	...
			West Germany									
1945	596	26,100	...	...	...	...	...	...	...	...	26.1	...
1946	696	31,500	...	...	...	...	...	...	...	...	24.1	...
1947	649	31,100	...	...	...	...	...	394	127	3,876	23.8	...
1948	645	30,600	...	...	...	...	...	310	177	4,800	22.2	...
1949	597	29,500	1,530	30,739	880	...	...	353	201	5,785	20.5	...
1950	545	26,400	1,472	30,264	954	18,576	...	616	257	7,142	17.4	...
1951	549	28,100	1,407	29,973	1,006	19,527	...	748	340	10,597	17.3[45]	...
1952	543	28,600	1,385	29,493	1,056	20,801	...	793	356	10,641	16.8	...
1953	496	25,900	1,398	31,754	997	20,529	...	870	364	10,669	16.5	...
1954	500	26,600	1,447	33,207	1,008	22,632	...	892	365	10,505	16.0	...
1955	509	27,800	1,555	35,919	1,016	22,905	13.9	1,002	367	10,277	16.8	...
1956	526	30,800	1,621[41]	38,811[41]	1,022	22,560	12.9	955	329	9,222	15.8	...
			1,670	39,748								
1957	552	32,600	1,685	41,384	1,011	22,785	11.9	916	356	10,417	16.5[23]	...
1958	553	32,300	1,562	39,718	980	21,399	11.1	867	399	11,889	11.7	525
1959	568	32,000	1,396	39,278	958	21,388	11.7	998	438	12,848	12.3	554
1960	570	32,000	1,399	38,402	943	21,288	11.4	1,030	485	14,324	11.1	567
1961	576	33,600	1,303	38,469	830	19,540	11.5	1,029	492	14,460	10.2	554
1962	579	35,800	1,246	38,415	691	16,791	11.5	1,044	523	15,560	9.8	542
1963	599	36,800	1,196	37,328	666	16,263	11.0	1,007	510	15,560	9.8	533
1964	608	37,800	1,178	37,378	685	17,378	11.2	1,078	527	16,223	9.3	536
1965	620	38,300	1,165	38,567	684	17,446	11.5	1,131	536	16,347	9.0	542
1966	628	38,400	1,066	35,672[42]	668	17,386	11.7	1,151	549	16,692	9.3	557
				36,483								
1967	624	38,380	1,018	33,877	649	17,462	11.7	1,150	561	16,772	8.9	546
1968	579	35,900	1,009	34,985	634	17,098	11.2	1,333	561	16,514	9.5	579
1969	607	39,060	1,024	37,156	636	17,610	11.8	1,437	549	16,391	10.0	589
1970	613	40,980	1,054	38,129	626	17,666	12.6	1,531	526	16,339	10.3	755
1971	608	41,140	1,053	36,892	630	18,407	13.3	1,635	505	15,888	11.0	783
1972	626	43,230	1,053	39,638	641	19,932	12.9	1,563	502	16,143	11.9	844
1973	620	44,700	1,093	39,765	633	20,851	12.7	1,571	493	16,038	12.7	875
1974	642	47,310	1,124	40,568	622	20,792	12.3	1,594	483	16,467	[11.4][45]	[694][45]
1975	658[40]	50,700[40]	1,079	37,727	634	21,305	12.5	1,553	463	15,823	13.9	899
	639	50,300										
1976	647	51,070	1,025	36,451	630	21,955	12.9	1,583	453	15,570	13.6	788
1977	665	51,990	1,029	36,543	631	22,350	13.4	1,623	435	15,396	14.7	876
1978	675	53,660	1,049	36,798	623	22,320	10.7	1,568	416	14,929	15.9	966
1979	680	53,740	1,085	38,016	613	22,284	10.4	1,531	402	14,612	17.9	1,113
1980	686	54,660	1,165	38,862	607	22,027	10.1	1,464	389	14,656	16.7	1,032
1981	698	55,840	1,170	40,268	601	21,644	10.4	1,515	374[44]	14,475[44]	15.4	995
									273	13,475		
1982	715	57,040	1,130	40,840	623	22,705	10.1	1,501	266	13,070	12.8	887
1983	736	58,600	1,124	39,097	620	22,605	10.6	1,546	237	11,104	13.0	846
1984	756	60,390	1,105	39,575	628	22,919	11.0	1,652	239	11,274	15.6	903
1985	777	62,070	1,134	43,451	623	22,451	11.2	1,731	235	11,209	20.1	1,023
1986	779	59,860	1,108	42,129	609	22,402	11.7	1,951	233	11,224	21.7	1,075
1987	782	59,970	1,088	39,965	603	22,563	11.8	1,973	230	11,324	24.9	1,196
1988	810	63,290	1,121	41,760	600	22,775	11.8	1,963	226	11,512	24.0	1,180
1989	840	64,490	1,134	42,023	592	23,588	13.0	2,011	228	11,871	24.6	1,226
1990	842	63,740	1,172	44,588	470	17,397	11.2	1,978	211	11,403	25.0	1,223
1991	...	62,300	1,530	57,034	**Included in**		11.2	1,995	190	9,861	25.6	1,243
1992	831	62,980	1,564	57,240	**West Germany**		11.4	2,004	173	9,183	26.8	1,222
1993	813	58,430	1,570	58,003			11.5	1,726	160	8,432	26.1	1,079
1994	821	58,930	1,592	61,962			10.0	1,399	166	8,508	26.7	1,260
1995	789	55,560	1,612	74,975			10.7	1,569	163	8,441	27.3	1,291
1996	846	59,770	1,661	75,975			11.7	1,752	170	8,582	27.4	1,295
1997	883	61,830	1,549	73,917			11.9	1,783	175	8,669	28.0	1,388
1998	906	64,450	1,600	72,389			10.5	1,552	182	8,884	...	...

F3 Passenger Traffic on Railways (in millions)

1935-1998

	Italy		Netherlands		Norway		Poland		Portugal		Romania[28]	
	P	PK	P	PK	P	PK	P	PK	P	PK	P	PK
1935	126.5	8,579	46.0	...	17.8	532	145	5,530	24.8	...	35.0	2,848
1936	136.1	9,806	44.5	...	19.6	597	174	5,941	25.7	848	39.1	3,141
1937	157.5	11,064	47.1	3,348	21.0	654	212	6,948	26.1	742	45.7	3,577
1938	167.0	11,773	47.8	3,423	21.8	703	228	7,493	21.7	714	48.7	3,788
1939	194.2	13,547	61.4	4,015	22.7	740	...	...	30.6	705	51.2	4,382
1940	222.6	17,135	62.3	4,236	17.7	596	...	...	26.3	768	...	5,094[29]
1941	284.6	21,932	66.0	4,641	25.5	767	...	...	25.5	738	...	3,266
1942	391.1	31,058	102.9	6,222	31.9	918	...	...	29.0	891	...	4,307
1943	217.9[46]	17,291	158.7	8,391	40.3	1,045	...	...	34.5	1,274	...	5,718
1944	114.0[46]	8,481	121.7	5,847	46.4	1,087	...	...	39.4	1,418	...	...[29]
1945	189.4[46]	12,552	43.0	2,026	47.7	1,069	...	...	42.0	1,233	...	...
1946	284.6[46]	18,467	127.0[48]	6,177	47.4[49]	1,305[49]	249	15,700	45.2	1,318	40.8	5,436[28]
			174.1									
1947	322.3[46]	21,262	180.0	6,776	42.2	1,485	336[50]	18,100[50]	68.0	1,677	...	...
	536.6[24]	24,960[24]										
1948	544.6	26,594	177.6	6,839	40.6	1,466	422	20,400	69.2	1,699	74.7	6,476
1949	514.0	23,850	166.6	6,478	42.9	1,694	488	21,540	61.5	1,476	...	...
1950	527.1	23,578	158.4	6,228	40.1	1,531	613	27,124	57.5	1,385	117	8,155
1951	522.3	24,476	156.8	6,291	39.9	1,558	714	31,557	60.3	1,443	173	9,873
1952	537.8	25,107	155.4	6,392	38.7	1,533	831	38,117	62.3	1,551	181	9,185
1953	557.4	25,784	160.7	6,621	38.5	1,519	849	36,477	63.8	1,574	222	11,971
1954	556.5	24,888	172.2	7,061	38.9	1,548	905	36,226	67.1	1,628	232	11,929
1955	564.8	26,071	184.5	7,573	40.1	1,628	940	36,981	69.6	1,673	252	12,460
1956	559.5	27,711	189.0	7,687	40.0	1,709	956	37,596	72.3	1,715	264	13,054
1957	531.5	28,114	189.4	7,612	40.2	1,738	956	38,262	78.4	1,840	265	13,323
1958	538.1	28,869	186.6	7,466	39.5	1,713	963	38,085	85.1	1,933	233	11,619
1959	539.6	28,953	187.3	7,416	39.1	1,752	905	34,894	91.6	2,037	214	10,558
1960	574.4	30,723	196.4	7,821	38.7[10]	1,735[10]	817	30,942	98.8	2,156	215	10,737
					42.4	1,831						
1961	542.5	31,449	200.5	7,991	41.4	1,830	836	30,850	104.3	2,307	224	11,457
1962	525.4	31,465	198.2	7,878	40.3	1,843	867	31,246	107.9	2,439	239	12,325
1963	503.5	32,026	198.8	7,911	39.1	1,762	895	32,139	114.1	2,606	253	12,836
1964	471.7	30,617	195.1	7,854	35.9	1,716	929	33,270	120.0	2,780	261	13,331
1965	448.7	29,034	192.0	7,715	34.5	1,716	972	34,318	126.5	2,970	262	13,535
1966	444.3	29,886	189.2	7,603	34.3	1,749	995	34,877	131.9	3,124	281	14,651
1967	446.4	30,385	183.7	7,412	32.6	1,712	1,012	35,447	138.0	3,266	302	15,775
1968	446.1	31,311	180.3	7,355	30.7	1,647	1,030	35,870	141.8	3,309	303	16,142
1969	444.0	31,946	179.8	7,502	29.3	1,568	1,048	37,035	144.7	3,441	306	16,719
1970	456.0	34,764	187.9	8,011	29.4	1,573	1,056	36,891	144.8	3,540	328	17,793
1971	462.5	36,298	187.6	8,114	29.4	1,600	1,066	37,228	145.7	3,569	338	18,811
1972	468.4	37,839	183.8	8,039	29.5	1,622	1,081	38,782	153.7	3,761	361	20,184
1973	482.4	38,805	181.3	8,173	29.5	1,640	1,088	39,647	166.3	4,106	367	21,228
1974	517.2	40,665	183.0	8,589	32.6	1,884	1,111	41,670	178.7	4,552	378	22,406
1975	490.7	39,055	176.3	8,501	33.5	1,948	1,118	42,819	182.5	4,856	367	22,380
1976	529.2[47]	42,003[47]	171.6	8,218	32.7	1,997	1,110	42,799	191.7	5,235	373	23,077
	374.4	39,118										
1977	376.9	38,361	170.8	8,013	33.6	2,004	1,152	44,312	196.3	5,235	371	23,206
1978	373.9	39,211	176.3	8,146	34.1	2,058	1,132	46,716	204.7	5,514	355	22,811
1979	374.9	39,688	186.5	8,514	35.4	2,265	1,099	45,473	210.7	5,635	351	22,724
1980	381.4	39,587	197.2	8,910	37.9	2,394	1,101	46,324	224.2	6,077	348	23,220
1981	395.8	40,096	205.2	9,230	38.9	2,425	1,114	48,238	213.4	5,856	378	24,379
1982	380.3	39,542	208.9	9,376	37.4	2,242	1,108	49,266	210.7	5,414	375	25,578
1983	388.6	38,840	202.0	9,052	35.9	2,175	1,042	50,153	208.0	5,195	414	27,676
1984	385.5	39,045	204.9	8,997	34.7	2,191	1,036	53,179	214.6	5,456	433	28,785
1985	364.0	37,401	208.2	9,007	34.8	2,241	1,005	51,978	221.5	5,725	460	31,082
1986	393.2	40,500	210.5	8,919	35.6	2,225	990	48,526	224.5	5,803	469	32,304
1987	394.2	41,395	222.0	9,396	36.7	2,187	977	48,285	228.0	5,907	472	33,520
1988	410.0	43,343	230.1	9,664	34.1	2,110	984	52,134	231.0	6,036	473	34,643
1989	418.7	44,443	239.4	10,235	34.5	2,136	951	55,888	229.4	5,908	481	35,456
1990	429.4	45,513	255.7	11,060	33.4	2,136	790	50,373	225.9	5,664	408	30,582
1991	438.0	46,427	304.2	12,796	35.8	2,153	652	40,115	223.6	5,692	363	25,429
1992	440.0	48,361	332.5	15,350	37.5	2,201	549	32,571	224.6	5,694	324	24,269
1993	438.0	47,101	333.8	15,245	37.9	2,316	541	30,865	...	...	225	19,402
1994	467.8	48,900	319.4	14,439	38.1	2,398	536	27,610	221.1	5,149	206	18,313
1995	470.5	49,700	311.6	13,977	37.9	2,381	524	26,635	207.1	4,840	219	18,879
1996	472.7	50,300	320.9	14,131	37.0	2,120	520	26,569	187.4	4,503	216	18,356
1997	494.6	51,600	322.5	14,485	38.1	2,426	501	25,806	188.9	4,563	198	15,795
1998	499.2	53,000	329.7	14,879	38.6	2,496	496	25,664	195.7	4,602	180	13,422

F3   Passenger Traffic on Railways (in millions)   1935–1998

	Russia/U.S.S.R		Spain		Sweden		Switzerland		U.K.:Great Britain[52]		Yugoslavia	
	P	PK thousand millions	P	PK	P	PK	P	PK	P	PK	P	PK
1935	919	67.9	58.3	3,425	73	2,702	151.5	3,134	856.2	...	39.7	2,224
1936	992	77.2	...	...	76	2,890	145.5	3,042	875.7	...	45.9	2,441
1937	1,143	90.9	...	...	80	3,103	152.4	3,296	906.1	...	54.7	2,860
1938	1,173	84.9	...	...	82	3,160	153.1	3,297	850.2	...	59.3	3,068
1939	1,267[11]	93.7[11]	...	...	88	3,565	159.4	3,561	844.9	30,566[53]	58.3	3,191
1940	1,344	98.0	...	...	98	4,494	169.5	3,659	691.1	...	...	...
1941	...	...	...	...	103	5,023	196.7	4,431	778.3	...	...	...
1942	...	...	107.8	7,529	117	5,743	217.5	4,800	944.4	...	...	...
1943	...	...	115.4	7,437	132	6,384	242.8	5,493	1,036.7	51,938	...	...
1944	...	...	114.4	7,343	145	6,580	262.5	5,915	1,039.1	51,583	...	...
1945	844	65.9	100.5	6,222	154	6,441	284.8	6,569	1,055.7	56,726	...	...
1946	1,078	97.9	99.0	6,867	154	6,405	285.7	6,315	901.1	47,043	78.4	3,969
1947	1,095	95.1	109.5	7,496	154	6,514	295.5	6,560	768.9[54]	37,039[54]	111	5,129
1948	1,049	82.5	115.1	7,567	151	6,578	285.3	6,724	700.3	34,213	136	6,102
1949	1,080	81.3	110.1	7,291	151	6,725	278.3	6,462	710.5	34,018	151	7,194
1950	1,164	88.0	107.5	7,093	150	6,637	267.6	6,428	704.0	32,472	179	8,304
1951	1,315	98.5	108.4	7,284	141	6,508	277.3	6,674	719.6	33,463	170	7,579
1952	1,441	107	114.6	7,851	134	6,333	284.1	6,878	710.8	32,926	104	4,815
1953	1,504	118	115.7	7,978	129	6,134	279.4	6,904	710.5	33,117	131	6,015
1954	1,574	129	114.4	7,879	126	6,138	280.4	6,954	744.7	33,333	148	6,536
1955	1,641	141	117.2	8,020	122	6,163	284.5	7,132	730.2	32,683	164	7,533
1956	1,658	142	123.3	8,552	118	6,237	290.9	7,307	740.1	34,010	159	7,314
1957	1,754	153	124.3	8,608	110	5,642	300.0	7,643	788.1	36,357	171	8,059
1958	1,835	158	127.6	8,730	103	5,312	304.3	7,843	777.3	35,647	184	8,877
1959	1,883	164	124.3	8,488	95	5,052	307.7	7,955	749.2	35,840	191	9,250
1960	1,950	171	108.8	7,341	91	5,180	310.7	7,974	721.3	34,677	212	10,449
1961	1,962	176	114.9	7,773	89	5,310	320.5	8,427	707.8	33,894	195	10,089
1962	2,037	189	128.5	8,789	87	5,353	330.2	8,812	670.5	31,749	193	9,908
1963	2,139	192	147.4	10,093	81	5,237	336.0	9,048	646.7	30,947	201	10,673
1964	2,250	195	168.6	11,820	77	5,371	344.5	9,659	629.0	31,984	226	12,308
1965	2,301	202	174.1	12,198	73	5,344	334.1	9,004	580.5	30,116	236	12,800
1966	2,450	219	176.2	12,523	67	5,133	332.0	9,027	547.3	29,697	213	12,196
1967	2,592	234	155.6	12,437	59	4,778	318.8	8,794	537.2	29,111	196	10,753
1968	2,746	254	148.0	11,836	61	4,603	320.2	8,992	532.3	28,703	183	10,284
1969	2,837	261	158.9	12,647	64	4,792	323.7	9,239	516.6	29,612	163	10,470
1970	2,930	265	164.4	13,293	64	4,693	322.6	9,339	526.4	30,408	157	10,939
1971	3,053	275	166.3	13,467	60	4,125	323.4	9,435	499.5	30,127	146	10,566
1972	3,167	286	177.9	14,391	69	4,553	316.6	9,502	445.8	29,100	141	10,578
1973	3,306	297	193.3	15,640	72	4,775	318.8	9,639	427.9	29,800	137	10,578
1974	3,389	306	198.7	16,079	81	5,499	313.8	9,538	436.5	30,900	135	10,429
1975	3,470	313	199.6	16,146	80	5,636	303.9	9,223	432.5	30,300	129	10,285
1976	3,545	315	157.0	12,731	81	5,636	301.8	9,357	403.9	28,400	126	9,941
1977	3,566	322	162.0	13,112	81	5,586	297.4	9,240	407.5	29,300	124	10,459
1978	3,603	332	158.0	12,797	82	5,524	295.2	9,308	430.2	30,000	113	10,445
1979	3,566	335	[156.4][51]	[12,671][51]	86	6,198	298.2	9,520	438.9	30,700	108	10,134
1980	3,551[35] 4,072	332[35] 342	167.2	13,527	95	7,019	314.2	10,505	439.0	30,300	107	10,392
1981	4,095	354	176.3	14,261	97	7,108	318.2	10,449	396.0	29,700	105	10,570
1982	4,098	358	181.7	14,703	93	6,612	316.2	10,310	361.9	27,200	111	11,265
1983	4,149	361	187.0	15,092	96	6,688	314.4	10,340	386.4	29,500	117	11,643
1984	4,155	364	193.0	15,574	90	6,690	315.9	10,394	387.2	29,800	118	11,734
1985	4,166	374	197.5	15,979	90	6,803	327.3	10,800	382.3	29,700	126	11,999
1986	4,345	390	194.0	15,693	86	6,363	332	10,753	380.2	30,800	132	12,398
1987	4,360	402	190.3	15,394	83	6,215	336	12,082	402.3	32,200	120	11,827
1988	4,396	414	194.3	15,716	87	6,289	375[60]	12,355[60]	398.5	34,400	116	11,449
1989	4,323	411	181.9	14,715	93	6,361	299	12,283	398.2	33,600	112	11,478
1990	2,660	...	274.4	15,476	94	6,353	324	12,678	397.5	33,200	112	11,052
1991	2,523[58]	...	316.3	15,022	95	5,745	336	13,834	379.0	32,500	...	2,935[61]
1992	...	...	358.6	16,302	101	5,583	328	13,209	383.5	31,700	...	2,800[61]
1993	2,324[59]	...	354.0	15,457	105	5,975	335	13,384	371.9	30,400	...	3,379[61]
1994	2,341	227	359.5	16,114	109	6,063	346	13,836	364.1	28,650	...	2,525[61]
1995	2,299	192	361.2	16,582	112	6,364	339	13,408	369.8	30,039	...	2,580[61]
1996	2,286	181	374.6	16,804	110	6,216	334	13,326	371.4	32,135	...	1,830[61]
1997	2,280	170	389.1	17,883	121	6,770	...	...	382.5	34,660	...	1,744[61]
1998	2,271	152	401.2	18,833	124	6,997	...	...	388.4	36,270	...	1,622[61]

F3 Passenger Traffic on Railways (in millions)

NOTE

SOURCES:- Finland to 1909—supplied by the Central Statistical Office of Finland; Germany to 1870—W. Fischer *et al*, *Social geschichtliches Arbeitsbuch* I (Munich, 1982); Sweden in 1862—supplied by the Swedish Central Office of Statistics; Great Britain to 1938 and Ireland to 1913—B.R. Mitchell, *British Historical Statistics* (Cambridge, 1988), where the original sources are given. All other statistics are taken from the official publications noted on p. xv.

FOOTNOTES

[1] Including Hungary to 1867 (1st line) and mixed lines subsequently until 1912. The Italian provinces are excluded throughout. From 1921 the statistics are for the Republic and relate to state-operated lines only. The Kaschau-Odenerger line, which carried 92 thousand passengers in 1870, is excluded in 1871.

[2] State-operated lines only to 1873 (1st line). To 1867 (1st line) passengers on return tickets were only counted once.

[3] State lines only (except as noted in footnote 16).

[4] Savoy and Nice are included subsequently.

[5] Revised figures are given here for 1900. In the source they are given at decennial intervals for the period 1841-91 as follows (in millions):-

	Passengers		Passengers	Passenger/Kilometres
1841	6.3	1871	94.1	no change
1851	19.6	1881	174	6,290
1861	61.1	1891	248	8,240

[6] Alsace-Lorraine is excluded from France for 1871-1920, and included in Germany for 1871-1917.

[7] Transleithania to 1918. The figures to 1888 (1st line) are for purely Hungarian lines only. Subsequently they include traffic on mixed Austro-Hungarian lines, which is also included in the Austrian statistics (see footnote 1). Statistics for 1915-1918 are for years ended 30 June.

[8] For 1843-48 the figures are for years ended 30 June.

[9] New bases of collection were adopted subsequently.

[10] First half-year only. Subsequent figures to 1960 (1st line) are for years ended 30 June.

[11] Figures to 1898 (1st line) apply to European Russia (exclusive of Finland). From 1898 (2nd line) to 1913 (1st line) they apply to the whole Empire, except Finland. From 1913 (2nd line) to 1939 they apply to the territory of the U.S.S.R. in 1923, and subsequently to the present territory.

[12] The territorial changes of the Balkan Wars were effective from 1914.

[13] From 1919-33 the figures are for years ended 31 March following that indicated. The 1934 figures are for 9 months.

[14] Excluding the Kosice-Bohumin line.

[15] Passengers on return tickets were only counted once to 1909 (1st line).

[16] Including private lines from 1899 (2nd line).

[17] Passengers on return tickets were only counted once to 1934.

[18] Memel, Danzig, Posen, West Prussia, parts of Pomerania and Schleswig, Eupen, Malmédy, etc., and Saarland are excluded from 1920, though Saarland is reincorporated in 1935.

[19] Eastern Upper Silesia is excluded from July 1922.

[20] Excluding the occupied Rhineland.

[21] Previously excluding some private narrow gauge lines.

[22] The territorial gains in the north are subsequently included.

[23] Subsequent statistics relate to railway systems based in southern Ireland, though including their traffic in Northern Ireland. From 1958 the latter ceased when the state took over the southern part of the Great Northern Railway.

[24] Statistics for 1905-1947 (1st line) are for years beginning 1 July and are for state-operated lines only. Figures for private lines are available as follows (in millions):-

	Passengers	Passenger/Kilometres		Passengers	Passenger/Kilometres		Passengers	Passenger/Kilometres
1906	19.6	412	1930	69.2	1,146	1938	102.0	1,653
1907	23.7	414	1931	63.5	1,121	1939	116.6	1,901
1908	28.2	476	1932	59.7	1,054	1940	136.2	...
1909	29.8	525	1933	61.0	1,081	1941	180.4	...
1910	32.5	550	1934	57.5	1,118			
1927	66.5	...	1935	72.9	1,211	1944	236.5	...
1928	69.1	1,208	1936	84.6	1,429	1945	220.0	...
1929	71.0	1,234	1937	92.2	1,490	1946	227.6	...

Figures for the state lines for the calendar year 1947 are as follows (in millions):- 311.4 passengers and 20,769 passenger/kilometres.

[25] Previously excluding season ticket holders.

[26] Previously excluding narrow gauge lines.

[27] The nature and size of this break is not given in the source.

[28] State-operated lines only. All remaining private lines were nationalised in 1946.

[29] For 1901-20 the figures are for years ended 31 March following that indicated. The newly acquired territories are included after 1920. Bessarabia, northern Bukovina, and southern Dobrudja are excluded from 1941, and northern Transylvania for 1941-44.

[30] The figure for 1922 is for 9 months to 30 September, and the figures for 1923-27 are for years ended 30 September.

F3 Passenger Traffic on Railways (in millions)

31   Figures to 1927 (1st line) are for state-operated lines plus the Southern Railway only.
32   Subsequently on standard gauge lines only.
33   Including non-paying passengers to 1915.
34   Subsequently excluding London Passenger Transport Board lines.
35   The reason for this break is not given in the source.
36   Bus traffic operated by the railways ceased in July.
37   Subsequently excluding local ferry crossings.
38   The following statistics are available for 1977–8:-

State lines for year ended 3 March 1977:	86.0 millions;	2,997 million	PKm
State lines for year ended 31 March 1978:	89.4 millions;	3,084 million	PKm
State lines for April–December 1978:	38.2 millions;	1,878 million	PKm
Private lines for calendar year 1977:	716 millions;	129 million	PKm
Private lines for calendar year 1978:	8.2 millions;	140 million	PKm

39   State railways only from 1938.
40   There was a change in the treatment of Paris suburban tickets.
41   Saarland is excluded to 1956 (1st line)
42   Subsequently including some private lines for the first time.
43   Subsequently excluding the Franco-Hellenic line.
44   Subsequently excluding the suburban railway.
45   Subsequent statistics for the state lines are for years beginning 1 April to 1973. The 1974 figures are for April–December.
46   Excluding Allied military traffic.
47   State railways only from 1976 (2nd line).
48   Excluding season ticket holders to 1946 (1st line)
49   From 1946/7 passengers carried jointly on a single journey by state and private lines are counted twice.
50   Subsequently including traffic on electric suburban lines.
51   Excluding the Basque Provinces and Catalonia.
52   The Passenger-Kilometres series includes estimates for season ticket holders, whereas the passenger-journeys series does not.
53   Year ended 31 August.
54   State railways only from 1948.
55   Subsequently including ferry passengers.
56   Czech Republic. Slovakia = 1993, 86.7(P);   2,498 (PKm)
57   Break in Source is unexplained.
58   Ex Soviet Union.
59   Russia Ex-USSR as follows:

		Total Numbers (Million)
Armenia	1992 1993	1.1
Azerbaijan	1992 1993	8.9
Belarus	1992 1993	201
Estonia	1994	11.5
Georgia	1992 1993	1000 (Passenger km)
Kazakhstan	1992 1993	47.3
Kyrgistan	1992 1993	2.3
Latvia	1994	55.7
Lithuania	1994	24.8
Moldova	1992 1993	12.7
Tajikistan	1992 1993	1.2

F3 Passenger Traffic on Railways (in millions)

		Total Numbers (Million)
Turkmenistan	1992	
	1993	273.1
Ukraine	1992	
	1993	66.7
Uzbekistan	1992	
	1993	18.6

[60] New evaluation method.
[61] Yugoslavia. Ex-Yugoslavia as follows: (Millions)

	Bosnia-Herc	Croatia	Macedonia	Slovenia
1991	554 (pkm)	...	...	...
1992	...	18.0 (Pass)	1.8 (Pass)	12.4 (Pass)
1993	...	18.7 (Pass)	1.21 (Pass)	11.9 (Pass)

F4 MERCHANT SHIPS REGISTERED

1788–1828   **1829–1879**

	United Kingdom[1]			
	Number of Ships		Thousand Tons	
	Sail	Steam	Sail	Steam
1788	12,464		1,278	
1789	12,801		1,308	
1790	13,557		1,383	
1791	13,960		1,415	
1792	14,334		1,437	
1793	14,440		1,453	
1794	14,590		1,456	
1795	14,317		1,426	
1796	14,458		1,361	
1797	14,405		1,454	
1798	14,631		1,494	
1799	14,883		1,551	
1800	15,734		1,699	
1801	16,552		1,797	
1802	17,207		1,901	
1803	18,068		1,986	
1804	18,870		2,077	
1805	19,027		2,093	
1806	19,315		2,080	
1907	19,373		2,097	
1808	19,580		2,130	
1809	19,882		2,167	
1810	20,253		2,211	
1811	20,478		2,247	
1812	20,637		2,263	
1813	20,951		2,349	
1814	21,449	1	2,414	...
1815	21,861	8	2,477	1
1816	22,014	12	2,503	1
1817	21,761	14	2,420	1
1818	22,005	19	2,450	2
1819	21,973	24	2,449	3
1820	21,935	34	2,436	3
1821	21,593	59	2,350	6
1822	21,153	85	2,307	9
1823	20,941	101	2,293	10
1824	21,164	116	2,338	12
1825	20,442	153	2,313	16
1826	20,738[2]	230[2]	2,387[2]	24[2]
1827	19,269	255	2,154	27
1828	19,372	274	2,165	28

	Austria-Hungary[3]				Belgium			
	Number of Ships		Thousand Tons		Number of Ships		Thousand Tons	
	Sail	Steam	Sail	Steam	Sail	Steam	Sail	Steam
1829	2,946	—	188	—	...	...	...	...
1830	2,927	—	190	—	...	...	...	...
1831	3,239	—	200	—	...	...	...	...
1832	3,157	—	195	—	...	...	...	...
1833	3,276	—	192	—	...	...	...	...
1834	3,231	—	187	—	...	...	...	...
1835	3,255	—	179	—	...	...	...	...
1836	3,266	—	166	—	...	...	...	...
1837	3,175	7	163	1	151	4	22	1
1838	3,283	10	164	2	146	5	22	2
1839	3,201	10	189	2	154	5	22	2
1840	3,228	10	197	2	155	6	22	1
1841	3,208	10	202	2	139	5	22	1
1842	3,400	11	205	2	145	7	23	5
1843	3,409	11	206	2	134	8	22	5
1844	3,382	13	208	3	134	...	23	...
1845	3,334	20	205	4	136	5	24	2
1846	3,393	20	215	4	137	6	25	3
1847	3,456	21	227	5	140	3	25	2
1848	3,465	26	234	6	151	4	29	2
1849	3,540	31	241	7	149	5	31	2
1850	3,564	32	252	8	156	5	33	2
1851	3,376[4]	35	238[4]	10	157	6	35	1
	9,868		262					
1852	9,645	39	272	11	155	5	34	1
1853	9,637	47	285	14	152	5	34	1
1854	9,843	50	305	15	151	7	37	1
1855	9,932	48	320	14	150	8	38	5
1856	9,600	53	339	18	140	8	36	6
1857	9,573	61	356	22	142	5	40	2
1858	9,596	60	352	22	136	6	39	3
1859	9,644	59	328	21	131	4	36	2
1860	...	...	...	...	108	8	29	4
1861	9,744	59	321	21	103	8	27	4
1862	9,766	59	310	21	96	7	26	3
1863	9,584	59	310	21	91	6	25	3
1864	9,428	63	312	24	99	8	31	4
1865	9,427	64	306	26	104	8	36	4
1866	9,045[3]	65[3]	318[3]	29[3]	91	7	33	5
	7,629		282					
1867	7,698	71	277	34	81	9	31	6
1868	7,756	74	290	34	68	11	23	9
1869	7,741	80	299	38	67	12	24	9
1870	7,750[3]	83[3]	316[3]	47[3]	55	12	21	10
	7,367	83	310	47				
1871	7,232	91	259	49	48	12	17	9
1872	6,528	95	224	53	40	19	16	16
1873	6,593	99	217	56	41	28	16	30
1874	6,556	99	204	58	33	24	15	30
1875	6,832	94	201	56	32	27	15	35
1876	...	...	...	...	25	23	15	30
1877	7,010	95	201	57	22	28	11	38
1878	7,290	91	200	58	24	34	10	50
1879	7,629	101	201	60	25	39	12	60

F4　Merchant Ships Registered

	Denmark[46]				Finland[7]				France				Germany			
	Number of Ships		Thousand Tons		Number of Ships		Thousand Tons		Number of Ships		Thousand Tons		Number Ships		Thousand Tons	
	Sail	Steam	Sail	Steam	Sail	Steam	Sail	Steam	Sail	Steam	Sail	Steam	Sail	Steam	Sail	Steam
1829	1,422		60		...	...	...	...	...	...	...	...				265
1830	1,435		63		...	...	...	...	...	...	...	...	...	...	...	
1831	1,466[46]		63[46]		...	...	...	...	...	...	...	...	...	...	...	
1832	1,626		65		...	...	...	...	...	...	...	...	...	...	...	
1833	1,645		66		...	...	...	...	...	...	...	...	...	...	...	
1834	1,626		64		...	...	...	...	...	...	...	...	...	...	...	282
1835	1,620		62		...	...	...	...	...	...	...	...	...	...	...	
1836	1,624		61		...	...	...	...	...	...	...	...	...	...	...	
1837	1,589		61		...	...	...	...	15,326		697		...	...	...	
1838	1,611		62		...	...	...	...	15,546	71	670	10	...	...	...	
1839	1,558		65		...	4	...	...	15,657	85	663	10	...	...	...	352
1840	1,634		69		...	6	...	...	15,511	89	653	10	...	...	...	
1841	1,633		74		...	...	...	...	13,276	107	580	10	...	...	...	
1842	1,650		76		1,286	8	120	- -	13,301	108	580	10	...	...	...	
1843	1,691		77		1,356		117		13,552	104	590	10	...	...	...	
1844	1,770	11	77	1	1,330	8	114	- -	13,578	101	595	9	...	...	...	406
1845	1,723	11	76	1	1,348		115		13,722	103	602	9	...	...	...	
1846	1,767	15	77	1	...		...		13,937	109	622	11	...	...	...	
1847	1,895	19	83	1	1,428		128		14,204	117	658	13	...	...	...	
1848	1,983	17	85	1	1,359	7	126	1	14,235	118	670	13	...	...	...	
1849	1,990	15	86	1	1,391		132		14,245	119	667	13	...	...	...	513
1850	2,002	16	90	1	1,349	9	131	1	14,229	126	674	14	3,655	22	496	4
1851	2,067	21	97	2	...	10	...	1	14,418	139	685	19	3,712	22	514	4
1852	2,077	26	101	2	...	10	...	1	14,456	151	699	22	3,682	20	519	3
1853	2,160	25	102	2	1,354	8	137	1	14,545	174	736	26	3,730	26	540	6
1854	2,403	25	113	2	...	...	...	...	14,199	197	785	35	3,853	32	595	11
1855	2,497	25	121	2	...	...	...	...	14,023	225	827	45	3,947	39	619	12
1856	2,624	27	130	2	...	...	...	...	14,448	273	935	64	4,118	49	673	14
1857	2,651	32	136	3	1,379		135		14,845	330	980	72	4,484	73	715	21
1858	2,698	35	139	4	...	24	...	...	14,863	324	983	67	4,636	80	752	29
1859	2,750	40	142	4	...	24	...	1	14,708	324	961	65	4,781	83	750	25
1860	2,727	43	135	4	1,523	27	169	1	14,608	314	928	68	4,672	70	754	23
1861	2,719	44	134	4	...	34	...	2	14,738	327	911	73	4,673	72	764	25
1862	2,719	44	133	4	...	34	...	2	14,794	338	904	79	4,842	73	811	26
1863	2,693[5]	47[5]	135[5]	4[5]	1,604	25	195	1	14,746	346	900	85	4,997	76	864	29
1864	3,028	51	144	5	1,526	35	187		14,820	364	901	98	4,879	81	861	29
1865	3,121	65	153	6	1,548	48	202		14,867	384	900	108	4,974	85	894	34
1866	3,054	77	163	8	1,675	56	225		15,230	407	915	128	5,078	88	889	41
1867	3,052[6]	80[6]	166[6]	10[6]	1,607	65	233		15,182	420	916	133	4,922	98	887	51
	2,686	76	164													
1868	2,867	79	168	10	1,641[7]	62[7]	241[7]		15,182	433	923	135	4,991	114	891	56
1869	2,719	89	168	10	...	...	...		15,324	454	932	143	4,876	126	890	67
1870	2,648	87	170	12	1,538	78	240		14,929	457	921	151	4,589	132	872	67
1871	2,655	91	173	16	...	...	...		14,786	473	917	160	4,354	175	856	80
1872	2,629	109	176	22	1,689[7]	97[7]	240[7]	6[7]	15,062	512	912	177	4,311	216	835	106
1873	2,723[5]	123[5]	185[5]	27[5]	1,512	100	239	6	15,043	516	883	185	4,242	253	831	137
1874	2,822	135	196	29	1,837	117	276	7	15,002	522	843	195	4,303	299	844	156
1875	2,909	167	205	39	1,813	134	293	7	14,904	537	823	205	4,426	319	865	151
1876	2,966	178	211	44	1,812	138	299	8	14,861	546	793	218	4,491	318	886	148
1877	2,966	187	207	45	1,836	161	294	9	14,884	565	758	231	4,469	336	898	150
1878	2,971	189	205	47	1,827	176	294	10	14,939	588	730	246	4,453	351	911	147
1879	2,953	192	203	49	1,673	201	275	10	14,434	599	678	256	4,403	374	936	161

F4   Merchant Ships Registered

	Greece				Hungary				Italy			
	Number of Ships		Thousand Tons		Number of Ships		Thousand Tons		Number of Ships		Thousand Tons	
	Sail	Steam	Sail	Steam	Sail	Steam	Sail	Steam	Sail	Steam	Sail	Steam
1829	...	...	...	...	...	...	...	...	...	...	...	...
1830	...	...	...	...	...	...	...	...	...	...	...	...
1831	...	...	...	...	...	...	...	...	...	...	...	...
1832	...	...	...	...	...	...	...	...	...	...	...	...
1833	...	...	...	...	...	...	...	...	...	...	...	...
1834	2,891	—	...	...	...	...	...	...	...	...	...	...
1835	...	...	...	...	...	...	...	...	...	...	...	...
1836	...	...	...	...	...	...	...	...	...	...	...	...
1837	...	...	...	...	...	...	...	...	...	...	...	...
1838	...	...	...	...	...	...	...	...	...	...	...	...
1839	...	...	...	...	...	...	...	...	...	...	...	...
1840	3,814	—	111	—	...	...	...	...	...	...	...	...
1841	...	...	...	...	...	...	...	...	...	...	...	...
1842	...	...	...	...	...	...	...	...	...	...	...	...
1843	...	...	...	...	...	...	...	...	...	...	...	...
1844	...	...	...	...	...	...	...	...	...	...	...	...
1845	3,581	—	164	—	...	...	...	...	...	...	...	...
1846	...	...	...	...	...	...	...	...	...	...	...	...
1847	...	...	...	...	...	...	...	...	...	...	...	...
1848	...	...	...	...	...	...	...	...	...	...	...	...
1849	3,970	—	265	—	...	...	...	...	...	...	...	...
1850	4,046	—	266	—	...	...	...	...	...	...	...	...
1851	...	...	...	...	...	...	...	...	...	...	...	...
1852	...	...	...	...	...	...	...	...	...	...	...	...
1853	4,230	—	248	—	...	...	...	...	...	...	...	...
1854	4,230	—	250	—	...	...	...	...	...	...	...	...
1855	...	...	...	...	...	...	...	...	...	...	...	...
1856	...	...	...	...	...	...	...	...	...	...	...	...
1857	4,339	...	295	...	...	...	...	...	...	...	...	...
1858	3,918	2	268	...	...	...	...	...	...	...	...	...
1859	3,984	—	274	—	...	...	...	...	...	...	...	...
1860	4,070	—	263	—	...	...	...	...	...	...	...	...
1861	4,152	1	256	- -	...	...	...	...	...	...	...	...
1862	4,334	1	257	- -	...	...	...	...	9,356	57	644	10
1863	4,451	1	262	- -	...	...	...	...	10,264	82	661_2	17
1864	4,527	1	280	- -	...	...	...	...	13,809	90	573	20
1865	5,743	1	327	- -	...	...	...	...	15,633	95	656	22
1866	5,501	11	324	5	...	...	...	...	16,111	99	695	22
1867	5,368	11	322	5	...	...	...	...	17,690	98	792	23
1868	5,411	11	330	5	...	...	...	...	17,858	101	860	23
1869	...	...	...	...	...	...	...	...	17,562	105	925	25
1870	...	...	...	...	...	...	...	...	$18,083_8$	118	980_8	32
1871	...	...	...	...	565	1	83	1	11,270	121	994	38
1872	...	...	...	...	...	...	...	...	10,951	118	993	38
1873	...	16	227	6	...	...	...	...	10,712	133	998	49
1874	5,182	20	242	8	...	...	...	...	10,791	138	980	52
1875	5,410	27	254	27	...	...	...	...	10,828	141	987	57
1876	...	...	...	...	505	5	68	—	10,903	142	1,020	58
1877	...	...	...	...	...	...	...	...	$10,742_2$	151	$1,010_2$	58
1878	...	...	...	...	...	3	...	—	8,438	152	966	63
1879	...	...	...	...	...	3	...	—	7,910	151	933	73

F4 Merchant Ships Registered

	Netherlands				Norway				Russia[11]			
	Number of Ships		Thousand Tons		Number of Ships		Thousand Tons		Number of Ships		Thousand Tons	
	Sail	Steam	Sail	Steam	Sail	Steam	Sail	Steam	Sail	Steam	Sail	Steam
1829	1,346		178		...		...		...	...	...	...
1830	...		...		2,031		135		...	...	...	...
1831	...		...		...		...		...	...	...	...
1832	...		...		...		...		...	...	...	...
1833	...		...		...		...		...	...	...	...
1834	...		...		...		...		...	...	...	...
1835	...		...		2,272		151		...	...	...	...
1836	...		...		2,293		153		...	...	...	...
1837	...		...		...		...		...	...	...	...
1838	...		...		2,427		170		...	...	...	...
1839	...		...		...		...		...	...	...	...
1840	...		...		2,509		205		...	...	...	...
1841	...		...		...		...		...	...	...	...
1842	...		...		...		...		...	...	...	...
1843	...		...		...		...		...	...	...	...
1844	...		...		...		...		...	...	...	...
1845	...		...		3,348		233		...	...	...	...
1846	1,931	5	378	2	...		...		...	...	...	...
1847	2,055	6	394	2	3,526		259		...	...	...	...
1848	2,140	6	408	2	...		...		...	...	...	...
1849	2,300[2]	10	430[2]	3	...		...		...	...	...	...
1850	1,781	12	331	3	3,696		284		...	...	...	...
1851	1,848	12	352	3	3,762		297		...	...	...	...
1852	1,958	13	375	3	4,089		320		...	...	...	...
1853	2,022	15	401	4	4,200		341		...	...	...	...
1854	2,139	17	435	4	4,309		375		...	...	...	...
1855	2,210	20	460	5	4,464		405		...	...	...	...
1856	2,312	31	492	9	4,851		456		...	...	...	...
1857	2,388	40	512	11	5,152		496		...	...	...	...
1858	2,397	41	512	11	5,247		514		...	...	...	...
1859	2,365	41	504	12	5,278		526		1,416		173	
1860	2,318	42	485	11	5,287		532			...		...
1861	2,292	40	474	11	5,493		552			...		...
1862	2,251	38	458	11	5,541		567			...		...
1863	2,191	40	445	12	5,621		604			...		...
1864	2,184	43	445	13	5,678		635			...		...
1865	2,161	42	443	13	5,407		706		2,045	87	181	
1866	2,135	43	443	14	6,155	60	790	6	...	...	...	
1867	2,114	45	443	14	6,381	76	830	7	...	...	...	
1868	2,074	43	438	14	6,811	98	894	10	...	...	...	
1869	2,016	43	433	14	6,727	106	921	11	2,534	114	230	
1870	1,937	48	430	17	6,875	118	961	13	...	...		...
1871	1,846[9]	56[9]	414[9]	26[9]	6,923	140	993	19	...	...		...
	1,843	59	417	31								
1872	1,790	66	400	39	7,019	170	1,038	29	2,325	189	260	
1873	1,731	73	390	51	7,248	199	1,149	37	...	...	...	...
1874	1,747	80	392	63	7,453	211	1,235	40	...	...	...	...
1875	1,749	86	400	68	7,596	218	1,310	42	...	...	...	...
1876	1,702[10]	84[10]	401[10]	64[10]	7,651	258	1,390	46	2,163	218	302	74
1877	1,168	79	307	58	7,791	273	1,446	47	3,051	222	271	69
1878	1,100	79	299	59	7,942	306	1,475	52	3,643	259	308	74
1879	1,044	76	289	59	7,823	324	1,456	55	4,120	296	368	91

F4 Merchant Ships Registered

1829–1879

Year	Spain				Sweden[26]				United Kingdom			
	Number of Ships		Thousand Tons		Number of Ships		Thousand Tons		Number of Ships		Thousand Tons	
	Sail	Steam	Sail	Steam	Sail	Steam	Sail	Steam	Sail	Steam	Sail	Steam
1829	...	...	...	...	...		...		18,821	289	2,170	30
1830	...	...	...	...	1,841		131		18,876	298	2,168	30
1831	...	...	...	...	1,917		133		19,126	324	2,192	33
1832	...	...	...	...	1,948		130		19,312	352	2,226	36
1833	...	...	...	...	1,882		126		19,302	387	2,233	39
1834	...	...	...	...	1,809		124		19,545	430	2,268	44
1835	...	...	...	...	1,740		118		19,797	503	2,307	53
1836	...	...	...	...	1,809		116		19,827	561	2,289	60
1837	...	...	...	...	1,828		121		19,912	624	2,264	70
1838	...	...	...	...	1,882		129		20,234	678	2,346	75
1839	...	...	...	...	2,068		146		20,947	723	2,491	80
1840	...	...	...	...	2,171		159		21,883	771	2,680	88
1841	...	...	...	...	2,196		163		22,668	793	2,839	96
1842	...	...	...	...	2,171		167		23,121	833	2,933	108
1843	...	...	...	...	2,112		165		23,040	858	2,898	110
1844	...	...	...	...	2,044		160		23,116	900	2,931	114
1845	...	...	...	...	2,093		160		23,471	917	3,004	119
1846	...	...	...	...	2,062		155		23,808	963	3,069	131
1847	...	...	...	...	2,409		173		24,167	1,033	3,167	141
1848	...	...	...	...	2,440		182		24,520	1,118	3,249	151
1849	...	...	...	...	2,624		195		24,753	1,149	3,326	160
1850	4,531	23	240	5	2,744		204		24,797	1,187	3,397	168
1851	...	...	...	...	2,771		207		24,816	1,227	3,476	187
1852	...	...	...	...	2,846		211		24,814	1,272	3,550	209
1853	...	...	...	...	2,826		208		25,224	1,385	3,780	250
1854	...	...	...	...	2,783		214		25,335	1,524	3,943	306
1855	...	...	...	...	2,874		229		24,274	1,674	3,969	381
1856	...	...	...	...	3,020		252		24,480	1,697	3,980	387
1857	5,118	57	345	5	3,190		268		25,273	1,824	4,141	417
1858	...	...	...	...	3,300		275		25,615	1,926	4,205	452
1859	...	...	...	...	3,364		287		25,784	1,918	4,226	437
1860	4,716	84	400	15	3,200		281		25,663	2,000	4,204	454
1861	4,739	101	347	21	3,313		289		25,905	2,133	4,301	506
1862	4,704	124	356	33	3,108		280		26,212	2,228	4,396	538
1863	4,732	127	356	39	3,236		283		26,339	2,298	4,731	597
1864	4,614	135	359	42	3,198		287		26,142	2,490	4,930	697
1865	4,593	140	368	42	2,867	288	254	12	26,069	2,718	4,937	823
1866	4,355	145	356	43	3,030	293	286		26,140	2,831	4,904	876
1867	4,363	151	345	46	2,991	310	303		25,842	2,931	4,853	901
1868	...	...	...	...	2,924	344	303		25,500	2,944	4,878	902
1869	...	...	...	...	2,999	358	337		24,187	2,972	4,765	948
1870	...	...	...	...	3,008	368	319	28	23,189	3,178	4,578	1,113
1871	4,326	...	360	...	3,089	406	345	24	22,510	3,382	4,374	1,320
1872	...	...	...	...	3,185	479	354	35	22,103	3,673	4,213	1,538
1873	...12	...12	...12	...12	3,335	565	383	52	21,698	3,863	4,091	1,714
1874	2,674	212	510	115	3,585	627	411	82	21,464	4,033	4,108	1,871
1875	2,886	212	625	115	3,573	664	424	83	21,291	4,170	4,207	1,946
1876	2,752	388	452	159	3,700	681	443	82	21,144	4,335	4,258	2,005
1877	...	...	...	...	3,701	691	447	84	21,169	4,564	4,261	2,139
1878	2,063	339	374	164	3,563	752	454	82	21,058	4,826	4,239	2,316
1879	...	...	...	...	3,550	752	447	84	20,538	5,027	4,069	2,511

F4 Merchant Ships Registered

1880–1934

	Austria				Belgium						Denmark					
	Number of Ships		Thousand Tons		Number of Ships			Thousand Tons			Number of Ships			Thousand Tons[14]		
	Sail	Steam	Sail	Steam	Sail	Steam	Motor	Sail	Steam	Motor	Sail	Steam	Motor	Sail	Steam	Motor
1880	7,608	107	198	64	24	42		10	65		2,881	201	...	198	52	...
1881	7,829	106	193	67	18	41		7	70		2,857	226	...	192	61	...
1882	8,166	112	184	74	16	46		7	76		2,829	239	...	186	71	...
1883	8,574	117	178	72	15	47		6	80		2,857	258	...	185	81	...
1884	8,589	118	179	75	13	51		6	75		2,854	274	...	182	91	...
1885	8,768	120	165	78	11	54		5	80		2,881	280	...	180	90	...
1886	9,124	128	155	86	12	55		6	81		2,874	279	...	176	88	...
1887	9,104	131	137	86	10	55		6	81		2,877	281	...	172	90	...
1888	9,291	135	121	85	9	50		4	73		2,889	290	...	167	96	...
1889	9,414	141	113	86	9	42		4	66		2,938	305	...	177	104	...
1890	9,778	135	108	87	10	46		4	72		3,054	322	...	182	112	...
1891	9,977	135	104	90	8	47		2	71		3,094	343	...	188	117	...
1892	10,151	141	99	89	6	47		1	69		3,114	349	...	193	119	...
1893	10,887	144	90	97	6	56		1	74		3,116	362	...	195	129	...
1894	11,140	139	85	96	5	50		1	78		3,009	377	...	186	142	...
1895	11,467	148	81	107	5	54		1	86		3,010	401	...	179	144	...
1896	11,658	162	75	122	5	54		1	85		3,000	418	...	173	163	...
1897	11,499	175	68	143	5	56		1	85		2,996	436	...	163	181	...
1898	12,134	174	62	146	6	60		2	89		3,020	476	...	158	223	...
1899	11,928	183	58	162	6	67		3	106		3,047	497	...	155	255	...
1900	12,440	199	54	191	4	69		1	113		3,017	483	...	147	247	...
1901	12,713	211	54	227	6	66		1	109		3,026	497	...	143	257	...
1902	12,792	229	58	244	5	68		1	105		3,087	502	...	144	270	...
1903	12,917	232	55	253	4	67		1	102		3,121	508	...	138	292	...
1904	13,304	250	52	262	4	65		3	100		3,130	549	...	136	318	...
1905	13,642	266	51	276	4	67		3	97		3,126	572	...	130	331	...
1906	13,680	278	51	284	2	73		1	112		3,161	606	...	122	373	...
1907	13,983	296	50	310	3	74		1	119		3,266[13]	641	...	121[13]	402	...
1908	14,189	316	47	335	4	84		3	149		2,497	645	690	108	402	8
1909	14,629	357	45	343	4	97		3	184		2,441	652	738	107	406	9
1910	15,114	359	46	368	5	99		3	188		2,251	643	754	101	412	9
1911	15,847	382	47	390	8	93		6	161		2,147	640	775	94	412	8
1912	16,370	394	49	422	8	97		8	174		2,062	642	860	91	415	16
1913	...	...	...	...	12	112		13	222		1,970	642	941	90	421	30
1914	...	...	...	...	...	...		...	...		1,906	672	1,060	86	434	42
1915	...	...	...	...	...	...		...	...		1,874	664	1,128	96	432	59
1916	...	...	...	...	...	...		...	...		1,773	634	1,163	121	412	62
1917	...	...	...	...	...	...		...	...		1,592	536	1,269	97	339	64
1918	...	...	...	...	...	...		...	...		1,559	496	1,311	96	313	61
1919	...	...	...	...	...	...		...	...		1,584	514	1,463	103	334	82
1920	...	...	...	...	13	180	...	7	337	...	1,595	571	1,583	101	392	100
1921	...	...	...	...	12	195	...	7	382	...	1,511[6]	615[6]	1,671[6,14]	94[6,14]	453[6,14]	122[6,14]
											574	609	714	92	764	179
1922	...	...	...	...	7	183	...	4	365	...	489	622	766	81	789	179
1923	...	...	...	...	3	180	...	3	379	...	396	623	816	60	770	209
1924	...	...	...	...	1	156	4	2	343	6	336	644	866	49	823	218
1925	...	...	...	...	1	150	5	2	328	12	285	659	931	40	841	236
1926	...	...	...	...	1	145	6	2	320	12	252	638	980	37	811	260
1927	...	...	...	...	1	142	6	2	301	12	204	617	1,007	31	762	286
1928	...	...	...	...	1	139	8	2	291	22	160	602	1,047	27	733	336
1929	...	...	...	...	1	149	10	2	321	33	136	595	1,081	21	734	351
1930	...	...	...	...	1	140	10	2	319	37	100	599	1,141	15	735	417
1931	...	...	...	...	1	137	10	2	315	37	73[6]	606[6]	1,202[6]	11[6]	736[6]	468[6]
1932	...	...	...	...	—	117	10	—	265	37	76	610	1,403	10	721	506
1933	...	...	...	...	—	103	10	—	230	37	59	591	1,410	8	672	512
1934	...	...	...	...	—	96	11	—	217	39	42	583	1,418	4	662	522

F4   Merchant Ships Registered

1880–1934

	Finland[7]						France				Germany			
	Number of Ships			Thousand Tons			Number of Ships		Thousand Tons		Number of Ships		Thousand Tons	
	Sail	Steam	Motor	Sail	Steam	Motor	Sail	Steam & Motor	Sail	Steam & Motor	Sail	Steam & Motor	Sail	Steam & Motor
1880	1,500	203	...	262	10	...	14,406	652	278	4,246	414	927	177	
1881	1,574	205	...	265	11	...	14,391	735	603	312	4,051	458	905	206
1882	1,670[7]	207[7]	...	272[7]	12[7]	...	14,368	832	567	416	3,855	515	878	255
1883	...	...	...	...	...	...	14,327	895	536	467	3,712	603	859	307
1884	...	...	...	...	...	...	14,414	938	523	511	3,607	650	845	339
1885	1,750	301	...	247	17	...	14,329	937	508	492	3,471	664	788	345
1886	1,835	318	...	251	17	...	14,400	951	493	500	3,327	694	798	372
1887	1,796[7]	312[7]	...	235[7]	17[7]	...	14,253	984	466	507	3,094	717	739	386
1888	...	...	...	...	...	...	14,263	1,015	451	510	2,885	750	702	412
1889	...	...	...	...	...	...	14,128	1,066	440	493	2,779	815	675	507
1890	...	...	...	...	...	...	14,001	1,110	444	500	2,757	896	682	593
1891	...	...	...	...	...	...	13,890	1,157	426	522	2,698	941	676	627
1892	1,776	417	...	232	26	...	14,117	1,161	407	499	2,742	986	696	645
1893	1,858	417	...	233	28	...	14,190	1,186	397	499	2,713	1,016	670	675
1894	1,964	404	...	238	28	...	14,332	1,196	399	492	2,622	1,043	635	732
1895	1,955	418	...	237	29	...	14,386	1,212	387	501	2,524	1,068	593	796
1896	1,921	447	...	237	36	...	14,301	1,235	390	504	2,552	1,126	576	862
1897	2,031	453	...	252	38	...	14,352	1,212	421	499	2,522	1,171	569	945
1898	2,171	495	...	276	44	...	14,406	1,209	415	496	2,490	1,223	586	1,010
1899	2,282	540	...	275	51	...	14,262	1,227	451	507	2,466	1,293	576	1,124
1900	2,411	588	...	287	54	...	14,313	1,272	510	528	2,493	1,390	584	1,319
1901	2,606	584	...	296	50	...	14,393	1,299	564	547	2,496	1,463	578	1,476
1902	2,594	595	...	292	50	...	14,691	1,330	669	549	2,500	1,545	574	1,591
1903	2,622	633	...	290	60	...	14,910	1,383	650	585	2,534	1,622	576	1,713
1904	2,696	662	...	294	62	...	15,057	1,457	653	696	2,567	1,657	574	1,743
1905	2,750	663	...	301	60	...	15,284	1,471	676	711	2,558	1,762	551	1,883
1906	2,793	709	...	303	64	...	15,488	1,511	677	723	2,597	1,833	532	2,063
1907	2,843	729	...	308	66	...	15,639	1,554	663	740	2,649	1,922	535	2,230
1908	3,025	805	...	327	74	...	15,768	1,608	648	808	2,685	1,955	517	2,280
1909	3,076	819	...	333	76	...	15,878	1,670	638	806	2,708	1,950	510	2,332
1910	3,171	828	...	333	78	...	15,895	1,726	636	816	2,702	1,973	507	2,383
1911	3,252	845	...	333	77	...	15,849	1,780	625	838	2,724	2,009	510	2,501
1912	3,349	852	...	349	77	...	15,813	1,857	614	904	2,752	2,098	498	2,643
1913	3,401	895	...	368	82	...	15,824	1,895	602	980	2,765	2,170	488	2,832
1914	3,569	950	...	393	86	...	15,682	1,935	586	1,043	...	...	...	...
1915	3,834	946	...	386	81	...	15,161	1,939	561	1,066	...	...	...	...
1916	4,094	988	...	418	87	...	14,470	1,942	520	1,027	...	...	...	...
1917	4,214	1,014	...	446	85	...	13,777	1,880	417	886	...	...	...	...
1918	4,401	1,120	...	436	102	...	13,378	1,842	409	850	...	...	...	...
1919	4,544	1,122	...	435	107	...	13,137	1,969	427	879	...	...	...	...
1920	4,064[7] / 788	1,144[7] / 809	123	380[7] / 108	108[7] / 144	22	13,292	2,246	433	1,085	...	...	...	...
1921	701	795	127	97	91	19	13,508	2,519	452	1,388	...	...	...	...
1922	633	637	125	92	88	17	13,693	2,693	451	1,698	...	...	...	...
1923	615	598	116	94	89	16	13,640	2,696	386	1,759	1,956	2,282	288	1,546
1924	590	575	107	88	93	14	13,602	2,690	357	1,750	1,987	2,283	287	1,633
1925	543	568	96	97	176	13	13,665	2,809	356	1,766	1,987	2,164	260	1,675
1926	520	547	91	81	110	11	13,650	2,911	291	1,784	1,970	2,075	241	1,811
1927	513	558	103	80	130	13	13,550	3,008	268	1,778	2,017	1,964	215	1,979
1928	481	564	144	79	145	17	13,378	3,072	237	1,797	2,064	1,892	200	2,166
1929	439	570	154	76	155	17	13,409	3,126	232	1,775	2,087	1,852	190	2,312
1930	328	538	149	66	157	24	13,294	3,290	233	1,831	2,074	1,839	183	2,373
1931	279	520	152	67	163	14	13,075	3,442	226	1,870	2,009	1,767	158	2,360
1932	256	530	163	67	211	19	12,764	3,551	220	1,839	1,890	1,700	140	2,153
1933	242	535	161	73	386	29	12,612	3,602	219	1,804	1,825	1,689	139	2,062
1934	206[15]	545	168[15]	66[15]	428	30[15]	12,423	3,620	214	1,593	1,837	1,699	135	2,020

F4 Merchant Ships Registered

1880–1934

	Greece				Hungary[18]				Italy			
	Number of Ships		**Thousand Tons**		**Number of Ships**		**Thousand Tons**		**Number of Ships**		**Thousand Tons**	
	Sail	Steam	Sail	Steam	Sail	Steam	Sail	Steam	Sail	Steam & Motor	Sail	Steam & Motor
1880	...	...	...	...	...	6	...	...	7,822	158	922	77
1881	...	...	...	...	465	6	67	...	7,639	176	895	94
1882	...	...	...	...	...	14	...	6	7,528	192	885	105
1883	...	...	...	...	...	17	...	6	7,270	201	866	...
1884	[3,141][16]	72	[225][16]	36	...	20	...	6	7,072	215	849	122
1885	...	...	...	...	...	24	...	7	7,111	225	829	125
1886	...	...	...	...	458	25	57	7	6,992	237	801	144
1887	5,074	83	227	31	...	28	...	10	6,727	254	732	163
1888	5,731	98	217	32	...	28	...	10	6,544	266	698	175
1889	5,809	82	223	41	457	30	48	10	6,442	279	642	186
1890	5,744	97	227	45	...	...	...	...	...	...	...	...
1891	5,675	105	214	55	445	40	41	13	6,312	305	626	200
1892	5,732	162	234	77	426	46	37	17	6,308	316	610	201
1893	6,002[17]	161[17]	231[17]	84[17]	433	59	36	32	6,341	327	588	208
1894	...	...	...	...	409	64	30	37	6,231	328	572	208
1895	1,164	112	251	81	440	64	28	38	6,166	345	556	221
1896	1,059	107	246	89	444	67	25	39	6,002	351	528	238
1897	1,165	109	246	92	432	70	22	46	5,872	366	527	260
1898	1,147	100	238	87	432	69	19	44	5,764	384	538	278
1899	972	108	197	91	424	80	16	47	5,665	409	558	315
1900	927[17]	122[17]	184[17]	115[17]	360	78	13	56	5,511	446	568	377
	673	122	176	143								
1901	630	134	148	163	347	79	1163	5,337	...	471	575	425
1902	595	184	145	201	333	91	885	5,205	...	485	570	448
1903	604	167	145	199	361	90	686	5,153	...	501	584	461
1904	560	179	146	200	339	95	392	5,083	...	513	570	462
1905	551	183	145	226	382	95	392	5,020	...	514	541	484
1906	571	201	147	247	379	97	393	4,981	...	548	503	498
1907	567	212	145	258	385	104	3	109	4,874	589	469	527
1908	701	224	146	295	381	113	3	113	4,701	626	453	567
1909	882	261	165	292	378	116	2	114	4,723	680	440	631
1910	804	298	145	313	341	114	2	110	4,741	718	433	674
1911	813	322	145	350	388	128	2	132	4,713	757	411	697
1912	807	346	142	407	400	133	2	137	4,693	839	375	762
1913	788	389	137	434	411	134	2	143	4,696	931	356	877
1914	...	450	...	493	412	137	2	148	4,773	949[19]	349	933[19]
1915	784	474	107	550	...	...	...	...	4,737	644	332	934
1916	...	...	...	...	407	130	2	144	4,464	659	262	1,036
1917	...	...	...	...	416	126	3	144	4,084	559	218	896
1918	700	205	120	291	...	...	...	...	...	448[19]	...	699[19]
1919	1,056	282	133	430	...	...	...	...	...	408	...	632
1920	1,079	335	138	494	...	...	...	...	...	495	...	835
1921	1,093	440	152	685	...	...	...	...	603	...	...	1,075
1922	1,089	418	133	737	...	...	...	...	...	856	...	1,509
1923	1,060	431	122	762	...	...	...	...	...	880[19]	...	1,636[19]
1924	1,018	437	114	829	*Southern Ireland*				3,432	1,304	191	...
1925	814	467	68	913	...	...	...	...	3,216	1,370	168	1,764
1926	735	472	60	930	166	152	232	9	52	4	3,089	1,410
1927	726	504	59	1,111	160	150	246	8	51	4	3,000	1,424
1928	729	528	59	1,257	151	150	253	7	51	5	2,827	1,454
1929	718	547	58	1,350	142	150	252	7	52	5	2,690	1,396
1930	708	559	56	1,413	116	152	249	6	48	6	2,629	1,434
1931	698	575	56	1,488	110	155	251	6	42	6	2,562	1,443
1932	697	558	56	1,430	105	152	260	5	41	6	2,482	1,407
1933	699	565	56	1,572	100	140	312	5	50	7	2,353	1,342
1934	709	600	56	1,755	95	147	329	5	50	7	2,261	1,301

F4 Merchant Ships Registered

	Netherlands				Norway						Poland		Portugal[23]
	Number of Ships		Thousand Tons		Number of Ships			Thousand Tons			Number	Thou	Thou
	Sail	Steam & Motor	Sail	Steam & Motor	Sail	Steam	Motor	Sail	Steam	motor	of ships	Tons	Tons
1880	917	79	264	64	7,761	334	…	1,461	58	…	…	…	…
1881	802	78	233	72	7,618	359	…	1,455	65	…	…	…	…
1882	751	86	217	85	7,506	407	…	1,447	83	…	…	…	…
1883	701	96	207	102	7,459	440	…	1,455	92	…	…	…	…
1884	673	107	198	110	7,397	487	…	1,478	105	…	…	…	…
1885	634	106	194	108	7,154	510	…	1,449	114	…	…	…	…
1886	586	106	177	109	6,942	502	…	1,411	113	…	…	…	…
1887	516	105	155	101	6,755	514	…	1,382	122	…	…	…	…
1888	502	107	140	105	6,697	536	…	1,397	138	…	…	…	…
1889	500	110	137	110	6,693	592	…	1,443	168	…	…	…	…
1890	500	118	127	128	6,760	672	…	1,503	203	…	…	…	…
1891	478	143	131	161	6,798	735	…	1,500	239	…	…	…	…
1892	447	150	123	169	6,739	767	…	1,494	251	…	…	…	…
1893	442	154	118	176	6,702	810	…	1,452	239	…	…	…	…
1894	424	157	110	183	6,453	859	…	1,335	264	…	…	…	…
1895	405	162	102	188	6,355	915	…	1,284	321	…	…	…	…
1896	440	172	98	196	6,230	962	…	1,215	352	…	…	…	…
1897	441	171	95	201	6,143	1,004	…	1,169	383	…	…	…	…
1898	429	176	88	214	5,981	1,068	…	1,121	437	…	…	…	…
1899	432	192	84	235	5,698	1,128	…	1,053	482	…	…	…	…
1900	425	213	78	268	5,642	1,171	…	1,003	505	…	…	…	…
1901	417	235	75	306	5,445	1,223	…	936	531	…	…	…	…
1902	436	257	73	331	5,569	1,290	…	884	567	…	…	…	…
1903	439	268	58	337	5,807	1,396	…	840	604	…	…	…	…
1904	463	269	58	341	5,843	1,477	…	809	642	…	…	…	…
1905	479	271	55	357	5,853	1,734	…	814	664	…	…	…	…
1906	492	283	53	377	5,813	1,493	305	793	752	3	…	…	…
1907	435	292	50	398	5,773	1,599	508	751	814	5	…	…	…
1908	403	283	44	414	5,742	1,645	1,165	725	847	9	…	…	…
1909	426	303	47	464	5,219[22]	1,671[22]	1,027[22]	702[22]	861[22]	9[22]	…	…	…
1910	440	324	46	488	1,205	1,738	104	630	893	3	…	…	…
1911	428	347	42	523	1,170	1,813	126	658	984	4	…	…	…
1912	413	367	41	577	1,106	1,973	153	633	1,081	4	…	…	…
1913	400	387	40	647	1,029	2,052	209	606	1,155	6	…	…	…
1914	402	407	47	720	947	2,107	271	561	1,214	9	…	…	…
1915	390	397	45	726	867	2,200	393	505	1,254	18	…	…	…
1916	364	422	35	726	740	2,142	613	428	1,273	29	…	…	…
1917	331	468	31	723	602	1,837	978	294	995	52	…	…	…
1918	332	575	32	770	547	1,763	1,164	257	898	69	…	…	…
1919	283	570	28	804	457	1,826	1,382	232	979	105	…	…	…
1920	241[20]	606[20]	24[20]	969[20]	409	1,922	1,497	204	1,199	125	…	…	236
	231	503	22	961									
1921	217	570	20[14]	1,167[14]	387	1,950	1,503	185	1,318	136	…	…	250
			25	1,869									
1922	214	577	24	2,069	361	1,906	1,473	172	1,300	147	…	…	237
1923	199	571	23	2,112	306	1,908	1,454	121	1,297	156	…	…	261
1924	173	575	20	2,089	256	1,928	1,451	62	1,324	181	…	…	264
1925	168	599	19	2,108	222	1,966	1,510	40	1,352	269	—	—	267
1926	149	645	17	2,116	216	1,956	1,547	30	1,325	340	6	11	251
1927	85[21]	681[21]	11[21]	2,115[21]	204	1,931	1,563	22	1,317	405	10	15	229
	231	545	33	2,152	187	1,893	1,608	13	1,315	515	18	22	219
1928	200	586	30	2,256	181	1,938	1,654	13	1,380	613	25	41	219
1930	161	638	24	2,397	181	1,991	1,781	12	1,414	868	31	65	239
1931	155	677	24	2,389	163	1,974	1,864	11	1,444	1,036	33	68	254
1932	152	665	24	2,228	158	1,944	1,921	9	1,392	1,059	39	66	245
1933	137	636	21	2,040	150	1,874	1,951	9	1,307	1,073	56	65	243
1934	140	617	22	1,968	140	1,776	2,002	8	1,169	1,125	57	65	241

F4 Merchant Ships Registered

1880–1934

	Russia/U.S.S.R.[11]				Spain						Sweden[26]			
	Number of Ships		Thousand Tons		Number of Ships			Thousand Tons			Number of Ships		Thousand Tons	
	Sail	Steam	Sail	Steam	Sail	Steam	Motor	Sail	Steam	motor	Sail	Steam & Motor	Sail	Steam & Motor
1880	4,276	326	379	89	1,889	347	...	326	234	...	3,581	752	462	81
1881	...	...	...	...	...	...	...	...	...	...	3,397	754	450	79
1882	...	...	...	...	1,555	252	...	316	248	...	3,356	785	440	88
1883	4,411[24]	379[24]	401[24]	99[24]	1,461	407	...	247	347	...	3,252	823	424	95
1884	2,608	342	351	120	1,395	430	...	231	383	...	3,158	886	422	108
1885	2,632	360	358	127	1,379	431	...	225	388	...	3,090	878	407	110
1886	2,614	369	362	130	1,336	431	...	216	384	...	3,033	903	386	115
1887	...	...	...	...	1,326	432	...	212	397	...	2,954	949	377	123
1888	...	...	...	...	1,277	421	...	205	393	...	2,885	959	375	125
1889	...	...	...	...	1,238	415	...	195	411	...	2,859	963	370	135
1890	...	...	...	...	1,342	411	...	210	408	...	2,858	1,016	370	141
1891	...	...	...	...	1,313	438	...	204	436	...	3,006	1,181	380	152
1892	...	...	...	...	1,233	474	...	197	455	...	2,927	1,209	377	172
1893	...	...	...	...	1,228	492	...	197	480	...	2,844	1,229	369	177
1894	...	...	...	...	1,237	502	...	199	489	...	2,914[26]	1,248[26]	371[26]	179[26]
1895	2,135	522	323	206	1,260	523	...	193	526	...	2,030	733	302	181
1896	2,207	567	336	241	1,256	543	...	192	564	...	2,013	756	291	206
1897	2,294	604	344	262	1,125	562	...	159	499	...	2,002	786	289	234
1898	2,143	657	254	300	...[12]	...[12]	...	...[12]	...[12]	...	2,004	817	291	266
1899	2,259	714	268	334	175	422	...	53	642	...	2,040	872	289	298
1900	2,293	745	269	364	163	469	...	51	735	...	2,076	911	289	325
1901	2,378	810	273	392	150	459	...	48	736	...	2,160	943	299	342
1902	2,489	840	285	397	136	459	...	44	721	...	2,035	952	279	357
1903	2,500	832	277	390	124	455	...	41	714	...	1,983	987	272	376
1904	2,533[25]	834[25]	284	383	119	450	...	38	689	...	1,950	1,019	266	408
1905	2,523	847	267	375	118	461	...	38	684	...	1,915	1,066	263	460
1906	...	...	...	...	110	468	...	35	673	...	1,852	1,090	254	488
1907	2,544	906	260	441	82	469	...	24	677	...	1,827	1,141	239	533
1908	2,465	898	258	443	80	479	...	23	687	...	1,751	1,187	213	564
1909	2,494	925	261	459	68	511	...	19	747	...	1,689	1,211	193	583
1910	2,504	943	260	463	65	526	...	17	758	...	1,635	1,214	177	593
1911	2,516	1,015	254	488	64	526	...	16	756	...	1,539	1,219	155	610
1912	2,577	1,068	257	500	60	547	...	15	826	...	1,539	1,254	154	651
1913	2,597	1,103	257[11]	526[11]	93	554	...	24	875	...	1,509	1,313	152	721
			184	790										
1914	...	...	...	...	94	548	...	25	875	...	1,509	1,336	152	749
1915	...	...	...	...	...	...	...	...	...	...	1,422	1,278	137	689
1916	...	...	...	...	...	...	...	...	...	...	1,378	1,267	130	666
1917	...	...	...	...	93	490	...	35	729	...	1,304	1,240	123	633
1918	...	...	...	...	149	452	...	47	692	...	1,295	1,238	119	621
1919	...	...	...	...	240	456	...	75	705	...	1,279	1,260	117	658
1920		...		510	314	548	...	83	875	...	1,316	1,274	121	712
1921		450		404	274	595	...	81	1,002	...	1,323	1,250	118	690
1922		424		360	263	630	...	79	1,072	...	1,337	1,296	121	766
1923		390		341	253	637	...	74	1,091	...	1,310	1,342	112	823
1924		381		331	248	642	...	73	1,109	...	1,266	1,364	101	854
1925		361		314	236	642	...	68	1,083	...	1,200	1,367	89	904
1926		354		315	236	642	...	67	1,073	...	1,152	1,382	83	925
1927		331		301	231	646	...	65	1,052	...	1,078	1,444	78	953
1928		349		374	214	637	4	59	1,040	12	1,054	1,457	73	1,025
1929		373		437	205	642	11	56	1,052	31	1,009	1,476	70	1,082
1930		344		529	179	626	32	43	1,035	79	997	1,502	72	1,144
1931		383		601	134	721	60	26	1,043	156	990	1,506	70	1,192
1932		446		682	130	774	83	24	1,016	184	964	1,482	67	1,156
1933		441		840	119	753	93	21	977	202	916	1,455	62	1,127
1934		489		939	119	732	100	20	936	220	906	1,409	62	1,074

F4   Merchant Ships Registered

1880–1899   **1900–1919**

| | United kingdom | | | | | United kingdom | | | |
| | Number of Ships | | Thousand Tons | | | Number of Ships | | Thousand Tons | |
	Sail	Steam	Sail	Steam		Sail	Steam	Sail	Steam
1880	19,938	5,247	3,851	2,724	1900	11,167	9,029	2,247	6,917
1881	19,325	5,505	3,688	3,004	1901	10,773	9,209	2,096	7,208
1882	18,892	5,814	3,622	3,335	1902	10,572	9,484	1,991	7,618
1883	18,415	6,260	3,514	3,728	1903	10,455	9,803	1,951	8,104
1884	18,053	6,601	3,465	3,944	1904	10,330	10,122	1,869	8,400
1885	17,018	6,644	3,457	3,973	1905	10,210	10,370	1,803	8,752
1886	16,179	6,653	3,397	3,965	1906	10,059	10,522	1,671	9,065
1887	15,473	6,663	3,250	4,085	1907	9,857	10,907	1,555	9,612
1888	15,025	6,871	3,114	4,350	1908	9,648	11,394	1,461	10,024
1889	14,640	7,139	3,041	4,718	1909	9,542	11,626	1,403	10,139
1890	14,181	7,410	2,936	5,043	1910	9,392	11,797	1,301	10,285
1891	13,823	7,720	2,972	5,307	1911	9,090	12,000	1,113	10,443
1892	13,578	7,950	3,080	4,565	1912	8,830	12,242	981	10,718
1893	13,239	8,088	3,038	5,740	1913	8,510	12,382	903	10,992
1894	12,943	8,263	2,987	5,969	1914	8,336	12,602[3]	847	11,273[3]
						8,203	12,862	794	11,622
1895									
1896	12,617	8,386	2,867	6,122	1915	8,019	12,771	779	11,650
1897	12,274	8,522	2,736	6,284	1916	7,669	12,405	715	11,037
1898	11,911	8,590	2,590	6,364	1917	7,186	11,534	625	9,608
1899	11,566	8,838	2,388	6,614	1918	6,856	11,334	604	9,497
					1919	6,555	11,791	593	10,335

1920–1934

| | United kingdom | | | | | | Yugoslavia | | | |
| | Number of Ships | | | Thousand Tons | | | Number of Ships | | Thousand Tons | |
	Sail	Steam	Motor	Sail	Steam	Motor	Sail	Steam & Motor	Sail	Steam & Motor
1920	6,309	12,307	...	584	10,777	...	...	...	...	...
1921	6,272	12,660	...	610	10,932	...	...	...	...	...
1922	6,184[27]	12,787[27]	...[27]	574[27]	11,223[27]	...[27]	...	...	...	...
1923	5,962	10,813	1,624	551	10,897	263	...	...	...	...
1924	5,842	10,690	1,823	522	10,810	385	...	...	...	...
1925	5,785	10,526	1,965	520	10,965	499	...	...	...	...
1926	5,678	10,262	2,170	517	10,760	629	...	...	...	...
1927	5,609	10,032	2,340	507	10,577	770	...	...	...	...
1928	5,408	9,959	2,681	496	10,754	1,009	702	224	12	284
1929	5,249	9,855	2,940	480	10,675	1,214	729	248	11	304
1930	5,098	9,729	3,237	468	10,561	1,425	700	253	9	314
1931	4,960	9,529	3,483	462	10,233	1,579	710	223	11	338
1932	4,773	9,248	3,650	472	9,774	1,617	704	246	13	376
1933	4,632	8,900	3,863	466	9,062	1,642	711	237	13	351
1934	4,435	8,622	4,168	432	8,621	1,692	705	238	14	327

F4 Merchant Ships Registered

1935–1998

	Belgium						Denmark					
	Number of Ships			Thousand Tons[28]			Number of Ships			Thousand Tons		
	Sail	Steam	Motor	Sail	Steam	Motor	Sail	Steam	Motor	Sail	Steam	Motor
1935	—	91	11	—	206	39	34	563	1,449	4	629	555
1936	—	89	11	—	201	40	26	549	1,497	2	602	586
1937	—	76	16	—	183	54	18	521	1,514	1	570	616
1938	—	67	28	—	164	88	16	518	1,558	2	584	647
1939	—	56	31	—	149	96	18	499	1,621	2	565	679
1940	—	59	34	—	159	94	15	465	1,607	1	526	679
1941	—	56	34	—	147	97	14	437	1,625	1	479	649
1942	—	...	...	—	...	...	...	...	...	...	...	...
1943	—	...	...	—	...[29]	...[28]	14	408	1,681	1	443	550
1944	—	30	22	—	109	90	...	...	...	...	...	...
1945	—	28	24	—	96	107	5	349	1,761	—	362	576
1946	—	34	27	—	118	130	5	339	1,778	—	348	593
1947	—	47	31	—	204	146	5[29]	383[29]	1,854[29]	—[29]	450[29]	648[29]
1948	—	52	39	—	216	176	4	373	1,920	—	469	746
1949	—	48	46	—	205	204	3	358	1,958	—	471	836
1950	—	45	49	—	199	226	2	344	2,010	—	447	939
1951	—	43	47	—	207	224	2	311	2,001	—	404	1,055
1952	—	40	51	—	200	237	2	268	2,017	—	370	1,162
1953	—	39	51	—	191	229	2	252	2,024	—	342	1,279
1954	—	32	50	—	198	232	2	218	2,015	—	282	1,395
1955	—	32	50	—	221	230	2	192	2,022	—	245	1,527
1956	—	34	52	—	241	262	2[30]	165	2,083[30]	—[30]	195	1,686[30]
1957	—	34	57	—	249	282	1,565	149	620	90	175	1,785
1958	—	34	65	—	266	354	1,609	140	685	92	162	1,932
1959	—	31	67	—	260	370	1,658	118	769	94	164	2,028
1960	—	27	70	—	283	394	1,708	99	882	95	159	2,135
1961	—	22	69	—	229	396	1,733	87	990	96	172	2,227
1962	—	21	76	—	239	429	1,724	74	1,044	95	182	2,250
1963	—	18	81	—	217	481	1,719	66	1,069	93	238	2,197
1964	—	15	85	—	219	509	1,717	55	1,132	93	287	2,281
1965	—	10	87	—	169	591	1,714	48	1,204	92	315	2,341
1966	—	9	80	—	161	610	1,720	45	1,294	91	465	2,487
1967	—	9	84	—	161	674	1,722	43	1,384	92	516	2,594
1968	—	9	83	—	161	724	1,700	43	1,465	89	669	2,566
1969	—	9	88	—	161	797	1,664	42	1,514	86	872	2,528
1970	—	9	80	—	161	812	1,629	35	1,569	85	800	2,530
1971	—	9	80	—	161	915	1,579	37	1,623	81	1,276	2,500
1972	—	9	86	—	161	930	1,542	36	1,683	79	1,465	2,605
1973	—	8	80	—	136	954	1,521	39	1,724	78	1,651	2,522
1974	—	8	82	—	136	1,115	1,506	36	1,753	77	1,979	2,706
1975	—	5	89	—	82	1,274	1,518	32	1,787	78	1,897	2,750
1976	—	2	89	—	37	1,373	1,498	37	1,821	76	2,225	2,886
		—2				—2						
		99			1,437							
1977		100			1,563		1,452	37	1,833	72	2,497	2,909
1978		90			1,628		1,407	33	1,805	69	2,419	3,068
1979		98			1,749		1,367	30	1,727	67	2,276	3,034
1980		100			1,771		1,283	28	1,656	62	2,120	3,032
1981		105			1,907		1,249	26	1,632	60	2,018	3,111
1982		105			2,086		1,227	24	1,635	59	1,874	3,312
1983		105			2,184		1,215	21	1,620	57	1,671	3,348
1984		106			2,230		1,200	16	1,616	56	1,521	3,673
1985		101			2,233		1,176	14	1,614	54	1,203	3,656
1986		96[2]			2,270[2]		1,145	12	1,638	53	1,172	3,816
		88			2,253							
1987		78			2,039		1,134	12	1,609	52	1,172	3,586
1988		75			2,015		1,037	10	1,620	48	838	4,080
1989		69			1,914		1,037	10	1,620	48	837	4,080
1990		70			1,919		1,000	10	1,632	47	837	4,601
1991		68			1,769		954	10	1,676	45	802	5,068
1992		73			1,809		...	...	...	...	...	...
1993		...			...		...	...	...	...	...	...
1994		...			...		...	...	1,732	...	...	5,698
1995		...			...		...	...	1,751	...	...	5,747
1996		...			...		...	...	1,763	...	...	5,885
1997		...			...		...	...	1,784	...	...	5,754
1998		...			...		...	...	...	...	...	5,687

F4   Merchant Ships Registered

	Finland						France			
	Number of Ships			Thousand Tons			Number of Ships		Thousand Tons	
	Sail	Steam	Motor	Sail	Steam	Motor	Sail	Steam & Motor	Sail	Steam & Motor
1935	298	528	31	72	418	14	12,125	3,713	199	1,588
1936	280	547	36	63	469	17	11,780	3,776	207	1,524
1937	262	567	37	56	537	17	11,320	3,842	200	1,484
1938	249	562	46	54	552	38	9,841	4,911	178	1,486
1939	227	560	50	49	557	43	9,079	5,373	171	1,546
1940	196	470	47	44	488	47	6,979	1,364	131	1,476
1941	180	429	42	31	379	30	8,517	5,437	158	1,608
1942	174	405	41	31	336	25	8,600	5,594	157	1,583
1943	172	400	42	31	336	25	8,585	5,668	156	1,579
1944	134_{15}	362	41_{15}	22_{15}	288	22_{15}	8,444	5,655	154	1,574
1945	15	312	167	14	232	21	8,257	5,781	153	1,546
1946	13	333	203	13	280	37	7,775	5,796	144	1,358
1947	11	386	247	13	411	66	7,403	6,258	94	1,671
1948	12_{15}	385	256_{15}	15_{15}	423	82_{15}	7,330	6,590	91	1,490
1949	162	387	108	27	429	79	7,218	$7,040_{31}$	86	$1,540_{32}$
								1,236		3,070
1950	153	376	123	20	458	90	...	1,234	...	3,207
1951	145	375	128	16	468	107	...	1,246	...	3,367
1952	131	360	135	13	473	147	...	1,251	...	3,638
1953	128	338	147	12	441	223	...	1,260	...	3,826
1954	125	327	150	12	425	285	...	1,257	...	3,841
1955	117	316	162	12	436	305	...	1,220	...	3,922
1956	117	293	173	12	424	331	...	1,201	...	3,943
1957	116	274	186	12	401	364	...	1,230	...	4,010
1958	103	252	183	10	362	329	...	1,307	...	4,338
1959	98	223	196	10	312	396	...	1,409	...	4,538
1960	88	216	217	9	314	478	...	1,456	...	4,809
1961	83	200	250	8	295	516	...	1,488	...	5,117
1962	78	192	287	8	298	575	...	1,462	...	5,162
1963	53	179	335	6	295	644	...	1,498	...	5,216
1964	38	157	369	5	268	690	...	1,532	...	5,116
1965	30	140	390	4	240	747	...	1,558	...	5,198
1966	25	123	393	3	211	793	...	1,539	...	5,260
1967	17	101	407	2	170	925	...	1,538	...	5,577
1968	14	78	414	2	109	972	...	$1,495_{33}$	...	$5,796_{33}$
								570		5,500
1969	12	59	437	2	67	1,174	...	554	...	5,725
1970	9	53	447	1	65	1,304	...	538	...	5,921
1971	5	44	441	1	51	1,366	...	550	...	6,982
1972	3	37	456	—	41	1,572	...	531	...	7,440
1973	3	28	435	—	21	1,492	...	498	...	8,177
1974	—	27	422	—	14	1,610	...	514	...	9,476
1975		450			2,048		...	525	...	10,291
1976		442			2,090		...	504	...	11,143
1977		446			2,275		...	502	...	11,860
1978		459			2,314		...	465	...	11,626
1979		466			2,420		...	424	...	11,581
1980		487			2,346		...	424	...	11,239
1981		483			2,479		...	393	...	10,319
1982		483			2,210		...	395	...	9,758
1983		484			2,360		...	388	...	9,123
1984		472			2,067		...	349	...	7,998
1985		439			1,650		...	311	...	5,830
1986		427			1,244		...	283	...	4,962
1987		415			841		...	261	...	4,389
1988		415			885		...	241	...	4,129
1989		441			1,053			223		3,870
1990		451			1,093			218		3,725
1991		464			1,031			216		3,833
1992		483			1,222			221		3,833
1993		493			1,429			215		3,928
1994		498			1,404			211		4,242
1995		511			1,519			207		4,086
1996		530			1,511			217		4,291
1997		539			1,559			223		4,570
1998		546			1,629			230		4,738

F4 Merchant Ships Registered

1935–1998

Year	Germany						East Germany[16]		Greece			
	Number of Ships			Thousand Tons			Number of Ships	Thousand Tons	Number of Ships		Thousand Tons	
	Sail	Steam & Motor		Sail	Steam & Motor				Sail	Steam	Sail	Steam
1935	1,692	1,825		132	2,006		...	...	700	600	54	1,759
1936	1,667	1,912		129	2,109		...	...	714	605	55	1,794
1937	1,636	2,032		127	2,243		...	...	...	615	...	1,875
1938	1,646	2,135		126	2,364		...	...	716	607	56	1,874
1939	...	...		...	...		...	...	...	577	...	1,837
1940	...	...		...	...		...	...	...	...	...	...
1941	...	...		...	...		...	...	...	...	...	...
1942	...	...		...	...		...	...	...	...	...	...
1943	...	...		...	...		...	...	...	...	...	...
1944	...	...		...	...		...	...	...	...	...	...
West Germany[16]												
1945	...	...		...	...		...	...		...		...[34]
1946	...	...		...	...		...	...		138		502
1947	...	...		...	...		...	...		270		1,204
1948	...	168		...	92		...	...		305		1,304
1949	847	186	381	87	143	73	...	...		327		1,335
1950	829	278	630	100	408	262	...	...		337		1,304
1951	751	288	844	87	494	604	...	...		331		1,259
1952	512	298	1,198	62	553	904	1	1		489		1,270
1953	484	283	1,337	60	621	1,249	2	1		461		1,187
1954	463	266	1,437	55	662	1,642	3	8		478		1,263
1955	438	257	1,616	52	719	2,127	9	10		486		1,296
1956	430	274	1,761	54	831	2,582	17	14		516		1,425
1957	413	263	1,929	49	858	2,981	21	35		549		1,563
1958	388	244	2,104	42	952	3,448	31	104		616[35]		1,905[35]
1959	366	224	2,175	40	1,039	3,664	33	148		827		3,344
1960	347	177	2,182	38	995	3,729	47	197		1,043		5,384
1961	304	160	2,240	35	1,026	3,972	61	238		1,165		6,393
1962	283	140	2,303	34	1,012	4,167	82	351		1,232		6,774
1963	254	116	2,321	29	1,033	4,277	97	421		1,314		6,938
1964	227	99	2,321	26	1,023	4,368	110	494		1,442		7,249
1965	177	82	2,383	21	971	4,764	127	570		1,570		7,256
1966	163	75	2,423	18	1,016	4,989	150	658		1,739		7,856
1967	150	70	2,473	17	1,052	5,478	162	756		1,848		8,050
1968	134	68	2,490	14	1,130	5,923	162	777		1,945		9,216
1969	128	57	2,547	13	1,084	6,381	169	878		2,104		11,139
1970	96	51	2,543	9	1,392	7,040	175	940		2,319		13,539
1971	1	42	2,288	...	1,357	7,059	179	961		2,543		15,441
1972	—	42	2,024	—	1,460	6,361	194	1,028		2,826		19,093
1973	—	58	1,803	—	1,676	6,167	190	1,008		3,113		23,400
1974	—	63	1,551	—	2,663	5,634	194	1,152		3,145		24,080
1975	—	69	1,494	—	3,026	5,663	198	1,200		3,216		24,820
1976	—			—			198	1,212		3,509		28,573
1977	—	53	1,590	—	3,335	5,978	200	1,259		3,886		33,475
1978	—	44	1,555	—	2,907	5,586	194	1,278		3,732		34,987
1979	—	44	1,496	—	2,726	5,140	194	1,308		3,951		38,842
1980	—	38	1,457	—	2,581	5,027	192	1,305		3,942		41,129
1981	—	35	1,378	—	2,505	4,898	177	1,290		3,896		42,488
1982	—	32	1,361	—	2,136	4,535	173	1,171		3,556		38,128
1983	—	28	1,362	—	1,741	4,567	174	1,234		3,263		36,806
1984	—	23	1,365	—	1,314	4,619	172	1,202		2,788		32,335
1985	—	19	1,385	—	696	4,594	171	1,222		2,456		28,646
1986	—	11	1,213	—	354	3,879	174	1,345		2,138		24,793
1987	—	10	1,014	—	329	3,439	170	1,332		2,061		22,706
1988	—	9	941	—	329	3,399	164	1,314		2,015		21,369
1989	—	9	913	—	329	4,005	...	...		7,004		20,898
Germany												
1990	—	9	1,055	—	330	5,105	Included in	West Germany		2,031		22,526
1991	—	7	1,047	—	273	5,349				2,062		24,090
1992	—	6	927	—	215	4,816				2,095		26,055
1993	—	3	869	—	71	4,847				2,166		29,672
1994	—	...	843	—	5,696					2,189		30,162
1995	—	...	831	—	5,626					2,213		29,435
1996	—	...	...	—	5,842					2,202		27,507
1997	—	...	...	—	6,950					2,184		25,288
1998	—	...	...	—	8,084					2,136		25,225

F4 Merchant Ships Registered

	Southern Ireland						Italy			
	Number of Ships			Thousand Tons			Number of Ships		Thousand Tons	
	Sail	Steam	Motor	Sail	Steam	Motor	Sail	Steam & Motor	Sail	Steam & Motor
1935	90	144	328	5	62	7	2,197	1,295	109	1,848
1936	88	136	334	5	61	7	2,093	1,284	104	1,832
1937	92	141	352	5	61	8	2,161	1,335	102	1,876
1938	93	137	364	5	59	51	2,263	1,346	99	1,940
1939	92	111	357	5	22	13	2,367	1,361	99[36]	1,998[36]
1940	85	87	360	5	16	9	2,403	1,341	145	3,353
1941	73	83	349	5	25	7	2,405	1,246	139	2,906
1942	66	88	345	5	40	7	2,442	1,129	133	2,431
1943	61	85	330	5	34	6	…	…	…	…
1944	58	85	323	4	34	6	…	…	…	…
1945	54	82	310	4	35	6	1,654	253	71	546
1946	50	76	313	4	28	6	2,569	646	106	1,160
1947	49	75	309	4	25	6	2,797	901	116	1,863
1948	50	78	320	4	30	12	2,993	1,074	118	2,287
1949	46	78	324	4	27	12	3,071	1,132	119	2,536
1950	46	82	340	4	30	12	3,072	1,189	112	2,809
1951	47	82	357	4	30	13	3,244	1,247	115	3,156
1952	43	76	368	4	30	14	3,310	1,275	116	3,413
1953	42	70	375	4	32	14	3,106	1,290	112	3,611
1954	41	68	381	4	31	15	2,946	1,323	105	3,933
1955	40	69	388	4	31	15	2,830	1,346	103	4,055
1956	39	67	396	4	35	21	2,643	1,437	98	4,407
1957	39	64	399	4	38	28	2,595	1,489	97	4,859
1958	39	63	409	4	44	34	2,539	1,474	105	5,019
1959	37	62	434	4	48	35	2,427	1,451	104	4,961
1960	37	58	426	4	40	36	2,360	1,479	104	5,161
1961	37	56	440	4	40	43	2,300	1,537	105	5,332
1962	34	53	467	3	39	57	2,293	1,643	108	5,369
1963	30	48	505	3	35	67	2,188	1,799	112	5,498
1964	30	47	537	3	36	67	2,151	1,819	119	5,472
1965	32	41	565	3	21	65	2,090	1,837	132	5,691
1966	33	40	609	3	20	66	2,100	1,879	139	5,864
1967	33	39	660	3	18	64	2,053	1,931	147	6,360
1968	34	38	755	3	18	70	2,001	1,968	154	6,710
1969	34	38	837	3	18	70	2,017	1,997	161	6,978
1970	35	38	920	3	18	90	2,028	2,108	170	7,467
1971	35	38	1,027	3	18	90	2,034	2,201	180	7,880
1972	35	37	1,111	3	14	92	2,022	2,297	182	8,304
1973	34	37	1,186	3	14	130	1,939	2,113	176	9,068
1974	24	3	1,317	1	1	144	1,932[37]	2,118[38]	172[37]	9,984[38]
							1,699	1,641	163	9,973
1975	26	3	1,384	1	1	144	1,663	1,626	160	10,673
1976	26	3	1,468	1	1	135	1,684	1,605	160	11,081
1977	33	3	1,566	1	1	155	1,617	1,603	154	11,398
1978	33	3	1,643	1	1	154	1,581	1,611	154	11,600
1979	44	3	1,698	1	1	147	1,535	1,602	151	11,134
1980	68	3	1,776	2	1	148	1,031	1,589	131	10,998
1981	89	3	1,831	2	1	187	893	1,553	120	10,284
1982	111	3	1,848	2	1	141	630	1,547	101	10,240
1983	124	3	1,866	2	1	156	599	1,516	94	9,526
1984	133	3	1,888	2	1	147	594	1,482	94	9,023
1985	134	3	1,890	2	1	130	580	1,465	91	7,913
1986	142	3	1,860	3	1	102	540	1,491	88	7,972
1987	142	3	1,883	3	1	107	530	1,520	86	7,938
1988	148	3	1,930	3	1	107	524	1,515	85	7,503
							Total		Total	
1989	154	2	1,927	3	—	107	1,403		7,853	
1990	163	1	1,958	2	—	120	1,486		8,630	
1991	177	1	1,962	3	—	124	1,490		8,416	
1992	190	1	1,983	3	—	121	1,516		8,096	
1993	203	1	1,995	3	—	111	1,443		7,489	
				Total						
1994	217	…	2,035	190			1,376		6,818	
1995	219	…	2,079	213			1,349		6,699	
1996	236	…	2,094	219			1,335		6,594	
1997	241	…	2,118	235			1,297		6,194	
1998	258	…	2,123	184			1,416		6,819	

F4 Merchant Ships Registered

1935–1998

	Netherlands				Norway					
	Number of Ships		Thousand Tons		Number of Ships			Thousand Tons		
	Sail	Steam & Motor	Sail	Steam & Motor	Sail	Steam	Motor	Sail	Steam	Motor
1935	131	622	21	1,907	127	1,733	2,081	7	1,153	1,220
1936	119	657	19	1,930	113	1,715	2,187	6	1,122	1,334
1937	123	698	19	2,039	88	1,680	2,413	5	1,094	1,563
1938	115	755	16	2,218	76	1,659	2,573	4	1,074	1,708
		1,028[20]		2,650[20]						
1939		1,102		2,764	64	1,590	2,737	3[39]	1,015[39]	1,815[39]
								5	1,758	3,083
1940		...		...	57	1,435	2,777	4	1,531	2,898
1941		...		...	46	1,307	2,824	3	1,299	2,702
1942		...		...	31	1,202	2,821	3	1,114	2,244
1943		...		...	30	1,161	2,895	3	1,013	2,019
1944		...		...	28	1,090	2,954	2	931	1,958
1945		...			28	1,078	3,036	2	892	2,134
1946		855		1,946	27	1,130	3,318	3	1,096	2,338
1947		921		2,366	23	1,198	3,636	2	1,495	2,677
1948		937		2,584	17	1,202	3,917	2	1,615	3,062
1949		1,035		2,796	14	1,172	4,212	1	1,640	3,659
1950		1,108		2,958	15	1,131	4,321	2	1,579	4,100
1951		1,141		2,983	...	1,057	4,500	...	1,448	4,527
1952		1,200		3,072	...	985	4,666	...	1,366	4,883
1953		1,226		3,166	...	935	4,856	...	1,332	5,304
1954		1,272		3,287	...	893	5,059	...	1,238	5,863
1955		1,338		3,608	...	834	5,272	...	1,204	6,562
1956		1,425		3,900	...	791	5,486	...	1,241	7,104
1957		1,549		4,242	...	707	5,691	...	1,330	7,710
1958		1,544		4,489	...	680	5,899	...	1,483	8,613
1959		1,533[24]		4,534[24]	...	644	5,996	...	1,657	9,320
		1,501		4,486						
1960		1,476		4,661	...	590	6,078	...	1,627	9,775
1961		1,482		4,787	...	545	6,109	...	1,686	10,479
1962		1,496		5,021	...	499	6,190	...	1,853	11,094
1963		1,455		4,950	...	464	6,195	...	1,985	11,875
1964		1,441		4,911	...	391	6,205	...	2,099	12,718
1965		1,402		4,686	...	348	6,155	...	2,140	13,836
1966		1,349		4,560	...	322	6,203	...	2,403	14,750
1967		1,297		4,545	...	268	6,275	...	2,249	16,902
1968		1,218		4,256	...	231	6,304	...	1,970	17,532
1969		1,088		4,089	...	206	6,250	...	2,143	16,703
1970		1,017		3,955	...	200	6,128	...	2,926	17,203
1971		941		3,878	...	199	6,029	...	3,743	18,556
1972		786		3,326	...	196	5,973	...	4,472	18,240
1973		702		3,355	...	184	5,790	...	5,575	18,156
1974		649		3,303	...	184	5,681	...	6,709	18,090
1975		615		3,223	...	173	5,599	...	7,811	17,970
1976		591		3,173	...	170	5,533	...	9,178	18,358
1977		553		3,041	...	154	5,352	...	9,385	17,899
1978		541		2,927	...	138	5,176	...	8,841	14,768
1979		557		3,305	...	121	5,027	...	7,767	14,242
1980		552		3,443	...	118	4,921	...	7,647	13,980
1981		550		3,417	...	104	4,832	...	7,711	14,478
1982		554		3,467	...	102	4,827	...	6,291	14,215
1983		562		3,563	...	100	4,738	...	5,315	13,284
1984		550		3,462	...	82	4,607	...	4,004	12,343
1985		558		3,387	...	64	4,473	...	1,234	10,027
1986		549		3,276	...	59	4,313	...	702	6,946
1987		473		2,892	...	53	4,156	...	392	3,234
1988		428		2,804	...	50	4,092	...	7	2,157
1989		418		2,771		4,015			1,982	
1990		412		2,845		3,995			2,019	
1991		410		2,857		3,903			1,911	
1992		399		2,875		3,738			2,039	
1993		367		2,648		3,654			2,137	
1994		307		3,149		...			...	
1995		329		3,409		...			...	
1996		389		3,995		...			...	
1997		376		3,880		...			...	
1998		405		4,263		...			...	

F4 Merchant Ships Registered

1935–1998

	Poland		Portugal[23]		Russia/U.S.S.R[11]	
	Number of Ships	Thousand Tons	Number of Ships	Thousand Tons	Number of Ships	Thousand Tons
1935	63	80	...	238	575	1,111
1936	58	95	...	238	649	95
1937	59	95	...	243	667	1,254
1938	71	102	...	250	680	1,273
1939	...	...	...	257	699	1,306
1940	...	...	...	...	...	...
1941	...	...	...	...	...	...
1942	...	...	...	...	...	...
1943	...	...	...	...	...	...
1944	...	...	...	...	...	...
1945	...	...	...	...	...	...
1946	26	94	232	179	...	...
1947	42	156	251	163	...	...
1948	43	160	270	263	966	2,097
1949	45	159	249	264	962	2,118
1950	52	171	216	230	967	2,125
1951	65	237	221	246	989	2,222
1952	69	249	216	258	1,019	2,261
1953	72	250	206	262	1,049	2,292
1954	78	265	205	271	1,101	2,371
1955	83	288	199	251	1,158	2,506
1956	83	287	189	255	1,228	2,636
1957	92	253	190	264	1,264	2,790
1958	106	407	185	275	1,390	2,966
1959	122	492	180	272	1,455	3,155
1960	138	578	178	286	1,138	3,429
1961	155	650	175	313	1,212	4,066
1962	178	764	170	322	1,313	4,684
1963	191	825	170	343	1,432	5,434
1964	196	853	164	342	1,674	6,958
1965	196	886	158	336	1,845	8,238
1966	211	991	157	357	2,024	9,492
1967	227	1,103	143	365	2,238	10,617
1968	237	1,191	147	384	4,206	12,062
1969	250	1,261	141	428	5,622	13,705
1970	259	1,319	142	433	5,924	14,832
1971	278	1,494	151	525	6,575	16,194
1972	283	1,610	156	547	6,851	16,774
1973	289	1,709	148	654	7,123	17,397
1974	307	2,083	148	704	7,342	18,176
1975	315	2,577	134	680	7,652	19,236
1976	320	2,719	118	796	7,945	20,668
1977	323	2,768	104	778	8,167	21,438
1978	323	2,827	96	765	7,991	22,262
1979	322	2,875	91	846	8,120	22,900
1980	331	2,904	82	841	8,279	23,444
1981	322	2,993	95	913	7,867	23,493
1982	317	3,005	100	925	7,713	23,789
1983	295	2,624	85	997	7,753	24,549
1984	278	2,667	87	999	7,095	24,492
1985	278	2,796	90	993	7,154	24,745
1986	261	2,826[47]	60	929	6,726	24,961
		4,231				
1987	251	4,101	...	...	6,705	25,232
1988	256	4,111	...	...	6,741	25,784
1989	249	4,061	...	...	6,555	25,854
1990	247	4,059	...	...	7,383	26,737
1991	234	4,049	...	...	...	...
1992	217	3,947	...	...	...	16,302[48]
1993	195	3,627	...	...	...	16,814[48]
1994	184	2,810	...	882	...	16,504[48]
1995	139	2,358	...	897	...	15,202[48]
1996	131	2,293	...	676	...	13,755[48]
1997	125	1,878	...	952	...	12,282[48]
1998	117	1,424	...	1,130	...	11,090[48]

F4 Merchant Ships Registered

	Spain						Sweden[26]			
	Number of Ships			Thousand Tons			Number of Ships		Thousand Tons	
	Sail	Steam	Motor	Sail	Steam	Motor	Sail	Steam & Motor	Sail	Steam & Motor
1935	118	731	106	20	925	233	897	1,375	61	1,041
1936	...	...	...	...	...	...	900	1,348	62	1,022
1937	...	...	...	...	...	...	923	1,342	62	1,020
1938	105	618	101	20	723	171	927	1,332	63	1,042
1939	...	...	...	...	...	...	922	1,320	63	1,055
1940	105	682	101	19	790	189	922	1,280	64	983
1941	106	708	106	20	846	191	893	1,227	62	949
1942	109	710	106	21	835	164	875	1,214	60	907
1943	122	720	105	19	823	168	847	1,229	59	923
1944	133	746	127	22	844	172	829	1,263	58	1,022
1945	150	759	155	26	834	209	814[42]	1,262	58[42]	1,052
1946	164	831	198	29	852	219	772	1,301	55	1,146
1947	168	847	235	30	858	232	754	1,378	55	1,274
1948	174	872	285	31	865	265	726	1,449	54	1,365
1949	181	888	323	33	874	291	702	1,493	52	1,394
1950	169	895	355	30	869	306	679[43]	1,522[43]	59[43 44]	1,432[43 44]
1951	173	884	392	31	852	331	644	1,260	67	2,261
1952	180	902	418	32	850	360	624	1,258	66	2,407
1953	175	906	448	31	870	401	599	1,260	63	2,590
1954	175[40]	901[40]	462[40]	30[40]	869[40]	445[40]	559	1,240	58	2,675
1955	171	911	490	29	879	472	516	1,123	55	2,735
1956	168	912	520	28	880	517	474	1,131	51	2,904
1957	165	912	569	27	878	602	432	1,151	46	3,141
1958	162	907	624	26	859	709	398	1,165	43	3,430
1959	164	896	682	26	820	797	1,508		3,628	
1960	162	894	769	26	797	957	1,486		3,851	
1961	167	893	857	27	780	1,098	1,409		3,978	
1962	168	897	972	27	777	1,195	1,373[26 43]		4,161[26 43]	
							1,073		4,139	
1963	164	880	1,071	26	757	1,267	1,001		4,095	
1964	154	820	1,191	25	693	1,303	943		4,136	
1965	143	727	1,508	22	573	1,606	900		4,117	
1966	142	682	1,679	22	561	1,800	872		4,454	
1967	76	618	1,965	11	596	2,046	833		4,561	
1968	84	567	2,103	13	561	2,346	819		4,746	
1969	72	513	2,216	10	748	2,579	795		4,750	
1970	71	456	2,330	10	579	2,992	763		4,634	
1971	62	418	2,401	9	539	3,332	719		4,950	
1972	58	382	2,522	8	459	4,031	688		5,351	
1973	65	341[41]	2,634	10	635[41]	4,196	650		5,788	
1974		1,041			4,331		629		6,991	
1975		1,032			5,200		613		7,711	
1976		1,062			5,691		562		7,008	
1977		1,082			7,102		545		6,833	
1978		1,111			7,712		513		5,508	
1979		1,107			7,632		513		4,305	
1980		1,109			7,700		510		3,979	
1981		1,115			7,688		484		3,629	
1982		1,109			7,299		468		3,313	
1983		1,109			6,613		471		3,258	
1984		1,105			6,377		476		3,043	
1985		1,058			5,444		444		2,620	
1986		1,017			4,929		434		2,209	
1987		952			4,652		454		2,467	
1988		930			3,843		409		2,028	
1989		875			3,386		435		2,463	
1990		842			3,288		446		2,920	
1991		969			2,865		455		3,203	
1992		942			2,722		436		3,045	
1993		...			...		417		2,339	
1994		...			...		442		2,797	
1995		...			...		456		2,955	
1996		...			...		467		3,002	
1997		...			...		466		2,754	
1998		...			...		450		2,552	

F4 Merchant Ships Registered

	United Kingdom						Yugoslavia			
	Number of Ships			Thousand Tons			Number of Ships		Thousand Tons	
	Sail	Steam	Motor	Sail	Steam	Motor	Sail	Steam & Motor	Sail	Steam & Motor
1935	4,351	8,306	4,494	414	8,253	1,819	699	244	14	356
1936	4,288	8,032	4,888	419	8,114	2,057	669	253	12	350
1937	4,185	7,702	5,294	415	7,902	2,236	667	256	12	361
1938	4,019	7,441	5,789	402	7,819	2,481	677[31]	262	13	404[31]
1939	...		13,303	...		10,511		185		401
1940	...		13,254	...		10,412	...		...	
1941	...		12,822	...		9,674	...		...	
1942	...		12,185	...		9,000	...		...	
1943	...		12,169	...		9,119	...		...	
1944	...		12,525	...		9,994	...		...	
1945	...		12,700	...		10,341	...		...	
1946	3,610		12,581	408		10,315		86		141
1947	3,250		12,481	380		10,371		99		164
1948	3,193		12,795	370		10,461		107		181
1949	3,149		13,103	367		10,453		115		201
1950	3,104		13,429	365		10,738		124		223
1951	3,056		13,473	349		10,606		134		246
1952	3,065		13,598	343		10,663		147		248
1953	2,835		13,649	321		10,811		176		256
1954	2,771		13,685	317		10,978		207		284
1955	2,676		13,671	316		10,966		222		291
1956	2,637		13,764	312		11,053		227		300
1957	2,600		13,837	312		11,207		251		395
1958	2,588		14,045	304		11,349		268		451
1959	2,496		14,202	294		11,627		290		575
1960	2,482		14,532	291		11,797		318		718
1961	2,493		15,008	279		12,001		325		806
1962	2,550		15,580	276		11,501		343		912
1963	2,596		16,115	270		11,462		346		930
1964	2,622		16,722	266		11,315		357		968
1965	2,829		17,483	272		11,426		360		996
1966	...		18,413	...		11,668		354		1,138
1967	...		19,277	...		11,736		356		1,183
1968	...		20,317	...		12,671		355		1,367
1969	...		21,647	...		13,574		365		1,434
1970	...		23,250[45]	...		14,700[45]		381		1,460
			1,977			24,061				
1971	...		1,875			25,177		390		1,514
1972	...		1,798	...		26,940		389		1,522
1973	...		1,776	...		29,106		387		1,600
1974	...		1,767	...		30,795		415		1,776
1975	...		1,682	...		31,489		426		1,865
1976	...		1,573	...		29,839		434		1,947
1977	...		1,545	...		30,061		445		2,208
1978	...		1,421	...		28,078		450		2,343
1979	...		1,305	...		25,232		455		2,414
1980	...		1,275	...		25,769		463		2,511
1981	...		1,118	...		22,117		454		2,524
1982	...		985	...		19,283		460		2,524
1983	...		866	...		15,894		454		2,547
1984	...		777	...		14,312		461		2,686
1985	...		693	...		12,208		472		2,774
1986	...		545[2]	...		7,711[2]		480		2,974
			546			8,046				
1987	...		506	...		7,059		472		3,066
1988	...		482	...		6,603				3,297
1989			450			6,025				3,681
1990			427			5,512				3,816
1991			409			4,963				3,293
1992			363			4,831		...		2[49]
1993			344			4,670		...		2[49]
1994			330			4,430		...		...
1995			329			4,413		...		...
1996			325			3,872		...		...
1997			313			3,486		...		...
1998			376			4,085		...		...

F4 Merchant Ships Registered

NOTES

1. SOURCES:- The official publications noted on p. xv except for the U.K. to 1969, which is taken from B.R. Mitchell *British Historical Statistics* (Cambridge, 1988), where the original sources are cited, and except also for the following material supplied by the respective national statistical offices:- Finland to 1863, Poland to 1955, Portugal to 1969, and Sweden to 1859. The U.N. Statistical Yearbook was also used.
2. Statistics relate to 31 December, except where otherwise indicated.
3. Tonnage figures refer to net capacity, British measure, except where otherwise indicated.
4. The minimum size of vessel included on the register has varied from time to time and from country to country. Where possible changes are indicated in footnotes. Where no limits are indicated the presumption is that all vessels are included.
5. The following statistics are available for years prior to 1829:-

Denmark

	Number of Ships	Thousand Tons		Number of Ships	Thousand Tons		Number of Ships	Thousand Tons
1814	1,495	65	1819	1,667	81	1824	1,405	61
1815	1,567	76	1820	1,627	79	1825	1,393	57
1816	1,665	85	1821	1,548	73	1826	1,408	58
1817	1,641	85	1822	1,494	67	1827	1,421	59
1818	1,663	83	1823	1,453	64	1828	1,417	61

Norway

	Number of Ships	Thousand Tons
1800	1,156	121
1815	1,673	148
1820	1,672	125
1825	1,761	113

Netherlands

	Number of Ships	Thousand Tons
1826	1,176	169
1828	1,302	178

Sweden

	Number of Ships	Thousand Tons
1795	721	83
1800	800	88
1805	864	96
1810	852	94
1815	994	117
1820	819	94
1825	700	87

The Swedish statistics relate only to ships registered in the 'staple towns' (i.e. the main ports)

FOOTNOTES

[1] At 30 September until 1824. Isle of Man and Channel Islands vessels are included.
[2] There was a revision in the register or in classification.
[3] Venetia is included to 1866 (1st line). From 1870 (2nd line) Hungary is excluded and shown separately.
[4] From 1851 (2nd line) fishing vessels are included.
[5] Figures for 1864–70 are for 31 March in the year following that indicated.
[6] From 1867 (2nd line) to 1921 (1st line) only ships of 4 net tons and over are included, and from 1921 (2nd line) only ships of 20 gross tons and over are included. Iceland and Faroe Islands ships are excluded from 1921 (2nd line) though the latter are reincluded from 1932, when they numbered 202 ships of 21 thousand GRT.
[7] The size of vessel included has varied as follows:- To 1868, ships of 5 lasts or over (approximately 9 net tons); for 1870–72, ships of 10 lasts or over; for 1874–82, ships of 50 net tons or over; for 1885–87, ships of 25 net tons or over, from 1892 to 1920 (1st line), all ships; and since 1920 (2nd line), ships of 19 net tons or over.
[8] Subsequently excluding ships which did not have a deed of nationality.
[9] Three ships were transferred from 'sail' to 'steam'.
[10] Statistics prior to 1877, when the register was revised, were later said to contain many errors.
[11] Vessels over 25 tons. Statistics to 1913 (1st line) are for the Russian Empire (exclusive of Finland), and subsequently they are for the U.S.S.R. and in gross measure.
[12] From 1874 to 1897 only vessels of 50 net tons or over are included. Subsequently only vessels of 100 net tons or over are included.
[13] Motor ships are previously included with sail.
[14] Gross measure from 1921 (2nd line).

F4   Merchant Ships Registered

15   Motor-assisted sailing vessels are included with the 'motor' category to 1935 and from 1945 to 1948, but with the 'sail' category at other times.
16   Vessels of 60 net tons or over.
17   From 1895 to 1900 (1st line) only ships of 50 net tons or over are included, and from 1900 (2nd line) only ships of 60 net tons or over are included.
18   i.e. Fiume.
19   For 1915–18 steamships of less than 250 net tons are not included, and for 1919–23 steamships of less than 50 net tons are not included.
20   From 1920 (2nd line) to 1938 (1st line) tugs and dredgers are excluded. Ships registered in the colonies are included for the first time from 1938 (2nd line).
21   Some motor-assisted vessels were transferred from the 'motor' to the 'sail' category.
22   In principle, to 1909 only vessels of 4 net tons or over are included, though ships as low as 1 ton were said to have been included "in some years". Subsequently only sailing ships of 50 gross tons or over and steamships of 25 gross tons or over are included.
23   Mechanically-propelled ships registered on the mainland at June each year. The tonnage figures are gross.
24   The reason for this break is not given in the source.
25   At 31 August.
26   The size of vessel has varied as follows:- To 1894, ships of 10 net tons or over; from 1895 to 1962 (1st line), ships of 20 net tons or over, and subsequently ships of 100 net tons or over.
27   Ships registered in Southern Ireland are excluded subsequently.
28   Gross measure from 1944.
29   At 30 September.
30   Motor-assisted sailing vessels are subsequently transferred from the 'motor' to the 'sail' category.
31   Subsequently vessels of 100 gross tons or over.
32   Gross measure from 1949 (2nd line).
33   Subsequently commercial ships only.
34   Gross measure from 1946.
35   Subsequently including ships with provisional registration papers.
36   Gross measure from 1940.
37   Motor-assisted sailing vessels are included, most of which comprised the fishing fleet. From 1974 (2nd line) the series relates entirely to the fishing fleet.
38   Subsequently excluding certain recreational vessels.
39   Gross measure from 1939 (2nd line).
40   At 1 November.
41   Subsequently excluding fishing vessels. The equivalent figures for 1973 are 1,032 ships and 4,002 thousand GRT.
42   Subsequently only motor-assisted vessels.
43   For 1951–1962 (1st line) fishing vessels are excluded.
44   Gross measure from 1951.
45   Subsequently statistics relate only to vessels of 500 GRT and over, and the tonnage figures are gross.
46   Excluding ferries and fishing vessels to 1831.
47   Deadweight tonnage subsequently.
48   Russian Federation. Ex USSR (tonnage) as follows.

	Azerbaijan	Estonia	Latvia	Lithuania	Ukraine
1992	637	680	1,207	668	5,222
1993	667	686	1,155	639	5,265
1994	621	695	1,034	661	5,279
1995	655	598	798	610	4,613
1996	636	545	723	572	3,825
1997	633	602	319	510	2,690
1998	651	522	118	481	2,033

49   Yugoslavia. Croatia (tonnage) = 1992, 210, 1993, 193.

F5 INLAND NAVIGATION TRAFFIC

a = Goods carried by Danube Steamship Co.; b = Goods Passing Customs on River Elbe; c = Goods carried by Inland Navigation; d = Loaded Ships Passing Customs on Rhine; e = Goods carried on River Danube.

	Austria[1]		Belgium		France	Germany[2]		Netherlands[3]
	a	b	c	p	c	c	c	d
	000 tons	000 tons	m ton/kms		m ton/kms	m ton/kms	000 tons	million tons
1835	2	...	...		...			...
1836	4	...	...		...			...
1837	5	...	...		...			...
1838	18	...	...		...			...
1839	20	...			...	...		...
1840	21	...	...		...	750		...
1841	29	...	...		...			...
1842	33	...	...		...			...
1843	47	...	...		...			...
1844	61	...	...		...			...
1845	86	...	...		1,813	850	...	...
1846	107	...	...		...	...		...
1847	178	...	...		...			...
1848	145	...	...		...			...
1849	70	...	...		...			...
1850	263	...	...		1,666		...	
1851	404	...	...		...	900	...	0.8
1852	597	...	...		...			0.9
1853	505	...	...		2,002			1.0
1854	771	...	...		...			1.0
1855	953	...	...		...	1,200		1.2
1856	712	...	...		...			1.1
1857	869	...	...		...			1.2
1858	949	...	...		...			1.1
1859	1,459[1]	...	...		...			1.2
1860	845	...	...		1,901	1,350		1.2
1861	850	...	...		1,936			1.4
1862	872	...	...		2,092			1.6
1863	986	...	...		2,132			1.6
1864	1,083	...	...		2,082			1.7
1865	963	...	...		2,059	1,550		1.6
1866	1,213	...	...		2,225			1.6
1867	1,188	...	...		2,024	1,700		1.9
1868	1,241	...	...		2,172	1,750		2.0
1869	1,247	...	...		1,999	1,800		2.2
1870	1,015	567	...		1,448[6]	1,650[6]		1.9
1871	918	456			1,558	1,730		1.9
1872	1,150	452			1,836	2,070	...	2.1
1873	1,011	408			1,847	2,199	12,300	2.8
1874	1,049	386			1,795	2,111	...	3.0
1875	1,189	562	...		1,964	2,373	...	2.6
1876	1,346	271	...		1,953	2,338		2.9
1877	1,271	405	...		2,034	2,486		3.1
1878	1,459	681	...		2,005	2,406	16,500	3.3
1879	1,356	948	...		2,023	2,558		3.6
1880	1,342	1,315	722		2,007	3,124		3.8
1881	1,444	1,267	703		2,174	2,920		4.1
1882	1,675	1,354	717		2,265	3,178		4.5
1883	1,644	1,337	726		2,383	3,524	21,900	4.6
1884	1,571	1,827	748		2,452	3,581		5.0
								5.3

F5 Inland Navigation Traffic

	Austria a (000 tons)	Austria b (000 tons)	Belgium c (m ton/kms)	Czechoslovakia c (000 tons)	Czechoslovakia c (m ton/kms)	France c (m ton/kms)	Germany c (m ton/kms)	Germany c (tons)	Netherlands[3] d (m tons)	Russia c (thou m ton/kms)	Russia c (m tons)
1885	1,694	1,649	760	...	...	2,453	3,801	...	5.2	...	...
1886	1,695	1,861	764	...	...	2,798	4,202	...	5.3	...	...
1887	1,710	1,851	857[5]	...	...	3,073	4,206	...	5.6	...	...
1888	1,855	2,375	588	...	...	3,180	4,693	28.0	6.1	...	...
1889	1,925	2,197	582	...	...	3,238	5,017	...	6.0	...	...
1890	[2,106][4]	2,765	578	...	...	3,216	5,586	...	6.6	...	...
1891	1,983	2,739	624	...	...	3,537	5,615	...	6.9	...	...
1892	1,830	2,543	623	...	...	3,609	5,193	...	7.3	...	...
1893	2,179	2,166	645	...	...	3,604	5,606	33.8	8.1	...	...
1894	2,030	3,035	696	...	...	3,912	6,339	...	9.3	...	...
1895	1,963	2,535	713	...	...	3,766	6,130	...	9.1	...	...
1896	2,241	2,969	800	...	...	4,191	7,447	...	12.4	...	...
1897	2,001	3,182	815	...	...	4,365	8,010	...	12.1	...	...
1898	1,910	3,001	882	...	...	4,577	8,413	46.2	14.0	...	...
1899	1,797	3,229	829	...	...	4,489	8,953	...	14.6	...	...
1900	2,012	2,740	894	...	...	4,675	9,371	...	15.6[3]	...	...
				...	...				13		
1901	2,073	3,028	852	...	...	4,380	9,257	...	13	...	...
1902	2,054	2,932	918	...	...	4,465	9,451	...	14	...	...
1903	1,997	3,964	1,035	...	...	4,955	11,644	56.2	18	...	...
1904	2,040	2,551	1,092	...	...	4,968	10,085	...	18	...	...
1905	2,256	3,422	1,143	...	...	5,085	11,692	...	21	...	...
1906	2,366	3,497	1,154	...	...	5,102	12,498	67.8	22	...	...
1907	2,218	3,435	1,198	...	...	5,371	12,674	68.8	23	...	...
1908	2,009	3,146	1,112	...	...	5,321	13,075	64.9	21	...	...
1909	2,249	3,350	1,200	...	...	5,471	13,470	73.4	25	...	...
1910	2,265	3,203	1,327	...	...	5,197	15,439	76.6	30	...	...
1911	2,436	2,161	1,404	...	...	5,767	12,953	80.0	31	...	...
1912	2,548	3,260	1,570	...	...	5,850	17,074	93.5	35	...	...
1913	2,311	3,096	1,636	...	...	6,185	17,888	99.6	38	28.5[7]	32.7[7]
1914	1,760	2,544	...	...	...	...	...	75.2	26	...	...
1915	981	1,629	...	...	...	2,167	...	40.5	9	...	...
1916	676	1,471	...	...	...	2,728	...	45.6	10	...	...
(Austria: e)	*000 tons*	*m ton/kms*									
1917	...	...	...	...	...	2,829	...	...	7	15.0	20.0
1918	295	...	...	...	...	3,268[6]	...[6]	...[6]	5	...	...
1919	...	...	649	...	...	2,682	...[10]	33.7[10]	6	...	...
1920	443	...	998	...	...	3,173	...	43.3	13	...	...
1921	830	...	942	...	...	2,799	...	41.6	16	...	...
1922	875[8]	...	1,322	...	...	4,691	...	58.8	21	...	...
1923	1,408	...	1,532	1,829	...	5,005	...	34.3	12	10.5	14.6
1924	1,387	...	1,610	3,297	...	5,229	11,531	70.9	32	8.8	13.5
1925	1,227	...	1,723	3,543	...	5,277	13,277	85.7	40	12.0	17.2
1926	1,584	...	1,766	3,799	1,724	5,720	14,736	102	52	15.5	21.7
1927	1,835	...	2,045	4,177	1,865	5,947	16,274	111	55	16.5	23.4
1928	2,308	...	2,266	4,167	1,777	6,980	15,170	108	51	17.5	25.5
1929	1,919	...	2,185	3,513	1,492	6,809	15,106	111	55	20.7	32.0
1930	2,508	...	2,407	3,586	1,572	7,266	14,702	105	52	...	41.1
1931	1,873	...	2,507	4,102	2,200	7,379	12,413	86.9	43	...	...
1932	1,622	...	2,513	2,952	1,554	7,589	10,927	73.5	33	...	...
1933	1,435	...	2,610	2,311	1,230	7,795	11,375	78.0	34	...	...
1934	1,507	...	2,785	2,465	1,127	8,377	13,532[10]	94.2[10]	41	...	...

F5 Inland Navigation Traffic

1935–2000

	Austria 000 tons (e)	Austria m ton/kms (e)	Belgium m ton/kms (c)	Czechoslovakia 000 tons (c)	Czechoslovakia m ton/kms (c)	France m ton/kms (c)	Germany / East Germany m ton/kms (c)	East Germany m tons (c)	West Germany m ton/kms (c)	Germany / West Germany m tons (c)	Netherlands million tons (d)	Russia thou m ton/kms (c)	Russia m tons (c)
1935	1,553	...	2,841	2,532	1,185	8,033	14,274			101	42	...	...
1936	1,833	...	2,831	2,951	1,400	8,093	17,112			116	46	...	...
1937	...	...	3,237	3,876	2,261	7,882	18,621			133	58	...	...
1938	...	...	2,939	3,787	...	8,256	18,653			177[11]	56	...	...
1939	...	...	2,931	3,677	...	6,908				170	42	...	...
1940	...	...		3,278	...	2,763				143	8	36.1	73.1
1941	...	...	1,892	3,258	...	3,084					19	...	...
1942	...	...		3,545	...	3,543					16	...	...
1943	...	...	2,105	3,503	...	3,749					16	...	...
1944	...	...	1,174	1,212	...	1,603					7	...	...
1945			1,389	817	...	2,616					2	18.8	36.9
1946			1,757	1,456	724	4,071					7	20.4	39.9
1947			2,020	1,532	...	4,767 9						25.1	48.2
1948			2,209	926	629	5,726[9]	...	...			16	32.1	63.5
1949			2,629	1,133	788	6,074	1,123	8.2	12,853	57.8	21	38.8	78.0
1950			2,998	1,336	764	6,693	1,579	10.0	16,752	71.9	29	46.2	91.8
1951			3,474	1,705	995	7,536	1,797	11.0	21,047	88.1	35	51.5	103
1952			3,389	1,943	1,138	7,772	1,707	12.5	22,452	95.3	37	58.2	110
1953			3,928	2,061	1,002	7,923	1,738	12.8	23,041	101	37	58.9	116
1954	2,558	430	4,116	2,058	1,260	8,282	1,742	11.6	25,054	109	41	62.4	128
1955	3,112	507	4,617	2,836	1,485	8,917	2,168	12.9	28,624	125	50	67.4	139
1956	4,113	546	4,493	2,651	1,472	9,265	2,268	13.5	32,270	136	58	70.5	147
1957	4,721	639	4,602	2,928	1,604	9,771	2,498	14.4	33,953	142	61	76.4	159
1958	5,058	698	4,326	3,247	1,784	9,425	2,398	14.9	32,768	137	59	85.5	178
1959	4,965	748	4,813	3,128	1,736	9,506	2,376	14.5	33,390	142	55	93.6	192
1960	6,202	962	5,226	3,530	1,962	10,773	2,252	12.6	40,390	171	71	99.6	210
1961	5,493	904	5,473	3,747	1,899	11,262	2,202	11.9	40,214	172	68	106	224
1962	5,390	919	5,421	3,925	1,975	11,234	2,162	11.4	39,936	171	66	110	230
1963	5,792	995	5,202	4,062	1,915	11,358	2,003	11.0	39,513	167	67	114	239
1964	5,907	1,032	6,107	4,498	2,170	12,470	2,138	12.0	40,609	184	73	124	252
1965	5,985	977	6,087	4,056	2,172	12,510	2,196	12.1	43,553	196	81	134	269
1966	6,741	2,104	5,970	4,346	2,412	12,652	2,556	13.4	45,072	208	88	138	279
1967	6,424	2,071	6,262	4,197	2,243	12,965	2,576	13.7	45,785	214	99	144	302
1968	8,067	2,500	6,651	4,340	2,360	13,235	2,443	13.1	47,932	233	110	155	322
1969	7,238	2,184	6,870	3,851	1,942	14,601	2,143	12.4	47,650	234	109	160	333
1970	7,593	2,367	6,734	4,464	2,434	14,183	2,358	13.7	48,813	240	112	174	358
1971	6,215	2,011	6,729	4,451	2,367	13,773	2,331	13.6	44,991	230	105	184	381
1972	6,684	2,076	6,758	4,868	2,626	14,156	2,304	13.2	43,969	228	102	180	396
1973	7,322	2,496	6,494	4,812	2,467	13,792	1,884	12.7	48,480	246	117	189	419
1974	7,273	7,012	6,853	4,924	2,812	13,738	2,326	14.7	50,972	252	128	212	452
1975	7,004	6,119	5,124	5,654	2,580	11,905	2,362	14.6	47,565	227	119	222	475
1976	6,393	5,614	6,072	5,866	2,568	12,156	1,947	13.9	45,804	230	118	223	485
1977	6,676	6,499	5,763	6,418	2,709	11,266	2,215	15.1	49,254	233	127	231	521
1978	6,908	6,877	5,936	7,884	3,192	11,594	2,265	15.6	51,489	246	140	244	546
1979	7,631	7,110	5,909	8,778	3,360	11,898	1,933	14.8	50,987	246	133	233	537
1980	7,615	7,161	5,853	10,457	3,593	12,151	2,159	16.3	51,435	241	129	245	568
1981	7,168	6,530	5,442	11,094	3,807	11,068	2,359	16.6	50,000	232	123	256	594
1982	6,622	6,831	5,004	11,393	3,782	10,190	2,290	16.8	49,401	222	124	262	604
1983	6,534	7,264	4,972	11,858	3,923	9,447	2,424	17.5			126	273	607
1984	8,094	8,976	5,242	13,374	4,431	8,880	2,642	18.7	51,996	236	137	264	619
1985	7,619	8,902	5,063	13,331	4,356	8,394	2,431	17.7	48,183	222	130	262	633
1986	7,814	9,047	5,205	14,217	4,825	7,767	2,477	18.5	52,185	229	137	256	649
1987	8,027	9,093	5,122	14,265	5,067	7,370	2,361	18.3	49,721	221	132	253	673
1988	8,832	10,276	5,435	15,216	5,403	7,334	2,532	20.3	52,854	233	139	251	691
1989	9,145	10,520	5,322	13,520	5,099	6,088	2,286	20.4	54,041	235	142	240	694
1990	8,140	9,012	5,448	9,847	4,199	7,582	1,924	13.6	54,802	232	143	233	669
1991	6,786	8,303	5,227	7,800	3,357	8,347	Included in West Germany		...	...	138	195	...
1992	6,705	7,810	5,083	5,130[13]	2,978[13]	8,631			57,239	230	135	136	...
1993	6,542	8,214	...	4,900[13]	1,261[13]	7,624			57,559	218	...	103[14]	215[14]
1994	5,969	...	...	4,811	...	5,607			...	...	98	...	...
1995	6,433	...	...	4,332	...	5,865					78		
1996	7,182	...	...	2,879	...	...			61,292	...	89	...	...
1997	7,245	...	...	1,554	...	5,682			61,153	...	97	...	...
1998	6,232	...	...	1,678	...	6,207			64,267	...	99	...	...
1999	6,436	...	...	1,877	...	6,829			62,692	...	...	...	...
2000	6,641	...	...	1,906	...	...			66,466	...	...	...	...

F5   Inland Navigation Traffic

NOTE

SOURCES:- The official publications noted on p. xv with German data to 1908 and Netherlands to 1900 (1st line) supplied by their respective national statistical offices.

FOOTNOTES

[1] The series to 1859 differs from that which follows. The latter is approximately half the former in the two years for which comparison is possible—1850 and 1855. The figures in the later series for these years are 137 and 532 thousand tons respectively. It is probable that inland traffic was only counted once in the later series, whilst it was double-counted in the earlier one.

[2] Information is available for earlier years but not in summary form.

[3] Data to 1900 (1 st line) relate to the capacity of loaded shipping (in million river-tons). Subsequently they are of goods carried (in million tons).

[4] Thirteen months ended 31 December. Previous figures are for years ended 30 November.

[5] Previous statistics include some traffic by sea-going ships.

[6] Alsace was part of Germany for 1871–1918.

[7] Data are for the boundaries of the interwar period.

[8] Inland traffic is subsequently counted twice.

[9] Figures to 1948 are of goods embarked. Subsequently they are of goods discharged.

[10] Saarland is excluded for 1920–1934.

[11] Earlier figures are calculated according to goods.

[12] Earlier figures are calculated according to goods classification, whilst later ones are derived from harbour records.

[13] Czech Republic.

[14] Russia. Other ex-USSR = 1993

	m tons
Belarus	8.9
Kazakhstan	4.0
Kyrgistan	0.1
Moldova	0.3
Ukraine	25.0

F6 MOTOR VEHICLES IN USE (thousands)

Key:—PC = Private Cars, CV = Commercial vehicles

1900–1949

	Austria		Belgium		Czechoslovakia		Denmark		Finland	
	PC	CV	PC	CV[7]	PC	CV	PC[12]	CV	PC	VC
1900	...	...	...		...	...	...		...	...
1901	...	...	...		...	...	...		...	...
1902	...	...	...		...	...	...		...	...
1903	...	...	...		...	...	...		...	...
1904	...	...	...		...	...	...		...	...
1905	...	...	...		...	...	...		...	...
1906	...	...	...		...	...	...		...	...
1907	...	...	...		...	...	...		...	...
1908	...	...	...		...	...	...		...	...
1909	...	...	...		...	...		0.7	...	...
1910	...	...	...		...	...		1.0	...	...
1911	7.7[1]	...	...		...	...		1.0	...	...
1912	...	...	...		...	...		1.6	...	...
1913	12.2[1]	...	9.6		...	...		...	...	...
1914	...	...	...		...	...	3.1	0.4	...	...
1915	...	...	...		...	...	3.8	0.6	...	...
1916	...	...	...		...	...	5.0	0.7	...	...
1917	...	...	...		...	...	6.4[13]	0.9[13]	...	...
1918	...[2]	...[2]	...		...	...	...		...	...
1919	...	...	...		...	...	...		...	...
1920	6.4	2.8	...		...	...	13.9[13]	3.8[13]	...	...
1921	7.8[3]	3.3[3]	20.7		...	...	17.6[10]	4.7[10]	...	...
1922	8.4	3.5	31.7		5.3[8]	2.1[8]	...		...	...
1923	10.1	4.1	47.3		...	...	...		1.9[1]	...
1924	9.7	5.1	67.8		...	...	37.9[14]	9.8[14]	3.3[1]	...
1925	11.0	6.2	86.7		12.7[9]	5.4[9]	46.4[14]	13.1[14]	6.6[1]	3.9[1]
1926	12.2	7.7	92.2		17.3[10]	7.1[10]	...[15]	...[15]	11.5	5.4
1927	14.1	9.6	96.9		——[11]	——[11]	59.1[8][16]	16.5[8][16]	17.0	7.5
1928	16.8	12.1	79.0	41.4	25.1	11.5	62.6	26.3	22.1	9.6
1929	19.6[4]	14.9[4]	92.2	51.2	32.1	15.9	69.2	29.1	24.5	11.7
1930	17.4	14.6	99.3	58.7	41.0	21.6	78.5[16]	31.8[16]	24.3	12.4
1931	22.3	16.6	110	64.8	48.6	25.8	85.2	35.1	23.8	12.1
1932	23.2	16.5	116	68.0	...	...	83.0	34.3	22.9	11.7
1933	23.3	16.1	123	69.1	67.8[11] 74.9	31.9[11] 32.5	84.1	35.5	20.7	11.9
1934	24.0	16.0	121	73.1	83.6	33.0	88.1	37.5	20.4	12.9
1935	26.8	16.4	124	73.3	88.3[1]	33.3[1]	91.7	38.9	20.9	14.2
1936	30.1	16.2	132	74.5	85.0	30.4	95.3	40.1	21.7	15.7
1937	32.4[3,5]	16.2[3,5]	144	78.3	90.9	31.5	101	41.7	24.4	18.8
1938	...	...	154	78.6	...	...	108	42.6	25.9	20.0
1939	...	...	155	79.0	...	...	117	45.3	30.1	23.2
1940	...	...	110	58.8	...	...	7.0[17]	23.3[17]	...	...
1941	...	...	15.4	30.7	...	...	7.6[18]	24.1[18]	...	...
1942	...	...	10.8	27.8	...	...	7.4	23.4	...	...
1943	...	...	8.8	25.4	...	...	7.2	21.7	...	...
1944	...	...	13.0	28.4	...	...	6.5[16,19]	21.2[16,19]	...	...
1945	...	...	46.1	60.5	...	...	44.5	28.3	...	...
1946	...	...	86.0	91.8	63.0	51.2	100	42.1	8.6	13.7
1947	...[6]	...[6]	129	112	...	...	104[19]	49.0[19]	12.9	28.1
1948	31.8	35.9	127	128	119	75.7	108	53.4	18.6	30.5
1949	41.2	41.2	227	133	...	...	111	57.8	23.2	28.9

F6   Motor Vehicles In Use (thousands)

	France		Germany		Greece		Hungary		Southern Ireland	
	PC	CV	PC	CV	PC	CV	PC	CV	PC	CV
1895	0.3	...	...	...	...	...	...	...	...	...
1896	0.5	...	...	...	...	...	...	...	...	...
1897	1.2	...	...	...	...	...	...	...	...	...
1898	1.5	...	...	...	...	...	...	...	...	...
1899	1.7	...	...	...	...	...	...	...	...	...
1900	2.9	...	...	...	...	...	...	...	...	...
1901	6.4	...	...	...	...	...	...	...	...	...
1902	9.2	...	...	...	...	...	...	...	...	...
1903	13.0	...	...	...	...	...	...	...	...	...
1904	17.1	...	...	...	...	...	...	...	...	...
1905	21.5	...	...	...	...	...	...	...	...	...
1906	26.3	...	10.1	1.2	...	...	...	...	...	...
1907	31.3	...	14.7	1.8	...	...	...	...	...	...
1908	37.6	...	18.5	2.3	...	...	...	...	...	...
1909	44.8	...	24.6	3.0	...	...	...	...	...	...
1910	53.7	...	31.7	4.2	...	...	...	...	...	...
1911	64.2	...	39.9	5.5	...	...	...	...	...	...
1912	76.8	...	49.8	7.7	...	...	...	...	...	...
1913	91.0	...	60.9[21]	9.7[21]	...	...	...	...	...	...
1914	108	...	55.3	9.1	...	...	...	...	...	...
1915	102	...	...	...	...	...	...	...	...	...
1916	101	...	...	...	...	...	...	...	...	...
1917	98.5	...	...	...	...	...	...	...	...	...
1918	94.9	...	...	...	...	...	...	...	...	...
1919	93.3	...	...	...	...	...	...	...	...	...
1920	157	79.4	...	...	...	...	1.4	0.3	...	...
1921	197[20]	92.9[20]	60.6[22]	30.3[22]	...	...	2.2	0.4	...	...
1922	243	121	80.9	45.5	...	...	2.3	0.5	...	...
1923	294	155	98.6	53.5	4.0	1.4	3.1	0.7	9.2	3.5
1924	374	201	130	62.4	5.6	2.8	4.0	1.0	13.4	4.5
1925	476	245	171	83.6	8.2	3.8	4.9[27]	1.5[27]	16.2	5.1[28]
1926	541	267	201	95.1	10.0	4.3	5.8	3.1	19.8	5.5
1927	643	307	261	108.6	12.3	5.0	8.2	4.4	22.4	6.0
1928	758	332	343	130.4	14.5	6.3	10.2	5.3	26.3	6.5
1929	930	366	422	155	17.1	8.0	11.6	6.8	29.4	7.2
1930	1,109	412	489	169	18.7	9.4	11.5	7.1	32.6	7.7
1931	1,252	438	511	173	19.8	11.2	9.8	6.9	35.7	8.3
1932	1,272	434	486	164	20.1	11.5	9.0	6.5	35.7	8.3
1933	1,397	458	511	167	20.3	11.7	5.8	5.7	36.7	8.4
1934	1,480	459	596[23]	180[23]	20.6[26]	12.4[26]	7.6	6.1	35.5	8.3
			662	205						
1935	1,547	458	787[24]	255[24]	...	...	8.9	6.5	38.0	8.7
			796	258						
1936	1,639	457	945	286[25]	...	...	10.9	6.9	40.8	9.3
1937	1,721	451	1,108	337	...	...	13.2	7.3	44.5	9.9
1938	1,818	451	1,272	384	...	...	15.7	7.6	48.6	11.2
1939	1,900	500	1,416	...	8.7	8.6	...	...	52.4	11.6
1940	1,800	500	...	...	...	...	...	...	50.2	11.7
1941	...	...	...	...	...	...	...	...	31.8	11.7
1942	...	...	...	...	...	...	...	...	8.0	12.1
1943	...	...	...	...	...	...	...	...	6.2	9.6
1944	680	230	...	...	...	...	...	...	6.6	9.6
1945	975	600	...	...	...	...	...	...	7.8	10.5
			West Germany							
1946	1,700		...	...	...	...	...	...	44.5	15.5
1947	1,750		...	...	4.6	15.2	36.4	11.9	52.2	19.7
1948	1,850		215	266	5.7	17.0	...	...	60.5	23.7
1949	1,950		352	329	8.2	21.1	...	...	71.9	24.9

F6 Motor Vehicles In Use (thousands)

1900–1949

	Italy		Netherlands		Norway		Poland		Portugal	
	PC	CV	PC	CV	PC	CV	PC	CV	PC	CV
1900	...	...	...	...	- -		...	...	...	...
1901	...	...	...	...	- -		...	...	...	...
1902	...	...	...	...	- -		...	...	...	...
1903	...	...	...	...	- -		...	...	...	...
1904	...	...	...	...	- -		...	...	...	...
1905	...	...	...	...	- -		...	...	...	...
1906	...	...	...	...	0.1		...	...	...	...
1907	...	...	...	...	0.1		...	...	...	...
1908	...	...	...	...	0.1		...	...	...	...
1909	...	...	...	...	0.2		...	...	...	...
1910	...	...	...	...	0.3		...	...	...	...
1911	...	...	...	...	0.4		...	...	...	...
1912	...	...	...	...	0.5		...	...	...	...
1913	...	...	4.0		0.7		...	...	...	...
1914	22.0	2.0	...		1.0	0.1	...	...	...	...
1915	22.7	2.1	4.7		1.3	0.2	...	...	...	...
1916	21.1	2.6	5.4		2.1	0.4	...	...	...	...
1917	17.1	4.0	5.2		2.5	0.6	...	...	...	...
1918	6.8	5.8	1.6		2.6	0.7	...	...	...	...
1919	23.9	10.9	6.6		3.9	1.2	...	...	...	...
1920	31.5	18.0	11		6.7	2.4	...	...	...	...
1921	34.1	23.4	15		8.2	3.1	...	...	...	...
1922	41.0	24.5	18		9.6	3.7	...	...	...	...
1923	53.8	24.5	23		12.8	4.9	...	...	...	...
1924	57.0	27.7	31		14.7	5.8	7.4[31]	2.4[31]	...	...
1925	84.8	32.8	19[29]	12[29]	17.6	7.6	8.8	6.0	...	...
1926	105	36.5	29[10]	18[10]	21.5[30]	8.9[30]	9.6	7.0	...	...
1927	119	34.1	45	26	17.4	15.3	12.8	9.1	...	...
1928	144	40.1	52	30	18.5	18.5	15.7	14.0	...	...
1929	170	52.7	60	36	20.3	21.5	18.9	18.5	...	...
1930	183	62.1	68	44	22.4	24.0	19.9	19.5	...	...
1931	186	65.0	75	48	24.2	25.5	14.0	14.7	25.1	7.9
1932	188	68.0	81	50	25.2	26.3	11.7	14.3	24.2	8.7
1933	219	74.4	85	51	27.3	27.1	13.7	13.4	25.4	8.9
1934	236	80.5	90	51	29.6	28.9	13.8	12.1	27.9	10.0
1935	244	82.1	88	48	32.1	30.8	13.9	11.9	31.0	10.5
1936	222	81.9	89	48	36.1	33.7	15.9	12.7	33.2	11.1
1937	271	82.1	91	49	43.0	36.6	19.5	14.8	36.4	11.4
1938	289	83.6	94	50	51.1	39.5	24.6	17.4	38.0	11.5
1939	290	101	100	53	56.2	42.9	...	...	39.5[32]	11.3[32]
1940	270	87.5	...	...	48.8	38.7	...	...	39.1	11.0
									61.4	
1941	97.6	86.5	...	...	45.9	38.0	...	...	61.6	
1942	73.8	75.0	...	...	44.4	38.4	...	...	52.2	
1943	...	...	...	...	43.1	37.9	...	...	47.8	
1944	...	...	...	...	38.0	36.2	...	...	47.4	
1945	...	...	...	...	41.9	40.6	...	...	47.0	
1946	150	137	47	42	49.7	47.4	...	...	29.9	15.5
1947	184	188	68	59	55.4	52.6	23.0	...	40.0	19.8
1948	219	196	86	67	56.6	54.1	23.1	30.1	49.6	24.0
1949	267	214	113	75	58.2	54.5	36.5	40.0	56.5	26.0

F6   Motor Vehicles In Use (thousands)

1900–1949

	Romania		Spain		Sweden		Switzerland		U.K.: G.B.		Yugoslavia	
	PC	CV	PC	CV	PC	CV	PC	CV	PC	CV	PC	CV
1900	...	...	...	...	...	...	...	...	...	...	...	...
1901	...	...	...	...	...	...	...	...	...	...	...	...
1902	...	...	...	...	...	...	...	...	...	...	...	...
1903	...	...	...	...	...	...	...	...	8	9	...	...
1904	...	...	...	...	...	...	...	...			...	...
1905	...	...	...	...	...	...	...	...	16	16	...	...
1906	...	...	...	...	...	...	...	...	23	22	...	...
1907	...	...	...	...	...	...	...	...	32	26	...	...
1908	...	...	...	...	...	...	...	...	41	33	...	...
1909	...	...	...	...	...	...	...	...	48	38	...	...
1910	...	...	...	...	...	...	2.3	0.3	53	54	...	...
1911	...	...	...	...	...	...	...	...	72	73	...	...
1912	...	...	...	...	...	...	...	...	88	88	...	...
1913	...	...	...	...	...	...	4.7	0.8	106	103	...	...
1914	...	...	...	...	...	...	5.4	0.9	132	133	...	...
1915	...	...	...	...	...	...	...	...	139	129	...	...
1916	...	...	...	...	3.0		...	...	142	133	...	...
1917	...	...	...	...	3.8		5.1	1.2	110	112	...	...
1918	...	...	...	...	4.1		...	...	78	83,	...	...
1919	...	...	...	...	8.5		...	...	110	10,6	...	...
1920	...	...	...	...	21.3		8.9	3.3	187[34]	176[34]	...	...
1921	...	...	...	...	30.4		...	...	243	21,1	...	...
1922	...	...	...	...	39.9		15	5.8	315	229	...	...
1923	...	...	...	...	37.8	12.6	16.7	6.3	384	259	...	...
1924	...	...	...	...	46.6	16.3	22.5	8.3	474	297	...	...
1925	...	...	...	...	59.1	20.5	28.7	8.3	580	323	...	...
1926	11.3	3.6	...	...	70.5	24.1	36.1	9.4	684	358	...	...
1927	15.0	5.7	...	...	81.5	28.1	42.4	10.9	787	378	...	...
1928	21.2	7.5	...	...	94.3	32.9	50.2	11.9	885	401	...	...
1929	25.9	9.3	...	...	99.1	37.1	55.1	14.4	981	428	8.4	3.8
1930	26.0	9.4	...	...	104	40.9	60.7	15.5	1,056	449	8.5	3.5
1931	24.5	8.6	...	...	105	44.0	63.9	18.0	1,083	448	8.7	4.0
1932	21.7	8.4	...	...	102	43.5	...	...	1,128	455	8.3	4.2
1933	21.5	8.1	...	...	98.9	42.3	66.4[33]	19.8[33]	1,203	472	7.8	4.3
1934	22.2	8.4	...	...	102	45.0	69.7	19.8	1,308	498	7.6	3.5
1935	23.2	8.8	...	...	109	46.0	70.8	19.7	1,477	520	7.3	3.1
1936	23.2	8.8	...	...	119	49.1	69.1	19.6	1,643	545	9.9	3.9
1937	24.7	9.7	...	...	134	57.7	71.5	20.6	1,798	565	11.3	4.3
1938	25.4	10.4	...	...	157	62.6	74.9	21.1	1,944	583	13.6	5.2
1939	...	...	...	...	181	68.1	77.9	21.6	2,034	578	...	...
1940	...	...	...	...	34.6	46.7	65.9	18.1	1,423	525	...	...
1941	...	...	...	...	31.9	42.5	16.2	18.2	1,503	535	...	...
1942	...	...	...	...	36.7	42.3	16.8	19.8	858	538	...	...
1943	...	...	...	...	36.2	41.9	17.0	20.2	718	536	...	...
1944	...	...	...	...	39.1	42.1	17.5	19.7	755	538	...	...
1945	...	...	...	...	50.1	45.9	18.3	21.7	1,487	572	...	...
1946	...	...	...	...	138	64.2	63.0	27.2	1,770	665	...	...
1947	...	...	...	...	161	76.9	82.2	30.6	1,944	784	...	14.0
1948	...	...	83	74	180	82.8	106	31.5	1,961	896	7.2	16.7
1949	...	...	86	80	194	86.5	123	35.8	2,131	978	7.2	17.0

F6 Motor Vehicles In Use (thousands)

	Austria		Belgium		Czechoslovakia		Denmark		Finland	
	PC	CV	PC	CV	PC	CV	PC	CV	PC	CV
1950	48.5	43.9	274	145	...	...	118	61.4	26.8	34.4
1951	56.6	46.3	304[35]	154[35]	...	...	122	67.0	36.2	40.0
1952	62.8	46.9	320[36]	150[36]	...	...	133	75.6	52.6	48.6
1953	71.8	48.5	368[36][37]	162[36][37]	...	...	158	85.0	59.2	49.1
1954	89.0	53.8	440[36]	135[36]	...	...	194	96.5	70.8	49.9
1955	140	61.1	...[38]	...[38]	140	105	221	103	85.4[40]	56.1[40]
1956	185	64.0	537	149	...	...	249	112	110	61.2
1957	230	65.4	...	...	...	...	280	118	127	58.0
1958	283	68.2	633	161	...	...	310	131	139	60.8
1959	337	70.9	...	...	...	...	354	150	160	65.2
1960	400	73.9	753	177	247	126	408	170	183	75.2
1961	471[6]	78.0[6]	...	...	287	133	470	189	217	85.8
1962	553	83.1	915	200	318	139	548	205	259	90.5
1963	623	87.1	...	...	352	141	605	217	303	92.9
1964	698	91.4	1,152	221	382	150	675	232	376	93.2
1965	786	95.6	...	...	413	153	744	237	455	90.0
1966	877	101	1,436[39]	236[39]	456	160	813	247	506	96.2
			1,503	320						
1967	960	104	...	...	521	171	888	254	551	104
1968	1,056	107	1,813	349	599	179	955	259	581	106
1969	1,119[46]	113	1,921	359	700	192	1,023	262	643	110
1970	1,197	121	2,060	376	826	218	1,077	252	712	116
1971	1,325	128	2,154	385	938	228	1,147	220	753	127
1972	1,460	138	2,273	395	1,084	238	1,203	204	818	130
1973	1,541	140	2,390	406	1,193	248	1,245	222	894	134
1974	1,636	144	2,502	419	1,328	265	1,256	221	937	140
1975	1,721	146	2,614	428	1,505	285	1,295	234	996	144
1976	1,828	151	2,738	436	1,677	301	1,338	256	1,033	149
1977	1,965	156	2,871	445	1,828	316	1,375	269	1,075	152
1978	2,040	162	2,973	453	1,982	336	1,408	272	1,115	156
1979	2,139	172	3,077	469	2,133	354	1,423	271	1,160	160
1980	2,247	184	3,159[53]	482[53]	2,274	370	1,390	260	1,226	167
1981	2,313	190	3,206	471	2,373	386	1,367	250	1,279	173
1982	2,361	193	3,231	474	2,441	390	1,358	244	1,352	181
1983	2,414	197	3,263	481	2,511	396	1,390	244	1,410	188
1984	2,468	203	3,300	487	2,640	413	1,440	253	1,474	194
1985	2,531	207	3,343	498	2,776	424	1,501	267	1,546	201
1986	2,609	212	3,409	511	2,812	437	1,558	283	1,620	209
1987	2,685	221	3,498	529	2,904	440	1,587	295	1,699	221
1988	2,785	235	3,614	547	3,000	461	1,596	302	1,796	238
1989	2,903	247	3,736	569	3,122	446	1,598	...	1,909	271
1990	2,991	253	3,864	591	3,242	462	1,590	301	1,940	294
1991	3,100	259	3,970	612	3,342	475	...	...	1,923	296
1992	3,245	269	4,021	619	2,523	336[59]	1,604	308	1,936	294
Czech Republic[59]										
1993	3,368	275	4,110	658	2,693	330[59]	1,618	325	1,873	278
1994	3,479	289	4,208	661	2,967	369	1,611	335	1,873	258
1995	3,599	297	4,270	674	3,113	390	1,679	348	1,901	260
1996	3,691	314	4,336	689	3,349	387	1,739	354	1,942	267
1997	3,782	327	4,412	695	3,547	362	1,783	360	1,948	275
1998	3,887	345	4,489	698	3,687	354	1,817	372	2,021	290

F6   Motor Vehicles In Use (thousands)

	France		West Germany		East Germany[55]		Greece		Hungary		Southern Ireland	
	PC	CV	PC	CV	PC	CV	PC	CV	PC	CV	PC	CV
1950	2,150		516	372	75.7	96.8	9.3	22.4	13.1	8.2[49]	85.1	26.6
1951	1,700	740	682[42]	431[42]		95.0	9.3	22.4	8.5	—	96.7	28.7
1952	1,800	876	900	512	89.2	96.2	10.1	23.4	9.5	—	105	29.5
1953	2,020[41]	1,038[41]	1,126	577	90.8	92.9	10.5	24.1	9.4	—	109	34.4
1954	2,677	1,125	1,393[24]	597[24]	102	93.9	16.6	25.5	10.1	—	117	38.3
			1,422	612								
1955	3,113	1,225	1,693	606	117	99.7	...	...	10.1	22.3	128	41.5
1956	3,477	1,278	2,065[43]	620[43]	139	109	24.7	28.1	10.5	—	136	43.3
			2,140	644								
1957	3,972	1,371	2,584	688	166	123	31.2	29.8	12.7	—	135	44.6
1958	4,512	1,464	3,097	676	194	126	36.4	31.9	17.9	—	143	44.8
1959	5,018	1,543	3,684	660	741	127	39.7	34.2	24.8	—	154	45.1
1960	5,546	1,634	4,489	703	299	132	43.2	37.0	31.3	46.7	170	45.0
1961	6,158	1,723	5,343	751	383	132	48.8	47.0	39.9	—	186	45.3
1962	7,010	1,823	6,335	796	446	139	56.9	51.8	53.1	—	207	46.4
1963	7,953	1,936	7,305	829	507	145	67.6	57.1	71.3	—	229	46.9
1964	8,800	2,069	8,274	862	581	159	81.6	65.8	86.2	—	254	48.5
1965	9,600	2,181	9,267	895	662	166	104	73.4	99.4	79.2	281	49.9
1966	10,400	2,302	10,302	931	721	173	122	81.4	117	87.1	196	48.6
1967	11,200	2,412	11,016	923	827	183	144	89.3	145	98.7	314	47.8
1968	11,800	2,407	11,683	941	920	194	170	97.7	164	121	337	48.0
1969	12,400	2,560	12,585	978	1,039	210	195	107	192	133	375	51.5
1970	12,900	2,745	13,941	1,038	1,160	229	227	118	240	89	389	51.2
1971	13,400	2,921	15,115	1,084	1,267	244	264	129	295	165	414	47.0
1972	13,900	3,092	16,055	1,110	1,400	255	303	143	340	165	440	47.2
1973	14,500	3,330	17,023	1,139	1,539	270	347	163	409	162	477	51.7
1974	15,500	3,565	17,341	1,136	1,703	282	380	183	481	173	489	55.6
1975	15,300	3,705[54]	17,898	1,121	1,880	301	439	211	568	161	512	55.2
		1,831										
1976	15,900	1,932	18,920	1,122	2,052	313	509	241	641	154	553	56.5
1977	16,990	1,976	20,020	1,146	2,237	333[52]	621	280	720	159	574	56.2
1978	17,720	2,092	21,212	1,175	2,392	327	728	322	820	164	641	62.6
1979	18,440	2,219	22,535	1,236	2,533	334	822	373	934	175	684	64.6
1980	19,130	2,332	23,192	1,277	2,678	348	859	406	1,013	163	736	68.2
1981	19,750	2,412	23,731	1,306	2,812	357	912	458	1,105	176	776	70.3
1982	20,300	2,515	24,104	1,291	2,922	356	996	514	1,181	184	710	71.5
1983	20,600	2,629	24,580	1,278	3,020	353	1,069	555	1,258	197	719	72.9
1984	20,800	2,739	25,218	1,278	3,157	355	1,155	589	1,344	213	711	87.2
1985	21,090	2,810	25,844	1,281	3,306	361	1,263	619	1,436	223	710	96.7
1986	21,500	2,868	26,917	1,295	3,462	367	1,359	646	1,539	238	711	105
1987	21,970	3,001	27,908	1,305	3,600	376	1,423	675	1,660	254	734	115
1988	22,520	3,087	28,878	1,322	3,764	389	1,504	709	1,789	259	749	124
1989	23,010	3,441	29,755	1,345	3,899[60]	407	1,605	750	1,732	268	773	136
			Germany									
1990	23,550	3,567	30,685	1,388	4,817[60]	438	1,736	793	1,945	289	796	150
1991	23,810	3,685	31,322	1,440	6,300[60]		1,778	819	2,016	290	837	155
1992	24,020	3,677	32,007	1,549	7,000[60]		1,829	825	2,058	289	858	152
1993	24,385	3,618	32,652	1,590	6,500[60]		1,959	854	2,092	296	891	143
			Included in Germany									
1994	24,900	5,314	39,765	2,619			2,074	873	2,177	319	947	144
1995	25,100	5,374	40,404	2,755			2,205	908	2,245	345	999	151
1996	25,500	5,437	40,987	2,851			2,339	939	2,264	351	1,068	156
1997	26,090	5,561	41,372	2,931			2,500	978	2,297	361	1,146	168
1998	26,810	5,680	41,673	3,068			2,676	1,014	2,218	355	1,209	181

F6 Motor Vehicles In Use (thousands)

	Italy		Netherlands		Norway		Poland		Portugal	
	PC	CV	PC	CV	PC	CV	PC	CV	PC	CV
1950	342	229	139	82	60.1	56.3	40.1	46.4	60.5	28.8
1951	425	249	157	89	64.4	64.9	33.3	41.6	66.2	30.3
1952	510	274	173	94	73.3	73.9	37.5	49.2	70.8	32.8
1953	613	305	188	95	85.3	80.2	38.1	63.2	77.3	33.8
1954	744	339	219	100	102	85.6	36.1	62.9	87.1	35.9
1955	879	367	268	112	116	90.1	40.3	73.2	95.2	40.2
1956	1,031	360	328	127	128	94.2	44.8	82.8	106	42.8
1957	1,231	373	376	134	147	99.7	61.9	93.5	116	44.9
1958	1,393	385	421	140	166	106	83.9	102	130	47.6
1959	1,644	426	457	148	186	112	105	107	145	48.7
1960	1,995	456	522	157	219	119	117	120	158	50.4
1961	2,444	489	616	172	269	124	135	132	171	51.3
1962	3,030	538	730	185	314	129	162	146	190	53.6
1963	3,913	596	866	205	357	133	188	164	196	55.1
1964	4,675	630	1,059	220	408	137	211	174	211	68.5
1965	5,473	650	1,273	235	458	139	246	183	319	61.9
1966	6,357	684	1,502	254	509[44]	142[44]	289	197	359	65.9
					516	135				
1967	7,311	718	1,725	275	569	138	332	210	401	76.1
1968	8,266	793	1,990	285	619	140	375	226	450	77.9
1969	9,174	851	2,290[50]	315[50]	700	146	423	245	514	81.7
1970	10,181	904	2,600[50]	302[50]	748[48]	152[48]	479	260	551	147
					695	140				
1971	11,299	972	2,800[50]	320[50]	742	146	557	274	621	163
1972	12,484	1,015[47]	3,050[50]	325[50]	788	156	657	293	697	185
		979						311[51]		
1973	13,424	1,028	2,957	326	838	156	781	346	770	214
1974	14,295	1,081	3,153	336	890	153	920	386	854	238
1975	15,061	1,128	3,399	342	954	147	1,078	425	937	259
1976	15,925	1,180	3,629	341	1,023	148	1,290	467	1,034	288
1977	16,371	1,209	3,851	337	1,107	153	1,547	509	1,110	333
1978	16,241	1,102	4,016	337	1,147	157	1,835	544	1,161	369
1979	17,073	1,204	4,312	360	1,190	163	2,117	584	1,212	408
1980	17,686	1,338	4,515	375	1,234	164	2,383	618	1,269	465
1981	18,603	1,457	4,594	387	1,279	172	2,634	641	1,346	527
1982	19,616	1,538	4,630	388	1,338	181	2,882	616	1,429	586
1983	20,389	1,654	4,728	390	1,383	195	3,179	655	1,578	618
1984	20,888	1,683	4,818	405	1,430	214	3,426	732	1,601	642
1985	22,495	1,794	4,901	428	1,514	250	3,671	780	1,702	669
1986	23,495	1,887	4,950	464	1,592	283	3,964	827	1,813	706
1987	24,320	2,068	5,118	507	1,623	303	4,232	866	1,947	608
1988	25,290	2,191	5,251	538	1,622	314	4,519	919	2,153	670
1989	26,267	2,311	5,371	557	1,613	320	4,846	977	2,343	739
1990	27,416	2,495	5,509	582	1,612	331	5,261	1,045	2,552	813
1991	28,519	2,599	5,569	605	1,615	334	6,112	1,151	2,775	881
1992	29,497	2,685	5,658	645	1,619	342	6,505	1,212	3,050	964
1993	...	...	5,755	679	1,633	353	6,771	1,235	3,295	1,050
1994	29,665	2,745	5,456	652	1,654	366	7,153	1,395	3,532	1,159
1995	30,149	2,864	5,581	654	1,684	382	7,517	1,442	3,751	1,219
1996	31,274	2,899	5,664	666	1,661	392	8,054	1,522	4,002	2,292
1997	32,485	2,945	5,810	695	1,758	412	8,534	1,579	4,273	1,384
1998	...	...	5,931	738	1,786	427	8,891	1,657	4,587	1,492

F6   Motor Vehicles In Use (thousands)

	Romania	Spain		Sweden		Switzerland		United Kingdom		Yugoslavia	
	CV	PC	CV	PC	CV	PC	CV	PC	CV	PC	CV
1950	...	89	83	252	94.5	147	38.5	2,258	1,032	6.4	17.1
1951	...	97[45]	87[45]	313	97.3	168	40.8	2,380	1,070	6.9	16.5
1952	...	102	89	361	105	188	42.7	2,508	1,097	8.5	19.3
1953	...	108	92	431	111	211	45.2	2,762	1,112	10.2	21.4
1954	...	118	114	536	116	238	48.9	3,100	1,140	11.3	22.4
1955	...	132	102	637	118	271	53.1	3,526	1,211	12.6	23.4
1956	5.2	153	111	735	121	309	58.6	3,888	1,273	14.7	23.8
1957	6.9	167	117	863	124	347	64.1	4,187	1,313	21.6	29.2
1958	9.1	188	124	972	126	386	68.7	4,549	1,364	28.4	32.4
1959	11.8	240	133	1,088	128	430	77.1	4,966	1,418	39.0	36.2
1960	22.1	291	159	1,194	130	485	82.3	5,526	1,491	53.3	38.7
1961	23.9	359	187	1,304	135	550	91.9	5,979	1,542	75.6	37.6
1962	23.9	441	220	1,424	138	630	108	6,556	1,563	97.9	43.8
1963	27.9	530	261	1,556	141	700	124	7,375	1,625	113	49.2
1964	31.2	652	315	1,666	144	779	144	8,247	1,673	142	56.3
1965	33.3	807	387	1,793	142	845	162	8,917	1,699	188	66.8
1966	34.0	1,053	467	1,890	143	919	180	9,513	1,647	253	80.0
1967	36.8	1,335	550	1,977	149	979	198	10,303	1,697	356	96.9
1968	38.1	1,634	620	2,072	150	1,061	219	10,816	1,644	430	103
1969	43.9	1,999	883	2,194	155	1,146	243	11,230	1,643	563	109
1970	45.1	2,378	741	2,289	159	1,239[52]	255[52]	11,515	1,694	721	122
1971	...	2,785	793	2,357	156	1,458	152	12,059	1,696	875	139
1972	...	3,255	852	2,458	160	1,557	162	12,717	1,721	1,002	158
1973	...	3,804	924	2,503	164	1,652	170	13,497	1,799	1,141	158 '
1974	...	4,310	988	2,639	170	1,723	176	13,639	1,869	1,333	171
1975	...	4,807	1,040	2,760	171	1,794	179	[13,747][58]	[1,887][58]	1,537	179
1976	...	5,351	1,092	2,881	178	1,864	181	[14,047][58]	[1,869][58]	1,732	191
								[13,792][58]	[2,124][58]		
1977	...	5,945	1,158	2,857	182	1,933	184[56]	...	...	1,924	199
1978	...	6,530	1,232	2,856	185	2,055	288	13,801	2,081	2,132	217
1979	...	7,057	1,303	2,868	191	2,154	302	14,307	2,150	2,260	218
1980	...	7,557	1,381	2,883	194	2,247	318	14,772	2,146	2,434	243
1981	...	7,943	1,440	2,893	199	2,394	330	14,943	2,146	2,568	257
1982	...	8,354	1,505	2,936	207	2,473	346	15,303	2,173	2,703	268
1983	...	8,714	1,573	3,007	215	2,521	367	15,543	2,193	2,771	278
1984	...	8,874	1,486	3,081	224	2,552	368	16,055	2,358	2,874	290
1985	...	9,274	1,571	3,151	231	2,617	386	16,454	2,410	2,824	278
1986	...	9,762	1,685	3,254	244	2,679[57]	402[57]	16,981	2,489	2,957	299
1987	...	10,218	1,865	3,367	260	2,733	410	17,421	2,566	3,024	307
1988	...	10,787	2,020	3,483	281	2,745	433	18,432	2,730	3,090	305
1989	...	11,468	2,162	3,578	310	2,900	451	19,248	2,826	3,324	321
1990	...	11,996	2,334	3,601	325	2,994	482	19,742	2,844	3,511	...
1991	...	12,537	...	3,619	325	3,066	491	19,737	2,773	...	...
1992	...	13,102	2,469	3,587	319	3,099	473[61]	19,870	2,721	...	...
1993	...	13,440	2,735	3,566	316	3,117	472[61]	20,102	2,733	...	...
1994	2,020	13,734	2,953	3,594	318	3,165	...	21,740	2,994	...	...
1995	2,197	14,212	3,072	3,631	322	3,229	...	21,949	2,987	...	...
1996	2,392	14,754	3,200	3,655	326	3,268	...	22,146	3,067	...	...
1997	2,605	15,297	3,360	3,703	337	3,323	...	22,794	3,125	...	...
1998	2,822	16,050	3,561	3,791	353	3,383	...	...	...	...	...

F6 Motor Vehicles In Use (thousands)

NOTES

1. SOURCES:- The official publications noted on p. xv with gaps filled from the League of Nations, *Statistical Yearbook*, except for Great Britain, which are taken from British Road Federation, *Basic Road Statistics*, and Greece 1923–34, which were supplied by the National Statistical Service of Greece.
2. So far as possible, and except as indicated in footnotes, buses and taxis are included with commercial vehicles.
3. Unless otherwise indicated, statistics relate to the year-end.

FOOTNOTES

[1] At 30 June.
[2] Previous figures are for Cisleithania, subsequent ones for the Republic.
[3] At 30 September for 1922–37.
[4] Buses (2.1 thousand in 1930) are included with private cars to 1929.
[5] Taxis (4.3 thousand in 1937) are included with private cars to 1937.
[6] At 31 October for 1948–61.
[7] Including tractors.
[8] In March.
[9] In August/September.
[10] At 1 October.
[11] In February for 1928–1933 (1st line).
[12] Including taxis.
[13] At 1 September previously, except 1917 which is at 20 May.
[14] At 1 July.
[15] Buses (0.9 thousand in 1927) are included with passenger cars to 1925.
[16] At 30 September for 1928–30 and 1942–44.
[17] At 1 September for 1931–40.
[18] At 1 December.
[19] At 31 October for 1945–47.
[20] Alsace-Lorraine is included from 1922.
[21] At 1 July subsequently. The 1914 figure is for the 1924 boundaries.
[22] Buses (1.8 thousand in 1922) are included with passenger cars to 1921.
[23] Figures to 1934 (1st line) are of vehicles operating on the roads; later figures are of all vehicles registered.
[24] Saarland is included in 1935 (2nd line) to 1939 and from 1954 (2nd line).
[25] Fuel lorries (1.4 thousand in 1936) are excluded in 1937 and 1938.
[26] The reason for this break is not given.
[27] Buses and taxis (1.1 thousand in 1926) are included with passenger cars to 1925.
[28] Previously including tractors.
[29] In January.
[30] Buses and taxis (3.7 thousand in 1927) are included with passenger cars to 1926.
[31] Buses are included with private cars in 1924.
[32] Previous figures are of vehicles registered, subsequently they are of all vehicles in existence.
[33] At 30 September subsequently.
[34] In March to 1920, and subsequently in August or September.
[35] Previous figures are of total vehicles taxed during the year.
[36] At 15 December.
[37] Dual purpose vehicles are included with commercial vehicles to 1953 and with private cars subsequently.
[38] At 1 August subsequently.
[39] Previous figures are of taxed vehicles only.
[40] Station wagons are included with commercial vehicles to 1955.
[41] A note in the source indicates that destroyed vehicles are subsequently deducted.
[42] Tax-exempt vehicles are not included in 1948–51.
[43] Subsequently including West Berlin.
[44] Taxis (7.8 thousand in 1966) are subsequently included with private cars.
[45] Previously including Spanish Morocco.
[46] Taxis (6.6 thousand in 1969) are subsequently included with private cars.
[47] Subsequently excluding buses.
[48] Subsequently excluding vehicles whose licences were cancelled during the year.
[49] Lorries only.
[50] Estimates (including special vehicles in commercial vehicles—10 thousand in 1968 and 1973).
[51] Subsequently including special vehicles.
[52] The basis of classification was changed.
[53] About 10 thousand vehicles were transferred from commercial to private in 1981.
[54] Subsequently excluding vehicles 10 years old and over and all buses and tractors.
[55] Statistics for 1949 (in thousands) are PC-63.8, CV-89.8.
[56] Subsequently including agricultural vehicles.
[57] About 5 thousand vehicles were transferred from commercial to private in 1987.

F6 Motor Vehicles In Use (thousands)

[58] From 1974 the census method underlying the count was changing as vehicle records were gradually transferred to the central licensing centre. Figures for 1975 and 1976 (1st line) are therefore not *strictly* comparable with each other or with 1974, nor are those for 1976 (2nd line) strictly comparable with those for 1978 and subsequently. No figures are available for 1977.

[59]

	Slovakia	
	PC	CV
1992	906	108
1993	995	114
1994	994	131
1995	1,016	132
1996	1,058	127
1997	1,136	135
1998	1,196	144

[60] Estimated figures. Technically, from 1990/91, East German statistics should be included with West German. However, since these figures were available, they have been included for the sake of continuity.

[61] Revised figure.

F7 COMMERCIAL AVIATION

A. Passenger Kilometres (in millions)   **1920–1944**

	Belgium	Czechoslovakia	Denmark	Finland	France	Germany	Ireland	Italy	Netherlands
1920	...	...	...	...	0.6	...	—	...	...
1921	...	...	...	...	4.1	...	—	...	...
1922	...	...	...	...	3.5	...	—	...	...
1923	...	...	...	...	4.2	2.1	—	...	...
1924	0.2	...	...	...	5.4	3.3	—	...	...
1925	0.4	...	...	...	6.3	11	—	...	...
1926	0.6	...	...	...	6.6	15	—	8	...
1927	0.8	...	...	...	7.9	27	—	20	...
1928	1.5	...	...	...	9.9	29	—	24	...
1929	1.6	...	0.5	0.8	12	24	—	40	7.1
1930	2.3	...	0.6	0.6	15	24	—	63	4.2
1931	3.2	...	0.7	0.5	18	26	—	54	5.2
1932	3.3	2.1	0.7	0.6	22	28	—	73	7.1
1933	4.4	2.9	1.0	0.8	30	38	—	72	14
1934	5.0	3.5	1.7	1.2	30	63	—	78	23
1935	8.0	3.7	2.6	1.4	38	86	—	99	26
1936	11	6.4	3.0	1.8	43	124	0.4	109	36
1937	14	9.2	3.3	2.2	60	121	1.4	187	46
1938	18	22	5.6	3.4	73	128	2.0	209	60
1939	13	...	7.6	4.2	...	114	0.9	246	61
1940	5.5	...	8.6	3.0	...	59	1.3	...	19
1941	5.4	...	11	2.4	...	...	1.4	...	17
1942	8.9	...	13	7.1	...	...	1.3	...	12
1943	9.8	...	11	10	...	...	1.5	...	17
1944	15	...	4.6	6.1	...	...	1.0	...	17

	Norway	Poland	Spain	Sweden	Switzerland	U.K.	Yugoslavia
1925	...	...	...	...	...	4.3	—
1926	...	...	...	...	...	6.0	—
1927	...	...	...	...	...	6.9	—
1928	...	...	...	1.0	3.5	10	—
1929	...	3.8	2.1	1.2	2.4	11	—
1930	...	3.2	3.0	1.1	2.7	10	0.6
1931	...	3.7	3.0	0.8	3.7	11	0.6
1932	...	2.9	3.0	1.9	3.8	26	0.3
1933	...	3.7	2.1	3.1	2.5	35	0.4
1934	0.1	4.9	3.4	4.6	3.8	47	0.7
1935	1.0	5.4	7.1	6.2	6.8	68	0.8
1936	1.8	8.8	...	5.7	9.2	66	0.9
1937	1.0	11	1.2	12	11	80	1.3
1938	2.4	9.4	11	14	14	86	2.0
1939	[2.5][2]	...	21	18	11	91	3.6
1940	—	...	18	13	0.9	68	4.5
1941	—	...	...	12	1.2	91	...
1942	—	...	...	14	6.9	164	—
1943	—	...	...	13	1.2	201	—
1944	—	...	15	12	0.4	288	—

F7   Commercial Aviation

B. Passenger Kilometres and Freight Ton/Kilometres (in millions)   1945–1998

	Austria		Belgium		Czechoslovakia		Denmark		Finland		France	
	PKM	TKM	PKM	TKM	PKM	TKM	PKM	TKM	PKM	TKM	PKM	TKM
1945	—	—	29	0.1	...	...	14	0.2	4.7	0.1	123	1.2
1946	—	—	153	0.9	46	1.7	45	...	7.8	0.1	343	5.6
1947	—	—	215	3.4	61	2.0	74	...	11	0.1	588	10
1948	—	—	173	3.3	55	2.3	108	1.1	21	0.3	815	19
1949	—	—	194	4.0	41	2.2	118	1.9	22	0.4	985	28
1950	—	—	235	6.8	46	2.7	149	3.4	27	0.5	1,118	33
1951	—	—	277	9.6	67	2.8	168	4.3	37	0.6	1,263	37
1952	—	—	344	12	64	1.9	189	4.2	46	0.2	1,460	49
1953	—	—	448	16	74	1.7	221	4.4	72	0.4	1,652	40
1954	—	—	489	19	77	1.1	240	5.1	95	0.6	2,711	67
1955	—	—	579	21	94	1.5	297	5.9	121	0.8	3,138	75
1956	—	—	679	24	117	1.9	356	6.5	143	1.3	3,616	79
1957	—	—	929	27	124	2.1	445	7.6	169	1.3	3,833	82
1958	19	0.1	1,198	28	172	2.3	509	8.5	177	1.5	4,144	85
1959	41	0.3	1,065	29	236	3.0	520	9.9	186	2.0	4,505	94
1960	66	0.4	1,264	34	344	4.9	602	12	228	3.4	5,229	108
1961	83	0.5	1,178	39	394	6.8	594	14	240	3.1	6,112	138
1962	103	0.6	1,384	35	506	14	640	16	287	3.7	6,116	136
1963	127	1.1	1,346	40	527	17	681	19	313	4.0	6,005	142
1964	181	1.7	1,488	47	610	15	783	22	311	4.3	6,697	153
1965	230	2.0	1,635	59	681	13	852	26	370	5.6	7,511	190
1966	271	2.3	1,654	64	752	12	903	30	410	6.3	8,987	227
1967	301	3.5	1,954	92	754	10	1,061	35	455	5.9	10,152	270
1968	312	4.5	1,977	119	776	10	1,202	49	440	7.8	9,678	325
1969	428	6.5	2,206	170	850	8.9	1,437	62	587	12	11,716	443
1970	452	5.9	2,447	184	887	12	1,616	63	773	21	13,587	475
1971	416	3.1	2,720	202	906	12	1,651	64	829	24	14,014	488
1972	477	5	3,093	225	1,132	15	1,956	78	936	25	17,484	619
1973	579	6	3,644	239	1,155	15	2,216	83	1,073	30	19,742	758
1974	598	7	3,975	286	1,313	15	2,229	94	1,158	30	21,745	871
1975	677	7	3,795	281	1,414	14	2,347	88	1,259	29	23,277	995
1976	823	8	3,893	317	1,364	14	2,603	101	1,380	30	25,192	1,279
1977	911	9	4,049	339	1,414	14	2,780	113	1,395	36	27,285	1,557
1978	1,035	10	4,497	376	1,584	15	3,060	125	1,644	38	30,215	1,697
1979	1,089	12	4,819	395	1,734	15	3,327	120	1,982	42	32,783	1,912
1980	1,120	12	4,852	395	1,539	12	3,296	116	2,139	48	34,130	1,986
1981	1,235	14	5,202	442	1,470	12	3,189	121	2,513	52	36,718	2,128
1982	1,236	16	5,277	479	1,592	14	3,193	115	2,589	61	37,846	2,185
1983	1,348	17	5,296	489	1,637	14	3,284	110	2,630	71	38,599	2,484
1984	1,407	20	5,478	525	1,696	14	3,587	114	2,991	72	38,687	2,798
1985	1,483	19	5,663	565	1,854	17	3,401	116	2,940	77	39,559	2,873
1986	1,429	20	5,561	575	1,870	17	3,508	117	2,936	86	39,470	3,080
1987	1,691	20	5,973	536	2,063	16	3,653	110	3,587	90	44,398	3,887
1988	2,031	23	6,528	657	2,242	17	3,935	114	3,169	97	31,982	3,484
1989	3,020	42	6,761	661	2,195	17	4,309	122	4,625	129	51,533	3,819
1990	3,828	54	7,642	656	2,030	15	4,657	124	4,859	135	52,912	3,996
1991	3,605	59	6,223	486	1,736	22	4,440	119	4,719	128	50,198	3,747
1992	4,867	568[3]	6,203	965[3]	2,135	219	4,495	536[3]	4,639	535[3]	56,701	9,293[3]
					Czech Republic[4]							
1993	5,629	669[3]	6,484	1,003[3]	1,900	196	4,913	580[3]	5,529	662[3]	59,455	9,753[3]
1994	5,933	703	7,496	1,209	1,976	201	5,112	603	6,720	804	68,225	11,404
1995	6,727	814	8,620	1,390	2,317	235	5,301	621	8,562	990	68,192	11,570
1996	8,791	1,035	9,011	1,419	2,368	237	5,466	679	8,731	1,031	81,594	13,151
1997	10,066	1,201	11,277	1,706	2,442	244	5,669	729	9,575	1,170	84,037	13,750
1998	11,923	1,411	15,338	1,853	2,637	264	5,658	725	10,714	1,250	90,225	14,033

F7 Commercial Aviation

	East Germany		West Germany		Greece		Ireland		Italy		Netherlands	
	PKM	TKM	PKM	TKM	PKM	TKM	PKM	TKM	PKM	TKM	PKM	TKM
1945	—	—	—	—			4.6	- -	...	...	31	0.1
1946	—	—	—	—			24	0.1	...	...	346	3.7
1947	—	—	—	—			47	0.3	...	...	473	8.0
1948	—	—	—	—			65	0.5	...	...	723	16
1949	—	—	—	—			68	0.6	...	...	608	13
1950	—	—	—	—	67	2.1	80	0.8	...	...	772	24
1951	—	—	—	—	65	1.6	97	1.1	185	3.5	876	28
1952	—	—	—	—	63	1.6	106	1.0	206	3.5	1,013	35
1953	—	—	—	—	44	1.1	106	1.4	229	3.3	1,179	38
1954	—	—	—	—	45	1.0	125	1.6	307	4.2	1,362	44
1955	—	—	78	1.0	58	1.0	139	1.7	369	5.7	1,485	51
1956	3.0	0.5	287	4.5	70	1.0	160	1.8	429	6.9	1,725	61
1957	4.4	1.8	488	7.0	99	1.1	162	1.7	555	8.0	1,975	67
1958	116	2.3	664	12	140	1.6	244	2.2	759	9.2	1,986	71
1959	128	2.8	842	18	209	2.6	314	2.7	1,039	15	2,229	87
1960	165	4.7	1,284	31	289	4.5	404	3.9	1,339	21	2,672	104
1961	159	5.0	1,699	51	358	5.9	508	6.1	1,864	36	2,795	118
1962	299	8.3	2,098	70	384	6.4	574	7.6	2,633	55	2,847	127
1963	306	9.4	2,583	84	401	6.8	639	11	3,050	72	2,563	128
1964	312	11	3,150	98	438	7.8	794	15	3,589	84	3,012	151
1965	373	13	3,785	133	542	8.3	896	22	3,967	106	3,367	199
1966	484	16	4,620	190	865	15	1,073	29	4,680	128	3,902	227
1967	606	22	5,623	236	1,146	22	1,224	29	5,247	139	4,311	247
1968	730	24	6,008	313	1,251	25	1,293	38	5,967	182	4,605	304
1969	843	23	6,922	424	1,717	32	1,456	59	7,121	250	4,799	355
1970	947	27	8,255	484	2,126	31	1,776	58	8,400	275	5,769	377
1971	1,073	30	8,610	533	2,343	32	1,791	65	9,502	302	6,444	408
1972	1,099	29	10,453	657	2,965	42	1,623	78	10,127	282	7,925	461
1973	1,120	31	11,106	827	3,729	54	1,757	88	11,129	406	9,211	499
1974	1,315	43	12,473	941	3,084	48	1,648	89	11,377	438	9,396	609
1975	1,490	53	13,634	921	3,430	33	1,487	69	10,799	397	10,323	587
1976	1,448	50	14,982	1,040	4,623	53	1,528	75	10,780	444	10,613	632
1977	1,586	68	15,905	1,204	4,356	53	1,558	86	12,793	504	11,741	719
1978	1,802	62	17,572	1,345	4,629	55	1,836	86	13,336	490	12,778	787
1979	1,848	67	19,844	1,513	5,132	62	2,212	98	12,859	483	14,013	868
1980	2,053	67	21,056	1,506	5,062	61	2,049	89	14,096	523	14,643	947
1981	2,130	66	21,635	1,495	5,197	68	2,270	84	13,720	476	15,652	1,046
1982	2,296	73	21,625	1,592	4,924	58	2,343	76	15,143	567	16,282	1,032
1983	2,307	72	22,704	1,941	5,326	66	2,121	85	14,983	614	16,463	1,194
1984	2,470	76	24,274	2,235	6,300	69	2,190	98	16,077	689	17,446	1,393
1985	2,541	72	24,431	2,378	7,460	103	2,474	82	17,652	757	18,715	1,404
1986	2,649	71	26,640	2,827	6,385	92	2,496	75	16,921	844	19,758	1,509
1987	2,846	79	31,756	3,248	7,122	104	2,738	81	18,647	912	22,605	1,734
1988	3,229	92	34,097	3,470	6,210	92	3,567	103	19,168	1,029	24,144	1,882
1989	...	...	36,316	3,840	8,015	103	4,299	118	21,493	1,119	25,896	2,003
1990	Included in		42,387	3,994	7,764	113	4,561	128	23,599	1,171	29,036	2,129
1991	West Germany		43,270	4,109	6,193	114	4,163	115	22,653	1, 215	28,197	2, 224
1992			48,965	9,166[3]	7,262	772[3]	4,461	501[3]	28,667	3,878[3]	33,351	5,556[3]
1993			52,941	10,109[3]	7,899	848[3]	4,209	467[3]	29,659	4,041[3]	38,544	6,512[3]
1994			58,263	11,365	8,429	904	4,920	537	31,757	4,259	42,435	7,320
1995			64,233	12,415	7,945	843	5,854	626	33,390	4,505	57,580	9,345
1996			77,765	13,850	8,533	933	6,732	700	36,157	5,060	62,397	9,959
1997			86,189	14,822	9,261	1,013	7,260	767	38,240	5,247	66,132	10,590
1998			90,393	15,301	8,561	936	8,510	889	38,122	5,261	68,597	10,864

F7 Commercial Aviation

	Norway		Poland		Portugal		Spain		Sweden		Switzerland		U.K.		Yugoslavia	
	PKM	TKM	PKM	TKM	PKM	TKM	PKM	TKM	PKM	TKM	PKM	TKM	PKM	TKM	PKM	TKM
1945	—	—	...	...			50	0.2	40	1.3	4.9	0.1	486	28	...	...
1946	30	0.2	17	...			78	0.2	83	2.1	39	0.4	584	13	3.6	- -
1947	85	1.0	18	...			102	0.3	150	2.5	54	0.6	710	17	11	0.1
1948	99	1.1	22	...			116	0.4	138	1.8	80	1.0	892	25	10	0.1
1949	135	2.6	22	...			181	0.5	181	3.0	120	1.4	989	30	11	0.1
1950	160	4.9	30	...			221	1.2	224	5.3	147	2.5	1,277	36	31	0.4
1951	200	7.2	28	0.8	40	0.3	245	1.2	258	6.6	197	3.5	1,717	46	31	0.4
1952	222	6.7	42	0.6	38	0.5	286	1.4	294	6.5	223	3.9	2,000	45	24	0.2
1953	260	6.9	40	0.6	44	0.6	320	1.5	346	6.8	328	4.5	2,308	50	29	0.3
1954	265	5.6	52	0.8	61	0.7	403	2.0	379	7.9	447	6.0	2,438	52	32	0.3
1955	327	6.0	63	0.8	81	0.8	537	2.7	474	9.2	516	9.0	2,899	70	49	0.4
1956	402	6.6	85	0.9	108	1.1	554	3.2	568	10	604	11	3,336	74	46[1]	0.5
1957	497	7.8	99	0.9	122	1.2	610	4.0	741	13	874	16	3,898	82	51	0.4
1958	566	8.7	71	0.7	162	1.4	661	4.8	849	15	1,015	21	4,107	83	59	0.4
1959	592	10	87	0.8	195	1.7	782	5.6	881	18	966	24	4,927	98	77	0.6
1960	685	12	101	0.9	244	2.1	947	7.0	1,012	21	1,138	27	7,289	131	103	0.7
1961	690	14	117	1.1	356	3.2	1,236	9.4	1,058	25	1,365	28	8,176	144	120	0.9
1962	780	17	140	1.3	400	2.8	1,468	14	1,177	29	1,686	31	8,760	175	127	1.1
1963	864	20	147	1.5	477	3.5	1,952	20	1,231	33	1,842	41	9,609	210	190	1.4
1964	1,014	22	189	1.8	571	4.1	2,395	26	1,420	36	2,143	46	10,867	247	246	2.0
1965	1,119	27	229	2.2	716	6.1	2,699	33	1,492	42	2,435	59	12,475	312	299	2.0
1966	1,211	31	309	3.0	932	8.5	3,071	41	1,560	49	2,688	71	13,969	389	299	2.5
1967	1,440	36	419	3.5	1,160	13	3,879	59	1,825	57	2,994	72	14,691	409	364	3.1
1968	1,608	50	451	4.5	1,495	21	4,837	83	2,027	77	3,335	106	14,943	437	460	4.0
1969	1,736	63	504	4.9	2,184	30	5,874	91	2,184	96	3,836	158	17,390	537	606	4.6
1970	1,954	64	550	6.2	2,455	37	7,067	132	2,449	98	4,420	169	18,953	508	774	5.8
1971	2,135	66	655	6.5	3,005	49	8,074	155	2,630	100	5,199	182	20,381	565	939	6.9
1972	2,464	79	815	8	3,419	55	9,573	172	3,007	120	5,782	198	24,319	715	1,029	6
1973	2,757	85	1,074	10	3,936	91	10,105	200	3,414	128	6,728	237	28,256	845	1,258	8
1974	2,738	96	1,075	10	4,272	106	10,695	215	3,477	143	7,089	272	27,656	848	1,419	10
1975	2,880	91	1,314	10	3,312	68	10,695	215	3,630	134	7,562	286	30,192	798	1,967	14
1976	3,180	105	1,425	11	2,841	68	11,130	264	4,041	155	8,493	321	34,044	866	2,150	19
1977	3,441	117	1,669	12	3,036	86	12,544	324	4,191	171	9,271	351	35,647	984	2,426	24
1978	3,789	129	2,088	14	3,410	106	14,601	359	4,729	188	10,148	403	45,132	1,153	2,719	28
1979	4,070	125	2,313	14	3,959	117	15,188	377	5,298	182	10,325	407	52,426	1,263	3,230	37
1980	4,068	120	2,232	14	3,459	106	15,517	390	5,342	175	10,831	422	56,746	1,427	2,984	38
1981	4,078	125	2,138	13	4,040	101	15,999	426	5,409	178	11,627	453	59,219	1,576	3,024	53
1982	4,118	121	778	4	4,174	98	16,457	448	5,573	173	11,773	461	53,645	1,511	2,870	54
1983	4,336	116	1,308	5	3,993	97	16,332	443	5,877	166	12,279	540	51,605	1,730	2,884	63
1984	4,533	121	1,777	7	4,314	117	17,460	483	6,230	173	12,127	634	56,874	2,191	3,108	74
1985	4,791	122	2,233	8	4,278	134	18,338	522	6,365	172	12,692	637	63,809	2,299	3,845	82
1986	5,009	124	2,199	10	4,512	123	19,113	533	6,811	174	12,977	674	65,500	2,547	4,284	97
1987	5,361	116	2,301	10	5,014	125	20,409	526	7,275	169	13,834	734	77,161	2,863	5,229	99
1988	5,632	121	2,701	14	5,673	141	22,272	598	7,830	175	14,525	814	83,042	3,134	5,667	124
1989	5,912	128	3,734	29	6,272	160	22,848	733	8,497	185	15,536	889	92,283	3,447	5,123	136
1990	6,502	130	3,479	49	6,881	167	24,157	760	9,118	191	16,016	929	104,999	3,825	5,678	135
1991	6,291	123	2,878	38	7,072	163	23,200	623	8,163	187	15,327	945	99,856	4,023	3,078	59
1992	6,584	718[3]	2,873	293[3]	7,790	882[3]	27,480	3,081[3]	8,247	932[3]	16,472	2,704[3]	115,199	15,710[3]	...[5]	...[5]
1993	7,266	791[3]	3,335	357[3]	7,917	897[3]	27,105	3,025[3]	8,428	993[3]	17,704	3,007[3]	124,882	17,387[3]	...[5]	...[5]
1994	7,664	836	3,690	396	7,880	904	26,919	3,025	9,417	1,064	18,858	3,288	139,088	19,699	...	...
1995	8,034	869	4,242	457	8,057	933	31,070	3,485	8,538	980	20,359	3,557	152,698	21,757	...	...
1996	8,688	969	3,917	430	8,423	985	34,102	3,807	8,925	1,073	22,264	3,743	167,577	24,104	...	...
1997	9,158	1,061	4,204	478	9,342	1,094	37,240	4,093	9,749	1,191	26,314	4,462	136,371	17,912	...	...
1998	9,480	1,082	4,255	483	10,107	1,157	40,042	4,378	10,249	1,234	29,415	4,897	151,880	19,589	...	...

F7 Commercial Aviation

NOTES

1. SOURCES:- The original source for most data is the records of the International Civil Aviation Organisation, but the immediate sources used are the United Nations, *Statistical Yearbooks* and the official publications noted on p. xv.
2. In principle, and except as otherwise indicated, data refer to the regular services of airlines based in the country concerned.

FOOTNOTES

[1] Previously including unscheduled traffic.
[2] To 31 August.
[3] = Total TON-KM
[4] Czech Republic.

	Slovakia	
	PKM	TKM
1993	10	1
1994	12	1
1995	43	4
1996	80	7
1997	103	10
1998	128	11

[5] Ex-Yugoslavia as follows.

	Croatia		Macedonia		Slovenia	
	PKM	TKM (Total)	PKM	TKM	PKM	TKM
1992	123	12	...	...	196	19
1993	255	26	292	28	278	28
1994	306	41	319	29	329	33
1995	405	41	340	31	357	36
1996	414	48	410	38	380	38
1997	486	45	285	27	375	37
1998	469	52	328	31	411	41

F8 POSTAL AND TELEGRAPH SERVICES (in millions, except as otherwise indicated)

	Austria[1]		Belgium		Denmark		Finland		France	
	Mail[2]	Telegrams	Mail	Telegrams	Mail[3]	Telegrams (thousands)	Mail[5]	Telegrams[6] (thousands)	Mail[5]	Telegrams
1830	18.6	—	...	—	...	...	...	...	104	...
1831	20.5	—	...	—	...	...	...	...	109	...
1832	24.0	—	...	—	...	...	...	...	143	...
1833	24.5	—	...	—	...	...	...	...	120	...
1834	25.6	—	...	—	...	...	...	...	120	...
1835	24.2	—	...	—	...	...	...	...	124	...
1836	24.7	—	...	—	...	...	...	...	125	...
1837	24.9	—	...	—	...	...	...	...	134	...
1838	26.3	—	...	—	...	...	...	...	136	...
1839	26.8	—	...	—	...	...	...	...	142	...
1840	29.3	—	...	—	...	...	...	...	147	...
1841	30.7	—	...	—	...	...	...	...	153	...
1842	30.1	—	...	—	...	...	...	...	158	...
1843	27.0	—	...	—	...	...	...	...	160	...
1844	28.7	—	...	—	...	...	...	...	169	...
1845	30.2	—	...	—	...	...	0.3	...	176	...
1846	32.2	—	...	—	...	...	...	...	189	...
1847	33.0	—	...	—	...	...	...	...	217	...
1848	32.1[1]	- -	...	—	...	...	...	...	252	...
	20.7									
1849	23.2	- -	...	—	...	...	...	...	305	...
1850	26.1	- -	22.6	—	...	...	...	...	254	...
1851	29.2	0.1	27.7	- -	...	...	...	...	199	...
1852	32.1	0.1	31.9	- -	...	...	...	...	276	...
1853	37.4	0.1	34.1	0.1	...	...	...	...	286	...
1854	43.4	0.2	36.6	0.1	...	...	...	...	329	...
1855	46.4	0.3	41.9	0.1	...	...	0.6	...	358	...
1856	47.7	0.3	45.7	0.1	...	...	...	...	380	...
1857	50.0	0.4	47.9	0.1	...	...	...	...	398	...
1858	54.5	0.5	49.0	0.1	...	...	...	...	406	0.5
1859	66.5[1]	0.7	56.0	0.2	...	...	...	...	426	0.6
1860	60.4	0.7	57.0	0.2	...	...	...	...	444	0.7
1861	65.6	0.9	59.7	0.3	6.7	...	...	...	464	0.9
1862	73.4	1.0	63.1	0.3	6.8	...	...	...	487	1.5
1863	73.8	1.1	65.5	0.4	7.2	...	...	...	505	1.8
1864	81.3	1.7	67.3	0.5	8.6[4]	...	...	...	568	2.2
					9.2					
1865	81.1[1]	1.9	74.5	0.7	9.3	203	0.7	...	592	2.5
1866	86.1	2.7	88.2	1.1	9.0	238	...	124	616	2.9
1867	107	2.4	90.3	1.3	9.3	316	...	...	652	3.3
1868	114	2.4	94.5	1.5	9.9	357	...	...	679	3.6
1869	128	3.1	100	1.7	10.7[3]	420	...	...	692	4.8
					12.1					
1870	148	3.4	111	2.0	13.0	525	...	131	733[7]	5.7[7]
1871	169	4.2	121	2.4	13.3	553	...	145	593	5.0
1872	205	4.9	131	2.4	15.2	600	...	184	649	6.2
1873	267	5.4	140	2.6	17.0	650	...	217	672	6.9
1874	245	4.7	154	2.7	18.8	763	...	299	719	6.9[8]
										7.3

F8 Postal and Telegraphs Services

	Germany		Greece		Hungary[9]		Italy		Netherlands		Norway	
	Mail[5]	Telegrams	Mail	Telegrams (thousands)	Mail[2]	Telegrams	Mail[5,11]	Telegrams	Mail[2]	Telegrams (thousands)	Mail[11]	Telegrams (thousands)
1830	...	...	...	—	...	...	...	...	...	—	...	...
1831	...	...	...	—	...	...	...	...	...	—	...	...
1832	...	...	...	—	...	...	...	...	...	—	...	...
1833	...	...	...	—	...	...	...	...	...	—	...	...
1834	...	...	...	—	...	...	...	...	...	—	...	...
1835	...	...	...	—	...	...	...	...	...	—	...	...
1836	...	...	...	—	...	...	...	...	...	—	...	...
1837	...	...	...	—	...	...	...	...	...	—	...	...
1838	...	...	...	—	...	...	...	...	...	—	...	...
1839	...	...	...	—	...	...	...	...	...	—	...	...
1840	...	...	...	0.8	...	...	...	...	...	—	...	...
1841	...	...	...	—	...	...	...	...	...	—	...	...
1842	...	...	...	—	...	...	...	...	...	—	...	...
1843	...	...	...	—	...	...	...	...	...	—	...	...
1844	...	...	...	—	...	...	...	...	...	—	...	...
1845	...	...	...	0.7	...	...	...	...	...	—	...	...
1846	...	...	...	—	...	...	...	...	...	—	...	...
1847	...	...	...	—	...	...	...	...	...	—	...	...
1848	...	...	...	—	...	...	...	...	...	—	1.0	...
1849	...	...	...	—	3.2	...	...	...	6	—	...	...
1850	85.9	0.04	0.8	—	5.5	...	...	...	7	—	1.5	...
1851	89.5	0.05	...	—	5.9[10]	...	...	...	11	—	...	...
1852	99.0	0.07	...	—	8.8	...	...	...	12	1	...	...
1853	111	0.15	...	—	10.6	...	...	...	13	46	...	...
1854	123	0.21	...	—	11.7	...	...	...	14	102	...	...
1855	133	0.32	1.0	—	14.3	...	...	...	15	104	2.3	23
1856	147	0.35	1.0	—	15.2	...	...	...	16	190	...	...
1857	155	0.44	1.1	—	16.3	...	...	...	17	225	...	...
1858	163	0.53	1.1	—	15.8	...	...	...	18	264	...	91
1859	170	0.57	1.2	5.5	54.7	...	...	...	19[12] / 26	389	...	117
1860	179	0.73	1.3	20	...	...	...	...	27	413	3.3	130
1861	187	0.81	1.3	29	...	...	108	0.1	28	479	...	128
1862	197	0.98	2.1	...	26.1	...	133	0.1	29	527	...	139
1863	210	1.32	2.1	57	26.7	...	154	0.1	30	653	3.9	167
1864	233	1.75	2.4	62	28.0	...	153	1.1	31	802	...	200
1865	253	2.65	2.7	85	28.0	...	156	1.3	33	966	...	218
1866	269	3.37	2.8	103	30.8	...	164	1.6	36	1,088	4.7	269
1867	307	4.26	2.9	107	38.2	...	174	1.4	...	1,113	...	310
1868	344	5.16	3.0	101	38.0	1.0	176	1.8	...	1,497	5.4	355
1869	371	6.07	3.1	112	45.0	1.2	103	1.9	...	1,632	...	392
1870	382[7]	8.66[7]	3.1	127	48.1	1.5	195	2.0	52	1,838	...	444
1871	463	8.88	3.3	145	58.3	3.4	230	2.6	66	2,038	...	604
1872	500	9.71	3.4	189	67.9	4.4	232	3.9	71	2,019	7.5	702
1873	563	10.8	3.5	195	74.4	4.4	234	4.5	78	2,064	...	615
1874	617	10.7	3.7	201	78.4	3.7	214	4.7	84	2,086[12] / 2,104	...	688

F8   Postal and Telegraph Services

	Portugal Telegrams[23] (thousands)	Russia Telegrams	Spain Mail	Telegrams (thousands)	Sweden Mail[5,13]	Telegrams (thousands)	Switzerland Mail[5]	Telegrams (thousands)	United Kingdom Mail[14]	Telegrams
1830	...	...	...	—	...	...	...	—	...	...
1831	...	...	...	...	...	...	...	—	...	...
1832	...	...	...	—	...	...	...	—	...	...
1833	...	...	...	—	...	...	...	—	...	...
1834	...	...	...	—	...	...	...	—	...	...
1835	...	...	...	—	...	...	...	—	...	...
1836	...	...	...	—	...	...	...	—	...	...
1837	...	...	...	—	...	...	...	—	...	...
1838	...	...	...	—	...	...	...	—	...	...
1839	...	...	...	—	...	...	...	—	82	...
1840	...	...	...	—	...	...	...	—	169	...
1841	...	...	...	—	...	...	...	—	196	...
1842	...	...	...	—	...	...	...	—	208	...
1843	...	...	...	—	...	...	...	—	219	...
1844	...	...	...	—	...	...	...	—	243	...
1845	...	...	...	—	...	...	...	—	272	...
1846	...	...	19.0	—	...	...	...	—	300	...
1847	...	...	19.8	—	...	...	...	—	321	...
1848	...	...	20.2	—	...	...	...	—	329	...
1849	...	...	20.5	—	...	...	...	—	338	...
1850	...	...	20.5	—	3.9	...	11.4	—	346	...
1851	...	...	20.8	—	4.0	...	16.2	—	361	...
1852	...	...	22.0	—	4.1	...	18.7	3	379	...
1853	...	...	23.2	—	4.4	...	21.0	...	411	...
1854	...	...	25.2	—	4.7	...	21.9	127	443	...
1855	...	...	28.8	3	4.8	61	23.1	159	457[14]	...
1856	...	...	30.2	...	5.3	117	25.2	210	552	...
1857	...	...	38.7	...	5.7	175	26.1	238	582	...
1858	...	...	42.6	...	5.8	174	27.3	228	602	...
1859	...	...	47.5	...	6.1	171	28.3	260	627	...
1860	...	...	54.4	316	6.3	159	28.8	277	646	...
1861	...	...	59.4	454	6.6	169	30.8	...	678	...
1862	...	...	63.5	496	6.9	210	31.3	...	692	...
1863	...	...	64.6	555	7.4	228	38.5	...	731	...
1864	...	0.9	64.0	747	8.2[13] 10.0	243	40.0	...	775	...
1865	...	1.0	65.0	956	11	328	43.4	560	817	...
1866	...	1.4	65.6	855	11	419	45.6	...	849	...
1867	...	1.6	66.9	742	12	490	48.7	...	877	...
1868	176	2.0	70.9	752	12	497	51.5	...	914	...
1869	454	2.4	76.8	748	13	561	49.3	...	933	...
1870	612	2.7	77.6	1,050	13	590	47.6	1,510	978	[8.6][15]
1871	674	3.0	78.2	...	14	655	57.0	...	1,069	11.8
1872	792	3.3	79.4	...	16	779	61.6	...	1,184	14.9
1873	908	3.4	82.9	...	17	910	69.1	...	1,233	17.3
1874	738	3.8	85.2	938	18	972	71.0	...	1,399	19.1

F8 Postal and Telegraphs Services

	Austria[1]		Belgium		Denmark		Finland		France	
	Mail	Telegrams	Mail	Telegrams	Mail[3]	Telegrams (thousands)	Mail[5]	Telegrams[6] (thousands)	Mail[5]	Telegrams
1875	242	4.9	169	2.9	20.7	887	...	493	743	8.0
1876	257	5.4	174	2.9	23.5	941	...	540	834	8.5
1877	263	5.8	181	2.9	25.2	937	...	598	866	9.6
1878	295	6.0	177	3.0	26.8	916	...	541	975	11[19]
1879	302	5.8	186[16] 197	3.2	28.3	969	2.6	521	1,122	14
1880	324	6.2	215	3.4	29.6	1,087	3.0	662	1,231	17
1881	342	6.7	239	3.8	32.7	1,161	3.1	892	1,361	20
1882	357	7.1	259	4.0[17] 6.9	34.7	1,192	3.2	1,001[6] 157	1,324	20
1883	384	7.0	268	7.0	35.9	1,247	3.6	162	1,390	21
1884	415	7.2	284	6.8	40.7	1,252	3.7	...	1,421	22
1885	437	7.2	295	6.8	41.0	1,256	4.3	178	1,524	23
1886	440	7.4	290	6.6	42.8	1,250	4.9	165	1,494	24
1887	449	7.7	286	6.8	45.4	1,293	5.5	171	1,527	25
1888	480	8.4	299	7.3	46.4	1,525	6.0[4] 7.7	...	1,794	26
1889	504	8.7	318	7.7	49.2	1,495	8.7	200	1,743	28
1890	538	9.1	326	8.1	53.6	1,503	10.0[16] 10.7	205	1,763	27
1891	568	9.7	341	8.4	55.3	1,629	11.2	209	1,802	28
1892	608	10.8	355	8.0	56.8	1,637	13.1	221	1,826	30
1893	647	12.1	360	8.3	62.4	1,765	13.6	225	1,902	31
1894	780	12.6	365	8.3	64.9	1,758	14.0	224	1,911	31
1895	788	13.2	388	8.5	67.9	1,811	15.1	218	2,046	34
1896	846	13.2	382	8.4	71.9	1,796	16.4	231	2,088	34
1897	923	13.8	410	9.2	74.6	1,860	17.7	251	2,223	34
1898	999	14.2	444	10.3	80.8	1,953	19.2	269	2,345	36
1899	1,112	14.7	470	12.3	84.9	2,057	21.1	...	2,361	38
1900	1,193	15.1	502	14.3	90.4	2,154	23.0	279	2,433	40
1901	1,239	15.4	530	14.2[18]	95.8	2,125	24.7	261	2,391	37
1902	1,298	16.1	568	14.0	100	2,245	27.2	261	2,227	41
1903	1,373	16.5	582	14.1	106	2,323	30.0	275	2,626	40
1904	1,421	17.2	604	15.6	112	2,406	32.4	283	2,812	42
1905	1,421	18.2	648	18.6	122	2,582	34.4	285	3,006	43
1906	1,436	18.8	667	19.2	134	2,728	38.6	328	3,217	45
1907	1,518	19.6	689	20.1	149	2,908	44.1	345	3,220	46
1908	1,598	19.8	708	18.1	157	2,982	47.4	349	3,419	47
1909	1,710	20.5	747	17.9	163	3,177	49.2	366	3,466	48
1910	1,797	21.0	808	20.7	172	3,302	53.1	388	3,758	50
1911	1,909	23.0	848	22.1	174	3,527	55.8	424	3,781	51
1912	1,968	23.9	873	23.7	185	3,760	56.5	454	3,897	...
1913	2,050	23.3	934	25.8	193	3,787	58.1	477	3,724	...
1914	...	21.0	...		199	4,517	53.9	483	3,128	52
1915	...	22.6	...	...	194	4,560	65.0	479	...	45
1916	...	20.6	...	...	203	4,593	67.3	531	...	47
1917	...	...	...	...	211	3,834	69.8	578	...	45
1918	...[1]	...[1]	...	...	214	3,814	61.5	445	...[7]	52[7]
1919	...	...	739		237	5,593	70.1	738	4,039	55

F8 Postal and Telegraph Services

| | Germany | | Greece | | Hungary[9] | | Italy[20] | | Netherlands | | Norway | |
	Mail[5]	Telegrams	Mail	Telegrams (thousands)	Mail[2]	Telegrams	Mail[5,11]	Telegrams	Mail[2]	Telegrams (thousands)	Mail[11]	Telegrams (thousands)
1875	654	11.0	3.9	240	80.5	3.7	239	4.7	...	2,215	...	709
1876	689	10.6	4.4	244	92.2	4.6	262	4.9	96	2,377	11.2	723
1877	717	11.3	4.6	...	95.8	4.7	315	4.9	103	2,405	13.0	794
1878	761	11.4	5.5	...	104	5.6	335	5.0	110	2,413	13.6	718
1879	794	12.4	5.5	367	111	5.3	307	5.3	117	2,705	14.3	680
1880	843	13.5	6.0	370	116	5.1	321	5.9	123	3,109	15.5	773
1881	905	14.3	7.1	481	132	5.3	362	6.0	131	3,282	17.5	847
1882	950	14.8	7.8	494	153	5.7	379	6.3	138	3,365	18.5	876
1883	1,042	15.2	8.3	543	162	5.9	401[20]	6.4[20]	148	3,380	20.4	874
1884	1,083	15.7	9.3	564	175	5.8	414	6.9	155	3,184	21.3	891
1885	1,150	15.8	10.1	550	183	5.8	431	7.0	165	3,183	22.2	860
1886	1,223	16.9	13.1	756	195	6.0	447	7.7	167	3,213	23.9	857
1887	1,303	17.9	11.4	734	242	6.2	364	7.9	166	3,375	24.5	830
1888	1,367	19.7	12.8	905	233	6.8	381	7.8	175	3,553	27.0	1,246
1889	1,493	21.3	11.1	875	245	7.1	388	8.0	182	3,695	28.4	1,373
1890	1,634	22.2	11.4	984	237	7.6	397	8.3	189	3,798	30.8	1,454
1891	1,736	24.5	12.1	899	250	8.3	418	8.2	195	4,014	32.3	1,594
1892	1,828	26.0	12.7	1,036	269	10.0	451	8.4	208	3,924	36.4	1,650
1893	1,917	27.8	12.7	1,163	280	11.6	484	7.9	218	4,021	37.9	1,729
1894	2,016	28.6	12.8	1,141	306	12.1	493	7.9	225	4,034	39.5	1,697
1895	2,104	32.0	12.8	...	318	12.9	522	8.1	243	4,237	42.4	1,799
1896	2,211	32.4	13.6	1,171	351	13.4	551	8.6	261	4,259	44.4	1,818
1897	2,357	34.1	13.9	1,209	373	13.4	597	8.6	268	4,459	47.8	1,941
1898	2,504	36.3	13.5	1,162	401	13.6	628	8.9	286	4,724	51.5	2,049
1899	2,724	38.3	13.4	...	441	13.9	628	9.2	302	4,923	56.6	2,049
1900	3,280	39.7	...	...	488	14.4	677	9.4	315	5,067	57.5	[2,677][21]
1901	3,557	38.9	19.3	1,205	512	14.7	747	9.6	340	5,392	60.9	2,195
1902	3,800	38.4	21.0	...	520	15.4	807	9.9	356	5,503	63.9	2,157
1903	4,019	39.3	23.0	1,308	559	15.9	906	10.1	393	5,671	70.0	2,221
1904	4,232	40.2	24.8	1,311	592	17.1	926	10.5	418	5,608	73.7	2,276
1905	4,423	42.7	23.9	1,413	638	17.8	873	11.1	441	5,919	77.0	2,250
1906	4,831	43.6	25.0	1,541	683	18.9	903	11.5	449	5,974	80.4	2,390
1907	5,339	45.8	27.1	1,608	752	20.4	994	11.7	483	5,970	90.0	2,520
1908	5,488	45.0	28.1	1,429	773	20.6	1,052	12.4	502	5,943	87.5	2,725
1909	5,821	46.8	30.1	1,516	806	22.2	1,137	12.7	527	6,171	90.4	2,774
1910	5,677	48.2	30.8	1,734	865	23.6	1,239	15.2	538	6,173	104	3,035
1911	5,994	49.6	...	1,701	922	25.3	1,464	18.9	558	6,404	109	3,270
1912	6,461	52.3	...	1,702	954	26.5	1,478	20.0	584	6,544	117	3,616
1913	7,024	52.3	...	...	1,020		1,515	21.0	610	6,477	124	3,727
1914	...	...	...	...	1,076	30.7	1,531	22.0	...	7,348	112	3,866
1915	...	...	53.3	2,931	...	41.4	2,052	22.3	673	8,195	127	4,572
1916	...	...	29.1	2,916	1,597	44.8	2,202	20.3	685	7,982	145	5,688
1917	...	...	33.5	3,450	1,648	42.3	2,533	19.8	705	7,256	138	6,283
1918	...[7]	...[7]	43.3	4,452	...	...	2,372	18.2	774	7,814	160	6,204
1919	4,346	82.8	55.6	4,773	...	...	2,127	21.9	838	10,259	174	6,560

F8 Postal and Telegraphs Services

	Portugal		Romania[39]		Russia		Serbia[25]	
	Mail	Telegrams[23] (thousands)	Mail	Telegrams (thousands)	Mail	Telegrams	Mail[2]	Telegrams (thousands)
1875	...	865	6.0	872	128[24]	4.2	...	...
1876	...	1,055	...	...	141	4.6	...	...
1877	...	...	11	960	188	5.4	...	...
1878	24	...	...	1,116	204	5.8	...	...
1879	26	1,117	...	...	200	6.4	...	...
1880	28	1,078	...	950	220	7.3	...	...
1881	34	1,122	13	1,150	239	8.9	...	...
1882	32	1,148	16	1,214	252	9.8	...	...
1883	34	1,206	17	1,244	255	10	...	...
1884	36	1,136	16	1,204	271	10	...	...
1885	39	1,191	19	1,224	292	11	...	...
1886	41	1,237	18	1,231	307	10	8.3	...
1887	43	1,105	19	1,257	329	9.9	8.6	396
1888	46	1,241	25	1,318	355	...	8.9	471
1889	51	1,355	...	1,328	371	...	11.3[25]	458[25]
1890	57	[2,172][22]	...	1,358	384	11	[14.7]	...
1891	60	[2,124][22]	28	1,523	418	12	14.5	617
1892	59	1,870	29	1,539	440	13	16.9	653
1893	56	1,711	34	1,593	464	13	17.3	888
1894	55	1,762	39	1,804	503	14	17.9[4] 14.4	885
1895	65	1,808	52	2,131	545	15	15.0	885
1896	61	1,762	55	2,195	593	16	15.7	901
1897	66	1,820	67	2,158	653	16	16.6	970
1898	64	1,961	73	2,399	711	18	17.4	1,018
1899	67	2,119	68	2,086	770	18	18.3	1,078
1900	67	2,199	62	2,063	849	20	21	1,172
1901	73	2,227	61	2,108	948	20	21	1,083
1902	77	2,337	89	2,342	1,007	20	21	1,169
1903	86	2,404	103	2,317	1,140	21	26	1,176
1904	91	2,641[23] 1,515	102	2,212	1,378	25	31	1,233
1905	94	1,533	222	2,651	1,529	26	40	1,332
1906	96	1,596	225	3,018	1,503	28	44	1,417
1907	107	1,611	151	2,925	1,634	30	55	1,563
1908	108	1,985	165	2,777	1,777	30	53	1,629
1909	104	1,821	153	2,937	1,944	34	55	1,814
1910	112	1,954	158	3,197	...	37	65	1,996
1911	108	2,024	167	3,492	...	41	65	1,463
1912	...	2,139[23]	175	3,685	...	45	76	...
1913	126	3,698	198	3,826	...	98	...	...
1914	...	3,740	...	3,865	...	...	...	...
1915	...	3,947	...	...	...	...	...	...
1916	...	4,378	...	...	...	...	...	...
1917	...	4,966	...	...	...	...	...	...
1918	...	5,749	...	...	...	...	...	...
1919	126	6,067	...	...	...	...	24	...

F8 Postal and Telegraph Services

	Spain		Mail[5,13]	Sweden Telegrams (thousands)	Mail[5]	Switzerland Telegrams (thousands)	Mail	United Kingdom Telegrams
	Mail	Telegrams						
1875	87.1	1.6	26	994	76.6	2,656	1,376	20.8
1876	88.6	1.6	28	983	70.1	2,706	1,411[27]	21.6[27]
1877	78.2	...	31[13]	1,016	70.4	2,527	1,478	22.2
			35					
1878	76.9	2.1	37	932	70.9	2,179	1,536	24.5
1879	...	...	36	860	75.7	2,325	1,588	26.5
1880	...	2.3	41	986	79.6	2,505	1,662	29.9
1881	95	2.6	43	1,118	84.7	2,717	1,776	31.4
1882	...	2.9	47	1,175	88.1	2,636	1,854	32.0
1883	111	3.2	49	1,209	90.0	2,586	1,914	32.7
1884	118	3.2	53	1,179	91.3	2,560	1,984	33.3
1885	...	3.3	59	1,167	96.3	2,623	2,065	39.1
1886	121	3.6	61	1,172	99.5	2,751	2,159	50.2
1887	124	3.8	62	1,190	98.4	2,825	2,243	53.3
1888	133	4.1	65	1,368	110	3,026	2,324	57.7
1889	164	4.2	66	1,709	111	3,226	2,469	62.3
1890	164	4.5	72	1,755	120	3,185	2,578	66.5
1891	194	4.9	75	1,850	126	3,214	2,667	69.8
1892	169	5.4	78	1,867	133	3,150	2,732	69.9
1893	167	4.3	78	1,863	144	3,181	2,800	70.9
1894	168	5.0	82	1,807	145	3,120	2,851	71.5
1895	173	5.4	86	1,905	155	3,252	2,970	78.8
1896	175	5.5	93	1,989	166	3,183	3,079	79.5
1897	...	5.4	101	2,120	173	3,153	3,250	83.1
1898	264	5.5	105	2,295	190	3,254	3,426	87.0
1899	332	5.1	112	2,489	208	3,359	3,514	90.4
1900	361	5.1	121	2,506	224[26]	3,272	3,642	89.6
					267			
1901	381	4.6	138	2,579	284	3,234	3,833	90.4
1902	411	4.7	163	2,556	298	3,274	4,056	92.5
1903	412	4.8	179	2,638	300	3,371	4,206	90.0
1904	...	4.9	188	2,749	325	3,485	4,383	89.0
1905	433	5.2	194	2,920	344	3,736	4,585	89.4
1906	435	5.2	205	3,195	365	3,949	4,759	89.5
1907	330	5.6	223	3,510	367	3,909	4,863	86.0
1908	292	6.0	216	3,574	380	2,904	4,922	84.8
1909	333	6.3	223	3,714	397	4,099	4,988	86.9
1910	361	6.7	237	3,900	419	4,396	5,161	86.7
1911	376	6.4	258	4,136	461	4,717	5,359	89.2
1912	393	7.0	270	4,636	480	4,862	5,479	88.5
1913	459	7.4	277	4,799	497	4,831	5,783	87.1
1914	491	7.6	276	5,504	373	5,282	5,520	91.2
1915	511	7.7	279	6,557	361	5,217	...	84.2
1916	518	8.9	287	6,967	395	5,076	...	79.0
1917	529	10.6	349	7,059	401	4,403	...	80.0
1918	551	11.0	391	6,887	386	5,273	...	89.0
1919	602	13.2	375	8,390	418	7,707	5,732	101.0

F8 Postal and Telegraphs Services

1920–1964

	Austria[1] Mail	Telegrams (thousands)	Belgium Mail	Telegrams	Czechoslovakia Mail	Telegrams	Denmark Mail[3]	Telegrams (thousands)	Finland Mail[5]	Telegrams[6] (thousands)	France Mail[5]	Telegrams
1920	...	...	788	24.0	762	23.0	264	5,175	65.1	836	4,162	51
1921	...	5,871	849	20.4	785	21.8	242	4,555	65.5	881	4,150	48
1922	742	...	950	19.0	750	17.3	230	4,400	68.5	875	4,467	49 28
												56
1923	674	6,903	1,020	20.3	719	14.5	236	4,760	74.1	924	4,958	57
1924	635	6,123	1,048	18.4	707	15.8	239	4,733	78.9	948 4	5,326	55
										858		
1925	773	5,481	1,084	14.7	798	15.7	253	4,721	84.7	863	5,678	54
1926	890	5,957	1,091	14.2	908	15.2	254	4,509	87.0	900	6,086	48
1927	886	5,448	1,130	12.2	909	15.7	254	4,475	95.1	883	5,920	45
1928	954	5,177	1,207	11.3	966	16.4	273	4,460	98.8	932	6,057	47
1929	968	4,883	1,390	11.9	1,084	17.1	273	4,614	105	848	6,146	48
1930	986	4,118	1,453	10.9	1,111	15.9	281	4,311	102	728	6,281	47
1931	846	3,162	1,351	9.8	998	14.1	275	3,969	94.7	597	6,308	45
1932	789	2,579	1,385	8.2	1,026	11.7	294	3,452	83.9	530	5,704	42
1933	770	2,425	1,313	7.6	940	9.9	286	3,432	84.4	523	5,625	40
1934	713	2,500	1,304	7.0	657	9.8	284	3,221	90.2	531	5,610	37
1935	770	2,540	1,292	7.1	661	10.5	289	3,160	93.2	542	5,582	39
1936	770	2,510	1,412	7.4	715	10.7	301	3,214	101	562	5,704	39
1937	...	...	1,430	7.7	710	11.3	321	3,166	113	581	5,707	38
1938	...	...	1,425	7.4	...	12.2	333	3,169	118	597	5,664	36
1939	...	...	1,397	7.6	...	...	342	3,388	119	660	5,261	40
1940	...	...	...	...	...	...	352	1,609	130	589	4,354	32
1941	...	...	662	1.0	...	...	292	1,583	185	597	4,572	27
1942	...	...	660	2.1	...	...	305	1,748	191	672	3,493	32
1943	...	...	696	3.9	...	...	325	3,917	202	777	3,723	40
1944	...	...	...	2.8	...	...	350	4,156	202	920	2,342	33
1945	...	...	...	5.6	...	...	354	3,296	180	975	3,694	56
1946	...	...	1,248	9.8	825	6.4	379	4,134	182	1,130	3,989	46
1947	478	6,069	1,492	10.3	...	...	430	4,260	195	1,161	3,841	39
1948	485	3,935	1,691	9.7	998	7.5	439	4,436	200	1,095	3,924	33
1949	484	4,355	1,825	9.2	927	7.8	431	4,491	184	1,031	3,838	24
1950	535	4,877	1,975	9.4	998	8.2	451 4	4,577	170	1,068	4,050	25
							415		182	1,158	4,293	25
1951	592	5,556	1,829	9.2	1,103	8.6	433	4,535	190	1,155	4,504	24
1952	557	4,794	1,851	8.7	1,149	8.7	437	4,310	241	1,080	4,493	24
1953	695	4,019	1,832	8.6	1,126	9.0	441	4,781	244	1,172	4,710	25
1954	734	4,251	1,942	8.6	1,174	9.4	459	4,864				
1955	670	4,510	2,093	8.8	1,261	9.7	466	4,755	246	1,235	4,996	26
1956	726	4,711	2,125	8.7	1,311	10.0	479	4,605	292	1,211	5,313	27
1957	781	4,821	2,323	8.3	1,353	10.1	483	4,488	314 4	1,171	5,629	27
1958	817	4,606	2,609	7.8	1,443	10.1	497	4,270	279	1,110	5,802	25
1959	895	4,646	2,405	7.3	1,543	10.5	533	4,294	304	1,164	6,062	23
1960	886	4,574	2,335	7.3	1,681	11.6	547	4,364	339	1,150	6,093	22
1961	933	4,619	2,388	7.0	1,836	12.7	571	4,262	372	1,174	6,471	23
1962	962	4,841	2,387	7.0	1,935	13.0	599	4,196	443	1,166	6,737	25
1963	991	4,967	2,354	7.0	1,960	12.9	620	4,183	401	1,129	6,954	25
1964	1,027	5,091	2,452	7.0	1,974	12.9	637	4,046	442	1,121	7,255	26

F8   Postal and Telegraph Services

	Germany			Greece		Hungary[9]		Ireland[32]		Italy[20]		Netherlands	
	Mail[5]	Telegrams		Mail	Telegrams	Mail[30]	Tele-grams	Mail[2]	Tele-grams	Mail[5,11]	Tele-grams	Mail[33]	Tele-grams (thousands)
1920	4,705	79.6		67.3	5,123	186	10.6	...	...	1,808	20.7	833	10,165
1921	4,821	81.5		67.5	5,042	216	14.7	...	...	1,809	19.4	804	9,804
1922	3,912	63.2		73.3	5,231	208	10.5	...	...	1,731	19.1	822	8,458
1923	3,225	57.1		68.6	5,050	183	5.0	...	...	1,801	23.5	776	7,915
1924	4,387	42.7		76.9	5,974	189[16] 202	4.7	204	3.8	1,829	26.7	791	8,692
1925	6,667	47.3		84.1	6,532	246	4.9	198	3.5	2,021	28.0	802	8,416
1926	6,763	43.7		86.7	5,928	276	5.3	201	3.3	2,005	28.7	810	8,443
1927	7,678	45.0		99.0	4,716	316	5.0	197	3.1	2,167	29.5	854	8,113
1928	7,771	41.1		107	4,663	333	5.0	203	3.0	2,173	31.6	915	8,030
1929	7,663	37.5		118	4,678	356	5.0	202	2.5	2,363	31.2	1,024	7,808
1930	6,461	31.7		122	4,578	353	4.5	...	2.1	2,406	29.6	1,081	7,191
1931	5,924	25.1		120	4,258	300	3.4	206	2.0	2,309	26.7	1,081	6,521
1932	5,600	21.3		113	4,463	274	2.6	...	1.8	2,236	25.7	1,016	5,529
1933	5,504	20.8		109	4,549	269	2.4	193	1.7	2,279	24.9	1,017	5,314
1934	5,564	19.3		115	4,650	339	2.3	191	1.6	2,445	24.5	1,016	4,901
1935	5,765	19.0		117	4,083	332	2.3	...	1.5	2,557	25.1	997	4,547
1936	6,434	19.7		118	5,239	358	2.4	197	1.5	2,598	25.3	990	4,715
1937	6,815	19.4		116	4,901	386[30] 471	2.6	219	1.5	2,767	26.4	1,078	5,306
1938	7,932[55]	26.5		113	4,884	510	2.9	...	1.5	2,856	28.5	1,120[33] 1,227	5,429 7,380[34]
1939	7,805[55]	29.8		111	5,088	610	3.7[31] 3.2	226	1.5	3,003	33.3	...	8,004
1940	8,288[55]	35.9		...	...	707	4.1	220	1.5	3,389	37.0	990	5,175
1941	...	...		...	...	953	6.1	...	1.4	3,657	40.6	941	2,450
1942	...	...		...	...	1,053	7.4	186	1.7	...	...	...	6,419
1943	...	...		...	...	...	...	...	1.9	...	...	...	10,863
1944	...	...		...	...	...	...	...	2.1	...	...	...	9,620

	East Germany		West Germany[29]										
	Mail	Telegrams	Mail[11]	Telegrams									
1945	...	...	...	...	35.7	...	...	...	228	2.2	...	18.8	...	5,034
1946	...	...	...	...	62.3	...	166	3.6	...	2.5	2,481	25.8	1,479	12,842
1947	...	...	...	...	80.9	5,079	408[30]	3.6	...	2.8	2,580	24.4	1,569	11,172
1948	...	...	...	...	85.8	4,942	339	4.7	...	2.9	2,651	26.0	1,697	11,857
1949	...	...	3,904	27	138	5,138	325	3.7	272	2.6	2,617	28.1	1,693	11,703
1950	1,120	9.8	4,181	28	137	5,880	395	4.0	276	2.6	2,797	30.2	1,702	11,522
1951	1,104	7.8	4,497	26	140	6,438	384	4.3	277	2.7	3,054	29.4	1,711	10,532
1952	1,097	7.3	4,949	27	146	5,934	440	4.9	287	2.4	3,185	29.7	1,839	9,832
1953	1,148	7.6	5,234	28	152	5,698	463	5.3	292	2.6	3,423	30.4	1,870	9,757
1954	1,226	7.5	5,551[29] 5,744	28[29] 29	180	5,995	495	5.8	318	2.4	3,565	32.2	1,974	9,612
1955	1,249	7.6	6,161	29	185	6,173	469	5.7	332	2.3	3,876	34.4	2,007	9,720
1956	1,246	8.0	6,687	30	188	6,331	430	6.2	...	1.9	4,339	35.1	2,124	9,785
1957	1,306	8.6	7,158	32	202	6,098	404	6.2	314	1.4	4,648	34.4	2,022	9,142
1958	1,335	8.6	7,637	31	210	6,041	429	6.5	326	1.3	4,834	33.0	2,032	8,595
1959	1,309	9.3	7,914[29]	32	211	5,986	492	6.9	...	1.2	4,867	33.5	2,068	8,603
1960	1,355	10.3	8,498	33	206	5,927	559	7.4	...	1.2	5,147	34.5	2,178	8,553
1961	1,136	10.7	9,092	32	221	6,392	566	7.6	352	1.1	5,116	36.4	2,240	8,164
1962	1,152	10.7	9,315	33	225	6,592	503	8.0	...	1.1	5,292	39.3	2,373	8,024
1963	1,341	11.4	9,056	32	239	7,183	537	8.6	360	1.0	5,664	40.9	2,490	7,972
1964	1,337	11.2	9,275	32	211	7,675	514	8.9	351	1.0	[2,869][20]	[21.6][20]	2,568[4]	8,029[34,35]

F8 Postal and Telegraphs Services

1920–1964

	Norway		Poland		Portugal		Romania[39]		Spain	
	Mail[11]	Telegrams (thousands)	Mail[11]	Telegrams	Mail	Telegrams (thousands)	Mail	Telegrams (thousands)	Mail	Telegrams[41]
1920	161	7,068	414	6.5	...	6,385	...[39]	5,807	549	14.6
1921	141	5,959	507	7.4	113	6,435	...	[6,670][39]	553	15.7
1922	148	5,557	595	7.6	139	6,818	...	5,443	656	15.1
1923	144	5,277	673	7.7	123	4,551	247	8,778	714	14.6
1924	143	5,078	584	7.8	...	3,988	322	9,224	563	16.0
1925	155	5,094	672	8.7	...	4,957	338	9,511	589	15.7
1926	145	4,836	736	7.7	...	5,155	324	9,945	605	15.7
1927	145	4,638	833	8.1	...	5,403	327	8,084	884	14.6
1928	149	4,515	934	7.7	135[37]	5,286[23] 2,939	407	8,006	709	14.0
1929	151	4,471	999	7.2	155	2,799	428	8,101	753	13.8
1930	154	4,448	978	6.3	159	...	376	7,619	772	13.5
1931	150	4,095	847	5.1	159	...	379	6,400	868	13.3[41] 24.5
1932	149	3,809	691	3.6	166	2,091	311	4,938	885	21.6
1933	148	3,649	677	3.1	152	2,420	278	4,277	884	21.8
1934	155	3,555	742	3.2	159	2,239	326	4,290	852	25.9
1935	159	3,509	735	3.5	174	2,293	386	4,125	948	26.9
1936	166	3,643	885	3.7	182	2,722	375	3,946	...	...
1937	183	3,927	908	3.9	...	2,772	455	4,413	...	...
1938	191	3,907	1,002	4.2	201	2,769	422	4,553	...	...
1939	195	3,930	...	...	[156][38]	2,910	462	5,448	...	...
1940	171	3,950	...	...	...	3,070	408	4,796	601	27.7
1941	195	3,568	...	...	[160][38]	3,458	344	6,420	690	31.3
1942	219	4,570	...	...	167	3,845	214	7,806[40]	653	26.3
1943	239	6,210	...	...	180	4,420	...	...	690	32.6
1944	245	7,553	...	...		4,961	...	...	769	33.8
1945	249	7,816	...	...	[187][38]	5,517	...	...	790	38.1
1946	273	7,966	510	6.1	[195][38]	6,230	...	...	832	42.8
1947	271	8,256	769	7.6	[218][38]	6,124	...	...	892	43.3
1948	274	7,576	818	6.0	[220][38]	5,370	190	3,056	1,019	42.2
1949	282	7,296	820	6.3	237	3,939	...	...	1,095	40.3
1950	288	6,956	844	7.2	263	3,639	318	3,504	1,195	40.9
1951	288	6,912	912	7.9	263	3,644	363	4,193	1,127	43.5
1952	304	6,699	1,025	8.7	286	3,502	478	3,771	1,210	45.4
1953	317	6,282	1,086	9.3	308	3,459	891	4,659	1,278	45.4
1954	327	6,121	1,177	9.9	325	3,417	900	4,670	1,377	43.8
1955	350	6,006	1,312[36] 716	10	364	3,536	908	4,486	1,422	41.2
1956	360	5,978	781	11	400	3,651	955	4,795	1,582	43.6
1957	382	5,912	829	11	425	3,661	958	4,847	1,784	45.1
1958	400	5,411	867	11[37] 10	442	3,739	1,066	4,715	2,129	43.6
1959	413	5,140	919	10	461	3,886	1,124	4,523	2,348	41.6
1960	435	5,055	953	9.9	483	3,887	1,218	4,635	2,437	39.1
1961	458	4,904	972	10	486	4,008	1,349	4,972	2,055	39.8
1962	462	4,746	1,016	11	497	4,049	1,405	5,304	2,152	42.5
1963	467	4,348	1,079	12	508	4,197	1,461	5,724	2,261	44.5
1964	490	4,057	1,155	12	522	4,336	1,497	5,901	2,607	46.4

F8 Postal and Telegraph Services

	Sweden		Switzerland		UK		Yugoslavia	
	Mail[5]	Telegrams (thousands)	Mail[5]	Telegrams (thousands)	Mail	Telegrams	Mail[47]	Telegrams (thousands)
1920	380	8,414	470	7,134	5,579	88	214	7,325
1921	366	6,833	456	5,423	5,231[44]	83[44]	228	8,708
1922	353	6,329	429	4,625	5,455	80	245	6,143
1923	397	6,259	455	4,644	5,585	78	185	...
1924	413	6,262	473	5,093	5,840	79	169	7,027
1925	420	6,409	520	5,103	6,060	77	189	6,556
1926	443	6,427	526	4,866	5,800	75	282	5,549
1927	454	6,460	542	4,916	6,200	74	295	5,700
1928	490	6,577	580	4,871	6,230	72	350	5,949
1929	511	6,556	593	4,756	6,400	71	370	6,204
1930	541	6,260	642	4,390	6,475	66	382	6,530
1931	552	5,911	660	4,002	6,540	61	417	6,027
1932	571	5,171	626	3,304	6,640	57	401	4,473
1933	563	5,011	631	3,168	6,753	58	377	4,087
1934	586	4,984	632	2,846	6,935	55	399	3,859
1935	622	5,061	650	2,679	7,345	65	406	4,005
1936	626	5,143	622	2,699	7,690	72	432	3,981
1937	660	5,388	649	2,814	7,990	71[45] 57	481	3,923
1938	704	5,348	656	2,720	8,150[46] 8,240	58	505	3,930
1939	713	5,913	620	3,031	7,460	63	528	4,276
1940	731	5,391	540	3,168	6,310	61	...	...
1941	753	5,151	589	3,004	6,150	67	...	...
1942	849	5,437	597	2,711	6,390	76	...	...
1943	895	5,909	620	2,871	6,480	71	...	...
1944	967	5,378	626	2,956	6,600	71	...	...
1945	975	7,278	689	3,545	6,550	74	...	...
1946	1,066	[4,021][42]	790	4,478	7,300	63	425	3,617
1947	1,010	8,340	859	4,961	7,600	58	542	4,502
1948	999	8,267	879	4,922	8,050	54	666	5,762
1949	1,021	8,210	925	4,586	8,350	52	775	6,900
1950	1,063	8,643	939	4,570	8,500	65	786	7,493
1951	1,080	8,785	960	4,723	8,750	62	634	6,101
1952	1,098	8,291	1,004	4,486	8,800	58	465	2,943
1953	1,119	7,911	1,045	4,581	9,100	56	467	3,408
1954	1,184[43] 1,082	7,887	1,080	4,652	9,500	48	459	3,858
1955	1,149	7,892	1,179	4,873	9,700	43	505	4,763
1956	1,231	7,861	1,216	4,956	9,700	39	566	5,400
1957	1,272	7,780	1,264	5,055	9,600	37	652	6,406
1958	1,287	7,132	1,337	4,945	9,700	35	745	7,187
1959	1,305	6,872	1,409	5,207	10,200	35	808	7,669
1960	1,425	6,857	1,503	5,267	10,600	35	912	8,943
1961	1,511	6,728	1,596	5,491	10,500	34	939	9,869
1962	1,598	6,614	1,702	5,615	10,600	33	974	10,580
1963	1,589	6,410	1,751	5,670	11,000	31	1,008	12,668
1964	1,730	6,410	1,756	5,738	11,200	32	1,151	14,410

F8 Postal and Telegraphs Services

1965–1993

	Austria[1]		Belgium		Czechoslovakia		Denmark		Finland		France	
	Mail	Telegrams (thousands)	Mail	Telegrams (thousands)	Mail[5]	Telegrams	Mail[3]	Telegrams (thousands)	Mail[5]	Telegrams[6] (thousands)	Mail[5]	Telegrams
1965	1,061	5,186	2,574	7,066	2,087	13	660	4,176	471	1,121	7,432	25
1966	1,075	5,064	2,522	7,092	2,132	13	697	4,030	526	1,115	7,854	26
1967	1,031	4,655	2,428	6,625	2,092	13	716	3,839	563	1,064	8,116	25
1968	1,024	4,489	2,584	6,388	2,068	14	749	3,627	619	1,074	7,726	25
1969	1,032	4,330	2,637	6,391	1,989	15	777	3,396	640	1,061	8,094	27[19] 23
1970	1,081	4,026	2,693	6,678	2,013	14	820	2,942	691	1,083	8,260	23
1971	1,122	3,819	2,818	4,772	2,045	14	870	2,623[48]	719	1,055	8,453	24
1972	1,148	3,603	2,647	4,464	2,031	14	911	1,954	783	1,052	8,965	23
1973	1,218	3,510	2,694	4,352	2,062	14	928	1,838	802	944	9,331	23
1974	1,292	3,364	2,601	4,167	2,178	14	964	1,672	738	940	8,641	21
1975	1,393	3,075	2,317	3,705	2,184	14	953	1,481	740	912	9,604	20
1976	1,369	2,665	2,463	3,219	2,231	14	960	1,361	725	854	9,660	19
1977	1,383	2,356	2,865	2,789	2,253	14	988	1,268	723	818	9,987	18
1978	1,414	2,237	3,224	2,555	2,306	14	1,020	1,070	768	832	10,161	18
1979	1,516	2,170	3,419	2,375	2,347	14	1,054	997	735	820	10,306	16
1980	1,593	2,124	3,268	2,306	2,337	11	1,093	943	870	797	10,514	14
1981	1,643	2,018	3,038	2,080	2,389	10	1,126	844	950	771	10,773	13
1982	1,741	1,852	2,803	1,877	2,451	10	1,108	710	999	752	11,012	12
1983	1,885	1,803	2,601	1,686	2,464	9.9	1,074	638	1,117[4]	725	11,100	12
1984	1,994	1,729	2,616	1,344	2,542	9.8	1,075	588	1,031	683	11,446	12
1985	2,069	1,756	2,655	1,174	2,648	9.5	1,034	331	1,094	661	11,797	13
1986	2,115	1,729	2,595	1,052	2,728	9.4	1,161	309	1,124	536	12,507[49] 13,881	12
1987	2,201	1,737	2,745	967	2,755	9.2	1,217	455	1,103	577	15,342	12
1988	2,316	1,721	2,988	891	2,840	8.9	1,252	421	1,202	544	16,487	12
1989	2,439	1,693	2,918	868	2,869	8.8	1,312	401	1,306	575	17,713	12
1990	2,424	1,691	2,973	816	3,778	8.1	1,337	338	1,335	477	18,577	12
1991	2,412	1,604	3,036	770	3,129	6.7	1,384	...	1,259	48	19,745	11
1992	2,362	1,496	2,940	643	2,334[57]	4.1	1,321	...	1,183	...	20,747	11
1993	2,494	1,145	...	...	1,481[57]	3.1	1,296	...	1,158	...	21,741	11

	East Germany		West Germany[29]		Greece		Hungary		Ireland[32]		Italy	
	Mail	Telegrams	Mail[11]	Telegrams	Mail	Telegrams	Mail[30]	Telegrams	Mail[2]	Telegrams	Mail[5,11]	Telegrams
1965	1,353	11.8	9,673	31	310	7,879	522[30] 1,465	8.9	358	0.9	5,600	37.5
1966	1,310	11.5	9,436	29	281	8,159	1,532	9.2	359	0.8	5,850	31.8
1967	1,390	11.4	9,358	26	251	7,862 7,480[51]	9.8	364	0.8	5,923	29.0
1968	1,334	11.8	9,787	25	262	6,203	1,678	10.0	372	0.8	5,936	26.4
1969	1,380	12.1	10,177	25	259	6,355	1,714	9.2	378	0.8	6,292	26.4
1970	1,376	12.3	10,680	24	270	6,246	1,776	9.7	387	0.8	6,356	25.9
1971	1,360	11.4	11,526	21	273	6,313	1,858	9.8	382	0.7	6,267	25.2
1972	1,272	10.6	11,102	18	367	6,254	1,932	10.1	382	0.7	6,589	25.5
1973	1,286	10.7	10,425	17	385	6,343	1,964	10.0	365	0.7	6,473	25.7
1974	1,257	10.6	10,490	16	[298][50]	6,637	2,023	10.7	382[32]	0.7[32]	6,432	24.3
1975	1,219	10.9	10,479	15	386	5,474	2,061[30] 1,990	11.3	387	0.7	5,889	23.0
1976	1,242	11.0	11,131	14	409	5,000	...	11.3	390	0.6	5,494	24.2
1977	1,279	11.2	11,460	14	431	5,272	2,196	11.8	408	0.6	5,000	22.1
1978	1,246	11.3	12,163	13	439	5,035	2,262	12.3	406	0.6	5,268	22.7
1979	1,242	12.0	12,176	13	454	4,626	2,082	12.6	241	0.4	5,567	23.8
1980	1,256	11.8	12,240	13	454	3,739	2,066	13.4	403	0.5	5,566	25.5
1981	1,249	12.0	12,738	12	438	3,666	2,056	11.8	426	0.5	5,841	24.6
1982	1,245	12.5	12,923	10[56] 6.3	427	3,117	2,097	11.5	378	0.4	6,042	23.8
1983	1,240	12.6	12,874	6.0	435	2,824	2,155	11.9	388	0.3	6,039	22.8
1984	1,238	12.8	12,712	5.9	443	2,818	2,217	12.3	415	0.3	6,362	22.3
1985	1,273	12.8	12,643	5.7	418	2,729	2,238	12.1	434	0.2	6,375	23.0
1986	1,271	13.3	13,279	5.4	425	2,406	2,272	12.4	447	0.1	6,653	22.7
1987	1,283	13.9	13,333	5.3	433	2,835	2,154	12.8	456	—	7,222	23.2
1988	1,279	14.4	13,808	5.2	451	2,585	2,171	12.8	465	—	7,574	23.0
1989	...	...	13,886	5.1	475	2,735	2,022	11.9	472	—	8,568	23.5
1990	Included in West Germany		14,244	6.3	438	2,725	2,131	10.7	482	—	8,554	23.5
1991			15,564	...	...	2,593	2,017	9.2	494	—	7,910	24.6
1992			16,600	...	...	2,399	2,093	8.0	484	—	7,843	24.4
1993			18,300	...	...	1,899	1,909	6.6	518	—	...	...

F8 Postal and Telegraph Services

1965–1993

	Netherlands Mail	Telegrams[35] (thousands)	Norway Mail	Telegrams (thousands)	Poland Mail	Telegrams[54] (thousands)	Portugal Mail	Telegrams (thousands)	Romania Mail	Telegrams (thousands)
1965	2,394	3,700	515	3,868	1,226	12	534	4,591	1,539	6,186
1966	2,462	3,527	522	3,147	1,315	13	544	4,738	1,566	6,714
1967	2,462	3,196	546	3,707	1,405	14	551	4,895	1,618	6,776
1968	2,597	3,051	554	3,520	1,478	15	560	4,977	1,654	6,688
1969	2,792	2,868	580	3,412	1,544	15	572	5,113	1,741	6,851
1970	2,941	2,771	601	3,169	1,587	15	583	5,090	1,730	5,860
1971	3,065	2,508	623	2,970	1,640	16	596	5,073	1,910	6,041
1972	3,057	2,134	655	2,705	1,665	16	656	4,925	2,067	6,352
1973	3,105	2,031	677	2,342	1,380	14	704	4,891	2,161	6,370
1974	3,260	1,989	703	1,958	1,437	14	711	4,542	1,958	6,501
1975	3,456	1,806	653	1,651	1,458	16	549	3,582	1,999	6,160
1976	3,602	1,617	694	1,555	1,482	18	528	3,053	2,010	5,664
1977	3,737	1,470	778	1,455	1,505	18	556	2,615	2,197	5,992
1978	3,913	1,360	839	1,352	1,542	19	518	2,224	2,287	5,602
1979	4,060	1,272	882	1,278	1,544	19	508	2,205	2,391	5,393
1980	4,210	1,202	943	1,146	1,502	19	520	2,134	2,410	5,389
1981	4,154	1,066	1,033	1,014	1,446	18[54] / 17	450	1,869	2,417	5,574
1982	4,187	968	1,037	854	1,334	12	459	1,849	1,919	4,329
1983	4,200	879	1,135	676	1,398	15	477	1,701	2,738	4,198
1984	...	...	1,169	606	1,369	16	466	1,475	1,726	4,116
1985	4,585	773	1,253	540	1,244	17	468	1,427	1,750	4,225
1986	4,789	733	1,382	433	1,239	18	491	1,405	...	...
1987	5,054	708	1,455	331	1,285	16	524	...	...	...
1988	5,361	658	1,515	274	1,335	16	565	...	...	...
1989	5,498	540	1,829	278	1,125	18	602	...		
1990	...	278	1,845	258	950	12	657	...		
1991	...	...	1,938	217	893	10	749	...		
1992	...	...	2,019	182	1,230	8	815	...		
1993	...	...	2,089	...	1,396	7	...	...		

	Spain Mail	Telegrams[41]	Sweden Mail[5]	Telegrams[42] (thousands)	Switzerland Mail[5]	Telegrams (thousands)	U.K. Mail	Telegrams	Yugoslavia Mail[47]	Telegrams
1965	2,992	50	1,732	6,314	1,813	5,721	11,300	31	1,158	12
1966	3,308	50	1,824	6,293	1,851	5,666	11,400	31	1,199	11
1967	3,641	46	1,829	5,935	1,844	5,555	11,500	31	1,244	11
1968	3,758	44	1,890	5,515	1,750	5,346	11,300	29	1,248	11
1969	3,891	44	1,915	5,162	1,799	5,331	11,400	29	1,260	13
1970	4,069	42	2,026	4,863	1,912	4,902	10,500	26	1,290	15
1971	4,191	40	1,979	4,438	1,998	4,750	10,550	27	1,279	15
1972	4,236	39	2,014	3,689[4] / 3,465	2,031	4,266	10,790	27	1,302	16
1973	4,362	37	2,153	3,329	1,970	4,158	11,010	28	1,288	15
1974	4,426	36	2,216	2,611	1,972	3,912	10,878	26	1,280	16
1975	4,535	35	2,295	2,298	1,950	3,286	9,903	21	1,255	16
1976	4,641	34	2,448	1,903	1,940	2,952	9,383	19	1,300	17
1977	4,327	36	2,446	1,480	2,108	2,791	9,485	17	1,293	18
1978	6,379	35	2,516	973	2,200	2,617	9,965	17	1,320	18
1979	4,698	36	2,694	841	2,337	2,519	10,207	16	1,363	18
1980	5,169	28	2,704	755	2,435	2,526	10,071	14	1,407	18
1981	4,747	25	2,701	688	2,498	2,417	9,985	12	1,424	17
1982	4,549	25	2,705	597	2,610	2,219	10,255	7.7[53]	1,402	17
1983	4,360	24	2,844	498	2,794	2,116	10,665	5.7	1,393	18
1984	4,196	24	2,872[52] / 2,615	442	2,823	2,205	11,439	...	1,425	18
1985	4,217	24	2,771	409[42]	2,926	2,137	11,721	...	1,429	18
1986	4,502	23	2,844	362	3,036[4]	2,043	12,535	...	1,410	18
1987	4,582	22	3,041	336	3,379	...	13,568	...	1,417	18
1988	5,210	25	3,242	312	3,507	...	13,741	...	1,385	16
1989	5,574	25	3,943	278	3,745	...	15,293	...	1,370	...
1990	5,626	26	4,061	236	3,871	...	15,902	...	1,239	...
1991	...	26	4,314	249	3,747	...	16,038	...	421	5
1992	...	26	4,099	117[58]	3,685	...	16,364	...	322	4
1993	...	25	4,267	113[58]	3,860	...	16,651	...	252	3

F8 Postal and Telegraphs Services

NOTES

1. SOURCES:- The official publications noted on p. xv with gaps filled from League of Nations and United Nations, *Statistical Yearbooks*, and the following data supplied by the respective national statistical offices: Finland mail to 1888 (1st line) and telegrams to 1917, and Poland telegrams 1938–57.
2. So far as possible, and except as indicated in footnotes, internal mail and telegrams are counted once, whilst international communications are counted both on sending and receipt.
3. The nature of the postal statistics differs considerably between countries. So far as possible the classifications used here are those which give the longest comparable series within each country.

FOOTNOTES

1. Austria-Hungary to 1848 (1st line); Cisleithania from 1848 (2nd line) to 1916, with Lombardy excluded from 1860 and Venetia from 1866; Republic of Austria from 1921.
2. Excluding registered mail.
3. Statistics are for years ended 31 March, and exclude newspapers, registered mail, and, to 1869 (1st line), outgoing international mail.
4. The reason for this break is not given in the source.
5. Excluding newspapers.
6. Statistics to 1882 (1st line) are of telegrams sent, received, and in transit. Subsequently they are of telegrams sent only.
7. Alsace-Lorraine was included in Germany rather than France from 1871 to 1918.
8. Previously excluding telegrams sent from railway stations.
9. Transleithania to 1917, and the territory established by the treaty of Trainon subsequently.
10. Previously internal mail only.
11. Letter post items.
12. Previously only paying communications.
13. Statistics to 1864 (1st line) are of internal letters only. From 1864 (2nd line) to 1877 (1st line) they are of all mail sent, but exclude incoming international mail.
14. Newspapers, packets, etc. are included for the first time in 1856.
15. From 5 February.
16. Subsequently including official mail.
17. Subsequently including official telegrams, other than those of the meteorological service.
18. Subsequently including telegrams on the railway companies' network. These numbered 134 thousand in 1900.
19. Including *correspondences pneumatiques* from 1879 to 1969 (1st line).
20. From 1884 to 1963 statistics are for years beginning 1 July. The 1964 figure is for July—December.
21. Subsequent statistics are for years ended 31 March. The 1900 figure is for a 15-month period.
22. Including service telegrams. They numbered 587 thousand in 1889 and 246 thousand in 1892.
23. Internal as well as external telegrams are counted twice up to 1904 (1st line) and in 1913–1928.
24. The first available figure is for 1874, and is 120 millions.
25. Statistics to 1889 are for years ended 31 October. The 1890 figure is for a 14-month period.
26. Previously excluding incoming international mail.
27. Subsequent statistics are for years ended 31 March following that indicated.
28. Subsequently including official telegrams and radio telegrams.
29. Statistics are for years ended 31 March following that indicated. Saarland is excluded to July 1959, and West Berlin to 1954 (1st line).
30. All items of mail to 1946, but excluding registered mail and newspapers to 1937 (1st line). From 1948 to 1965 statistics are of letters carried. Subsequently they are of all letter post sent, but excluding small packets from 1975 (2nd line).
31. Excluding incoming international telegrams from 1939 (2nd line).
32. Statistics are for the Republic and are for years ended 31 March to 1974. The 1975 figures are for the calendar year. Data for April—December are as follows: letters 289; telegrams 0.6.
33. Excluding registered mail to 1937 (1st line).
34. Internal telegrams are counted twice from 1938 (2nd line) to 1964.
35. Excluding incoming international telegrams from 1965.
36. The reason for this break is not clear, but is probably the previous double-counting of internal mail.
37. Previously mail received only.
38. Internal mail only.
39. Statistics are for years ended 31 March following that indicated to 1920. The 1921 figures are for 9 months.
40. Excluding incoming international telegrams from 1943.
41. Internal telegrams are counted twice from 1931 (2nd line).
42. The 1946 figure is for the first half year. Subsequent statistics to 1985 are for years ended 30 June. The calendar year figure for 1985 is 394.
43. Subsequently excluding certain printed papers.
44. Subsequently does not include southern Ireland.
45. Subsequently excluding telegrams sent via private cable companies.
46. Subsequent statistics are of mail forwarded rather than delivered.
47. Ordinary mail sent.
48. Subsequently excluding giro advices and similar telegrams.
49. A new classification was adopted in 1986.
50. Excluding incoming international mail, which came to 82 million in each of 1973 and 1975.
51. Telegrams received from 1968 (2nd line).
52. Subsequently excluding payment orders.

F8   Postal and Telegraph Services

[53]   The inland service ceased in October 1982.
[54]   Inland telegrams only from 1981 (2nd line).
[55]   Data are for years beginning 1 April.
[56]   Subsequently only telegrams sent.
[57]   Czech Republic.
[58]   Revised figure.

F9 TELEPHONE SERVICES

Key:- A = Telephones in use (in thousands), B = Telephone calls (in millions)

1883–1934

	Austria[1]		Belgium		Bulgaria	Czechoslovaka		Denmark		Finland	
	A	B[2]	A[3]	B	A	A	B	A[5]	B	A	B[6]
1883	—	—	...	...	...	...	...	...	...	...	...
1884	1.2	1.9	...	...	...	...	...	...	...	...	...
1885	2.5	2.5	...	...	...	...	...	...	...	...	...
1886	3.4	3.8	...	...	...	...	...	...	...	...	...
1887	4.0	4.8	...	...	...	...	...	...	...	...	...
1888	5.0	5.9	...	...	...	...	...	...	...	...	...
1889	6.6	7.7	...	...	...	...	...	...	...	...	...
1890	9.2	12.8	...	13.3	...	...	...	...	...	...	...
1891	12	17.0	...	...	...	...	...	...	...	...	...
1892	13	22.4	...	...	...	...	...	...	...	...	...
1893	15	38.7	...	...	...	...	...	...	...	...	...
1894	17	57.3	...	...	...	...	...	...	...	...	...
1895	19	62.8	...	19.5	...	...	...	...	...	...	...
1896	22	75.3	10	22.3	...	...	...	...	...	...	...
1897	25	91.2	11	26.6	...	...	...	...	...	...	...
1898	27	<u>101</u>	12	29.8	...	...	...	...	...	...	...
1899	29	82.2[2]	14	33.5	...	...	...	...	...	...	...
1900	33	94.1	15[3] 17	38.4[4]	...	...	...	27	52.9	...	...
1901	35	104	19	37.2	...	...	...	30	59.2	...	...
1902	38	114	20	37.0	0.5	...	...	33	73.4	...	...
1903	44	134	22	43.0	0.6	...	...	36	80.9	...	...
1904	49	158	24	47.7	0.9	...	...	43	97.6	...	...
1905	54	166	27	55.0	1	...	...	48	109	...	...
1906	60	185	31	64.5	1.3	...	...	55	125	...	...
1907	70	156	34	73.0	1.6	...	...	63	143	...	...
1908	82	182	38	88.0	2.0	...	...	...	149	...	...
1909	97	215	42	100	2.2	...	...	75	164	...	...
1910	112	270	49	112	2.5	...	...	82	186	...	...
1911	127	327	51	123	2.8	...	...	91	210	...	...
1912	145	361	57	135	3.0	...	...	100	227	...	...
1913	162	388	66	145	3.6	...	...	110	257	...	...
1914	172	403	...	...	...	...	...	119	283	...	...
1915	174	384	...	...	...	...	...	134	309	...	...
1916	193	374	...	...	...	...	...	156	345	...	...
1917	...	...	...	...	...	...	...	175	385	...	...
1918	...	...	...	...	...	...	...	194	422	...	...
1919	...[1]	...[1]	40	23	...	...	...	207[5] 239	448	...	0.1
1920	...	...	64	76	...	78	155	255	387	22	0.2
1921	...	...	82	99	8	82	167	271	397	...	0.3
1922	84	...	101	122	6	86	177	277	399	...	0.4
1923	138	...	117	145	7.3	92	189	293	416	...	0.6
1924	145	...	136	160	8.3	101	174	308	443	...	0.8
1925	153	...	157	144	8.8	110	190	317	462	...	1.1
1926	158	...	174	155	13	115	215	321	474	...	1.5
1927	166	...	194	158	15	120	211	325	486	102	2.0
1928	213	...	224	178	17	129	224	330	503	108	2.4
1929	223	...	257	202	18	136	237	342	546	114	3.7
1930	234	...	293	222	19	144	243	354	542	...	4.7
1931	240	...	299	229	19	147	251	366	563	...	5.6
1932	240	...	300	229	20	143	246	360	549	135	5.8
1933	241	...	317	239	22	145	241	369	515	135	6.3[6] 28.6
1934	259	...	323	245	22	143	237	382	610	140	64.4

F9   Telephone Services

	France[8]		Germany		Hungary[10]		Ireland		Italy	
	A	**B[46]**	**A[8]**	**B**	**A**	**B**	**A**	**B**	**A[5]**	**B[11]**
1883	...	...		8	...	...	...	...	6	...
1884	...	...		16	...	...	...	...	8	...
1885	...	...		34	...	...	...	...	...	...
1886	...	...		57	...	...	...	...	9	...
1887	...	...		84	...	...	...	...	9	...
1888	...	...	37	130	...	...	...	...	11	...
1889	12	...	48	155	...	...	...	...	11	...
1890	16	...	58	182	...	...	...	...	12	...
1891	20	...	70	200	...	...	...	...	12	...
1892	24	21	80	238	...	...	...	...	12	...
1893	27	30	91	285	...	...	...	...	12	...
1894	30	44	115	326	...	...	...	...	11	...
1895	35	78	132	382	...	...	...	...	12	...
1896	39	94	157	434	...	...	...	...	12	...
1897	44	106	174	500	...	...	...	...	13	...
1898	51	142	212	563	...	...	...	...	14	...
1899	60	170	229	621	...	...	...	...	17	...
1900	70	193	290[8] 306	691	...	...	...	...	17	...
1901	80	178	358	766	16	42.6	...	...	18	...
1902	94	189	412	843	18	49.0	...	...	21	...
1903	109	203	470	927	20	54.5	...	...	23	...
1904	123	219	538	1,069	23	62.8	...	...	26	0.2
1905	138	236	618	1,207	26	83.0	...	...	30	...
1906	152	239	705	1,353	30	104	...	...	36	2.4
1907	168	266	797	1,467	35	120	...	...	43	2.9
1908	182	237	883	1,519	40	125	...	...	50	3.8
1909	199	254	975	1,670	45	136	...	...	58	4.6
1910	219	264	1,076	1,851	51	161	...	...	66	5.6
1911	245	331	1,193	2,074	58	183	...	...	76	5.5
1912	276	396	1,310	2,327	68	202	...	...	84	6.9
1913	310	430	1,428	2,518	76	234	...	...	90	7.3
1914	328	375	...	...	84	245	...	...	94	7.1
1915	330	227	...	...	...	...	...	...	100	4.6
1916	343	254	...	...	...	231	...	...	100	7.4
1917	354	...	...	...	...	260	...	...	104	8.1
1918	368[7]	...[7]	...[7,9]	...[7]	...[10]	...[10]	...	...	98	7.6
1919	406	...	1,767	...	...	...	...	...	104[5] 109	8.6
1920	439	...	1,818	3,180	...	3.3	...	...	115	10.9
1921	488	...	1,946	2,971	...	5.0	...	...	120	11.8
1922	524	...	2,073	2,068	50	6.0	...	...	124	12.3
1923	579	...	2,242	1,852	59	5.2	...	...	136	14.9
1924	634	...	2,385	1,820	79	4.4	21	16	143	17.3
1925	709	788	2,588	2,039	78	3.8	22	18	161	18.7
1926	789	687	2,688	2,052	80	3.9	24	19	172	22.2
1927	849	703	2,815	2,595	86	4.1	26	20	298	21.9
1928	929	740	2,950	2,426	94	4.6	27	21	339	25.2
1929	1,018	782	3,182	2,599	101	5.0	28	21	390	27.0
1930	1,113	836	3,247	2,541	115	4.7	29	22	440	28.7
1931	1,185	852	3,114	2,375	116	4.3	31	22	481	30.3
1932	1,292	861	2,960[9]	2,167	111	3.6	32	23	482	31.4
1933	1,349	847	2,954	2,176	110	3.4	33	25	483	31.5
1934	1,400	877	3,134	2,289	121	3.6	33	26	505	32.0

F9 Telephone Services

1883–1934

	Netherlands		Norway		Poland		Portugal		Romania	
	A	B[33]	A	B[35][37]	A	B	A[13]	B	A	B[15]
1883	...	...	...	...	...	...	...	...	...	...
1884	...	...	...	...	...	...	...	...	...	...
1885	...	...	...	...	...	...	...	...	...	...
1886	...	...	...	...	...	...	...	...	...	...
1887	...	...	...	...	...	...	...	...	...	...
1888	...	...	...	...	...	...	...	...	...	...
1889	...	...	...	...	...	...	...	...	...	...
1890	...	...	...	...	...	...	...	...	...	...
1891	...	...	...	...	...	...	...	...	...	...
1892	...	...	...	...	...	...	...	...	...	...
1893	...	0.1	...	...	...	...	...	...	...	...
1894	...	0.1	...	...	...	...	...	...	...	...
1895	...	0.1	...	...	...	...	...	...	...	...
1896	...	0.1	...	...	...	...	...	...	...	0.4
1897	...	0.2	...	...	...	...	...	...	...	0.8
1898	...	0.3	...	...	...	...	...	...	...	1.0
1899	...	0.5	...	...	...	...	...	...	...	1.9
1900	18	0.7	36	...	...	...	...	...	2.7	1.5
1901	20	0.9	37	1.5	...	...	...	...	...	4.0
1902	23	1.1	38	1.7	...	...	...	...	5.5	2.0
1903	27	1.2	40	1.9	...	...	...	...	5.9	2.8
1904	30	1.5	41	2.1	...	...	...	...	6.6	2.5
1905	33	1.9	43	2.2	...	...	...	...	7.5	3.2
1906	38	2.4	46	2.4	...	...	...	...	9.2	4.9
1907	45	2.8	49	2.5	...	...	...	...	10	9.4
1908	49	3.0	53	2.9	...	...	...	...	11	6.7
1909	54	3.7	57	3.2	...	...	...	...	15	12.4
1910	60	4.5	64	3.9	...	...	...	...	19	13.5
1911	66	5.5	74	4.3	...	...	...	...	20	17.9
1912	73	6.7	80	5.0	...	...	...	...	20	17.8
1913	80[12] 37	7.3	89	5.6	...	...	...	...	22	22.0
1914	40	8.1[14]	...	6.3	...	...	...	27	...	26.1
1915	43	8.1	...	6.9	...	...	...	30	...	...
1916	62	8.8	...	8.2	...	...	...	35	...	...
1917	68	9.1	...	9.2	...	...	...	35	...	...
1918	74	9.5	...	9.6	...	...	...	35	...	...
1919	88[12] 146	11.0	132	10.3	...	...	...	39	...	...
1920	163	11.3	147	11.1	...	...	...	20	26	21.3
1921	178	12.1	158	11.3	49	121	...	22	27	[21.8][15]
1922	187	12.4	163	11.4	60	158	12	30	30	57.6
1923	195	13.4	165	11.9	68	475	13	28	32	63.3
1924	205	15.0	170	12.7	66	497	13	31[14]	39	67.4
1925	216	15.8	172	13.2	52	...	18	44	46	50.1
1926	227	17.3	178	13.4	135	...	19	46	53	70.7
1927	241	18.9	183	13.4	150	615	21	46	56	...
1928	258	20.9	187	13.5	166	544	27[13]	53	58	81.3
1929	284	22.9	191	13.7	178	723	52	59	58	99.4
1930	307	26.4	192	14.1	...	792	42	70	57[14] 50	105[14]
1931	326	30.1	195	14.1	...	565	45	80	51	81.6
1932	333	29.6	195	13.7	188	527	45	92	52	85.1
1933	343	30.9	197	13.4	194	532	49	94	57	97.8
1934	353	31.9	200	13.7	211	526	53	129	63	112

F9 Telephone Services

	Spain		Sweden		Switzerland		U.K.		Serbia/Yugoslavia[19]	
	A	B	A[16]	B	A	B	A	B[45]	A	B
1883	...	...	...	...		1.7	...	...	...	...
1884	...	...	...	...		2.1	...	...	...	...
1885	...	...	1.3	...		3.6	...	...	...	...
1886	...	...	...	...		6.7	...	...	...	...
1887	...	...	...	...		8.2	...	...	...	...
1888	...	...	...	...		8.5	...	...	...	...
1889	...	...	...	...		7.7	...	...	...	...
1890	...	...	5	...		5.8	...	...	...	...
1891	...	...	...	...		7.4	...	...	...	...
1892	...	...	...	...		8.0	...	...	...	...
1893	...	...	...	...		9.6	...	...	...	...
1894	...	...	...	...		11.7	1.8	...	...	...
1895	...	...	23	...		14.6	1.9	...	...	...
1896	...	...	...	58		16.2	2.0	...	...	...
1897	...	...	...	76		19.0	2.0	5.9	...	...
1898	...	...	...	97		19.7	2.1	7.1	...	...
1899	...	...	...	119		23.5	2.2	8.1	...	...
1900	...	...	52	136	42	25.4	2.7	9.0	...	...
1901	...	...	...	155	45	26.8	3.9	10.1	...	...
1902	14	...	...	169	47	28.5	14	11.6	...	0.6
1903	15	...	...	178	50	30.8	22	13.5	...	0.8
1904	16	...	...	193	53	33.2	33	15.5	...	1.2
1905	17	...	82	234	56	36.5	45	18.1	...	2.4
1906	18	...	...	271	61	39.3	54	19.9	...	3.0
1907	19	...	...	301	66	42.4	79	22.1	...	4.7
1908	20	...	...	314	70	44.8	87	23.6	...	3.9
1909	22	...	...	322	75	50.3	98	26.7	...	4.1
1910	23	...	128	337	80	56.4	122	30.2	...	4.2
1911	25	...	...	309	84	62.2	701	33.7	...	4.6
1912	28	...	...	313	91	68.5	731	36.0[45] 833	...	6.0
1913	32	...	...	322	97	72.6	775	872	...	...
1914	34	...	...	334	100	71.0	796	856	...	...
1915	37	...	181	347	98	66.5	787	816	...	...
1916	46	...	207	352	104	78.7	774	740	...	...
1917	...	...	236	355	112	88.7	779	744	...	...
1918	...	...	260[16] 364	494	124	103	797	763	...	...
1919	...	...	377	607	139	118	888	902	...	...[19]
1920	58	...	380	603	152	120	980[17] 988	901	...	...
1921	60	...	376	538	164	118	1,005	734[18]	...	...
1922	60	...	383	555	170	126	1,061[18]	790	...	...
1923	64	...	391	571	180	133	1,169	902	...	...
1924	67	...	407	609	189	145	1,285	930	23	48
1925	103	...	423	639	200	152	1,402	1,017	26	49
1926	114	...	438	662	210	160	1,521	1,101	27	51
1927	125	...	454	694	224	172	1,644	1,174	30	61
1928	135	7.4	472	718	244	191	1,768	1,266	33	81
1929	174	10.1	495	752	269	212	1,896	1,323	34	67
1930	212	12.8	522	790	298	228	1,996	1,371	38	101
1931	242	14.2	563	822	324	248	2,069	1,431	48	116
1932	271	16.8	577	830	346	256	2,137	1,491	46	131
1933	281	18.3	602	832	364	268	2,225	1,581	44	144
1934	304	19.5	628	877	383	275	2,388	1,681	47	167

F9 Telephone Services

	Austria	Belgium		Bulgaria	Czechoslovakia		Denmark		Finland		France	
	A	A	B[20]	A	A	B	A	B	A	B[24]	A	B[46]
1935	272	340	274	23	142	236	394	639	149	62.8	1,441	903
1936	280	362	295	[22][21]	150	250	409	663	160	65.4	1,482	940
1937	...	394	315	155[22] / 213	268[23] / 18.1		425	692	171	82.4	1,514	962
1938	...	422	320	27	...	17.9	442	702	185	89.5	1,590	960
1939	...	429	328	28	...	...	459	732	186	...	1,622	852
1940	...	205	156	29	...	...	467	729	187	92.3	1,634	592
1941	...	305	205	33	...	...	489	752	201	99.6	1,705	774
1942	...	360	294	35	...	...	512	823	219	95.5	1,768	1,008
1943	...	393	363	36	...	...	537	894	...	107	1,809	1,156
1944	...	304	294	39	...	...	558	969	230	111	1,849	1,099
1945	...	375	289	29	...	...	567	1,027	243	124	1,913	1,358
1946	...	450	368	45	303	33.9	592	1,059	264	129	1,997	1,457
1947	317	535	408	54	351	42.1	616	1,044	282	134	2,109	1,491
1948	351	602	428	58	386	35.8	644	1,040	304	132	2,233	1,534
1949	383	650	448	68	420	44.5	646	1,023	314	132	2,319	1,441
1950	413	687	485	78	451	51.5	722	1,082	328	138	2,406	1,537
1951	427	715	502	87	478	56.9	758	1,083	359	137	2,521	1,729
1952	449	744	505	94	519	59.4	789	1,088	384	137	2,645	1,766
1953	458	777	521	100	555	62.7	824	1,118	409	141	2,769	1,913
1954	479	830	548	110	607	68.2	862	1,187	483	141	2,946	2,108
1955	507	878	580	112	662	71.6	894	1,195	462	155	3,117	2,347
1956	541	931	622	120	703	75.5	920	1,237	496	151	3,313	2,624
1957	578	987	642	128	743	78.8	951	1,226	525	150	3,499	2,935[46] / 2,799
1958	615	1,032	668	140	790	84.0	978	1,267	545	...	3,704	3,100
1959	653	1,079	686	158	936	92.7	1,019	1,307	571	134[24] / 37.2	4,085	3,405
1960	701	1,137	735	172	1,016	101	1,072	1,381	607	141	4,358	3,849
1961	750	1,205	785	190	1,114	104	1,132	1,484	654	166	4,649	4,389
1962	805	1,279	842	206	1,207	107	1,194	1,570	682	252	4,978	5,012
1963	866	1,364	922	225	1,300	109	1,248	1,634	729	389	5,336	5,703
1964	936	1,461	970[20] / 945	249	1,399	114	1,311	1,681	778	664	5,704	6,171
1965	1,009	1,558	999	279	1,492	122	1,369	1,744	836	855	6,117	6,773[46] / 9.2
1966	1,087	1,658	1,041	306	1,583	128	1,411	1,752	892	1,031	6,554	10.0
1967	1,163	1,746	1,073	338	1,679	133	1,469	1,773	950	1,517	7,003	10.6
1968	1,243	1,839	1,129	378	1,789	139	1,517	1,796	1,009	1,816	7,503	11.7
1969	1,334	1,931	1,173	414	1,895	143	1,603	1,891	1,090	2,357	8,114	13.8
1970	1,427	2,036	1,220	473	2,003	152	1,700	2,001	1,181	2,882	8,774	15.5
1971	1,547	2,180	1,241	534	2,112	166	1,798	2,078	1,290	3,317	9,546	17.4
1972	1,694	2,324	1,284	582	2,233	176	1,918	2,204	1,412	3,772	10,338	19.8
1973	1,841	2,503	1,218[20] / 1,065	641	2,354	191	2,047	2,195	1,535	4,847	11,337	22.7
1974	1,987	2,667	1,075	718	2,481	204	2,164	2,290	1,679	6,411	12,405	24.4
1975	2,133	2,798	1,075	777	2,616	218	2,295	2,329	1,834	8,956[24] / 3,600	13,833	29.2
1976	2,281	2,949	1,155	853	2,743	236	2,505	2,565	1,936	5,240	15,554	32.7
1977	2,443	3,100	1,205	946	2,863	252	2,718	2,773	2,032	6,360	17,519	37.3
1978	2,618	3,271	1,248	1,032	2,981	279	2,907	2,947	2,127	6,803	19,870	42.4
1979	2,813	3,447	1,356	1,136	3,073	282	3,114	3,104	2,244	7,603	22,212	49.2
1980	3,010	3,636	1,395	1,255	3,150	283	3,283	3,114	2,374	8,473	24,686	55.8
1981	3,178	3,819	1,483	1,382	3,226	301	3,453	3,217	2,511	9,010	26,940	62.4
1982	3,330	3,959	1,574	1,514	3,306	316	3,595	3,371	2,644	6,867	29,374	67.4
1983	3,469	4,111	1,630	1,655	3,402	333	3,676	3,493	2,777	7,534	31,220	73.6
1984	3,594	4,243	1,721	1,810	3,499	350	3,828	3,689	2,899	9,515	32,693	78.0
1985	3,720	4,346	...	1,946	3,591	381	4,005	3,955	3,028	10,422	33,993	81.6
1986	3,834	4,556	...	2,079	3,707	...	4,195	4,141	...	7,917	...	87.0
1987	3,979	4,719	...	2,229	3,838	...		4,343	2,365[52]	8,490	...	94.2
1988	4,128	4,841	...	2,386	3,980	...	4,509	4,560	2,470[52]	...	...	96.7
1989	4,310	5,138	...	2,515	4,131	...	4,398	4,615[51]	2,582[52]	...	...	82.0[52]
1990	4,541	5,429	...	2,635	4,278	...	5,000	4,467[51]	2,678[52]	...	...	86.0
1991	4,732	5,691	...	2,727	1,707[49]	...	2,973[50]	4,598[51]	...	...	...	87.6
1992	4,957	5,898	...	2,839	1,819[49]	...	3,003[50]	3,864[51]	...	...	...	90.6
1993	5,195	...	...	...	1,961[49]	...	...	...	...	...	...	95.0
1994	5,371	5,816	...	2,984	2,178	...	3,123	...	2,791	...	31,700	...
1995	5,568	5,934	...	3,625	2,444	...	3,193	...	2,799	...	32,400	...
1996	5,724	5,995	...	3,772	2,817	...	3,251	...	2,802	...	32,900	...
1997	5,891	6,182	...	3,963	3,280	...	3,341	...	2,850	...	33,700	...
1998	5,964	6,273	...	3,998	3,741	...	3,496	...	2,842	...	34,099	...

F9 Telephone Services

Note: For the Germany columns, 1935–1944 refer to unified Germany; 1945–1990 the first two columns (A, B) refer to **East Germany** (A[25], B) and the next two columns to **West Germany** (A[26], B[27]); 1991 onward all four columns refer to **Germany**, with East Germany "Included in West Germany".

Year	Germany A	Germany B	W. Ger A	W. Ger B	Greece A	Greece B	Hungary[10] A	Hungary B	Ireland A[31]	Ireland B	Italy A	Italy B[11]
1935	3,270	2,433			26	...	130	4.1	35	27	525	32.2
1936	3,431	2,562			32	...	137	4.3	36	29	537	35.1
1937	3,624	2,722			45	...	149	4.7	38	31	568	36.6
1938	4,146	2,973			49	...	163	5.6[10]	40	35	611	39.6
1939	4,382	3,175			...	...	178[28] / 181	...	44	37	650	45.4
1940	4,959	...			...	...	201		45	39	695	54.2
1941	...	...			...	...	233		47	41	751	54.0
1942	...	...			...	...	248		49	44	836	64.4
1943	...	...			...	...	266[28]		50	45	879	...
1944	...	...			...	...	...[29]		52	48	...	...
	East Germany A[25]	**B**	**West Germany A[26]**	**B[27]**								
1945					...		40	...	54	53	...	49.1
1946	...	...			57	...	79	...	57	58	787 / 895[14]	68.1
1947	...	...	1,753	...	63	...	107	...	61	62	932	76.5
1948	...	...	1,856	...	69	...	...	...	68	64	1,014	81.1
1949	336	...	2,113	1,828	76	...	115[29] / 91	187	76	68	1,119	87.5
1950	357	717	2,393	2,039	82	...	110	231	84	74	1,244	101
1951	378	736	2,700	2,197	88	...	132	264	92	82	1,304	121
1952	401	792	2,977[26] / 3,017	2,363	101	276	153	319	99	86	1,410	143
1953	425	799	3,301	2,531	104	276	159	382	105	89	1,652	164
1954	457	855	3,494	2,674[27]	110	285	169	419	110	93	1,883	193[11]
1955	481[25] / 1,043	855	4,041	3,147	122	308	183	442	111	96	2,187	206
1956	1,067	859	4,383	3,377	137[14] / 108	336	192	463	125	112	2,444	239
1957	1,123	880	4,732	3,531	119	376	206	443	131	106	2,750	307
1958	1,175	907	5,090	3,734	131	411	221	473	139	102	2,988	349
1959	1,238	933	5,516	4,118[27]	148	460	233	504	149	123	3,331	402
1960	1,296	985	5,994	4,561	173	520	243	538	160	135	3,861	445
1961	1,366	1,007	6,509	4,880	267	618	255	558	181	149	4,235	517
1962	1,436	1,024	7,047	5,198	303	713	266[14] / 479	572	184	159	4,654	603
1963	1,515	1,041	7,600	5,679	356	794	505	596	193	170	5,058	716
1964	1,587	1,051	8,168	5,749	431	899	539	606	206	182	5,529	787
1965	1,659	1,074	8,802	6,331	508	1,133	566	553	217	199	5,981	869
1966	1,724	1,114	9,532	6,903	579	1,480	597	570	230	221	6,468	936
1967	1,780	1,149	10,321	7,427	660	1,773	635	597	253	237	7,057	1,070
1968	1,896	1,200	11,249	8,141	762	1,953	684	618	274	262	7,752	1,185
1969	1,986	1,246	12,456	9,107	881	2,375	778	645	287	293	8,528[47]	1,380
1970	2,089	1,304	13,835	10,216	1,045	2,994	824	660[30]	307	302	9,371	1,609
1971	2,165	1,367	15,246	11,679	1,230	4,149	873	674	324	329	10,322	1,839
1972	2,232	1,419	16,521	13,132	1,438	5,295	924	687	341	367	11,345	1,974
1973	2,326	1,544	17,803	14,045	1,670	6,577	968	709	366	405[14] / 623	12,612	2,128[14] / 1,971
1974	2,451	1,575	18,767	13,897	1,862	8,008	1,014	669	394	711	13,700	2,231
1975	2,570	1,608	19,603	14,063	2,009	7,819	1,048	456	444	809	14,501	2,384
1976	2,751	1,748	21,162	15,299	2,180	9,252	1,076	329	480	863	15,246	2,679
1977	2,860	1,850	22,932	16,267	2,320	10,849	1,104	291	519	1,023	16,125	2,871
1978	2,956	1,888	24,743	17,726	2,487	11,842	1,143	281	554	1,161	17,088	3,181
1979	3,072	2,046	26,632	19,301	2,664	13,285	1,187	259	556	1,467	18,092	3,610
1980	3,156	1,957	28,554	21,903	2,796	15,308	1,261	181	650	1,657	19,277	3,832
1981	3,252	1,983	30,122	22,779	2,957	17,232	1,297	151	720	1,729[32]	20,453	4,146
1982	3,344	2,015	31,370	24,164	3,113	15,179	1,338	149	779	1,731	21,680	...
1983	3,441	2,071	35,137	25,408	3,313	17,716	1,383	146	824	2,004	22,992	...
1984	3,527	2,142	36,582	26,432	3,529	20,393	1,433	138[30]	894	2,218	24,331	...
1985	3,630	2,084	37,899	27,616	3,721	23,298	1,485	1,060	942[31] / 703	2,313[32]	25,615	...
1986	3,755	2,142	39,128	28,989	3,920	24,716	1,541	1,109	751	2,550[32]	26,874	...
1987	3,875	2,220	40,288	30,326	4,126	...	1,609	1,139	796	2,808[32]	28,052	...
1988	3,977	2,297	41,735	30,419	4,303	...	1,676	1,226	843	...	29,300	...
1989	1,826	...	43,095	31,710	4,523	...	1,770	1,429	903	...	30,716	...
1990	1,906	...	—	33,856	4,699	...	1,872	1,312	916	...	32,037	...
			Germany									
1991	Included in	West Germany	33,600	41,900	4,980	...	1,954	1,428	983	...	...	...
1992			35,400	45,600	5,289	...	2,052	1,802	1,048	...	...	...
1993			37,000	51,400	5,571	...	...	2,033	1,113	...	...	...
1994			38,800	52,000	4,976	...	1,774	2,305	1,240	...	...	...
1995			42,000	53,100	5,163	...	2,157	2,476	1,310	...	...	...
1996			44,100	53,750	5,329	...	2,651	2,561	1,390	...	...	...
1997			45,200	54,500	5,431	...	3,095	2,678	1,500	...	...	...
1998			46,600	55,670	5,536	...	3,423	2,850	1,600	...	...	...

F9 Telephone Services

	Netherlands		Norway		Poland		Portugal		Romania		Russia/U.S.S.R
	A	B[33,34]	A	B[35,36,37]	A	B[39]	A	B	A	B	A
1935	366	35.8	210	14.2	231	518	56	116	63	131	861
1936	382	41.1	222	15.2	249	530	61	116	71	155	...
1937	404	49.7	235	16.7	272	561	66	106	81	200	...
1938	434	58.1	250	17.6	—	619[39] 29	69	104	93	214	...
1939	461	68.5	256	18.1	...	...	73	108	102	249	...
1940	458	67.4	245	18.6	...	...	76	114	...	...	...
1941	498	70.9	269	20.3	...	...	81	125	...	...	...
1942	498	84.9	288	24.0	...	...	87	138	...	...	...
1943	...	98.8	301	27.9	...	...	90	130	...	...	...
1944	...	...	307	29.4	...	...	93	113	...	...	...
1945	...	...	323	29.0[35] 462	83	...	98	122	...	...	...
1946	514	99.3	372	465	170	32	104	133	...	...	...
1947	576	122	379	508	189	42	115	152	...	...	...
1948	633	134	406	504	207	40	125	161	...	12.0	...
1949	692	144	431	506	225	39	133	162	...	...	...
1950	782	161	452	498	230	47	153	169	...	22.7	...
1951	821	175	477	502	230	56	169	186	...	26.3	...
1952	896	189[33] 848	503	527	235	68	187	205	...	30.2	...
1953	920	921	531	506	240	78	209	222	...	33.9	...
1954	1,021	1,000	558	508	250	89	232	244	...	30.3	...
1955	1,117	1,083	588	520	...	97	257	273	...	34.9	...
1956	1,229	1,179	615	571	378	101	280	302	...	38.4	...
1957	1,318	1,234	647	576	406	94	305	326	...	40.5	...
1958	1,402	1,288	672	588	446	95	332	348	...	43.9	...
1959	1,501	1,387	694	566[36]	812	102	365	430	...	45.3	...
1960	1,613	1,510[34] 1,505	724	598	881	109	395	474	...	47.8	...
1961	1,740	1,600	773	635	957	115	427	520	217	51.7	...
1962	1,888	1,732	808	656	1,031	119	455	585	347	56.4	...
1963	2,023	1,870	838	672	1,089	123	485	671	377	60.9	...
1964	2,180	1,944	869	673	1,193	124	522	789	427	63.9	7,100
1965	2,352	2,037	908	679	1,294	132[39] 225	550	804	473	70.0	7,700
1966	2,515	2,155	946	722[37] 718	1,411	257	582	896	510	74.8	7,872
1967	2,719	2,218	987	769	1,530	273	616	975	552	76.4	9,680
1968	2,910	2,386	1,036	803	1,651	347	653	1,092	569	...	10,800
1969	3,120	2,521	1,091	843	1,756	396	698	1,284	606	...	11,000
1970	3,410	2,717	1,145	876	1,867	434	758	1,495	639	...	11,000
1971	3,721	...	1,204	921	1,971	472	809	1,728	727	...	12,078
1972	4,003	...	1,262	954	2,087	489	873	1,969	807	...	13,199
1973	4,317	...	1,308	997	2,238	553	948	2,292	886	...	14,463
1974	4,687	...	1,355	1,026[48]	2,399	617	1,011	2,410	1,076	...	15,782
1975	5,047	3,447	1,407	2,376	2,578	653	1,066	2,435	1,196	...	16,949
1976	5,410	...	1,476	2,657	2,753	723	1,119	2,524	...	...	18,000
1977	5,845	...	1,555	2,980	2,925	787	1,175	2,782	...	...	19,600
1978	6,341	...	1,634	3,253	3,095	892	1,254	2,931	...	...	20,943
1979	6,853	...	1,726	3,573	3,244	950	1,306	3,081	...	...	22,464
1980	7,357	4,821	1,881	3856	3,387	1,011	1,372	3,439	...	...	23,707
1981	7,697	5,106	1,992	4,254	3,506	1,000	1,456	3,730	...	...	25,069
1982	8,023	5,333	2,204	4,620	3,648	894	1,567	4,288	...	...	26,667
1983	8,272	5,526	2,395	4,971	3,846	1,084	1,625	4,445	...	...	...
1984	8,544	5,776	2,579	5,403	4,028	1,142	1,764	4,646	...	...	29,462
1985	8,840	6,007	...	6,138	4,215	1,239	1,835	5,038	...	...	31,100
1986	9,080	6,196	...	6,745	4,418	1,309	1,936	...	...	...	32,900
1987	9,410	6,401	1,948[52]	7,668	4,618	1,392	2,072	...	...	...	35,300
1988	9,750	6,609	2,016	8,280	4,830	1,466	2,258	...	...	...	37,500
1989	6,691[52]	7,188	2,070[52]	8,557	5,039	1,530	...	...	...	...	...
1990	6,940[52]	7,672	2,132[52]	8,138	5,232	1,533	2,769	...	...	...	...
1991	...	...	...	7,830	5,480	1,674	...	...	...	...	...
1992	...	...	...	8,524	5,854	1,858	...	...	...	...	...
1993	...	...	...	...	6,274	2,082	...	...	...	...	...
1994	7,859	...	2,401	...	6,391	2,271	3,474	...	2,806	...	...
1995	8,124	...	2,476	...	6,542	2,364	3,643	...	2,968	...	...
1996	8,431	...	2,589	...	6,673	2,475	3,822	...	3,176	...	...
1997	8,860	...	2,735	...	6,811	2,671	4,002	...	3,398	...	...
1998	9,337	...	2,935	...	6,904	2,783	4,117	...	3,599	...	...

F9 Telephone Services

	Spain		Sweden		Switzerland		U.K.		Yugoslavia	
	A	B[41]	A	B[42,44]	A	B	A	B	A	B
1935	329	21.8	628	930	400	278	2,570	1,824	47	125
1936	...	18.1	672	983	412	277	2,827	1,983	51	137
1937	275	16.0	726	1,046	431	288	3,050	2,167	54	147
1938	...	23.8	787	1,117	450	302	3,235	2,237	60	153
1939	[295][40]	20.0	845	1,170	462	322	3,339	2,215	62	164
1940	327	27.7	890	1,193	474	324	3,311	2,092	...	...
1941	345	31.6	960	1,236	498	340	3,316	2,035	...	...
1942	365	30.2	1,015	1,377	530	374	3,536	2,103	...	...
1943	...	39.1	1,071	1,452	568	410	3,764	2,151	...	...
1944	...	41.7	1,146	1,576	605	457	3,889	2,228	...	...
1945	444	42.4	1,221	1,694	645	521	3,937	2,368	...	...
1946	481	43.0	...	[902][42]	698	569	4,319	2,714	91	126
1947	497	46.0	1,316	1,871	745	601	4,653	2,898	96	191
1948	512	47.7	1,428	1,941	795	607	4,919	3,047	101	242
1949	592	50.9	1,508	1,989	245	626	5,171	3,175	110	263
1950	652	56.3	1,615	2,099[14]	896	657	5,426	3,326	111	270
1951	733	63.1	1,683	2,087	952	703	5,715	3,492	111	249
1952	810	67.3	1,787	2,138	1,013	736	5,873	3,429	119	206
1953	893	70.8	1,994	2,174	1,074	775	6,094	3,648	128	242
1954	981	74.4	2,098	2,218	1,141	823	6,436	3,921	149	265
1955	1,076	80.5	2,220	2,564	1,215	881	6,830	4,198	160	291
1956	1,188	91.4	2,313	2,927	1,294	939	7,167	4,064	175	307
1957	1,328	96.3	2,312	3,256	1,385	994	7,300	3,998	198	339
1958	1,478	105	2,409	3,713	1,475	1,047	7,469	4,043	217	368
1959	1,628	112	2,526	4,039	1,562	1,112	7,790	4,287	236	402
1960	1,779	104	2,637	4,670	1,659	1,211	8,208	4,726	260	450
1961	1,930	111	2,761	5,506[44]	1,762	1,299	8,544	4,977	276	475
				5,426						
1962	2,082	120	2,904	6,223	1,875	1,395	8,841	5,295	303	487
1963	2,268	117	3,054	7,221	1,998	1,513	9,272	5,724	322	509
1964	2,509	133[41]	3,223	8,120	2,132	1,598	9,883	6,336	370	557
		164								
1965	2,772	176	3,387	9,488	2,259	1,689	10,621	6,891	415	568
1966	3,054	206	3,573	10,683	2,395	1,790	11,289	7,380	452	679
1967	3,359	242	3,757	12,067	2,534	1,881	12,009	7,944	506	799
1968	3,702	277	3,935	12,655	2,686	1,999	12,805	8,627	549	977
1969	4,093	377	4,111	13,631	2,847	2,139	13,844	9,622	623	1,177
1970	4,569	445	4,307	14,489	3,026	2,152	14,858	10,747	736	1,447
1971	5,129	540	4,506	15,332	3,213	...	16,025	12,029	821	1,872
1972	5,713	636	4,680	15,936	3,404	...	17,441	12,144	911	2,299
1973	6,331	734	4,829	16,233	3,604	...	18,955	13,238	1,004	2,615
1974	7,043	902	5,178	17,001	3,790	...	20,191	14,313	1,143	2,999
1975	7,836	1,077	5,423	18,175	3,913	...	20,884	15,156	1,300	3,365
1976	8,605	1,327	5,673	19,287	4,016	...	21,516	15,956	1,431	3,745
1977	9,528	1,496	5,930	20,191	4,145	...	23,016	17,303	1,556	4,415
1978	10,311	1,684	6,160	21,022	4,310	...	24,760	19,122	1,733	5,348
1979	11,707	1,896	6,407	21,972	4,465	...	26,807	19,857	1,913	6,517
1980	11,845	2,072	6,621	23,010[42]	4,612	...	27,870	20,175	2,133	7,470
1981	12,386	2,169	6,888	24,395	4,802	...	28,450	20,806	2,304	8,456
1982	12,820	2,299	7,132	25,353	4,955	...	28,882	21,403	2,544	9,691
1983	13,345	2,487	7,410[31]	26,195	5,113	...	29,336	22,696	2,796	11,285
			5,017							
1984	13,825	2,644	5,128	27,696	5,270	...	...	...	3,031	13,510
1985	14,259	2,907	5,242	30,194	5,436	...	...	...	3,322	15,994
1986	14,748	3,097	5,372	33,031	5,623	...	...	...	3,598	18,150
1987	15,477	3,437	5,480	35,854	5,783	...	...	...	3,909	20,160
1988	10,522[52]	3,804	5,601	37,122	5,879	...	...	...	4,243	
1989	11,292[52]	4,196	5,716	39,960	6,050	...	...	...	4,550	32,707
1990	12,603[52]	4,577	5,849	44,640	6,153	...	...	...	...	...
1991	13,264[52]	4,540	5,913	47,553	6,227	...	...	...	2,028[53]	11,565[53]
1992	13,792[52]	4,261	5,922	49,960	6,081	...	...	...	2,160[53]	19,589[53]
1993	14,253[52]	4,278	5,907	52,300	5,975	...	...	...	2,274[53]	24,163[53]
1994	14,685	4,364	5,967	54,000	4,258	...	28,358	...	...	...
1995	15,095	4,571	6,013	55,100	4,480	...	29,411	...	...	...
1996	15,413	4,827	6,032	56,350	4,571	...	30,678	...	...	...
1997	15,854	4,965	6,010	56,870	4,688	...	31,879	...	...	...
1998	16,289	5,076	5,965	56,900	4,803	...	32,829	...	...	...

F9 Telephone Services

NOTES

1. SOURCES:- The official publications noted on p. xv and League of Nations and United Nations, *Statistical Yearbooks*. In addition, Polish calls to 1938 (1st line) were supplied by the National Statistical Office, and those for Romania for 1948–67 were supplied by Mr.G. Radulescu of the *Enciclopedica Romana*.
2. Except as indicated in footnotes, the number of telephones shown refers to apparatus installed.
3. So far as possible, and except as indicated in footnotes, internal telephone calls are counted once, and international calls both incoming and outgoing.

FOOTNOTES

[1] Cisleithania to 1916, the Republic subsequently.
[2] Double-counting was not eliminated until 1899.
[3] Number of subscribers to 1900 (1st line).
[4] In 1905 a revised figure of 42.3 million was given for 1900. The series given here for the years before 1905 may therefore be too low.
[5] Number of subscribers to 1919 (1st line).
[6] Figures are of inland trunk calls only, in 3-minute units. To 1933 (1st line) they relate only to the state network.
[7] Alsace-Lorraine was included in Germany to 1913 and in France from 1919.
[8] Including instruments in exchanges only from 1900 (2nd line).
[9] Excluding Saarland from 1919 to 1932.
[10] Transleithania to 1917. Local telephone calls are excluded from 1920 to 1938.
[11] Years beginning 1 July to 1954.
[12] Subscribers to the state network or in large communes only from 1913 (2nd line) to 1919 (1st line).
[13] Lisbon and Porto only to 1928.
[14] The reason for this break is not given.
[15] Years beginning 1 April to 1920. The 1921 figure is for 9 months.
[16] Excluding railway telephones to 1918 (1st line).
[17] From 1920 (2nd line) private network instruments are included provided that they are connected, directly or indirectly, to the public exchange system.
[18] Excluding southern Ireland from 1922 (for calls) or 1923 (for apparatus).
[19] Serbia to 1912, Yugoslavia from 1924.
[20] International calls are given in minutes after 1964 and cannot be aggregated with internal calls, whilst interzonal calls are excluded from 1973 (2nd line).
[21] Excluding public call boxes.
[22] Numbers of subscribers to 1937 (1st line).
[23] Interurban calls only from 1937 (2nd line).
[24] Measured in automatic system impulses from 1959 (2nd line). The impulses are of 5p. to 1975 (1st line) and of 20p. subsequently.
[25] Principal connections only to 1955 (1st line).
[26] Excluding Saarland to 1952 (1st line).
[27] Figures are for years beginning 1 April. West Berlin is excluded to 1954 (1st line), and Saarland to July 1959.
[28] Figures for 1939 (2nd line) to 1943 are for the temporarily enlarged wartime territory, which included Subcarpathian Ruthenia in 1939–40, plus northern Transylvania in 1941–43.
[29] Data for 1945 to 1949 (1st line) are for connections.
[30] From 1971 to 1984 calls made on the automatic system are excluded. They are as follows, in million charging units:-

1971	14	1975	578	1979	1,336	1982	2,007
1972	21	1976	785	1980	1,645	1983	2,231
1973	72	1977	1,015	1981	1,836	1984	2,574
1974	238	1978	1,141				

[31] Numbers of connections from 1985 (2nd line) for Ireland and 1983 (2nd line) for Sweden.
[32] Estimated.
[33] Excluding local calls to 1952 (1st line).
[34] Excluding incoming international calls from 1960 (2nd line).
[35] Excluding local calls to 1945 (1st line).
[36] Excluding free calls from 1959.
[37] Figures are for years ended 31 March to 1960 and subsequently for calendar years.
[38] International calls are given in minutes after 1966 and cannot be aggregated with internal calls.
[39] Long-distance calls only from 1938 (2nd line), excluding calls made automatically to 1965 (1st line).
[40] Excluding Giupuzcoa Province.
[41] Excluding calls made automatically to 1964 (1st line).
[42] The 1946 figure as for the first half-year. Subsequently to 1980 the data are for years ended 30 June.
[43] Numbers of connections from 1983 (2nd line).
[44] Measured in automatic system impulses from 1961 (2nd line).
[45] Excluding local calls to 1912 (1st line).
[46] To 1957 (1st line) statistics are the sums of metered calls (in units of basic price) and longer-distance calls in 3-minute units. From then to 1965 (1st line) they are numbers of calls made, and subsequently numbers of units of charge (in thousand million).
[47] Subsequently including San Marino.

F9　Telephone Services

[48]　Measured in automatic system impulses from 1975.
[49]　Czech Republic.

	Slovakia (Telephones in Use)
1991	669
1992	711
1993	759
1994	1,004
1995	1,118
1996	1,246
1997	1,392
1998	1,539

[50]　Number of subscribers.
[51]　Inland calls only.
[52]　Main lines only.
[53]　Yugoslavia. Ex-Yugoslavia : No. of Telephones (000's).

	Bosnia-Herc.	Croatia	Macedonia	Slovenia
1991	...	...	...	...
1992	...	...	323	770
1993	...	1,216	...	...
1994	250	1,205	337	577
1995	238	1,287	351	615
1996	272	1,389	367	664
1997	303	1,488	408	722
1998	333	1,558	439	757

F10 RADIO AND TELEVISION RECEIVING LICENCES (in thousands)

	Austria		Belgium		Bulgaria		Czechoslovakia		Denmark[5]		Finland	
	Radio	TV	Radio	TV	Radio	TV	Radio	TV	Radio	TV	Radio	TV
1923	...	—	...	—	...	—	- -	—	...	—	—	—
1924	...		...		...	—	2					
1925	...	—	...	—	...	—	15	—	...	—	—	—
1926	...	—	...	—	...	—	175	—	...	—	4	—
1927	...	—	...	—	...	—	220	—	131	—	37	—
1928	...	—	...	—	...	—	238	—	212	—	74	—
1929	...	—	...	—	...	—	268	—	254	—	98	—
1930	...	—	...	—	...	—	315	—	340	—	107	—
1931	...	—	...	—	...	—	385	—	438	—	117	—
1932	...	—	...	—	...	—	472	—	472	—	120	—
1933	507	—	...	—	...	—	573	—	493	—	121	—
1934	527	—	600	—	9	—	694	—	523	—	129	—
1935	560	—	744	—	17	—	848	—	549	—	145	—
1936	594	—	891	—	21	—	928	—	586	—	177	—
1937	620	—	957[1]	—	32	—	1,044[4]	—	620	—	231	—
							1,034					
1938	682	—	1,081[1]	—	47	—	764	—	668	—	294	—
1939	...	—	1,113[1]	—	60	—	...	—	713	—	333	—
1940	...	—	...	—	83	—	...	—	761	—	348	—
1941	...	—	...	—	...	—	...	—	792	—	375	—
1942	...	—	...	—	...	—	...	—	822	—	425	—
1943	...	—	...	—	...	—	...	—	866	—	479	—
1944	...	—	...	—	...	—	...	—	895	—	497	—
1945	...	—	...	—	...	—	...	—	905	—	542	—
1946	880	—	...	—	...	—	1,662	—	906	—	561	—
1947	970	—	1,081	—	205	—	1,891	—	968	—	602	—
1948	1,106	—	1,227	—	210	—	2,108	—	1,015	—	622	—
1949	1,210	—	1,395	—	212	—	2,259	—	1,058	—	664	—
1950	1,319	—	1,548	—	226	—	2,421	—	1,087	—	722	—
1951	1,440	—	1,637	—	...	—	2,545	—	1,114	—	785	—
1952	1,550	—	1,794	—	225	—	2,638	—	1,162	—	853	—
1953	1,624	—	1,863	—	445[3]	—	2,676	—	1,205	—	905	—
1954	1,683	- -	2,000	—	350	—	2,744	4	1,240	—	968	—
1955	1,736	1	2,135	72[2]	627	—	2,839	32	1,209	4	1,021	—
1956	1,790	4	2,229	150	754	...	2,915	76	1,218	16	1,066	—
1957	1,842	16	2,307	250	898	...	2,971	173	1,256	62	1,112	2
1958	1,893	50	2,409	223	1,059	...	3,055	328	1,297	137	1,140	8
1959	1,944	113	2,477	392	1,246	1	3,085	519	1,326	251	1,187	34
1960	1,988	193	2,588	618	1,431	5	3,104	795	1,350	388	1,228	93
1961	2,036	291	2,734	821	1,601	11	3,141	1,089	1,362[6]	583	1,290	190
1962	2,079	377	2,896	1,018	1,733	31	3,132	1,356	735	726	1,330	336
1963	2,110	465	2,935	1,206	1,843	66	3,112	1,630	592	860	1,397	476
1964	2,134	586	2,919	1,375	1,959	122	3,094	1,899	508	939	1,456	622
1965	2,154	711	3,026	1,543	2,055	185	3,100	2,113	383	1,031	1,541	732
1966	2,171	853	3,047	1,660	2,144	288	3,179	2,375	380	1,097	1,605	822
1967	2,146	978	3,120	1,779	2,218	420	3,185	2,600	302	1,145	1,663	899
1968	2,071	1,129	3,200	1,894	2,245	621	3,287	2,864	267	1,188	1,701	958
1969	2,044	1,277	3,313	2,000	2,271	829	3,221	2,996	236	1,228	1,744	1,015
1970	2,026	1,426	3,396	2,100	2,292	1,028	3,174	3,091	207	1,311	1,783	1,058
1971	2,160	1,586	3,497	2,203	2,305	1,181	3,140	3,187	183	1,375	1,817	1,099
1972	2,154	1,695	3,560	2,289	2,302	1,286	3,127	3,305	164	1,411	1,896	1,183
1973	2,157	1,779	3,662	2,376	2,266	1,383	3,115	3,404	151	1,442	1,944	1,224
1974	2,170	1,856	3,768	2,464	2,273	1,457	3,237	3,602	144	1,527	1,997	1,261
1975	2,170	1,910	3,891	2,547	2,512	1,508	3,245	3,689	137	1,556	2,099	1,558
1976	2,191	1,974	4,044	2,646	2,750	1,546	3,265	3,793	119	1,637	2,200	1,779

F10 Radio and Television Receiving Licences (in thousands)

	France		Germany[7]		East Germany		Hungary		Ireland[9]		Italy	
	Radio	TV	Radio	TV	Radio	TV	Radio	TV	Radio	TV	Radio	TV
1923	...	—	—	—	...	—	—	—	1	—	—	—
1924	...	—	9	—	...	—	—	—	1	—	—	—
1925	...	—	1,022	—	...	—	17	—	8	—	—	—
1926	...	—	1,377	—	...	—	60	—	19	—	—	—
1927	...	—	2,010	—	...	—	83	—	24	—	—	—
1928	...	—	2,235	—	...	—	169	—	26	—	63	—
1929	...	—	2,838	—	...	—	267	—	26	—	...	—
1930	...	—	3,238	—	...	—	308	—	26	—	176	—
1931	...	—	3,732	—	...	—	325	—	29	—	239	—
1932	...	—	4,168	—	...	—	322	—	33	—	305	—
1933	1,368	—	4,533	—	...	—	328	—	51	—	373	—
1934	1,756	—	5,425[8]	—	...	—	340	—	66	—	431	—
1935	2,626	—	6,725	—	...	—	353	—	88	—	529	—
1936	3,219	—	7,584	—	...	—	365	—	105	—	697	—
1937	4,164	—	8,512	—	...	—	384	—	140	—	826	—
1938	4,706	—	9,598	—	...	—	419	—	155	—	978	—
1939	5,220	—	...	—	...	—	499	—	170	—	1,142	—
1940	5,089	—	...	—	...	—	[409][15]	—	184	—	1,321	—
1941	5,098	—	...	—	...	—	[731][15]	—	176	—	1,583	—
1942	5,180	—	...	—	...	—	[812][15]	—	171[9]	—	1,827	—
1943	5,248	—	...	—	...	—	[891][15]	—	169	—	1,784	—
1944	5,117	—	...	—	...	—	...	—	171	—	1,608	—
1945	5,346	—	...	—	...	—	...	—	173	—	1,646	—
			West Germany[8]									
1946	5,668	—	...	—	...	—	...	—	180	—	1,850	—
1947	5,750	—	...	—	...	—	386	—	187	—	1,982	—
1948	6,104	—	7,299	—	...	—	475	—	261	—	2,205	—
1949	6,421	- -	...	—	...	—	539	—	280	—	2,566	—
1950	6,889	4	...	—	3,489	—	606	—	298	—	3,135	—
1951	7,407	11	9,493	—	3,813	—	701	—	327	—	3,683	—
1952	7,923	24	10,182	—	4,210	—	887	—	383	—	4,228	—
1953	8,368	60	11,108	2	4,511	—	1,080	—	406	—	4,800[6]	—
1954	8,853	125	11,730	22	4,776	2	1,236	—	428	—	5,391	88
1955	9,266	261	12,238[8] / 13,160	121[8] / 127	5,009	14	1,432	—	445	—	5,637	179
1956	9,715	442	13,672	393	5,218	71	1,587	1[10]	461	—	5,869	366
1957	10,199	683	14,531	835	5,306	159	1,774	1	477	—	6,009	673
1958	10,646	989	15,194[7]	1,513[7]	5,378	318	1,963	16	485	—	6,042	1,096
1959	10,793	1,368	15,900	3,375	5,489	594	2,102	53	486	—	6,014	1,573
1960	10,981[6]	1,902	15,892	4,635	5,574	1,035	2,224	104	494	—	5,882	2,124
1961	10,411	2,555	16,270	5,888	5,602	1,459	2,314	206	495[6]	—	5,726	2,762
1962	10,349	3,427	16,696	7,213	5,670	1,893	2,390	325	389	127	5,580	3,458
1963	10,151	4,400	17,099	8,539	5,739	2,379	2,452	471	337	201	5,279	4,285
1964	9,567	5,414	17,494	10,024	5,759	2,801	2,484	675	293	259	4,886	5,216
1965	8,937	6,489	17,878	11,379	5,743	3,216	2,484	831	259	297	4,571	6,045
1966	8,390	7,471	18,232	12,720	5,820	3,600	2,485	996	230	320	4,196	6,855
1967	6,940	8,316	18,587	13,806	5,881	3,933	2,479	1,169	210	389	3,844	7,666
1968	6,306	9,252	18,988	14,958	5,942	4,173	2,514	1,397	185	395	2,553	8,347
1969	5,675	10,121	19,368	15,909	5,983	4,337	2,531	1,596	161	433	2,197	9,016
1970	5,027	10,968	19,622[12]	16,675[12]	5,985	4,499	2,531	1,769	138	438	1,823	9,717
1971	4,371	11,655	19,026	16,669	6,016	4,649	2,543	1,943	123	474	1,506	10,344
1972	3,841	12,279	19,199	17,100	6,050	4,820	2,542	2,085	—	514	1,253	10,951
1973	3,474	12,955	19,329	17,351	6,082	4,966	2,533	2,199	—	514	1,022	11,426
1974	...	...	19,396	17,556	6,114	5,096	2,541	2,295	—	556	825	11,816
1975	...	...	19,958	17,796	6,167	5,224	2,537	2,390	—	565	715	12,103
1976	...	...	20,244	18,489	6,205	5,351	2,559	2,477	—	573	647	12,377

F10 Radio and Television Receiving Licences (in thousands)

	Netherlands		Norway		Poland		Portugal		Romania	
	Radio	TV	Radio	TV	Radio	TV	Radio	TV	Radio	TV
1923	...	—		—	—	—	...	—	...	—
1924	...	—		—	—	—	...	—	...	—
1925	...	—	—	—	5	—	...	—	...	
1926	...	—	46[1]	—	48	—	...	—	...	
1927	...	—	63	—	120	—	...	—	...	
1928	...	—	64	—	184	—	...	—	...	
1929	...	—	77	—	203	—	...	—	...	
1930	429	—	84	—	246	—	...	—	...	
1931	524	—	102	—	310	—	...	—	...	
1932	560	—	123	—	296	—	...	—	...	
1933	648	—	138	—	311	—	16	—	...	
1934	909	—	157	—	374	—	28	—	101	
1935	947	—	189	—	492	—	40	—	132	—
1936	989	—	240	—	677	—	54	—	162	—
1937	1,072	—	305	—	922	—	69	—	218	—
1938	1,109	—	365	—	...	—	81	—	274	—
1939	1,438	—	423	—	...	—	89	—	317	—
1940	...	—	429	—	...	—	98	—	...	
1941	...	—	468[1]	—	...	—	114	—	...	
1942	...	—	...	—	...	—	120	—	...	
1943	...	—	...	—	...	—	123	—	...	
1944	...	—	...	—	...	—	129	—	...	
1945	...	—	226	...	168	—	136	—	...	
1946	...	—	373	...	475	—	142	—	...	
1947	1,467	—	539	...	667	—	145	—	219	
1948	1,615	—	654	...	974	—	179	—	258	
1949	1,816	—	737	...	1,176	—	212	—	...	
1950	1,957	—	786	...	1,464	—	228	—	313	—
1951	2,106	—	824	...	1,747	—	310	—	...	—
1952	2,216	1	860	...	2,001	—	354	—	...	—
1953	2,333	3	895	...	2,211	—	393	—	750	—
1954	2,487	9	925	...	2,661	—	443	—	...	—
1955	2,691	41	948	...	3,057	—	479	—	1,164	—
1956	2,878	99	968	...	3,624	5[10]	534	—	1,326	- -
1957	2,888	239	985	—	4,005	22	596	1	1,499	3
1958	2,998	391	997	- -	4,465	85	689	13	1,655	16
1959	3,095	585	1,008	6	4,931	238	791	28	1,841	30
1960	3,126	801	1,021	49	5,268	426	848	46	2,008	55
1961	3,064	1,040	1,034	107	5,487	648	902	68	2,165	88
1962	3,072	1,275	1,038	204	5,620	959	1,005	90	2,372	110[2]
1963	3,097	1,574	1,060	292	5,701	1,295	1,068	119	2,549	245
1964	3,130	1,836	1,071	407	5,788	1,698	1,127	151	2,684	357
1965	3,093	2,113	1,089	490	5,646	2,078	1,173	180	2,790	501
1966	3,134	2,370	1,110	574	5,593	2,540	1,240	214	2,925	712
1967	3,154	2,559	1,135	662	5,539	2,934	1,345	271	3,019	916
1968	3,174	2,717	1,152	739	5,598	3,389	1,391	293	3,031	1,115
1969	...	2,939	1,171	796	5,649	3,828	1,406	347	3,050	1,288
1970	...	3,086	1,191	854	5,658	4,215	1,405	388	3,075	1,484
1971	...	3,240	1,204	895	5,709	4,709	1,447	472	3,106	1,703
1972	...	3,353	1,235	951	5,795	5,200	1,484	543	3,112	1,944
1973	...	3,462	1,255	986	5,872	5,687	1,506	609	3,077	2,145
1974	...	3,545	1,277	1,021	...	6,100	1,516	675	3,066	2,405
1975	...	3,640	1,300	1,051	...	6,472	1,519	722	3,084	2,692
1976	...	3,764	1,313	1,037	...	6,820	...	914	3,104	2,963

F10   Radio and Television Receiving Licences (in thousands)

1923–1976

	Spain[11]		Sweden		Switzerland		United Kingdom[5]		Yugoslavia	
	Radio	TV	Radio	TV	Radio	TV	Radio	TV	Radio	TV
1923	...	—	5	—	—	—	125	—	—	—
1924	...	—	40	—	17	—	748	—	—	—
1925	...	—	126	—	34	—	1,350	—	—	—
1926	...	—	243	—	51	—	1,960	—	—	—
1927	...	—	328	—	59	—	2,270	—	—	—
1928	...	—	381	—	70	—	2,483	—	—	—
1929	...	—	428	—	84	—	2,730	—	—	—
1930	...	—	482	—	104	—	3,091	—	45	—
1931	...	—	550	—	151	—	3,647	—	48	—
1932	...	—	609	—	231	—	4,620	—	57	—
1933	...	—	666	—	300	—	5,497	—	59	—
1934	213	—	733	—	357	—	6,260	—	67	—
1935	304	—	834	—	418	—	7,012	—	83	—
1936	...	—	944	—	464	—	7,618	—	96	—
1937	...	—	1,074	—	504	—	8,131	—	112	—
1938	...	—	1,227	—	549	—	8,589	—	135	—
1939	...	—	1,358	—	593	—	8,968	—	155	—
1940	281	—	1,470	—	634	—	8,951	—	...	—
1941	...	—	1,551	—	680	—	8,752	—	...	—
1942	...	—	1,628	—	729	—	8,683	—	...	—
1943	...	—	1,709	—	780	—	9,242	—	...	—
1944	...	—	1,784	—	820	—	9,555	—	...	—
1945	...	—	1,840	—	855	—	9,711	—	180	—
1946	...	—	...[13]	—	891	—	10,396[6]	—	198	—
1947	552	—	1,895	—	923	—	10,763	15	223	—
1948	657	—	1,959	—	970	—	11,134	46	252	—
1949	...	—	2,025	—	1,008	—	11,621	127	301	—
1950	...	—	2,095	—	1,037	—	11,876	344	336	—
1951	...	—	2,153	—	1,079	—	11,605	764	357	—
1952	...	—	2,205	—	1,120	—	11,304	1,449	387	—
1953	1,313	—	2,256	—	1,158	1	10,750	2,142	422	—
1954	1,622	—	2,317	—	1,199	4	10,188	3,249	497	—
1955	...	...	2,391	—	1,233	11	9,477	4,504	592	—
1956	1,839	3	2,462	—	1,268	20	8,522	5,740	711	4[10]
1957	2,105	3	2,548	13	1,308	31	7,559	6,966	890	4
1958	2,293	21	2,608	76	1,350	50	6,556	8,090	1,088	7
1959	2,464	140	2,651	244	1,388	79	5,481	9,255	1,309	12
1960	2,717	250	2,686	599	1,445	129	4,535	10,470	1,428	30
1961	3,174	...	2,744	1,030	1,490	194	3,909	11,268	1,672	61
1962	3,491	375	2,843	1,327	1,538	274	3,538	11,834	1,896	124
1963	4,000	850	2,938	1,626	1,583	366	3,256	12,443	2,073	208
1964	4,000	1,100	2,950	1,821	1,619	492	2,999	12,885	2,294	387
1965	4,550	1,750	2,947	1,964	1,654	621	2,794	13,253	2,462	563
1966	5,920	2,325	2,954	2,085	1,677	752	2,611	13,567	2,604	752
1967	6,475	2,685	2,925	2,160	1,725	868	2,506	14,267	2,715	972
1968	6,951	...	2,928	2,268	1,752	1,011	2,557	15,089	2,794	1,255
1969	7,042	...	2,927	2,345	1,800	1,144	2,464	15,496	2,892	1,483
1970	...	4,115	—	2,420	1,852	1,274	2,301	15,883	2,786	1,692
1971	7,174	4,520	—	2,513	1,900	1,403	—	16,658	2,880	1,939
1972	...	5,200	—	2,619	1,958	1,536	—	17,125	2,904	2,201
1973	8,000	5,719	—	2,701	2,003	1,627	—	17,325	2,995	2,322
1974	8,050	6,125	—	2,758	2,036	1,714	—	17,701	3,437	2,533
1975	8,075	6,525	—	2,841	2,076	1,759	—	17,788	3,561	2,747
1976	...	6,640	—	2,909	2,108	1,809	—	18,056	3,839	3,100

F10 Radio and Television Receiving Licences (in thousands)

1977–1997

	Austria Radio	Austria TV	Belgium Radio	Belgium TV	Bulgaria Radio	Bulgaria TV	Czechoslovakia Radio	Czechoslovakia TV	Denmark Radio	Denmark TV	Finland TV	East Germany Radio	East Germany TV
1977	2,219	2,027	4,077	2,811	...	1,584	3,721	3,903	106	1,721	1,454[14]	6,261	5,450
1978	2,246	2,068	4,212	2,866	...	1,655	3,778	4,048	97	1,771	1,500	6,288	5,540
1979	2,287	2,121	4,451	2,925	2,176	1,634	3,799	4,092	91	1,815	1,505	6,342	5,634
1980	2,404	2,233	4,508	2,934	2,149	1,652	4,082	4,292	87	1,856	1,538	6,409	5,731
1981	2,413	2,247	4,596	2,963	2,115	1,659	4,100	4,296	88	1,864	1,614	6,459	5,811
1982	2,505	2,329	4,617	2,976	2,085	1,683	4,133	4,308	91	1,873	1,678	6,439	5,847
1983	2,538	2,356	4,607	2,981	2,055	1,691	4,165	4,323	116	1,889	1,738	6,490	5,928
1984	2,613	2,419	4,558	2,983	...	...	4,209	4,346	124	1,894	1,770	6,551	6,005
1985	2,627	2,426	4,526	2,972	2,018	1,697	4,234	4,368	174	2,005	1,784	6,646	6,079
1986	2,639	2,434	4,516	2,984	...	...	3,935	4,387	146	1,976	1,822	6,699	6,139
1987	2,691	2,484	4,608	3,173	1,983	1,692	3,966	4,425	86	1,941	1,843	6,758	6,199
1988	2,694	2,487	2,066[3]	3,258	...	...	4,229	4,662	80	1,942	1,862	6,781	6,233
1989	2,700	2,495	2,162	3,274	1,941	1,663	4,217	4,661	75	1,962	1,732	...	...
1990	2,701	2,500	2,252	3,296	1,909	1,633	4,321	4,781	81	1,983	1,775	Included in West Germany	
1991	2,703	2,508	2,331	3,304	1,857	1,591	4,369	4,952	88	2,016	1,801		
1992	2,814	2,638	3,297	3,297	1,780	1,550	2,883[4]	3,184[4]	92	2,039	1,809		
1993	2,853	2,677	...	3,316	...	...	2,919[4]	3,256[4]	94	2,054	1,802		
							Czech Republic						
1994	3,065	2,745	3,458	3,472	1,892	1,671	3,276	3,381	96	2,161	1,932		
1995	3,197	2,861	3,562	3,582	1,946	1,735	3,482	3,425	99	2,374	1,989		
1996	3,306	2,914	3,599	3,711	1,992	1,846	3,572	3,613	103	2,486	2,347		
1997	3,412	2,987	3,768	3,847	2,175	1,938	3,616	3,887	107	2,538	2,459		

	West Germany Radio	West Germany TV	Hungary Radio	Hungary TV	Ireland TV	Italy Radio	Italy TV	Netherlands TV	Norway TV	Poland TV	Portugal TV
1977	20,724	19,019	2,577	2,557	593	611	12,705	3,878	1,120	7,170	1,137
1978	21,152	19,422	2,590	2,633	590	533	12,868	4,033	1,147	7,474	1,175
1979	22,771	20,763	2,608	2,702	556	464	13,170	4,111	1,173	7,708	1,150
1980	23,323	23,749	...	2,766	643	420	13,361	4,181	1,205	7,954	1,382
1981	23,748	21,491	...	2,806	648	402	13,436	4,294	1,233	8,188	1,461
1982	24,158	21,836	...	2,838	660	378	13,645	4,367	1,295	8,347	1,501
1983	24,604	22,132	...	2,864	677	382	13,831	4,454	1,316	8,542	1,523
1984	25,046	22,434	...	2,895	705	368	13,951	4,516	1,339	8,765	1,567
1985	25,483	22,705	...	2,911	717	308	14,521	4,514	1,369	9,468	1,605
1986	25,916	23,011	...	2,930	752	212	14,605	4,641	1,443	9,692	1,618
1987	26,391	23,378	...	2,958	788	230	14,687	4,703	1,454	9,868	1,626
1988	26,892	23,742	...	2,940	760	...	14,717	4,763	1,472	10,031	...
1889	27,427	24,142	...	2,944	950		14,851[5]	4,838	1,467	...	1,671
1990	28,062	24,694	...	2,930	...		15,001	4,879	1,496	9,919	1,706
1991	34,760	31,031	...	2,852	829		15,094	5,242	1,482	9,809	...
1992	35,302	31,516	...	2,863	849		15,267	5,618	1,496	10,043	...
1993	35,736	31,888	...	2,819	930		15,675	5,675	1,522	10,111	1,687
	Germany										
1994	36,249	32,067	...	2,781	945	...	15,737	5,713	1,603	10,247	1,725
1995	36,786	32,289	...	2,702	977	...	15,898	5,892	1,725	10,368	1,801
1996	37,145	32,458	...	2,670	992	...	15,937	5,936	1,781	10,472	1,868
1997	38,006	32,891	...	2,601	1,025	...	16,089	5,992	1,836	10,673	1,913

	Romania Radio	Romania TV	Sweden TV	Switzerland Radio	Switzerland TV	U.K. TV	Yugoslavia Radio	Yugoslavia TV
1977	3,086	3,161	2,988	2,134	1,846	18,149	3,919	3,285
1978	3,141	3,409	3,051	2,172	1,890	18,381	3,995	3,449
1979	...	...	3,077	2,210	1,937	18,285	4,088	3,552
1980	3,205	3,714	3,103	2,253	1,980	18,667	4,242	3,735
1981	3,218	3,813	3,165	2,291	2,013	18,554	4,278	3,843
1982	3,214	3,862	3,221	2,337	2,057	18,494	4,698	3,976
1983	3,223	3,912	3,236	2,379	2,095	18,632	4,689	4,001
1984	3,224	3,935	3,245	2,423	2,140	18,716	4,699	4,075
1985	3,208	3,879	3,251	2,467	2,186	18,705	4,706	4,062
1986	3,192	3,856	3,257	2,512	2,241	18,953	4,794	4,127
1987	3,150	3,801	3,278	2,553	2,289	19,354	4,772	4,089
1988	3,112	3,740	3,293	2,590	2,338	19,396	4,735	4,092
1989	3,073	3,696	3,314	2,629	2,385	19,645	4,703	4,074
1990	2,983	3,645	3,327	2,670	2,435	19,546	...	...
1991	2,828	3,587	3,309	2,701	2,476	19,631	1,877[6]	1,699[6]
1992	2,577	3,542	3,331	2,727	2,513	20,067	1,786[6]	1,624[6]
1993	2,402	3,485	3,327	2,764	2,547	20,413	1,738[6]	1,582[6]
1994	2,380	3,407	3,346	2,811	2,596	20,539	1,692	1,573
1995	2,311	3,368	3,471	2,869	2,671	20,724	1,604	1,498
1996	2,268	3,217	3,499	2,906	2,723	21,325	1,533	1,409
1997	2,146	3,124	3,562	2,985	2,814	21,562	1,498	1,364

F10   Radio and Television Receiving Licences (in thousands)

NOTES

1. SOURCES:- The official publications noted on p. xv with gaps filled from United Nations, *Statistical Yearbooks*, and the following data supplied by the respective national statistical offices:- Finland 1926–29; 1931–33, and 1936–37; Italy 1942–46; Netherlands 1930–39; Poland 1924–36; and Portugal 1933–34.
2. So far as possible the data apply to 31 December in each year.
3. There was a change in the method of calculation.
4. Czech Republic.
5. Television & Radios from this point.
6. Yugoslavia only.

FOOTNOTES

[1]   At 30 June.
[2]   Estimates of number of receivers in October.
[3]   This is a later revised figure.
[4]   The figures from 1937 (2nd line) are for the post-Second World War territory.
[5]   At 31 March.
[6]   Television licences subsequently included radio licences.
[7]   Figures to 1958 are at 1 April.
[8]   Saarland is excluded up to 1934 and from 1948 to 1955 (1st line), and West Berlin is also excluded from 1948 to 1955 (1st line).
[9]   Figures to 1942 are of licences issued during the year ended 31 March following that indicated.
[10] Estimates of the number of receivers.
[11] At 1 July.
[12] Subsequently only taxed receivers.
[13] Subsequently at 30 June.
[14] Separate monochroma and colour licences were no longer required.
[15] Including the territorial gains of 1940/1.

G FINANCE

1.	Banknote Circulation	page 783
2.	Deposits in Commercial Banks	page 793
3.	Deposits in Savings Banks	page 800
4.	Money Supply	page 811
5.	Total Central Government Expenditure	page 816
6.	Central Government Revenue and Main Tax Yields	page 825

Financial statistics exhibit great contrasts regarding availability. Some were collected and published from a very early date. Some may have been collected but were regarded as state secrets. Others were not collected for a long time because they were regarded as private secrets whose publication was beyond the competence of state compulsion. Finally, in the period since World War II, the centrally-planned economies of eastern Europe have returned to the old policy of treating many financial statistics as state secrets.

The first three tables in this section showing various banking statistics point some of these contrasts very well. The banknote issues of the Bank of England are available from the beginning of our period, yet publication of those of other British banks was not compelled until 1833. Experience in most other countries was similar with publication from the start by the central bank (where it existed) but little or no information from other issuers for a long time. In general, however, this has been of much less importance than in the British case because in many countries the privilege of note issue has always been confined to a single bank. Where it was not, such restriction has usually been imposed before bank notes became an important part of the money supply. The Netherlands was a major exception.

Table G2, showing commercial bank deposits, demonstrates both the scarcity of such data before the interwar period outside north-western Europe and the secretive reactions of regimes in eastern Europe since World War II. Unfortunately, it also displays a lack of uniformity in what was regarded as a commercial bank deposit in different countries. Savings bank data in Table G3, on the other hand, are both more homogeneous and more readily available for earlier periods. Not being part of the world of high finance, there was no reluctance to compel publication of their statistics. Indeed, they were more likely to be seen as something of which a government could be proud, indicating the prosperity of ordinary citizens. In recent years the distinction between savings and commercial banks has become blurred in a number of countries and the continuity of these series has tended to be broken in these cases.

Two tables are given showing some of the many public finance statistics of central governments. Table G5 gives total expenditures, including capital items which are normally financed by borrowing. Table G6 shows the current revenues exclusive of loans, with their main tax constituents. Both these tables are taken from closed accounts rather than budget statements. There is very much more data available, both on details of receipts and outlays, than it has been possible to find space for here. The most reluctant omission has been any disaggregation of government expenditure. The material is generally so heterogeneous, changes in nature so often, and is frequently not available in a really meaningful form. In most cases it would require considerable research effort to put the statistics of even a single country onto a reasonably uniform basis. Therefore, regretfully, only expenditure totals are shown. Tax yields, on the other hand, exhibit less disguise and less change—at any rate until fairly recently, so the most important of these are given. However, in using them it is necessary to be alert to changes in definitions.

It is noteworthy that statistics of public finances for very few countries are available much before the middle of the nineteenth century. Only for Great Britain, and for the Habsburg monarchy in summary form, are there any usable eighteenth-century data. Both of these are the results of retrospective exercises by government statisticians in the middle of the nineteenth century. It is fair to say that in general consistent and fairly full information on state finances only became available when the various parliamentary regimes had established some sort of control over taxation. Even then, accounting systems often remained archaic. There were several changes in them and it was often still in the government's interest to hide or disguise some of their income as well as, more frequently, some of their expenditures. It would be unwise to assume that all the figures in Tables G5 and G6 are fully comprehensive or that all of their inconsistencies and breaks in continuity have been identified in the footnotes.

G1 BANKNOTE CIRCULATION

key:- A = Central Bank issues; B = other bank issues; C = total issues

	1750-1774			**1775-1799**	
	Sweden **A** (kroner) million	**U.K.:E & W** **A**[1] (pounds) million		**Sweden** **A** (kroner) million	**U.K.:E & W** **A**[1] (pounds) million
1750	2.7	4.3	1775	11	8.8
1751	3.0	5.2	1776	12	8.6
1752	3.4	4.7	1777	11	8.0
1753	3.3	4.4	1778	10	7.1
1754	3.4	4.1	1779	9.2	8.1
1755	3.4	4.1	1780	8.5	7.4
1756	4.3	4.5	1781	8.4	6.7
1757	6.1	5.1	1782	8.9	7.4
1758	7.3	4.9	1783	8.9	7.0
1759	9.2	4.8	1784	7.9	5.9
1760	8.3	4.9	1785	7.7	6.2
1761	10	5.2	1786	7.4	7.9
1762	11	5.9	1787	8.0	9.0
1763	11	5.3	1788	9.1	9.8
1764	11	6.2[1]	1789	8.3	10.5
1765	9.6	...	1790	5.6	10.7
1766	9.6	5.8	1791	4.5	11.6
1767	9.1	5.5	1792	3.8	11.2
1768	8.2	5.8	1793	3.1	11.4
1769	7.9	5.7	1794	2.8	10.5
1770	8.8	5.2	1795	2.6	12.4
1771	9.1	6.8	1796	2.2	10.0
1772	9.4	6.0	1797	1.9	10.4
1773	10	6.0	1798	1.7	12.6
1774	11	...[1]	1799	1.5	13.2

G1 Banknote Circulation

	Austria[3] A (gulden) million	Denmark[11] A (rigsdaler)	Finland[3] A (markkaa) thousand	France[4] A (francs)	Ireland[5] B (pounds)	Netherland[7] C (gulden)	Norway A	Sweden A (kroner)	Sweden B	UK:GB A[1] (pounds)	UK:GB B[1]
							millions				
1800	—	...	—	—	...	...	...	1.5		15.9	...
1801	—	...	—	—	...	...	...	1.5		15.4	...
1802	—	...	—	—	...	...	...	1.5		16.1	...
1803	—	...	—	—	...	...	...	2.4		15.7	...
1804	—	...	—	—	...	...	...	5.3		17.1	...
1805	—	...	—	—	...	...	...	8.4		17.1	...
1806	—	...	—	—	...	...	...	10	...	19.4	...
1807	—	...	—	85	...	...	...	13	...	18.3	...
1808	—	...	—	96	...	...	...	25	...	17.6	...
1809	—	...	—	95	...	...	...	31	...	19.1	...
1810	—	...	—	101	...	...	...	32	...	22.9	...
1811	—	...	—	101	...	...	...	34	...	23.3	...
1812	—	...	—	111	...	...	...	34	...	23.2	...
1813	—	...	2	81	...	...	...	30	...	24.0	...
1814	—	...	4	28	...	...	...	29	...	26.6	...
1815	—	...	11	41	...	1.8	...	29	...	27.3	...
1816	—	...	15	69	...	3.7	...	31	...	26.9	...
1817	—	...	16	84	...	5.3	...	35	...	28.5	...
1818	26.7	...	15	100	...	5.0	...	37	...	27.0	...
1819	43.8	31	16	102	...	5.8	13	36	...	25.2	...
1820	51.9	24	18[3]	154	...	8.7	13	36	...	23.9	...
1821	34.8	23	23	180	...	13	14	36	...	22.1	...
1822	48.3	22	18	187	...	11	14	35	...	18.1	...
1823	51.0	22	16	189	...	14	14	35	...	18.8	...
1824	68.1	21	16	222	...	20	15	37	...	19.9	...
1825	82.1	21	15	218	...	14	16	37	...	20.1	...
1826	82.3	21	15	169	...	12	16	37	...	23.5	...
1827	87.4	20	14	191	...	12	16	36	...	22.3	...
1828	95.7	20	11	199	...	14	17	36	...	21.7	...
1829	108	19	12	201	...	20	18	37	...	19.7	...
1830	112	19	11	224	...	26	19	37	...	20.8	...
1831	124	18	10	217	...	14	19	38	...	19.1	...
1832	120	18	9	233	...	14	19	38	...	18.0	...
1833	125	17	9	212	5.3	20	20	37	...	19.5	13.0[6]
1834	136	17	11	206	5.2	23	20	36	1.3	19.0 / 18.8	13.4
1835	151	16	12	222	5.2	24	21	38	1.5	18.1	13.8
1836	154	17	14	214	5.5	23	22	41	2.5	17.8	15.0
1837	146	17	14	205	5.1	21	21	43	4.1	18.3	13.7
1838	167	17	14	212	5.6	26	20	40	7.3	18.9	14.5
1839	167	16	15	214	5.8	24	22	40	9.1	17.7	15.0
1840	167	17	20	223	5.4	24	22	40	10.0	16.8	13.7
1841	167	17	127	227	5.4[7]	31	23	38	10.7	16.9	12.9
1842	173	17	178	233	5.1	27	23	33	9.8	18.4	11.1
1843	179	17	172	237	5.2	29	23	31	9.5	19.5	10.4
1844	198	16	181	254	5.9	34	22	30	9.8	21.2	11.1
1845	215	17	177	267	6.9	37	23	36	12	20.7	11.0
1846	214	17	184	272	7.3	32	23	39	13	20.3	11.1
1847	219	20	204	251	6.0	32	22	43	16	19.1	10.9
1848	223	20	168	342	4.8	37	19	39	16	18.1	9.5
1849	250	20	153	422	4.3	44	19	34	15	18.4	9.3

G1   Banknote Circulation

	Austria[2] A (gulden) million	Belgium A (francs) million	Bulgaria A (leva) thousand	Denmark[11] A (rigsdaler) million	Finland A (markkaa) thousand	France[4] A (francs) million	Germany C[12] (marks) million	Ireland B (pounds) million	Italy C (lire) million	Netherlands[7] C (gulden) million	Norway A (kroner) million
1850	255	—	—	20	143	486		4.5	...	49	
1851	216	53	—	20	147	530	102	4.5	...	51	20
1852	195	67	—	20	163	621	113	4.8	...	67	21
1853	188	82	—	20	177	660	113	5.6	...	78	21
1854	383	95	—	20	184	614	119	6.3	...	94	27
											31
1855	378	100	—	24	188	638	129	6.4	...	92	31
1856	380	99	—	24	225	620	245	6.7	...	91	29
1857	383	105[10]	—	24	222	594	288	6.8	...	81	27
1858	389	119	—	24	163	625	320	6.2	...	76	26
1859	467	114	—	24	184	716	366	6.9	...	87	24
1860	475	118	—	24	224	750	463	6.8	...	99	26
1861	467	118	—	24	292	745	533	6.3	...	104	25
1862	427	123	—	24	304	805	521	5.7	...	95	27
1863	397	117	—	24	267	796	524	5.4	...	99	27
1864	376	113	—	27	276	762	527	5.6	...	92	26
1865	351	125	—	24	261	839	579	6.0	...	105	29
1866	284	124	—	24	219	937	564	5.9	...	113	28
1867	247	138	—	24	237	1,082	637	5.8	...	109	29
1868	276	172	—	25	284	1,233	684	6.2	...	119	26
1869	284	199	—	22	329	1,355	703	6.6	...	136	27
1870	297	203	—	24	366	1,544	854	6.9	...	132	28
1871	317	229	—	25	420	2,075	1,074	7.5	1,207	143	34
1872	318	298	—	28	498	2,401	1,378	7.7	1,363	168	39
1873	359	321	—	32	609	2,857	1,368	7.1	1,454	165	47

m kroner[11]

	Austria[2] A (gulden) million	Belgium A (francs) million	Bulgaria A (leva) thousand	Denmark[11] A (rigsdaler) million	Finland A (markkaa) thousand	France[4] A (francs) million	Germany C[12] (marks) million	Ireland B (pounds) million	Italy C (lire) million	Netherlands[7] C (gulden) million	Norway A (kroner) million
1874	294	329	—	64	735	2,597	1,325	6.8	1,513	166	46
1875	286	340	—	61	575	2,461	1,054	7.1	1,561	175	37
1876	296	365	—	66	527	2,484	990[12] 1,118	7.5	1,586	184	40
1877	282	342	—	60	442	2,490	1,045	7.4	1,569	187	36
1878	289	314	—	65	384	2,339	988	7.0	1,612	200	31
1879	317	335	—	70	370	2,199	1,112	6.1	1,672	188	33
1880	329	340	—	70	486	2,305	1,130	5.7	1,689	191	39
1881	354	355	—	78	448	2,576	1,182	6.6	1,676	194	38
1882	369	356	—	70	451	2,732	1,167	7.3	1,672	195	41
1883	380	358	—	72	471	2,926	1,159	7.1	1,512	186	41
1884	376	358	—	71	450	2,928	1,192	6.5	1,510	186[7]	39
1885	364	367	—	71	410	2,846	1,183	6.1	1,442	186	37
1886	372	379	49	75	400	2,789	1,336	6.0	1,479	198	39
1887	391	389	1,036	77	431	2,719	1,323	5.9	1,471	195	40
1888	426	376	183	80	488	2,676	1,402	6.1	1,421	193	44
1889	435	402	402	76	553	2,876	1,461	6.7	1,461	204	49
1890	446	405	1,958	77	525	3,060	1,401	6.8	1,469	208	50
1891	455	422	1,303	77	489	3,085	1,416	6.5	1,464	195	48
1892	478	428	472	...	460	3,151	1,430	6.2	1,480	189	45
1893	487	451	1,231	81	444	3,445	1,398	6.3	1,573[13]	193	47
1894	508	470	825	78	491	3,476	1,503	6.3	1,618	200	48
1895	620	477	1,681	83	563	3,527	1,621	6.4	1,595	204	51

m kroner[9]

	Austria[2] A (gulden) million	Belgium A (francs) million	Bulgaria A (leva) thousand	Denmark[11] A (rigsdaler) million	Finland A (markkaa) thousand	France[4] A (francs) million	Germany C[12] (marks) million	Ireland B (pounds) million	Italy C (lire) million	Netherlands[7] C (gulden) million	Norway A (kroner) million
1896	1,319	493	2,397	85	640	3,607	1,553	6.3	1,572	200	53
1897	1,400	513	1,957	88	715	3,687	1,621	6.2	1,662	202	57
1898	1,475	545	3,156	91	768	3,694	1,655	6.1	1,686	203	63
1899	1,458	590	7,972	96	734	3,820	1,661	6.4	1,674	219	63

G1 Banknote Circulation

	Portugal C (escudos) million	Romania[14] A (lei) million	Russia C (rubels) million	Spain A (pesetas) million	Spain B (pesetas) million	Sweden A (kroner) million	Sweden B (kroner) million	Switzerland C (Francs) million	UK: GB A[1] (pounds) million	UK: GB B[8] (pounds) million
1850	...	...	...	...	...	34	15	...	19.4	9.6
1851	...	...	...	...	...	34	16	...	19.5	9.5
1852	...	...	...	...	...	34	17	...	21.9	9.8
1853	...	...	...	...	...	41	21	...	22.6	10.6
1854	...	...	...	...	...	50	25	...	20.7	10.9
1855	...	...	...	—	...	59	32	...	19.8	11.0
1856	...	...	...	40	17	52	27	...	19.7	10.9
1857	...	...	...	46	26	47	21	...	19.5	10.7
1858	1.9	...	...	52	34	40	25	...	20.2	9.9
1859	2.9	...	...	67	45	37	26	...	21.3	10.5
1860	2.4	...	...	63	55	39	30	...	21.3	10.7
1861	2.1	...	...	45	55	37	32	...	20.0	10.3
1862	2.6	...	...	52	48	36	30	...	20.8	10.3
1863	2.5	...	...	68	50	31	27	...	20.7	10.2
1864	2.3	...	...	72	53	32	28	...	20.6	10.2
1865	2.5	...	664	62	53	31	33	...	21.1	10.2
1866	2.3	...	662	45	45	27	32	...	23.2	9.6
1867	2.1	...	697	49	46	26	34	...	23.4	9.7
1868	2.2	...	675	55	48	26	31	...	23.9	9.7
1869	2.4	...	703	53	43	27	35	...	23.5	9.8
1870	2.6	...	694	61	38	29	40	...	23.3	9.8
1871	2.9	...	695	79	43	31	48	24.8	24.4	10.2
1872	3.3	...	752	68	47	45	57	...	25.5	10.4
1873	3.4	...	748	55	42	45	67	...	25.6	10.7
1874	4.7	...	774	72	...	...	64	...	26.3	10.9
1875	4.8	...	764	128	—	36	60	77.3	27.3	10.9
1876	...	...	752	158	—	30	61	...	27.7	10.8
1877	...	...	767	157	—	27	51	...	27.9	10.7
1878	4.7	...	1,015	174	...	27	46	...	28.1	10.2
1879	5.6	...	1,153	193	...	32	49	...	29.2	9.1
1880	6.0	—	1,130	245	...	39	51	92.9	26.9	9.0
1881	7.3	34	1,085	350	...	38	49	99.4	26.3	8.9
1882	6.8	73	1,028	334	...	37	53	98.2	26.0	9.1
1883	6.3	93	973	364	...	36	52	102	25.6	9.2
1884	6.6	89	959	383	...	38	52	115	25.4	9.0
1885	7.1	92	900	469	...	39	50	123	24.7	8.7
1886	7.8	101	907	527	...	42	48	127	24.7	8.4
1887	9.6	106	941	612	...	40	50	135	24.3	8.1
1888	11.7	113	971	720	...	44	56	140	24.3	8.2
1889	12.1	94	973	735	...	44	59	145	24.4	8.3
1890	10.5	106	928	734	...	45	59	152	24.6	8.6
1891	37.9	124	907	812	...	44	59	163	25.1	8.7
1892	53.4	114	1,055	884	...	44	58	163	25.9	8.6
1893	...	131	1,074	928	...	48	59	167	25.9	8.5
1894	...	117	1,072	910	...	52	61	171	25.3	8.4
1895	...	119	1,048	994	...	57	61	179	25.8	8.7
1896	...	133	1,055	1,031	...	63	66	190	26.5	8.8
1897	...	139	1,134	1,206	...	69	72	199	27.2	8.7
1898	...	161	1,128	1,444	...	71	79	208	27.4	8.9
1899	...	141	1,235	1,518	...	75	80	215	27.8	9.2

G1 Banknote Circulation

	Austria A (kroner) million	Belgium A (francs) million	Bulgaria A (leva) million	Czecho C (koruna) million	Denmark A (kroner) million	Finland A (markka) thousand	France[4] A (francs) million	Germany C (marks) million	Greece A[22] (drachmae) million
1900	1,494	632	22	…	97	712	4,034	1,715	…
1901	1,585	649	27	…	99	624	4,116	1,756	…
1902	1,635	676	25	…	103	703	4,162	1,777	…
1903	1,771	671	33	…	110	724	4,310	1,843	…
1904	1,751	694	40	…	111	725	4,283	1,858	…
1905	1,847	724	37	…	118	927	4,408	1,927	…
1906	1,982	770	45	…	124	924	4,659	2,023	…
1907	2,028	798	49	…	129	951	4,800	2,096	…
1908	2,113	807	72	…	133	860	4,853	2,187	…
1909	2,188	845	72	…	134	1,117	5,080	2,287	…
1910	2,376	905	82	…	137	1,239	5,198	2,291	…
1911	2,541	970	111	…	148	1,153	5,243	2,492	…
1912	2,816	1,035	164	…	155	1,175	5,323	2,778	…
1913	2,494	1,067	189	…	165[11] 152	1,130	5,665	2,902	245
1914	5,137	1,614	227	…	207	1,417	7,325	5,862	265
1915	7,162	1,320	370	…	220	2,316	12,280	8,360	392
1916	10,889	1,282	834	…	285	4,213	15,552	11,438	569
1917	18,440	1,268	1,493	…	338	7,645	19,845	18,246	865
						million			
1918	…	3,210	2,299	…	450	12	27,536	33,073	1,274
1919	…	4,786	2,858	4,723	489	11	34,744	50,065	1,382
1920	30,646	6,260	3,354	11,289	557	13	38,186	81,398	1,508
1921	227,016[15]	6,415	3,615	10,323	471	14	37,679	122,500	2,161
1922	4,080,177	6,876	3,886	10,064	459	14	36,352	1,295,228[21]	3,149
1923	7,125,755	7,357	4,139	9,599	473	14	37,356	2,274	4,681
	million schilling								
1924	839	7,873	4,530	8,810	478	13	39,938	3,891	4,866
1925	890	7,814	3,655	8,408	438	13	44,071	4,627	5,339
1926	937	9,432[18][19]	3,481	8,203	386	13	53,420	5,081	4,865
1927	998	10,035	3,727	8,417	354	15	53,490	5,470	4,966
1928	1,064	11,512	4,173	8,466	360	15	60,061	5,653	5,690
1929	1,094	13,437	3,609	8,230	367	14	64,647	5,635	5,193
1930	1,090	15,818	3,296	7,824	360	13	72,119	5,409	4,803
1931	1,183	18,015	2,919	7,679	346	13	79,033	5,389	4,003
1932	914	18,053	2,635	6,816[20] 6,267	332	11	82,139	4,163	4,714
1933	952	16,981	2,984	5,906	375	12	83,065	4,220	5,449
1934	964	17,591	2,449	5,640	386	13	81,037	4,471	5,686
1935	976	20,637	2,497	5,761	384	14	82,163	4,865	5,988
1936	944	22,452	2,571	6,478	399	16	84,069	5,354	6,203
1937	944	21,460	2,569	6,902	417	21	88,308	5,884	6,776
1938	…	22,018	2,800	…	441	21	101,556	8,605	7,239
1939	…	27,898	4,245	…	600	40	128,514	12,756	9,453
1940	…	34,426	6,518	…	741	56	181,807	15,135	15,369
	thousand million						thousand million		
1941	…	48.2	13,467	…	842	73	240	20,577	48,798
1942	…	67.7	18,922	…	983	96	313	25,639	335,000
1943	…	83.7	…	…	1,359	108	435	34,702	3,199,000
1944	…	38.8	…	…	1,658	157	568	51,110	…

G1 Banknote Circulation

	Hungary[25] A (kroner) million	Ireland[5] B (pounds) million	N.Ireland[26] B (pounds) million	Italy C (lire) million	Netherland[7] C (gulden) million	Norway A (kroner) million	Poland A (marks) thousand million	Portugal C (escudos) million	Romania[14] A (lei) million
1900	...	6.8	...	1,602	214	66	...	...	117
1901	...	6.8	...	1,606	222	63	...	...	130
1902	...	6.8	...	1,624	222	63	...	...	164
1903	...	7.3	...	1,682	234	61	...	...	175
1904	...	6.7	...	1,722	236	60	...	...	179
1905	...	6.4	...	1,849	259	66	...	...	196
1906	...	6.5	...	2,043	277	69	...	...	239
1907	...	6.8	...	2,289	260	73	...	...	273
1908	...	6.7	...	2,299	266	73	...	...	263
1909	...	6.9	...	2,365	274	78	...	...	272
1910	...	7.4	...	2,469	281	84	...	...	299
1911	...	7.6	...	2,678	283	93	...	...	382
1912	...	7.4	...	2,711	299	99	...	...	463
1913	...	8.3	...	2,783	310	108	...	87	424[14] 437
1914	...	9.1	...	3,593	313	134	...	96	578
1915	...	13.6	...	5,050	472	162	...	115	762
1916	...	17.6	...	6,329	618	251	...	140	1,452
1917	...	20.9	...	10,265	746	326	...	193	4,110
1918	...	27.5	—	14,087	890	436	1	274	4,638
1919	...	30.6	...	18,814	1,023	454	5	370	6,364
1920	14,308	26.9	...	22,277	1,052	492	49	611	10,455
1921	25,175	20.6	...	21,754	1,052	419	230	737	13,908
1922	75,887	18.1	...	20,496	996	395	793	1,054	15,162
1923	931,000	17.1	...	19,810	966	406	125,372	1,420	17,917
							million zlotys		
1924	4,514,000	16.6	...	20,514	1,018	401	642	1,763	19,356
	million pengos[24]								*thousand million*
1925	416	15.9	...	21,450	915	365	663	1,821	20.1
1926	471	15.0	...	20,134[13]	852	337	880	1,854	21.0
1927	487	14.7	...	18,776	819	331	1,170	1,857	21.0
1928	513		...	17,456	810	315	1,394	1,990	21.2
1929	501	161	...	16,854	833	318	1,404	2,046	21.1
1930	469	17	...	15,681	837	312	1,331	1,994	19.6
1931	423	16.6	...	14,295	860	334	1,220	2,062	23.7
1932	353	16.2	...	13,672	1,006	315	1,003	2,001	21.6
1933	369	16.8	...	13,243	990	327	1,004	1,989	21.2
1934	381	16.8	...	13,145	937	333	981	2,137	22.3
1935	417	17.5	...	16,944	889	348	1,007	2,205	23.1
1936	436	18.5	...	17,831	792	428	1,034	2,257	25.7
1937	466	19.5	...	18,818	823	449	1,059	2,224	29.4
		Southern Ireland							
1938	863	15.9	5.3	20,811	934[7] 992	477	1,406	2,279	34.9
1939	975	18.0	5.6	26,880	1,152	575	1,928[27]	2,550	48.8
1940	1,387	21.2	7.6	34,204	1,552	...	...	2,903	64.3
1941	1,984	24.5	10.8	53,759	2,116	...	...	4,488	96.6
1942	2,958	30.3	14.2	78,778	3,034	...	...	5,481	117
1943	4,392[24]	33.1	16.0	180,823	3,478	...	...	6,910	160[14]
1944	12,424	37.8	16.3	318,985	5,078	...	...	7,642	374

G1 Banknote Circulation

	Russia C (rubels) million	Spain A (pesetas) million	Sweden		Switzerland		U.K:G.B.		Yugoslavia A (dinari) million
			A (kroner) million	B (kroner) million	A (francs) million	B (francs) million	A[1] (pounds) million	B[8] (pounds) million	
1900	491	1,592	72	82	—	217	29.4	9.2	...
1901	555	1,639	101	56	—	214	29.6	9.0	...
1902	542	1,623	137	26	—	223	29.4	8.7	...
1903	554	1,609	166	4	—	222	28.9	8.5	...
1904	578	1,599	173	3	—	228	28.3	8.1	...
1905	854	1,550	185	1	—	233	29.0	8.0	
1906	1,208	1,525	202	—	—	235	28.9	7.9	
1907	1,195	1,557	190	—	159	196	28.9	7.9	
1908	1,155	1,643	201	—	204	98	28.8	7.5	
1909	1,087	1,671	202	—	262	48	29.3	7.4	
1910	1,174	1,715	206	—	297	—	28.3	7.3	
1911	1,234	1,763	218	—	315	—	28.6	7.3	
1912	1,326	1,863	228	—	339	—	28.8	7.5	
1913	1,495	1,932	234	—	314	—	28.7	7.7	
1914	1,665	1,974	304	—	456	—	31.6[30] 61	8.6	
1915	2,947	2,100	328	—	466	—	90	11	...
1916	5,617	2,360	418	—	537	—	157	14	...
1917	9,104[29]	2,799	573	—	702	—	206	17	...
1918	...	3,334	814	—	976	—	311	23	...
1919	...	3,867	748	—	1,036	—	413	27	...
1920	...	4,326	760	—	1,024	—	449	29	3,344
1921	...	4,244	628	—	1,009	—	437	27	4,688
1922	...	4,137	584	—	976	—	400	24	5,040
1923	220	4,353	576	—	982	—	388	23	5,790
1924	523	4,547	537	—	914	—	391	22	6,002
1925	958	4,440	530	—	876	—	384	22	6,063
1926	1,282	4,339	525	—	874	—	376	21	5,812
1927	1,502	4,202	526	—	917	—	375	21	5,743
1928	...	4,397	546	—	953	—	372	21	5,528
1929	...	4,458	569	—	999	—	362	21	5,818
1930	...	4,767	594	—	1,062	—	359	21	5,397
1931	...	4,993	583	—	1,609	—	355	21	5,172
1932	...	4,834	598	—	1,613	—	360	21	4,773
1933	...	4,825	648	—	1,510	—	371	21	4,327
1934	...	4,696	708	—	1,440	—	379	21	4,384
1935	...	4,837	786	—	1,366	—	395	22	4,890
1936	...	...	893	—	1,482	—	431	22	5,409
1937	...	...	980	—	1,531	—	480	23	5,834
1938	...	...	1,061	—	1,751	—	485	24	6,921
1939	...	...	1,422	—	2,050	—	506	25	9,698
1940	...	...	1,482	—	2,273	—	574	29	13,834
1941	...	13,536	1,700	—	2,337	—	650	34	15,281[31]
1942	...	15,738	2,016	—	2,637	—	807	44	...
1943	...	16,381	2,266	—	3,049	—	965	54	...
1944	...	17,729	2,492	—	3,548	—	1,134	61	...

G1   Banknote Circulation

	Austria	Belgium	Denmark	Finland	France[4]	West Germany	East	Greece	Ireland[5]	N. Ireland[26]
	A	**A**	**A**	**A**	**A**	**C**	**A**	**A**	**C**	**B**
	(schilling) thousand million	(francs) thousand million	(kroner) million	(markka) million	(francs) thousand million	(marks) thousand million	(marks) million	(drachmae) thousand million[23]	(pounds) million	(pounds) million
1945	...	69.9	1,561	136	541	...	...	...	42.8	15.7
1946	5.7	72.2	1,633	182	638	...	...	0.54	45.0	16.0
1947	4.3[16][17]	78.3[19] 80.4	1,641	252	808	...	...	0.97	48.7	14.7
1948	5.6	84.9	1,614	274	849	6.6	...	1.2	504	1.2
1949	5.7	87.9	1,627	296	1,110	7.7	3,288	1.9	545	11.2
1950	6.3	88.6	1,709	344	1,389	8.2	3,363	1.9	57.3	10.0
1951	8.0	95.0	1,817	448	1,679	9.2	3,331	2.2	62.4	9.2
1952	9.0	97.8	1,966	462	1,934	10.5	3,353	2.5	67.4	8.9
1953	10.5	102	2,118	450	2,133	11.5	3,564	3.5[33]	71.7	8.2
1954	12.3	103	2,145	479	2,348	12.3	4,298	3.9	75.3	8.3
1955	13.0	108	2,217	559	2,604	13.6	4,123	4.9	77.2	8.4
1956	14.3	112	2,372	607	2,895	14.5	4,496	5.9	76.4	9.5
1957	15.4	113	2,432	606	3,135	16.1	3,479	6.8	80.7	9.9
1958	16.6	117	2,642	651	3,296[32]	17.1	3,756	7.4	79.4	9.4
1959	17.7	118	2,892	694	33.5	19.0	4,161	8.6	77.8	8.9
1960	18.7	124	3,006	727	35.3	20.5	4,543	10.2	81.5	8.7
1961	20.9	129	3,318	837	40.1	23.0	4,225	11.6	86.8	8.5
1962	22.4	138	3,504	774	45.3	24.1	4,413	13.8	91.3	7.9
1963	24.0	151	3,835	944	51.0	25.4	4,512	16.1	99	7.4
1964	25.7	160	4,117	1,003	55.7	27.7	4,503	19.3	114	7.2
1965	27.5	170	4,442	1,029	64.2	29.5	5,162	22.3	112	7.4
1966	29.6	175	4,906	1,106	67.6	30.8	5,466	25.1	119	7.8
1967	31.2	177	5,084	1,052	70.5	31.6	5,844	32.3	125	8.9
1968	32.4	183	5,444	1,160	72.2	32.5	6,428	31.9	138	10.9
1969	34.1	183	5,816	1,298	72.4[4] 70.1	34.6	7,045	34.2	144	12.9
1970	35.7	188	5,387	1,344	73.4	36.5	7,407	37.5	159	15.3
1971	39.0	202	5,382	1,479	74.8	39.5	7,684	41.6	169	22.0
1972	44.7	223	5,874	1,730	80.4	44.5	8,778	49.0	188	27.1
1973	48.9	239	6,523	1,907	85.6	46.2	9,181	62.9	221	28.4
1974	52.4	256	6,732	2,260	93.6	50.3	9,581	78.0	248	29.6
1975	56.0	288	8,206	2,617	102	55.1	10,139	89.1	295	33.8
1976	58.9	307	8,939	2,635	110	59.0	10,488	109	339	36.3
1977	62.2	335	10,245	2,892	114	65.6	11,313	129	389	40.5
1978	67.4	360	11,150	3,509	124	74.8	11,909	157	469	45
1979	72.0	372	12,317	4,020	129	79.4	12,372	179	600	48
1980	76.8	376	12,949	4,572	136	83.7	12,250	205	680	51[24] 53
1981	77.7	382	14,018	5,152	152	83.8	12,315	255	752	65
1982	80.5	382	14,601	5,572	168	88.6	12,534	294	832	86
1983	88.7	396	15,644	6,029	180	96.1	13,034	335	924	126
1984	89.9	398	17,237	6,744	188	101	13,352	392	997	164
1985	90.5	395	18,599	7,304	195	105	13,651	496	1,026	184
1986	93.9	415	19,702	7,856	201	114	14,330	531	1,067	208
1987	98.4	418	21,093	9,117	210	126	15,014	617	1,130	233
1988	104	422	22,094	10,601	222	144	15,623	722	1,246	271
1989	113	420	23,290	13,129	252	151	...	952	1,394	324
1990	119	419	24,453	14,555	257	167		1,142	1,507	360
1991	128	423	25,565	14,528	255	181		1,233	1,546	417
1992	135	422	25,391	14,508[37]	252	213		1,382	1,421	510
1993	143	427	26,880	14,994[37]	249	224		1,476	1,577	558
1994	...	431	...	14,315	270	250		...	1,907	...
1995	...	466	...	15,611	275	263		...	2,092	...
1996	...	486	...	16,891	278	276		...	2,287	...
1997	...	501	...	17,817	283	276		...	2,619	...
1998	...	506	...	17,689	287	271		...	3,040	...

G1 Banknote Circulation

	Italy C (lire) thousand million	Netherlands C (gulden) million	Norway A (kroner) million	Poland[28] A (zloty) thousand million	Portugal C (escudos) thousand million	Spain A (pesetas) thousand million	Sweden A (kronor) million	Switzerland A (francs) million	UK A[1] (pounds) million	GB B[8] (pounds) million	Yugoslavia A (dinari) thousand million
1945	382	1,386	...	...	8.2	19.0	2,782	3,835	1,283	65	17.8
1946	505	2,748	1,953	0.06	8.8	22.8	2,877	4,091	1,357	68	20.5
1947	788	3,010	2,111	0.09	8.8	26.0	2,895	4,383	1,382	72	29.5
1948	963	3,115	2,191	0.13[28] 3.9	8.7	26.5	3,113	4,594	1,252	66	39.3
1949	1,048	3,036	2,334	5.2	8.5	27.6	3,287	4,566	1,264	69	45.1
1950	1,165	2,911	2,415	4.6	8.5[35] 7.7	31.7	3,513	4,664	1,283	70	40.0
1951	1,292	2,991	2,667	5.6	8.4	36.2	...	4,927	1,341	74	38.3
1952	1,381	3,118	2,916	6.2	8.6	38.5	...	5,122	1,434	81	50.0
1953	1,449	3,330	3,128	8.4	8.9	38.8	...	5,229	1,530	90	67.6
1954	1,538	3,579	3,321	10.1	9.4	43.0	...	5,412	1,628	96	87.8
1955	1,671	3,955	3,305	11.6	9.9	47.0	5,319	5,516	1,758	102	88
1956	1,818	4,073	3,502	17.4	10.3	55.8	5,598	5,810	1,873	109	95
1957	1,914	4,187	3,469	19.7	10.9	66.7	5,840	5,931	1,964	117	126
1958	2,061	4,418	3,511	22.6	11.5	72.5	6,059	6,109	2,033	119	140
1959	2,237	4,513	3,675	23.2	12.2	74.1	6,266	6,344	2,104	121	176
1960	2,424	4,900	3,823	26.3	12.8	78.9	6,559	6,854	2,210	125	193
1961	2,779	5,278	4,043	30.5	14.8	88.6	6,870	7,656	2,305	128	246
1962	3,234	5,565	4,287	32.6	15.7	104	7,330	8,506	2,326	126	284
1963	3,699	6,019	4,517	33.2	16.5	120	7,869	9,035	2,397	126	360
1964	3,914	6,742	4,756	36.7	17.5	142	8,386	9,722	2,561	129	460[36]
1965	4,282	7,479	5,118	39.4	19.7	165	8,746	10,043	2,726	130	5.1
1966	4,595	8,060	5,501	44.1	19.9	187	9,297	10,651	2,892	134	6.9
1967	5,126	8,350	5,918	48.4	20.3	209	9,965	11,327	2,971	136	8.0
1968	5,390	8,442	6,257	53.3	19.8	227	11,243	12,047	3,119	142	9.6
1969	6,100	8,865	6,644	57.4	26.7	253	10,962	12,518	3,240	148	11.9
1970	6,619	9,316	7,365	58.6	29.7	274	11,319	13,106	3,409	155	14.9
1971	7,281	9,763	8,070	67.3	31.9	309	12,704	14,310	3,678[1] 3,785	164	18.0[36] 18.3
1972	8,747	10,684	8,801	78.2	36.1	350	13,925	16,635	4,379	177	23.5
1973	10,029	11,244	9,536	96.3	38.3	418	15,229	18,296	4,788	196	29.0
1974	11,160	12,153	10,866	117	69.7	488	17,274	19,436	5,520	227	34.8
	million million	thousand million	thousand million				thousand million	thousand million			
1975	12.9	13.8	12.5	141	110[35]	580	20.1	19.1	6,138	266	41.9
1976	14.6	15.2	14.3[34] 14.8	164	109	681	22.1	19.7	6,858	299	49.1
1977	16.5	16.6	16.7	182	113	851	24.4	20.4	8,019	333	58.3
1978	19.6	17.8	17.8	209	121	1,048	27.7	22.5	9,122	390[88] 382	75.0
1979	22.6	19.0	18.6	239	142	1,161	316	23.8	10,089	422	90.7
1980	26.6	20.8	19.8	297	165	1,322	34.4	24.1	10,611	468	116
1981	31.0	21.0	21.1	409	188	1,470	37.1	23.3	11,001		149
1982	34.7	22.0	22.0	615	219	1,672	39.0	24.5	11,271		196
1983	33.8	24.9	23.0	731	240	1,841	42.7	24.8	12,152		249
1984	43.8	26.3	24.5	839	267	2,038	46.5	26.5	12,610		327
1985	47.7	27.1	27.2	1,031	319	2,261	48.1	25.9	12,612		551
1986	51.3	28.2	29.0	1,188	399	2,604	54.0	27.0	14,119		1,161
1987	55.2	31.7 33.3	30.8	1,339	458	2,973	56.3	27.3	14,654		2,153
1988	59.8	34.6	30.9	2,728	510	3,413	59.5	29.0	16,071		5,852
1989	65.9	36.0	31.6	12,779	...	4,003	66.1	29.2	16,849		12,375
1990	69.4	36.4	32.7	48,079	...	4,717	69.6	29.6	17,283		42,047
1991	76.4	37.0	34.3	...	...	5,791	73.1	29.2	17,466		69,400[38]
1992	85.6	37.0	34.7	...	...	6,210	73.9[37]	29.3	17,542		458,330
1993	89.8	37.6	38.0	...	...	6,682	75.7[37]	29.3	18,218		518,188
1994	...	40.93	...	...	...	7,165	...	...	...		...
1995	...	41.30	...	...	...	7,535	...	...	...		...
1996	...	41.67	...	...	...	7,942	...	...	...		...
1997	...	42.10	...	...	...	8,378	...	...	...		...
1998	...	40.90	...	...	...	8,437	...	...	...		...

G1   Banknote Circulation

NOTES

1. SOURCES:- The main sources were the official publications noted on p. xv with gaps filled from League of Nations, *Statistical Yearbooks*, *Memorandum on Currency and Central Banks, Money and Banking*, and *Monthly Bulletin of Statistics*. The Germany figures to 1913 are taken from W.G. Hoffman, *Das Wachstum der Deutschen Wirtschaft seit der Mitte des 19 Jahrhunderts* (Berlin, etc., 1965); the British and Irish figures to 1978 from B.R. Mitchell; *British Historical Statistics* (Cambridge, 1988), where the original sources are given, or the Bank of England, *Statistical Summary* (for Irish and legal tender notes); the Russian figures to 1917 from P.A. Khromov, *Economic Development of Russia in the 19th and 20th Centuries, 1800–1917* (Moscow, 1950); the Bank of Spain figures to 1873 from J.A. Galvarriato, *El Banco de España*; (Madrid, 1932) and the private Spanish issues from Albert Carreras *et al*, *Estadisticas Historicas de España*; the Swedish total note circulation 1750–1803 from L. Jorberg, *A History of Prices in Sweden 1732–1914* (2 vols., Lund, 1972). In addition the following data were supplied by the respective national statistical offices:- Belgium to 1857; Finland to 1899; and Netherlands to 1864.
2. Unless otherwise indicated, the statistics are of circulation at the end of each year.

FOOTNOTES

1. Figures to 1764 are at 31 August. For 1766–73 they are at 28/29 February. From 1775 to 1834 (1st line) they are averages of end-February and end-August figures. From 1834 (2nd line) to 1841 they are averages of 12 monthly figures. From 1842–44 they are averages of average weekly circulation in thirteen 4-week periods. From 1845 to 1971 (1st line) they are averages of 52 weekly figures. Subsequently they are for a day in December.
2. The circulation in the Italian provinces is not included. In 1857 it amounted to 25 million gulden.
3. Figures to 1820 are at 31 March. The original currency units have been converted into markkaa.
4. Averages of 52 weekly figures. From 1969 (2nd line) figures relate to notes in the hands of the public.
5. Averages of 12 monthly figures to 1841, and averages of average weekly circulation in 13 4-week periods from 1842 to 1938 (1st line). Figures from 1938 (2nd line) are at 31 December. Note: *All* Irish banks are included up to 1938 (1st line), and only southern Irish banks subsequently. Irish legal tender notes are included from their issue in 1929.
6. September–December only.
7. Averages of 12 month-end figures for years ended 31 March up to 1884. Circulation at 31 March from 1885 to 1938 (1st line), and year-end figures subsequently.
8. Country bank and Scottish bank issues, being averages of 12 monthly figures to 1841, and averages of average weekly circulation in 13 4-week periods from 1842 to 1978 (1st line). Subsequently they are averages of 12 figures on a day in the middle of each month.
9. Two kroner = 1 gulden.
10. Figures to 1857 are averages of monthly figures. The year-end figures for 1851 and 1855 are 50 and 96 respectively.
11. Figures to 1913 (1st line) are at 31 July. 2 kroner = 1 rigsdaler.
12. Excluding state note issues to 1876 (1st line), for which only isolated figures are available previously, viz:- 1850 154; 1862 98; 1863 101; 1864 104; 1865 108; and 1872 184.
13. At 1 June or 1 July for 1894–1926.
14. Averages of 12 monthly figures to 1913 (1st line), and year-end figures subsequently. A small amount of coin is included after 1943. Circulation at end 1945 was 1,232 and at end 1946 6,397 million lei.
15. January 1922.
16. At 7 December.
17. The figures are subsequently averages of 12 month-end figures.
18. At 25 October.
19. For 1927–1947 (1st line) at 25 December.
20. Excluding 10 and 20 koruna notes from 1932 (2nd line). Circulation in 1945–7 was as follows in million koruna:- 1945 24, 1946 44, 1947 59.
21. 1 new mark = 1 million million old marks.
22. Including the issues of the Bank of Crete and the Ionian Bank up to 1919 when they ceased.
23. 1 new (1944) drachma = 50 thousand million old drachmae.
24. 1 pengo = 12, 500 paper koruna. A small amount of coin is included after 1943.
25. Circulation at the end of 1945 was 765,446 million pengos. In 1946–49 it was as follows in million forints (1 forint = 400, 000 quadrillion pengos):- 1946 1,024, 1947 2,099, 1948 2,947, 1949 2,761
26. Averages of average weekly circulation in 13 4-week periods to 197.
27. August.
28. The figures from 1948 (2nd line) are of total monetary circulation. Figures from 1945 are in new (1950) zloties, one of which equalled 100 old zloties.
29. On 1 October 1917 (according to P.I. Lyaschenko, *History of the National Economy of Russia*) the circulation was 17,175 million rubels.
30. Treasury-issued currency notes are included from 1914 (2nd line) until 1928, when they were absorbed into the Bank of England issue.
31. March.
32. From 1959 in new francs (1 new = 100 old francs).
33. From 1954 in new drachmae (1 new = 1, 000 old drachmae).
34. Subsequently including a small amount of coin.
35. Subsequently notes in the hands of the public. There was a change in the scope of the series in 1976.
36. From 1965 in new dinari (1 new = 100 old dinari). A small amount of coin is included from 1971 (2nd line).
37. Including coinage.
38. Yugoslavia only.

G2 DEPOSITS IN COMMERCIAL BANKS (in millions of stated unit)

	Belgium[1] (Francs)	Denmark[13] (Kroner)	Finland[2] (markkaa)	Germany[3] (marks)	Norway[4] (kroner)	Russia[5] (rubels)	Spain[27] (pesetas)	Sweden[6] (kroner)	U.K.[7] (pounds)
1848	...	1	...	...	0.1	...	...	...	...
1849	...	1	...	...	0.3	...	...	...	...
1850	...	1	...	...	0.3	...	...	...	...
1851	...	1	...	...	...	...	...	...	...
1852	...	1	...	6	...	...	...	...	...
1853	...	1	...	19	...	...	...	...	...
1854	...	1	...	22	...	...	...	...	...
1855	...	3	...	30	1.5	...	...	...	...
1856	...	4	...	42	...	...	15	...	...
1857	...	4	...	51	...	...	17	...	...
1858	...	4	...	58	...	...	18	...	...
1859	...	9	...	52	...	...	25	...	...
1860	...	13	...	157	16.4	...	26	...	...
1861	...	16	...	180	...	...	18	...	...
1862	...	17	1.8	202	...	...	18	...	...
1863	...	19	5.7	...	...	...	19	...	...
1864	...	19	11.2	...	...	...	16	...	...
1865	...	17	15.2	...	25	...	21	...	...
1866	...	18	13.5	...	...	...	29	...	...
1867	...	21	15.5	...	...	...	33	...	...
1868	...	26	18.0	...	...	...	29	...	...
1869	...	25	17.6	220	...	...	36	...	...
1870	...	27	18.6	230	35	...	42	...	427
1871	...	27	19.3	250	...	...	52	...	475
1872	...	35	20.2	498	...	...	51	...	504
1873	...	54	22.4	716	...	275	35	...	499
1874	...	59	28.7	648	...	300	62	...	519
1875	455	71	30.9	542	55	278	81	201	539
1876	423	71	34.5	479	68	227	80	235	538
1877	430	67	31.8	385	64	275	92	235	515
1878	468	55	28.3	424	65	254	92	230	475
1879	562	61	27.1	527	70	197	87	242	485
1880	537	78	33.1	529	81	207	175	269	495
1881	653	102	39.0	678	85	227	160	275	509
1882	687	120	43.5	626	97	212	121	288	522
1883	766	117	46.7	780	99	214	125	306	525
1884	700	123	50.0	921	100	219	116	326	526
1885	701	129	54.1	1,034	100	264	112	333	539
1886	639	120	56.0	1,084	98	255	119	348	539
1887	646	167	55.8	1,058	101	235	125	354	555
1888	643	152	62.5	1,142	105	212	141	354	579
1889	694	160	77.1	1,558	117	230	173	354	599
1890	705	176	89	1,509	120	288	117	371	614
1891	690	155	98	1,548	114	320	132	385	640
1892	673	161	106	1,531	123	285	121	391	645
1893	676	168	118	1,558	127	268	128	405	635
1894	703	184	132	1,999	136	308	107	420	668
1895	736	214	167	2,242	151	305	136	435	695
1896	804	233	197	2,251	153	354	151	453	733
1897	1,044	244	232	2,547	179	448	177	510	762
1898	915	255	256	2,995	203	551	278	583	788
1899	1,033	283	282	3,449	219	548	244	688	313

G2   Deposits in Commercial Banks (in millions of stated unit except as otherwise indicated)

	Austria[8] (kronen)	Belgium[1] (francs)	Bulgaria[10] (leva)	Czech[12] (koruna)	Denmark[13] (kroner)	Finland[2] (markkaa)	France[15] (francs) thousand million	Germany[3] (marks)	Greece[19] (drachma)	Hungary[20] (pengoes)	Ireland[21] (pounds)	Italy[22] (lire)
1900	...	1,128	...	...	310	289	4.5	3,742	...	...	...	...
1901	...	1,079	...	...	328	306	5.0	3,730	...	...	...	...
1902	...	1,085	...	...	387	301	4.7	4,141	...	...	...	...
1903	...	1,168	...	...	423	326	5.3	4,409	...	...	...	...
1904	...	1,240	...	...	451	336	6.6	5,182	...	...	...	...
1905	...	1,455	...	...	509	398	6.5	6,060	...	...	...	...
1906	...	1,707	...	...	571	394	7.1	6,876	...	...	...	...
1907	...	1,666	...	...	659	456	7.4	7,662	...	...	...	...
1908	...	1,846	...	...	733	478	8.5	8,027	...	...	...	...
1909	...	1,938	...	...	683	517	9.2	8,915	...	...	53	...
1910	...	2,150	...	...	701	544	9.7	10,025	...	...	55	...
1911	...	2,362	...	...	778	582	10.1	10,344	...	...	57	...
1912	...	2,512[1]	...	...	801	591	10.3	10,369	...	...	58	...
1913	4,181[8] / 2,720	2,335	170	...	899	619	11.4	10,606[3] / 9,720	207	4,739[20]	62	1.7
1914	...	...	...	...	957	640	...	...	...	...	66	...
1915	...	...	...	...	1,077	724	...	...	...	...	67	...
1916	...	...	...	...	1,372	917	...	...	...	...	75	...
1917	...	...	...	...	2,175	1,470[2]	...	...	...	...	91	...
1918	9,974	...	...	...	2,669	2,846	...	...	439	...	121	7.7
1919	16,378	...	...	...	3,550	3,385	25.1	...	636	...	153	12.4
1920	37,204[8] / 77,908	8,271	1,578	9,207	4,037 / 4,168[13]	3,613	25.3	...	797	...	183	16.5
1921	370,410	8,518	2,247	11,616	1,195	2,788	26.3	...	1,053	...	194	18.5
1922	7,452,300	9,506	2,461[10] / 3,266	13,091	1,067	4,136	27.9	...	1,138	...	193	...
	schillings											
1923	1,378	10,156	4,729	12,048	910	4,746	30.6	1,995[17]	1,669	...	178[21] / 147	12.3
1924	1,856	9,815	5,394	10,629	612	5,402	28.0	5,086	2,104	...	141	14.5
1925	2,093	11,264	6,497	10,646	589	5,464	39.0	7,103	2,232	1,125	133	15.0
1926	2,667	14,294	7,139	10,777	515	6,102	47.0	9,678	2,617	1,502	128	15.9[22]
1927	2,947	18,159	8,635	11,675	618	6,982	54.0	11,666	2,941	2,123	128	18.3
1928	3,219	20,734	11,726	12,711	554	7,380	72.9	13,197	5,289 / 11,287[18]	2,703	128	19.6[22] / 22.4
1929	2,714	21,290	12,678	12,566	551	7,481	74.3	13,831	11,192	2,820	124	22.4
1930	3,210	...	12,492	12,993	614	7,698	79.9	12,653	11,950	2,970	123	21.8
1931	...	20,037	12,256	11,221	545	7,378	75.2	8,902	10,610	2,413	122	19.8
1932	1,691	17,506	11,983	10,832	533[18] / 514	7,155	74.4	7,575	9,778	2,164	131	19.8
1933	1,449	18,083	11,280	10,884	554	7,498	67.8	6,953	10,714	2,099	124	20.4
1934	1,372	...	11,823	11,471	559	7,635	66.9	7,297	11,877	2,100	120	20.3
1935	1,374	16,067[9]	12,306	10,857	560	7,966	54.3	7,876	12,021	2,182	118	20.6
1936	1,307	17,312[9] / 24,100[1]	13,135	10,946	610	8,598	62.3	8,560[3] / 6,573	12,597	2,183	119	22.6
	thousand million	thousand million				thousand million						
1937	1,180[8]	23.0	14.3	11,115	674	10.0	70.4	7,263	13,737	2,352	117[21] / 21.8	24.1[22] / 19.0
1938	...	19.7	15.2	...	670	10.8	85.4[15] / 80	8,298	12,381	2,403	22.4	21.1
1939	...	16.0	16.4[10] / 12.1	...	833	10.4[14] / 9.4	107	...	12,753[19]	2,685[20] / 1,038	24.3	26.6
1940	...	20.1	13.2	...	949	12.2	114	...	...	1,219	26.6	36.8
1941	...	24.0	15.7	...	1,239	13.4	...	...	...	1,637	32.1	47
1942	...	29.9	23.7	...	1,475	15.8	...	...	...	2,074	37.9	63
1943	...	41.2	34.4	...	1,823	18.6	...	...	...	2,869	44.4	88
1944	...	24.0	41.7	...	2,467	21.8	260[16]	...	...	3,664	50.7	185

G2 Deposits in Commercial Banks (in millions of stated unit)

1900–1944

	Netherlands[23] (gulden)	Norway[24] (kroner)	Poland[24] (marks)	Portugal[25] (esudos)	Romania[26] (lei)	Russia[5] (rubels)	Spain[27] (pesetes)	Sweden[6] (kroner)	Switzerland[28] (francs)	U.K.[7] (pounds)	Yugo[2] (dinari)
					thousand million						
1900	...	257	...	...	...	536	246	772	...	839	...
1901	...	284	...	...	...	545	279	838	...	834	...
1902	...	281	...	...	...	613	225	874	...	841	...
1903	...	291	...	...	...	722	239	915	...	815	...
1904	...	298	...	...	...	776	242	957	...	826	...
1905	...	302	...	...	...	671	238	1,042	...	846	...
1906	...	339	...	...	...	761	275	1,174	1,179	867	...
1907	...	373	...	...	...	818	276	1,314	1,221	887	...
1908	...	391	...	...	...	977	300	1,395	1,295	909	...
1909	...	428	...	...	...	1,262	325	1,414	1,494	919	...
1910	...	449	...	...	...	1,675	372	1,465	1,585	956	...
1911	...	482	...	...	...	1,817	388	1,516	1,717	976	...
1912	...	520	...	...	...	2,293	384	1,602	1,844	1,017	...
1913	292	592	...	...	...	2,539	381	1,692	1,837	1,064	...
1914	...	630	...	...	...	2,873	346	1,794	1,863	1,168	...
1915	...	856	...	...	...	3,931	482	1,999	2,260	1,287	...
1916	...	1,441				6,748	650	2,497	2,797	1,499	...
1917	...	2,200	...	63	...	...	950	3,221	3,416	1,763	...
1918	1,001	2,720	...	101	...	...	4,595	4,502	3,906	2,075	...
1919	1,265	2,973	1,895	328	...	...	1,951	5,018	4,308	2,424	...
1920	1,351	3,113	6,733	...	8.1	...	2,273	5,095	4,440	2,573	4,461
1921	1,328	2,982	32,626	...	13.1	...	2,311	4,853	4,050	2,562[7] 2,276	5,353
1922	1,207	2,697	136,603	...	18.4	...	2,641	4,325	3,789	1,245[7]	6,962
1923	1,235	2,261	...	...	17.7	...	2,616	3,869	3,863	1,208	7,464
			(zlotys)								
1924	1,201	2,065	183	707	20.4	...	2,290	3,675	4,117	1,199	8,713
1925	1,261	1,993	306	736	28.3	...	2,239	3,484	4,251	1,170	10,898
1926	1,293	1,993	458	815	33.5	...	2,376	3,453	4,708	1,173	10,682
1927	1,367	1,765	661	867	39.3	...	2,876	3,484	5,247	1,193	11,448
1928	1,390	1,645	716	984	46.9	...	3,232	3,431	5,738	1,230	12,226
1929	1,355	1,596	679	1,048	57.3	...	3,240	3,481	6,462	1,152	13,185
1930	1,473	1,498	642	883	53.3	...	3,470	3,631	6,781[28]	1,201	14,172
1931	1,242	1,373	486	811	30.2	...	2,764	3,554	3,267	1,064	11,733
1932	1,112	1,245	448	818	26.2	...	2,963	3,556	3,035	1,210	9,556
1933	996	1,137	456	838	23.0	...	3,026	3,629	2,731	1,248	8,682
1934	944	1,048	496	965	18.3	...	3,240	3,552	2,544	1,287	8,060
1935	776	864	487	956	21.0	...	3,588	3,632	2,094	1,406	7,713
1936	964 917	840	602 3,680	1,133[25]	20.0	...	3,198	3,833	2,712[28]	1,529	7,745
1937	1,489	939	737	3,770	21.9[26] 23	...	...	3,999	3,868	1,530	7,311
1938	1,493	1,011	776	3,680	25	...	...	4,260	3,789	1,506	5,940
1939	1,189	985	...	4,170	24	...	...	4,401	2,986	1,659	6,452
1940	1,634	1,401	...	5,020	26	...	...	4,321	3,649	2,067	5,819[29]
1941	2,046	1,844	...	7,420	45	...	...	4,879	3,827	2,511	...
1942	2,063	2,161	...	10,280	71	...	11,048 5,352	5,157[14]	4,047	2,826	...
1943	2,922	2,555	...	11,840	87	...	12,395	5,958	4,206	3,163	...
1944	3,678[23]	2,782	...	14,870	138	...	14,623	6,377	4,196	3,549	...

G2 Deposits in Commercial Banks (in thousand millions of stated unit except as otherwise indicated)

1945–2000

	Austria[8] (shilling)	Belgium[1] (francs)	Denmark[13] (kroner)	Finland[2] (markkaa)	France[15] (francs)	West Germany[18] (marks)	Greece[19] (drachmae)	Ireland[21] (pounds)	Italy[22] (lire)
								million	
1945	...	50.9	2,984	28.1	436	...	...	56.3	290
1946	...	63.6[1]	2,714	31.3	617	...	0.24	62.1	532
1947		58.5	2,258	37.8	755	...	0.52	67.0	745
1948	...	61.6	2,138	44.1	1,172	5.42	0.72	71.9	1,044
1949	7.2	64.9	2,069	54.4	1,403	6.74	1.48	78.9	1,226
			million						
1950	7.3	62.9[1] / 38.5	2,041	61.0	1,530	8.11	1.97	79.8	1,372[14]
1951	8.9	42.8	2,058	89.5	1,795	9.79	2.64	87.0	1,659
1952	9.5[8]	45.7	2,139	87.8	2,035	10.49	...	88.3	2,019
1953	9.3	46.2	2,232	103	2,320	11.4	1.94	90.6	2,226
1954	12.0	47.6	2,136	118	2,715	13.7	2.18	105	2,442
1955	11.0	51.5	2,201	134	3,059	15.2	2.69	98.8	2,760
1956	10.9	54.5	2,341	135	3,404	16.4	2.51	101	2,980
1957	11.3	52.3	2,414	141	3,794	18.6	3.23	107	3,143
1958	12.8	56.3	2,968	162	4,026[16] / 39.8	21.8	3.58	113	3,496[14]
1959	14.5	59.8	3,184	206	48.2	25.1	4.28	120	4,102
1960	15.2	57.4	3,272	236	55.3	26.6	5.00	129	4,786
1961	15.9	65.1	3,706	268	65.0	31.3	5.61	139	5,550
1962	18.4	69.3	4,103	291	79.1	33.8	6.19	155	6,666
			(p)						
1963	20.1	78.5	5,062	3,156	90.8	36.5	6.81	174	7,525
1964	21.3	86.3	5,831	3,500	99.0	39.5	8.02	181	8,143
1965	23.5	95.1	6,623	3,826	110	42.9	9.06	189	9,649
1966	23.7	104	7,757	4,262	119	43.0	9.76	199	11,088
1967	25.7	113	8,545	4,731	125	49.7	9.97	217	8,401
1968	28.4	123	10,545	5,413	140	55.4	12.1	233	10,602
1969	31.5	109	11,531	6,262	137	58.6	13.5	249	13,295
1970	34.2	124	10,596	7,241	157	65.4	15.4	275	20,149
1971	41.5	144	11,219	8,305	181	75.0	18.8	256	24,722
			thousand million	million	76.0[14]				million million
1972	53.3	173	12.3	9.9	217	87.1	25.5	302	28.5
1973	58.3	186	14.0	11.1[14]	240	87.7	28.3	303	35.0
1974	59.1	195	14.3[13]	13.6	282	98.2	31.3	310	38.0
1975	73.9	236	33.2	16.1	323	115	37.2	379	46.4
1976	81.4	248	35.2	16.9	347	116	48.3	431	57.6
1977	83.0	279	37.8	18.7	393	131	54.8	570	72.8
					443[15]				
1978	89.1	292	44.7	21.7	443	151	68.4	739	93.8
1979	73.6	297	48.4	25.4	610	154	81.6	740	120
1980	83.6	294	55.1	28.9	656	159	103	817	138
1981	76.7	307	62.0	33.0	737	155	125	845	154
1982	87.7	335	72.2	37.4	805	167	171	844[21]	182
1983	97.8	394	91.9	42.3	913	181	193	907	204
1984	103	383	107	49.1	1,016	194	251	1,049	230
1985	107	428	139	60.5	1,102	210[31]	292	1,033	254
1986	113	468	154	63.1	1,190	227	338	1,077	285
1987	129	503	162	69.6[31]	1,245	241	418	1,198	308
1988	142	546	195	94.0	1,293	265	467	1,327	335
1989	147	575	192	100	1,383	283	548	1,533	373
1990	156	585	206	111	1,439	392	719	1,651	402
1991	171	...	233	118	1,351	402	850	1,709	450
1992	181	...	230	119	1,349	440	...	1,681	447
1993	207	...	255	180[33]	1,367	485	...	2,166	477
				thousand million					
1994	201	1,111	248	291	1,415	506	1,647	3,539	471
1995	244	1,153	260	307	1,557	546	1,922	6,808	471
1996	255	1,200	287	297	1,554	633	2,370	7,552	499
1997	274	1,237	304	304	1,670	651	2,705	5,199	532
1998	...	...	321	315	...	749	3,109	6,802	601
	thousand million euros			thousand milion euros				milion euros	thousand milion euros
1999	42.2	50.2	336	60.5	242	420	4,503	12,649	385
							thousand milion euros		
2000	42.9	53.7	...	60.9	265	442	4,348	15,032	408

G2 Deposits in Commercial Banks (in thousand millions of stated unit, except as otherwise indicated)

1945–2000

	Netherlands[23] (gulden)	Norway[4] (Kroner)	Portugal[25] (escudos)	Spain[27] (pesetas)	Sweden[6] (Kroner)	Switzerland[28] (Francs)	U.K.[7] (pounds)	Yugoslavia[29] (dinari)
	million	million			million	million	million	...
1945	2,714	3,538	17.1	17.2	7,062	4,677	3,820	...
1946	3,392	3,255	18.5	22.4	7,328	5,133	4,436	...
1947	3,892	3,914	18.0	25.1	7,725	5,341	4,603	...
1948	4,164	3,987	17.8	26.8	7,848	5,449	4,812	...
1949	4,467	3,998	16.4	30.2	8,609	6,201	4,808	...
1950	4,148[23] / 3,842	3,923	17.1	34.3	9,141	6,423	4,909	...
1951	3,945	4,633	19.3	41.4	10,728[14] / 10,513	6,640	4,920	...
1952	4,526	4,807	20.3	47.7	10,358	6,824	4,804	...
1953	4,830	4,831	21.0[25] / 19.17	53.8	11,839	7,227[28] / 5,290	4,890	88
1954	5,100	4,952	21.4	60.9	12,727	5,400	5,082	139
1955	5,482	5,146	22.1	71.3	12,609	5,540	4,894	115
1956	5,014	5,252	23.7	87.1	13,090	5,790	4,808	146
1957	4,703	5,369	25.2	100	14,263	5,980	4,707	240
1958	5,557	5,335	27.4	118	15,987	6,870	4,802	250
1959	5,913	5,629	30.1	124	18,950	7,420	5,052	301
1960	6,225	6,047	32.2	123	18,524	8,470	4,928	339
1961	6,711	6,316	30.6	140	19,415	8,820	4,760	481
1962	7,155	6,719	33.1	168	22,080	10,720	4,996	660[30]
						thousand million		
1963	7,890	7,145	38.8	198	24,410	11.4	5,447	10.9
1964	8,285[23] / 8,269	7,921	46.3[14]	237	26,649	11.8	5,646	13.8
1965	9,197	8,548	48.7	276	27,731	12.1	5,708	14.0
1966	9,784	9,297[14] / 9,969	52.8	303	30,303	11.9	5,592	13.7
1967	10,573	11,074	57.0	345	35,017	12.5	6,064	13.2
1968	12,642	12,823	63.9	392	40,442	14.3	6,264	15.8
1969	13,812	14,488	64.3	456	41,050	13.5	6,128	17.2
1970	15,279	16,857	62.5	472	43,098	15.8	6,502	19.4
1971	16,981	19,174	72.4	624	47,493	20.5	7,560	22.1[29]
	thousand million	thousand million			thousand million		thousand million	20.8
1972	19.2	21.5	85.6	811	54.4	21.2	8.8	29.8
1973	25.3	25.0	127	1,025	63.4	20.3[28]	9.2	45.8
1974	32.2	28.0	111	1,211	89.9	17.8	9.9	59.7
1975	32.4 / 41.1[14]	32.7 / 38.5[14]	115[25]	1,451 / 1,769[14]	99.6	19.6	12.6[7] / 14.1	834
1976	43.0	18.0	146	1,788	101	23.0	16.1	149
1977	41.6	20.7	172	2,082	109	24.2	19.9	183
1978	42.6	22.1	204	2,378	138	33.3	22.6	210
1979	47.1	24.7	270	2,611	152	27.9	26.6	244
1980	46.8	25.5	300	2,911	165	27.2	26.9	330
1981	51.1	31.1	360	3,274	196	27.5[28]	30.4	412
1982	56.0	36.7	415	3,394	213	34.1	37.3[7]	518
1983	59.3[23] / 94.7	42.8	444	3,561	225	36.8[28]	46.0	621
1984	92.6	57.7	528	3,786	251	32.8	53.6[7]	917
1985	115	71.9	696	4,271	262	34.5	66.2	1,240
1986	123	73.8	1,002	5,574	295	35.4	84.6	2,639
1987	126	123	1,119	6,509	293	43.2	101	5,417
1988	143	157	1,284	7,897	327	44.0	113	17,980
1989	191	173	3,363	9,684	336	40.3	157	38,840
1990	202	193	3,801	11,059	365	38.6	170	79,644
1991	212	207	4,928	11,486	395	38.8	172	...
1992	200	235	6,136	10,944	387	40.8	180	...
1993	222[34]	246	6,937[34]	10,878	391[35]	46.0	195[36]	...
1994	114	315	3,060	10,291	644	62.2	623	...
1995	135	316	3,436	10,484	664	67.6	707	...
1996	156	350	3,915	11,319	746	93.6	784	...
1997	171	372	4,640	13,598	753	105.5	814	...
1998	...	453	5,412	16,959	748	113.9	876	...
	thousand million euros		thousand million euros					
1999	116	479	39.6	130.76	814	124.0	912	...
2000	128	521	42.2	144.86	821	122.3	1,015	...

G2 Deposits in Commercial Banks

NOTES

1. SOURCES:- The main sources were the League of Nations, *Memorandum on Commercial Banks, Money and Banking*, and *Statistical Yearbooks*; United Nations, *Statistical Yearbooks*; International Monetary Fund, *International Financial Statistics*; and the official publications noted on p. xv. German statistics to 1913 are taken from W.G. Hoffman, *Das Wachstum der Deutschen Wirtschaft seit der Mitte des 19 Jahrhunderts* (Berlin, etc., 1965), and data for the U.K. to 1975 (1st line) are taken from Forrest Capie & Alan Webber, *A Monetary History of the United Kingdom, 1870-1982*, (London, 1985). Belgian data to 1912 were supplied by the Belgian National Institute of Statistics, and Norwegian data for 1848-50, 1865, 1870, and 1875 were supplied by the Norwegian Central Office of Statistics.
2. So far as possible interbank deposits and savings account deposits are excluded.
3. Except as otherwise indicated the statistics are for the end of each year.

FOOTNOTES

[1] Figures to 1912 are of all deposits. From 1913 to 1936 (1st line) they are of deposits of less than 1 month's notice in commercial banks (including overseas branches and agencies). From 1936 (2nd line) to 1946 they are of all deposits in commercial banks. From 1947 to 1950 (1st line) they are of all 'bank money', and subsequently they are of demand deposits in commercial banks, with Luxembourg included.

[2] All deposits in commercial banks, though the coverage of some accounts is incomplete until 1917.

[3] Figures to 1913 (1st line) are of all deposits in the credit banks, as they are also from 1936 (2nd line) to 1938 (excluding interbank deposits). From 1913 (2nd line) to 1936 (1st line) they are of all deposits in commercial banks (excluding interbank deposits).

[4] All deposits in commercial banks (excluding interbank deposits) to 1976 (1st line). Demand deposits (including Post Office chequeing deposits) subsequently.

[5] All deposits in commercial banks.

[6] All deposits by the public in commercial banks.

[7] Statistics to 1922 (1st line) are of all bank deposits, whilst those from 1922 (2nd line) to 1975 (1st line) are of demand deposits, both including interbank deposits. From 1975 (1st line) they are of sterling demand deposits from a wide range of institutions, including the TSB and the Banking Department of the Bank of England from 1983. Southern Ireland is excluded from 1922. The figures relate to the end of December to 1975 (1st line) and from 1985. From 1975 (2nd line) to 1734 they relate to the second Wednesday in December.

[8] Cisleithamia in 1913 (1st line), subsequently the Republic Statistics are of all deposits in commercial banks to 1937 (including from 1920, deposits in agricultural credit institutions). From 1949 they are of demand deposits, excluding those of the government from 1953.

[9] Including one bank operating mainly in the Congo, which had not been included previously.

[10] Figures to 1922 (1st line) are of all deposits in the ten main commercial banks and in the Agricultural and Cooperative Central Banks. From 1922 (2nd line) to 1939 (1st line) the Popular Banks and the smaller commercial banks are also included. Subsequently only commercial banks are covered.

[11] The following postwar figures are available:- 1945 53.6, 1946 66.6, June 1947 103 million leva.

[12] Figures to 1937 are of current account deposits in commercial banks. Subsequently they are of all unblocked accounts. The following postwar figures are available:- 1945 11.5, 1946 42.5, 1947 54.3, 1948 53.3, 1949 126.8 million koruna.

[13] All deposits in commercial banks to 1921 (1st line) and sight deposits subsequently. Foreign accounts are excluded from 1932 (2nd line). A much broader definition was adopted in 1975.

[14] There was a change in the coverage of the series.

[15] Statistics to 1978 (1st line) are of total bank money, excluding interbank deposits. Thereafter they are of all demand deposits in a wider range of institutions. The figures to 1938 (1st line) are estimated by the I.N.S.E.E., and the 1939 and 1940 figures are official estimates.

[16] Saarland is included from 1945 to 1958 (1st line). Subsequent figures are in the new currency (1 new = 100 old francs).

[17] At 1 January 1924 in the new currency.

[18] All chequeing deposits (excluding interbank and government deposits).

[19] Figures to 1928 (1st line) are of all non-savings deposits in the five main commercial banks. From 1928 (2nd line) to 1939 all commercial banks are covered. From 1946 figures are of all chequeing deposits (excluding interbank and government deposits).

[20] Statistics to 1939 (1st line) are of all deposits in commercial banks. Subsequently they are of demand deposits (excluding the government's). The 1913 figure is for Transleithania. The following postwar figures are available: 1946 406, 1947 1,110, 1948 3,740, 1949 6,494 million forints.

[21] Figures to 1923 (1st line) are of all deposits of joint stock banks. From 1923 (2nd line) to 1937 (1st line) they are of all deposits in financial institutions (excluding interbank deposits) in southern Ireland. From 1937 (2nd line) they are of demand deposits in commercial banks (excluding interbank and government deposits), with accounts of non-residents excluded from 1982.

[22] Figures to 1926 (1st line) are of all deposits in the four main banks. From 1926 (2nd line) to 1928 (1st line) they are of all deposits in commercial banks (excluding interbank deposits, with deposits in public credit institutions added from 1928 (2nd line) to 1937 (1st line). From 1937 (2nd line) they are of all chequeing deposits (excluding interbank and government deposits).

[23] Figures to 1936 (1st line) are of all deposits in the six main banks (including agencies and branches overseas). Subsequently they are of all chequeing deposits (excluding interbank and government deposits). From 1945 to 1950 blocked accounts are included, and non-residents' balances in giro accounts are excluded from 1964 (2nd line). From 1983 (2nd line) coverage was extended to a much wider range of institutions.

[24] Current account deposits in commercial banks.

[25] Figures to 1936 (1st line) are of all deposits in commercial banks operating mainly in Portugal. From 1936 (2nd line) to 1953 (1st line) they are of chequeing deposits in banks based in Portugal (excluding interbank and government deposits). Subsequently they are of sight deposits in the hands of the public. Coverage was widened in 1976.

[26] Figures to 1937 (1st line) are of all deposits in commercial banks having a capital of 40 million lei or more (excluding interbank deposits). Subsequently they are of all deposits in commercial banks (excluding interbank and government deposits).

[27] Demand deposits in commercial banks. In principle, interbank deposits are excluded, but it is not clear that this was possible in the early years of the series.

G2 Deposits in Commercial Banks

[28] Figures to 1930 are of all deposits other than in savings accounts. From 1931 to 1936 (1st line) they are of chequeing accounts and deposit accounts in the big banks and in the cantonal banks they are of chequeing deposits (including deposits in the central bank). From 1953 (2nd line) they are of demand deposits in deposit money banks, though from 1974 to 1981 and from 1984 they relate only to banks which were subject to a minimum reserve on foreign liabilities.

[29] Statistics to 1940 are of all deposits in commercial banks (excluding interbank deposits). Figures from 1953 are of chequeing deposits (excluding interbank and government deposits). From 1971 (2nd line) the statistics relate to "business banks" only.

[30] Subsequent figures are in the new currency (1 new = 100 old dinari).

[31] Including deposits in the Post Office Bank.

[32] Subsequently including the Cooperative Banks.

[33] Cheque accounts.

[34] Demand deposits.

[35] Demand, time, savings and foreign currency deposits in deposit money banks.

[36] Demand, time, savings and foreign currency deposits in banking institutions.

G3 DEPOSITS IN SAVINGS BANKS (in millions of stated unit)

Key: All = all savings banks; CGE = Caisse Génerale d'Epargne; Gen = general savings banks; Nat = National Savings Bank; PO = Post Office banks PRIV = private savings banks; Reg = regulated savings banks; TSB = Trustee Savings Banks

1817–1869

	Austria	Belgium[3]	Denmark	France	Germany	Hungary[5]	Netherlands	Norway	Sweden	United Kingdom	
	Reg	CGE	All[4]	Priv.	All	All	Gem	All	Priv	TSB	PO
	(gulden)	(francs)	(kroner)	(francs)	(marks)	(gulden)	(gulden)	(kroner)	(kroner)	(pounds)	(pounds)
1817	...	—	...	—	...	...	—	...	...	0.2	—
1818	...	—	...	—	...	...	—	...	...	1.7	—
1819	...	—	...	—	...	...	—	...	...	2.8	—
1820	...	—	...	—	...	...	—	...	...	3.5	—
1821	...	—	...	—	...	...	—	...	...	4.7	—
1822	...	—	...	—	...	...	—	...	...	6.5	—
1823	...	—	1	—	...	...	—	...	...	8.7	—
1824	...	—	1	—	...	...	—	...	...	11.7	—
1825	...	—	2	—	...	...	—	...	...	13.3	—
1826	...	—	2	—	...	...	—	...	...	13.1	—
1827	...	—	2	—	...	...	—	...	...	14.2	—
1828	...	—	3	—	...	...	—	...	...	15.4₇	—
1829	...	—	3	—	...	...	—	...	...	14.3	—
1830	...	—	3	—	...	...	—	...	...	14.6	—
1831	...	—	4	—	...	...	—	...	...	14.6	—
1832	...	—	4	—	...	...	—	...	...	14.4	—
1833	...	—	4	—	...	...	—	...	...	15.3	—
1834	...	—	4	—	...	...	—	...	2.3	16.3	—
1835	...	—	5	62	...	...	—	...	...	17.4	—
1836	...	—	5	97	...	...	—	...	...	18.8	—
1837	...	—	4	108	...	...	—	...	...	19.6	—
1838	...	—	5	145	85	...	—	...	...	21.4	—
1839	...	—	5	171	95	...	1.1	...	...	22.4	—
1840	...	—	6	192	108	...	1.2	...	5.2	23.5	—
1841	...	—	7	250	122	...	1.3	...	...	24.5	—
1842	40	—	8	302	134	...	1.4	...	...	25.3	—
1843	46	—	9	347	149	1.0	1.6	...	...	27.2	—
1844	51	—	10	393	159	1.7	1.8	...	...	29.5	—
1845	54	—	12	394	167	...	1.9	...	7.7	30.7	—
1846	59	—	14	396	180	...	2.1	...	...	31.7	—
1847	61	—	17	358	191	...	2.2	...	...	30.3	—
1848	48	—	16	...	179	...	2.0	...	...	28.2	—
1849	...	—	15	74	195	...	3.5	...	...	28.6	—
1850	...	—	16	135	212	...	3.8	17	13	28.9	—
1851	67	—	19	158	230	...	4.1	...	...	30.3	—
1852	...	—	21	245	247	...	3.2	...	...	31.8	—
1853	...	—	26	286	270	...	3.5	...	...	33.4	—
1854	75	—	32	272	295	...	3.7	...	...	33.7	—
1855	...	—	41	272	322	...	4.0	35	22	34.3	—
1856	...	—	47	275	354	...	...	...	...	35.0	—
1857	83	—	48	279	388	...	...	...	...	35.2	—
1858	93	—	44	311	419	...	...	...	...₆	36.4	—
1859	96	—	50	337	441	...	...	...	25	39.2	—
1860	107	—	57	377	477	...	5.5	44	27	41.5	—
1861	107	—	64	401	529	...	...	...	30	41.7	—
1862	112	—	68	424	578	...	...	...	31	40.8	1.7
1863	113	—	72	448	648	...	...	...	32	41.2	3.4
1864	112	—	75	462	667	...	6.5	...	33	39.5	5.0
1865	113	0.3	83	493	714	...	8.0	68	36	39.0	6.5
1866	...	2	90	529	720	...	8.3	...	38	36.7	8.1
1867	[157]²	7	102	571	755	64	9.0	...	40	36.8	9.7
1868	[200]²	15	111	633	786	85₅ 86	10.1	...	43	37.2	11.7
1869	245	17	112	711	849	110	11.1	...	47	37.9	13.5

G3 Deposits in Savings Banks (in millions of stated unit)

	Austria[1]		Belgium[3]		Bulgaria	Czechoslovakia		Denmark	Finland	
	Reg (gulden)	PO (gulden)	CGE (francs)	PO (francs)	PO (leva)	Reg (koruna)	PO (koruna)	All (kroner)	PO (markkaa)	Other (markkaa)
									thousands	
1870	286	—	20	1	—	...	...	118	—	...
1871	341	—	22	2	—	...	...	133	—	...
1872	403	—	27	3	—	...	...	153	—	...
1873	483	—	34	5	—	...	...	174	—	...
1874	539	—	37	7	—	...	...	197	—	...
1875	589	—	45	9	—	...	...	214	—	...
1876	610	—	66	13	—	...	...	221	—	...
1877	625	—	79	17	—	...	...	208	—	...
1878	649	—	92	21	—	...	...	201	—	...
1879	699	—	108	24	—	...	...	218[10]	—	...
1880	745	—	125	30	—	...	...	254	—	...
1881	792	—	128	37	—	...	...	338	—	...
1882	826	—	128	45	—	...	...	350	—	...
1883	868	4	142	53	—	...	...	366	—	...
1884	926	11	159	65	—	...	...	377	—	...
1885	986	25	189	83	—	...	...	378	—	...
1886	1,054	39	217	102	—	...	...	424	—	...
1887	1,091	41	240	122	—	...	...	462	338	...
1888	1,154	43	260	142	—	...	...	481	711	...
1889	1,236	50	283	163	—	...	...	501	1,102	...
1890	1,283	55	325	192	—	...	...	510	1,310	...
1891	1,336	62	333	205	—	...	...	520	1,253	...
1892	1,407	72	351	225	—	...	...	540	1,107	...
1893	1,462	83	390	258	—	...	...	564[4]	948	...
								438		
1894	1,531	91	427	289	—	...	...	465	981	...
	kronen	kronen								
1895	3,195	198	453	318	—	...	...	487	1,129	...
1896	3,320	228	481	347	1	...	...	509	1,386	...
1897	3,435	287	532	387	2	...	...	522	2,001	...
1898	3,518	323	564	420	3	...	...	533	2,640	...
1899	3,603	338	608	459	4	...	...	519	3,056	...
1900	3,718	360	662	504	4	...	...	514	3,731	...
1901	3,900	387	735	562	6	...	...	526	4,008	...
1902	4,155	420	731	564	7	...	...	568	4,328	...
1903	4,369	451	735	575	10	...	...	593	5,084	...
1904	4,574	456	764	601	14	...	...	615[11]	5,358	...
								674		
1905	4,748	516	786	629	19	...	...	703	5,205	...
1906	4,904	606	812	655	24	...	...	717	6,290	...
1907	5,077	586	844	695	27	...	...	723	7,309	...
1908	5,394	549	886	734	29	...	...	739	7,424	...
1909	5,720	584	920	771	34	...	...	768	7,107	...
1910	6,045	622	965	814	37	...	...	803	7,238	...
1911	6,360	671	1,008	862	43	...	...	844	7,932	...
1912	6,416	644	1,058	909	46	...	...	838	8,513	...
1913	6,590	590	1,099	954	51[8]	...	...	858	8,857	...
1914	6,515	1,058	1,068	...	49	...	...	894	6,952	...
1915	6,673	1,171	1,048	...	56	...	...	981	9,550	...
									millions	
1916	...[1]	1,635[1]	1,052	...	92	...	...	1,109	15.68	...
1917	4,072	...	1,090	...	184	...	...	1,253	24.23	...
1918	5,192	...	1,214	...	248	...	...	1,452	28.19	...
1919	5,255	3,425	1,306	1,121	232	5,326	1,402	1,459	33.92	360

G3 Deposits in Savings Banks (in millions of stated unit)

	France		Germany	Greece	Hungary[5]	Italy		Netherlands		Norway
	Priv	Nat	All	PO	All	Priv	P.O.	Gem	PO	All
	(francs)	(francs)	(marks)	(drachmae)	(gulden)	(lire)	(lire)	(gulden)	(gulden)	(kronen)
				thousands						
1870	632[12]	—	908[14]	—	121	...	—	11.1	—	82
1871	538	—	1,031	—	147	...	—	13.2	—	...
1872	515	—	1,200	—	162	447	—	14.8	—	...
1873	545	—	1,427	—	161	450	—	16.6	—	109
1874	574	—	1,663	—	169	467	—	18.9	—	125
1875	660	—	1,878	—	185	527	—	23	—	128
1876	769	—	2,051	—	203	553	2	27	—	134
1877	863	—	2,190	—	206	574	6	30	—	137
1878	1,016	—	2,294	—	216	602	11	33	—	136
1879	1,155	—	2,434	—	243	657	26	33	—	133
1880	1,280	—	2,615	—	260	687	46	37	—	139
1881	1,409	—	2,774	—	284	715	67	40	1	144
1882	1,754	48	2,962	—	294	744	85	42	2	152
1883	1,816	77	3,179	—	314	801	117	44	3	159
1884	2,022	115	3,415	—	325	888	156	47	5	166
1885	2,211	154	3,658	—	336	954	184	49	6	168
1886	2,314	191	3,943	—	357	1,033	229	53	9	169
1887	2,365	224	4,234	—	364	1,077	249	56	11	170
1888	2,495	267	4,545	—	389	1,112	276	58	14	175
1889	2,684	332	4,863	—	423	1,139	300	60	18	187
1890	2,912	431	5,134	—	458	1,166	323	62	21	194
1891	3,053	506	5,340	—	490	1,177	348	62	24	197
1892	3,227	616	5,587	—	521	1,215	380	63	28	201
1893	3,140	611	5,925	—	534	1,258[16]	416[16]	66	32	207
1894	3,287	691	6,270	—	554	1,307	441	70	38	217
					(kronen)					
1895	3,395	754	6,792	—	1,151	1,344	481	73	44	226
1896	3,382	785	7,244	—	1,185	1,347	496	76	53	235
1897	3,427	844	7,707	—	1,246	1,361	555	78	62	252
1898	3,400	875	8,162	—	1,311	1,382	586	79	70	271
1899	3,407	930	8,486	—	1,330	1,431	644	77	78	288
1900	3,264	1,010	8,824	—	1,366	1,467	696	80	85	306
1901	3,349	1,080	9,541	—	1,435	1,505	734	79	94	322
1902	3,283	1,107	10,313	88	1,496	1,572	796	82	102	334
1903	3,188	1,118	11,089	209	1,577	1,630	878	84	110	349
1904	3,246	1,187	11,895	256	1,668	1,718	992	88	120	365
1905	3,377	1,278	12,663	197	1,763	1,811	1,085	92	130	374
1906	3,434	1,339	13,414	247	1,860	1,898	1,228	93	140	403
1907	3,543	1,434	13,908	258	1,946	2,041	1,435	91	145	430
1908	3,580	1,539	14,547	306	2,054	2,165	1,524	97	152	452
1909	3,833	1,640	15,646	279	2,207 [3,413][15]	2,305	1,604	107	160	478
1910	3,933	1,710	16,782	293	[3,782][15]	2,397	1,792	111	164	507
1911	3,909	1,704	17,820	305	[4,229][15]	2,463	1,890	119	171	539
1912	3,947	1,746	18,682	323	[4,146][15]	2,492	1,965	124	177	567
1913	4,011[13]	1,818	19,687	584	[4,236][15]	2,595	2,108	130	184	607
1914	3,939	1,807	20,500	719	[3,684][15]	2,546	2,021	118	185	638
1915	3,692	1,656	20,400	1,180	[4,226][15]	2,561	1,990	121	189	724
1916	3,342	1,429	21,400	1,375	[5,419][15]	2,975	2,193	136	207	952
1917	3,563	1,455	25,400[14]	1,246	...	3,430	2,708	152	223	1,244
1918	3,910[12,13]	1,612[12]	31,800	1,686	...	4,428	3,478	176	242	1,566[17]
1919	5,144	2,087	37,000	5,012	...	5,454	5,189	205	268	1,838

G3 Deposits in Savings Banks (in millions of stated unit)

| | Romania | Russia | Spain | | Sweden | | Switzerland | United Kingdom | |
| | Nat | All | Priv | PO | Priv | PO | All | TSB | PO |
	(lei)	(rubel)	(pesetas)	(pesetas)	(kronor)	(kronor)	(francs)	(pounds)	(pounds)
1870	—	5	...	—	57	—	...	38.3	15.1
1871	—	...	...	—	71	—	...	39.2	17.0
1872	—	...	...	—	87	—	...	40.3	19.3
1873	—	...	...	—	106	—	...	41.2	21.2
1874	—	...	16	—	124	—	...	42.3	23.2
1875	—	5	23	—	133	—	...	43.5	25.2
1876	—	...	28	—	143	—	...	44.6	27.0
1877	—	...	38	—	145	—	...	45.6	28.7
1878	—	...	43	—	139	—	...	45.9	30.4
1879	—	...	50	—	135	—	...	45.6	32.0
1880	—	8	57	—	146	—	...	46.0	33.7
1881	1	9	61	—	160	—	...	46.4	36.2
1882	2	11	68	—	173	—	...	47.2	39.0
1883	4	13	71	—	190	—	...	47.8	41.8
1884	5	17	74	—	204	0.8	...	48.9	44.8
1885	6	25	81	—	219	1.5	...	49.7	47.7
1886	7	42	81	—	231	2.1	...	50.4	50.9
1887	9	65	99	—	240	2.9	...	51.1	54.0
1888	10	88	82	—	253	4.7	...	50.4	58.6
1889	12	111	104	—	268	8.5	...	49.1	63.0
1890	15	139	95	—	275	13	...	48.0	67.6
1891	18	191	139	—	284	16	...	47.0	71.6
1892	18	239	128	—	291	20	...	46.7	75.9
1893	21	283	136	—	308	23	...	46.7	80.6
1894	21	330	149	—	324	30	...	48.1	89.3
1895	23	368	155	—	339	38	...	50.0	97.9
1896	24	409	161	—	360	50	...	51.4	108
1897	27	466	155	—	384	58	...	53.1	116
1898	32	537	153	—	403	64	...	54.6	123
1899	29	608	172	—	415	60	...	56.0	130
1900	29	662	179	—	437	56	...	56.0	136
1901	32	723	191	—	467	54	...	56.5	140
1902	37	784	218	—	496	54	...	57.1	145
1903	42	861	239	—	531	54	...	57.2	146
1904	45	911	260	—	568	55	...	57.2	148
1905	52	831	283	—	602	55	...	58.3	152
1906	59	1,035	299	—	645	54	1,367	59.4	156
1907	62	1,149	310	—	682	51	1,402	59.3	158
1908	61	1,208	376	—	714	46	1,490	59.9	161
1909	60	1,283	395	—	760	45	1,592	62.0	165
1910	63	1,397	420	—	809	46	1,691	63.3	169
1911	64	1,503	448	—	857	47	1,753	65.2	177
1912	54	1,595	478	—	904	48	1,763	67.2	182
1913	58	1,685	500	—	953	48	1,771	68.7	187
1914	57	1,835	479	—	987	45	1,800	69.5	191
1915	57	2,449	529	—	1,065	48	1,841	66.8	186
1916	50	3,890	574	16	1,207	54	1,935	68.5	197
1917	51	...	650	32	1,382	64	2,079	66.5	203
1918	67	...	742	47	1,624	75	2,337	75.1	235
1919	105	...	849	66	1,871	83	2,621	86.8	266

G3 Deposits in Savings Banks (in millions of stated unit)

	Austria		Belgium			Bulgaria	Czechoslovakia		Denmark
	Reg (kronen)	PO (kronen)	CGE (francs)	PO (francs)	Priv (francs)	PO (leva)	Reg (koruna)	PO$_9$ (koruna)	All (kronen)
1920	6,781	7,776	1,504	1,322	...	224	5,887	2,213	1,517
1921	11,304	34,666	1,712	1,486	...	278	7,407	2,399	1,620
1922	138,343	742,238	1,845	1,609	...	279	8,706	2,343	1,785
1923	880,000	1,715,437	1,971	1,777	...	256	10,421	2,355	1,823
	(schillings)								
1924	267	209	2,235	2,022	...	279	11,565	1,954	1,872
1925	529$_{18}$ 536	246	2,571	2,339	...	299	12,489	2,057	1,931
1926	766	288	2,760	2,475	...	356	13,772	1,825	1,949
1927	987	314	3,516	3,144	...	508	15,497	2,164	1,967
1928	1,246	356	4,267	3,838	...	638	17,030	2,635	2,018
1929	1,414	381	5,549	5,011	...	684	18,033	2,275	2,097
1930	1,635	396	7,768	7,060	...	874	19,656	2,289	2,179
1931	1,479	321	9,248	8,435	...	1,268	21,742	1,953	2,169
1932	1,520	303	9,864	9,106	...	1,486	21,904	1,823	2,162
1933	1,512	290	10,054	9,252	...	1,706	20,688	1,681	2,185
1934	1,584	350	10,589	9,698	...	2,024	20,620	1,626	2,190
1935	1,677	368	10,809	9,812	...	2,252	21,350	1,768	2,181
1936	1,733	366	11,966	10,330	...	2,520	21,252	2,072	2,190
1937	...	390	13,022	11,608	...	2,858	20,922	2,256	2,198
1938	...	...	13,158	11,806	...	3,330	...	2,382	2,264
1939	...	...	12,404	11,163	...	3,613	...	...	2,180
1940	...	...	11,934	10,753	...	4,047	...	...	2,203
1941	...	...	12,255	10,831	...	5,061	...	...	2,439
1942	...	...	13,667	11,926	...	6,632	...	...	2,728
1943	...	...	17,248	14,998	...	8,400	...	...	3,158
1944	...	...	20,672	18,081	...	9,363	...	...	3,769
1945	...	2,191	19,404	16,766	...	11,169	...	...	4,272
1946	...	3,615	21,459	18,434	3,833	...	7,280	11,273	4,539
1947	1,137	2,394	25,835	21,716	4,263	...	11,931	13,934	4,718
			(thousand million)					(thousand million)	
1948	1,487	1,024	30.4	25.5	4.8	...	...	...	4,814
1949	1,739	1,239	33.7	28.4	5.5	...	...	...	4,983
1950	2,103	1,292	35.6	30.4	6.0	...	...	...	4,993
1951	2,389	1,552	38.5	32.3	6.8	...	...	...	4,991
1952	3,114	1,753	44.7	37.7	8.3	...	...	...	5,169
1953	4,223	2,577	49.9	42.2	9.9	...	...	...	5,408
1954	5,806	2,882	53.8	45.9	11.5	...	...	6,145	5,510
1955	7,038	3,413	56.8	48.7	13.8	...	...	7,041	5,688
1956	8,586	3,872	61.2	52.3	15.7	...	...	8,306	5,961
1957	10,482	4,456	64.9	56.0	17.6	...	...	9,000	6,299
1958	12,860	5,605	72.4	61.9	20.0	...	...	10,045	6,853
1959	16,241	6,838	78.8	68.8	23.5	...	...	11,080	7,436
1960	19,090	6,846	83.0	72.9	25.8	...	...	11,971	7,876
1961	21,131	7,567	88.7	78.0	29.5	...	...	11,329	8,461
1962	24,511	8,768	97.5	85.0	34.8	...	...	12,035	9,083
1963	28,402	9,835	103	89.6	41.3	...	...	12,607	9,946
1964	33,470	9,996	108	93.1	46.7	...	...	12,850	10,787
	(thousand million)								
1965	37.8	11.0	118	96.8	54.5	...	...	12,525	11,722
1966	41.9	11.0	126	106	63.0	...	...	12,812	12,898
1967	46.8	12.0	138	113	69.1	...	...	13,225	13,995
1968	52.1	12.5	152	119	78.1	...	...	13,599	15,611
1969	58.7	12.6	164	122	86.3	...	...	14,069	17,026

G3 Deposits in Savings Banks (in millions of stated unit)

	Finland			France		Germany	East Germany	Greece	Hungary[5]
	PO	Priv	Coop	Priv	Nal	All	All	PO	All
	(markkaa)	(markkaa)	(markkaa)	(francs)	(francs)	(marks)	(marks)	(drachmae)	(kronen)
1920	60.32	1,010	8.7	5,833	2,354	44,600	...	5.6	...
1921	86.52	1,190	11.6	6,993	2,697	...	...	10.0	...
1922	108	1,390	15.9	7,799	3,052	new marks		15.1	...
1923	127	1,590	21.7	8,287	3,272	5	...	33.8	49,441
									(penges)
1924	147	1,820	28.1	8,577	3,419	595	...	62.8	261
1925	162	2,110	46.1	9,854	3,936	1,693	...	103	341
1926	184	2,340	82.4	11,237	4,418	3,182	...	120	330
1927	198	3,120	156	14,607	6,674	4,839	...	176	417
1928	209	3,710	274	17,962	9,085	7,205	...	260	472
1929	225	3,930	349	20,314	11,659	9,314	...	385	541
1930	242	4,180	400	23,570	15,033	10,752	...	673	561
1931	279	4,224	420	30,175	20,686	10,123	...	1,084	533
1932	299	4,223	420	33,669	23,614	10,195	...	1,256	547
1933	327	4,410	450	34,739	24,120	11,953	...	1,767	536
1934	356	4,770	520	35,337	24,696	12,814	...	2,139	364
1935	376	5,200	620	36,575	25,456	13,819	...	2,402	316
1936	402	5,870	790	34,921	23,975	14,615	...	2,871	316
1937	455	6,930	1,150	36,256	25,112	16,062	...	3,203	358
1938	502	7,580	1,380	37,563[12]	26,028[12]	18,009	...	3,624	419
1939	453	7,720	1,480	39,294	27,456	...	...	3,211	490
1940	1,170[19]	8,140	1,720	40,013	27,672	...	...	3,713[22]	606[23]
									499
1941	1,870	8,180	1,920	44,829	31,761	...	...	3,553	582
1942	2,970	9,370	2,430	53,405	39,166	...	...	...	541
1943	5,450	11,510	3,430	69,640	52,678	...	...	...	807
1944	7,990	13,700	4,500	96,554	81,713	...	...	...	...[23]
	(thousand million)			(thousand million)					
1945	11.37	18.83		6.93	139	131	...	...	...
				West Germany					
				(D. marks)					
1946	13.65	20.78	8.39	152	140	...	...	...	...
1947	19.93	24.92	11.37	162	147	...	...	...	...
1948	21.94	29.33	14.03	206	192	1,159	...	...	...
1949	27.24	37.46	18.19	249	238	2,197	...	...	...
									(forints)
1950	32.30	41.90	21.61	317	301	2,898	1,093	...	289
1951	42.24	55.26	31.76	357[12]	337[12]	3,563	1,231	...	...
1952	48.86	68.96	39.25	450	389	5,314	1,729	...	...
1953	51.31	80.62	44.52	560	469	8,120	2,130	...	...
								(new drachmae)	
1954	55.7	97.1	54.6	669	560	11,930	2,988	29	...
1955	58.5	114	63.9	850	664	14,791	3,861	123	722
1956	64.7	118	66.0	991	755	16,963	4,763	295	...
1957	59.1	123	70.2	1,098	823	20,487	7,080	743	...
1958	68.8	137	77.7	1,283	942	25,168	8,885	1,141	...
1959	70.9	160	89.9	1,519[20]	1,091[20]	31,309	11,079	1,855	...
1960	77.3	189	110	17.3	12.1	36,998	13,925	2,447	5,542
1961	87.0	217	129	19.7	13.3	42,280	15,989	3,191	6,658
1962	100.5	232	138	22.9	14.9	48,611	17,158	4,229	8,801
	(new markkaa)					(thousand million)			
1963	1,117	2,448	1,503	26.4	16.8	56.5	18,902	5,682	12,288
1964	1,227	2,750	1,738	31.8	19.8	64.9	21,913	6,997	16,804
1965	1,322	3,104	2,010	36.3	22.2	75.1	25,044	8,101	20,411
1966	1,471	3,510	2,301	41.5	25.0	84.9	27,677	10,111	23,029
1967	1,595	3,810	2,493	45.7	27.1	96.0	30,885	11,156	24,797
1968	1,803	4,161	2,781	50.5	29.3	109	34,453	14,614	29,152
1969	2,055	4,547	3,166	60.5	33.2	120[21]	38,412	17,667	35,097
						121			

G3 Deposits in Savings Banks (in millions of stated unit)

	Southern Ireland		Italy		Netherlands		Norway	Poland	Portugal
	PO	TSB	Priv	PO	Gen	PO	All	All	All
	(pounds)	(pounds)	(lire)	(live)	(gulden)	(gulden)	(kroner)	(zloty)	(escudos)
1920	...	...	6,234	6,980	217	273	2,053	...	215
1921	...	...	7,428	8,148	240	283	2,295	...	308
1922	...	...	8,530	8,720	...	298	2,439	...	358
1923	1.6	1.1	10,211	9,078	...	305	2,528	...	463
1924	2.1	1.1	11,925	9,912	...	307	2,555	...	487[25]
1925	2.4	1.2	12,784	10,619	281	312	2,541	164	615
1926	2.6	1.2	12,954[16]	10,633[16]	306	321	2,527	307	789
1927	2.8	1.2	13,766	10,139	327	329	2,423	583	1,043
1928	3.1	1.2	15,685	10,819	354	341	2,352	889	1,447
1929	3.2	1.2	16,459	11,774	381	351	2,287	1,172	1,822
1930	3.4	1.2	17,372	13,032	430	375	2,234	1,431	1,983[25]
									1,622
1931	3.7	1.3	18,181	14,675	449	439	2,150	1,467	1,868
1932	4.2	1.3	18,743	17,016	446	511	2,114	1,568	2,208
1933	4.8	1.5	19,524	19,403	466	529	2,051	1,672	2,319
1934	5.6	1.6	19,617	20,427	485	540	1,980	1,795	2,517
1935	6.5	1.8	18,637	19,958	484	540	1,990	1,873	2,550
1936	7.5	1.9	18,803	22,309	495	546	1,863	1,896	2,611
1937	8.5	2.0	19,064	25,520	622	603	1,889	2,168	2,637
1938	9.6	2.1	17,601	29,233	628	679	1,971	2,302	2,750
1939	10.7	2.3	17,550	32,008	558	670	1,926	...	2,953
1940	11.8	2.4	19,424	37,302	481	516	1,820	...	3,215
1941	13.6	2.6	23,460	46,911	471	479	2,066	...	3,850
1942	16.7	2.9	28,255	59,465	545	543	2,424	...	5,366
1943	20.9	3.4	31,250	61,317	717	793	2,838	...	5,823
1944	26.4	4.0	43,124	65,030	848	1,008	3,325	...	7,073
1945	32.7	4.7	76,803	91,896	1,175	1,803	4,118	...[24]	7,930
			(thousand million lire)						
1946	36.4	5.3	121	140	1,105	1,545	4,004	1.4	8,168
1947	36.9	5.4	176	199	1,147	1,514	4,019	4.2	8,139
1948	39.0	5.7	275	342	1,156	1,445	4,280	9.5	8,039
1949	43.9	6.6	350	522	1,238	1,440	4,488	46	7,393
1950	48.1	7.3	401	688	1,246	1,365	4,600	77	7,419
1951	53.4	8.2	451	796	1,236	1,298	4,753	190	8,330
1952	57.1	8.8	538	962	1,328	1,338	5,008	276	9,054
1953	61.8	9.5	626	1,150	1,504	1,402	5,338	436	9,587
1954	66.7	10.6	753	1,268	1,753	1,503	5,671	751	9,957
1955	71.2	11.2	887	1,363	1,996	1,697	5,961	1,274	10,508
1956	73.5	11.8	1,044	1,457	2,147	1,913	6,325	2,230	11,011
1957	76.0	12.1	1,218	1,562	2,124	1,956	6,723	5,399	11,617
1958	78.7	12.7	1,377	1,694	2,329	2,142	7,023	7,202	12,303
1959	82.5	13.9	1,622	1,869	2,654	2,369	7,414	10,987	12,998
1960	86.7	15.1	1,882	2,066	3,006	2,646	7,898	14,307	13,472
1961	91.5	16.5	2,210	2,308	3,408	2,896	8,345	16,384	13,343
1962	97.2	17.7	2,603	2,611	3,857	3,230	8,898	21,506	14,347
1963	102	18.4	2,977	2,951	4,365	3,568	9,423	28,649	15,294
1964	107	19.6	3,318	3,252	4,859	3,880	9,928	35,016	17,203
1965	110	19.8	3,904	3,627	5,426	4,209	10,769	42,256	18,500
1966	111	20.6	4,553	4,011	6,025	4,491	11,741	51,951	19,307
1967	116	21.8	5,153	4,358	6,743	4,840	12,773	63,021	20,509
1968	118	22.8	5,798	4,697	7,305	5,246	14,080	73,412	23,085
1969	121	27.5	6,344	5,018	8,059	5,594	15,282	86,890	27,203

G3 Deposits in Savings Banks (in millions of stated unit)

	Romania		Spain		Sweden		Switzerland	United Kingdom		Yugoslavia
	Nat	other	Priv	PO	Priv	PO	All	TSB	PO	PO[32]
	(lel)	(lel)	(pesetas)	(pesetas)	(kroner)	(kroner)	(francs)	(pounds)	(pounds)	(dinari)
1920	137	...	939	85	2,024	84	2,731	91.3	267	...
1921	165	...	1,283	105	2,130	100	2,831	92.4	264	...
1922	175[26]	503	1,515	122	2,243	119	3,034	98.3[30]	268[30]	...
1923	167	791	1,617	138	2,359	135	3,248	103	273	...
1924	157	996	1,734	157	2,399	149	3,266	107	280	405
1925	146	1,471	1,846	177	2,489	165	3,410	110	286	447
1926	166	1,900	2,571	194	2,621	190	3,655	111	284	475
1927	183	2,172	3,012	216	2,706	206	3,873	114	285	646
1928	187	2,761	3,547	239	2,793	223	4,064	121	289	703
1929	198	4,246	4,000	252	2,884	284	4,304	124	285	1,020
							4,723[25]			
1930	255	4,553	4,672	265	2,961	338	5,339	133	290	1,188
1931	624	4,740	4,646	278	3,051	382	5,569	143	289	1,134
1932	809[27]	4,565	4,981	299	3,142	451	5,913	155	306	1,387
1933	1,539	5,061	5,380	318	3,206	440	5,877	171	327	1,722
1934	2,260	...	5,825	...	3,312	473	5,888	182	355	1,858
1935	3,091	3,667	6,500	370	3,351	497	5,766	197	390	2,030
1936	3,767	2,965	...	367	3,402	514	5,680	212	432	2,449
1937	5,301	2,712	...	391	3,523	558	5,981	224	471	3,090
1938	5,405	2,773	...	450	3,685	618	6,232	239	509	2,995
1939	5,316	...	7,020	370	3,679	628	6,138	252	551	...
1940	5,387	...	7,876[28]	318	3,596	649	5,847	276	654	...
1941	10,096	...	[5,717][29]	344	3,807	743	5,948	323	823	...
1942	18,166	...	[6,012][29]	[466][29]	4,137	908	6,274	379	1,005	...
1943	...	...	[7,063][29]	421	4,611	1,111	6,715	448	1,241	...
			6,549							
1944	...	...	8,644	475	5,106	1,269	7,166	527	1,494	...[32]
1945	...	...	10,940	542	5,606	1,422	7,368	603	1,777	478
1946	...	...	12,721	606	6,034	1,589	7,706	670	1,982	767
1947	...	...	15,697	698	6,357	1,722	8,104	732	1,943	1,075
1948	...	...	17,527	809	6,751	1,923	8,363	799	1,948	1,847
1949	...	...	20,409	910	7,231	2,083	8,893	857	1,948	2,268
1950	...	...	24,623	1,028	7,619	2,143	9,274	909	1,934	2,442
1951	...	...	29,393	1,185	8,060	2,325	9,700	932	1,876	2,549
1952	...	...	35,131	1,393	8,703	2,639	10,295	954	1,812	3,861
1953	...	...	40,646	1,653	9,343	2,851	11,093	969	1,747	5,797
1954	...	...	47,446	1,966	9,978	3,026	11,929	1,020	1,727	9,439
			(thousand million)							
1955	...	...	55.3	2,362	10,696	3,225	12,677	1,054	1,700	14,088
1956	...	...	64.1	2,771	11,509	3,436	13,267	1,094	1,688	18,793
1957	...	...	74.4	3,402	12,459	3,723	13,810	1,140	1,677	31,651
1958	...	...	86.3	3,932	13,442	4,036	14,945	1,165	1,646	46,657
1959	...	...	95.3	4,433	14,337	4,368	16,561	1,239	1,680	67,342
1960	...	...	122	5,266	15,403	4,725	18,082	1,315	1,710	91,681
1961	...	...	146	6,480	16,391	5,016	20,153	1,501	1,737	122,750
1962	...	...	176	8,178	17,699	5,478	22,325	1,517	1,760	148,412
1963	...	...	210	10,684	18,957	5,931	24,510	1,685	1,792	213,300
1964	...	...	269	13,355	20,531	6,342	26,344	1,881	1,814	296,700[33]
1965	...	...	334	16,532	22,263	6,696	28,547	2,022	1,823	3,523
1966	...	...	463	19,715	24,511	7,240	30,832	2,149	1,740	5,863
1967	...	...	545	23,572	27,259	7,762	33,676	2,266	1,673	7,549
1968	...	...	642	27,298	29,685[17]	8,261	37,250	2,365	1,590[31]	9,697
1969	...	...	766	31,703	30,779	8,829	40,286	2,417[31]	1,757	12,927

G3 Deposits in Savings Banks (in thousand millions of stated unit except as otherwise indicated)

1970-1993

	Austria[1]		Belgium			Czechoslovakia	Denmark		Finland	
	Reg	**PO**	**CGE**	**PO**	**Priv**	**Nat**	**All**	**PO**	**Priv**	**Coop**
	(schilling)	(schilling)	(francs)	(francs)	(francs)	(koruna)	(kroner)		(markkaa)	
1970	65.7	13.4	177	123	94.9	13.6	18.1	2.3	5.1	3.6
1971	75.0	16.7	208	133	114	14.3	19.9	2.7	5.7	4.1
1972	83.8	21.3	242	146	141	14.9	22.4	3.4	6.5	4.7
1973	94.3	25.9	273	157	167	15.5	24.8	4.2	7.6[25]	5.5[25]
1974	109	22.5	301	165	187	15.9	27.4	5.0	8.3	6.7
		All[38]								
1975		277	358	190	227	16.1	30.3	6.4	9.8	8.1
1976		331	406	196	264	16.4	33.6	6.8	11.1	9.3
1977		370	457	204	291	16.9	37.9	7.3	12.7	10.6
1978		433	507	204	328	17.4	41.1	8.0	14.7	12.1
1979		472	548	110	361	17.8	45.3	9.3	17.2	14.4
1980		538	599	100	366	18.1	49.1	10.1	20.0	17.0
1981		619	653	91.9	399	17.4	53.9	11.8	22.9	19.9
1982		683	683	—	437	17.8	58.9	13.2	25.9	22.9
1983		721	739	—	493	18.1	73.7	14.8	29.3	26.3
1984		773	806	—	561	18.3	85.8	17.6	33.3	30.3
1985		819	902	—	521	18.8	102	19.7	38.2	34.9
1986		886	1,002	—	600	19.2	114	20.5	42.5	39.1
1987		946	1,080	—	669	19.7	119	22.3	48.4	45.2
1988		988	1,164	—	769	20.2	137	...[38]	60.4	55.7
1989		1,051	1,262		...	20.4	143		65.4	61.3
1990		1,155	...		...	21.1	...		61.8	66.7
1991		1,264	...		...	...	...		62.6	71.8
1992		1,356	...		...	26.6[40]	...		57.4	75.8
1993		1,421	...		...	34.5[40]	...		52.0	89.5

	France		West Germany	East Germany	Greece	Hungary[5]	Southern Ireland	
	Priv	**Nat**	**All**	**All**	**Priv**	**All**	**PO**	**TSB**
	(francs)	(francs)	(marks)	(marks)	(drachmae)	(forints)	(pounds) million	(pounds) million
1970	69.9	36.6	132	42.0	21.7	42.1	139	45.5
1971	81.1	44.9	147	45.2	26.5	48.4	140	45.2
1972	92.6	50.5	165	49.0	30.9	54.5	147	55.5
1973	106	54.9	173	53.5	32.6	62.0	154	63.6
1974	124	64.6	191	58.0	39.4	70.8	165	76.9
1975	153	79.4	224	62.5	52.0	81.3	180	95.1
		—[39]						
		318						
1976	379		244	66.8	66.2	92.9	205	129
1977	377		259	72.1	81.5	108	223	176
1978	444		275	77.4	102	125	239	195
1979	512		283	80.9	119	136	249	215
1980	577		287	83.3	145	145	259	253
1981	658		287	86.2	186	160	281	319
1982	750		310	90.2	241	176	306	380
1983	831[39]		327	95.2	286	197	330	443
1984	920		342	99.8	362	219	357	541
1985	950		361	105	446	244	388	643
1986	1,001		384	111	511	275	382	647
1987	1,061		403	120	603	287	388	...
1988	1,119		416	128	728	313	384	...
1989	1,296		404	...	862	325	383	...
1990	1,259		447		967	384	391	...
1991	1,239		442		1,057	481	399	...
1992	1,204		409[41]		1,164	657	413	...
1993	1,229		456		1,312	779	412	...

G3 Deposits in Savings Banks (in thousand millions of stated unit (except as otherwise indicated

1970–1993

	Italy		Netherlands		Norway	Poland	Portugal
	Priv	**PO**	**Gen**	**PO**	**All**	**All**	**All**
	(lire)	(lire)	(gulden)	(gulden)	(kroner)	(zlotys)	(escudos)
1970	6,110	5,184	8.8	6.0	17.4	97.2	32.7
1971	6,999	6,258	9.8	6.7	19.8	113	34.4
1972	8,279	7,612	11.0	7.6	22.0	140	38.1
1973	9,760	9,191	12.0	8.3	24.5	174	35.9
1974	11,596	9,787	11.7	9.0	27.3	216	42.7
	million[2]	million[2]					
1975	15.8	11.8	13.0	10.4	30.7	251	...
1976	18.9	14.1	14.3	11.5	35.5	276	...
1977	23.1	16.5	16.1	13.0	41.3	303	...
1978	27.4	20.3	17.6	13.9	46.9	332	...
1979	31.9	24.8	18.7	15.2	53.8	370	...
1980	35.5	28.5	19.9	16.3	60.8	399	...
1981	38.9	30.4	21.5	17.4	69.3	537	...
1982	46.5	33.3	23.3	19.7	76.6	682	...
1983	...	37.0	23.8	20.7	85.7	838	...
1984	...	42.9	24.6	21.5	102	978	...
1985	...	50.7	24.7	21.5	125	1,316	...
1986	...	61.3	25.5	23.0	132	1,664	...
1987	...	73.4	24.8	24.5	147	2,003	...
1988	...	86.7	25.4	25.8	166	3,695	...
			All				
1989	...	100	165		149	7,971	...
1990	...	115	179		136	32,762[42]	...
1991	...	127	189		197	6,277	...
1992	...	136	207		146	9,499	...
1993	...	149	213		146	11,487	...

	Spain		Sweden		Switzerland	U.K.		Yugoslavia
	Priv	**PO**	**Priv**	**PO**	**All**	**PO**	**TSB**	**All**
	(pesetas)	(pesetas)	(kronor)	(kronor)	(francs)	(pounds)	(pounds)	(dinari)
1970	862	37.3	32.1	9.6	43.7	1,797	2,779	16.8
1971	1,052	45.8	35.0	10.0	52.3[36]	1,882	2,916	21.1
					41.3			
1972	1,286	54.3	38.0	10.4	48.6	2,047	3,270	25.0
1973	1,537	63.7	41.9	11.2	53.9	2,086	3,413	31.3
1974	1,738	74.5	46.9	11.6[35]	56.9	2,121	3,599	40.3
1975	2,183	88.3	52.2	—	64.8	2,185	3,982	52.5
		All[25]						
1976	1,887		56.6	—	73.9	2,220	4,295	70.6
1977	2,272		61.9	—	80.8	3,256	4,710	90.0
1978	2,751		69.8	—	87.8	3,152	5,429	125
1979	3,258		78.5	—	93.2	3,426	...[37]	152[25]
								118
1980	3,714		86.5	—	90.3	4,060	...	128
1981	4,354		95.7	—	85.7	4,697	...	150
1982	5,100		103	—	95.9	5,685	...	198
1983	5,916		108	—	107	6,510	...	218
1984	6,739		114	—	110	6,861	...	366
1985	7,804		117	—	114	7,281	...	657
1986	10,725		128	—	120	8,072	...	1,297
1987	12,281		135	—	131	9,037	...	2,397
1988	17,886		146	—	142	9,353	...	8,008
1989	19,521		144	—	135	9,562	...	33,879
1990	21,870		170	—	129	10,100	...	37,724
1991	25,171		167	—	137	10,373	...	...
1992	28,208		198	—	148	10,358	...	...
1993	32,053		209	—	182	10,622	...	...

G3   Deposits in Savings Banks (in millions of stated unit)

NOTES

1. SOURCES:- The main sources are the official publications noted on p.xv with gaps filled from the League of Nations, *Statistical Yearbooks*. German statistics to 1913 are taken from W.G. Hoffman, *Das Wachstum der Deutschen Wirtschaft seit der Mitte des 19 Jahrhunderts* (Berlin, etc., 1965); Russian statistics to 1915 are taken from P.A. Khromov, *Economic Development of Russia in the 19th and 20th Centuries, 1800–1917* (Moscow, 1950). Spanish statistics to 1940 are taken from the *Anuario Financiero Sociedades Anonimos*. The U.K. statistics to 1938 are taken from H. Oliver Horne, *A History of Savings Banks* (Oxford, 1947). The Greek data for 1902–5 and 1954–55 were supplied by the National Statistical Service of Greece.
2. In principle, this table relates to all deposits in institutions which are described as savings banks, with government (or post office) savings banks shown separately; but there are exceptions indicated in the footnotes.
3. Except where otherwise indicated the statistics are for the end of each year.

FOOTNOTES

[1] Cisleithania (excluding the Italian provinces) to 1916, Republic of Austria subsequently.
[2] Excluding certain districts in Galicia.
[3] There are, in addition, two savings banks run by communes. In 1862 they had deposits of 5 million francs, rising to 12 million francs in 1913, 63 million francs in 1938, and 500 million francs in 1969.
[4] All savings accounts to 1893 (1st line): subsequently in savings banks only.
[5] Transleithania to 1918, but excluding Croatia-Slavonia up to 1868 (2nd line). Subsequent figures are for the territory established by the treaty of Trianon.
[6] Previous statistics are known to be incomplete.
[7] Previous statistics are of the amounts due by the National Debt Commissioners to trustees. In 1829 this was £0.5 million greater than the amount owing to depositors.
[8] A figure given later is 66, which may apply to the postwar territory.
[9] With the establishment of the Communist government this became the National Savings Bank.
[10] Subsequent figures are at 31 March in the year following that indicated.
[11] Statistics back to 1905 were revised upward at a later date.
[12] For 1871–1918 and 1939–51 Alsace-Lorraine is excluded.
[13] For 1914–18 includes Algeria.
[14] For 1871–1917 including Alsace-Lorraine.
[15] These figures are of all savings deposits rather than deposits in Savings Banks.
[16] From 1894 to 1926 at 1 June or 1 July.
[17] Subsequently excluding interbank deposits.
[18] Subsequently includes banks in Burgenland.
[19] Giro accounts began in 1940.
[20] Subsequently in the new currency (1 new = 100 old francs).
[21] Subsequently excluding Central Giro.
[22] At 31 July.
[23] The Post Office Bank only from 1940 (2nd line) to 1943.
[24] Subsequently deposits in the General Savings Bank.
[25] There was a change in the scope of the series.
[26] Previous figures are at 31 March in the year following that indicated.
[27] Current accounts began in 1933.
[28] This break occurs on a change of source (see note 1).
[29] Including blocked accounts.
[30] Subsequently excluding Southern Ireland.
[31] Subsequently at 31 March in the year following that shown.
[32] Savings deposits in all institutions from 1945.
[33] Subsequently in the new currency (1 new = 100 old dinari).
[34] Subsequently excluding personal accounts.
[35] At 30 June.
[36] This break is apparently caused by the exclusion of *livrets de depots*.
[37] The Trustee Savings Bank subsequently became an ordinary commercial bank.
[38] Included with deposits in commercial banks.
[39] Subsequently all time and savings deposits in non-deposit-money banks, or, from 1984, non-commercial banks.
[40] Czech Republic.
[41] Giro accounts were scrapped.
[42] Change in method of calculation.

G4 MONEY SUPPLY (in thousand millions of stated unit, unless otherwise indicated)

1950–1974

	Austria (shillings)		Belgium (francs)		Denmark (kroner)		Finland (markkaa)		France (francs)		West Germany (marks)		Greece (drachmae)		Ireland (million pounds)	
	M1	M2	M1	M2	M1	M2	M1	M2	M1	M2	M1	M2	M1	M2	M1	M2
1950	12.8	...	156.1	170.7	6.53	10.18	0.70	1.80	31.29	31.89	16.8	...	2.64	...	122.5	287.3
1951	16.1	...	168.7	184.2	6.17	11.91	0.99	2.45	36.95	37.75	19.1	27.2	3.26	...	131.6	298.8
1952	17.1	...	174.6	194.8	6.57	12.58	0.88	2.74	41.88	42.87	21.1	32.8	3.58	...	137.4	305.3
1953	19.5	27.3	180.4	202.4	7.06	13.43	0.91	3.08	46.58	47.94	23.2	39.7	5.38	6.93	145.2	324.4
1954	24.0	35.4	183.7	206.9	6.93	13.63	1.00	3.57	52.98	54.65	26.4	47.4	6.49	9.15	152.3	337.2
1955	23.8	38.9	192.6	218.4	7.11	14.07	1.08	4.08	59.69	61.69	29.1	54.4	8.01	11.35	154.7	337.2
1956	24.8	41.8	198.2	223.7	7.44	14.86	1.16	4.23	65.85	68.17	30.8	60.6	8.75	13.64	154.7	336.6
1957	26.3	48.2	198.0	224.5	7.80	15.71	1.17	4.39	71.37	75.35	35.1	72.1	10.56	18.96	165.5	343.7
1958	29.0	58.1	209.5	239.5	8.84	17.70	1.30	5.01	74.58	79.96	39.7	83.4	11.45	22.21	164.7	359.5
1959	31.8	67.4	216.3	252.2	9.80	19.73	1.45	5.81	83.11	90.66	44.4	97.0	13.4	27.3	170.7	371.4
1960	33.5 / 31.1	74.9 / 70.6	220.5	262.5	10.03	20.74	1.49	6.65	94.87	106	107.8 / 47.5	114.5	31.9 / 15.6	29.5	203	413
1961	33.8	78.6	237.5	289.1	11.14	22.72	1.64	7.63	110	124	54.4	129.5	18.1	34.9	219	445
1962	37.2	89.2	254.5	310.4	12.21	24.76	1.72	8.14	130	147	58.1	145.4	20.8	41.9	241	482
1963	40.4	99.8	279.2	343.3	13.86	27.84	1.99	8.87	148	168	62.3	161.4	24.2	49.9	278	519
1964	43.3	113.7	297.4	367.6	15.23	30.68	2.04	9.87	161	184	67.6	181.6	28.7	57.5	287	544
1965	47.3	127.7	318.6	400.4	16.97	33.67	2.08	10.93	176	204	72.8	203.4	32.3	63.2	298	572
1966	49.6	140.9	339.6	434.3	19.34	38.02	2.22	12.28	189	226	74.2	225.6	36.6	73.9	315	620
1967	52.9	154.7	350.5	466.7	21.12	41.61	2.18	13.30	198	256	81.6	255.7	44.0	85.2	341	693
1968	56.2	169.9	375.9	510.4	24.06	46.92	2.67	14.96	214	285	90.6	276.6	46.5	97.9	364	793
1969	60.8	190.6	353.5	538.8	27.13	51.88	3.13	16.91	210	300	95.4	305.2	48.9	112.6	389	873
1970	64.8	215.1	378.1	582.5	27.47	54.39	3.44	19.48	232	344	103.7	332.3	54.6	133.0	415	956
1971	73.7	247.0	420.3	660.4	29.61	59.21	4.02	21.98	260	407	116.9	376.9	63.6	162.5	440	1,038
1972	89.2	285.8	484.2	768.1	33.64	67.12	4.96	25.71	299	484	133.4	429.8	75.9	201.8	518	1,172
1973	95.9	323.2	520.3	875.6	37.59	76.27	6.11	29.67	328	555	135.7	467.6	93.7	236.9	572	1,396
1974	101.4	363.6	552.6	951.7	39.36	82.70	7.27	34.90	378	654	150.2	501.4	112.2	285.2	624	1,666

G4 Money Supply (in thousand millions of stated unit, unless otherwise indicated)

1975–2000

Year	Austria (shillings) M1	M2	Belgium (francs) M1	M2	Denmark (kroner) M1	M2	Finland (markkaa) M1	M2	France (francs) M1	M2	West Germany (marks) M1	M2	Greece (drachmae) M1	M2	Ireland (million pounds) M1	M2
1975	115.9	430.5	639.4	1,097	51.27	105.0	9.77	42.70	425	757	171.7	558.8	130.6	353.9	748	2,028
1976	125.5	503.2	684.1	1,235	54.51	117.3	9.60	46.67	457	850	177.3	601.0	159.6	439.0	875	2,292
1977	127.3	548.9	741.0	1,338	58.85	128.2	9.87	51.99	506	974	198.6	663.2	186.6	538.4	1,072	2,764
1978	137.9	627.4	784.4	1,438	68.30	136.4	11.50	59.92	666	1,681	227.5	731.2	228.2	666.7	1,367	3,415
1979	125.4	678.3	804.1	1,527	75.05	150.4	14.09	70.75	751	1,923	234.1	768.9	265.4	781.8	1,479	3,878
1980	145.1	765.0	806.1	1,577	83.21	168.0	14.98	81.40	801	2,102	243.4	803.9	308.8	946.0	1,686	4,678
1981	141.6	843.6	823.5	1,677	88.03	186.2	17.19	94.38	900	2,323	239.6	833.5	377.4	1,242	1,743	5,183
1982	153.3	936.1	855.8	1,797	91.67	206.8	19.92	107.1	985	2,578	256.7	890.9	459.1	1,577	1,838	5,534
1983	170.4	984.7	929.8	1,947	113.3	247.6	21.43	121.3	1,108	2,861	278.2	941.7	525.6	1,909	2,048	5,903
1984	176.4	1,047	932.5	2,035	128.1	309.8	24.94	140.2	1,219	3,107	294.8	994.5	630.9	2,400	2,245	6,432
1985	181.9	1,110	962.4	2,142	156.5	366.7	27.69	165.6	1,312	3,318	314.5	1,074	743.3	2,954	2,288	6,753
1986	193.5	1,206	1,037	2,366	168.0	401.2	27.84	178.7	1,407	3,571	340.2	1,144	896.0	3,537	2,382	7,841
1987	213.5	1,296	1,086	2,581	188.5	417.8 / 427.3	30.34	200.3	1,471	3,805	365.7	1,213	1,058	4,159	2,640	8,532
1988	232.2	1,372	1,146	2,719	225.1	450.9	35.92	246.4	1,532	4,016	408.3	1,283	1,206	5,047	2,826	9,084
1989	235.0	1,469	1,207	2,995	226.1	456.9	41.44	269.8	1,633	4,112	431.6	1,348	1,486	6,198	3,112	10,357
1990	247.3	1,611	1,217	3,117	244.5	486.7	44.43	283.3	1,703	4,212	551.9	1,599	1,848	7,077	3,346	11,280
1991	265.8	1,731	...	...	258.3	505.8	130.65	295.9	1,609	4,173	575.0	1,701	2,098	7,716	3,390	12,571
1992	283.0	1,850	...	...	256.0	502.1	134.83	293.1	1,608	4,226	641.0	1,836	2,377	8,324	3,253	14,164
1993	308.7	1,952	...	...	283.0	601.1	141.76	297.5	1,623	4,385	697.6	2,048	2,644	8,895	3,996	16,876
1994	355.6	2,077	1,543	6,249	279.1	541.3	157.86	305.08	1,671	3,003	703.0	1,279	3,487	15,412	5,446	19,294
1995	409.2	2,180	1,619	6,555	292.0	574.9	179.13	322.84	1,800	3,246	729.0	1,207	3,983	17,668	8,900	29,394
1996	431.2	2,243	1,686	7,177	325.5	621.7	208.08	313.62	1,815	3,363	805.0	1,225	4,621	19,960	9,839	34,163
1997	452.3	2,293	1,738	7,654	344.1	664.1	219.37	321.56	1,933	3,624	872.9	1,266	5,156	21,861	7,818	40,708
1998	...	...	...	...	360.7	686.2	229.32	332.87	1,993	3,781	930.6	1,322	5,629	22,193	9,842	47,950
1999	...	...	63,700	221,309	381.8	680.0	41,627	63,837	293,231	926,012	568.2	2003.8	7,657	25,632	18,177	77,400
2000	...	...	67,197	221,336	...	...	40,369	64,192	314,932	951,713	584.0	2016.3	7,446	26,610	20,400	87,435

Unit notes for the 1999–2000 figures: Belgium — million euros; Finland — million euros; France — million euros; West Germany/Germany — thousand million euros; Greece — thousand million euros; Ireland — million euros. (West Germany figures become "Germany" from 1990.)

G4 Money Supply (in thousand millions of stated unit, unless otherwise indicated)

1950–1974

Year	Italy (million million lira) M1	Italy M2	Netherlands (guilders) M1	Netherlands M2	Norway (kroner) M1	Norway M2	Portugal (escudos) M1	Portugal M2	Spain (pesetas) M1	Spain M2	Sweden (Kroner) M1	Sweden M2	Switzerland (Francs) M1	Switzerland M2	U.K. (pounds) M1	U.K. M2	Yugoslavia (dinars) M1	Yugoslavia M2
1950	2.57	3.46	6.80	9.18	4.82	10.86	23.6	...	66	...	6.89	22.13	11.43	23.89	...	...	...	...
1951	2.98	3.44	7.04	9.85	5.61	12.05	26.2	...	78	...	8.58	25.08	11.92	19.95	...	...	...	...
1952	3.45	4.90	7.76	10.87	6.00	12.89	26.9	...	88	139	8.87	26.01	12.31	21.03	5.67	8.40	...	...
1953	3.82	5.60	8.26	11.53	6.25	13.57	28.3	29.8	94	155	9.25	28.68	12.84	22.63	5.85	8.75	...	...
1954	4.13	6.25	8.85	12.57	6.51	14.27	31.1	32.8	105	175	9.40	30.41	13.20	23.81	6.08	9.11	...	...
1955	4.52	7.01	9.58	13.76	6.68	15.01	32.6	34.7	121	204	9.59	31.51	13.63	25.28	6.01	8.84	...	...
1956	4.88	7.86	9.23	13.64	6.89	15.89	34.7	37.3	144	239	10.37	33.72	14.61	26.99	6.04	8.98	...	...
1957	5.13	8.59	9.05	14.01	6.86	16.60	36.7	39.6	167	275	10.72	36.80 / 13.33	15.00 / 30.54	28.39	5.94	9.27	5.32	9.09
1958	5.71	9.84	10.13	16.06	7.05	17.14	39.4	43.1	191	313	10.91	39.16	14.80	33.10	6.09	9.59	5.84	10.37
1959	6.52	11.4	10.59	17.81	7.35	18.06	43.0	47.4	201	335	12.66	44.06	15.52	35.81	6.60	10.14	6.94	12.83
1960	7.41 / 2.65	13.0	11.30	19.82 / 25.43	7.77	19.27	45.7	51.7	205	389	12.66 / 6.53	44.55 / 38.27	17.11	39.95	6.63	10.42	7.97	14.19
1961	3.03	15.0	12.16	27.69	8.13	20.32	46.2	53.1	227	451	6.82	39.93	19.71	45.3	6.76	10.71	10.07	17.80
1962	5.49	19.7	13.09	30.53	8.77	21.71	49.5	58.7	271	546	7.26	44.15	21.91	50.48	6.40	10.48	13.73	24.85
1963	9.42	20.9	14.29	34.12	9.26	23.20	56.0	67.1	311	637	7.77	48.01	23.51	55.14	7.32	11.40	17.26	28.12
1964	10.9	23.5	15.45	37.68	9.83	25.00	64.4	78.3	372	774	8.30	51.35	25.04	59.34	7.56	12.03	20.83	31.64
1965	12.7	27.1	16.99	41.72	10.61	27.53	68.8	88.9	429	913	8.70	54.42	26.01	63.67	7.85	12.93	21.2	41.5
1966	14.2	30.6	18.16	45.11	11.42	29.85	73.1	96.7	480	1,043	9.25	59.24	26.99	68.52	7.84	13.40	22.6	51.4
1967	16.4	34.8	19.29	50.59	12.26	32.78	77.9	108.5	545	1,204	10.00	66.97	28.99	73.97	8.44	14.84	21.6	56.1
1968	19.0	39.4	21.49	57.25	14.12	36.76	84.5	122.8	612	1,430	10.46	77.03	32.59	82.78	8.78	15.91	26.7	70.1
1969	22.5	44.3	23.23	63.82	15.27	40.59	93.9	144.9	701	1,698	10.94	81.86	36.39	94.67	8.81	16.40	30.3	84.1
1970	29.9	51.4	25.95	71.31	17.20	46.70	100.5	166.5	743	1,955	11.40	84.98	40.38	104.4	9.64	17.95	35.8	104.0
1971	35.6	60.2	29.85	81.08	19.21	52.93	104.9	189.0	920	2,424	12.82	95.31	47.51	115.6	11.09	20.18	41.5	126.7
1972	42.2	71.6	35.13	92.43	22.39	59.57	122.3	234.8	1,142	2,985	14.15	107.6	50.09	128.1	12.66	25.67	58.8	156.2
1973	52.5	88.2	35.14	106.1	25.81	67.61	165.6	301.3	1,410	3,710	15.38	121.9	49.68	135.1	13.30	32.84	81.4	206.7
1974	57.2	101	39.43	121.5	28.87	75.09	18.25	342.3	1,654	4,419	17.32	132.7	48.03	117.6	14.74	37.11	102	255

G4 Money Supply (in thousand millions of stated unit, unless otherwise indicated)

1975–2000

	Italy (million million lira)		Netherlands (guilders)		Norway (Kroner)		Portugal (escudos)		Spain (pesetas)		Sweden (Kroner)		Switzerland (Francs)		U.K. (pounds)		Yugoslavia (dinars)	
	M1	M2	M1	M2	M1	M2	M1	M2	M1	M2	M1	M2	M1	M2	M1	M2	M1	M2
1975	64.0	125	47.20	137.5	33.65	86.59	227.3	385.5	1,963	5,257	20.15	148.1	50.11	128.7	17.48	40.10	135	338
1976	76.3	151	51.05	159.7	32.42	93.71	256.2	470.7	2,392	6,270	22.19	157.2	55.96	140.5	19.47	44.74	217	467
1977	92.7	183	57.77	180.5	37.00	109.9	286.0	578.6	2,836	7,441	24.43	171.3	56.43	149.8	23.52	48.99	247	571
1978	117	225	60.19	201.5	40.19	123.0	326.5	738.2	3,325	8,953	27.58	200.1	69.69	167.0	27.36	56.12	291	732
1979	145	272	61.88	223.6	43.25	139.7	414.8	1,012	3,610	10,551	30.97	233.8	68.40	182.5	29.86	63.13	341	895
1980	165	306	65.58	236.2	45.56	154.7	497.3	1,126	4,098	12,319	33.61	257.2	68.33	183.4	31.04	74.79	452	1,232
1981	189	322	64.03	254.5	52.38	175.3	540.4	1,391	4,630	14,269	36.11	293.6	64.79	195.2	36.53	95.55	568	1,620
1982	221	379	72.30	268.1	58.81	194.6	628.1	1,714	4,850	16,259	38.46	315.1	69.35	229.9	40.66	106.4	727	2,151
1983	250	429	79.66	281.3	65.92	215.6	679.3	1,996	5,277	16,082	87.0	385.2	75.82	253.3	42.46	120.0	874	2,988
1984	280	479	85.00	299.7	82.00	257.0	784.0	2,490	5,746	16,883	96.8	425.1	75.8	273.9	48.05	134.9	1,252	4,360
																	(million new dinars)	
1985	310	530	90.77	320.1	98.65	295.5	1,000	3,084	6,589	18,867	100.4	439.4	73.9	285.2	56.67	150.5	182	7,021
1986	344	575	97.21	337.2	101.8	301.9	1,359	3,690	7,996	24,026	112.2	504.7	75.5	294.7	69.27	183.8	383	1,279
1987	372	618	103.7	343.5	152.6	359.7	1,537	4,215	9,271	26,056	115.4	529.8	86.0	325.8	154.1	377.7	764	2,960
1988	401	664	111.3	368.8	187.1	377.4	1,804	4,751	11,165	29,051	116.9	574.1	88.0	343.4	170.7	394.0	2,407	10,122
1989	452	738	119.0	406.3	218.3	409.8	1,903	5,266	13,546	33,068	…	633.1	85.7	365.2	195.3	473.3	51,030	247,683
1990	483	802	123.9	434.4	237.6	432.7	2,455	6,256	15,682	37,553	…	638.1	84.3	368.2	214.9	523.1	126,283	344,968
1991	538	878	129.3	455.0	255.8	445.3	2,872	7,800	17,179	42,350	…	667.0	82.9	376.8	229.2	531.8	…	…
1992	546	921	135.1	477.4	323.3	483.6	3,416	9,553	17,003	45,212	…	686.8	86.2	386.6	238.7	565.3	…	…
1993	579	986	149.6	504.8	340.1	480.1	3,775	10,712	17,409	49,462	…	716.9	91.2	421.0	252.1	601.7	…	…
1994	581	1,079	155.1	509.0	355.0	504.2	3,589	10,586	17,456	51,948	…	728.1	94.9	438.5	…	643.0	…	…
1995	585	1,105	176.0	539.3	358.7	523.3	3,901	11,435	18,019	55,416	…	750.6	100.7	458.7	…	728.3	…	…
1996	614	1,130	197.3	569.5	392.7	559.5	4,302	12,468	19,261	56,840	…	817.1	128.2	502.6	…	806.5	…	…
1997	645	1,056	212.7	607.8	417.0	567.5	4,882	13,316	21,976	57,655	…	826.3	139.8	535.8	…	837.4	…	…
1998	728	1,074	…	…	497.5	655.3	5,757	14,401	25,396	61,742	…	822.7	149.3	563.2	…	895.0	…	…
	thousand million euros		thousand million euros						thousand million euros									
1999	457	648	134.5	362.8	525.3	666.3	…	…	192.1	502.8	…	892.7	163.4	637.9	…	933.4		
2000	484	675	147.1	404.6	565.2	724.3	…	…	204.7	564.0	…	909.9	160.0	529.9	…	1,038.6		

G4   Money Supply

NOTES

1. SOURCES:- I.M.F., International Financial Statistics
2. On the I.M.F. definitions M.1 equals currency in circulation plus demand deposits (other than those of central government). M.2 additionally includes time and savings deposits and foreign currency deposits of residents.
3. Changes have occurred quite frequently in reporting systems and in the institutions covered. These are indicated by "break" lines in the table, two figures being given for the year in which the break occurred if possible.

G5 TOTAL CENTRAL GOVERNMENT EXPENDITURE (in millions, except as otherwise indicated)

1750–1799	Austria[1] (gulden)[6]	U.K.[2,3] (pounds)		1800–1849	Austria (gulden)[6]	Belgium (francs)	France (francs)	Greece (drachmae)	Netherlands (guilders)	Russia (paper rubels)	Switzerland (francs)	U.K.[2,3] (pounds)
1750	...	7[3]		1800	167	...	...	...	...	...	...	[63][3]
1751	...	6[3]		1801	150	...	...	...	...	...	...	65
1752	...	7[3]		1802	118	...	...	...	...	...	...	55
1753	...	6		1803	115	...	...	...	...	109	...	53
1754	...	6		1804	114	...	...	...	...	122	...	63
1755	...	7		1805	146	...	...	...	...	125	...	71
1756	...	10		1806	163	...	...	...	...	122	...	73
1757	...	11		1807	207	...	...	...	...	159	...	73
1758	...	13		1808	190	...	...	...	...	248	...	78
1759	...	15		1809	262	...	...	...	...	278	...	82
1760	...	18		1810	351	...	...	...	...	279	...	82
1761	...	21		1811	118	...	...	...	...	272	...	87
1762	...	20		1812	96	...	...	...	...	342	...	95
1763	...	14		1813	111	...	...	...	...	423	...	111
1764	...	11		1814	112	...	...	...	...	457	...	113
1765	...	11		1815	117	...	931	...	...	391	...	99
1766	...	10		1816	131	...	1,056	...	...	428	...	71
1767	...	10		1817	128	...	1,189	...	...	438	...	59
1768	...	9		1818	127	...	1,434	...	...	443	...	58
1769	...	10		1819	160	...	896	...	...	476	...	58
1770	...	11		1820	215	...	907	...	...	500	...	58
1771	...	10		1821	186	...	908	...	...	482	...	58
1772	...	11		1822	157	...	949	...	...	456	...	56
1773	...	10		1823	189	...	1,118	...	...	479	...	54
1774	...	10		1824	151	...	986	...	...	417	...	55
1775	...	10		1825	146	...	982	...	...	413	...	54
1776	...	14		1826	146	...	977	...	...	404	...	56
1777	...	15		1827	146	...	987	...	...	422	...	56
1778	...	18		1828	140	...	1,024	...	...	407	...	53
1779	...	20		1829	146	...	1,015	...	...	428	...	54
1780	...	23		1830	138	[31][4]	1,095	...	...	428	...	52
1781	65	26		1831	187	119	1,219	...	...	447	...	51
1782	81	29		1832	161	164	1,174	...	...	497	...	51
1783	71	24		1833	160	97	1,134	14	...	495	...	49
1784	78	18		1834	160	101	1,064	29	...	528	...	49
1785	84	16		1835	164	90	1,047	16	...	587	...	48[5]
1786	81	17		1836	156	103	1,066	16	...	583	...	50[5]
1787	82	15		1837	153	106	1,079	18	...	573	...	51
1788	112	16		1838	158	121	1,136	16	...	597	...	52
1789	120	16		1839	162	124	1,179	16	...	628	...	53
1790	113	17								(silver rubels)		
1791	112	18										
1792	91	17		1840	165	166	1,364	16	...	188	...	53
1793	116	20		1841	163	115	1,425	16	...	196	...	54
1794	151	27		1842	157	129	1,441	16	...	211	...	55
				1843	165	120	1,445	14	...	212	...	55
1795	136	38		1844	168	195	1,428	14	...	222	...	55
1796	158	38		1845	171	134	1,489	14	75	224	...	54
1797	132	46		1846	177	123	1,567	15	74	245	...	55
1798	133	47		1847	204	128	1,630	15	76	245	...	59
1799	154	47		1848	182	135	1,771	16	78	284	...	59
				1849	255	112	1,646	16	72	270	3	55

G5 Total Central Government Expenditure (in thousand millions except as otherwise indicated)

1850–1899

	Austria[1,7] (gulden)[6]	Belgium (francs)	Bulgaria (leva)	Denmark[10] (kroner)	Finland (markkaa)	France (francs)	Germany[11] (marks)	Greece (drachmae)	Hungary[12] (gulden)	Italy[13] (lire)
1850	269	119	...	...	...	1,473	...	17	...	...
1851	296	119	...	...	...	1,461	...	16	...	...
1852	310	132	...	...	...	1,513	...	16	...	...
1853	321	135	...	...	...	1,548	...	16	...	...
1854	407	143	...	51	...	1,988	...	18	...	...
1855	441	147	...	54	...	2,309	...	19	...	...
1856	371	150	...	52	...	2,196	...	19	...	...
1857	371	146	...	57	...	1,893	...	20	...	...
1858	367[6]	145	...	57	...	1,859	...	23	...	...
1859	542	153	...	51	...	2,208	...	23	...	...
1860	524	159	...	55	...	2,084	...	24	...	...
1861	500	163	...	54	...	2,171	...	25	...	...
1862	395	177	...	57	...	2,213	...	26	...	936
1863	402	187	...	51	...	2,287	...	24	...	916
1864	411[1] 670[7]	186	...	80	...	2,257	...	25	...	971
1865	618	189	...	73[10]	...	2,147	...	29	...	987
1866	940	203	...	48	...	2,203	...	28	...	1,371
1867	943[1]	192	...	51	...	2,170	...	38	...	956
1868	344	192	...	49	...	1,903	...	45	169	1,129
1869	394	200	...	57	...	1,904	...	37	178	1,105
1870	422	217	...	45	...	3,173	...	36	192	1,195
1871	422	238	...	46	...	3,047	...	37	220	1,130
1872	421	252	...	43	...	2,723	1,407	33	239	1,183
1873	469	351	...	47	...	2,874	1,370	33	257	1,232
1874	471[1] 730	302	...	48	...	2,782	673	46	254	1,174
1875	717	292	...	65	...	2,936	634	35	234	1,210
1876	719	294	...	47	...	3,031	[679][11]	35	244	1,272
1877	881	386	...	50	...	3,027	569	35	245	1,312
1878	898	349	...	44	...	3,348	784	37	279	1,260
1879	832	344	20[9]	42	...	3,322	550	96	386	1,265
1880	674	383	27[9]	44	...	3,365	550	89	290	1,261
1881	780	402	27	48	...	3,616	612	103	505	1,303
1882	812	423	39	50	35	3,687	604	64	383	2,017
1883	770	406	33	51	37	3,715	587	68	399	1,382
1884	814	362	34	50	39	3,539	615	91	431	[679][13]
1885	764	351	45	48	44	3,467	638	123	487	[1,508][13]
1886	880	350	55[9]	50	40	3,294	694	130	348	1,467[13]
1887	967	346	48	58	43	3,261	877	107	368	1,499
1888	883	356	120	60	38	3,221	1,020	108	362	1,606
1889	782	373	74	60	37	3,247	1,111	169	814	1,768
1890	813	418	84	62	37	3,285	1,354	142	387	1,675
1891	787	402	93[9] 93	66	39	3,258	1,245	123	406	1,657
1892	611	406	107	65	40	3,380	1,244	108	418	1,613
1893	630	395	95	63	42	3,451	1,270	92	495	1,653
	kronen[8]								kronen[8]	
1894	1,384	403	107	62	47	3,480	1,337	85	2,051	1,743
1895	1,487	410	97	61	54	3,434	1,307	92	1,009	1,655
1896	1,457	438	101	74	53	3,445	1,366[11] 1,629	91	1,032	1,727
1897	1,525	511	99	66	54	3,524	1,746	137	1,096	1,652
1898	1,607	694	111	135	95	3,528	1,856	312	1,049	1,648
1899	1,681	570	100	76	67	3,589	1,961	105	1,027	1,650

G5 Total Central Government Expenditure (in thousand millions, except as otherwise indicated)

	Netherlands (guilders)	Norway[14] (kroner)	Portugal[29] (escudos)	Romania[15] (lei)	Russia (silver rubels)	Serbia (dinari)	Spain (pesetas)	Sweden (kronor)	Switzerland (francs)	U.K. (pounds)
1850	72	13	...	...	287	...	320	...	5	55
1851	76	15	...	...	281	...	347	...	5	54
1852	71	16	...	...	280	...	344	...	5	55
1853	71	14	...	...	313	...	353	...	5	56
1854	83	17	...	...	384	...	360	...	6	[83][3]
1855	86	17	...	...	526	...	354	...	5	93
1856	94	17	...	...	619	...	449	...	6	76
1857	95	19	...	...	348	...	485	...	6	68
1858	87	20	...	...	363	...	490	...	7	65
1859	102	21	...	...	351	...	506	...	10	70
1860	87	23	...	...	438	...	594	...	9	73
1861	98	20	...	...	414	...	630	...	9	72
1862	92	20	...	44	393	...	650	...	8	70
1863	99	21	...	44	432	...	657	...	8	68
1864	100	24	...	62	437	...	684	...	9	67
1865	99	20	...	64	428	...	694	...	10	66
1866	106	22	...	68	438	...	640	...	11	67
1867	112	22	...	61	460	...	634	...	9	72
1868	96	21	...	78	492	...	639	...	9	75[2]
1869	94	21	...	81	535	...	644	...	9	67
1870	99	20	...	72	564	...	670	...	18	68
1871	94	22	...	74	557	...	574	...	10	70
1872	109	21	...	85	583	...	501	...	11	69
1873	108	22	...	92	612	...	526	...	14	75
1874	99	31	...	90	602	...	611	...	15	73
1875	119	38	...	99	605	...	711	...	19	75
1876	113	44	...	101	704	...	641	...	20	76
1877	118	50	...	105	1,121	...	728	...	20	80
1878	116	[26][14]	35	122	1,076	...	755	...	20	83
1879	115	49	37	114	812	...	791	...	20	82
1880	113	44	34	...	793	...	811	...	22	81
1881	124	44	35	[141][15]	840	...	784	80	23	83
1882	130	46	35	131	788	...	795	80	23	87
1883	138	43	35	137	804	...	843	83	24	85
1884	133	42	40	136	816	...	843	83	25	89
1885	122	41	40	130	913	...	884	85	25	92
1886	124	43	42	130	945	...	889	87	25	90
1887	122	43	45	129	931	...	828	91	28	87
1888	127	45	51	140	927	...	833	90	31	87
1889	125	44	54	161	963	...	822	93	34	91
1890	166	46	51	159	1,057	...	823	98	38	93
1891	130	53	55	162	1,116	...	821	102	43	96
1892	152	52	48	168	1,125	...	754	101	54	96
1893	135	60	46	179	1,061	...	688	105	54	98
1894	133	61	49	199	1,155	57	753	101	48	101
1895	133	62	55	210	1,521	64	782	103	47	105
1896	134	71	58	215	1,484	64	783	106	48	110
1897	139	78	58	210	1,495	69	848	118	52	112
1898	150	81	56	217	1,772	79	878	125	56	118
1899	150	91	62	225	1,785	81	822	135	59	144

G5 Total Central Government Expenditure (in thousand millions except as otherwise indicated)

1900–1949

	Austria[1,7] (kronen)	Belgium (francs)	Bulgaria[18] (leva)	Czechoslovakia (koruna)	Denmark[10] (kroner)	Finland (markkaa)	France (francs)	Germany[11] (marks)
1900	1,755	574	109	...	78	66	3,747	2,197
1901	1,877	604	103	...	79	112	3,756	2,324
1902	1,819	615	111	...	77	109	3,699	2,321
1903	1,886	628	105	...	78	103	3,597	2,357
1904	2,017	688	113	...	79	120	3,639	2,068
1905	1,999	626	149	...	99	120	3,707	2,195
1906	2,018	772	147	...	85	112	3,852	2,392
1907	2,376	768	181	...	114	130	3,880	2,810
1908	2,562	770	228	...	94	168	4,021	2,683
1909	3,081	786	191	...	108	178	4,186	3,266
1910	3,137	829	230	...	133	156	4,322	3,024
1911	3,235	811	205	...	139	160	4,548	2,897
1912	3,657	896	288	...	173[20] 108	166	4,743	2,893
1913	3,962	...	350	...	106	185	5,067	3,521
1914	[2,193][7]	...	291	...	111	186	10,065	9,651
1915	17,357[7]	...	314	...	156	199	20,925	26,689
1916	...	...	476	...	185	268	28,113	28,780
1917	...	...	973	...	251	488	35,320	53,261
1918	...	...	1,294	...	369	1,085	41,897	45,514
1919	...[1]	...	1,316[13]	8,615	616	1,682	39,970	54,867
1920	...	10,944	2,026	11,604	533	2,090	39,644	145,255[11]
1921	...	9,808	3,861	21,890	555	2,700	32,845	298,766
1922	(schillings)	8,749	4,518	23,076	499	2,560	45,188	...
1923	1,062	8,863	5,481	23,371	424	3,500	38,293	...
1924	1,361	9,849	8,387	19,223[19]	402	3,150	42,511	5,027
1925	1,411	13,398	7,157	17,300	417	3,950	36,275	5,683
1926	1,602	14,630	6,785	17,978	382	4,080	41,976	6,616
1927	1,835	9,286	6,696	17,374	362	3,990	45,869	7,168
1928	1,977	10,747	7,726	17,600	332	5,040	44,248	8,517
1929	1,990	12,259	10,449	17,994	323	4,510	[59,335][21]	8,187
1930	2,289	12,695	8,188	18,201	324	4,740	55,712[21]	8,392
1931	2,331	12,074	6,568	18,903	317	4,250	53,428[21]	6,995
1932	1,924[1] 1,290	11,740	5,567	18,249	333	3,000	[40,666][21]	5,965
1933	1,494	11,190	5,497	16,500	328	3,250	54,945	6,270
1934	1,574	11,384	[4,213][18]	14,800	393	4,100	49,883	8,221
1935	1,450	13,568	5,685	15,159	393	4,530	49,868	...
1936	1,413	13,847	6,274	15,262	405	4,860	55,789	...
1937	[1,400][1,17]	14,175	7,171	15,906	442	5,900	72,759	...
1938	...	14,482	7,202	...	497	5,430	82,345	...
1939	...	15,797	8,354	...	523	8,360	150,116	...
		thousand millions				thousand millions	thousand millions	
1940	...	...	9,873	...	611	21	204	...
1941	...	16.0	16,952	...	822	31	121	...
1942	...	17.7	...	...	892	28	133	...
1943	...	20.0	...	...	1,081	34	160[22]	...
1944	...	24.2	...	...	1,121	44	259[22]	...
								West Germany[35]
1945	...	49.2	...	...	1,249	43	465	...
1946	...	77.1	...	...	1,503	100	521	...
1947	...	76.5	...	...	1,883	88	690	...
1948	5,725	141	...	...	1,980	105	992	...
1949	8,214	90.4	...	...	2,070	133	1,205	1,592

G5   Total Central Government Expenditure (in thousand millions, except as otherwise indicated)

1900–1949

	Greece (drachmae)	Hungary[12] (kronen)	S Ireland[26] (pounds)	Italy[13] (lire)	Netherlands (guilders)	Norway[14] (kroner)	Poland[27] (zlotys)	Portugal[29] (escudos)
1900	109	1,084	...	1,659	155	77	...	56
1901	114	1,102	...	1,692	153	110	...	58
1902	125	1,111	...	1,809	162	105	...	60
1903	116	2,176	...	1,793	166	105	...	...
1904	116	1,215	...	1,776	190	101	...	...
1905	116	1,192	...	1,820	176	97	...	...
1906	122	1,245	...	2,414	182	101	...	...
1907	132	1,399	...	2,079	184	111	...	...
1908	134	1,616	...	2,179	189	108	...	...
1909	137	1,722	...	2,431	193	138	...	...
1910	141	1,902	...	2,448	199	117	...	...
1911	181	1,768	...	2,650	204	121	...	...
1912	208	2,013	...	2,841	220	133	...	...
1913	261	2,319	...	3,137	232	154	...	...
1914	482	[1,444][12]	...	3,009	354	123	...	...
1915	376	6,659	...	5,795	507	165	...	...
1916	215	12,248	...	12,543	543	158	...	163
1917	317	10,911	...	21,622	704	234	...	204
1918	...	12,251[12]	...	26,502	1,074	502	...	242
1919	[1,446][23]	[11,200][24]	...	33,335	852	619	...	...
1920	1,354	[10,092][25]	...	27,827	935	648	...	...
1921	1,683	45,920	...	37,488	1,032	746	...	577
1922	2,476	54,085	30	37,206	1,123	585	...	1,045
1923	3,460	264,304	39	24,090	807	550	...	1,072
1924	5,000	8,644,649	27	24,240	737	478	1,663	1,608
		(pengos)						
1925	5,498	1,005	26[26] 28	21,930	699	486	1,884	1,492
1926	6,841	1,145	28.3	22,755	689	445	1,975[27]	1,953
1927	8,687	1,250	31.4	24,592	645	395	2,556	1,824
1928	7,770	1,354	29.1	29,649	698	397	2,841	2,049[28] 1,889
1929	9,446	1,473	30.1	20,841	729	387	2,993	2,043
1930	18,355	1,478	31.1	20,858	738	376	2,814	1,883
1931	11,176	1,628	27.9	25,856	865	374	2,468	1,857
1932	11,099	1,388	36.9	25,235	883	361	2,245	1,949
1933	9,117	1,184	33.0	22,855	993	309	2,231	2,069
1934	7,706	1,185	32.2	28,137	932	302	2,302	...[29]
1935	8,746	1,188	33.1	21,871	989	341	2,337	2,886
1936	10,049	1,230	33.5	66,923	935	384	2,213	2,734
1937	12,683	1,305	35.6	48,065	938	422	2,335[27]	2,070
1938	13,412	1,381	52.2	40,632	1,045	472	...	2,299
1939	12,652	1,723	45.7	42,627	1,182	567	...	2,400
			thousand million					
1940	14,016	4,033	39.2	70	2,310	714	...	2,423
1941	...	...	48.6	106	3,666	1,132	...	2,820
1942	...	...	45.2	123	3,474	2,042	...	2,595
1943	...	...	47.5	160	3,686	1,896	...	3,985
1944	...	...	50.7	247	4,281	2,274	...	3,684
	thousand million							
1945	...[23]	...	56.2	319	4,439	1,224	...	3,929
1946	314	...	62.1	622	4,501	2,008	...	4,630
1947	1,659	...	73.5	1,215	5,095	2,936	10,508	5,694
1948	3,422	...	99.2	1,907	5,209	2,556	20,852	5,699
1949	3,950	...	103	1,735	4,454	2,980	30,871	5,661

G5 Total Central Government Expenditure (in thousand millions except as otherwise indicated)

	Romania[15]	Russia/U.S.S.R.[31]	Spain	Sweden[33]	Switzerland	U.K.[23]	Serbia/ Yugoslavia[34]
	(lei)	(rubels)	(pesetas)	(kroner)	(francs)	(pounds)	(dinari)
1900	235	1,883	833	151	60	193	78
1901	237	1,874	906	153	61	205	80
1902	218	2,167	902	167	61	194	79
1903	218	2,108	971	185	63	155	92
1904	230	2,738	945	188	66	150	110
1905	252	3,205	933	189	66	147	92
1906	263	3,213	964	196	72	144	89
1907	265	2,583	978	209	81	143	...
1908	269	2,661	981	216	88	145	...
1909	417	2,608	1,062	232	94	157	...
1910	482	2,597	1,077	236	91	168	112
1911	525	2,846	1,122	249[28]	99	174	120
1912	533	3,171	1,101	254	101	184	118
1913	522	3,383	1,374	259	106	192	131
1914	543	4,865	1,379	271	210[28] 224	559	214
1915	747	...	1,888	413	300	1,559	...
1916	...	...	1,520	434	346	2,198	...
1917	1,027	...	2,200	650	466	2,696	...
1918	787	...	1,733	1,718	547	2,579	...
1919	1,646	...	2,798[32]	849	573	1,666	...
1920	4,331	...	2,514	945	616	1,188	...
1921	6,037	...	3,384	1,116	540	1,070	...
1922	6,818	...	3,131	938	426	812	...
1923	13,639	...[30]	3,309	[389][33]	428	749	...
1924	21,403	2,318	3,129[32]	775	376	751	...
1925	[17,942][15]	2,970	3,131[32]	714	376	776	10,540[34]
1926	28,499	4,051	2,344[32]	758	383	782	11,777
1927	33,137	5,335	2,818	810	361	774	11,593
1928	35,224	6,465	2,925	740	366	761	10,983
1929	34,607	8,241	3,207	792	377	782	11,147
1930	31,579	12,335[30]	3,330	811	483	814	11,817
1931	34,702	23,146	3,476	819	404	819	12,470
1932	[24,891][15]	30,740[31] 34,402	3,894	894	432	833	11,530
1933	20,741	39,905	4,116	1,067	450	770	9,969
1934	19,864	52,398	4,270	973	497	785	9,663
1935	20,699	...	4,162	1,148	505	829	9,379
1936	23,060	...	...	1,108[28] 1,118	518	889	9,562
1937	26,762	...	...	1,199	537	909	10,059
1938	30,287	123,996	...	1,372	604	1,006	11,083
1939	...	...	...	1,578	964	1,401	11,814
		(new rubels)					
1940	...	17.4	5,594	2,880	1,807	3,954	11,920[34]
1941	...	...	6,383	3,878	2,142	4,876	...
1942	...	...	7,322	4,085	2,261	5,726	...
1943	...	...	8,928	4,503	2,482	5,899	...
1944	...	...	10,400	4,618	2,594	6,174	...
							thousand millions
1945	...	...	10,625	5,232	2,323	5,592	...
1946	...	...	11,258	4,537	2,213	4,192	32.4
1947	...	...	13,533	4,108	1,947	3,354	58.1
1948	...	...	15,374	4,844	1,947	3,314	74.3
1949	...	...	16,155	5,675	1,581	3,531	114

G5   Total Central Government Expenditure (in thousand millions, except as otherwise indicated)

	Austria[1] (schillings)	Belgium (francs)	Denmark[10] (kroner)	Finland (markkaa)	France (francs)	W Germany[35] (marks)	E. Germany (marks)	Greece (drachmae)	S Ireland[26] (pounds)	Italy[13] (lire)
									millions	
1950	12.3	80.8	2.17	143	2,357	11.6	24.1	5,439	109	1,948
1951	17.4	89.8	2.39	207	2,914	17.8[35] 17.9	27.3	6,039	129	2,213
1952	21.4	101	2.55	204	3,656	19.8[28]	32.3	6,612	154	2,434
								(new drachmae)		
1953	22.6	94.5	2.83	221	3,801	22.7	34.7	8.1	178	2,429
1954	24.9	96.4	3.27	214	3,702	23.7	36.1	9.8	180	2,510
1955	28.9	95.3	3.08[20] 3.97	243	3,945	22.9	38.3	11.7	193	2,759
1956	31.1	98.7	4.08	279	4,648	27.8	35.9	[19.6][23]	213	2,901
1957	36.3	108	4.50	301	5,640	31.8	36.4	15.4	237	3,069
1958	41.4	123	4.80	333	5,490	33.9[35]	42.2	15.8	236	3,715
1959	42.0	135	5.22	355	5,946	38.1	46.5	17.5	244	3,621
					(new francs)					
1960	45.2	142	5.83	400	60.0	30.8[12]	49.5	19.1	299	4,612
1961	50.0	144	6.25	447	66.5	47.9	50.8	21.8	345	4,634
1962	54.1	152	7.87	497	76.9	51.8	55.5	24.1	423	5,369
				(new markkaa)						
1963	59.1	167	9.2	4.9	90.8	56.1	56.1	25.4	450	6,106
1964	62.7	181	10.2	5.7	90.6	63.3	56.3	29.8	530	6,759[13]
1965	66.6	203	11.3	6.8	98.2	67.5	55.8	33.9	731	8,464
1966	72.3	236	13.1	7.2	106	70.7	60.8	39.0	685	9,517
1967	80.1	255	15.5	8.1	122	79.4	59.0	45.6	744	10,322
1968	86.2	285	18.2	9.8	134	[82.2][36]	59.5	52.1	875	11,841
1969	93.2	296	24.0	10.2	148	81.7	65.0	65.5	1,039	14,014
										million million
1970	102	352	27.6	10.8	162	87.6	70.0	65.1	1,036	14.3
1971	113	372	35.6	11.9	175	98.4	79.1	73.9	1,440	17.6
1972	128	423	41.1	13.7	194	112	85.7	89.1	1,599	19.1
1973	141	491	46.6	17.0	220	123	93.3	105	1,899	23.8
1974	167	576	53.3	21.3	254	135	103	129	[1,772][26]	29.6
1975	197	729	66.5	27.5	320	160	114	171	3,440	40.2
1976	222	836	77.1[10]	31.1	364	166	117	212	3,598	48.5
1977	237	951	99.5	35.1	404	174	124	255	3,988	62.2
1978	266	1,126	117	38.9	466	191	132	300	4,874	83.4
1979	288	1,212	135	45.0	532	205	140	376	7,044	104
1980	306	1,332	151	50.8	624	218	160	423	8,414	143
1981	339	1,551	178	57.8	757	235	167	733	11,470	179
1982	373	1,675	210	68.0	859	247	182	794	15,603	209
1983	408	1,828	240	77.2	954	249	192	1,055	15,329	260
1984	435	1,877	260	85.7	1,027	254	212	1,470	18,365	296
1985	465	1,970	269	95.8	1,058	259	234	1,777	21,118	353
1986	498	2,015	269	105	1,114	264	246	2,166	20,087	406
1987	514	1,959	274	117	1,123	271	260	2,755	20,444	440
1988	518	1,991	297	117	1,154	278	269	3,718	23,021	493
1989	541	1,461	312	129	1,213	292	282	4,592	18,810	488
1990	565	1,465	323	141	1,282	311		6,698	20,576	541
1991	620	1,546	340	168	1,336	406		9,811	23,766	580
1992	658	1,664	359	186	1,425	432		11,965	31,597	628
1993	700	1,635	387	202	1,502	463		16,035	43,072	635
	million US $								million US $	
1994	917	...	412	223	...	...		11,242	11,999	601
1995	994	...	418	232	...	...		10,366	12,683	617
1996	1,013	...	424	231	...	...		10,861	13,320	653
1997	979	...	425	...	...	...		11,691	14,819	595
1998	1,058	...	434	...	...	...		12,538	15,949	611

G5 Total Central Government Expenditure (in thousand millions except as otherwise indicated)

1950–1998

	Neth'l	Norway[14]	Poland	Portugal	Romania[15]	Russia/ U.S.S.R.[31]	Spain	Sweden[33]	Swit- zerland	U.K.[3]	Yugo- slavia
	(guilders)	(kroner)	(zlotys)	(escudos)	(lei)	(rubels)	(pesetas)	(kroner)	(francs)	(pounds)	(dinari)
1950	5.0	3.04	39.6	5.1	19.1	41.3	18.7	5.8	1,637	3,417	107
1951	6.2	2.93	43.8	5.6	21.7	...	20.3	6.4	1,786	4,222	99
1952	6.0	3.54	52.6	5.9	29.0	46.0	22.6	7.8	2,162	4,531	228
1953	6.6	4.27	82.6	6.4	35.6	51.5	23.9	9.5	1,884	4,477	203
1954	7.1	4.62	100	6.7	38.4	...	27.2	10.1	1,959	4,517	246
1955	8.1	4.60	105	7.3	42.9	54.0	30.2	10.7	1,949	4,727	213
1956	8.6	4.85	111	7.6	42.0	56.4	37.7	12.0	1,964	5,136	203
1957	8.9	4.76	120	8.2	43.9	...	42.9	13.0	2,238	5,218	211
1958	9.0	5.16	128	8.7	44.7	64.3	55.6	14.6	2,643	5,435	289
1959	9.7	5.35	136	9.7	48.3	70.4	63.1	15.2	2,482	5,590	336
1960	10.4	5.76[14]	147	11.3	55.4	73.1	70.2	16.4	2,601	6,157	409
1961	11.7	6.40	176	13.4	63.7	76.3	78.8	17.4	3,267	6,195	539
1962	12.2	7.23	183	14.8	73.1	82.2	93.2	18.8	3,684	6,401	587
1963	13.2	8.08	180	15.7	77.7	87.0	113	21.5	4,083	6,776	581
											(new dinari)
1964	16.0	8.9	200	17.2	87.1	92.2	126	22.5	4,856	7,265	6.8
1965	19.5	10.0[14] 10.1	210	18.3	93.1	102	151	26.8	4,920	7,974[28] 8,456	8.4
1966	21.0	10.4	234	19.4	105	106	187	30.8	5,683	9,541	8.1
1967	23.9	11.7	235	23.4	124	115	215	35.1	5,874	11,525[28] 10,871	10.0
1968	27.1	13.1	236	25.2	132	129	240	37.6	6,447	11,615	10.8
1969	29.8	15.3	253	27.4	143	138	281	40.2	7,081	12,822	11.5
									thousand millions	thousand millions	
1970	35.0	18.4	279	31.7	131	155	313	45.3	7.8	14.1	14.2
1971	41.3	21.2	281	36.6	134	164	382	49.3	9.0	15.5	18.4
1972	46.4	24.1	295	40.9	145	173	424	57.6	10.4	17.7	25.5
1973	53.8	26.7	321	48.9	168	184	491	61.9	11.6	20.0	32.9
1974	62.0	30.5	418	63.4	207	197	506	72.1	13.1	26.8	48.3
1975	76.5	38.6	531	86.6	236	214	708	84.3	13.5	36.0	59.9
1976	91.9	46.6	604	125	250	227	872	99.4	15.9	39.4	78.4
1977	98.7	56.8[28] 58.0	687	159	280	243	1,133	118	15.5	44.0	93.4
1978	111	64.3	776	215	299	260	1,571[28] 1,368	140	15.8	51.5	82.0
1979	132	68.7	869	281	...[28]	276	1,686[28]	162	16.6	61.0	102
1980	145	84.2	978	375	276	295	2,026	189	17.4	76.2	132
1981	156	93.4	1,138	507	250	310	2,362	215	17.6	84.8	166
1982	168	104[37] 138	1,709	624	234	343	2,820	235	19.3	90.5	198
1983	176	153	1,770	802	212	354	3,409	278	20.3	97.5	262
1984	182	167	2,292	1,019	236	371	3,974	298	21.6	106	391
1985	186	182	2,733	1,334	340	386	4,981	329	22.9	110	696
1986	188	203	3,244	1,597	356	417	5,746	322	23.2	116	1,375
1987	192	228	3,825	1,835	344	431	6,462	335	23.9	121	3,009
1988	173	236	8,431	2,325	314	459	...	337	26.6	127	7,597
1989	167	254	29,618	2,728	321	483	...	350	27.4	134	52,150
1990	182	279	172,165	3,439	290	513	...	398	31.6	158	282,540
1991	190	309	241,858	4,596	780	...	...	438	35.5	178	23,420[38]
1992	195	319	381,890	4,776	2,406	2,102[37]	...	478	37.1	212	1,640,806[38]
1993	197	327	502,428	...	...	...	...	565	39.7	222	2,678,359[38]
1994	218	357	...	6,138	...	...	16,438	553	36.7	284	...
1995	255	362	...	6,613	...	...	17,242	619	37.4	295	...
1996	197	375	...	6,975	...	...	18,322	659	39.4	307	...
1997	209	387	...	7,242	...	...	18,694	665	38.1	306	...
1998	218	...	...	7,795	...	...	18,633	699	41.6	313	...

G5   Total Central Government Expenditure (in thousand millions, except as otherwise indicated)

NOTES

1. SOURCES:- The official publications noted on p. xv with a few gaps filled from the League of Nations, *Public Finance Statistics.* In addition statistics for Ireland and the U.K. to 1979 are taken from B.R. Mitchell, *British Historical Statistics* (Cambridge, 1988), where the original sources are given; and statistics for Russia to 1914 are taken from P.A. Khromov, *Economic Development of Russia in the 19th and 20th Centuries, 1800–1917* (Moscow, 1950).
2. So far as possible, all kinds of central government expenditure are included in this table, in contrast to G6, showing state revenue, in which the aim has been to exclude capital receipts.
3. Except where otherwise indicated, statistics are from the closed accounts.
4. It must be stressed that in some countries, especially those with federal constitutions, central government expenditure may be no more important than the outlays of lower levels of administration.

FOOTNOTES

[1] Austria-Hungary to 1867, Cisleithania from 1868 to 1915, and the Republic from 1920. Statistics to 1874 (1st line) are of cash payments from the Treasury. From then to 1915 they include obligations undertaken and the change in the Treasury's cash balance. Figures to 1864 (1st line) and from 1932 to 1937 do not include expenditure on tax-collection.

[2] Net expenditure of Great Britain to 1800, gross expenditure of the U.K. subsequently. Capital items (including debt redemption) are excluded throughout. Figures to 1868 include expenditure out of the Indian Military Contribution and the Army & Navy Extra Receipts.

[3] Figures for 1750 and 1751 are for years ended 29 September. From 1752 to 1799 they are for years ended 10 October. The 1800 figure is for 15 months ended 5 January 1801. The figures for 1801–53 are for years ended 5 January following that indicated. The figure for 1854 is for the period 6 January—31 March 1855, and all subsequent figures are for years ended 31 March following that indicated.

[4] Fourth quarter-year only.

[5] Exclusive of compensation paid to West Indian slaveowners.

[6] Convention gulden to 1858 and standard gulden thereafter. The difference is negligible.

[7] Statistics to 1864 are for years ended 31 October. From 1865 to 1913 they are for Calendar years (expenditure in Nov–Dec 1864 being 179 million gulden). The 1914 figure is for the first half-year and that for 1915 is for the year ended 30 June.

[8] 2 kronen = 1 gulden.

[9] Revised figures were later published for each year back to 1891, but only for three years before that. The original series is given here to 1891 (1st line). Earlier revised figures are 1879 21; 1880 26; 1886 36.

[10] Statistics to 1976 are for years ended 31 March. Subsequently they are for calendar years. Expenditure for the calendar year 1976 was 86.1 thousand million kroner. The Duchies of Schleswig, Holstein, and Lauenburg are included to 1865.

[11] The figure for 1876 is for 15 months ended 31 March 1877. Subsequent statistics are for years ended 31 March following that shown. Up to 1896 (1st line) and from 1921 onwards, the expenditure of public enterprises was entered net of receipts.

[12] Transleithania (including Croatia-Slavonia) to 1918, and the territory established by the treaty of Trianon subsequently. The figure for 1914 is for the first half year, and subsequent figures (to 1940) are for years ended 30 June, except as indicated in footnote[24] and [25]. Expenditure for Transleithania for 1 July—31 October 1918 was 6,906 million kroner.

[13] The figure for 1884 is for 8 months ended 31 August. That for 1885 is for 10 months ended 30 June, and all subsequent figures to 1964 are for years ended 30 June. Later statistics are for calendar years.

[14] Net expenditure excluding debt redemptions to 1965 (1st line). The figure for 1878 is for the first half-year. Later statistics (to 1960) are for years ended 30 June, and subsequently they are for calendar years.

[15] The figure for 1881 is for 15 months ended 31 March. From 1882 to 1924 the figures are for years ended 31 March. The 1925 figure is for 9 months. From 1926 to 1931 the figures are for calendar years. The 1932 figure is for 15 months to 31 March 1933, and subsequent figures (to 1939) are for years ended 31 March following that indicated.

[16] Footnote suppressed.

[17] Budget estimate.

[18] Figures from 1919 to 1933 are for years ended 31 March following that indicated. The 1934 figure is for 9 months.

[19] The expenditure of public enterprises is subsequently entered net of receipts.

[20] From 1912 (2nd line) to 1955 (1st line) the figures are of current account expenditure only.

[21] The figure for 1929 is for 15 months ended 31 March 1930. Those for 1930 and 1931 are for years ended 31 March following that indicated. The figure for 1932 is for 9 months.

[22] Including the budget of the Comité Francaise de Libéeration Nationale in 1943, and of the provisional government in 1944.

[23] The figure for 1919 is for 15 months ended 31 March. Figures for 1920–40 are for years ended 31 March. Those for 1946–55 are for years ended 30 June, and the 1956 figure is for 18 months to 31 December.

[24] 1 November 1918–6 August 1919.

[25] 7 August 1919–30 June 1920.

[26] Statistics to 1925 (1st line) are of expenditure on current account only. Figures to 1973 are for years ended 31 March in the year following that shown. The 1974 figure is for April–December, and subsequent statistics are for calendar years.

[27] Figures for 1926–37 are for years ended 31 March following that indicated.

[28] This break is caused by a change in methods of accounting.

[29] Figures to 1933 are for years ended 30 June following that indicated. The 1935 figure is for 18 months to 31 December.

[30] Figures from 1924 to 1930 are for years ended 30 September. Expenditure in the fourth quarter of 1930 was 4,616 million rubels.

[31] Statistics from 1932 include local government expenditure.

[32] Footnote suppressed.

[33] The figure for 1923 is for the first half-year only. Subsequent figures are for years ended 30 June.

[34] Serbia to 1914, Yugoslavia subsequently. Figures for 1925–40 are for years ended 31 March.

[35] West Berlin is included from 1957 (2nd line) and Saarland from 1959.

[36] Subsequently excluding special financial transactions.

[37] Russian Federation.

[38] Yugoslavia.

G6 CENTRAL GOVERNMENT REVENUE AND MAIN TAX YIELDS

Key:- Consum = Consumption taxes; Ded Profits = Deductions from profits; I & P = Income & Property taxes; I & T = Industrial & Turnover taxes; P & T Mon = Petrol and tobacco monopolies; Prop = Property tax; Reg = Registration Tax; S & T Mon = Salt and tobacco monopolies; Trans = Transactions tax; VAT = Value added tax

1750-1799

	Austria[1,8]		U.K.[2,3]			
	Total (million gulden)	Direct	Total	Customs (thousand pounds)	Excise	Land & I & P
1750	...	...	7,467	1,537	3,454	2,212
1751	...	...	7,097	1,588	3,468	1,769
1752	...	...	6,992	1,635	3,402	1,685
1753	...	...	7,338	1,770	3,582	1,728
1754	...	...	6,827	1,587	3,692	1,288
1755	...	...	6,938	1,782	3,660	1,236
1756	...	...	7,006	1,699	3,649	1,375
1757	...	...	7,969	1,872	3,303	2,043
1758	...	...	7,946	1,918	3,477	2,139
1759	...	...	8,155	1,830	3,615	2,216
1760	...	...	9,207	2,113	4,218	2,407
1761	...	...	9,594	2,191	4,671	2,253
1762	...	...	9,459	1,824	4,816	2,386
1763	...	...	9,793	2,283	4,793	2,288
1764	...	...	10,221	2,282	5,027	2,316
1765	...	...	10,928	2,324	4,935	2,243
1766	...	...	10,276	2,514	4,879	2,225
1767	...	...	9,868	2,460	4,521	2,174
1768	...	...	10,131	2,453	4,746	1,895
1769	...	...	11,130	2,675	4,961	1,814
1770	...	...	11,373	2,841	5,139	1,796
1771	...	...	10,987	2,739	4,842	1,834
1772	...	...	11,033	2,457	4,995	2,092
1773	...	...	10,487	2,702	5,141	1,843
1774	...	...	10,613	2,557	4,922	1,821
1775	...	...	11,112	2,756	5,106	1,756
1776	...	...	10,576	2,684	5,383	1,875
1777	...	...	11,105	2,411	5,252	2,299
1778	...	...	11,436	2,348	5,369	2,497
1779	...	...	11,853	2,523	5,625	2,450
1780	...	...	12,524	2,774	6,081	2,523
1781	66	25	13,280	3,019	6,111	2,635
1782	75	25	13,765	2,898	6,420	2,724
1783	64	24	12,677	2,949	5,480	2,596
1784	69	25	13,214	3,026	6,139	2,460
1785	77	25	15,527	4,537	6,142	2,666
1786	74	24	15,246	3,783	6,413	2,774
1787	76	25	16,453	4,094	7,043	2,909
1788	87	27	16,779	3,996	7,257	3,013
1789	84	26	16,669	3,647	7,301	3,006
1790	86	23	17,014	3,462	7,698	2,993
1791	89	23	18,506	4,018	8,433	2,914
1792	87	23	18,607	4,100	8,741	3,020
1793	86	22	18,131	3,557	8,559	2,952
1794	93	22	18,732	4,348	8,387	3,034
1795	68	22	19,053	3,419	9,915	2,946
1796	66	20	19,391	3,645	9,096	3,021
1797	71	21	21,380	3,940	10,303	3,365
1798	73	21	26,946	4,741	11,571	4,591
1799	80	21	31,783	7,056	11,862	8,117

G6   Central Government Revenue and Main Tax Yields

	Austria[1]					Belgium				France		
	Total	Customs	Consum	Direct	S & T Mon	Total[4]	Customs	Excise	Direct	Total	Customs	Direct
		(million gulden)					(million francs)				(million francs)	
1800	86	...	...	26	...	...	...	...	...	...	...	...
1801	95	...	...	26	...	...	...	...	...	...	...	...
1802	86	...	...	30	...	...	...	...	...	...	...	...
1803	101	...	...	31	...	...	...	...	...	...	...	...
1804	108	...	...	36	...	...	...	...	...	...	...	...
1805	112	...	...	32	...	...	...	...	...	...	...	...
1806	87	...	...	27	...	...	...	...	...	...	...	...
1807	140	...	...	46	...	...	...	...	...	...	...	...
1808	162	...	...	59	...	...	...	...	...	...	...	...
1809	95	...	...	35	...	...	...	...	...	...	...	...
1810	136	...	...	30	...	...	...	...	...	...	...	...
1811	71	...	...	18	...	...	...	...	...	...	...	...
1812	87	...	...	34	...	...	...	...	...	...	...	...
1813	102	...	...	31	...	...	...	...	...	...	...	...
1814	76	...	...	21	...	...	...	...	...	...	...	...
1815	96	...	...	27	...	...	...	...	...	729	...	...
1816	125	...	...	33	...	...	...	...	...	879	...	...
1817	125	...	...	44	...	...	...	...	...	900	...	...
1818	127	...	...	53	...	...	...	...	...	938	...	...
1819	124	...	...	53	...	...	...	...	...	895	...	...
1820	121	...	...	50	...	...	...	...	...	933	...	...
1821	128	...	...	50	...	...	...	...	...	928	...	...
1822	139	...	...	50	...	...	...	...	...	933	...	...
1823	131	...	...	52	...	...	...	...	...	919	...	...
1824	128	...	...	52	...	...	...	...	...	960	...	...
1825	125	...	...	51	...	...	...	...	...	979	...	...
1826	121	...	...	47	...	...	...	...	...	983	...	...
1827	127	...	...	49	...	...	...	...	...	948	...	...
1828	121	...	...	48	...	...	...	...	...	978	...	...
1829	122	...	...	50	...	...	...	...	...	992	...	...
1830	126	...	...	48	...	[30][5]	[1][5]	[4][5]	[8][5]	971	...	...
1831	123	...	...	45	...	120	4	16	28	949	...	...
1832	133	...	...	47	...	158	7	19	27	985	...	...
1833	131	...	...	48	...	93	8	45	31	990	...	...
1834	130	...	...	47	...	101	9	21	32	1,008	...	...
1835	133	...	...	47	...	94	8	18	29	1,021	...	...
1836	140	...	...	48	...	106	8	17	29	1,053	...	...
1837	144	...	...	47	...	104	9	17	29	1,076	...	...
1838	142	...	...	47	...	125	11	19	30	1,111	...	293
1839	145	...	...	48	...	116	9	19	33	1,124	...	...
1840	147	...	...	47	...	169[4]	10	18	30	1,160	...	295
1841	144	...	...	47	...	101	10	18	30	1,198	...	...
1842	146	...	...	47	...	104	11	18	30	1,256	...	297
1843	150	...	...	48	...	105	11	19	30	1,270	...	...
1844	153	...	...	48	...	110	12	21	30	1,298	...	299
1845	154	18	22	47	38	113	12	20	31	1,330	...	...
1846	155	19	22	48	37	113	11	19	31	1,352	...	298
1847	153	20	20	48	39	113	11	17	32	1,343	139	...
1848	101	10	14	26	21	109	10	20	32	1,207	91	301
1849	101	11	15	27	24	114	12	21	31	1,257	130	...

G6 Central Government Revenue and Main Tax Yields

1800–1849

	Netherlands				Russia/U.S.S.R.[6]				United Kingdom[2]			
	Total	Customs	Excise	Direct	Total	Customs	Excise[7]	Direct	Total	Customs	Excise	Land & I & P
	(million guilders)				(million paper rubles)				(thousand pounds)			
1800	...	...	...	...	...	...	...	...	31,585[3]	6,785[3]	10,594[3]	9,606[3]
1801	...	...	...	...	...	...	...	...	39,086	8,758	11,573	10,453
1802	...	...	...	...	...	...	...	...	41,168	7,699	15,475	8,645
1803	...	...	...	...	102	...	...	...	42,442	8,158	18,795	6,182
1804	...	...	...	...	103	...	...	...	50,206	9,425	21,451	9,710
1805	...	...	...	...	107	12	26	45	55,031	10,130	23,156	10,849
1806	...	...	...	...	106	10	35	44	60,084	10,799[3]	24,053[3]	12,552
1807	...	...	...	...	115	9	34	44	64,843	12,648	26,711	17,180
1808	...	...	...	...	123	6	36	48	68,174	12,607	27,628	19,023
1809	...	...	...	...	134	8	37	53	69,170	14,575	24,750	20,849
									(million pounds)			
1810	...	...	...	...	178	11	37	82	73	14	27	21
1811	...	...	...	...	233	16	75	81	71	13	28	21
1812	...	...	...	...	236	19	73	88	70	14	26	21
1813	...	...	...	...	270	32	75	103	75	14	27	22
1814	...	...	...	...	297	26	84	118	78	15	29	23
1815	...	...	...	...	323	26	100	133	79	14	30	24
1816	...	...	...	...	347	27	115	132	69	12	27	19
1817	...	...	...	...	357	43	110	127	58	13	23	11
1818	...	...	...	...	367	44	109	130	60	14	26	9
1819	...	...	...	...	422	44	155	133	58	13	27	8
1820	...	...	...	...	447	52	157	132	60	12	30	8
1821	...	...	...	...	410	50	152	119	62	13	30	8
1822	...	...	...	...	391	41	139	125	60	13	29	8
1823	...	...	...	...	399	41	131	134	59	14	27	7
1824	...	...	...	...	380	50	121	118	60	14	28	5
1825	...	...	...	...	397	54	117	121	58	19	23	5
1826	...	...	...	...	390	57	117	118	55	19	21	5
1827	...	...	...	...	393	63	105	126	55	20	20	5
1828	...	...	...	...	384	63	107	119	57	19	22	5
1829	...	...	...	...	404	67	112	124	55	19	21	5
1830	...	...	...	...	393	66	109	116	54	19	20	5
1831	...	...	...	...	407	68	115	118	51	18	18	5
1832	...	...	...	...	451	82	118	142	51	19	18	5
1833	...	...	...	...	429	82	117	121	50	18	18	5
1834	...	...	...	...	430	81	122	115	50	20	16	5
1835	...	...	...	...	495	78	131	157	50	22	14	4
1836	...	...	...	...	520	82	139	159	53	23	16	4
1837	...	...	...	...	527	90	140	162	50	22	15	4
1838	...	...	...	...	543	87	147	163	51	22	15	4
1839	...	...	...	...	558	89	153	162	52	23	15	4
					(million silver rubels)							
1840	...	...	...	...	155	26	44	42	52	23	15	4
1841	...	...	...	...	161	27	47	43	52	23	15	5
1842	...	...	...	...	173	30	50	45	51	23	14	5
1843	...	...	...	...	179	30	55	46	57	23	14	10
1844	...	...	...	...	186	32	57	47	58	24	14	10
1845	56	5	20	18	185	30	59	44	57	22	15	10
1846	56	5	19	18	192	30	63	45	58	22	15	10
1847	56	5	18	196	29	64	46	56	22	14	10	
1848	55	4	19	19	195	30	64	44	58	23	15	10
1849	55	5	19	19	198	30	64	45	57	22	15	10

G6   Central Government Revenue and Main Tax Yields

1850–1899

	Austria[1,8]					Belgium				Bulgaria			
	Total	Customs	Consum	Direct	S & T Mon	Total	Customs	Excise	Direct	Total	Customs	Excise[29]	Direct
	(million gulden)					(million francs)				(million leva)			
1850	197	21	23	63	38	117	12	21	32	...	...	...	...
1851	225	19	25	77	40	118	12	21	32	...	...	...	...
1852	230	22	28	83	43	123	14	21	32	...	...	...	...
1853	238	20	29	83	45	128	13	22	33	...	...	...	...
1854	250	19	29	87	50	132	12	22	33	...	...	...	...
1855	283	19	29	91	53	139	12	22	34	...	...	...	...
1856	290	20	32	92	57	142	12	23	34	...	...	...	...
1857	317	18	37	95	55	146	13	25	34	...	...	...	...
1858	315[1]	19[1]	41[1]	96[1]	57[1]	155	16	28	34	...	...	...	...
1859	261	12	43	96	48	156	16	29	35	...	...	...	...
1860	305	12	52	101	68	155	16	28	35	...	...	...	...
1861	305	12	47	98	70	156	15	25	35	...	...	...	...
1862	320	13	53	117	74	161	15	26	35	...	...	...	...
1863	329	13	59	120	65	163	14	28	35	...	...	...	...
1864	335[1]	12	53	123	[81][3]	164	13	28	36	...	...	...	...
	454[8]	___[8]	___[8]	___[8]	___[8]								
1865	447	12[1]	55[1]	119[1]	64[1]	169	14	29	36	...	...	...	...
1866	472	10	50	104	67	169	13	30	37	...	...	...	...
1867	460[1]	11[1]	44[1]	112[1]	61[1]	173	14	30	37	...	...	...	...
		10	35	68	...								
1868	325	11	47	74	43	176	15	28	37	...	...	...	...
1869	323	16	45	78	44	185	16	31	37	...	...	...	...
1870	356	14	48	82	50	191	22	29	38	...	...	...	...
1871	356	18	53	88	53	208	20	25	39	...	...	...	...
1872	367	18	57	90	50	213	19	27	40	...	...	...	...
1873	386	16	59	92	50	227	18	31	41	...	...	...	...
1874	380	16	53	92	49	243	18	31	44	...	...	...	...
1875	385[1]	11	54	92	51	246	18	33	42	...	...	...	...
	510												
1876	524	6	54	91	53	255	19	33	42	...	...	...	...
1877	568	5	58	91	53	258	18	32	43	...	...	...	...
1878	623	4	59	92	53	260	18	30	43	...	...	...	...
1879	592	3	61	90	55	270	19	33	44	29	5		20
1880	547	6	69	95	59	292	22	32	45	33[9]	6[8]		24[9]
1881	608	−1	80	93	58	297	23	34	45	24	7		14
1882	655	17	74	95	63	301	24	34	46	27	7		16
1883	653	18	76	97	64	303	23	35	47	31	8		18
1884	681	21	76	99	63	306	22	34	49	29	7		18
1885	663	5	86	100	65	313	24	39	49	27	6		16
1886	668	19	87	100	65	316	24	40	49	49[9]	10[9]		33[9]
1887	727	8	78	105	68	324	26	40	49	55	9		38
1888	696	38	46	104	67	333	28	41	50	55	11		35
1889	694	39	89	105	71	338	27	41	51	70	13		43
1890	725	39	94	108	70	341	24	42	50	70	14		43
1891	601	41	94	111	71	346	24	43	52	81[9]	16[9]		51[9]
										87	14		48
1892	618	42	101	112	70	347	24	42	51	84	15		46
	(million kronen)												
1893	1,318	96	207	223	146	352	26	43	51	78	20		39
1894	1,321	102	214	215	157	363	27	44	51	98	21		40
1895	1,397	101	224	237	160	373	30	45	52	76	26		31
1896	1,416	101	221	240	159	389	39	50	53	79	26		30
1897	1,482	117	244	243	164	431	38	69	54	78	30		32
1898	1,564	128	235	256	163	439	37	59	57	80	33		30
1899	1,598	108	252	263	170	469	41	64	57	70	29		27

G6 Central Government Revenue and Main Tax Yields

	Denmark[10]				Finland			France				
	Total[11]	Customs	Excise[12]	I & P	Total	Customs	Excise	Total	Customs[13]	Excise	Reg.	Direct
	(million kroner)				(million markaa)			(million francs)				
1850	...	...		...	...	...	...	1,297	128	...	...	301
1851	...	...		...	...	...	...	1,273	120	...	...	301
1852	...	...		...	...	...	...	1,336	142	...	...	277
1853	49	9		8	...	...	...	1,391	143	...	...	277
1854	54	9		8	...	...	...	1,418	152	...	...	279
1855	57	11		8	...	...	...	1,536	192	...	...	282
1856	60	11		9	...	...	...	1,638	179	...	...	285
1857	54	11		9	...	...	...	1,683	185	...	...	291
1858	49	9		8	...	...	...	1,747	188	...	...	294
1859	50	9		8	...	...	...	1,728	194	...	...	297
1860	53	9		8	...	...	...	1,722	135	...	...	301
1861	60	10		8	...	...	...	1,780	128	...	...	304
1862	59	10		8	...	...	...	1,882	153	...	...	310
1863	70[10]	11		8	...	...	...	1,959	167	...	...	313
1864	78	11		10	...	...	...	1,923	134	...	...	317
1865	44	15		9	...	...	...	1,965	125	...	...	320
1866	53	15		7	...	...	...	2,018	123	...	...	325
1867	49	15		9	...	...	...	1,964	121	...	...	329
1868	58	17		10	...	...	...	1,818	124[13] 77	306	364	336
1869	45[11] 37	16		8	...	...	...	1,865	74	317	368	340
1870	39	18		9	...	...	...	1,662	82	276	286	343
1871	43	19		10	...	...	...	2,014	106	317	337	331
1872	42	20		8	...	...	...	2,497	110	426	433	345
1873	43	21		8	...	...	...	2,680	162	463	422	409
1874	46	22		8	...	...	...	2,518	157	516	430	403
1875	48	25		8	...	...	...	2,705	182	602	453	408
1876	46	24		8	...	...	...	2,778	200	608	471	413
1877	46	22		9	...	...	...	2,780	196	601	470	417
1878	44	22		9	...	...	...	2,853	217	612	487	421
1879	46	23		9	...	...	...	2,966	237	595	520	424
1880	49	24		9	...	...	...	2,957	262	615	550	401
1881	51	26		9	...	...	...	2,988	285	595	571	401
1882	52	27		9	36	...	...	2,980	289	590	559	414
1883	54	28		9	37	11	6	3,038	300	608	549	420
1884	55	29		9	38	11	6	3,032	291	612	524	425
1885	52	28		9	38	12	7	3,057	294	598	524	429
1886	51	27		9	40	12	7	2,940	309	590	522	434
1887	51	28		9	36	13	6	2,968	325	589	517	438
1888	54	30		9	35	13	5	3,108	362	591	514	443
1889	56	30		9	38	14	6	3,108	351	616[14]	506	446
1890	56	30		9	38	14	6	3,229	355	612	541	480
1891	56	27	4[12]	9	40	15	6	3,364	385	624	545	474
1892	55	24	7	10	45	16	6	3,370	410	601	551	469
1893	57	25	7	10	42	17	5	3,366	431	586	522	497
1894	58	25	7	10	43	17	4	3,458	446	575	529	501
1895	62	28	8	10	46	18	5	3,416	387	588	529	506
1896	64	29	8	10	49	18	6	3,436	407	596	508	512
1897	68	31	9	10	51	19	5	3,528	426	612	522	518
1898	70	33	9	10	55	22	5	3,620	470	632	533	505
1899	69	33	10	11	58	25	7	3,657	430	639	543	517

G6 Central Government Revenue and Main Tax Yields

1850-1899

	Germany[16]			Greece				Hungary[17]		
	Total[15]	Customs	Excise	Total	Customs	Excise	Direct	Total[18]	Consum	Direct
	(million marks)			(million drachmae)				(million gulden)		
1850	...	...	...	...	...	...	...	...	...	...
1851	...	...	...	...	...	...	...	...	...	...
1852	...	...	...	...	...	...	...	...	...	...
1853	...	...	...	...	...	...	...	...	...	...
1854	...	...	...	...	...	...	...	...	...	...
1855	...	...	...	...	...	...	...	...	...	...
1856	...	...	...	...	...	...	...	...	...	...
1857	...	...	...	...	...	...	...	...	...	...
1858	...	...	...	...	...	...	. ...	...	...	...
1859	...	...	...	...	...	...	...	...	...	...
1860	...	...	...	...	...	...	...	...	...	...
1861	...	...	...	...	...	...	...	...	...	...
1862	...	...	...	...	...	...	...	...	...	...
1863	...	...	...	...	...	...	...	...	...	...
1864	...	...	...	...	...	...	...	...	...	...
1865	...	...	...	...	...	...	...	...	...	...
1866	...	...	...	...	...	...	...	...	...	...
1867	...	...	...	...	...	...	...	...	...	...
1868	...	...	...	...	...	...	...	170	13	59
1869	...	...	...	...	...	...	...	167	13	57
1870	...	...	...	...	...	...	...	176	13	63
1871	...	...	...	...	...	...	...	148	14	62
1872	182	95	74	...	...	...	...	156	13	61
1873	263	123	140	...	...	...	...	175	13	60
1874	253	104	138	...	...	...	...	183	12	68
1875	253	111	132	...	...	...	...	188	13	71
1876	[311][16]	[135][16]	[162][16]	...	...	...	...	203	12	80
1877	244	100	133	...	...	...	...	214	12	82
1878	242	101	130	...	...	...	...	218	14	82
1879	282	135	134	...	...	...	...	247	19	80
1880	294	164	117	...	...	...	...	245	20	82
1881	367	181	165	...	...	...	...	285	25	88
1882	362	187	149	...	...	...	...	280	24	90
1883	355	191	136	...	...	...	...	295	27	94
1884	375	209	137	...	...	...	...	300	28	96
1885	369	216	123	...	...	...	...	322	36	98
1886	388	232	121	...	...	...	...	312	32	94
1887	417	252	130	...	...	...	...	323	35	97
1888	507	283	183	...	...	...	...	335	35	101
1889	629	350	236	...	...	...	...	342	44	99
1890	661	368	257	...	...	...	...	373	48	101
1891	675	378	263	...	...	...	...	414	51[19]	106
1892	631	360	260	...	...	...	...	425	74	103
								(million kronen)		
1893	638	337	270	...	...	...	...	932	162	209
1894	691	363	279	...	...	...	...	951	165	215
1895	706	383	287	...	...	...	...	955	158	214
1896	790	434	298	97	27.9	34.4	18.5	1,001	167	220
1897	792	441	292	92	...	...	...	1,022	167	221
1898	847	476	306	105	...	...	...	1,018	164	221
1899	852	462	324	111	...	...	...	1,007	159	224

G6 Central Government Revenue and Main Tax Yields

	Italy[20]				Netherlands			
	Total	Customs	S & T Mon	Direct	Total	Customs	Excise	Direct
		(million lire)				(million guilders)		
1850	...	...	...	...	57	5	20	19
1851	...	...	...	...	57	5	20	19
1852	...	...	...	...	57	5	20	19
1853	...	...	...	...	58	5	20	19
1854	...	...	...	...	60	5	20	19
1855	...	...	...	...	61	5	21	19
1856	...	...	...	...	57	4	17	19
1857	...	...	...	...	58	4	18	20
1858	...	...	...	...	60	4	18	20
1859	...	...	...	...	59	4	18	20
1860	...	...	...	...	60	5	18	20
1861	...	...	...	...	61	5	18	20
1862	480	59	99	129	62	5	18	21
1863	524	60	109	131	63	5	19	21
1864	577	59	120	148	65	4	20	21
1865	647	63	128	198	65	4	19	21
1866	617	67	141	157	69	5	24	21
1867	715	66	140	227	72	4	26	21
1868	748	75	168	166	71	4	26	21
1869	871	81	140	291	74	5	28	21
1870	866	74	142	271	75	5	28	21
1871	966	81	147	320	78	5	28	22
1872	1,010	88	149	334	82	5	30	22
1873	1,047	97	148	340	85	6	32	22
1874	1,077	101	154	344	89	6	33	23
1875	1,096	104	165	347	91	6	34	23
1876	1,123	101	165	350	96	6	37	23
1877	1,243	103	172	356	95	5	38	24
1878	1,191	108	176	354	96	5	39	24
1879	1,223	134	184	361	98	4	39	24
1880	1,222	126	185	365	103	5	39	25
1881	1,278	157	189	373	106	5	40	25
1882	1,300	159	190	383	105	5	41	25
1883	1,333	179	193	385	104	5	40	26
1884	[658][20]	[86][20]	[124][20]	[191][20]	104	5	41	26
1885	[1,413][20]	[204][20]	[259][20]	[392][20]	107	5	43	27
1886	1,409	191	254	394	109	5	43	27
1887	1,453	205	249	394	110	5	44	27
1888	1,500	212	246	390	112	5	43	27
1889	1,501	206	247	461	114	5	44	28
1890	1,562	231	249	407	114	6	44	28
1891	1,540	211	252	416	118	6	44	28
1892	1,528	204	254	425	120	6	45	29
1893	1,551	204	255	427	115	6	43	32
1894	1,517	188	259	427	118	6	43	35
1895	1,570	195	261	481	121	7	43	35
1896	1,633	198	261	483	122	8	44	35
1897	1,615	202	261	483	123	9	45	33
1898	1,629	209	261	481	125	9	47	33
1899	1,658	214	270	483	131	9	47	34

G6   Central Government Revenue and Main Tax Yields

1850-1899

	Norway[21]				Portugal[22]				Romania[24]		
	Total	Customs	Consum	I & P	Total[23]	Customs	Prop	Business	Total	Customs	Prop
		(million kroner)				(million escudos)				(million lei)	
1850	14	...	...	—	...	...	...	...	...	...	...
1851	14	9	2	—	...	...	...	...	...	...	...
1852	13	...	...	—	...	...	...	...	...	...	...
1853	14	...	...	—	...	...	...	...	...	...	...
1854	16	...	...	—	...	...	...	...	...	...	...
1855	16	9	3	—	...	...	...	...	...	...	...
1856	17	...	...	—	...	...	...	...	...	...	...
1857	18	...	...	—	...	...	...	...	...	...	...
1858	17	...	...	—	...	...	...	...	...	...	...
1859	18	...	...	—	...	...	...	...	...	...	...
1860	17	11	3	—	...	...	...	...	...	...	...
1861	18	...	...	—	...	...	...	...	...	...	...
1862	19	...	...	—	...	...	...	...	...	3	...
1863	20	...	...	—	...	...	...	...	...	4	3
1864	20	...	...	—	...	...	...	...	...	5	3
1865	20	13	3	—	...	...	...	...	...	6	2
1866	21	...	...	—	...	...	...	...	...	5	2
1867	20	...	...	—	...	...	...	...	...	8	2
1868	21	...	...	—	...	...	...	...	...	9	...
1869	20	...	...	—	...	...	...	...	...	8	3
1870	20	12	4	—	...	...	...	...	...	7	3
1871	21	...	...	—	...	...	...	...	...	8	4
1872	22	...	...	—	...	...	...	...	...	10	6
1873	25	...	...	—	...	...	...	...	...	8	6
1874	27	...	...	—	...	8	...	...	...	9	6
1875	28	18	5	—	...	10	...	...	...	8	6
1876	28	...	...	—	...	9	...	...	...	8	5
1877	31	...	...	—	...	10	...	...	...	10	6
1878	[17][21]	...	...	—	...	10	...	...	...	16	5
1879	28	...	...	—	29	12	2.2	0.8	...	13	5
1880	34	19	6	—	24	9	2.3	0.8	...	[16][24]	[6][24]
1881	35	16	7	—	26	10	3.0	1.1	...	16	8
1882	39	18	6	—	29	11	3.2	1.1	...	16	9
1883	43	21	7	—	38	11	2.5	1.1	147	20	9
1884	41	19	7	—	30	12	3.0	1.1	127	16	9
1885	45	...	...	—	31	12	3.1	1.1	124	17	9
1886	44	20	6	—	32	13	3.0	1.1	137	18	11
1887	43	...	...	—	35	15	3.1	1.2	140	21	11
1888	44	21	6	—	38	14	3.1	1.2	159	22	11
1889	45	20	6	—	38	14	3.1	1.1	160	23	11
1890	50	23	7	—	39	15	3.1	1.0	170	24	11
1891	51	23	9	—	40	13	3.1	1.1	180	29	13
1892	51	22	8	—	38	10	3.1	1.2	182	30	13
1893	53	21	8	3	42	14	2.9	1.0	220	37	13
1894	54	21	8	3	46	14	3.1	1.1	200	30	13
1895	55	22	9	3	46	16	3.0	1.1	203	31	13
1896	57	23	9	4	52	15	3.1	1.9	...	34	16
1897	65	27	10	4	50	13	3.1	1.5	211	32	16
1898	74	32	11	5	49	12	3.2	1.8	237	36	16
1899	83	37	12	5	50	15	3.1	1.7	200	22	16

G6 Central Government Revenue and Main Tax Yields

1850-1899

	Russia/U.S.S.R.[6]			Serbia				Spain[25]				
	Total	Customs	Excise[7]	Direct	Total	Direct	Indirect	State Mon	Total	Customs	Consum	Tobacco Monopoly	Direct
	(million rubels)				(million dinari)				(million pesetas)				
1850	202	30	63	45	...	...	...	...	318	42	...	44	86
1851	212	31	75	45	...	...	...	...	314	40	...	47	90
1852	222	32	79	48	...	...	...	...	335	43	...	47	91
1853	220	28	82	48	...	...	...	...	350	40	...	48	93
1854	213	20	77	46	...	...	...	...	362	38	...	50	93
1855	209	18	81	47	...	...	...	...	371	44	...	52	93
1856	232	30	91	51	...	...	...	...	451	49	...	56	109
1857	241	36	92	55	...	...	...	...	492	53	...	62	110
1858	248	34	100	53	...	...	...	...	464	53	...	66	122
1859	279	33	123	55	...	...	...	...	497	56	...	69	124
1860	278	34	128	58	...	...	...	...	577	59	...	73	125
1861	330	33	130	58	...	...	...	...	569	66	...	78	126
1862	291	33	134	56	...	...	...	...	[791][25]	[95][25]	...	[125][25]	[188][25]
1863	344	34	135	73	...	...	...	...	577	65	...	89	126
1864	324	27	120	75	...	...	...	...	877	58	...	91	134
1865	356	26	129	79	...	...	...	...	601	57	...	90	132
1866	345	32	127	74	...	...	...	...	575	53	...	87	135
1867	402	37	143	89	...	...	...	...	767	54	...	80	148
1868	406	37	144	99	...	...	...	...	746	44	...	68	136
1869	436	42	147	104	...	...	...	...	595	51	...	56	140
1870	460	43	175	110	...	...	...	...	683	52	...	61	158
1871	488	49	187	108	...	...	...	...	522	56	...	70	170
1872	490	55	186	108	...	...	...	...	488	53	...	71	176
1873	510	56	194	108	...	...	...	...	600	62	...	65	154
1874	531	58	217	109	...	...	...	...	688	67	...	66	173
1875	558	64	212	134	...	...	...	...	636	72	...	79	184
1876	540	73	208	132	...	...	...	...	1,165	83	...	91	198
1877	526	53	210	134	...	...	...	...	885	88	...	97	206
1878	601	81	232	137	...	...	...	...	955	107	...	102	204
1879	645	93	248	136	...	...	...	...	706	111	...	107	203
1880	629	96	241	128	...	...	...	...	735	114	...	114	213
1881	652	86	242	140	...	...	...	...	1,081	121	...	120	221
1882	704	94	276	136	...	...	...	...	819	145	...	125	215
1883	699	97	282	132	...	...	...	...	821	130	...	130	220
1884	705	97	277	126	...	...	...	...	815	123	...	133	216
1885	762	95	265	131	...	...	...	...	799	126	...	132	228
1886	781	112	272	125	...	...	...	...	866	133	...	129	235
1887	830	107	305	82	...	...	...	...	787	134	...	90	242
1888	899	141	320	84	...	...	...	...	731	100	...	90	221
1889	927	138	335	88	...	...	...	...	746	127	...	90	223
1890	944	142	333	89	...	...	...	...	747	134	...	89	225
1891	892	128	312	87	...	...	...	...	745	134	...	93	220
1892	970	131	344	91	...	...	...	...	707	129	36	95	223
1893	1,046	166	346	100	56	19	9	13	736	144	35	89	237
1894	1,154	184	398	102	59	19	9	14	728	127	39	88	233
1895	1,256	179	420	106	59	19	7	16	733	113	39	90	232
1896	1,369	182	428	99	60	19	8	16	793	121	36	95	233
1897	1,416	196	453	101	62	20	9	16	775	93	30	95	229
1898	1,585	219	518	104	66	22	9	17	868	104	35	95	230
1899	1,673	219	560	121	72	24	11	19	[483][25]	[75][25]	[19][25]	[48][25]	[114][25]

G6   Central Government Revenue and Main Tax Yields

	Sweden				Switzerland		United Kingdom[2]			
	Total	Customs	Excise	I & P	Total[27]	Customs	Total	Customs	Excise	Land & I & P
	(million kronor)				(million francs)		(million pounds)			
1850	...	...	...	...	4.7	4	57	22	15	10
1851	...	...	...	...	5.6	5	56	22	15	9
1852	...	...	...	...	6.3	6	57	22	16	9
1853	...	...	...	...	6.3	6	59	23	16	9
1854	...	...	...	...	5.9	6	62[2]	22[2]	17[2]	14[2]
1855	...	...	...	...	6.2	6	70	23	17	18
1856	...	...	...	...	6.7	6	72	24	18	19
1857	...	...	...	...	7.1	6	67	23	18	15
1858	...	...	...	...	8.1	7	64	24	18	10
1859	...	...	...	...	9.4	7	70	24	20	13
1860	...	...	...	...	8.4	8	70	23	19	14
1861	...	13	8	10	8.8	8	69	24	18	14
1862	...	12	8	10	8.8	8	69	24	17	14
1863	...	13	9	10	9.2	9	68	23	18	12
1864	...	14	9	10	9.3	9	69	23	20	11
1865	...	14	10	10	9.3	9	66	21	20	10
1866	...	13	9	10	9.2	9	68	22	21	9
1867	...	13	8	10	9.0	8	68	23	20	10
1868	...	15	7	11	9.6	9	71	22	20	12
1869	...	14	8	10	9.5	9	74	22	22[28]	15[28]
1870	...	16	11	10	9.2	9	68	20	23	9
1871	...	19	12	10	13	11	73	20	23	11
1872	...	19	13	11	13	13	75	21	26	10
1873	...	24	14	9	15	14	75	20	27	8
1874	...	29	14	14	16	15	74	19	27	7
1875	...	24	15	10	19	17	75	20	28	7
1876	...	26	15	11	19	17	77	20	28	8
1877	...	26	13	11	19	16	78	20	27	8
1878	...	23	13	11	20	16	81	20	27	11
1879	...	25	12	12	22	17	73	19	25	12
1880	...	28	15	12	23	17	82	19	25	13
1881	87	30	17	13	23	17	84	19	27	13
1882	86	31	13	13	23	19	87	20	27	15
1883	88	34	13	11	25	20	86	20	27	14
1884	88	34	14	10	26	21	88	20	27	15
1885	88	33	16	11	27	21	90	20	25	18
1886	84	32	16[26] 21	9	28	22	91	20	25	19
1887	75	30	15	9	31	25	90	20	26	17
1888	91	37	22	9	33	26	90	20	26	16
1889	97	42	21	9	35	28	95	20	27	16
1890	101	42	24	10	39	31	97	20	29	16
1891	94	37	23	10	39	32	99	20	30	16
1892	95	37	24	10	43	36	98	20	30	16
1893	98	36	26	11	46	38	98	20	30	18
1894	110	38	28	14	49	41	102	20	31	18
1895	116	39	31	14	51	43	109	21	32	19
1896	121	42	34	10	55	46	112	21	32	19
1897	137	43	38	9	56	48	116	22	33	20
1898	144	51	36	9	57	49	118	21	34	20
1899	155	59	39	9	62	51	130	24	37	21

G6 Central Government Revenue and Main Tax Yields

	Austria[1,8]					Belgium			
	Total	Customs	Consum	Direct	S & T Mon	Total	Customs	Excise	Direct
			(million kronen)					(million francs)	
1900	1,654	111	275	268	176	494	44	67	58
1901	1,687	102	275	283	169	501	43	73	60
1902	1,728	105	267	279	171	504	42	72	60
1903	1,758	112	271	289	172	514	44	61	60
1904	1,798	119	304	288	177	533	46	70	61
1905	1,882	127	301	298	179	581	52	89	63
1906	2,008	135	327	310	193	597	53	81	65
1907	2,253	144	329	335	193	618	54	77	68
1908	2,388	149	338	349	198	617	54	80	68
1909	2,796	170	340	366	197	645	58	82	70
1910	2,895	171	355	370	205	682	64	78	73
1911	3,083	190	384	384	229	695	63	94	74
1912	3,173	195	370	408	247	755	71	91	76
1913	3,486	228	414	432	254	...	...	...	...
1914	[1,704][8]	...[8]	...[8]	[207][8]	...[8]	...	...	...	...
1915	10,039	...	488	426	286	...	...	...	...
1916	...	...	...	437	...	...	...	...	...
1917	...	...	...	...	...	...	...	...	...
1918	...[1,8]	...[1,8]	...[1,8]	...[1,8]	...[1,8]	...	...	...	...
1919	...	...	...	...	...	...	...	...	...
					Turnover				
1920	...	...	249	1,555	35	3,766	200	115	422
1921	...	...	1,376	15,835	164	4,626	195	189	465
1922	...	260	46,018	139,605	111,230	6,720	256	205	490
1923	6,069,600	1,124,133	674,676	1,611,759	1,047,421	7,165	364	369	1,477
			(million schillings)						
1924	834	148	80	283	239	8,118	433	425	1,412
1925	901	201	85	285	226	8,304	551	435	1,899
1926	967	214	89	325	230	9,299	709	636	2,436
1927	1,024	241	86	327	241	10,763	901	802	2,737
1928	1,086	263	91	353	253	12,413	1,097	910	3,217
1929	1,164	286	102	385	257	13,714	1,319	1,001	3,668
1930	1,170	290	126	373	250	11,045	1,336	997	2,868
1931	1,142	273	185	343	220	10,767	1,303	1,036	2,678
1932	1,049	230	177	321	207	8,989	1,556	1,119	2,338
1933	970	180	160	276	252	10,357	1,496	1,280	2,883
1934	1,020	204	177	275	262	9,973	1,497	1,254	2,797
1935	1,075	211	185	298	278	10,015	1,456	1,336	2,610
1936	1,086	215	193	289	266	10,635	1,554	1,295	3,007
1937	1,134	215	194	321	281	11,102	1,587	1,429	2,828
1938	...	...	...	...	...	11,108	1,543	1,518	3,132
1939	...	...	...	...	...	11,339	1,438	1,541	3,439
1940	...	...	...	...	...	9,911	679	1,650	3,679
1941	...	...	...	...	...	13,574	583	2,007	4,872
1942	...	...	...	...	...	16,344	372	2,444	6,236
1943	...	...	...	...	...	16,802	272	2,000	7,513
1944	...	...	...	...	...	17,748	168	1,906	9,506
1945	638	6	72	476	69	20,887	188	2,383	8,392
1946	1,651	10	554	810	200	47,133	2,146	5,071	15,351
1947	3,542	17	1,150	1,722	462	46,910	3,701	6,204	12,971
1948	4,111	45	1,233	1,813	754	62,543	3,159	8,211	24,641
1949	6,520	143	1,188	3,275	1,403	66,857	3,332	8,117	27,759

G6 Central Government Revenue and Main Tax Yields

	Bulgaria[30]				Czechoslovakia				
	Total	Customs	Excise[29]	Direct	Total[15]	Customs	Excise	Direct	Turnover
	(million leva)				(million korunas)				
1900	74	23		35	...	...	...	...	...
1901	92	28		31	...	...	...	...	...
1902	97	31		32	...	...	...	...	...
1903	99	33		34	...	...	...	...	...
1904	115	40		36	...	...	...	...	...
1905	128		46[29]	38	...	...	...	...	...
		15	25						
1906	134	17	22	41	...	...	...	...	...
1907	146	22	29	39	...	...	...	...	...
1908	149	22	29	40	...	...	...	...	...
1909	163	27	31	33	...	...	...	...	...
1910	172	28	31	40	...	...	...	...	...
1911	199	30	45	34	...	...	...	...	...
1912	170	31	42	18	...	...	...	...	...
1913	169	26	47	14	...	...	...	...	...
1914	224	32	52	29	...	...	...	...	...
1915	195	15	51	26	...	...	...	...	...
1916	193	14	42	33	...	...	...	...	...
1917	338	19	79	39	...	...	...	...	...
1918	567[30]	24[30]	174[30]	58[30]	...	...	...	...	...
1919	844	40	149	104	1,957	160	413	760	—
1920	2,006	423	300	288	5,453	408	1,734	1,217	500
1921	2,846	665	406	378	8,630	768	2,641	1,819	1,349
1922	4,423	1,298	653	331	8,924	947	2,106	1,853	1,631
1923	5,362	1,275	746	206	8,111	785	1,493	1,788	1,434
1924	6,858	1,470	1,006	343	8,723	871	1,368	2,187	1,553
1925	6,364	1,402	1,152	402	9,162	848	1,349	2,397	1,780
1926	6,234	1,184	1,171	465	9,939	1,010	1,420	2,494	1,934
1927	6,687	1,263	1,184	568	11,135	1,399	1,782	2,545	2,102
1928	6,282	1,374	1,338	779	11,045	1,503	1,885	1,971	2,341
1929	6,713	1,407	1,396	625	11,316	1,429	1,938	2,032	2,346
1930	5,597	853	1,323	603	10,870	1,240	1,898	1,893	2,357
1931	5,212	961	1,252	490	10,836	1,331	2,171	1,771	2,214
1932	4,751	883	1,098	392	10,651	879	2,120	2,067	2,227
1933	4,987[30]	626[30]	1,002[30]	456[30]	10,043	651	2,016	1,855	2,311
1934	[3,713]	[537]	[977]	[418]	10,077	666	1,996	1,719	2,391
1935	5,399	672	1,302	394	9,818	673	1,984	1,763	2,313
1936	6,020	823	1,445	527	10,234	743	2,106	1,868	2,365
1937	6,847	1,124	1,513	590	10,014	787	2,272	1,979	2,792
1938	7,188	1,138	1,671	608	...	...	...	...	...
1939	7,708	1,173	1,771	656	...	...	...	...	...
1940	8,994	1,178	1,969	1,012	...	...	...	...	...
1941	13,094	1,163	3,088	2,430	...	...	...	...	...
1942	...	...	...	...	...	...	...	...	...
1943	...	...	...	...	...	...	...	...	...
1944	...	...	...	...	...	...	...	...	...
1945	...	...	...	...	[12,017][31]	...	...	[7,685][31]	[1,430][31]
1946	...	...	...	...	35,211	602	5,729	15,620	6,955
1947	...	...	...	...	...	...	...	...	...
1948	...	...	...	...	...	...	...	...	...
1949	...	...	...	...	...	...	...	...	...

G6 Central Government Revenue and Main Tax Yields

	Denmark[10]				Finland				
	Total	Customs	Excise	I & P	Total	Customs	Excise	I & P	Sales
		(million kroner)					(million markaa)		
1900	67	33	10	11	61	27	7	...	—
1901	66	32	10	11	92	30	7	...	—
1902	74	35	10	11	93	31	6	...	—
1903	79	37	10	11	100	36	6	...	—
1904	96	38	10	13	103	36	6	...	—
1905	87	37	12	14	106	38	8	...	—
1906	102	39	13	13	122	47	7	...	—
1907	96	42	13	15	133	49	8	...	—
1908	93	41	15	15	144	48	9	...	—
1909	82	29	14	16	144	49	12	...	—
1910	91	32	13	18	152	51	13	...	—
1911	102	33	15	20	158	53	10	...	—
1912	114	36	18	20	171	57	14	...	—
1913	124	35	21	24	181	58	14	...	—
1914	122	33	22	26	168	46	13	...	—
1915	142	37	23	31	194	42	4	...	—
1916	242	41	25	35	304	46	20	...	—
1917	375	30	41	74	440	34	13	...	—
1918	462	25	59	71	470	17	- -	...	—
1919	594	73	98	102	1,039	239	75	...	—
1920	499	59	116	336	1,734	334	153	...	—
1921	409	56	100	259	2,283	551	127	...	—
1922	427	72	103	138	2,669	799	141	...	—
1923	390	89	122	120	3,063	1,058	181	...	—
1924	432	80	137	132	3,158	1,042	171	...	—
1925	383	80	130	141	3,316	1,175	179	...	—
1926	369	88	120	126	3,424	1,021	184	...	—
1927	338	88[10]	117[10]	103	3,908	1,227	197	...	—
1928	312	90	113	93	4,476	1,390	215	...	—
1929	336	102	123	97	4,302	1,337	221	...	—
1930	343	108	121	104	4,275	1,405	210	...	—
1931	333	105	122	104	3,756	1,130	216	...	—
1932	335	83	128	91	2,438	1,021	217	...	—
1933	376	94	198	86	2,873	1,243	278	...	—
1934	411	104	240	100	3,367	1,490	330	580	—
1935	419	105	233	116	3,482	1,480	400	570	—
1936	469	106	248	121	3,725	1,620	400	...	—
1937	521	109	263	130	4,316	1,720	470	740	—
1938	543	114	273	193	4,862	1,830	480	1,090	—
1939	621	123	308	227	4,709	1,560	590	...	—
1940	879	105	417	348	5,182	920	940	1,440	—
1941	927	75	458	363	11,967	1,380	1,370	1,760	1,410
1942	1,125	58	541	442	17,185	1,660	1,650	3,380	3,510
1943	1,161	47	584	494	22,039	1,050	1,740	4,860	4,000
1944	1,237	49	729	562	23,640	660	1,930	4,890	4,020
1945	1,291	28	633	641	33,734	400	2,270	10,710	6,870
1946	1,901	125	966	751	66,400	2,440	4,430	17,280	13,530
1947	2,020	102	1,205	875	70,207	4,560	5,370	22,140	18,290
1948	2,170	96	1,367	1,014	99,434	9,110	7,770	28,770	27,680
1949	2,189	127	1,406	935	111,402	12,450	9,280	23,040	29,740

G6   Central Government Revenue and Main Tax Yields

	France						Germany[16]				
	Total	Customs	Excise	Reg.	Turnover & Trans	Direct	Total[15]	Customs	Excise	Income	Turnover
	(million francs)						(million marks)				
1900	3,815	415	668	573	—	524	887	466	341	...	...
1901	3,576	383	576	550	—	532	901	494	323	...	...
1902	3,582	365	557	567	—	533	909	498	320	...	...
1903	3,668	402	580	592	—	541	906	508	311	...	...
1904	3,739	401	614	592	—	549	928	490	345	...	...
1905	3,766	410	586[32]	626	—	555	1,055	626	326	...	...
1906	3,837	478	590	609	—	560	1,075	557	375	...	...
1907	3,968	509	603	646	—	561	1,206	645	422	...	...
1908	3,966	494	618	643	—	570	1,121	546	406	...	...
1909	4,141	526	623	686	—	577	1,360	660	464	...	...
1910	4,274	586	645	690	—	587	1,499	663	548	...	...
1911	4,689	768	680	805	—	599	1,676	734	635	...	...
1912	4,857	685	680	811	—	612	1,662	728	617	...	...
1913	5,092	778	697	834	—	634	1,665[34] 2,095	679	660	...	...
1914	4,549	603	581	611	—	611	2,399	561	776	...	...
1915	4,131	786	495	464	—	547	1,769	360	581	...	...
1916	5,259	1,422	506	525	—	608	2,045	348	679	...	...
1917	6,943	1,599	651	719	—	839	7,682	...	...	...	...
1918	7,621	1,258	780	929	—	1,460	6,830	...	...	...	...
1919	13,282	1,580	1,314	1,879	—	1,735	9,712	...	...	...	...
1920	22,502	1,916	1,888	2,724	1,757	1,910	53,046	2,163	8,994	11,195	4,988
1921	23,119	1,521	3,223	2,699	1,927	3,457	149,570	5,952	15,264	32,773	11,474
1922	23,888	2,003	2,771	2,965	2,314	3,386	...	...	...	...	...
1923	26,224	2,058	3,070	3,394	3,045	4,533	...	...	...	...	...
1924	30,568	2,153	3,567	4,614	4,120	5,838	4,650	357	1,193	2,527	1,918
1925	33,455	2,114	3,946	5,134	4,583	6,075	4,731	591	1,371	2,440	1,416
1926	41,902	2,899	5,513	6,029	7,517	8,052	5,313	940	1,520	2,636	876
1927	45,746	3,972	6,207	3,701	8,645	10,020	6,357	1,251	1,688	3,262	878
1928	48,177	4,658	6,751	4,471	9,318	9,936	6,568	1,105	1,771	3,718	1,000
1929	64,268	6,958	8,987	6,534	12,403	11,036	6,741	1,095	1,804	3,584	1,013
1930	50,794	6,139	7,041	4,879	8,744	10,531	6,634	1,083	1,980	3,211	996
1931	47,944	7,379	6,911	4,046	7,558	10,060	5,704	1,147	1,637	2,447	994
1932	36,038	5,226	4,792	2,625	5,152	8,841	4,994	1,106	1,514	1,438	1,354
1933	43,536	6,297	6,408	3,560	6,897	7,997	6,850	1,070	1,720	1,503	1,516
1934	41,070	6,575	4,970	3,245	6,387	7,841	8,220	1,149	1,945	2,040	1,873
1935	39,485	6,161	5,217	3,013	5,857	5,984	9,650	1,249	2,225	3,097	2,020
1936	38,676	6,522	5,173	2,851	6,123	5,717	11,492	1,333	2,315	4,256	2,389
1937	44,224	7,754	4,963	3,226	6,985	6,815	13,964	1,595	2,542	5,612	2,754
1938	54,606	8,823	5,120	4,094	9,848	9,245	17,712	1,818	2,828	7,769	3,357
1939	63,005	10,184	5,440	3,970	13,490	11,434	23,575	1,697	4,422	11,453	3,735
1940	71,953	8,053	5,776	2,991	18,201	13,636	27,221	1,414	5,578	14,211	3,929
1941	80,195	2,576	6,503	5,185	20,914	19,823	32,258	1,121	6,189	18,208	4,149
1942	97,320	1,610	4,731	7,450	26,005	28,548	34,700	832	6,176	19,831	4,160
1943	124,246[33]	998	4,365	8,807	37,502	40,918	...	640	5,943	20,038	4,177
1944	129,934[33]	584	4,139	7,680	35,137	44,274	...	...	...	...	...
	(thousand million francs)						West Germany[35]				
1945	222	4	9	11	66	61	...	...	...	...	...
1946	434	18	16	31	153	78	12,004	25	1,927	5,727	1,769
1947	670	37	25	40	230	163	14,377	174	2,259	6,273	2,302
1948	1,021	54	42	49	396	263	4,877[36] 8,977	72[36] 99	697[36] 1,705	2,211[36] 4,176	842[36] 2,199
1949	1,441	101	53	80	625	357	15,410	278	3,425	6,234	3,835

G6 Central Government Revenue and Main Tax Yields

1900–1949

	Greece[37]				Hungary[17]				
	Total	Customs	Consum	Direct	Total[18]	Consum	Turnover	Direct	Customs
	(million drachmae)				(million kronen)				
1900	112	...	...	...	1,042	177	...	226	...
1901	115	...	...	...	1,039	175	...	228	...
1902	114	...	...	...	1,064	178	...	230	...
1903	115	34.4	45.2	19.3	1,027	185	...	187	...
1904	116	...	...	...	1,177	190	...	266	...
1905	126	...	...	...	1,015	175	...	124	...
1906	126	...	...	...	1,335	206	...	311	...
1907	126	...	...	...	1,370	219	...	295	...
1908	128	...	...	...	1,409	236	...	277	...
1909	130	...	...	...	1,452	233	...	277	...
1910	142	...	...	...	1,543	248	...	277	...
1911	136	...	62.1	23.5	1,703	268	...	310	...
1912	131	...	...	...	1,804	301	...	306	...
1913	174	...	...	...	1,839	300	...	326	...
1914	218	...	...	...	[889][17]	[153][17]	...	[133][17]	...
1915	222	...	...	...	1,829	322	...	302	...
1916	226	...	...	...	2,283	387	...	359	...
1917	234	...	...	...	2,772	312	...	495	...
1918	...[37]	...[37]	...[37]	...[37]	5,015[17]	362[17]	...	1,206[17]	...
1919	516	...	...	117	...	...	...	...	...
1920	586	...	...	...	...	...	...	...	...
1921	725	165	97	148	13,831	4,045	...	4,587	1,523
1922	978	192	...	...	33,029	3,882	...	3,223	5,629
1923	1,895	471	...	...	194,572	8,577	...	20,751	13,850
1924	3,712	1,039	...	...	4,676,719	249,361	...	365,499	263,613
					(million pengos)				
1925	5,091[37]	886	...	898	...	59	224	95	...
1926	6,045	2,151	...	...	...	83	238	159	...
1927	...	...	...	1,197	1,334	86	265	166	129
1928	9,448	2,605	1,694	1,763	1,422	97	270	191	133
1929	9,602	2,579	1,646	1,871	1,467	102	265	226	107
1930	10,322	2,709	1,654	1,755	1,372	96	232	222	78
1931	10,096	2,660	1,606	1,595	1,242	85	191	219	61
1932	9,506	3,514	1,649	1,756	1,151	78	201	252	35
1933	8,360	2,826	1,628	1,551	1,041	79	194	230	21
1934	8,476	2,739	1,763	1,656	1,102	84	198	228	24
1935	9,237	2,931	1,927	2,051	1,102	85	203	225	29
1936	10,647	3,464	2,017	2,201	1,180	93	219	230	29
1937	13,244	3,669	2,104	2,655	1,294	101	246	250	29
1938	14,131	3,893	2,524	2,988	1,352	105	251	255	50
1939	12,655	3,753	2,730	3,284	1,606	109	271	274	52
1940	12,620	...	...	...	[3,229][38]	[199][38]	[570][38]	[522][38]	[107][38]
1941	...	...	...	...	...	...	...	...	...
1942	...	...	...	...	...	...	...	...	...
1943	...	...	...	...	...	...	...	...	...
1944	...	...	...	...	...	...	...	...	...
1945	...	...	...	...	...	...	...	...	...
1946	...	...	...	...	...	...	...	...	...
1947	...	...	...	...	...	...	...	...	...
1948	...	...	...	...	...	...	...	...	...
1949	...	...	...	...	...	...	...	...	...

G6 Central Government Revenue and Main Tax Yields

	Southern Ireland[39]				Italy[20]				
	Total	Customs	Excise	I & P	Total	Customs	S & T Mon	Direct	Profits Tax
		(million pounds)					(million lire)		
1900	...	...	...	...	1,671	203	270	484	—
1901	...	...	...	...	1,721	187	276	485	—
1902	...	...	...	...	1,744	183	285	487	—
1903	...	...	...	...	1,795	179	285	490	—
1904	...	...	...	...	1,787	176	293	491	—
1905	...	...	...	...	1,853	170	303	494	—
1906	...	...	...	...	1,946	198	312	494	—
1907	...	...	...	...	1,954	232	319	459	—
1908	...	...	...	...	1,946	240	340	436	—
1909	...	...	...	...	2,134	256	355	452	—
1910	...	...	...	...	2,237	249	376	464	—
1911	...	...	...	...	2,403	270	388	481	—
1912	...	...	...	...	2,475	259	407	500	—
1913	...	...	...	...	2,529	271	423	519	—
1914	...	...	...	...	2,524	259	440	541	—
1915	...	...	...	...	2,560	193	462	592	—
1916	...	...	...	...	3,734	310	607	659	—
1917	...	...	...	...	5,345	470	724	695	—
1918	...	...	...	...	7,533	535	958	751	
1919	...	...	...	...	9,676	530	1,294	752	—
1920	...	...	...	...	15,207	513	1,706	986	—
1921	...	...	...	...	18,820	527	2,597	1,306	—
1922	28	2	16	5	19,701	620	2,816	1,922	—
1923	31	8	9	6	18,803	517	2,923	2,203	144
1924	27	8	8	6	20,582	523	3,006	3,217	592
1925	25	7	6	6	20,440	913	3,076	3,361	753
1926	25	7	7	6	21,043	663	3,255	4,008	873
1927	24	7	7	5	21,450	645	3,465	4,612	787
1928	24	7	7	5	20,072	1,458	3,479	4,224	644
1929	24	7	6	4	20,201	2,095	2,647	4,117	704
1930	24	7	6	5	19,838	1,848	2,786	4,147	424
1931	25	8	5	5	20,387	1,670	2,947	4,080	911
1932	30	9	5	6	19,324	1,943	2,894	4,010	1,103
1933	30	10	5	6	18,217	1,873	2,859	3,791	1,037
1934	29	9	6	6	18,057	1,836	2,816	3,705	1,052
1935	31	10	6	6	18,817	1,733	2,791	3,663	1,115
1936	31	10	6	6	20,371	1,410	2,827	3,641	1,312
1937	31	10	6	6	24,702	1,302	2,965	3,882	1,552
1938	32	10	6	6	27,468	1,365	3,245	4,278	2,241
1939	32	11	6	7	27,576	1,158	3,424	4,671	2,476
1940	35	12	7	8	32,350	1,255	3,744	4,976	3,317
1941	37	11	7	10	34,234	1,119	4,270	5,360	5,023
1942	40	11	7	13	41,224	1,159	5,808	5,737	5,988
1943	44	11	8	15	50,376	1,248	7,893	6,781	5,801
1944	46	11	9	17	47,236	499	6,993	7,655	6,272
1945	51	13	10	18	64,635	133	10,019	8,899	10,271
					(thousand million lire)				
1946	54	17	9	17	160	1	35	20	48
1947	65	22	11	18	382	4	62	40	102
1948	72	24	13	20	851	13	111	84	191
1949	74	25	13	19	1,138	7	171	112	256

G6 Central Government Revenue and Main Tax Yields

	Netherlands					Norway[21]				Poland[42]			
	Total	Customs	Excise	Direct	Turnover	Total	Customs	Consum	I & P	Total	Customs	Consum	Direct
		(million guilders)					(million kroner)				(million zlotys)		
1900	138[40]	10	49	35[41]	...	64	28	9	6	...	...	...	...
	120			58									
1901	119	10	51	55	...	83	35	12	6	...	...	...	...
1902	125	10	52	61	...	86	36	13	6	...	...	...	...
1903	128	11	53	64	...	84	34	13	6	...	...	...	...
1904	130	11	55	64	...	86	35	12	5	...	...	...	...
1905	132	12	55	67	...	83	33	11	5	...	...	...	...
1906	139	12	57	70	...	92	36	12	5	...	...	...	...
1907	138	12	58	71	...	99	40	11	6	...	...	...	...
1908	139	12	57	74	...	107	44	12	7	...	...	...	...
1909	145	13	59	77	...	134	53	16	7	...	...	...	...
1910	151	13	62	83	...	116	49	10	8	...	...	...	...
1911	154	14	63	88	...	123	51	10	8	...	...	...	...
1912	158	16	64	90	...	131	54	11	9	...	...	...	...
1913	166	17	67	96	...	143	51	8	13	...	...	...	...
1914	165	14	69	103	...	102	52	12	17	...	...	...	...
1915	195	15	71	123	...	112	53	13	35	...	...	...	...
1916	272	17	79	192	...	144	55	19	52	...	...	...	...
1917	503	13	89	262	...	243	65	18	390	...	...	...	...
1918	506	10	85	287	...	443	52	15	384	...	...	...	...
1919	611	33	105	370	...	488	67	19	365	...	...	...	...
1920	744	52	123	527	...	562	127	25	197	...	...	...	...
1921	666	41	132	613	...	448	69	27	196	...	...	...	...
1922	592	42	141	564	...	372	64	31	283	404	31	184	150
1923	531	39	140	492	...	317	94	41	140	674	100	229	281
1924	506	40	139	461	...	313	103	45	118	1,182	238	384	291
1925	540	45	149	467	...	378	126	61	120	1,329[42]	285[42]	508[42]	363[42]
1926	569	54	154	477	...	371	111	71	127	1,754	213	776	513
1927	596	58	156	483	...	363	111	67	120	2,222	372	964	615
1928	571	57	161	463	...	363	118	92	103	2,628	425	1,072	766
1929	606	62	156	500	...	351	106	92	83	2,622	395	1,078	786
1930	583	66	156	500	...	356	111	94	82	2,271	258	988	718
1931	502	70	153	460	...	330	104	92	79	1,859	157	849	589
1932	460	61	147	392	...	317	104	90	79	1,610	108	781	539
1933	455	100	156	375	...	259	99	97	71	1,595	94	800	516
1934	476	81	136	381	...	278	106	101	72	1,588	80	794	539
1935	499	89	135	383	...	293	113	108	71	1,640	83	816	522
1936	507	84	132	372	...	350	126	139	82	1,851	92	821	648[42]
1937	582	91	138	404	...	413	140	170	90	2,049	168	856	723
1938	600	98	142	437	...	474	145	188	117	...	...	...	...
1939	645	123	154	448	89	533	154	201	175	...	...	...	...
1940	683	80	195	497	109	562	150	198	192	...	...	...	...
1941	1,142	22	249	856	178	940	129	480	259	...	...	...	...
1942	1,481	...	...	1,042	...	1,220	78	686	320	...	...	...	...
1943	1,460	9	161	1,083	196	1,406	61	753	394	...	...	...	...
1944	1,356	6	135	1,027	173	1,450	46	791	399	...	...	...	...
1945	645	8	85	452	116	1,353	37	760	389	...	...	...	...
1946	2,422	54	247	1,859	342	1,426	120	790	359	...	...	...	...
1947	3,328	68	316	2,331	518	2,270	218	1,114	411	...	...	...	...
1948	5,374	230	349	2,258	689	2,415	179	1,176	675	...	...	...	...
1949	4,288	258	405	2,496	746	2,769	151	1,133	1,172	...	...	...	...

G6   Central Government Revenue and Main Tax Yields

	Portugal[22]				Romania[24]			Russia/U.S.S.R.[6]				
	Total[23]	Customs	Prop	Business	Total	Customs	Prop	Total	Customs	Excise[7]	Direct	
	(million escudos)							(million new rubels)				
1900	53	16	3.1	1.7	210	18	16	1,704	204	572	132	
1901	55	15	3.2	1.8	239	25	17	1,799	219	630	131	
1902	53	14	3.3	1.8	250	26	17	1,905	225	688	133	
1903	54	16	3.0	1.7	247	25	17	2,032	241	741	135	
1904	...	17	...	...	259	23	17	2,018	219	743	135	
1905	...	17	...	...	308	36	17	2,025	213	805	127	
1906	...	17	...	...	292	40	19	2,272	241	950	163	
1907	...	16	...	...	316	50	18	2,342	260	956	183	
1908	...	17	...	...	469	49	18	2,418	279	956	194	
1909	...	16	...	...	459	49	18	2,526	274	974	199	
1910	...	16	...	...	583	58	18	2,781	301	1,059	216	
1911	...	16	...	...	644	73	19	2,952	328	1,086	224	
1912	...	17	4.8	2.7	621	66	18	3,106	327	1,148	243	
1913	...	22	6.5	2.8	639	67	18	3,417	353	1,254	273	
1914	...	25	6.9	3.0	755	44	...	2,898	304	861	281	
1915	...	23	6.7	3.1	...	34	...	...	...	...	...	
1916	...	17	6.8	3.2	379	90	...	...	...	...	...	
1917	86	19	6.8	3.3	187	2	...	...[6]	...[6]	...[6]	...[6]	
1918	100	19	6.9	...	419	8	...	...	...	...	...	
1919	128	19	8.3	...	1,115	93	...	...	...	...	...	
									I & T		Ded Profits	
1920	...	25	...	...	3,554	1,083	...	...	...	...	...	—
1921	...	51	...	...	7,708	1,501	...	...	...	...	...	—
1922	388	50	...	...	15,114	3,816	...	...	...	...	...	—
1923	544	84	...	...	[18,792][24]	[5,778][24]	...	...[45]	...[45]	...[45]	...[45]	—
1924	842	114	...	...	27,744	8,085	...	2,134	113	241	296	—
1925	1,365	133	...	...	34,039	7,325	...	2,872	157	508	421	—
1926	1,369	280	109	121	31,224	8,753	...	3,893	229	842	403	—
1927	1,312	350	104	97	36,008	9,252	...	5,056	349	1,210	550	—
1928	1,642	445	109	116	32,768	6,890	...	5,888	373	1,491	586	—
1929	2,165[23]	653[43]	179	127	36,018	5,727	...	7,497	1,056	1,803	735	—
		633										
								11,521[45]	1,941[45]	2,643[45]	1,020[45]	
1930	2,072	682	191	206	31,155	4,306	...	19,886	10,730	—	803	—
1931	1,969	664	192	176	27,643	2,518	...	27,109[45]	17,693[45]	—	704[45]	—[45]
1932	1,889	672	194	169	17,848[24]	2,019[24]	...	33,050	17,693	—	2,699	1,657
1933	1,908	658	199	162	18,364	1,869	...	43,191	23,167	—	3,310	2,072
1934	1,981	712	181	155	18,809	1,824	...	54,155	30,242	—	3,621	2,375
1935	[3,049][22]	[1,163][22]	[286][22]	[248][22]	23,096[44]	1,354	...	...	...	—	...	...
1936	2,047	818	231	199	27,184	1,518	...	...	...	—	...	...
1937	2,153	806	233	204	30,345	1,511	...	...	...	—	...	...
1938	2,259	845	237	195	31,649	1,325	...	127,571	80,411	—	5,047	10,598
1939	2,177	770	230	204	35,109	...	...	...	...	—	...	...
								(million new rubels)				
1940	2,223	724	248	217	40,813	...	...	16.9	10.6	—	0.9	2.2
1941	2,447	819	263	223	66,763	...	...	...	...	—	...	...
1942	2,967	984	263	243	112,820	...	...	...	...	—	...	...
1943	3,269	1,011	264	257	[139,960][38][24]	...[24]	...	...	...	—	...	...
1944	3,340	864	266	321	...	...	...	...	...	—	...	...
1945	3,328	839	271	371	...	...	...	...	...	—	...	...
1946	3,900	1,245	275	378	...	...	...	...	...	—	...	...
1947	4,433	1,528	297	460	...	...	...	...	...	—	...	...
1948	4,433	1,436	304	525	...	...	...	...	...	—	...	...
1949	4,692	1,564	322	542	...	...	...	...	...	—	...	...

G6 Central Government Revenue and Main Tax Yields

1900–1949

	Spain[25]					Sweden[50]				
	Total	Customs	Consum	P & T Mon	Direct	Total	Customs	Excise	I & P	Automobile
			(million pesetas)					(million kronor)		
1900	914	168	120	118	254[47]	152	57	44	9	—
1901	959[46] 952	166	131	125	380	140	49	45	6	—
1902	961	140	128	132	395	147	55	40	12	—
1903	989	144	136	134	402	171	56	42	27[49]	—
1904	990	141	138	132	404	176	59	47	21	—
1905	990	164	128	130	393	185	59	50	22	—
1906	1,051	183	133	133	405	187	59	44	24	—
1907	1,027	160	138	133	407	204	59	57	27	—
1908	1,021	156	138	136	410	200	57	64	25	—
1909	1,015	157	135	137	417	189	58	52	28	—
1910	1,066	169	145	143	420	221	60	63	31	—
1911	1,079	177	147	138	438	236	60	67	36	—
1912	1,111	181	143	151	447	249	64	68	37	—
1913	1,286	225	148	151	456	264	69	66	41	—
1914	1,227	196	137	153	445	261	58	68	45	—
1915	1,159	134	132	149	452	365	55	73	44	—
1916	1,231	150	129	164	475	413	61	79	67	—
1917	1,267	137	128	169	497	636	43	54	114	—
1918	1,303	120	140	162	531	766	36	56	259	—
1919	1,542[25]	206[25]	169[25]	159[25]	576[25]	891	100	108	277	—
1920	1,793	312	163	133	664	892	145	143	307	—
1921	2,163	402	207	186	770	767	102	173	298	—
1922	2,360	511	204	223	799	672	111	172	188	—
1923	2,569	524	232	258	902	[277][50]	[62][50]	[85][50]	[9][50]	—
1924	2,758[25]	587[25]	225[25]	263[25]	944[25]	672	149	155	143	9
1925	2,816	579	239	260	951	653	140	171	145	19
1926	[1,396][25]	[261][25]	[128][25]	[135][25]	[475][25]	653	125	169	152	22
1927	3,096	576	244	279	1,119	673	141	175	151	25
1928	3,396	624	241	398	1,166	707	142	174	150	32
1929	3,568	655	258	441	1,203	733	154	166	149	40
1930	3,585	568	262	480	1,246	779	154	181	151	44
1931	3,373	490	263	503	1,241	783	148	173	166	51
1932	3,633	518	272	572	1,234	736	138	184	163	59
1933	3,701	481	280	604	1,299	741	117	213	148	73
1934	3,643	470	…	618	1,249	783	113	231	140	79
1935	3,854	472	…	662	1,350	903	136	247	156	88
1936	…	…	…	[203][48]	…	995[51] 831	148	268	183	97
1937	…	…	…	[137][48]	…	949	167	276	233	107
1938	…	…	…	[270][48]	…	1,069	180	308	264	117
1939	…	…	…	[482][48]	…	1,244	207	330	366	130
1940	4,443	207	…	893	2,016	1,570	223	441	513	127
1941	6,454	249	1,260	826	2,672	1,730	149	619	750	30
1942	7,785	467	1,615	688	3,237	1,942	109	810	794	30
1943	9,674	718	2,158	865	3,471	2,330	117	1,023	930	31
1944	10,180	637	2,365	924	3,636	2,687	122	1,165	1,178	34
1945	9,460	423	2,292	1,164	3,927	2,875	96	1,226	1,330	32
1946	9,888 —[67]	619	2,334	1,482	3,975	3,173	151	1,321	1,408	83
1947	11.9	805	2,717	1,533	4,957	3,237	296	1,347	1,178	203
1948	12.8	871	3,296	1,472	5,425	4,179	329	1,250	2,056	263
1949	13.7	718	3,672	2,296	5,784	4,626	243	1,471	2,077	436

G6 Central Government Revenue and Main Tax Yields

	Switzerland				United Kingdom[2]				Serbia/Yugoslavia[54]			
	Total[27]	Customs	Consum	I & P	Total	Customs	Excise	Land & I & P[53]	Total	Direct	Indirect	State Monoplies
	(million francs)				(million pounds)				(million dinari)			
1900	59	48	—	—	140	27	38	29	75	29	10	20
1901	58	46	—	—	153	31	37	37	72	26	10	20
1902	62	50	—	—	161	35	37	41	74	23	11	21
1903	66	53	—	—	151	34	37	33	78	23	12	22
1904	66	54	—	—	153	36	36	34	88	30	13	24
1905	78	64	—	—	154	35	36	34	88	28	13	25
1906	77	62	—	—	155	33	36	34	91	26	15	27
1907	87	72	—	—	157	32	36	35	...	...	...	...
1908	85	70	—	—	152	29	34	37	...	...	...	...
1909	91	74	—	—	132	30	31	14	...	...	...	...
1910	96	81	—	—	204	33	40	66	117	...	...	...
1911	99	81	—	—	185	34	38	48	120	...	...	...
1912	103	87	—	—	189	33	38	48	128	...	...	...
1913	100	85	—	—	198	33	40	50	131	...	...	...
1914	79	65	—	—	227	39	42	72	214	...	...	...
1915	78	55	—	—	337	60	61	131	...	...	...	...
1916	150	60	—	80	573	71	56	348	...	...	...	...
1917	211	52	—	136	707	71	39	462	...	...	...	...
1918	254	44	—	202	889	103	59	579	...	...	...	...
1919	322	67	—	218	1,340	149	134	652	...[54]	...[54]	...[54]	...[54]
1920	265	98	—	163	1,426	134	200	616	3,884	...	...	...
1921	247	113	—	87	1,125	130	194	445	6,258	...	...	...
1922	340	159	—	23	914	123	157	403	8,135	...	...	...
1923	283	179	—	48	837	120	148	356	10,344	...	...	...
1924	308	200	—	41	799	99	135	355	10,405	...	...	...
1925	346	213	—	35	812	103	135	342	10,508	1,960	3,857	2,520
1926	405	222	—	160	806	108	133	310	12,504	1,828	3,577	2,529
1927	359	225	—	45	843	112	139	314	11,319	1,754	3,594	2,388
1928	399	252	—	31	836	119	134	296	7,541	1,775	3,227	2,305
1929	436	267	—	61	815	120	128	297	9,018	2,393	3,693	2,374
1930	569	289	—	182	858	121	124	327	8,476	2,094	3,587	2,325
1931	455	308	—	45	851	136	120	367	6,758	1,785	2,802	2,133
1932	442	293	—	39	827	162	121	315	6,132	1,793	2,504	1,894
1933	418	291	—	23	809	179	107	284	6,467	2,104	2,302	1,866
1934	456	299	11	43	805	185	105	283	6,698	2,199	2,457	1,840
1935	490	299	29	62	845	197	107	291	6,950	2,196	2,551	1,911
1936	518	280	37	59	897	211	110	312	10,571	2,390	2,732	1,918
1937	528	283	41	56	949	222	114	356	11,987	2,705	3,171	2,070
1938	546	291	33	60	1,006	226	114	420	12,387	...	...	...
1939	603	331	34	66	1,132	262	138	487	12,786	...	...	...
1940	795	265[52]	40	53	1,495	305	224	696	15,116	...	...	...
1941	903[27] 877	178	55	567	2,175	378	326	1,114	...	...	...	...
									(thousand million dinari)			
1942	793	160	179	381	2,922	460	425	1,460	...	...	...	...
1943	788	139	255	323	3,149	561	482	1,760	...	...	...	...
1944	919	100	303	445	3,355	579	497	1,901	...	...	...	...
1945	897	104	340	373	3,401	570	541	1,897	...	...	...	...
1946	1,633	293	418	836	3,623	621	564	1,590	32	...	...	...
1947	1,516	437	519	459	4,011	791	630	1,570	58	...	...	...
1948	1,634	435	566	534	4,168	823	733	1,744	74	...	...	...
1949	1,319	388	541	296	4,098	813	706	1,850	114	...	...	...

G6 Central Government Revenue and Main Tax Yields

1950–1993

	Austria					Belgium			
	Total	Customs	Consum	Direct	Turnover	Total	Customs	Excise	Direct
	(thousand million schillings)					(thousand million francs)			
1950	8.7	0.2	1.4	4.3	2.1	63.3	4.0	7.8	23.6
1951	12.3	0.3	1.9	5.6	3.5	76.9	4.4	8.1	34.3
1952	14.6	0.4	2.0	3.3	4.5	77.6	4.4	9.3	31.6
1953	16.4	0.6	2.0	7.5	4.6	76.7	4.4	8.8	32.6
1954	17.5	1.0	2.2	7.6	5.0	75.8	4.6	8.8	30.2
1955	18.9	1.4	2.4	7.0	5.9	82.1	5.0	10.7	32.3
1957	25.0	1.7	3.0	10.6	7.0	96.3	17.5		38.6
1958	26.3	1.8	3.3	11.1	7.2	99.6	18.2		36.8
1959	27.9	2.2	3.7	11.1	7.8	102	19.6		38.8
1960	30.8	2.8	3.8	12.2	8.6	109	22.0		41.6
1961	36.3	3.3	4.6	14.8	9.5	120	23.8		43.5
1962	40.1	3.4	5.1	16.7	10.3	131	24.5		50.3
1963	43.2	3.6	5.6	18.0	11.1	140	25.8		52.8
1964	48.6	4.0	6.1	20.2	12.8	158	28.2		60.5
1965	53.2	4.3	6.8	22.5	13.7	174	30.1		67.6
1966	59.1	4.8	7.7	25.1	14.9	201	34.2		77.6
1967	62.0	4.6	8.6	26.6	15.2	223	37.1		87.2
1968	66.8	4.8	9.3	26.6	18.0	240	38.6		95.8
1969	74.5	4.8	9.9	30.6	20.3	268	42.8		110
1970	83.9	5.5	10.8	35.8	22.0	300	46.0		131
1971	95.1	6.0	12.4	40.7	25.5	326	46.5		151
1972	116	6.9	14.1	47.7	30.1	367	49.4		175
1973	116	6.9	14.4	52.4	37.2	411	47.2		212
1974	141	7.0	14.9	64.4	49.3	490	45.1		267
1975	149	5.7	14.5	65.5	57.0	581	58.4		336
1976	163	5.0	16.4	69.4	64.8	633	62.0		374
1977	180	4.4	18.2	78.5	68.1	748	64.4		433
1978	201	2.9	19.4	93.9	73.1	877	71.7		514
1979	218	3.1	21.3	100	79.6	941	75.6		564
1980	236	3.6	22.5	110	84.8	1,004	77.2		589
1981	260	3.5	24.1	123	92.6	1,011	70.3		603
1982	268	3.6	25.2	125	96.1	1,153	79.9		697
1983	282	4.0	26.9	128	105	1,143	95.1		717
1984	313	4.3	27.5	139	120	1,236	96.8		796
1985	337	4.5	28.9	155	124	1,314	101		864
1986	352	4.9	29.9	164	129	1,343	104		870
1987	356	5.6	30.7	160	134	1,391	107		891
1988	375	6.3	30.9	171	138	1,450	109		915
1989	387	6.7	31.9	170	147	996	120		703
1990	425	6.6	32.6	194	157	1,041	134		730
1991	465	7.3	34.1	220	166	1,063	150		726
1992	509	7.7	40.3	245	174	1,102	166		733
1993	512	7.6	40.6	246	176	1,133	172		741

G6   Central Government Revenue and Main Tax Yields

	Denmark[10]					Finland				
	Total	**Customs**	**Excise**	**I & P**	**VAT**	**Total**[56]	**Customs**	**Excise**	**I & P**	**Sales**
			(million kroner)				(thousand million markkaa)			
1950	2,403	145	1,499	1,091	—	130	13	11	36	34
						121				
1951	2,576	132	1,613	1,396	—	168	16	12	47	62
1952	2,844	145	1,713	1,599	—	163	21	13	52	59
1953	3,295[55]	183	1,889	1,740	—	174	17	13	52	53
	3,315									
1954	3,455	210	1,986	1,823	—	180	19	14	49	57
1955	3,881	211	2,238	1,967	—	193	27	15	57	50
1956	4,252	251	2,376	2,427	—	237[56]	41	17	68	62
						220				
1957	4,537	280	2,622	2,544	—	242	42	19	72	69
1958	5,378	285	2,891	2,652	—	248	39	28	63	66
1959	6,032	374	3,296	2,916	—	282	42	35	75	76
1960	6,498	436	3,555	3,126	—	314	46	39	79	89
1961	7,087	468	3,945	3,638	—	328	47	41	84	100
1962	8,745	531	4,792	4,595	355	366[57]	43[57]	45[57]	104[57]	105[57]
1963	9,829	506	5,664	4,763	1,143	3.5	0.3	0.5	1.0	1.0
1964	11,159	557	6,538	5,366	1,399	4.4	0.4	0.6	1.3	1.2
1965	13,082	556	7,598	6,456	1,925	4.9	0.5	0.7	1.5	1.3
1966	15,400	600	9,003	7,744[52]	2,230	5.5	0.5	0.9	1.7	1.4
				7,356						
1967	16,566	551	9,969	7,752	3,302	6.5	0.5	1.0	1.9	1.9
1968	21,725	561	12,137	9,454	5,298	7.7	0.9	1.1	2.3	2.1
1969	24,457	635	14,736	9,852	6,786	8.5	0.5	1.6	2.3	2.4
	(thousand million kroner)									
1970	34.3	0.7	16.7	17.7	8.3	9.4	0.5	1.8	2.6	2.8
1971	38.9	0.6	17.2	17.7	10.4	10.4	0.4	2.1	3.0	3.2
1972	44.9	0.8	19.8	20.5	11.8	12.4	0.5	2.3	3.9	3.8
1973	51.8	0.8	24.5	24.7	13.6	15.1	0.6	2.6	5.1	4.5
1974	55.2	0.8	25.9	28.4	13.8	18.5	0.5	3.1	6.8	5.4
1975	56.0	0.8	29.2	24.9	15.4	21.7	0.6	3.8	7.8	6.1
1976	67.8	1.0	34.3	29.8	18.8	28.0	0.6	4.8	11.5	6.7
1977	75.8	0.9	41.2	31.3	22.1	29.7	0.6	5.8	10.5	8.3
1978	[61.6][10]	0.8	48.7	[22.6][10]	27.0	30.9	0.6	6.8	9.3	9.6
1979	94.6	0.9	57.1	36.3	32.8	33.7	0.6	8.2	9.5	10.6
1980	101	1.0	60.4	40.0	36.1	39.4	0.8	9.2	12.3	12.3
1981	109	1.1	65.5	43.6	40.5	46.9	0.8	10.4	15.6	14.4
1982	124	1.2	72.1	51.3	44.8	52.2	1.0	12.2	16.7	15.9
1983	146	1.4	81.3	63.5	49.5	56.3	0.9	10.8	19.1	17.8
1984	164	1.6	89.3	73.3	53.5	65.9	0.9	11.7	21.9	22.1
1985	186	1.7	98.9	85.8	60.2	73.9	0.8	12.7	25.1	24.8
1986	218	1.8	114	101	64.7	80.1	0.9	13.2	27.5	27.6
1987	228	1.6	117	110	67.1	87.0	1.0	12.0	28.8	33.3
1988	226	1.7	120	113[70]	66.6	102	1.4	13.9	34.5	37.3
1989	242	1.8	120	193	70.5	116	1.4	15.1	38.5	43.6
1990	245	1.8	124	198	72.1	121	1.4	17.3	41.5	45.5
1991	249	2.2	118	203	74.1	134	1.5	19.4	41.6	52.9
1992	262	2.1	117	221	84.2	105	1.3	19.4	35.1	47.0
1993	274	1.9	114	226	86.1	100	1.7	20.4	29.1	39.3

G6 Central Government Revenue and Main Tax Yields

	France						West Germany[35]				
	Total	Customs	Excise	Reg	Turnover & Trans	Direct	Total[15]	Customs	Excise	Income	Turn-over
	(thousand million francs)						(thousand million marks)				
1950	2,076	150	48	91	745	555[52] 580	16.1[35]	0.6[35]	3.0[35]	5.3[35]	4.8[35]
1951	2,515	204	52	107	1,008	679	21.7	0.8	4.5	7.4	6.8
1952	2,888	228	56	120	1,099	811	27.0	1.1	4.6	10.4	8.4
1953	3,103	248	59	123	1,091	955	29.6	1.3	4.7	11.6	8.9
1954	3,356	271	53	123	1,153	951	30.8	1.5	4.5	11.5	9.6
1955	3,450	326	54	123	1,161	975	34.2	1.8	5.2	11.9	11.1
1956	3,878	395	58	140	1,209	1,148	38.4	2.0	5.7	13.8	12.2
1957	4,985	519	79	166	1,376	1,353	40.9	2.0	6.1	15.7	12.6
1958	5,228	647	78	194	1,531	1,748	42.9	2.1	6.4	16.6	13.0
1959	6,014[58]	677[58]	100[58]	234[58]	1,754[58]	1,938[58]	48.0	2.5	7.3	18.3	14.2
1960	62.0	7.2	1.1	2.5	19.6	20.6	56.3[35] 57.0	2.8[35] 2.8	8.2[35] 8.3	23.3[35] 23.6	15.9[35] 16.1
1961	67.8	7.9	3.4	2.7	21.6	20.2	66.2	3.1	9.5	28.7	17.9
1962	74.5	8.9	3.8	3.1	24.3	23.6	73.3	3.4	10.3	32.3	19.2
1963	85.1	10.0	4.3	3.5	28.3	26.3	78.0	3.6	11.1	35.0	20.0
1964	94.7	11.0	5.1	3.7	32.2	31.2	85.5	3.0	13.3	38.2	21.9
1965	102	11.7	5.0	4.1	33.9	36.6	91.4	2.9	15.0	39.7	24.2
1966	108	12.3	5.2	4.4	38.0	36.5	97.1	2.8	16.2	42.8	25.1
1967	117	13.1	5.4	4.7	40.4	39.5	99.3	2.7	18.6	42.4	24.7
1968	126	11.3	6.5	5.5	51.2	37.4	106	2.4	19.4	46.9	25.7
1969	157	12.7	7.4	6.3	68.5	45.4	128	3.0	20.6	54.9	36.8
1970	175	14.4	7.6	7.3	71.8	52.5	137	2.9	21.9	59.8	38.1
1971	188	15.1	7.9	7.3	82.1	54.0	153	3.1	23.4	68.3	42.9
1972	213	16.2	8.9	8.5	95.3	61.6	175	3.2	26.8	81.4	43.0
1973	242	18.1	10.4	10.1	103	74.1	199	3.2	30.6	98.6	49.8
1974	293	19.0	10.7	10.7	123	99.2	213	3.3	30.2	109	51.9
1975	316	19.3	11.4	13.1	137	100	215	3.3	31.1	109	54.1
1976	381	21.6	12.7	13.7	164	129	237	3.7	32.9	123	58.5
1977	421	28.4	12.2	15.7	171	150	265	3.7	34.8	143	62.7
1978	477	36.1	13.0	17.8	195	166	284	3.7	37.0	149	83.3
1979	553	47.6	14.4	21.9	228	188	307	4.1	38.2	158	84.2
1980	647	49.0	17.0	25.4	262	232	329	4.6	38.9	170	93.4
1981	748	54.6	19.2	31.0	299	270	337	4.9	40.4	170	97.8
1982	806	61.7	22.8	32.2	350	318	344	4.7	41.9	175	97.7
1983	859	67.2	24.3	36.5	386	339	362	4.7	44.1	181	106
1984	929	74.7	23.9	41.1	417	369	378	5.3	45.1	189	110
1985	1,014	110	27.5	51.0	453	389	398	5.4	45.5	208	110
1986	1,092	114	29.3	57.0	475	427	411	5.2	46.9	214	111
1987	1,162	122	30.5	64.4	510	449	428	5.5	47.6	222	119
1988	1,238	115	33.2	70.7	553	462	488	6.3	52.7	231	123
1989	1,321	117	36.6	72.0	595	494	536	6.8	61.3	253	139
1990	1,395	117	33.7	77.6	625	532	550	7.2	65.9	244	147
1991	1,453	128	38.2	79.2	642	563	661	8.3	93.6	287	183
1992	1,484	116	41.2	78.5	654	549	732	7.7	105.1	320	203
1993	1,430	117	44.0	78.5	622	547	749	7.2	93.7	319	191

G6   Central Government Revenue and Main Tax Yields

	Greece[37]					Southern Ireland[39]				
	Total	Customs	Consum	Direct	Trans	Total	Customs	Excise	I & P	VAT
	(million drachmae)					(million pounds)				
1950	...	...	...	...	...	77	27	13	20	—
1951	...	1,033	1,613	865	495	84	29	14	23	—
1952	...	1,222	1,921	1,295	511	96	34	16	26	—
1953	...	1,395	2,280	1,551	598	103	37	17	25	—
1954	7,729	1,792	1,539	1,677	698	107	37	17	26	—
1955	8,967	1,963	1,750	1,930	838	112	39	17	28	—
1956	[16,207][37]	[4,207][37]	[2,935][37]	[3,230][37]	[1,489][37]	118	45	17	27	—
1957	15,162	4,123	2,623	2,429	1,487	123	47	17	28	—
1958	15,721	4,440	3,051	2,724	1,647	126	48	17	28	—
1959	17,449	4,258	3,272	2,502	1,696	130	45	24	27	—
1960	18,925	4,635	3,547	2,615	1,865	139	41	30	31	—
1961	21,769	5,278	3,765	3,222	2,054	152	45	34	35	—
1962	24,036	5,907	4,065	3,591	2,290	163	47	35	41	—
1963	24,823	6,481	4,683	3,606	2,650	184	50	38	48	4
1964	24,749	7,550	5,298	4,467	3,071	219	56	43	56	13
1965	28,188	9,116	6,200	4,493	3,494	241	58	49	64	14
1966	34,081	11,043	7,732	5,666	4,052	273	68	55	73	17
1967	38,941	11,814	8,858	6,729	4,882	305	70	62	82	23
1968	44,416	12,687	9,541	8,248	7,026	345	76	73	94	27
1969	57,066	14,136	10,392	9,523	8,332	411	88	88	93	41
	(thousand million drachmae)									
1970	55.3	15.2	11.3	10.8	9.8	482	92	91	117	66
1971	62.9	16.2	12.2	13.2	11.1	569	101	97	153	80
1972	72.6	18.9	13.5	15.6	13.3	659	116	104	174	101
1973	87.3	23.9	16.2	18.8	16.3	793	139	116	222	137
1974	104	24.8	18.2	28.4	18.9	[651][39]	[109][39]	[89][39]	[170][39]	[112][39]
1975	137	34.6	23.6	29.6	26.6	1,091	175	157	332	175
1976	174	41.3	29.5	47.9	36.2	1,470	27	417	462	254
1977	209	57.9	36.3	49.0	43.9	1,757	29	449	522	321
1978	248	15.5	92.0	60.9	52.3	2,023	34	493	605	415
1979	312	22.1	109	80.7	65.7	2,384	39	602	731	421
1980	358	19.1	118	104	72.6	3,155	46	857	1,014	472
1981	634	11.5	148	124	85.8	3,973	58	1,060	1,243	620
1982	602	10.4	214	175	121	4,908	62	11,132	1,459	946
1983	828	9.7	281	201	154	5,711	76	1,182	1,664	1,193
1984	1,245	9.5	353	253	203	5,952	93	1,241	1,966	1,362
1985	1,491	7.1	399	303	286	6,331	96	1,316	2,103	1,402
1986	1,852	2.4	580	386	352	6,709	81	1,380	2,388	1,527
1987	2,434	2.3	367	439	748	7,152	86	1,391	2,713	1,585
1988	3,342	52.8	338	520	828	7,690	105	1,482	3,050	1,805
1989	4,150	88.9	334	581	911	7,755	132	1,617	2,890	1,942
1990	6,212	104.9	487	822	1,208	8,269	113	1,674	3,095	1,979
1991	9,183	117.7	691	1,024	1,481	8,776	120	1,722	3,330	2,013
1992	11,218	129.8	945	1,192	1,749	9,360	124	1,734	3,510	2,177
1993	15,285	100.2	1,115	1,359	1,866	10,140	157	1,757	3,798	2,331

G6 Central Government Revenue and Main Tax Yields

	Italy[20]							Netherlands				
	Total	Customs	S & T Mon	Direct	Profits Tax	Petroleum Tax	VAT	Total[15]	Customs	Excise	I & P	Turnover
	(thousand million lire)							(million guilders)				
1950	1,419	6	202	133	252	67	—	4,125	355	433	2,569	870
1951	1,720	57	220	163	311	96	—	5,686	410	516	2,938	1,213
1952	1,737	74	244	201	337	115	—	6,254	362	532	3,654	1,101
1953	1,804	88	266	184	372	133	—	6,087	430	550	3,321	1,169
1954	2,001	109	285	212	414	170	—	6,303	542	562	3,223	1,315
1955	2,296	118	305	245	468	209	—	6,538	609	591	3,375	1,296
1956	2,527	133	328	283	518	244	—	7,644	721	637	4,315	1,299
1957	2,807	149	347	335	579	268	—	8,058	869	708	4,676	1,425
1958	3,102	157	366	365	616	298	—	7,691	817	733	4,396	1,393
1959	3,207	151	389	416	657	348	—	8,282	856	773	4,703	1,550
1960	3,585	185	420	452	749	390	—	9,359	956	813	5,374	1,788
1961	3,913	202	445	514	827	415	—	10,308	1,048	843	6,019	1,890
1962	4,496	224	479	590	909	499	—	10,881	1,157	872	6,342	1,987
1963	5,194	257	521	698	1,053	596	—	11,514	1,180	951	6,575	2,197
1964	5,952[20]	273[20]	557[20]	837[20]	1,126[20]	746[20]	—	13,742	1,547	974	7,806	2,643
1965	6,858	223	584	1,056	1,282	906	—	15,543	1,577	1,165	9,013	2,961
1966	7,418	227	627	1,152	1,408	1,022	—	17,563	1,914	1,208	10,197	3,400
1967	8,404	252	657	1,192	1,557	1,188	—	19,892	2,152	1,356	11,557	3,913
1968	9,301	199	693	1,336	1,660	1,303	—	21,996	2,233	1,410	12,405	4,980
1969	10,007	210	747	1,491	1,848	1,509	—	24,830	2,407	1,520	14,589	4,877
1970	10,990	235	793	1,532	2,045	1,717	—	29,020	2,680	1,592	16,076	6,657
1971	12,162	220	800	1,796	2,212	1,872	—	33,670	2,653	1,581	19,334	8,385
1972	13,359	233	862	2,045	2,140	1,981	—	39,295	3,045	1,853	22,596	9,827
1973	15,250	267	761	2,333	323	1,999	4,032	45,423	3,398	2,023	26,233	11,152
1974	19,625	334	863	4,490	699	2,517	5,018	50,741	3,621	2,191	30,310	12,064
	(million million lire)							(thousand million guilders)				
1975	23.8	- -	1.0	5.0	- -	2.9	5.0	57.9	3.8	2.4	34.7	13.8
1976	35.8	- -	1.1	7.2	0.1	3.6	7.1	66.2	4.1	2.7	38.6	16.3
1977	44.1	- -	1.3	10.5	- -	4.5	9.3	73.7	4.3	2.9	41.9	19.3
1978	55.1	- -	1.5	12.1	- -	5.0	10.9	79.9	4.5	3.1	45.4	21.3[59]
1979	68.5	- -	1.8	15.8	- -	5.8	11.9	81.5	3.3	3.3	48.4	21.2
1980	93.4	- -	2.0	23.5	...	6.7	17.4	88.9	3.5	3.5	53.5	23.1
1981	113	- -	2.5	31.2	...	7.1	20.7	88.6	3.4	3.6	52.9	23.6
1982	149	0.1	3.3	38.7	...	8.6	24.2	89.8	3.3	4.0	53.8	23.4
1983	184	0.1	3.9	50.6	...	11.2	30.1	89.6	3.7	4.2	51.3	24.5
1984	205	0.1	4.3	56.4	...	13.1	36.0	92.5	4.0	4.2	50.0	26.4
1985	228	...	4.9	64.5	...	14.3	38.8	96.4	3.9	4.1	51.7	28.2
1986	259	...	5.2	69.6	...	19.1	40.3	104	4.1	4.2	56.5	29.3
1987	284	...	5.4	78.9	...	21.8	47.0	111	4.8	4.2	59.5	31.1
1988	318	...	5.7	92.8	...	24.3	55.7	116	4.8	4.6	63.1	32.6
1989	359	...	6.2	101.8	...	25.3	62.0	117	—	4.0	63.7	31.3
1990	408	...	6.3	113.9	...	30.7	68.8	134	—	4.3	66.4	34.5
1991	455	...	6.8	206.0	...	36.2	76.7	148	—	4.4	86.7	35.0
1992	513	...	7.2	247.2	...	37.1	78.6	150	—	4.6	77.0	36.5
1993	480	...	8.5	257.5	...	37.5	77.0	159	—	5.1	99.5	35.9

G6 Central Government Revenue and Main Tax Yields

	Norway[21]				Portugal					Romania	
	Total	Customs	Consum	I & P	Total	Customs	Prop	Business	Trans	Total	Trans
	(million kroner)				(million escudos)					(thousand million lei)	
1950	2,727	179	1,306	984	4,826	1,629	336	564	—	17.1	8.5
1951	3,092	174	1,471	1,151	5,527	1,943	346	574	—	20.5	11.3
1952	3,778	267	1,946	1,163	5,808	2,135	363	599	—	28.9	13.5
1953	4,368	328	2,179	1,356	6,226	1,928	378	647	—	32.7	15.1
1954	4,315	317	2,228	1,240	6,347	2,099	391	664	—	35.9	15.5
1955	4,591	383	2,392	1,228	6,731	2,301	400	676	—	38.6	17.2
1956	4,860	330	2,627	1,401	7,303	2,443	410	737	—	36.3	15.9
1957	5,264	398	2,935	1,572	7,933	2,574	421	788	—	38.6	17.1
1958	5,637	414	3,082	1,726	8,378	2,619	436	870	—	38.1	16.0
1959	5,989	395	3,210	1,785	8,835	2,788	458	881	—	41.1	15.4
1960	6,462[21]	438[21]	3,462[21]	1,500[21]	9,590	3,150	473	927	—	48.6[52]	18.0
										44.6	
1961	6,943	489	4,007	1,463	10,812	3,663	497	951	—	48.8	20.2
1962	7,607	476	4,348	1,691	11,355	3,522	521	1,098	—	55.5	21.7
1963	8,317	480	4,686	1,925	12,709	3,733	554	1,142	—	64.9	25.0
1964	9,213	520	5,217	2,054	13,120	3,797[60]	704	1,128	—	72.3	27.0
1965	10,225	544	5,974	2,264	15,184	4,550	721	1,419	—	76.3	28.7
1966	11,321[40]	537	6,596	2,426	16,957	4,803	776	1,526	428	86.4	31.4
	9,559										
1967	10,591	501	7,377	2,713	19,896	5,154	923	1,575	2,212	99.0	34.3
1968	11,345	408	7,917	3,020	21,828	5,322	964	2,058	2,625	10.1	36.2
1969	13,064	380	9,163	3,521	...	5,994	1,029	2,504	2,898	10.2	37.5
1970	15,158	378	11,995	2,785	29,729	7,755	1,128	2,836	3,424	10.5	40.5
1971	17,932	348	14,689	2,895	32,285	7,593	1,245	2,458	4,351	108	44.0
1972	20,647	356	16,326	3,965	36,214	8,259	1,382	2,526	5,206	116	45.1
1973	22,864	358	17,633	4,872	43,387	8,623	1,547	2,860	6,565	129	48.0
1974	25,737	351	19,323	6,063	50,286	11,001	1,731	4,170	8,658	165	46.0
	(thousand million kroner)				(thousand million escudos)						
						9.2[68]		18.8[41]			
1975	29.2	0.4	22.5	6.3	54.9	9.2		18.8	10.4	193	42.1
1976	35.6	0.3	27.0	8.3	...	12.6		24.7	14.9	200	44.9
1977	41.1[52]	0.4	31.2[52]	9.5[52]	98.4	16.9		33.6	22.6	...	32.5
	42.3		32.5	9.4							
1978	46.7	0.3	35.2	11.2	122	16.0		42.9	29.6	...	34.4
1979	52.1	0.2	37.3	14.5	157	15.5		63.0	37.0	...[28]	35.7
1980	72.0	0.7	44.5	26.8	208	18.9		77.4	56.9	279	39.4
1981	87.2	0.7	52.2	34.2	276	23.5		109	71.7	260	34.9
1982	93.3	0.8	56.9	35.6	347	27.7		141	83.1	255	65.3
1983	101	0.8	64.9	35.4	486	31.4		200	104	237	221
1984	115	0.9	71.5	42.1	559	29.5		239	117	289	261
1985	134	1.0	86.0	47.0	663	34.4		310	137	361	271
1986	139	1.2	95.9	41.9	858	38.6		295	282	392	...
1987	135	1.2	104	29.4	1,083	52.1		295	316	404	...
1988	131	1.2	102	29.1	1,368	...		...	...	364	...
1989	132	1.1	102	30.3	2,031	...		...	...	386	...
1990	145	1.3	106	39.7	2,726	...		...	...	298	...
1991	154	1.4	109	44.5	3,216	...		...	...	823	...
1992	151	1.5	119	32.2	3,870	...		...	...	2,201	...
1993	...	...	...	...	4,594	...		...	...	...	...

G6 Central Government Revenue and Main Tax Yields

1950–1993

	Russia/U.S.S.R.[6]				Spain					Sweden[50]				
	Total	I & T	Direct	Ded Profits	Total	Customs	Consum	P & T Mon	Direct	Total	Customs	Excise	I & P	Auto-mobile
	(million new rubels)				(thousand million pesetas)					(million kroner)				
1950	39.2	23.6	3.6	4.0	15.9	0.7	4.5	3.0	6.6	4,474	241	1,398	2,035	444
1951	...	...	...	...	18.4	0.7	5.1	3.3	8.0	5,426	367[61] 355	1,448[61] 1,461	2,754	472
1952	45.6	24.7	4.7	5.8	22.4	1.0	6.7	4.0	9.5	7,507	362	1,763	4,124	411
1953	51.0	24.4	4.6	7.0	24.9	1.2	7.4	4.4	10.8	7,808	379	1,839	4,100	520
1954	...	...	...	...	27.6	1.2	8.0	5.0	12.0	8,535	433	1,899	4,492	602
1955	52.7	24.2	4.8	10.3	30.5	1.4	9.1	5.3	13.1	8,907	505	2,007	4,600	819
1956	54.2	25.9	5.1	10.3	36.0	2.2	10.5	5.9	14.2	10,072	553	2,268	5,212	1,043
1957	...	...	...	...	42.4[52]	2.4[52]	12.6[52]	8.4	16.7	10,691	608	2,369	5,600	1,018
1958	66.1	30.5	5.2	13.5	53.2	2.7	14.5	11.0	20.9[52] 22.2	12,019	652	2,908	6,210	1,062
1959	72.5	31.1	5.5	16.0	57.6	2.9	16.6	11.9	23.2	12,605	654	3,284	6,401	1,086
1960	76.2	31.3	5.6	18.6	66.3	5.5	19.0	14.0	24.9	13,657	811	3,819	6,468	1,182
1961	77.3	30.9	5.8	20.7	76.7	8.4	20.3	6.8	27.5	16,641	826	5,086	8,016	1,265
1962	83.1	32.9	6.0	23.9	88.7	10.4	26.6	7.6	30.2	18,007	856	5,696	8,620	1,227
1963	88.2	34.5	6.3	25.7	10.2	12.2	25.4	8.4	33.2	19,869	867	6,679	9,025	1,587
1964	94.3	36.7	6.8	28.7	117	14.1	30.6	9.5	36.5	20,927	959	7,418	8,952	1,820
1965	102	38.7	7.7	30.9	140	14.5	28.4	10.7	45.4	24,257	1,058	7,926	11,088	1,962
1966	106	39.3	8.4	35.7	174	19.4	32.3	14.1	53.3	28,015	1,088	9,759	11,928	2,215
1967	117	40.1	9.3	41.8	196	18.0	38.4	17.4	60.6	30,441	984	11,119	12,669	2,384
1968	130	40.8	10.5	48.0	207	17.6	43.6	18.5	60.7	32,101	950	12,219	12,885	2,562
1969	131	44.5	11.6	48.0	246	21.0	51.7[69]	23.4	72.3	34,836	953	12,956	14,078	2,762
1970	15.7	49.4	12.7	54.2	279	22.4	98.6	23.4	82.0	38,887	1,046	13,110	17,048	3,044
1971	166	54.5	13.7	55.6	316	23.9	113	21.8	98.6	44,378	1,036	15,875	18,441	3,223
1972	175	55.6	14.8	60.0	375	31.5	128	26.6	118	50,303	956	19,057	19,772	3,329
1973	188	59.1	15.8	60.0	452	38.8	155	35.2	148	52,647	979	20,785	18,266	3,450
1974	201	63.5	17.1	64.4	524	42.3	180	9.0	190	59,133	1,022	22,289	20,957	3,616
										(thousand million kroner)				
1975	219	66.6	18.4	69.7	621	45.9	192	24.9	246	70.0	1.2	24.3	28.1	3.7
1976	232	70.7	19.6	70.6	741	55.2	185	42.8	315	91.4	1.1	29.8	40.6	3.9
1977	248	74.6	20.8	78.4	944	76.7	219	43.9	414	102	1.2	34.0	45.0	4.6
1978	268	84.1	22.1	78.6	1,214	66.8	285	56.9	589	109	0.9	40.0	46.1	4.9
1979	281	88.3	23.2	84.2	1,436[28]	71.4[28]	322[28]	76.8[28]	709[28]	116	0.9	42.9	51.8	6.4
1980	303	94.1	24.5	89.8	1,891	139	328	185	849	129[62]	1.1	46.9	57.6	7.0
1981	321	100	25.5	92.4	2,233	157	337	234	948	155	1.3	54.5	67.9	8.5
1982	353	101	26.6	102	2,491	208	434	209	964	167	1.4	60.8	67.5	9.2
1983	358	103	27.6	107	3,057	247	516	327	1,276	191	1.7	68.0	75.6	10.6
1984	377	103	25.8	116	3,476	266	637	390	1,491	221	1.7	74.8	96.0	10.3
1985	391	97.7	30.0	120	4,439	363	1,335	137	1,884	261	1.9	88.7	110	13.3
1986	419	91.5	31.2	130	5,708	256	2,228	342	2,111	275	1.8	93.8	111	17.8
1987	435	94.4	32.5	127	6,722	281	2,491	112	3,075	320	2.1	105	136	17.3
1988	469	101	35.9	120	...	...	...	...	...	333	2.8	115	139	18.8
1989	402	111	41.7	115	...	...	...	...	...	367	2.9	129	156	19.8
1990	472	121	48.4	116	...	...	...	...	...	402	3.2	169	162	22.0
1991	...	...	...	...	...	...	...	...	...	404	3.0	166	134	22.8
1992	...	...	...	...	...	...	...	...	...	398	4.8	165	114	21.5
1993	...	...	...	...	...	...	...	...	...	378	4.9	173	103	21.9

G6　Central Government Revenue and Main Tax Yields

1950–1993

	Switzerland				United Kingdom[2]					Yugoslavia
	Total[15]	Customs	Consum	I & P	Total	Customs	Excise	VAT	Land & I & P[53]	Total
	(million francs)				(million pounds)					(thousand) million dinari
1950	1,668	478	526	550	4,157	905	725	—	1,973	111
1951	1,485	493	546	324	4,629	999	753	—	2,114	88
1952	1,672	473	578	495	4,654	1,024	739	—	2,247	217
1953	1,599	514	599	318	4,606	1,042	722	—	2,118	189
1954	1,968	567	623	592	4,987	1,100	772	—	2,277	256
1955	1,842	645	659	351	5,160	1,149	865	—	2,293	203
1956	2,197	740	664	592	5,462	1,199	902	—	2,472	177
1957	2,043	770	723	350	5,679	1,208	942	—	2,617	227
1958	2,428	783	737	688	5,850	1,262	930	—	2,763	271
1959	2,302	858	719	482	6,016	1,373	909	—	2,686	378
1960	2,806	1,061	810	640	6,344	1,456	933	—	2,886	510
1961	2,978	1,281	918	452	6,645	1,616	978	—	3,286	547
1962	3,629	1,362	1,056	867	6,794	1,639	1,028	—	3,385	556
1963	3,647	1,538	1,179	581	6,890	1,723	1,043	—	3,313	681[66]
1964	4,481	1,697	1,325	1,076	7,727	2,008	1,166	—	3,695	7.8
1965	4,410	1,800	1,407	818	8,674		3,401	—	4,319	8.1
1966	5,129	1,889	1,480	1,349	9,716		3,536	—	4,613	8.7
1967	5,151	2,067	1,588	1,151	11,227		3,721	—	5,338	10.0
1968	5,916	2,231	1,664	1,551	13,363		4,601	—	5,962	10.8
1969	6,349	2,436	1,831	1,508	15,267		4,953	—	6,965	11.6
1970	7,241	2,354	2,342	1,967	15,843		4,709	—	7,699	15.2
1971	7,814	2,556	2,619	2,015	16,932		5,325	—	8,513	18.5
1972	9,283	2,921	3,185	2,505	17,178		5,744[65]	—	8,558	25.5
1973	9,807	2,987	3,552	2,594	18,226		4,793	1,471	10,030	28.6
1974	10,922	2,803	3,942	3,547	23,570		4,920	2,510	13,656	37.7
1975	11,026	2,939	3,792	3,510	29,417		5,803	3,455	17,548	37.6
1976	12,868	2,833	4,076	5,069	33,778		7,124	3,770	24,053	44.2
1977	12,623	2,921	4,388	4,382	38,773		8,064	4,235	21,135	56.0
1978	13,451	2,990	4,639	4,677	43,088		8,953	4,838	23,081	46.4
1979	13,256	3,002	4,904	4,139	54,331		10,071	8,189	25,643	58.9
					(thousand million pounds)					
1980	14,619	3,171	5,438	4,772	66.2		11.0	11.0	29.5	66.9
1981	15,745	3,244	5,948	5,197	76.8		13.4	11.9	34.2	95.2
1982	17,382	3,266	6,361	6,219	83.3		14.2	13.8	36.7	117
1983	18,000	3,382	6,740	5,999	88.4		16.2	15.2	38.4	161
1984	19,683	3,393	7,260	6,979	98.2		17.0	18.5	41.6	243
1985	20,558	3,449	7,671	6,697	106		18.1	19.3	47.0	415
1986	23,426	3,758[63]	8,202[64]	8,242	111		19.7	21.4	53.0	809
1987	23,315	3,738	8,753	7,410	121		20.6	24.1	58.5	1,698
1988	25,956	3,925	9,366	9,340	132		22.4	27.3	64.3	4,931
1989	26,147	4,089	9,226	8,366	141		22.8	29.3	72.1	68,695
1990	28,815	4,260	9,871	8,801	144		24.2	30.5	78.6	477,447
1991	29,169	4,418	10,006	8,783	143		25.6	33.7	76.9	29,492[71]
1992	30,406	4,476	9,817	10,295	148		26.6	37.7	73.6	1,714,066[71]
1993	28,589	5,129	9,381	10,065	166		28.3	37.8	74.0	2,984,333[71]

G6 Central Government Revenue and Main Tax Yields

NOTES

1. SOURCES:- The official publications noted on p. xv with a few gaps filled from the League of Nations, *Public Finance Statistics*. In addition, statistics for the UK to 1978 are taken from B.R. Mitchell, *British Historical Statistics* (Cambridge, 1988) where the original sources are given; and statistics for Russia to 1914 are taken from P.A. Khromov, *Economic Development of Russia in the 19th and 20th Centuries, 1800–1917* (Moscow, 1950).
2. Total revenue, unless otherwise stated, means total ordinary revenue exclusive of loan receipts. Whether or not receipts from public enterprises are included (and, if so, whether net or gross) varies from country to country. Changes in composition are indicated in footnotes.
3. Except where otherwise indicated statistics are from the closed accounts.
4. See also note 4 to table G5.

FOOTNOTES

[1] Austria-Hungary to 1867 (1st line); Cisleithania from 1867 (2nd line) to 1916; and Republic of Austria from 1920. Lombardy is excluded from 1859 and Venetia from 1866. Figures to 1858 are in convention gulden, subsequently in standard gulden, kronen or schillings. Total yields to 1864 (1st line) are of fiscal receipts only. From then to 1875 (1st line) they are of all ordinary receipts, whilst subsequently (to 1915) they include certain extraordinary receipts, but not the proceeds of loans. All yields are net.

[2] Figures for 1750 and 1751 are for years ended 29 September. From 1752 to 1799 they are for years ended 10 October. From 1800 to 1853 they are for years ended 5 January following that indicated, and subsequently they are for years ended 31 March following that indicated. Figures for the periods 11 October 1799–5 January 1800 and 6 January–31 March 1854 are not shown here.

[3] Figures to 1800 are for Great Britain, and are of net receipts. Subsequently they are for the U.K. and are of gross receipts, though Irish Customs and Excise receipts are not included under these headings until 1807. Their combined totals were as follows (in thousands of pounds):-

1801	2,350	1803	2,801	1805	3,056
1802	3,226	1804	3,062	1806	3,482

[4] Total revenue to 1840 includes the proceeds of loans.

[5] Fourth quarter only.

[6] Statistics to 1914 are for the Russian Empire exclusive of Finland. Subsequently they are for the U.S.S.R.

[7] Including profits from the state spirit monopoly.

[8] Figures to 1864 are for years ended 31 October (though the 1864 figure for Monopolies is for 14 months to 31 December). From 1865 to 1913 the figures are for calendar years. The 1914 figure is for the first half-year only, and those for 1915 and 1916 are for years ended 30 June. Figures for the Republic are for calendar years.

[9] Revised figures were later published for each year back to 1891, but only for three years before that. The original series is given here for 1879–1891 (1st line). Revised figures are available for this period as follows:-

	Total	Customs & Excise	Direct Taxes
1879	21	6	13
1880	31	8	21
1886	41	12	22

[10] Statistics are for Denmark proper, except that total revenue to 1863 includes that of the Duchies of Schleswig, Holstein, and Lauenburg. Figures to 1977 are for years ended 31 March following that indicated, except that Customs, Excise and VAT yields from 1928 are for calendar years. With the same exceptions, the figures for 1978 are for April-December. All subsequent statistics are for calendar years.

[11] Total net revenue includes the proceeds of loans to 1869 (1st line).

[12] Including navigation tax to 1891.

[13] Figures to 1868 (1st line) are of receipts by the Customs Administration. Subsequently they are of receipts from import duties.

[14] Subsequently excluding the tax on matches.

[15] Tax revenue only.

[16] The 1876 figures are for 15 months ended 31 March 1877. Subsequent statistics are for years ended 31 March following that indicated

[17] Transleithania to 1918, and the territory established by the treaty of Trianon subsequently. The figures to 1913 are for calendar years. That for 1914 is for the first half-year only, and subsequent figures are for years ended 30 June.

[18] Ordinary' revenue, which includes a small amount of the proceeds from loans in some years.

[19] Subsequently including the net revenue of state monopolies.

[20] Figures for 1884 are for 9 months ended 31 August. For 1885 they are for 10 months ended 30 June. From 1886 to 1964 they are for years ended 30 June, and subsequently for calendar years.

[21] Figures for 1878 are for the first half-year only. From 1879 to 1960 they are for years ended 30 June, and subsequently for calendar years.

[22] Figures to 1934 are for years ended 30 June. The 1935 figure is for 18 months, and subsequent figures are for calendar years.

[23] All current revenue exclusive of the proceeds of loans to 1929. Ordinary revenue subsequently.

[24] Figures for 1880 are for 15 months ended 31 March 1881. From 1881 to 1922 they are for years ended 31 March following that indicated. The 1923 figures are for 9 months, and those for 1924–32 are for calendar years. Figures for 1933–43 are for years ended 31 March following that indicated.

[25] Statistics to 1862 are for 18 months to 30 June 1863. For 1863-98 they are for years beginning 1 July. The 1899 figures are for the second half-year only. Statistics for 1919–23 are for years ended 31 March following that indicated and those for 1924-5 are for years ended 30 June following that indicated. The 1926 figures are for the second half-year only, and subsequent statistics are for calendar years, as are those for 1900-18.

[26] Subsequently including the tax on the sale of spirits.

G6   Central Government Revenue and Main Tax Yields

27   Figures are of total ordinary receipts plus extraordinary tax receipts to 1941 (1st line). Subsequently they are of tax revenue only.

28   From 1870/1 most assessed taxes which had been included with land tax were replaced by excise licences.

29   Figures to 1905 (1st line) include the net revenue from monopolies.

30   Figures for 1919–33 are for years ended 31 March following that indicated. The figures for 1934 are for 9 months.

31   May-December only.

32   Subsequently including the tax on salt.

33   Including the budget of the Comité Francaise de Libération Nationale in 1943, and of the provisional government in 1944.

34   The definition of tax revenue was enlarged in scope.

35   Figures are for calendar years. West Berlin is included from 1951 and Saarland from 1960 (2nd line).

36   The first line for 1948 is to 20 June and is in million Reichsmarks; the second line is from 21 June and is in million Deutschmarks.

37   Statistics from 1919 to 1955 are for years ended 31 March. The figure for 1956 is for 21 months. Figures to 1924/5 are of budgetary receipts (excluding loans). Subsequently they are of ordinary receipts.

38   Budget estimates.

39   Figures to 1973 are for years ended 31 March following that indicated. Those for 1974 are for April-December, and subsequently they are for calendar years.

40   Subsequently tax revenue only.

41   Subsequently all income and property taxes.

42   Figures for 1926–37 are for years ended 31 March following that indicated. A new income tax system operated in 1937.

43   From 1929 (2nd line) accessory duties are excluded from customs revenue.

44   Subsequently including arrears received during the year.

45   Figures for 1924–30 are for years ended 30 September. Total ordinary revenue excluding loans in the fourth quarter of 1930 was 4,315 million rubels. From 1932 (2nd line) local government revenue is included.

46   Subsequently receipts from taxes and state enterprises only.

47   Income tax is included subsequently.

48   Petrol monopoly only.

49   The old property tax, which had declined to negligible proportions, is subsequently excluded.

50   Figures for 1923 are for the first half-year only. Subsequent figures are for years ended 30 June.

51   Some items previously included were subsequently excluded from current ordinary revenue.

52   This break is caused by a change in classification.

53   Including corporation, profits and excess profits taxes, surtax, and capital gains tax.

54   Serbia to 1914, Yugoslavia from 1920.

55   Subsequently tax revenue only. The fact that this is higher than total revenue in 1953 is due to the inclusion in the latter of losses made by public enterprises.

56   Tax revenue only, though the surplus of the tobacco monopoly is included to 1956 (1st line).

57   Subsequently in the new currency (1 new = 100 old markkaa).

58   Subsequently in the new currency (1 new = 100 old francs).

59   Subsequently excluding the part going to the European Commission.

60   From 1965 revenue from stamps for customs purposes is included.

61   Coffee tax was transferred from customs to excise in 1951.

62   Subsequently total budget revenue, including capital receipts.

63   Some small supplementary duties (31 million francs in 1985) are excluded subsequently.

64   Subsequently excluding beer tax (55 million francs in 1985).

65   Subsequently actual receipts rather than payments into the Consolidated Fund.

66   Subsequently in the new currency (1 new = 100 old dinari).

67   Subsequently in thousand million pesetas.

68   Subsequently import duties.

69   Subsequently including general sales tax and VAT (37.8 in 1970).

70   Change in calculation method

71   Yugoslavia

H PRICES

1.   Wholesale Price Indices   page 856
2.   Cost-of-Living/Consumer Prices Indices   page 863

There is a considerable array of material on prices available for most countries far back in time, before the period covered here. Most of this, however, is intractable in the extreme and it has been decided to exclude it from this work. Instead, there are two sets of indices, based on this material, but reducing it to some sort of readily comprehensible order. It was felt that annual averages of prices in local currencies of (say) a kilogram of wheat were unlikely to be of use except to the specialist, and that a general indication of overall price levels would be more widely useful. Of course, there is oversimplification and distortion in the process. Like all index numbers, those presented here require careful interpretation. In order to achieve exact comparability of an index over long periods of time the commodities and their weighting must remain unchanged. However, in a changing economy first the weightings and then probably the commodities themselves will cease to be appropriate representations of the quantities and of the things actually used. All indices, therefore, must compromise between continuity and relevance, and the more rapid is economic change the more frequent must be the breaks in continuity.

In the period since World War II, the official indices in some countries have been changed very frequently indeed. This has especially been true of cost-of-living indices as statisticians have striven to produce indices capable of measuring material welfare over time, rather than some fixed basket of goods. At the other extreme, some of the eighteenth and nineteenth-century indices remained unchanged for very long periods. Usually this does not involve much danger of lack of representativeness. Commodity consumption patterns changed very little in most countries until the second half of the nineteenth century, when increasing incomes and increasing urbanisation both began to have effects.

A more serious problem in some of the earlier indices is lack of sufficient variety of information. Price series exist only for the most important commodities traded. Most of the series, certainly for the eighteenth century, are of prices paid by institutions, often on long-term contracts, rather than of prices paid in the market place. It seems likely that these institutional prices were rather rigid in the short run, and insulated from some of the ordinary fluctuations. However, as a measure of long-term secular trends in the price level indices based on wholesale prices, even with a large element based on institutional records, should be reasonably reliable.

Genuine retail price or cost-of-living indices cannot generally be carried as far back in time as wholesale prices because of lack of enough information about the prices themselves and about typical consumption patterns. It is perhaps worth pointing out *en passant* that there is always something artificial about such 'typical' patterns for, like the 'average man', they are something of a myth, or at any rate a bloodless conceptual tool. Leaving that on one side, and accepting that averages do serve a purpose, the problem of establishing expenditure patterns and assembling retail price data remains. It is probably fair to say that most of the indices shown in Table H2 for periods before the late nineteenth century are based on too little information to be fully representative. Certainly they rarely include any element to represent the cost of housing, and mostly they cover the prices of only a few basic foodstuffs, fuel, and some proxy for clothing.

Perhaps too much should not be made of these problems for it is likely that the more readily available wholesale prices, even on contracts, did not vary very much from retail prices in the long run. Changes in costs of distribution or in retailers' profit margins could produce such variation. It is very probable that both of these declined as means of transport improved and, partly as a consequence, competition between suppliers increased. But the effect is unlikely to have been very pronounced or other than very gradual.

One further point is worth making about both sorts of price index. Until some time in the twentieth century most of the underlying data were derived from a few cities, often only the capital city, in each country. There may well have been quite wide regional variations of which the indices take no account.

In order to facilitate comparisons between countries—though it must be understood that these are necessarily inexact owing both to the nature of indices and to the variety of consumption patterns—many of the indices shown here have been converted to common base-years. Anyone wanting to use these indices for further calculations should bear in mind this shifting of the base-year, and also the fact that different indices have, where necessary, been crudely spliced together.

H1 WHOLESALE PRICE INDICES
1750–1799   **1800–1849**

	France	Germany	Spain[1]	U.K.[2]		Belgium	France	Germany	Spain[1]	Switzerland	U.K.[2]
	1820 = 100	1913 = 100	1726–50 = 100	1770 = 100		1913 = 100	1820 = 100	1913 = 100	1726–50 = 100	1914 = 100	1821–5 = 100
1750	...	...	...	94	1800	...	118	135	194	...	151
1751	...	...	111	90	1801	...	105	134	...	...	156
1752	...	...	115	80	1802	...	104	131	...	...	122
1753	...	...	126	80	1803	...	111	139	...	...	124
1754	...	...	137	95	1804	...	104	136	...	...	124
1755	...	...	131	97	1805	...	114	156	...	...	136
1756	...	...	116	99	1806	...	125	157	...	152	134.5
1757	...	...	111	100	1807	...	122	148	...	14	131
1758	...	...	115	107	1808	...	161	176	...	158	144.5
1759	...	...	109	107	1809	...	161	156	...	13	155
1760	...	...	111	109	1810	...	166	132	...	141	153
1761	...	...	108	107	1811	...	164	123	...	126	145
1762	...	...	112	109							
1763	...	...	121	109					1913 = 100		
1764	...	...	128	107	1812	...	171	137	224	156	164
1765	...	...	138	105	1813	...	160	120	180	147	169
1766	...	...	134	105	1814	...	122	110	143	136	154
1767	...	...	130	105	1815	...	116	112	160	132	130
1768	...	...	131	104	1816	...	120	124	162	153	119
1769	...	...	133	98	1817	...	129	148	173	178	132
1770	...	...	128	100	1818	...	123	130	150	134	139
1771	...	...	129	100	1819	...	105	103	129	107	128
1772	...	...	130	104							
1773	...	...	128	105				1901–10 = 100			
1774	...	...	131	104	1820	...	153	90	111	103	115
1775	...	...	128	104	1821	...	143	85	104	105	100
1776	...	...	130	107	1822	...	138	84	114	101	88
1777	...	...	130	109	1823	...	143	82	104	93	98
1778	...	...	134	111	1824	...	133	72	108	94	102
1779	...	...	136	117	1825	...	146	76	108	98	113
1780	...	...	140	120	1826	...	136	72	103	88	100
1781	...	...	145	117	1827	...	134	77	88	87	99
1782	...	...	145	128	1828	...	129	78	86	94	96
1783	...	...	144	124	1829	...	130	77	76	92	96
1784	...	...	149	115	1830	...	130	78	75	90	94.5
1785	...	...	153	114	1831	...	124	82	81	96	95
1786	...	...	156	120	1832	79	125	80	83	104	91.5
1787	...	...	153	118	1833	77	126	76	80	94	89
1788	...	...	159	120	1834	77	128	76	89	94	86.5
1789	...	...	160	114	1835	81	132	77	96	94	84.5
1790	...	...	166	114	1836	85	135	78	96	103	95
					1837	84	126	74	98	92	94
			1821–5 = 100[3]		1838	87	131	78	91	96	98
					1839	91	130	81	91	102	104
1790	...	...	...	89	1840	91	135	80	81	98	102.5
1791	...	...	161	90	1841	92	134	78	78	91	98
1792	...	98	165	88	1842	89	131	78	82	95	89
1793	...	98	171	97	1843	82	121	77.5	70	96	80
1794	...	101	173	98.5	1844	77	118	76	76	96	81
1795	...	122	187	115	1845	79	121	82	73	98	83
1796	...	114	187	116	1846	87	129	88	83	112	86
1797	...	108	206	106	1847	96	136	97	92	117	97
1798	118	116	215	108	1848	80	112	76	89	81	82
1799	117	132	205	125	1849	77	111	70	75	79	74

H1 Wholesale Price Indices

	Austria-Hungary 1867–77 = 100	Belgium 1913 = 100	Denmark 1891–1900 = 100	France 1901–10 = 100	Germany 1913 = 100	Italy 1913 = 100	Norway 1913 = 100	Spain 1913 = 100	Sweden 1913 = 100	Switzerland 1914 = 100	U.K.[2] 1821–5 = 100
1850	...	83	...	111	71	...	...	76	...	89	73.5
											1913 = 100[3]
1851	...	80	...	110	75	...	...	80	...	92	91
1852	...	75	...	119	82	...	...	78	...	96	92
1853	...	89	...	139	92	...	...	73	...	108	112
1854	...	97	...	148	100	...	...	79	...	118	120
1855	...	100	...	154	105	...	...	86	...	112	119
1856	...	101	...	156	105	...	...	96	...	112	119
1857	...	99	...	151	101	...	...	98	...	114	124
1858	...	97	...	137	91	...	...	83	...	98	107
1859	...	91	...	137	89	...	...	97	...	106	111
1860	...	94	...	144	94	...	...	95	99	115	116
1861	...	97	...	142	94	98	...	95	97	113	115
1862	...	96	...	142	94	91	...	102	102	112	119
1863	...	93	...	143	92	87	...	116	107	120	121
1864	...	96	...	141	91	87	...	120	108	126	124
1865	...	94	...	132	89	86	...	111	103	119	119
1866	...	95	...	134	90	90	...	120	97	121	120
1867	104.1	95	...	131	97	90	...	111	96	121	118
1868	97.7	93	...	132	97	96	...	98	95	114	116
1869	99.6	93	...	130	92	89	...	100	93	111	115
1870	102.4	94	...	133	92	88.5	...	109	92	111	113
1871	105.6	98	...	138	100	91.5	...	91	95	118	113[3]
											116
1872	105.1	102	...	144	114	99	...	90	106	132	125
1873	103.5	103	...	144	120	105	...	90	113	135	130
1874	99.0	102	...	132	112	105	...	93	107	117	126
1875	91.2	100	...	129	100	93	...	84	101	112	121
1876	94.5	98	145	130	95	90	...	91	98	117	118
1877	97.8	98	135	131	91	102	...	96	97	115	121
1878	89.2	92	122	120	83	99	...	93	88	107	113
1879	84.5	91	120	117	81	93	...	95	86	103	107
1880	89.3	98	128	120	87	93	...	90	91	106	111
1881	87.1	99	129	117	85	87	...	91	89	101	109
1882	86.0	98	127	114	81	90	...	94	88	102	110
1883	86.1	96	126	110	80	84	...	89	85	96	108
1884	84.5	93	120	101	78	80	...	81	82	92	98
1885	79.8	86	109	99	75	85	...	81	78	87	92
1886	76.9	81	101	95	72	85	...	80	75	86	87
1887	76.7	81	99	92	73	79	...	77	72	87	85
1888	77.1	83	105	96	75	81	...	78	79	85	87
1889	77.0	84	109	100	82	85	...	80	79	90	89
1890	77.0	86	109	100	86.5	88	...	84[3]	82	91	89
								74			
1891	78.0	86	112	98	86	85	80	78	82	89	92
1892	74.1	82	101	95	80	81	76	80	77	85	87
1893	75.2	80	100	94	77	76	76	78	74	85	85
1894	72.0	78	94	87	73	74	71	75	71	81	80
1895	72.4	74	92	85	72	78	71	80	70	80	78
1896	70.5	75	93	82	72	78	71	76	71	81	76
1897	72.1	75	95	83	76	77	71	82	72	84	77
1898	74.7	76	99	86	79	79	76	91	76	84	80
1899	76.4	82	105	93	83	81	76	92	81	87	79

H1 Wholesale Price Indices

	Austria-Hungary	Belgium	Bulgaria	Czecho-slovakia	Denmark	Finland	France	Germany	Greece	Hungary	S. Ireland
	1867–77 = 100	1913 = 100	1913 = 100	1929 = 100	1891–1900 = 100	1929 = 100	1901–10 = 100	1913 = 100	1929 = 100	1929 = 100	1953 = 100
1900	81.5	87	57	...	110	...	99	90	...	...	...
1901	79.8	86	57	...	106	...	95	83	...	...	...
1902	77.9	84	59	...	108	...	94	81	...	...	...
1903	80.0	83	61	...	105	...	96	82	...	...	...
1904	81.8	86	63	...	107	...	94	82	...	...	...
1905	85.3	88	69	...	110	...	98	86	...	...	...
1906	90.5	95	73	...	114	...	104	92	...	...	...
1907	94.5	96	75	...	118	...	109	97	...	...	...
1908	91.0	96	77	...	113	...	101	90	...	...	...
1909	94.4	90	80	...	115	...	101	91	...	...	...
1910	...	95	82	...	120	...	108	93	...	...	...
1911	...	96	86	...	123	...	113	94	...	...	...
1912	...	100	95	...	131	...	118	102	...	...	...
1913	...	100	100	...	129	9	116	100	...	...	...
1914	Austria		103	...	145	10	118	105			...
	1929 = 100	1929 = 100	1929 = 100	1929 = 100	1929 = 100		1929 = 100	1929 = 100			
1914	79	[14]7	2.9	[11]11	97		17	74			...
1915	...	...	...	...	123	13	23	99	...	...	...
1916	...	...	...	...	163	19	31	106	...	...	...
1917	...	...	...	...	215	31	43	125	...	...	...
1918	...	...	...	...	261	55	56	152	...	...	...
1919	...	...	...	...	281	69	58	291	...	...	...
1920	...	...	...	166	335	112	83	1,040	...	...	...
1921	...	43[8]	...	156[3]	192	119	57	1,338	...	...	...
1922	78[4]	43	...	145	147	115	54	23,927	...	...	...
1923	98	58	...	106	160	104	69	11,634,000	...	[101]4,15	...
								million			
1924	107	67	84	108	127	104	80	86[4]	...	116	...
1925	107	66	95	109	141[3]	106	90	91[3]	...	116	...
1926	95	87	87	103	109	103	115	92	...	102	...
1927	102	100	88	106	102	104	101	96	...	109	...
1928	100	99	94	106	102	105	102	99	95	112	...
1929	100	100	100	100	100	100	100	100	100	100	...
1930	91	87	82	89	87	92	87	91	91	87	...
1931	84	74	67	81	76	86	74	81	81	82	...
1932	86	61	59	74	78	93	65	70	98	82	...
1933	83	59	53	72	83	92	62	68	110	71	...
1934	85	56	54	74	88	92	59	72	109	71	...
1935	85	63	55	77	97[3]	93	56	74	111	78	...
1936	84	69	56	77	97	96	65	76	113	80	...
1937	87[3]	80	63	82	110	113	90	77	126	86	...
1938	86	74	65	81[3]	104	106	103	77	124	87	33
1939	87	76	66	93	109	111	108	78	123	86	35
1940	90	[98]9	76	113	159	149	142	80	145	100	44
1941	91	...	97	121	188	182	174	82	162	123	49
1942	91	...	123	124	197	225	203	83	...	150	57
1943	92	...	156	125	198	256	236	85	...	204	63
1944	92	...	227	126	201	282	266	85	...	274	66
1945	[92]5	...	363	140	197	406	376	...	...	...	66
										1948 = 100[3]	
1946	...	[246]3,10	413	245	195	635	648	...	18,610[3]	[76]8	66
1947	[261]6	264	470	[263]2	215	764	986	...	22,320	89	73
1948	275	289	...	...	236	1,009	1,699	...	31,000	100[11]	78

H1 Wholesale Price Indices

	Italy 1913 = 100	Nether- lands	Norway 1913 = 100	Poland	Portugal	Romania	Spain 1913 = 100	Sweden	Switzerland 1914 = 100	UK[2] 1913 = 100	Yugo- slavia
1900	84.5	...	85	...	...	...	97	84	85	86	...
1901	84	65	85	...	...	...	97	82	84	83	...
1902	81	65	80	...	...	...	95	81	85	83	...
1903	81	65	80	...	...	...	98	81	89	83	...
1904	77	67	80	...	...	...	100	82	88	84	...
1905	80	69	85	...	...	...	100	83	90	84	...
1906	83	69	89	...	...	...	97	88	94	87	...
1907	90	71	95	...	...	...	101	92	102	91	...
1908	87	71	95	...	...	...	99	88	94	88	...
1909	88	73	89	...	...	...	97	89	96	89	...
1910	88	71	89	...	...	...	98	91	100	93	...
1911	95	78	89	...	...	...	95	94	104	94	...
1912	103	80	100	...	...	...	99	98	102	99	...
1913	10	75	100	87	...	...	100	100	104	100	...
							1929 = 100				
1913							58[3]	102[3]			
1914	96	80	105	...	...	...	59	1929 = 100	100	101	...
	1929 = 100		1929 = 100							1929 = 100	
1914	20		69					72		72	
1915	26	108	100	...	...	...	71	104	119	88	...
1916	38	165	150	...	...	...	84	132	163	114	...
1917	57	186	222	...	...	...	99	174	202	148	...
1918	85	210	228	...	...	...	122	242	296	164	...
1919	93	212	216	...	...	...	122	236	305	181	...
1920	122	196	256	...	...	...	132	256	294	225[3]	...
1921	112	153	200	...	...	...	113	159	222	144	...
									1929 = 100[3]		
									142		
1922	112	120	156	...	...	...	103	124	112	116	...
1923	113	112	156[3]	...	...	...	102	116	120	116	...
1924	113	118	178	...	...	...	108	116	121	122	...
1925	126	118	172	...	...	...	110	115	114	117	...
1926	129	106	134	91	...	...	104	106	102	108	101
1927	108	102	113	103	97	...	100	104	101	104	104
1928	105	102	106	104	101	...	97	106	102	103	107
1929	100	100	100	100	100	100	100	100	100	100	100
1930	90	88	94	89	95	78	100	87	90	88[3]	86
1931	78	75	84	78	85	60	101	79	78	77	73
1932	73	65	84	68	86	54	99	78	68	75	65
1933	66	63	84	61	84	52	95	76	65	75	64
1934	65	63	84	58	90	52	97	81	64	78	63
1935	71	61	88	55	83	60	98	86	64	78	66
1936	80	63	94	56	86	69	100	87	68	83	68
1937	93	75	106	62	102	78	112	98	79	96	74
1938	100	71	103	58	99	78	126	95	76	89	78
1939	104	73	106	[57][16]	100	88	144	99	79	90	79
1940	122	92	138	...	127	133	172	96	101	120	114
1941	136	104	169	...	148	[186][17]	204	102	130	134	...
1942	152	110	175	...	171	...	224	164	149	140	...
1943	229	112	178	...	213	...	250	172	155	143	...
1944	857	114	181	...	239	...	269	172	158	146	...
1945	2,058	125	181	...	233	...	298	169	157	149	...
1946	2,881	175	175	...	228	...	358	162	152	154	...
1947	5,154	188	178	...	239	...	420	175	159	169	...
1948	5,437	196	188	...	238	...	450	188	165	193	...

H1   Wholesale Price Indices

(1953 = 100)

	Austria	Belgium	Denmark	Finland	France	West Germany	Greece	Southern Ireland	Italy
1948	42	94	74	63	65	[90][14]	58		104
1949	53	89	76	63	72	88	68	77	98
1950	82	93	86	74	78	85	71[3]	82	93
1951	103	113	109	103	100	100	86	95	106
1952	106	107	106	104	105	103	86	100	100
1953	100	100	100	100	100	100	100	100	100
1954	105	99	100	99	98	98	112	99	99
1955	108	101	103	97	98	101[3]	120	102	100
1956	110	104	106[3]	103	102	102	131	103	102
1957	114	106	106	111	108	104	131	110	103
1958	111	102	105	120	121	103	128	114	101
1959	114	101	105	121	126	103	130	113	98
1960	113	102	105	126	130	104	132	113	99
1961	115	102	107	126	132	105[3]	134	114	99
1962	122	103	109	129	136	106	133	118	102
1963	120	106	113	133	141	106	141	120	107
1964	127	111	115	143	143	106	145	127	111
1965	131	112	120	149	145	109	148	132	113
1966	133	115	123	152	148	110	153	135	114
1967	136	113	124	157	148	109[18]	154	138	114
1968	137	114	128	174	153	103	154	147	115
1969	141	119	132	180	166	106	159	158	119
1970	147	125[21]	143	188	177	112	165	167	128
1971	154	124	149	197	188	117	172	175	132
1972	160	129	156	214	199	121	181	195[22]	137[20]
1973	163	145	179	252	225	131	224	230	161
1974	188	169	219	313	270	148	307	256	227
1975	199	172	232	355	278[24]	153	327	321	246
1976	211	184	250	395	310	162	372	384	303
1977	217	188	270	437	328	165	424	450	353
1978	219	185	282	460	341	164	467	490	382
1979	229	196	307	501	407	170	565	550	442
1980	248	208	358	582	435	189	726	607	530
1981	268	224	412	660	463	204	914	713	618
1982	277	242	455	710	530	215	1,060	792	704
1983	278	254	480	752	601	215	1,270	841	764
1984	289	273	516	797	674	221	1,542	906	842
1985	296	273	530	837	681	222	1,859	934	908
1986	281	256	495	799	622	206	2,192	914	907
1987	275	249	495	810	614	198	2,393	919	936
1988	274	252	513	838	700	200	2,651	957	970
1989	279	267	542	885	732	209	3,014	1,006	1,033
						Germany			
1990	286	270	549	914	729	207	3,493	981	1,052
1991	289	266	553	914	733	207	4,231	994	1,165
1992	286	266	549	926	751	209	4,713	1,000	1,191
1993	286	264	545	955	762	205	5,256	1,048	1,250
					1995 = 100				
1994	99.7	96.8	97.3	99.3	...	98.3	92.8	98.0	92.7
1995	100.0	100.0	100.0	100.0	100.0	100.0	100.0	100.0	100.0
1996	100.0	102.0	101.1	99.1	...	99.6	106.1	100.4	101.9
1997	100.4	105.8	103.0	100.6	...	100.7	109.6	100.0	103.2
1998	99.8	103.8	102.4	99.2	...	100.3	113.9	101.5	103.3
1999	99.0	104.0	102.9	99.1	...	99.3	116.3	102.6	103.1
2000	103.0	115.1	109.1	107.3	...	102.5	125.4	...	109.3

H1 Wholesale Price Indices

(1953 = 100)

	Netherlands	Norway	Portugal	Spain	Sweden	Switzerland	U.K.[3]	Yugoslavia
1948	74	67	93	57	72	102	73	...
1949	78[3]	68	97	61	72	97	82	...
1950	87	77	99	72	76	96	93[23]	...
1951	107	96	106	93	100	107	128	...
1952	104	101	107	93	106	104	110	103
1953	100	100	100	100	100	100	100	100
1954	101	102	103	100	100	101	99	100
1955	102	104	103	104	104	101	105[3]	102
1956	104	109	107	114	110[3]	104	109	104
1957	107	113	108	133	111	105	110	103
1958	105	111	108	146	109	102	103	104
1959	106	111	107	149[3]	109	100	104	103
1960	104	112	110	152	112	101	104	105
1961	103	113	110	156	114	101	103	111
1962	104	116	111	164	117	105	103	114
1963	106	117	112	171	120	109	105[3]	116
1964	113	121	113	176	125	111[3]	110	121
1965	116	124	117	194	131	111	111	143
1966	122	127	121	199	135	113	114	170
1967	122	129	126	200	135	113	113	186
1968	123	130	130	205	136	113	124[3]	192
1969	124[19]	135	135	211	142	118	128	202
1970	131	144	140	214	151	124	135	218
1971	135	151	143	227	156	126	141	250
1972	149	155	151	242	165	131	147	288
1973	156	168	168	268	183	145	195	335
1974	177	200	216	316	223	169	291	463
1975	195	218	244	344	243	165	335	591
1976	212	235	291	391	262	164	425	634
1977	226	250	375	470	284	164	488	698
1978	236	262	493	547	302	159	484	752
1979	246	285	640	626	335	165	561	887
1980	263	327	681	735	379	173	673[3]	1,294
1981	307	364	828	850	418	183	735	1,987
1982	318	386	986	956	468	188	788	2,589
1983	316	411	1,232	1,090	520	189	843	3,632
1984	338	437	1,570	1,223	564	195	911	5,844
1985	339	458	1,903	1,320	596	199	926[3]	10,829
1986	266	461	2,079	1,332	608	192	856	20,044
1987	254	499	...	1,344	627	188	883	40,630
1988	253	522	...	1,384	665	192	911	127,862
1989	236	551	...	1,443	717	201	953	1,901,282
1990	263	568	...	1,479	778	202	945	10,000,000
1991	274	587	...	1,494	790	204	921	21,367,948
1992	263	587	...	1,516	778	204	923	...
1993	246	587	...	1,552	836	204	966	...
			1995 = 100					
1994	98.5	97.5	...	94.0	90.0	100.1	96.1	...
1995	100.0	100.0	100.0	100.0	100.0	100.0	100.0	...
1996	102.0	108.5	...	101.7	...	98.2	102.6	...
1997	103.8	109.7	...	102.7	177.0	97.5	103.6	...
1998	103.6	95.8	...	102.0	205.0	96.3	104.2	...
1999	104.7	113.8	...	102.7	242.0	95.4	105.4	...
2000	109.8	157.1	...	108.3	350.0	96.3	108.1	...

H1   Wholesale Price Indices

NOTES

1. SOURCES:- The statistics mainly are based on the official publications noted on p. xv and on the League of Nations and United Nations, *Statistical Yearbooks*. In addition, the following have been used:- Austria-Hungary—B. Von Jankovich, in *Bulletin de l'Institut Internationale de Statistique*, XIX, 3 (1911); Belgium to 1913—an unweighted average of the indices of agricultural and industrial prices in P. Schöller, "La transformation économique de la Belgique de 1832 à 1844", *Bulletin de l'Institut de Recherche Economique* (Louvain, 1948), spliced on to similar indices in F. Loots, "Les mouvements fondamentaux des prix de gros en Belgique de 1822 à 1913", *ibid.* (1936); Denmark to 1948—based on H.C. Johanson, *Denmarks Historie*, vol. 9. (Copenhagen, 1985); France to 1819—A. Chabert, *Essai sur les mouvements des prix et des revenus en France de 1798 à 1820* (Paris, 1945); Germany to 1913—A. Jacobs & H. Richter, *Die Grosshandelpreise in Deutschland von 1792 bis 1934* (Sonderhefte des Instituts fur Konjunctforschung, No. 37, Berlin, 1935); Great Britain to 1978—B.R. Mitchell *British Historical Statistics* (Cambridge, 1988), quoting Schumpeter, Gayer Rostow & Schwartz, Sauerbeck, and the Board of Trade; Spain to 1800—Earl J. Hamilton, *War and Prices in Spain, 1651-1800* (Cambridge, Mass., 1947); Spain 1812-1913 (1st line)—Juan Sarda, *La Politica Monetaria y las Fluctuaciones de la Economiá Española en el Siglo XIX* (Madrid, 1948); and Sweden to 1913—Åmark, "En svensk prisindex för åren 1860-1913", *Kommersiella meddelanden*, III, 18 (1921). Data after 1993 are compiled from the IMF International Financial Statistics Year book.
2. Various indices have been crudely spliced together in the case of certain countries to give a rough indicator of the long-term movement of prices. The differences in the construction of these indices should be borne in mind if they are used in further calculations.

FOOTNOTES

[1] New Castile to 1800.
[2] England to 1790 (1st line), Great Britain subsequently.
[3] A new index has been spliced on to the old. Where this appears to be accompanied by a discontinuity a "break" line has been inserted.
[4] In prices based on gold.
[5] First two months only.
[6] Fourth-quarter year only.
[7] April.
[8] Last five months only.
[9] First four months only.
[10] Last two months only.
[11] July.
[12] Excluding December.
[13] Previous figures are for end-July rather than annual averages.
[14] Second half-year only. The figure for 1938 on the same basis is 49.
[15] At end-December.
[16] First seven months of 1949 = 95.
[17] First half-year only.
[18] Subsequently excluding Value Added Tax.
[19] No general index was published subsequently. Later statistics relate to the process of manufacturing inputs.
[20] Value Added Tax was imposed from January, 1973.
[21] Whereas transmission tax is included previously, the subsequent Value Added Tax is excluded.
[22] Value Added Tax is included from November 1972.
[23] No general index was published subsequently. Later statistics relate to the prices of materials and fuel purchased by manufacturing industry.
[24] No general index was published subsequently. Later statistics relate to the producer prices of metal products.

H2 COST-OF-LIVING/CONSUMER PRICES INDICES

1781–1814

	U.K.: England[1] 1857 = 100
1781	111
1782	111
1783	113
1784	110
1785	104
1786	102
1787	105
1788	108
1789	114
1790	118
1791	114
1792	112
1793	120
1794	123
1795	146
1796	153
1797	133
1798	131
1799	149
1800	200
1801	209
1802	154
1803	150
1804	154
1805	177
1806	169
1807	161
1808	173
1809	197
1810	207
1811	196
1812	227
1813	222
1814	193

1815–1864

	Belgium 1913 = 100	Denmark 1913 = 100	France[2] 1914 = 100	Germany 1913 = 100	Italy 1913 = 100	Sweden 1914 = 100	U.K.: England[1] 1851 = 100
1815	...	321	...	...	...	...	164
1816	...	321	...	...	...	...	181
1817	...	288	...	...	...	...	187
1818	...	180	...	...	...	...	179
1819	...	182	...	...	...	...	167
1820	...	119	...	44	...	...	151
1821	...	100	...	38	...	...	138
1822	...	86	...	38	...	...	126
1823	...	92	...	40	...	...	134
1824	...	79	...	30	...	...	144
1825	...	81	...	29	...	...	151
1826	...	78	...	33	...	...	136
1827	...	82	...	39	...	...	132
1828	...	76	...	40	...	...	135
1829	...	79	...	40	...	...	139
1830	...	80	...	43	...	62	135
1831	...	83	...	50	...	65	137
1832	...	80	...	47	...	65	130
1833	...	74	...	44	...	64	122
1834	...	70	...	37	...	64	116
1835	88	73	...	38	...	65	109
1836	95	86	...	37	...	65	126
1837	89	75	...	38	...	67	129
1838	95	75	...	44	...	70	139
1839	94	77	...	46	...	69	144
1840	96	76	76	45	...	68	140
1841	97	75	76	43	...	69	135
1842	99	77	78	47	...	70	126
1843	85	72	78	49	...	66	113
1844	85	70	77	44	...	62	118
1845	92	73	81	49	...	65	115
1846	94	82	82	60	...	67	121
1847	98	88	82	71	...	69	141
1848	91	78	80	47	...	67	115
1849	90	75	79	41	...	66	105
1850	88	74	76	40	...	66	102
1851	87	75	76	47	...	67	100[1]
1852	88	75	76	55	...	69	102
1853	90	83	80	61	...	72	115
1854	108	92	83	73	...	77	122
1855	113	94	85	78	...	82	121
1856	113	98	86	76	...	91	121
1857	105	96	85	62	...	91	124
1858	101	88	83	59	...	81	113
1859	96	86	83	59	...	77	115
1860	100	88	85	63	...	80	120
1861	107	91	86	66	82	83	119
1862	110	90	86	66	82.5	86	120
1863	102	88	87	60	80	81	122
1864	97	89	87	56	78	78	122

H2 Cost-of-living/Consumer Prices Indices

1865–1914

	Belgium 1913 = 100	Denmark 1913 = 100	France[2] 1914 = 100	Germany 1913 = 100	Italy 1913 = 100	Netherlands 1913 = 100	Norway[3]	Sweden 1914 = 100	Switzerland 1914 = 100	U.K: 1851 = 100
1865	101	90	89	58	77	...	...	78	...	120
1866	106	93	91	63	77	...	...	80	...	121
1867	109	97	91	76	79	...	...	85	...	121
1868	105	96	91	76	82.5	...	...	88	...	120
1869	104	90	89	69	83	...	...	83	...	118
1870	101	<u>88</u>	91	70	84	...	...	80	...	117
1871	103	91	95	<u>76</u>9	87	...	...	82	...	120
				69					1st ½1914 = 100	
										113
1872	107	90	94	72	98	...	...	85	...	120
1873	115	100	94	80	104	...	...	92	...	122
1874	110	104	94	83	106.5	...	...	95	...	115
1875	106	100	92	76	91	...	...	94	...	111
1876	112	101	95	70	96.5	...	...	95	...	110
1877	112	102	95	77	100	...	...	94	...	110
1878	107	94	93	73	97	...	...	88	...	104
1879	104	88	93	72	95.5	...	...	83	...	101
1880	99	95	94	76	99	109	...	87	...	105
1881	99	97	93	77	93	109	...	89	...	103
1882	98	96	93	75	90	106	...	87	...	102
1883	99	91	95	75	87.5	103	...	86	...	102
1884	92	89	95	72	86	103	...	83	...	97
1885	89	86	93	70	88	94	...	79	...	91
1886	82	82	93	68	88	90	...	75	...	89
1887	87	82	92	68	87	90	...	72	...	88
1888	85	80	93	70	88.5	88	...	75	...	88
1889	87	83	92	73	90	94	...	78	...	89
1890	90	84	92	75	93	95	...	80	84	89
1891	90	92	93	77	93	97	...	83	85	89
1892	87	87	92	76	92	102	...	81	85	90
1893	84	82	91	75	90	91	...	78	84	89
1894	82	80	92	74	90	89	...	74	83	85
1895	80	78	91	73	89	86	...	75	83	83
1896	77	76	91	72	89	83	...	75	82	83
1897	78	76	89	74	89	84	...	77	83	85
1898	78	80	90	76	89	84	...	81	84	88
1899	79	82	90	76	88	84	...	84	83	86
1900	89	84	91	77	88	86	...	85	83	91
1901	91	87	91	78	88	91	85	83	83	90
1902	89	87	91	78	88	89	82	84	83	90
1903	89	84	90	78	90	89	82	85	84	91
1904	78	84	90	79	91	91	80	84	84	92
1905	80	86	90	82	91.5	91	80	86	85	92
1906	88	87	91	87	93	91	82	88	87	93
1907	90	92	92	88	98	91	85	92	91	95
1908	91	94	93	88	97	95	87	94	93	93
1909	90	91	93	90	94	94	87	93	94	94
1910	92	92	94	92	96.5	97	88	93	96	96
1911	98	91	98	95	99	97	92	92	99	97
1912	105	96	98	100	100	98	97	98	101	100
1913	100	100	98	100	100	100	100	98	100	102
1914	...	103	100	103	100	100	...	100	100	[100]

H2 Cost-of-living/Consumer Prices Indices

1929 = 100 or 1953 = 100

1914–1965

Year	Austria[6]	Belgium	Bulgaria	Czech.[11]	Denmark	Finland[13]	France	Germany		Greece[14]	Hungary[17]	S. Ireland[18]
1914	90	[11][1]	3	13	60	9	17	67		5	...	57
1915	142	...	4	...	71	9	20	84		6	...	...
1916	303	...	...	...	83	12	23	110		8	...	...
1917	605	...	...	...	96	22	27	164		8	...	...
1918	1,047	...	...	...	113	57	35	196		19	...	...
1919	2,243	...	41	...	134	83[13]	44	269		17	...	...
1920	4,604	52	62	...	159	80	61	661		18	...	...
1921	8,984	46	64	...	135	95	53	870		21	...	...
1922	237,568	43	87	...	115	93	51	9,766		33	...	106
1923	68[4]	49	83	[93][12]	120	93	57	10,324 billion		61	...	103
1924	77	57	94	93	127	95	65	83[4]		64	[99][16]	105
1925	87	59	100	97	123	99	69	91		74	93	108
1926	93	71	96	96	105	97	90	92		85	87	105
1927	95	90	93	100	101	98	94	96		93	95	98
1928	97	94	9.7	101	101	101	94	99		97	100	99
1929	100	100	100	100	100	100	100	100		100	100	100
1930	100	100	92	98	95	92	101	96		87	91	97
1931	95	91	80	94	90	85	97	88		87	86	90
1932	97	82	74	92	89	84	88	78		92	83	88
1933	95	81	68	91	92	81	85	77		99	77	86
1934	95	76	64	90	95	80	82	79		101	76	87
1935	95	75	60	93	99	81	75	80		102	78	90
1936	95	78	57	94	100	81	80	81		105	82	91
1937	95	84	58	95	104	85	101	81		112[14]	87	98
1938	[94][5]	87	60	99	105	88	115	82		113	88	99
1939	93	88[8]	62	109	108	89	122	82		112	86	99
1940	95	[98][9]	69	134	134	107	145	85		124	93	118
1941	96	...	83	156	154	126	170	87		[142][9]	111	131
1942	97	...	110	169	159	149	205	89		...	129	144
1943	98	...	139	167	160	168	254	90		...	155	163
1944	98	...	209	168	164	178	311	92		[445][15]	191	170
								West	*East*	2,140		
								1953 = 100	1960 = 100	1953 = 100		
1945	104	...	314	178	166	250	461	68	...	5	...	168
1946	132	[270][10]	353	323	165	398	703	75	...	37	358	166
1947	259	285	392	309		517	1,049	80	...	44	402	183
1948	422	326	...	305[11]	174	696	1,664	92	...	63	421	181
	1953 = 100	1953 = 100		1953 = 100	1953 = 100	1953 = 100	1953 = 100					
(1948)	43[6]	95		...	80	70	63				61	79
1949	56	92	...	...	82	71	71	99	...	72	56	80
1950	70	91	...	...	85	81	78	92	202	78	59	80
1951	89[6]	100	...	...	94	95	91	100	...	87	72	89
1952	101	100	...	...	99	99	102	102	...	92	100	98
1953	100	100	...	100	100	100	100	100	...	100	100	100
1954	103	101	...	97	100	98	100	100	...	116	94	102
1955	105	101	...	94	105	95	101	102	112	122	93	104
1956	108	104	...	92	111	106	104	110	126	92	105	
1957	112	107	...	90	115	120	109	107	109	130	95	114
1958	114[6]	108	...	90	116	131	125	109	104	132[14]	95	117
1959	115	110	...	88	119	133	133	110	101	136	94	116
1960	117	110	...	81	121	138	138	112	100	139	94	117
1961	122	111	...	81	123	140	142	114	100	141	94	121
1962	127	113	...	82	128	146	149	118	100	141	95	126
1963	130	115	...	82	135	153	156	121	100	145	94	127
1964	135	120	...	83	140	169	161	124	100	146	95	136
1965	142	125	...	84	147	178	166	128	100	151	99	143

H2 Cost-of-living/Consumer Prices Indices

1914–1965

	Italy	Neth'l	Norway	Poland[19]	Portugal[22]	Romania[24]	Russia/USSR	Spain[26]	Sweden	Switzer-land	U.K.	Yugo-slavia
1914	22	71	60	[81][16]	[4][23]	...	...	55	59	63	[61][16]	
1915	24	83	69	...	...			60	68	70	75	
1916	30	91	83	...	...			64	[82][27]	81	89	
1917	43	97	103	...	...			70	[98][28]	101	107	
1918	59	117	145	...	...			85	133	127	124	
1919	60	126	155	...	...			96	154	138	131	
1920	79	137	180	[9,084][20]	...	...	...	105	159	139	152	...
1921	94	120	167	20,902	...	31	...	104	143	124	138	...
1922	93	106	139	42[4]	...	40	...	100	115	102	112	...
1923	93	103	131	51	...	59	...	98	105	102	106	...
1924	96	103	144	103	...	70	...	102	103	105	107	...
1925	108	103	147	119	...	77		104	104	104	107	...
1926	116	100	124	145	...	84		103	102	101	105	...
1927	106	100	112	93	...	91		104	101	99	102	...
1928	98	100	105	100	...	93		97	101	100	101	99
1929	130	100	100	100	100	100	...	100	100	100	100	100
1930	97	94	97	92	95	99	...	103	97	98	96	92
1931	87	89	92	83	84	71	...	107	94	93	90	85
1932	85	83	90	75	82	59	...	103	92	86	88	77
1933	80	83	89	67	82	55	...	100	91	81	85	66
1934	76	83	89	63	84	53	...	102	91	80	86	61
1935	77	80	91	60	84	57	...	99[26]	92	80	87	60
1936	83	77	93	58	86	60	...	...	93	81	90	61
1937	91	80	100	62	89	65	...	...	96	85	94	65
1938	98	83	103	61	86	68	...	...	98	85	95	69
1939	100	80	105	[61][21]	81	73	...	1953 = 100	101	86	96	71
							1953 = 100	[27][12]				
1940	119	94	122	...	85	99	72	31	114	94	112	93
1941	138	106	143	...	96	142	...	40	129	108	121	126
1942	159	114	151	...	117	209	...	43	140	120	122	...
1943	267	117	155	...	132	282	...	43	141	126	121	...
1944	1,187	120	157	...	136	423	...	45	143	129	123	...
1945	2,338	140	160	4,687	147	2,506	...	48	143	130	124	...
1946	2,759	151	164	5,620	169	15,416	...	63	144	129	124	...
1947	4,471	160	165	7,487	174	197,464	[237][25]	74	152	135	124	...
1948	4,734	166	164	7,786[19]	164	...	197	79	154	139	134	...
	1953 = 100	1953 = 100	1953 = 100	1953 = 100	1953 = 100				1953 = 100	1953 = 100	1953 = 100	
	86	76	74	44	99				77	96	77	
1949	87	82	74	46	100		168[5]	83	78	95	79	
												1953 = 100
1950	86	88	78	56	98		135[5]	92	79	94	81	
1951	94	100	90	61	99		123[5]	100	92	98	89	124
1952	98	100	98	70	99		117[7]	98	99	101	97	95
1953	100	100	100	100	100		106	100	100	100	100	100
1954	103	104	104	94	101		100	101	101	101	102	98
1955	106	105	105	92	104		100	105	104	102	106	110
1956	111	108	109	91	109		100	111	109	103	110	119
1957	113	114	112	97	109		100	123	114	105	114	122
1958	118	117	118	100	110		102	140	118	107	117	128
1959	118	117	120	101	112		101	150	120	106	118	131
1960	121	121	121	103	114		101	152	125	108	119	143
1961	125	122	124	104	114		100	156	127	110	123	155
1962	131	126	130	106	114		101	165	133	115	128	171
1963	141	132	134	107	117		102	179	137[28]	119	131	180
1964	149	139	141	108	121		102	192	141	122	135	201
1965	156	146	147	109	125		101	217	149	127	141	271

H2 Cost-of-living/Consumer Prices Indices

1965–2000

	Austria	Belgium	Czecho-slavakia	Denmark	Finland	France	East Germany	West Germany	Greece	Hungary	S. Ireland[18]
1965	85	84	92	73	66	81	101	88	89	97	77
1966	87	88	92	78	71	84	101	92	93	97	79
1967	90	90	93	84	77	86	101	92	95	98	82
1968	93	92	95	91	83	89	101	94	95	98	86
1969	96	96	98	94	86	95	101	97	97	99	92
1970	100	100	100	100	100	100	100	100	100	100	100
1971	105	104	100	106	106	106	100	105	103	102	109
1972	111	110	99	113	114	112	100	111	107	105	118
1973	120	118	100	123	127	120	98	119	124	109	132
1974	131	133	100	142	150	137	99	127	157	111	155
1975	142	152	100	156	176	153	99	135	178	115	159[18]
1976	153	164	101	170	201	168	99	140	202	121	184
1977	161	176	102	189	227	183	99	146	227	125	209
1978	167	184	102	208	244	200	99	150	255	131	227
1979	173	192	104	228	262	221	99	156	304	143	257
1980	184	205	106	256	292	251	99	164	379	156	306
1981	196	220	106	286	328	285	100	175	472	163	367
1982	207	239	116	314	358	319	100	184	571	174	430
1983	214	254	117	336	389	349	100	190	686	187	473
1984	226	273	118	357	416	375	100	195	813	202	510
1985	233	286	121	374	440	397	99	199	970	216	538
1986	230	290	122	388	456	408	99	198	1,193	228	555
1987	233	294	122	403	473	421	99	199	1,389	247	573
1988	238	298	122	422	496	432	99	201	1,577	286	585
1989	245	308	124	443	528	447	100	206	1,660	334	609
1990	252	318	136	453	560	462		211	1,743	431	630
1991	261	329	215	465	584	477		219	1,816	581	651
1992	272	337	238	476	598	487		227	1,844	715	669
1993	281	345	…	481	610	500		237	1,862	876	681

			Czech Republic				Germany				

1995 = 100.0

	Austria	Belgium	Czech Republic	Denmark	Finland	France		Germany	Greece	Hungary	S. Ireland[18]
1994	97.8	98.6	91.6	97.9	99.0	98.3		98.3	91.8	77.9	97.5
1995	100.0	100.0	100.0	100.0	100.0	100.0		100.0	100.0	100.0	100.0
1996	101.8	102.1	108.8	102.1	100.6	102.0		101.4	108.2	123.5	101.7
1997	103.2	103.7	118.1	104.4	101.8	103.2		103.3	114.2	146.1	103.2
1998	104.1	104.7	103.7	106.3	103.2	103.9		104.3	119.6	166.7	105.7
1999	104.7	105.9	133.5	108.9	104.4	104.5		104.9	122.8	183.4	107.4
2000	107.2	108.3	138.7	112.1	108.0	106.2		107.0	126.6	201.4	113.4

	Italy	Netherlands	Norway	Poland	Portugal[22]	Spain	Sweden	Switzerland	U.K.	Yugo-slavia
1965	88	78	79	93	73	78	81	84	80	61
1966	90	83	81	95	77	83	86	88	83	75
1967	92	85	85	96	82	88	89	92	85	80
1968	93	89	88	97	86	92	91	94	89	84
1969	95	96	91	99	94	95	93	97	94	90
1970	100	100	100	100	100	100	100	100	100	100
1971	105	107	106	100	112	108	108	107	109	116
1972	111	116	114	100	124	117	114	114	117	135
1973	123	125	122	103	136	131	122	124	128	161
1974	146	137	134	109	175	151	134	136	148	195
1975	171	151	149	111	202	177	147	145	184	243
1976	199	165	163	115	244[22]	208	162	147	215	271
1977	233	175	178	121	311	259	181	149	249	312
1978	262	183	192	131	380	310	199	151	270	356
1979	300	190	202	140	471	359	213	156	306	429
1980	364	228	224	152	550	414	242	162	361	559
1981	429	243	254	180	659	474	271	173	404	786
1982	499	257	283	377	807	543	294	183	438	1,036
1983	573	264	307	460	1,013	609	321	188	458	1,459
1984	635	272	326	527	1,309	672	346	194	481	2,236

(continued overleaf)

H2 Cost-of-living/Consumer Prices Indices (contd.)

	Italy	Netherlands	Norway	Poland	Portugal[22]	Spain	Sweden	Switzerland	U.K.	Yugo-slavia
1985	693	278	344	602	1,562	731	372	200	511	3,879
1986	734	279	369	709	1,745	795	388	202	528	7,335
1987	768	278	401	875	1,909	837	404	205	540	16,158
1988	807	280	428	1,401	2,095	877	428	209	566	47,602
1989	858	284	446	4,918	2,359	934	454	217	608	646,629
1990	913	291	466	33,728	2,673	996	503	228	669	4,401,123
1991	971	303	482	57,363	2,975	1,057	549	242	708	…
1992	1,018	312	492	82,138	…	1,118	561	251	732	…
1993	1,065	319	504	111,132	…	1,168	587	259	747	…
					1995 = 100.0					
1994	95.0	98.1	97.6	78.1	96.0	95.5	98.0	98.2	96.7	…
1995	100.0	100.0	100.0	100.0	100.0	100.0	100.0	100.0	100.0	…
1996	104.0	102.0	101.3	119.8	103.1	103.6	101.0	100.8	102.4	…
1997	106.1	104.2	103.9	137.9	105.3	105.6	101.0	101.3	105.7	…
1998	108.2	106.3	106.2	154.1	108.3	107.5	101.0	101.4	109.3	…
1999	110.0	108.6	108.7	165.3	110.8	110.0	110.0	102.2	111.0	…
2000	112.8	111.4	112.0	182.1	114.0	113.8	102.0	103.8	114.2	…

NOTES

1. SOURCES:- The statistics are mainly based on the official publications noted on p. xv and the League of Nations and United Nations, *Statistical Yearbooks.* In addition the following have been used:-Belgium to 1913—index of retail prices in F. Michelotte, "L'évolution des prix de détail en Belgique de 1830 á 1913", *Bulletin de l'Institute de Recherche Economique* (Louvain, 1937); France to 1914 (1st line)—Jeanne Singer-Kérel, *Le Coût de la Vie á Paris de 1840 a 1954* (Paris, 1961); Germany to 1871—J. Kuczynski, *Die Geschichte der Lage der Arbeiter unter dem Kapitalismus* (Berlin, 1961); Germany 1871 (2nd line) to 1914—Ashok V. Desai, *Real Wages in Germany 1871–1913* (Oxford, 1968); Germany 1914 to 1924—G. Bry, *Wages in Germany, 1871–1945* Princeton, 1960); Denmark to 1970—based on H.G. Johansen; *Danmarks Historie*, vol. 9 (Copenhagen, 1985); Sweden to 1914—G. Myrdal, *The Cost of Living in Sweden, 1830–1930* (London, 1933); U.K. to 1914 (1st line)—B.R. Mitchell, *British Historical Statistics* (Cambridge, 1988), quoting Lindert & Williamson and Bowley.
2. Where a cost-of-living index is not available, an index of retail (or consumer) prices has been given instead.
3. Various indices have been crudely spliced together in the case of certain countries to give a rough indicator of the long-term movement of the cost-of-living. The differences in the construction of these indices should be borne in mind if they are used in further calculations.

FOOTNOTES

[1] The "best guess" cost-of-living index with Southern Urban weight to 1851.
[2] Cost-of-living in Paris to 1914 (1st line).
[3] Cost of living in Oslo to 1913.
[4] Based on prices in terms of gold following currency stabilisation.
[5] March.
[6] Purchasing power of money, based on retail prices, for 1939–48; retail prices for 1949–51 and cost-of-living in Vienna only for 1952–58.
[7] April.
[8] This is a weighted average of the old index to April and the new one from May.
[9] First four months.
[10] Last five months.
[11] Cost-of-living in Prague to 1948.
[12] Second half-year.
[13] July only to 1919.
[14] Cost-of-living in Athens for 1938–1958.
[15] November.
[16] July.
[17] Cost-of-living in Budapest.
[18] June, July or August to 1974, November subsequently.
[19] Cost-of-living in Warsaw to 1948 (1st line).
[20] December.
[21] First seven months.
[22] Cost-of-living in Lisbon to 1976.
[23] June.
[24] Cost-of-living in Bucharest.
[25] Fourth quarter.
[26] Retail prices in Madrid to 1935.
[27] Excluding December.
[28] Excluding September.
[29] Subsequently the consumers' price index.

I EDUCATION

1.   Children and Teachers in Schools   page 870
2.   Number of Students in Universities   page 894

Of all the subjects on which statistical material exists, none (not even crime) shows less uniformity, both over time and between countries, than education. There is no universal definition of what constitutes a primary school or a general secondary school. Even the definition of a university has shown some flexibility, especially in recent years. Moreover, there has been a minimum of two major reorganisations of school systems in every country of Europe in the twentieth century; there were others earlier; and minor changes have been very frequent. Furthermore, the statistics of pupils and teachers have not always been collected in a consistent manner, even within the same school system. The date in the school-year to which they relate has been altered on various occasions. The exact meaning of the statistics has been changed, sometimes referring to all pupils on the registers, sometimes to those in regular attendance, sometimes to those present on a particular day, and sometimes to those present when the inspector visited. Nevertheless, in spite of all the inconsistencies and other obstacles in the way of precise comparisons, when used with care these statistics do provide useful intertemporal comparative material, even if of a rough nature. Comparisons between countries may sometimes be made on the basis of the data provided here but often they require more detailed information on the precise composition of the statistics than can be given in the space available.

I1　CHILDREN AND TEACHERS IN SCHOOLS (in thousands, except as otherwise indicated)

Key:- P = Pupils; T = Teachers; * = actual numbers, not thousands

1830–1869

	Austria[1]				Belgium			France		
	Primary		Secondary		Primary		Secondary	Primary		Secondary
	P	T	P	T	P	T	P	T*	P	P
1830	...	...	...	...	293	...	...	...	...	42.2
1831	...	...	...	...	355					...
1832	...	...	...	...	372					...
1833	...	...	...	...	399					...
1834	...	...	...	...	412					...
1835	...	...	...	...	408					...
1836	...	...	...	...	421					...
1837	...	...	...	...	430₂					...
1838	...	...	...	...	440					...
1839	...	...	...	...	...					...
1840	...	...	...	...	453					41.9
1841	...	...	20.5	0.6	...					...
1842	1,365	27.3	20.4	0.6	...					...
1843	1,359	27.8	20.6	0.6	...					...
1844	1,386	28.2	...	...	...					...
1845	...	...	21.0	0.7	426					...
1846	1,426	28.4	21.5	0.7	429					...
1847	1,434	28.7	...	...	436	...	...	...	...	...
1848	...	...	20.6	0.7	451	8.0	4.4	330	...	...
1849	1,435	28.7	23.8	1.0	...	...	...	...	...	...
1850	1,426	28.4	24.3	1.3	...	...	7.0₃	...₃	3,322	47.9
1851	1,458	27.4	23.3	1.1	487	8.9	...	...	...	45.6
1852	1,484	26.4	23.5	1.4	492	...	9.4	733	...	45.0
1853	1,518	27.6	22.9	1.4	498	...	9.4	...	...	45.4
1854	1,513	25.8	25.1	1.5	492	8.8	9.5	919	...	46.4
1855	1,502	26.3	26.2	1.5	...	...	10.2	...	...	48.0
1856	1,530	26.3	28.3	1.6	...		10.6			50.6
1857	1,569	26.5	30.7	1.6	499₄ / 511	9.1	11.1			52.9
1858	1,610	26.6	33.0	1.7	...	...	11.7	...	...	53.5
1859	1,644	27.2	34.4	1.7	...	...	11.9	...	...	54.1
1860	1,656	27.6	36.7	1.8	516	9.2	12.0	972	...	55.9
1861	1,651	27.6	37.6	1.9	...		14.0			58.3
1862	1,637	27.3	38.4	2.0	...	...	14.5	...	...	61.5
1863	1,650	27.2	41.5	2.2	545	9.6	14.5₃	...₃	...	63.0
1864	1,450	33.5	43.0	2.3	...	...	15.1	...	...	64.8
1865	1,669	33.8	43.6	2.3	...	...	16.1	1,142	4,437	65.7
1866	1,689	34.4	42.9	2.4	564	10.4	15.8	...	...	67.4
1867	1,682	34.6	42.7	2.4	...	...	15.9	...	...	68.6
1868	1,691	35.0	43.4	2.6	...	...	16.5	...	...	71.3
1869	...	...	43.7	2.7	593	9.5	17.1	...	...	...

I1 Children and teachers in schools (in thousands, except as otherwise indicated)

	Hungary[5]				Croatia-Slavonia		Ireland		Italy			Netherlands			
	Primary		Secondary		Primary		Primary		Primary[8]		Secondary	Primary		Secondary	
	P	T	P	T	P	T	P[7]	T	P	T	P	P	T	P	T*
1830	...	...	...	...	...	...	...	...	...	...	...	...	...	...	...
1831	...	...	...	...	...	...	...	...	...	...	...	...	...	...	...
1832	...	...	...	...	...	...	...	...	...	...	...	...	...	...	...
1833	...	...	...	...	...	...	...	...	...	...	...	...	...	...	...
1834	...	...	...	...	...	...	...	...	...	...	...	...	...	...	...
1835	...	...	...	...	...	...	...	...	...	...	...	...	...	...	...
1836	...	...	...	...	...	...	...	...	...	...	...	...	...	...	...
1837	...	...	...	...	...	...	...	...	...	...	...	...	...	...	...
1838	...	...	...	...	...	...	...	...	...	...	...	...	...	...	...
1839	...	...	...	...	...	...	...	...	...	...	...	...	...	1.4	...
1840	...	...	...	...	...	...	...	...	...	...	...	...	...	1.3	...
1841	...	...	26.6	0.8	...	...	...	...	...	...	...	...	...	1.3	...
1842	...	...	27.1	0.8	...	...	...	...	...	...	...	...	...	1.4	...
1843	...	...	...	...	...	...	...	...	...	...	...	...	...	1.5	...
1844	...	...	...	...	...	...	...	...	...	...	...	...	...	1.5	...
1845	...	...	...	...	...	...	...	...	...	...	...	...	...	1.5	...
1846	...	...	...	...	...	...	...	...	...	...	...	...	...	1.5	...
1847	...	...	...	...	...	...	...	...	...	...	...	...	...	1.5	...
1848	...	...	...	...	...	...	...	...	...	...	...	...	...	1.8	...
1849	...	...	...	...	...	...	...	...	...	...	...	...	6.2	1.8	244
1850	...	...	18.3	1.2	...	...	...	...	...	...	...	...	6.4	1.8	252
1851	...	...	19.5	1.4	...	...	...	4.6	...	...	...	397	6.5	1.8	251
1852	...	...	20.6	1.5	...	...	280	...	...	...	...	398	6.9	1.8	245
1853	...	...	20.1	1.5	...	...	271	4.9	...	...	...	392	7.0	1.8	255
1854	[900][6]	[20.6][6]	22.9	1.6	...	...	267	5.1	...	...	...	326	7.2	1.8	252
1855	...	...	24.1	1.7	...	...	252	5.0	...	...	...	388	7.3	1.8	252
1856	...	...	25.6	1.8	...	...	258	5.4	...	...	...	394	7.4	1.9	258
1857	...	...	27.3	1.8	...	...	268	5.5	...	...	...	406	7.4	1.8	260
1858	...	...	28.1	1.9	...	...	266	5.6	...	...	...	399	8.0	1.8	254
1859	[935][6]	[20.8][6]	...	...	...	...	269	5.6	...	...	...	405	7.9	1.8	255
1860	...	...	...	...	...	...	263	6.0	...	...	...	401	8.4	1.8	253
1861	...	...	...	...	...	...	285	6.4	1,009	28.2	15.8	391	9.0	1.8	254
1862	...	...	32.1	1.7	...	...	285	7.0	1,109	31.4	18.2	441	9.6	1.3	261
1863	...	...	...	...	...	...	297	7.2	1,175	34.3	17.3	453	10.2	1.8	254
1864	...	...	36.0	1.9	...	...	315	7.5	1,194	33.3	18.6	450	10.4	1.8	244
1865	985	17.8	37.0	2.0	99	1.6	321	7.8	1,214	32.4	19.6	432	10.2	1.3	243
1866	...	...	...	...	...	...	316	7.8	1,409	35.2	23.3	437	10.3	1.3	245
1867	...	...	...	...	...	...	322	8.0	1,484	38.0	22.9	434	10.4	1.3	243
1868	...	...	38.2	1.7	...	...	355	8.3	1,529	39.2	23.0	437	10.4	1.3	236
1869	...	...	38.1	1.7	...	...	359	8.6	1,573	40.3	22.8	451	10.7	1.3	231

I1 Children and teachers in schools (in thousands, except as otherwise indicated)

| | Norway | | Portugal | | Spain | | Sweden | U.K.:E. & W. | | U.K.:Scotland | |
| | Primary[16] | | Primary | | Primary | Secondary | Primary | Primary | | Primary | |
	P	T*	P	T*	P	P	P	P	T	P	T
1830	...	...	...	...	...	...	...	...	...	...	...
1831	...	...	...	...	...	...	...	...	...	...	...
1832	...	...	...	...	...	...	...	...	...	...	...
1833	...	...	...	...	...	...	...	...	...	...	...
1834	...	...	...	...	...	...	...	...	...	...	...
1835	...	...	...	...	...	...	...	...	...	...	...
1836	...	...	...	...	...	...	...	...	...	...	...
1837	178	2,142	...	...	...	...	...	...	...	...	...
1838	...	...	...	...	...	...	...	...	...	...	...
1839	...	...	...	...	...	...	...	...	...	...	...
1840	180	2,236	...	...	...	...	...	...	...	...	...
1841	...	...	...	...	...	...	...	...	...	...	...
1842	...	...	...	...	...	...	...	...	...	...	...
1843	...	...	...	...	...	...	...	...	...	...	...
1844	...	...	...	...	...	...	...	...	...	...	...
1845	...	...	...	...	...	...	...	...	...	...	...
1846	...	...	...	...	...	...	...	...	...	...	...
1847	...	...	...	...	...	...	...	...	...	...	...
1848	...	...	37	...	...	...	...	...	...	...	...
1849	...	...	42	1,169	...	...	...	...	...	28	...
1850	...	...	...	...	...	...	...	250	...	32	...
1851	...	...	...	...	...	...	...	323	...	64	...
1852	...	...	...	...	...	...	...	...	2.0	...	...
1853	196	2,575	...	...	...	...	...	394	2.4	68	...
1854	...	...	...	...	...	...	...	447	3.0	91	...
1855	...	...	...	...	1,005	...	...	480	3.7	92	...
1856	...	...	...	...	...	...	...	531	4.4	95	...
1857	...	...	...	...	...	17.6	...	636	5.1	125	...
1858	...	...	...	...	...	19.9	...	675	6.0	127	...
1859	...	...	...	...	1,047	20.9	...	751	6.7	133	...
1860	...	...	...	...	1,252	21.5	...	774	7.6	146	...
1861	...	...	...	...	...	23.2	...	799[9]	8.0	151	...
1862	...	...	...	...	...	24.6	...	826	8.8	162	...
1863	...	...	...	...	...	27.1	...	829[10] / 797	9.7[11] / 9.1	148	...
1864	...	...	...	...	...	28.8	...	848	10.3	156	1.9
1865	...	...	...	...	...	26.4	462	863	10.9	162	2.0
1866	...	...	...	...	...	27.0	...	912	11.7	169	2.2
1867	236	3,533	...	...	1,425	28.7	...	979	12.4	182	2.3
1868	...	...	...	...	...	...	521	1,063	13.0	179	2.2
1869	...	...	...	...	...	...	...	1,152	13.7	198	2.5

I1 Children and teachers in schools (in thousands, except as otherwise indicated)

	Austria[1]				Belgium				Bulgaria			
	Primary		Secondary		Primary		Secondary		Primary		Secondary	
	P	T	P	T	P	T	P	T*	P	T	P	T*
1870	1,821	35.3	46.3	2.9	...	...	17.8	1,218	...	...	...	...
1871	...	...	49.8	3.3	...	...	17.7	...	...	...	...	...
1872	...	...	52.0	3.5	619	9.8	18.3	...	...	...	...	...
1873	...	...	54.1	3.8	...	...	19.3	...	...	...	...	...
1874	2,135	31.2	55.7	3.8	...	...	20.1	...	...	...	...	...
1875	...	...	57.6	4.0	669	10.8	21.0	1,319	...	...	...	...
1876	...	...	59.7	4.2	...	...	20.2	...	...	...	...	...
1877	...	...	62.0	4.2	...	...	20.6	...	...	...	...	...
1878	...	...	64.1	4.4	688[14]	11.8[14]	20.7	...	...	...	...	...
					598	9.4						
1879	2,378	52.2[12]	65.9	4.4	...	...	22.8	...	...	...	...	...
		48.3										
1880	2,438	48.4	66.3	4.6	...	...	26.6	...	...	...	...	...
1881	2,591	51.2	65.9	4.6	340	8.3	25.7	...	...	...	...	...
1882	2,642	52.3	67.1	4.7	...	8.6	28.3	...	...	...	...	...
1883	2,696	53.0	68.4	4.8	346	8.7	28.2	...	...	...	...	...
1884	2,781	54.4	69.6	4.8	326	...	28.5	...	...	...	...	...
1885	2,862	55.8	71.3	4.9	589[14]	...	29.3	...	...	...	...	...
1886	2,856	57.2	70.6	4.9	600	...	28.9	...	...	...	...	...
1887	2,899	58.8	70.2	4.8	604	...	28.9	...	...	...	...	...
1888	2,939	60.1	70.5	4.8	601	...	28.8	...	...	...	...	...
1889	3,078	61.4[12]	71.3	4.9	615	...	28.6	...	...	...	...	...
1890	3,157	63.2	72.1	4.9	616	...	28.4	...	[197][16]	[4.3][16]	...	...
1891	3,220	65.3	73.4	5.0	627	...	28.7	...	...	...	...	...
1892	3,276	67.4	75.7	5.2	641	...	28.8	...	...	...	...	...
1893	3,313	68.0	77.6	5.2	652	...	28.9	...	...	...	...	...
1894	3,379	69.8	79.8	5.3	695	...	29.4	...	...	...	...	...
1895	3,430	71.6	82.3	5.5	720	...	29.9	...	341	8.3	42	1,357
1896	3,424	72.6	84.4	5.5	752	...	30.0	...	340	7.8	44	1,428
1897	3,484	74.8	87.0	5.8	764	...	30.1	...	343	8.0	43	1,502
1898	3,542	76.6	91.0	5.9	775	...	30.3	...	340	8.0	41	1,477
1899	3,619	78.0	95.9	6.2	786	...	30.7	...	329	7.9	35	1,596
1900	3,693	79.9	100	6.4	794	...	31.3	...	318	7.8	34	1,501
1901	3,742	81.5	106	6.8	810	...	30.1	...	312	7.6	30	1,384
1902	3,822	83.1	111	7.1	827	...	32.5	...	341	7.8	29	1,408
1903	3,908	85.1	116	7.4	843	...	32.4	...	359	8.1	31	1,535
1904	4,014	87.0	120	7.8	859	...	33.1	...	378	8.4	33	1,641
1905	4,207	94.8[12]	124	8.1	871	...	33.2	...	400	8.8	36	1,613
		100										
1906	4,284	102	127	8.6	884	...	32.7	...	416	9.0	39	1,691
1907	4,378	103	129	8.9	897	...	34.2	...	430	9.4	46	1,976
1908	4,454	105	134	9.2	915	...	35.0	...	436	9.9	53	2,111
1909	4,520	108	141	9.8	923	...	35.4	...	445	10.3	62	2,513
1910	4,534	110	157	11.7	929	...	35.5	...	454	10.4	71	2,917
1911	4,616	113	163	12.5	935	...	37.1	...	475	10.7	80	3,158
1912	4,634	115	165	12.8	935	...	38.2	...	241	6.3	64	2,147
1913	4,561	108	[125][13]	[10.3][13]	939	...	39.1	...	504	10.8	87	3,353
1914	4,123	100	111	9.5	[891][15]	...	25.8	...	554	11.5	92	3,710
1915	...	...	...	...	...	...	33.7	...	453	8.8	94	2,806
1916	...	...	...	...	...	...	37.8	...	534	9.6	98	2,966
1917	913	22.7	40.1	3.1	...	...	37.8	...	555	9.6	117	3,266
1918	903	26.9	40.2	3.2	...	...	36.1	...	539	11.8	134	4,249
1919	909	32.6	40.3	3.2	961	...	47.2	...	572	12.9	130	4,659

I1   Children and Teachers in Schools (in thousands, except as otherwise indicated)

	Denmark			Finland				France		
	Primary	Secondary	All Schools	Primary		Secondary		Primary		Secondary
	P	P	T	P	T*	P	T*	P	T	P
1870	...	...	...	...	...	...	...	...[20]	...	...[20]
1871	...	...	...	...	...	...	...	...	...	64.7
1872	...	...	...	...	...	...	...	...	...	69.5
1873	...	...	...	...	...	...	...	...	...	71.6
1874	...	...	...	...	...	...	...	...	...	72.3
1875	...	...	...	18	474	...	...	4,610	...	73.9
1876	...	...	...	...	...	...	...	...	...	79.2
1877	...	...	...	...	...	...	...	4,717	...	79.1
1878	...	...	...	...	...	...	...	4,870	...	80.2
1879	...	...	...	...	...	...	...	4,950	120	83.2
1880	...	...	...	29	787	...	...	5,049	123	86.8
1881	...	...	...	29	858	8.0	858	5,341	125	89.5
1882	...	...	...	33	918	8.3	911	5,442	130	90.9
1883	...	...	...	36	993	8.9	1,005	5,469	133	93.4
1884	...	...	...	38	1,069	8.9	1,020	5,531	134	92.9
1885	...	...	...	39	1,131	9.0	1,085	5,517	135	93.0
1886	...	...	...	43	1,213	9.3	1,133	5,521	137	94.6
1887	...	...	...	45	1,264	9.6	1,163	5,617	141	95.7
1888	...	...	...	47	1,332	9.7	1,192	5,623	143	93.0
1889	...	...	...	50	1,385	9.7	1,191	5,602	143[21]	91.5
1890	...	...	... 53	55[10]	1,492	10.2	1,216	5,594	146	90.8
1891	...	...	...	57	1,628	10.6	1,232	5,556	147	91.9
1892	...	...	...	61	1,736	10.7	1,231	5,554	148	94.0
1893	335	5.9	...	67	1,850	10.9	1,216	5,548	149	95.9
1894	...	...	...	74	1,967	11.7	1,278	5,540	151	95.9
1895	...	...	...	81	2,120	12.4	1,356	5,534	152	96.5
1896	...	...	...	87	2,297	12.9[19]	1,416	5,532	152	96.2
1897	357	6.8	...	94	2,503	11.5	1,418	5,535	154	96.2
1898	...	...	...	99	2,698	12.4	1,453	5,539	155	95.8
1899	...	...	...	103	2,889	13.5	1,548	5,530	157	96.8
1900	...	...	...	110	3,076	14.4	1,519	5,526	158	98.7
1901	...	...	...	117	3,263	15.5	1,609	5,550	159	102
1902	376	7.0	...	116	3,463	16.5	1,699	5,553	156	107
1903	...	...	...	124	3,596	17.1	1,767	5,555	153	112
1904	385	8.1	...	126	3,708	17.6	1,776	5,568	152	117
1905	390[17] 380	8.3[17] 17.9	10.9	132	3,987	18.8[19]	1,832	5,567	152	120
1906	389	20.2	10.9	141	4,102	19.7	1,858	5,585	152	123
1907	394	21.1	11.2	147	4,377	21.4	1,918	5,600	153	123
1908	397	23.1	11.3	158	4,679	22.3[19]	2,042[19]	5,630	155	124
1909	402	25.1	11.5	163	5,068	23.5	1,890	5,639	156	126
1910	406	25.6	11.5[18]	177	5,512	24.4	1,919	5,655	157	126
1911	409	26.5	14.1	183	5,738	24.8	1,953	5,682	158	128
1912	413	26.7	14.2	188	5,890	25.2	2,036	5,669	160	131
1913	418	28.7	14.3	194	6,079	25.3	2,031	...[22]	...[22]	133[22]
1914	422	28.8	14.4	197	6,199	25.2	2,131	...	...	97
1915	427	30.0	14.7	200	6,322	25.5	2,153	...	...	109
1916	431	30.8	14.7	204	6,413	26.1	2,134	...	...	118
1917	...	...	...	215	6,554	26.7	2,107	4,072	99	124
1918	435	34.5	15.1	212	7,058	27.2	2,158	3,893	99	121[22]
1919	437	36.1	15.3	248	7,556	30.0	2,340	3,836	102	140

I1 Children and Teachers in Schools (in thousands, except as otherwise indicated)

1870–1919

	Germany				Greece		Hungary[5]			
	Primary[23]		Secondary		Primary		Primary		Secondary[25]	
	P	T	P	T	P	T*	P	T	P	T
1870	...	...	...	...	...	...	1,156	18.5	33.0	2.0
1871	...	...	...	...	...	...	...	...	34.0	2.0
1872	...	...	...	...	...	...	...	...	35.6	2.3
1873	...	...	...	...	...	...	...	...	36.3[6]	2.4[6]
1874	...	...	...	...	...	...	...	...	36.5[6]	2.5[6]
1875	...	...	...	...	...	...	1,493	19.9	36.9[6]	2.7[6]
1876	...	...	...	...	...	...	1,507	20.1	37.9[6]	2.6[6]
1877	...	...	...	...	...	...	1,560	20.7	36.1	2.4
1878	...	...	...	...	...	...	1,625	21.2	37.1	2.4
1879	...	...	...	...	...	...	1,645	21.4	37.8	2.4
1880	...	...	...	...	...	...	1,620	21.7	38.6	2.5
1881	...	...	...	...	...	...	1,656	22.0	38.4	2.4
1882	...	...	...	...	...	...	1,698	22.4	38.4	2.5
1883	...	...	...	...	...	...	1,757	22.7	38.0	2.5
1884	...	...	...	...	...	...	1,801	23.1	37.5	2.7
1885	...	...	...	...	...	...	1,831	23.4	37.9	2.7
1886	...	...	...	...	...	...	1,868	24.0	38.7	2.9
1887	...	...	...	...	...	...	1,951	24.1	39.3	2.9
1888	...	...	...	...	...	...	2,016	24.4	40.0	2.9
1889	...	...	...	...	...	...	2,058	24.6	40.7	2.9
1890	...	...	...	...	...	...	2,118[24]	...	42.1	...
							2,030			
1891	...	...	...	...	...	...	2,075	25.5	43.9	...
1892	...	...	...	...	...	...	2,134	25.8	45.9	3.2
1893	...	...	...	...	...	...	2,174	26.1	48.3	3.3
1894	...	...	...	...	...	...	2,239	26.4	49.7	3.3
1895	...	...	...	...	...	...	2,224	26.7	51.7	3.4
1896	...	...	...	...	...	...	2,239	27.2	53.2	3.5
1897	...	...	...	...	...	...	2,232	27.7	54.7	3.5
1898	...	...	...	...	...	...	2,250	28.0	56.4	3.6
1899	...	...	...	...	...	...	2,278	28.6	58.0[25]	3.7[25]
									62.9	4.1
1900	8,966	147	...	...	...	...	2,315	29.1	64.2	4.2
1901	...	...	...	...	190	4,055	2,369	29.4	65.5	4.3
1902	...	...	...	...	211	4,346	2,399	30.1	66.6	4.4
1903	...	...	...	...	...	...	2,337[26]	31.4[26]	67.3	4.5
							2,281	29.2		
1904	...	...	...	...	...	...	2,294	29.9	67.7	4.6
1905	9,779	167	...	...	...	...	2,345	30.3	69.6	4.7
1906	...	...	...	...	...	...	2,376	30.8	71.1	4.6
1907	...	...	...	...	...	...	2,415	31.4	71.9	4.8
1908	...	...	...	...	241	4,346	2,441	31.9	73.7	4.9
1909	...	...	...	...	...	...	2,457	32.4	75.4	5.0
1910	10,310	187	1,016	47.4	260	4,641	2,471	33.0	77.6	5.2
1911	...	...	...	...	...	...	2,488	33.9	79.5	5.1
1912	...	...	...	...	...	...	...	...	...	...
1913	...	...	...	...	...	...	...	35.3	84.3	4.8
1914	...	...	...	...	...	...	...	...	...	...
1915	...	...	...	...	...	...	2,012	29.0	86.5	3.3
1916	...	...	...	...	...	...	2,113	29.6	89.8	3.3
1917	...	...	...	...	...	...	2,037[5,27]	28.9[5,27]	92.1[5,27]	3.7[5,27]
1918	...	...	...	...	...	...	776	14.4	56.5	2.5
1919	...	...	...	...	...	...	813	16.3	56.5	2.7

I1 Children and Teachers in Schools (in thousands, except as otherwise indicated)

	Croatia-Slavonia				Ireland		Italy				Netherlands			
	Primary		Secondary		Primary		Primary[8]		Secondary		Primary		Secondary	
	P	T	P	T	P[7]	T	P	T	P[29]	T	P	T	P	T*
1870	...	...	...	...	359	8.8	1,605	41.0	23.2	...	467	11.0	1.4[30]	230[30]
													4.8	747
1871	...	...	...	...	364	9.0	1,723	43.4	23.8	...	474	10.9	5.1	793
1872	...	...	...	...	356	9.4	1,798	44.4	24.6	...	484	11.1	5.6	[841][31]
1873	...	...	...	...	373	9.5	1,842	45.6	25.6	...	500	11.5	5.4	[865][31]
1874	...	...	...	...	395	9.9	1,896	46.8	27.3	...	499	11.7	5.4	872
1875	...	...	...	...	390	10.1	1,932	47.1	28.5	...	510	12.0	5.8	913
1876	...	...	...	...	417	10.3	1,968	47.3	29.7	...	515	12.6	6.1	944
1877	...	...	...	...	418	10.5	2,003	47.6	31.6	...	523	12.3	6.4	964
1878	...	...	...	...	437	10.7	2,058	48.5	33.0	...	523	12.7	6.6	996
1879	...	...	...	...	435	10.8	2,031	48.4	33.2	...	531	13.3	6.9	1,073
1880	...	...	...	...	469	10.7	2,003	48.3	32.5	...	541	14.2	7.4	1,131
1881	...	...	...	...	454	10.6	1,976	48.2	35.4	...	545	15.1	7.8	1,189
1882	...	...	...	...	469	10.5	2,037	51.8	36.2	...	562	15.9	8.1	1,254
1883	...	...	...	...	468	10.6	2,153	54.1	38.1	...	563	16.3	8.5	1,300
1884	...	...	...	...	493	10.7	2,206	54.8	38.8	...	579	17.2	8.7	1,322
1885	...	...	...	...	502	11.0	2,253	55.3	40.5	...	594	17.3	8.9	1,311
1886	...	...	...	...	490	11.0	2,279	55.6	42.9	...	607	17.3	8.9	1,278
1887	150	...	3.5	...	515	11.2	2,308	56.9	46.8	...	617	17.6	9.0	1,291
1888	153	...	3.6	...	494	11.1	2,326	57.1	48.5	...	627	17.5	9.4	1,310
1889	160	...	3.6	...	508	11.2	2,374	58.1	57.6	...	636	17.5	9.6	1,314
1890	169	...	3.8	...	489	11.1	2,419	59.0	63.5[29]	...	643	18.1	9.9	1,341
1891	175	2.2	4.0	0.3	506	11.3	2,454	59.8	78.2	...	652	18.5	10.2	1,369
1892	180	2.2	4.4	0.3	495	11.4	2,488	60.4	80.1	...	659	19.0	10.6	1,375
1893	185	2.3	4.0	0.3	527	11.6	2,526	61.1	82.9	...	672	19.8	10.7	1,371
1894	187	2.4	4.3	0.3	526	11.8	2,567	61.8	84.7	...	684	20.3	11.0	1,403
1895	195	2.5	5.2	0.4	520	11.9	2,589	62.1	88.3	...	691	21.4	11.2	1,385
1896	199	2.5	5.6	0.4	535	12.0	2,564	62.2	88.0	...	702	21.8	11.4	1,393
1897	196	2.5	5.9	0.4	[521][28]	12.0	2,538	62.4	87.8	...	709	22.8	11.6	1,401
1898	197	2.6	6.0	0.4	[519][28]	12.0	2,637	62.6	87.3	...	719	23.5	12.0	1,442
1899	198	2.6	6.1	0.4	[514][28]	12.1	2,682	64.3	90.1	...	731	24.2	12.6	1,450
1900	199	2.6	6.3	0.4	478	11.9	2,708	65.0	91.6	...	740	24.7	13.1	1,481
1901	205	2.7	6.3	0.4	482	11.9	2,733	65.7	92.0	...	755	25.1	13.2	1,510
1902	211	2.7	6.4	0.4	487	12.0	2,810	66.0	98.6	...	802	25.7	13.7[32]	1,543
													16.0	
1903	216[26]	2.7[26]	6.3	0.4	482	12.0	2,878	66.5	101	...	820	26.1	16.1	1,651
	213	2.6												
1904	219	2.6	6.1	0.4	484	12.3	2,962	66.9	105	...	832	26.6	16.6	1,699
1905	230	2.7	6.1	0.4	500	12.5	3,032	67.0	112	...	845	26.7	17.1	1,747
1906	238	2.8	6.2	0.4	494	12.6	3,102	67.0	116	...	857	27.3	18.2	1,852
1907	250	2.9	6.3	0.5	486	12.7	3,150	66.4	127	...	867	27.5	19.0	1,889
1908	255	3.0	6.3	0.5	495	12.7	3,210	68.7	141	...	879	28.6	19.2	1,911
1909	260	3.0	6.6	0.5	501	12.8	3,250	70.5	156	...	892	29.3	19.8	1,992
1910	266	3.1	6.7	0.5	496	12.8	3,309	72.8	164	...	904	30.1	20.3	2,028
1911	271	3.1	6.9	0.5	513	13.0	3,354	75.1	...	...	917	31.2	30.7	2,038
1912	282	...	6.7	...	499	13.2	3,387	76.9	...[29]	...	929	32.1	21.3	2,143
1913	290	3.5	7.1	0.6	503	13.3	3,484	80.1	282	20.3	943	32.9	22.0	2,222
1914	...	...	...	...	508	13.5	3,583	83.5	294	21.4	959	33.5	23.1	2,290
1915	223	3.1	6.6	0.5	500	13.5	3,684	87.3	305	21.9	981	34.2	24.7	2,344
1916	...	...	...	...	494	13.4	3,773	90.5	322	22.5	994	34.5	26.5	2,433
1917	...	...	...	...	489	13.4	3,869	94.0	325	23.1	1,008	34.6	28.1	2,589
1918	...	...	...	...	488	13.4	3,971	97.7	354	24.1	1,019	34.7	30.6	2,738
1919	...	...	...	...	488	13.3	4,069	102	383	25.9	1,022	35.3	31.6	3,246

I1 Children and Teachers in Schools (in thousands, except as otherwise indicated)

	Norway				Portugal				Romania		
	Primary[16]		Secondary[29]		Primary[16]		Secondary		Primary[16]		Secondary
	P	T	P	T*	P	T*	P[35]	T*[16]	P	T	P
1870	237	3.7	...	...	...	...	...	...	...	...	...
1871	...	...	...	...	...	...	...	...	...	...	...
1872	...	...	...	...	125	...	...	...	...	...	...
1873	...	...	...	...	...	...	...	...	...	...	...
1874	...	...	...	...	...	...	...	...	...	...	...
1875	245	3.9	4.0	401	...	...	...	...	...	...	...
1876	247	4.0	4.4	450	...	...	...	...	...	...	...
1877	247	4.1	3.4	455	...	...	...	...	...	...	...
1878	249	4.2	5.4	504	...	...	...	...	...	...	...
1879	248	4.3	5.8	519	...	...	...	...	...	...	...
1880	247	4.4	6.5	576	...	...	...	...	108	3.0	...
1881	244[33] 226	4.4	6.3	556	...	...	...	...	...	...	...
1882	227	4.5	6.4	577	...	...	...	...	...	...	...
1883	239	4.6	6.7	639	236	3,649	...	...	...	...	...
1884	238	4.5	7.0	643	240	3,624	...	...	...	...	...
1885	244	4.7	7.6	692	237	3,776	...	...	135	3.6	...
1886	249	4.9	8.0[29]	759[29]	240	3,883	...	...	...	...	...
1887	255	4.9	10.0	1,043	246	3,954	2.4	...	...	...	...
1888	258	5.0	10.5	1,084	238	4,069	2.9	...	...	...	...
1889	262	5.0	10.4	1,004	...	...	3.0	...	...	...	...
1890	265[33] 287	5.1	11.0	1,113	...	...	3.5	...	191	4.4	...
1891	288	5.3	11.0	1,051	...	...	3.6	...	...	...	...
1892	301	6.1	11.2	1,085	...	...	3.6	222	...	...	...
1893	307	6.3	11.3	1,103	...	...	3.6	229	...	...	...
1894	311	6.4	11.3	1,077	...	...	3.7	222	...	...	...
1895	320[34]	6.5	12.0	1,113	...	...	4.1	234	259	5.2	...
1896	323	6.6	12.4	1,040	...	...	4.6	247	...	...	...
1897	327	6.8	9.8	1,129	...	...	5.1	264	...	...	...
1898	331	6.9	9.6	1,119	...	...	5.0	272	...	...	...
1899	333	7.1	9.9	1,114	231	...	4.8	283	...	...	...
1900	336[34]	7.3	10.4	1,088	...	...	5.2	315	352	5.9	17.8
1901	341	7.4	11.2	1,244	...	...	6.0	337	364	6.0	16.6
1902	345	7.5	11.7	1,253	...	...	6.7[35] 5.5	362	446	6.0	15.4
1903	350	7.6	12.1	1,312	...	...	5.8	364	474	6.1	14.2
1904	354	7.7	12.0	1,326	...	...	5.9	411	497	6.2	14.0
1905	359	7.7	11.0	1,319	...	...	7.1	487	505	6.4	14.8
1906	361	7.7	12.4	1,321	...	...	7.5	456	515	6.4	15.6
1907	365	8.0	11.5	1,337	...	...	8.3	484	530	6.9	15.9
1908	370	8.1	13.1	1,313	...	...	9.1	468	561	7.7	15.6
1909	374	8.3	13.9	1,357	...	...	9.7	510	585	7.8	16.4
1910	377	8.6	15.0	1,415	...	...	10.6	512	587	7.9	17.2
1911	379	8.7	16.1	1,424	...	...	11.7	531	677	8.2	...
1912	379	9.1	17.3	1,366	...	...	11.1	540	681	8.3	...
1913	382	9.3	18.1	1,519	...	...	11.0	557	683	8.2	...
1914	382	9.4	20.0	1,582	...	...	11.6	613	721	9.0	...
1915	382	9.6	18.5	1,539	...	...	12.7	607	...	...	...
1916	383	10.1	22.2	1,695	...	...	13.4	649	...	...	...
1917	379	10.5	22.6	1,697	...	...	13.7	572	...	...	...
1918	378	10.7	24.2	1,683	...	...	12.7	695	...	...	...
1919	380	10.9	25.4	1,678	...	...	...	...	778	13.1	22.7

I1 Children and Teachers in Schools (in thousands, except as otherwise indicated)

	Serbia/Yugoslavia				Spain			Sweden			
	Primary		Secondary		Primary		Secondary	Primary		Secondary	
	P	T	P	T*	P	T	P	P	T	P	T
1870	23.3	0.6	1.8	99	...	...	...	556	7.8	...	...
1871	25.7	0.6	2.0	116	...	...	...	...	...	...	...
1872	25.9	0.6	2.1	134	...	...	...	...	...	...	...
1873	26.6	0.6	1.8	134	...	...	...	...	...	...	...
1874	28.1	0.6	2.6	135	...	...	...	...	...	...	...
1875	28.3	0.7	2.3	149	...	...	...	613	9.3	...	...
1876	28.0	0.7	2.3	163	...	...	...	...	...	...	...
1877	...	0.7	...	156	...	...	...	...	...	...	...
1878	23.6	0.6	1.8	157	...	...	...	...	...	...	...
1879	29.7	0.7	2.2	169	...	...	...	...	...	...	...
1880	36.3	0.8	2.8	205	1,769	...	...	...	...	...	...
1881	39.7	0.9	3.3	214	...	...	...	...	...	...	...
1882	39.1	0.9	4.1	232	...	...	...	...	...	...	...
1883	39.9	0.9	4.5	267	...	...	...	...	...	...	...
1884	45.4	0.9	4.6	285	...	...	...	...	...	...	...
1885	47.8	0.9	5.0	267	1,843	...	...	...	...	...	...
1886	47.8	0.9	5.2	275	...	...	...	677	12.6	...	...
1887	57.8	1.1	6.0	306	...	...	...	...	...	...	...
1888	58.9	1.2	6.3	337	...	...	...	...	...	14	...
1889	61.9	1.3	6.6	360	...	...	...	...	...	14	...
1890	65.7	1.3	6.8	363	...	...	...	690	13.5	14	...
1891	68.0	1.4	7.3	346	...	...	...	...	...	15	...
1892	73.3	1.5	7.1	379	...	...	...	...	...	15	...
1893	76.6	1.6	7.5	402	...	...	...	...	...	15	...
1894	83.5	1.7	7.8	405	...	...	...	...	...	15	...
1895	90.0	1.8	7.8	499	...	...	...	...	...	15	...
1896	92.1	1.9	8.0	471	...	...	...	...	...	16	...
1897	93.8	1.9	7.8	473	...	...	...	...	...	16	...
1898	98.1	2.0	8.0	464	...	...	...	740	15.9	17	...
1899	101	1.9	5.3	324	...	...	...	741	16.3	17	...
1900	102	1.9	4.5	322	...	...	...	742	16.6	18	...
1901	105	2.0	4.5	333	...	...	...	743	17.2	18	...
1902	110	2.0	4.6	350	...	...	...	748	17.4	19	...
1903	112	2.1	6.2	368	...	...	...	753	17.8	20	...
1904	122	2.2	6.1	374	...	...	...	759	18.3	21	...
1905	128	2.3	6.7	392	...	...	...	762	18.8	22	...
1906	129	2.3	7.1	429	...	...	...	765	19.3	22	...
1907	132	2.4	...	...	...	...	...	772	19.9	23	...
1908	136	2.5	...	...	1,526	...	...	778	20.5	23	...
1909	138	2.6	...	...	...	...	...	785	21.0	24	1,648
1910	146	2.5	...	...	...	...	...	791	21.5	24	1,681
1911	...	...	...	...	...	...	...	795	22.0	25	1,720
1912	...	...	...	...	...	...	...	802	22.5	26	1,750
1913	...	...	...	...	...	...	...	808	23.0	26	1,798
1914	...	...	...	...	1,812	37.0	48.8	813[36]	23.5	27	1,807
1915	...	...	...	...	...	...	48.3	704	24.2	27	1,851
1916	...	...	...	...	1,712	35.2	52.0	706	24.8	28	1,892
1917	...	...	...	...	...	...	52.5	708	25.3	29	1,942
		Yugoslavia									
1918	...	...	42.7	2,053	...	...	51.8	707	25.9	30	1,960
1919	801	12.5	55.5	2,656	...	...	52.4	709	26.4	32	2,048

I1 Children and Teachers in Schools (in thousands, except as otherwise indicated)

	Switzerland				U.K.: England & Wales				U.K.: Scotland			
	Primary[16]		Secondary		Primary		Secondary[16]		Primary		Secondary[16]	
	P	T	P	T*	P	T	P	T	P	T	P	T
1870	...	...	...	...	1,231	14.4	...	...	201	2.4	...	...
1871	...	...	...	...	1,336	16.4	...	...	206	2.6	...	...
1872	...	...	...	...	1,482	18.8	...	...	213	2.7	...	...
1873	...	...	...	...	1,679	21.2	...	...	275[9]	3.2[9]	...	...
1874	...	...	...	...	1,837	23.7	...	...	312	3.9	...	...
1875	...	...	...	...	1,985	26.8	...	...	333	4.3	...	...
1876	...	...	...	...	2,151	30.0	...	...	360	4.9	...	...
1877	...	...	...	...	2,405	34.5	...	...	377	5.2	...	...
1878	...	...	...	...	2,595	38.5	...	...	385	5.5	...	...
1879	...	...	...	...	2,751	41.4	...	...	405	5.8	...	...
1880	...	...	...	...	2,864	44.6	...	...	410	6.1	...	...
1881	434	...	25.5	...	3,015	48.1	...	...	421	6.4	...	...
1882	...	...	...	...	3,127	52.7	...	...	433	6.9	...	...
1883	...	...	...	...	3,273	57.8	...	...	448	7.2	...	...
1884	456	8.8	...	...	3,371	61.6	...	...	456	7.4	...	...
1885	...	...	...	...	3,438	64.3	...	...	477	7.9	...	...
1886	...	...	...	...	3,527	66.5	...	...	492	8.2	...	...
1887	471	9.0	33.8	...	3,615	68.7	...	...	496	8.5	...	...
1888	475	9.2	35.2	2,008	3,683	70.8	...	...	503	8.8	...	...
1889	476	9.2	35.4	2,028	3,718	73.5	...	...	513	9.1	...	...
1890	468	9.3	36.6	2,060	3,750	77.0	...	...	538	9.6	...	...
1891	470	9.4	38.3	2,085	3,871	79.3	...	...	539	9.9	...	...
1892	470	9.5	40.5	2,190	4,100	83.0	...	...	543	10.2	...	...
1893	471	9.6	41.3	2,207[37]	4,226	87.0	...	...	567	10.7	...	...
1894	469	9.5	41.5	2,018	4,325	92.6	...	...	575	10.9	...	...
1895	471	9.7	42.7	2,052	4,423	94.9	...	...	593	11.5	...	...
1896	479	9.8	43.9	2,123	4,489	101	...	...	605	11.9	...	...
1897	484	9.9	44.4	2,150	4,554	102	...	...	606	12.2	...	...
1898	473	10.1	44.4	2,181	4,637	109	...	...	612	12.7	18.3	...
1899	472	10.3	47.8	2,389	4,666	114	...	...	626	13.3	18.2	...
1900	473	10.5	49.2	2,447	4,754	119	...	...	633	13.9	17.7	0.9
1901	477	10.6	51.8	2,489	4,923	122	...	...	643	14.2	17.9	0.9
1902	485	10.8	53.9	2,531	5,057	127	...	...	665	14.8	17.9	1.0
1903	493	11.0	55.7	2,613	5,177	134	...	...	672	15.5	18.1	1.0
1904	502	11.2	59.7	2,686	5,258	141	94.7	...	682	16.3	18.2	1.0
1905	517	11.5	55.8	2,491	5,312	149	116	...	689	17.0	18.1	1.0
1906	526	11.7	59.3	2,678	5,302	153	126	...	693	17.6	18.3	1.0
1907	522	11.8	67.3	2,876	5,301	156	138	...	692	18.1	19.0	1.1
1908	530	12.0	69.3	3,103	5,355	160	151	9.3	705	19.0	20.9	1.1
1909	538	12.2	71.5	3,194	5,375	162	156	9.5	719	19.7	21.0	1.1
1910	544	12.5	73.2	3,245	5,382	164	160	9.8	732	20.0	20.5	1.1
1911	543	12.3	74.0	4,638	5,367	164	166	10.1	734	20.4	20.5	1.2
1912	...	...	...	...	5,376	165	174	10.4	729	20.6	19.6	1.2
1913	...	...	...	...	5,393	166	188	10.8	728	20.8	19.8	1.2
1914	...	...	...	...	...	...	199	...	725	21.3	19.9	1.2
1915	559	13.0	...	...	...	...	209	...	716	21.9	20.3	1.3
1916	563	13.1	76.6	4,474	...	...	219	12.0	715	22.0	21.0	1.5
1917	557	13.1	76.5	4,546	...	...	239	...	713	22.1	22.3	1.3
1918	555	13.4	76.0	4,694	...[38]	...	270	14.5	694[39]	21.7[39]	24.0[39]	1.4[39]
1919	545	13.4	80.2	4,501	5,199[38] 5,187	166	308	16.0	620	18.3	155.0	6.1

I1   Children and Teachers in Schools (in thousands, except as otherwise indicated)

1920–1969

	Austria[1]				Belgium		Bulgaria			
	Primary		Secondary		Primary	Secondary	Primary		Secondary	
	P	T	P	T	P	P	P	T	P	T
1920	868	31.4	38.2	3.0	968	50.8	560	13.6	122	5.1
1921	819[40]	31.0[40]	38.6	3.5	955	56.3	587	14.5	137	6.1
1922	873	31.8	39.0[40]	3.4[40]	911	57.6	595	15.5	155	7.5
1923	819	31.1	41.7	3.4	856	55.0	541	16.0	175	8.9
1924	749	29.2[41] 21.4	44.5	3.6	805	52.1	496	15.7	176	8.5
1925	718	21.5	46.1	3.7	795	48.7	462	14.9	166[44] 169	7.4[44] 7.7
1926	712	21.3	47.5	3.8	800	46.9	474	15.2	173	7.9
1927	710	21.2	49.2	4.1	804	45.3	514	15.6	181	8.3
1928	723	21.5	50.3	4.2	811	43.8	554	16.1	166	8.1
1929	748	21.8	52.0	4.3	835	46.1	609	16.6	154	7.5
1930	793	22.2	55.8	4.6	871	48.4	656	17.4	168	7.7
1931	835	22.1	59.4	4.6	917	53.7	693	18.2	207	8.6
1932	875	22.1	62.6	4.7	957	61.2	714	18.4	253	9.7
1933	887	21.4	64.4	4.8	974	68.8	726	18.1	281	9.1
1934	866	20.7	65.3	4.9	974	73.7	725	18.0	291	8.8
1935	850	20.8	64.0	4.9	968	75.1	710	18.0	303	9.0
1936	823	…	…	…	965	79.2	694	18.0	326	9.8
1937	…	…	…	…	960	83.7	662	17.5	367	10.2
1938	…	…	…	…	955	86.3	647	17.3	369	10.8
1939	…	…	…	…	954	86.5	639[45] 927	17.2[45] 26.0	371[45] 83	11.0[45] 3.2
1940	…	…	…	…	939	78.5	950	25.9	89	3.2
1941	…	…	…	…	917	81.7	1,063	28.5	102	3.5
1942	…	…	…	…	886	81.2	…	…	…	…
1943	…	…	…	…	865	81.5	…	…	…	…
1944	…	…	…	…	…	83.5	894	24.6	159	5.1
1945	716	27.5	49.0	3.3	829	83.9	…	…	…	…
1946	…	…	49.0	3.3	…	85.8	…	…	…	…
1947	797	29.5	48.3	3.4	789	…	…	…	…	…
1948	829	34.1	47.3	3.5	771	90.7[43] 118	876	30.2	144	5.0
1949	847	35.9	50.1	3.6	768	125	…	…	…	…
1950	867	36.4	55.2	3.4	780	129	…	…	…	…
1951	857	37.3	61.5	3.9	784	135	…	…	…	…
1952	844	37.2	67.2	…	801	139	871	31.7	121	4.8
1953	828	37.0	73.0	…	836[42] 886	141	…	…	…	…
1954	794	36.6	78.1	…	909	147	…	…	…	…
1955	764	35.8	80.6	4.6	933	153	…	…	…	…
1956	748	34.9	81.7	4.9	945	163	961	39.2	165	7.4
1957	735	34.0	84.2	5.1	955	175	…	…	…	…
1958	725	34.0	85.4	5.2	956	196	1,008	41.1	167	8.0
1959	734	34.3	85.1	5.3	960	218	…	…	…	…
1960	744	34.6	83.4	5.3	969	241	1,054	43.0	158	8.0
1961	742	34.7	81.5	5.4	969	252	…	…	…	…
1962	747	34.9	80.7	5.2	970	263	1,123	46.8	158	
1963	758	35.6	84.4	6.5	980	272	1,137	47.9	145	7.2
1964	774	36.3	90.0	7.0	990	277	1,155	48.8	119	6.7
1965	794	37.1	95.3	7.3	998	283	1,129	49.4	125	7.0
1966	869	40.0	103	7.7	1,004	289	1,108	49.5	123	7.1
1967	892	41.5	112	7.8	1,016	300	1,096	49.5	117	6.9
1968	913	42.6	120	7.9	1,019	310	1,079	48.7	108	6.7
1969	944	42.9	131	8.7	1,022	314	1,064	48.1	103	6.2

I1 Children and Teachers in Schools (in thousands, except as otherwise indicated)

1920–1969

	Czechoslovakia				Denmark			Finland			
	Primary		Secondary		Primary	Secondary	All Schools	Primary		Secondary	
	P	T	P	T	P	P	T	P	T	P	T
1920	2,152	...	...	...	437	38.9	15.3	264	8.0	32.5	2.4
1921	2,186	45.8	91.9	...	464	41.2	16.0	309	8.9	35.4	2.5
1922	2,070	45.6	95.0	...	461	42.7	16.1	327	9.6	38.1	2.6
1923	1,951	45.4	100.3	...	453	47.3	16.1	326	10.1	40.4	2.8
1924	1,781	44.9	102.8	...	448	47.8	15.9	331	10.4	42.6	2.9
1925	1,718	42.3	100.1	...	445	47.8	16.0	330	10.7	44.6	2.9
1926	1,711	42.9	94.3	...	439	47.8	16.0	334	11.1	45.8	3.0
1927	1,729	44.0	88.4	6.4	444	48.0	16.1	343	11.4	46.8	3.1
1928	1,770	45.4	83.8	6.3	444	49.2	16.1	352	12.0	47.8	3.1
1929	1,839	47.8	81.0	6.3	445	50.1	16.2	365	12.4	48.6	3.2
1930	1,953	50.3	85.2	6.5	446	51.5	16.3	379	12.9	49.6	3.2
1931	2,086	52.8	96.3	6.8	446	53.5	16.4	395[50]	12.9[50]	49.9	3.2
1932	2,215	54.9	107	6.6	446	55.4	16.6	394	12.6	49.6	3.2
1933	2,271	56.5	118	6.9	447	58.2	16.7	400	12.9	49.7	3.2
1934	2,269	57.8	126	7.1	438	59.7	17.1	470	13.1	49.7	3.2
1935	2,249	58.4	133	7.4	429	61.6	17.2	477	13.4	50.3	3.3
1936	2,189	59.1	...	...	422	63.3	17.2	480	13.5	50.6	3.3
1937	1,534	60.4	...	...	415	64.8	17.3	492	14.0[51]	52.3	3.3
1938	1,313	...	...	...	408	66.1	17.3	496	18.5	53.8	3.4
1939	1,309	...	...	...	397	67.1	17.4	426	[12.4][51]	53.9	3.1
1940	1,280	...	...	...	392	67.4	17.3	481	17.3	56.3	3.3
1941	1,261	...	...	...	390	68.9	17.5	428	[12.6][51]	57.1	3.6
1942	1,233	...	...	...	389	69.3	17.6	437	[13.8][51]	61.9	3.7
1943	1,190	...	...	...	386	69.8	17.6	448	17.9	68.8	4.1
1944	1,115	...	...	...	389	69.9	17.9	425	16.0	72.8	3.9
1945	1,381[46]	48.0	...[46]	5.7	401	70.8	18.1	442	17.3	77.5	4.3
	1,478		109								
1946	1,510	...	109	...	408	73.4	18.5	462	18.3	81.2	4.6
1947	1,550	...[47]	98	...	412	75.4	18.7	466	18.8	84.8	4.9
1948	1,594[46]	63.9	93[46]	...[47]	416	78.6	19.1	484	19.6	87.7	5.1
	1,523		163								
1949	1,633	66.2	141	...[47]	428	83.4	19.4	484	20.1	91.7	5.4
1950	1,686	...	145	...	443	88.9	20.0	489	20.8	95.0	5.6
1951	1,731	...	150	...	442	93.6	20.6	495	21.3	99.9	5.8
1952	1,807	70.3	157	...[47]	485	97.1	21.2	516	22.3	107	5.9
1953	1,787	72.4[47]	190	...[47]	509	102	21.9	541	22.7	115	6.1
1954	1,802	64.2	233	11.9[48]	527	108	22.8	565	23.3	123	6.5
1955	1,847	66.4	258	13.3	536	118	23.5	591	24.2	134	6.9
1956	1,867	69.9	285	14.3	537	127	24.4	605	24.8	146	7.6
1957	1,917	73.5	291	15.2	533	140	25.3	622	25.2	162	8.2
1958	1,954	74.8[47]	293	15.3	521	156	26.3	629	26.3	181	8.8
1959	2,053	96.0	297	...[47]	547	139[49]	27.5	633	27.1	200	9.7
1960	2,153	103[47]	312	...[47]	577	112	28.7	626	27.3	215	10.4
1961	2,278	91.8	335	15.8	578	109	30.0	612	27.3	228	11.2
1962	2,273	91.9	380	16.8	580	106	31.1	596	27.2	240	12.0
1963	2,260	91.1	407	18.2	583	106	32.2	583	26.8	249	12.7
1964	2,241	93.7	422	20.1[48]	569	105	...	565	26.5	258	13.5
1965	2,221	96.0	411	20.5	573	105	...	544	26.2	268	14.1
1966	2,164	97.8	395	21.1	572	110	...	523	25.5	282	14.8
1967	2,109	97.5	384	21.3	576	116	[34.8][101]	507[36]	24.7[36]	292	15.4
1968	2,053	98.4	387	21.8	580	121	[37.4][101]	511	25.2	305	16.2
1969	2,002	98.6	390	22.2	583	124	45.5	522	26.0	316	16.9

I1   Children and Teachers in Schools (in thousands, except as otherwise indicated)

	France			Germany				East Germany			Greece			
	Primary		Secondary	Primary[23]		Secondary		Primary	Secondary	All Schools	Primary		Secondary	
	P	T	P	P	T	P	T	P	P	T	P	T	P	T
1920	3,697[22]	119[22]	146[52]	...	...	...	...	...	...	...	...	...	...	...
	4,452		243[20]											
1921	4,614	120[20]	255	8,894	196	1,081	49.9	...	...	...	...	...	...	...
1922	3,995[20]	...	260	...	...	...	...	...	...	...	...	...	...	...
	4,210													
1923	3,973	121	270	...	...	...	...	...	...	...	...	...	...	...
1924	3,828	121	277	...	...	...	...	...	...	...	...	...	...	...
1925	3,754	120	281	6,662	187	1,080	57.3	...	...	...	...	...	...	...
1926	3,854	119	279	...	...	...	...	...	...	...	726	13.9	48.2	2.3
1927	3,917	119	282	...	...	...	...	...	...	...	738	14.6	49.4	2.2
1928	4,099	119	286	...	...	...	...	...	...	...	734[58]	15.2[58]	52.7[58]	2.2[58]
1929	4,359	120	298	...	...	...	...	...	...	...	733	14.7	72.2	3.3
1930	4,635	133	330	7,590	190	1,016	56.4	...	...	...	772	14.6	68.7	3.4
1931	4,915	137	363	...	...	...	...	...	...	...	817	14.6	67.0	3.5
1932	5,111	138	403	...	...	...	...	...	...	...	857	14.4	70.1	3.6
1933	5,200	141	425	...	...	...	...	...	...	...	889	14.5	74.0	3.7
1934	5,230	141	446	...	...	...	...	...	...	...	917	15.4	74.7	4.1
1935	5,261	142	465	7,892	185	907	53.1	...	...	...	951	16.0	78.1	4.3
1936	5,332	147	475	7,758	181	943	52.6	...	...	...	1,001	16.3	...	...
1937	5,437	150	506	...	...	944	52.6	...	...	...	985	15.6	...	4.6
1938	5,422[53]	151	...[53]	7,487	177	935	52.9	...	...	...	...	...	...	...
1939	5,032	168	432	7,289	171	958	53.9	...	...	...	...	...	...	...
1940	4,913	154	432	...	...	...	...	...	...	...	...	...	...	...
1941	4,924	152	485[53]	...	...	...	...	...	...	...	...	...	...	...
1942	4,865	152	...	...	...	...	...	...	...	...	...	...	...	...
1943	4,666	150	600[53]	...	...	...	...	...	...	...	...	...	...	...
1944	4,576[53]	154	...	...	...	...	...	...	...	...	...	...	...	...

West Germany[56]

	France			Germany				East Germany			Greece			
	P	T	P	P	T	P	T	P	P	T	P	T	P	T
1945	4,746	154	625[53]	...	...	...	...	...	...	...	...	...	...	...
1946	4,702	156	734	...	...	...	...	...	...	...	...	...	...	...
1947	4,635	155	747	...	...	...	...	...	...	...	...	...	...	...
1948	4,882	157	729	...	...	...	...	...	...	...	...	...	...	...
1949	4,669	159	746	...	...	...	...	...	...	...	...	...	...	...
1950	4,726	159	788	6,330	131	801	33.9	...	...	...	...	...	...	...
1951	4,798	160	797	6,142	135	879	36.7	2,374	101	75.1	936	18.9	207	6.4
1952	5,075	163	844	5,720	136	948	39.9	2,174	113	77.1	...	...	...	...
1953	5,282	167	871	5,340	137	1,018	42.1	1,981	123	77.5	982	...	219	...
1954	5,573	172	922	5,135	137	906	44.3	1,840	125	78.7	...	...	...	...
1955	5,873	182	969	4,936	136	924	46.0	1,703[57]	128[57]	75.6	972	21.2	...	6.7
								1,724	107					
1956	6,146	192	1,064	4,867	135	912	48.5	1,682	96.4	77.4	965	20.8	212	7.0
1957	6,355	201	1,129	4,847[27]	132[27]	1,072[27]	52.5[27]	1,687	91.3	79.5	989	21.2	...	7.0
				4,775		1,144								
1958	6,537	210	1,196	4,783[56]	144[56]	1,134[56]	54.1	1,671	89.4	78.5	923	21.8	215	7.6
				4,883		1,150								
1959	6,738[54]	218	1,265	4,998[56]	144	1,170[56]	57.0	1,806	...	...	901	23.1	233	7.9
	5,720			5,138		1,221								
1960	5,708	226	1,493	5,291	145	1,222	58.2	1,922	82.5	86.4	896	23.3	247	8.4
1961	5,681	225	1,608	5,343	145	1,233	62.3	2,026	80.7	102	908	24.0	272	8.2
1962	5,681	241	1,715[54]	5,445	150	1,254	65.2	2,128	76.2	105	911	24.3	284	8.6
1963	5,669	255[55]	1,560	5,469	152	1,326	68.5	2,202	76.5	113	912	25.7	294	9.1
1964	5,714	191	1,693	5,525	158	1,388	70.5	2,248	81.1	118	953	26.6	334	11.0
1965	5,650	187	1,827	5,607	161	1,497	71.8	2,274	85.3	122	964	27.4	352	11.3
1966	5,576	186	1,955	5,711	167	1,628	76.7	2,301	92.5	125	969	27.5	365	12.1
1967	5,496	189	2,143	5,755	173	1,889	84.5	2,367	72.4	128	964	28.0	384	12.5
1968	5,346	194	2,390	5,887	177	2,032	90.1	2,437	50.5	131	948	28.2	386	12.4
1969	5,218	196	2,619	6,077	181	2,187	97.8	2,485	51.9	134	938	28.1	400	12.7

I1 Children and Teachers in Schools (in thousands, except as otherwise indicated)

	Hungary[5]				Southern Ireland				Italy				Netherlands			
	Primary		Secondary		Primary		Secondary		Primary[8]		Secondary		Primary		Secondary	
	P	T	P	T	P[7]	T	P	T	P	T	P	T	P	T	P	T
1920	857	17.6	56.9	3.0	482[60]	...	...	...	4,166	105	382	26.0	1,032	...	32.6	3.8
1921	905	18.3	56.0	3.0	365	...	...	...	4,267	109	390	26.4	1,040	...	36.2	4.1
1922	821	17.5	56.8	3.0	356	...	...	...	4,167	108	383	25.6	1,039	35.3	40.0	4.3
1923	770	17.4	57.8	3.0	369	...	...	...	3,981	105	327	20.9	1,063	35.2	41.3	4.3
1924	694	16.6	60.8	3.0	363	...	22.9	...	3,759	100	290	18.5	1,089	34.5	42.7	4.4
1925	656	16.7	61.8	3.0	...	13.2	25.5	2.1	3,622	98	292	19.5	1,078	34.0	43.6	4.5
1926	689	17.0	61.0	3.0	399	13.2	24.8	2.3	3,635	99	372	20.9	1,077	33.4	42.2	4.6
1927	748	17.6	60.3	3.0	413	13.3	25.6	2.3	3,838	100	366	21.0	1,067	33.9[65] 31.1	42.4[65] 95.7	4.7
1928	833	18.4	59.5	3.0	424	13.6	26.8	2.4	4,052	102	371	22.0	1,103	31.6	97.7	4.7[65]
1929	908	19.1	60.8	3.0	420	13.7	27.6	2.4	4,340	101	332	26.8	1,161	34.9	102	...
1930	967	19.3	64.2	3.0	421	13.6	29.0	2.6	4,595	105	312	28.0	1,183	36.1	106	...
1931	1,004	19.4	65.1	3.0	417	13.7	30.0	2.6	4,762	107	379	32.7	1,201	36.8	114	...
1932	997	19.4	65.3	3.1	417	13.6	31.0	2.6	4,799	109	441	35.4	1,200	36.5	125	...
1933	989	19.5	66.8	3.2	422	13.8	32.4	2.7	4,818	110	499	43.8	1,176	35.5	134	...
1934	969	19.6	67.8	3.2	422	13.7	33.5	2.8	4,841	111	543	41.1	1,149	32.5	141	...
1935	962	19.7	69.0	3.3	413	13.6	35.1	2.9	5,074	117	593	46.9	1,142	31.2	146	...
1936	962	19.8	69.8	3.4	405	13.5	35.9	2.9	5,187	123	675	49.8	1,143	30.1	151	...
1937	963	20.1	70.0	3.5	393	13.4	36.1	2.9	5,051	117	744	52.3	1,144	30.0	157	...
1938	...	...	...	...	393	13.4	36.7	3.0	5,095	120	809	60.7	1,143	30.1	161	...
1939	...	...	...	...	385	13.3	37.7	3.0	5,149	122	850	64.8	1,144	30.5	162	...
1940	...	...	...	...	389	13.3	38.7	3.1	5,213	127	908	76.5	1,143	30.4	164	...
1941	...	...	...	...	381	13.1	39.5	3.2	[5,110][61]	[121][61]	972	81.4	...	...	...	...
1942	...	...	...	...	382	13.1	39.8	3.3	...	...	...	...	1,129	31.8	...	...
1943	...	...	...	...	381	13.1	40.0	3.4	...	...	...	...	1,172	34.0	185	...
1944	...	...	...	...	373	12.9	41.2	3.4	...	...	...	...	...	...	...	...
1945	...	...	...	...	375	12.8	41.8	3.5	4,360	133	879	77.8	1,172	33.8	193	...
1946	...	...	...	...	371	12.8	42.9	3.5	4,703	145	894	82.7	1,182	33.9	209	...
1947	...	...	...	...	355	12.8	43.8	3.6	4,836	157	896	83.5	1,154	34.2	213	10.7
1948	...	...	...	...	374	12.6	45.4	3.7	4,878	165	941	89.1	1,154	34.4[66]	213	...
1949	1,202[59]	35.0[59]	94	6.3	377	12.7	47.1	3.9	4,815	168	996	100	1,167	34.0	210	11.4
1950	1,230	35.2	108	6.2	382	12.9	48.6	3.8	4,640	170	1,101	106	1,216	34.4	211	11.6
1951	1,205	38.1	122	5.9	377	12.8	50.2	3.9	4,443	170	1,206	112	1,240	35.0	216	11.8
1952	1,196	39.9	139	6.1	393	12.9	52.2	4.0	4,477	173	1,317	118	1,289	36.2	226	...
1953	1,203	43.1	164	7.0	401	13.0	54.0	4.2	4,556	177	1,378	117	1,357	37.6	240	...
1954	1,207	46.0	162	7.5	405	13.1	56.4	4.1	4,614	175	1,464	126	1,413	39.4	256	13.7
1955	1,226	50.3	155	7.8	405	13.2	59.3	4.4	4,693[62] 4,741	175[62] 180	1,511[63] 906	129[63] 75.7	1,452	40.7	278	15.2
1956	1,255	52.2	173	7.9	419	13.3	62.4	4.6	4,828	184	930	84.5	1,470	41.5	305	16.5
1957	1,259	53.7	159	8.1	424	13.4	66.2	4.7	4,768	190	1,020	80.8	1,479	41.9	332	17.2
1958	1,269	55.1	178	8.4	420	13.6	69.6	5.0	4,676	192	1,150	91.3	1,476	42.1	368	18.8
1959	1,314	56.4	204	8.4	425	13.8	73.4	5.0	4,498	197	1,311	105	1,448	42.0	407	...
1960	1,392	57.3	241	8.8	431	13.9	76.8	5.2	4,418	200	1,414	118	1,416	41.6	435	...
1961	1,445	58.3	284	9.2	428	14.0	80.4	5.3	4,421	201	1,539	133	1,398	41.5	453	...
1962	1,473	59.9	334	9.6	421	14.1	84.9	5.6	4,391	205	1,594	139	1,395	42.0	462	22.8
1963	1,469	61.5	385	10.6	428	14.2	89.2	5.9	4,420	205	1,685	147	1,395	43.1	470	...
1964	1,445	62.1	417	11.6	435	14.3	93.0	6.2	4,468	206	1,732	151	1,398	43.9	478	24.2
1965	1,414	62.2	407	12.0	449	14.5	98.7	6.5	4,520	207	1,795	155	1,409	45.0	487	25.4
1966	1,380	62.2	376	12.3	434	14.6	104	6.8	4,556	210	1,821	160	1,419	45.6	493	...
1967	1,331	62.3	351	...	447	14.7	119	7.2	4,620	213	1,891	166	1,428	46.0	509	...
1968	1,255	62.5	335	...	444	14.8	134	8.2	4,673[64] 4,652	216[64] 213	1,982	172[64] 168	1,439	46.5	537	...
1969	1,178	62.8	337	...	445	14.7	144	9.1	4,750	217	2,064	178	1,451	47.8	562	...

I1 Children and Teachers in Schools (in thousands, except as otherwise indicated)

1920–1969

	Norway				Poland				Portugal				Romania			
	Primary[69]		Secondary		Primary		Secondary		Primary[70]		Secondary[71]		Primary[16]		Secondary	
	P	T	P	T*	P	T	P	T	P	T	P	T*	P	T	P	T*
1920	386	11.1	27.0	1,815	...	...	...	...	...	...	11.7	707	834[72] 1,516	13.7[72] 25.8	27.4[72]	...
1921	390	11.4	25.1	1,755	...	...	...	...	...	...	11.4	731	[1,589][73]	[24.6][73]	...	...
1922	394	11.6	24.3	1,773	3,132	62.0	227	...	...	...	11.5	774	1,389	24.7	...	...
1923	395	11.6	24.9	1,797	3,173	65.6	227	...	...	...	12.4	787	1,390	26.8	...	...
1924	396	11.6	23.9	1,767	3,137	66.2	220	14.7	...	...	12.8	756	[1,460][74]	[30.6][74]	...	...
1925	396	11.5	23.7	1,763	3,152	69.0	217	14.7	317	8.5	14.3	836	1,537	33.2	195	10.4
1926	394	11.4	22.7	1,684	3,245	68.4	215	14.8	318	8.4	16.5	935	1,599	35.2	177	11.6
1927	399	11.1	21.9	1,624	3,256	70.2	209	14.8	321	8.6	17.1	892	1,674	37.3	192	12.2
1928	399	11.1	22.2	1,605	3,359	73.1	204	14.7	341	9.0	15.6	768	1,787	37.8	175	12.4
1929	402	11.1	22.5	1,596	3,570	76.2	203	14.3	367	9.5	15.7	788	1,692	37.4	162	12.3
1930	404	11.2	22.6	1,602	3,833	...	205	...	423	9.3	18.5	877	2,111	37.8	173	13.9
1931	403	11.1	23.4	1,584	4,113	...	203	...	442	9.7	20.9	808	2,207	41.3	166	14.4
1932	398	10.8	24.7	1,619	4,385	...	187	...	420	9.7	24.5	869	2,330	41.7	163	16.5
1933	392	10.7	25.9	1,675	4,491	...	161	...	423	9.7	25.4	920	2,394	45.4	164	14.9
1934	380	10.6	27.7	1,716	4,517	...	166	...	429	9.8	27.0	976	2,480	47.4	178	15.8
1935	370	10.5	29.1	1,798	4,539	...	181	...	445	10.3	19.8[35]	873	2,478	46.9	185	16.1
1936	358	10.5	30.7	1,856	4,593	...	201	...	449	9.8	32.8	926	2,480	49.0	190	17.0
1937	353	11.1	32.4	1,977	4,701	76.6	221	...	458	10.1	33.4	958	2,491[75] 1,575	49.6[75] 39.9	201[75] 49.3	17.4[75] 10.4
1938	345	11.4	32.9	2,046	...	...	...	...	463	10.1	34.2	993	...	...	...	...
1939	338	11.5	32.9	2,074	...	...	...	...	468[70]	10.7[70]	34.4	1,022	...	...	...	...
1940	326	11.2	32.0	2,037	...	...	...	...	588	13.0	32.3	993	...	...	...	...
1941	317	11.2	30.5	2,047	...	...	...	...	574	13.9[70]	33.2	1,047	...	...	...	...
1942	298	10.8	29.7	2,031	...	...	...	...	574[70] 555	13.4	37.7	982	...	...	...	...
1943	294	10.5	32.2	2,071	...	...	...	...	542	13.4	40.5	996	...	...	...	...
1944	292	10.7	32.5	2,055	...	...	...	...	546	13.3	42.4	1,040	...	...	...	...
1945	287	10.7	35.7	2,240	3,004	58.6	224	10.6	556	13.9	43.6	1,123	...	...	...	...
1946	295	11.1	37.1	2,383	3,283	66.6	228	11.0	555	13.7	45.8	1,154	...	...	...	...
1947	296	11.4	35.6	2,505	3,405	74.7	202	...	573	14.1	45.6	1,063	...	...	...	...
1948	300	11.5	33.1	2,527	3,375	76.3	219	...	582	14.4	45.3	1,096	1,791	61.5	69.4	4.6
1949	309	11.7	31.9[68]	2,560[68]	3,353	76.5	221	...	606	14.8	46.5	1,112	1,790	...	...	...
1950	321	11.9	37.4	2,450	3,282	81.7	194	10.1	632	14.8	48.5	1,158	1,778	67.0	93.3	5.1
1951	337	12.2	38.3	2,482	3,177	85.8	186	9.6	666	15.7	51.6	1,199	1,766	69.5	99.1	5.2
1952	356	12.7	40.3	2,564	3,038	89.5	187	9.5	759	17.6	54.4	1,196	1,672	74.1	98.5	5.1
1953	379	13.2	43.8	2,743	3,087	93.3	188	9.6	795	19.0	58.7	1,293	1,664	76.4	117	5.7
1954	401	13.8	46.5	2,779	3,203	96.2	195	10.1	813	20.0	62.7	1,315	1,614	79.2	117	5.9
1955	421	14.3	49.1	2,941	3,386	103	201	10.4	829	20.9	68.9	1,408[71]	1,603	76.3	13	7.8
1956	432	14.8	53.5	3,092	3,655	110	203	11.1	842	23.4	76.6	4,919	1,714	79.5	148	8.7
1957	439	15.2	60.1	3,278	3,924	120	195	11.5	852	24.4	83.0	4,484	1,819	84.2	159	6.6
1958	440	15.3	70.7	3,648	4,240	130	199	11.6	857	24.9	91.0	5,216	1,964	87.5	185	7.9
1959	441	15.7	80.0	4,007	4,574	140	214	11.8	869	25.7	102	5,459	2,135	88.0	208	9.5
1960	436	16.5	92.5	4,443	4,828	146	260	12.2	887	26.1	112	5,702	2,346	93.1	251	11.5
1961	...	...	...	...	4,994	151	298	12.7	887	26.8	118	5,757	2,540	98.8	268	12.0
1962	438[69]	17.3[69]	103	4,719	5,117	156	340	13.7	...	...	...	...	2,694	106	334	13.2
1963	444	18.4	106	4,918	5,182	160	379	14.9	883	27.3	139	6,782	2,682	111	377	14.2
1964	448	19.1	107	5,060	5,208	166	405	15.5	894	27.8	145	6,965	2,992	123	330	12.6
1965	458	20.1	107	5,276	5,177	172	427	15.9	893	28.0	150	7,145	2,987	128	372	14.2
1966	473	21.5	103	5,243	5,527	189	323	15.4	891	27.7	155	7,141	2,956	130	407	15.7
1967	487	23.0	98.3	5,176	5,706	201	306	15.1	904	28.4	160	7,361	2,928	131	402	16.9
1968	503	24.5	91.2	4,942	5,604	207	311	15.0	962	29.3	144	7,548	2,909	132	478	19.5
1969	519	26.2	83.8	4,562	5,443	210	310	15.4	990	29.8	120	7,225	2,934	134	498	21.5

I1 Children and Teachers in Schools (in thousands, except as otherwise indicated)

1920–1969

	Spain				Sweden				Switzerland			
	Primary		Secondary		Primary		Secondary		Primary[16]		Secondary	
	P	T	P	T	P	T	P	T	P	T	P	T
1920	...	...	52.3	...	708	27.1	34	2.2	536	13.5	81.7	4,524
1921	...	...	54.6	...	705	27.7	35	2.2	531	13.5	82.9	4,503
1922	...	...	57.7	...	700	28.0	36	2.2	522	13.5	88.4	5,191
1923	...	...	63.1	...	686	28.4	36	2.2	510	13.4	85.0	5,197
1924	...	...	68.9	...	680	28.7	36	2.2	496	13.4	88.0	5,144
1925	...	...	74.3	...	665	28.9	35	2.3	491	13.6	84.4	4,892
1926	1,800	...	76.3	...	661	29.1	34	2.3	483	13.4	82.1	5,302
1927	...	...	63.4	...	665	29.5	34	2.3	474	13.2	81.2	4,468
1928	1,837	...	66.4	...	675	29.9	35	2.6	472	13.0	77.2	5,250
1929	...	...	70.9	...	673	30.3	38	2.8	472	13.2	79.5	5,212
1930	...	...	76.1	...	672	30.7	42	3.0	472	13.4	76.5	5,061
1931	...	...	106	...	664	31.0	46	3.2	475	13.3	82.4[81]	4,497[81]
											48.1	2,396
1932	2,262	49.2	115	...	663	31.0	50	3.1	480	13.4	46.2	1,834
1933	2,398	53.0	131	...	642	30.8	53	3.2	480	13.6	48.5	1,850
1934	2,500	46.8	125	...	619	30.6	55	3.4	477	13.6	52.2	1,866
1935	2,502	47.9	125	...	599	30.6	56	3.5	476	13.7	51.0	1,899
1936	...	...	...	...	581	30.7	57	3.7	471	13.7	50.5	1,891
1937					568	30.7	59	3.9	464	13.6	50.2	1,884
1938	...	...	...	...	558	30.7	61	4.0	460	13.6	50.0	1,902
1939	...	...	...	...	549	30.4	61	3.9	456	13.6	49.3	1,907
1940	2,410	51.1	158	...	538	29.0	62	4.1	453	13.5	49.2	1,917
1941	2,376	51.6	171	...	530	28.6	63	4.1	448	13.5	49.3	1,923
1942	2,446	52.4	180	...	524	28.5	64	4.1	443	13.4	49.0	1,944
1943	2,906	52.3	178	...	519	28.6	66	4.3	441	13.5	49.4	1,970
1944	2,531	53.2	186	...	523	29.1	70	4.5	441	13.4	49.9	1,979
1945	2,600	53.2	195	...	528	29.6	73	4.8	431	13.5	50.4	2,045
1946	2,426	55.1	203	...	544	30.6	78	5.2	430	13.7	50.0	2,086
1947	2,436[76]	55.8	212	...	556	31.2	85	5.6	431	13.9	50.0	2,065
1948	2,064	57.5	214	...	590	32.6	94	6.0	434	14.1	55.0	2,305
1949	2,111	58.3	215	...	612	33.7	95	5.9	...	...	...	...
1950	2,123	59.9	223	...	651	34.7[77]	101[77]	6.1[78]	...	...	...	...
1951	2,119	60.6	236	...	685	36.6	107	9.6	476	14.5	56.1	2,365
1952	2,158	61.2	252	15.4	726	38.1	115	10.1	...	...	...	...
1953	2,510[76]	61.6	266	17.9	754	39.7	122	10.6	518	15.2	59.3	2,462
1954	2,575[76]	63.8	300	18.7	785	41.3	132	11.0	...	...	...	...
1955	2,647[76]	66.2	338	18.8	805	42.9	143	11.6	...	...	...	...
1956	2,425	68.5	382	19.0	815	44.3	157	12.5	557	16.4	77.3	2,963
1957	2,446	73.3	417	19.6	814	45.0	170[77]	13.1	...	...	...	...
							195					
1958	2,465[76]	...	434	19.7	806	45.7	211	13.8	...	...	...	...
	3,335											
1959	3,370	...	463	20.5	794	46.5	235	14.8	572	17.2	90.0	3,423
1960	3,387	...	497	21.6	778	53.4	263	15.9	...	...	...	...
1961	3,410	...	594	22.7	746[79]	53.6	290	16.2	557	17.7	88.5	3,175
1962	3,453	...	653	23.7	714	55.4	314	17.3	...	...	...	...
1963	3,505	...	718	25.6	699	60.7	332	17.8	...	...	...	...
1964	3,763	...	790	27.0	688	61.5	339	17.1	...	...	...	...
1965	3,942	...	854	28.6	676	63.7	345	17.5	...	...	...	...
1966	4,025	...	985	31.0	661	66.1[80]	368	16.9	...	...	...	...
1967	4,179	...	1,165	34.1	654	84.5	386	...	...	...	...	...
1968	4,390	...	1,239	36.0	640	85.0	397	...	...	...	...	...
1969	4,555	...	1,393	...	644	86.4	412	...	...	...	...	...

I1 Children and Teachers in Schools (in thousands, except as otherwise indicated)

1920–1969

	U.K.: England & Wales				U.K.: Northern Ireland				U.K.: Scotland				Yugoslavia			
	Primary		Secondary[16]		Primary		Secondary		Primary		Secondary		Primary		Secondary	
	P	T	P	T	P	T	P	T	P	T	P	T	P	T	P	T
1920	5,206	167	337	17.7	...	...	...	...	627	17.9	154	5.7	908	14.8	69.7	3.3
1921	5,181	168	355	19.0	...	...	...	...	615	17.8	155	5.7	989	16.2	74.9_{90} 132	3.5_{90} 6.9
1922	5,136	164	354	18.5	153	4.2	...	...	608	17.8	155	6.0	968	17.7	145	7.5
1923	5,025	163	349	18.7	156	4.3	...	...	588	17.8	153	6.1	894	17.2	163	8.1
1924	4,934	165	353	19.1	157	4.3	8.5	...	584	18.1	149	6.1	786	17.6	166	8.7
1925	4,950	166	361	19.6	165	4.3	9.0	0.6	587	18.4	150	6.2	768	18.2	170	9.2
1926	4,967	166	371	19.3	170	4.4_{84} 5.7	9.9	0.6	591	18.7	151	6.3	800	19.4	173	9.8
1927	4,981	...	378	20.1	169	5.3	10.6	0.6	587	18.8	153	6.4	881	20.3	162	9.6
1928	4,909	167	387	20.5	169	5.3	11.6	0.6	585	19.1	151	6.5	984	21.3	149	10.2
1929	4,941	168	394	21.2	168	5.4	12.1	0.7	591	19.5	151	6.6	1,088	22.5	161	10.4
1930	4,930	169	411	21.7	172	5.3	12.3	0.7	595	19.5	154	6.6	1,185	22.8	166	10.6
1931	5,006	170	432	22.3	174	5.4	12.3	0.7	601	19.4	160	6.7	1,245	25.1	157	10.8
1932	5,049	171	442	22.8	177	5.4	12.7	0.7	606	19.4	162	6.7	1,275	27.4	165	8.1
1933	5,066	171	448	23.0	177	5.5	13.0	0.7	607	19.4	159	6.7	1,317	29.4	163	11.2
1934	4,907	171	457	23.4	174	5.4	13.2	0.7	592	19.4	157	6.7	1,341	30.9	171	11.0
1935	4,748	170	464	24.0	172	5.4	13.4	0.8	581	19.5	154	6.8	1,342	31.1	180	11.9
1936	4,588	168	466	24.5	171	5.3	13.7	0.8	567	19.7	152	6.8	1,363	31.4	192	12.3
1937	4,527	167	470	25.0	167	5.3	14.1	0.8	557	19.6	153	6.9	1,393	32.1	203	12.6
1938	...	...	...	...	166	5.3	...	...	...	...	...	...	1,471	34.7	213	13.5
1939	...	...	...	...	...	...	...	...	...	...	...	...	...	...	...	...
1940	...	...	...	...	...	...	...	...	...	...	...	...	...	...	...	...
1941	...	...	...	...	...	...	...	...	...	...	...	...	...	...	...	...
1942	...	...	...	...	...	...	...	...	...	...	...	...	...	...	...	...
1943	...	...	...	...	...	...	...	...	...	...	...	...	...	...	...	...
1944	$..._{82}$	$..._{82}$	$..._{82}$	$..._{82}$	...		...	...	$..._{82}$	$..._{82}$	$..._{82}$	$..._{82}$	...		...	...
1945	3,736	117	1,269	...	185	4.9	19.9	1.1	383	...	348	...	1,442	24.3	138	14.5
1946	3,700	123	1,335	63.7	187	4.9	21.0	1.1	361	...	367	...	1,725	25.7	137	16.6
1947	3,812	126	1,545	69.4	185_{86}	5.4	22.0_{86}	1.1_{86}	364	...	403	...	1,916	27.6	173	19.4
1948	3,874	128	1,654	75.2	184	5.7	33.7	1.4	363	...	417	...	1,977	26.8	241	24.4
1949	3,955	130	1,695	78.7	187	5.7	37.2	1.5	367_{87}	$..._{87}$	419_{87}	$..._{87}$	1,988	26.9	285	27.8
1950	4,005	134	1,733	82.1	189	5.8	39.7	1.7	557	18.9	233	...	1,931	32.1	296	28.3
1951	4,214	138	1,756	84.4	194	5.9	41.3	1.8	566	19.4	236	13.8	1,815	40.0	252	24.6
1952	4,436	142	1,770	86.1	200	6.1	42.5	1.8	586	19.9	237	14.0	1,809	46.0	242	20.9
1953	4,554	144	1,822	88.6	204	6.1	44.2	1.8	595	20.0	225	14.2	1,847	51.1	242	22.7
1954	4,601	149	1,914	92.4	205	6.3	49.6	1.9	603	19.7	227	14.5	1,918	55.6	250	22.9
1955	4,592	150	2,057	97.2_{88} 99.4	207	6.3	50.1	2.0	607	19.8	232	15.1	2,036	61.3	267	22.9
1956	4,590	151	2,187	101	208	6.5	52.9	2.3	608	20.2	240	15.4	2,175	65.9	280	23.5
1957	4,508	150	2,330	112	206	6.4	63.5	2.7	610	20.1	239	15.5	2,316	71.8	291	23.9
1958	4,308	146	2,593	123	203	6.4	77.0	3.3	608	20.2	249	15.9	2,427	79.7	309	24.1
1959	4,201	145	2,723	132	197	6.4	84.5	3.6	598	19.7	272	16.8	2,590	79.5	334	25.4
1960	4,133	144	2,829	139	196	6.4	89.2	3.9	589	20.1	288	17.9	2,764	84.3	363	27.6
1961	4,130	145	2,835	144	192	6.4	97.0	4.3	587_{89} 581	19.9	292	18.2	2,896	89.6	403	30.0
1962	4,145	144	2,781	144	192	6.4	100	4.5	584	20.2	286	18.8	2,960	93.4	448	31.2
1963	4,204	146	2,830	147	193	6.4	103	4.7	589	20.8	288	19.2	2,980	96.4	503	33.0
1964	4,273	151	2,819	151	192	6.5	108	5.0	595	20.8	285	19.3	2,972	100	571	35.5
1965	4,366	156	2,817	153	194	6.7	112	5.4	601	21.4	284	19.7	2,946	102	611	34.4
1966	4,495	161	2,833	156	197	6.9	117	5.8	606	21.3	288	20.0	2,922	106	627	35.7
1967	4,647	167	2,895	160	202	7.1	124	6.1	615	21.8	296	20.0	2,894	109	640	36.7
1968	4,789	173	2,960	164	207	7.2	129	6.5	623	22.0	307	20.7	2,875	114	662	36.8
1969	4,914	180	3,009	170	211	7.4	133	6.8	631	23.2	317	20.4	2,853	117	678	39.3

I1 Children and Teachers in Schools (in thousands, except as otherwise indicated)

1970–1998

	Austria				Belgium		Bulgaria			
	Primary		Secondary		Primary	Secondary	Primary		Secondary	
	P	T	P	T	P	P	P	T	P	T
1970	964	44.5	141	9.5	1,029	327	1,054	47.8	101	6.3
1971	975	46.5	151	10.3	1,022	342	1,028	48.5	104	6.5
1972	979	48.3	160	10.6	1,010	313	1,009	47.6	109	6.9
1973	984	50.7	166	11.0	995	305₉₁ / 434	993	47.7	115	7.2
1974	985	52.4	168	11.6	979	465	979	47.7	117	7.5
1975	978	54.9	172	…	957	495	982	48.4	117	7.6
1976	975	54.9	174	…	937	518	983	49.3	113	7.8
1977	935	62.4	177	13.7	919	528	986	49.5	108	7.6
1978	904	59.8	180	14.0	873	548	973	50.0	103	7.6
1979	868	62.2	182	14.7	877	563	977	50.8	99	7.3
1980	831	63.6	181	15.1	823	584	995	51.6	97	7.4
1981	799	64.6	180	15.8	803	608	1,031	57.7	104	8.0
1982	766	65.6	178	15.9	812	633	1,054	60.2	117	8.5
1983	736	66.2	174	15.5	789	661	1,064	61.9	138	8.6
1984	701	67.2	172	15.9	768	683	1,073	61.4	157	9.2
1985	676	67.8	170	16.4	758	698	1,081	61.2	163	9.4
1986	658	68.6	166	16.9	755	699	1,097	62.2	164	9.6
1987	650	68.6	164	17.3	757	700	1,092	62.1	168	9.8
1988	650	68.4	160	17.4	756	696	1,075	64.4	159	9.4
1989	647	68.4	159	17.6	752	698	989	61.1	158	9.4
1990	649	68.9	158	17.8	744	697	958	62.4	153	9.8
1991	668	70.3	163	18.1	739	709	918	61.9	150	10.8
1992	682	70.9	168	18.6	739	724	875	61.1	153	11.3
1993	686	72.1	172	18.9	…	…	836	58.6	152	11.8
1994	689	73.2	173	19.0	739	757	838	58.4	150	11.7
1995	691	74.0	176	19.2	742	763	841	58.1	149	11.5
1996	694	74.1	179	19.4	746	769	837	58.0	147	11.4
1997	699	74.6	181	19.4	747	771	340	57.6	149	11.5
1998	702	75.0	180	19.5	748	774	341	57.7	150	11.6

	Czechoslovakia				Denmark			Finland			
	Primary		Secondary		Primary	Secondary	All Schools	Primary		Secondary	
	P	T	P	T	P	P	T	P	T	P	T
1970	1,966	97.7	396	23.3	591	126	43.9	461	23.7	324	17.5
1971	1,940	97.2	400	23.3	599	131	51.4	461	24.0	332	18.2
1972	1,912	96.7	402	23.8	613	139	52.7	472	25.5	319	17.9
1973	1,890	96.8	405	24.1	629	145	54.3	500	26.5₃₆ / 28.2	296	16.9
1974	1,884	96.1	412	24.6	633	150	58.4	546	31.7	244	15.1
1975	1,881	95.6	422₃₆ / 418	24.9	631₃₆	153₃₆	59.4	588	34.3	196	12.6
1976	1,882	93.2	434	25.0	667	114	63.6	628	37.5	144	10.7
1977	1,884	92.6	444	25.0	704₉₂ / 761	72₉₂ / 160	66.1	642	36.2	115	7.7
1978	1,878	91.9	461	25.5	750	174	…	625	37.0	117	6.9
1979	1,875	90.4	475	25.7	744	186	…	604	36.9	120	6.8
1980	1,904	90.4	479	26.1	734	200	…	583	38.3	120	6.8
1981	1,931	90.3	475	26.3	722	209	…	569	39.2	121	6.5
1982	1,957	90.7	461	26.2	709	217	…	561	39.6	120	6.6
1983	1,992	92.4	435	26.1	691	212	…	554₉₃ / 569	40.6₉₄ / 38.0	120₉₅ / 102	6.9₉₄ / 6.2
1984	2,037	94.4	410	26.1	677	222	…	564	38.1	102	6.3
1985	2,074	96.4	396	26.2	666	224	…	564	39.2	99.6	6.3
1986	2,089	97.4	392	26.8	654	227	…	564	40.0	96.9	6.3
1987	2,062	97.7	398	27.4	638	228	…	567	40.8	93.6	6.2
1988	2,014	97.9	416	28.4	618	229	…	572	41.4	91.2	6.2
1989	1,962	98.0	427	29.4	600	225	…	584	42.2	87.9	6.2
1990	1,916	100.1	451	30.5	581	222	…	589	42.6	88.2	6.2
1991	1,883	101.9	464	30.1	561	226	…	592	42.2	92.3	6.3
Czech Republic											
1992[102]	1,115	65.1	291	22.7	552	229	…	590	41.2	99.5	6.3
1993[102]	1,061	63.7	301	26.6	550	223	…	587	…	105.1	…
1994	1,058	62.9	307	26.9	548	225	…	585	40.7	106.0	6.9
1995	1,056	62.1	305	26.8	549	230	…	584	40.5	107.2	7.1
1996	1,050	60.7	304	26.7	551	231	…	579	40.0	108.1	7.4
1997	1,051	60.8	309	27.1	558	229	…	581	40.3	109.4	7.9
1998	1,057	61.2	311	28.0	559	228	…	584	41.0	109.0	7.8

I1   Children and Teachers in Schools (in thousands, except as otherwise indicated)

1970–1998

	France			West Germany				East Germany			Greece			
	Primary		Secondary	Primary		Secondary		Primary	Secondary	All Schools	Primary		Secondary	
	P	T	P	P	T	P	T	P	P	T	P	T	P	T
1970	5,147	198	2,771	6,347	188	2,243	104	2,534	54.7	138	907	29.3	422	13.0
1971	5,042	198	2,916	6,477	196	2,355	108	2,571	57.3	145	906	29.3	457	13.4
1972	5,038	197	2,977	6,510	210	2,548	116	2,598	55.1	147	909	28.2	470	14.9
1973	5,013	199	2,984	6,500	218	2,730	126	2,608	51.6	152	922	29.8	485	16.6
1974	4,976	190	2,968	6,481	226	2,890	131	2,602	49.2	156	928	30.5	501	17.6
1975	4,964	191	2,989	6,425	236	3,011	137	2,579	47.9	159	936	31.0	529	18.7
1976	4,971	191	3,014	6,278	240	3,163	148	2,533	47.6	161	938	32.6	546	21.8
1977	5,034	192	2,980	6,019	244	3,288	155	2,481	46.8	166	933	34.7	565	24.3
1978	5,074	193	2,958	5,722	245	3,364	163	2,420	46.0	167	922	35.7	572	26.9
1979	5,077	195	2,964	5,354	247	3,454	171	2,314	46.5	169	899	36.2	608	29.7
1980	5,017	198	2,950	5,044	248	3,470	180	2,204	46.9	169	901	37.3	631	31.7
1981	4,903	198	2,961	4,775	245	3,430	187	2,106	46.1	170	891	37.9	659	33.6
1982	4,390[96]	196	3,031	4,501	243	3,329	188	2,024	45.3	171	890	37.3	667	36.0
1983	4,557	194	3,115	4,247	239	3,174	189	1,974	45.0	172	888	36.8	680	37.8
1984	4,419	191[36]	3,180	4,006	235	2,983	189	1,951	44.3	173	890	37.9	685	39.4
1985	4,340	221	3,191	3,828	234	2,798	187	1,943	42.6	174	888	...	...	...
1986	4,335	221	3,204[36]	3,722	232	2,631	186	1,943	40.8	170	...	...	...	...
1987	4,336	224	3,170	3,661	230	2,511	184	1,948	40.5	167	...	...	...	...
1988	4,107	222	3,224	3,653	230	2,438	180	1,953	40.8	167	...	...	...	...
1989	4,096	222	3,157	3,704	228	2,403	179				...	...	...	...
1990	4,084	298[103]	3,134	3,807	231	2,414	178				...	...	...	...
				Germany										
1991	4,047	299[103]	3,168	4,834	271	2,905	189				...	...	...	...
1992	4,002	300[103]	3,228	4,902	311	3,104	205				...	...	...	...
1993	3,961	301[103]	3,285	4,953	311	3,222	206				...	...	...	...
1994	3,901	303[103]	3,296	4,989	313	3,276	208				...	...	...	...
1995	3,879	304[103]	3,294	5,013	316	3,307	211				...	...	...	...
1996	3,860	303[103]	3,281	5,034	319	3,342	215				...	...	...	...
1997	3,851	301[103]	3,280	5,107	325	3,391	219				...	...	...	...
1998	3,849	300[103]	3,272	5,145	330	3,408	221				...	...	...	...

	Hungary				Southern Ireland				Italy			
	Primary		Secondary		Primary		Secondary		Primary		Secondary	
	P	T	P	T	P[7]	T	P	T	P	T	P	T
1970	1,116	63.1	347	13.4	453	14.9	151	9.6	4,841	222	2,168	198
1971	1,078	63.4	352	...	458	15.1	157	10.3	4,913	229	2,287	...
1972	1,044	64.0	347	...	463	15.4	162	10.7	4,965	238	2,422	...
1973	1,033	64.6	349	...	464	15.6	167	11.2	4,963	249	2,530	...
1974	1,040	65.7	375	13.7	465	16.1	173	12.1	4,923	251	2,629	...
1975	1,051	66.9	382	14.1	474	16.7	183	11.8	4,835	253	2,762	...
1976	1,072	68.4	373	14.5	481	17.1	189	12.2	4,785	...	2,867	...
1977	1,090	70.0	364	14.7	488	17.3	193	12.7	4,649	...	2,939	...
1978	1,107	71.9	352	15.0	496	17.6	197	13.2	4,562	...	2,923	...
1979	1,128	73.5	342	15.2	497	18.4	199	13.4	4,518	...	2,904	...
1980	1,162	75.4	334	15.5	503[7] 556	18.8	201	13.5	4,423	...	2,885	...
1981	1,213	78.1	327	16.0	559	19.4	204	13.8	4,333	...	2,856	...
1982	1,244	80.8	319	16.4	565	19.9	206	14.1	4,204	...	2,850	...
1983	1,270	83.5	317	16.9	564	20.4	209	14.1	4,063	...	2,816	...
1984	1,287	86.4	319	17.5	567	20.7	212	13.9[94] 12.1	3,904	...	2,789	...
1985	1,298	88.1	321	17.9	567	20.9	214	11.9	3,716	...	2,757	...
1986	1,299	89.6	319	18.5	568	21.1	216	12.0	3,518	...	2,705	...
1987	1,277	90.9	322	19.2	565	21.2	214	12.1	3,371	...	2,613	...
1988	1,243	90.6	329	20.1	560	21.2	214	12.0	3,237	...	2,506	...
1989	1,183	90.6	349	21.4	552	20.4	214	11.6	3,140	...	2,395	...
1990	1,130	90.5	360	22.9	544	20.3	213	11.5	3,060	...	2,262	...
1991	1,081	89.3	376	24.0	534	20.4	217	11.9	3,005	...	2,151	...
1992	1,044	88.9	393	25.3	521	20.7	221	12.3	2,939	...	2,059	...
1993	1,009	89.7	407	26.8	506	20.8	224	12.5	2,863	...	1,996	...
1994	1,000	90.1	421	27.3	500	20.9	226	12.6	2,854	...	1,902	...
1995	989	89.7	423	28.1	491	20.8	229	12.8	2,806	...	1,868	...
1996	976	89.6	434	28.9	487	20.7	233	12.9	2,823	...	1,849	...
1997	981	90.0	439	29.2	484	20.7	237	13.0	2,800	...	1,807	...
1998	983	90.1	445	29.6	481	20.5	236	13.0	2,775	...	1,800	...

I1 Children and Teachers in Schools (in thousands, except as otherwise indicated)

1970–1998

	Netherlands				Norway				Poland			
	Primary		Secondary		Primary		Secondary		Primary		Secondary	
	P	T	P	T	P	T	P	T	P	T	P	T
1970	1,462	49.2	591	...	536	28.1	76.9	4.3	5,257	211	401	17.5
1971	1,464	50.1	626	...	555	30.5	72.5	4.2	5,052	211	439	...
1972	1,462	50.2	662	...	569	32.1	68.7	4.1	4,841	207	451	21.8
1973	1,455	51.0	707	...	576	31.4	66.1	...	4,634	201	471	22.8
1974	1,448	52.5	740	...	583	29.8	64.2	3.8	4,453	179	483	23.0
1975	1,453	53.4	766	...	585	29.3	66.1_{90} 152	3.9_{90} 10.8	4,310	191	472	23.0
1976	1,448	53.8	795	...	590	28.9	158	11.0	4,199	185	452	23.0
1977	1,435	...	812	...	589	30.4	165	12.2	4,137	180	421	22.9
1978	1,413	54.9	821	53.4	592	31.3	174	13.5	4,105	182	389	22.1
1979	1,380	56.0	824	54.0	594	30.6	179	14.2	4,113	188	364	21.3
1980	1,333	56.5	824	54.4	591	30.8	184	14.9	4,162	196	345	21.3
1981	1,270	55.9	829	54.9	586	30.1	184	15.0	4,250	216	336	21.0
1982	1,202	54.0	836	55.9	577	30.0	188	15.5	4,372	235	329	21.4
1983	1,140	51.4	833	53.8	565	30.0	196	16.4	4,530	260	326	22.1
1984	$1,095_{97}$ 1,494	50.5_{97} 82.1	823	53.4	550	30.8	204	17.1	4,671	265	330	21.6
1985	1,469	88.4	804	53.4	534	31.5	210	18.2	4,795	268	338	21.3
1986	1,448	85.0	776	52.5	520	33.0	206	18.1	4,923	263	353	21.1
1987	1,431	84.0	747	...	506	34.4	200	18.2	5,030	266	373	21.6
1988	1,429	82.6	718	...	493	34.7	209	18.3	5,081	263	393	21.9
1989	1,433	82.5	697	...	483	34.0	224	19.1	5,141	282	414	22.5
1990	1,443	84.0	684	...	473	34.0	237	20.6	5,189	317	446	24.3
1991	1,408	...	674	...	467	35.4	244	21.0	5,218	310	499	25.8
1992	1,415	87.4	668	...	464	36.4	244	20.7	5,232	309	555	27.5
1993	1,427	88.7	668	...	467	36.2	241	21.7	5,194	311	601	29.5
1994	1,429	89.1	669	...	469	36.7	239	22.4	5,176	302	647	30.1
1995	1,433	90.2	673	...	474	37.0	236	23.7	5,171	299	682	32.4
1996	1,428	89.0	667	...	478	37.9	240	22.8	5,203	307	870	31.9
1997	1,425	88.6	665	...	473	37.2	242	22.4	5,213	314	865	31.2
1998	1,419	87.2	661	...	468	36.8	237	21.9	5,224	316	851	30.5

	Portugal				Romania				Spain			Sweden		
	Primary		Secondary		Primary		Secondary		Primary	Secondary		Primary	Secondary	
	P	T	P	T	P	T	P	T	P	P	T	P	T	P
1970	992	29.6	137	7.4	2,934	136	506	23.1	4,749	1,538	62.3	649	92.0	414
1971	989	28.3	156	8.3	2,824	136	502	24.5	4,942	1,333	60.8	669	95.4	542
1972	971	31.3	179	9.1	2,720	135	505	25.1	5,262	1,274	60.9	685	99.2	540
1973	947	32.0	212	10.3	2,733	133	510	25.1	5,775	1,013	56.4	702	104	529
1974	933	34.6	238	13.6	2,882	137	708	31.8	6,215	792	49.1	716	106	521
1975	922	88.7	216_{90} 323	14.9_{90}	3,020	142	902	41.6	6,374	818	48.7	723	107	524
1976	914	39.8	369	...	3,117	145	1,016	46.4	6,501	844	48.8	718	...	536
1977	926	40.0	409	...	3,145	146	1,039	51.5	6,588	878	51.5	700	124	560
1978	931	...	407	...	3,414	148	1,055	52.6	6,668	999	59.4	688	128	592
1979	929	42.2	416_{98} 453	... 26.8	3,289	154	1,030	50.2	6,767	1,056	63.6	678	134	615
1980	946	43.7	455	35.6	3,308	157	980	46.6	6,789	1,091	66.2	668	141	633
1981	938	44.2	460	39.5	3,285	158	1,021	47.3	6,828	1,124	67.9	664	143	639
1982	932	44.7	519	33.9	3,140	152	1,205	47.1	6,821	1,118	69.8	658	143	644
1983	923	43.3	535	40.7	3,067	151	1,272	49.2	6,804	1,142	71.3	648	142	643
1984	899	43.7	571	42.9	3,035	148	1,238	47.0	6,787	1,182	73.4	631	142	639
1985	...	44.0	615	...	3,031	147	1,227	47.7	6,722	1,230	75.6	613	145	634
1986	839	41.5	569	...	3,017	145	1,197	46.1	6,660	1,266	75.6	600	144	626
1987	791	...	...	...	3,027	142	1,228	43.8	6,452	1,355	81.5	589	140	623
1988	...	...	...	...	3,005	146	1,271	41.3	6,274	1,426	87.2	580	141	618
1989	716	...	...	...	2,922	146	1,346	42.5	6,081	1,471	92.2	579	143	614
1990	669	...	...	...	2,730	145	995	51.7	5,887	1,499	96.4	578	144	608
1991	635	41.5	...	...	2,639	140	778	55.0	5,675	1,505	99.7	584	144	601
1992	...	...	...	...	2,572	134	714	58.2	5,521	1,488	...	595	138	602
1993	...	...	...	...	2,533	128	722	59.5	...	...	...	600	134	607
1994	...	...	...	...	2,501	126	785	61.4	...	...	...	602	140	609
1995	...	...	...	...	2,490	121	860	62.3	...	...	...	613	142	611
1996	...	...	...	...	2,414	118	873	62.8	...	...	...	618	139	607
1997	...	...	...	...	2,400	115	865	61.9	...	...	...	624	138	606
1998	...	...	...	...	2,425	123	852	61.0	...	...	...	627	140	613

I1 Children and Teachers in Schools (in thousands, except as otherwise indicated)

1970–1998

Year	E&W Primary P	E&W Primary T	E&W Secondary P	E&W Secondary T	N. Ireland Primary P	N. Ireland Primary T	N. Ireland Secondary P	N. Ireland Secondary T	Scotland Primary P	Scotland Primary T	Scotland Secondary P	Scotland Secondary T	Yugoslavia Primary P	Yugoslavia Primary T	Yugoslavia Secondary P	Yugoslavia Secondary T
1970	5,023	188	3,089	173	215	7.6	137	7.2	636	23.2	328	21.3	2,835	120	697	40.9
1971	5,115	197	3,176	182	218	7.8	139	7.5	643	24.1	338	22.3	2,835	121	717	42.8
1972	5,151	204	3,239	191	217	7.9	141	7.8	644	25.5	352	23.8	2,856	124	737	44.6
1973	5,149	209	3,551	204	217	8.1	152	8.5	643	26.4	385[100]	25.4[100]	2,869	126	763	45.6
1974	5,100	213	3,619	213	216	8.2	154	8.7	635	28.0	407	26.1	2,867	128	790	47.4
1975	5,048	214	3,712	220	216	8.3	158	9.0	629	26.1	412	27.3	2,856	131	833	49.2
1976	4,943	211	3,793[99]	225[99]	213	8.6	161	9.5	619	27.1	416	27.9	2,851	132	886	51.8[36]
1977	4,800[99] / 4,876	207[99]	4,024 / 4,079	236 / 241	210	8.9	162	10.0	601	27.3	420	28.4	2,831	132	919	56.2
1978	4,738	206	4,101	245	207	8.8	163	10.3	576	26.7	422	28.8	2,825	130	969	59.9
1979	4,569	202	4,094	247	202	8.6	164	10.4	552	26.6	422	29.1	2,818	131	985	60.9
1980	4,371	195	4,067	245	199	8.5	164	10.4	525	25.5	419	29.1	2,809	132	1,008	62.3
1981	4,184	187	4,023	242	194	8.3	164	10.4	499	24.3	416	28.8	2,803	134	1,003	65.1
1982	3,923	180	3,965	241	190	8.2	163	10.4	474	23.0	410	28.5	2,807	134	987	64.8
1983	3,915	177	3,865	239	188	8.1	162	10.3	454	22.1	401	27.9	2,817	135	964	63.4
1984	3,799	176	3,740	232	188	8.1	160	10.2	444	21.4	387	27.8	2,824	135	938	62.6
1985	3,805	172	3,606	226	188	8.1	157	10.2	436	21.2	361	27.1	2,834	137	910	62.8
1986	3,835	174	3,448	220	189	8.2	153	10.0	434	21.3	345	27.1	2,833	139	901	63.7
1987	3,880	177	3,269	221	191	8.4	149	9.8	431	21.3	328	26.4	2,828	141	…	…
1988	3,935	179	3,137	205	193	8.5	147	9.7	433	21.3	312	24.6	2,843	140	946	57.8
1989	4,009	183	3,048	203	194	8.5	145	9.5	437	22.2	299	24.1	…	…	…	…
1990	4,059	185	3,147	206	195	8.6	145	9.5	441	22.6	294	24.1	2,799	141	968	60.1
1991	4,090	186	3,094	200	195	8.7	147	9.4	441	22.6	296	23.8	936	51	347	24.9[104]
1992	4,160	187	3,157	200	196	8.9	149	9.6	439	22.7	303	24.0	923	52	348	25.6[104]
1993	4,231	188	3,128	196	197	9.0	152	9.7	438	22.5	311	24.3	…	…	…	…
1994	4,248	189	3,121	195	198	9.1	154	9.3	437	22.3	315	24.5	…	…	…	…
1995	4,278	191	3,118	193	199	9.2	157	9.4	435	22.2	318	24.7	…	…	…	…
1996	4,301	193	3,113	192	200	9.4	155	9.8	438	22.5	321	24.9	…	…	…	…
1997	4,352	196	3,127	196	203	9.6	153	9.7	441	22.9	319	24.6	…	…	…	…
1998	4,387	198	3,140	200	205	9.8	150	9.7	444	23.2	314	24.3	…	…	…	…

I1 Children and Teachers in Schools

NOTES

1. SOURCES:- The official publications noted on p. xv. Ireland to 1920—*Reports of the Commissioners of National Education*. Polish data on pupils for 1922–48 and on teachers for 1937, 1945, 1947, and 1948 were supplied by the Polish Central Statistical Office. Romanian data for 1938, 1948, and 1950–59 were kindly supplied by Mr.G. Radulescu, Editor in Chief of the *Enciclopedica Romana*.
2. The definition of the different sorts of schools varies from country to country and from time to time, and is not always clear. Nor is it always clear to exactly what time of year the statistics relate, and which pupils are covered by them (e.g. whether it is all registered pupils, or only those attending school regularly, or those there on a certain day). So far as possible changes in the scope of the statistics are indicated in the footnotes, but there are believed to be many which were not recorded in the sources.
3. So far as possible, the statistics relate to the school year beginning in that indicated.

FOOTNOTES

[1] Cisleithania (excluding the Italian provinces) to 1914, and the Republic of Austria subsequently.

[2] Previous figures include the part of Limburg ceded to the Netherlands, and this figure also includes the Grand Duchy of Luxembourg. Subsequent figures exclude both.

[3] Subsequent figures have a more complete coverage of private schools.

[4] *Pensionnats primaires* were previously not included.

[5] Transleithania (excluding Croatia-Slavonia) to 1917, and subsequently the territory established by the Treaty of Trianon.

[6] Including Croatia-Slavonia.

[7] Statistics are of average attendance to 1980 (1st line). Earlier figures are available for numbers registered as follows (in thousands):-

1833	107	1839	193	1844	396	1849	481
1835	146	1840	233	1845	433	1850	511
1836	154	1841	282	1846	456	1851	520
1837	167	1842	320	1847	403	1852	545
1838	170	1843	355	1848	507	1853	551

[8] The source says that exact comparisons over time are impossible owing to different meanings for the term 'elementary', but that this series is an attempt to provide as consistent a series as possible. A number of the figures is estimated-viz. 1864, 1868, 1876, 1880, 1896, 1901, 1902–6, and 1908–25.

[9] Children at Roman Catholic schools in Scotland are included in the English statistics to 1862, and not included in the Scottish statistics until 1875.

[10] Previous figures include night schools.

[11] Previous figures refer to certificated and assistant teachers employed in all schools.

[12] From 1879 to 1905 the number of teachers in private Primary schools is not known, except in 1889 when it was 5 thousand.

[13] Excluding Galicia.

[14] Subsequent figures are for inspected schools only. There was a great fall in the number of schools covered between 1878 and 1881, which was regained in 1885 and 1886.

[15] Excluding Dixmunde canton.

[16] State schools only, including state-aided schools in the United Kingdom (though not "direct grant" schools).

[17] Previously only lycées were classed as Secondary schools, and all others were classed as Primary.

[18] Previously excluding Eksamensret schools.

[19] From 1897 to 1908 certain schools were not included in the annual series published at the time, and from 1909 ancillary teachers were excluded. Statistics were given later for 1900 and 1905 as follows:-

	Pupils	Teachers
1900	14,698	1,352
1905	19,370	1,657

[20] Alsace-Lorraine is excluded from 1871 to 1922.

[21] Auxiliary teachers temporarily in charge of a class are subsequently included.

[22] From 1914 to 1918 (and 1920 for Primary schools) the invaded departments are excluded.

[23] Public Primary schools only to 1939. In 1910 there were 26 thousand pupils in private Primary schools, and in 1921 there were 36 thousand pupils and 1.8 thousand teachers.

[24] An element of double-counting was subsequently eliminated.

[25] Excluding girls' high schools to 1899 (1st line).

[26] Previous figures are of all Volksschulen. Subsequently only elementary schools are covered.

[27] New Organisation schools, previously wholly included in the Primary category, are subsequently divided.

[28] These figures are for the "results year" of each school examined.

[29] State schools only to 1886 in the case of Norway, and to 1910 including teachers' training schools from 1891 in the case of Italy.

[30] Previous figures refer only to athenées, gymnasia, and Latin schools.

[31] These figures are known to be slightly defective.

[32] Previous figures do not include pupils at gymnasia who were not doing a complete course.

[33] From 1881 (2nd line) to 1890 (1st line) the figures exclude pupils in 'ambulant schools'.

[34] Revised figures, which do not, however, fit into the series, are available for 1895 and 1900. They are 331 and 339 respectively.

I1   Children and Teachers in Schools

[35]   Figures to 1902 (1st line) refer to registered pupils of state and private licees. From 1902 (2nd line) to 1935 they refer to registered pupils of state licees plus pupils of private licees taking state examinations. From 1936 onwards they refer to registered pupils at all licees plus external students taking state examinations.

[36]   There was a change in the basis of collection of the statistics.

[37]   There was a change in coverage in Aargau canton.

[38]   Subsequently state schools only.

[39]   Some schools were transferred from the Primary to the Secondary category.

[40]   Burgenland is included subsequently.

[41]   Subsequently excludes teachers of handicrafts and of religion.

[42]   Subsequent figures include uninspected schools.

[43]   Subsequently including private schools, but excluding preparatory departments, which had previously been included.

[44]   Some special schools are subsequently included.

[45]   Progymnasia are subsequently transferred from the Secondary to the Primary category.

[46]   From 1945 (2nd line) to 1949 (1st line) pupils in the 'Eleven-year Schools' are included in the Primary rather than the Secondary category.

[47]   From 1948 to 1953 and from 1959 to 1960 all teachers in Primary and Secondary schools are included.

[48]   From 1953 to 1964 certain teachers of practical subjects are included who are omitted at other times.

[49]   The subsequent decline was caused by the lapsing of certain classes following a new Education Act.

[50]   'People's High Schools' are subsequently excluded.

[51]   Assistant teachers are excluded in these years and prior to 1938.

[52]   Previous figures are for state lycees and colleges only. Subsequently pupils in private Secondary schools are included.

[53]   For 1939–44 (for Primary school pupils) and for 1940–45 (for Secondary schools) Alsace-Lorraine and Corsica (Primary schools only) are excluded. Algeria is also excluded for state Secondary schools in 1943–45 and for private Secondary schools in 1939–41.

[54]   Subsequently pupils in elementary and special classes, though such classes in lycées etc. are not transferred from the Secondary category until 1963.

[55]   Subsequently excludes teachers of complementary courses and of infant classes.

[56]   Saarland is not included until 1958 (2nd line in the case of pupils). West Berlin teachers are included throughout, but pupils only from 1959 (2nd line). Only full-time qualified teachers are included.

[57]   Middle schools were transferred from the Secondary to the Primary category.

[58]   'Hellenic' schools were counted as Primary to 1929/30 and subsequently divided between Primary and Secondary.

[59]   Subsequently including gygogypedagoiai schools which had 18 thousand pupils and 1.4 thousand teachers in 1950/1.

[60]   The figure is for all Ireland, and is comparable with earlier statistics.

[61]   Excluding Cagliari, Caltanissetta, and Messina.

[62]   Certain private schools, which were not covered previously, are subsequently included.

[63]   Subsequent figures are for Secondary schools, properly so-called, only.

[64]   Certain private schools are excluded from 1968 (2nd line).

[65]   Higher Primary schools are subsequently transferred to the Secondary category.

[66]   Previously excluding teachers at private gymnasia.

[67]   Subsequently excluding teachers of continuation classes.

[68]   Previously only schools with 'examination right' are covered. Statistics for all Secondary general schools are available for earlier years as follows:-

	Pupils	Teachers		Pupils	Teachers		Pupils	Teachers
	(thousands)			(thousands)			(thousands)	
1875	14.6	1,085	1900	20.1	1,478	1925	28.5	1,676
1880	16.0	1,213	1905	20.7	1,671	1930	25.3	1,457
1885	18.0	1,450	1910	22.5	1,321	1935	31.6	1,627
1890	18.7	1,572	1915	26.1	1,403	1940	36.1	1,936
1895	19.3	1,474	1920	34.0	1,643	1945	44.4	2,208

Note: In these statistics, from 1910 onwards only full-time teachers are covered.

[69]   State schools only to 1962.

[70]   State schools only to 1939. Subsequently all schools (including night schools in 1940 to 1941 or 1942).

[71]   State schools only to 1955.

[72]   Subsequently including the newly acquired territories.

[73]   Excluding Cetatea—Alba department.

[74]   Excluding Ilfov and Dambovitza departments.

[75]   Statistics from 1938 relate to the postwar territory. There was a change in the definition of Secondary schools.

[76]   From 1948 to 1958 (1st line) the figures refer to state schools only. Figures for 1953–55 derive from the Central Inspectorate for Primary Education, and are not comparable with the rest of the series.

[77]   There were changes in the organization of schools which affect comparability.

[78]   This break probably results mainly from the subsequent inclusion of private Secondary schools.

[79]   Subsequently excluding middle school classes attached to Primary schools.

[80]   All school teachers from 1967.

[81]   Subsequent figures are for middle schools only. Previously they included Secondary schools (so-called).

[82]   Comparability across the years of the Second World War is impossible owing to the re-organisation following the 1944 Education Act. The figures of pupils, which are of average attendance prior to the War, are subsequently of numbers registered.

[83]   Part-time teachers are included subsequently, on a full-time equivalent basis.

[84]   Figures to 1926 (1st line) relate only to teachers receiving personal salaries from the Ministry of Education.

[85]   Subsequently including state-maintained nursery and special schools.

I1 Children and Teachers in Schools

86 Subsequently including technical schools and voluntary schools.
87 Primary departments in Secondary schools were transfered from the Secondary to the Primary sector.
88 Subsequently including part-time teachers on a full-time equivalent basis.
89 Subsequently including state-maintained nursery schools.
90 Subsequently all kinds of Secondary education, previously academic schools only.
91 There was a reorganisation of the Secondary education system.
92 Subsequently including vocational education at gymnasium level.
93 Subsequently comprehensive schools but excluding pre-Primary education.
94 Subsequently full-time teachers only.
95 Subsequently academic Secondary schools only.
96 Excluding certain special schools.
97 Subsequently including nursery schools.
98 Subsequently including 12th year pupils.
99 Subsequent statistics are calculated from U.K. data and contain elements of estimation. There was also an expansion of the coverage of Secondary schools from 1976 (2nd line).
100 A change in the date at which the data were collected may have resulted in some increase in the figures.
101 Excluding gymanesen, where there were 3.9 thousand teachers in 1969.
102 Czech Republic.
103 Includes pre-elementary.
104 Yugoslavia.

I2 NUMBER OF STUDENTS IN UNIVERSITIES

1817–1869

	Austria[1]	Belgium	Finland[4]	Hungary[5]	Italy	Netherlands	Norway	Portugal[7]	Spain	Sweden
1817	...	679	...	...	...	...	...	1,426	...	...
1818	...	744	...	...	...	702	...	1,524	...	...
1819	...	773	...	...	...	735	...	1,430	...	...
1820	...	730	...	...	...	786	300	1,419	...	...
1821	...	813	...	...	...	843	...	1,288	...	...
1822	...	940	...	...	...	971	...	1,351	...	...
1823	...	996	...	...	...	1,069	...	1,204	...	...
1824	...	1,055	...	...	...	1,111	...	1,111	...	...
1825	...	1,450	...	...	...	1,223	...	1,184	...	...
1826	...	1,566	...	...	...	1,316	...	1,226	...	...
1827	...	1,627	...	...	...	1,373	...	1,262	...	...
1828	...	1,620	329	...	...	1,441	...	...	...	...
1829	...	1,612	423	...	...	1,477	...	521	...	...
1830	...	1,071	407	...	...	1,444	600	478	...	1,265
1831	...	970	—	...	...	1,624	...	...	...	...
1832	...	1,007	425	...	...	1,568	...	...	...	...
1833	...	1,139	389	...	...	1,622	...	...	...	...
1834	...	1,178	401	...	...	1,597	...	446	...	...
1835	...	1,173	438	...	...	1,527	...	665	...	...
1836	...	1,310	414	...	...	1,588	...	777	...	...
1837	...	1,312	424	...	...	1,503	...	708	...	...
1838	...	1,283	451	...	...	1,450	...	843	...	...
1839	...	1,496	444	...	...	1,397	...	782	...	...
1840	...	1,459	403	...	...	1,410	600	928	...	...
1841	[11,235][2]	1,513	414	1,250	...	1,425	...	998	...	...
1842	8,590	1,533	429	1,134	...	1,296	...	1,086	...	...
1843	8,338	1,589	433	...	...	1,223	...	1,082	...	...
1844	...	1,604	414	...	...	1,250	...	1,102	...	...
1845	7,843	1,659	400	...	...	1,214	...	989	...	...
1846	8,508	1,660	422	...	...	1,077	...	...	...	...
1847	8,372[3]	1,652	385	...	...	1,025	...	900	...	...
1848	12,815	1,708	...	...	...	1,040	...	928	...	...
1849	12,627	1,808	476	...	...	1,037	...	1,008	...	...
1850	11,439	1,773	460	838	...	1,082	550	898	...	...
1851	11,424	1,821	492	843	...	1,226	...	884	...	...
1852	10,622	1,731	464	1,135	...	1,438	...	956	...	...
1853	10,115	1,742	410	1,104	...	1,396	...	894	...	...
1854	9,328	1,864	276	1,241	...	1,414	...	1,034	...	...
1855	9,119	2,113	338	1,063	...	1,413	605	990	...	...
1856	9,365	2,204	417	1,069	...	1,429	...	740	...	...
1857	8,168	2,221	363	1,010	...	1,327	...	796	7,528	...
1858	8,654	2,222	369	1,095	...	1,352	...	905	7,842	...
1859	8,026	2,336	402	1,133	...	1,395	...	801	7,977	...
1860	7,993	2,473	389	1,179	...	1,375	550	861	8,611	...
1861	8,043	2,440	387	1,228	6,504	1,224	...	990	7,679	...
1862	8,408	2,427	407	1,593	5,793	1,241	...	888	7,941	...
1863	8,706	2,409	411	1,831	6,316[6]	1,265	...	911	8,305	...
1864	8,798	2,466	405	1,909	...	1,283	...	789	9,704	...
1865	9,421	2,431	430	1,999	...	1,205	701	803	16,545	...
1866	9,181	2,384	471	...	9,340	1,212	...	698	12,104	...
1867	10,166	2,453	503	2,417	10,599	1,331	...	697	12,269	...
1868	10,605	2,457	528	2,538	10,765	1,217	...	779	...	...
1869	11,166	2,521	587	2,518	10,888	1,273	...	780	...	...

I2 Number of Students in Universities

	Austria[1]	Belgium	Bulgaria	Denmark[27]	Finland	France[29]	Germany	Greece[34]	Hungary[5]	Southern Ireland
1870	11,561	2,631	...	...	685	...	...	...	2,629	...
1871	12,497	2,751	...	...	508	...	...	...	2,678	...
1872	12,292	2,861	...	...	673	...	20,576	...	3,178	...
1873	12,434	3,025	...	...	664	...	...	...	3,295	...
1874	12,797	3,156	...	...	640	...	...	...	3,836	...
1875	12,356	3,256	...	...	627	...	22,892	...	3,990	...
1876	12,655	3,722	...	...	627	...	...	...	4,233[5]	...
									4,103	
1877	12,497	3,863	...	...	647	...	...	...	4,120	...
1878	12,315	4,051	...	...	619	...	...	...	4,268	...
1879	12,797	4,324	...	...	662	...	...	...	4,037	...
1880	13,264	4,568	...	...	736	...	26,254	...	4,396	...
1881	13,572	4,880	...	...	811	...	...	...	4,019	...
1882	14,252	5,182	...	...	805	...	...	...	4,183	...
1883	14,391	5,564	...	...	812[11]	...	...	...	4,401	...
					1,477					
1884	15,295	5,624	...	...	1,527	...	...	...	4,572	...
1885	15,909	5,768	...	...	1,662	...	31,418	...	4,473	...
1886	16,581	5,957	...	...	1,799	...	...	...	4,530	...
1887	17,175	5,860	...	...	1,820	...	...	...	4,690	...
1888	17,286	5,837	...	...	1,745	...	...	...	4,816	...
1889	16,919	6,203	...	...	1,816	16,587	...	...	4,723[5]	...
1890	17,492	5,663	...	...	1,863	19,821	[28,359][14]	...	...	...
1891	17,562	5,226	...	...	1,868	22,336	33,992	...	5,218	...
1892	17,894	4,937	...	...	1,888	23,295	...	...	5,266	...
1893	18,916	4,886	...	430	1,905	24,795	...	...	5,800	...
1894	19,413	4,844	...	472	1,979	24,855	...	...	6,135	...
1895	20,206	5,031	310	456	2,037	26,941	...	...	6,651	...
1896	20,992	4,830	313	475	2,194	26,819	40,286	...	7,319	...
1897	21,598	4,951	354	414	2,282	28,543	...	...	7,952	...
1898	22,134	5,113	338	407	2,384	28,254	...	...	8,758	...
1899	23,204	5,265	409	452	2,606	29,377	46,520	...	9,298	...
1900	24,140	5,389	483	414	2,727	29,901	47,986	...	9,700	...
1901	25,548	5,459	495	383	2,795	30,370	51,042	...	10,122	...
1902	27,363	5,708	578	450	2,880	31,277	52,538	...	10,530	...
1903	28,689	5,888	796	463	2,908	32,407	53,806	...	11,018	...
1904	30,631	6,130	1,014	451	3,034	33,618	55,053	...	11,351	...
1905	31,802	6,426	1,151	521	2,285	35,670	57,375	...	11,616	...
1906	34,391	6,662	1,324	546	2,474	38,197	59,360	...	11,968	...
1907	35,095	6,998	812	585	2,724	39,890	61,946	...	12,255	...
1908	36,605	7,319	1,569	582	2,315	40,767	64,490	...	11,887	...
1909	38,817	7,661	...	745	3,099	41,044	67,877	...	12,643	2,254
1910	39,416	7,910	...	829	3,238	41,190	70,183	...	12,951	2,531
1911	40,455	8,157	2,380	839	3,468	41,194	72,194	...	13,227	2,638
1912	40,252	8,300	...	862	3,690	41,109	77,378	774	13,445	2,751
1913	42,392	8,532	2,455	918	3,849	42,037[12]	79,557	844	14,249[16]	2,507
1914	17,396	...	2,887	963	3,951	11,231	66,568	782	...	2,362
1915	13,705[1]	...	2,110	937	4,067	12,566	64,384	1,036	5,890	2,321
	6,123									
1916	[7,901][9]	...	1,304	1,022	3,811	14,121	71,809	1,274	5,504	2,431
1917	9,322	...	[1,408][10]	1,094	3,172	19,381[12]	80,100[15]	2,448	6,983[5]	2,725
1918	19,394	10,797	[5,897][10]	1,140	2,915	29,890[13]	95,986	1,795	16,984	3,383
1919	21,495	8,709	8,677	1,099	3,310	45,114	117,772	1,864	12,990	3,647

I2 Number of Students in Universities

	Italy	Netherlands	Norway	Portugal	Romania	Serbia	Spain	Sweden	Switzerland
1870	12,069	1,240	1,026	801	...	224	...	...	...
1871	12,446	1,357	1,050	913	...	237	...	...	...
1872	12,013	1,354	1,010	953	...	226	...	...	...
1873	11,821	1,491	980	926	...	208	...	...	...
1874	10,666	1,556	830	903	...	207	...	...	...
1875	9,554	1,537	833	898	...	209	...	...	...
1876	9,431	1,603	880	864	...	151	...	...	...
1877	9,940	1,606	900	815	...	...	...	...	...
1878	10,601	1,564	770	794	...	146	...	...	...
1879	11,233	1,425	730	748	...	100	...	...	...
1880	11,871[17]	1,493	750	766	...	130	...	...	...
1881	12,481	1,543	810	768	...	157	...	...	...
1882	13,856	1,538	880	818	...	158	...	...	...
1883	14,675	1,852	840	948	...	192	15,732	...	...
1884	15,089	1,978	1,240	958	...	206	...	...	...
1885	16,131	2,110	1,350	1,035	...	225	...	...	...
1886	16,980	2,237	1,510	1,115	...	366	...	...	...
1887	17,191	2,418	1,720	1,097	...	233	...	...	1,966
1888	17,584	2,501	1,650	1,126	...	293	...	...	2,039
1889	17,605	2,488	1,620	1,183	...	355	...	...	2,172
1890	18,145	2,815	1,537	1,180	...	466	...	...	2,315
1891	18,685	2,915	1,460	1,157	...	565	...	...	2,532
1892	19,802	3,053	1,370	1,200[8] 905	...	472	...	...	2,758
1893	20,925	3,097	1,290	918	...	460	...	...	2,903
1894	22,230	3,112	1,190	948	...	480	...	...	3,119
1895	23,112	3,076	1,140	1,065	...	432	...	...	3,112
1896	24,318	3,046	1,200	1,021	...	491	...	...	3,272
1897	24,705	2,938	1,220	1,066	...	482	...	...	3,492
1898	24,632	3,021	1,330	1,084	...	466	...	...	3,589
1899	25,242	3,028	1,350	1,118	...	438	...	...	3,841
1900	26,033	3,135	1,400	1,181	5,074	415	...	...	4,208
1901	26,613	3,178	1,400	1,106	3,433[18]	405	...	...	4,315
1902	25,748	3,235	1,500	1,028	4,769	395	...	...	4,790
1903	25,436	3,294	1,600	944	5,271	465	...	...	4,942
1904	25,098	3,409	1,600	911	4,950	490	...	...	5,219
1905	25,573	3,552	1,300	953	5,075	618	...	...	5,612
1906	26,621	3,621	1,470	1,050	4,101	780	...	...	6,444
1907	26,766	3,655	1,560	1,085	[4,628][19]	...	...	...	6,906
1908	27,304	3,732	1,580	1,195	3,821	...	...	...	6,752
1909	27,005	3,945	1,550	1,262	4,144	...	...	...	6,958
1910	26,850	4,128	1,540	...	3,817	...	...	7,659	6,831
1911	27,783	4,180	1,550	1,212	[5,425][20]	...	...	8,092	7,134
1912	27,142	4,292	1,500	1,822	[5,571][20]	...	...	8,310	7,019
1913	28,026	4,450	1,500	2,285	[5,901][20]	...	...	8,373	8,110
1914	29,624	3,650	1,500	2,573	[5,940][20]	...	20,497	8,123	6,814
1915	28,968	3,985	1,500	3,073	...	...	21,467	8,075[21] 8,176	6,787
1916	32,882	4,471	1,500	2,743	...	...	23,683	8,617	7,710
1917	38,691	4,810	1,550	2,493	...	...	23,586	9,078[21] 8,987	7,894
1918	46,114	5,396	1,550	2,472	...	...	23,660	8,928	7,307
1919	53,670	5,645	1,550	2,747	...	...	23,403	9,195	7,501

I2 Number of Students in Universities

1920–1969

	Austria[1]	Belgium	Bulgaria	Czecho-slovakia	Denmark[27]	Finland	France[29]	Germany / East Germany[32]	West Germany[33]	Greece[34]	Hungary
1920	...[22]	9.3	5.5	28.2	1.1[27] 0.7	3.4	49.9	119[30]		1.6	12.9
1921	22.0	9.0	3.4	28.3	0.8	3.6	50.9	119		2.2	15.7
1922	21.0	9.0	4.4	25.5	0.8	3.7	50.4	122		2.7	16.7
1923	18.4[22] 19.5	9.8	4.2	26.2	0.8	3.9	50.9	114		3.7	13.9
1924	18.4	9.8	4.8	27.4	0.9[27] 4.9	4.1	53.1	93.5		3.1	12.1
1925	17.7	9.0	5.2	27.7	5.0	4.4	58.5	90.3		4.4	11.6
1926	17.7	9.2	5.4	27.8	5.3	4.8	61.0	94.8		2.0	11.4
1927	18.6	9.4	6.5	28.9	5.0	5.2	64.5	101		1.3[34] 6.6	11.9
1928	19.3	9.9	6.3	29.8	5.1	5.9	67.0	112		7.1	12.3
1929	20.1	11.4	6.9	31.2	5.0	6.4	73.6	121		6.7	12.1
1930	21.4	10.8	7.2	32.5	5.3	7.0	78.7	128		6.8	12.6
1931	22.5	11.4	7.9	34.1	6.1	7.4	82.7	126		7.8	12.4
1932	22.8	11.5	9.0	33.3	6.2	7.7	84.7	121		8.6	12.1
1933	19.8	11.7	9.3	32.3	6.5	8.2	87.2	107		8.6	12.4
1934	18.5	11.0	8.7	31.6	6.4	8.1	82.1	86.1		9.2	11.7
1935	17.8	10.7	7.9	29.3	6.7	8.2	73.8	76.3		8.2	10.8
1936	16.8[23] 18.7	10.3	8.1	23.4	6.5	8.2	72.1	64.5		8.9	10.4
1937	...	10.8	7.9	25.7	6.8	8.0	75.3	56.4		7.9	9.7[35] 11.7
1938	...	11.6	[6.0][25]	...	7.0	8.0	79.0	55.9		...	...
1939	...	11.1	10.2	...	7.2	8.2	55.5	47.4[31]		...	...
1940	...	12.3[24] 12.9	[9.2][25]	...	7.4	8.3	76.5	49.7		...	...
1941	...	15.7	[9.7][25]	...	7.8	6.3	89.9	52.3		...	...
1942	...	15.4	...	...	8.2	5.9	106	63.6		...	...
1943	...	13.5	...[26]	...	...	6.8	90.7	64.8		...	...
1944	...	15.1	26.4	...	...	10.4	97.0	...		...	...
1945	26.8	18.6	...	54.9	8.6	12.2	123	...	...	...	...
1946	...	17.5	...	60.3	8.7	12.9	129	...	...	...	...
1947	35.2	18.3	...	60.7	9.1	13.3	129	...	...	...	...
1948	32.0	19.2	39.2	57.7	9.2	13.6	129	...	...	...	...
1949	28.2	20.0	38.5	43.2	9.2	12.4	137	...	[110][11]	...	...
1950	24.8	20.7	33.0	38.9	9.1	12.1	140	...	[117][11]	...	32.5
1951	22.7	21.3	31.7	39.1	8.4	12.1	142	31.5	[118][11]	...	40.4
1952	20.8	21.8	31.4	42.7	8.3	12.1	148	42.2	[120][11]	...	49.4
1953	20.0	22.5	...	47.2	8.2	12.1	151	55.2	117	...	53.3
1954	20.0	23.3	...	48.6	8.4	12.5	156	70.7	123	...	47.5
1955	21.1	24.5	37.0	49.5	8.3	12.7	157	74.7	130[33]	...	45.4
1956	22.8	25.7	37.5	52.5	8.7	13.4	170	80.0	145	...	42.6
1957	27.3	27.1	41.2	53.8	8.6	14.4	181	85.7	161	...	35.9
1958	32.6	28.3	43.1	54.0	9.4	15.9	192	82.8	181	...	34.0
1959	36.1	29.1	48.8	58.6	10.0	17.5	202[29]	89.1	196	16.3	38.0
1960	40.8	30.7	54.8	67.3	10.8	19.1	211	99.9	212	17.2	44.6
1961	45.1	32.7	61.4	78.1	12.7	21.6	233	111	229	19.7	53.3
1962	48.3	35.4	71.6	87.4	14.7	23.5	271	113	244	22.9	67.3
1963	50.3	38.4	78.0	94.7	16.9	25.3	308	114	256	28.8	82.3
1964	51.4	42.4	82.8	92.7	21.4	27.4	349	114	263	35.2	91.9
1965	52.2	48.8	85.0	95.0	25.4	29.2[28] 40.9	394	112	267	38.3	94.0
1966	52.4	53.8	83.2	96.1	28.1	44.9	433	111	281	42.0	89.5
1967	55.5	59.2	81.8	99.3	31.7	50.8	478	111	286	47.2	83.9
1968	52.5	64.8	80.3	104	33.2	53.9	540	115	304	50.1	78.7
1969	53.8	69.6	...	104	35.4	57.3	615	128	376	52.8	78.9

I2 Number of Students in Universities

	Southern Ireland	Italy	Netherlands	Norway	Poland	Portugal	Romania	Spain	Sweden	Switzer-land	U.K.[45]	Yugo-slavia[49]
1920	3.7	53.2	5	1.8	25.9	3.0	13.6[36]	23.5	9.1	6.9	...	...
1921	3.5	49.1	6.0	2.0	35.2	3.4	14.4	23.1	8.8	6.5	...	...
1922	3.4	46.6	6.8[3] 9.5	2.3	38.0	3.4	[14.1][37]	25.7	9.1	6.0	59.0	10.6
1923	3.3	43.2	9.4	2.5	39.3	3.6	18.8	27.8	9.0	6.3	57.1	11.0
1924	3.2	43.8	9.3	2.8	38.0	3.9	19.5	29.6	9.4	6.6	55.9	10.8
1925	3.2	45.2	9.4	3.2	37.5	4.1	22.4	31.6	9.1	6.7	56.3	10.8
1926	3.0	42.9	10.0	3.1	40.7	4.5	27.6	39.7	9.5	6.5	57.1	12.2
1927	3.2	42.4	10.4	3.6	41.7	5.0	29.8	45.5	9.7	6.5	57.8	11.9
1928	3.5	40.4	11.1	3.5	43.6	5.0	31.1	41.2	10.2	6.6	58.5	12.3
1929	3.9	44.9	11.5	3.5	45.5	4.9	32.0	33.6	10.1	6.6	59.5	13.1
1930	4.3	46.3	12.1	3.5	48.2	5.6	28.6	35.7	10.1	6.9	62.3	14.2
1931	4.6	47.6	12.7	3.6	49.8	6.0	31.2	33.6	10.6	7.4	62.5	15.0
1932	5.0	53.7	13.5	3.7	51.8	...	30.1	31.9	11.1	7.8	64.1	14.2
1933	5.0	57.3	13.7	3.9	49.6	...	40.9	30.8	11.3	8.6	64.4	15.6
1934	5.1	62.0	13.1	4.0	47.9	...	41.3	34.5	11.4	8.8	64.0	15.3
1935	5.0	64.9	12.6	3.9	47.0	...	38.2	29.2	11.7	8.7	63.6	14.5
1936	5.2	71.5	12.4	4.0	48.0	...	34.1	...	12.5	8.7	62.5	14.7
1937	5.3	74.9	12.5	4.0	49.5	5.8	30.8[26,38]	...	12.5[40] 11.7	9.1	62.3	15.4
1938	5.4	77.4	12.6	4.2	...	6.2	26.5	...	12.1	9.5	63.4	17.0
1939	5.4	85.5	11.3	4.1	...	6.6	...	54.3	12.1	9.0	49.8	21.3
1940	5.4	127	10.4	4.2	...	8.7	...	33.8	11.4	9.6	44.0	...
1941	5.5	146	10.9	3.9	...	6.8	...	[34.7][39]	12.4[41] 11.5	10.1	46.5	...
1942	5.8	168	...	3.1	...	8.9	...	37.7	11.8	10.7	48.0	...
1943	5.9	157	...	4.2	...	10.1	...	41.8	12.3	11.8	48.9	...
1944	6.3	171	...	...	...[26]	10.8	...	39.4	13.0	12.1	49.8	...
1945	6.6	190	14.6	6.0	56.0	11.9	...	40.4	13.7	12.2	67.2	...
1946	7.0	191	24.7	6.2	86.5	12.0	...	42.6	13.7	12.8	86.3	39.2
1947	7.0	180	26.0	6.1	94.8	12.0	...	46.9	13.9	13.2	96.5	46.1
1948	7.3	168	27.0	5.5	103	12.0	48.7	50.0	14.4	13.2	102[45] 105	58.7
1949	7.5	146	28.6	5.3	116	12.8	48.6	50.3	15.4	12.9	106	60.0
1950	7.2	145	29.7	5.4	125	13.5[3] 15.8	53.0	51.6	16.4	12.8	105	59.8
1951	7.5	143	29.9	4.0	142	16.2	61.1	53.4	[17.8][42]	12.7	103	54.8
1952	7.6	139	28.7	4.0	131	16.4	71.5	58.1	[18.6][42]	12.5	100	54.4
1953	7.7	138	28.0	3.7	140	17.0	30.6	59.6	[19.9][42]	12.4	99.1	57.5
1954	8.0	136	28.8	3.8	155	17.7	78.9	58.7	21.5	11.8	101	70.0
1955	8.1	139	29.6	3.7	157	18.5	77.6	57.0	23.1	11.9	104	69.6
1956	8.4	145	30.9	4.3	170	18.8	81.2	62.2	26.3	12.1	109	71.9
1957	8.8	155	32.6	4.7	163	19.5	80.9	64.3	27.7	12.8	115	82.9
1958	9.4	164	35.1	5.8	157	20.5	67.8	63.0	30.6	13.7	119	96.9
1959	10.0	176	37.7	6.1	161	22.2	63.2	63.8	33.4	14.6	124	105
1960	10.9	192	40.7	6.6	166	23.9	72.0	62.1	37.4	15.7	130	141
1961	11.8	206	43.9	7.7	172	25.1	83.7	64.0	40.7[43]	17.3	136	158
1962	12.7	226	47.8	8.9	190	...	98.9	69.4	45.0	19.1	140	160
1963	13.8	240	52.4	10.8	213	29.8	113	80.1	49.3	20.7	148	161
1964	14.7	259	58.4	12.8	231	31.6	123	85.1	60.2[44] 59.8	22.9	162	170
1965	16.2	298	64.4	14.4	252	34.0	131	930	68.3	24.8	187	185
1966	17.2	339	71.3	15.5	274	35.9	137	105	75.5	25.8	207	195
1967	18.1	370	77.9	16.2	289	38.6	142	116	89.5	27.8	225	211
1968	19.9	426	84.8	17.5	306	42.0	148	135	100	29.8	240	231
1969	21.3	488	93.6	20.4	322	47.3	152	150	114	31.3	234	240

I2 Number of Students in Universities

1970–1998

	Austria	Belgium	Bulgaria[26]	Czecho-slavakia	Denmark	Finland	France	East Germany[32]	West Germany	Greece	Hungary[35]
1970	57.3	75.1	88.6	106	41.4	58.7	651	143	412	53.7	80.5[35] / 44.7
1971	62.9	81.0	93.1	106	41.6	60.7	698	158	466	50.9	44.4
1972	70.7	78.3	101	107	45.4	62.1	735	161	534	56.7	44.5
1973	77.0	79.5	104	112	48.7	66.7	742	154	589	59.7	46.2
1974	82.4	81.0	106	117	51.0	69.9	760	145	640	66.7	47.2
1975	89.6	83.4	107	123	54.2	75.8	806	137	676	68.8	48.5
1976	97.4	86.8	105	130	56.9	78.2	826[46] / 820	130	700	71.7	48.5
1977	105	89.3	95.1	138	55.8	81.9	838	130	725	74.1	48.0
1978	114	89.6	93.0	140	...	82.4	857	127	751	73.5	47.5
1979	123	92.5	88.1	146	...	83.5	861	129	774	63.2	47.0
1980	121	95.2	85.8	152	49.1	84.2	864	130	818	64.2	45.4
1981	132	95.9	84.9	156	48.9	86.0	894	131	880	66.2	44.6
1982	140	96.8	82.7	154	49.8	88.5	918	130	928	73.4	44.0
1983	149	100	85.1	149	51.0	88.2	932	130	971	79.3	43.0
1984	159	102	91.1	145	52.2	89.7	953	130	999	91.9	42.2
1985	168	104	99.1	141	52.9	92.2	969	130	1,014	...	42.4
1986	176	104	107	140	53.4	96.0	965	132	1,033	...	42.5
1987	184	104	114	140	55.1	99.2	985	133	1,060	...	43.4
1988	180	105	126	142	56.8	104	1,031	132	1,105	...	44.8
1989	186	108	133	143	55.4	108	1,105		1,399	...	45.5
1990	193	111	152	154	57.8	113	1,171		1,650	...	47.5
1991	202	116	152	151	62.3	115	1,225		1,699	...	51.3
1992	206	...	162	114[50]	65.02	122	1,296		1,731	...	54.0
1993	211	...	176	127[50]	67.2	124	1,395		1,751	...	58.3
				Czech Republic				**Germany**			
1994	224	201	192	179	72.1	136	1,427		1,849	202	62.7
1995	233	246	207	191	76.4	139	1,498		1,937	219	64.5
1996	238	352	223	207	83.0	145	1,560		2,042	290	67.9
1997	240	358	250	213	85.3	151	1,577		2,098	329	69.2
1998	242	359	262	217	87.2	163	1,591		2,156	363	70.1

	Southern Ireland	Italy	Netherlands	Norway	Poland	Portugal	Romania	Spain	Sweden	Switzer-land	U.K.	Yugo-slavia[49]
1970	21.7	561	103	23.0	331[26]	49.5	152	169	120	32.3	259	261
1971	22.2	631	113	24.9[48] / 32.9	98 / 102	57.5	148	196	116	34.4	266	283
1972	22.4	658	...[47]	35.4	107	54.0	144	217	114	36.6	270	302
1973	22.4	675	...[47]	37.3	119	58.6	144	252	110	37.9	276	329
1974	23.5	709	113	39.3	131	56.9	153	291	109	39.8	283	360
1975	23.7	736	122	40.8	147	70.8	165	346	110	41.8	295	394
1976	23.5	758	128	40.6	156	86.2	175	370	114	43.3	307	406
1977	24.3	748	136	39.3	152	82.0	182	428	148	44.9	317	424
1978	24.3	778	142	39.5	147	79.6	191	406	157	46.3	325	440
1979	24.7	768	150	40.6	139	81.3		415	155	47.7	332	448
1980	25.9	764	153	40.6	131	84.1	193	424	158	49.7	340	411
1981	26.3	725	152	39.8	125	86.3	191	441	158	51.8	343	402
1982	26.9	717	156	41.0	119	90.0	181	465	163	53.4	339	386
1983	27.6	745	164	41.4	113	90.3	174	507	164	56.0	337	374
1984	28.0	767	167	42.4	111	102	166	536	165	57.7	346	359
1985	28.4	763	169	41.7	117	92.5	160	579	163	58.9	352	349
1986	29.5	784	172	42.9	115	...	157	607	161	59.6	361	350
1987	29.8	813	178	44.0	120	...	157	646	163	60.6	367	347
1988	31.4	846	171	47.9	126	...	159	673	166	62.0	384	340
1989	32.0	866	174	56.6	135	...	165	703	164	63.4	405	343
1990	34.9	961	172	63.3	158	...	193	721	173	66.0	429	327
1991	38.4	1,019	179	68.2	160	...	215	...	189	68.9	468	133[51]
1992	41.7	1,044	181	73.8	169	...	236	...	209	70.2	511	142[51]
1993	...	1,093	187	77.9	172	...	250	...	256	70.4	554	141[51]
1994	56.2	1,140	191	80.3	177	...	251	817	246	71.2	567	140
1995	59.9	1,210	195	85.7	179	...	259	829	261	72.0	583	144
1996	66.3	1,275	199	90.6	184	...	265	856	275	72.8	596	...
1997	69.8	1,311	206	97.8	189	...	271	880	281	73.1	611	...
1998	74.2	1,334	213	102.2	196	...	274	906	287	73.7	627	...

I2 Number of Students in Universities

NOTES

1. SOURCES:- The official publications noted on p. xv. Finnish data to 1883 were compiled at the Department of Economic and Social History of the University of Helsinki, and made available through the Central Statistical Office of Finland. The Romanian figure for 1938 was kindly supplied by Mr. G. Radulescu, Editor in Chief of the *Enciclopedica Romana*.
2. Institutions of higher education other than universities are covered in some of the statistics in this table. These are indicated in footnotes.
3. Unless otherwise indicated, the statistics refer to the autumn (or winter) term or semester.

FOOTNOTES

[1] Cisleithania (excluding the Italian provinces) to 1915 (1st line), and Republic of Austria subsequently. During the period of Austrian rule the numbers at the University of Padua were as follows:-

1841	1,825	1846	1,941	1851	1,630	1856	1,348	1861	952
1842	1,905	1847	...	1852	1,751	1857	1,282	1862	1,080
1843	1,935	1848	...	1853	1,587	1858	1,568	1863	1,381
1844	...	1849	...	1854	1,388	1859	827	1864	1,433
1845	1,941	1850	1,574	1855	1,300	1860	829		

[2] Including philosophy students who were subsequently omitted.
[3] Students at Technical High Schools are subsequently included.
[4] Annual averages of the number of students in residence for five-year periods from 1861 to 1805 have been supplied by the Central Statistical Office of Finland, taken from S.E. Astrom, *Studentfrekvensen vid de svenska universiteten under 1700-talet*. They are as follows:-

1761-65	198	1776-80	189	1791-95	165
1766-70	159	1781-85	178	1796-1800	179
1771-75	161	1786-90	178	1801-05	228

[5] Transleithania to 1917, and the territory established by the treaty of Trianon subsequently. Agram (Zagreb) University is excluded from 1876 (2nd line) to 1889.
[6] Previously excluding the University of Naples.
[7] Previous figures for Portugal are as follows:-

1800	1,148	1805	850	1810	...	1815	1,068
1801	1,093	1806	871	1811	427	1816	1,215
1802	1,078	1807	748	1812	489		
1803	939	1808	576	1813	611		
1804	932	1809	517	1814	848		

[8] Figures to 1892 (1st line) are the sums of students registered in the separate faculties, and there is an element of double-counting which is subsequently eliminated.
[9] This includes students at various high schools not included in other years.
[10] Summer semester.
[11] Including those on leave of absence (from 1883 (2nd line) in the case of Finland).
[12] The University of Lille is excluded for 1914-17.
[13] Subsequently including the University of Strasbourg.
[14] Male students at universities only.
[15] Subsequently excluding the University of Strasbourg.
[16] Subsequently excluding the University of Agram (Zagreb).
[17] Subsequently excluding the School of Obstrectrics.
[18] Previously excluding students in the theological, veterinary and pharmacy faculties.
[19] Excluding students in the faculty of letters at the University of Jassy.
[20] Excluding students in the faculty of science at the University of Jassy.
[21] This break results from a change in the method of counting at the Karolin Medico-Surgical Institute.
[22] From 1921 to 1923 (1st line) Graz Technischehochschule is excluded.
[23] Subsequently including students at Arts High Schools.
[24] Subsequently including the Institut St. Louis, College Nôtre Dame de la Paix (Namur), and the Polytechnic Faculty at Mons.
[25] Excluding students at the Free University, who numbered 2,336 in 1937 and 2,775 in 1939.
[26] All higher education students from 1945 (to 1970 (1st line) in the case of Poland).
[27] Figures to 1920 (1st line) are of candidates for all examinations. From 1920 (2nd line) to 1924 (1st line) only those who passed the obligatory entrance examination are covered. Subsequently the figures are of all matriculated students.
[28] Subsequently including certain other institutions of equivalent status.
[29] Including the University of Algiers to 1959.
[30] Subsequently excluding the University of Danzig.
[31] First term of 1940.
[32] Including teachers' training colleges.
[33] Including West Berlin throughout, but only including Saarland from 1956.
[34] Statistics to 1927 (1st line) are for Athens University only.
[35] All higher education students from 1936 (2nd line) to 1970 (1st line).

I2 Number of Students in Universities

[36] Subsequently including the University of Cluj.
[37] Excluding students in the faculties of medicine and pharmacy at the University of Jassy.
[38] Subsequent statistics relate to the postwar territory.
[39] Excluding students in the law faculty at the University of Barcelona and in the science faculty at the University of Oviedo.
[40] This break results from a change in the method of counting at the University of Uppsala.
[41] Subsequently including the Central Gymnastic Institute and excluding the Karolin Medico-Surgical Institute.
[42] Excluding students at Music and Art High Schools, who numbered 294 in 1950.
[43] The basis of reckoning was changed from net numbers registered to numbers actually present.
[44] Subsequently excluding the Music High School.
[45] Great Britain to 1948 (1st line). Northern Ireland is included subsequently.
[46] The basis of reckoning was changed.
[47] A new Act on tuition fees resulted in considerable numbers of students refraining from enrolment. Since this undermined the basis for compiling reliable statistics no data are available for these years.
[48] The State College for Teachers became the University of Trondheim.
[49] All higher education students.
[50] Czech Republic.
[51] Yugoslavia.

J NATIONAL ACCOUNTS

1. National Accounts Total page 905
2. Proportions of National Product by Sector of Origin (%) page 929
3. Balances of Payments page 937

While it has been the general principle in most sections of this work, other than the last, to prefer 'raw' data to those which have been processed, there are no such things as raw national accounts statistics. Everything in this section is 'synthetic'—the result of elaborate calculations by sophisticated statisticians. It is really impossible to summarise briefly all the complex operations involved, and the user who requires description of them is advised to consult the latest United Nations *Yearbook of National Accounts Statistics*, or for more detail the United Nations *National Accounting Practices in Sixty Countries*

Interest in the nation's wealth and income can be traced as far back as the later middle ages in a number of countries, and the balance of trade was of great concern to many by the seventeenth century but the beginnings of the modern national accounts concepts date from the interwar period. Their refinement into something close to the present-day concepts came after World War II. Since then a great deal of work has been done in many countries, not only to improve the concepts and the collection of statistical material with which to clothe them but also to produce retrospective estimates going back, in some cases, a long way into the nineteenth century. Much work in this field is still going on, and in this connection, I am very grateful to those scholars who have allowed me to reproduce part of their work here.

Three main concepts of overall product were used for Table J1. These differ considerably, making comparison between them extremely difficult. There are related differences in the concepts of capital formation employed. National income (which equals net national product) was the first concept to be much used, and is characteristic of most estimates made before the end of the 1940s. It relates to the disposable income of individuals, institutions and governments, after providing for the maintenance and depreciation of capital stocks. Gross national product (and gross domestic product, which is not very different in most countries, and even at its maximum divergence, in the United Kingdom just before World War I, was over ninety per cent of G.N.P.) is the other main concept used for western Europe. This includes depreciation and maintenance outlays. All of these concepts can be expressed in terms of either market prices or factor cost with the latter excluding the excess of indirect taxes over government subsidies. The choice of which series to show in Table J1 has usually depended on which is available for the longest continuous period. Neither is intrinsically preferable to the other.

In the centrally-planned economies of eastern Europe, the most commonly used concept has been net material product. This not only excludes depreciation and maintenance, but also expenditures on what were deemed to be 'unproductive' services—a category which has not been constant. In recent years, some of these countries have begun to produce estimates using western concepts. It is to be expected that eventually these will be extended backwards to the immediate post-war period.

In making comparisons both over time and between countries, it is worth remembering that no national product concept includes the majority of income in kind, amongst which is the rental value of owner-occupied buildings, and the consumption of home-produced goods, including farmers' consumption of their own products. These have always tended to be proportionately more important the less developed has been a country's economy and the more dependent it is on agriculture. Another warning is in order in relation to estimates given in terms of constant prices. Aside from the technical problems associated with price index numbers, it is impossible in practice to reflect completely the changes which take place in the *quality* of goods having the same designation. These changes may be either improvements or deteriorations but it seems to be generally accepted that the former predominate on balance, especially in the twentieth century, except perhaps in times of war and its aftermath.

Table J2 takes gross domestic product (or gross material product in the centrally-planned economies) as its base, and shows estimates of the proportion contributed by each of the major sectors of the economy. Once again, it is necessary to be cautious in making comparisons between countries owing to differences in definitions. These are such as to render meaningless comparisons between market and centrally-planned economies but are not usually of very great importance for comparisons between different countries of each type.

While the modern balance of payments concepts grew out of the disruptions to international trade and payments mechanisms that became evident in the interwar years, concern about the balance of trade and monetary reserves (or 'treasure') goes back long before that. Consequently it has been possible for latter-day analysts to reconstruct something reasonably close to a modern balance of payments for some countries for a long way back into the nineteenth century. Table J3 shows rather more of the components of these estimates than in previous editions, in particular including something on changes in international reserves. In using the figures in the first part of this table, it should be borne in mind that the modern practice of treating both imports and exports 'free on board' was not generally employed before the 1950s.

For the last five decades, balance of payments estimates calculated on a uniform basis with the most recent revisions and in a common currency are available from the publications of the International Monetary Fund for all the market economies and, for limited periods, for some of the eastern European countries. In the second part of Table J3 these have been preferred to national statistics because they facilitate comparisons. Statistics on national definitions, continuing those in the first part of the table, are generally available in national sources.

It must be stressed that all these statistics are estimates, and sometimes pretty rough ones. Since World War II they are probably adequately reliable, though significant revisions are apt to be made to a figure for any year for at least a decade afterwards. The nineteenth century figures are no doubt generally less reliable because the data on which they are based were collected for totally different purposes, and much information that would be desirable is lacking. Nevertheless, they have been carefully made, after prolonged study of the sources. The same applies to most of the interwar statistics, and probably most of them, certainly in Table J1, are better than those for earlier years. But some of the interwar balance of payments estimates are probably the least reliable of all. *The Banker* described those made in the United Kingdom at the time as 'little more than the vaguest haphazard guessing'[1] and whilst it is now possible to replace these with Feinstein's more carefully calculated estimates, the strictures probably apply to some of the other countries' interwar figures, which have not been subjected to recalculation.

[1] March 1948 issue.

J1 NATIONAL ACCOUNTS TOTALS

Key:- CF = Capital formation (gross excluding stocks, except as indicated in footnotes); GDP = gross domestic product; GNP = gross national product; NMP = Net material product; NNP = net national product (national income)

1815–1849

	Denmark (in million kroner at factor cost)				France[1] (in million francs at factor cost)		United Kingdom (in million pounds at factor cost)			
	Current Prices		Constant Prices		Current Prices	Constant Prices	Current Prices		Constant Prices	
	GDP	CF	GDP	CF	GDP	GDP	GDP	CF	GDP	CF
			1929 Prices			1905–13 Prices		1900 Prices		
1815	...	...	...	...	7,378	8,473	...	...	...	...
1816	...	...	...	...	8,895	8,798	...	...	...	...
1817	...	...	...	...	10,594	9,410	...	...	...	...
1818	230	...	441	...	9,554	9,410	...	...	...	...
1819	221	...	454	...	8,866	10,265	...	...	...	...
1820	188	...	456	...	8,966	9,980	...	...	...	...
1821	169	...	480	...	9,268	10,794	...	...	...	...
1822	153	...	487	...	9,045	10,387	...	...	...	...
1823	157	...	486	...	10,082	11,080	...	...	...	...
1824	156	...	502	...	9,817	11,283	...	...	...	...
1825	175	...	503	...	10,218	10,794	...	...	...	...
1826	173	...	511	...	10,284	11,161	...	...	...	...
1827	185	...	526	...	10,449	11,120	...	...	...	...
1828	183	...	535	...	10,498	11,405	...	...	...	...
1829	185	...	522	...	11,323	11,731	...	...	...	...
1830	194	...	526	...	11,422	11,650	440	25	432	26
1831	200	...	523	...	11,082	12,098	442	28	452	31
1832	199	...	536	...	11,581	13,035	419	21	445	23
1833	188	...	534	...	11,440	12,790	412	21	452	23
1834	184	...	562	...	11,582	13,035	440	25	472	28
1835	198	...	560	...	12,197	13,483	471	39	497	41
1836	216	...	558	...	12,452	13,524	508	42	505	39
1837	216	...	573	...	11,967	14,012	484	46	502	46
1838	220	...	576	...	12,921	14,827	519	53	530	53
1839	229	...	585	...	12,546	14,705	549	56	554	55
1840	236	...	602	...	13,466	15,683	510	55	538	55
1841	234	...	603	...	14,067	15,845	481	35	517	36
1842	236	...	607	...	13,745	15,479	459	31	514	33
1843	239	...	637	...	13,612	16,171	459	27	530	31
1844	251	29	670	83	13,866	16,660	506	30	559	33
1845	269	33	690	82	14,013	15,968	537	46	589	47
1846	314	39	704	100	14,925	15,764	580	69	630	66
1847	321	41	702	103	17,352	17,964	604	88	614	82
1848	311	38	738	98	12,992	17,108	580	71	634	73
1849	303	37	779	97	14,087	17,190	588	60	642	69

J1   National Accounts Totals

	Denmark (in million kroner at factor cost)				Finland (Current in million, constant in thousand millions 1963 markkaa at market prices)				France (in million francs at market prices)		Germany[38] (in million marks at market prices)			
	Current prices		Constant prices		Current prices		Constant prices	Index 1926=100	Current prices	Constant prices	Current prices		Constant prices	
	GDP	CF	GDP	CF	GDP	CF	GDP	CF	GDP	GDP	NNP	CF²	NNP³	CF²
			1929 Prices				1985 Prices		1905–13 Prices		1913 Prices			
1850	315	44	823	111	...	...	...	...	14,279	17,353	6,070	500	10,534	700
1851	319	47	785	123	...	...	...	...	14,154	17,067	6,431	570	10,568	740
1852	346	48	812	130	...	...	...	...	15,986	18,004	7,296	990	11,121	1,300
1853	407	54	816	135	...	...	...	...	16,286	16,579	7,189	470	10,630	600
1854	426	66	819	156	...	...	...	...	18,396	17,679	8,203	920	10,961	920
1855	469	67	912	155	...	...	...	...	18,488	17,190	7,882	260	10,316	370
1856	478	73	861	160	...	...	...	...	20,011	17,801	9,139	1,190	11,553	1,200
1857	492	77	874	152	...	...	...	...	19,947	19,226	8,581	560	11,845	680
1858	455	64	867	139	...	...	...	...	18,474	20,041	8,334	670	12,053	750
1859	467	59	924	145	...	...	...	...	17,815	18,127	8,134	710	12,219	880
1860	464	62	917	148	3.1	0.33	7.8	15.4	20,684	19,715	9,630	1,260	13,604	1,530
1861	500	67	934	159	3.4	0.33	7.8	15.3	21,260	19,023	9,379	720	13,002	890
1862	492	72	963	170	3.3	0.32	7.4	16.2	21,934	21,426	10,050	1,320	13,731	1,670
1863	495	71	1,022	174	3.4	0.33	8.0	17.0	21,746	22,404	10,372	1,500	14,639	1,970
1864	505	69	1,013	153	3.4	0.35	8.2	17.2	21,740	22,974	10,207	1,220	14,677	1,630
1865	575	79	1,050	180	3.5	0.41	8.1	18.5	20,910	22,404	10,279	1,050	14,858	1,440
1866	591	81	1,049	180	3.4	0.38	8.2	17.4	22,727	23,137	10,714	1,060	15,106	1,460
1867	634	75	1,050	170	3.0	0.34	7.6	16.9	22,536	21,956	11,558	1,850	15,108	1,070
1868	652	73	1,068	157	3.4	0.41	8.3	20.4	25,040	24,644	11,558	1,850	15,108	1,070
1869	641	79	1,129	173	3.6	0.47	8.9	22.8	25,335	25,540	11,750	860	15,660	1,140
1870	669	81	1,175	176	3.7	0.46	9.3	23.0	23,959	23,626	12,876	1,590	16,706	1,870
1871	685	85	1,191	175	3.9	0.48	9.4	23.3	23,682	22,526	14,013	1,480	17,395	1,520
1872	722	93	1,243	170	4.2	0.54	9.7	25.1	24,955	24,603	16,627	2,600	19,133	2,440
1873	781	108	1,239	178	4.6	0.59	10.3	26.2	24,220	22,852		17,950	2,370	19,768
1874	809	117	1,273	200	5.0	0.61	10.5	26.1	25,993	25,785	19,544	3,370	21,316	3,180
1875	808	118	1,296	207	5.0	0.62	10.7	27.2	26,237	26,640	18,242	2,480	21,070	2,570
1876	832	114	1,322	202	5.4	0.57	11.3	24.9	24,604	24,481	17,966	2,390	20,890	2,750
1877	773	97	1,285	194	5.2	0.50	11.1	22.8	25,623	25,785	17,414	1,830	20,705	2,240
1878	758	84	1,336	173	4.5	0.42	10.8	20.6	24,964	25,439	17,874	1,820	21,803	2,310
1879	759	84	1,380	184	4.3	0.41	11.0	21.0	22,947	23,870	16,678	1,210	21,193	1,820
1880	840	93	1,412	197	4.7	0.45	11.0	21.9	25,409	25,988	16,902	1,330	20,576[3] 19,874	1,860
1881	839	105	1,425	227	4.8	0.48	10.7	23.1	26,494	27,007	17,330	1,590	20,616	2,160
1882	850	111	1,478	231	5.1	0.50	11.7	24.6	27,850	28,269	17,489	1,530	20,444	2,110
1883	868	120	1,527	254	5.1	0.56	12.2	26.6	27,243	28,351	18,014	1,810	21,909	2,460
1884	839	119	1,535	260	5.1	0.51	12.3	26.7	26,031	28,025	18,540	1,960	22,712	2,730
1885	820	109	1,545	242	5.0	0.55	12.6	29.1	25,100	27,536	18,731	1,960	23,452	2,740
1886	819	93	1,609	212	4.9	0.56	13.2	29.2	25,226	27,984	18,935	1,980	24,142	2,830
1887	827	102	1,664	227	4.8	0.48	13.4	26.1	25,144	28,188	19,280	2,230	24,558	3,030
1888	841	106	1,678	235	5.1	0.53	13.9	28.2	25,684	28,473	20,716	2,400	25,840	2,960
1889	892	119	1,689	238	5.6	0.64	14.4	29.4	27,426	29,165	22,749	2,940	26,478	3,600
1890	965	130	1,801	262	6.0	0.72	15.2	35.2	28,928	29,858	23,676	3,360	27,754	4,050
1891	1,008	133	1,835	285	6.3	0.72	15.1	36.1	29,331	30,550	22,624	2,080	26,822	2,900
1892	1,005	131	1,830	278	6.1	0.72	14.6	36.9	28,698	31,324	24,061	3,140	28,390	3,980
1893	1,000	132	1,915	274	6.2	0.65	15.2	33.2	28,151	31,854	24,357	2,930	30,606	4,080
1894	990	130	1,955	277	6.4	0.64	16.4	33.9	28,408	33,035	24,361	2,530	30,196	3,710
1895	1,039	148	2,065	318	6.6	0.69	17.3	35.6	27,166	32,343	25,254	2,830	32,079	4,010
1896	1,059	180	2,141	370	7.2	0.83	18.4	40.4	28,758	33,891	26,979	3,590	33,377	4,860
1897	1,097	208	2,192	430	8.0	0.94	19.3	44.0	30,420	33,443	28,714	4,150	34,739	5,360
1898	1,157	261	2,227	508	8.8	1.24	20.1	54.5	31,900	35,072	28,714	4,150	34,739	5,360
1899	1,217	280	2,323	517	9.0	1.32	19.7	55.1	32,571	37,068	31,761	5,390	36,860	6,010

J1 National Accounts Totals

	Italy (in thousand million lire at market prices)				Norway (in million kroner at market prices)				Sweden (in million kroner at market prices)				United Kingdom[6] (in million pounds at factor cost)			
	Current prices		Constant prices		Current prices		Constant prices		Current prices		Constant prices		Current prices		Constant prices	
	GNP	CF[4]	GNP	CF[4]	GNP	CF[5]	GDP	CF[5]	GDP	CF	GDP	CF	GDP	CF	GDP	CF
			1938 Prices				1910 Prices				1908/9 Prices				1900 Prices	
1850	...	...	...	...	...	...	...	...	...	...	...	...	534	47	631	57
1851	...	...	...	...	...	...	...	...	...	...	...	...	565	46	659	58
1852	...	...	...	...	...	...	...	...	...	...	...	...	572	53	672	64
1853	...	...	...	...	...	...	...	...	...	...	...	...	646	59	691	63
1854	...	...	...	...	...	...	...	...	...	...	...	...	686	64	704	64
1855	...	...	...	...	...	...	...	...	...	...	...	...	707	62	715	61
1856	...	...	...	...	...	...	...	...	...	...	...	...	734	56	745	56
1857	...	...	...	...	...	...	...	...	...	...	...	...	741	53	753	55
1858	...	...	...	...	...	...	...	...	...	...	...	...	705	51	741	55
1859	...	...	...	...	...	...	...	...	...	...	...	...	765	54	793	60
1860	...	...	...	...	...	...	...	...	...	...	...	...	761	59	787	64
1861	7.7	0.57	49.6	3.0	...	...	...	...	776	50	879	51	820	63	820	70
1862	8.1	0.84	51.3	4.0	...	...	...	...	815	76	910	76	828	68	822	76
1863	7.5	0.66	50.1	3.4	...	...	...	...	811	67	935	68	992	78	861	86
1864	7.7	0.88	51.4	4.8	...	...	...	...	797	72	954	75	935	88	875	92
1865	8.0	0.99	53.0	5.5	480	62	601	76	796	62	975	64	975	91	919	96
1866	8.7	0.96	55.3	5.1	492	66	613	79	827	76	1,011	79	1,019	89	926	92
1867	8.3	0.76	51.4	3.9	518	67	628	79	855	63	1,019	67	1,009	80	926	85
1868	9.3	1.06	52.8	5.1	524	68	627	81	851	39	964	43	76	957	82	
1869	9.0	1.06	54.4	5.6	537	65	651	80	842	74	1,012	80	1,015	77	977	82
1870	9.0	0.83	54.2	4.3	542	66	650	82	914	105	1,128	117	1,079	87	1,063	90
1871	9.3	0.83	55.0	4.2	562	70	661	86	967	95	1,169	101	1,133	99	1,084	100
1872	10.4	0.87	54.7	4.1	640	96	704	96	1,091	120	1,240	123	1,194	118	1,074	107
1873	11.8	1.38	57.1	6.0	729	123	721	109	1,281	155	1,311	139	1,262	125	1,087	105
1874	11.3	1.04	55.9	4.3	790	145	748	119	1,357	188	1,326	168	1,312	141	1,155	119
1875	10.0	1.02	58.1	4.7	771	140	769	121	1,305	178	1,300	155	1,236	137	1,146	126
1876	10.0	0.63	57.7	3.2	799	136	792	124	1,399	170	1,380	148	1,201	139	1,145	132
1877	11.2	0.87	58.1	4.0	797	136	798	128	1,371	168	1,379	155	1,157	135	1,132	132
1878	10.6	0.91	58.5	4.1	706	111	770	113	1,261	144	1,374	140	1,226	120	1,204	124
1879	10.4	1.06	58.7	5.3	662	98	777	108	1,229	125	1,461	126	1,078	106	1,131	114
1880	11.2	1.50	60.9	7.2	720	106	802	117	1,287	126	1,471	127	1,297	107	1,276	110
1881	10.1	0.61	57.5	3.1	739	108	809	120	1,349	137	1,491	144	1,222	109	1,246	116
1882	10.9	1.55	60.6	7.5	760	114	808	124	1,335	122	1,495	130	1,244	110	1,258	115
1883	10.2	1.26	60.0	6.2	750	113	805	125	1,384	133	1,576	139	1,315	113	1,332	119
1884	10.1	1.24	60.6	6.8	721	106	819	121	1,358	147	1,577	156	1,287	106	1,338	117
1885	10.8	1.58	60.6	5.9	679	97	827	117	1,343	135	1,597	146	1,228	96	1,315	109
1886	11.2	1.91	62.8	9.3	667	92	831	114	1,286	144	1,618	158	1,228	85	1,332	100
1887	10.4	1.52	62.5	8.6	659	94	842	119	1,231	103	1,595	118	1,262	86	1,374	103
1888	10.3	1.39	62.2	7.7	710	104	881	131	1,302	125	1,659	138	1,272	90	1,389	107
1889	10.5	0.56	59.7	4.7	770	126	915	148	1,385	146	1,679	160	1,330	100	1,432	114
1890	11.5	1.20	63.9	6.5	780	139	940	152	1,442	149	1,729	157	1,373	106	1,453	116
1891	12.0	0.89	65.7	7.0	802	138	949	155	1,516	122	1,800	137	1,399	107	1,478	122
1892	10.8	1.19	62.6	4.4	799	130	967	152	1,529	126	1,825	148	1,392	108	1,470	125
1893	11.0	0.72	64.6	6.8	809	132	993	157	1,527	140	1,876	169	1,357	109	1,441	127
1894	10.6	0.71	64.1	4.9	816	134	999	162	1,533	136	1,926	171	1,434	111	1,557	132
1895	11.0	0.91	65.2	5.3	832	140	1,011	173	1,633	190	2,039	223	1,439	115	1,586	138
1896	11.0	0.55	66.4	5.4	875	143	1,040	170	1,706	215	2,110	245	1,520	127	1,659	150
1897	10.8	1.32	68.7	3.1	919	162	1,095	189	1,837	241	2,195	263	1,506	144	1,625	167
1898	12.1	1.20	69.5	7.3	998	189	1,104	208	1,972	249	2,254	262	1,616	172	1,738	193
1899	12.2	1.81	73.1	6.1	1,065	220	1,138	223	2,131	288	2,299	283	1,750	192	1,858	204

J1   National Accounts Totals

	Austria (in thousand million schillings at market prices)				Belgium (in thousand million francs at market prices)		Bulgaria (in thousand million leva at market prices		Czechoslovakia (in thousand million korunas at market prices)	
	Current Prices		Constant prices		Current Prices	Constant Prices	Current Prices	Constant Prices	Constant	Prices
	GNP	CF[7]	GNP	CF[7]	NNP	GNP	NNP	NNP	GDP	CF
	1937 Prices				1948 Prices				1929 Prices	
1913	10.12	1.31	10.80	1.47	6.5	...	...	...	48.2	...
1914	...	...	...	...	...	...	...	...	...	...
1915	...	...	...	...	...	...	...	...	...	...
1916	...	...	...	...	...	...	...	...	...	...
1917	...	...	...	...	...	...	...	...	...	...
1918	...	...	...	...	...	...	...	...	...	...
1919	...	...	...	...	...	...	...	...	...	...
1920	...	...	7.17	...	...	...	...	...	43.6	4.4
1921	...	...	7.94	...	...	...	...	...	47.1	3.8
1922	...	...	8.66	...	...	...	...	...	45.8	4.2
1923	...	...	8.56	...	...	...	...	...	49.7	4.5
1924	9.26	0.63	9.57	0.63	31.3	176	44	47	54.8	5.5
1925	10.29	0.84	10.21	0.78	...	...	50	50	61.3	6.5
1926	10.28	0.96	10.38	0.89	...	...	49	51	61.0	7.1
1927	11.11	0.89	10.70	0.84	48.2	173	53	57	65.6	7.7
1928	11.68	1.14	11.19	1.03	...	...	56	58	71.4	9.6
1929	12.09	1.27	11.36	1.14	...	...	56	56	73.4	10.3
1930	11.56	1.09	11.04	1.01	66.5	215	49	53	70.9	9.9
1931	10.36	0.89	10.15	0.81	...	...	45	56	68.5	9.7
1932	9.55	0.58	9.11	0.54	...	...	39	53	65.8	8.4
1933	9.02	0.47	8.80	0.46	...	...	36	53	63.0	6.9
1934	8.98	0.51	8.88	0.50	49.4	209	35	55	60.6	6.8
1935	9.14	0.57	9.06	0.57	50.7	219	37	62	60.0	7.3
1936	9.32	0.65	9.32	0.65	59.8	246	40	70	64.9	8.2
1937	9.82	0.72	9.82	0.72	65.3	250	47	81	72.2	8.8
	1954 Prices									
			63.61	6.14	65.2	241	51	85		
1938	...	...	...	...	65.2	241	51	85	...	...
1939	...	...	...	...	65	...	59	95	...	...
1940	...	...	...	...	...	...	65[8]	94[8]	...	...
							67	97	...	...
1941	...	...	...	...	46	...	89	107	...	...
1942	...	...	...	...	...	...	122	111	...	...
1943	...	...	...	...	55	...	162	117	...	...
1944	...	...	...	...	...	...	250	120	...	...

J1 National Accounts Totals

	Denmark (in million kroner at factor cost)				Finland (current in million constant in thousand million 1763 marketed at market prices)				France[1] (in million francs at market prices)	
	Current Prices		Constant Prices		Current Prices		Constant Prices		Current Prices	Constant Prices
	GDP	CF	GDP	CF	GDP	CF	GDP	CF	GDP	GDP
			1929 Prices				1985 Prices	Index 1926 = 100		1905–13 Prices
1900	1,322	288	2,402	526	9.7	1.27	20.6	53.8	32,806	36,661
1901	1,372	276	2,503	536	9.4	1.15	20.3	50.6	30,938	36,090
1902	1,396	301	2,563	580	9.2	1.14	19.9	50.3	31,880	35,479
1903	1,462	309	2,714	590	10.1	1.20	21.2	52.4	33,891	36,253
1904	1,479	310	2,774	594	10.4	1.26	22.1	53.7	33,071	36,538
1905	1,558	305	2,820	583	10.9	1.34	22.4	54.8	33,215	37,149
1906	1,627	365	2,900	664	11.6	1.46	22.3	56.5	35,615	37,842
1907	1,739	386	3,007	668	12.3	1.58	24.1	62.5	38,741	39,471
1908	1,773	362	3,103	640	12.5	1.65	24.4	70.4	37,326	39,268
1909	1,828	356	3,222	630	12.9	1.51	25.5	64.3	40,101	40,897
1910	1,922	362	3,320	636	13.3	1.42	26.0	58.9	40,914	38,412
1911	2,051	374	3,497	625	14.1	1.58	26.8	66.1	45,089	42,160
1912	2,159	412	3,498	659	15.2	1.75	28.3	84.3	49,360	45,663
1913	2,301	443	3,629	702	16.0	1.91	29.8	80.6	49,571	45,378
1914	2,529	381	3,857	598	15.7	2.08	28.5	79.9	...	...
1915	2,887	...	3,590	...	17.3	2.06	27.0	61.3	...	...
1916	3,767	...	3,742	...	24.3	2.93	27.4	56.3	...	...
1917	4,003	...	3,520	...	37.7	4.26	23.0	46.6	...	...
1918	4,766	...	3,405	...	54.0	5.55	20.0	45.5	...	...
1919	5,821	...	3,843	...	85.8	8.66	24.1	57.9	...	...
1920	7,396	...	4,025	...	137	15.6	27.0	57.9	175,371	41,426
1921	5,794[9]	...[9]	3,909[9]	...[9]	161	17.0	27.9	58.9	133,729	39,716
	6,057	1,071	4,055	612						
1922	5,406	991	4,497	787	177	21.0	30.8	70.3	155,636	46,844
1923	6,030	1,080	4,971	836	190	26.2	33.1	80.7	188,961	49,288
1924	6,566	1,140	4,987	885	201	28.5	33.9	85.2	217,288	55,480
1925	6,153	1,112	4,873	849	217	28.3	35.8	83.2	247,945	55,724
1926	5,529	984	5,159	941	226	34.1	37.2	100	323,766	57,190
1927	5,318	887	5,259	885	253	38.7	40.1	109.0	304,506	55,968
1928	5,437	877	5,438	893	273	53.3	42.9	145.8	330,369	59,879
1929	5,802	1,070	5,802	1,070	265	43.8	43.4	121.5	346,426	63,912
1930	5,705	1,185	6,149	1,185	240	33.2	42.8	96.7	334,083	62,079
1931	5,369	1,098	6,216	1,134	213	22.9	41.8	79.1	298,785	58,372
1932	5,112	817	6,052	851	215	24.8	41.6	83.7	266,224	54,584
1933	5,506	923	6,247	860	231	23.8	44.4	86.6	248,740	58,453
1934	5,967	1,112	6,434	1,081	261	31.2	49.4	105.3	229,990	57,883
1935	6,380	1,210	6,579	1,165	275	38.9	51.6	125.5	204,412	56,417
1936	6,690	1,224	6,742	1,149	303	46.4	55.0	142.0	246,318	58,535
1937	7,141	1,288	6,905	1,103	357	64.3	58.2	163.1	346,764	61,956
1938	7,514	1,407	7,073	1,114	385	70.4	61.2	177.5	413,952	61,671
1939	8,127	1,569	7,409	1,304	374	74.5	58.6	175.5	...	...
1940	8,620	1,377	6,370	1,117	429	96.4	55.5	187	...	...
1941	9,788	1,586	5,740	1,048	531	53.5	57.3	81	...	...
1942	11,020	1,890	5,870	1,144	658	72.4	57.5	94	...	...
1943	12,480	2,058	6,520	1,216	843	90.5	64.1	109	...	...
1944	13,850	1,944	7,200	1,185	946	78.3	64.2	86	...	...

J1   National Accounts Totals

1900–1944

	Germany (in million marks at market prices)				Greece (in thousand million drachmae at market prices)		Hungary[10] (in million crowns/pengos)				Southern Ireland (in million pounds at market prices)
	Current Prices		Constant Prices		Current Prices	Constant Prices	Current Prices		Constant Prices		Current Prices
	NNP	CF[2]	NNP	CF[2]	NNP	NNP	NNP	CF[7]	NNP	CF[7]	NNP/ GNP[13]
			1913 prices		1929 Prices				1938/9 Prices	1937 Prices	
1900	32,448	5,100	36,466	5,330	...	...	1,825[11]	...	2,913[11]	...	...
1901	31,617	3,890	36,197	4,470	...	...	...	...	...	...	...
1902	31,928	3,520	36,918	4,060	...	...	...	...	...	...	...
1903	34,402	4,960	40,132	5,890	...	...	...	...	...	...	...
1904	36,284	5,630	42,263	6,630	...	...	...	...	...	...	...
1905	38,878	6,050	43,346	6,710	...	...	...	...	...	...	...
1906	40,643	6,680	44,299	7,040	...	...	...	...	...	...	...
1907	42,976	7,610	46,181	7,740	...	...	...	...	...	...	...
1908	42,441	5,610	46,410	6,020	...	...	...	...	...	...	...
1909	44,358	6,040	47,512	6,700	...	...	...	...	...	...	...
1910	45,785	6,100	47,457	6,610	...	...	...	...	...	...	...
1911	48,106	7,270	49,648	7,830	...	...	...	...	million pengos		...
1912	51,563	8,570	51,914	8,590	...	...	3,328[11]	...	3,900[11]	...	...
1913	52,440	8,170	52,440	8,170	...	...	...	...	...	...	...
1914	...	...	...	...	...	...	...	...	...	...	...
1915	...	...	...	...	...	...	...	...	...	...	...
1916	...	...	...	...	...	...	...	...	...	...	...
1917	...	...	...	...	...	...	...	...	...	...	...
1918	...	...	...	...	...	...	...	...	...	...	...
1919	...	...	...	...	...	...	...	...	...	...	...
							in million pengos		in million pengos		
1920	...	...	...	...	...	...	...	...	...	...	...
1921	...	...	...	...	...	...	4,258[12]	...	3,300	...	...
1922	...	...	...	...	...	...	...	...	...	...	...
1923	...	...	...	...	...	...	...	...	...	...	...
1924	...	...	...	...	...	...	...	...	...	...	...
1925	67,346	8,620	46,897	5,380	...	...	4,966	358	3,842	311	...
1926	65,472	4,280	46,587	3,300	...	...	5,786	479	4,596	424	154
1927	80,466	12,240	53,108	8,070	44	47	5,567	624	4,402	566	...
1928	83,964	10,980	53,950	6,880	46	47	5,853	808	4,596	703	...
1929	79,491	5,770	51,694	3,550	45	45	6,435	862	4,999	740	161
1930	71,862	2,630	49,289	2,790	43	49	6,304	643	5,164	560	...
1931	58,484	−3,150	43,913	−1,360	39	45	5,649	484	5,050	438	147
1932	50,782	−2,060	41,760	−680	44	48	4,900	418	4,807	403	...
1933	56,764	1,940	47,375	2,310	49	49	4,512	308	4,678	324	134
1934	64,604	4,730	52,102	3,250	53	52	4,434	238	5,101	258	...
1935	72,015	7,510	58,658[3] 60,352	5,790	55	54	4,577	235	5,136	255	...
1936	78,941	9,000	66,226	7,260	59	56	4,935	286	5,393	309	154
1937	87,862	13,580	73,167	11,200	68	61	5,371	389	5,755	402	156[13]
1938	97,990	14,070	81,335	11,950	67	59	5,576	455	5,626	449	184
1939	...	...	...	...	67	60	5,913	510	5,913	496	...
1940	...	...	...	...	...	...	6,782	579	6,360	546	...
1941	...	...	...	...	...	...	7,515	...	5,927	...	...
1942	...	...	...	...	...	...	9,165	...	5,961	...	...
1943	...	...	...	...	...	...	11,490	...	6,260	...	...
1944	...	...	...	...	...	...	...	...	...	...	...

J1 National Accounts Totals

	Italy (in thousand million lire at market prices)				Netherlands (in million guilders at market prices)		
	Current Prices		Constant Prices		Current Prices		Constant Prices
	GNP	CF[4]	GNP	CF[4]	NNP	CF[15]	NNP
			1938 Prices				1963 Prices
1900	13.0	2.26	73.1	9.0	1,796	...	8,980
1901	13.4	1.59	77.9	11.5	1,863	...	8,468
1902	12.8	1.86	76.3	8.3	1,901	...	9,052
1903	14.0	1.84	79.9	10.4	1,952	...	9,295
1904	13.8	1.89	79.6	9.3	1,993	...	9,059
1905	14.5	2.13	83.2	10.0	2,058	...	9,355
1906	15.4	3.67	84.6	10.8	2,156	...	9,800
1907	17.3	2.94	92.9	17.4	2,195	...	9,977
1908	16.6	3.75	90.0	13.8	2,255	...	10,250
1909	18.0	2.70	95.7	18.3	2,322	...	10,555
1910	17.8	2.70	90.1	13.0	2,408	...	10,470
1911	19.7	3.64	97.1	17.0	2,511	...	10,463
1912	20.6	3.71	98.5	16.8	2,688	...	11,200
1913	21.4	3.99	102	18.4	2,807	...	11,696
1914	20.6	2.27	99.2	11.9	2,730	...	11,375
1915	23.4	1.36	101	5.3	3,227	...	11,952
1916	32.0	0.56	102	1.4	3,692	...	12,307
1917	42.6	1.59	98.6	1.6	3,666	...	11,456
1918	53.0	2.05	96.4	2.4	4,100	...	10,789
1919	63.9	5.54	96.4	6.2	5,530	...	13,488
1920	94.8	15.0	101	13.3	6,285	...	13,663
1921	96.2	10.6	101	9.1	5,780	327	14,821
1922	106	15.5	110	13.9	5,380	106	14,944
1923	115	21.0	116	18.3	5,304	141	15,600
1924	120	24.4	117	19.4	5,542	301	16,301
1925	150	32.7	124	23.7	5,724	317	16,835
1926	160	30.3	125	21.1	5,855	390	17,742
1927	139	21.8	124	17.9	5,965	294	18,646
1928	140	29.6	134	27.0	6,358	431	19,267
1929	139	27.7	136	26.8	6,496	543	19,685
1930	125	19.5	128	19.3	6,237	195	20,119
1931	111	16.4	127	16.9	5,490	−197	18,931
1932	107	16.4	132	19.5	4,928	−267	18,252
1933	99.1	14.4	131	17.7	4,779	−117	17,700
1934	99.8	15.3	131	19.2	4,754	−107	17,607
1935	112	23.3	144	29.2	4,682	−114	18,008
1936	119	21.7	142	25.2	4,807	−56	18,488
1937	141	30.3	143	32.2	5,310	224	19,666
1938	153	28.7	153	28.7	5,395	60	19,981
1939	169	34.9	162	34.1	5,743[14] 5,207	6	20,511
1940	195	32.1	154	25.9	5,264	...	...
1941	228	31.2	151	23.5	5,924	...	...
1942	283	26.2	144	18.2	5,592	...	...
1943	375	18.0	129	11.2	5,635	...	...
1944	686	8.1	95.3	8.0	3,930	...	...

J1   National Accounts Totals

	Norway (in million kroner at market prices)				Russia (in thousand million rubels at factor cost)				Spain (in thousand million pesetas at market prices)	
	Current Prices		Constant Prices		Current Prices		Constant Prices		Current Prices	Constant Prices
	GDP	CF[4]	GDP	CF[4]	GNP[16]	CF[17]	GNP[16]	CF[17]	NNP	NNP
	1910 prices									1958 Prices
1900	1,115	208	1,152	206	...	...	...	...	...	...
1901	1,101	194	1,181	208	...	...	...	...	10.2	163
1902	1,088	183	1,199	193	...	...	...	...	10.4	168
1903	1,081	172	1,192	185	...	...	...	...	10.7	173
1904	1,081	182	1,194	196	...	...	...	...	11.1	178
1905	1,105	174	1,203	183	...	...	...	...	11.2	183
1906	1,187	206	1,253	208	...	...	...	...	11.3	188
1907	1,265	243	1,307	238	...	...	...	...	11.7	191
1908	1,299	248	1,349	242	...	...	...	...	11.9	196
1909	1,316	228	1,378	232	...	...	...	...	12.3	202
1910	1,435	263	1,435	263	...	...	...	...	12.0	199
1911	1,530	317	1,491	305	...	...	...	...	12.7	213
1912	1,680	359	1,564	336	...	...	...	...	12.6	209
1913	1,857	384	1,649	349	...	...	...	...	13.1	215
1914	1,919	396	1,683	349	...	...	...	...	14.4	229
1915	2,594	513	1,757	372	...	...	...	...	16.4	228
1916	3,871	811	1,825	378	...	...	...	...	20.0	234
1917	4,489	1,086	1,659	335	...	...	...	...	25.5	253
1918	5,048	792	1,592	217	...	...	...	...	27.3	236
1919	6,195	2,218	1,865	606	...	...	...	...	33.7	239
1920	7,500	2,297	1,987	505	...	...	...	...	32.9	242
1921	5,448	1,290	1,795	330	...	...	...	...	26.9	240
1922	4,980	961	1,987	336	...	...	...	...	25.7	245
1923	4,997	961	2,041	371	...	...	...	...	26.9	251
1924	5,576	1,020	2,040	383	...	...	...	...	28.9	257
1925	5,633	1,052	2,166	417	...	...	...	...	31.3	276
1926	4,646	797	2,198	382	...	...	...	...	31.1	282
1927	4,218	685	2,281	387	...	...	1937 prices		31.2	298
1928	4,221	793	2,382	476	14.2	4.95	123.7	9.56	31.0	305
1929	4,345	847	2,607	527	15.9	6.40	127.0	12.19	31.8	313
	1938 prices									
1930	4,377	1,005	4,746	79	18.8	9.26	134.5	17.68	31.5	312
1931	3,842	741	4,368	961	27.0	14.16	137.2	18.81	31.9	317
1932	3,862	649	4,595	840	49.4	17.79	135.7	20.77	32.9	329
1933	3,866	654	4,699	849	77.0	15.59	141.3	18.46	32.3	326
1934	4,068	771	4,870	995	99.8	20.27	155.2	21.04	34.9	342
1935	4,362	923	5,114	1,154	148.6	25.06	178.6	26.26	34.4	335
1936	4,850	1,081	5,459	1,283	189.7	34.23	192.8	36.08	...	...
1937	5,581	1,414	5,697	1,483	212.3	32.51	212.3	32.51	...	...
1938	5,827	1,473	5,827	1,473	216.1	34.34	216.1	32.97	...	...
1939	6,253	1,600	6,110	1,535	234.1	36.64	229.5	32.95	...	...
1940	...	...	...	...	315.6	39.73	250.5	32.19	44.9	249
1941	...	...	...	...	...	30.50	...	21.57	56.7	252
1942	...	...	...	...	...	18.26	...	32.19	65.5	270
1943	...	...	...	...	...	20.48	...	10.58	68.8	270
1944	...	...	...	...	...	34.28	...	17.92	74.8	276

J1 National Accounts Totals

1900–1944

Year	Sweden (in million kronor at market prices)				Switzerland (in million francs at market prices)		United Kingdom[6] (in million pounds at factor cost)				Yugoslavia (in thousand million dinari at market prices)	
	Current Prices		Constant Prices		Current Prices	Constant Prices	Current Prices		Constant Prices		Current Prices	Constant Prices
	GDP	CF	GDP	CF	NNP	NNP	GDP	CF	GDP	CF	GDP	GDP
			1908/9 Prices		1938 Prices		1900 Prices				1938 Prices	
1900	2,248	300	2,356	290	...	...	1,794	205	1,787	205	...	...
1901	2,186	262	2,330	277	...	...	1,913	210	1,919	216	...	...
1902	2,191	257	2,418	275	...	...	1,854	213	1,890	227	...	...
1903	2,372	316	2,542	341	...	...	1,842	208	1,871	225	...	...
1904	2,396	332	2,624	362	...	...	1,876	203	1,911	223	...	...
1905	2,485	329	2,675	357	...	...	1,936	198	1,974	220	...	...
1906	2,790	386	2,912	399	...	...	1,957	192	1,976	207	...	...
1907	2,981	411	3,033	406	...	...	1,997	176	1,984	185	...	...
1908	3,039	357	3,045	358	...	...	1,977	145	1,944	156	...	...
1909	3,061	324	3,052	323	...	...	2,011	154	2,010	167	...	...
1910	3,298	366	3,240	360	...	...	2,052	158	2,047	169	...	...
1911	3,375	446	3,378	441	...	...	2,163	163	2,124	172	...	...
1912	3,619	462	3,507	448	...	...	2,206	171	2,103	172	...	...
									2,229	189	...	...
							1938 Prices					
1913	3,930	558	3,649	523	3,960	5,390	2,354	192	4,121	325	...	...
1914	3,984	659	3,658	585	...	...	2,383	193	4,204	325	...	...
1915	4,734	836	3,595	643	...	...	2,975	170	4,637	256	...	...
1916	5,960	1,296	3,794	783	...	...	3,449	159	4,673	201	...	...
1917	7,031	1,559	3,375	641	...	...	4,399	203	4,736	215	...	...
1918	9,099	1,484	3,358	459	...	...	5,225	286	4,763	261	...	...
1919	10,696	1,437	3,520	426	...	...	5,546	434	4,308	342	...	...
1920	12,318	1,672	3,751	463	...	...	5,970[18]	578[18]	3,860[18]	397[18]	...	...
							5,612	482	3,607	326		
1921	9,418	1,177	3,866	430	...	...	4,732	458	3,402	326	...	...
1922	7,624	1,059	4,079	528	...	...	4,140	381	3,542	300	...	...
1923	7,637	1,036	4,264	500	...	...	3,931	334	3,657	308	65.2	34.5
1924	7,886	1,068	4,352	519	8,150	6,580	3,989	374	3,765	359	70.1	36.5
1925	8,515	1,220	4,757	605	...	...	4,215	420	3,966	410	63.3	40.1
1926	8,686	1,242	5,061	626	...	...	3,947	401	3,769	397	56.2	38.7
1927	8,921	1,393	5,288	736	...	...	4,134	426	4,045	442	53.3	37.6
1928	9,062	1,325	5,303	693	...	...	4,166	420	4,117	438	59.6	41.1
1929	9,640	1,616	5,711	862	10,000	8,470	4,251	442	4,216	461	60.0	43.5
1930	9,770	1,673	6,038	884	9,950	8,560	4,228	435	4,210	463	50.4	43.1
1931	8,539	1,320	5,614	698	9,170	3,900	408	3,980	454	45.1	42.1	
1932	8,009	1,074	5,482	574	8,140	8,140	8,060	3,786	347	4,008	396	36.5
1933	7,966	1,124	5,609	650	8,190	8,510	3,773	357	4,046	409	36.1	38.9
1934	8,715	1,400	5,957	798	8,110	8,560	4,006	427	4,334	498	34.1	40.4
1935	9,369	1,608	6,301	895	8,040	8,560	4,199	456	4,496	518	34.6	39.3
1936	10,176	1,808	6,704	1,020	8,020	8,580	4,348	517	4,633	565	40.7	44.9
1937	11,129	2,078	6,810	1,083	8,780	8,780	4,707	574	4,834	584	45.0	45.1
1938	11,759	2,321	7,033	1,171	8,870	8,870	4,985	592	4,985	592	48.5	48.5
1939	12,785	2,646	7,277	1,320	9,040	8,950	5,318	540	5,190	530	52.8	51.0
1940	14,041	2,503	6,958	1,116	9,690	8,780	6,718	520	6,036	460	...	...
1941	15,604	2,639	6,954	1,107	10,640	8,400	7,781	480	6,414	370	...	...
1942	16,814	3,277	7,173	1,283	11,490	8,170	8,440	450	6,487	320	...	...
1943	18,147	3,753	7,294	1,401	12,440	8,410	8,990	360	6,612	220	...	...
1944	19,046	3,964	7,561	1,445	12,960	8,560	9,060	300	6,284	170	...	...

J1 National Accounts Totals

Year	Austria (in thousand million schillings at market prices) Current Prices GNP	CF[7]	Constant Prices GNP	CF[7]	Belgium (in thousand million francs at market prices) Current Prices NNP /GDP /GNP[19]	CF[20]	Constant Prices NNP /GDP /GNP[19]	CF[20]	Bulgaria (in thousand million leva at market prices) Current Prices NNP /NMP[21]	CF[2]	Czechoslovakia (in thousand million kotura at market prices) Current Prices NMP	CF	Constant Prices NMP	CF[2]
	1954 Prices				*1948 Prices*						*April 1955 Prices*			
1945	...	...	...	...	...	...	...	...	286	...	...	...	...	...
1946	...	...	40.7	...	194	...	...	...	334[21]	...	...	...	...	...
1947	...	...	44.9	...	218	...	250	...	...	...	...	...	...	...
1948	32.1	4.20	56.9	8.49	248[19] 339	48.1	248[19] 339	48.1	1,577	...	59.1	11.7	70.2	5.2
1949	41.5	6.48	67.7	11.7	347	52.5	358	54.2	1,655	...	74.9	16.1	77.2	8.8
1950	51.9	9.21	76.1	14.6	354	60.2	369	62.8	1,877		85.4	14.0	85.0	4.9
1951	69.1	13.7	81.3	17.6	408	63.1	388	60.0	2,355		103	22.5	93.1	10.9
1952	80.0	15.7	81.3	17.3	429	68.7	405	64.9	2,443	...	116	25.1	103	15.5
1953	82.5	14.9	84.9	15.1	433[19]	69.4[20]	410[19]	65.7[20]	2,780	200	129	31.6	110	18.0
					1970 Prices									
					411	68.4	640	117						
1954	93.6	19.0	93.6	19.0	428	76.0	667	131	2,708	344	123	19.8	114	10.4
	1964 Prices													
			130	24.5										
1955	107	23.9	145	30.8	457	77.8	700	131	2,820	481	134	25.6	125	17.7
1956	119	25.8	155	31.3	487	92.1	722	149	2,745	369	133	16.4	132	16.8
1957	132	29.8	164	35.4	517	97.7	736	150	3,209	380	141	21.3	142	21.0
1958	137	30.9	170	36.0	521	86.4	734	130	3,486	366	149	25.8	153	28.5
1959	146	34.3	175	39.5	537	97.1	755	148	4,220	597	152	26.7	163	32.2
1960	163	40.7	191	45.7	571	108	797	163	4,489	642	163	27.8	176	33.5
											April 1960 Prices			
													162	29.6
1961	181	47.3	201	51.4	606	126	835	186	4,716	687	172	34.7	173	37.3
1962	192	49.6	205	52.9	648	135	879	194	5,158	697	175	31.6	175	34.5
1963	207	53.9	214	54.7	696	144	917	195	5,676	986	173	22.8	172	25.0
1964	227	59.9	227	59.9	778	183	981	235	6,204	1,226	170	17.0	173	23.7
1965	246	67.4	233	63.0	849	190	1,019	235	6,636	983	174	15.4	179	23.7
1966	269	74.8	246	68.6	913	213	1,050	255	7,274	1,188	191[23]	24.4[23]	195[23]	34.3[23]
											Jan 1967 Prices			
											196	31.3	219	43.5
1967	286	76.0	254	68.6	978	224	1,092	257	7,853	1,623	234	50.7	231	46.0
1968	307	78.9	265	70.6	1,046	229	1,139	259	8,556	1,612	258	58.6	248	50.5
1969	335	85.9	282	74.1	1,160	264	1,212	285	9,350	2,041	294	70.9	266	54.1
1970	376	97.2	302	81.3	1,292	308	1,292	308	10,527	1,948	312	80.8	281	63.1
	1976 Prices				*1980 Prices*									
			571	144			2,570	621						
1971	420	117	601	163	1,412	325	2,661	608	10,411	1,379	328	79.7	296	62.7
1972	480	145	638	183	1,581	338	2,806	608	11,242	1,774	346	85.0	313	67.5
1973	543	155	669	184	1,792	399	2,967	679	12,147	...	363	94.1	330	75.8
1974	619	176	696	191	2,103	573	3,092	749	13,093	...	390	109	349	86.6
1975	656	175	693	182	2,326	499	3,048	650	14,289	...	410[23]	118[23]	371[23]	44.6[23]
											Jan 1977 Prices			
											408	117	369	93.8
1976	725	189	725	189	2,650	575	3,225	701	15,145	...	418	120	384	104
			1983 Prices											
			1,036	279										
1977	796	213	1,083	293	2,859	614	3,236	706	15,486	...	415	103	411	99.6
1978	842	216	1,084	281	3,068	654	3,325	722	16,338	...	438	108	427	99.1
1979	919	232	1,136	291	3,261	687	3,382	724	17,666	...	461	112	444	101

J1 National Accounts Totals

	Denmark (in thousand million kroner at factor cost)				Finland (in thousand million 1963 markkaa at market prices)				France (in million francs to 1949 1st line and thousand million new (1959) francs subsequently)			
	Current Prices		Constant Prices		Current Prices		Constant Prices		Current Prices		Constant Prices	
	GDP	CF	GDP	CF	GDP	CF	GDP	CF	GNP/ GDP[24]	CF	GNP/ GDP[25]	CF
			1929 Prices				1985 Prices	Index 1926 = 100			1963 Prices	
1945	14.0	1.98	6.66	1.10	1.46	0.18	60.5	116	...	...	...	...
1946	14.8	2.79	7.70	1.60	2.19	0.37	65.4	163	...	...	...	...
1947	16.3	3.63	8.13	1.53	2.97	0.53	66.9	194	...	...	...	...
1948	17.7	4.45	8.40	1.77	4.10	0.89	72.2	216	...	...	...	...
1949	18.9	4.67	8.79	1.78	4.44	0.99	76.5	236	88.1	21.4	207	49.7
1950	21.6	5.88	9.41	2.15	5.47	1.22	79.5	248	102	23.9	222	51.8
								1970 Prices				
								3.5				
1951	23.4	5.83	9.47	1.80	8.28	1.82	86.3	4.6	125	28.5	235	51.3
1952	25.0	6.20	9.62	1.79	8.15	2.16	89.1	5.2	147	32.9	243	50.7
1953	26.5	7.08	10.2	2.12	9.04	2.20	89.8	5.1	153	31.8	249	48.6
1954	27.6	7.38	10.5	2.21	10.1	2.36	97.6	5.5	162	34.9	259	53.8
1955	28.7	6.97	10.6	2.02	11.1	2.54	103	5.8	173	38.2	272	57.8
1956	30.6	7.97	10.8	2.23	12.2	2.86	106	6.1	193	46.0	288	66.3
1957	32.7	8.94	11.3	2.42	13.2	2.92	111	5.8	216	51.3	305	69.0
1958	34.0	8.57	11.6	2.27	14.2	3.22	111	5.9	249	60.7	313	74.8
1959	37.4	11.0	12.3	2.94	16.0	3.59	118	6.5	273[24]	61.5[24]	323[25]	71.8[25]
											1970 Prices	
									267	54.0	425	80.2
1960	40.5	12.7	13.1	3.33	16.2[23]	4.32[23]	129[23]	7.5[23]	297	59.5	455	86.3
1961	45.4	13.8	13.8	3.38	18.4	5.13	138	8.5	323	68.5	480	95.7
1962	50.8	16.2	14.4	3.84	19.7	5.42	143	8.7	361	77.1	512	104
1963	53.5	15.3	14.8	3.34	21.4	5.46	147	8.4	405	89.5	540	113
1964	61.1	19.8	16.0	4.26	24.1	6.07	155	9.0	449	103	575	125
1965	68.3	22.4	16.8	4.53	26.6	7.02	163	10.2	483	113	602	134
1966	74.7	23.6	17.2	4.50	28.6	7.56	167	10.1	523	124	634	143
1967	81.9	25.5	17.9	4.56	31.3	7.86	171	10.0	565	135	664	152
1968	89.3	27.4	18.9	4.73	35.9	8.29	175	8.9	615	143	692	160
1969	100	32.3	20.5	5.33	41.0	9.77	191	10.0	701	164	740	175
1970	112	35.6	21.3	5.47	45.7	12.0	206	12.0	783	183	783	183
			1975 Prices				1985 Prices					
			170	51.4			56.9					
1971	112	32.5	175	51.5	50.3	13.8	210	60.3	872	206	825	196
1972	129	37.3	184	55.5	58.6	16.4	226	64.3	981	232	874	210
1973	149	45.1	191	60.2	71.4	20.6	241	69.7	1,114	265	920	223
1974	170	48.8	193	54.4	90.1	26.9	248	772.2	1,278	311	950	225
1975	189	45.2	189	45.2	104	32.9	251	77.0	1,452	338	952	218
			1980 Prices									
			272	70								
1976	218	60.2	287	85	118	33.2	251	70.0	1,678	391	1,001	226
1977	240	63.8	294	83	130	35.5	251	67.6	1,885[23]	420[23]	1,052[23]	224[23]
											1980 Prices	
									1,918	439	2,590	598
1978	265	67.0		80	143	34.8	257	62.9	2,183	488	2,677	610
1979	292	74.0	313	82	167	39.3	276	64.8	2,481	555	2,763	629

J1   National Accounts Totals

	East Germany (in thousand million marks at market prices)		West Germany[27,28] (in thousand million marks at market prices)				Greece (in thousand million drachmae at market prices)			
	Current Prices		Current Prices		Constant Prices		Current Prices		Constant Prices	
	NMP	CF[2]	GDP	CF[7]	GDP	CF[7]	GDP	CF	GDP	CF
				1954 Prices					1929 Prices	
1945	...	...	...	...	...	...	...	...	...	...
1946	...	...	...	...	...	...	6.4	0.4	41	...
1947	...	...	...	...	...	...	10.2	1.2	54	...
1948	...	...	...	...	...	...	15.9	2.2	59	...
									1954 Prices	
1949	22.3[26]	2.86	...	...	...	...	21.8	3.0	39.0	5.9
1950	29.1[26]	3.60	97.8	21.8	113	25.7	25.8	5.1	38.4	8.2
1951	35.3	4.55	119	26.0	126	26.4	30.5	4.7	42.5	6.9
1952	40.1	5.81	136	30.7	136	29.3	31.7	4.7	41.7	6.6
1953	42.4	6.98	147	31.0	147	30.6	42.7	5.7	47.6	6.5
1954	46.1	7.14	158	35.6			49.1	8.0	49.1	8.0
1955	50.0[26]	8.13	181	46.2	177	45.0	58.3	9.8	55.5	9.3
1956	52.3	10.2	199	48.8	189	46.3	67.6	12.0	58.5	10.9
1957	56.0	10.6	216	51.8	200	47.7	72.2	13.2	63.5	11.3
1958	62.0	12.1	231	54.1	207	48.7	75.6	17.0	65.6	16.1
									1958 Prices	
1959	67.5	14.6	251	62.2	221	55.1	78.6[29]	19.5[29]	79.6[29]	19.1[29]
							86.4	21.2	86.5	20.8
1960	71.5[23]	16.3[23]	279[28]	75.0[28]	240[28]	64.6[28]	92.5	27.8	88.9	26.1
	79.4	21.9	303	81.4	255	68.2				
				1962 Prices						
					329	89.7				
1961	80.7	22.2	331	90.7	344	95.8	105	27.8	98.4	26.0
1962	82.8	22.8	360	97.8	360	97.8	110	28.0	101	25.4
1963	85.8	23.1	381	101	370	98.2	120	27.2	107	24.1
1964	90.0	25.3	418	119	395	112	137	35.0	119	30.0
1965	94.2	27.6	456	132	416	122	154	38.6	129	32.9
1966	98.8	29.3	486	130	428	117	169	43.1	136	36.6
1967	104	32.0	492	113	428	103	183	43.6	144	36.1
1968	109	35.4	535	136	458	124	197	54.0	153	43.3
1969	115	40.9	597	162	494	141	220	65.1	167	50.9
1970	122	43.7	679[23]	189[23]	524[23]	149[23]	247[23]	68.4[23]	181[23]	52.2[23]
									1970 Prices	
			675	186	521	146	258	70.7	258	70.7
1971	127	44.4	751	201	537	145	286	83.3	278	80.6
1972	134	46.7	824	214	557	149	330	105	304	93.0
1973	142	50.6	917	232	586	155	428	136	329	100
1974	151	53.3	985	218	588	135	507	125	323	74.5
				1980 Prices						
					1,080	293				
1975	158	55.8	1,027	204	1,255	264	593	140	340	74.7
1976	164	59.9	1,122	243	1,323	304	729	175	360	79.7
1977	172	63.1	1,198	252	1,362	304	845	221	371	85.9
1978	178	64.8	1,285	275	1,401	313	1,017	278	395	91.1
1979	185	65.6	1,392	331	1,459	352	1,245	369	409	99.1

J1 National Accounts Totals

	Hungary[10] (in million forints at market prices)				Southern Ireland (in million pounds at market prices)				Italy (in million million lire at market prices)			
	Current Prices		Constant Prices		Current Prices		Constant Prices		Current Prices		Constant Prices	
	NMP	CF[2]	NMP	CF[2]	GNP	CF	GNP	CF	GNP /GDP[31]	CF[4]	GNP /GDP[31]	CF[4]
										1958 Prices		1938 Prices
1945	...	...	...	...	...	...	...	...	1.25	0.04	76.6	0.006
1946	...	...	...	...	...	...	...	...	2.98	0.63	0.121	0.025
1947	...	...	...	...	332	31.5	505	43.2	5.99	1.62	0.140	0.037
1948	...	...	...	...	365	40.9	529	51.9	7.07	1.34	0.149	0.026
1949	...	...	...	...	391	54.2	551	69.4	7.61	1.43	0.160	0.028
			1949 Prices									
1950	46.5	5.1	45.5	5.8	398	64.5	562	81.6	8.44	1.65	0.171	0.032
1951	65.3	7.8	53.2	8.9	420	77.5	573	93.6	9.75[31]	2.08[4]	0.182[31]	0.036[4]
											1963 Prices	
									10.5	2.09	15.4	2.26
1952	73.8	9.6	52.2	10.7	478	81.5	586	92.3	11.3	2.13	16.0	2.57
1953	83.0	11.4	59.1	11.7	524	81.4	601	92.5	12.5	2.44	17.2	2.92
1954	85.6	9.5	56.7	9.5	528	86.3	607	99.3	13.3	2.65	17.9	3.27
			1959 Prices									
1955	94.3	10.2	104	12.7	551	91.9	619	103	14.6	3.18	19.1	3.67
1956	82.5	8.9	83.1	8.9	559	91.6	610	97.0	15.9	3.42	19.9	3.92
1957	107[30]	9.2[30]	113[30]	10.7[30]	581	80.2	614	81.4	17.0	3.80	20.9	4.26
1958	110	14.2	120	16.3	601	83.0	600	83.0	18.3	3.89	22.0	4.38
1959	128	20.0	128	20.0	639	83.3	627	83.2	19.4	4.23	23.4	4.77
1960	142	24.3	139	25.2	676	90.3	659	88.5	210[23]	5.07[23]	24.9[23]	5.77[23]
			1968 Prices									
			150	20.8					21.7	5.24	25.7	6.0
1961	149	21.8	158	19.2	727	109	692	103	24.2	6.0	27.8	6.7
1962	157	23.3	167	20.8	784	129	714	118	27.2	6.9	29.5	7.3
1963	165	28.5	176	25.8	840	148	744	133	31.1	8.0	31.1	8.0
1964	173	29.3	184	26.5	952	173	771	147	34.0	8.1	32.0	7.5
							1975 Prices					
							2,532	458				
1965	170	26.4	185	26.7	999	200	2,545	522	36.6	7.5	33.1	6.9
1966	190	24.7	199	25.5	1,052	200	2,582	521	39.6	8.0	35.1	7.2
1967	207	31.9	216	33.2	1,148	221	2,715	554	43.6	9.1	37.5	8.0
1968	225	32.3	226	32.3	1,300	258	2,940	623	47.0	10.3	39.8	8.9
1969	253	37.4	244	36.3	1,494	332	3,106	737	51.7	11.7	42.1	9.5
1970	272	55.5	256	52.7	1,675[23]	361[23]	3,154[23]	720[23]	57.9	13.4	44.2	9.8
					1,648	36.2	3,104	735			1970 Prices	
1971	294	57.7	273	54.0	1,881	435	3,204	793	73.0	17.5	68.1	16.3
1972	319	66.4	287	58.1	2,257	497	3,391	805	78.9	18.5	69.3	16.3
1973	354	72.8	309	60.9	2,725	656	3,542	959	96.7	24.1	76.1	18.1
1974	370	71.2	330	57.4	3,010	753	3,681	901	122	31.7	81.1	
							1980 Prices					
1975	394	101	347	78.6	3,796	885	7,499	1,798	139	34.6	78.3	17.1
			1981 Prices									
			519	115								
1976	432	930	535	100	4,585	1,159	7,485	1,991	175	41.8	83.7	17.4
1977	476	98.1	573	99.2	5,533	1,414	7,974	2,083	214	50.3	86.2	17.6
1978	513	112	596	109	6,529	1,862	8,513	2,464	254	57.7	89.4	18.0
1979	556	120	604	113	7,634	2,430	8,757	2,828	310	70.8	94.4	19.1

J1 National Accounts Totals

Netherlands (in thousand million guilders at market prices) · Norway (in thousand million kroner at market prices) · Poland (in thousand million zlotys at market prices)

	Netherlands				Norway				Poland			
	Current Prices		Constant Prices		Current Prices		Constant Prices		Current Prices		Constant Prices	
Year	NNP /GDP[32]	CF[32]	NNP /GDP[32]	CF	GDP	CF[4]	GDP	CF[4]	NMP	CF[2]	NMP	CF[2]
							1955 Prices				*1961 Prices*	
1945	4.2	...	...	...	...	...	...	...	...	...	...	...
1946	9.3[14] / 9.9	...	...	...	10.8	3.35	16.5	5.81	...	...	...	15.5
1947	12.1	...	...	...	12.7	4.72	18.8	7.68	...	...	104	19.6
			1963 Prices	*1953 Prices*								
1948	14.2[32] / 15.0	1.9[32] / 3.2	26.9[32] / 28.3	... / 4.1	13.9	5.08	20.1	7.61	...	...	136	23.9
1949	16.8	3.4	29.5	4.4	14.9	5.66	20.6	7.99	...	...	159	28.0
1950	19.4	3.9	31.3	4.6	16.4	5.81	21.6	7.81	183	...	183	38.6
1951	21.5	4.2	30.6	4.4	20.5	7.11	22.8	8.33	197	...	198	43.2
1952	22.4	4.2	31.1	4.1	22.6	7.83	23.6	8.36	209	...	209	51.4
			1963 Prices									
1953	23.8	5.0	33.8	7.1	22.9	8.07	24.6	8.53	231	...	231	59.4
1954	26.6	5.7	35.5	7.9	24.8	9.14	25.8[23]	9.31[4,23]	255	49.1	255	63.2
							1963 Prices					
1955	29.7	6.8	38.5	8.4	24.2	7.37	30.4	10.0	223	52.6	277	65.7
1956	32.3	8.1	40.4	9.4	26.4[23] / 27.3	9.67[4,23] / 7.61	32.3	9.2	252	51.4	297	68.6
1957	35.1	9.0	41.6	9.8	29.0	8.39	32.8	9.6	301	74.2	328	73.5
1958	35.4	8.1	41.2	8.8	28.9	9.30	32.9	9.9	321	77.5	346	80.7
1959	37.8	8.9	43.1	9.8	30.7	9.04	33.3	9.5	345	87.4	365	94.4
1960	42.4	10.1	47.1	10.9	32.7	9.30	35.8	9.7	375	90.0	380	100
1961	44.7	10.9	48.5	11.6	35.6	10.5	37.6	10.9	411	102	411	108
1962	48.1	11.6	50.6	12.1	38.4	11.2	39.4	11.4	426	101	419	119
1963	52.2	12.3	52.2	12.3	41.5	12.3	41.5	12.3	460	113	449	123
1964	61.5	15.4	56.9	14.6	45.9	12.8	43.8	12.8	497	120	479	128
1965	68.7	17.0	60.1	15.3	50.9	14.4	46.0	13.5	531	137	512	141
1966	74.9	19.3	61.8	16.6	55.5	15.9	48.1	14.4	567	150	549	153
1967	82.3	21.3	65.2	18.0	61.0	18.2	50.8	16.0	606	153	580	170
1968	91.2[23]	24.0	69.8[23]	19.9	65.5	17.6	52.8	14.7	669	175	632	185
			1970 Prices									
	89.8		100	27.3								
1969	102	24.9	107	26.7	70.9	17.4	55.5	13.7	696	174	650	201
1970	115	29.4	115	29.4	79.9	21.2	56.1	15.2	738[23]	143[23]	684[23]	148[23]
							1970 Prices				*1971 Prices*	
							79.9	21.2	149	139	791	167
1971	130	33.4	120	30.4	89.1	26.7	85.3	25.4	855	184	855	184
1972	147	34.8	124	29.4	98.4	27.6	87.8	24.4	951	235	946	235
1973	168	38.7	132	31.0	112	33.0	91.5	27.6	1,065	300	1,048	299
1974	190	41.4	137	29.9	130	39.6	96.2	29.1	1,209	354	1,158	367
1975	209	436	136	36.0	149	50.8	99.6	33.1	1,350	394	1,238	382
			1980 Prices				*1975 Prices*				*1977 Prices*	
			156	62.2						394	150	470
1976	238	46.4	193	61.2	171	62.0	159	59.1	1,593	459	1,606	461
1977	261[23] / 275	54.8[23] / 57.9	226[23] / 318	67.2[23] / 70.9	192	71.1	165	58.0	1,736	485	1,686	486
1978	297	63.3	326	72.7	213	67.7	172	51.5	1,903	510	1,741	465
1979	316	66.5	334	71.5	239	66.2	181	48.9	1,935	447	1,701	389

J1 National Accounts Totals

	Portugal (in thousand million escudos at market prices)				Russia/U.S.S.R. (in thousand million rubels)				Spain (in thousand million pesetas at market prices)			
	Current Prices		Constant Prices		Current Prices		Constant Prices		Current Prices		Constant Prices	
	GDP	CF	GDP	CF	GNP /NMP[33]	CF[33]	GNP /NMP[33]	CF[33]	NNP /GDP[34]	CF	NNP /GDP[34]	CF
							1937 Prices				1958 Prices	
1945	...	...	...	...	334	40.8	199	21.3	197	...	270	...
1946	...	...	...	...	470	50.2	198	26.7	111	...	300	...
1947	...	...	...	...	763	58.8	220	31.0	133	...	305	...
1948	...	...	...	...	752	74.2	251	37.9	141	...	303	...
1949	...	...	...	...	744	122	278	45.8	151	...	307	...
1950	40.1	...	...	...	676	124	304	55.2	182	...	322	...
1951	...	...	...	...	674	135	327	60.8	241	...	357	...
1952	...	...	...	...	697	140	352	64.6	257	...	381	...
			1963 Prices									
1953	49.2	6.8	55.6	7.3	674	149	375	71.3	273	...	387	...
1954	50.5	7.1	57.6	7.7	687	172	404	81.8	295[34]	...	415[34]	...
											1970 Prices	
									369	65.1	1,027	137
1955	53.4	7.2	60.2	7.8	151[33]	180[33]	442[33]	94.0[33]	413	73.8	1,081	150
							1958 Prices	July 1955 Prices				
					98.5	25.1	95.8	19.6				
1956	57.4	7.9	62.7	8.4	107	29.1	106	22.4	474	89.0	1,159	163
1957	60.1	8.7	65.4	9.1	113	26.4	114	25.3	556	108	1,208	170
1958	61.9	9.7	66.5	10.3	128	34.6	128	29.4	642	121	1,258	180
1959	66.1	10.6	70.2	11.2	136	35.6	138	33.3	662	115	1,245	171
1960	72.4	12.5	74.9	13.0	145	38.9	148	35.9	679	121	1,261	183
1961	77.3	13.5	79.1	13.8	153	42.9	158	37.5	777	144	1,411	213
1962	83.1	13.8	84.3	13.9	165	45.0	167	39.3	906	170	1,547	236
1963	88.6	16.0	88.5	16.0	169	42.3	174	41.3	1,069	203	1,693	265
1964	95.8	16.6	94.1	16.7	181	49.3	190	45.0	1,202	245	1,792	306
1965	107	18.5	101	18.4	193	50.2	203	48.7	1,399	295	1,905	354
1966	117	22.3	105	21.6	207	54.2	220	52.4	1,618	335	2,040	393
1967	131	26.5	114	22.9	225	59.4	239	56.7	1,818	347	2,128	400
							1960 Prices	1969 Prices				
							233	66.0				
1968	147	24.4	124	20.7	244	64.8	252	71.2	2,037	377	2,272	412
1969	162	27.3	127	22.6	262	69.4	265	73.6	2,317	441	2,475	464
										482[29]		482[29]
1970	177	31.3	138	25.2	290	84.2	290	82.1	2,576	597	2,576	597
1971	199	37.3	147	27.7	305	87.1	307	88.0	2,920	618	2,704	579
1972	231	47.5	159	31.4	314	85.3	319	94.3	3,432	762	2,924	671
1973	281	57.3	176	34.4	338	97.6	348	98.7	4,140	976	3,154	767
1974	338	66.8	178	32.0	354	98.1	365	106	5,102	1,258	3,334	818
1975	376	74.0	171	28.4	363	96.6	...	115	6,018	1,400	3,371	786
1976	468	88.9	182	28.6	386	103	...	...	7,234	1,578	3,472	771
1977	626	125[29]	193	320[29]	406	107	...	...	9,178	1,927	3,586	769
		166	1977 Prices				...					
1978	787	220	647	178	426	113	...	...	11,231	2,236	3,651	751
1979	993	264	687	174	441	109	...	...	13,131	2,481	3,658	717

J1   National Accounts Totals

	Sweden (in thousand million Kronor at market prices)				Switzerland (in thousand million Francs at market prices)			
	Current Prices		Constant Prices		Current Prices		Constant Prices	
	GDP	CF	GDP	CF	NNP/GNP[37]	CF	NNP/GNP[37]	CF
	1908/9 Prices						*1938 Prices*	
1945	20.7	4.63	8.1	1.71	13.9	...	9.1	...
1946	22.7	4.84	8.5	1.67	15.4	...	10.2	...
1947	25.0	5.77	8.8	1.85	17.4	...	11.0	...
1948	27.6	5.70	9.2	1.73	18.1	...	11.1	...
1949	29.3	6.40	9.7	1.96	17.5	...	10.8	...
1950	31.9[36]	6.87[36]	10.2[36]	2.02[36]	18.5[37]	...	11.6[37]	...
	1970 Prices						*1958 Prices*	
	32.1	5.9	78.1	13.5	19.9	3.18	23.2	3.97
1951	39.6	7.8	80.4	14.2	21.6	4.60	24.8	5.25
1952	43.2	8.4	81.8	13.5	22.7	4.04	25.1	4.40
1953	44.4	9.3	84.4	15.7	23.7	3.97	26.1	4.44
1954	47.3	10.1	89.5	13.6	25.1	4.82	27.5	5.45
1955	50.8	10.6	92.2	17.6	26.9	5.86	29.0	6.46
1956	55.2	11.5	95.2	18.2	28.9	6.97	30.8	7.44
1957	59.0	11.9	97.5	18.0	30.5	7.60	31.7	7.80
1958	62.3	13.3	99.8	20.2	31.2	5.94	31.2	5.94
1959	66.2	14.6	105	22.1	33.4	7.50	33.3	7.49
1960	72.2	15.9	109	22.9	36.6	9.67	35.2	9.30
1961	78.5	17.8	115	24.7	41.0	12.3	37.8	11.2
1962	85.2	19.7	120	26.2	45.5	13.8	39.7	11.8
1963	92.1	21.8	126	27.9	49.8	15.1	41.6	12.1
1964	103	24.7	135	30.3	54.9	17.2	43.7	13.1
1965	113	27.4	141	31.9	59.1	17.0	45.3	12.7
1966	123	29.8	144	33.0	63.5	17.5	46.4	12.6
1967	133	32.5	149	34.8	67.7	17.9	47.2	12.7
1968	142	33.2	155	35.3	72.7[23]	19.0[23]	48.9[23]	13.2[23]
							1970 Prices	
					74.9	19.2	81.5	21.9
1969	153	34.9	163	36.7	81.5	21.0	85.8	23.1
	1980 Prices							
1970	172	38.8	433	100	90.7	25.0	90.7	25.0
1971	186	41.0	436	99.9	103	30.1	94.4	27.4
1972	204	45.2	447	104	117	34.6	97.4	28.8
1973	227	49.6	464	107	130	38.2	100	29.6
1974	256	55.0	479	103	141	38.9	102	28.4
1975	301	62.9	492	106	140	33.7	94.4	24.5
1976	340	72.0	497	108	142	29.2	93.1	21.9
1977	370	78.0	489	105	146	30.2	95.3	22.3
1978	412	80.1	497	98.1	152	32.5	95.7	23.6
1979	462	91.6	516	102	159	34.6	98.1	24.8

J1 National Accounts Totals

| | United Kingdom[6] (in thousand million pounds at factor cost) | | | | Yugoslavia (in million dinari at market prices) | | | |
| | Current Prices | | Constant Prices | | Current Prices | | Constant Prices | |
	GDP	CF	GDP	CF	NMP	CF	NMP	CF
			1938 Prices					
1945	8.67	0.35	5.84	0.19	...	...		
1946	8.77	0.92	5.79	0.48	...	...		
1947	9.31	1.20	5.64	0.56	...	...		
1948	10.3	1.42	5.81	0.60	...	...		
			1958 Prices					
			15.7	2.13				
1949	10.9	1.58	16.2	2.33				
1950	11.4	1.71	16.8	2.47				
1951	12.6	1.90	17.4	2.49				
1952	13.8	2.13	17.4	2.51	827	276	5,470	1,560
1953	14.9	2.39	18.2	2.79	999	361	6,368	1,930
1954	15.7	2.59	18.9	3.03	1,130	407	6,558	2,087
1955	16.9	2.88	19.5	3.21	1,398	424	7,449	2,037
1956	18.3	3.16	19.9	3.36	1,444	441	7,048	1,976
1957	19.4	3.45	20.3	3.54	1,829	536	8,510	2,357
1958	20.2	3.57	20.2	3.57	1,834	646	8,638	2,710
1959	21.3	3.82	20.9	3.85	2,269	801	10,050	3,124
1960	22.6	4.19	21.9	4.20	2,686	1,020	10,776	3,634
1961	24.4	4.70	22.9	4.61	3,115	1,279	11,381	4,166
1962	25.5	4.90	23.5	4.67	3,470	1,425	11,741	4,496
1963	27.2	5.14	24.2	4.80	4,200	1,699	13,147	4,963
1964	29.5	6.12	25.7	5.61	5,593	2,175	14,647	5,718
					(in thousand million new dinari)			
1965	32.0	6.63	27.0	5.84	73.6	23.4	149	50.1
1966	33.5	7.06	26.8	5.99	91.7	26.3	161	52.8
			1985 Prices					
			208	43.8				
1967	35.4	7.71	214	47.6	94.3	30.3	164	53.8
1968	38.1	8.51	223	50.6	102	35.0	170	57.9
1969	40.1	8.83	227	50.3	120	42.2	186	61.6
1970	44.2	9.74	232	51.6	143	53.5	197	69.5
1971	50.4	10.9	238	52.5	186	65.9	212	72.7
1972	56.3	11.9	242	52.4	221	76.1	221	74.9
1973	65.6	14.7	261	55.8	276	86.7	232	77.1
1974	76.2	17.5	260	54.5	363	119	251	84.1
1975	96.5	21.0	258	53.4	454	166	261	92.2
1976	115	24.5	267	54.3	528	210	271	99.7
1977	130	27.0	270	53.3	662	271	292	109
1978	150	31.1	277	54.9	812	363	312	121
1979	173	36.9	283	56.4	1,053	455	334	128

J1 National Accounts Totals

	Austria (in thousand million schillings at market prices)				Belgium (in thousand million francs at market prices)				Bulgaria (in thousand million leva at market prices)		Czechoslovakia (in thousand million kotura at market prices)			
	Current Prices		Constant Prices		Current Prices		Constant Prices		Current Prices		Current Prices		Constant Prices	
	GNP	CF[7]	GNP	CF[7]	GNP	CF[20]	GNP	CF[20]	NNP	CF[2]	NMP	CF	NMP	CF[2]
			1983 Prices				1985 Prices						Jan 1977 Prices	
1980	995	255	1,169	299	3,451	756	4,649	959	20,509	...	486	124	453	109
1981	1,056	268	1,165	295	3,641	640	4,601	762	21,933	...	473	91.8	453	85.5
1982	1,134	263	1,178	271	3,984	680	4,640	763	22,849	...	491	96.6	454	82.5
1983	1,201	270	1,201	270	4,127	642	4,655	597	23,479	...	503	94.4	464	76.5
1984	1,277	283	1,218	275	4,437	727	4,761	762	24,907	...	534	83.6	480	70.8
1985	1,348	304	1,248	289	4,746	707	4,792	707	25,451	...	549	91.3	495	74.7
													Jan 1984 Prices	
													525	83.1
1986	1,422	323	1,262	299	4,994	753	4,811	752	26,861	...	562	94.0	539	78.5
1987	1,481	341	1,286	307	5,212	845	4,906	832	28,338	...	575	76.1	549	58.5
1988	1,566	371	1,335	327	5,564	1,002	5,147	967	29,423	...	599	82.3	564	64.6
1989	1,673	406	1,386	348	6,032	1,178	5,256	1,083	30,840	...	609	64.7	566	49.9
1990	1,801	442	1,445	368	6,422	1,303	5,499	1,165	34,481	...	665	63.3	561	43.7
1991	1,928	488	1,487	391	6,743	1,306	5,623	1,150	99,006	...	...	...	...	...
1992	2,046	511	1,515	396	7,102	1,357	5,727	1,169	...	...	...	...	...	...
													Czech Republic	
1993	2,118	511	1,514	388	7,285	1,286	5,630	1,093	...	...	...	...	...	...
						1990 = 100							1995 = 100	
						GFCF	GNI	GFCF	GNI	GFCF	GDP	CF		
1994	2,242	534	...	...	7,925	1,558	...	1,235	515	72	1,182	339	94.4	...
1995	2,338	564	...	...	8,224	1,643	...	1,286	858	134	1,374	443	100.0	...
1996	2,428	581	...	...	8,443	1,674	...	1,293	1,680	238	1,555	501	104.3	...
1997	2,528	...	...	...	8,797	1,802	...	1,363	16,466	1,932	1,648	515	103.5	...
1998	2,618	...	...	...	9,147	1,896	...	...	21,078	2,496	1,772	532	102.3	...

	Denmark (in thousand million kroner at factor cost)				Finland (in thousand million 1963 markkaa at market prices)				France (in thousand million new (1959) francs)			
	Current Prices		Constant Prices		Current Prices		Constant Prices		Current Prices		Constant Prices	
	GDP	CF	GDP	CF	GDP	CF	GDP	CF	GDP	CF	GDP	CF
			1980 Prices				1985 Prices				1970 Prices	
1980	316	69.2	316	69	193	49.1	291	71.6	2,808	646	2,808	646
1981	345	63	315	56	219	55.3	295	73.1	3,165	701	2,841	634
1982	397	76	325	62	246	68.2	306	76.4	3,626	774	2,914	625
1983	513	82	391	62	271	69.4	315	79.5	4,007	810	2,934	603
1984	565	104	408	70	305	74.5	326	77.8	4,362	840	2,972	587
1985	615	120	426	79	331	78.9	337	80.1	4,700	905	3,028	606
1986	666	143	441	92	355	80.7	344	80.1	5,069	977	3,098	626
1987	700	133	443	89	387	91.6	358	83.7	5,337	1,055	3,158	649
1988	732	131	448	83	434	112.3	374	91.1	5,735	1,188	3,270	698
1989	767	141	450	84	487	142.6	515	153.0	6,160	1,315	3,458	785
1990	799	138	457	82	515	142.1	515	142.1	6,509	1,391	3,545	807
1991	828	136	463	77	491	100.6	479	101.4	6,776	1,437	3,573	807
1992	851	130	467	72	477	82.1	462	86.2	7,010	1,402	3,621	782
1993	873	124	474	70	480	68.6	455	72.9	7,083	1,319	3,567	737
		GFCF	1995 = 100			GFCF	1995 = 100			GFCF	1995 = 100	
1994	965	168	97.3	...	522	80.85	96.3	...	7,488	1,428	98.4	...
1995	1,009	189	100.0	...	564	91.97	100.0	...	7,758	1,458	100.0	...
1996	1,061	198	102.5	...	586	99.73	104.0	...	7,955	1,470	101.5	...
1997	1,116	198	105.6	...	635	114.30	110.6	...	8,205	1,473	102.7	...
1998	1,169	220	108.5	...	689	128.91	116.5	...	8,564	1,578	103.6	...

J1 National Accounts Totals

	East Germany (in thousand million marks at market prices)		West Germany[27,28] (in thousand million marks at market prices)				Greece (in thousand million Drachmae at market prices)			
	Current Prices		Current Prices		Constant Prices		Current Prices		Constant Prices	
	NMP	CF[2]	GDP	CF[7]	GDP	CF[7]	GDP	CF	GDP	CF
					1980 Prices				1970 Prices	
1980	194	65.7	1,479	350	1,479	350	1,524	414	418	92.7
1981	203	67.3	1,535	331	1,481	309	2,050	456	418	85.7
1982	208	63.9	1,587	324	1,472	293	2,575	514	421	84.1
1983	218	63.7	1,667	341	1,494	311	3,079	624	477	83.0
1984	230	60.6	1,750	351	1,536	320	3,806	703	491	78.3
1985	242	62.6	1,826	356	1,566	314	4,618	880	506	82.3
1986	252	65.9	1,936	374	1,603	329	5,575	1,018	514	77.2
1987	261	71.2	2,003	386	1,633	339	6,272	1,075	512	73.3
1988	268	77.0	2,108	410	1,693	366	7,572	1,318	535	79.8
					1991 Prices					
1989			2,249	449	2,384	490	8,805	1,690	554	87.9
1990			2,448	508	2,520	532	10,551	2,072	548	96.1
1991			2,668	563	2,648	563	12,889	2,376	566	91.7
1992			2,820	587	2,694	565	14,832	2,696	571	93.1
1993			2,843	552	2,649	518	16,760	2,910	573	91.3
			Germany							
			GFCF		1995 = 100				1995 = 100	
1994			3,394	785	98.3	...	...	...	98.1	...
1995			3,523	790	100.0	...	...	...	100.0	...
1996			3,586	779	100.8	...	...	...	102.4	...
1997			3,666	785	102.2	...	...	...	106.0	...
1998			3,784	797	104.4	...	...	...	109.2	...

J1 National Accounts Totals

1980–1998

	Hungary[10] (in million forints at market prices)				Southern Ireland (in million pounds at market prices)				Italy (in million lire at market prices)			
	Current Prices		**Constant Prices**		**Current Prices**		**Constant Prices**		**Current Prices**		**Constant Prices**	
	NMP	CF[2]	NMP	CF[2]	GNP	CF	GNP	CF	GDP	CF[4]	GDP	CF[4]
	1981 Prices				*1980 Prices*				*1970 Prices*			
1980	583	110	598	105	9,003	2,718	9,003	2,718	388	94.0	97.9	21.1
1981	635	101	613	89.2	10,854	3,350	9,242	2,917	469	111	100	20.6
1982	696	96.1	630	75.2	12,455	3,531	9,208	2,819	545	122	98.8	19.5
											1980 Prices	
											396	87.3
1983	738	121	631	86.6	14,779	3,419	9,104	2,565	634	135	400	87.2
1984	804	123	647	78.7	16,407	3,516	9,443	2,505	726	153	409	89.4
1985	842	105	638	49.6	17,790	3,387	9,300	2,312	811	168	420	90.6
					1985 Prices							
1986	881	154	643	82.2	18,874	3,394	18,631	3,351	900	177	430	92.1
1987	1,000	150	670	66.5	21,704	3,470	19,499	3,313	984	194	443	98.3
1988	1,153	145	...	...	22,657	3,670	20,331	3,327	1,091	219	461	103
											1985 Prices	
											895	192
1989	1,414[38]	...	...	...	25,393	4,364	21,387	3,753	1,193	241	922	200
1990	2,089	401	...	...	27,093	4,943	23,709	4,205	1,312	266	941	208
1991	2,308[39]	441	...	...	28,189	4,661	24,392	3,829	1,429	282	952	209
1992	2,935	577	...	...	29,987	4,761	25,614	3,824	1,504	287	960	205
1993	3,538	661	...	...	32,290	4,819	26,632	3,726	1,560	267	953	183
					Ireland							
		GFCF	*1995 = 100* GDP			GFCF	*1995 = 100* GDP			GFCF	*1995 = 100* GDP	
1994	4,364	878	98.5	...	32,908	6,043	91.1	...	1,653	297	97.2	...
1995	5,614	1,125	100.0	...	36,725	7,072	100.0	...	1,787	327	100.0	...
1996	6,894	1,476	101.3	...	40,487	8,512	107.7	...	1,902	348	101.1	...
1997	8,541	1,899	106.0	...	46,428	10,650	119.3	...	1,987	362	103.1	...
1998	10,087	2,384	111.1	...	53,193	13,275	129.5	...	2,077	385	105.0	...

1980–1998

	Netherlands (in thousand million guilders at market prices)				Norway (in thousand million kroner at market prices)				Poland (in thousand million zlotys at market prices)			
	Current Prices		**Constant Prices**		**Current Prices**		**Constant Prices**		**Current Prices**		**Constant Prices**	
	GDP	CF[32]	GDP	CF	GDP	CF[4]	GDP	CF[4]	NMP	CF[2]	NMP	CF[2]
	1980 Prices				*1975 Prices*				*1977 Prices*			
1980	337	70.8	337	70.8	285	70.8	189	48.5	1,936[30]	348	1,639[30]	285
					1980 Prices				*1982 Prices*			
									1,992		5,508	1,326
1981	353	67.6	334	58.8	328	91.8	288	83.5	2,160	225	4,848	1,005
1982	369	67.2	330	60.2	362	92.3	289	74.3	4,753	800	4,581	805
1983	381	69.5	334	62.1	402	103	302	78.6	5,924	1,054	4,856	881
1984	400	74.3	344	65.4	453	118	319	87.2	7,182	1,275	5,128	990
					1984 Prices				*1984 Prices*			
1985	418	80.2	351	69.7	500	110	476	101	8,658	1,534	7,030	838
	1990 Prices											
1986	437	89.3	456	95.9	514	146	496	125	10,697	1,950	7,376	688
1987	441	91.5	462	96.9	561	157	506	123	14,013	2,612	7,520	933
1988	457	97.3	474	101.2	583	170	504	124	24,995	4,785	7,885	1,019
1989	484	104.0	496	106.2	621	169	506	119	104,952	16,695	7,869	944
1990	516	107.9	516	107.9	661	124	515	87	506,253	76,922	6,695	682
1991	542	110.5	528	108.1	687	127	523	89	...	...	...	...
1992	563	114.2	535	109.3	703	135	541	93	...	...	...	...
1993	574	113.0	536	106.9	734	161	559	105	...	...	...	...
		GFCF	*1995 = 100* GDP			GFCF	*1995 = 100*		GDP[38]	GFCF	*1995 = 100* GDP	
1994	608	117.3	97.7	...	867	179	96.3	...	225	40	93.4	...
1995	639	124.8	100.0	...	928	192	100.0	...	308	57	100.0	...
1996	661	131.6	103.1	...	1,016	216	104.9	...	387	80	106.0	...
1997	703	142.4	106.9	...	1,096	252	109.8	...	472	110	113.3	...
1998	750	149.9	110.8	...	1,109	276	112.0	...	553	139	118.8	...

J1 National Accounts Totals

1980–1998

	Portugal (in thousand million escudos at market prices)				Russia/U.S.S.R. (in thousand million rubels)		Spain (in thousand million pesetas at market prices)			
	Current Prices		Constant Prices		Current Prices		Current Prices		Constant Prices	
	GDP	CF	GDP	CF	NMP	CF	GDP	CF	GDP	CF
	1977 Prices								1970 Prices	
1980	1,256	359	720	189	462	109	15,185[23]	2,943[23]	3,714[23]	727[23]
							1980 Prices			
							15,168	3,368	15,209	3,308
1981	1,501	463	729	198	487	113	17,045	3,729	15,171	3,259
1982	1,850	575	746	204	523	134	19,723	4,264	15,356	3,275
							1986 Prices			
1983	2,302	672	744	199	548	143	22,532	4,686	30,083	5,804
1984	2,816	664	732	155	570	152	25,520	4,779	30,524	5,402
1985	3,524	768	756	150	578	150	28,201	5,409	31,322	5,730
	1985 Prices									
1986	4,420	977	3,670	851	587	148	32,324	6,297	32,324	6,297
1987	5,026	1,591	4,438	1,253	600	144	36,144	7,518	34,148	7,181
1988	5,892	1,950	4,695	1,392	631	153	40,159	9,083	35,910	8,179
1989	6,910	2,237	4,965	1,452	666	151	45,044	10,868	37,611	9,290
1990	8,140	2,612	5,177	1,551	...	...	50,145	12,261	39,018	9,906
1991	9,585	2,988	5,288	1,589	...	...	54,901	13,041	39,893	10,035
1992	11,184	3,426	5,346	1,675	...	...	59,002	12,859	40,169	9,620
1993	12,829	3,414	5,285	1,594	...	...	60,904	12,040	39,726	8,674
		GFCF	1995 = 100		GDP[38]	GFCF		GFCF	1995 = 100	
1994	14,617	3,439	97.2	...	610	113	64,812	12,860	97.4	...
1995	15,802	3,743	100.0	...	1,540	327	69,780	14,494	100.0	...
1996	16,809	4,005	103.2	...	2,145	454	73,743	14,976	102.4	...
1997	17,859	4,516	106.8	...	2,478	482	77,897	16,029	106.0	...
1998	19,246	4,992	110.5	...	2,696	472	82,650	19,800	110.1	...

J1   National Accounts Totals

	Sweden (in thousand millions Kronor at market prices)				Switzerland (in thousand million Francs at market prices)			
	Current Prices		Constant Prices		Current Prices		Constant Prices	
	GDP	CF	GDP	CF	GDP	CF	GDP	CF
	1980 Prices				*1970 Prices*			
1980	525	106	525	106	170	40.5	103	27.3
							1980 Prices	
1981	573	110	524	100	185	44.6	173	41.6
1982	628	118	528	99.2	196	45.3	171	40.5
1983	712	132	541	101	204	47.5	173	42.2
1984	797	148	562	106	213	49.8	176	43.9
1985	867	167	574	112	228	54.2	182	46.3
1986	947	176	580	112	243	59.0	188	49.9
1987	1,024	198	594	119	255	64.4	192	53.6
1988	1,114	225	607	125	269	71.5	197	57.3
	1985 Prices							
			935	192				
1989	1,233	271	957	215	290	79.9	205	60.7
1990	1,360	292	970	217	314	84.5	209	62.2
1991	1,447	280	<u>959</u>	<u>198</u>	331	84.8	209	60.7
1992	1,442	245	1,426	250	339	80.4	209	57.6
1993	1,442	206	1,390	206	343	77.0	207	55.9
		GFCF	*1995 = 100*			GFCF	*1995 = 100*	
1994	1,596	240	96.4	...	357	78	99.5	...
1995	1,713	265	100.0	...	363	77	100.0	...
1996	1,756	276	101.1	...	365	74	100.3	...
1997	1,813	269	103.1	...	371	73	102.0	...
1998	1,890	298	106.1	...	381	76	104.4	...

	United Kingdom[6] (in thousand million pounds at factor cost)				Yugoslavia (in thousand million dinari at market prices)			
	Current Prices		Constant Prices		Current Prices		Constant Prices	
	GDP	CF	GDP	CF	NMP	CF	NMP	CF
	1985 Prices							
1980	201	41.6	278	53.4	1,399	554	342	121
1981	220	41.3	276	48.3	2,003	695	346	109
1982	238	44.8	280	50.9	2,595	857	348	103
1983	261	48.6	290	53.5	3,597	1,036	344	92.9
1984	280	55.0	294	58.1	5,633	1,472	350	84.0
1985	308	60.7	306	60.3	10,112	2,676	351	80.9
1986	328	65.0	316	61.5	19,896	5,108	364	83.7
1987	361	75.1	329	66.9	43,578	9,993	359	79.4
1988	401	91.5	<u>342</u>	<u>75.7</u>	131,479	27,193	353	77.0
	1940 Prices							
			535	105				
1989	442	105.4	547	111	197,791	99,991	398	54.5
1990	479	107.6	549	107	1,147,787	253,153	...	...
1991	496	97.7	538	97.4	...	...	...	...
1992	516	93.6	536	96.3	...	...	...	...
1993	547	94.6	547	96.6	...	...	...	...
		GFCF	*1995 = 100*					
1994	677	107.5	97.3	...	...	...	...	...
1995	713	116.2	100.0	...	...	...	...	...
1996	756	125.4	102.6	...	...	...	...	...
1997	805	134.2	106.2	...	...	...	...	...
1998	851	148.5	109.0	...	...	...	...	...

J1 National Accounts Totals

NOTES

1. SOURCES:- The main sources used have been the official and other publications noted on p. xv and the United Nations, *Yearbooks of National Accounts Statistics*, whichever seems to have the latest revisions. In addition, the following have been used:-

Belgium 1913–1948 (1st line)—F. Baudhuin, "Prix, consommation, balance et revenus en 1957", *Bulletin des Recherches Economiques et Sociales* (1958). Conversion to constant prices to 1953 was by using the cost-of-living index in table H2.

Bulgaria 1924–46—United Nations, *National Income Statistics* (1950). Conversion to constant prices to 1946 was by using the cost-of-living index in table H2.

Czechoslovakia 1913–37—based on Frederic L. Pryor *et al*, "Czechoslovak Aggregate Production in the Interwar Period", *Review of Income and Wealth* (1971).

Finland 1860–1950—Riitta Hjerppe, *The Finish Economy 1860–1985* (Helsinki, 1989).

France 1915–1938—J-C. Toutain, "Le Produit intérieur brut de la France de 1789 à 1982", *Economi et Sociétés* XXI (1987).

Germany—W.G. Hoffman, *Das Wachstum der Deutschen Wirtschaft seit der Mitte des 19 Jahrhunderts* (Berlin, 1965).

Greece 1927–39—United Nations, *National Income Statistics* (1950).

Hungary 1899–1949—Alexander Eckstein, "National Income and Capital Formation in Hungary, 1900–1950", *Income and Wealth* (series V).

Italy to 1951 (1st line)—*Indagine sullo sviluppo del reddito nazionale dell'Italia del 1861 al 1956* (ISTAT, Rome, 1957).

Norway to 1955 (1st line)—Statistisk Sentralbyra, *Nasjonalregnskap 1865–1960 and Langtislinjer i Norsk Okonomie 1865–1960*.

U.S.S.R. 1928–55—A. Bergson, *The Real National Income of Soviet Russia since 1928* (Cambridge, Mass., 1961) for G.N.P. at current prices, and R. Moorsteen & R.P. Powell, *The Soviet Capital Stock 1928–1962* (Homewood, Ill., 1966) for other series.

Sweden to 1950 (1st line)—O. Krantz & C-A. Nilsson, *Swedish National Product 1861–1970* (Lund, 1975)

Switzerland 1913—Colin Clark, *The Conditions of Economic Progress* (3rd edition, London, 1957).

U.K. to 1948—B.R. Mitchell, *British Historical Statistics* (Cambridge, 1988), quoting estimates by Charles Feinstein.

2. For definitions of the concepts see the United Nations publications on national accounts. However, it should be noted that not all countries use precisely the U.N. concepts.
3. Wherever possible G.N.P. or G.D.P. figures are shown, whichever provides the lengthiest and best-authenticated series. Statistics for other concepts are often available in the sources, especially for the period since 1950.

FOOTNOTES

[1] Alternative estimates at current prices for 1820–1913, which include estimates of capital formation, are available in M. L'évy-Leboyer & F. Bourguignon, *Léconomie Française au XIXe siècle* (Paris, 1985). Toutain only gives estimates of capital formation in the form of annual averages for mainly decennial periods in million current francs and, as an index, in constant 1905–13 francs. The following figures are derived from these:-

	Current Prices	Constant Prices		Current Prices	Constant Prices
1815–24	805	703	1885–94	3,527	3,834
1825–34	1,086	959	1895–1904	4,933	5,304
1835–44	1,521	1,406	1905–13	6,390	6,390
1845–54	1,629	1,661	1920–24	39,426	8,307
1855–64	2,415	2,300	1925–34	58,788	10,863
1865–74	2,831	2,748	1935–38	58,149	9,777
1875–84	3,451	3,451			

Estimates of N.N.P. at 1938 prices are available in official publications for 1938–49 as follows (in million francs):-

1938	3,800	1941	2,660	1944	1,910	1947	3,410
1939	4,070	1942	2,380	1945	2,070	1948	3,660
1940	3,360	1943	2,260	1946	3,150	1949	4,140

These are based on work by Alfred Sauvy.

[2] Net, including stocks.

[3] Estimates for the balance of payments at constant prices are incomplete to 1880 (1st line) and in 1936–38.

[4] Including stocks to 1951 (1st line).

[5] Including stocks to 1954 or 1955 (1st line).

[6] The estimates constructed from expenditure sources are shown here because they are available for a longer period and because such G.D.P. statistics are the appropriate complement to those of capital formation. Different estimates, using income sources, and a 'compromise' estimate may be preferable for some purposes and are available in the sources.

[7] Including stocks.

[8] This break occurs on a change in the original source used by the United Nations.

[9] Subsequently South Jutland is included.

[10] All statistics relate to the territory established by the Treaty of Trianon, as subsequently altered. For 1920–48 they are for years ended 30 June.

J1 National Accounts Totals

11 Annual averages for three-year periods 1899–1902 and 1911–13.
12 In 1924/5 prices.
13 N.N.P. to 1937, G.N.P. subsequently.
14 At factor cost from 1939 (2nd line) to 1946 (1st line).
15 Net, including stocks, but excluding investment by public authorities.
16 At factor cost.
17 At factor cost, including stocks, but excluding repairs.
18 Southern Ireland is excluded from 1920 (2nd line).
19 Net National product to 1948 (1st line), G.D.P. from then to 1953 (1st line), and G.N.P. subsequently.
20 Including stocks from 1953 (2nd line).
21 Net national product to 1946, net material product subsequently.
22 Net, excluding stocks.
23 These breaks occur because of small changes in the concepts.
24 G.N.P. to 1959 (1st line), G.D.P. subsequently.
25 G.N.P. from then to 1959 (1st line), and G.D.P. subsequently.
26 Figures for N.M.P. on the post-1960 basis have been published for these years as follows:- 1949 24.9, 1950 30.4, and 1955 56.2. Revised capital formation statistics are available on this bases for 1949–59, as follows:-

1949	3.8	1952	7.7	1955	10.9	1958	16.4
1950	4.8	1953	9.3	1956	13.7	1959	19.9
1951	6.0	1954	9.5	1957	14.2		

27 The following estimates, comparable with statistics for 1938 and earlier (except for the change from Reichsmarks to Deutschmarks) have been made for 1950 (in million DM):-

	Current Prices		1913 Prices	
	N.N.P.	N.C.F.	N.N.P.	N.C.F.
	92,063	15,820	44,904	6.970.

28 Saarland and West Berlin are excluded until 1960 (2nd line).
29 There was a change in the basis of calculation.
30 The definition of N.M.P. was broadened subsequently.
31 G.N.P. to 1951 (1st line), G.D.P. subsequently.
32 N.N.P. and N.C.F. to 1948 (1st line), G.D.P. and G.C.F. subsequently.
33 G.N.P. and G.C.F., including stocks but excluding repairs to 1955 (1st line); N.M.P. and N.C.F. subsequently. All later figures are in new (1961) rubels.
34 N.N.P. to 1954 (1st line), G.D.P. subsequently.
35 Albert Carreras, in P. Martin Acena & L. Prados de la Escosura (eds), *La Nueva Historia Economica en Espana* (Madrid, 1985), gives the following series of gross capital formation as a percentage of G.N.P.:-

1850	1.9	1871	3.8	1892	6.3	1913	11.9	1934	9.9
1851	2.0	1872	3.6	1893	5.2	1914	8.5	1935	11.2
1852	1.9	1873	2.7	1894	5.5	1915	6.7		
1853	2.0	1874	3.5	1895	5.9	1916	6.3	1940	12.3
1854	1.9	1875	3.9	1896	5.9	1917	6.1	1941	11.1
1855	1.6	1876	4.3	1897	6.6	1918	6.2	1942	10.8
1856	2.2	1877	4.6	1898	4.4	1919	7.2	1943	11.9
1857	3.1	1878	4.4	1899	7.7	1920	8.9	1944	9.8
1858	3.9	1879	5.2	1900	9.6	1921	9.4	1945	11.6
1859	3.8	1880	5.6	1901	7.8	1922	9.6	1946	13.0
1860	5.5	1881	5.9	1902	6.4	1923	11.1	1947	13.4
1861	6.6	1882	6.9	1903	7.1	1924	12.5	1948	13.8
1862	6.5	1883	6.8	1904	7.6	1925	12.4	1949	14.8
1863	6.6	1884	6.5	1905	6.9	1926	12.6	1950	15.2
1864	6.0	1885	5.7	1906	6.5	1927	14.2	1951	15.0
1865	4.1	1886	6.1	1907	8.2	1928	14.4	1952	14.7
1866	3.2	1887	5.9	1908	8.1	1929	17.1	1953	16.0
1867	3.1	1888	6.4	1909	7.9	1930	14.7	1954	17.2
1868	3.7	1889	6.6	1910	7.7	1931	12.6	1955	19.1
1869	3.0	1890	7.3	1911	8.2	1932	9.7	1956	20.1
1870	4.2	1891	7.0	1912	8.9	1933	9.7		

36 This break occurs on a change of source (see note 1).
37 N.N.P. to 1950 (1st line), G.D.P. subsequently.
37 Revised estimats of N.N.P. at intervals are given in W. Fischer, J. Krengel, & J. Wietag, *Sozialgeschichtliches Arbeitsbuch*, vol. 1 (Munich, 1982) as follows (in million marks at 1913 prices):

| 1800 | 5,700 | 1850 | 9,449 | 1860 | 11,577 | 1870 | 14,169 |
| 1825 | 7,300 | 1855 | 9,657 | 1865 | 13,167 | | |

38 G.D.P. subsequently.
39 Change in calculation method.

J2 PROPORTIONS OF NATIONAL PRODUCT BY SECTOR OF ORIGIN (%)

Key: A = agriculture (usually including forestry and fisheries); I = manufacturing, mining, and construction (usually including utilities); T & C = transport and communications; C = commerce (usually excluding financial and other services)

1788–1998

	Austria				Belgium[7]				Bulgaria[10]				Czechoslovakia[12]			
	A	I	T&C	C	A	I	T&C	C	A	I	T&C	C	A	I	T&C	C
1788/9	...	...	...	...	...	...	...	...	...	...	...	...	...	...	...	...
1801	...	...	...	...	...	...	...	...	...	...	...	...	...	...	...	...
1811	...	...	...	...	...	...	...	...	...	...	...	...	...	...	...	...
1815	...	...	...	...	...	...	...	...	...	...	...	...	...	...	...	...
1818–9	...	...	...	...	...	...	...	...	...	...	...	...	...	...	...	...
1820–4	...	...	...	...	...	...	...	...	...	...	...	...	...	...	...	...
1825–9	...	...	...	...	...	...	...	...	...	...	...	...	...	...	...	...
1830–4	...	...	...	...	...	...	...	...	...	...	...	...	...	...	...	...
1835–9	...	...	...	...	...	...	...	...	...	...	...	...	...	...	...	...
1840–4	...	...	...	...	...	...	...	...	...	...	...	...	...	...	...	...
1845–9	...	...	...	...	...	...	...	...	...	...	...	...	...	...	...	...
1850–4	...	...	...	...	...	...	...	...	...	...	...	...	...	...	...	...
1855–9	...	...	...	...	...	...	...	...	...	...	...	...	...	...	...	...
1860–4	...	...	...	...	...	...	...	...	...	...	...	...	...	...	...	...
1865–9	...	...	...	...	...	...	...	...	...	...	...	...	...	...	...	...
1870–4	...	...	...	...	...	...	...	...	...	...	...	...	...	...	...	...
1875–9	...	...	...	...	...	...	...	...	...	...	...	...	...	...	...	...
1880–4	...	...	...	...	...	...	...	...	...	...	...	...	...	...	...	...
1885–9	...	...	...	...	...	...	...	...	...	...	...	...	...	...	...	...
1890–4	...	...	...	...	...	...	...	...	...	...	...	...	...	...	...	...
1895–9	...	...	...	...	...	...	...	...	...	...	...	...	...	...	...	...
1900–4	...	...	...	...	...	...	...	...	...	...	...	...	...	...	...	...
1905–9	...	...	...	...	...	...	...	...	...	...	...	...	...	...	...	...
1910–4	11[1]	45[1]	6[1]	14[1]	...	...	...	...	...	...	...	...	27[1]	31[1]	9[1]	10[1]
1915–9	...	...	...	...	...	...	...	...	...	...	...	...	...	...	...	...
1920–4	15[2]	45[2]	7[2]	15[2]	...	...	...	...	...	...	...	...	25	31	10	9
1925–9	14	46	8	15	...	...	...	...	...	...	...	...	24	36	10	10
1930–4	14	42	8	14	...	...	...	...	...	...	...	...	26	34	8	10
1935–9	14[3]	41[3]	8[3]	14[3]	...	...	...	...	42[8]	17[8]	4[8]	15[8]	24[3]	35[3]	8[3]	10[3]
1940–4	...	...	...	...	...	...	...	...	39	18	4	21	...[12]	...[12]	...[12]	...[12]
1945–9	16[4]	46[4]	6[4]	11[4]	9[4]	46[4]	8[4]	13[4]	40[9,10]	25[9,10]	4[9,10]	14[9,10]	18[4]	68[4]	4[4]	7[4]
1950–4	17	48	6	11	8[6,7]	44[6,7]	9[6,7]	12[6,7]	30[11]	41[11]	4[11]	22[11]	12	75	3	7
1955–9	13	49	6	12	7	41	7	11	32	46	4	14	15	73	3	7
1960–4	10[5]	49[5]	6[5]	14[5]	7	41	7	11	33	52	4	9	14	74	4	7
1965–9	8	45	6	18	5[5]	42[5]	8[5]	12[5]	30	55	5	8	13	72	4	10
1970–4	6	45	6	18	4	41	7	18	23	60	7	6	11	74	3	11
1975–9	5	40	6	17	2	36	8	17	20	69	9	8	9	75	3	12
1980–4	4	38	6	17	2	32	8	16	18	62	8	9	8	72	4	15
1985–8	3	37	6	16	2	31	8	17	14	70	7	7	8	72	4	16
1989–93	3	35	6	17	2	30	8	18	12	44	7	10	9	70	3	17
1994–98	2	31	7	17	1	29	9	19	18	31	7	11	5	41	7	13

J2   Proportions of National Product by Sector of Origin (%)

1788–1998

	Denmark				Finland				France				Germany			
	A	I	T&C	C	A	I	T&C	C	A	I	T&C	C	A	I	T&C	C
1788/9	...	...	...	...	...	...	...	...	49	18	...	12	...	...	...	...
1801	...	...	...	...	...	...	...	...	...	...	...	...	...	...	...	...
1811	...	...	...	...	...	...	...	...	...	...	...	...	...	...	...	...
1815	...	...	...	...	...	...	...	...	51	22	...	7	...	...	...	...
1818–9	60	16	2	5	...	...	...	...	...	...	...	...	...	...	...	...
1820–4	51	21	2	7	...	...	...	...	43	40	3	11	...	...	...	...
1825–9	53	19	2	7	...	...	...	...	43	40	3	11	...	...	...	...
1830–4	54	18	2	7	...	...	...	...	44	37	3	12	...	...	...	...
1835–9	53	20	2	8	...	...	...	...	42	38	3	14	...	...	...	...
1840–4	52	21	2	8	...	...	...	...	40	39	3	14	...	...	...	...
1845–9	51	21	2	8	...	...	...	...	38	39	4	14	...	...	...	...
1850–4	51	21	2	8	...	...	...	...	37	41	4	15	45	21	1	7
1855–9	51	22	2	9	...	...	...	...	40	37	5	15	44	23	1	7
1860–4	47	23	2	9	61	16	4	4	40	37	5	16	45	24	1	7
1865–9	49	21	3	10	58	17	5	4	39	36	5	17	43	27	2	8
1870–4	49	20	3	12	58	19	5	4	41	33	6	16	38	32	2	8
1875–9	44	20	4	13	57	18	5	5	40	34	6	16	37	33	2	8
1880–4	42	20	4	14	55	19	4	5	38	35	6	17	36	33	3	8
1885–9	37	22	5	16	53	19	4	5	36	36	6	19	36	34	3	9
1890–4	37	22	5	16	53	20	4	6	35	38	6	17	32	37	4	9
1895–9	31	25	6	18	51	21	4	6	34	39	7	17	31	38	4	9
1900–4	31	26	6	19	48	23	5	7	34	41	7	19	29	40	5	9
1905–9	30	25	7	21	45	24	5	7	33	40	7	20	26	42	6	9
1910–4	30	24	7	21	43	24	6	8	32[14]	41[14]	7[14]	20[14]	23[14]	44[14]	6[14]	9[14]
1915–9	30	24	10	21	45	23	6	8	...	...	...	...	...	...	...	...
1920–4	25	23	9	25	42	26	5	7	...	...	...	...	...	...	...	...
1925–9	22	25	9	23	35	29	5	8	...	...	...	...	16	48	7	10
1930–4	19	30	9	22	30	28	6	8	...	...	...	...	20	41	6	10
1935–9	18	32	9	22	32	30	6	9	[22][15]	[36][15]	[7][15]	[14][15]	16	50	6	9
1940–4	...	...	...	...	29	27	5	8	...	...	...	...	...	...	...	...

West Germany[17]

	Denmark				Finland				France				West Germany[17]			
1945–9	21[13]	37[13]	9[13]	19[13]	35	34	6	8	[18][16]	[36][16]	[9][16]	[12][16]	...	...	...	...
1950–4	21	36	9	19	26	39	7	10	13	48	6	12	10	51	7	13
1955–9	17	36	10	18	21_5	39_5	7_5	10_5	10	48	6	13	7	53	7	13
1960–4	13	39	9	19	17	38	8	10	8	48	5	12	5	53	6	13
1965–9	10_5	40_5	10_5	18_5	14	37	8	10	7_5	48_5	5_5	11_5	4_5	52_5	6_5	14_5
1970–4	7	34	9	21	11	40	8	10	6	38	5	13	3	48	6	11
1975–9	6_5	29_5	8_5	21_5	10	39	8	10	5	36	5	13	3	44	6	11
1980–4	5	24	8	16	9	38	8	10	4	32	6	14	2	42	6	11
1985–8	5	24	8	15	7	36	7	11	4	30	6	15	2	40	6	10
1989–93	3	14	5	7	6	31	7	11	3	46	6	15	1	38	6	10
1994–98	4	27	13	9	4	34	9	11	2	28	6	16	1	32	6	...

J2 Proportions of National Product by Sector of Origin (%)

	Greece[19]				Hungary[20]				Southern Ireland[25]			
	A	I	T&C	C	A	I	T&C	C	A	I	T&C	C
1788/9	...	...	...	...	...	...	...	...	...	...	...	...
1801	...	...	...	...	...	...	...	...	...	...	...	...
1811	...	...	...	...	...	...	...	...	...	...	...	...
1815	...	...	...	...	...	...	...	...	...	...	...	...
1818-9	...	...	...	...	...	...	...	...	...	...	...	...
1820-4	...	...	...	...	...	...	...	...	...	...	...	...
1825-9	...	...	...	...	...	...	...	...	...	...	...	...
1830-4	...	...	...	...	...	...	...	...	...	...	...	...
1835-9	...	...	...	...	...	...	...	...	...	...	...	...
1840-4	...	...	...	...	...	...	...	...	...	...	...	...
1845-9	...	...	...	...	...	...	...	...	...	...	...	...
1850-4	...	...	...	...	...	...	...	...	...	...	...	...
1855-9	...	...	...	...	...	...	...	...	...	...	...	...
1860-4	...	...	...	...	...	...	...	...	...	...	...	...
1865-9	...	...	...	...	...	...	...	...	...	...	...	...
1870-4	...	...	...	...	...	...	...	...	...	...	...	...
1875-9	...	...	...	...	...	...	...	...	...	...	...	...
1880-4	...	...	...	...	...	...	...	...	...	...	...	...
1885-9	...	...	...	...	...	...	...	...	...	...	...	...
1890-4	...	...	...	...	...	...	...	...	...	...	...	...
1895-9	...	...	...	...	...	...	...	...	...	...	...	...
1900-4	...	...	...	...	43[21]	20[21]	8[21]	6[21]	...	...	...	...
1905-9	...	...	...	...	...	...	...	...	...	...	...	...
1910-4	...	...	...	...	44[22]	24[22]	8[22]	6[22]	...	...	...	...
1915-9	...	...	...	...	...	...	...	...	...	...	...	...
1920-4	...	...	...	...	...	...	...	...	...	...	...	...
1925-9	...	...	...	...	33	30	9	8	33[26][27]	18[26][27]	16[26][27]	
1930-4	...	...	...	...	33	29	7	7	26[28]	21[28]	16[28]	
1935-9	40[18]	21[18]	6[18]	12[18]	31	31	7	8	26[25]	23[25]	16[25]	
1940-4	...	...	...	...	...	...	...	...	...	...	...	
1945-9	39[19]	24[19]	7[19]	11[19]	27[23][20]	37[23][20]	7[23][20]	7[23][20]	35[13]	28[13]	21[13]	
1950-4	31	21	7	11	26	63	4	11	30	28	17	
1955-9	29[5]	24[5]	6	11	35/29[24]	58/64[24]	4/4[24]	3/2[24]	29/26[25]	28/29[25]	16/17[25]	
1960-4	22	22	6	11	21	72	5	...	23	31	17	
1965-9	19	24	6	11	21[5]	62[5]	6[5]	9[5]	19	34	18	
1970-4	17	28	7	11	18	55	6	20	17	35	18	
1975-9	16	27	7	12	15	58	8	14	16	35	17	
1980-4	16	27	7	12	14[20]	47[20]	8[20]	12[20]	12	35	17	
					17	43	8	9				
1985-8	15	27	7	13	16	42	8	10	11	35	20	
1989-93	13	23	6	11	12	35	7	12	13	56	29	
					7	30	8	12				
1994-98	11	23	7	18	7	31	9	13	6	38	5	11

J2   Proportions of National Product by Sector of Origin (%)

1788–1998

	Italy[29]				Netherlands[32]				Norway				Poland			
	A	I	T&C	C	A	I	T&C	C	A	I	T&C	C	A	I	T&C	C
1788–9	...	...	...	...	...	...	...	...	...	...	...	...	...	...	...	...
1801	...	...	...	...	...	...	...	...	...	...	...	...	...	...	...	...
1811	...	...	...	...	...	...	...	...	...	...	...	...	...	...	...	...
1815	...	...	...	...	...	...	...	...	...	...	...	...	...	...	...	...
1818–9	...	...	...	...	...	...	...	...	...	...	...	...	...	...	...	...
1820–4	...	...	...	...	...	...	...	...	...	...	...	...	...	...	...	...
1825–9	...	...	...	...	...	...	...	...	...	...	...	...	...	...	...	...
1830–4	...	...	...	...	...	...	...	...	...	...	...	...	...	...	...	...
1835–9	...	...	...	...	...	...	...	...	...	...	...	...	...	...	...	...
1840–4	...	...	...	...	...	...	...	...	...	...	...	...	...	...	...	...
1845–9	...	...	...	...	...	...	...	...	...	...	...	...	...	...	...	...
1850–4	...	...	...	...	...	...	...	...	...	...	...	...	...	...	...	...
1855–9	...	...	...	...	...	...	...	...	...	...	...	...	...	...	...	...
1860–4	57[30]	18[30]	2[30]	15[30]	...	...	...	...	...	...	...	...	...	...	...	...
1865–9	57	20	2	15	...	...	...	...	34[36]	21[36]	...	...	...	...	...	...
1870–4	58	19	2	16	...	...	...	...	...	...	...	...	...	...	...	...
1875–9	55	19	3	16	...	...	...	...	33[37]	21[37]	...	...	...	...	...	...
1880–4	53	20	3	17	...	...	...	...	...	...	...	...	...	...	...	...
1885–9	50	21	4	17	...	...	...	...	...	...	...	...	...	...	...	...
1890–4	51	19	4	17	...	...	...	...	27[38]	23[38]	...	...	...	...	...	...
1895–9	50	19	4	17	...	...	...	...	...	...	...	...	...	...	...	...
1900–4	50	20	5	16	...	...	...	...	22[39]	24[39]	...	...	...	...	...	...
1905–9	46	24	5	16	...	...	...	...	...	...	...	...	...	...	...	...
1910–4	44	24	6	16	...	...	...	...	23[40]	26[40]	11[40]	16[40]	...	...	...	...
1915–9	45	29	5	14	...	...	...	...	...	...	...	...	...	...	...	...
1920–4	43	29	4	17	...	...	...	...	...	...	...	...	...	...	...	...
1925–9	37	30	7	16	...	...	...	...	...	...	...	...	...	...	...	...
1930–4	30	28	8	20	...	...	...	...	14	29	13	14	...	...	...	...
1935–9	29	31	8	18	8[33]	35[33]	11[33]	12[33]	13	33	14	16	...	...	...	...
1940–4	44	25	6	16	11[34]	38[34]	10[34]	12[34]	...	...	...	...	...	...	...	...
1945–9	42	33	5	15	13[35,32]	37[35,32]	11[35,32]	13[35,32]	15[35]	36[35]	15[35]	14[35]	...	...	...	...
1950–4	30/22[31]	37/36[31]	7/7[31]	14/11[31]	13	41	9	13	13	36	18	16	35[5]	52[5]	...	...
1955–9	18[5]	36[5]	7[5]	11[5]	11	41	9	13	11	34	18	17	27	59	3	9
1960–4	13	41	6	13	8	44	8	13	9	35	17	18	24	58	6	10
1965–9	11	41	6	14	7[5]	43[5]	8[5]	12[5]	7[5]	35[5]	17[5]	18[5]	21[5]	59[5]	6[5]	10[5]
1970–4	8	43	6	16	5	37	7	14	5	32	13	14	18	64	7	10
1975–9	7	43	6	15	4	34	6	13	5	35	10	12	16	66	7	9
1980–4	5	37	5	19	4	33	6	13	4	41	9	12	20[41]	59[41]	6[41]	13[41]
1985–8	4	35	6	19	4	33	7	14	3	38	8	12	15	60	6	16
1989–93	4	36	6	19	4	28	6	15	3	35	10	11	8	52	5	13
1994–98	3	30	7	18	3	28	7	15	3	34	10	12	7	39	7	20

J2 Proportions of National Product by Sector of Origin (%)

1788–1998

	Portugal				Romania				Russia/U.S.S.R[43]				Spain			
	A	I	T&C	C	A	I	T&C	C	A	I	T&C	C	A	I	T&C	C
1788/9	...	...	...	...	...	...	...	...	...	...	...	...	...	...	...	...
1801	...	...	...	...	...	...	...	...	...	...	...	...	...	...	...	...
1811	...	...	...	...	...	...	...	...	...	...	...	...	...	...	...	...
1815	...	...	...	...	...	...	...	...	...	...	...	...	...	...	...	...
1818–9	...	...	...	...	...	...	...	...	...	...	...	...	...	...	...	...
1820–4	...	...	...	...	...	...	...	...	...	...	...	...	...	...	...	...
1825–9	...	...	...	...	...	...	...	...	...	...	...	...	...	...	...	...
1830–4	...	...	...	...	...	...	...	...	...	...	...	...	...	...	...	...
1835–9	...	...	...	...	...	...	...	...	...	...	...	...	...	...	...	...
1840–4	...	...	...	...	...	...	...	...	...	...	...	...	...	...	...	...
1845–9	...	...	...	...	...	...	...	...	...	...	...	...	...	...	...	...
1850–4	...	...	...	...	...	...	...	...	...	...	...	...	...	...	...	...
1855–9	...	...	...	...	...	...	...	...	...	...	...	...	...	...	...	...
1860–4	...	...	...	...	...	...	...	...	...	...	...	...	...	...	...	...
1865–9	...	...	...	...	...	...	...	...	...	...	...	...	...	...	...	...
1870–4	...	...	...	...	...	...	...	...	...	...	...	...	...	...	...	...
1875–9	...	...	...	...	...	...	...	...	...	...	...	...	...	...	...	...
1880–4	...	...	...	...	...	...	...	...	...	...	...	...	...	...	...	...
1885–9	...	...	...	...	...	...	...	...	...	...	...	...	...	...	...	...
1890–4	...	...	...	...	...	...	...	...	...	...	...	...	...	...	...	...
1895–9	...	...	...	...	...	...	...	...	...	...	...	...	...	...	...	...
1900–4	...	...	...	...	...	...	...	...	...	...	...	...	...	...	...	...
1905–9	...	...	...	...	...	...	...	...	...	...	...	...	...	...	...	...
1910–4	...	...	...	...	...	...	...	...	...	...	...	...	...	...	...	...
1915–9	...	...	...	...	...	...	...	...	...	...	...	...	...	...	...	...
1920–4	...	...	...	...	...	...	...	...	...	...	...	...	...	...	...	...
1925–9	...	...	...	...	...	...	...	...	45[44]	...	...	...	...	...	...	...
1930–4	...	...	...	...	...	...	...	...	34	...	...	...	...	...	...	...
1935–9	...	...	...	...	...	...	...	...	29	...	...	...	...	...	...	...
1940–4	...	...	...	...	...	...	...	...	29[45]	...	...	...	...	...	...	...
1945–9	...	...	...	...	...	...	...	...	28	...	...	...	...	...	...	...
1950–4	31[42]	32[42]	5[42]	12[42]	31	49	4	11	22	...	...	...	22[46]	35[46]	7[46]	12[46]
1955–9	28	33	5	12	37	49	4	7	21[43]	...[43]	...[43]	...	23	36	7	11
									23	60	4					
1960–4	21	35	5	12	31	55	4	7	21	62	5	11	21	34	6	10
1965–9	18	38	5	12	28	61	4	5	22	61	6	11	15[5]	33[5]	6[5]	16[5]
1970–4	15	40	6	10	...	...	...	...	20	62	6	12	10	37	6	15
1975–9	13	39	6	18	...	...	...	...	17	63	6	14	9[5]	36[5]	6[5]	17[5]
1980–4	9	40	7	22	...	...	...	...	17	59	6	18	6	38	6	19
1985–8	7	38	7	21	...	...	...	...	...	...	...	...	5[48]	38[48]	6[48]	21[48]
1989–93	...	...	...	...	20	41	7	13	...	...	...	...	5	36	5	20
1994–98	4	36	6	17	20	44	9	10	8	38	11	17	3	8	...	...

J2 Proportions of National Product by Sector of Origin (%)

1788-1998

	Sweden				U.K.				Yugoslavia			
	A	I	T&C	C	A	I	T&C	C	A	I	T&C	C
1788/9	...	...	...	...	40[48]	21[48]	12[48]		...	...	...	...
1801	...	...	...	...	33	23	17		...	...	...	...
1811	...	...	...	...	36	21	17		...	...	...	...
1815	...	...	...	...	...	...	...		...	...	...	...
1818-9	...	...	...	...	...	...	...		...	...	...	...
1820-4	...	...	...	...	26[49]	32[49]	16[49]		...	...	...	...
1825-9	...	...	...	...	...	...	...		...	...	...	...
1830-4	...	...	...	...	24[49]	35[49]	18[49]		...	...	...	...
1835-9	...	...	...	...	...	...	...		...	...	...	...
1840-4	...	...	...	...	22[49]	35[49]	19[49]		...	...	...	...
1845-9	...	...	...	...	...	...	...		...	...	...	...
1850-4	...	...	...	...	21[49]	35[49]	19[49]		...	...	...	...
1855-9	...	...	...	...	...	...	...		...	...	...	...
1860-4	37[30]	20[30]	2[30]	22[30]	18[49]	38[49]	20[49]		...	...	...	...
1865-9	38	19	3	21	...	...	...		...	...	...	...
1870-4	38	21	4	20	15[49]	40[49]	23[49]		...	...	...	...
1875-9	36	22	5	20	...	...	...		...	...	...	...
1880-4	36	21	6	21	11[49]	40[49]	24[49]		...	...	...	...
1885-9	32	22	6	22	...	...	...		...	...	...	...
1890-4	32	23	6	22	9[49]	41[49]	24[49]		...	...	...	...
1895-9	29	26	6	22	...	...	...		...	...	...	...
1900-4	26	32	6	22	7[49]	43[49]	25[49]		...	...	...	...
1905-9	24	33	7	22	6[50]	38[50]	10	19[50]	...	...	...	...
1910-4	23	33	7	22	...	...	...	...	...	...	...	...
1915-9	25	35	8	22	...	...	...	...	...	...	...	...
1920-4	19	32	9	24	6	39	10	13	...	...	...	...
1925-9	15	39	9	21	4	37	10	14	...	...	...	...
1930-4	13	38	9	21	4	34	9	14	...	...	...	...
1935-9	13	41	9	21	4[51]	36[51]	9[51]	14[51]	...	...	...	...
1940-4	11	42	9	19	...	...	...	...	...	...	...	...
1945-9	10[47]	45[47]	8[47]	20[47]	6[35]	44[35]	8[35]	14[35]	...	...	...	...
1950-4	13	45	9	10	5	47	9	13	28[5]	51[5]	5[5]	8[5]
1955-9	10	45	9	11	4	48	8	12	31	48[5]	5[5]	10
1960-4	7	40	6	9	4	47	8	12	25	54	8	12
1965-9	5	39	6	10	3	46	8	11	23[5]	49[5]	7[5]	15[5]
1970-4	4	36	6	11	3	44	8	11	16	41	8	11
1975-9	4	33	6	11	2	42	8	13	13	41	7	11
1980-4	3	31	6	11	2	41	7	13	13	43	7	11
1985-8	3	30	6	11	2	37	7	14	12	46	7	11
1989-93	2	28	6	10	2	29	7	12	12[55]	41[55]	15[55]	13[55]
1994-98	2	30	6	11	2	30	8	14	18	37	7	13

J2 Proportions of National Product by Sector of Origin (%)

NOTES

1. SOURCES:- The main sources used were the official publications noted on p. xv and the U.N., *Yearbook of National Accounts Statistics*. In addition the following were used:- Finland—Riitta Hjerppe, *The Finnish Economy 1860-1985* (Helsinki, 1989); France 1820-1914—M. Lévy-Leboyer & R. Bourguignon, *L'économie Francaise au XIXe siécle* (Paris, 1985). Germany—W.G. Hoffman, *Das Wachstum der Deutschen Wirtscahft seit der Mitte des 19 Jahrhunderts* (Berlin, etc., 1965); Hungary 1899-1949—Alexander Eckstein, "National Income and Capital Formation in Hungary, 1900-1950", *Income and Wealth* (series V); Italy to 1951—*Annali di Statistica* (serie VIII, 9); Russia to 1958 (1st line)—based on R. Moorsteen and R.P. Powell, *The Soviet Capital Stock, 1928-1962* (Homewood, I11., 1966); Sweden to 1950—based on O. Johansson, *The Gross Domestic Product of Sweden and its Composition, 1861-1955* (Stockholm, 1967); U.K. 1688-1907—based on Phyllis Deane & W.A. Cole, *British Economic Growth, 1688-1959* (Cambridge, 1962); U.K. 1920-38—based on C.H. Feinstein, *National Income, Expenditure and Output of the United Kingdom, 1855-1965* (Cambridge, 1972).
2. Except as indicated in footnotes, the proportions shown in this table are of gross domestic product.

FOOTNOTES

[1] 1913 only.
[2] 1924 only.
[3] 1935-37.
[4] 1948-49.
[5] These breaks result from changes in the concepts used.
[6] 1950-53.
[7] Proportions of N.D.P. prior to 1955.
[8] 1939 only.
[9] 1945-46.
[10] Proportions of N.D.P. to 1946, of N.M.P. subsequently.
[11] 1953 only.
[12] Proportions of N.M.P. from 1948.
[13] 1947-49.
[14] 1910-13.
[15] 1938 only. The proportions are of N.D.P.
[16] 1946-49. The proportions are of N.D.P. in 1938 prices.
[17] The following figures of proportions of N.M.P. are available for East Germany:-

1951	28	53	7	10
1955	20	59	7	14
1960	17	65	6	13
1965-9	14	70	5	13
1970-4	11	72	5	13
1986	13	74	5	9

[18] 1939 only.
[19] Proportions of N.D.P. to 1949.
[20] Statistics throughout relate to the territory established by the Treaty of Trianon, as modified by the cession of the Bratislava Bridgehead, For 1925-48 they are for years ended 30 June and are proportions of N.D.P. in 1938/9 prices. Subsequently they are proportions of N.M.P. to 1980/4 (1st line) and of G.D.P. thereafter.
[21] 1899-1901.
[22] 1911-13.
[23] 1947-48.
[24] The first figure is for 1955-57, the second is for 1958-59. The definition of N.M.P. was broadened after 1957.
[25] Proportions of N.N.P. to 1937, and of N.D.P. from 1947 to 1957. The first figure for 1955-9 is for 1955-57, the second is for 1958-59.
[26] 1926 and 1929.
[27] 1931 and 1933.
[28] 1936-37.
[29] Data are for the 1914 territory to 1919, the 1924 territory from 1920 to 1939, and for the 1953 territory subsequently.
[30] 1861-64.
[31] The first figure is for 1950-51 on the old concepts, the second is for 1951-54 on the new ones.
[32] Proportions of N.D.P. to 1949.
[33] 1938-39.
[34] 1940-43.
[35] 1946-49.
[36] 1865.
[37] 1875.
[38] 1890.
[39] 1900.
[40] 1911.
[41] The averages for 1980-4 are much affected by the many stoppages in industry in 1981, which raised the agricultural share to 30% and reduced that of industry to 49%.
[42] 1953-54.

J2   Proportions of National Product by Sector of Origin (%)

[43]   Proportions of G.N.P. to 1955–9 (1st line) and of N.M.P. subsequently.
[44]   1928–29.
[45]   1940 only.
[46]   1954 only.
[47]   This break occurs on a change of source (see note 1). The major difference is the inclusion of financial and catering services with commerce in the statistics up to 1949.
[48]   England & Wales only.
[49]
[50]   1821, 1831, 1841, etc. to 1901.
[51]   1907.
[52]   1935–38.
[53]   1985–87.
[54]   Change in calculation method.
[55]   1989–91

J3 BALANCE OF PAYMENTS

Key:- CB = change in bullion & specie; CTR change in total foreign exchange reserves; EC = exports of capital (net); ELTC = exports of long-term capital (net); IIB = investment income balance; OCB = overall current balance; TIB = total invisible balance; TTB = tourism and travel balance; VB = visible balance

A   **National Definitions and Currencies**   **1816-1859**

	France (in million francs)					United Kingdom (in million pounds)[7]				
	VB	TIB	*IIB*[1]	OCB	EC	VB	TIB	*IIB*	OCB	CB
1816	...	...	...	...	...	4.1	15.5	0.6	19.6	−5.0
1817	...	...	...	...	...	−9.1	18.3	1.5	9.2	−2.9
1818	...	...	...	...	...	−21.9	22.7	1.9	0.8	3.9
1819	...	...	...	...	...	−10.6	16.5	2.1	5.9	1.4
1820	13	79	...	92	...	−7.4	16.0	2.6	8.6	−5.4
1821	−46	73	...	27	...	0.6	15.4	2.8	16.0	−2.2
1822	26	82	...	108	...	0.2	15.9	3.6	16.1	−2.8
1823	84	81	...	165	...	−9.4	17.8	4.4	8.4	−2.5
1824	58	90	...	148	...	−5.3	18.1	4.7	12.8	3.5
1825	141	108	...	249	...	−26.5	23.5	5.7	−3.0	5.4
1826	18	93	...	111	...	−11.6	18.0	5.4	6.4	−4.0
1827	90	94	...	184	...	−14.8	18.4	5.0	3.6	−3.6
1828	40	94	...	134	...	−14.0	17.5	4.5	3.5	0.3
1829	10	92	...	102	...	−11.7	16.7	4.2	5.0	1.1
1830	−43	88	...	45	...	−12.0	16.1	3.9	4.0	−3.5
1831	—	86	...	86	...	−18.1	17.0	3.9	−1.1	3.5
1832	−5	89	...	84	...	−8.7	16.0	4.3	7.3	−1.2
1833	48	97	...	145	45	−12.3	18.3	4.8	6.0	−2.4
1834	1	105	...	106	13	−15.1	19.9	6.1	4.8	2.3
1835	28	112	...	140	92	−11.4	23.3	7.8	11.9	0.8
1836	80	127	...	207	197	−21.8	25.8	8.6	4.0	1.5
1837	−66	113	...	47	−81	−19.0	23.3	8.4	4.3	−2.0
1838	−6	119	...	113	−6	−20.8	25.6	8.1	4.8	—
1839	−6	149	9	143	46	−28.4	27.1	7.7	−1.3	4.4
1840	−65	149	10	84	−60	−29.8	26.6	7.1	−3.2	0.9
1841	−73	145	8	72	−37	−22.4	24.5	6.2	2.1	−1.0
1842	−207	135	7	−72	−155	−20.6	22.9	6.3	2.3	−2.9
1843	−127	134	2	7	−58	−10.9	23.8	7.0	12.9	−3.6
1844	−39	140	—	101	21	−12.3	25.7	8.3	13.4	−3.0
1845	40	152	1	192	111	−19.0	29.3	9.7	10.3	−1.0
1846	−56	171	5	115	73	−20.3	29.7	10.2	9.4	−1.4
1847	−227	185	8	−42	−94	−41.6	35.2	10.6	−6.4	5.3
1848	216	148	4	364	115	−26.9	28.0	9.0	1.1	1.0
1849	214	184	9	398	142	−25.7	29.6	8.2	3.9	1.0
1850	77	224	14	301	409	−19.6	31.2	9.4	11.6	−1.0
1851	393	260	30	643	493	−22.6	33.0	10.4	−1.2	
1852	268	305	51	573	563	−18.9	34.4	10.9	15.5	−7.8
1853	346	372	74	718	557	−32.8	42.6	11.8	9.8	−6.5
1854	122	412	97	534	259	−36.6	46.0	12.6	9.4	−3.6
1855	−37	447	115	410	394	−25.9	47.6	12.9	11.7	−7.8
1856	−98	463	116	365	278	−32.1	55.8	14.9	23.7	−1.9
1857	−8	484	127	476	438	−40.4	61.0	16.2	20.6	6.5
1858	323	507	157	930	425	−23.8	56.1	15.9	32.3	−9.9
1859	624	574	176	1,198	898	−22.6	60.1	16.9	37.5	−1.4

J3 Balance of Payments

1860–1914

	Denmark (in million kroner)				France (in million francs)					Germany (in million marks)				
	VB	TIB	OCB	CTR	VB	TIB	IIB[1]	OCB	EC	VB	TIB	IIB[1]	OCB	CB
1860	...	...	...	...	379	658	226	1,037	979	...	...	...	...	...
1861	...	...	...	...	−417	718	271	301	242	...	...	...	...	...
1862	...	...	...	...	43	739	282	782	809	...	...	...	...	...
1863	...	...	...	...	217	826	319	1,043	1,280	...	...	...	...	...
1864	...	...	...	...	395	956	378	1,351	1,382	...	...	...	...	...
1865	...	...	...	...	443	1,005	432	1,448	1,351	...	...	...	...	...
1866	...	...	...	...	386	994	423	1,380	997	...	...	...	...	...
1867	...	...	...	...	−203	1,034	440	831	323	...	...	...	...	...
1868	...	...	...	...	−516	1,112	529	596	367	...	...	...	...	...
1869	...	...	...	...	−80	1,134	541	1,054	749	...	...	...	...	...
1870	...	...	...	...	−66	1,167	619	1,101	1,007	...	...	...	...	...
1871	...	...	...	...	−696	1,251	670	555	−468	...	...	...	...	...
1872	...	...	...	...	210	1,313	647	1,523	129	...	...	...	...	...
1873	...	...	...	...	229	1,318	653	1,547	−741	...	...	...	...	...
1874	−56	47	−9	7	190	1,268	616	1,458	739	...	...	...	...	...
1875	−59	50	−9	−13	333	1,256	597	1,589	983	...	...	...	...	...
1876	−51	47	−4	−3	−415	1,202	545	787	267	...	...	...	...	...
1877	−64	49	−15	4	−234	1,267	648	1,033	540	...	...	...	...	...
1878	−40	45	5	−6	−999	1,307	650	306	2	...	...	...	...	...
1879	−44	44	—	−7	−1,367	1,282	620	−80	91	...	...	...	...	...
1880	−33	43	10	−7	−1,566	1,286	616	−280	−11	120	168	60	288	12
1881	−65	50	−15	−8	−1,304	1,309	615	5	19	67	290	80	357	38
1882	−69	59	−10	10	−1,248	1,318	604	70	95	126	329	100	455	20
1883	−94	64	−30	−1	−1,352	1,320	604	−32	137	39	224	110	263	37
1884	−100	65	−35	4	−1,008	1,301	611	293	158	−46	535	130	489	41
1885	−94	64	−30	—	−1,001	1,264	612	262	201	−68	575	150	507	3
1886	−53	63	10	−6	−960	1,283	616	343	285	101	385	170	486	−1
1887	−72	67	−5	−15	−782	1,305	630	523	737	28	403	190	431	−21
1888	−92	62	−30	5	−864	1,364	659	500	609	−57	743	220	686	−16
1889	−100	65	−35	4	−618	1,436	658	818	721	−825	1,415	240	590	−6
1890	−79	64	−15	−1	−690	1,406	664	716	913	−819	1,249	250	430	−44
1891	−92	72	−20	1	−1,202	1,387	679	185	127	−978	1,312	260	334	−71
1892	−79	64	−15	—	−731	1,324	667	593	358	−1,065	1,250	270	185	−13
1893	−91	71	−20	−7	−622	1,293	670	671	517	−870	1,231	280	361	−19
1894	−62	46	−16	1	−777	1,261	667	584	222	−977	1,618	300	641	−257
1895	−109	88	−21	−6	−363	1,321	670	958	979	−803	1,140	310	337	−19
1896	−122	95	−27	3	−414	1,347	703	933	1,118	−782	1,372	340	590	−22
1897	−82	68	−14	6	−374	1,398	727	1,024	948	−1,046	1,712	360	666	−33
1898	−129	68	−61	−3	−979	1,455	769	476	464	−1,324	2,139	390	815	−105
1899	−130	76	−54	5	−382	1,515	795	1,127	1,110	−1,276	1,650	400	374	−140
1900	−134	73	−61	1[2]	−609	1,622	838	1,013	824	−1,155	1,566	400	411	−136
1901	−105	72	−33	−13	−376	1,621	884	1,245	1,076	−990	1,408	410	418	−208
1902	−116	77	−39	2	−159	1,667	941	1,508	1,323	−953	1,447	430	494	−40
1903	−92	77	−15	—	−565	1,755	1,010	1,190	1,060	−988	1,432	440	444	−202
1904	−107	72	−35	−15	−66	1,816	1,052	1,650	1,279	−1,131	1,770	440	639	−407
1905	−92	71	−21	−9	71	1,951	1,127	1,880	1,427	−1,397	2,702	480	1,305	−197
1906	−165	78	−87	−1	−398	2,148	1,226	1,750	1,615	−1,663	2,181	490	518	−297
1907	−184	81	−103	29	−645	2,304	1,315	1,659	1,320	−1,903	2,059	490	156	−3
1908	−111	49	−62	−10	−607	2,356	1,372	1,749	802	−1,268	1,825	500	557	−329
1909	−123	48	−75	−4	−545	2,449	1,390	1,904	1,812	−1,933	2,350	510	417	−69
1910	−87	42	−45	−6	−958	2,600	1,483	1,642	1,709	−1,459	2,211	530	752	−206
1911	−86	46	−40	−6	−2,011	2,728	1,547	1,717	633	−1,601	2,244	540	643	−183
1912	−142	60	−82	−12	−1,539	2,862	1,573	1,323	1,223	−1,735	2,188	550	453	−183
1913	−140	62	−78	6	−1,556	2,991	1,657	1,435	1,001	−673	1,612	570	939	−335
1914	62	68	130	−35	...	...	...	...	...	...	...	...	...	...

J3 Balance of Payments

	Italy (in million lire)						Norway (in million kroner)				
	VB	TIB	*IIB*	*TTB*	OCB	CB	VB	TIB	*IIB*	OCB	CTR
1860	...	...	...	...	...	...	...	...	...	...	...
1861	−313	−14	*−57*	*−52*	−325	...	...	...	...	...	...
1862	−223	−21	*−76*	*63*	−244	...	...	...	...	...	...
1863	−231	−24	*−89*	*71*	−255	...	...	...	...	...	...
1864	−367	−43	*−107*	*72*	−410	...	...	...	...	...	...
1865	−367	−25	*−110*	*83*	−392	...	...	...	*−5*	−9	−5
1866	−219	−43	*−135*	*87*	−262	...	−35	25	*−4*	−10	5
1867	−109	−49	*−149*	*84*	−158	...	−28	28	*−5*	—	−2
1868	−71	−45	*−155*	*88*	−116	...	−37	28	*−5*	−9	4
1869	−101	−12	*−155*	*123*	−113	...	−15	31	*−5*	16	−1
1870	−101	6	*−138*	*120*	−95	...	−22	35	*−5*	15	−2
1871	152	−8	*−144*	*117*	144	...	−23	40	*−5*	17	−10
1872	35	9	*−137*	*129*	44	41	−33	50	*−4*	17	−3
1873	−96	59	*−109*	*139*	−37	−14	−45	56	*−4*	11	−4
1874	−264	82	*−93*	*144*	−182	—	−65	57	*−3*	−8	—
1875	−132	112	*−78*	*146*	−20	47	−73	46	*−3*	−27	10
1876	−62	120	*−94*	*160*	58	−4	−49	53	*−4*	4	−7
1877	−171	99	*−114*	*152*	−72	5	−81	51	*−4*	−30	11
1878	6	95	*−121*	*153*	101	−9	−48	47	*−5*	−1	2
1879	−121	90	*−127*	*162*	−31	−1	−44	47	*−5*	3	−7
1880	−35	123	*−135*	*188*	88	−33	−42	50	*−6*	8	−7
1881	−27	115	*−147*	*189*	88	−133	−44	46	*−6*	2	4
1882	−36	104	*−162*	*185*	68	−455	−37	57	*−5*	20	−3
1883	−51	123	*−154*	*177*	72	24	−46	50	*−4*	4	−2
1884	−204	127	*−173*	*214*	−77	42	−47	51	*−3*	4	1
1885	−452	94	*−187*	*215*	−358	111	−42	42	*−3*	—	6
1886	−373	80	*−191*	*209*	−293	15	−33	41	*−2*	8	−2
1887	−524	72	*−233*	*256*	−452	29	−27	42	*−1*	15	−10
1888	−220	88	*−238*	*255*	−132	—	−36	54	—	18	−5
1889	−363	168	*−175*	*260*	−195	3	−58	72	*−2*	14	−2
1890	−362	159	*−209*	*249*	−203	27	−76	67	*2*	−9	8
1891	−194	220	*−226*	*247*	26	−36	−93	60	*1*	−33	4
1892	−161	219	*−244*	*259*	58	18	−73	55	—	−18	−4
1893	−172	211	*−222*	*264*	39	9	−68	52	—	−15	7
1894	−9	211	*−195*	*264*	202	−116	−73	51	*−2*	−23	−1
1895	−84	252	*−164*	*267*	168	−40	−84	49	*−3*	−35	−3
1896	−68	277	*−162*	*271*	209	−30	−93	53	*−5*	−40	2
1897	−18	310	*−149*	*276*	292	−4	−97	56	*−7*	−40	−13
1898	−101	360	*−128*	*283*	259	−24	−119	57	*−9*	−62	3
1899	29	400	*−150*	*286*	429	95	−148	62	*−14*	−86	2
							−133₃	64₃			
1900	−244	436	*−137*	*284*	192	28	−138	70	*−17*	−69	6
1901	−246	639	*−145*	*291*	393	−18	−122	42	*−22*	−80	−4
1902	−166	613	*−138*	*307*	467	−36	−109	46	*−22*	−63	7
1903	−240	654	*−132*	*344*	414	−265	−100	42	*−22*	−58	2
1904	−214	655	*−129*	*375*	442	−7	−99	50	*−25*	−49	−5
1905	−234	976	*−129*	*418*	742	−202	−95	49	*−25*	−45	−1
1906	−494	1,044	*−127*	*449*	550	−174	−98	57	*−26*	−41	−8
1907	−813	942	*−121*	*454*	129	−266	−133	69	*−26*	−64	−3
1908	−1,059	956	*−122*	*535*	−103	−107	−136	66	*−25*	−70	—
1909	−1,098	881	*−131*	*533*	−217	−47	−122	66	*−25*	−56	−2
1910	−1,028	1,059	*−131*	*565*	31	−17	−119	89	*−19*	−30	−5
1911	−10,35	1,057	*−135*	*546*	22	−82	−170	109	*−22*	−61	−5
1912	−1,155	1,049	*−150*	*579*	−106	−53	−189	136	*−20*	−53	−2
1913	−991	1,086	*−140*	*602*	95	5	−160	159	*−18*	−1	−12
1914	−459	758	*−131*	*571*	299	−51	−157	125	*−17*	−32	5

J3 Balance of Payments

	Sweden (in million kronor)					United Kingdom (in million pounds)				
	VB	TIB	*IIB*	OCB	CTR[4]	VB	TIB	*IIB*	OCB	CB
1860	...	...	...	...	...	−45.5	66.7	*18.7*	21.2	2.5
1861	−34	5	*−7*	−29	−4	−57.6	69.9	*19.9*	12.3	2.1
1862	−18	5	*−7*	−13	−3	−58.8	72.6	*20.7*	13.7	−2.3
1863	−12	5	*−7*	−7	1	−51.4	81.4	*21.3*	30.0	−3.5
1864	−10	5	*−7*	−5	—	−61.5	88.9	*22.9*	27.4	−4.6
1865	−6	5	*−7*	−1	—	−51.2	92.5	*24.1*	41.3	−6.4
1866	−15	2	*−12*	−13	1	−55.2	100.9	*26.4*	45.7	−12.7
1867	−17	3	*−12*	−14	−1	−48.6	100.3	*28.2*	51.7	−9.5
1868	−28	1	*−12*	−27	−5	−65.5	106.6	*31.1*	41.1	−4.6
1869	−21	—	*−12*	−21	—	−57.5₅	108.3₅	*33.1*	50.8₅	−4.1
1870	−2	6	*−12*	4	−8	−33	88	*35*	55	−10.5
1871	−2	8	*−13*	6	−7	−19	95	*39*	76	−4.4
1872	−4	11	*−13*	7	−8	−8	105	*44*	97	0.7
1873	−38	14	*−13*	−24	−17	−27	113	*52*	86	−4.7
1874	−67	18	*−13*	−49	2	−40	118	*57*	78	−7.5
1875	−51	13	*−13*	−38	2	−61	118	*58*	57	−5.6
1876	−53	12	*−18*	−41	−12	−88	119	*57*	31	−7.6
1877	−78	14	*−18*	−64	14₄	−110	120	*55*	10	2.6
1878	−45	11	*−18*	−34	−3	−92	115	*55*	23	−5.7
1879	−25	7	*−18*	−18	−4	−83	114	*56*	31	4.4
1880	−31	7	*−18*	−24	−7	−88	121	*58*	33	2.6
1881	−54	−2	*−24*	−56	5	−62	122	*59*	60	5.6
1882	−37	−1	*−24*	−38	—	−67	128	*63*	61	−2.6
1883	−66	3	*−24*	−63	3	−83	132	*64*	49	−0.8
1884	−78	2	*−24*	−76	−7	−60	130	*67*	70	1.6
1885	−87	—	*−24*	−87	2	−69	131	*70*	62	−0.2
1886	−67	−4	*−25*	−71	−3	−52	130	*74*	78	0.6
1887	−45	−5	*−25*	−50	−2	−50	138	*79*	88	−0.6
1888	−45	2	*−25*	−43	−7	−55	146	*84*	91	0.6
1889	−77	13	*−25*	−64	3	−70	153	*89*	83	−2.0
1890	−83	15	*−25*	−68	1	−53	160	*94*	107	−8.8
1891	−54	13	*−21*	−41	1	−87	159	*94*	72	−2.4
1892	−46	12	*−21*	−34	3	−95	158	*95*	63	−3.4
1893	−3	11	*−21*	8	−9	−92	149	*95*	57	−3.7
1894	−28	19	*−21*	−9	−12	−99	149	*93*	50	−10.8
1895	−11	16	*−21*	5	−1	−93	148	*94*	55	−14.9
1896	1	24	*−19*	25	−4	−103	153	*96*	50	6.4
1897	−21	26	*−19*	5	−3	−115	156	*97*	41	0.6
1898	−86	30	*−19*	−56	−5	−131	160	*101*	29	−6.2
1899	−129	36	*−19*	−93	−15	−115	162	*103*	47	−9.8
1900	−118	42	*−19*	−76	−8	−129	163	*104*	34	−7.5
1901	−93	26	*−25*	−67	−6	−136	155	*106*	19	−6.2
1902	−110	26	*−25*	−84	2	−141	165	*109*	24	−5.3
1903	−88	32	*−25*	−56	2	−144	187	*112*	43	0.3
1904	−157	41	*−25*	−116	−2	−140	192	*113*	52	0.7
1905	−124	45	*−25*	−79	−12	−118	206	*123*	88	−6.2
1906	−134	51	*−31*	−83	−2	−106	227	*134*	121	−1.8
1907	−150	58	*−34*	−92	3	−84	246	*144*	162	−5.3
1908	−116	49	*−39*	−67	−17	−93	243	*157*	150	6.8
1909	−142	48	*−39*	−96	10	−111	253	*158*	142	−6.5
1910	−78	59	*−40*	−19	−17	−96	270	*170*	174	−6.7
1911	−29	62	*−43*	33	−39	−75	279	*177*	204	−6.0
1912	−39	70	*−44*	31	−10	−94	297	*187*	203	−4.6
1913	−50	83	*−46*	33	−24	−82	317	*200*	235	−11.9
1914	46	64	*−47*	110	−3	−120	254	*190*	134	−29.1

J3 Balance of Payments

1924-1937

	Bulgaria (in million leva)						Czechoslovakia (in million koruna)						
	VB	TIB	*IIB*	OCB	ELTC	CTR	VB	TIB	*IIB*	*TTB*	OCB	ELTC	CTR
1924	386	−618	−451	−232	140	−22	...	...	...	...	...	...	...
1925	−160	−775	−559	−935	59	522	1,212	−644	−739	−280	568	597	−465
1926	−193	−738	−478	−931	172	601	2,575	−714	−814	−239	1,861	−302	−884
1927	937	−1,430	−1,144	−493	1,049	−810	2,172	−104	−697	70	2,066	−2,060	−430
1928	−236	−701	−767	−937	3,107	−1,480	2,023	33	−571	70	2,064	−1,719	−235
1929	−1,774	−1,159	−1,089	−2,933	808	1,562	520	361	−361	100	881	−1,182	156
1930	1,208	−1,327	−1,141	−119	826	299	1,779	−61	−572	95	1,718	244	−461
1931	839	−1,458	−1,121	−619	565	480	1,373	−357	−356	−180	1,016	−528	−492
1932	531	−595	−509	−64	—	126	−144	−123	−281	—	−267	1,118	−28
1933	429	−331	−193	98	−18	−44	21	−69	−330	−121	−47	201	104
1934	273	−278	−219	−5	−1	17	898	−62	−331	−252	836	−170	−786
1935	910	−248	−251	662	100	−370	680	−502	−478	−39	178	−63	136
1936	1,134	−191	−214	943	−399	−337	99	−658	−546	140	−559	−535	253
1937	...	...	...	...	...	...	992	−692	−514	110	300	−166	5

1915-1948

	Denmark (in million kroner)						Finland (in million markka)					
	VB	TIB	*IIB*	*TTB*	OCB	CTR	VB	TIB	*IIB*	*TTB*	OCB	CTR
1915	−50	...	...	...	...	−23	...	...	...	...	...	...
1916	−73	...	...	...	...	−104	...	...	...	...	...	...
1917	−54	...	...	...	...	−80	...	...	...	...	...	...
1918	−200	...	...	...	...	−33	...	...	...	...	...	...
1919	−1,654	...	...	...	...	61	...	...	...	...	...	...
1920	−1,352	...	...	...	...	30	...	...	...	...	...	...
1921	−139	136	...	...	−3	11	...	...	...	...	...	...
1922	−280	129	...	...	−151	36	428	−25	−238	−22	403	−558
1923	−368	168	−57	−5	−200	14	−283	36	−234	−13	−247	177
1924	−242	199	−45	−5	−43	−32	225	4	−258	−16	229	50
1925	−148	167	−70	−5	19	−39	−15	106	−325	20	91	−709
1926	−122	137	−55	−15	15	63	−116	136	−284	−5	19	162
1927	−131	144	−50	−5	13	−43	−72	105	−318	10	33	−203
1928	−102	120	−50	−5	18	−8	−1,778	175	−350	−10	−1,603	556
1929	−81	112	−63	−10	31	23	−576	98	−410	−30	−478	66
1930	−113	66	−51	−10	−47	−8	183	29	−412	−30	212	−259
1931	−135	43	−70	−10	−92	92	981	−23	−436	30	958	345
1932	−6	24	−74	−10	18	24	1,124	37	−583	50	1,161	−149
1933	−64	64	−72	−10	—	14	1,370	−20	−530	10	1,350	−607
1934	−119	81	−95	−5	−38	−5	1,461	110	−425	20	1,571	−112
1935	−62	133	−95	−15	71	13	913	315	−325	10	1,228	−38
1936	−104	109	−90	−15	5	1	1,028	290	−270	−60	1,318	−504
1937	−95	205	−80	−20	110	−58	238	580	−195	−20	818	−366
1938	−83	194	−75	−15	111	−86	−72	600	−150	−10	528	−754
1939	−155	243	−80	−12	88	127	135	745	−110	−80	880	605
1940[6]	147	151	−75	—	298	−834	−6,780	2,750	−145	−50	−4,030	1,660
1941[6]	−27	79	−65	—	52	−886	−5,910	1,125	−200	−20	−4,785	2,580
1942[6]	−156	48	−50	3	−108	−683	−5,770	765	−135	15	−5,005	1,267
1943[6]	112	72	−30	3	184	−830	−4,185	920	−130	20	−3,265	824
1944[6]	196	2,556[6]	−15	2	2,752[6]	−2,732	−2,415	105	−45	20	−2,310	−2,800
1945[6]	206	670[6]	−40	—	876[6]	6,849[7]	...	...	...	...	...	...
1946	−1,231	338	−60	−15	−893	17	4,760	2,370	−890	110	7,130	2,460
1947	−780[8]	362[8]	−75	−15	−418	31	7,510	3,080	−1,290	210	10,590	490
1948	−338	126	−67	−40	−212	−27	500	4,480	−1,260	—	4,980	1,120

J3 Balance of Payments

1920-1948

	France (in million gold francs)						Germany (in million marks)						
	VB	TIB	IIB	TTB	OCB	CB/CTR[10]	VB	TIB	IIB	TTB	OCB	ELTC	CTR
1920	-35,910	8,217	2,800	3,850	-27,693	830	...	...	...	...	...	...	...
1921	-435	9,224	3,591	5,300	8,789	400	...	...	...	...	...	...	...
1922	-4,890	10,466	4,055	6,200	5,576	-100	...	...	...	...	...	...	...
1923	-4,760	9,502	3,082	6,160	4,742	27	...	...	...	...	...	...	...
1924	400	9,794	2,904	6,340	10,194	150	...	...	...	...	...	...	...
1925	-1,560	9,988	2,150	10,008	8428	≡10	-2,444	456	-6	-55	-1,988	-1,214	90
1926	-2,000[9]	11,255[9]	2,274	10,530	9,255[9]	1,458	793	359	-173	-65	1,152	-1,454	-568
1927	467	8,050	3,000	6,000	7,746	-15,182	-2,960	300	-345	-110	-2,660	-1,778	-452
1928	-4,237	10,200	3,500	7,500	5,720	-13,280	-1,311	109	-563	-120	-1,202	-1,788	931
1929	-9,000	14,500	5,500	8,500	4,489	-3,208	-44	-88	-800	-120	-132	-660	-165
1930	-11,473	13,281	5,100	8,500	308	-7,390	1,558	-462	-1,000	-25	1,096	-1,119	-120
1931	-12,762	10,250	4,000	6,000	-3,012	-12,150	2,778	-750	-1,200	-9	2,038	-180	-1,653
1932	-10,015	3,700	600	2,500	-6,315	844	1,052	-635	-900	-47	417	-14	-256
1933	-9,241	6,050	2,000	3,000	-2,950	4,732	666	-385	-698	52	281	50	-447
1934	-5,500	5,600	2,500	2,500	-1,250	-1,300	-373	-161	-625	208	-534	200	-424
1935	-5,000	5,600	4,000	750	-400	15,000	-9	-99	-550	195	-108	33	-30
1936	-7,130	5,520	3,840	850	-2,820	20,700	...	...	...	...	...	...	...
1937	-9,150	6,055	3,925	1,300	-3,995	6,500	...	...	...	...	...	...	...
1938	-5,025	5,980	3,500	1,550	-120	-3,000	...	...	...	...	...	...	...
1939-44	...	...	...	...	...								
	(in million U.S. dollars)												
1945	-861	-255	...	...	-1,496	680	...	...	...	...	...	...	...
1946	-1,527	-225	72	-19	-2,049	1,105	...	...	...	...	...	...	...
1947	-1,452	-61	86	9	-1,676	-368	...	...	...	...	...	...	...
1948	-1,428	-102	57	70	-1,738	335	...	...	...	...	...	...	...

1923-1948

	Greece (in million Swiss gold francs)						Hungary (in million gold pengos)						
	VB	TIB	IIB	TTB	OCB	CTR	VB	TIB	IIB	TTB	OCB	ELTC	CTR
1923	-87	17	...	...	-70	...	-97	24	5	-6	-73	9	-8
1924	...	...	...	...	...	...	-148	—	-16	-7	-148	-15	-207
1925	...	...	...	...	...	...	...	...	...	...	...	...	...
1926	-294	112	...	...	-182	...	-76	-71	-87	-11	-148	167	-13
1927	...	...	...	...	...	...	-377	-130	-117	-32	-507	278	13
1928	...	...	...	...	...	...	-385	-141	-148	-18	-526	315	110
1929	-421	190	38	11	-231	...	-44	-188	-162	-30	-232	218	52
1930	-332	154	3	1	-178	...	73	-191	-187	-30	-119	-43	12
1931	-308	117	-81	—	-191	...	27	-235	-208	-30	-207	19	105
1932	-157	97	16	14	-60	...	-9	-13	-18	-11	-21	1	9
1933	-89	105	-22	46	16	...	66	-32	-28	-19	34	—	5
1934	-95	63	-27	23	-32	...	48	-39	-41	-13	10	—	-2
1935	-102	67	10	10	-35	-18	50	-23	-25	-5	28	2	-37
1936	-127	38	-8	12	-89	-22	67	-2	-25	-11	65	-2	25
1937	-193	108	—	12	-85	3	95	5	-27	-10	100	1	-17
1938	-152	86	—	10	-66	-2	...	...	...	...	...	...	...
	(in million U.S. dollars)												
1946	-295	290	3	—	-5	1							
1947	-191	84	-1	—	-107	96							
1948	-248	140	-3	2	-108	24							

J3   Balance of Payments

	Southern Ireland (in million pounds)					Netherlands (in million guilders)					
	VB	**TIB**	*IIB*	**OCB**	**CB**	**VB**	**TIB**	*IIB*	*TTB*	**OCB**	**CTR**
1930	...	...	...	...	...	−456	500	...	−32	44	−6
1931	−14.1	10.8	5.7	−3.3	—	−391	382	...	−24	−9	−300
1932	...	...	...	...	...	−326	311	...	−23	−15	−131
1933	−16.8	15.5	6.0	−1.3	—	−375	254	...	−25	−121	181
1934	−21.2	16.9	6.3	−4.3	—	−236	201	94	−31	−35	80
1935	−17.4	18.0	5.6	0.6	—	−181	260	125	−31	78	198
1936	−17.4	15.9	5.2	−2.5	—	−181	339	155	−33	158	−77
1937	−21.3	18.8	5.3	−2.5	—	−237	451	157	−36	214	−649
1938	−17.2	19.2	6.3	2.0	−2.0	−232	337	157	−36	105	−94
1939	−16.5	16.0	6.5	−0.5	−1.0	−398	387	176	−23	−11	449
1940	−13.8	16.1	7.0	2.3	—	...	...	...	...	...	...
1941	2.3	12.0	4.8	14.3	—	...	...	...	...	...	...
1942	−2.0	28.1	4.9	26.1	—	...	...	...	...	...	...
1943	1.4	33.8	6.6	32.4	—	...	...	...	...	...	...
1944	1.4	34.0	7.1	32.6	—	...	...	...	...	...	...
1945	−5.4	40.0	6.7	34.6	—	...	...	...	...	...	...
1946	−33.1	52.8	8.6	19.7	—	−1,330	18	124	...	−1,312	834
1947	−91.8	62.0	8.8	−29.8	—	−1,862	195	124	12	−1,667	1,730
1948	−87.0	67.4	10.2	−19.6	—	−1,770	323	132	−12	−1,447	468

J3 Balance of Payments

	Italy (in million lire)						Norway (in million kroner)				
	VB	TIB	*IIB*	*TTB*	OCB	CB/CTR[11]	VB	TIB	*IIB*	OCB	CTR
1915	−590	−323	−132	508	−913	5	−191	320	−15	129	−62
1916	−3,140	−724	−223	583	−3,863	207	−365	757	−10	392	−72
1917	−6,883	−1,848	−381	522	−8,731	−29	−866	780	−15	−86	7
1918	−7,826	−2,767	−632	570	−10,593	272	−488	590	−20	102	1
1919	−7,774	356	−1,122	605	−7,418	42	−793	724	−20	−69	−29
1920	−13,802	2,932	−1,316	828	−10,870	−371	−1,772	909	−25	−864	19
1921	−8,496	3,457	−1,145	1,399	−5,039	−49	818	277	−35	−541	15
1922	−6,627	4,199	−977	1,823	−2,428	−81	−519	223	−46	−296	−10
1923	−5,767	4,227	−1,362	2,035	−1,541	−7[11] / 734	−505	237	−52	−268	25
1924	−5,074	5,460	−1,390	2,555	386	50	−463	265	−62	−198	−19
1925	−7,315	6,128	−1,038	3,212	−1,187	−108	−323	248	−62	−74	−14
1926	−7,264	6,220	−451	2,787	−1,034	−1,391	−272	268	−51	−5	−2
1927	−4,919	4,223	−266	2,282	−696	−5,543	−295	234	−60	−63	16
1928	−7,432	4,180	−258	2,355	−3,252	1,047	−336	217	−70	−120	6
1929	−6,505	4,103	−284	2,197	−2,402	753	−316	276	−69	−40	−18
1930	−5,220	3,700	53	1,831	−1,520	746	−377	309	−72	−68	20
1931	−1,386	3,154	79	1,638	1,768	1,839	−394	275	−70	−117	14
1932	−1,383	2,155	130	1,285	772	652	−116	173	−86	55	−2
1933	−2,644	2,076	−53	1,578	−568	−253	−103	189	−83	86	26
1934	−2,378	1,751	−90	1,450	−627	1,514	−155	193	−71	38	−26
1935	−2,874	1,284	−109	1,272	−1,590	2,489	−216	238	−70	22	−47
1936	−1,701	1,962	−203	1,643	261	−628	−239	304	−74	75	−90
1937	−4,384	2,392	−423	2,537	−1,992	−6	−465	507	−65	42	−62
1938	−2,281	1,734	−583	2,052	−547	202	−401	452	−60	51	−25
1939	−908	899	−448	1,276	−9	695[11] / 936	−553	523	−57	−30	105
1940	−2,060	−820	−418	472	−2,880	456	...	...	...	...	...
1941	3,409	−2,079	...	356	1,330	−67	...	...	...	...	...
1942	2,800	−2,624	...	205	176	−324	...	...	...	...	...
1943	2,846	−5,333	...	...	−2,487	436	...	...	...	...	...
1944	−30,221	−5,358	...	...	−35,579	1,774	...	...	...	...	...
	(in thousand million lire)										
1945	−121	−15	...	...	−135	—	...	...	...	...	...
1946	−119	−25	...	...	−144	−0.1[11] / −8.7	−998	469	−35	−529	
1947	−510	155	−1	3	−355	−4.1	−1,990	765	−47	−1,225	340
1948	−208	219	−7	14	11	−5.1	−1,632	1,106	−63	−526	152

J3 Balance of Payments

	Poland (in million zlotys)							Spain (in million U.S. dollars)				
	VB	TIB	*IIB*	*TTB*	OCB	CTR		VB	TIB	OCB	ELTC	CTR
1923	87	117	−37	−48	204	−30	**1931**	−82.5	48.4	−34.0	−0.3	34.3
1924	−481	75	−114	−86	−406	−61	**1932**	−87.6	48.7	−38.9	−2.9	41.8
							1933	−63.0	28.8	−34.2	4.5	12.1
1925	−524	−59	−118	−93	−582	391	**1934**	−93.4	21.4	−71.8	4.3	40.4
1926	759	112	−169	−16	647	−228						
1927	−308	−174	−229	−51	−481	−960	**1940**	−72.8	13.8	−59.0	14.2	0.8
1928	−872	−127	−284	−71	−999	77	**1941**	−13.5	35.1	21.5	9.2	−73.5
1929	−462	−57	−380	2	−519	108	**1942**	17.2	42.8	59.9	−11.2	−20.9
							1943	−13.1	32.1	19.0	−1.4	−67.9
1930	90	−238	−451	−88	−148	252	**1944**	30.4	56.9	87.3	−14.7	−15.8
1931	314	−209	−417	−91	105	162						
1932	124	−99	−285	−42	25	174	**1945**	−8.2	36.9	28.8	−44.4	−7.6
1933	99	−18	−213	−38	81	75	**1946**	−26.4	21.9	−4.5	−14.7	18.7
1934	176	−10	−167	−9	166	33	**1947**	−55.7	12.2	−43.4	88.5	82.1
							1948	−62.5	7.1	−55.3	172.4	−91.6
1935	68	−5	−145	−15	62	60						
1936	21	−11	−172	−36	10	48						
1937	−62	−12	−177	−47	−84	−48						

	Sweden (in million kronor)							United Kingdom (in million pounds)					
	VB	TIB	*IIB*	*TTB*	OCB	ELTC	CTR	VB	TIB	*IIB*	*TTB*	OCB	CB/CTR[3]
1915	144	146	−46	…	290	…	−159	−340	285	165	…	−55	28
1916	338	280	−42	…	618	…	−59	−350	440	200	…	90	
1917	471	195	−37	…	666	…	−37	−420	470	195	…	50	…
1918	−13	346	−35	…	333	…	−33	−630	415	175	…	−275	…
1919	−958	353	−35	…	−605	…	−2	−470	425	165	…	−45	…
1920	−1,038	310	−31	…	−726	…	−222	−176[12]	493[12]	254[12]	…[12]	317[12]	42
								−148	485	246	28	337	
1921	−161	107	−26	…	−54	…	215	−148	341	178	31	193	10
1922	40	78	−12	−43	118	…	−78	−63	264	177	22	201	10
1923	−137	142	3	−25	5	−34	106	−97	280	176	23	183	13
1924	−148	150	6	−20	2	80	41	−214	292	196	23	78	14
1925	−88	165	3	−20	77	−28	−58	−265	317	232	18	52	8
1926	−71	191	7	−20	120	−11	1	−346	328	237	20	−18	−11
1927	29	213	19	−24	242	51	−62	−270	368	239	26	98	−3
1928	−135	215	25	−28	80	−179	−42	−237	361	240	23	124	13
1929	37	240	30	−30	277	−2	−59	−263	359	243	22	96	15
1930	−116	214	20	−25	98	−392	−121	−283	319	215	27	36	−5
1931	−304	176	−6	2	−128	−138	376	−322	219	163	8	−103	35
1932	−205	294	128	4	−89	124	−165	−216	165	127	9	−51	−18
1933	−15	227	78	−2	212	55	−396	−192	184	154	3	−8	−191
1934	−4	206	67	−9	202	−48	−68	−220	198	167	7	−22	−134
1935	−183	244	87	3	61	22	−133	−183	206	181	8	23	−70
1936	−120	241	79	−3	121	23	−209	−261	234	195	10	−27	−228
1937	−126	311	109	−7	185	−92	−277	−336	289	205	14	−47	−80
1938	−243	316	104	−7	73	−12	66	−285	230	196	10	−55	63
1939	−617	348	84	1	−269	54	477	−300	50	160	…	−250	322
1940	−677	375	…	…	−302	…	146	−600	−200	160	…	−800	630
1941	−321	560	…	…	239	…	−174	−700	−120	140	…	−820	4
1942	−457	710	…	…	253	…	−257	−500	−160	100	…	−660	−57
1943	−667	860	100	…	193	…	−286	−560	−120	90	…	−680	−23
1944	−818	647	60	…	−171	…	−163	−630	−30	80	…	−660	−132
1945	669	624	45	…	1,293	…	−425	−250	−620	80	…	−870	−19[13]
1946	−853	747	30	…	−106	…	540	−103	37	85	…	−66	−54
1947	−1,984	536	22	−12	−1,448	…	1,304	−361	139	150	…	−222	152
1948	−962	564	19	−53	−398	…	176	−151	411	235	…	260	55

J3   Balance of Payments

B   IMF Definitions, in million U.S. dollars.   1948–2000

	Austria							Belgium						
	VB	TIB	*IIB*	*TTB*	OCB	ELTC	CTR	VB	TIB	*IIB*	*TTB*	OCB	ELTC	CTR
1948	−283	43	—	−1	−240[14]	...	...	72	37	*35*	*−42*	109	...	−44
1949	−312	26	−1	1	−286[14]	...	...	102	−53	*6*	*−26*	49	...	9
1950	−150	29	−1	11	−121[14]	...	−12	−100	−82	*4*	*−28*	−182	...	−131
1951	−201	36	—	18	−165[14]	...	−6	464	−144	*19*	*−42*	320	...	−261
1952	−147	51	*1*	25	−96[14]	...	−77	270	−74	*17*	*−30*	196	...	−22
1953	−10	86	*2*	53	76[14]	...	−171	98	−28	*22*	*−16*	70	...	−11
1954	−46	115	*1*	64	69[14]	...	−108	30	−6	*22*	*−2*	24	...	46
1955	−182	52	*1*	62	−130	−3	15	190	120	*42*	*6*	310	...	−105
1956	−35	−4	*2*	92	−39	27	−46	94	172	*70*	*20*	266	−160	−16
1957	−59	57	*4*	120	−2	51	−106	−46	246	*66*	*22*	200	−120	58
1958	−68	87	*−3*	133	7	129	−155	90	284	*50*	*66*	374	−98	−395[15]
1959	−93	104	*−4*	162	10	72	−18[15]	−48	120	*22*	*−28*	72	−38	247
1960	−210	121	*−8*	171	−89	−8	−19	14	96	*46*	*−28*	110	8	−201
1961	−217	192	*−12*	217	−36	87	−131	−40	90	*26*	*−42*	50	−22	−307
1962	−235	316	*−15*	281	81	89	−235	—	84	*2*	*−44*	84	28	61
1963	−297	286	*−16*	314	11	126	−147	−80	−24	*20*	*−64*	−104	124	−218
1964	−394	408	*−21*	386	14	70	−89	22	−24	*18*	*−68*	−2	286	−252
1965	−472	427	*−21*	420	−45	52	7	−90	262	*12*	*−82*	152	18	−111
1966	−596	402	*−23*	424	−194	167	−21	−352	256	*22*	*−90*	−96	−76	−15
1967	−483	369	*−34*	396	−114	263	−152	−124	320	*24*	*−128*	196	49	−241
1968	−469	373	*−56*	430	−96	183	−27	−261	289	*34*	*−124*	28	−114	403
1969	−353	442	*−44*	489	89	−28	−26	−97	339	*16*	*−138*	242	272	−198
1970	−679	604	*−46*	693	−75	14	−221[16]	464	253	*68*	*−144*	717	−363	−462[16]
1971	−932	841	*−51*	920	−91	−18	−503	215	432	*86*	*−210*	647	−546	−420
1972	−1,127	970	*−84*	1,200	−157	80	−380	792	516	*165*	*−277*	1,308	−898	−435
1973	−1,566	1,312	*−134*	1,555	−254	−227	−65	879	516	*187*	*−428*	1,395	−730	−1,087
1974	−1,308	1,105	*−107*	1,417	−203	402	−543	22	809	*311*	*−462*	831	−211	−219
1975	−1,955	1,724	*−137*	1,693	−231	1,062	−1,048	−828	1,009	*442*	*−545*	181	−280	−531
1976	−2,581	1,462	*−215*	1,629	−1,119	−73	23	−1,242	1,677	*607*	*−586*	435	149	578
1977	−3,826	1,626	*−336*	1,647	−2,200	604	209	−2,979	2,425	*537*	*−729*	−554	−312	−465
1978	−3,283	2,577	*−487*	2,261	−706	1,404	−1,696	−2,644	1,821	*623*	*−1,080*	−823	−271	−10
1979	−4,272	3,131	*−484*	2,041	−1,141	−521	972	−4,627	1,547	*355*	*−1,332*	−3,080	511	−1,477
1980	−6,617	4,892	*−528*	3,337	−1,725	550	−1,205	−5,154	223	*−70*	*−1,473*	−4,931	3,986	−2,380
1981	−5,043	3,579	*−466*	2,897	−1,464	919	−5	−3,474	537	*−5,865*	*−1,259*	−4,168	3,747	2,871
1982	−3,450	4,091	*−408*	2,888	641	−558	−15	−2,300	1,063	*−180*	*−615*	−2,394	1,611	1,025
1983	−3,639	3,885	*−369*	2,371	246	−1,343	785	−666	1,378	*−108*	*−384*	−495	−2,339	−787
1984	−4,014	3,750	*−352*	2,443	−178	−308	271	−191	959	*8*	*−293*	−55	−2,229	150
1985	−4,406	4,133	*−255*	2,345	−158	−93	−523	492	854	*−21*	*−389*	669	−4,557	−285
1986	−4,612	4,698	*−672*	2,935	204	602	−1,395	2,305	1,451	*−245*	*−712*	3,035	−6,776	−689
1987	−4,809	5,481	*−862*	3,268	−263	1,880	−1,370	1,294	2,445	*485*	*−941*	2,794	897	−4,082
1988	−4,765	5,473	*−908*	3,693	−242	598	164	2,705	2,148	*496*	*−1,171*	3,594	−691	287
1989	−5,552	6,850	*−934*	4,457	248	−757	−1,230	2,575	527	*2,684*	*−1,197*	3,197	218	−1,433
1990	−6,969	9,083	*−942*	5,669	1,166	−1,288	−778	2,602	1,836	*2,317*	*−1,753*	4,950	5,734	−1,385
1991	−8,560	10,227	*−1,475*	6,492	61	−2,339	−956	2,079	1,794	*3,178*	*−1,922*	4,731	7,957	−29
1992	−8,443	9,849	*−1,168*	6,355	−631	−1,463	−2,051	3,510	2,659	*2,986*	*−1,433*	6,468	−3,865	−1,621
1993	−7,281	8,173	*−847*	5,163	−762	−1,422	−2,228	6,126	3,371	*4,873*	*−2,647*	12,588	11,072	2,386
1994	−7,914				−2,992			6,901				12,571		
1995	−6,656		...		−5,448		...	9,555		...		14,232		...
1996	−7,315		...		−4,890		...	8,690		...		13,762		...
1997	−4,274		...		−5,221		...	7,703		...		13,914		...
1998	−3,684		...		−5,258		...	6,981		...		12,168		...
1999	−3,629		...		−6,655		...	6,642		...		13,374		...
2000	−2,732		...		−5,205		...	5,335		...		11,851		...

J3 Balance of Payments (in million U.S. dollars)

1948–2000

	Denmark							Finland						
	VB	TIB	*IIB*	*TTB*	OCB	ELTC	CTR	VB	TIB	*IIB*	*TTB*	OCB	ELTC	CTR
1948	-70	—	-14	-8	-70	...	-9	2	20	-5	—	22	...	...
1949	-45	-9	-15	-10	-54	...	-3	34	21	-6	-4	55	...	-5
1950	-101	-20	-13	-9	-121	...	-10	1	8	-10	-7	9	...	-6
1951	-68	108	-10	-4	40	...	-21	187	14	-10	-22	201	...	-105
1952	-15	38	-10	-4	23	...	-32	-77	20	-12	-15	-57	...	77
1953	-26	45	-8	—	19	...	-17	35	18	-10	-13	53	-2	-12
1954	-113	38	-11	—	-75	...	-23	27	29	-11	-8	56	-1	-64
1955	-16	46	-11	—	30	...	-4	17	57	-9	-7	64	9	-9
1956	-83	70	-7	7	-13	...	-2	-52	-5	-11	-8	-57	15	39
1957	-67	113	-7	10	46	...	-34	-5	-6	-11	-10	-11	10	8
1958	18	112	-1	25	130	-5	-58	96	18	-12	-11	78	-4	-79
1959	-109	125	3	19	16	27	-99[15]	59	31	-6	-17	28	1	-8[15]
1960	-211	152	4	33	-59	47	44	-2	-41	-6	-23	-43	3	1
1961	-241	132	-5	30	-109	80	3	-28	-50	-7	-30	-78	39	-2
1962	-363	121	-3	21	-241	105	27	25	-68	-15	-35	-93	54	38
1963	-111	135	-8	24	24	181	-214	14	-36	-22	-31	-22	116	-47
1964	-379	176	-10	30	-203	204	-170	-123	-53	-31	-36	-176	189	-93
1965	-368	185	-13	25	-183	117	58	-125	-63	-41	-36	-188	12	69
1966	-403	193	-18	15	-210	57	-10	-123	-74	-47	-30	-197	61	101
1967	-458	171	-23	-6	-287	163	62	-69	-94	-60	-26	-163	79	5
1968	-454	238	-28	3	-216	107	92	129	-81	-66	-2	48	72	-154
1969	-630	220	-39	12	-410	184	-22	76	-55	-76	1	21	19	11
1970	-760	216	-45	41	-544	111	-62[16]	-177	-73	-94	34	-240	79	-127[16]
1971	-712	288	-71	76	-424	384	-234	-275	-66	-113	59	-341	378	-199
1972	-430	367	-121	115	-63	265	-133	-55	-62	-142	81	-117	334	-44
1973	-1,189	721	-161	79	-468	511	-461	-250	-136	-199	91	-386	108	73
1974	-1,787	806	-259	118	-981	344	389	-881	-329	-268	87	-1,210	236	-22
1975	-1,304	814	-324	100	-490	134	55	-1,715	-428	-385	29	-2,143	428	163
1976	-2,878	964	-363	55	-1,914	1,863	-38	-666	-451	-454	6	-1,117	955	-29
1977	-2,715	993	-664	-2	-1,722	2,479	-748	442	-547	-604	-1	-105	449	-69
1978	-2,356	854	-884	-24	-1,502	2,434	-1,540	1,095	-421	-660	39	674	882	-692
1979	-3,392	420	...	...	-2,972	2,129	-107	366	-535	-729	49	-169	247	-317
1980	-2,023	-443	...	...	-2,466	2,545	-151	-658	-752	-882	92	-1,410	-150	-330
1981	-927	1,189	-1,981	35	-1,875	1,349	839	377	-762	-1,024	100	-385	525	387
1982	-794	872	-2,155	138	-2,259	2,400	282	215	-978	-1,129	-49	-763	235	-34
1983	236	630	-2,020	92	-1,176	2,465	-1,355	162	-1,097	-1,043	-125	-935	363	280
1984	-206	748	-2,240	64	-1,637	1,900	612	1,491	-1,501	-1,125	-193	-10	1,031	-1,517
1985	-771	835	-2,462	-83	-2,728	4,451	-2,420	878	-1,644	-1,014	-277	-766	852	-996
1986	-1,050	307	-3,461	-359	-4,490	3,563	465	1,642	-2,373	-1,423	-460	-731	263	1,963
1987	795	547	-4,161	-640	-3,002	8,153	-5,102	1,379	-3,191	-1,706	-688	-1,812	68	-4,630
1988	1,883	1,195	-4,333	-669	-1,340	2,909	-699	1,136	-4,134	-1,920	-863	-2,998	1,553	48
1989	2,425	931	-4,331	-627	-1,118	161	4,368	-228	-2,607	-2,654	-1,024	-5,781	741	1,258
1990	4,875	2,612	-5,708	-353	1,372	3,435	-4,195	718	-3,020	-3,685	-1,588	-6,939	5,236	-4,533
1991	4,748	3,844	-5,744	72	1,983	-3,448	3,187	2,309	-3,387	-4,611	-1,492	-6,741	3,591	2,036
1992	7,204	3,599	-5,655	466	4,268	-4,559	-3,640	3,944	-2,715	-5,357	-1,080	-4,922	417	2,395
1993	7,812	2,186	-4,779	-803	4,711	5,391	743	6,384	-1,816	-4,497	-368	-959	2,570	-197
1994	7,441				3,189			7,723				1,110		
1995	6,528	...			1,855	...		12,437	...			5,231	...	
1996	7,532	...			3,090	...		11,314	...			5,003	...	
1997	5,369	...			921	...		11,544	...			6,633	...	
1998	3,886	...			-2,008	...		12,490				7,340	...	
1999	6,689	...			3,042	...		12,168	...			7,661	...	
2000	7,199	...			3,353	...		13,684	...			8,890	...	

J3   Balance of Payments

1948–2000

	France[9] (in million U.S. dollars)							West Germany (in thousand million U.S. dollars)						
	VB	TIB	*IIB*	*TTB*	OCB	ELTC	CTR	VB	TIB	*IIB*	*TTB*	OCB	ELTC	CTR
1948	−234	−1,209	*57*	*70*	−1,651	...	252	−0.32	0.31	...	..	0.01	...	−0.09
1949	−456	−79	*22*	*121*	−702	...	−152	−0.22	0.18	—	..	−0.04	...	0.03
1950	−78	−15	*25*	*141*	316	...	−281	−0.55	0.45	—	*0.01*	−0.10	...	0.01
1951	−770	283	*30*	*73*	−573	...	175	0.36	0.25	—	*0.01*	0.61	...	−0.24
1952	−618	343	*19*	*24*	−343	...	−70	0.32	0.34	—	*0.01*	0.66	...	−0.42
1953	−338	558	*23*	*−6*	117	...	−143	0.88	0.09	*−0.01*	—	0.97	...	−0.74
1954	−169[9]	928[9]	*25*	*61*	691[9]	...	−435	0.95	−0.09	*−0.12*	*0.04*	0.86	...	−0.90
1955	36	911	*4*	*26*	947	−52	−711	0.77	−0.28	*−0.14*	*0.07*	0.49	−0.09	−0.44
1956	−933	198	*50*	*−78*	−735	12	664	1.40	−0.35	*−0.10*	*0.16*	1.05	−0.18	−0.90
1957	−1,134	−191	*41*	*−90*	−1,325	84	666	1.81	−1.69	*−0.09*	*0.12*	1.40	−0.16	−0.99
1958	−211	37	*−5*	*57*	−174	124	−405	1.84	−1.39	*−0.14*	*−0.03*	1.45	−0.28	−0.70
1959	405	307	*−7*	*185*	712	512	−686	1.89	−0.89	*−0.23*	*−0.11*	1.00	−0.33	−1.08[15]
1960	−20	594	*37*	*234*	574	162	−536	2.11	−1.00	*−0.19*	*−0.16*	1.11	0.07	−2.24
1961	371	632	*19*	*208*	1,003	327	−1,093	2.53	−1.79	*−0.31*	*−0.32*	0.74	−0.43	−0.11
1962	612	183	*42*	*194*	795	−201	−684	1.71	−2.25	*−0.33*	*−0.53*	−0.54	0.04	0.21
1963	346	85	*66*	*121*	431	79	−859	2.41	−2.20	*−0.31*	*−0.48*	0.21	0.39	−0.71
1964	−159	57	*91*	*33*	−102	451	−616	2.48	−2.43	*−0.40*	*−0.50*	0.05	−0.43	−0.23
1965	724	37	*120*	*−28*	761	116	−619	1.38	−3.05	*−0.44*	*−0.69*	−1.67	−0.06	−0.48
1966	154[9]	17[9]	*119[9]*	*11[9]*	171[9]	18[9]	−390[9]	3.07	−2.97	*−0.36*	*−0.85*	0.10	−0.22	−1.80
1967	200	80	*479*	*−5*	180	29	−261	5.16	−2.66	*−0.40*	*−0.76*	2.50	−0.37	−0.10
1968	−83	−988	*346*	*−133*	−1,071	−1,201	2,793	5.67	−2.70	*−0.12*	*−0.78*	2.97	−2.48	−1.17
1969	−932	737	*313*	*128*	−1,669	−311	368	5.13	−3.23	*0.04*	*−1.00*	1.90	−4.90	2.92
1970	258	−462	*378*	*210*	−204	103	−1,127[16]	5.69	−4.84	*0.06*	*−1.47*	0.85	0.25	−6.57[16]
1971	858	−693	*408*	*312*	165	7	−3,000	6.66	−5.72	*0.30*	*−2.10*	0.94	1.28	−4.60
1972	1,059	−1,158	*362*	*350*	−99	−651	−1,761	8.40	−7.21	*0.29*	*−2.48*	1.19	4.56	−5.19
1973	435	1,002	*719*	*216*	1,437	−2,476	1,921	15.84	−10.65	*0.45*	*−3.56*	5.19	5.24	−8.88
1974	−4,795	938	*789*	*209*	−3,857	−261	−258	21.90	−10.27	*0.30*	*−3.99*	10.63	−2.28	0.85
1975	1,129	1,614	*580*	*299*	2,743	−1,499	−3,931	16.91	−12.50	*0.75*	*−4.91*	4.41	−7.19	1.14
1976	−4,993	1,620	*731*	*88*	−3,373	−2,195	2,837	16.02	−12.30	*1.13*	*−5.03*	3.72	−0.75	−3.80
1977	−3,289	2,881	*660*	*459*	−408	898	−252	19.47	−15.49	*0.16*	*−6.05*	3.98	−5.37	−4.69
1978	100	6,964	*1,427*	*1,638*	7,064	−3,433	−3,406	24.16	−15.00	*1.52*	*−7.54*	9.16	−1.37	−13.77
1979	−3,220	8,362	*2,451*	*1,655*	5,142	−5,201	−8,301	16.45	−10.80	*0.73*	*−9.10*	−5.65	6.63	−4.07
1980	−13,419	9,211	*3,721*	*2,228*	−4,208	−8,483	−9,761	8.89	−22.79	*1.48*	*−9.56*	−13.90	2.99	3.96
1981	−10,139	7,974	*1,606*	*1,498*	−4,811	−8,887	5,078	16.18	−19.47	*0.44*	*−8.72*	−3.29	3.52	4.87
1982	−15,449	7,805	184	*1,832*	−12,082	1,239	5,731	24.73	−19.75	*−1.07*	*−9.12*	4.98	−4.99	−1.04
1983	−8,412	8,583	1,522	*2,901*	−5,166	9,313	−3,320	21.42	−16.01	*1.52*	*−8.48*	5.41	−3.23	2.09
1984	−4,484	8,902	2,387	*3,327*	−876	5,216	−1,089	22.29	−12.54	*3.51*	*−7.94*	9.75	−6.80	2.53
1985	−4,814	9,667	2,260	*3,401*	−35	3,846	−5,649	28.51	−11.51	*2.89*	*−7.97*	17.00	−4.64	−4.24
1986	−1,347	10,050	1,684	*3,202*	2,430	−7,469	−4,865	55.74	−15.65	*3.42*	*−10.02*	40.09	14.66	−7.35
1987	−7,775	10,382	1,642	*3,372*	−4,446	2,211	−1,595	69.88	−23.76	*3.01*	*−12.07*	46.12	−13.36	−27.02
1988	−7,649	10,476	948	*4,063*	−4,795	220	7,685	79.41	−19.94	*3.39*	*−12.30*	50.47	−49.72	20.23
1989	−10,240	13,395	285	6,549	−4,726	−5,405	753	75.04	−19.4	11.12	−14.98	57.33	0.88	−21.81
1990	−13,230	15,449	3,893	7,941	−9,942	−386	−12,167	68.62	−13.08	17.10	−19.01	48.46	−156.01	−71.93
1991	−9,594	16,632	5,727	8,940	−6,469	−2,839	5,494	18.51	−17.12	18.31	−20.36	−18.62	202.20	49.01
1992	2,344	19,378	8,885	11,353	3,934	−10,065	4,256	26.94	−27.60	14.37	−25.99	−21.59	−18.16	−27.97
1993	7,749	17,561	8,968	10,588	10,301	−7,446	4,559	39.68	−31.40	11.02	−26.94	−15.44	−79.21	13.32
1994	7,250				7,420			50.92				−20.94		
1995	11,000		...		10,840		...	65.11		...		−18.93		...
1996	14,940		...		20,560		...	69.38		...		−7.97		...
1997	26,900		...		37,800		...	70.81		...		−2.90		...
1998	24,940		...		37,700		...	78.89		...		−4.56		...
1999	17,990		...		35,040		...	72.00		...		−19.31		...
2000	1,130		...		20,470		...	57.29		...		−18.71		...

J3 Balance of Payments (in million U.S. dollars)

1948–2000

	Greece							Southern Ireland						
	VB	**TIB**	*IIB*	*TTB*	**OCB**	**ELTC**	**CTR**	**VB**	**TIB**	*IIB*	*TTB*	**OCB**	**ELTC**	**CTR**
1948	−248	173	−3	2	−75	...	22	−357	234	41	133	−117	...	−7
1949	−236	231	−2	−4	−5	...	−8	−254	200	34	103	−54	...	10
1950	−268	238	−2	−2	−30	...	−8	−222	126	25	59	−96	...	−49
1951	−273	251	−2	1	−22	...	−4	−315	127	30	62	−188	...	59
1952	−130	131	−1	2	1	...	−7	−172	124	28	55	−48	...	14
1953	−91	131	−1	16	40	...	−46	−164	120	30	49	−44	...	−17
1954	−135	129	−1	17	−16	...	−8	−154	125	33	50	−29	...	−29
1955	−130	137	−3	19	7		−52	−235	127	28	53	−108	−8	33
	−274₃	205₃												
1956	−220	151	2	18	−69		−3	−185	133	29	58	−52	14	49
1957	−237	152	2	26	−85		11	−125	137	35	52	12	—	−14
1958	−221	146	2	21	−75		23	−165	142	35	52	−23	14	−10
1959	−191	180	5	26	−11	62	−55	−202	152	32	63	−50	36	−19
1960	−250	195	3	31	−55	72	−13	−178	167	35	69	−11	1	1
1961	−283	222	−3	43	−61	102	−26	−195	182	38	76	−13	36	−18
1962	−368	279	−4	54	−89	97	−19	−244	175	38	74	−69	65	−17
1963	−366	315	−3	68	−51	108	−6	−271	175	37	76	−96	65	−47
1964	−473	269	—	52	−204	207	11	−304	193	36	92	−111	96	−40
1965	−583	307	−10	66	−276	233	31	−361	230	55	110	−131	64	36
1966	−616	351	−23	103	−265	244	−22	−295	220	49	94	−75	116	−84
1967	−574	338	−25	86	−236	153	−13	−223	237	51	107	14	72	55
1968	−640	375	−29	78	−265	225	−36	−309	231	56	95	−78	46	−106
1969	−739	378	−34	102	−361	262	−15	−437	233	44	96	−204	77	−146
1970	−897	475	−50	139	−422	280	6₁₆	−432	234	43	82	−198	150	−6₁₆
1971	−1,100	756	−68	231	−344	235	−218	440	240	37	88	−200	382	−297
1972	−1,326	926	−56	274	−400	496	−487	−378	228	59	41	−150	32	−131
1973	−2,352	1,163	−47	337	−1,189	795	—	−527	273	14	61	−254	284	102
1974	−2,351	1,208	−73	255	−1,143	759	117	−1,082	394	23	69	−688	541	−240
1975	−2,360	1,483	−80	388	−877	789	−182	−486	362	−47	52	−124	387	−266
1976	−2,694	1,766	−98	583	−928	544	83	−609	181	−167	68	−428	772	−305
1977	−3,164	2,086	−122	700	−1,078	862	−167	−820	298	−265	85	−522	854	−533
1978	−3,499	2,544	−114	875	−955	1,040	−257	−1,065	216	−542	61	−849	965	−317
1979	−5,015	3,128	−122	1,050	−1,887	1,331	−38	−2,320	220	−724	13	−2,100	1,294	456
1980	−5,557	3,348	−200	1,091	−2,209	1,994	−3	−2,222	90	−902	−3	−2,132	1,491	−648
1981	−5,377	2,969	−502	1,312	−2,408	1,589	324	−2,255	−346	−965	−18	−2,601	2,291	209
1982	−4,769	2,877	−592	1,052	−1,892	1,239	161	−1,162	−773	−1,452	11	−1,935	2,107	29
1983	−4,294	2,416	−745	767	−1,878	2,110	−40	−252	−967	−1,594	32	−1,219	560	−18
1984	−4,230	2,098	−716	957	−2,132	1,773	−53	237	−1,275	−1,873	69	−1,038	800	288
1985	−5,053	1,777	−1,093	1,036	−3,276	2,766	86	631	−1321	−2,191	124	−690	836	−587
1986	−4,423	2,747	−1,082	1,125	−1,676	2,151	−651	1,142	−1,822	−2,764	−26	−680	1,050	296
1987	−5,500	4,277	−1,099	1,364	−1,223	1,387	−1,162	2,615	−2,245	−3,054	12	100	826	−1,460
1988	−6,072	5,114	−1,097	1,253	−958	1,438	−938	3,822	−3,178	−4,020	38	224	−261	−291
1989	−7,327	2,930	−1,631	1,160	−2,561	1,189	396	4,003	−1,387	−4,702	76	−381	−1,951	1,030
1990	−10,106	2,413	−1,709	1,498	−3,537	1,970	−189	3,969	−1,240	−5,301	287	146	−2,900	−1,166
1991	−10,022	3,560	−1,764	1,552	−1,574	2,452	−1,777	4,167	−1,192	−4,717	373	1,541	−1,569	−517
1992	−11,561	4,029	−2,050	2,084	−2,140	1,047	395	6,813	−1,608	−5,716	265	2,555	−927	2,300
1993	−10,499	4,996	−1,440	2,331	−747	4,374	−2,997	8,172	−1,637	−5,705	372	3,735	−1,112	−2,485
1994	−11,273				−146			9,366				1,577		
1995	−14,425	...	...		−2,864	...		13,557	...			1,721	...	
1996	−15,505	...	...		−4,554	...		15,754	...			2,049	...	
1997	−15,375	...	...		−4,860	...		18,625	...			1,866	...	
1998	...	...	...		...	...		25,390	...			1,016	...	
1999	...	...	...		...	...		24,256	...			354	...	
2000	...	...	...		...	...		25,416	...			−593	...	

J3   Balance of Payments (in million U.S. dollars)

1948–2000

	Italy							Netherlands						
	VB	TIB	*IIB*	*TTB*	OCB	ELTC	CTR	VB	TIB	*IIB*	*TTB*	OCB	ELTC	CTR
1948	−323	396	−12	24	73	...	...	−608	485	50	−5	−223	...	1
1949	−248	402	−16	34	154	...	−299	−278	−142	57	−3	−420	...	−53
1950	−120	342	−17	67	222	...	−18	−456	478	35	−4	22	...	−153
1951	−268	335	−7	72	67	...	−45	−275	376	49	−9	101	...	−5
1952	−755	402	−13	75	−353	...	64	162	390	60	−2	552	−42	−406
1953	−736	523	−7	131	−213	−3	−126	39	354	61	−3	393	−36	−282
1954	−636	558	−12	138	−78	66	−114	−226	298	78	−4	72	−35	−115
1955	−672	598	−18	190	−74	157	−205	−173	376	83	−3	203	−58	1
1956	−732	637	−27	215	−95	146	−96	−496	299	64	−13	−197	12	213
1957	−769	803	−25	323	34	191	−216	−461	301	63	−17	−160	81	76
1958	−373	938	−34	411	565	162	−799	32	383	86	2	415	−9	−509
1959	−133	889	−5	448	756	278	−842[15]	19	448	150	3	467	50	117[15]
1960	−649	929	−30	548	280	291	−131	−116	463	106	5	347	−42	−419
1961	−581	1,054	−51	647	473	477	−541	−347	528	167	5	181	−203	−92
1962	914	1,191	−91	724	2,105	278	−268	−279	420	105	6	141	−89	12
1963	−1,902	1,186	−114	749	−716	904	449	−443	562	178	−1	119	−124	−156
1964	−645	1,272	−98	846	627	844	−205	−719	565	204	−24	−154	93	−250
1965	645	1,567	−89	1,061	2,212	269	−976	−559	608	203	−12	49	−178	−58
1966	336	1,794	−40	1,199	2,130	−691	−90	−680	466	161	−51	−214	7	−34
1967	−21	1,621	−13	1,126	1,600	−342	−552	−580	500	248	−80	−80	−126	−180
1968	1,048	1,576	34	1,113	2,624	−349	122	−338	403	192	−116	65	−135	161
1969	542	2,193	106	1,139	2,735	−1,016	363	−404	381	217	−192	−23	−43	−57
1970	−381	1,181	−22	913	800	376	−306[16]	−904	316	127	−176	−588	573	−725[16]
1971	119	1,485	−31	1,048	1,604	−80	−1,224	−613	383	101	−143	−230	514	−270
1972	54	2,002	−87	1,558	2,056	−2,754	735	438	746	211	−129	1,184	−941	−1,002
1973	−3,961	1,496	−241	1,651	−2,465	−2,769	1	997	1,422	430	−218	2,419	−1,821	−1,527
1974	−8,512	508	−784	1,779	−8,004	−176	−453	594	2,445	565	−330	3,039	−2,149	−377
1975	−1,149	624	−1,172	2,353	−525	−1,116	2,100	893	1,480	−92	−664	2,373	−1,816	−254
1976	−4,241	1,400	−1,100	2,471	−2,841	−29	−1,917	1,343	2,107	231	−918	3,450	−4,066	−294
1977	−131	2,618	−1,079	3,863	2,487	407	−4,881	−243	1,474	702	−1,343	1,231	−1,875	−564
1978	2,912	3,340	−1,104	5,078	6,252	250	−3,005	−1,488	280	76	−2,142	−1,208	−2,655	654
1979	−989	6,492	−540	6,889	5,503	−2,796	−7,088	−1,428	1,643	2,225	−2,625	215	−4,063	−2,503
1980	−16,934	6,977	−670	7,010	−9,957	2,868	−4,929	−1,415	379	1,613	−3,016	−1,036	−1,902	−4,054
1981	−12,141	2,441	−3,207	5,832	−9,700	7,995	2,992	3,887	191	470	−1,907	3,696	−3,052	2,306
1982	−8,911	2,523	−3,928	6,569	−6,388	4,888	6,043	4,663	176	433	−1,867	4,487	−4,044	−793
1983	−2,508	3,889	−3,915	7,180	1,381	340	−6,014	4,254	715	1,178	−1,811	4,969	−3,220	−39
1984	−5,818	3,317	−3,901	6,483	−2,501	1,155	−690	5,656	915	1,450	−1,588	6,571	−4,279	934
1985	−6,083	2,543	−3,973	6,476	−3,540	1,969	5,200	5,462	−1,435	−451	−1,770	4,027	−2,598	−1,545
1986	4,525	−1,613	−6,227	6,967	2,912	−3,702	−4,392	7,168	−3,548	−758	−2,684	3,620	−6,609	−409
1987	−73	−1,590	−6,618	7,607	−1,663	3,349	−10,227	5,141	−1,464	777	−3,715	3,677	−2,554	−4,812
1988	−768	−4,678	−7,134	6,354	−5,446	7,607	−4,501	9,741	−3,019	−480	−3,837	5,468	3,119	−72
1989	−1,664	−331	−7,320	5,132	−12,812	18,996	−12,005	9,148	−72	2,962	−3,412	9,889	4,920	−433
1990	1,373	−1,154	−14,640	6,333	−17,586	38,458	−16,207	11,654	1,099	−580	−3,740	9,158	2,773	−976
1991	−445	−184	−17,152	6,665	−24,649	15,899	14,248	12,417	−1,112	−635	−3,903	7,764	2,876	−314
1992	3,085	−4,438	−20,607	4,792	28,727	−1,730	21,036	13,083	−1,262	−461	−4,412	6,885	−2,111	−4,139
1993	32,825	50	−16,293	7,986	9,411	−6,413	98	14,411	−297	645	−4,284	10,201	−1,929	−9,407
1994	31,568				13,209			18,686				17,294		
1995	38,729		...		25,076		...	23,812		...		25,761		...
1996	54,118		...		39,999		...	22,767		...		22,049		...
1997	39,878		...		32,403		...	20,937		...		25,239		...
1998	35,631		...		19,998		...	21,055		...		12,720		...
1999	23,437		...		8,111		...	17,939		...		16,505		...
2000	10,717		...		−5,670		...	19,022		...		16,307		...

J3 Balance of Payments (in million U.S. dollars)

1948–2000

	Norway							Portugal[17]						
	VB	**TIB**	*IIB*	*TTB*	**OCB**	**ELTC**	**CTR**	**VB**	**TIB**	*IIB*	*TTB*	**OCB**	**ELTC**	**CTR**
1948	−269	150	−13	−3	−119	...	33	−220	17	5	6	−193	...	...
1949	−265	145	—	−12	−120	...	39	−161	53	4	6	−108	...	82
1950	−232	267	−9	−9	35	...	−21	−55	55	4	5	—	...	−40
1951	−172	237	−11	−14	65	...	−38	−1	53	7	4	52	...	−94
1952	−240	238	−9	−11	−2	...	—	−53	40	2	2	−13	...	−12
1953	−337	209	−10	−8	−128	...	8	−15	46	3	4	31	...	−62
1954	−377	209	−14	−10	−168	...	5	−14	50	4	5	36	...	−49
1955	−382	258	−19	−13	−124	117	−28	−50	47	3	6	−3	2	−16
1956	−353	357	−25	−8	4	46	−13	−71	78	2	10	7	4	−24
1957	−396	410	−26	−10	14	24	−5	−83	48	3	14	−35	1	4
1958	−513	355	−31	−7	−158	143	−59	−85	112	2	12	27	−1	151₁₅
1959	−457		−33	−8	−69	150	−25	−87	97	1	13	10	3	−37
1960	−515	380	−38	−3	−125	74	−26	−106	93	3	11	−13	4	1
1961	−626	416	−40	−1	−210	186	−4	−184	40	−3	13	−144	24	84
1962	−624	411	−33	1	−213	114	—	−152	117	−7	28	−35	120	−129
1963	−692	512	−58	−7	−180	185	−50	−164	143	−6	43	−21	76	−52
1964	−625	550	−65	5	−75	92	−33	−182₁₇	198₁₇	−13₁₇	70₁₇	16₁₇	99₁₇	−139
1965	−702	532	−71	6	−170	211	−89	−297	168	−8	81	−129	54	−67
1966	−774	539	−77	10	−235	144	−52	−341	301	−5	178	−40	125	−139
1967	−962	655	−94	−89	−307	441	−150	−332	361	−3	187	29	130	−157
1968	−720	728	−93	−99	8	56	−25	−382	345	−6	135	−37	122	−129
1969	−679	807	−75	−95	128	−134	−14	−389	432	−5	93	43	17	−82
1970	−1,153	911	−80	−86	−242	138	−101₁₆	−515	538	—	124	23	53	−59₁₆
1971	−1,459	934	−183	−95	−525	354	−336	−647	800	−10	185	153	96	−343
1972	−1,015	956	−258	−109	−59	294	−170	−699₁₇	998₁₇	−12₁₇	238₁₇	297₁₇	43₁₇	−343₁₇
								−734	1,088	22	264	354	−105	−346
1973	−1,532	1,168	−383	−162	−364	851	−246	−910	1,251	86	319	341	−141	−385
1974	−2,336	1,218	−646	−209	−1,118	990	−353	−1,995	1,164	129	259	−831	290	515
1975	−2,871	393	−345	−344	−2,478	2,582	−310	−1,603	848	−27	101	−755	−82	763
1976	−3,561	−185	−531	−401	−3,746	3,122	7	−2,169	887	−132	182	−1,282	28	222
1977	−4,053	−981	−878	−566	−5,034	4,303	−6	−1,995	1,038	−179	267	−957	94	−190
1978	−512	−1,591	−1,365	−675	−2,103	3,188	−665	−2,045	1,582	−328	427	−463	716	−505
1979	146	−1,190	−1,823	−712	−1,044	2,270	−1,356	−2,634	2,580	−435	695	−54	735	−60
1980	1,896	−798	−1,917	−720	1,098	−1,833	−4,029	2,965	−616	855	−1,064	710	136	
1981	3,035	−858	−1,806	−843	2,177	−740	−205	−5,060	2,455	−972	783	−2,605	1,230	261
1982	2,386	−1,672	−1,923	−1,036	662	714	−621	−4,863	1,613	−1,230	616	−3,250	2,118	87
1983	4,351	−2,365	−1,718	−1,025	1,986	−1,503	244	−2,400	1,396	−1,059	585	−1,004	1,242	62
1984	5,158	−2,239	−1,550	−936	2,919	33	−2,736	−2,026	1,512	−1,203	729	−514	1,150	−131
1985	4,728	−1,676	−1,033	−1,075	3,052	−1,115	−4,552	−1,457	1,867	−1,217	938	410	951	−879
1986	−2,115	−2,430	−1,137	−1,549	−4,545	2,809	1,392	−1,634	2,778	−1,004	1,219	1,144	−501	−61
1987	−759	−3,346	−1,208	−1,896	−4,105	88	−1,752	−3,375	4,015	−944	1,722	640	−98	−1,871
1988	−209	−3,570	−1,910	−2,138	−3,896	5,145	1,009	−5,137	4,505	−788	1,881	−1,066	753	−1,800
1989	3,770	−541	−2,570	−1,639	212	−183	−517	−4,742	958	−603	2,100	153	94	−4,825
1990	7,761	146	−2,700	−2,109	3,992	−1,358	−1,548	−6,684	1,092	97	2,689	−181	166	−4,533
1991	8,696	407	−2,753	−1,767	5,032	2,339	2,100	−7,688	811	−186	2,689	−716	118	−6,144
1992	9,303	630	−3,417	−2,059	2,982	1,279	1,292	−9,387	766	−611	2,555	−184	1,015	1,500
1993	7,995	−1,147	−3,337	−1,852	2,152	534	−7,682	−6,636	785	−83	2,323	947	306	3,289
1994	7,496				3,760			−8,321				−2,196		
1995	8,571		...		4,854	...		−8,910		...		−132	...	
1996	12,931		...		10,240	...		−9,722		...		−5,216	...	
1997	11,152		...		8,017	...		−10,342		...		−6,465	...	
1998	1,799		...		−1,318	...		−13,221		...		−8,789	...	
1999	10,119		...		6,014	...		−13,766		...		−9,629	...	
2000	25,500		...		22,986	...		−14,143		...		−10,632	...	

J3 Balance of Payments (in million U.S. dollars)

1948-2000

	Spain[18]							Sweden						
	VB	TIB	*IIB*	*TTB*	OCB	ELTC	CTR	VB	TIB	*IIB*	*TTB*	OCB	ELTC	CTR
1948	-62	-7	...	...	-55	172	-1	-270	157	*5*	*-15*	-113	...	39
1949	-15	-10	...	...	-25	66	-2	-30	142	*4*	*-4*	112	...	-36
1950	62	-9	...	...	53	-3	1	-84	112	*3*	*-4*	28	...	-20
1951	117	-3	...	...	114	-2	-1	-2	174	*10*	*-5*	172	...	-231
1952	-52	15	...	...	-38	-2	-12	-164	193	*14*	*-12*	29	...	16
1953	-56	78	...	*92*	21	68	-16	-95	163	*13*	*-12*	68	...	-55
	-91[18]	118[18]			27[18]	-27[18]								
1954	-102	125	*-3*	*87*	23	11	-55	-190	160	*18*	*-19*	-30	...	16
1955	-243	174	*-7*	*94*	-69	31	-20	-272	191	*17*	*-30*	-81	-8	21
								-268[8]	238[8]					
1956	-304	178	*-4*	*91*	-126	46	70	-101	71	*25*	*-18*	-30	-23	-13
1957	-380	189	*-5*	*74*	-191	12	49	-111	83	*29*	*-21*	-28	-7	34
1958	-315	153	*-9*	*69*	-162	14	40	-86	35	*29*	*-22*	-51	-3	-15
1959	-247	219	*-14*	*138*	-28	95	134[3]	-15	16	*27*	*-21*	1	-5	38[15]
1960	41	349	*-14*	*247*	390	122	-341	-113	28	*29*	*-20*	-85	-12	-50
1961	-294	514	*-3*	*329*	220	225	-346[7]	42	1	*28*	*-37*	43	16	-207
1962	-653	641	*-13*	*466*	-12	195	-159	50	-44	*37*	*-52*	6	41	-67
1963	-1,026	843	*-15*	*611*	-183	227	-102	73	-99	*36*	*-71*	-26	-67	44
1964	-1,077	1,109	*-21*	*852*	32	260	-366	119	-103	*53*	*-80*	16	105	-207
1965	-1,759	1,279	*-31*	*1,027*	-487	311	82	-62	-123	*45*	*-113*	-185	63	-7
1966	-1,992	1,428	*-73*	*1,202*	-564	341	169	35	-196	*44*	*-143*	-161	164	-55
1967	-1,781	1,325	*-92*	*1,111*	-456	521	153	171	-218	*31*	*-178*	-47	104	186
1968	-1,575	1,378	*-110*	*1,111*	-197	586	-49	177	-293	*19*	*-203*	-116	117	26
1969	-1,871	1,479	*-166*	*1,195*	-392	514	-132	224	-421	*6*	*-266*	-197	-40	119
1970	-1,874	1,955	*-184*	*1,343*	79	668	-536[16]	303	-568	*18*	*-338*	-265	139	-65[16]
1971	-1,599	2,455	*-148*	*1,879*	856	500	-1,408	895	-543	*-21*	*-377*	352	10	-332
1972	-2,316	2,897	*-176*	*2,238*	581	848	-1,746	1,218	-675	*-27*	*-543*	567	223	-465
1973	-3,504	4,089	*-85*	*2,868*	585	765	-1,697	2,031	-602	*8*	*-515*	1,429	173	-926
1974	-7,047	3,814	*121*	*2,867*	-3,233	1,767	296	392	-944	*-16*	*-503*	-552	424	797
1975	-7,410	3,895	*-231*	*3,099*	-3,515	1,809	368	1,078	-1,420	*-57*	*-610*	-342	1,361	-1,352
1976	-7,305	3,013	*-496*	*2,681*	-4,292	2,011	802	162	-1,810	*-184*	*-729*	-1,648	376	584
1977	-6,187	4,054	*-709*	*3,460*	-2,133	3,011	-1,273	275	-2,456	*-469*	*-803*	-2,181	915	-1,160
1978	-4,081	2,547	*-1,049*	*4,894*	1,634	1,717	-4,135	2,574	-2,825	*-704*	*-890*	-251	-739	-709
1979	-5,690	4,562	*-1,070*	*4,260*	1,128	3,233	-3,112	-695	-1,719	*-787*	*-1,133*	-2,414	-781	610
1980	-11,728	6,555	*-1,486*	*5,715*	-5,173	4,205	1,361	-2,198	-2,206	*-1,303*	*-1,133*	-4,404	-333	94
1981	-10,113	5,124	*-2,323*	*5,760*	-4,989	4,232	1,058	163	-2,684	*-2,168*	*-1,245*	-2,847	-1,057	-183
1982	-9,254	5,009	*-2,311*	*6,121*	-4,245	1,773	3,150	-223	-3,217	*1,807*	*894*	-3,440	-1,587	88
1983	-7,701	4,955	*-2,463*	*5,960*	-2,746	3,122	253	1,899	-2,933	*-1,903*	*-518*	-1,034	-4,489	521
1984	-4,271	2,253	*-2,390*	*6,904*	2,018	3,274	-4,553	3,420	-3,174	*-2,189*	*-587*	246	-6,294	189
1985	-4,171	1,320	*-1,808*	*7,101*	2,851	-1,372	780	2,384	-3,992	*-2,339*	*-778*	-1,608	-4,789	-1,948
1986	-6,524	2,559	*-1,996*	*10,465*	3,965	-1,634	-3,580	5,036	-6,304	*-2,303*	*-1,268*	62	-4,132	-758
1987	-12,986	12,753	*-2,776*	*12,800*	-233	9,290	-15,914	4,485	-6,227	*-2,607*	*-1,748*	-21	-479	-1,623
1988	-17,998	14,214	*-3,517*	*14,193*	-3,784	9,610	-6,405	4,880	-6,978	*-3,076*	*-2,230*	-534	-1,931	-318
1989	-25,406	12,634	*-2,768*	*13,121*	-10,924	1,935	-4,393	4,015	-3,033	*-2,335*	*-2,529*	-3,104	1,560	-1,067
1990	-30,952	13,288	*-3,787*	*14,329*	-18,653	2,958	-9,761	3,402	-3,357	*-4,448*	*-3,381*	-6,338	-6,893	-8,429
1991	-30,536	12,021	*-4,520*	*14,478*	-20,137	8,418	-14,594	6,359	-2,637	*-6,368*	*-3,612*	-4,632	12,282	-343
1992	-30,572	12,250	*-6,069*	*17,793*	-21,996	15,557	20,318	6,723	-2,890	*-10,012*	*-3,970*	-8,790	17,434	-4,293
1993	-15,020	11,108	*-3,788*	*14,594*	-6,048	8,813	4,459	7,669	-784	*-9,156*	*-1,817*	-4,078	14,209	3,574
1994	-14,892				-6,389			-9,558				743		
1995	-18,415		...		792	...		15,978		...		4,940	...	
1996	-16,283		...		407	...		18,636		...		5,892	...	
1997	-13,407		...		2,512	...		17,999		...		7,406	...	
1998	-20,758		...		-3,135	...		17,632		...		4,639	...	
1999	-30,339		...		-13,761	...		15,714		...		5,982	...	
2000	-32,755		...		-17,257	...		15,215		...		6,617	...	

J3 Balance of Payments (in million U.S. dollars)

1948–2000

	Switzerland							United Kingdom						
	VB	TIB	*IIB*	*TTB*	OCB	ELTC	CTR	VB	TIB	*IIB*	*TTB*	OCB	ELTC	CTR
1948	−370	266	...	...	−104	...	−63	−609	851	*359*	*−133*	242	...	219
1949	−91	222	...	...	131	...	−31	−506	798	*347*	*−122*	292	...	257
1950	−154	226	...	...	72	...	113	−143	1,028	*431*	*−67*	885	...	−1,691
1951	−295	266	...	...	−29	...	−90	−1,929	801	*361*	*−81*	−1,128	...	1,068
1952	−122	276	*78*	*82*	154	...	−35	−781	1,156	*255*	*−8*	375	−476	419
1953	24	305	*94*	*105*	329	...	−101	−683	1,106	*207*	*−3*	423	−577	−715
1954	−82	325	*117*	*117*	243	...	−69	−571	910	*221*	*−17*	339	−599	−364
1955	−186	337	*95*	*133*	151	...	−10	−876	436	*216*	*−39*	−440	−420	642
1956	−300[8] −257	329[8] 286	*133*	*145*	29	−74	−63	148	437	*325*	*−31*	585	−745	116
1957	−334	289	*133*	*168*	−45	−44	−39	−81	686	*224*	*−48*	605	−862	−2[15]
1958	−92	314	*127*	*176*	222	−40	−161	90	833	*820*	*−48*	923	−524	6
1959	−159	334	*140*	*195*	175	−115	—	−325	695	*739*	*−62*	370	−778	268
1960	−260	354	*157*	*217*	94	−217	−258	−1,142	419	*666*	*−48*	−723	−661	−920
1961	−545	333	*164*	*249*	−212	−276	−431	−427	416	*683*	*−53*	−11	251	401
1962	−670	332	*182*	*279*	−338	−304	−160	−285	599	*908*	*−76*	314	−618	10
1963	−694	334	*197*	*298*	−360	−147	−201	−197	508	*1,109*	*−49*	311	−433	160
1964	−807	396	*212*	*347*	−411	−43	−200	−1,411	344	*1,145*	*−199*	−1,067	−835	833
1965	−553	483	*259*	*365*	−70	32	−119	−615	396	*1,238*	*−272*	−219	−315	−689
1966	−467	588	*317*	*382*	121	−8	−104	−160	386	*1,100*	*−217*	226	−451	−95
1967	−423	696	*355*	*395*	273	−444	−148	−1,566	464	*1,049*	*−105*	−1,102	−497	404
1968	−272	995	*441*	*404*	723	−775	−602	−1,637	454	*799*	*27*	−1,183	−624	273
1969	−434	1,224	*519*	*431*	790	−1,182	−132	−422	1,634	*1,194*	*84*	1,212	−811	−105
1970	−1,071	1,430	*705*	*478*	359	−947	−706	−5	1,990	*1,343*	*120*	1,985	−1,066	−300[16]
1971	−1,233	1,658	*837*	*552*	425	−1,939	−1,407[16]	533	2,186	*1,237*	*114*	2,719	−715	−6,513
1972	−1,317	1,956	*1,037*	*669*	639	−2,887	−591	−1,854	2,362	*1,357*	*101*	508	−2,266	3,144
1973	−1,777	2,620	*1,496*	*833*	843	−2,756	−608	−6,253	3,835	*3,090*	*73*	−2,419	−794	−741
1974	−2,200	3,404	*1,987*	*850*	1,204	−1,584	−439	−12,239	4,758	*3,307*	*456*	−7,481	3,380	−450
1975	−4,918	2,479	*2,422*	*973*	−2,439	−3,709	−1,573	−7,272	3,855	*1,705*	*660*	−3,417	−740	1,441
1976	−4,463	3,069	*2,247*	*979*	−1,394	−7,117	−2,587	−7,070	5,387	*2,430*	*1,235*	−1,683	−2,764	1,230
1977	−5,202	3,653	*2,662*	*839*	−1,569	−5,757	−683	−4,006	3,797	*166*	*2,036*	−209	−1,716	−16,740
1978	−7,803	4,247	*3,392*	*791*	−3,556	−8,478	−7,474	−3,064	4,922	*1,583*	*1,834*	1,858	−8,634	4,080
1979	−2,453	3,720	*3,800*	*557*	1,267	−13,586	1,328	−7,087	6,222	*2,521*	*1,473*	−875	−10,064	−3,710
1980	−5,891	4,336	*4,309*	*789*	−1,555	−11,213	779	3,343	4,177	*−224*	*508*	7,520	−11,861	−910
1981	−3,318	4,774	*4,662*	*893*	1,456	−9,622	1,677	7,155	7,345	*2,450*	*−592*	14,500	−17,759	5,410
1982	−2,107	6,035	*5,950*	*819*	3,928	−13,605	−1,481	3,710	4,331	*2,511*	*−792*	8,041	−16,387	2,840
1983	−5,393	6,602	*6,160*	*868*	1,209	−5,087	426	−1,676	7,507	*4,316*	*−139*	5,831	−16,011	1,060
1984	−1,079	7,231	*6,710*	*895*	6,152	−3,944	−262	−6,109	8,717	*5,862*	*−77*	2,608	−22,928	1,900
1985	−1,562	7,601	*6,754*	*758*	6,039	−7,036	−2,720	−2,653	7,418	*3,801*	*751*	4,765	−25,979	−3,420
1986	−4,960	9,614	*8,496*	*880*	4,654	3,554	−3,770	−12,801	12,959	*7,846*	*−785*	158	−31,881	−5,560
1987	−5,427	11,712	*10,502*	*1,032*	6,280	−4,396	−5,690	−17,926	10,553	*8,783*	*−1,668*	−7,373	11,827	−23,300
1988	−4,576	12,931	*12,962*	*622*	8,326	−3,061	3,273	−36,976	10,243	*10,272*	*−3,625*	−26,733	−11,696	−3,380
1989	−4,576	4,994	*10,396*	*665*	8,042	−3,169	−1,073	−40,544	5,527	*5,611*	*−3,927*	−36,862	9,876	9,330
1990	−4,323	5,875	*9,788*	*998*	6,942	−4,617	−3,947	−32,742	6,563	*1,883*	*−3,790*	−33,037	11,851	−1,080
1991	−6,391	845	*9,985*	*1,371*	10,325	−1,093	219	−18,274	6,588	*−395*	*−4,671*	−14,643	24,251	−6,040
1992	−3,806	7,147	*9,550*	*1,434*	14,190	−578	−3,438	−23,428	7,121	*7,564*	*−6,055*	−17,850	1,675	5,250
1993	490	7,789	*9,530*	*1,220*	16,696	−149	790	−20,146	7,783	*2,440*	*−5,588*	−17,776	26,571	−140
1994	3,346				−17,587			−16,890				−2,040		
1995	3,259		...		21,804		...	−18,530		...		−5,970		...
1996	1,868		...		21,053		...	−20,230		...		−720		...
1997	2,738		...		26,679		...	−19,490		...		10,830		...
1998	933		...		26,535		...	−34,010		...		−150		...
1999	723		...		29,119		...	−42,350		...		−15,980		...
2000	...		...		...		...	−43,580		...		−24,460		...

J3 Balance of Payments (in million U.S. dollars)

1970–2000

	Hungary					Poland				
	VB	TIB	OCB	ELTC	CTR	VB	TIB	OCB	ELTC	CTR
1970	−102	77	−25	—	...	...	...	...	...	...
1971	−342	−5	−347	217	...	...	...	...	...	...
1972	96	−1	95	137	−172	...	...	...	...	...
1973	370	−114	256	5	−448	...	...	...	...	...
1974	−400	61	−339	143	−220	...	...	...	...	...
1975	−512	−139	−651	413	1	...	...	...	...	...
1976	−486	−134	−620	428	−18	−2,757	−36	−2,793	−2,785	−185
1977	−619	−194	−813	637	−94	−2,218	−174	−2,392	−2,619	372
1978	−1,187	−250	−1,437	1,143	−365	−2,292	−253	−2,545	−2,181	−129
1979	−560	−382	−942	943	145	−2,384	−981	−3,365	−3,603	−275
1980	−143	−434	−577	782	−434	−1,776	−1,641	−3,417	−2,652	636
1981	46	−939	−893	990	617	−2,181	−1,805	−3,986	−1,107	−35
1982	410	−944	−534	55	1,008	−84	−1,857	−1,941	−5,210	−370
1983	434	−614	−180	−55	−467	303	−1,884	−1,581	−3,790	−118
1984	780	−741	39	1,314	−307	659	−1,742	−1,083	−2,651	−341
1985	448	−903	−455	1,695	−611	347	−1,329	−982	−1,732	236
1986	−465	−897	−1,362	893	−26	467	−1,573	−1,106	−2,949	173
1987	80	−756	−676	937	437	790	−1,169	−379	−1,892	−797
1988	583	−1,155	−572	421	−96	1,089	−1,196	−107	−2,616	−561
1989	1,043	−367	−588	1,280	221	47	148	−1,409	−1,656	−259
1990	534	425	379	241	176	3,589	353	3,067	−3,989	−2,178
1991	358	534	403	759	−2,866	−711	693	−2,146	−3,195	−860
1992	−11	764	352	1,696	−492	−131	728	−3,104	−935	−467
1993	−4,021	216	−4,262	133	−2,343	−3,505	570	−5,788	−14	8
1994	−3,716	...	−4,054	...	...	−575	...	954	...	...
1995	−2,433	...	−2,530	...	...	−1,646	...	854	...	...
1996	−2,652	...	−1,689	...	...	−7,287	...	−3,264	...	...
1997	−1,962	...	−982	...	...	−9,822	...	−5,744	...	...
1998	−2,354	...	−2,304	...	...	−12,836	...	−6,901	...	...
1999	−2,189	...	−2,106	...	...	−15,072	...	−12,487	...	...
2000	−2,106	...	−1,494	...	...	...	...	...	...	...

J3 Balance of Payments (in million U.S. dollars)

	Romania					Yugoslavia				
	VB	TIB	OCB	ELTC	CTR	VB	TIB	OCB	ELTC	CTR
1956	...	...	...	...	...	−125	124	129	...	−29
1957	...	...	...	...	...	−217	109	−108	...	−1
1958	...	...	...	...	...	−178	90	−88	...	−4
1959	...	...	...	...	...	−159	137	−22	...	43[15]
1960	...	...	...	...	...	−199	76	−123	...	21
1961	...	...	...	...	...	−269	52	−217	...	−20
1962	...	...	...	...	...	−124	76	−48	...	−39
1963	...	...	...	...	...	−188	108	−80	...	−25
1964	...	...	...	...	...	−323	120	−203	...	23
1965	...	...	...	...	...	−90	158	67	...	−29
1966	...	...	...	...	...	−222	176	−46	...	−12
1967	...	...	...	...	...	−314	218	−96	...	35
1968	...	...	...	...	...	−385	265	−120	...	−52
1969	...	...	...	...	...	−484	400	−84	...	−121
1970	...	...	...	...	...	−958	586	−372	...	113[16]
1971	−51	−56	−107	121	38	−1,171	776	−395	...	−68
1972	−72	−53	−125	113	−5	−727	1,158	431	...	−518
1973	−68	−112	−180	130	121	−1,284	1,787	502	...	−601
1974	−326	−190	−516	659	−32	−3,117	2,168	−951	...	191
1975	−111	−149	−260	385	−259	−2,984	2,359	−625	...	274
1976	76	−137	−61	21	144	−1,863	2,049	186	1,099	−1,179
1977	−83	−190	−273	91	348	−3,782	2,453	−1,329	1,404	−54
1978	−592	−187	−779	384	−127	−3,768	2,495	−1,273	1,609	−344
1979	−1,155	−513	−1,668	1,065	−167	−6,058	2,399	−3,659	1,299	131
1980	−1,534	−865	−2,399	1,810	202	−4,899	2,582	−2,317	1,954	−127
1981	204	−1,022	−818	896	185	−3,163	2,204	−959	578	−213
1982	1,525	−870	655	602	−90	−2,022	1,549	−473	−93	822
1983	1,688	−766	922	−99	330	−1,231	1,506	275	941	−201
1984	2,186	−650	1,536	−1,039	−194	−789	1,267	478	−265	−182
1985	1,445	−530	915	−1,118	415	−588	1,421	833	78	63
1986	1,917	−509	1,408	−1,001	−522	−702	1,802	1,100	−1,406	−365
1987	2,178	255	2,043	−1,512	−820	82	1,166	1,248	−892	762
1988	3,750	370	3,922	−3,619	622	779	1,708	2,487	−932	−1,600
1989	2,050	384	2,514	−1,707	−1,079	58	2,099	2,427	−314	−3,908
1990	−3,344	−177	−3,524	58	1,235	−2,676	2,625	−2,364	−47	−1,339
1991	−1,106	139	−1,012	245	−113	512	365	−1,161	−386	2,792
1992	−1,194	287	−1,506	1,134	−178	...	...	...	...	...
1993	−1,128	111	−1,162	825	−179	...	...	...	...	...
1994	−411	...	−455	...	...	...	...	...	...	...
1995	−1,577	...	−1,780	...	...	...	...	...	...	...
1996	−2,470	...	−2,579	...	...	...	...	...	...	...
1997	−1,980	...	−2,137	...	...	...	...	...	...	...
1998	−2,625	...	−2,918	...	...	...	...	...	...	...
1999	−1,092	...	−1,297	...	...	...	...	...	...	...
2000	−1,684	...	−1,359	...	...	...	...	...	...	...

J3 Balance of Payments

C. Changes in Gold Reserves (in million fine Troy ounces and million U.S. dollars)[19]

	Austria		Belgium		Denmark		Finland		France	
	m.oz.	m.$	m.oz.	m.$	m.oz.	m.$	m.oz.	m.$	m.oz.	m.$
1971	−0.43	−44	−2.11	−253	0.03	−3	−0.58	−20	0.25	−293
1972	−0.03	−19	1.04	51	—	−1	—	−1	−0.03	−1
1973	−0.03	−130	0.91	−98	—	−8	0.58	19	−0.22	−435
1974	—	−144	—	—	—	−8	—	−3	−0.02	—
1975	—	78	—	—	—	7	—	3	—	−9,872
1976	—	−101	—	—	—	−9	—	−1	−0.09	1,293
1977	−0.12	−123	−0.28	−13	−0.12	−13	−0.08	−1	−0.65	−3,877
1978	−0.05	−1,018	−0.15	−4	−0.05	−17	−0.05	−10	−0.32	−5,623
1979	−0.06	−969	8.38	352	0.34	25	−0.04	−246	20.07	−11,855
1980	—	319	−0.03	2	0.01	−450	—	10	0.07	−15,996
1981	—	375	—	—	—	−242	−0.28	−38	—	16,114
1982	−0.01	119	—	—	—	216	—	56	—	−2,971
1983	−0.01	325	—	—	—	−5	—	23	—	6,062
1984	—	251	—	—	—	28	—	26	—	3,954
1985	−0.01	−490	—	—	—	−86	−0.64	−172	—	−748
1986	—	−605	—	—	—	−19	—	−50	—	−6,352
1987	−0.01	−635	0.55	22	—	−117	−0.05	−105	—	−7,564
1988	—	370	−0.04	—	—	54	—	29	—	7,810
1989	—	−1,228	3.44	144	—	2	0.05	−27	—	−296
1990	—	−815	—	—	—	−69	—	−63	—	2,661
1991	—	−901	—	−9,497	—	142	—	73	—	−385
1992	—	−1,851	5.19	2,453	—	58	—	112	—	5,391
1993	—	−2,360	—	—	—	102	—	38	—	4,416
1994	0.26	−2,142	0	1473	0	−225	−0.001	−83	0	−1
1995	6.35	−1,859	4.86	1,176	0	−11	0.40	60	0	−928
1996	1.24	−3,994	5.22	1,135	0	124	0	25	0	1290
1997	2.88	3,256	0	1,031	0	45	0	54	−0.04	5,366
1998	−1.77	−2,313	5.8	2,575	0	−132	−0.40	−106	−20.48	−4,869
1999	−3.46	6,902	1.22	152	0	146	0.43	−31	5.13	1,587
2000	0.96	524	0	136	0	−38	0	26	−0.01	1,595

	West Germany		Greece		Hungary		Ireland		Italy	
	m.oz.	m.$	m.oz.	m.$	m.oz.	m.$	m.oz.	m.$	m.oz.	m.$
1971	−2.77	−500	0.52	18	...	...	—	−1	0.08	3
1972	−0.89	130	−0.69	−35	...	...	—	—	0.03	−246
1973	−0.25	−815	—	−15	...	...	0.03	−1	−0.11	−352
1974	—	−631	−0.11	−7	...	...	−0.02	−1	—	—
1975	—	471	−0.02	6	...	...	—	1	—	—
1976	—	−587	−0.02	—	...	...	—	—	—	−583
1977	−0.69	−758	−0.08	—	...	...	−0.02	−2	−0.43	−1,939
1978	−0.34	−2,660	−0.04	−13	...	...	0.02	—	−0.21	−3,074
1979	23.39	1,438	−0.04	−4	...	...	0.07	2	16.41	−5,791
1980	0.07	918	−0.03	4	...	...	0.02	2	0.04	−16,597
1981	—	917	−0.01	14	...	...	—	−101	—	7,729
1982	—	310	−0.02	8	...	...	—	21	—	5,308
1983	—	735	−0.01	7	...	...	—	−10	—	−2,467
1984	—	677	−0.23	1	−0.53	−120	—	18	—	4,515
1985	—	−1,213	−0.01	−722	−0.27	−174	—	−7	—	−1,921
1986	—	−1,492	0.81	22	−0.02	−111	—	−10	—	−2,497
1987	—	−1,602	−0.03	−216	0.71	226	—	−34	—	−7,995
1988	—	966	−0.06	132	0.05	15	—	25	—	5,529
1989	—	−373	—	23	1.0	31	—	6	—	2,024
1990	—	−1,100	—	68	1.197	382	—	—	—	1,583
1991	—	133	−0.03	27	0.04	14	—	5	—	1,683
1992	—	548	−0.01	61	0.16	50	—	−5	—	55
1993	—	552	—	−110	0.01	−12	—	−14	—	−418
1994	0	−909	−0.005	5	0.004	3	0	−18	0	−2,749
1995	0	−711	−0.013	−21	−0.001	−1	−0.001	4	0	772
1996	0	745	−0.008	39	0.01	6	0	−6	0	201
1997	0	1,166	−0.175	149	0	8	0	27	0	3,563
1998	−23.8	−2,589	0.021	−1	0	0	−0.09	−16	−16.69	−2,905
1999	7.46	−22,209	−0.614	−97	0	0	0.275	80	4.53	1,831
2000	0	1,830	−0.025	29	0	1	0	8	0	1245

J3 Balance of Payments

1971–2000

	Netherlands		Norway		Poland		Portugal		Romania	
	m.oz.	m.$	m.oz.	m.$	m.oz.	m.$	m.oz.	m.$	m.oz.	m.$.
1971	−3.47	−320	−0.28	−13	...	...	−0.54	−98	...	...
1972	0.36	−7	−0.03	−1	...	...	−0.57	−21	...	...
1973	−0.16	−308	—	−4	...	...	−0.66	−42	...	...
1974	—	−307	—	−4	...	...	−0.30	−30	−0.17	−9
1975	—	184	—	3	...	...	0.12	57	−0.15	−1
1976	—	−240	—	−3	...	...	0.05	11	−0.15	−6
1977	−0.30	−233	−0.10	−5	...	...	3.56	100	−0.31	−18
1978	−0.15	−3,469	−0.05	−3	...	...	−0.02	16	−0.29	−23
1979	10.81	1,107	—	−4	...	...	—	−11	−0.19	−10
1980	0.03	569	—	3	0.53	−36	−0.04	−4,632	−0.17	−3
1981	—	−390	—	6	0.29	115	0.03	8	0.12	20
1982	—	309	—	9	—	−1	0.05	13	0.04	9
1983	—	703	—	3	—	—	1.66	422	−0.07	4
1984	—	−4,510	—	5	—	—	0.13	35	−0.11	5
1985	—	−2,441	—	−6	—	—	0.07	15	−0.09	−18
1986	—	−2,948	—	−1	—	—	0.07	20	0.57	7
1987	—	−1,441	—	−7	—	—	0.10	25	1.88	23
1988	—	1,725	—	2	—	—	3.99	−76	−0.09	−1,215
1989	—	−606	—	0.3	—	—	0.02	6	0.725	−609
1990	—	−306	—	−5.1	—	—	0.22	71	0.03	1,065
1991	—	176	—	0.5	0.01	—	0.04	−12	0.04	114
1992	—	831	—	6.5	—	—	0.19	−63	−0.06	−714
1993	8.89	6,073	—	3.3	—	—	—	1	0.06	−144
1994	0.28	−838	0	−4.2	0	0	−0.01	4	−0.255	−41
1995	0	−691	0	−3	0	0	0	−4	−0.078	185
1996	0	546	0	0.9	0	0	0	196	−0.115	260
1997	7.7	2,821	0	5.4	−0.431	−73	0	1,728	−0.201	62
1998	−6.76	−1,498	0	1.3	−2.401	−688	−4.02	−124	−0.205	100
1999	2.26	−1,884	0	−237	−0.001	−9	0.58	−2,284	−0.099	−609
2000	2.25	3,830	0	17.4	0	58	0	320	−0.051	47

	Spain		Sweden		Switzerland		United Kingdom		Yugoslavia	
	m.oz.	m.$	m.oz.	m.$	m.oz.	m.$	m.oz	m.$	m.oz	m.$
1971	—	—	−0.06	−20	−5.08	−390	16.34	508	—	−4
1972	—	−43	—	—	—	−1	1.10	41	−0.03	−1
1973	−0.04	−61	−0.01	−24	−0.09	−572	0.07	−88	0.03	−6
1974	—	—	—	−4	—	−1,016	−0.02	—	−0.01	—
1975	—	—	—	11	—	143	—	—	0.01	—
1976	—	—	—	2	−0.08	−321	—	—	—	—
1977	−0.17	−7	−0.14	−17	—	1,092	−1.20	−50	—	−2
1978	−0.08	−4	−0.07	−22	—	−1,396	−0.60	−26	−0.12	−5
1979	−0.09	−4	−0.07	−6	—	−186	4.58	−2,300	−0.09	−4
1980	—	—	—	9	—	784	−0.59	−3,730	−0.13	−5
1981	—	−3,736	—	24	—	131	−0.19	−340	—	—
1982	—	687	—	13	—	651	0.02	2,770	—	—
1983	—	−161	—	12	—	506	—	−1,350	—	−1
1984	−0.02	−5	—	14	—	857	−0.02	430	—	—
1985	−0.02	110	—	−25	—	−1,128	—	...	—	—
1986	−0.17	−63	—	−27	—	−1,599	0.02	...	—	—
1987	2.90	18	—	−41	—	−1,983	—	...	—	—
1988	−2.12	−999	—	15	—	1,400	0.01	...	−0.03	−1
1989	−1.68	−2,940	—	7	—	218	0.01	...	−0.01	—
1990	0.11	−11,596	—	−23	—	−1,492	0.05	...	−0.04	−1
1991	0.01	−7,535	—	−2	—	407	0.05	...	−0.1	—
1992	—	−21,900	—	12	—	606	0.28	...	...	...
1993	—	−48,769	—	—	—	130	0.16	...	...	...
1994	0	0	0	−18	0	−1,031	0.01	−750	...	...
1995	−0.01	−4	1.367	65	0	−1,270	0.01	70	...	...
1996	0	0	—	8	0	1,506	0	−240	...	...
1997	0	82	−0.02	14	0	659	0.01	670	...	...
1998	−3.91	−1,478	0	−10	0	−485	−4.58	−270	...	...
1999	2.71	722	−1.239	−53	0	1,203	2.45	−880	...	...
2000	0	276	0	14	5.49	−13,755	4.88	1,690	...	...

J3 Balance of Payments

NOTES

1. SOURCES:- Part A-the official publications noted on p. xv, with the following additions: Bulgaria, Czechoslovakia, Finland (to 1938), Greece (to 1938), Hungary, Netherlands (change in reserves), Norway (change in reserves), Poland, and Sweden (1924-35)-League of Nations, *Memorandum on Balances of Payments* and *Statistical Yearbooks*; France (to 1913)-M. Lévy-Leboyer & F. Bourguignon, L'èconomie française au XIX siècle (Paris, 1985); Germany-W. G. Hoffman *et al, Das Wachstum der Deutschen Wirtschaft seit der Mitte des 19 Jahrhunderts* (Berlin, etc., 1965); Sweden (to 1923)-E. Lindahl *et al, National Income of Sweden, 1861-1930* (London, 1937); U.K. (to 1869 and change in bullion to 1913)-A.H. Imlah, *Economic Elements in the Pax Britannica* (Cambridge, Mass., 1958); U.K. (remainder)-based on C.H. Feinstein, *National Income, Expenditure and Output of the United Kingdom, 1855-1965* (Cambridge, 1972), with bullion movements from 1914 taken from the *Annual Statement of Trade* and changes in total reserves from the *Annual Abstract of Statistics*.
   Parts B and C-I.M.F., *Balances of Payments Yearbook, and International Financial Statistics*.
2. In all parts, a minus sign indicates an outward payment. Thus, net export of capital and acquisition of reserves both carry a minus sign, and net import of capital and loss of reserves carry an (implicit) plus sign.
3. The total invisible balance includes unrequited transfer payments except as indicated in footnotes.
4. Where possible, the statistics for reserves in Part B are taken from the "International Liquidity" section of the I.M.F. publications, since these provide longer and more consistent series.
5. To convert statistics in parts B and C to national currencies, the following annual average exchange rates (national currency per U.S. dollar) may be used, though it should be noted that (except as indicated in the footnote) changes in currency are not taken into account and the national currency of 1989 is the unit employed:-

	Austria	Belgium	Denmark	Finland	France	West Germany	Greece	Hungary	Ireland	Italy
1948	10.14	43.96	4.81	2.31	2.6616	3.33	10	...	0.2481	575
1949	11.2946	50	5.0571	2.31	3.49	3.5243	11.37	...	0.2715	625
1950	19.996	50	6.9071	2.31	3.499	4.195	15	...	0.3571	625
1951	21.358	50	6.9071	2.31	3.5	4.195	15	...	0.3571	625
1953	24.414	50	6.9071	2.31	3.5	4.2	26.34	...	0.3571	625
1954	26	50	6.9071	2.31	3.5	4.2	30	...	0.3571	625
1955	26	50	6.9071	2.31	3.5	4.2	30	...	0.3571	625
1956	26	50	6.9071	2.31	3.6789	4.2	30	...	0.3571	625
1957	26	50	6.9071	2.525	4.1974	4.2	30	...	0.3571	625
1958	26	50	6.9071	3.2	4.9371	4.2	30	...	0.3571	624.7
1959	26	50	6.9071	3.2	4.9371	4.2	30	...	0.3571	621.1
1960	26	50	6.9071	3.2	4.9371	4.2	30	...	0.3571	624
1961	26	50	6.9071	3.2	4.9371	4.0333	30	...	0.3571	625
1962	26	50	6.9071	3.2	4.9371	4	30	...	0.3571	625
1963	26	50	6.9071	3.2	4.9371	4	30	...	0.3571	625
1964	26	50	6.9071	3.2	4.9371	4	30	...	0.3571	625
1965	26	50	6.9071	3.2	4.9371	4	30	...	0.3571	625
1966	26	50	6.9071	3.2	4.9371	4	30	...	0.3571	625
1967	26	50	9.565	3.45	4.9371	4	30	...	0.3614	625
1968	26	50	7.5	4.2	4.9371	4	30	...	0.4167	625
1969	26	50	7.5	4.2	5.1942	3.9433	30	...	0.4167	625
1970	26	50	7.5	4.2	5.5542	3.66	30	60	0.4167	625
1971	24.96	48.87	7.4169	4.1843	5.5426	3.4908	30	59.822	0.4108	619.9
1972	23.115	44.015	6.9493	4.1463	5.0497	3.1886	30	55.26	0.3997	583.2
1973	19.58	38.977	6.0495	3.8212	4.4578	2.6726	29.625	48.966	0.4078	583
1974	18.693	38.952	6.0949	3.7738	4.8141	2.5878	30	46.752	0.4275	650.3
1975	17.417	36.779	5.7462	3.6787	4.2862	2.4603	32.051	43.971	0.4501	652.8
1976	17.94	38.605	6.045	3.8644	4.779	2.518	36.518	41.575	0.5536	832.3
1977	16.527	35.843	6.0032	4.0294	4.9136	2.3222	36.838	40.961	0.5729	882.4
1978	14.522	31.492	5.5146	4.1173	4.5131	2.0086	36.745	37.911	0.521	848.7
1979	13.368	29.319	5.261	3.8953	4.2544	1.8329	37.038	35.578	0.4884	830.9
1980	12.938	29.242	5.6359	3.7301	4.2256	1.8177	42.617	32.532	0.4859	856.4
1981	15.927	37.129	7.1234	4.3153	5.4346	2.26	55.408	34.314	0.6185	1,136.8
1982	17.059	45.691	8.3324	4.8204	6.5721	2.4266	66.803	36.631	0.7031	1,352.5
1983	17.963	51.132	9.145	5.5701	7.6213	2.5533	88.064	42.671	0.8012	1,518.8
1984	20.009	57.784	10.3566	6.01	8.7391	2.8459	112.717	48.042	0.9199	1,757
1985	20.69	59.378	10.5964	6.1979	8.9852	2.944	138.119	50.119	0.9384	1,909.4
1986	15.267	44.672	8.091	5.0695	6.9261	2.1715	139.981	45.832	0.7454	1,490.8
1987	12.643	37.334	6.8403	4.3956	6.0107	1.7974	135.43	46.971	0.672	1,296.1
1988	12.348	36.768	6.7315	4.1828	5.9569	1.7562	141.861	50.413	0.6553	1,301.6
1989	13.231	39.404	7.310	4.2912	6.3801	1.8800	162.42	59.066	0.7047	1,372.1
1990	11.370	34.148	6.189	3.8235	5.4453	1.6157	158.51	63.206	0.6029	1,198.1
1991	11.676	33.148	6.396	4.0440	5.6421	1.6595	182.27	74.735	0.6190	1,240.6
1992	10.989	32.150	6.036	4.4794	5.2938	1.5617	190.62	78.988	0.5864	1,232.4
1993	11.632	34.597	6.484	5.7123	5.6632	1.6533	229.25	91.933	0.6816	1,573.7
1994	11.422	33.456	6.361	5.2235	5.5520	1.6228	242.60	105.160	...	1,612.4
1995	10.081	29.480	5.602	4.3667	4.9915	1.4331	231.66	125.681	...	1,628.9
1996	10.587	30.962	5.799	4.5936	5.1155	1.5048	240.71	152.647	...	1,542.9
1997	12.204	35.774	6.604	5.1914	5.8367	1.7341	273.06	186.789	...	1,703.1
1998	12.379	36.299	6.701	5.3441	5.8995	1.7597	295.53	214.402	...	1,736.2
1999	...	...	6.976	...	...	...	305.65	237.146	...	...
2000	...	...	8.083	...	...	...	282.179	...	...	...

J3 Balance of Payments

	Nether-lands	Norway	Poland	Portugal	Romania	Spain	Sweden	Switzer-land	U.K.	Yugoslavia
1948	2.653	4.97	...	25.065	...	21.9	3.6	4.373	0.2481	...
1949	3.8	5.0355	...	26.085	...	23.43	4.0439	4.373	0.2715	...
1950	3.8	7.1429	...	28.75	...	39.8	5.1728	4.373	0.3571	...
1951	3.8	7.1429	...	28.75	...	39.65	5.1732	4.373	0.3571	...
1952	3.8	7.1429	...	28.75	...	39.65	5.1732	4.373	0.3571	...
1953	3.8	7.1429	...	28.75	...	39.65	5.1732	4.373	0.3571	...
1954	3.8	7.1429	...	28.75	...	38.95	5.1732	4.373	0.3571	...
1955	3.8	7.1429	...	28.75	...	38.95	5.1732	4.373	0.3571	...
1956	3.8	7.1429	...	28.75	...	38.95	5.1732	4.373	0.3571	3.0
1957	3.8	7.1429	...	28.75	...	41.3	5.1732	4.373	0.3571	3.0
1958	3.8	7.1429	...	28.75	...	42	5.1732	4.373	0.3571	3.0
1959	3.8	7.1429	...	28.75	...	51	5.1732	4.373	0.3571	3.0
1960	3.8	7.1429	...	28.75	...	60	5.1732	4.373	0.3571	3.0
1961	3.65	7.1429	...	28.75	...	60	5.1732	4.373	0.3571	3.0
1962	3.62	7.1429	...	28.75	...	60	5.1732	4.373	0.3571	3.0
1963	3.62	7.1429	...	28.75	...	60	5.1732	4.373	0.3571	3.0
1964	3.62	7.1429	...	28.75	...	60	5.1732	4.373	0.3571	3.0
1965	3.62	7.1429	...	28.75	...	60	5.1732	4.373	0.3571	6.958
1966	3.62	7.1429	...	28.75	...	60	5.1732	4.373	0.3571	12.5
1967	3.62	7.1429	...	28.75	...	61.67	5.1732	4.373	0.3571	12.5
1968	3.62	7.1429	...	28.75	...	70	5.1732	4.373	0.4167	12.5
1969	3.62	7.1429	...	28.75	...	70	5.1732	4.373	0.4167	12.5
1970	3.62	7.1429	...	28.75	...	70	5.1732	4.373	0.4167	12.5
1971	3.5024	7.0418	...	28.312	...	69.47	5.1168	4.1339	0.4108	14.875
1972	3.2095	6.5882	...	27.053	...	64.27	4.7624	3.8193	0.3997	17.0
1973	2.7956	5.7658	...	24.515	20.253	58.26	4.3673	3.1648	0.4078	16.242
1974	2.6884	5.5397	...	25.408	20	57.69	4.4394	2.9793	0.4275	15.913
1975	2.529	5.2269	...	25.553	20	57.41	4.1522	2.5813	0.4501	17.344
1976	2.6439	5.4565	...	30.229	20	66.9	4.3559	2.4996	0.5536	18.178
1977	2.4543	5.3235	3.32	38.277	20	75.96	4.4816	2.4035	0.5729	18.289
1978	2.1636	5.2423	33.2	43.937	18.355	76.67	4.5185	1.788	0.521	18.637
1979	2.006	5.0641	40.16	48.923	18	67.13	4.2871	1.6627	0.4713	18.973
1980	1.9881	4.9392	44.22	50.062	18	71.7	4.2296	1.6757	0.4299	24.639
1981	2.4952	5.7395	51.15	61.546	15	92.32	5.0634	1.9642	0.4931	34.966
1982	2.6702	6.454	84.82	79.473	15	109.86	6.2826	2.0303	0.5713	50.276
1983	2.8541	7.2964	91.55	110.78	17.179	143.43	7.6671	2.0991	0.6592	92.839
1984	3.2087	8.1615	113.24	146.39	21.28	160.76	8.2718	2.3497	0.7483	152.822
1985	3.3214	8.5972	147.14	170.395	17.14	170.04	8.6039	2.4571	0.7714	270.163
1986	2.45	7.3947	175.29	149.587	16.153	140.05	7.1236	1.7989	0.6817	<u>379.222</u>*
1987	2.0257	6.7375	265.08	140.882	14.56	123.48	6.3404	1.4912	0.6102	0.074
1988	1.9766	6.517	430.55	143.954	14.28	116.49	6.1272	1.4633	0.5614	<u>0.252</u>

* Subsequently new dinars per dollar.

1989	2.1207	6.9045	<u>1,439.20</u>	157.46	14.92	118.38	6.4469	1.6359	0.6099	2.876
1990	1.8209	6.2597	.95	142.55	22.43	101.93	5.9188	1.3892	0.5603	11.318
1991	1.8697	6.4824	1.06	144.48	<u>76.39</u>	103.91	6.0475	1.4340	0.5651	19.638
1992	1.7585	6.2145	1.36	135.00	307.95	102.38	5.8238	1.4062	0.5664	...
1993	1.8573	7.0941	1.81	160.80	760.05	127.26	7.7834	1.4776	0.6657	...
1994	1.8200	7.0576	2.27	165.99	1655.1	133.96	7.7160	1.3677	...	...
1995	1.6057	6.3352	2.42	151.11	2033.3	124.69	7.1333	1.1825	...	...
1996	1.6859	6.4498	2.70	154.24	3084.2	126.66	6.7060	1.2360	...	...
1997	1.9513	7.0734	3.28	175.31	7167.9	146.41	7.6349	1.4513	...	...
1998	1.9837	7.5451	3.48	180.10	8875.6	149.40	7.9499	1.4498	...	...
1999	...	7.7992	3.97	...	15332.8	...	8.2624	1.5022	...	...
2000	...	8.8018	4.35	...	12708.7	...	9.1622	1.6888	...	...

FOOTNOTES

[1] Balance of *all* factor incomes.
[2] Silver is not included in the reserves subsequently.
[3] There was a change in the system of calculation.
[4] Movements of industrial gold are included to 1877.
[5] This break occurs on a change in source (see note 1 above). Feinstein treats all visible trade f.o.b., whereas Imlah takes imports c.i.f. Feinstein has also adjusted the trade returns to include diamonds and second-hand ships.

J3   Balance of Payments

[6]   Expenditure on German occupation forces was not included in current items except in 1944 and 1945, when respectively 2,497 and 620 million kroner were included with invisibles.

[7]   Claims on the German occupation forces were transferred to a government settlement account.

[8]   Imports are taken f.o.b. subsequently

[9]   French overseas territories are included from 1926 to 1954. The difference between col. 5 and the sum of cols 1 and 2 in this period represents the overall balance of current payments of these territories. From 1955 to 1966 the statistics relate to the whole of the franc area. There is no break in cols 3, 4, and 7 in 1954/55.

[10]   Gold only to 1925.

[11]   Gold and silver only to 1923 (1st line) and from 1939 (2nd line) to 1946 (1st line).

[12]   Subsequently excluding southern Ireland.

[13]   Movement of gold bullion and specie to 1945. Feinstein *op. cit.* in note 1 above) has the following estimates of the changes in central government total reserves:-

1920	36	1925	−8	1930	3	1935	77
1921	—	1926	7	1931	−43	1936	205
1922	−2	1927	−2	1932	28	1937	134
1923	9	1928	3	1933	156	1938	−260
1924	12	1929	−4	1934	−1		

(N.B. Signs changed to accord with the notation used in this table.)

[14]   Excluding the following amounts (in million dollars) of extraordinary economic aid:-

1948	274	1950	183	1952	103	1954	20
1949	298	1951	222	1953	38		

[15]   Previously including the net position in the European Payments Union.

[16]   Subsequent statistics are of reserves minus gold. For gold movements in 1971–88 see part C of this table.

[17]   Escudo area to 1964, and Portugal exclusive of transactions with the rest of the escudo area from 1965 to 1972 (1st line). There is no break in col. 7 in 1964/65.

[18]   Statistics to 1954 (1st line) are from national sources and use national definitions.

[19]   Values are derived from national valuations.